SUGGESTIONS FOR FAST, EFFECTIVE
USE OF THE INDEX

1. PLEASE **READ THE FOREWORD** TO THE INDEX WHICH APPEARS IN THIS VOLUME.

2. STOP AND THINK ABOUT YOUR SUBJECT; TAKE A MOMENT TO **SELECT THE TERMS MOST DESCRIPTIVE OF YOUR RESEARCH SUBJECT.** IT HELPS TO SELECT THE PRINCIPAL SUBJECT RATHER THAN THE SECONDARY SUBJECT AND TO LOOK FOR NOUNS RATHER THAN ADJECTIVES.

3. IF YOUR SEARCH DOES NOT LEAD YOU TO THE CODE SECTION SOUGHT, OR IF YOU HAVE QUESTIONS ABOUT OR SUGGESTIONS FOR THE INDEX, PLEASE FEEL WELCOME TO **CONTACT THE INDEXERS.** THE INDEXERS MAY BE REACHED DIRECTLY BY **INTERNET E-MAIL** ADDRESSED TO **lng-cho-indexing@ lexisnexis.com.**

DISTRICT OF COLUMBIA
OFFICIAL CODE
2001 EDITION

Containing the Laws, general and permanent in their nature,
relating to or in force in the District of Columbia (Except such
laws as are of application in the General and Permanent
Laws of the United States) as of March 31, 2017.

2017 Replacement Index

Indexed by the Editorial Staff of the Publishers

LexisNexis®

4636514

ISBN 978-1-5221-3712-2

Matthew Bender & Company, Inc.
701 East Water Street, Charlottesville, VA 22902
www.lexisnexis.com
Customer Service: 1-800-833-9844

(Pub. No. 45948)

TITLES OF DISTRICT OF COLUMBIA CODE OFFICIAL CODE, 2001 EDITION

DIVISION I. GOVERNMENT OF DISTRICT

Title
1. Government Organization.
2. Government Administration.
3. District of Columbia Boards and Commissions.
4. Public Care Systems.
5. Police, Firefighters, and Chief Medical Examiner.
6. Housing and Building Restrictions and Regulations.
7. Human Health Care and Safety.
8. Environmental and Animal Control and Protection.
9. Transportation Systems.
10. Parks, Public Buildings, Grounds and Space.

DIVISION II. JUDICIARY AND JUDICIAL PROCEDURE

*11. Organization and Jurisdiction of the Courts.
*12. Right to Remedy.
*13. Procedure Generally.
*14. Proof.
*15. Judgments and Executions; Fees and Costs.
*16. Particular Actions, Proceedings and Matters.
*17. Review.

DIVISION III. DECEDENTS' ESTATES AND FIDUCIARY RELATIONS

*18. Wills.
*19. Descent, Distribution, and Trusts.
*20. Probate and Administration of Decedents' Estates.
*21. Fiduciary Relations and Persons with Mental Illness.

DIVISION IV. CRIMINAL LAW AND PROCEDURE AND PRISONERS

22. Criminal Offenses and Penalties.
*23. Criminal Procedure.
24. Prisoners and Their Treatment.

---

*Title has been enacted as law.

Title

DIVISION V. LOCAL BUSINESS AFFAIRS

*25. Alcoholic Beverages Regulation.
 26. Banks and Other Financial Institutions.
 27. Civil Recovery by Merchants for Criminal Conduct.
*28. Commercial Instruments and Transactions.
*29. Business Organizations.
29A. Corporations [Repealed].
 30. Hotels and Lodging Houses.
 31. Insurance and Securities.
 32. Labor.
 33. Partnerships [Repealed].
 34. Public Utilities.
 35. Railroads and Other Carriers.
 36. Trade Practices.
 37. Weights, Measures, and Markets.

DIVISION VI. EDUCATION, LIBRARIES, AND PUBLIC INSTITUTIONS

38. Educational Institutions.
39. Libraries and Cultural Institutions.

DIVISION VII. PROPERTY

40. Liens.
41. Personal Property.
42. Real Property.

DIVISION VIII. GENERAL LAWS

 43. Cemeteries and Crematories.
 44. Charitable and Curative Institutions.
 45. Compilation and Construction of Code.
 46. Domestic Relations.
*47. Taxation, Licensing, Permits, Assessments, and Feed.
 48. Foods and Drugs.
 49. Military.
 50. Motor and Non-Motor Vehicles and Traffic.
 51. Social Security.

---

*Title has been enacted as law.

Foreword to the Index

This general index has been revised and updated to include index treatment of the laws compiled in the District of Columbia Official Code, 2001 Edition, in force as of March 31, 2017. The volume also contains two additional indexes, a Popular Names Index and a Legislative Highlights Index, which have also been updated through the March 31, 2017 legislation.

This index contains treatment of the District of Columbia Official Code, the Constitution of the United States and the various rules of court promulgated by the local courts of the District. Statutory provisions are referred to in the index by section number (e.g., §28-4604). The Constitution, which is set out in Volume 1, and the court rules, which are set out in two soft-bound volumes are identified by abbreviations, a table of which follows this foreword.

The general index is a topical index, not a random word index. Random entries in an index to statutes are misleading since they result in split or partial treatment. Therefore, we have chosen to use a systematic arrangement of main topical headings in order to avoid this split treatment. Main headings in the general index treat subject matter exhaustively, unless cross references are made to other main headings.

Main headings were derived from the language of the District of Columbia Official Code, 2001 Edition, from phraseology commonly used in the courts of the District and from terminology commonly used in the legal profession. In addition, an effort was made to employ phrases and terms commonly applied to District of Columbia Code sections, such as frequently used nonlegal terms.

We solicit your help in keeping this index as usable as possible and ask that you inform us of any popular names that may have eluded us, errors we have made or improvements you think we should make. You may reach the Indexers by **E-mail (lng-cho-indexing@lexisnexis.com)**. All suggestions, questions or comments receive serious consideration. For non-index questions and comments, or to place orders, Customer Service may be reached by **toll-free telephone number (1-800-833-9844)**.

LexisNexis

June 2017

Table of Abbreviations

Amd . . . . Amendment
Appx. . . . . Appendix
Art . . . . Article
Adoption Rule . . . . Rules Governing Adoption Proceedings
Arbitration Rule . . . . Superior Court Civil Arbitration Program Rules
CivPro . . . . Superior Court Rules of Civil Procedure
CJC Canon. . . . . Code of Judicial Conduct
CrimPro. . . . . Superior Court Rules of Criminal Procedure
DCBar . . . . District of Columbia Bar Rules
DCCtApp . . . . Rules of the District of Columbia Court of
            Appeals
DomesticViolence Rule . . . . Rules Governing Proceedings in the Domestic Violence
            Unit
DomRel . . . . Rules Governing Domestic Relations Proceedings
FamDiv . . . . General Rules of the Family Division
FRAP . . . . Federal Rules of Appellate Procedure and
            Corresponding Circuit Rules of the District
            of Columbia Circuit
IndigentRep. Plan for Furnishing Representation to Indigents
JuvProc . . . . Rules Governing Juvenile Proceedings
LandlordTenant. . . . . Superior Court Rules of Procedure for the Landlord and
            Tenant Branch
MentalHealth Rule . . . . Superior Court Rules of Procedure for Mental Health
MentalRetardation Rule. . . . . Superior Court Rules for Mental Retardation Proceed-
            ings
NeglectProc . . . . Rules Governing Neglect and Abuse Proceedings
PostConvRel . . . . Rules Governing Proceedings under D.C. Code § 23-11C
Probate. . . . . Superior Court Rules of the Probate Division
ProfCond Rule. . . . . Rules of Professional Conduct
SmallClaims . . . . Superior Court Rules of Procedure for the Small Claims
            and Conciliation Branch
Tax . . . . Rules of Practice and Procedure Before the Tax Division
            of the Superior Court
US Const . . . . Constitution of the United States
USCtApp . . . . Federal Rules of Appellate Procedure and
            Corresponding Circuit Rules of the District
            of Columbia Court
USCtApp HPIP Rule. . . . . Handbook of Practice and Internal Procedures, United
            States Court of Appeals for the District of Columbia
            Circuit
USDistCt LCrR. . . . . U.S. District Court Local Criminal Rules
USDistCt LCvR. . . . . U.S. District Court Local Civil Rules
USDistDCBank. . . . . Local Rules for United States Bankruptcy Court for the
            District of Columbia
VictComp Rule. . . . . Superior Court Crime Victims Compensation Program

2017 LEGISLATIVE HIGHLIGHTS INDEX

A

ABUSED ADULTS.
Criminal abuse, neglect and financial exploitation of vulnerable adults and elderly persons, §§22-931 to 22-938.

ACCIDENT AND HEALTH INSURANCE.
Liens.
  Health care benefits lien reduction, §31-3551.

ADVERTISING.
Schools and education.
  My School DC EdFest sponsorship and advertising, §38-196.01.

AGED PERSONS.
Criminal abuse, neglect and financial exploitation of vulnerable adults and elderly persons, §§22-931 to 22-938.

ANATOMICAL BOARD, §§3-201 to 3-209.

ANIMAL CONTROL.
Animal and pet owners.
  Prohibited conduct, §8-1778.45.

APPRENTICES.
Youth apprenticeship advisory council, §32-1412.01.

ARRESTS.
Resisting arrest, §22-405.01.

ASSAULT AND BATTERY.
Police officer, assault on.
  Resisting arrest, §22-405.01.

ATTORNEY GENERAL FOR DISTRICT OF COLUMBIA.
Challenge to statutes, rule, regulation, program or policy.
  Reporting on, §1-301.89a.
Consumer protection.
  Investigative powers.
    Subpoenas, authority to issue, §1-301.88d.
Independent government agency.
  Judicial or administrative proceeding in which agency party.
    Notification of office, §1-301.89b.
Special counsel, §1-301.89.

ATTORNEY GENERAL FOR DISTRICT OF COLUMBIA.
  —Cont'd
Subpoena powers, §1-301.88c.
  Consumer protection matters, authority to issue, §1-301.88d.

AUDITOR FOR DISTRICT OF COLUMBIA.
Compliance unit, §1-301.183.

AUTOMATED EXTERNAL DEFIBRILLATORS.
Usage by public.
  CPR and AED program, §44-232.03.

B

BICYCLES.
Bicycle and pedestrian priority area program, §50-2371.
Bicycle insurance policies, §§50-531 to 50-535.
Complete streets policy, §50-2381.

BID PARKING ABATEMENT FUND, §1-325.341.

BONUS PAY AND SPECIAL AWARDS PAY ACT OF 2016, §§1-551.01 to 1-551.06.

BUILDING CODE.
Fireproof buildings, §§6-601.05 to 6-601.09.
Height of buildings, §§6-601.05 to 6-611.02.
Smoke detectors, §§6-751.01, 6-751.02.
Unsafe structures or excavations, §§6-801 to 6-808.

BUILDING PERMITS.
Third party plan review, §6-1405.02.

BUSINESS AND ECONOMIC DEVELOPMENT.
H Street, N.E., Retail Priority Area.
  Funding for eligible development projects, §1-325.311.
Incarceration to incorporation entrepreneurship program.
  Effective date, §2-1210.55.
Local food economy study, §48-411.

BUSINESS IMPROVEMENT DISTRICTS.
Term of, §2-1215.18.

C

CAMPAIGN FINANCE.
Constituent services.
Mayor and chairman and members of
  council.
  Contributions for purposes of
    services, §1-1163.38.

CHARTER SCHOOLS.
Public charter schools.
Conflicting interest transactions,
  §38-1802.04.
School management contracts,
  §38-1802.04.
Services of public schools extended to,
  §38-1802.09.
Street safety education, §38-3401.

CHILD ABUSE AND NEGLECT.
Reasonable and prudent parent
  standard.
Application or failure to apply.
  Immunity from civil damages,
    §4-1303.03f.
Defined, §4-1301.02.

CHILDREN AND MINORS.
Employment of minors.
Programs for employment and training
  of domiciliaries of District,
  §32-241.

CLEAN AND AFFORDABLE
  ENERGY, §§8-1773.01 to 8-1774.16.

CONSUMER PROTECTION.
Attorney general.
Investigative powers.
  Subpoenas, authority to issue,
    §1-301.88d.
Bicycle insurance policies, §§50-531
  to 50-535.

CORRECTIONS, DEPARTMENT OF.
Inmate and returning citizen
  assistance, §24-211.71.

CRIMES AND OFFENSES.
Criminal abuse, neglect and
  financial exploitation of
  vulnerable adults and elderly
  persons, §§22-931 to 22-938.
Salvage, flood and junk vehicles.
Unlawful acts, §50-1331.08.

CRIMINAL ABUSE, NEGLECT AND
  FINANCIAL EXPLOITATION OF
  VULNERABLE ADULTS AND
  ELDERLY PERSONS, §§22-931 to
  22-938.

CRIMINAL CODE REFORM
  COMMISSION, §§3-151 to 3-156.

D

DISABILITIES, PERSONS WITH.
Criminal abuse, neglect and
  financial exploitation of
  vulnerable adults and elderly
  persons, §§22-931 to 22-938.

DISPOSABLE FOOD SERVICE
  WARE, MANAGEMENT.
Compostable or recyclable food
  service ware.
Compostable, defined, §8-1531.

DOMESTIC PARTNERSHIPS.
Bigamy, §22-501.
Parentage proceedings, §§16-909 to
  16-909.03.

DOMESTIC RELATIONS.
Hospital discharge planning,
  §§21-2231.01 to 21-2231.05.

DRIVERS' LICENSES.
Vehicle-for-hire drivers' licenses,
  §47-2829.

DRIVING UNDER THE
  INFLUENCE.
Penalties, §50-2206.13.

E

ECONOMIC DEVELOPMENT.
Walter Reed Medical Center site
  development, §§2-1227.01 to
  2-1227.06.

ELECTIONS.
Initiative and referendum,
  §1-1001.16.
Mobile application.
Defined, §1-1001.02.
Mobile device.
Defined, §1-1001.02.
Recall of elected public officials,
  §1-1001.17.
Voter identification for voting,
  §1-1001.07.

ELECTRONIC WASTE.
Definitions, §8-1031.08.
Fees.
Shortfall fees, §8-1041.04.
Violations of act.
Civil fines and penalties, §8-1041.12.

EMERGENCY MEDICAL SERVICES.
Firefighters.
Fire and emergency services
department personnel.
Service longevity, §5-544.01.
Hospital discharge planning,
§§21-2231.01 to 21-2231.05.
Presumptive disability or death.
Applicability, §5-656.
Maintaining eligibility, §5-655.01.
Physical examination, §5-655.01.
Preemployment physical examination,
defined, §5-651.
Reporting requirements, §5-655.02.
Rules, §5-655.03.

EMISSIONS.
Inspection of motor vehicles,
§§50-1101 to 50-1110.

ENERGY CONSERVATION.
Commercial property energy
conservation, §§8-1772.01 to
8-1772.04.
National capital energy fund.
Administrators.
Contract to obtain, §8-1778.45.

ENVIRONMENTAL PROTECTION.
Department of the environment.
Organization, §8-151.06.
Rulemaking, §8-151.11.

ETHICS AND GOVERNMENT
ACCOUNTABILITY BOARD.
Compensation, §1-1162.03.

EX-OFFENDERS.
Hiring of ex-offenders.
Fair criminal record screening.
Rules, §32-1346.

F

FINANCIAL EXPLOITATION OF
VULNERABLE ADULTS AND
ELDERLY PERSONS.
Criminal abuse, neglect and
financial exploitation of
vulnerable adults and elderly
persons, §§22-931 to 22-938.
FIRE AND EMERGENCY MEDICAL
SERVICES DEPARTMENT.
Integrated health care task force,
§5-404.02.
Paramedics, EMTs and EMS
specialists.
Service longevity, §5-544.01.
Public duty doctrine, §5-401.02.

FIRE DEPARTMENTS.
Paramedics and emergency medical
technicians/specialists.
Fire and emergency services
department personnel.
Service longevity, §5-544.01.
Pilot civilian technical services
program, §5-451.
Third-party contractors.
Quarterly reports, §5-401.

FIRES AND FIRE PREVENTION.
Height of buildings, §§6-601.05 to
6-611.02.
Smoke detectors, §§6-751.01, 6-751.02.

FOOD.
Local food economy study, §48-411.

FOR-HIRE VEHICLES.
Impoundment of vehicles, §50-331.

G

GEOTHERMAL ENERGY.
Sustainable energy, §§8-1773.01 to
8-1774.16.

GREEN BUILDINGS.
Privately-owned buildings and
projects, §6-1451.03.
Publicly-owned, leased and financed
buildings and projects,
§6-1451.02.

H

HEALTH.
Flame retardants.
Prohibitions on chlorinated flame
retardants, §8-108.02a.
Replacement of regulated flame
retardants, §8-108.02b.
Perchloroethylene in dry cleaning,
§§8-108.03 to 8-108.05.

HEALTH CARE FINANCE
DEPARTMENT.
Violence prevention and health
equity office, establishment,
§7-781.

HEALTH DEPARTMENT.
Disparities.
Commission on health equity,
§§7-756.01 to 7-756.03.

HEALTH EQUITY, COMMISSION
ON, §§7-756.01 to 7-756.03.

HEALTH INSURANCE.
Liens.
Health care benefits lien reduction, §31-3551.
Spouse or domestic partner equity.
Compliance with court orders, §1-523.03.

HIGHWAYS.
Complete streets policy, §50-2381.

HISTORIC DISTRICTS, §§6-1104 to 6-1108.

HISTORIC LANDMARKS.
New construction, §6-1105.

HOMELESS SERVICES.
Flexible rent subsidy pilot program, §4-751.05.

HOME PURCHASE ASSISTANCE FUND.
Repayment structure, revision by mayor, §42-2602.01.

HOSPITAL DISCHARGE PLANNING, §§21-2231.01 to 21-2231.05.

HOSPITALS.
Discharge planning, §§21-2231.01 to 21-2231.05.
Medicaid.
Hospital inpatient rate supplement 2016-2017, §§44-662.11 to 44-662.18.
Hospital outpatient supplemental payment 2016-2017, §§44-661.11 to 44-661.19.

HOURS OF WORK.
Building service employees.
Minimum work hours, §§32-1051.01 to 32-1051.17.

HOUSING.
Height of buildings, §§6-601.05 to 6-611.02.
Smoke detectors, §§6-751.01, 6-751.02.

H STREET RETAIL PRIORITY AREA GRANT FUND.
Grants.
Award of grants to qualified high technology companies (QHTCs), §1-325.172.

I

IMPOUNDMENT OF VEHICLES.
For-hire vehicles, §50-331.

INCAPACITATED PERSONS.
Hospital discharge planning, §§21-2231.01 to 21-2231.05.

INCOME TAXES.
District and non-District income, allocation and apportionment of, §§47-1810.01 to 47-1810.08.

INSPECTOR GENERAL, OFFICE OF.
Annual budget for office, §1-301.115a.

INSURANCE.
Bicycle insurance policies, §§50-531 to 50-535.
Taxicabs, §50-301.14.

INTELLECTUAL DISABILITIES, PERSONS WITH.
Criminal abuse, neglect and financial exploitation of vulnerable adults and elderly persons, §§22-931 to 22-938.

J

JUNK VEHICLES.
Generally, §§50-1331.01 to 50-1331.09.

L

LABOR AND EMPLOYMENT RELATIONS.
Child labor.
Programs for employment and training of domiciliaries of District, §32-241.
Public employment service, §32-241.

LANDLORD AND TENANT.
Commercial tenancy.
Notice to quit, §42-3202.

LAW ENFORCEMENT OFFICERS.
Resisting arrest, §22-405.01.

LIENS.
Health care benefits lien reduction, §31-3551.

LOTTERIES.
Lottery and charitable games control board, §§3-1301 to 3-1336.

M

MADE IN DC PROGRAM, §§2-1208.31 to 2-1208.35.

MAYOR.
Deputy Mayor for planning and economic development.
Grant-making authority, §1-328.04.
Deputy Mayor for public safety and justice.
Report on felony crime statistics, §1-301.191.
Executive service.
Subordinate agency heads in the executive service.
Mayoral nominees, §1-523.01.
Powers and duties generally.
Additional governmental powers, §1-301.86b.
Unsafe structures or excavations.
Power to take immediate action regarding, §6-801.

MEDICAID.
District of Columbia medical assistance program.
Council review of plan Federal financial assistance under Title XIX, §1-307.02.
Hospital inpatient rate supplement 2016-2017, §§44-662.11 to 44-662.18.
Hospital outpatient supplemental payment 2016-2017, §§44-661.11 to 44-661.19.

MEDICAL DIRECTIVES.
Hospital discharge planning, §§21-2231.01 to 21-2231.05.

MEDICAL LIABILITY CAPTIVE INSURANCE AGENCY.
Authority of the agency, §1-307.85.
Captive trust fund, §§1-307.82, 1-307.91.
Exemption from certain laws, §1-307.92.
Insurance coverage, §1-307.90.
Limit of agency's liability, §1-307.82.

MENTAL ILLNESS, PERSONS WITH.
Criminal abuse, neglect and financial exploitation of vulnerable adults and elderly persons, §§22-931 to 22-938.

MERIT SYSTEM.
Disability compensation.
Employees' compensation fund, §1-623.42.
Excepted service.
Officeholders who serve at the pleasure of the appointing authority, §1-609.08.

MERIT SYSTEM —Cont'd
Rules and regulations.
Appropriate personnel authority.
Who may issue for specific agency personnel, §§1-604.04, 1-604.06.

METROPOLITAN POLICE.
Assault on member of police force.
Resisting arrest, §22-405.01.
Community crime prevention team, §5-132.31.
Community policing working group, §5-132.32.
Records.
Contacts, frisks and stops, §5-113.01.
Resisting arrest, §22-405.01.

MOTOR VEHICLE ACCIDENTS.
Major crash review task force, §50-1831.
Open access to collision data and information, §§50-1951.01 to 50-1951.07.

MOTOR VEHICLE INSURANCE.
Taxicabs, §50-301.14.

MOTOR VEHICLE REGISTRATION.
Emissions.
Inspection of motor vehicles.
Self-service exhaust emissions testing pilot program, §50-1110.

MOTOR VEHICLES.
Aggressive driving, §50-2204.
Salvage, flood and junk vehicles, §§50-1331.01 to 50-1331.09.

N

NEGLIGENCE.
Non-motorized user contributory negligence, §§50-2204.51 to 50-2204.53.
Vulnerable adults and elderly persons.
Criminal abuse, neglect and financial exploitation.
Criminal negligence, §22-934.

NEW COLUMBIA STATEHOOD FUND.
Statehood Delegation members.
Use of funds by, §§1-129.32, 1-129.35.

P

PEDESTRIANS.
Bicycle and pedestrian priority area program, §50-2371.

PEDESTRIANS —Cont'd
Complete streets policy, §50-2381.
Motor vehicle accidents.
Open access to data and information.
General provisions, §§50-1951.01 to
50-1951.07.
**Non-motorized user contributory
negligence,** §§50-2204.51 to
50-2204.53.

PENSIONS AND RETIREMENT.
Creditable service.
Defined for purposes of vesting
pursuant to §1-626.10(b),
§1-626.04.
Spouse or domestic partner equity.
Compliance with court orders,
§1-523.03.

**PERSONAL DELIVERY DEVICES
PILOT PROGRAM,** §§50-1551 to
50-1555.

PERSONAL INJURY PROTECTION.
Health care benefits lien reduction,
§31-3551.

PREGNANCY.
Teen pregnancy prevention fund.
Grant-managing entity, §§1-325.322 to
1-325.326.

PRIVATE VEHICLES-FOR-HIRE.
Impoundment of vehicles, §50-331.

PROCUREMENT PRACTICES.
**Construction projects and related
services.**
Estimate of construction costs,
§2-356.05.
Security in non-construction service
contracts, §2-357.02a.
Contract appeals board.
Protest procedures, §2-360.08.
**Function closely associated with an
inherently governmental
function.**
Defined, §2-351.04.
Inherently governmental functions.
Contracts for performance, prohibition,
§2-352.05a.
Defined, §2-351.04.
Labor organization.
Defined, §2-351.04.
**Office of contracting and
procurement.**
Inherently governmental functions.
Contracts for performance,
prohibition, §2-352.05a.

PROCUREMENT PRACTICES
—Cont'd
**Office of contracting and
procurement** —Cont'd
Review of contracts.
Multiyear contracts and contracts in
excess of one million dollars,
§2-352.02.
**Ombudsman for contracting and
procurement,** §2-352.07.
Restricted period.
Defined, §2-351.04.
**Source selection and contract
formation.**
Prohibited contacts during source
selection, §2-354.01a.
Transparency in contracting,
§2-361.04.

PUBLIC BUILDINGS.
Height of buildings, §§6-601.05 to
6-611.02.

PUBLIC CONTRACTS.
Quick payment provisions.
Interest penalty payments.
Change order clause, §2-221.02.
Failure to pay discounted price
within specified period,
§2-221.03.
Filing of claims, §2-221.04.

**PUBLIC OFFICERS AND
EMPLOYEES.**
**Bonus pay and special awards pay
act of 2016,** §§1-551.01 to 1-551.06.
Hatch act.
Political activity authorized,
§1-1171.02.

**PUBLIC-PRIVATE PARTNERSHIP
ADMINISTRATION FUND,**
§2-272.04.

PUBLIC-PRIVATE PARTNERSHIPS.
**Solicitation through requests for
proposals,** §2-273.03.

PUBLIC SPACE.
Naming, §9-204.09.
Designation of official names,
§9-204.22.
Symbolic names.
Designation for public spaces,
streets and alleys, §§9-204.23,
9-204.24.

PUBLIC UTILITIES.
Sustainable energy, §§8-1773.01 to
8-1774.16.

R

REAL PROPERTY TAX EXEMPTIONS.
Jubilee Ontario Apartments, LP, Lot 805, Square 2565, §47-1099.

RECALL OF ELECTED PUBLIC OFFICIALS, §1-1001.17.

RETAIL DEVELOPMENT INCENTIVES.
Retail priority areas.
Corridor revitalization programs, §2-1217.73b.

S

SALVAGE, FLOOD AND JUNK VEHICLES, §§50-1331.01 to 50-1331.09.

SCHOOLS AND EDUCATION.
District of Columbia public schools (DCPS) funds.
Relocation and use, §38-2955.
Funding.
Uniform per-student funding formula.
Per capita funding.
Supplement to foundation level funding, §38-2905.
My School DC EdFest sponsorship and advertising, §38-196.01.
Street safety education, §38-3401.
Traffic control devices.
Installation, §38-3101.

SECURITY CAMERAS.
Private security camera system incentive program.
Established, §7-2831.
Private security camera incentive fund, §7-2832.

SENIOR CITIZENS.
Criminal abuse, neglect and financial exploitation of vulnerable adults and elderly persons, §§22-931 to 22-938.

SENTENCING AND CRIMINAL CODE REVISION COMMISSION.
Meetings and hearings, §3-103.

SOLAR ENERGY.
Solar for All program, §8-1774.16.
Sustainable energy, §§8-1773.01 to 8-1774.16.

STREETS AND ALLEYS.
Complete Streets policy, §50-2381.

STREETS AND ALLEYS —Cont'd
Naming of public spaces.
Designation of official names.
Official name, defined, §9-201.01.
Procedural requirements, §9-204.21.
Public spaces other than alley or street, §§9-204.22, 9-204.24.
Symbolic names.
Designation for public spaces, streets and alleys, §§9-204.23, 9-204.24.

STUDENT HEALTH CARE.
Medication.
Student access to epinephrine, §38-651.04a.

SURGERY.
Hospital discharge planning, §§21-2231.01 to 21-2231.05.

SUSTAINABLE ENERGY, §§8-1773.01 to 8-1774.16.

T

TAXICABS.
For-hire vehicles department, §§50-301.04 to 50-301.11.
Insurance, §50-301.14.

TITLING OF MOTOR VEHICLES.
Salvage, flood and junk vehicles.
Generally, §§50-1331.01 to 50-1331.09.

TRAFFIC LAWS.
Aggressive driving, §50-2204.
Impoundment of vehicles.
For-hire vehicles, §50-331.
Unlawfully parked or abandoned vehicles, §50-2637.

TRAFFIC TICKET ADJUDICATION.
Reports to DPW and DDOT, §50-2301.10.
Study of parking infraction adjudications, §50-2301.11.

TRAINING.
Employment and training of domiciliaries of District, §32-241.
Public employment service, §32-241.

TRANSIT RIDER ADVISORY COUNCIL, §§50-2361.01 to 50-2361.03.

TRANSPORTATION.
Complete streets policy, §50-2381.
Department of transportation.
Personal delivery devices pilot program, §§50-1551 to 50-1555.

TRANSPORTATION —Cont'd
Mulitmodal accessibility advisory council, §§50-2361.31, 50-2361.32.
Transit rider advisory council, §§50-2361.01 to 50-2361.03.

U

UNEMPLOYMENT COMPENSATION.
Administrative expenses, payment of, §51-114.
Benefits and refunds, payment of, §51-108.
"Unemployed" construed for purposes of earnings, §51-101.
UNIFIED COMMUNICATIONS, OFFICE OF.
Emergency medical application.
  Development to aid in providing cardiopulmonary resuscitation, §1-327.54a.
Interagency coordination, §1-327.56.
Organization.
  Primary organizational functions, §1-327.55.
UNSAFE STRUCTURES OR EXCAVATIONS, §§6-801 to 6-808.
URBAN FOREST PRESERVATION.
Advisory council, §8-651.09.
Hazardous trees.
  Defined, §8-651.02.
Heritage trees.
  Protection, §8-651.04a.
  Removal permit requirement, §8-651.04a.
Urban forestry advisory council, §8-651.09.

V

VITAL RECORDS.
Fund, §7-221.

VULNERABLE ADULTS AND ELDERLY PERSONS.
Criminal abuse, neglect and financial exploitation, §§22-931 to 22-938.

W

WALTER REED MEDICAL CENTER SITE DEVELOPMENT, §§2-1227.01 to 2-1227.06.
WALTER REED REDEVELOPMENT FUND, §2-1227.06.
WALTER REED REINVESTMENT FUND, §2-1227.05.
WASHINGTON METROPOLITAN AREA TRANSIT AUTHORITY.
WMATA operations support fund, §1-325.311.
WASTE AND WASTE DISPOSAL.
Compost drop-off program, §8-761.
Trash compactor grant program, §§8-751 to 8-753.
WILDLIFE PROTECTION.
Wildlife control operator.
  License fees, §8-2209.
WIND ENERGY.
Sustainable energy, §§8-1773.01 to 8-1774.16.

Y

YOUTH APPRENTICESHIP ADVISORY COUNCIL, §32-1412.01.

Index

___

A

ABANDONED AND DETERIORATED PROPERTY.
Acquisition and disposal by District,
 §§42-3171.01 to 42-3171.04.
 Acquisition and redevelopment,
 §42-3171.02.
 Definitions, §42-3171.01.
 Displaced occupants or tenants.
 Assistance, §42-3171.04.
 Disposal, §42-3171.03.
Demolition or enclosure of deteriorated property,
 §§42-3173.01 to 42-3173.12.
 Action by interested parties after
 initial notice, time, §42-3173.06.
 Amount collected.
 Use and deposit, §42-3173.11.
 Assessment of cost to demolish or
 enclose as tax, §42-3173.10.
 Authority of mayor, §42-3173.02.
 Cost to demolish or enclose.
 Recovery, §42-3173.10.
 Definitions, §42-3173.01.
 Final determination structure
 deteriorated, §42-3173.07.
 Judicial review, §42-3173.09.
 Historic structures.
 Designation of potential historic
 structure, §42-3173.04.
 Initial determination structure
 deteriorated, §42-3173.05.
 Notice of final determination structure
 deteriorated, §42-3173.07.
 Notice of initial determination
 structure deteriorated,
 §42-3173.05.
 Redevelopment feasibility analysis,
 §42-3173.03.
 Remedies cumulative, §42-3173.12.
 Tax on property.
 Assessment of cost to demolish or
 enclose, §42-3173.10.
Trespass.
 Prima facie evidence, §22-3302.
Vacant property.
 Special disposal procedures, §§10-831
 to 10-839.
 See VACANT AND ABANDONED
 PROPERTY.
Wells, abandonment, §8-103.13a.

ABANDONED INFANTS.
Newborn safe haven, §§4-1451.01 to
 4-1451.08.
 See NEWBORN SAFE HAVEN.

ABANDONED VEHICLES.
Blue Plains impoundment lot,
 §50-2405.
Junk vehicles, §§50-2401 to 50-2406.
 Abandoned and junk vehicle division.
 Established, §50-2402.
 Blue Plains impoundment lot.
 Jurisdiction over, §50-2405.
 Definitions, §50-2401.
 Disposal of junk vehicles, §50-2623.
 Notice of vehicle being taken into
 custody, §50-2622.
 Rulemaking, §50-2406.
 Sale at public auction, §50-2623.
Scrap vehicle title authorization,
 §§50-2701 to 50-2708.
 See SCRAP VEHICLE TITLE
 AUTHORIZATION.
Unclaimed property.
 General provisions, §§41-101 to
 41-142.
 See UNCLAIMED PROPERTY.
Unlawfully parked vehicles,
 §§50-2421.01 to 50-2421.15.
 Applicability of provisions,
 §50-2421.15.
 Definitions, §50-2421.02.
 Disposal of unclaimed vehicle,
 §50-2421.10.
 Owners' and lienholders' remedies,
 §50-2421.11.
 Impoundment, §50-2421.07.
 Post-removal disposition, §50-2421.06.
 Prohibited acts, §50-2421.03.
 Reclamation of impounded vehicle.
 Procedures, §50-2421.09.
 Time period, §50-2421.08.
 Removal from private property,
 §50-2421.05.
 Removal from public space,
 §50-2421.04.
 Repeal of provisions, effect of,
 §50-2421.14.
 Rulemaking authority, §50-2421.12.
 Short title, §50-2421.01.
 Tampering with, §50-2421.04.

ABANDONMENT OF DISABLED, INJURED, OR SICK ANIMALS,
 §22-1012.

ABANDONMENT OF PROSECUTION.
Dismissal of proceedings.
Criminal cases, CrimPro Rule 48.
ABANDONMENT OF RAILROAD SUBSTATION, §35-121.
ABANDONMENT OF STREETS.
Reversion of title upon, §9-101.08.
ABATEMENT.
Alcoholic beverage violations, places of, §25-805.
Asbestos abatement.
Project prohibitions, §8-111.04.
Task force, §§44-732 to 44-734.
Building code.
Failure to fireproof building.
Abatement of nuisance, §6-601.08.
Drug, firearm, or prostitution-related nuisance abatement, §§42-3101 to 42-3114.
See CRIME-RELATED NUISANCE ABATEMENT.
E-commerce companies.
Qualified social electronic commerce companies tax abatements, §§47-1818.01 to 47-1818.08.
Graffiti, §§42-3141.01 to 42-3141.11.
See GRAFFITI.
Homestead housing preservation abatement agreements, §42-2108.
Prostitution.
Drug, firearm, or prostitution-related nuisance abatement, §§42-3101 to 42-3114.
See CRIME-RELATED NUISANCE ABATEMENT.
Houses of prostitution.
See PROSTITUTION.
Public assistance.
Nonabatement of causes of action, §4-220.02.
Public space.
Abatement of dangerous conditions on public space, §§10-1181.01 to 10-1181.07.
See PUBLIC SPACE.
Rodent abatement program, §§8-2103.01 to 8-2103.05.
Social media.
Qualified social electronic commerce companies tax abatements, §§47-1818.01 to 47-1818.08.
Solid waste nuisance abatement fund, §8-807.01.
Steam boilers or vessels.
Use as nuisance, §2-113.

ABATEMENT —Cont'd
Tax abatement.
Abatement or refund of tax assessed against exempt property, §47-1008.
Greater Southeast Community Hospital, §47-1050.
Hadley Memorial Hospital, §47-1050.
High technology commercial real estate database and service providers, §47-4630.
Homeowners in enterprise zones, §§47-858.01 to 47-858.05.
Lower income home ownership tax abatement and incentives, §§47-3501 to 47-3508.
New residential developments, §§47-857.01 to 47-857.10, 47-859.01 to 47-859.05.
Nonprofit organizations locating in emerging commercial neighborhoods, §§47-857.11 to 47-857.16.
See REAL PROPERTY TAXES.
Penalty and interest, §47-811.04.
Rental housing.
Conversion and sale, §42-3402.09.
New or rehabilitated vacant units, §42-3508.02.
Section 8 and other affordable housing, §§47-865, 47-866.
Special assessments, §47-1203.
The Advisory Board Company, §§47-4665.01 to 47-4665.05.
Urban Institute properties, §47-4624.
Vector-borne disease control, §8-2131.05.
Corrective actions by the District, §8-2131.06.
ABLE SAVINGS ACCOUNTS, §§47-4901, 47-4902.
ABORTION.
Crime victims' compensation.
Medical expenses, VictComp Rule 24.
Health care durable powers of attorney, §21-2211.
ABSENCE FOR SEVEN YEARS.
Presumption of death, §§14-701, 14-702.
ABUSED ADULTS.
Adult protective services, §§7-1901 to 7-1913.
See ADULT PROTECTIVE SERVICES.

ABUSED ADULTS —Cont'd
Assisted living residences.
Abuse, neglect and exploitation, §44-105.09.
Criminal abuse, neglect and financial exploitation of vulnerable adults and elderly persons, §§22-931 to 22-938.
See CRIMINAL ABUSE, NEGLECT AND FINANCIAL EXPLOITATION OF VULNERABLE ADULTS AND ELDERLY PERSONS.

ABUSED CHILDREN, §§4-1301.02 to 4-1362, NeglectProc Rules 1 to 47.
See CHILD ABUSE AND NEGLECT.

ABUTTING PROPERTY OWNERS.
Business improvement districts, §2-1215.09a.
Curbs, sidewalks or alleys laid on streets being improved.
No assessment to property owner, §9-401.04.

ACCELERATION CLAUSES.
Interest, §28-3312.

ACCESSIONS.
Secured transactions.
Perfection and priority of security interests, §28:9-335.

ACCESSORIES AFTER THE FACT, §22-1806.

ACCESSRX PHARMACEUTICAL RESOURCE CENTER, §48-831.42.

ACCESSRX PROGRAM, §§48-831.01 to 48-831.42.

ACCESS TO JUSTICE FOR BICYCLISTS.
Assault or battery of bicyclist by motorist.
Right of civil action for damages, §50-1621.

ACCESS TO JUSTICE INITIATIVE PROGRAM, §§4-1701.01 to 4-1704.07.
Annual financial audit, §4-1702.02.
ATJ program.
Annual financial audit, §4-1702.02.
Defined, §4-1701.01.
Grant to bar foundation, §4-1703.01.
Reporting on administration and performance, §4-1702.02.
Definitions, §4-1701.01.
Establishment, §4-1702.01.

ACCESS TO JUSTICE INITIATIVE PROGRAM —Cont'd
LRAP program.
Administrator, §4-1704.01.
Duties, §4-1704.02.
Annual financial audit, §4-1702.02.
Bar foundation funding, §4-1704.01.
Defined, §4-1701.01.
Eligibility to participate, §4-1704.03.
Funding, §4-1704.01.
Involuntary termination from eligible employment, §4-1704.05.
Loans to participants to repay educational expenses, §4-1704.02.
Award, §4-1704.04.
Disbursement, §4-1704.06.
Maximum amount, §4-1704.04.
Preference, §4-1704.04.
Semi-annual repayment assistance payments, §4-1704.06.
Obligations of participants, §4-1704.05.
Purpose, §4-1704.01.
Reporting on administration and performance, §4-1702.02.
Rules, §4-1704.07.
Service obligation, §4-1704.05.
Purposes, §4-1702.01.

ACCIDENT AND HEALTH INSURANCE.
Casualty and other insurance rates.
General provisions, §§31-2701 to 31-2714.
See INSURANCE.
Clinical trials insurance coverage, §§31-2993.01 to 31-2993.03.
COBRA, §§31-3301.01 to 31-3303.14.
See HEALTH INSURANCE PORTABILITY AND ACCOUNTABILITY.
Credit life, accident and health insurance.
General provisions, §§31-5101 to 31-5112.
See CREDIT LIFE, ACCIDENT AND HEALTH INSURANCE.
Domestic partner benefits, §§32-701 to 32-710.
See DOMESTIC PARTNER BENEFITS.
Employer's health benefits plans.
Continuation of coverage.
Employees and dependents, §§32-731 to 32-734.
Generally.
See HEALTH INSURANCE.

ACCIDENT AND HEALTH INSURANCE —Cont'd

Health maintenance organizations.
General provisions, §§31-3401 to 31-3431.
See HEALTH MAINTENANCE ORGANIZATIONS.

Hospital and medical services corporations, §§31-3501 to 31-3524.
See HOSPITAL AND MEDICAL SERVICES CORPORATIONS.

Liens.
Health care benefits lien reduction, §31-3551.

Life and health insurance guaranty association.
General provisions, §§31-5401 to 31-5416.
See LIFE AND HEALTH INSURANCE GUARANTY ASSOCIATION.

Long-term care insurance, §§31-3601 to 31-3612.
See LONG-TERM CARE INSURANCE.

Medicare supplement insurance.
General provisions, §§31-3701 to 31-3710.
See MEDICARE SUPPLEMENT INSURANCE.

Newborn health insurance.
General provisions, §§31-3801 to 31-3805.
See NEWBORN HEALTH INSURANCE.

Public officers and employees, §§1-621.01 to 1-621.17.
See MERIT SYSTEM.

Rates.
Casualty and other insurance rates.
General provisions, §§31-2701 to 31-2714.
See INSURANCE.

Reimbursement, health benefits plans.
Claims by providers, §§31-3131 to 31-3138.
See HEALTH INSURANCE.

Voluntary withdrawal by health benefit plan carriers, §§31-3151 to 31-3154.

ACCIDENTS.
Motor vehicles.
See MOTOR VEHICLE ACCIDENTS.
Public utilities.
Report, investigation, §34-401.

ACCORD AND SATISFACTION.
Negotiable instruments.
Use of instrument, §28:3-311.

ACCOUNTANTS.
Board of accountancy, §§47-2853.06 to 47-2853.10.
Business licenses, §§47-2853.41 to 47-2853.49.
Disciplinary action, §47-2853.48.
Eligibility requirements, §47-2853.42.
Firms.
Registration, §47-2853.44.
Permits, §47-2853.47.
Revocation, §47-2853.48.
Practice privilege.
Licensees from other states, §47-2853.49.
Prohibited representations, §47-2853.43.
Registration.
Firms, §47-2853.44.
Revocation, §47-2853.48.
Scope of practice, §47-2853.41.
Substantially equivalent qualifications, §47-2853.49.

ACCOUNTS AND ACCOUNTING.
ABLE savings accounts, §§47-4901, 47-4902.
Action of account, §16-101.
Administration of estates.
Records and accounts.
See ADMINISTRATION OF ESTATES.
Advisory neighborhood commissions.
Funding and accounts, §§1-309.13, 1-309.14.
Assignments for benefit of creditors.
Settlement by assignee or trustee, §28-2106.
Attorneys at law.
Client's property, ProfCond Rule 1.15.
Interest on Lawyers Trust Account (IOLTA), DCBar Appx A, DCBar Rule X, ProfCond Rule 1.15.
Approved depositories, DCBar Rule XI.
Verification of participation, DCBar Rule XIV.
Bar association, DCBar Rule VIII.
Cable television special account, §34-1252.03.
Captive insurance companies.
Liquidation and rehabilitation, §31-3931.05.

ACCOUNTS AND ACCOUNTING
—Cont'd
Captive insurance companies
—Cont'd
Protective cell captive insurers,
§31-3931.04.
Protective cells, defined, §31-3931.01.
Committees.
Bond of committee.
Discharge only after accounting,
§28-2504.
Complaint on an account, CivPro
Form CA 4.
Condominiums.
Escrow accounts, §42-1904.09.
Conservators, Probate Rule 330.
Audit of accounts, Probate Rule 331.
Missing persons, Probate Rule 351.
Protection of property, §21-2065.
Termination of conservatorship,
Probate Rule 334.
Consistency of systems, §1-204.47.
Constitution of the United States.
Receipts and expenditures of public
money.
Publication of statement and
account, US Const Art I §9.
**Consumer credit service
organizations.**
Trust account in lieu of bond,
§28-4604.
**Continuing care retirement
communities.**
Entrance fee.
Escrow accounts, §44-151.09.
Court ordered property sales, CivPro
Rule 308.
Probate proceedings, Probate Rule
203.
Custodial trustee, §19-1115.
Limitation of action against trustee,
§19-1116.
Custodians.
Bond of custodian.
Discharge only after accounting,
§28-2504.
Executors and administrators.
Bond of executor or administrator.
Discharge only after accounting,
§28-2504.
Fiduciaries, CivPro Rule 305.
Bond of fiduciary.
Discharge only after accounting,
§28-2504.
Fund-type accounting, §§47-371 to
47-377.

ACCOUNTS AND ACCOUNTING
—Cont'd
**Generally accepted accounting
principles (GAAP),** §§47-372,
47-374.
Guardian ad litem.
Bond of guardian.
Discharge only after accounting,
§28-2504.
Guardians.
Bond of guardian.
Discharge only after accounting,
§28-2504.
Housing finance agency.
Payments out of accounts,
§42-2704.11.
**Interest on Lawyers Trust Account
(IOLTA),** DCBar Appx A, DCBar
Rule X, ProfCond Rule 1.15.
Approved depositories, DCBar Rule XI.
Verification of participation, DCBar
Rule XIV.
Intervention proceedings.
Conservators, Probate Rule 330.
Audit of accounts, Probate Rule 331.
Missing persons, Probate Rule 351.
Termination of conservatorship,
Probate Rule 334.
Joint accounts, §§26-801 to 26-804.
Masters.
Statement of accounts, CivPro Rule
53.
Domestic relations actions, DomRel
Rule 53.
Mayor's duties, §1-204.49.
Mortgage lenders and brokers.
Escrow accounts, §26-1115.
Multiple-party accounts.
Nonprobate transfers on death,
§§19-601.01 to 19-602.27.
See NONPROBATE TRANSFERS.
Opportunity accounts, §§1-307.61 to
1-307.74.
Probate proceedings.
Death before January 1, 1981, Probate
Rule 19.
Death between January 1, 1981 and
June 30, 1995, Probate Rules 114
to 119.
Death on or after July 1, 1995,
Probate Forms 18 to 20, Probate
Rules 414 to 419.
Financial account information, Probate
Form 27.
Exclusion from filed documents,
Probate Rule 5.1.

ACCOUNTS AND ACCOUNTING
—Cont'd
Probate proceedings —Cont'd
Guardians, conservators, trustees, etc.,
involved, Probate Rules 204, 221.
Costs for accounts, Probate Rule
206.
Failure to account, Probate Rule
207.
Fiduciaries authorized to file
consents, Probate Rule 205.
Missing persons, Probate Rule 351.
Sale of property, Probate Rule 203.
Personal representatives.
See PERSONAL
REPRESENTATIVES.
Revolving credit accounts, §§28-3701,
28-3702.
Consumers' remedies, §§28-3812,
28-3813.
Defined, §28-3802.
Trusts and trustees.
Bond of trustee.
Discharge only after accounting,
§28-2504.
Custodial trustee, §19-1115.
Limitation of actions against
trustee, §19-1116.

**ACHIEVING A BETTER LIFE
EXPERIENCE (ABLE) ACT.**
ABLE savings accounts, §§47-4901,
47-4902.

ACKNOWLEDGMENTS.
Assignments for benefit of creditors,
§28-2103.
**Guam, Samoa, and Panama Canal
Zone,** §42-111.
**Improperly executed or
acknowledged instruments,**
§42-407.
Notarial acts, §§42-141 to 42-148.
Parentage.
Voluntary acknowledgment based on
genetic testing, §16-909.01.
Philippines and Puerto Rico, §42-112.
Power of attorney, §42-101.
Superior court judges.
Judges' oaths, §11-905.
Power to administer oaths, §11-945.

**ACQUIRED IMMUNE DEFICIENCY
SYNDROME.**
General provisions.
See AIDS.

ACQUITTAL, CrimPro Rule 29.
Delinquent minors, JuvProc Rule 29.

ACQUITTAL —Cont'd
Insanity defense, §24-501.
Joinder of parties.
Discharge or acquittal of joint
defendant in order to be witness,
§23-107.

ACTIONS.
Account, actions of, §16-101.
Aliens.
Suits against state, US Const Amd 11.
Anti-SLAPP, §§16-5501 to 16-5505.
Applicability of provisions, §16-5505.
Definitions, §16-5501.
Dismissal motions, §16-5502.
Fees and costs, §16-5504.
Quash motions, §16-5503.
Arbitration.
General provisions, §§16-4401 to
16-4432.
See ARBITRATION.
Asbestos contractors.
Civil actions, §8-111.10.
Civil I calendar cases, CivPro Rule
40-II.
Criminal actions, §8-111.09.
Summary actions, §8-111.07.
Assignment of choses in action,
§§28-2301 to 28-2305.
Assignments for benefit of creditors.
Assignee's actions, §28-2106.
Assistive technology warranty.
Recovery of damages, §28-4034.
Attachment.
See ATTACHMENT.
**Attorney discipline or disability
proceedings,** DCBar Rule XI,
USDistCt LCrR 57.27, USDistCt
LCvR 83.16.
Family court proceedings generally,
FamDiv Rule S.
Attorneys' fees.
See ATTORNEYS' FEES.
Benefit corporations.
Benefit enforcement proceedings,
§29-1303.05.
Defined, §29-1301.02.
Restrictions on actions against
corporation, §29-1303.05.
Bicycles.
Assault or battery of bicyclist by
motorist.
Right of civil action for damages,
§50-1621.
Bonds, surety.
Actions on bonds.
Bonds in a penal sum containing an
avoidance condition, §28-2502.

ACTIONS —Cont'd
Bonds, surety —Cont'd
Actions on bonds —Cont'd
Bond to United States, §28-2503.
Building code.
Failure to fireproof building.
Injunctive relief, §6-601.08.
Business licenses.
Action to enforce provisions, §47-2844.
Charitable solicitations, §44-1712.
Child custody.
De facto parent, action brought by, §16-831.03.
Minor parent, right to initiate action, §16-914.
Third-party, action brought by, §16-831.02.
Child fatality or near fatality.
Public disclosure of findings and information.
Civil action to compel disclosure, §4-1303.33.
Children, actions involving, §21-120.
Child support enforcement, §46-224.
Choses in action.
Assignment of choses in action, §§28-2301 to 28-2305.
"Civil action" as single form of action, CivPro Rule 2.
Civil procedure rules generally.
See Court Rules Volume.
Class actions, CivPro Rule 23-I, USDistCt LCvR 23.1.
Joinder of parties exception, CivPro Rule 19.
Unincorporated associations, CivPro Rule 23.2.
Commencement of action.
See COMMENCEMENT OF ACTIONS.
Common carrier employees, actions for injuries to, §§35-301 to 35-305.
Condemnation of property, CivPro Rule 71A.
Condominiums, §42-1904.12.
Conservation easements.
Persons eligible to bring actions, §42-203.
Constitution of the United States.
Actions to which United States a party, US Const Art III §2.
Consumer credit sales.
Consumers' remedies, §28-3813.
Creditors' actions, §28-3812.
Consumer credit service organizations.
Recovery of damages.
Violations of chapter, §28-4607.

ACTIONS —Cont'd
Consumer protection.
Consumers' remedies, §28-3813.
Creditors' actions, §28-3812.
Damages, §28-3905.
Continuing care retirement communities.
Violations.
Recovery allowed, limitation of action, §44-151.14.
Cooperative associations.
Powers, §29-905.
Corporations.
Powers, §29-303.02.
Counterclaims, §§13-501 to 13-505.
Court costs.
See COSTS.
Crime investigation records.
Cause of action for willful or malicious tampering with records, §5-113.33.
Crime victims' compensation.
Preservation of civil actions, §4-509, VictComp Rule 40.
Criminal procedure.
See CRIMINAL PROCEDURE.
Criminal proceedings.
Applicability of civil division rules, CrimPro Rule 57.
Custodial trustees, claims for relief against.
Limitation of actions, §19-1116.
Damages.
See DAMAGES.
Death, survival of rights of action following, §12-101.
Derivative actions.
See DERIVATIVE ACTIONS.
Derivative actions by shareholders, CivPro Rule 23.1.
Discovery.
See DISCOVERY.
Dishonored checks.
Merchants.
Civil recovery by, §28-3152.
Dismissal of actions.
See DISMISSAL OF ACTIONS.
Dog bites, §8-1812.
Dangerous dog.
Generally, §§8-1901 to 8-1908.
See DANGEROUS DOGS.
Domestic relations actions.
Court rules, DomRel Rules 1 to 406.
See DOMESTIC RELATIONS ACTIONS.
Private right of action, §16-1002.
Drug, firearm, or prostitution-related nuisance abatement, §42-3102.

ACTIONS —Cont'd

Drug haven, action for possession of rental unit used as, §42-3602.

Ejectment, §§16-1101 to 16-1124.
See EJECTMENT.

Emergency medical services.
Continuation of existing actions and proceedings, §7-2341.28.

Eminent domain.
General provisions, §§16-1301 to 16-1385.
See EMINENT DOMAIN.

Employee paid leave.
Cause of action for violations, §32-131.12.

Environmental covenants.
Enforcement, §8-671.10.

Evidence.
See EVIDENCE.

Federal benefit payments under District programs, §§1-815.01 to 1-815.04.

Financial Responsibility and Management Assistance Authority, §§47-391.04, 47-391.05.

Forcible entry and detainer.
Generally, §§16-1501 to 16-1505.

Foreclosure rescue services.
Private right of action, §42-2434.

Foreign judgment enforcement, §15-356.

Frivolous actions.
Appeals, DCCtApp Rule 38.
Attorney not to assert frivolous claims, ProfCond Rule 3.1.
Sanctions, CivPro Rule 11.
Domestic relations actions, DomRel Rule 11.

Gaming losses, recovery, §16-1702.

Garnishment.
See GARNISHMENT.

Gas station marketing agreements, §36-303.06.

Gross sales tax collections, §§47-2004, 47-2007.

Habeas corpus.
General provisions, §§16-1901 to 16-1909.
See HABEAS CORPUS.

Hate crimes, §22-3704.

Hazardous materials transportation.
Strict liability for releases during transport.
Action to recover costs, §8-1444.

Hazardous substance releases.
Compliance, §8-634.07.

ACTIONS —Cont'd

Hazardous substance releases —Cont'd
Contribution, §8-634.09.

Hearing commissioners, CivPro Rule 73.
Assignment of civil actions to commissioners, CivPro Rule 40-I.
Collection and subrogation cases, CivPro Rule 40-III.

Insanitary building actions under prior law, §6-919.

Installment loans.
Consumers' remedies, §28-3813.
Creditors' actions, §28-3812.

Insurance companies.
Unauthorized entities.
Administrative and judicial enforcement, §31-233.

Intellectual disabilities, persons with.
Actions to compel rights, §7-1305.13.

Interest.
Action to recover usury paid, §28-3304.
Parties compelled to testify, §28-3306.
Unlawful interest credited on principal debt, §28-3305.

Interpleader, CivPro Rule 22.
Complaint for interpleader, CivPro Form CA 18.
Counterclaim for interpleader, CivPro Form CA 21.

Intrafamily proceedings.
Private right of action, §16-1002.

Joint contracts, §§16-2101 to 16-2106.

Judicial directives, CivPro Rule 83.

Jury trials.
See JURIES AND JURY TRIALS.

Landlord's use and occupation actions, §42-3221.

Lead-hazard prevention and elimination.
Action against District not authorized by provisions, §8-231.17.

Lease-purchase agreements.
Consumer remedies, §42-3671.12.
Limitation of action, §42-3671.13.

Limitation of actions, §§12-301 to 12-311.
See LIMITATION OF ACTIONS.

Limited cooperative associations.
See LIMITED COOPERATIVE ASSOCIATIONS.

Limited liability partnerships.
Liability for improper distributions, §29-610.03.

ACTIONS —Cont'd
Limited partnerships.
See LIMITED PARTNERSHIPS.
Lis pendens notice, §42-1207.
Marriage of party, effect of, §12-104.
Medical malpractice.
General provisions, §§16-2801 to
16-2841.
See MEDICAL MALPRACTICE.
**Metropolitan police actions taken
based on citizen complaints,**
§5-1112.
Mortgages and deeds of trust.
Foreclosure rescue services.
Private right of action, §42-2434.
Pending actions involving, §§42-805 to
42-807.
Motions.
See MOTIONS.
Negotiable instruments.
Accrual and limitation of actions,
§28:3-118.
Nonprofit corporations, §29-403.02.
Not-for-profit hospital corporations.
Notice requirements, §44-951.14.
Notice.
Pendency of action (lis pendens),
§42-1207.
One form of action, CivPro Rule 2.
Domestic relations actions, DomRel
Rule 2.
Open meetings act violation, §2-579.
Paid leave.
Cause of action for violations,
§32-131.12.
Parentage proceedings.
General provisions, §§16-2341 to
16-2348.
See PARENTAGE PROCEEDINGS.
Parties.
See PARTIES.
Partnerships, §§29-603.07, 29-604.08.
Court action to require person to sign
or file record, §29-601.10.
**Pensions and retirement for public
officers and employees,**
§§1-626.14, 1-747, 1-748.
Phosphate cleaners, §8-107.03.
Pleadings.
See PLEADINGS.
Police complaints, office of, §5-1112.
**Pregnant and nursing workers,
reasonable accommodations for.**
Civil action, enforcement by,
§32-1231.09.
**Prescription drugs, excessive
pricing,** §28-4555.

ACTIONS —Cont'd
Pretrial conferences.
See PRETRIAL CONFERENCES.
Private detectives.
Suits by injured parties against,
§5-121.01.
Private right of action.
See PRIVATE RIGHT OF ACTION.
Procurement violations, §2-381.03.
Public assistance.
Nonabatement of causes of action,
§4-220.02.
Public records management, §2-1713.
Quo warranto.
General provisions, §§16-3501 to
16-3548.
See QUO WARRANTO.
Real estate tax sales, §47-1313.
Real property actions.
Form of pleadings, CivPro Rule 3-I.
**Real property tax assessments, class
actions as to,** §47-827.
Rental housing.
Conversion and sale, §§42-3405.03 to
42-3405.03b.
Drug haven, action for possession of
rental unit used as, §42-3602.
Rent control.
Tenant organization.
Right to assert claim in name of
member, §42-3502.16a.
Replevin.
General provisions, §§16-3701 to
16-3713.
See REPLEVIN.
Restraints of trade, §28-4507.
Indirect purchasers, §28-4509.
Judgment in favor of District of
Columbia as prima facie evidence,
§28-4510.
Limitation on actions, §28-4511.
Relief for private parties, §28-4508.
Remedies cumulative, §28-4514.
**Retirement Board fiduciary
responsibilities,** §§1-747, 1-748.
Revolving credit accounts.
Consumers' remedies, §28-3813.
Limitation on creditors' remedies,
§28-3812.
Security agents and brokers.
Civil liability, §31-5606.04.
Service of process.
Generally, §§13-301 to 13-341.
See SERVICE OF PROCESS AND
PAPERS.
Long-arm statute, §§13-401 to 13-434.
See LONG-ARM STATUTE.

ACTIONS —Cont'd
Shoplifting.
Merchant's recovery of civil damages, §§27-101 to 27-106.
Spam deterrence, §28-5003.
Statutory trusts, §29-1203.08.
Beneficial owners.
Action for improper distribution, §29-1206.16.
Derivative actions, §29-1206.10.
Complaint, contents, §29-1206.12.
Proceeds, costs and fees, §29-1206.13.
Proper plaintiff, §29-1206.11.
Settlement requiring court approval, §29-1206.13.
Special litigation committee, §29-1206.14.
Direct actions, §29-1206.09.
Trust management and trustees, §29-1205.03.
Stay of proceedings.
See STAYS.
Substitution of parties, §12-102.
Summons.
See SUMMONS AND PROCESS.
Survival of rights of action following death, §12-101.
Taxation.
Levy for failure to pay.
Wrongful distraint, §47-4479.
Telecommunications competition, §34-2003.01.
Telephone solicitation.
Private right of action, §22-3226.11.
Tenant organization.
Right to assert claim on behalf of member, §42-3502.16a.
Termination of parental rights.
General provisions, §§16-2351 to 16-2365.
See TERMINATION OF PARENTAL RIGHTS.
Testimony.
Perpetuation by action.
Depositions not limiting power of court to entertain action, CivPro Rule 27, DomRel Rule 27.
Theft of electric or natural gas utility service.
Civil liability in addition to criminal penalties, §22-3218.04.
Unclaimed property.
Action to compel delivery of, §41-133.

ACTIONS —Cont'd
Unclaimed property —Cont'd
Reciprocal actions and agreements, §41-134.
Unemployment compensation, §51-121.
Usury.
Recovery of usury paid, §28-3304.
Parties compelled to testify, §28-3306.
Unlawful interest credited on principal debt, §28-3305.
Water pollution, §§8-103.18, 8-103.19.
Workplace fraud.
Private right of action to enforce provisions, §32-1331.09.
Wrongful death.
Generally, §§16-2701 to 16-2703.

ACTS OF CONGRESS.
Congress generally.
See CONGRESS.
Interpretation of provisions, §45-401.

ACTS OF TERRORISM.
See TERRORISM.

ACT TO SECURE THE ATTENDANCE OF WITNESSES FROM WITHOUT A STATE IN CRIMINAL PROCEEDINGS, §§23-1501 to 23-1504.

ACUPUNCTURE.
Advisory committee, §7-743.02.
Board of medicine.
Advisory committee on acupuncture, §3-1202.03.
Definition of practice of, §3-1201.02.
Health occupations boards.
General provisions, §§3-1201.01 to 3-1213.01.
See HEALTH OCCUPATIONS BOARDS.
Health occupations licensure, registration or certification, §§3-1205.01 to 3-1205.24.
See HEALTH OCCUPATIONS LICENSURE, REGISTRATION OR CERTIFICATION.
Registered acupuncture therapists, §3-1209.03.
Titles and terms prohibited as misrepresentation without license to practice, §3-1210.03.

**ADAMS MORGAN HOTEL
DEVELOPMENT PROJECT.**
Real property tax exemptions,
§47-4652.

ADDICTION COUNSELORS,
§§3-1208.51 to 3-1208.54.
**Advanced practice addiction
counselor,** §3-1208.53.
Board of professional counseling,
§3-1202.13.
Certified addiction counselor I,
§3-1208.51.
Certified addiction counselor II,
§3-1208.52.
**Definition of practice of addiction
counseling,** §3-1201.02.
**Health occupations licensure,
registration or certification,**
§§3-1205.01 to 3-1205.24.
See HEALTH OCCUPATIONS
LICENSURE, REGISTRATION
OR CERTIFICATION.
**Titles and terms prohibited as
misrepresentation without
license to practice,** §3-1210.03.
Waiver of requirements, §3-1208.54.

ADDICTION RECOVERY FUND,
§7-3004.

ADDICTION SERVICES.
Pay-for-success contracts, §§2-211.01
to 2-211.03.

**ADJUDICATION OF TRAFFIC
TICKETS,** §§50-2301.01 to
50-2305.02.
See TRAFFIC TICKET
ADJUDICATION.

ADMINISTRATION OF ESTATES,
§§20-701 to 20-753.
After-discovered property, §20-1304.
Appraisal.
Reappraisal, §20-713.
Supervised administration, §§20-712,
20-713.
Unsupervised administration,
§20-713.01.
Certificate of completion, filing,
§20-735.
**Closing, subsequent administration
after,** §20-1304.
Decedents' estates.
See DECEDENTS' ESTATES.
Inventory, §20-711.
Revision of, §20-714.
Rights of heir or legatee regarding,
§20-733.

ADMINISTRATION OF ESTATES
—Cont'd
Inventory —Cont'd
Successor personal representative,
§20-715.
Supplemental inventory, §20-713.
Unsupervised administration,
§20-713.01.
Waiver on filing, §20-731.
Notice.
Appointment of personal
representative, §20-704.
Sale or transfer of property, §20-703.
Personal representatives, §§20-401 to
20-406.
See PERSONAL
REPRESENTATIVES.
**Priorities and preferences,
establishing,** §20-703.
Probate proceedings.
General provisions, §§16-3101 to
16-3112, Probate Rules 1 to 430.
See PROBATE PROCEEDINGS.
Reappraisal, §20-713.
Records and accounts.
Certificate of completion, filing,
§20-735.
Duty to account, §20-721.
Failure to render account, §20-725.
Filing revised or corrected documents,
§20-705.
Finality, §20-736.
Initial account, §20-722.
Inventory. See within this heading,
"Inventory."
Objections to accounts, filing, §20-726.
Rights of heir or legatee regarding,
§20-733.
Subsequent account, §20-723.
Supervised administration, §§20-721
to 20-726.
Time to render account, §20-724.
Unsupervised administration, §20-734.
Waiver of audit of account, §20-732.
Sale or transfer of property, §20-703.
Statutory rule against perpetuities,
§§19-901 to 19-907.

ADMINISTRATIVE FINES,
§§2-1801.01 to 2-1803.03.
Administrative agency review,
§§2-1803.01 to 2-1803.03.
Administrative law judges,
§2-1801.03.
Answer to notice of infraction,
§2-1802.02.
Appeals, §§2-1803.01 to 2-1803.03.
Costs, §2-1803.02.

ADMINISTRATIVE FINES —Cont'd
Appeals —Cont'd
Jurisdiction to hear, §2-1803.01.
Right to, §2-1803.02.
Scope, §2-1803.03.
Asbestos contractors, §8-111.09.
Attorney examiners, §2-1801.03.
Bees.
Enforcement of subchapter,
§8-1825.09.
Business licenses.
Unpaid fines or penalties.
Computer record-keeping and
reporting system, §47-2866.
Definitions, §47-2861.
Right to appeal denial, §47-2865.
Self-certification of lack of
outstanding debt, §47-2863.
Falsification of certification,
penalty, §47-2864.
Definitions, §§2-1801.02, 2-1801.03.
Final decisions as to, §2-1802.04.
Hearings, §2-1802.03.
**Issuance of rules and regulations
regarding,** §2-1801.05.
**Natural disaster consumer
protection.**
Overcharging, §28-4103.
Notice of infraction, §2-1802.01.
Policy declaration, §2-1801.01.
Procedures, §§2-1802.01 to 2-1802.05.
Schedule of, §2-1801.04.
Schools and education.
Testing integrity in public schools.
Sanctions for violations, §38-771.04.
Service of notice or order regarding,
§2-1802.05.
Summary actions, §2-1801.06.
Testing integrity in public schools.
Sanctions for violations, §38-771.04.
Workplace fraud.
Complaints, investigation,
§32-1331.05.
Penalties for violation of provisions,
§32-1331.07.
Zoning.
Inclusionary zoning.
Civil infractions, §6-1041.04.

**ADMINISTRATIVE HEARINGS,
OFFICE OF,** §§2-1831.01 to
2-1831.18.
Administrative law judges.
Appointment, qualifications, term,
compensation, §2-1831.08.
Chief judge serving as, authority,
§2-1831.05.

**ADMINISTRATIVE HEARINGS,
OFFICE OF** —Cont'd
Administrative law judges —Cont'd
Commission on selection and tenure of
administrative law judges,
§2-1831.07.
Discipline and removal, §2-1831.10.
Power, duties and liability, §2-1831.09.
Reappointment, §2-1831.10.
Rules governing appointment,
reappointment and discipline,
§2-1831.11.
Senior administrative law judge.
Former chief administrative law
judge, §2-1831.04.
Advisory committee to office,
§2-1831.17.
Agencies.
Representation in case before office,
§2-1831.14.
Appeals from orders.
Retention of jurisdiction by agency,
§2-1831.16.
Attorneys.
Representation of parties in case
before office, §2-1831.14.
Audit and examination of office,
§2-1831.13.
Chief administrative law judge.
Head of office, appointment and
removal, term, compensation,
§2-1831.04.
Powers and duties, §2-1831.05.
Summary of caseload, §2-1831.13.
Clerk and deputy clerks, §2-1831.12.
**Commission on selection and tenure
of administrative law judges.**
Established, §2-1831.06.
Indemnification, §2-415.
Members, §2-1831.07.
Conflicts with other authority.
Act to take precedence, §2-1831.15.
Contempt.
Show cause orders.
Authority of administrative law
judge to apply for, §2-1831.09.
Continuing education.
Administrative law judge to
participate in program,
§2-1831.09.
**Cooperation of other government
agencies,** §2-1831.13.
Corporations.
Representation in case before office,
§2-1831.14.
Declaration in lieu of oath.
Filing with office, §2-1831.13.

ADMINISTRATIVE HEARINGS, OFFICE OF —Cont'd
Definitions, §2-1831.01.
Effective date for commencing activities, §2-1831.02.
Established as independent agency, §2-1831.02.
Executive director.
Appointment, qualifications, §2-1831.12.
Fiscal and operational impact of proposed agency rules.
Rules affecting types of cases heard by office, §2-1831.13.
Hearing officers in agencies.
Eligibility to be appointed administrative law judge, §2-1831.08.
Homeless services.
Fair hearings, §4-754.41.
Administrative review, §4-754.42.
Influencing decisionmaking, prohibition, §2-1831.13.
Judicial review of order, §2-1831.16.
Jurisdiction, §2-1831.03.
Limited partnerships.
Representation in case before office, §2-1831.14.
Orders or interlocutory orders of administrative law judges.
Effective upon issuance, §2-1831.16.
Failure to comply, §2-1831.09.
Other personnel, §2-1831.12.
Partnerships.
Representation in case before office, §2-1831.14.
Practice of law.
Administrative law judges, prohibition, §2-1831.09.
Procurement practices act.
Applicability to office, §2-1831.02.
Public review of document filed with office, §2-1831.13.
Reconsideration of order, motion, §2-1831.16.
Representation of parties in cases before office, §2-1831.14.
Self-representation in case before office, §2-1831.14.
Senior administrative law judge.
Former chief administrative law judge, §2-1831.04.
Summary of caseload.
Chief administrative law judge to prepare, §2-1831.13.
Taxation.
Assessments, protest of, §47-4312.

ADMINISTRATIVE HEARINGS, OFFICE OF —Cont'd
Taxation —Cont'd
Intermediate care facilities for persons with intellectual disabilities.
Appeal of assessments, §47-1276.
Jeopardy assessments, protest of, §47-4451.
Nursing facility assessments.
Appeals, §47-1266.
Refund offsets, protest of, §47-4312.

ADMINISTRATIVE LAW JUDGES.
Office of administrative hearings, §§2-1831.01 to 2-1831.18.
See ADMINISTRATIVE HEARINGS, OFFICE OF.

ADMINISTRATIVE PROCEDURE, §§2-501 to 2-562.
Appeal of administrative orders and decisions, §§17-303, 17-304.
Bond, DCCtApp Rule 19.
Conditions pending appeal, DCCtApp Rule 19.
Costs, DCCtApp Rule 39.
Fees, DCCtApp Rule 15.
Indigent persons.
Proceedings in forma pauperis, DCCtApp Rule 24.
Intervention, DCCtApp Rule 15.
Judicial review of administrative procedure, §2-510.
Merit system decisions, CivPro Agency Review Rule 1.
Final decision affecting performance rating, §1-606.03.
Petition for review, CivPro Agency Review Rule 1.
Petitions for review, DCCtApp Rule 15.
Record on review, DCCtApp Rules 16, 17.
Records access, administrative appeals regarding, §2-537.
Rules applicable, DCCtApp Rule 20.
Stay pending appeal, DCCtApp Rule 18.
Traffic adjudication appeals board decisions, CivPro Agency Review Rule 2.
Application for leave to appeal, CivPro Agency Review Rule 2.
Appeal of administrative orders and decisions, federal rules.
Applicability of rules, FRAP 20.
Application for enforcement, FRAP 15.

ADMINISTRATIVE PROCEDURE
—Cont'd
Appeal of administrative orders and decisions, federal rules —Cont'd
Docketing of appeals, USCtApp HPIP Rule IV(b).
Docketing statement, USCtApp Rule 15.
Enforcement of orders.
How obtained, USCtApp HPIP Rule III(f)(1).
Timing, USCtApp HPIP Rule III(f)(2).
Extension of time for filing petition, etc., FRAP 26(b).
Federal Labor Relations Authority proceedings.
Briefs and oral argument, USCtApp Rule 15.1.
National Labor Relations Board proceedings.
Briefs and oral argument, FRAP 15.1, USCtApp Rule 15.1.
Petition, FRAP 15, FRAP Form 3.
Record.
Filing, FRAP 17, USCtApp Rule 17.
Generally, FRAP 16.
Review of orders.
How obtained, USCtApp HPIP Rule III(e)(1).
Intervention, USCtApp HPIP Rule III(e)(3).
Timing, USCtApp HPIP Rule III(e)(2).
Rules to govern, FRAP 1.
Settlement of judgments enforcing orders, FRAP 19.
Stay and emergency relief pending review, FRAP 18, USCtApp Rule 18.
Applicability of provisions, §2-501.
Compilation of rules and regulations, §2-507.
Consumer protection.
Department of consumer and regulatory affairs, §28-3902.
Contested cases, §2-509.
Office of administrative hearings, §§2-1831.01 to 2-1831.18.
See ADMINISTRATIVE HEARINGS, OFFICE OF.
Declaratory orders, §2-508.
Definitions, §2-502.
Emergency medical services.
Rulemaking, §7-2341.23.
Emergency rules, §2-505.

ADMINISTRATIVE PROCEDURE
—Cont'd
Establishment of, §2-503.
Freedom of information, §§2-531 to 2-540.
See FREEDOM OF INFORMATION.
Housing finance agency, §42-2705.01.
Interpreters, §2-1902.
Judicial review, §2-510.
Lead-hazard prevention and elimination.
Rulemaking, incorporating federal regulations by reference, §8-231.18.
Legal publication of documents, §§2-551 to 2-562.
Office of administrative hearings, §§2-1831.01 to 2-1831.18.
See ADMINISTRATIVE HEARINGS, OFFICE OF.
Open meeting requirement, §1-207.42.
Publication of documents, §§2-504, 2-551 to 2-562.
See PUBLICATION.
Public participation in rulemaking, §2-505.
Rental housing conversion and sale, §42-3405.08.
Testing integrity in public schools.
Sanctions for violations.
Administrative review, §38-771.05.
Transcripts of meetings, §1-207.42.

ADMINISTRATIVE SEARCH WARRANTS, CivPro Rule 204.

ADMIRALTY.
Constitution of the United States, US Const Art I §8.
Jurisdiction of courts, US Const Art III §2.
Interpretation of principles of admiralty, §45-401.

ADMISSIONS.
Discovery.
Requests for admission, CivPro Rule 36.
Adoption proceedings, Adoption Rule 36.
Domestic relations actions, DomRel Rule 36.
Form, CivPro Form CA 25.
General provisions governing discovery, CivPro Rule 26, USDistCt LCvR 26.2.

ADOPTION, §§16-301 to 16-317.
Abused and neglected children, §§4-1361, 4-1362.
Admission to courtroom, Adoption Rule 53.
Appeal of grant or denial of petition.
Expedited review in court of appeals, §11-721.
Attorneys at law.
Appearance and withdrawal of attorney, Adoption Rule 101.
Appointment and compensation, §16-316.
Confidentiality requirements, Adoption Rule 79-I.
Birth certificates, §16-314.
New certificates of birth, §7-210.
Case summaries, Adoption Rule 79-I.
Child custody.
Uniform child custody proceedings, §§16-4601.01 to 16-4605.03.
See CHILD CUSTODY AND CHILD CUSTODY PROCEEDINGS.
Child equivalent to adopted child in instruments, §16-313.
Confidentiality.
Notice of adoption proceedings, Adoption Rule 4.
Records, Adoption Rule 79-I.
Show cause hearings, Adoption Rule 39.
Consent required for, §16-304.
Contact with birth parents.
Post-adoption contact agreements, §4-361.
Costs, Adoption Rule 54.
Exempt petitioners, §15-719.
Failure to attend deposition, Adoption Rule 30.
Decree of adoption, Adoption Rules 7, 52.
Entry of decree, Adoption Rule 58.
Relief from decree, Adoption Rule 60.
Definitions, Adoption Rule 2.
Disabled children.
Interstate compact on adoption and medical assistance, §§4-321 to 4-328.
Discovery and disclosure of information, Adoption Rule 26.
Depositions, Adoption Rules 30, 31.
Persons before whom depositions may be taken, Adoption Rule 28.
Use of depositions, Adoption Rule 32.

ADOPTION —Cont'd
Discovery and disclosure of information —Cont'd
Interrogatories, Adoption Rule 33.
Noncompliance, Adoption Rule 37.
Physical and mental examination of persons, Adoption Rule 35.
Production of documents and things, Adoption Rule 34.
Requests for admission, Adoption Rule 36.
Stipulations regarding discovery procedure, Adoption Rule 29.
Domestic partnerships, §16-909.
Eligibility to adopt, §16-302.
Eligibility to be adopted, §16-303.
Expedited response, Adoption Rules 4, 7.
Family and medical leave for, §32-502.
Family court proceedings, §11-1101.
Fees by child-placing agencies, §4-1410.
Filing of papers with court, Adoption Rule 5.
Final decrees, §§16-309, 16-310.
Findings of the court, Adoption Rule 52.
Foreign adoptions.
New certificates of birth, §7-210.
Forms, §7-209.
Funds.
Adoption support fund, §4-344.01.
Adoption voucher fund, §4-344.
Guardian ad litem.
Appointment and compensation, §16-316.
Harmless error, Adoption Rule 61.
Incentive program and special funds, §§4-341 to 4-346.
Administration, §4-346.
Adoption support fund, §4-344.01.
Adoption voucher fund, §4-344.
Benefits, §4-345.
Definitions, §4-342.
Establishment, §4-343.
Legislative findings, §4-341.
Inspection of adoption records, §16-311.
Interpreters, Adoption Rule 43.
Interstate compact on adoption and medical assistance, §§4-321 to 4-328.
Compacts authorized, §4-325.
Contents, §§4-326, 4-327.
Definitions, §4-321.

ADOPTION —Cont'd
Interstate compact on adoption and medical assistance —Cont'd
Federal participation, §4-328.
Findings, §4-322.
Medical assistance, §4-324.
Purposes, §4-323.
Interstate compact on placement of children, §§4-1421 to 4-1424.
Agreements with other state for placement, §4-1423.
Authority to enter into and execute compact, §4-1422.
Definitions, §4-1421.
Delinquent children.
Administrative hearing on placement, review, §4-1424.
Intervention, Adoption Rule 24.
Invalidation of final decrees of, §16-310.
Investigations, §§16-307, 16-308.
Judge's bias, prejudice, or inability to proceed, Adoption Rule 63.
Jurisdiction, §16-301.
Legal effects of, §16-312.
Motions, Adoption Rule 8.
Amendment of decree, Adoption Rule 60.
Appearance and withdrawal of attorneys, Adoption Rule 101.
Compelling discovery or disclosure, Adoption Rule 37.
New trial, Adoption Rule 60.
Terminating or limiting deposition, Adoption Rule 30.
Natural parenthood, establishing relationship of, §16-312.
Notice of proceedings, §16-306, Adoption Rule 4.
Opposition to adoption, Adoption Rule 12.
Motions, Adoption Rule 8.
Parent-child relationship, proof of, §16-909.
Parties, Adoption Rule 17.
Death or incompetency of party, Adoption Rule 25.
Persons who may adopt, §16-302.
Persons who may be adopted, §16-303.
Petition for, §16-305, Adoption Rule 7.
Physical and mental examination of persons, Adoption Rule 35.
Pleadings, Adoption Rule 7.
Amended and supplemental pleadings, Adoption Rule 15.

ADOPTION —Cont'd
Pleadings —Cont'd
Form and content, Adoption Rules 10, 11.
Post-adoption contact agreements, §4-361.
Prior proceedings, effect of current law on, §16-315.
Proceedings, §16-309.
Protective orders, Adoption Rule 26.
Public welfare institutions, from, §§4-301, 4-302.
Recommendation, §16-307, Adoption Rule 7.
Records, §16-311, Adoption Rules 79, 79-I, FamDiv Rule P.
Reference orders, Adoption Rules 4, 7.
Reports, §16-307, Adoption Rule 7.
Physical and mental examination of persons, Adoption Rule 35.
Revocation of consent or relinquishment, Adoption Rule 70.
Schedule of proceedings, Adoption Rule 16.
Show cause hearings, Adoption Rule 39.
Scope of rules, Adoption Rule 1.
Service of process, Adoption Rule 5.
Motions, Adoption Rule 8.
Notice of adoption proceedings, Adoption Rule 4.
Time for service, Adoption Rule 6.
Show cause hearings, Adoption Rule 39.
Special needs children.
Interstate compact on adoption and medical assistance, §§4-321 to 4-328.
Spouse of natural parent, by, §16-308.
Stays, Adoption Rule 62.
Stipulations, Adoption Rule 8.
Discovery procedures, Adoption Rule 29.
Subpoenas, Adoption Rule 45.
Time periods contained in rules, Adoption Rule 6.
Transcripts of proceedings, Adoption Rule 201.
Depositions, Adoption Rule 30.
Trials, Adoption Rule 43.
Consolidation or bifurcation, Adoption Rule 42.
Findings of the court, Adoption Rule 52.
Proof of official record, statute, etc., Adoption Rule 44.

ADOPTION —Cont'd
Vital records, §7-209.
  Birth certificates, §§7-210, 16-314.

**ADOPTION OF IMPOUNDED
  ANIMALS,** §8-1807.

ADOPTION OF PARKS, §10-304.

ADOPTIVE SEIZURES.
Civil asset forfeiture, §41-311.

ADULT EDUCATION PROGRAMS.
DC promise grant awards, §38-2757.
Employment services department.
  Job training and adult education
    programs.
    Quarterly reporting by department,
      §32-771.
School board, §§38-1001 to 38-1003.
**Uniform per-student funding
  formula,** §§38-2901 to 38-2914.

**ADULTERATION OF FOOD OR
  DRUGS,** §§48-101 to 48-110.
**Administrative remedies for
  enforcement,** §48-108.01.
Analysis of samples, §§48-106, 48-107.
Complaints, investigation of, §48-105.
Definitions, §§48-102, 48-103.
Disposition of adulterated goods,
  §48-101.
Enforcement of provisions, §48-104.
  Administrative remedies, §48-108.01.
**Interference with officials,
  prohibition of,** §48-108.
Interpretation of provisions, §48-110.
Investigations, §48-105.
Penalties, §48-109.
Possession of adulterated goods,
  §48-101.
Prosecutions, §48-109.
Repeal of inconsistent acts, §48-110.
Rulemaking, §48-104.

**ADULT GUARDIANSHIP AND
  PROTECTIVE PROCEEDINGS
  JURISDICTION ACT,**
  §§21-2401.01 to 21-2405.03.
See GUARDIAN AND WARD.

ADULT LITERACY.
Reports, §38-192.01.

ADULT PROTECTIVE SERVICES,
  §§7-1901 to 7-1913.
Criminal procedure, §7-1912.
Definitions, §7-1901.
Entitlement not created, §7-1905.
Fines, §7-1912.
Immunity, §7-1908.

ADULT PROTECTIVE SERVICES
  —Cont'd
Indigents, representation for,
  §7-1906.
Investigations, §7-1904.
Issuance of rules, §7-1909.
Orders for protection.
  Ex parte temporary protection orders,
    §7-1907.
  Provisional protection orders, §7-1906.
**Payment or reimbursement for
  costs,** §7-1910.
**Police officer to accompany APS
  worker when providing services,**
  §7-1905.
Protective order.
  When required to provide services,
    §7-1905.
Refusal of service by adult, §7-1905.
Reports, §§7-1903, 7-1913.
Required provision of services,
  §7-1905.
Waiver of privilege by professionals,
  §7-1911.

**ADVANCED REGISTERED
  NURSING,** §§3-1206.01 to
  3-1206.04.
Authorized acts, §§3-1206.01,
  3-1206.04.
Collaboration, §§3-1206.01, 3-1206.03.
Definition of practice of, §3-1201.02.
Health occupations boards.
  General provisions, §§3-1201.01 to
    3-1213.01.
    See HEALTH OCCUPATIONS
      BOARDS.
**Health occupations licensure,
  registration or certification,**
  §§3-1205.01 to 3-1205.24.
  See HEALTH OCCUPATIONS
    LICENSURE, REGISTRATION
    OR CERTIFICATION.
**Titles and terms prohibited as
  misrepresentation without
  license to practice,** §3-1210.03.

ADVANCEMENTS.
Corporations, §29-306.53.
  Court-ordered, §29-306.54.
Intestate succession, §19-319.
Limited partnerships.
  General partners, §29-704.09.
Nonprofit corporations, §29-406.53.
  Court-ordered, §29-406.54.
Partnerships, §29-604.01.
Statutory trustees, §29-1205.09.

ADVANCEMENTS —Cont'd
Unincorporated nonprofit associations.
Managers and members, §29-1123.
Wills, §18-307.

ADVERSE POSSESSION.
Ejectment, §§16-1103, 16-1113.
Quiet title, §16-3301.
Service by publication on nonresidents, §13-336.

ADVERTISING.
Alcoholic beverage licenses, §§25-763 to 25-766.
Exterior signs, §25-763.
False statements, §25-766.
Generally, §25-764.
Price displays.
Windows and doors, §25-765.
Signs, restrictions on use, §25-763.
Attorneys at law, ProfCond Rule 7.1.
Firm names and letterhead, ProfCond Rule 7.5.
Breastmilk bank and lactation support, §7-881.09.
Bus shelters.
Commercial advertising space, §9-1154.
Compensation to district government from advertising revenues, §9-1155.
Exemption from building code provisions pertaining to outdoor signs, §9-1159.
Capitol grounds, on, §10-503.14.
Condominium public offering statement, §42-1904.04.
Emergency medical services.
Advertising restrictions, §7-2341.20.
Food sold by false advertising, §37-201.22a.
Foreclosure rescue transactions or services, §42-2432.
Fraudulent, §22-1511.
Prosecution, §22-1512.
Hearing aid dealers.
Dishonest or misleading advertising.
Grounds for revocation and suspension of registration, §28-4006.
Lease-purchase agreements, §42-3671.10.
Legalized gambling and lotteries, §22-1718.
Life and health insurance guaranty association, §31-5416.
Life insurance companies, §31-4310.

ADVERTISING —Cont'd
Medicare supplement insurance filing requirements, §31-3708.
Misleading trade practices, §28-3904.
Mortgage lenders and brokers, §26-1116.
Mortgages and deeds of trust.
Foreclosure rescue transactions or services, §42-2432.
Outdoor signs, §§1-303.21 to 1-303.23.
Pawnbrokers, §47-2884.08.
Prescription drug pricing, §48-802.01.
Prison industries program, §24-231.05.
Real estate tax sales, §47-1309.
Schools and education.
Event sponsorships, §38-174.01.
My School DC EdFest sponsorship and advertising, §38-196.01.
State athletic activities, programs, and office fund.
Advertisements and sponsorships, §38-2671.
Turkey Bowl revenue generation and sponsorship, §38-2981.
Security agents and brokers.
Filing of sales and advertising literature, §31-5604.05.
Unlawful trade practices, §28-3904.

ADVISORY BOARD COMPANY.
Real property tax abatement, §§47-4665.01 to 47-4665.05.
Certification by mayor, §47-4665.05.
Community benefits, §47-4665.04.
Compliance with incentive and agreement, §47-4665.03.
Definitions, §47-4665.01.
Tax abatement, §47-4665.02.

ADVISORY JURIES, CivPro Rule 39.

ADVISORY NEIGHBORHOOD COMMISSIONS, §§1-309.01 to 1-309.36.
Alcoholic beverage control board.
Notice of applications, §1-309.10.
Allocations, §1-309.13.
Audit, §1-309.13.
Boundaries, §§1-309.01, 1-309.02, 1-309.08.
Bylaws, §1-309.11.
Checking and other accounts, establishing, §1-309.13.
Citizens' advisory mechanisms established by District agencies, §1-309.12.

ADVISORY NEIGHBORHOOD COMMISSIONS —Cont'd
Council assistance, §1-309.12.
Depository for funds, designating, §1-309.13.
Division of District into, §§1-309.01, 1-309.02.
Election of members, §§1-207.38, 1-309.06, 1-309.07, 1-309.09, 1-309.34.
Election ward task forces, §§1-1041.01, 1-1041.02.
Employees of, §1-309.13.
Establishment, §1-207.38.
Executive director.
  Office of ANC, §1-309.15.
Financial reports, §1-309.13.
Funding and accounts, §§1-309.13, 1-309.14.
Funds transferred from office of ANC, §1-309.15.
Meetings, §§1-309.11, 1-309.12.
  Open meeting act.
    Report as whether provision applicable, §2-575.
Membership generally, §§1-309.06, 1-309.33, 1-309.34.
Neighborhood groups, involving, §1-309.12.
Nomination of members by petition, §§1-309.05, 1-309.33.
Office of ANC.
  Executive director, §1-309.15.
  Report to council, §1-325.172.
Officers, §1-309.11.
Pawnbroker licenses.
  Notice to commissions prior to issuance, §47-2884.03.
Petitions for establishment of, §§1-309.04, 1-309.32.
Petty cash fund, §1-309.13.
Powers and duties, §§1-207.38, 1-309.10.
Publications of, §1-309.13.
Qualifications for membership, §§1-309.05, 1-309.33.
Regulations, §1-309.36.
Reports, §1-309.13.
Service area managers and coordinators, §1-309.12.
Single-member districts, §1-309.03.
Streets and alleys.
  Closing procedures, §9-202.02.
  Naming of public spaces, §9-204.07.
Subsequently established commissions, §1-309.35.

ADVISORY NEIGHBORHOOD COMMISSIONS —Cont'd
Succession, §1-309.03.
Winners of election, determining, §1-309.07.

ADVISORY NEIGHBORHOOD COMMISSIONS, OFFICE OF.
Executive director, §1-309.15.
Report to council, §1-325.172.

AED (AUTOMATED EXTERNAL DEFIBRILLATOR).
Usage, §§44-231 to 44-235.

AFDC.
Temporary assistance to needy families.
  General provisions, §§4-205.01 to 4-205.191.
  See TEMPORARY ASSISTANCE FOR NEEDY FAMILIES (TANF).

AFFIDAVITS.
Appeals, D.C. courts.
  Indigent persons.
    Proceedings in forma pauperis, DCCtApp Forms 7a, 7b, DCCtApp Rule 24.
  Release in criminal cases, DCCtApp Rule 9.
Appeals, federal cases.
  In forma pauperis proceedings, FRAP 24, USCtApp Rule 24.
  Motion for stay.
    Pending appeal, FRAP 8(a).
    Pending review of administrative orders, FRAP 18, USCtApp Rule 18.
  Release in criminal cases, FRAP 9.
  Supporting motions, FRAP 27(a).
Arbitration.
  Evidence at hearings, Arbitration Rule IX.
Attachment, §§16-501, 16-506.
Bail bondsmen.
  Authorization of sureties, CrimPro Rule 116.
Child custody proceedings.
  Initial pleading, §16-4602.09.
Disbarment, DCBar Rule XI.
Domestic life insurance company disbursements, §31-4439.
Fiduciary accounts and reports.
  Audit and examination where bank is fiduciary, CivPro Rule 305.
Garnishment.
  Prejudgment garnishment, §16-501.

AFFIDAVITS —Cont'd
Indigent persons.
In forma pauperis motions, CivPro Form CA 106.
In forma pauperis proceedings, FRAP 24, USCtApp Rule 24.
Judge's bias or prejudice, CivPro Rule 63-I.
Adoption proceedings, Adoption Rule 63.
Domestic relations actions, DomRel Rule 63.
Probate proceedings.
Death between January 1, 1981 and June 30, 1995, Probate Rule 126.
New trial motions, CivPro Rule 59.
Domestic relations actions, DomRel Rule 59.
Notaries public taking, §1-1210.
Pleadings, CivPro Rule 9-I.
Probate proceedings.
Accounts of administrators, executors and collectors.
Death before January 1, 1981, Probate Rule 19.
Notice of petitions.
Death before January 1, 1981, Probate Rules 10, 11.
Release in criminal cases.
Appeals, federal cases, FRAP 9.
Rental housing.
Action for declaratory relief, §42-3405.03a.
Replevin, §16-3703.
Service of process.
Landlord and tenant court.
Affidavit of service by special process server, CivPro Rule 6.
Time for service, CivPro Rule 6.
Criminal procedure, CrimPro Rule 45.
Hospitalization of persons with mental illness, MentalHealth Rule 13.
Juvenile proceedings, JuvProc Rule 45.
Summary judgment, CivPro Rule 56.
Domestic relations actions, DomRel Rule 56.
Voluntary leave transfer program.
Application to receive transferred leave, §1-612.33.

AFFIRMATIONS.
See OATHS.

AFFIRMATIVE ACTION, §2-1402.53.
Cable television franchises.
Affirmative action in employment, §34-1262.02.
Condominiums, §42-1904.14.
Merit system.
Equal employment opportunity, §§1-607.01 to 1-607.08.
See MERIT SYSTEM.
Public officers and employees, §§1-521.01 to 1-521.08.
See PUBLIC OFFICERS AND EMPLOYEES.

AFFORDABLE HOUSING.
Community development by financial institutions, §§26-431.01 to 26-431.08.
Inventory.
Comprehensive tracking plan for affordable housing inventory.
Definitions, §42-2141.
Requirements for tracking, §42-2142.
Partnership program for affordable housing, §6-227.
Preservation and rehabilitation of government-supported housing, §§42-2851.01 to 42-2851.08.
Real property tax abatement.
Section 8 and other affordable housing, §§47-865, 47-866.

AFFORDABLE HOUSING CLEARINGHOUSE DIRECTORY, §§42-2131 to 42-2136.
Affordable housing development request for inclusion, §42-2134.
Agency submission of data to mayor, §42-2133.
Contents of inventory information, §42-2135.
Definitions, §§42-2131, 42-2151.01.
Inventory, §§42-2132, 42-2135.
List of developments, §42-2136.
Locator, §42-2132.

AFFORDABLE HOUSING OPPORTUNITIES, INC.
Real property tax exemptions, §§47-1078, 47-1084, 47-1086.

AFFRAYS, §22-1301.

AFRICAN AFFAIRS, §§2-1391 to 2-1395.
Commission on African affairs.
Established, §2-1393.
Functions, §2-1395.

AFRICAN AFFAIRS —Cont'd
Commission on African affairs
  —Cont'd
  Meetings, §2-1394.
  Members, §2-1394.
  Vacancies, §2-1394.
Office on African affairs.
  Established, §2-1391.
  Executive director, §2-1392.
  Staff, §2-1392.

AFRICAN-AMERICAN AFFAIRS
  COMMISSION.
Established, §3-1441.
Organization, §3-1442.

AFTER-ACQUIRED PROPERTY.
Secured transactions.
  Security interest in after-acquired
    property, §28:9-204.
Wills, devises and bequests, §18-305.

AFTER-DISCOVERED PROPERTY.
Decedents' estates, §§20-355, 20-1304.

AGE.
Child support enforcement.
  Age of majority, §46-101.
Congress.
  Representatives, US Const Art I §2.
  Senators, US Const Art I §3.
Elections.
  Right to vote.
    Not to be abridged on account of
      age, US Const Amd 26.
    Persons eighteen years of age, US
      Const Amd 26.
Metropolitan police.
  Original appointment, §5-105.07.
President of the United States, US
  Const Art II §1.
Vice-president, US Const Amd 12.

AGED PERSONS.
AccessRx for the elderly, §§48-831.21
  to 48-831.23.
Adult protective services.
  General provisions, §§7-1901 to
    7-1913.
    See ADULT PROTECTIVE
      SERVICES.
Assisted living residences,
  §§44-101.01 to 44-113.01.
    See ASSISTED LIVING
      RESIDENCES.
Commission on aging, §§7-504.01 to
  7-504.10.
  Chairperson, §7-504.07.
  Compensation and expenses,
    §7-504.08.

AGED PERSONS —Cont'd
Commission on aging —Cont'd
  Duties, §7-504.10.
  Established, §7-504.01.
  Members, §7-504.02.
  Qualifications, §7-504.03.
  Rules of procedure, §7-504.06.
  Staff, technical assistance, §7-504.09.
  Term of office, §7-504.04.
  Vacancies, §7-504.05.
Crimes and offenses with senior
  citizen victims, enhanced
  penalties for, §22-3601.
  Identity theft, §22-3227.03.
Criminal abuse, neglect and
  financial exploitation of
  vulnerable adults and elderly
  persons, §§22-931 to 22-938.
Discrimination against elderly
  tenants.
  Rental housing providers, §42-3505.05.
Health services.
  Innovation fund, §§1-325.221 to
    1-325.226.
HIV/AIDS education and outreach
  program, §§7-1631 to 7-1633.
Home for aged and infirm, §44-716.
  Admission of paying patients to,
    §44-717.
  Sale of surplus products of, §44-716.
Home repair and improvement
  program fund, §§42-2201 to
  42-2207.
Identity theft.
  Enhanced penalty for committing
    offense against individuals 65
    years of age or older, §22-3227.03.
Innovation fund.
  Health services for seniors,
    §§1-325.221 to 1-325.226.
Landlord discrimination against,
  §42-3505.05.
Medicare.
  Health benefit plan grievance
    procedures not applicable to,
    §44-301.02.
  Powers of attorney, §21-2114.
  Supplement insurance, §§31-3701 to
    31-3710.
    See MEDICARE SUPPLEMENT
      INSURANCE.
Motor vehicle accidents.
  General provisions, §§50-2001 to
    50-2003.
Office on aging, §§7-503.01 to 7-503.06.
  Established, §7-503.01.

AGED PERSONS —Cont'd
Office on aging —Cont'd
Executive director, §§7-503.02, 7-503.03.
Impact of proposed policy or program on aged.
Submission to office, §7-503.04.
Standards for making decisions, award of grants and contracts, §7-503.04.
Transfer of funds and positions from division of services to aging, §7-503.05.
Pet ownership restriction in assisted housing, §§8-2031 to 8-2035.
Policy declaration, §7-501.01.
Prescription drugs.
AccessRx for the elderly, §§48-831.21 to 48-831.23.
Real property taxes.
Deferral for low-income seniors, §47-845.03.
Reduced liability for, §47-863.
Rental housing.
Conversion and sale, §42-3402.08.
Discrimination against elderly tenants, providers, §42-3505.05.
Rent control, §§42-3502.06, 42-3502.08.
Rent supplement program, §6-226.
Capital-based assistance, §6-229.
Tenant-based assistance, §6-228.
Voucher assistance, §6-227.
Senior citizens' home repair and improvement program fund, §§42-2201 to 42-2207.
Telephone solicitation.
Targeting elderly or aged persons, §22-3226.09.
Tenant assistance program, §42-3503.03.
Volunteer Service Credit Program, §§7-531.01 to 7-531.11.
Vulnerable adults and elderly persons.
Crimes and offenses with senior citizen victims, enhanced penalties for, §22-3601.
Identity theft, §22-3227.03.
Criminal abuse, neglect and financial exploitation, §§22-931 to 22-938.

AGENTS.
Art dealers.
Agency relationship with artist, §28-5102.
Athlete agents, §§47-2887.01 to 47-2887.18.

AGENTS —Cont'd
Insurance agents and brokers.
Managing general agents, §§31-1501 to 31-1506.
See INSURANCE AGENTS AND BROKERS.
Producer licensing, §§31-1131.01 to 31-1131.19.
See INSURANCE PRODUCER LICENSING.
Interstate banking and branch banks, agency agreements between affiliated depository institutions, §26-739.
Investment securities.
Effect of signature of transfer agent, §28:8-208.
Registration.
Obligations of transfer agent, §28:8-407.
Limited cooperative associations.
No agency created by reason of becoming member, §29-1005.03.
Limited liability companies.
Members not deemed agents, §29-803.01.
Limited partnerships.
General partners as, §29-704.02.
No agency relationship created by limited partnership, §29-703.02.
Money lenders, resident agent required for, §26-901.
Motor vehicle safety responsibility, operator deemed to be agent of owner for purposes of, §50-1301.08.
Negotiable instruments.
Signature by authorized representative, §28:3-403.
Nonprobate transfers.
Designation, §19-602.05.
Payment to designated agent, §19-602.24.
Partners as agents of partnership, §29-603.01.
Prison work release program participants not regarded as District agents, §24-241.10.
Real estate brokers and salespersons.
General provisions, §§42-1701 to 42-1709.
See REAL ESTATE BROKERS AND SALESPERSONS.
Registered agents, §§29-104.01 to 29-104.14.
See BUSINESS ORGANIZATIONS.

AGENTS —Cont'd

Savings and loan acquisitions, registered agent requirement, §26-1216.

Security agents and brokers, §§31-5601.01 to 31-5608.04.
See SECURITY AGENTS AND BROKERS.

Trusts and trustees.
Uniform trust code.
Personal representatives, §19-1303.03.

AGE OF MAJORITY.

Child support enforcement, §46-101.

AGGRAVATING CIRCUMSTANCES.

Murder.
Sentencing procedure for first degree murder, §22-2104.01.

AGRICULTURE.

Real property taxes.
Reduced liability for agricultural uses, §47-868.

Sustainable urban agriculture apiculture act of 2012, §§8-1825.01 to 8-1825.09.
See BEES.

Urban gardens program, §§48-401 to 48-403.

AIDING AND ABETTING.

Bingo games, raffles, or Monte Carlo Night parties, unauthorized, §3-1332.

Crimes and offenses, §22-1805.
Murder, §22-2101.
Sexual abuse, §22-2101.

Discrimination, §§2-1402.61, 2-1402.62.

District guardianship of minor, §4-125.

Insurance companies.
Unauthorized entities.
Aiding or assisting authorized activity, §31-232.

Tax return preparer aiding and abetting taxpayer in understating liability.
Penalties, §47-4217.

AIDS.

AIDS health care, §§7-1601 to 7-1606.
Comprehensive health-care response plan, §7-1602.
Definitions, §7-1601.
Privacy and confidentiality of medical records, §7-1605.

AIDS —Cont'd

AIDS health care —Cont'd
Program coordination office, §7-1604.
Residential health-care facilities, §7-1603.
Rulemaking, §7-1606.

Delinquent minors.
Testing, §16-2315, JuvProc Rule 110.

District of Columbia general hospital hospice program, §§4-1101 to 4-1105.

Effi Slaughter Barry AIDS/HIV initiative, §§7-1611 to 7-1617.

HIV/AIDS crisis area capacity building fund, §§1-325.51 to 1-325.53.
Building fund report, §1-325.53.
Established, §1-325.51.
Rulemaking, §1-325.52.

HIV screening test while receiving emergency medical services.
Health insurance coverage, §31-2803.

HIV testing of persons convicted of sexual offenses, §§22-3901 to 22-3903.
At request of victim, §22-3902.
Collection of blood sample, §22-3902.
Court order to furnish blood sample, §22-3902.
Definitions, §22-3901.
Disclosure of results by victim, §22-3902.
Notification to victim and person tested of results, §22-3902.
Results not evidence, §22-3902.
Rules, §22-3903.

Insurance discrimination based upon AIDS tests, §§31-1601 to 31-1610.

Needle exchange programs, §48-1103.01.

Prevention.
Communicable and chronic disease prevention and treatment fund, §7-736.02.
Fees for prevention and treatment, §7-736.03.
Grants, §7-736.01.

Prisoners, HIV testing of, §§22-3901 to 22-3903.

Senior education and outreach, §§7-1631 to 7-1633.
Administration of program, §7-1633.
Contract with community provider to train seniors, §7-1633.
Definitions, §7-1631.

AIDS —Cont'd
Senior education and outreach
   —Cont'd
   Establishment of program, §7-1632.
   Purpose, §7-1632.
   Stipend to participants, §7-1633.
Treatment for sexual partners,
   §§7-2081.01 to 7-2081.04.

AID TO FAMILIES WITH
   DEPENDENT CHILDREN.
Temporary assistance for needy
   families.
   General provisions, §§4-205.01 to
   4-205.19l.
   See TEMPORARY ASSISTANCE
      FOR NEEDY FAMILIES
      (TANF).

AIR CONDITIONER MECHANICS.
Board of industrial trades,
   §§47-2853.06 to 47-2853.10.
Business licenses, §§47-2853.201 to
   47-2853.203.
   Eligibility, §47-2853.202.
   Representations prohibited,
      §47-2853.203.
   Scope of practice, §47-2853.201.

AIRCRAFT.
Foreign missions, owned by
   members of, §6-1304.01.
High school courses in aviation,
   §§38-920 to 38-922.

AIR-DRIVEN PIPES.
Drug paraphernalia, §§48-904.10,
   48-1101 to 48-1104.

AIR POLLUTION, §§8-101.05 to
   8-101.14.
Administrative appeals, §8-101.05h.
Alternative fuel technology, §§50-701
   to 50-715.
   See ALTERNATIVE FUEL
      TECHNOLOGY.
Cease and desist orders, §8-101.05g.
Compliance orders, §8-101.05g.
Comprehensive program, §§8-101.05,
   8-101.05a, 8-101.06.
Crimes and offenses, §8-101.05d.
Definitions.
   Demand response generating sources,
      §8-101.11.
Demand response generating
   sources, §§8-101.11 to 8-101.14.
   Definitions, §8-101.11.
   Fees, §8-101.14.
   Generators.
      Internal combustion engine owners,
         disclosures, §8-101.12.

AIR POLLUTION —Cont'd
Demand response generating
   sources —Cont'd
   Generators —Cont'd
      Limitation on use, §8-101.13.
      Rules, §8-101.14.
False statements, §8-101.05e.
Fines and civil penalties, §8-101.05c.
Rules, §8-101.06.
   Demand response generating sources,
      §8-101.14.
Sanctions, §8-101.05f.
Violations, §8-101.05b.

AIRPORTS.
Dulles international airport, §§9-801
   to 9-813.
   See DULLES INTERNATIONAL
      AIRPORT.
Helicopter landing pads, §9-1211.01.
Metropolitan Washington airports
   authority, §§9-901 to 9-926, 9-1001
   to 9-1011.
   See METROPOLITAN WASHINGTON
      AIRPORTS AUTHORITY.
Ronald Reagan Washington national
   airport, §§9-701 to 9-707.
   See RONALD REAGAN
      WASHINGTON NATIONAL
      AIRPORT.

AIRSPACE.
Rental of air space, §§10-1121.01 to
   10-1121.13.
   See RENTAL OF AIRSPACE.

ALABAMA AVENUE AFFORDABLE
   RENTAL HOUSING PROJECT.
Real property tax exemptions,
   §47-4641.

ALARM SYSTEMS.
Security and fire alarm contractors.
   General provisions, §§7-2801 to
   7-2815.
   See SECURITY AND FIRE ALARM
      CONTRACTORS.

ALCOHOL AND DRUG ABUSE.
Addiction counselors, §§3-1208.51 to
   3-1208.54.
Attorney discipline or disability
   proceedings, DCBar Rule XI,
   USDistCt LCrR 57.30, USDistCt
   LCvR 83.19.
Child abuse and neglect.
   Exposure of children to drug-related
      activity, §§4-1301.06a, 4-1301.07.

ALCOHOL AND DRUG ABUSE
—Cont'd
Children and youth.
Juveniles and young adults,
rehabilitation programs for,
§24-612.
Pilot substance abuse program for
youth, §§7-3101 to 7-3103.
**Controlled substances, §§48-901.02 to
48-931.02.**
See CONTROLLED SUBSTANCES.
Corrections department.
Employee drug and alcohol testing,
§§24-211.21 to 24-211.24.
Criminal offenses.
Controlled substances, §§48-901.02 to
48-931.02.
See CONTROLLED SUBSTANCES.
Drivers' licenses.
Alcohol violation, suspension of
minor's license for, §50-1403.03.
Drug offenses, revocation for,
§50-1403.02.
Driving under the influence.
See DRIVING UNDER THE
INFLUENCE.
Firearms.
Pistols, license to carry, §7-2509.06.
Possession by addict unlawful,
§22-4503.
**Health insurance coverage, §§31-3101
to 31-3112, 44-1209.**
See HEALTH INSURANCE.
Marijuana.
Consumption in public space or
impairment, §48-911.01.
Needle exchange programs,
§48-1103.01.
Nurses.
Impaired nurses, treatment and
rehabilitation, §§3-1251.01 to
3-1251.15.
See NURSES.
**Pay-for-success contracts, §§2-211.01
to 2-211.03.**
Prisons and prisoners.
Alcoholics, rehabilitation of, §§24-601
to 24-615.
See PRISONS AND PRISONERS.
Drug addicts, rehabilitation of,
§§24-701 to 24-715.
See PRISONS AND PRISONERS.
Mandatory testing of Corrections
Department employees,
§§24-211.21 to 24-211.24.
Public intoxication, §§24-604, 25-1001.

ALCOHOL AND DRUG ABUSE
—Cont'd
Public officers and employees.
Drug and alcohol testing.
Commercial motor vehicle drivers,
§1-620.11.
Corrections department, §§24-211.21
to 24-211.24.
Department of mental health and
department of human services
employees, §§1-620.21 to
1-620.25.
District employees who serve
children, §§1-620.31 to 1-620.37.
District of Columbia housing
authority, §6-217.
Rehabilitation programs, §24-610.
**Tax check-off, drug prevention and
children at risk, §§47-4001 to
47-4005.**
**Temporary assistance for needy
families (TANF) program for
drug felons, §4-205.71.**
**Treatment and prevention, §§44-1201
to 44-1210.**
Appropriations for programs,
§44-1210.
Definitions, §44-1201.
Eligibility for treatment, §44-1202.
Entitlement not created by provisions,
§44-1208.
Facilities.
Certification, §44-1204.
Establishment, §44-1203.
Financial assistance program,
§44-1204.
Fees, §44-1207.
Financial assistance program,
§44-1205.
Fines for violations, §44-1207.
Insurance, §44-1209.
Privatization of residential treatment,
§44-1203.01.
Public information and education
program, §44-1206.
Rulemaking for prevention and
treatment programs, §44-1207.
Violations of provisions, §44-1207.
**ALCOHOLIC BEVERAGE CONTROL
BOARD, §§25-201 to 25-212.**
**Advisory neighborhood
commissions.**
Notice of applications, §1-309.10.
**Alcoholic beverage regulation
administration (ABRA).**
Director, §25-207.

ALCOHOLIC BEVERAGE CONTROL BOARD —Cont'd
Alcoholic beverage regulation administration (ABRA) —Cont'd
Established, §25-202.
Funding, §25-210.
General counsel, §25-208.
Staff, §25-207.
Transfer of functions from alcoholic beverage control division of the department of consumer regulatory affairs, §25-203.
Application proceedings.
Notice by board, §25-421.
Review of applications, §§25-431 to 25-434.
Procedures, §§25-441 to 25-447.
Authority to grant licenses, §25-104.
Community resource officer, §25-209.
Conflicts of interest, §25-206.
Decisions.
Written decisions.
Time limit, §25-433.
Duties, §§25-201, 25-204.
Enforcement authority, §25-801.
Established, §25-201.
Establishments.
Substantial changes.
Approval, §25-762.
False swearing before board.
Perjury, §25-442.
General counsel, §25-208.
Hours of operation.
Board restrictions, §25-724.
Members, §25-206.
Moratoria on licenses, §§25-351 to 25-354.
Notice.
Application proceedings, §25-421.
Open meetings, §25-204.01.
Orientation classes for new licensees and general public, §25-212.
Panels.
Review of applications, §§25-431 to 25-434.
Perjury.
False swearing before board, §25-442.
Records, §25-205.
Reports, §25-205.
Subpoenas.
Witnesses, §25-443.
Terms of office, §25-206.
Transfer of functions from alcoholic beverage control division of the department of consumer regulatory affairs, §25-204.
Transfer to ABRA, §25-203.

ALCOHOLIC BEVERAGE CONTROL BOARD —Cont'd
Witnesses.
Perjury.
False swearing before board, §25-442.
Subpoenas, §25-443.

ALCOHOLIC BEVERAGE LICENSES.
Admission into licensed premises.
Restrictions, §25-782.
Advertising, §§25-763 to 25-766.
Exterior signs, §25-763.
False statements, §25-766.
Generally, §25-764.
Price displays.
Windows and doors, §25-765.
Signs, restrictions on use, §25-763.
Advisory neighborhood commissions.
Notice of applications, §1-309.10.
Protest hearings.
ANC recommendations, §25-609.
Settlement agreements submitted to board, §25-609.
Amendments.
Fees, §25-510.
Appeals.
Summary revocation or suspension, §25-826.
Applications, §§25-401 to 25-447.
Approval of substantial change in operation, §25-404.
Brew pubs, §25-407.
Denial.
Successive applications limited after initial denial, §25-338.
False statements on applications, §25-401.
Form of application, §25-401.
Importation permits, §25-409.
Influencing application process, §25-434.
Manager's license, §25-410.
Manufacturers.
New license applications, §25-402.
Renewal, §25-403.
New license applications.
Manufacturers, wholesalers and retailers, §25-402.
Notice of proceedings, §§25-421 to 25-423.
Board's notice, §25-421.
Posted notice outside of establishment, §25-423.
Petition for reconsideration, §25-433.

ALCOHOLIC BEVERAGE LICENSES
—Cont'd

Applications —Cont'd

Pool buying group retail agents, §25-411.

Qualifications for applicants, §§25-301 to 25-303.

Renewal.

Manufacturers, wholesalers and retailers, §25-403.

Required, §25-104.

Requirements generally, §§25-401 to 25-410.

Retailers.

New license applications, §25-402.

Renewal, §25-403.

Review of applications, §§25-431 to 25-434.

Attempt to influence process, §25-434.

Decision of board, §25-433.

General procedures, §25-431.

Notice to public, opportunity to protest, §25-431.

Panels for conducting hearings and taking actions, §25-431.

Proceedings, §§25-441 to 25-447.

Protest received, actions by board, §25-432.

Reconsideration, petition, §25-433.

Scheduling administrative review, §25-431.

Time, §25-432.

Standard review procedures, §25-432.

Separate application for each license, §25-401.

Solicitor's license, §25-406.

Substantial change in operation, §25-404.

Successive applications.

Limitation after initial denial, §25-338.

Tasting permits, §25-408.

Transfers of ownership, §25-405.

Wholesalers.

New license applications, §25-402.

Renewal, §25-403.

Appropriateness standard.

Moratoria based on public interest, §§25-351 to 25-354.

Qualifications for establishments, §25-313.

Arena licenses, §25-114.

Fees, §25-505.

ALCOHOLIC BEVERAGE LICENSES
—Cont'd

Assault on police officer, government inspector or investigator.

Summary revocation or suspension, §25-826.

Authority to grant, §25-104.

Back-up drinks.

Prohibited, §25-741.

Bankruptcy.

Involuntary transfer of license, §25-361.

Brew pubs, §25-117.

Applications, §25-407.

Fees, §25-508.

Taxation, §25-902.

Bribes, §25-434.

Caterers.

Application procedure, §25-313.

On-premises retailers, §25-113.

Cease and desist orders, §25-829.

Chief of police.

Suspension or revocation at request of chief of police, §25-827.

Children and minors.

Entrance into licensed premises.

Restrictions, §25-782.

Legal drinking age.

Posting of signs, §25-713.

Classifications and types of, §§25-110 to 25-126.

Clubs.

Consumption license for, §25-113.

Credit sales.

Exemption, §25-734.

Defined, §25-101.

Common carriers.

On-premises retailers, §25-113.

Taxation, §25-905.

Complaints.

Noise restrictions.

ABRA to maintain complaint program, §25-725.

Compliance record.

Qualifications for establishments.

Renewal, additional considerations, §25-315.

Conditions, §25-104.

Conflicts of interest, §25-303.

Consumption license for clubs, §25-113.

Containers.

Limitations on size, §25-751.

Contents, §25-104.

Controlled substance violations.

Denial, §25-335.

ALCOHOLIC BEVERAGE LICENSES
—Cont'd
Controlled substance violations
—Cont'd
Mandatory revocation, §25-822.
Credit sales, §§25-731 to 25-736.
Payment defined, §25-731.
Records.
Delivery and payment, §25-733.
Restrictions, §25-731.
Sales by retailers prohibited, §25-734.
Subsequent sales.
Failure to make payment, §25-731.
Crimes and offenses.
Employees.
Notice of criminal conviction,
§25-702.
Influencing application process,
§25-434.
Suspension or revocation at request of
chief of police, §25-827.
Unlawful importation, §25-772.
Death of licensee.
Involuntary transfer of license,
§25-361.
Denial, §§25-331 to 25-339.
Controlled substance violations,
§25-335.
Georgetown historic district.
Special restrictions, §25-339.
Off-premises retailers.
Distance between licensees,
limitation, §25-333.
Moratoria, §25-332.
Quotas, §25-331.
Public health and safety restrictions,
§25-335.
Retail licenses.
Residential-use districts, §25-336.
Successive applications, limitation,
§25-338.
Wholesaler's license.
Residential-use districts, §25-337.
Disasters.
Safekeeping.
Temporary surrender, §25-791.
Disciplinary actions.
Revocation or suspension, §§25-821 to
25-832. See within this heading,
"Revocation or suspension."
Discontinuance.
Temporary surrender, §25-791.
Distance between licensees,
limitation.
Off-premises retailers, §25-333.
Duration of, §25-104.

ALCOHOLIC BEVERAGE LICENSES
—Cont'd
Education.
Manager's license, §25-120.
Programs, §25-121.
Employees.
Notice of criminal conviction, §25-702.
Endorsements, §25-113a.
Entertainment endorsements,
§25-113a.
Entrance into licensed premises.
Restrictions, §25-782.
Establishments.
Employees.
Notice of criminal conviction,
§25-702.
Examination of books, records and
premises, §25-802.
Qualifications, §§25-311 to 25-317.
Standards of operation, §§25-701 to
25-798.
Structural requirements, §25-761.
Substantial changes.
Approval, §25-762.
Exceptions, §25-103.
Failure to obtain, §25-102.
False statements on applications,
§25-401.
Farmer's market licenses, §25-128.
Farm wineries, §25-123.
Fees.
Alteration.
Proposal by mayor, §25-502.
Amendments, §25-510.
Annual charge and collection of,
§25-501.
Arena licenses, §25-505.
Brew pubs, §25-508.
Farmer's market licenses, §25-128.
Festival licenses, §25-127.
Importation permits, §25-508.
Manager's license, §25-508.
Manufacturers, §25-503.
Off-premises retailers, §25-503.
On-premises retailers, §25-504.
Revocation or suspension.
Not returnable, §25-821.
Safekeeping fee, §25-791.
Schedules for, §§25-501 to 25-511.
Solicitor's license, §25-507.
Tasting permits, §25-508.
Temporary licenses, §25-506.
Transfers of licenses, §25-316.
Transfers to new owner, §25-509.
Wholesalers, §25-503.
Festival licenses, §25-127.

ALCOHOLIC BEVERAGE LICENSES
—Cont'd
Fines.
Civil penalties for violations, §25-830.
Failure to ascertain valid
identification, §25-783.
Influencing application process,
§25-434.
No specific penalty specified, §25-831.
Pregnant women, warnings for.
Failure to post, §25-712.
Foreclosure.
Involuntary transfer of license,
§25-361.
General public orientation classes,
§25-212.
Georgetown historic district.
Special restrictions, §25-339.
Gifts.
Manufacturers.
Gifts and loans for manufacturer
prohibited, §25-735.
Wholesalers.
Gifts and loans for wholesaler
prohibited, §25-736.
Go-cups.
Prohibited, §25-741.
Grocery stores.
Retail licenses for stores in certain
location, §25-336.
Health and safety violations.
Summary revocation or suspension,
§25-826.
Hearings, §§25-441 to 25-447.
Continuances, §25-441.
Protest hearings, §25-444.
Settlement agreements, §25-446.
Enforceable provisions, §25-446.01.
Unenforceable provisions,
§25-446.02.
Settlement conference, §25-445.
Show cause, §25-447.
Violation of settlement agreement,
§25-446.
Subpoenas, §25-443.
Summary revocation or suspension,
§25-826.
Witnesses, §25-442.
Subpoenas, §25-443.
**Holding more than one classification
or type,** §25-303.
Hotels.
Credit sales.
Exemption, §25-734.
Hours of sale and service, §25-723.
Mini bars, §25-723.

ALCOHOLIC BEVERAGE LICENSES
—Cont'd
Hotels —Cont'd
On-premises retailers, §25-113.
Hours of operation, §§25-721 to
25-724.
Board may further restrict, §25-724.
Hotel mini bars, §25-723.
Manufacturers, §25-721.
Off-premises retailers, §25-722.
On-premises retailers, §25-723.
Suspension, §25-827.
Temporary licenses, §25-721.
Wholesalers, §25-721.
Identification.
Valid identification required, §25-783.
**Importation of beverages into
District,** §25-772.
Importation permits, §25-119.
Applications, §25-409.
Fees, §25-508.
Taxation, §25-904.
Influencing application process,
§25-434.
Injunctions.
Cease and desist orders, §25-829.
Investigations.
Examination of books, records and
premises, §25-802.
Involuntary transfers, §25-361.
Keg restrictions, §25-753.
Law enforcement officers.
Availability for inspection, §25-711.
Legal drinking age.
Posting of signs, §25-713.
Valid identification required, §25-783.
Legitimate theater.
Nudity.
Exceptions, §25-372.
Litter control, §25-726.
Loans.
Manufacturers.
Gifts and loans for manufacturer
prohibited, §25-735.
Wholesalers.
Gifts and loans for wholesaler
prohibited, §25-736.
Manager conduct, §25-703.
Manager's license, §25-120.
Applications, §25-410.
Board-approved manager required,
§25-701.
Exemptions, §25-701.
Fees, §25-508.
Revocation or suspension.
Effect, §25-821.

ALCOHOLIC BEVERAGE LICENSES
—Cont'd
Manager's license —Cont'd
Traffic offenses.
Notice to board of conviction,
§25-701.
**Manufacture or sale of alcohol
without,** §25-102.
Manufacturers, §25-110.
Applications.
New license applications, §25-402.
Renewal, §25-403.
Beer sampling, §25-118.
Containers.
Limitations on size, §25-751.
Credit sales, §§25-731 to 25-736.
Fees, §25-503.
Gifts and loans for manufacturer
prohibited, §25-735.
Hours of sale and delivery, §25-721.
Records, §25-773.
Reports, §25-771.
Revocation or suspension.
Undue influence of wholesaler or
retailer, §25-824.
Tie-in purchases.
Prohibited, §25-743.
**Manufacturer with substantial
interest in retailer,** §§25-735,
25-824.
Misdemeanors.
Influencing application process,
§25-434.
Unlawful importation, §25-772.
Moratoria, §§25-351 to 25-354.
Board review of request, §25-354.
Determination of affected area,
§25-352.
Effect on existing licenses, §25-351.
Hearing on request, §25-354.
Notice requirements, §25-353.
Nude dancing establishments,
§§25-371 to 25-374.
Off-premises retailers, §25-332.
Procedures to request, §25-352.
Standard for declaring, §25-351.
Mt. Pleasant.
Restrictions for off-premises retailers,
§25-344.
Multiple violations.
Mandatory revocation, §25-822.
Multi-purpose facilities.
On-premises retailers, §25-113.
Music.
Noise restrictions, §25-725.

ALCOHOLIC BEVERAGE LICENSES
—Cont'd
Neighborhood.
Qualifications for establishments.
Initial issuance, additional
considerations, §25-314.
New licensee orientation classes,
§25-212.
Nightclubs.
Georgetown historic district.
Special restrictions, §25-339.
On-premises retailers, §25-113.
Noise restrictions, §25-725.
Orientation classes for new licensees
and general public, §25-212.
Notice.
Application proceedings, §§25-421 to
25-423.
Employees.
Notice of criminal conviction,
§25-702.
Enforcement actions, §25-804.
Revocation or suspension, §25-828.
Nude dancers.
Exceptions, §25-371.
Legitimate theater, §25-372.
Performance space, §25-372.
Grandfather clause, §25-371.
Moratorium on nude dancing
establishments, §§25-371 to
25-374.
Prohibited generally, §§25-113, 25-371.
Transfer of location of establishment,
§25-374.
Transfer of ownership of
establishment, §25-373.
Off-premises retailers, §25-112.
Containers.
Limitations on size, §25-751.
Distance between licensees, limitation,
§25-333.
Fees, §25-503.
Go-cups prohibited, §25-741.
Hours of sale and delivery, §25-722.
Keg restrictions, §25-753.
Moratoria, §25-332.
Quotas, §25-331.
Records, §25-773.
Reports, §25-771.
Restrictions on individual containers.
Mt. Pleasant, §25-344.
Ward 2, §25-345.
Ward 6, §25-346.
Ward 7, §25-342.
Ward 8, §25-343.
Tasting permits.
Applications, §25-408.

ALCOHOLIC BEVERAGE LICENSES
 —Cont'd
Off-premises retailers —Cont'd
 Tie-in purchases.
  Prohibited, §25-743.
 Wine pubs, §25-124.
On-premises retailers.
 Back-up drinks prohibited, §25-741.
 Fees, §25-504.
 Hours of sale and service, §25-723.
  Suspension, §25-827.
 Records, §25-773.
 Removal of partially consumed bottle
  of wine, §25-113.
 Reports, §25-771.
 Solicitation of drinks prohibited,
  §25-742.
On-site sales consumption permit,
 §25-126.
**Orientation classes for new
 licensees and general public,**
 §25-212.
Owner conduct, §25-703.
Panels.
 Review of applications, §§25-431 to
  25-434.
Petition for reconsideration.
 Applications, §25-433.
Physical space.
 Structural requirements, §25-761.
 Substantial changes.
  Approval, §25-762.
**Posted notice outside of
 establishment.**
 Application proceedings, §25-423.
Posting, §25-711.
Pregnant women, warnings for,
 §25-712.
Prison terms.
 No specific penalty specified, §25-831.
Protest hearings, §25-444.
Protests, §§25-601 to 25-609.
 ANC recommendations.
  Settlement agreements submitted to
   board, §25-609.
 Contracts of licensee.
  Access by ANC or citizens
   associations to documents
   obtained by board or ABRA,
   §25-601.01.
 Filing requirements, §25-602.
 Incident logs.
  Access by ANC or citizens
   associations to documents
   obtained by board or ABRA,
   §25-601.01.

ALCOHOLIC BEVERAGE LICENSES
 —Cont'd
Protests —Cont'd
 Settlements.
  ANC submitting settlement
   agreement to board, §25-609.
 Standing to file, §25-601.
 Timing, §25-602.
Qualifications for applicants,
 §§25-301 to 25-303.
Qualifications for establishments,
 §§25-311 to 25-317.
 Appropriateness standard, §25-313.
  Presumption of appropriateness,
   §25-315.
 Boundaries, §25-312.
 Certificate of occupancy, required,
  §25-311.
 Community effect.
  Initial issuance, additional
   considerations, §25-314.
 Compliance record.
  Renewal, additional considerations,
   §25-315.
 General provisions, §25-311.
 Initial issuance, additional
  considerations, §25-314.
 Neighborhood.
  Initial issuance, additional
   considerations, §25-314.
  Presumption of appropriateness,
   §25-315.
 Proximity to certain schools or
  recreation areas, §25-314.
 Renewal, additional considerations,
  §25-315.
 Size of relevant area, §25-312.
 Transfer of establishment to new
  location.
  Additional considerations, §25-317.
  Settlement agreements, §25-317.
 Transfer of establishment to new
  owner.
  Additional considerations, §25-316.
Quotas.
 Off-premises retailers, §25-331.
Records, §§25-205, 25-773.
 Credit sales.
  Delivery and payment, §25-733.
 Examination of books, records and
  premises, §25-802.
 Noise restrictions, complaints,
  §25-725.
Reimbursable details, §25-798.
**Removal of partially consumed
 bottle of wine.**
 On-premises retailers, §25-113.

ALCOHOLIC BEVERAGE LICENSES
—Cont'd
Reports, §25-771.
Incident reports, §25-804.
Required, §25-102.
Exceptions, §25-103.
Residential districts.
Denial of retail licenses, §25-336.
Denial of wholesaler's license, §25-337.
Restaurants.
Brew pub licenses, §25-117.
On-premises retailers, §25-113.
Wine pub permits, §25-124.
Retailers.
Applications.
New license applications, §25-402.
Renewal, §25-403.
Arena, §25-114.
Brew pubs, §25-117.
Credit sales, §§25-731 to 25-736.
Sales by retailers prohibited,
§25-734.
Denial.
Residential-use districts, §25-336.
Grocery stores.
Retail licenses for stores in certain
location, §25-336.
Off-premises, §25-112.
Containers.
Limitations on size, §25-751.
Distance between licensees,
limitation, §25-333.
Fees, §25-503.
Go-cups prohibited, §25-741.
Hours of sale and delivery, §25-722.
Keg restrictions, §25-753.
Moratoria, §25-332.
Quotas, §25-331.
Records, §25-773.
Reports, §25-771.
Restrictions on individual
containers.
Mt. Pleasant, §25-344.
Ward 2, §25-345.
Ward 6, §25-346.
Ward 7, §25-342.
Ward 8, §25-343.
Tasting permits.
Applications, §25-408.
Tie-in purchases.
Prohibited, §25-743.
On-premises, §25-113.
Back-up drinks prohibited, §25-741.
Endorsements, §25-113a.
Fees, §25-504.
Hours of sale and service, §25-723.
Suspension, §25-827.

ALCOHOLIC BEVERAGE LICENSES
—Cont'd
Retailers —Cont'd
On-premises —Cont'd
Solicitation of drinks prohibited,
§25-742.
Qualifications, §25-302.
Records, §25-773.
Reports, §25-771.
Wine pubs, §25-124.
Review of applications, §§25-431 to
25-434.
Proceedings, §§25-441 to 25-447.
Revocation or suspension, §§25-821
to 25-832.
Cease and desist orders, §25-829.
Criminal activity.
Suspension or revocation at request
of chief of police, §25-827.
Failure to ascertain valid
identification, §25-783.
Fees.
Not returnable, §25-821.
Generally, §25-821.
Grounds, §25-823.
Investigative reports, prompt notice of,
§25-832.
Manager's license.
Effect, §25-821.
Mandatory revocation, §25-822.
Manufacturers.
Undue influence of wholesaler or
retailer, §25-824.
Misuse of premises, §25-823.
Multiple violations.
Mandatory revocation, §25-822.
Notice, §25-828.
Safekeeping.
Temporary surrender, §25-791.
Summary revocation or suspension,
§25-826.
Wholesalers.
Undue influence of retailer, §25-825.
Safekeeping.
Temporary surrender, §25-791.
Sales.
Credit sales, §§25-731 to 25-736.
Restrictions on sales, promotions and
service, §§25-741 to 25-743.
Safekeeping.
Temporary surrender, §25-791.
Security plans of licensees, §§25-402,
25-403.
Contracting with third party for
security, prohibited, §25-797.
On-premises retailers, §25-113.

ALCOHOLIC BEVERAGE LICENSES
  —Cont'd
Settlement conference, §25-445.
Settlement of disputes, §25-446.
  Enforceable provisions, §25-446.01.
  Unenforceable provisions, §25-446.02.
Show cause hearings, §25-447.
  Violation of settlement agreement,
    §25-446.
Sidewalk cafe endorsements,
  §25-113a.
Signs.
  Advertising, §§25-763 to 25-766.
  Application proceedings.
    Posted notice outside of
      establishment, §25-423.
  Legal drinking age, §25-713.
  Posting of license, §25-711.
  Pregnant women, warnings for,
    §25-712.
  Proof of valid identification, §25-713.
  Revocation or suspension, notice,
    §25-828.
Solicitation of drinks.
  Retailers.
    Prohibited, §25-742.
Solicitor's license, §25-116.
  Applications, §25-406.
  Fees, §25-507.
Staff requirements, §§25-701, 25-702.
Standards of operation, §§25-701 to
  25-798.
  Hours of operation, §§25-721 to
    25-724.
  Signs, §§25-711 to 25-713.
  Staff requirements, §§25-701, 25-702.
  Structural requirements, §25-761.
Storage of alcoholic beverages,
  §25-754.
Structural requirements for
  establishments, §25-761.
  Substantial changes.
    Approval, §25-762.
Substantial change in operation.
  Applications, §25-404.
Summary revocation or suspension,
  §25-826.
Summer garden endorsements,
  §25-113a.
Tasting permits, §25-118.
  Applications, §25-408.
  Fees, §25-508.
Taverns.
  Brew pub licenses, §25-117.
  Georgetown historic district.
    Special restrictions, §25-339.

ALCOHOLIC BEVERAGE LICENSES
  —Cont'd
Taverns —Cont'd
  On-premises retailers, §25-113.
  Wine pub permits, §25-124.
Taxation.
  Qualifications for applicants.
    Failure to file District tax returns,
      effect of, §25-301.
Tax sales.
  Involuntary transfer of license,
    §25-361.
Temporary licenses.
  Fees, §25-506.
  Hours of sale and delivery.
    Manufacturers and wholesalers,
      §25-721.
  Requirements, §25-115.
Temporary surrender, §25-791.
Term, §§25-104, 25-206.
Tie-in purchases.
  Prohibited, §25-743.
Training.
  Manager's license, §25-120.
  Programs, §25-121.
Transfers of establishments.
  Safekeeping.
    Temporary surrender, §25-791.
  To new location.
    Additional considerations, §25-317.
    Nude dancing establishments,
      §25-374.
    Settlement agreements, §25-317.
  To new owner.
    Additional considerations, §25-316.
    Applications, §25-405.
    Fees, §25-509.
    Nude dancing establishments,
      §25-373.
Transfers of licenses.
  Involuntary transfers, §25-361.
Transportation of beverages into
  District, §25-772.
Transportation of liquor into
  District.
  Importation permits, §25-119.
Validity, §25-104.
Ward 2.
  Restrictions on individual containers,
    §25-345.
Ward 4.
  Restrictions on licenses issued or
    transferred, §25-340.01.
  Targeted moratorium zone, §25-341.01.
Ward 6.
  Restrictions on individual containers,
    §25-346.

ALCOHOLIC BEVERAGE LICENSES
—Cont'd
Ward 7.
Restrictions on individual containers,
§25-342.
Ward 8.
Restrictions on individual containers,
§25-343.
Wholesalers, §25-111.
Applications.
New license applications, §25-402.
Renewal, §25-403.
Containers.
Limitations on size, §25-751.
Credit sales, §§25-731 to 25-736.
Denial.
Residential-use districts, §25-337.
Fees, §25-503.
Gifts and loans for wholesaler
prohibited, §25-736.
Hours of sale and delivery, §25-721.
Keg restrictions, §25-753.
Qualifications, §25-302.
Records, §25-773.
Reports, §25-771.
Revocation or suspension.
Undue influence of retailer, §25-825.
Temporary licensees, deliveries to,
§25-115.
Tie-in purchases.
Prohibited, §25-743.
**Wholesaler with substantial interest
in retailer, §§25-736, 25-825.**
Wine pubs, §25-124.
Zoning restrictions.
Retail licenses, §25-336.
Wholesale licenses, §25-337.

**ALCOHOLIC BEVERAGE
REGULATION
ADMINISTRATION.**
Director, §25-207.
Established, §25-202.
Funding, §25-210.
General counsel, §25-208.
Staff, §25-207.
**Transfer of functions from alcoholic
beverage control division of the
department of consumer
regulatory affairs, §25-203.**

**ALCOHOLIC BEVERAGES, §§25-101
to 25-1003.**
Abatement of nuisances, §25-805.
ABRA.
See ALCOHOLIC BEVERAGE
REGULATION
ADMINISTRATION.

ALCOHOLIC BEVERAGES —Cont'd
Advertising, §§25-763 to 25-766.
Exterior signs, §25-763.
False statements, §25-766.
Generally, §25-764.
Price displays.
Windows and doors, §25-765.
Signs, restrictions on use, §25-763.
Back-up drinks.
Prohibited, §25-741.
Beer.
Defined, §25-101.
Taxation, §25-902.
Board.
Control board, §§25-201 to 25-212.
See ALCOHOLIC BEVERAGE
CONTROL BOARD.
Boats and other watercraft.
Operating under the influence,
§§50-2206.31 to 50-2206.36.
Chemical testing, §§50-1908 to
50-1912.
Brew pubs.
Licenses, §25-117.
Applications, §25-407.
Fees, §25-508.
Taxation, §25-902.
**Children and minors, §§25-781 to
25-785.**
Contributing to the delinquency of a
minor, §22-811.
Delivery, offer, or making available to,
§25-785.
Diversion program, §25-1002.
Drivers' licenses.
Suspension or revocation, §25-1002.
Entrance into licensed premises.
Restrictions, §25-782.
Legal drinking age.
Posting of signs, §25-713.
Misrepresentation of age, §25-1002.
Purchase, possession, or consumption
by, §25-1002.
Sale or distribution by, §25-784.
Sale to, §25-781.
Valid identification required, §25-783.
Constitution of the United States,
US Const Amds 18, 21.
Containers, §§25-751 to 25-754.
Kegs, §25-753.
Labeling, §25-752.
Limitations on size, §25-751.
**Contraband, seizure and forfeiture
of, §25-911.**
Control board, §§25-201 to 25-212.
See ALCOHOLIC BEVERAGE
CONTROL BOARD.

ALCOHOLIC BEVERAGES —Cont'd

Convention center and sports arena, beverage containers not permitted in, §25-1003.

Credit sales, §§25-731 to 25-736.

Crimes and offenses.

Enforcement generally, §§25-801 to 25-805.

Open container law, §25-1001.

On-premises retailer knowingly allowing customer to exit with an open container, §25-113.

Public intoxication, §25-1001.

Definitions, §25-101.

Distillery pubs.

Permit requirements and qualifications, §25-125.

District of Columbia housing authority.

Drug and alcohol testing of employees, §6-217.

Driving under the influence.

See DRIVING UNDER THE INFLUENCE.

Enforcement generally, §§25-801 to 25-805.

False statements.

Advertising, §25-766.

Farm wineries.

Licenses, §25-123.

Fees.

Schedules for, §§25-501 to 25-511.

Transfers of licenses, §25-316.

Fines and penalties.

Children and minors.

Delivery, offer, or making available to, §25-785.

Purchase, possession, or consumption by, §25-1002.

Sale to minors or intoxicated persons, §25-781.

Failure to perform certain required acts, §25-831.

Open container law, §25-1001.

Prohibited act for which no specific penalty is provided, §25-831.

Public intoxication, §25-1001.

Sale to minors or intoxicated persons, §25-781.

Taxation, §25-907.

Gifts.

Manufacturers.

Gifts and loans for manufacturer prohibited, §25-735.

Wholesalers.

Gifts and loans for wholesaler prohibited, §25-736.

ALCOHOLIC BEVERAGES —Cont'd

Go-cups.

Prohibited, §25-741.

Gross sales tax, §47-2002.02.

Rate of tax, §47-2002.

Growlers.

Brew pubs selling, §25-117.

Defined, §25-101.

Off-premises retailers selling, §25-112.

Illegal beverages.

Search warrants, §25-803.

Importation of liquor into District, §25-772.

Injunctions, §25-805.

Intoxicated persons, sales to, §25-781.

Investigations.

Examination of books, records and premises, §25-802.

Issuance of rules and regulations, §25-211.

Kegs, §25-753.

Labeling.

Keg restrictions, §25-753.

Requirements, §25-752.

Legal drinking age.

Posting of signs, §25-713.

Licenses.

See ALCOHOLIC BEVERAGE LICENSES.

Manufacture of.

Defined, §25-101.

Labeling requirements, §25-752.

License restrictions on manufacturer with substantial interest in retailer, §§25-735, 25-824.

Licenses, §25-110.

License, without, §25-102.

Records, §25-773.

Reports, §25-771.

Manufacturers.

See ALCOHOLIC BEVERAGE LICENSES.

Motor vehicles operated under the influence of.

See DRIVING UNDER THE INFLUENCE.

Nonbeverage purposes, provisions not applicable to alcohol intended for, §25-211.

Notice.

Enforcement actions, §25-804.

Nude dancers not allowed on licensed premises, §25-113.

Nuisance, place of violation declared as, §25-805.

ALCOHOLIC BEVERAGES —Cont'd
Open container law, §25-1001.
On-premises retailer knowingly
allowing customer to exit with an
open container, §25-113.
Pool buying groups.
Creation, §25-122.
Importation permits, §25-119.
Fee, §25-511.
Retail agent permits, §25-411.
Sales licenses, §25-102.
Pregnant women, warnings for,
§25-712.
Price displays.
Windows and doors, §25-765.
Prohibition.
Constitutional amendment, US Const
Amd 18.
Repeal, US Const Amd 21.
Prosecutions, §25-831.
Public intoxication, §§24-604, 25-1001.
Records, §25-773.
Control board, §25-205.
Examination of books, records and
premises, §25-802.
Licenses, §25-205.
**Removal of partially opened bottle
of wine.**
On-premises retailers, §25-113.
Reports, §25-771.
Incident reports, §25-804.
Retailers.
See ALCOHOLIC BEVERAGE
LICENSES.
Rules and regulations, §25-211.
Enforcement, §25-201.
Sales.
Children and minors.
Sales by, §25-784.
Sales to, §25-781.
Credit sales, §§25-731 to 25-736.
Defined, §25-101.
Implied warranty of merchantability,
§28:2-314.
Individual containers.
Mt. Pleasant sales restrictions,
§25-344.
Ward 2 sales restrictions, §25-345.
Ward 6 sales restrictions, §25-346.
Ward 7 sales restrictions, §25-342.
Ward 8 sales restrictions, §25-343.
Intoxicated persons, sales to, §25-781.
Labeling requirements, §25-752.
License, sales without, §25-102.
Pool buying groups, §25-102.
Records, §25-773.

ALCOHOLIC BEVERAGES —Cont'd
Sales —Cont'd
Reports, §25-771.
Restrictions on sales, promotions and
service, §§25-741 to 25-743.
Wholesalers.
See ALCOHOLIC BEVERAGE
LICENSES.
Samples.
Solicitor's license.
Transportation of samples to and
from establishment, §25-116.
**Search warrants for illegal
beverages,** §25-803.
Signs.
Advertising, §§25-763 to 25-766.
Solicitation of drinks.
Retailers.
Prohibited, §25-742.
Stamps, redemption of, §47-2411.
Storage, §25-754.
Warehouse receipts.
Storage under government bond,
§28:7-201.
Tasting permits, §25-118.
Applications, §25-408.
Fees, §25-508.
Taxation, §§25-901 to 25-911.
Appeals, §25-910.
Beer, §25-902.
Collection and payment, §§25-901,
25-903, 25-908.
Common carriers, §25-905.
Exemptions, §25-906.
Fines and penalties.
Contraband, seizure and forfeiture
of, §25-911.
Failure to pay tax, §25-907.
Importation permits, §25-904.
Personal debt, liability deemed as,
§25-907.
Protests, §25-907.
Refunds, §25-909.
Severability of provisions, §25-911.
Wine and spirits, §25-901.
Temporary licenses.
Requirements, §25-115.
Tie-in purchases.
Prohibited, §25-743.
**Transportation of liquor into
District,** §25-772.
Importation permits, §25-119.
Vessels.
Operating under the influence,
§§50-2206.31 to 50-2206.36.
Chemical testing, §§50-1908 to
50-1912.

ALCOHOLIC BEVERAGES —Cont'd
Warehouses.
Receipts.
Storage under government bond,
§28:7-201.
Warranties.
Implied warranty of merchantability,
§28:2-314.
Wholesalers.
See ALCOHOLIC BEVERAGE
LICENSES.
Wine pubs.
Permits, §25-124.
Zoning restrictions on licenses.
Retailer licenses, §25-336.
Wholesale licenses, §25-337.

ALIAS WRITS, §15-303.

ALIBI OF CRIMINAL DEFENDANT,
CrimPro Rule 12.1.
Delinquent minors, JuvProc Rule 12.1.

ALIENATION OF AFFECTIONS.
Abolition of action for, §16-923.

ALIENATION OF PROPERTY.
Statutory rule against perpetuities,
§§19-901 to 19-907.

ALIENS.
Actions.
Suits against state, US Const Amd 11.
Congress.
Eligibility to be representative, US
Const Art I §2.
Criminal procedure, §16-713.
**Disability compensation for public
officers and employees,**
§§1-623.37, 1-623.38.
**Intestate succession by descent
through alien ancestor,** §19-321.
Naturalization, US Const Art I §§8, 9.
President of the United States.
Ineligible for presidency, US Const Art
II §1.
Real property, ownership of,
§§42-901, 42-902.
Sentencing, §16-713.
Suits against state, US Const Amd 11.
**Temporary assistance for needy
families (TANF) program,**
§4-205.24.

**ALIEN TERRORIST REMOVAL
COURT.**
Appeals from, USCtApp Rule 47.6.

ALIMONY.
Spousal support.
See SPOUSAL SUPPORT.

ALIMONY —Cont'd
Support generally.
See SUPPORT AND MAINTENANCE.

ALLEN CHAPEL A.M.E. CHURCH.
Senior residential rental project.
Real property tax exemptions,
§47-4641.

ALLEYS.
Streets and alleys.
See STREETS AND ALLEYS.

ALLOCUTION, CrimPro Rule 32.

ALL-TERRAIN VEHICLES.
Defined, §50-2201.02.
Public property.
Operation on prohibited, §50-2201.04b.
Registration not required,
§50-2201.04b.

**ALTERNATIVE DISPUTE
RESOLUTION.**
Arbitration, §§16-4401 to 16-4432.
See ARBITRATION.
General provisions.
See ARBITRATION.
Family court proceedings.
Use to greatest extent possible,
§11-1102.
Mediation.
See MEDIATION.

**ALTERNATIVE FUEL
TECHNOLOGY,** §§50-701 to
50-715.
Choice of fuels, who makes, §50-710.
Clean-fuel fleets.
Incentives for operating, §50-714.
Commercial vehicle restrictions,
§50-704.
Compliance with requirements of,
§50-703.
Converted vehicles, §50-708.
Definitions, §50-702.
Emission credit trading program,
§50-713.
Emission standards for, §50-707.
**Exemptions from compliance with
requirements of,** §50-703.
Fines, §§50-703, 50-712.
Fuel providers, requirements for,
§50-709.
Incentives.
Alternative fuels, using, §50-715.
Clean-fuel fleets, operating, §50-714.
Income taxes.
Alternative fuel infrastructure credit.
Corporations, §47-1807.10.

ALTERNATIVE FUEL TECHNOLOGY —Cont'd
Income taxes —Cont'd
Alternative fuel infrastructure credit —Cont'd
Residents and nonresidents, §47-1806.12.
Unincorporated businesses, §47-1808.10.
Alternative fuel vehicle conversion credit.
Corporations, §47-1807.11.
Residents and nonresidents, §47-1806.13.
Unincorporated businesses, §47-1808.11.
Issuance of rules regarding, §50-705.
Labeling regulations, §50-711.
Motor vehicle registration.
Fees, §50-1501.03.
Motor vehicle titling tax.
Exemption, §50-2201.03.
Penalties, §§50-703, 50-712.
Policy regarding encouragement of, §50-701.
Private right of action regarding, §50-706.
Public-owned vehicles.
Fleet management.
Plan to expand use of alternative fuel, §50-211.06.
Records, §50-703.
Registration of operators of covered fleets, §50-703.
Reports, §§50-703, 50-704.01.

AMBASSADORS AND CONSULS.
Constitution of the United States,
US Const Art II §§2, 3, Art III §2.

AMBULANCE CHASING, ProfCond Rule 7.1.

AMBULANCES.
Business licenses, §47-2829.
Cardiopulmonary resuscitation in case of cardiac arrest.
Non-resuscitation procedures for EMS, §§7-651.01 to 7-651.16.
See EMERGENCY MEDICAL SERVICES.
Crimes and offenses.
Obstruction, prevention, or interference with request for ambulance or emergency medical assistance, §22-1931.
Emergency medical services system generally.
See EMERGENCY MEDICAL SERVICES.

AMBULANCES —Cont'd
Service fees, §5-416.

AMBULATORY SURGICAL TREATMENT CENTERS.
Criminal background checks for unlicensed personnel, §§44-551 to 44-554.
Licenses, §§44-501 to 44-509.
Malpractice.
Medical malpractice, §§16-2801 to 16-2841.
See MEDICAL MALPRACTICE.

AMERICAN ACADEMY OF ACHIEVEMENT.
Real property tax exemptions, §47-1093.

AMERICAN ASSOCIATION OF UNIVERSITY WOMEN.
Real property tax exemptions, §47-1041.

AMERICAN COLLEGE OF CARDIOLOGY.
Real property tax exemptions, §47-1059.

AMERICAN INSTITUTE OF ARCHITECTS FOUNDATION.
Real property tax exemptions, §47-1044.

AMERICANIZATION, EVENING, AND SUMMER SCHOOLS, §38-1903.

AMERICAN LEGION.
Real property tax exemptions, §§47-1035, 47-1046.

AMERICAN PSYCHOLOGICAL ASSOCIATION.
Real property tax exemptions.
Lot 146, square 677, §47-1069.

AMERICAN RECOVERY AND REINVESTMENT ACT OF 2009.
Grants.
Jobs listing, §2-219.52.
Reports, §2-219.51.

AMERICAN SIGN LANGUAGE.
Educational opportunities, §§38-2431 to 38-2433.

AMICI CURIAE.
Appeals, District of Columbia court of appeals.
Briefs, DCCtApp Rule 29.
Appeals, federal cases, FRAP 29, USCtApp Rule 29.
Briefs, USCtApp HPIP Rule IX(a)(4).

AMICI CURIAE —Cont'd

Appeals, federal cases —Cont'd
Docketing statement, USCtApp Rule 12.
Oral argument, USCtApp HPIP Rule XI(e).

AMMUNITION.

Child abuse and neglect.
Injuries caused by bullets.
Reporting requirements, §4-1321.02.

Defined, §7-2501.01.

Display of weapons or ammunition by firearms dealers, §7-2504.07.

Fraud and deceit, §7-2507.04.

Large capacity ammunition feeding device.
Possession, sale or transfer prohibited, §7-2506.01.

Metropolitan police ammunition feeding devices, prohibition on transfer of, §5-133.16.

Pawnbrokers.
Ammunition prohibited as pawns, §7-2507.01.

Possession of, §7-2506.01.

Reporting injuries caused by, §7-2603.
Child abuse and neglect.
Injuries caused by bullets, §4-1321.02.

Restricted pistol bullets, §7-2507.06.

Sale and transfer of ammunition.
Permissible sales and transfers, §7-2505.02.
Prohibited sales and transfers, §7-2505.01.

Security, prohibition on use as, §7-2507.01.

Voluntary surrender of, §7-2507.05.

AMNESTY PROGRAMS.

Basic business licenses.
Amnesty period, §47-2851.19.

Water and sewer services, §§34-2301 to 34-2306.

AMUSEMENT PARKS.

Business licenses, §47-2823.

AMUSEMENT PLACES.

Discrimination in admission, §47-2901.
Increase in penalty, §47-2903.
Recovery of fine, §47-2904.

AMVETS (AMERICAN VETERANS OF WORLD WAR II).

Real property tax exemptions, §47-1038.

ANACOSTIA.

Uniontown's name changed to, §1-108.

ANACOSTIA BRIDGE, §9-305.

ANACOSTIA PARK, §10-155.

ANACOSTIA RIVER.

Cleanup and protection, §§8-102.01 to 8-102.07.
Anacostia pilot program.
Pilot program allowing entities to adopt sections of the Anacostia River for purposes of removing litter, §8-102.06a.
Definitions, §8-102.01.
Disposable carryout bags.
Credit for consumer-provided bags, §8-102.03.
Fees, §8-102.03.
Recycling requirements, §8-102.02.
Rulemaking authority, §8-102.04.
Violations, §8-102.04.
Fertilizer, §§8-104.01 to 8-104.07.
Fund.
Establishment and authorized uses, §8-102.05.
Income tax check-off, §47-1812.11d.
License plate fees, §50-1501.03.
Sales tax exemption, §47-2005.
License plates, commemorative, §8-102.07.
Fees, §50-1501.03.
Pilot program allowing entities to adopt sections of the Anacostia River for purposes of removing litter, §8-102.06a.
Public information and outreach campaigns, §8-102.06.
Toxics remediation.
Remediation of contaminated sediment, §8-104.31.

Fertilizer.
Anacostia River cleanup and protection fertilizer act, §§8-104.01 to 8-104.07.
Definitions, §8-104.02.
Enforcement, §8-104.07.
Fertilizer application requirements, §8-104.03.
Fertilizer labeling requirements, §8-104.05.
Fertilizer public education program, §8-104.04.
Penalties, §8-104.06.
Rules, §8-104.07.
Short title, §8-104.01.

ANACOSTIA RIVER —Cont'd
Private conduits in, §34-2504.
Toxics remediation.
Remediation of contaminated
sediment, §8-104.31.
**United States title to lands or
waters of,** §10-102.

**ANACOSTIA WATERFRONT
CORPORATION.**
Reorganization, §§2-1225.01 to
2-1225.42.
Assets and liabilities, transfer,
§2-1225.12.
Capital funds, §2-1225.22.
Contracts and procurement,
§2-1225.13.
Dissolution of boards, §2-1225.01.
Economic development special account,
§2-1225.21.
Eminent domain authority not
impaired, §2-1225.41.
Skyland eminent domain area,
§2-1225.42.
Employees, §2-1225.02.
Transition to District control,
§2-1225.02.
Urban renewal plan modifications,
§2-1225.31.

**ANACOSTIA WATERFRONT
DEVELOPMENT ZONE,**
§§2-1226.01 to 2-1226.41.
Defined, §2-1226.04.
Environmental standards,
§§2-1226.31 to 2-1226.41.
Applicability of provisions, §2-1226.33.
DDOE, power and authority,
§2-1226.40a.
Definitions, §2-1226.32.
Exemptions, §2-1226.39.
Green building standards, §2-1226.35.
Integrated design standards,
§2-1226.34.
Marina standards, §2-1226.37.
Relationship to other laws, §2-1226.40.
Rules, §2-1226.41.
Savings clause, §2-1226.40b.
Site planning and preservation,
§2-1226.38.
Stormwater control, §2-1226.36.
Title of act, §2-1226.31.
Transition provisions, §2-1226.40b.
Hiring requirements.
Workforce intermediary, §2-1226.03.
Implementation of framework plan,
§2-1226.01.
Project requirements, §2-1226.02.

**ANACOSTIA WATERFRONT
DEVELOPMENT ZONE** —Cont'd
Workforce intermediary, §2-1226.03.

ANALOGUES.
Controlled substance analogues,
§48-902.14.

ANATOMICAL BOARD, §§3-201 to
3-209.

ANATOMICAL GIFTS, §§7-1531.01 to
7-1531.28.
Advance health-care directive.
Effect on, §7-1531.20.
Amendment of gift.
Before donor's death, §7-1531.05.
Decedent's body or parts, §7-1531.09.
Donor registry.
Effect upon registry, §7-1531.19d.
Preclusive effect, §7-1531.07.
Applicability of provisions,
§7-1531.02.
Uniformity of application and
construction, §7-1531.23.
Chief medical examiner.
Cooperation with procurement
organizations, §7-1531.21.
Decedent whose body is under
jurisdiction of.
Facilitation of anatomical gift from,
§7-1531.22.
Construction of provisions.
Uniformity of application and
construction, §7-1531.23.
**Coordination of procurement and
use,** §7-1531.14.
Corporations.
Tax credit.
Provision of paid leave to employee
serving as donor, §47-1807.08.
Decedent's body or parts.
Amendment of gift, §7-1531.09.
Chief medical examiner.
Decedent whose body is under
jurisdiction of.
Facilitation of anatomical gift
from, §7-1531.22.
Hospitals and hospices, duties of,
§7-1531.24.
Certificate requirement, §7-1531.26.
Rulemaking, §7-1531.27.
Manner of making gift, §7-1531.09.
Preservation of organs, §7-1531.25.
Revocation of gift, §7-1531.09.
Who may make gift, §7-1531.08.
Definitions, §§7-1531.01, 7-1531.20.
Document of gift.
Choice of law as to execution,
§7-1531.18.

ANATOMICAL GIFTS —Cont'd
Document of gift —Cont'd
Delivery not required, §7-1531.12.
Examination.
Right to examine, §7-1531.12.
Law governing validity, §7-1531.18.
Presumption of validity, §7-1531.18.
Search for, §7-1531.11.
Donees.
Persons who may receive anatomical gift, §7-1531.10.
Donor registry.
Access to information in, §7-1531.19a.
Amendment of gift.
Effect upon registry, §7-1531.19d.
Confidentiality of information, §7-1531.19b.
Department of motor vehicles.
Transfer of information, §7-1531.19c.
Donor status not dependent on being listed in, §7-1531.19e.
Establishment, §7-1531.19.
Revocation of gift.
Effect upon registry, §7-1531.19d.
Rulemaking, §7-1531.19f.
Sources of information, §7-1531.19b.
Electronic signatures in global and national commerce act.
Relation of provisions to act, §7-1531.28.
Government employee serving as donor.
Donor leave, §1-612.03b.
Hospitals and hospices, duties of, §7-1531.13.
Decedent's body or parts, §7-1531.24.
Certificate requirement, §7-1531.26.
Rulemaking, §7-1531.27.
Human tissue banks.
General provisions, §§7-1541.01 to 7-1551.01.
See HUMAN TISSUE BANKS.
Immunity, §7-1531.17.
Decedent's body or parts.
Organ preservation, §7-1531.25.
Manner of making gift.
Before donor's death, §7-1531.04.
Decedent's body or parts, §7-1531.09.
Preclusive effect of gift, amendment or revocation, §7-1531.07.
Presumptions.
Document of gift.
Presumption of validity, §7-1531.18.
Procurement organizations.
Cooperation with chief medical examiner, §7-1531.21.

ANATOMICAL GIFTS —Cont'd
Procurement organizations —Cont'd
Duties, §7-1531.13.
Human tissue banks.
Authority of organization acting on behalf of, §7-1541.05a.
Prohibited acts, §7-1531.16.
Sale or purchase of parts, §7-1531.15.
Purposes of anatomical gift, §7-1531.10.
Refusal to make gift, §7-1531.06.
Revocation of gift.
Before donor's death, §7-1531.05.
Decedent's body or parts, §7-1531.09.
Donor registry.
Effect upon registry, §7-1531.19d.
Preclusive effect, §7-1531.07.
Rulemaking.
Decedent's body or parts.
Duties of hospitals and hospices, §7-1531.27.
Donor registry, §7-1531.19f.
Sale or purchase of parts prohibited, §7-1531.15.
Search and notification, §7-1531.11.
Trafficking in human body parts, §§7-1501.01 to 7-1501.03.
Unincorporated businesses.
Tax credits.
Provision of paid leave to employee serving as donor, §47-1808.08.
Who may make gift.
Before donor's death, §7-1531.03.
Decedent's body or parts, §7-1531.08.

ANESTHESIOLOGIST ASSISTANTS.
Advisory committee, §7-743.03.
Board of medicine.
Advisory committee on anesthesiologist assistants, §3-1202.03.
Council hearing, §3-1206.34.
Definition of practice by, §3-1201.02.
Health occupations licensure, registration or certification, §§3-1205.01 to 3-1205.24.
See HEALTH OCCUPATIONS LICENSURE, REGISTRATION OR CERTIFICATION.
Licenses, §3-1206.31.
Renewal, §3-1206.32.
Scope of practice, §3-1206.31.
Titles and terms prohibited as misrepresentation without license to practice, §3-1210.03.
Transition, §3-1206.33.

ANIMAL CONTROL.
Animal and pet owners.
Prohibited conduct, §8-1778.45.
Cruelty to animals.
See CRUELTY TO ANIMALS.
Generally, §§8-1801 to 8-1813.
See ANIMALS.
Sustainable urban agriculture apiculture act of 2012,
§§8-1825.01 to 8-1825.09.
See BEES.
Wildlife protection, §§2201 to 8-2211.
See WILDLIFE PROTECTION.

ANIMAL FIGHTING, §22-1009.
Penalty, §22-1006.01.
Urging dogs to fight or create disorder, §22-1310.

ANIMALS.
Adoption of impounded animals,
§8-1807.
Animal care and control agency,
§8-1802.
Animal control license fees fund,
§8-1804.
Assisted housing.
Pet ownership restriction in assisted housing, §§8-2031 to 8-2035.
Definitions, §8-2031.
Discrimination by reason of owning pets, §8-2032.
Ownership policy, §8-2032.
Removal of pets constituting threat or nuisance, §8-2033.
Rules, §8-2035.
Violation civil infraction, fine, §8-2034.
At large.
Allowing animal to go at large.
Prohibition, §§8-1808, 22-1311.
Baby rabbits, chicks or ducks.
Sale, restrictions, §8-1808.
Bees.
Sustainable urban agriculture apiculture act of 2012, §§8-1825.01 to 8-1825.09.
See BEES.
Circus, carnival or other special event animals.
Permit required to display, §8-1808.
Classroom animals, §§8-1851.01, 8-1851.02.
Commercial animal care or breeder license.
Pet care facilities, §8-1821.02.
Requirements, §8-1821.01.

ANIMALS —Cont'd
Cruelty to animals.
General provisions, §§22-1001 to 22-1013.
See CRUELTY TO ANIMALS.
Dangerous dogs, §§8-1901 to 8-1908.
Definitions, §§8-1801, 22-1013.
District sales of animals and materials, proceeds from,
§47-132.
Dog park.
At large does not include dog in dog park, §8-1801.
Defined, §8-1801.
Establishment, requirements, §8-1808.01.
Dogs generally.
See DOGS.
Dyeing fur, hair, or feathers of,
§8-1808.
Education and incentive program,
§8-1810.
Emergency preparedness plan,
§8-1861.01.
Fees, §8-1804.
Fighting, §22-1009.
Penalty, §22-1006.01.
Urging dogs to fight or create disorder, §22-1310.
Fines, §8-1811.
Fish and game laws, §§22-4328 to 22-4333.
Hobby permits, §8-1809.
Horses.
Footways in public grounds, driving or riding on, §22-1318.
Horse-drawn carriages, §§8-2001 to 8-2013.
See HORSE-DRAWN CARRIAGES.
Public works, use in, §9-1209.03.
Importing into district.
Restrictions, §8-1808.
Impounded animals, §8-1805.
Adoption of, §8-1807.
Food and water supplied to, §22-1007.
Owner, release to, §8-1806.
Relief of, §22-1008.
Leash laws, §§1-303.41, 8-1808, 22-1311.
Liabilities of owners, §8-1812.
Licenses, §8-1804.
Commercial animal care or breeder license, §§8-1821.01, 8-1821.02.
Issuance by veterinarian, §47-2888.06.
Livestock.
Inspector of, §7-179.

ANIMALS —Cont'd
Livestock —Cont'd
Secured transactions.
When security interest attaches, §28:9-204.
Metropolitan police property clerk.
Sale of unclaimed animals, §5-119.12.
Notice of violations, §8-1813.
Ownership of animal.
Falsely denying, §8-1808.
Permits.
Animal hobby permits, §8-1809.
Circus, carnival or other special event animals, display of, §8-1808.
Pet care facilities.
Commercial animal care or breeder license, §8-1821.02.
Pleuropneumonia, §1-333.01.
Police animals.
Harassing, interfering with, injuring or obstructing, §22-861.
Prohibitions regarding, §8-1808.
Railroad transportation, §22-1003.
Release from entity having custody and control or charged with protection of animal, §8-1831.01.
Release to owner, §8-1806.
Research animals, release, §8-1831.01.
Scientific experiments, §22-1012.
Spaying and neutering incentive program, §8-1810.
Sterilization fund, §8-1804.
Sustainable urban agriculture apiculture act of 2012, §§8-1825.01 to 8-1825.09.
Targets, used as, §47-2841.
Trust for care of animals.
Uniform trust code, §19-1304.08.
Unborn young.
Sale of goods.
Definition of "goods," §28:2-105.
Vaccination requirements, §8-1803.
Veterinary facilities, §§47-2888.01 to 47-2888.08.
See VETERINARY FACILITIES.
Veterinary medicine, §§3-1208.61 to 3-1208.65.
See VETERINARY MEDICINE.
Wildlife protection, §§8-2201 to 8-2211.
See WILDLIFE PROTECTION.
Wrestling or fighting, prohibition, §8-1808.

ANNUAL LEAVE BANK, §§1-612.04 to 1-612.11.
Definitions, §1-612.04.

ANNUAL LEAVE BANK —Cont'd
Donations, §1-612.06.
Establishment, §1-612.05.
Medical emergency, termination of, §1-612.10.
Rulemaking, §1-612.11.
Use of leave, §1-612.09.
Withdrawals, §§1-612.07, 1-612.08.

ANNUITIES.
Life insurance company annuity contracts, filing, §31-4705.
Teachers' retirement.
After June 30, 1946, §§38-2021.01 to 38-2023.16.
Prior to June 30, 1946, §§38-2001.01 to 38-2001.19.

ANNULMENT OF MARRIAGE.
Appointment of counsel, §16-918.
Decree, §16-903.
Defaults, §16-919.
Divorce.
See DIVORCE.
Domestic relations actions generally, DomRel Rules 1 to 406.
See DOMESTIC RELATIONS ACTIONS.
Effective date of decree, §16-920.
Evidence, §16-919.
Family court jurisdiction, §11-1101.
Grounds, §16-904.
Persons allowed to institute proceedings, §46-404.
Property rights, §16-910.
Registration, §7-216.
Residence requirements, §16-902.
Spousal support.
See SPOUSAL SUPPORT.
Validity of alleged marriage, denial of, §16-921.

ANOMALOUS INDORSEMENTS.
Negotiable instruments, §28:3-205.

ANSWERS.
Appeals, federal cases.
Administrative review of enforcement, FRAP 15(b).
Bankruptcy proceedings, FRAP 6(b).
Permissive appeals, FRAP 5(b).
Petition.
Prohibition, mandamus, or other extraordinary writs, FRAP 21, USCtApp Rule 21.
Rehearing, FRAP 40(a).
Attachment.
Post-judgment attachment, CivPro Rule 69-I.
Wages, CivPro Rule 69-II.

ANSWERS —Cont'd
Attachment —Cont'd
Pre-judgment attachment, CivPro Rule 64-I.
Domestic relations actions, DomRel Rule 64.
Attorneys at law.
Appointment of attorney.
Domestic relations actions, DomRel Rule 101.
Discipline or disability proceedings, DCBar Rule XI.
Condemnation of property, CivPro Rule 71A.
Defenses generally.
See DEFENSES.
Domestic relations actions, DomRel Rules 8, 12.
Parentage proceedings, DomRel Rule 405.
Reciprocal enforcement of support proceedings, DomRel Rule 401.
Forms.
Defense under Rule 12(b), CivPro Form CA 20.
Money had and received, CivPro Form CA 21.
Interrogatories, CivPro Rule 33.
Adoption proceedings, Adoption Rule 33.
Domestic relations actions, DomRel Rule 33.
Parentage proceedings, DomRel Rule 405.
Pleadings generally.
See PLEADINGS.
Post-conviction proceedings.
Superior court proceedings, PostConvRel Rule 5.
Probate proceedings.
Death on or after July 1, 1995.
Response to petition for claim against an estate, Probate Rule 410.
Rule to show cause response, Probate Rule 413.
Guardians, conservators, trustees, etc., involved.
Rule to show cause response, Probate Rule 211.
Reciprocal enforcement of support proceedings, DomRel Rule 401.
Requests for admission, CivPro Rule 36.
Adoption proceedings, Adoption Rule 36.

ANSWERS —Cont'd
Requests for admission —Cont'd
Domestic relations actions, DomRel Rule 36.
Form, CivPro Form CA 25.
Tax proceedings, Tax Rule 7.
Replies, Tax Rule 8.
Time for filing, CivPro Rule 12.
Domestic relations actions, DomRel Rule 12.

ANTENUPTIAL AGREEMENTS,
§§19-113, 46-501 to 46-510.
Statutory rule against perpetuities.
Exclusions from rule, §19-904.

ANTENUPTIAL CHILDREN.
Intestate succession, §19-318.

ANTICIPATORY REPUDIATION.
Sales under UCC, §28:2-610.
Proof of market price, §28:2-723.
Retraction, §28:2-611.

ANTI-GRAFFITI MURAL ASSISTANCE PROGRAM FUND,
§1-325.101.

ANTI-SLAPP, §§16-5501 to 16-5505.
Applicability of provisions, §16-5505.
Definitions, §16-5501.
Dismissal motions, §16-5502.
Fees and costs, §16-5504.
Quash motions, §16-5503.

ANTI-TERRORISM ACT OF 2002,
§§22-3151 to 22-3156.

ANTITRUST.
Limited cooperative associations.
Relation to law, §29-1001.08.
Restraint of trade.
General provisions, §§28-4501 to 28-4518.
See RESTRAINTS OF TRADE.

APARTMENTS.
Bicycle parking spaces requirements, §50-1641.05.
Condominiums.
General provisions, §§42-1901.01 to 42-1904.18.
See CONDOMINIUMS.
Deposits.
Return of deposit, SmallClaims Forms 9, 10.
Horizontal property regimes,
§§42-2001 to 42-2031.
See HORIZONTAL PROPERTY REGIMES.

APARTMENTS —Cont'd
Landlord and tenant.
General provisions, §§42-3201 to 42-3232.
See LANDLORD AND TENANT.
Rental housing act, §§42-3501.01 to 42-3509.08.
See LANDLORD AND TENANT.
Lead level water testing.
Multiple dwelling residences, §§42-3251 to 42-3255.
Master-metered apartment buildings.
General provisions, §§42-3301 to 42-3307.
Rental housing act, §§42-3501.01 to 42-3509.08.
See LANDLORD AND TENANT.
Small claims court forms.
Return of deposit, SmallClaims Forms 9, 10.

APICULTURE.
Sustainable urban agriculture apiculture act of 2012, §§8-1825.01 to 8-1825.09.
See BEES.

APPALACHIAN STATE UNIVERSITY.
Real property tax exemptions.
Lot 42 in square 871, §47-1068.

APPEAL CONFERENCES, DCCtApp Rule 14, FRAP 33.

APPEALS, D.C. COURTS.
Administrative fines, §§2-1803.01 to 2-1803.03.
Administrative hearings, office of.
Administrative appeal and judicial review of orders, §2-1831.16.
Administrative orders and decisions.
See ADMINISTRATIVE PROCEDURE.
Adoption petition.
Expedited review in court of appeals, §11-721.
Alcoholic beverage licenses.
Summary revocation or suspension, §25-826.
Alcoholic beverages tax, §25-910.
Amicus curiae, DCCtApp Rule 29.
Appeal as of right, DCCtApp Rules 3, 4.
Application for appeal, DCCtApp Rules 5, 6.
Forms, DCCtApp Forms 3, 4.

APPEALS, D.C. COURTS —Cont'd
Apprenticeship agreement determinations, §32-1410.
Arbitration.
Trial de novo, Arbitration Rule XI.
Arbitration, revised act, §16-4427.
Assessments, §47-3303.
Assisted living residences, §44-103.08.
Actions of mayor, §44-112.01.
Attorneys at law.
Admission to the bar, DCCtApp Rule 46.
Appearance and withdrawal of attorney, DCCtApp Rule 42.
Discipline or disability proceedings, DCBar Rule XI.
Law student practice, DCCtApp Rule 48.
Number of counsel at oral argument, DCCtApp Rule 34.
Banks and financial institutions.
Cease and desist orders issued by commissioner, §26-551.20.
Final orders of commissioner or final action of department, §26-551.20.
Bicycle insurance policies.
Cancellation or refusal to renew.
Agency review of insured disputes, §50-533.
Bonds, CivPro Rule 62-I, DCCtApp Rules 7, 8.
Administrative orders and decisions, DCCtApp Rule 19.
Briefs.
Amicus curiae, DCCtApp Rule 29.
Appendix, DCCtApp Rule 30.
Form of appendix, DCCtApp Rule 32.
Contents, DCCtApp Rule 28.
Filing and service, DCCtApp Rule 31.
Form of brief, DCCtApp Rule 32.
Calendaring of cases, DCCtApp Rule 33.
Captive insurance companies.
Judicial review of commissioner, §31-3931.20.
Certificate of counsel, DCCtApp Rule 28.
Child abuse and neglect, §16-2329.
Child care facility decisions, §7-2045.
Child custody proceedings.
Enforcement of foreign custody determinations, §16-4603.14.
Child support.
Expedited hearing by magistrate judge, §16-924.

APPEALS, D.C. COURTS —Cont'd
Child support —Cont'd
Hearing commissioner's judgment,
FamDiv Rule D.
Class actions, CivPro Rule 23.
Collection of taxes.
Refund offsets, §47-4437.
Commission on judicial disabilities and tenure.
Proceedings of, §11-1529.
Condominiums, §42-1904.16.
Conferences, DCCtApp Rule 14.
Conservators, §21-2024.
Consolidated appeals, DCCtApp Rule 3.
Motions, DCCtApp Rule 27.
Constitutional questions.
Notice requirements, DCCtApp Rule 44.
Review of facts tried by jury, US Const Amd 7.
Consumer protection.
Complaint procedures, §28-3905.
Contract appeals board, §2-360.07.
Costs, DCCtApp Rule 39.
Fee schedule, DCCtApp Rule 50-Fee Schedule.
Frivolous appeals, DCCtApp Rule 38.
Court of appeals.
Generally, §§11-701 to 11-745, 17-301 to 17-307.
See COURT OF APPEALS.
Crime victims' compensation.
Board review of determinations, VictComp Rule 20.
Judicial review, VictComp Rule 21.
Modification of determination, VictComp Rule 19.
Request for reconsideration, VictComp Rule 18.
Criminal procedure.
Government appeal, §23-104.
Hearing commissioners, CrimPro Rule 117.
Notice of appeal.
Fee for filing notice of appeal, CrimPro Rule 37.
Time for filing, DCCtApp Rule 4.
Notice of right to appeal, CrimPro Rule 32.
Hearing commissioners, CrimPro Rule 117.
Release pending appeal, CrimPro Rule 46, DCCtApp Rule 9.
Required information, DCCtApp Form 6.

APPEALS, D.C. COURTS —Cont'd
Criminal procedure —Cont'd
Rules governing criminal appeals, CrimPro Rule 37.
Sealing of arrest records, CrimPro Rule 118.
Stay of execution, CrimPro Rule 38.
Transcript on appeal, CrimPro Rule 36-I.
Definitions, DCCtApp Rule 1.
Delinquent minors, §§16-2328, 16-2329.
Detention or release upon conditions, JuvProc Rule 107.
Expedited appeals, DCCtApp Rule 4.
Notice of right to appeal, JuvProc Rule 32.
Sealing arrest records, FamDiv Rule P, JuvProc Rule 118.
Forms, FamDiv Forms 2 to 6, JuvProc Forms 8 to 10.
Deposition pending appeal, CivPro Rule 27.
Domestic relations actions, DomRel Rule 27.
Disability compensation for public officers and employees, §1-623.28.
Disciplinary grievances and appeals under merit system, §1-616.52.
Dismissal of appeal, DCCtApp Rule 13.
District of Columbia court of appeals.
See COURT OF APPEALS.
Docketing the appeal, DCCtApp Rule 12.
Domestic relations actions.
Deposition pending appeal, DomRel Rule 27.
Injunction pending appeal, DomRel Rule 62.
Stay upon appeal, DomRel Rule 62.
Transcript on appeal, DomRel Rule 201.
Motion for free transcript, DomRel Rule 54-II.
Domestic violence unit proceedings, DomesticViolence Rule 13.
Drivers' license revocation for refusal to take blood alcohol test, §50-1907.
Emergency appeals, DCCtApp Rule 4.
Emergency medical services.
Appeal of decisions regarding certification, §7-2341.18.
Eminent domain as to real property for United States, §16-1365.

APPEALS, D.C. COURTS —Cont'd
En banc hearings.
Petitions for hearing or rehearing, DCCtApp Rule 35.
Environmental impact statements, §8-109.08.
Ethics and government accountability board decisions, §1-1162.17.
Evidence.
Statement of proceedings and evidence, DCCtApp Rule 10.
Administrative orders and decisions, DCCtApp Rule 17.
Excise tax assessment on titling vehicles, §50-2201.22.
Expedited appeals, DCCtApp Rule 4.
Extension of time, DCCtApp Rule 26.
Extraordinary writs, DCCtApp Rule 21.
Family court proceedings generally.
Hearing commissioner's judgment, FamDiv Rule D.
Federal cases.
See APPEALS, FEDERAL CASES.
Fees, DCCtApp Rule 50-Fee Schedule.
Filing of documents, DCCtApp Rule 25.
Briefs, DCCtApp Rules 31, 32.
Amicus curiae briefs, DCCtApp Rule 29.
Form of filed documents, DCCtApp Rule 32.
Firefighter retirement while under disciplinary investigation, §5-1056.
First amendment assemblies.
Notice and plan approval process. Denial of application, §5-331.06.
Fraternal benefit societies, §31-5334.
Freedom of information.
Denial of right to inspect, §2-537.
Frivolous appeals, DCCtApp Rule 38.
Funeral directors, §3-410.
Gross sales tax, §47-2021.
Hazardous substance releases, §§8-634.11, 8-636.03.
Hazardous waste management, §8-1308.
Health benefit plan carriers.
Voluntary withdrawal, §31-3153.
Health benefit plan grievance procedures, §§44-301.01 to 44-304.01.
See HEALTH BENEFITS PLANS.
Health occupations licensure, registration or certification, §3-1205.20.

APPEALS, D.C. COURTS —Cont'd
Hearing commissioner orders and judgments, CivPro Rule 73, CrimPro Rule 117.
Historic landmarks and districts.
Enforcement actions, §6-1110.
Hospital and medical services corporations, §31-3522.
Human rights commission hearings.
Judicial review of, §2-1403.14.
Income taxes.
Right of appeal, §47-1815.01.
Indigent persons.
Plan for furnishing representation to indigents, IndigentRep Rules I to IV.
Proceedings in forma pauperis, DCCtApp Rule 24.
Form of affidavit, DCCtApp Form 7b.
Waiver of prepayment of court costs and fees, motion for, DCCtApp Form 7a.
Insanitary buildings, condemnation of, §§6-913, 6-914.
Insurance company standard for determining hazardous financial conditions, §31-2103.
Insurance holding companies, §31-714.
Insurance regulatory trust fund assessments, §31-1205.
Insurance underwriting, §31-5009.
Intellectual disabilities, persons with.
Commitment to mental health facility, §§7-1304.10, 7-1304.12, MentalRetardation Rule 4C.
Intercepted oral or wire communications.
Government appeal of suppression of, §23-552.
Interest on lower court judgment, DCCtApp Rule 37.
Intermediate care facilities for persons with intellectual disabilities.
Assessments on facilities, §47-1276.
Joint appeals, DCCtApp Rule 3.
Administrative orders and decisions, DCCtApp Rule 15.
Judgments, DCCtApp Rule 36.
Juvenile offenders in receipt of no-further-benefit notice, §24-905.
Labor-management relations under merit system, §1-617.13.

APPEALS, D.C. COURTS —Cont'd
Law student practice, DCCtApp Rule
48.
Life insurance companies, §31-4332.
Limitation of actions, §17-307.
Litter control, §8-809.
Mandamus, DCCtApp Rule 21.
Mandate of the court, DCCtApp Rule
41.
Medicaid service provider fraud,
§4-803.
Merit system, §§1-606.01 to 1-606.11,
CivPro Agency Review Rule 1.
Disciplinary grievances and appeals,
§1-616.52.
Final agency decision affecting
performance rating, §1-606.03.
Labor-management relations under
merit system, §1-617.13.
Motions, DCCtApp Rule 27.
Form and copies of motions, DCCtApp
Rule 32.
Indigent persons.
Proceedings in forma pauperis,
DCCtApp Rule 24.
Stays pending appeal, DCCtApp Rule
8.
Motor fuel tax, §47-2319.
Notice of appeal, DCCtApp Rules 3, 4.
Fee for filing in criminal case,
CrimPro Rule 37.
Forms, CivPro Form CA 27, DCCtApp
Forms 1, 2.
Nursing homes.
Assessments on nursing facilities,
§47-1266.
Discharge, transfer, or relocation of
residents of, §44-1003.12.
Occupational safety and health,
§32-1116.
Occupations and professions
licensure, §47-2853.23.
Office of administrative hearings.
Administrative appeal and judicial
review of orders, §2-1831.16.
Opinions of court, DCCtApp Rule 36.
Oral arguments, DCCtApp Rule 34.
Amicus curiae, DCCtApp Rule 29.
Overpayments of tax, §47-3310.
Pawnbrokers, §47-2884.07.
Personal property taxes, §47-1533.
Petition for rehearing by division,
DCCtApp Rule 40.
Petition for review, DCCtApp Form 5.
Pharmacists and pharmacies,
§47-2885.21.

APPEALS, D.C. COURTS —Cont'd
Post-conviction relief.
Superior court proceedings.
Time of appeal, PostConvRel Rule
11.
Probate proceedings, Probate Rule 8.
Stays pending appeal, Probate Rule 9.
Procurement contracts.
Contract appeals board.
See PROCUREMENT PRACTICES.
Pro hac vice arguments.
Application for admission pro hac vice,
DCCtApp Form 8.
Prohibition, writ of, DCCtApp Rule
21.
Pro se representation, DCCtApp Rule
42.
Public assistance.
Notification of right to judicial review,
§4-210.13.
Public utilities, §§34-604 to 34-609,
34-901.
Questions of law.
Certification, DCCtApp Rule 22.
Real property taxes, §47-3305.
Denials of exemption, §47-1009.
New residential developments,
§47-859.04a.
New structures and existing
structures, §§47-829, 47-830.
Real property tax appeals commission,
§47-825.01a.
Reassessment or redistribution,
§47-834.
Reclassification, §47-813.
Special assessments, §47-1202.
Supplemental assessments, §§47-829,
47-830.
Transfer tax, §47-914.
Recordation tax, §42-1114.
Record on appeal, DCCtApp Rule 10.
Administrative decisions reviewed,
DCCtApp Rules 16, 17.
Application for appeal, DCCtApp Rule
6.
Expedited appeals, DCCtApp Rule 4.
Indigent persons.
Proceedings in forma pauperis,
DCCtApp Rule 24.
Sealing of records, DCCtApp Rule 12.
Transmission of record, DCCtApp Rule
11.
Records access, administrative
appeals regarding, §2-537.
Reductions in force for public
officers and employees, §1-624.04.

APPEALS, D.C. COURTS —Cont'd
Rental housing conversion and sale,
§42-3405.09.
Rent control, §42-3502.19.
Schools and education.
Testing integrity in public schools.
Sanctions for violations, §38-771.07.
Scope of review, §17-305.
Security agents and brokers.
Judicial review of commissioner's
actions, §31-5608.03.
Service of process, DCCtApp Rule 25.
Administrative orders and decisions,
DCCtApp Rule 15.
Briefs, DCCtApp Rule 31.
State health planning and
development agency certificates
of need, §§44-412 to 44-414.
Stay of proceedings, DCCtApp Rule 8.
Administrative orders and decisions,
DCCtApp Rule 18.
Adoption proceedings, Adoption Rule
62.
Application for permission to appeal,
DCCtApp Rule 5.
Bonds, CivPro Rule 62-I, DCCtApp
Rules 7, 8.
Administrative orders and decisions,
DCCtApp Rule 19.
Civil procedure, CivPro Rule 62.
Criminal cases, CrimPro Rule 38.
Family court proceedings generally.
Hearing commissioner proceedings,
FamDiv Rule D.
Mandate of the court, DCCtApp Rule
41.
Probate proceedings, Probate Rule 9.
Substitution of parties, DCCtApp
Rule 43.
Summary disposition, DCCtApp Rule
27.
Tax proceedings, §§47-3301 to 47-3310.
See TAX PROCEEDINGS.
Termination of parental rights
order.
Expedited review in court of appeals,
§11-721.
Testing integrity in public schools.
Sanctions for violations, §38-771.07.
Time computation and extension,
DCCtApp Rule 26.
Tobacco tax, §47-2413.
Traffic adjudication appeals board
decisions, CivPro Agency Review
Rule 2.
Application for leave to appeal, CivPro
Agency Review Rule 2.

APPEALS, D.C. COURTS —Cont'd
Unclaimed property claim
determinations, §41-127.
Unemployment compensation,
§§51-111, 51-112.
Wastewater disposal system,
§8-105.10.
Workers' compensation orders,
§32-1522.
Compensation order review board,
§32-1521.01.

APPEALS, FEDERAL CASES.
Abbreviated dispositions, USCtApp
Rule 36.
ABBS.
Electronic public access to information,
USCtApp HPIP Rule II(b)(3).
Administrative orders.
Answer, FRAP 15(b).
Applicability of rules, FRAP 20.
Application for enforcement, FRAP 15.
Docketing of appeals, USCtApp HPIP
Rule IV(b).
Docketing statement, USCtApp Rule
15.
Enforcement of orders.
How obtained, USCtApp HPIP Rule
III(f)(1).
Timing, USCtApp HPIP Rule
III(f)(2).
Extension of time for filing petition,
etc., FRAP 26(b).
Federal Labor Relations Authority
proceedings.
Briefs and oral argument, USCtApp
Rule 15.1.
National Labor Relations Board
proceedings.
Briefs and oral argument, FRAP
15.1, USCtApp Rule 15.1.
Petition, FRAP 15, FRAP Form 3.
Record for review.
Filing, FRAP 17, USCtApp Rule 17.
Generally, FRAP 16.
Review of orders.
How obtained, USCtApp HPIP Rule
III(e)(1).
Intervention, USCtApp HPIP Rule
III(e)(3).
Timing, USCtApp HPIP Rule
III(e)(2).
Rules to govern, FRAP 1.
Settlement of judgments enforcing
orders, FRAP 19.
Stay and emergency relief pending
review, FRAP 18, USCtApp Rule
18.

APPEALS, FEDERAL CASES
—Cont'd

Admission, disbarment, and suspension of attorneys, FRAP 46, USCtApp Rule 46.

Advisory committee on procedures, USCtApp Rule 47.4.

Affidavits.
In forma pauperis proceedings, FRAP 24, USCtApp Rule 24.
Motion for stay.
Pending appeal, FRAP 8(a).
Pending review of administrative orders, FRAP 18, USCtApp Rule 18.
Release in criminal cases, FRAP 9.
Supporting motions, FRAP 27(a).

Affiliated corporations.
Corporate disclosure statements, FRAP 26.1, USCtApp Rule 26.1.

Affirmance of orders.
Costs, FRAP 39(a).
Interest on judgment, FRAP 37.

Alien terrorist removal court.
Appeals from, USCtApp Rule 47.6.

Amicus curiae.
Briefs, FRAP 29, USCtApp HPIP Rule IX(a)(4), USCtApp Rule 29.
Docketing statement, USCtApp Rule 12.
Oral argument, USCtApp HPIP Rule XI(e).

Answer.
Administrative review of enforcement, FRAP 15(b).
Appeals by allowance in bankruptcy proceedings, FRAP 6(b).
Permissive appeals, FRAP 5(b).
Petition.
Prohibition, mandamus, or other extraordinary writs, FRAP 21, USCtApp Rule 21.
Rehearing, FRAP 40(a).

Appeal conference, FRAP 33.

Appearance and non-appearance.
Attorneys and counselors, FRAP 46(a).
Law students, FRAP 46(g), USCtApp Rule 46.
Parties.
Oral argument, FRAP 34(e).

Appellate mediation program, USCtApp Appx I.

Appendices to briefs, FRAP 30, USCtApp Rule 30.
Contents, USCtApp HPIP Rule IX(b)(1).

APPEALS, FEDERAL CASES
—Cont'd

Appendices to briefs —Cont'd
Copies of agreed statement filed as, FRAP 10(d).
Cost of producing, FRAP 39(c).
Deferred appendix, USCtApp HPIP Rule IX(b)(3).
Format, USCtApp HPIP Rule IX(b)(4).
In forma pauperis appeals, USCtApp HPIP Rule IX(b)(6).
Mailing as time deemed filed, FRAP 25(a).
Number of copies, USCtApp HPIP Rule IX(b)(5).
Preparation, USCtApp HPIP Rule IX(b)(2).
Preservation by clerk, FRAP 45(d).
Seals.
Appendix containing matters under seal, USCtApp HPIP Rule IX(b)(7).
Timing, USCtApp HPIP Rule IX(b)(3).

Appointment of counsel.
Criminal justice act plan, USCtApp Appx II.

Associations.
Corporate disclosure statements, FRAP 26.1, USCtApp Rule 26.1.

Attorney general.
Statutes challenged on constitutional grounds.
Federal statute, FRAP 44(a).
State statute, FRAP 44(b).

Attorneys at law.
Admission to practice, FRAP 46(b).
Exclusion from practice, USCtApp HPIP Rule II(a)(3).
Obtaining admission, USCtApp HPIP Rule II(a)(2).
When required, USCtApp HPIP Rule II(a)(1).
Appearance before the court, FRAP 46(a).
Law students, FRAP 46(g).
Appendices to briefs.
Sanctions against attorneys for inclusion of unnecessary material, FRAP 30(b).
Change of address, FRAP 46(c).
Change of name of attorney after admission, FRAP 46(d).
Clerk or deputy clerk not to practice, FRAP 45(a).
Committee on admissions and grievances, FRAP 46(f).

APPEALS, FEDERAL CASES
—Cont'd
Attorneys at law —Cont'd
Death of counsel, effect on service of notice of appeal, FRAP 3(d).
Death of party, filing notice of appeal, FRAP 43(a).
Disciplinary actions.
Failure to comply with rules, USCtApp Rule 38.
Rules of disciplinary enforcement, USCtApp Appx I.
Suspension or disbarment, FRAP 46(e).
Disciplinary power of court over, FRAP 46(e).
In forma pauperis.
Appointment of counsel, USCtApp HPIP Rule VI(d).
Oral argument, non-appearance of parties, FRAP 34(e).
Representation statement, filing, FRAP 12(b).
Suspension or disbarment, FRAP 46(e).
Attorneys' fees.
Plan to implement criminal justice act of 1964, USCtApp Appx II.
AVIS.
Electronic public access to information, USCtApp HPIP Rule II(b)(3).
Bankruptcy.
Appeals from district courts, FRAP 6.
Bill of costs, FRAP 39(d).
Bonds, surety.
Clerk of court of appeals, FRAP 45(a).
Costs.
Civil cases, FRAP 7.
Permission under 28 USCS 1292(b), FRAP 5(d).
Motion for additional security, record for preliminary hearing in court of appeals, FRAP 11(g).
Motion for stay pending review of administrative orders, filing, FRAP 18.
Release of prisoner pending review of habeas corpus decision, FRAP 23.
Stay.
Mandate, condition to grant or continuance, FRAP 41(d).
Pending appeal, FRAP 8(b).
Supersedeas bond.
Application for approval, FRAP 8(a).
Motion for additional security, record for preliminary hearing in court of appeals, FRAP 11(g).

APPEALS, FEDERAL CASES
—Cont'd
Briefs, FRAP 28 to 32, USCtApp HPIP Rule IX(a), USCtApp Rules 28 to 32.1.
Amici curiae, FRAP 29, USCtApp HPIP Rule IX(a)(4), USCtApp Rule 29.
Appellant's brief, FRAP 28(a).
Appellee's brief, FRAP 28(b).
Appendix, FRAP 30, USCtApp HPIP Rule IX(b), USCtApp Rule 30.
Citation of authorities, FRAP 28(j), USCtApp Rule 28.
Judicial dispositions, USCtApp Rule 32.1.
Consolidated and joint appeals, USCtApp HPIP Rule IX(a)(2).
Contents, USCtApp HPIP Rule IX(a)(8).
Costs, FRAP 39(c).
Cross appeals, FRAP 28.1(c), USCtApp HPIP Rule IX(a)(3).
Cover, FRAP 28.1(d).
Length, FRAP 28.1(e).
Time to file and serve, FRAP 28.1(f).
Failure to file, consequence, FRAP 31(c).
Federal labor relations authority proceedings, USCtApp Rule 15.1.
Filing, FRAP 25(a), 31.
Cross appeals, FRAP 28.1(f).
Form, FRAP 32(a).
Appendix and other papers, USCtApp Rule 32.
Certificate of compliance, FRAP Form 6.
Format, USCtApp HPIP Rule IX(a)(6).
Generally, FRAP 28, USCtApp Rule 28.
Intervenors, USCtApp HPIP Rule IX(a)(4).
Length, USCtApp HPIP Rule IX(a)(7).
Mailing as time deemed filed, FRAP 25(a).
Mandamus, prohibition, etc., petition for writ of, FRAP 21, USCtApp Rule 21.
Multiple appellants or appellees, cases involving, FRAP 28(i).
National labor relations board proceedings, FRAP 15.1, USCtApp Rule 15.1.
Non-appearance of parties, decision on briefs, FRAP 34(e).
Number of copies, FRAP 31(b), USCtApp HPIP Rule IX(a)(5), USCtApp Rule 31.

APPEALS, FEDERAL CASES
—Cont'd
Briefs —Cont'd
Preservation by clerk, FRAP 45(d).
References to parties, FRAP 28(d).
References to the record, FRAP 28(e).
Reply brief.
Time for serving and filing, FRAP 31(a).
Cross appeals, FRAP 28.1(f).
Reproduction of statutes.
Rules, regulations, etc., FRAP 28(f).
Seals.
Briefs containing material under seal, USCtApp HPIP Rule IX(a)(10).
Service, FRAP 31.
Cross appeals, FRAP 28.1(f).
Shortening time for serving and filing, FRAP 31(a).
Submission for decision on, FRAP 34(f).
Supplemental briefs and letters, USCtApp HPIP Rule IX(a)(9).
Supporting motions, FRAP 27(a).
Timing, FRAP 31(a), USCtApp HPIP Rule IX(a)(1).
Cross appeals, FRAP 28.1(f).
Unpublished opinions, USCtApp HPIP Rule IX(a)(8).
Calendar, USCtApp HPIP Rule X.
Arguments.
Scheduling cases for argument, USCtApp HPIP Rule X(d).
Caseload and case mix, USCtApp HPIP Rule X(c).
Merits panel, USCtApp HPIP Rule X(b).
Preparation of, FRAP 45(b).
Scheduling of cases.
Argument, USCtApp HPIP Rule X(d).
Particular cases, USCtApp HPIP Rule X(e).
Related cases, USCtApp HPIP Rule X(e)(2).
Remands to this court, USCtApp HPIP Rule X(e)(3).
Special panel, USCtApp HPIP Rule X(e)(1).
Stipulated stand-by pool, USCtApp HPIP Rule X(e)(4).
Scheduling sitting periods, USCtApp HPIP Rule X(a).
Certificates.
Certificate of appealability, FRAP 22(b).

APPEALS, FEDERAL CASES
—Cont'd
Certificates —Cont'd
Certificate of temporary retention of record in district court, FRAP 12(c).
Probable cause for appeal, necessity, habeas corpus, FRAP 22(b).
Temporary retention of record in district court, filing of certificate as to, FRAP 12(c).
Certiorari.
Duty of counsel.
Criminal Justice Act plan, USCtApp Appx II.
Stay of mandate pending application for, FRAP 41(d).
Chambers, USCtApp HPIP Rule I(a)(1).
Circuit executive.
Generally, USCtApp HPIP Rule I(b)(4).
Office, USCtApp HPIP Rule I(a)(2).
Civil appeals management plan, USCtApp HPIP Rule II(b)(5).
Multiparty cases, USCtApp HPIP Rule V(b).
Civil cases.
Appeals as of right, when taken, FRAP 4(a).
Interest on judgments, FRAP 37.
Clerk of court.
Administrative review or enforcement, duties, FRAP 15.
Attorney's application for admission to bar, filing, FRAP 46(b).
Bond, FRAP 45(a).
Calendar, preparation, FRAP 45(b).
Computerized records, FRAP 45(b).
Costs inserted in mandate, FRAP 39(d).
District court appeals, duties, FRAP 3, 11(b).
Transmitting the record on appeal, FRAP 11(b).
Docket, FRAP 12(a), 45(b).
Duties, generally, FRAP 45, USCtApp Rule 45.
District court appeals, FRAP 3.
Transmitting the record on appeal, FRAP 11(b).
Entry of judgment, FRAP 36.
Fees, USCtApp HPIP Rule II(d).
Filing and service of papers, duties, FRAP 25, USCtApp Rule 25.
Filing record, partial record, or certificate on appeal, FRAP 12(c).

APPEALS, FEDERAL CASES
—Cont'd
Clerk of court —Cont'd
Index of docket, FRAP 45(b).
Martin Luther King, Jr.'s birthday,
office to be closed on, FRAP 45(a).
Motions.
Clerk may dispose of certain
motions, FRAP 27(e).
Disposition by clerk, USCtApp HPIP
Rule VII(c), USCtApp Rule 27.
Oath, FRAP 45(a).
Office, USCtApp HPIP Rule I(a)(3).
Staff, USCtApp HPIP Rule I(b)(5).
When open, FRAP 45(a).
Petition for appeal.
Permission under 28 USCS 1292(b)
filed with, FRAP 5(a).
Preservation and custody of papers
and records, FRAP 45(d).
Tax court, notice of appeal filed with,
FRAP 13(b).
Transmission of record on appeal to,
FRAP 11(b).
Petition for hearing or hearing en
banc, FRAP 35(b).
U.S. tax court, notice of appeal filed
with, FRAP 13(b).
Commencing appeal.
Preliminary matters, USCtApp HPIP
Rule III(a).
Committees, USCtApp HPIP Rule
I(c)(3).
Complaints against judges, USCtApp
HPIP Rule II(e).
Complex cases.
Appeals management plan, USCtApp
HPIP Rule II(b)(5).
Composition of record.
Appeal, FRAP 10(a).
Review or enforcement of
administrative orders, FRAP
16(a).
Computation of time, FRAP 26,
USCtApp Rule 26.
Filing notice of appeal as of right,
FRAP 4.
Computerized docket, FRAP 45(b).
Conference, prehearing or appeal,
FRAP 33.
Consolidation of appeals, FRAP 3(b).
Multiparty cases, USCtApp HPIP Rule
V(a).
**Constitutional challenges to
statutes.**
Federal statute, FRAP 44(a).

APPEALS, FEDERAL CASES
—Cont'd
Constitutional challenges to statutes
—Cont'd
State statute, FRAP 44(b).
Copies.
Agreed statement as record on appeal,
FRAP 10(d).
Appeals by permission under 28 USCS
1292(b), FRAP 5(c), USCtApp Rule
5.
Appendix, number, FRAP 30(a).
Application for writ of mandamus,
prohibition, etc., FRAP 21,
USCtApp Rule 21.
Briefs, number, filed and served,
FRAP 31(b).
Costs, FRAP 39(c).
Docket entries, composition of record
on appeal, FRAP 10(a).
Exhibits in appendix, reproduction,
FRAP 30(e).
Motions, FRAP 27(d).
Record on appeal, FRAP 10(b).
Statutes.
Rules, regulations, etc., in briefs or
pamphlets, FRAP 28(f).
Corporate disclosure statement,
FRAP 26.1, USCtApp Rule 26.1.
Correction of record.
Appeal, FRAP 10(e).
Review or enforcement of
administrative orders, FRAP
16(b).
Costs, FRAP 39, USCtApp Rule 39.
Appendix, production of, FRAP 30(b).
Bill of costs inserted in mandate or
added later, FRAP 39(d).
Briefs and appendices, FRAP 39(c).
District courts, appeals from
judgments and orders.
Taxable costs, FRAP 39(e).
Frivolous appeals, FRAP 38.
Production of appendix to briefs,
FRAP 30(b).
Record on appeal, FRAP 10(b), 39.
Sanctions against attorneys for
including unnecessary material in
appendices, FRAP 30(b).
Transcript, payment, FRAP 10(b).
Court organization, USCtApp HPIP
Rule I(c).
Court reporters.
Payment for cost of transcript, FRAP
10(b).
Transcripts' preparation and filing,
FRAP 11(b).

APPEALS, FEDERAL CASES
—Cont'd

Criminal law and procedure.

Appeals as of right, when taken, FRAP 4(b).

Direct appeals of criminal cases.

Handling not delayed for consideration of postconviction proceedings in district court, USCtApp Rule 47.5.

Release in, FRAP 9, USCtApp Rule 9.

Record on appeal, preliminary motions, FRAP 11(g).

Service of process and papers.

Notice of filing of notice of appeal as of right, FRAP 3(d).

Stays pending appeal, FRAP 8(c).

Cross appeals, FRAP 28.1, USCtApp HPIP Rule III(I).

Argument, FRAP 34(d).

Briefs, FRAP 28.1(c).

Cover, FRAP 28.1(d).

Length, FRAP 28.1(e).

Time to serve and file, FRAP 28.1(f).

Permissive appeals, FRAP 5(b).

Cross-application for enforcement of administrative orders, FRAP 15(b).

Custody of records and papers, FRAP 45(d).

Damages for delay, FRAP 38.

Death of party.

Service of notice of appeal, FRAP 3(d).

Substitution, FRAP 43(a).

Decisions.

Appendix to brief, FRAP 30(a).

Briefs, submission for decision on, FRAP 34(f).

Case conferences, USCtApp HPIP Rule XII(b).

Forms of decision, USCtApp HPIP Rule XII(a).

Notice, USCtApp HPIP Rule XII(e).

Preparation of opinions, USCtApp HPIP Rule XII(c).

Suspension of rules to expedite, FRAP 2, USCtApp Rule 2.

Timing of decisions, USCtApp HPIP Rule XII(d).

Unpublished opinions, USCtApp HPIP Rule XII(a).

Default.

Administrative review or enforcement, FRAP 15(b).

Delay.

Damages, FRAP 38.

APPEALS, FEDERAL CASES
—Cont'd

Disclosure of interest of parties, FRAP 26.1, USCtApp Rule 26.1.

Disclosure statement, corporate, FRAP 26.1, USCtApp Rule 26.1.

Dismissal of actions.

Content of notice of appeal, FRAP 3(c).

Failure to file briefs, FRAP 31(c).

Voluntary dismissal, FRAP 42.

District Court, appeals from orders of.

See UNITED STATES DISTRICT COURT FOR THE DISTRICT OF COLUMBIA.

Dockets and docketing, FRAP 12.

Bankruptcy proceedings, FRAP 6(b).

Book to be kept, FRAP 45(b).

Computerized format, FRAP 45(b).

District court and tax court, USCtApp HPIP Rule IV(a).

Entries.

Appendix to brief, FRAP 30(a).

Arrangement, FRAP 30(d).

Certified copy transmitted in lieu of entire record, FRAP 11(e).

Composition of record on appeal, FRAP 10(a).

Permission under 28 USCS 1292(b), FRAP 5(d).

Petition for writs of mandamus, prohibition, and other extraordinary writs, FRAP 21, USCtApp Rule 21.

Representation statement.

Attorneys at law, FRAP 12(b).

Review of decisions of U.S. Tax court, FRAP 13(d).

Documents.

Certified lists, filing of record, administrative review or enforcement, FRAP 17(b).

Transmission of record on appeal, FRAP 11(b).

Electronic service, FRAP 25(c).

Additional time after service, FRAP 26(c).

Proof of service, FRAP 25(d).

Emergency relief pending appeal or review, FRAP 18, USCtApp Rules 8, 18.

En banc proceedings, FRAP 35, USCtApp Rule 35.

Petitions for hearing or rehearing, USCtApp Rule 35.

Entry of judgment.

Settlement of judgments enforcing orders, FRAP 19.

APPEALS, FEDERAL CASES
—Cont'd
Evidence.
Composition of record on review or
enforcement of administrative
orders, FRAP 16(a).
Record on appeal, FRAP 10(b).
References in briefs to, FRAP 28(e).
Statement of when no report made or
transcript unavailable, FRAP
10(c).
Exhibits.
Certified lists, filing as filing of record,
administrative review or
enforcement, FRAP 17(b).
Composition of record on appeal,
FRAP 10(a).
Physical exhibits, use in argument,
FRAP 34(g).
Record on appeal, FRAP 10(a), 11(b).
Reproduction in appendix, FRAP 30(e).
Expedited appeals, USCtApp HPIP
Rule III(j), USCtApp Rule 47.2.
Expenses.
Criminal justice act plan, USCtApp
Appx II.
Extension of time, FRAP 26, USCtApp
Rule 26.
Notice of appeal, filing, FRAP 4, 26(b).
Record on review or enforcement of
administrative orders, filing,
FRAP 17(a).
Rehearing petition, FRAP 40(a).
Transmission of record on appeal,
FRAP 11(b).
Extraordinary writs, FRAP 21,
USCtApp Rule 21.
Certiorari, stay of mandate pending
application for, FRAP 41(d).
Fees, USCtApp Appx I, USCtApp Rule
45.
Administrative orders, FRAP 15(e).
Clerks of court, USCtApp HPIP Rule
II(d).
Docketing.
Notice of appeal, FRAP 3(e).
Petition for mandamus, prohibition,
and other extraordinary writs,
FRAP 21, USCtApp Rule 21.
Permissive appeals, FRAP 5(d).
Filing of documents and papers.
Administrative orders, review or
enforcement of, FRAP 17.
Amicus curiae brief, FRAP 29.
Appendices to briefs, FRAP 30.
Attorneys at law.
Application for admission to bar of
court of appeals, FRAP 46(b).

APPEALS, FEDERAL CASES
—Cont'd
Filing of documents and papers
—Cont'd
Attorneys at law —Cont'd
Representation statement, FRAP
12(b).
Briefs, FRAP 25(a), 31.
Cross appeals, FRAP 28.1(f).
Compliance with rules, USCtApp
HPIP Rule II(c)(1).
Dockets, USCtApp HPIP Rule II(c)(4).
Mailing papers, FRAP 25(a).
Motion for stay or injunction pending
appeal, FRAP 8(a).
Notice of appeal.
As of right, FRAP 3(a).
Death of party, FRAP 43(a).
Extension of time prohibited, FRAP
26(b).
Review of U.S. Tax Court decisions,
FRAP 13a.
Papers, FRAP 25(a).
Petition, time for filing.
Allowance of or permission to
appeal, extension of time
prohibited, FRAP 26(b).
Mandamus, prohibition, and other
extraordinary writs, FRAP 21,
USCtApp Rule 21.
Rehearing, time, FRAP 40(a).
Service, USCtApp HPIP Rule II(c)(3).
Special delivery, FRAP 25(a).
Timeliness, USCtApp HPIP Rule
II(c)(2).
Findings.
Composition of record on review or
enforcement of administrative
orders, FRAP 16(a).
Form of briefs.
Appendix and other papers, USCtApp
Rule 32.
Forms.
Agency, board, commission, or officer,
petition for review, FRAP Form 3.
Application for writ of mandamus,
prohibition, etc., FRAP 21,
USCtApp Rule 21.
Briefs, appendix, and other papers,
FRAP 32, USCtApp Rule 32.
Certificate of compliance with brief
form requirements, FRAP Form
6.
In forma pauperis, affidavit to
accompany motion for leave to
appeal, FRAP Form 4.

APPEALS, FEDERAL CASES
—Cont'd
Forms —Cont'd
Notices of appeal from district court, FRAP Form 1.
Bankruptcy court decisions and orders, FRAP Form 5.
Notices of appeal from tax court, FRAP Form 2.
Papers.
Appeals by permission under 28 USCS 1292(b), FRAP 5(c).
Frivolous actions.
Damages for, FRAP 38.
Sanctions against attorneys, USCtApp Rule 38.
Good faith.
In forma pauperis proceedings, FRAP 24.
Habeas corpus proceedings, FRAP 22, USCtApp Rule 47.2.
Certificate of appealability, FRAP 22(b).
Certificate of probable cause, necessity of, FRAP 22(b).
Custody of prisoners, FRAP 23.
Modification of initial order respecting custody, FRAP 23(d).
Original writ, application for, FRAP 22(a).
Recognizance, FRAP 23(b), (c).
Release of prisoners, FRAP 23(b), (c).
Service, notice of filing of notice of appeal as of right, FRAP 3(d).
Hearing.
Appeal on original record without appendix, FRAP 30(f).
En banc, FRAP 35.
Prehearing conference, FRAP 33.
Record for preliminary hearing in court of appeals, FRAP 11(g).
Sanction against attorney for inclusion of unnecessary material in appendix to brief, FRAP 30(b).
Holidays.
Clerk of court's office closed, FRAP 45(a).
Computation of time, FRAP 26(a).
Hours of clerk, FRAP 45(a).
Immigration and naturalization.
Record for review in agency action.
Filing, USCtApp Rule 17.
Inclement weather.
Court operations during, USCtApp HPIP Rule II(b)(4).
Oral arguments.
Weather closings, USCtApp HPIP Rule XI(g).

APPEALS, FEDERAL CASES
—Cont'd
Index of docket, clerk of court's duties, FRAP 45(b).
In forma pauperis proceedings, FRAP 24, USCtApp HPIP Rule VI, USCtApp Rule 24.
Affidavits, FRAP 24, FRAP Form 4.
Appendix, USCtApp HPIP Rule IX(b)(6).
Appointment of counsel, USCtApp HPIP Rule VI(d).
Compensation, USCtApp HPIP Rule VI(d)(4).
Duties in criminal cases, USCtApp HPIP Rule VI(d)(3).
Time and manner of appointment, USCtApp HPIP Rule VI(d)(1).
Withdrawal, USCtApp HPIP Rule VI(d)(2).
District court dismissal of suits brought in forma pauperis, USCtApp HPIP Rule VI(b).
Good faith, FRAP 24.
Leave to appeal, FRAP 24(a).
Procedural consequences of, USCtApp HPIP Rule VI(c).
When permitted, USCtApp HPIP Rule VI(a).
Inmate confined in institution.
Appeal as of right, when taken, FRAP 4(c).
Filing and service, FRAP 25(a).
Interest on judgments, FRAP 37.
Interlocutory appeals from district court, FRAP 5(a).
How taken, USCtApp HPIP Rule III(c)(1).
Timing, USCtApp HPIP Rule III(c)(2).
Intervention.
Administrative review, FRAP 15(d).
Briefs, USCtApp HPIP Rule IX(a)(4).
Docketing statement of intervenor, USCtApp Rule 12.
Joint appeals, USCtApp HPIP Rule III(h).
Administrative review, FRAP 15(a).
As of right, FRAP 3(b).
Judges.
Complaints against judges, USCtApp HPIP Rule II(e).
Generally, USCtApp HPIP Rule I(b)(1).
Masters, appointment of, FRAP 48.
Promulgation of rules by, FRAP 47.
Single judge to entertain motions, FRAP 27(c).

APPEALS, FEDERAL CASES
—Cont'd

Judges —Cont'd

Staffs, USCtApp HPIP Rule I(b)(2).

Writs of mandamus and prohibition directed to, FRAP 21, USCtApp Rule 21.

Judgments.

Affirmance, reversal, etc., costs, FRAP 39(a).

Briefs.

Citing judicial dispositions, USCtApp Rule 32.1.

Conviction, release pending appeal, FRAP 9(b).

Entry of, FRAP 36.

Administrative orders, judgment enforcing, FRAP 19.

Issuance of mandate after, FRAP 41(b).

Interest, FRAP 37.

Notice of, FRAP 45(c).

Settlements of judgment enforcing administrative orders, FRAP 19.

Judicial conference, USCtApp HPIP Rule I(c)(4), USCtApp Rule 47.3.

Judicial counsel, USCtApp HPIP Rule I(c)(1).

Jurisdiction.

Administrative agency cases, USCtApp HPIP Rule III(a)(2).

Collateral review of local court decisions, USCtApp HPIP Rule III(a)(4).

Commencing appeal, USCtApp HPIP Rule III(a).

District court cases, USCtApp HPIP Rule III(a)(1).

Original jurisdiction, USCtApp HPIP Rule III(a)(3).

Rules not to affect, FRAP 1.

Law students.

Appearance by, FRAP 46(g), USCtApp Rule 46.

Leave to appeal.

Bond.

In forma pauperis proceedings, FRAP 24, USCtApp Rule 24.

Brief of amicus curiae, FRAP 29.

In forma pauperis proceedings, FRAP 24(a).

Legal division.

Office, USCtApp HPIP Rule I(a)(4).

Personnel, USCtApp HPIP Rule I(b)(3).

Length of rehearing petition, FRAP 40(b).

APPEALS, FEDERAL CASES
—Cont'd

Libraries.

Generally, USCtApp HPIP Rule I(a)(5).

Librarians, USCtApp HPIP Rule I(b)(6).

Local rules.

Advisory committee on procedures, USCtApp Rule 47.4.

Clerk of court's office closed on legal holidays, FRAP 45(a).

Expedited appeals, USCtApp Rule 47.2.

Habeas corpus proceedings, USCtApp Rule 47.2.

Judicial conference, USCtApp Rule 47.3.

Maximum rate of costs of briefs, appendices, and copies, FRAP 39(c).

Oral argument, FRAP 34(a).

Process for rulemaking, USCtApp Rule 47.

Promulgated by courts of appeals, FRAP 47.

Sanctions against attorneys including unnecessary material in appendix to brief, FRAP 30(b).

Sealed matters, USCtApp Rule 47.1.

Sentencing appeal, USCtApp Rule 47.2.

Mail.

Additional time to act after service by, FRAP 26(c).

Briefs and appendices, time deemed filed, FRAP 25(a).

Copy of opinion to parties, FRAP 36.

Notice of appeal, decisions of U.S. Tax court, FRAP 13(b).

Service.

Additional time to act after, FRAP 26(c).

Generally, FRAP 25(a).

Notice of filing of notice of appeal as of right, FRAP 3(d).

Papers.

Generally, FRAP 25(c).

Mandamus writs, FRAP 21, USCtApp Rule 21.

Mandates, FRAP 41, USCtApp Rule 41.

Clerk to insert costs in, FRAP 39(d).

Contents, FRAP 41(a).

Effective date, FRAP 41(c).

Interest on judgment, FRAP 37.

Petition of party for rehearing en banc not to stay, FRAP 35(c).

APPEALS, FEDERAL CASES
—Cont'd
Mandates —Cont'd
Staying of mandate, FRAP 41(d).
When issues, FRAP 41(b).
Masters.
Appointment of, FRAP 48.
Mediation.
Docketing of appeals, USCtApp HPIP
Rule IV(d).
Mediation program, USCtApp Appx I.
Meetings of court.
Executive session, USCtApp HPIP
Rule I(c)(2).
Misstatements.
Record on review or enforcement of
administrative orders, FRAP
16(b).
Mistaken filing in court of appeals.
Appeal as of right, FRAP 4(d).
Modification.
Initial order respecting custody,
habeas corpus, FRAP 23(d).
Interest on judgment, FRAP 37.
Procedural orders, determination of
motions for, FRAP 27(b).
Record on appeal, FRAP 10(e).
Motions, FRAP 27, USCtApp Rule 27.
Administrative orders.
Motion for stay pending review of
administrative orders, filing,
FRAP 18, USCtApp Rule 18.
Admission of attorney to practice,
FRAP 46(a).
Brief of amicus curiae, leave to file,
FRAP 29.
Clerk may dispose of certain motions,
FRAP 27(e).
Consolidation of appeals, FRAP 3(b).
Dismissal of appeal.
Failure to file briefs, FRAP 31(c).
Record for hearing in court of
appeals, FRAP 11(g).
Disposition by clerk, USCtApp HPIP
Rule VII(c).
Disposition by merits panel, USCtApp
HPIP Rule VII(e).
Disposition by panel, USCtApp HPIP
Rule VII(d).
Distribution of orders, USCtApp HPIP
Rule VII(f).
Expedite consideration of appeal,
USCtApp HPIP Rule VIII(b).
Extensions of time, FRAP 26(b).
Filing notice of appeal as of right,
FRAP 4.

APPEALS, FEDERAL CASES
—Cont'd
Motions —Cont'd
Extensions of time —Cont'd
Transmission of record on appeal,
FRAP 11(b).
Filing, FRAP 25(a).
Formal requirements, USCtApp HPIP
Rule VII(a).
Form of papers, FRAP 32(c).
Intervention.
Administrative review or
enforcement, FRAP 15(d).
Leave to proceed in forma pauperis,
FRAP 24.
Oral arguments.
Amicus curiae, FRAP 29.
Postponement of, FRAP 34(b).
Preliminary hearing in court of
appeals, record for, FRAP 11(g).
Procedural orders, motions for, FRAP
27(b).
Processing, USCtApp HPIP Rule
VII(b).
Release in criminal cases, FRAP 9,
USCtApp HPIP Rule VIII(c).
Remand, USCtApp HPIP Rule VIII(e).
Single judge, power to entertain,
FRAP 27(c).
Stay or injunction pending appeal,
FRAP 8, USCtApp HPIP Rule
VIII(a), USCtApp Rule 8.
Summary disposition, USCtApp HPIP
Rule VIII(g).
Suspension of rules, FRAP 2.
Transfer, USCtApp HPIP Rule VIII(f).
Unsealing sealed records, USCtApp
HPIP Rule VIII(h).
Voluntary dismissal, FRAP 42,
USCtApp HPIP Rule VIII(d).
Multiparty cases.
Briefs in cases involving, FRAP 28(i).
Civil appeals management plan,
USCtApp HPIP Rule V(b).
Consolidation, USCtApp HPIP Rule
V(a).
Name, USCtApp Rule 1.
Name or title of public officer
substituted as party, FRAP 43(c).
**National labor relations board
proceedings.**
Briefs and oral argument, FRAP 15.1,
USCtApp Rule 15.1.
Neglect.
Extension of time to file notice of
appeal as of right, FRAP 4.

APPEALS, FEDERAL CASES
—Cont'd
Non-appearance of parties for argument, FRAP 34(e).
Notice.
Argument, FRAP 34(b).
As of right, FRAP 3, 4.
Death of party, filing notice of appeal, FRAP 43(a).
Decisions, USCtApp HPIP Rule XII(e).
Decisions of U.S. Tax court, FRAP 13, FRAP Form 2.
Docketing fee, FRAP 3(e).
Entry of judgment, date of, FRAP 36.
Filing of record.
Appeal, FRAP 12(c).
Review or enforcement of administrative orders, FRAP 17(a).
Form.
Bankruptcy court, FRAP Form 5.
District court orders, FRAP Forms 1, 5.
Tax court orders, FRAP Form 2.
Motion for stay or injunction, FRAP 18.
Pending appeal, FRAP 8(a).
Oral argument, USCtApp HPIP Rule XI(a).
Orders or judgments, FRAP 45(c).
Partial transcript ordered, notice to appellee, FRAP 10(b).
Release in criminal cases, appeal or motion, FRAP 9(a).
Sanction against attorney for inclusion of unnecessary material in appendix to brief, FRAP 30(b).
Substitution of parties before or after filing, FRAP 43(a).
Number of copies.
Appeals by permission under 28 USCS 1292(b), FRAP 5(c), USCtApp Rule 5.
Appendix, FRAP 30(a).
Application for writ of mandamus, prohibition, etc., FRAP 21.
Briefs, USCtApp Rule 31.
To be filed and served, FRAP 31(b).
Motions, FRAP 27(d).
Papers.
Application for writ of mandamus, prohibition, etc., FRAP 21.
Motions, FRAP 27(d).
Oaths and affirmations.
Attorneys, admission to practice, FRAP 46(b).

APPEALS, FEDERAL CASES
—Cont'd
Oaths and affirmations —Cont'd
Clerks of court of appeals, FRAP 45(a).
Objections.
Bill of costs, FRAP 39(d).
Statement when transcript unavailable, service of objections, FRAP 10(c).
Omissions.
Record on review or enforcement of administrative orders, FRAP 16(b).
Opinions of court, USCtApp Rule 36.
Briefs.
Citing judicial dispositions, USCtApp Rule 32.1.
Entry of judgments following receipt of, FRAP 36.
Settlement of judgments enforcing orders, FRAP 19.
Oral argument, FRAP 34, USCtApp Rule 34.
Amicus curiae, USCtApp HPIP Rule XI(e).
Motions, FRAP 29.
Appellee not heard, failure to file brief, FRAP 31(c).
Argument time, USCtApp HPIP Rule XI(c).
Rule 34(j) dispositions, USCtApp HPIP Rule XI(c)(2).
Screening by the panel, USCtApp HPIP Rule XI(c)(1).
Briefs, FRAP 28(a).
Federal labor relations authority proceedings, USCtApp Rule 15.1.
Form and content, USCtApp HPIP Rule XI(f).
Mandamus, prohibition, etc., petition for writ of, FRAP 21, USCtApp Rule 21.
National labor relations board proceedings, FRAP 15.1, USCtApp Rule 15.1.
Notice, USCtApp HPIP Rule XI(a).
Number of counsel, USCtApp HPIP Rule XI(d).
Order and content of argument, FRAP 34(c).
Permissive appeals, FRAP 5(b).
Petition for extraordinary writ, FRAP 21, USCtApp Rule 21.
Postponements, USCtApp HPIP Rule XI(b).
Procedures, USCtApp HPIP Rule XI(h).

APPEALS, FEDERAL CASES
　—Cont'd
Oral argument —Cont'd
　Transcription of arguments, USCtApp
　　HPIP Rule XI(i).
　Weather closings, USCtApp HPIP Rule
　　XI(g).
Orders of court.
　Answer to petition for writ of
　　mandamus, prohibition, etc., order
　　directing, FRAP 21, USCtApp
　　Rule 21.
　Briefs.
　　Citing judicial dispositions,
　　　USCtApp Rule 32.1.
　Extension of time to file petition for
　　rehearing, FRAP 40(a).
　Hearing or rehearing en banc, FRAP
　　35.
　Interlocutory orders, appeals from by
　　permission under 28 USCS
　　1292(b), FRAP 5(a).
　Notice of, clerk to serve, FRAP 45(c).
・　Prehearing or appeal conference,
　　recitation of action at, FRAP 33.
　Transfer of custody pending review in
　　habeas corpus proceedings, FRAP
　　23(a).
Original proceedings, USCtApp HPIP
　Rule III(g).
　Docketing of appeals, USCtApp HPIP
　　Rule IV(c).
　How taken, USCtApp HPIP Rule
　　III(g)(1).
　Timing, USCtApp HPIP Rule III(g)(2).
　Writs of mandamus.
　　Challenging district court transfers,
　　　USCtApp HPIP Rule III(g)(3).
　　Petitions alleging unreasonable
　　　agency delay, USCtApp HPIP
　　　Rule III(g)(4).
Panels.
　Disclosure of panels and dates,
　　USCtApp HPIP Rule II(b)(8).
Papers.
　Appeals by permission under 28 USCS
　　1292(b), FRAP 5(c).
　Custody of clerk of court of appeals,
　　FRAP 45(d).
　Form, FRAP 32(c).
　　Motions, FRAP 27(d).
　Preservation by clerk, FRAP 45(d).
　Supporting motions, FRAP 27(a).
Partial transcript, FRAP 10(b).
Parties.
　Multiple appellants or appellees, briefs
　　in cases involving, FRAP 28(i).

APPEALS, FEDERAL CASES
　—Cont'd
Parties —Cont'd
　Non-appearance of parties, decision on
　　briefs, FRAP 34(e).
　Petition for hearing or rehearing en
　　banc, FRAP 35(b).
　References in briefs to, FRAP 28(d).
　Statutes challenged on constitutional
　　grounds.
　　Federal statute, FRAP 44(a).
　　State statute, FRAP 44(b).
　Substitution of parties, FRAP 43.
Partnerships.
　Corporate disclosure statements,
　　FRAP 26.1, USCtApp Rule 26.1.
Pending cases, USCtApp HPIP Rule
　II(b)(7).
Permissive appeals, FRAP 5,
　USCtApp Rule 5.
Personal representatives.
　Substitution as party, FRAP 43(a).
Personnel, USCtApp HPIP Rule I(b).
Petitions.
　Administrative review, FRAP 15.
　Extension of time to file prohibited,
　　FRAP 26(b).
　Hearing or rehearing en banc, FRAP
　　35(b).
　Joint petition.
　　Administrative review, FRAP 15(a).
　Mandamus, prohibition, and other
　　extraordinary writs, FRAP 21,
　　USCtApp Rule 21.
　Motions practice generally, USCtApp
　　Rule 27.
　Permission to appeal under 28 USCS
　　1292(b).
　　Extension of time to file prohibited,
　　　FRAP 26(b).
　Permissive appeals, FRAP 5.
　　Certificate of parties and amici
　　　attached, USCtApp Rule 5.
　　Discovery statement attached,
　　　USCtApp Rule 5.
　Rehearing, USCtApp Rule 35.
　Review of administrative order, FRAP
　　Form 3.
Physical exhibits.
　Use in argument, FRAP 34(g).
Physical facilities, USCtApp HPIP
　Rule I(a).
Pleadings.
　Appendix, FRAP 30(a).
　Composition of record on review or
　　enforcement of administrative
　　orders, FRAP 16(a).

APPEALS, FEDERAL CASES
—Cont'd
Postconviction proceedings.
Direct criminal appeals not delayed to handle postconviction proceedings in district court, USCtApp Rule 47.5.
Post-decision procedures.
Reconsiderations.
Rehearing by panel, USCtApp HPIP Rule XIII(b)(1).
Review by Supreme Court, USCtApp HPIP Rule XIII(c).
Terminating case.
Costs, USCtApp HPIP Rule XIII(a)(4).
Enforcement judgments, USCtApp HPIP Rule XIII(a)(1).
Mandates, USCtApp HPIP Rule XIII(a)(2).
Remands, USCtApp HPIP Rule XIII(a)(3).
Sealed records, disposal, USCtApp HPIP Rule XIII(a)(5).
Postponement of argument, FRAP 34(b).
Preferences.
Application for writ of mandamus, prohibition, etc., FRAP 21, USCtApp Rule 21.
Cases on calendar, FRAP 45(b).
Prehearing conference, FRAP 33.
Preliminary matters.
Admission to practice, FRAP 46, USCtApp HPIP Rule II(a), USCtApp Rule 46.
Filings, USCtApp HPIP Rule II(c).
Requests for information, USCtApp HPIP Rule II(b).
Preservation of copies of briefs, appendices and other papers by clerk, FRAP 45(d).
Press relations, USCtApp HPIP Rule II(b)(9).
Printing costs.
Maximum rate taxable, FRAP 39(c).
Prisons and prisoners.
Appeal as of right, when taken, FRAP 4(c).
Filing and service, FRAP 25(a).
Habeas corpus proceedings, FRAP 22, 23.
Procedural orders.
Motions for, FRAP 27(b).
Requests for information, USCtApp HPIP Rule II(b)(1).

APPEALS, FEDERAL CASES
—Cont'd
Process and service of process. See within this heading, "Service of process and papers."
Prohibition, writ of, FRAP 21, USCtApp Rule 21.
Directed to judge, FRAP 21.
Promulgation of rules by courts of appeals, FRAP 47.
Public officers and employees.
Death or separation from office. Substitution, FRAP 43(c).
Successor in public office. Substitution as party, FRAP 43(c).
Recognizance.
Release of prisoner pending review of habeas corpus decision, FRAP 23.
Recollection of appellant.
Unavailable record, FRAP 10(c).
Reconsideration.
Procedural orders.
Determination of motions for, FRAP 27(b).
Record for review in agency action.
Filing, USCtApp Rule 17.
Record on appeal, FRAP 10 to 12.
Composition of record.
Review or enforcement of administrative orders, FRAP 16(a).
Copies, cost of, FRAP 39(c).
Extension of time for transmission, FRAP 11(b).
Filing, FRAP 12.
Bankruptcy proceedings, appeals in, FRAP 6(b).
Papers, FRAP 25(a).
U.S. Tax court, review of decisions of, FRAP 13(d).
Lists, documents, transcripts, etc.
Filing as filing of record, administrative review or enforcement, FRAP 17(b).
Motion for stay or injunction pending appeal, filing with, FRAP 8(a).
Parts relied on in briefs, FRAP 28(a).
Permissive appeals, FRAP 5(d).
Preliminary hearing in court of appeals, FRAP 11(g).
References in briefs to, FRAP 28(e).
Release in criminal cases, FRAP 9(a).
Retention in district court by order of court, FRAP 11(e).
Service of papers, FRAP 25.
Stipulation that parts be retained in district court, FRAP 11(f).

APPEALS, FEDERAL CASES
—Cont'd
Record on appeal —Cont'd
Temporary retention in district court
for use in preparing appellate
papers, FRAP 11(c).
Transmission, FRAP 11, USCtApp
Rule 11.
Review of decisions of U.S. tax
court, FRAP 13(d).
Records.
Availability, USCtApp HPIP Rule
II(b)(2).
Electronic public access to information,
USCtApp HPIP Rule II(b)(3).
Rehearings.
En banc, FRAP 35, USCtApp HPIP
Rule XIII(b)(2).
Panel, USCtApp HPIP Rule XIII(b)(1).
Petition for panel rehearing, FRAP 40.
Stay of mandate upon filing, FRAP
41(b).
Release in criminal cases, FRAP 9,
22, 23, USCtApp Rule 9.
Record for preliminary hearing in
court of appeals, FRAP 11(g).
Remands, USCtApp Rule 41.
Calendar.
Scheduling of cases.
Cases on remand to this court,
USCtApp HPIP Rule X(e)(3).
Motions for remand, USCtApp HPIP
Rule VIII(e).
Terminating case, USCtApp HPIP
Rule XIII(a)(3).
Removal of exhibits after argument,
FRAP 34(g).
Reply.
Permissive appeals, USCtApp Rule 5.
Reports.
Statement of evidence or proceedings
when no report made or transcript
unavailable, FRAP 10(c).
Representation statement.
Attorneys at law.
Filing, FRAP 12(b).
Reproductions.
Exhibits in appendix, FRAP 30(e).
Requests for information.
General information, USCtApp HPIP
Rule II(b)(6).
Resignation of public officers.
Substitution of party, FRAP 43(c).
Response to motions, FRAP 27(a).
Retention of record in district court.
Preparing appellate papers, use in,
FRAP 11(c).

APPEALS, FEDERAL CASES
—Cont'd
Retention of record in district court
—Cont'd
Stipulation of parties, FRAP 11(f).
Reversal.
Costs, FRAP 39(a).
Interest on judgment, FRAP 37.
Rulemaking process.
Local rules by courts of appeals, FRAP
47, USCtApp Rule 47.
Rules and regulations.
Reproduction in briefs, FRAP 28(f).
Rules of court, USCtApp HPIP Rule
I(d).
Sanctions against attorneys.
Failure to comply with rules,
USCtApp Rule 38.
Inclusion of unnecessary material in
appendix, FRAP 30(b).
Rules of disciplinary enforcement,
USCtApp Appx I.
Saturday.
Clerk's office not open except as
provided by local rule or order,
FRAP 45(a).
Computation of time, FRAP 26(a).
Schedule of clerk's fees, USCtApp
Rule 45.
Fee schedule generally, USCtApp
Appx I.
Scope of rules, FRAP 1, USCtApp Rule
1.
Sealed records, USCtApp HPIP Rule
III(k), USCtApp Rule 47.1.
Appendix containing matters under
seal, USCtApp HPIP Rule
IX(b)(7).
Briefs containing material under seal,
USCtApp HPIP Rule IX(a)(10).
Motion to unseal, USCtApp HPIP Rule
VIII(h).
Post-decision procedures.
Disposal of sealed records, USCtApp
HPIP Rule XIII(a)(5).
Seal of court, USCtApp Rule 1.
Sentencing appeal, USCtApp Rule
47.2.
Separate appeals.
Argument, FRAP 34(d).
Service of process and papers, FRAP
25, USCtApp Rule 25.
Acknowledgment, service of papers,
FRAP 25(d).
Administrative review or enforcement,
FRAP 15(c).

APPEALS, FEDERAL CASES
—Cont'd
Service of process and papers
—Cont'd
Appendix to briefs, FRAP 30(a).
Application for enforcement of
administrative orders, FRAP 15(c).
Briefs, FRAP 31.
Cross appeals, FRAP 28.1(f).
District courts, appeals from
judgments and orders, FRAP 3(d).
Electronic service, FRAP 25(c).
Additional time after service, FRAP
26(c).
Proof of service, FRAP 25(d).
Filed papers, service of, required,
FRAP 25(b).
Motion for stay or injunction pending
appeal, USCtApp Rule 8.
Notice.
Orders or judgments by clerk, FRAP
45(c).
Notice of appeal.
Appeal as of right, FRAP 3(d).
Review of decisions of U.S. Tax
Court, FRAP 13(c), FRAP Form
2.
Petition.
Administrative review or
enforcement, FRAP 15(c).
Mandamus, prohibition or other
extraordinary writs, FRAP 21,
USCtApp Rule 21.
Rehearing, FRAP 40(b).
Proof of service, FRAP 25(d).
Statement of appellant when no
transcript available, FRAP 10(c).
Sessions of court, USCtApp Rule 1.
Settlements.
Judgments enforcing administrative
orders, FRAP 19.
Simplification of issues.
Prehearing or appeal conference,
FRAP 33.
Special delivery, FRAP 25(a).
Special master.
Appointment of, FRAP 48.
**Statement of evidence or
proceedings.**
No report made or transcript
unavailable, statement of, FRAP
10(c).
**Statutes challenged on
constitutional grounds.**
Federal statute, FRAP 44(a).
State statute, FRAP 44(b).

APPEALS, FEDERAL CASES
—Cont'd
Statutes noted in briefs, FRAP 28(a).
Reproduction, FRAP 28(f).
Stays or injunctions.
Criminal cases, FRAP 8(c).
Mandate, FRAP 41, USCtApp Rule 41.
Pending application for certiorari,
FRAP 41(d).
Pending appeal or review, FRAP 8,
USCtApp Rule 8.
Administrative orders, FRAP 18,
USCtApp Rule 18.
Record for preliminary hearing in
court of appeals, FRAP 11(g).
Petition of party for rehearing en banc
not to stay mandate, FRAP 35(c).
Stipulations.
Correction of record on review or
enforcement of administrative
orders, FRAP 16(b).
Dismissal of appeal in district court,
FRAP 42(a).
Parts of record to be retained in
district court, FRAP 11(f).
Record or parts thereof to be filed,
administrative review or
enforcement, FRAP 17(b).
Submission for decision on briefs,
FRAP 34(f).
Subsidiary corporations.
Corporate disclosure statements,
FRAP 26.1, USCtApp Rule 26.1.
Substitution of parties, FRAP 43.
Successor in public office.
Substitution as party, FRAP 43(c).
Supplemental authorities.
Briefs, FRAP 28(j), USCtApp Rule 28.
Supreme Court of the United States.
DC Circuit court of appeals.
Review by supreme court, USCtApp
HPIP Rule XIII(c).
Survival of action.
Death of party, substitution, FRAP 43.
Suspension of attorney, FRAP 46(e).
Rules of disciplinary enforcement,
USCtApp Appx I.
Suspension of rules, FRAP 2,
USCtApp Rule 2.
Table of authorities.
Reply brief, FRAP 28(c).
Table of contents.
Briefs, FRAP 28.
Taxation of costs, FRAP 39, USCtApp
Rule 39.
Appeal, costs on, FRAP 39.

APPEALS, FEDERAL CASES
—Cont'd
Taxation of costs —Cont'd
Appendix, production of, FRAP 30(b).
Bill of costs inserted in mandate or added later, FRAP 39(d).
Tax court, FRAP 13, USCtApp HPIP Rule III(d).
Applicability of other rules, FRAP 14.
Docketing of appeal, USCtApp HPIP Rule IV(a).
Preliminary record on appeal and preparation of transcripts, USCtApp HPIP Rule IV(a)(1).
How taken, USCtApp HPIP Rule III(d)(1).
Leave to proceed in forma pauperis, FRAP 24(b).
Notice of appeal, FRAP Form 2.
Timing, USCtApp HPIP Rule III(d)(2).
Terminating case.
Post-decision procedures, USCtApp HPIP Rule XIII(a).
Terrorism.
Alien terrorist removal court.
Appeals from, USCtApp Rule 47.6.
Time and date.
Additional time after service by mail, FRAP 26(c).
Briefs and appendix to briefs, FRAP 30, 31(a).
Cross appeals, FRAP 28.1(f).
Clerk's office, hours open to public, FRAP 45(a).
Computation and extension, FRAP 26, USCtApp Rule 26.
Filing notice of appeal as of right, FRAP 4.
Entry of judgment, FRAP 36.
Filing.
Appendix to briefs, FRAP 30.
Briefs, FRAP 31(a).
Cross appeals, FRAP 28.1(f).
Notice of appeal, appeal as of right, FRAP 4.
Petition for rehearing, FRAP 40(a).
Record on review or enforcement of administrative orders, FRAP 17(a).
Mail, additional time after service by, FRAP 26(c).
Mandate, issuance of, FRAP 41(b).
Petition of party for rehearing en banc, FRAP 35(c).
Service by mail, additional time after, FRAP 26(c).

APPEALS, FEDERAL CASES
—Cont'd
Time and date —Cont'd
Service of briefs and appendix to briefs, FRAP 30(a), 31(a).
Cross appeals, FRAP 28.1(f).
Shortening period for serving and filing briefs, FRAP 31(a).
Sundays and holidays, FRAP 26(a), 45(a).
Transmission of record on appeal, FRAP 11(a).
Extension of time, FRAP 11(b).
Title of action.
Docketing of appeal, FRAP 12(a).
Title of rules, FRAP 1, USCtApp Rule 48.
Transcripts, FRAP 10(b).
Agreed statement as record on appeal, FRAP 10(d).
Appellant's duty to order, FRAP 10(b).
Certified list, filing as constituting filing of record, administrative review or enforcement, FRAP 17(b).
Composition of record on appeal, FRAP 10(a).
Correction of record on appeal, FRAP 10(e).
Modification of record on appeal, FRAP 10(e).
Reporter's duty to prepare and file, FRAP 11(b).
Statement of evidence when unavailable, FRAP 10(c).
Transmitting the record on appeal, FRAP 11.
Transmission of record on appeal, FRAP 11, USCtApp Rule 11.
Review of decisions of U.S. tax court, FRAP 13(d).
Unauthorized practice of law.
Clerk or deputy clerk not to practice, FRAP 45(a).
Court employees, USCtApp Rule 1.
United States.
Costs for and against, FRAP 39(b).
Unpublished opinions.
Briefs, USCtApp HPIP Rule IX(a)(8).
Decisions of the court, USCtApp HPIP Rule XII(a).
Vacation of judgments.
Costs, FRAP 39(a).
Procedural orders, determination of motions for, FRAP 27(b).
Voluntary dismissal, FRAP 42.

APPEALS, FEDERAL CASES
—Cont'd
Weather.
Court operation during inclement
weather, USCtApp HPIP Rule
II(b)(4).
Oral arguments.
Weather closings, USCtApp HPIP
Rule XI(g).
Weight of record on appeal, FRAP
11(b).
Writs of mandamus.
Petitions alleging unreasonable agency
delay, USCtApp HPIP Rule
III(g)(4).
Petitions challenging district court
transfers, USCtApp HPIP Rule
III(g)(3).

APPEARANCES.
Adoption proceedings, Adoption Rule
101.
Appeals, D.C. courts, DCCtApp Rule
42.
Appeals, federal cases.
Attorneys and counselors, FRAP 46(a).
Law students, FRAP 46(g), USCtApp
Rule 46.
Oral argument, parties, FRAP 34(e).
Arbitration, Arbitration Rule XIV.
**Child abuse and neglect
proceedings.**
Initial appearance.
Matters addressed, NeglectProc Rule
12.
Notice, NeglectProc Rule 5.
Report, NeglectProc Rule 7.
Child custody proceedings.
Parities and child, §16-4602.10.
Special appearance immunity,
§16-4601.08.
Civil procedure, CivPro Rule 101,
USDistCt LCvR 83.2, USDistCt
LCvR 83.6.
Criminal procedure, USDistCt LCrR
44.1, USDistCt LCrR 44.5.
Appearance by non-District attorney,
CrimPro Rule 115.
Domestic relations actions, DomRel
Rule 101.
Intervention proceedings, Probate
Rule 305.
Judges.
Governmental bodies, appearances
before.
Conflicts with office, avoiding, CJC
Canon 3.2.

**APPELLATE MEDIATION
PROGRAM,** USCtApp Appx I.

APPLICATION FOR APPEAL,
DCCtApp Rules 5, 6.
Forms, DCCtApp Forms 3, 4.

APPOINTMENT OF COUNSEL.
See RIGHT TO COUNSEL.

APPORTIONMENT.
Congress, US Const Art I §§2, 3, Amds
14, 17.

APPRAISALS.
Conservators, Probate Rule 333.
Corporations.
Appraisal and payment for shares,
§§29-311.01 to 29-311.50.
See CORPORATIONS.
Court ordered property sales, CivPro
Rule 308.
Probate proceedings, Probate Rule
203.
Eminent domain.
Objections or exceptions to
appraisement, §§16-1317, 16-1318.
Fiduciary held property, CivPro Rule
305.
Probate proceedings.
Death before January 1, 1981.
Securities' registration and
appraisal, Probate Rule 16.
Death between January 1, 1981 and
June 30, 1995, Probate Rule 109.
Death on or after July 1, 1995,
Probate Rule 409.
Limited use of appraisals, Probate
Rule 412.
Guardians, conservators, trustees, etc.,
involved, Probate Rules 204, 333.
Failure to appraise, Probate Rule
207.
Sale of property, Probate Rule 203.
Personal representatives, §§20-711 to
20-715.

APPRENTICES, §§32-1402 to 32-1413.
Administration.
Associate director of apprenticeship,
duties, §32-1405.
Agreements.
Appeals of decisions regarding,
§32-1410.
Approval, §32-1409.
Contents, §32-1408.
Hearings on, §32-1410.
Majority, agreement extending into,
§32-1409.

APPRENTICES —Cont'd
Agreements —Cont'd
Registration, §32-1409.
Violations, §32-1410.
Appeals of determinations regarding agreements, §32-1410.
Applicability of provisions, §32-1411.
Associate director of apprenticeship, §32-1403.
Duties, §32-1405.
Committees, §32-1406.
Council.
Organization and membership, §32-1402.
Procedures, §32-1404.
Definitions, §32-1407.
Director of apprenticeship, §1-202.04.
Funeral directors, §3-407.
Hearings on agreements, §32-1410.
Issuance of rules and regulations, §32-1404.
Majority, agreement extending into, §32-1409.
Pre-apprenticeship program, §32-1332.
Registration.
Agreements, §32-1409.
Programs, §§32-1431, 36-409.
Reports, §32-1404.
Severability of provisions, §32-1413.
Transfer of functions, §1-202.04.
Youth apprenticeship advisory council, §32-1412.01.

APPROPRIATIONS.
Administrative expenses, §1-321.06.
Advances.
Bonds, surety, §47-3401.03.
Definitions, §47-3401.05.
Liquidation of deficit, intermediate-term advances for, §47-3401.01.
Reimbursement of, §47-3401.04.
Seasonal cash-flow management, short-term advances for, §47-3401.02.
Transitional provision for short-term advances, §47-3401.
Alcohol and drug abuse prevention and treatment programs, §44-1210.
Antideficiency provisions, §47-105.
Bathing pools and beaches, §10-164.
Building lines, §6-406.
Capital outlay, §47-137.
Capitol police, §10-505.06.
Charitable institutions' appropriations as liens on property, §44-711.

APPROPRIATIONS —Cont'd
Charitable solicitations, §44-1714.
Claims against the District, settlement of, §2-404.
Congress, US Const Art I §§7, 9.
Constitution of the United States, US Const Art I §9.
Army, US Const Art I §8.
Revenue bills, US Const Art I §7.
Contingent expenses, §§47-106, 47-107.
Convention center and sports arena, §§47-396.01 to 47-398.06.
Convention center and sports arena preconstruction, §47-398.03.
Corrections, Department of, §24-211.05.
Crime victims' compensation, §4-518.
Deficiencies, §47-3404.
Definitions, §47-3401.05.
Demonstrations to influence legislation or governmental actions, §47-138.
Department of Motor Vehicles, appropriations transferred to, §§50-905, 50-906.
Disclosure, §47-3409.
District of Columbia General Hospital hospice program, §4-1103.
Dulles International Airport, §9-812.
Dulles International Airport Sanitary Sewer, §34-2133.
Elections, §1-1001.13.
Emergency management, §7-2207.
Employees retirement program management, §1-724.
Enactment by council, §1-204.46.
Increase in amount appropriated, §1-204.46a.
Excess property for development of seat of government, §16-1335.
Excess property for United States, §16-1383.
Federal City College, §§38-1106 to 38-1110.
Federal contribution, §§47-3402, 47-3406.02.
Federal provisions, repeal of, §§47-108, 47-109.
Fire departments, §5-406.
Gallaudet University, §38-2402.11.
Indigent blind children formerly instructed at, §38-2301.
Health occupations boards, §3-1213.01.

APPROPRIATIONS —Cont'd
Home purchase assistance fund,
  §§42-2602, 42-2605.
Homestead housing preservation,
  §42-2110.
Inaugural ceremonies of the
  President of the United States,
  §§2-810, 2-823.
Increases to appropriations,
  §47-369.02.
Indigent blind children formerly
  instructed at Gallaudet
  University, §38-2301.
Indigent criminal defendants,
  counsel for, §11-2608.
Industrial home school, §44-1304.
Insanitary buildings, §6-917.
Intellectual disabilities, persons
  with, §7-1306.03.
Intermediate-term advances for
  liquidation of deficit, §47-3401.01.
Issuance of rules and regulations,
  §47-3407.
Lapsed appropriations, restoration
  of, §47-136.
Latino community development,
  §2-1341.
Law revision commission, §45-304.
Library expenses, §39-106.
Liens on motor vehicles and trailers,
  §50-1216.
Liquidation of deficit, intermediate-
  term advances for, §47-3401.01.
Mental health services
  administration, §44-908.
Meritorious service awards for fire,
  police, and corrections
  departments, §5-904.
Merit system, §1-633.01.
Metabolic disorders, screening
  newborns for, §7-839.
Metropolitan police.
  Band, §5-131.05.
  Uniforms, §5-111.03.
Metrorail and metrobus.
  See METRORAIL AND METROBUS.
Motor vehicles.
  Inspection facilities, §50-1103.
  Safety responsibility provisions,
    §50-1301.80.
National Capital Housing Authority,
  §6-101.03.
National Capital Planning
  Commission, §§2-1008, 2-1010.
National Institute of Justice,
  §22-4201.

APPROPRIATIONS —Cont'd
Notaries public, §1-1217.
Old Georgetown Market, §6-1207.
Parking, §50-2608.
Parole, §24-134.
Police and firefighters medical care
  reimbursement, §5-609.
Police and firefighters retirement
  and disability, §5-732.
Powers and obligations, §1-301.01.
Printing schedules or lists of
  supplied and materials,
  §1-333.06.
Privacy and confidentiality,
  §47-3409.
Public assistance, §4-219.01.
Public building repairs and
  improvements, §10-703.
Public defender service, §2-1607.
Public officers and employees,
  §1-503.
Public Service Commission, §34-805.
Public welfare institutions
  supported by Congressional
  appropriations, §4-111.
Public works, §9-401.07.
Rapid rail transit, §9-1105.02.
Receptions for eminent persons,
  §1-333.09.
Recordation tax, §42-1124.
Recorder of deeds, §42-1213.
Reimbursable appropriation to
  district, §1-207.22.
Reimbursement of advances,
  §47-3401.04.
Religious institutions, §44-715.
Restoration of lapsed
  appropriations, §47-136.
Scholarships for opportunity and
  results (SOAR) act, §38-1853.14.
School food services, §§38-805,
  38-809.
Schools and education, §§38-911,
  38-914, 38-915, 38-1806.08.
Senior citizens' home repair and
  improvement program fund,
  §42-2203.
Severability of provisions, §47-3408.
Short-term advances.
  Seasonal cash-flow management,
    §47-3401.02.
  Transitional, §47-3401.
Statehood Constitutional
  Convention, §1-127.
Surplus funds, §47-369.01.
Tax Enforcement Act of 1982,
  §47-3410.

APPROPRIATIONS —Cont'd
Teachers' retirement.
Prior to June 30, 1946, §38-2001.07.
Tenant assistance program,
§42-3503.02.
Theodore Roosevelt Island, §§10-159,
10-160.
**Transitional provision for short-
term advances,** §47-3401.
Unclaimed property, §41-139.
United States, US Const Art I §9.
Annual payment by, §§47-3402,
47-3406.02.
**University of the District of
Columbia,** §§38-1203.01,
38-1204.05.
Wage increases, §47-3403.
**Washington Asylum and Jail
Superintendent, failure to make
appropriation for,** §24-201.17.
Water supply and waterworks,
§§1-204.88, 34-2401.26.
Workers' compensation, §32-1543.
World Class Schools Task Force,
§38-1803.15.
Zoning, §6-641.13.

AQUATIC ANIMALS AND PLANTS.
**Protection while regulating against
water pollution,** §8-103.03.

ARBITRATION, §§16-4401 to 16-4432.
Agreement to arbitrate.
Effect, §16-4404.
Jurisdiction to enforce, §16-4426.
Validity, §16-4406.
Appeals, §16-4427.
Applicability of provisions, §16-4403.
Applications for proceedings, CivPro
Rule 70-I.
Arbitration organizations.
Regulation, §16-4430.
Arbitrators.
Appointment, §16-4411.
Assignment, Arbitration Rule IV.
Authority generally, §16-4415.
Compensation, Arbitration Rule V.
Authority to award, §16-4421.
Conduct of arbitration, §16-4415.
Conflicts of interest, §16-4411.
Damages, fees and expenses.
Authority to award, §16-4421.
Disclosure of facts affecting
impartiality, §16-4412.
Immunity from liability, §16-4414.
Multiple arbitrators, §16-4413.
Powers, Arbitration Rule VI.
Qualifications, Arbitration Rule III.

ARBITRATION —Cont'd
Arbitrators —Cont'd
Recusal, Arbitration Rule IV.
Removal, Arbitration Rule III.
Small claims court, SmallClaimsArb
Rule 1.
Assignment of case to arbitration,
Arbitration Rule I.
Attorneys at law.
Appearance and withdrawal of
attorney, Arbitration Rule XIV.
Fee disputes, DCBar Rule XIII.
Lawyer serving as a third-party
neutral, ProfCond Rule 2.4.
Representation by counsel, §16-4416.
Representation in case where attorney
was arbitrator, ProfCond Rule
1.12.
Small claims court, SmallClaimsArb
Rule 3.
Award and judgment, Arbitration Rule
X.
Confirmation, §16-4422.
Motion for confirmation, CivPro
Form CA 107.
Correction, §§16-4420, 16-4424,
Arbitration Rule XIII.
Judgment on award, §16-4425.
Modification, §§16-4420, 16-4424,
Arbitration Rule XIII.
Objections, Arbitration Rule XII.
Record of award, §16-4419.
Small claims court, SmallClaimsArb
Rules 5, 6.
Vacation, §16-4423.
Binding arbitration, Arbitration Rule
I.
Civil procedure rules.
Applicability of rules, Arbitration Rule
XV.
Confirmation of awards, §16-4422,
CivPro Rule 70-I.
Motion for confirmation, CivPro Form
CA 107.
Consolidation of proceedings,
§16-4410.
**Construction of statutory
provisions,** §16-4428.
Damages, fees and expenses,
§16-4421.
Compensation, Arbitration Rule V.
Disclosure of costs, §16-4431.
Definitions, §16-4401.
Depositions, §16-4417.
Disclosure of costs, §16-4431.

ARBITRATION —Cont'd
Discovery, §16-4417, Arbitration Rule VII.
   Suspension of discovery rules, Arbitration Rule VI.
Electronic signatures in global and national commerce act.
   Relationship to, §16-4429.
Eligibility of cases, Arbitration Rule I.
Employment agencies, §32-413.
Evictions, §§42-3505.03, 42-3505.04.
Existing agreements, §16-4432.
Fees, §16-4421, Arbitration Rules IV, V.
   Small claims court, SmallClaimsArb Rule 1.
Filing procedures, Arbitration Rule VIII.
Hearings, Arbitration Rule IX.
   Small claims court, SmallClaimsArb Rule 3.
Initiation of proceeding, §16-4409.
Judges.
   Acting as arbitrators, avoiding conflicts with office, CJC Canon 3.9.
Judgment and award, §16-4425, Arbitration Rule X.
   Modification or correction of award, Arbitration Rule XIII.
   Objections, Arbitration Rule XII.
   Small claims court, SmallClaimsArb Rules 5, 6.
Judicial enforcement of pre-award ruling, §16-4418.
Judicial relief, application for, §16-4405.
Jurisdiction to enforce agreement, §16-4426.
Landlord and tenant.
   Rental housing providers and tenant disputes, §§42-3505.03, 42-3505.04.
Lemon law, §§50-503, 50-509.
Lie detector tests, §32-903.
Merit system, §1-606.07.
Minors affected by settlement or judgment, Arbitration Rule VI.
Motions, Arbitration Rule VIII, CivPro Rule 70-I.
   Motion to compel, §16-4407.
   Pending motions at time of assignment, Arbitration Rule VI.
Multi-door dispute resolution division.
   Filing of papers, Arbitration Rule VIII.
No-fault motor vehicle insurance, §31-2405.

ARBITRATION —Cont'd
Non-binding unless otherwise stated, Arbitration Rule I.
Notice provisions, §16-4402.
Objections, Arbitration Rule XII.
Polygraphs, §32-903.
Pre-award ruling, §16-4418.
Probate proceedings, §16-3111.
Provisional remedies, §16-4408.
Record of award, §16-4419.
Regulation of arbitration organizations, §16-4430.
Rehearing, CivPro Rule 70-I.
   Vacation of award, §16-4423.
Removal of case from arbitration, Arbitration Rule II.
Rental housing providers and tenant disputes, §§42-3505.03, 42-3505.04.
Retaliatory actions against tenants, §§42-3505.03, 42-3505.04.
Rules of civil procedure.
   Applicability of rules, CivPro Rule 81.
Savings clause, §16-4432.
Small claims court, §11-1322, SmallClaimsArb Rules 1 to 6.
Stay, motion for, §16-4407.
Summary disposition, requests, §16-4415.
Trial de novo, Arbitration Rule XI.
Waiver by agreement to arbitrate, §16-4404.
Witnesses.
   Subpoena and discovery procedures, §16-4417.

ARCHITECT OF THE CAPITOL, §10-503.11.

ARCHITECTS.
Board of architecture and interior designers, §§47-2853.06 to 47-2853.10.
Business licenses, §§47-2853.61 to 47-2853.63.
   Eligibility, §47-2853.62.
   Representations prohibited, §47-2853.63.
   Scope of practice, §47-2853.61.
Public procurement, §2-356.04.

ARCHIVES.
Filing acts and resolutions with, §2-604.

ARCH TRAINING CENTER.
Real property exempt from taxation, §47-1047.

ARENAS.
Alcoholic beverage licenses, §25-114.

ARENA STAGE PROJECT.
Economic assistance to, §39-403.

ARMED CARJACKING, §22-2803.

ARMED FORCES.
See MILITARY AFFAIRS.

ARMORY BOARD, §§3-301 to 3-344.
Audits, §3-310.
Barriers and restricted zones at Armory and RFK Stadium, §3-343.
Chairperson, election of, §3-302.
Disposable containers prohibited at Armory and RFK Stadium, §3-343.01.
Establishment of, §3-302.
Fiscal year, §1-204.41.
Funds.
Transfer of assets held in various funds, §3-308.
Jurisdiction over Armory, §3-303.
Organization and membership, §3-302.
Parking, §3-304.
Policy declaration, §3-301.
Powers and duties, §3-303.
Repair and maintenance responsibilities, §3-303.
Reports and financial statements by, §3-310.
Robert F. Kennedy Memorial Stadium, §§3-322 to 3-330.
Barriers and restricted zones, §3-343.
Bond issues, §3-323.
Definition of stadium for purposes of, §3-330.
Disposable containers prohibited at, §3-343.01.
Leased from United States to District, §3-326.
Payment of costs to construct and operate, §3-323.
Playing field, unauthorized entry onto, §3-343.02.
Secretary of Interior authorized to acquire property for, §3-322.
Title vested to United States, §3-326.
Transfer of assets held in various funds, §3-308.
Use by National Guard, §3-305.

ARRAIGNMENT, CrimPro Rule 10.
Continuance of jury trial, CrimPro Rule 102.

ARRAIGNMENT —Cont'd
Felonies, CrimPro Rule 108.
Misdemeanors, CrimPro Rules 109, 110.
Presence of defendant, CrimPro Rule 43.
Tax cases, CrimPro Rule 104.

ARREST OF JUDGMENT, CrimPro Rule 34.

ARRESTS.
Advance information passed regarding, §23-1109.
Attachment after judgment.
Failure to appear upon summons, CivPro Rule 69-I.
Citation, release on, §23-584.
Failure to appear, §23-585.
Violation of condition, §23-585.
Communicable diseases, carriers of, §7-137.
Confessions made by arrested persons, §5-115.01.
Congress.
Arrest of members, US Const Art I §6.
Privilege from, US Const Art I §6.
Controlled substances, §48-921.01.
Cruelty to animals, arrest without warrant for, §22-1004.
District of Columbia housing authority police department.
Powers, §6-223.
Domestic violence, for, §16-1031.
Dulles International Airport, §9-808.
Duties and prohibitions regarding, §5-121.05.
Extradition.
General provisions, §§23-701 to 23-707.
See EXTRADITION.
Federal law enforcement officers.
Arrest for nonfederal offenses, §§5-301 to 5-303.
Field arrests, §23-584.
First amendment assemblies, §5-331.07.
Documentation of arrests, §5-331.10.
Physical restraints.
Use on persons arrested, §5-331.11.
Release.
Notice of options, §5-331.13.
Promptness, §5-331.12.
Fresh pursuit, §§23-901 to 23-903.
Fugitives from justice, arrest procedures for, §23-702.
Gambling house, keeping, §5-115.06.

ARRESTS —Cont'd

Habeas corpus.
General provisions, §§16-1901 to 16-1909.
See HABEAS CORPUS.

Initial proceedings before the court, CrimPro Rule 5.
Statement by the court, CrimPro Rule 5.

Inspector general, office of.
Employees making felony investigations.
Authority to make, §1-301.115a.

Interpreters, §2-1902.

Lottery tickets, keeping premises for sale of, §5-115.06.

Metropolitan police, §§5-115.01 to 5-115.07.

Military courts, warrants for arrest issued by, §49-509.

Neglectful failure to make, §5-115.03.

Notice.
Duty to make known to duty officer, §5-115.02.
Return notice, §5-115.02.

Officers of other states arresting person in District.
Fresh pursuit, §§23-901 to 23-903.

Out-of-state witnesses, exemption for, §23-1504.

Outside District of Columbia, CrimPro Rule 5-I.

Panhandling, disclosure of arrests and convictions for, §22-2306.

Park police, §5-206.

Private detectives, §§5-121.02, 5-121.05.

Privilege from arrest.
Congress, US Const Art I §6.

Processing arrests, §23-583.

Prosecution of arrested persons, §5-115.07.

Prostitution, keeping house of, §5-115.06.

Questioning and, §5-115.01.

Release on citation, §23-584.
Failure to appear, §23-585.
Violation of condition, §23-585.

Release without charge following, §5-115.01.

Request for production of arrest record, §2-1402.66.

Resisting arrest, §22-405.01.

Rights, advising of, §5-115.01.

Sealing arrest records, §§16-801 to 16-807, CrimPro Rule 118.
Actual innocence as grounds, §16-802.

ARRESTS —Cont'd

Sealing arrest records —Cont'd
Availability of sealed records, §16-806.
Decriminalized or legalized offenses, §16-803.02.
Definitions, §16-801.
Delinquent minors, FamDiv Rule P, JuvProc Rule 118.
Motion to seal records, JuvProc Form 8.
Notice of motion to seal records, JuvProc Form 9.
Notice of opposition, FamDiv Form 3.
Notice of proposal, FamDiv Form 2.
Order denying application, FamDiv Form 6.
Order for hearing, FamDiv Form 4.
Order to seal records, FamDiv Form 5, JuvProc Form 10.
Fugitives from justice, §16-803.01.
Grounds, §§16-802, 16-803.
Hearing, §16-805.
Motions, §16-804.
Dismissal or denial, §16-805.
Grounds, §§16-802, 16-803.
Response to, §16-805.
Savings provision, §16-807.

Summons upon complaint, CrimPro Rule 4.
Failure to appear upon summons.
Attachment after judgment, CivPro Rule 69-I.
Indictments and informations, CrimPro Rule 9.
Reprosecution, CrimPro Rule 4-I.

Unnecessary or wanton force, use of, §5-123.02.

Warrants for arrest.
General provisions, §§23-561 to 23-563.
See ARREST WARRANTS.

Washington National Airport, §9-704.

Wrongful arrest cases.
Legal assistance for police involved in, §5-115.04.

ARREST WARRANTS, §§23-561 to 23-563.

Advance information passed regarding, §23-1109.

Child neglect and abuse, §23-563.

Contents of, §23-561.

Definitions, §23-501.

Executions, §23-562, CrimPro Rules 4, 9.

Form and content, §23-561, CrimPro Rules 4, 9.

ARREST WARRANTS —Cont'd
Fugitives from justice, §23-701,
CrimPro Rule 40-I.
Indictment or information, CrimPro
Rule 9.
Issuance, §23-561, CrimPro Rule 4.
Limitation of actions, §23-563.
Metropolitan police execution of,
§5-127.05.
Military courts, issued by, §49-509.
Probable cause requirement,
CrimPro Rule 4.
Returns, §23-562, CrimPro Rules 4, 9.
Superior court, §11-941.
Territorial limits on, §23-563.

ARSON.
**Aged persons, offense committed
against.**
Enhanced penalties, §22-3601.
**Another's property, malicious
burning of,** §22-303.
Defined, §22-301.
Felony murder, §22-2101.
**Fraudulent burning of own
property,** §22-302.
**Injury, burning of own property
with intent to cause,** §22-302.
Investigations, §5-417.01.
Own property, §22-302.
Reports, §5-417.

ART GALLERIES.
Real property exempt from taxation,
§47-1002.

ARTICLES OF INCORPORATION.
Cooperative associations.
See COOPERATIVE ASSOCIATIONS.

ARTIFICIAL INSEMINATION.
**Presumptions and proof of
parentage,** §16-909.
Surrogate parenting contracts,
§§16-401, 16-402.

ARTISAN'S LIEN, §§40-307.01 to
40-307.03.

ARTIST PROTECTION, §§28-5101 to
28-5108.
Dealers.
Agency relationship with artist,
§28-5102.
Creditors' claims, §28-5104.
Duties, §28-5106.
Liability for loss or damage to work of
art, §28-5106.
Penalties for violations, §28-5108.
Purchase of art for own account,
§28-5103.

ARTIST PROTECTION —Cont'd
Dealers —Cont'd
Written contract with artist, §28-5105.
Definitions, §28-5101.
Loss or damage to work of art.
Dealer liability, §28-5106.
Penalties for violations by dealers,
§28-5108.
Proceeds of sale.
Holding in trust, §28-5103.
Trust property.
Creditors of dealer, §28-5104.
Proceeds of sale, §28-5103.
Purchase for dealer's own account,
§28-5103.
Work of fine art as, §28-5102.
Use or display of work of art.
Notice to users or viewers, §28-5106.
Prior written consent, §28-5106.
Waiver of statutory provisions void,
§28-5107.

ARTS AND HUMANITIES.
Artist protection, §§28-5101 to
28-5108.
Commission on arts and humanities,
§§39-201 to 39-206.
Defacement of art works, §22-3306.
District of Columbia cultural plan,
§39-231.
**Economic assistance to arts, cultural
and educational facilities,**
§§39-401 to 39-405.
Museum of city of Washington,
§§39-301 to 39-309.
Musicians.
Metropolitan police, §§5-131.01 to
5-131.05.
National guard, §49-903.
Music piracy, §22-3214.
Real property exempt from taxation.
Art galleries, §47-1002.
Historic music cultural institutions,
§47-4662.
Museums, §47-1002.
Studio theatre housing, §47-1082.
Theatre Downtown, Inc, §47-1074.
Theatrical performances.
See THEATRICAL PERFORMANCES.

**ARTS AND HUMANITIES,
COMMISSION ON,** §§39-201 to
39-206.
Accounting system, establishment,
§39-206.
Administration, §39-205.
**Arts and humanities enterprise
fund,** §39-205.01.

ARTS AND HUMANITIES, COMMISSION ON —Cont'd

Authority of council, §39-201.

Conflicts of interest in handling grants.

Development of procedure, §39-206.

Definitions, §39-202.

Established, §39-203.

Membership, §39-203.

Powers, §39-204.

Residency requirement for nominees, §39-206.

ARTS, CULTURAL AND EDUCATIONAL FACILITIES.

Economic assistance to, §§39-401 to 39-405.

Arena stage project, §39-403.

Authorization to provide support, §39-402.01.

Definitions, §39-401.

Purposes, §39-401.

Report to council, §39-405.

Rules and regulations, promulgation, §39-404.

ART WORKS.

Defacement of, §22-3306.

ASBESTOS.

Abatement.

Contractors, §§8-111.01 to 8-111.14. See ASBESTOS CONTRACTORS.

Prohibitions regarding, §8-111.04.

Task force, §§44-732 to 44-734.

Appropriations, §44-733.

Established, §44-731.

Rules, §44-732.

Civil I calendar cases, CivPro Rule 40-II.

ASBESTOS CONTRACTORS, §§8-111.01 to 8-111.14.

Business licenses for asbestos worker, §§47-2853.51 to 47-2853.53.

Eligibility, §47-2853.52.

Representations prohibited, §47-2853.53.

Scope of practice, §47-2853.51.

Cease and desist orders against, §8-111.08.

Civil actions, §8-111.10.

Criminal actions, §8-111.09.

Definitions, §8-111.01.

Fees, §8-111.10.

Fines, §8-111.10.

Inspections, §8-111.05.

Investigations, §8-111.05.

ASBESTOS CONTRACTORS —Cont'd

Issuance of rules, §8-111.13.

Licenses.

Application forms, §8-111.12.

Asbestos workers, §8-111.02.

Business entities, §8-111.03.

Renewals, §8-111.12.

Requirements, §8-111.04.

Revocation or suspension, §8-111.06.

Summary actions regarding, §8-111.07.

Limitation of actions for death or injury caused by exposure to asbestos, §12-311.

Mayor's responsibilities regarding, §8-111.12.

Penalties, §8-111.10.

Permits.

Business entities, §8-111.03.

Revocation or suspension, §8-111.06.

Summary actions regarding, §8-111.07.

Records, §8-111.11.

Remedies, cumulative nature of, §8-111.14.

Reprimands, §8-111.06.

Summary actions, §8-111.07.

ASBESTOSIS.

Workers' compensation, §32-1510.

ASIANS AND PACIFIC ISLANDERS.

Chinese, Vietnamese and Korean language.

Government publications translated in.

Publications concerning health, safety and welfare of Asian and Pacific Islander resident, §2-1375.

Commission on Asian and Pacific Islander community development, §§2-1374, 2-1376.

Office of Asian and Pacific Islander affairs, §§2-1371 to 2-1376.

Definitions, §2-1372.

Establishment, §2-1373.

Findings, §2-1371.

Health, safety and welfare.

Translation of publications relating to, §2-1375.

Transition provisions, §2-1376.

ASPHALT.

Inspector of asphalts and cements, §1-333.02.

ASSAULT AND BATTERY, §§22-401 to 22-407.

Aged persons, offenses committed against.

Enhanced penalties, §22-3601.

ASSAULT AND BATTERY —Cont'd
Aggravated assault, §22-404.01.
Public vehicle inspection officer,
§22-404.03.
Alcoholic beverage licenses.
Assault on police officer, government
inspector or investigator.
Summary revocation or suspension,
§25-826.
**Bicyclist, assault or battery by
motorist.**
Right of civil action for damages,
§50-1621.
Common law assault, §§22-404,
22-3312.02.
Crime investigation records.
Retention of records in open
investigations, §5-113.32.
Dangerous weapon, with, §22-402.
Domestic violence.
Intrafamily offenses.
Generally, §§16-1001 to 16-1034.
See INTRAFAMILY
PROCEEDINGS.
**Emergency care for sexual assault
victims,** §§7-2121 to 7-2125.
Firefighter, assault on, §22-405.
Homicide, intent to commit, §22-401.
Law enforcement officers.
Alcoholic beverage licenses.
Assault on police officer, government
inspector or investigator.
Summary revocation or
suspension, §25-826.
Mayhem, intent to commit, §22-402.
**Offense of any kind, intent to
commit,** §22-403.
Poison, assault with intent to,
§22-401.
Police officer, assault on, §22-405.
Resisting arrest, §22-405.01.
Public officials, §22-851.
Public vehicle inspection officer,
§22-404.02.
Aggravated assault, §22-404.03.
Robbery, intent to commit, §22-401.
Sexual abuse, with intent to commit,
§22-401.
Stalking.
See STALKING.
Threats and menaces, §22-404.

ASSAULT WEAPONS, §§7-2501.01,
7-2551.01 to 7-2551.03.

ASSEMBLIES.
**Federal government, assemblies in
District relating to.**
Reimbursement of costs, §1-207.37.

ASSEMBLIES —Cont'd
First amendment assemblies,
§§5-331.01 to 5-331.17.
See FIRST AMENDMENT
ASSEMBLIES.
Right of assembly, US Const Amd 1.
Smoking.
"No Smoking" signs, §7-1704.
Public assembly or hearing room,
§7-1703.
Unlawful assembly, §22-1321.
Capitol grounds, §10-503.17.

ASSESSMENTS.
Administrative hearings, office of.
Protest of assessments, §47-4312.
Appeals, §47-3303.
**Budget estimates for costs of real
property assessments,** §47-211.
Building code.
Correction of conditions violative of
law, §42-3131.01.
Fire violations, correction of,
§6-703.08.
Insanitary buildings, repair or
demolition of, §6-907.
Unsafe structures, correction of,
§§6-805, 6-806.
Cigarette tax, §47-4312.
Condominiums.
Common expenses, §42-1903.12.
Horizontal property regimes, §42-2017.
Liens, §42-1903.13.
Crime victims' compensation, §4-516.
Curbs and gutters, §§9-401.04,
9-411.01 to 9-411.04, 9-421.02.
**Emergency and non-emergency
number telephone calling
systems fund.**
Subscribers, §34-1803.
Gross sales tax, §§47-2019, 47-4312.
**Health benefit plan grievance
procedures.**
Assessment of insurers to cover,
§44-301.09.
**Health maintenance organization
bankruptcy and insolvency.**
Protecting against, §31-3430.
Horizontal property regimes,
§42-2017.
Income taxes, §§47-1812.05, 47-4312.
Inheritance and estate taxes,
§§47-3717, 47-4312.
**Insanitary buildings, repair or
demolition of,** §6-907.
Insurance regulatory trust fund,
§§31-1202 to 31-1205.

ASSESSMENTS —Cont'd

Insurers rehabilitation and liquidation proceedings, §31-1329.

Intermediate care facilities for persons with intellectual disabilities, §§47-1270 to 47-1278.

Medicaid, hospital assessments.
See MEDICAID.

Motor fuel tax.
Procedures, §47-2316.
Street paving, §§47-2323, 47-2324.

Nursing facilities, §§47-1261 to 47-1269.

Personal property taxes, §§47-1528, 47-4312.

Property and liability insurance guaranty association, §31-5513.

Public works.
See PUBLIC WORKS.

Real property taxes.
Designation of property for assessment, §§47-701 to 47-709.
Generally, §§47-820 to 47-828.
See REAL PROPERTY TAXES.

Refunds, §2-403.

Sidewalks, §9-401.04.

Tax assessor, §§47-601, 47-602.

Titling vehicles, excise tax assessment on, §50-2201.22.

Tobacco tax, §47-2410.

Toll telecommunication service tax, §§47-3908, 47-4312.

Water supply and waterworks mains and sewers, §§34-2405.01 to 34-2405.08.

Witnesses in condemnation proceedings, assessment officials as, §14-308.

ASSIGNMENT OF CASES, CivPro Rule 40-I, USDistCt LCrR 57.8 to USDistCt LCrR 57.15, USDistCt LCvR 40.1 to USDistCt LCvR 40.9.

Arbitration, Arbitration Rule IV.

Civil I calendar, CivPro Rule 40-II.

Classification of cases, USDistCt LCrR 57.9, USDistCt LCvR 40.2.

Collection and subrogation cases, CivPro Rule 40-III.

Criminal proceedings.
Certification of jury trial to criminal assignment commissioner, CrimPro Rule 102.
Duties and operation of Assignment Section, CrimPro Rule 101.
Felony cases, CrimPro Rule 105.

ASSIGNMENT OF CASES —Cont'd

Criminal proceedings —Cont'd
Notice, CrimPro Rule 107.
Related cases, CrimPro Rule 105, USDistCt LCrR 57.12, USDistCt LCvR 40.5.
Special assignment, CrimPro Rule 106.

Domestic relations actions, DomRel Rule 40.

Manner of assignment, USDistCt LCrR 57.10, USDistCt LCvR 40.3.

Motions judges, USDistCt LCvR 40.8.

Probate proceedings.
Contested estate cases.
Death before January 1, 1981, Probate Rule 15.

Related cases, USDistCt LCrR 57.12, USDistCt LCvR 40.5.

Sanctions, USDistCt LCrR 57.15, USDistCt LCvR 40.9.

Suspension of new assignments, USDistCt LCrR 57.11, USDistCt LCvR 40.4.

Transfers and reassignments, USDistCt LCrR 57.13, USDistCt LCvR 40.6.

ASSIGNMENT OF CHOSES IN ACTION, §§28-2301 to 28-2305.

Future wages and salaries, contract to assign, §28-2305.

General assignments, §28-2304.

Judgment or money decree, §28-2301.

Nonnegotiable contract, §28-2303.

Securities, §28-2302.

ASSIGNMENTS.

Assignments for benefit of creditors, §§28-2101 to 28-2110.
See ASSIGNMENTS FOR BENEFIT OF CREDITORS.

Bankruptcy and insolvency.
Assignments for benefit of creditors, §§28-2101 to 28-2110.
See ASSIGNMENTS FOR BENEFIT OF CREDITORS.

Bills of exchange.
Nonnegotiable bills of exchange, §28-2303.

Bonds, surety, §28-2302.

Child support rights of persons receiving public assistance, §4-205.19.

Choses in action.
Bond or obligation under seal, §28-2302.

ASSIGNMENTS —Cont'd
Choses in action —Cont'd
General assignments including choses
in action, §28-2304.
Judgments or money decrees,
§28-2301.
Nonnegotiable contracts, §28-2303.
**Condominium limited common
elements,** §42-1902.13.
Consumer credit sales.
Assignment of earnings prohibited,
§28-3804.
Seller's assignees subject to defenses
of consumer, §28-3808.
Consumer protection.
Assignment of earnings prohibited,
§28-3804.
Seller's assignees subject to defenses
of consumer, §28-3808.
Contracts.
Future salary or wages.
Contract to assign prohibited,
§28-2305.
Nonnegotiable contracts, §28-2303.
Sale of goods, §28:2-210.
Counterclaims, §13-502.
Creditors.
Assignments for benefit of creditors,
§§28-2101 to 28-2110.
See ASSIGNMENTS FOR BENEFIT
OF CREDITORS.
Decrees.
Money decrees, §28-2301.
Defined, §28-2901.
**Disability compensation for public
officers and employees,** §1-623.30.
Fiduciaries.
Securities, §28-2903.
Transfers.
Defined, §28-2901.
Fiduciary's commission, CivPro Rule
301.
Fiduciary security transfers,
§§28-2903, 28-2904.
Foster care requirements, §§4-217.07
to 4-217.11.
Fraudulent transfers.
General provisions, §§28-3101 to
28-3111.
See FRAUDULENT TRANSFERS.
Gas station marketing agreements,
§36-303.05.
Industrial life insurance, §31-4804.
Installment loans.
Assignment of earnings prohibited,
§28-3804.

ASSIGNMENTS —Cont'd
Judgments, §28-2301.
Letters of credit.
Proceeds, §28:5-114.
Market employees, §37-205.01.
Motor vehicle titling.
Assignment of lien, §§50-1208,
50-1209.
**No-fault motor vehicle insurance,
future benefits from,** §31-2410.
Nonnegotiable contracts, §28-2303.
Obligations under seal, §28-2302.
Penalties.
Contract to assign future salary or
wages, §28-2305.
**Police and firefighters retirement
and disability.**
Funds not assignable, §5-723.05.
Probate proceedings.
Death before January 1, 1981, Probate
Rule 21.
Death between January 1, 1981 and
June 30, 1995, Probate Rule 120.
Death on or after July 1, 1995,
Probate Rule 420.
Promissory notes.
Nonnegotiable notes, §28-2303.
Public assistance, §4-215.01.
Recipients, §§4-213.01, 4-213.05,
4-213.06, 4-217.07 to 4-217.11.
Real estate tax sales, §47-1303.04.
Revised real property tax sale.
Certificate of sale, §§47-1349,
47-1354.
**Rental housing conversion and sale
rights,** §§42-3404.06, 42-3404.31,
42-3404.36.
Salaries.
Consumer credit sales or direct
installment loans.
Assignment of earnings prohibited,
§28-3804.
Contract to assign future salary
prohibited, §28-2305.
Seals and sealed instruments.
Obligations under seal, §28-2302.
**Secondary market, sale or
assignment of instruments on,**
§42-1102.01.
Secured transactions.
Filing officer's duties, §28:9-514.
Teachers' retirement.
After June 30, 1946, §38-2021.17.
Prior to June 30, 1946, §38-2001.17.
**Temporary assistance for needy
families (TANF) program,**
§§4-217.07 to 4-217.11.

ASSIGNMENTS —Cont'd
Trust, §28-3503.
Wages.
Consumer credit sales or direct
installment loans.
Assignment of earnings prohibited,
§28-3804.
Contract to assign future wages
prohibited, §28-2305.
Workers' compensation, §32-1517.

**ASSIGNMENT SECTION OF
CRIMINAL DIVISION.**
Authorization of sections, CrimPro
Rule 1.
Creation, CrimPro Rule 100.
Duties and operation, CrimPro Rule
101.

**ASSIGNMENTS FOR BENEFIT OF
CREDITORS,** §§28-2101 to
28-2110.
Accounts and accounting.
Settlement by assignee or trustee,
§28-2106.
Acknowledgments, §28-2103.
Actions.
Assignee's actions, §28-2106.
Amount of creditors' demands.
List required, §28-2101.
Assignee, §§28-2102 to 28-2106.
Actions, §28-2106.
Assent to assignment, §28-2103.
Assignment to hinder or defraud
creditors.
Appointment of trustee, §28-2109.
Bond of assignee, §28-2104.
Conveyances by assignee, §28-2106.
Death of assignee, §28-2105.
Disposal of assets, §28-2106.
Distribution among creditors,
§28-2106.
Duties, §28-2106.
Failure or refusal to comply with
requirements.
Removal and appointment of
trustee, §28-2105.
Nonperformance by assignee.
Removal and appointment of
trustee, §28-2105.
Notice to creditors, §28-2110.
Qualifications, §28-2103.
Removal, §28-2105.
Residence, §28-2103.
Resignation, §28-2105.
Settlement of accounts, §28-2106.
Vesting of property of debtor in
assignee, §28-2102.

**ASSIGNMENTS FOR BENEFIT OF
CREDITORS** —Cont'd
Bonds, surety.
Assignee, §28-2104.
Trustee, §28-2105.
Claims.
Notice to creditors to produce and
prove, §28-2110.
Consumer credit, §28-3804.
Conveyances.
Assignee's conveyances, §28-2106.
Death.
Assignee or trustee, §28-2105.
Defrauding creditors.
Assignment to defraud, §28-2109.
Disposal of assets, §28-2106.
Distribution among creditors,
§28-2106.
Preferences prohibited, §28-2107.
Proceedings for benefit of all creditors,
§28-2108.
Equity.
Proceedings for benefit of all creditors,
§28-2108.
Executors and administrators.
Death of trustee or assignee, §28-2105.
Exempt assets, §28-2102.
Extent of assignment, §28-2102.
**Fiduciary's bond, undertaking in
lieu of,** §16-601.
Form of assignment, §28-2101.
Fraud and deceit, §28-2109.
Fraudulent conveyances.
Assignment to hinder or defraud
creditors, §28-2109.
Orders to prevent, §28-2106.
Hindering creditors.
Assignment to hinder or defraud
creditors, §28-2109.
Injunctions.
Assignment to hinder or defraud
creditors, §28-2109.
Inventory of estate.
Required, §28-2101.
Liens.
Priorities not affected, §28-2107.
List of creditors.
Required, §28-2101.
Notice to creditors, §28-2110.
Oaths.
Examination of assignor under oath,
§28-2106.
Powers and duties of assignee,
§28-2106.
Preferences.
Prohibited, §28-2107.

ASSIGNMENTS FOR BENEFIT OF CREDITORS —Cont'd
Priorities.
Not affected, §28-2107.
Proceedings deemed for benefit of all creditors equally, §28-2108.
Recordation, §28-2103.
Residence.
Assignee, §28-2103.
Sales.
Disposal of assets, §28-2106.
Trustees.
Appointment, §§28-2105, 28-2109.
Assignment to hinder or defraud creditors.
Appointment of trustee, §28-2109.
Bond, §28-2105.
Death of trustee, §28-2105.
Duties, §28-2106.
Notice to creditors, §28-2110.
Removal, §28-2105.
Resignation, §28-2105.
Settlement of account, §28-2106.
Void assignments.
Assignment to hinder or defraud creditors, §28-2109.

ASSISTANCE ANIMALS.
Definitions, §7-1009.
Housing accommodations.
Full and equal access, §7-1006.
Public places accommodations, and conveyances.
Right to be accompanied by, §7-1002.

ASSISTED LIVING ADMINISTRATOR.
Titles and terms prohibited as misrepresentation without license to practice, §3-1210.03.
Transition provisions.
Persons already practicing, §3-1210.05.

ASSISTED LIVING RESIDENCES, §§44-101.01 to 44-113.01.
Abuse, neglect and exploitation, §44-105.09.
Right to be free from, §44-105.03.
Accommodation of needs, §44-105.04.
Admissions, §44-106.01.
Pre-admission medication management assessment, §44-109.02.
Appeals, §44-103.08.
Actions of mayor, §44-112.01.
Bathrooms.
Requirements, §§44-110.06, 44-110.11.
Bedrooms.
Requirements, §§44-110.08, 44-110.11.

ASSISTED LIVING RESIDENCES —Cont'd
Buildings.
Facility regulations generally, §§44-110.01 to 44-110.12.
Certificate of need not required, §44-110.12.
Changes in licensees, §44-103.05.
Civil penalties, §44-104.02.
Confidentiality of information.
Residents' rights, §44-105.06.
Correspondence.
Right to receive and send, §44-105.03.
Criminal penalties, §44-104.03.
Definitions, §44-102.01.
Dignity, §44-105.03.
Emergency placement, §44-108.05.
Emergency suspension of license, §44-104.04.
Exterior of building, requirements, §44-110.03.
Facility regulations, §§44-110.01 to 44-110.12.
Fire safety, §44-110.02.
Grievances and complaints.
Representation and resolution, §44-105.05.
Health and social services.
Access, §44-105.04.
Heating and air conditioning, §44-110.07.
Inspections, §44-103.06.
Insurance, §44-111.01.
Interior of building, requirements, §44-110.04.
Light and ventilation, §44-110.07.
Kitchens.
Requirements, §44-110.09.
Laundry facility, §44-110.10.
Licenses, §§44-103.01 to 44-103.05, 44-103.07.
Appeals, §44-103.08.
Application and fee, §44-103.02.
Emergency suspension, §44-104.04.
Initial licensure, §44-103.02.
Pre-licensure inspection, §44-103.02.
Renewal, §44-103.04.
Restrictions, §44-103.07.
Revocation or suspension, §§44-104.01, 44-104.04.
Unlawful to operate without license, §44-103.01.
Light and ventilation, §44-110.07.
Living units in good repair and operable, §44-110.01.

ASSISTED LIVING RESIDENCES
—Cont'd
Medication management, §§44-109.01
to 44-109.07.
Administration of medications,
§44-109.05.
Control of medication, §44-109.07.
On-site medication review, §44-109.03.
Pre-admission assessment, §44-109.02.
Responsibilities of ALR personnel,
§44-109.01.
Storage, §44-109.04.
Training program, §44-109.06.
Philosophy of care, §44-101.02.
Privacy.
Residents' rights, §§44-105.02,
44-105.06.
Purpose of provisions, §44-101.01.
Refusal to participate.
Right, §44-105.04.
Religious services.
Right to attend or not attend,
§44-105.03.
Residential occupancy.
Classification as, §44-110.01.
Residents.
Admissions, §44-106.01.
Pre-admission medication
management assessment,
§44-109.02.
Agreements, §44-106.02.
Financial agreements, §44-106.03.
Shared responsibility agreements,
§44-106.05.
Assessment, §§44-108.01 to 44-108.05.
Discharge, §44-106.08.
Emergency placement, §44-108.05.
Functional assessment, §44-108.03.
Individualized service plans,
§44-106.04.
Medical, rehabilitation, psychosocial
assessment, §44-108.02.
Medication management, §§44-109.01
to 44-109.07.
Records, §44-106.06.
Rights, §§44-105.02 to 44-105.07.
Notice of, §44-105.08.
Services to be provided to, §44-106.07.
Short-term residential care,
§44-108.04.
Transfer, §44-106.08.
Wheelchairs, residents who use.
Accessibility, §§44-110.03, 44-110.05.
Restraints.
Right to be free from, §44-105.04.
Rights of residents, §§44-105.02 to
44-105.07.
Notice of, §44-105.08.

ASSISTED LIVING RESIDENCES
—Cont'd
Roommates.
Right to approve, §44-105.03.
Rulemaking.
Mayor, §44-113.01.
Sanctions for violations, §§44-104.01
to 44-104.04.
Civil penalties, §44-104.02.
Criminal penalties, §44-104.03.
Emergency suspension of license,
§44-104.04.
Generally, §44-104.01.
Short-term residential care,
§44-108.04.
Staff, §44-107.01.
Training, §44-107.02.
Medication management training
program, §44-109.06.
Standard of care, §44-105.01.
Training for staff, §44-107.02.
Medication management training
program, §44-109.06.
Unlawful to operate without license,
§44-103.01.
Visitors.
Free access, §44-105.03.
Wheelchairs, residents who use.
Accessibility, §§44-110.03, 44-110.05.
Bathrooms, §44-110.06.
**Zoning, building, housing, sewer,
etc. codes, rules and regulations.**
Duty to meet, §44-110.01.

**ASSISTIVE TECHNOLOGY DEVICE
WARRANTY,** §§28-4031 to 28-4034.
Action to recover damages, §28-4034.
Definitions, §28-4031.
Implied warranty, §28-4032.
Exclusion or limitation void, §28-4032.
Irresponsibility for repair, §28-4032.
Refund, §28-4032.
Return or replacement, §28-4032.
Selling or leasing returned devices.
Disclosure required, §28-4033.
Selling or leasing returned devices.
Disclosure required, §28-4033.
Waiver of rights void, §28-4032.

ASSOCIATIONS.
Appeals, federal cases.
Corporate disclosure statements,
FRAP 26.1, USCtApp Rule 26.1.
Building and loan associations.
Direct-reduction loans for veterans,
§42-3002.

ASSOCIATIONS —Cont'd
Building and loan associations
—Cont'd
Mortgages and deeds of trust.
General provisions, §§42-804 to
42-820.
See MORTGAGES AND DEEDS
OF TRUST.
Saturdays.
Designated holiday, §28-2701.
Building associations.
General provisions, §§26-201 to
26-232.
See BUILDING ASSOCIATIONS.
**Cemeteries and cemetery
associations.**
General provisions, §§43-101 to
43-131.
See CEMETERIES AND
CEMETERY ASSOCIATIONS.
Class actions.
Unincorporated associations, CivPro
Rule 23.2.
Cooperative associations, §§29-901 to
29-939.
See COOPERATIVE ASSOCIATIONS.
General provisions.
See CEMETERIES AND
CEMETERY ASSOCIATIONS.
Cooperative housing associations.
See COOPERATIVE HOUSING
ASSOCIATIONS.
Savings and loan associations.
Acquisition of, §§26-1201 to 26-1217.
See SAVINGS AND LOAN
ACQUISITIONS.
Generally.
See SAVINGS AND LOAN
ASSOCIATIONS.
Service of process on association.
Summons, CivPro Rule 4.
**Unincorporated nonprofit
associations,** §§29-1101 to 29-1127.
See NONPROFIT ASSOCIATIONS,
UNINCORPORATED.

ASSUMPTION OF RISK.
Helmets.
Failure of bicycle operator or
passenger to wear, §50-1606.

ATHLETE AGENTS, §§47-2887.01 to
47-2887.18.
Administrative penalty, §47-2887.16.
Agency contracts.
Acting without certificate of
registration, §47-2887.03.

ATHLETE AGENTS —Cont'd
Agency contracts —Cont'd
Contract in violations of provisions
void, §47-2887.03.
Notice of existence of contract given to
educational institution,
§47-2887.10.
Prohibited conduct, §47-2887.13.
Required form, §47-2887.09.
Right of student-athlete to cancel,
§47-2887.11.
Civil penalties, §47-2887.15.
Criminal penalties, prosecution.
Prohibited conduct, §47-2887.14.
Definitions, §47-2887.01.
**Electronic signatures in global and
national commerce act,**
§47-2887.18.
Prohibited conduct, §47-2887.13.
Administrative penalty, §47-2887.16.
Civil penalties, §47-2887.15.
Criminal penalties, prosecution,
§47-2887.14.
Records, §47-2887.12.
Registration.
Application, §47-2887.04.
Fees, rules establishing, §47-2887.08.
Individual registered or licensed in
another state, §47-2887.04.
Issuance of certificate, §47-2887.05.
Refusal to issue certificate,
§47-2887.05.
Renewal of certificate, §47-2887.05.
Required, §47-2887.03.
Suspension, revocation, refusal to
renew, §47-2887.06.
Temporary registration, §47-2887.07.
Service of process.
Mayor appointed agent for service,
§47-2887.02.
Subpoenas.
Issuance for relevant material,
§47-2887.02.
**Uniformity of application and
construction,** §47-2887.17.

ATHLETIC COACHES.
Child abuse and neglect.
Reporting requirements, §4-1321.02.

**ATHLETIC CONCUSSION
PROTECTION,** §§7-2871.01 to
7-2871.05.
Definitions, §7-2871.01.
**Materials development and
distribution,** §7-2871.04.
Removal from athletic activity.
Athletes suspected of sustaining
concussion, §7-2871.02.

ATHLETIC CONCUSSION PROTECTION —Cont'd
Return to athletic activity.
Athletes suspected of sustaining concussion, §7-2871.02.
Rules, §7-2871.05.
Training program, §7-2871.03.

ATHLETIC CONTESTS.
District of Columbia interscholastic athletic association (DCIAA).
Turkey Bowl revenue generation and sponsorship, §38-2981.
Gambling on, §§22-1708, 22-1713.
Interscholastic athletic events.
Medical coverage, requirement, §38-621.
State athletic activities, programs, and office fund, §§38-2671 to 38-2674.

ATHLETIC EQUITY.
Schools and education, §§38-841.01 to 38-841.08.

ATHLETIC FIELD PERMIT COORDINATION COMMITTEE, §10-308.

ATHLETIC TRAINERS.
Qualifications for licensure, §3-1205.04.
Titles and terms prohibited as misrepresentation without license to practice, §3-1210.03.
Transition provisions.
Persons already practicing, §3-1210.05.

ATMS, §§26-131.01 to 26-131.13.
See AUTOMATED TELLER MACHINES.

AT-RISK CHILDREN, YOUTH, AND FAMILIES.
Schools and education.
Interagency collaboration and services integration commission, §§2-1591 to 2-1597.

ATTACHMENT, §§16-501 to 16-584.
Additional attachments, §16-504.
Administrator, by, §§16-516, 16-549.
Affidavits, §§16-501, 16-506.
Alternatives to, §16-532.
Answers to interrogatories, §16-522.
Bills of lading.
Attachment of goods covered by a negotiable document, §28:7-602.
Bonds, surety, §§16-501, 16-505.
Claims to attached property, §§16-523, 16-554.

ATTACHMENT —Cont'd
College savings program.
Seizure of accounts prohibited, §47-4510.
Condemnation of attached property, §§16-524, 16-555.
Cooperative associations.
Exemption of share and membership certificates, §29-928.
Credits, on, §§16-511, 16-546.
Debts not due, for, §16-503.
Defenses, §§16-519, 16-520, 16-551.
Dismissal of attachment, CivPro Form CA 109.
Docket, §16-531.
Documents of title.
Attachment of goods covered by a negotiable document, §28:7-602.
Eligible property, §16-507.
Examinations, oral, §§16-521, 16-552.
Executor, by, §§16-516, 16-549.
Fraternal benefit society benefits, §31-5315.
Habeas corpus violations, §16-1904.
Index of attachments, §16-531.
Insurers rehabilitation and liquidation proceedings, §31-1355.
Interlocutory order, sale under, §§16-525, 16-555.
Interrogatories, §§16-521, 16-522, 16-552.
Investment securities.
Creditor's legal process, §28:8-112.
Judgment, §16-524.
Against garnishee, §§16-526, 16-556.
Attachment prior to, §§16-501, 16-583.
Execution, attachment and garnishment after judgment in aid of, §§16-541 to 16-556.
See EXECUTION OF JUDGMENTS.
Protection of garnishee by, §16-528.
Undertakings, §16-527.
Liens, §§16-507, 16-523.
Marshal of District, in hands of, §§16-515, 16-548.
Multiple attachments against same debtor, §16-545.
Notice of attachment, CivPro Form CA 105.
Oral examinations, §§16-521, 16-552.
Partnership interests, §16-511.
Personal property, §16-509.
Police and firefighters retirement and disability.
Funds not subject to execution, §5-723.05.

ATTACHMENT —Cont'd
Post-judgment attachment, CivPro
Rule 69-I.
Pre-judgment attachment, CivPro
Rule 64-I.
Domestic relations actions, DomRel
Rule 64.
Preservation of attached property,
§§16-518, 16-550.
Probate proceedings, §§16-3104 to
16-3107.
Property subject to, §16-507.
Public officers and employees.
Wages subject to attachment and
garnishment for support and
maintenance payments, §1-507.
Quashing writ of, §16-506.
Real property, §16-508.
Receivers, §16-518.
Release from, §16-510.
Replevin, §16-517, CivPro Rule 64-II.
Domestic relations actions, DomRel
Rule 64.
**Representative capacity, credits or
property held for two or more
persons in,** §16-514.
**Retention of attached property and
credits by garnishee,** §16-547.
Sale of attached property, §§16-518,
16-525, 16-550, 16-555.
Secured transactions.
Security interest attachment,
§28:9-203.
Financial asset.
Security interest arising in
purchase or delivery of,
§28:9-206.
Perfection.
Security interest perfected upon
attachment, §28:9-309.
**Service by publication on
nonresidents,** §13-336.
Service of process, §16-502.
Sufficiency of bond, §16-505.
Superior court proceedings, §16-533.
Support orders, enforcement,
§16-571.01.
Teachers' retirement.
After June 30, 1946.
Funds not assignable or subject to
execution, §38-2021.17.
Traverse.
Affidavits, §16-506.
Answers of garnishee, §§16-522,
16-553.
Trials, §§16-506, 16-522, 16-530, 16-551,
16-552.

ATTACHMENT —Cont'd
Trusts and trustees.
Uniform trust code.
Creditor's claims, §19-1305.01.
**Two or more persons in
representative capacity, credits
or property held for,** §16-514.
Undertakings, §§16-509, 16-527.
Wages and salaries.
See WAGES AND SALARIES.
Warehouse receipts.
Attachment of goods covered by a
negotiable document, §28:7-602.
**Writ of attachment on wages, salary
and commissions,** CivPro Form CA
123.
**Writ of attachment other than
wages, salary and commissions,**
CivPro Form CA 122.

ATTAINDER.
Bill of attainder, US Const Art I §§9,
10, Art III §3.

ATTEMPTS TO COMMIT CRIMES,
§22-1803.
Aggravated assault, §22-404.01.
Controlled substances, §48-904.09.
Robbery, §22-2802.
Sexual offenses, §22-3018.

ATTORNEY EXAMINERS.
Administrative fines, §2-1801.03.

**ATTORNEY GENERAL FOR
DISTRICT OF COLUMBIA.**
Appeals, federal cases.
Statutes challenged on constitutional
grounds.
State statute, FRAP 44(b).
Appointment, §1-301.82.
Assistant attorneys general,
§1-301.87.
Budgets, §1-301.86.
**Challenge to statutes, rule,
regulation, program or policy.**
Reporting on, §1-301.89a.
Charitable solicitations.
Actions, §44-1712.
Chief deputy attorney general,
§§1-301.87, 1-301.90.
Child custody proceedings.
Enforcement of foreign custody
determinations.
Role of under Hague Convention,
§§16-4603.15, 16-4603.17.
Civil protection orders.
Representation of petitioner,
DomesticViolence Rule 9.

ATTORNEY GENERAL FOR DISTRICT OF COLUMBIA
—Cont'd

Compensation, §1-301.85.

Condominiums, §42-1904.17.

Consumer credit reporting agencies.
Consumer security freeze.
Enforcement of provisions, §28-3864.

Consumer protection.
Investigative powers, §28-3910.
Subpoenas, authority to issue, §1-301.88d.

Contingency fee contracts, §1-301.86a.

Contributing to the delinquency of a minor.
Prosecution of violations, §22-811.

Crimes and offenses.
Forfeiture of position, §1-301.84.

Criminal prosecutions, §23-101.

Deputy attorneys general, §1-301.87.

Domestic violence unit proceedings.
Civil protection orders.
Representation of petitioner, DomesticViolence Rule 9.

Driving under the influence.
Prosecution of violations, §50-2206.53.

Duties, §1-301.81.

Elections, §§1-204.35, 1-1001.08.

Financial exploitation of vulnerable adults and elderly persons.
Subpoena authority, §1-301.88e.

Foreclosure rescue services and transactions.
Prosecutions for violations of provisions, §42-2435.

Forfeiture of position, §1-301.84.

Hazardous materials transportation.
Strict liability for releases during transport.
Action to recover costs, §8-1444.

Health care entity conversion approval, §44-603.

Inability to carry out duties, §1-301.90.

Independent government agency.
Judicial or administrative proceeding in which agency party.
Notification of office, §1-301.89b.

Lead-hazard prevention and elimination.
Injunction of violations, §8-231.15.

Legal service, §§1-608.51 to 1-608.66.
See LEGAL SERVICE.

Litigation support fund, §1-301.86b.

ATTORNEY GENERAL FOR DISTRICT OF COLUMBIA
—Cont'd

Mortgages and deeds of trust.
Foreclosure rescue services and transactions.
Prosecutions for violations of provisions, §42-2435.

Oaths and affirmations, administration of, §1-301.88.

Opinions, §1-301.81.

Parental kidnapping prosecuted by, §16-1025.

Pedestrians.
Right-of-way at crosswalks.
Prosecution of violations, §50-2201.28.

Personnel.
Authority over personnel, §1-301.88a.

Practice of law.
Forfeiture of position, §1-301.84.

Procurement.
Authority for procurement of goods and services, §1-301.88b.
Contingency fee contracts, §1-301.86a.
Procurement claims, §2-381.03.

Public utilities investigations, §34-905.

Qualifications, §1-301.83.

Recordation of false financing statements, §41-204.

Reporting on challenges to statutes, rule, regulation, program or policy, §1-301.89a.

Restraints of trade.
Civil investigative demand, §28-4505.

Schools and education.
Tuition of nonresidents.
Prosecution of violations, §38-303.

Special counsel, §1-301.89.

Staff.
Authority over personnel, §1-301.88a.

Subpoena powers, §1-301.88c.
Consumer protection matters, authority to issue, §1-301.88d.

Terms of office, §§1-204.35, 1-301.82.

Vacancies in office, §1-204.35.

Wages and salaries, §1-611.09.

Workers' compensation court proceedings, §32-1523.

ATTORNEY GENERAL, UNITED STATES.

Appeals, federal cases.
Statutes challenged on constitutional grounds.
Federal statute, FRAP 44(a).

ATTORNEY IN FACT.

Condominium attorney in fact to grant and accept beneficial easements, §42-1903.08.

Durable powers of attorney, §§21-2081 to 21-2085.
See DURABLE POWERS OF ATTORNEY.

Healthcare decisions.
See HEALTHCARE DURABLE POWERS OF ATTORNEY.

Heath-care decisions, §§21-2201 to 21-2213.

ATTORNEYS AT LAW.

Access to justice initiative program, §§4-1701.01 to 4-1704.07.
See ACCESS TO JUSTICE INITIATIVE PROGRAM.

Accounts and accounting.
Client's property, ProfCond Rule 1.15.
Interest on Lawyers Trust Account (IOLTA), DCBar Appx A, DCBar Rule X, ProfCond Rule 1.15.
Approved depositories, DCBar Rule XI.
Verification of participation, DCBar Rule XIV.

Administrative representation, ProfCond Rule 3.9.

Admission to bar, §11-2501, DCCtApp Rule 46, USDistCt LCrR 57.21, USDistCt LCvR 83.8.
False statements, etc., ProfCond Rule 8.1.

Adoption proceedings.
Appearance and withdrawal of attorney, Adoption Rule 101.
Appointment and compensation, §16-316.
Confidentiality requirements, Adoption Rule 79-I.

Advancing money to clients, ProfCond Rule 1.8.

Advertising, ProfCond Rule 7.1.
Firm names and letterhead, ProfCond Rule 7.5.

Advising client, ProfCond Rule 2.1.

Advocacy, ProfCond Rules 3.1 to 3.9.

Appeals, D.C. courts.
Appearance and withdrawal of attorney, DCCtApp Rule 42.
Discipline or disability proceedings, DCBar Rule XI.
Number of counsel at oral argument, DCCtApp Rule 34.

ATTORNEYS AT LAW —Cont'd

Appeals, federal cases.
Admission to practice, FRAP 46(b).
Exclusion from practice, USCtApp HPIP Rule II(a)(3).
Obtaining admission, USCtApp HPIP Rule II(a)(2).
When required, USCtApp HPIP Rule II(a)(1).
Appearance before the court, FRAP 46(a).
Law students, FRAP 46(g).
Appendices to briefs.
Sanctions against attorneys for inclusion of unnecessary material, FRAP 30(b).
Change of address, FRAP 46(c).
Change of name of attorney after admission, FRAP 46(d).
Clerk or deputy clerk not to practice, FRAP 45(a).
Committee on admissions and grievances, FRAP 46(f).
Death of counsel, effect on service of notice of appeal, FRAP 3(d).
Death of party, filing notice of appeal, FRAP 43(a).
Disciplinary actions.
Failure to comply with rules, USCtApp Rule 38.
Rules of disciplinary enforcement, USCtApp Appx I.
Suspension or disbarment, FRAP 46(e).
Disciplinary power of court over, FRAP 46(e).
In forma pauperis.
Appointment of counsel, USCtApp HPIP Rule VI(d).
Oral argument, non-appearance of parties, FRAP 34(e).
Representation statement, filing, FRAP 12(b).
Sanctions against attorneys.
Failure to comply with rules, USCtApp Rule 38.
Suspension or disbarment, FRAP 46(e).

Appearances generally.
See APPEARANCES.

Appointment of counsel.
See RIGHT TO COUNSEL.

Arbitration.
Appearance and withdrawal of attorney, Arbitration Rule XIV.
Fee disputes, DCBar Rule XIII.

ATTORNEYS AT LAW —Cont'd
Arbitration —Cont'd
Representation in case where attorney was arbitrator, ProfCond Rule 1.12.
Small claims court, SmallClaimsArb Rule 3.
Arbitration, revised act.
Representation by counsel, §16-4416.
Bail bond business, involvement with, §§23-1103, 23-1104.
Bankruptcy proceedings.
Admission to practice before bankruptcy court, USDistDCBank Rule 2090-1.
Names, addresses and telephone numbers required on pleadings, USDistDCBank Rule 5005-1.
Notice of appearance, USDistDCBank Rule 9010-1.
Withdrawal, USDistDCBank Rule 2091-1.
Bar admission, §11-2501, DCCtApp Rule 46, USDistCt LCrR 57.21, USDistCt LCvR 83.8.
Bar association.
See DISTRICT OF COLUMBIA BAR.
Bar examination, DCCtApp Rule 46.
Board on professional responsibility, DCBar Rule XI.
Candor toward the tribunal, ProfCond Rule 3.3.
Censure, suspension, or disbarment, §§11-2502 to 11-2504.
Certificate of good standing.
Government lawyers.
Required for attorneys employed at level of DS-13 or above, §1-608.81.
Child abuse and neglect proceedings, NeglectProc Rule 42.
Appointment.
Shelter care hearing or initial appearance, NeglectProc Rule 12.
Practice standards, NeglectProc Appx.
Reports by attorney, NeglectProc Rule 21.
Child clients, ProfCond Rule 1.14.
Civility in professional conduct.
Voluntary standards, DCBar Appx B.
Client-lawyer relationship, ProfCond Rules 1.1 to 1.18.
Communication with client, ProfCond Rule 1.4.
Competent representation, ProfCond Rule 1.1.

ATTORNEYS AT LAW —Cont'd
Client-lawyer relationship —Cont'd
Confidentiality of information, ProfCond Rule 1.6.
Conflicts of interest, ProfCond Rules 1.7 to 1.9.
Imputed disqualification, ProfCond Rule 1.10.
Declining representation, ProfCond Rule 1.16.
Diligent representation required, ProfCond Rule 1.3.
Diminished capacity, clients with, ProfCond Rule 1.14.
Disqualification from representation, ProfCond Rules 1.10 to 1.12.
Prospective clients, ProfCond Rule 1.18.
Fees.
See ATTORNEYS' FEES.
Former clients.
Representation of adverse interest, ProfCond Rule 1.9.
Government to private employment, ProfCond Rule 1.11.
Organization as client, ProfCond Rule 1.13.
Prohibited transactions, ProfCond Rule 1.8.
Prospective clients, duties to, ProfCond Rule 1.18.
Safekeeping property, ProfCond Rule 1.15.
Sale of law practice, ProfCond Rule 1.17.
Scope of representation, ProfCond Rule 1.2.
Soliciting clients, ProfCond Rule 7.1.
Terminating representation, ProfCond Rule 1.16.
Zealous representation required, ProfCond Rule 1.3.
Clients' Security Trust Fund, DCBar Rule XII.
Confidential files of bar counsel.
Access by trustees of client security fund, DCBar Appx C.
Restitution to fund by attorney, DCBar Rule XI.
Collaborative law disqualification, §16-4009.
Confidentiality of information.
Client information, ProfCond Rule 1.6.
Discipline or disability proceedings, DCBar Rule XI.
Lawyer counseling panel, USDistCt LCrR 57.31, USDistCt LCvR 83.20.

ATTORNEYS AT LAW —Cont'd
Conflicts of interest, ProfCond Rules
1.7 to 1.9.
Imputed disqualification, ProfCond
Rule 1.10.
Counseling clients, ProfCond Rules 2.1
to 2.4.
**Court-annexed limited legal service
programs,** ProfCond Rule 6.5.
Court appointed counsel.
See RIGHT TO COUNSEL.
Crimes and offenses, §11-2503.
Criminal law and procedure.
Counsel for accused, US Const Amd 6.
Death, disappearance, etc.
Protection of clients' interests, DCBar
Rule XI.
Decorum of a tribunal, ProfCond Rule
3.5.
Delaying proceedings, ProfCond Rule
3.2.
Diminished capacity, clients with.
Client-lawyer relationship, ProfCond
Rule 1.14.
Disbarment, §§11-2501 to 11-2504,
DCBar Rule XI, USDistCt LCrR
57.27, USDistCt LCvR 83.16.
Disciplinary actions, DCBar Rule XI.
Appeals, federal cases.
Failure to comply with rules,
USCtApp Rule 38.
Rules of disciplinary enforcement,
USCtApp Appx I.
Suspension or disbarment, FRAP
46(e).
Authority to initiate proceedings,
CivPro Rule 102.
False statements, etc., in connection
with disciplinary matter,
ProfCond Rule 8.1.
Family court proceedings generally,
FamDiv Rule S.
Jurisdiction and choice of law,
ProfCond Rule 8.5.
Legal service attorneys, §1-608.56.
Nonpayment of bar dues, DCBar Rule
II.
United States District Court.
See UNITED STATES DISTRICT
COURT FOR THE DISTRICT
OF COLUMBIA.
Discrimination in employment,
ProfCond Rule 9.1.
**Dismissal of action for failure to
prosecute.**
Referral to disciplinary board, CivPro
Rule 41-I.

ATTORNEYS AT LAW —Cont'd
**Disqualification from
representation,** ProfCond Rules
1.10 to 1.12.
Diversion programs, DCBar Rule XI.
Domestic relations actions, DomRel
Rule 101.
Pretrial procedures, DomRel Rule 16-I.
Employment discrimination,
ProfCond Rule 9.1.
Ethics.
Admission to bar, DCCtApp Rule 46.
Rules of professional conduct, DCBar
Rule X, ProfCond Rules 1.0 to 9.1.
**Evaluation of matter affecting client
for third persons,** ProfCond Rule
2.3.
**Ex parte communications with
tribunal,** ProfCond Rule 3.5.
Expediting litigation, ProfCond Rule
3.2.
**Fairness to opposing party and
counsel,** ProfCond Rule 3.4.
False statements or evidence.
Bar admission and disciplinary
matters, ProfCond Rule 8.1.
Candor to tribunal, ProfCond Rule 3.3.
Family court proceedings.
Standards of practice for appointed
counsel, §11-1103.
Fiduciary eligibility requirements,
CivPro Rule 304.
Firms.
Imputed disqualification, ProfCond
Rules 1.10, 1.11.
Name of firm, ProfCond Rule 7.5.
Non-lawyers sharing fees, managing
firm, etc., ProfCond Rule 5.4.
Partner's or supervisory lawyer's
responsibilities, ProfCond Rule
5.1.
Non-lawyer assistants, ProfCond
Rule 5.3.
Sale of law practice, ProfCond Rule
1.17.
Subordinate lawyer's responsibilities,
ProfCond Rule 5.2.
Garnishment.
Post-judgment garnishment in aid of
execution.
Trial on traverse of garnishee's
answers.
Costs and attorneys' fees may be
awarded in judgment
favorable to garnishee,
§16-553.

ATTORNEYS AT LAW —Cont'd
Garnishment —Cont'd
Prejudgment garnishment.
Fee awarded in judgment in favor of garnishee, §16-522.
Government lawyers.
"Attorney for the government" defined, CrimPro Rule 54.
Certificate of good standing.
Required for attorneys employed at level of DS-13 or above, §1-608.81.
Legal service, §§1-608.51 to 1-608.66. See LEGAL SERVICE.
Prosecutors, ProfCond Rule 3.8.
Scope of representation, ProfCond Rule 1.2.
Successive government and private employment, ProfCond Rule 1.11.
Unauthorized practice of law exceptions, DCCtApp Rule 49.
Guardian ad litem to be member of bar, CivPro Rule 304.
Intervention proceedings, Probate Rule 306.
Probate proceedings.
Death on or after July 1, 1995, Probate Rule 422.
Guardians, conservators, trustees, etc., involved, Probate Rule 202.
Impartiality of the tribunal, ProfCond Rule 3.5.
Imputed disqualification, ProfCond Rule 1.10.
Incompetent or incapacitated attorneys, DCBar Rule XI, USDistCt LCrR 57.30, USDistCt LCvR 83.19.
Competent representation requirement, ProfCond Rule 1.1.
Independence of lawyer, ProfCond Rule 5.4.
Indigent persons.
Access to justice initiative program, §§4-1701.01 to 4-1704.07. See ACCESS TO JUSTICE INITIATIVE PROGRAM.
Right to counsel.
See RIGHT TO COUNSEL.
Intellectual disability proceedings, MentalRetardation Rule 11.
Interest on Lawyers Trust Account (IOLTA), DCBar Appx A, DCBar Rule X, ProfCond Rule 1.15.
Approved depositories, DCBar Rule XI.
Verification of participation, DCBar Rule XIV.

ATTORNEYS AT LAW —Cont'd
International wills.
Persons authorized to act in relation to international wills, §18-709.
Interstate family support.
Private counsel, §46-353.09.
Intervention proceedings.
See INTERVENTION PROCEEDINGS.
Judges.
Law practice prohibited, avoiding conflicts with office, CJC Canon 3.10.
Judgments.
Consent of counsel, CivPro Rule 68-I.
Juvenile proceedings.
Practice by attorneys no members of District bar, JuvProc Rule 115.
Right to and assignment of counsel, JuvProc Rule 44.
Work-product rule, JuvProc Rule 16.
Landlord and tenant court, LandlordTenant Rule 9.
Limitation of cases, LandlordTenant Rule 8.
Law-related services.
Responsibilities regarding, ProfCond Rule 5.7.
Lawyer counseling panel, USDistCt LCrR 57.31, USDistCt LCvR 83.20.
Legal service, §§1-608.51 to 1-608.66. See LEGAL SERVICE.
Legal service programs.
Nonprofit or court-annexed limited legal service programs, ProfCond Rule 6.5.
Legal services organizations.
Serving as director, officer, etc., ProfCond Rule 6.3.
Legislative representation, ProfCond Rule 3.9.
Letterhead, ProfCond Rule 7.5.
Literary rights.
Drafting instruments giving attorney rights, ProfCond Rule 1.8.
Malpractice.
Agreements or settlement with client, ProfCond Rule 1.8.
Media rights to story.
Drafting instruments giving attorney rights, ProfCond Rule 1.8.
Meritorious claims and contentions, ProfCond Rule 3.1.
Merit system.
Legal service, §§1-608.51 to 1-608.66. See MERIT SYSTEM.

ATTORNEYS AT LAW —Cont'd

Misconduct, ProfCond Rule 8.4.

Grounds for disciplinary proceedings, DCBar Rule XI, USDistCt LCrR 57.2, USDistCt LCrR 57.27, USDistCt LCvR 83.15, USDistCt LCvR 83.16.

Reporting misconduct, ProfCond Rule 8.3.

Non-adjudicative representation, ProfCond Rule 3.9.

Non-compete agreements, ProfCond Rule 5.6.

Non-lawyers sharing fees, managing firm, etc., ProfCond Rule 5.4.

Nonprofit limited legal service programs, ProfCond Rule 6.5.

Notice.

See NOTICE.

Number of attorneys at trial, CivPro Rule 39-II, USDistCt LCrR 44.2, USDistCt LCvR 83.3.

Appellate arguments, DCCtApp Rule 34.

Obstructing access to evidence, ProfCond Rule 3.4.

Opposing party or counsel.

Communications with opposing party, ProfCond Rule 4.2.

Fairness to opposition, ProfCond Rule 3.4.

Unrepresented parties, ProfCond Rule 4.3.

Organizations as clients, ProfCond Rule 1.13.

Patent office practice.

Orders as to admission or exclusion, review of, USDistCt LCvR 83.7.

Plea bargains.

Communication of proffer of plea bargain to client, ProfCond Rule 1.4.

Poverty lawyer loan repayment assistance program, §§4-1704.01 to 4-1704.07.

See ACCESS TO JUSTICE INITIATIVE PROGRAM.

Pro bono cases, ProfCond Rule 6.1.

Appearances by attorneys, CivPro Rule 101.

Certification of practice pro bono publico, DCCtApp Form 9.

Unauthorized practice of law exceptions, DCCtApp Rule 49.

ATTORNEYS AT LAW —Cont'd

Pro hac vice appearances, CivPro Rule 101, CrimPro Rule 115, USDistCt LCrR 44.1, USDistCt LCvR 83.2.

Adoption proceedings, Adoption Rule 101.

Application for admission pro hac vice, DCCtApp Form 8.

Domestic relations actions, DomRel Rule 101.

Juvenile proceedings, JuvProc Rule 115.

Unauthorized practice of law exceptions, DCCtApp Rule 49.

Property of client, ProfCond Rule 1.15.

Prosecutors.

Special responsibilities, ProfCond Rule 3.8.

Pro se litigants.

Dealings with unrepresented persons, ProfCond Rule 4.3.

Prospective clients, duties to, ProfCond Rule 1.18.

Public defender service, §§2-1601 to 2-1608.

See PUBLIC DEFENDER SERVICE.

Publicity of trial, ProfCond Rule 3.6.

Referrals to attorney, ProfCond Rule 7.1.

Reforming the law.

Law reform activities affecting client interests, ProfCond Rule 6.4.

Reinstatement, DCBar Rule XI, USDistCt LCrR 57.27, USDistCt LCrR 57.29, USDistCt LCrR 57.30, USDistCt LCvR 83.16, USDistCt LCvR 83.18, USDistCt LCvR 83.19.

Release of information relating to pending criminal proceedings, USDistCt LCrR 57.7.

Rights of third persons, ProfCond Rule 4.4.

Right to counsel.

See RIGHT TO COUNSEL.

Rules of professional conduct, DCBar Rule X, ProfCond Rules 1.0 to 9.1.

Advocate for client, ProfCond Rules 3.1 to 3.9.

Client-lawyer relationship, ProfCond Rules 1.1 to 1.18.

Communications concerning a lawyer's services, ProfCond Rules 7.1, 7.5.

Counseling client, ProfCond Rules 2.1 to 2.4.

ATTORNEYS AT LAW —Cont'd
Rules of professional conduct
—Cont'd
Definitions, ProfCond Rule 1.0.
Discrimination in employment,
ProfCond Rule 9.1.
Law firms and associations, ProfCond
Rules 5.1 to 5.7.
Maintaining the integrity of the
profession, ProfCond Rules 8.1 to
8.5.
Public service, ProfCond Rules 6.1 to
6.5.
Transactions with non-clients,
ProfCond Rules 4.1 to 4.4.
Sale of law practice, ProfCond Rule
1.17.
Sanctions generally.
See SANCTIONS.
Scheduling conflicts, CivPro Rule 104,
USDistCt LCrR 57.5, USDistCt
LCvR 16.2.
Service upon attorney, CivPro Rule 5.
Domestic relations actions, DomRel
Rule 5.
Settlement.
Communication of offer of settlement
to client, ProfCond Rule 1.4.
Signing of pleadings, CivPro Rule 11.
Small claims court, SmallClaims Rule
9.
Arbitration, SmallClaimsArb Rule 3.
Soliciting clients, ProfCond Rule 7.1.
Special education student rights.
Restriction of practice by attorney
based on pattern of frivolous
pleadings, §38-2572.04.
Special legal consultants, DCCtApp
Rule 46.
**Third-party neutral, lawyer serving
as,** ProfCond Rule 2.4.
Trade names, ProfCond Rule 7.5.
Truthfulness.
Candor toward the tribunal, ProfCond
Rule 3.3.
Statements to third persons, ProfCond
Rule 4.1.
Unauthorized practice of law,
DCCtApp Rule 49, ProfCond Rule
5.5.
United States District Court.
Practice by attorneys, USDistCt LCrR
44.1, USDistCt LCvR 83.2.
**Voluntary standards for civility in
professional conduct,** DCBar
Appx B.

ATTORNEYS AT LAW —Cont'd
Wills.
Drafting instruments giving attorney
gift, ProfCond Rule 1.8.
Withdrawing from case, ProfCond
Rule 1.16.
Appeals, DCCtApp Rule 42.
Bankruptcy proceedings,
USDistDCBank Rule 2091-1.
Child abuse and neglect proceedings,
NeglectProc Rule 42.
Domestic relations actions, DomRel
Rule 101.
Intellectual disability proceedings,
MentalRetardation Rule 11.
Witness at trial, ProfCond Rule 3.7.
Work-product.
Discovery scope and limits, CivPro
Rule 26.
Adoption proceedings, Adoption Rule
26.
Criminal procedure, CrimPro Rule
16.
Delinquent minors, JuvProc Rule 16.
Domestic relations actions, DomRel
Rule 26.
Liens on client files, ProfCond Rule
1.8.
Zealous representation required,
ProfCond Rule 1.3.

ATTORNEYS' FEES.
Address of party changed.
Failure to provide notice, CivPro Rule
10-I.
Adoption proceedings, Adoption Rule
54.
Appointed counsel, compensation of,
§16-316.
Discovery or disclosure violations,
Adoption Rules 30, 37.
Scheduling order noncompliance,
Adoption Rule 16.
Advance payment of, §15-704.
Appeals, federal cases.
Plan to implement criminal justice act
of 1964, USCtApp Appx II.
**Appointment of counsel in criminal
proceedings,** §11-2604.
Arbitration for disputes, DCBar Rule
XIII.
Arbitration, revised act.
Authority to award, §16-4421.
Judgment on award, §16-4425.
**Attachment and garnishment after
judgment in aid of execution,**
§§16-542, 16-553.

ATTORNEYS' FEES —Cont'd
Attachment of wages.
Noncompliance by judgment creditor, CivPro Rule 69-II.
Basis of fee statements, ProfCond Rule 1.5.
Bicyclist, assault or battery by motorist.
Right of civil action for damages, §50-1621.
Child abuse and neglect, §§16-2326, 16-2326.01, NeglectProc Rule 42.
Child custody proceedings.
Enforcement of foreign custody determinations, §16-4603.12.
Compensation of attorney as costs, §15-701.
Consumer credit, §28-3806.
Consumer credit reporting agencies.
Consumer security freeze.
Willful violations, §28-3864.
Consumer credit sales, §§28-3806, 28-3813.
Consumer credit service organizations.
Action for damages, §28-4607.
Consumer protection violations, §28-3905.
Consumers' remedies, §28-3813.
Contingent fees, ProfCond Rule 1.5.
Hiring by attorney general for the District of Columbia, §1-301.86a.
Continuing care retirement communities.
Civil liability of providers for violations, recovery, §44-151.14.
Corporations.
Derivative actions, §29-305.56.
Costs, attorneys' fees as, §15-702.
Court appointed counsel in criminal proceedings, §11-2604.
Crime victims' compensation, VictComp Rule 39.
Death of attorney.
Appointment of counsel to protect clients' interest upon death, etc., of other attorney, DCBar Rule XI.
Delinquent minors, §§16-2326, 16-2326.01, JuvProc Rule 113.
Determination, USDistCt LCvR 54.2.
Disability compensation for public officers and employees, §1-623.27.
Discovery, CivPro Rules 26, 37, USDistCt LCvR 26.2.
Adoption proceedings, Adoption Rules 30, 37.

ATTORNEYS' FEES —Cont'd
Discovery —Cont'd
Depositions, CivPro Rule 30.
Domestic relations actions, DomRel Rules 30, 37.
District of Columbia exempt from, §15-705.
Division of fees with outside attorneys, ProfCond Rule 1.5.
Domestic relations actions, DomRel Rule 54.
Discovery or disclosure violations, DomRel Rules 30, 37.
Offer of judgment, DomRel Rule 68.
Drug-related evictions, §42-3608.
Ejectment, §16-1114.
E-mail, spam, §28-5003.
Fiduciaries, CivPro Rule 301.
Conservators and guardians of minors, Probate Rule 225.
Death before January 1, 1981, Probate Rules 19, 22.
Foreclosure rescue services and transactions.
Private right of action, §42-2434.
Frivolous, dilatory, etc., pleadings, CivPro Rule 11.
Domestic relations actions, DomRel Rule 11.
Hospitalization of persons with mental illness.
Court-order hospitalization, §21-543.
Human trafficking, §22-1840.
Indigent persons.
In forma pauperis proceedings, §15-712.
Plan for furnishing representation to indigents.
Court of appeals procedures, IndigentRep Rule III.
Superior court procedures, IndigentRep Rule II.
Table of guideline fees, IndigentRep Form.
In forma pauperis proceedings, §15-712.
Installment loans.
Provision for attorneys' fees, §28-3806.
Intervention proceedings.
Compensation of attorneys, etc., Probate Rule 308.
Judgments and decrees, enforcement of, §15-111.
Delay of entry, CivPro Rule 58.
Juvenile proceedings, JuvProc Rule 113.

ATTORNEYS' FEES —Cont'd
Landlord and tenant, §42-3509.02.
Liens, ProfCond Rule 1.8.
Merit system, §§1-606.08, 1-617.03.
Mortgages and deeds of trust.
   Foreclosure rescue services and
     transactions.
     Private right of action, §42-2434.
Motions for fees, CivPro Rule 54.
New parties, §12-103.
No-fault motor vehicle insurance,
   §31-2410.
Non-client paying fees, ProfCond Rule
   1.8.
Nonprofit corporations.
   Derivative actions, §29-411.07.
Nonresidents, security bond for,
   §§15-703, 15-711.
Nursing homes.
   Discharge, transfer, or relocation of
     residents of, §44-1004.04.
Personal representatives, §20-752.
Prescription drugs, excessive
   pricing, §28-4555.
Pretrial conference violations,
   CivPro Rule 16.
   Adoption proceedings, Adoption Rule
     16.
   Domestic relations actions, DomRel
     Rule 16-I.
   Tax proceedings, Tax Rule 13.
Probate fees, §§15-707, 15-708.
Probate proceedings, §§16-3106,
   16-3112.
   Conservators and guardians of minors,
     Probate Rule 225.
   Death before January 1, 1981, Probate
     Rules 19, 22.
Procedures for obtaining fees, CivPro
   Rule 54, USDistCt LCvR 54.2.
Procurement practices violations.
   Action seeking relief from retaliatory
     actions, §2-381.04.
   Qui tam actions, §2-381.03.
Prompt payment.
   Private contractor and subcontractor
     prompt payment act.
     Failure to make prompt payments,
       §27-133.
      Subcontractors, payments to,
       §27-135.
Rate of fee statements, ProfCond Rule
   1.5.
Reasonableness, ProfCond Rule 1.5.
Rental properties, §42-3509.02.
Rent control, §42-3509.02.

ATTORNEYS' FEES —Cont'd
Replevin, §16-3701.
Residential drug-related evictions.
   Recovery of court cost, §42-3608.
Restraints of trade, §28-4507.
Sharing fees with non-lawyers,
   ProfCond Rule 5.4.
Shoplifting, §27-106.
Small claims court, §§16-3902,
   16-3903, 16-3909, SmallClaims Rule
   19.
Smoking in public places.
   Employee rights and protections,
     §7-741.06.
Spam deterrence, §28-5003.
Subpoenas.
   Protection of persons subject to
     subpoenas, CivPro Rule 45.
   Domestic relations actions, DomRel
     Rule 45.
Summary judgment motions, CivPro
   Rule 56.
Superior court, §§15-709, 15-711,
   15-713, 15-714.
Tax proceedings, Tax Rule 13.
Telephone number of party changed.
   Failure to provide notice, CivPro Rule
     10-I.
Tenant assistance program,
   §42-3509.02.
Tenant organizations.
   Violation of provisions, §42-3505.06.
Termination of parental rights,
   §16-2326.01, NeglectProc Rule 42.
Trade secrets, §36-404.
Trusts and trustees.
   Uniform trust code.
     Judicial proceedings, §19-1310.04.
United States exempt from, §15-705.
Workers' compensation, §32-1530.
Workplace fraud.
   Private right of action to enforce
     provisions, §32-1331.09.

ATTORNMENT, FRAUDULENT.
Landlord and tenant, §42-3232.

ATV'S.
Defined, §50-2201.02.
Public property.
   Operation on prohibited, §50-2201.04b.
Registration not required,
   §50-2201.04b.

AT WILL ESTATES, §§42-504, 42-522.

AT WILL TENANTS, §42-3203.

AUCTIONS AND AUCTIONEERS.
Abandoned and unlawfully parked vehicles.
Disposal of unclaimed vehicle, §50-2421.10.
Bankruptcy proceedings, USDistDCBank Rule 6005-1.
Court ordered property sales.
Compensation of auctioneer, CivPro Rule 308.
Probate proceedings, Probate Rule 203.
Mortgages and deeds of trust.
Foreclosure sales.
See MORTGAGES AND DEEDS OF TRUST.
Procurement practices.
Reverse auctions, §2-381.23.
Public auctions.
See PUBLIC AUCTIONS.
Sale of goods, §28:2-328.

AUDIOLOGISTS, §§28-4001 to 28-4007.
Assistants.
Registration, §3-1209.09.
Transition provisions.
Persons already practicing, §3-1212.05.
Board of audiology and speech-language pathology, §3-1202.18.
Defined, §28-4001.
Health occupations licensure, registration or certification, §§3-1205.01 to 3-1205.24.
See HEALTH OCCUPATIONS LICENSURE, REGISTRATION OR CERTIFICATION.
Hearing aid dealers, §§28-4001 to 28-4007.
See HEARING AID DEALERS.
Practice of audiology, defined, §3-1201.02.
Qualifications for licensure, §3-1208.41.
Renewal of license, §3-1208.41.
Titles and terms prohibited as misrepresentation without license to practice, §3-1210.03.

AUDIO RECORDINGS.
Depositions, CivPro Rule 30.
Superior court proceedings, CivPro Rule 201.
Family division, FamDiv Rule N.

AUDITA QUERELA.
Writ abolished, CivPro Rule 60.

AUDITOR FOR DISTRICT OF COLUMBIA.
Appointment, §1-204.55.
Compliance unit, §1-301.183.
Established, §1-301.181.
List of noncompliant contractors, §1-301.183.
Powers, §1-301.182.
Reports, §§1-301.183, 1-301.184.
Site visits, §1-301.182.
Testimony to council, §1-301.183.
Contempt.
Subpoena and oath authority, §1-301.172.
Legal fund, §1-301.174.
Powers and duties, §1-204.55.
Subpoena and oath authority, §§1-301.171 to 1-301.173.
Public procurements, §2-354.18.
Records, §1-204.55.
Reports, §1-204.55.
TANF reduction statements, §4-205.11c.
Wages and salaries, §1-204.55.

AUDITOR-MASTERS, CivPro Rules 53 to 53-II.
Domestic relations actions, DomRel Rule 53.
Probate proceedings.
Sale of real property.
Death before January 1, 1981, Probate Rule 18.

AUDITS.
Access to justice program, §4-1702.02.
Armory board, §3-310.
Banks and financial institutions, §26-102.
Closed special funds, §47-131.
College savings program.
Program depository or manager, §47-4506.
Submission of audit report, §47-4512.
Comptroller General, audit of District accounts by, §1-204.55.
Cooperative associations, §29-933.
Court auditor-master, §11-1724.
Disbursing officer's accounts, §47-111.
District accounts.
Auditor of District of Columbia, by, §1-204.55.
Independent annual auditor, by, §47-119.
District of Columbia School of Law records, §38-1205.09.

AUDITS —Cont'd
Fiduciary accounts and reports,
CivPro Rule 305.
Decedents' estates.
Death between January 1, 1981 and
June 30, 1995, Probate Rules
117, 118.
Death on or after July 1, 1995,
Probate Form 20, Probate Rules
417, 418.
Guardians, conservators, trustees, etc.,
involved, Probate Rules 204, 331.
Missing persons, Probate Rule 350.
Gallaudet University, §38-2402.03.
**Health benefits for public
employees,** §1-621.12.
Home purchase assistance fund,
§42-2605.
Horizontal property regimes,
§42-2015.
Housing finance agency, §42-2705.04.
**Independent annual audit of
District accounts,** §47-119.
Inmate welfare fund, §24-282.
Inspector general, §1-301.115a.
**Insurance company annual audited
financial reports,** §§31-301 to
31-314.
See INSURANCE COMPANIES.
Insurance regulatory trust fund,
§31-1209.
**Insurers rehabilitation and
liquidation proceedings,**
§31-1347.
**Intermediate care facilities for
persons with intellectual
disabilities.**
Stevie Sellows quality improvement
fund, §§47-1271, 47-1275.
**Lottery and charitable games
control board,** §3-1319.
**Mental health disclosures for
purposes of,** §7-1203.05.
Merit system.
Other post-employment benefits fund,
annual audit, §1-621.09e.
**Metropolitan Washington Airports
Authority,** §9-919.
**Motor fuel tax and International
Fuel Tax Agreement,** §47-2353.
**Motor vehicle registration,
international registration plan
agreements,** §50-1507.05.
Nursing facilities.
Assessment on nursing facilities,
§47-1265.

AUDITS —Cont'd
Pensions and retirement funds,
§1-903.06.
Pre-kindergarten programs.
Enhancement and expansion of
programs.
Capacity audit, §38-271.04.
High quality standards for existing
programs.
Audit of program in relation to high
quality standards, §38-272.02.
Producer controlled insurers.
Business transactions with, §31-405.
Public defender service, §2-1606.
Public procurements, §2-354.18.
**Public schools, capital
improvements,** §38-2973.05.
**Public space, public rights of way,
and public structures, permits to
occupy,** §10-1141.05.
Public utilities, accounts of, §34-1114.
Schools and education.
Calculation of number of students,
§38-1804.02.
Capital improvements to public
schools.
Expenditure accountability,
§38-2973.05.
School food services accounts, §38-807.
Step Up program, §42-2622.
**Stevie Sellows quality improvement
fund,** §§47-1271, 47-1275.
Title insurance producers,
§31-5041.03.
**Tobacco settlement financing
corporation,** §7-1831.03.
Unemployment compensation,
§51-122.
**United States District Court for the
District of Columbia,** §11-521.
**Washington convention and sports
authority,** §10-1203.05.
Workers' compensation funds.
Administration fund, §32-1541.
Special fund, §32-1540.

**AUTHENTICATION OF OFFICIAL
RECORDS.**
Adoption proceedings, Adoption Rule
44.
Civil cases, CivPro Rule 44.
Criminal cases, CrimPro Rule 27.
Delinquent minors, JuvProc Rule 27.
Domestic relations actions, DomRel
Rule 44.
Foreign judgments, CivPro Rule 72.

AUTOMATED EXTERNAL DEFIBRILLATORS.
Usage by public, §§44-231 to 44-235.
CPR and AED program, §44-232.03.
Definitions, §44-231.
Immunity, §44-233.
Public access, §44-232.
Recreational facilities, program for, §44-232.01.
Registration fee fund, §44-234.
Rules, §44-235.
Study to expand AED program, §44-232.02.

AUTOMATED TELLER MACHINES, §§26-131.01 to 26-131.13.
Complaints against operator, §26-131.09.
Definitions, §26-131.02.
Establishment, §26-131.03.
Lighting, §26-131.06.
Penalties for violation, §26-131.12.
Point-of-sale terminal, §26-131.04.
Defined, §26-131.02.
Surcharge disclosure, §26-131.08.
Records, §26-131.11.
Registration, §26-131.10.
Rules and regulation, issuance, §26-131.13.
Safety evaluation, §26-131.05.
Satellite device, §26-131.04.
Defined, §26-131.02.
Short title of act, §26-131.01.
Surcharge disclosure, §26-131.07.
Point-of-sale terminal, §26-131.08.

AUTOMATED TRAFFIC ENFORCEMENT, §§50-2209.01 to 50-2209.11.

AUTOMATIC DATA PROCESSING, §§2-213.01, 2-213.02.

AUTONOMOUS VEHICLES, §§50-2351 to 50-2354.
Conversion of vehicle into.
Limited liability of original manufacturer, §50-2353.
Model years authorized to convert, §50-2353.
Definitions, §50-2351.
Permissible, §50-2352.
Requirements for operating on public roadway, §50-2352.
Rulemaking by mayor, §50-2354.

AUTOPSIES.
Medical examiners.
General provisions, §§5-1401 to 5-1419.
See MEDICAL EXAMINERS.

AVIATION.
Aircraft.
Foreign missions, owned by members of, §6-1304.01.
High school courses in aviation, §§38-920 to 38-922.
Dulles international airport, §§9-801 to 9-813.
See DULLES INTERNATIONAL AIRPORT.
Helicopter landing pads, §9-1211.01.
High school courses in, §§38-920 to 38-922.
Metropolitan Washington airports authority, §§9-901 to 9-926, 9-1001 to 9-1011.
See METROPOLITAN WASHINGTON AIRPORTS AUTHORITY.
Ronald Reagan Washington national airport, §§9-701 to 9-707.
See RONALD REAGAN WASHINGTON NATIONAL AIRPORT.

AWARDS.
Crime victim's compensations, §§4-507, 4-510.
Incentive awards.
Public officers and employees, §§1-619.01 to 1-619.03.
Single-room-occupancy housing development, §42-3508.06.
Teachers' retirement, §38-2041.01.
Public safety officers.
Awards for meritorious service, §§5-901 to 5-904.

B

BABY DROP-OFF LAW.
Newborn safe haven, §§4-1451.01 to 4-1451.08.
See NEWBORN SAFE HAVEN.

BACKGROUND CHECKS.
See CRIMINAL BACKGROUND CHECKS.

BACKPAY.
Employment discrimination award.
Income averaging for tax purposes, §47-1806.10.
Workplace fraud.
Private right of action to enforce provisions, §32-1331.09.

BAD CHECKS.
Courts.
Payments to courts, liability for non-payment, §11-1748.

BAD CHECKS —Cont'd
Real estate tax sales.
  Revised real property tax sale.
    Payment by bad check, §47-1342.01.
Sales.
  Power to transfer title, §28:2-403.

BADGES.
Insignia of police and fire and emergency medical services departments.
  Unauthorized use, §22-1409.

BAIL AND RECOGNIZANCE,
  §§16-704, 23-1321 to 23-1333.
Addicts, detention prior to trial,
  §23-1323.
Appeals, D.C. courts.
  Release pending appeal, DCCtApp
    Rule 9.
  Required information, DCCtApp
    Form 6.
Applicability of law, §23-1332.
Bail bondsmen.
  General provisions, §§23-1101 to
    23-1112.
    See BAIL BONDSMEN.
Bail determinations.
  Defined, §23-1302.
  Reports used in making, §23-1303.
Collateral as security for, §16-704.
  Criminal procedure, §16-704.
  Out-of-District property, collateral
    accepted for appearance before
    Magistrate regarding violations
    involving, §10-509.04.
  Washington National Airport.
    Collateral deposited by violators of
      rules regarding, §9-706.
Conditions of pretrial release,
  §23-1321, USDistCt LCrR 46.1.
Constitution of the United States.
  Excessive bail, US Const Amd 8.
Corporate sureties, CrimPro Rule 116.
Definitions, §23-1331.
Detention prior to trial.
  Addicts, §23-1323.
  Conditions requiring, §23-1322.
Excessive bail, US Const Amd 8.
Execution on, §16-709.
Exoneration and release of bail,
  CrimPro Rule 116.
Forfeitures, §16-709, CrimPro Rules
  35, 116.
Fugitives from justice, CrimPro Rule
  40-I.
Habeas corpus, §16-1906.

BAIL AND RECOGNIZANCE —Cont'd
Pretrial release, §23-1321, USDistCt
  LCrR 46.1.
Pretrial services agency.
  General provisions, §§23-1301 to
    23-1309.
    See PRETRIAL SERVICES
      AGENCY.
Private sureties, CrimPro Rule 116.
Release prior to trial.
  Appeal from conditions of, §23-1324.
  Assault with intent to kill while armed
    cases, §23-1325.
  Conditions of, §23-1321, USDistCt
    LCrR 46.1.
  Contempt for violation of conditions of,
    §§23-1329, 23-1330.
  Conviction, following, §23-1325.
  First degree murder cases, §23-1325.
  Juvenile history, consideration of,
    §23-1333.
  Material witnesses, §23-1326.
  Offenses committed during release,
    §23-1328.
  Second degree murder, §23-1325.
Releasing officials, §23-1110.
Temporarily detained.
  Revocation of conditional release,
    §23-1321.

BAIL BONDSMEN, §§23-1101 to
  23-1112.
Advance information passed to,
  §23-1109.
**Attorney, business involvement
  with,** §§23-1103, 23-1104.
Authorization of sureties, CrimPro
  Rule 116.
Corporate sureties, CrimPro Rule 116.
Definitions, §23-1101.
Disqualification as, §23-1108.
Duties of sureties, CrimPro Rule 116.
Enforcement of provisions, §23-1112.
Fees, §23-1105.
Fines, §§23-1108, 23-1111.
**Notice to prisoners of authorized
  bondsmen,** §23-1106.
Penalties, §§23-1108, 23-1111.
Private sureties, CrimPro Rule 116.
**Procuring business through official
  or attorney,** §23-1103.
**Public interest, bonding business
  impressed with,** §23-1102.
**Public official, business involvement
  with,** §§23-1103, 23-1104, 23-1109.
Qualification requirements, §23-1108.
Records kept by, §23-1108.

BAIL BONDSMEN —Cont'd
Releasing officials, §23-1110.
Schedule of bonds and collateral security, CrimPro Rule 116.
Visits to places of detention, §23-1107.

BAILMENTS.
Garage keepers' liens, §§40-102 to 40-105.
Pawnbrokers.
General provisions, §§47-2884.01 to 47-2884.19.
See PAWNBROKERS.

BALLET.
Washington ballet, real property tax exemption, §47-4655.

BALLOON PAYMENTS, §28-3803.

BALLPARK.
Alternative ballpark site.
Requirement to review costs and pursue, §10-1601.07.
Apprentice requirements, §10-1601.04.
Ballpark revenue fund, §10-1601.02.
Baseball financing review fund, §10-1601.06.
Bond issues, §10-1601.03.
Community benefit fund, §10-1602.03.
Community benefit fund, §§10-1602.01 to 10-1602.04.
Construction administration agreement, §10-1601.05.
Required provisions, §10-1601.08.
Construction hard and soft costs cap, §§10-1601.31 to 10-1601.34.
Definitions, §10-1601.31.
Development rights, §10-1601.34.
Limitations on contributions of bond proceeds and fund expenditures, §10-1601.32.
Payment in excess of expenditure limits, §10-1601.33.
Definitions, §§10-1601.03, 10-1601.05.
Development and construction, §10-1601.05.
Construction hard and soft costs cap, §§10-1601.31 to 10-1601.34.
Development rights, §10-1601.04.
Disadvantaged business enterprise requirements, §10-1601.04.
Findings, §10-1601.01.
First source employment requirements, §10-1601.04.
Parking structures not subject to zoning, §1-306.07.

BALLPARK —Cont'd
Performance parking zones.
Ballpark performance parking pilot zone, §50-2532.
Private financing.
Requirement to invite and evaluate, §10-1601.06.
Small business requirements, §10-1601.04.
Taxation without representation federal tax pay-out message board, §10-1701.
TIF area, §2-1217.12.

BALLPARK FEE, §§47-2761 to 47-2763.
Amount, computation, §47-2762.
Ballpark revenue fund.
Deposit of revenue received, §47-2762.
Basis of fee.
District gross receipts of feepayer, §47-2762.
Definitions, §47-2761.
Failure to file return or pay.
Enforcement provisions, §47-2763.
Remission, time, §47-2762.

BALLPARK SALES TAXES, §47-2002.05.

BANK DEPOSITS AND COLLECTIONS, §§28:4-401 to 28:4-504.
Alteration of customer's account.
Customer's duty to discover and report, §28:4-406.
Applicability of provisions, §28:4-102.
Depositary and collecting banks.
Collection of items, §28:4-201.
Variation by agreement, §28:4-103.
Bankruptcy and insolvency.
Collection of items.
Depositary and collecting banks.
Insolvency and preference, §28:4-216.
Branch offices.
Separate office of bank, §28:4-107.
Burden of proof.
Stop payment orders.
Losses resulting from violation of orders, §28:4-403.
Charge-back, §28:4-214.
Charging account of customer.
When bank may charge, §28:4-401.
Citation of article.
Short title, §28:4-101.
Collecting banks.
Security interest in items, documents and proceeds, §28:4-210.

**BANK DEPOSITS AND
  COLLECTIONS** —Cont'd
Collection of items.
  Depositary and collecting banks. See
    within this heading, "Depositary
    and collecting banks."
  Liability of secondary party, §28:4-212.
  Presentment of items by notice of item
    not payable by, through or at
    bank, §28:4-212.
Conflict of laws, §28:4-102.
Construction and interpretation.
  Applicability of article, §28:4-102.
  Depositary and collecting banks.
    Collection of items, §28:4-201.
  Variation by agreement, §28:4-103.
Contracts.
  Variation of article provisions by
    agreement, §28:4-103.
Customer relationship.
  Payor banks. See within this heading,
    "Payor banks."
Damages.
  Measure of damages, §28:4-103.
  Wrongful dishonor, §28:4-402.
Death of customer.
  Effect, §28:4-405.
Definitions, §28:4-104.
  Bank, §28:4-105.
  Collecting bank, §28:4-105.
  Depositary bank, §28:4-105.
  General commercial code definitions,
    §28:1-201.
    Course of dealing, §28:1-303.
    Reasonable time and seasonably,
      §28:1-205.
    Usage of trade, §28:1-303.
  Intermediary bank, §28:4-105.
  Payor bank, §28:4-105.
  Presenting bank, §28:4-105.
Delays, §28:4-109.
Depositary and collecting banks.
  Collection of items, §§28:4-201 to
    28:4-216.
    Agency status of collecting items,
      §28:4-201.
    Charge-back, §28:4-214.
    Credits for items.
      Availability for withdrawal,
        §28:4-215.
      Provisional status, §28:4-201.
      When provisional credits become
        final, §28:4-215.
    Death or incompetence of customer.
      Effect, §28:4-405.
    Debits for items.
      When provisional credits become
        final, §28:4-215.

**BANK DEPOSITS AND
  COLLECTIONS** —Cont'd
Depositary and collecting banks
  —Cont'd
  Collection of items —Cont'd
    Endorsements.
      "Pay any bank," §28:4-201.
      Generally, §28:4-201.
    Holders in due course.
      When bank gives value, §28:4-211.
    Insolvency and preference,
      §28:4-216.
    Instructions of transferor.
      Effect, §28:4-203.
    "Pay any bank."
      Items so endorsed, §28:4-201.
    Payment of item by payor bank.
      Final payment, §28:4-215.
    Presentment of items.
      Methods, §28:4-204.
    Refunds, §28:4-214.
    Responsibility required, §28:4-202.
    Security interest of collecting bank.
      Items accompanying documents
        and proceeds, §28:4-210.
    Sending items.
      Methods, §28:4-204.
    Settlement of items.
      Medium and time of settlement,
        §28:4-213.
      Provisional status, §28:4-201.
      When provisional credits become
        final, §28:4-215.
    Transfer of items.
      Between banks, §28:4-206.
    Unendorsed items.
      Depositary bank holder of,
        §28:4-205.
    When action timely, §28:4-202.
  Encoding and retention warranties,
    §28:4-209.
  Presentment warranties, §28:4-208.
  Unendorsed items.
    Depositary bank holder of,
      §28:4-205.
  Warranties.
    Documents of title, §28:7-508.
    Encoding and retention warranties,
      §28:4-209.
    Presentment warranties, §28:4-210.
    Transfer warranties, §28:4-207.
Documentary drafts.
  Dishonor.
    Duty to notify customer, §28:4-501.
    Privilege of presenting bank to deal
      with goods, §28:4-504.
      Security interests for expenses,
        §28:4-504.

BANK DEPOSITS AND COLLECTIONS —Cont'd
Documentary drafts —Cont'd
Dishonor —Cont'd
Reporting reasons for dishonor, §28:4-503.
Presentment.
Duty to send for presentment, §28:4-501.
"On arrival" drafts, §28:4-502.
Documents of title.
Negotiation and transfer.
Delivery without endorsement, §28:7-506.
Endorser not guarantor for other parties, §28:7-505.
Right to compel endorsement, §28:7-506.
Electronic presentment, §28:4-110.
Encoding warranties, §28:4-209.
Endorsements.
Collection of items.
Depositary and collecting banks.
Items endorsed "pay any bank," §28:4-201.
Funds transfers.
General provisions, §§28:4A-101 to 28:4A-507.
See FUNDS TRANSFERS.
General provisions, §§28:1-101 to 28:1-310.
See COMMERCIAL CODE.
Good faith.
Obligation of good faith, §28:1-304.
Holders in due course.
Collection of items.
Depositary and collecting banks.
When bank gives value for purposes of holder in due course, §28:4-211.
Incapacitated persons.
Effect of incompetence of customer, §28:4-405.
Interpretation of provisions, §§28:10-103, 28:10-104.
Liability.
Collection of items.
Depositary and collecting banks.
Liability of secondary parties, §28:4-212.
Wrongful dishonor.
Payor bank's liability to customer, §28:4-402.
Limitation of actions.
Deposits and collections.
Unauthorized signature or alteration.
Claims against bank, §28:4-406.

BANK DEPOSITS AND COLLECTIONS —Cont'd
Mental illness.
Incompetency of customer.
Authority of payor or collecting bank, §28:4-405.
Negotiable instruments.
General provisions, §§28:3-101 to 28:3-605.
See NEGOTIABLE INSTRUMENTS.
Ordinary care.
Action constituting, §28:4-103.
Payable through or at banks, §28:4-106.
Payor banks.
Collection of items.
Death or incompetence of customer.
Effect, §28:4-405.
Deferred posting, §28:4-301.
Dishonor of items.
Time of dishonor, §28:4-301.
Items subject to notice, stop payment order, legal process or setoff, §28:4-303.
Return of items.
Late return, §28:4-302.
Method of recovery of payment, §28:4-301.
Customer relationship.
Alteration of instruments.
Customer's duty to discover and report, §28:4-406.
Charging customer's account.
When allowed, §28:4-401.
Death of customer.
Effect, §28:4-405.
Dishonor, wrongful.
Liability to customer, §28:4-402.
Incompetency of customer.
Effect, §28:4-405.
Stale checks.
Obligation to bank to pay, §28:4-404.
Stop payment orders.
Customer's right to issue, §28:4-403.
Subrogation on improper payment.
Right of payor bank, §28:4-407.
Unauthorized signatures.
Customer's duty to discover and report, §28:4-406.
Subrogation rights on improper payment, §28:4-407.
Presentment.
Electronic presentment, §28:4-110.

BANK DEPOSITS AND COLLECTIONS —Cont'd
Presentment —Cont'd
Responsibility of presenting banks, §28:4-503.
Warranties, §28:4-208.
Receipt of items.
Delay, §28:4-109.
Time, §28:4-108.
Refunds, §28:4-214.
Retention warranties, §28:4-209.
Secured transactions.
Depositary and collecting banks.
Collection of items.
Security interests of collecting banks.
Items accompanying documents and proceeds, §28:4-210.
Documentary drafts.
Dishonor.
Privilege of presenting bank to deal with goods.
Security interest for expenses, §28:4-504.
Statute of limitations, §28:4-111.
Deposits and collections.
Unauthorized signature or alteration.
Claims against bank, §28:4-406.
Transitional provisions, §§28:11-101 to 28:11-108.
See COMMERCIAL CODE.

BANK FEES SPECIAL FUND, §1-325.231.

BANKING REGULATORY TRUST FUND.
Established, §31-107.

BANKRUPTCY AND INSOLVENCY.
Abandonment of estate property, USDistDCBank Rule 6007-1.
Administration of system, USDistDCBank Appx B.
Administrative expenses, payment of, USDistDCBank Rule 2016-4.
Adversary proceedings.
Amended pleadings, USDistDCBank Rule 7015-1.
Appeal bonds, USDistDCBank Rule 7062-1.
Costs, USDistDCBank Rule 7054-1.
Default, USDistDCBank Rule 7055-1.
Depositions, USDistDCBank Rule 7030-1.
Discovery, USDistDCBank Rule 7026-1.

BANKRUPTCY AND INSOLVENCY —Cont'd
Adversary proceedings —Cont'd
Dismissal, USDistDCBank Rule 7041-1.
Injunctions, USDistDCBank Rule 7065-1.
Intervention, USDistDCBank Rule 7024-1.
Registry fund, USDistDCBank Rule 7067-1.
Summary judgment, USDistDCBank Rule 7056-1.
Alcoholic beverage licenses.
Involuntary transfer of license, §25-361.
Appeals, federal cases.
Appeals from district courts, FRAP 6.
Applicability of local rules, USDistDCBank Rule 9029-3.
Assignment of cases, USDistCt LCvR 40.3.
Assignments for benefit of creditors, §§28-2101 to 28-2110.
See ASSIGNMENTS FOR BENEFIT OF CREDITORS.
Attorneys.
Admission to practice, USDistDCBank Rule 2090-1.
Names, addresses and telephone numbers required on pleadings, USDistDCBank Rule 5005-1.
Notice of appearance, USDistDCBank Rule 9010-1.
Withdrawal, USDistDCBank Rule 2091-1.
Auctioneers, USDistDCBank Rule 6005-1.
Automatic stays.
Relief from, USDistDCBank Rule 4001-1.
Bankruptcy abuse prevention and consumer protection act.
Interim rules, adoption of, USDistDCBank Appx E.
Calendars, USDistDCBank Rule 5070-1.
Captive insurance companies, §31-3931.16.
Chapter 11.
Final report and final decree, USDistDCBank Rule 3022-1.
Voting on plans, USDistDCBank Rule 3018-1.
Chapter 13.
Plan, USDistDCBank Rule 3015-1.
Amendments to plan, USDistDCBank Rule 3015-2.

BANKRUPTCY AND INSOLVENCY
—Cont'd
Chapter 13 —Cont'd
Plan —Cont'd
Confirmation, USDistDCBank Rule
3015-3.
Claims.
Objections, USDistDCBank Rule
3007-1.
Clerk of court.
Office hours, USDistDCBank Rule
5005-1.
Operation of clerk's office.
Standing order, USDistDCBank
Appx C.
Procedure for payment of fees,
USDistDCBank Rule 1006-1.
Compensation of professionals,
USDistDCBank Rule 2016-1.
Auctioneers, USDistDCBank Rule
6005-1.
**Compensation to debtor's officers,
partners and directors,**
USDistDCBank Rule 2016-3.
Congress.
Powers of congress, US Const Art I §8.
Contested matters, USDistDCBank
Rule 9014-1.
Continuances, USDistDCBank Rule
5070-1.
Costs.
Adversary proceedings,
USDistDCBank Rule 7054-1.
Creditors.
Meetings, USDistDCBank Rule
2003-1.
Notice to creditors and other
interested parties, USDistDCBank
Rule 2002-1.
Undeliverable addresses,
USDistDCBank Appx F.
Default.
Adversary proceedings,
USDistDCBank Rule 7055-1.
Depositions.
Adversary proceedings,
USDistDCBank Rule 7030-1.
Discharge, objections to,
USDistDCBank Rule 4004-2.
Discovery, USDistDCBank Rule
7026-1.
Dismissal.
Adversary proceedings,
USDistDCBank Rule 7041-1.
Involuntary petitions, USDistDCBank
Rules 1013-1, 1017-2.

BANKRUPTCY AND INSOLVENCY
—Cont'd
Electronic case filing, USDistDCBank
Appx D.
Notice re bounced back ECF e-mails,
USDistDCBank Appx G.
Practice and procedure,
USDistDCBank Appx H.
Examination of documents,
USDistDCBank Rule 2004-1.
Exemptions, objections to,
USDistDCBank Rule 4003-1.
Exhibits, USDistDCBank Rule 9070-1.
Filing of papers, USDistDCBank Rule
5005-1.
Forms.
Local official forms, USDistDCBank
Appx A.
Fraudulent conveyances, §28-3102.
Health maintenance organizations.
See HEALTH MAINTENANCE
ORGANIZATIONS.
**Health professional recruitment
program.**
Damages for breach of service
obligation contract.
Not dischargeable, §7-751.13.
Hearings, USDistDCBank Rule 9073-1.
Injunctions.
Adversary proceedings,
USDistDCBank Rule 7065-1.
Intervention.
Adversary proceedings,
USDistDCBank Rule 7024-1.
Involuntary petitions.
Dismissal, USDistDCBank Rules
1013-1, 1017-2.
Judicial notice, USDistDCBank Rule
9073-1.
Jury trial, USDistDCBank Rule 9015-1.
**Life and health insurance guaranty
association,** §§31-5409, 31-5411.
Lists, schedules and statements,
USDistDCBank Rule 1007-1.
Amendments, USDistDCBank Rule
1009-1.
Mailing matrix, USDistDCBank Rules
1007-1, 1007-2.
Mediation.
Referral to mediation, USDistCt LCvR
84.4.
**Meetings of creditors and equity
security holders,** USDistDCBank
Rule 2003-1.
Motion practice, USDistDCBank Rule
9013-1.

BANKRUPTCY AND INSOLVENCY
—Cont'd
Motor vehicle judgments,
§50-1301.48.
Names, addresses and telephone
numbers required on pleadings,
USDistDCBank Rule 5005-1.
Notice.
Creditors and other interested parties,
USDistDCBank Rule 2002-1.
Electronic case filing.
Bounced back ECF e-mails,
USDistDCBank Appx G.
Undeliverable addresses,
USDistDCBank Appx F.
United States, federal agencies, and
District of Columbia,
USDistDCBank Rule 2002-2.
Objections to claims, USDistDCBank
Rule 3007-1.
Objections to discharge,
USDistDCBank Rule 4004-2.
Objections to exemptions,
USDistDCBank Rule 4003-1.
Office hours of clerk of court,
USDistDCBank Rule 5005-1.
Orders.
Proposed orders, USDistDCBank Rule
9072-1.
Payment of fees, procedure for,
USDistDCBank Rule 1006-1.
Petitions.
Dismissal of involuntary petitions,
USDistDCBank Rules 1013-1,
1017-2.
Generally, USDistDCBank Rule
1002-1.
Partnerships, USDistDCBank Rule
1004-1.
Plans.
Chapter 11.
Final report and final decree,
USDistDCBank Rule 3022-1.
Voting on plans, USDistDCBank
Rule 3018-1.
Chapter 13, USDistDCBank Rule
3015-1.
Amendments to plan,
USDistDCBank Rule 3015-2.
Confirmation, USDistDCBank Rule
3015-3.
Pleadings.
Adversary proceedings,
USDistDCBank Rule 7015-1.
Form of pleadings and other papers,
USDistDCBank Rule 5005-1.

BANKRUPTCY AND INSOLVENCY
—Cont'd
Production of documents,
USDistDCBank Rule 2004-1.
Proof of service, USDistDCBank Rule
5005-1.
Property and liability insurance
guaranty association, §§31-5501
to 31-5515.
See PROPERTY AND LIABILITY
INSURANCE GUARANTY
ASSOCIATION.
Property of estate.
Abandonment, USDistDCBank Rule
6007-1.
Use, sale or lease, USDistDCBank
Rule 6004-1.
Proposed orders, USDistDCBank Rule
9072-1.
Publication, USDistDCBank Rule
9008-1.
Registry fund, USDistDCBank Rule
7067-1.
Reimbursement of professionals,
USDistDCBank Rule 2016-1.
Rules for the United States
bankruptcy court for the
District of Columbia.
Applicability of local rules,
USDistDCBank Rule 9029-3.
Scope of rules, USDistDCBank Rule
1001-1.
Suspension of local rules,
USDistDCBank Rule 9029-1.
Title of rules, USDistDCBank Rule
1001-1.
Sale of goods.
Buyer's insolvency.
Seller's remedies on discovery,
§28:2-702.
Schedules, lists and statements,
USDistDCBank Rule 1007-1.
Amendments, USDistDCBank Rule
1009-1.
Scheduling hearings, USDistDCBank
Rule 5070-1.
Standing orders, USDistDCBank Appx
C.
Issuance, USDistDCBank Rule 9029-2.
Stays.
Relief from automatic stay,
USDistDCBank Rule 4001-1.
Stipulations, USDistDCBank Rule
9071-1.
Summary judgment.
Adversary proceedings,
USDistDCBank Rule 7056-1.

BANKRUPTCY AND INSOLVENCY
—Cont'd
Suspension of local rules,
USDistDCBank Rule 9029-1.
Tax refunds and setoffs,
USDistDCBank Rule 6070-1.
Title insurers, §31-5031.09.
Trial.
Jury trial, USDistDCBank Rule
9015-1.
Use, sale or lease of estate property,
USDistDCBank Rule 6004-1.
Witnesses, USDistDCBank Rule 9070-1.

BANKS AND FINANCIAL
INSTITUTIONS, §§26-101 to
26-323.
Affordable housing.
Community development, §§26-431.01
to 26-431.08.
Appeal of orders of commissioner or
department, §26-551.20.
Applicability of acts of congress to
national banks in District,
§47-2508.
Approval required for, §26-103.
Association of notary public with,
§26-110.
ATMs, §§26-131.01 to 26-131.13.
See AUTOMATED TELLER
MACHINES.
Audits, §26-102.
Automated teller machines and
point of sale terminals,
§§26-131.01 to 26-131.13.
See AUTOMATED TELLER
MACHINES.
Bank fees special fund, §1-325.231.
WMATA momentum fund, §1-325.241.
Branch banks.
General provisions, §§26-731 to
26-741.
See INTERSTATE BANKING AND
BRANCH BANKS.
Building associations.
General provisions, §§26-201 to
26-232.
See BUILDING ASSOCIATIONS.
Cease and desist orders, §26-551.16.
Judicial review, §26-551.20.
Misdemeanor for violating final order,
§26-551.21.
Temporary order, §26-551.17.
Certification.
Universal banks, §§26-1401.01 to
26-1401.31.

BANKS AND FINANCIAL
INSTITUTIONS —Cont'd
Check cashers.
General provisions, §§26-301 to
26-323.
See CHECK CASHING
BUSINESSES.
Checks of District, cashing,
§47-351.14.
Child support enforcement.
Data match requirements for financial
institutions, §§26-531 to 26-533.
Definitions, §26-531.
Disclosure of person's financial
reports by IV-D agency,
unauthorized disclosure,
§26-533.
Fee paid by IV-D agency, §26-532.
Obligations, §26-532.
Violations, penalties, §26-532.
Commissioner of banking and
financial institutions.
Abolished, §26-551.03.
Common trust funds, §§26-401 to
26-404.
Court accountings, rendering, §26-403.
Establishment of, §26-401.
Interpretation of provisions, §26-403.
Taxation, §26-402.
Community development, §§26-431.01
to 26-431.08.
Community development plan.
Monitoring compliance, §26-431.05.
Requirement, §26-431.04.
Definitions, §26-431.02.
Examination and evaluation of
performance.
Cooperation with other regulators,
§26-431.07.
Obligation to meet needs of local
communities, §26-431.03.
Rating system for community
development performance,
§26-431.06.
Rules and regulations, §26-431.08.
Short title, §26-431.01.
Comptroller of the Currency,
supervision by, §26-101.
Confidentiality of information.
Examinations and investigations by
commissioner, §26-551.18.
Credit unions.
General provisions, §§26-501 to
26-504.
See CREDIT UNIONS.
Definitions, §26-1201.

BANKS AND FINANCIAL INSTITUTIONS —Cont'd
Department of banking and financial institutions.
Abolished, §26-551.03.
Department of insurance, securities, and banking, §§26-551.01 to 26-551.25.
Administration of banking code, §26-551.03.
Commissioner.
Investigation, examination and enforcement powers, §§26-551.10 to 26-551.21.
Rules, issuance, §26-551.23.
Definitions, §26-551.02.
Department and commissioner of banking and financial institutions abolished, §26-551.03.
General powers, §26-551.05.
Investigation, examination and enforcement powers, §§26-551.10 to 26-551.21.
Merchant banks, §§26-831.01 to 26-831.22.
Short title.
General provisions of the 21st century financial modernization act of 2000, §26-551.01.
Deposits.
Adverse claims to, §26-803.
Joint accounts, §26-801.
Dissolution, §26-103.
District funds deposited and invested in, §§47-351.01 to 47-351.16.
Dividends, §26-106.
Drafts.
Negotiable instruments.
Generally, §§28:3-101 to 28:3-605.
See NEGOTIABLE INSTRUMENTS.
Electronic funds transfers.
Generally, §§28:4A-101 to 28:4A-507.
Money transmissions, §§26-1001 to 26-1027.
See MONEY TRANSMISSIONS.
Enforcement of commissioner's order, §26-551.19.
Examination of financial institution, §§26-102, 26-551.10.
Examiners.
Commissioner to hire, §26-551.10.
Federal provisions applicable to, §§26-102 to 26-104, 26-109.
Fees.
Bank fees special fund, §1-325.231.

BANKS AND FINANCIAL INSTITUTIONS —Cont'd
Financial institutions advisory board, §§26-551.06 to 26-551.09.
Financial literacy council, §§38-731.01 to 38-731.05.
Financial reports, §26-551.11.
Fines, §26-103.
Fingerprint-based background checks.
Confidentiality of information, §31-633.
Definitions, §31-631.
Requirement of, §31-632.
Rules, §31-634.
Fraudulent activity prohibited, §26-551.22.
International banking corporations, §§26-103, 26-631 to 26-643.
Application of District of Columbia banking code, §26-633.
Assets held in District of Columbia, §26-638.
Banking business requirements, §26-634.
Branch bank establishment, §26-635.
Certification of financial capital, surplus and profits, §26-639.
Construction of legal and financial terms, §26-632.
Conversion of office, §26-635.
Deposits received within the District, §26-635.
Dissolution and liquidation, §26-642.
Examination by commissioner, §26-641.
License, §26-635.
Application, §26-636.
Surrender upon dissolution, §26-642.
Suspension or revocation, §26-641.
Liquidation, §26-642.
Loans and investments.
Applicability of banking code, §26-639.
Permissible activities, §26-635.
Powers of commissioner generally, §26-643.
Records, §26-640.
Examination by commissioner, §26-641.
Registered office and agent, §26-637.
Reports, §26-640.
Time deposits or loans.
Interest rate provision inapplicable, §28-3301.

BANKS AND FINANCIAL INSTITUTIONS —Cont'd

Interstate banking and branch banks.
General provisions, §§26-731 to 26-741.
See INTERSTATE BANKING AND BRANCH BANKS.

Investigation of financial institution, §26-551.12.
Final decision and order, §26-551.13.
Misdemeanor for violating final order, §26-551.21.
Modification or rescission, §26-551.15.
Notice of charges, hearing, subpoenas, §26-551.13.
Referral for appropriate action, notice to other agencies, §26-551.14.

Joint accounts, §§26-801 to 26-804.
Deposits, §§26-201, 26-801.
Safe deposit boxes, §26-802.
Shares of stock issued in names of 2 or more persons, §26-801.

Liquidation, §26-103.

Management of institutional funds.
General provisions.
See PRUDENT INVESTOR ACT.

Merchant banks, §§26-831.01 to 26-831.22.

Misdemeanor for violating final order, §26-551.21.

Money lenders, §§26-901 to 26-912.
See MONEY LENDERS.

Money transmissions, §§26-1001 to 26-1027.
See MONEY TRANSMISSIONS.

Mortgage lenders and brokers.
General provisions, §§26-1101 to 26-1121.
See MORTGAGE LENDERS AND BROKERS.

Mortgages and deeds of trust.
General provisions, §§42-804 to 42-820.
See MORTGAGES AND DEEDS OF TRUST.

Negotiable instruments.
General provisions, §§28:3-101 to 28:3-605.
See NEGOTIABLE INSTRUMENTS.

Notaries public associated with, §26-110.

Office of banking and financial institutions.
References deemed to mean department, §26-551.03.

BANKS AND FINANCIAL INSTITUTIONS —Cont'd

Opportunity accounts.
Establishing, requirements, §1-307.65.

Payment on death (POD) accounts.
TOD security registration, §§19-603.01 to 19-603.11.
See NONPROBATE TRANSFERS.

Penalties, §26-103.

Personal property taxes, §47-2510.

Point of sale terminals, §§26-131.01 to 26-131.13.
See AUTOMATED TELLER MACHINES.

Powers of attorney, §21-2108.

Prior law, validity, §26-551.25.

Public utility bill payment services offered by, §26-111.

Quarterly financial reports, §26-551.11.

Real property taxes, §47-2514.

Receivers, §26-103.

Regional bank holding companies.
Acquisitions, §26-702.

Regional interstate banking, §§26-702 to 26-714.
Regional bank holding companies.
Acquisitions, §26-702.
United States branch domestication, §§31-2301 to 31-2307.
Use of women-owned banks, §26-711.

Reports, §§26-101, 26-103.

Reserves, §26-102.

Revolving credit accounts, §§28-3701, 28-3702.

Safe deposit boxes.
Unclaimed property in.
See UNCLAIMED PROPERTY.

Saturdays.
Designated holiday, §28-2701.

Savings and loan acquisitions.
Use of minority-owned associations, §26-1217.

Savings and loan associations.
Acquisitions, §§26-1201 to 26-1217.
See SAVINGS AND LOAN ACQUISITIONS.
General provisions.
See SAVINGS AND LOAN ASSOCIATIONS.

Secured transactions.
Definition of bank, §28:9-102.
Rights of banks and financial institutions.
Control agreement.
Refusal to enter into or disclose existence of, §28:9-342.

BANKS AND FINANCIAL INSTITUTIONS —Cont'd
Secured transactions —Cont'd
Security interests in deposit accounts.
Control agreements.
Rights of banks and financial institutions with respect to agreements, §28:9-342.
Perfection and priority, §28:9-304.
Rules of priority, §28:9-327.
Rights and duties of banks and financial institutions, §28:9-341.
Set-off or recoupment, §28:9-340.
Transfer of funds from deposit account, §28:9-332.
Security agents and brokers.
General provisions, §§31-5601.01 to 31-5608.04.
See SECURITY AGENTS AND BROKERS.
Shareholder liability, §§26-104, 26-105.
Small business financing.
Community development, §§26-431.01 to 26-431.08.
Special financial reports, §26-551.11.
Superintendent of office of banking and financial institutions.
References deemed to mean Commissioner, §26-551.03.
Taxation, §§47-2503 to 47-2515.
Applicability of acts of congress to national banks in District, §47-2508.
Effective date of provisions, §47-2515.
Estimated tax, §47-2509.
Information requests about delinquent obligors, §47-4481.
Issuance of rules and regulations, §47-2513.
Note brokers, §§47-2505, 47-2506.
Payment of tax, §47-2506.
Personal property taxes, §47-2510.
Private banks, §§47-2503, 47-2506.
Real property taxes, §47-2514.
Savings clause, §47-2512.
Severability of provisions, §47-2511.
Transitional rules, §47-2507.
Washington Stock Exchange, §47-2504.
Termination of charter, §26-103.
Termination of shareholder liability, §26-105.
Terms "bank" and "trust company" restrictions on use of, §26-107.
Trust accounts, payment on death of trustee, §26-804.

BANKS AND FINANCIAL INSTITUTIONS —Cont'd
Trust, loan, mortgage, safe deposit and title corporations.
General provisions, §§26-1301 to 26-1336.
See TRUST, MORTGAGE AND TITLE CORPORATIONS.
Unclaimed property.
General provisions, §§41-101 to 41-142.
See UNCLAIMED PROPERTY.
Uniform fiduciaries act, §§21-1701 to 21-1712.
See FIDUCIARIES.
Universal banks.
Certification, §§26-1401.01 to 26-1401.31.
WMATA momentum fund, §1-325.241.

BANQUETS.
Alcoholic beverage licenses.
Temporary licenses, §25-115.

BAR ASSOCIATION.
See DISTRICT OF COLUMBIA BAR.

BARBED-WIRE FENCES, §§9-1213.01 to 9-1213.05.

BARBERS.
Board of barber and cosmetology, §§47-2853.06 to 47-2853.10.
Business licenses, §§47-2853.71 to 47-2853.73.
Eligibility, §47-2853.72.
Representations prohibited, §47-2853.73.
Scope of practice, §47-2853.71.

BARBERSHOPS.
Business licenses, §§47-2809, 47-2810.
Well-behaved persons.
Required to serve, §47-2907.

BAR EXAMINATION, DCCtApp Rule 46.

BARROOMS.
Price list.
Charging greater price, §47-2911.
Posting required, §47-2908.
Failure, §47-2911.
Transmission to assessor, §47-2909.
Service of well-behaved persons, §47-2910.
Failure to serve, §47-2911.

BARTENDERS.
Minimum wage for persons receiving gratuities, §32-1003.

BATH HOUSES.
Business licenses, §47-2812.
Well-behaved persons.
Required to serve, §47-2907.

BATHING POOLS AND BEACHES,
§§10-162 to 10-165.

BAWDY HOUSES.
Houses of prostitution.
See PROSTITUTION.

BAZAARS.
Alcoholic beverage licenses.
Temporary licenses, §25-115.

BEACH PARKWAY.
Exchange of property to extend,
§10-117.
Dedication and conveyances, §10-118.
Power of Secretary of Interior to sell
not curtailed, §10-119.

BEARER PAPER.
Negotiable instruments, §28:3-109.

**BEATTY AND HAWKINS'S
ADDITION TO GEORGETOWN.**
Street connections for, §9-101.07.

BEAUTICIANS.
Business licenses, §§47-2809,
47-2853.71 to 47-2853.73.

BEER.
Alcoholic beverages.
General provisions, §§25-101 to
25-1003.
See ALCOHOLIC BEVERAGES.
Brew pubs.
Alcoholic beverage licenses, §25-117.
Defined, §25-101.
Taxation, §25-902.

BEER FESTIVALS.
Tasting permits, §25-118.

BEES, §§8-1825.01 to 8-1825.09.
Definitions, §8-1825.02.
Diseased colonies or equipment,
§8-1825.07.
Enforcement of chapter, §8-1825.09.
General authorization, §8-1825.03.
Infractions, §8-1825.09.
Injunctions.
Enforcement of chapter, §8-1825.09.
Nuisance colonies.
Remediation of swarms and nuisance
conditions, §8-1825.04.
Registration of colonies, §8-1825.04.
Reimbursement of costs, §8-1825.09.
Remediation of diseased colonies,
§8-1825.07.

BEES —Cont'd
**Remediation of swarms and
nuisance conditions,** §8-1825.04.
Responsibilities of beekeepers,
§8-1825.04.
Restrictions, §8-1825.03.
Rules and regulations, §8-1825.09.
Short title, §8-1825.01.
**Sustainable urban agriculture
apiculture act of 2012,** §8-1825.01.
Swarming.
Remediation of swarms and nuisance
conditions, §8-1825.04.
Written warning notice of violation.
Enforcement of chapter, §8-1825.09.

BEGGING.
Capitol grounds, on, §10-503.14.
Panhandling, §§22-2301 to 22-2306.

**BEHAVIORAL HEALTH
DEPARTMENT,** §§7-1141.01 to
7-1141.09.
Behavioral health access project,
§§7-1142.01 to 7-1142.03.
Definitions, §7-1141.01.
**Department of behavioral health
enterprise fund,** §1-325.281.
Director.
Appointment, §7-1141.03.
Duties, §7-1141.04.
Establishment, §7-1141.02.
Powers and duties, §7-1141.06.
Purpose, §7-1141.05.
Rules and regulations.
Continuation, §7-1141.08.
Statutory construction, §7-1141.09.
Transitional provisions, §7-1141.07.

BENEFIT CORPORATIONS,
§§29-1301.01 to 29-1304.01.
Accountability, §§29-1303.01 to
29-1303.05.
Actions.
Benefit enforcement proceedings,
§29-1303.05.
Defined, §29-1301.02.
Restrictions on actions against
corporation, §29-1303.05.
Applicability of provisions,
§29-1301.03.
Articles of incorporation.
Election by business corporation to
become benefit corporation.
Amendment of articles, §29-1301.05.
Statement of status as benefit
corporation, §29-1301.04.
Termination of status as benefit
corporation.
Amendment of articles, §29-1301.06.

BENEFIT CORPORATIONS —Cont'd
Benefit director.
  Defined, §29-1301.02.
  Powers and duties, §29-1303.02.
  Report, §29-1303.02.
  Selection, §29-1303.02.
  Standard of conduct, §29-1303.02.
Benefit enforcement proceedings,
  §29-1303.05.
  Defined, §29-1301.02.
Benefit officer.
  Defined, §29-1301.02.
  Designation, §29-1303.04.
  Powers and duties, §29-1303.04.
Definitions, §29-1301.02.
Directors.
  Benefit director.
    Defined, §29-1301.02.
    Powers and duties, §29-1303.02.
    Report, §29-1303.02.
    Selection, §29-1303.02.
    Standard of conduct, §29-1303.02.
  Immunity from personal liability for
    damages, §29-1303.01.
  Standards of conduct of directors and
    board, §29-1303.01.
Election by business corporation to
  become benefit corporation,
  §29-1301.05.
Formation.
  Applicable provisions, §29-1301.04.
General public benefits.
  Corporate purpose to be creation of
    general public benefit,
    §29-1302.01.
  Defined, §29-1301.02.
Minimum status votes.
  Defined, §29-1301.02.
  Election by business corporation to
    become benefit corporation,
    §29-1301.06.
  Termination of status as benefit
    corporation, §29-1301.06.
Officers.
  Benefit officer.
    Defined, §29-1301.02.
    Designation, §29-1303.04.
    Powers and duties, §29-1303.04.
  Immunity from personal liability for
    damages, §29-1303.03.
  Standard of conduct for officers,
    §29-1303.03.
Reports.
  Annual benefit report, §29-1304.01.

BENEFIT CORPORATIONS —Cont'd
Short title of provisions, §29-1301.01.
Statutory construction, §29-1301.03.
Termination of status as benefit
  corporation, §29-1301.06.

BENNING BRIDGE, §9-314.

BEQUESTS.
See WILLS.

BEULAH BAPTIST CHURCH.
Real property tax exemption,
  §47-4654.

BEVERAGES.
Alcoholic beverages, §§25-101 to
  25-1003.
  See ALCOHOLIC BEVERAGES.
Bottles, §§36-101, 36-102.
Business licenses, §47-2827.
Gross sales tax, §47-2002.02.
Milk container registration, §§36-121
  to 36-157.
  See MILK CONTAINER
    REGISTRATION.
Sales.
  Implied warranty of merchantability,
    §28:2-314.
Warranties.
  Implied warranty of merchantability,
    §28:2-314.

BIAS.
Judges, CJC Canon 2.3, CivPro Rule
  63-I.
  Adoption proceedings, Adoption Rule
    63.
  Domestic relations actions, DomRel
    Rule 63.
  Probate proceedings.
    Death between January 1, 1981 and
      June 30, 1995, Probate Rule
      126.

BIAS-RELATED CRIMES, §§22-3701
  to 22-3704.

BICYCLE RENTALS.
Information required on rental
  forms, §50-1612.

BICYCLES, §§50-1601 to 50-1652.
Assault or battery of bicyclist by
  motorist.
  Right of civil action for damages,
    §50-1621.
Bicycle and pedestrian priority area
  program, §50-2371.

BICYCLES —Cont'd

Bicycle insurance policies, §§50-531 to 50-535.

Cancellation or refusal to renew, §50-532.

Agency review of insured disputes, §50-533.

General policy provisions, §50-532.

Rights and policy terms, §50-535.

Definitions, §50-531.

Good faith immunity, §50-534.

Private right of action, prohibition, §50-534.

Bicycle registry.

Voluntary registration of bicycle through, §50-1611.

Bicycle sharing fund, §50-921.16.

Commercial bicycle operators, §§50-1631 to 50-1634.

Definitions, §50-1631.

Employers of, responsibilities of, §50-1633.

Enforcement, §50-1634.

Fees, §50-1632.

Fines, §50-1634.

Identification numbers, §50-1632.

Licenses, §50-1632.

Violations, §50-1632.

Commuter and parking expansion, §§50-1641.01 to 50-1641.09. See within this heading, "Parking."

Complete streets policy, §50-2381.

Comprehensive Bicycle Transportation and Safety Program, §50-1602.

Crosswalks, right-of-way at, §50-2201.28.

Definitions, §50-1609.

District of Columbia Bicycle Advisory Council, §50-1604.

Helmet requirements, §§50-1605, 50-1651.

Child safety education program, §50-1607.

Child safety helmet assistance program, §50-1608.

Effective date for enforcement, §50-1652.

Failure to wear.

Not negligence per se, contributory negligence, assumption of risk, §50-1606.

Identification numbers.

Commercial bicycle operators, §50-1632.

BICYCLES —Cont'd

Identification numbers —Cont'd

Metropolitan police.

Duty to check recovered bicycle's number with bike registry, §50-1611.

Tampering with or removing, §22-3234.

Labor and employment relations.

Transportation benefits.

Reducing single occupancy vehicle use by encouraging transit benefits, §§32-151 to 32-153.

National bike registry.

Voluntary registration of bicycle through, §50-1611.

Office of Bicycle Transportation and Safety, §50-1603.

Parking, §§50-1641.01 to 50-1641.09.

Applicability of provisions, §50-1641.08.

Definitions, §50-1641.01.

District government buildings.

Mayor's report regarding parking at, §50-1641.04.

Enforcement of provisions, §50-1641.07a.

John A. Wilson building.

Increase in bicycle parking requirements, §50-1641.03.

Office, retail, and service uses, §50-1641.06.

Parking space requirements generally, §50-1641.02.

Residential building parking requirements, §50-1641.05.

Rules promulgation, §50-1641.07.

Zoning regulations, effect, §50-1641.09.

Policy declaration, §50-1601.

Public-owned heavy duty vehicles.

Bicycle safety enhancements, §50-205.

Public structures in public space.

Safe accommodation for pedestrians and cyclists required when path is obstructed, §§10-1141.03, 10-1141.04.

Registration.

Voluntary registration, §50-1611.

Rentals.

Information required on rental forms, §50-1612.

Right-of-way at crosswalks, §50-2201.28.

Sellers.

Information on voluntary registration provided purchaser, §50-1611.

BICYCLES —Cont'd
Tampering with or removing identifying numbers, §22-3234.
Traffic signals.
Pedestrian crossing signals, crossing with, §50-2201.04d.

BID PARKING ABATEMENT FUND, §1-325.341.

BIDS AND BIDDING.
Business improvement districts.
See BUSINESS IMPROVEMENT DISTRICTS.
Procurement practices.
General provisions.
See PROCUREMENT PRACTICES.
Public contracts, §§2-201.01 to 2-223.07.
See PUBLIC CONTRACTS.

BIFURCATION OF TRIALS, CivPro Rule 42.
Adoption, Adoption Rule 42.
Counterclaims and cross-claims, CivPro Rule 13.
Domestic relations actions, DomRel Rule 42.

BIGAMY, §§22-501, 46-401.01.

BILLIARD TABLES.
Business licenses, §47-2821.

BILL OF COSTS, CivPro Form CA 121.
Appellate procedure, FRAP 39(d).

BILL OF PARTICULARS.
Child abuse and neglect proceedings, NeglectProc Rule 9.
Delinquent minors, JuvProc Rule 7.
Indictments and informations, CrimPro Rule 7.

BILL OF RIGHTS, US Const Amds 1 to Amd 10.

BILLS OF ATTAINDER, US Const Art I §§9, 10, Art III §3.

BILLS OF EXCHANGE.
Assignments.
Nonnegotiable bills of exchange, §28-2303.
Notaries public, §§1-1207, 1-1208.

BILLS OF LADING.
Attachment.
Goods covered by a negotiable document, §28:7-602.
Damages.
Limitations of liability, §28:7-309.

BILLS OF LADING —Cont'd
Documents of title.
General provisions, §§28:7-101 to 28:7-702.
See DOCUMENTS OF TITLE.
Injunctions.
Enjoining negotiations of document, §28:7-602.
Interpleader.
Determination of conflicting claims, §28:7-603.
Lost and unclaimed property.
Missing bills, §28:7-601.
Overpayment liabilities, §47-112.

BILLS OF REVIEW.
Abolished, CivPro Rule 60.

BINGO GAMES.
Lottery and charitable games control board, §§3-1322 to 3-1332.
Operated for educational and charitable purposes.
Advertising and promoting, §22-1718.
Permissible activity, §22-1717.

BIOLOGICAL AGENTS.
Terrorism, §§22-3151 to 22-3156.

BIRTH.
Artificial insemination.
Presumptions and proof of parentage, §16-909.
Family and medical leave for, §32-502.
Maternity, proof of, §16-909.
Newborns.
See NEWBORNS.
Paternity, proof of, §16-909.

BIRTH DEFECTS.
Alcoholic beverage licenses.
Signs.
Pregnant women, warnings for, §25-712.

BIRTHING HOSPITALS, PARENTAGE.
Acknowledgment programs required of, §16-909.03.

BIRTH RECORDS.
Adopted children, birth certificates for, §16-314.
Parentage proceedings, new birth record following, §§16-2345, 16-2346.
Registration of births, §§7-205 to 7-210.
See VITAL RECORDS.

BISPHENOL-A, §§8-108.01, 8-108.04, 8-108.05.

BLACKMAIL, §22-3252.

BLANK INDORSEMENTS.
Negotiable instruments, §28:3-205.

BLIGHTED AREAS.
Community development.
General provisions, §§6-1001 to 6-1007.
See COMMUNITY DEVELOPMENT.
Housing and community development reform advisory commission, §§6-1031 to 6-1037.
Economic development zone incentives.
General provisions, §§6-1501 to 6-1506.
See ECONOMIC DEVELOPMENT ZONE INCENTIVES.
Housing redevelopment.
General provisions, §§6-311.01 to 6-341.05.
See URBAN RENEWAL.
National Capital Housing Authority.
General provisions, §§6-101.01 to 6-103.01.
See NATIONAL CAPITAL HOUSING AUTHORITY.
Urban renewal.
General provisions, §§6-311.01 to 6-341.05.
See URBAN RENEWAL.

BLIND AND VISUALLY IMPAIRED.
Assistive technology device warranty, §§28-4031 to 28-4034.
Braille printers.
Assistive technology warranty, §§28-4031 to 28-4034.
Defined terms, §§7-903, 7-1009.
Employment discrimination, §7-1005.
Employment opportunities, §§32-301 to 32-305.
Equal access.
Employment, §7-1005.
Housing, §7-1006.
Public places, accommodations, and conveyances, §§7-1001, 7-1002.
Fines for interfering with or discriminating against, §7-1007.
Guide dogs.
Defined, §7-1009.
Housing accommodations.
Full and equal access, §7-1006.

BLIND AND VISUALLY IMPAIRED
—Cont'd
Guide dogs —Cont'd
Public places accommodations, and conveyances.
Right to be accompanied by, §7-1002.
Infants and newborns, screening, §§7-801 to 7-803.
Inflammation of the eyes, report, treatment, §7-802.
Prophylactic solution administered, §7-801.
Treatment by other than registered physician, §7-803.
Violations, penalty, §7-804.
Motor vehicle drivers, safety standards for, §7-1004.
Penalties for interfering with or discriminating against, §7-1007.
Public places, accommodations, and conveyances.
Equal access to, §§7-1001, 7-1002.
Register of blind persons, §§7-901 to 7-904.
Taxicabs.
Digital dispatch for individuals with disabilities, §50-301.25a.
White Cane Safety Day, §7-1008.

BLOCKING PASSAGE.
Public or private building, enclosure, road or sidewalk, §22-1307.

BLOCK PARTIES.
Department of transportation, §§9-631 to 9-634.
Applications, §9-632.
Criteria for review, §9-634.
Duties of department, §9-633.
Criteria for review, §9-634.
Definitions, §9-631.
Duties of department, §9-633.
Requirements, §9-632.

BLOOD BANKS.
Human tissue banks, §§7-1541.01 to 7-1551.01.
See HUMAN TISSUE BANKS.

BLOOD DONORS.
Minors, donations by.
Consent of parent or guardian, §7-1551.31.
Rulemaking, §7-1551.32.

BLOOD TESTS.
Marriage requirements.
See MARRIAGE.

BLOOD TESTS —Cont'd
Parentage proceedings, DomRel Rule 405.

BLUE PLAINS IMPOUNDMENT LOT.
Jurisdiction over, §50-2405.

BOARD OF EDUCATION.
Bonds, surety, §38-104.
Budgeting.
School-based budgeting and accountability, §§38-2801.01 to 38-2807.
Budget submission requirements, §38-2831.
Child labor, §§32-214, 32-224.
Classification of academic subjects, §38-108.
Class size limitations, §38-109.
Continuation, §1-207.19.
Coordination of educational programs, §38-153.
Elections, §1-1001.08.
Food services.
Powers regarding, §38-802.
Gifts, §38-907.
Heads of department, §38-109.
Head teachers, §38-109.
Intellectual disabilities, persons with.
Authority of board, §7-1306.04.
Junior Reserve Officers' Training Program, §38-158.
Manual training, supervisor of, §38-107.
Merit system.
Delegation of authority, §1-604.03.
Educational employees, applicability to, §1-602.03.
Non-educational employees.
Preference for resident applicants, §1-602.03.
Normal schools.
Powers and duties regarding, §38-151.
Pages, education of, §38-152.
Personal liability, exemption from, §38-104.
Policy declaration, §38-102.
Real property exempt from taxation, §47-1027.
Recreation board, relationship to, §10-223.
Reduction-in-force procedures, §1-525.01.
Schedule A submission, §38-160.

BOARD OF EDUCATION —Cont'd
School-based budgeting and accountability, §§38-2801.01 to 38-2807.
Select adult, community and continuing education courses.
Course fees, §§38-1001 to 38-1003.
Staffing, §38-102.
State board.
Budget estimates for board operations, §38-2652.
Establishment, §38-2651.
Functions, §38-2652.
Internal operation, §38-2652.
Meetings, §38-2652.
Members, §38-2651.
Wards comprising districts, §38-2651.
State personnel and merit system.
See MERIT SYSTEM.
Student health care administration, §38-608.
Supervisor of manual training, §38-107.
Taxation.
Real property exempt from taxation, §47-1027.
Teacher investigations and trials, §38-111.
Wages and salaries, §1-611.10.

BOARDS AND COMMISSIONS.
Administrative law judges.
Commission on selection and tenure of administrative law judges, §§2-1831.06, 2-1831.07.
Advisory neighborhood commissions.
See ADVISORY NEIGHBORHOOD COMMISSIONS.
African-American affairs commission.
Established, §3-1441.
Organization, §3-1442.
Aging, Commission on, §§7-504.01 to 7-504.10.
Aging, Office on, §§7-501.01 to 7-503.06.
Alcoholic beverage control board, §§25-201 to 25-212.
Armory board, §§3-301 to 3-344.
See ARMORY BOARD.
Arts and humanities, commission on, §§39-201 to 39-206.
Asians and Pacific Islanders.
Commission on Asian and Pacific Islander community development, §§2-1374, 2-1376.

BOARDS AND COMMISSIONS
—Cont'd
Attorneys at law.
Bar association board of governors, DCBar Rule IV.
Recommendations to the board of governors, DCBar Rule VI.
Board on professional responsibility, DCBar Rule XI.
Audiology and speech-language pathology, board of, §3-1202.18.
Board of education.
General provisions.
See BOARD OF EDUCATION.
Boards of allied health.
Executive director, §3-1202.19.
Boards of behavioral health.
Executive director, §3-1202.20.
Boxing and wrestling commission, §§3-601 to 3-610.
See BOXING AND WRESTLING COMMISSION.
Bullying, §2-1535.02.
Business and economic development.
See BUSINESS AND ECONOMIC DEVELOPMENT.
Business improvement district boards of directors, §2-1215.07.
Cable television.
Office of cable television, film, music, and entertainment, §§34-1252.01 to 34-1252.03.
Charter schools.
Board of trustees, §38-1802.05.
Public Charter School Board, §38-1802.14.
Charter schools admissions task force, §38-1802.14a.
Child support guideline commission, §16-916.02.
Chiropractic, board of, §3-1202.16.
City of Washington museum, §§39-304, 39-305.
Clinical laboratories advisory board, §44-206.
Commission on Latino community development, §§2-1321 to 2-1330.
Compensation, §1-611.08.
Compensation order review board, §32-1521.01.
Condemnation Review Board, §6-902.
Contract appeals board.
General provisions.
See PROCUREMENT PRACTICES.
Crime victims' compensation.
Advisory commission, VictComp Rule 5.

BOARDS AND COMMISSIONS
—Cont'd
Crime victims' compensation
—Cont'd
Appeals board, VictComp Rule 6.
Review of determination, VictComp Rule 20.
Crime victims' compensation advisory commission, §4-504.
Crime victims' compensation appeals board, §4-505.
Dentistry, Board of, §3-1202.01.
Dietetics and nutrition, board of, §3-1202.02.
Directors or trustees, board of.
Hospital and medical services corporations.
See HOSPITAL AND MEDICAL SERVICES CORPORATIONS.
Donations.
Authority to accept, §1-329.01.
Education, board of.
See BOARD OF EDUCATION.
Elections and Ethics, Board of, §§1-1001.02 to 1-1001.06.
Enterprise zone study commission, §§2-1211.01 to 2-1211.06.
Ethics and government accountability board, §§1-1161.01 to 1-1164.01.
See ETHICS AND GOVERNMENT ACCOUNTABILITY BOARD.
Ex-offenders.
Commission on re-entry and ex-offender affairs, §24-1303.
Fashion arts and events, commission on, §§3-651 to 3-653.
Fathers, men and boys, commission on, §§3-731 to 3-733.
Federal City College board of higher education, §§38-1102 to 38-1104.
Fees, §§1-321.03 to 1-321.06.
Applicability of subchapter, §1-321.02.
Appropriations, §1-321.06.
Proration of fees, authority, §1-321.04.
References to boards, commissions and committees, §1-321.05.
Refund of unearned fees, §1-321.03.
Financial institutions advisory board, §§26-551.06 to 26-551.09.
Fine arts commission.
Building heights, review of, §§6-611.01, 6-611.02.
Fire protection study commission, §§3-1101 to 3-1108.
See FIRE PROTECTION STUDY COMMISSION.

BOARDS AND COMMISSIONS
—Cont'd
Flag design advisory commission,
§1-153.
Foreign Missions, Office of, §6-1303.
Gallaudet University board of
trustees, §38-2401.03.
Gas station advisory board,
§36-304.01.
Gifts.
Authority to accept, §1-329.01.
Health, Board of (defunct), §§7-174 to
7-177.
Health care disparities.
Commission on health equity,
§§7-756.01 to 7-756.03.
Health Care System Development
Commission, §§7-2901 to 7-2906.
Health occupations boards.
General provisions, §§3-1201.01 to
3-1213.01.
See HEALTH OCCUPATIONS
BOARDS.
Healthy youth and schools
commission, §§38-827.01 to
38-827.04.
Higher education licensure
commission, §§38-1301 to 38-1313.
Historic districts Board of Review,
§6-1203.
Historic Preservation Review Board,
§6-1103.
Historic Rhodes Tavern Advisory
Board, §§6-1132, 6-1133.
Homeland security and emergency
management agency, §§7-2202 to
7-2209.
See EMERGENCY MANAGEMENT.
Homeland security commission,
§§7-2271.01 to 7-2271.07.
See EMERGENCY MANAGEMENT.
Honoraria, §§1-321.01, 1-321.02.
Housing and community
development reform advisory
commission, §§6-1031 to 6-1037.
Housing production trust fund
board, §42-2802.01.
Human rights commission,
§§2-1401.01 to 2-1404.04.
See HUMAN RIGHTS COMMISSION.
Industrial safety.
See WORKPLACE SAFETY.
Insanitary Buildings.
Board for the Condemnation of,
§6-902.
Interpreters, §§2-1901 to 2-1912.01.
See INTERPRETERS.

BOARDS AND COMMISSIONS
—Cont'd
Interstate compact on educational
opportunity for military
children.
Interstate commission, §§49-1101.09 to
49-1101.12.
Judicial disabilities and tenure,
§§11-1521 to 11-1530.
See COMMISSION ON JUDICIAL
DISABILITIES AND TENURE.
Judicial nomination commission,
§1-204.34.
Lactation commission, §§7-881.05,
7-881.06.
Latino community development,
Commission on, §§2-1321 to
2-1330.
Law revision commission, §§45-301 to
45-305.
Libraries, §§39-104, 39-105.
Licenses, §§1-321.03 to 1-321.06.
Applicability of subchapter, §1-321.02.
Appropriations, §1-321.06.
Fixing and changing licensing period,
authority, §1-321.04.
References to boards, commissions and
committees, §1-321.05.
Long-term care administration,
board of, §3-1202.05.
Lottery and charitable games
control board.
General provisions, §§3-1301 to
3-1336.
See LOTTERY AND CHARITABLE
GAMES CONTROL BOARD.
Marriage and family therapy, board
of, §3-1202.17.
Massage therapy, board of,
§3-1202.15.
Mayor and council compensation
advisory committee, §§1-611.51 to
1-611.57.
See MAYOR AND COUNCIL
COMPENSATION ADVISORY
COMMITTEE.
Mayor's official residence
commission, §§1-331.01 to
1-331.05.
Medicine, board of, §3-1202.03.
Mental Health, Commission on,
§§7-1208.03, 21-502, 21-503.
Metabolic disorders, committee on,
§§7-835 to 7-837.
Minimum wage and industrial safety
board.
See WORKPLACE SAFETY.

BOARDS AND COMMISSIONS
—Cont'd
Motor vehicle theft prevention commission, §§3-1351 to 3-1358.
Multimodal accessibility advisory council, §§50-2361.31, 50-2361.32.
Naming rights, §9-204.09.
National capital planning commission.
General provisions, §§2-1001 to 2-1011.
See NATIONAL CAPITAL PLANNING COMMISSION.
New Columbia statehood commission, §§1-129.31 to 1-129.35.
Nursing, board of, §3-1202.04.
Occupational safety and health.
Board, §32-1105.
Commission, §32-1106.
Occupational therapy, board of, §3-1202.06.
Occupations and professions.
Non-health related, §§47-2853.06 to 47-2853.10.
Official correspondence, §§2-701 to 2-710.
Optometry, board of, §3-1202.07.
Parole.
See PAROLE.
Pay equity and training commission, §§32-601 to 32-609.
Pharmacy, board of, §3-1202.08.
Physical therapy, board of, §3-1202.09.
Podiatry, board of, §3-1202.10.
Police and firefighters retirement and disability, §5-722.
Police complaints, office of.
General provisions, §§5-1101 to 5-1115.
See OFFICE OF POLICE COMPLAINTS.
Procurement contract appeals board.
See PROCUREMENT PRACTICES.
Professional counseling, board of, §3-1202.13.
Professions and occupations, non-health related, §§47-2853.06 to 47-2853.10.
Psychology, board of, §3-1202.11.
Public defender service, §2-1603.
Public employee relations board, §§1-605.01 to 1-605.04.
Public Health, Commissioner of, §7-101.

BOARDS AND COMMISSIONS
—Cont'd
Public Health Coordination Advisory Committee, §7-154.
Public Parking Authority Board.
Board of directors, §50-2504.
Public records management, §§2-1701 to 2-1714.
See PUBLIC RECORDS MANAGEMENT.
Public schools.
Interagency collaboration and services integration commission, §§2-1591 to 2-1597.
State board of education.
See BOARD OF EDUCATION.
Public Welfare, Board of, §§4-105 to 4-126, 24-211.03.
See PUBLIC WELFARE, BOARD OF.
Real property tax appeals commission, §47-825.01a.
Recreation Assistance Board.
Rules, §10-307.
Recreation board, §§10-201 to 10-226.
See RECREATION BOARD.
Rental housing commission, §§42-3502.01 to 42-3502.02a.
Report on, §1-315.07.
Respiratory care, board of, §3-1202.14.
Retirement Board, §1-711.
Safety.
See WORKPLACE SAFETY.
Sentencing and criminal code revision commission, §§3-101 to 3-108.
See SENTENCING AND CRIMINAL CODE REVISION COMMISSION.
Social work, board of, §3-1202.12.
State board of education.
General provisions.
See BOARD OF EDUCATION.
Sustainable energy utility advisory board, §§8-1774.03, 8-1774.04.
Taxicab Commission.
See TAXICABS.
Tax revision commission.
General provisions, §§47-461 to 47-464.
See TAX REVISION COMMISSION.
Temporary commission on pay equity and training.
General provisions, §§32-601 to 32-609.
Transit rider advisory council, §§50-2361.01 to 50-2361.03.

BOARDS AND COMMISSIONS
—Cont'd
Truth in sentencing commission,
§§24-111 to 24-114.
Unemployment compensation,
§51-121.
**University of District of Columbia
community college transition to
independence advisory board.**
Funding, §38-1271.03.
Membership, §38-1271.01.
Transition plan, §38-1271.02.
**University of the District of
Columbia board of trustees and
university,** §§38-1202.01 to
38-1202.11, 38-1204.01 to
38-1204.07.
Veterinary medicine, board of,
§3-1202.21.
Wages and salaries, §1-611.08.
**Washington Technical Institute
board of vocational education,**
§§38-1122 to 38-1124.
Women, commission for, §§3-701 to
3-704.
Workers' compensation.
Compensation order review board,
§32-1521.01.
Workers' compensation insurance
study commission, §32-1542.01.
Workforce investment council,
§32-1603.
Authority to make grants for job
development, §1-328.05.
Workplace safety, §§32-801 to 32-812.
See WORKPLACE SAFETY.
Youth residential facilities, §7-2104.
Youth services.
See YOUTH SERVICES.
**Zoning Commission and Office of
Zoning.**
See ZONING.

BOARDS OF ALLIED HEALTH.
Executive director, §3-1202.19.

**BOARDS OF BEHAVIORAL
HEALTH.**
Executive director, §3-1202.20.

**BOATING UNDER THE
INFLUENCE,** §§50-2206.31 to
50-2206.36.
Chemical testing, §§50-1908 to
50-1912.
Arrest, testing after, §50-1910.
Breath test, preliminary, §50-1909.
Definitions, §50-1908.

BOATING UNDER THE INFLUENCE
—Cont'd
Chemical testing —Cont'd
Refusal or failure to submit to testing,
§50-1911.
Penalties, §50-1912.
Impaired operation, §50-2206.33.
Minor in watercraft, §50-2206.36.
Marijuana.
Articulable suspicion, §48-921.02a.
Offense generally, §50-2206.31.
Penalties, §50-2206.32.
Impaired operation, §50-2206.34.
Minor in watercraft, §50-2206.36.
**Public awareness campaign by
harbor master,** §50-2206.35.

BOATS AND OTHER WATERCRAFT.
Alcoholic beverage licenses.
On-premises retailers, §25-113.
Taxation, §25-905.
Alcoholic beverages.
Operating under the influence,
§§50-2206.31 to 50-2206.36.
Chemical testing, §§50-1908 to
50-1912.
Bridges.
Tugboat power boat requirements for
going under, §9-309.
Constitution of the United States.
Bound to and from one state not to be
obliged to clear, etc., in another,
US Const Art I §9.
Fire, casualty and marine insurance.
General provisions, §§31-2501.01 to
31-2502.42.
See FIRE AND CASUALTY
INSURANCE.
**Foreign missions, owned by
members of,** §6-1304.01.
Marine insurance.
Fire, casualty and marine insurance.
General provisions, §§31-2501.01 to
31-2502.42.
See FIRE AND CASUALTY
INSURANCE.
Investments, §§31-1373.01 to
31-1373.12.
See INSURANCE INVESTMENTS.
Prohibitions, §31-2601.01.
Tidal basin boathouses, licenses for,
§10-151.
**Uniform certificates of title for
vessels,** §§50-1541.01 to 50-1541.28.
Access to files, §50-1541.10.
Applicability.
Scope of chapter, §50-1541.02.

BOATS AND OTHER WATERCRAFT
—Cont'd
Uniform certificates of title for vessels —Cont'd
Applications, §50-1541.06.
  Rejection, §50-1541.07.
  Transfer of ownership without certificate of title, §50-1541.20.
  When delivered, §50-1541.05.
Attachment.
  Effect of possession of certificate, §50-1541.13.
Cancellation, §50-1541.07.
Construction and interpretation.
  Principles of law and equity, §50-1541.03.
  Uniformity of application and construction, §50-1541.26.
Contents of applications, §50-1541.06.
Contents of certificate of title, §50-1541.08.
Creation, §50-1541.07.
  Actions required of Harbor Master, §50-1541.11.
Definitions, §50-1541.01.
Duties of Harbor Master, §50-1541.24.
Effect of certificate, §50-1541.12.
Effect of possession of certificate, §50-1541.13.
Electronic signatures in global and national commerce act, relation to, §50-1541.27.
Fees.
  Applications, §50-1541.06.
Foreign countries.
  Contents of certificate of title, §50-1541.08.
Garnishment.
  Effect of possession of certificate, §50-1541.13.
Harbor Master, duties, §50-1541.24.
Hull damaged.
  Contents of certificate of title, §50-1541.08.
  Title brand, §50-1541.09.
Incorrect information, effect, §50-1541.17.
Judicial process.
  Effect of possession of certificate, §50-1541.13.
Jurisdiction.
  Law governing vessel covered by certificate of title, §50-1541.04.
Law governing vessel covered by certificate of title, §50-1541.04.
Levy.
  Effect of possession of certificate, §50-1541.13.

BOATS AND OTHER WATERCRAFT
—Cont'd
Uniform certificates of title for vessels —Cont'd
Lost, stolen, mutilated, or destroyed certificates.
  Replacement certificates of title, §50-1541.21.
Missing information, effect, §50-1541.17.
Perfection of security interests, §50-1541.14.
Possession of certificate, effect, §50-1541.13.
Previously registered or titled vessels.
  Contents of certificate of title, §50-1541.08.
Principles of law and equity, §50-1541.03.
Records.
  Access to files, §50-1541.10.
  Applications, §50-1541.06.
  Maintenance, §50-1541.10.
Replacement certificates of title, §50-1541.21.
Replevin.
  Effect of possession of certificate, §50-1541.13.
Required, §50-1541.05.
Rights of purchaser other than secured party, §50-1541.22.
Rights of secured party, §50-1541.23.
Rules, promulgation, §50-1541.25.
Savings clause, §50-1541.28.
Scope of chapter, §50-1541.02.
Security interests.
  Contents of certificate of title, §50-1541.08.
  Perfection, §50-1541.14.
  Rights of purchaser other than secured party, §50-1541.22.
  Rights of secured party, §50-1541.23.
  Termination of security interest without certificate of title, §50-1541.20.
  Transfer of ownership by secured party's transfer statement, §50-1541.18.
Specific performance, right of transferee.
  Transfer of ownership, §50-1541.16.
Termination of security interest without certificate of title, §50-1541.20.
Termination statement, §50-1541.15.

BOATS AND OTHER WATERCRAFT
—Cont'd
Uniform certificates of title for
vessels —Cont'd
Title brand, §50-1541.09.
Transfer of ownership, §50-1541.16.
Application for transfer of ownership
without certificate of title,
§50-1541.20.
By operation of law, §50-1541.19.
Secured party's transfer statement,
§50-1541.18.
Transfer-by-law statement,
§50-1541.19.
Water pollutants discharged from,
§8-103.08.

BODY ARTISTS AND BODY ART
ESTABLISHMENTS.
Board of barber and cosmetology,
§§47-2853.06 to 47-2853.10.
Business licenses.
Body artists, §§47-2853.76a to
47-2853.76e.
Establishments, §47-2809.01.
Children or minors.
Consent, §47-2853.76e.
Duties and responsibilities,
§47-2853.76d.
Eligibility, §47-2853.76c.
Exceptions.
Scope of practice, §47-2853.76a.
Fines, §47-2853.76d.
Criminal penalties, §47-2853.76e.
Intoxicated persons.
Consent, §47-2853.76e.
Penalties, §47-2853.76e.
Prohibitions, §47-2853.76e.
Qualifications, §47-2853.76c.
Regulation of, §47-2853.76b.
Scope of practice, §47-2853.76a.

BODY-WORN CAMERA PROGRAM.
Metropolitan police, §§5-116.31 to
5-116.33.

BOILER INSPECTIONS, §§2-101 to
2-118.
Boiler inspection service, §2-103.
Boiler inspectors, §§2-103, 2-104.
Building inspectors.
Duties of assistant inspector of
buildings, §2-138.
Certificate of inspection.
Cessation of insurance, §2-110.
Display, §2-107.
Exempt boilers or vessels, §2-109.
Invalidation of certificate, §2-110.

BOILER INSPECTIONS —Cont'd
Certificate of inspection —Cont'd
Issuance, §2-107.
Required for boiler operation, §§2-105,
2-106.
Revocation, §2-108.
Citation of act, §2-101.
Construction of act.
Effective date, §2-118.
Repeal of inconsistent provisions,
§2-116.
Severability of provisions, §2-117.
Electrical inspectors, §§2-131 to
2-133.
Elevator inspectors, §2-139.
Enforcement of act, §2-118.
Exempt boilers or vessels, §§2-109,
2-131.
Cessation of insurance, §2-110.
Inspection fees, §§2-110, 2-115.
Nuisances.
Abatement of use as nuisance, §2-113.
Person, defined, §2-102.
Plumbing inspectors, §§2-134 to
2-137.
Public utilities.
Exemption from act, §2-131.
Recordkeeping requirements, §2-112.
Regulatory violations, §2-114.
Right of entry for inspection, §2-111.
Rulemaking authority, §§2-115, 2-140.

BOLLING AIR FORCE BASE.
Real property tax exemptions.
Housing on base, §47-1080.

BOMB DISPOSAL DUTY.
Police and firefighters, additional
compensation for, §5-542.02.

BOMBS.
Weapons of mass destruction.
False reports, §22-1319.
Hoax weapons, §22-1319.
False report, §22-1319.
Manufacture or possession, §22-3154.
See EXPLOSIVES.
Use, dissemination or detonation,
§22-3155.

BOMB SCARES, §22-1319.

BOND ANTICIPATION NOTES,
§1-204.75.

BONDING COMPANIES.
Taxation, §47-2502.

BOND ISSUES.
Appropriations.
Borrowing to meet, §1-204.71.

BOND ISSUES —Cont'd
Authority to issue and redeem for capital projects, §1-204.61.
Ballpark, §10-1601.03.
Community benefit fund, §10-1602.03.
Bond anticipation notes, §1-204.75.
Building associations exchanging securities or real property for federal bonds, §26-232.
City Market at O Street tax increment financing, §§2-1217.33a to 2-1217.33m.
See CITY MARKET AT O STREET TAX INCREMENT FINANCING.
Community benefit fund, §10-1602.03.
Contents of borrowing legislation, §1-204.62.
Convention center hotel, §§10-1221.05 to 10-1221.15.
Washington convention and sports authority, §§10-1202.04, 10-1202.09.
Debt service amount, borrowing limitation.
Amount, §47-335.02.
Definitions, §47-334.
Deposit and investments of District funds.
General provisions, §§47-351.01 to 47-351.16.
See BUDGETS AND BUDGET ESTIMATES.
District of Columbia housing authority, §§6-209, 6-210.
Electric company infrastructure improvement, §§34-1311.01 to 34-1314.04.
See ELECTRIC COMPANY INFRASTRUCTURE IMPROVEMENT FINANCING.
Energy conservation, §§8-1778.21 to 8-1778.31.
See ENERGY CONSERVATION.
Fiduciary investments in, §1-204.86.
Fiduciary security transfers, §§28-2901 to 28-2909.
See FIDUCIARY SECURITY TRANSFERS.
Financial Responsibility and Management Assistance Authority, §§47-392.11 to 47-392.15.
Full faith and credit of District, §1-204.82.
Full faith and credit of United States, §§1-204.84, 47-392.15.

BOND ISSUES —Cont'd
General obligation bonds, §§1-204.61 to 1-204.90.
Highways.
Transportation infrastructure improvement GARVEE bonds, §§9-107.51 to 9-107.62.
Housing finance agency, §§42-2704.02 to 42-2704.10.
See HOUSING FINANCE AGENCY.
Housing production trust fund, §§42-2812.01 to 42-2812.12.
Howard Theatre redevelopment project TIF area, §§2-1217.34a to 2-1217.34n.
H Street, N.E. retail priority area incentive, §§1-325.171 to 1-325.173.
Income tax secured bonds, §§47-340.26 to 47-340.36.
See INCOME TAX SECURED BONDS.
Industrial revenue bond fees, §§47-340.20 to 47-340.23.
Allocation of funds, §47-340.22.
Assessment of fees, §47-340.20.
Deposit, §47-340.21.
Use of allocated funds, §47-340.23.
Industrial revenue bond forward commitment program, §§47-340.01 to 47-340.16.
Bond authorization, §47-340.02.
Conflict of laws, §47-340.16.
Council review for each project, §47-340.03.
Definitions, §47-340.01.
Delegation of authority, §47-340.08.
Disclaimer, §47-340.13.
District officials not personally liable, §47-340.10.
Expiration of authorization, §47-340.14.
Financing and closing documents, §47-340.07.
Form, content, designation, terms, §47-340.04.
Limited liability, §47-340.09.
Payment, §47-340.06.
Records, §47-340.11.
Reporting, §47-340.12.
Sale of bonds, §47-340.05.
Security, §47-340.06.
Severability, §47-340.15.
Investments in, fiduciary legality of, §1-204.86.
Issuance, §1-204.90.
Execution, §1-204.65.

BOND ISSUES —Cont'd

Metropolitan Washington Airports Authority, §§9-910 to 9-916, 9-1006.

Metrorail and metrobus.
See METRORAIL AND METROBUS.

New communities initiative, §42-2812.03.

Pay-for-success contracts, §§2-211.01 to 2-211.03.

Payment of bonds and notes.
General obligation bonds, §§1-204.81, 1-204.83.
Industrial revenue bond forward commitment program, §47-340.06.
Revenue bonds, §1-204.90.

Period of limitations for taking acting on authorizing act, §1-204.64.

Philanthropic bonds.
Pay-for-success contracts, §§2-211.01 to 2-211.03.

PILOT agreements, §§1-308.01 to 1-308.10.
Amount of bonds.
Limitation, §1-308.05.
Approval by council, §1-308.03.
Contents, §1-308.02.
Default in payment of bonds, §1-308.08.
Definitions, §1-308.01.
Execution of bonds, §1-308.06.
Generally, §1-308.02.
Issuance of bonds.
Approval by council, §1-308.03.
Authorized, §1-308.05.
Liability on bonds, §1-308.09.
Payments in lieu of taxes, §1-308.04.
Prior legislation not affected, §1-308.10.
Rhode Island Metro Plaza PILOT agreement.
Sales tax exemption, §47-4613.
Saving clause.
Prior legislation not affected, §1-308.10.
Security for bonds, §1-308.07.
Taxation.
Payments in lieu of taxes, §1-308.04.
Terms and conditions of bonds, §1-308.06.

Publication of act authorizing bonds, §1-204.63.

Public Parking Authority.
Authority to issue revenue bonds, §50-2512.

BOND ISSUES —Cont'd

Public Parking Authority —Cont'd
Tax exemption for bonds issued by, §50-2513.

Qualified zone academy revenue bond project forward commitment approval act, §§2-1217.101 to 2-1217.108.
See QUALIFIED ZONE ACADEMY REVENUE BOND PROJECT FORWARD COMMITMENT APPROVAL ACT.

Redemption.
General obligation bonds, §1-204.73.

Retail development incentives, §2-1217.77.
Default, §2-1217.80.
Details of bonds, §2-1217.78.
Liability, §2-1217.81.
Limitations on issuance, §2-1217.72.
Proceeds, use of, §2-1217.75.
Security for bonds, §2-1217.79.

Revenue anticipation notes, §1-204.72.

Revenue bonds, §1-204.90.

Rhode Island Metro Plaza PILOT (payments in lieu of taxes) agreement.
Sales tax exemption, §47-4613.

Robert F. Kennedy Memorial Stadium, §3-323.

Sale at private sale, §1-204.66.

Schools modernization fund.
Authorization to issue bonds, §1-325.43.
Criteria for use of revenue, §1-325.44.

Security for, §47-335.

Security interest in district revenues, §1-204.67.

Security interests, §1-204.67.

Skyland TIF area, §§2-1217.35a to 2-1217.35l.
See SKYLAND TIF AREA.

Southwest waterfront bond financing, §§2-1217.131 to 2-1217.151.
See SOUTHWEST WATERFRONT.

Sursum Corda.
New communities initiative, §42-2812.03.

Tax exemption for, §1-204.85.

Tax increment financing, §§2-1217.02, 2-1217.06.

Tobacco settlement financing corporation.
Revenue bonds.
Delegation of council authority to issue, §§1-204.90, 7-1831.03.

BOND ISSUES —Cont'd

Transfer of securities by fiduciaries, §§28-2901 to 28-2909.
See FIDUCIARY SECURITY TRANSFERS.

Transportation infrastructure improvement GARVEE bonds, §§9-107.51 to 9-107.62.

Union Market district tax increment financing, §§2-1217.36a to 2-1217.36d.

Washington convention and sports authority, §§10-1202.09 to 10-1202.14.

Water and Sewer Authority.
See WATER AND SEWER AUTHORITY.

Woodrow Wilson bridge and tunnel compact, §9-1115.03.

BONDS, SURETY.
Actions.
Avoidance condition, bonds in penal sum containing, §28-2502.
Bonds in a penal sum containing an avoidance condition, §28-2502.
Bond to United States, §28-2503.
Counterclaims, §13-503.
United States, bonds in which private persons are interested executed to, §28-2503.

Advances on appropriations, §47-3401.03.

Appeals, D.C. courts, CivPro Rule 62-I, DCCtApp Rules 7, 8.
Administrative orders and decisions, DCCtApp Rule 19.

Appeals, federal cases.
Clerk of court of appeals, FRAP 45(a).
Costs.
Civil cases, FRAP 7.
Permission under 28 USCS 1292(b), FRAP 5(d).
Motion for additional security, record for preliminary hearing in court of appeals, FRAP 11(g).
Motion for stay pending review of administrative orders, filing, FRAP 18.
Release of prisoner pending review of habeas corpus decision, FRAP 23.
Stay.
Mandate, condition to grant or continuance, FRAP 41(d).
Pending appeal, FRAP 8(b).
Supersedeas bond.
Application for approval, FRAP 8(a).

BONDS, SURETY —Cont'd
Appeals, federal cases —Cont'd
Supersedeas bond —Cont'd
Motion for additional security, record for preliminary hearing in court of appeals, FRAP 11(g).

Approval, etc., of bonds.
Clerk of superior court, CivPro Rule 77-II.
United States District Court clerk, USDistCt LCrR 57.4, USDistCt LCvR 65.1.1.

Assignments, §28-2302.
Assignees, §28-2104.
Choses in action, §28-2302.

Assignments for benefit of creditors.
Assignee, §28-2104.
Trustee, §28-2105.

Assistant disbursing officers, §47-115.

Attachment, §§16-501, 16-505.

Attorneys' fees and costs for nonresidents, §§15-703, 15-711.

Avoidance condition.
Action on bonds in a penal sum containing an avoidance condition, §28-2502.

Bail bondsmen, §§23-1101 to 23-1112.
See BAIL BONDSMEN.

Bingo licenses, §3-1325.

Board of Education, §38-104.

Boiler inspectors, §2-104.

Building association advancements, §26-208.

Business licenses, §47-2844.

Bus shelters.
Franchisee, §9-1156.

Cable television franchise.
Performance bond, §34-1256.05.
Security fund, §34-1256.02.

Captive insurance companies.
Special purpose financial captive insurance companies.
Contested case by a third party, §31-3932.14.

Check cashing businesses, §26-306.

Clerk of superior court.
Approval, etc., of bonds, CivPro Rule 77-II.

Collection of taxes, §47-401.

Committees.
Discharge only after accounting, §28-2504.

Compensating-use tax, §47-2208.

Condominiums.
Escrow deposits, §42-1904.09.

Conservators, Probate Rule 332.
Missing persons, Probate Rule 350.

BONDS, SURETY —Cont'd

Conservators appointed for protection of property, §§21-2058, 21-2077.

Consumer credit service organizations.
Trust account in lieu of, §28-4604.

Contractors' bonds.
Prompt payment, private contractors and subcontractors.
Prohibition on requiring waiver of right to claim mechanics' lien, §27-134.

Cooperative associations.
Officers and employees, §29-932.

Costs of litigation.
Premiums on bonds, CivPro Rule 54-I.

Counter surety, §16-4101.

Custodians.
Discharge only after accounting, §28-2504.

Dead bodies, schools and boards receiving, §3-204.

Defined, §28-2501.

Deputy disbursing officers, §47-115.

Disbursing officer, §47-111.

Domestic life insurance companies, §31-4402.

Drug, firearm, or prostitution-related nuisance abatement.
Injunctions, not required for, §42-3107.
Violation of orders, §42-3112.

Educational licensure commission, §38-1311.

Employment agencies, §32-403.

Executive officer of District of Columbia courts, §11-1704.

Executors and administrators.
Discharge only after accounting, §28-2504.

Fiduciaries, CivPro Rule 303.
Discharge of bond, §28-2504.
Discharge only after accounting, §28-2504.
Undertaking in lieu of bond, §16-601.

Garnishment.
Prejudgment garnishment, §16-501.
Sufficiency of plaintiff's bond, §16-505.

Green buildings, §6-1451.05.
Performance bond, §6-1451.05.

Guardian ad litem.
Discharge only after accounting, §28-2504.

Guardianship of minors, §§21-114 to 21-118.

BONDS, SURETY —Cont'd

Habeas corpus, §16-1906.

Home improvement contractors, §§47-2883.01 to 47-2883.07.
See HOME IMPROVEMENT CONTRACTORS.

Hospitalization of persons with mental illness, court-ordered, §21-550.

Housing finance agency, §42-2702.05.

Injunctions, CivPro Rule 65.
Domestic relations actions, DomRel Rule 65.

Insurance adjuster licensing, §31-1631.05.

Internet telecommunications franchise agreement.
Furnishing digitally-disadvantaged residents services.
Performance bond.
Requiring franchisee to obtain, §34-1731.04.

Judgments and decrees assessed in actions on, §15-106.

Life insurance companies, §§31-4315 to 31-4317.

Lottery and charitable games control board, §3-1304.
Bingo and raffle operators, §3-1325.
Suppliers, §3-1327.

Metropolitan police, §5-133.12.

Military supplies issued for use in schools, §38-908.

Money lenders, §26-902.

Money transmitters, §26-1007.

Mortgage lenders and brokers, §26-1103.

Motor fuel importers, §47-2303.

Motor vehicle financing, §50-603.

Motor vehicle safety responsibility.
Clerk of superior court may approve, CivPro Rule 77-II.

Notaries public, §1-1203.

Pawnbrokers, §47-2884.04.

Penal sum, bonds in, §28-2502.

Pensions and retirement funds, §1-909.08.

Personal representatives, §20-502.

Persons prohibited as surety upon bond, §1-317.01.

Power to make or modify regulations regarding requirement of, §1-301.01.

Private detectives, §5-121.01.

Probate proceedings.
Guardians, conservators, trustees, etc., involved, Probate Rules 201, 332.
Missing persons, Probate Rule 350.

BONDS, SURETY —Cont'd
Probate proceedings —Cont'd
Personal representative of decedent.
Death between January 1, 1981 and
June 30, 1995, Probate Rule
104.
Death on or after July 1, 1995,
Probate Forms 5 to 8, Probate
Rules 404, 412.
Proceedings against sureties, CivPro
Rule 65.1.
Appeals, DCCtApp Rule 8.
Domestic relations actions, DomRel
Rule 71.
Procurement practice.
Construction bonds.
See PROCUREMENT PRACTICES.
**Prostitution, bond for abatement of
nuisances of houses of,** §22-2719.
Public contracts, §§2-201.01 to
2-201.11.
Public officers and employees,
§47-103.
Agency not allowed to require bonds
on, §1-630.01.
Prohibited from being surety on bond,
§1-317.01.
Surety bonds on officers and
employees, §1-207.37.
Raffle licenses, §3-1325.
**Recordability of bonds relating to
land,** §42-409.
Relief from suretyship, §16-4101.
**Removal from office for failure to
obtain,** §16-4101.
Replevin, §16-3708, CivPro Rule 64-II.
Restraining orders, CivPro Rule 65.
Retirement Board, §1-745.
Special administrators, §20-532.
**Subrogation of surety satisfying
judgment,** §16-4102.
Supersedeas bonds, CivPro Rule 62-I,
DCCtApp Rules 7, 8.
Administrative orders and decisions
reviewed, DCCtApp Rule 19.
Suppliers of bingo equipment,
§3-1327.
Taxation.
Stay of collection, §47-4452.
Taxicabs, §50-301.15.
Telephone solicitors, §22-3226.03.
Security in lieu of bond, §22-3226.04.
Transfers to minors, §21-315.
Trusts and trustees.
Discharge only after accounting,
§28-2504.

BONDS, SURETY —Cont'd
Trusts and trustees —Cont'd
Trustee's bond, §19-1307.02.
United States.
Action on bond to United States,
§28-2503.
Weights and measures, Director of,
§37-201.02.
Workers' compensation, §32-1534.

BONDS TO KEEP THE PEACE.
Threats to do bodily harm, §22-407.

BONE MARROW DONATION.
Corporations.
Tax credit.
Provision of paid leave to employee
serving as donor, §47-1807.08.
**Government employee serving as
donor.**
Donor leave, §1-612.03b.
Unincorporated businesses.
Tax credit.
Provision of paid leave to employee
serving as donor, §47-1808.08.

BONFIRES, §22-1313.

BONGS.
Drug paraphernalia, §§48-1101 to
48-1104.

**BONUS PAY AND SPECIAL AWARDS
PAY ACT OF 2016,** §§1-551.01 to
1-551.06.

BOOKMAKING, §22-1708.

BOOKS.
Defacement of, §22-3306.
Libraries.
General provisions, §§39-101 to
39-124.
See LIBRARIES.

BOOT CAMP, §§24-921 to 24-932.
**Agreement as to terms and
conditions,** §24-928.
Definitions, §24-921.
Educational requirements, §24-924.
Elements of, §24-924.
Establishment of, §24-922.
Evaluation of progress, §24-925.
Graduation from, §24-930.
Grooming requirements, §24-927.
Location of, §24-923.
Physical training requirements,
§24-924.
**Post-BOOT CAMP supervision of
juveniles,** §24-931.
Removal of juvenile from, §24-929.

BOOT CAMP —Cont'd
Reports, §24-932.
Standards required in, §§24-926,
24-927.
Vocational training requirements,
§24-924.

BOTANIC GARDENS.
Tunnel under, §§10-511.01 to
10-511.07.

BOTTLES.
Beverage bottle registration,
§§36-101, 36-102.
Milk containers, §§36-121 to 36-157.
See MILK CONTAINER
REGISTRATION.

BOUNDARIES.
Advisory neighborhood commission,
§§1-309.01, 1-309.02, 1-309.08.
Destroying boundary markers,
§22-3309.
District of Columbia, §1-101.
Election wards, §1-1041.03.
Fire departments, §5-401.
Lots, §1-1319.
Metropolitan police, §5-101.02.
Schools and education.
Attendance zone boundaries, §38-221.
Surveyor of the District recording,
§§1-1318, 1-1319.
United States Park Police, §5-208.

BOUNTY ON ILLEGAL DUMPING,
§8-904.

BOWLING ALLEYS.
Business licenses, §47-2821.

BOXING AND WRESTLING
COMMISSION, §§3-601 to 3-610.
Administrative procedure, §3-607.
Council's authority to establish,
§3-603.
Definitions, §3-602.
Establishment of, §3-604.
Fines, §3-608.
Issuance of rules by, §3-610.
Jurisdiction of, §3-605.
Liability of members, §3-609.
Licenses, §3-606.
Penalties, §3-608.
Permits, §3-606.
Policy declaration, §3-601.
Powers and duties, §3-606.
Protective equipment requirements,
§3-610.

BRAILLE PRINTERS.
Assistive technology warranty,
§§28-4031 to 28-4034.

BRAIN DEATH, §7-601.

BRANCH BANKS, §§26-731 to 26-741.
See INTERSTATE BANKING AND
BRANCH BANKS.

BRANDING.
Body art establishments.
Business licenses, §47-2809.01.
Body artists.
Business licenses, §§47-2853.76a to
47-2853.76e.

BRANDS, COMMERCIAL.
Forgery, §22-1502.

BREACH OF FIDUCIARY DUTY.
Personal representatives, §20-743.

BREACH OF PROMISE.
Abolition of action for, §16-923.

BREAD.
Weights and measures.
General provisions, §§37-201.13 to
37-201.22a.
See WEIGHTS AND MEASURES.

BREAD FOR THE CITY
COMMUNITY GARDEN.
Real property tax exemptions,
§47-1062.

BREAKING AND ENTERING.
Burglary, §22-801.

BREAKING INTO DEVICES
DESIGNED TO RECEIVE
CURRENCY, §22-601.

BREAST CANCER.
Mammograms, health insurance
coverage for, §§31-2901 to 31-2903.
Reconstructive surgery following
mastectomies.
Women's rights to health insurance
coverage, §§31-3831 to 31-3837.

BREASTFEEDING MOTHERS,
RIGHTS OF, §§2-1402.81 to
2-1402.83.
Discrimination, §2-1401.05.
Employment discrimination.
Pregnant and nursing workers,
reasonable accommodations for,
§§32-1231.01 to 32-1231.15.

BREASTMILK BANK AND
LACTATION SUPPORT,
§§7-881.01 to 7-881.11.
Advertising, §7-881.09.
Applicability, §7-881.08.
Contingency, §7-881.11.

**BREASTMILK BANK AND
   LACTATION SUPPORT** —Cont'd
Center.
Defined, §7-881.01.
Established, §7-881.02.
Comprehensive plan, §7-881.04.
Definitions, §7-881.01.
Education and outreach campaign,
   §7-881.03.
Lactation commission.
Establishment, §7-881.05.
Meetings, §7-881.06.
Members, §7-881.06.
Procedures, §7-881.06.
Milk banks.
Regulation, §7-881.07.
Penalties, §7-881.09.
Prohibited activities, §7-881.09.
Purpose, §7-881.02.
Restrictions on distribution,
   §7-881.09.
Rules, §7-881.10.

BREEDERS.
Commercial animal care or breeder
   license, §§8-1821.01, 8-1821.02.

BRENTWOOD RETAIL CENTER.
Real property tax exemption,
   §47-4608.

BREW PUBS.
Alcoholic beverage licenses, §25-117.
Fees, §25-508.
Smoking, §§7-741.02, 7-741.03.
Taxation, §25-902.

BRIBERY, §§22-704 to 22-713.
Alcoholic beverage licensing,
   §25-434.
Constitution of the United States,
   US Const Art II §4.
Definitions, §22-711.
Prohibited actions regarded as,
   §22-712.
Public officers and employees,
   §22-704.
Security agents and brokers.
Grounds for disciplinary actions,
   §31-5602.07.
Vice-president of the United States,
   US Const Art II §4.
Witnesses, §22-713.

BRIDGES.
Anacostia Bridge, §9-305.
Benning Bridge, §9-314.
Calvert Street Bridge, §9-324.
Connecticut Avenue Bridge over
   Klingle Valley, §9-313.

BRIDGES —Cont'd
Drawbridge openings, submarine
   cables used at, §9-1207.02.
Francis Case Memorial Bridge,
   §9-325.
Francis Scott Key Bridge, §9-311.
Highway Bridge over Potomac
   River, §9-307.
John Philip Sousa Bridge, §9-306.
Mayor's control of, §9-301.
Monroe Street Bridge, §9-310.
Obstructing bridges connecting
   District of Columbia and
   Virginia, §22-1323.
Pennsylvania Avenue Bridge, §9-304.
Power boat requirements for going
   under, §9-309.
Rights-of-way over canals and
   railways, §9-302.
Rochambeau Bridge, §9-308.
Rock Creek bridges, §9-303.
South Dakota Avenue Bridge, §9-312.
Theodore Roosevelt Island, access
   to, §10-159.
Tugboat requirements for going
   under, §9-309.
Washington Channel Bridge, §9-326.

BRIEFS.
Amicus curiae.
Appeals, District of Columbia court of
   appeals, DCCtApp Rule 29.
Appeals, federal cases, FRAP 29,
   USCtApp HPIP Rule IX(a)(4),
   USCtApp Rule 29.
Docketing statement, USCtApp Rule
   12.
Appeals, D.C. courts.
Amicus curiae, DCCtApp Rule 29.
Appendix, DCCtApp Rule 30.
   Form of appendix, DCCtApp Rule
     32.
Contents, DCCtApp Rule 28.
Filing and service, DCCtApp Rule 31.
Form of brief, DCCtApp Rule 32.
Appeals, federal cases, FRAP 28 to 32,
   USCtApp HPIP Rule IX(a),
   USCtApp Rules 28 to 32.1.
Amicus curiae brief, FRAP 29,
   USCtApp HPIP Rule IX(a)(4),
   USCtApp Rule 29.
Appellant's brief, FRAP 28(a).
Appellee's brief, FRAP 28(b).
Appendix to briefs, FRAP 30,
   USCtApp HPIP Rule IX(b),
   USCtApp Rule 30.

BRIEFS —Cont'd
Appeals, federal cases —Cont'd
Citation of authorities, FRAP 28(j), USCtApp Rule 28.
Judicial dispositions, USCtApp Rule 32.1.
Consolidated and joint appeals, USCtApp HPIP Rule IX(a)(2).
Contents, USCtApp HPIP Rule IX(a)(8).
Costs, FRAP 39(c).
Cross appeals, FRAP 28.1(c), USCtApp HPIP Rule IX(a)(3).
Cover, FRAP 28.1(d).
Length, FRAP 28.1(e).
Time to file and serve, FRAP 28.1(f).
Failure to file, consequence, FRAP 31(c).
Federal labor relations authority proceedings, USCtApp Rule 15.1.
Filing, FRAP 25(a), 31.
Cross appeals, FRAP 28.1(f).
Form, FRAP 32(a).
Appendix and other papers, USCtApp Rule 32.
Certificate of compliance, FRAP Form 6.
Format, USCtApp HPIP Rule IX(a)(6).
Generally, FRAP 28, USCtApp Rule 28.
Intervenors, USCtApp HPIP Rule IX(a)(4).
Length, USCtApp HPIP Rule IX(a)(7).
Mailing as time deemed filed, FRAP 25(a).
Mandamus, prohibition, etc., petition for writ of, FRAP 21, USCtApp Rule 21.
Multiple appellants or appellees, cases involving, FRAP 28(i).
National labor relations board proceedings, FRAP 15.1, USCtApp Rule 15.1.
Non-appearance of parties, decision on briefs, FRAP 34(e).
Number of copies, FRAP 31(b), USCtApp HPIP Rule IX(a)(5), USCtApp Rule 31.
Preservation by clerk, FRAP 45(d).
References to parties, FRAP 28(d).
References to the record, FRAP 28(e).
Reply brief, FRAP 28(c).
Time for serving and filing, FRAP 31(a).
Cross appeals, FRAP 28.1(f).
Reproduction of statutes.
Rules, regulations, etc., FRAP 28(f).

BRIEFS —Cont'd
Appeals, federal cases —Cont'd
Seals.
Briefs containing material under seal, USCtApp HPIP Rule IX(a)(10).
Service, FRAP 31.
Cross appeals, FRAP 28.1(f).
Shortening time for serving and filing, FRAP 31(a).
Submission for decision on, FRAP 34(f).
Supplemental briefs and letters, USCtApp HPIP Rule IX(a)(9).
Supporting motions, FRAP 27(a).
Time for serving and filing, FRAP 31(a), USCtApp HPIP Rule IX(a)(1).
Cross appeals, FRAP 28.1(f).
Unpublished opinions, USCtApp HPIP Rule IX(a)(8).

BROADCASTING COURT PROCEEDINGS.
Superior court proceedings, CivPro Rule 203, CrimPro Rule 53.
Child abuse and neglect proceedings, NeglectProc Rule 45.
Juvenile proceedings, JuvProc Rule 53.
United States District Court proceedings, USDistCt LCrR 53.1.1, USDistCt LCvR 83.1.

BROADCASTING INDUSTRY EMPLOYMENT CONTRACTS, §§32-531 to 32-533.
Defined, §32-531.
Unenforceability of contract provisions restricting employment after expiration of contract or termination of employment, §32-532.
Liability of employers violating provisions, §32-533.

BROKERS AND BROKER-DEALERS.
Mortgage lenders and brokers, §§26-1101 to 26-1121.
See MORTGAGE LENDERS AND BROKERS.
Real estate brokers and salespersons.
General provisions, §§42-1701 to 42-1709.
See REAL ESTATE BROKERS AND SALESPERSONS.
Security agents and brokers, §§31-5601.01 to 31-5608.04.
See SECURITY AGENTS AND BROKERS.

BROTHERS AND DESCENDANTS OF BROTHERS.
Intestate succession, §§19-309, 19-310, 19-315.

BROWNFIELD REVITALIZATION.
Hazardous substances releases.
Liability, cleanup, response, §§8-631.01 to 8-638.01.
See HAZARDOUS SUBSTANCES RELEASES.

BUDGETS AND BUDGET ESTIMATES, §§47-201 to 47-215.
Adoption of budget by council, §1-204.46.
Agency-by-agency accounting of expenditures, §§47-318 to 47-318.05a.
Annual budget, submission of, §§1-204.42, 47-301.01.
Agency enhancement requests, §47-318.05a.
Agency performance measures, §38-121.02.
Private funds used by public schools, §38-121.01.
Annual federal payment, deposit of, §47-392.05.
Antideficiency provisions, §§47-355.01 to 47-355.08.
Definitions, §47-355.01.
Limits on expenditures and obligations, §47-355.02.
Notice of provisions, §47-355.08.
Report of spending plan, §47-355.04.
Reports of actual expenditures and obligations, §47-355.05.
Review board, §47-355.07.
Spending projections, §47-355.03.
Violations, §47-355.06.
Appropriations.
See APPROPRIATIONS.
Attorney general, §1-301.86.
Borrowing.
Control year, during, §47-392.04.
Convention center and sports arena, §§47-398.01, 47-398.02, 47-398.05.
Limitations, §§1-206.03, 47-392.04.
Treasury borrowings in anticipation of revenues, §47-309.
Business improvement districts, §2-1215.12.
Capital funds.
Prohibition on expending for operating expenses, §1-301.77.
Capital projects, §47-339.01.

BUDGETS AND BUDGET ESTIMATES —Cont'd
Capital review and debt affordability committee, §§47-336 to 47-340.
Cash flow statements, §47-318.05.
Chief financial officer.
Contingency cash reserve notification, §1-301.152.
Control periods, powers during, §47-317.03a.
Department of housing and community development, §1-301.141.
Duties, §1-204.24d.
Economic change analysis, §47-318.06.
General provisions, §§1-204.24a to 1-204.24f.
Health care analysis and overtime plan, §1-301.151.
Claims against District, §47-210.
Comprehensive financial management policy, §1-204.50b.
Consistency of systems, §1-204.47.
Contingency reserve fund, §1-204.50a.
Control budget, §47-307.
Control periods, §47-392.09.
Chief financial officer.
Powers during control periods, §47-317.03a.
Control years.
Transmission to President during control years, §1-204.46.
Council, §47-318.01b.
Court-appointed receivers, submission of annual expense estimates by, §47-301.01.
Courthouse protection force wages and salaries, §47-201.
Courts, §11-1743.
Deficiency recommendations, submission of, §1-204.42.
Deposits and investment in financial institutions, §§47-351.01 to 47-351.16.
Disbursement control, §§47-381 to 47-385.
District budget, §§47-201 to 47-215.
Emergency reserve fund, §1-204.50a.
Ethic and government accountability board, §1-1162.07.
Existing provisions, preservation of, §1-206.03.
Expenses of employees, §47-313.01.

INDEX

BUDGETS AND BUDGET ESTIMATES —Cont'd

Financial accountability and management, §§47-318 to 47-318.05a.

Comprehensive financial management policy, §1-204.50b.

Financial responsibility and management assistance authority.

General provisions, §§47-391.01 to 47-395.

See FINANCIAL RESPONSIBILITY AND MANAGEMENT ASSISTANCE AUTHORITY.

Fiscal impact statements.

Council, §1-301.47a.

Fiscal year, §1-204.41.

Fiscal year 1996 special rules, §47-392.08.

Freedom of information, §2-536.

Fund-type accounting, §§47-371 to 47-377.

Gap-closing actions, §§47-318.03, 47-318.04.

Government of District, §47-213.

Grants.

Acceptance of grant amounts not included in annual budget, §1-204.46b.

Gross planning budget, §47-306.

Highways, §47-209.

Increases to appropriations, §47-369.02.

Independent agencies, reductions in budgets of, §1-204.53.

Indigent criminal defendants, counsel for, §11-2607.

Initiative implementation monitoring committee, §§47-319.01 to 47-319.04.

Compensation and expenses, §47-319.03.

Composition, §47-319.02.

Establishment, §47-319.01.

Reports, §47-319.04.

Insurance regulatory trust fund, §31-1202.

Investment in financial institutions, §§47-351.01 to 47-351.16.

Items included in annual estimates.

Assignment of market employees, report, §47-207.

Bridges and approaches, employees, supplies, expenses, §47-209.

Claims against District, expenses incurred, §47-210.

BUDGETS AND BUDGET ESTIMATES —Cont'd

Items included in annual estimates —Cont'd

Real estate assessments, §47-211.

Sewer maintenance, employees and supplies, §47-208.

Water department expenses, §47-212.

Lottery and charitable games control board, §3-1311.

Mayor's financial duties, §§1-204.48, 1-204.49, 47-318.01 to 47-318.05a.

Metrorail and metrobus.

Washington metropolitan area transit authority compact on, §9-1107.01.

Modification.

Reprogramming, §§47-361 to 47-366.

Monitoring committee, §§47-319.01 to 47-319.04.

Multiyear capital improvements plan, §§1-204.44, 47-339.

Multiyear plans, §§1-204.43, 47-318.02.

National Capital Planning Commission, §2-1011.

Not-for-profit hospital corporations, §44-951.09.

Notice.

Expenditure of funds from emergency reserve fund, §1-204.50a.

Obligations and expenditures not authorized under budget, §1-204.46.

Organization of fund structure, §47-373.

Parks and recreation, §10-214.

Performance and financial accountability, §§1-204.56a to 1-204.56e.

See DEPARTMENTS AND AGENCIES.

Performance based budgets, §47-308.01.

Performance accountability reporting, §47-308.03.

Relevant performance measures, §47-308.02.

Policy.

Comprehensive financial management policy, §1-204.50b.

Pretrial services agency, §23-1308.

Prison system exemption from personnel and budget ceilings under federal control, §24-142.

Public access corporation, §34-1253.02.

Publication of, §47-215.

BUDGETS AND BUDGET ESTIMATES —Cont'd

Public-private partnerships, §2-272.03.

Public records management, §2-1712.

Public schools.
DCPS budget, §38-2907.01.
Mayor submission of agency budget, §38-173.

Public Welfare, Board of, §4-121.

Real property assessments, §47-211.

Recreation board, §10-214.

Reprogramming of amounts, restrictions, §1-204.46.

Reprogramming policy, §§47-361 to 47-366.
Appropriated funds.
Reprogramming, §47-365.
Approval of reprogramming, §47-363.
Budget modification of $500,000 or more, §47-361.
Definitions, §47-361.
Non-departmental account.
Notice of reprogramming, transfer, budget modification, §47-366.
Policies enumerated, §47-362.

Request for budget submitted by mayor, §47-318.02.

Reserve funds, §1-204.50a.

Rights of way.
Revenue from public rights of way.
Inclusion in budget submission, §47-305.01.

Schedule of funds available, §47-214.

School buildings and grounds, §§47-202, 47-203.

Schools and education, §§38-1804.01, 38-1807.53.
Public schools.
DCPS budget, §38-2907.01.
Mayor submission of agency budget, §38-173.

Sentencing, Advisory Commission on, §3-107.

Sewer maintenance workers, §47-209.

Spending limitations, §1-206.03.

Statehood initiatives budgeting, §1-301.154.

Stormwater management.
Compliance estimates to be included in budgets, §8-152.01.

Structure of budget.
Establishing, §47-308.

Submission of annual budget, §§1-204.42, 47-301.01.
Agency enhancement requests, §47-318.05a.

BUDGETS AND BUDGET ESTIMATES —Cont'd

Superintendent of Washington Asylum and Jail.
Salary of, §47-201.

Supplemental recommendations, submission of, §1-204.42.
Agency enhancement requests, §47-318.05a.

Unified economic development budget transparency and accountability, §§2-1208.01 to 2-1208.04.
Definitions, §2-1208.01.
FOIA disclosure, §2-1208.04.
Performance measures, §2-1208.03.
Reports, §2-1208.02.
Strategic plan, §2-1208.03.

University of the District of Columbia tuition grants, §38-1207.07.

Water department expenses, §47-212.

Youth services, §2-1510.

BUILDING ASSOCIATIONS, §§26-201 to 26-232.

Advancements, §§26-207 to 26-214.
Bonds, surety, §26-208.
Equal participation of all shares advanced in profits, §26-209.
Foreclosure on security, §26-214.
Premium payments, §26-207.
Redemption on failure to bid, §26-210.
Repayment of, §26-212.
Security, §§26-208, 26-214.

Approval required for, §26-103.

Bonds, federal.
Exchanging securities or real property for, §26-232.

Bonds, surety on advancements, §26-208.

Bonus paid by late subscribers, §26-203.

Certificate of incorporation, §26-201.

Comptroller of the currency, §26-251.

Direct-reduction loans for veterans, §42-3002.

Federal bonds.
Exchanging securities or real property for, §26-232.

Federal home loan bank board powers over, §26-204.

Federal securities, §§26-231, 26-232.

Fines, §26-204.

Foreign associations, §26-206.

Formation of, §26-201.

BUILDING ASSOCIATIONS —Cont'd

Mortgages and deeds of trust.

General provisions, §§42-804 to
42-820.

See MORTGAGES AND DEEDS OF
TRUST.

Penalties, §26-204.

Powers and duties, §§26-201, 26-202.

Premium payments, §26-207.

Purpose of, §§26-201, 26-204.

Real property.

Exchanging real property for federal
bonds, §26-232.

Purchase of, §26-215.

Recordation of instruments, §26-201.

Repayment of advances, §26-212.

Reports, §26-204.

Saturdays.

Designated holiday, §28-2701.

Securities.

Exchanging securities for federal
bonds, §26-232.

Purchasing federal securities, §26-231.

**Servicemen's readjustment for
mortgages and deeds of trust,**
§§42-3001, 42-3002.

Stock and stockholders.

Advancements, §§26-207 to 26-214.
See within this heading,
"Advancements."

Bonus paid by late subscribers,
§26-203.

Forfeitures, §26-213.

Powers as to stock, §26-202.

Premium payments, §26-207.

Redemption, §26-210.

Withdrawal by shareholder, §26-211.

Veterans.

Direct-reduction loans for veterans,
§42-3002.

**BUILDING BRIDGES ACROSS THE
RIVER, INC.**

Real property tax exemptions,
§47-1083.

BUILDING CODE.

Assault on code inspectors, §22-405.

Assessments.

Correction of conditions violative of
law, §42-3131.01.

Fire violations, correction of,
§6-703.08.

Insanitary buildings, repair or
demolition of, §6-907.

Unsafe structures, correction of,
§§6-805, 6-806.

BUILDING CODE —Cont'd

Construction codes, §§6-1401 to
6-1409.

See CONSTRUCTION CODES.

Correction of violative conditions,
§§42-3131.01 to 42-3131.03.

Fireproof buildings, §§6-601.05 to
6-601.09.

Fires and fire prevention.

Enforcement, regulations authorized
for, §6-703.03.

Fines, §6-703.06.

Inspections. See within this heading,
"Inspections."

Notice. See within this heading,
"Notice."

Rental unit alterations to occupied
units after notice to vacate,
§§6-731.01 to 6-731.04.

Restraints on use and occupancy of
building violating requirements,
§§6-703.04, 6-703.09.

Smoke detectors, §§6-751.01, 6-751.02.
See SMOKE DETECTORS.

Flood hazards, §§6-501 to 6-506.

Annual report, §6-505.

Building permit applications.
Review, §6-501.

Design and construction requirements.
Building site located in flood hazard,
§6-501.

Excavation, grading, filing,
construction permits.
Review, §6-504.

Mudslide hazards.
Review of site and improvements,
§6-504.

Penalties for violations of provisions,
§6-506.

Subdivision and other new
development proposals.
Review, §6-502.

Water and sanitary sewage systems.
Design, §6-503.
Location of on-site waste disposal
system, §6-503.

Height of buildings, §§6-601.05 to
6-611.02.

Common nuisances, §6-601.08.

Congressional right to alter, appeal, or
amend provisions, §6-601.09.

Federal property, buildings fronting
on, §§6-611.01, 6-611.02.

Fine Arts Commission review,
§§6-611.01, 6-611.02.

Maximum permissible height,
§6-641.06.

BUILDING CODE —Cont'd
Height of buildings —Cont'd
Street width, controlled by, §6-601.05.
Structures above top story, §6-601.05.
Insanitary buildings, §§6-901 to 6-919.
See INSANITARY BUILDINGS.
Inspections, §42-3131.02.
Assault on code inspectors, §22-405.
Fees, §6-703.01.
Insanitary buildings, §§6-901, 6-911.
Interference with, §42-3131.02.
Unsafe structures or excavations, §6-801.
Notice.
Failure to comply with, §6-703.08.
Installations required, §6-703.05.
Occupancy after receipt of, §6-703.04.
Rental unit alterations to occupied units after notice to vacate, §§6-731.01 to 6-731.04.
Required fire safety measures, §6-703.05.
Service of notice, §6-703.07.
Unlawful conditions, requirement to correct, §§6-703.05, 42-3131.03.
Unsafe structures, §§6-804, 6-807.
Violations of fire safety requirements, §§6-703.05, 42-3131.03.
Occupancy.
Condemned insanitary buildings, §§6-903, 6-904.
Fire safety violations, §6-703.04.
Unsafe structures, §6-808.
Power to issue regulations regarding, §1-303.04.
Rental unit alterations to occupied units after notice to vacate, §§6-731.01 to 6-731.04.
Prohibited, §6-731.01.
Exemption, consent of tenants, §6-731.02.
Exemption, mayor granting, §6-731.03.
Penalty for violation, §6-731.04.
Smoke detectors, §§6-751.01, 6-751.02.
See SMOKE DETECTORS.
Unsafe structures or excavations, §§6-801 to 6-808.
Assessment of cost to correct, §§5-605, 6-805.
Correction of conditions violative of law, §§42-3131.01 to 42-3131.03.
Dangerous nuisance, classification as, §6-804.
Failure of owner to make safe, §§5-603, 6-803, 6-804.

BUILDING CODE —Cont'd
Unsafe structures or excavations —Cont'd
Historic districts and landmarks, §6-1111.
Inspections, §§5-601, 6-801.
Mayor's power to take immediate action regarding, §6-801.
Notice, §§6-804, 6-807.
Occupancy, §6-808.
Removal or securing of, §§6-801, 6-803.
Sale for nonpayment of cost to correct, §6-806.
Survey of premises, §5-602.
Vacant lots, §6-804.
Vacant buildings, §§42-3131.05 to 42-3131.17.
See VACANT BUILDINGS.
Zoning, §§6-621.01 to 6-661.02.
See ZONING.

BUILDING CONTRACTORS.
Asbestos contractors.
General provisions, §§8-111.01 to 8-111.14.
See ASBESTOS CONTRACTORS.
Construction codes, §§6-1401 to 6-1409.
See CONSTRUCTION CODES.
Home improvement contractors.
Bonding requirements, §§47-2883.01 to 47-2883.07.
See HOME IMPROVEMENT CONTRACTORS.
Mechanics' and materialmen's liens.
General provisions, §§40-301.01 to 40-307.03.
See MECHANIC'S LIENS.
Parking.
Contractor daytime parking permit, §50-2635.
Plumbing inspections, §§2-134 to 2-137.
Private contractor and subcontractor prompt payment act, §§27-131 to 27-136.
See PROMPT PAYMENT.
Radon contractor proficiency, §§28-4201 to 28-4203.
Security and fire alarm contractors.
General provisions, §§7-2801 to 7-2815.
See SECURITY AND FIRE ALARM CONTRACTORS.

BUILDING INSPECTOR.
Assistant inspector of buildings, §2-138.

BUILDING PERMITS.
Cancellation of, §6-661.02.
Construction codes generally,
§§6-1401 to 6-1412.
See CONSTRUCTION CODES.
Fees for, §§6-661.01, 6-661.02.
Freedom of information, §2-536.
Rent control certificate of assurance
issued with, §42-3502.21.
Requirement to have, §6-641.09.
Third party inspectors, §6-1405.04.
Third party plan review, §6-1405.02.

BUILDING REHABILITATION
CODE, §6-1410.
Advisory council, §6-1411.

BUILDINGS.
Alcoholic beverage licenses.
Structural requirements for
establishments, §25-761.
Assisted living residences.
Facility regulations generally,
§§44-110.01 to 44-110.12.
Construction codes generally,
§§6-1401 to 6-1412.
See CONSTRUCTION CODES.
Construction contracts.
Prompt payment.
Private contractor and subcontractor
prompt payment act, §§27-131
to 27-136.
See PROMPT PAYMENT.
Demolition or enclosure of
deteriorated structures,
§§42-3173.01 to 42-3173.12.
Graffiti abatement, §§42-3141.01 to
42-3141.11.
See GRAFFITI.
Green buildings, §§6-1451.01 to
6-1451.11.
See GREEN BUILDINGS.
Indoor mold assessment and
remediation, §§8-241.01 to
8-241.09.
See INDOOR MOLD ASSESSMENT
AND REMEDIATION.
Public buildings.
See PUBLIC BUILDINGS.
Vacant buildings.
Fires and fire prevention, §§42-3131.05
to 42-3131.17.
See VACANT BUILDINGS.
Workplace fraud, §§32-1331.01 to
32-1331.12.
See WORKPLACE FRAUD.

BULK TRANSFERS.
Pharmacies, bulk sales or transfers
by, §47-2885.12.

BULK TRANSFERS —Cont'd
Taxation.
Notice of bulk sales for tax liability
determination, §§47-4461 to
47-4463.

BULLETS.
Ammunition generally.
See AMMUNITION.
Firearms generally.
See FIREARMS.
Weapons generally.
See WEAPONS.

BULLYING, §§2-1535.01 to 2-1535.09.
Defined terms, §2-1535.01.
Investigation appeals, §2-1535.04.
Policies, §2-1535.03.
Programs, §2-1535.06.
Remedies, §2-1535.08.
Reports, §2-1535.07.
Retaliation, §2-1535.05.
Rules, §2-1535.09.
Task force, §2-1535.02.

BURDEN OF PROOF.
Abandoned and unlawfully parked
vehicles.
Disposal of unclaimed vehicle.
Owners' and lienholders' remedies,
§50-2421.11.
AIDS health care.
Standard for disclosing medical
records regarding, §7-1605.
Arrest records, requests to seal.
Burden to deny relief, §16-803.
Attorneys at law.
Admission to the bar, DCCtApp Rule
46.
Discipline or disability proceedings.
Incompetent or incapacitated
attorneys, DCBar Rule XI.
Child custody.
Third-party custody proceedings.
Modification or termination of award
of custody to third party,
§16-831.11.
Parental presumption, rebutting,
§16-831.06.
Civil asset forfeiture, §41-308.
Competence to proceed.
Incompetent criminal defendants.
Party asserting incompetence,
§24-531.04.
Controlled substances, §48-905.03.
Crime victims' compensation.
Appeal of determination, VictComp
Rule 20.

BURDEN OF PROOF —Cont'd
Driving under the influence.
Mandatory-minimum periods of incarceration, proof required, §50-2206.57.
Drug, firearm, or prostitution-related nuisance abatement, §42-3108.
Emergency medical services.
Prosecution of violations, burden of proving exemption, §7-2341.25.
Hospitalization of persons with mental illness, MentalHealth Rule 5.
Incompetent criminal defendants.
Competence to proceed.
Party asserting incompetence, §24-531.04.
Insurance compliance self-evaluation privilege.
Burden of proof of applicability, §31-857.
Limited partnerships.
Actions, special litigation committee, §29-709.06.
Prescription drugs.
Burden of proving price not excessive, §28-4554.
Procurement practices.
Claims against the District, §2-381.05.
Real property transfers.
Compulsory recordation of, §47-1432.
Real property transfer tax, §47-907.
Recordation tax exemptions, §42-1107.
Secured transactions.
Purchase-money security interest.
Burden of establishing, §28:9-103.
Tax proceedings, Tax Rule 12.
Trusts and trustees.
Uniform trust code.
Oral trusts, evidence, §19-1304.07.
Unjust imprisonment, §2-422.

BUREAU OF BANKING AND FINANCIAL INSTITUTIONS.
Director, §31-106.
Established, §31-106.

BUREAU OF NATIONAL AFFAIRS.
Real property tax deferrals, §47-845.01.

BUREAU OF PRISONS.
Corrections information council, §24-101.01.
Transfer of system to federal authority, §24-101.

BUREAU OF RODENT CONTROL, §§8-2101.01, 8-2101.02.
Rodent abatement program, §§8-2103.01 to 8-2103.05.

BUREAU OF TRAFFIC ADJUDICATION.
Study on improving quality of adjudications, §2-1831.18.

BURGLARY, §22-801.
Aged persons, offenses committed against.
Enhanced penalties, §22-3601.
Crime investigation records.
Retention of records in open investigations, §5-113.32.
Implements of crime, possession of, §22-2501.

BURIAL.
Burial assistance program, §4-1001.
Cemeteries.
See CEMETERIES AND CEMETERY ASSOCIATIONS.
Communicable diseases, opening graves of persons deceased from, §43-123.
Crime victims' compensation, VictComp Rule 25.
Depth of grave, §43-116.
Disinterment, §§43-123, 43-128.
Funeral directors.
General provisions, §§3-401 to 3-421.
See FUNERAL DIRECTORS.
Grave robbery, §§3-206, 22-3303.
Medical examiner's release of body for, §5-1411.
Park reservation 13 transferred for use as indigent burial ground, §10-135.
Place of burial, requirements regarding, §43-121.
Police and firefighters retirement and disability, §5-720.
Public assistance claims, §§4-214.01 to 4-214.04.
Public expense, at, §3-202.
Public officers and employees, §1-623.34.
Registers, §43-117.
Size of grave, §43-116.
Vault requirements, §43-122.

BURNING CROSSES, §22-3312.02.

BUSES.
Charter buses.
Registration, §50-1501.02.
International registration plan agreements, §50-1507.03.

BUSES —Cont'd
Charter buses —Cont'd
Registration —Cont'd
Penalties, §50-1501.04.
DC Circulator bus service,
§§50-921.31 to 50-921.38.
Labor and employment relations.
Transportation benefits.
Reducing single occupancy vehicle
use by encouraging transit
benefits, §§32-151 to 32-153.
Metrorail and metrobus, §§9-1101.01
to 9-1115.04.
See METRORAIL AND METROBUS.
Right of way at intersections,
§50-2201.29.
School buses.
Business licenses, §47-2829.
Smoking, §7-1703.
"No Smoking" signs, §7-1704.

**BUSINESS AND ECONOMIC
DEVELOPMENT,** §§2-1201.01 to
2-1217.84.
**Access to capital for businesses and
nonprofit organizations,**
§§2-1210.01 to 2-1210.12.
Annual report, §2-1210.10.
Capital access fund.
Audit, §2-1210.10.
Established, §2-1210.02.
Capital access program.
Capital access loans, §§2-1210.04,
2-1210.05.
Reserve accounts, §2-1210.06.
District's rights, §2-1210.08.
Limitations on District's
contribution, §2-1210.07.
Established, §2-1210.03.
Financial institutions.
Minimum eligibility to participate
in capital access program,
§2-1210.04.
Reports, §2-1210.09.
Definitions, §2-1210.01.
District not liable, §2-1210.11.
Rules, §2-1210.12.
Business improvement districts.
General provisions, §§2-1215.01 to
2-1215.71.
See BUSINESS IMPROVEMENT
DISTRICTS.
Business incubator facilitation,
§§2-1209.01 to 2-1209.14.
Admissions policy, §2-1209.04.
Annual report, §2-1209.14.

**BUSINESS AND ECONOMIC
DEVELOPMENT** —Cont'd
Business incubator facilitation
—Cont'd
Contract for outside management,
§2-1209.06.
Definitions, §2-1209.02.
Eligibility criteria, §2-1209.03.
First source employment agreement,
§2-1209.08.
Location of business incubators,
§2-1209.10.
Maximum stay policy, §2-1209.09.
Priority to residents, §2-1209.07.
Purposes, §2-1209.01.
Services, §2-1209.05.
Capital access program, §§2-1210.01
to 2-1210.12.
**Economic development liaison
office,** §§2-1203.01 to 2-1203.03.
Established, §2-1203.01.
Functions, §2-1203.02.
Transfer of functions assigned to
Office of Tourism and
Promotions, §2-1203.03.
**Economic development zone
incentives.**
General provisions, §§6-1501 to
6-1506.
See ECONOMIC DEVELOPMENT
ZONE INCENTIVES.
Enterprise zone study commission,
§§2-1211.01 to 2-1211.06.
Grocery store development program,
§§2-1212.21 to 2-1212.24.
Ambassador program, §2-1212.23.
Definitions, §2-1212.01.
Established, §2-1212.21.
Participation, §2-1212.22.
Rules, §2-1212.41.
Zoning incentives, §2-1212.24.
Healthy food retail program,
§§2-1212.31 to 2-1212.34.
Definitions, §2-1212.01.
Distribution, §2-1212.33.
Energy efficiency, §2-1212.34.
Established, §2-1212.31.
Requirements, §2-1212.32.
Rules, §2-1212.41.
H Street, N.E., Retail Priority Area.
Funding for eligible development
projects, §1-325.311.
**Incarceration to incorporation
entrepreneurship program.**
Effective date, §2-1210.55.

BUSINESS AND ECONOMIC DEVELOPMENT —Cont'd
Local food economy study, §48-411.
National Capital Revitalization Corporation.
General provisions.
See NATIONAL CAPITAL REVITALIZATION CORPORATION.
Office of business and economic development, §§2-1201.01 to 2-1201.05.
Executive director, §2-1201.04.
Findings of council, purpose of subchapter, §2-1201.01.
Functions, §2-1201.03.
Funding, §2-1201.05.
Retail development incentives, §§2-1217.71 to 2-1217.84.
See RETAIL DEVELOPMENT INCENTIVES.
Tax increment financing.
General provisions, §§2-1217.01 to 2-1217.12.
See TAX INCREMENT FINANCING.

BUSINESS CORPORATION ACT OF 2010, §§29-301.01 to 29-314.02.
See CORPORATIONS.

BUSINESS, DISCRIMINATION BASED ON PLACE OF, §2-1401.01.

BUSINESS HIGH SCHOOL, §38-408.

BUSINESS HOLIDAYS.
Designation, §28-2701.
Extension of time for performing acts, §28-2701.

BUSINESS IMPROVEMENT DISTRICTS, §§2-1215.01 to 2-1215.71.
Accounting requirements, §2-1215.12.
Adams Morgan BID, §2-1215.56.
Adjacent or abutting properties, §2-1215.09a.
Amendment of plans for, §2-1215.08.
Anacostia BID, §2-1215.59.
Application for status as, §2-1215.04.
Articles of incorporation, §2-1215.08.
Boards of directors, §2-1215.07.
Budget, §2-1215.12.
Bylaws, §2-1215.08.
Capital riverfront BID, §2-1215.58.
Capitol Hill BID, §2-1215.54.
Categories of taxable real property, expanding, §2-1215.09b.
Newly established BID, §2-1215.09c.

BUSINESS IMPROVEMENT DISTRICTS —Cont'd
City services, maintenance of, §2-1215.20.
Definitions, §2-1215.02.
Dispute resolution procedures, §2-1215.16.
Dissolution of, §§2-1215.16, 2-1215.18.
Downtown BID, §2-1215.51.
Duration of, §2-1215.18.
Establishment of, §§2-1215.04, 2-1215.51 to 2-1215.60.
Provisions not to prohibit establishment in other areas, §2-1215.71.
Exempt real property in, §2-1215.21.
Expanding taxable real property within, §2-1215.09b.
Newly established BID, §2-1215.09c.
Expansion of geographic area of, §2-1215.09.
Adjacent or abutting properties, §2-1215.09a.
Functions, §2-1215.03.
Funds.
BID parking abatement fund, §1-325.341.
Georgetown BID, §2-1215.53.
Golden triangle BID, §2-1215.52.
Hearings on applications, §2-1215.06.
Inspections, §2-1215.12.
Issuance of rules and regulations, §2-1215.22.
Liability regarding, §2-1215.14.
Litter cleanup assistance fund, §1-325.111.
Meetings, §2-1215.10.
Mount Vernon triangle BID, §2-1215.55.
Newly established BID.
Categories of taxable real property, expanding, §2-1215.09c.
NoMa improvement association BID, §2-1215.57.
Parking.
BID parking abatement fund, §1-325.341.
Policy declaration, §2-1215.01.
Powers and duties, §§2-1215.07, 2-1215.16.
Prohibited acts, §2-1215.19.
Records, §2-1215.12.
Reports, §2-1215.13.
Review of applications, §2-1215.05.
Southwest BID, §2-1215.60.
Taxation, §§2-1215.15, 2-1215.17.
Collection and disbursement of BID taxes, §2-1215.15.

BUSINESS IMPROVEMENT DISTRICTS —Cont'd
Termination of, §2-1215.18.
Term of, §§2-1215.16, 2-1215.18.
Voting, §2-1215.11.

BUSINESS INCUBATORS.
Facilitation, §§2-1209.01 to 2-1209.14.

BUSINESS LICENSE CENTER, §§47-2851.05, 47-2851.06.

BUSINESS LICENSES, §§47-2805.01 to 47-2881.
Accountants, §§47-2853.41 to 47-2853.49.
Action to enforce provisions, §47-2844.
Additional licenses, §47-2851.12.
Air conditioner mechanics, §§47-2853.201 to 47-2853.203.
Ambulances, §47-2829.
Amusement parks, §47-2823.
Application for, §§47-2805.01, 47-2851.04.
Architects, §§47-2853.61 to 47-2853.63.
Armed forces personnel.
    Waiver of business license renewal fees for, §1-301.01.
Asbestos workers, §§47-2853.51 to 47-2853.53.
Athlete agents, §§47-2887.01 to 47-2887.18.
Auctioneers, §47-2808.
Barbers, §§47-2853.71 to 47-2853.73.
Barbershops, §§47-2809, 47-2810.
Basic business licenses, §§47-2851.01 to 47-2851.20.
    Amnesty period, §47-2851.19.
    Denial of, §47-2851.11.
    Departments and agencies, §47-2851.18.
    Fees, §47-2851.08.
    Fund, establishment of, §47-2851.13.
Bath houses, §47-2812.
Beauticians, §§47-2809, 47-2853.71 to 47-2853.73.
Beverages, §47-2827.
Billiard tables, §47-2821.
Body art establishments, §47-2809.01.
Body artists, §§47-2853.76a to 47-2853.76e.
Bonds, surety, §47-2844.
Bowling alleys, §47-2821.
Carnivals, §§47-2823, 47-2826.
Cease and desist order.
    Violations, §47-2844.01.
Center, §§47-2851.05, 47-2851.06.

BUSINESS LICENSES —Cont'd
Circuses, §47-2825.
Clean hands requirement, §§47-2861 to 47-2866.
Clubs, §47-2827.
Construction/construction manager license, §47-2851.03d.
Controlled substances, transactions involving, §47-2844.
Cosmetologists, §§47-2809, 47-2810, 47-2853.81 to 47-2853.83.
Council powers, §§47-2842, 47-2844.
Criteria, §47-2853.02.
Dairies, §47-2827.
Dangerous weapons, dealers in, §47-2838.
Debt owed District.
    Computer record-keeping and reporting system, §47-2866.
    Definitions, §47-2861.
    Issuance prohibited, §47-2862.
    Right to appeal denial of license, §47-2865.
    Self-certification of lack of outstanding debt, §47-2863.
    Falsification of certification, penalty, §47-2864.
Definitions, §§47-2807, 47-2851.01.
Denial.
    Applicant owing outstanding debt to state, §47-2862.
    Computer record-keeping and reporting system, §47-2866.
    Definitions, §47-2861.
    Right to appeal denial of license, §47-2865.
    Self-certification of lack of outstanding debt, §47-2863.
    Falsification of certification, penalty, §47-2864.
Disciplinary actions authorized against licensee, §47-2844.
Dry cleaners, §47-2817.
Dyeing establishments, §47-2817.
Electricians, §§47-2853.91 to 47-2853.93.
Elevator contractors, mechanics and inspectors.
    Eligibility, §47-2853.96.
    Fees, §47-2853.99.
    Temporary licenses, §47-2853.98.
Elimination.
    Existing licenses, §47-2851.03a.
    Requirements, §47-2842.
Endorsements, §47-2851.03.
    Third party inspections, §47-2851.16.

BUSINESS LICENSES —Cont'd

Engineers, §§47-2853.131 to 47-2853.133, 47-2853.211 to 47-2853.213.

Entertainment, §§47-2820 to 47-2826.

Exemptions, §47-2844.

Existing licenses.

Basic business license system, §47-2851.15.

Elimination of, §47-2851.03a.

Expiration dates, §§47-2805.01, 47-2851.09.

Explosives, §47-2814.

Fairs, §47-2826.

Fees, §§47-2844, 47-2851.04.

Armed forces personnel.

Waiver of business license renewal fees for, §1-301.01.

Basic business licenses, §47-2851.08.

Disposition of, §47-2851.13.

Erroneously paid, §47-2849.

Prorating fees for late application, §47-2805.01.

Refunds, §47-2849.

Renewal, §47-2851.08.

Trade names, §§47-2855.04, 47-2855.05.

Vehicles for hire, §47-2829.

Fines and civil penalties, §47-2844.

Disposition of, §47-2851.13.

Unpaid fines, penalties, and interest.

Computer recordkeeping and reporting system, §47-2866.

Definitions, §47-2861.

Issuance prohibited, §47-2862.

Right to appeal denial of license, §47-2865.

Self-certification of lack of outstanding debt, §47-2863.

Falsification of certification, penalty, §47-2864.

Firearm dealers, §§7-2504.01 to 7-2504.10.

See FIREARMS.

Fireworks, §47-2814.

Fish dealers, wholesale, §47-2827.

Food, §47-2827.

Funeral hearses, §47-2829.

Games establishments, §47-2821.

Gas-fitters, §§47-2853.121 to 47-2853.123.

Gas sales or storage, §47-2814.

General business license, §47-2851.03d.

Generally, §§47-2853.01 to 47-2853.30.

Groceries, §47-2827.

BUSINESS LICENSES —Cont'd

Guides, §47-2836.

Hairdressers, §§47-2809, 47-2810.

Hotline, §47-2881.

Identifying numbers, §47-2851.03b.

Illegal transactions, §47-2844.

Inspections, §47-2851.03c.

Third party, §47-2851.16.

Interagency computer system, §47-2866.

Interior designers, §§47-2853.101 to 47-2853.103.

Interns of surveyors, §47-2853.113.

Interpretation of provisions, §47-2807.

Issuance of licenses, §47-2851.07.

Issuance of rules and regulations, §47-2844.

Kerosene sales or storage, §47-2814.

Lapsed, §47-2851.10.

Late application for, §47-2805.01.

Laundries, §47-2817.

Massage parlors, §47-2811.

Mattresses, §47-2818.

Modification of requirements, §47-2842.

Motion pictures, §47-2820.

Motor vehicles, §§47-2829 to 47-2832.

See MOTOR VEHICLES.

MPD overtime reimbursement fund, §47-2826.

Oil sales or storage, §47-2814.

Operating engineers, §§47-2853.211 to 47-2853.213.

Parking establishments, §47-2832.01.

Passenger vehicles for hire, §47-2829.

Penalties, §47-2846.

Plumbers, §§47-2853.121 to 47-2853.123.

Pool tables, §47-2821.

Posting on premises, §47-2806.

Private clubs, §47-2827.

Private detectives, §47-2839.

Professional sports, §47-2823.

Professions and occupations, non-health related, §§47-2853.01 to 47-2853.224.

Property managers, §§47-2853.141 to 47-2853.143, 47-2853.181 to 47-2853.198.

Prorating fees for late application, §47-2805.01.

Prosecutions, §47-2845.

Public baths, §47-2812.

Public education and information programs, §47-2851.06.

BUSINESS LICENSES —Cont'd
Pyroxylin, §47-2815.
Real estate appraisers, §§47-2853.151 to 47-2853.154.
Real estate brokers and salespersons, §§47-2853.161 to 47-2853.198.
　See REAL ESTATE BROKERS AND SALESPERSONS.
Refrigerator mechanics, §§47-2853.201 to 47-2853.203.
Regulated non-health occupations and professions, §47-2853.04.
　Appeal and review, §47-2853.23.
　Boards.
　　Abolished board.
　　　Service of members until term expires, §47-2853.222.
　　　Transfer of personnel, property, records, funds, §47-2853.221.
　　Appointment, tenure, §47-2853.07.
　　Compensation and expenses, §47-2853.09.
　　Establishment of boards for regulated occupations and professions, §47-2853.06.
　　Immunity for actions taken, §47-2853.09.
　　Meetings, §47-2853.09.
　　Powers, §47-2853.08.
　　Quorum, §47-2853.09.
　　Staffing and administration, §47-2853.10.
　　Transfer from abolished boards, §47-2853.224.
　　Uniform procedures, adoption, §47-2853.09.
　Cease and desist order.
　　Issuance, §47-2853.17.
　Change of address.
　　Notice, §47-2853.16.
　Civil fines, penalties, fees, §§47-2853.17, 47-2853.29.
　Continuing education requirements.
　　Establishment by rule, §47-2853.12.
　Conviction bearing on fitness of person to be licensed, §§47-2853.12, 47-2853.17.
　Criminal violations, §47-2853.27.
　　Prosecutions, §47-2853.28.
　Criteria.
　　Waiver, §47-2853.12.
　Denial, §§47-2853.12, 47-2853.17.
　Display, §47-2853.16.
　Exceptions, §47-2853.04.
　Exemptions, federal services, §47-2853.05.

BUSINESS LICENSES —Cont'd
Regulated non-health occupations and professions —Cont'd
　Expired license.
　　Reinstatement, §47-2853.15.
　False representations of authority to practice, §47-2853.26.
　Final decision, §47-2853.22.
　Fines and penalties.
　　Civil alternatives, §47-2853.29.
　　Criminal penalties, §47-2853.27.
　　Prosecutions, §47-2853.28.
　Foreign graduates.
　　Granting license to, §47-2853.12.
　Hearings, §47-2853.22.
　Inactive status, §47-2853.14.
　Injunctions, §47-2853.30.
　License or certificate issued prior to effective date of subchapter, §47-2853.25.
　Licensure special account, §47-2853.11.
　Limitation of practice.
　　Voluntary, §47-2853.21.
　Mental or physical examination, §47-2853.17.
　Notice of hearing, §47-2853.22.
　Pending proceedings not to abate, §47-2853.223.
　Previously enacted rules to continue in effect, §47-2853.223.
　Probation, §47-2853.17.
　Reinstatement.
　　Expired license, §47-2853.15.
　　Suspended or revoked license, §47-2853.24.
　Remediation, course of, requiring, §47-2853.17.
　Renewal of license, certificate or registration, §47-2853.13.
　Reprimand of licensee, §47-2853.17.
　Requirements, §47-2853.12.
　Restriction without hearing, §47-2853.18.
　Revocation, §47-2853.17.
　　Reinstatement, §47-2853.24.
　Revocation of, §§47-2853.17 to 47-2853.24.
　Summary suspension, §47-2853.18.
　Surrender.
　　Voluntary surrender, §§47-2853.20, 47-2853.21.
　Suspension, §47-2853.17.
　　Reinstatement, §47-2853.24.
　Suspension of, §§47-2853.17 to 47-2853.24.
　Term, §47-2853.12.

BUSINESS LICENSES —Cont'd
Regulated non-health occupations and professions —Cont'd
Waiver of requirements, §47-2853.12.
Reinstated, §47-2851.10.
Rental properties, §47-2828.
Rental vehicles, §47-2830.
Requirements, §47-2851.02.
Restaurants, §47-2827.
Revocation of, §§47-2844, 47-2851.03c.
Savings clause, §47-2847.
School buses, §47-2829.
Scope of subchapter, §47-2853.03.
Sealing of premises, §47-2844.
Secondhand dealers, §47-2837.
Security agencies, §47-2839.01.
Severability of provisions, §47-2848.
Skating rinks, §47-2820.
Social security numbers, §47-2805.02.
Solicitations, door-to-door, §47-2835.
Special events, §47-2826.
Sports, §47-2823.
Steam engineers, §§47-2853.211 to 47-2853.213.
Stolen goods, transactions involving, §47-2844.
Supermarkets, §47-2827.
Surveyors, §§47-2853.111 to 47-2853.114.
Suspension of, §47-2844.
Swimming pools, §47-2824.
Targets, persons or animals used as, §47-2841.
Tax delinquency.
Computer record-keeping and reporting system, §47-2866.
Definitions, §47-2861.
Issuance prohibited, §47-2862.
Right to appeal denial of license, §47-2865.
Self-certification of lack of outstanding debt, §47-2863.
Falsification of certification, penalty, §47-2864.
Taxicabs, §47-2829.
Theatrical performances, §47-2820.
Third party inspections, §47-2851.16.
Tire dealers, §47-2832.02.
Trade names, §§47-2855.01 to 47-2855.05.
Unique identifying numbers, §47-2851.03b.
Vehicles for hire, §47-2829.
Wholesale fish dealers, §47-2827.
Workers' compensation.
Proof of coverage requirement, §47-2851.07.

BUSINESS OPERATIONS.
Powers of attorney, §21-2109.

BUSINESS ORGANIZATIONS, §§29-101.01 to 29-1304.01.
Administrative dissolution, §§29-106.01 to 29-106.04.
Effect of, §29-106.02.
Grounds, §29-106.01.
Procedures, §29-106.02.
Reinstatement, §29-106.03.
Judicial review of denial, §29-106.04.
Amendments.
Reservation of power to amend or repeal, §29-107.01.
Applicability of law, §29-101.03.
Benefit corporations, §§29-1301.01 to 29-1304.01.
See BENEFIT CORPORATIONS.
Certificates of good standing or registration, §29-102.08.
Construction of act.
Applicability, §29-107.03.
Reservation of power to amend or repeal, §29-107.01.
Rules applicable to organizations formed prior to effective date of act, §29-107.01.
Savings clause, §29-107.05.
Short title, §29-101.01.
Supplemental principles of law, §29-107.02.
Uniformity, §29-107.03.
Conversion.
Amendment or abandonment, §29-204.04.
Approval, §29-204.03.
Authorization, §29-204.01.
Foreign entities.
Withdrawal of registration to do business.
Domestic entity, conversion to, §29-105.09.
Nonfiling entity, conversion to, §29-105.10.
Plans, §29-204.02.
Statement of conversion, §29-204.05.
Cooperative associations, §§29-901 to 29-939.
See COOPERATIVE ASSOCIATIONS.
Corporate recordation fund, §29-102.03.
Corporations, §§29-301.01 to 29-314.02.
See CORPORATIONS.
Definitions, §29-101.02.

BUSINESS ORGANIZATIONS
—Cont'd
Delivery of records, §29-101.04.
Mayor, §29-102.10.
Dissolution.
Administrative dissolution,
§§29-106.01 to 29-106.04.
Effect of, §29-106.02.
Grounds, §29-106.01.
Procedures, §29-106.02.
Reinstatement, §29-106.03.
Judicial review of denial,
§29-106.04.
Cooperative associations, §29-934.
Corporations, §§29-312.01 to
29-312.40.
Foreign entities.
Withdrawal of registration,
§29-105.10.
Limited cooperative associations,
§§29-1012.01 to 29-1012.13.
See LIMITED COOPERATIVE
ASSOCIATIONS.
Limited liability companies,
§§29-807.01 to 29-807.07.
Limited partnerships, §§29-708.01 to
29-708.11.
Nonprofit corporations, §§29-412.01 to
29-412.30.
See NONPROFIT CORPORATIONS.
Partnerships, §§29-608.01 to
29-608.12.
See PARTNERSHIPS.
Professional corporations, §29-516.
Series trusts, §29-1204.04.
Statutory trusts, §§29-1208.01 to
29-1208.06.
Title insurers, §31-5031.09.
Unincorporated nonprofit associations,
§29-1124.
Domestication, §§29-205.01 to
29-205.06.
Amendment or abandonment,
§29-205.04.
Approval, §29-205.03.
Authorization, §29-205.01.
Corporations, §§29-307.01 to
29-307.06.
See CORPORATIONS.
Effect of, §29-205.06.
Limited liability companies,
§§29-809.06 to 29-809.11.
See LIMITED LIABILITY
COMPANIES.
Nonprofit corporations, §§29-407.01 to
29-407.06.
See NONPROFIT CORPORATIONS.

BUSINESS ORGANIZATIONS
—Cont'd
Domestication —Cont'd
Plans, §29-205.02.
Statement of domestication,
§29-205.05.
Entity transactions, §§29-201.01 to
29-205.06.
See ENTITY TRANSACTIONS.
E-SIGN Act.
Relation to, §29-107.04.
Filing, §§29-102.01 to 29-102.13.
Biennial report, §29-102.11.
Certificates of good standing or
registration, §29-102.08.
Corporate recordation fund,
§29-102.03.
Corrections to filed record, §29-102.05.
Deceased individual, signing entity
filing on behalf of, §29-102.09.
Delivery of records by mayor,
§29-102.10.
Duty of mayor, §29-102.06.
Effective date, §29-102.03.
Effectiveness without signature,
§29-102.09.
Electronic transmission of record or
notice, §29-102.10.
Evidentiary effect of copy of filed
record, §29-102.07.
Failure of individual to sign or deliver
entity filing.
Remedies, §29-102.09.
Fees, §29-102.12.
Disposition, §29-102.13.
Forms, §29-102.02.
Incorrect information within record.
Recovery from signer with
knowledge that information was
incorrect, §29-102.09.
Registered agents.
Addresses, §29-104.03.
Requirements, §29-102.01.
Review of refusal to file, §29-102.06.
Signing as affirmation, §29-102.09.
Withdrawal of filed record, §29-102.04.
Fines and civil penalties, §29-101.06.
Foreign entities, §§29-105.01 to
29-105.12.
Activities not constituting doing
business, §29-105.05.
Attorney general actions, §29-105.12.
Conversion to domestic filing entity or
domestic LLP.
Effect as withdrawal of registration,
§29-105.08.

BUSINESS ORGANIZATIONS
—Cont'd
Foreign entities —Cont'd
Foreign registration statement,
§29-105.03.
Amendments, §29-105.04.
Governing law, §29-105.01.
Merger with nonregistered foreign
entity.
Transfer of registration, §29-105.10.
Name registration, §29-103.04.
Noncomplying names, §29-105.06.
Registration to do business,
§29-105.02.
Termination of, §29-105.11.
Transfer of, §29-105.10.
Withdrawal of, §29-105.07.
Conversion to domestic entity,
§29-105.09.
Conversion to nonfiling entity,
§29-105.10.
Dissolution, §29-105.10.
Interest exchanges, §§29-203.01 to
29-203.06.
Amendment or abandonment,
§29-203.04.
Approval, §29-203.03.
Authorization, §29-203.01.
Corporations.
Share exchanges, §§29-309.01 to
29-309.08.
See CORPORATIONS.
Effect of, §29-203.06.
Nonprofit corporations.
Membership exchanges, §§29-409.01
to 29-409.08.
See NONPROFIT
CORPORATIONS.
Partnerships, §29-609.05.
Plans, §29-203.02.
Statement of interest exchange,
§29-203.05.
Limited cooperative associations,
§§29-1001.01 to 29-1015.08.
See LIMITED COOPERATIVE
ASSOCIATIONS.
Limited liability companies,
§§29-801.01 to 29-810.01.
See LIMITED LIABILITY
COMPANIES.
Limited partnerships, §§29-701.01 to
29-711.01.
See LIMITED PARTNERSHIPS.
Mergers and consolidations,
§§29-202.01 to 29-202.06.
Names, §§29-103.01 to 29-103.04.
Consent to use of name by another
registered entity, §29-103.01.

BUSINESS ORGANIZATIONS
—Cont'd
Names —Cont'd
Foreign entities.
Noncomplying names, §29-105.06.
Registration of name, §29-103.04.
Misleading names prohibited,
§29-103.01.
Permitted names, §29-103.01.
Registration of, §29-103.04.
Requirements, §29-103.02.
Reservation of, §29-103.03.
Words prohibited in entity name,
§29-103.01.
Nonprofit corporations, §§29-401.01
to 29-401.03.
See NONPROFIT CORPORATIONS.
Partnerships, §§29-601.01 to 29-611.01.
See PARTNERSHIPS.
Procedures, §29-101.05.
Professional corporations, §§29-501
to 29-516.
See PROFESSIONAL
CORPORATIONS.
Registered agents, §§29-104.01 to
29-104.14.
Addresses.
Filing, §29-104.03.
Change of agent, §29-104.07.
Change of name, address, type of
entity or jurisdiction of formation.
Commercial registered agents,
§29-104.09.
Noncommercial registered agents,
§29-104.08.
Commercial registered agents.
Change of name, address, type of
entity or jurisdiction of
formation, §29-104.09.
Listing, §29-104.05.
Termination of listing, §29-104.06.
Definitions, §29-104.01.
Designation, §29-104.04.
Nonregistered foreign entity or
nonfiling domestic entity,
§29-104.11.
Duties, §29-104.13.
Entities required to designate and
maintain, §29-104.02.
Mayor as entity for service where no
agent designated, §29-104.12.
Noncommercial registered agents.
Change of name, address, type of
entity or jurisdiction of
formation, §29-104.08.
Personal jurisdiction, §29-104.14.

BUSINESS ORGANIZATIONS
—Cont'd
Registered agents —Cont'd
Resignation of, §29-104.10.
Service of process and papers,
§29-104.12.
Reinstatement, §29-106.03.
Judicial review of denial, §29-106.04.
Rulemaking, §29-101.05.
**Rules applicable to organizations
formed prior to effective date of
act,** §29-107.01.
Short title, §29-101.01.
Statutory trusts, §§29-1201.01 to
29-1209.01.
See STATUTORY TRUSTS.
**Unincorporated nonprofit
associations,** §§29-1101 to 29-1127.
See NONPROFIT ASSOCIATIONS,
UNINCORPORATED.

BUSINESS RECORDS.
Civil proceedings, CivPro Rule 43-I.
Family court proceedings generally,
FamDiv Rule Q.
Interrogatories.
Option to produce business records,
CivPro Rule 33.
Domestic relations actions, DomRel
Rule 33.

BUSINESS START UP COSTS.
Opportunity accounts.
Generally, §§1-307.61 to 1-307.74.
Use for, §1-307.68.

BUS SHELTERS, §§9-1151 to 9-1161.
Advertising space, §9-1154.
Compensation to district government
from advertising revenues,
§9-1155.
Exemption from building code
provisions pertaining to outdoor
signs, §9-1159.
Findings of council, §9-1151.
**Franchise agreement for installation
and maintenance,** §9-1152.
Advertising space.
Exemption from building code
provisions pertaining to outdoor
signs, §9-1159.
Sale by franchisee, §9-1154.
Compensation to district
government, §9-1155.
Bonds, surety, §9-1156.
Compensation to district government
under, §9-1155.
Insurance, §9-1156.

BUS SHELTERS —Cont'd
**Franchise agreement for installation
and maintenance** —Cont'd
Selection of franchisee, §9-1158.
Termination, §9-1157.
Locations, §9-1153.
Purpose of provisions, §9-1151.
Regulations, §9-1160.
Severability of provisions, §9-1161.

BUS STOPS.
Smoking restrictions, §7-1703.
Bus stop defined, §7-1702.

BUY-AMERICAN PROVISIONS.
**Mental health services
administration,** §44-909.

BUZZARDS POINT.
Railroad track extensions,
§9-1203.01.

BYLAWS.
Advisory neighborhood commission,
§1-309.11.
Bar association, DCBar Rule IX.
Amendment, DCBar Rule XV.
Business improvement districts,
§2-1215.08.
**Cemeteries and cemetery
associations,** §43-110.
Condominiums, §§42-1902.04,
42-1903.01, 42-1904.10.
Credit unions, §26-503.
Fraternal benefit societies, §31-5302.
Horizontal property regimes,
§§42-2013, 42-2014.
**Trust, mortgage and title
corporations,** §26-1325.

C

CABLE TELEVISION, §§34-1251.01 to
34-1264.06.
Accounts.
Cable television special account,
§34-1252.03.
Affirmative action.
Employment, §34-1262.02.
Bonds, surety.
Franchises.
Performance bond, §34-1256.05.
Security fund, §34-1256.02.
**Broadcasting industry employment
contracts,** §§32-531 to 32-533.
Cable television special account,
§34-1252.03.
Compliance required, §34-1263.01.

CABLE TELEVISION —Cont'd
Construction and operation of cable system, §§34-1257.01 to 34-1257.06.
Bandwidth requirement, §34-1257.01.
Best efforts, duty to exercise, §34-1257.02.
Construction generally, §34-1257.04.
Construction notice to public, §34-1257.05.
Construction schedule, §34-1257.03.
Excavation work in public right of way, §34-1257.04.
General requirements, §34-1257.02.
Jurisdictional parity, §34-1257.01.
Locating underground, §34-1257.04.
Removal, replacement of facilities, §34-1257.04.
Use of existing poles and other facilities, §34-1257.04.
Use of system by District during emergency or disaster, §34-1257.06.
Consumer protection, §34-1260.01.
Competition and consumer choice, §34-1261.01.
Protection of privacy, §34-1260.02.
Correspondence with federal or District agencies, §34-1259.06.
Crimes and offenses.
Cable theft, §34-1264.02.
Definitions.
Office of cable television, film, music, and entertainment amendment act of 2015, §34-1251.03.
Disasters.
Use of system during emergencies or disasters, §34-1257.06.
Discrimination prohibition, §§34-1262.01 to 34-1262.03.
Affirmative action in employment, §34-1262.02.
Employment, §34-1262.01.
District residents, §34-1262.03.
Tenants of rental property, §34-1261.01.
Educational channels.
PEG Channels, §§34-1258.01 to 34-1258.03.
Emergencies.
Use of system during emergencies or disasters, §34-1257.06.
Employment.
Affirmative action, §34-1262.02.
District residents, §34-1262.03.
Non-discrimination, §34-1262.01.
Enforcement.
Compliance required, §34-1263.01.

CABLE TELEVISION —Cont'd
Enforcement —Cont'd
Specific performance, §34-1263.02.
Willful repeated violations, §34-1263.03.
Executive director.
Cable television special account, §34-1252.03.
Office of cable television, film, music, and entertainment, §34-1252.01.
Facilities.
Construction, §34-1257.04.
Fees.
Franchises, §34-1256.01.
Subscriber fees, §34-1259.08.
Franchises, §§34-1254.01 to 34-1254.08.
Application for initial franchise, §34-1254.02.
Evaluation, §34-1254.03.
Arbitration.
Purchase price upon purchase of cable system by District, §34-1255.07.
Fees, §34-1256.01.
Franchise agreement.
Minimum contents, §34-1254.05.
Negotiation of initial agreement, §34-1254.04.
Required, §34-1254.01.
Indemnification of District, §34-1256.03.
Insurance requirements, §34-1256.04.
Open video systems.
Franchise required for operation, §34-1251.04.
Operator as trustee.
Termination or revocation of franchise, §34-1255.06.
Renewal of franchise, §34-1254.07.
Transfer or purchase of franchise upon denial, §34-1255.05.
Required, §34-1254.01.
Review and approval of initial franchise, §34-1254.06.
Review prior to expiration of franchise, §34-1254.08.
Revocation, §34-1255.04.
Operator as trustee, §34-1255.06.
Willful repeated violations, §34-1263.03.
Security fund, §34-1256.02.
Transfer of franchise to District.
Mandatory transfer, §34-1255.03.
Revocation of franchise, §34-1255.04.
Transfer of franchise to person other than District.
Approval required, §34-1255.01.

CABLE TELEVISION —Cont'd
Franchises —Cont'd
Transfer of franchise to person other
than District —Cont'd
Procedure, §34-1255.02.
Transfer or purchase of franchise upon
denial of renewal, §34-1255.05.
Government channels.
PEG Channels, §§34-1258.01 to
34-1258.03.
Indemnification of District,
§34-1256.03.
Inspections.
Records, §34-1259.05.
Right to inspect, §34-1259.01.
Insurance.
Franchises, §34-1256.04.
Landlord and tenant.
Interference by landlord with
installation, maintenance, etc.,
§34-1261.01.
Non-discrimination.
Employment, §34-1262.01.
Notice to public.
Construction, §34-1257.05.
Obscenity laws.
Compliance, §34-1264.01.
Office.
Maintenance of business office,
§34-1260.01.
**Office of cable television, film,
music, and entertainment,**
§§34-1252.01 to 34-1252.03.
Cable television special account,
§34-1252.03.
Established, §34-1252.01.
Executive director, §34-1252.01.
Powers and responsibilities,
§34-1252.02.
**Office of cable television, film,
music, and entertainment
amendment act of 2015,**
§§34-1251.01 to 34-1264.06.
Open video systems.
Applicability of chapter, §34-1251.04.
Defined, §34-1251.03.
Franchise required for operation,
§34-1251.04.
Other cable entities, §§34-1253.02,
34-1253.03.
PEG Channels, §§34-1258.01 to
34-1258.03.
Performance evaluations,
§34-1259.03.
Public access.
PEG Channels, §§34-1258.01 to
34-1258.03.
Allocation, §34-1258.03.

CABLE TELEVISION —Cont'd
Public access —Cont'd
PEG Channels —Cont'd
Carriage requirements, §34-1258.01.
Funding, §34-1258.02.
Public access corporation,
§34-1253.02.
Public service commission.
Generally.
See PUBLIC SERVICE
COMMISSION.
Regulation of rights of way,
§34-1253.03.
Rates.
Regulation of, §34-1259.07.
Records.
Correspondence with federal or
District agencies, §34-1259.06.
Inspection, §34-1259.05.
Retention, §34-1259.04.
Reports, §34-1259.09.
Rights of way.
Public service commission.
Regulation of rights of way,
§34-1253.03.
Rights reserved by District,
§34-1264.03.
Rules, §34-1264.04.
Service offerings.
Regulation, §34-1259.07.
Short title.
Office of cable television, film, music,
and entertainment amendment
act of 2015, §34-1251.01.
Specific performance, §34-1263.02.
Subscriber fees, §34-1259.08.
System.
Construction and operation of cable
system, §§34-1257.01 to
34-1257.06.
Regulation, oversight and inspection,
§§34-1259.01 to 34-1259.09.
System monitor tests, §34-1259.02.
Taxation, §47-2501.01.
Technical performance tests,
§34-1259.02.
Tests and monitoring, §34-1259.02.
Performance evaluations, §34-1259.03.
Theft.
Cable theft, §34-1264.02.
Toll telecommunication service tax,
§§47-3901 to 47-3922.
See TOLL TELECOMMUNICATION
SERVICE TAX.
Transition provisions, §34-1264.05.
Additional transition provisions,
§34-1264.06.

CABLE TELEVISION SPECIAL ACCOUNT, §34-1252.03.

CADET PROGRAM.
Fire departments, §§5-418, 5-419.
Metropolitan police, §§5-109.01, 5-109.02.
Minimum and maximum ages, §2-1402.12.

CALIFORNIA VEHICLE EMISSIONS STANDARDS.
Low-emissions vehicle program.
Adoption of California standards and compliance requirements, §50-731.
Vehicle not in compliance.
Registering prohibited, §50-732.

CALL BEFORE YOU DIG, §§34-2701 to 34-2709.
See MISS UTILITY.

CALVERT STREET BRIDGE, §9-324.

CAMERAS.
Metropolitan police.
Body-worn camera program, §§5-116.31 to 5-116.33.

CAMERAS IN THE COURTROOM.
Superior court proceedings, CivPro Rule 203, CrimPro Rule 53.
Child abuse and neglect proceedings, NeglectProc Rule 45.
Juvenile proceedings, JuvProc Rule 53.
United States District Court proceedings, USDistCt LCrR 53.1.1, USDistCt LCvR 83.1.

CAMPAIGN FINANCE, §§1-1163.01 to 1-1163.38.
Advisory opinions, §1-1163.06.
Board of elections, §§1-1001.02 to 1-1001.06.
Campaign literature identification, §1-1163.15.
Certifications.
Reports, §1-1163.13.
Citation of provisions, §1-1163.01.
Committees, §§1-1163.07 to 1-1163.27.
Aggregate and individual contribution limits to exploratory committees, §1-1163.19.
Campaign literature identification, §1-1163.15.
Contributions to exploratory committees, §1-1163.20.
Contributions to inaugural committees, §1-1163.22.
Contributions to transition committees, §1-1163.26.

CAMPAIGN FINANCE —Cont'd
Committees —Cont'd
Depositories, §1-1163.08.
Duration of exploratory committees, §1-1163.21.
Duration of inaugural committees, §1-1163.24.
Duration of transition committees, §1-1163.27.
Expense exemptions, §1-1163.14.
Financial liabilities, §1-1163.16.
Fund balance requirements of exploratory committees, §1-1163.18.
Fund balance requirements of inaugural committees, §1-1163.23.
Fund balance requirements of transition committees, §1-1163.25.
Organization, §1-1163.07.
Organization statements, §1-1163.11.
Principal campaign committee, §1-1163.10.
Organization statements, §1-1163.11.
Registration statements of candidates, §1-1163.12.
Reports, §1-1163.09.
Receipts and expenditures, §1-1163.17.
Constituent services.
Mayor and chairman and members of council.
Contributions for purposes of services, §1-1163.38.
Contributions.
Limitations on, §1-1163.33.
Director of campaign finances, §§1-1163.02 to 1-1163.06.
Duties, §1-1163.04.
Enforcement of chapter, §1-1163.02.
Office established, §1-1163.02.
Powers, §1-1163.03.
Elections board created, §1-1163.05.
Enforcement of provisions, §1-1163.02.
Expense exemptions, §1-1163.14.
Exploratory committees.
Aggregate and individual contribution limits, §1-1163.19.
Contributions, §1-1163.20.
Duration, §1-1163.21.
Fund balance requirements of, §1-1163.18.
Financial liabilities of candidate, §1-1163.16.
Fund balance requirements.
Exploratory committees, §1-1163.18.

CAMPAIGN FINANCE —Cont'd
Fund balance requirements —Cont'd
Inaugural committees, §1-1163.23.
Principal campaign committees,
§1-1163.10a.
Transition committees, §1-1163.25.
**Government employees engaging
political activities,** §§1-1171.01 to
1-1171.07.
See POLITICAL ACTIVITIES BY
GOVERNMENT EMPLOYEES.
Government resource prohibitions,
§1-1163.36.
Identifications.
Reports, §1-1163.13.
Inaugural committees.
Contributions to, §1-1163.22.
Duration, §1-1163.24.
Fund balance requirements,
§1-1163.23.
Legal defense committees,
§§1-1163.28, 1-1163.29.
Receipt and expenditure reports,
§§1-1163.31, 1-1163.32.
Legal defense depositories,
§1-1163.30.
Oaths and affirmations, §1-1163.37.
**Office of director of campaign
finances,** §§1-1163.02 to 1-1163.06.
Partnership contributions,
§1-1163.34.
Penalties, §1-1163.35.
Principal campaign committee.
Fund balance requirements,
§1-1163.10a.
**Registration statements of
candidates,** §1-1163.12.
Reports, §§1-1163.09, 1-1163.13.
Legal defense committees, §§1-1163.31,
1-1163.32.
Persons other than political
committees and candidates,
§1-1001.07.
Preservation of copy of report filed,
§1-1001.08.
Receipts and expenditures, §1-1163.17.
Requirements, §1-1001.08.
Verified by oath or affirmation of
person filing, §1-1001.08.
Statehood initiative.
Senators or representative elected to
represent District, §1-135.
Transition committees.
Contributions to, §1-1163.26.
Duration of, §1-1163.27.
Fund balance requirements,
§1-1163.25.

CAMPBELL HEIGHTS PROJECT.
Real property tax exemptions,
§47-4632.

CANADA.
**Insurance company annual audited
financial reports,** §31-314.

CANALS.
Bridges as rights-of-way over, §9-302.
**Public spaces resulting from filling
in of,** §10-139.

CANCER.
Cervical cancer.
Human papillomavirus vaccination,
§§7-1651.01 to 7-1651.05.
Chemotherapy pill coverage,
§§31-2995.01 to 31-2995.03.
Colorectal cancer screening.
Health insurance coverage, §31-2931.
**District of Columbia general
hospital hospice program,**
§§4-1101 to 4-1105.
Grants, §7-736.01.
Mammograms, §§31-2901 to 31-2903.
Applicability, §31-2903.
Definitions, §31-2901.
Payable benefits, §31-2902.
**Presumption as to disability or
death resulting from.**
Fire and emergency medical services
employees, §5-653.
Prevention and monitoring, §§7-301
to 7-304.
Prostate cancer screening.
Health insurance coverage, §§31-2951
to 31-2954.
Reporting, §§7-301 to 7-304.
Confidentiality of records reporting
disease, §7-302.
Medial examination or treatment not
required by chapter, §7-303.
Rules to prevent and monitor
occurrence on District, §7-301.
Violations, penalties, prosecution,
§7-304.

C. & F.
Sale of goods, UCC, §§28:2-320,
28:2-321.

CAPACITY.
Attorneys at law.
Clients with diminished capacity.
Client-lawyer relationship, ProfCond
Rule 1.14.
Incompetent or incapacitated
attorneys, DCBar Rule XI,
USDistCt LCrR 57.30, USDistCt
LCvR 83.19.

CAPACITY —Cont'd
Law determining capacity, CivPro Rule 17.
Domestic relations actions, DomRel Rule 17.
Pleading special matters, CivPro Rule 9.
Domestic relations actions, DomRel Rule 9.
Real property transfers on death.
Capacity of transferor, §19-604.08.
Trusts and trustees.
Uniform trust code.
Revocable trusts.
Settlor's capacity, §19-1306.01.

CAPITAL ACCESS PROGRAM.
Capital access fund, §2-1210.02.
Definitions, §§1-325.171, 2-1210.01.
District liability prohibited, §2-1210.11.
Establishment of program, §§1-325.173, 2-1210.03.
Fees to be paid by borrowers, §2-1210.06.
Financial institutions.
Fees to be paid by borrowers, §2-1210.06.
Minimum eligibility requirements, §2-1210.04.
Reports.
Financial institution reports, §2-1210.09.
Mayor's status report, §2-1210.10.
Reserve accounts, §2-1210.06.
District's rights, §2-1210.08.
Limitations on District's contribution, §2-1210.07.
Rules, §2-1210.12.
Fund.
Establishment, §1-325.172.
Use of funds, §1-325.172.
Line of credit.
Minimum requirements, §2-1210.04.
Loans.
Ineligible loans, §2-1210.05.
Minimum requirements, §2-1210.04.
Sale of enrolled loan on secondary market, §2-1210.05.
Mayor's authority, §§1-325.172, 1-325.173.
Participation agreements, §2-1210.04.
Reports.
Quarterly and annual, §2-1210.09.
Reserve accounts.
District's rights, §2-1210.08.
Establishment by financial institutions, §2-1210.06.

CAPITAL ACCESS PROGRAM —Cont'd
Reserve accounts —Cont'd
Limitations on District's contribution, §2-1210.07.

CAPITAL FUNDS.
Expending on operating expenses, prohibition, §1-301.77.

CAPITAL OFFENSES.
Appeals.
Stay of execution, CrimPro Rule 38.
Indictments and information.
Capital offenses to be prosecuted by indictment, CrimPro Rule 7.

CAPITAL PROJECT SUPPORT FUND, §§1-325.151 to 1-325.156.
Alley rehabilitation project, §1-325.156.
Capital budget memoranda of understanding, closure, §1-325.153a.
Definitions, §1-325.151.
Established, §1-325.152.
Expenditures, §1-325.153.
Reporting requirements, §1-325.154.
Surplus capital funds, transfer, §§1-325.153a, 1-325.153b.
Washington Metropolitan Area Transit Authority project.
Funds reprogramed for, §1-325.155.

CAPITAL REVIEW AND DEBT AFFORDABILITY COMMITTEE, §§47-336 to 47-340.
Bonds and capital lease financing.
Duties, §47-338.
Chairperson, §47-337.
Definitions, §47-336.
Duties, §47-338.
Established, §47-337.
Members, §47-337.

CAPITATION TAX.
Constitution of the United States,
US Const Art I §9.
Elections.
Denial or abridgement of right to vote for failure to pay poll tax prohibited, US Const Amd 24.

CAPITOL GROUNDS, §§10-503.01 to 10-503.26.
Advertising on, §10-503.14.
Architect of the Capitol, §10-503.11.
Assemblages on, §10-503.17.
Begging on, §10-503.14.
Boundaries, §10-503.11.

CAPITOL GROUNDS —Cont'd

Capitol employees' duty to assist enforcement authorities, §10-503.21.

Concerts, §10-503.24.

Definitions, §10-503.26.

Demonstrations on, §10-503.17.

Explosives prohibition, §10-503.16.

Fines, §10-503.18.

Firearms prohibition, §10-503.16.

Issuance of rules and regulations, §10-503.01.

Mayor's responsibilities regarding, §10-503.11.

Obstruction of roads, prohibition of, §10-503.13.

Parades on, §10-503.17.

Penalties, §10-503.18.

Police.
See CAPITOL POLICE.

Prohibited acts, §§10-503.02 to 10-503.17.

Property on, removal or injury of, §10-503.15.

Prosecution of violations, §10-503.18.

Public travel restricted to roads, walks, and places, §10-503.12.

Real property tax special assessments to improve streets around, §47-1207.

Restoration of grounds following construction of tunnel under, §10-511.04.

Sale of goods on, §10-503.14.

Suspension of prohibitions regarding, §§10-503.22, 10-503.23.

Traffic laws, §10-503.25.

Tunnel under, §§10-511.01 to 10-511.07.

Weapons prohibition, §10-503.16.

CAPITOL HILL COMMUNITY GARDEN LAND TRUST.

Real property tax exemptions, §47-1054.
Lot 0109 in square 1100, §47-1061.

CAPITOL POLICE.

Appropriations, §10-505.06.

Capitol employees' duty to assist, §10-503.21.

Congressional employee, creditable service as, §10-505.03.

Congressional personnel, protection of, §10-503.20.

Definitions, §10-505.05.

Effective date of provisions, §10-505.07.

CAPITOL POLICE —Cont'd

Federal law enforcement officer cooperative agreements, §§5-301 to 5-303.

Lateral police career appointments, §§1-610.71 to 1-610.76.

Metropolitan police detailed to, §§10-505.01 to 10-505.07.

Police and firefighters retirement and disability, §10-505.04.

Powers and duties of, §§10-503.02, 10-503.19, 10-503.20.

Suspension of prohibitions regarding Capitol grounds, §§10-503.22, 10-503.23.

Traffic laws, §10-503.25.

Transfer of detailed Metropolitan police member to, §§10-505.02, 10-505.03.

CAPPER/CARROLLSBURG PILOT.

Payments in lieu of taxes, §47-4611.

CAPTIONS FOR PLEADINGS, MOTIONS, ETC., CivPro Rule 10, USDistCt LCvR 5.1, USDistCt LCvR 11.1.

Adoption proceedings, Adoption Rule 10.

Domestic relations actions, DomRel Rule 10.

Hospitalization of persons with mental illness, MentalHealth Rule 14.

CAPTIVE INSURANCE AGENCY ESTABLISHMENT ACT OF 2008, §§1-307.81 to 1-307.95.
See MEDICAL LIABILITY CAPTIVE INSURANCE AGENCY.

CAPTIVE INSURANCE COMPANIES, §§31-3931.01 to 31-3931.23.

Appeals.
Judicial review of commissioner, §31-3931.20.

Applicable laws, §31-3931.22.

Capital requirements, §31-3931.06.
Special purpose financial captive insurance companies, §31-3932.05.

Captive insurance agency establishment act of 2008, §§1-307.81 to 1-307.95.
See MEDICAL LIABILITY CAPTIVE INSURANCE AGENCY.

Certificate of authority.
Application for, §31-3931.09.
Required, §31-3931.11.

CAPTIVE INSURANCE COMPANIES
—Cont'd
Certificate of authority —Cont'd
Revocation or suspension, §31-3931.15.
Definitions, §31-3931.01.
Examinations of financial condition by commissioner, §31-3931.14.
Fines.
Imposition by commissioner, §31-3931.15.
Incorporation, §31-3931.03.
Insolvency, §31-3931.16.
Investments, §31-3931.07.
Mandamus, §31-3931.20.
Medical liability captive insurance agency, §§1-307.81 to 1-307.95.
See MEDICAL LIABILITY CAPTIVE INSURANCE AGENCY.
Names, §31-3931.10.
Prohibited activities, §31-3931.02.
Protected cell captive insurers, §31-3931.04.
Protective cells.
Defined, §31-3931.01.
Liquidation and rehabilitation, §31-3931.05.
Rating organizations.
Joining not required, §31-3931.18.
Redomestication, §31-3931.17.
Regulations, §31-3931.21.
Regulatory and supervision trust account, §31-3931.19.
Reinsurance, §31-3931.08.
Reports.
Annual report, §31-3931.13.
Segregated accounts.
Capital and surplus, §31-3932.05.
Special purpose financial captive insurance companies, §§31-3932.01 to 31-3932.15.
Applicability of provisions, §31-3932.03.
Authorized contracts, §31-3932.07.
Capital and surplus requirements, §31-3932.05.
Certificate of authority.
Application requirements, §31-3932.04.
Contents of applications, §31-3932.04.
Grounds for denial, §31-3932.04.
Satisfaction of capital requirements, §31-3932.05.
Confidentiality of examination reports, §31-3932.10.
Contested case by a third party.
Standards and criteria applicable, §31-3932.14.

CAPTIVE INSURANCE COMPANIES
—Cont'd
Special purpose financial captive insurance companies —Cont'd
Discount on reserves, §31-3932.13.
Dividends and distributions, §31-3932.09.
Examination reports.
Disclosure of information, §31-3932.10.
Exemption from provisions, §31-3932.03.
Goals of legislation, §31-3932.01.
Letters of credit.
Satisfaction of capital requirements, §31-3932.05.
Liquidation and rehabilitation, §31-3932.12.
Public policy, §31-3932.01.
Reinsurance, §31-3932.11.
Report on reserves, §31-3932.13.
Reserves, §31-3932.13.
Rulemaking authority, §31-3932.15.
Securities of SPFCs, §31-3932.06.
SPFC strategic business plan, §31-3932.04.
Swap transaction.
Change and substitution in a counterparty, §31-3932.04.
Termination or cancellation of an SPFC contract.
Effect on certificate of authority, §31-3932.04.
Trust requirements, §31-3932.08.
Surplus requirements, §31-3931.06.
Special purpose financial captive insurance companies, §31-3932.05.
Taxation.
Premiums collected, §31-3931.12.
Transacting business.
Authority to do business, §31-3931.02.
Organizational requirements, §§31-3931.03, 31-3931.11.
Transitional provisions, §31-3931.23.

CAPTIVE INSURANCE COMPANY REGULATORY AND SUPERVISION TRUST ACCOUNT, §31-3931.19.

CARBON MONOXIDE DETECTORS.
Funding of purchase of detectors and batteries, §6-751.05c.
Outreach program to test and install detectors, §6-751.05a.
Report on detector and battery program from previous year, §6-751.05b.

CARBURETION TUBES AND DEVICES.
Drug paraphernalia, §§48-904.10, 48-1101 to 48-1104.

CARDIAC ARREST.
Automated external defibrillators.
Usage, §§44-231 to 44-235.
Non-resuscitation procedures for EMS.
Comfort care orders, §§7-651.01 to 7-651.16.
See EMERGENCY MEDICAL SERVICES.
Presumption as to disability or death resulting from.
Fire and emergency medical services employees, §5-652.

CARDIOPULMONARY RESUSCITATION.
Non-resuscitation procedures for EMS.
Comfort care orders, §§7-651.01 to 7-651.16.
See EMERGENCY MEDICAL SERVICES.

CAREER SERVICE, §§1-608.01, 1-611.02, 1-611.04.

CAREFIRST.
Tax credit for wages, sales tax exemption, §47-4602.

CARJACKING, §22-2803.
Aged persons, offenses committed against.
Enhanced penalties, §22-3601.

CARNIVALS.
Business licenses, §§47-2823, 47-2826.
Display of circus, carnival or other special event animals.
Permit required, §8-1808.
Recycling, §47-2826.

CAROTID ARTERY HOLDS.
Metropolitan police restrictions, §5-125.03.

CARRIAGEWAYS.
Parks and recreation, §10-138.

CARRIERS.
Commercial drivers' licenses, §§50-401 to 50-409.
See COMMERCIAL DRIVERS' LICENSES.
Damages.
Limitation of liability.
Carrier issuing bill of lading, §28:7-309.

CARRIERS —Cont'd
Liens, §28:7-307.
Enforcement, §28:7-308.
Negligence.
Contractual limitation of liability.
Bill of lading, §28:7-309.
Duty of carrier.
Carrier issuing bill of lading, §28:7-309.

CAR SERVICES.
Impoundment of vehicles, §50-331.
Private vehicles-for-hire, §§50-301.29a to 50-301.29g.
Public vehicles for hire exclusive of taxicabs and limousines, §50-301.29.

CARSHARING SERVICE.
Private vehicles-for-hire, §§50-301.29a to 50-301.29g.

CARVER 2000 LOW-INCOME AND SENIOR HOUSING PROJECT.
Tax exemptions, §47-4605.

CASA VOLUNTEERS, §§16-2371, 16-2372.

CASE MANAGEMENT/ELECTRONIC CASE FILING SYSTEM.
United States District Court, USDistCt LCvR 5.4.

CASEY MANSION.
Designation as mayor's official resident, §1-331.10.

CASH FLOW STATEMENTS.
Budgets and budget estimates, §47-318.05.

CASHIER'S CHECKS.
Defined, §28:3-104.
Payment.
Obligation of issuer, §28:3-412.
Refusal to pay, §28:3-411.

CASUALTY INSURANCE.
Fire and casualty insurance.
See FIRE AND CASUALTY INSURANCE.

CATERERS.
Alcoholic beverage licenses.
Application procedure, §25-313.
On-premises retailers, §25-113.

CATHOLIC UNIVERSITY OF AMERICA'S SOLDERS' AND AIRMEN'S HOME.
Real property tax exemptions, §47-1066.

CATHY L. LANIER.
Police chief.
Length of service award, §5-544.01.
Separation pay, §1-610.58.
Term of office, §5-105.01.
Voluntary retirement, §5-712.

CATS.
Animal control, §§8-1801 to 8-1813.
Assisted housing.
Pet ownership restriction in assisted housing.
See PETS.
Assisted housing for elderly or persons with disabilities.
Pet ownership restriction in assisted housing, §§8-2031 to 8-2035.
Cruelty to animals.
General provisions, §§22-1001 to 22-1013.
See CRUELTY TO ANIMALS.
Feral cats, §8-2206.
Veterinary facilities, §§47-2888.01 to 47-2888.08.
See VETERINARY FACILITIES.
Veterinary medicine, §§3-1208.61 to 3-1208.65.
See VETERINARY MEDICINE.

CATV, §§34-1251.01 to 34-1264.06.
See CABLE TELEVISION.

CEASE AND DESIST ORDERS.
Air pollution, §8-101.05g.
Alcoholic beverage licenses, §25-829.
Asbestos contractors, against, §8-111.08.
Banks and financial institutions.
Interstate banking and branch banks, §26-712.
Issuance by commission, §§26-551.16, 26-551.17.
Judicial review, §26-551.20.
Business licensees.
Issuance, §47-2853.17.
Violations, §47-2844.01.
Check cashing businesses, §26-321.
Child care facilities, §7-2042.
Condominiums, §§42-1904.14, 42-1904.15.
Drug manufacture and distribution licensure, §48-713.
Employment agencies, §32-412.
Energy efficiency standards.
Manufacturers, distributors and retailers in violation, §8-1771.05.
Health occupations licensure, registration or certification, §3-1205.16.

CEASE AND DESIST ORDERS
—Cont'd
Interstate banking and branch banks, §26-712.
Prescription drug pricing, §48-804.03.
Security agents and brokers, §31-5606.02.

CEDAR HILL (FREDERICK DOUGLASS MEMORIAL AND HISTORICAL ASSOCIATION).
Real property exempt from taxation, §47-1025.

CEDAR STREET SUBWAY, §9-319.

CELLULAR PHONES.
Distracted driving, §§50-1731.01 to 50-1731.10.
See DISTRACTED DRIVING.
911 systems.
Prepaid wireless E911 charge.
Collection and remittance, §34-1803.02.
Schools and education.
Testing integrity in public schools, prohibited acts, §38-771.03.
Toll telecommunication service tax, §§47-3901 to 47-3922.
See TOLL TELECOMMUNICATION SERVICE TAX.

CEMENT.
Inspector of asphalts and cements, §1-333.02.

CEMETERIES AND CEMETERY ASSOCIATIONS, §§43-101 to 43-131.
Bylaws, §43-110.
Communicable diseases, opening graves of persons deceased from, §43-123.
Cremation.
See CREMATION.
Dedication of land for use as cemetery, §43-112.
Depth of grave, §43-116.
Disinterment, §§43-123, 43-128.
Distance from city and dwellings established, §43-114.
Election of officers of associations, §43-108.
Embalming, §43-125.
Enclosure requirements, §§43-104, 43-105.
Equipment, purchasing, §43-104.
Exhibiting dead bodies, §43-120.

CEMETERIES AND CEMETERY ASSOCIATIONS —Cont'd

Fines, §43-126.

Funeral directors.

General provisions, §§3-401 to 3-421. See FUNERAL DIRECTORS.

Gifts.

Dedication of land for use as cemetery, §43-112.

Grave robbery, §§3-206, 22-3303.

Graves.

Communicable diseases, opening graves of persons deceased from, §43-123.

Disinterment, §§43-123, 43-128.

Size and depth requirements, §43-116.

Vault requirements, §43-122.

Human tissue banks, §§43-119, 43-125.

Incorporation of, §43-101.

Keeping and exhibiting dead bodies, §43-120.

Licensing of lands for cemetery purposes, §43-115.

Lots.

Grants and bequests for care of, §43-113.

Marking of, §43-116.

Owners as voting members of associations, §43-109.

Plats, recording, §43-116.

Officers of associations, §§43-107, 43-108.

Ornamentation of land, §43-104.

Penalties, §43-126.

Place of burial, requirements regarding, §43-121.

Platting and surveying, §§43-103, 43-116.

Powers and duties, §§43-101 to 43-105.

Prosecutions, §43-127.

Railings, destroying, §22-3314.

Real property.

Acquisition and sale of, §43-102.

Tax exemption, §§47-1002, 47-1015.

Records, §43-117.

Register of burials, §43-117.

Registration of cemetery superintendent, §43-118.

Rights of way through, §1-1315.

Sale on execution, not liable to, §43-111.

Sales.

Power to acquire and sell real property, §43-102.

Use of proceeds from sale of lots, §43-106.

CEMETERIES AND CEMETERY ASSOCIATIONS —Cont'd

Size of grave, §43-116.

Tax exemptions, §43-111.

Tombs, destroying, §22-3314.

Underdraining requirements, §43-105.

Use of proceeds from sale of lots, §43-106.

Voting members, lot owners as, §43-109.

CENSURE OF ATTORNEY, DCBar Rule XI, USDistCt LCrR 57.27, USDistCt LCvR 83.16.

CENSUS.

Constitution of the United States, US Const Art I §§2, 9.

CENSUS OF STUDENTS.

School attendance purposes, §38-204.

School funding purposes, §38-159.

CENTER FOR PUBLIC ADMINISTRATION AND SERVICE.

Real property exempt from taxation, §47-1010.01.

CENTER LEG FREEWAY (INTERSTATE 395).

Pilot area.

Real property taxes.

Payments in lieu of taxes, §47-4641.

CENTRAL DETENTION FACILITY.

Inspections, §24-211.02.

Maximum number of inmates, §24-201.71.

Processing and release of prisoners, §24-211.02a.

CENTRAL UNION MISSION DEVELOPMENT PROJECT.

Real property tax exemptions, §47-4651.

CERTIFICATE OF GOOD STANDING.

Person previously convicted of crime, §24-1304.

CERTIFICATES OF AUTHORITY.

Domestic life insurance companies, §31-4403.

Fire and casualty insurance, §§31-2502.02, 31-2502.03, 31-2502.21.

Health maintenance organizations, §§31-3403, 31-3419.

CERTIFICATES OF AUTHORITY
—Cont'd
Life insurance companies, §§31-4304, 31-4305, 31-4403.
Penalty for engaging in business without, §47-2604.
Public utilities stock and securities, certificate of authority to issue, §§34-502, 34-503.
Revocation for failure to pay tax, §47-2608.

CERTIFICATES OF DEPOSIT.
Bank deposits and collections.
General provisions, §§28:4-101 to 28:4-504.
See BANK DEPOSITS AND COLLECTIONS.

CERTIFIED BUSINESS ENTERPRISES.
Small and certified business enterprise development and assistance, §§2-218.01 to 2-218.75.
See SMALL AND CERTIFIED BUSINESS ENTERPRISE DEVELOPMENT AND ASSISTANCE.

CERTIFIED CAPITAL COMPANIES, §§31-5231 to 31-5239.
Certification, §31-5232.
Continuance.
Requirements, §31-5235.
Decertification, §31-5237.
Definitions, §31-5231.
Disqualification, §31-5238.03.
Distributions.
One hundred percent investment requirement, §31-5236.
Economic impact studies, §31-5238.02.
Information provided, §31-5238.02.
Insurance regulatory trust fund.
Fees deposited in fund, §31-5238.01.
Premium tax credit, §31-5233.
Aggregate limitations on, §31-5234.
Allocation requests, §31-5234.
Transferability, §31-5238.
Rulemaking, §31-5239.
Waivers, §31-5238.03.

CERTIFIED CHECKS.
Defined, §28:3-409.
Refusal to pay, §28:3-411.

CERTIFIED PUBLIC ACCOUNTANTS.
Board of accountancy, §§47-2853.06 to 47-2853.10.

CERTIFIED PUBLIC ACCOUNTANTS —Cont'd
Business licenses, §§47-2853.41 to 47-2853.49.

CERTIFIED RECREATIONAL VOLUNTEERS.
Criminal background checks.
See PARKS AND RECREATION.

CERTIORARI.
Appellate procedure.
Duty of counsel.
Criminal Justice Act plan, USCtApp Appx II.
Stay of mandate pending application for, FRAP 41(d).

CERVICAL CANCER.
Human papillomavirus vaccination, §§7-1651.01 to 7-1651.05.

CESTUI QUE USE, LEGAL ESTATE IN, §42-1501.

CFO.
Office of the chief financial officer.
See CHIEF FINANCIAL OFFICER.

CHANGE OF GENDER, §§16-2501, 16-2503.

CHANGE OF NAME, §§16-2501, 16-2503, CivPro Rule 205.
Divorce, DomRel Rule 13.
Insurance producer licensing, §31-1131.08a.
Notice of application, CivPro Form CA 111.

CHARCOAL.
Sale by weight, §37-201.11.

CHARITABLE INSTITUTIONS.
Appropriations as liens on property, §44-711.
Conflicts of interest of trustees or directors of, §44-714.
Health care entity conversion act, §44-604.
Investigations, §§44-709, 44-710.
Lottery and charitable games control board, §§3-1301 to 3-1336.
See LOTTERY AND CHARITABLE GAMES CONTROL BOARD.
Mayor's responsibilities, §§44-709, 44-710.
Monte Carlo night parties, §3-1322.01.
Pay-for-success contracts, §§2-211.01 to 2-211.03.

CHARITABLE INSTITUTIONS —Cont'd
Real property exempt from taxation, §§47-1002, 47-1010.01.
Reports, §§44-709, 44-710.
Restraints of trade.
Exclusions from chapter, §28-4504.
Wastewater and sewage works, §34-2111.

CHARITABLE SOLICITATIONS, §§44-1701 to 44-1714.
Actions, §44-1712.
Advisory committee, §44-1709.
Application for registration, §44-1704.
Appropriations, §44-1714.
Council powers and duties regarding, §44-1702.
Definitions, §44-1701.
Findings by mayor, representation of registration certificate or solicitor information card as, §44-1707.
Fines, §44-1712.
Issuance of registration, §44-1704.
Issuance of regulations, §44-1710.
Mayor's powers and duties regarding, §44-1702.
Names of other persons, using, §44-1711.
Penalties, §44-1712.
Prosecutions, §44-1712.
Publication of names of contributors, §44-1711.
Registration requirements, §§44-1703, 44-1704.
Reports, §44-1706.
Severability of provisions, §44-1713.
Solicitor information cards, §44-1705.
Telephone solicitation.
Compensation prohibited, §44-1708.

CHARITABLE TRUSTS, §21-1801.
Health care entity conversion act, §44-604.

CHARLES H. RAMSEY.
Police chief.
Separation pay, §1-610.58.
Term of office, §5-105.01.
Voluntary retirement, §5-712.

CHARTER REFERENDUM, §§1-207.01 to 1-207.04.
Ballot, §1-207.03.
Certification of result, §1-207.04.
Conducted by board of elections, §1-207.02.

CHARTER REFERENDUM —Cont'd
Date referendum conducted, §1-207.01.
Majority vote required to accept, §1-207.04.

CHARTER SCHOOLS.
Admissions task force, §38-1802.14a.
Admission to, §38-1802.06.
Applicability of provisions, §38-1802.10.
Approval of petition for, §38-1802.03.
Athletics plan, §38-824.02a.
Biennial evaluation of authorizing boards, §38-1835.01.
Board of trustees of, §38-1802.05.
Charter petitions.
Contents, §38-1802.02.
Civil rights applicable, §38-1802.04.
Content standards, §§38-1803.11 to 38-1803.15.
Contracting authority, §38-1802.04.
Core curriculum, §§38-1803.11 to 38-1803.15.
Definitions, §38-1800.02.
Denial of petition for, §38-1802.03.
Direct loan fund for charter school improvement, §38-1833.02.
Disposition of excess facilities, §38-1802.09.
Drug free zones, §48-904.07a.
Duties and responsibilities of, §38-1802.04.
Education data warehouse, participation, §§38-1802.04, 38-2609.
Effective date, §38-1800.03.
Elementary and Secondary Education Act of 1965, §38-1802.10.
Eligible chartering authorities, §38-1802.11.
Employees of DC public schools accepting positions at, §38-1802.07.
Enrollment in, §38-1802.06.
Escrow funds, §38-1804.03.
Evaluation of authorizing boards, §38-1835.01.
Existing schools.
Exemption from petition requirement, §38-1802.01.
Facilities.
School buildings and grounds, §38-1802.09.
Sharing facilities with public schools, §38-1831.01.

CHARTER SCHOOLS —Cont'd
Facilities —Cont'd
Uniform per student funding formula.
Facilities allowance for public
charter schools, §38-2908.
Facilities allotment task force.
Establishment, §38-1837.01.
Members, §38-1837.02.
Oversight, §38-1837.02.
Federal agency assistance,
§38-1802.15.
Foundation level.
Uniform per student funding formula,
§38-2903.
Education costs excluded from,
§38-2907.
Revenue unavailability.
Procedure for adjusting
appropriation, §38-2910.
Supplement.
Special education, summer school
and residential school
students, §38-2905.
Funding.
General provisions.
See SCHOOLS AND EDUCATION.
Funds.
District of Columbia public charter
school board fund, §38-1802.14.
**Government employer-assisted
housing program,** §§42-2501 to
42-2507.
See GOVERNMENT EMPLOYER-
ASSISTED HOUSING
PROGRAM.
Health and safety powers,
§38-1802.04.
Immunity from civil liability,
§38-1802.04.
**Leasing or purchasing of public
school facilities, preferences to
eligible entities,** §38-1802.09.
Long-term reform plan, §38-1801.01.
Mandatory dissolution, §38-1802.13a.
Meridian Public Charter School.
Real property tax exemption,
§47-1088.
New charter school fund,
§38-1804.03.
Ombudsman for public education.
Cooperation with, §38-1802.04.
Payments to schools, §38-1804.03.
Per capita funding, §38-2906.02.
Per capita funding.
Calculation of number of students,
§38-1804.02.

CHARTER SCHOOLS —Cont'd
Per capita funding —Cont'd
Facilities allowance, §38-2908.
Payment to public charter schools,
§38-2906.02.
Per student funding formula.
General provisions, §§38-2901 to
38-2914.
See SCHOOLS AND EDUCATION.
Petitions, §§38-1802.01 to 38-1802.03.
Powers and duties, §38-1802.04.
Procurement contracts, notice,
§38-1802.04.
Promotion gates, §§38-1803.11 to
38-1803.15.
Public charter school board,
§38-1802.14.
Public charter schools.
Charter petitions.
Approval or denial process,
§38-1802.03.
Process for filing, §38-1802.01.
Conflicting interest transactions,
§38-1802.04.
Duties and powers, §38-1802.04.
Existing schools.
Exemption from petition
requirement, §38-1802.01.
Office of public charter school
financing and support,
§38-1833.01.
Qualified zone academy revenue bond
project forward commitment
approval act, §§2-1217.101 to
2-1217.108.
See QUALIFIED ZONE ACADEMY
REVENUE BOND PROJECT
FORWARD COMMITMENT
APPROVAL ACT.
School management contracts,
§38-1802.04.
Services of public schools extended to,
§38-1802.09.
Street safety education, §38-3401.
Student admission, enrollment and
withdrawal, §38-1802.06.
Public school enrollment census,
§38-159.
Real property tax rebate.
Public charter school leasing facility
from entity subject to tax,
§47-867.
Reclamation of excess facilities,
§38-1802.09.
Reform program, §§38-1800.01 to
38-1803.21.

CHARTER SCHOOLS —Cont'd
Renewal of charter, §38-1802.12.
  Mandatory dissolution when not
    renewed, §38-1802.13a.
Repairs and maintenance,
  §38-1802.09.
Reports.
  Annual report, §38-1802.04.
Requirements, §38-1802.04.
Residency requirements, §§38-301 to
  38-313.
Revocation of charter, §38-1802.13.
  Mandatory dissolution, §38-1802.13a.
School buildings and grounds,
  §38-1802.09.
  Sharing facilities with public schools,
    §38-1831.01.
**Services of public schools extended
  to,** §38-1802.09.
**Sharing facilities with public
  schools,** §38-1831.01.
Taxes or bonds, prohibition,
  §38-1802.04.
Transportation, §38-1802.08.
**Tuition, fees or other payments,
  charging,** §38-1802.04.
**Uniform per student funding
  formula.**
  Supplement to foundation level
    funding, §38-2905.
Withdrawal from, §38-1802.06.
World Class Schools Task Force,
  §§38-1803.11 to 38-1803.15.

CHATTEL PAPER.
Secured transactions.
  General provisions, §§28:9-101 to
    28:9-809.
  See SECURED TRANSACTIONS.

CHATTELS REAL.
Pur autre vie estates, §42-505.
Years, estates in, §42-504.

CHEATING AT GAMBLING, §16-1704.

CHECK CASHING BUSINESSES,
  §§26-301 to 26-323.
Bond, surety, §26-306.
Capital required, §26-307.
Cease and desist orders, §26-321.
Change in location, §26-315.
Definitions, §26-301.
Examination of operations,
  §26-311.01.
Exemptions from provisions, §26-303.
Fees.
  Cashing checks, §26-317.
  Examination of licensees, §26-311.01.

CHECK CASHING BUSINESSES
  —Cont'd
Fees —Cont'd
  Licenses, §26-305.
Fines, §26-323.
Investigations, §§26-308, 26-320.
Issuance of rules and regulations,
  §26-322.
Licenses.
  Application for, §26-304.
  Bond, surety, §26-306.
  Change in location, §26-315.
  Criteria for granting, §26-308.
  Display of, §26-310.
  Duration of, §26-311.
  Fees, §26-305.
  Form of, §26-309.
  Issuance of, §26-308.
  Limited stations, §26-314.
  Number of locations covered by,
    §26-313.
  Renewal of, §26-311.
  Requirements regarding, §26-302.
  Revocation or suspension, §26-316.
  Transferability, §26-312.
Limitations on business, §26-319.
Limited stations.
  Defined, §26-301.
  Licenses, §26-314.
Mobile units.
  Change in business area, §26-315.
  Defined, §26-301.
  Number of locations covered by
    license, §26-313.
**Number of locations covered by
  license,** §26-313.
Prohibited acts, §26-319.
Records, §26-318.

CHECK FORGERY, §22-3242.

CHECKS.
Bad checks.
  Sales.
    Power to transfer title, §28:2-403.
Check cashing businesses, §§26-301
  to 26-323.
  See CHECK CASHING BUSINESSES.
Commercial code.
  Negotiable instruments.
    General provisions, §§28:3-101 to
      28:3-605.
    See NEGOTIABLE
      INSTRUMENTS.
Courts.
  Authority to accept certain types of
    payments, §11-1748.

CHECKS —Cont'd

Credit card information used for payment by check, §47-3152.

Dishonored checks.

Merchants.

Civil recovery by, §28-3152.

Defined, §28-3151.

Forgery, §22-3242.

Insufficient funds, §22-1510.

Merchants.

Dishonored checks.

Civil recovery for, §28-3152.

Definition of merchant, §28-3151.

Metropolitan police.

Depositing of seized currency, §§23-531 to 23-534.

Negotiable instruments.

General provisions, §§28:3-101 to 28:3-605.

See NEGOTIABLE INSTRUMENTS.

Sale of goods, UCC.

Payment by check, §28:2-511.

Sales.

Bad checks.

Power to transfer title, §28:2-403.

Worthless checks.

Sales.

Power to transfer title, §28:2-403.

CHECK SELLERS.

Money transmissions, §§26-1001 to 26-1027.

See MONEY TRANSMISSIONS.

CHECKS OF DISTRICT.

Banks and financial institutions cashing, §47-351.14.

CHEMOTHERAPY PILL COVERAGE, §§31-2995.01 to 31-2995.03.

Definitions, §31-2995.01.

Group health plans, applicability, §31-2995.03.

Mandated insurance coverage, §31-2995.02.

CHERRY.

Official fruit of the District of Columbia, §1-171.

CHESAPEAKE AND OHIO CANAL.

Real property exempt from taxation, §47-1014.

CHESAPEAKE REGIONAL OLYMPIC GAMES AUTHORITY, §§2-1131 to 2-1138.

Additional powers, §2-1136.

CHESAPEAKE REGIONAL OLYMPIC GAMES AUTHORITY —Cont'd

Commitments of signatories, §2-1138.

Composition, §2-1133.

Definitions, §2-1131.

Established, §2-1132.

Funding, §2-1135.

Indemnification, §2-1137.

Local laws, compliance, §2-1134.

Order of business, §2-1133.

Oversight responsibility, §2-1136.

CHIEF FINANCIAL OFFICER.

Appointment, §1-204.24b.

Bank fees special fund, §1-325.231.

Capital assets of district.

Replacement schedule, §47-308.04.

College saving program trust.

Implementation, administration, §47-4505.

Trustee, §47-4502.

Comprehensive annual financial report, §47-310.02.

Contingency cash reserve notification, §1-301.152.

Control periods.

Powers during, §47-317.03a.

Definitions, §1-204.24f.

Department of housing and community development, §1-301.141.

Duties, §1-204.24d.

Economic changes, analysis of, §47-318.06.

Establishment of office, §1-204.24a.

Estate taxes.

Marriage equality estate tax clarification, §1-301.153.

Financial reporting, §1-301.155.

Five-year financial plan and report, §1-204.56c.

Functions, §1-204.24d.

Treasurer, §1-204.24e.

Health care analysis and overtime plan, §1-301.151.

Maintenance of effort and matching funds, §§47-387.51, 47-387.52.

Marriage equality estate tax clarification, §1-301.153.

Personnel, §1-204.25.

Procurement authority, §1-204.26.

Removal, §1-204.24c.

Reports, §1-301.155.

Statehood initiatives budgeting, §1-301.154.

CHIEF FINANCIAL OFFICER
—Cont'd
Streamlined sales and use tax agreement.
Authority to enter into agreement, §1-301.123.
Taxation.
Revenue estimates and other revenue duties, §1-204.24d.
Tax increment financing, authorization to enter into financing documents, §2-1217.02.
Tax preference review, §1-301.157.
Transparency, §1-301.156.
Tax preference review, §1-301.157.
Definitions, §1-301.156.
Tax transparency, §1-301.156.
Term, §1-204.24b.
Treasurer.
Duties, §1-204.24e.
Unified economic development budget transparency and accountability, §§2-1208.01 to 2-1208.04.
Definitions, §2-1208.01.
FOIA disclosure, §2-1208.04.
Performance measures, §2-1208.03.
Reports, §2-1208.02.
Strategic plan, §2-1208.03.
Vacancy in office.
Treasurer or deputy as acting CFO, §1-204.24b.
WMATA momentum support fund, §1-325.311.

CHIEF JUDGES.
Designation, §§1-204.31, 11-1503.
Responsibilities of, §11-1702.
United States District Court, USDistCt LCrR 57.14, USDistCt LCvR 40.7.

CHIEF MANAGEMENT OFFICER.
Financial Responsibility and Management Assistance Authority, §47-391.09.

CHIEF TECHNOLOGY OFFICER, §§1-1401 to 1-1406.
Applicability, §1-1406.
Establishment of office, §1-1401.
Function, §1-1403.
Organization, §1-1405.
Purpose, §1-1402.
Transfers, §1-1404.

CHIEF TENANT ADVOCATE, §42-3531.06.
Rental accommodations fee fund, §42-3504.01.

CHILD ABUSE AND NEGLECT, §§4-1301.02 to 4-1362.
Admission to neglect proceedings, NeglectProc Rule 45.
Adoption of abused and neglected children, §§4-1361, 4-1362.
Appeals, §16-2329.
Arrest warrants, §23-563.
Attorneys at law, NeglectProc Rule 42.
Appointment.
Shelter care hearing or initial appearance, NeglectProc Rule 12.
Compensation of appointed counsel, §16-2326.01, NeglectProc Rule 42.
Practice standards, NeglectProc Appx.
Reports by attorney, NeglectProc Rule 21.
Right to counsel, §16-2304.
Advisement of right, NeglectProc Rule 12.
Attorneys' fees and costs, §§16-2326, 16-2326.01, NeglectProc Rule 42.
Behavioral health screenings and assessments, §4-1303.03e.
Bill of particulars, NeglectProc Rule 9.
Child and family services agency, §§4-1303.01 to 4-1303.09.
Establishment of, §4-1303.01a.
Medical treatment, authorization of, §4-1303.05.
Neighborhood-based services.
Provision of, §4-1303.03a.
Obstructing or interfering with reports to child welfare agencies, §22-1931.
Organization of, §4-1303.02a.
Policy declaration, §4-1303.01.
Powers and duties, §§4-1303.03, 4-1303.04.
Privacy and confidentiality, §4-1303.06.
Purposes, §4-1303.01a.
Rapid housing program.
Duties, §4-1303.03d.
Records.
Privacy and confidentiality, §4-1303.06.
Unauthorized disclosure, §4-1303.07.
Reports, handling, §4-1301.04.
Services performed by, §4-1303.04.
Single reporting line, §4-1303.03b.
Child custody.
Uniform child custody proceedings, §§16-4601.01 to 16-4605.03.
See CHILD CUSTODY AND CHILD CUSTODY PROCEEDINGS.

CHILD ABUSE AND NEGLECT
—Cont'd
Child fatality or near fatality.
Public disclosure of findings and
information, §4-1303.32.
Action to compel disclosure,
§4-1303.33.
Definitions, §4-1303.31.
Freedom of Information Act requests
not limited or restricted,
§4-1303.35.
Immunity, §4-1303.34.
Rules, §4-1303.36.
**Child-placing agencies required to
check enumerated registers for,**
§4-1407.01.
Child pornography.
Sexual performances using minors,
§§22-3101 to 22-3104.
Child Protection Register,
§§4-1302.01 to 4-1302.09.
Children's trust fund, §§4-1341.01 to
4-1341.08.
Board of Directors, §§4-1341.03,
4-1341.04.
Corporate powers of, §4-1341.06.
Definitions, §4-1341.01.
Dissolution of, §4-1341.07.
Establishment of, §4-1341.02.
Service of process, designated agent
for, §4-1341.05.
Taxation, §4-1341.08.
Citizen review panel, §§4-1303.51 to
4-1303.55.
Access to information, §4-1303.54.
Confidentiality of information,
§4-1303.54.
Conflicts of interest, §4-1303.55.
Establishment, §4-1303.51.
Meetings, §4-1303.53.
Members, §4-1303.52.
Conflicts of interest, §4-1303.55.
Purposes, §4-1303.51.
Quorum, §4-1303.53.
Staff support, §4-1303.53.
Civil procedure rules applicable,
NeglectProc Rule 1.
Confidentiality of information.
Children's advocacy center,
§4-1301.52.
Citizen review panel, §4-1303.54.
**Consolidation of related family
matters,** NeglectProc Rule 3.
Construction of rules, NeglectProc
Rule 2.
**Contributing to the delinquency of a
minor,** §22-811.

CHILD ABUSE AND NEGLECT
—Cont'd
Costs and expenses, NeglectProc Rule
47.
Court-appointed special advocates,
§§16-2371, 16-2372.
Crime victims' compensation.
Eligibility for compensation, VictComp
Rule 7.
**Criminal matters transferred to
family court,** §16-2307.
Cruelty to children, §§22-1101,
22-1102.
Custody orders, NeglectProc Rule 4A.
Ex parte orders for custody,
NeglectProc Rule 4.
Definitions, §§4-1301.02, 16-2301.
Delinquency.
See DELINQUENT MINORS.
**Director of Social Services,
additional powers of,** §16-2337.
Discovery, NeglectProc Rules 14, 15.
Disposition of child, §16-2320.
Findings, NeglectProc Rule 25.
Intermediate disposition, §16-2312.
Limitation of actions, §16-2322.
Mentally ill or intellectually disabled
child, §16-2321.
Order of disposition, NeglectProc Rule
25.
Parental visitations, §16-2323.
Predisposition study and report,
§16-2319.
Filing of disposition report,
NeglectProc Rule 21.
Review of orders, §16-2323.
Scheduling of fact finding and
dispositional hearings,
§16-2316.01.
Stipulated disposition, NeglectProc
Rule 23.
Support and maintenance, §16-2325.
Time for disposition hearing,
NeglectProc Rule 20.
**Drugs and drug-related activity,
exposure of children to,**
§4-1301.06a.
Emergency medical treatment,
§16-2338.
Expert witnesses, NeglectProc Rule 47.
Factfinding hearings, NeglectProc
Rule 19.
Scheduling, §16-2316.01.
Family assessments.
Child and family services agency.
Handling of reports, §4-1301.04.

CHILD ABUSE AND NEGLECT
—Cont'd
Family court of superior court.
Delinquency, neglect or children in need of supervision proceedings, §§16-2301 to 16-2340.
References to family division to refer to, §16-2301.01.
Family team meeting.
Evaluation of process, §16-2312a.
Safety plan, development, §16-2312.
Finality of judgments, §16-2329.
Guardian ad litem.
Appointment.
Child taken into custody, §16-2312.
Guardianship of minors.
Permanent guardianship, §§16-2381 to 16-2399.
See GUARDIAN AND WARD.
Guardian's neglect or refusal to provide for child under 14, §22-1102.
Health care providers' child neglect reports, §§4-1321.01 to 4-1321.07.
Hearings.
See HEARINGS.
Initial appearance.
Matters addressed, NeglectProc Rule 12.
Notice of appearance, NeglectProc Rule 5.
Report, NeglectProc Rule 7.
Intellectual disabilities, persons with.
Commitment to mental health facility, §21-1114.
Interpreters, §2-1902.
Intrafamily offenses.
Generally, §§16-1001 to 16-1034.
See INTRAFAMILY PROCEEDINGS.
Investigations, §§4-1301.06, 4-1301.07, 4-1301.09.
Child and family services agency.
Handling of reports, §4-1301.04.
Multidisciplinary investigation team, §4-1301.51.
Social investigation, §4-1301.09.
Jurisdiction, retention of, §16-2303.
Juvenile curfew, §§2-1541 to 2-1543.
Juvenile proceeding's effect on neglect case, NeglectProc Rule 3.
Law student practice, FamDiv Rule M.
Limitation of actions, §§16-2322, 16-2330.

CHILD ABUSE AND NEGLECT
—Cont'd
Media coverage of proceedings, NeglectProc Rule 45.
Medical examinations, §4-1301.08.
Motions generally, NeglectProc Rule 43.
Multidisciplinary investigation team, §4-1301.51.
Newborn safe haven, §§4-1451.01 to 4-1451.08.
See NEWBORN SAFE HAVEN.
Obstructing, preventing, or interfering with reports of acts of child abuse or neglect, §22-1931.
Parties, NeglectProc Rule 10.
Permanency planning.
Hearings, NeglectProc Rules 32 to 34.
Notice, NeglectProc Rule 12.
Petitions, NeglectProc Rule 9.
Reading of petition, NeglectProc Rule 12.
Photographs and radiological examinations, §4-1301.08.
Pretrial proceedings, NeglectProc Rule 17.
Privilege not grounds for excluding evidence of, §4-1321.05.
Protective supervision, revocation or modification of terms of, NeglectProc Rule 26.
Purpose of rules, NeglectProc Rule 2.
Reasonable and prudent parent standard.
Application or failure to apply.
Immunity from civil damages, §4-1303.03f.
Defined, §4-1301.02.
Records.
Absconding juveniles, §16-2333.02.
Case records, §16-2331.
Disclosure, §§16-2331 to 16-2333.02, 16-2336, NeglectProc Rule 46.
Fingerprints, §16-2334.
Inspections, §§16-2331 to 16-2333.02, NeglectProc Rule 46.
Permitted disclosures, §16-2333.01.
Person reporting to turn over certain records, §4-1301.06b.
Police and other law enforcement records, §§16-2333, 16-2334.
Privacy and confidentiality, §§16-2331 to 16-2333.02.
Sealing of, §16-2335.
Social records, §16-2332.

CHILD ABUSE AND NEGLECT
—Cont'd

Records —Cont'd
Transcripts of proceedings, §16-2329.
Unlawful disclosure, §16-2336.
Registers, child-placing agencies required to check, §4-1407.01.
Removal of children from environment, §4-1301.07.
Reasonable efforts criteria, §4-1301.09a.
Reports.
Child and family services agency, handling by, §4-1301.04.
Contents of, §4-1321.03.
Defined, §4-1301.02.
Disposition reports.
Contents, NeglectProc Rule 22.
Filing, NeglectProc Rule 21.
Failure to make, §4-1321.07.
Fines, §4-1321.07.
Health care providers, §§4-1321.01 to 4-1321.07.
Immunity from liability in making, §4-1321.04.
Initial investigation, NeglectProc Rule 7.
Presentation, NeglectProc Rule 14.
Metropolitan police, handling by, §4-1301.05.
Obstructing, preventing, or interfering with reports of abuse or neglect, §22-1931.
Oral, §4-1321.03.
Penalties, §4-1321.07.
Permanency hearings.
Contents, NeglectProc Rule 33.
Filing, NeglectProc Rule 32.
Persons required to make, §4-1321.02.
Photographs and radiological examinations, §4-1301.08.
Policy declaration, §4-1321.01.
Privilege not grounds for excluding evidence, §4-1321.05.
Procedures for making, §4-1321.02.
Records to be turned over by person reporting, §4-1301.06b.
Review hearings.
Contents, NeglectProc Rule 29.
Filing, NeglectProc Rule 28.
Social investigation, §4-1301.09.
Spiritual means, children treated solely by, §4-1321.06.
Written, §4-1321.03.
Review hearings, NeglectProc Rules 28 to 30.

CHILD ABUSE AND NEGLECT
—Cont'd

Revocation of protective supervision, NeglectProc Rule 26.
Right to counsel, §16-2304.
Advisement of right, NeglectProc Rule 12.
Rulemaking authority, §4-1306.01.
Safety plan, development.
Family team meeting, convening, §16-2312.
Scope of rules, NeglectProc Rule 1.
Service of process, §16-2306, NeglectProc Rule 11.
Motions, NeglectProc Rule 43.
Sexual abuse.
Generally.
See CHILD SEXUAL ABUSE.
Multidisciplinary investigation team, §4-1301.51.
Reporting of abuse, §§22-3020.51 to 22-3020.55.
Shelter care.
Conditional release.
Revocation and modification, NeglectProc Rule 16.
Conduct of hearing, NeglectProc Rule 14.
Criteria for shelter care, NeglectProc Rule 13.
Findings, NeglectProc Rule 15.
Matters addressed, NeglectProc Rule 12.
Notice of shelter care, NeglectProc Rule 6.
Orders, NeglectProc Rule 15.
Probable cause, NeglectProc Rule 14.
Report for first hearing, NeglectProc Rule 7.
Time of hearing, NeglectProc Rule 8.
Shelter care hearing, §16-2312.
Social investigation, §4-1301.09.
Spiritual means, children treated solely by, §4-1321.06.
Stipulations.
Disposition, NeglectProc Rule 23.
Fact-finding, NeglectProc Rule 18.
Subpoenas, FamDiv Rule E.
Summons and process, §16-2306, NeglectProc Rule 11.
Superior court, family court.
Delinquency, neglect or children in need of supervision proceedings, §§16-2301 to 16-2340.
Support and maintenance, §16-2325.
Taking child into custody, §16-2312.

CHILD ABUSE AND NEGLECT
—Cont'd

Tax check-off, drug prevention and children at risk, §§47-4001 to 47-4005.

Termination of parental rights.
General provisions, §§16-2351 to 16-2365.
See TERMINATION OF PARENTAL RIGHTS.

Termination or vacation of orders regarding, §16-2324.

Transcripts of proceedings, §16-2329.

Vacation or termination of orders regarding, §16-2324.

Washington Humane Society, §§44-1501 to 44-1511.

CHILD AND FAMILY SERVICES AGENCY, §§4-1303.01 to 4-1303.09.

Child abuse and neglect.
Reporting requirements, §4-1321.02.

Compulsory school attendance.
Tenth unexcused absence, referrals to social services agencies, §38-208.

Criminal background checks, §§4-1305.01 to 4-1305.09.
Application process, §4-1305.03.
Confidentiality of information, §4-1305.08.
Penalties for violations, §4-1305.09.
Definitions, §4-1305.01.
Failure to request, effect, §4-1305.07.
Person for which required, §4-1305.02.
Processing fees and costs, §4-1305.04.
Processing of applications, §4-1305.05.
Records, §4-1305.06.
Timing of application, §4-1305.03.

Definitions.
Criminal records check, §4-1305.01.

Director.
Powers and duties, §4-1303.03.

Establishment, §4-1303.01a.

Foster care.
Rights and responsibilities for youth in foster care, §§4-1303.71 to 4-1303.74.
Voluntary foster care registry, §4-1303.08.
Fund, §4-1303.09.

Neighborhood-based services.
Provision of, §4-1303.03a.

Organization, §4-1303.02a.

Policy declaration, §4-1303.01.

Powers and duties, §§4-1303.03, 4-1303.04.

Privacy and confidentiality, §4-1303.06.

CHILD AND FAMILY SERVICES AGENCY —Cont'd

Purposes, §4-1303.01a.

Rapid housing program.
Duties, §4-1303.03d.

Records.
Privacy and confidentiality, §4-1303.06.
Unauthorized disclosure, §4-1303.07.

Reports, handling, §4-1301.04.

Services performed by, §4-1303.04.

Single reporting line, §4-1303.03b.

CHILD CARE FACILITIES, §§4-401 to 4-415, 7-2031 to 7-2050.

Access rights, §7-2043.

After-school day care program, §4-402.01.

Appeals regarding, §7-2045.

Applicability of provisions, §7-2032.

Cease and desist orders, §7-2042.

Child abuse and neglect reports.
Day care workers required to make, §4-1321.02.

Child care services assistance fund, §§7-2001 to 7-2008.

Child development homes.
Defined, §4-401.
Payments to, §4-410.
Satellite programs, grants for, §4-414.

Compliance with District regulations, §4-412.

Comprehensive child development programs, §4-415.

Corporate income tax credit for, §47-1807.06.

Crimes and offenses, §7-2046.

Definitions, §§4-401, 7-2031.

Drug-free zones, §48-904.07a.

Early care and education administration.
Transfer of functions from, §7-2033.01.

Early intervention program.
Transfer of functions from, §7-2033.01.

Employees' child care facilities, §§4-901 to 4-905.

Exemptions to provisions regarding, §7-2033.

Existing and prior law.
Licenses issued pursuant to, §7-2035.
Pending actions and proceedings, §7-2050.
Repeal of existing regulations, §7-2049.

Fines, §7-2046.

CHILD CARE FACILITIES —Cont'd
Firearms.
Enhanced penalties and fines for carrying guns into gun free zones, §22-4502.01.
Funding, §4-402.
After-school day care program, §4-402.01.
Supplemental payments by Mayor, §4-404.01.
Government buildings and facilities.
Facilities located in, §§4-901 to 4-905.
Hearings, §7-2044.
Housing production trust fund, §§42-2801 to 42-2804.
In-home providers, §4-411.
Insurance coverage, §§31-4001 to 31-4003.
Payment, §4-410.
Injunctions, §7-2048.
Inspections, §7-2043.
Issuance of rules and regulations regarding, §7-2036.
Judicial review of final decisions, §7-2045.
Licenses, §§7-2034, 7-2035.
Denial, revocation, or suspension, §§7-2039 to 7-2041.
Denial, §7-2039.
Refusal to issue, revoke, suspend, deny renewal, §7-2040.
Summary suspension, §7-2041.
Existing and prior law, issued pursuant to, §7-2035.
Renewals, §7-2038.
Requirement to have, §7-2034.
Summary suspension, §7-2041.
Mayor's powers and duties regarding, §7-2036.
Supplemental payments by Mayor, §4-404.01.
Monitoring, §4-413.
Payments.
Child development homes, §4-410.
Human Services, payment by Department of, §4-406.
In-home caregivers, §4-410.
Overpayments, §§4-407, 4-408.
Public contracts with licensed centers, §4-409.
Schedule of parental payments, §4-405.
Penalties, §7-2046.
Firearms.
Enhanced penalties and fines for carrying guns into gun free zones, §22-4502.01.

CHILD CARE FACILITIES —Cont'd
Pending actions and proceedings under existing and prior law, §7-2050.
Program for, §4-402.
Prosecutions, §7-2047.
Public contracts with licensed centers, §4-409.
Public officers and employees.
Facilities located in government buildings, §§4-901 to 4-905.
Quality improvement network (QIN), pilot community-based.
Establishment, §4-415.
Repeal of existing regulations, §7-2049.
Satellite child development home programs, grants to develop, §4-414.
Scope of provisions, §7-2032.
Summary actions, §7-2041.
Variances, §7-2037.

CHILD CARE SERVICES ASSISTANCE FUND, §§7-2001 to 7-2008.
Annual report, §7-2008.
Definitions, §7-2001.
Eligibility for loan or grant, §7-2004.
Established, §7-2002.
Funding, §7-2003.
Person receiving loan or grant not agent or employee, §7-2006.
Repayment of loan or grant, §7-2005.
Rules, §7-2007.

CHILD CUSTODY AND CHILD CUSTODY PROCEEDINGS, §§16-4601.01 to 16-4605.03.
Abduction prevention measures, §§16-4604.01 to 16-4604.10.
Action for abduction prevention measures.
Who may make, §16-4604.04.
Contents of petition, §16-4604.06.
Cooperation and communication among courts, §16-4604.03.
Definitions, §16-4604.02.
Duration of order, §16-4604.10.
Jurisdiction, §16-4604.05.
Order seeking to prevent abduction, §16-4604.08.
Duration of order, §16-4604.10.
Risk of abduction, factors to determine, §16-4604.07.
Short title, §16-4604.01.
Warrant to take physical custody of child, §16-4604.09.

CHILD CUSTODY AND CHILD CUSTODY PROCEEDINGS
—Cont'd
Affidavits.
  Initial pleading, §16-4602.09.
Appearances.
  Parities and child, §16-4602.10.
  Special appearance status,
    §16-4601.08.
Appointment of counsel, §16-918.
  Third-party custody cases, §16-831.06.
Best interests of child standard,
    §16-914.
  Third-party custody.
    Factors to consider in determining,
      §16-831.08.
    Presumption in favor of parental
      custody, §16-831.05.
Child abuse and neglect.
  Notice of taking into custody,
    NeglectProc Rule 6.
  Orders for custody, NeglectProc Rule
    4A.
  Ex parte orders, NeglectProc Rule 4.
Child-custody determinations.
  Defined, §16-4601.01.
  Effect of, §16-4601.05.
  Notice requirements, §16-4602.05.
  Opportunity to be heard, §16-4602.05.
  Simultaneous proceedings,
    §16-4602.06.
Communication between courts,
    §16-4601.09.
Construction of act.
  Applicability to Indian tribes,
    §16-4601.03.
  Emergency medical care for a child,
    §16-4601.02.
  International application, §16-4601.04.
  Uniformity of application, §16-4605.01.
Cooperation between states,
    §16-4601.11.
Custodial power of attorney.
  Parents authorized to create,
    §21-2301.
Definitions, §16-4601.01.
  Enforcement of foreign custody
    determinations, §16-4603.01.
  Record, §16-4601.09.
Depositions.
  Testimony in another state,
    §16-4601.10.
Divorce proceedings, generally,
    §16-914.
Domestic abuse victims.
  Privacy protection in proceedings,
    §16-925.

CHILD CUSTODY AND CHILD CUSTODY PROCEEDINGS
—Cont'd
Electronic records.
  Testimony in another state,
    §16-4601.10.
Electronic signatures in global and national commerce act, relation to, §16-4605.02.
Emergency medical care.
  Inapplicability of act, §16-4601.02.
Enforcement of foreign custody determinations, §§16-4603.01 to 16-4603.17.
  Appeals from final orders, §16-4603.14.
  Attorney general, role of,
    §§16-4603.15, 16-4603.17.
  Cost, fees and expenses, §16-4603.12.
  Definitions, §16-4603.01.
  District's duty to enforce, §16-4603.03.
  Enforcement of registered custody
    determination, §16-4603.06.
  Expedited enforcement, §16-4603.08.
  Hague Convention, international child
    abduction, §16-4603.02.
  Hearing and order, §16-4603.10.
  Law enforcement, role of,
    §§16-4603.16, 16-4603.17.
  Recognition and enforcement,
    §16-4603.13.
  Registration criteria, §16-4603.05.
  Remedies available under District law,
    §16-4603.03.
  Service of petition and order,
    §16-4603.09.
  Simultaneous proceedings,
    §16-4603.07.
  Temporary visitation, §16-4603.04.
  Warrant to take physical custody of
    child, §16-4603.11.
Factors to be considered, §16-914.
Family court proceedings, §11-1101.
First pleading.
  Verified pleading or affidavit,
    §16-4602.09.
Former testimony.
  Testimony in another state,
    §16-4601.10.
Forum non conveniens, §16-4602.07.
Full faith and credit.
  Enforcement of foreign custody
    determinations, §16-4603.13.
Guardianship of minors.
  Permanent guardianship, §§16-2381 to
    16-2399.
  See GUARDIAN AND WARD.

CHILD CUSTODY AND CHILD CUSTODY PROCEEDINGS
—Cont'd
Inconvenient forum, §16-4602.07.
Indian tribes.
  Inapplicability of act, §16-4601.03.
Infants of unknown parentage.
  Birth registration information, §7-206.
Initial child-custody jurisdiction.
  Criteria for exercising jurisdiction, §16-4602.01.
  Exclusive, continuing jurisdiction, §16-4602.02.
  Initial determination, defined, §16-4601.01.
  Modification of determination, §16-4602.03.
Initial pleading.
  Verified pleading or affidavit, §16-4602.09.
International application, §16-4601.03.
Joinder of parties, §16-4602.05.
Jurisdiction.
  Decline for reason of conduct, §16-4602.08.
  Exercise of personal jurisdiction, §16-4601.07.
  Immunity from personal jurisdiction, §16-4601.08.
  Initial child-custody jurisdiction, §§16-4602.01 to 16-4602.03.
  Temporary emergency jurisdiction, §16-4602.04.
Jurisdiction, retention of, §16-914.01.
  Third-party custody orders, §16-831.12.
Leaving jurisdiction of court.
  Writ of ne exeat, DomRel Rule 406.
Military personnel during deployment, §16-914.02.
Minor parent.
  Right to initiate action, §16-914.
Parental kidnapping, §§16-1021 to 16-1026.
Pendente lite, §16-911.
  Third-party custody proceedings, §16-831.09.
Power of attorney, custodial.
  Parents authorized to create, §21-2301.
Preservation of records, §16-4601.11.
Priority calendaring, §16-4601.06.
Prior testimony.
  Testimony in another state, §16-4601.10.

CHILD CUSTODY AND CHILD CUSTODY PROCEEDINGS
—Cont'd
Procedure generally, DomRel Rules 1 to 406.
  See DOMESTIC RELATIONS ACTIONS.
Proceedings involving child custody generally, §§16-4601.01 to 16-4605.03.
Service by publication on nonresidents, §13-336.
Sexual abuse, child conceived as result of.
  Prohibition of custody or visitation, §16-914.
Simultaneous proceedings, §16-4602.06.
  Enforcement of foreign custody determinations, §16-4603.07.
Social service referrals, DomRel Rule 404.
Superior court jurisdiction, §11-925.
Temporary emergency jurisdiction, §16-4602.04.
Temporary visitation, §16-4603.04.
Third-party custody, §§16-831.01 to 16-831.13.
  Actions.
    De facto parent, action brought by, §16-831.03.
    Third party, action brought by, §16-831.02.
  Award of custody to third party, §16-831.06.
  Best interests of child.
    Factors to consider in determining, §16-831.08.
    Parental presumption, §16-831.05.
  Custody orders.
    Contents, §16-831.04.
    Effect of third-party custody order, §16-831.10.
    Modification or termination of orders, §16-831.11.
  Definitions, §16-831.01.
  Effect of third-party custody order, §16-831.10.
  Jurisdiction, §16-831.12.
  Modification or termination of orders, §16-831.11.
  Orders.
    Contents, §16-831.04.
    Effect of third-party custody order, §16-831.10.
    Modification or termination of orders, §16-831.11.

CHILD CUSTODY AND CHILD CUSTODY PROCEEDINGS
—Cont'd
Third-party custody —Cont'd
Other actions not abolished, diminished, or preempted, §16-831.13.
Pendente lite relief, §16-831.09.
Presumption in favor of parental custody, §16-831.05.
Rebuttal.
Burden of proof, §16-831.06.
Findings necessary to rebut, §16-831.07.
Transitional provisions, §16-4605.03.
Uniformity of application, §16-4605.01.
Venue.
Inconvenient forum, §16-4602.07.
Verified pleading or affidavit.
Initial pleading, §16-4602.09.
Warrant to take physical custody of child, §16-4603.11.

CHILD DEVELOPMENT FACILITIES.
Child and adult food program.
Office of state superintendent of education (OSSE) requirements, §38-283.
Participation in, §38-282.01.

CHILD DEVELOPMENT HOMES.
Defined, §4-401.
Payments to, §4-410.
Satellite programs, grants for, §4-414.

CHILD FATALITY OR NEAR FATALITY.
Public disclosure of findings and information, §§4-1303.31 to 4-1303.36.

CHILD FATALITY REVIEW COMMITTEE, §§4-1371.01 to 4-1371.14.
Access to information, §4-1371.06.
Appointment of members, §4-1371.04.
Approaches for reviewing cases, §4-1371.05.
Child defined, §4-1371.02.
Child fatality review committee establishment act of 2001.
Subchapter cited as, §4-1371.01.
Co-chairs.
Selection, §4-1371.04.
Composition, §4-1371.04.

CHILD FATALITY REVIEW COMMITTEE —Cont'd
Confidentiality of information, §§4-1371.08, 4-1371.09.
Unlawful disclosure, §4-1371.11.
Confidentiality of proceedings, §4-1371.08.
Current law enforcement investigation information.
Withholding from committee, §4-1371.06.
Definitions, §4-1371.02.
Destruction of information and records obtained, §4-1371.06.
Disclosure of information, §4-1371.09.
Information presented at committee proceeding, restrictions, §4-1371.08.
Unlawful disclosure, §4-1371.11.
Entities and agencies outside District.
Seeking information from, §4-1371.06.
Established, §4-1371.03.
Facilities and support, providing, §4-1371.03.
Full multidisciplinary/multi-agency reviews.
Fatalities conducted on, §4-1371.05.
Immunity for providing information to committee, §4-1371.10.
Immunity of persons making reports, §4-1371.13.
Nonresidents, reviewing death of, §4-1371.05.
Purposes, §4-1371.03.
Quorum and other procedure requirements, committee to establish, §4-1371.04.
Report of child's death.
Failure to make, §4-1371.14.
Immunity of persons making, §4-1371.13.
Persons required to make, §4-1371.12.
Responsibility to review child death, §4-1371.05.
Review teams.
Establishment to conduct reviews, §4-1371.05.
Service of subpoenas, §4-1371.07.
Subpoena power, §4-1371.07.
Unlawful disclosure of information, §4-1371.11.
Vacancies, §4-1371.04.
Witnesses.
Power to compel appearance, §4-1371.07.

CHILD HEALTH SCREENING,
§§7-875.01 to 7-875.06.
Applicability of provisions, §7-875.06.
Definitions, §7-875.02.
Payment for screenings, §7-875.04.
Purpose of act, §7-875.01.
Rulemaking, §7-875.05.
Uniform requirements and forms,
establishment, §7-875.03.

CHILD HOME DAY CARE.
Insurance coverage for providers,
§§31-4001 to 31-4003.

CHILD LABOR, §§32-201 to 32-224.
Age 10, children under, §32-215.
Age 12, children under, §32-215.
Age 14, children under, §32-201.
Age 16, children under.
Loitering around business
establishments during school
hours, §32-221.
Newspaper sales and distribution,
§32-215.
Power machinery, maintenance or
operation of, §32-204.
Street-trade badges required for,
§32-216.
Age 17, children under, §32-215.
Age 18, children under, §32-202.
Freight or nonautomatic elevator
operation, §32-205.
Newspaper sales and distribution,
§32-215.
Professional sports, §32-206.
Theatrical performances, §32-206.
Age, evidence of, §§32-210, 32-212.
Applications for street trade badges,
§32-217.
Board of Education, §§32-214, 32-224.
Dangerous work, §32-203.
Employer duty to furnish proof of
age on demand, §32-212.
Evidence of age, §§32-210, 32-212.
Fines, §32-213.
Inspections, §32-214.
Irregular or causal work.
Work or vacation permit not required,
§32-207.
List of child employees, §32-202.
Loitering around business
establishments during school
hours, §32-221.
Newspaper sales and distribution,
§§32-201, 32-215.
Notice, §32-202.
Penalties, §32-213.

CHILD LABOR —Cont'd
Political literature, distribution of,
§32-215.
Professional sports, §32-206.
Prosecutions for violations of
provisions, §32-222.
Records, §§32-202, 32-218.
Resale, merchandise sold to minor
for, §32-220.
Severability of provisions, §32-223.
Street trades and street-trade badge
requirements, §§32-215 to 32-220.
Theatrical performances, §32-206.
Violations, §32-213.
Work or vacation permits, §§32-207 to
32-211, 32-219.
Application by minor desiring
employment, §32-209.
Contents, §32-208.
Evidence of age, §32-210.
Issued by board of education, §32-208.
Vacation permits, §32-211.
Records of applicants, §32-208.
Required by employer, §32-207.
Exception, §32-207.
Revocation, §32-219.
Vacation permits, §32-211.
Violations, §32-219.

CHILD-PLACING AGENCIES,
§§4-1401 to 4-1410.
Criminal background checks,
§§4-1305.01 to 4-1305.09.
See CHILD AND FAMILY SERVICES
AGENCY.
Interstate compact on placement of
children, §§4-1421 to 4-1424.

CHILD PORNOGRAPHY.
Sexual performances using minors,
§§22-3101 to 22-3104.
Affirmative defenses regarding,
§22-3104.
Definitions, §22-3101.
Fines, §22-3103.
Penalties, §22-3103.
Prohibited acts, §22-3102.

CHILD PROTECTION REGISTER,
§§4-1302.01 to 4-1302.09.
Access to register, §4-1302.03.
Challenges to information,
§4-1302.06.
Duties of staff maintain register,
§4-1302.01.
Established, §4-1302.01.
Expungement of information,
§4-1302.07.

CHILD PROTECTION REGISTER —Cont'd

Information to be retained, §4-1302.02.

Notification of persons identified in report, §4-1302.05.

Prosecution of violations, §4-1302.09.

Purpose, §4-1302.01.

Release of information.
Criteria for disclosure, §4-1302.03.
Research and evaluation, §4-1302.04.
Unauthorized release, penalties, §4-1302.08.

Report on plan to implement, §4-1302.01.

Twenty-four hour intake components, §4-1302.01.

Twenty-four hour, seven days a week telephone lines, §4-1302.01.

CHILD RAPE.

Aggravating circumstances, §22-3020.

Defenses, §22-3011.

First and second degree, §§22-3008 to 22-3010.

State of mind.
Proof requirement, §22-3012.

CHILDREN AND MINORS.

Actions involving, §21-120.

Age of majority.
Child support enforcement, §46-101.

Alcohol and drug abuse.
Pilot substance abuse program for youth, §§7-3101 to 7-3103.

Alcoholic beverages, §§25-781 to 25-785.
Contributing to the delinquency of a minor, §22-811.
Delivery, offer, or making available to, §25-785.
Diversion program, §25-1002.
Drivers' licenses.
Suspension or revocation, §25-1002.
Entrance into licensed premises.
Restrictions, §25-782.
Legal drinking age.
Posting of signs, §25-713.
Misrepresentation of age, §25-1002.
Purchase, possession, or consumption by, §25-1002.
Sale or distribution by, §25-784.
Valid identification required, §25-783.

Apprentices, §§32-1402 to 32-1413.
See APPRENTICES.

Arbitration.
Settlement or judgment involving minor, Arbitration Rule VI.

CHILDREN AND MINORS —Cont'd

Attorneys at law.
Client-lawyer relationship with minor client, ProfCond Rule 1.14.

Behavioral health.
Early childhood and school-based behavioral health infrastructure, §§2-1517.31, 2-1517.32.

Bicycles.
Helmet requirements.
Child safety helmet assistance program, §50-1608.
Child safety helmet education program, §50-1607.
Failure to wear.
Not negligence per se, contributory negligence, assumption of risk, §50-1606.
Persons under 16 years, §§50-1605, 50-1651.

Blood donations.
Consent of parent or guardian, §7-1551.31.
Rulemaking, §7-1551.32.

Body artists.
Consent, §47-2853.76e.

Bullying, §§2-1535.01 to 2-1535.09.
See BULLYING.

Census of minors for school attendance purposes, §38-204.

Child abuse and neglect.
General provisions, §§4-1301.02 to 4-1362.
See CHILD ABUSE AND NEGLECT.

Child care facilities.
General provisions, §§4-401 to 4-415, 7-2031 to 7-2050.
See CHILD CARE FACILITIES.

Child labor.
General provisions, §§32-201 to 32-224.
See CHILD LABOR.

Child welfare and juvenile justice behavioral health infrastructure.
Family resource guide, §2-1517.51.
Reports, §2-1517.52.

Commercial paper.
Defenses against holder in due course, §§28:3-305.

Communicable diseases, carriers of, §7-134.

Contempt.
Delinquent act, JuvProc Rule 42.

Contributing to the delinquency of a minor, §22-811.

CHILDREN AND MINORS —Cont'd
Controlled substances.
  Distribution to minors, §48-904.06.
  Drug-free zones, §48-904.07a.
  Enlistment of minors to distribute,
    §48-904.07.
Conveyances or assurances by,
  §§42-408, 42-808, 42-809.
Crimes by juvenile offenders,
  §§24-901 to 24-941.
  See JUVENILE OFFENDERS.
**Crimes of violence committed
  against minors.**
  Enhanced penalties, §22-3611.
Crime victims' rights.
  Generally, §§23-1901 to 23-1911.
  See VICTIMS OF CRIME.
Cruelty to children, §§22-1101,
  22-1102.
Custodianship of minors.
  Probate proceedings, Probate Rules
    231, 232.
Death of child.
  Child fatality review committee,
    §§4-1371.01 to 4-1371.14.
  Public disclosure of findings and
    information, §§4-1303.31 to
    4-1303.36.
Deaths, fetal, §§7-213, 7-214.
**Debt incurred during infancy,
  acknowledgment or new
  promise of,** §28-3505.
Deeds, §42-408.
Default judgment against minors,
  CivPro Rule 55.
Delinquent minors.
  See DELINQUENT MINORS.
**Detained and committed youth
  under supervision of DYRS.**
  Education, §38-3301.
Drivers' licenses.
  Alcoholic beverage offenses.
    Suspension or revocation.
      See DRIVERS' LICENSES.
Driving under the influence.
  Minor in vehicle, impaired driving
    with.
    Additional penalty, §50-2206.18.
Drug abuse.
  Pilot substance abuse program for
    youth, §§7-3101 to 7-3103.
**Early childhood and school-based
  behavioral health infrastructure,**
  §§2-1517.31, 2-1517.32.
**Emergency medical services for
  children,** §7-2341.21.

CHILDREN AND MINORS —Cont'd
Employment of minors.
  General provisions, §§32-201 to
    32-224.
    See CHILD LABOR.
  Programs for employment and training
    of domiciliaries of District,
    §32-241.
Fetal deaths, §§7-213, 7-214.
Firearms.
  Pistol, license to carry, §7-2509.02.
  Sale prohibition, §22-4507.
Gambling by, §§3-1334, 3-1335.
Guardianship.
  General provisions, §§21-101 to
    21-182.
    See GUARDIAN AND WARD.
  Intervention proceedings, Probate
    Rules 301 to 361.
    See INTERVENTION
      PROCEEDINGS.
  Standby guardianship, §§16-4801 to
    16-4810.
    See GUARDIAN AND WARD.
Hate crimes.
  Parental liability for damages,
    §22-3704.
**Health care expenses, recoupment
  of,** §1-307.43.
Health insurance, §1-307.05.
  Dependent child coverage,
    §31-2996.02.
  Habilitative services coverage,
    §§31-3271, 31-3272.
Helmet requirements.
  Riding certain vehicles.
    Child safety helmet assistance
      program, §50-1608.
    Child safety helmet education
      program, §50-1607.
    Failure to wear.
      Not negligence per se,
        contributory negligence,
        assumption of risk, §50-1606.
    Persons under 16 years, §§50-1605,
      50-1651.
**Hospitalization of persons with
  mental illness.**
  Minors admitted in emergency.
    Notice to parent or guardian,
      §21-522.
  Minors released.
    Notice to parent or guardian,
      §21-527.
Human trafficking, §22-1834.
Infants. See within this heading,
  "Newborns."

CHILDREN AND MINORS —Cont'd

Inheritances, §20-1106.

Interstate compact for juveniles, §§24-1101 to 24-1106.

Alteration, amendment or repeal of provisions, §24-1106.

Compact administrator, §24-1103.

Congressional findings, §24-1101.

Construction of compact, §24-1105.

Enforcement, §24-1104.

Entry into and execution of compact, §24-1102.

Interstate compact on placement of children, §§4-1421 to 4-1424.

Agreements with other state for placement, §4-1423.

Authority to enter into and execute compact, §4-1422.

Definitions, §4-1421.

Delinquent children.

Administrative hearing on placement, review, §4-1424.

Intestate succession.

See INTESTATE SUCCESSION.

Juvenile curfew, §§2-1541 to 2-1543.

Juvenile offenders, §§24-901 to 24-941.

See JUVENILE OFFENDERS.

Juvenile proceedings.

See DELINQUENT MINORS.

Landlord and tenant, §§42-3225 to 42-3228.

Lead poisoning screening and reporting, §§7-871.01 to 7-871.06.

Definitions, §7-871.02.

Enforcement, §7-871.04.

Requirements, §7-871.03.

Rules, §7-871.06.

Short title, §7-871.01.

Violations, penalties, §7-871.05.

Leases, §§42-3225 to 42-3228.

Legitimacy and illegitimacy, §§16-907, 16-908.

Libraries.

Books from birth program, §39-115.

Books from birth fund, §39-116.

Life insurance companies.

Contracting with, §31-4330.

Limitation of actions, §12-302.

Marriage of.

See MARRIAGE.

Medical consent, §16-4901.

Mental health consumer's rights, §7-1231.14.

Sexual orientation change efforts for minors, §7-1231.14a.

CHILDREN AND MINORS —Cont'd

Missing children.

See MISSING PERSONS.

Mortgages and deeds of trust.

Conveyances or assurances, §§42-808, 42-809.

Property of infants, §21-158.

Servicemen's readjustment, §42-3001.

Motion pictures, §47-2820.

Motor vehicle restraint seats.

General provisions, §§50-1701 to 50-1708.

See SEAT BELTS.

National Children's Island, §§10-1401 to 10-1406.

Newborns.

At-home postpartum treatment, §31-3802.01.

Health insurance coverage, §§31-3801 to 31-3805.

Hearing screening, §§7-851 to 7-855.

Newborn screening, §§7-831 to 7-840.

Ophthalmia in newborns, §§7-801 to 7-804.

Nonprobate transfers.

Payment to minor by financial institution, §19-602.25.

Parental kidnapping, §§16-1021 to 16-1026.

Parental leave to attend school-related events, §§32-1201 to 32-1206.

Parental rights.

Termination of, §§16-2351 to 16-2365.

See TERMINATION OF PARENTAL RIGHTS.

Parent-child relationship, §§16-907 to 16-909.03.

Parent locator service, §46-224.02.

Parents' intestate succession, §19-308.

Parent-teacher conferences, §38-1809.01.

Parties, CivPro Rule 17.

Domestic relations actions, DomRel Rule 17.

Posthumous children.

Decedents' estates, §42-704.

Intestate succession, §19-314.

Powers of appointment.

General provisions, §§42-1001 to 42-1019.

See POWERS OF APPOINTMENT.

Prisons and prisoners, §§24-901 to 24-941.

See JUVENILE OFFENDERS.

CHILDREN AND MINORS —Cont'd
Probate proceedings.
Costs for administration of minors'
estates.
Death between January 1, 1981 and
June 30, 1995, Probate Rule
125.
Distributions to minors.
Death between January 1, 1981 and
June 30, 1995, Probate Rule
108.
Death on or after July 1, 1995,
Probate Rule 408.
Property of.
See GUARDIAN AND WARD.
Public assistance.
See PUBLIC ASSISTANCE.
**Public officers and employees,
transportation in District-owned
vehicles of children of,** §1-333.08.
Public welfare institutions, §§4-114 to
4-125.
Service of process, §13-332.
Domestic relations actions, DomRel
Rule 4.
Summons, CivPro Rule 4.
Sex trafficking, §22-1834.
Sexual abuse.
See CHILD SEXUAL ABUSE.
Skating rinks, §47-2820.
Special education.
Nonpublic schools, §§38-2561.01 to
38-2561.16.
Task force, §§38-2551 to 38-2555.
Statute of frauds.
New promise or acknowledgment of
debt incurred during infancy,
§28-3505.
Substance abuse.
Pilot substance abuse program for
youth, §§7-3101 to 7-3103.
Surrogate parenting contracts,
§16-402.
Theatrical performances, §47-2820.
Tobacco.
False identification, use of, §7-1721.03.
Purchases by minors, §7-1721.02.
Sales to minors, §7-1721.02.
School campuses, tobacco-free,
§38-826.05.
Transfers to minors.
General provisions, §§21-301 to
21-324.
See TRANSFERS TO MINORS.
Violent crimes committed against.
Enhanced penalties, §§22-3611.

CHILDREN AND MINORS —Cont'd
**Witness testimony of, corroboration
not required for,** §23-114.
**Workforce investment
implementation.**
Youth employment and training
services, §32-1610.01.
**Youth behavioral health
epidemiology reports.**
Citation of provisions, §2-1517.01.
Definitions, §2-1517.02.
Youth behavioral health program,
§7-1131.17.
Youth council, §§2-1561 to 2-1564,
2-1565.01 to 2-1565.06.
Youth leadership institute, §§2-1571
to 2-1574.
**Youth rehabilitation services,
department of,** §§2-1515.01 to
2-1515.54.
See YOUTH REHABILITATION
SERVICES, DEPARTMENT OF.
Youth residential facilities, §§7-2101
to 7-2108.
See YOUTH RESIDENTIAL
FACILITIES.
Youth services, §§2-1501 to 2-1511.
See YOUTH SERVICES.

**CHILDREN'S ISLAND
DEVELOPMENT PLAN.**
Submission and approval of plan,
§10-1431.
Development plan defined, §10-1432.

CHILDREN'S TRUST FUND,
§§4-1341.01 to 4-1341.08.
Board of Directors, §§4-1341.03,
4-1341.04.
Corporate powers of, §4-1341.06.
Definitions, §4-1341.01.
Dissolution of, §4-1341.07.
Establishment of, §4-1341.02.
**Service of process, designated agent
for,** §4-1341.05.
Taxation, §4-1341.08.

**CHILDREN'S TUBERCULOSIS
SANATORIUM,** §44-702.

CHILD RESTRAINT SEATS.
Motor vehicles, §§50-1701 to 50-1708.

CHILD SEXUAL ABUSE.
Aggravating circumstances, §22-3020.
**Arranging for a sexual contact with
a real or fictitious child,**
§22-3010.02.
Assault with intent to commit,
§22-401.

CHILD SEXUAL ABUSE —Cont'd
Child custody and visitation.
Prohibition where child conceived as result of sexual abuse, §16-914.
Defenses to, §22-3011.
Enticing a child or minor, §22-3010.
Felony murder, §22-2101.
First degree, §22-3008.
Secondary education students, §22-3009.03.
Sexual abuse of a minor, §22-3009.01.
Indictments.
Fictitious name indictments, §23-331.
Knowledge of child's age or age difference between perpetrator and child, §22-3012.
Lewd, indecent, or obscene acts, §22-1312.
Limitation of actions, §23-113.
Multidisciplinary investigation team, §4-1301.51.
Prostitution, §22-2704.
Reporting of abuse, §§22-3020.51 to 22-3020.55.
Defense to non-reporting, §22-3020.53.
Definitions, §22-3020.51.
Exemptions, §22-3020.52.
Failure to make report, §22-3020.54.
Immunity of person making good faith report, §22-3020.55.
Requirements generally, §22-3020.52.
Second degree, §22-3009.
Secondary education students, §22-3009.04.
Sexual abuse of a minor, §22-3009.02.
Sexually suggestive conduct with child or minor, §22-3010.01.
Sexual performances using minors, §§22-3101 to 22-3104.
Affirmative defenses regarding, §22-3104.
Definitions, §22-3101.
Fines, §22-3103.
Penalties, §22-3103.
Prohibited acts, §22-3102.
Wards.
Defenses to sexual abuse of, §22-3017.
First degree sexual abuse of, §22-3013.
Second degree sexual abuse of, §22-3014.

CHILD SUPPORT, §16-916.
Adjusted gross income.
Determination of, §16-916.01.
Appeals.
Expedited hearing by magistrate judge, §16-924.

CHILD SUPPORT —Cont'd
Assignment of rights.
Foster care, §§4-217.07 to 4-217.11.
Public assistance recipients, §§4-205.19, 4-217.07 to 4-217.11.
Temporary assistance for needy families (TANF) program, §§4-217.07 to 4-217.11.
Child care expenses, §16-916.01.
Crime victims' compensation.
Loss of support, VictComp Rule 30.
Definitions, §16-901.
Delinquency of payments, §16-916.
Domestic abuse victims.
Privacy protection in proceedings, §16-925.
Enforcement of child support.
General provisions, §§46-201 to 46-231.
See CHILD SUPPORT ENFORCEMENT.
Expedited judicial hearing on, §16-924.
Family court proceedings, §11-1101.
Financial institutions.
Data match requirements.
Providing IV-D agency, §§26-531 to 26-533.
Foreign ex parte divorce, §16-916.
Formulae, §§16-916.01, 16-916.01a.
Foster care, §§4-217.07 to 4-217.11.
Gross income.
Determination of adjusted gross income, §16-916.01.
Guardianship of minors.
Permanent guardianship.
Support from child's parent, §16-2396.
Guideline commission, §16-916.02.
Guidelines for setting, §§16-916.01, 16-916.01a.
Health insurance, §16-916.
Medical support enforcement, §§46-251.01 to 46-251.10.
Hearing commissioners, FamDiv Rule D.
Imputed income, §16-916.01.
Income taxes.
Credit, §47-1806.04.
Interpreters, §2-1902.
Interstate family support.
General provisions, §§46-351.01 to 46-359.03.
See INTERSTATE FAMILY SUPPORT.
Reciprocal enforcement of support proceedings, DomRel Rule 401.

CHILD SUPPORT —Cont'd
Intestate succession.
Surviving spouse and children,
§§19-101.01 to 19-101.06.
Jurisdiction, retention of, §16-914.01.
Leaving jurisdiction of court.
Writ of ne exeat, DomRel Rule 406.
Magistrate judge.
Expedited hearing, §16-924.
Medical care expenses.
Extraordinary medical expenses,
§16-916.01.
Recoupment of, §1-307.43.
Medical insurance, §16-916.
Medical expenses, coverage,
§16-916.01.
Medical support enforcement,
§§46-251.01 to 46-251.10.
Payment of moneys through court,
DomRel Rule 403.
Pendente lite support, §16-916.
Parentage proceeding, §16-2349.01.
Presumptions, §16-916.01.
Procedure generally, DomRel Rules 1
to 406.
See DOMESTIC RELATIONS
ACTIONS.
Proceedings considering, §16-916.03.
Public assistance recipients,
§4-205.19.
Public officers and employees.
Wages subject to attachment and
garnishment for, §1-507.
Public utilities.
Furnishing IV-D agency with financial
information, §34-1131.
**Reciprocal enforcement of support
proceedings,** DomRel Rule 401.
Self-support reserve, §16-916.01.
**Sentencing of individual to period of
imprisonment for criminal or
probation violation.**
Modification or suspension of support
payments.
Individuals being sentenced subject
to support order, §23-112a.
Petition, when deemed filed,
§46-204.
Shared physical custody.
Worksheet, §16-916.01a.
Social security disability insurance.
Effect of receipt by child, §16-916.01.
Sole physical custody.
Worksheet, §16-916.01a.
**Subsistence needs of parents,
allowing for,** §16-916.01.

CHILD SUPPORT —Cont'd
**Tax returns or other tax
information.**
Disclosure for support purposes,
§47-1805.04.
Temporary support obligation.
Expedited hearing by magistrate
judge, §16-924.
Unemployment compensation,
§51-118.
**Wages and salary, consideration
given to,** §16-916.01.
Withholding, enforcement by,
§§46-207 to 46-223.
See CHILD SUPPORT
ENFORCEMENT.
Worksheets, §16-916.01a.

CHILD SUPPORT ENFORCEMENT,
§§46-201 to 46-231.
Actions, §46-224.
Amendments to orders, §46-204.
Caretakers, notice to, §46-203.
Choice of law, §46-228.
Collection and disbursement unit,
§46-202.01.
Orders for payments to be made to
unit, §16-911.
Collection of taxes.
Refund offsets.
Applicability of provisions, §47-4436.
Protest and notice, §47-4433.
Right to credit overpayments,
§47-4431.
Contents of orders, §46-205.
**Criminal contempt for failure to
pay,** §46-225.02.
Definitions, §46-201.
Delinquent payments.
Liability limitations, §46-226.
Lottery prizes, intercepting,
§46-224.01.
Penalties, §46-225.01.
Reports and publications, §46-225.
Sanctions, §46-225.01.
Drivers' licenses, §46-225.01.
Effective date of provisions, §46-231.
Funding, §46-226.01.
Health insurance.
Medical support enforcement,
§§46-251.01 to 46-251.10.
Identifying information.
Parties to parentage and support
proceedings, §46-226.02.
Issuance of rules and regulations,
§§46-227, 46-229.
Liability limitations, §46-226.

CHILD SUPPORT ENFORCEMENT
—Cont'd
Liens, §46-224.
Lottery prizes, §46-224.01.
Medical support enforcement,
§§46-251.01 to 46-251.10.
Defined terms, §46-251.01.
Employer's duties, §46-251.04.
Failure to withhold.
Sanctions, §46-251.10.
Health insurance coverage.
Liability for contributions,
§46-251.09.
Objections to withholding,
§46-251.09.
Selection of options, §46-251.06.
Withholding, §46-251.07.
Objections to withholding,
§46-251.09.
Priority of withholding,
§46-251.08.
Insurer's duties, §46-251.05.
Limitations on liability for employer,
§46-251.10.
Medical support notice.
Contents, §46-251.03.
Employer's duties, §46-251.04.
Format, §46-251.03.
Reciprocity, §46-251.03.
Submission to employer, §46-251.02.
Use, §46-251.02.
Options for coverage, selection,
§46-251.06.
Sanctions, §46-251.10.
Withholding for health insurance
coverage, §46-251.07.
Priority of withholding, §46-251.08.
Motor vehicle registration,
§46-225.01.
Notice.
Caretakers, §46-203.
Hearing commissioner's judgment,
FamDiv Rule D.
Withholding.
Notice to holder, §46-211.
Notice to obligor, §46-209.
Parentage and support proceedings.
Access to locate system, §46-226.05.
Administrative enforcement in
interstate cases, §46-226.07.
Automated procedures, §46-226.10.
Court-ordered work requirements,
§46-226.09.
Directory of new hires, §46-226.06.
District-wide jurisdiction over parties,
§46-226.11.

CHILD SUPPORT ENFORCEMENT
—Cont'd
Parentage and support proceedings
—Cont'd
Expedited process by IV-D agency,
§46-226.03.
Filing of identifying information by
parties, §46-226.02.
Fraudulent transfers, §46-226.08.
Other state IV-D agency.
Recognition and enforcement of
authority of, §46-226.04.
Parent locator service, §46-224.02.
Penalties for delinquent payments,
§46-225.01.
Policy declaration, §46-202.
**Public education and information
program,** §46-230.
Reciprocity.
Medical support enforcement.
Medical support notice, §46-251.03.
Sanctions for delinquent payments,
§46-225.01.
**Sanctions for medical support
enforcement,** §46-251.10.
Service of process, §46-224.01.
Social Security numbers.
Inclusion in records, §46-205.01.
Subrogation of District, §46-203.
Withholding, enforcement by,
§§46-207 to 46-223.
Determining amount, §46-208.
Discrimination in employment for,
§46-219.
Duty of holder to withhold and make
payments, §46-212.
Failure of holder to comply with order
to withhold, §46-213.
Implementation of withholding,
§46-207.01.
Installment payments, §46-220.
Interstate.
Other jurisdictions, initiation of
withholding in, §46-223.
Procedures and provisions, §46-222.
Lapse of order of withholding, §46-215.
Limitations on withholding, §46-217.
Means other than withholding,
§46-224.
Medical support enforcement.
Withholding for health insurance
coverage, §46-251.07.
Objections to withholding,
§46-251.09.
Priority of withholding,
§46-251.08.

CHILD SUPPORT ENFORCEMENT
—Cont'd
Withholding, enforcement by
—Cont'd
Multiple withholding orders, §46-217.
Notice of withholding to holder,
§46-211.
Notice of withholding to obligor,
§46-209.
Objections to withholding, §46-210.
Withholding for health insurance
coverage, §46-251.09.
Priorities as to withholding, §46-217.
Medical support enforcement.
Withholding for health insurance
coverage, §46-251.08.
Quashing, §46-221.
Termination of employment, §46-216.
Termination of withholding, §46-214.
Voluntary withholding, §46-218.

**CHILD SUPPORT GUIDELINE
COMMISSION,** §16-916.02.

CHILD SUPPORT GUIDELINES,
§§16-916.01, 16-916.01a.

CHILLERS.
Drug paraphernalia, §§48-904.10,
48-1101 to 48-1104.

CHINESE LANGUAGE.
**Foreign language services and
documents,** §§2-1931 to 2-1936.
See FOREIGN LANGUAGE
SERVICES AND DOCUMENTS.
**Government publications translated
in.**
Publications concerning health, safety
and welfare of Asian and Pacific
Islander resident, §2-1375.

CHIROPRACTIC.
Board of, §3-1202.16.
Child abuse and neglect reports.
Chiropractors required to make,
§4-1321.02.
Definition of practice of, §3-1201.02.
Health occupations boards.
General provisions, §§3-1201.01 to
3-1213.01.
See HEALTH OCCUPATIONS
BOARDS.
**Health occupations licensure,
registration or certification,**
§§3-1205.01 to 3-1205.24.
See HEALTH OCCUPATIONS
LICENSURE, REGISTRATION
OR CERTIFICATION.

CHIROPRACTIC —Cont'd
**Titles and terms prohibited as
misrepresentation without
license to practice,** §3-1210.03.

CHLAMYDIA.
Treatment for sexual partners,
§§7-2081.01 to 7-2081.04.

CHOICE OF LAW.
Anatomical gifts.
Execution of document of gift,
§7-1531.18.
Attorney disciplinary proceedings,
ProfCond Rule 8.5.
Child support enforcement, §46-228.
Interstate family support.
Registration for enforcement of
support orders, §46-356.04.
Investment securities, §28:8-110.
Letters of credit, §28:5-116.

CHOKEHOLDS.
**Metropolitan police prohibitions
and restrictions,** §§5-125.01 to
5-125.03.

CHOKING.
Respiratory arrest.
Non-resuscitation procedures for EMS.
Comfort care orders, §§7-651.01 to
7-651.16.
See EMERGENCY MEDICAL
SERVICES.

CHOSES IN ACTION.
Assignment of choses in action,
§§28-2301 to 28-2305.
See ASSIGNMENTS.

CHRISTMAS DAY.
Appeals in federal cases, FRAP 26(a),
45(a).
Designated holiday, §§1-612.02,
28-2701.
**Extension of time for performing
acts,** §28-2701.

CHURCHES.
See RELIGIOUS INSTITUTIONS.

CIC.
**District of Columbia corrections
information council,** §24-101.

C.I.F.
Sale of goods, UCC, §§28:2-320,
28:2-321.

CIGARETTE ROLLING PAPERS.
Drug paraphernalia, §§48-1101 to
48-1104.

CIGARETTES.
Fire-standard-compliant cigarettes,
§§7-1751 to 7-1757.
Free cigarettes.
Prohibition on distribution of, §7-1731.
Minors.
Purchase of tobacco by, §7-1721.03.
Sale of tobacco to, §7-1721.02.
Sales below cost, §§28-4521 to 28-4527.
Damages, §28-4525.
Definitions, §28-4521.
Discontinuance of trade and stock.
Exceptions from acts prohibitions,
§28-4523.
Evidence.
Effect of judgment, §28-4526.
Exceptions, §28-4523.
Injunctions, §28-4525.
Issuance of rules and regulations,
§28-4527.
Judgment.
Effect of, §28-4526.
License.
Suspension or revocation of,
§28-4525.
Mayor.
Rulemaking authority, §28-4527.
Penalties, §28-4525.
Presumptive wholesale markup,
§28-4522.
Price gouging, §28-4522.
Prohibitions, §28-4522.
Exceptions, §28-4523.
Rulemaking authority.
Mayor, §28-4527.
Unfair trade practices, §28-4524.
Penalties, §28-4525.
Secret payments, §28-4524.
Wholesalers and retailers.
Unfair trade practices, §28-4524.
Penalties, §28-4525.
Smoking, §§7-1701 to 7-1731.
See SMOKING.

CIGARETTE TAX.
See TOBACCO TAX.

CINCINNATI, SOCIETY OF THE.
Real property exempt from taxation,
§47-1037.

CIRCUSES.
Business licenses, §47-2825.
Display of circus, carnival or other
special event animals.
Permit required, §8-1808.

CITIZEN PATROL MEMBERS.
Enhanced penalty for committing
certain crimes against, §22-3602.

CITIZENSHIP, US Const Art IV §2,
Amd 14.

CITY MARKET AT O STREET TAX
INCREMENT FINANCING,
§§2-1217.33a to 2-1217.33m.
Bond issues.
Authorization, §2-1217.33d.
Grant authorization, §2-1217.33m.
Information reporting, §2-1217.33l.
Issuance, §2-1217.33g.
Limited liability of District,
§2-1217.33i.
Maintenance of documents,
§2-1217.33k.
Payment and security, §2-1217.33e.
Personal liability of officials,
§2-1217.33j.
Terms and conditions, §2-1217.33f.
Creation of fund, §2-1217.33b.
Creation of TIF area, §2-1217.33c.
Definitions, §2-1217.33a.
Financing and closing documents,
§2-1217.33h.
Grant authorization, §2-1217.33m.

CITY OF WASHINGTON.
Museum, §§39-301 to 39-309.
Ordinances of, §45-402.

CITYWIDE TECHNOLOGY
SUPPORT SERVICES, §§1-1431 to
1-1433.
DC-NET services support fund,
§1-1432.
Definitions, §1-1431.
Technology infrastructure services
support fund, §1-1433.

CIVIL ASSET FORFEITURE.
Definitions, §41-301.

CIVIL DEFENSE.
Defined, §7-2201.
Interstate civil defense compacts,
§7-2209.

CIVIL DIVISION, SUPERIOR
COURT.
See ACTIONS.

CIVIL DOCKET, CivPro Rule 79.
Domestic relations actions, DomRel
Rule 79.

CIVIL INFRACTIONS, §§2-1801.01 to
2-1803.03.
See ADMINISTRATIVE FINES.

CIVIL INVESTIGATIVE DEMAND.
Restraints of trade, §28-4505.

CIVIL PROCEDURE.
Actions generally.
  See ACTIONS.
Commencement of action.
  See COMMENCEMENT OF
    ACTIONS.
Discovery.
  See DISCOVERY.
Domestic relations actions, DomRel
  Rules 1 to 406.
  See DOMESTIC RELATIONS
    ACTIONS.
Intervention proceedings.
  See INTERVENTION
    PROCEEDINGS.
Jury trials.
  See JURIES AND JURY TRIALS.
Motions.
  See MOTIONS.
Parties.
  See PARTIES.
Pleadings.
  See PLEADINGS.
Pretrial conferences.
  See PRETRIAL CONFERENCES.
Service of process.
  See SERVICE OF PROCESS AND
    PAPERS.
Stay of proceedings.
  See STAYS.
Trials generally.
  See TRIALS.

CIVIL PROCEDURE RULES.
Amendments or additions to rules,
  CivPro Rule 83-I.
  Effective date, CivPro Rule 86-I.
Applicability of rules, CivPro Rule 81.
  Arbitration, Arbitration Rule XV.
  Child abuse and neglect proceedings,
    NeglectProc Rule 1.
  Domestic relations actions, DomRel
    Rule 1.
  Landlord and tenant court,
    LandlordTenant Rule 2.
  Probate proceedings, Probate Rule 1.
  Small claims court, SmallClaims Rule
    2.
  Tax proceedings, Tax Rule 3.
Citation of rules, CivPro Rule 85.
**"Civil action" as single form of
  action,** CivPro Rule 2.
Effective date of rules, CivPro Rule
  86.
  Amendments or additions, CivPro Rule
    86-I.
Generally.
  See Court Rules Volume I.

CIVIL PROCEDURE RULES —Cont'd
**Jurisdiction of superior court not
  extended by rules,** CivPro Rule 82.
One form of action, CivPro Rule 2.
Scope of rules, CivPro Rule 1.
Title of rules, CivPro Rule 85.

CIVIL SERVICE.
Annual leave bank, §§1-612.04 to
  1-612.11.
  See ANNUAL LEAVE BANK.
Leave transfer program, §§1-612.31 to
  1-612.38.
Legal service, §§1-608.51 to 1-608.66.
  See LEGAL SERVICE.
Merit system.
  General provisions, §§1-601.01 to
    1-636.03.
  See MERIT SYSTEM.
Pensions and retirement, §§1-626.01
  to 1-626.14.
  See PENSIONS AND RETIREMENT.
Voluntary leave transfer program,
  §§1-612.31 to 1-612.38.

CIVIL UNION.
See DOMESTIC PARTNERSHIPS.

CLAIMS AGAINST ESTATES,
  §§20-901 to 20-914.
Action required on claims, §20-908.
Closure of estate, after, §20-901.
Execution of judgments, §20-914.
Exempt assets, §20-904.
Failure to act on, §20-908.
Funeral expenses, §20-907.
Future claims, §20-911.
Heirs and legatees, claims against,
  §20-1303.
Insurance, §20-903.
Levy, §20-914.
Liens, §20-903.
Limitation of actions, §§20-902,
  20-903.
Meeting of creditors, convening,
  §20-910.
Opening estate, prior to, §20-901.
Payment of claims, §§20-906, 20-909.
**Personal representatives, claims
  against,** §20-1303.
Priority of payments, §20-906.
Probate proceedings.
  General provisions, §§16-3101 to
    16-3112, Probate Rules 1 to 430.
  See PROBATE PROCEEDINGS.
Procedures, §20-905.
Secured claims, §20-912.
Unsecured claims, §20-911.

CLAIMS AGAINST THE DISTRICT,
§§2-401 to 2-425.
Appropriations for settlement of,
§2-404.
Budgets and budget estimates,
§47-210.
Compromise, §2-406.
Constitution of the United States,
US Const Amd 11.
Discipline of public employees
stemming from, §2-415.
Effective date of provisions
regarding, §2-405.
Excessive verdicts, §2-414.
Indemnification of medical
employees, §2-415.
Judgment against District, action
against District employee barred
by, §2-413.
Negligent damage to District
property by District employees,
§2-416.
Negligent operation of vehicles,
§§2-412, 2-415.
Occupational safety and health,
§32-1122.
Procurement practices.
General provisions, §§2-381.01 to
2-381.10.
See PROCUREMENT PRACTICES.
Public officers and employees,
nonliability of, §§2-411 to 2-416.
Refund of assessments held void,
§2-403.
Reports, §2-404.
Service of process, §2-401.
Settlements, §§2-402, 2-404.
Unjust imprisonment, §§2-421 to
2-425.
Applicability to person entering guilty
plea, §2-425.
Damages, §2-423.
Effective date, §2-424.
Proof required, §2-422.
Right to present claim, §2-421.
CLASS ACTIONS, CivPro Rule 23-I,
USDistCt LCvR 23.1.
Consumer protection.
Public interest organizations.
Actions for relief from trade
practices, §28-3905.
Joinder of parties exception, CivPro
Rule 19.
Public assistance, §4-210.16.
Real property tax assessments,
§47-827.

CLASS ACTIONS —Cont'd
Restraints of trade, §28-4508.
Unincorporated associations, CivPro
Rule 23.2.

CLASSIFICATION OF WORKERS.
Workplace fraud, §§32-1331.01 to
32-1331.12.
See WORKPLACE FRAUD.

CLASSROOM ANIMALS, §§8-1851.01,
8-1851.02.

CLEAN AND AFFORDABLE
ENERGY, §§8-1773.01 to 8-1774.16.
See SUSTAINABLE ENERGY.

CLEAN CARS.
Low-emissions vehicle program.
Establishment.
Adoption of California emissions
standards and compliance
requirements, §50-731.
Vehicle not in compliance.
Registering prohibited, §50-732.

CLEAN-FUEL VEHICLES.
Alternative fuel technology, §§50-701
to 50-715.
See ALTERNATIVE FUEL
TECHNOLOGY.
Motor vehicle registration.
Fees, §50-1501.03.
Motor vehicle titling tax.
Exemption, §50-2201.03.

CLEAN LAND FUND.
Brownfield revitalization, §8-633.08.

CLEANUP OF CONTAMINATED
PROPERTY.
Hazardous substances releases.
Liability, cleanup, response, §§8-631.01
to 8-638.01.
See HAZARDOUS SUBSTANCES
RELEASES.

CLERGY.
See RELIGION, MINISTERS OF.

CLERGY-PENITENT PRIVILEGE,
§14-309.

CLERKS OF COURT.
Appeals in federal cases.
Administrative review or enforcement,
duties, FRAP 15.
Attorney's application for admission to
bar, filing, FRAP 46(b).
Bond, FRAP 45(a).
Calendar, preparation, FRAP 45(b).
Computerized records, FRAP 45(b).

CLERKS OF COURT —Cont'd

Appeals in federal cases —Cont'd

Costs inserted in mandate, FRAP 39(d).

District court appeals, duties, FRAP 3, 11(b).

Transmitting the record on appeal, FRAP 11(b).

Docket, FRAP 12(a), 45(b).

Duties, generally, FRAP 45, USCtApp Rule 45.

District court appeals, FRAP 3.

Transmitting the record on appeal, FRAP 11(b).

Entry of judgment, FRAP 36.

Filing and service of papers, duties, FRAP 25, USCtApp Rules 1, 25.

Filing record, partial record, or certificate on appeal, FRAP 12(c).

Index of docket, FRAP 45(b).

Martin Luther King, Jr.'s birthday, office to be closed on, FRAP 45(a).

Motions.

Clerk may dispose of certain motions, FRAP 27(e).

Disposition of, USCtApp Rule 27.

Oath, FRAP 45(a).

Office, when open, FRAP 45(a).

Petition for appeal.

Permission under 28 USCS 1292(b) filed with, FRAP 5(a).

Preservation and custody of papers and records, FRAP 45(d).

Tax court, notice of appeal filed with, FRAP 13(b).

Transmission of record on appeal to, FRAP 11(b).

Petition for hearing or hearing en banc, FRAP 35(b).

Bankruptcy court.

Office hours of clerk of court, USDistDCBank Rule 5005-1.

Court of appeals.

See COURT OF APPEALS.

Landlord and tenant court.

Preliminary proceedings by clerk, LandlordTenant Rule 11.

Release of information relating to pending criminal proceedings, USDistCt LCrR 57.7.

Superior court.

See SUPERIOR COURT.

CLIENTS' SECURITY TRUST FUND, DCBar Rule XII.

Restitution to fund by attorney, DCBar Rule XI.

CLIMATE CHANGE AND RESILIENCY COMMISSION.

Definitions, §8-181.01.

CLINICAL HEALTH SERVICES.

Fees, §44-731.

Lead poisoning.

Childhood lead poisoning screening and reporting, §§7-871.01 to 7-871.06.

CLINICAL LABORATORIES, §§44-201 to 44-213.

Advisory board, §44-206.

Clinical laboratory practitioner.

Defined, §3-1201.01.

Qualifications for licensure, §3-1207.61.

Cytology screening, §44-210.

Definitions, §44-201.

Directors, §44-203.

Enforcement of provisions, §44-212.

Inspections, §44-207.

Issuance of rules and regulations, §44-213.

Licenses, §44-202.

Penalties, §44-212.

Privacy and confidentiality, §44-211.

Proficiency testing programs, §44-209.

Quality assurance, §44-208.

Technical personnel, qualifications for, §44-204.

Titles and terms prohibited as misrepresentation without license to practice, §3-1210.03.

Violations, §44-212.

CLINICAL TRIALS INSURANCE COVERAGE.

Health insurance, §§31-2993.01 to 31-2993.03.

Covered trials, §31-2993.02.

Defined terms, §31-2993.01.

Right to file grievance, independent review, §31-2993.03.

CLOSED PROCEEDINGS.

Child fatality review committee, §4-1371.08.

CLOSING ARGUMENTS.

Criminal procedure, CrimPro Rule 29.1.

CLOSING ESTATES, §§20-1301 to 20-1305.

CLOSING-OUT SALES, §§47-2101 to 47-2110.

Addition of new stock during, §47-2104.

CLOSING-OUT SALES —Cont'd
Applicability of provisions, §47-2107.
Definitions, §47-2101.
Delegation of powers, §47-2110.
Fraud and deceit, §47-2106.
Interpretation of provisions,
§47-2110.
Issuance of rules and regulations,
§47-2109.
Jurisdiction, §47-2108.
Penalties, §47-2106.
Prosecutions, §47-2106.
Public officers and employees,
§47-2107.
Purchase of new stock for, §47-2103.
Superior court, §47-2108.
**Termination date, continuation of
sale beyond,** §47-2105.

CLOTHING.
Crime victims' compensation.
Replacement of clothing, VictComp
Rule 27.
**Execution of judgment, property
exempt from,** §15-503.
Private vehicles-for-hire.
Trade dress requirements,
§50-301.29d.

CLUBS.
Alcoholic beverage licenses.
Credit sales.
Exemption, §25-734.
On-premises retailers, §25-113.
Business licenses, §47-2827.
Smoking, §§7-741.02, 7-741.03.

COACHES.
Child abuse and neglect.
Reporting requirements, §4-1321.02.

COAL.
Weights and measures.
General provisions, §§37-201.01 to
37-201.33.
See WEIGHTS AND MEASURES.

COAL TAR.
Stormwater management.
Coal tar pavement product limitations,
§8-153.01.

COASTERS.
Helmet requirement for riders.
Persons under 16 years, §50-1651.

COBRA.
Health insurance, §§31-3301.01 to
31-3303.14.
See HEALTH INSURANCE
PORTABILITY AND
ACCOUNTABILITY.

COCAINE FREEBASE KITS.
Drug paraphernalia, §§48-904.10,
48-1101 to 48-1104.

COCKFIGHTING, §22-1009.
Penalty, §22-1006.01.

C.O.D.
Buyer not entitled to inspect goods,
§28:2-513.

**CODE OF THE DISTRICT OF
COLUMBIA,** §§45-102, 45-201.
Disabilities, persons with.
Respectful language modernization,
§§2-631, 2-632.
Evidence, CivPro Rule 44-I.
Adoption proceedings, Adoption Rule
44.
Domestic relations actions, DomRel
Rule 44.
Full faith and credit clause, US
Const Art IV §1.
International law.
Power of congress to punish offenses
against, US Const Art I §8.
President.
Approval of laws by president, US
Const Art I §7.
Veto, US Const Art I §7.
Respectful language modernization.
Definitions, §2-631.
References to persons with disabilities.
Terms to avoid, terms to use and
how to use, §2-632.
Retroactive laws.
Ex post facto laws.
Prohibited, US Const Art I §§9, 10.
Statutory construction generally.
See STATUTORY CONSTRUCTION.
Supreme law of the land.
Constitution of the United States, US
Const Art VI.
United States.
Approval of laws by president, US
Const Art I §7.
Ex post facto laws, US Const Art I §§9,
10.
Full faith and credit, US Const Art IV
§1.
Limitations on legislation, US Const
Art I §9.
Proof, US Const Art IV §1.
Revenue bills, US Const Art I §7.
Supreme law of the land, US Const
Art VI.
Veto, US Const Art I §7.

COERCION.
Judges.
Coercing parties into settlement
prohibited, CJC Canon 2.6.

COERCION OF DISCRIMINATION,
§2-1402.61.

COIN TELEPHONES.
Breaking and entering, §22-601.

COKE.
Weights and measures.
General provisions, §§37-201.01 to
37-201.33.
See WEIGHTS AND MEASURES.

COLLABORATIVE LAW, §§16-4001 to
16-4022.
Agreements, §16-4004.
Approval, §16-4008.
Applicability of provisions,
§§16-4003, 16-4021.
Appropriateness of, §16-4014.
Beginning the process, §16-4005.
Citation of provisions, §16-4001.
Coercive relationships, §16-4015.
Concluding the process, §16-4005.
Confidentiality of information,
§§16-4012, 16-4016.
Construction and interpretation,
§16-4021.
Definitions, §16-4002.
Disclosure of information, §§16-4012,
16-4016.
Disqualification of lawyers, §16-4009.
Effective date of provisions,
§16-4003.
Electronic signatures and, §16-4022.
Emergency orders, §16-4007.
Government as party, §16-4011.
Low-income parties, §16-4010.
Mandatory reporting, §16-4013.
Noncompliance, §16-4020.
Privileged communications,
§16-4017.
Limits, §16-4019.
Waiver and preclusion, §16-4018.
Proceedings prior to, §16-4006.
Professional responsibility
standards, §16-4013.
Status reports, §16-4006.
Violent relationships, §16-4015.

COLLATERAL.
Cross-collateral, §28-3805.
District funds invested or deposited
in banks and financial
institutions, §47-351.08.

COLLATERAL RELATIVES.
Intestate succession, §19-311.

COLLECTION AGENCIES.
Consumer protection against
generally, §28-3814.
Tax payment collection, §47-4405.

COLLECTION OF TAXES, §§47-401 to
47-433.
Account books, §§47-404, 47-408.
Administrative hearings, office of.
Jeopardy assessments, protest of,
§47-4451.
Refund offsets, protest of, §47-4312.
Agreement of liability, §47-4403.
Amnesty program, §47-4407.
Bonds, surety, §47-401.
Stay of collection, §47-4452.
Cashier of collector's office, §47-403.
Certificate of taxes and assessments
due, §47-405.
Adjustment rates charged for issuing
certificates for real estate taxes,
§47-406.
Collection agencies, contracting
with, §47-4405.
Collector of taxes, §47-402.
Compensating-use tax, §§47-2202.02,
47-2203.
Compromise as to liability, §47-4404.
Confidentiality of returns, §47-4406.
Corporations, personal liability of
officers, §47-4491.
Credit card payment, §47-4402.
Deputy collector of taxes, §47-402.
Electronic funds transfer payment,
§47-4402.
Gross sales tax, §§47-2002.03, 47-2004,
47-2007.
Holidays, §47-412.01.
Jeopardy assessments, §47-4451.
Levy for failure to pay, §§47-4471 to
47-4481.
See TAXATION.
Lien for taxes.
Duration, §47-4422.
Establishment, §47-4421.
Priority, §47-4423.
Payment, §47-4401.
Personal property.
Distraint or levy.
See PERSONAL PROPERTY
TAXES.
Privatization of, §47-317.04a.
Procedural rules, CivPro Rule 40-III.
Reciprocal recovery of taxes,
§§47-431 to 47-433.
Definitions, §47-433.

COLLECTION OF TAXES —Cont'd
Reciprocal recovery of taxes —Cont'd
Multistate tax compact, §§47-441 to 47-445.
Right of District to sue in states.
Mayor's authority to secure services, §47-432.
Right of states to sue in District.
Proof of authority, §47-431.
Recordation tax, §42-1122.
Recorder of deeds fees deposited with collector of taxes, §42-1212.
Records, §§47-404, 47-408.
Refund offsets.
Additional remedies available, §47-4439.
Appeal of determinations, §47-4437.
Applicability of provisions, §47-4436.
Deposit of offset amounts, §47-4435.
Joint returns, §47-4432.
Notice, §47-4433.
Priority of application, §47-4435.
As against federal offsets, §47-4438.
Protest, right to, §47-4433.
Real property refund for multiple owners of property, §47-4432.
Reciprocal rights of credit, §47-4440.
Return of excess offsets, §47-4434.
Right to credit overpayments, §47-4431.
Refunds of erroneous collections, §47-3306.
Regulations, promulgation, §47-415.
Saturdays, §47-412.01.
Sundays, §47-412.01.
Uncollectible taxes and assessments, §47-408.

COLLECTIVE BARGAINING.
Merit system.
Labor-management relations, §§1-617.01 to 1-617.18.
See MERIT SYSTEM.
Minimum wages.
Right of collective bargaining, §32-1014.
Office of labor relations and collective bargaining, §1-531.01.
Funding for provided in budget, §1-531.02.
Public officers and employees.
Office of labor relations and collective bargaining, §1-531.01.
Funding for provided in budget, §1-531.02.

COLLEGE ACCESS ASSISTANCE.
Students at public and private schools, §§38-2701 to 38-2706.

COLLEGES.
College access assistance, §§38-2701 to 38-2706.
College savings program, §§47-4501 to 47-4512.
DC promise program, §§38-2751 to 38-2759.
See UNIVERSITIES AND COLLEGES.
Dental colleges.
General provisions, §§38-1401 to 38-1419.
See MEDICAL AND DENTAL COLLEGES.
Drug free zones, §48-904.07a.
Federal City College.
General provisions, §§38-1101 to 38-1112.
See FEDERAL CITY COLLEGE.
Successor institution, §§38-1201.01 to 38-1207.07.
See UNIVERSITY OF THE DISTRICT OF COLUMBIA.
Gallaudet University.
General provisions, §§38-2301 to 38-2402.11.
See GALLAUDET UNIVERSITY.
General provisions.
See UNIVERSITIES AND COLLEGES.
Insurance holding companies.
Supervisory colleges, §31-707.01.
Law school, §§38-1205.01 to 38-1205.12.
See DISTRICT OF COLUMBIA SCHOOL OF LAW.
Management of institutional funds.
General provisions.
See PRUDENT INVESTOR ACT.
Medical colleges.
General provisions, §§38-1401 to 38-1419.
See MEDICAL AND DENTAL COLLEGES.
Student health care.
General provisions, §§38-601 to 38-651.12.
See STUDENT HEALTH CARE.
University of the District of Columbia.
General provisions, §§38-1201.01 to 38-1207.07.
See UNIVERSITY OF THE DISTRICT OF COLUMBIA.

COLLEGE SAVINGS PROGRAM, §§47-4501 to 47-4512.
Administration of program, §47-4505.

COLLEGE SAVINGS PROGRAM
—Cont'd
Audit.
Program depository or manager, §47-4506.
Submission of audit report, §47-4512.
College savings accounts.
Application for, §47-4503.
Authorized, §47-4502.
Designated beneficiary.
  Change, §47-4503.
Distributions.
  Reporting to IRS, §47-4503.
Establishment, §47-4503.
Fee for maintenance of account, §47-4503.
Information disclosed to account owner, §47-4503.
Interest in account.
  Prohibited uses, §47-4503.
Transfer to another account, §47-4503.
Withdrawals, notice required, §47-4503.
College savings program trust.
Designated as, §47-4502.
Definitions, §47-4501.
Established, §47-4502.
Examination of program manager, §47-4506.
Financial organizations.
Implementation through, §47-4506.
Implementation, §§47-4505, 47-4506.
Limitations, §47-4507.
Local tax exemption, §47-4509.
Management contract, §47-4506.
Obligation or guarantee of District.
Program not to create, §47-4507.
Payroll deductions to remit payments to accounts, §47-4511.
Reports.
Submission of audit report, §47-4512.
Seizure of accounts prohibited, §47-4510.
Tax exemption, §47-4509.
Termination of program manager or depository, §47-4506.
Trustee.
Chief financial officer, §47-4502.

COLONIAL DAMES OF AMERICA.
Real property exempt from taxation, §47-1004.

COLORECTAL CANCER SCREENING.
Health insurance coverage, §31-2931.

COLUMBIA HOSPITAL FOR WOMEN.
Conveyance of property to, §44-751.

COLUMBIA HOSPITAL FOR WOMEN —Cont'd
Lien in favor of United States, §44-753.

COLUMBUS DAY.
Appeals in federal cases, FRAP 26(a), 45(a).
Designated holiday, §1-612.02.

COMFORT CARE BRACELETS OR NECKLACES.
Comfort care orders.
Non-resuscitation procedures for EMS, §§7-651.01 to 7-651.16.
See EMERGENCY MEDICAL SERVICES.

COMFORT CARE ORDERS.
Non-resuscitation procedures for EMS, §§7-651.01 to 7-651.16.
See EMERGENCY MEDICAL SERVICES.

COMMEMORATIVE WORKS.
Public space, §§9-204.11 to 9-204.19.

COMMENCEMENT OF ACTIONS,
CivPro Rule 3.
Domestic relations actions, DomRel Rule 3.
Parentage proceedings, DomRel Rule 405.
Landlord and tenant court, LandlordTenant Rule 3.
Parentage proceedings, DomRel Rule 405.
Probate proceedings.
Contested estate cases, Probate Rule 407.
  Death before January 1, 1981, Probate Rule 15.
  Death between January 1, 1981 and June 30, 1995, Probate Rule 107.
  Guardians, conservators, trustees, etc., involved, Probate Rule 208.
Reciprocal enforcement of support proceedings, DomRel Rule 401.
Small claims court, SmallClaims Rule 3.

COMMERCIAL BICYCLE OPERATORS, §§50-1631 to 50-1634.

COMMERCIAL CODE, §§28:1-101 to 28:11-108.
Bank deposits and collections, §§28:4-101 to 28:4-504.
Agreement for electronic presentment.
  Defined, §28:4-110.

COMMERCIAL CODE —Cont'd
Bank deposits and collections
—Cont'd
Payor banks —Cont'd
Customer relationship.
Alteration of instruments.
Customer's duty to discover and
report, §28:4-406.
Charging customer's account.
When allowed, §28:4-401.
Death of customer.
Effect, §28:4-405.
Dishonor, wrongful.
Liability of customer, §28:4-402.
Incompetency of customer.
Effect, §28:4-405.
Stale checks.
Obligation of bank to pay,
§28:4-404.
Stop payment orders.
Customer's right to issue,
§28:4-403.
Subrogation on improper payment.
Right of payor bank, §28:4-407.
Unauthorized signatures.
Customer's duty to discover and
report, §28:4-406.
Subrogation rights on improper
payment, §28:4-407.
Presentment.
Electronic presentment, §28:4-110.
Responsibility of presenting banks,
§28:4-503.
Receipt of items.
Delay, §28:4-109.
Time, §28:4-108.
Refunds, §28:4-214.
Statute of limitations, §28:4-111.
Deposits and collections.
Unauthorized signature or
alteration.
Claims against bank, §28:4-406.
Warranties.
Documents of title, §28:7-508.
Conflict of laws.
Parties' power to choose applicable
law, §28:1-301.
Construction and interpretation.
Bills of lading.
Third party documents, prima facie
evidence, §28:1-307.
Course of dealing, §28:1-303.
Definitions.
General commercial code definitions,
§28:1-201.
Course of dealing, §28:1-303.

COMMERCIAL CODE —Cont'd
Construction and interpretation
—Cont'd
Definitions —Cont'd
General commercial code definitions
—Cont'd
Reasonable time and seasonably,
§28:1-205.
Usage of trade, §28:1-303.
Evidence.
Bills of lading.
Third party documents, prima
facie evidence, §28:1-307.
General repealer, §28:10-103.
General rules of construction,
§28:1-103.
Good faith.
Obligation of good faith, §28:1-304.
Implicit repeal.
Construction against, §28:1-104.
Parties' power to choose applicable
law, §28:1-301.
Reasonable time, §28:1-205.
Remedies to be liberally administered,
§28:1-305.
Saving of certain provisions,
§28:10-104.
Seasonably, §28:1-205.
Severability of provisions, §28:1-105.
Supplementary general principles of
law.
Applicable, §28:1-103.
Territorial application of act,
§28:1-301.
Time, §28:1-205.
Usage of trade, §28:1-303.
Construction of code, §§28:10-103,
28:10-104.
Contributory negligence.
Negotiable instruments.
Forged signature or alteration of
instrument, §28:3-406.
Documents of title, §§28:7-101 to
28:7-702.
Agriculture.
Warehouse receipts.
Storage of commodities under
government bond, §28:7-201.
Alcoholic beverages.
Warehouse receipts.
Storage under government bond,
§28:7-201.
Alteration.
Bills of lading, §28:7-306.
Warehouse receipts, §28:7-208.
Applicability of provisions.
Effective date, §28:7-701.

COMMERCIAL CODE —Cont'd
Documents of title —Cont'd
Applicability of provisions —Cont'd
Savings clause, §28:7-702.
Attachment of goods.
Goods covered by negotiable
document, §28:7-602.
Bills of lading.
Altered bills, §28:7-306.
Care owing from carrier, §28:7-309.
Consignments.
Reconsignment, §28:7-303.
Contractual limitation of carrier's
liability, §28:7-309.
Delivery of goods, §28:7-303.
Good faith delivery pursuant to
bill, §28:7-404.
Obligation of carrier to deliver,
§28:7-403.
Description of goods.
Liability for misdescription,
§28:7-301.
"Said to contain," §28:7-301.
"Shipper's weight, load and
count," §28:7-301.
Destination bills, §28:7-305.
Diversion of goods, §28:7-303.
Duplicates, §28:7-402.
Generally, §§28:7-301 to 28:7-309.
Handling of goods.
Improper handling, §28:7-301.
Instructions.
Change, §28:7-303.
Irregularities in issue or conduct of
issuer, §28:7-401.
Liability.
Contractual limitation of carrier's
liability, §28:7-309.
Good faith delivery pursuant to
bill, §28:7-404.
Nonreceipt or misdescription of
goods, §28:7-301.
Lien of carrier, §28:7-307.
Enforcement, §28:7-308.
Negotiability, §28:7-104.
Negotiation.
Generally, §§28:7-501 to 28:7-509.
See within this subheading,
"Negotiation and transfer."
Overissue, §28:7-402.
Overseas shipments, §28:2-323.
Receipt of goods.
Liability for nonreceipt, §28:7-301.
Sets, §28:7-304.
Third party documents.
Prima facie evidence, §28:1-307.

COMMERCIAL CODE —Cont'd
Documents of title —Cont'd
Bills of lading —Cont'd
Through bills and similar
documents, §28:7-302.
Transfer.
Generally, §§28:7-501 to 28:7-509.
See within this subheading,
"Negotiation and transfer."
Certain laws not repealed, §28:10-104.
Citation of article.
Short title, §28:7-101.
Claims.
Conflicting claims.
Interpleader, §28:7-603.
Consignor and consignee.
Bills of lading.
Reconsignment, §28:7-303.
Construction and interpretation.
Certain laws not repealed,
§28:10-104.
Relation of article to treaty, statute,
tariff, classification or
regulation, §28:7-103.
Contracts.
Bills of lading.
Limitation of carrier's liability,
§28:7-309.
Warehouse receipts.
Limitation of liability of
warehouse, §28:7-204.
When adequate compliance with
obligations of commercial
contract, §28:7-509.
Crops.
Warehouse receipts.
Storage under government bond,
§28:7-201.
Definitions, §28:7-102.
Duly negotiated, §28:7-501.
General commercial code definitions,
§28:1-201.
Course of dealing, §28:1-303.
Reasonable time and seasonably,
§28:1-205.
Usage of trade, §28:1-303.
Index of definitions, §28:7-102.
Delivery of goods.
Bills of lading, §28:7-303.
Good faith delivery pursuant to
bill, §28:7-404.
Obligation of carrier to deliver,
§28:7-403.
Excuses, §28:7-403.
Negotiation and transfer.
Seller's stoppage of delivery.
Rights acquired in absence of
due negotiation, §28:7-504.

COMMERCIAL CODE —Cont'd
Documents of title —Cont'd
Delivery of goods —Cont'd
Warehouse receipts.
Good faith delivery pursuant to receipt, §28:7-404.
Obligation of warehouse to deliver, §28:7-403.
Warranties, §28:7-507.
Description of goods.
Bills of lading.
Liability for misdescription, §28:7-301.
"Said to contain," §28:7-301.
"Shipper's weight, load and count," §28:7-301.
Warehouse receipts.
Liability for misdescription, §28:7-203.
Diversion of goods.
Bills of lading, §28:7-303.
Negotiation and transfer.
Rights acquired in absence of due negotiation.
Effect of diversion, §28:7-504.
Duplicates, §28:7-402.
Electronic documents.
Control, §28:7-106.
Reissuance in alternative medium, §28:7-105.
Endorsements.
Negotiation and transfer.
Delivery without endorsement, §28:7-506.
Endorser not guarantor for other parties, §28:7-505.
Right to compel endorsement, §28:7-506.
Forms.
Warehouse receipts, §28:7-202.
Fungible goods.
Warehouse receipts, §28:7-207.
Good faith.
Obligation of good faith, §28:1-304.
Guaranty.
Negotiation and transfer.
Endorser not guarantor for other parties, §28:7-505.
Handling of goods.
Bills of lading.
Improper handling, §28:7-301.
Liability.
Carrier's liability.
Contractual limitation of carrier's liability, §28:7-309.
Description of goods.
Liability for misdescription, §28:7-301.

COMMERCIAL CODE —Cont'd
Documents of title —Cont'd
Liability —Cont'd
Carrier's liability —Cont'd
Good faith delivery of goods pursuant to bill.
No liability, §28:7-404.
Receipt of goods.
Liability for nonreceipt, §28:7-301.
Warehouse liability.
Contractual limitation of warehouseman's liability, §28:7-204.
Good faith delivery of goods pursuant to receipt.
No liability, §28:7-404.
Nonreceipt or misdescription of goods, §28:7-203.
Liens.
Carrier's lien, §28:7-307.
Enforcement, §28:7-308.
Warehouse lien, §§28:7-209, 28:7-210.
Lost instruments and records, §28:7-601.
Missing documents, §28:7-601.
Negotiability, §28:7-104.
Negotiation and transfer, §§28:7-501 to 28:7-509.
Commercial contracts.
When document adequately complies with obligations of, §28:7-509.
Delivery of goods.
Seller's stoppage of delivery.
Rights acquired in absence of due negotiation, §28:7-504.
Diversion of goods.
Rights acquired in absence of due negotiation.
Effect of diversion, §28:7-504.
Due negotiation.
Requirements, §28:7-501.
Rights acquired, §28:7-502.
Endorsements.
Delivery without endorsement, §28:7-506.
Endorser not guarantor for other parties, §28:7-505.
Right to compel endorsement, §28:7-506.
Form of negotiation, §28:7-501.
Rights acquired.
Absence of due negotiation, §28:7-504.

COMMERCIAL CODE —Cont'd
Documents of title —Cont'd
Negotiation and transfer —Cont'd
Rights acquired —Cont'd
Due negotiation, §28:7-502.
Title to goods defeated in certain
cases, §28:7-503.
Warranties.
Collecting bank's warranties as to
documents, §28:7-508.
Overissues, §28:7-402.
Receipt of goods.
Bills of lading.
Liability for nonreceipt, §28:7-301.
Warehouse receipts.
Liability for nonreceipt, §28:7-203.
Separation of goods.
Warehouse receipts, §28:7-207.
Stolen records, §28:7-601.
Substitute documents for electronic
documents, §28:7-105.
Title of article.
Short title, §28:7-101.
Transfer.
Generally, §§28:7-501 to 28:7-509.
See within this subheading,
"Negotiation and transfer."
United States treaty or statute.
Relation of article, §28:7-103.
Warehouse receipts.
Altered receipts, §28:7-208.
Care owing from warehouse,
§28:7-204.
Contractual limitation of liability of
warehouse, §28:7-204.
Delivery of goods.
Good faith delivery pursuant to
receipt, §28:7-404.
Obligation of warehouse to
deliver, §28:7-403.
Description of goods.
Liability for misdescription,
§28:7-203.
Duplicates, §28:7-402.
Forms, §28:7-202.
Fungible goods, §28:7-207.
Generally, §§28:7-202 to 28:7-210.
Government bond.
Storage under, §28:7-201.
Irregularities in issue or conduct of
issuer, §28:7-401.
Liability.
Contractual limitation of
warehouse liability, §28:7-204.
Good faith delivery of goods
pursuant to receipt, §28:7-404.

COMMERCIAL CODE —Cont'd
Documents of title —Cont'd
Warehouse receipts —Cont'd
Liability —Cont'd
Nonreceipt or misdescription of
goods, §28:7-203.
Lien of warehouse, §28:7-209.
Enforcement, §28:7-210.
Negotiability, §28:7-104.
Negotiation.
Generally, §§28:7-501 to 28:7-509.
See within this subheading,
"Negotiation and transfer."
Overissue, §28:7-402.
Receipt of goods.
Liability for nonreceipt, §28:7-203.
Separation of goods, §28:7-207.
Termination of storage.
Option of warehouse, §28:7-206.
Terms.
Essential terms, §28:7-202.
Optional terms, §28:7-202.
Title defeated in certain cases,
§28:7-205.
Transfer.
Generally, §§28:7-501 to 28:7-509.
See within this subheading,
"Negotiation and transfer."
Who may issue, §28:7-201.
Warranties.
Negotiation and transfer, §28:7-507.
Negotiation or delivery, §28:7-507.
Collecting bank's warranties as to
documents, §28:7-508.
Funds transfers, §§28:4A-101 to
28:4A-507.
Applicability of article, §28:4A-102.
Federal electronic fund transfer act.
Relationship between UCC
provision and federal
provision, §28:4A-108.
Attachment and garnishment.
Creditor process served on receiving
bank, §28:4A-502.
Beneficiary.
Defined, §28:4A-103.
Payment order misdescription,
§28:4A-207.
Beneficiary's bank.
Defined, §28:4A-103.
Payment orders.
Misdescription, §28:4A-208.
Obligation to pay and give notice
to beneficiary, §28:4A-404.
Payment to beneficiary,
§28:4A-405.

COMMERCIAL CODE —Cont'd
Funds transfers —Cont'd
Beneficiary's bank —Cont'd
Setoff by, §28:4A-502.
Choice of law, §28:4A-507.
Citation of title, §28:4A-101.
Conflict of laws.
Choice of law, §28:4A-507.
Federal electronic fund transfer act.
Relationship between UCC
provision and federal
provision, §28:4A-108.
Federal reserve regulations and
operating circulars, §28:4A-107.
Creditor process served on receiving
bank, §28:4A-502.
Definitions.
Authorized account, §28:4A-105.
Bank, §28:4A-105.
Beneficiary, §28:4A-103.
Beneficiary's bank, §28:4A-103.
Creditor process, §28:4A-502.
Customer, §28:4A-105.
Executed, §28:4A-301.
Execution date, §28:4A-301.
Funds-transfer business day,
§28:4A-105.
Funds transfers, §28:4A-104.
Funds-transfer system, §28:4A-105.
Funds-transfer system rule,
§28:4A-501.
Index of definitions, §28:4A-105.
Intermediary bank, §28:4A-104.
Originator, §28:4A-104.
Originator's bank, §28:4A-104.
Payment date, §28:4A-401.
Payment order, §28:4A-103.
Prove, §28:4A-105.
Receiving bank, §28:4A-103.
Security procedure, §28:4A-201.
Sender, §28:4A-103.
Federal electronic fund transfer act.
Relationship between UCC provision
and federal provision,
§28:4A-108.
Federal reserve regulations and
operating circulars, §28:4A-107.
Funds-transfer system rule.
Defined, §28:4A-501.
Effect of, §28:4A-501.
Variation by agreement, §28:4A-501.
Injunctive relief, §28:4A-503.
Interest.
Rate of interest, §28:4A-506.
Intermediary bank.
Defined, §28:4A-104.

COMMERCIAL CODE —Cont'd
Funds transfers —Cont'd
Intermediary bank —Cont'd
Payment order misdescription,
§28:4A-208.
Notice.
Payment orders.
Obligation of beneficiary's bank to
give notice to beneficiary,
§28:4A-404.
Rejection of payment order,
§28:4A-210.
Payment orders.
Acceptance, §28:4A-209.
Amendment, §28:4A-211.
Authorized payment orders,
§28:4A-202.
Cancellation, §28:4A-211.
Cut-off time, §28:4A-106.
Defined, §28:4A-103.
Discharge of underlying obligation,
§28:4A-406.
Erroneous payment orders,
§28:4A-205.
Execution by receiving bank.
Erroneous execution, §28:4A-303.
Duty of sender to report,
§28:4A-304.
"Executed" defined, §28:4A-301.
"Execution date" defined,
§28:4A-301.
Failure to execute.
Liability for, §28:4A-305.
Improper execution.
Liability for, §28:4A-305.
Late execution.
Liability for, §28:4A-305.
Obligations of receiving bank,
§28:4A-302.
Misdescription.
Beneficiary, §28:4A-207.
Beneficiary's bank, §28:4A-208.
Intermediary bank, §28:4A-208.
Objection to debit of customer's
account.
Preclusion of objection,
§28:4A-505.
Obligation of beneficiary's bank,
§28:4A-404.
Obligation of sender to pay receiving
bank, §28:4A-402.
Order in which payment orders may
be charged to account,
§28:4A-504.
Order of withdrawals from account,
§28:4A-504.

COMMERCIAL CODE —Cont'd
Funds transfers —Cont'd
Payment orders —Cont'd
Payment by beneficiary's bank to
beneficiary, §28:4A-405.
Payment by originator to
beneficiary, §28:4A-406.
Payment by sender to receiving
bank, §28:4A-403.
Payment date.
Defined, §28:4A-401.
Preclusion of objection to debit of
customer's account, §28:4A-505.
Rejection, §28:4A-210.
Liability and duty of receiving
bank regarding unaccepted
payment order, §28:4A-212.
Security procedure.
Defined, §28:4A-201.
Time of acceptance, §28:4A-209.
Time received, §28:4A-106.
Transmission through
communications system,
§28:4A-206.
Transmission through funds-transfer
system, §28:4A-206.
Unauthorized payment orders.
Duty of customer to report,
§28:4A-204.
Refund of payment, §28:4A-204.
Verified payment orders, §28:4A-202.
Unenforceability of, §28:4A-203.
Scope of article, §28:4A-102.
Service of process.
Creditor process on receiving bank,
§28:4A-502.
Setoff by beneficiary's bank,
§28:4A-502.
Short title, §28:4A-101.
Statutory construction.
Federal electronic fund transfer act.
Relationship between UCC
provision and federal
provision, §28:4A-108.
Title of article, §28:4A-101.
General definitions, §28:1-201.
Notice and knowledge, §28:1-202.
General provisions, §§28:1-101 to
28:1-310.
Acceleration at will.
Options, §28:1-309.
Acceptance under reservation of
rights, §28:1-308.
Agreements.
Variation of code, §28:1-302.
Applicability of article, §28:1-102.

COMMERCIAL CODE —Cont'd
General provisions —Cont'd
Applicable law.
Parties' power to choose, §28:1-301.
Supplementary general principles of
law, §28:1-103.
Captions of sections.
Construction, §28:1-107.
Citation of title.
Short title, §28:1-101.
Claims under code.
Waiver of renunciation of claim after
breach, §28:1-306.
Construction and interpretation.
Course of dealing, §28:1-303.
Gender, §28:1-106.
General rules of construction,
§28:1-103.
Implicit repeal.
Construction against, §28:1-104.
Parties' power to choose applicable
law, §28:1-301.
Plural includes singular, §28:1-106.
Reasonable time, §28:1-205.
Remedies to be liberally
administered, §28:1-305.
Section captions, §28:1-107.
Singular and plural, §28:1-106.
Creditors.
Subordination of right to
performance, §28:1-310.
Definitions, §28:1-201.
Course of dealing, §28:1-303.
Discover, §28:1-202.
Knowledge, §28:1-202.
Learn, §28:1-202.
Notice, §28:1-202.
Notifies, §28:1-202.
Receives, §28:1-202.
Seasonably, §28:1-205.
Usage of trade, §28:1-303.
Electronic signatures in global and
national commerce act.
Effect of commercial code on act,
§28:1-108.
Evidence.
Third party documents.
Prima facie evidence, §28:1-307.
Gender.
Construction and interpretation,
§28:1-106.
Good faith obligations, §28:1-304.
Disclaimer by agreement prohibited,
§28:1-302.
Leases.
Security interest distinguished from
lease, §28:1-203.

COMMERCIAL CODE —Cont'd
General provisions —Cont'd
Option to accelerate at will, §28:1-309.
Performance under reservation of
rights, §28:1-308.
Plural includes singular.
Construction and interpretation,
§28:1-106.
Presumptions.
Effect to be given by trier of fact,
§28:1-206.
Purposes of code, §28:1-103.
Reasonableness.
Disclaiming by agreement
prohibited, §28:1-302.
Remedies to be liberally administered,
§28:1-305.
Renunciation of claims or rights after
breach, §28:1-306.
Section captions, §28:1-107.
Security interests.
Lease distinguished from security
interest, §28:1-203.
Subordination of obligation does not
create security interest,
§28:1-310.
Severability of provisions, §28:1-105.
Short title, §28:1-101.
Singular and plural.
Construction and interpretation,
§28:1-106.
Subordination of obligations,
§28:1-310.
Value.
Giving value described, §28:1-204.
Variation of code by agreement,
§28:1-303.
Waiver of claims or rights after
breach, §28:1-306.
Investment securities, §§28:8-101 to
28:8-601.
Acquisition of security or interest
therein, §28:8-104.
Adverse claims.
Defined, §28:8-102.
Notice, §28:8-105.
Securities intermediary and others
not liable to adverse claimant,
§28:8-115.
Security entitlements.
Assertion of adverse claim against
entitlement holder, §28:8-502.
Rights of purchaser of security
entitlement from entitlement
holder, §28:8-510.
Alteration of security certificate,
§28:8-206.

COMMERCIAL CODE —Cont'd
Investment securities —Cont'd
Applicable law, §28:8-110.
Choice of law, §28:8-110.
Citation of article.
Short title, §28:8-101.
Clearing corporations.
Defined, §28:8-102.
Rules, §28:8-111.
Completion of security certificate,
§28:8-206.
Control, §28:8-106.
Creditor's legal process, §28:8-112.
Defenses.
Issuer's defenses.
Generally, §28:8-202.
Notice of defense, §§28:8-202,
28:8-203.
Definitions, §28:8-210.
Appropriate evidence of appointment
or incumbency, §28:8-402.
General commercial code definitions,
§28:1-201.
Course of dealing, §28:1-303.
Reasonable time and seasonably,
§28:1-205.
Usage of trade, §28:1-303.
Guaranty of the signature,
§28:8-402.
Index of definitions, §28:8-102.
Issuers, §28:8-201.
Overissue, §28:8-104.
Protected purchaser, §28:8-303.
Securities account, §28:8-501.
Destroyed securities.
Registration, §28:8-405.
Destroyed security certificates.
Notification to issuer, §28:8-406.
Replacement, §28:8-405.
Endorsements.
Registration of securities.
Duty of issuer to register transfer,
§28:8-401.
Entitlement orders.
Defined, §28:8-102.
Effectiveness, §28:8-107.
Evidence.
Rules concerning certificated
securities, §28:8-114.
Financial assets.
Defined, §28:8-102.
Security interest arising in purchase
or delivery of, §28:9-206.
Good faith.
Obligation of good faith, §28:1-304.
Indorsements, §28:8-304.
Assurance that indorsement is
effective, §28:8-402.

COMMERCIAL CODE —Cont'd
Investment securities —Cont'd
  Indorsements —Cont'd
    Defined, §28:8-102.
    Effectiveness, §28:8-107.
    Guaranteeing indorsement.
      Effect, §28:8-306.
  Instructions, §28:8-305.
    Assurance that instructions are
      effective, §28:8-402.
    Defined, §28:8-102.
    Effectiveness, §28:8-107.
    Guaranteeing instruction.
      Effect, §28:8-306.
  Issuers.
    Defenses.
      Generally, §28:8-202.
      Notice of defense, §§28:8-202,
        28:8-203.
    Defined, §28:8-201.
    Liens, §28:8-209.
    Registration.
      Demand that issuer not register
        transfer, §28:8-403.
      Duty to register transfer,
        §28:8-401.
      Notification to issuer of lost,
        destroyed or wrongfully taken
        security certificate, §28:8-406.
    Transfer of security.
      Duty of issuer, §28:8-401.
    Responsibility, §28:8-202.
    Rights with respect to registered
      owners, §28:8-207.
    Transfer restrictions.
      Effect, §28:8-204.
  Issues.
    Overissues.
      Defined, §28:8-210.
      Effect, §28:8-210.
  Liens.
    Issuer's lien, §28:8-209.
  Lost security certificates.
    Notification to issuer, §28:8-406.
    Replacement, §28:8-405.
  Notice.
    Adverse claims, §28:8-105.
    Defects or defenses, §§28:8-202,
      28:8-203.
  Overissues.
    Defined, §28:8-210.
    Effect, §28:8-210.
  Purchaser.
    Delivery to, §28:8-301.
    Protected purchaser, §28:8-303.
    Rights acquired, §28:8-302.

COMMERCIAL CODE —Cont'd
Investment securities —Cont'd
  Purchaser —Cont'd
    Right to requisites for registration of
      transfer, §28:8-307.
  Registration.
    Assurance that indorsements or
      instructions are effective,
      §28:8-402.
    Authenticating trustee.
      Obligations, §28:8-407.
    Issuer.
      Demand that issuer not register
        transfer, §28:8-403.
      Duty to register transfer,
        §28:8-401.
      Notification of lost, destroyed or
        wrongfully taken security
        certificate, §28:8-406.
      Rights with respect to registered
        owners, §28:8-207.
    Purchaser's right to requisites for
      registration of transfer,
      §28:8-307.
    Registrar.
      Obligations, §28:8-407.
    Replacement of lost, destroyed or
      wrongfully taken security
      certificates, §28:8-405.
    Signature of registrar.
      Effect, §28:8-208.
    Transfer.
      Duty of issuer to register transfer,
        §28:8-401.
    Transfer agent.
      Obligations, §28:8-407.
    Wrongful registration, §28:8-404.
  Rules for determining whether certain
    obligations and interests are
    securities or financial assets,
    §28:8-103.
  Savings clause, §28:8-601.
  Secured transactions.
    Attachment and enforceability of
      security interests, §28:9-203.
    Financial asset.
      Security interest arising in
        purchase or delivery of,
        §28:9-206.
    Security entitlements.
      Priority among security interests
        and entitlement holders,
        §28:8-511.
  Securities intermediaries.
    Defined, §28:8-102.
    Liability.
      Not liable to adverse claimant,
        §28:8-115.

COMMERCIAL CODE —Cont'd
Investment securities —Cont'd
Warranties.
Direct holding, §28:8-108.
Effect of signature of authenticating trustee, registrar or transfer agent, §28:8-208.
Indirect holding, §28:8-109.
Wrongfully taken security certificates.
Notification to issuer, §28:8-406.
Replacement, §28:8-405.
Leases, §§28:2A-101 to 28:2A-532.
Acceptance of goods, §28:2A-515.
Accessions.
Lessor's and lessee's rights when goods become accessions, §28:2A-310.
Burden of establishing default after acceptance, §28:2A-516.
Damages.
Lessor's damages for nonacceptance, §28:2A-528.
Effect, §28:2A-516.
Nonconforming goods or delivery of goods, §28:2A-509.
Notice of default, §28:2A-516.
Rejection of goods. See within this subheading, "Shipment and delivery."
Revocation of acceptance, §28:2A-517.
Damages, §28:2A-519.
Justifiable revocation, §28:2A-517.
Lessee's rights and remedies, §28:2A-508.
Wrongful revocation, §28:2A-523.
Accessions.
Defined, §28:2A-310.
Lessor's and lessee's rights.
When goods become accessions, §28:2A-310.
Alienability of interest.
Lessor's residual interest in goods, §28:2A-303.
Party's interest under lease contract, §28:2A-303.
Animals.
Unborn young.
Definition of "goods," §28:2A-103.
Identification, §28:2A-217.
Anticipatory repudiation, §28:2A-402.
Retraction, §28:2A-403.
Applicability of article.
Certificates of title.
Territorial application of article to goods covered by certificates, §28:2A-105.

COMMERCIAL CODE —Cont'd
Leases —Cont'd
Applicability of article —Cont'd
Leases subject to other statutes, §28:2A-104.
Scope, §28:2A-102.
Assignments, §28:2A-303.
Attorneys at law.
Fees.
Unconscionable lease contracts or clauses, §28:2A-108.
Buyer in ordinary course of business.
Defined, §28:2A-103.
Cancellation.
Defined, §28:2A-103.
Effect on rights and remedies, §28:2A-505.
Lessor's remedies, §28:2A-523.
Casualty to identified goods, §28:2A-221.
Citation of article, §28:2A-101.
Claims.
Limitation of actions, §28:2A-506.
Notice of claim to person answerable over, §28:2A-516.
Rent.
Action by lessor, §28:2A-529.
Third parties.
Standing to sue for injury to goods, §28:2A-531.
Waiver or renunciation, §28:2A-107.
Commercial units.
Defined, §28:2A-103.
Conflict of laws.
Leases subject to other statutes, §28:2A-104.
Limitation on power of parties to choose applicable law and judicial forum, §28:2A-106.
Conforming.
Defined, §28:2A-103.
Construction of lease agreements.
Course of performance, §28:1-303.
Consumer leases.
Choice of judicial forum, §28:2A-106.
Defined, §28:2A-103.
Option to accelerate at will, §28:2A-109.
Unconscionability, §28:2A-108.
Cover by lessor, §28:2A-518.
Creditors' special rights, §28:2A-308.
Damages.
Acceptance of goods.
Nonacceptance.
Lessor's damages, §28:2A-528.
Consequential damages, §28:2A-520.

COMMERCIAL CODE —Cont'd
Leases —Cont'd
  Damages —Cont'd
    Cover by lessor.
      Effect, §28:2A-518.
    Incidental damages, §28:2A-520.
      Lessor's damages, §28:2A-530.
    Lessee's incidental and
        consequential damages.
      Generally, §28:2A-520.
    Lessor's damages.
      Generally, §28:2A-523.
      Incidental damages, §28:2A-530.
      Nonacceptance or repudiation by
        lessee, §28:2A-528.
    Liquidation, §28:2A-504.
    Nondelivery of goods, §28:2A-519.
    Rejection of goods, §28:2A-519.
    Repudiation by lessee.
      Lessor's damages, §28:2A-528.
    Repudiation by lessor, §28:2A-519.
    Revocation of acceptance of goods,
        §28:2A-519.
    Warranties.
      Breach of warranty, §§28:2A-508,
        28:2A-519.
  Default.
    Anticipatory repudiation,
        §§28:2A-402, 28:2A-403.
    Cover.
      Right of lessor, §28:2A-518.
    Installment lease contracts.
      Lessee's rights and remedies,
        §28:2A-508.
      Rejection and default, §28:2A-510.
    Limitation of actions, §28:2A-506.
    Modification or impairment,
        §28:2A-503.
    Notice, §§28:2A-502, 28:2A-516.
    Procedure generally, §28:2A-501.
    Replevin of goods, §§28:2A-508,
        28:2A-521.
    Rights and remedies.
      Default by lessee.
        Disposal of goods by lessor,
          §§28:2A-523, 28:2A-524,
          28:2A-527.
        Identification of goods to lease
          contract, §28:2A-524.
        Possession of goods,
          §§28:2A-523, 28:2A-525.
        Rent action by lessor,
          §28:2A-529.
      Default by lessor.
        Cover, §28:2A-518.
        Lessee's rights and remedies
          generally, §28:2A-508.

COMMERCIAL CODE —Cont'd
Leases —Cont'd
  Default —Cont'd
    Rights and remedies —Cont'd
      Default by lessor —Cont'd
        Nonconforming goods or
          delivery of goods,
          §§28:2A-509, 28:2A-510.
        Replevy of goods, §§28:2A-508,
          28:2A-521.
        Specific performance,
          §§28:2A-508, 28:2A-521.
        Substitute goods, §28:2A-518.
        Waiver or renunciation of rights
          after default, §28:2A-107.
    Risk of loss.
      Effect of default on risk,
          §28:2A-220.
  Defenses.
    Unconscionability, §28:2A-108.
  Definitions, §28:2A-103.
    Accessions, §28:2A-310.
    Fixtures, §28:2A-309.
    Index of definitions, §28:2A-103.
  Delegation of performance,
      §28:2A-303.
  Delivery of goods.
    Generally. See within this
        subheading, "Shipment and
        delivery."
  Disposal of goods.
    Lessor's rights and remedies,
        §§28:2A-523, 28:2A-524,
        28:2A-527.
  Enforcement of lease contract,
      §28:2A-301.
  Evidence.
    Extrinsic evidence, §28:2A-202.
  Excused performance, §28:2A-405.
    Procedure on excused performance,
        §28:2A-406.
  Express warranties.
    Generally, §28:2A-210.
    Third party beneficiaries,
        §28:2A-216.
  Extrinsic evidence, §28:2A-202.
  Fault.
    Defined, §28:2A-103.
  Finance leases.
    Defined, §28:2A-103.
    Irrevocable promises, §28:2A-407.
    Lessee under finance lease as
        beneficiary of supply contract,
        §28:2A-209.
  Losses.
    Casualty to identified goods,
        §28:2A-221.

COMMERCIAL CODE —Cont'd
Leases —Cont'd
Finance leases —Cont'd
Losses —Cont'd
Risk of loss, §28:2A-219.
Supply contracts.
Lessee under finance lease as beneficiary, §28:2A-209.
Warranties.
Implied warranty of fitness for particular purpose, §28:2A-213.
Implied warranty of merchantability, §28:2A-212.
Warranty against infringement, §28:2A-211.
Firm offers, §28:2A-205.
Fitness for particular purpose.
Implied warranties, §28:2A-213.
Fixtures.
Defined, §28:2A-309.
Lessor's and lessee's rights.
When goods become fixtures, §28:2A-309.
Formation.
Firm offers, §28:2A-205.
Generally, §28:2A-204.
Offer and acceptance.
Firm offers, §28:2A-205.
Generally, §28:2A-206.
Fraud.
Effect on rights and remedies, §28:2A-505.
Goods.
Defined, §28:2A-103.
Identification of goods, §28:2A-217.
Casualty to identified goods, §28:2A-221.
Insurable interest in existing goods.
Vesting in lessee, §28:2A-218.
Lessor's right to identify goods upon lessee's default, §28:2A-524.
Implied warranties.
Fitness for particular purpose, §28:2A-213.
Merchantability, §28:2A-212.
Third party beneficiaries, §28:2A-216.
Infringement.
Warranty against, §28:2A-211.
Insecurity.
Adequate assurance of performance, §28:2A-401.
Insolvency of lessor.
Lessee's rights to goods, §28:2A-522.

COMMERCIAL CODE —Cont'd
Leases —Cont'd
Installment lease contracts.
Default.
Lessee's rights and remedies, §28:2A-508.
Rejection and default, §28:2A-510.
Defined, §28:2A-103.
Insurance, §28:2A-218.
Interference with goods.
Warranty against interference, §28:2A-211.
Lease agreements.
Defined, §28:2A-103.
Lease contracts.
Defined, §28:2A-103.
Leasehold interest.
Defined, §28:2A-103.
Lessee in ordinary course of business.
Defined, §28:2A-103.
Lessees.
Defined, §28:2A-103.
Lessors.
Defined, §28:2A-103.
Lessor's residual interest.
Defined, §28:2A-103.
Liens.
Defined, §28:2A-103.
Priority of certain liens arising by operation of law, §28:2A-306.
Priority of liens arising by attachment or levy on, security interest in and other claims to goods, §28:2A-307.
Limitation of actions.
Action for default, §28:2A-506.
Losses.
Casualty to identified goods, §28:2A-221.
Risk of loss, §28:2A-219.
Effect of default, §28:2A-220.
Lot.
Defined, §28:2A-103.
Market rent.
Proof, §28:2A-507.
Merchantability.
Implied warranties, §28:2A-212.
Merchant lessees.
Defined, §28:2A-103.
Rightfully rejected goods.
Duties, §28:2A-511.
Modification, §28:2A-208.
Notice.
Default, §§28:2A-502, 28:2A-516.
Objections to goods.
Waiver of lessee's objections, §28:2A-514.

COMMERCIAL CODE —Cont'd
Leases —Cont'd
Offer and acceptance.
Firm offers, §28:2A-205.
Generally, §28:2A-206.
Parol evidence, §28:2A-202.
Payment or performance.
Course of performance.
Construction of lease agreements, §28:1-303.
Delegation of performance, §28:2A-303.
Excused performance, §28:2A-405.
Procedure on excused performance, §28:2A-406.
Insecurity.
Adequate assurance of performance, §28:2A-401.
Option to accelerate at will, §28:2A-109.
Repudiation. See within this subheading, "Repudiation."
Substituted performance, §28:2A-404.
Possession of goods, §28:2A-302.
Lessor's rights and remedies, §§28:2A-523, 28:2A-525.
Present value.
Defined, §28:2A-103.
Priorities.
Liens.
Certain liens arising by operation of law, §28:2A-306.
Liens arising by attachment or levy on, security interest in and other claims to goods, §28:2A-307.
Subordination of priority, §28:2A-311.
Promises.
Irrevocable promises, §28:2A-407.
Purchase.
Defined, §28:2A-103.
Rejection of goods. See within this subheading, "Shipment and delivery."
Remedies. See within this subheading, "Rights and remedies."
Rent.
Action by lessor for rent, §28:2A-529.
Proof of market rent, §28:2A-507.
Replevy of goods, §§28:2A-508, 28:2A-521.
Repudiation.
Anticipatory repudiation, §28:2A-402.
Retraction, §28:2A-403.

COMMERCIAL CODE —Cont'd
Leases —Cont'd
Repudiation —Cont'd
Damages.
Lessee's damages, §28:2A-519.
Lessor's damages, §28:2A-528.
Insecurity.
Failure to provide adequate assurance of performance, §28:2A-401.
Lessee's rights and remedies.
Damages for repudiation, §28:2A-519.
Lessor's remedies, §28:2A-523.
Rescission, §28:2A-208.
Effect on rights and remedies, §28:2A-505.
Rights and remedies.
Cancellation, termination, rescission or fraud.
Effect on rights and remedies, §28:2A-505.
Default by lessee.
Disposal of goods by lessor, §§28:2A-523, 28:2A-524, 28:2A-527.
Identification of goods to lease contract, §28:2A-524.
Lessor's remedies generally, §28:2A-523.
Possession of goods, §§28:2A-523, 28:2A-525.
Rent.
Action by lessor, §28:2A-529.
Stoppage of delivery of goods, §§28:2A-523, 28:2A-526.
Default by lessor.
Lessee's rights and remedies generally, §28:2A-508.
Nonconforming goods or delivery of goods, §§28:2A-509, 28:2A-510.
Replevin of goods, §28:2A-508.
Specific performance, §28:2A-508.
Installment lease contracts.
Lessee's rights and remedies, §28:2A-508.
Modification or impairment, §28:2A-503.
Risk of loss, §28:2A-219.
Effect of default, §28:2A-220.
Sales.
Sale of goods by lessee, §28:2A-305.
Scope of article, §28:2A-102.
Seals.
Inoperative to render lease a sealed instrument, §28:2A-203.

COMMERCIAL CODE —Cont'd
Leases —Cont'd
Secured transactions.
　Distinguishing between security
　　interest and lease, §28:1-203.
　Security interests arising under
　　provisions, §28:9-110.
Shipment and delivery.
　Acceptance of goods, §28:2A-515.
　Accessions.
　　Lessor's and lessee's rights
　　　when goods become,
　　　§28:2A-310.
　Burden of establishing default
　　after acceptance, §28:2A-516.
　Damages.
　　Lessor's damages for
　　　nonacceptance, §28:2A-528.
　Effect, §28:2A-516.
　Nonconforming goods or delivery,
　　§28:2A-509.
　Notice of default, §28:2A-516.
　Revocation of acceptance,
　　§28:2A-517.
　　Damages, §28:2A-519.
　　Justifiable revocation,
　　　§§28:2A-508, 28:2A-517.
　　Wrongful revocation,
　　　§28:2A-523.
　Casualty to identified goods,
　　§28:2A-221.
　Failure to deliver goods.
　　Lessee's rights and remedies,
　　　§28:2A-508.
　Identification of goods, §28:2A-217.
　Improper tender or delivery.
　　Burden of establishing default
　　　after acceptance of goods,
　　　§28:2A-516.
　　Cure by lessor, §28:2A-513.
　　Lessee's rights.
　　　Installment lease contracts,
　　　　§28:2A-510.
　　Notice of default after acceptance
　　　of goods, §28:2A-516.
　　Objection by lessee.
　　　Waiver, §28:2A-514.
　Notice of default.
　　Accepted goods, §28:2A-516.
　Rejection of goods.
　　Accepted goods.
　　　Rejection precluded, §28:2A-516.
　　Cure by lessor, §28:2A-513.
　　Damages, §28:2A-519.
　　Installment lease contracts,
　　　§28:2A-510.

COMMERCIAL CODE —Cont'd
Leases —Cont'd
Shipment and delivery —Cont'd
　Rejection of goods —Cont'd
　　Replacement of rejected goods.
　　　Cure by lessor, §28:2A-513.
　　Rightfully rejected goods,
　　　§28:2A-509.
　　　Lessee's duties generally,
　　　　§28:2A-512.
　　　Lessee's rights and remedies,
　　　　§28:2A-508.
　　　Merchant lessee's duties,
　　　　§28:2A-511.
　　Wrongfully rejected goods.
　　　Lessor's remedies, §28:2A-523.
　Revocation of acceptance of goods,
　　§28:2A-517.
　　Damages, §28:2A-519.
　　Justifiable revocation, §28:2A-517.
　　　Lessee's rights and remedies,
　　　　§28:2A-508.
　　Wrongful revocation, §28:2A-523.
　Stoppage of delivery.
　　Failure of agreed means or
　　　manner of payment,
　　　§28:2A-404.
　　Lessor's remedies, §§28:2A-523,
　　　28:2A-526.
　Subsequent lease of goods by lessor,
　　§28:2A-304.
　Withholding delivery.
　　Failure of agreed means or
　　　manner of payment,
　　　§28:2A-404.
Special rights of creditors, §28:2A-308.
Specific performance, §§28:2A-208,
　28:2A-521.
Statute of frauds, §28:2A-201.
Sublease by lessee, §28:2A-305.
　Definition of sublease, §28:2A-103.
Subsequent lease of goods by lessor,
　§28:2A-304.
Substituted performance, §28:2A-404.
Substitute goods, §28:2A-518.
　Cover by lessor, §28:2A-518.
Suppliers.
　Definition of sublease, §28:2A-103.
Supply contracts.
　Beneficiaries.
　　Lessee under finance lease,
　　　§28:2A-209.
　Defined, §28:2A-103.
Termination.
　Defined, §28:2A-103.
　Effect on rights and remedies,
　　§28:2A-505.

COMMERCIAL CODE —Cont'd
Leases —Cont'd
Third parties.
Standing to sue for injury to goods, §28:2A-531.
Warranties.
Third party beneficiaries, §28:2A-216.
Title of article.
Short title, §28:2A-101.
Title to goods, §28:2A-302.
Infringement.
Warranty against, §28:2A-211.
Unconscionability, §28:2A-108.
Waiver.
Claims, rights after default or breach of warranty, §28:2A-107.
Generally, §28:2A-208.
Objections by lessee to goods, §28:2A-514.
Warranties.
Breach of warranty.
Damages, §§28:2A-508, 28:2A-519.
Notice of claim or litigation answerable over, §28:2A-516.
Waiver or renunciation of rights after breach, §28:2A-107.
Cumulation and conflict, §28:2A-215.
Damages.
Breach of warranty, §§28:2A-508, 28:2A-519.
Exclusion, §28:2A-214.
Express warranties.
Generally, §28:2A-210.
Third party beneficiaries, §28:2A-216.
Fitness for particular purpose.
Implied warranties, §28:2A-213.
Implied warranties.
Fitness for particular purpose, §28:2A-213.
Merchantability, §28:2A-212.
Third party beneficiaries, §28:2A-216.
Infringement.
Warranty against, §28:2A-211.
Interference with goods.
Warranty against, §28:2A-211.
Merchantability.
Implied warranties, §28:2A-212.
Modification, §28:2A-214.
Third party beneficiaries, §28:2A-216.
Letters of credit, §§28:5-101 to 28:5-120.
Adviser, §28:5-107.
Defined, §28:5-102.

COMMERCIAL CODE —Cont'd
Letters of credit —Cont'd
Amendment, §28:5-106.
Applicability of provisions, §28:5-120.
Applicant.
Defined, §28:5-102.
Subrogation, §28:5-117.
Assignment of proceeds, §28:5-114.
Cancellation, §28:5-106.
Choice of law and forum, §28:5-116.
Citation of article.
Short title, §28:5-101.
Confirmer, §28:5-107.
Defined, §28:5-102.
Consideration, §28:5-105.
Contracts.
Sale of goods, §28:2-325.
Definitions, §28:5-102.
General commercial code definitions, §28:1-201.
Reasonable time and seasonably, §28:1-205.
Index of definitions, §28:5-102.
Proceeds of a letter of credit, §28:5-114.
Dishonor.
Defined, §28:5-102.
Remedies for wrongful dishonor, §28:5-111.
Duration, §28:5-106.
Forgery, §28:5-109.
Formal requirements, §28:5-104.
Fraud, §28:5-109.
Good faith.
Obligation of good faith, §28:1-304.
Issuance, §28:5-106.
Issuer.
Defined, §28:5-102.
Rights and obligations, §28:5-108.
Subrogation, §28:5-117.
Nominated person, §28:5-107.
Defined, §28:5-102.
Subrogation, §28:5-117.
Remedies, §28:5-111.
Sale of goods.
Contracts, §28:2-325.
Savings clause, §28:5-119.
Scope of article, §28:5-103.
Signatures, §28:5-104.
Statute of limitations, §28:5-115.
Subrogation.
Issuer, applicant and nominated person, §28:5-117.
Title of article.
Short title, §28:5-101.
Transfer, §28:5-112.
Operation of law, §28:5-113.

COMMERCIAL CODE —Cont'd
Letters of credit —Cont'd
Warranties, §28:5-110.
Negotiable instruments, §§28:3-101 to
28:3-605.
Acceptance.
Defined, §28:3-409.
Drafts, §28:3-409.
Acceptance varying drafts,
§28:3-410.
Obligation of acceptor, §28:3-413.
Incomplete drafts, §28:3-409.
Mistake, §28:3-418.
Obligation of acceptor, §28:3-413.
Preparation of, §28:3-409.
Presentment.
Time allowed for acceptance,
§28:3-501.
Unaccepted draft.
Drawee not liable, §28:3-408.
Varying of draft, §28:3-410.
Writing required, §28:3-409.
Accommodation party.
Discharge of secondary obligors,
§28:3-605.
Reimbursement, §28:3-419.
Actions.
Accrual of actions, §28:3-118.
Limitation of actions, §28:3-118.
Alteration of instruments, §28:3-604.
Ambiguous terms, §28:3-114.
Applicability of article, §28:3-102.
Bearer.
Payable to bearer, §28:3-109.
Cancellation.
Discharge, §28:3-604.
Cashier's checks.
Defined, §28:3-104.
Lost, destroyed or stolen cashier's
check, §28:3-312.
Payment.
Obligation of issuer, §28:3-412.
Refusal to pay, §28:3-411.
Certificates of deposit.
Defined, §28:3-104.
Certified checks.
Lost, destroyed or stolen certified
check, §28:3-312.
Refusal to pay, §28:3-411.
Checks.
Defined, §§28:3-104, 28:3-312.
Citation of article.
Short title, §28:3-101.
Claims.
Claims in recoupment, §28:3-305.
Claim to the instrument, §28:3-306.

COMMERCIAL CODE —Cont'd
Negotiable instruments —Cont'd
Consideration.
Absence of, §28:3-303.
Defined, §28:3-303.
Consumer transactions.
Defenses and claims in recoupment.
Applicable provisions, §28:3-305.
Defined, §28:3-103.
Contributory negligence.
Forged signature or alteration of
instrument, §28:3-406.
Conversion.
When instrument converted,
§28:3-420.
Date.
Antedating, §28:3-113.
Failure to date, §28:3-113.
Postdating, §28:3-113.
Defenses.
Burden of establishing signature
and status of holder in due
course, §28:3-308.
Generally, §28:3-305.
Definitions, §28:3-103.
Acceptance, §28:3-409.
Alteration, §28:3-407.
Certified check, §28:3-409.
Checks, §§28:3-104, 28:3-312.
Claimant, §28:3-312.
Consideration, §28:3-303.
Declaration of loss, §28:3-312.
Employee.
Fraudulent endorsement,
§28:3-405.
Fiduciary, §28:3-307.
Fraudulent endorsement, §28:3-405.
Holder in due course, §28:3-302.
Incomplete instrument, §28:3-115.
Indorsement, §28:3-204.
Instruments, §28:3-104.
Issue, §28:3-105.
Negotiation, §28:3-201.
Obligated bank, §28:3-312.
Person entitled to enforce, §28:3-301.
Presentment, §28:3-501.
Represented person, §28:3-307.
Responsibility.
Fraudulent endorsement,
§28:3-405.
Demand.
Date of payment, §28:3-113.
Overdue instruments, §28:3-304.
Demand paper.
Generally, §28:3-108.
Destroyed instruments.
Cashier's check, teller's check or
certified check, §28:3-312.

COMMERCIAL CODE —Cont'd
Negotiable instruments —Cont'd
Destroyed instruments —Cont'd
  Enforcement, §28:3-309.
Discharge.
  Accord and satisfaction.
    Use of instrument, §28:3-311.
  Certification of check, §28:3-310.
  Effect of discharge, §28:3-601.
  Generally, §28:3-601.
  Holder in due course.
    Effect of discharge against,
      §28:3-601.
  Payment.
    Discharge upon payment,
      §28:3-602.
    Tender of payment, §28:3-603.
  Renunciation, §28:3-604.
  Secondary obligors, §28:3-605.
Dishonor.
  Evidence of dishonor, §28:3-505.
  Generally, §28:3-502.
  Notice of dishonor, §§28:3-503 to
    28:3-505.
  Obligation of drawer, §28:3-414.
  Obligation of indorser, §28:3-415.
  When instrument is dishonored,
    §28:3-502.
Drafts.
  Dishonor, §28:3-502.
  Unaccepted drafts.
    Drawee not liable on, §28:3-408.
Effect of instrument on obligation for
  which taken, §28:3-310.
Evidence.
  Dishonor.
    Evidence of dishonor, §28:3-505.
  Notice of dishonor, §28:3-505.
Fiduciaries.
  Breach of fiduciary duty.
    Notice, §28:3-307.
  Defined, §28:3-307.
Foreign money.
  Instrument payable in, §28:3-107.
Fraud.
  Indorsements.
    Responsibility of employer for
      fraudulent indorsement by
      employee, §28:3-405.
Holder in due course.
  Defined, §28:3-302.
  Discharge.
    Effect of discharge against holder
      in due course, §28:3-302.
    Effect of discharge against parties,
      §28:3-601.

COMMERCIAL CODE —Cont'd
Negotiable instruments —Cont'd
Holder in due course —Cont'd
  Free of claim to the instrument,
    §28:3-306.
  Proof of status as, §28:3-308.
Identification.
  Person to whom instrument payable,
    §28:3-110.
Incomplete instruments, §28:3-115.
Indorsement.
  Anomalous indorsement, §28:3-205.
  Blank indorsement, §28:3-205.
  Discharge of secondary obligors,
    §28:3-605.
  Fraud.
    Responsibility of employer for
      fraudulent indorsement of
      employee, §28:3-405.
  Generally, §28:3-204.
  Impostors, §28:3-404.
  Obligation of indorser, §28:3-415.
  Reacquisition, §28:3-207.
  Restrictive indorsements, §28:3-206.
  Signatures.
    Proof of signature, §28:3-308.
  Special indorsement, §28:3-205.
  Transfer of security interest,
    §28:3-204.
Interest.
  Payment, §28:3-112.
  Rate, §28:3-112.
Issue.
  Defined, §28:3-105.
Issuer.
  Defined, §28:3-105.
Liability of parties.
  Employers.
    Responsibility for fraudulent
      indorsement by an employee,
      §28:3-405.
  Fictitious payees, §28:3-404.
  Impostors, §28:3-404.
  Signatures.
    Authorized representative,
      §28:3-402.
    Person not liable unless signature
      appears, §28:3-401.
    Signing of instrument, §28:3-401.
  Unaccepted draft.
    Drawee not liable, §28:3-408.
Limitation of actions, §28:3-118.
Lost instruments.
  Cashier's check, teller's check or
    certified check, §28:3-312.
  Enforcement, §28:3-309.

COMMERCIAL CODE —Cont'd
Negotiable instruments —Cont'd
Negligence.
Contributing to forged signature alteration or alteration of instrument, §28:3-406.
Negotiability.
Incomplete instruments, §28:3-115.
Other writings affecting instrument, §28:3-117.
Negotiation.
Defined, §28:3-201.
Rescission, §28:3-202.
Notes.
Dishonor, §28:3-502.
Notice.
Breach of fiduciary duty, §28:3-307.
Third parties.
Right to defend action, §28:3-119.
Notice of dishonor.
Delay.
Excused delay, §28:3-504.
Evidence of, §28:3-505.
Excused notice of dishonor, §28:3-504.
Generally, §28:3-503.
Protests, §28:3-505.
When necessary, §28:3-503.
Order.
Payable to order, §28:3-109.
Unconditional.
When order unconditional, §28:3-106.
Other agreements affecting instrument, §28:3-117.
Payment.
Bearer.
Payable to bearer, §28:3-109.
Demand.
Date of payment, §28:3-113.
Payment on demand or at a definite time, §28:3-108.
Discharge, §§28:3-602, 28:3-603.
Foreign money, §28:3-107.
Identification of person to whom instrument payable, §28:3-110.
Interest, §28:3-112.
Mistakes, §28:3-418.
Money.
Foreign currency, §28:3-107.
Obligation of issuer.
Note or cashier's check, §28:3-412.
Order.
Payable to order, §28:3-109.
Overdue instruments, §28:3-304.
Place of payment, §28:3-111.

COMMERCIAL CODE —Cont'd
Negotiable instruments —Cont'd
Payment —Cont'd
Refusal to pay.
Cashier's checks, teller's checks and certified checks, §28:3-411.
Time.
When payable at definite time, §28:3-108.
Presentment.
Acceptance.
Time allowed for acceptance, §28:3-501.
Defined, §28:3-501.
Dishonor.
When instrument is dishonored, §28:3-502.
Excused presentment, §28:3-504.
How made, §28:3-501.
Place of presentment, §28:3-501.
Rights of party to whom presentment made, §28:3-501.
Time of presentment, §28:3-501.
Unconditional.
When promise unconditional, §28:3-106.
Warranties, §28:3-417.
Recoupment.
Claims in recoupment, §28:3-305.
Remotely created consumer items.
Defined, §28:3-103.
Presentment warranties, §28:3-417.
Transfer warranties, §28:3-416.
Renunciation.
Discharge, §28:3-604.
Rescission.
Negotiation subject to rescission, §28:3-202.
Restrictive indorsements, §28:3-206.
Secondary obligors.
Defined, §28:3-103.
Discharge, §28:3-605.
Signatures.
Accommodation party, §28:3-419.
How made, §28:3-401.
Impostors, §28:3-404.
Liability.
Person not liable unless signature appears, §28:3-401.
Signature by authorized representative, §28:3-402.
Negligence.
Contributing to forged signature, §28:3-406.
Proof of signature, §28:3-308.

COMMERCIAL CODE —Cont'd
Negotiable instruments —Cont'd
Signatures —Cont'd
Representative, §28:3-402.
Trade or assumed name, §28:3-401.
Unauthorized signature, §28:3-403.
Ratification, §28:3-403.
Stolen instruments.
Cashier's check, teller's check or
certified check, §28:3-312.
Enforcement, §28:3-309.
Teller's checks.
Defined, §28:3-104.
Lost, destroyed or stolen teller's
check, §28:3-312.
Refusal to pay, §28:3-411.
Third parties.
Notice of right to defend action,
§28:3-119.
Title of article.
Short title, §28:3-101.
Transfer.
Generally, §28:3-203.
Reacquisition, §28:3-207.
Rights vested in transferee,
§28:3-203.
Warranties on transfer, §28:4-207.
Transfer warranties, §28:3-416.
Traveler's checks.
Defined, §28:3-104.
Unconditional promises or orders,
§28:3-106.
Value.
Issued or transferred for value,
§28:3-303.
Warranties.
Negligence contributing to,
§28:3-406.
Presentment warranties, §§28:3-417,
28:3-418, 28:4-208.
Transfers, §28:4-207.
What constitutes, §28:3-407.
Sale of goods, §§28:2-101 to 28:2-725.
Acceptance of goods.
Breach in regard to accepted goods.
Buyer's damages, §28:2-714.
Effect of acceptance, §28:2-607.
Nonacceptance.
Seller's damages, §28:2-708.
Obligation of buyer, §28:2-301.
Revocation in whole or in part,
§§28:2-607, 28:2-608.
Buyer's remedies.
Enumerated, §28:2-711.
Seller's remedies.
Enumerated, §28:2-703.

COMMERCIAL CODE —Cont'd
Sale of goods —Cont'd
Acceptance of goods —Cont'd
What constitutes, §28:2-606.
Action for price.
Seller's remedies, §28:2-709.
Affirmations.
Express warranties, §28:2-313.
Antecedent breach.
Effect of cancellation or rescission on
claims, §28:2-720.
Anticipatory repudiation, §28:2-610.
Proof of market price, §28:2-723.
Retraction, §28:2-611.
Approval.
Sale on approval, §§28:2-326,
28:2-327.
Assignment of rights, §28:2-210.
Assortment of goods.
Buyer's option, §28:2-311.
Assurance of performance.
Right to adequate assurance,
§28:2-609.
Auction sales, §28:2-328.
Breach of obligation.
Antecedent breach.
Effect of cancellation or rescission
on claims, §28:2-720.
Installment contracts, §28:2-612.
Limitation of actions, §28:2-725.
Notice requirements, §28:2-607.
Burden of proof.
Breaches with respect to accepted
goods, §28:2-607.
Cancellation of contract.
Buyer's remedies, §28:2-711.
Seller's remedies, §28:2-703.
C. & F. terms, §§28:2-320, 28:2-321.
Casualty to identified goods, §28:2-613.
C.I.F. terms, §§28:2-320, 28:2-321.
Citation of article, §28:2-101.
Collateral contracts.
Remedies for breach unimpaired,
§28:2-701.
Consignment sales, §28:2-326.
Cooperation respecting performance,
§28:2-311.
Course of dealing.
Implied warranties, §28:2-314.
Cover.
Buyer's procurement of substitute
goods, §28:2-712.
Credit.
Confirmed credit, §28:2-325.
Letters of credit, §28:2-325.
Creditors' rights and remedies.
Sale on approval and sale or return
transactions, §28:2-326.

COMMERCIAL CODE —Cont'd
Sale of goods —Cont'd
Creditors' rights and remedies
—Cont'd
Sold goods.
Rights of seller's creditors,
§28:2-402.
Cure.
Improper tender or delivery of
goods.
Seller's right to cure, §28:2-508.
Damages.
Acceptance of goods.
Buyer's damages for breach in
regard to accepted goods,
§28:2-714.
Antecedent breach.
Effect of cancellation or rescission
on claims, §28:2-720.
Consequential damages.
Buyer's consequential damages,
§28:2-715.
Contractual limitations, §28:2-719.
Cover by buyer.
Right to recover, §28:2-712.
Deduction from price, §28:2-717.
Delivery of goods.
Buyer's damages for nondelivery,
§28:2-713.
Incidental damages.
Buyer's incidental damages,
§28:2-715.
Recovery by person in position of
seller, §28:2-707.
Seller's incidental damages,
§28:2-710.
Limitation, §28:2-718.
Liquidation, §28:2-718.
Nonacceptance of goods.
Seller's damages, §28:2-708.
Repudiation by seller.
Buyer's damages, §28:2-713.
Repudiation of buyer.
Seller's damages, §28:2-708.
Resale of goods by seller, §§28:2-703,
28:2-706.
Warranty breaches, §28:2-714.
Definitions.
Agreement, §28:2-106.
Banker's credit, §28:2-325.
Between merchants, §28:2-104.
Buyer, §28:2-103.
Cancellation, §28:2-106.
Commercial unit, §28:2-105.
Confirmed credit, §28:2-325.
Conforming to contract, §28:2-106.

COMMERCIAL CODE —Cont'd
Sale of goods —Cont'd
Definitions —Cont'd
Contract, §28:2-106.
Contract for sale, §28:2-106.
Cover, §28:2-712.
Entrusting, §28:2-403.
Financing agency, §28:2-104.
Future goods, §28:2-105.
General commercial code definitions,
§28:1-201.
Course of dealing, §28:1-303.
Reasonable time and seasonably,
§28:1-205.
Usage of trade, §28:1-303.
Goods, §28:2-105.
Identification, §28:2-501.
Index of definitions, §28:2-103.
Installment contract, §28:2-612.
Letter of credit, §28:2-325.
Lot, §28:2-105.
Merchant, §28:2-104.
Overseas, §28:2-323.
Person in position of seller,
§28:2-707.
Present sale, §28:2-106.
Receipt, §28:2-103.
Sale, §28:2-106.
Sale on approval, §28:2-326.
Sale or return, §28:2-326.
Seller, §28:2-103.
Termination, §28:2-106.
Delegation of performance, §28:2-210.
Description of goods.
Express warranties by description,
§28:2-313.
Detinue.
Right of buyer, §28:2-716.
Disputed goods.
Preservation of evidence, §28:2-515.
Documents against which draft is
drawn.
When deliverable, §28:2-514.
Entrusters and entrustees, §28:2-403.
Evidence.
Breaches with respect to accepted
goods, §28:2-607.
Disputed goods.
Preserving evidence, §28:2-515.
Price.
Admissibility of market
quotations, §28:2-724.
Proof of market price, §28:2-723.
Excludable security and other
transactions, §28:2-102.
Exclusive dealings, §28:2-306.

COMMERCIAL CODE —Cont'd
Sale of goods —Cont'd
Executory portion of contract.
  Waiver, §28:2-209.
Extrinsic evidence, §28:2-202.
Failure of buyer to pay.
  Seller's remedies.
    Action for price, §28:2-709.
Finality of written expression,
  §28:2-202.
Financing agencies.
  Shipment of goods.
    Drafts paid or purchased by
      agency.
      Rights of agency, §28:2-506.
Firm offers, §28:2-205.
Fitness for particular purpose.
  Implied warranties, §28:2-315.
    Exclusion or modification,
      §§28:2-316, 28:2-316.01.
Formation of contract.
  Generally, §28:2-204.
  Offer and acceptance, §28:2-206.
    Auctions, §28:2-328.
    Firm offers, §28:2-205.
Fraud.
  Remedies for fraud, §28:2-721.
Good faith.
  Good faith purchasers, §28:2-403.
  Obligation of good faith, §28:1-304.
Goods severed from realty, §28:2-107.
Identification of goods, §28:2-501.
  Casualty to identified goods,
    §28:2-613.
  Seller's right notwithstanding
    breach of contract, §28:2-704.
Improper tender or delivery.
  Buyer's right on improper delivery,
    §28:2-601.
Infringement of enjoyment of goods.
  Warranty against infringement,
    §28:2-312.
Insolvency of buyer.
  Remedies of seller on discovery,
    §28:2-702.
Insolvency of seller.
  Buyer's right to goods, §28:2-502.
Inspection of goods.
  Buyer's right, §28:2-513.
    Inspection after arrival of goods
      but before payment is due,
      §28:2-310.
  Payment by buyer before inspection,
    §28:2-512.
Installment contracts, §28:2-612.
Insurable interest in goods, §28:2-501.

COMMERCIAL CODE —Cont'd
Sale of goods —Cont'd
Interpretation and construction.
  Cancellation.
    Effect of term on claims for
      antecedent breach, §28:2-720.
  Course of performance, §28:1-303.
  Delivery of goods.
    Absence of specified place for
      delivery, §28:2-308.
    Time for delivery.
      Absence of specified time,
        §28:2-309.
  Open price terms, §28:2-305.
  Rescission.
    Effect of term on claims for
      antecedent breach, §28:2-720.
  Risks.
    Allocation or division, §28:2-303.
  Shipment of goods.
    Time for shipment.
      Absence of specified time,
        §28:2-309.
Letters of credit, §28:2-325.
  Contracts for sale of goods,
    §28:2-325.
Merchantability of goods.
  Implied warranties, §28:2-314.
    Exclusion or modification,
      §§28:2-316, 28:2-316.01.
Minerals.
  Applicability of chapter, §28:2-107.
Modification of contract, §28:2-209.
Notice, §28:2-607.
  Breach of obligations, §28:2-607.
  Termination of contract, §28:2-309.
Obligations of parties.
  Generally, §28:2-301.
Offer and acceptance, §28:2-206.
  Auctions, §28:2-328.
  Firm offers, §28:2-205.
Oil and gas.
  Applicability of chapter, §28:2-107.
Open price terms, §28:2-305.
Options respecting performance,
  §28:2-311.
Output contracts, §28:2-306.
Parol evidence, §28:2-202.
Payment.
  Accepted goods, §28:2-607.
  Before inspection, §28:2-512.
  By check, §28:2-511.
  Confirmed credit, §28:2-325.
  Credit.
    Running of credit, §28:2-310.

COMMERCIAL CODE —Cont'd
Sale of goods —Cont'd
  Payment —Cont'd
    Failure of buyer to pay.
      Person in position of seller.
        Recovery of incidental damages,
          §28:2-707.
        Seller's remedies.
          Action for price, §28:2-709.
          Enumerated, §28:2-703.
          Incidental damages, §28:2-710.
    Letters of credit, §28:2-325.
    Obligation of buyer, §28:2-301.
    On arrival of goods, §28:2-321.
    Open time for payment, §28:2-310.
    Price payable in money, goods,
      realty, etc., §28:2-304.
    Tender by buyer, §28:2-511.
    When due, §28:2-310.
  Performance.
    Assurance.
      Right to adequate assurance of
        performance, §28:2-609.
    Cooperation, §28:2-311.
    Course of performance,
      interpretation of agreement,
      §28:1-303.
    Delegation, §28:2-210.
    Generally, §§28:2-501 to 28:2-515.
    Options, §28:2-311.
    Substituted performance, §28:2-614.
    Suspension until adequate
      assurance of performance,
      §28:2-609.
  Price.
    Action for price.
      Seller's remedies, §§28:2-703,
        28:2-709.
    Deduction of damages, §28:2-717.
    Failure of buyer to pay.
      Person in position of seller.
        Recovery of incidental damages,
          §28:2-707.
        Seller's remedies.
          Action for price, §28:2-703.
          Incidental damages, §28:2-710.
    Net landed weights, §28:2-321.
    Open price terms, §28:2-305.
    Payable in money, goods, realty, etc.,
      §28:2-304.
    Proof of market price, §28:2-723.
      Admissibility of market
        quotations, §28:2-724.
  Promises.
    Express warranties, §28:2-313.
  Reclamation of goods.
    Seller's remedies on discovery of
      buyer's insolvency, §28:2-702.

COMMERCIAL CODE —Cont'd
Sale of goods —Cont'd
  Rejection of goods.
    Rightful rejection.
      Buyer's options as to salvage of
        rightfully rejected goods,
        §28:2-604.
      Buyer's remedies.
        Enumerated, §28:2-711.
      Effect, §28:2-602.
      Manner, §28:2-602.
      Merchant buyer's duties as to
        rightfully rejected goods,
        §28:2-603.
      Waiver of buyer's objections by
        failure to particularize,
        §28:2-605.
    Wrongful rejection.
      Seller's remedies.
        Enumerated, §28:2-703.
  Remedies.
    Buyer's remedies.
      Acceptance of goods.
        Breach in regard to accepted
          goods, §28:2-714.
      Collateral contracts.
        Remedies for breach
          unimpaired, §28:2-701.
      Consequential damages,
        §28:2-715.
      Cover, §28:2-712.
      Detinue, §28:2-716.
      Fraud, §28:2-721.
      Incidental damages, §28:2-715.
      Modification or limitation by
        contract, §28:2-719.
      Nondelivery of goods, §28:2-713.
      Options and cooperation
        respecting performance.
        Additional remedies, §28:2-311.
      Repudiation of contract by seller,
        §28:2-713.
      Restitution, §28:2-718.
      Specific performance, §28:2-716.
    Person in position of seller,
      §28:2-707.
    Seller's remedies.
      Action for price, §28:2-709.
      Buyer's insolvency, §28:2-702.
      Collateral contracts.
        Remedies for breach
          unimpaired, §28:2-701.
      Delivery of goods.
        Stoppage in transit or
          otherwise, §28:2-705.
      Fraud, §28:2-721.

COMMERCIAL CODE —Cont'd
Sale of goods —Cont'd
Remedies —Cont'd
Seller's remedies —Cont'd
Generally, §28:2-703.
Identification of goods.
Seller's right notwithstanding
breach of contract,
§28:2-704.
Modification or limitation by
contract, §28:2-719.
Nonacceptance of goods by buyer,
§28:2-708.
Options and cooperation
respecting performance.
Additional remedies, §28:2-311.
Repudiation of contract by buyer,
§28:2-708.
Resale of goods, §28:2-706.
Salvaging unfinished goods,
§28:2-704.
Repudiation.
Anticipatory repudiation,
§§28:2-610, 28:2-611.
Proof of market price, §28:2-723.
Buyer's damages, §28:2-713.
Buyer's repudiation of contract.
Enumeration of seller's remedies,
§28:2-703.
Seller's damages, §28:2-708.
Seller's repudiation of contract.
Buyer's remedies.
Enumerated, §28:2-711.
Requirements contracts, §28:2-306.
Resale of goods.
Remedy of person in position of
seller, §28:2-707.
Seller's remedies, §28:2-706.
Rescission of contract, §28:2-209.
Restitution.
Buyer's remedies, §28:2-718.
Return of goods.
Sale or return transactions,
§§28:2-326, 28:2-327.
Risk of loss.
Absence of breach, §28:2-509.
Casualty to identified goods,
§28:2-613.
Effect of breach, §28:2-510.
Sale on approval transactions,
§§28:2-326, 28:2-327.
Sale or return transactions,
§§28:2-326, 28:2-327.
Salvaging unfinished goods.
Right of seller, §28:2-704.
Samples of goods.
Express warranties by samples,
§28:2-313.

COMMERCIAL CODE —Cont'd
Sale of goods —Cont'd
Scope of chapter, §28:2-102.
Seals.
Inoperability, §28:2-203.
Secured transactions.
Security interests arising under
provisions, §28:9-110.
Security interests arising under
sales chapter, §28:9-110.
Shipment and delivery.
C. & F. terms.
Bill of lading required in overseas
shipments, §28:2-323.
Casualty to identified goods,
§28:2-613.
C.I.F. terms.
Bill of lading required in overseas
shipments, §28:2-323.
Condition.
Delivery on, §28:2-507.
Cure by seller of improper tender or
delivery, §28:2-508.
Delay in delivery.
Excuse by failure of presupposed
conditions, §§28:2-615,
28:2-616.
Ex-ship delivery, §28:2-322.
F.A.S. terms, §28:2-319.
Financing agency's rights.
Drafts paid or purchased by
agency, §28:2-506.
F.O.B. terms, §28:2-319.
Bill of lading required in overseas
shipments, §28:2-323.
Improper tender or delivery.
Cover by buyer, §28:2-712.
Cure by seller, §28:2-508.
Damages of buyer for nondelivery,
§28:2-713.
Excuse by failure of presupposed
conditions, §§28:2-615,
28:2-616.
Inspection of goods, §§28:2-512,
28:2-513.
Net landed weights, §28:2-321.
No arrival, no sale terms, §28:2-324.
Casualty to identified goods,
§28:2-613.
Obligation of seller to transfer and
deliver goods, §28:2-301.
Overseas shipments, §28:2-323.
Payment on arrival, §28:2-321.
Place for delivery.
Absence of specified place,
§28:2-308.

COMMERCIAL CODE —Cont'd
Sale of goods —Cont'd
Shipment and delivery —Cont'd
Refusal of delivery.
Buyer's remedies.
Enumerated, §28:2-711.
Seller's remedies on discovery of
buyer's insolvency, §28:2-702.
Reservation.
Authority to ship under
reservation, §28:2-310.
Risk of loss.
Absence of breach, §28:2-509.
Effect of breach, §28:2-510.
Sale on approval transactions,
§§28:2-326, 28:2-327.
Sale or return transactions,
§§28:2-326, 28:2-327.
Seller's option.
Specifications or arrangements
relating to shipment,
§28:2-311.
Shipment by seller, §28:2-504.
Under reservation, §28:2-505.
Single lot or several lots, §28:2-307.
Stoppage of goods in transit or
otherwise.
Remedy of person in position of
seller, §28:2-707.
Remedy of seller, §§28:2-703,
28:2-704.
Substituted performance, §28:2-614.
Tender of delivery.
Buyer's rights on improper
delivery, §28:2-601.
Cover by buyer where tender
improper, §28:2-712.
Cure by seller of improper tender,
§28:2-508.
Effect of seller's tender, §28:2-507.
Excuse by failure of presupposed
conditions, §§28:2-615,
28:2-616.
Manner of seller's tender,
§28:2-503.
Time for shipment or delivery.
Absence of specified time,
§28:2-309.
Warranty of condition on arrival,
§28:2-321.
Withholding delivery.
Seller's remedies, §28:2-703.
Specific performance.
Right of buyer, §28:2-716.
Statute of limitations, §28:2-725.
Substituted performance, §28:2-614.

COMMERCIAL CODE —Cont'd
Sale of goods —Cont'd
Termination of contract.
Contracts of indefinite duration,
§28:2-309.
Definition of "termination,"
§28:2-106.
Notice of termination, §28:2-309.
Third party actions.
Who can sue third parties for injury
to goods, §28:2-722.
Third party beneficiaries.
Warranties, §28:2-318.
Timber.
Applicability of chapter, §28:2-107.
Title of article.
Short title, §28:2-101.
Title to goods.
Passing of title, §28:2-401.
Power to transfer title, §28:2-403.
Reservation for security, §28:2-401.
Warranty of title, §28:2-312.
Transfer of goods.
Requisites, §28:2-105.
Unconscionability, §28:2-302.
Unfinished goods.
Seller's right to salvage, §28:2-704.
Usage of trade.
Implied warranties, §28:2-314.
Waiver of executory portion of
contract, §28:2-209.
Warranties.
Damages for breach, §28:2-714.
Express warranties, §28:2-313.
Cumulation and conflict,
§28:2-317.
Exclusions.
Generally, §§28:2-316,
28:2-316.01.
Modification.
Generally, §§28:2-316,
28:2-316.01.
Third party beneficiaries,
§28:2-318.
Implied warranties.
Course of dealing or usage of
trade, §28:2-314.
Cumulation and conflict,
§28:2-317.
Exclusions.
Generally, §§28:2-316,
28:2-316.01.
Fitness for particular purpose,
§28:2-315.
Exclusion or modification,
§§28:2-316, 28:2-316.01.

COMMERCIAL CODE —Cont'd
Sale of goods —Cont'd
Warranties —Cont'd
Implied warranties —Cont'd
Merchantability.
Exclusion or modification,
§§28:2-316, 28:2-316.01.
Modification.
Generally, §§28:2-316,
28:2-316.01.
Third party beneficiaries,
§28:2-318.
Infringement of enjoyment of goods.
Warranty of title and against
infringement, §28:2-312.
Merchantability, §28:2-314.
Shipment and delivery of goods.
Warranty of condition on arrival,
§28:2-321.
Third party beneficiaries, §28:2-318.
Title.
Warranty of title and against
infringement, §28:2-312.
Sales.
See SALE OF GOODS, UCC.
Secured transactions, §§28:9-101 to
28:9-809.
Accessions.
Perfection and priority of security
interest in, §28:9-335.
Accounting.
Defined, §28:9-102.
Request for, §28:9-210.
After-acquired property, §28:9-204.
Security interest in, §28:9-204.
Agricultural liens.
Defined, §28:9-102.
Perfection and priority.
Filed financing statement
providing certain incorrect
information.
Priority of agricultural lien
perfected by, §28:9-338.
Filing.
When required to perfect lien,
§28:9-310.
Interests that take priority over or
take free of agricultural lien,
§28:9-317.
Law governing, §28:9-302.
Priorities among agricultural liens
on same collateral, §28:9-322.
When perfected, §28:9-308.
Applicability of provisions, §§28:9-109,
28:9-110.
Assignments.
Filing officer's duties, §28:9-514.

COMMERCIAL CODE —Cont'd
Secured transactions —Cont'd
Attachment of security interest,
§28:9-203.
Effect on delegation of performance
and assignment of rights,
§28:9-210.
Financial asset.
Security interest arising in
purchase or delivery of,
§28:9-206.
Perfection.
Security interests perfected upon
attachment, §28:9-309.
Bank.
Control agreement.
Refusal to enter into or disclose
existence of, §28:9-342.
Defined, §28:9-102.
Rights of banks and financial
institutions.
Deposit accounts, §§28:9-340,
28:9-341.
Bank deposits and collections.
Documentary drafts.
Dishonor.
Privilege of presenting bank to
deal with goods, §28:4-504.
Chattel paper.
Perfection of security interests in,
§28:9-312.
Purchaser of chattel paper or
instrument.
Priority, §28:9-330.
Citation of article.
Short title, §28:9-101.
Citation of provisions, §28:9-101.
Collateral.
Control of collateral.
Rights and duties of secured party
having, §§28:9-207, 28:9-208.
Default.
Acceptance in full or partial
satisfaction of obligation,
§§28:9-620 to 28:9-622.
Disposition after default,
§§28:9-610 to 28:9-617.
Redemption.
Right to redeem collateral,
§28:9-623.
Transfer of record or legal title,
§28:9-619.
Description.
Sufficiency, §28:9-108.
Disposition.
Permissible, §28:9-205.

COMMERCIAL CODE —Cont'd
Secured transactions —Cont'd
Collateral —Cont'd
Disposition —Cont'd
Rights of secured party on,
§28:9-315.
Without accounting, §28:9-205.
List of collateral.
Request regarding, §28:9-210.
Possession of collateral.
Rights and duties of secured party
having, §28:9-207.
Rights and duties when collateral in
secured party's possession,
§28:9-207.
Title immaterial to applicability of
article, §28:9-202.
Transferred collateral.
Priority of security interests in,
§28:9-325.
Use.
Without accounting, §28:9-205.
Use permissible, §28:9-205.
Commingled goods, §28:9-336.
Construction and interpretation.
Sales article of UCC.
Security interests arising under,
§28:9-110.
Title to collateral immaterial to
applicability of article,
§28:9-202.
Crops.
Priority of security interests in,
§28:9-334.
Debtor.
Defined, §28:9-102.
Location, §28:9-307.
Default.
Acceptance of collateral in full or
partial satisfaction of obligation,
§28:9-620.
Effect, §28:9-622.
Notification, §28:9-621.
Agricultural lien.
Time of default, §28:9-606.
Collateral.
Acceptance in full or partial
satisfaction of obligation,
§§28:9-620 to 28:9-622.
Disposition after default,
§§28:9-610 to 28:9-617.
Redemption.
Right to redeem collateral,
§28:9-623.
Transfer of record or legal title,
§28:9-619.

COMMERCIAL CODE —Cont'd
Secured transactions —Cont'd
Default —Cont'd
Collection and enforcement by
secured party, §28:9-607.
Application of proceeds, §28:9-608.
Commercially reasonable conduct.
Determination whether conduct
commercially reasonable,
§28:9-627.
Disposition of collateral after,
§28:9-610.
Compulsory disposition, §28:9-620.
Deficiency.
Action in which deficiency is in
issue, §28:9-626.
Explanation of calculation of,
§28:9-616.
Liability for, §28:9-615.
Notification before, §28:9-611.
Contents and form, §§28:9-613,
28:9-614.
Timeliness, §28:9-612.
Proceeds.
Application, §28:9-615.
Surplus.
Action in which surplus is in
issue, §28:9-626.
Explanation of calculation of,
§28:9-616.
Right to, §28:9-615.
Transferee of collateral.
Rights, §28:9-617.
Fixtures.
Procedure if security agreement
covers, §28:9-604.
Judicial enforcement, §28:9-601.
Noncompliance with provisions by
secured party.
Remedies, §28:9-625.
Possession.
Rights of secured party to take
possession after default,
§28:9-609.
Real property.
Procedure if security agreement
covers, §28:9-604.
Rights after default, §28:9-601.
Agreement on standards
concerning, §28:9-603.
Waiver and variance, §28:9-602.
Secondary obligor.
Liability, §28:9-628.
Limitation on liability of secured
party, §28:9-628.
Rights and duties, §28:9-618.

COMMERCIAL CODE —Cont'd
Secured transactions —Cont'd
Default —Cont'd
Security agreement.
Generally, §§28:9-601 to 28:9-628.
See within this subheading,
"Security agreement."
Unknown debtor or secondary
obligor, §28:9-605.
Waiver of certain rights, §28:9-624.
Definitions, §§28:9-102, 28:9-103.
General commercial code definitions,
§28:1-201.
Course of dealing, §28:1-303.
Reasonable time and seasonably,
§28:1-205.
Usage of trade, §28:1-303.
Deposit account.
Bank's rights and duties with
respect to, §28:9-341.
Right of recoupment or set-off
against deposit account.
Effectiveness, §28:9-340.
Control, §28:9-104.
Defined, §28:9-102.
Perfection and priority of security
interest in, §28:9-312.
Law governing, §28:9-304.
Perfection by control, §28:9-314.
Priority of security interests,
§28:9-327.
Transfer of funds from deposit
account.
Transferee takes funds free of
security interest, §28:9-332.
Description of property.
Sufficiency, §28:9-108.
Duties of secured party.
Account debtor notified of
assignment, §28:9-209.
Control or possession of collateral.
Secured party having, §§28:9-207,
28:9-208.
Effective date of provisions, §28:9-701.
Action taken before.
Effectiveness, §28:9-705.
Financing statement.
Pre-effective-date financing
statement, §28:9-707.
Security interest perfected before
effective date, §28:9-703.
Security interest unperfected before
effective date, §28:9-704.
Electronic chattel paper.
Control, §28:9-105.
Perfection by control, §28:9-314.

COMMERCIAL CODE —Cont'd
Secured transactions —Cont'd
Electronic chattel paper —Cont'd
Defined, §28:9-102.
Perfection and priority of security
interests in.
Perfection by control, §28:9-314.
Electronic documents.
Control.
Perfection by control, §28:9-314.
Rights and duties of secured party
having, §28:9-208.
Enforceability of security interest,
§28:9-203.
Fees.
Financing statements.
Filing, §28:9-512.
Assignment of security
interests, §28:9-514.
Filing office, §28:9-501.
Delay by, §28:9-524.
Destruction of records, §28:9-522.
Duties, §§28:9-519, 28:9-520,
28:9-522, 28:9-523.
Fees, §28:9-525.
Information from, §28:9-523.
Refusal to accept record, §§28:9-520,
28:9-521.
Reports on operation, §28:9-527.
Rules, §28:9-526.
Uniform form of written financing
statement and amendment,
§28:9-521.
Filing officers.
Assignment of security interests.
Duties, §28:9-514.
Duties, §§28:9-512, 28:9-514.
Financial asset.
Priority of certain interests in,
§28:9-331.
Purchase or delivery of.
Security interest arising in,
§28:9-206.
Financing statements.
Amendment, §§28:9-501, 28:9-502,
28:9-512.
Pre-effective-date financing
statement, §28:9-707.
Assignment, §28:9-501.
Collateral.
Indication of collateral, §28:9-504.
Contents, §28:9-502.
Duration of effectiveness,
§§28:9-501, 28:9-515.
Effective date of provisions.
Pre-effective-date financing
statement, §28:9-707.

COMMERCIAL CODE —Cont'd
Secured transactions —Cont'd
Financing statements —Cont'd
Effectiveness, §28:9-516.
Errors and omissions.
Claims concerning inaccurate or
wrongfully filed record,
§28:9-518.
Effect, §28:9-506.
Indexing errors, §28:9-517.
Events with impact on effectiveness,
§28:9-507.
Filing, §§28:9-501, 28:9-502,
28:9-505.
Assignment of security interests,
§28:9-514.
Continuation statement.
Persons entitled to file,
§28:9-708.
Duration, §28:9-512.
Effectiveness of filed record,
§28:9-510.
Fees, §28:9-512.
Assignment of security
interests, §28:9-514.
Filing officers.
Assignment of security
interests, §28:9-514.
Duties, §§28:9-512, 28:9-514.
Initial financing statement.
Persons entitled to file,
§28:9-708.
When filing suffices to continue
effectiveness of financing
statement, §28:9-706.
Lapsed filing.
Effect, §28:9-512.
Persons entitled to file, §28:9-509.
Place of filing, §28:9-501.
Termination statement, §28:9-513.
What constitutes, §§28:9-512,
28:9-516.
Wrongfully filed record.
Claims concerning, §28:9-518.
Lapsed financing statement.
Effect, §28:9-515.
Mortgage as financing statement,
§28:9-502.
Name of debtor and secured party,
§28:9-503.
Errors and omissions.
Effect, §28:9-506.
New debtor becoming bound by
security agreement.
Effectiveness of financing
statement, §28:9-508.

COMMERCIAL CODE —Cont'd
Secured transactions —Cont'd
Financing statements —Cont'd
Replacement financing statement,
§28:9-501.
Secured party of record, §28:9-511.
Assignment of powers of,
§28:9-514.
Termination statement, §28:9-513.
Time of filing, §28:9-502.
Transitional provisions, 2012
amendments, §§28:9-805 to
28:9-808.
Fixtures.
Priority of security interests in,
§28:9-334.
Forms.
Financing statement, §28:9-502.
Future advances, §28:9-204.
Priority of security interests,
§28:9-323.
Security interest in, §28:9-204.
Good faith.
Obligation of good faith, §28:1-304.
Healthcare insurance receivables.
Defined, §28:9-102.
Third party assignments.
Modification of assigned contract,
§28:9-405.
Restrictions on, §§28:9-406,
28:9-408.
Identification and proof of assignment,
§28:9-406.
Identification of property.
Sufficiency of description, §28:9-110.
Investment property.
Control, §28:9-106.
Defined, §28:9-102.
Perfection and priority of security
interests in, §28:9-312.
Law governing, §28:9-305.
Perfection by control, §28:9-314.
Priority of security interests,
§28:9-328.
Investment securities.
Attachment and enforceability of
security interests, §28:9-203.
Financial asset.
Security interest arising in
purchase or delivery of,
§28:9-206.
Security entitlements.
Priority among security interests
and entitlement holders,
§28:8-511.
Leases.
Distinguishing between security
interest and lease, §28:1-203.

INDEX

COMMERCIAL CODE —Cont'd
Secured transactions —Cont'd
Leases —Cont'd
Restrictions on security interest in
leasehold interest or in lessor's
residual interest, §28:9-407.
Letter-of-credit right.
Assignment.
Restrictions on assignment
ineffective, §28:9-409.
Control, §28:9-107.
Defined, §28:9-102.
Perfection and priority of security
interests in, §28:9-312.
Law governing, §28:9-306.
Perfection by control, §28:9-314.
Priority of security interests,
§28:9-329.
Limitation of actions.
Duration of financing statements,
§28:9-512.
Location of debtor.
Perfection of security interests.
Continuity of perfection, change in
location, §28:9-316.
Mortgages and deeds of trust.
Mortgage as financing statement,
§28:9-502.
Perfection of security interests.
Attachment.
Security interests perfected upon
attachment, §28:9-309.
Chattel paper.
Security interests in, §28:9-312.
Continuity of perfection, §§28:9-303,
28:9-308.
Change in governing law,
§28:9-316.
Control.
Perfection by, §28:9-314.
Delivery to secured party.
Perfection of security interest
without filing, §28:9-313.
Deposit accounts.
Perfection by control, §28:9-314.
Security interests in, §28:9-312.
Documents.
Security interests in, §28:9-312.
Effective date of provisions.
Security interest perfected before,
§28:9-703.
Security interest unperfected
before, §28:9-704.
Effect on delegation of performance
and assignment of rights,
§28:9-210.

COMMERCIAL CODE —Cont'd
Secured transactions —Cont'd
Perfection of security interests
—Cont'd
Filing.
Not required to perfect security
interest in property subject to
certain statutes, regulations,
and treaties, §28:9-311.
Permissive filing, §28:9-312.
When required, §28:9-310.
Instruments, §28:9-304.
Security interests in, §28:9-312.
Investment property.
Perfection by control, §28:9-314.
Security interests in, §28:9-312.
Law governing, §28:9-301.
Agricultural liens, §28:9-302.
Deposit accounts, §28:9-304.
Goods covered by certificate of
title, §28:9-303.
Investment property, §28:9-305.
Letter-of-credit rights, §28:9-306.
Letter-of-credit rights.
Law governing, §28:9-306.
Perfection by control, §28:9-314.
Security interests in, §28:9-312.
Money.
Security interests in, §28:9-312.
Possession by secured party.
Perfection of security interest
without filing, §28:9-313.
Transitional provisions, 2012
amendments, §28:9-803.
Treaties.
Security interest in property
subject to certain treaties,
§28:9-311.
When perfected, §28:9-308.
Preferences and priorities.
Unperfected security interests,
§28:9-301.
Priority of security interests.
Accessions, §28:9-335.
Agricultural liens.
Agricultural liens on same
collateral, §28:9-322.
Filed financing statement
providing certain incorrect
information.
Agricultural lien perfected by,
§28:9-338.
Interests that take priority over or
take free of, §28:9-317.
Law governing, §28:9-302.
Buyer of goods, §28:9-320.

I-221

COMMERCIAL CODE —Cont'd
Secured transactions —Cont'd
Priority of security interests —Cont'd
Certificate of title.
Security interest in goods covered
by, §28:9-337.
Chattel paper or instrument.
Priority of purchaser, §28:9-330.
Commingled goods, §28:9-336.
Conflicting security interests,
§28:9-322.
Consignee.
Rights and title with respect to
creditors and purchasers,
§28:9-319.
Crops.
Security interest in, §28:9-334.
Deposit account, §28:9-327.
Transfer of funds from, §28:9-332.
Filed financing statement providing
certain incorrect information.
Security interest perfected by,
§28:9-338.
Financial asset.
Priority of certain interests in,
§28:9-331.
Fixtures.
Security interest in, §28:9-334.
Future advances, §28:9-323.
Investment property, §28:9-328.
Law governing, §28:9-301.
Agricultural liens, §28:9-302.
Deposit accounts, §28:9-304.
Goods covered by certificate of
title, §28:9-303.
Investment property, §28:9-305.
Letter-of-credit rights, §28:9-306.
Lessee of goods in ordinary course of
business, §28:9-321.
Letter-of-credit right, §28:9-329.
Law governing, §28:9-306.
Licensee of general intangible,
§28:9-321.
Liens arising by operation of law,
§28:9-333.
New debtor.
Security interests created by,
§28:9-326.
Purchase-money security interests,
§28:9-324.
Purchasers of instruments,
documents, and securities under
other provisions.
Priority of rights of, §28:9-331.
Sale of right to payment, §28:9-318.
Subordination.
Priority subject to, §28:9-339.

COMMERCIAL CODE —Cont'd
Secured transactions —Cont'd
Priority of security interests —Cont'd
Transfer of money.
Transferee takes money free of
security interest, §28:9-332.
Transferred collateral, §28:9-325.
Transitional provisions, 2012
amendments, §28:9-809.
Transition provisions, §28:9-709.
Unperfected security interest.
Interests that take priority over or
take free of, §28:9-317.
Proceeds.
Rights of secured party in,
§28:9-315.
Purchase-money security interests,
§28:9-103.
Priority, §28:9-324.
Sales article of UCC.
Security interests arising under,
§28:9-110.
Savings clause, §28:9-702.
Scope of provisions, §§28:9-109,
28:9-110.
Security agreement.
Default.
Collateral.
Acceptance as discharge of
obligation, §28:9-620.
Collection rights of secured
party, §28:9-607.
Debtor's right to redeem
collateral, §28:9-623.
Disposition after default,
§28:9-620.
Possession after default,
§28:9-609.
Secured party's rights,
§§28:9-609, 28:9-610.
Collections.
Secured party's rights,
§28:9-607.
Liability of secured party for
noncompliance, §28:9-628.
Procedure when agreement covers
both realty and personalty,
§28:9-604.
Validity generally, §28:9-201.
Statement of account.
Request regarding, §28:9-210.
Third parties.
Alienability of debtor's rights,
§28:9-401.
Assignments.
Agreement not to assert defenses
against assignee, §28:9-403.

COMMERCIAL CODE —Cont'd
Secured transactions —Cont'd
Third parties —Cont'd
Assignments —Cont'd
Claims and defenses against
assignee, §28:9-404.
Discharge of account debtor,
§28:9-406.
Modification of assigned contract,
§28:9-405.
Restrictions on certain
assignments, §28:9-406.
Certain restrictions ineffective,
§§28:9-408, 28:9-409.
Rights acquired by assignee,
§28:9-404.
Contract of debtor.
Secured party not obligated on,
§28:9-402.
Torts of debtor.
Secured party not obligated on,
§28:9-402.
Title of article.
Short title, §28:9-101.
Transitional provisions.
Effective date, §28:11-101.
Filing, §§28:11-104, 28:11-105.
Required refilings, §28:11-106.
General rule for transition,
§28:11-103.
Presumption that rule of law
continues unchanged,
§28:11-108.
Priorities, §28:11-107.
Transitional provisions, 2012
amendments, §§28:9-801 to
28:9-809.
Applicability date.
Defined, §28:9-801.
Financing statements.
Actions taken before date, effect,
§28:9-805.
Amendment of pre-effective date
statement, §28:9-807.
Initial statement, entitlement to
file, §28:9-808.
Initial statement, when
sufficient to continue
effectiveness, §28:9-806.
Perfection of security interest
before applicability date,
§28:9-803.
Priorities determined before
applicability date, applicable
provisions, §28:9-809.
Transactions or liens commenced
before date.
Savings clause, §28:9-802.

COMMERCIAL CODE —Cont'd
Secured transactions —Cont'd
Transitional provisions, 2012
amendments —Cont'd
Applicability date —Cont'd
Unperfected security interest
before applicability date,
§28:9-804.
Definitions, §28:9-801.
Savings clause, §28:9-802.
Unperfected security interests.
Priorities, §28:9-301.
Transitional provisions, 2012
amendments, §28:9-804.
Security entitlements.
Security interests.
Priority among security interests
and entitlement holders,
§28:8-511.
Severability of provisions, §28:1-105.
Territorial application of subtitle,
§28:1-301.
Transfer warranties, §28:4-207.
Transitional provisions, §§28:11-101
to 28:11-108.
General repealer, §28:10-103.
Laws not repealed, §28:10-104.
Secured transactions.
Effective date, §28:11-101.
Filing, §§28:11-104, 28:11-105.
Required refilings, §28:11-106.
General rule for transition,
§28:11-103.
Presumption that rule of law
continues unchanged,
§28:11-108.
Priorities, §28:11-107.

COMMERCIAL COUNTERFEITING,
§§22-901, 22-902.

COMMERCIAL DRIVERS'
LICENSES, §§50-401 to 50-409.
Definitions, §50-401.
Disqualification from holding,
§50-406.
Driver responsibilities, §50-403.
Driving while intoxicated, §50-405.01.
Employer responsibilities, §50-404.
Fees, §50-408.
Issuance of rules regarding, §50-409.
Medical standards for holders of,
§50-407.
Penalties, §50-405.
Railroad crossings, §50-405.01.
Requirements regarding, §50-402.
Violation of out-of-service order,
§50-405.01.

COMMERCIAL GUARD DOGS,
§§8-1841.01 to 8-1841.09.

COMMERCIAL PAPER.
Metropolitan police.
Depositing of seized currency,
§§23-531 to 23-534.
Negotiable instruments.
General provisions, §§28:3-101 to
28:3-605.
See COMMERCIAL CODE.

**COMMERCIAL PROPERTY
ENERGY CONSERVATION.**
Definitions, §8-1772.01.
Penalties for violations, §8-1772.03.
Requirements, §8-1772.02.

COMMERCIAL VEHICLES.
**Alternative fuel technology
restrictions,** §50-704.
Drivers' licenses, §§50-401 to 50-409.
See COMMERCIAL DRIVERS'
LICENSES.

COMMINGLED GOODS.
Secured transactions, §28:9-336.

COMMISSION FOR WOMEN, §§3-701
to 3-704.
Administrative procedure, §3-704.
Establishment of, §3-702.
Policy declaration, §3-701.
Powers and duties of, §3-703.

**COMMISSION ON FATHERS, MEN
AND BOYS,** §§3-731 to 3-733.
Duties, §3-733.
Establishment, §3-731.
Members, §3-732.
Terms of office and removal, §3-732.

**COMMISSION ON JUDICIAL
DISABILITIES AND TENURE,**
§§1-204.31, 11-1521 to 11-1530.
Appeals, §11-1529.
Appointment, §1-204.31.
Confidentiality and privilege.
Information furnished commission,
§1-204.31.
Privacy and confidentiality of
proceedings, §11-1528.
Continuation, §1-207.18.
Employees, §11-1525.
Established, §§1-204.31, 11-1521.
**Financial and administrative
services,** §11-1525.
Financial statements required by,
§11-1530.
Involuntary retirement, ordering,
§11-1526.

**COMMISSION ON JUDICIAL
DISABILITIES AND TENURE**
—Cont'd
Issuance of rules and regulations,
§11-1525.
Judicial review of proceedings,
§11-1529.
Meetings, §1-204.31.
Membership, §§1-204.31, 11-1522,
11-1523.
Powers, §1-204.31.
Procedures of, §§11-1526, 11-1527.
**Qualifications for appointment to
commission,** §1-204.31.
Removal or suspension of judges by,
§11-1526.
Rules of procedure, adoption,
§1-204.31.
Term, §1-204.31.
Vacancies, §1-204.31.
Wages and salaries, §11-1524.

**COMMISSION ON MENTAL
HEALTH SERVICES.**
Department of mental health.
Generally, §§7-1131.01 to 7-1131.21.
See MENTAL HEALTH
DEPARTMENT.

**COMMITMENT OF PERSONS WITH
INTELLECTUAL DISABILITIES,**
§§7-1303.01 to 7-1303.14, 21-1114,
21-1115.
**Advocates for the intellectually
disabled,** §7-1304.13.
Appeals, §§7-1304.11, 7-1304.12,
MentalRetardation Rule 4C.
Child abuse and neglect cases,
§21-1114.
Civil procedure rules incorporated,
MentalRetardation Rules 8A, 8B.
**Commencement of commitment
proceedings,** §7-1304.01.
Individuals who are not competent to
refuse commitment,
MentalRetardation Rule 4A.
Respondents found incompetent to
participate in criminal
proceedings, MentalRetardation
Rule 4B.
Comprehensive evaluations reports,
MentalRetardation Rule 7.
Individuals who are not competent to
refuse commitment,
MentalRetardation Rule 4A.
Respondents found incompetent to
participate in criminal
proceedings, MentalRetardation
Rule 4B.

COMMITMENT OF PERSONS WITH INTELLECTUAL DISABILITIES
—Cont'd
Conduct of hearings.
Hearing and review procedures, §§7-1304.01 to 7-1304.13. See within this heading, "Hearing and review procedures."
Individuals who are not competent to refuse commitment, MentalRetardation Rule 4A.
Respondents found incompetent to participate in criminal proceedings, MentalRetardation Rule 4B.
Construction of rules, MentalRetardation Rule 1.
Continuances, MentalRetardation Rule 13.
Court committal.
Competence to refuse irrelevant, §7-1303.01.
Effect of determination of incompetency to refuse commitment, §7-1303.13.
Person found to be incompetent in a criminal case, §7-1303.04, MentalRetardation Rule 4B.
Hearing procedures, §7-1304.06a.
Crimes and offenses, inquiry into, §21-1115.
Criminal procedure, incompetent to stand trial.
Competence to refuse irrelevant, §7-1303.01.
Person found to be incompetent in a criminal case, §7-1303.04, MentalRetardation Rule 4B.
Hearing procedures, §7-1304.06a.
Discharge from facility, MentalRetardation Rule 6.
Discovery.
Periodic review of orders for commitment and admission, MentalRetardation Rule 7.
Respondents found incompetent to participate in criminal proceedings, MentalRetardation Rule 8C.
Dismissal of proceedings upon death of resident, MentalRetardation Rule 17.
Entry of judgment, MentalRetardation Rule 16.
Evaluation report and rehabilitation plan requirements, §7-1304.03, MentalRetardation Rules 4A, 4B.

COMMITMENT OF PERSONS WITH INTELLECTUAL DISABILITIES
—Cont'd
Findings of fact and conclusions of law, MentalRetardation Rule 15.
Hearing and review procedures, §§7-1304.01 to 7-1304.13.
Advocates, §7-1304.13.
Appeal of commitment order, §7-1304.10.
Closed hearings, §7-1304.08.
Conduct of hearings.
Individuals who are not competent to refuse commitment, MentalRetardation Rule 4A.
Respondents found incompetent to participate in criminal proceedings, MentalRetardation Rule 4B.
Court hearing required prior to commitment, §7-1303.12.
Disposition orders following, §7-1304.09.
Informal manner, conducted in, §7-1304.06.
Open hearings, §7-1304.08.
Payment of costs and expenses of, §7-1304.12.
Periodic review of commitment order, §7-1304.11.
Procedural rights at, §7-1304.06.
Prompt conduct of hearing, §7-1304.05.
Public, closed to, §7-1304.08.
Representation by counsel, right to, §7-1304.02.
Standard of proof, §7-1304.07.
Individual rehabilitation plans, MentalRetardation Rule 7.
Individuals who are not competent to refuse commitment, MentalRetardation Rule 4A.
Respondents found incompetent to participate in criminal proceedings, MentalRetardation Rule 4B.
Judgments.
Entry of judgment, MentalRetardation Rule 16.
Law student practice, FamDiv Rule M.
Legal representation, §7-1304.02, MentalRetardation Rule 11.
Magistrate judges, MentalRetardation Rule 2.
Mental health information, §§7-1201.01 to 7-1208.07.
See MENTAL HEALTH DISCLOSURES.

COMMITMENT OF PERSONS WITH INTELLECTUAL DISABILITIES
—Cont'd
Mental retardation advocates, MentalRetardation Rule 12.
Motions practice, MentalRetardation Rule 10.
Order of commitment.
Entry of judgment, MentalRetardation Rule 16.
Individuals who are not competent to refuse commitment, MentalRetardation Rule 4A.
Respondents found incompetent to participate in criminal proceedings, MentalRetardation Rule 4B.
Parent or guardian filing petition for commitment of individual 14 years or older, §7-1303.04.
Time limit for filing, §7-1303.12a.
Parent or guardian filing petition for commitment of individual under 14 years, §7-1303.06.
Periodic review of commitment order, MentalRetardation Rule 7.
Individuals who are not competent to refuse commitment, MentalRetardation Rule 4A.
Petition for commitment.
Filing, §7-1304.01.
Individuals who are not competent to refuse commitment, MentalRetardation Rule 4A.
Placement pending petition and commitment proceedings, §7-1303.12a.
Respondents found incompetent to participate in criminal proceedings, §7-1303.04, MentalRetardation Rule 4B.
Status hearing, §7-1304.05.
Placement pending petition and commitment proceedings, §7-1303.12a.
Refusal of, competence regarding, §7-1303.01.
Effect of determination of incompetency to refuse commitment, §7-1303.13.
Respite care.
Rules and regulations, §7-1303.14.
Review of, §§7-1304.11, 7-1304.12.
Scope of rules, MentalRetardation Rule 1.
Service of process, MentalRetardation Rule 9.

COMMITMENT OF PERSONS WITH INTELLECTUAL DISABILITIES
—Cont'd
Transfers between facilities, §7-1303.09, MentalRetardation Rule 5.
Voluntary admission to facility, §7-1303.02.

COMMITMENT OF PERSONS WITH MENTAL ILLNESS, §§21-501 to 21-592.
See HOSPITALIZATION OF PERSONS WITH MENTAL ILLNESS.

COMMITTEES.
Accounts and accounting.
Bond of committee.
Discharge only after accounting, §28-2504.
Bonds, surety.
Discharge only after accounting, §28-2504.
Fiduciary security transfers, §§28-2901 to 28-2909.
See FIDUCIARY SECURITY TRANSFERS.

COMMODITIES COST RESERVE FUND, §47-368.04.

COMMON CARRIERS.
Actions for injuries to employees.
Employer's liability, §§35-301 to 35-305.
Alcoholic beverage licenses.
On-premises retailers, §25-113.
Taxation, §25-905.
Buses.
General provisions, §§9-1101.01 to 9-1115.04, 35-201 to 35-253.
See METRORAIL AND METROBUS.
Contributory negligence, §35-301.
Defined, §34-203.
Employers' liability, §§35-301 to 35-305.
Liability for injuries or death to employees, §35-301.
Commencement of action, time limitation, §35-304.
Contract, insurance, relief benefit or indemnity not bar to recovery, §35-303.
Contributory negligence no bar to recovery, §35-302.
Safety Appliance Act.
Provisions not limit employer's duties or impair employee's rights under act, §35-305.

COMMON CARRIERS —Cont'd
Employers' liability —Cont'd
Liability for injuries or death to
employees —Cont'd
Statute of limitations, §35-304.
**Injuries to employees, employer
liability for,** §35-301.
Insurance, §35-301.
Railroads.
General provisions, §§35-101 to
35-124.
See RAILROADS.
Street railways.
General provisions, §§35-201 to
35-253.
See METRORAIL AND
METROBUS.
Traffic laws, §50-2201.03.

COMMON LAW.
Constitution of the United States.
Suits at common law, US Const Amd
7.
Evidentiary considerations.
Criminal procedure, CrimPro Rule 26.
Delinquent minors, JuvProc Rule 26.
Interpretation of provisions, §45-401.
Trusts and trustees.
Uniform trust code.
Common law of trusts, applicability,
§19-1301.06.

COMMON LAW ASSAULT, §22-404.

COMMON TRUST ACCOUNTS,
§§26-401 to 26-404.

COMMUNICABLE DISEASES.
Access to premises for inspection,
§7-138.
AIDS.
See AIDS.
Carriers, persons believed to be.
Arrest of, §7-137.
Children and minors, §7-134.
Continuation of order for removal,
§7-134.
Detention, §§7-134, 7-135.
Examination of, §7-135.
Expiration of order for removal,
§7-134.
Hearings for, §7-135.
Leaving detention without discharge,
§7-136.
Order for removal, §7-133.
Spiritual means to cure disease,
persons relying on, §7-141.
**Communicable and chronic disease
prevention and treatment fund,**
§7-736.02.

COMMUNICABLE DISEASES
—Cont'd
Defined terms, §7-132.
Emergency.
Public health emergency executive
order, §7-2304.01.
Fees for prevention and treatment,
§7-736.03.
Fines, §7-140.
Graves, reopening, §43-123.
Health emergency.
Public health emergency executive
order, §7-2304.01.
Hospitals for treatment of, §44-701.
Inspection, access to premises for,
§7-138.
**Interference with duties or
functions regarding,** §7-139.
Interpretation of provisions, §7-144.
Penalties, §7-140.
Pleuropneumonia, §1-333.01.
**Presumption as to disability or
death resulting from.**
Fire and emergency medical services
employees, §5-654.
Preventing spread of, §7-131.
**Public health emergency executive
order,** §7-2304.01.
**Spiritual means to cure disease,
persons relying on,** §7-141.

COMMUNITY BENEFIT FUND,
§§10-1602.01 to 10-1602.04.
Bond issues, §10-1602.03.
Community investment plan,
§10-1602.04.
Creation, §10-1602.02.
Findings of council, §10-1602.01.

**COMMUNITY CENTER AND
PLAYGROUNDS DEPARTMENT.**
Recreation board, transfers to,
§§10-221, 10-226.

COMMUNITY DEVELOPMENT,
§§6-1001 to 6-1007.
Acquisition of real property, §6-1005.
**Annual preparation and submission
of program,** §6-1002.
**Community-based violence
reduction fund,** §1-325.121.
**Comprehensive plan for the
National Capital, community
input on,** §1-306.04.
**Department of housing and
community development unified
fund,** §42-2857.01.
Disposition of real property, §6-1005.

COMMUNITY DEVELOPMENT
—Cont'd
District funds invested or deposited in banks and financial institutions, §§47-351.07, 47-351.09.
Economic development zone incentives.
General provisions, §§6-1501 to 6-1506.
See ECONOMIC DEVELOPMENT ZONE INCENTIVES.
Financial institutions, §§26-431.01 to 26-431.08.
Grants, §6-1006.
Housing and community development reform advisory commission, §§6-1031 to 6-1037.
Implementation of program after approval, §6-1004.
Insurance, §6-1006.
Interpretation of provisions, §6-1007.
Latino community development, §§2-1301 to 2-1341.
See LATINO COMMUNITY DEVELOPMENT.
Loans, §6-1006.
Permissible program activities, §6-1003.
Policy declaration, §6-1001.
Rehabilitation of private property, §6-1006.
Severability of provisions, §6-1007.
Youth services, neighborhood planning councils for.
See YOUTH SERVICES.

COMMUNITY EDUCATION COURSES, §§38-1001 to 38-1003.

COMMUNITY PROPERTY.
Nonprobate transfers.
Rights at death, §19-602.12.

COMMUNITY RESIDENCE FACILITIES.
Clinical privileges and staff membership.
Reduction, suspension, revocation, not renewed.
Reporting, §44-508.
Standards, §44-507.
Crimes and offenses.
Failure to report certain deaths, §5-1406.
Criminal background checks for unlicensed personnel, §§44-551 to 44-554.
Confidentiality, §44-552.
Rules, §44-554.

COMMUNITY RESIDENCE FACILITIES —Cont'd
Criminal background checks for unlicensed personnel —Cont'd
Confidentiality —Cont'd
Unauthorized release, penalties, §44-553.
Convictions prohibiting employment, §44-552.
Definitions, §44-551.
Required, §44-552.
Dead bodies.
Duty to report certain deaths to medical examiner, §5-1405.
Failure to report certain deaths, §5-1406.
Enjoining violations, §44-509.
Fines and penalties, §44-509.
Health-care facility licensure, §§44-501 to 44-509.
Licenses, §§44-501 to 44-509.
Applications, §44-502.
Definitions, §44-501.
Inspection, §44-505.
Mayor's authority, §44-503.
Provisional and restricted licenses, §44-506.
Requirements, §44-502.
Rules, §44-504.
Unlawful to operate without, §44-502.
Public assistance recipients, §4-205.49.
Violations, penalties, enforcement, §44-509.

COMMUNITY RESOURCE OFFICER.
Alcoholic beverage control board, §25-209.

COMMUNITY SCHOOLS.
Administration, §38-754.03.
Citation of provisions, §38-754.01.
Definitions, §38-754.02.
Fund establishment, §38-754.04.
Rules, §38-756.01.

COMMUNITY SERVICE.
Criminal procedure, §16-712.
Delinquent minors, JuvProc Rule 112.
Juvenile offenders, §24-903.
Parental kidnapping, §16-1024.

COMPACTS.
Adoption.
Interstate compact on adoption and medical assistance, §§4-321 to 4-328.

COMPACTS —Cont'd

Detainers.

Interstate agreement on detainers, §§24-801 to 24-805.

Driver license compact, §§50-1001, 50-1002.

Duties and imposts.

Duty of tonnage, US Const Art I §10.

Tonnage, US Const Art I §10.

Education.

Compact for education of the education commission of the states, §§38-3001 to 38-3004.

Interstate agreement on qualification of educational personnel, §§38-2101 to 38-2104.

Interstate compact on educational opportunity for military children, §§49-1101.01 to 49-1101.20.

See SCHOOLS AND EDUCATION.

Emergency management assistance compact, §§7-2331, 7-2332.

Interstate agreement on qualification of educational personnel, §§38-2101 to 38-2104.

Interstate civil defense compacts, §7-2209.

Interstate insurance product regulation compact.

Authority to enter, §31-1391.

Interstate parole and probation compact, §§24-451 to 24-453.

Mass transportation compact.

National capital region transportation, §§9-1103.01 to 9-1103.07.

See METRORAIL AND METROBUS.

Mental illness, persons with.

Interstate compact on mental health, §§7-1101 to 7-1106.

Military.

Interstate compact on educational opportunity for military children, §§49-1101.01 to 49-1101.20.

See SCHOOLS AND EDUCATION.

Minors.

Interstate compact for juveniles, §§24-1101 to 24-1106.

Alteration, amendment or repeal of provisions, §24-1106.

Compact administrator, §24-1103.

Congressional findings, §24-1101.

Construction of compact, §24-1105.

Enforcement, §24-1104.

Entry into and execution of compact, §24-1102.

COMPACTS —Cont'd

Minors —Cont'd

Interstate compact on adoption and medical assistance, §§4-321 to 4-328.

Interstate compact on educational opportunity for military children, §§49-1101.01 to 49-1101.20.

See SCHOOLS AND EDUCATION.

Interstate compact on placement of children, §§4-1421 to 4-1424.

Agreements with other state for placement, §4-1423.

Authority to enter into and execute compact, §4-1422.

Definitions, §4-1421.

Delinquent children.

Administrative hearing on placement, review, §4-1424.

National capital region transportation.

Mass transportation compact, §§9-1103.01 to 9-1103.07.

Washington metropolitan area transit authority compact, §§9-1107.01 to 9-1107.12.

Parole.

Interstate parole and probation compact, §§24-451 to 24-453.

Police.

Reciprocal police mutual aid agreements, §§2-209.01 to 2-209.04.

Potomac river basin compact, §§8-1601, 8-1602.

Prisons and prisoners.

Interstate corrections compact, §§24-1001, 24-1002.

Sewerage.

Agreements with Maryland and Virginia, §1-204.87.

State.

Compacts between the states or with foreign powers, US Const Art I §10.

Taxation.

Multistate tax compact, §§47-441 to 47-445.

Washington metropolitan area transit authority safety regulation.

Joint state oversight agency for creation of rail fixed guideway system, §§9-1109.01 to 9-1109.07.

Woodrow Wilson bridge and tunnel compact, §§9-1115.01 to 9-1115.04.

COMPENSATING-USE TAX, §§47-2201 to 47-2214.

Applicability of provisions, §47-2212.

Assumption of tax by vendor, §47-2209.

Beverages, §47-2202.01.

Bonds, surety, §47-2208.

Collection of taxes, §§47-2202.02, 47-2203.

Definitions, §47-2201.

Exemptions, §47-2206.

Food, §47-2202.01.

Incorporation of other provisions, §47-2213.

Lincoln Square Theater.
Exemption, §47-4601.

Lodging places, §47-2202.01.

Monthly returns, §47-2211.

Nonresident vendors, §47-2204.

Payment of tax.
Monthly returns, §47-2211.
Purchaser, by, §47-2205.
Vendors and retailers, payment over by, §47-2210.

Rates, §§47-2202, 47-2202.01.

Refunds, §47-2209.

Registration, §47-2212.

Rental vehicles, §47-2202.01.

Returns, §§47-2210, 47-2211.

Vender, collection of taxes by, §47-2203.

Washington convention and sports authority, transfer of proceeds to, §47-2202.02.

COMPENSATION.

Arbitrators, Arbitration Rule V.

Attorney general, §1-301.85.

Attorneys' fees generally.
See ATTORNEYS' FEES.

Conservators.
Probate proceedings, Probate Rule 225.

Crime victims' compensation program, §§4-501 to 4-518, VictComp Rules 1 to 41.
See CRIME VICTIMS' COMPENSATION.

Elected officials generally.
Mayor and council compensation advisory committee, §§1-611.51 to 1-611.57.
See MAYOR AND COUNCIL COMPENSATION ADVISORY COMMITTEE.

Fiduciaries generally, CivPro Rule 301.

COMPENSATION —Cont'd

Guardian ad litem.
Adoption proceedings, §16-316.
Conservatorship proceedings, CivPro Rule 302.
Intervention proceedings, Probate Rule 308.
Probate proceedings.
Death between January 1, 1981 and June 30, 1995, Probate Rule 122.
Death on or after July 1, 1995, Probate Rule 422.

Guardians of minors.
Probate proceedings, Probate Rule 225.

Hospitals.
Benefits in lieu of pay, §44-708.
Patients, stipends for, §44-707.
Resident employees, stipends for, §44-707.

Interpreters, CivPro Rule 43.
Adoption proceedings, Adoption Rule 43.
Criminal procedure, CrimPro Rule 28.
Domestic relations actions, DomRel Rule 43.
Juvenile proceedings, JuvProc Rule 28.

Intervention proceedings, Probate Rule 308.

Juror fees, §§11-1912, 15-718.

Masters, CivPro Rule 53-I, USDistCt LCvR 53.1.
Domestic relations actions, DomRel Rule 53.

Merit system.
Compensation of employees, §§1-611.01 to 1-611.21.
See MERIT SYSTEM.
General provisions, §§1-601.01 to 1-636.03.
See MERIT SYSTEM.

Minimum wages.
General provisions, §§32-1001 to 32-1015.
See MINIMUM WAGES.

National Guard.
Pay and allowances, §§49-901 to 49-906.
See NATIONAL GUARD.

Probate proceedings.
Conservators and guardians of minors, Probate Rule 225.
Guardian ad litem.
Conservatorship proceedings, Probate Rule 224.

COMPENSATION —Cont'd
Probate proceedings —Cont'd
Guardian ad litem —Cont'd
Death between January 1, 1981 and June 30, 1995, Probate Rule 122.
Death on or after July 1, 1995, Probate Rule 422.
Request for compensation of personal representative, Probate Rule 124.
Review of compensation, Probate Rule 424.
Sale of property.
Proceedings involving guardians, conservators, etc., Probate Rule 203.
Sale of property by court order, CivPro Rule 308.
Probate proceedings, Probate Rule 203.
Teachers.
Foreign exchange program participants, §38-1922.
Installment payments, §38-1902.
Research assistants classified as teachers for purposes of, §38-1906.
Retirement, salary deductions for, §38-2001.01.
Sex discrimination, §38-1901.
Unemployment compensation.
General provisions, §§51-101 to 51-151.
See UNEMPLOYMENT COMPENSATION.
Wages and salaries.
See WAGES AND SALARIES.
Whistleblowers, compensation restrictions for interference with rights, §1-615.58a.
Witness fees.
See WITNESSES.
Workers' compensation.
General provisions, §§32-1501 to 32-1545.
See WORKERS' COMPENSATION.

COMPENSATORY TIME OFF.
Merit system compensation policy, §1-611.03.

COMPETENCE TO PROCEED, §§24-531.01 to 24-531.13.
Appearance for examination and treatment.
Ordering defendant, §24-531.02.
Burden of proving incompetence, §24-531.04.

COMPETENCE TO PROCEED —Cont'd
Civil commitment proceedings.
Status hearing, §24-531.07.
Commitment of defendant.
Civil commitment proceedings.
Status hearing, §24-531.07.
Escape from hospital, §24-531.13.
Full competence examination, §24-531.03.
Release ordered, civil commitment petition filed.
Remand to facility, §24-531.07.
Remand to facility.
Release ordered but civil commitment petition filed, §24-531.07.
Treatment for restoration of defendant's competence, §24-531.05.
Extending pending completion of civil commitment proceeding, §24-531.07.
Competence defined, §24-531.01.
Computing time periods prescribed.
Tolling periods, §24-531.11.
Defendant determined incompetent, §24-531.02.
Definitions, §24-531.01.
Delinquent minors, §16-2307.
Treatment when child determined to be incompetent, JuvProc Rule 110A.
Dismissal without prejudice.
Failure of defendant to obtain competence, §24-531.08.
Escape from hospital, §24-531.13.
Examination to determine defendant's competence, §24-531.03.
Independent experts.
Prosecutor or defense attorney engaging, §24-531.12.
Statements made during, admissibility, §24-531.10.
Federal statutes superseded, §24-531.13.
Findings by court.
Initial competence determination, §24-531.04.
Full competence examination, §24-531.03.
Habeas corpus.
Establishing eligibility for release, §24-531.13.
Hearings during and after treatment, §24-531.06.

COMPETENCE TO PROCEED
—Cont'd
Hearing to determine competence of defendant, §24-531.04.
Incompetent defined, §24-531.01.
Independent experts.
Prosecutor or defense attorney engaging, §24-531.12.
Initial competence determination, §24-531.04.
Involuntary administration of medication to incompetent defendant, §24-531.09.
Motions in underlying proceedings.
Prosecutor or defense attorney may file, §24-531.02.
Preliminary screening examination.
Ordered before full competence examination, §24-531.03.
Presumption defendant competent, §24-531.04.
Pretrial release, eligibility for, determination.
Competency determination not to delay, §24-531.02.
Probable cause determination.
Competency determination not to delay, §24-531.02.
Report by treatment provider, §24-531.06.
Report defendant incompetent, §24-531.03.
Tolling periods.
Computing time periods prescribed, §24-531.11.
Treatment for restoration of defendant's competence, §24-531.05.
Dismissal without prejudice.
Failure of defendant to obtain competence, §24-531.08.
Extending pending completion of civil commitment proceeding, §24-531.07.
Hearings during and after treatment, §24-531.06.
Involuntary medication, §24-531.09.
Statements made during, admissibility, §24-531.10.

COMPLAINTS.
Accounts, CivPro Form CA 4.
Claim for debt, CivPro Form CA 13.
Class actions, CivPro Rule 23-I, USDistCt LCvR 23.1.
Commencement of action.
Domestic relations actions, DomRel Rule 3.

COMPLAINTS —Cont'd
Commencement of civil action, CivPro Rule 3.
Condemnation of property, CivPro Form CA 29, CivPro Rule 71A.
Conversion, CivPro Form CA 11.
Criminal procedure, CrimPro Rule 3.
Declaratory relief, CivPro Form CA 18.
Delinquent minors, JuvProc Rule 3.
Verified complaint requirement, §16-2305, JuvProc Rule 3.
Derivative actions by shareholders, CivPro Rule 23.1.
Electronic filing.
Mandatory eFiling in civil division, CivPro Appx IV.
Forcible entry and detainer.
Verified complaint, §16-1501.
Fraudulent conveyance set aside, CivPro Form CA 13.
Goods sold and delivered, CivPro Form CA 5.
Interpleader, CivPro Form CA 18.
Landlord and tenant court,
LandlordTenant Rule 3.
Form.
Commercial property, LandlordTenant Form 1D.
Nonpayment of rent, LandlordTenant Form 1A.
Other grounds for eviction in addition to nonpayment of rent, LandlordTenant Form 1C.
Violation of obligations of tenancy or other grounds for eviction, LandlordTenant Form 1B.
Money had and received, CivPro Form CA 8.
Answer to complaint, CivPro Form CA 21.
Money lent, CivPro Form CA 6.
Money paid by mistake, CivPro Form CA 7.
Negligence, CivPro Forms CA 9, CA 10.
Pleadings generally.
See PLEADINGS.
Promissory notes, CivPro Form CA 3.
Replevin.
Form of complaint, §16-3702.
Specific performance to convey land, CivPro Form CA 12.
Support and maintenance, DomRel Form 13.
Third party complaints, CivPro Form CA 22-A.

COMPLAINTS —Cont'd
Workplace fraud.
Investigation of complaints,
§32-1331.05.

**COMPREHENSIVE HOUSING
STRATEGY TASK FORCE,**
§§6-1051 to 6-1054.
Composition, §6-1051.
**Development of comprehensive
housing strategy,** §6-1052.
Established, §6-1051.
**Presentation of comprehensive
housing strategy,** §6-1053.
Public meetings, §6-1053.
Reports, §§6-1054, 42-3502.23.

COMPREHENSIVE PLAN, §§1-306.01
to 1-306.07, 2-1003.
Community input, §1-306.04.
**Housing linkage requirement of the
housing element,** §§1-306.31 to
1-306.45.
Affordable housing.
Building permit issued for required
amount, §1-306.42.
Creating required housing, §1-306.35.
Housing trust fund, §§1-306.36,
1-306.37.
Contribution schedule, §1-306.43.
Inapplicability of provisions, §1-306.41.
Issuance of building permits and
certificate of occupancy.
Satisfaction of part required,
§1-306.44.
Objective, §1-306.31.
Policies, §1-306.33.
Purpose, §1-306.32.
Regulations, §1-306.45.
Required housing ratio, §1-306.34.
Zoning consistent with plan,
§1-306.40.
Zoning density increase, §1-306.38.
Zoning requirements not supplanted,
§1-306.39.
Land use element.
Mayor to submit, §1-306.02.
Review of issuance of building and
construction permits, §1-306.06.
Land use maps.
Mayor to submit, §1-306.02.
Publication, §1-306.05.
Purpose of elements, §1-306.01.
Small area action plans, §1-306.03.
Ten district elements, §1-306.01.
Zoning conformity, §1-306.07.

COMPROMISE OR SETTLEMENT.
See SETTLEMENT OR COMPROMISE.

**COMPTROLLER GENERAL OF
UNITED STATES.**
**Metrorail and metrobus acquisition
of mass transit bus systems,**
§9-1113.07.

**COMPTROLLER OF THE
CURRENCY.**
**Banks and financial institutions
under supervision of,** §26-101.
Building associations, §26-251.

**COMPULSORY NO-FAULT MOTOR
VEHICLE INSURANCE,**
§§31-2401 to 31-2408.01.
See NO-FAULT MOTOR VEHICLE
INSURANCE.

**COMPULSORY SCHOOL
ATTENDANCE,** §§38-201 to
38-213.
**Absence of students for certain
amount of times.**
Reporting to child and family services
agency, §4-1321.02.
Attendance zone boundaries,
§38-221.
Census of minors for, §38-204.
**Contributing to the delinquency of a
minor.**
Encouraging, causing, or allowing
truancy, §22-811.
Definitions, §38-201.
End-of-year report.
Absences, §§38-203, 38-209.
Enforcement, §38-203.
Enrollment reports, §38-205.
Fines, §38-203.
Jurisdiction, §38-213.
Notice.
Tenth unexcused absence as trigger for
notice.
Parental notice, §38-207.
Police and superintendent of
education, §38-208.
Penalties, §§38-203, 38-206.
Police authority over truant child,
§38-207.
Reports.
End-of-year report, §§38-203, 38-209.
Enrollment reports, §38-205.
Truancy referrals and enforcement,
§38-208.
Withdrawal reports, §38-205.
Requirements regarding, §38-202.
School-based student support teams.
Role, §38-203.
Superior court, §38-213.

COMPULSORY SCHOOL ATTENDANCE —Cont'd
Taking child into custody.
Child not in school on day school in session, §16-2309.
Tenth unexcused absence.
Notice to parents.
Triggering notice upon 10th absence, §38-207.
Notice to police and superintendent of education.
Triggering notice upon 10th absence, §38-208.
Referrals to social services agencies, §38-208.
Truancy and Dropout Prevention Program, §38-241.
Withdrawal reports, §38-205.

COMPUTATION OF TIME.
Appeals, DCCtApp Rule 26.
Civil cases, CivPro Rule 6.
Criminal procedure, CrimPro Rule 45.
Daylight savings time as standard time for District, §28-2711.
Delinquent minors, JuvProc Rule 45.
Domestic relations actions, DomRel Rule 6.
Hospitalization of persons with mental illness, MentalHealth Rule 13.

COMPUTERS.
Assistive technology warranty, §§28-4031 to 28-4034.
Business licenses.
Interagency computer system, §47-2866.
Civil docket maintained electronically, CivPro Rule 79.
Domestic relations actions, DomRel Rule 79.
Defined, §2-213.01.
Electronic transactions, uniform act, §§28-4901 to 28-4918.
Electronic waste, §§8-1041.01 to 8-1041.12.
See ELECTRONIC WASTE.
Internet.
Compensating-use tax, §§47-2201 to 47-2214.
See COMPENSATING-USE TAX.
Definition of Internet access service, §47-2201.
Franchise agreement.
Furnishing services to digitally-disadvantaged residents, §§34-1731.01 to 34-1731.11.
See INTERNET.

COMPUTERS —Cont'd
Internet —Cont'd
Toll telecommunication service tax, §§47-3901 to 47-3922.
See TOLL TELECOMMUNICATION SERVICE TAX.

CONCEALED WEAPONS, CARRYING, §§22-4504 to 22-4505.

CONCERTS ON CAPITOL GROUNDS, §10-503.24.

CONCILIATION.
Discrimination, complaints of, §2-1403.06.
Discriminatory practices, §2-1402.63.
Evictions, §42-3505.03.
Metropolitan police citizen complaint review, office, §5-1110.
Retaliatory actions against tenants, §42-3505.03.
Small claims court, §11-1322, SmallClaims Conciliation Rules 1 to 4.

CONCURRENT SENTENCES.
Criminal proceedings, §23-112.

CONCUSSIONS.
Athletic concussion program, §§7-2871.01 to 7-2871.05.
Defined terms, §7-2871.01.
Materials development and distribution, §7-2871.04.
Removal from athletic activity.
Athletes suspected of sustaining concussion, §7-2871.02.
Return to athletic activity.
Athletes suspected of sustaining concussion, §7-2871.02.
Rules, §7-2871.05.
Training program, §7-2871.03.

CONDEMNATION PROCEEDINGS.
Assessments.
Witnesses in condemnation proceedings, assessment officials as, §14-308.
Attachment.
Condemnation of attached property, §§16-524, 16-555.
Condemnation Review Board, §6-902.
Deposits in court, CivPro Rule 71A.
District-owned real property, §§16-1312 to 16-1320.
Dulles International Airport, §9-803.
Eminent domain.
General provisions, §§16-1301 to 16-1385.
See EMINENT DOMAIN.

CONDEMNATION PROCEEDINGS
—Cont'd
Execution of judgments.
Attachment and garnishment after
judgment in aid of execution,
§16-555.
Forms.
Complaint, CivPro Form CA 29.
Notice, CivPro Form CA 28.
Garnishment.
Prejudgment garnishment of attached
property, §§16-524, 16-525.
Highways, §§9-101.05, 9-101.09,
9-101.18.
Resubdivision affected by highway
plans, §9-101.09.
Insanitary buildings.
See INSANITARY BUILDINGS.
Joinder of parties, CivPro Rule 71A.
Judges.
Assignment for, §16-1302.
Metrorail and metrobus.
Acquisition of mass transit bus
systems, §9-1113.06.
National Capital Housing Authority,
§6-101.02.
Railroads, §9-1203.06.
Real estate tax sales, §47-1204.
Streets and alleys.
Construction materials, §9-1219.01.
Opening, extending, widening, or
straightening, §9-203.02.
Repealed laws, condemnations or
closings pursuant to, §9-206.01.
Telephone and telegraph companies,
§34-1921.08.

CONDOMINIUMS, §§42-1901.01 to
42-1904.18.
Actions, §42-1904.12.
Additional land, §42-1902.23.
Affirmative action, §42-1904.14.
Annual updating report, §42-1904.07.
Appeals, §42-1904.16.
Applicability of provisions,
§42-1901.01.
Assessments.
Common expenses, §42-1903.12.
Horizontal property regimes, §42-2017.
Liens, §42-1903.13.
Attorney general, §42-1904.17.
Attorney in fact to grant and accept
beneficial easements, §42-1903.08.
Bicycle parking spaces
requirements, §50-1641.05.
Bonds, surety.
Escrow deposits, §42-1904.09.

CONDOMINIUMS —Cont'd
Boundaries of units, §§42-1902.06,
42-1902.25.
Bylaws, §§42-1902.04, 42-1903.01,
42-1904.10.
Cease and desist orders,
§§42-1904.14, 42-1904.15.
Common elements.
Allocation of interests in,
§§42-1902.11, 42-1902.12.
Conveyances, §42-1903.20.
Easements, §42-1902.21.
Encumbrances, §42-1903.20.
Liens, §§42-1902.02, 42-1903.09.
Limited common elements.
Assignment of, §42-1902.13.
Provisions applicable to,
§42-1902.14.
Model units, §42-1902.22.
Relocated boundaries affecting,
§42-1902.25.
Sales offices, §42-1902.22.
Single unit, serving, §42-1902.06.
Undivided interest included in
individual units, §42-1902.03.
Common expenses, §42-1903.12.
Compliance with provisions,
§42-1902.09.
Contiguity of units, §42-1902.01.
Contractible condominiums.
Allocation of interests in common
elements, §42-1902.12.
Contraction of condominiums,
§42-1902.20.
Declaration, §42-1902.10.
Defined, §42-1901.02.
Control, §42-1903.02.
Conversion condominiums.
Council allowed to prohibit
conversions to condominiums,
§42-2051.
Defined, §42-1901.02.
Notice, §42-1904.12.
Offer or disposition, §42-1904.08.
Warranty limitations, §42-1903.16.
Convertible lands.
Allocation of interests in common
elements, §42-1902.12.
Conversion of, §42-1902.17.
Declaration, §42-1902.10.
Defined, §42-1901.02.
Convertible spaces, conversion of,
§42-1902.18.
Conveyances of common elements,
§42-1903.20.
Declarant, control by, §42-1903.02.

CONDOMINIUMS —Cont'd
Declaration, §§42-1902.04, 42-1902.10, 42-1904.10.
Deeds, §42-2006.
Definitions, §§42-1901.01, 42-1901.02.
Descriptions required, §§42-1902.03, 42-1902.10.
Easements, §42-1902.10.
Attorney in fact to grant and accept beneficial easements, §42-1903.08.
Declarant's easement over common elements for purposes of improvement, §42-1902.21.
Encroachments and support, for, §42-1902.16.
Electronic notice of meetings, §42-1903.03.
Eminent domain, §42-1901.06.
Encumbrances of common elements, §42-1903.20.
Enforcement of provisions, §42-1904.13.
Escrow accounts, §42-1904.09.
Establishment of, §§42-1902.01 to 42-1902.30.
Executive board, §§42-1903.02, 42-1903.04.
Expandable condominiums.
Allocation of interests in common elements, §§42-1902.12, 42-1902.19.
Declaration, §42-1902.12.
Defined, §42-1901.02.
Expansion of condominiums, §42-1902.19.
Financial records, §42-1903.14.
Fines, §42-1904.17.
First refusal, right of, §42-1903.15.
Home purchase assistance fund, §§42-2601 to 42-2626.
See HOME PURCHASE ASSISTANCE FUND.
Homestead deduction.
Real property taxes, §47-850.
Homestead housing preservation, §§42-2101 to 42-2111.
See HOMESTEAD HOUSING PRESERVATION.
Horizontal property regimes, §§42-2001 to 42-2031.
See HORIZONTAL PROPERTY REGIMES.
Improvements and alterations, §§42-1902.21, 42-1902.23, 42-1902.24.
Individual units, ownership of, §42-1901.03.

CONDOMINIUMS —Cont'd
Inspection of books and records, §42-1903.14.
Instruments.
Amendments to, §42-1902.27.
Compliance with, §42-1902.09.
Conflicts between, §42-1902.07.
Interpretation of provisions in, §§42-1902.06, 42-1902.07.
Recordation. See within this heading, "Recordation of instruments."
Severability of provisions, §42-1902.08.
Insurance, §42-1903.10.
Interpretation of provisions.
Chapter, §42-1901.08.
Control, §42-1903.02.
Instruments, §42-1902.06.
Investigations, §42-1904.13.
Issuance of rules and regulations, §42-1904.12.
Land use planning, §42-1901.05.
Leasehold condominiums, §§42-1902.10, 42-1902.29.
Letters of credit.
Escrow deposits, §42-1904.09.
Liens.
Assessments, §42-1903.13.
Common elements, §§42-1902.02, 42-1903.09.
Individual units, §42-1903.09.
Release prior to conveyance of first unit, §42-1902.02.
Limitation of actions on warranties, §42-1903.17.
Master associations, §42-1903.18.
Mayor's administration of provisions, §42-1904.12.
Meetings of owners' association, §42-1903.03.
Mergers and consolidations, §42-1903.19.
Model units, §42-1902.22.
Noncompliance with provisions, §42-1902.09.
Notice.
Cease and desist and affirmative action orders, §42-1904.14.
Conversion condominiums, §42-1904.12.
Electronic notice of meetings, §42-1903.03.
Insurance, §42-1903.10.
Registration, filing for, §42-1904.06.
Registration, rejection of, §42-1904.06.
Offer or disposition, §§42-1904.01 to 42-1904.18.
Abbreviated public offering statement, §42-1904.12.

CONDOMINIUMS —Cont'd
Offer or disposition —Cont'd
Actions, §42-1904.12.
Bylaws, furnishing copy of,
§42-1904.10.
Changes to, §42-1904.04.
Conversion condominiums,
§42-1904.08.
Declaration, furnishing copy of,
§42-1904.10.
Escrow of deposits, §42-1904.09.
Exemptions, §42-1904.01.
Fraud and deceit, §42-1904.02.
Language of public offering statement,
§42-1904.02.
Public offering statement,
§§42-1904.02, 42-1904.04.
Registration, no offer or disposition
prior to, §42-1904.02.
Resale, §42-1904.11.
Officers, §42-1903.06.
Owners' associations, §42-1903.08.
Attorney in fact to grant and accept
beneficial easements, §42-1903.08.
Control in absence of, §42-1903.02.
Electronic transmission of votes,
§42-1903.05.
Executive board, §§42-1903.02,
42-1903.04.
Insurance obtained by, §42-1903.10.
Liability, §42-1903.09.
Master associations, §42-1903.18.
Meetings, §42-1903.03.
Officers, §42-1903.06.
Powers and duties, §42-1903.08.
Quorum, §42-1903.04.
Surplus funds, §42-1903.11.
Trustees, as, §42-1903.21.
Votes, allocation of, §42-1903.05.
Ownership of individual units,
§42-1901.03.
Penalties, §42-1904.17.
Plat and plans, §42-1902.01.
Recordation and filing of,
§§42-1902.14, 42-1902.15.
Prior law superseded, §42-1901.01.
Real property taxes.
Homestead deduction, §47-850.
Reduced tax liability for seniors and
persons with disabilities, §47-863.
Recordation of instruments.
Amendments and certifications,
§42-1902.05.
Bylaws, §42-1903.01.
Contraction of condominiums,
§42-1902.20.

CONDOMINIUMS —Cont'd
Recordation of instruments —Cont'd
Convertible lands, conversion of,
§42-1902.17.
Establishment of condominiums,
§42-1902.01.
Expansion of condominiums,
§42-1902.19.
Limited common elements, assignment
of, §42-1902.13.
Plat and plans, §§42-1902.14,
42-1902.15.
Records, §42-1903.14.
**Reduction in number of units, effect
of,** §42-1902.12.
Registration, §§42-1904.01 to
42-1904.18.
Acceptance of application, §42-1904.06.
Additional units, later registration of,
§42-1904.03.
Annual updating report, §42-1904.07.
Application for, §§42-1904.03,
42-1904.05.
Exemptions, §42-1904.01.
Fees, §42-1904.03.
Hearings, §§42-1904.06, 42-1904.15.
Investigations, §42-1904.05.
No offer or disposition prior to,
§42-1904.02.
Notice of filing for, §42-1904.06.
Notice of rejection, §42-1904.06.
Public inspection of application for,
§42-1904.03.
Rejection of application, §42-1904.06.
Revocation of, §42-1904.15.
Rental housing conversion and sale.
General provisions, §§42-3401.01 to
42-3405.13.
See RENTAL HOUSING.
Repair and maintenance.
General provisions, §42-1903.07.
Horizontal property regimes.
See HORIZONTAL PROPERTY
REGIMES.
Reports, §42-1904.07.
Resale, §42-1904.11.
Right of first refusal, §42-1903.15.
Sales offices, §42-1902.22.
Severability of provisions,
§42-1904.18.
Instruments, §42-1902.08.
Special declarant rights.
Defined, §42-1901.02.
Transfer of, §42-1902.30.
Step Up program, §42-2622.
Structural defects, warranty for,
§§42-1903.16, 42-1903.17.

CONDOMINIUMS —Cont'd
Subdivision of units, §42-1902.26.
Surplus funds, §42-1903.11.
Taxation.
    Convertible lands, §42-1901.02.
    Individual units, separate taxation of, §42-1901.04.
Termination of, §42-1902.28.
Updating report, annual, §42-1904.07.
Variances, §42-1901.07.
Warranties, §§42-1903.16, 42-1903.17.
Withdrawable land, §42-1902.23.
Zoning, §42-1901.05.

CONDUCT, STANDARDS OF.
Attorneys at law.
    Admission to bar, DCCtApp Rule 46.
    Rules of professional conduct, DCBar Rule X, ProfCond Rules 1.0 to 9.1.
    See ATTORNEYS AT LAW.
Disorderly conduct, §22-1321.
    Prosecutions, §22-1809.
Labor unions, for, §1-617.03.
Metropolitan police, §5-127.01.
Metrorail and metrobus, §§35-251 to 35-253.
Public officers and employees.
    See MERIT SYSTEM.
Unfair labor practices, §1-617.04.

CONDUITS.
Defined, §34-2001.
Permits, §§1-301.01, 34-1406.
Public utilities.
    Electric light and power companies.
        See ELECTRIC LIGHT AND POWER COMPANIES.
    Private conduits.
        See PUBLIC UTILITIES.
Telecommunications companies.
    See TELECOMMUNICATIONS COMPANIES.

CONFERENCES.
Appeal conferences, DCCtApp Rule 14, FRAP 33.
Duty to confer, USDistCt LCvR 16.3.
Judicial Conference of the District of Columbia, DCCtApp Rule 50.
Pretrial conferences generally.
    See PRETRIAL CONFERENCES.

CONFESSION OF JUDGMENT,
    CivPro Rule 68-I.
Consumer credit sales.
    Authorization to confess judgment prohibited, §28-3804.
Consumer protection.
    Authorization to confess judgment prohibited, §28-3804.

CONFESSION OF JUDGMENT
    —Cont'd
Installment loans.
    Authorization to confess judgment. Prohibited, §28-3804.

CONFIDENCE GAMES, §22-1706.

CONFIDENTIALITY OF INFORMATION.
Adoption.
    Notice of adoption proceedings, Adoption Rule 4.
    Records, Adoption Rule 79-I.
    Show cause hearings, Adoption Rule 39.
AIDS, §7-1605.
Anatomical gifts.
    Donor registry, §7-1531.19b.
Appropriations, §47-3409.
Arrest.
    Congress, US Const Art I §6.
Arrest records.
    Delinquent minors, JuvProc Rule 118.
Assignment of felony cases and related cases, CrimPro Rule 105.
Assisted living residences.
    Residents' rights, §44-105.06.
Attorneys at law.
    Client information, ProfCond Rule 1.6.
    Discipline or disability proceedings, DCBar Rule XI.
    Lawyer counseling panel, USDistCt LCrR 57.31, USDistCt LCvR 83.20.
Banks and financial institutions.
    Examinations and investigations by commissioner, §26-551.18.
Blind persons, registration of, §7-902.
Cancer, §7-302.
Captive insurance companies.
    Special purpose financial captive insurance companies.
    Examination reports, §31-3932.10.
Child abuse and neglect.
    Children's advocacy center, §4-1301.52.
    Citizen review panel, §4-1303.54.
Child and family services agency.
    Criminal background checks, §4-1305.08.
        Penalties for violations, §4-1305.09.
    Records and information, §4-1303.06.
Child fatality or near fatality.
    Proceedings, §4-1371.08.
    Public disclosure of findings and information, §§4-1303.31 to 4-1303.36.

CONFIDENTIALITY OF INFORMATION —Cont'd
Child fatality review committee,
§§4-1371.08, 4-1371.09.
Unlawful disclosure, §4-1371.11.
Choice in drug treatment program,
§7-3006.
Clinical laboratories, §44-211.
Collaborative law, §§16-4012, 16-4016.
Collection of taxes.
Returns, §47-4406.
Commission on judicial disabilities and tenure.
Information furnished commission, §1-204.31.
Proceedings of, §11-1528.
Controlled substances, §48-905.01.
Crime victims' compensation, §4-511, VictComp Rule 4.
Criminal background checks.
Child and family services agency, §4-1305.08.
Penalties for violations, §4-1305.09.
Child or youth services providers, §4-1501.08.
Penalties for disclosure, §4-1501.10.
Criminal procedure.
Privacy protection for filings made with the court, CrimPro Rule 49.1.
Criminal proceedings.
Release of information relating to pending criminal proceedings, USDistCt LCrR 57.7.
Detoxification center records, §24-604.
Domestic violence counselors.
Disclosure of confidential communication between victim and counselor.
Prohibition, exceptions, §14-310.
Disclosure of confidential information acquired.
Prohibited without consent of client, §14-307.
Domestic violence fatality review board, §16-1056.
Electronic waste.
Extended manufacturer responsibility, §8-1041.08.
Employment agencies, §32-409.
Fingerprint-based background checks, §31-633.
Grand jury secrecy, CrimPro Rule 6, USDistCt LCrR 6.1.
Discovery of transcripts, CrimPro Rule 16.
Delinquent minors, JuvProc Rule 16.

CONFIDENTIALITY OF INFORMATION —Cont'd
Gross sales tax returns, §47-2018.
Guardianship of minors.
Permanent guardianship, §§16-2393, 16-2394.
Hazardous waste and toxic chemicals.
Business information regarding, §8-1321.
Health care ombudsman program, §7-2071.07.
Health data privacy.
Generally, §§7-241 to 7-248.
See HEALTH DATA PRIVACY.
Mental health disclosures, §§7-1201.01 to 7-1208.07.
See MENTAL HEALTH DISCLOSURES.
Health insurance.
Regulatory standards, §31-3451.08.
Health maintenance organizations, §31-3426.
Homeland security commission.
Confidential information, 7-2271.05.
Confidential proceedings, 7-2271.04.
Homeless services.
Client rights, §4-754.11.
Human trafficking counselors, §14-311.
Disclosure prohibited without consent of client, §14-307.
Income tax returns, §47-1805.04.
Inheritance and estate tax returns, §47-3719.
Insurance companies.
Insurance industry material transactions disclosures, §31-1004.
Insurance holding companies, §31-708.
Intellectual disabilities, persons with, §§7-1305.05, 7-1305.12.
Intermediate care facilities for persons with intellectual disabilities.
Stevie Sellows quality improvement fund, §47-1275.
Judges.
Disclosure of nonpublic information, CJC Canon 3.5.
Jury selection, §16-5102.
Penalties for violations, §16-5103.
Juvenile records, §§16-2331 to 16-2333.02.
Lawyer counseling panel, USDistCt LCrR 57.31, USDistCt LCvR 83.20.

CONFIDENTIALITY OF INFORMATION —Cont'd

Library circulation records, §39-108.

Lie detector tests, §32-903.

Long-term care ombudsman, §7-702.06.

Malignant neoplastic diseases, §7-302.

Marriage blood test, §46-420.

Mediation, §16-4207.

Confidential mediation statements, USDistCt LCvR 84.6.

Medical malpractice, §16-2827.

Proceedings, USDistCt LCvR 84.9.

Medical malpractice.

Mediation, §16-2827.

Medical records, §44-804.

Mental health consumer's rights, §7-1231.10.

Mental health information, §§7-1201.01 to 7-1208.07.

See MENTAL HEALTH DISCLOSURES.

Mental illness, persons with.

Hospitalization, MentalHealth Rule 12.

Mortgage lenders and brokers, §26-1120.01.

NAIC insurance regulatory information system, §31-1903.

Neoplastic diseases, malignant, §7-302.

Nurse's rehabilitation program.

Committee on impaired nurses.

Closed meetings, §3-1251.07.

Minutes of meetings, §3-1251.03.

Records of committee, §3-1251.03.

Disclosure, restrictions, §3-1251.07.

Nursing facilities.

Assessment on nursing facilities, §47-1265.

Occupational safety and health, §32-1119.

Paint stewardship, §8-233.05.

Parentage proceedings, §16-2348.

Polygraphs, §32-903.

Prescription drugs.

Marketing costs, §48-833.05.

Monitoring program, §48-853.05.

Pretrial services agency, information obtained by, §23-1303.

Probate proceedings.

Exclusion of personal identification from filed documents, Probate Rule 5.1.

CONFIDENTIALITY OF INFORMATION —Cont'd

Public assistance applicants, §§4-209.01, 4-209.04.

Public procurements, §2-354.17.

Public records management, §2-1707.

Public welfare institutions.

Children and minors, §4-117.

Risk-based capital, insurance companies, §31-2008.

Scholarships for opportunity and results (SOAR) act.

Personal information, disclosure prohibited, §38-1853.10.

Security agents and brokers.

Privileged information, §31-5607.03.

Use of information by commission, §31-5607.02.

Sexual assault victim advocates.

Disclosure of confidential information prohibited without consent of client, §14-307.

Privileged communications, §14-312.

Stroke system of care, §44-1157.

Subpoenas.

Quashing or modifying subpoena, CivPro Rule 45.

Domestic relations actions, DomRel Rule 45.

Substance abuse.

Choice in drug treatment program, §7-3006.

Termination of parental rights, §§16-2363, 16-2364.

Trade secrets, §36-405.

Unauthorized practice of law committee, DCCtApp Rule 49.

Unclaimed property records, §41-131.

Vital records, §7-219.

Voting secrecy requirements, §1-1001.09.

Wastewater disposal systems, §8-105.09.

Youth rehabilitation services, department of.

Youth records, §2-1515.06.

CONFLICT OF LAWS.

Attorney disciplinary proceedings, ProfCond Rule 8.5.

Capacity to sue or be sued, CivPro Rule 17.

Domestic relations actions, DomRel Rule 17.

Construction codes, §6-1405.

Consumer credit, §28-3816.

Consumer credit sales, §28-3816.

CONFLICT OF LAWS —Cont'd
Consumer protection, §28-3816.
Environmental covenants.
Electronic signatures in global and
national commerce act.
Relation to federal act, §8-671.14.
Other land-use law.
Relationship of provisions to,
§8-671.05.
Fiduciary security transfers.
Territorial application of chapter,
§28-2908.
Foreign-money claims, §15-912.
Funds transfers.
Federal electronic fund transfer act.
Relationship between UCC provision
and federal provision,
§28:4A-108.
Home Rule act, §1-207.61.
Horizontal property regimes,
§42-2027.
**Industrial revenue bond forward
commitment program,** §47-340.16.
Installment loans, §28-3816.
**Interstate compact on educational
opportunity for military
children,** §49-1101.19.
Investment securities, §28:8-110.
Parties' power to choose applicable
law, §28:1-301.
Security entitlements.
Duties of securities intermediary.
Specification by statute or
regulation, §28:8-509.
Leases, UCC.
Leases subject to other statutes,
§28:2A-104.
Limitation on power of parties to
choose applicable law and judicial
forum, §28:2A-106.
Mental health disclosures,
§§7-1208.02, 7-1208.06.
**Metropolitan Washington Airports
Authority,** §9-926.
Negotiable instruments, §28:3-102.
Uniform trust code, §19-1301.05.
Governing law, §19-1301.07.
**Youth rehabilitation services,
department of.**
Conflicting orders repealed,
§2-1515.10.

CONFLICTS OF INTEREST.
Alcoholic beverage control board,
§25-206.
Alcoholic beverage licenses, §25-303.

CONFLICTS OF INTEREST —Cont'd
Arbitration, revised act.
Arbitrators, §16-4411.
Disclosure of facts affecting
impartiality, §16-4412.
Attorneys at law, ProfCond Rules 1.7
to 1.9.
Banks and financial institutions.
Notaries public associated with,
§26-110.
Charitable institutions.
Trustees or directors of, §44-714.
Charter schools.
Public charter schools.
Conflicting interest transactions,
§38-1802.04.
Child abuse and neglect.
Citizen review panel, §4-1303.55.
**Conservators appointed for
protection of property,** §21-2068.
Corporations.
Conflicting interest transactions,
§§29-306.70 to 29-306.73.
Definitions, §29-306.70.
Directors' actions, §29-306.72.
Judicial action, §29-306.71.
Shareholders' actions, §29-306.73.
**Crime victims' compensation
appeals board,** VictComp Rule 6.
**District of Columbia housing
authority,** §§6-220, 6-221.
Domestic life insurance companies,
§31-4430.
**Ethics and government
accountability,** §1-1162.23.
**Examination of insurance
companies,** §31-1405.
Fiduciaries, CivPro Rule 304.
Probate proceedings.
Death on or after July 1, 1995,
Probate Rule 422.
Guardians, conservators, trustees,
etc., involved, Probate Rule 202.
**Guardianship of incapacitated
persons,** §21-2043.
Health benefit exchange authority,
§31-3171.10.
Housing finance agency, §42-2702.04.
Insurance demutualization, §31-912.
Insurance investments, §31-1371.06.
Judges.
Arbitrators or mediators, acting as,
CJC Canon 3.9.
Avoiding conflicts with office, CJC
Canon 3.
Disclosure of nonpublic information,
CJC Canon 3.5.

CONFLICTS OF INTEREST —Cont'd
Judges —Cont'd
Discriminatory organizations,
affiliation with, CJC Canon 3.6.
Dual office holding.
Appointment to governmental
position.
Conflicts with office, avoiding, CJC
Canon 3.4.
Fiduciary positions, appointment to,
CJC Canon 3.8.
Participation in educational,
charitable, civic, etc. activities,
CJC Canon 3.7.
Extrajudicial activities.
Activities prohibited, CJC Canon
3.1.
Financial, business or remunerative
activities, CJC Canon 3.11.
Government appearance or
consultation, CJC Canon 3.2.
Law practice prohibited, avoiding
conflicts with office, CJC Canon
3.10.
Management of investments, CJC
Canon 3.11.
Witnesses, acting as, CJC Canon 3.3.
Lead-hazard prevention and
elimination.
Clearance examinations, §8-231.11.
Limited cooperative associations.
Directors, §29-1008.19.
Lottery and charitable games
control board, §3-1305.
Mediators, §16-4208.
Metrorail and metrobus.
Washington metropolitan area transit
authority compact on, §9-1107.01.
Mortgage lenders and brokers
acting in dual capacity, §26-1114.
Nonprofit corporations.
Conflicting interest transactions,
§29-406.70.
Notaries public, §1-1201.
Notaries public associated with
banks and financial institutions,
§26-110.
Personal representatives, §20-743.01.
Probate proceedings.
Death on or after July 1, 1995.
Guardian ad litem, Probate Rule
422.
Guardians, conservators, trustees, etc.,
involved, Probate Rule 202.
Public contracts, §1-207.32.
Public officers and employees,
§§1-615.05, 1-618.02.

CONFLICTS OF INTEREST —Cont'd
Public Parking Authority, §50-2514.
Public Welfare, Board of, §4-113.
Statehood initiative.
Senators or representative elected to
represent District, §1-135.
Volunteers used by District of
Columbia, §1-319.03.
Weights and measures sold by
director of weights, measures,
and markets, §§37-201.01 to
37-201.03, 37-201.23.
Witnesses.
Judges acting as witnesses, CJC
Canon 3.3.
Youth services, §2-1508.

CONGRESS.
Absent members, US Const Art I §5.
Action on District matters, §1-206.04.
Acts of Congress, §45-401.
Adjournment, US Const Art I §§5, 7,
Art II §3.
Admiralty, US Const Art I §8.
Age.
Representative in congress, US Const
Art I §2.
Senator, US Const Art I §3.
Aliens.
Eligibility to be representative, US
Const Art I §2.
Amendments to the constitution, US
Const Art V.
Senate.
Equal suffrage in senate, US Const
Art V.
Apportionment, US Const Art I §§2, 3,
Amds 14, 17.
Appropriations, US Const Art I §§7, 9.
Approval by president of order.
Resolution or vote, US Const Art I §7.
Army and navy.
Powers of congress, US Const Art I §8.
Arrest.
Arrest of members, US Const Art I §6.
Privilege from, US Const Art I §6.
Bankruptcy and insolvency.
Powers of congress, US Const Art I §8.
Borrowing money, US Const Art I §8.
Capitol police.
Congressional employee.
Creditable service as, §10-505.03.
Congressional personnel.
Protection of, §10-503.20.
Changing meeting of congress, US
Const Amd 20.
Charitable institutions.
Trustees or directors of, §44-712.

CONGRESS —Cont'd
Commerce, US Const Art I §§8, 9.
Compensation of members, US Const Art I §6, Amd 27.
Consists of senate and house of representatives, US Const Art I §1.
Constitution of the United States, US Const Art I §1.
Absent members, US Const Art I §5.
Adjournment, US Const Art I §§5, 7, Art II §3.
Admiralty, US Const Art I §8.
Amendments to the constitution, US Const Art V.
Appropriations, US Const Art I §9.
Approval of order.
Resolution or vote by president, US Const Art I §7.
Army and navy.
Powers of congress, US Const Art I §8.
Arrest, US Const Art I §6.
Bankruptcy.
Powers of congress, US Const Art I §8.
Borrowing money, US Const Art I §8.
Commerce, US Const Art I §§8, 9.
Compensation of members, US Const Art I §6, Amd 27.
Consists of senate and house of representatives, US Const Art I §1.
Copyright, US Const Art I §8.
Counterfeiting.
Powers of congress, US Const Art I §8.
Courts.
Power to constitute tribunals inferior to supreme court, US Const Art I §8.
Customs, US Const Art I §§8 to 10.
Debate, US Const Art I §6.
Debt.
Powers of congress, US Const Art I §8.
Declaration of war, US Const Art I §8.
Defense.
Powers of congress, US Const Art I §8.
District of Columbia, US Const Art I §8.
Duties and imposts.
Powers of congress, US Const Art I §8.
Elections.
House of representatives, US Const Art I §§2, 4.

CONGRESS —Cont'd
Constitution of the United States —Cont'd
Elections —Cont'd
Senate, US Const Art I §4, Amd 17.
Excises.
Powers of congress, US Const Art I §8.
Foreign commerce, US Const Art I §8.
Freedom of speech, US Const Art I §6.
Holding other office, US Const Art I §6.
House of representatives, US Const Art I §§1, 2, 4, 5.
Absent members, US Const Art I §5.
Arrest of members, US Const Art I §6.
Compensation of members, US Const Art I §6, Amd 27.
Debate, US Const Art I §6.
Elections.
Election of representatives, US Const Art I §2.
Times, places and manner of holding, US Const Art I §4.
Expulsion of member, US Const Art I §5.
Holding other office, US Const Art I §6.
Impeachment, US Const Art I §2.
Journal, US Const Art I §§5, 7.
Libel and slander.
Privilege of members, US Const Art I §6.
Officers, US Const Art I §2.
Presidential elector.
Representative ineligible, US Const Art II §1.
Punishment of members, US Const Art I §5.
Qualifications.
Electors, US Const Art I §2.
Members, US Const Art I §2.
Judge of qualifications, US Const Art I §5.
Revenue bills, US Const Art I §7.
Rules of procedure, US Const Art I §5.
Speaker, US Const Art I §2.
Term, US Const Art I §2.
Vacancies, US Const Art I §2.
Vice-president.
Vacancy in office.
Confirmation of nomination of president, US Const Amd 25.

CONGRESS —Cont'd
Constitution of the United States
   —Cont'd
Insurrections, US Const Art I §8.
International law.
   Power of congress to punish offenses
      against, US Const Art I §8.
Interstate commerce, US Const Art I
   §§8, 9.
Invasions, US Const Art I §8.
Journals, US Const Art I §§5, 7.
Legislative powers vested in congress,
   US Const Art I §1.
Letters of marque and reprisal, US
   Const Art I §8.
Libel and slander.
   Privilege of members of congress,
      US Const Art I §6.
Messages to congress, US Const Art II
   §3.
Militia.
   Powers of congress, US Const Art I
      §8.
Money.
   Powers of congress, US Const Art I
      §8.
Naturalization, US Const Art I §8.
Navy.
   Powers of congress, US Const Art I
      §8.
Patents, US Const Art I §8.
Piracy.
   Powers of congress, US Const Art I
      §8.
Post office and post roads, US Const
   Art I §8.
Powers of congress, US Const Art I §8.
   Limitations on powers, US Const
      Art I §9.
President of the United States.
   Declaration of disability.
      Determination of issue, US Const
         Amd 25.
Qualifications of members of congress,
   US Const Art I §§2, 3, 5.
Rules of procedure, US Const Art I §5.
Senate.
   Absent members, US Const Art I §5.
   Arrest of members, US Const Art I
      §6.
   Compensation of members, US
      Const Art I §6, Amd 27.
   Debate, US Const Art I §6.
   Elections.
      Election of senators, US Const
         Amd 17.

CONGRESS —Cont'd
Constitution of the United States
   —Cont'd
Senate —Cont'd
   Elections —Cont'd
      Times, places and manner of
         holding, US Const Art I §4.
   Expulsion of member, US Const Art
      I §5.
   Freedom of speech, US Const Art I
      §6.
   Holding other office, US Const Art I
      §6.
   Impeachment, US Const Art I §3.
   Journal, US Const Art I §§5, 7.
   Libel and slander.
      Privilege of members, US Const
         Art I §6.
   Officers, US Const Art I §3.
   President, US Const Art I §3.
      Pro tempore, US Const Art I §3.
   Presidential elector.
      Senator ineligible, US Const Art II
         §1.
   Punishment of members, US Const
      Art I §5.
   Qualifications.
      Judge of qualifications, US Const
         Art I §5.
      Qualifications of electors, US
         Const Amd 17.
      Qualifications of senators, US
         Const Art I §§3, 5.
   Quorum, US Const Art I §5.
   Revenue bills, US Const Art I §7.
   Rules of procedure, US Const Art I
      §5.
   Vacancies, US Const Amd 17.
   Vice-president of the United States.
      Vacancy in office.
         Confirmation of nominee of
            president, US Const Amd
            25.
Sessions, US Const Art I §4, Amd 20.
   Special sessions, US Const Art II §3.
Taxation.
   Powers of congress, US Const Art I
      §8.
Territories, US Const Art IV §3.
Vice-president.
   Vacancy in office.
      Nomination by president.
         Confirmation by congress, US
            Const Amd 25.
War.
   Articles of war, US Const Art I §8.

CONGRESS —Cont'd
Constitution of the United States
—Cont'd
War —Cont'd
Declaration of war, US Const Art I
§8.
Weights and measures, US Const Art I
§8.
Copyright, US Const Art I §8.
Counterfeiting.
Powers of congress, US Const Art I §8.
Courts.
Power to constitute tribunals inferior
to supreme court, US Const Art I
§8.
Debate, US Const Art I §6.
Debts.
Powers of congress, US Const Art I §8.
Declaration of war, US Const Art I §8.
Defense.
Powers of congress, US Const Art I §8.
District of Columbia, US Const Art I
§8.
Delegate, §§1-401, 1-402.
Home Rule act.
Reservation of Congressional
authority, §§1-206.01 to
1-206.04.
Duties and imposts.
Powers of congress, US Const Art I §8.
Elections.
Payment of poll tax not required, US
Const Amd 24.
Proclamation by governor of names of
members of congress elected.
Judge of elections, returns,
qualifications of members, US
Const Art I §5.
Excises.
Powers of congress, US Const Art I §8.
Foreign commerce, US Const Art I §8.
Freedom of speech.
Members of congress, US Const Art I
§6.
Holding other office, US Const Art I
§6.
Insurrections, US Const Art I §8.
International law.
Power to punish offenses against, US
Const Art I §8.
Interstate commerce, US Const Art I
§§8, 9.
Invasions, US Const Art I §8.
Legislative powers vested in, US
Const Art I §1.
Letters of marque and reprisal, US
Const Art I §8.

CONGRESS —Cont'd
Libel and slander.
Privilege of members of congress, US
Const Art I §6.
**Mental health services
administration plan review,**
§44-904.
Messages to congress, US Const Art II
§3.
Militia.
Powers of congress, US Const Art I §8.
Money.
Powers of congress, US Const Art I §8.
**National banks in District,
applicability of acts of congress
to,** §47-2508.
Naturalization, US Const Art I §§8, 9.
Navy.
Powers of congress, US Const Art I §8.
Oath of office, US Const Art VI.
Parking for members of congress,
§§50-2201.03, 50-2631.
**Park land buildings, Congressional
approval required for,** §10-128.
Patents, US Const Art I §8.
Piracy.
Powers of congress, US Const Art I §8.
Post offices and post roads, US Const
Art I §8.
Powers of congress, US Const Art I
§8.
Limitations on powers, US Const Art I
§9.
President of the United States.
Adjourning congress, US Const Art II
§3.
Convening congress, US Const Art II
§3.
Declaration of president's disability.
By two-thirds vote of both houses,
US Const Amd 25.
Determination of issue, US Const
Amd 25.
Messages to congress, US Const Art II
§3.
Special sessions of congress, US Const
Art II §3.
**Public utility balance sheets
supplied to,** §34-1113.
**Qualifications of members of
congress,** US Const Art I §§2, 3, 5.
Religious institutions.
Appropriations for, §44-715.
Rules of procedure, US Const Art I §5.
Sessions, US Const Art I §4, Amd 20.
Special sessions, US Const Art II §3.

CONGRESS —Cont'd
Statehood constitutional convention, §§1-121 to 1-128.
Suffrage, US Const Art V, Amds 15, 19, 26.
Tag plates for members of congress, §§50-2201.25, 50-2201.26.
Taxation.
Powers of congress, US Const Art I §8.
Territories, US Const Art IV §3.
War.
Articles of war, US Const Art I §8.
Declaration of war, US Const Art I §8.
Weights and measures, US Const Art I §8.
Welfare.
Power of congress to provide for general welfare, US Const Art I §8.

CONNECTICUT AVENUE BRIDGE OVER KLINGLE VALLEY, §9-313.

CONSECUTIVE SENTENCES, CrimPro Rule 32.
Criminal proceedings, §23-112.
Theft, §22-3203.

CONSENT JUDGMENTS, CivPro Rule 68-I.
Delinquent minors, JuvProc Rule 104.
Form, JuvProc Form 4.
Delinquent minors, supervision without commitment, §16-2314.
Landlord and tenant court, LandlordTenant Rule 11-I.
Consent judgment praecipe, LandlordTenant Forms 4, 4a.
Addendum, list of repairs, LandlordTenant Form 4A.
Consent settlement agreement, LandlordTenant Form 4b.
Addendum, list of repairs, LandlordTenant Form 4A.

CONSENT TO MENTAL HEALTH SERVICES.
Consumer's informed consent, requirement, §7-1231.07.
Administering medication, §7-1231.08.
Intellectual disabilities, persons with, §7-1305.06a.
Health care decision-makers, substitute consent, §7-1305.07a.
Minors receiving services and supports, §7-1231.14.

CONSERVATION.
Energy conservation.
District of Columbia energy plan, §§8-171.01 to 8-171.07, 8-1779.01 to 8-1779.03.
See DISTRICT OF COLUMBIA.
Energy efficiency standards, §§8-1771.01 to 8-1771.06.
Green buildings, §§6-1451.01 to 6-1451.11.
See GREEN BUILDINGS.
Historic districts, §§6-1201 to 6-1207.
Historic landmarks, §§6-1101 to 6-1115.
Historic property tax relief, §§47-842 to 47-844.
Historic Rhodes Tavern, §§6-1131 to 6-1133.
Soil and water conservation, §§8-1701 to 8-1721.
See SOIL AND WATER CONSERVATION DISTRICTS.

CONSERVATION EASEMENTS, §§42-201 to 42-205.
Actions, persons eligible to bring, §42-203.
Applicability of provisions, §§42-204, 42-205.
Covered interests, §42-204.
Definitions, §42-201.
Interpretation of provisions, §42-205.
Recordation tax exemption, §42-202.
Rights of holders of, §42-202.01.

CONSERVATORS, §§21-2001 to 21-2034.
Accounts, Probate Rule 330.
Audit of accounts, Probate Rule 331.
Adult guardianship and protective proceedings jurisdiction, §§21-2401.01 to 21-2405.03.
See GUARDIAN AND WARD.
Appeals, §21-2024.
Applicability of other laws, §21-2002.
Appraisals, Probate Rule 333.
Bonds, Probate Rule 332.
Continuation of existing conservatorship proceedings, Probate Rule 301.
Counsel, duty of, §21-2033.
Court rules, governance of, §21-2022.
Definitions, §21-2011.
Evidence required in proceedings, §21-2003.

CONSERVATORS —Cont'd
Fiduciaries generally.
See FIDUCIARIES.
Fiduciary security transfers,
§§28-2901 to 28-2909.
See FIDUCIARY SECURITY
TRANSFERS.
Final distributions, Probate Rule 331.
Foreign conservators, Probate Rule
361.
**Geographic applicability of
provisions,** §21-2021.
Guardian ad litem, §§21-2031,
21-2033.
Conservatorship proceedings, CivPro
Rule 302.
**Guardianship of incapacitated
persons,** §§21-2041 to 21-2049.
See GUARDIAN AND WARD.
Incapacity, effect of finding of,
§21-2004.
Interpretation of provisions,
§21-2001.
Intervention proceedings generally.
See INTERVENTION
PROCEEDINGS.
Inventories, Probate Rule 329.
Missing persons, Probate Rules 350,
351.
Notice, §21-2031.
Account of conservator, Probate Rule
330.
Missing persons, Probate Rule 350.
Protection of property, §21-2053.
Request by interested person for,
§21-2034.
Waiver of, §21-2032.
Orders for appointment, CivPro Rule
310.
Petition for appointment, CivPro
Rule 310.
Plans, Probate Rule 329.
Powers of attorney.
See DURABLE POWERS OF
ATTORNEY.
Presumption of competence,
§21-2002.
**Probate proceedings involving
conservators,** Probate Rules 201 to
225.
See PROBATE PROCEEDINGS.
Protection of property.
Acceptance of appointment, effect of,
§21-2059.
Accounts, §21-2065.
Administration, powers of conservator
in, §21-2070.

CONSERVATORS —Cont'd
Protection of property —Cont'd
Authorization of protective
arrangements and single
transactions, §21-2056.
Bonds, surety, §§21-2058, 21-2077.
Conflicts of interest, §21-2068.
Court orders, §21-2055.
Death, resignation, or removal of
conservator, §21-2061.
Distributive powers and duties,
§21-2071.
Eligibility for conservatorship,
§21-2057.
Enlargement of powers and duties,
§21-2072.
Estate plan, §21-2073.
Expenses, §21-2060.
Foreign conservators, §§21-2076,
21-2077.
Hearing and order on original petition,
§21-2054.
Inventory, §21-2064.
Letters of conservatorship, recordation
of, §21-2067.
Limitation of powers and duties,
§21-2072.
Notice requirements, §21-2053.
Original petition for, §§21-2052,
21-2054.
Personal liability of conservator,
§21-2074.
Persons assisting or dealing with
conservator, §21-2069.
Petitions for orders subsequent to
appointment of conservator,
§21-2062.
Powers and duties, §21-2063.
Administration, in, §21-2070.
Distributive, §21-2071.
Enlargement of, §21-2072.
Limitation of, §21-2072.
Priorities as to conservator, §21-2057.
Proceedings, §21-2051.
Records, §§21-2064, 21-2065, 21-2067.
Single transactions, §21-2056.
Termination of proceedings, §21-2075.
Title to all property by appointment,
§21-2066.
Wages and salaries, §21-2060.
Reports, Probate Rule 330.
Security transfers, §§28-2901 to
28-2909.
See FIDUCIARY SECURITY
TRANSFERS.

CONSERVATORS —Cont'd
Trusts and trustees.
  Uniform trust code.
    Personal representatives,
      §19-1303.03.
Uniform fiduciaries act, §§21-1701 to
  21-1712.
  See FIDUCIARIES.
Visitors, appointment of, §21-2033.
Waiver of notice, §21-2032.

CONSIGNMENT.
Works of fine art, §§28-5101 to
  28-5108.
  See ARTIST PROTECTION.

CONSOLIDATION OF TRIALS,
  CivPro Rule 42.
Adoption, Adoption Rule 42.
Appeals, DCCtApp Rule 3.
  Motions, DCCtApp Rule 27.
Assignment of criminal trials,
  CrimPro Rule 105.
**Child abuse and neglect
  proceedings,** NeglectProc Rule 3.
Domestic relations actions, DomRel
  Rule 42.
Related cases, USDistCt LCvR 40.5.

CONSPIRACY.
**Aged persons, offenses committed
  against.**
  Enhanced penalties, §22-3601.
Controlled substances, §48-904.09.
Crime, conspiracy to commit,
  §22-1805a.
**Interception of wire or oral
  communications,** CrimPro Rule
  41-I.
Kidnapping, §22-2001.
Monopolization, §28-4503.
Restraints of trade, §§28-4501 to
  28-4518.
  See RESTRAINTS OF TRADE.

CONSTITUENT SERVICES.
**Mayor and chairman and members
  of council.**
  Contributions for purposes of services,
    §1-1163.38.

**CONSTITUTION OF THE STATE OF
  NEW COLUMBIA.**
Approval and ratification, §1-132.
Proposed constitution.
  See Vol. 1.

**CONSTITUTION OF THE UNITED
  STATES.**
Absence.
  Congress.
    Members of congress, US Const Art
      I §5.
  Vice-president.
    Senate to choose president pro tem,
      US Const Art I §3.
Accounts and accounting.
  Receipts and expenditures of public
    money.
    Publication of statement and
      account, US Const Art I §9.
**Actions to which United States a
  party,** US Const Art III §2.
Admiralty, US Const Art I §8.
  Jurisdiction of courts, US Const Art
    III §2.
Age.
  Congress.
    Representatives, US Const Art I §2.
    Senators, US Const Art I §3.
  Elections.
    Right to vote not to be abridged on
      account of age, US Const Amd
      26.
    Voting by persons eighteen years of
      age, US Const Amd 26.
  President of the United States, US
    Const Art II §1.
  Vice-president, US Const Amd 12.
Alcoholic liquors, US Const Amds 18,
  21.
Aliens.
  Eligibility to be representative, US
    Const Art I §2.
  Naturalization, US Const Art I §8.
  Presidency.
    Ineligibility for presidency, US
      Const Art II §1.
  Suits against state, US Const Amd 11.
Ambassadors and consuls, US Const
  Art II §§2, 3, Art III §2.
Amendments, US Const Art V.
  Bail, US Const Amd 8.
  Congress.
    Sessions, US Const Amd 20.
    Terms of office, US Const Amd 20.
    Time of convening, US Const Amd
      20.
  Criminal law, US Const Amds 5, 6.
  Due process of law, US Const Amds 5,
    14.

CONSTITUTION OF THE UNITED STATES —Cont'd

Amendments —Cont'd

Effect of enumeration of rights, US Const Amd 9.

Eminent domain, US Const Amd 5.

Freedom of religion, speech and press, US Const Amd 1.

Guarantees in criminal cases, US Const Amds 5, 6.

House of representatives.

Terms of representatives, US Const Amd 20.

Income tax, US Const Amd 16.

Intoxicating liquors, US Const Amds 18, 21.

Lame duck amendment, US Const Amd 20.

Manner of making amendments, US Const Art V.

Poll tax.

Denial or abridgement of right to vote upon failure to pay.

Prohibited, US Const Amd 24.

President.

Death, US Const Amd 20.

Election, US Const Amds 12, 20.

Failure to qualify, US Const Amd 20.

Succession upon death, resignation or removal of president, US Const Amd 25.

Terms of office, US Const Amds 20, 22.

Limitation on terms, US Const Amd 22.

Proposal and ratification of amendments, US Const Art V.

Punishments, US Const Amd 8.

Quartering soldiers in houses, US Const Amd 3.

Ratification of amendment, US Const Art V.

Repeal of the eighteenth amendment, US Const Amd 21.

Restriction of judicial power, US Const Amd 11.

Rights and immunities of citizens, US Const Amd 14.

Right to bear arms, US Const Amd 2.

Right to vote, US Const Amds 15, 26.

Searches and seizures, US Const Amd 4.

Self-incrimination, US Const Amd 5.

Senate.

Election of senators, US Const Amd 17.

CONSTITUTION OF THE UNITED STATES —Cont'd

Amendments —Cont'd

Senate —Cont'd

Terms of senators, US Const Amd 20.

Slavery, US Const Amd 13.

Suits against state, US Const Amd 11.

Terms of office, US Const Amd 20.

Limitation on terms of president, US Const Amd 22.

Trial by jury, US Const Amds 6, 7.

Vice-president.

Death, US Const Amd 20.

Election, US Const Amds 12, 20.

Failure to qualify, US Const Amd 20.

Terms of office, US Const Amd 20.

Weapons.

Right to bear arms, US Const Amd 2.

Woman suffrage, US Const Amd 19.

Appeals.

Review of facts tried by jury, US Const Amd 7.

Apportionment.

Congress, US Const Amds 14, 17.

Appropriations, US Const Art I §9.

Army, US Const Art I §8.

Revenue bills, US Const Art I §7.

Approval of laws by president, US Const Art I §7.

Arms.

Right to bear, US Const Amd 2.

Army and navy, US Const Art I §8.

Commander in chief, US Const Art II §2.

Arrest.

Privilege from arrest, US Const Art I §6.

Assembly.

Right of, US Const Amd 1.

Attainder, US Const Art III §3.

Attorneys at law.

Right to counsel, US Const Amd 6.

Authors.

Protection of rights, US Const Art I §8.

Autrefois, acquit or convict, US Const Amd 5.

Bail.

Excessive bail, US Const Amd 8.

Bankruptcy.

Powers of congress, US Const Art I §8.

Bill of attainder, US Const Art I §§9, 10.

Bill of rights, US Const Amds 1 to Amd 10.

CONSTITUTION OF THE UNITED STATES —Cont'd

Congress —Cont'd

Senate —Cont'd

Vice-president of the United States. Vacancy in office.

Confirmation of nomination of president, US Const Amd 25.

Sessions, US Const Art I §4, Amd 20.

Special sessions, US Const Art II §3.

Taxation.

Powers of congress, US Const Art I §8.

Territories, US Const Art IV §3.

Vice-president of the United States. Vacancy in office.

Nomination by president, US Const Amd 25.

Confirmation by majority of both houses of congress, US Const Amd 25.

War.

Articles of war, US Const Art I §8.

Declaration of war, US Const Art I §8.

Weights and measures, US Const Art I §8.

Construction and interpretation.

Effect of enumeration of rights, US Const Amd 9.

Consuls, US Const Art II §§2, 3, Art III §2.

Contracts.

Impairment of obligations of contracts, US Const Art I §10.

Copyright, US Const Art I §8.

Corruption of blood.

Attainder of treason not to work, US Const Art III §3.

Counsel for defense, US Const Amd 6.

Counterfeiting, US Const Art I §8.

Courts.

Congress.

Power to constitute tribunals inferior to supreme court, US Const Art I §8.

Inferior courts, US Const Art III §1.

Judges.

Compensation, US Const Art III §1.

Tenure, US Const Art III §1.

Restriction of judicial power, US Const Amd 11.

Criminal procedure.

Cruel and unusual punishment, US Const Amd 8.

CONSTITUTION OF THE UNITED STATES —Cont'd

Criminal procedure —Cont'd

Excessive bail, US Const Amd 8.

Extradition, US Const Art IV §2.

Fugitives from justice, US Const Art IV §2.

Guarantees in criminal cases, US Const Amds 5, 6.

Public trial, US Const Amd 6.

Self-incrimination, US Const Amd 5.

Speedy trial, US Const Amd 6.

Cross-examination, US Const Amd 5.

Cruel and unusual punishment, US Const Amd 8.

Customs, US Const Art I §§8 to 10.

Congress.

Power to lay and collect, US Const Art I §8.

Exportations from any state.

Duties not to be laid on, US Const Art I §9.

Importation of persons, US Const Art I §9.

Death.

President and vice-president of the United States.

Duty of congress, US Const Art II §1, Amd 25.

President elect.

Provisions in case of, US Const Amd 20.

Debts.

Aid of rebellion, US Const Amd 14.

Debts and engagements contracted before adoption, US Const Art VI.

Not to be questioned, US Const Amd 14.

Powers of congress, US Const Art I §8.

Declaration of rights, US Const Amds 1 to Amd 10.

Defense.

Power of congress, US Const Art I §8.

Discrimination, US Const Amds 14, 15.

District of Columbia.

Constitutional provisions, US Const Art I §8.

Double jeopardy, US Const Amd 5.

Due process of law, US Const Amds 5, 14.

Duties and imposts.

Powers of congress, US Const Art I §8.

States, US Const Art I §§9, 10.

Elections.

Age.

Right to vote not to be abridged on account of age, US Const Amd 26.

CONSTITUTION OF THE UNITED STATES —Cont'd

Elections —Cont'd

Age —Cont'd

Voting by persons eighteen years of age, US Const Amd 26.

House of representatives, US Const Art I §§2, 4.

President and vice-president, US Const Art II §1, Amds 12, 14, 23.

Racial minorities, US Const Amd 15.

Senate, US Const Art I §4, Amd 17.

Suffrage, US Const Amds 15, 19.

Eminent domain, US Const Amd 5.

Emoluments, US Const Art I §9.

Equal protection of the laws, US Const Amd 14.

Equity.

Judicial power to extend to cases in, US Const Art III §2.

Excessive bail, US Const Amd 8.

Excessive fines, US Const Amd 8.

Excises.

Powers of congress, US Const Art I §8.

Execution of laws, US Const Art II §3.

Expenditures.

Necessity for appropriations, US Const Art I §9.

Publication of statement, US Const Art I §9.

Exports and imports, US Const Art I §§9, 10.

Ex post facto laws, US Const Art I §§9, 10.

Extradition, US Const Art IV §2.

Fines.

Excessive fines, US Const Amd 8.

Foreign presents, US Const Art I §9.

Forgery and counterfeiting, US Const Art I §8.

Former jeopardy, US Const Amd 5.

Freedom of conscience, US Const Amd 1.

Freedom of speech, US Const Amd 1.

Members of congress, US Const Art I §6.

Freedom of the press, US Const Amd 1.

Fugitives, US Const Art IV §2.

Full faith and credit clause, US Const Art IV §1.

Gifts.

Foreign presents to United States officials, US Const Art I §9.

Grand jury.

Presentments by, US Const Amd 5.

CONSTITUTION OF THE UNITED STATES —Cont'd

Habeas corpus, US Const Art I §9.

Immigration, US Const Art I §9.

Immunities, US Const Art IV §2.

Impairment of obligations of contracts, US Const Art I §10.

Impeachment, US Const Art I §§2, 3, Art II §4, Art III §2.

Imports and exports, US Const Art I §§9, 10.

Income tax, US Const Amd 16.

Indictments, informations and presentments, US Const Amd 5.

Insurrection or rebellion, US Const Art I §8.

International law.

Power of congress to punish offenses against, US Const Art I §8.

Interstate commerce, US Const Art I §§8, 9.

Intoxicating liquors.

Prohibition, US Const Amds 18, 21.

Repeal of the eighteenth amendment, US Const Amd 21.

Invasions, US Const Art I §8.

Involuntary servitude, US Const Amd 13.

Jeopardy.

Double jeopardy, US Const Amd 5.

Journals.

Congress, US Const Art I §§5, 7.

Judges.

Compensation, US Const Art III §1.

Tenure, US Const Art III §1.

Judgments.

Full faith and credit clause, US Const Art IV §1.

Proof, US Const Art IV §1.

Jury.

Jury of vicinage, US Const Amd 6.

Lame duck amendment, US Const Amd 20.

Legal tender, US Const Art I §10.

Letters of marque and reprisal, US Const Art I §§8 to 10.

Libel and slander.

Congress.

Privilege of members of congress, US Const Art I §6.

Limitations on powers of states, US Const Art I §10.

Liquors, US Const Amds 18, 21.

Messages to congress, US Const Art II §3.

Militia.

Powers of congress, US Const Art I §8.

**CONSTITUTION OF THE UNITED
  STATES** —Cont'd
Militia —Cont'd
Quartering soldiers, US Const Amd 3.
Ministers.
Jurisdiction of cases affecting, US
  Const Art III §2.
Receiving, US Const Art II §3.
Money, US Const Art I §§8, 10.
Coinage, US Const Art I §§8, 10.
Counterfeiting, US Const Art I §8.
Powers of congress, US Const Art I §8.
Naturalization, US Const Art I §8.
Navy.
Powers of congress, US Const Art I §8.
New states, US Const Art IV §3.
Nonresidents.
Jurisdiction of suits against state, US
  Const Amd 11.
Pardons, US Const Art II §2.
Patents, US Const Art I §8.
Payments.
Legal tender, US Const Art I §10.
Petitions.
Right of, US Const Amd 1.
Piracy.
Powers of congress, US Const Art I §8.
Poll tax.
Failure to pay poll or other tax.
  Denial or abridgement of right to
    vote.
    Prohibited, US Const Amd 24.
Post offices, US Const Art I §8.
Post roads, US Const Art I §8.
Powers of congress, US Const Art I
  §8.
**Powers reserved to states and
  people,** US Const Amd 10.
President.
Age, US Const Art II §1.
Aliens.
  Ineligible for presidency, US Const
    Art II §1.
Ambassadors and consuls, US Const
  Art II §§2, 3.
Appointment of officers, etc., US Const
  Art II §2.
Approval of laws by president, US
  Const Art I §7.
Approval of order, resolution or vote of
  congress, US Const Art I §7.
Bribery, US Const Art II §4.
Commander in chief, US Const Art II
  §2.
Compensation, US Const Art II §1.
Congress.
  Adjourning congress, US Const Art
    II §3.

**CONSTITUTION OF THE UNITED
  STATES** —Cont'd
President —Cont'd
Congress —Cont'd
  Convening congress, US Const Art II
    §3.
  Messages to congress, US Const Art
    II §3.
  Special sessions of congress, US
    Const Art II §3.
Death, US Const Art II §1, Amd 20.
  Succession upon death, US Const
    Amd 25.
Disability, US Const Art II §1.
  Declaration by president.
    Inability to perform duties, US
      Const Amd 25.
  Declaration by vice-president and
    other officers, US Const Amd 25.
  Determination of issue by
    congress, US Const Amd 25.
Duties, US Const Art II §3.
  Declaration by president of inability
    to perform duties, US Const
    Amd 25.
  Transmittal to senate and house
    of representatives, US Const
    Amd 25.
Elections, US Const Art II §1, Amds
  12, 14, 23.
Eligibility, US Const Art II §1.
Execution of laws, US Const Art II §3.
Executive power, US Const Art II §1.
Failure to qualify, US Const Amd 20.
Impeachment, US Const Art I §3, Art
  II §4.
Inability, US Const Art II §1.
Limitation on terms, US Const Amd
  22.
Message to congress, US Const Art II
  §3.
Ministers.
  Receiving, US Const Art II §3.
Opinions from principal officers in
  executive departments, US Const
  Art II §2.
Pardons, US Const Art II §2.
Powers of president, US Const Art II
  §§2, 3.
Public officers.
  Commissions, US Const Art II §3.
Qualifications, US Const Art II §1.
Removal, US Const Art II §§1, 4.
  Succession upon removal, US Const
    Amd 25.
Resignation, US Const Art II §1.
  Succession upon resignation, US
    Const Amd 25.

CONSTITUTION OF THE UNITED STATES —Cont'd

President —Cont'd

Signing of bills, US Const Art I §7.

Statutes.

Veto, US Const Art I §7.

Succession to office, US Const Art II §1, Amd 20.

Upon death, resignation or removal of president, US Const Amd 25.

Supreme court.

Appointment of justices, US Const Art II §2.

Terms of office, US Const Art II §1, Amds 20, 22.

Limitation on terms, US Const Amd 22.

Time of taking office, US Const Amd 20.

Treason, US Const Art II §4.

Treaties, US Const Art II §2.

Vacancy in office, US Const Art II §1, Amd 20.

During senate recess, US Const Art II §2.

Veto, US Const Art I §7.

Press.

Freedom of the press, US Const Amd 1.

Privileges.

Privileged from arrest, US Const Art I §6.

Prohibition, US Const Amds 18, 21.

Protection and aid of states, US Const Art IV §4.

Public debt, US Const Art I §8.

Public officers and employees.

Appointment, US Const Art II §2.

Senate recess, US Const Art II §2.

Bribery, US Const Art II §4.

Commissions, US Const Art II §3.

Emoluments, US Const Art I §9.

Foreign office or title, US Const Art I §9.

Holding more than one office, US Const Art I §6.

Impeachment, US Const Art II §4.

Ineligibility of members of congress, US Const Art I §6.

Presents from foreign states, US Const Art I §9.

Presidential electors.

Eligibility, US Const Art II §1.

Religious tests, US Const Art VI.

Removal, US Const Art II §4.

Treason, US Const Art II §4.

CONSTITUTION OF THE UNITED STATES —Cont'd

Public officers and employees —Cont'd

Vacancies during senate recess, US Const Art II §2.

Public trial, US Const Amd 6.

Punishment.

Cruel and unusual punishment, US Const Amd 8.

Quartering soldiers in houses, US Const Amd 3.

Racial minorities, US Const Amds 14, 15.

Ratification, US Const Art VII.

Records.

Full faith and credit clause, US Const Art IV §1.

Proof, US Const Art IV §1.

Redress of grievances.

Right to petition for, US Const Amd 1.

Religious test, US Const Art VI.

Republican form of government, US Const Art IV §4.

Reservation of rights of the people, US Const Amd 9.

Revenue bills, US Const Art I §7.

Right of assembly, US Const Amd 1.

Right of trial by jury, US Const Art III §2, Amds 6, 7.

Right to bear arms, US Const Amd 2.

Right to counsel, US Const Amd 6.

Right to petition for a redress of grievances, US Const Amd 1.

Searches and seizures, US Const Amd 4.

Self-incrimination, US Const Amd 5.

Sentence and punishment, US Const Amd 8.

Capital punishment, US Const Amd 5.

Sessions of congress, US Const Art I §4.

Special sessions, US Const Art II §3.

Slavery.

Civil War amendments, US Const Amds 13 to 15.

Importation, US Const Art I §9, Amd 14.

Congressional apathy to prohibit, US Const Art I §9.

Prohibition, US Const Amd 13.

Compensation, illegal and void, US Const Amd 14.

Runaway slaves.

Congressional authority to return, US Const Art IV §2, Amd 13.

CONSTITUTION OF THE UNITED STATES —Cont'd

Slavery —Cont'd

Suffrage, US Const Amd 15.

Taxation, US Const Art I §§2, 9, Amd 14.

Three-fifths rule, US Const Art I §2, Amd 14.

Soldiers.

Quartering prohibited, US Const Amd 3.

Speech.

Freedom of speech, US Const Amd 1.

Members of congress, US Const Art I §6.

Speedy trial, US Const Amd 6.

States.

Admission of new states, US Const Art IV §3.

Bill of attainder, US Const Art I §10.

Bills of credit, US Const Art I §10.

Commerce, US Const Art I §§8, 9.

Compacts between the states or with foreign powers, US Const Art I §10.

Contracts.

Impairing obligations of contracts, US Const Art I §10.

Controversies between citizens of different states, US Const Art III §2.

Controversies between states, US Const Art III §2.

Duties and imposts, US Const Art I §10.

Equal suffrage in senate, US Const Art V.

Exports, US Const Art I §§9, 10.

Ex post facto laws, US Const Art I §10.

Full faith and credit clause, US Const Art IV §1.

Gold and silver coin tender in payment of debts, US Const Art I §10.

Impairing obligations of contracts, US Const Art I §10.

Imports and exports, US Const Art I §10.

Invasion.

Protection against, US Const Art IV §4.

Legal tender, US Const Art I §10.

Letters of marque and reprisal, US Const Art I §10.

Limitations on powers of states, US Const Art I §10.

CONSTITUTION OF THE UNITED STATES —Cont'd

States —Cont'd

Money.

Coining money, US Const Art I §10.

New states, US Const Art IV §3.

Powers, US Const Art I §10.

Reserved to states, US Const Amd 10.

Protection and aid of states, US Const Art IV §4.

Republican form of government guaranteed, US Const Art IV §4.

Reservation of powers to states, US Const Amd 10.

Right to coin money, US Const Art I §10.

Suits against state, US Const Amd 11.

Tender in payment of debts, US Const Art I §10.

Tonnage, US Const Art I §10.

Treaties, US Const Art I §10.

Troops or ships of war in time of peace, US Const Art I §10.

War, US Const Art I §10.

Statutes.

Approval of laws by president, US Const Art I §7.

Ex post facto laws, US Const Art I §§9, 10.

Full faith and credit clause, US Const Art IV §1.

Limitations on legislation, US Const Art I §9.

Proof, US Const Art IV §1.

Revenue bills, US Const Art I §7.

Supreme law of the land, US Const Art VI.

Veto, US Const Art I §7.

Suits against state, US Const Amd 11.

Suits against United States, US Const Art III §2.

Supreme court.

Chief justice presides in impeachment of president, US Const Art I §3.

Jurisdiction, US Const Art III §2.

Justices.

Appointment, US Const Art II §2.

Compensation, US Const Art III §1.

Tenure, US Const Art III §1.

Supreme law of the land, US Const Art VI.

Taxation.

Capitation tax, US Const Art I §9.

Elections.

Denial or abridgement of right to vote for failure to pay poll tax prohibited, US Const Amd 24.

CONSTITUTION OF THE UNITED STATES —Cont'd

Taxation —Cont'd

Excises.

Powers of congress, US Const Art I §8.

Exports, US Const Art I §§9, 10.

Income tax, US Const Amd 16.

Limitations on powers of states, US Const Art I §10.

Powers of congress, US Const Art I §8.

Revenue bills, US Const Art I §7.

Tender, US Const Art I §10.

Territories, US Const Art IV §3.

Time when constitution effective, US Const Art VII.

Titles of nobility, US Const Art I §§9, 10.

Tonnage, US Const Art I §10.

Treason, US Const Art I §6, Art II §4, Art III §3.

Trial.

Jury, US Const Art III §2, Amds 6, 7.

Public trial, US Const Amd 6.

Speedy trial, US Const Amd 6.

Venue, US Const Art III §2.

Vessels and boats.

Bound to and from one state not to be obliged to clear, etc., in another, US Const Art I §9.

Veto, US Const Art I §7.

Vice-president of the United States.

Age, US Const Amd 12.

Bribery, US Const Art II §4.

Death, US Const Art II §1.

Election, US Const Art II §1, Amd 12.

Failure to qualify, US Const Amd 20.

Impeachment, US Const Art II §4.

Oaths, US Const Art VI, Amd 14.

President of senate, US Const Art I §3.

Qualifications, US Const Amd 12.

Removal, US Const Art II §4.

Succession to office of president, US Const Art II §1, Amds 20, 25.

Upon death, resignation or removal of president, US Const Amd 25.

Treason, US Const Art II §4.

Vacancy in office, US Const Art II §1, Amd 20.

Nomination by president, US Const Amd 25.

Confirmation by congress, US Const Amd 25.

War.

Articles of war, US Const Art I §8.

Declaration by congress, US Const Art I §8.

CONSTITUTION OF THE UNITED STATES —Cont'd

War —Cont'd

Grand jury.

Presentment as dispensable in certain cases, US Const Amd 5.

Quartering of soldiers in times of war, US Const Amd 3.

State engaging in, US Const Art I §10.

Treason.

Levying against the United States, US Const Art III §3.

Warrants.

Searches and seizures.

Conditions for issuance, US Const Amd 4.

Weapons.

Right to bear arms, US Const Amd 2.

Weights and measures, US Const Art I §8.

Welfare.

General welfare.

Powers of congress, US Const Art I §8.

Witnesses.

Confrontation with witnesses, US Const Amd 6.

Process to obtain, US Const Amd 6.

Self-incrimination, US Const Amd 5.

Treason.

Number in treason cases, US Const Art III §3.

Woman suffrage, US Const Amd 19.

CONSTITUTION SQUARE DEVELOPMENT PROJECT.

Tax abatements, §47-4612.

CONSTRUCTION AND INTERPRETATION.

Statutory construction.

General provisions, §§45-601 to 45-606.

See STATUTORY CONSTRUCTION.

United States District Court rules, USDistCt LCrR 1.1, USDistCt LCvR 1.1.

CONSTRUCTION BONDS.

Procurement practices.

See PROCUREMENT PRACTICES.

CONSTRUCTION CODES, §§6-1401 to 6-1409.

Administrative procedure, §6-1405.01.

Amendments to, §6-1409.

Applicability and coverage, §6-1403.

Approval by council, §6-1402.

CONSTRUCTION CODES —Cont'd
Building code officials.
Duties, §6-1405.01.
Building rehabilitation code,
§6-1410.
Advisory council, §6-1411.
Compliance letter fees, §6-1406.02.
Conflicts of law, §6-1405.
Definitions, §6-1401.
Denial of building permit.
Period during which permit may be
denied, §6-1407.01.
Editions, §6-1409.
Enforcement, §6-1405.01.
Fines, §6-1406.
Green building practices.
Revisions of codes for, §6-1412.
Injunctions, §6-1407.
Inspections.
Third party plan review.
Third party inspectors, §6-1405.04.
Intent of codes, §6-1404.
Interpretation of provisions, §6-1404.
Office of documents, §6-1408.
Penalties, §6-1406.
Rehabilitation.
Building rehabilitation code, §6-1410.
Advisory council, §6-1411.
Scope of codes, §6-1403.
Supplements, §6-1409.
Third party plan review, §6-1405.02.
Third party inspectors, §6-1405.04.

CONSTRUCTION CONTRACTS.
Prompt payment of private
contractors and subcontractors
generally, §§27-131 to 27-136.
See PROMPT PAYMENT.

CONSTRUCTION PROJECTS.
Bathing pools and beaches, §10-163.
Electric light and power plants,
permission to construct, §34-302.
Gas plant, permission for
construction of, §34-302.
Grade crossing elimination projects.
Construction of viaducts and subways
as part of, §9-1201.15.
Authority of mayor, §9-1203.05.
Highway construction program
authorization, §9-101.16.
Historic districts, new construction
in, §6-1107.
Historic landmarks, new
construction in, §6-1107.
Judiciary square detention facility
construction, §§24-1201 to
24-1203.

CONSTRUCTION PROJECTS
—Cont'd
Labor and employment.
Workplace fraud, §§32-1331.01 to
32-1331.12.
See WORKPLACE FRAUD.
Metropolitan Washington Airports
Authority, §9-1005.
Metrorail and metrobus adopted
regional system.
Approval of construction for,
§9-1111.04.
Federal contributions, §§9-1111.11,
9-1111.14.
Motor vehicle moving infractions in
work zones, §50-2201.04c.
National Capital Planning
Commission consultation on,
§2-1005.
Parking facilities, §50-2603.
Park land buildings, Congressional
approval required for, §10-128.
Public building loans for, §§10-603 to
10-620.
See PUBLIC BUILDINGS.
Public procurement, §§2-356.01 to
2-356.04.
Architectural and engineering
services, §2-356.04.
Authorized, §2-356.01.
Estimate of construction costs,
§2-356.05.
Performance and payment bonds,
§2-357.02.
Prequalification, §2-356.03.
Security, §2-357.01.
Security in non-construction service
contracts, §2-357.02a.
Source selection methods, §2-356.02.
Public works, §9-401.01.
Railroad switch connections,
§§9-1205.01 to 9-1205.05.
Recycling.
Construction and demolition waste
recycling accountability, §§8-1071
to 8-1077.
Riparian permits, §47-2711.
School buildings and grounds,
§38-402.
Small, local and disadvantaged
business enterprise development
and assistance.
Contracts and procurement,
§§2-218.41 to 2-218.55.
Tunnel under Capitol grounds and
botanic gardens, §10-511.02.

CONSTRUCTION PROJECTS
—Cont'd
Water quality, affecting, §8-103.13.
Well construction, maintenance and abandonment, §8-103.13a.
Permit fees, §8-103.13b.
Water supply and waterworks, assessments for constructing mains and sewers, §§34-2405.01 to 34-2405.08.
Work zones.
Motor vehicle moving infractions, §50-2201.04c.

CONSULAR.
Constitution of the United States, US Const Art II §§2, 3, Art III §2.
Foreign missions, §§6-1301 to 6-1315. See FOREIGN MISSIONS.

CONSUMER AND REGULATORY AFFAIRS, DEPARTMENT OF.
Complaint procedures, §§28-3901 to 28-3913.
Advisory committee on consumer protection, §28-3907.
Definitions, §28-3901.
Policy declaration, §28-3901.
Powers and duties of department, §28-3903.
Procedural outline, §28-3905.
Public education and information programs, §28-3906.
Restraint of prohibited acts, §28-3909.
Role of department, §28-3902.
Severability of provisions, §28-3908.
Unfair trade practices, §28-3904.
Construction and demolition waste recycling accountability, §§8-1071 to 8-1077.
Office of tenant advocate, §§42-3531.01 to 42-3531.10.
Recycling.
Construction and demolition waste recycling accountability, §§8-1071 to 8-1077.
Rental accommodations and rental conversions and sales.
Transfer of functions to housing and community development department, §42-3502.03.
CONSUMER CREDIT, §§28-3801 to 28-3819.
Actions.
Consumers' remedies, §28-3813.
Creditors' actions, §28-3812.
Applicability of provisions, §28-3801.

CONSUMER CREDIT —Cont'd
Assertion of rights of consumer or lessee, §28-3808.
Assignees of rights of seller or lessor, §28-3808.
Assignments.
Earnings.
Prohibited, §28-3804.
Seller's assignees subject to defenses of consumer, §28-3808.
Attorneys at law.
Consumers' remedies.
Attorneys' fees, §28-3813.
Fees, §28-3806.
Consumers' remedies, §28-3813.
Attorneys' fees and costs, §28-3806.
Authorization to confess judgment, §28-3804.
Balloon payments, §28-3803.
Cancellation.
Home solicitation sales.
Buyer's right to cancel, §28-3811.
Collection of debt, §28-3814.
Confession of judgment.
Authorization to confess judgment prohibited, §28-3804.
Conflicts of law, §28-3816.
Consolidation of debts.
Termination of security interests in property, §28-3805.
Consumer credit service organizations, §§28-4601 to 28-4608.
See CONSUMER CREDIT SERVICE ORGANIZATIONS.
Consumer protection, §§28-3801 to 28-3819.
See CONSUMER PROTECTION.
Consumer security breach notification, §§28-3851 to 28-3853.
Consumer security freeze, §§28-3861 to 28-3864.
Creditors' remedies.
Limitation on creditors' remedies, §28-3812.
Cross-collateral.
Debts secured by cross-collateral, §28-3805.
Defined, §28-3802.
Cure of default by debtor, §28-3812.
Damages.
Consumers' remedies, §28-3813.
Debt collection.
Restrictions on creditors or debt collectors, §28-3814.
Default.
Limitation on creditors' remedies, §28-3812.

CONSUMER CREDIT —Cont'd
Defenses.
Lender subject to defenses arising
from sales, §28-3809.
Seller's assignees subject to defenses
of consumer, §28-3808.
Definitions, §28-3802.
Discounts.
Referral sales, §28-3810.
Enforcement.
Administrative enforcement, §28-3815.
Equal payments, §28-3803.
Health spa sales, §28-3817.
Home solicitation sales, §28-3811.
Interest rate.
Applicability of provisions, §28-3301.
Layaway plans, §28-3818.
**Lenders making direct installment
loans,** §28-3809.
**Lender subject to defenses arising
from sales,** §28-3809.
Loan sharking.
Repayment unenforceable, §28-3812.
Negotiable instruments, §28-3807.
Seller not permitted to take negotiable
instrument, §28-3807.
Notice.
Default.
Required notice by creditor,
§28-3812.
Punitive damages.
Violations of chapter, §28-3813.
Rebates.
Referral sales, §28-3810.
**Redemption of collateral after
default,** §28-3812.
Referral sales, §28-3810.
Rebates, discounts, etc., prohibited,
§28-3810.
Remedies.
Consumers, §28-3813.
Creditors, §28-3812.
Limitation on creditors' remedies,
§28-3812.
Rental housing locators, §28-3819.
Rent-to-own.
Commercial code leases, §§28:2A-101
to 28:2A-532.
See LEASES, UCC.
Repossession of collateral, §28-3812.
Salaries.
Assignment of earnings prohibited,
§28-3804.
Service organizations, §§28-4601 to
28-4608.
See CONSUMER CREDIT SERVICE
ORGANIZATIONS.

CONSUMER CREDIT —Cont'd
Unconscionable agreements,
§28-3812.
Violations.
Punitive damages, §28-3813.
Wages.
Assignment of earnings prohibited,
§28-3804.

**CONSUMER CREDIT REPORTING
AGENCIES.**
**Consumer security breach
notification,** §§28-3851 to 28-3853.
Definitions, §28-3851.
Enforcement agency, §28-3853.
Notification of security breach.
Conduct constituting notice,
§28-3852.
Defined, §28-3851.
Electronic notice, §28-3851.
Who required to give notice,
§28-3852.
Rights and remedies, §28-3853.
Consumer security freeze, §§28-3861
to 28-3864.
Agency prompt response to request,
§28-3862.
Definitions, §28-3861.
Enforcement of provisions, §28-3864.
Fees and charges, §28-3862.
Form of notice of rights, §28-3863.
Internet-based method of requesting,
§28-3862.
Lifting freeze, §28-3862.
Notice of rights, §28-3863.
Persons not required to place security
freeze, §28-3862.
Promotion by reporting agencies,
§28-3863.
Responsibilities of reporting agencies,
§28-3862.
Telephone or mail requests, §28-3862.
Third party requests for information,
§28-3862.
Written confirmation to consumer,
§28-3862.

**CONSUMER CREDIT SERVICE
ORGANIZATIONS,** §§28-4601 to
28-4608.
Accounts and accounting.
Trust account in lieu of bond,
§28-4604.
Actions.
Violations of provisions.
Actions for damages, §28-4607.

CONSUMER CREDIT SERVICE ORGANIZATIONS —Cont'd

Attorneys' fees.
Violations of provisions.
Judgments for damages.
Provision for attorneys' fees, §28-4607.

Bonds, surety, §28-4604.
Trust account in lieu of, §28-4604.

Burden of proof.
Exemption or exception, §28-4606.

Contracts.
Disclosure statement required, §28-4605.
Notice of cancellation.
Contract to be accompanied by, §28-4605.
Written agreements required, §28-4605.

Damages.
Violations of provisions.
Actions for damages, §28-4607.

Definitions, §28-4601.

Disclosure statements.
Prerequisite to contract or agreement, §28-4605.

Enforcement of provisions, §28-4606.

Extension of credit.
Defined, §28-4601.

Fines, §28-4607.

Issuance of rules and regulations, §28-4608.

Mayor.
Rules and regulations, §28-4608.

Penalties, §28-4607.
Violations of provisions, §28-4607.

Prohibited acts, §28-4603.

Punitive damages.
Violations of provisions, §28-4607.

Registration, §28-4602.
Requirements, §28-4602.
Revocation or suspension of registration.
Procedural requirements, §28-4606.
Statement, §28-4602.

Rules and regulations, §28-4608.

Violations of provisions.
Damages.
Actions for damages, §28-4607.
Penalties, §28-4607.
Prohibited acts, §28-4603.

Written agreement requirement, §28-4605.

CONSUMER IDENTIFICATION, §§47-3151 to 47-3154.

CONSUMER LEASES.
Commercial code leases.
Generally, §§28:2A-101 to 28:2A-532.
See LEASES, UCC.

CONSUMER PROTECTION.
Actions.
Consumers' remedies, §28-3813.
Creditors' actions, §28-3812.
Damages, §28-3905.

Administrative law judges or attorney examiners.
Appointment, §28-3902.
Powers, §28-3902.

Advisory committee, §28-3907.
Composition, §28-3907.
Definition of "committee," §28-3901.
Duties, §28-3907.
Terms of members, §28-3907.

Ambiguity as to material fact, §28-3904.

Appeals.
Complaint procedures, §28-3905.

Application of chapter, §28-3801.

Assignments.
Earnings.
Assignment prohibited, §28-3804.
Seller's assignees subject to defenses of consumer, §28-3808.

Assistive technology device warranty, §§28-4031 to 28-4034.

Attorney general.
Investigative powers, §28-3910.
Subpoenas, authority to issue, §1-301.88d.

Attorneys at law.
Consumers' remedies.
Attorneys' fees, §28-3813.
Provision for attorneys' fees, §§28-3806, 28-3905.

Balloon payments, §28-3803.

Bicycle insurance policies, §§50-531 to 50-535.

Cable television, §34-1260.01.
Protection of privacy, §34-1260.02.

Class actions.
Public interest organizations.
Actions for relief from trade practices, §28-3905.

Complainant.
Defined, §28-3901.

Complaint procedures, §28-3905.

Confession of judgment.
Authorization to confess judgment prohibited, §28-3804.

Conflict of laws, §28-3816.

Construction of act, §28-3901.

CONSUMER PROTECTION —Cont'd
Consumer.
Defined, §28-3901.
Consumer and regulatory affairs, department of.
Complaint procedures, §§28-3901 to 28-3913.
Consumer credit.
General provisions, §§28-3801 to 28-3819.
See CONSUMER CREDIT.
Consumer credit sales.
Defined, §28-3802.
Consumer credit service organizations.
General provisions, §§28-4601 to 28-4608.
See CONSUMER CREDIT SERVICE ORGANIZATIONS.
Credit line deeds of trust, §28-3904.
Creditors' remedies.
Limitation on creditors' remedies, §28-3812.
Credit service organizations, §§28-4601 to 28-4608.
See CONSUMER CREDIT SERVICE ORGANIZATIONS.
Cross-collateral.
Debts secured by cross-collateral, §28-3805.
Defined, §28-3802.
Cure of default by debtor, §28-3812.
Damages.
Consumers' remedies, §28-3813.
Violations of chapter, §28-3905.
Debt collection.
Restrictions on collectors, §28-3814.
Deception.
Unlawful trade practices, §28-3904.
Deeds of trust.
Credit line deeds of trust, §28-3904.
Default.
Limitation on creditors' remedies, §28-3812.
Defenses.
Seller's assignees subject to defenses of consumer, §28-3808.
Definitions, §§28-3802, 28-3901.
Consumer protection procedures, §28-3901.
Debt collection, §28-3814.
Health spa sales, §28-3817.
Layaway plans, §28-3818.
Natural disasters, §28-4101.
Rental housing locators, §28-3819.
Delinquent debts owed District, recovery, §1-350.10.

CONSUMER PROTECTION —Cont'd
Department of consumer and regulatory affairs.
Definition of "department," §28-3901.
Director.
Defined, §28-3901.
Powers, §28-3902.
Duties, §§28-3902, 28-3903.
Fines and civil penalties, §28-3903.
Investigations.
Complaint procedure, §28-3905.
Powers of department, §28-3903.
Office of adjudication.
Defined, §28-3901.
Office of compliance.
Chief.
Appointment, §28-3902.
Defined, §28-3901.
Duties, §28-3902.
Office of consumer protection.
Defined, §28-3901.
Duties, §28-3906.
Plans.
Submission to the council, §28-3912.
Powers, §28-3903.
Principal consumer protection agency, §28-3902.
Reports, §28-3903.
Rulemaking, §28-3913.
Subpoenas.
Powers of department, §28-3903.
Direct installment loans.
Defined, §28-3802.
Direct motor vehicle installment loans, §§28-3601 to 28-3603.
Disciplinary actions against licensees.
Overcharging during natural disaster, §28-4103.
Dodd-Frank Wall Street reform and consumer protection act.
Filings under, USDistCt LCvR 85.
Door-to-door sales.
Home solicitation sales, §28-3811.
Education.
Consumer education and information, §28-3906.
Electric light and power companies.
Disconnection of service in extreme temperature, prohibition, §34-1506.01.
Retail electric competition and consumer protection, §§34-1501 to 34-1522.
Enforcement.
Administrative enforcement, §28-3815.

CONSUMER PROTECTION —Cont'd
Fiduciary status of public officers and employees, §1-615.04.
Gas companies.
Disconnection of service in extreme temperature, prohibition, §34-1671.06a.
Natural gas suppliers.
Retail natural gas supplier licensing and consumer protection, §§34-1671.01 to 34-1671.14.
See GAS COMPANIES.
Goods and services.
Defined, §28-3901.
Health spa sales, §28-3817.
Hearing aid dealers.
General provisions, §§28-4001 to 28-4007.
See HEARING AID DEALERS.
Hearings.
Complaint procedures, §28-3905.
Home solicitation sales, §28-3811.
Buyer's right to cancel, §28-3811.
Injunctions.
Restraining prohibited acts, §28-3909.
Innuendo as to material fact, §28-3904.
Insurance.
Unfair insurance trade practices, §§31-2231.01 to 31-2231.25.
See INSURANCE.
Interest rates, §28-3310.
Investigations.
Complaint procedures, §28-3905.
Department of consumer and regulatory affairs.
Powers, §28-3903.
Layaway plans, §28-3818.
Violation of provisions, §28-3904.
Lease-purchase agreements, §§42-3671.01 to 42-3671.14.
See LEASE-PURCHASE AGREEMENTS.
Lender subject to defenses arising from sales, §28-3809.
Loan sharking.
Repayment unenforceable, §28-3812.
Mayor.
Administrative enforcement, §28-3815.
Mental health.
See MENTAL HEALTH CONSUMERS PROTECTION ACT OF 2001.
Merchant.
Defined, §28-3901.
Misleading trade practices, §28-3904.
Misrepresentation.
Unlawful trade practices, §28-3904.

CONSUMER PROTECTION —Cont'd
Motor vehicle financing.
Installment sales, §§50-601 to 50-610.
See MOTOR VEHICLE FINANCING.
Motor vehicles.
New car warranties, §§50-501 to 50-510.
See LEMON LAW.
Natural disasters, §§28-4101 to 28-4103.
Declaration of state of emergency, §28-4102.
Definitions, §28-4101.
Overcharging, §28-4102.
Natural gas suppliers.
Retail natural gas supplier licensing and consumer protection, §§34-1671.01 to 34-1671.14.
See GAS COMPANIES.
Negotiable instruments.
Prohibited in consumer credit sales, §28-3807.
No-fault motor vehicle insurance, §31-2409.
Nonprofit organizations.
Actions for relief from trade practices, §28-3905.
Defined, §28-3901.
Notice.
Complaint procedures, §28-3905.
Default.
Required notice by creditor, §28-3812.
Office of consumer protection.
Defined, §28-3901.
Duties, §28-3906.
Hearing aid dealers.
Powers and duties of office, §28-4002.
Penalties.
Department of consumer and regulatory affairs.
Fines and civil penalties, §28-3903.
Overcharging.
Natural disasters, §28-4103.
Violations, §28-3905.
Civil fines, penalties and fees, §28-3815.
Person.
Defined, §28-3901.
Prescription drugs, excessive pricing, §§28-4551 to 28-4555.
Price gouging.
Natural disaster, §§28-4101 to 28-4103.

CONSUMER PROTECTION —Cont'd
Procedures, §§28-3901 to 28-3913.
Public interest organizations.
Actions for relief from trade practices, §28-3905.
Defined, §28-3901.
Punitive damages.
Violations of chapter, §§28-3813, 28-3905.
Radon contractors.
Proficiency requirements, §§28-4201 to 28-4203.
Real property credit line deed of trust.
Unlawful trade practices, §28-3904.
Redemption of collateral after default, §28-3812.
Referral sales.
Rebates, discounts, etc., prohibited, §28-3810.
Remedies.
Consumers' remedies, §28-3813.
Creditors' remedies.
Limitation on creditors' remedies, §28-3812.
Rental housing locators, §28-3819.
Violations of provisions, §28-3904.
Reports.
Department of consumer and regulatory affairs, §28-3903.
Repossession of collateral, §28-3812.
Respondent.
Defined, §28-3901.
Restraint of trade.
General provisions, §§28-4501 to 28-4518.
See RESTRAINTS OF TRADE.
Revolving credit accounts, §§28-3701, 28-3702.
Defined, §28-3802.
Salaries.
Assignment of earnings prohibited, §28-3804.
Scope of chapter, §28-3801.
Settlement of complaints, §28-3905.
Severability of procedural provisions, §28-3908.
Social media.
Unlawful trade practices, §28-3904.
Statute of frauds, §§28-3501 to 28-3505.
Subpoenas.
Department of consumer and regulatory affairs.
Powers, §28-3903.
Trade practices.
Defined, §28-3901.

CONSUMER PROTECTION —Cont'd
Truthful information from merchants.
Enforceable right, §28-3901.
Unconscionable agreements, §28-3812.
Unlawful trade practices, §28-3904.
Complaint procedures, §28-3905.
Penalties, §28-3905.
Restraining prohibited acts, §28-3909.
Violations, §28-3904.
Complaint procedures, §28-3905.
Penalties, §28-3905.
Punitive damages, §28-3813.
Unlawful trade practices, §28-3904.
Wages.
Assignment of earnings prohibited, §28-3804.

CONSUMERS' RIGHTS PROTECTION.
Mental health, §§7-1231.01 to 7-1231.15.

CONTAGIOUS DISEASES.
Biological agents.
Anti-terrorism act of 2002, §§22-3151 to 22-3156.
See COMMUNICABLE DISEASES.

CONTAMINATION OF PROPERTY.
Hazardous substances releases.
Liability, cleanup, response, §§8-631.01 to 8-638.01.
See HAZARDOUS SUBSTANCES RELEASES.

CONTEMPT.
Administrative law judges.
Show cause orders.
Authority of administrative law judge to apply for, §2-1831.09.
Assignment of felony cases and related cases, CrimPro Rule 105.
Auditor for District of Columbia.
Subpoena and oath authority, §§1-301.171 to 1-301.173.
Building code.
Failure to fireproof building.
Violation of injunction, §6-601.08.
Child support enforcement.
Criminal contempt for failure to pay, §46-225.02.
Hearing commissioner proceedings, FamDiv Rule D.
Court of appeals, §11-741.
Criminal contempt, CrimPro Rule 42.
Child support, failure to pay, §46-225.02.

CONTEMPT —Cont'd

Delinquent minors, JuvProc Rule 42.
Subpoena noncompliance, JuvProc Rule 17.

Discovery noncompliance, CivPro Rule 37.

Domestic relations actions.
Judgment for specific act not complied with, DomRel Rule 70.

Domestic violence unit proceedings, DomesticViolence Rule 12.

Drug, firearm, or prostitution-related nuisance abatement, §42-3112.

Ethics and government accountability, §1-1162.21.

Family court proceedings generally.
Hearing commissioner proceedings, FamDiv Rule D.

Habeas corpus violations, §16-1904.

Hearing commissioner proceedings, CivPro Rule 73, CrimPro Rule 117.

Minors.
Criminal contempt brought against child.
Delinquent act, JuvProc Rule 42.

Parentage proceedings.
Failure to submit to blood test, DomRel Rule 405.

Probate proceedings, §16-3103.

Public utilities investigations, §34-918.

Release prior to trial, violating conditions of, §§23-1329, 23-1330.

Service of process, CivPro Rule 4.1.

Subpoena noncompliance.
Adoption proceedings, Adoption Rule 45.
Civil procedure, CivPro Rule 45.
Criminal cases, CrimPro Rule 17.
Delinquent minors, JuvProc Rule 17.
Domestic relations actions, DomRel Rule 45.

Summary judgment.
Bad faith affidavits, CivPro Rule 56.

Superior court, §11-944.

CONTINGENCY CASH RESERVE FUND, §1-204.50a.

Short-term borrowing, §47-369.03.

CONTINGENCY PLANS.

Water pollution emergencies, §8-103.08.

CONTINGENT FEES.

Attorneys at law, ProfCond Rule 1.5.

Public procurements, §2-354.16.

CONTINUANCES.

Arbitration hearings, Arbitration Rule IX.

Bankruptcy proceedings, USDistDCBank Rule 5070-1.

Child abuse and neglect proceedings.
Factfinding hearings, NeglectProc Rule 19.
Initial appearances, NeglectProc Rule 14.

Civil trials generally, CivPro Rule 40-I, USDistCt LCvR 16.1.

Court-ordered commitment of persons with mental illness.
Appointed counsel, continuances granted to, §21-543.

Criminal procedure, CrimPro Rule 111, USDistCt LCrR 57.2.
Jury trials at arraignment, CrimPro Rule 102.

Domestic violence unit proceedings, DomesticViolence Rule 4.

Family court proceedings, FamDiv Rule G.

Intellectual disability proceedings, MentalRetardation Rule 13.

Landlord and tenant court, LandlordTenant Rule 11.

Pretrial conferences, CivPro Rule 16.

Small claims court, SmallClaims Rule 7.

Summary judgment motions, CivPro Rule 56.

CONTINUING CARE RETIREMENT COMMUNITIES, §§44-151.01 to 44-151.18.

Accommodations, requirements, §44-151.10.

Action for violations, §44-151.14.

Assisted living services contracted for.
Bed not available when resident needs promised care, §44-151.06.

Civil liability for violations, §44-151.14.

Civil penalties, authority to impose, §44-151.14.

Comprehensive nursing care services.
Contract proving for.
Bed not available when resident needs promised care, §44-151.06.

CONTINUING CARE RETIREMENT COMMUNITIES —Cont'd
Continuing care providers.
License, §44-151.02.
Revocation and suspension, §44-151.03.
Continuing care retirement community regulatory and supervision trust fund account, §§31-1202, 44-151.18.
Contracts for continuing care, §44-151.06.
Criminal penalties for violation, §44-151.15.
Definitions, §44-151.01.
Disclosure statement.
Delivered prior to contract to provide services, §44-151.05.
Revised statement setting forth current information, §44-151.07.
Entrance fee.
Escrow accounts, §44-151.09.
Refund upon termination of agreement, §44-151.06.
Examination of providers books and records, §44-151.13.
False or misleading statements.
Criminal penalties for violation, §44-151.15.
Fraud.
First degree, §44-151.15.
Second degree, §44-151.15.
Investigations.
Subpoenas, issuance authorized, §44-151.12.
Meetings with residents.
Duty of board of directors to hold, §44-151.10.
Operating reserves, §44-151.08.
Other licensing or regulation authority, §44-151.16.
Records, examination and preservation, §44-151.13.
Rehabilitation or liquidation, §44-151.11.
Resident included on governing body, §44-151.10.
Rules and regulations, §44-151.17.
Sale or transfer of ownership, §44-151.04.
Self-organization.
Right of resident to, §44-151.10.
Visits by commissioner or designee, §44-151.13.

CONTINUING EDUCATION COURSES, §§38-1001 to 38-1003.

CONTRABAND.
Gray-market cigarettes, §47-2423.
Mattresses, §8-508.
Prison grounds, §§22-2603.01 to 22-2603.04.
Definitions, §22-2603.01.
Detention of persons on grounds, §22-2603.04.
Employee's failure to report violation, §22-2603.02.
Penalties, §22-2603.03.
Prohibited acts, §22-2603.02.

CONTRACT APPEALS BOARD, §§2-360.01 to 2-360.08.
Creation, §2-360.01.
Decisions, §2-360.05.
Judicial review, §2-360.07.
Jurisdiction, §2-360.03.
Members, §2-360.02.
Powers, §2-360.06.
Procedures, §2-360.08.
Right to appeal, §2-360.04.

CONTRACTORS.
Apprenticeship programs.
Registration by contractors and subcontractors contracting with District, §32-1431.
Asbestos licensing and control, §§8-111.01 to 8-111.14.
See ASBESTOS CONTRACTORS.
Claims against the District, §§2-359.08, 2-359.09.
Interest, §2-359.09.
Construction codes, §§6-1401 to 6-1409.
See CONSTRUCTION CODES.
Daytime parking permit, §50-2635.
Debarment or suspension, §2-359.07.
Deferred compensation program, §47-3603.
Elevators, §§47-2853.95 to 47-2853.99.
See ELEVATORS.
Home improvement contractors.
Bonding requirements, §§47-2883.01 to 47-2883.07.
See HOME IMPROVEMENT CONTRACTORS.
Mechanics' and materialmen's lien.
General provisions, §§40-301.01 to 40-307.03.
See MECHANIC'S LIENS.
Parking.
Contractor daytime parking permit, §50-2635.

CONTRACTORS —Cont'd

Prompt payment, private contractors and subcontractors, §§27-131 to 27-136.
See PROMPT PAYMENT.

Radon contractor proficiency, §§28-4201 to 28-4203.

Security and fire alarm contractors.
General provisions, §§7-2801 to 7-2815.
See SECURITY AND FIRE ALARM CONTRACTORS.

Tax returns or other tax information.
Disclosure to contractors obligated to store government documents, §§47-1805.04, 47-4406.

CONTRACTS.

Artists placing works of art with art dealers.
Written contract requirement, §28-5105.

Assignment of choses in action, §§28-2303, 28-2305.

Assignments.
Future salary or wages.
Contract to assign prohibited, §28-2305.
Nonnegotiable contracts, §28-2303.

Athlete agents, §§47-2887.01 to 47-2887.18.

Breach of contract.
Small claims court forms, SmallClaims Form 3.

Captive insurance companies.
Special purpose financial captive insurance companies.
Authorized contracts, §31-3932.07.
Reinsurance, §31-3932.11.
Trust agreements, §31-3932.08.

Charter schools.
Public charter schools.
School management contracts, §38-1802.04.

Collaborative law, §16-4004.
Approval, §16-4008.

Collection of taxes.
Agreement of liability, §47-4403.

Commercial code.
Secured transactions.
General provisions, §§28:9-101 to 28:9-809.
See SECURED TRANSACTIONS.

Condominium owners' associations, liabilities of, §42-1903.09.

CONTRACTS —Cont'd

Constitution of the United States.
Impairment of obligations of contracts, US Const Art I §10.

Construction contracts.
Prompt payment.
Private contractor and subcontractor prompt payment act, §§27-131 to 27-136.
See PROMPT PAYMENT.

Consumer credit service organizations.
Disclosure statement required, §28-4605.
Notice of cancellation.
Contract to be accompanied by, §28-4605.
Written agreements required, §28-4605.

Continuing care retirement communities.
Specifications, §44-151.06.

Corporations.
Officers.
Contract rights, §29-306.44.
Powers, §29-303.02.

Corrections, Department of, §24-211.05.

Defenses.
Unconscionability.
Sale of goods, §28:2-302.

Department of corrections.
Delivery of inmate health care, §24-1401.

Department of general services.
Representative to provide real estate brokerage and consulting services, §10-551.07.

Direct motor vehicle installment loans, §§28-3601 to 28-3603.

Documents of title.
Bills of lading.
Limitation of carrier's liability, §28:7-309.
Warehouse receipts.
Limitation of warehouse liability, §28:7-204.
When adequate compliance with obligations of commercial contract, §28:7-509.

Dulles International Airport, §9-806.

Ejectment, performance of contract and, §16-1106.

Electronic transactions, uniform act, §§28-4901 to 28-4918.

CONTRACTS —Cont'd
Evidence.
Sales contracts.
Parol and extrinsic evidence,
§28:2-202.
Food service contracts.
Prompt payment.
Private contractor and subcontractor
prompt payment act, §§27-131
to 27-136.
See PROMPT PAYMENT.
Forgery, §22-3242.
Gaming contracts invalid, §16-1701.
Garnishment.
Prejudgment garnishment.
Damages for breach, §16-501.
Guardianship of minors.
Property subject to executory contract,
§21-145.
Sale of real estate on behalf of
guardian and infant, §21-146.
**Health benefits for public officers
and employees, §1-621.04.**
**Health professional recruitment
program.**
Service obligation contract.
Breach, §7-751.13.
Conditions of participation,
provision of contract, §7-751.07.
No-compete clause prohibited,
§7-751.07.
Renewal, §7-751.07.
Waiver of contract terms and
conditions.
Mental or physical disability or
death, §7-751.15.
**Healthy DC and health care
expansion fund and program.**
Contract requirements, §4-635.
Homeless services.
Authority of mayor, §4-756.01.
Impairing obligations of contracts,
US Const Art I §10.
Inspector general.
Contract with auditor not employee of
office, §1-301.115a.
Insurance adjusters, §31-1631.08.
Interest.
Maximum rate of interest, §28-3301.
Interest on judgments, §§15-109,
15-110.
Interest rate expressed in, §28-3301.
Joint contracts, §§16-2101 to 16-2106,
28-3504.
Death of defendant after action
brought.
Representation, §16-2104.

CONTRACTS —Cont'd
Joint contracts —Cont'd
Death of party.
Executors, administrators, heirs
bound by contract, §16-2102.
Definition, §16-2101.
Judgment rendered if others not
joined, §16-2105.
Proof of joint liability unnecessary,
§16-2105.
Separate composition or compromise
with creditors, §16-2106.
Service of process on some of parties
to contract.
Judgment against parties served not
extinguishment or merger of
action, §16-2103.
Lie detector tests, §32-903.
**Life insurance benefits for public
officers and employees, §1-622.05.**
Limitation of actions.
Sale of goods.
Breach of contract, §28:2-725.
Limitations by agreements may be
reduced to less than one year,
§28:2-725.
Limited cooperative associations.
Marketing contracts, §§29-1007.01 to
29-1007.04.
Authorization, §29-1007.01.
Breach of contract, §29-1007.04.
Defined, §29-1007.01.
Duration of, §29-1007.03.
Effect of, §29-1007.02.
Metropolitan police department.
Fleet management services, §2-381.42.
Nonprofit corporations.
Officers.
Contract rights, §29-406.44.
Powers, §29-403.02.
Nurse's rehabilitation program.
Contract by participating nurse,
§3-1251.09.
Oral, §28-3504.
Parol evidence.
Sales contracts, §28:2-202.
Pay-for-success contracts, §§2-211.01
to 2-211.03.
**Pensions and retirement benefits for
public officers and employees,**
§1-626.06.
Polygraphs, §32-903.
**Private fire hydrant responsibility
agreements, §34-2410.02.**
Public contracts, §§2-201.01 to
2-223.07.
See PUBLIC CONTRACTS.

CONTRACTS —Cont'd
Public procurements, §§2-355.01 to
2-355.04.
Appeals board, §§2-360.01 to 2-360.08.
Creation, §2-360.01.
Decisions, §2-360.05.
Judicial review, §2-360.07.
Jurisdiction, §2-360.03.
Members, §2-360.02.
Powers, §2-360.06.
Procedures, §2-360.08.
Right to appeal, §2-360.04.
Authorized, §2-355.03.
Cost-plus-a-percentage-of-cost
contracts, §2-355.01.
Cost-reimbursement contracts,
§2-355.02.
Improper contracts, §2-359.02.
Multiyear contracts, §2-355.04.
Oral agreements, §2-359.01.
Punitive damages, §2-359.05.
Sovereign immunity, §2-359.04.
Termination, §2-359.03.
Real property.
Recordability of contracts relating to,
§42-409.
Rehabilitation services program.
Authority, §32-331.01.
Rental housing conversion and sale,
§§42-3404.05, 42-3404.34.
Rental housing locators, §28-3819.
Restraints of trade, §28-4502.
Revolving credit accounts, §§28-3701,
28-3702.
Sale of goods, commercial code.
General provisions, §§28:2-101 to
28:2-725.
See SALE OF GOODS, UCC.
Secured transactions.
General provisions, §§28:9-101 to
28:9-809.
See SECURED TRANSACTIONS.
Sales contracts.
Seals and sealed instruments.
Seals inoperative, §28:2-203.
Small claims court.
Breach of contract, SmallClaims Form
3.
Surrender of contracts, SmallClaims
Rule 16.
Social services.
Pay-for-success contracts, §§2-211.01
to 2-211.03.
Specific performance.
Complaint for specific performance to
convey land, CivPro Form CA 12.

CONTRACTS —Cont'd
States.
Impairing obligations of contracts, US
Const Art I §10.
Statute of frauds, §§28-3501 to
28-3505.
Statute of limitations.
Sale of goods.
Breach of contract, §28:2-725.
Limitations by agreements may be
reduced to less than one year,
§28:2-725.
Surrogate parenting contracts,
§§16-401, 16-402.
Sustainable energy utilities,
§§8-1774.01, 8-1774.02, 8-1774.05.
Unconscionability.
Sale of goods, §28:2-302.
University of the District of
Columbia, §38-1204.05.
Waiver.
Sale of goods.
Waiver of executory portion of
contract, §28:2-209.
Washington convention and sports
authority marketing service
contracts, §10-1202.08a.
Workplace fraud.
Waiver of protections of law by
agreement, prohibited,
§32-1331.08.
Written requirement, §28-3504.

CONTRIBUTING TO
DELINQUENCY OF MINOR,
§22-811.

CONTRIBUTORY NEGLIGENCE.
Child restraint seats, §50-1707.
Common carriers, §35-301.
Helmets.
Failure of bicycle operator or
passenger to wear, §50-1606.
Negotiable instruments.
Forged signature or alteration of
instrument, §28:3-406.
Seat belts, §50-1807.

CONTROLLED SUBSTANCE
ANALOGUES, §48-902.14.

CONTROLLED SUBSTANCES,
§§48-901.02 to 48-931.02.
Administration of provisions,
§48-902.01.
Alcoholic beverage licenses.
Denial.
Controlled substance violations on
premises, §25-335.

CONTROLLED SUBSTANCES
—Cont'd
Alcoholic beverage licenses —Cont'd
Violations, mandatory revocation,
§25-822.
Analogues, §48-902.14.
Arrests, §48-921.01.
Attempt to commit offenses,
§48-904.09.
Burden of proof, §48-905.03.
Business licenses.
Disciplinary actions against licensees,
§47-2844.
Chemist reports, §48-905.06.
Children and minors.
Contributing to the delinquency of a
minor, §22-811.
Distribution to, §48-904.06.
Drug-free zones, §48-904.07a.
Enlistment of minors to distribute,
§48-904.07.
Conspiracy, §48-904.09.
Cooperative agreements, §48-905.01.
Definitions, §48-901.02.
Dispensing.
Regulation, §§48-903.01 to 48-903.09.
Distribution of.
Regulation, §§48-903.01 to 48-903.09.
**District of Columbia Housing
Authority.**
Drug and alcohol testing of employees,
§6-217.
Drug-free zones, §48-904.07a.
Drug paraphernalia, §§48-904.10,
48-1101 to 48-1104.
Distribution of needles or syringes
near schools, §48-1121.
**Emergency medical services
technicians.**
Administering, supervision required,
§48-931.02.
Enforcement of provisions,
§§48-905.01 to 48-905.07.
Evidence, §48-905.03.
**Federal law, acquittal or conviction
under,** §48-904.05.
Felony murder, §22-2101.
Forfeitures, §48-905.02.
Fraud and deceit, §48-904.03.
Inspections, §48-905.05.
Inventories, §48-903.06.
Issuance of rules and regulations,
§48-906.02.
Manufacturing.
Regulation, §§48-903.01 to 48-903.09.
Marijuana.
Consumption in public space
prohibited, §48-911.01.

CONTROLLED SUBSTANCES
—Cont'd
Marijuana —Cont'd
Impairment prohibited, §48-911.01.
Medical marijuana, §§7-1671.01 to
7-1671.13.
See MEDICAL MARIJUANA.
Monitoring prescription drugs,
§§48-853.01 to 48-853.10.
See PRESCRIPTION DRUGS.
Needle exchange programs,
§48-1103.01.
Nomenclature, §48-902.02.
Nurses.
Administering, supervision required,
§48-931.02.
Offenses and penalties, §48-904.01.
**Overdose victim, seeking medical
attention for.**
Mitigating factor in sentencing for
certain offenses, §7-403.
Penalties.
Attempts to commit offenses,
§48-904.09.
Children and minors.
Distribution to, §48-904.06.
Drug-free zones, §48-904.07a.
Enlistment of minors to distribute,
§48-904.07.
Conspiracy to commit offenses,
§48-904.09.
Drug-free zones, §48-904.07a.
Drug paraphernalia, §§48-904.10,
48-1101 to 48-1104.
Distribution of needles or syringes
near schools, §48-1121.
Federal law, acquittal or conviction
under, §48-904.05.
Forfeitures, §48-905.02.
Fraud and deceit, §48-904.03.
Knowing or intentional manufacture,
distribution, or possession,
§§48-904.01, 48-904.03a.
Other laws, penalties under,
§48-904.04.
Registered manufacturers,
distributors, and dispensers,
§§48-903.09, 48-904.02.
Second or subsequent offenses,
§48-904.08.
Pending proceedings, §48-906.01.
Physician-patient privilege,
§48-931.01.
Prescription drugs, §48-903.08.
Prisons and prisoners.
Contraband on prison grounds,
§§22-2603.01 to 22-2603.04.

CONTROLLED SUBSTANCES
—Cont'd
Privacy and confidentiality,
§48-905.01.
Public information and education
programs, §48-905.04.
Records, §48-903.06.
Registration of dispensers,
distributors, manufacturers,
§§48-903.01 to 48-903.09.
Civil infractions, §48-903.09.
Exceptions, §48-903.02.
Fees.
Mayor may charge, §48-903.01.
Forfeiture of substances, §48-903.04.
Inspection of registrants, §48-903.02.
Order forms.
Required to distribute from
registrant to registrant,
§48-903.07.
Public interest limitations, §48-903.03.
Records and inventories, §48-903.06.
Renewal, §48-903.02.
Required, §48-903.02.
Rules and regulations, §48-903.01.
Suspension or revocation, §48-903.04.
Procedural rights, §48-903.05.
Waiver of requirement, §48-903.02.
Reports, §48-905.06.
Residential housing.
Drug, firearm, or prostitution-related
nuisance abatement, §§42-3101 to
42-3114.
See CRIME-RELATED NUISANCE
ABATEMENT.
Drug-related evictions, §§42-3601 to
42-3610.
See DRUG-RELATED EVICTIONS.
Schedule I, §§48-902.03, 48-902.04.
Schedule II, §§48-902.05, 48-902.06.
Schedule III, §§48-902.07, 48-902.08.
Schedule IV, §§48-902.09, 48-902.10.
Schedule V, §§48-902.11, 48-902.12.
Schedule revision and publication,
§48-902.13.
Search and seizure without warrant,
§48-921.01.
Search warrants, §§48-921.01,
48-921.02.
Marijuana, articulable suspicion,
§48-921.02a.
Second or subsequent offenses,
§§48-904.08.
Severability of provisions, §48-906.03.
Subpoenas, §48-905.07.
Supervision of administration by
licensed practitioner, §48-931.02.

CONTROLLED SUBSTANCES
—Cont'd
Warrantless arrests, §48-921.01.

CONVENTION CENTER.
Convention center hotel.
See CONVENTION CENTER HOTEL.
Washington convention and sports
authority, §§10-1202.01 to
10-1221.15.
See WASHINGTON CONVENTION
AND SPORTS AUTHORITY.
Washington convention center.
See WASHINGTON CONVENTION
CENTER.

CONVENTION CENTER HOTEL.
Bond issues, §§10-1221.05 to
10-1221.07.
Authorization, §10-1221.05.
Federal recovery act reimbursement,
§10-1221.15.
Financing and closing documents,
§10-1221.09.
Issuance, §10-1221.07.
Limited liability, §§10-1221.10,
10-1221.11.
Payment and security, §10-1221.08.
Recordkeeping, §10-1221.12.
Recovery zone designation,
§10-1221.14.
Terms and conditions, §10-1221.06.
Transcript of proceedings, §10-1221.13.
Washington convention and sports
authority, §§10-1202.04,
10-1202.09.
Construction of hotel, §§10-1202.41 to
10-1202.44.
Apprenticeship program, §10-1202.43.
Contracting requirements,
§10-1202.41.
First source agreement, §10-1202.42.
Internship program, §10-1202.44.
D.C. citizens' job program,
§10-1221.05.
Definitions, §10-1221.01.
Eminent domain, §10-1202.31.
Eminent domain, §§10-1202.31 to
10-1202.33.
Definitions, §10-1202.31.
Exercise, §10-1202.33.
Findings, §10-1202.32.
Findings, §10-1221.02.
Eminent domain, §10-1202.32.
Lease of land, §10-1202.21.
Fund.
Creation of new convention center
hotel fund, §10-1221.03.

CONVENTION CENTER HOTEL
—Cont'd
Leases.
Land lease authority for hotel,
§§10-1202.21 to 10-1202.24.
Findings, §10-1202.21.
Mayor's authority, §10-1202.22.
Washington convention and sports
authority, §10-1202.23.
Air or vault space adjacent to
property subject to lease.
Grant of easement,
§10-1202.23b.
Permit for, §10-1202.24.
Use of space, §10-1202.23a.
Real property transfer tax.
Exempt transfers, §47-4609.
Recordation tax.
Exemption, §47-4609.
TIF area.
Creation of new convention center
hotel TIF area, §10-1221.04.
Washington convention and sports
authority.
Land lease authority for hotel,
§10-1202.23.
Air or vault space adjacent to
property subject to lease.
Grant of easement,
§10-1202.23b.
Permit for, §10-1202.24.
Use of space, §10-1202.23a.

CONVERSION.
Complaint for conversion, CivPro
Form CA 11.
Negotiable instruments, §28:3-420.

CONVEYANCES.
Adverse possession, effect of,
§42-305.
Assignments for benefit of creditors.
Assignee's conveyances, §28-2106.
Children and minors.
Conveyances or assurances by,
§§42-408, 42-808, 42-809.
Columbia hospital.
Conveyance of property to hospital,
§§44-751, 44-753.
**Complaint for specific performance
to convey land,** CivPro Form CA
12.
Condominium common elements,
§42-1903.20.
Contingent interests, §§42-1401 to
42-1404.

CONVEYANCES —Cont'd
Court ordered sales of property,
CivPro Rule 308.
Probate proceedings. See within this
heading, "Probate proceedings."
Deeds.
See DEEDS.
Express trusts not contained in,
§42-1503.
Fiduciaries.
Sale of estate property, CivPro Rule
305.
Probate proceedings. See within this
heading, "Probate proceedings."
Fraudulent conveyances.
General provisions, §§28-3101 to
28-3111.
See FRAUDULENT TRANSFERS.
Garnishment.
Prejudgment garnishment.
Fraudulent conveyances, §16-529.
**Intellectual disabilities, persons
with,** §42-820.
Interests conveyable, §42-301.
Judgment enforcement, CivPro Rule
70.
Domestic relations actions, DomRel
Rule 70.
**Limitations on leases of more than
one year.**
Deed or will required for, §42-306.
Mental illness, persons with, §42-820.
Mortgages and deeds of trust.
General provisions, §§42-804 to
42-820.
See MORTGAGES AND DEEDS OF
TRUST.
Notarial acts, §§42-141 to 42-148.
Probate proceedings.
Death before January 1, 1981.
Personal property, Probate Rule 17.
Real property, Probate Rule 18.
Death between January 1, 1981 and
June 30, 1995, Probate Rule 112.
Guardians, conservators, trustees, etc.,
involved, Probate Rules 203, 222,
223.
Public lands.
Exchange of District-owned land,
§§10-901 to 10-904.
Real property transfer tax, §§47-901
to 47-920.
Residential home sales disclosures,
§§42-1301 to 42-1311.
See HOME SALES.
**Title claim, conveyance by anyone
with,** §42-305.

CONVEYANCES —Cont'd
Transfer tax on real property,
§§47-901 to 47-920.
See REAL PROPERTY TRANSFER
TAX.

CONVULSIVE THERAPY.
**Health care durable powers of
attorney,** §21-2211.
**Intellectual disabilities, persons
with.**
Prohibited therapy, §7-1305.06.

COOPERATIVE AGREEMENTS.
Controlled substances, §48-905.01.
Fire protection study commission,
§3-1105.
Insurance rates, §31-2705.
**Metropolitan police and federal
agencies, cooperative
agreements between,** §5-133.17.
Pesticides, §8-416.
Restraints of trade, prosecuting,
§28-4513.
Savings and loan acquisitions,
§26-1214.
Sentencing.
Advisory Commission on, §3-108.
Soil and water conservation, §8-1709.

COOPERATIVE ASSOCIATIONS,
§§29-901 to 29-939.
Actions, §29-905.
Administrative dissolution.
Generally, §§29-106.01 to 29-106.04.
See BUSINESS ORGANIZATIONS.
Admission to membership, §29-923.
Applicability of provisions, §29-938.
Articles of incorporation.
Amendment, §29-907.
Filing, §29-935.
Contents of, §29-906.
Audits, §29-933.
Bylaws.
Adoption, amendment or repeal,
§29-908.
Filing, §29-935.
Contents of, §29-909.
Capital, limitations on return on,
§§29-922, 29-931.
Certificates of share.
Contents, §29-925.
Exemption for legal process, §29-928.
Issuance, §29-925.
Recall, §29-927.
Compliance with chapter, §29-937.
Definitions, §29-902.
Delegates.
Voting, §29-917.

COOPERATIVE ASSOCIATIONS
—Cont'd
Directors, §29-918.
Referenda on acts of, §29-921.
Removal of, §29-920.
Dissolution of corporations, §29-934.
Distributions, §29-934.
Net savings, §29-931.
Employees.
Surety bonds, §29-932.
Existing cooperatives, §29-935.
Fees, §29-939.
Filing.
Generally, §§29-102.01 to 29-102.13.
See BUSINESS ORGANIZATIONS.
Foreign corporations, §29-936.
Foreign entities.
Generally, §§29-105.01 to 29-105.12.
See BUSINESS ORGANIZATIONS.
Incorporators, §29-903.
Liability of members, §29-929.
Licenses.
Fees, §29-939.
Limited cooperative associations,
§§29-1001.01 to 29-1015.08.
See LIMITED COOPERATIVE
ASSOCIATIONS.
Meetings, §29-910.
Notice, §29-911.
Units of membership, §29-912.
Membership.
Admission to, §29-923.
Certificates.
Contents, §29-925.
Exemption for legal process,
§29-928.
Issuance, §29-925.
Recall, §29-927.
Eligibility for, §29-923.
Expulsion of, §29-930.
Liability, §29-929.
Transfer of, §29-926.
Voting, number permitted per
member, §29-913.
Mortgages and deeds of trust.
Powers, §29-905.
Names.
Generally, §§29-103.01 to 29-103.04.
See BUSINESS ORGANIZATIONS.
Net savings.
Allocation of, §29-931.
Distributions, §29-931.
Notice.
Meetings, §29-911.
Officers, §29-919.
Removal of, §29-920.

COOPERATIVE ASSOCIATIONS
—Cont'd
Officers —Cont'd
Surety bonds, §29-932.
Personal property.
Powers, §29-905.
Powers, §29-905.
Purposes of, §29-904.
Real property.
Powers, §29-905.
Registered agents.
Generally, §§29-104.01 to 29-104.14.
See BUSINESS ORGANIZATIONS.
Rental housing conversions,
§42-3402.06.
Restraints of trade.
Not deemed, §29-937.
Seals.
Powers, §29-905.
Shares and shareholders.
Certificates of share.
Contents, §29-925.
Exemption for legal process,
§29-928.
Issuance, §29-925.
Recall, §29-927.
Transfer of shares, §29-926.
Short title, §29-901.
Subscribers, §29-924.
Taxation, §29-939.
Units of membership, §29-912.
Voting.
Delegates, §29-917.
Electronic mail, §§29-915, 29-916.
Mail, §§29-915, 29-916.
Number permitted per member,
§29-913.
Proxy arrangements.
Prohibitions, §29-914.

COOPERATIVE HOUSING ASSOCIATIONS.
Condominiums, §§42-1901.01 to
42-1904.18.
See CONDOMINIUMS.
Home purchase assistance fund,
§§42-2601 to 42-2626.
See HOME PURCHASE ASSISTANCE
FUND.
Homestead deduction.
Lower income home ownership tax
abatement and incentives,
§47-3503.
Residential property tax relief,
§§47-850.01 to 47-850.04.

COOPERATIVE HOUSING ASSOCIATIONS —Cont'd
Homestead housing preservation,
§§42-2101 to 42-2111.
See HOMESTEAD HOUSING
PRESERVATION.
Horizontal property regimes,
§§42-2001 to 42-2031.
See HORIZONTAL PROPERTY
REGIMES.
Income tax credits.
Long term homeowner credit,
§§47-1806.09 to 47-1806.09f.
Interest.
Maximum rate on share, §28-3301.
**Lower income home ownership tax
abatement and incentives,**
§§47-3503, 47-3506.
**Persons sixty five years of age or
older.**
Reduced tax liability, §47-863.
Persons with disabilities.
Reduced tax liability, §47-863.
Real property taxes, §§47-820.01,
47-850, 47-873.
Exemption.
Property transfer to qualified lower
income homeowner, §47-3503.
Administration and enforcement,
§47-3504.
Transfers exempt from tax, §47-802.
Rental housing conversion and sale,
§§42-3401.01 to 42-3405.13.
See RENTAL HOUSING.
Secondary financing.
Required conditions, §28-3301.
Step Up program, §42-2622.

COPARCENARY ESTATES.
Abolition of, §42-517.

COPYRIGHTS.
Authors.
Protection of rights, US Const Art I §8.

CORAM NOBIS.
Writ abolished, CivPro Rule 60.

CORAM VOBIS.
Writ abolished, CivPro Rule 60.

CORCORAN GALLERY OF ART.
Real property exempt from taxation,
§§47-1016, 47-1017.

CORD OF WOOD.
Weights and measures, §37-201.17.

CORN.
Barrel of corn, defined, §37-203.01.

CORONERS.
Autopsies, §§5-1409, 5-1410, 5-1414.
Medical examiners.
General provisions, §§5-1401 to
5-1419.
See MEDICAL EXAMINERS.

**CORPORATE DISCLOSURE
STATEMENT.**
Appeals in federal cases, FRAP 26.1,
USCtApp Rule 26.1.
Filing generally, CivPro Rule 7.1,
USDistCt LCrR 44.6, USDistCt
LCvR 7.1.

CORPORATION COUNSEL.
See ATTORNEY GENERAL FOR
DISTRICT OF COLUMBIA.

CORPORATIONS, §§29-301.01 to
29-314.02.
Acquisition of own shares,
§29-304.41.
Actions, §29-303.02.
Administrative dissolution.
Generally, §§29-106.01 to 29-106.04.
See BUSINESS ORGANIZATIONS.
After-acquired shares.
Appraisal and payment for shares,
§29-311.15.
Appraisal and payment for shares,
§§29-311.01 to 29-311.50.
After-acquired shares, §29-311.15.
Beneficial owners, §29-311.03.
Definitions, §29-311.01.
Demand.
Notice, §29-311.11.
Dissatisfied shareholders, §29-311.16.
Injunctions, §29-311.50.
Judicial appraisal.
Costs, §29-311.31.
Judicial proceedings, §29-311.30.
Limitation of remedies, §29-311.50.
Nominees, §29-311.03.
Notice, §29-311.12.
Payment, §29-311.14.
Procedures, §§29-311.10 to 29-311.16.
Rescission, §29-311.50.
Right to, §29-311.02.
Notice, §29-311.10.
Perfection of, §29-311.13.
Withdrawal, §29-311.13.
Articles of incorporation.
Amendment, §§29-308.01 to 29-308.09.
Articles of amendment, §29-308.06.
Authority, §29-308.01.
Before issuance of shares,
§29-308.02.

CORPORATIONS —Cont'd
Articles of incorporation —Cont'd
Amendment —Cont'd
Directors, §29-308.05.
Directors and shareholders,
§29-308.03.
Reorganization, upon, §29-308.08.
Voting groups, §29-308.04.
Contents, §29-302.02.
Effect of, §29-308.09.
Restatement, §29-308.07.
Attorneys at law.
Organizations as client, ProfCond Rule
1.13.
Authorized shares, §29-304.01.
Bail and recognizance.
Corporate sureties, CrimPro Rule 116.
Benefit corporations.
Election by business corporation to
become benefit corporation,
§29-1301.05.
Generally, §§29-1301.01 to 29-1304.01.
See BENEFIT CORPORATIONS.
Board of directors, §§29-306.01 to
29-306.11. See within this heading,
"Directors."
Bylaws.
Amendment.
Directors, §29-308.20.
Election, §29-308.22.
Quorum, §29-308.21.
Voting, §29-308.21.
Shareholders, §29-308.20.
Contents, §29-302.06.
Emergency bylaws, §29-302.07.
Certificates of shares, §29-304.25.
Certified capital companies,
§§31-5231 to 31-5239.
See CERTIFIED CAPITAL
COMPANIES.
Commencement of existence,
§29-302.03.
Conflicting interest transactions,
§§29-306.70 to 29-306.73.
Definitions, §29-306.70.
Directors' actions, §29-306.72.
Judicial action, §29-306.71.
Shareholders' actions, §29-306.73.
Contracts.
Powers, §29-303.02.
Custodians.
Judicial dissolution, §§29-312.21,
29-312.22.
Shareholders.
Appointment, §29-305.70.
Deeds, §42-602.

CORPORATIONS —Cont'd
Definitions, §§28-2901, 29-301.02.
Derivative actions, §§29-305.50 to
    29-305.57, CivPro Rule 23.1.
  Attorneys' fees, §29-305.56.
  Costs, §29-305.56.
  Definitions, §29-305.50.
  Demand, §29-305.52.
  Discontinuances, §29-305.55.
  Dismissal of actions, §29-305.54.
  Expenses, §29-305.56.
  Foreign corporations, §29-305.57.
  Settlement or compromise, §29-305.55.
  Standing, §29-305.51.
  Stays, §29-305.53.
Directors, §§29-306.01 to 29-306.80.
  Action without meeting, §29-306.21.
  Articles of incorporation.
    Amendment, §§29-308.03, 29-308.05.
  Board, §§29-306.01 to 29-306.11.
  Business opportunities, §29-306.80.
  Bylaws.
    Amendment, §29-308.20.
  Classes of shares.
    Determination, §29-304.02.
  Committees, §29-306.25.
  Compensation, §29-306.11.
  Conflicting interest transactions,
    §§29-306.70 to 29-306.73.
    Definitions, §29-306.70.
    Directors' actions, §29-306.72.
    Judicial action, §29-306.71.
    Shareholders' actions, §29-306.73.
  Election, §29-306.03.
    Bylaws.
      Amendment, §29-308.22.
    Classes of shareholders, §29-306.04.
    Voting by shareholders, §29-305.28.
  Indemnification, §§29-306.50 to
    29-306.59. See within this
    heading, "Indemnification."
  Insurance, §29-306.57.
  Liability, §29-306.31.
    Unlawful distributions, §29-306.32.
  Meetings, §§29-306.20 to 29-306.25.
    See within this heading,
    "Meetings of directors."
  Number of, §29-306.03.
  Powers, §29-306.01.
  Qualifications, §29-306.02.
  Qualified director, §29-301.21.
  Records.
    Inspection, §29-313.05.
  Removal of.
    Judicial proceedings, §29-306.09.
    Shareholders, §29-306.08.

CORPORATIONS —Cont'd
Directors —Cont'd
  Requirements, §29-306.01.
  Resignation of, §29-306.07.
  Standards of conduct, §29-306.30.
  Terms of office, §29-306.05.
    Staggered terms, §29-306.06.
  Vacancies in office, §29-306.10.
  Voluntary dissolution, §§29-312.01,
    29-312.02.
  Duties, §29-312.09.
  Voting, §29-306.24.
    Bylaws.
      Amendment, §29-308.22.
Disclosure statements, filing, CivPro
    Rule 7.1, USDistCt LCrR 44.6,
    USDistCt LCvR 7.1.
Disposition of assets.
  Shareholder approval, §29-310.02.
  Not required, §29-310.01.
Dissolution, §§29-312.01 to 29-312.40.
  Deposit of assets with mayor,
    §29-312.40.
  Judicial dissolution, §§29-312.20 to
    29-312.24. See within this
    heading, "Judicial dissolution."
  Voluntary dissolution, §§29-312.01 to
    29-312.09. See within this
    heading, "Voluntary dissolution."
Distributions, §29-304.60.
  Unlawful distributions.
    Liability, §29-306.32.
Domestication, §§29-307.01 to
    29-307.06.
  Abandonment, §29-307.06.
  Approval, §29-307.02.
  Articles of domestication, §29-307.03.
  Authorization, §29-307.01.
  Effect of, §29-307.05.
  Plans, §§29-307.01, 29-307.02.
  Surrender of charter, §29-307.04.
Duration of, §29-303.02.
E-commerce companies.
  Qualified social electronic commerce
    companies tax abatements,
    §§47-1818.01 to 47-1818.08.
Emergency bylaws, §29-302.07.
Emergency powers, §29-303.03.
Fiduciary security transfers.
  General provisions, §§28-2901 to
    28-2909.
  See FIDUCIARY SECURITY
    TRANSFERS.
Filing.
  Generally, §§29-102.01 to 29-102.13.
  See BUSINESS ORGANIZATIONS.

CORPORATIONS —Cont'd
Financial statements, §29-313.07.
Foreign corporations.
See FOREIGN CORPORATIONS.
Foreign entities.
Generally, §§29-105.01 to 29-105.12.
See BUSINESS ORGANIZATIONS.
Fractional shares, §29-304.04.
Gifts.
Powers, §29-303.02.
Income tax, §§47-1805.02, 47-1807.01
to 47-1807.12.
E-commerce companies.
Qualified social electronic commerce
companies tax abatements,
§§47-1818.01 to 47-1818.08.
Incorporation, §§29-302.01 to
29-302.07.
Incorporators, §29-302.01.
Voluntary dissolution, §29-312.01.
Indemnification, §§29-306.50 to
29-306.59.
Advancements, §29-306.53.
Court-ordered, §29-306.54.
Authorization, §29-306.55.
Court-ordered indemnification,
§29-306.54.
Definitions, §29-306.50.
Determinations, §29-306.55.
Exclusivity of provisions, §29-306.59.
Mandatory indemnification,
§29-306.52.
Officers, §29-306.56.
Permissible indemnification,
§29-306.51.
Variation of, §29-306.58.
Insurance, §29-306.57.
Investments.
Powers, §29-303.02.
Investment securities, §§28:8-101 to
28:8-601.
See INVESTMENT SECURITIES.
Judicial appraisal of shares.
Costs, §29-311.31.
Judicial proceedings, §29-311.30.
Judicial dissolution, §§29-312.20 to
29-312.24.
Custodians, §§29-312.21, 29-312.22.
Decree of dissolution, §29-312.23.
Election to purchase in lieu of,
§29-312.24.
Grounds, §29-312.20.
Injunctions, §29-312.21.
Procedures, §29-312.21.
Receivers, §§29-312.21, 29-312.22.
Landlord and tenant court.
Attorneys appearing in representative
capacity, LandlordTenant Rule 9.

CORPORATIONS —Cont'd
Liability.
Directors, §29-306.31.
Unlawful distributions, §29-306.32.
Preincorporation transactions,
§29-302.04.
Shares, §29-304.22.
Loans.
Powers, §29-303.02.
Mediation.
Attendance requirements, USDistCt
LCvR 84.8.
Meetings of directors, §§29-306.20 to
29-306.25.
Action without meeting, §29-306.21.
Notice, §29-306.22.
Waiver, §29-306.23.
Quorum, §29-306.24.
Bylaws.
Amendment, §29-308.22.
Regular meetings, §29-306.20.
Special meetings, §29-306.20.
Voting, §29-306.24.
Bylaws.
Amendment, §29-308.22.
Meetings of shareholders, §§29-305.01
to 29-305.09.
Action without meeting, §29-305.04.
Annual meetings, §29-305.01.
Remote participation, §29-305.09.
Conduct of, §29-305.08.
Court-ordered meetings, §29-305.03.
Notice, §29-305.05.
Waiver, §29-305.06.
Record date, §29-305.07.
Special meetings, §29-305.02.
Remote participation, §29-305.09.
Mergers and share exchanges,
§§29-309.01 to 29-309.08.
Abandonment, §29-309.08.
Approval, §29-309.04.
Articles of merger or share exchange,
§29-309.06.
Authorization, §§29-309.02, 29-309.03.
Definitions, §29-309.01.
Effect of, §29-309.07.
Mergers, §29-309.02.
Parents and subsidiaries, §29-309.05.
Plans, §§29-309.02, 29-309.03.
Share exchanges, §§29-309.02,
29-309.03.
Mortgages and deeds of trust.
Powers, §29-303.02.
Names.
Generally, §§29-103.01 to 29-103.04.
See BUSINESS ORGANIZATIONS.

CORPORATIONS —Cont'd
Names —Cont'd
Requirements, §29-103.02.
Nominees.
Voting by shareholders, §29-305.23.
Nonprofit corporations, §§29-401.01
to 29-401.03.
See NONPROFIT CORPORATIONS.
Notice, §29-301.03.
Appraisal and payment for shares,
§29-311.12.
Demand, §29-311.11.
Right to, §29-311.10.
Common address, §29-301.22.
Consent to electronic notice,
§29-301.03.
Meetings of directors, §29-306.22.
Waiver, §29-306.23.
Meetings of shareholders, §29-305.05.
Waiver, §29-305.06.
Methods of sending notice and other
communications, §29-301.03.
Records.
Exception, §29-313.06.
Officers, §§29-306.40 to 29-306.44.
Contract rights, §29-306.44.
Indemnification, §29-306.56.
Insurance, §29-306.57.
Powers, §29-306.41.
Removal of, §29-306.43.
Requirements, §29-306.40.
Resignation of, §29-306.43.
Standards of conduct, §29-306.42.
Organization, §29-302.05.
Outstanding shares, §29-304.03.
Pensions and retirement.
Powers, §29-303.02.
Perpetual existence, §29-303.02.
Personal property.
Powers, §29-303.02.
Pledges.
Powers, §29-303.02.
Powers, §29-303.02.
Emergency powers, §29-303.03.
Ultra vires, §29-303.04.
Preemptive rights, §29-304.40.
Preincorporation transactions.
Liability, §29-302.04.
Professional corporations, §§29-501
to 29-516.
See PROFESSIONAL
CORPORATIONS.
Purposes of, §29-303.01.
Qualified director, §29-301.21.
Real property.
Powers, §29-303.02.

CORPORATIONS —Cont'd
Receivers.
Judicial dissolution, §§29-312.21,
29-312.22.
Shareholders.
Appointment, §29-305.70.
Records, §§29-313.01 to 29-313.07.
Financial statements, §29-313.07.
Inspection.
Court-ordered, §29-313.04.
Directors, §29-313.05.
Scope of right, §29-313.03.
Shareholders, §29-313.02.
Notice.
Exception, §29-313.06.
Retention, §29-313.01.
Reference to extrinsic facts,
§29-301.04.
Registered agents.
Generally, §§29-104.01 to 29-104.14.
See BUSINESS ORGANIZATIONS.
Reports, §29-313.07.
Scrip, §29-304.04.
Seals.
Powers, §29-303.02.
Service of process.
Domestic relations actions, DomRel
Rule 4.
Summons, CivPro Rule 4.
Share dividends, §29-304.23.
Share exchanges, §§29-309.01 to
29-309.08. See within this heading,
"Mergers and share exchanges."
Shareholders, §§29-305.01 to
29-305.70.
Action without meeting, §29-305.04.
Articles of incorporation.
Amendment, §29-308.03.
Bylaws.
Amendment, §29-308.20.
Conflicting interest transactions.
Shareholders' actions, §29-306.73.
Custodians.
Appointment, §29-305.70.
Derivative actions, §§29-305.50 to
29-305.57. See within this
heading, "Derivative actions."
Directors.
Removal of, §29-306.08.
Distributions, §29-304.60.
Financial statements, §29-313.07.
Meetings, §§29-305.01 to 29-305.09.
See within this heading,
"Meetings of shareholders."
Number of, §29-301.20.
Preemptive rights, §29-304.40.

CORPORATIONS —Cont'd
Shareholders —Cont'd
Receivers.
Appointment, §29-305.70.
Records.
Inspection, §29-313.02.
Voluntary dissolution, §29-312.02.
Voting, §§29-305.20 to 29-305.29. See within this heading, "Voting by shareholders."
Voting agreements, §§29-305.41, 29-305.42.
Voting trusts, §29-305.40.
Share options, §29-304.24.
Shares, §§29-304.01 to 29-304.41.
Acquisition of own shares, §29-304.41.
Appraisal and payment, §§29-311.01 to 29-311.50. See within this heading, "Appraisal and payment for shares."
Authorized shares, §29-304.01.
Certificates, §29-304.25.
Classes of, §29-304.01.
Determination, §29-304.02.
Expenses, §29-304.28.
Fractional shares, §29-304.04.
Issuance, §29-304.21.
Articles of incorporation.
Amendment before, §29-308.02.
Liability, §29-304.22.
Outstanding shares, §29-304.03.
Preemptive rights, §29-304.40.
Restrictions on transfer, §29-304.27.
Scrip, §29-304.04.
Share dividends, §29-304.23.
Share options, §29-304.24.
Subscription for shares, §29-304.20.
Voting entitlement of shares, §29-305.21.
Without certificates, §29-304.26.
Short title, §29-301.01.
Small claims court.
Attorneys appearing in representative capacity, SmallClaims Rule 9.
Stock and stockholders.
Fiduciary security transfers, §§28-2901 to 28-2909.
See FIDUCIARY SECURITY TRANSFERS.
Investment securities, §§28:8-101 to 28:8-601.
See INVESTMENT SECURITIES.
Transfer of securities by fiduciaries, §§28-2901 to 28-2909.
See FIDUCIARY SECURITY TRANSFERS.

CORPORATIONS —Cont'd
Transitional provisions.
Existing domestic corporations, §29-314.01.
Registered foreign corporations, §29-314.02.
Ultra vires, §29-303.04.
Universities and colleges.
See UNIVERSITIES AND COLLEGES.
Unlawful distributions.
Liability, §29-306.32.
Voluntary dissolution, §§29-312.01 to 29-312.09.
Articles of dissolution, §29-312.03.
Court proceedings on claims, §29-312.08.
Directors, §29-312.01.
Duties, §29-312.09.
Directors and shareholders, §29-312.02.
Effect of, §29-312.05.
Incorporators, §29-312.01.
Known claims, §29-312.06.
Other claims, §29-312.07.
Revocation, §29-312.04.
Voting agreements, §§29-305.41, 29-305.42.
Voting by directors, §29-306.24.
Bylaws.
Amendment, §29-308.22.
Voting by shareholders, §§29-305.20 to 29-305.29.
Acceptance of votes, §29-305.24.
Articles of incorporation.
Amendment.
Voting groups, §29-308.04.
Cumulative voting, §29-305.28.
Directors.
Election, §29-305.28.
Inspectors, §29-305.29.
Multiple voting groups, §29-305.26.
Nominees, §29-305.23.
Proxy arrangements, §29-305.22.
Quorum, §29-305.25.
Alteration of, §29-305.27.
Requirements, §29-305.25.
Alteration of, §29-305.27.
Shareholders' list, §29-305.20.
Single voting groups, §29-305.26.
Voting entitlement of shares, §29-305.21.
Voting trusts, §29-305.40.

CORRECTIONAL OFFICERS.
Deadly force.
Correctional treatment facilities, §24-261.02.

CORRECTIONS, DEPARTMENT OF.
Appropriations, §24-211.05.
Awards for meritorious service,
§§5-901 to 5-904.
Central detention facility.
Inspections, §24-211.02.
Maximum number of inmates,
§24-201.71.
Processing and release of prisoners,
§24-211.02a.
Continuance of prior regulations,
contracts, and appropriations,
§§24-211.04, 24-211.05.
Contracts, §24-211.05.
Delivery of inmate health care,
§24-1401.
Corrections information council,
§24-101.01.
Criminal background investigations
of employees, §24-211.41.
Department of corrections inmate
and returning citizen assistance
grant, §24-211.71.
Department of corrections
reimbursement fund, §1-325.21.
Drug and alcohol testing for
employees, §§24-211.21 to
24-211.24.
Breathalyzer deemed positive,
§24-211.23.
Contractor to perform, §24-211.23.
Definitions, §24-211.21.
Employees tested, §24-211.22.
Grounds for termination, §24-211.24.
Implied consent by employees
operating motor vehicles,
§24-211.23.
Methodology, §24-211.23.
Notice of confirmed positive urinalysis,
§24-211.23.
Notice of implementation of program,
§24-211.22.
Policy issued in advance, §24-211.24.
Program for all employees, §24-211.24.
Random testing.
Employees subject to, §24-211.22.
On-site testing, §24-211.23.
Turning results over to law
enforcement.
Employee consent required,
§24-211.24.
Establishment of, §24-211.01.
Federal control of prison system,
§§24-101 to 24-142.
See PRISON SYSTEM, FEDERAL
CONTROL.

CORRECTIONS, DEPARTMENT OF
—Cont'd
Hospitals.
Correction department's use of D.C.
General Hospital's campus,
§24-211.61.
Inmate and returning citizen
assistance, §24-211.71.
Issuance of rules, §24-211.02.
Juvenile offenders.
BOOT CAMP, §§24-921 to 24-932.
See BOOT CAMP.
General provisions, §§24-901 to
24-907.
See JUVENILE OFFENDERS.
Meritorious service awards, §§5-901
to 5-904.
Powers and duties, §24-211.02.
Prison industries.
General provisions, §§24-231.01 to
24-231.15.
See PRISON INDUSTRIES.
Prison personnel subject to,
§24-201.11.
Prisons and prisoners.
General provisions, §§24-201.02 to
24-261.05.
See PRISONS AND PRISONERS.
Reimbursement fund, §1-325.21.
Transfers from (abolished) Board of
Public Welfare, §24-211.03.
United States prisoners, §§24-201.10,
24-211.06.

CORRUPT INFLUENCE.
Athletic contests, in connection
with, §22-1713.
Bribery, §§22-704 to 22-713.
See BRIBERY.
Elections, §1-1001.14.
Public officers and employees,
§22-704.

CORRUPTION OF BLOOD.
Constitution of the United States.
Attainder of treason not to work, US
Const Art III §3.

COSMETICS.
Drug manufacture and distribution
licensure exception for, §48-715.

COSMETOLOGISTS.
Board of barber and cosmetology,
§§47-2853.06 to 47-2853.10.
Business licenses, §§47-2809, 47-2810,
47-2853.81 to 47-2853.83.
Eligibility, §47-2853.82.

COSMETOLOGISTS —Cont'd
Business licenses —Cont'd
Representations prohibited,
§47-2853.83.
Scope of practice, §47-2853.81.

COST BENEFIT ANALYSES.
Procurement practices.
Training for contracting manager or
contracting officer performing,
§2-381.43.

COST-OF-LIVING ADJUSTMENTS.
**Disability compensation for public
officers and employees,** §1-623.41.
**Police and firefighters retirement
and disability,** §§5-718, 5-719.

COSTS.
Address of party changed.
Failure to provide notice, CivPro Rule
10-I.
Adoption proceedings, Adoption Rule
54.
Failure to attend deposition, Adoption
Rule 30.
Anti-SLAPP actions, §16-5504.
Appeals, D.C. courts, DCCtApp Rule
39.
Fee schedule, DCCtApp Rule 50-Fee
Schedule.
Frivolous appeals, DCCtApp Rule 38.
Appeals, federal cases, FRAP 39,
USCtApp Rule 39.
Appendix, production of, FRAP 30(b).
Bill of costs inserted in mandate or
added later, FRAP 39(d).
Briefs and appendices, FRAP 39(c).
District courts, appeals from
judgments and orders.
Taxable costs, FRAP 39(e).
Frivolous appeals, FRAP 38.
Production of appendix to briefs,
FRAP 30(b).
Record on appeal, FRAP 10(b), 39.
Sanctions against attorneys including
unnecessary material in
appendices to briefs, FRAP 30(b).
Transcript, payment, FRAP 10(b).
Arbitration, Arbitration Rules IV, X.
Attachment of wages.
Noncompliance by judgment creditor,
CivPro Rule 69-II.
Attorneys at law.
Advancing money to clients, ProfCond
Rule 1.8.
Discipline or disability proceedings,
DCBar Rule XI.

COSTS —Cont'd
Attorneys' fees.
See ATTORNEYS' FEES.
**Bicyclist, assault or battery by
motorist.**
Right of civil action for damages,
§50-1621.
Bill of costs, CivPro Form CA 121.
Bond premiums, CivPro Rule 54-I.
**Child abuse and neglect
proceedings,** NeglectProc Rule 47.
Child custody proceedings.
Enforcement of foreign custody
determinations, §§16-4603.12,
16-4603.17.
Class actions.
Cost of notice, CivPro Rule 23.
**Continuing care retirement
communities.**
Civil liability of providers for
violations, recovery, §44-151.14.
Corporations.
Derivative actions, §29-305.56.
Judicial appraisal of shares,
§29-311.31.
**Court fees for superior court
actions,** CivPro Rule 202.
Delinquent minors, JuvProc Rule 113.
Depositions, JuvProc Rule 15.
Discovery, CivPro Rule 26, USDistCt
LCvR 26.2.
Compelling discovery, CivPro Rule 37.
Domestic relations actions, DomRel
Rule 37.
Depositions, CivPro Rules 30, 54-I.
Adoption proceedings, Adoption Rule
30.
Criminal procedure, CrimPro Rule
15.
Delinquent minors, JuvProc Rule 15.
Domestic relations actions, DomRel
Rule 30.
Dismissal of actions, CivPro Rule 41.
**District of Columbia housing
authority.**
Exemption from court fees and costs,
§6-208.
Domestic relations actions, DomRel
Rule 54.
Compelling discovery, DomRel Rule
37.
Failure to attend deposition, DomRel
Rule 30.
Offer of judgment, DomRel Rule 68.
Waiver of costs, fees or security,
DomRel Rule 54-II.

COSTS —Cont'd

E-mail, spam, §28-5003.

Expert witnesses.

Child abuse and neglect proceedings, NeglectProc Rule 47.

Discovery of facts known and opinions, CivPro Rule 26.

Fees generally.

See FEES.

Fiduciary accounts.

Court costs for District real estate, CivPro Rule 305.

Foreclosure rescue services and transactions.

Private right of action, §42-2434.

Frivolous, dilatory, etc., actions, CivPro Rule 11.

Appeals, DCCtApp Rule 38.

Domestic relations actions, DomRel Rule 11.

Garnishment.

Post-judgment garnishment in aid of execution, §16-542.

Trial on traverse of garnishee's answers, §16-553.

Prejudgment garnishment.

Favorable judgment for garnishee, §16-522.

Gas station violations.

Franchise purchase rights, §36-304.14.

Human trafficking, §22-1840.

Indigent persons.

In forma pauperis proceedings.

See IN FORMA PAUPERIS PROCEEDINGS.

Interpreters, CivPro Rule 43.

Adoption proceedings, Adoption Rule 43.

Domestic relations actions, DomRel Rule 43.

Interstate family support.

Filing fees and other costs, prohibition, §46-353.13.

Intervention proceedings, Probate Rule 310.

Landlord and tenant court, LandlordTenant Rule 15.

Service of process, LandlordTenant Rule 4.

Licenses.

Business licenses.

See BUSINESS LICENSES.

Generally.

See LICENSES.

COSTS —Cont'd

Masters, USDistCt LCvR 53.1.

Deposit for expenses, CivPro Rule 53-II.

Domestic relations actions, DomRel Rule 53.

Medical malpractice.

Mediation, §16-2822.

Mortgages and deeds of trusts.

Foreclosure rescue services and transactions.

Private right of action, §42-2434.

Nonprofit corporations.

Derivative actions, §29-411.07.

Prescription drugs, excessive pricing, §28-4555.

Pretrial conference violations, CivPro Rule 16.

Adoption proceedings, Adoption Rule 16.

Domestic relations actions, DomRel Rule 16-I.

Tax proceedings, Tax Rule 13.

Prevailing party allowed costs, CivPro Rule 54, USDistCt LCvR 54.1.

Probate proceedings.

Death between January 1, 1981 and June 30, 1995, Probate Rule 125.

Death on or after July 1, 1995, Probate Form 1, Probate Rule 425.

Guardians, conservators, trustees, etc., involved.

Costs for accounts, Probate Rule 206.

Expenses of guardian ad litem, Probate Rule 209.

Procurement practices.

Action for violations by qui tam plaintiff, §2-381.03.

Action seeking relief from retaliatory actions, §2-381.04.

Prompt payment.

Private contractor and subcontractor prompt payment act.

Failure to make prompt payments, §27-133.

Subcontractors, payments to, §27-135.

Small claims court, SmallClaims Rule 15.

Attorneys' fees, SmallClaims Rule 19.

Spam deterrence, §28-5003.

Summary judgment motions, CivPro Rule 56.

COSTS —Cont'd
Tax proceedings, Tax Rule 13.
Telephone number of party changed.
Failure to provide notice, CivPro Rule 10-I.
Transcripts on appeal, CivPro Rule 54-I.
Waiver of costs, fees, or security, CivPro Rule 54-II.
Appeals.
Motion for waiver of prepayment of costs and fees, DcCtApp Form 7a.
Application to proceed without prepayment of costs, fees or security, CivPro Form CA 106A.
Domestic relations actions, DomRel Rule 54-II.
Workers' compensation.
Frivolous proceedings, §32-1528.
Workplace fraud.
Private right of action to enforce provisions, §32-1331.09.

COTTAGE FOOD BUSINESSES.
Conditions for sale of products, §7-742.02.
Definitions, §7-742.01.

COUNCIL.
Access to justice initiative, §1-204.13.
Acts and resolutions, §§1-204.12, 1-206.02.
Definition of terms, §1-301.47.
Enacting and resolving clauses, §1-301.46.
Numbering of sections, §1-301.46.
Advisory neighborhood commission.
Assisting, §1-309.12.
Alcoholic beverages.
Issuance of rules and regulations regarding, §25-211.
Bills and resolutions.
Fiscal impact statements, §1-301.47a.
Boxing and wrestling commission.
Authority to establish, §3-603.
Budget adopted by, §1-204.46.
Fiscal impact statements, §1-301.47a.
Budget submissions by, §47-318.01b.
Business license requirements, §§47-2842, 47-2844.
Chairperson, §1-204.11.
Challenge to statutes, rule, regulation, program or policy.
Attorney general report to council regarding, §1-301.89a.
Charitable solicitations.
Powers and duties regarding, §44-1702.

COUNCIL —Cont'd
Community development program.
Annual preparation and submission to, §6-1002.
Compensation, determination.
Mayor and council compensation advisory committee, §§1-611.51 to 1-611.57.
See MAYOR AND COUNCIL COMPENSATION ADVISORY COMMITTEE.
Construction and interpretation of act.
Acts and resolutions of council, §1-301.45.
Construction codes.
Approval of, §6-1402.
Conversions to condominiums.
Allowed to prohibit, §42-2051.
Crimes and offenses.
Electronic communications.
Disclosure, §1-301.44a.
Definitions, §1-301.41.
District of Columbia corporation.
Officers of, §1-103.
Elections, §1-1001.08.
Authority regarding, §1-207.52.
Designation by member of employee to solicit, accept, receive contributions while on leave, §1-1171.02.
Electronic communications.
Access for performance official duties, §1-301.44c.
Disclosure, §1-301.44a.
Management of, §1-301.44b.
Emergency preparedness plan transmitted to, §7-2303.
Energy plan submitted to, §8-1779.01.
Establishment of, §1-204.01.
Expenditures.
Approval of, §1-333.10.
Expulsion, §1-204.01.
Fines and civil penalties.
Electronic communications.
Disclosure, §1-301.44a.
Fire protection.
Approval required for changes in, §5-401.
Fiscal impact statements, §1-301.47a.
Fish and game laws.
Authority regarding, §22-4328.
Gross sales tax, §47-2024.
Home purchase assistance fund, §§42-2604, 42-2605.
Housing finance agency.
Delegation of powers to, §42-2702.06.

COUNCIL —Cont'd
Housing finance agency —Cont'd
Review and approval of proposals,
§42-2702.07.
Immunity, legislative, §1-301.42.
**Independent branch of District of
Columbia government, as,**
§1-301.44.
Information technology, §1-301.44b.
Interest.
Changing rates of interest.
Council authorized to change,
§28-3309.
Exemption of certain loans.
Council authorized to exempt,
§28-3309.
Interest rates.
Council authorized to change or
exempt, §28-3309.
Investigation of municipal matters,
§5-1021.
Investigations.
Obstruction of, §1-301.43.
Power to investigate, §1-204.13.
Legal publication of documents,
§§2-551 to 2-562.
See ADMINISTRATIVE
PROCEDURE.
**Mayor and council compensation
advisory committee,** §§1-611.51 to
1-611.57.
See MAYOR AND COUNCIL
COMPENSATION ADVISORY
COMMITTEE.
Membership, §1-204.01.
Metropolitan police.
Powers regarding, §5-127.01.
Motor vehicle financing.
Powers regarding, §50-605.
Motor vehicle registration and,
§50-1501.05.
Naming and renaming powers,
§1-301.01.
Oaths and affirmations.
Authority to administer, §§1-301.22,
5-1021.
Power to administer, §1-204.13.
Obstruction of proceedings,
§1-301.43.
Official correspondence, §§2-701 to
2-710.
Organization and structure,
§1-204.01.
Out-of-District property.
Issuance of rules and regulations
regarding, §10-509.02.

COUNCIL —Cont'd
Personnel, §1-204.01.
Police and firefighters.
Authority to regulate wages of,
§§5-545.04, 5-545.06a.
Political contributions.
Designation by member of employee to
solicit, accept, receive
contributions while on leave,
§1-1171.02.
Powers and duties generally,
§§1-204.04, 1-301.01.
Public lands.
Exchanges, §§10-903, 10-904.
Public spaces.
Naming, §9-204.01.
Qualifications for holding office,
§1-204.02.
Quorum, §1-204.12.
Receptions for eminent persons,
§1-333.09.
Regulations.
Power to make and modify.
Building regulations, §1-303.04.
Dogs, keeping and leashing of,
§1-303.41.
Elevators, construction, repair, and
operation of, §1-303.44.
Firearms, explosives and weapons,
§1-303.43.
Police regulations, §1-303.01.
Protection of life, health, and
property, §1-303.03.
Publication, §1-303.02.
**Resocialization furlough program
report,** §24-251.07.
Seal, §1-301.48.
Streets and alleys.
Closing, §9-202.01.
Naming, §9-204.01.
Subpoenas.
Power to issue, §1-204.13.
**Tax increment financing
development project.**
Approval of, §2-1217.04.
Traffic ticket adjudication report to,
§50-2301.08.
**University of the District of
Columbia,** §38-1204.06.
Wages and salaries, §§1-204.03,
1-611.09.
**Washington metropolitan area
transit authority compact.**
Authority to amend, §§9-1107.02,
9-1107.03.
Water supply and waterworks.
Powers regarding, §34-2401.03.

COUNCIL —Cont'd
Workplace safety rules and regulations.
Power to make, §32-804.
Youth advisory council, §§2-1561 to 2-1564, 2-1565.01 to 2-1565.06.
Youth behavioral health epidemiology reports.
Citation of provisions, §2-1517.01.
Definitions, §2-1517.02.

COUNCIL TECHNOLOGY PROJECTS FUND, §1-325.201.

COUNSELING.
Addiction counselors, §§3-1208.51 to 3-1208.54.
Domestic violence counselors.
Child abuse and neglect.
Counselors to report, §4-1321.02.
Confidential communication between victim and counselor.
Disclosure prohibited, exceptions, §14-310.
Confidential information acquired in professional capacity.
Disclosure prohibited without consent of client, §14-307.
Defined, §14-310.
Employment.
See EMPLOYMENT AGENCIES.
Professional counseling.
Board of professional counseling, §3-1202.13.
Definition of practice of professional counseling, §3-1201.02.
Health occupations boards.
General provisions, §§3-1201.01 to 3-1213.01.
See HEALTH OCCUPATIONS BOARDS.
Health occupations licensure, registration or certification, §§3-1205.01 to 3-1205.24.
See HEALTH OCCUPATIONS LICENSURE, REGISTRATION OR CERTIFICATION.
Licenses, §§3-1207.10 to 3-1207.12.
Titles and terms prohibited as misrepresentation without license to practice, §3-1210.03.
School counselors, §38-2807.

COUNTERCLAIMS, §§13-501 to 13-505.
Administrator, action by or against, §13-505.
Assignment, effect of, §13-502.

COUNTERCLAIMS —Cont'd
Class actions, CivPro Rule 23-I, USDistCt LCvR 23.1.
Default judgments applicable, CivPro Rule 55.
Domestic relations actions, DomRel Rule 55.
Dismissal of actions, CivPro Rule 41.
Domestic relations actions, DomRel Rule 13.
Executor, action by or against, §13-505.
Interpleader, CivPro Form CA 21.
Joinder of claims and remedies, CivPro Rule 18.
Landlord and tenant court, LandlordTenant Rule 5.
Pleadings generally.
See PLEADINGS.
Principal and sureties, action against, §13-503.
Setoff, by way of, §13-501.
Small claims court, §16-3904.
Third party practice, CivPro Rule 14.
Trustee, action by, §13-504.

COUNTERFEITING.
Commercial counterfeiting, §§22-901, 22-902.
Drivers' licenses.
Seizure of suspect documents, §50-1401.04.
Trademark counterfeiting, §22-902.

COURIER SERVICES.
Commercial bicycle operators, §§50-1631 to 50-1634.

COURSE OF DEALING.
Sale of goods, UCC.
Implied warranties, §28:2-314.

COURT APPOINTED COUNSEL.
Generally.
See RIGHT TO COUNSEL.

COURT-APPOINTED SPECIAL ADVOCATES, §§16-2371, 16-2372.

COURT COSTS.
See COSTS.

COURT DUTY.
Police and firefighters, §5-1304.

COURTHOUSES.
Attorneys at law.
Soliciting clients near courthouse, ProfCond Rule 7.1.

COURT OF APPEALS.
Absent, disabled, or disqualified judges, replacing, §11-706.

COURT OF APPEALS —Cont'd

Administrative orders and decisions, jurisdiction over, §11-722.

Administrative procedure, appeals from, §§17-303, 17-304.

Admission to bar, DCCtApp Rule 46.

False statements, etc., ProfCond Rule 8.1.

Appeals heard by, §§17-301 to 17-307.

Appellate procedure.

See APPEALS, D.C. COURTS.

Application for allowance of appeals, §17-301.

Assignment of judges, §§11-705, 11-707.

Calendaring of cases, DCCtApp Rule 33.

Certification of questions of law, jurisdiction over, §11-723.

Clerk's duties, §11-708, DCCtApp Rule 45.

Granting procedural motions, DCCtApp Rule 27.

Notice of appeal, DCCtApp Rule 3.

Transmission of record on appeal, DCCtApp Rule 11.

Composition, §11-702.

Conducting proceedings outside District.

Emergency authority, §11-710.

Conferences, judicial, §11-744.

Contempt powers, §11-741.

Continuation, §§1-207.18, 11-701.

Definitions, DCCtApp Rule 1.

Delay of proceedings.

Emergency authority to toll or delay proceedings, §11-745.

Denial of application for appeal, §17-301.

Divisions, §11-705.

Emergency authority to toll or delay proceedings, §11-745.

Employees not to practice law, DCCtApp Rule 50.

En banc hearings.

Petitions for hearing or rehearing, DCCtApp Rule 35.

Expedited review.

Adoption or termination of parental rights orders, §11-721.

Family court order.

Expedited review.

Adoption or termination of parental rights orders, §11-721.

Federal Rules of Civil Procedure and Federal Rules of Criminal Procedure, use of, §11-743.

COURT OF APPEALS —Cont'd

Hearings, §11-705.

Hearings for application for appeal, §17-301.

Judges, §§11-702 to 11-709.

Chief judge.

Designation, terms, §1-204.31.

Mandatory retirement, §1-204.31.

Nomination and appointment, §1-204.33.

Reappointment, §1-204.33.

Removal, suspension, involuntary retirement, §1-204.32.

Term, §1-204.31.

Judicial Conference of the District of Columbia, DCCtApp Rule 50.

Judicial power invested in, §§1-204.31, 11-101.

Jurisdiction, §§1-204.31, 11-721 to 11-723.

Limitation of actions, §17-307.

Mandate of the court, DCCtApp Rule 41.

Oaths and affirmations.

Judges' oaths, §11-704.

Power of court to administer, §11-742.

Opinions of court, DCCtApp Rule 36.

Permissible actions on appeal, §17-306.

Petition for rehearing by division, DCCtApp Rule 40.

Quorum, §11-706.

Record on appeal, §17-302.

Regulation of appeals by, §17-302.

Reimbursement for expenses of, §47-206.

Reports of judges, §11-709.

Scope of review by, §17-305.

Seal, §11-701, DCCtApp Rule 2.

Secretaries, §11-708.

Status of, §11-102.

Superior court.

Application for allowance of appeals from, §17-301.

Assignment of judges to and from, §§11-705, 11-707.

Orders and judgments, jurisdiction over, §11-721.

Toll of proceedings.

Emergency authority to toll or delay proceedings, §11-745.

Unauthorized practice of law committee, DCCtApp Rule 49.

Wages and salaries of judges, §11-703.

COURT REGISTRY INVESTMENT SYSTEM.
United States District Court, USDistCt LCvR 67.1.

COURT REPORTERS.
Admissibility of report or transcript, CivPro Rule 80.
  Adoption proceedings, Adoption Rule 201.
  Domestic relations actions, DomRel Rule 201.
Appeals, D.C. courts.
  Duty of court reporter, DCCtApp Rule 10.
Appeals, federal cases.
  Payment for cost of transcript, FRAP 10(b).
  Transcripts' preparation and filing, FRAP 11(b).
Arbitration hearings, Arbitration Rule IX.
Crime victims' compensation.
  Appeal of determination, VictComp Rule 20.
Criminal proceedings, CrimPro Rule 36-I.
Family division of superior court, FamDiv Rule N.

COURTS.
Administration, §§11-1701 to 11-1704.
Appeals court, §§11-701 to 11-745, 17-301 to 17-307.
  See COURT OF APPEALS.
Auditor-master, §11-1724.
Autopsies performed under court order, §5-1414.
Bad checks.
  Payments to courts, liability for non-payment, §11-1748.
Budgets and budget estimates, §11-1743.
Certification of copies of papers or documents filed in, §11-1746.
Checks.
  Authority to accept certain types of payments, §11-1748.
Clerks, §11-1721.
  Court of appeals, §11-708.
  Register of wills, §11-2103.
  Superior court, §11-910.
Commitment of persons with mental illness ordered by, §§21-541 to 21-551.

COURTS —Cont'd
Constitution of the United States.
  Congress.
    Power to constitute tribunals inferior to supreme court, US Const Art I §8.
  Inferior courts, US Const Art III §1.
  Judges.
    Compensation, US Const Art III §1.
    Tenure, US Const Art III §1.
  Restriction of judicial power, US Const Amd 11.
Continuation of court system, §1-207.18.
  Court of appeals, §11-701.
  Superior court, §11-901.
Contracts for procurement of severable services, §11-1742a.
Court of appeals.
  See COURT OF APPEALS.
Court orders and proceedings.
  Certified copies of, §34-611.
Credit cards.
  Authority to accept certain types of payments, §11-1748.
Delegation of powers, §11-1747.
District court, §§11-501 to 11-521.
  See UNITED STATES DISTRICT COURT FOR THE DISTRICT OF COLUMBIA.
Electronic funds transfer.
  Authority to accept certain types of payments, §11-1748.
Employees, §§11-1721 to 11-1733.
  Appointment of nonjudicial personnel, §11-1725.
  Auditor-master, §11-1724.
  Clerks, §11-1721.
    Court of appeals, §11-708.
    Register of wills, §11-2103.
    Superior court, §11-910.
  Debts and erroneous payments made to employees, collection by executive officer, §11-1733.
  Fiscal officer, §11-1723.
  Marshal of District, service provided by, §11-1729.
  Practice of law, USDistCt LCrR 44.4, USDistCt LCvR 83.5.
  Recruitment, §11-1728.
  Release of information relating to pending criminal proceedings, USDistCt LCrR 57.7.
  Reporters, §11-1727.

COURTS —Cont'd
Employees —Cont'd
Reports, §§11-1730, 11-1731.
Social Services, Director of, §11-1722.
Training, §11-1728.
Wages and salaries, §11-1726.
Executive officer, §§11-1703, 11-1704,
11-1741 to 11-1748.
Authority to accept certain forms of
payment, §11-1748.
Certification of copies, §11-1746.
Collection of debts and erroneous
payments made to employees,
§11-1733.
Contracts for procurement of severable
services, §11-1742a.
Delegation of authority, §11-1747.
Disbursing and payroll officer,
§11-1742.
Duties, §11-1741.
Information and liaison services,
§11-1744.
Management of buildings and space,
§11-1742.
Multiyear leasing agreements,
§11-1742a.
Procurement of equipment, supplies,
services and uniforms, §11-1742.
Reports and records, §11-1745.
False personation before, §§22-1403,
22-1404.
Fiscal officer, §11-1723.
Home Rule act.
Continuation of court system,
§1-207.18.
District of Columbia courts' budget,
§1-204.45.
Judiciary, §§1-204.31 to 1-204.34.
**Hospitalization of persons with
mental illness ordered by.**
See HOSPITALIZATION OF
PERSONS WITH MENTAL
ILLNESS.
**Information and statistics,
compiling and publishing,**
§11-1744.
Interpreters, §§2-1901 to 2-1912.01.
See INTERPRETERS.
Judicial power of District, §§1-204.31
to 1-204.34, 11-101.
Jury selection, §§11-1901 to 11-1918.
See JURY SELECTION.
**Lease agreements for
accommodation of courts.**
Multiyear leasing agreements,
§11-1742a.

COURTS —Cont'd
Levy court ordinances, §45-402.
Magistrate judges, §11-1732.
Family court and domestic violence
unit.
Special rules, §11-1732a.
Marshal of District, §11-1729.
**Mental health disclosures, court-
related,** §§7-1204.01 to 7-1204.05.
See MENTAL HEALTH
DISCLOSURES.
Military courts.
General provisions, §§49-501 to
49-509.
See COURTS-MARTIAL.
News media privilege, §§16-4701 to
16-4704.
Operations and organization,
§11-1741.
Payments.
Authority to accept certain types of
payments, §11-1748.
Powers and duties, §§11-1741 to
11-1748.
**Probate court powers regarding
trust, mortgage and title
corporations,** §26-1334.
**Protection force, wages and salaries
of,** §47-201.
**Public education and information
programs,** §11-1744.
Records, §§11-1745, 11-1746.
Register of wills, §§11-2101 to 11-2106.
See WILLS.
Reporters, §11-1727.
Reports, §§11-1730, 11-1731, 11-1745.
Service of process rules, §13-331.
**Sex offender registration, duties
regarding,** §5-1304.
Small claims court, §§11-1301 to
11-1323.
See SMALL CLAIMS COURT.
Social Services, Director of, §11-1722.
Superior court.
See SUPERIOR COURT.

COURTS-MARTIAL, §§49-501 to
49-509.
Compulsory attendance before,
§49-507.
Constitution of, §49-504.
General courts-martial, §49-503.
Inquiry, courts of, §49-502.
Jurisdiction of, §§49-504, 49-506.
Members of courts, prosecution of,
§49-505.
Sentences, execution of, §49-508.

COURTS-MARTIAL —Cont'd
Types of, §49-501.
Warrants for arrest, §49-509.
Witnesses, §49-507.

COVENANTS.
Encumbered land, against having,
§42-607.
Environmental covenants, §§8-671.01
to 8-671.14.
See ENVIRONMENTAL
COVENANTS.
Further assurances, for, §42-608.
Quiet enjoyment, §42-606.
Use of term, §42-603.

COVER.
Sales under UCC.
Buyer's procurement of substitute
goods, §28:2-712.

CPA'S.
Board of accountancy, §§47-2853.06 to
47-2853.10.
Business licenses, §§47-2853.41 to
47-2853.49.

CPR.
Non-resuscitation procedures for
EMS.
Comfort care orders, §§7-651.01 to
7-651.16.
See EMERGENCY MEDICAL
SERVICES.

CRACK HOUSES.
Drug-related evictions.
Action for possession of rental unit,
§42-3602.

CREDIT.
Alcoholic beverages.
Credit sales, §§25-731 to 25-736.
Bills of credit.
Constitutional provisions, US Const
Art I §10.
Consumer credit, §§28-3801 to
28-3819.
See CONSUMER CREDIT.
Consumer protection, §§28-3801 to
28-3819.
See CONSUMER PROTECTION.
Financial literacy council,
§§38-731.01 to 38-731.05.
Gross sales tax, expenses of
collecting, §47-2004.
Income taxes.
See INCOME TAXES.
Inheritance and estate taxes,
§47-3702.

CREDIT —Cont'd
Letters of credit.
Commercial code, §§28:5-101 to
28:5-120.
See COMMERCIAL CODE.
Real property taxes, §47-872.
Reinsurance, §§31-501 to 31-503.
Revolving credit accounts, §§28-3701,
28-3702.
Secured transactions.
Commercial code, §§28:9-101 to
28:9-809.
See COMMERCIAL CODE.
Toll telecommunication service tax,
§47-3907.

CREDIT CARDS.
Address and phone number requests
prohibited, §47-3153.
Consumer credit, §§28-3801 to
28-3819.
See CONSUMER CREDIT.
Consumer protection, §§28-3801 to
28-3819.
See CONSUMER PROTECTION.
Courts.
Authority to accept certain types of
payments, §11-1748.
Fraud and deceit, §22-3223.
Information used for payment by
check, §47-3152.
Information used for payment by
credit card, §47-3153.
Revolving credit accounts, §§28-3701,
28-3702.
Service charge, §28-3702.
Taxes, payment, §47-4402.

CREDIT LIFE, ACCIDENT AND
HEALTH INSURANCE, §§31-5101
to 31-5112.
Administrative review or judicial
review of orders and actions,
§31-5112.
Amount of credit life insurance.
Limitation, §31-5104.
Amount of indemnity payable by
credit accident and health
insurance.
Limitation, §31-5104.
Applicability, §31-5101.
Casualty and other insurance rates.
General provisions.
See INSURANCE.
Claims, §31-5109.
Definitions, §31-5102.
Filing requirements, §31-5107.

CREDIT LIFE, ACCIDENT AND HEALTH INSURANCE —Cont'd
Forms authorized to be issued, §31-5103.
Filing required, §31-5107.
Policies or certificates.
Filing required, §31-5107.
Required, contents, applications, notice, §31-5106.
Rates.
Approval, §31-5107.
Casualty and other insurance rates.
General provisions, §§31-2701 to 31-2714.
See INSURANCE.
Refunds, credits, charges, §31-5108.
Short title, §31-5101.
Term of coverage, §31-5105.
Title of provisions, §31-5101.
Violations, §31-5111.

CREDIT LINE DEEDS OF TRUST, §§42-2301 to 42-2303.
Consumer protection, §28-3904.

CREDIT MEMOS.
Unclaimed property, §41-114.

CREDITORS.
Assignments for benefit of creditors, §§28-2101 to 28-2110.
See ASSIGNMENTS FOR BENEFIT OF CREDITORS.
Attachment.
See ATTACHMENT.
Consumer credit, §§28-3801 to 28-3819.
See CONSUMER CREDIT.
Consumer credit service organizations.
General provisions, §§28-4601 to 28-4608.
See CONSUMER CREDIT SERVICE ORGANIZATIONS.
Consumer protection, §§28-3801 to 28-3819.
See CONSUMER PROTECTION.
Debtors and creditors generally.
See DEBTORS AND CREDITORS.
Fraudulent transfers.
General provisions, §§28-3101 to 28-3111.
See FRAUDULENT TRANSFERS.
Garnishment.
See GARNISHMENT.
Installment loans.
See INSTALLMENT LOANS.
Limited partnerships.
Transferable interests.
Rights, §29-707.03.

CREDITORS —Cont'd
Money lenders, §§26-901 to 26-912.
See MONEY LENDERS.
Mortgage lenders and brokers, §§26-1101 to 26-1121.
See MORTGAGE LENDERS AND BROKERS.
Mortgages and deeds of trust.
General provisions, §§42-804 to 42-820.
See MORTGAGES AND DEEDS OF TRUST.
Motor vehicle financing.
Installment sales, §§50-601 to 50-610.
See MOTOR VEHICLE FINANCING.
Nonprofit corporations.
Rights and obligations of members, §29-404.14.
Secured transactions.
Commercial code, §§28:9-101 to 28:9-809.
See COMMERCIAL CODE.
Statutory trusts.
No rights in property, §29-1203.05.
Trusts and trustees.
Uniform trust code.
Creditor's claims, §19-1305.01.
Overdue distributions, §19-1305.06.
Personal obligations of trustee, §19-1305.07.
Settlor, claims against, §19-1305.05.

CREDIT UNIONS, §§26-501 to 26-504.
Approval of, §26-502.
Bylaws, §26-503.
Federal unions, conversion of District unions into, §§26-501 to 26-503.
Fees, §26-503.
Liquidation of existing loans, §26-503.
Mortgages and deeds of trust.
General provisions, §§42-804 to 42-820.
See MORTGAGES AND DEEDS OF TRUST.
Repeal of District act, §26-504.
Unclaimed property.
General provisions, §§41-101 to 41-142.
See UNCLAIMED PROPERTY.

CREMATION.
Building and maintaining a crematory, §43-124.

CREMATION —Cont'd

Crime victims' compensation, VictComp Rule 25.

Disposal of ashes, §43-128.

Indigent persons, §7-178.

CRIME-RELATED NUISANCE ABATEMENT, §§42-3101 to 42-3114.

Action to abate, §42-3102.

Bonds, surety.
Injunctions, not required for, §42-3107.
Violation of orders, §42-3112.

Burden of proof, §42-3108.

Complaints, §42-3103.

Contempt proceedings, §42-3112.

Conviction not required to demonstrate existence of nuisance, §42-3106.

Damages, §42-3111.

Definitions, §42-3101.

Evidence.
Burden of proof, §42-3108.
Conviction not required to demonstrate existence of nuisance, §42-3108.
Reputation, §42-3109.
Witnesses, §42-3105.

Fund, §42-3111.01.

Injunctions.
Bonds, surety, §42-3107.
Permanent, §42-3110.
Preliminary, §42-3104.
Violating, §42-3112.

Law enforcement records.
Authority to obtain, §42-3102.01.

Remedies, §§42-3110, 42-3111, 42-3114.

Reputation as evidence of nuisance, §42-3109.

Statutory construction, §42-3113.

Violating injunction or abatement order, §42-3112.

Witnesses, §42-3105.

CRIMES AND OFFENSES.

Abandoned and unlawfully parked vehicles.
Purchaser of salvaged vehicle, abandoning vehicle, §50-2421.10.

Abuse, neglect and financial exploitation of vulnerable adults and elderly persons, §§22-931 to 22-938.

Accessories after the fact, §22-1806.

Adult protective services, §7-1912.

Advising criminal offenses, §22-1805.

Affrays, §22-1301.

CRIMES AND OFFENSES —Cont'd

Aged persons.
Enhanced penalties for certain offenses against, §22-3601.

Aggravated assault, §22-404.01.

Aiding and abetting.
See AIDING AND ABETTING.

Air pollution, §8-101.05d.

Airspace, rental of, §10-1121.10.

Alcoholic beverage licenses.
Influencing application process, §25-434.

Alcoholic beverages.
Enforcement generally, §§25-801 to 25-805.
Open container law, §25-1001.
On-premises retailer knowingly allowing customer to exit with an open container, §25-113.
Public intoxication, §25-1001.
Unlawful importation, §25-772.

Animal fighting, §22-1009.
Penalty, §22-1006.01.
Urging dogs to fight or create disorder, §22-1310.

Animals, cruelty to.
General provisions, §§22-1001 to 22-1013.
See CRUELTY TO ANIMALS.

Animals, release from entity having custody and control, §8-1831.01.

Anti-terrorism act of 2002, §§22-3151 to 22-3156.

"Anything of value" defined, §22-1802.

Appropriations for National Institute of Justice, §22-4201.

Arson, §§22-301 to 22-303.

Asbestos contractors, §8-111.09.

Assault, §§22-401 to 22-407.
See ASSAULT AND BATTERY.

Assembly, unlawful, §22-1321.

Athlete agents, §47-2887.14.

Attempts to commit crime, §22-1803.

Attorney general.
Forfeiture of position, §1-301.84.

Attorneys at law, committed by, §11-2503.

Banks and financial institutions.
Violation of final order of commissioner, §26-551.21.

Bias-related crimes, §§22-3701 to 22-3704.

Bicycle identifying numbers.
Tampering with or removing, §22-3234.

CRIMES AND OFFENSES —Cont'd

Bigamy, §22-501.

Blindness in newborns, prevention of, §7-804.

Blocking passage.
Public or private building, enclosure, road or sidewalk, §22-1307.

Boating under the influence, §§50-2206.31 to 50-2206.36.
Refusal or failure to submit to chemical testing, §50-1912.

Bodily harm, threat to do, §22-407.

Boiler inspections.
Regulatory violations, §2-114.

Bonfires.
Kindling, §22-1313.

Bribery, §§22-704 to 22-713.
See BRIBERY.

Bridges.
Obstructing bridges connecting District of Columbia and Virginia, §22-1323.

Building code requirements for fire prevention, §6-703.06.

Burglary, §22-801.

Burning crosses, §22-3312.02.

Cable television.
Cable theft, §34-1264.02.

Cancer prevention and monitoring, §7-304.

Capitol grounds, §10-503.18.

Carjacking, §22-2803.

Certificate of good standing.
Person previously convicted of crime, §24-1304.

Child abuse and neglect.
See CHILD ABUSE AND NEGLECT.

Child care facilities, §7-2046.

Child fatality report.
Failure to make, §4-1371.14.

Child fatality review committee investigations.
Unlawful disclosure of information, §4-1371.11.

Children, violent crimes committed against.
Enhanced penalties, §22-3611.

Collection of taxes.
Divulging information about returns, §47-4406.

Comfort care orders.
Non-resuscitation procedures for EMS.
Forgery, concealment, withholding or placement causing resuscitation to be withheld and death results, §7-651.12.

CRIMES AND OFFENSES —Cont'd

Commercial counterfeiting, §§22-901, 22-902.

Communicable diseases, §7-140.

Community residence facilities.
Failure to report certain deaths, §5-1406.

Compulsory school attendance, §§38-203, 38-206.

Conniving at criminal offenses, §22-1805.

Conspiracy to commit crime, §22-1805a.

Construction codes, §6-1406.

Continuing care retirement communities, §44-151.15.

Contraband on prison grounds, §§22-2603.01 to 22-2603.04.

Contributing to the delinquency of a minor, §22-811.

Controlled substances, §§48-901.02 to 48-931.02.
See CONTROLLED SUBSTANCES.

Corrupt influence.
Athletic contests, in connection with, §22-1713.
Bribery, §§22-704 to 22-713.
See BRIBERY.
Elections, §1-1001.14.
Public officers and employees, §22-704.

Council.
Electronic communications.
Disclosure, §1-301.44a.

Crime victims' compensation.
Victims of violent crime, §§4-501 to 4-518, VictComp Rules 1 to 41.
See CRIME VICTIMS' COMPENSATION.

Crime victims' rights, §§23-1901 to 23-1911.
See VICTIMS OF CRIME.

Criminal abuse, neglect and financial exploitation of vulnerable adults and elderly persons, §§22-931 to 22-938.

Criminal background checks.
Child or youth services providers.
Disclosing confidential information, §4-1501.10.

Criminal justice coordinating council, §§22-4231 to 22-4244.

Criminal procedure.
See CRIMINAL PROCEDURE.

Cross-burning, §22-3312.02.

Cruelty to animals.
General provisions, §§22-1001 to 22-1013.
See CRUELTY TO ANIMALS.

CRIMES AND OFFENSES —Cont'd

Cruelty to children, §§22-1101, 22-1102.

Dead bodies.
Failure to report certain deaths, §5-1406.

Delinquent minors.
See DELINQUENT MINORS.

Detention by force, §22-3301.

Disfigurement, malicious, §22-406.

Disorderly conduct, §22-1321.

District of Columbia or similar designation, prohibition of, §§22-3401 to 22-3403.

District, offenses committed outside of, §22-1808.

DNA collection.
Qualifying offenses, §22-4151.

DNA testing.
Pre-conviction and post-conviction, §§22-4131 to 22-4135.

Dogs.
Allowing fierce or dangerous dogs to go at large, §22-1311.
Urging dogs to fight or create disorder, §22-1310.

Do not resuscitate procedures.
Comfort care orders.
Falsification, forgery, other actions causing resuscitation to be withheld causing death, §7-651.12.

Drug addict rehabilitation patients not deemed to be criminals, §24-711.

Drug manufacture and distribution licensure, §48-711.

Drug offenders.
Non-violent drug offenders, treatment instead of jail.
See DRUG ABUSE.

Drug offenses.
Controlled substances, §§48-901.02 to 48-931.02.
See CONTROLLED SUBSTANCES.

Due process, threatening, injuring, intimidating, or interfering with persons in order to deprive, §§22-3312.02 to 22-3312.04.

Elections.
Circulators of nominating petitions, §1-1001.08.

Embalmers.
Failure to report certain deaths, §5-1406.

Emblems of certain types, displaying, §22-3312.02.

CRIMES AND OFFENSES —Cont'd

Emergency medical services, §7-2341.24.
Failure to notify medical examiner of certain deaths, §5-1406.

Employees retirement program management, §1-739.

Extortion.
See EXTORTION.

False fire alarms, §22-1319.

False personation, §§22-1402 to 22-1406.

False report to police, §5-117.05.

Family court, transferred to, §16-2307.

Federal benefit payments under District programs, misappropriation of, §1-815.04.

Felonies.
Firearms.
Unlawful possession of firearms, §22-4503.
Third felony conviction, §22-1804a.

Fighting or baiting fowl or animals, §22-1009.
Penalty, §22-1006.01.
Urging dogs to fight or create disorder, §22-1310.

Fines for criminal offenses, §§22-3571.01, 22-3571.02.

Fire alarms, false, §22-1319.

Firearms, §§22-4501 to 22-4517.
See FIREARMS.

Fire balloons, §22-1317.

Fish and game.
General provisions, §§22-4328 to 22-4333.
See FISH AND GAME.

Flood hazards, §6-506.

Food, sale of unwholesome.
See FOOD.

Footways in public grounds, driving or riding on, §22-1318.

Forced entry, §22-3301.

Forgery.
See FORGERY.

Fraud and deceit, §§22-1502 to 22-1514, 22-3221 to 22-3225.14.
See FRAUD AND DECEIT.

Freedom of information violations.
Arbitrary or capricious violations, §2-537.

Funeral directors.
Failure to report certain deaths, §5-1406.
Regulatory violations, §3-417.

CRIMES AND OFFENSES —Cont'd
Gambling.
General provisions, §§22-1701 to
22-1718.
See GAMBLING.
Games played in street, §22-1308.
Gangs, §22-951.
Graffiti, §22-3312.04.
Harbor and ports, §§22-4402 to
22-4404.
Hate crimes, §§22-3701 to 22-3704.
See HATE CRIMES.
Health care facilities, §44-509.
Failure to notify medical examiner of
certain deaths, §5-1406.
Interference with or obstruction of,
§§22-1314.01, 22-1314.02.
Health data privacy.
Unlawful use or disclosure of
information, §7-246.
**Health occupations licensure,
registration or certification,**
§3-1210.07.
Historic landmarks, §6-1110.
Hoax weapons of mass destruction,
§22-1319.
Defined, §22-3152.
Homicide.
See HOMICIDE.
Hoods, wearing, §22-3312.03.
**Hospitalization of persons with
mental illness,** §21-591.
Hospitals.
Failure to notify medical examiner of
certain deaths, §5-1406.
Human trafficking, §§22-1831 to
22-1843.
See HUMAN TRAFFICKING.
Identity theft, §§22-3227.01 to
22-3227.08.
Implements of crime, possession of,
§22-2501.
Incest, §22-1901.
Incitement.
Criminal offenses, §22-1805.
Prostitution, §22-2705.
Riots, §22-1322.
Indecency.
See OBSCENITY.
Injury to property.
General provisions, §§22-3312.01 to
22-3322.
See VANDALISM.
Insanitary buildings, §6-916.
**Insignia of police and emergency
medical services departments.**
Unauthorized use, §22-1409.

CRIMES AND OFFENSES —Cont'd
Insurance fraud, §§22-3225.01 to
22-3225.15.
See INSURANCE FRAUD.
**Intellectual disabilities, persons
with.**
Commitment proceedings, §21-1115.
**Interception of oral or wire
communications,** §§23-541 to
23-556.
See INTERCEPTION OF ORAL OR
WIRE COMMUNICATIONS.
Jails.
Failure to report certain deaths,
§5-1406.
Jury selection.
Confidentiality violations, §16-5103.
Juvenile offenders, §§24-901 to
24-941.
See JUVENILE OFFENDERS.
Juvenile records.
Unlawful disclosure, §16-2336.
Kidnapping, §§22-1810, 22-2001.
Language, profane or indecent,
§22-1321.
Law enforcement officers.
Failure to notify medical examiner of
certain deaths, §5-1406.
**Lead-hazard prevention and
elimination,** §8-231.16.
Lead poisoning.
Childhood lead poisoning screening
and reporting, failure to comply,
§7-871.05.
Lie detector tests, §32-903.
Living wills, §§7-627, 7-628.
Lottery tickets.
Forged, altered, or counterfeit,
§3-1333.
Malice.
See MALICE.
Manslaughter, §22-2105.
Marijuana.
Consumption in public space or
impairment, §§48-911.01.
Medical marijuana, §7-1671.08.
Possession decriminalization,
§§48-1201 to 48-1213.
See MARIJUANA.
Masks, wearing, §22-3312.03.
Mattresses, §8-505.
Mayhem, §22-406.
Assault with intent to commit,
§22-402.
Medicaid fraud, §§4-801 to 4-805.
Medical examiners.
Failure to notify of deaths, §5-1406.

CRIMES AND OFFENSES —Cont'd
Medical marijuana, §7-1671.08.
Mental health disclosures,
§7-1207.02.
Mentally illness, hospitalization of
persons with, §21-591.
Metropolitan police records,
§§5-113.02 to 5-113.04.
Metrorail station managers.
Enhanced penalties, §22-3751.01.
Offenses for which penalties apply,
§22-3752.
Minors.
Contributing to the delinquency of,
§22-811.
Juvenile offenders, §§24-901 to 24-941.
See JUVENILE OFFENDERS.
Violent crimes committed against.
Enhanced penalties, §22-3611.
Motor vehicle identification
numbers.
Altering or removing, §22-3233.
Motor vehicle registration.
Unlawful acts, §50-1501.04.
Motor vehicles.
Unlawful entry, §22-1341.
Murder.
See MURDER.
National Institute of Justice
Appropriations, §22-4201.
Nazi swastikas, displaying,
§22-3312.02.
Non-covered offenses, penalties for,
§22-1807.
Nurses.
Failure to notify medical examiner of
certain deaths, §5-1406.
Nursing homes.
Failure to report certain deaths,
§5-1406.
Obscenity.
General provisions, §§22-2201 to
22-3104.
See OBSCENITY.
Obstructing justice, §§22-721 to
22-723.
Occupational safety and health,
§32-1121.
Official correspondence violations,
§§2-708, 2-709.
Official mail.
Unauthorized use, §2-708.
Unintentional violations, §2-709.
Oral communications, interception
of, §§23-541 to 23-556.
See INTERCEPTION OF ORAL OR
WIRE COMMUNICATIONS.

CRIMES AND OFFENSES —Cont'd
Panhandling, §§22-2301 to 22-2306.
Parachutes, §22-1317.
Parentage proceedings.
Disclosure of information, §16-2348.
Peace, disturbing, §§22-1301 to
22-1323.
Perjury, §§22-2402 to 22-2405.
See PERJURY.
Physicians and surgeons.
Failure to notify medical examiner of
certain deaths, §5-1406.
Poison, assault with intent to,
§22-401.
Polygraphs, §32-903.
Possession of implements of crime,
§22-2501.
Prison breach, §22-2601.
Prisons and prisoners.
Failure to report certain deaths,
§5-1406.
Privies, §8-604.
Profane language, §22-1321.
Prosecution of, §22-1809.
Prostitution.
General provisions, §§22-2701 to
22-2725.
See PROSTITUTION.
Protection of innocence act,
§§22-4131 to 22-4135.
Public assistance, §§4-218.01 to
4-218.06.
Public officers and employees.
Threatening, stalking, assaulting, etc.,
§22-851.
Public or private building,
enclosure, road or sidewalk.
Blocking passage, §22-1307.
Real estate brokers and
salespersons, §42-1708.
Religious symbols, defacing or
burning, §22-3312.02.
Rental of public space, §10-1104.04.
Repeal of statutory crime.
Common law crime not reinstated,
§45-401.
Research animals, release,
§8-1831.01.
Restraints of trade, §28-4506.
Riot or incitement to riot, §22-1322.
Robbery, §§22-2801 to 22-2803.
See ROBBERY.
Salvage, flood and junk vehicles.
Unlawful acts, §50-1331.08.
Second conviction of criminal
offense.
Gambling premises, keeping, §22-1705.

CRIMES AND OFFENSES —Cont'd

Second conviction of criminal offense —Cont'd

General provisions, §22-1804.

Senior citizen victims, enhanced penalties for, §22-3601.

Sexual offenses.

General provisions, §§22-3001 to 22-3024.

See SEXUAL OFFENSES.

Sexual psychopaths, §§22-3803 to 22-3811.

See SEXUAL PSYCHOPATHS.

Shoplifting, §§22-3213, 27-101 to 27-106.

See SHOPLIFTING.

Small and certified business enterprise development and assistance.

Falsification of certificates of registration, §2-218.64.

Smoking, §7-1706.

Stalking, §§22-3131 to 22-3135.

Stolen property, §§22-3231, 22-3232.

Stones, throwing, §22-1309.

Street, playing games in, §22-1308.

Tampering with physical evidence, §22-723.

Taxation.

Attempt to evade or defeat tax, §47-4101.

Attempt to interfere with administration of revenue laws, §47-4107.

Failure to collect or pay over, §47-4102.

Failure to pay tax ,make return, keep records or supply information, §47-4103.

Fraud and false statements, §47-4106.

Fraudulent statements or failure to make statements to employee, §47-4104.

Fraudulent withholding information or failure to supply information to employer, §47-4105.

Taxicab drivers.

Crimes against, enhanced penalties, §22-3751.

Applicability, §22-3752.

Fleeing from public vehicle inspection officer in public vehicle for hire, §50-301.34.

Telephone solicitation fraud, §22-3226.10.

Termination of parental rights.

Unlawful disclosures, §16-2364.

CRIMES AND OFFENSES —Cont'd

Terrorism.

Anti-terrorism act of 2002, §§22-3151 to 22-3156.

Theft.

Burglary, §22-801.

Cable television.

Cable theft, §34-1264.02.

Criminal trespass, via, §§22-3301 to 22-3311.

See VANDALISM.

General provisions, §§22-3201 to 22-3216.

See THEFT.

Identity theft, §§22-3227.01 to 22-3227.08.

Robbery, §§22-2801 to 22-2803.

See ROBBERY.

Third felony conviction, §22-1804a.

Threats.

See THREATS.

Throwing stones or other missiles, §22-1309.

Tobacco.

Minors, sales to, §7-1721.02.

Prohibited sellers, §7-1721.06.

Self-service displays, §7-1721.04.

Toilets, §8-604.

Towing services.

Rules governing business of furnishing.

Violation, §47-2850.

Trademark counterfeiting, §22-902.

Transit operators.

Enhanced penalties for offenses committed against, §22-3751.01.

Notice of enhanced penalties, §35-261.

Offenses for which penalties apply, §22-3752.

Trespass.

General provisions, §§22-3301 to 22-3311.

See VANDALISM.

Unlawful assembly, §22-1321.

Unlawful discharge of a firearm, §22-4503.01.

Utility service theft, §§22-3218.01 to 22-3218.04.

Vandalism.

See VANDALISM.

Vehicle identification numbers.

Altering or removing, §22-3233.

Vending machines, breaking and entering, §22-601.

Vital records, §7-225.

CRIMES AND OFFENSES —Cont'd
Voyeurism, §22-3531.
Washington National Airport, §9-705.
Water pollution, §8-103.16.
Weapons.
General provisions, §§22-4501 to
22-4517.
See WEAPONS.
Weapons of mass destruction.
False reports, §22-1319.
Manufacture or possession, §22-3154.
Use, dissemination or detonation,
§22-3155.
**Wire communications, interception
of,** §§23-541 to 23-556.
See INTERCEPTION OF ORAL OR
WIRE COMMUNICATIONS.
Witnesses with criminal records,
§14-305.
Youth residential facilities, §7-2108.

CRIME VICTIMS' COMPENSATION,
§§4-501 to 4-518, VictComp Rules 1
to 41.
Administration of program, §4-503,
VictComp Rule 3.
Advisory commission, §4-504,
VictComp Rule 5.
Amount of award, §§4-507, 4-508.
Appeal of determination.
Board review of determinations,
VictComp Rule 20.
Judicial review, VictComp Rule 21.
Modification of determination,
VictComp Rule 19.
Request for reconsideration, VictComp
Rule 18.
Appeals board, §4-505, VictComp Rule
6.
Meetings closed to public, VictComp
Rule 4.
Review of determination, VictComp
Rule 20.
Applications.
Contents, VictComp Rule 9.
Processing, VictComp Rule 10.
Submitting, VictComp Rule 8.
Appropriations, §4-518.
Assessments, §4-516.
Attorneys' fees, VictComp Rule 39.
Availability of funds, VictComp Rule
38.
Awards of, §§4-507, 4-510.
Claims.
Verification, VictComp Rules 11 to 16.
Cleaning crime scene, VictComp Rule
26.

CRIME VICTIMS' COMPENSATION
—Cont'd
Clothing replacement, VictComp Rule
27.
Computation of award, VictComp
Rule 23.
Confidentiality, VictComp Rule 4.
Definitions, §4-501.
Denial of claims, VictComp Rule 16.
Disqualification for, §4-508.
Domestic violence victims.
Shelter and transitional housing for
victims of domestic violence fund,
§4-521.
Earnings lost, VictComp Rule 28.
Request for employment information,
VictComp Rule 14.
Eligibility for, §4-506, VictComp Rule
7.
Emergency awards, §4-510, VictComp
Rule 37.
Establishment of program, §4-502.
False claims, VictComp Rule 41.
Filing claims, procedures for, §4-512.
Food on temporary basis, VictComp
Rule 29.
Fraud and deceit, §4-513.
Funds.
Crime victims assistance fund,
§4-515.01.
Crime victims compensation fund,
§4-515.
**Funeral, burial, or cremation
expenses,** VictComp Rule 25.
Request for information, VictComp
Rule 15.
Housing on temporary basis,
VictComp Rule 29.
**Law enforcement officers'
responsibilities regarding,**
§4-517.
Law enforcement verification,
VictComp Rule 11.
Limitation on compensation,
VictComp Rule 22.
Medical expenses, VictComp Rule 24.
Request for information, VictComp
Rule 13.
Modification of determination,
VictComp Rule 19.
Moving expenses, VictComp Rule 34.
Notice of determination, VictComp
Rule 17.
Payment of claims, VictComp Rule 36.
Preservation of civil actions, §4-509,
VictComp Rule 40.

CRIME VICTIMS' COMPENSATION
—Cont'd
Privacy and confidentiality, §4-511.
Purpose of rules, VictComp Rule 1.
Reductions in amounts, §4-508.
Rental cars, VictComp Rule 33.
Reports, §4-514.
Restitution, VictComp Rule 40.
Scope of rules, VictComp Rule 2.
Securing residence, VictComp Rule 32.
Services provided for dependents, VictComp Rule 31.
Subrogation, §4-509, VictComp Rule 40.
Support for dependents, VictComp Rule 30.
Temporary emergency food and housing, VictComp Rule 29.
Transportation expenses, VictComp Rule 35.
Verification of claims, VictComp Rules 11 to 16.
Victims assistance, §4-517.01.
Victims of violent crimes, §§4-501 to 4-518, VictComp Rules 1 to 41.

CRIMINAL ABUSE, NEGLECT AND FINANCIAL EXPLOITATION OF VULNERABLE ADULTS AND ELDERLY PERSONS, §§22-931 to 22-938.
Criminal abuse, §22-933.
Penalties, §22-936.
Criminal negligence, §22-934.
Penalties, §22-936.
Definitions, §22-932.
Financial exploitation, §22-933.01.
Asset protection, §22-938.
Attorney general for District of Columbia.
Subpoena authority, §1-301.88e.
Civil penalties, §22-937.
Criminal penalties, §22-936.01.
Injunctive relief, §22-938.
Penalties, §22-936.
Short title, §22-931.
Treatment by spiritual means through prayer.
Exception, §22-935.
Vulnerable adult defined, §22-931.

CRIMINAL BACKGROUND CHECKS.
Certificate of good standing.
Person previously convicted of crime, §24-1304.

CRIMINAL BACKGROUND CHECKS
—Cont'd
Child and family services agency, §§4-1305.01 to 4-1305.09.
Application process, §4-1305.03.
Confidentiality of information, §4-1305.08.
Penalties for violations, §4-1305.09.
Definitions, §4-1305.01.
Failure to request, effect, §4-1305.07.
Person for which required, §4-1305.02.
Processing fees and costs, §4-1305.04.
Processing of applications, §4-1305.05.
Records, §4-1305.06.
Timing of application, §4-1305.03.
Child or youth services providers, §§4-1501.01 to 4-1501.11.
Agencies to submit positions subject to, §4-1501.06.
Assessment of information, §§4-1501.05a, 4-1501.07.
Citation of act, §4-1501.01.
Confidentiality of information, §4-1501.08.
Penalty for disclosure, §4-1501.10.
Definitions, §4-1501.02.
False information.
Prosecution for providing, §4-1501.09.
Procedure, §4-1501.05.
Records.
Authorization to obtain, §4-1501.04.
Required for certain individuals, §4-1501.03.
Rulemaking, §4-1501.11.
Title of act, §4-1501.01.
Volunteers, §4-1501.03.
Defined, §4-1501.02.
Corrections Department employees, §24-211.41.
Health care personnel, unlicensed, §§44-551 to 44-554.
Health occupations licensure, registration or certification, §3-1205.22.
Insurance, securities and banking, fingerprinting for background checks.
Confidentiality of information, §31-633.
Definitions, §31-631.
Requirement of, §31-632.
Rules, §31-634.
Labor and employment relations.
Limited liability for employers regarding criminal history of employees, §24-1351.

CRIMINAL BACKGROUND CHECKS
—Cont'd
Private vehicles-for-hire.
Operators, §50-301.29a.
Registration of operators, §50-301.29b.
Public officers and employees,
§§1-620.41 to 1-620.44.
Definitions, §1-620.41.
Implementation of provisions,
§1-620.44.
Limitations on disqualification,
§1-620.43.
Pre-employment inquiries, §1-620.42.
Recreational volunteers.
See PARKS AND RECREATION.

**CRIMINAL CODE REFORM
COMMISSION,** §§3-151 to 3-156.

CRIMINAL CONTEMPT, CrimPro
Rule 42.

Child support, failure to pay,
§46-225.02.

CRIMINAL CONVERSATION.
Abolition of action for, §16-923.

**CRIMINAL DIVISION, SUPERIOR
COURT.**
See CRIMINAL PROCEDURE.

CRIMINAL FINANCE OFFICE.
Hours of office, CrimPro Rule 56.

CRIMINAL INVESTIGATIONS.
**Freedom of information act
exemptions,** §2-534.
Records.
Preservation of crime investigation
records, §§5-113.31 to 5-113.34.

CRIMINAL JUSTICE ACT.
Plan to implement, generally,
USCtApp Appx II.
Record on appeal, FRAP 10(b).

**CRIMINAL JUSTICE
COORDINATING COUNCIL,**
§§22-4231 to 22-4244.
Administrative support, §22-4235.
Annual report, §22-4242.
Criminal justice agency.
Designation, §22-4234.
Definitions, §22-4231.
Duties, §22-4234.
Established, §22-4232.
Federal participation, §22-4241.
Annual report, §22-4242.
Appropriation for federal contribution,
§22-4243.

**CRIMINAL JUSTICE
COORDINATING COUNCIL**
—Cont'd
Federal participation —Cont'd
District of Columbia criminal justice
coordinating council defined,
§22-4244.
Membership, §22-4233.

CRIMINAL PROCEDURE.
Abandonment of prosecution,
§23-102, CrimPro Rule 48.
Acquittal, CrimPro Rule 29.
Delinquent minors, JuvProc Rule 29.
Insanity defense, §24-501.
Joinder of parties.
Discharge or acquittal of joint
defendant in order to be
witness, §23-107.
Actual innocence.
Motion to vacate conviction or grant
new trial, §22-4135.
Adult protective services, §7-1912.
Alibi of defendant, CrimPro Rule 12.1.
Aliens, §16-713.
Allocution, CrimPro Rule 32.
Anatomical gifts.
Prosecution of violations of act, §3-209.
Anti-terrorism act of 2002.
Jurisdiction and venue to prosecute,
§22-3156.
Appeals, D.C. courts.
Governmental appeals, §23-104.
Hearing commissioner's orders or
judgments, CrimPro Rule 117.
Notice of appeal.
Fee for filing, CrimPro Rule 37.
Time for filing, DCCtApp Rule 4.
Notice of right to appeal, CrimPro
Rule 32.
Hearing commissioners, CrimPro
Rule 117.
Release pending appeal, CrimPro Rule
46, DCCtApp Rule 9.
Required information, DCCtApp
Form 6.
Rules governing criminal appeals,
CrimPro Rule 37.
Sealing of arrest records, CrimPro
Rule 118.
Stay of execution, CrimPro Rule 38.
Transcript on appeal, CrimPro Rule
36-I.
Appeals, federal cases.
Appeals as of right, when taken, FRAP
4(b).

CRIMINAL PROCEDURE —Cont'd

Appeals, federal cases —Cont'd

Direct appeals of criminal cases.

Handling not delayed for consideration of postconviction proceedings in district court, USCtApp Rule 47.5.

Release in, FRAP 9, USCtApp Rule 9.

Record on appeal, preliminary motions, FRAP 11(g).

Service of process and papers.

Notice of filing of notice of appeal as of right, FRAP 3(d).

Stays pending appeal, FRAP 8(c).

Appearance of defendant before the court, CrimPro Rule 5.

Extradition, CrimPro Rule 40-I.

Application of terms, CrimPro Rule 54.

Arraignment.

See ARRAIGNMENT.

Arrests.

Generally.

See ARRESTS.

Warrants for arrest, §§23-561 to 23-563.

See ARREST WARRANTS.

Arrest without warrant, §§23-581, 23-582.

See WARRANTLESS ARRESTS.

Asbestos contractors, criminal actions against, §8-111.09.

Assignment of cases, USDistCt LCrR 57.8 to USDistCt LCrR 57.15, USDistCt LCvR 40.1 to USDistCt LCvR 40.9.

Certification of jury trial to criminal assignment commissioner, CrimPro Rule 102.

Duties and operation of Assignment Section, CrimPro Rule 101.

Felony cases, CrimPro Rule 105.

Notice, CrimPro Rule 107.

Related cases, CrimPro Rule 105, USDistCt LCrR 57.12, USDistCt LCvR 40.5.

Special assignment, CrimPro Rule 106.

Assignments.

Contracts for future salary or wages, §28-2305.

Assignment section of criminal division, CrimPro Rule 101.

Attorneys at law.

Counsel for accused, US Const Amd 6.

CRIMINAL PROCEDURE —Cont'd

Bail and recognizance.

General provisions, §§23-1321 to 23-1333, USDistCt LCrR 46.1.

See BAIL AND RECOGNIZANCE.

Bail bondsmen.

General provisions, §§23-1101 to 23-1112.

See BAIL BONDSMEN.

Biological materials, preservation of evidence, §22-4134.

Branches, sections, etc., of criminal division, CrimPro Rules 1, 100 to 104.

Child support orders.

Modification or suspension of payments.

Individual sentenced to period of imprisonment subject of order, §23-112a.

Petition, when deemed filed, §46-204.

Civil procedure.

Applicability of civil division rules, CrimPro Rule 57.

Closing arguments, CrimPro Rule 29.1.

Commencement of prosecution, §23-113.

Communications by counsel to judge, CrimPro Rule 49.

Community service, §16-712.

Competence to proceed, §§24-531.01 to 24-531.13.

See COMPETENCE TO PROCEED.

Competency to stand trial.

Mental examination of defendant, CrimPro Rule 120.

Complaints, CrimPro Rule 3.

Concurrent sentences, §23-112.

Conduct of prosecutions, §23-101.

Consecutive sentences, §23-112.

Constitution of the United States.

Cruel and unusual punishment, US Const Amd 8.

Excessive bail, US Const Amd 8.

Extradition, US Const Art IV §2.

Fugitives from justice, US Const Art IV §2.

Guarantees in criminal cases, US Const Amds 5, 6.

Public trial, US Const Amd 6.

Self-incrimination, US Const Amd 5.

Speedy trial, US Const Amd 6.

Construction of rules, CrimPro Rule 2.

CRIMINAL PROCEDURE —Cont'd
Consumer credit service organizations, §28-4607.
Contempt of court, CrimPro Rule 42.
Continuances, CrimPro Rule 111.
Jury trials at arraignment, CrimPro Rule 102.
Continuing care retirement communities.
Prosecution upon information, §44-151.15.
Contracts.
Assignment of future salary or wages, §28-2305.
Court trial, §16-705.
Crime victims' compensation.
Victims of violent crime, §§4-501 to 4-518, VictComp Rules 1 to 41.
See CRIME VICTIMS' COMPENSATION.
Crime victims' rights, §§23-1901 to 23-1911.
See VICTIMS OF CRIME.
Criminal justice coordinating council, §§22-4231 to 22-4244.
Cruelty to animals, §22-1006.
Delinquent minors, JuvProc Rules 1 to 119.
See DELINQUENT MINORS.
Depositions, CrimPro Rule 15.
Detention prior to trial.
Addicts, §23-1323.
General provisions, §23-1322.
Discovery, CrimPro Rule 16.
Depositions, CrimPro Rule 15.
Informal discovery, CrimPro Rule 16-II.
Prosecutor's responsibilities, ProfCond Rule 3.8.
Dismissal of proceedings, CrimPro Rule 48.
Assignment of felony cases and related cases, CrimPro Rule 105.
District of Columbia section of criminal division, CrimPro Rule 102.
DNA collection, §22-4151.
DNA testing.
Definitions, §22-4131.
Motion to vacate conviction or grant new trial.
Actual innocence, §22-4135.
Post-conviction testing, §22-4133.
Pre-conviction testing, §22-4132.
Preservation of DNA evidence, §22-4134.

CRIMINAL PROCEDURE —Cont'd
Effective date of rules, CrimPro Rule 59.
Enforcement of judgments, §16-706.
Evidence at trial, CrimPro Rule 26.
Notice of intent to use evidence, CrimPro Rule 12.
Theft of electric or natural gas utility service.
Presumptions and rebuttal evidence, §22-3218.03.
Exceptions to rulings or orders, CrimPro Rule 51.
Execution of judgments, §16-709.
Exhibits' custody, preservation, or destruction, CrimPro Rule 119.
Expert witnesses, CrimPro Rule 28.
Insanity defense, CrimPro Rule 12.2.
Extension of time to undertake prosecution, §23-102.
Extradition.
General provisions, §§23-701 to 23-707.
See EXTRADITION.
Failure to appear, §§23-703, 23-1327.
Federal offenders.
Release or detention, CrimPro Rule 40.
Fees, §16-703.
Fictitious name indictments.
First or second degree sexual abuse or child sexual abuse, §23-331.
Filings with the court.
Privacy protection for filings made with the court, CrimPro Rule 49.1.
Findings in trial without jury, CrimPro Rule 23.
Fines.
Disposition of, §16-707.
Imprisonment on nonpayment of, §16-706.
Wrongful conversion of, §16-708.
Firearms.
Dealers, ban on use of evidence obtained from, §7-2504.09.
Registration information, ban on use of, §7-2502.11.
Fish and game, §22-4331.
Foreign law determinations, CrimPro Rule 26.1.
Forfeitures.
Bail and recognizance, §16-709.
Wrongful conversion of, §16-708.
Fresh pursuit, §§23-901 to 23-903.
Fugitives from justice, §§23-701 to 23-707.

CRIMINAL PROCEDURE —Cont'd
Funeral directors.
Prosecutions for regulatory violations, §3-418.
Gag orders, CrimPro Rule 53.
Governmental appeals, §23-104.
Grand juries.
See GRAND JURIES.
Habeas corpus.
General provisions, §§16-1901 to 16-1909.
See HABEAS CORPUS.
Harmless error, CrimPro Rule 52.
Health care practitioners.
Prosecution for licensing violations, §3-1210.08.
Hearing commissioners, CrimPro Rule 117.
Imprisonment on nonpayment of fine, §16-706.
Incompetent criminal defendants.
Competence to proceed, §§24-531.01 to 24-531.13.
See COMPETENCE TO PROCEED.
Indictments and informations.
General provisions, §§23-301 to 23-331.
See INDICTMENTS AND INFORMATIONS.
Information, prosecution by, §16-702.
Innocence protection act of, §§22-4131 to 22-4135.
Insanity defense, CrimPro Rule 12.2.
General provisions, §§24-501 to 24-503.
Mental examination of defendant, CrimPro Rule 120.
Interception of oral or wire communications, §§23-541 to 23-556.
See INTERCEPTION OF ORAL OR WIRE COMMUNICATIONS.
Interest.
Consumer protection, §28-3313.
Interpreters, §2-1902, CrimPro Rule 28.
Interrogatories.
Criminal procedure, CrimPro Rule 15.
Intrafamily offenses.
Generally, §§16-1001 to 16-1034.
See INTRAFAMILY PROCEEDINGS.
Investigators assigned to United States Attorney, powers of, §23-109.
Issuance of rules and regulations regarding, §16-701.

CRIMINAL PROCEDURE —Cont'd
Joinder of offenses or defendants,
CrimPro Rules 8, 13.
Pretrial requests for severance, CrimPro Rule 12.
Relief from prejudicial joinder, CrimPro Rule 14.
Verdicts, CrimPro Rule 31.
Judge's disability, CrimPro Rule 25.
Judgments, CrimPro Rule 32.
Arrest of judgment, CrimPro Rule 34.
Clerical mistakes, CrimPro Rule 36.
Juror challenges, §23-105.
Jury trials, §16-705, CrimPro Rules 23, 24.
Certification to criminal assignment commissioner, CrimPro Rule 102.
Continuance at arraignment, CrimPro Rule 102.
Instructions to the jury, CrimPro Rule 30.
Polling the jury, CrimPro Rule 31.
Presence of defendant when impaneling jury, CrimPro Rule 43.
Juvenile proceedings.
See DELINQUENT MINORS.
Lesser included offenses, CrimPro Rule 31.
Limitation of actions, §23-113.
Identity theft, §22-3227.07.
Tolling, §23-113.
Media coverage of proceedings, CrimPro Rule 53.
Medicaid service provider fraud.
Prosecutions, investigations, subpoenas, §4-804.
Mental examinations of defendants, CrimPro Rule 120.
Miranda warnings.
Initial proceedings before the court. Statement by the court, CrimPro Rule 5.
Mistrials.
Comments before order, CrimPro Rule 26.3.
Witness statements not produced, CrimPro Rule 26.2.
Motions, CrimPro Rules 47, 47-I.
Acquittal, CrimPro Rule 29.
Actual innocence.
Motion to vacate conviction or grant new trial, §22-4135.
Continuances, CrimPro Rule 111.
Pretrial motions, CrimPro Rule 12.
Sealing arrest records, §§16-802 to 16-805, CrimPro Rule 118.

CRIMINAL PROCEDURE —Cont'd
Motions —Cont'd
Time for service, CrimPro Rule 45.
New trial, CrimPro Rule 33.
Actual innocence.
Motion to vacate conviction or grant new trial, §22-4135.
No controlling law, CrimPro Rule 57.
Nolle prosequi, CrimPro Rule 110.
Nonparties to case.
Application for relief by persons not parties to case, USDistCt LCrR 57.6.
Out-of-state witnesses.
Compelling attendance at hearings, §§23-1501 to 23-1504.
Certificate providing for attendance in criminal prosecutions in District, §23-1502.
Exemption from arrest, §23-1503.
Hearing on recall of out-of-state witness by state court, §23-1501.
Panhandling, §22-2305.
Parental kidnapping.
Prosecution by attorney general, §16-1025.
Phosphate cleaners, §8-107.03.
Plain error, CrimPro Rule 52.
Pleas, CrimPro Rule 11.
Hearing commissioners' power to accept plea, CrimPro Rule 117.
Presence of defendant, CrimPro Rule 43.
Withdrawal of guilty or nolo contendere pleas, CrimPro Rule 32.
Praecipe submitted by defense counsel.
Continuing effect of praecipe, CrimPro Rule 112.
Preliminary examination of defendant, CrimPro Rule 5.
Extradition, CrimPro Rule 40-I.
Hearing commissioners, CrimPro Rule 117.
Time of hearing, CrimPro Rule 110.
Presence of defendant, CrimPro Rule 43.
Presentments, CrimPro Rule 109.
Preservation of evidence.
Biological materials, §22-4134.
Presumptions.
Theft of electric or natural gas utility service.
Presumptions and rebuttal evidence, §22-3218.03.

CRIMINAL PROCEDURE —Cont'd
Pretrial motions and pleadings, CrimPro Rule 12.
Closure of pretrial proceedings, USDistCt LCrR 17.2.
Hearing commissioners, CrimPro Rule 117.
Pretrial services agency.
General provisions, §§23-1301 to 23-1309.
See PRETRIAL SERVICES AGENCY.
Previous convictions, establishing, §23-111.
Privacy protection for filings made with the court, CrimPro Rule 49.1.
Probable cause hearings, CrimPro Rule 5.
Extradition, CrimPro Rule 40-I.
Probation.
General provisions, §§24-303 to 24-306.
See PROBATION.
Professional bail bondsmen.
General provisions, §§23-1101 to 23-1112.
See BAIL BONDSMEN.
Prosecution of criminal offenses, §22-1809.
Prosecutors.
Special responsibilities, ProfCond Rule 3.8.
Prostitution, abatement of nuisance of house of, §22-2715.
Purpose of rules, CrimPro Rule 2.
Recording of court proceedings, CrimPro Rule 36-I.
Records.
Clerical mistakes, CrimPro Rule 36.
Pleas in criminal cases, CrimPro Rule 11.
Proof of official records, CrimPro Rule 27.
Release of transcripts, CrimPro Rule 36-I.
Release from custody or detention, CrimPro Rule 46, USDistCt LCrR 46.1.
Release prior to trial.
See BAIL AND RECOGNIZANCE.
Restitution or reparation, requiring, §16-711.
Enforcement, §16-711.01.
Restraint of trade, §28-4506.
Right to counsel.
See RIGHT TO COUNSEL.

CRIMINAL PROCEDURE —Cont'd
Scope of rules, CrimPro Rule 1, USDistCt LCrR 1.1.
Tax proceedings, Tax Rule 2.
Sealing arrest records, §§16-801 to 16-807, CrimPro Rule 118.
Delinquent minors, FamDiv Rule P, JuvProc Rule 118.
Searches and seizures.
See SEARCHES AND SEIZURES.
Search warrants.
General provisions, §§23-521 to 23-525.
See SEARCH WARRANTS.
Sentencing.
See SENTENCING.
Service of process, §16-703, CrimPro Rule 49.
Motions, CrimPro Rules 45, 47-I.
Summons, CrimPro Rules 4, 9.
Sex offender registration, §§22-4001 to 22-4017.
See SEX OFFENDER REGISTRATION.
Sexual psychopaths.
General provisions, §§22-3803 to 22-3811.
See SEXUAL OFFENSES.
Shoplifting, §27-103.
Speedy trial, USDistCt LCrR 45.1, US Const Amd 6.
Dismissal of criminal proceedings, CrimPro Rule 48.
Subpoenas, CrimPro Rule 17, USDistCt LCrR 17.1.
Summons, §§23-561 to 23-563, CrimPro Rule 4.
Indictments and informations, CrimPro Rule 9.
Reprosecution, CrimPro Rule 4-I.
Superior court jurisdiction, §11-923.
Taxation.
Criminal provisions, §§47-4101 to 47-4111.
Tax division of superior court, CrimPro Rule 104.
Applicability of criminal procedure rules, Tax Rule 2.
Terrorism.
Anti-terrorism act of 2002.
Jurisdiction and venue to prosecute, §22-3156.
Theft of electric or natural gas utility service.
Presumptions and rebuttal evidence, §22-3218.03.

CRIMINAL PROCEDURE —Cont'd
Title of rules, CrimPro Rule 60.
Traffic section of criminal division, CrimPro Rule 103.
Transcripts, CrimPro Rule 36-I.
Correcting errors, CrimPro Rule 36.
Trial, CrimPro Rules 23 to 31.
Trial by court or jury, §16-705.
Unanimity of verdict, CrimPro Rule 31.
United States District Court for the District of Columbia.
Criminal jurisdiction of, §11-502.
Usury.
Consumer protection, §28-3313.
Vacation of conviction.
Actual innocence.
Motion to vacate conviction or grant new trial, §22-4135.
Venue, CrimPro Rule 20.
Verdicts, CrimPro Rule 31.
Presence of defendant, CrimPro Rule 43.
Victim impact statements, CrimPro Rule 32.
Warrants.
Arrest warrants.
See ARREST WARRANTS.
Search warrants.
See SEARCH WARRANTS.
Witnesses.
Child witness testimony, corroboration of, §23-114.
Defense, for, §23-106.
Depositions, §23-108.
Joint defendant discharged or acquitted in order to be witness, §23-107.
Material witnesses, release of, §23-1326.
Out-of-state witnesses, compelling attendance, §§23-1501 to 23-1504.
Certificate providing for attendance in criminal prosecutions in District, §23-1502.
Exemption from arrest, §23-1503.
Hearing on recall of witness by state courts, §23-1501.
Right to be confronted by witnesses, US Const Amd 6.
Witness statements.
Production of statements, CrimPro Rule 26.2.
Probation modification hearings, CrimPro Rule 32.1.
Release from custody or detention, CrimPro Rule 46.

CRIMINAL PROCEDURE —Cont'd
Witness statements —Cont'd
Production of statements —Cont'd
Sentencing hearings, CrimPro Rule 32.
Wrongful conversion of fines and forfeitures, §16-708.

CRIMINAL STREET GANGS, §22-951.

CRISIS ASSISTANCE AND SERVICE PROGRAM, §4-206.02.

CRISPUS ATTUCKS DEVELOPMENT CORPORATION.
Real property tax exemptions, §47-1058.

CROPS.
Contracts.
Sale of goods.
Definition of "goods," §28:2-105.
Documents of title.
Warehouse receipts.
Storage under government bond, §28:7-201.
Secured transactions.
Description of land, §28:9-203.
Financing statement, §28:9-502.
Place of filing, §28:9-501.
Priority of security interests in, §28:9-334.
When security interest attaches, §28:9-204.
Warehouse receipts.
Storage under government bond, §28:7-201.

CROSS APPEALS.
Appeals in federal cases, FRAP 28.1.
Argument, FRAP 34(d).
Briefs, FRAP 28.1(c).
Permissive appeals, FRAP 5(b).

CROSS-BURNING, §22-3312.02.
Hate crimes, §§22-3701 to 22-3704.

CROSS-CLAIMS, CivPro Rule 13.
Appeals.
Administrative orders and decisions, DCCtApp Rule 15.
Briefs, DCCtApp Rule 28.
Class actions, CivPro Rule 23-I, USDistCt LCvR 23.1.
Default judgments applicable, CivPro Rule 55.
Dismissal of actions, CivPro Rule 41.
Joinder of claims and remedies, CivPro Rule 18.

CROSS-CLAIMS —Cont'd
Pleadings generally.
See PLEADINGS.
Third party practice, CivPro Rule 14.

CROSS-COLLATERAL.
Consumer credit, §28-3805.

CROSSWALKS.
Rights-of-way, §50-2201.28.

CRUELTY TO ANIMALS, §§22-1001 to 22-1013.
Abandonment of sick, injured, or disabled animals, §22-1011.
Arrest without warrant for, §22-1004.
Criminal penalties, §22-1001.
Disposition of fines, §22-1006.
Defined, §§22-1001, 22-1002, 22-1013.
Disabled, injured, or sick animals.
Abandonment of, §22-1012.
Neglect of, §22-1011.
Disposition of fines imposed for, §22-1006.
Fighting or baiting fowl or animals, §22-1009.
Dogs urged to fight or create disorder, §22-1310.
Keeping place for, §22-1009.
Penalty, §22-1006.01.
Horse-drawn carriages, §§8-2010, 8-2012.
Humane society.
Child abuse and neglect.
Humane officers.
Reporting requirements, §4-1321.02.
Prosecution of violations.
Duties of humane officers, §22-1006.
Taking possession of animals, §22-1004.
Impounded animals.
Food and water supplied to, §22-1007.
Relief of, §22-1008.
Intrafamily offenses.
Protective orders, §16-1005.
Neglect of sick or disabled animals, §22-1011.
Prosecution of offenders, §22-1006.
Railroad transportation of animals, §22-1003.
Reporting, §22-1002.01.
Scientific experiments, §22-1012.
Search warrants, §22-1005.
Issuance, §22-1005.
Seizure of animals.
Notice to owner, §22-1004.
Warrantless arrests.
Authorization, §22-1004.

CRUELTY TO ANIMALS —Cont'd
Washington humane society,
§44-1510.
Witness fees, §15-715.

CRUELTY TO CHILDREN.
Child abuse generally.
See CHILD ABUSE AND NEGLECT.

CULTURAL RESOURCES.
District of Columbia cultural plan,
§39-231.

CURATORS.
Security transfers, §§28-2901 to
28-2909.
See FIDUCIARY SECURITY
TRANSFERS.

CURBS AND GUTTERS.
Assessments, §§9-401.04, 9-411.01 to
9-411.04, 9-421.02.
Computation, §9-411.02.

CURFEWS.
Juvenile curfew, §§2-1541 to 2-1543.

CURTESY.
Abolishment, §19-102.

CUSTODIAL TRUSTS, §§19-1101 to
19-1120.
Acceptance of property by trustee.
Effect, §19-1104.
Administration of trust for
incapacitated beneficiary,
§19-1110.
Augmenting property, §19-1102.
Beneficial interest in property,
§19-1102.
Multiple beneficiaries, §19-1106.
Breach of duty.
Limitations of action against trustee,
§19-1116.
Checking, savings or other accounts.
Establishment, §19-1109.
Claims for relief against trustee.
Limitations of action, §19-1116.
Compensation and expenses of
trustee, §19-1114.
Creation, §19-1102.
Law governing creation, §19-1119.
Methods and forms, §19-1118.
Upon future event, §19-1103.
Custodial trustee's receipt and
acceptance.
Effect, form, §19-1104.
Death of trustee, §19-1113.
Declaration of trust under District
of Columbia's uniform custodial
trust act, §19-1118.

CUSTODIAL TRUSTS —Cont'd
Declination to serve by trustee,
§19-1113.
Definitions, §19-1101.
Determination that beneficiary
incapacitated, §19-1110.
Directions of beneficiary.
Duty of trustee to follow, §19-1107.
Distribution on termination,
§19-1117.
Durable power of attorney for
incapacitated person.
Not effective to terminate or direct
administration or distribution,
§19-1107.
Duties generally of trustee, §19-1107.
Evidence of trustee's acceptance,
§19-1104.
Exemption of third person from
liability, §19-1111.
Forms.
Custodial trustee's receipt and
acceptance, §19-1104.
Declaration of trust under District of
Columbia's uniform custodial trust
act, §19-1118.
Transfer under District of Columbia's
uniform custodial trust act,
§19-1118.
Future event.
Creation upon occurrence, §19-1103.
Generally, §19-1102.
Incapacitated beneficiaries.
Determination on incapacity, §19-1110.
Incapacity of trustee, §19-1113.
Law governing creation, §19-1119.
Liability to third persons, §19-1112.
Limitations of action against
trustee, §19-1116.
Methods and forms for creating,
§19-1118.
Multiple beneficiaries.
Beneficial interest in property,
§19-1106.
Notice of resignation, §19-1113.
Obligations of trustee.
Arise on acceptance of property,
§19-1104.
Personal jurisdiction of court.
Trustee subject to, §19-1104.
Petition for accounting by trustee,
§19-1115.
Petition to determine incapacity,
§19-1110.
Powers generally of trustee,
§19-1108.

CUSTODIAL TRUSTS —Cont'd
Property kept separate, §19-1107.
Prudent person standard of care, §19-1107.
Records of transactions, duty to keep, §19-1107.
Removal of trustee, §19-1113.
Accounting, §19-1115.
Reporting and accounting by trustee, §19-1115.
Limitations of action against trustee, §19-1116.
Resignation by trustee, §19-1113.
Rights and powers over property, §19-1108.
Separate accounting to beneficiaries.
Property held for more than one beneficiary, §19-1106.
Separate trusts.
Multiple trustees, beneficial interest, §19-1106.
Single trust.
Property held by same trustee for same beneficiary, §19-1106.
Statement of administration by trustee, §19-1115.
Substitute trustee, §19-1113.
Successor trustee, §19-1113.
Designation, §19-1102.
Termination, §19-1102.
Distribution on termination, §19-1117.
Third persons.
Exemption from liability, §19-1111.
Liability to, §19-1112.
Title to property, §19-1102.
Transfer creating trust, §19-1118.
Transfer of property to trustee or member of beneficiary's family.
Use and benefit of incapacitated individual, §19-1105.
Trustee for future payment or transfer.
Designating, trust upon future event, §19-1103.
Uniformity of application and construction, §19-1120.
Use of trust property, §19-1109.

CUSTODIANS.
Corporations.
Judicial dissolution, §§29-312.21, 29-312.22.
Shareholders.
Appointment, §29-305.70.
Nonprofit corporations.
Judicial dissolution, §29-412.22.

CUSTODIANSHIP OF MINORS.
Generally.
See CHILD CUSTODY AND CHILD CUSTODY PROCEEDINGS.
Probate proceedings, Probate Rules 231, 232.
Proceedings, §§16-4601.01 to 16-4605.03.
See CHILD CUSTODY AND CHILD CUSTODY PROCEEDINGS.

CUSTODIANS OF PROPERTY.
Reports, §1-502.

CUSTOMER SERVICE OPERATIONS UNIT, §§1-327.31 to 1-327.34.
Applicability, §1-327.34.
Duties, §1-327.32.
Establishment, §1-327.32.
Short tile, §1-327.31.
Transfer of personnel and property to, §1-327.33.

CUSTOMS.
Constitutional provisions, US Const Art I §§8 to 10.

CUTS.
Sharps injury protection.
Safe needle distribution, §§7-2851 to 7-2858.

CY PRES DOCTRINE.
Trusts and trustees.
Uniform trust code.
Modification or termination, §19-1304.13.

CYTOLOGY SCREENING.
Clinical laboratories, §44-210.
Mammogram coverage, §31-2901.

CYTOTECHNOLOGY.
Definition of practice, §3-1201.02.
Health occupations licensure, registration or certification, §§3-1205.01 to 3-1205.24.
Qualifications for licensure, §3-1207.61.
Exemption, §3-1207.63.
Transition provision, §3-1207.64.
Waiver, §3-1207.62.
Titles and terms prohibited as misrepresentation without license to practice, §3-1210.03.

D

DAIRIES AND DAIRY FARMS.
Business licenses, §47-2827.

DAIRIES AND DAIRY FARMS
—Cont'd
Inspector of, §7-179.
Milk and milk products.
Sale by weight, §37-201.14.
Registration of milk containers,
§§36-121 to 36-157.
See MILK CONTAINER
REGISTRATION.

DAMAGES.
Adult protective services, §7-1912.
Appeals.
Frivolous appeals, DCCtApp Rule 38.
Arbitration, revised act.
Authority to award, §16-4421.
Bicyclist, assault or battery by
motorist.
Right of civil action for damages,
§50-1621.
Bills of lading.
Limitations of liability in bill of lading,
§28:7-309.
Business organizations.
Incorrect information within filed
record.
Recovery from signer with
knowledge that information was
incorrect, §29-102.09.
Carriers.
Limitation of liability.
Carrier issuing bill of lading,
§28:7-309.
Child restraint seat law not basis for
civil action for, §50-1706.
Cigarette sales below cost, §28-4525.
Comparative negligence.
Bank deposits and collections.
Unauthorized signature or
alteration, customer's duty to
report, §28:4-406.
Consumer credit reporting agencies.
Consumer security freeze.
Willful violations, §28-3864.
Consumer credit sales.
Consumers' remedies, §28-3813.
Consumer credit service
organizations.
Actions for damages, §28-4607.
Consumer protection.
Consumers' remedies, §28-3813.
Violations of chapter, §28-3905.
Continuing care retirement
communities.
Civil liability of providers for
violations, §44-151.14.

DAMAGES —Cont'd
Contributory fault.
Bank deposits and collections.
Unauthorized signature or
alteration, customer's duty to
report, §28:4-406.
Dishonored checks.
Merchants.
Civil recovery by, §28-3152.
Distress for rent, §42-3217.
Dog bites, §8-1812.
Drug, firearm, or prostitution-
related nuisance abatement,
§42-3111.
Ejectment, §§16-1109 to 16-1112,
16-1116 to 16-1120.
E-mail, spam, §28-5003.
Excess property for United States,
§16-1384.
Flood hazards, §6-506.
Foreclosure rescue services and
transactions.
Private right of action, §42-2434.
Foreign missions, fee for unsatisfied
judgments or damages,
§6-1304.01.
Gaming contracts.
Cheating at gambling, §§16-1702,
16-1704.
Hate crimes.
Parental liability for minor, §22-3704.
Hazardous waste management,
§8-1311.
Hazardous materials transportation.
Strict liability for releases during
transport, §8-1446.
Health professional recruitment
program.
Breach of service obligation contract,
§7-751.13.
Installment loans.
Consumers' remedies, §28-3813.
Interception of oral or wire
communications, §23-554.
Interest on judgments, §15-109.
Landlord's use and occupation
actions, §42-3221.
Long-term care ombudsman, civil
actions, §7-705.02.
Mental health disclosures,
§§7-1207.01, 7-1207.02, 7-1208.01.
Mesne profits and damages, §16-1109.
Metropolitan police property clerk,
§5-119.11.
Miss Utility.
See MISS UTILITY.

DAMAGES —Cont'd

Money lenders' contracts, §26-909.

Mortgages and deeds of trust.
Foreclosure rescue services and transactions.
Private right of action, §42-2434.

Nursing homes.
Discharge, transfer, or relocation of residents of, §44-1004.03.

Partnerships.
Liability for inaccurate information in filed record, §29-601.11.

Pleading special matters, CivPro Rule 9.

Prescription drugs, excessive pricing, §28-4555.

Presumption of death.
Person presumed dead found living, §14-702.

Procurement claims, §2-381.02.
Qui tam plaintiff, actions by, §2-381.03.
Relief from retaliatory actions, §2-381.04.

Punitive damages.
Consumer credit reporting agencies.
Consumer security freeze.
Willful violations, §28-3864.
Consumer credit sales, §28-3813.
Consumer credit service organizations, §28-4607.
Consumer protection, §§28-3813, 28-3905.
Debt collectors, §28-3814.
Hate crimes, §22-3704.
Hazardous waste management.
Hazardous materials transportation.
Strict liability for releases during transport, §8-1446.
Installment loans, §28-3813.
Procurement claims, §2-381.02.
Real property, waste of, §42-1601.
Revolving credit accounts.
Violations, §28-3813.

Quo warranto, §16-3548.

Real property, waste of, §§42-1601, 42-1602.

Replevin, §§16-3710 to 16-3713.

Restraints of trade, §§28-4507, 28-4508.
Indirect purchasers, §28-4509.
Injuries to or within the District of Columbia, §28-4507.
Relief for private parties, §28-4508.

Revolving credit accounts.
Consumers' remedies, §28-3813.

DAMAGES —Cont'd

Sale of goods, UCC.
Acceptance of goods.
Buyer's damages for breach in regard to, §28:2-714.
Antecedent breach.
Effect of cancellation or rescission on claims, §28:2-720.
Consequential damages.
Buyers, §28:2-715.
Contractual limitations, §28:2-719.
Cover by buyer, §28:2-712.
Deduction from price, §28:2-717.
Delivery of goods.
Buyer's damages for nondelivery, §28:2-713.
Incidental damages.
Buyers, §28:2-715.
Recovery by person in position of seller, §28:2-707.
Sellers, §28:2-710.
Limitation, §28:2-718.
Liquidation, §28:2-718.
Nonacceptance of goods.
Sellers, §28:2-708.
Repudiation by sellers.
Buyers' remedies, §28:2-713.
Repudiation of buyer.
Seller's damages, §28:2-708.
Resale of goods by seller, §§28:2-703, 28:2-706.
Warranty breaches, §28:2-714.

Seat belt law not basis for civil action for, §50-1807.

Secured transactions.
Defaults.
Noncompliance with provisions, §28:9-625.

Security agents and brokers.
Civil liability, §31-5606.04.

Shoplifting, §27-102.
Merchant's recovery of civil damages, §§27-101 to 27-106.

Spam deterrence, §28-5003.

Streets and alleys, closing, §9-202.11.

Tenant organizations.
Violation of provisions, §42-3505.06.

Tobacco tax.
Enforcement of provisions, §47-2425.

Trade secrets, §36-403.

Unjust imprisonment, §2-423.

Unliquidated damages against District.
Limitation of actions involving, §12-309.

Waste, writ of.
Prohibition of waste without written license, §42-1602.

DAMAGES —Cont'd
Workplace fraud.
Private right of action to enforce provisions, §32-1331.09.
Wrongful death, §§16-2701, 16-2703.

DANCE THERAPY, §3-1209.02.
Board of occupational therapy, §3-1202.06.
Health occupations licensure, registration or certification, §§3-1205.01 to 3-1205.24.
See HEALTH OCCUPATIONS LICENSURE, REGISTRATION OR CERTIFICATION.

DANGEROUS DOGS, §§8-1901 to 8-1908.
Allowing fierce or dangerous dogs to go at large, §22-1311.
Consequences resulting from dangerous dog determination, §8-1903.
Definitions, §8-1901.
Determination of dangerousness, §8-1902.
Educational program regarding, §8-1907.
Fines, §8-1906.
Humane destruction of, §8-1903.
Issuance of rules, §8-1908.
Licenses, §8-1907.
Owner responsibilities regarding, §8-1905.
Registration, §8-1904.

DAUGHTERS OF 1812.
Real property exempt from taxation, §47-1033.

DAUGHTERS OF AMERICAN REVOLUTION.
Real property exempt from taxation, §§47-1028 to 47-1032.

DAY CARE.
See CHILD CARE FACILITIES.

DAYLIGHT-SAVING TIME.
Alcoholic beverage licensees.
Hours of sale and delivery, §25-722.
Provision for, §28-2711.
Standard time for District, §28-2711.

DC ARENA.
Alcoholic beverage licenses, §25-114.
Authorizations, §§47-396.01 to 47-398.06.
Beverage containers not permitted, §25-1003.

DC ARENA —Cont'd
Borrowing, §§47-398.01, 47-398.02, 47-398.05.
Interpretation of provisions, §47-398.05.
Preconstruction, §§47-398.03, 47-398.04.
Special public safety fees, §§47-2751 to 47-2753.

DC CIRCUIT COURT OF APPEALS.
Federal rules of appellate procedure and DC Circuit local rules.
See APPEALS, FEDERAL CASES.

DC CIRCULATOR BUS SERVICE, §§50-921.31 to 50-921.38.
Consolidation with WMATA, §50-921.36.
Crimes and offenses.
Enhanced penalties for offenses committed against transit operators and station managers, §22-3751.01.
Notice of enhanced penalties, §35-261.
Offenses for which penalties apply, §22-3752.
Definitions, §50-921.31.
Enforcement powers, §50-921.35.
Expansion beyond jurisdiction of DC, §§50-921.37, 50-921.38.
Fares, §50-921.34.
Fund, §50-921.33.
Powers of department, §50-921.32.
Rulemaking to implement, §50-921.35.
Service structure, §50-921.34.
Territorial operation, §§50-921.37, 50-921.38.

DC CITIZENS' JOB PROGRAM.
Convention center hotel, §10-1221.05.

DC ONE CARD, §§1-327.71 to 1-327.73.

DCPS.
Cabinet-level agency, public schools, §§38-171 to 38-175.

DC STREETCAR SERVICE, §§50-921.71 to 50-921.77.
Coordination with Washington Metropolitan Area Transit Authority, §50-921.77.
Definitions, §50-921.71.
Discounted or free tickets, §50-921.74.
Fund.
Establishment, §50-921.73.

DC STREETCAR SERVICE —Cont'd
Labor negotiations with employees of program, §50-921.75.
Penalties for violations of rules, §50-921.76.
Powers of department, §50-921.72.
Quality service, §50-921.74.
Rates and fares, §50-921.74.
Rulemaking, §50-921.76.

DC-USA PROJECT.
Tax exemptions, §47-4606.

DDOT.
District department of transportation, §§50-921.01 to 50-921.22.
See TRANSPORTATION.

DDOT STORMWATER RETENTION CREDIT FUND, §50-921.22.

DEAD BODIES.
Anatomical gifts.
General provisions.
See ANATOMICAL GIFTS.
Autopsies, §§5-1409, 5-1410, 5-1414.
Medical examiners.
General provisions, §§5-1401 to 5-1419.
See MEDICAL EXAMINERS.
Burial.
See BURIAL.
Cemeteries and cemetery associations, §§43-101 to 43-131.
See CEMETERIES AND CEMETERY ASSOCIATIONS.
Cremation.
See CREMATION.
Crimes and offenses.
Failure to report certain deaths, §5-1406.
Defined, §7-201.
Embalming, §43-125.
Exhibiting, §43-120.
Final disposition, §7-214.
Funeral directors, §§3-401 to 3-421.
See FUNERAL DIRECTORS.
Funeral expenses.
See FUNERAL EXPENSES.
Grave robbery, §§3-206, 22-3303.
Indigent persons.
Cremation, §7-178.
Park reservation 13 transferred for use as indigent burial ground, §10-135.
Public assistance, burial on, §§4-214.01 to 4-214.04.
Keeping, §43-120.

DEAD BODIES —Cont'd
Medical examiners, §§5-1401 to 5-1419.
See MEDICAL EXAMINERS.
Place of burial, requirements regarding, §43-121.
Public expense, buried at, §3-202.
Public officers and employees, transportation of body as part of death benefits, §1-623.34.
Sale or purchase of, §3-206.
Trafficking in human body parts, §§7-1501.01 to 7-1501.03.

DEAF AND HEARING IMPAIRED.
ABLE savings accounts, §§47-4901, 47-4902.
Assistive technology device warranty, §§28-4031 to 28-4034.
Defined terms, §7-1009.
Equal access.
Employment, §7-1005.
Housing, §7-1006.
Public places, accommodations, and conveyances, §§7-1001, 7-1002.
Fines for interfering with or discriminating against, §7-1007.
Gallaudet University.
General provisions, §§38-2301 to 38-2402.11.
See GALLAUDET UNIVERSITY.
Guide dogs.
Defined, §7-1009.
Housing accommodations.
Full and equal access, §7-1006.
Public places accommodations, and conveyances.
Right to be accompanied by, §7-1002.
Hearing aid dealers, §§28-4001 to 28-4007.
See HEARING AID DEALERS.
Hearing aids.
Assistive technology device warranty, §§28-4031 to 28-4034.
Interpreters, §§2-1901 to 2-1912.01.
See INTERPRETERS.
Motor vehicle drivers, safety standards for, §7-1004.
National technical institute for the deaf, §§38-2401.11, 38-2401.12, 38-2402.01 to 38-2402.11.
See NATIONAL TECHNICAL INSTITUTE FOR THE DEAF.
Newborn hearing screening, §§7-851 to 7-855.
Definitions, §7-851.

DEAF AND HEARING IMPAIRED
—Cont'd
Newborn hearing screening —Cont'd
Health benefit plans, reimbursement,
§7-853.
Effective date, §7-855.
Rules, §7-854.
Screening programs, §7-852.
Effective date, §7-855.
**Penalties for interfering with or
discriminating against,** §7-1007.
Taxicabs.
Digital dispatch for individuals with
disabilities, §50-301.25a.
**Visual recording of proceedings
involving,** §2-1910.

DEATH, §§7-601 to 7-630.
**Absence for seven years as evidence
of,** §§14-701, 14-702.
Alcoholic beverage licenses.
Involuntary transfer of license,
§25-361.
Appeals in federal cases.
Service of notice of appeal, FRAP 3(d).
Substitution, FRAP 43(a).
Asbestos exposure.
Limitation of actions for death or
injury caused by exposure to
asbestos, §12-311.
Assignments for benefit of creditors.
Assignee or trustee, §28-2105.
Attorneys at law.
Protection of clients' interests, DCBar
Rule XI.
Brain death, §7-601.
Child fatality or near fatality.
Child fatality review committee,
§§4-1371.01 to 4-1371.14.
Public disclosure of findings and
information, §§4-1303.31 to
4-1303.36.
Community residence facilities.
Duty to report certain deaths to
medical examiner, §5-1405.
Failure to report certain deaths,
§5-1406.
**Conservators appointed for
protection of property,** §21-2061.
Constitution of the United States.
President and vice-president of the
United States.
Duty of Congress, US Const Art II
§1, Amd 25.
President-elect.
Provision in case of, US Const
Amd 20.

DEATH —Cont'd
Crimes and offenses.
Failure to report certain deaths,
§5-1406.
**Elected official, filling vacancy left
by,** §1-1001.10.
Embalmers.
Suspicious deaths.
Duty to report certain deaths to
medical examiner, §5-1405.
Failure to report certain deaths,
§5-1406.
Emergency medical services.
Duty to report certain deaths to
medical examiner, §5-1405.
Failure to report certain deaths,
§5-1406.
Presumptive disability or death,
§§5-651 to 5-656.
**Evidence of, absence for seven years
as,** §§14-701, 14-702.
Execution of judgments.
Death of judgment debtor after
delivery of writ of execution,
§15-309.
Execution of final decree after,
§15-319.
Marshal, death of, §15-315.
Fiduciaries.
Death of represented person, CivPro
Rule 305.
Guardianship reports, Probate Rule
328.
Fire departments and firefighters.
Presumptive disability or death,
§§5-651 to 5-656.
Health care facilities.
Duty to report certain deaths to
medical examiner, §5-1405.
Failure to report certain deaths,
§5-1406.
Intellectual disability proceedings.
Dismissal of proceedings,
MentalRetardation Rule 17.
Substitution of petitioner,
MentalRetardation Rule 4A.
Intervention proceedings.
Death of guardian's ward, Probate
Rule 328.
Intestate estate.
Death of distributee before
distribution of, §19-313.
Jails.
Duty to report certain deaths to
medical examiner, §5-1405.
Failure to report certain deaths,
§5-1406.

DEATH —Cont'd

Joint contract, party to, §§16-2102, 16-2104.

Law enforcement officers.
Duty to report certain deaths to medical examiner, §5-1405.
Failure to report certain deaths, §5-1406.

Living wills, §§7-621 to 7-630.
See LIVING WILLS.

Medical examiners.
General provisions, §§5-1401 to 5-1419.
See MEDICAL EXAMINERS.

Metropolitan police property clerk.
Custody of property of deceased persons, §5-119.09.

Natural death act, §§7-621 to 7-630.
See LIVING WILLS.

Negligence causing, §§16-2701 to 16-2703.

Notaries public, custody of records of, §1-1215.

Notice of, §32-1513.

Nurses.
Duty to report certain deaths to medical examiner, §5-1405.
Failure to report certain deaths, §5-1406.

Nursing homes.
Duty to report certain deaths to medical examiner, §5-1405.
Failure to report certain deaths, §5-1406.

Opportunity accounts.
Disposition upon account holders death, §1-307.70.

Parentage proceedings, death of respondent in, §16-2347.

Parents.
Standby guardianship for child, §§16-4801 to 16-4810.
See GUARDIAN AND WARD.

Partnerships.
Transferable interests of partners.
Deceased partner, power of legal representative, §29-605.05.

Party substitution, CivPro Rule 25.
Adoption proceedings, Adoption Rule 25.
Appeals, DCCtApp Rule 43.
Domestic relations actions, DomRel Rule 25.
Intellectual disability proceedings, MentalRetardation Rule 4A.
Suggestion of death upon record, CivPro Form CA 30.

DEATH —Cont'd

Personal representatives, §20-524.

Person presumed dead found to be alive, §14-702.

Physicians and surgeons.
Duty to report certain deaths to medical examiner, §5-1405.
Failure to report certain deaths, §5-1406.

President of the United States.
Duty of congress, US Const Art II §1.
President-elect.
Provision in case of, US Const Amd 20.
Succession upon death, US Const Amd 25.

Presumption of, §§14-701, 14-702.
Emergency medical services or fire department employees.
Presumptive disability or death, §§5-651 to 5-656.

Prisons and prisoners.
Duty to report certain deaths to medical examiner, §5-1405.
Failure to report certain deaths, §5-1406.

Records of workplace deaths, §32-1531.

Reports of workplace deaths, §32-1532.

Rights of action, survival of, §12-101.

Teachers' retirement.
After June 30, 1946, §§38-2021.09, 38-2021.10, 38-2021.23, 38-2023.02.
Prior to June 30, 1946, §§38-2001.10, 38-2001.10a.

Transfers to minors, custodian of, §21-318.

Vice-president, US Const Art II §1.

Will, devisee legatee of, §18-308.

Witness testimony involving deceased persons, §§14-302, 14-303.

Workplace safety reports, §32-808.

Wrongful, §§16-2701 to 16-2703.

DEATH BENEFITS.

Public officers and employees, §1-623.33.

Workers' compensation, §32-1509.

DEATH BY WRONGFUL ACT.

Generally, §§16-2701 to 16-2703.
See WRONGFUL DEATH.

DEATH CERTIFICATES.

Copies.
Assessment and collection of fees, §1-301.01.

DEATH CERTIFICATES —Cont'd
Death registration generally, §§7-211 to 7-214, 7-224.
Funeral directors.
Courtesy cards for purpose of filing death certificates, §3-415.
Medical examiners.
Responsibilities of chief medical examiner, §5-1412.
No removal of tissue or embalming until after issuance of, §43-125.

DEATH PENALTY.
Appeals.
Stay of execution, CrimPro Rule 38.
Indictments and information.
Capital offenses to be prosecuted by indictment, CrimPro Rule 7.

DEATH REGISTRATION, §§7-211 to 7-214, 7-224.

DEATH WITH DIGNITY.
Natural death act, §§7-621 to 7-630.
See LIVING WILLS.

DEBENTURES.
Fiduciary security transfers, §§28-2901 to 28-2909.
See FIDUCIARY SECURITY TRANSFERS.

DEBTORS AND CREDITORS.
Alcoholic beverages tax liability deemed personal debt, §25-907.
Answer to complaint for money had and received, CivPro Form CA 21.
Artist protection.
Creditors of art dealer, §28-5104.
Assignments for benefit of creditors, §§28-2101 to 28-2110.
See ASSIGNMENTS FOR BENEFIT OF CREDITORS.
Attachment.
See ATTACHMENT.
Capital review and debt affordability committee, §§47-336 to 47-340.
Childhood, debt incurred during, §28-3505.
Collectors or creditors.
Definitions, §28-3814.
Installment loans.
Restriction on collectors, §28-3814.
Prohibited practices, §28-3814.
Punitive damages, §28-3814.
Telephone calls.
Time for making, §28-3814.
Threats, §28-3814.

DEBTORS AND CREDITORS
—Cont'd
Complaints.
Claim on debt, CivPro Form CA 13.
Money had and received, CivPro Form CA 8.
Answer to complaint, CivPro Form CA 21.
Money lent, CivPro Form CA 6.
Congress.
Powers of congress, US Const Art I §8.
Constitution of the United States.
Aid of rebellion, US Const Amd 14.
Debts and engagements contracted before adoption, US Const Art VI.
Not to be questioned, US Const Amd 14.
Powers of congress, US Const Art I §8.
Consumer credit, §§28-3801 to 28-3819.
See CONSUMER CREDIT.
Consumer protection, §§28-3801 to 28-3819.
See CONSUMER PROTECTION.
Contracts.
Sale of goods.
Creditors' rights and remedies.
Sale on approval and sale or return transactions, §28:2-326.
Sold goods.
Rights of seller's creditors, §28:2-402.
Credit line deeds of trust, §§42-2301 to 42-2303.
Credit service organizations, §§28-4601 to 28-4608.
See CONSUMER CREDIT SERVICE ORGANIZATIONS.
Delinquent debts to the District, recovery, §§1-350.01 to 1-350.12.
Consumer protection, §1-350.10.
Costs, §1-350.03.
Defined terms, §1-350.01.
Discharge, §1-350.06.
Fees, §1-350.03.
Fund, §1-350.04.
License suspension, §1-350.07.
Liens, §1-350.05.
Offsets, §1-350.09.
Payment plans, §1-350.06.
Permit suspension, §1-350.07.
Reciprocity, §1-350.08.
Referrals for collection, §1-350.02.
Reports to Council, §1-350.11.
Reports to credit agencies, §1-350.06.

DEBTORS AND CREDITORS
—Cont'd
Delinquent debts to the District, recovery —Cont'd
Rules, §1-350.12.
Sale of, §1-350.06.
Transfer for collection, §1-350.02.
Financial literacy council, §§38-731.01 to 38-731.05.
Fraudulent transfers.
General provisions, §§28-3101 to 28-3111.
See FRAUDULENT TRANSFERS.
Heir or legatee, liabilities of, §20-1302.
Indebtedness of District of Columbia, §47-102.
Installment loans.
See INSTALLMENT LOANS.
Interest on judgment for liquidated debt, §15-108.
Intervention proceedings.
Creditor's claims, Probate Rule 307.
Joint contracts, §§16-2101 to 16-2106.
Money lenders, §§26-901 to 26-912.
See MONEY LENDERS.
Mortgage lenders and brokers, §§26-1101 to 26-1121.
See MORTGAGE LENDERS AND BROKERS.
Mortgages and deeds of trust.
General provisions, §§42-804 to 42-820.
See MORTGAGES AND DEEDS OF TRUST.
Motor vehicle financing.
Installment sales, §§50-601 to 50-610.
See MOTOR VEHICLE FINANCING.
Procedural rules in debt collection actions, CivPro Rule 40-III.
Prostitution compelled for debt, §22-2709.
Public officers and employees.
Debt set-offs for, §§1-629.01 to 1-629.04.
Revolving credit accounts, §§28-3701, 28-3702.
Secured transactions.
Commercial code, §§28:9-101 to 28:9-809.
See COMMERCIAL CODE.
Wills, creditors as witnesses to, §18-106.
Workers' compensation exempt from creditors' claims, §32-1517.

DECEDENTS' ESTATES, §§20-101 to 20-109.
Administration of the estate.
General provisions, §§20-701 to 20-753.
See ADMINISTRATION OF ESTATES.
After-discovered property, §§20-355, 20-1304.
Appraisals, §§20-711 to 20-715.
Child equivalent to adopted child in instruments, §16-313.
Claims against the estate.
General provisions, §§20-901 to 20-914.
See CLAIMS AGAINST ESTATES.
Closing the estate, §§20-1301 to 20-1305.
Counterclaims, action by or against executor or administrator, §13-505.
Definitions, §20-101.
Descent and distributions.
General provisions, §§19-101.01 to 19-701.
See INTESTATE SUCCESSION.
Devolution of property at death, §20-105.
Disclaimer of property interest.
Generally, §§19-1501 to 19-1518.
See DISCLAIMER OF PROPERTY INTERESTS.
Dower, Probate Rule 6.
Effective date of provisions, §20-109.
Estates in land.
General provisions, §§42-501 to 42-523.
See ESTATES IN LAND.
Fee simple estates, §42-701.
Firearms as part of, §7-2503.01.
Fraud and deceit, §20-108.01.
Fraudulent transfers.
General provisions, §§28-3101 to 28-3111.
See FRAUDULENT TRANSFERS.
Incompetent or incapacitated persons, guardian ad litem for, §20-108.
Inheritance and estate taxes.
General provisions, §§47-3701 to 47-3722.
See INHERITANCE AND ESTATE TAXES.
Intestate succession.
General provisions, §§19-101.01 to 19-701.
See INTESTATE SUCCESSION.

DECEDENTS' ESTATES —Cont'd
Inventory, §§20-711 to 20-715.
Investments by fiduciaries, Probate
    Rule 5.
Joint contracts, §§16-2101 to 16-2106.
Liability of heir or legatee to
    creditor after closing, §20-1302.
Life estates, Probate Rule 6.
Limitation of actions in actions
    against, §12-305.
Motor vehicles, §20-357.
Notice requirements, §20-103.
Opening the estate.
    General provisions, §§20-301 to
        20-357.
    See OPENING ESTATES.
Opportunity accounts.
    Transfer to contingent beneficiary on
        death of holder, §1-307.70.
Parentage proceedings, liability in,
    §16-2347.
Personal representatives, §§20-401 to
    20-406.
    See PERSONAL
        REPRESENTATIVES.
Posthumous children, §42-704.
Powers of appointment.
    General provisions, §§42-1001 to
        42-1019.
    See POWERS OF APPOINTMENT.
Presumptions, rebuttability of,
    §20-104.
Principal and income act,
    §§28-4801.01 to 28-4806.02.
    See PRINCIPAL AND INCOME.
Priority or preference between real
    and personal property, lack of,
    §20-106.
Private right of action to resolve,
    §20-107.
Probate proceedings.
    General provisions, §§16-3101 to
        16-3112, Probate Rules 1 to 430.
    See PROBATE PROCEEDINGS.
Public assistance claims on,
    §§4-214.01 to 4-214.04.
Real property, §§42-701 to 42-705.
    Uniform real property transfers on
        death, §§19-604.01 to 19-604.19.
Receivers administering estate.
    Rules governing, CivPro Rule 66.
Register of wills, §§11-2101 to 11-2106.
    See REGISTER OF WILLS.
Remainder to heirs of life tenant,
    §42-703.

DECEDENTS' ESTATES —Cont'd
Secured transactions.
    Name of debtor and secured party,
        §28:9-503.
Shelley's case rule, abolition of,
    §42-703.
Simultaneous deaths, §§19-501 to
    19-506.
Small estates, §§20-351 to 20-357.
    See SMALL ESTATES.
Special administrators, §§20-531 to
    20-534.
    See PERSONAL
        REPRESENTATIVES.
Statutory rule against perpetuities,
    §§19-901 to 19-907.
Supervised and unsupervised
    administration.
    General provisions, §§20-401 to
        20-406.
    See PERSONAL
        REPRESENTATIVES.
Survival of rights of action following
    death, §12-101.
Terminology used in creating.
    "Bargain and sell" whole estate and
        interest passed by, §42-702.
    Fee simple estates, no word of
        inheritance necessary to create,
        §42-701.
    "Grant" whole estate and interest
        passed by, §42-702.
    Want or failure of issue, words
        purporting, §42-705.
Uniform real property transfers on
    death, §§19-604.01 to 19-604.19.
Uniform TOD security registration,
    §§19-603.01 to 19-603.11.
    See NONPROBATE TRANSFERS.
Verifications, form of, §20-102.
Veterans estates.
    Filing pleadings or orders affecting
        estate, CivPro Rule 5-I.
Wills.
    General provisions, §§18-101 to
        18-308.
    See WILLS.
    International wills, §§18-701 to
        18-710.
    See INTERNATIONAL WILLS.

DECLARATION OF WAR.
Powers of congress, US Const Art I
    §8.

DECLARATIONS.

Unsworn declaration supplement, CivPro Form CA 101-A.

DECLARATORY JUDGMENTS, §2-508, CivPro Rule 57.

Complaint for interpleader and declaratory relief, CivPro Form CA 18.

Domestic relations actions, DomRel Rule 57.

Rental housing, §42-3405.03a.

State health planning and development agency, §44-607.

DECORUM.

Judges, CJC Canon 2.8.

DECREES.

See JUDGMENTS AND DECREES.

DEDUCTIBLES.

No-fault motor vehicle insurance, §31-2410.

DEDUCTIONS.

Income taxes.

See INCOME TAXES.

Money lenders, deductions from principal, §26-905.

Police and firefighters retirement and disability, §§5-706, 5-717.

Prison industries wages, §24-231.11.

Teachers' retirement, salary deductions for.

After June 30, 1946, §§38-2021.01, 38-2021.11.

Prior to June 30, 1946, §§38-2001.01, 38-2001.11.

Toll telecommunication service tax, §47-3903.

DEEDS.

Acknowledgments, §§42-101, 42-111, 42-112.

See ACKNOWLEDGMENTS.

Address change, notice of, §42-405.

Bonds, surety.

Relating to land, §42-409.

Children and minors, conveyances by, §42-408.

Condominiums, §42-2006.

Contracts relating to land, §42-409.

Corporate deeds, §42-602.

Covenant, use of, §42-603.

Credit line deeds of trust, §§42-2301 to 42-2303.

Defective.

Formal requisites, failures in, §42-404.

On or after April 27, 1994, §42-403.

DEEDS —Cont'd

Defective —Cont'd

Prior to April 27, 1994, §42-402.

Effective date, §42-401.

Electronic recording, §§42-1231 to 42-1235.

Evidence, as, §14-502.

First recorded deed, preference for, §42-406.

Forgery, §22-3242.

Formal requisites, failures in, §42-404.

Form for, §§42-601, 42-602.

Horizontal property regime units, §42-2006.

Improperly executed or acknowledged instruments, §42-407.

Interests conveyable by deed, §42-301.

Mortgages and deeds of trust.

General provisions, §§42-804 to 42-820.

See MORTGAGES AND DEEDS OF TRUST.

Name change, notice of, §42-405.

Notarial acts, §§42-141 to 42-148.

Preference for first recorded deed, §42-406.

Real estate tax sales, §§47-1303.03, 47-1304.

Real property transfers on death, §§19-604.01 to 19-604.19.

Real property transfer tax, §§47-901 to 47-920.

Recordation tax on deeds.

General provisions, §§42-1101 to 42-1124.

See RECORDATION TAX.

Real property transfer tax, §§47-901 to 47-920.

Recorder of deeds.

General provisions, §§42-1202 to 42-1218.

See RECORDER OF DEEDS.

Trustees of infants, conveyances by, §42-408.

Uniform real property transfers on death, §§19-604.01 to 19-604.19.

DEFACING PROPERTY.

See VANDALISM.

DEFAMATION.

Libel and slander.

Congress.

Privilege of members of congress, US Const Art I §6.

DEFAULT.

Consumer credit sales.
Limitation on creditors' remedies, §28-3812.

Consumer protection.
Limitation on creditors' remedies, §28-3812.

Drug-related evictions, §42-3605.

Installment loans.
Limitation on creditors' remedies, §28-3812.

Layaway plans.
Seller's default, §28-3818.

Life and health insurance guaranty association, §31-5415.

Residential mortgage foreclosure default, right to cure, §42-815.01.

Workers' compensation payments, §32-1519.

DEFAULT JUDGMENTS.

Annulment, §16-919.

Appeals in federal cases.
Administrative review or enforcement, FRAP 15(b).

Appearance at trial.
Defendant's failure to appear, CivPro Rule 39-I.

Deficiency judgments, CivPro Rule 55-II.

Demand for judgment.
Default judgment not to exceed demand, CivPro Rule 54.
Domestic relations actions, DomRel Rule 54.

Divorce, §16-919.

Domestic relations actions, DomRel Rule 55.
Default judgment not to exceed demand, DomRel Rule 54.

Entry of judgment, CivPro Rule 55.
Domestic relations actions, DomRel Rule 55.

Failure to appear.
In obedience to order of publication, §13-340.

Forfeiture of property, CivPro Rule 71A-I.

Jury demand withdrawal, CivPro Rule 55-I.

Landlord and tenant court, LandlordTenant Rule 11.

Motion to vacate default, CivPro Rule 12-I.

Motor vehicle judgments, §50-1301.51.

Parentage proceedings, §16-2343.03.

DEFAULT JUDGMENTS —Cont'd

Pecuniary loss.
Proof of loss, CivPro Rule 55-II.

Pleading defenses and objections, CivPro Rule 12.

Pretrial conferences.
Failure to attend, CivPro Rule 16-II.
Tax proceedings, Tax Rule 13.

Property damage.
Proof of loss, CivPro Rule 55-II.

Public utility's daily default constituting separate and distinct offense, §34-708.

Quo warranto, §16-3543.

Replevin, §16-3707.

Residential drug-related evictions.
Failure to appear, §42-3605.

Service by order of publication.
Failure to appear in obedience to order, §13-340.

Setting aside default, CivPro Rule 55.
Domestic relations actions, DomRel Rule 55.

Small claims court, §§16-3902, 16-3906, SmallClaims Rule 11.

Tax increment financing bonds, payment on, §2-1217.08.

Vacating default by consent, CivPro Rule 55-III.

DEFENSES.

Aged persons, offenses committed against.
Enhanced penalties.
Affirmative defense, §22-3601.

Alibi, CrimPro Rule 12.1.
Delinquent minors, JuvProc Rule 12.1.

Children, violent crimes committed against.
Enhanced penalties.
Affirmative defense, §22-3601.

Comparative negligence.
Bank deposits and collections.
Unauthorized signature or alteration, customer's duty to report, §28:4-406.

Consolidation of defenses, CivPro Rule 12.
Domestic relations actions, DomRel Rule 12.

Consumer credit sales.
Lender subject to defenses arising from sales, §28-3809.
Seller's assignees subject to defenses of consumer, §28-3808.

Consumer protection.
Seller's assignees subject to defenses of consumer, §28-3808.

DEFENSES —Cont'd
Contracts.
Statute of frauds, §§28-3501 to
28-3505.
Unconscionability.
Sale of goods, §28:2-302.
Contributory fault.
Bank deposits and collections.
Unauthorized signature or
alteration, customer's duty to
report, §28:4-406.
Contributory negligence.
Child restraint seats, §50-1707.
Common carriers, §35-301.
Negotiable instruments.
Forged signature or alteration of
instrument, §28:3-406.
Seat belts, §50-1807.
Criminal procedure.
Alibi of defendant, CrimPro Rule 12.1.
Insanity defense, CrimPro Rule 12.2.
Pretrial motions, CrimPro Rule 12.
Delinquent minors, JuvProc Rule 12.
Alibi defense, JuvProc Rule 12.1.
Domestic relations actions, DomRel
Rules 8, 12.
**Fleeing from a law enforcement
officer in a motor vehicle,**
§50-2201.05b.
Fraudulent transfers, §28-3108.
Garnishment.
Prejudgment garnishment.
Garnishees' defenses, §16-519.
**Guardianship of incapacitated
persons.**
Sexual abuse of a ward, §22-3017.
Hazardous materials transportation.
Strict liability for releases during
transport, §8-1445.
Healing arts practitioners.
Sexual abuse of patient or client,
§22-3017.
Insanity defense, §§24-501 to 24-503,
CrimPro Rule 12.2.
Installment loans.
Lender subject to defenses arising
from sales, §28-3809.
Interstate family support.
Nonparentage as defense, §46-353.15.
Spousal privilege, inapplicable,
§46-353.16.
Investment securities.
Issuers' defenses.
Generally, §28:8-202.
Notice of defense, §§28:8-202,
28:8-203.

DEFENSES —Cont'd
Landlord and tenant court,
LandlordTenant Rule 5.
Leaving after colliding, §50-2201.05c.
Negotiable instruments.
Burden of establishing effectiveness of
signature and holder in due
course, §28:3-308.
Defenses generally, §28:3-305.
Object falling or flying from vehicle,
§50-2201.05d.
Permitted defenses, CivPro Rule 12.
Domestic relations actions, DomRel
Rule 12.
Pleading, CivPro Rule 12.
Answer presenting defense under Rule
12(b), CivPro Form CA 20.
Domestic relations actions, DomRel
Rule 12.
Pornography.
Nonconsensual pornography, §22-3056.
Preliminary hearings, CivPro Rule 12.
Domestic relations actions, DomRel
Rule 12.
Rape.
Various degrees of sexual abuse,
§§22-3002 to 22-3006.
Sexual abuse.
Various degrees of sexual abuse,
§§22-3002 to 22-3006.
Statute of frauds, §§28-3501 to
28-3505.
Waiver, CivPro Rule 12.
Domestic relations actions, DomRel
Rule 12.

**DEFERRED COMPENSATION
PROGRAM.**
Public officers and employees,
§§1-611.17, 47-3601 to 47-3604.
Annual report, §47-3604.
Contract for services, §47-3603.
Eligibility to participate, §47-3601.
Established, §47-3601.
Regulations, §47-3602.

DEFIBRILLATORS.
Usage by public, §§44-231 to 44-235.
Definitions, §44-231.
Immunity, §44-233.
Public access, §44-232.
Recreational facilities, program for,
§44-232.01.
Registration fee fund, §44-234.
Rules, §44-235.
Study to expand AED program,
§44-232.02.

DEFICIENCY JUDGMENTS.
Proof of deficiency, CivPro Rule 55-II.

DEFINED TERMS.
Abandon.
Water pollution, §8-103.01.
Abandoned.
Uniform child custody proceedings,
§16-4601.01.
Abandoned property.
Acquisition and disposal, §42-3171.01.
Abandoned vehicles.
Abandoned and unlawfully parked
vehicles, §50-2421.02.
Removal of abandoned and junk
vehicles, §50-2401.
Scrap vehicle title authorization,
§50-2701.
Abate, §8-1051.
Graffiti, §22-3312.05.
Graffiti abatement, §42-3141.01.
Rodent abatement program,
§8-2103.01.
Vector-borne disease control,
§8-2131.01.
Abatement.
Lead-hazard prevention and
elimination, §8-231.01.
Abatement costs.
Graffiti abatement, §42-3141.01.
Abatement date.
Taxation, waiver or abatement,
§47-4222.
Abatement period.
Qualified social electronic commerce
companies tax abatements,
§47-1818.01.
The Advisory Board Company, real
property tax abatement,
§47-4665.01.
Abbreviated probate proceedings,
§20-101.
Abduction.
Uniform child abduction prevention
act, §16-4604.02.
ABLE account.
ABLE savings accounts, §47-4901.
ABLE account savings agreement.
ABLE savings accounts, §47-4901.
ABLE savings accounts, §47-4901.
Above-the-line crew.
Motion pictures, §2-1204.11c.
ABRA.
Alcoholic beverages, §25-101.
ABRA fund.
Alcoholic beverages, §25-101.
Abstract.
Title insurers, §31-5031.01.

DEFINED TERMS —Cont'd
Abstract of title.
Title insurance producers,
§31-5041.01.
Title insurers, §31-5031.01.
Abuse, §7-1901.
Mental health consumer's rights,
§7-1231.02.
Abused, §§4-1301.02, 16-2301.
Abuse or threatened abuse of law or
legal process.
Human trafficking, §22-1831.
Abusive drug, §48-901.02.
Academic year.
DC promise program, §38-2751.
Higher education financial aid
assistance, §38-2731.
Acceptable collateral.
Insurance investments, §31-1371.02.
Acceptable level of school
attendance.
Mayor's youth leadership institute,
§2-1571.
Acceptable private mortgage
insurance.
Insurance investments, §31-1371.02.
Acceptance.
Negotiable instruments, §28:3-409.
Acceptor.
Negotiable instruments, §28:3-103.
Access.
Foreign language services and
documents, §2-1931.
Access area.
Automated teller machines,
§26-131.02.
Access device, §4-218.05.
Automated teller machines,
§26-131.02.
Accessible.
Health care ombudsman program,
§7-2071.01.
Accession.
Secured transactions, §28:9-102.
AccessRx.
Access to prescription drugs,
§48-831.02.
Accident, §31-2402.
Public employees disability
compensation, §1-623.01.
Vehicle insurance enforcement,
§5-114.01.
Accident and health insurance.
Insurance investments, §31-1371.02.
Accident and health insurer.
Insurance investments, §31-1371.02.

DEFINED TERMS —Cont'd

Accident report.
Personal information from motor vehicle records and accident reports, §50-1401.01b.

Accident vehicle.
Scrap vehicle title authorization, §50-2701.

Accommodation.
Rental housing, §42-3401.03.

Account, §31-5501.
Bank deposits and collections, §28:4-104.
College savings program, §47-4501.
Data match requirements for financial institutions, §26-531.
Delinquent taxpayers, §47-4481.
Life and health insurance guaranty association, §31-5401.
Nonprobate transfers on death, §19-602.01.

Accountant, §31-301.

Account debtors.
Secured transactions, §28:9-102.

Account group, §47-372.

Account holder.
Opportunity accounts, §1-307.61.

Account holder of interest.
Delinquent taxpayers, §47-4481.

Accounting.
Secured transactions, §28:9-102.

Accounting period.
Principal and income, §28-4801.02.

Account owner.
College savings program, §47-4501.

Accredited, §38-1302.

Accredited investor.
Securities brokers and dealers, §31-5601.01.

Accredited state, §31-401.

Accredited training provider.
Lead-hazard prevention and elimination, §8-231.01.

Accumulated new district resident hires.
The Advisory Board Company, real property tax abatement, §47-4665.01.

Acknowledgment, §42-141.

Acquire, §26-732.
Savings and loan acquisitions, §26-1201.

Acquired corporation.
Corporations, §29-309.01.

Acquired entity.
Entity transactions, §29-201.02.

DEFINED TERMS —Cont'd

Acquiring authority.
Eminent domain, §16-1351.

Acquiring corporation.
Corporations, §29-309.01.

Acquiring effective control.
Health planning and development agency, §44-401.

Acquiring entity.
Entity transactions, §29-201.02.

Acquisition.
Alternative fuels technology, §50-702.

Acquisition of a branch, §26-732.

Across-the-board increase.
Merit system, disability compensation, §1-623.41.

Act, §2-601.
Home Rule act, §1-201.03.

Act in furtherance of the right of advocacy on issues of public interest.
Anti-SLAPP, §16-5501.

Action, §§8-109.02, 15-901, 34-2602.
Family court, §11-1101.
UCC, §28:1-201.
Uniform trust code, §19-1301.03.

Active business operations.
Employees retirement program management, §1-335.01.

Active duty.
Interstate compact on educational opportunity for military children, §49-1101.03.

Active ingredient, §8-401.

Active metabolite.
Impaired operation or driving, §50-2206.01.

Activities of daily living.
Assisted living residences, §44-102.01.

Activity.
Performance based budget, §47-308.01.

Activity and use limitations.
Environmental covenants, §8-671.01.

Act of physical violence, §10-503.26.

Act of terrorism.
Anti-terrorism act of 2002, §22-3152.

Actor.
Sexual abuse, §22-3001.

Acts of Congress, §7-2501.01.
Criminal procedure, CrimPro Rule 54.

Actual income.
Truth in affordability reporting, §42-2131.
Housing, §42-2151.01.

Actual innocence.
Protection of innocence act, §22-4131.

DEFINED TERMS —Cont'd

Actually innocent.
Protection of innocence act, §22-4131.

Actuary, §§31-1501, 31-1801.

Acupuncture, practice of, §3-1201.02.

Acute stroke ready hospital.
Stroke system of care, §44-1151.

ADA.
Disability rights, §2-1431.01.
Regulation of for-hire vehicles, §50-301.03.

ADA compliance program.
Disability rights, §2-1431.01.

Addict, §48-901.02.
Bail and pretrial detention, §23-1331.

Addiction counseling, practice of, §3-1201.02.

Addiction prevention and recovery administration (APRA).
Choice in drug treatment, §7-3002.

Addition.
Building rehabilitation code, §6-1410.
Green buildings, §6-1451.01.

Additional benefits eligibility period.
Unemployment compensation, §51-107.

Additional benefits period.
Unemployment compensation, §51-107.

Additional bonds.
Income tax secured bonds, §47-340.26.

Additional charges.
Compensating use tax, §47-2201.
Gross sales tax, §47-2001.

Adequate notice.
Access to justice initiative program, §4-1701.01.

Adjacent.
Medical marijuana, §7-1671.01.

Adjoining property, §47-1303.01.

Adjoining residential neighborhood.
Business improvement districts, §2-1215.02.

Adjudicated case.
Office of administrative hearings, §2-1831.01.

Adjudication, §2-502.

Adjusted average pay, §5-701.

Adjusted for inflation.
Tobacco master settlement agreement, §7-1801.01.

Adjusted gross income.
Access to justice initiative program, §4-1701.01.
Income tax, §47-1803.02.
Real property tax deferral, §47-845.03.
Reduced real property tax liability for seniors and persons with disabilities, §47-863.

DEFINED TERMS —Cont'd

Adjusted maximum special assessment.
Southwest waterfront special assessment district, §47-895.01.

Adjusted RBC report, §31-2001.
Health insurance regulatory standards, §31-3451.01.

Adjustment process, §16-2305.02.

Administer, §§21-1201, 48-901.02.
Medical marijuana, §7-1671.01.
Monitoring prescription drugs, §48-853.01.

Administering.
Public assistance applicants, confidentiality of information, §4-209.04.

Administering organization.
Opportunity accounts, §1-307.61.

Administration.
Medical marijuana, §7-1671.01.

Administration payments.
Walter Reed Medical Center site development, §2-1227.01.

Administrative costs.
Low-income housing tax credit, §47-4801.
Low-income housing tax credit fund, §42-2853.01.

Administrative decision.
Ethics and government accountability, §1-1161.01.

Administrative fines, §2-1801.02.

Administrative information, §7-1201.01.

Administrative law judge.
Office of administrative hearings, §2-1831.01.

Administrative procedure, §2-502.

Administrative procedure act.
Ethics and government accountability, §1-1161.01.
Office of administrative hearings, §2-1831.01.
Public-Private Partnership Administration Fund, §2-271.01.

Administrative review.
Alcoholic beverages, §25-101.

Administrative services provider status, §31-3401.

Administrative value, §2-1701.

Administrative workweek.
Police and fire departments, §5-1304.

Administrator, §§7-701.01, 21-501, 44-1001.01.
Access to justice initiative program, §4-1701.01.

DEFINED TERMS —Cont'd
Administrator —Cont'd
Energy efficiency financing,
§8-1778.02.
Metropolitan Washington airport,
§9-1003.
Southwest waterfront special
assessment district, §47-895.01.
Washington National Airport, §9-701.
Admission, §7-1301.03.
Admitted assets, §§31-2501.03,
31-4202.
Insurance investments, §31-1371.02.
Adopt.
Parks and recreation, §10-301.
Adopted regional system, §9-1111.01.
Adoption assistance state.
Interstate compact on adoption and
medical assistance, §4-321.
Adoption or adopted, §32-1501.
Adoptive family.
Adoption subsidy payments, §4-301.
Adult.
Alcoholic beverage control, §25-101.
Anatomical gifts, §7-1531.01.
Child and family services agency.
Criminal record checks, §4-1305.01.
Custodial trusts, §19-1101.
Family court proceedings, §16-2301.
Funeral directors, §3-402.
Homeless services, §4-751.01.
Public assistance, §4-201.01.
Transfers to minors, §21-301.
Tuition of nonresidents, §38-304.
Uniform adult guardianship and
protective proceedings jurisdiction
act, §21-2401.02.
Adult education.
Uniform per student funding formula,
§38-2901.
Adulterated article, §48-103.
Adulteration, §8-401.
Adult in need of protective services,
§7-1901.
Adult protective services worker,
§7-1901.
Adult student, §§38-304, 38-601.
Advanced airway management.
Non-resuscitation procedures for EMS,
§7-651.01.
Advanced life support.
Non-resuscitation procedures for EMS,
§7-651.01.
Advanced metering infrastructure.
Electric light and power companies,
§34-1561.

DEFINED TERMS —Cont'd
Advanced practice registered nurse,
§31-3101.
Medical marijuana, §7-1671.01.
Rights of persons with intellectual
disability, §7-1301.03.
Advance fee, §42-1702.
Advance health-care directive.
Anatomical gifts, §7-1531.20.
Advance registered nursing,
practice of, §3-1201.02.
Adverse benefit determination.
Health benefit plan members bill of
rights, §44-301.01.
Adverse claim.
Investment securities, §28:8-102.
Adverse decision.
Habilitative services for children,
health care coverage, §31-3271.
Adverse event.
Health occupations licensure,
registration or certification.
Mandatory adverse event reporting,
§7-161.
Adverse impact, §42-3101.
Adverse impact on adjoining
residential neighborhood.
Business improvement districts,
§2-1215.02.
Adverse party.
Uniform fiduciaries act, §21-1722.
Advertisement.
Lease-purchase agreements,
§42-3671.01.
Security agents and broker,
§31-5601.01.
Adviser.
Letters of credit, §28:5-102.
Advisory board.
Sustainable energy, §8-1773.01.
Advisory council.
Medical liability captive insurance
agency, §1-307.81.
Advocate for a person with an
intellectual disability.
Rights of persons with intellectual
disability, §7-1301.03.
AED.
Defibrillator usage, §44-231.
Affected party.
Prescription drugs, excessive pricing,
§28-4552.
Sidewalk design and installation,
§9-425.02.
Affected unit.
Shared work unemployment
compensation program, §51-171.

DEFINED TERMS —Cont'd
Affidavit.
Appeals, DCCtApp Rule 1.
Domestic relations actions, DomRel
Rule 2.
Affiliate, §§28-3101, 31-701, 31-5501,
44-1001.01.
Annual audited financial reports,
§31-301.
Banks and financial institutions,
§26-551.02.
Certified capital companies, §31-5231.
Corporations, §29-311.01.
Fraudulent transfers, §28-3101.
Insurance investments, §31-1371.02.
Merchant bank, §26-831.02.
Office of cable television, film, music,
and entertainment amendment
act of 2015, §34-1251.03.
Procurement practices, §2-351.04.
Retail electric competition and
consumer protection, §34-1501.
Retail natural gas supplier licensing
and consumer protection,
§34-1671.02.
Security agents and broker,
§31-5601.01.
Title insurance producers,
§31-5041.01.
Title insurers, §31-5031.01.
Tobacco master settlement agreement,
§7-1801.01.
Universal banks, §26-1401.02.
Affiliated.
Security agents and broker,
§31-5601.01.
Affiliated company.
Captive insurance companies,
§31-3931.01.
Affiliated employee.
Living wage act, §2-220.02.
Affiliated entity.
Ethics and government accountability,
§1-1161.01.
Affiliated group.
Gross sales tax, §47-2001.
Income tax, §47-1801.04.
Affiliated organization.
Ethics and government accountability,
§1-1161.01.
Affiliated person.
Annual audited financial reports,
§31-301.
Statutory trusts, §29-1205.12.
Affiliation period, §31-3301.01.
**Afflicted with a communicable
disease,** §7-132.

DEFINED TERMS —Cont'd
Affordable.
Anacostia waterfront development
zone, §2-1226.02.
Affordable care act.
Health insurance ratemaking,
§31-3311.11.
Affordable housing development.
Affordable housing clearinghouse
directory, §42-2131.
Truth in affordability reporting,
§42-2131.
Housing, §42-2151.01.
Affordable housing inventory.
Affordable housing clearinghouse
directory, §42-2131.
Affordable housing locator.
Affordable housing clearinghouse
directory, §42-2131.
Affordable housing unit.
Affordable housing clearinghouse
directory, §42-2131.
Affordable housing inventory
comprehensive tracking plan,
§42-2141.
**Affordable multifamily housing
property.**
Preservation and rehabilitation of
government-supported housing,
§42-2851.02.
Affordable rental housing project.
Allen Chapel A.M.E. residential rental
project, real property tax
exemptions, §47-4641.
Parkside Terrace development project
tax exemptions, §47-4607.
Affordable units.
Georgia commons.
Real property transfer tax
exemption, §47-4610.
Real property tax exemptions,
§§47-4628, 47-4630.
Rental housing conversion,
opportunity to purchase,
§42-3404.32.
Africanized bee.
Bees, §8-1825.02.
Aftercare.
Hospital discharge planning,
§21-2231.01.
Aftercare placement.
Taking delinquent children into
custody, §16-2309.
Aftercare plan.
Choice in drug treatment, §7-3002.
Aftercare services.
Youth rehabilitation services,
department of, §2-1515.01.

DEFINED TERMS —Cont'd
Afternoon.
  Bank deposits and collections,
    §28:4-104.
Aged, §7-502.01.
Agency.
  Appeals, DCCtApp Rule 1.
  Budgets and budget estimates,
    §47-355.01.
  Bullying, §2-1535.01.
  Child and family services agency.
    Criminal record checks, §4-1305.01.
  Disability rights, §2-1431.01.
  Fee collection incentive fund,
    §1-325.61.
  Governmental reorganization,
    §1-315.02.
  Health data privacy, §7-241.
  Homeland security commission,
    §7-2271.01.
  Homeland security program,
    §7-2231.02.
  Leave of absence, §1-612.04.
  Legal service, §1-608.51.
  Medical liability captive insurance
    agency, §1-307.81.
  Merit system, §§1-603.01, 1-614.11.
  Office of administrative hearings,
    §2-1831.01.
  Office of unified communications,
    §1-327.51.
  Official correspondence, §2-701.
  Procurement practices, §2-351.04.
  Sex offender registration, §22-4001.
  Small and certified business enterprise
    development and assistance,
    §2-218.02.
  Voluntary leave transfer program,
    §1-612.31.
Agency captive insurer, §31-3931.01.
Agency contract.
  Athlete agents, §47-2887.01.
Agency contracting officer.
  Small and certified business enterprise
    development and assistance,
    §2-218.02.
Agency funding source.
  Budget reprogramming policy,
    §47-361.
**Agency having responsibility for the
  child.**
  Permanent guardianship, §16-2382.
Agent, §47-2807.
  Anatomical gifts, §7-1531.01.
  Controlled substances, §48-901.02.
  Educational licensure commission,
    §38-1302.

DEFINED TERMS —Cont'd
Agent —Cont'd
  General license law, §47-2807.
  Health maintenance organizations,
    §31-3401.
  Income tax, §47-1801.04.
  Insurance rate regulation, §31-2701.
  Life insurance, §31-4202.
  Nonprobate transfers on death,
    §19-602.01.
  Prescription drugs, §48-804.51.
  Security agents and broker,
    §31-5601.01.
  Unfair insurance trade practices,
    §31-2231.01.
Aggregate attachment point.
  Stop-loss health insurance for
    employers, §31-3821.
Aggregated effective tax rate.
  Income tax, §47-1801.04.
Aggregation program.
  Retail electric competition and
    consumer protection, §34-1501.
Aggregator.
  Retail electric competition and
    consumer protection, §34-1501.
Aggressive manner, §22-2301.
Aggrieved party.
  Title insurance producers,
    §31-5041.01.
  UCC, §28:1-201.
Aggrieved person, §23-541.
Aging in place.
  Assisted living residences, §44-102.01.
Agreement.
  Electronic transactions, uniform act,
    §28-4901.
  Employer-assisted housing program,
    §42-2501.
  Sales, §28:2-106.
  UCC, §28:1-201.
  Uniform certificates of title for vessels,
    §50-1541.01.
  Washington metropolitan area transit
    authority safety regulation,
    §9-1109.01.
**Agreement for electronic
  presentment.**
  Bank deposits and collections,
    §28:4-110.
Agricultural lien.
  Secured transactions, §28:9-102.
Agricultural products, §37-101.
Agricultural use.
  Real property taxes, reduced liability
    for agricultural uses, §47-868.

DEFINED TERMS —Cont'd
Agriculture.
Pesticide education and control,
§8-431.
AIDS, §§7-1601, 31-1601.
Air conditioner.
Commercial property energy
conservation, §8-1772.01.
Airport, §9-701.
Airports authority.
Metropolitan Washington airport,
§9-1003.
Airspace, §10-1121.01.
**Alabama Ave. Affordable Housing,
L.P.**
Allen Chapel A.M.E. residential rental
project, real property tax
exemptions, §47-4641.
**Alabama Avenue affordable rental
housing project.**
Allen Chapel A.M.E. residential rental
project, real property tax
exemptions, §47-4641.
Alarm agent, §7-2802.
Alarm dealer, §7-2802.
Alarm system, §7-2802.
Alarm user, §7-2802.
Alcohol, §25-101.
Impaired operation or driving,
§50-2206.01.
Traffic regulation, §50-2201.02.
Alcohol abuse, §31-3101.
Alcoholic beverage, §25-101.
Alien, §47-2601.
Alien captive insurer, §31-3931.01.
Alien company, §§31-2501.03, 31-4202.
Alley, §§6-101.07, 9-201.01.
Alley dwelling, §6-101.07.
Alley rehabilitation project.
Capital project support fund,
§1-325.151.
Allied health professional, §1-623.01.
All jobs.
First source employment, §2-219.01.
Allocable share.
Tobacco master settlement agreement,
§7-1801.01.
Allocated fund.
Housing production trust fund, bond
issues, §42-2812.01.
Allocation date.
Certified capital companies, §31-5231.
All-terrain vehicle, §50-2201.02.
Alternate standby guardian,
§16-4802.
Alternative fuel, §50-702.
Fleet management, publicly-owned
vehicles, §50-211.01.

DEFINED TERMS —Cont'd
Alternative fuel —Cont'd
Regulation of for-hire vehicles,
§50-301.03.
Alternative-fuel vehicle, §50-702.
Alternative program.
Uniform per student funding formula,
§38-2901.
Alternative technical concept.
Procurement practices, §2-351.04.
Alter or alteration.
Building rehabilitation code, §6-1410.
Historic landmarks, §6-1102.
Negotiable instruments, §§28:3-405,
28:3-407.
Ambulance.
Emergency medical services,
§7-2341.01.
Fees, §5-416.
Ambulatory surgical facility.
Health-care facility, hospice and home
care licensure, §44-501.
Amend, amendment, §6-641.12.
American health benefit exchange.
Health benefit exchange authority,
§31-3171.01.
American sign language.
American sign language education,
§38-2432.
American vessel, §51-101.
AMI.
Affordable housing clearinghouse
directory, §42-2131.
Electric light and power companies,
§34-1561.
Real property tax exemptions,
§47-4631.
Ammunition, §7-2501.01.
Anacostia nonprofit zone.
Nonprofit corporations locating in
emerging commercial
neighborhoods, §47-857.11.
**Anacostia waterfront development
zone,** §2-1226.04.
Anatomical gift, §7-1531.01.
ANC.
Alcoholic beverages, §25-101.
ANC 3/4G.
Alcoholic beverage licenses, §25-336.
ANC 4C07.
Alcoholic beverage licenses,
§25-340.01.
Ancillary agreement.
Electric company infrastructure
improvement financing,
§34-1311.01.

DEFINED TERMS —Cont'd
Ancillary services, §31-2801.
Ancillary state, §31-1301.
Anesthesiologist, §§3-1201.02, 3-1206.31.
Anesthesiologist assistants, practice by, §3-1201.02.
Animal, §§8-401, 22-1013.
Penalty for fighting or baiting animals, §22-1006.01.
Animal at large, §8-1801.
Animal care and control agency.
Wildlife protection, §8-2201.
Animal control officer, §8-2001.
Animal shelter, §§8-1801, 47-2888.01.
Annual additions.
Police and firefighters retirement and disability, §5-723.01.
Teachers' retirement, maximum benefit computations, §38-2021.27.
Annual adjusted income, §42-3503.01.
Annual fair market rental amount, §42-3501.03.
Annual implementation plan.
Health planning and development agency, §44-401.
Annual percentage rate, §28-3601.
Mortgage loan protection, §26-1151.01.
Annual reporting date.
The Advisory Board Company, real property tax abatement, §47-4665.01.
Annuitant, §5-701.
Merit system.
Health benefits, §1-621.03.
Life insurance, §1-622.04.
Annuity contract.
Unfair insurance trade practices, §31-2231.01.
Anomalous indorsement.
Negotiable instruments, §28:3-205.
Anticipated litigation.
Condominiums, §42-1903.14.
Anticompetitive conditions.
Retail electric competition and consumer protection, §34-1501.
Retail natural gas supplier licensing and consumer protection, §34-1671.02.
Anticompetitive conduct.
Retail electric competition and consumer protection, §34-1501.
Retail natural gas supplier licensing and consumer protection, §34-1671.02.

DEFINED TERMS —Cont'd
Antimicrobial drug.
Sexually transmitted diseases, treatment for sexual partners, §7-2081.01.
Antique firearm, §7-2501.01.
Antiques, §37-101.
Any device.
Stalking, §22-3132.
Any means.
Stalking, §22-3132.
Anything of value, §22-1802.
Apartment house, §42-3301.
Apartment improvement program, §42-3501.03.
Apartment style.
Homeless services, §4-751.01.
Apiary.
Bees, §8-1825.02.
Apparent owner, §41-102.
Appeal, §47-3301, DCCtApp Rule 1.
Health benefit plan members bill of rights, §44-301.01.
Appellant, DCCtApp Rule 1.
Appellee, DCCtApp Rule 1.
Appliance, §8-171.02.
Applicability date.
Secured transactions, transitional provisions (2012 amendments), §28:9-801.
Applicable schools.
Athletic equity, §38-841.01.
Applicant.
Access to justice initiative program, §4-1701.01.
Alcoholic beverages, §25-101.
Anacostia waterfront environmental standards, §2-1226.32.
Brownfield revitalization, §8-631.02.
Child and family services agency.
Criminal record checks, §4-1305.01.
Clean hands before receiving a license or permit, §47-2861.
Corrections employee mandatory substance abuse testing, §24-211.21.
Criminal background checks for the protection of children act, §4-1501.02.
Fingerprint-based background checks, §31-631.
Green buildings, §6-1451.01.
Health care entity conversion, §44-602.
Hiring of ex-offenders, fair criminal record screening, §32-1341.
Industrial revenue bonds, §47-340.01.

DEFINED TERMS —Cont'd
Applicant —Cont'd
Letters of credit, §28:5-102.
Long-term care insurance, §31-3601.
Mandatory drug and alcohol testing, §1-620.31.
Mandatory drug and alcohol testing of certain employees, §1-620.21.
Medicare supplement insurance, §31-3701.
Money transmissions, §26-1001.
Public assistance applicants, confidentiality of information, §4-209.04.
Real property tax abatement for qualified high technology companies, §47-811.03.
Retail natural gas supplier licensing and consumer protection, §34-1671.02.
Telephone solicitation fraud, §22-3226.01.
Applicant hospital.
Stroke system of care, §44-1151.
Applicant's or recipient's record.
Public assistance applicants, confidentiality of information, §4-209.04.
Application.
Interstate family support, §46-357.01.
Voluntary withdrawal by health benefit plan carriers, §31-3151.
Application distribution.
Elections, §1-1001.02.
Application distribution agency.
Elections, §1-1001.02.
Appointed representative.
Tuition of nonresidents, §38-304.
Appointing authority.
Interpreters, §2-1901.
Apportioned net operating loss.
Income tax, §47-1801.04.
Apportioned operator, §50-1507.01.
Apportionment.
Budgets and budget estimates, §47-355.01.
Apportionment and apportionable vehicle.
International registration plan agreements, §50-1507.01.
Appraised value.
Rental housing, §42-3401.03.
Apprehension.
District of Columbia housing authority, §6-201.
Apprentice, §32-1407.

DEFINED TERMS —Cont'd
Apprentice funeral director, §3-402.
Appropriate, §22-3201.
Appropriate authority, §4-1421.
Appropriate congressional committees.
Charter schools, §38-1800.02.
Appropriate court.
Interstate agreement on detainers, §24-802.
Appropriate evidence of appointment or incumbency.
Investment securities, §28:8-402.
Appropriate federal financial institutions agency.
Banks and financial institutions, §26-551.02.
Universal banks, §26-1401.02.
Appropriate financial institutions agency.
Merchant bank, §26-831.02.
Appropriately trained and qualified.
Homeless services, §4-751.01.
Appropriate permanent housing.
Homeless services, §4-751.01.
Approve.
Entity transactions, §29-201.02.
Approved clinical trial.
Health insurance, clinical trials insurance coverage, §31-2993.01.
APTA manual, §9-1109.01.
Aquatic animals and plants, §8-103.01.
Arbitration organization.
Arbitration, revised act, §16-4401.
Arbitrator.
Arbitration, revised act, §16-4401.
ARC, §31-1601.
Architectural and engineering services.
Procurement practices, §2-351.04.
Archival quality, §2-1701.
Archival record, §2-1701.
Area median income.
Affordable housing inventory comprehensive tracking plan, §42-2141.
Anacostia waterfront development zone, §2-1226.02.
DC promise program, §38-2751.
District of Columbia housing authority, §6-201.
Historic landmarks, §6-1102.
Housing production trust fund, §42-2801.
Housing, truth in affordability reporting, §42-2151.01.

DEFINED TERMS —Cont'd
Area median income —Cont'd
Preservation and rehabilitation of government-supported housing, §42-2851.02.
Solar for All program, §8-1774.16.
Tax abatement for homeowners in enterprise zones, §47-858.01.
Tax abatement for new residential developments, §47-857.01.
Truth in affordability reporting, §42-2131.
Housing, §42-2151.01.
Arena stage project.
Arts, cultural and educational facilities, economic assistance to, §39-401.
Arm bar hold, §5-125.02.
Armored car service.
Gross sales tax, §47-2001.
Armory.
Washington convention and sports authority, §10-1202.01.
Army.
Walter Reed Medical Center site development, §2-1227.01.
ARRA.
Electric light and power companies, §34-1561.
Arranging for prostitution, §22-2701.01.
Arrest.
District of Columbia housing authority, §6-201.
Hiring of ex-offenders, fair criminal record screening, §32-1341.
Arrest record.
Request for production of arrest record, §2-1402.66.
Arson, §22-301.
Art dealer, §28-5101.
Arterial road, §8-1051.
Articles.
Cooperative associations, §29-902.
Artificial insemination, §16-401.
Artificial ventilation.
Non-resuscitation procedures for EMS, §7-651.01.
Artist, §§28-5101, 37-101.
Arts.
Arts and humanities commission, §39-202.
Asbestos, §8-111.01.
Asbestos abatement, §8-111.01.
Asbestos worker, §8-111.01.

DEFINED TERMS —Cont'd
Ascertainable standard relating to the trustee's health, education, support and maintenance.
Uniform fiduciaries act, §21-1722.
As-extracted collateral.
Secured transactions, §28:9-102.
Asian.
Office of Asian and Pacific Islander affairs, §2-1372.
Ask, beg, or solicit, alms, §22-2301.
ASL.
American sign language education, §38-2432.
ASLTA.
American sign language education, §38-2432.
ASRH.
Stroke system of care, §44-1151.
Assault weapon, §§7-2501.01, 7-2551.01.
Assessable year, §31-1201.
Assessed value.
Business improvement districts, §2-1215.02.
Mortgage loan protection, §26-1151.01.
Rental of public space, §10-1101.01.
Assessor, §2-1217.01.
Superior court, tax division, §47-3301.
Asset, §28-3101.
Fraudulent transfers, §28-3101.
Asset-backed security.
Insurance investments, §31-1371.02.
Assignment, §28-2901.
Fiduciary security transfers, §28-2901.
Assistance unit, §4-201.01.
Assistant living administrator.
Assisted living residences, §44-102.01.
Assisted living.
Continuing care retirement communities, §44-151.01.
Assisted living administration, practice of, §3-1201.02.
Assisted living residence, §§7-701.01, 44-102.01.
Assist in the transmission.
Spam deterrence, §28-5001.
Assistive device dealer.
Assistive technology device warranty, §28-4031.
Assistive device lessor.
Assistive technology device warranty, §28-4031.
Assistive technology device.
Assistive technology device warranty, §28-4031.

DEFINED TERMS —Cont'd
Associate commissioner for securities and banking.
Insurance, securities, and banking, department of, §31-101.
Association.
Captive insurance companies, §31-3931.01.
Cooperative associations, §29-902.
Domestic limited cooperative associations, §29-1001.02.
Life and health insurance guaranty association, §31-5401.
Savings and loan acquisitions, §26-1201.
Association captive insurer, §31-3931.01.
Athlete.
Athletic concussion program, §7-2871.01.
Athlete agent, §47-2887.01.
Athletic activity.
Athletic concussion program, §7-2871.01.
Athletic contests, §22-1708.
Athletic director.
Athlete agents, §47-2887.01.
Athletic program.
Athletic equity, §38-841.01.
Athletic training, practice of, §3-1201.02.
ATJ.
Access to justice initiative program, §4-1701.01.
At least a moderate intellectual disability, §7-1301.03.
At-risk.
School-based budgeting and accountability, §38-2801.01.
Uniform per student funding formula, §38-2901.
Attachment point.
Stop-loss health insurance for employers, §31-3821.
Attending clinician.
Standby guardianship, §16-4802.
Attending physician, §7-621.
Non-resuscitation procedures for EMS, §7-651.01.
Attends school.
Sex offender registration, §22-4001.
Attest services.
Certified public accountants, §47-2853.41.
Attorney.
Legal service, §1-608.51.

DEFINED TERMS —Cont'd
Attorney —Cont'd
Title insurance producers, §31-5041.01.
Title insurers, §31-5031.01.
Attorney for the government.
Criminal procedure, CrimPro Rule 54.
Attorney general, §41-102.
Criminal abuse, neglect and financial exploitation of vulnerable adults and elderly persons, §22-932.
Department of health care finance, §7-771.01.
Elections, §1-1001.02.
Health occupations, §3-1201.01.
Home Rule act, §1-204.35.
Intrafamily offenses, §16-1001.
Merit system, §1-603.01.
Non-health related occupations and professions licensure, §47-2853.01.
Tuition of nonresidents, §38-303.
Attorney in fact, §21-2202.
Mental health consumer's rights, §7-1231.02.
Attorneys' fees.
Adoption voucher fund, §4-342.
Audiologist, §28-4001.
Hearing aid dealers, §28-4001.
Audiology assistant, practice by, §3-1201.02.
Audiology, practice of, §3-1201.02.
Audit committee.
Annual audited financial reports, §31-301.
Audited financial report, §31-301.
Authenticate.
Secured transactions, §28:9-102.
Authority.
Health benefit exchange authority, §31-3171.01.
Office of inspector general, §1-301.115a.
Authority facilities.
Washington metropolitan airports authority, §9-901.
Authorized.
Life and health insurance guaranty association, §31-5406.
Authorized account.
Funds transfers, §28:4A-105.
Authorized company, §31-2501.03.
Authorized control level event.
Health insurance regulatory standards, §31-3451.01.
Authorized control level RBC, §31-2001.
Health insurance regulatory standards, §31-3451.01.

DEFINED TERMS —Cont'd

Authorized dealer.
Assistive technology device warranty, §28-4031.

Authorized decision-maker.
Non-resuscitation procedures for EMS, §7-651.01.

Authorized delegate.
City Market at O Street tax increment financing, §2-1217.33a.
Electric company infrastructure improvement financing, §34-1311.01.
Energy efficiency financing, §8-1778.02.
Housing production trust fund, bond issues, §42-2812.01.
Howard Theatre redevelopment project, §2-1217.151.
Howard Theatre redevelopment project TIF area, §2-1217.34a.
Income tax secured bonds, §47-340.26.
Money transmissions, §26-1001.
New convention center hotel, §10-1221.01.
Qualified zone academy revenue bond project forward commitment approval act, §2-1217.102.
Skyland TIF area, §2-1217.35a.
Southwest waterfront bond financing, §2-1217.131.

Authorized employee representative, §32-1101.

Authorized person, §44-602.

Authorized personnel.
Testing integrity in public schools, §§38-771.01, 38-2602.

Authorized practitioner.
Medical marijuana, §7-1671.01.

Authorized receiving facility.
Newborn safe haven, §4-1451.01.

Authorized representative.
Hospital discharge planning, §21-2231.01.

Authorized shares.
Corporations, §29-301.02.

Authorized signatory.
Transportation infrastructure improvement GARVEE bonds, §9-107.51.

Authorizing official.
Police and fire departments, §5-1304.

Automated data system, §2-213.01.

Automated external defibrillator.
Defibrillator usage, §44-231.

DEFINED TERMS —Cont'd

Automated parking enforcement system.
Traffic ticket adjudication, §50-2303.02a.

Automated teller machine, §26-131.02.

Automated traffic enforcement system, §50-2209.01.

Automated transaction.
Electronic transactions, uniform act, §28-4901.

Automatic data processing, §2-213.01.

Automotive product, §36-301.01.

Autonomous vehicle, §50-2351.

Available business franchise tax revenue.
Income tax secured bonds, §47-340.26.

Available income tax revenues.
Income tax secured bonds, §47-340.26.

Available increment.
City Market at O Street tax increment financing, §2-1217.33a.
Skyland TIF area, §2-1217.35a.
Southwest waterfront bond financing, §2-1217.131.

Available real property tax increment.
Howard Theatre redevelopment project TIF area, §2-1217.34a.

Available real property tax increment revenues.
Howard Theatre redevelopment project, §2-1217.151.

Available real property tax revenues, §2-1217.01.
City Market at O Street tax increment financing, §2-1217.33a.
New convention center hotel, §10-1221.01.
Qualified zone academy revenue bond project forward commitment approval act, §2-1217.102.
Retail development incentives, §2-1217.71.
Skyland TIF area, §2-1217.35a.

Available revenue.
Revenue bonds, notes or other obligations, §1-204.90.

Available sales tax increment revenues.
Howard Theatre redevelopment project, §2-1217.151.
Howard Theatre redevelopment project TIF area, §2-1217.34a.

DEFINED TERMS —Cont'd

Available sales tax revenues,
§2-1217.01.
City Market at O Street tax increment
financing, §2-1217.33a.
New convention center hotel,
§10-1221.01.
Retail development incentives,
§2-1217.71.
Skyland TIF area, §2-1217.35a.
Southwest waterfront bond financing,
§2-1217.131.

Available tax increment.
City Market at O Street tax increment
financing, §2-1217.33a.
Howard Theatre redevelopment
project, §2-1217.151.
Howard Theatre redevelopment project
TIF area, §2-1217.34a.
New convention center hotel,
§10-1221.01.
Skyland TIF area, §2-1217.35a.

Available tax revenues.
Income tax secured bonds, §47-340.26.

**Average annual net backpay or
frontpay.**
Employment discrimination, income
average, §47-1806.10.

Average daily attendance.
Charter schools, §38-1800.02.

Average daily membership.
Charter schools, §38-1800.02.

Average pay, §5-701.

Average salary.
Teachers' retirement, §38-2021.13.

Aversive intervention.
Nonpublic schools, §38-2561.01.

Backhaul.
Wireless network antennae franchise
agreement, §34-1731.02.

Backpay.
Employment discrimination, income
average, §47-1806.10.

Backpay period.
Employment discrimination, income
average, §47-1806.10.

Back-up drink.
Alcoholic beverages, §25-101.

Bad debt.
Health planning and development
agency, §44-401.

Bail determination, §23-1302.

Bailee.
Warehouse receipts, §28:7-102.

Baiting.
Penalty for fighting or baiting animals,
§22-1006.01.

DEFINED TERMS —Cont'd

Ballast.
Energy efficiency standards,
§8-1771.01.

Ballpark, §10-1601.05.
Ballpark construction hard and soft
costs cap, §10-1601.31.
Ballpark fee, §47-2761.
Ballpark sales taxes, §47-2002.05.

Ballpark revenue fund.
Ballpark fee, §47-2761.
Ballpark sales taxes, §47-2002.05.

Ballpark site.
Ballpark construction hard and soft
costs cap, §10-1601.31.

Bank, §26-551.02.
Automated teller machine, §26-131.02.
Fiduciaries, §26-1311.01.
Funds transfers, §28:4A-105.
Interstate banking and branching,
§26-732.
Investment and deposit of District
funds, §47-351.01.
Secured transactions, §28:9-102.
Uniform commercial code, §28:1-201.
Uniform fiduciaries act, §21-1701.

Bank holding company.
Banks and financial institutions,
§26-551.02.
Universal banks, §26-1401.02.

Banking business.
International banking corporations,
§26-631.
Investment and deposit of District
funds, §47-351.01.

Banking day.
Bank deposits and collections,
§28:4-104.

Banking organization, §41-102.
Bank-offered spot rate, §15-901.
Bar-arm hold, §5-125.02.

Bar counsel.
Attorney discipline or disability
proceedings, DCBar Rule XI.

Bar foundation.
Access to justice initiative program,
§4-1701.01.

Barge.
Uniform certificates of title for vessels,
§50-1541.01.

Barrel of corn.
Weights and measures, §37-203.01.

Bartender.
Alcoholic beverages, §25-101.

BAS agreement.
Qualified social electronic commerce
companies tax abatements,
§47-1818.01.

DEFINED TERMS —Cont'd
Baseball site.
Ballpark, §10-1601.05.
Baseball stadium.
Armory board, §3-342.01.
Baseball stadium agreement.
Ballpark, §10-1601.05.
Base calculation year, §42-3501.03.
Base closure act.
Walter Reed Army Medical Center,
§10-1901.
Walter Reed Medical Center site
development, §2-1227.01.
Base infrastructure investment.
Motion pictures, §2-1204.11c.
Base jurisdiction, §50-1507.01.
Baseline mammogram, §31-2901.
Base period, §51-101.
Base plate, §50-1507.01.
Base rent, §42-3501.03.
Base year.
Fee collection incentive fund,
§1-325.61.
Basic business license, §47-2851.01.
Basic business license application,
§47-2851.01.
Basic component of AccessRx.
Access to prescription drugs,
§48-831.02.
Basic health care services, §31-3401.
Basic life support.
Fire departments, §5-401.
Basic necessities.
Homeless services, §4-751.01.
Basic property insurance, §31-5002.
Basic salary, §5-701.
Basic service.
Office of cable television, film, music,
and entertainment amendment
act of 2015, §34-1251.03.
Basic skills program.
Adult literacy task force, §32-1661.
Basic workweek.
Police and fire departments, §5-1304.
Basis, §47-1401.
Bearer.
UCC, §28:1-201.
Bearer form.
Investment securities, §28:8-102.
Bee disease.
Bees, §8-1825.02.
Beer, §25-101.
Bees, §8-1825.02.
Behavioral health.
Behavioral health department,
§7-1141.01.

DEFINED TERMS —Cont'd
Behavioral health —Cont'd
Child abuse and neglect, §4-1301.02.
Early childhood and school-based
behavioral health infrastructure,
§2-1517.31.
Mental health department, §7-1131.02.
Youth behavioral health epidemiology
reports, §2-1517.02.
Behavioral health assessment.
Child abuse and neglect, §4-1301.02.
Mental health department, §7-1131.02.
Behavioral health ombudsman.
Mental health department, §7-1131.02.
**Behavioral health ombudsman
program.**
Mental health department, §7-1131.02.
Behavioral health screening.
Child abuse and neglect, §4-1301.02.
Mental health department, §7-1131.02.
Behavioral health services.
Behavioral health department,
§7-1141.01.
Behavioral plan.
Rights of persons with intellectual
disability, §7-1301.03.
Belief.
Rules of professional conduct,
ProfCond Rule 1.0.
Believes.
Rules of professional conduct,
ProfCond Rule 1.0.
Below-the-line crew.
Motion pictures, §2-1204.11c.
Beneficial owner.
Corporations, §29-311.01.
Statutory trusts, §29-1201.02.
Beneficial shareholder.
Corporations, §§29-311.01, 29-312.20.
Beneficiary, §§4-601, 31-2402,
31-3301.01.
Custodial trusts, §19-1101.
First source employment, §2-219.01.
Funds transfers, §28:4A-103.
Letters of credit, §28:5-102.
Nonprobate transfers on death,
§19-602.01.
Principal and income, §28-4801.02.
Small and certified business enterprise
development and assistance,
§2-218.02.
Uniform real property transfers on
death, §19-604.02.
Uniform trust code, §19-1301.03.
Beneficiary form.
TOD securities registration,
§19-603.01.

DEFINED TERMS —Cont'd

Beneficiary's bank.
Funds transfers, §28:4A-103.
Benefit contract, §31-5301.
Benefit corporations, §29-1301.02.
Benefit director.
Benefit corporations, §29-1301.02.
Benefit enforcement proceeding.
Benefit corporations, §29-1301.02.
Benefit, foreign missions, §6-1302.
Benefit member, §31-5301.
Benefit officer.
Benefit corporations, §29-1301.02.
Benefit period.
Real property tax abatement for
qualified high technology
companies, §47-811.03.
Benefit plan, §21-301.
Life and health insurance guaranty
association, §31-5401.
Benefits, §§4-801, 51-101.
Veterans' affairs, office of, §49-1001.
Benefits system.
Merit system, other post-employment
benefits system, §1-621.09b.
Benefit year, §51-101.
**Best available control technology
(BACT), §8-1051.**
Air pollution, demand response
generating sources, §8-101.11.
Best interests.
Guardianship, etc., §21-2011.
Rights of persons with intellectual
disability, §7-1301.03.
Best management practices.
Wastewater disposal systems,
§8-105.02.
Between merchants, §28:2-104.
Beverage.
Alcoholic beverages, §25-101.
Bias-related crime, §22-3701.
Bicycle parking space.
Bicycles commuter and parking
expansion, §50-1641.01.
Bicycles, §50-1609.
Identifying numbers, tampering with
or removing, §22-3234.
Bicyclist.
Bicycle insurance policies, §50-531.
BID.
Business improvement districts,
§2-1215.02.
BID activity.
Business improvement districts,
§2-1215.02.
Bid bond.
Procurement practices, §2-351.04.

DEFINED TERMS —Cont'd

BID corporation.
Business improvement districts,
§2-1215.02.
Bidder.
Procurement practices, §2-351.04.
Bid off property, §47-1303.01.
Bid premium.
Retail electric competition and
consumer protection, §34-1501.
Bid price.
Procurement practices, §2-351.04.
Bid proposal.
Chesapeake regional Olympic games
authority, §2-1131.
BID tax.
Business improvement districts,
§2-1215.02.
Biennial report.
Business organizations, §29-101.02.
Bi-fuel vehicle, §50-702.
Bigamy, §22-501.
Bikeshare.
Fleet management, publicly-owned
vehicles, §50-211.01.
Billed assessed value.
Real property tax abatement for
qualified high technology
companies, §47-811.03.
Billiard parlor.
Gross sales tax, §47-2001.
Bill of lading.
UCC, §28:1-201.
Biological agent.
Anti-terrorism act of 2002, §22-3152.
Biological material.
Crime investigation records, §5-113.31.
Protection of innocence act, §22-4131.
Birthing hospital.
Parentage, §16-909.03.
Birth parent.
Adoption, Adoption Rule 2.
Black liquor.
Renewable energy portfolio standards,
§34-1431.
Blighted area.
Acquisition and disposal of abandoned
and deteriorated property,
§42-3171.01.
Blighted vacant building.
Fire safety, §42-3131.05.
Blind, §§7-903, 32-302.
Income tax, §47-1801.04.
Blind person, §7-1009.
Block.
Business improvement districts,
§2-1215.02.

DEFINED TERMS —Cont'd

Block parties, §9-631.

Blue Plains.
Wastewater disposal systems, §8-105.02.

Blunt wrap.
Drug paraphernalia, §48-1101.

Board, §47-2853.01.
Automobile consumer protection, §50-501.
Certified public accountants, §47-2853.41.
Forensic sciences department, §5-1501.01.
Government employee engagement in political activity, §1-1171.01.
Not-for-profit hospital corporations, §44-951.01.

Board of directors.
Limited cooperative associations, §29-1001.02.
Nonprofit corporations, §29-401.02.

Board of judges, §11-1902.

Boards and commissions.
Governmental reorganization, §1-315.02.
Merit system, §1-603.01.

Boards of allied health.
Health occupations, §3-1201.01.

Boards of behavioral health.
Health occupations, §3-1201.01.

Bodily injury.
Sexual abuse, §22-3001.

Body art.
Body art establishments, business licenses, §47-2809.01.

Body art establishments.
Business licenses, §47-2809.01.

Body artist.
Body art establishments, business licenses, §47-2809.01.

Body art procedure.
Body art establishments, business licenses, §47-2809.01.

Body piercings.
Body art establishments, business licenses, §47-2809.01.

Bona fide association, §31-3301.01.

Bona fide loan discount points.
Mortgage loan protection, §26-1151.01.

Bona fide offer of sale.
Rental housing, §42-3401.03.

Bona fide physician-patient relationship.
Medical marijuana, §7-1671.01.

Bona fide prospective purchaser.
Brownfield revitalization, §8-631.02.

DEFINED TERMS —Cont'd

Bond act.
Verizon center sales tax, §47-2002.06.

Bond counsel.
City Market at O Street tax increment financing, §2-1217.33a.
Electric company infrastructure improvement financing, §34-1311.01.
Energy efficiency financing, §8-1778.02.
Housing production trust fund, bond issues, §42-2812.01.
Howard Theatre redevelopment project, §2-1217.151.
Howard Theatre redevelopment project TIF area, §2-1217.34a.
Income tax secured bonds, §47-340.26.
New convention center hotel, §10-1221.01.
Qualified zone academy revenue bond project forward commitment approval act, §2-1217.102.
Skyland TIF area, §2-1217.35a.
Southwest waterfront bond financing, §2-1217.131.
Transportation infrastructure improvement GARVEE bonds, §9-107.51.

Bonding business, §23-1101.

Bonds.
Ballpark, §10-1601.03.
Ballpark construction hard and soft costs cap, §10-1601.31.
Ballpark fee, §47-2761.
Bonds and undertakings, §28-2501.
Capper/Carrollsburg PILOT.
Payments in lieu of taxes, §47-4611.
City Market at O Street tax increment financing, §2-1217.33a.
Electric company infrastructure improvement financing, §34-1311.01.
Energy efficiency financing, §8-1778.02.
Green buildings, §6-1451.01.
Housing finance agency, §42-2701.02.
Housing production trust fund, bond issues, §42-2812.01.
Howard Theatre redevelopment project, §2-1217.151.
Howard Theatre redevelopment project TIF area, §2-1217.34a.
Income tax secured bonds, §47-340.26.
Industrial revenue bonds, §47-340.01.
New convention center hotel, §10-1221.01.

DEFINED TERMS —Cont'd
Bonds —Cont'd
Payments in lieu of taxes, §47-1052.
PILOT agreements, §1-308.01.
Procurement practices, §2-351.04.
Public parking authority, §50-2502.
Qualified zone academy revenue bond project forward commitment approval act, §2-1217.102.
Real property taxes.
  Special energy assessments, §47-895.31.
Retail development incentives, §2-1217.71.
Rhode Island Metro Plaza PILOT.
  Payments in lieu of taxes, sales tax exemption, §47-4613.
Skyland TIF area, §2-1217.35a.
Southwest waterfront bond financing, §2-1217.131.
Southwest waterfront special assessment district, §47-895.01.
Tobacco settlement financing, §7-1831.01.
Transportation infrastructure improvement GARVEE bonds, §9-107.51.
Washington convention and sports authority, §10-1202.01.
Washington metropolitan airports authority, §9-901.
Bondsman, §23-1101.
Book.
District of Columbia housing authority, §6-201.
BOOT CAMP, §24-921.
Born in wedlock, §16-907.
Born out of wedlock, §16-907.
Borrower, §26-1101.
Foreclosure mediation, §42-815.02.
Mortgage loan protection, §26-1151.01.
Bottle-type water dispenser.
Energy efficiency standards, §8-1771.01.
Boundaries of the United States.
Unsworn foreign declarations, §16-5302.
Bowling alley.
Gross sales tax, §47-2001.
Branch, §26-732.
Savings and loan acquisitions, §26-1201.
UCC, §28:1-201.
Branch business.
Captive insurance companies, §31-3931.01.

DEFINED TERMS —Cont'd
Branch captive insurer, §31-3931.01.
Branch office.
Savings and loan acquisitions, §26-1201.
Branch operations.
Captive insurance companies, §31-3931.01.
Brand.
Extended manufacturer responsibility for electronic waste, §8-1041.01.
Brand family.
Tobacco master settlement agreement enforcement, §7-1803.02.
Branding.
Body art establishments, business licenses, §47-2809.01.
BRC.
Building rehabilitation code, §6-1410.
Breastfeeding.
Breastmilk bank and lactation support, §7-881.01.
Breastmilk.
Breastmilk bank and lactation support, §7-881.01.
Brew pub, §25-101.
Bridge loan.
Mortgage loan protection, §26-1151.01.
Broker, §§21-301, 31-2501.03, 31-4202.
Investment securities, §28:8-102.
Retail electric competition and consumer protection, §34-1501.
Unfair insurance trade practices, §31-2231.01.
Brokerage relationship, §42-1702.
Broker-dealer.
Security agents and broker, §31-5601.01.
Brood.
Bees, §8-1825.02.
Brother, §§1-623.01, 32-1501.
Brownfield.
Brownfield revitalization, §8-631.02.
Brush.
Renewable energy portfolio standards, §34-1431.
Budget.
Budget reprogramming policy, §47-361.
Home Rule act, §1-201.03.
Budget category.
Budget reprogramming policy, §47-361.
Budget gap, §47-318.
Budget modification, §47-318.
Builder's certificate.
Uniform certificates of title for vessels, §50-1541.01.

DEFINED TERMS —Cont'd

Building, §8-171.02.
Green buildings, §6-1451.01.
Submetering, §34-1551.
Building code, §8-171.02.
Building code official, §6-1401.
Building improvement plan,
§42-3501.03.
Building materials.
Supermarket tax incentives, §47-3801.
Building owner, operator or
manager.
Submetering, §34-1551.
Building systems monitoring
method.
Green buildings, §6-1451.01.
Bullying, §2-1535.01.
Bundled.
Ethics and government accountability,
§1-1161.01.
Bundling.
Ethics and government accountability,
§1-1161.01.
Burden of establishing.
UCC, §28:1-201.
Burglary, §22-801.
Business.
Business licenses, §47-2851.01.
Ethics and government accountability,
§1-1161.01.
Gross sales tax, §47-2001.
Human trafficking, §22-1831.
Partnerships, §29-601.02.
Procurement practices, §2-351.04.
Trade names, §47-2855.01.
Trash compactor grant program,
§8-751.
Business associate.
Mental health department, §7-1131.02.
Business association, §41-102.
Business concern.
Quick payment provisions, §2-221.01.
Business contributor.
Ethics and government accountability,
§1-1161.01.
Business corporation.
Business organizations, §29-101.02.
Business day.
Alcoholic beverages, §25-101.
Child support enforcement, §46-201.
Business enterprise.
Small and certified business enterprise
development and assistance,
§2-218.02.
Business entity, §8-111.01.
Ethics and government accountability,
§1-1161.01.

DEFINED TERMS —Cont'd

Business entity —Cont'd
Insurance investments, §31-1371.02.
Insurance producers, §31-1131.02.
Lead-hazard prevention and
elimination, §8-231.01.
Title insurance producers,
§31-5041.01.
Title insurers, §31-5031.01.
Business franchise tax.
Income tax secured bonds, §47-340.26.
Business improvement district,
§2-1215.02.
Business improvement district
activity, §2-1215.02.
Business income.
Income tax, §47-1801.04.
Business incubator, §2-1209.02.
Business license center, §47-2851.01.
Business of banking.
Banks and financial institutions,
§26-551.02.
Business of insurance, §22-3225.01.
Business of title insurance.
Title insurance producers,
§31-5041.01.
Title insurers, §31-5031.01.
Business operations.
Employees retirement program
management, §1-335.01.
Business trust, §29-101.02.
Business with which he or she is
associated.
Ethics and government accountability,
§1-1161.01.
Bus stop.
Smoking restrictions, §7-1702.
Buyer, §28-3701.
Revolving credit accounts, §28-3701.
Sales, §28:2-103.
Uniform certificates of title for vessels,
§50-1541.01.
Buyer agency.
Capital project support fund,
§1-325.151.
Buyer in ordinary course of
business.
Leases, UCC, §28:2A-103.
UCC, §28:1-201.
Uniform certificates of title for vessels,
§50-1541.01.
Bylaws.
Corporations, §29-301.02.
Limited cooperative associations,
§29-1001.02.
Nonprofit corporations, §29-401.02.

DEFINED TERMS —Cont'd
By operation of law.
Uniform certificates of title for vessels, §50-1541.19.
By type of property.
Civil asset forfeiture, §41-301.
Cable, §34-2001.
Cable facility.
Office of cable television, film, music, and entertainment amendment act of 2015, §34-1251.03.
Cable operator.
Cable television operators, protection of customer privacy, §34-1260.02.
Cable theft, §34-1264.02.
Office of cable television, film, music, and entertainment amendment act of 2015, §34-1251.03.
Cable service.
Cable theft, §34-1264.02.
Office of cable television, film, music, and entertainment amendment act of 2015, §34-1251.03.
Cable system.
Office of cable television, film, music, and entertainment amendment act of 2015, §34-1251.03.
Calendar day.
Appeals, DCCtApp Rule 1.
Calendar quarter, §51-101.
Call center.
Office of unified communications, §1-327.51.
Call center technology.
Office of unified communications, §1-327.51.
Called.
Life and health insurance guaranty association, §31-5406.
Call option.
Insurance investments, §31-1371.02.
Campus police officer, §47-2839.01.
Canadian broker-dealer.
Securities brokers and dealers, §31-5601.01.
Cancel.
Uniform certificates of title for vessels, §50-1541.01.
Cancellation.
Leases, UCC, §28:2A-103.
Sales, §28:2-106.
C. & F.
Sales, §28:2-320.
Candidate.
Ethics and government accountability, §1-1161.01.

DEFINED TERMS —Cont'd
Candidate —Cont'd
Government employee engagement in political activity, §1-1171.01.
Grant administration, §1-328.11.
Candlefoot power.
Automated teller machine, §26-131.02.
Cannabis, §48-901.02.
Cap.
Insurance investments, §31-1371.02.
Capable of being centrally fueled, §50-702.
Capacity.
Mental health consumer's rights, §7-1231.02.
Capital.
Banks and financial institutions, §26-551.02.
Merchant bank, §26-831.02.
Universal banks, §26-1401.02.
Capital accounts.
Universal banks, §26-1401.02.
Capital and surplus.
Insurance investments, §31-1371.02.
Capital asset.
Income tax, §47-1801.04.
Capital budget.
Budget reprogramming policy, §47-361.
Capital City Business and Industrial Area, §2-1217.01.
Capital City Market, §6-1062.02.
Workforce housing production program, §6-1061.02.
Capital City Market Area, §2-1217.01.
Capital City Plan.
Regulation of for-hire vehicles, §50-301.03.
Capital costs.
Arts, cultural and educational facilities, economic assistance to, §39-401.
Capital expenditure.
Health planning and development agency, §44-401.
Capital improvement, §§2-1217.01, 42-3501.03.
Capital lease financing, §47-336.
Capital project.
Budget reprogramming policy, §47-361.
Capital project support fund, §1-325.151.
Home Rule act, §1-201.03.
Income tax secured bonds, §47-340.26.
Capital stock.
Universal banks, §26-1401.02.

DEFINED TERMS —Cont'd

Capitated basis, §31-3401.

Capitol buildings, §10-503.26.

Capitol exclusion zone.
Hazardous materials transportation, terrorism prevention, §8-1422.

Capitol riverfront nonprofit zone.
Nonprofit corporations locating in emerging commercial neighborhoods, §47-857.11.

Capper/Carrollsburg PILOT area.
Payments in lieu of taxes, §47-4611.

Capper/Carrollsburg public improvements.
District of Columbia housing authority, §6-201.

CapStat.
Department of the environment, §8-151.01.

Captive insurers, §§31-401, 31-3931.01.

Captive manager.
Medical liability captive insurance agency, §1-307.81.

Cardiac arrest.
Non-resuscitation procedures for EMS, §7-651.01.

Cardiopulmonary resuscitation.
Non-resuscitation procedures for EMS, §7-651.01.

Career pathways.
Adult literacy task force, §32-1661.

Career service.
Merit system, §1-603.01.

CareFirst.
CareFirst tax credit for wages, sales tax exemption, §47-4602.

CareFirst project.
CareFirst tax credit for wages, sales tax exemption, §47-4602.

Caregiver, §§7-1901, 7-2031, 31-4001.
Medical marijuana, §7-1671.01.

Caretaker.
Child support enforcement, §46-201.

Caretaker relative, §4-201.01.

Carotid artery hold, §5-125.02.

Car pool, §8-171.02.

Carriage, §8-2001.

Carrier, §32-1501.
Merit system, health benefits, §1-621.03.
Strict liability for release of hazardous waste during transport, §8-1441.
Voluntary withdrawal by health benefit plan carriers, §31-3151.
Warehouse receipts, §28:7-102.

DEFINED TERMS —Cont'd

Carrying charge subsidies.
Real property assessment, §47-802.

Case jacket.
Crime investigation records, §5-113.31.

Case mix reimbursement methodology.
Nursing homes, §47-1261.

Case plan.
Child abuse and neglect, §4-1301.02.

Case review subcommittee.
Victims of crime, sexual assault response, §4-561.01.

Cash and carry, §28-4521.

Cash equivalent.
Insurance investments, §31-1371.02.

Cashier's checks.
Negotiable instruments, §28:3-104.

Cash medical support.
Divorce, annulment, separation, support, §16-901.

Cash price.
Lease-purchase agreements, §42-3671.01.

Cash proceeds.
Secured transactions, §28:9-102.

Casting a vote.
Corporations, §29-301.02.
Nonprofit corporations, §29-401.02.

Categorical eligibility.
Food stamps, §4-261.01.

Categorical preference.
Chief financial officer, tax transparency, §1-301.156.

Categorical pretreatment standards.
Wastewater disposal systems, §8-105.02.

Categorical standards, §8-105.02.

Categorical wastewater.
Wastewater disposal systems, §8-105.02.

Caterers.
Alcoholic beverages, §25-101.

Cause injury to others as a result of the individual's intellectual disability.
Rights of persons with intellectual disability, §7-1301.03.

CBE agreement.
Skyland TIF area, §2-1217.35a.

CBO.
Pre-kindergarten programs, §38-271.01.

CDC.
Human papillomavirus vaccination, §7-1651.01.

DEFINED TERMS —Cont'd

Ceased to attend school, §4-205.61.

Cellular telephone.
Prison contraband, §22-2603.01.

Cellular telephone or other portable communication device and accessories thereto.
Prison contraband, §22-2603.01.

Census tracts.
Wireless network antennae franchise agreement, §34-1731.02.

Center.
Breastmilk bank and lactation support, §7-881.01.

Center hall, §37-101.

Center Leg Freeway (interstate 395) PILOT area.
Payments in lieu of taxes, §47-4637.

Central administration.
Uniform per student funding formula, §38-2901.

Central alarm station, §7-2802.

Central authority.
Interstate family support, §46-357.01.

Central business district.
Personal delivery devices pilot program, §50-1551.

Central collection unit.
Delinquent debts to the District, recovery, §1-350.01.

Central labor council.
District of Columbia housing authority, §6-201.

Centrally fueled, §50-702.

Certificate, §§31-3701, 31-5301, 38-1302, 47-2853.01.
Certified public accountants, §47-2853.41.
Liens on motor vehicles or trailers, §50-1201.
Long-term care insurance, §31-3601.

Certificated security, §28:8-102.

Certificate form, §31-3701.

Certificate of approval.
Nonpublic schools, §38-2561.01.

Certificate of eligibility, §42-3503.01.

Certificate of limited partnership.
Limited partnerships, §29-701.02.

Certificate of occupancy.
Green buildings, §6-1451.03.
Waterfront park special assessment district, §47-895.21.

Certificate of organization.
Limited liability companies, §29-801.02.

Certificate of origin.
Uniform certificates of title for vessels, §50-1541.01.

DEFINED TERMS —Cont'd

Certificate of registration.
Telephone solicitation fraud, §22-3226.01.

Certificate of title.
Secured transactions, §28:9-102.
Uniform certificates of title for vessels, §50-1541.01.

Certificate of trust.
Statutory trusts, §29-1201.02.

Certificates of deposit.
Negotiable instruments, §28:3-104.

Certification, §31-3301.01.
Choice in drug treatment, §7-3002.

Certification standard.
Energy efficiency financing, §8-1778.02.

Certified applicator, §8-401.

Certified automated system.
Streamlined sales and use tax agreement, §1-301.121.

Certified business enterprise.
Skyland TIF area, §2-1217.35a.
Small and certified business enterprise development and assistance, §2-218.02.
Walter Reed Medical Center site development, §2-1227.01.

Certified capital.
Certified capital companies, §31-5231.

Certified capital company, §31-5231.

Certified checks.
Negotiable instruments, §28:3-409.

Certified equity participant.
Small and certified business enterprise development and assistance, §2-218.02.

Certified facility.
Construction and demolition waste recycling accountability, §8-1071.

Certified investor.
Certified capital companies, §31-5231.

Certified joint venture.
Small and certified business enterprise development and assistance, §2-218.02.

Certified nurse practitioner, §38-601.

Certified service provider.
Streamlined sales and use tax agreement, §1-301.121.

Certify, certified and certification, §47-2853.01.

Certifying entity.
Stroke system of care, §44-1151.

CFBR.
Cottage food business registry, §7-742.01.

DEFINED TERMS —Cont'd
CFO.
ABLE savings accounts, §47-4901.
Business improvement districts,
§2-1215.02.
Chief financial officer, tax
transparency, §1-301.156.
Community development by financial
institutions, §26-431.02.
Delinquent taxpayers, §47-4481.
District of Columbia housing
authority, §6-201.
Procurement practices, §2-351.04.
Retail development incentives,
§2-1217.71.
CFR.
Wastewater disposal systems,
§8-105.02.
CFSA.
Newborn safe haven, §4-1451.01.
Chain of stores.
Commercial property energy
conservation, §8-1772.01.
Chairman.
Howard Theatre redevelopment
project, §2-1217.151.
Howard Theatre redevelopment project
TIF area, §2-1217.34a.
Skyland TIF area, §2-1217.35a.
Chancellor.
Early childhood education, §38-755.01.
Metropolitan police school safety
division, §5-132.01.
Chancery, §6-1302.
Change of occupancy.
Building rehabilitation code, §6-1410.
Change of ownership.
Assisted living residences, §44-102.01.
Nurse staffing agencies, §44-1051.02.
Change order.
Procurement practices, §2-351.04.
Charitable.
Charitable solicitations, §44-1701.
Charitable corporation.
Nonprofit corporations, §29-401.02.
Charitable purpose.
Nonprofit corporations, §29-401.02.
Prudent management of institutional
funds, §44-1631.
Charitable trust.
Uniform trust code, §19-1301.03.
Chartering authority.
Tuition of nonresidents, §38-304.
Charter school, §38-1800.02.
Charter school facility incubator,
§38-1800.02.

DEFINED TERMS —Cont'd
Chattel paper.
Secured transactions, §28:9-102.
Chauffeur.
Fleet management, publicly-owned
vehicles, §50-211.01.
Check, §26-301.
Negotiable instruments, §§28:3-104,
28:3-312.
Check cashing, §26-301.
Chemical restraint.
Assisted living residences, §44-102.01.
Chemical test, §50-1901.
Impaired operation or driving,
§50-2206.01.
Chief.
Firefighter retirement while under
disciplinary investigation, §5-1051.
Chief clinical officer.
Hospitalization of persons with mental
illness, §21-501.
Chief election officer.
National popular vote interstate
agreement, §1-1051.01.
Chief executive.
National popular vote interstate
agreement, §1-1051.01.
Chief financial officer.
ABLE savings accounts, §47-4901.
Ballpark fee, §47-2761.
Capital project support fund,
§1-325.151.
City Market at O Street tax increment
financing, §2-1217.33a.
District of Columbia housing
authority, §6-201.
Electric company infrastructure
improvement financing,
§34-1311.01.
Energy efficiency financing,
§8-1778.02.
Housing production trust fund, bond
issues, §42-2812.01.
Howard Theatre redevelopment
project, §2-1217.151.
Howard Theatre redevelopment project
TIF area, §2-1217.34a.
H Street, N.E. retail priority area
incentive, §1-325.171.
Income tax secured bonds, §47-340.26.
Job growth tax credit, §47-1807.51.
New convention center hotel,
§10-1221.01.
New Town at Capital City Market
revitalization, §6-1062.02.
New York avenue metrorail benefit
area, §47-881.

DEFINED TERMS —Cont'd
Chief financial officer —Cont'd
Procurement practices, §2-351.04.
Qualified zone academy revenue bond project forward commitment approval act, §2-1217.102.
Real property taxes, special energy assessments, §47-895.31.
Rental of public space, §10-1101.01.
Skyland TIF area, §2-1217.35a.
Southeast water and sewer improvement benefit district, §47-891.
Southwest waterfront bond financing, §2-1217.131.
Southwest waterfront special assessment district, §47-895.01.
Transportation infrastructure improvement GARVEE bonds, §9-107.51.
Unified economic development budget transparency and accountability, §2-1208.01.
Washington convention and sports authority, §10-1202.01.
Waterfront Park at the Yards, §10-1801.
Workforce housing production program, §6-1061.02.
Chief judge, §11-1902.
Chief of police.
Metropolitan police.
School safety division, §5-132.21.
Chief of service, §21-501.
Chief of the office of compliance.
Consumer protection procedures, §28-3901.
Chief procurement officer.
Procurement practices, §2-351.04.
Chief program director, §7-1301.03.
Chief property management officer, §37-101.
Child.
Child care facilities, §4-401.
Child fatality review committee, §4-1371.02.
Childhood lead poisoning screening and reporting, §7-871.02.
Criminal background checks for the protection of children act, §4-1501.02.
Disability compensation, §1-623.01.
Family leave, §1-612.03c.
Interstate family support, §46-351.02.
License to carry pistol, §7-2509.01.
Reporting of child sexual abuse, §22-3020.51.

DEFINED TERMS —Cont'd
Child —Cont'd
Retirement, §11-1561.
Sexual abuse, §22-3001.
Standby guardianship, §16-4802.
Teachers' retirement, deferred or survivor annuity, §38-2021.09.
Tuition of nonresidents, §38-304.
Uniform child abduction prevention act, §16-4604.02.
Uniform child custody proceedings, §16-4601.01.
Voluntary leave transfer program, §1-612.31.
Workers' compensation, §32-1501.
Child abuse, §4-1341.01.
Child and adult care food program, §38-281.
Child care.
Public assistance, §4-205.61.
Child-custody determination.
Uniform child custody proceedings, §16-4601.01.
Child-custody proceeding.
Uniform child abduction prevention act, §16-4604.02.
Uniform child custody proceedings, §16-4601.01.
Child development associate credential.
Child care facilities, §4-401.
Child development center, §7-2001.
Child care facilities, §4-401.
Child development facility, §§7-2031, 42-2801.
Child and adult food program funding, §38-281.
Child development home, §§7-2001, 31-4001.
Child care facilities, §4-401.
Child development program, §31-4001.
Child fatality.
Public disclosure of findings and information, §4-1303.31.
Child in need of supervision, §16-2301.
Child neglect, §4-1341.01.
Child-occupied facilities.
Lead-hazard prevention and elimination, §8-231.01.
Pesticide education and control, §8-431.
Pre-kindergarten programs, §38-271.01.
Child-placing agencies, §4-1402.

DEFINED TERMS —Cont'd
Child protection register, §4-1301.02.
Child-related educational program.
Child health screening, §7-875.02.
Child-related health program.
Child health screening, §7-875.02.
Child-related human or social services program.
Child health screening, §7-875.02.
Children at risk, §47-4001.
Children of families who are at-risk.
Child care facilities, §4-401.
Children of military families.
Interstate compact on educational opportunity for military children, §49-1101.03.
Children or youth with mental health problems.
Department of mental health, §7-1131.02.
Children with special needs who reside or are receiving care in another state.
Child health screening, §7-875.02.
Child restraint seat, §50-1702.
Child-support order.
Interstate family support, §46-351.02.
Child with a disability.
Special education student rights, §38-2571.02.
State superintendent of education, office of, §38-2601.02.
Child with special needs.
Adoption subsidy payments, §4-301.
Guardianship of minors, §16-2399.
Chiropractic, practice of, §3-1201.02.
Choice of electricity suppliers.
Retail electric competition and consumer protection, §34-1501.
Chronic absenteeism.
Compulsory school attendance, §38-201.
Chronic alcoholic, §24-602.
Church plan, §31-3301.01.
C.I.F.
Sales, §28:2-320.
Cigar.
Gross sales tax, §47-2001.
Tobacco tax, §47-2401.
Cigarettes, §28-4521.
Fire-standard-compliant cigarettes, §7-1751.
Tobacco master settlement agreement, §7-1801.01.
Tobacco master settlement agreement enforcement, §7-1803.02.

DEFINED TERMS —Cont'd
Cigarettes —Cont'd
Tobacco tax, §47-2401.
Circumference.
Urban forest preservation, §8-651.02.
City administrator.
New convention center hotel, §10-1221.01.
Citywide messaging program.
Citywide technology support services, §1-1431.
City-wide resident council advisory board.
District of Columbia housing authority, §6-201.
Citywide security program.
Citywide technology support services, §1-1431.
Civic association, §42-3601.
Civil action.
Criminal procedure, CrimPro Rule 54.
Delinquent minors, JuvProc Rule 101.
Civil celebrant.
Marriage solemnization, §46-406.
Civil defense, §7-2201.
CJCC.
Criminal justice coordinating council, §22-4231.
Claim.
Anti-SLAPP, §16-5501.
Claimant, §§1-623.01, 4-501, 31-5501.
Income tax, §47-1806.06.
Negotiable instruments, §28:3-312.
No-fault motor vehicle insurance, §31-2407.01.
Claimant's insurer.
No-fault motor vehicle insurance, §31-2407.01.
Claim of beneficial interest, §28-2901.
Fiduciary security transfers, §28-2901.
Claims.
Debt collection protection, §28-3814.
Fraudulent transfers, §28-3101.
Guardianship, etc., §21-2011.
Medicaid provider fraud, §4-801.
Procurement practices, §2-381.01.
Veterans' affairs, office of, §49-1001.
Class A contraband.
Prison contraband, §22-2603.01.
Class B contraband.
Prison contraband, §22-2603.01.
Class C contraband.
Prison contraband, §22-2603.01.
Class F(I) historic motor vehicle.
Motor vehicle registration, §50-1501.01.

DEFINED TERMS —Cont'd

Class F(II) historic motor vehicle.
Motor vehicle registration,
§50-1501.01.

Class one bond mutual fund.
Insurance investments, §31-1371.02.

Class one money market mutual fund.
Insurance investments, §31-1371.02.

Clean air act, §50-702.

Clean claim.
Health benefit plans reimbursement,
§31-3131.

Clean fuel, §50-702.

Clean fuel fleet vehicle (CFFV),
§50-702.

Clean fuel vehicle, §50-702.

Cleaning agent, §8-107.02.

Cleansing product.
Body art establishments, business
licenses, §47-2809.01.

Clean water act.
Wastewater disposal systems,
§8-105.02.

Clearance examination.
Lead-hazard prevention and
elimination, §8-231.01.

Clearance report.
Lead-hazard prevention and
elimination, §8-231.01.

Clearing corporation.
Investment securities, §28:8-102.

Clearing house.
Bank deposits and collections,
§28:4-104.

Clerical tasks.
Mortgage lenders and brokers,
§26-1101.

Clerk.
Adoption, Adoption Rule 2.
Appeals, DCCtApp Rule 1.
Criminal records sealing, §16-801.
Domestic relations actions, DomRel
Rule 2.
Jury, §11-1902.

Client, §§7-1201.01, 42-1702.
Choice in drug treatment, §7-3002.
Homeless services, §4-751.01.
Nurse staffing agencies, §44-1051.02.

Client representative, §7-1201.01.

Clinical laboratory, §44-201.

Clinical laboratory practitioners,
§3-1201.01.
Qualifications for licensure, transition
provision, §3-1207.64.

Clinically significant, §31-3101.

DEFINED TERMS —Cont'd

Clinical program.
Law student practice in appeals,
DCCtApp Rule 48.

Closed investigation.
Crime investigation records, §5-113.31.

Close friend.
Health care durable powers of
attorney, §21-2202.

Closing costs, §42-2621.

Closing documents.
City Market at O Street tax increment
financing, §2-1217.33a.
Electric company infrastructure
improvement financing,
§34-1311.01.
Energy efficiency financing,
§8-1778.02.
Housing production trust fund, bond
issues, §42-2812.01.
Howard Theatre redevelopment
project, §2-1217.151.
Howard Theatre redevelopment project
TIF area, §2-1217.34a.
Income tax secured bonds, §47-340.26.
New convention center hotel,
§10-1221.01.
Qualified zone academy revenue bond
project forward commitment
approval act, §2-1217.102.
Skyland TIF area, §2-1217.35a.
Southwest waterfront bond financing,
§2-1217.131.
Transportation infrastructure
improvement GARVEE bonds,
§9-107.51.

Closing-out sale, §47-2101.

Closure, §42-3601.

Club.
Alcoholic beverages, §25-101.

CMPA.
Department of health care finance,
§7-771.01.

CNG.
Regulation of for-hire vehicles,
§50-301.03.

CNG vehicle.
Regulation of for-hire vehicles,
§50-301.03.

Coal tar pavement products.
Stormwater management, §8-153.01.

COBRA continuation provision,
§31-3301.01.

Cocaine, §48-901.02.

Code.
Insurance investments, §31-1371.02.

DEFINED TERMS —Cont'd

Code of conduct.

Ethics and government accountability, §1-1161.01.

Coding guidelines.

Health benefit plans reimbursement, §31-3131.

Coercion.

Human trafficking, §22-1831.

Cognitive impairment.

Assisted living residences, §44-102.01.

Collaboration, §3-1201.01.

Collaborative law communication, §16-4002.

Collaborative law participation agreement, §16-4002.

Collaborative law process, §16-4002.

Collaborative lawyer, §16-4002.

Collaborative matter, §16-4002.

Collaborative practice agreement.

Practice of pharmacy, §3-1201.02.

Collar.

Insurance investments, §31-1371.02.

Collateral.

Secured transactions, §28:9-102.

Collateral costs.

Assistive technology device warranty, §28-4031.

Collateralized mortgage obligations.

Investment and deposit of District funds, §47-351.01.

Collateral source, §4-501.

Collecting bank.

Bank deposits and collections, §28:4-105.

Collection agent.

Income tax secured bonds, §47-340.26.

Qualified zone academy revenue bond project forward commitment approval act, §2-1217.102.

Collection agreement.

Qualified zone academy revenue bond project forward commitment approval act, §2-1217.102.

Collection and disbursement unit.

Child support enforcement, §46-201.

Collection event.

Extended manufacturer responsibility for electronic waste, §8-1041.01.

Collection site.

Extended manufacturer responsibility for electronic waste, §8-1041.01.

Collector.

Gross sales tax, §47-2001.

Solid waste reduction and recovery, §8-1031.01.

DEFINED TERMS —Cont'd

College, §3-602.

Collision.

Chemical testing for driving under the influence, §50-1901.

Implied consent to blood alcohol tests. Watercraft, §50-1908.

Open access to collision data and information, §50-1951.01.

Traffic regulation, §50-2201.02.

Colony.

Bees, §8-1825.02.

Comb.

Bees, §8-1825.02.

Combination packages.

Unit pricing, §28-5202.

Combined gross vehicle weight (CGVW), §50-1507.01.

Combined group.

Income tax, §47-1801.04.

Combined sewage, §34-2101.

Combined sewer, §§8-103.01, 34-2101.

Combined sewer system, §34-2101.

Comfort care order.

Non-resuscitation procedures for EMS, §7-651.01.

Commemorative work.

Public space, §9-204.11.

Commencement.

Uniform child custody proceedings, §16-4601.01.

Commencement date.

Southwest waterfront bond financing, §2-1217.131.

Commercial animal breeder, §8-1821.01.

Commercial applicator, §8-401.

Commercial bicycle operator, §50-1631.

Commercial domicile.

Income tax, §47-1801.04.

Commercial driver's license, §50-401.

Commercial driver's license information system, §50-401.

Commercial electronic mail message.

Spam deterrence, §28-5001.

Commercial guard dogs, §8-1841.01.

Commercial hot food holding cabinet.

Energy efficiency standards, §8-1772.01.

Commercial loans.

Health professional recruitment program, §7-751.01.

DEFINED TERMS —Cont'd

Commercially useful function.
Small and certified business enterprise development and assistance, §2-218.02.

Commercial mortgage loan.
Insurance investments, §31-1371.02.

Commercial motor vehicle, §50-401.

Commercial pet care facilities, §8-1821.02.

Commercial property.
Commercial property energy conservation, §8-1772.01.
Homestead housing provision, §42-2103.

Commercial purpose, §8-901.

Commercial registered agent.
Business organizations, §29-101.02.

Commercial sex act.
Human trafficking, §22-1831.

Commercial tenant.
Business improvement districts, §2-1215.02.

Commercial tort claim.
Secured transactions, §28:9-102.

Commercial trash compactor.
Trash compactor grant program, §8-751.

Commercial unit.
Leases, UCC, §28:2A-103.
Sales, §28:2-105.
Vacant buildings, §42-3131.05.

Commercial vehicle.
Chemical testing for driving under the influence, §50-1901.
Impaired operation or driving, §50-2206.01.
Traffic regulation, §50-2201.02.

Commingled goods.
Secured transactions, §28:9-336.

Commissary.
Inmate welfare fund, §24-281.

Commission of fine arts.
Historic landmarks, §6-1102.

Commitment, §§7-1301.03, 26-1101.

Committed.
Youth rehabilitation services, department of, §2-1515.01.

Committed a registration offense.
Sex offender registration, §22-4001.

Committed relationship, §32-701.

Committed youth offender, §24-901.

Commodities.
Ethics and government accountability, §1-1161.01.
Unit pricing, §28-5202.

DEFINED TERMS —Cont'd

Commodity account.
Secured transactions, §28:9-102.

Commodity contracts.
Secured transactions, §28:9-102.

Commodity customers.
Secured transactions, §28:9-102.

Commodity Exchange Act.
Security agents and broker, §31-5601.01.

Commodity intermediary.
Secured transactions, §28:9-102.

Common carrier, §34-203.

Common elements.
Condominiums, §42-1901.02.

Common expenses, §42-2002.
Condominiums, §42-1901.02.

Common household pet.
Pet ownership restriction in assisted housing, §8-2031.

Common-interest community.
Environmental covenants, §8-671.01.

Common-law business trust, §29-101.02.

Common-law trust.
Statutory trusts, §29-1201.02.

Common ownership and control.
Captive insurance companies, §31-3931.01.

Common profits, §42-2002.

Common source information company, §42-1702.

Common space.
Green buildings, §6-1451.01.

Communicable disease, §7-132.

Communicate.
Investment securities, §28:8-102.
Secured transactions, §28:9-102.

Communicating.
Stalking, §22-3132.

Communication common carrier, §23-541.

Communication-impaired person.
Interpreters, §2-1901.

Community.
Victims of crime, §23-1905.

Community arts center, §37-101.

Community association, §42-3601.

Community-based organization, §42-3101.
Pre-kindergarten programs, §38-271.01.

Community-based services, §7-1301.03.
Disability services, department on, §7-761.02.

DEFINED TERMS —Cont'd

Community benefits agreements.
The Advisory Board Company, real
property tax abatement,
§47-4665.01.
Community development.
Financial institutions, §26-431.02.
Community development loan.
Financial institutions, §26-431.02.
Community garden.
Urban gardens program, §48-401.
Community group, §37-101.
Community health reinvestment.
Hospital and medical services
corporation, §31-3501.
Community impact statement.
Victims of crime, §23-1905.
Community net metering.
Retail electric competition and
consumer protection, §34-1501.
**Community-oriented healthcare
services model.**
Inmate health care, §24-1401.
Community partner.
Community schools, §38-754.02.
Community reinvestment act.
Community development by financial
institutions, §26-431.02.
Investment and deposit of District
funds, §47-351.01.
Universal banks, §26-1401.02.
**Community renewable energy
facility.**
Retail electric competition and
consumer protection, §34-1501.
Community residence facility,
§§4-205.49, 44-1001.01.
Health-care facility, hospice and home
care licensure, §44-501.
Community schools, §38-754.02.
Community service.
Homestead housing provision,
§42-2103.
Compact.
Interstate compact on educational
opportunity for military children,
§49-1101.03.
Compact commissioner.
Interstate compact on educational
opportunity for military children,
§49-1101.03.
Compact vehicle.
Fleet management, publicly-owned
vehicles, §50-211.01.
Company.
Employees retirement program
management, §§1-335.01,
1-336.01.

DEFINED TERMS —Cont'd

Company —Cont'd
Fire, casualty and marine insurance,
§31-2501.03.
Insurance compliance self-evaluation
privilege, §31-851.
Insurance examinations, §31-1401.
Insurance rate regulation, §31-2701.
Life insurance, §31-4202.
Savings and loan acquisitions,
§26-1201.
Theft of utility service, §22-3218.01.
Company action level event.
Health insurance regulatory
standards, §31-3451.01.
Company action level RBC, §31-2001.
Health insurance regulatory
standards, §31-3451.01.
Compatible or complementary uses,
§37-101.
Compensating balances.
Investment and deposit of District
funds, §47-351.01.
Compensation.
Defibrillator usage, §44-231.
Disability compensation, §1-623.01.
Ethics and government accountability,
§1-1161.01.
Income tax, §47-1801.04.
Competence.
Incompetent criminal defendants,
§24-531.01.
Competency evaluation.
Emergency medical services,
§7-2341.01.
Competent, §7-1301.03.
Competition levels.
Athletic equity, §38-841.01.
Competitive billing.
Retail electric competition and
consumer protection, §34-1501.
Competitive sealed proposals.
Procurement practices, §2-351.04.
Competitive service, §34-2001.
**Competitive telecommunications
service provider,** §34-2001.
Competitive transition charge.
Retail electric competition and
consumer protection, §34-1501.
Compilation service.
Certified public accountants,
§47-2853.41.
Complainant, §28-3901.
Consumer protection procedures,
§28-3901.
Complaint examiner.
Office of police complaints, §5-1103.

DEFINED TERMS —Cont'd

Completed operations liability,
§31-4101.

Complete stormwater management plan.
Anacostia waterfront environmental standards, §2-1226.32.

Complete streets policy, §50-2381.

Completion of the sentence.
Criminal records sealing, §16-801.

Complicit.
Employees retirement program management, §1-335.01.

Component, §38-1201.03.

Component developer.
Walter Reed Medical Center site development, §2-1227.01.

Compost.
Solid waste reduction and recovery, §8-1031.01.

Compostable.
Disposable food service ware, management, §8-1531.
Solid waste reduction and recovery, §8-1031.01.

Compost collection program.
Solid waste reduction and recovery, §8-1031.01.

Composted.
Solid waste reduction and recovery, §8-1031.01.

Composting.
Solid waste reduction and recovery, §8-1031.01.

Composting facility, §8-1051.

Comprehensive evaluation,
§7-1301.03.

Comprehensive, multi-disciplinary assessment.
Interagency collaboration and services integration commission, §2-1592.

Comprehensive psychiatric emergency program.
Behavioral health department, §7-1141.01.

Comprehensive stroke center.
Stroke system of care, §44-1151.

Compressed schedule.
Public officers and employees, §1-510.

Computation date, §51-101.

Computer, §2-213.01.

Computer program.
Electronic transactions, uniform act, §28-4901.

Concealed pistol.
License to carry pistol, §7-2509.01.

DEFINED TERMS —Cont'd

Concussion.
Athletic concussion program, §7-2871.01.

Condemnation.
Adulteration of food and drugs, §48-102.

Conditional license, §48-701.

Conditional offer.
Hiring of ex-offenders, fair criminal record screening, §32-1341.

Conditional retirement.
Firefighter retirement while under disciplinary investigation, §5-1051.
Police retirement while under disciplinary investigation, §5-801.

Conditions of participation, §4-801.

Condominium, §42-1901.02.
Horizontal property regime, §42-2002.
Real property assessment, §47-803.
Real property taxes, classes of property, §47-813.
Trash collection tax credit, §47-871.

Condominium association.
Homestead housing provision, §42-2103.

Condominium conversion,
§42-3401.03.

Condominium instruments,
§42-1901.02.

Condominium project, §§42-1901.01, 42-2002.

Condominium unit, §§42-1901.02, 42-2002.

Condominium unit owners' association.
Rental of public space, §10-1101.01.

Conduit, §§10-1141.01, 34-2001.

Confer, §38-1302.

Conference of state bank supervisors.
Mortgage lenders and brokers, §26-1101.

Confidential communication.
Domestic violence counselors, §14-310.
Human trafficking counselors, §14-311.
Sexual assault victim advocates, §14-312.
Victims of crime, §23-1907.

Confined.
Prisoners, use of restraints on pregnant women, §24-276.01.
Youth rehabilitation services department, use of restraints on pregnant youths, §2-1515.51.

Confirmed credit.
Sales, §28:2-325.

DEFINED TERMS —Cont'd
Confirmer.
Letters of credit, §28:5-102.
Conforming.
Leases, UCC, §28:2A-103.
Sales, §28:2-106.
Congenital birth defect.
Habilitative services for children,
health care coverage, §31-3271.
Connectivity.
Wireless network antennae franchise
agreement, §34-1731.02.
Consensus commission.
Charter schools, §38-1800.02.
Consent.
Sexual abuse, §22-3001.
Standby guardianship, §16-4802.
Conservation, §8-1702.
Conservation easement, §42-201.
Conservator, §§21-301, 21-2011.
Custodial trusts, §19-1101.
Uniform adult guardianship and
protective proceedings jurisdiction
act, §21-2401.02.
Uniform trust code, §19-1301.03.
Consideration, §§42-1101, 47-901,
47-1401.
Negotiable instruments, §28:3-303.
Consignee.
Secured transactions, §28:9-102.
Warehouse receipts, §28:7-102.
Consignment.
Secured transactions, §28:9-102.
Consignor.
Secured transactions, §28:9-102.
Warehouse receipts, §28:7-102.
Consolidator.
Retail electric competition and
consumer protection, §34-1501.
Conspicuous.
Corporations, §29-301.02.
Nonprofit corporations, §29-401.02.
UCC, §28:1-201.
Uniform certificates of title for vessels,
§50-1541.01.
Constituent association.
Limited cooperative associations,
§29-1015.01.
**Constituent association
organization.**
Unincorporated nonprofit associations,
§29-1126.
Constituent company.
Limited liability companies,
§29-809.01.

DEFINED TERMS —Cont'd
**Constituent limited cooperative
association.**
Limited cooperative associations,
§29-1015.01.
Constituent limited partnership.
Limited partnerships, §29-710.01.
Constituent statutory trust.
Statutory trusts, §29-1207.01.
Construction, §§8-171.02, 38-2402.01,
47-2302.
Procurement practices, §2-351.04.
Construction and demolition wastes,
§8-1051.
Construction and demolition waste
recycling accountability, §8-1071.
Construction codes, §6-1401.
Energy efficiency standards,
§8-1771.01.
Green buildings, §6-1451.01.
Smoke detectors, §6-751.01.
Construction codes supplement,
§6-1401.
Smoke detectors, §6-751.01.
Construction documents.
Construction codes, §6-1401.
Green buildings, §6-1451.01.
Construction in progress.
Real property taxes, supplemental
assessment, §47-830.
Construction loan, §42-2701.02.
Insurance investments, §31-1371.02.
**Construction loan deed of trust or
mortgage,** §42-1101.
Construction management at-risk.
Procurement practices, §2-351.04.
Construction permit application.
Building rehabilitation code, §6-1410.
Green buildings, §6-1451.01.
Construction services.
Workplace fraud, §32-1331.01.
Constructively received.
Income tax withholding, §47-1812.08.
Constructive receipt.
Income tax withholding, §47-1812.08.
Consult.
Rules of professional conduct,
ProfCond Rule 1.0.
Consultant.
Victims of crime, sexual assault
response, §4-561.01.
Consultation.
Rules of professional conduct,
ProfCond Rule 1.0.
Consumer, §3-402.
Arbitration, revised act, §16-4401.

DEFINED TERMS —Cont'd
Consumer —Cont'd
Assistive technology device warranty, §28-4031.
Consumer protection procedures, §28-3901.
Credit service organizations, §28-4601.
Disability services, department on, §7-761.02.
Food delivery insurance requirements, §50-101.
Health care ombudsman program, §7-2071.01.
Lease-purchase agreements, §42-3671.01.
Mental health consumer's rights, §7-1231.02.
Retail electric competition and consumer protection, §34-1501.
Telephone solicitation fraud, §22-3226.01.
Tobacco tax, §47-2401.
UCC, §28:1-201.
Consumer accounts.
Negotiable instruments, §28:3-103.
Consumer arbitration agreement.
Arbitration, revised act, §16-4401.
Consumer credit sale, §28-3802.
Consumer protection, §28-3802.
Consumer credit service organization, §28-4601.
Consumer debtor.
Secured transactions, §28:9-102.
Consumer goods, §28-3818.
Secured transactions, §28:9-102.
Uniform certificates of title for vessels, §50-1541.01.
Consumer-goods transaction.
Secured transactions, §28:9-102.
Consumer lease.
Leases, UCC, §28:2A-103.
Consumer obligor.
Secured transactions, §28:9-102.
Consumer price index.
Income tax, §47-1806.06.
Southwest waterfront bond financing, §2-1217.131.
Uniform per student funding formula, §38-2901.
Consumers of mental health services.
Department of mental health, §7-1131.02.
Consumer testing.
Fire-standard-compliant cigarettes, §7-1751.

DEFINED TERMS —Cont'd
Consumer transaction.
Negotiable instruments, §28:3-103.
Secured transactions, §28:9-102.
Consummation.
Lease-purchase agreements, §42-3671.01.
Containment.
Lead-hazard prevention and elimination, §8-231.01.
Contaminant, §34-2202.01.
Contaminated property, §2-1217.01.
Tax increment financing authorization, §2-1217.01.
Contamination.
Brownfield revitalization, §8-631.02.
Content area.
Promotion or retention of students, §38-781.01.
Contents, §23-541.
Contested case, §2-502.
Adoption, Adoption Rule 2.
Office of administrative hearings, §2-1831.01.
Continuation statement.
Secured transactions, §28:9-102.
Continuing care, §7-2101.
Continuing care facility.
Continuing care retirement communities, §44-151.01.
Continuing care retirement community regulatory and supervision trust account, §31-1201.
Continuing care services.
Continuing care retirement communities, §44-151.01.
Continuum of care.
Homeless services, §4-751.01.
Contraband.
Controlled substances, §48-901.02.
Contract, §2-223.01.
Athlete agents, §47-2887.01.
Electronic transactions, uniform act, §28-4901.
Labor-peace agreement for public projects, §32-852.
Living wage act, §2-220.02.
Nurse's rehabilitation program, §3-1251.01.
Pensions and retirement, §1-801.02.
Private contractor and subcontractor prompt payment act, §27-131.
Sales, §28:2-106.
UCC, §28:1-201.
Whistleblower protection, §1-615.52.

DEFINED TERMS —Cont'd

Contractable condominium.
Condominiums, §42-1901.02.

Contracted provider.
Youth rehabilitation services,
department of, §2-1515.01.

Contract for sale.
Sales, §28:2-106.

Contract fueling, §50-702.

Contractholder.
Hospital and medical services
corporation, §31-3501.

Contracting officer.
Procurement practices, §2-351.04.

Contracting provider, §31-3401.

Contract modification.
Procurement practices, §2-351.04.

Contractor.
Private contractor and subcontractor
prompt payment act, §27-131.
Procurement practices, §2-351.04.
Quick payment provisions, §2-221.01.

Contractual obligation.
Life and health insurance guaranty
association, §31-5401.

Contributing factor, §2-223.01.
Whistleblower protection, §1-615.52.

Contribution.
Charitable solicitations, §44-1701.
Ethics and government accountability,
§1-1161.01.
Grant administration, §1-328.11.
Limited cooperative associations,
§29-1001.02.
Limited liability companies,
§29-801.02.
Limited partnerships, §29-701.02.
Partnerships, §29-601.02.
Statutory trusts, §29-1201.02.

Contribution period.
Waterfront Park at the Yards,
§10-1801.
Waterfront Park special assessment
district, §47-895.21.

Contribution to costs of supports.
Disability services, department on,
§7-761.02.

Control, §31-401.
Automated teller machine, §26-131.02.
Corporations, §29-306.70.
Ethics and government accountability,
§1-1161.01.
Insurance holding company system,
§31-701.
Insurance investments, §31-1371.02.
Money transmissions, §26-1001.

DEFINED TERMS —Cont'd

Control —Cont'd
Office of cable television, film, music,
and entertainment amendment
act of 2015, §34-1251.03.
Property and liability insurance
guaranty association, §31-5501.
Savings and loan acquisitions,
§26-1201.
Security agents and broker,
§31-5601.01.
Special purpose financial captive
insurance companies, §31-3932.02.

Control budget, §47-382.

Control center.
Budgets and budget estimates,
§47-382.

Controlled by.
Corporations, §29-306.70.
Qualified social electronic commerce
companies tax abatements,
§47-1818.01.
Special purpose financial captive
insurance companies, §31-3932.02.

Controlled dangerous substance,
§42-3601.

Controlled insurer, §31-401.

Controlled substances, §48-901.02.
Drug, firearm, or prostitution-related
nuisance abatement, §42-3101.
Family court proceedings, §16-2301.
Monitoring prescription drugs,
§48-853.01.

Controlled substances act.
Medical marijuana, §7-1671.01.

Controlling.
Qualified social electronic commerce
companies tax abatements,
§47-1818.01.
Special purpose financial captive
insurance companies, §31-3932.02.

Controlling interest.
Banks and financial institutions,
§26-551.02.
Ethics and government accountability,
§1-1161.01.

Controlling person, §31-1801.
Money transmissions, §26-1001.

Controlling producer, §31-401.

Control period, §47-393.
Miscellaneous provisions, §47-3401.05.

Control year.
Budgets and budget estimates,
§1-204.46.
Chief financial officer, §1-204.24f.
Office of inspector general,
§1-301.115a.

DEFINED TERMS —Cont'd

Convention.
Interstate family support, §46-351.02.

Convention support order.
Interstate family support, §46-357.01.

Conversion, §§42-3401.03, 44-602.
Entity transactions, §29-201.02.
Real property taxes, supplemental
assessment, §47-830.

Conversion condominium.
Condominiums, §42-1901.02.

Conversion date, §15-901.

Converted entity.
Entity transactions, §29-201.02.

Converted stock company, §31-901.

Converted vehicle, §50-702.

Converter.
Office of cable television, film, music,
and entertainment amendment
act of 2015, §34-1251.03.

Convertible land.
Condominiums, §42-1901.02.

Convertible space.
Condominiums, §42-1901.02.

Converting entity.
Entity transactions, §29-201.02.

Conveyance.
Rental housing conversion,
opportunity to purchase,
§42-3404.02.

Convicted.
HIV testing of certain criminal
offenders, §22-3901.

Conviction.
Child and family services agency.
Criminal record checks, §4-1305.01.
Criminal records sealing, §16-801.
Hiring of ex-offenders, fair criminal
record screening, §32-1341.
Sentencing, §24-901.
Youth rehabilitation services,
department of, §2-1515.01.

Cooling water.
Wastewater disposal systems,
§8-105.02.

Cooperating employer.
Unemployment compensation, §51-107.

Cooperative, §§42-2701.02, 42-3401.03.
Limited cooperative associations,
§29-1001.02.

Cooperative agreement.
Alcoholic beverages, §25-101.

Cooperative basis.
Cooperative associations, §29-902.

Cooperative conversion, §42-3401.03.

DEFINED TERMS —Cont'd

Cooperative housing association,
§42-3501.03.
Homestead housing provision,
§42-2103.
Real property assessment, §47-803.
Real property taxes, classes of
property, §47-813.

Cooperative purchasing.
Procurement practices, §2-351.04.

Coordinate.
Ethics and government accountability,
§1-1161.01.

Coordinating council.
Pre-kindergarten programs,
§38-271.01.

Coordination.
Ethics and government accountability,
§1-1161.01.

Co-owner, §42-2002.
Condominiums, §42-1901.01.

**Co-owners with right of
survivorship.**
Simultaneous deaths, §19-501.

Copayment, §31-3401.

Core curriculum.
Charter schools, §38-1800.02.

Core services agency.
Department of mental health,
§7-1131.02.
Hospitalization of persons with mental
illness, §21-501.

Corner store.
Grocery and retail stores development,
§2-1212.01.

Corporate action.
Nonprofit corporations, §29-401.20.

Corporation, §§29-301.02, 29-306.50,
29-311.01.
Fiduciary security transfers, §28-2901.
Hospital and medical services
corporation, §31-3501.
Income tax, §§47-1801.04, 47-1807.01.
Nonprofit corporations, §§29-401.02,
29-406.50.
Not-for-profit hospital corporations,
§44-951.01.
Public utilities, §34-204.
Tobacco settlement financing,
§7-1831.01.

Correctional facility, §24-231.01.
Gun offender registry, §7-2508.01.
Inmate welfare fund, §24-281.

Corrective order, §31-2001.
Health insurance regulatory
standards, §31-3451.01.

DEFINED TERMS —Cont'd

Cost, §§9-901, 28-4521, 34-2202.01.

Citywide technology support services, §1-1431.

Revised real property tax sale, §47-1330.

Washington convention and sports authority, §10-1202.01.

Cost of abandonment.

Public utility relocation expenses, §9-107.02.

Cost-of-living adjustment.

Income tax, §47-1801.04.

Inheritance and estate taxes, §47-3701.

Real property assessment, §47-802.

Cost of relocation, adjustment, replacement or removal, §9-107.02.

Cost-plus incentive fee contract.

Procurement practices, §2-351.04.

Cost-reimbursement contract.

Procurement practices, §2-351.04.

Cottage food business, §7-742.01.

Cottage food product, §7-742.01.

Council, §1-301.41.

Arts and humanities commission, §39-202.

Automobile consumer, §50-501.

Business improvement districts, §2-1215.02.

City Market at O Street tax increment financing, §2-1217.33a.

Home Rule act, §1-201.03.

Howard Theatre redevelopment project, §2-1217.151.

Howard Theatre redevelopment project TIF area, §2-1217.34a.

Inheritance and estate taxes, §47-3701.

Merit system, §1-603.01.

Real property assessment, §47-802.

Skyland TIF area, §2-1217.35a.

Streets and alleys, §9-201.01.

Transportation infrastructure improvement GARVEE bonds, §9-107.51.

Council of co-owners, §42-2002.

Condominiums, §42-1901.01.

Council year, §2-601.

Counsel, §21-2011.

Counterfeit mark, §22-901.

Counterfeit substance, §48-901.02.

Counterparty.

Special purpose financial captive insurance companies, §31-3932.02.

DEFINED TERMS —Cont'd

Counterparty exposure amount.

Insurance investments, §31-1371.02.

Courier company, §50-1631.

Court, §21-2011.

Appeals, DCCtApp Rule 1.

Arbitration, revised act, §16-4401.

Automobile consumer, §50-501.

Chemical testing for driving under the influence, §50-1901.

Civil asset forfeiture, §41-301.

Crime victims' rights, §23-1905.

Criminal abuse, neglect and financial exploitation of vulnerable adults and elderly persons, §22-932.

Criminal defendant's initial appearance before court, CrimPro Rule 5.

Criminal records sealing, §16-801.

Custodial trusts, §19-1101.

Delinquent minors, JuvProc Rule 101.

Department of mental health, §7-1131.02.

Divorce, annulment, separation, support, §16-901.

Drug paraphernalia, §48-1101.

Impaired operation or driving, §50-2206.01.

Incompetent criminal defendants, §24-531.01.

Intrafamily offenses, §16-1001.

Jury, §§11-1902, 16-5101.

Medical malpractice, §16-2801.

Mental health consumer's rights, §7-1231.02.

Pleas in criminal cases, CrimPro Rule 11.

Release from custody or detention, CrimPro Rule 46.

Sex offender registration, §22-4001.

Sexual psychopaths, §22-3803.

Standby guardianship, §16-4802.

Superior court, tax division, §47-3301.

Traffic regulation, §50-2201.02.

Uniform child custody proceedings, §16-4601.01.

Court day.

Police and fire departments, §5-1304.

Court of the District of Columbia.

Bribery, §22-711.

Obstructing justice, §22-721.

Court order.

Spouse or domestic partner equity in retirement benefits, §1-529.02.

Court reporter division.

Appeals, DCCtApp Rule 1.

DEFINED TERMS —Cont'd

Covenants.

Real property tax exemptions, §47-4632.

Covered.

Insurance investments, §31-1371.02.

Covered area, §50-702.

Covered benefits, §31-3101.

Covered child or youth services provider.

Criminal background checks for the protection of children act, §4-1501.02.

Covered claim, §31-5501.

Covered creditor.

Statutory trusts, §29-1206.06.

Covered District employee, §§1-801.02, 1-901.02.

Covered electronic equipment.

Extended manufacturer responsibility for electronic waste, §8-1041.01.

Covered electronic equipment stewardship program.

Extended manufacturer responsibility for electronic waste, §8-1041.01.

Covered employer.

Reducing single occupancy vehicle use by encouraging transit benefits, §32-151.

Covered entity.

Access to prescription drugs, §48-831.02.

Extended manufacturer responsibility for electronic waste, §8-1041.01.

Foreign language services and documents, §2-1931.

Covered entity with major public contact.

Foreign language services and documents, §2-1931.

Covered fleet, §50-702.

Covered fleet operator, §50-702.

Covered individual.

Access to prescription drugs, §48-831.02.

Continuation of health benefits plan coverage, §32-731.

Covered loan.

Mortgage loan protection, §26-1151.01.

Covered party.

Statutory trusts, §29-1205.07.

Covered policy.

Life and health insurance guaranty association, §31-5401.

Covered recipient.

Grant administration, §1-328.11.

DEFINED TERMS —Cont'd

Covered services, §31-3401.

Covered voter.

Military and overseas voters, §1-1061.02.

CPEP.

Behavioral health department, §7-1141.01.

CPI.

Inheritance and estate taxes, §47-3701.

Tenant organizations, §42-3505.06.

Uniform per student funding formula, §38-2901.

Waterfront Park at the Yards, §10-1801.

CPMO, §37-101.

CPO.

Procurement practices, §2-351.04.

CPR.

Defibrillator usage, §44-231.

CPR and AED program.

Defibrillator usage, §44-231.

Crafter, §37-101.

Cramming.

Retail natural gas supplier licensing and consumer protection, §34-1671.02.

Credentialing.

Emergency volunteer health practitioners, §7-2361.06.

Credentialing intermediary.

Health insurers, §31-3251.

Credible evidence, §4-1301.02.

Creditable District service.

Merit system, health benefits, §1-621.03.

Creditable service, §1-626.04.

Police and firefighters retirement and disability, §5-712.

Credit accident and health insurance, §31-5102.

Credit card.

Alcoholic beverages, §25-101.

Credit certificate.

Job growth tax credit, §47-1807.51.

Credit life insurance, §31-5102.

Credit line deed of trust, §42-2301.

Creditor, §§28-3101, 31-1301, 31-5102.

Debt collection protection, §28-3814.

Fraudulent transfers, §28-3101.

UCC, §28:1-201.

Credit period.

Job growth tax credit, §47-1807.51.

Credit report.

Consumer security freeze, §28-3861.

DEFINED TERMS —Cont'd

Credit reporting agency.
Child abuse and neglect, §4-1301.02.
Consumer security freeze, §28-3861.

Credit service charge, §28-3701.
Revolving credit accounts, §28-3701.

Credit tenant loan.
Insurance investments, §31-1371.02.

Credit union.
Banks and financial institutions, §26-551.02.
Investment and deposit of District funds, §47-351.01.

CREF.
Retail electric competition and consumer protection, §34-1501.

CREF credit rate.
Retail electric competition and consumer protection, §34-1501.

Crime of violence.
Bail and pretrial detention, §23-1331.
Compensation of crime victims, §4-501.
Firearms control, §7-2501.01.
Protection of innocence act, §22-4131.
Weapons, §22-4501.

Crime scene examination case file.
Crime investigation records, §5-113.31.

Crime victim.
Crime victims' rights, §23-1905.

Criminal accusation.
Hiring of ex-offenders, fair criminal record screening, §32-1341.

Criminal background check.
Criminal background checks for the protection of children act, §4-1501.02.
Temporary assistance for needy families.
Grandparent caregiver subsidies, §4-251.01.

Criminal investigation.
Obstructing justice, §22-721.

Criminal investigator.
Obstructing justice, §22-721.

Criminal justice coordinating council, §22-4231.

Criminal proceeding, §22-3803.

Criminal record check.
Child and family services agency, §4-1305.01.

Criminal street gang, §22-951.

Crisis intervention.
Homeless services, §4-751.01.

Criteria, §8-103.01.

Critical congenital heart disease.
Newborn heart screening, §7-857.01.

DEFINED TERMS —Cont'd

Critical infrastructure.
Freedom of information, §2-539.

Critical infrastructure information.
Freedom of information, §2-539.

Cross-collateral, §28-3802.
Consumer protection, §28-3802.

Crosswalk.
Personal delivery devices pilot program, §50-1551.

Cruelty to animals, §22-1001.

CSA.
Alcoholic beverages, §25-101.

CSC.
Stroke system of care, §44-1151.

CTC program.
Trash compactor grant program, §8-751.

CTE grant program.
Career and technical education, §38-2601.02.

Cultivation center.
Medical marijuana, §7-1671.01.

Cultural competence.
Department of mental health, §7-1131.02.

Culturally competent.
Homeless services, §4-751.01.

Culturing.
Breastmilk bank and lactation support, §7-881.01.

Curfew hours, §2-1542.

Currency.
Civil asset forfeiture, §41-301.

Current assessed value, §2-1217.01.

Current edition.
Anacostia waterfront environmental standards, §2-1226.32.
Green buildings, §6-1451.01.

Current value, §§1-702, 1-901.02.

Current value of the assets in the fund.
Employees retirement program management, §1-722.

Custodial property, §21-301.

Custodial trustee, §19-1101.

Custodial trust property, §19-1101.

Custodian, §8-2001.
Child support enforcement, §46-201.
Family court proceedings, §16-2301.
Intrafamily offenses, §16-1001.
Medical support enforcement, §46-251.01.
Procurement claims, §2-381.01.
Public records, §2-1701.
Transfers to minors, §21-301.

DEFINED TERMS —Cont'd
Custodian —Cont'd
Tuition of nonresidents, §38-304.
Custody.
Youth rehabilitation services,
department of, §2-1515.01.
Customer, §§7-1301.03, 42-1702.
Automated teller machine, §26-131.02.
Bank deposits and collections,
§28:4-104.
Electric light and power companies,
§34-1561.
Funds transfers, §28:4A-105.
Portable electronics insurance,
§31-5051.01.
Retail electric competition and
consumer protection, §34-1501.
Retail natural gas supplier licensing
and consumer protection,
§34-1671.02.
Toll telecommunication service tax,
§47-3901.
Customer choice.
Retail electric competition and
consumer protection, §34-1501.
Customer generation.
Renewable energy portfolio standards,
§34-1431.
Customer service.
Office of unified communications,
§1-327.51.
Cytologic screening, §31-2901.
Cytotechnologist, §44-201.
Cytotechnology, practice of,
§3-1201.02.
Dangerous animal, §8-1801.
Dangerous articles, §22-4517.
Dangerous crime.
Bail and pretrial detention, §23-1331.
Weapons, §22-4501.
Dangerous dog, §8-1901.
Dangerous vehicle.
Abandoned and unlawfully parked
vehicles, §50-2421.02.
Dangerous weapon, §10-503.26.
Data collector, §7-1201.01.
Data processing service, §47-2201.
Gross sales tax, §47-2001.
Date of the tax sale.
Revised real property tax sale,
§47-1330.
Day, §§3-1201.01, 7-201, 47-382.
District of Columbia housing
authority, §6-201.
Lead-hazard prevention and
elimination, §8-231.01.

DEFINED TERMS —Cont'd
Day program.
Homeless services, §4-751.01.
D.C. arena.
Alcoholic beverages, §25-101.
DC Circulator, §50-921.31.
DC Circulator fund, §50-921.31.
D.C. citizens' job program.
New convention center hotel,
§10-1221.01.
DC collaborative.
Pre-kindergarten programs,
§38-271.01.
D.C. federal pension fund, §1-801.02.
**DC general family shelter
replacement unit.**
Homeless services, §4-751.01.
DCHAPD.
District of Columbia housing
authority, §6-201.
**DC leveraging educational
assistance partnership program.**
Higher education financial aid
assistance, §38-2731.
DC-Net.
Wireless network antennae franchise
agreement, §34-1731.02.
DC-NET program.
Citywide technology support services,
§1-1431.
D.C. official code.
Administrative procedure, legal
publication of documents, §2-551.
DC One Card.
One Card service support, §1-327.71.
DCPS.
Charter schools, §38-1800.02.
Early childhood education, §38-755.01.
Metropolitan police.
School safety division, §5-132.01.
Nonpublic schools, §38-2561.01.
School-based budgeting and
accountability, §38-2801.01.
Uniform per student funding formula,
§38-2901.
DCRA.
Building rehabilitation code, §6-1410.
DC SANE program.
Victims of crime, §23-1907.
Victims of crime, sexual assault
response, §4-561.01.
**DC sexual assault nurse examiner
program.**
Sexual assault victim advocates,
§14-312.
Victims of crime, §23-1907.

DEFINED TERMS —Cont'd
DC sexual assault nurse examiner program —Cont'd
Victims of crime, sexual assault response, §4-561.01.
DCSS.
Procurement practices, §2-351.04.
DC streetcar, §50-921.71.
Streetcar safety oversight, §5-401.01.
Transportation department, §50-921.04.
DC Streetcar fund, §50-921.71.
DC TAG.
Tuition assistance, §38-2751.
DC-USA project, §47-4606.
DDOE.
Anacostia waterfront environmental standards, §2-1226.32.
Department of the environment, §8-151.01.
Electric light and power companies, §8-1776.01.
Regulation of for-hire vehicles, §50-301.03.
DDOT.
Electric company infrastructure improvement financing, §34-1311.01.
Open access to collision data and information, §50-1951.01.
Personal delivery devices pilot program, §50-1551.
Streets and alleys, §9-201.01.
DDOT underground electric company infrastructure improvement.
Electric company infrastructure improvement financing, §34-1311.01.
DDOT underground electric company infrastructure improvement activity.
Electric company infrastructure improvement financing, §34-1311.01.
DDOT underground electric company infrastructure improvement annual revenue requirement.
Electric company infrastructure improvement financing, §34-1311.01.
DDOT underground electric company infrastructure improvement charge.
Electric company infrastructure improvement financing, §34-1311.01.

DEFINED TERMS —Cont'd
DDOT underground electric company infrastructure improvement costs.
Electric company infrastructure improvement financing, §34-1311.01.
DDOT underground electric company infrastructure improvement fund.
Electric company infrastructure improvement financing, §34-1311.01.
DDOT underground electric company infrastructure improvement property.
Electric company infrastructure improvement financing, §34-1311.01.
DDOT underground electric company infrastructure improvement revenue.
Electric company infrastructure improvement financing, §34-1311.01.
DDS.
Disability services, department on, §7-761.02.
Incompetent criminal defendants, §24-531.01.
Dead body, §7-201.
Deadly force, §24-261.01.
Deaf.
American sign language education, §38-2432.
Deaf people.
American sign language education, §38-2432.
Deaf person, §7-1009.
Dealer in residential real property, §47-1401.
Dealers, §§7-2531.01, 7-2551.01, 47-2807.
Motor vehicle registration, §50-1501.01.
Uniform certificates of title for vessels, §50-1541.01.
Dealer's license, §7-2501.01.
Death, §32-1501.
Debilitation.
Standby guardianship, §16-4802.
Debris.
Rodent abatement program, §8-2103.01.
Debris removal operations.
Garbage collection, §8-741.

DEFINED TERMS —Cont'd

Debt, §28-3101.

Fraudulent transfers, §28-3101.

Debt bondage.

Human trafficking, §22-1831.

Debt collection.

Consumer protection, §28-3814.

Debt collector.

Consumer protection, §28-3814.

Debtor, §§28-3101, 31-5102.

Fraudulent transfers, §28-3101.

Secured transactions, §28:9-102.

Uniform certificates of title for vessels, §50-1541.01.

Debtor in bankruptcy.

Business organizations, §29-101.02.

Debt service.

Bond issues, borrowing limitation, §47-334.

Electric company infrastructure improvement financing, §34-1311.01.

Energy efficiency financing, §8-1778.02.

Real property taxes.

Special energy assessments, §47-895.31.

Skyland TIF area, §2-1217.35a.

Southwest waterfront bond financing, §2-1217.131.

Southwest waterfront special assessment district, §47-895.01.

Transportation infrastructure improvement GARVEE bonds, §9-107.51.

Decedent.

Anatomical gifts, §7-1531.01.

Inheritance and estate taxes, §47-3701.

Deceit.

Security agents and broker, §31-5601.01.

Decent, safe, and sanitary housing, §42-3503.01.

Deck.

Center Leg Freeway (interstate 395) PILOT area.

Payments in lieu of taxes, §47-4637.

Declarant.

Condominiums, §42-1901.02.

Rental of public space, §10-1101.01.

Declaration.

Anatomical gifts, §7-1531.20.

Declaration of advance instructions.

Mental health consumer's rights, §7-1231.02.

DEFINED TERMS —Cont'd

Declaration of loss.

Negotiable instruments, §28:3-312.

Declared conversion fee.

Rental housing conversion and sale, §42-3402.04.

Dedicated funding source.

Washington metropolitan area transit authority compact, §9-1107.01.

Dedicated taxes and fees.

Revenue bonds, notes or other obligations, §1-204.90.

Washington convention and sports authority, §10-1202.01.

Dedicated vehicle, §50-702.

Deductible, §31-3401.

Deed, §§42-1101, 47-901.

Deed recordation tax, §47-1401.

Deed to property.

Recordation tax, §42-1102.

De facto parent.

Third-party child custody, §16-831.01.

Default.

Self-service storage facilities, §40-401.

Default environmental preference standard.

Procurement practices, §2-351.04.

Defendant.

Incompetent criminal defendants, §24-531.01.

UCC, §28:1-201.

Deferred deposit, §26-301.

Deferred payment loan.

Employer-assisted housing program, §42-2501.

Defibrillator, §44-231.

Deficiency.

Income tax, §47-1801.04.

Real property transfer excise tax, §47-1401.

Real property transfer tax, §47-901.

Recorder of deeds, §42-1101.

Defined benefit dollar limit.

Police and firefighters retirement and disability, §5-723.01.

Teachers' retirement, maximum benefit computations, §38-2021.27.

Defined parking area.

Automated teller machine, §26-131.02.

Definitive contract.

Procurement practices, §2-351.04.

Defoliant, §8-401.

Defraud.

Security agents and broker, §31-5601.01.

Degree, §38-1302.

DEFINED TERMS —Cont'd

Delegate.
Elections, §1-1001.02.
Nonprofit corporations, §29-401.02.
Delinquency proceeding, §31-1301.
Delinquent act, §16-2301.
Delinquent child, §16-2301.
Delinquent debt.
Delinquent debts to the District, recovery, §1-350.01.
Delinquent taxes.
Collection of taxes, §47-4405.
Delivered by electronic means.
Electronic delivery and posting of insurance documents, §31-651.01.
Delivery.
UCC, §28:1-201.
Delivery order.
Warehouse receipts, §28:7-102.
Demand response generating sources.
Air pollution, §8-101.11.
Demolish, §§8-111.01, 34-2701.
Historic landmarks, §6-1102.
Demolition, §§8-111.01, 34-2701.
Historic landmarks, §6-1102.
Demolition by neglect.
Historic landmarks, §6-1102.
Demonstrations.
Protests targeting a residence, §22-2751.
Demurrer.
Criminal procedure, CrimPro Rule 54.
De novo branch, §26-732.
Dental assistant, §3-1209.05.
Dental hygiene, practice of, §3-1201.02.
Dentistry, practice of, §3-1201.02.
Dentists.
Health professional recruitment program, §7-751.01.
Medical marijuana, §7-1671.01.
Department activity.
Parks and recreation, §10-301.
Department CFO.
Department of health care finance, §7-771.01.
Dependent, §31-3301.01.
Income tax, §47-1801.04.
Military and overseas voters, §1-1061.02.
Dependent child.
Child support enforcement, §46-201.
Health insurance coverage, §31-2996.01.
Merit system.
Health benefits, §1-621.03.

DEFINED TERMS —Cont'd

Dependent child —Cont'd
Merit system —Cont'd
Life insurance, §1-622.04.
Dependent father.
Teachers' retirement, deferred or survivor annuity, §38-2021.09.
Dependent mother.
Teachers' retirement, deferred or survivor annuity, §38-2021.09.
Dependent parents.
Teachers' retirement, deferred or survivor annuity, §38-2021.09.
Dependent relative, §51-101.
Deployment.
Interstate compact on educational opportunity for military children, §49-1101.03.
Deposit.
Investment and deposit of District funds, §47-351.01.
Merchant bank, §26-831.02.
Savings and loan acquisitions, §26-1201.
Deposit accounts.
Secured transactions, §28:9-102.
Depositary bank.
Bank deposits and collections, §28:4-105.
Depository institution.
Mortgage lenders and brokers, §26-1101.
Security agents and broker, §31-5601.01.
Depository institution affiliate, §26-732.
Deposit-receiving institution.
Community development by financial institutions, §26-431.02.
Depreciation.
Principal and income, §28-4805.03.
Deprive, §22-3201.
Deputy chief financial officer.
Graffiti abatement, §42-3141.01.
Deputy commissioner.
Insurance, securities, and banking, department of, §31-101.
Deputy mayor.
Access to justice initiative program, §4-1701.01.
Derivative.
Principal and income, §28-4804.14.
Derivative instrument.
Insurance investments, §31-1371.02.
Derivative proceeding.
Corporations, §29-305.50.

DEFINED TERMS —Cont'd
Derivative proceeding —Cont'd
Nonprofit corporations, §29-411.01.
Derivative transaction.
Insurance investments, §31-1371.02.
Desiccant, §8-401.
Design.
Historic landmarks, §6-1102.
Designated act, §22-3701.
Designated agent, §42-1702.
Designated beneficiary.
ABLE savings accounts, §47-4901.
College savings program, §47-4501.
Uniform real property transfers on
death, §19-604.02.
Designated body.
Nonprofit corporations, §29-401.02.
Designated nonprofit zone.
Nonprofit corporations locating in
emerging commercial
neighborhoods, §47-857.11.
Designated organizations.
Parks and recreation, §10-301.
Designated payment office.
Quick payment provisions, §2-221.01.
Designated state official.
Interstate agreement on qualification
of educational personnel,
§38-2102.
Designation.
Standby guardianship, §16-4802.
Designation of agent.
Business organizations, §29-104.01.
Designator.
Standby guardianship, §16-4802.
Design-bid-build.
Procurement practices, §2-351.04.
Design-build.
Procurement practices, §2-351.04.
**Design-build-finance-operate-
maintain.**
Procurement practices, §2-351.04.
Design-build-operate-maintain.
Procurement practices, §2-351.04.
Designee, §7-701.01.
Design requirements.
Procurement practices, §2-351.04.
Destructive device, §7-2501.01.
Detain.
Criminal procedure, CrimPro Rule 54.
Detained.
Youth rehabilitation services,
department of, §2-1515.01.
Detective, §47-2839.
Detention officer, §1-626.04.
Detention or shelter care hearing,
§16-2301.

DEFINED TERMS —Cont'd
Deteriorated paint.
Lead-hazard prevention and
elimination, §8-231.01.
Deteriorated property.
Acquisition and disposal, §42-3171.01.
Deteriorated structure.
Demolition, §42-3173.01.
Determination of incapacity.
Standby guardianship, §16-4802.
Determinations and findings.
Procurement practices, §2-351.04.
Developer, §42-2002.
Condominiums, §42-1901.01.
Constitution square development
project.
Tax abatements, §47-4612.
DC-USA project tax exemptions,
§47-4606.
Eckington One residential project tax
exemptions, §47-4618.
Low-income housing tax credit,
§47-4801.
Low-income housing tax credit fund,
§42-2853.01.
New Town at Capital City Market
revitalization, §6-1062.02.
Real property tax exemptions,
§§47-4629, 47-4636.
Skyland TIF area, §2-1217.35a.
Walter Reed Medical Center site
development, §2-1227.01.
Workforce housing production
program, §6-1061.02.
Developer sponsor.
H Street, N.E. retail priority area
incentive, §1-325.171.
Jenkins Row Development tax
exemption, §47-4603.
Parkside Terrace development project
tax exemptions, §47-4607.
Third and H Streets, N.E.
development project, tax
exemption, §47-4634.
Development, §6-102.01.
Supermarkets, §47-3801.
Development agreement.
Howard Theatre redevelopment
project, §2-1217.151.
Howard Theatre redevelopment project
TIF area, §2-1217.34a.
Developmental disability, §21-1201.
Development costs, §2-1217.01.
City Market at O Street tax increment
financing, §2-1217.33a.
District of Columbia housing
authority, §6-201.

DEFINED TERMS —Cont'd
Development costs —Cont'd
  Howard Theatre redevelopment project
    TIF area, §2-1217.34a.
  PILOT agreements, §1-308.01.
  Skyland TIF area, §2-1217.35a.
  Southwest waterfront bond financing,
    §2-1217.131.
  Union Market district tax increment
    financing, §2-1217.36a.
Development plan.
  Children's island development plan,
    §10-1432.
Development sponsor, §2-1217.01.
  City Market at O Street tax increment
    financing, §2-1217.33a.
  DC-USA project tax exemptions,
    §47-4606.
  Howard Theatre redevelopment
    project, §2-1217.151.
  Howard Theatre redevelopment project
    TIF area, §2-1217.34a.
  Real property tax exemptions,
    §§47-902, 47-1002.
  Recordation tax, §42-1102.
  Skyland TIF area, §2-1217.35a.
  Union Market district tax increment
    financing, §2-1217.36a.
Device, §8-401.
  Detection device, §22-1211.
DFHV.
  Regulation of for-hire vehicles,
    §50-301.03.
DFS.
  Victims of crime, sexual assault
    response, §4-561.01.
DHCD.
  New Town at Capital City Market
    revitalization, §6-1062.02.
  Workforce housing production
    program, §6-1061.02.
DHCF.
  Disability services, department on,
    §7-761.02.
DHS.
  Disability services, department on,
    §7-761.02.
Diagnostic health care facility.
  Health planning and development
    agency, §44-401.
Diagnostic information, §7-1201.01.
Dialing parity, §34-2001.
Dietetics and nutrition, practice of,
    §3-1201.02.
Digital, §2-1701.
Digital dispatch.
  Regulation of for-hire vehicles,
    §50-301.03.

DEFINED TERMS —Cont'd
Digitally-disadvantaged areas.
  Wireless network antennae franchise
    agreement, §34-1731.02.
Digitally-disadvantaged population.
  Wireless network antennae franchise
    agreement, §34-1731.02.
**Digitally-disadvantaged resident
  household.**
  Wireless network antennae franchise
    agreement, §34-1731.02.
Digitally-disadvantaged residents.
  Wireless network antennae franchise
    agreement, §34-1731.02.
Diploma, §38-1302.
Direct.
  Insurance investments, §31-1371.02.
Direct and predictable effect.
  Ethics and government accountability,
    §1-1161.01.
Direct gross receipts, §31-1201.
  Health benefit exchange authority,
    §31-3171.01.
Direct holdings.
  Employees retirement program
    management, §§1-335.01,
    1-336.01.
Direct installment loan, §28-3802.
  Consumer protection, §28-3802.
Direct labor, §32-302.
Direct labor costs.
  First source employment, §2-219.01.
Directly.
  Insurance investments, §31-1371.02.
Directly related entity.
  Real property tax exemptions,
    qualified high technology company
    interior renovation tax rebate,
    §47-4665.
Direct operations.
  Title insurers, §31-5031.01.
Director.
  Abandoned and unlawfully parked
    vehicles, §50-2421.02.
  Banks and financial institutions,
    §26-551.02.
  Corporations, §29-306.50.
  Fleet management, publicly-owned
    vehicles, §50-211.01.
  Forensic sciences department,
    §5-1501.01.
  General license law, §47-2851.01.
  Liens on motor vehicles or trailers,
    §50-1201.
  Limited cooperative associations,
    §29-1001.02.

DEFINED TERMS —Cont'd
Director —Cont'd
Motor vehicle registration,
§50-1501.01.
Nonprofit corporations, §§29-401.02,
29-406.50.
Personal delivery devices pilot
program, §50-1551.
Trade names, §47-2855.01.
Traffic adjudication, §50-2301.02.
Unemployment compensation, §51-101.
Universal banks, §26-1401.02.
Weights and measures, §37-201.29.
**Director's conflicting interest
transaction.**
Corporations, §29-306.70.
Direct request.
Interstate family support, §46-357.01.
Direct rollover.
Police and firefighters retirement and
disability, §5-706.
Teachers' retirement, service credit
purchase and rollovers,
§38-2021.26.
Direct supervision, §3-402.
Audiology assistants, §3-1209.09.
Dental assistants, §3-1209.05.
Pharmacy technicians, §3-1207.51.
Speech-language pathology assistants,
§3-1209.10.
Dirt bike, §50-2201.02.
Disability, §2-1431.01.
Human rights, §2-1401.02.
Interim disability assistance,
§4-204.07.
Limitation of asbestos actions,
§12-311.
Police and firefighters retirement and
disability, §§5-701, 5-710.
Public assistance, §4-205.42.
Respectful language modernization,
§2-631.
Workers' compensation, §32-1501.
Disabled, §5-701.
Disadvantaged business enterprise.
Small and certified business enterprise
development and assistance,
§2-218.02.
Disadvantaged investor.
Small and certified business enterprise
development and assistance,
§2-218.02.
Disappearing association.
Unincorporated nonprofit associations,
§29-1126.
Disaster relief organization.
Emergency volunteer health
practitioners, §7-2361.01.

DEFINED TERMS —Cont'd
Disbursal year.
Fee collection incentive fund,
§1-325.61.
Disbursement of loan funds,
§42-2401.
**Disbursement of settlement
proceeds, §42-2401.**
Discharge, §§8-103.01, 8-105.02.
Hospital discharge planning,
§21-2231.01.
Disciplinary action.
Nurse's rehabilitation program,
§3-1251.01.
Disciplinary investigation.
Firefighter retirement while under
disciplinary investigation, §5-1051.
Police retirement while under
disciplinary investigation, §5-801.
Disciplining court.
Attorney discipline or disability
proceedings, DCBar Rule XI.
Disc jockey.
Alcoholic beverages, §25-101.
Disclaimant.
Uniform disclaimer of property
interests act, §19-1502.
Disclaimed interest.
Uniform disclaimer of property
interests act, §19-1502.
Disclaimer.
Uniform disclaimer of property
interests act, §19-1502.
Disclose, §7-1201.01.
Nonconsensual pornography, §22-3051.
Disclosing official.
Child fatality or near fatality,
§4-1303.31.
Disclosure.
Health data privacy, §7-241.
Public assistance applicants,
confidentiality of information,
§4-209.04.
Discover.
UCC, §28:1-202.
Discriminatory wage differential,
§32-601.
**Discriminatory wage-setting
practices, §32-601.**
Dishonor.
Letters of credit, §28:5-102.
Disinterested director.
Nonprofit corporations, §29-406.50.
Disinterested witness.
Anatomical gifts, §7-1531.01.
Dispatch.
Regulation of for-hire vehicles,
§50-301.03.

DEFINED TERMS —Cont'd

Dispensary.
  Medical marijuana, §7-1671.01.
Dispense, §§47-2885.02, 48-901.02.
  Medical marijuana, §7-1671.01.
  Monitoring prescription drugs,
    §48-853.01.
Dispenser, §48-901.02.
  Monitoring prescription drugs,
    §48-853.01.
Disperse.
  Metropolitan police.
    School safety division, §5-132.21.
Disposable carryout bag.
  Anacostia river clean up and
    protection, §8-102.01.
Disposable food service ware.
  Management, §8-1531.
Disposable wages, §16-571.
Disposal, §§8-1302, 8-1501.
Dispose, §8-901.
Disposition.
  Condominiums, §42-1901.02.
  Solid waste reduction and recovery,
    §8-1031.01.
Dispositional hearing, §16-2301.
Disqualify, §50-401.
Disqualifying arrest or conviction.
  Criminal records sealing, §16-801.
Disrupted corridor.
  Qualified social electronic commerce
    companies tax abatements,
    §47-1818.01.
Dissolved corporation.
  Corporations, §29-312.03.
Distillery pub, §25-101.
Distracted driving, §50-1731.02.
Distressed neighborhood.
  Housing production trust fund,
    §42-2801.
Distressed property, §42-3501.03.
Distribute, §§8-401, 48-701, 48-901.02.
  Medical marijuana, §7-1671.01.
Distributee.
  Police and firefighters retirement and
    disability, §5-706.
  Teachers' retirement, service credit
    purchase and rollovers,
    §38-2021.26.
  Uniform trust code, §19-1301.03.
Distribution.
  Corporations, §29-301.02.
  Limited cooperative associations,
    §29-1001.02.
  Limited liability companies,
    §29-801.02.

DEFINED TERMS —Cont'd

Distribution —Cont'd
  Limited partnerships, §29-701.02.
  Partnerships, §29-601.02.
  Statutory trusts, §29-1201.02.
Distributional interest.
  Business organizations, §29-101.02.
Distribution proceeding, §15-901.
Distribution service.
  Retail natural gas supplier licensing
    and consumer protection,
    §34-1671.02.
**Distribution service customer class
  cost allocations.**
  Electric company infrastructure
    improvement financing,
    §34-1311.01.
Distributor, §§36-301.01, 47-2302,
  48-901.02.
  Paint stewardship, §8-233.01.
District.
  Access to prescription drugs,
    §48-831.02.
  Automated teller machine, §26-131.02.
  Automobile consumer, §50-501.
  Banks and financial institutions,
    §26-551.02.
  Business improvement districts,
    §2-1215.02.
  Choice in drug treatment, §7-3002.
  City Market at O Street tax increment
    financing, §2-1217.33a.
  Compulsory school attendance,
    §38-201.
  Criminal procedure, CrimPro Rule 54.
  Department of mental health,
    §7-1131.02.
  District of Columbia housing
    authority, §6-201.
  Foreign judgments, §15-351.
  Health maintenance organizations,
    §31-3401.
  Howard Theatre redevelopment project
    TIF area, §2-1217.34a.
  Inheritance and estate taxes,
    §47-3701.
  Installment sales of motor vehicles,
    §50-601.
  Insurance companies, §47-2601.
  Insurance demutualization, §31-901.
  Insurance fraud, §22-3225.01.
  Interstate banking and branching,
    §26-732.
  Interstate family support, §46-351.02.
  Investment and deposit of District
    funds, §47-351.01.

DEFINED TERMS —Cont'd

District —Cont'd

Merchant bank, §26-831.02.

Merit system, §1-603.01.

Mortgage loan protection, §26-1151.01.

National Children's Island, §10-1401.

Non-health related occupations and professions licensure, §47-2853.01.

Notarial acts, §42-141.

Office of cable television, film, music, and entertainment amendment act of 2015, §34-1251.03.

Parking regulation, §50-2602.

Pawnbrokers, §47-2884.01.

Pet ownership restriction in assisted housing, §8-2031.

Portable electronics insurance, §31-5051.01.

Preservation and rehabilitation of government-supported housing, §42-2851.02.

RBC report, §31-2001.

Recorder of deeds, §42-1101.

Redomestication of insurer, §31-1701.

Rental housing, §42-3401.03.

Rental of airspace, §10-1121.01.

Rental of public space, §10-1101.01.

Self-government, §1-201.03.

State of entry for non-United States insurers, §31-2201.

Streets and alleys, §9-201.01.

Superior court, tax division, §47-3301.

Tax check-off, drug prevention and children at risk, §47-4001.

Tax increment financing authorization, §2-1217.01.

Tobacco settlement financing, §7-1831.01.

Tobacco tax, §47-2401.

Traffic adjudication, §50-2301.02.

Transportation infrastructure improvement GARVEE bonds, §9-107.51.

Unemployment compensation, §51-101.

Universal banks, §26-1401.02.

Vector-borne disease control, §8-2131.01.

Women's rights regarding certain health insurance coverage, §31-3831.

District agency.

Delinquent debts to the District, recovery, §1-350.01.

Quick payment provisions, §2-221.01.

District-assisted facility, §8-171.02.

District association, §26-1201.

DEFINED TERMS —Cont'd

District bank, §26-732.

Automated teller machine, §26-131.02.

Banks and financial institutions, §26-551.02.

District-based wireless telecommunication service.

Toll telecommunication service tax, §47-3901.

District bond issuance.

Bond issues, borrowing limitation, §47-334.

District bonds.

Bond issues, borrowing limitation, §47-334.

District CFO.

Department of health care finance, §7-771.01.

District Court.

Criminal procedure, CrimPro Rule 54.

District credit union.

Automated teller machine, §26-131.02.

Banks and financial institutions, §26-551.02.

District department of the environment.

Sustainable energy, §8-1773.01.

District employee.

Mandatory drug and alcohol testing of certain employees who serve children, §1-620.31.

District-financed.

Anacostia waterfront environmental standards, §2-1226.32.

Green buildings, §6-1451.01.

District funds.

Investment and deposit of District funds, §47-351.01.

District government.

Chief financial officer, §1-204.24f.

Clean hands before receiving a license or permit, §47-2861.

District of Columbia housing authority, §6-201.

Miscellaneous provisions, §47-3401.05.

Office of inspector general, §1-301.115a.

District government employee, §32-701.

District gross receipts, §47-2751.

Ballpark fee, §47-2761.

Small and certified business enterprise development and assistance, §2-218.02.

District instrumentality.

Revenue bonds, notes or other obligations, §1-204.90.

DEFINED TERMS —Cont'd
District instrumentality-financed.
Anacostia waterfront environmental standards, §2-1226.32.
Green buildings, §6-1451.01.
District of Columbia banking code.
Automated teller machine, §26-131.02.
Banks and financial institutions, §§26-551.02, 26-631.
Insurance, securities, and banking, department of, §31-101.
Merchant bank, §26-831.02.
Universal banks, §26-1401.02.
District of Columbia building rehabilitation code advisory council, §6-1410.
District of Columbia courts.
Home Rule act, §1-201.03.
District of Columbia emancipation day.
Parental leave, §32-1201.
District of Columbia median family income.
Truth in affordability reporting, §42-2131.
Housing, §42-2151.01.
District of Columbia median income.
Opportunity accounts, §1-307.61.
District of Columbia payment.
Offset program, §47-143.
District of Columbia public record.
Identity theft, §22-3227.05.
District of Columbia public schools.
Tuition of nonresidents, §38-304.
Uniform per student funding formula, §38-2901.
District of Columbia supply schedule.
Procurement practices, §2-351.04.
Small and certified business enterprise development and assistance, §2-218.02.
District of Columbia undertaking.
Historic landmarks, §6-1102.
District of Columbia water and sewer authority service fees.
Clean hands before receiving a license permit, §47-2861.
District-owned parkland.
Animal control, §8-1801.
District premium tax liability.
Certified capital companies, §31-5231.
District pretreatment standards.
Wastewater disposal systems, §8-105.02.
District property.
Pesticide education and control, §8-431.

DEFINED TERMS —Cont'd
District resident.
The Advisory Board Company, real property tax abatement, §47-4665.01.
District restricted use.
Pesticide education and control, §8-431.
District revenues.
Home Rule act, §1-201.03.
District saving institution.
Banks and financial institutions, §26-551.02.
Universal banks, §26-1401.02.
District savings and loan holding company, §26-1201.
District sports and entertainment facility.
Washington convention and sports authority, §10-1202.01.
District state bank, §26-732.
District telecommunications assets.
Wireless network antennae franchise agreement, §34-1731.02.
District waters, §8-103.01.
Districtwide assessments.
Charter schools, §38-1800.02.
Testing integrity in public schools, §§38-771.01, 38-2602.
Diversion payment, §4-205.81.
Dividend.
Income tax, §47-1801.04.
Division.
Delinquent minors, JuvProc Rule 101.
DMH.
Incompetent criminal defendants, §24-531.01.
DMPED.
H Street, N.E. retail priority area incentive, §1-325.171.
DNA.
Crime investigation records, §5-113.31.
Protection of innocence act, §22-4131.
DNA testing.
Crime investigation records, §5-113.31.
Protection of innocence act, §22-4131.
Document.
Drivers' licenses, §50-1401.04.
Letters of credit, §28:5-102.
Real property electronic recording, §42-1231.
Documentary draft.
Bank deposits and collections, §28:4-104.
Documentary material.
Procurement claims, §2-381.01.

DEFINED TERMS —Cont'd

Documented.
Presumptive disability or death of fire and emergency medical services employees, §5-651.

Documented vessel.
Uniform certificates of title for vessels, §50-1541.01.

Document having general applicability and legal effect.
Administrative procedure, legal publication of documents, §2-551.

Document of gift.
Anatomical gifts, §7-1531.01.

Document of title.
UCC, §28:1-201.

DOES.
Pregnant and nursing workers, reasonable accommodations for, §32-1231.01.
Pregnant workers, protecting, §32-1231.01.

Dog park, §8-1801.

DOH.
Department of health care finance, §7-771.01.
Sexually transmitted diseases, treatment for sexual partners, §7-2081.01.
Stroke system of care, §44-1151.

Doing business, §31-1301.
Income tax, §47-1801.04.

Dollar limit.
Police and firefighters retirement and disability, §5-723.01.
Teachers' retirement, maximum benefit computations, §38-2021.27.

Dollar roll transaction.
Insurance investments, §31-1371.02.

Domestic, §47-2601.
Business organizations, §29-101.02.

Domestic association.
Domestic limited cooperative associations, §29-1001.02.

Domesticated company.
Limited liability companies, §29-809.01.

Domesticated corporation.
Nonprofit corporations, §29-407.01.

Domesticated entity.
Entity transactions, §29-201.02.

Domesticating company.
Limited liability companies, §29-809.01.

Domesticating corporation.
Nonprofit corporations, §29-407.01.

DEFINED TERMS —Cont'd

Domesticating entity.
Entity transactions, §29-201.02.

Domestication.
Entity transactions, §29-201.02.
Nonprofit corporations, §29-407.01.
United States branch domestication of insurers, §31-2301.

Domestic business corporation.
Corporations, §29-301.02.

Domestic (fire and casualty) company, §31-2501.03.

Domestic (life insurance) company, §31-4202.

Domestic corporation.
Corporations, §29-301.02.
Nonprofit corporations, §29-401.02.

Domestic entity.
Entity transactions, §29-201.02.

Domestic health organization.
Health insurance regulatory standards, §31-3451.01.

Domestic insurer, §31-2001.
United States branch domestication, §31-2301.

Domestic jurisdiction.
Insurance investments, §31-1371.02.

Domestic liability partnership.
Partnerships, §29-601.02.

Domestic limited cooperative association, §29-1001.02.

Domestic nonprofit corporation.
Nonprofit corporations, §29-401.02.

Domestic partner, §32-701.
Adoption, §16-909.
Anatomical gifts, §7-1531.01.
Bigamy, §22-501.
Boxing and wrestling commission, §3-602.
Condominiums, §42-1901.02.
Conservators, §21-2011.
Crime investigation records, §5-113.31.
Custodial trusts, §19-1101.
District of Columbia housing authority, §6-201.
Divorce, annulment, separation, support, §16-901.
Employees retirement program management, §1-702.
Ethics and government accountability, §1-1161.01.
Execution of judgments, §15-503.
Family court proceedings, §16-2301.
Garnishment of wages, §16-571.
Habeas corpus, §16-1908.
Health care durable powers of attorney, §21-2202.

DEFINED TERMS —Cont'd
Domestic partner —Cont'd
Health occupations, §3-1201.01.
Hospitalization of persons with mental illness, §21-501.
Hospitalization of the mentally ill, §21-501.
Human rights, §2-1401.02.
Income tax, §47-1801.04.
Inheritance and estate taxes, §47-3701.
Interception of oral or wire communications, §23-541.
Intestate succession, §§19-115, 19-322.
Joint bank accounts, §§26-801, 26-802.
Life insurance, §31-4202.
Lottery and charitable games control board, §§3-1320, 3-1328.
Merit system, §1-603.01.
Metropolitan police, §5-131.03.
Mortgages, §15-502.
Nonprobate transfers on death, §19-602.01.
Personal representatives, §20-303.
Police and firefighters retirement and disability, §§1-901.02, 5-701.
Powers of attorney, §21-2113.
Premarital agreements, §46-501.
Priest-penitent privilege, §14-309.
Principal and income, §28-4801.02.
Prostitution, §22-2701.01.
Real property assessment, §47-802.
Rule against perpetuities, §19-904.
Sexual abuse, §22-3001.
Spousal privilege, §14-306.
Spousal property rights, §46-601.
Spouse or domestic partner equity in retirement benefits, §1-529.02.
Teachers' retirement, §38-2021.13.
Teachers' retirement, deferred or survivor annuity, §38-2021.09.
Vital records, §7-201.
Voluntary leave transfer program, §1-612.31.
Workers' compensation, §32-1501.
Wrongful death, §16-2701.
Domestic partnership, §32-701.
Adoption, §16-909.
AIDS health care, §7-1601.
Bigamy, §22-501.
Child abuse and neglect, §4-1301.02.
COBRA health insurance coverage, §31-3301.01.
Conservators, §21-2011.
Divorce, annulment, separation, support, §16-901.

DEFINED TERMS —Cont'd
Domestic partnership —Cont'd
Employment agencies, §32-408.
False personation, §22-1403.
Health care durable powers of attorney, §21-2202.
Health occupations, §3-1201.01.
Human rights, §2-1401.02.
Intestate succession, §19-115.
Intrafamily offenses, §16-1001.
Life insurance, §31-4202.
Mental health consumer's rights, §7-1231.02.
Merit system, §1-603.01.
Natural death act, §7-621.
Parental leave, §32-1201.
Parent-child relationship, §16-907.
Partnerships, §29-601.02.
Police and firefighters retirement and disability, §5-701.
Premarital agreements, §46-501.
Principal and income, §28-4801.02.
Rule against perpetuities, §19-904.
Sexual abuse, §22-3001.
Spousal property rights, §46-601.
Spouse or domestic partner equity in retirement benefits, §1-529.02.
Vital records, §7-201.
Workers' compensation, §32-1501.
Domestic unincorporated entity.
Corporations, §29-301.02.
Nonprofit corporations, §29-401.02.
Domestic violence.
Domestic violence hotline, §4-551.
Reporting of child sexual abuse, §22-3020.53.
Right to sick and safe leave, §32-131.01.
Unemployment compensation, §51-131.
Domestic violence counselor, §14-310.
Domestic violence hotline, §4-551.
Domestic violence fatality.
Domestic violence fatality review board, §16-1051.
Domestic violence program.
Domestic violence counselors, §14-310.
Domestic violence hotline, §4-551.
Domestic violence unit.
Intrafamily offenses, §16-1001.
Domicile, §§31-4101, 41-102.
Merit system, §1-603.01.
Domiciliary state, §31-1301.
Donor, §7-1541.02.
Anatomical gifts, §7-1531.01.
Donor registry.
Anatomical gifts, §7-1531.01.

DEFINED TERMS —Cont'd

Dormitory, §42-3501.03.

Downpayment, §42-2621.

Downtown area, §2-1217.01.

Downtown retail priority area.
Retail development incentives, §2-1217.71.

DPAH.
District of Columbia housing authority, §6-201.

DPW.
Fleet management, publicly-owned vehicles, §50-211.01.

Drafts.
Bank deposits and collections, §28:4-104.

Drawee.
Bank deposits and collections, §28:4-104.
Negotiable instruments, §28:3-103.

Drawer.
Consumer identification, §47-3151.
Negotiable instruments, §28:3-103.

Dredge and fill activity, §8-103.01.

Drive, §8-2001.

Driver.
Autonomous vehicles, §50-2351.

Driver or operator, §§2-2001, 50-1301.02.

Driver safety course, §50-101.

Driver's license.
Anatomical gifts, §7-1531.01.

Drop-in center.
Homeless services, §4-751.01.

Dropout, §4-205.61.

Drug.
Adulteration, §48-102.
Chemical testing for driving under the influence, §50-1901.
Choice in drug treatment, §7-3002.
Drug manufacture and distribution licensure, §48-701.
Homeless services, §4-751.01.
Impaired operation or driving, §50-2206.01.
Mandatory drug and alcohol testing of certain employees who serve children, §1-620.31.
Monitoring prescription drugs, §48-853.01.
Pharmacists and pharmacies, §47-2885.02.

Drug abuse, §31-3101.

Drug, firearm, or prostitution-related nuisance, §42-3101.

Drug haven, §42-3601.

DEFINED TERMS —Cont'd

Drug paraphernalia, §§42-3101, 48-1101.

Drug prevention.
Tax check-off, drug prevention and children at risk, §47-4001.

Drug-related activity, §4-1301.02.
Family court proceedings, §16-2301.

Drug-related eviction, §42-3601.

Drug used as a restraint.
Mental health consumer's rights, §7-1231.02.

Drug user, §24-702.

DSM-IV.
Department of mental health, §7-1131.02.
Rights of persons with intellectual disability, §7-1301.03.

DSM-IV V codes.
Department of mental health, §7-1131.02.
Rights of persons with intellectual disability, §7-1301.03.

Dual agent, §42-1702.

Dual diagnosis.
Choice in drug treatment, §7-3002.

Dual representative, §42-1702.

Duly registered voter.
Elections, §1-1001.02.

Dunnage.
Renewable energy portfolio standards, §34-1431.

Durable power of attorney for health care, §21-2202.

Durable powers of attorney, §21-2081.

Dust action level.
Lead-hazard prevention and elimination, §8-231.01.

Dust sampling technician.
Lead-hazard prevention and elimination, §8-231.01.

Duty of support, §46-201.
Interstate family support, §46-351.02.

Dwelling, §6-101.07.

Dwelling unit, §6-751.01.
Homestead housing provision, §42-2103.
Indoor mold assessment and remediation, §8-241.01.
Lead-hazard prevention and elimination, §8-231.01.
Lead level water testing, §42-3251.
Real property assessment, §47-803.
Real property taxes, classes of property, §47-813.

DEFINED TERMS —Cont'd
Dwelling unit —Cont'd
Vacant buildings, §42-3131.05.
DYRS.
Mental health, §7-1131.02.
Earned income, §4-205.05.
Earnest money contract, §42-2621.
Earnings, §§46-201, 51-101.
Eastern market, §37-101.
Eastern market community advisory committee, §37-101.
Eastern market special use area, §37-101.
Eastern market square, §37-101.
Eastern market tenants council, §37-101.
EATF.
Sustainable energy, §8-1773.01.
EBL child.
Lead-hazard prevention and elimination, §8-231.01.
Ecgonine, §48-901.02.
Eckington One residential property, §47-4618.
Economically disadvantaged individual.
Small and certified business enterprise development and assistance, §2-218.02.
Economic assistance.
Arts, cultural and educational facilities, economic assistance to, §39-401.
Economic development incentive.
Unified economic development budget transparency and accountability, §2-1208.01.
Economic development purpose.
Chief financial officer, tax transparency, §1-301.156.
Economic impact study.
Certified capital companies, §31-5231.
Economic loss, §4-501.
EDC agreement.
Walter Reed Medical Center site development, §2-1227.01.
Edge act.
International banking corporations, §26-631.
Education, §7-1301.03.
Educational channel.
Office of cable television, film, music, and entertainment amendment act of 2015, §34-1251.03.
Educational employee.
Merit system, §1-603.01.

DEFINED TERMS —Cont'd
Educational facility, §7-1702.
Green buildings, §6-1451.01.
Educational institution, §§2-1401.02, 38-1301.
Bullying, §2-1535.01.
Compulsory school attendance, §38-201.
Educational records.
Interstate compact on educational opportunity for military children, §49-1101.03.
Educational specification.
School-based budgeting and accountability, §38-2801.01.
Effective.
Limited liability companies, §29-801.02.
Effective competition.
Retail electric competition and consumer protection, §34-1501.
Effective date, §47-1401.
Business organizations, §29-101.02.
Effort, §32-601.
EHA.
Brownfield revitalization, §8-631.02.
Elderly.
Pet ownership restriction in assisted housing, §8-2031.
Elderly person.
Criminal abuse, neglect and financial exploitation of vulnerable adults and elderly persons, §22-932.
Elderly resident.
Community development by financial institutions, §26-431.02.
Elderly tenant, §42-3501.03.
Elections, §1-1001.02.
Official correspondence, §2-701.
Rent control, §42-3502.06.
Elected official.
Elections, §1-1001.02.
Election.
Ethics and government accountability, §1-1161.01.
Grant administration, §1-328.11.
Home Rule act, §1-201.03.
Election code.
Ethics and government accountability, §1-1161.01.
Election observers, §1-1001.02.
Elections board.
Ethics and government accountability, §1-1161.01.
Elector slate.
National popular vote interstate agreement, §1-1051.01.

DEFINED TERMS —Cont'd

Electric company.
Electric light and power companies, §34-1561.
Infrastructure improvement financing, §34-1311.01.
Retail electric competition and consumer protection, §34-1501.
Sustainable energy, §8-1773.01.

Electric company infrastructure improvement activity.
Financing, §34-1311.01.

Electric company infrastructure improvement costs.
Financing, §34-1311.01.

Electric company infrastructure improvement revenue.
Financing, §34-1311.01.

Electric company infrastructure improvements.
Financing, §34-1311.01.

Electric corporation, §34-207.

Electricity supplier.
Renewable energy portfolio standards, §34-1431.
Retail electric competition and consumer protection, §34-1501.

Electric personal assistive mobility device, §50-2201.01.

Electric plant, §34-206.
Infrastructure improvement financing, §34-1311.01.

Electric vehicle.
Motor vehicle registration, §50-1501.01.

Electronic.
Corporations, §29-301.02.
Electronic transactions, uniform act, §28-4901.
Nonprofit corporations, §29-401.02.
Real property electronic recording, §42-1231.
Uniform certificates of title for vessels, §50-1541.01.

Electronic agent.
Electronic transactions, uniform act, §28-4901.

Electronically transmitted.
Corporations, §29-301.02.
Nonprofit corporations, §29-401.02.

Electronic certificates of title.
Uniform certificates of title for vessels, §50-1541.01.

Electronic chattel paper.
Secured transactions, §28:9-102.

Electronic chip.
One Card service support, §1-327.71.

DEFINED TERMS —Cont'd

Electronic communication.
Bullying, §2-1535.01.
Council, §1-301.44a.

Electronic data transfer system.
Charter schools, §38-1800.02.

Electronic device.
Voyeurism, §22-3531.

Electronic document.
Real property electronic recording, §42-1231.

Electronic funds transfer.
Collection of taxes, §47-4402.
Courts, authority to accept certain types of payments, §11-1748.

Electronic instrument.
Money transmissions, §26-1001.

Electronic mail.
Spam deterrence, §28-5001.

Electronic mail service provider.
Spam deterrence, §28-5001.

Electronic record.
Electronic transactions, uniform act, §28-4901.

Electronic signature.
Electronic transactions, uniform act, §28-4901.
Real property electronic recording, §42-1231.

Electronic smoking device.
Health department, §7-741.01.

Electronic transmission.
Condominiums, §42-1901.02.
Corporations, §29-301.02.
Nonprofit corporations, §29-401.02.

Elementary and secondary education.
Pre-kindergarten programs, §38-271.01.

Elementary school.
Charter schools, §38-1800.02.
Scholarships for opportunity and results (SOAR) act, §38-1853.13.

Elevated blood lead level.
Childhood lead poisoning screening and reporting, §7-871.02.
Lead-hazard prevention and elimination, §8-231.01.

Elevator contractor, §47-2853.95.

Elevator inspector, §47-2853.95.

Elevator mechanic, §47-2853.95.

Eligibility period.
Unemployment compensation, §51-107.

Eligible applicant.
Charter schools, §38-1800.02.

Eligible area.
Grocery and retail stores development, §2-1212.01.

DEFINED TERMS —Cont'd

Eligible area —Cont'd

New residential development tax
abatement, §47-859.01.

Supermarket tax incentives, §47-3801.

Eligible area #1.

Tax abatement for new residential
developments, §47-857.01.

Eligible area #2.

Tax abatement for new residential
developments, §47-857.01.

Eligible area #3.

Tax abatement for new residential
developments, §47-857.01.

Eligible area #4.

Tax abatement for new residential
developments, §47-857.01.

Eligible building.

Real property tax abatement for
qualified high technology
companies, §47-811.03.

Real property tax exemptions,
qualified high technology company
interior renovation tax rebate,
§47-4665.

Eligible caretaker relative,
§38-1207.01.

Eligible chartering authority.

Charter schools, §38-1800.02.

Eligible child.

Child and adult food program funding,
§38-281.

Eligible consortium.

Community schools, §38-754.02.

Eligible debt.

Access to justice initiative program,
§4-1701.01.

Eligible District youth.

Mayor's youth leadership institute,
§2-1571.

Eligible employee, §31-3301.01.

Family leave, §1-612.03c.

Eligible employment.

Access to justice initiative program,
§4-1701.01.

Eligible entity.

Charter schools, §38-1800.02.

Nonprofit corporations, §29-401.02.

Eligible family, §42-3503.01.

Eligible felony.

Criminal records sealing, §16-801.

Eligible financial institution.

Investment and deposit of District
funds, §47-351.01.

Eligible foods.

Gross sales tax, §47-2001.

DEFINED TERMS —Cont'd

Eligible household.

Housing production trust fund,
§42-2801.

Reduced real property tax liability for
seniors and persons with
disabilities, §47-863.

Eligible individual, §31-3301.01.

ABLE savings accounts, §47-4901.

Eligible institution.

College access assistance, public school
program, §38-2702.

College savings program, §47-4501.

Higher education financial aid
assistance, §38-2731.

Eligible interests.

Corporations, §29-301.02.

Nonprofit corporations, §29-401.02.

Eligible legal guardian, §38-1207.01.

**Eligible low-income housing
development.**

Preservation and rehabilitation of
government-supported housing,
§42-2851.02.

Eligible member, §31-901.

Eligible misdemeanor.

Criminal records sealing, §16-801.

Eligible nonprofit zone.

Nonprofit corporations locating in
emerging commercial
neighborhoods, §47-857.11.

Eligible organization.

Arts, cultural and educational
facilities, economic assistance to,
§39-401.

Eligible owner.

Real property tax deferral, §47-845.02.

Tax abatement for homeowners in
enterprise zones, §47-858.01.

Eligible parent, §38-1207.01.

Eligible person, §§7-531.01,
42-2701.02.

Eligible premises.

Real property tax abatement for
qualified high technology
companies, §47-811.03.

Real property tax exemptions,
qualified high technology company
interior renovation tax rebate,
§47-4665.

Eligible production company.

Motion pictures, §2-1204.11c.

Eligible project, §2-1217.01.

Emergency highway relief, §9-109.01.

Qualified zone academy revenue bond
project forward commitment
approval act, §2-1217.102.

DEFINED TERMS —Cont'd
Eligible project —Cont'd
Union Market district tax increment financing, §2-1217.36a.
Eligible property.
Brownfield revitalization, §8-631.02.
Eligible real property.
New residential development tax abatement, §47-859.01.
Tax abatement for new residential developments, §47-857.01.
Eligible recipient.
Small business capital access fund, §2-218.75.
Eligible retirement plan.
Police and firefighters retirement and disability, §5-706.
Teachers' retirement, service credit purchase and rollovers, §38-2021.26.
Eligible rollover distribution.
Police and firefighters retirement and disability, §5-706.
Teachers' retirement, service credit purchase and rollovers, §38-2021.26.
Eligible services.
Community schools, §38-754.02.
Teachers' retirement, §38-2021.13.
Eligible state or local government unit, §42-2701.02.
Eligible student.
College access assistance, public school program, §38-2702.
Higher education financial aid assistance, §38-2731.
Scholarships for opportunity and results (SOAR) act, §38-1853.13.
Eligible training provider.
Workforce investment implementation, §32-1602.
ELL.
Testing integrity (public schools), §38-771.01.
Emancipated minor.
Mental health consumer's rights, §7-1231.02.
Emancipation day parade, §1-181.
Embargo.
Adulteration of food and drugs, §48-102.
EMCAC, §37-101.
Emergencies involving the safety of human life or the protection of property.
Budgets and budget estimates, §47-355.01.

DEFINED TERMS —Cont'd
Emergency, §§2-1542, 5-1306.
Emergency medical services, §7-2341.01.
Emergency volunteer health practitioners, §7-2361.01.
Garbage collection, §8-741.
Hazardous materials transportation, terrorism prevention, §8-1422.
Mental health consumer's rights, §7-1231.02.
Uniform adult guardianship and protective proceedings jurisdiction act, §21-2401.02.
Emergency care, §7-2101.
Guardianship, §21-2011.
Emergency circumstances.
Student health care, §38-651.01.
Emergency contraception.
Emergency care for sexual assault victims, §7-2121.
Emergency declaration.
Emergency volunteer health practitioners, §7-2361.01.
Emergency management assistance compact.
Emergency volunteer health practitioners, §7-2361.01.
Emergency medical condition, §44-301.01.
Emergency medical response vehicle.
Emergency medical services, §7-2341.01.
Emergency medical services.
Non-resuscitation procedures for EMS, §7-651.01.
Emergency medical services agency, §7-2341.01.
Non-resuscitation procedures for EMS, §7-651.01.
Emergency medical services instructor, §7-2341.01.
Emergency medical services personnel, §7-2341.01.
Non-resuscitation procedures for EMS, §7-651.01.
Emergency medical services training facility, §7-2341.01.
Emergency operations plan, §7-2301.
Emergency run, §2-411.
Emergency services, §31-2801.
Emergency situation.
Metropolitan police, §5-101.04.
Emergency vehicle, §§2-411, 50-702.
Fleet management, publicly-owned vehicles, §50-211.01.

DEFINED TERMS —Cont'd
Emerging neighborhood nonprofit zone.
Nonprofit corporations locating in emerging commercial neighborhoods, §47-857.11.
Emotional distress.
Stalking, §22-3132.
Employ, §32-1002.
Employee, §§32-601, 32-1002, 32-1101.
Budgets and budget estimates, §47-355.01.
Bullying, §2-1535.01.
Corporations, §29-301.02.
Criminal background checks for the protection of children act, §4-1501.02.
Disability compensation, §1-623.01.
Discrimination, §32-1361.
Ethics and government accountability, §1-1161.01.
Government employee engagement in political activity, §1-1171.01.
Health care benefits expansion, §32-701.
Human rights commission, §2-1401.02.
Income tax, §47-1801.04.
Leave of absence, §1-612.04.
Lie detectors, §32-901.
Mandatory drug and alcohol testing of certain employees who serve children, §1-620.31.
Merit system, §1-603.01.
Health benefits, §1-621.03.
Life insurance, §1-622.04.
Metropolitan Washington airport, §9-1003.
Negotiable instruments, §28:3-405.
Nonprofit corporations, §§29-401.02, 29-406.91.
Protection of District public officials, §22-851.
Public officers and employees, §1-319.05.
Reducing single occupancy vehicle use by encouraging transit benefits, §32-151.
Retirement, §1-626.04.
Right to sick and safe leave, §32-131.01.
Spouse or domestic partner equity in retirement benefits, §1-529.02.
Voluntary leave transfer program, §1-612.31.
Wages and salaries, §32-1301.
Wage transparency, §32-1451.

DEFINED TERMS —Cont'd
Employee —Cont'd
Whistleblower protection, §1-615.52.
Workplace fraud, §32-1331.01.
Employee benefit trust distribution, §41-102.
Employee contributions, §1-901.02.
Employee organization, §§1-702, 1-901.02.
Employees retirement program management, §1-702.
Employer, §§32-401, 32-1002, 32-1101.
Discrimination, §32-1361.
Health care benefits expansion, §32-701.
Hiring of ex-offenders, fair criminal record screening, §32-1341.
Human rights commission, §2-1401.02.
Income tax, §47-1801.04.
Labor-peace agreement for public projects, §32-852.
Lie detectors, §32-901.
Parental leave, §32-1201.
Reducing single occupancy vehicle use by encouraging transit benefits, §32-151.
Right to sick and safe leave, §32-131.01.
Unemployment compensation, §51-101.
Wages and salaries, §32-1301.
Wage transparency, §32-1451.
Workplace fraud, §32-1331.01.
Employer-paid personnel service, §32-401.
Employing unit, §51-101.
Employment, §51-101.
Hiring of ex-offenders, fair criminal record screening, §32-1341.
Employment agency, §§2-1401.02, 32-401.
Discrimination, §32-1361.
Employment agreement.
First source employment, §2-219.01.
Employment benefit, §32-501.
Employment counseling service, §32-401.
Employment counselor, §32-401.
Employment discrimination backpay or frontpay.
Income averaging, §47-1806.10.
Employment office, §51-101.
Employment security law.
Shared work unemployment compensation program, §51-171.
EMS.
Department of the environment, §8-151.01.

DEFINED TERMS —Cont'd
EMS —Cont'd
Non-resuscitation procedures for EMS, §7-651.01.
EMS agency.
Non-resuscitation procedures for EMS, §7-651.01.
EMS employee.
Presumptive disability or death of fire and emergency medical services employees, §5-651.
EMS personnel.
Non-resuscitation procedures for EMS, §7-651.01.
Encapsulate, §8-111.01.
Encapsulation.
Lead-hazard prevention and elimination, §8-231.01.
Enclose.
Deteriorated property, §42-3173.01.
Enclosed area.
Health department, §7-741.01.
Enclosure.
Lead-hazard prevention and elimination, §8-231.01.
Encumbrance.
Secured transactions, §28:9-102.
Endocrine disruptor compounds, §34-2202.01.
Endorsement.
Health occupations licensure, registration or certification, §3-1205.07.
Endorsement contract.
Athlete agents, §47-2887.01.
Endorsing prescriber.
Prescription drugs, §48-804.51.
Endowment fund.
Prudent management of institutional funds, §44-1631.
Energy, §8-171.02.
Energy allocation equipment.
Submetering, §34-1551.
Energy assistance trust fund.
Sustainable energy, §8-1773.01.
Energy audit, §8-171.02.
Energy auditor, §8-171.02.
Energy burden.
Solar for All program, §8-1774.16.
Energy conservation, §8-171.02.
Energy distributor, §8-171.02.
Energy efficiency audit.
Energy efficiency financing, §8-1778.02.
Energy efficiency financing act.
Real property taxes.
Special energy assessments, §47-895.31.

DEFINED TERMS —Cont'd
Energy efficiency guidelines, §8-171.02.
Energy efficiency improvement.
Energy efficiency financing, §8-1778.02.
Energy efficiency loan.
Energy efficiency financing, §8-1778.02.
Real property taxes.
Special energy assessments, §47-895.31.
Energy efficiency loan agreement.
Real property taxes.
Special energy assessments, §47-895.31.
Energy information, §8-171.02.
Energy resources, §8-171.02.
ENERGY STAR portfolio manager.
Green buildings, §6-1451.01.
Sustainable energy, §8-1773.01.
ENERGY STAR target finder.
Green buildings, §6-1451.01.
Engaged in the business, §7-2531.01.
Engaging in business, §47-2001.
Engaging in business in the District, §47-2201.
Engaging in the retail sale of motor fuel, §36-301.01.
Engineered sharps injury protection.
Safe needle distribution, §7-2851.
Enhanced efficiency fertilizer.
Anacostia River cleanup and protection fertilizer act, §8-104.02.
Enhanced zip code.
Toll telecommunication service tax, §47-3901.
Enrolled actuary, §§1-702, 1-801.02, 1-901.02.
Enrolled customers.
Portable electronics insurance, §31-5051.01.
Enrollee, §31-3401.
Enrollment.
Retail natural gas supplier licensing and consumer protection, §34-1671.02.
Enrollment agreement.
Retail natural gas supplier licensing and consumer protection, §34-1671.02.
Enrollment date, §31-3301.01.
Enrollment fees, §31-3401.
Enterprise fund.
Revenue bonds, notes or other obligations, §1-204.90.

DEFINED TERMS —Cont'd

Enterprise risk.
Insurance holding companies, §31-701.

Enterprise zone.
Small and certified business enterprise development and assistance, §2-218.02.
Tax abatement for homeowners in enterprise zones, §47-858.01.

Entertainment.
Alcoholic beverages, §25-101.

Entertainment industry.
Office of cable television, film, music, and entertainment amendment act of 2015, §34-1251.03.

Entitled to vote.
Nonprofit corporations, §29-401.02.

Entitlement holder.
Investment securities, §28:8-102.

Entitlement order.
Investment securities, §28:8-102.

Entity.
Business organizations, §29-101.02.
Child support enforcement, §46-201.
Emergency volunteer health practitioners, §7-2361.01.
Ethics and government accountability, §1-1161.01.
Principal and income, §28-4804.01.
Trade names, §47-2855.01.

Entity filing.
Business organizations, §29-101.02.

Entity of the District of Columbia government.
Gifts and donations, §1-329.01.

Entrance fee.
Continuing care retirement communities, §44-151.01.

Environment, §§8-109.02, 8-401, 34-2602.
Department of the environment, §8-151.01.

Environmental agency.
Environmental covenants, §8-671.01.

Environmental conditions.
Health department, §7-731.

Environmental covenant, §8-671.01.

Environmental hazard, §31-5002.

Environmental impact statement, §8-109.02.

Environmental law.
Uniform trust code, §19-1301.03.

Environmentally preferable product or service.
Procurement practices, §2-351.04.

Environmentally sound management practices.
Paint stewardship, §8-233.01.

DEFINED TERMS —Cont'd

Environmental management system.
Department of the environment, §8-151.01.

Environmental residual, §8-171.02.

Environmental response project.
Environmental covenants, §8-671.01.

Environs of the District of Columbia.
United States park police, §5-208.

EPA.
Brownfield revitalization, §8-631.02.
Lead-hazard prevention and elimination, §8-231.01.

EPPS.
Procurement practices, §2-351.04.

EPT.
Sexually transmitted diseases, treatment for sexual partners, §7-2081.01.

Equipment, §§8-401, 36-301.01.
Secured transactions, §28:9-102.

Equitable job evaluation technique, §32-601.

Equitable title, §47-1401.

Equity, §42-3501.03.

Equity interest.
Insurance investments, §31-1371.02.

Equity securities.
Universal banks, §26-1401.02.

Equivalent securities.
Insurance investments, §31-1371.02.

Equivalent unit.
Southwest waterfront special assessment district, §47-895.01.

Error rate.
Post-election audits, §1-1001.09a.

Escrow.
Title insurance producers, §31-5041.01.
Title insurers, §31-5031.01.

Escrow funds, §42-1702.

Escrow officer.
Title insurance producers, §31-5041.01.
Title insurers, §31-5031.01.

Escrow, settlement, or closing fee.
Title insurers, §31-5031.01.

Established geographic service area, §31-3301.01.

Established place of business, §§47-2302, 50-1507.01.

Established practices.
Unincorporated nonprofit associations, §29-1102.

Establishment, §2-1542.
Alcoholic beverages, §25-101.

DEFINED TERMS —Cont'd
Estate, §21-2011.
Estimated market value.
Real property assessment, §47-802.
Ethics board.
Ethics and government accountability,
§1-1161.01.
Evaluated bid price.
Procurement practices, §2-351.04.
**Event site for organized sporting
events,** §7-1702.
Evidence-based program.
Interagency collaboration and services
integration commission, §2-1592.
**Evidence-based treatment
guidelines.**
Stroke system of care, §44-1151.
Evidence of coverage, §31-3401.
Examiner, §§21-2011, 31-1401.
Excavation, §34-2701.
Excepted benefits, §31-3301.01.
Excepted service.
Merit system, §1-603.01.
Exceptional circumstances.
Excepted service, domicile
requirements, §1-609.06.
Merit system, §1-603.01.
Excess.
Charter schools, §38-1800.02.
School-based budgeting and
accountability, §38-2801.01.
**Excess workers' compensation
insurance.**
Captive insurance companies,
§31-3931.01.
Exchanging entity.
Nonprofit corporations, §29-409.01.
Excise, §47-1401.
Excise tax, §47-1401.
Excluded shares.
Corporations, §29-311.01.
Exclusive control.
Construction codes, §6-1403.
Execute.
District of Columbia housing
authority, §6-201.
Executed.
Trade names, §47-2855.01.
Execution date.
Funds transfers, §28:4A-301.
Executive agency.
Ethics and government accountability,
§1-1161.01.
Executive board.
Condominiums, §42-1901.02.
Executive director.
District of Columbia housing
authority, §6-201.

DEFINED TERMS —Cont'd
Executive director —Cont'd
Office of first source compliance,
§2-219.32.
Executive office of the mayor.
Governmental reorganization,
§1-315.02.
Executive officer.
Banks and financial institutions,
§26-551.02.
Money transmissions, §26-1001.
Executive service.
Merit system, §1-603.01.
Exempt commercial risk.
Insurance rate regulation, §31-2701.
Exempted vendor.
Internet tax, §47-3931.
Exempt household.
Reduced real property tax liability for
seniors and persons with
disabilities, §47-863.
Exempt person.
Workplace fraud, §32-1331.01.
Exempt purposes.
Real property taxes, §47-1005.01.
Exhaustee.
Unemployment compensation, §51-107.
Existing building.
Building rehabilitation code, §6-1410.
Green buildings, §6-1451.01.
Existing convention center.
Washington convention and sports
authority, §10-1202.01.
Existing electricity programs.
Sustainable energy, §8-1773.01.
Existing low-income programs.
Sustainable energy, §8-1773.01.
Existing natural gas programs.
Sustainable energy, §8-1773.01.
Existing solid waste facility, §8-1051.
Ex-offenders, §24-1301.
Expandable condominium.
Condominiums, §42-1901.02.
Expanded polystyrene.
Disposable food service ware,
management, §8-1531.
**Expanded polystyrene food service
products.**
Disposable food service ware,
management, §8-1531.
Ex parte contract.
Health planning and development
agency, §44-401.
Expected claims.
Stop-loss health insurance for
employers, §31-3821.

DEFINED TERMS —Cont'd

Expected death, §7-201.

Expedited administrative review.
Health planning and development agency, §44-401.

Expedited partner therapy.
Sexually transmitted diseases, treatment for sexual partners, §7-2081.01.

Expendable budget.
Small and certified business enterprise development and assistance, §2-218.02.

Expenditure.
Ethics and government accountability, §1-1161.01.

Expenses.
Corporations, §29-301.02.
Nonprofit corporations, §29-406.50.
Revised real property tax sale, §47-1330.

Explanation.
Secured transactions, §28:9-616.

Exploitation, §7-1901.

Exploratory committee.
Ethics and government accountability, §1-1161.01.

Explosive, §10-503.26.

Exposure incident.
Safe needle distribution, §7-2851.

Ex-ship.
Sales, §28:2-322.

Extended benefit period.
Unemployment compensation, §51-107.

Extended benefits.
Unemployment compensation, §51-107.

Extension of benefits, §31-3401.

Extension of credit, §28-4601.
Credit service organizations, §28-4601.

Extension or extensions.
Public utilities, §34-205.

Exterior surfaces.
Lead-hazard prevention and elimination, §8-231.01.

External provider, §31-3401.

Extra-contractual claims.
Life and health insurance guaranty association, §31-5401.

Extracurricular activities.
Interstate compact on educational opportunity for military children, §49-1101.03.

Extremely-low income.
Affordable housing inventory comprehensive tracking plan, §42-2141.

DEFINED TERMS —Cont'd

Extremely-low income —Cont'd
District of Columbia housing authority, §6-201.
Housing production trust fund, §42-2801.

Extremely low-income household.
Preservation and rehabilitation of government-supported housing, §42-2851.02.
Tax abatement for new residential developments, §47-857.01.

Eye bank.
Anatomical gifts, §7-1531.01.

Facilities.
Brownfield revitalization, §8-631.02.
Charter schools, §38-1805.50.
Educational licensure commission, §38-1302.
Health-care facility unlicensed personnel criminal background checks, §44-551.
Nursing homes, etc., §44-1001.01.
Rights of persons with intellectual disabilities, §7-1301.03.
Underground storage tank management, §8-113.01.
Youth rehabilitation services, department of, §2-1515.01.
Youth residential facilities, §7-2101.

Facility AED Coordinator.
Defibrillator usage, §44-231.

Factfinding hearing, §16-2301.

Failure to renew, §36-301.01.

Fair consideration, §31-1301.

Fair market value, §47-1401.
Office of cable television, film, music, and entertainment amendment act of 2015, §34-1251.03.

Fair to the corporation.
Corporations, §29-306.70.

Fair value.
Corporations, §29-311.01.
Special purpose financial captive insurance companies, §31-3932.02.

Faith-based initiative.
Grants, §7-736.01.

False alarm, §7-2802.

False claims law.
Procurement claims, §2-381.01.

False claims law investigations.
Procurement claims, §2-381.01.

False claims law investigator.
Procurement claims, §2-381.01.

Familial status, §2-1401.02.

Family, §§4-205.05, 7-1601.
Crime investigation records, §5-113.31.

DEFINED TERMS —Cont'd
Family —Cont'd
Homeless services, §4-751.01.
Family assessment.
Child abuse and neglect, §4-1301.02.
Family counseling, §16-2301.
Family court, §16-2301.
Appeals, DCCtApp Rule 1.
Family member, §§32-501, 32-701.
Collaborative law, §16-4002.
Family leave, §1-612.03c.
Human rights commission, §2-1401.02.
Protection of District public officials,
§22-851.
Right to sick and safe leave,
§32-131.01.
Family preservation services.
Child abuse and neglect, §4-1301.02.
Family resource center.
Charter schools, §38-1800.02.
Family responsibilities, §2-1401.02.
Family support services.
Child abuse and neglect, §4-1301.02.
Farm cooperative.
Urban gardens program, §48-401.
Farmer, §37-101.
Farmers' line, §37-101.
Farmers market.
Alcoholic beverages, §25-101.
Grocery and retail stores development,
§2-1212.01.
Farming operation.
Secured transactions, §28:9-102.
Farm products.
Secured transactions, §28:9-102.
Farm-to-preschool programs.
Child and adult food program funding,
§38-281.
Farm tractors, §50-1501.01.
Farm winery.
Alcoholic beverages, §25-101.
F.A.S.
Free alongside sales, §28:2-319.
Fault.
Leases, UCC, §28:2A-103.
UCC, §28:1-201.
FCC.
Office of cable television, film, music,
and entertainment amendment
act of 2015, §34-1251.03.
FDA.
Off-label use of prescription
medication, §48-841.02.
Feasibility study, §31-4101.
Federal ABLE Act.
ABLE savings accounts, §47-4901.

DEFINED TERMS —Cont'd
Federal act, §26-1201.
Brownfield revitalization, §8-631.02.
Health benefit exchange authority,
§31-3171.01.
Workforce investment implementation,
§32-1602.
Federal agency.
Banks and financial institutions,
§26-551.02.
International banking corporations,
§26-631.
Universal banks, §26-1401.02.
Federal association.
Savings and loan acquisitions,
§26-1201.
Federal benefit payment, §§1-801.02,
1-901.02.
Federal branch.
International banking corporations,
§26-631.
Federal cable act.
Office of cable television, film, music,
and entertainment amendment
act of 2015, §34-1251.03.
Federal court consent decree,
§44-902.
Federal covered adviser.
Security agents and broker,
§31-5601.01.
Federal covered security.
Security agents and broker,
§31-5601.01.
Federal credit.
Inheritance and estate taxes,
§47-3701.
Federal credit union.
Automated teller machine, §26-131.02.
**Federal financial institutions
agency.**
Universal banks, §26-1401.02.
**Federal financial supervisory
agency.**
Community development by financial
institutions, §26-431.02.
Federal fleet, §50-702.
Federal governmental plan,
§31-3301.01.
Federal international act.
International banking corporations,
§26-631.
Federal international bank office.
International banking corporations,
§26-631.
Federally-approved seller-services,
§26-1101.

DEFINED TERMS —Cont'd

Federally assisted housing accommodation.
Preservation and rehabilitation of government-supported housing, §42-2851.02.

Federally chartered savings institutions.
Universal banks, §26-1401.02.

Federally insured bank or savings and loan association.
Installment loans, §28-3308.

Federally qualified health center.
Medical liability captive insurance agency, §1-307.81.

Federal official.
Offset program, §47-143.

Federal post card application.
Military and overseas voters, §1-1061.02.

Federal share.
Employees retirement program management, §1-724.

Federal student loan programs.
Collection of taxes, §47-4431.

Federal write-in absentee ballot.
Military and overseas voters, §1-1061.02.

Fee-based use permit.
Parks and recreation, §10-301.

Feeder pattern.
School-based budgeting and accountability, §38-2801.01.

Feeder school group.
Early warning and support system, §38-751.02.

Feepayer, §47-2751.
Ballpark fee, §47-2761.

Fees and charges.
Employment agencies, §32-401.
Rental housing locators, §28-3819.

Fees and fines.
Fee collection incentive fund, §1-325.61.

Felony.
Elections, §1-1001.02.

FEMS.
Stroke system of care, §44-1151.

Fertilizer.
Anacostia River cleanup and protection fertilizer act, §8-104.02.

Fetal death, §7-201.

FHVAC.
Regulation of for-hire vehicles, §50-301.03.

FICA taxes.
Job growth tax credit, §47-1807.51.

DEFINED TERMS —Cont'd

Fiduciary.
Employees retirement program management, §1-702.
Fiduciary security transfers, §28-2901.
Income tax, §47-1801.04.
Pensions and retirement, §1-626.04.
Police and firefighters retirement and disability, §1-901.02.
Principal and income, §28-4801.02.
Uniform disclaimer of property interests act, §19-1502.

Field arrest.
Warrants, §23-501.

Field test.
State superintendent of education, office of, §38-2601.02.

FIFRA.
Pesticide education and control, §8-431.

.50 BMG rifle, §7-2501.01.

Fighting.
Penalty for fighting or baiting animals, §22-1006.01.

File, §7-201.

Filed.
Security agents and broker, §31-5601.01.

Filed document.
Corporations, §29-301.04.
Nonprofit corporations, §29-401.04.

Filed record.
Business organizations, §29-101.02.
Nonprofit corporations, §29-401.04.

File number.
Secured transactions, §28:9-102.

Filing entity.
Business organizations, §29-101.02.

Filing office.
Secured transactions, §28:9-102.

Filing-office rule.
Secured transactions, §28:9-102.

Final conversion fee.
Rental housing conversion and sale, §42-3402.04.

Final disposal, §8-1051.

Final disposition, §7-201.

Finance charge, §§28-3601, 50-601.
Installment loans, §§28-3308, 28-3603.

Finance lease.
Leases, UCC, §28:2A-103.

Financial advisor.
Electric company infrastructure improvement financing, §34-1311.01.

Financial asset.
Investment securities, §28:8-102.

DEFINED TERMS —Cont'd
Financial injury.
Identity theft, §22-3227.01.
Stalking, §22-3132.
Financial institution, §§21-301,
26-551.02, 28-3701, 38-1201.03.
Automated teller machine, §26-131.02.
Community development by financial
institutions, §26-431.02.
Data match requirements for financial
institutions, §26-531.
Delinquent taxpayers, §47-4481.
Income tax, §47-1801.04.
Merchant bank, §26-831.02.
Nonprobate transfers on death,
§19-602.01.
Revolving credit accounts, §28-3701.
Universal banks, §26-1401.02.
Financial interest.
Arbitration, revised act, §16-4401.
Limited cooperative associations,
§29-1012.07.
Financial literacy, §38-731.01.
Financial literacy council,
§38-731.01.
Financial organization, §41-102.
Opportunity accounts, §1-307.61.
Financial or institutional investor.
Security agents and broker,
§31-5601.01.
Financial plan and budget, §§47-393,
47-3401.05.
Miscellaneous provisions, §47-3401.05.
Financial rights.
Limited cooperative associations,
§29-1001.02.
Financial services.
Investment and deposit of District
funds, §47-351.01.
Financial transition period, §44-902.
Financing agency.
Sales, §28:2-104.
Financing agreement, §26-1101.
Financing costs.
Electric company infrastructure
improvement financing,
§34-1311.01.
Financing documents.
City Market at O Street tax increment
financing, §2-1217.33a.
Electric company infrastructure
improvement financing,
§34-1311.01.
Energy efficiency financing,
§8-1778.02.
Housing production trust fund, bond
issues, §42-2812.01.

DEFINED TERMS —Cont'd
Financing documents —Cont'd
Howard Theatre redevelopment
project, §2-1217.151.
Howard Theatre redevelopment project
TIF area, §2-1217.34a.
Income tax secured bonds, §47-340.26.
New convention center hotel,
§10-1221.01.
Qualified zone academy revenue bond
project forward commitment
approval act, §2-1217.102.
Skyland TIF area, §2-1217.35a.
Southwest waterfront bond financing,
§2-1217.131.
Transportation infrastructure
improvement GARVEE bonds,
§9-107.51.
Financing order.
Electric company infrastructure
improvement financing,
§34-1311.01.
Financing statement.
Secured transactions, §28:9-102.
**Findings and information related to
a child fatality or near fatality,**
§4-1303.31.
Fingerprint.
Background checks, §31-631.
Fire and casualty act.
Title insurers, §31-5031.01.
Fire and casualty insurance,
§31-2501.03.
Firearm, §§7-2501.01, 7-2531.01,
10-503.26.
Crimes and offenses, §22-4501.
Drug, firearm, or prostitution-related
nuisance abatement, §42-3101.
Firearms dealer.
Microstamping of semiautomatic
pistols, §7-2505.03.
Firearms instructor, §7-2501.01.
Fire department.
Civil defense, §7-2204.
Fire protection systems.
Building code, §6-1401.
Fire-standard-compliant cigarette,
§7-1751.
Firm.
Certified public accountants,
§47-2853.41.
Rules of professional conduct,
ProfCond Rule 1.0.
First amendment activities.
Metropolitan police.
Investigations concerning first
amendment activities,
§5-333.02.

DEFINED TERMS —Cont'd
First amendment assembly,
  §5-331.02.
  Metropolitan police.
    Investigations concerning first
      amendment activities,
      §5-333.02.
First building permits.
  Anacostia waterfront environmental
    standards, §2-1226.32.
  Green buildings, §6-1451.01.
First source agreement.
  Grocery and retail stores development,
    §2-1212.01.
  Skyland TIF area, §2-1217.35a.
  Walter Reed Medical Center site
    development, §2-1227.01.
First source employment, §2-219.01.
First source employment agreement.
  Office of first source compliance,
    §2-219.32.
First source register.
  First source employment, §2-219.01.
First-time homebuyer, §42-2901.
  Employer-assisted housing program,
    §42-2501.
Fiscal agent.
  Sustainable energy, §8-1773.01.
Fiscal value, §2-1701.
Fiscal year.
  Business improvement districts,
    §2-1215.02.
  Income tax, §47-1801.04.
  Nursing facility assessment, §47-1261.
  Office of administrative hearings,
    §2-1831.01.
Fish market.
  Southwest waterfront bond financing,
    §2-1217.131.
Fit for occupancy.
  Vacant buildings, §42-3131.05.
Fitting and selling of hearing aids,
    §28-4001.
  Hearing aid dealers, §28-4001.
Fixed asset, §47-372.
Fixed obligation, §2-381.01.
Fixed-price contract.
  Procurement practices, §2-351.04.
Fixed-price incentive contract.
  Procurement practices, §2-351.04.
Fixture filing.
  Secured transactions, §28:9-102.
Fixtures.
  Secured transactions, §28:9-102.
Fleet, §47-2302.
  International registration plan
    agreements, §50-1507.01.

DEFINED TERMS —Cont'd
Fleet —Cont'd
  Rental vehicle tax, §50-1505.01.
  Traffic ticket adjudication,
    §50-2303.04a.
Fleetshare.
  Fleet management, publicly-owned
    vehicles, §50-211.01.
Flexible-fueled vehicle, §50-702.
Flight emergency medical services
    personnel, §7-2341.01.
Flood vehicle, §50-1331.01.
Floor.
  Insurance investments, §31-1371.02.
F.O.B.
  Free on board sales, §28:2-319.
Follow-on investment.
  Certified capital companies, §31-5231.
Food.
  Urban gardens program, §48-401.
Food access.
  Food policy council, §48-311.
Food assets.
  Food policy council, §48-311.
Food commodity.
  Income tax credits, farm to food
    donations, §47-1806.14.
    Corporations and financial
      institutions, §47-1807.12.
  Real property taxes, reduced liability
    for agricultural uses, §47-868.
  Tax credit for farm to food donations,
    unincorporated businesses,
    §47-1808.12.
Food delivery service, §50-101.
Food desert.
  Food policy council, §48-311.
Food establishment.
  Adulteration of food and drugs,
    §48-102.
Food merchant, §37-101.
Food or drink, §47-2201.
  Adulteration, §48-102.
  Alcoholic beverage control, §25-101.
  Gross sales tax, §47-2001.
Food or drink prepared for
    immediate consumption.
  Gross sales tax, §47-2001.
Food procurement.
  Food policy council, §48-311.
Food service entity.
  Disposable food service ware,
    management, §8-1531.
Food stamp coupon, §4-218.05.
Food stamp program, §4-261.01.
Food wholesaler, §37-101.

DEFINED TERMS —Cont'd
Force.
Sexual abuse, §22-3001.
Forcible entry and detainer,
§16-1501.
Forecast of extreme temperature.
Gas companies, §34-1671.06a.
Retail electric competition and
consumer protection, §34-1506.01.
Foreclosure rescue service.
Home equity protection, §42-2431.
Foreclosure rescue transaction.
Home equity protection, §42-2431.
Foreign, §47-2601.
Business organizations, §29-101.02.
Foreign business corporation.
Nonprofit corporations, §29-401.02.
Foreign central authority.
Interstate family support, §46-357.01.
Foreign company, §§31-2501.03,
31-4202.
Foreign cooperative.
Limited cooperative associations,
§29-1001.02.
Foreign corporation.
Corporations, §29-301.02.
Foreign country, §§31-1301, 47-2601.
International banking corporations,
§26-631.
Interstate family support, §46-351.02.
Judgments, §15-362.
Foreign-country judgment, §15-362.
Foreign currency.
Insurance investments, §31-1371.02.
Foreign-documented vessel.
Uniform certificates of title for vessels,
§50-1541.01.
Foreign health organization.
Health insurance regulatory
standards, §31-3451.01.
Foreign insurer, §31-2001.
United States branch domestication,
§31-2301.
Foreign investment.
Insurance investments, §31-1371.02.
Foreign judgment, §15-351.
Foreign jurisdiction.
Insurance investments, §31-1371.02.
Interstate depositions and discovery,
§13-442.
Foreign limited liability company.
Limited liability companies,
§29-801.02.
Foreign limited liability limited
partnership.
Limited partnerships, §29-701.02.

DEFINED TERMS —Cont'd
Foreign limited liability
partnership.
Partnerships, §29-601.02.
Foreign limited partnership.
Limited partnerships, §29-701.02.
Foreign milk bank.
Breastmilk bank and lactation
support, §7-881.01.
Foreign mission, §§6-1302, 6-1304.01.
Foreign money, §15-901.
Foreign-money claim, §15-901.
Foreign nonprofit corporation.
Corporations, §29-301.02.
Nonprofit corporations, §29-401.02.
Foreign partnership.
Partnerships, §29-601.02.
Foreign protection order.
Interstate enforcement of domestic
violence proceedings, §16-1041.
Foreign statutory trust.
Statutory trusts, §29-1201.02.
Foreign subpoena.
Interstate depositions and discovery,
§13-442.
Foreign support agreements.
Interstate family support, §46-357.01.
Foreign support order.
Interstate family support, §46-351.02.
Foreign title insurer.
Title insurers, §31-5031.01.
Foreign tribunal.
Interstate family support, §46-351.02.
Foreign unincorporated entity.
Corporations, §29-301.02.
Nonprofit corporations, §29-401.02.
Forensic nurse examiner.
Victims of crime, §23-1907.
Forensic sciences services.
Forensic sciences department,
§5-1501.01.
Forestry.
Pesticide education and control,
§8-431.
Forfeitable offense.
Civil asset forfeiture, §41-301.
Forged written instrument, §22-3241.
Formal delinquency proceeding,
§31-1301.
Former spouse or domestic partner.
Spouse or domestic partner equity in
retirement benefits, §§1-529.03,
1-529.04.
Formula.
Uniform per student funding formula,
§38-2901.

DEFINED TERMS —Cont'd
Formula grant, §47-382.
For-profit activities.
District of Columbia housing authority, §6-201.
For-profit entity, §44-602.
Forward.
Insurance investments, §31-1371.02.
Forward commitment mortgage purchase program, §42-2701.02.
Foster care.
Adoption voucher fund, §4-342.
Foster care and adoption assistance.
Medicaid and special education reform fund, §4-204.52.
Office of Medicaid operations reform, §4-204.12.
Tobacco settlement trust fund, §7-1811.03.
Foster child.
Adoption voucher fund, §4-342.
Foster family home.
Child and family services agency.
Criminal record checks, §4-1305.01.
Foster parent.
Adoption voucher fund, §4-342.
Rights and responsibilities of foster parents, §4-1303.81.
Foundation.
Uniform per student funding formula, §38-2901.
Foundation level.
Uniform per student funding formula, §38-2901.
IV-D agency, §4-201.01.
Child support enforcement, §46-201.
Data match requirements for financial institutions, §26-531.
Divorce, annulment, separation, support, §16-901.
Medical support enforcement, §46-251.01.
Vital records, §7-201.
IV-D case.
Divorce, annulment, separation, support, §16-901.
14W and the YMCA Anthony Bowen project.
Real property tax exemptions, §47-4627.
14W and the YMCA Anthony Bowen property.
Real property tax exemptions, §47-4627.
Franchise.
Gas stations, §36-304.11.

DEFINED TERMS —Cont'd
Franchise —Cont'd
Office of cable television, film, music, and entertainment amendment act of 2015, §34-1251.03.
Franchise agreement.
Office of cable television, film, music, and entertainment amendment act of 2015, §34-1251.03.
Franchisee.
Gas stations, §36-304.11.
Wireless network antennae franchise agreement, §34-1731.02.
Franchise relationship.
Gas stations, §36-304.11.
Franchisor.
Gas stations, §36-304.11.
Fraternal benefit societies, §31-5301.
Fraud, §27-101.
Rules of professional conduct, ProfCond Rule 1.0.
Security agents and broker, §31-5601.01.
Fraudulent.
Rules of professional conduct, ProfCond Rule 1.0.
Fraudulent endorsement.
Negotiable instruments, §28:3-405.
Free appropriate public education.
Nonpublic schools, §38-2561.01.
Freedom of information act.
Public-Private Partnership Administration Fund, §2-271.01.
Freeze date, §1-801.02.
Fresh pursuit, §23-903.
Friable asbestos material, §8-111.01.
Friends groups.
Parks and recreation, §10-301.
Fringe benefits.
Shared work unemployment compensation program, §51-171.
Frontpay.
Employment discrimination backpay or frontpay, income averaging, §47-1806.10.
Frontpay period.
Employment discrimination backpay or frontpay, income averaging, §47-1806.10.
FTE.
The Advisory Board Company, real property tax abatement, §47-4665.01.
Fuel economy.
Fleet management, publicly-owned vehicles, §50-211.01.

DEFINED TERMS —Cont'd
Fuel input.
Renewable energy portfolio standards, §34-1431.
Fuel provider, §50-702.
Full-building commissioning.
Green buildings, §6-1451.01.
Full-funded cost estimate.
School-based budgeting and accountability, §38-2801.01.
Full range of duties.
Police and firefighters retirement and disability, §§5-631, 5-701.
Presumptive disability or death of fire and emergency medical services employees, §5-651.
Full school day.
Compulsory school attendance, §38-201.
Full-time employee, §3-402.
Full-time employment.
Access to justice initiative program, §4-1701.01.
Full-time equivalent.
Uniform per student funding formula, §38-2901.
Full-time students, §38-1419.
Fully allocated cost.
Procurement practices, §2-351.04.
Functional assessment.
Assisted living residences, §44-102.01.
Functional equivalent, §8-109.02.
Function closely associated with an inherently governmental function.
Procurement practices, §2-351.04.
Fund, §§1-901.02, 47-372.
Anacostia river clean up and protection fund, §8-102.01.
Arts and humanities commission, §39-202.
Capital project support fund, §1-325.151.
Climate change and resiliency commission, §8-181.01.
CTE grant program, §38-2601.02.
DC promise program, §38-2751.
DC Streetcar service, §50-921.71.
District of Columbia housing authority, §6-201.
Emancipation day fund, §1-183.
Inmate welfare fund, §24-281.
Innovation fund, §1-325.221.
LGBTQ homeless youth training grants, §2-1381.
Medical liability captive insurance agency, §1-307.81.

DEFINED TERMS —Cont'd
Fund —Cont'd
Motor vehicle theft prevention commission, §3-1351.
New Columbia statehood initiative, §1-129.21.
Not-for-profit hospital corporations, §44-951.01.
Regulation of for-hire vehicles, §50-301.03.
Retirement, §11-1561.
Shelter and transitional housing for victims of domestic violence fund, §4-521.
Small business capital access fund, §2-218.75.
Strict liability for release of hazardous waste during transport, §8-1441.
Tax check-off, drug prevention and children at risk, §47-4001.
Unemployment compensation, §51-101.
Fundamental transaction.
Corporations, §29-301.02.
Nonprofit corporations, §29-401.02.
Fund balance.
Self-government, §1-201.03.
Fund category, §47-372.
Funds-transfer business day.
Funds transfers, UCC, §28:4A-105.
Funds-transfer system.
Funds transfers, UCC, §28:4A-105.
Funeral director, §3-402.
Funeral provider, §3-402.
Funeral services establishment, §3-402.
Fungible goods.
UCC, §28:1-201.
Fungus, §8-401.
Furlough, §24-251.01.
Future.
Insurance investments, §31-1371.02.
Sales, §28:2-105.
Future interest.
Uniform disclaimer of property interests act, §19-1506.
Future sales price.
Housing production trust fund, §42-2801.
Future value, §1-702.
Gain, §47-1401.
Galactosemia, §7-832.
Gallery place project.
Sales tax exemption, §47-2005.
Gaming premises, §22-1705.
Gaming tables, §22-1707.
Gap-closing action, §47-318.

DEFINED TERMS —Cont'd

Gap coverage.

Medical liability captive insurance agency, §1-307.81.

Garaged under normal operations at personal residence, §50-702.

Garnishment, §16-571.

GARVEE.

Transportation infrastructure improvement GARVEE bonds, §9-107.51.

GARVEE bonds.

Transportation infrastructure improvement GARVEE bonds, §9-107.51.

GARVEE revenues.

Transportation infrastructure improvement GARVEE bonds, §9-107.51.

Gas company, §34-209.

Electric company infrastructure improvement financing, §34-1311.01.

Retail natural gas supplier licensing and consumer protection, §34-1671.02.

Sustainable energy, §8-1773.01.

Gas plant, §34-210.

Electric company infrastructure improvement financing, §34-1311.01.

Gateway Market center and residences.

Real property tax exemptions, §47-4621.

GBA.

Southwest waterfront special assessment district, §47-895.01.

Gender identity or expression.

AIDS discrimination in the provision of insurance, §31-1601.

Bias-related crimes, §22-3701.

Divorce, annulment, separation, support, §16-901.

Elections, §1-1001.02.

Employment agencies, §32-401.

Health occupations, §3-343.02.

Homeless services, §4-751.01.

Mental health consumer's rights, §7-1231.02.

Office of police complaints, §5-1103.

Retail electric competition and consumer protection, §34-1501.

Unfair insurance trade practices, §31-2231.01.

General agent, §31-4202.

DEFINED TERMS —Cont'd

General assets, §31-1301.

General common elements, §42-2002.

Condominiums, §42-1901.01.

General cooperative association.

Business organizations, §29-101.02.

General counsel.

District of Columbia housing authority, §6-201.

General intangible.

Secured transactions, §28:9-102.

Generally-accepted accounting principles (GAAP), §47-372.

General obligation bonds.

New York avenue metrorail benefit area, §47-881.

General partner.

Limited partnerships, §29-701.02.

Partnerships, §29-609.01.

General partnership.

Business organizations, §29-101.02.

General population housing.

District of Columbia housing authority, §6-201.

General public benefit.

Benefit corporations, §29-1301.02.

General supervision, §21-1201.

Veterinary technicians, §3-1208.65.

Generation, §8-1302.

Generator, §§8-1302, 8-1501.

Generic drug.

Access to prescription drugs, §48-831.02.

Genetic birth defect.

Habilitative services for children, health care coverage, §31-3271.

Genetic information.

Human rights commission, §2-1401.02.

Genetic test.

Human rights commission, §2-1401.02.

Genuine.

UCC, §28:1-201.

Georgia Avenue area, §2-1217.01.

Georgia commons.

Real property transfer tax exemption, §47-4610.

GERC.

Athletic equity, §38-841.01.

Geriatric inmate, §24-461.

Gift.

Ethics and government accountability, §1-1161.01.

Gift instrument.

Prudent management of institutional funds, §44-1631.

GMP.

Procurement practices, §2-351.04.

DEFINED TERMS —Cont'd
Go-cup.
Alcoholic beverages, §25-101.
Godparent.
Child abuse and neglect, §4-1301.02.
Temporary assistance for needy
   families.
    Grandparent caregiver subsidies,
      §4-251.01.
Good faith, §41-102.
Foreclosure mediation, §42-815.02.
Letters of credit, §28:5-102.
Overdose, seeking help for victim,
   §7-403.
UCC, §28:1-201.
Uniform certificates of title for vessels,
   §50-1541.01.
Warehouse receipts, §28:7-102.
Goods, §28-3901.
Consumer protection procedures,
   §28-3901.
Leases, UCC, §28:2A-103.
Procurement practices, §2-351.04.
Sales, §28:2-105.
Secured transactions, §28:9-102.
Telephone solicitation fraud,
   §22-3226.01.
Warehouse receipts, §28:7-102.
Goodwill, §36-301.01.
Governance interest.
Business organizations, §29-101.02.
Governing authority.
Employees retirement program
   management, §1-702.
Governing instrument.
Simultaneous deaths, §19-501.
Statutory trusts, §29-1201.02.
Governing law.
Statutory trusts, §29-1207.01.
Governing principles.
Unincorporated nonprofit associations,
   §29-1102.
Governing statute.
Limited liability companies,
   §29-809.01.
Limited partnerships, §29-710.01.
Government, §5-701.
Governmental agency.
Electronic transactions, uniform act,
   §28-4901.
Governmental charges, §50-601.
Governmental plan, §31-3301.01.
Governmental unit.
Secured transactions, §28:9-102.
Government assistance.
Auditor compliance unit, §1-301.181.

DEFINED TERMS —Cont'd
Government assistance —Cont'd
Living wage act, §2-220.02.
Government assisted contract.
First source employment, §2-219.01.
Government assisted project.
First source employment, §2-219.01.
Small and certified business enterprise
   development and assistance,
   §2-218.02.
Government channel.
Office of cable television, film, music,
   and entertainment amendment
   act of 2015, §34-1251.03.
Government employee.
Official correspondence, §2-701.
**Government money market mutual
   fund.**
Insurance investments, §31-1371.02.
Government of Iran.
Employees retirement program
   management, §1-336.01.
Government of Sudan.
Employees retirement program
   management, §1-335.01.
Government service, §5-701.
Government-sponsored enterprise.
Insurance investments, §31-1371.02.
Governor, §23-707.
Business organizations, §29-101.02.
Interstate agreement on detainers,
   §24-802.
GPS.
Regulation of for-hire vehicles,
   §50-301.03.
Graffiti, §22-3312.05.
Abatement, §42-3141.01.
Graffiti material, §22-3312.05.
Grandchild, §§1-623.01, 32-1501.
Grandparent.
Temporary assistance for needy
   families.
    Grandparent caregiver subsidies,
      §4-251.01.
Grant, §§38-1302, 47-382.
Grant administration, §1-328.11.
Grant administration act.
Trash compactor grant program,
   §8-751.
Grantee, §1-328.11.
Bullying, §2-1535.01.
Job opportunity bank, §32-751.
Trash compactor grant program,
   §8-751.
Grant funds, §47-382.

DEFINED TERMS —Cont'd
Granting body.
Unified economic development budget transparency and accountability, §2-1208.01.
Grant-making agency, §47-382.
Grant-managing authority.
Teen pregnancy prevention fund, §1-325.321.
Grant-managing entity.
Innovation fund, §1-325.221.
Grantor, §1-328.11.
Trash compactor grant program, §8-751.
Grant program, §1-328.11.
Gratuities, §32-1002.
Grease.
Rodent abatement program, §8-2103.01.
Green building, §6-1451.01.
Green building act.
Anacostia waterfront environmental standards, §2-1226.32.
Green building checklist, §6-1451.01.
Green-collar jobs.
Sustainable energy, §8-1773.01.
Green communities, §6-1451.01.
Grievance, §44-301.01.
Mental health consumer's rights, §7-1231.02.
Merit system, §1-603.01.
Grievance decision, §44-301.01.
Grocery store.
Grocery and retail stores development, §2-1212.01.
Gross annual food sales.
Alcoholic beverages, §25-101.
Gross annual receipts.
Alcoholic beverages, §25-101.
Gross building area.
Southeast water and sewer improvement benefit district, §47-891.
Southwest waterfront special assessment district, §47-895.01.
Gross charge.
Toll telecommunication service tax, §47-3901.
Gross estate.
Inheritance and estate taxes, §47-3701.
Gross floor area, §2-1217.01.
Green buildings, §6-1451.01.
Gross income, §4-205.05.
Child support guidelines, §16-916.01.
Mortgage loan protection, §26-1151.01.

DEFINED TERMS —Cont'd
Gross planning budget, §47-382.
Gross receipts, §47-2201.
Gross sales tax, §47-2001.
Gross resident revenue.
Nursing facility assessment, §47-1261.
Gross revenues.
Office of cable television, film, music, and entertainment amendment act of 2015, §34-1251.03.
Stevie Sellows quality improvement fund, §47-1270.
Gross valuation misstatement.
Taxation penalties, §47-4211.
Gross vehicle weight rating (GVWR), §47-2302.
Grounds.
Prison contraband, §22-2603.01.
Groundwater, §8-103.01.
Group contract, §31-3401.
Group contract holder, §31-3401.
Group health insurance coverage, §31-3301.01.
Group health plan, §31-3301.01.
Chemotherapy pill coverage, §31-2995.01.
Health insurance for dependents, §31-2996.01.
Women's rights regarding certain health insurance coverage, §31-3831.
Group home.
Homeless services, §4-751.01.
Group home for intellectually disabled persons.
Healthcare facility, hospice and home care licensure, §44-501.
Group insurers.
Annual audited financial reports, §31-301.
Group long-term care insurance, §31-3601.
Group practice, §44-801.
Group session, §7-1201.01.
Growler.
Alcoholic beverages, §25-101.
Guaranteed maximum price.
Procurement practices, §2-351.04.
Guaranteed or insured.
Insurance investments, §31-1371.02.
Security agents and broker, §31-5601.01.
Guarantor, §§8-113.01, 8-1302.
Guaranty association, §31-1301.
Guaranty of the signature.
Investment securities, §28:8-402.

DEFINED TERMS —Cont'd

Guardian, §§2-1542, 21-2011, 38-304.
Anatomical gifts, §7-1531.01.
Custodial trusts, §19-1101.
Uniform adult guardianship and
protective proceedings jurisdiction
act, §21-2401.02.
Uniform trust code, §19-1301.03.
Guardian ad litem, §§4-1301.02,
21-2011.
**Guardianship of the person of a
minor,** §16-2301.
Guardianship order.
Permanent guardianship, §16-2382.
Uniform adult guardianship and
protective proceedings jurisdiction
act, §21-2401.02.
Guardianship proceeding.
Uniform adult guardianship and
protective proceedings jurisdiction
act, §21-2401.02.
Guide dog, §7-1009.
Gun offender.
Registry, §7-2508.01.
Gun offense.
Gun offender registry, §7-2508.01.
Habilitation, §§7-1301.03, 21-2011.
Disability services, department on,
§7-761.02.
Habilitative services.
Health benefit exchange authority,
§31-3171.09.
Health insurance coverage for
habilitative services for children,
§31-3271.
Hand-crafted goods, §37-101.
Handgun, §7-2551.01.
Handicapped person, §42-3503.01.
Hands-free accessory.
Distracted driving, §50-1731.02.
HAP contract.
Preservation and rehabilitation of
government-supported housing,
§42-2851.02.
Harborage.
Rodent abatement program,
§8-2103.01.
Harbor Master.
Uniform certificates of title for vessels,
§50-1541.01.
Hard costs.
Ballpark construction hard and soft
costs cap, §10-1601.31.
Hard of hearing.
American sign language education,
§38-2432.

DEFINED TERMS —Cont'd

Hard to employ.
First source employment, §2-219.01.
Hard to fill position.
Excepted service, domicile
requirements, §1-609.06.
Merit system, §1-603.01.
Hardware, §2-213.01.
Hardware cloth.
Rodent abatement program,
§8-2103.01.
Harm.
Nonconsensual pornography, §22-3051.
Hashish, §48-901.02.
Hazardous financial condition,
§31-4101.
Continuing care retirement
communities, §44-151.01.
Hazardous materials, §8-1402.
Hazardous substance, §§8-103.01,
8-109.02.
Brownfield revitalization, §8-631.02.
Hazardous substances report plan.
Brownfield revitalization, §8-631.02.
Hazardous tree.
Urban forest preservation, §8-651.02.
Hazardous waste, §§8-901, 8-1051,
8-1302.
Wastewater disposal systems,
§8-105.02.
Head.
Merit system, §1-603.01.
Voluntary leave transfer program,
§1-612.31.
Header information.
Spam deterrence, §28-5001.
Head of assistance unit, §4-201.01.
Head of household, §42-3401.03.
Income tax, §47-1801.04.
**Health and human services
information.**
Health data privacy, §7-241.
**Health benefit exchange authority
establishment act.**
Health insurance portability and
accountability, §31-3301.01.
Health benefit plan, §§31-2901,
31-3301.01, 44-301.01.
Child health screening, §7-875.02.
Continuation of health benefits plan
coverage, §32-731.
Credentialing intermediary, §31-3251.
Diabetes health insurance coverage,
§31-3001.
Gender equality in ratemaking,
§31-3161.

DEFINED TERMS —Cont'd
Health benefit plan —Cont'd
Health benefit exchange authority,
§31-3171.01.
Health benefit plans reimbursement,
§31-3131.
Health care ombudsman program,
§7-2071.01.
Health insurance, clinical trials
insurance coverage, §31-2993.01.
Health insurance coverage for
habilitative services for children,
§31-3271.
HIV screening test while receiving
emergency medical services,
§31-2803.
Human rights commission, §2-1401.02.
Merit system, health benefits,
§1-621.03.
Newborn hearing screening, §7-851.
Newborn heart screening, §7-857.01.
Prostate cancer screening, §31-2951.
Substance abuse insurance coverage,
§31-3101.
Telehealth reimbursement, §31-3861.
Uniform consultation referral forms,
§31-3231.
Voluntary withdrawal by health
benefit plan carriers, §31-3151.
Women's rights regarding certain
health insurance coverage,
§31-3831.
Health care.
Permanent guardianship, §16-2382.
Health care agency.
Nurse staffing agencies, §44-1051.02.
Health-care assistance, §4-601.
Health care benefit program.
Doctor-patient privilege, §14-307.
Health-care decision.
Anatomical gifts, §7-1531.20.
Health care facility, §§7-1702, 44-801.
Ambulance fees, §5-416.
Childhood lead poisoning screening
and reporting, §7-871.02.
Emergency medical services,
§7-2341.01.
Health planning and development
agency, §44-401.
Nurse staffing agencies, §44-1051.02.
Unused pharmaceutical safe disposal,
§48-851.01.
Health-care-insurance receivable.
Secured transactions, §28:9-102.
Health care ombudsman, §7-2071.01.
Health care ombudsman program,
§7-2071.01.

DEFINED TERMS —Cont'd
Healthcare practitioner.
Assisted living residences, §44-102.01.
Sexually transmitted diseases,
treatment for sexual partners,
§7-2081.01.
Health care provider, §§21-2202,
44-801.
Assisted living residences, §44-102.01.
Childhood lead poisoning screening
and reporting, §7-871.02.
Credentialing intermediary, health
insurers, §31-3251.
Family and medical leave, §32-501.
Health occupations licensure,
registration or certification.
Mandatory adverse event reporting,
§7-161.
Medical malpractice, §16-2801.
Mental health disclosures within
mental health facility, §7-1203.01.
Health care services, §44-301.01.
Health care ombudsman program,
§7-2071.01.
Health carrier.
Health benefit exchange authority,
§31-3171.01.
Health center.
Medical liability captive insurance
agency, §1-307.81.
Health club services.
Gross sales tax, §47-2001.
Health education standards.
Early childhood and school-based
behavioral health infrastructure,
§2-1517.31.
Health facility.
Emergency volunteer health
practitioners, §7-2361.01.
Health food.
Grocery and retail stores development,
§2-1212.01.
Health insurance.
Coverage for habilitative services for
children, §31-3271.
Health insurance coverage,
§31-3301.01.
Chemotherapy pill coverage,
§31-2995.01.
Divorce, annulment, separation,
support, §16-901.
Health insurance for dependents,
§31-2996.01.
Medical support enforcement,
§46-251.01.
Women's rights regarding certain
health insurance coverage,
§31-3831.

DEFINED TERMS —Cont'd

Health insurance portability and accountability act.

Public assistance applicants, confidentiality of information, §4-209.04.

Health insurer, §31-3301.01.

Chemotherapy pill coverage, §31-2995.01.

Child health screening, §7-875.02.

Continuation of health benefits plan coverage, §32-731.

Credentialing intermediary, §31-3251.

Diabetes health insurance coverage, §31-3001.

Health benefit plans reimbursement, §31-3131.

Health insurance, clinical trials insurance coverage, §31-2993.01.

Health insurance for dependents, §31-2996.01.

Healthy DC and health care expansion fund and program, §4-631.

HIV screening test while receiving emergency medical services, §31-2803.

Human rights commission, §2-1401.02.

Medical support enforcement, §46-251.01.

Newborn hearing screening, §7-851.

Newborn heart screening, §7-857.01.

Prostate cancer screening, §31-2951.

Substance abuse insurance coverage, §31-3101.

Telehealth reimbursement, §31-3861.

Uniform consultation referral forms, §31-3231.

Women's rights regarding certain health insurance coverage, §31-3831.

Health maintenance organization producers, §31-3401.

Health maintenance organizations (HMOs), §31-3401.

AIDS discrimination in the provision of insurance, §31-1601.

Health insurance portability and accountability, §31-3301.01.

Health planning and development agency, §44-401.

Medical assistance program, §1-307.02.

Substance abuse and mental illness insurance coverage, §31-3101.

Health occupation, §3-1201.01.

Administrative fines, §2-1801.02.

DEFINED TERMS —Cont'd

Health occupations board.

Monitoring prescription drugs, §48-853.01.

Health organization.

Health insurance regulatory standards, §31-3451.01.

Health practitioner.

Emergency volunteer health practitioners, §7-2361.01.

Health professional, §§3-1201.01, 22-1314.01, 44-801.

Health benefit exchange authority, §31-3171.01.

Health professional association, §44-801.

Health professional shortage area.

Health professional recruitment program, §7-751.01.

Health services.

Emergency volunteer health practitioners, §7-2361.01.

Health planning and development agency, §44-401.

Health spa sales, §28-3817.

Health status-related factor, §31-3301.01.

Healthy DC and health care expansion fund.

Hospital and medical services corporation, §31-3501.

Healthy schools and youth commission.

Schools and education, §38-821.01.

Healthy schools fund.

Schools and education, §38-821.01.

Hearing aid, §28-4001.

Hearing aid dispenser, §28-4001.

Hearing aid dealers, §28-4001.

Hearing-impaired person.

Interpreters, §2-1901.

Hearing impairment.

Newborn hearing screening, §7-851.

Hearing officer.

Office of administrative hearings, §2-1831.01.

Hearing test evaluation, §28-4001.

Hearing aid dealers, §28-4001.

Hearing tribunal, §2-1401.02.

Heavy duty vehicle (HDV), §50-702.

Heavy equipment.

Fleet management, publicly-owned vehicles, §50-211.01.

Hedge agreement.

Income tax secured bonds, §47-340.26.

Hedging transaction.

Insurance investments, §31-1371.02.

DEFINED TERMS —Cont'd
HEIG fund.
Pre-kindergarten programs,
§38-271.01.
**Heights on Georgia Avenue
developer.**
Real property tax exemptions,
§47-4630.
Heights on Georgia Avenue project.
Real property tax exemptions,
§47-4630.
HEI program.
Pre-kindergarten programs,
§38-271.01.
Heir, §20-101.
HEI scholarship program.
Pre-kindergarten programs,
§38-271.01.
Held by.
Corporations, §29-306.73.
Help America Vote Act of 2002,
§1-1001.02.
HFA.
District of Columbia housing
authority, §6-201.
**High-demand occupations or
sectors.**
Adult literacy task force, §32-1661.
Higher education act.
Higher education financial aid
assistance, §38-2731.
Highest and best use.
Rental housing, §42-3401.03.
High grade investment.
Insurance investments, §31-1371.02.
High income country.
Prescription drugs, excessive pricing,
§28-4552.
High intensity discharge lamp.
Energy efficiency standards,
§8-1771.01.
High level policy form, §31-3301.01.
Highly rated.
Insurance investments, §31-1371.02.
High-occupancy vehicle lanes,
§50-702.
High potential risk employee.
Corrections employee mandatory
substance abuse testing,
§24-211.21.
Mandatory drug and alcohol testing of
certain employees, §1-620.21.
High school equivalency diploma,
§4-205.61.
High strength wastes.
Wastewater disposal systems,
§8-105.02.

DEFINED TERMS —Cont'd
**High technology commercial real
estate database and service
provider.**
Tax abatement, §47-4630.
Highway, §§31-2402, 47-2302.
Chemical testing for driving under the
influence, §50-1901.
Complete streets policy, §50-2381.
Impaired operation or driving,
§50-2206.01.
Traffic regulation, §50-2201.02.
Highway plan, §9-201.01.
Highway trust fund.
Budget reprogramming policy,
§47-361.
HIPAA.
Health data privacy, §7-241.
Voluntary withdrawal by health
benefit plan carriers, §31-3151.
Hiring procedure, §32-901.
Histologic technicians, practice of,
§3-1201.02.
Historical value, §2-1701.
Historic district.
Historic landmarks, §6-1102.
Historic landmark, §6-1102.
Historic preservation office.
Historic landmarks, §6-1102.
Historic preservation review board.
Historic landmarks, §6-1102.
Historic tax credits.
Rental housing conversion,
opportunity to purchase,
§42-3404.02.
Histotechnology, practice of,
§3-1201.02.
HIV, §31-1601.
Hive.
Bees, §8-1825.02.
HIV screening test.
Health insurance coverage, §31-2803.
HIV test.
HIV testing of certain criminal
offenders, §22-3901.
Hoax weapon of mass destruction.
Anti-terrorism act of 2002, §22-3152.
Holder.
Child support enforcement, §46-201.
Conservation easements, §42-201.
Corporations, §29-306.73.
Environmental covenants, §8-671.01.
Unclaimed property, §41-102.
Uniform commercial code, §28:1-201.
Holder in due course.
Negotiable instruments, §28:3-302.

DEFINED TERMS —Cont'd

Hold harmless, §31-3401.

Holding company system, §31-401.

Holding period, §47-1401.

Hold out as authorized or competent to practice law in the District of Columbia.

Unauthorized practice of law, DCCtApp Rule 49.

Holidays.

Merit system, §1-603.01.

Police and fire departments, §5-521.02.

Home.

Income tax, §47-1806.06.

Home and community-based services waiver.

Disability services, department on, §7-761.02.

Home and community-based services waiver provider.

Rent control, §42-3501.03.

Home care agency.

Health-care facility, hospice and home care licensure, §44-501.

Home health aide.

Nurse staffing agencies, §44-1051.02.

Home health care administration, practice of, §3-1201.02.

Home improvement.

Mechanics' and materialmen's liens, §40-301.03.

Home improvement business, §47-2883.01.

Home improvement contract.

Mechanics' and materialmen's liens, §40-301.03.

Homeless, §4-751.01.

Affordable housing inventory comprehensive tracking plan, §42-2141.

Homelessness, §22-3701.

Homeless submission.

Walter Reed Army Medical Center, §10-1901.

Home mortgage disclosure act.

Investment and deposit of District funds, §47-351.01.

Home office.

Certified public accountants, §47-2853.41.

Homeowners association, §47-871.

Homeownership program, §42-2701.02.

Homeowner's insurance, §31-5002.

Home Rule act.

Bond issues, borrowing limitation, §47-334.

DEFINED TERMS —Cont'd

Home Rule act —Cont'd

City Market at O Street tax increment financing, §2-1217.33a.

Electric company infrastructure improvement financing, §34-1311.01.

Energy efficiency financing, §8-1778.02.

Ethics and government accountability, §1-1161.01.

Housing production trust fund, bond issues, §42-2812.01.

Howard Theatre redevelopment project, §2-1217.151.

Howard Theatre redevelopment project TIF area, §2-1217.34a.

New convention center hotel, §10-1221.01.

PILOT agreements, §1-308.01.

Qualified zone academy revenue bond project forward commitment approval act, §2-1217.102.

Retail development incentives, §2-1217.71.

Skyland TIF area, §2-1217.35a.

Southwest waterfront bond financing, §2-1217.131.

Transportation infrastructure improvement GARVEE bonds, §9-107.51.

Union Market district tax increment financing, §2-1217.36a.

Home school student.

DC promise program, §38-2751.

Home service provider.

Toll telecommunication service tax, §47-3901.

Home solicitation sale.

Consumer protection, §28-3811.

Home state.

Insurance producers, §31-1131.02.

Interstate family support, §46-351.02.

Uniform adult guardianship and protective proceedings jurisdiction act, §21-2401.02.

Uniform child custody proceedings, §16-4601.01.

Homestead.

Residence property tax relief, §47-849.

Homesteader (commercial).

Homestead housing provision, §42-2103.

Homesteader (residential).

Homestead housing provision, §42-2103.

DEFINED TERMS —Cont'd

Homestudy.

Adoption voucher fund, §4-342.

Homocystinuria, §7-832.

Homozygous sickle cell disease,
§7-832.

Honey bee.

Bees, §8-1825.02.

Honor.

Letters of credit, §28:5-102.

Honoraria, §1-321.01.

Horizontal development.

Walter Reed Medical Center site
development, §2-1227.01.

Horizontal property regime.

Condominiums, §42-1901.01.

Real property assessment, §47-803.

Horse, §8-2001.

Horse-drawn carriage trade, §8-2001.

Horticultural techniques.

Urban gardens program, §48-401.

Hospice.

Anatomical gifts, §7-1531.01.

Health-care facility, hospice and home
care licensure, §44-501.

Hospital.

Anatomical gifts, §7-1531.01.

Department of mental health,
§7-1131.02.

Emergency care for sexual assault
victims, §7-2121.

Health-care facility, hospice and home
care licensure, §44-501.

Hospital discharge planning,
§21-2231.01.

Medicaid hospital inpatient 2016-2017
rate supplement, §44-662.18.

Medicaid hospital outpatient 2016-
2017 supplemental payment,
§44-661.11.

Newborn heart screening, §7-857.01.

Not-for-profit hospital corporations,
§44-951.01.

Substance abuse and mental illness
insurance coverage, §31-3101.

Unemployment compensation, §51-101.

Victims of crime, §23-1907.

Victims of crime, sexual assault
response, §4-561.01.

Hospitality industry.

Regulation of for-hire vehicles,
§50-301.03.

Hospital service plan.

Hospital and medical services
corporation, §31-3501.

DEFINED TERMS —Cont'd

Hospital service plan —Cont'd

Insurance holding companies, §31-701.

Hospital system.

Medicaid hospital inpatient 2016-2017
rate supplement, §44-662.18.

Medicaid hospital outpatient 2016-
2017 supplemental payment,
§44-661.11.

Host city.

Chesapeake regional Olympic games
authority, §2-1131.

Host entity.

Emergency volunteer health
practitioners, §7-2361.01.

Host state, §26-732.

Hotel.

Alcoholic beverages, §25-101.

Waterfront Park special assessment
district, §47-895.21.

Hotline.

Domestic violence hotline, §4-551.

Hours of darkness.

Automated teller machine, §26-131.02.

Hours of daylight.

Execution of search warrant, §23-523.

Household.

Affordable housing clearinghouse
directory, §42-2131.

Ethics and government accountability,
§1-1161.01.

Home purchase assistance step up
program, §42-2621.

Rental housing, §42-3401.03.

Household adjusted gross income.

Real property tax deferral,
§§47-845.02, 47-845.03.

Reduced real property tax liability for
seniors and persons with
disabilities, §47-863.

Household goods.

Warehouse receipts, §28:7-209.

Household gross income.

Income tax, §47-1806.06.

Household income.

Income tax, §47-1806.06.

Preservation and rehabilitation of
government-supported housing,
§42-2851.02.

Tax abatement for new residential
developments, §47-857.01.

**Household interest and dividend
income.**

Reduced real property tax liability for
seniors and persons with
disabilities, §47-863.

DEFINED TERMS —Cont'd

Housing accommodation,
§§42-3401.03, 42-3501.03, 42-3601.
Preservation and rehabilitation of
government-supported housing,
§42-2851.02.

Housing act of 1937.
District of Columbia housing
authority, §6-201.

Housing business, §2-1401.02.

Housing choice voucher program.
District of Columbia housing
authority, §6-201.

Housing element.
Georgia commons.
Real property transfer tax
exemption, §47-4610.
Real property tax exemptions,
§§47-4628, 47-4630.

Housing expenses.
Rental housing conversion and sale
relocation assistance, §42-3403.04.

Housing finance agency, §42-2701.02.
District of Columbia housing
authority, §6-201.

Housing finance agency act.
District of Columbia housing
authority, §6-201.

Housing first.
Homeless services, §4-751.01.

Housing production, §42-2801.

Housing project, §§6-102.01,
42-2701.02.

Housing property.
District of Columbia housing
authority, §6-201.

Housing provider, §§42-3501.03,
42-3601.

Housing regulations, §42-3501.03.

Housing unit, §42-2901.
Employer-assisted housing program,
§42-2501.

Howard Theatre parking garage.
Howard Theatre redevelopment project
TIF area, §2-1217.34a.

**Howard Theatre redevelopment
project.**
Howard Theatre redevelopment project
TIF area, §2-1217.34a.

**Howard Theatre redevelopment
project TIF area,** §2-1217.151.

HPO.
Historic landmarks, §6-1102.

HPV.
Human papillomavirus vaccination,
§7-1651.01.

DEFINED TERMS —Cont'd

HQ standards.
Pre-kindergarten programs,
§38-271.01.

H Street, N.E. retail priority area,
§1-325.171.

**H Street real property tax
increment revenue.**
H Street, N.E. retail priority area
incentive, §1-325.171.

H Street retail developer.
H Street, N.E. retail priority area
incentive, §1-325.171.

**H Street sales tax increment
revenue.**
H Street, N.E. retail priority area
incentive, §1-325.171.

HUD.
District of Columbia housing
authority, §6-201.
Lead-hazard prevention and
elimination, §8-231.01.

Hull damaged.
Uniform certificates of title for vessels,
§50-1541.01.

Hull identification number.
Uniform certificates of title for vessels,
§50-1541.01.

Human body parts, §7-1501.01.

Human care agreement.
Procurement practices, §2-351.04.

Humanities.
Arts and humanities commission,
§39-202.

Human remains, §3-402.

Human rights act.
Disability rights, §2-1431.01.

Human services.
Health data privacy, §7-241.

Human trafficking counselor,
§14-311.

Human trafficking offense, §14-311.

Human trafficking program, §14-311.

HVAC&R.
Green buildings, §6-1451.01.

Hyperthermia shelter.
Homeless services, §4-751.01.

Hypothermia shelter.
Homeless services, §4-751.01.

Hypothyroidism, §7-832.

IBF.
Income tax, §47-1801.04.

IBF loan.
Income tax, §47-1801.04.

IBF time deposit.
Income tax, §47-1801.04.

DEFINED TERMS —Cont'd
ICC.
Green buildings, §6-1451.01.
ICD-9-CM.
Department of mental health, §7-1131.02.
Rights of persons with intellectual disability, §7-1301.03.
ICF-IDD.
Stevie Sellows quality improvement fund, §47-1270.
IDEA.
Charter schools, §38-1800.02.
Mental health consumer's rights, §7-1231.02.
Nonpublic schools, §38-2561.01.
Special education student rights, §38-2571.02.
State superintendent of education, office of, §38-2601.02.
Identification card, §8-2001.
Anatomical gifts, §7-1531.01.
Identification number.
Bicycles, §§22-3234, 50-1609.
Identified individual.
Health data privacy, §7-241.
Identifying information.
Jury selection, §16-5101.
Traffic regulation, §50-2201.02.
Identifying number.
Condominiums, §42-1901.02.
IECC.
Green buildings, §6-1451.01.
IEP.
Charter schools, §38-1800.02.
Nonpublic schools, §38-2561.01.
Special education student rights, §38-2571.02.
State superintendent of education, office of, §38-2601.02.
Testing integrity (public schools), §38-771.01.
IFSP.
Special education student rights, §38-2571.02.
Illegal dumping, §8-901.
Illegal order, §2-223.01.
Whistleblower protection, §1-615.52.
Illegal sale, §7-2531.01.
IMA.
Public assistance applicants, confidentiality of information, §4-209.04.
IMA programs.
Public assistance applicants, confidentiality of information, §4-209.04.

DEFINED TERMS —Cont'd
Immediate birth family member.
Voluntary foster care registry, §4-1303.08.
Immediate family.
Ethics and government accountability, §1-1161.01.
Grant administration, §1-328.11.
Immediate family member.
Family court proceedings, §16-2301.
Immediately available.
Anesthesiologist assistants, §3-1206.31.
Immediate precursor, §48-901.02.
Immediate relative.
Voluntary leave transfer program, §1-612.31.
Immediate supervision, §3-402.
Imminent risk of becoming homeless.
Homeless services, §4-751.01.
Imminent threat to the health or safety.
Homeless services, §4-751.01.
Impaired.
Chemical testing for driving under the influence, §50-1901.
Impaired operation or driving, §50-2206.01.
Impaired health professional, §3-1201.01.
Impaired insurer.
Life and health insurance guaranty association, §31-5401.
Impaired nurse.
Nurse's rehabilitation program, §3-1251.01.
Impervious area stormwater user fee.
Department of the environment, §8-151.01.
Impervious surface.
Department of the environment, §8-151.01.
Importer, §§7-2531.01, 7-2551.01, 47-2302.
Tobacco tax, §47-2401.
Importers of handcrafted and indigenous goods, §37-101.
Impound, §8-1901.
Impounded.
Abandoned and unlawfully parked vehicles, §50-2421.02.
Improper means, §36-401.
Improvement, §47-2302.
Real property taxes, supplemental assessment, §47-830.

DEFINED TERMS —Cont'd
Improvement parcels.
Capper/Carrollsburg PILOT area.
Payments in lieu of taxes, §47-4611.
Inactive.
Capital project review and
reconciliation, §50-921.51.
Inactive business activities.
Employees retirement program
management, §1-336.01.
Inactive business operations.
Employees retirement program
management, §1-335.01.
Inactive public record, §2-1701.
In a representative capacity, §42-141.
Inaugural committee, §§2-801, 2-821.
Ethics and government accountability,
§1-1161.01.
Inaugural period, §§2-801, 2-821.
Incapacitated.
Custodial trusts, §19-1101.
**Incapacitated individual, §§21-2011,
21-2202.**
**Incapacitated individual for
healthcare decisions.**
Conservators, §21-2011.
Incapacitated person.
Uniform adult guardianship and
protective proceedings jurisdiction
act, §21-2401.02.
Incapacity, §4-205.42.
Standby guardianship, §16-4802.
Incentive.
Unified economic development budget
transparency and accountability,
§2-1208.01.
Incentive agreement.
The Advisory Board Company, real
property tax abatement,
§47-4665.01.
Incest, §22-1901.
Incineration.
Solid waste reduction and recovery,
§8-1031.01.
Inclusionary development.
Zoning, §6-1041.01.
Inclusionary unit.
Zoning, §6-1041.01.
**Inclusionary zoning program,
§6-1041.01.**
Income, §4-205.05.
Ethics and government accountability,
§1-1161.01.
Insurance investments, §31-1371.02.
Interstate family support, §46-351.02.
Principal and income, §28-4801.02.

DEFINED TERMS —Cont'd
Income beneficiary.
Principal and income, §28-4801.02.
Income generation transaction.
Insurance investments, §31-1371.02.
Income interest.
Principal and income, §28-4801.02.
Income-producing property.
Waterfront Park special assessment
district, §47-895.21.
**Income tax secured bond fund,
§47-340.26.**
Income-withholding order.
Interstate family support, §46-351.02.
Incompetent.
Incompetent criminal defendants,
§24-531.01.
Incompetent to proceed.
Family court proceedings, §16-2301.
Incomplete instruments.
Negotiable instruments, §28:3-115.
Inconclusive report.
Child abuse and neglect, §4-1301.02.
Incorporated protected cell.
Captive insurance companies,
§§31-3931.01, 31-3931.04.
**Incumbent local exchange carrier,
§34-2001.**
In custody or under supervision.
Sex offender registration, §22-4001.
Indebtedness, §31-5102.
Indemnification.
Annual audited financial reports,
§31-301.
Indemnity.
Title insurance producers,
§31-5041.01.
Title insurers, §31-5031.01.
Indemnity deposit.
Title insurance producers,
§31-5041.01.
Title insurers, §31-5031.01.
Indenture.
Electric company infrastructure
improvement financing,
§34-1311.01.
Energy efficiency financing,
§8-1778.02.
Indenture of trust.
Southwest waterfront special
assessment district, §47-895.01.
Special energy assessments,
§47-895.31.
Independent.
Benefit corporations, §29-1301.02.
Independent agency, §2-502.
Criminal justice coordinating council,
§22-4231.

DEFINED TERMS —Cont'd
Independent agency —Cont'd
Merit system, §1-603.01.
Office of administrative hearings, §2-1831.01.
Voluntary leave transfer program, §1-612.31.
Independent certified public accountants, §31-301.
Independent contractor.
Mortgage lenders and brokers, §26-1101.
Independent evidentiary value.
Seized-currency, §23-531.
Independent expenditure.
Ethics and government accountability, §1-1161.01.
Independent expenditure committee.
Ethics and government accountability, §1-1161.01.
Independent expert consultant.
Victims of crime, sexual assault response, §4-561.01.
Independent living.
Continuing care retirement communities, §44-151.01.
Independent review organization, §44-301.01.
Indigent.
Civil asset forfeiture, §41-301.
Indirect discharge.
Wastewater disposal systems, §8-105.02.
Indirect holdings.
Employees retirement program management, §§1-335.01, 1-336.01.
Indirect labor costs.
First source employment, §2-219.01.
Individual, §31-2402.
Income tax, §47-1801.04.
Insurance producers, §31-1131.02.
Stalking, §22-3132.
Title insurance producers, §31-5041.01.
Title insurers, §31-5031.01.
Individual attachment point.
Stop-loss health insurance for employers, §31-3821.
Individual billing meter.
Retail electric competition and consumer protection, §34-1501.
Individual career path.
Charter schools, §38-1800.02.
Individual contract, §31-3401.

DEFINED TERMS —Cont'd
Individual found incompetent in a criminal case.
Rights of persons with intellectual disability, §7-1301.03.
Individual health insurance coverage, §31-3301.01.
Individual health plan.
Chemotherapy pill coverage, §31-2995.01.
Women's rights regarding certain health insurance coverage, §31-3831.
Individualized education plan.
Nonpublic schools, §38-2561.01.
Individualized education program.
Charter schools, §38-1800.02.
Special education student rights, §38-2571.02.
State superintendent of education, office of, §38-2601.02.
Individualized family service plan.
Special education student rights, §38-2571.02.
Individualized service plan.
Assisted living residences, §44-102.01.
Individual market, §31-3301.01.
Substance abuse insurance coverage, §31-3101.
Individual plan of care.
Department of mental health, §7-1131.02.
Mental health consumer's rights, §7-1231.02.
Individual preference.
Chief financial officer, tax transparency, §1-301.156.
Individual recovery plan.
Department of mental health, §7-1131.02.
Mental health consumer's rights, §7-1231.02.
Individual's representative.
Public assistance applicants, confidentiality of information, §4-209.04.
Individual taxable properties.
Business improvement districts, expanding taxable real property within, §§2-1215.09b, 2-1215.09c.
Individual training account.
Workforce investment implementation, §32-1602.
Individual vehicle mileage record (IVMR), §50-1507.01.
Individual with a disability.
Homeless services, §4-751.01.

DEFINED TERMS —Cont'd
Individual with a severe disability, §32-302.
Indoor mold, §8-241.01.
Indoor mold assessment professional, §8-241.01.
Indoor mold contamination, §8-241.01.
Indoor mold remediation professional, §8-241.01.
Indorsement.
Investment securities, §28:8-102.
Negotiable instruments, §28:3-204.
Indorser.
Negotiable instruments, §28:3-204.
Industrial life insurance, §31-4202.
Industrial user.
Wastewater disposal systems, §8-105.02.
Industrial wastewater, §8-103.01.
Industry member.
Regulation of for-hire vehicles, §50-301.03.
Industry placement facility, §31-5002.
Ineligible felony.
Criminal records sealing, §16-801.
Ineligible misdemeanor.
Criminal records sealing, §16-801.
I-Net.
Office of cable television, film, music, and entertainment amendment act of 2015, §34-1251.03.
Infant, §§7-2031, 31-4001.
Child and adult food program funding, §38-281.
Infant or toddler with a disability.
Special education student rights, §38-2571.02.
Infectious waste, §8-1051.
Wastewater disposal systems, §8-105.02.
Informant.
Metropolitan police.
Investigations concerning first amendment activities, §5-333.02.
Information.
Electronic transactions, uniform act, §28-4901.
Information form.
Child and family services agency.
Criminal record checks, §4-1305.01.
Information processing system.
Electronic transactions, uniform act, §28-4901.

DEFINED TERMS —Cont'd
Information relating to legal presence.
Personal information from motor vehicle records and accident reports, §50-1401.01b.
Information service, §47-2201.
Gross sales tax, §47-2001.
Information systems, §2-213.01.
Information systems technology, §2-213.01.
Informed consent, §7-1301.03.
Infraction, §§2-1801.02, 50-2301.02.
Inhabited alley, §6-101.07.
Inherently governmental functions.
Procurement practices, §2-351.04.
Inherently low-emission vehicle (ILEV), §50-702.
In-home care.
Child care facilities, §4-401.
Initial assessed value, §2-1217.01.
Initial determination.
Uniform child custody proceedings, §16-4601.01.
Initial discounted price.
Access to prescription drugs, §48-831.02.
Initial enrollment period, §31-3301.01.
Initial implementation date.
Retail electric competition and consumer protection, §34-1501.
Initial investment.
Certified capital companies, §31-5231.
Initial leasing period, §42-3501.03.
Initial margin.
Insurance investments, §31-1371.02.
Initial PILOT period.
Payments in lieu of taxes, §47-1052.
Initial sales tax amount, §2-1217.01.
Initiating state.
Interstate family support, §46-351.02.
Initiative.
Access to justice initiative program, §4-1701.01.
Elections, §1-1001.02.
Home Rule act, §1-204.101.
Injury.
Doctor-patient privilege, §14-307.
No-fault motor vehicle insurance, §31-2402.
Public employees disability compensation, §1-623.01.
Workers' compensation, §32-1501.
Inpatient net patient revenue.
Medicaid hospital inpatient 2016-2017 rate supplement, §44-662.18.

DEFINED TERMS —Cont'd
Inpatient services, §31-3101.
Inpatient treatment facility.
Incompetent criminal defendants,
§24-531.01.
In place transfer.
Assisted living residences, §44-102.01.
Inquiry.
Hiring of ex-offenders, fair criminal
record screening, §32-1341.
Insanitary buildings, §6-918.
Insect, §8-401.
Insider, §28-3101.
Fraudulent transfers, §28-3101.
Insolvency or insolvent, §§31-1301,
31-3401.
Fraudulent transfers, §28-3102.
Special purpose financial captive
insurance companies, §31-3932.02.
UCC, §28:1-201.
Insolvency proceedings.
UCC, §28:1-201.
Insolvent insurer, §31-5501.
Life and health insurance guaranty
association, §31-5401.
Inspection, §32-1101.
Inspection bureau, §31-5002.
Inspector.
Lead-hazard prevention and
elimination, §8-231.01.
Installation.
Office of cable television, film, music,
and entertainment amendment
act of 2015, §34-1251.03.
Installment lease contracts.
Leases, UCC, §28:2A-103.
Institute.
Mayor's youth leadership institute,
§2-1571.
Institution, §§7-201, 47-2886.02.
Prudent management of institutional
funds, §44-1631.
Institutional control.
Brownfield revitalization, §8-631.02.
Institutional fund.
Prudent management of institutional
funds, §44-1631.
Institutional lender.
Condominiums, §42-1901.02.
Institutional network.
Office of cable television, film, music,
and entertainment amendment
act of 2015, §34-1251.03.
Institutional pharmacy.
Unused pharmaceutical safe disposal,
§48-851.01.

DEFINED TERMS —Cont'd
Institution of higher education,
§§38-2402.01, 51-101.
College access assistance, public school
program, §38-2702.
DC promise program, §38-2751.
Higher education financial aid
assistance, §38-2731.
Instruction.
Investment securities, §28:8-102.
Instrument.
Liens on motor vehicles or trailers,
§50-1201.
Secured transactions, §28:9-102.
**Instrumental activities of daily
living.**
Assisted living residences, §44-102.01.
Instrumentality, §2-223.01.
Instrument of security, §50-601.
Insurance, §§22-3225.01, 31-2701,
31-4101.
Insurance producers, §31-1131.02.
Insurance bureau.
Insurance, securities, and banking,
department of, §31-101.
Insurance business.
Unfair insurance trade practices,
§31-2231.01.
Insurance compliance audit.
Insurance compliance self-evaluation
privilege, §31-851.
**Insurance compliance self-
evaluative audit document,**
§31-851.
Insurance consultation services,
§32-1501.
Insurance documents.
Electronic delivery and posting of
insurance documents, §31-651.01.
Insurance future.
Insurance investments, §31-1371.02.
Insurance futures option.
Insurance investments, §31-1371.02.
Insurance holding company system,
§31-701.
Insurance identification card,
§31-2402.
Vehicle insurance enforcement,
§5-114.01.
Insurance policy.
Unfair insurance trade practices,
§31-2231.01.
**Insurance premium finance
company,** §31-1102.
Insurance producer, §31-1131.02.
Insurance professional, §22-3225.01.

DEFINED TERMS —Cont'd
Insurance securitization.
Special purpose financial captive
insurance companies, §31-3932.02.
Insurance transaction, §7-1201.01.
Insured, §31-2402.
Diabetes health insurance coverage,
§31-3001.
HIV screening test while receiving
emergency medical services,
§31-2803.
Security agents and broker,
§31-5601.01.
Unfair insurance trade practices,
§31-2231.01.
Insured financial institution.
Investment and deposit of District
funds, §47-351.01.
Insured work, §51-101.
Insurer.
AIDS discrimination in the provision
of insurance, §31-1601.
Annual audited financial reports,
§31-301.
Bicycle insurance policies, §50-531.
Business transacted with producer
controlled insurer, §31-401.
Child development homes insurance,
§31-4001.
Health benefit plan members bill of
rights, §44-301.01.
Holding company system, §31-701.
Insurance fraud, §22-3225.01.
Insurance holding company system,
§31-704.
Insurance producers, §31-1131.02.
Insurance regulatory trust fund,
§31-1201.
Managing general agents, §31-1501.
No-fault motor vehicle insurance,
§31-2402.
Rehabilitation and liquidation
procedures, §31-1301.
Reinsurance intermediary, §31-1801.
Security agents and broker,
§31-5601.01.
Title insurance producers,
§31-5041.01.
Title insurers, §31-5031.01.
Unfair insurance trade practices,
§31-2231.01.
Vehicle insurance enforcement,
§5-114.01.
Intake screening and assessment.
Choice in drug treatment, §7-3002.
Intangible expense.
Income tax, §47-1801.04.

DEFINED TERMS —Cont'd
Intangible personal property,
§41-102.
Intangible property.
Income tax, §47-1801.04.
Integrated pest management.
Pesticide education and control,
§8-431.
Integrated service plan.
Interagency collaboration and services
integration commission, §2-1592.
Intellectual disability, §§7-1301.03,
21-1201.
Disability services, department on,
§7-761.02.
Intellectual property, §22-901.
Intelligence section.
Metropolitan police.
Investigations concerning first
amendment activities,
§5-333.02.
Intelligence section file.
Metropolitan police.
Investigations concerning first
amendment activities,
§5-333.02.
**Intensive program of special
education services.**
Uniform per student funding formula,
§38-2901.
Intercept, §23-541.
Intercepting device, §23-541.
Intercollegiate sport.
Athlete agents, §47-2887.01.
Interest, §28-3311.
Alcoholic beverages, §25-101.
Business organizations, §29-101.02.
Corporations, §29-311.01.
Interest and usury, §28-3311.
Interested party.
Demolition or enclosure of deteriorated
property, §42-3173.01.
Workplace fraud, §32-1331.01.
Interested person, §20-101.
Corporations, §29-311.01.
Statutory trusts, §29-1205.12.
Interested transaction.
Corporations, §29-311.01.
Interest exchange.
Entity transactions, §29-201.02.
Interest expense.
Income tax, §47-1801.04.
Interest holder.
Business organizations, §29-101.02.
Interest holder liability.
Entity transactions, §29-201.02.

DEFINED TERMS —Cont'd
Interest holder liability —Cont'd
Nonprofit corporations, §29-401.02.
Interest in real property, §26-1101.
Interest payments, §42-3501.03.
Interests of the beneficiaries.
Uniform trust code, §19-1301.03.
Interference, §8-105.02.
Interim controls.
Lead-hazard prevention and
elimination, §8-231.01.
Interim eligibility replacement.
Homeless services, §4-751.01.
Interjurisdictional movement.
International registration plan
agreements, §50-1507.01.
Interlocutory orders.
Office of administrative hearings,
§2-1831.01.
Intermediary bank.
Bank deposits and collections,
§28:4-105.
Funds transfers, §28:4A-104.
Intermediary interpreter, §2-1901.
Intermediary processing facility.
Solid waste reduction and recovery,
§8-1031.01.
**Intermediate care facility for
persons with intellectual or
developmental disabilities.**
Stevie Sellows quality improvement
fund, §47-1270.
**Intermediate materials recycling
facility,** §8-1051.
**Internal control over financial
reporting.**
Annual audited financial reports,
§31-301.
Internal revenue code.
College savings program, §47-4501.
Ethics and government accountability,
§1-1161.01.
Police and firefighters retirement and
disability, §5-701.
Teachers' retirement, §38-2021.13.
Uniform fiduciaries act, §21-1722.
Internal Revenue Code of 1954.
Income tax, §47-1801.04.
Inheritance and estate taxes,
§47-3701.
Internal Revenue Code of 1986.
Health benefit exchange authority,
§31-3171.01.
Income tax, §47-1801.04.
Teachers' retirement, §38-2021.13.
International agency.
International banking corporations,
§26-631.

DEFINED TERMS —Cont'd
**International banking corporation
office.**
International banking corporations,
§26-631.
International banking facility.
Income tax, §47-1801.04.
**International banking facility
extension of credit.**
Income tax, §47-1801.04.
**International banking facility time
deposit.**
Income tax, §47-1801.04.
International branch.
International banking corporations,
§26-631.
International commercial mediation,
§16-4210.
International financing corporation.
International banking, §26-631.
International Fuel Tax Agreement,
§47-2302.
International Olympic committee.
Chesapeake regional Olympic games
authority, §2-1131.
**International registration plan
(IRP),** §50-1507.01.
International representative office.
International banking corporations,
§26-631.
International student, §38-2402.01.
Internet.
Nonconsensual pornography, §22-3051.
Internet access service, §47-2201.
Gross sales tax, §47-2001.
Internet Protocol-enabled service,
§34-2001.
Internet publication.
Respectful language modernization,
§2-631.
Interoperability.
Monitoring prescription drugs,
§48-853.01.
Interpersonal violence.
Intrafamily offenses, §16-1001.
Interscholastic athletics program.
Athletic equity, §38-841.01.
**Interstate commission on
educational opportunity for
military children.**
Interstate compact on educational
opportunity for military children,
§49-1101.03.
Interstate merger transaction,
§26-732.
Intervention proceeding, §21-2011.

DEFINED TERMS —Cont'd

Interview.
  Hiring of ex-offenders, fair criminal record screening, §32-1341.
  Victims of crime, §23-1907.

Intestate decedent, §20-101.

In the District, §47-2201.
  Unauthorized practice of law, DCCtApp Rule 49.

Intimate partner violence.
  Intrafamily offenses, §16-1001.

Intimidate, threaten or coerce.
  Voluntary leave transfer program, §1-612.31.

Intoxicated.
  Chemical testing for driving under the influence, §50-1901.
  Impaired operation or driving, §50-2206.01.

Intra-district transfer.
  Budget reprogramming policy, §47-361.

Intrafamily offense, §16-1001.
  Domestic violence counselors, §14-310.
  Firearms, §7-2501.01.
  Human trafficking counselor, §14-311.
  Sexual assault victim advocates, §14-312.
  Third-party child custody, §16-831.01.

Intrafamily violence, §16-1001.

Intrajurisdictional movement, §50-1507.01.

Inventory.
  Secured transactions, §28:9-102.

Invest.
  Investment and deposit of District funds, §47-351.01.

Investigation, §32-1101.
  Whistleblower protection, §1-615.52.

Investigative officer, §23-541.

Investigative or law enforcement officer.
  Criminal procedure, CrimPro Rule 54.

Investment.
  Investment and deposit of District funds, §47-351.01.

Investment adviser.
  Security agents and broker, §31-5601.01.

Investment adviser representative.
  Security agents and broker, §31-5601.01.

Investment Advisers Act of 1940.
  Security agents and broker, §31-5601.01.

Investment company.
  Insurance investments, §31-1371.02.

DEFINED TERMS —Cont'd

Investment Company Act of 1940.
  Security agents and broker, §31-5601.01.

Investment company series.
  Insurance investments, §31-1371.02.

Investment grade obligation.
  Investment and deposit of District funds, §47-351.01.

Investment practices.
  Insurance investments, §31-1371.02.

Investment property.
  Secured transactions, §28:9-102.

Investment securities.
  Universal banks, §26-1401.02.

Investment strategy.
  Insurance investments, §31-1371.02.

Investment subsidiary.
  Insurance investments, §31-1371.02.

Investor member.
  Limited cooperative associations, §29-1001.02.

Invitation for bids.
  Procurement practices, §2-351.04.

In vitro fertilization, §16-401.

Involuntary termination.
  Access to justice initiative program, §4-1701.01.

In writing.
  Procurement practices, §2-351.04.

IOC.
  Chesapeake regional Olympic games authority, §2-1131.

IPM.
  Pesticide education and control, §8-431.

Iran.
  Employees retirement program management, §1-336.01.

IRLA.
  Title insurers, §31-5031.01.

Islands.
  National Children's Island, §10-1401.

Isomer, §48-901.02.

Issuance costs.
  Qualified zone academy revenue bond project forward commitment approval act, §2-1217.102.

Issue.
  Negotiable instruments, §28:3-105.

Issue date, §§26-301, 48-804.51.
  Prescription drugs, §48-804.51.

Issue of public interest.
  Anti-SLAPP, §16-5501.

Issuer, §31-3701.
  Investment securities, §28:8-201.

DEFINED TERMS —Cont'd

Issuer —Cont'd

Letters of credit, §28:5-102.

Negotiable instruments, §28:3-105.

Warehouse receipts, §28:7-102.

Issuing court.

Uniform child custody proceedings, §16-4601.01.

Issuing foreign country.

Interstate family support, §46-351.02.

Issuing state.

Interstate enforcement of domestic violence proceedings, §16-1041.

Uniform child custody proceedings, §16-4601.01.

Issuing tribunal.

Interstate family support, §46-351.02.

Item.

Bank deposits and collections, §28:4-104.

It ServUS program.

Citywide technology support services, §1-1431.

Jenkins Row project.

Jenkins Row Development tax exemption, §47-4603.

Jenkins Row property.

Jenkins Row Development tax exemption, §47-4603.

Jobber, §36-301.01.

Job growth tax credit.

Income tax, §47-1807.51.

Job listing service, §32-401.

Job-seeker, §32-401.

Job skills-deficient resident.

Job opportunity bank, §32-751.

Joint and several contracts, §16-2101.

Joint commission.

Stroke system of care, §44-1151.

Joint consent.

Department of mental health, §7-1131.02.

Mental health disclosures, §7-1201.01.

Jointly held property.

Uniform disclaimer of property interests act, §19-1502.

Joint owner.

Uniform real property transfers on death, §19-604.02.

Joint rates, public utilities, §34-211.

Joint state oversight agency, §9-1109.01.

Joint-use sewerage facilities, §34-2202.01.

DEFINED TERMS —Cont'd

Joint venture, §24-231.01.

Small and certified business enterprise development and assistance, §2-218.02.

Judge, §§1-702, 1-901.02, 11-1561, 23-541.

Judge of competent jurisdiction, §23-541.

Judgment, §16-541, CivPro Rule 54.

Domestic relations actions, DomRel Rule 54.

Enforcement, §15-301.

Motor vehicle safety responsibility, §50-1301.36.

Judicial officer, §23-1302.

Bail and pretrial detention, §23-1331.

Intrafamily offenses, §16-1001.

Warrants, §23-501.

Judicial service, §11-1561.

Junk vehicle certificate.

Salvage, flood and junk vehicles, §50-1331.01.

Junk vehicles.

Removal of abandoned and junk vehicles, §50-2401.

Salvage, flood and junk vehicles, §50-1331.01.

Jurisdiction.

Business organizations, §29-101.02.

Rental vehicle tax, §50-1505.01.

Uniform trust code, §19-1301.03.

Jurisdictional base, §47-2302.

Jurisdiction of formation.

Business organizations, §29-101.02.

Jurisdiction of organization.

Secured transactions, §28:9-102.

Juror, §§11-1902, 22-711.

Jury, §11-1902.

Jury system plan, §11-1902.

Juvenile, §27-101.

Juvenile case records.

Child abuse and neglect, §16-2331.

Juvenile social records.

Child abuse and neglect, §16-2332.

Keg, §25-101.

Key shareholder.

Money transmissions, §26-1001.

Kidnapping, §22-2001.

Kinship caregiver.

Child abuse and neglect, §4-1301.02.

Know.

Anatomical gifts, §7-1531.01.

Rules of professional conduct, ProfCond Rule 1.0.

Knowing.

Procurement claims, §2-381.01.

DEFINED TERMS —Cont'd

Knowingly, §§22-2201, 22-3101.
Business licenses, §47-2844.
Procurement claims, §2-381.01.
Rules of professional conduct,
ProfCond Rule 1.0.
Unemployment compensation, §51-104.
Workplace fraud, §32-1331.01.

Knowledge.
Arbitration, revised act, §16-4401.
UCC, §28:1-202.
Uniform certificates of title for vessels,
§50-1541.01.
Uniform trust code, §19-1301.04.

Known, §50-501.
Rules of professional conduct,
ProfCond Rule 1.0.

**Known violent or dangerous
offender.**
Metropolitan police.
School safety division, §5-132.21.

Knuckles.
Weapons, §22-4501.

K street building.
Tax abatement for mixed-income
housing projects, §47-857.06.

Labeler.
Access to prescription drugs,
§48-831.02.
Practice of pharmaceutical detailing,
§3-1201.02.

Label, labeling, §47-2885.02.
Pesticide operations, §8-401.

Labor.
Human trafficking, §22-1831.
Prisoners, use of restraints on
pregnant women, §24-276.01.
Youth rehabilitation services
department, use of restraints on
pregnant youths, §2-1515.51.

Laboratory director, §44-201.
Clinical laboratory practitioners,
qualifications for licensure,
exemption, §3-1207.63.

Laboratory reference system,
§44-201.

Labor organization, §2-1401.02.
Labor-peace agreement for public
projects, §32-852.
Procurement practices, §2-351.04.

Land, §8-401.
Condominiums, §42-1901.02.

Land area.
Southeast water and sewer
improvement benefit district,
§47-891.

DEFINED TERMS —Cont'd

Land area —Cont'd
Southwest waterfront special
assessment district, §47-895.01.

Land disposition lease.
Alcoholic beverages, §25-101.

Landlord.
Real property tax abatement for
qualified high technology
companies, §47-811.03.

Land records.
Mechanics' and materialmen's liens,
§40-301.03.

Landscaping.
Gross sales tax, §47-2001.

Land trust plan.
Housing production trust fund,
§42-2801.

Language access director.
Foreign language services and
documents, §2-1931.

**Large capacity ammunition feeding
device,** §7-2506.01.

Large employer, §31-3301.01.
Hospital and medical services
corporation, §31-3501.
Substance abuse insurance coverage,
§31-3101.

Large group market, §31-3301.01.
Substance abuse insurance coverage,
§31-3101.

Large multi-family dwelling,
§42-2103.

Large vehicle.
Fleet management, publicly-owned
vehicles, §50-211.01.

Last known address, §41-102.
Self-service storage facilities, §40-401.

Late enrollee, §31-3301.01.

Lateral feeder.
Electric company infrastructure
improvement financing,
§34-1311.01.

Lateral law enforcement officer,
§1-610.71.

Latino, Latino community, §2-1302.

Law.
Criminal procedure, CrimPro Rule 54.
Interstate family support, §46-351.02.
Unsworn foreign declarations,
§16-5302.

Law clerk.
Rules of professional conduct,
ProfCond Rule 1.0.

Law enforcement agency,
§§7-2531.01, 7-2551.01.
Crime investigation records, §5-113.31.

DEFINED TERMS —Cont'd

Law enforcement agency —Cont'd
Protection of innocence act, §22-4131.
Law enforcement officer.
Assault weapon manufacturer liability, §7-2551.01.
Chemical testing for driving under the influence, §50-1901.
Child abuse and neglect, §4-1301.02.
Firearm transfers, §7-2531.01.
Fleeing from a law enforcement officer, §50-2201.05b.
Impaired operation or driving, §50-2206.01.
Interception of oral or wire communications, §23-541.
License to carry pistol, §7-2509.01.
Resisting arrest, §22-405.01.
Traffic regulation, §50-2201.02.
Vehicle insurance enforcement, §5-114.01.
Warrants, §23-501.
Law enforcement retirement status.
Corrections employee mandatory substance abuse testing, §24-211.21.
Law enforcement vehicle, §50-702.
Law firm.
Collaborative law, §16-4002.
Rules of professional conduct, ProfCond Rule 1.0.
Lawful custodian, §16-1021.
Lawyer.
Access to justice initiative program, §4-1701.01.
Layaway plan, §28-3818.
Consumer protection, §28-3818.
Lay caregiver.
Hospital discharge planning, §21-2231.01.
LDA.
Walter Reed Medical Center site development, §2-1227.01.
LEA.
Athletic equity, §38-841.01.
School-based budgeting and accountability, §38-2801.01.
Special education student rights, §38-2571.02.
State superintendent of education, office of, §38-2601.02.
Testing integrity in public schools, §§38-771.01, 38-2602.
Lead agency, §8-109.02.
Lead-based paint.
Lead-hazard prevention and elimination, §8-231.01.

DEFINED TERMS —Cont'd

Lead-based paint activities.
Lead-hazard prevention and elimination, §8-231.01.
Lead-based paint hazard.
Lead-hazard prevention and elimination, §8-231.01.
Lead-based paint inspector.
Lead-hazard prevention and elimination, §8-231.01.
Lead-contaminated dust.
Lead-hazard prevention and elimination, §8-231.01.
Lead-contaminated soil.
Lead-hazard prevention and elimination, §8-231.01.
Lead-disclosure form.
Lead-hazard prevention and elimination, §8-231.01.
Lead-free property.
Lead-hazard prevention and elimination, §8-231.01.
Lead-free unit.
Lead-hazard prevention and elimination, §8-231.01.
Lead-poisoned child.
Childhood lead poisoning screening and reporting, §7-871.02.
Lead-safe work practices.
Lead-hazard prevention and elimination, §8-231.01.
Learn.
UCC, §28:1-202.
Lease, §21-2011.
Leases, UCC, §28:2A-103.
Uniform certificates of title for vessels, §50-1541.01.
Lease agreements.
Leases, UCC, §28:2A-103.
Lease commencement.
Real property tax exemptions, qualified high technology company interior renovation tax rebate, §47-4665.
The Advisory Board Company, real property tax abatement, §47-4665.01.
Lease contracts.
Leases, UCC, §28:2A-103.
Leased marketing premises.
Gas stations, §36-304.11.
Leased space.
Self-service storage facilities, §40-401.
Lease execution.
The Advisory Board Company, real property tax abatement, §47-4665.01.

DEFINED TERMS —Cont'd
Leasehold condominium.
Condominiums, §42-1901.02.
Leasehold interest.
Leases, UCC, §28:2A-103.
Lease-purchase agreement,
§42-3671.01.
Least restrictive alternative,
§7-1301.03.
Least restrictive environment.
Nonpublic schools, §38-2561.01.
Leave contributor.
Voluntary leave transfer program,
§1-612.31.
Leave donor.
Leave of absence, §1-612.04.
Leave recipient.
Leave of absence, §1-612.04.
LEED.
Anacostia waterfront environmental
standards, §2-1226.32.
Green buildings, §§6-1451.01,
6-1451.03.
LEED-H.
Green buildings, §6-1451.01.
**LEED standard for commercial and
institutional buildings,**
§6-1451.01.
Anacostia waterfront environmental
standards, §2-1226.32.
Legacy, §20-101.
Legal custody, §16-2301.
Child custody, §16-914.
Third-party child custody, §16-831.01.
Legal defense committee.
Ethics and government accountability,
§1-1161.01.
Legal drinking age.
Alcoholic beverages, §25-101.
Legal holiday, §47-1401.
Domestic relations actions, DomRel
Rule 2.
Legally binding agreement.
Walter Reed Army Medical Center,
§10-1901.
Walter Reed Medical Center site
development, §2-1227.01.
Legal representation.
Custodial trusts, §19-1101.
Legal representative, §21-301.
Legal service.
Merit system, §1-603.01.
Legal title, §47-1401.
Legal value, §2-1701.
Legatee, §20-101.
Legislative action.
Ethics and government accountability,
§1-1161.01.

DEFINED TERMS —Cont'd
Legislative branch agency.
Council, §1-301.44a.
Legislative duties.
Council, §1-301.41.
**Legitimate law enforcement
objective.**
Metropolitan police.
Investigations concerning first
amendment activities,
§5-333.02.
Legitimate, legitimated, §16-907.
Legitimate theater.
Alcoholic beverages, §25-101.
Lender, §42-2401.
Foreclosure mediation, §42-815.02.
Mortgage loan protection, §26-1151.01.
LEP/NEP.
Uniform per student funding formula,
§38-2901.
**Lesbian, gay, bisexual, transgender,
and questioning,** §2-1381.
Lessee, §§6-321.08, 6-341.05.
Leases, UCC, §28:2A-103.
**Lessee in ordinary course of
business.**
Leases, UCC, §28:2A-103.
Lessor.
Lease-purchase agreements,
§42-3671.01.
Leases, UCC, §28:2A-103.
Traffic adjudication, §50-2301.02.
Uniform certificates of title for vessels,
§50-1541.01.
Lessor's residual interest.
Leases, UCC, §28:2A-103.
Letter contract.
Procurement practices, §2-351.04.
Letter of credit, §28:5-102.
Insurance investments, §31-1371.02.
Sales, §28:2-325.
Letter-of-credit right.
Secured transactions, §28:9-102.
Letters, §§20-101, 21-2011.
Levy.
Taxation, §47-4471.
LGBTQ, §2-1381.
Homeless services, §4-751.01.
Liability, §§31-2501.03, 31-4101,
31-4202.
Corporations, §29-306.50.
Nonprofit corporations, §29-406.50.
License, §§31-2402, 38-1302.
Administrative procedure, §2-502.
Chemical testing for driving under the
influence, §50-1901.

DEFINED TERMS —Cont'd
License —Cont'd
Clean hands before receiving a license permit, §47-2861.
Emergency volunteer health practitioners, §7-2361.01.
General license law, §47-2851.01.
Insurance adjusters, §31-1631.02.
Insurance producers, §31-1131.02.
Insurance, securities, and banking, department of, §31-101.
License to carry pistol, §7-2509.01.
Motor vehicle registration, §50-1501.31.
Motor vehicle safety responsibility, §50-1301.02.
Non-health related occupations and professions licensure, §47-2853.01.
Professional corporations, §29-502.
Licensed, §47-2853.01.
Licensed child-placing agency.
Adoption proceedings, §4-1406.
Child and family services agency.
Criminal record checks, §4-1305.01.
Licensed insurer, §31-401.
Licensed nurse.
Nurse's rehabilitation program, §3-1251.01.
Licensed practitioner, §21-1201.
Licensed producer, §31-1801.
Licensed professional, §44-551.
Licensed securities, commodities or investment broker.
Telephone solicitation fraud, §22-3226.01.
Licensed veterinarian, §8-2001.
Licensed wildlife rehabilitator.
Wildlife protection, §8-2201.
Licensee.
Administrative fines, §2-1801.02.
Assisted living residences, §44-102.01.
Child development facilities, §7-2031.
Insurance adjusters, §31-1631.02.
Insurance premium finance companies, §31-1102.
License to carry pistol, §7-2509.01.
Money transmissions, §26-1001.
Mortgage lenders and brokers, §26-1101.
Real estate licenses, §42-1702.
Licensee in ordinary course of business.
Secured transactions, §28:9-321.
License information packet, §47-2851.01.
License service area.
Toll telecommunication service tax, §47-3901.

DEFINED TERMS —Cont'd
Licensing.
Administrative procedure, §2-502.
LID.
Department of the environment, §8-151.01.
Lie detector test, §32-901.
Lien.
Fraudulent transfers, §28-3101.
Leases, §28:2A-103.
Leases, UCC, §28:2A-103.
Motor vehicle liens, §50-1201.
Lien creditor.
Secured transactions, §28:9-102.
Uniform certificates of title for vessels, §50-1541.01.
Lien information, §50-1201.
Lien instrument.
Mortgage loan protection, §26-1151.01.
Life-cycle cost, §8-171.02.
Life-cycle cost analysis, §8-171.02.
Life insurance corporation, §41-102.
Life or health insurer, §31-2001.
Life-sustaining procedure, §7-621.
Lifetime registration offense.
Sex offender registration, §22-4001.
Light duty truck (LDT), §50-702.
Light duty vehicle (LDV), §50-702.
LIHEAP.
Food stamps, §4-261.01.
Limited common elements, §42-2002.
Condominiums, §42-1901.02.
Limited cooperative association, §29-1001.02.
Business organizations, §29-101.02.
Limited duty.
Police and firefighters retirement and disability, §5-631.
Limited English proficient/non-English proficient.
Foreign language services and documents, §2-1931.
Uniform per student funding formula, §38-2901.
Limited English speaking person.
Interpreters, §2-1901.
Limited-equity cooperative.
Real property assessment, §47-802.
Limited liability company.
Business organizations, §29-101.02.
Insurance investments, §31-1371.02.
Limited liability limited partnership.
Business organizations, §29-101.02.
Limited partnerships, §29-701.02.
Limited liability partnership.
Business organizations, §29-101.02.

DEFINED TERMS —Cont'd
Limited liability partnership
—Cont'd
Partnerships, §29-601.02.
Limited line of insurance.
Insurance producers, §31-1131.02.
Limited lines producer.
Insurance producers, §31-1131.02.
Limited partner.
Limited partnerships, §29-701.02.
Partnerships, §29-609.01.
Limited partnership, §29-701.02.
Business organizations, §29-101.02.
Partnerships, §29-609.01.
Limited station, §26-301.
Limousine.
Regulation of for-hire vehicles,
§50-301.03.
Linked deposit.
Investment and deposit of District
funds, §47-351.01.
Liquidating asset.
Principal and income, §28-4804.10.
**Liquid-immersed distribution
transformer.**
Energy efficiency standards,
§8-1771.06.
Literacy.
Charter schools, §38-1800.02.
Live birth, §7-201.
Living unit.
Continuing care retirement
communities, §44-151.01.
Living wage, §2-220.02.
Living Wage Act.
Wages and salaries, §32-1301.
Loan, §42-2701.02.
Universal banks, §26-1401.02.
Loan application, §26-1101.
Loan closing, §42-2401.
Loan documents, §42-2401.
Loan funds, §42-2401.
Loan officer.
Mortgage lenders and brokers,
§26-1101.
Loan processor or underwriter.
Mortgage lenders and brokers,
§26-1101.
Lobbying.
Ethics and government accountability,
§1-1161.01.
Lobbyist.
Ethics and government accountability,
§1-1161.01.
Local business enterprise.
Small and certified business enterprise
development and assistance,
§2-218.02.

DEFINED TERMS —Cont'd
Local education agency, §32-501.
Athletic equity, §38-841.01.
Interstate compact on educational
opportunity for military children,
§49-1101.03.
Nonpublic schools, §38-2561.01.
School-based budgeting and
accountability, §38-2801.01.
Special education student rights,
§38-2571.02.
State superintendent of education,
office of, §38-2601.02.
Testing integrity in public schools,
§§38-771.01, 38-2602.
Local exchange carrier, §34-2001.
Emergency and non-emergency
telephone system assessments
fund, §34-1801.
Local exchange service, §34-2001.
Emergency and non-emergency
telephone system assessments
fund, §34-1801.
Local food economy.
Food policy council, §48-311.
Locality.
Alcoholic beverages, §25-101.
Local law enforcement officer.
Killing law enforcement officer,
§22-2106.
Local limits.
Wastewater disposal systems,
§8-105.02.
**Locally assisted housing
accommodation for elderly
persons or persons with
disabilities.**
Pet ownership restriction in assisted
housing, §8-2031.
Locally grown.
Child and adult food program funding,
§38-281.
Food policy council, §48-311.
Schools and education, §38-821.01.
**Locally grown and unprocessed
foods.**
Healthy schools fund, §38-821.02.
Locally processed.
Schools and education, §38-821.01.
Local participating governments,
§9-1111.01.
**Local streets ward-based capital
projects.**
Budgets and budget estimates,
reprogramming policy, §47-362.
Capital project review and
reconciliation, §50-921.51.

DEFINED TERMS —Cont'd

Local telephone service.
Gross sales tax, §47-2001.

Location, §50-702.
Portable electronics insurance, §31-5051.01.

Lodge, §31-5301.

Lodge system, §31-5301.

Loitering.
Taxicabs, §50-301.28.

Long-term care facility, §7-701.01.

Long-term care insurance, §31-3601.

Long-term care ombudsman, §44-1001.01.

Long-term reform plan.
Charter schools, §38-1800.02.

Longtime resident business.
Small and certified business enterprise development and assistance, §2-218.02.

Loss, §31-2402.

Loss mitigation analysis.
Foreclosure mediation, §42-815.02.

Lot.
Business improvement districts, §2-1215.02.
Leases, UCC, §28:2A-103.
Sales, §28:2-105.
Southwest waterfront special assessment district, §47-895.01.
Special energy assessments, §47-895.31.

Lottery winnings.
Income tax withholding, §47-1812.08.

Low- and moderate-income area, §26-1201.

Low barrier shelter.
Homeless services, §4-751.01.

Low-emission vehicle (LEV), §50-702.

Lower grade investment.
Insurance investments, §31-1371.02.

Low Impact Development.
Department of the environment, §8-151.01.

Low-income, §§42-2801, 42-3401.03.
Affordable housing inventory comprehensive tracking plan, §42-2141.
Community development by financial institutions, §26-431.02.
Solar for All program, §8-1774.16.
Universal banks, §26-1401.02.

Low-income area.
Community development by financial institutions, §26-431.02.

Low-income District resident.
Job opportunity bank, §32-751.

DEFINED TERMS —Cont'd

Low-income families, §42-3503.01.
District of Columbia housing authority, §6-201.

Low-income household.
Anacostia waterfront development zone, §2-1226.02.
Inclusionary zoning, §6-1041.01.
Preservation and rehabilitation of government-supported housing, §42-2851.02.
Tax abatement for new residential developments, §47-857.01.

Low-income housing tax credit program, §47-4801.

Low-income individual.
Rental housing conversion and sale, §42-3402.04.

Low income persons, §§42-2103, 42-2701.02.

Low-income resident.
Wireless network antennae franchise agreement, §34-1731.02.

Low level policy form, §31-3301.01.

Low-level radioactive waste, §8-1501.

Low-performing school.
Early warning and support system, §38-751.02.

Low phosphorous fertilizer.
Anacostia River cleanup and protection fertilizer act, §8-104.02.

Low-to-moderate income area.
Investment and deposit of District funds, §47-351.01.

LRA.
Walter Reed Army Medical Center, §10-1901.

LRAP.
Access to justice initiative program, §4-1701.01.

LSDBE.
Retail development incentives, §2-1217.71.

L street building.
Tax abatement for mixed-income housing projects, §47-857.06.

Lump-sum credit for retirement, §11-1561.

Lump-sum credit for survivor annuity, §11-1561.

Lump-sum payments and settlements, §4-205.30.

MAA.
Department of health care finance, §7-771.01.

Machine gun, §7-2551.01.
Firearms control, §7-2501.01.

DEFINED TERMS —Cont'd
Machine gun —Cont'd
Weapons, §22-4501.
Machine-readable and searchable.
Procurement practices, §2-351.04.
Mail cover.
Metropolitan police.
Investigations concerning first
amendment activities,
§5-333.02.
Mail opening.
Metropolitan police.
Investigations concerning first
amendment activities,
§5-333.02.
Mainline primary feeder.
Electric company infrastructure
improvement financing,
§34-1311.01.
Maintenance accountability method.
Green buildings, §6-1451.01.
Maintenance agreement.
Waterfront Park at the Yards,
§10-1801.
Maintenance or use, §§31-2402,
47-2302.
Major action, §8-109.02.
Major appliances, §47-1401.
Major construction.
School-based budgeting and
accountability, §38-2801.01.
Majority interest.
Clean hands before receiving a license
or permit, §47-2861.
Majority of co-owners, §42-2002.
Major medical equipment.
Health planning and development
agency, §44-401.
Make public, §2-1401.02.
Maker.
Negotiable instruments, §28:3-103.
Malice, §22-3225.01.
Maltreatment, §16-2301.
Mammogram, §31-2901.
Managed care organization,
§1-623.01.
Managed care provider.
Medical assistance program,
§1-307.02.
Managed care system.
Coverage for habilitative services for
children, §31-3271.
Substance abuse insurance coverage,
§31-3101.
Manage financial resources, §21-2011.
Management.
Special purpose financial captive
insurance companies, §31-3932.02.

DEFINED TERMS —Cont'd
Management employee.
Merit system, §1-614.11.
Management fee, §42-3501.03.
Management supervisory service.
Merit system, §1-603.01.
Manager.
Budgets and budget estimates,
§47-355.01.
Limited liability companies,
§29-801.02.
Unincorporated nonprofit associations,
§29-1102.
**Manager-managed limited liability
company.**
Limited liability companies,
§29-801.02.
Managing general agent, §31-1501.
Mandarin Oriental Hotel project.
Real property tax exemptions,
§§47-902, 47-1002.
Recordation tax, §42-1102.
Sales tax exemption, §47-2005.
Mandarin TIF bonds.
Real property tax exemptions,
§§47-902, 47-1002.
Recordation tax, §42-1102.
Sales tax exemption, §47-2005.
Mandatory control level event.
Health insurance regulatory
standards, §31-3451.01.
Mandatory control level RBC,
§31-2001.
Health insurance regulatory
standards, §31-3451.01.
Mandatory deductions, §4-205.05.
Mandatory income interest.
Principal and income, §28-4801.02.
**Mandatory-minimum term of
incarceration.**
Impaired operation or driving,
§50-2206.01.
Manufacture.
Alcoholic beverage control, §25-101.
Controlled substances, §48-901.02.
Drug manufacture and distribution
licensure, §48-701.
Drug-related evictions, §42-3601.
Medical marijuana, §7-1671.01.
Manufactured home.
Secured transactions, §28:9-102.
Manufactured-home transaction.
Secured transactions, §28:9-102.
Manufacturer, §7-2531.01.
Access to prescription drugs,
§48-831.02.

DEFINED TERMS —Cont'd

Manufacturer —Cont'd

Assistive technology device warranty, §28-4031.

Deceptive labeling, §22-3214.01.

Extended manufacturer responsibility for electronic waste, §8-1041.01.

Fire-standard-compliant cigarettes, §7-1751.

Microstamping of semiautomatic pistols, §7-2505.03.

Practice of pharmaceutical detailing, §3-1201.02.

Tobacco tax, §47-2401.

Manufacturing, §42-3101.

Maple syrup urine disease, §7-832.

Marginalized populations of Sudan.

Employees retirement program management, §1-335.01.

Margin of victory.

Post-election audits, §1-1001.09a.

Marijuana, §48-901.02.

Medical marijuana, §7-1671.01.

Marital status, §2-1401.02.

Marketer.

Retail electric competition and consumer protection, §34-1501.

Marketing.

Access to prescription drugs, §48-831.02.

Marketing agreement, §36-301.01.

Marketing contract.

Limited cooperative associations, §29-1007.01.

Market manager, §37-101.

Market participants.

Retail electric competition and consumer protection, §34-1501.

Market power, §34-2001.

Market share.

Extended manufacturer responsibility for electronic waste, §8-1041.01.

Market value.

Insurance investments, §31-1371.02.

Market vendor, §37-101.

Mark, marks, §36-151.

Marriage and family therapy, practice of, §3-1201.02.

Mask.

Protests targeting a residence, §22-2751.

Massage therapy, practice of, §3-1201.02.

Mass mailing.

Official correspondence, §2-701.

DEFINED TERMS —Cont'd

Mastectomy.

Women's rights regarding certain health insurance coverage, §31-3831.

Master association.

Condominiums, §42-1901.02.

Master developer.

Southwest waterfront bond financing, §2-1217.131.

Southwest waterfront special assessment district, §47-895.01.

Master juror list, §11-1902.

Master settlement agreement.

Tobacco master settlement agreement, §7-1801.01.

Tobacco master settlement agreement enforcement, §7-1803.02.

Tobacco settlement financing, §7-1831.01.

Master tenant.

Rental housing conversion, opportunity to purchase, §42-3404.02.

Matching contributions.

Employer-assisted housing program, §42-2501.

Material.

Procurement claims, §2-381.01.

Material change.

Small and certified business enterprise development and assistance, §2-218.02.

Material default.

Public-Private Partnership Administration Fund, §2-271.01.

Material fact, §42-1702.

Material financial interest.

Corporations, §29-306.70.

Material interest.

Corporations, §29-301.21.

Nonprofit corporations, §29-401.02.

Material involvement.

Ethics and government accountability, §1-1161.01.

Material litigation.

Money transmissions, §26-1001.

Material mechanical defect, §50-501.

Material relationship.

Corporations, §29-301.21.

Nonprofit corporations, §29-401.02.

Material support or resources.

Anti-terrorism act of 2002, §22-3152.

Maternal health facility.

Breastmilk bank and lactation support, §7-881.01.

INDEX

DEFINED TERMS —Cont'd
Maternity center, §7-832.
Health-care facility, hospice and home
care licensure, §44-501.
Newborn heart screening, §7-857.01.
Matriculation, §2-1401.02.
Matter.
Rules of professional conduct,
ProfCond Rule 1.0.
Matter-of-right.
Rental housing, §42-3401.03.
Mattress, §8-501.
Maximum possible rental income,
§42-3501.03.
Maximum special assessment.
Southwest waterfront special
assessment district, §47-895.01.
**Maximum standard utility
allowance.**
Food stamps, §4-261.01.
Mayor.
Adoption, Adoption Rule 2.
Arts and humanities commission,
§39-202.
Automobile consumer, §50-501.
Business improvement districts,
§2-1215.02.
Charitable solicitation, §44-1701.
Chemical testing for driving under the
influence, §50-1901.
Civil asset forfeiture, §41-301.
Clean hands before receiving a license
permit, §47-2861.
College access assistance, public school
program, §38-2702.
Controlled substances act, §48-901.02.
District of Columbia housing
authority, §6-201.
Electric company infrastructure
improvement financing,
§34-1311.01.
Emergency volunteer health
practitioners, §7-2361.01.
Fish and game, §22-4332.
Gross sales tax, §47-2001.
Historic landmarks, §6-1102.
HIV testing of certain criminal
offenders, §22-3901.
Hospital and medical services
corporation, §31-3501.
Impaired operation or driving,
§50-2206.01.
Inheritance and estate taxes,
§47-3701.
Installment sales of motor vehicles,
§50-601.

DEFINED TERMS —Cont'd
Mayor —Cont'd
Insurance companies, §47-2601.
Interstate family support, §46-351.02.
Investment and deposit of District
funds, §47-351.01.
Job growth tax credit, §47-1807.51.
Life and health insurance guaranty
association, §31-5401.
Motor fuel tax, §47-2302.
Motor vehicle safety responsibility,
§50-1301.02.
Nonprofit corporations locating in
emerging commercial
neighborhoods, §47-857.11.
Parking regulation, §50-2602.
Pawnbrokers, §47-2884.01.
Real property assessment, §47-802.
Rental of airspace, §10-1121.01.
Rental of public space, §10-1101.01.
Scholarships for opportunity and
results (SOAR) act, §38-1853.13.
Smoking restrictions, §7-1702.
Streets and alleys, §9-201.01.
Superior court, tax division, §47-3301.
Temporary assistance for needy
families.
Grandparent caregiver subsidies,
§4-251.01.
Tobacco tax, §47-2401.
Traffic regulation, §50-2201.02.
Transportation infrastructure
improvement GARVEE bonds,
§9-107.51.
Wages and salaries, §32-1301.
Weights and measures, §37-201.29.
Workplace fraud, §32-1331.01.
**Mayor's committee on persons with
disabilities,** §2-1431.01.
Meals.
Schools and education, §38-821.01.
Measurable amount.
Chemical testing for driving under the
influence, §50-1901.
Impaired operation or driving,
§50-2206.01.
Mediation, §16-4201.
Foreclosure, §42-815.02.
United States District Court mediation
program, USDistCt LCvR 84.2.
Mediation administrator.
Foreclosure mediation, §42-815.02.
Mediation certificate.
Foreclosure mediation, §42-815.02.
Mediation communication, §16-4201.
Mediation election form.
Foreclosure mediation, §42-815.02.

I-412

DEFINED TERMS —Cont'd
Mediation party, §16-4201.
Mediation report.
Foreclosure mediation, §42-815.02.
Mediation services.
Foreclosure mediation, §42-815.02.
Mediator, §16-4201.
Medicaid.
Medicaid and special education reform fund, §4-204.52.
Medicaid hospital inpatient 2016-2017 rate supplement, §44-662.18.
Medicaid hospital outpatient 2016-2017 supplemental payment, §44-661.11.
Nursing facility assessment, §47-1261.
Office of Medicaid operations reform, §4-204.12.
Stevie Sellows quality improvement fund, §47-1270.
Tobacco settlement trust fund, §7-1811.03.
Medicaid legislation, §4-801.
Medicaid program, §4-801.
Department of mental health, §7-1131.02.
Disability services, department on, §7-761.02.
Medicaid services, §44-551.
Medical assistance administration.
Department of mental health, §7-1131.02.
Disability services, department on, §7-761.02.
Medical assistance program.
Department of mental health, §7-1131.02.
Disability services, department on, §7-761.02.
Medical care, §31-3301.01.
Medical clearance, §28-4001.
Hearing aid dealers, §28-4001.
Medical control system.
Emergency medical services, §7-2341.01.
Medical device, §47-2885.02.
Medical emergency, §31-2801.
Leave of absence, §1-612.04.
Opportunity accounts, §1-307.61.
Medical employees of the District of Columbia, §2-411.
Medical expenses, §4-501.
Medical facility, §22-1314.01.
Health occupations licensure, registration or certification.
Mandatory adverse event reporting, §7-161.

DEFINED TERMS —Cont'd
Medical facility —Cont'd
Prisoners, use of restraints on pregnant women, §24-276.01.
Youth rehabilitation services department, use of restraints on pregnant youths, §2-1515.51.
Medical laboratory technicians, practice of, §3-1201.02.
Medical laboratory technology, practice of, §3-1201.02.
Medical liability captive trust fund, §1-307.81.
Medically or psychologically necessary, §31-3101.
Medically underserved area.
Health professional recruitment program, §7-751.01.
Medical malpractice insurer.
Insurance rate regulation, §31-2701.
Medical marijuana, §7-1671.01.
Medical marijuana product, §7-1671.01.
Medical or surgical benefits.
Substance abuse insurance coverage, §31-3101.
Medical professional.
Chemical testing for driving under the influence, §50-1901.
Medical service plan.
Hospital and medical services corporation, §31-3501.
Insurance holding companies, §31-701.
Medical support notice.
Medical support enforcement, §46-251.01.
Medical, surgical, and hospitals services and supplies, §1-623.01.
Medical waste, §8-901.
Wastewater disposal systems, §8-105.02.
Medicare, §31-3701.
Medicaid and special education reform fund, §4-204.52.
Office of Medicaid operations reform, §4-204.12.
Tobacco settlement trust fund, §7-1811.03.
Voluntary withdrawal by health benefit plan carriers, §31-3151.
Medicare supplement policy, §31-3701.
Medication, §21-1201.
Student health care, §38-651.01.
Medication action plan.
Student health care, §38-651.01.

DEFINED TERMS —Cont'd
Medication advisory committee.
Medication advisory committee receiving gifts or remuneration prohibition act, §48-842.02.
Medicinal chemicals, §47-2885.02.
Medicine, practice of, §3-1201.02.
Medium grade investment.
Insurance investments, §31-1371.02.
Meet essential requirements for physical health or safety, §21-2011.
Meeting.
Alcoholic beverage control board, §25-204.01.
Open meetings act, §2-574.
Member.
Business improvement districts, §2-1215.02.
Cooperative associations, §29-902.
Health benefit plan members bill of rights, §44-301.01.
Limited cooperative associations, §29-1001.02.
Limited liability companies, §29-801.02.
Nonprofit corporations, §29-401.02.
Police and firefighters retirement and disability, §§5-631, 5-701.
Presumptive disability or death of fire and emergency medical services employees, §5-651.
Unincorporated nonprofit associations, §29-1102.
Member agency.
Homeless services, §4-751.01.
Member-governed corporation.
Nonprofit corporations, §29-401.50.
Member insurer, §31-5501.
Life and health insurance guaranty association, §31-5401.
Member jurisdiction, §§47-2302, 50-1507.01.
Member-managed limited liability company.
Limited liability companies, §29-801.02.
Member of a religious order or diocesan priest, §21-2202.
Member of family.
Merit system.
Health benefits, §1-621.03.
Life insurance, §1-622.04.
Member of record.
Business improvement districts, §2-1215.02.

DEFINED TERMS —Cont'd
Member of the beneficiary's family.
Custodial trusts, §19-1101.
Member of the minor's family, §21-301.
Member organization.
Captive insurance companies, §31-3931.01.
Member representative, §44-301.01.
Membership.
Nonprofit corporations, §29-401.02.
Membership corporation.
Nonprofit corporations, §29-401.02.
Membership exchange.
Nonprofit corporations, §29-409.01.
Member's interest.
Limited cooperative associations, §29-1001.02.
Members meeting.
Limited cooperative associations, §29-1001.02.
Members of the DCHAPD.
District of Columbia housing authority, §6-201.
Members of the decedent's family.
Rental housing conversion, opportunity to purchase, §42-3404.02.
Member state.
Interstate compact on educational opportunity for military children, §49-1101.03.
Memorandum of agreement.
Walter Reed Army Medical Center, §10-1901.
Walter Reed Medical Center site development, §2-1227.01.
Memorandum of understanding.
Capital project support fund, §1-325.151.
Mental health benefits.
Substance abuse insurance coverage, §31-3101.
Mental health facility, §7-1201.01.
Mental health information, §7-1201.01.
Mental health professional, §7-1201.01.
Mental health services.
Department of mental health, §7-1131.02.
Mental health consumer's rights, §7-1231.02.
Mental health supports.
Department of mental health, §7-1131.02.

DEFINED TERMS —Cont'd
Mental health supports —Cont'd
Hospitalization of persons with mental illness, §21-501.
Mental health consumer's rights, §7-1231.02.
Mental illness, §§21-501, 31-3101.
Hospitalization of persons with mental illness, Federal reservations, persons found in, §21-901.
Rights of persons with intellectual disability, §7-1301.03.
Mental incapacity, §4-205.42.
Mental injury.
Family court proceedings, §16-2301.
Mentally ill person.
Financial responsibility for care of hospitalized person, §21-586.
Merchandise, §47-2807.
Merchant, §§27-101, 28-3901.
Consumer protection procedures, §28-3901.
Sales, §28:2-104.
Merchantable product, §36-301.01.
Merchant bank, §26-831.02.
Merchant lessee.
Leases, UCC, §28:2A-103.
Merger.
Corporations, §29-309.01.
Entity transactions, §29-201.02.
Nonprofit corporations, §29-409.01.
Merging entity.
Entity transactions, §29-201.02.
Merit personnel act.
Ethics and government accountability, §1-1161.01.
Merit system, §1-603.01.
Metabolic disorder, §7-832.
Metal halide lamp.
Energy efficiency standards, §8-1771.01.
Metal level.
Health benefit exchange authority, §31-3171.01.
Meter data management system.
Electric light and power companies, §34-1561.
Methamphetamine, §48-901.02.
Metropolitan police department.
Civil defense, §7-2204.
District of Columbia housing authority, §6-201.
Metropolitan police force, §10-505.05.
Metropolitan Washington airport, §9-1003.
Microreproduction equipment, §2-1701.

DEFINED TERMS —Cont'd
Microstamp-ready.
Microstamping of semiautomatic pistols, §7-2505.03.
Mid-high performing school.
Early warning and support system, §38-751.02.
Midnight deadline.
Bank deposits and collections, §28:4-104.
Military equipment.
Employees retirement program management, §1-335.01.
Military installation.
Interstate compact on educational opportunity for military children, §49-1101.03.
Military-overseas ballot.
Military and overseas voters, §1-1061.02.
Military service, §5-701.
Milk bank.
Breastmilk bank and lactation support, §7-881.01.
Mineral extraction activities.
Employees retirement program management, §1-335.01.
Miniature.
Alcoholic beverages, §25-101.
Minimization procedures.
Metropolitan police.
Investigations concerning first amendment activities, §5-333.02.
Minimum custody status, §24-251.01.
Minimum risk.
Pesticide education and control, §8-431.
Minimum status vote.
Benefit corporations, §29-1301.02.
Minimum Wage Revision Act.
Wages and salaries, §32-1301.
Ministerial acts, §42-1702.
Minnesota-Benning nonprofit zone.
Nonprofit corporations locating in emerging commercial neighborhoods, §47-857.11.
Minor.
Anatomical gifts, §7-1531.01.
Child custody, §16-914.
Compulsory school attendance, §38-201.
Criminally negligent storage of firearms, §7-2507.02.
Domestic relations actions, DomRel Rule 2.

DEFINED TERMS —Cont'd
Minor —Cont'd
Domestic relations proceedings, DomRel Rule 2.
Family court proceedings, §16-2301.
Graffiti, §22-3312.05.
Impaired operation or driving, §50-2206.01.
Intrafamily offenses, §16-1001.
Juvenile curfew act, §2-1542.
Medical marijuana, §7-1671.01.
Mental health consumer's rights, §7-1231.02.
Non-resuscitation procedures for EMS, §7-651.01.
Obscenity, §22-2201.
Public assistance, §4-201.01.
Sex offender registration, §22-4001.
Sexual abuse, §22-3001.
Sexual performances using minors, §22-3101.
Transfers to minors, §21-301.
Minority.
Minority and women-owned business assessment program, §2-214.01.
Minority group.
Community development by financial institutions, §26-431.02.
Minority-owned business.
Community development by financial institutions, §26-431.02.
Minor offense.
Criminal records sealing, §16-801.
Minor student, §38-601.
Charter schools, §38-1800.02.
Misappropriation, §36-401.
Misbranded, §8-401.
Mixed-income community.
District of Columbia housing authority, §6-201.
Mixed population housing.
District of Columbia housing authority, §6-201.
Mixed-use building.
Real property tax abatement for qualified high technology companies, §47-811.03.
Real property tax exemptions, qualified high technology company interior renovation tax rebate, §47-4665.
Mixed-use space.
Green buildings, §6-1451.01.
MLB team.
Ballpark, §10-1601.05.
Ballpark construction hard and soft costs cap, §10-1601.31.

DEFINED TERMS —Cont'd
Mobile application.
Elections, §1-1001.02.
Mobile device.
Elections, §1-1001.02.
Mobile telecommunication service.
Toll telecommunication service tax, §47-3901.
Mobile telephone.
Distracted driving, §50-1731.02.
Mobile unit, §26-301.
Model codes.
Construction codes, §6-1401.
Model law.
Mediation, §16-4210.
Model year, §50-702.
Moderate-income, §42-2801.
Community development by financial institutions, §26-431.02.
Universal banks, §26-1401.02.
Moderate-income area.
Community development by financial institutions, §26-431.02.
Moderate-income families.
District of Columbia housing authority, §6-201.
Moderate-income household.
Anacostia waterfront development zone, §2-1226.02.
Inclusionary zoning, §6-1041.01.
Moderate income persons, §§42-2103, 42-2701.02.
Moderate-to-vigorous physical activity.
Schools and education, §38-821.01.
Modification.
Uniform child custody proceedings, §16-4601.01.
Modified guarantee contracts.
Insurance investments, §31-1371.02.
Money, §15-901.
UCC, §28:1-201.
Money market mutual fund.
Insurance investments, §31-1371.02.
Money of the claim, §15-901.
Money transmissions, §26-1001.
Monitor, §21-1201.
Month, §51-101.
Monthly pay, §1-623.01.
Moody's corporate bond yield average.
Life and health insurance guaranty association, §31-5401.
Mortgage, §§21-2011, 42-2701.02.
Foreclosure mediation, §42-815.02.
Secured transactions, §28:9-102.

DEFINED TERMS —Cont'd

Mortgage broker, §26-1101.
  Mortgage loan protection, §26-1151.01.
Mortgage lender, §§26-1101,
  42-2701.02.
Mortgage loan, §§26-1101, 42-2701.02.
  Community development by financial
    institutions, §26-431.02.
  Insurance investments, §31-1371.02.
  Investment and deposit of District
    funds, §47-351.01.
  Mortgage loan protection, §26-1151.01.
Mortgage loan originator.
  Mortgage lenders and brokers,
    §26-1101.
Mortgage uniform licensing form.
  Mortgage lenders and brokers,
    §26-1101.
**Most commonly used prescription
  drugs,** §48-804.51.
Most recent work, §51-101.
Motion to quash.
  Criminal procedure, CrimPro Rule 54.
Motor carrier, §§47-2302, 50-1507.01.
Motorcycle, §31-2402.
Motor fuel, §36-301.01.
Motor vehicle, §50-1501.01.
  Abandoned and unlawfully parked
    vehicles, §50-2421.02.
  Automobile consumer protection,
    §50-501.
  Chemical testing for driving under the
    influence, §50-1901.
  Child restraint system, §50-1702.
  Driver's license, §50-1401.01.
  Food delivery insurance, §50-101.
  Gross sales tax, §47-2001.
  Illegal dumping enforcement, §8-901.
  Impaired operation or driving,
    §50-2206.01.
  Installment sales, §50-601.
  Liens on motor vehicles or trailers,
    §50-1201.
  Mandatory seat belt usage, §50-1801.
  Motor fuel tax, §47-2302.
  Motor vehicle theft prevention
    commission, §3-1351.
  No-fault motor vehicle insurance,
    §31-2402.
  Non-motorized user contributory
    negligence, §50-2204.51.
  Open access to collision data and
    information, §50-1951.01.
  Parking regulation, §50-2602.
  Regional transportation, §9-1103.01.
  Rental vehicle tax, §50-1505.01.

DEFINED TERMS —Cont'd

Motor vehicle —Cont'd
  Safety responsibility act, §50-1301.02.
  Salvage, flood and junk vehicles,
    §50-1331.01.
  Strict liability for release of hazardous
    waste during transport, §8-1441.
  Traffic adjudication, §50-2301.02.
  Traffic regulation, §50-2201.02.
  Unauthorized use of motor vehicle,
    §22-3215.
  Vehicle inspection fee, §50-1108.
  Vehicle insurance enforcement,
    §5-114.01.
Motor vehicle accident victim,
  §31-2402.
Motor vehicle fleet owner.
  Traffic ticket adjudication,
    §50-2303.04a.
Motor vehicle fuels, §47-2302.
Motor vehicle record.
  Personal information from motor
    vehicle records and accident
    reports, §50-1401.01b.
**Mount Vernon Triangle nonprofit
  zone.**
  Nonprofit corporations locating in
    emerging commercial
    neighborhoods, §47-857.11.
MPD.
  Alcoholic beverage licenses,
    reimbursable details, §25-798.
  First amendment assemblies,
    §5-335.01.
  Forensic sciences department,
    §5-1501.01.
  License to carry pistol, §7-2509.01.
  Metropolitan police.
    School safety division, §§5-132.01,
      5-132.21.
  Open access to collision data and
    information, §50-1951.01.
  Sexual assault victim advocates,
    §14-312.
  Victims of crime, §23-1907.
  Victims of crime, sexual assault
    response, §4-561.01.
MS4.
  Department of the environment,
    §8-151.01.
MS4 permit.
  DDOT stormwater retention credit
    fund, §50-921.22.
  Department of the environment,
    §8-151.01.
Multilateral development bank.
  Insurance investments, §31-1371.02.

DEFINED TERMS —Cont'd
Multiple dwelling.
Lead level water testing, §42-3251.
Multiple-party account.
Nonprobate transfers on death,
§19-602.01.
Multiunit.
Bees, §8-1825.02.
**Multiyear capital improvements
plan,** §47-336.
Multiyear plan, §47-318.
Multiyear plan modification, §47-318.
Municipal matter.
Mayors, §1-301.21.
Municipal wastewater, §8-103.01.
Murder, §22-2101.
Mutual aid.
Emergency medical services,
§7-2341.01.
Mutual foreign protection order.
Interstate enforcement of domestic
violence proceedings, §16-1041.
Mutual fund.
Insurance investments, §31-1371.02.
Mutual insurer.
Captive insurance companies,
§31-3931.01.
NAIC, §31-301.
Health insurance regulatory
standards, §31-3451.01.
Insurance investments, §31-1371.02.
Insurance producers, §31-1131.02.
Risk-based capital, §31-2001.
Named insured, §31-2402.
Bicycle insurance policies, §50-531.
Name of the settlor or testator,
§28:9-503.
Narcotic drugs, §§24-702, 48-901.02.
Narcotic trafficking, §2-1542.
National bank.
Universal banks, §26-1401.02.
National bike registry, §50-1609.
National certifying organization.
Air conditioner and refrigeration
mechanics, business licenses,
§47-2853.202.
National Children's Island, §10-1401.
**National drug code registration
number.**
Access to prescription drugs,
§48-831.02.
Nationally approved examination,
§3-402.
**National pretreatment standards for
wastewater,** §8-105.02.
National register.
Historic landmarks, §6-1102.

DEFINED TERMS —Cont'd
National register of historic places.
Historic landmarks, §6-1102.
**Nationwide mortgage licensing
system and registry.**
Mortgage lenders and brokers,
§26-1101.
Natural conditions.
Department of the environment,
§8-151.01.
Natural disaster, §28-4101.
Natural gas supplier.
Retail natural gas supplier licensing
and consumer protection,
§34-1671.02.
Natural gas supplier choice.
Retail natural gas supplier licensing
and consumer protection,
§34-1671.02.
Natural outlet.
Wastewater disposal systems,
§8-105.02.
Natural parent.
Adoption, Adoption Rule 2.
Naturopathic medicine, practice of,
§3-1201.02.
Naturopathic physician.
Medical marijuana, §7-1671.01.
Navigator.
Health benefit exchange authority,
§31-3171.01.
Near fatality.
Child fatality or near fatality,
§4-1303.31.
Necessary in the public interest.
Historic landmarks, §6-1102.
Negative trend, §31-2001.
Neglect, §7-1901.
Mental health consumer's rights,
§7-1231.02.
Neglected child, §16-2301.
Child abuse and neglect, §4-1301.02.
Negligence.
Taxation penalties, §47-4211.
Negligently.
Health data privacy, §7-245.
Negligent treatment, §16-2301.
Negotiable instrument, §28:3-104.
Uniform commercial code, §28:3-104.
Negotiate.
Insurance producers, §31-1131.02.
Negotiation.
Negotiable instruments, §28:3-201.
Procurement practices, §2-351.04.
Neighborhood cluster.
School-based budgeting and
accountability, §38-2801.01.

DEFINED TERMS —Cont'd

Neighborhood planning council,
§2-1501.

Nematode, §8-401.

Net charges.
Compensating use tax, §47-2201.
Gross sales tax, §47-2001.

Net direct premiums.
Captive insurance companies,
§31-3931.01.

Net direct written premiums,
§31-5501.

Net energy metering.
Retail electric competition and
consumer protection, §34-1501.

Net income, §47-1803.01.
Principal and income, §28-4801.02.

Net job growth.
Job growth tax credit, §47-1807.51.

Net landed weights.
Sales, §28:2-321.

Net new District FTE.
The Advisory Board Company, real
property tax abatement,
§47-4665.01.

Net operating loss.
Income tax, §47-1801.04.

Net operating loss deduction.
Income tax, §47-1801.04.

Net premium receipts, §§31-4202,
47-2601.

**Net premium receipts or
consideration received,** §31-1201.
Health benefit exchange authority,
§31-3171.01.

Net rentable square feet.
Business improvement districts,
§2-1215.02.

Net resident revenue.
Nursing facility assessment, §47-1261.

Net retained liability.
Title insurers, §31-5031.01.

Net savings.
Cooperative associations, §29-902.

Network.
Automated teller machine, §26-131.02.

Network element, §34-2001.

Network plan, §31-3301.01.

Net worth, §31-3401.

Newborn, §7-832.
Newborn safe haven, §4-1451.01.

New communities initiative.
Housing production trust fund, bond
issues, §42-2812.01.

New communities initiative projects.
Income tax secured bonds, §47-340.26.

DEFINED TERMS —Cont'd

New construction.
Anacostia waterfront environmental
standards, §2-1226.32.
Green buildings, §6-1451.01.

New convention center.
Washington convention and sports
authority, §10-1202.01.
Eminent domain, §10-1202.31.

New convention center hotel.
Washington convention and sports
authority, §10-1202.01.
Eminent domain, §10-1202.31.
Financing, §10-1221.01.

New convention center hotel fund.
Washington convention and sports
authority.
Financing, §10-1221.01.

New convention center hotel site.
Washington convention and sports
authority.
Eminent domain, §10-1202.31.
Financing, §10-1221.01.

**New convention center hotel TIF
area,** §47-4609.
Washington convention and sports
authority.
Financing, §10-1221.01.

New debtor.
Secured transactions, §28:9-102.

New evidence.
Protection of innocence act, §22-4131.

New hire.
Qualified social electronic commerce
companies tax abatements,
§47-1818.01.

New hire wage credit.
Qualified social electronic commerce
companies tax abatements,
§47-1818.01.

New hire wage credit cap.
Qualified social electronic commerce
companies tax abatements,
§47-1818.01.

Newly hired.
Qualified social electronic commerce
companies tax abatements,
§47-1818.01.

New motor vehicle, §50-501.

News media, §16-4701.

New value.
Secured transactions, §28:9-102.

New York avenue metro project.
New York avenue metrorail benefit
area, §47-881.

**New York avenue metrorail benefit
area,** §47-881.

DEFINED TERMS —Cont'd
New York avenue metrorail benefit area account, §47-881.
Nexus-vendor.
Gross sales tax, §47-2001.
Nightclub.
Alcoholic beverages, §25-101.
911 system.
Emergency and non-emergency telephone system assessments fund, §34-1801.
NMLSR.
Mortgage lenders and brokers, §26-1101.
No arrival, no sale.
Sales, §28:2-324.
NoMa nonprofit zone.
Nonprofit corporations locating in emerging commercial neighborhoods, §47-857.11.
Nominated person.
Letters of credit, §28:5-102.
Non-appropriated budget, §47-382.
Nonbinding reservation agreement.
Condominiums, §42-1901.02.
Nonbusiness income.
Income tax, §47-1801.04.
Noncash proceeds.
Secured transactions, §28:9-102.
Noncommercial registered agent.
Business organizations, §29-101.02.
Nonconformity.
Assistive technology device warranty, §28-4031.
Noncontrolling interest.
Rental housing conversion, opportunity to purchase, §42-3404.02.
Non-conventional mortgage loan, §26-1101.
Non-deadly force, §24-261.01.
Non-depository financial institution.
Banks and financial institutions, §26-551.02.
Noneconomic loss, §31-2402.
Non-English proficiency.
Foreign language services and documents, §2-1931.
Non-English speaking person.
Interpreters, §2-1901.
Multilingual election materials, §1-1031.01.
Nonessential.
Pesticide education and control, §8-431.
Nonfederal governmental plan, §31-3301.01.

DEFINED TERMS —Cont'd
Nonfiling entity.
Business organizations, §29-101.02.
Nonforfeiture benefit.
Long-term care insurance, §31-3601.
Nonhospital residential facility, §31-3101.
Noninsured financial institution.
Investment and deposit of District funds, §47-351.01.
Non-issuer transactions.
Security agents and broker, §31-5601.01.
Nonmanagement personnel.
Merit system, §1-614.11.
Nonmembership corporation.
Nonprofit corporations, §29-401.02.
Nonmember state.
Interstate compact on educational opportunity for military children, §49-1101.03.
Non-motorized user.
Non-motorized user contributory negligence, §50-2204.51.
Non-participating manufacturer.
Tobacco master settlement agreement enforcement, §7-1803.02.
Nonparty participant.
Collaborative law, §16-4002.
Mediation, §16-4201.
Nonpoint source, §8-103.01.
Nonprobate transfers.
Liability of nonprobate transferees for creditor claims and statutory allowances, §19-601.02.
Nonprofit, §§38-1302, 38-1419.
Nonprofit corporation, §§26-1101, 29-401.02.
Business organizations, §29-101.02.
Nonprofit corporation act.
Charter schools, §38-1800.02.
Nonprofit developer.
Homestead housing provision, §42-2103.
Nonprofit housing developer, §42-2801.
Nonprofit organization.
Consumer protection procedures, §28-3901.
Nonpublic special education school or program, §38-2561.01.
Nonqualified foreign entity.
Business organizations, §29-104.01.
Nonqualified withdrawal.
College savings program, §47-4501.
Nonrecord, §2-1701.

DEFINED TERMS —Cont'd

Nonregional association, §26-1201.

Nonregional savings and loan holding company, §26-1201.

Nonregistered foreign corporation.
Nonprofit corporations, §29-401.02.

Nonregistered foreign entity.
Business organizations, §29-101.02.

Nonresidential.
Green buildings, §6-1451.01.

Nonresidential building, §8-171.02.

Nonresidential rental unit.
Submetering, §34-1551.

Nonresident insurance producer, §31-1131.02.

Nonresidents, §§50-1301.02, 50-1901.
Chemical testing for driving under the influence, §50-1901.
Income tax, §47-1801.04.
Inheritance and estate taxes, §47-3701.

Nonresident's operating privilege, §§50-1301.02, 50-1901.

Nonresident student.
Charter schools, §38-1800.02.

Non-responsible person.
Brownfield revitalization, §8-631.02.

Nonroad vehicle, §50-702.

Nonscheduled benefits.
Workers' compensation, §32-1501.

Nonschool-based personnel.
Merit system, §1-603.01.

Nontransient.
Real property assessment, §47-803.
Real property taxes, classes of property, §47-813.

Non-tuition expenses.
DC promise program, §38-2751.

Non-U.S. insurer, §31-2201.
United States branch domestication, §31-2301.

Non-U.S. title insurer.
Title insurers, §31-5031.01.

Nonviolent offenses, §16-2305.02.
Sentencing, §24-403.01.

Normal average retail price, §28-4101.

Normalization principle, §7-1301.03.

Normal weekly hours of work.
Shared work unemployment compensation program, §51-171.

North hall, §37-101.

North plaza, §37-101.

Notarial officer, §42-141.

Note, §42-2701.02.
Mortgage loan protection, §26-1151.01.

DEFINED TERMS —Cont'd

Notice, §7-2802.
Mortgage loan protection, §26-1151.01.
Taxation, waiver or abatement, §47-4222.
UCC, §28:1-202.
Uniform certificates of title for vessels, §50-1541.01.

Notice amount.
Mechanics' and materialmen's liens, §40-301.03.

Notice of default on residential mortgage.
Foreclosure mediation, §42-815.02.

Notice of intent.
Mechanics' and materialmen's liens, §40-301.03.

Notice of intention to foreclose residential mortgage.
Foreclosure mediation, §42-815.02.

Notice to withhold.
Child support enforcement, §46-201.

Notification date.
Secured transactions, §28:9-611.

Notifies.
UCC, §28:1-202.

NPDES.
Wastewater disposal systems, §8-105.02.

NPDES permit.
Wastewater disposal systems, §8-105.02.

NTID.
National technical institute for the deaf, §38-2402.01.

Nuclear material.
Anti-terrorism act of 2002, §22-3152.

Nude performance.
Alcoholic beverages, §25-101.

Nudity, §22-2201.

Nuisance, §42-3601.
Litter control, §8-803.

Number portability, §34-2001.

Nurse-midwife.
Newborn heart screening, §7-857.01.

Nurse staffing agencies, §44-1051.02.

Nursing facility, §47-1261.

Nursing home, §44-1001.01.
Continuing care retirement communities, §44-151.01.
Health-care facility, hospice and home care licensure, §44-501.
Practice of nursing home administration, §3-1201.02.

Nursing home administration, practice of, §3-1201.02.

DEFINED TERMS —Cont'd
Nursing personnel.
Nurse staffing agencies, §44-1051.02.
OAG.
First amendment assemblies,
§5-335.01.
Oak Hill youth center, §7-1131.02.
Oath.
Criminal procedure, CrimPro Rule 54.
Delinquent minors, JuvProc Rule 101.
Domestic relations actions, DomRel
Rule 2.
Object category.
Budget reprogramming policy,
§47-361.
Object class.
Budget reprogramming policy,
§47-361.
Objectionable color, wastewater,
§8-105.02.
Obligated bank.
Negotiable instruments, §§28:3-312,
28:3-411.
Obligations.
District of Columbia housing
authority, §6-201.
Insurance investments, §31-1371.02.
Procurement claims, §2-381.01.
Obligee.
Child support enforcement, §46-201.
Interstate family support, §46-351.02.
Obligor, §46-201.
Delinquent taxpayers, §47-4481.
Interstate family support, §46-351.02.
Secured transactions, §28:9-102.
Occupant, §42-3601.
Self-service storage facilities, §40-401.
Occupation, §32-1002.
Occupational therapy, practice of,
§3-1201.02.
Occupied.
Real property taxes, classes of
property, §47-813.
Vacant buildings, §42-3131.05.
OCE.
Regulation of taxicabs, §50-301.03.
OCFO.
Capital project support fund,
§1-325.151.
OCME.
Victims of crime, sexual assault
response, §4-561.01.
OCP.
Procurement practices, §2-351.04.
OCS.
Regulation of taxicabs, §50-301.03.

DEFINED TERMS —Cont'd
OCTO.
Wireless network antennae franchise
agreement, §34-1731.02.
Off-duty days.
Police and fire departments, §5-1304.
Offense.
Bail and pretrial detention, §23-1331.
HIV testing of certain criminal
offenders, §22-3901.
Offer, §38-1302.
Condominiums, §42-1901.02.
Offeror.
Procurement practices, §2-351.04.
Office.
Office of first source compliance,
§2-219.32.
Office building.
Minimum wage, §32-1002.
Office of adjudication.
Consumer protection procedures,
§28-3901.
Office of consumer protection.
Consumer protection procedures,
§28-3901.
Office of human rights.
Disability rights, §2-1431.01.
Office of the Attorney General.
Interstate family support, §46-351.02.
Officer, §31-2501.03.
Condominiums, §42-1901.02.
Corporations, §29-306.50.
District of Columbia housing
authority, §6-201.
Nonprofit corporations, §§29-401.02,
29-406.50.
Police and fire departments, §5-1304.
Professional corporations, §29-508.
Official.
Protection of District public officials,
§22-851.
Official action, §22-711.
Official capacity.
Corporations, §29-306.50.
Nonprofit corporations, §29-406.50.
Official custody.
Sexual abuse, §22-3001.
Official duty, §22-711.
Official in the executive branch.
Ethics and government accountability,
§1-1161.01.
Official in the legislative branch.
Ethics and government accountability,
§1-1161.01.
Official mail.
Official correspondence, §2-701.

DEFINED TERMS —Cont'd
Official name.
Streets and alleys, §9-201.01.
Official of a political party.
Ethics and government accountability,
§1-1161.01.
Official proceeding, §22-711.
Obstructing justice, §22-721.
Official residence.
Mayor's official residence commission,
§1-331.02.
Off-label use.
Off-label use of prescription
medication, §48-841.02.
Offset agreement, §47-143.
Offsetting.
Budget reprogramming policy,
§47-361.
Offshore facility, §8-103.01.
OHCR.
Regulation of taxicabs, §50-301.03.
Oil-related activities.
Employees retirement program
management, §1-335.01.
OIML.
Sustainable energy, §8-1773.01.
Olmstead compliance plan.
Disability rights, §2-1431.01.
Olympic games.
Chesapeake regional Olympic games
authority, §2-1131.
Ombudsman, §7-701.01.
Insurance, securities, and banking,
department of, §31-101.
Mental health department, §7-1131.02.
Ombudsman program.
Mental health department, §7-1131.02.
On consignment.
Artist protection, §28-5101.
On-cycle tax preference.
Chief financial officer, tax
transparency, §1-301.156.
On duty.
Government employee engagement in
political activity, §1-1171.01.
One-call center, §34-2701.
Ongoing financing costs.
Electric company infrastructure
improvement financing,
§34-1311.01.
Online instruction.
Educational licensure commission,
§38-1302.
Online presence.
Educational licensure commission,
§38-1302.

DEFINED TERMS —Cont'd
Onshore facility, §8-103.01.
OPC.
Electric company infrastructure
improvement financing,
§34-1311.01.
Open container.
Alcoholic beverages, §25-101.
Open government office.
Open meetings act, §2-574.
Open investigation.
Crime investigation records, §5-113.31.
Open meetings act.
Ethics and government accountability,
§1-1161.01.
Public-Private Partnership
Administration Fund, §2-271.01.
Open solid waste facility, §8-1051.
Open video system.
Office of cable television, film, music,
and entertainment amendment
act of 2015, §34-1251.03.
Operate and operated.
Motor vehicle registration,
§50-1501.01.
Operate, operating, §38-1302.
Operating agency.
Performance based budget, §47-308.01.
Operating agreement.
Limited liability companies,
§29-801.02.
Operating budget.
Budget reprogramming policy,
§47-361.
Operating expenses, §42-3501.03.
Shelter and transitional housing for
victims of domestic violence fund,
§4-521.
Operational.
Medical liability captive insurance
agency, §1-307.81.
Operation area, §8-1051.
Operations and maintenance.
Procurement practices, §2-351.04.
Operator, §§31-2402, 50-1501.01.
Automated teller machine, §26-131.02.
Bicycles, §50-1609.
Body art establishments, business
licenses, §47-2809.01.
Child restraint seats, §50-1702.
Horse-drawn carriages, §8-2001.
Juvenile curfew, §2-1542.
Personal delivery devices pilot
program, §50-1551.
Public-Private Partnership
Administration Fund, §2-271.01.

DEFINED TERMS —Cont'd
Operator —Cont'd
Self-service storage facilities, §40-401.
Traffic adjudication, §50-2301.02.
Underground storage tanks, §8-113.01.
Vehicle insurance enforcement,
§5-114.01.
Water pollution, §8-103.01.
Opiate, §48-901.02.
Opioid antagonist.
Overdose, seeking help for victim,
§7-403.
Opium, §48-901.02.
Opium poppy, §48-901.02.
OPM, §37-101.
Opportunity account, §1-307.61.
Opportunity account office,
§1-307.61.
Opportunity account program,
§1-307.61.
Opportunity account reserve fund,
§1-307.61.
Option.
Insurance investments, §31-1371.02.
Optometry, practice of, §3-1201.02.
Oral communications, §23-541.
Oral language services.
Foreign language services and
documents, §2-1931.
Order, §2-502.
Banks and financial institutions,
§26-551.02.
Negotiable instruments, §28:3-103.
Office of administrative hearings,
§2-1831.01.
Order to withhold.
Child support enforcement, §46-201.
Ordinary care.
Negotiable instruments, §28:3-103.
Ordinary wear and tear.
Rent control, §42-3502.17.
Organ, §1-623.01.
Organic fertilizer.
Anacostia River cleanup and
protection fertilizer act, §8-104.02.
Organic law.
Business organizations, §29-101.02.
Organic record.
Nonprofit corporations, §29-401.02.
Organic rules.
Business organizations, §29-101.02.
Organization, §§7-2501.01, 21-2011.
Statutory trusts, §29-1207.01.
UCC, §28:1-201.
Organizational document.
Special purpose financial captive
insurance companies, §31-3932.02.

DEFINED TERMS —Cont'd
Organizational document —Cont'd
Statutory trusts, §29-1207.01.
Organized health care arrangement.
Department of mental health,
§7-1131.02.
Organized sporting events, §7-1702.
Organizer.
Limited cooperative associations,
§29-1001.02.
Limited liability companies,
§29-801.02.
**Organizing committee for the
Olympic games.**
Chesapeake regional Olympic games
authority, §2-1131.
Organ procurement organization.
Anatomical gifts, §7-1531.01.
Original debtor.
Secured transactions, §28:9-102.
Original package.
Tobacco tax, §47-2401.
Original source.
Procurement claims, §2-381.01.
Originator.
Funds transfers, §28:4A-104.
Originator's bank.
Funds transfers, §28:4A-104.
Orphan, §38-304.
ORPP.
Regulation of taxicabs, §50-301.03.
OSSE.
Athletic equity, §38-841.01.
Pre-kindergarten programs,
§38-271.01.
Special education student rights,
§38-2571.02.
Student health care, medication,
§38-651.01.
Testing integrity in public schools,
§38-771.01.
Other electronic device.
Distracted driving, §50-1731.02.
Other health professional.
Health professional recruitment
program, §7-751.01.
Other income.
Child support enforcement, §46-201.
**Other income which is derived from
the housing accommodation,**
§42-3501.03.
Other obligations, §42-2701.02.
Other primary caregiver.
Tuition of nonresidents, §38-304.
Other programming service.
Office of cable television, film, music,
and entertainment amendment
act of 2015, §34-1251.03.

DEFINED TERMS —Cont'd
Other public right-of-way.
Bicycles, §50-1609.
Other tobacco product.
Tobacco, §7-1721.01.
Tobacco tax, §47-2401.
**OTO Hotel at Constitution Square
project.**
Real property tax exemptions,
§47-4636.
**OTO Hotel at Constitution Square
property.**
Real property tax exemptions,
§47-4631.
Otolaryngologist, §28-4001.
Hearing aid dealers, §28-4001.
OUC.
Stroke system of care, §44-1151.
Out-of-school suspension.
Pre-kindergarten programs,
§38-271.01.
Out of service order.
Commercial drivers' licenses, §50-401.
Uniform classification and commercial
driver's license, §50-401.
Out-of-state.
Automated teller machine, §26-131.02.
Out-of-state bank, §26-732.
Automated teller machine, §26-131.02.
Out-of-state credit union.
Automated teller machine, §26-131.02.
Out-of-state national bank, §26-732.
Out-of-state state bank, §26-732.
Outpatient gross patient revenue.
Medicaid hospital outpatient 2016-
2017 supplemental payment,
§44-661.11.
Outpatient services, §31-3101.
Outpatient treatment facility,
§31-3101.
Outside the District.
Interstate family support, §46-351.02.
Outstanding debt.
Income tax secured bonds, §47-340.26.
Outstanding payment instrument.
Money transmissions, §26-1001.
Overconcentration.
Alcoholic beverages, §25-101.
Overdose.
Overdose, seeking help for victim,
§7-403.
Overissue.
Investment securities, §28:8-210.
Overseas.
Sales, §28:2-323.
Overseas voter.
Military and overseas voters,
§1-1061.02.

DEFINED TERMS —Cont'd
Over-the-counter drug, §47-2885.02.
OVS.
Victims of crime, sexual assault
response, §4-561.01.
Owner, §§31-2402, 47-2302.
Acquisition and disposal of abandoned
and deteriorated property,
§42-3171.01.
Animal control, §8-1801.
Apparent owner of unclaimed
property, §41-102.
Business improvement districts,
§2-1215.02.
Capper/Carrollsburg PILOT.
Payments in lieu of taxes, §47-4611.
Center Leg Freeway (interstate 395)
PILOT area.
Payments in lieu of taxes, §47-4637.
Civil asset forfeiture, §41-301.
Commercial piracy, §22-3214.
Dangerous dogs, §8-1901.
Drug, firearm, or prostitution-related
nuisance abatement, §42-3101.
Graffiti abatement, §42-3141.01.
Horse-drawn carriages, §8-2001.
Human Rights Commission,
§2-1401.02.
Insanitary buildings, §6-918.
International motor vehicle
registration plan agreements,
§50-1507.01.
Lead-hazard prevention and
elimination, §8-231.01.
Lead level water testing, §42-3251.
Liens on motor vehicles and trailers,
§50-1201.
Life and health insurance guaranty
association, §31-5401.
Mechanics' and materialmen's liens,
§40-301.03.
Motor vehicle registration,
§50-1501.01.
Motor vehicle safety responsibility,
§50-1301.02.
Payments in lieu of taxes, §47-1052.
PILOT agreements, §1-308.01.
Private contractor and subcontractor
prompt payment act, §27-131.
Real property taxes, §47-802.
Rental housing conversion and sale,
§42-3401.03.
Rental of public space, §10-1101.01.
Rental vehicle tax, §50-1505.01.
Rhode Island Metro Plaza PILOT.
Payments in lieu of taxes, sales tax
exemption, §47-4613.

DEFINED TERMS —Cont'd
Owner —Cont'd
Salvage, flood and junk vehicles,
§50-1331.01.
Smoke detectors, §6-751.01.
Southwest waterfront special
assessment district, §47-895.01.
Streets and alleys, §9-201.01.
Unclaimed property, §41-102.
Underground storage tanks, §8-113.01.
Uniform certificates of title for vessels,
§50-1541.01.
Vacant buildings, §42-3131.05.
Vehicle insurance enforcement,
§5-114.01.
Water and sewer services amnesty
program, §34-2301.
Waterfront Park special assessment
district, §47-895.21.
Water pollution, §8-103.01.
Owner liability.
Corporations, §29-301.02.
Owner of record.
Uniform certificates of title for vessels,
§50-1541.01.
Owner-paid areas.
Submetering, §34-1551.
Ownership.
Income tax, §47-1801.04.
Owner's property.
Business improvement districts,
§2-1215.02.
Pacific Islander.
Office of Asian and Pacific Islander
affairs, §2-1372.
**Package of services for digitally-
disadvantaged residents.**
Wireless network antennae franchise
agreement, §34-1731.02.
Paid leave.
Right to sick and safe leave,
§32-131.01.
Paint.
Paint stewardship, §8-233.01.
Paint stewardship assessment,
§8-233.01.
Panel.
Child abuse and neglect, §4-1301.02.
Nonpublic schools, §38-2561.01.
Paper, §22-1801.
Paper document.
Real property electronic recording,
§42-1231.
Paraphernalia.
Medical marijuana, §7-1671.01.
Parcel.
Payments in lieu of taxes, §47-1052.

DEFINED TERMS —Cont'd
Parent, §32-1501.
Anatomical gifts, §7-1531.01.
Captive insurance companies,
§31-3931.01.
Charter schools, §38-1800.02.
Compulsory school attendance,
§38-201.
Disability compensation, §1-623.01.
Parental leave, §32-1201.
Promotion or retention of students,
§38-781.01.
Public assistance, §4-201.01.
Scholarships for opportunity and
results (SOAR) act, §38-1853.13.
Special education student rights,
§38-2571.02.
Standby guardianship, §16-4802.
Tuition of nonresidents, §38-304.
Parent and child relationship,
§16-2352.
Parenting classes, §16-2301.
**Parent who is principal household
income earner,** §4-201.01.
Parity bonds.
Income tax secured bonds, §47-340.26.
Park.
Traffic regulation, §50-2201.02.
Parking.
Alcoholic beverages, §25-101.
Drainage, §8-205.
Public space rental and utilization,
§10-1101.01.
Parking facilities, §§50-2502, 50-2602.
Parking garage unit.
DC-USA project tax exemptions,
§47-4606.
Park partner agreement.
Parks and recreation, §10-301.
**Park Place at Petworth, Highland
Park, and Highland Park Phase
II projects.**
Real property tax exemptions,
§47-4629.
Parkside Terrace project.
Parkside Terrace development project
tax exemptions, §47-4607.
Parkside Terrace property.
Parkside Terrace development project
tax exemptions, §47-4607.
Part.
Anatomical gifts, §7-1531.01.
Partially covered fleet, §50-702.
Participant, §§1-702, 3-602, 31-3301.01.
Access to justice initiative program,
§4-1701.01.

DEFINED TERMS —Cont'd
Participant —Cont'd
Athletic equity, §38-841.01.
Brownfield revitalization, §8-631.02.
Captive insurance companies,
§31-3931.01.
Employer-assisted housing program,
§42-2501.
Participant contract.
Captive insurance companies,
§31-3931.01.
Participate.
Foreign language services and
documents, §2-1931.
Participating eligible student.
Scholarships for opportunity and
results (SOAR) act, §38-1853.13.
Participating employer.
Shared work unemployment
compensation program, §51-171.
Participating manufacturer.
Tobacco master settlement agreement
enforcement, §7-1803.02.
Participating private school.
Schools and education, §38-821.01.
Participating provider, §31-3401.
Department of mental health,
§7-1131.02.
Participating retail pharmacy.
Access to prescription drugs,
§48-831.02.
Participation rate.
Athletic equity, §38-841.01.
Particular matter.
Ethics and government accountability,
§1-1161.01.
Parties, §42-2401.
Parties in interest.
Uniform fiduciaries act, §21-1722.
Partisan.
Government employee engagement in
political activity, §1-1171.01.
Partisan political group.
Government employee engagement in
political activity, §1-1171.01.
Partisan political office.
Government employee engagement in
political activity, §1-1171.01.
Partner.
Limited partnerships, §29-701.02.
Partnerships, §§29-601.02, 29-609.01.
Rules of professional conduct,
ProfCond Rule 1.0.
Partnership, §29-601.02.
Extended manufacturer responsibility
for electronic waste, §8-1041.01.

DEFINED TERMS —Cont'd
Partnership —Cont'd
Income tax, §47-1801.04.
New Town at Capital City Market
revitalization, §6-1062.02.
Workforce housing production
program, §6-1061.02.
Partnership agreement, §29-601.02.
Limited partnerships, §29-701.02.
Partnership at will, §29-601.02.
Partnership council.
Department of mental health,
§7-1131.02.
Partnership interest, §29-601.02.
**Partnership program for affordable
housing.**
District of Columbia housing
authority, §6-201.
**Partner's interest in the
partnership.**
Partnerships, §29-601.02.
Party, §2-502.
Attorneys communicating with
opposing party, ProfCond Rule
4.2.
Bullying, §2-1535.01.
Collaborative law, §16-4002.
Corporations, §29-306.50.
Delinquent minors, JuvProc Rule 101.
Electronic delivery and posting of
insurance documents, §31-651.01.
Insurance holding companies, §31-701.
Negotiable instruments, §28:3-103.
Nonprobate transfers on death,
§19-602.01.
Nonprofit corporations, §29-406.50.
Office of administrative hearings,
§2-1831.01.
UCC, §28:1-201.
Uniform adult guardianship and
protective proceedings jurisdiction
act, §21-2401.02.
Party in interest.
Police officers, firefighters and
teachers retirement, §1-901.02.
Public employees retirement,
§1-626.04.
Public employees retirement program
management, §1-702.
Party to a membership exchange.
Nonprofit corporations, §29-409.01.
Party to a merger.
Corporations, §29-309.01.
Nonprofit corporations, §29-409.01.
Party to a share exchange.
Corporations, §29-309.01.

DEFINED TERMS —Cont'd
Party who is not related or subordinate.
Uniform fiduciaries act, §21-1722.
Par value.
Condominiums, §42-1901.02.
Passenger.
Bicycles, §50-1609.
Passenger surcharge.
Regulation of for-hire vehicles, §50-301.03.
Passenger vehicle, §31-2402.
Fleet management, publicly-owned vehicles, §50-211.01.
Passing grade.
Promotion or retention of students, §38-781.01.
Pass through, §8-105.02.
Pasteurization.
Breastmilk bank and lactation support, §7-881.01.
Patient, §§22-3803, 24-702.
Monitoring prescription drugs, §48-853.01.
Non-resuscitation procedures for EMS, §7-651.01.
Patient care report.
Fire departments, §5-401.
Patronage.
Limited cooperative associations, §29-1001.02.
Patron member.
Limited cooperative associations, §29-1001.02.
Pawnbroker, §§7-2531.01, 47-2884.01.
Pay-for-success contracts, §2-211.01.
Paying agent.
Income tax secured bonds, §47-340.26.
Payment, §4-801.
Alcoholic beverages, credit sales, §25-731.
Income tax withholding, §47-1812.08.
Nonprobate transfers on death, §19-602.01.
Payment bond.
Procurement practices, §2-351.04.
Payment date.
Funds transfers, §28:4A-401.
Payment in lieu of taxes, §47-1052.
Capper/Carrollsburg PILOT, §47-4611.
Rhode Island Metro Plaza PILOT.
Payments in lieu of taxes, sales tax exemption, §47-4613.
Payment instrument.
Money transmissions, §26-1001.
Payment intangible.
Secured transactions, §28:9-102.

DEFINED TERMS —Cont'd
Payment on arrival.
Sales, §28:2-321.
Payment order.
Funds transfers, §28:4A-103.
Payments in lieu of taxes.
PILOT agreements, §1-308.01.
Payor.
Income tax withholding, §47-1812.08.
Simultaneous deaths, §19-501.
Payor bank.
Bank deposits and collections, §28:4-105.
Payroll period.
Income tax, §47-1801.04.
Pedestrian.
Non-motorized user contributory negligence, §50.2204.51.
Personal delivery devices pilot program, §50-1551.
Pediatric health facility.
Breastmilk bank and lactation support, §7-881.01.
Pediatric health provider.
Breastmilk bank and lactation support, §7-881.01.
Peer review, §§31-3101, 44-801.
Peer review body, §44-801.
PEG.
Office of cable television, film, music, and entertainment amendment act of 2015, §34-1251.03.
Penal institution.
Prison contraband, §22-2603.01.
Prisoners, use of restraints on pregnant women, §24-276.01.
Pending.
Home Rule act, §1-201.03.
PERB.
District of Columbia housing authority, §6-201.
Performance, §22-3101.
Performance-based budget.
Budget and financial management, §47-308.01.
Performance bond.
Procurement practices, §2-351.04.
Performance measures.
Merit system, §1-614.11.
Performance plan.
Merit system, §1-614.11.
Performance report.
Merit system, §1-614.11.
Performance standards, §8-171.02.
Perjury, §22-2402.
Permanent guardianship.
Guardianship of minors, §16-2382.

DEFINED TERMS —Cont'd
Permanently incapacitated inmate,
§24-461.
Permanent supportive housing.
Homeless services, §4-751.01.
Permissible distributee.
Uniform trust code, §19-1301.03.
Permissible investments.
Money transmissions, §26-1001.
Permit.
Clean hands before receiving a license
permit, §47-2861.
Permitted investments.
Special purpose financial captive
insurance companies, §31-3932.02.
Person, §21-2011.
Administrative fines, §2-1801.02.
Administrative procedure, §2-502.
Adult protective services, §7-1901.
Alcoholic beverages, §25-101.
Alternative fuel technology, §50-702.
Anatomical gifts, §7-1531.01.
Arbitration, revised act, §16-4401.
Asbestos contractors, §8-111.01.
Athlete agent, §47-2887.01.
Automated teller machine, §26-131.02.
Banks and financial institutions,
§26-551.02.
Bees, §8-1825.02.
Bicycle insurance policies, §50-531.
Boiler inspections, §2-102.
Boxing and wrestling commission,
§3-602.
Brownfield revitalization, §8-631.02.
Business improvement districts,
§2-1215.02.
Business licenses, §§47-2807,
47-2851.01.
Business organizations, §29-101.02.
Captive insurance companies,
§31-3931.01.
Certified capital companies, §31-5231.
Charitable solicitations, §44-1701.
Check cashing businesses, §26-301.
Child care facilities, §7-2031.
Child care services assistance fund,
§7-2001.
Child home day care insurance
coverage, §31-4001.
Childhood lead poisoning screening
and reporting, §7-871.02.
Closing-out sales, §47-2101.
Collaborative law, §16-4002.
Commercial property energy
conservation, §8-1772.01.
Compensating-use tax, §47-2201.

DEFINED TERMS —Cont'd
Person —Cont'd
Condominiums, §42-1901.02.
Construction and demolition waste
recycling accountability, §8-1071.
Consumer credit service organizations,
§28-4601.
Consumer protection procedures,
§28-3901.
Controlled substances, §48-901.02.
Credit service organizations, §28-4601.
Custodial trusts, §19-1101.
Delinquent debts to the District,
recovery, §1-350.01.
Educational licensure commission,
§38-1302.
Electronic transactions, uniform act,
§28-4901.
Emergency and non-emergency
telephone system assessments
fund, §34-1801.
Emergency volunteer health
practitioners, §7-2361.01.
Energy plan of District of Columbia,
§8-171.02.
Environmental covenants, §8-671.01.
Ethics and government accountability,
§1-1161.01.
Examination of insurance companies,
§31-1401.
Fiduciary security transfers, §28-2901.
Fire and casualty insurance,
§31-2501.03.
Foreign-money claim, §15-901.
Fraudulent conveyances, §28-3101.
Fraudulent transfers, §28-3101.
Funeral directors, §3-402.
Gas stations, §36-301.01.
Grant administration, §1-328.11.
Gross sales tax, §47-2001.
Hazardous materials transportation,
terrorism prevention, §8-1422.
Hazardous waste management,
§8-1302.
Health benefit plans reimbursement,
§31-3131.
Health care entity conversion act,
§44-602.
Health care facilities, interference
with or obstruction of,
§22-1314.01.
Health data privacy, §7-241.
Health maintenance organizations,
§31-3401.
Health occupation boards, §3-1201.01.
Health planning and development
agency, §44-401.

DEFINED TERMS —Cont'd
Person —Cont'd

Hearing aid dealers, §28-4001.

Horizontal property regimes, §42-2002.

Horse-drawn carriages, §8-2001.

Human Rights Commission, §2-1401.02.

Illegal dumping, §8-901.

Income taxes, §47-1801.04.

Insurance fraud, §22-3225.01.

Insurance holding companies, §31-701.

Insurance investments, §31-1371.02.

Insurance producers, §31-1131.02.

Insurers rehabilitation and liquidation proceedings, §31-1301.

Interstate depositions and discovery, §13-442.

Interstate family support, §46-351.02.

Landlord and tenant, §42-3501.03.

Liens on motor vehicles and trailers, §50-1201.

Life and health insurance guaranty association, §31-5401.

Life insurance companies, §31-4202.

Long-arm statute, §13-421.

Long-term care ombudsman, §7-701.01.

Mattresses, §8-501.

Mediation, §16-4201.

Medicaid service provider fraud, §4-801.

Mental health disclosures, §7-1201.01.

Milk container registration, §§36-128, 36-151.

Miss Utility, §34-2701.

Mortgage lenders and brokers, §26-1101.

Mortgage loan protection, §26-1151.01.

Motor vehicle financing, §50-601.

Motor vehicle registration, §50-1501.01.

Motor vehicle safety responsibility, §50-1301.02.

National Capital Housing Authority, §6-101.07.

Natural disaster price gouging, §28-4101.

No-fault motor vehicle insurance, §31-2402.

Nursing homes, §44-1001.01.

Office of cable television, film, music, and entertainment amendment act of 2015, §34-1251.03.

Offset program, §47-143.

Pawnbrokers, §47-2884.01.

Pensions and retirement funds, §1-801.02.

DEFINED TERMS —Cont'd
Person —Cont'd

Personal property taxes, §47-1521.

Pesticides, §8-401.

Pharmacists and pharmacies, §47-2885.02.

Police and firefighters medical care reimbursement, §5-601.

Prescription drugs, §48-804.51.

Principal and income, §28-4801.02.

Probate proceedings, Probate Rule 25.

Procurement claims against the District, §2-381.01.

Procurement practices, §2-381.07.

Property and liability insurance guaranty association, §31-5501.

Prudent management of institutional funds, §44-1631.

Public assistance penalties, §4-218.05.

Public utilities, §34-212.

Real estate brokers and salespersons, §42-1702.

Real property electronic recording, §42-1231.

Real property transfer tax, §47-901.

Recordation tax, §42-1101.

Rental housing, §42-3501.03.

Reporting of child sexual abuse, §22-3020.51.

Residential real property transfer excise tax, §47-1401.

Restraint of trade, §28-4501.

Retail natural gas supplier licensing and consumer protection, §34-1671.02.

Revolving credit accounts, §28-3701.

Safe needle distribution, §7-2851.

Salvage, flood and junk vehicles, §50-1331.01.

Savings and loan acquisitions, §26-1201.

Security agents and broker, §31-5601.01.

Security and fire alarm contractors, §7-2802.

Smoking, §7-1702.

Solid waste facility permits, §8-1051.

Statutory trusts, §29-1201.02.

Streamlined sales and use tax agreement, §1-301.121.

Strict liability for release of hazardous waste during transport, §8-1441.

Tax proceedings, §47-3301.

Theft of utility service, §22-3218.01.

Title insurance producers, §31-5041.01.

DEFINED TERMS —Cont'd
Person —Cont'd
Title insurers, §31-5031.01.
Tobacco tax, §§47-2401, 47-2402.01.
Toll telecommunication service tax, §47-3901.
Trade names, §47-2855.01.
Trade secrets, §36-401.
Transfers to minors, §21-301.
Transportation department, §50-921.01a.
UCC, §28:1-201.
Unauthorized practice of law, DCCtApp Rule 49.
Unclaimed property, §41-102.
Underground storage tanks, §8-113.01.
Unemployment compensation, §51-104.
Unfair insurance trade practices, §31-2231.01.
Uniform adult guardianship and protective proceedings jurisdiction act, §21-2401.02.
Uniform certificates of title for vessels, §50-1541.01.
Uniform child custody proceedings, §16-4601.01.
Uniform disclaimer of property interests act, §19-1502.
Uniform real property transfers on death, §19-604.02.
Uniform trust code, §19-1301.03.
Unit pricing, §28-5202.
Universal banks, §26-1401.02.
Vector-borne disease control, §8-2131.01.
Vital records, §7-201.
Wastewater disposal systems, §8-105.02.
Water pollution, §8-103.16.
Weapons, §22-4501.
Weights and measures, §37-201.30.
Workers' compensation, §32-1501.
Person acting as a parent.
Uniform child custody proceedings, §16-4601.01.
Personal appearance, §2-1401.02.
Personal care.
Voluntary leave transfer program, §1-612.31.
Personal care aide.
Nurse staffing agencies, §44-1051.02.
Personal fitness trainer, §3-1209.08.
Personal identifying information.
Anti-SLAPP, §16-5501.
Identity theft, §22-3227.01.
Stalking, §22-3132.

DEFINED TERMS —Cont'd
Personal information.
Personal information from motor vehicle records and accident reports, §50-1401.01b.
Personal injury, §4-501.
Personal injury protection, §31-2402.
Personal liability.
Limited liability companies, §29-809.01.
Limited partnerships, §29-710.01.
Personally identifiable information.
Cable television operators, protection of customer privacy, §34-1260.02.
Personal mobility device.
Impaired operation or driving, §50-2206.01.
Traffic regulation, §50-2201.02.
Personal notes, §7-1201.01.
Public assistance applicants, confidentiality of information, §4-209.04.
Personal or private information.
Child fatality or near fatality, §4-1303.31.
Personal property.
Self-service storage facilities, §40-401.
Title insurance producers, §31-5041.01.
Title insurers, §31-5031.01.
Personal representative.
Custodial trusts, §19-1101.
Department of mental health, §7-1131.02.
Inheritance and estate taxes, §47-3701.
Probate and administration proceedings, §20-101, Probate Rule 25.
Public assistance applicants, confidentiality of information, §4-209.04.
Transfers to minors, §21-301.
Personal risk liability, §31-4101.
Person at risk.
Lead-hazard prevention and elimination, §8-231.01.
Person closely affiliated with the employee.
Ethics and government accountability, §1-1161.01.
Person dissociated as a general partner.
Limited partnerships, §29-701.02.
Person entitled to enforce.
Negotiable instruments, §28:3-301.

DEFINED TERMS —Cont'd
Person entitled under the document.
 Documents of title, §28:7-102.
 Warehouse receipts, §28:7-403.
Person in the position of a seller.
 Sales, §28:2-707.
Personnel act.
 District of Columbia housing
  authority, §6-201.
Personnel authority, §1-604.06.
 Leave of absence, §1-612.04.
 Merit system, §1-603.01.
 Office of administrative hearings,
  §2-1831.01.
Person related to.
 Secured transactions, §28:9-102.
Person responsible, §8-1302.
Persons of low income.
 District of Columbia housing
  authority, §6-201.
Persons of moderate income.
 District of Columbia housing
  authority, §6-201.
**Persons with intellectual
 disabilities.**
 Disability services, department on,
  §7-761.02.
Persons with mental illness.
 Department of mental health,
  §7-1131.02.
**Persons with physical or mental
 disabilities, §7-1009.**
Person with a disability.
 Pet ownership restriction in assisted
  housing, §8-2031.
 Tenant assistance program,
  §42-3503.01.
Per student funding formula.
 Uniform per student funding formula,
  §38-2901.
Pest, §8-401.
 Pesticide education and control,
  §8-431.
Pesticide application.
 Pesticide education and control,
  §8-431.
Pesticide applicator, §8-401.
 Pesticide education and control,
  §8-431.
Pesticide dealer, §8-401.
Pesticide operator, §8-401.
 Pesticide education and control,
  §8-431.
Pesticide registration fee.
 Pesticide education and control,
  §8-431.

DEFINED TERMS —Cont'd
Pesticides, §8-401.
 Pesticide education and control,
  §8-431.
Pest management.
 Pesticide education and control,
  §8-431.
Petition.
 Charter schools, §38-1800.02.
 Conservators, §21-2011.
 Delinquent minors, JuvProc Rule 101.
 Uniform child abduction prevention
  act, §16-4604.02.
Petitioner.
 Intrafamily offenses, §16-1001.
Petroleum, §8-113.01.
Petroleum product, §36-301.01.
Petroleum resources.
 Employees retirement program
  management, §1-336.01.
Pharmaceutical company.
 Medication advisory committee
  receiving gifts or remuneration
  prohibition act, §48-842.02.
Pharmaceutical product, §3-1201.02.
 Pharmaceutical education program,
  §48-843.02.
 SafeRX evaluation act of 2008,
  §48-844.02.
 Unused pharmaceutical safe disposal,
  §48-851.01.
Pharmacist, §47-2885.02.
Pharmacy.
 Business licenses, §3-1201.02.
 Prescription drugs, §48-804.51.
Pharmacy benefits management.
 Access to prescription drugs,
  §48-831.02.
Pharmacy benefits manager.
 Access to prescription drugs,
  §48-831.02.
Pharmacy intern, §47-2885.02.
Pharmacy, practice of, §3-1201.02.
**Pharmacy technician trainee,
 §3-1207.51.**
Phased-in assessed value.
 Real property assessment, §47-802.
Phencyclidine, §48-901.02.
Phenmetrazine, §48-901.02.
Phenylketonuria, §7-832.
Phlebotomist, §3-1209.12.
Phonorecords, §22-3214.
Phosphate cleaners, §8-107.02.
PHSA.
 Health benefit exchange authority,
  §31-3171.01.

DEFINED TERMS —Cont'd

Physical characteristics of an abandoned vehicle.
Abandoned and unlawfully parked vehicles, §50-2421.02.

Physical custody.
Child custody, §16-914.
Third-party child custody, §16-831.01.
Uniform child custody proceedings, §16-4601.01.

Physical impairment, §32-1501.

Physical incapacity, §4-205.42.

Physical injury.
Bail and pretrial detention, §23-1331.
Family court proceedings, §16-2301.

Physical restraint.
Assisted living residences, §44-102.01.
Mental health consumer's rights, §7-1231.02.

Physical therapy assistants, practice by, §3-1201.02.

Physical therapy, practice of, §3-1201.02.

Physician, §§31-3101, 32-1501.
Anatomical gifts, §7-1531.01.
Department of mental health, §7-1131.02.
Disability compensation, §1-623.01.
Health professional recruitment program, §7-751.01.
Medical marijuana, §7-1671.01.

Physician assistant.
Medical marijuana, §7-1671.01.

Physician assistants, practice by, §3-1201.02.

PILOT.
Payment in lieu of taxes, §47-1052.
Center Leg Freeway (interstate 395) PILOT area, §47-4637.

PILOT agreement, §1-308.01.

PILOT parcel, §1-308.01.

PILOT period, §1-308.01.
Capper/Carrollsburg PILOT.
Payments in lieu of taxes, §47-4611.
Low-income housing tax credit, §47-4801.
Payment in lieu of taxes, §47-1052.
Center Leg Freeway (interstate 395) PILOT area, §47-4637.
Rhode Island Metro Plaza Pilot Area.
Payments in lieu of taxes, sales tax exemption, §47-4613.

Pilot program.
Retail electric competition and consumer protection, §34-1501.

PILOT revenues.
Southwest waterfront special assessment district, §47-895.01.

DEFINED TERMS —Cont'd

Pipeline company, §34-213.

Pistol, §7-2501.01.
Weapons, §22-4501.

PJM interconnection.
Renewable energy portfolio standards, §34-1431.

Placed for adoption, placement or being placed for adoption, §31-3301.01.

Placement disruption.
Child abuse and neglect, §4-1301.02.

Place of business.
Firearms, §7-2501.01.
Secured transactions, location of debtor, §28:9-307.
Weapons, §22-4501.

Place of employment, §32-802.
Health department, §7-741.01.

Place of primary use.
Toll telecommunication service tax, §47-3901.

Place of public accommodation, §2-1401.02.

Plan, §32-1101.
Corporations, §29-301.04.
Entity transactions, §29-201.02.
Hospital and medical services corporation, §31-3501.
Nonprofit corporations, §29-401.04.

Planned unit development.
Parks and recreation, §10-301.

Plan of conversion, §31-901.
Entity transactions, §29-201.02.

Plan of domestication.
Entity transactions, §29-201.02.

Plan of interest exchange.
Entity transactions, §29-201.02.

Plan of merger.
Entity transactions, §29-201.02.

Plan of operation, §31-4101.

Plan sponsor, §31-202.
Life and health insurance guaranty association, §31-5401.

Plant regulator, §8-401.

Plat, §10-1401.

Plat of condominium subdivision, §42-2002.

Playground, §§10-1401, 48-901.02.
Smoking restrictions, §7-1702.
Weapons, §22-4501.

Playing field.
Robert F. Kennedy Memorial Stadium, §3-343.02.

Plea in abatement.
Criminal procedure, CrimPro Rule 54.

DEFINED TERMS —Cont'd

Plea in bar.
Criminal procedure, CrimPro Rule 54.

PMD.
Impaired operation or driving, §50-2206.01.
Traffic regulation, §50-2201.02.

Pneumatic tires, §50-1501.01.

POD designation.
Nonprobate transfers on death, §19-602.01.

Podiatry, practice of, §3-1201.02.

Point.
Interest and usury, §28-3301.
Mortgage loan protection, §26-1151.01.

Point of care testing.
Clinical laboratory practitioners, qualifications for licensure, exemption, §3-1207.63.

Point-of-sale terminal, §26-131.02.

Point of service plan, §31-3401.

Point source, §8-103.01.

Police.
Child abuse and neglect, §4-1301.02.
Child and family services agency.
  Criminal record checks, §4-1305.01.
Reporting of child sexual abuse, §22-3020.51.

Police officer, §§8-2001, 42-2901.

Police or fire service, §5-701.

Police service, §10-505.05.

Policy.
Fire and casualty insurance, §31-2501.03.
Insurance demutualization, §31-901.
Long-term care insurance, §31-3601.
Regulation of casualty and other insurance rates, §31-2701.
Respectful language modernization, §2-631.
Title insurers, §31-5031.01.

Policy form, §31-3701.

Policy-writing agent, §31-2501.03.

Political action committee.
Ethics and government accountability, §1-1161.01.

Political activity.
Government employee engagement in political activity, §1-1171.01.

Political affiliation, §2-1401.02.

Political committee.
Ethics and government accountability, §1-1161.01.
Grant administration, §1-328.11.

Political contribution.
Government employee engagement in political activity, §1-1171.01.

DEFINED TERMS —Cont'd

Political party.
Ethics and government accountability, §1-1161.01.
Government employee engagement in political activity, §1-1171.01.
Grant administration, §1-328.11.

Political purpose.
Government employee engagement in political activity, §1-1171.01.

Pollutant, §§8-103.01, 8-105.02.

Polysomnographic technician, §3-1201.02.

Polysomnographic technologist, §3-1201.02.

Polysomnographic trainee, §3-1201.02.

Polysomnography, practice of, §3-1201.02.

Pooled or commingled real estate investment vehicle.
Employees retirement program management, §1-702.

Poppy straw, §48-901.02.

Portable communication device.
Prison contraband, §22-2603.01.

Portable electronics.
Portable electronics insurance, §31-5051.01.

Portable electronics insurance, §31-5051.01.

Portable electronics transactions.
Portable electronics insurance, §31-5051.01.

Portion.
Alcoholic beverages, §25-101.

Position, §32-601.

Position classification, §32-601.

Possess.
Sexual performances using minors, §22-3101.

Possessing.
Sexual performances using minors, §22-3101.

Possession.
Sexual performances using minors, §22-3101.
Tobacco tax, §47-2401.

Post-accident employee, §1-620.31.
Corrections employee mandatory substance abuse testing, §24-211.21.
Mandatory drug and alcohol testing of certain employees, §1-620.21.

Post-and-forfeit procedure.
First amendment assemblies, §5-335.01.

DEFINED TERMS —Cont'd

Postconsumer paint.
Paint stewardship, §8-233.01.

Post employment benefit programs.
Employees retirement program management, §1-702.
Police officers, firefighters and teachers retirement, §1-901.02.

Postpartum recovery.
Prisoners, use of restraints on pregnant women, §24-276.01.
Youth rehabilitation services department, use of restraints on pregnant youths, §2-1515.51.

Postproduction expenditure.
Motion pictures, §2-1204.11c.

Postsecondary, §38-1302.

Post-secondary institution.
Post-secondary preparation plan, §38-752.02.

Potential employee.
Discrimination, §32-1361.

Potential exposure.
Insurance investments, §31-1371.02.

Potentially competitive service.
Retail electric competition and consumer protection, §34-1501.

Potentially dangerous dog, §8-1901.

POTW.
Wastewater disposal systems, §8-105.02.

POTW treatment plant.
Wastewater disposal systems, §8-105.02.

Poverty line.
Scholarships for opportunity and results (SOAR) act, §38-1853.13.

Power, §§4-201.01, 42-1001.

Power boats, §9-309.

Power of arrest.
District of Columbia housing authority, §6-201.

Power of sale.
Foreclosure mediation, §42-815.02.

Power of withdrawal.
Uniform trust code, §19-1301.03.

Power production activities.
Employees retirement program management, §1-335.01.

PPA.
Department of health care finance, §7-771.01.

PPD.
Personal delivery devices pilot program, §50-1551.

Practical alternative route.
Hazardous materials transportation, terrorism prevention, §8-1422.

DEFINED TERMS —Cont'd

Practical nursing, practice of, §3-1201.02.

Practice by anesthesiologist assistants, §3-1201.02.

Practice by audiologist assistant, §3-1201.02.

Practice by nursing assistive personnel, §3-1201.02.

Practice by physical therapy assistants, §3-1201.02.

Practice by physician assistants, §3-1201.02.

Practice by physicians-in-training, §3-1201.02.

Practice by speech-language pathology assistant, §3-1201.02.

Practice by speech-language pathology clinical fellow, §3-1201.02.

Practice by surgical assistants, §3-1201.02.

Practice by trauma technologists, §3-1201.02.

Practice of acupuncture, §3-1201.02.

Practice of addiction counseling, §3-1201.02.

Practice of advanced practice registered nursing, §3-1201.02.

Practice of assisted living administration, §3-1201.02.

Practice of athletic training, §3-1201.02.

Practice of audiology, §3-1201.02.

Practice of certified public accounting, §47-2853.41.

Practice of chiropractic, §3-1201.02.

Practice of dental hygiene, §3-1201.02.

Practice of dentistry, §3-1201.02.

Practice of dietetics and nutrition, §3-1201.02.

Practice of funeral directing, §3-402.

Practice of home health care administration, §3-1201.02.

Practice of law.
Unauthorized practice of law, DCCtApp Rule 49.

Practice of marriage and family therapy, §3-1201.02.

Practice of massage therapy, §3-1201.02.

Practice of medicine, §3-1201.02.

Practice of naturopathic medicine, §3-1201.02.

Practice of nursing home administration, §3-1201.02.

DEFINED TERMS —Cont'd

Practice of occupational therapy, §3-1201.02.

Practice of optometry, §3-1201.02.

Practice of pharmaceutical detailing, §3-1201.02.

SafeRX evaluation act of 2008, §48-844.02.

Practice of pharmacy, §47-2885.02.

Practice of physical therapy, §3-1201.02.

Practice of podiatry, §3-1201.02.

Practice of polysomnography, §3-1201.02.

Practice of practical nursing, §3-1201.02.

Practice of professional counseling, §3-1201.02.

Practice of psychology, §3-1201.02.

Practice of registered nursing, §3-1201.02.

Practice of respiratory care, §3-1201.02.

Practice of social work, §3-1201.02.

Practice of speech-language pathology, §3-1201.02.

Practice of veterinary medicine, §3-1201.02.

Practice test.

State superintendent of education, office of, §38-2601.02.

Practitioner, §§22-3225.01, 47-2885.02, 48-901.02.

Monitoring prescription drugs, §48-853.01.

Preceding year.

Rental vehicle tax, §50-1505.01.

Pre-effective-date financing statement.

Secured transactions, §28:9-707.

Preemployment physical examination.

Fire and emergency medical services employees, §5-651.

Presumptive disability or death of fire and emergency medical services employees, §5-651.

Preexisting conditions, §31-3301.01.

Preexisting equity.

Housing production trust fund, §42-2801.

Preferred claim, §31-1301.

Preferred shares.

Corporations, §29-311.01.

Preferred stock.

Insurance investments, §31-1371.02.

DEFINED TERMS —Cont'd

Pregnant or parenting teen, §4-205.61.

Pre-k.

Pre-kindergarten programs, §38-271.01.

Pre-k act of 2008.

Child care facilities, §7-2031.

Pre-k age, §38-271.01.

Pre-k education services, §38-271.01.

Pre-k program, §38-271.01.

Premarital agreement, §46-501.

Premises address.

Revised real property tax sale, §47-1330.

Premium (insurance), §22-3225.01.

Premium cigar.

Cigarette tax, §47-2401.

Gross sales tax, §47-2001.

Tobacco tax, §47-2401.

Premium finance agreement, §31-1102.

Premium pay.

Police and fire departments, §5-1304.

Premium pay program.

Right to sick and safe leave, §32-131.01.

Premiums, §§31-3301.01, 31-5301, 47-2601.

Life and health insurance guaranty association, §31-5401.

Premiums written, §31-5002.

Premium tax credit.

Certified capital companies, §31-5231.

Premium tax credit allocation request.

Certified capital companies, §31-5231.

Preschool.

Child and adult food program funding, §38-281.

Preschooler.

Child and adult food program funding, §38-281.

Prescriber.

Monitoring prescription drugs, §48-853.01.

Off-label use of prescription medication, §48-841.02.

Prescription drugs, §48-804.51.

Prescription, §21-1201.

Health occupations boards, §3-1201.02.

Practice of pharmacy, §3-1201.02.

Prescription drug monitoring program, §48-853.01.

Presentation.

Letters of credit, §28:5-102.

DEFINED TERMS —Cont'd

Presenter.
Letters of credit, §28:5-102.

Presenting bank.
Bank deposits and collections, §28:4-105.

Presentment.
Negotiable instruments, §28:3-501.

Present sales.
Sales, §28:2-106.

Present value.
Leases, UCC, §28:2A-103.
UCC, §28:1-201.

Presidential elector.
National popular vote interstate agreement, §1-1051.01.

Presidential elector certifying official.
National popular vote interstate agreement, §1-1051.01.

Presidential slate.
National popular vote interstate agreement, §1-1051.01.

Presumed lead-based paint.
Lead-hazard prevention and elimination, §8-231.01.

Pretreatment, §8-105.02.

Pretreatment requirements, §8-105.02.

Prevention program, §4-1341.01.

Price amendment.
Security agents and broker, §31-5601.01.

Primacy.
Department of the environment, §8-151.01.

Primary care provider, §31-3401.
Medical assistance program, §1-307.02.

Primary health record, §44-801.
Health occupations licensure, registration or certification.
Mandatory adverse event reporting, §7-161.

Primary stroke center.
Stroke system of care, §44-1151.

Principal, §21-2202.
Mortgage lenders and brokers, §26-1101.
Principal and income, §28-4801.02.
Promotion or retention of students, §38-781.01.
Uniform fiduciaries act, §21-1701.

Principal asset.
Rental housing conversion, opportunity to purchase, §42-3404.02.

DEFINED TERMS —Cont'd

Principal balance.
Mortgage loan protection, §26-1151.01.

Principal base period employer, §51-101.

Principal business operations.
Certified capital companies, §31-5231.

Principal obligor.
Negotiable instruments, §28:3-103.

Principal office.
Business organizations, §29-101.02.

Principal place of business.
Certified public accountants, §47-2853.41.
Life and health insurance guaranty association, §31-5401.

Principal place of business of an association, §26-1201.

Principal place of business of a savings and loan holding company, §26-1201.

Principal residence, §47-1401.

Principle balance, §50-601.

Printed.
Elections, §1-1001.02.

Priority development area, §2-1217.01.
Supermarket tax incentives, §47-3801.
Tax abatement, §47-4630.

Prior offense.
Chemical testing for driving under the influence, §50-1901.
Impaired operation or driving, §50-2206.01.
Traffic regulation, §50-2201.02.

Prisoner, §24-231.01.

Prison industries, §24-231.01.

Private applicator, §8-401.

Private area.
Nonconsensual pornography, §22-3051.
Voyeurism, §22-3531.

Private collection property.
Solid waste reduction and recovery, §8-1031.01.

Private communication service.
Gross sales tax, §47-2001.

Private corporations.
Foreign trade zones, §36-501.

Private correctional officer, §24-261.01.

Private dwelling.
Unlawful entry on property, §22-3302.

Private entity.
Public-Private Partnership Administration Fund, §2-271.01.

Private fire hydrant, §34-2410.01.

DEFINED TERMS —Cont'd
Private hospital, §21-501.
Private investigation service.
Gross sales tax, §47-2001.
Private operator, §24-261.01.
Private organic rules.
Business organizations, §29-101.02.
Private property.
Abandoned and unlawfully parked
vehicles, §50-2421.02.
Private room.
Homeless services, §4-751.01.
Private-sector employee, §24-231.01.
Private structure, §10-1141.01.
Abatement of dangerous conditions on
public space, §10-1181.01.
Private vehicle-for-hire.
Regulation of for-hire vehicles,
§50-301.03.
Private vehicle-for-hire company.
Regulation of for-hire vehicles,
§50-301.03.
Private vehicle-for-hire operator.
Regulation of for-hire vehicles,
§50-301.03.
Privatization contract.
Procurement practices, §2-351.04.
Privilege.
Insurance compliance self-evaluation,
§31-851.
Privileging.
Emergency volunteer health
practitioners, §7-2361.06.
Probable cause.
Mandatory drug and alcohol testing of
certain employees, §1-620.21.
Mandatory drug and alcohol testing of
certain employees who serve
children, §1-620.31.
Probable cause referral.
Mandatory drug and alcohol testing of
certain employees, §1-620.21.
Probate, §20-101.
Probate Court.
Intestate succession, §19-115.
Probation, §16-2301.
Probe-start metal halide ballast.
Energy efficiency standards,
§8-1771.01.
Proceeding, §2-502.
Business organizations, §29-101.02.
Collaborative law, §16-4002.
Corporations, §29-306.50.
Mediation, §16-4201.
Nonprofit corporations, §29-406.50.
Proceeds, §2-381.01.
Secured transactions, §28:9-102.

DEFINED TERMS —Cont'd
Proceeds of a letter of credit,
§28:5-114.
Processing.
Breastmilk bank and lactation
support, §7-881.01.
Procurement.
Procurement practices, §2-351.04.
Procurement act.
District of Columbia housing
authority, §6-201.
Procurement organization.
Anatomical gifts, §7-1531.01.
Producer, §§31-401, 31-1501.
Paint stewardship, §8-233.01.
Title insurance producers,
§31-5041.01.
Title insurers, §31-5031.01.
Producer licensing act.
Title insurance producers,
§31-5041.01.
Production, §48-901.02.
Product label.
Extended manufacturer responsibility
for electronic waste, §8-1041.01.
Product liability, §31-4101.
**Professional and convenience
services,** §48-804.51.
Professional athletic team.
Ballpark sales taxes, §47-2002.05.
Professional certification.
American sign language education,
§38-2432.
Professional corporation, §29-502.
Professional counseling, practice of,
§3-1201.02.
Professional development.
Pre-kindergarten programs,
§38-271.01.
**Professional indoor mold
assessment.**
Indoor mold assessment and
remediation, §8-241.01.
**Professional indoor mold
remediation.**
Indoor mold assessment and
remediation, §8-241.01.
**Professional limited liability
company.**
Business organizations, §29-101.02.
Professional service, §7-1201.01.
Professional corporations, §29-502.
**Professional-sports-services
contract.**
Athlete agent, §47-2887.01.
Proficiency testing program, §44-201.

DEFINED TERMS —Cont'd

Program, §§7-701.01, 21-1201.

Brownfield revitalization, §8-631.02.

Budget reprogramming policy, §47-361.

Budgets and budget estimates, §47-355.01.

Homeland security program, §7-2231.02.

Medical marijuana, §7-1671.01.

Monitoring prescription drugs, §48-853.01.

Nurse's rehabilitation program, §3-1251.01.

Program participant, §21-1201.

Program-related asset.

Prudent management of institutional funds, §44-1631.

Program rules.

Homeless services, §4-751.01.

Progress notes.

Mental health disclosures within mental health facility, §7-1203.01.

Prohibited discharge standards, §8-105.02.

Prohibited personnel action, §2-223.01.

Whistleblower protection, §1-615.52.

Prohibited source.

Ethics and government accountability, §1-1161.01.

Project.

Anacostia waterfront environmental standards, §2-1226.32.

City Market at O Street tax increment financing, §2-1217.33a.

Construction codes, §6-1401.

Green buildings, §6-1451.01.

Job growth tax credit, §47-1807.51.

Mechanics' and materialmen's liens, §40-301.03.

New convention center hotel, §§10-1221.01, 47-4609.

Skyland TIF area, §2-1217.35a.

Southwest waterfront bond financing, §2-1217.131.

Southwest waterfront special assessment district, §47-895.01.

Tax increment financing authorization, §2-1217.01.

The Advisory Board Company, real property tax abatement, §47-4665.01.

Union Market district tax increment financing, §2-1217.36a.

Woodrow Wilson Bridge and Tunnel Compact, §9-1115.03.

DEFINED TERMS —Cont'd

Project area.

Ballpark, §10-1601.03.

National capital revitalization corporation, §2-1217.12.

Project-based voucher assistance.

District of Columbia housing authority, §6-201.

Project developer.

Waterfront Park at the Yards, §10-1801.

Waterfront Park special assessment district, §47-895.21.

Prolonged absence.

Voluntary leave transfer program, §1-612.31.

Promise.

Negotiable instruments, §28:3-103.

Promissory note.

Secured transactions, §28:9-102.

Promote, §22-3101.

Promoted.

Promotion or retention of students, §38-781.01.

Promoter.

Security agents and broker, §31-5601.01.

Promotion gate.

Charter schools, §38-1800.02.

Proof of financial responsibility for the future, §50-1301.35.

Proof of insurance.

Vehicle insurance enforcement, §5-114.01.

Proper enclosure, §8-1901.

Proper invoice.

Quick payment provisions, §2-221.01.

Properly payable.

Bank deposits and collections, §28:4-104.

Properly registered vehicle, §47-2302.

International registration plan agreements, §50-1507.01.

Properly restrained, §50-1702.

Seat belts, §50-1801.

Property.

Bees, §8-1825.02.

Business organizations, §29-101.02.

Drainage, §8-205.

Drug, firearm, or prostitution-related nuisance abatement, §42-3101.

Fraudulent transfers, §28-3101.

Guardianship, etc., §21-2011.

Horizontal property regime, §42-2002.

Identity theft, §22-3227.01.

DEFINED TERMS —Cont'd
Property —Cont'd
Premarital agreements, §46-501.
Probate and administration
proceedings, §20-101, Probate
Rule 5.
Search warrants, CrimPro Rule 41.
Skyland TIF area, §2-1217.35a.
The Advisory Board Company, real
property tax abatement,
§47-4665.01.
Theft and related offenses, §22-3201.
Unclaimed property, §§41-102, 41-106.
Uniform real property transfers on
death, §19-604.02.
Uniform trust code, §19-1301.03.
Vector-borne disease control,
§8-2131.01.
Property and casualty insurer.
Risk-based capital, §31-2001.
Property disposition by lease.
Green buildings, §6-1451.01.
Property disposition by sale.
Green buildings, §6-1451.01.
Property line, §8-205.
Public space rental and utilization,
§10-1101.01.
Transportation department,
§50-921.01a.
Property management, §42-1702.
Property of another, §22-3201.
Property owner, §31-5002.
Energy efficiency financing,
§8-1778.02.
Property taxes, §42-3501.03.
Proportionately.
Southwest waterfront special
assessment district, §47-895.01.
Proposal.
Secured transactions, §28:9-102.
Proposal development.
Procurement practices, §2-351.04.
Proposer.
Elections, §1-1001.02.
Public-Private Partnership
Administration Fund, §2-271.01.
Proprietary information, §22-3214.
Proprietary school, §38-1302.
Proprietor of a pharmacy,
§47-2885.02.
Prosecutor, CrimPro Rule 54.
Warrants, §23-501.
Prospective donor.
Anatomical gifts, §7-1531.01.
Prospective party.
Collaborative law, §16-4002.

DEFINED TERMS —Cont'd
Prostitution, §22-2701.01.
Drug, firearm, or prostitution-related
nuisance abatement, §42-3101.
Prostitution-related offenses,
§22-2701.01.
Protected agreement.
Entity transactions, §29-201.02.
Protected cell.
Captive insurance companies,
§§31-3931.01, 31-3931.04.
Protected cell captive insurer.
Captive insurance companies,
§§31-3931.01, 31-3931.04.
Protected classes, §32-601.
Protected disclosure, §2-223.01.
Whistleblower protection, §1-615.52.
Protected health information.
Public assistance applicants,
confidentiality of information,
§4-209.04.
Protected individual, §21-2011.
Interstate enforcement of domestic
violence proceedings, §16-1041.
**Protected mental health
information.**
Department of mental health,
§7-1131.02.
Protected person.
Uniform adult guardianship and
protective proceedings jurisdiction
act, §21-2401.02.
Protected purchaser.
Investment securities, §28:8-303.
Protection order.
Domestic violence fatality review
board, §16-1051.
Interstate enforcement of domestic
violence proceedings, §16-1041.
Protective bicycle helmet, §50-1609.
Protective order.
Uniform adult guardianship and
protective proceedings jurisdiction
act, §21-2401.02.
Protective proceeding, §21-2011.
Uniform adult guardianship and
protective proceedings jurisdiction
act, §21-2401.02.
Protective services, §7-1901.
Protective supervision, §16-2301.
Protest.
Alcoholic beverages, §25-101.
Protest hearing.
Alcoholic beverages, §25-101.
Protest period.
Alcoholic beverages, §25-101.

DEFINED TERMS —Cont'd

Prove.

Funds transfers, §28:4A-105.

Negotiable instruments, §28:3-103.

Provider, §§4-801, 31-3401.

Continuing care retirement communities, §44-151.01.

Department of mental health, §7-1131.02.

Health benefit plans reimbursement, §31-3131.

Homeless services, §4-751.01.

Hospitalization of persons with mental illness, §21-501.

Mental health consumer's rights, §7-1231.02.

Nurse's rehabilitation program, §3-1251.01.

Telehealth reimbursement, §31-3861.

Provider agreement, §4-801.

Provider of services, §4-501.

Provider panel, §31-3401.

Credentialing intermediary, health insurers, §31-3251.

Health benefit plans reimbursement, §31-3131.

Provisional certificate of authority.

Captive insurance companies, §31-3931.01.

Provisional certification.

American sign language education, §38-2432.

Provision of material support.

Anti-terrorism act of 2002, §22-3152.

PSC.

Stroke system of care, §44-1151.

Psychiatrist.

Family court proceedings, §16-2301.

Hospitalization of persons with mental illness, §21-501.

Psychological impact, §42-1702.

Psychologist, §31-3101.

Psychology, practice of, §3-1201.02.

Psychotropic medication.

Rights of persons with intellectual disability, §7-1301.03.

Public.

Criminal records sealing, §16-801.

Public access channel.

Office of cable television, film, music, and entertainment amendment act of 2015, §34-1251.03.

Public agency.

Special education student rights, §38-2571.02.

Public applicator, §8-401.

DEFINED TERMS —Cont'd

Public art.

Arts and humanities commission, §39-202.

Public assistance, §§4-201.01, 46-201.

Homeless services, §4-751.01.

Publications.

Home Rule act, §1-201.03.

Respectful language modernization, §2-631.

Public benefit.

Real property tax exemptions, qualified high technology company interior renovation tax rebate, §47-4665.

Public bicycle path, §50-1609.

Public body, §2-223.01.

Open meetings act, §2-574.

Respectful language modernization, §2-631.

Whistleblower protection, §1-615.52.

Public charter school, §38-1800.02.

Nonpublic schools, §38-2561.01.

Schools and education, §38-821.01.

Tuition of nonresidents, §38-304.

Uniform per student funding formula, §38-2901.

Public charter school board, §38-1800.02.

Public collection property.

Solid waste reduction and recovery, §8-1031.01.

Public corporation.

Corporations, §29-301.02.

Foreign trade zones, §36-501.

Public emergency, §7-2301.

Public employee relations board.

District of Columbia housing authority, §6-201.

Public entity.

Public-Private Partnership Administration Fund, §2-271.01.

Public-finance transaction.

Secured transactions, §28:9-102.

Public funds.

Employees retirement program management, §§1-335.01, 1-336.01.

Merit system, §1-614.11.

Public health nuisance.

Vector-borne disease control, §8-2131.01.

Public high school.

Post-secondary preparation plan, §38-752.02.

DEFINED TERMS —Cont'd
Public highway, §§50-1301.02, 50-1501.01.
Non-motorized user contributory negligence, §50-2204.51.
Public hospital, §21-501.
Public-housing-assisted unit.
District of Columbia housing authority, §6-201.
Public infrastructure facility.
Procurement practices, §2-351.04.
Public insurance adjuster, §31-1631.02.
Public interest organizations.
Consumer protection procedures, §28-3901.
Publicly funded.
Merit system, §1-614.11.
Publicly owned treatment works.
Wastewater disposal systems, §8-105.02.
Public market.
Vending regulation, §37-131.01.
Public notice.
Procurement practices, §2-351.04.
Public-private partnership administration fund, §2-271.01.
Public official.
Ethics and government accountability, §1-1161.01.
Public organic record.
Business organizations, §29-101.02.
Secured transactions, §28:9-102.
Public or private property.
Graffiti, §22-3312.05.
Public parking.
Urban forest preservation, §8-651.02.
Public place, §§2-1542, 22-2701.01.
Health department, §7-741.01.
Public-private partnerships, §2-271.01.
Hospital and medical services corporation, §31-3501.
Public purpose program.
Retail electric competition and consumer protection, §34-1501.
Public record, §§2-502, 2-1701.
Child fatality or near fatality, §4-1303.31.
Public recreational facility.
Smoking restrictions, §7-1702.
Public rights of way, §10-1141.01.
Abatement of dangerous conditions on public space, §10-1181.01.
Office of cable television, film, music, and entertainment amendment act of 2015, §34-1251.03.

DEFINED TERMS —Cont'd
Public rights of way —Cont'd
Transportation department, §50-921.01a.
Public roadway, §50-1609.
Autonomous vehicles, §50-2351.
Public safety agency, §32-501.
Public safety answering point.
Emergency and non-emergency telephone system assessments fund, §34-1801.
Public safety facility.
Historic landmarks, §6-1102.
Public school.
Charter schools, §38-1800.02.
Green buildings, §6-1451.01.
Schools and education, §38-821.01.
Student health care, medication, §38-651.01.
Public sector comparator.
Public-private partnership administration fund, §2-271.01.
Public servant, §22-711.
Public service event.
Garbage collection, §8-741.
Public space, §§8-205, 10-1141.01.
Abandoned and unlawfully parked vehicles, §50-2421.02.
Abatement of dangerous conditions on public space, §10-1181.01.
Commemorative work, §9-204.11.
Rental and utilization, §10-1101.01.
Transportation department, §50-921.01a.
Public structure, §10-1141.01.
Public thoroughfare.
Personal delivery devices pilot program, §50-1551.
Public utilities commission act.
Electric company infrastructure improvement financing, §34-1311.01.
Public utility, §34-214.
Public Utility Holding Company Act of 1935.
Security agents and broker, §31-5601.01.
Public utility operator, §34-2701.
Public vehicle-for-hire.
Assault of public vehicle inspection officer, §§22-404.02, 22-404.03.
Public vehicle-for-hire industry.
Regulation of for-hire vehicles, §50-301.03.
Public vehicle inspection officer.
Assault of public vehicle inspection officer, §§22-404.02, 22-404.03.

DEFINED TERMS —Cont'd
Public way, §34-2001.
Publish.
Administrative procedure, §2-502.
Home Rule act, §1-201.03.
Nonconsensual pornography, §22-3051.
Pulse oximetry.
Newborn heart screening, §7-857.01.
Purchase, §47-2201.
Alternative fuels technology, §50-702.
Leases, UCC, §28:2A-103.
UCC, §28:1-201.
Uniform certificates of title for vessels, §50-1541.01.
Weapons, §22-4501.
Purchase agreement.
Tobacco settlement financing, §7-1831.01.
Purchase card program.
Procurement practices, §2-351.04.
Purchased, §47-2201.
Purchase-money collateral.
Secured transactions, §28:9-103.
Purchase money mortgage or purchase money deed of trust, §42-1101.
Purchase-money obligation.
Secured transactions, §28:9-103.
Purchaser.
Compensating use tax, §47-2201.
Condominiums, §42-1901.02.
Gross sales tax, §47-2001.
Revised real property tax sale, §47-1330.
Uniform certificates of title for vessels, §50-1541.01.
Uniform commercial code, §28:1-201.
Purchaser's certificate, §47-2201.
Gross sales tax, §47-2001.
Purchasing group, §31-4101.
Pure captive insurer, §31-3931.01.
Pursuant to commitment.
Secured transactions, §28:9-102.
Put option.
Insurance investments, §31-1371.02.
Qualified.
Small and certified business enterprise development and assistance, §2-218.02.
Qualified apprenticeship program.
Energy efficiency financing, §8-1778.02.
Qualified area.
Preservation and rehabilitation of government-supported housing, §42-2851.02.

DEFINED TERMS —Cont'd
Qualified asset.
Income taxes.
Qualified high technology companies, §47-1817.01.
Qualified bank.
Insurance investments, §31-1371.02.
Qualified beneficiary.
Uniform trust code, §19-1301.03.
Qualified business.
Certified capital companies, §31-5231.
Qualified business entity.
Insurance investments, §31-1371.02.
Qualified business property.
Income taxes.
Qualified high technology companies, §47-1817.01.
Qualified capital gain.
Income taxes.
Qualified high technology companies, §47-1817.01.
Qualified certification.
American sign language education, §38-2432.
Qualified clearinghouse.
Insurance investments, §31-1371.02.
Qualified debt instrument.
Certified capital companies, §31-5231.
Qualified dental plan.
Health benefit exchange authority, §31-3171.01.
Qualified developmental disability professional, §§7-1301.03, 21-2011.
Qualified disability expense.
ABLE savings accounts, §47-4901.
Qualified distribution.
Certified capital companies, §31-5231.
Qualified donor.
Breastmilk bank and lactation support, §7-881.01.
Qualified elector.
Elections, §1-1001.02.
Qualified employee.
CareFirst tax credit for wages, sales tax exemption, §47-4602.
Income taxes.
Qualified high technology companies, §47-1817.01.
Qualified employer.
Health benefit exchange authority, §31-3171.01.
Qualified escrow fund.
Tobacco master settlement agreement, §7-1801.01.
Tobacco master settlement agreement enforcement, §7-1803.02.

DEFINED TERMS —Cont'd
Qualified exchange.
Insurance investments, §31-1371.02.
**Qualified film and digital media
infrastructure project.**
Motion pictures, §2-1204.11c.
Qualified financial institution.
Title insurance producers,
§31-5041.01.
Title insurers, §31-5031.01.
Qualified foreign exchange.
Insurance investments, §31-1371.02.
Qualified guarantor.
Insurance investments, §31-1371.02.
Qualified health care professional.
Emergency medical services,
§7-2341.01.
Qualified health plan.
Health benefit exchange authority,
§31-3171.01.
Qualified health professional,
§44-1201.
**Qualified higher education
expenses.**
College savings program, §47-4501.
Higher education financial aid
assistance, §38-2731.
Qualified high technology company.
Income taxes, §47-1817.01.
Qualified social electronic commerce
companies tax abatements,
§47-1818.01.
Real property tax abatement for
qualified high technology
companies, §47-811.03.
Real property tax exemptions,
qualified high technology company
interior renovation tax rebate,
§47-4665.
Qualified individual.
Health benefit exchange authority,
§31-3171.01.
Health insurance, clinical trials
insurance coverage, §31-2993.01.
Qualified interpreter.
Interpreters, §2-1901.
Qualified interviewer.
Interpreters, §2-1901.
Qualified investments.
Certified capital companies, §31-5231.
Community development by financial
institutions, §26-431.02.
Qualified job training expenditure.
Motion pictures, §2-1204.11c.
**Qualified long-term care insurance
contract,** §31-3601.

DEFINED TERMS —Cont'd
Qualified military service.
Teachers' retirement, deferred or
survivor annuity, §38-2021.09.
Qualified milk.
Breastmilk bank and lactation
support, §7-881.01.
**Qualified nonprofit agency for the
blind and other individuals with
severe disabilities,** §32-302.
Qualified nonprofit organization.
Nonprofit corporations locating in
emerging commercial
neighborhoods, §47-857.11.
Qualified partnership interest.
Income taxes.
Qualified high technology
companies, §47-1817.01.
Qualified patient, §7-621.
Qualified personnel expenditure.
Motion pictures, §2-1204.11c.
Qualified physician.
Hospitalization of persons with mental
illness, §21-501.
Qualified primary credit source.
Insurance investments, §31-1371.02.
Qualified production.
Motion pictures, §§2-1204.11c,
1204.11c.
Qualified production expenditure.
Motion pictures, §2-1204.11c.
Qualified project.
Low-income housing tax credit,
§47-4801.
Public-private partnership
administration fund, §2-271.01.
Qualified psychologist, §21-501.
Family court proceedings, §16-2301.
Health-care durable powers of
attorney, §21-2202.
Qualified public accountant, §§1-702,
1-901.02.
Qualified real property.
Qualified social electronic commerce
companies tax abatements,
§47-1818.01.
Qualified registered elector.
Elections, §1-1001.02.
Qualified resident.
Access to prescription drugs,
§48-831.02.
Qualified restaurant or retail store.
Tax incentives, §47-3801.
Qualified second market vehicle,
§50-702.
Qualified shares.
Corporations, §29-306.73.

DEFINED TERMS —Cont'd

Qualified social e-commerce company.
Qualified social electronic commerce companies tax abatements, §47-1818.01.

Qualified stock.
Income taxes.
Qualified high technology companies, §47-1817.01.

Qualified substance abuse counselor.
Choice in drug treatment, §7-3002.

Qualified supermarket.
Tax incentives, §§47-3801, 47-3805.

Qualified tenant improvement.
Real property tax exemptions, qualified high technology company interior renovation tax rebate, §47-4665.

Qualified theater company.
Payment in lieu of taxes, §47-1052.

Qualified third party.
Intrafamily offenses.
Notice of lease termination by tenant who is victim, §42-3505.07.

Qualified transportation project.
Transportation infrastructure improvement GARVEE bonds, §9-107.51.

Qualified transportation project costs.
Transportation infrastructure improvement GARVEE bonds, §9-107.51.

Qualified United States financial institution, §31-1801.
Special purpose financial captive insurance companies, §31-3932.02.

Qualified withdrawal.
College savings program, §47-4501.

Qualifying biomass.
Renewable energy portfolio standards, §34-1431.

Qualifying court order.
Spouse or domestic partner equity in retirement benefits, §1-529.02.

Qualifying event.
Family leave, §1-612.03c.

Qualifying income.
Rental housing conversion and sale, §42-3402.08.

Qualifying medical condition.
Medical marijuana, §7-1671.01.

Qualifying medical treatment.
Medical marijuana, §7-1671.01.

DEFINED TERMS —Cont'd

Qualifying patient.
Medical marijuana, §7-1671.01.

Qualifying school.
Qualified zone academy revenue bond project forward commitment approval act, §2-1217.102.

Qualifying tenant-purchasers.
Rental housing conversion and sale, §42-3402.04.

Quality assurance program.
Energy efficiency financing, §8-1778.02.

Quality control and quality assurance program.
Fire-standard-compliant cigarettes, §7-1751.

Quality of care improvements.
Stevie Sellows quality improvement fund, §47-1270.

Quality of care initiatives.
Nursing facility assessment, §47-1261.

Quasi-governmental corporation.
Investment and deposit of District funds, §47-351.01.

QZAB pledged account.
Qualified zone academy revenue bond project forward commitment approval act, §2-1217.102.

Radioactive hazardous waste, §8-1051.

Radio communication.
Toll telecommunication service tax, §47-3901.

Radiopharmaceuticals, §47-2885.02.

Radio technology.
Office of unified communications, §1-327.51.

Rail car.
Strict liability for release of hazardous waste during transport, §8-1441.

Rail fixed guideway system, §9-1109.01.

Random selection, §11-1902.

Random testing, §1-620.31.
Corrections employee mandatory substance abuse testing, §24-211.21.
Mandatory drug and alcohol testing of certain employees, §1-620.21.

Rated credit instrument.
Insurance investments, §31-1371.02.

Rate of basic compensation.
Police and fire departments, §5-1304.

Rate of exchange, §15-901.

Rate of insured unemployment.
Unemployment compensation, §51-107.

DEFINED TERMS —Cont'd

Rates.

Nonpublic schools, §38-2561.01.

RBC, §31-2001.

RBC instructions, §31-2001.

Health insurance regulatory standards, §31-3451.01.

RBC level, §31-2001.

Health insurance regulatory standards, §31-3451.01.

RBC plan, §31-2001.

Health insurance regulatory standards, §31-3451.01.

RBC report, §31-2001.

Health insurance regulatory standards, §31-3451.01.

Real covenant, §47-1401.

Real estate, §42-1702.

Condominiums, §42-1901.02.

Insurance investments, §31-1371.02.

Real estate brokerage activity.

Mortgage lenders and brokers, §26-1101.

Real estate broker or salesperson, §2-1401.02.

Real estate franchise, §42-1702.

Real property.

Controlled substances, §48-901.02.

Foreign missions, §6-1302.

Mortgage loan protection, §26-1151.01.

Qualified social electronic commerce companies tax abatements, §47-1818.01.

Real property assessment, §47-802.

Recorder of deeds, §42-1101.

Sale of public lands, §10-801.01.

Transfer tax, §47-901.

Vacant buildings, §42-3131.05.

Real property maintenance, §47-2201.

Gross sales tax, §47-2001.

Real property tax base year.

Howard Theatre redevelopment project, §2-1217.151.

Howard Theatre redevelopment project TIF area, §2-1217.34a.

Real property tax increment revenues, §2-1217.01.

Real-time electronic records.

Medical marijuana, §7-1671.01.

Reasonable.

Rules of professional conduct, ProfCond Rule 1.0.

Reasonable accommodation.

Pregnant and nursing workers, reasonable accommodations for, §32-1231.01.

DEFINED TERMS —Cont'd

Reasonable accommodation —Cont'd

Pregnant workers, protecting, §32-1231.01.

Reasonable and prudent parent standard.

Child abuse and neglect, §4-1301.02.

Reasonable attempt to repair.

Assistive technology device warranty, §28-4031.

Reasonable educational expenses.

Access to justice initiative program, §4-1701.01.

Reasonable education expenses.

Health professional recruitment program, §7-751.01.

Reasonable efforts.

Breastfeeding mothers, rights of, §2-1402.82.

Reasonable notice.

Access to dwelling unit by housing provider, §42-3505.51.

Reasonable purpose.

Access to dwelling unit by housing provider, §42-3505.51.

Reasonable suspicion.

Corrections employee mandatory substance abuse testing, §24-211.21.

Mandatory drug and alcohol testing of certain employees who serve children, §1-620.31.

Metropolitan police.

Investigations concerning first amendment activities, §5-333.02.

Reasonable suspicion referral.

Mandatory drug and alcohol testing of certain employees who serve children, §1-620.31.

Reasonable time.

Access to dwelling unit by housing provider, §42-3505.51.

Reasonably.

Rules of professional conduct, ProfCond Rule 1.0.

Reasonably ascertainable.

Business improvement districts, §2-1215.02.

Reasonably available.

Anatomical gifts, §7-1531.01.

Business improvement districts, §2-1215.02.

Reasonably determined.

Business improvement districts, §2-1215.02.

DEFINED TERMS —Cont'd

Reasonably should know.
Rules of professional conduct,
ProfCond Rule 1.0.

Rebuilt salvage title.
Salvage, flood and junk vehicles,
§50-1331.01.

Rebuilt salvage vehicle.
Salvage, flood and junk vehicles,
§50-1331.01.

Recall.
Elections, §§1-204.111, 1-1001.02.

Recall of elected public officials,
§1-204.111.

Receipt.
Business organizations, §29-101.02.
Sales, §28:2-103.

Receive.
Business organizations, §29-101.02.
Nonprobate transfers on death,
§19-602.01.
UCC, §28:1-202.

Receiver, §31-1301.
District of Columbia housing
authority, §6-201.

Receivership court.
Life and health insurance guaranty
association, §31-5401.

Receiving bank.
Funds transfers, §28:4A-103.

Receiving state.
Interstate compact on educational
opportunity for military children,
§49-1101.03.

Recipient, §§4-201.01, 4-801, 46-201.
Anatomical gifts, §7-1531.01.
Living wage act, §2-220.02.
Public assistance applicants,
confidentiality of information,
§4-209.04.
Unified economic development budget
transparency and accountability,
§2-1208.01.

Recipient employee.
Voluntary leave transfer program,
§1-612.31.

Reciprocal, §31-2501.03.

Reciprocal insurance company,
§31-751.

Reciprocal insurer.
Captive insurance companies,
§31-3931.01.

Reciprocal state, §31-1301.

Reciprocity, §§47-2302, 50-1507.01.
Health occupations licensure,
registration or certification,
§3-1205.07.

DEFINED TERMS —Cont'd

Reciprocity agreement.
Educational licensure commission,
§38-1302.

**Recognized equivalent of secondary
school diploma.**
DC promise program, §38-2751.

Reconstruction, §47-2302.
Building rehabilitation code, §6-1410.

Reconveyance.
Rental housing conversion,
opportunity to purchase,
§42-3404.02.

Record.
Anatomical gifts, §7-1531.01.
Arbitration, revised act, §16-4401.
Athlete agent, §47-2887.01.
Business organizations, §29-101.02.
Collaborative law, §16-4002.
Documents of title, §28:7-102.
Electronic transactions, uniform act,
§28-4901.
Environmental covenants, §8-671.01.
Health occupations licensure,
registration or certification,
§3-1210.11.
Interstate family support, §46-351.02.
Letters of credit, §28:5-102.
Long-term care ombudsman program,
§7-701.01.
Mediation, §16-4201.
Medicaid provider fraud, §4-801.
Prudent management of institutional
funds, §44-1631.
Public assistance applicants,
confidentiality of information,
§4-209.04.
Secured transactions, §28:9-102.
Unclaimed property, §41-102.
Uniform adult guardianship and
protective proceedings jurisdiction
act, §21-2401.02.
Uniform certificates of title for vessels,
§50-1541.01.
Uniform child abduction prevention
act, §16-4604.02.
Uniform commercial code, §28:1-201.
Uniform disclaimer of property
interests act, §19-1505.
Unsworn foreign declarations,
§16-5302.

Record date.
Corporations, §29-301.02.
Nonprofit corporations, §29-401.02.

Recorder.
Liens on motor vehicles or trailers,
§50-1201.

DEFINED TERMS —Cont'd
Records disposition, §2-1701.
Record shareholder.
Corporations, §29-311.01.
Records management officer,
§2-1701.
Records retention schedule, §2-1701.
Crime investigation records, §5-113.31.
Recovery.
Behavioral health department,
§7-1141.01.
Recovery support services.
Behavioral health department,
§7-1141.01.
Recreation facility.
Defibrillator usage, §44-231.
Recreation facility certificate.
Defibrillator usage, §44-231.
Recreation park, §10-1401.
Recyclable.
Disposable food service ware,
management, §8-1531.
Solid waste reduction and recovery,
§8-1031.01.
Recyclable material, §8-1051.
Gross sales tax, §47-2001.
Recycle.
Solid waste reduction and recovery,
§8-1031.01.
Recycled.
Solid waste reduction and recovery,
§8-1031.01.
Recycling.
Construction and demolition waste
recycling accountability, §8-1071.
Paint stewardship, §8-233.01.
Solid waste reduction and recovery,
§8-1031.01.
Redevelopment, §§6-321.08, 6-341.05.
Redevelopment company, §§6-321.08,
6-341.05.
Red flag warning disclosure notice.
Mortgage loan protection, §26-1151.01.
Redomestication, §31-1701.
Captive insurance companies,
§31-3931.01.
Reduced leave schedule, §32-501.
Reduced risk.
Pesticide education and control,
§8-431.
Referendum.
Elections, §1-1001.02.
Home Rule act, §1-204.101.
Referral source.
Title insurers, §31-5031.01.
Refiner.
Gas stations, §36-304.11.

DEFINED TERMS —Cont'd
Refiner, producer, or manufacturer,
§36-301.01.
Refusal.
Anatomical gifts, §7-1531.01.
Region.
Savings and loan acquisitions,
§26-1201.
Regional association, §26-1201.
Regional authority.
Chesapeake regional Olympic games
authority, §2-1131.
Regional authority advisory
committee.
Chesapeake regional Olympic games
authority, §2-1131.
Regional facility, §8-1501.
Regional governmental entity.
Small and certified business enterprise
development and assistance,
§2-218.02.
Regional savings and loan holding
company, §26-1201.
Register.
Interstate family support, §46-351.02.
TOD securities registration,
§19-603.01.
Registered acupuncture therapist,
§3-1209.03.
Registered agent.
Business organizations, §29-101.02.
Registered agent filing.
Business organizations, §29-104.01.
Registered employee, §8-401.
Registered foreign cooperative.
Limited cooperative associations,
§29-1001.02.
Registered foreign entity.
Business organizations, §29-101.02.
Registered foreign limited liability
partnership.
Partnerships, §29-601.02.
Registered foreign statutory trust.
Statutory trusts, §29-1201.02.
Registered form.
Investment securities, §28:8-102.
Registered land surveyor.
Condominiums, §42-1901.02.
Registered loan officer.
Mortgage lenders and brokers,
§26-1101.
Registered mortgage loan
originator.
Mortgage lenders and brokers,
§26-1101.
Registered nursing, practice of,
§3-1201.02.

DEFINED TERMS —Cont'd
Registered organization.
Secured transactions, §28:9-102.
Registered pharmacy technician,
§3-1207.51.
Registered qualified elector,
§1-1001.02.
Registering entity.
TOD securities registration,
§19-603.01.
Registering tribunal.
Interstate family support, §46-351.02.
Register of wills.
Probate proceedings, Probate Rule 25.
Registrant.
Charitable solicitations, §44-1701.
Ethics and government accountability,
§1-1161.01.
Hearing aid dealers, §28-4001.
Voluntary foster care registry,
§4-1303.08.
Weapons, §22-4501.
Registrar.
Income tax secured bonds, §47-340.26.
Registration.
Athlete agent, §47-2887.01.
Motor vehicle safety responsibility,
§50-1301.02.
Non-health related occupations and
professions, §47-2853.01.
Vital records, §7-201.
Registration certificate.
Firearms control, §7-2501.01.
No-fault motor vehicle insurance,
§31-2402.
Registration offense.
Sex offender registration, §22-4001.
Registration system.
Emergency volunteer health
practitioners, §7-2361.01.
Registry.
Anatomical gifts, §7-1531.01.
Voluntary foster care registry,
§4-1303.08.
Regular benefits.
Unemployment compensation, §51-107.
Regular rate, §32-1002.
Regulate.
Department of mental health,
§7-1131.02.
Health department functions, §7-731.
Regulated activity.
Banks and financial institutions,
§26-551.02.
Regulated substance, §8-113.01.
Regulation.
Administrative procedure, §2-502.

DEFINED TERMS —Cont'd
Regulation —Cont'd
Business license, §47-2851.01.
Codification of acts, §2-601.
Real property assessment, §47-802.
Respectful language modernization,
§2-631.
Regulatory action level event.
Health insurance regulatory
standards, §31-3451.01.
Regulatory action level RBC,
§31-2001.
Health insurance regulatory
standards, §31-3451.01.
Regulatory agency, §47-2851.01.
Regulatory asset.
Electric light and power companies,
§34-1561.
Rehabilitation.
Building rehabilitation code, §6-1410.
Rehabilitation act.
Charter schools, §38-1800.02.
Disability rights, §2-1431.01.
Rehabilitation plan.
Choice in drug treatment, §7-3002.
Rehabilitative services.
Youth rehabilitation services,
department of, §2-1515.01.
Reimbursable details.
Alcoholic beverage licenses, §25-798.
Reimbursement methodology.
Stevie Sellows quality improvement
fund, §47-1270.
Reinsurance intermediary, §31-1801.
**Reinsurance intermediary-broker
(RB),** §31-1801.
**Reinsurance intermediary-manager
(RM),** §31-1801.
Reinsurer, §31-1801.
Related cases.
Assignment of criminal cases, CrimPro
Rule 105, USDistCt LCrR 57.12,
USDistCt LCvR 40.5.
Related entity.
Income tax, §47-1801.04.
Qualified social electronic commerce
companies tax abatements,
§47-1818.01.
Related facility, §42-3501.03.
Related member.
Income tax, §47-1801.04.
Related owners.
Vacant buildings, §42-3131.05.
Related ownership.
Vacant buildings, §42-3131.05.
Related party.
Statutory trusts, §29-1201.02.

DEFINED TERMS —Cont'd

Related person, §7-2031.
Corporations, §29-306.70.
Related services, §42-3501.03.
Nonpublic schools, §38-2561.01.
Related sibling group.
Adoption voucher fund, §4-342.
Related to a collaborative matter.
Collaborative law, §16-4002.
Related vehicle conveyance fee.
Traffic adjudication, §50-2301.02.
Relative.
Civil asset forfeiture, §41-301.
Fraudulent transfers, §28-3101.
Merit system, §1-608.01a.
Parental kidnapping, §16-1021.
Resocialization furlough programs,
§24-251.01.
Relative caregiver.
Temporary assistance for needy
families.
Grandparent caregiver subsidies,
§4-251.01.
Release, §8-113.01.
Brownfield revitalization, §8-631.02.
Criminal procedure, CrimPro Rule 54.
Released claims.
Tobacco master settlement agreement,
§7-1801.01.
Release on citation.
Warrants, §23-501.
Releasing official.
Bail and recognizance, §23-1110.
First amendment assemblies,
§5-335.01.
Warrants, §23-501.
Releasing parties.
Tobacco master settlement agreement,
§7-1801.01.
Relevant cost drivers.
Performance based budget, §47-308.01.
Relevant performance measures.
Performance based budget, §47-308.01.
Relevant time.
Corporations, §29-306.70.
Relief, §2-502.
Religious.
Marriage solemnization, §46-406.
Religious corporation.
Nonprofit corporations, §29-401.02.
Religious superior, §21-2202.
Relocation costs.
Income tax credits, qualified high
technology companies,
§47-1817.02.
Relocation expenses.
Lead-hazard prevention and
elimination, §8-231.01.

DEFINED TERMS —Cont'd

Remain, §2-1542.
Remainder beneficiary.
Principal and income, §28-4801.02.
Remainder certificate.
Tobacco settlement financing,
§7-1831.01.
Remedy.
UCC, §28:1-201.
Remit.
Money transmissions, §26-1001.
Remitter.
Negotiable instruments, §28:3-103.
Remitting bank.
Bank deposits and collections,
§28:4-105.
Remotely created consumer items.
Negotiable instruments, §28:3-103.
Remote sales taxes.
Internet tax, §47-3931.
Remote vendor.
Internet tax, §47-3931.
Remuneration.
Police and firefighters retirement and
disability, §5-723.01.
Teachers' retirement, maximum
benefit computations, §38-2021.27.
Renal dialysis facility.
Health-care facility, hospice and home
care licensure, §44-501.
Renewable energy credit.
Renewable energy portfolio standards,
§34-1431.
Retail electric competition and
consumer protection, §34-1501.
**Renewable energy portfolio
standard,** §34-1431.
**Renewable energy resource
measure,** §8-171.02.
Renewable energy source, §8-171.02.
Renewable natural resources,
§8-1702.
Renewable on-site generator.
Renewable energy portfolio standards,
§34-1431.
Renewal application, §47-2851.01.
Renovation.
Building rehabilitation code, §6-1410.
Lead-hazard prevention and
elimination, §8-231.01.
Renovator.
Lead-hazard prevention and
elimination, §8-231.01.
Rent, §42-3501.03.
Rental agreement.
Self-service storage facilities, §40-401.

DEFINED TERMS —Cont'd

Rental captive insurer, §31-3931.01.

Rental fleet, §50-1505.01.

Rental housing.
Preservation and rehabilitation of government-supported housing, §42-2851.02.

Rental housing locator, §28-3819.
Consumer protection, §28-3819.

Rental housing locator contract, §28-3819.
Consumer protection, §28-3819.

Rental operator, §50-1505.01.

Rental property, §34-2301.

Rental transaction, §50-1505.01.

Rental unit.
Drug-related evictions, §42-3601.
Preservation and rehabilitation of government-supported housing, §42-2851.02.
Rental housing, §§42-3401.03, 42-3501.03.
Rental housing locators, §28-3819.

Rental vehicles, §50-1505.01.

Rent ceiling, §42-3501.03.

Rent constituting property taxes accrued.
Income tax, §47-1806.06.

Rent paid.
Income tax, §47-1806.06.

Rent supplement program.
District of Columbia housing authority, §6-201.

Reorganization, §1-315.02.

Repair and improvement, §38-1805.50.
Building rehabilitation code, §6-1410.
Credit service organizations, §28-4603.

Repeatability.
Fire-standard-compliant cigarettes, §7-1751.

Replacement coverage, §31-3401.

Replication transaction.
Insurance investments, §31-1371.02.

Reply.
Graffiti abatement, §42-3141.01.

Reportable transactions.
Other post-employment benefits fund, annual audit, §1-621.09e.

Reporting agency.
Adoption, Adoption Rule 2.

Representative.
International banking corporations, §26-631.
UCC, §28:1-201.
Uniform certificates of title for vessels, §50-1541.01.

DEFINED TERMS —Cont'd

Representative form of government, §31-5301.

Representative of a resident, §7-701.01.

Representative organization.
Extended manufacturer responsibility for electronic waste, §8-1041.01.
Paint stewardship, §8-233.01.

Representative with settlement authority.
Medical malpractice.
Mediation, §16-2824.

Represented entity.
Business organizations, §29-104.01.

Reproductive health decisions.
Discrimination based on pregnancy, childbirth, related medical conditions, or breastfeeding, §2-1401.05.

Reprogramming.
Budget reprogramming policy, §47-361.

Repurchase transaction.
Insurance investments, §31-1371.02.

Request.
Nonprobate transfers on death, §19-602.01.
Secured transactions, §§28:9-210, 28:9-616.

Request for an accounting.
Secured transactions, §28:9-210.

Request for information.
Public-Private Partnership Administration Fund, §2-271.01.

Request for lease approval, §42-3503.01.

Request for proposals.
Procurement practices, §2-351.04.
Public-private partnership administration fund, §2-271.01.
Sustainable energy, §8-1773.01.

Request for qualifications.
Procurement practices, §2-351.04.
Public-private partnership administration fund, §2-271.01.

Request regarding a list of collateral.
Secured transactions, §28:9-210.

Request regarding a statement of account.
Secured transactions, §28:9-210.

Required disclosure.
Corporations, §29-306.70.

Required information.
Limited cooperative associations, §29-1001.02.

DEFINED TERMS —Cont'd
Required information —Cont'd
Limited partnerships, §29-701.02.
Required liabilities.
Insurance investments, §31-1371.02.
Required occupancy.
Waterfront Park special assessment
district, §47-895.21.
Resale restricted properties.
Real property taxes, §47-820.02.
Resale restrictions.
Housing production trust fund,
§42-2801.
Rescission.
Health benefit plan members bill of
rights, §44-301.01.
Reseller.
Toll telecommunication service tax,
§47-3901.
Reserve agreement.
City Market at O Street tax increment
financing, §2-1217.33a.
Howard Theatre redevelopment
project, §2-1217.151.
Howard Theatre redevelopment project
TIF area, §2-1217.34a.
Skyland TIF area, §2-1217.35a.
Southwest waterfront bond financing,
§2-1217.131.
Residence.
Elections, §1-1001.02.
Hospital discharge planning,
§21-2231.01.
Medical marijuana, §7-1671.01.
Protests targeting, §22-2751.
Real property tax deferral, §47-845.03.
Reduced real property tax liability for
seniors and persons with
disabilities, §47-863.
Residence property tax relief, §47-849.
Residence state.
Interstate compact on adoption and
medical assistance, §4-321.
Resident.
Assisted living residences, §44-102.01.
Choice in drug treatment, §7-3002.
Continuing care retirement
communities, §44-151.01.
District of Columbia housing
authority, §6-201.
Income tax, §47-1801.04.
Inheritance and estate taxes,
§47-3701.
Life and health insurance guaranty
association, §31-5401.
Long-term care ombudsman program,
§7-701.01.

DEFINED TERMS —Cont'd
Resident —Cont'd
Merit system, §1-603.01.
Nursing facility assessment, §47-1261.
Nursing homes, etc., §44-1001.01.
Qualified social electronic commerce
companies tax abatements,
§47-1818.01.
Resocialization furlough programs,
§24-251.01.
Stevie Sellows quality improvement
fund, §47-1270.
Substance abuse treatment and
prevention, §44-1201.
Youth residential facilities, §7-2101.
Resident agreement.
Assisted living residences, §44-102.01.
Resident association, §42-3601.
Resident employment baseline.
The Advisory Board Company, real
property tax abatement,
§47-4665.01.
Resident employment credit.
Qualified social electronic commerce
companies tax abatements,
§47-1818.01.
Resident hiring factor.
Qualified social electronic commerce
companies tax abatements,
§47-1818.01.
Residential, §8-171.02.
Green buildings, §6-1451.01.
Residential aid discount.
Sustainable energy, §8-1773.01.
Residential child care facility.
Nonpublic schools, §38-2561.01.
Residential condominium.
Waterfront Park special assessment
district, §47-895.21.
Residential districts.
Alcoholic beverages, §25-101.
Residential essential service.
Sustainable energy, §8-1773.01.
Residential facility.
Mandatory drug and alcohol testing of
certain employees, §1-620.21.
Residential mortgage.
Foreclosure mediation, §42-815.02.
Residential real property, §47-1401.
Mortgage loan protection, §26-1151.01.
Residential school.
Uniform per student funding formula,
§38-2901.
Residential street, §8-1051.
Residential tenant.
Business improvement districts,
§2-1215.02.

DEFINED TERMS —Cont'd

Resident insurance producer,
§31-1131.02.

Resident of the District.
Department of mental health,
§7-1131.02.
Homeless services, §4-751.01.
Mental health consumer's rights,
§7-1231.02.
Veterans' affairs, office of, §49-1001.

Resident of the District of Columbia,
§11-1902.
Disability services, department on,
§7-761.02.
Rights of persons with intellectual
disability, §7-1301.03.

Resident-owned business.
Small and certified business enterprise
development and assistance,
§2-218.02.

Resident's representative,
§44-1001.01.

Resident student.
Uniform per student funding formula,
§38-2901.

Resides.
Gun offender registry, §7-2508.01.

Residing and domiciled, §42-3503.01.

Residual bond.
Tobacco settlement financing,
§7-1831.01.

Residual bond purchase agreement.
Tobacco settlement financing,
§7-1831.01.

Residual interest.
Tobacco settlement financing,
§7-1831.01.

**Residual parental rights and
responsibilities,** §16-2301.

Residuary legatee, §20-101.

Residue, §§8-105.02, 8-1051.

Resign.
Firefighter retirement while under
disciplinary investigation, §5-1051.

Resignation.
Police retirement while under
disciplinary investigation, §5-801.

Resolution, §2-601.

Resources, §7-2301.
Home Rule act, §1-201.03.

RESPA.
Title insurance producers,
§31-5041.01.

Respiratory arrest.
Non-resuscitation procedures for EMS,
§7-651.01.

DEFINED TERMS —Cont'd

Respiratory care, practice of,
§3-1201.02.

Respite care.
Rights of persons with intellectual
disability, §7-1301.03.

Respondent.
Civil infractions, §2-1801.02.
Consumer protection procedures,
§28-3901.
Interstate enforcement of domestic
violence proceedings, §16-1041.
Intrafamily offenses, §16-1001.
Rights of persons with intellectual
disability, §7-1301.03.
Transportation department,
§50-921.01a.
Uniform adult guardianship and
protective proceedings jurisdiction
act, §21-2401.02.

Responding state.
Interstate family support, §46-351.02.

Responding tribunal.
Interstate family support, §46-351.02.

Response.
Brownfield revitalization, §8-631.02.

Responsibility, §32-601.
Procurement practices, §2-351.04.

Responsibility center.
Budgets and budget estimates,
§47-382.

Responsible.
Procurement practices, §2-351.04.

**Responsible condominium unit
owners' association.**
Rental of public space, §10-1101.01.

Responsible party, §8-113.01.
Nurse staffing agencies, §44-1051.01.

Responsible person.
Brownfield revitalization, §8-631.02.
Student health care, medication,
§38-651.01.

Responsible relative.
Child support enforcement, §46-201.

Responsive bidder or offeror.
Procurement practices, §2-351.04.

Restaurant, §§7-1702, 50-101.
Alcoholic beverages, §25-101.

Restraint.
Mental health consumer's rights,
§7-1231.02.
Prisoners, use of restraints on
pregnant women, §24-276.01.
Youth rehabilitation services
department, use of restraints on
pregnant youths, §2-1515.51.

DEFINED TERMS —Cont'd
Restricted period.
  Procurement practices, §2-351.04.
Restricted pistol bullet, §7-2501.01.
Restricted recipient.
  Medical assistance program,
    §1-307.02.
Restricted use.
  Pesticide education and control,
    §8-431.
Restricted use pesticides, §8-401.
Resuscitate.
  Non-resuscitation procedures for EMS,
    §7-651.01.
Retail dealer, §§8-171.02, 36-301.01.
  Fire-standard-compliant cigarettes,
    §7-1751.
Retail development costs.
  Retail development incentives,
    §2-1217.71.
Retail development project.
  Retail development incentives,
    §2-1217.71.
Retail element.
  Georgia commons.
    Real property transfer tax
      exemption, §47-4610.
Retailer, §§28-4521, 47-2201.
  Extended manufacturer responsibility
    for electronic waste, §8-1041.01.
  Gas stations, §36-304.11.
  Gross sales tax, §47-2001.
Retail establishment, §47-2201.
  Anacostia river clean up and
    protection, §8-102.01.
  Gross sales tax, §47-2001.
Retail installment contract, §50-601.
Retail installment transaction,
    §50-601.
Retail pharmacy.
  Access to prescription drugs,
    §48-831.02.
  Unused pharmaceutical safe disposal,
    §48-851.01.
Retail priority area.
  Retail development incentives,
    §2-1217.71.
Retail sale, §§36-301.01, 47-2201.
  Gross sales tax, §47-2001.
Retail service station, §36-301.01.
Retail store, §7-1702.
Retail value, §§22-901, 48-901.02.
Retained.
  Promotion or retention of students,
    §38-781.01.
Retaliating.
  Whistleblower protection, §1-615.52.

DEFINED TERMS —Cont'd
Retention.
  Promotion or retention of students,
    §38-781.01.
Retention period, §2-1701.
Retire, §11-1561.
  Firefighter retirement while under
    disciplinary investigation, §5-1051.
Retirement, §1-307.61.
  Police retirement while under
    disciplinary investigation, §5-801.
Retirement program, §§1-702,
    1-901.02.
Return, §47-2201.
  Gross sales tax, §47-2001.
Reusable carryout bag.
  Anacostia river clean up and
    protection, §8-102.01.
Reuse.
  Extended manufacturer responsibility
    for electronic waste, §8-1041.01.
  Paint stewardship, §8-233.01.
**Revenue bonds, notes or other
    obligations,** §§1-204.90, 9-901,
    34-2202.01.
Revenue funds, §47-382.
Reverse 911 system.
  Emergency and non-emergency
    telephone system assessments
    fund, §34-1801.
Reverse auction.
  Procurement practices, §2-351.04.
Reverse repurchase transaction.
  Insurance investments, §31-1371.02.
Review board.
  Historic landmarks, §6-1102.
Revised RBC plan.
  Health insurance regulatory
    standards, §31-3451.01.
**Revitalization initiative and
    development plan.**
  New Town at Capital City Market
    revitalization, §6-1062.02.
  Workforce housing production
    program, §6-1061.02.
Revocable.
  Uniform trust code, §19-1301.03.
Revocation.
  Anatomical gifts, §7-1531.01.
  Health occupations, §3-1201.01.
Revolving credit account, §§28-3701,
    28-3802.
  Commercial instruments, §28-3701.
  Consumer protection, §28-3802.
RFI.
  Wireless network antennae franchise
    agreement, §34-1731.02.

DEFINED TERMS —Cont'd

RFP.
Procurement practices, §2-351.04.
Sustainable energy, §8-1773.01.
Wireless network antennae franchise
agreement, §34-1731.02.

RFQ.
Procurement practices, §2-351.04.

**Rhode Island Metro Plaza PILOT
area.**
Payments in lieu of taxes, sales tax
exemption, §47-4613.

Rifle, §7-2501.01.

Rights.
UCC, §28:1-201.

Risk and protective factors.
Interagency collaboration and services
integration commission, §2-1592.

Risk assessment.
Lead-hazard prevention and
elimination, §8-231.01.

Risk assessor.
Lead-hazard prevention and
elimination, §8-231.01.

Risk officer.
Medical liability captive insurance
agency, §1-307.81.

Risk retention group, §31-4101.

RLA.
Alcoholic beverages, §25-101.

Robbery, §22-2801.

**Robert F. Kennedy Memorial
Stadium.**
Washington convention and sports
authority, §10-1202.01.

Rodent-proof.
Rodent abatement program,
§8-2103.01.

Rodent-proofing.
Rodent abatement program,
§8-2103.01.

Roll-call time.
Police and fire departments, §5-1304.

Room remarketer.
Compensating use tax, §47-2201.
Gross sales tax, §47-2001.

Rough order of magnitude estimate.
School-based budgeting and
accountability, §38-2801.01.

Routine patient care costs.
Health insurance, clinical trials
insurance coverage, §31-2993.01.

RSA.
Disability services, department on,
§7-761.02.

RS fund.
Hospital and medical services
corporation, §31-3501.

DEFINED TERMS —Cont'd

Rule.
Administrative procedure, §2-502.
Codification of acts, §2-601.
Fraternal benefit societies, §31-5301.
Governmental reorganization,
§1-315.02.
Interstate compact on educational
opportunity for military children,
§49-1101.03.
Respectful language modernization,
§2-631.

Rulemaking, §2-502.

Rules of operation.
Retail development incentives,
§2-1217.71.

Sado-masochistic abuse, §22-2201.

Safe housing.
Homeless services, §4-751.01.

Safe or safety, §32-802.

Safety-related defect, §50-501.

Safety-sensitive position.
Mandatory drug and alcohol testing of
certain employees who serve
children, §1-620.31.

Salaried company employee,
§31-2501.03.

Sale at retail, §47-2201.
Gross sales tax, §47-2001.

Sale or sell, §§28-4001, 42-3404.02,
47-2201.
Alcoholic beverages, §25-101.
Consumer identification, §47-3151.
Fire-standard-compliant cigarettes,
§7-1751.
Gross sales tax, §47-2001.
Income tax, §47-1801.04.
Paint stewardship, §8-233.01.
Security agents and broker,
§31-5601.01.
Tobacco tax, §47-2401.
UCC, §28:2-106.
Uniform certificates of title for vessels,
§50-1541.01.
Weapons, §22-4501.

Sale proceeds.
Civil asset forfeiture, §41-301.

Sales price, §47-2201.
Gross sales tax, §47-2001.

Sales tax.
Streamlined sales and use tax
agreement, §1-301.121.

Sales tax base year.
Howard Theatre redevelopment
project, §2-1217.151.
Howard Theatre redevelopment project
TIF area, §2-1217.34a.

DEFINED TERMS —Cont'd

Sales tax increment revenues,
§2-1217.01.

Sales tax revenue.
Waterfront Park at the Yards,
§10-1801.

Salvage title.
Salvage, flood and junk vehicles,
§50-1331.01.

Salvage vehicle, §50-1331.01.

Sanction, §2-502.
Homeless services, §4-751.01.

Sanitary sewage, §§8-103.01, 34-2101.

Sanitary sewage works, §34-2101.

Sanitary sewer, §§8-103.01, 34-2101.

Sanitization.
Body art establishments, business
licenses, §47-2809.01.
Breastmilk bank and lactation
support, §7-881.01.

Sanitize.
Procurement practices, §2-351.04.

SART.
Victims of crime, sexual assault
response, §4-561.01.

Satellite service.
Automated teller machines,
§26-131.02.

Satisfactory academic progress.
DC promise program, §38-2751.

Saving institution.
Banks and financial institutions,
§26-551.02.
Universal banks, §26-1401.02.

Savings and loan association.
Investment and deposit of District
funds, §47-351.01.

Savings and loan holding company,
§26-1201.

Savings bank.
Investment and deposit of District
funds, §47-351.01.

Savings returns.
Cooperative associations, §29-902.

Sawed-off shotgun, §7-2501.01.
Weapons, §22-4501.

Scarification.
Body art establishments, business
licenses, §47-2809.01.

Scene, §7-2802.

Schedule.
Retail electric competition and
consumer protection, §34-1501.

School, §3-602.
Athletic concussion program,
§7-2871.01.

DEFINED TERMS —Cont'd

School —Cont'd
Defibrillator usage, §44-231.
Pesticide education and control,
§8-431.
Student health care, medication,
§38-651.01.

School administrators.
Merit system, §1-603.01.

School-based clinician.
Interagency collaboration and services
integration commission, §2-1592.

School-based educational position.
Preservation of school-based staffed
positions, §38-1807.57.

School-based student support team.
Compulsory school attendance,
§38-201.

School day.
Metropolitan police.
School safety division, §5-132.21.

School facility.
Charter schools, §38-1800.02.
School-based budgeting and
accountability, §38-2801.01.

School management organization.
Charter schools, §38-1800.02.

School of dentistry, §38-1419.

School of medicine, §38-1419.

School readiness.
Pre-kindergarten programs,
§38-271.01.

School-related event, §32-1201.

School resource officer.
Metropolitan police.
School safety division, §5-132.01.

School security guards.
Metropolitan police.
School safety division, §5-132.01.

School security personnel.
Metropolitan police.
School safety division, §5-132.01.

School year.
Compulsory school attendance,
§38-201.
Promotion or retention of students,
§38-781.01.

Scope of practice.
Emergency volunteer health
practitioners, §7-2361.01.

Scrap title.
Scrap vehicle title authorization,
§50-2701.

Screened.
Rules of professional conduct,
ProfCond Rule 1.0.

DEFINED TERMS —Cont'd
Screening, §7-1301.03.
  Breastmilk bank and lactation support, §7-881.01.
Screening mammogram, §31-2901.
Scrutinized business activities.
  Employees retirement program management, §1-336.01.
Scrutinized companies list.
  Employees retirement program management, §1-335.01.
Scrutinized company.
  Employees retirement program management, §§1-335.01, 1-336.01.
SDWA.
  Department of the environment, §8-151.01.
SEA.
  Nonpublic schools, §38-2561.01.
Seasonably.
  UCC, §28:1-205.
SEC, §31-301.
Seclusion.
  Mental health consumer's rights, §7-1231.02.
Secondary discounted price.
  Access to prescription drugs, §48-831.02.
Secondary feeder.
  Electric company infrastructure improvement financing, §34-1311.01.
Secondary obligor.
  Negotiable instruments, §28:3-103.
  Secured transactions, §28:9-102.
Secondary school.
  Charter schools, §38-1800.02.
  College access assistance, public school program, §38-2702.
  Scholarships for opportunity and results (SOAR) act, §38-1853.13.
Secondary victim, §4-501.
Secretary.
  Corporations, §29-301.02.
  Health benefit exchange authority, §31-3171.01.
  Metropolitan Washington airport, §9-1003.
  Miscellaneous provisions, §47-3401.05.
  National Children's Island, §10-1401.
  Nonprofit corporations, §29-401.02.
  Scholarships for opportunity and results (SOAR) act, §38-1853.13.
Secretary of the interior, §22-4332.
Section.
  Alcoholic beverages, §25-101.

DEFINED TERMS —Cont'd
Section 6 of the pistols and other dangerous weapons act.
  License to carry pistol, §7-2509.01.
Section 404 and section 404 report.
  Annual audited financial reports, §31-301.
Secured claim, §31-1301.
Secured facility.
  Mandatory drug and alcohol testing of certain employees, §1-620.21.
Secured location.
  Insurance investments, §31-1371.02.
Secured party, §50-601.
  Secured transactions, §28:9-102.
  Uniform certificates of title for vessels, §50-1541.01.
Secured party of record.
  Uniform certificates of title for vessels, §50-1541.01.
Secured party's transfer statement.
  Uniform certificates of title for vessels, §50-1541.18.
Secure facilities.
  Youth rehabilitation services department, §7-1131.02.
Secure juvenile residential facility.
  Prison contraband, §22-2603.01.
  Youth rehabilitation services department, use of restraints on pregnant youths, §2-1515.51.
Securities.
  Special purpose financial captive insurance companies, §31-3932.02.
Securities Act of 1933.
  Security agents and broker, §31-5601.01.
Securities and banking bureau.
  Insurance, securities, and banking, department of, §31-101.
Securities Exchange Act of 1934.
  Security agents and broker, §31-5601.01.
Securities intermediary.
  Investment securities, §28:8-102.
Securities lending transaction.
  Insurance investments, §31-1371.02.
Security, §21-2011.
  Employees retirement program management, §1-702.
  Ethics and government accountability, §1-1161.01.
  Fiduciary security transfers, §28-2901.
  Investment securities, §28:8-102.
  Security agents and broker, §31-5601.01.

DEFINED TERMS —Cont'd
Security —Cont'd
TOD securities registration,
§19-603.01.
Security account.
Investment securities, §28:8-501.
TOD securities registration,
§19-603.01.
Security agency, §47-2839.01.
Security agreements.
Secured transactions, §28:9-102.
Uniform certificates of title for vessels,
§50-1541.01.
Security and fire alarm contractors,
§7-2802.
Security certificate.
Investment securities, §28:8-102.
Security entitlement.
Investment securities, §28:8-102.
Securityholder, §31-701.
Security interest, §50-601.
UCC, §28:1-201.
Uniform certificates of title for vessels,
§50-1541.01.
Security interest instrument,
§42-1101.
Security officer, §47-2839.01.
Minimum wage, §32-1002.
Whistleblower protection, §2-223.01.
Security procedure.
Electronic transactions, uniform act,
§28-4901.
Funds transfers, §28:4A-201.
Security services, §47-2839.01.
Gross sales tax, §47-2001.
Sedan-class vehicle.
Regulation of for-hire vehicles,
§50-301.03.
Seized-currency.
Metropolitan police, §23-531.
**Select adult, community and
continuing education course,**
§38-1001.
Self-administration of medication,
§21-1201.
**Self-contained (dedicated) special
education school.**
Uniform per student funding formula,
§38-2901.
Self-insurer, §31-2402.
Vehicle insurance enforcement,
§5-114.01.
Self-regulatory organization.
Security agents and broker,
§31-5601.01.
Self-service display.
Tobacco, §7-1721.01.

DEFINED TERMS —Cont'd
Self-service storage facility, §40-401.
Self-sufficiency.
Workforce investment implementation,
§32-1602.
Seller, §28-3701.
Revolving credit accounts, §28-3701.
Sales, §28:2-103.
Streamlined sales and use tax
agreement, §1-301.121.
Telephone solicitation fraud,
§22-3226.01.
Uniform certificates of title for vessels,
§50-1541.01.
Seller agency.
Capital project support fund,
§1-325.151.
Selling, sell, or sale, §36-301.01.
Gross sales tax, §47-2001.
Hearing aid dealers, §28-4001.
Insurance producers, §31-1131.02.
Semiautomatic pistol.
Microstamping of semiautomatic
pistols, §7-2505.03.
Semipublic institution, §47-2201.
Gross sales tax, §47-2001.
Send.
Secured transactions, §28:9-102.
UCC, §28:1-201.
Uniform certificates of title for vessels,
§50-1541.01.
Sender.
Funds transfers, §28:4A-103.
Sending state.
Interstate compact on educational
opportunity for military children,
§49-1101.03.
Senior.
AIDS/HIV education and outreach,
§7-1631.
Senior executive.
Corporations, §29-311.01.
**Senior executive attorney service
position.**
Legal service, §1-608.51.
Senior's household.
Real property tax deferral, §47-845.03.
Septic tank, §8-105.02.
Series company.
Insurance investments, §31-1371.02.
Series trust.
Statutory trusts, §29-1201.02.
Serious bodily injury, §2-1542.
Pre-kindergarten programs,
§38-271.01.
Sexual abuse, §22-3001.

DEFINED TERMS —Cont'd
Serious crime.
Attorney discipline or disability
proceedings, DCBar Rule XI.
Serious harm.
Human trafficking, §22-1831.
Serious health condition, §32-501.
Voluntary leave transfer program,
§1-612.31.
Serious injury, §8-1901.
Serious misconduct.
Firefighter retirement while under
disciplinary investigation, §5-1051.
Police retirement while under
disciplinary investigation, §5-801.
Server operations program.
Citywide technology support services,
§1-1431.
Service animal.
Disabilities, persons with, §7-1009.
Service animal in training.
Disabilities, persons with, §7-1009.
Service charge, §28-3818.
Layaway consumer protections,
§28-3818.
Service coordination period, §44-902.
Service corporation, §26-1201.
Service credit, §7-531.01.
Service fees.
Clean hands before receiving a license
permit, §47-2861.
Service-level budgets.
Performance based budget, §47-308.01.
Service location.
Special education student rights,
§38-2571.02.
Service obligation.
Access to justice initiative program,
§4-1701.01.
Service obligation site.
Health professional recruitment
program, §7-751.01.
Service plan.
Homeless services, §4-751.01.
Mental health consumer's rights,
§7-1231.02.
Service provider.
Health data privacy, §7-241.
Servicer.
Mortgage loan protection, §26-1151.01.
Services, §§5-701, 22-3201, 34-215.
Consumer identification, §47-3151.
Human trafficking, §22-1831.
Performance based budget, §47-308.01.
Procurement practices, §2-351.04.
Telephone solicitation fraud,
§22-3226.01.

DEFINED TERMS —Cont'd
Service sewer, §§34-2202.01,
34-2405.08.
Services to the aged, §7-502.01.
Services to the Asian and Pacific
communities.
Office of Asian and Pacific Islander
affairs, §2-1372.
Services to the Latino community,
§2-1302.
Servicing agreement.
Electric company infrastructure
improvement financing,
§34-1311.01.
Serving carrier.
Toll telecommunication service tax,
§47-3901.
SETF.
Sustainable energy, §8-1773.01.
Settle.
Bank deposits and collections,
§28:4-104.
Settlement, §42-2401.
Settlement agent, §42-2401.
Settlement agreement.
Foreclosure mediation, §42-815.02.
Settlement conference.
Alcoholic beverages, §25-101.
Settlor.
Uniform trust code, §19-1301.03.
Settlor's successors in interest.
Uniform trust code, §19-1301.03.
SEU.
Sustainable energy, §8-1773.01.
Severe weather conditions.
Homeless services, §4-751.01.
Severe weather shelter.
Homeless services, §4-751.01.
Sewage collection, treatment, and
disposal systems, §34-2202.01.
Sewer, §§34-2101, 34-2202.01.
Department of the environment,
§8-151.01.
Sex offender.
Sex offender registration, §22-4001.
Sex offenses.
Rights of persons with intellectual
disability, §7-1301.03.
Sexual abuse.
Family court proceedings, §16-2301.
Reporting of child sexual abuse,
§22-3020.51.
Right to sick and safe leave,
§32-131.01.
Sexual act.
Family court proceedings, §16-2301.

DEFINED TERMS —Cont'd
Sexual act —Cont'd
Human trafficking, §22-1831.
Prostitution, §22-2701.01.
Sex offender registration, §22-4001.
Sexual abuse, §22-3001.
Sexual assault.
Sexual assault victim advocates,
§14-312.
Victims of crime, §23-1907.
Victims of crime, sexual assault
response, §4-561.01.
Sexual assault victim.
Sexual assault victim advocates,
§14-312.
Victims of crime, §23-1907.
Victims of crime, sexual assault
response, §4-561.01.
Sexual assault victim advocate,
§14-312.
Victims of crime, §23-1907.
Sexual conduct, §§22-2201, 22-3101.
Nonconsensual pornography, §22-3051.
Sex offender registration, §22-4001.
Sexual contact.
Family court proceedings, §16-2301.
Human trafficking, §22-1831.
Sexual abuse, §22-3001.
Sexual excitement, §22-2201.
Sexual exploitation, §16-2301.
Sexual image.
Nonconsensual pornography, §22-3051.
Sexually explicit conduct.
Family court proceedings, §16-2301.
Sexually suggestive conduct,
§22-3010.01.
Sexual orientation, §2-1401.02.
Sexual orientation change efforts.
Mental health consumer's rights,
§7-1231.02.
Sexual performance, §22-3101.
Sexual psychopath, §22-3803.
Shared responsibility.
Assisted living residences, §44-102.01.
Shared responsibility agreement.
Assisted living residences, §44-102.01.
Shared work benefit.
Shared work unemployment
compensation program, §51-171.
Shared work plan.
Shared work unemployment
compensation program, §51-171.
**Shared work unemployment
compensation program,** §51-171.
Share exchange.
Corporations, §29-309.01.

DEFINED TERMS —Cont'd
Shareholder.
Corporations, §§29-301.02, 29-305.50,
29-311.01, 29-313.02.
Nonprofit corporations, §29-401.02.
Shares.
Corporations, §§29-301.02, 29-304.27,
29-304.40.
Nonprofit corporations, §29-401.02.
Sharps.
Body art establishments, business
licenses, §47-2809.01.
Safe needle distribution, §7-2851.
Sharps injury.
Safe needle distribution, §7-2851.
Shell business entity.
Insurance investments, §31-1371.02.
Shelter.
Homeless services, §4-751.01.
Shelter care, §16-2301.
Shippers.
Documents of title, §28:7-102.
SHOP Exchange.
Health benefit exchange authority,
§31-3171.01.
Shoplifting, §27-101.
Short barreled rifle, §7-2501.01.
Short-term.
Insurance investments, §31-1371.02.
Shotgun, §7-2501.01.
Weapons, §22-4501.
SHPO.
Historic landmarks, §6-1102.
Sick and safe leave act.
Wages and salaries, §32-1301.
Sickle cell anemia, §7-832.
Sickle hemoglobinopathy, §7-832.
Sidewalk market, §37-101.
Sidewalk market stall, §37-101.
Sign, §4-801.
Alcoholic beverages, §25-101.
Anatomical gifts, §7-1531.01.
Business organizations, §29-101.02.
Collaborative law, §16-4002.
Documents of title, §28:7-102.
Graffiti, §22-3312.05.
Mediation, §16-4201.
Uniform certificates of title for vessels,
§50-1541.01.
Uniform disclaimer of property
interests act, §19-1505.
Unsworn foreign declarations,
§16-5302.
Signal.
Fleeing from a law enforcement officer,
§50-2201.05b.

DEFINED TERMS —Cont'd

Signatory.
Chesapeake regional Olympic games
authority, §2-1131.

Signed.
UCC, §28:1-201.

Significant activities.
Merit system, §1-614.11.

Significant-connection state.
Uniform adult guardianship and
protective proceedings jurisdiction
act, §21-2401.02.

Significant industrial user.
Wastewater disposal systems,
§8-105.02.

Significantly impair, §50-501.

Significantly underused.
School-based budgeting and
accountability, §38-2801.01.

Significant noncompliance.
Wastewater disposal systems,
§8-105.02.

Significant relationship.
Sexual abuse, §22-3001.

Single family dwelling.
Homestead housing provision,
§42-2103.

Single family home, §42-2621.

Single family residential property,
§42-2301.
Real property assessment, §47-803.
Tax abatement for homeowners in
enterprise zones, §47-858.01.

Single-room-occupancy housing,
§42-3501.03.

Single-use.
Body art establishments, business
licenses, §47-2809.01.

**Single-voltage external AC to DC
power supply.**
Energy efficiency standards,
§8-1771.01.

Sinking fund stock.
Insurance investments, §31-1371.02.

Sister, §§1-623.01, 32-1501.

Site, §8-1051.
Demolition or enclosure of deteriorated
property, §42-3173.01.
Not-for-profit hospital corporations,
§44-951.01.
Payment in lieu of taxes, §47-1052.

SIU.
Wastewater disposal systems,
§8-105.02.

Size.
Condominiums, §42-1901.02.

DEFINED TERMS —Cont'd

Skill, §32-601.

Slamming.
Retail natural gas supplier licensing
and consumer protection,
§34-1671.02.

Slash.
Renewable energy portfolio standards,
§34-1431.

Sleeper hold, §5-125.02.

SLS license.
Insurance, securities, and banking,
department of, §31-101.

Sludge, §§8-103.01, 8-105.02.

Slug discharge.
Wastewater disposal systems,
§8-105.02.

Slug load.
Wastewater disposal systems,
§8-105.02.

Slum and blight.
Acquisition and disposal of abandoned
and deteriorated property,
§42-3171.01.

Slum area.
National capital revitalization
corporation, §2-1217.12.

Small business.
Investment and deposit of District
funds, §47-351.01.

Small business enterprise.
Small and certified business enterprise
development and assistance,
§2-218.02.

Small business loan.
Community development by financial
institutions, §26-431.02.

Small employer, §31-3301.01.
Health benefit exchange authority,
§31-3171.01.
Hospital and medical services
corporation, §31-3501.
Substance abuse insurance coverage,
§31-3101.

Small food retailer.
Grocery and retail stores development,
§2-1212.01.

Small group market.
Substance abuse insurance coverage,
§31-3101.

Small investor.
Small and certified business enterprise
development and assistance,
§2-218.02.

Small multi-family dwelling.
Homestead housing provision,
§42-2103.

DEFINED TERMS —Cont'd
Small store.
Commercial property energy
conservation, §8-1772.01.
Smart grid.
Electric light and power companies,
§34-1561.
Smoke.
Marijuana, consumption in public
space or impairment, §48-911.01.
Smokeless tobacco.
Tobacco tax, §47-2401.
Smoking, §7-1702.
Health department, §7-741.01.
SNAP benefits.
Grocery and retail stores development,
§2-1212.01.
Social development company.
Employees retirement program
management, §1-335.01.
Social impact funding instrument.
Pay-for-success contracts, §2-211.01.
Social Security Act.
Health benefit exchange authority,
§31-3171.01.
Social service intermediary.
Pay-for-success contracts, §2-211.01.
Social worker, §31-3101.
Social work, practice of, §3-1201.02.
Society, §31-5301.
Marriage solemnization, §46-406.
Soft costs.
Ballpark construction hard and soft
costs cap, §10-1601.31.
Soft drink.
Gross sales tax, §47-2001.
Software, §2-213.01.
Secured transactions, §28:9-102.
Soil and water conservation, §8-1702.
Soil test.
Anacostia River cleanup and
protection fertilizer act, §8-104.02.
Solar energy.
Renewable energy portfolio standards,
§34-1431.
Solar system.
Solar for All program, §8-1774.16.
Solar thermal systems.
Sustainable energy, §8-1773.01.
Sold at retail, §47-2201.
Sole source.
Procurement practices, §2-351.04.
Solicit.
Charitable solicitations, §44-1701.
Insurance producers, §31-1131.02.
Solicitation, §3-402.
Anti-terrorism act of 2002, §22-3152.

DEFINED TERMS —Cont'd
Solicitation —Cont'd
Charitable solicitation, §44-1701.
Solicit for prostitution, §22-2701.01.
Soliciting agent, §31-2501.03.
Solicitor, §§31-4202, 47-1401.
**Solicitor of residential real
property,** §47-1401.
Solid waste.
Illegal dumping enforcement, §8-901.
Solid waste facility permit act,
§8-1051.
Solid waste reduction and recovery,
§8-1031.01.
Solid waste disposal facility, §8-1051.
Solid waste facility, §8-1051.
Solid waste handling facility,
§8-1051.
Solid waste stream.
Solid waste reduction and recovery,
§8-1031.01.
SOS administrator.
Retail electric competition and
consumer protection, §34-1501.
Source.
Child abuse and neglect, §4-1301.02.
Source of income, §2-1401.02.
Source reduction, §8-1302.
Source selection.
Procurement practices, §2-351.04.
Source separated, §8-1051.
Source separation.
Solid waste reduction and recovery,
§8-1031.01.
Southeast Federal center.
Alcoholic beverages, §25-101.
**Southeast Federal Center Navy Yard
area,** §2-1217.01.
**Southeast water and sewer
improvement benefit district,**
§47-891.
**Southeast water and sewer
improvement project,** §47-891.
South hall, §37-101.
Southwest waterfront fund.
Southwest waterfront bond financing,
§2-1217.131.
Southwest waterfront special
assessment district, §47-895.01.
**Southwest waterfront improvement
benefit district.**
Southwest waterfront bond financing,
§2-1217.131.
Southwest waterfront special
assessment district, §47-895.01.
Southwest waterfront pilot.
Southwest waterfront bond financing,
§2-1217.131.

DEFINED TERMS —Cont'd
Southwest waterfront pilot base amount.
Southwest waterfront bond financing, §2-1217.131.
Southwest waterfront pilot base increment.
Southwest waterfront bond financing, §2-1217.131.
Southwest waterfront pilot/TIF area.
Southwest waterfront bond financing, §2-1217.131.
Southwest waterfront special assessment.
Southwest waterfront bond financing, §2-1217.131.
SOX compliance entity.
Annual audited financial reports, §31-301.
Special administrator, §20-101.
Special appraiser, §20-101.
Special assessment.
Energy efficiency financing, §8-1778.02.
Southwest waterfront special assessment district, §47-895.01.
Special energy assessments, §47-895.31.
Special assessment annual collection account.
New York avenue metrorail benefit area, §47-881.
Special assessment credit.
Southwest waterfront special assessment district, §47-895.01.
Special assessment factor.
New York avenue metrorail benefit area, §47-881.
Special assessment requirement.
Southwest waterfront special assessment district, §47-895.01.
Special assessment total collection account.
New York avenue metrorail benefit area, §47-881.
Special assignment.
Police and fire departments, §5-1304.
Special credit rated instrument.
Insurance investments, §31-1371.02.
Special declarant right.
Condominiums, §42-1901.02.
Special deposit claim, §31-1301.
Special education.
Medicaid and special education reform fund, §4-204.52.
Nonpublic schools, §38-2561.01.

DEFINED TERMS —Cont'd
Special education —Cont'd
Tobacco settlement trust fund, §7-1811.03.
Uniform per student funding formula, §38-2901.
Special education capacity fund.
Uniform per student funding formula, §38-2901.
Special education compliance fund.
Uniform per student funding formula, §38-2901.
Special education payment.
Uniform per student funding formula, §38-2901.
Special education school.
Uniform per student funding formula, §38-2901.
Special education services.
Procurement practices, §2-351.04.
Special energy assessment fund.
Real property taxes.
Special energy assessments, §47-895.31.
Special events.
Gross sales tax, §47-2001.
Police and fire departments, §5-1304.
Specialized vehicle.
Fleet management, publicly-owned vehicles, §50-211.01.
Special merits, §2-1217.01.
Historic landmarks, §6-1102.
Special plea in bar.
Criminal procedure, CrimPro Rule 54.
Special police officer, §47-2839.01.
Special purpose financial captive or SPFC.
Captive insurance companies, §31-3932.02.
Special real property tax levy, §47-336.
Special tree.
Urban forest preservation, §8-651.02.
Specification.
Procurement practices, §2-351.04.
Specific individual.
Stalking, §22-3132.
Specific public benefit.
Benefit corporations, §29-1301.02.
Specified offense.
Anti-terrorism act of 2002, §22-3152.
Specimen, §§44-201, 50-1901.
Impaired operation or driving, §50-2206.01.
Speech-language pathology assistant, practice by, §3-1201.02.

DEFINED TERMS —Cont'd

Speech-language pathology clinical fellow, practice by, §3-1201.02.

Speech-language pathology, practice of, §3-1201.02.

Spendthrift provision.
Uniform trust code, §19-1301.03.

SPFC contract.
Special purpose financial captive insurance companies, §31-3932.02.

SPFC securities.
Special purpose financial captive insurance companies, §31-3932.02.

Spirits, §25-101.

Sponsor, §§7-531.01, 42-2701.02.
Commemorative work, §9-204.11.
Mortgage lenders and brokers, §26-1101.
Parks and recreation, §10-301.

Sponsor-based voucher assistance.
District of Columbia housing authority, §6-201.

Spot rate, §15-901.

Spousal support.
Child support enforcement, §46-201.

Spousal-support order.
Interstate family support, §46-351.02.

Spouse.
Teachers' retirement, deferred or survivor annuity, §38-2021.09.

SRCC.
Sustainable energy, §8-1773.01.

SRR.
Mortgage lenders and brokers, §26-1101.

Stable, §8-2001.

Stacking, §31-2402.

Stadium, §3-330.

Stakeholders.
Performance based budget, §47-308.01.

Stamp.
Tobacco tax, §47-2401.

Standard, §32-1101.
Merit system, §1-603.01.

Standard agent, §42-1702.

Standard deduction.
Income tax, §47-1801.04.

Standardized plan.
Health benefit exchange authority, §31-3171.01.

Standard offer service.
Retail electric competition and consumer protection, §34-1501.

Standard probate proceeding, §20-101.

Standby guardian, §16-4802.

DEFINED TERMS —Cont'd

Standing appraiser, §20-101.

State.
Anatomical gifts, §7-1531.01.
Athlete agent, §47-2887.01.
Business organizations, §29-101.02.
Controlled substances act, §48-901.02.
Criminal procedure, CrimPro Rule 54.
Custodial trusts, §19-1101.
Emergency volunteer health practitioners, §7-2361.01.
Environmental covenants, §8-671.01.
Extradition and fugitives from justice, §23-707.
Foreign-money claim, §15-901.
Income tax, §47-1801.04.
Inheritance and estate taxes, §47-3701.
Insurance companies, §47-2601.
Insurance investments, §31-1371.02.
International banking corporations, §26-631.
Interstate compact on adoption and medical assistance, §4-321.
Interstate compact on educational opportunity for military children, §49-1101.03.
Interstate depositions and discovery, §13-442.
Interstate enforcement of domestic violence proceedings, §16-1041.
Interstate family support, §46-351.02.
Life and health insurance guaranty association, §31-5401.
Military and overseas voters, §1-1061.02.
Motor vehicle safety responsibility, §50-1301.36.
National technical institute for the deaf, §38-2402.01.
Out-of-state witness, §23-1501.
Real property electronic recording, §42-1231.
Savings and loan acquisitions, §26-1201.
Secured transactions, §28:9-102.
Security agents and broker, §31-5601.01.
Sex offender registration, §22-4001.
UCC, §28:1-201.
Unemployment compensation, §51-101.
Uniform adult guardianship and protective proceedings jurisdiction act, §21-2401.02.
Uniform certificates of title for vessels, §50-1541.01.

DEFINED TERMS —Cont'd
State —Cont'd
Uniform child custody proceedings, §16-4601.01.
Uniform disclaimer of property interests act, §19-1502.
Uniform trust code, §19-1301.03.
Unsworn foreign declarations, §16-5302.
State bank.
Universal banks, §26-1401.02.
State council.
Interstate compact on educational opportunity for military children, §49-1101.03.
State education agency.
Nonpublic schools, §38-2561.01.
State education office.
Tuition of nonresidents, §38-304.
State enforcement agency.
Interstate family support, §46-351.02.
State financial institutions agency.
Universal banks, §26-1401.02.
State historic preservation officer.
Historic landmarks, §6-1102.
Statehood delegation.
New Columbia statehood initiative, §1-129.21.
Statehood fund.
New Columbia statehood initiative, §1-129.21.
State law.
Unemployment compensation, §51-107.
State law enforcement officer.
Killing law enforcement officer, §22-2106.
State level costs.
Uniform per student funding formula, §38-2901.
Statement.
Partnerships, §29-601.02.
Production of witness statements, CrimPro Rule 26.2.
Delinquent minors, JuvProc Rule 26.2.
Statement of authority.
Unincorporated nonprofit associations, §29-1107.
Statement of conversion.
Entity transactions, §29-201.02.
Statement of domestication.
Entity transactions, §29-201.02.
Statement of interest exchange.
Entity transactions, §29-201.02.
Statement of merger.
Entity transactions, §29-201.02.

DEFINED TERMS —Cont'd
Statement of qualifications.
Procurement practices, §2-351.04.
State of principal use.
Uniform certificates of title for vessels, §50-1541.01.
State or local government loan, §42-2701.02.
State plan, §47-382.
State-regulated incandescent reflector lamp.
Energy efficiency standards, §8-1771.01.
Statewide popular election.
National popular vote interstate agreement, §1-1051.01.
Status as unemployed.
Discrimination, §32-1361.
Statute of limitations.
Crime investigation records, §5-113.31.
Statutory trust, §29-1201.02.
Business organizations, §29-101.02.
STEM.
Qualified social electronic commerce companies tax abatements, §47-1818.01.
Stepparent, §4-201.01.
Sterilization.
Body art establishments, business licenses, §47-2809.01.
STI.
Sexually transmitted diseases, treatment for sexual partners, §7-2081.01.
Still or motion picture.
Sexual performances using minors, §22-3101.
Stock insurance company, §31-601.
Stock insurer.
Captive insurance companies, §31-3931.01.
Stolen property, §22-3201.
Stolen vehicle.
Scrap vehicle title authorization, §50-2701.
Stop-loss insurance.
Health insurance for employers, §31-3821.
Stop work orders.
Workplace fraud, §32-1331.01.
Storage, §§8-1302, 47-2201.
Breastmilk bank and lactation support, §7-881.01.
Store, §47-2201.
Stormwater best management practice.
DDOT stormwater retention credit fund, §50-921.22.

DEFINED TERMS —Cont'd
**Stormwater best management
  practice** —Cont'd
Department of the environment,
  §8-151.01.
Stormwater permit.
Department of the environment,
  §8-151.01.
Stormwater retention credit.
DDOT stormwater retention credit
  fund, §50-921.22.
Stormwater sewage, §34-2101.
Stormwater sewer, §34-2101.
Stormwater sewer system, §34-2101.
Stormwater user fee.
Department of the environment,
  §8-151.01.
Street, §§8-205, 9-201.01.
Public space rental and utilization,
  §10-1101.01.
Street railroad, §34-216.
Street railroad corporation, §34-217.
Stroke.
Stroke system of care, §44-1151.
Stroke triage assessment tool.
Stroke system of care, §44-1151.
Structural member, §8-111.01.
Structured settlement annuity.
Life and health insurance guaranty
  association, §31-5401.
Student, §32-1501.
Interstate compact on educational
  opportunity for military children,
  §49-1101.03.
Right to sick and safe leave,
  §32-131.01.
Student-athlete.
Athlete agent, §47-2887.01.
Student child, §5-701.
Student education loan.
Insurance, securities, and banking,
  department of, §31-101.
Student with a disability.
Nonpublic schools, §38-2561.01.
Student with special needs.
Charter schools, §38-1800.02.
Subcontractor.
Private contractor and subcontractor
  prompt payment act, §27-131.
Quick payment provisions, §2-221.01.
Subdivide.
Historic landmarks, §6-1102.
Subdivision.
Historic landmarks, §6-1102.
Subject.
Promotion or retention of students,
  §38-781.01.

DEFINED TERMS —Cont'd
Sublease.
Leases, UCC, §28:2A-103.
Submetering equipment, §34-1551.
Subordinate agency, §2-502.
Merit system, §1-603.01.
Subordinated bonds.
Income tax secured bonds, §47-340.26.
Subpart F income.
Income tax, §47-1801.04.
Subpoena.
Interstate depositions and discovery,
  §13-442.
Subrogee.
Health care benefits lien reduction,
  §31-3551.
Subscriber.
Corporations, §29-301.02.
Hospital and medical services
  corporation, §31-3501.
Office of cable television, film, music,
  and entertainment amendment
  act of 2015, §34-1251.03.
Retail electric competition and
  consumer protection, §34-1501.
Security and fire alarm systems
  regulations, §7-2802.
Subscriber contract.
Hospital and medical services
  corporation, §31-3501.
Subscriber organization.
Retail electric competition and
  consumer protection, §34-1501.
Subscription.
Retail electric competition and
  consumer protection, §34-1501.
Subsidiary.
Banks and financial institutions,
  §26-551.02.
Benefit corporations, §29-1301.02.
Hospital and medical services
  corporation, §31-3501.
Insurance holding company system,
  §31-701.
Merchant bank, §26-831.02.
Mortgage loan protection, §26-1151.01.
Savings and loan acquisitions,
  §26-1201.
Title insurance producers,
  §31-5041.01.
Title insurers, §31-5031.01.
Universal banks, §26-1401.02.
Subsidy, §42-2701.02.
Substance abuse, §44-1201.
Behavioral health department,
  §7-1141.01.

DEFINED TERMS —Cont'd

Substance abuse —Cont'd

Choice in drug treatment, §7-3002.

Substantial.

Rules of professional conduct, ProfCond Rule 1.0.

Substantial action.

Employees retirement program management, §1-335.01.

Substantial action specific to Iran.

Employees retirement program management, §1-336.01.

Substantial change.

Mental health consumer's rights, §7-1231.02.

Substantial completion.

Waterfront Park special assessment district, §47-895.21.

Substantial improvement.

Anacostia waterfront environmental standards, §2-1226.32.

Green buildings, §6-1451.01.

Sustainable energy, §8-1773.01.

Substantially alter, §8-1051.

Substantially rehabilitated.

Bicycle commuter and parking expansion, §50-1641.05.

Substantially rehabilitates.

Tax abatement for homeowners in enterprise zones, §47-858.01.

Substantially similar securities.

Insurance investments, §31-1371.02.

Substantial nongovernment in-kind contributions.

Mayor's official residence commission, §1-331.02.

Substantial rehabilitation, §42-3501.03.

Substantial understatement of income tax.

Taxation penalties, §47-4211.

Substantial valuation misstatement.

Taxation penalties, §47-4211.

Substantial violation, §42-3501.03.

Substantiated report.

Child abuse and neglect, §4-1301.02.

Substitute aide.

Right to sick and safe leave, §32-131.01.

Substituted judgment.

Conservators, §21-2011.

Rights of persons with intellectual disability, §7-1301.03.

Substitute drug product.

Prescription drugs, §48-804.51.

DEFINED TERMS —Cont'd

Substitute health care decision-maker.

Mental health consumer's rights, §7-1231.02.

Substitute teacher.

Right to sick and safe leave, §32-131.01.

Successor of a beneficiary.

Letters of credit, §28:5-102.

Suitable work.

Unemployment compensation, §51-107.

Summer school.

Uniform per student funding formula, §38-2901.

Summons.

Out-of-state witness, §23-1501.

Sums on deposit.

Nonprobate transfers on death, §19-602.01.

Superintendent.

Metropolitan police.

School safety division, §5-132.01.

Savings and loan acquisitions, §26-1201.

Superior court.

Bail and recognizance, §23-1110.

Business organizations, §29-101.02.

Criminal procedure, CrimPro Rule 54.

Family court proceedings, §16-2301.

First amendment assemblies, §5-335.01.

Foreign judgments, §15-351.

Incompetent criminal defendants, §24-531.01.

Interstate depositions and discovery, §13-442.

Merchant bank, §26-831.02.

Nursing facility assessment, §47-1261.

Revised real property tax sale, §47-1330.

Uniform adult guardianship and protective proceedings jurisdiction act, §21-2401.02.

Universal banks, §26-1401.02.

Supermarket.

Tax incentives, §47-3801.

Supervised.

Criminal background checks for the protection of children act, §4-1501.02.

Supervised administration, §20-101.

Supervised personal representative, §20-101.

Supervising entity.

Portable electronics insurance, §31-5051.01.

DEFINED TERMS —Cont'd
Supervising federal agency.
Mortgage loan protection, §26-1151.01.
Supervising lawyer.
Appeals, DCCtApp Rule 48.
Civil procedure, CivPro Rule 101.
Criminal procedure, CrimPro Rule 44-I.
Family court proceedings, FamDiv Rule M.
Supervising surgeon.
Surgical assistants, §3-1206.41.
Supervision.
Anesthesiologist assistants, §3-1206.31.
Speech-language pathology clinical fellows, §3-1209.11.
Supervision status.
Overdose, seeking help for victim, §7-403.
Supervisor, §2-223.01.
Whistleblower protection, §1-615.52.
Supplemental benefit, §31-3101.
Supplemental component of AccessRx.
Access to prescription drugs, §48-831.02.
Supplemental contract.
Life and health insurance guaranty association, §31-5401.
Supplementary revenue.
Fee collection incentive fund, §1-325.61.
Suppliers.
Leases, UCC, §28:2A-103.
Supply contracts.
Leases, UCC, §28:2A-103.
Supporting obligation.
Secured transactions, §28:9-102.
Supportive housing.
District of Columbia housing authority, §6-201.
Homeless services, §4-751.01.
Supportive services.
Homeless services, §4-751.01.
Support order.
Child support enforcement, §46-201.
Divorce, annulment, separation, support, §16-901.
Interstate family support, §46-351.02.
Medical support enforcement, §46-251.01.
Surcharge.
Automated teller machines, §26-131.02.
Surety.
Procurement practices, §2-351.04.

DEFINED TERMS —Cont'd
Surety —Cont'd
UCC, §28:1-201.
Surplus, §§31-2501.03, 31-4202.
Hospital and medical services corporation, §31-3501.
Revised real property tax sale, §47-1330.
Surplus capital funds.
Capital project support fund, §1-325.151.
Surplus goods.
Procurement practices, §2-351.04.
Surplus note.
Special purpose financial captive insurance companies, §31-3932.02.
Surplus property fund.
Procurement practices, §2-351.04.
Surrender.
Newborn safe haven, §4-1451.01.
Surrogate.
Assisted living residences, §44-102.01.
Non-resuscitation procedures for EMS, §7-651.01.
Surrogate parenting contract, §16-401.
Survey.
National Children's Island, §10-1401.
Surveyor.
Streets and alleys, §9-201.01.
Surviving association.
Limited cooperative associations, §29-1015.01.
Unincorporated nonprofit associations, §29-1126.
Surviving company.
Limited liability companies, §29-809.01.
Surviving corporation.
Nonprofit corporations, §29-407.01.
Surviving entity.
Entity transactions, §29-201.02.
Surviving limited cooperative association.
Limited cooperative associations, §29-1015.01.
Surviving limited partnership.
Limited partnerships, §29-710.01.
Surviving organization.
Statutory trusts, §29-1207.01.
Surviving partnership.
Partnerships, §29-601.02.
Surviving spouse.
Income tax, §47-1801.04.
Surviving spouse or domestic partner.
Disability compensation, §1-623.01.

DEFINED TERMS —Cont'd
Surviving spouse or domestic partner —Cont'd
Workers' compensation, §32-1501.
Survivor, §§5-701, 31-2402.
Corporations, §29-309.01.
Nonprofit corporations, §29-409.01.
Survivor annuitant, §5-701.
Suspends payments.
Bank deposits and collections, §28:4-104.
Suspension.
Health occupations, §3-1201.01.
Sustainable agriculture.
Child and adult food program funding, §38-281.
Schools and education, §38-821.01.
Sustainable energy trust fund.
Sustainable energy, §8-1773.01.
Sustainable energy utility.
Sustainable energy, §8-1773.01.
Sustainable energy utility advisory board.
Sustainable energy, §8-1773.01.
Sustainable solid waste management hierarchy.
Solid waste reduction and recovery, §8-1031.01.
SVO.
Insurance investments, §31-1371.02.
Swap.
Insurance investments, §31-1371.02.
Swing space.
School-based budgeting and accountability, §38-2801.01.
Sworn declaration.
Unsworn foreign declarations, §16-5302.
Sworn police personnel.
Metropolitan police, §5-101.04.
SWW development.
Southwest waterfront special assessment district, §47-895.01.
System, §47-2851.01.
System implementation plan, §44-902.
System of care for adults.
Department of mental health, §7-1131.02.
Mental health consumer's rights, §7-1231.02.
System of care for children, youth and their families.
Department of mental health, §7-1131.02.
Mental health consumer's rights, §7-1231.02.

DEFINED TERMS —Cont'd
System of vital records, §7-201.
Table.
Alcoholic beverages, §25-101.
Tail coverage.
Medical liability captive insurance agency, §1-307.81.
Takes a residential mortgage loan application.
Mortgage lenders and brokers, §26-1101.
TANF.
Child care facilities, §4-401.
Food stamps, §4-261.01.
Public assistance, §4-201.01.
TANF-related Medicaid recipient.
Medical assistance program, §1-307.02.
Tangible chattel paper.
Secured transactions, §28:9-102.
Tangible personal property, §§47-1521, 47-2201.
Gross sales tax, §47-2001.
Tanning studio.
Gross sales tax, §47-2001.
Target development area, §26-1201.
Target economic development project, §26-1201.
Targeted moratorium zone.
Alcoholic beverages, §25-341.01.
Targeted population, §42-2801.
Targeted service, §7-531.01.
Task force.
Adult literacy task force, §32-1661.
Victims of crime, sexual assault response, §4-561.01.
Tattoo.
Body art establishments, business licenses, §47-2809.01.
Tavern, §25-101.
Tax.
Clean hands before receiving a license permit, §47-2861.
Ethics and government accountability, §1-1161.01.
Gross sales tax, §47-2001.
Income tax, §47-1801.04.
Multistate tax compact, §47-441.
Real property transfer excise tax, §47-1401.
Revised real property tax sale, §47-1330.
Superior court, §47-3301.
Tax collection, §47-433.
Taxable assessment.
Reduced real property tax liability for seniors and persons with disabilities, §47-863.

DEFINED TERMS —Cont'd

Taxable estate.
Inheritance and estate taxes, §47-3701.

Taxable income, §47-1807.01.
Income tax, §47-1801.04.
Unincorporated businesses, §47-1808.02.

Taxable period, §47-1807.01.
Unincorporated businesses, §47-1808.02.

Taxable property.
Business improvement districts, §2-1215.02.

Taxable situs.
Inheritance and estate taxes, §47-3701.

Tax check-off, §47-4001.

Tax expenditure.
Unified economic development budget transparency and accountability, §2-1208.01.

Tax haven.
Income tax, §47-1801.04.

Taxicab.
Regulation of for-hire vehicles, §50-301.03.

Taxicab association.
Regulation of for-hire vehicles, §50-301.03.

Taxicab company.
Regulation of for-hire vehicles, §50-301.03.

Taxicab fleet.
Regulation of for-hire vehicles, §50-301.03.

Taxicab industry.
Regulation of for-hire vehicles, §50-301.03.

Taxicab operator.
Regulation of for-hire vehicles, §50-301.03.

Taxicab owner.
Regulation of for-hire vehicles, §50-301.03.

Taxicab rate structure.
Regulation of for-hire vehicles, §50-301.03.

Taxicab service.
Regulation of for-hire vehicles, §50-301.03.

Tax increment.
Union Market district tax increment financing, §2-1217.36a.

Tax increment financing, §2-1217.01.

Tax increment revenues.
Retail development incentives, §2-1217.71.

DEFINED TERMS —Cont'd

Tax increments.
Revenue bonds, notes or other obligations, §1-204.90.

Taxing agency.
Revised real property tax sale, §47-1330.

Taxi or taxicab, §31-2402.

Tax liability.
Income tax, §47-1801.04.

Tax lot.
New York avenue metrorail benefit area, §47-881.

Taxpayer.
Gross sales tax, §47-2001.
Income tax, §47-1801.04.
Job growth tax credit, §47-1807.51.
Multistate tax compact, §47-441.
Real property assessment, §47-802.
Real property transfer tax, §47-901.
Recorder of deeds, §42-1101.

Tax preference.
Chief financial officer, tax transparency, §1-301.156.

Tax regime.
Income tax, §47-1801.04.

Tax return preparer.
Taxation penalties, §47-4217.

Tax sale date.
Revised real property tax sale, §47-1330.

Tax year.
CareFirst tax credit for wages, sales tax exemption, §47-4602.
Gross sales tax, §47-2001.
Personal property tax, §47-1521.
Real property assessment, §47-802.
Real property taxes.
Special energy assessments, §47-895.31.

Teacher.
Employees retirement program management, §1-702.
Police and firefighters retirement and disability, §1-901.02.
Teacher retirement, prior to June 30, 1946, §38-2001.13.
Teachers' retirement, §38-2021.13.

Technical assistance.
Pre-kindergarten programs, §38-271.01.

Technician.
Anatomical gifts, §7-1531.01.

Telecommunications, §34-2001.

Telecommunications carrier, §34-2001.

DEFINED TERMS —Cont'd
Telecommunications equipment,
§34-2001.
Telecommunications industry,
§34-2001.
Telecommunications relay service,
§34-2001.
Telecommunications service,
§34-2001.
Telecommunications system,
§34-2001.
Telegraph corporation, §34-218.
Telegraph line, §34-219.
Telehealth.
Telehealth reimbursement, §31-3861.
Telemarketing.
Telephone solicitation fraud,
§22-3226.01.
Telephone corporation, §34-220.
Telephone line, §34-221.
Telephone option, §28-4001.
Hearing aid dealers, §28-4001.
Telephone solicitor.
Telephone solicitation fraud,
§22-3226.01.
Teller's checks.
Negotiable instruments, §28:3-104.
Temporary assistance for needy
families.
Grandparent caregiver subsidies,
§4-251.01.
Temporary electricity programs.
Sustainable energy, §8-1773.01.
Temporary officiant.
Marriage solemnization, §46-406.
Temporary shelter.
Homeless services, §4-751.01.
Tenancy interest.
Lis pendens, §42-1207.
Tenant.
Acquisition and disposal of abandoned
and deteriorated property,
§42-3171.01.
Drug, firearm, or prostitution-related
nuisance abatement, §42-3101.
Drug-related evictions, §42-3601.
Eastern market, §37-101.
Master-metered apartment buildings,
§42-3301.
Preservation and rehabilitation of
government-supported housing,
§42-2851.02.
Real property tax abatement for
qualified high technology
companies, §47-811.03.

DEFINED TERMS —Cont'd
Tenant —Cont'd
Real property tax exemptions,
qualified high technology company
interior renovation tax rebate,
§47-4665.
Rental housing, §§42-3401.03,
42-3501.03.
Rental housing conversion,
opportunity to purchase,
§42-3404.02.
Water and sewer services amnesty
program, §34-2301.
Tenant assistance contract,
§42-3503.01.
Tenant association.
Homestead housing provision,
§42-2103.
Tenant organization, §42-3401.03.
Tenant organizer, §42-3505.06.
Tenant with a disability.
Rent control, §42-3502.06.
Tenement house, §6-701.12.
Term.
UCC, §28:1-201.
Term contract.
Procurement practices, §2-351.04.
Terminal condition, §§4-1101, 7-621.
Non-resuscitation procedures for EMS,
§7-651.01.
Terminally ill inmate, §24-461.
Terminate.
Insurance producers, §31-1131.02.
Termination.
Leases, UCC, §28:2A-103.
Sales, §28:2-106.
Termination of employment.
Child care facilities, §4-401.
Termination of parent and child
relationship, §16-2352.
Termination statement.
Secured transactions, §28:9-102.
Term sheet.
Walter Reed Medical Center site
development, §2-1227.01.
Terms of a trust.
Principal and income, §28-4801.02.
Uniform trust code, §19-1301.03.
Terms of the account.
Nonprobate transfers on death,
§19-602.01.
Testate decedent, §20-101.
Testing integrity and security
agreement.
Testing integrity in public schools,
§38-2602.

DEFINED TERMS —Cont'd

Testing integrity and security notification statement.
Testing integrity in public schools, §38-771.01.

Testing laboratory.
Medical marijuana, §7-1671.01.

Test integrity coordinator.
Testing integrity in public schools, §§38-771.01, 38-2602.

Test monitor.
Testing integrity in public schools, §§38-771.01, 38-2602.

Text or texting.
Distracted driving, §50-1731.02.

The Heights on Georgia Avenue developer.
Real property tax exemptions, §§47-4628, 47-4630.

The Heights on Georgia Avenue project.
Real property tax exemptions, §§47-4628, 47-4630.

The mayor's maximum income levels for the local medical assistance program, §1-307.02.

Therapeutically equivalent drug product.
Prescription drugs, §48-804.51.

Therapeutic care, §7-2101.

Therapeutic interchange.
Prescription drugs, §48-804.51.

Therapeutic interchange list.
Prescription drugs, §48-804.51.

Therapeutic service.
Healthcare facility, hospice and home care licensure, §44-501.

Third and H Streets, N.E. project.
Tax exemption, §47-4634.

Third and H Streets, N.E. property.
Tax exemption, §47-4634.

Third party, §§4-601, 47-1401.
Third-party child custody, §16-831.01.

Third-party payor, §7-1201.01.

Third party plan reviewer.
Construction codes, §6-1401.

Third party right of enforcement, §42-201.

Third-party standard.
Benefit corporations, §29-1301.02.

This chapter.
Traffic regulation, §50-2201.02.

This subchapter.
Impaired operation or driving, §50-2206.01.

Threatening letter or communication.
Council, §1-301.41.

DEFINED TERMS —Cont'd

Three fourths of co-owners, §42-2002.

311 system.
Emergency and non-emergency telephone system assessments fund, §34-1801.

Three-year cycle.
Real property assessment, §47-802.

Ticket.
Ballpark sales taxes, §47-2002.05.
DC Circulator bus service, §50-921.31.
DC Streetcar service, §50-921.71.
Verizon center sales tax, §47-2002.06.

Tier one qualified business.
Certified capital companies, §31-5231.

Tier one renewable source.
Renewable energy portfolio standards, §34-1431.

Tier three qualified business.
Certified capital companies, §31-5231.

Tier two qualified business.
Certified capital companies, §31-5231.

Tier two renewable source.
Renewable energy portfolio standards, §34-1431.

TIF.
City Market at O Street tax increment financing, §2-1217.33a.
Howard Theatre redevelopment project, §2-1217.151.
Howard Theatre redevelopment project TIF area, §2-1217.34a.
New convention center hotel, §10-1221.01.
Retail development incentives, §2-1217.71.
Skyland TIF area, §2-1217.35a.

TIF act.
Retail development incentives, §2-1217.71.
Union Market district tax increment financing, §2-1217.36a.

TIF area.
Retail development incentives, §2-1217.71.

TIF bonds.
Union Market district tax increment financing, §2-1217.36a.

TIF revenues.
Southwest waterfront special assessment district, §47-895.01.

Time-limited family reunification services.
Child abuse and neglect, §4-1301.02.

Timely, §4-205.55.

Time of distribution.
Uniform disclaimer of property interests act, §19-1506.

DEFINED TERMS —Cont'd

Time out, §7-1301.03.

Time share.

Condominiums, §42-1901.02.

Tissue.

Anatomical gifts, §7-1531.01.

Tissue Bank.

Anatomical gifts, §7-1531.01.

Tissue removal.

Body art establishments, business licenses, §47-2809.01.

Title brand.

Uniform certificates of title for vessels, §50-1541.01.

Title-holding entity.

Real property tax exemptions, §47-1002.

Title insurance business.

Title insurance producers, §31-5041.01.

Title insurers, §31-5031.01.

Title insurance commitment.

Title insurance producers, §31-5041.01.

Title insurers, §31-5031.01.

Title insurance policy.

Title insurance producers, §31-5041.01.

Title insurers, §31-5031.01.

Title insurance producer.

Title insurance producers, §31-5041.01.

Title insurers, §31-5031.01.

Title insurer.

Title insurance producers, §31-5041.01.

Title insurers, §31-5031.01.

Title IX.

Athletic equity, §38-841.01.

Title IX regulations.

Athletic equity, §38-841.01.

Title plant.

Title insurers, §31-5031.01.

Title XIX maximum income levels.

Medical assistance program, §1-307.02.

Tobacco bar.

Health department, §7-741.01.

Tobacco product, §7-1702.

Tobacco product manufacturer.

Tobacco master settlement agreement, §7-1801.01.

Tobacco master settlement agreement enforcement, §7-1803.02.

Tobacco specialty store.

Tobacco, §7-1721.01.

DEFINED TERMS —Cont'd

To be in violation, §31-1801.

Toddler, §7-2031.

Child and adult food program funding, §38-281.

To engage in course of conduct.

Stalking, §22-3132.

Toll telecommunication company.

Toll telecommunication service tax, §47-3901.

Toll telecommunication service.

Toll telecommunication service tax, §47-3901.

Toll telephone service.

Gross sales tax, §47-2001.

Ton, §37-201.08.

Tongue bifurcation.

Body art establishments, business licenses, §47-2809.01.

Top.

Urban forest preservation, §8-651.02.

To record, §42-2002.

Tortfeasor.

No-fault motor vehicle insurance, §31-2407.01.

Total adjusted capital, §31-2001.

Health insurance regulatory standards, §31-3451.01.

Total employment baseline.

The Advisory Board Company, real property tax abatement, §47-4665.01.

Total expenditures.

Bond issues, borrowing limitation, §47-334.

Total project cost.

Green buildings, §6-1451.01.

Total system efficiency.

Renewable energy portfolio standards, §34-1431.

Total value of qualified tenant improvements.

Real property tax exemptions, qualified high technology company interior renovation tax rebate, §47-4665.

Toxic.

Anti-terrorism act of 2002, §22-3152.

Toxic chemical, §8-1302.

Toxic or poisonous chemical.

Anti-terrorism act of 2002, §22-3152.

Trace quantity of phosphorus, §8-107.02.

Trachea hold, §5-125.02.

Tracking, §8-1051.

Trademark, §36-301.01.

DEFINED TERMS —Cont'd
Trade name, §47-2855.01.
Trade or business, §47-1521.
Income tax, §47-1801.04.
Unemployment compensation, §51-104.
Trade practice, §28-3901.
Consumer protection procedures, §28-3901.
Trade secret, §36-401.
Traffic, §50-2201.02.
Impaired operation or driving, §50-2206.01.
Traffic control device.
Autonomous vehicles, §50-2351.
Traffic offense.
Delinquent minors, JuvProc Rule 101.
Trailer, §§31-2402, 50-1501.01.
Gross sales tax, §47-2001.
Strict liability for release of hazardous waste during transport, §8-1441.
Trained employee, §21-1201.
Trained medication employee.
Assisted living residences, §44-102.01.
Training.
Garbage collection, §8-741.
Transaction.
Electronic transactions, uniform act, §28-4901.
Transaction in real property, §2-1401.02.
Transactions in securities or commodities.
Ethics and government accountability, §1-1161.01.
Transaction total.
Consumer protection, §28-3813.
Transfer.
Business organizations, §29-101.02.
Fiduciary security transfers, §28-2901.
Fraudulent transfers, §28-3101.
Insurers rehabilitation and liquidation procedures, §31-1301.
Real property transfer excise tax, §47-1401.
Real property transfer tax, §47-901.
Retail natural gas supplier licensing and consumer protection, §34-1671.02.
Transfers to minors, §21-301.
Transferable interest.
Limited liability companies, §29-801.02.
Partnerships, §29-601.02.
Transferable records.
Electronic transactions, uniform act, §28-4915.

DEFINED TERMS —Cont'd
Transfer agent, §28-2901.
Fiduciary security transfers, §28-2901.
Transfer-by-law statement.
Uniform certificates of title for vessels, §50-1541.19.
Transferee, §§47-901, 47-1401.
Limited liability companies, §29-801.02.
Limited partnerships, §29-701.02.
Partnerships, §29-601.02.
Transfer of economic interest, §42-1102.02.
Transfer of ownership.
Uniform certificates of title for vessels, §50-1541.01.
Transfer on death deed.
Uniform real property transfers on death, §19-604.02.
Transferor, §§21-301, 47-901, 47-1401.
Custodial trusts, §19-1101.
Uniform real property transfers on death, §19-604.02.
Transfer proceedings.
Incompetent criminal defendants, §24-531.01.
Rights of persons with intellectual disability, §7-1301.03.
Transferring insurer, §31-1701.
Transformer.
Energy efficiency standards, §8-1771.06.
Transient.
Compensating use tax, §47-2201.
Gross sales tax, §47-2001.
Transition.
Interstate compact on educational opportunity for military children, §49-1101.03.
Transitional housing.
Homeless services, §4-751.01.
Transition committee.
Ethics and government accountability, §1-1161.01.
Transition costs.
Retail electric competition and consumer protection, §34-1501.
Transit pass.
Reducing single occupancy vehicle use by encouraging transit benefits, §32-151.
Transmission.
Sexual performances using minors, §22-3101.
Transmit.
Sexual performances using minors, §22-3101.

DEFINED TERMS —Cont'd

Transmitting utility.
Secured transactions, §28:9-102.

Transplant hospital.
Anatomical gifts, §7-1531.01.

Transport, §§8-1302, 50-1702.
Strict liability for release of hazardous waste during transport, §8-1441.

Trash.
Solid waste reduction and recovery, §8-1031.01.

Trauma technologists, practice by, §3-1201.02.

Travel document.
Uniform child abduction prevention act, §16-4604.02.

Traveler's checks.
Negotiable instruments, §28:3-104.

Treatment, §8-1302.
Incompetent criminal defendants, §24-531.01.
Sentencing, §24-901.

Treatment facility, §§8-103.01, 8-1302, 44-1201.
Emergency medical services, §7-2341.01.
Nurse's rehabilitation program, §3-1251.01.

Treatment provider.
Choice in drug treatment, §7-3002.
Incompetent criminal defendants, §24-531.01.

Tree fund.
Urban forest preservation, §8-651.02.

Tribunal.
Collaborative law, §16-4002.
Interstate enforcement of domestic violence proceedings, §16-1041.
Interstate family support, §46-351.02.
Rules of professional conduct, ProfCond Rule 1.0.

Triggering event.
Standby guardianship, §16-4802.

Trip pass, §47-2302.

Trip permits, §50-1507.01.

True and real name.
Trade names, §47-2855.01.

Trust, §§1-626.04, 1-901.02.
ABLE savings accounts, §47-4901.
Statutory trusts, §29-1201.02.
Uniform disclaimer of property interests act, §19-1502.

Trust company, §21-301.
Custodial trusts, §19-1101.

Trust document.
Employees retirement program management, §1-702.

DEFINED TERMS —Cont'd

Trustee.
Electric company infrastructure improvement financing, §34-1311.01.
Energy efficiency financing, §8-1778.02.
Foreclosure mediation, §42-815.02.
Income tax secured bonds, §47-340.26.
Principal and income, §28-4801.02.
Statutory trusts, §29-1201.02.
Uniform trust code, §19-1301.03.

Trust instrument.
Statutory trusts, §29-1201.02.
Uniform trust code, §19-1301.03.

Truth in lending act.
Mortgage loan protection, §26-1151.01.

Tuition grant, §38-1207.01.

Turf.
Anacostia River cleanup and protection fertilizer act, §8-104.02.

2012 act.
Secured transactions, transitional provisions (2012 amendments), §28:9-801.

Two thirds of co-owners, §42-2002.

Two-way radio communications, §§5-1306 to 5-1309.

Type of entity.
Business organizations, §29-101.02.

UEA plan.
Student health care, medication, §38-651.01.

Ultimate user, §48-901.02.
Monitoring prescription drugs, §48-853.01.

Ultra low-emission vehicle (ULEV), §50-702.

Unacceptable hazardous condition, §9-1109.01.

Unallocated annuity contract.
Life and health insurance guaranty association, §31-5401.

Unauthorized company, §31-2501.03.

Unauthorized signature.
UCC, §28:1-201.

Uncertificated security, §28:8-102.

Unclaimed property, §41-102.

Unclaimed vehicle.
Abandoned and unlawfully parked vehicles, §50-2421.02.

Uncollected rent, §42-3501.03.

Uncompensated care.
Health planning and development agency, §44-401.

Uncovered expenditures, §31-3401.

DEFINED TERMS —Cont'd

Under common control with.
Qualified social electronic commerce companies tax abatements, §47-1818.01.
Special purpose financial captive insurance companies, §31-3932.02.
Underground facility, §34-2701.
Underground infrastructure improvement projects plan.
Electric company infrastructure improvement financing, §34-1311.01.
Underground injection.
Water pollution, §8-103.01.
Underground project charge.
Electric company infrastructure improvement financing, §34-1311.01.
Underground storage tank, §8-113.01.
Underinsured motor vehicle, §31-2402.
Underlying condition.
Lead-hazard prevention and elimination, §8-231.01.
Underlying interest.
Insurance investments, §31-1371.02.
Underserved area.
Regulation of for-hire vehicles, §50-301.03.
Savings and loan acquisitions, §26-1201.
Understatement.
Taxation penalties, §47-4211.
Understatement of liability.
Taxation penalties, §47-4217.
Undertaking.
Bonds and undertakings, §28-2501.
Under the direct supervision of, §8-401.
Underwater land, §8-103.01.
Underwrite, §31-1501.
Title insurance producers, §31-5041.01.
Title insurers, §31-5031.01.
Underwriter.
Security agents and broker, §31-5601.01.
Undesignated epinephrine auto-injector.
Student health care, medication, §38-651.01.
Undisputed amount.
Private contractor and subcontractor prompt payment act, §27-131.
Undistributed income.
Principal and income, §28-4803.03.

DEFINED TERMS —Cont'd

Undue hardship.
Breastfeeding mothers, rights of, §2-1402.82.
Pregnant and nursing workers, reasonable accommodations for, §32-1231.01.
Pregnant workers, protecting, §32-1231.01.
Unemployed, §51-101.
Unemployed District resident.
First source employment, §2-219.01.
Unemployment compensation.
Collection of taxes, §47-4431.
Unfair trade practices.
Unfair insurance trade practices, §31-2231.01.
Unfounded report.
Child abuse and neglect, §4-1301.02.
Unified communications center.
Office of unified communications, §1-327.51.
Uniform business entity application.
Insurance producers, §31-1131.02.
Uniform credentialing form.
Credentialing intermediary, health insurers, §31-3251.
Uniformed service.
Interstate compact on educational opportunity for military children, §49-1101.03.
Military and overseas voters, §1-1061.02.
Uniformed-service voter.
Military and overseas voters, §1-1061.02.
Uniform health form.
Child health screening, §7-875.02.
Uniform individual application.
Insurance producers, §31-1131.02.
Uniform mileage schedule, §50-1507.01.
Unincorporated business, §47-1808.01.
Unincorporated entity.
Corporations, §29-301.02.
Nonprofit corporations, §29-401.02.
Unincorporated nonprofit association, §29-1102.
Business organizations, §29-101.02.
Unique identifier.
Mortgage lenders and brokers, §26-1101.
Unit, §42-2002.
Condominiums, §42-1901.02.
Rental housing, §42-3401.03.

DEFINED TERMS —Cont'd
Unitary business.
Income tax, §47-1801.04.
United States.
Income tax, §47-1801.04.
Military and overseas voters,
§1-1061.02.
United States attorney, §23-541.
Criminal abuse, neglect and financial
exploitation of vulnerable adults
and elderly persons, §22-932.
**United States branch, §§31-2201,
31-2301.**
Domestication of insurers, §31-2301.
United States central authority.
Interstate family support, §46-357.01.
**United States government agency,
§8-1702.**
United States housing act.
Preservation and rehabilitation of
government-supported housing,
§42-2851.02.
United States Olympic committee.
Chesapeake regional Olympic games
authority, §2-1131.
United States representative.
New Columbia statehood initiative,
§1-129.21.
United States senator.
New Columbia statehood initiative,
§1-129.21.
Unit of government.
Anti-terrorism act of 2002, §22-3152.
Unit owner.
Condominiums, §42-1901.02.
Unit owner in good standing.
Condominiums, §42-1901.02.
Unit owners association.
Homestead housing provision,
§42-2103.
Unit price, §28-5202.
Unit pricing, §28-5202.
Units sold.
Tobacco master settlement agreement,
§7-1801.01.
Tobacco master settlement agreement
enforcement, §7-1803.02.
Unity health center.
Walker Jones/Northwest One Unity
health center tax exemption,
§47-4619.
Universal bank, §26-1401.02.
Merchant bank, §26-831.02.
Universal service, §34-2001.
University, §3-602.
Collection of taxes, §47-4431.

DEFINED TERMS —Cont'd
University —Cont'd
National technical institute for the
deaf, §38-2402.01.
Pesticide education and control,
§8-431.
**Unlawful discriminatory practice,
§2-1401.02.**
Unprocessed.
Child and adult food program funding,
§38-281.
Schools and education, §38-821.01.
Unreasonable economic hardship.
Historic landmarks, §6-1102.
**Unregulated contaminant,
§34-2202.01.**
Unrelated entity.
Qualified social electronic commerce
companies tax abatements,
§47-1818.01.
Unrestricted surplus.
Insurance investments, §31-1371.02.
**Unsupervised personal
representative, §20-101.**
Unsworn declaration.
Unsworn foreign declarations,
§16-5302.
Upfront financing costs.
Electric company infrastructure
improvement financing,
§34-1311.01.
Urban agriculture.
Food policy council, §48-311.
Urban gardens program, §48-401.
Urban farm.
Urban gardens program, §48-401.
Urban farming.
Urban gardens program, §48-401.
Urgent medical condition, §44-301.01.
U.S. candidate city.
Chesapeake regional Olympic games
authority, §2-1131.
Use, §47-2201.
Distracted driving, §50-1731.02.
Health data privacy, §7-241.
Used hearing aid, §28-4001.
Hearing aid dealers, §28-4001.
Used motor vehicle, §50-501.
Use in a trade or business, §47-1521.
User, §§7-2802, 8-105.02, 47-2302.
User fee.
Low-income housing tax credit,
§47-4801.
Low-income housing tax credit fund,
§42-2853.01.
Use tax.
Streamlined sales and use tax
agreement, §1-301.121.

DEFINED TERMS —Cont'd
USGBC.
Green buildings, §6-1451.01.
USOC.
Chesapeake regional Olympic games authority, §2-1131.
Usury, §28-3303.
Interest and usury, §28-3303.
Utility, §41-102.
Public utility relocation expenses, §9-107.02.
Utility facility.
Public utility relocation expenses, §9-107.02.
Utility line, §34-2701.
Utility or energy company.
Sustainable energy, §8-1773.01.
Utility trailer, §50-1505.01.
Utilization.
School-based budgeting and accountability, §38-2801.01.
Utilization review, §§1-623.01, 32-1501.
Utter.
Forgery, §22-3241.
Vacancy loss, §42-3501.03.
Vacant, §47-1401.
Vacant building.
Fire safety, §42-3131.05.
Vacant lot.
Urban gardens program, §48-401.
Vaccinated, §8-1801.
Valet parking service business.
Gross sales tax, §47-2001.
Valid identification document.
Alcoholic beverages, §25-101.
Valid lien, §28-3101.
Fraudulent transfers, §28-3101.
Valuation date.
Real property assessment, §47-802.
Value.
Fraudulent transfers, §28-3103.
Inheritance and estate taxes, §47-3701.
Theft and related offenses, §22-3201.
UCC, §28:1-204.
Uniform certificates of title for vessels, §50-1541.01.
Value-for-money analysis.
Public-private partnership administration fund, §2-271.01.
Vanpool.
Reducing single occupancy vehicle use by encouraging transit benefits, §32-151.
Vapor product.
Tobacco tax, §47-2401.

DEFINED TERMS —Cont'd
Variable contracts.
Insurance investments, §31-1371.02.
Variety packages.
Unit pricing, §28-5202.
Vault.
Public space rental and utilization, §10-1101.01.
Vault rent year.
Rental of public space, §10-1101.01.
Vector.
Vector-borne disease control, §8-2131.01.
Vehicle.
Abandoned and unlawfully parked vehicles, §50-2421.02.
Chemical testing for driving under the influence, §50-1901.
Claims against District, §2-411.
Fleet management, publicly-owned vehicles, §50-211.01.
Impaired operation or driving, §50-2206.01.
Motor vehicle safety responsibility, §50-1301.02.
No-fault motor vehicle insurance, §31-2402.
Traffic regulation, §50-2201.02.
Vehicle conveyance fee.
Traffic adjudication, §50-2301.02.
Traffic regulation, §50-2201.02.
Vehicle for hire.
Chemical testing for driving under the influence, §50-1901.
Impaired operation or driving, §50-2206.01.
Traffic regulation, §50-2201.02.
Vehicle-for-hire industry.
Regulation of for-hire vehicles, §50-301.03.
Vehicle inspection officer.
Regulation of for-hire vehicles, §50-301.03.
Vending locations.
Vending regulation, §37-131.01.
Vending site permit, §37-131.01.
Vending machine.
Tobacco tax, §47-2401.
Vendor, §47-2201.
Gross sales tax, §47-2001.
Internet tax, §47-3931.
Portable electronics insurance, §31-5051.01.
Venture.
Human trafficking, §22-1831.
Verification.
Green buildings, §6-1451.01.

DEFINED TERMS —Cont'd

Verification upon oath or affirmation, §42-141.

Verizon center.
Gross sales tax, §47-2002.06.

Vertical development.
Walter Reed Medical Center site development, §2-1227.01.

Very-low income, §42-2701.02.
Affordable housing inventory comprehensive tracking plan, §42-2141.
Housing production trust fund, §42-2801.

Very low-income household.
Preservation and rehabilitation of government-supported housing, §42-2851.02.
Tax abatement for new residential developments, §47-857.01.

Vessel number.
Uniform certificates of title for vessels, §50-1541.01.

Vessel, vessels, §36-151.
Uniform certificates of title for vessels, §50-1541.01.

Veteran.
Interstate compact on educational opportunity for military children, §49-1101.03.
License plates, §50-1501.02a.
Veterans' affairs, office of, §49-1001.

Veteran-owned business enterprise.
Small and certified business enterprise development and assistance, §2-218.02.

Veterinarian, §3-1201.01.

Veterinary euthanasia technician, §3-1201.01.

Veterinary facility, §§3-1201.01, 47-2888.01.

Veterinary medicine, practice of, §3-1201.02.

Veterinary services.
Emergency volunteer health practitioners, §7-2361.01.

Veterinary technician, §3-1201.01.

V hold, §5-125.02.

Viatical settlement.
Merit system, life insurance, §1-622.04.

Victim.
Crime victims' compensation, §4-501.
Crime victims' rights, §23-1905.
Domestic violence counselors, §14-310.
Family court proceedings, §16-2301.

DEFINED TERMS —Cont'd

Victim —Cont'd
HIV testing of certain criminal offenders, §22-3901.
Human trafficking counselor, §14-311.
No-fault motor vehicle insurance, §31-2402.
Sexual abuse, §22-3001.

Video arcade, §48-901.02.
Weapons, §22-4501.

Video programming.
Office of cable television, film, music, and entertainment amendment act of 2015, §34-1251.03.

View 14 project.
Real property tax exemptions, §47-4629.

View 14 property.
Real property tax exemptions, §47-4629.

Vintage goods or collectibles, §37-101.

Violates or attempts to violate.
Unemployment compensation, §51-104.

Violent misdemeanor.
Criminal street gangs, §22-951.

Visitor, §21-2011.

Vital documents.
Foreign language services and documents, §2-1931.

Vital records, §7-201.

Vital statistics, §7-201.

Voice over Internet Protocol service, §34-2001.

Volunteer, §§1-319.05, 7-531.01.
Criminal background checks for the protection of children act, §4-1501.02.

Volunteer health practitioner.
Emergency volunteer health practitioners, §7-2361.01.

Volunteer service provider.
Medical liability captive insurance agency, §1-307.81.

Vote.
Corporations, §29-301.02.
Nonprofit corporations, §29-401.02.

Voter registration agency.
Elections, §1-1001.02.

Voting.
Corporations, §29-301.02.
Nonprofit corporations, §29-401.02.

Voting group.
Corporations, §29-301.02.
Limited cooperative associations, §29-1001.02.

DEFINED TERMS —Cont'd
Voting group —Cont'd
Nonprofit corporations, §29-401.02.
Voting member.
Limited cooperative associations,
§29-1001.02.
Voting power.
Corporations, §29-301.02.
Limited cooperative associations,
§29-1001.02.
Nonprofit corporations, §29-401.02.
Voting security, §31-701.
Voting shares, §31-751.
Voting system.
Elections, §1-1001.02.
Voucher.
Procurement practices, §2-351.04.
Vulnerable adult.
Criminal abuse, neglect and financial
exploitation of vulnerable adults
and elderly persons, §22-932.
Wage, §§32-1002, 32-1301.
Garnishment, §16-571.
Income tax, §47-1801.04.
Minimum wage, §32-1002.
Unemployment compensation, §51-101.
Wage transparency, §32-1451.
Workers' compensation, §32-1501.
Waiting period, §31-3301.01.
Walk-in refrigerator or freezer.
Energy efficiency standards,
§8-1771.01.
**Walter Reed Army Medical Center
site,** §10-1901.
**Walter Reed common area
association.**
Walter Reed Medical Center site
development, §2-1227.01.
Walter Reed LRA.
Walter Reed Army Medical Center,
§10-1901.
Walter Reed Medical Center site
development, §2-1227.01.
Walter Reed LRA committee.
Walter Reed Army Medical Center,
§10-1901.
Walter Reed redevelopment site.
Walter Reed Medical Center site
development, §2-1227.01.
Walter Reed reuse plan.
Walter Reed Army Medical Center,
§10-1901.
Walter Reed Medical Center site
development, §2-1227.01.
Ward, §21-2011.
Elections, §1-1001.02.

DEFINED TERMS —Cont'd
Warehouse.
Documents of title, §28:7-102.
Warehouse receipt.
UCC, §28:1-201.
Warrant.
Insurance investments, §31-1371.02.
Uniform child custody proceedings,
§16-4601.01.
Warranty, §50-501.
Washington beef properties.
New Town at Capital City Market
revitalization, §6-1062.02.
Workforce housing production
program, §6-1061.02.
**Washington convention center
authority act.**
New convention center hotel,
§10-1221.01.
**Washington Dulles International
airport,** §9-1003.
Washington Metropolitan area.
Regulation of for-hire vehicles,
§50-301.03.
Washington metropolitan region,
§32-1002.
Washington National airport,
§9-1003.
Waste diversion.
Solid waste reduction and recovery,
§8-1031.01.
Waste diversion rate.
Solid waste reduction and recovery,
§8-1031.01.
Wastewater, §§8-103.01, 8-105.02.
Wastewater and sewage works,
§34-2101.
Wastewater disposal systems,
§8-105.02.
Wastewater system, §8-105.02.
Wastewater treatment systems,
§8-205.
Water and sewer rates, §34-2202.01.
Waterbody.
Anacostia River cleanup and
protection fertilizer act, §8-104.02.
Pesticide education and control,
§8-431.
Waterbody-contingent property.
Pesticide education and control,
§8-431.
Watercraft.
Impaired operation or driving,
§50-2206.01.
Implied consent to blood alcohol tests,
§50-1908.

DEFINED TERMS —Cont'd

Water dispenser.
Energy efficiency standards, §8-1771.01.

Water distribution system, §34-2202.01.

Waterfront Park, §10-1801.

Waterfront Park benefit district, §§10-1801, 47-895.21.

Waterfront Park retail area, §10-1801.

Waterfront Park special assessment, §10-1801.

Water pollution, §8-103.01.

Water's edge combined group.
Income tax, §47-1801.04.

Waters of the District, §8-103.01.

Wax museum developer.
Tax abatement for mixed-income housing projects, §47-857.06.

WBRC.
Chesapeake regional Olympic games authority, §2-1131.

Weapon.
District of Columbia housing authority, §6-201.
Homeless services, §4-751.01.
Schools and education, §38-234.

Weapon of mass destruction.
Anti-terrorism act of 2002, §22-3152.

Weapons offense.
Family court proceedings, §16-2301.
Firearms control, §7-2501.01.

Weed, §8-401.

Week, §51-101.

Weekly benefit amount.
Unemployment compensation, §51-107.

Weighted average, §31-3301.01.

Weighting.
Uniform per student funding formula, §38-2901.

Well.
Water pollution, §8-103.01.

Wetlands, §8-103.01.

Wheelchair-accessible vehicle.
Regulation of for-hire vehicles, §50-301.03.

Whistleblower, §§1-615.52, 2-223.01.

Wholesale dealer.
Fire-standard-compliant cigarettes, §7-1751.

Wholesale electricity supplier.
Retail electric competition and consumer protection, §34-1501.

Wholesale price.
Cigarette tax, §47-2401.

DEFINED TERMS —Cont'd

Wholesaler, §§28-4521, 36-301.01, 48-701.
Tobacco master settlement agreement enforcement, §7-1803.02.

WIC.
Child and adult food program funding, §38-281.
Workforce investment implementation, §32-1602.

WIC benefits.
Grocery and retail stores development, §2-1212.01.

Widow.
Police and firefighters retirement and disability, §5-701.
Retirement of judges, §11-1561.
Workers' compensation, §32-1501.

Widower.
Police and firefighters retirement and disability, §5-701.
Retirement of judges, §11-1561.
Workers' compensation, §32-1501.

Wild animals, §22-4328.

Wildlife, §8-2201.

Wildlife control, §8-2201.

Wildlife control services provider, §8-2201.

Wildlife rehabilitation facility, §47-2888.01.

Wine, §25-101.

Wire communications, §23-541.

Wireless telecommunication company.
Toll telecommunication service tax, §47-3901.

Wireless telecommunication equipment.
Toll telecommunication service tax, §47-3901.

Withdraw.
Voluntary withdrawal by health benefit plan carriers, §31-3151.

Within the District, §47-2201.

Witness.
Out-of-state witness, §23-1501.

WMATA, §9-1109.01.
DC Circulator bus service, §50-921.31.

Women-owned, §26-1201.
Savings and loan acquisitions, §26-1201.

Women-owned business.
Community development by financial institutions, §26-431.02.

Workforce act.
First source employment, §2-219.01.

DEFINED TERMS —Cont'd
Workforce development.
Pre-kindergarten programs,
§38-271.01.
Workforce housing.
New Town at Capital City Market
revitalization, §6-1062.02.
Workforce housing production
program, §6-1061.02.
Workforce housing land trust.
Housing production trust fund,
§42-2801.
**Workforce housing production
program approval act.**
Housing production trust fund,
§42-2801.
Working conditions, §32-601.
Working day.
Wages and salaries, §32-1301.
Working time, §32-1002.
Work of fine art, §28-5101.
Works.
Sex offender registration, §22-4001.
Works of art, §37-101.
Work zone.
Traffic regulation, §50-2201.02.
Worldwide combined report.
Income tax, §47-1801.04.
Writing, §22-1801.
Rules of professional conduct,
ProfCond Rule 1.0.
UCC, §28:1-201.
Written.
Business organizations, §29-101.02.
Procurement practices, §2-351.04.
Rules of professional conduct,
ProfCond Rule 1.0.
Written certificate of title.
Uniform certificates of title for vessels,
§50-1541.01.
Written instrument.
Forgery, §22-3241.
Written listing contract, §42-1702.
Wrongfully obtains or uses.
Theft, §22-3211.
Wrongful removal.
Uniform child abduction prevention
act, §16-4604.02.
Wrongful retention.
Uniform child abduction prevention
act, §16-4604.02.
Year 2000 compliance or compliant.
Immunity for district system failure,
§2-381.31.
Year 2000 system failure.
Immunity for district system failure,
§2-381.31.

DEFINED TERMS —Cont'd
Youth, §2-1501.
Bullying, §2-1535.01.
Child abuse and neglect, §4-1301.02.
Criminal background checks for the
protection of children act,
§4-1501.02.
Homeless services, §4-751.01.
Mandatory drug and alcohol testing of
certain employees who serve
children, §1-620.31.
Mental health department, §7-1131.02.
Rights and responsibilities for youth in
foster care, §4-1303.71.
Rights and responsibilities of foster
parents, §4-1303.81.
Youth advisory council, §2-1561.
Youth behavioral health epidemiology
reports, §2-1517.02.
Youth council, §2-1565.01.
Youth center, §48-901.02.
Weapons, §22-4501.
Youth council, §§2-1561, 2-1565.01.
Youth offender, §24-901.
Youth residential facility, §7-2101.
Youth rehabilitation services,
department of, §2-1515.01.
Youth services, §2-1501.
Youth services center.
Youth rehabilitation services
department, §7-1131.02.
Zero bracket amount.
Inheritance and estate taxes,
§47-3701.
Zero-emission vehicle (ZEV), §50-702.
Zoning, §6-641.12.

DELAY.
Appeals.
Frivolous appeals, DCCtApp Rule 38.
Appeals in federal cases.
Damages, FRAP 38.
Attorneys at law.
Expediting litigation, ProfCond Rule
3.2.
Criminal procedure.
Dismissal of proceedings, CrimPro
Rule 48.
**Pleadings causing unnecessary
delay, etc., CivPro Rule 11.**
Domestic relations actions, DomRel
Rule 11.
Hospitalization of persons with mental
illness, MentalHealth Rule 14.

DELINQUENT DEBT FUND,
§1-350.04.

DELINQUENT MINORS.

Abscondence review committee, §16-2333.02.

Acquittal, JuvProc Rule 29.

Actual innocence.
Sealing of records, §16-2335.02.
Vacation of adjudication, §16-2335.01.

Adjustment process, §16-2305.02.

Adult detention facilities.
Hearing on transfer to facility, JuvProc Rule 107.

Alibi defense, JuvProc Rule 12.1.

Appeals, §§16-2328, 16-2329.
Detention or release upon conditions, JuvProc Rule 107.
Expedited appeals, DCCtApp Rule 4.
Notice of right to appeal, JuvProc Rule 32.
Sealing arrest records, FamDiv Rule P, JuvProc Rule 118.
Forms, FamDiv Forms 2 to 6, JuvProc Forms 8 to 10.

Attorneys at law.
Compensation of appointed counsel, §16-2326.01.
Practice by attorneys no members of District bar, JuvProc Rule 115.
Right to and assignment of counsel, JuvProc Rule 44.
Right to counsel, §16-2304.
Work-product rule, JuvProc Rule 16.

Attorneys' fees and costs, §§16-2326, 16-2326.01.

Bill of particulars, JuvProc Rule 7.

Calendaring, JuvProc Rule 50.

Child abuse and neglect.
Juvenile proceeding's effect on neglect case, NeglectProc Rule 3.
Multiple delinquency petitions filed against a child 13 or younger.
Institution of neglect investigation, §16-2305.

Community service.
Order to perform in lieu of restitution, JuvProc Rule 112.

Competency to proceed, §16-2307.
Definition of incompetent to proceed, §16-2301.
Mental examination, §16-2315.

Complaints, JuvProc Rule 3.

Compulsory school attendance.
Tenth unexcused absence.
Referrals to social services agencies, §38-208.

Consent decree to supervise child without commitment, §16-2314.

DELINQUENT MINORS —Cont'd

Construction of rules, JuvProc Rule 2.

Contempt, JuvProc Rule 42.
Subpoena noncompliance, JuvProc Rule 17.

Contributing to the delinquency of a minor, §22-811.

Costs, JuvProc Rule 113.
Depositions, JuvProc Rule 15.

Court-appointed special advocates, §§16-2371, 16-2372.

Courtroom conduct, JuvProc Rule 53.

Crimes and offenses.
Convicted minors.
See JUVENILE OFFENDERS.

Criminal charge transferred to family division, §16-2302.

Custody, taking child into, §16-2309.
Consent decree to supervise child without commitment, §16-2314.
Dangerous crime or crime of violence.
Rebuttable presumption that detention required, §16-2310.
Detention of, criteria for, §16-2310, JuvProc Rule 106.
Forms, JuvProc Forms 1 to 3.
Hearing as to detention or shelter care, §16-2312, JuvProc Rule 107.
Issuance of rules and regulations, §16-2311.01.
Parental visitation of children in custody, §16-2310.
Physical and mental examinations, §16-2315.
Place of detention or shelter, §16-2313.
Release or delivery of child, §16-2311.
Support and maintenance, §16-2325.
Younger children physically separated from children 13 or older, §16-2310.01.

Defenses and objections, JuvProc Rule 12.
Alibi defense, JuvProc Rule 12.1.

Definitions, JuvProc Rule 101.

Detention and shelter care procedures, JuvProc Rule 105.
Criteria used, §16-2310, JuvProc Rule 106.
Forms, JuvProc Forms 1 to 3.
Hearings, §16-2312, JuvProc Rule 107.
Place of detention or shelter, §16-2313.
Younger children physically separated from children 13 or older, §16-2310.01.

Director of Social Services, additional powers of, §16-2337.

DELINQUENT MINORS —Cont'd
Discovery, JuvProc Rule 16.
   Depositions, JuvProc Rule 15.
   Informal discovery, JuvProc Rule 16-I.
   Subpoenas, JuvProc Rule 17.
   Witness statements, JuvProc Rule
     26.2.
Dismissal of actions, JuvProc Rule 48.
Disposition of child, §16-2320,
   JuvProc Rule 32.
   Clerical mistakes, JuvProc Rule 36.
   Director of Social Services, additional
     powers of, §16-2319.
   Evaluations, §16-2323.
   Failure to appear at hearing.
     Consideration of, §16-2320.
   Forms, JuvProc Forms 5 to 7.
   Individualized treatment plans,
     §16-2319.
   Limitation of actions, §16-2322.
   Mentally ill or intellectually disabled
     child, §16-2321.
   Modification of dispositional orders,
     §16-2323.
   Predisposition study and report,
     §16-2319, JuvProc Rule 32.
   Review of orders, §16-2323.
Emergency medical treatment,
   §16-2338.
**Employment, education or housing
   application.**
   Juvenile's right to refuse disclosure of
     delinquency history, §16-2335.
Evidence, §16-2316, JuvProc Rule 26.
   Actual innocence.
     New evidence, §16-2335.01.
   Alibi of respondent, JuvProc Rule 12.1.
   Consent decree violations, JuvProc
     Rule 104.
   Deposition's use, JuvProc Rule 15.
   Extra-judicial statements, JuvProc
     Rule 111.
   Newly discovered evidence, JuvProc
     Rule 33.
   Notice of intent to use evidence,
     JuvProc Rule 12.
   Questioning minor on unrelated
     offense, JuvProc Rule 105.
   Search warrants.
     Motion to suppress evidence,
       JuvProc Rule 41.
   Transfer for criminal prosecution,
     JuvProc Rule 109.
Examinations, physical and mental,
   §16-2315.
Exceptions unnecessary, JuvProc
   Rule 51.

DELINQUENT MINORS —Cont'd
Failure to appear at hearing.
   Disposition of child.
     Consideration of failure to appear,
       §16-2320.
   Report on failure to appear,
     §16-2325.02.
Finality of judgments, §16-2329.
Forms.
   Consent decree, JuvProc Form 4.
   Detention order, JuvProc Form 1.
   Dispositional order.
     Commitment to social services
       administration, JuvProc Form 7.
     Medical or private placement,
       JuvProc Form 5.
     Probation, JuvProc Form 6.
   Illustrative nature of forms, JuvProc
     Rule 58.
   Release upon conditions order,
     JuvProc Form 3.
   Sealing records.
     Motion to seal records, JuvProc
       Form 8.
     Notice of motion to seal records,
       JuvProc Form 9.
     Notice of opposition, FamDiv Form
       3.
     Notice of proposal, FamDiv Form 2.
     Order denying application, FamDiv
       Form 6.
     Order for hearing, FamDiv Form 4.
     Order to seal records, FamDiv Form
       5, JuvProc Form 10.
   Shelter care order, JuvProc Form 2.
Gag orders, JuvProc Rule 53.
Goals for delinquency cases,
   §16-2301.02.
Guilty pleas, JuvProc Rules 11, 12.
   Withdrawal of plea, JuvProc Rule 32.
Harmless error, JuvProc Rule 52.
Hearings.
   Competency treatment, report on,
     JuvProc Rule 110A.
   Conduct of, §16-2316.
   Detention or shelter care, §16-2312.
   Dismissal, §16-2317, JuvProc Rule 48.
   Factfinding hearings, §16-2317.
     Actual innocence, §16-2335.01.
   Findings at, §16-2317.
   Mental health examination, request
     for, JuvProc Rule 110.
   Restitution hearing, JuvProc Rule 112.
   Transfer hearing, JuvProc Rule 109.
     Time to hold transfer hearing and
       enter order, JuvProc Rule 108.

DELINQUENT MINORS —Cont'd
HIV/AIDS testing, JuvProc Rule 110.
Respondent's test results to be
disclosed to victims, §16-2315.
Immunity, §16-2339.
Incompetence to proceed, §16-2307.
Definition of incompetent to proceed,
§16-2301.
Mental examination, §16-2315.
Treatment when child determined to
be incompetent, JuvProc Rule
110A.
Initial appearance before judge,
§16-2308.
Initial hearings, JuvProc Rule 10.
Intake procedures, JuvProc Rule 102.
Criteria for intake, JuvProc Rule 103.
Interlocutory appeals, §16-2328.
Interpreters, §2-1902, JuvProc Rule 28.
Interstate compact for juveniles,
§§24-1101 to 24-1106.
Alteration, amendment or repeal of
provisions, §24-1106.
Compact administrator, §24-1103.
Congressional findings, §24-1101.
Construction of compact, §24-1105.
Enforcement, §24-1104.
Entry into and execution of compact,
§24-1102.
**Interstate compact on placement of
children,** §§4-1421 to 4-1424.
Agreements with other state for
placement, §4-1423.
Authority to enter into and execute
compact, §4-1422.
Definitions, §4-1421.
Delinquent children.
Administrative hearing on
placement, review, §4-1424.
**Joinder of offenses and of
respondents,** JuvProc Rules 8, 13.
Relief from prejudicial joinder,
JuvProc Rule 14.
Judge's disability, JuvProc Rule 25.
Judgments and decrees, JuvProc Rule
32.
Clerical mistakes, JuvProc Rule 36.
Consent decrees, JuvProc Rule 104.
Form, JuvProc Form 4.
Findings by division, JuvProc Rule 31.
Restitution, JuvProc Rule 112.
Jurisdiction, §16-2303.
Law student practice, FamDiv Rule
M.
Limitation of actions, §§16-2322,
16-2330.

DELINQUENT MINORS —Cont'd
Media coverage of proceedings,
JuvProc Rule 53.
Medical examinations, §16-2315.
Mistrials.
Comments before order, JuvProc Rule
26.3.
Failure to produce witness statement,
JuvProc Rule 26.2.
Modification of dispositional orders,
§16-2323.
Motions, JuvProc Rule 47-I.
Actual innocence.
Sealing of records, §16-2335.02.
Vacation of adjudication,
§16-2335.01.
Mental health examination, request
for, JuvProc Rule 110.
Pretrial motions, JuvProc Rule 12.
Sealing records, FamDiv Rule P,
JuvProc Rule 118.
Form, JuvProc Form 8.
Witness statement production,
JuvProc Rule 26.2.
New factfinding hearings, JuvProc
Rule 33.
Noncriminal orders and decrees,
§16-2318.
Not guilty pleas, JuvProc Rule 12.
Notice of initial appearance, JuvProc
Rule 9.
Order for custody, JuvProc Rule 4.
Participation orders, §16-2325.01,
JuvProc Rule 119.
Parties to cases involving, §16-2304.
Petitions, §16-2305, JuvProc Rules 7,
12.
Reinstituting charges, JuvProc Rule 5.
Physical and mental examinations,
§16-2315, JuvProc Rule 110.
Transfer for criminal prosecution,
JuvProc Rule 108.
Plain error, JuvProc Rule 52.
Policy declaration, §16-2305.01.
Preliminary probation conferences,
§16-2305.02.
**Presence of respondent at hearings,
etc.,** JuvProc Rule 43.
Detention and shelter care hearings,
JuvProc Rule 107.
Transfer for criminal prosecution
hearings, JuvProc Rule 109.
Pretrial procedures, JuvProc Rule 12.
Conferences, JuvProc Rule 17.1.
Probation, JuvProc Forms 3, 6, JuvProc
Rule 32.
Detention or shelter care, JuvProc
Rule 107.

DELINQUENT MINORS —Cont'd
Probation —Cont'd
Preliminary probation conferences, §16-2305.02.
Revocation of, §16-2327.
Public access to proceedings, JuvProc Rule 53.
Purpose of rules, JuvProc Rule 2.
Records.
See RECORDS.
Rehabilitation, parent or guardian required to participate in, §16-2325.01, JuvProc Rule 119.
Reinstituting charges, JuvProc Rule 5.
Reports.
Competency treatment, JuvProc Rule 110A.
Failure to appear at hearings, §16-2325.02.
Mental examination, results of, §16-2315, JuvProc Rule 110.
Predisposition investigation reports, §16-2319, JuvProc Rule 32.
Restitution, §16-2320.01, JuvProc Rule 112.
Right to counsel, §16-2304.
School grounds.
Expulsion of students for bringing weapons onto, §38-232.
Scope of rules, JuvProc Rule 1.
Sealing arrest records, FamDiv Rule P, JuvProc Rule 118.
Forms, FamDiv Forms 2 to 6, JuvProc Forms 8 to 10.
Search and seizure, JuvProc Rule 41.
Self-incrimination privilege, JuvProc Rule 111.
Service of process, §16-2306, JuvProc Rule 49.
Motions procedure, JuvProc Rule 47-I.
Summons and other notices of hearings, JuvProc Rule 9.
Time for service, JuvProc Rule 45.
Sexual abuse of prisoner.
First degree, §22-3013.
Second degree, §22-3014.
Subpoenas, JuvProc Rule 17.
Summons, JuvProc Rule 9.
Reinstituting charges, JuvProc Rule 5.
Transfer for criminal prosecution, JuvProc Rule 108.
Support and maintenance, §16-2325.
Termination or vacation of orders regarding, §16-2324.
Time.
Computation, JuvProc Rule 45.

DELINQUENT MINORS —Cont'd
Time —Cont'd
Transfer for criminal prosecution.
Time to conduct transfer hearing and enter order, JuvProc Rule 108.
Title of rules, JuvProc Rule 60.
Transcripts of proceedings, §16-2329.
Transfer for criminal prosecution, §16-2307, JuvProc Rules 108, 109.
Transfer of criminal charge to family division, §16-2302.
Vacation of adjudication.
Actual innocence, §16-2335.01.
Sealing of records, §16-2335.02.
Vacation or termination of orders regarding, §16-2324.
Victims.
Defined, §16-2301.
HIV/AIDS testing.
Respondent's test results to be disclosed to victim, §16-2315, JuvProc Rule 110.
Impact statements, §§16-2319, 16-2320, JuvProc Rule 32.
Notice of disposition and post-disposition hearings, §16-2317.
Rights of victims or eyewitnesses in delinquency proceedings, §16-2340.
Witnesses, §16-2339.
Alibi defense, JuvProc Rule 12.1.
Expert witnesses, JuvProc Rule 28.
Production of witness statements, JuvProc Rule 26.2.
Rights of victims or eyewitnesses, §16-2340.
Youth rehabilitation, §§24-901 to 24-907.

DELINQUENT REAL ESTATE TAX SALES, §§47-1301 to 47-1321.
See REAL ESTATE TAX SALES.

DEMAND FOR JUDGMENT, CivPro Rule 54.

DEMAND FOR TRIAL BY JURY, CivPro Rule 38.
Default judgments.
Withdrawal of jury demand after default, CivPro Rule 55-I.
Granting of trial by jury, CivPro Rule 39.
Landlord and tenant court, LandlordTenant Rule 6.
Parentage proceedings.
No right to jury trial, §16-2343.04.

DEMAND FOR TRIAL BY JURY
—Cont'd
Small claims court, SmallClaims Rule
6.

DEMOLITIONS.
Defined, §§6-1102, 34-2702.
Deteriorated property, §§42-3173.01
to 42-3173.12.
**Displaced tenants, relocation
assistance for,** §§42-3507.01 to
42-3507.05.
**Historic districts and historic
landmarks,** §6-1104.
Demolition by neglect.
Prevention, §6-1109.03.
**Injunctions against improper
demolitions,** §34-2708.
**Insanitary buildings, repair or
demolition of,** §§6-905, 6-907.
**Lodging places, rental housing
demolished for construction or
expansion of,** §42-3506.02.
Miss Utility.
See MISS UTILITY.
Public utility damages caused by,
§34-2707.
Washington Convention Center.
Neighborhood demolition permits.
See WASHINGTON CONVENTION
CENTER.

DEMONSTRATIONS.
Capitol grounds, §10-503.17.
**Federal government,
demonstrations in District
relating to.**
Reimbursement of costs, §1-207.37.
Residence targeted, §§22-2751,
22-2752.
Warrantless arrest, §23-581.

DEMURRERS.
Abolished, CivPro Rule 7.

DENATURED ALCOHOL.
Alcoholic beverage licenses.
Exceptions to license requirements,
§25-103.

DENIALS.
Effect of failure to deny, CivPro Rule
8.
Domestic relations actions, DomRel
Rule 8.
Requests for admission, CivPro Rule
36.
Adoption proceedings, Adoption Rule
36.

DENIALS —Cont'd
Requests for admission —Cont'd
Domestic relations actions, DomRel
Rule 36.
Form, CivPro Form CA 25.

DENTAL COLLEGES, §§38-1401 to
38-1419.
See MEDICAL AND DENTAL
COLLEGES.

DENTAL HYGIENE.
Definition of practice of, §3-1201.02.
Health occupations boards.
General provisions, §§3-1201.01 to
3-1213.01.
See HEALTH OCCUPATIONS
BOARDS.
**Health occupations licensure,
registration or certification,**
§§3-1205.01 to 3-1205.24.
See HEALTH OCCUPATIONS
LICENSURE, REGISTRATION
OR CERTIFICATION.
**Titles and terms prohibited as
misrepresentation without
license to practice,** §3-1210.03.

DENTISTS.
Alcoholic beverage licenses.
Exceptions to license requirements,
§25-103.
Board of dentistry, §3-1202.01.
Child abuse and neglect reports,
§4-1321.02.
Definition of practice of dentistry,
§3-1201.02.
Dental assistants.
Health occupations licensure,
registration or certification,
§3-1209.05.
Requirements, §3-1209.05.
Health occupations boards.
General provisions, §§3-1201.01 to
3-1213.01.
See HEALTH OCCUPATIONS
BOARDS.
**Health occupations licensure,
registration or certification,**
§§3-1205.01 to 3-1205.24.
See HEALTH OCCUPATIONS
LICENSURE, REGISTRATION
OR CERTIFICATION.
**Health professional recruitment
program,** §§7-751.01 to 7-751.16.
See HEALTH PROFESSIONAL
RECRUITMENT PROGRAM.
**Titles and terms prohibited as
misrepresentation without
license to practice,** §3-1210.03.

DEPARTMENT OF EDUCATION, §§38-191 to 38-193.
Ombudsman for public education, §§38-351 to 38-356.

DEPARTMENT OF GENERAL SERVICES, §§10-551.01 to 10-551.10.
See GENERAL SERVICES, DEPARTMENT OF.

DEPARTMENT OF HEALTH CARE FINANCE, §§7-771.01 to 7-771.11.
See HEALTH CARE FINANCE DEPARTMENT.

DEPARTMENT OF INSURANCE, SECURITIES, AND BANKING, §§26-551.01 to 26-551.25.
See BANKS AND FINANCIAL INSTITUTIONS.

DEPARTMENT OF MENTAL HEALTH ENTERPRISE FUND, §7-1131.21.

DEPARTMENT OF THE ENVIRONMENT, §§8-151.01 to 8-151.15.
See ENVIRONMENTAL PROTECTION.

DEPARTMENT OF TRANSPORTATION, §§50-921.01 to 50-921.22.
See TRANSPORTATION.

DEPARTMENTS AND AGENCIES.
Abandoned and junk vehicles division, §50-2402.
Administrative fines.
Administrative agency review of, §§2-1803.01 to 2-1803.03.
Administrative hearings.
Office of administrative hearings, §§2-1831.01 to 2-1831.18.
See ADMINISTRATIVE HEARINGS, OFFICE OF.
Administrative law judges.
Commission on selection and tenure of administrative law judges, §§2-1831.06, 2-1831.07.
Affirmative action plans, §§1-521.01 to 1-521.08.
See PUBLIC OFFICERS AND EMPLOYEES.
Aging, office on, §§7-501.01 to 7-503.06.
Animal care and control agency, §8-1802.

DEPARTMENTS AND AGENCIES —Cont'd
Appeal of administrative orders and decisions.
See ADMINISTRATIVE PROCEDURE.
Asians and Pacific Islanders.
Office of Asian and Pacific Islander affairs, §§2-1371 to 2-1376.
Banking and financial institutions.
Department of insurance, securities, and banking, §§26-551.01 to 26-551.25.
See BANKS AND FINANCIAL INSTITUTIONS.
Basic business license program participation, §47-2851.18.
Bicycle advisory council, §50-1604.
Bicycle transportation and safety, office of, §50-1603.
Budgets, anti-deficiency provisions, §§47-355.01 to 47-355.08.
Definitions, §47-355.01.
Limits on expenditures and obligations, §47-355.02.
Notice of provisions, §47-355.08.
Report of spending plan, §47-355.04.
Reports of actual expenditures and obligations, §47-355.05.
Review board, §47-355.07.
Spending projections, §47-355.03.
Violations, §47-355.06.
Business and economic development.
See BUSINESS AND ECONOMIC DEVELOPMENT.
Chief financial officer.
Office of chief financial officer.
See CHIEF FINANCIAL OFFICER.
Child and family services agency, §§4-1303.01 to 4-1303.09.
See CHILD ABUSE AND NEGLECT.
Community center and playgrounds department, §§10-221, 10-226.
Consumer and regulatory affairs.
See CONSUMER AND REGULATORY AFFAIRS, DEPARTMENT OF.
Corrections, department of.
General provisions, §§24-211.01 to 24-211.41.
See CORRECTIONS, DEPARTMENT OF.
Court services and offender supervision agency, §24-133.
Customer service operations unit, §§1-327.31 to 1-327.34.

DEPARTMENTS AND AGENCIES
—Cont'd
Delinquent debts owed District, recovery transfers, §1-350.02.
Donations.
Independent agencies authorized to accept, §1-329.01.
Education department, §§38-191 to 38-193.
Public schools agency, §§38-171 to 38-175.
Emergency preparedness, office of.
See EMERGENCY MANAGEMENT.
Employer-assisted housing program, §§42-2501 to 42-2507.
Environment.
District department of the environment, §§8-151.01 to 8-151.15.
See ENVIRONMENTAL PROTECTION.
Environmental services, department of, §34-2401.08.
False personation of inspectors of District departments, §22-1405.
Financial accountability and performance, §§1-204.56a to 1-204.56e.
Financial responsibility and management assistance authority.
General provisions, §§47-391.01 to 47-395.
See FINANCIAL RESPONSIBILITY AND MANAGEMENT ASSISTANCE AUTHORITY.
Foreign missions, office of, §6-1303.
General services, §§10-551.01 to 10-551.10.
See GENERAL SERVICES, DEPARTMENT OF.
Gifts.
Independent agencies authorized to accept, §1-329.01.
Health care finance department, §§7-771.01 to 7-771.11.
See HEALTH CARE FINANCE DEPARTMENT.
Health, department of.
Functions, §§7-731 to 7-737.
Health care safety net administration, §§7-1401 to 7-1405.01.
Smoking in public places, §§7-741.01 to 7-741.07.
Homeland security and emergency management agency, §§7-2202 to 7-2209.

DEPARTMENTS AND AGENCIES
—Cont'd
Housing finance agency.
General provisions, §§42-2701.01 to 42-2706.05.
See HOUSING FINANCE AGENCY.
Human rights and business development, department of, §§2-1411.04, 2-1411.06.
Human services, department of, §§7-103 to 7-171.
Independent agencies, reductions in budgets of, §1-204.53.
Insurance, securities, and banking, §§26-551.01 to 26-551.25.
See BANKS AND FINANCIAL INSTITUTIONS.
Insurance, securities, and banking, department of.
General provisions, §§31-101 to 31-108.
See INSURANCE, SECURITIES, AND BANKING, DEPARTMENT OF.
Legal aid agency redesignated as public defender service, §§2-1601, 2-1608.
Licenses, investigations, and inspections, director of department of, §1-301.03.
Loans from productivity bank fund, §§1-325.01, 1-325.02.
Meetings, §§2-571 to 2-580.
Mental health department, §§7-1131.01 to 7-1131.21.
See MENTAL HEALTH DEPARTMENT.
Motor vehicle parking agency, §50-2608.
Motor vehicles.
Department of motor vehicles, §§50-901 to 50-907.
See MOTOR VEHICLES DEPARTMENT.
National capital housing authority.
General provisions, §§6-101.01 to 6-103.01.
See NATIONAL CAPITAL HOUSING AUTHORITY.
Nominees by mayor to serve as subordinate agency heads, §1-523.01.
Office of chief financial officer.
See CHIEF FINANCIAL OFFICER.
Office of human rights, §§2-1411.01 to 2-1411.06.

DEPARTMENTS AND AGENCIES
—Cont'd
Office of police complaints.
General provisions, §§5-1101 to 5-1115.
See OFFICE OF POLICE
COMPLAINTS.
Office of veterans' affairs, §§49-1001
to 49-1006.
Office on aging, §§7-503.01 to 7-503.06.
Official correspondence, §§2-701 to
2-710.
Open government office, §§2-591 to
2-593.
Open meetings, §§2-571 to 2-580.
Opportunity account office,
§1-307.62.
**Performance and financial
accountability,** §§1-204.56a to
1-204.56e.
Performance based budgets,
§47-308.01.
Performance accountability reporting,
§47-308.03.
Relevant performance measures,
§47-308.02.
Placement of orders with, §1-301.01.
Pretrial services agency, §§23-1301 to
23-1309.
See PRETRIAL SERVICES AGENCY.
Procurement.
Applicability of provisions, §§2-351.02,
2-351.05.
Construction of provisions, §2-351.01.
Definitions, §2-351.04.
Exemption from provisions, §2-351.05.
Good faith, §2-351.03.
Public defender service, §§2-1601 to
2-1608.
See PUBLIC DEFENDER SERVICE.
Public health department.
See PUBLIC HEALTH,
DEPARTMENT OF.
Public-owned vehicles, §§50-202 to
50-205.
Bicycle safety enhancements, §50-205.
EPA miles per gallon requirement,
§50-203.
Fleet management, §§50-211.01 to
50-211.07.
Official use, §50-202.
Restrictions on use, §50-204.
Public parking authority.
General provisions, §§50-2501 to
50-2514.
See PUBLIC PARKING
AUTHORITY.

DEPARTMENTS AND AGENCIES
—Cont'd
Public records management,
§§2-1701 to 2-1714.
See PUBLIC RECORDS
MANAGEMENT.
Public works department.
Parks and recreation responsibilities
of, §10-166.
**Recreation and parks, department
of,** §§10-137.01, 10-166, 10-302.
RLA revitalization corporation.
General provisions, §6-341.05.
Schools and education.
Food services department, §38-801.
General services department, §§38-924
to 38-926.
**Small and local business
development, department of,**
§§2-218.11 to 2-218.13.
Soil and water conservation district,
§§8-1701 to 8-1721.
**State health planning and
development agency.**
General provisions, §§44-401 to
44-421.
See STATE HEALTH PLANNING
AND DEVELOPMENT
AGENCY.
Titles and tags, office of registrar of,
§50-2201.24.
Transportation, department of,
§§50-921.01 to 50-921.22,
50-2201.03.
See TRANSPORTATION.
Unclaimed property held by, §41-112.
Veterans' affairs, office of, §§49-1001
to 49-1006.
Water and sewer authority,
§§34-2201.01 to 34-2202.41.
See WATER AND SEWER
AUTHORITY.
**Weights, measures, and markets,
department of,** §§37-201.01 to
37-201.03.
**Youth rehabilitation services,
department of,** §§2-1515.01 to
2-1515.54.
See YOUTH REHABILITATION
SERVICES, DEPARTMENT OF.
Youth services.
See YOUTH SERVICES.

DEPENDENT CHILDREN.
Adoption.
Adoption subsidy payments, §4-301.
Limitation on number, §4-115.

DEPENDENT CHILDREN —Cont'd

Adoption —Cont'd

Mayor's powers, §§4-115, 4-302.

Annual budget, §4-121.

Board of Public Welfare.

Child placement, §4-118.

Classes of children, §4-116.

Confidentiality of records, §4-302.

Discharge from guardianship, §4-123.

Duties and powers, §4-124.

Transfer of duties of board of trustees of National Training School for Girls, §4-120.

Visitation of ward, §4-122.

Child abuse and neglect.

See CHILD ABUSE AND NEGLECT.

Child custody.

Uniform child custody proceedings, §§16-4601.01 to 16-4605.03.

See CHILD CUSTODY AND CHILD CUSTODY PROCEEDINGS.

Delinquent minors.

See DELINQUENT MINORS.

Discharge from guardianship, §4-123.

Escape from institution, §4-125.

Family court of superior court.

Commitment of children, §§4-118, 4-119.

Delinquency, neglect or children in need of supervision proceedings, §§16-2301 to 16-2340.

Termination of parental rights, §§16-2351 to 16-2365.

Foster care.

General provisions, §§4-217.01 to 4-217.11.

See FOSTER CARE.

Guardianship of minors.

Permanent guardianship, §§16-2381 to 16-2399.

See GUARDIAN AND WARD.

Mandated studies, §§4-117, 4-121.

National Training School for Girls.

Transfer of trustees' functions to Board of Public Welfare, §4-120.

Service of process, §16-2306.

Summons and process, §16-2306.

DEPOSIT AND INVESTMENT OF DISTRICT FUNDS, §§47-351.01 to 47-351.16.

Banking services in low to moderate income area, §47-351.10.

Bids.

Eligibility to submit, §47-351.04.

Information provided in bid, §47-351.04.

DEPOSIT AND INVESTMENT OF DISTRICT FUNDS —Cont'd

Bids —Cont'd

Joint bid, §47-351.04.

Solicitation for bids, §47-351.04.

Check cashing, identification, §47-351.14.

Collateral, §47-351.08.

Community development score for eligible financial institution, §47-351.07.

Competition for District banking business, §47-351.05.

Definitions, §47-351.01.

Financial score for eligible financial institution, §47-351.06.

General deposit and investment requirements, §47-351.03.

Insured institutions.

Reservation of funds for, §47-351.11.

Investments authorized, §47-351.03.

Linked deposits for community development lending, §47-351.09.

Mayor's powers, §47-351.02.

Penalties, §47-351.15.

Protection of funds at risk, §47-351.13.

Public disclosure, §47-351.12.

Restriction on amount deposited in single financial institution, §47-351.03.

Rules, §47-351.16.

DEPOSITIONS, §14-103.

Adoption proceedings, Adoption Rules 30, 31.

Persons before whom depositions may be taken, Adoption Rule 28.

Use of depositions, Adoption Rule 32.

Appeal pending, CivPro Rule 27.

Domestic relations actions, DomRel Rule 27.

Arbitration, revised act.

Subpoena and discovery procedures, §16-4417.

Bankruptcy proceedings, USDistDCBank Rule 7030-1.

Certificates regarding discovery, CivPro Rule 5.

Child custody proceedings.

Testimony in another state, §16-4601.10.

Costs, CivPro Rule 54-I.

Criminal procedure, CrimPro Rule 15.

Delinquent minors, JuvProc Rule 15.

Criminal procedure, §23-108, CrimPro Rule 15.

DEPOSITIONS —Cont'd
Delinquent minors, JuvProc Rule 15.
Domestic relations actions, DomRel
Rules 30, 31.
Appeal pending, DomRel Rule 27.
Persons before whom depositions may
be taken, DomRel Rule 28.
Prior to action, DomRel Rule 27.
Use of depositions, DomRel Rules 27,
32.
Errors and irregularities, CivPro Rule
32.
Domestic relations actions, DomRel
Rule 32.
Failure to attend, CivPro Rule 37.
Adoption proceedings, Adoption Rule
37.
Domestic relations actions, DomRel
Rule 37.
Filing of requests, CivPro Rule 5.
**General provisions governing
discovery,** CivPro Rule 26,
USDistCt LCvR 26.2.
Interstate deposition and discovery,
§§13-441 to 13-448.
See INTERSTATE DEPOSITIONS
AND DISCOVERY.
Interstate family support.
Special rules of evidence, §46-353.16.
Non-District of Columbia cases,
CivPro Rule 28-I.
Nonresidents, §14-104.
Notaries public taking, §1-1210.
Notice, service of, USDistCt LCvR
30.1.
Oral examination, CivPro Rule 30.
Adoption proceedings, Adoption Rule
30.
Domestic relations actions, DomRel
Rule 30.
Outside District of Columbia, CivPro
Rule 28-I.
Adoption proceedings, Adoption Rule
28.
Domestic relations actions, DomRel
Rule 28.
**Persons before whom depositions
may be taken,** CivPro Rule 28.
Adoption proceedings, Adoption Rule
28.
Domestic relations actions, DomRel
Rule 28.
Pre-action depositions, CivPro Rule
27.
Domestic relations actions, DomRel
Rule 27.

DEPOSITIONS —Cont'd
Public utilities investigations,
§34-920.
Recordings, CivPro Rule 30.
Adoption proceedings, Adoption Rule
30.
Domestic relations actions, DomRel
Rule 30.
Use of expert's videotaped deposition,
CivPro Rule 32.
Service of notice, USDistCt LCvR
30.1.
Stipulations regarding procedures,
CivPro Rule 29.
Adoption proceedings, Adoption Rule
29.
Domestic relations actions, DomRel
Rule 29.
Subpoenas, CivPro Rule 30.
Criminal cases, CrimPro Rule 17.
Delinquent minors, JuvProc Rule 17.
Use in court proceedings, CivPro
Rule 32.
Adoption proceedings, Adoption Rule
32.
Criminal procedure, CrimPro Rule 15.
Delinquent minors, JuvProc Rule 15.
Domestic relations actions, DomRel
Rules 27, 32.
Written questions, CivPro Rule 31.
Adoption proceedings, Adoption Rule
31.
Domestic relations actions, DomRel
Rule 31.

DEPOSITS WITH COURT.
Condemnation proceedings, CivPro
Rule 71A.
Masters.
Deposit for expenses, CivPro Rule
53-II.
Domestic relations actions, DomRel
Rule 53.
Small claims court forms.
Return of deposits, SmallClaims
Forms 8 to 10.
Superior court.
Deposits with court, CivPro Rule 67-I.
Domestic relations actions, DomRel
Rule 67.

DEPRECIATION.
Income tax deduction for,
§47-1811.04.
Public utilities, §34-1115.

DERIVATIVE ACTIONS.
Benefit corporations.
Benefit enforcement proceedings,
§29-1303.05.
Definition of benefit enforcement
proceeding, §29-1301.02.
Corporations, §§29-305.50 to
29-305.57.
See CORPORATIONS.
Limited cooperative associations,
§29-1013.01.
Limited liability companies,
§29-808.02.
Limited partnerships, §29-709.02.
Nonprofit corporations, §§29-411.01 to
29-411.09.
See NONPROFIT CORPORATIONS.
Statutory trusts, §§29-1206.10 to
29-1206.14.

DESERTION AND NONSUPPORT.
Child support enforcement, §§46-201
to 46-231.
See CHILD SUPPORT
ENFORCEMENT.
Interstate family support, §§46-351.01
to 46-359.03.
See INTERSTATE FAMILY
SUPPORT.
Medical support enforcement,
§§46-251.01 to 46-251.10.

DETAINERS, INTERSTATE
AGREEMENT ON, §§24-801 to
24-805.
Definitions, §24-802.
Enactment, §24-801.
Enforcement and cooperation,
§24-803.
Regulation, §24-804.
Right to alter, amend, repeal
reserved, §24-805.

DETECTION DEVICE.
Tampering by persons required to
wear, §22-1211.

DETENTION FACILITY
CONSTRUCTION.
Judiciary Square, §§24-1201 to
24-1203.

DETENTION OF PERSONS BY
FOREIGN POWERS.
Property, protection of.
See CONSERVATORS.

DETERGENTS.
Phosphate cleaners, §§8-107.01 to
8-107.04.

DETERIORATED PROPERTY.
Acquisition and disposal by District.
Eliminating slum and blight,
§§42-3171.01 to 42-3171.04.
Demolition or enclosure of
deteriorated property,
§§42-3173.01 to 42-3173.12.

DETINUE.
Sale of goods, UCC.
Buyer's right to detinue of goods,
§28:2-716.

DEVELOPMENTAL DISABILITIES.
ABLE savings accounts, §§47-4901,
47-4902.
Disability services, department on,
§§7-761.01 to 7-761.12.
See DISABILITY SERVICES,
DEPARTMENT ON.
Early intervention program,
§§7-863.01 to 7-863.04.
Intermediate care facilities.
Stevie Sellows quality improvement
fund, §§47-1270 to 47-1278.

DEVISES.
See WILLS.

DIABETES.
Health insurance coverage, §§31-3001
to 31-3004.
Applicability, §31-3004.
Definitions, §31-3001.
Nondiscrimination, §31-3003.
Payable benefits, §31-3002.

DIAMONDS.
Public auction permit requirements,
§47-2705.

DIETETICS AND NUTRITION.
Board of, §3-1202.02.
Definition of practice of, §3-1201.02.
Examinations, §§3-1207.01, 3-1207.02.
Health occupations boards.
General provisions, §§3-1201.01 to
3-1213.01.
See HEALTH OCCUPATIONS
BOARDS.
Health occupations licensure,
registration or certification,
§§3-1205.01 to 3-1205.24.
See HEALTH OCCUPATIONS
LICENSURE, REGISTRATION
OR CERTIFICATION.
Intellectual disabilities, persons
with.
Rights of persons regarding diet,
§7-1305.05.

DIETETICS AND NUTRITION
—Cont'd
Licenses, §§3-1207.01, 3-1207.02.
Qualifications for practitioners,
§3-1207.01.
Titles and terms prohibited as
misrepresentation without
license to practice, §3-1210.03.
Waiver of examination, §3-1207.02.

DIGITAL TELECOMMUNICATIONS.
Internet-related
telecommunications.
Franchise agreement.
Furnishing digitally-disadvantaged
residents, §§34-1731.01 to
34-1731.11.

DIGITAL TRANSACTIONS.
Collection of taxes.
Certificate of taxes and assessments
due, §47-405.
Electronic transactions, uniform act,
§§28-4901 to 28-4918.

DILATORY PLEADINGS, CivPro Rule
11.
Domestic relations actions, DomRel
Rule 11.
Hospitalization of persons with
mental illness, MentalHealth Rule
14.

DINOSAUR OF DISTRICT OF
COLUMBIA.
Capitalsaurus dinosaur, §1-161.

DIPHTHERIA.
Immunization of school students,
§§38-501 to 38-508.
Interstate compact on educational
opportunity for military children.
Time to obtain immunizations,
§49-1101.05.

DIPLOMATIC OFFICES.
Foreign missions, §§6-1301 to 6-1315.
See FOREIGN MISSIONS.

DIRECT DEPOSIT, §1-611.20.

DIRECTED VERDICTS, CivPro Rule
50.
Domestic relations actions, DomRel
Rule 50.
Stay of proceedings, CivPro Rule 62.

DIRECT INSTALLMENT LOANS.
Consumer credit, §28-3809.
Finance charges on, §§28-3308,
28-3602.
Motor vehicles, §§28-3601 to 28-3603.

DIRECT-REDUCTION LOANS.
Veterans, §42-3002.

DIRT BIKES.
Defined, §50-2201.02.
Public property.
Operation on prohibited, §50-2201.04b.
Registration not required,
§50-2201.04b.

DISABILITIES, PERSONS WITH.
ABLE savings accounts, §§47-4901,
47-4902.
Adoption.
Interstate compact on adoption and
medical assistance, §§4-321 to
4-328.
Assistive technology device
warranty, §§28-4031 to 28-4034.
Attorneys at law.
Clients with diminished capacity.
Client-lawyer relationship, ProfCond
Rule 1.14.
Incompetent or incapacitated
attorneys, DCBar Rule XI,
USDistCt LCrR 57.30, USDistCt
LCvR 83.19.
Criminal abuse, neglect and
financial exploitation of
vulnerable adults and elderly
persons, §§22-931 to 22-938.
See CRIMINAL ABUSE, NEGLECT
AND FINANCIAL
EXPLOITATION OF
VULNERABLE ADULTS AND
ELDERLY PERSONS.
Decedents' estates.
Conflicts.
Appointment of guardian for person
with a legal disability, §20-108.
Nonprobate transfers.
Agent on accounts.
Appointment, §19-602.05.
Payment to designated agent,
§19-602.24.
Financial institutions, protection of.
Discharges from claims,
§19-602.26.
POD designation, payment on,
§19-602.23.
Multiple-party accounts.
Payment by financial institution,
§19-602.22.
Defined terms.
Rights of blind persons and persons
with physical disabilities, §7-1009.

DISABILITIES, PERSONS WITH
—Cont'd
Department on disability services,
§§7-761.01 to 7-761.12.
See DISABILITY SERVICES,
DEPARTMENT ON.
District of Columbia Code, rules,
regulations, publications,
Internet publications.
Respectful language modernization,
§§2-631, 2-632.
Employment discrimination, §7-1005.
Employment opportunities, §§32-301
to 32-305.
Committee for purchase of products
and services of the blind and other
individuals with severe
disabilities, §§32-303, 32-304.
Definitions, §32-302.
Procurement requirements for District
government, §32-305.
Purpose of chapter, §32-301.
Equal access.
Housing, §7-1006.
Public places, accommodations, and
conveyances, §§7-1001, 7-1002.
Fines for interfering with or
discriminating against, §7-1007.
Interim program for disability
assistance, §4-204.08.
Judges.
Commission on judicial disabilities
and tenure, §§11-1521 to 11-1530.
See COMMISSION ON JUDICIAL
DISABILITIES AND TENURE.
Disability of judge, CJC Canon 2.14.
Landlord discrimination against,
§42-3505.05.
Limitation of actions, §12-302.
Mayor's committee on persons with
disabilities.
Transfer of functions to office of
disability rights, §2-1431.06.
Merit system.
Disability compensation, §§1-623.01 to
1-623.47.
See MERIT SYSTEM.
Metrorail and metrobus adopted
regional system facilities for,
§9-1111.17.
Minimum wage for workers with
disabilities, §32-1003.
Motor vehicle registration for
disabled American veterans,
§50-1503.01.
National Guard.
Excuse from duty for disability,
§49-104.

DISABILITIES, PERSONS WITH
—Cont'd
National Guard —Cont'd
Retirement of commissioned officer for
disability, §49-309.
Office of disability rights, §2-1431.03.
Establishment, §2-1431.03.
Mayor's committee on persons with
disabilities.
Transfer of functions to office,
§2-1431.06.
Office of risk management.
Transfer of functions to office,
§2-1431.06.
Powers and duties, §2-1431.04.
Parole for medical and geriatric
reasons, §§24-461 to 24-468.
See PAROLE.
Penalties for interfering with or
discriminating against, §7-1007.
Personal representatives, §20-524.
Distributions.
Fiduciary of incompetent or
incapacitated nonresident, to,
§20-1107.
Pet ownership restriction in
assisted housing, §§8-2031 to
8-2035.
Prohibition of discrimination
against, §2-1401.01.
Public assistance.
Incapacitated person, defined,
§4-205.42.
Payments to, §4-212.01.
Protective or vendor payments on
behalf of dependent children,
§4-212.02.
Protective payments on behalf of adult
recipients, §4-212.03.
Public officers and employees.
Equal employment opportunity,
§1-607.02.
Public places, accommodations, and
conveyances.
Equal access to, §§7-1001, 7-1002.
Real estate transactions.
Unlawful discriminatory practices in,
§2-1402.21.
Real property taxes.
Reduced tax liability, §47-863.
Rehabilitation services program.
Establishment, §32-331.
Grant and contract authority,
§32-331.01.
Rulemaking to implement, §32-332.
Rental housing conversion and sale,
§42-3402.08.

DISABILITIES, PERSONS WITH
—Cont'd
Rent control, §§42-3502.06, 42-3502.08.
Rent supplement program, §6-226.
  Capital-based assistance, §6-229.
  Tenant-based assistance, §6-228.
  Voucher assistance, §6-227.
Rights, §§2-1431.01 to 2-1431.08.
  ADA compliance program, §2-1431.02.
  Definitions, §2-1431.01.
  Interagency agreements, §2-1431.08.
  Mayor's committee on persons with
    disabilities.
    Transfer of functions to office of
      disability rights, §2-1431.06.
  Office of disability rights, §2-1431.03.
    Mayor's committee on persons with
      disabilities.
      Transfer of functions to office,
        §2-1431.06.
    Office of risk management.
      Transfer of functions to office,
        §2-1431.06.
    Powers and duties, §2-1431.04.
  Office of risk management.
    Transfer of functions to office of
      disability rights, §2-1431.06.
  Public availability of plans and
    reports, §2-1431.05.
  Rulemaking, §2-1431.08.
  Transfer of functions from office of risk
    management, §2-1431.07.
  Transfer of functions to office of
    disability rights, §2-1431.06.
Schools and education, §38-913.
  Medicaid and special education reform
    fund, §§4-204.51 to 4-204.56.
  Nonpublic schools for students with
    disabilities.
    See SPECIAL EDUCATION.
  Special education task force, §§38-2551
    to 38-2555.
Taxicabs.
  Accessible taxicabs, §50-301.25.
  Digital dispatch for individuals with
    disabilities, §50-301.25a.
  Training of employees and operators,
    §50-301.25b.
Tenant assistance program,
  §42-3503.03.
Volunteer Service Credit Program,
  §§7-531.01 to 7-531.11.

DISABILITIES, PERSONS WITH
—Cont'd
Vulnerable adults and elderly
  persons.
  Criminal abuse, neglect and financial
    exploitation, §§22-931 to 22-938.
    See CRIMINAL ABUSE, NEGLECT
      AND FINANCIAL
      EXPLOITATION OF
      VULNERABLE ADULTS AND
      ELDERLY PERSONS.

DISABILITY INCOME.
Emergency medical services or fire
  department employees.
  Presumptive disability or death,
    §§5-651 to 5-656.
Interim disability assistance (IDA),
  §4-204.07.
  Fund, §4-204.09.
Merit system.
  Disability income protection program,
    §§1-622.02, 1-622.15.
  Generally, §§1-623.01 to 1-623.47.
  See MERIT SYSTEM.
Police and firefighters retirement
  and disability.
  General provisions, §§5-631 to 5-762.
  See POLICE AND FIREFIGHTERS
    RETIREMENT AND
    DISABILITY.
Public officers and employees.
  See MERIT SYSTEM.
Teachers' retirement.
  After June 30, 1946, §§38-2021.04,
    38-2021.06.
  Prior to June 30, 1946, §§38-2001.04
    to 38-2001.06.
Workers' compensation, §32-1508.

DISABILITY SERVICES,
  DEPARTMENT ON, §§7-761.01 to
  7-761.12.
Accounts, §7-761.08.
Conflicts, rescission, §7-761.11.
Contracting authority, §7-761.09.
Contribution to costs of supports.
  Defined, §7-761.02.
Definitions, §7-761.02.
Delegation of authority, §7-761.10.
Director, §7-761.06.
Duties, §7-761.05.
Establishment, §7-761.03.
Family support council, §7-761.12.

**DISABILITY SERVICES,
    DEPARTMENT ON** —Cont'd
Medicaid services, §7-761.07.
Notice, §7-761.06b.
Organization, §7-761.04.
Purpose, §7-761.03.
Reports, §7-761.06a.
    Public availability, §7-761.06b.
Rulemaking, §7-761.09.
Staff and resources, §7-761.04.
Title of provisions, §7-761.01.
Transfers of authority, §7-761.08.

DISABLED AMERICAN VETERANS.
Real property exempt from taxation,
    §47-1003.

**DISABLED, INJURED, OR SICK
    ANIMALS.**
Abandonment of, §22-1012.
Horse-drawn carriage trade horses,
    §8-2010.
Neglect of, §22-1011.

DISABLED PERSONS.
See DISABILITIES, PERSONS WITH.

**DISADVANTAGED BUSINESS
    ENTERPRISES.**
Ballpark.
    Requirements, §10-1601.04.
**Small and certified business
    enterprise development and
    assistance,** §§2-218.01 to 2-218.75.
    See SMALL AND CERTIFIED
        BUSINESS ENTERPRISE
        DEVELOPMENT AND
        ASSISTANCE.

DISAPPEARED PERSONS.
Property, protection of.
    See CONSERVATORS.

DISASTERS.
Alcoholic beverage licenses.
    Safekeeping.
        Temporary surrender, §25-791.
Cable television.
    Use of system during emergencies or
        disasters, §34-1257.06.
Emergency management.
    General provisions, §§7-2201 to
        7-2404.
    See EMERGENCY MANAGEMENT.
**Emergency volunteer health
    practitioners,** §§7-2361.01 to
    7-2361.12.
    See EMERGENCY VOLUNTEER
        HEALTH PRACTITIONERS.

DISASTERS —Cont'd
**Homeland security and emergency
    management agency,** §§7-2201 to
    7-2209.
    See EMERGENCY MANAGEMENT.
**Natural disaster consumer
    protection,** §§28-4101 to 28-4103.

DISBARMENT.
Attorneys at law, §§11-2501 to 11-2504,
    DCBar Rule XI, USDistCt LCrR
    57.27, USDistCt LCvR 83.16.

DISBURSING OFFICER, §§47-111,
    47-113 to 47-116.
Appointment of, §47-111.
Audits, §47-111.
Bonds, surety, §47-111.
**Deputy disbursing and assistant
    disbursing officers,** §§47-113 to
    47-115.
    Appointment, §47-113.
    Authority and powers, §47-114.
    Misconduct, liability, §47-115.
Outstanding checks, §§47-125, 47-126.
Powers and duties, §47-111.
Suspension of items in accounts of,
    §47-116.

DISCHARGE OF EMPLOYEE.
See TERMINATION OF
    EMPLOYMENT.

DISCIPLINARY ACTIONS.
Asbestos contractors, §§8-111.06,
    8-111.07.
Boiler inspections.
    Revocation or suspension of certificate,
        §2-108.
Child care facilities, §§7-2039 to
    7-2041.
**Claims against the District,
    stemming from,** §2-415.
**Fire and emergency medical
    services department,** §§5-1031 to
    5-1057.
    Commencement of action, §5-1031.
Funeral directors.
    Grounds, §3-408.
    Hearing procedures, §3-409.
Heath care practitioners.
    Administrative agency review,
        §3-1205.20.
    Ground, §3-1205.14.
    Reinstatement of license, §3-1205.21.
    Summary actions, §3-1205.15.
Judges.
    Cooperation of judge with authorities,
        CJC Canon 2.16.

DISCIPLINARY ACTIONS —Cont'd
Legal service, §1-608.56.
Merit system, under, §§1-616.51 to
1-616.54.
Metropolitan police, §5-1114.
Commencement of action, §5-1031.
National guard, §49-804.
Pesticide operators, §8-410.
Pharmacists.
Grounds, §47-2885.10.
Security agents and brokers.
Licensing, §31-5602.07.
Lack of qualification, §31-5602.08.
Registration of securities, §31-5603.07.
Teachers.
Testing integrity in public schools.
Sanctions for violations, §38-771.04.
Underground storage tanks,
§8-113.07.
Whistleblower protection, §§1-615.55,
2-223.04.

DISCLAIMER OF PROPERTY
INTERESTS, §§19-1501 to 19-1518.
Applicability and scope of
provisions, §19-1503.
Bar to right to disclaim, §19-1513.
Beneficiary designation.
Defined, §19-1512.
Delivery of disclaimer of interest
created by, §19-1512.
Chapter supplemental to other law,
§19-1504.
Definitions, §19-1502.
Beneficiary designation, §19-1512.
Future interest, time of distribution,
§19-1506.
Record, sign, §19-1505.
Delivery of disclaimer, §19-1512,
Probate Rule 6.1.
Effective date, §19-1506.
Electronic signature in global and
nation commerce act.
Chapter modifies, limits or supersedes,
§19-1517.
Fiduciaries.
Power to disclaim, §19-1505.
Filing disclaimer, §19-1512, Probate
Rule 6.1.
Recording disclaimer, §19-1515.
Future exercise of right.
Disclaimer not barred by previous
exercise, §19-1513.
Interests or powers existing on
effective date of chapter.
Effect, §19-1516.
Jointly held property.
Defined, §19-1502.

DISCLAIMER OF PROPERTY
INTERESTS —Cont'd
Jointly held property —Cont'd
Disclaimer of right of survivorship in,
§19-1507.
Limitation on right, §19-1513.
Partial disclaimers.
Power to disclaim, expression,
§19-1505.
Passage of disclaimer interest,
§19-1506.
Persons to whom delivery of
disclaimer made, §19-1512.
Power held in fiduciary capacity,
§19-1511.
Power of appointment or other
power not held in fiduciary
capacity.
Appointee, object or taker in default of
exercise.
Disclaimer by, §19-1510.
Rules applicable to disclaimer,
§19-1509.
Power to disclaim, §19-1505.
Recording disclaimer, §19-1515.
Requirements for disclaimer to be
effective, §19-1505.
Right to waive, release, disclaim or
renounce interest.
Chapter not to limit, §19-1504.
Rules applicable to disclaimer,
§19-1506.
Short title.
Uniform disclaimer of property
interest act, §19-1501.
Spendthrift provision or similar
restriction imposed by creator.
Power to disclaim, §19-1505.
Tax qualified disclaimer, §19-1514.
Time disclaimer effective, §19-1506.
Transfer, assignment, release.
Disclaimer not, §19-1505.
Trustee disclaiming interest that
would have become trust
property.
Interest not trust property, §19-1508.
Uniform disclaimer of property
interest act.
Short title, §19-1501.
Uniformity of application and
construction, §19-1518.
Waiver of right.
Bar to disclaimer, §19-1513.

DISCLOSURE OF INFORMATION.
Adoption proceedings, Adoption Rules
26, 37.

DISCLOSURE OF INFORMATION
   —Cont'd
Appropriations, §47-3409.
Arbitration, revised act.
   Arbitrators, disclosure of facts
      affecting impartiality, §16-4412.
   Disclosure of costs, §16-4431.
**Assignment of felony cases and
   related cases,** CrimPro Rule 105.
Attorneys at law.
   Client information, ProfCond Rule 1.6.
   Discipline or disability proceedings,
      DCBar Rule XI.
**Cancer prevention and monitoring
   requirements,** §§7-302, 7-304.
**Child abuse and neglect
   proceedings.**
   Inspection and disclosure of neglect
      records, NeglectProc Rule 46.
Child and family services agency.
   Records and information, §4-1303.07.
Child Protection Register,
   §§4-1302.01 to 4-1302.09.
**Commission on judicial disabilities
   and tenure.**
   Proceedings of, §11-1528.
**Consumer credit service
   organizations,** §28-4605.
Discovery generally.
   See DISCOVERY.
**District funds invested or deposited
   in banks and financial
   institutions,** §47-351.12.
Domestic relations actions, DomRel
   Rules 26, 37.
**Employees retirement program
   management,** §§1-731 to 1-739.
Fair trials in superior court, CivPro
   Rule 203, CrimPro Rule 53.
   Juvenile proceedings, JuvProc Rule 53.
Freedom of information, §§2-531 to
   2-540.
   See FREEDOM OF INFORMATION.
Gas station marketing agreements,
   §36-303.02.
Grand jury secrecy, CrimPro Rule 6,
   USDistCt LCrR 6.1.
   Discovery of transcripts, CrimPro Rule
      16.
   Delinquent minors, JuvProc Rule 16.
**Health insurance portability and
   accountability.**
   Group insurance provisions,
      §31-3303.08.
**Housing finance agency board and
   employees,** §42-2702.04.

DISCLOSURE OF INFORMATION
   —Cont'd
Income tax returns, §47-1805.04.
**Insurance industry material
   transactions disclosures,**
   §§31-1001 to 31-1004.
**Intercepted oral or wire
   communications,** §§23-551 to
   23-553.
   Use of intercepted communications,
      CrimPro Rule 41-I.
**Internal Revenue Service
   information,** §47-3409.
Juvenile proceedings, JuvProc Rule
   53.
Juvenile records, §§16-2331 to
   16-2333.02, 16-2336.
Lemon law.
   Rights of consumer under, §50-504.
   Used vehicles, damages or defects in,
      §50-505.
**Lottery and charitable games
   control board,** §3-1302.
Medical records, §44-802.
Medicare supplement insurance,
   §31-3705.
Mental health information,
   §§7-1201.01 to 7-1208.07.
   See MENTAL HEALTH
      DISCLOSURES.
**Mortgage lenders and brokers, loans
   by,** §26-1113.
Naturopaths, §3-1206.22.
News media privilege, §§16-4702,
   16-4703.
**Panhandling, disclosure of arrests
   and convictions for,** §22-2306.
Parentage proceedings, §16-2348.
Pensions and retirement funds,
   §§1-909.01 to 1-909.05.
Pornography.
   Nonconsensual pornography,
      §§22-3051 to 22-3057.
   See OBSCENITY.
Prescription drug pricing,
   §§48-801.01 to 48-801.06.
Producer controlled insurers.
   Business transactions with, §31-407.
**Public Parking Authority board
   members, financial disclosure
   statements made by,** §50-2505.
Public utilities under investigation,
   §34-1118.
**Real estate brokers and
   salespersons,** §§42-1703,
   47-2853.196, 47-2853.198.

DISCLOSURE OF INFORMATION
—Cont'd
Residential home sales disclosures,
§§42-1301 to 42-1311.
See HOME SALES.
Sentencing.
Presentence investigation reports,
CrimPro Rule 32, USDistCt LCrR
32.2.
Delinquent minors, JuvProc Rule 32.
Termination of parental rights,
§16-2364.
Trade secrets, §36-410.
Unemployment compensation,
§51-113.
Witness statements.
Criminal procedure, CrimPro Rule
26.2.
Delinquent minors, JuvProc Rule 26.2.
Probation modification hearings,
CrimPro Rule 32.1.
Release from custody or detention,
CrimPro Rule 46.
Sentencing hearings, CrimPro Rule 32.
Delinquent minors, JuvProc Rule 32.

**DISCLOSURE OF INTEREST OF
PARTIES.**
Appeals in federal cases, FRAP 26.1,
USCtApp Rule 26.1.

**DISCLOSURE STATEMENT,
CORPORATE.**
Appeals in federal cases, FRAP 26.1,
USCtApp Rule 26.1.

DISCOUNTS.
Consumer credit sales.
Referral sales, §28-3810.
Metrorail and metrobus.
Student fares, §35-234.
Motor vehicle insurance.
Senior citizen accident prevention
course certification, §50-2003.
**Public contract quick payment
provisions,** §2-221.03.

DISCOVERY.
Adoption proceedings generally,
Adoption Rules 26 to 37.
See ADOPTION.
Arbitration, Arbitration Rule VII.
Suspension of discovery rules,
Arbitration Rule VI.
Arbitration proceedings, CivPro Rule
70-I.
Arbitration, revised act.
Subpoena and discovery procedures,
§16-4417.

DISCOVERY —Cont'd
Attachment.
Post-judgment attachment, CivPro
Rule 69-I.
Domestic relations actions, DomRel
Rule 69.
Pre-judgment attachment, CivPro Rule
64-I.
Domestic relations actions, DomRel
Rule 64.
Attorneys at law.
Discipline or disability proceedings,
DCBar Rule XI.
Fairness to opposing party and
counsel, ProfCond Rule 3.4.
Bankruptcy proceedings,
USDistDCBank Rule 7026-1.
Certificates regarding discovery,
CivPro Rules 5, 37.
**Child abuse and neglect
proceedings,** NeglectProc Rules 14,
15.
Compelling discovery, CivPro Rule 37.
Criminal procedure, CrimPro Rule 16.
Domestic relations actions, DomRel
Rule 37.
Conferences, CivPro Rule 16, USDistCt
LCvR 16.3.
Authority to set conference, CivPro
Rule 309.
Failure to appear, CivPro Rule 16-II.
Criminal procedure, CrimPro Rule 16,
USDistCt LCrR 16.1.
Depositions, CrimPro Rule 15.
DNA testing.
Defendants rights, §22-4132.
Informal discovery, CrimPro Rule
16-II.
Presentence investigation reports,
CrimPro Rule 32.
Pretrial requests for discovery,
CrimPro Rule 12.
Prosecutor's responsibilities, ProfCond
Rule 3.8.
Delinquent minors, JuvProc Rule 16.
Depositions, JuvProc Rule 15.
Informal discovery, JuvProc Rule 16-I.
Presentence investigation reports,
JuvProc Rule 32.
Subpoenas, JuvProc Rule 17.
Witness statements, JuvProc Rule
26.2.
Depositions generally.
See DEPOSITIONS.
Disclosures.
Required disclosures, CivPro Rule 26.

DISCOVERY —Cont'd
DNA testing.
Defendants rights, §22-4132.
Documents and tangible things,
CivPro Rule 34.
Adoption proceedings, Adoption Rule
34.
Domestic relations actions, DomRel
Rule 34.
Request for production of documents,
CivPro Form CA 24.
Accompanying deposition notice,
CivPro Rule 30.
Domestic relations actions
generally, DomRel Rules 26 to 37.
See DOMESTIC RELATIONS
ACTIONS.
Domestic violence unit proceedings,
DomesticViolence Rule 8.
Electronically stored information.
Production, CivPro Rule 34.
Entry upon land for inspection, etc.,
CivPro Rule 34.
Domestic relations actions, DomRel
Rule 34.
Request for entry, CivPro Form CA 24.
Examination of person, CivPro Rule
35.
Criminal procedure, CrimPro Rule 16.
Delinquent minors, JuvProc Rule 16.
Experts.
Adoption proceedings, Adoption Rule
26.
Civil cases, CivPro Rule 26.
Criminal procedure, CrimPro Rule 16.
Delinquent minors, JuvProc Rule 16.
Domestic relations actions, DomRel
Rule 26.
Failure to cooperate, CivPro Rule 37.
Fiduciary accounts and reports,
CivPro Rule 305.
Filing of requests, CivPro Rule 5,
USDistCt LCvR 5.2.
Insurance agreements, CivPro Rule
26.
No-fault motor vehicle insurance,
§31-2403.01.
Intellectual disability proceedings.
Periodic review of orders for
commitment and admission,
MentalRetardation Rule 7.
Interrogatories.
See INTERROGATORIES.
Interstate deposition and discovery,
§§13-441 to 13-448.
See INTERSTATE DEPOSITIONS
AND DISCOVERY.

DISCOVERY —Cont'd
Interstate family support.
Assistance with discovery, §46-353.18.
Intervention proceedings, Probate
Rule 312.
Judgments and decrees.
Execution of judgment, CivPro Rule
69.
Landlord and tenant court,
LandlordTenant Rule 10.
Certification to civil division,
LandlordTenant Rule 13-I.
Mediation, effect of use at, §16-4203.
Meetings to resolve disputes, CivPro
Rules 26, 37.
Mental illness, persons with.
Hospitalization.
Limited discovery in a commitment
trial, MentalHealth Rule 17.
Methods of discovery, CivPro Rule 26,
USDistCt LCrR 16.1, USDistCt
LCvR 26.2.
Domestic relations actions, DomRel
Rule 26.
No-fault motor vehicle insurance.
Pre-litigation discovery of insurance,
§31-2403.01.
Post-conviction proceedings.
Superior court proceedings,
PostConvRel Rule 6.
Probate proceedings.
Contested estate cases, Probate Rule
407.
Death between January 1, 1981 and
June 30, 1995, Probate Rule
107.
Guardians, conservators, trustees,
etc., involved, Probate Rule 208.
Procurement practices.
Action for violations by qui tam
plaintiff, §2-381.03.
Protective orders, CivPro Rules 26, 37.
Adoption proceedings, Adoption Rule
26.
Criminal procedure, CrimPro Rule 16.
Delinquent minors, JuvProc Rule 16.
Domestic relations actions, DomRel
Rule 26.
Requests for admission, CivPro Rule
36.
Adoption proceedings, Adoption Rule
36.
Domestic relations actions, DomRel
Rule 36.
Form, CivPro Form CA 25.
Restraints of trade.
Civil investigative demand, §28-4505.

DISCOVERY —Cont'd
Sanctions, CivPro Rules 26, 37, USDistCt LCvR 26.2.
Adoption proceedings, Adoption Rule 37.
Domestic relations actions, DomRel Rule 37.
Scope and limitations, CivPro Rule 26, USDistCt LCvR 26.2.
Domestic relations actions, DomRel Rule 26.
Sentencing.
Presentence investigation reports, CrimPro Rule 32.
Delinquent minors, JuvProc Rule 32.
Sequence of discovery, CivPro Rule 26, USDistCt LCvR 26.2.
Domestic relations actions, DomRel Rule 26.
Service of process.
Certificates regarding discovery.
Domestic relations actions, DomRel Rule 5.
Signing requests, responses, and objections, CivPro Rule 26.
Small claims court, SmallClaims Rule 10.
Certification to civil division, SmallClaims Rule 13-I.
Stipulations regarding procedures, CivPro Rule 29.
Adoption proceedings, Adoption Rule 29.
Domestic relations actions, DomRel Rule 29.
Supplementation of responses.
Domestic relations actions, DomRel Rule 26.
Time limits, CivPro Rule 26, USDistCt LCvR 26.2.
Domestic relations actions, DomRel Rule 26.
No-fault motor vehicle insurance.
Pre-litigation discovery of insurance, response time, §31-2403.01.
Witness statements.
Criminal cases, CrimPro Rule 26.2.
Delinquent minors, JuvProc Rule 26.2.
Probation modification hearings, CrimPro Rule 32.1.
Release from custody or detention, CrimPro Rule 46.
Sentencing hearings, CrimPro Rule 32.
Work-product rule, CivPro Rule 26.
Adoption proceedings, Adoption Rule 26.

DISCOVERY —Cont'd
Work-product rule —Cont'd
Criminal procedure, CrimPro Rule 16.
Delinquent minors, JuvProc Rule 16.
Domestic relations actions, DomRel Rule 26.
DISCRIMINATION.
Age discrimination.
Exceptions for practices with discriminatory effects.
Cadet programs, age requirements for, §2-1402.12.
Educational institutions, age requirements for, §2-1402.42.
Prohibition of, §2-1401.01.
Aiding and abetting, §2-1402.62.
Athletic equity.
Schools and education, §§38-841.01 to 38-841.08.
Attorneys at law.
Employment discrimination, ProfCond Rule 9.1.
Bases for, §2-1401.01.
Blind and visually impaired.
See BLIND AND VISUALLY IMPAIRED.
Breastfeeding mothers, rights of, §§2-1402.81 to 2-1402.83.
Discrimination based on sex, §2-1401.05.
Cable television operators, §§34-1262.01 to 34-1262.03.
Affirmative action in employment, §34-1262.02.
Non-discrimination in employment, §34-1262.01.
Tenants of rental property, §34-1261.01.
Child support withholding.
Employment discrimination based on, §46-219.
Coercion, §2-1402.61.
Color discrimination.
Prohibition of, §2-1401.01.
Complaints, procedure for handling, §§2-1403.02 to 2-1403.17.
Conciliation agreements, §2-1402.63.
Constitution of the United States, US Const Amds 14, 15.
District of Columbia government.
Applicability of chapter, §2-1402.73.
Educational institutions, §§2-1402.41, 2-1402.42.
Employment agencies, §32-408.

DISCRIMINATION —Cont'd
Employment discrimination,
§§2-1402.01 to 2-1402.13.
See EMPLOYMENT
DISCRIMINATION.
Equal employment opportunity.
See EQUAL EMPLOYMENT
OPPORTUNITY.
Exceptions for practices with
discriminatory effects,
§2-1401.03.
Age requirements.
Cadet programs, §2-1402.12.
Educational institutions, §2-1402.42.
Educational institutions, §2-1402.42.
Employment discrimination,
§2-1402.12.
Real estate transactions.
Unlawful discriminatory practices
in, §2-1402.24.
Seniority systems, §2-1402.12.
Sex discrimination in educational
institution admissions policies,
§2-1402.42.
Familial status or responsibilities
discrimination.
Prohibition of, §2-1401.01.
Real estate transactions.
Unlawful discriminatory practices
in, §2-1402.21.
Fire and casualty insurance,
§31-2502.29.
Fraud and deceit, §2-1402.65.
Gas station wholesalers.
Nondiscrimination requirements,
§36-302.03.
Genetic information.
Defined, §2-1401.02.
Exceptions for certain practices,
§2-1401.03.
Prohibited acts, §2-1402.11.
Hate crimes, §§22-3701 to 22-3704.
Health insurance ratemaking,
§§31-3161 to 31-3163.
Applicability, §31-3163.
Requirements, §31-3161.
Rules, §31-3162.
Homeless services.
Limitations on use of District monies,
§4-755.02.
Housing accommodation
discrimination complaints.
Posting notice of, §2-1403.08.
Human rights commission,
§§2-1401.01 to 2-1404.04.
See HUMAN RIGHTS COMMISSION.

DISCRIMINATION —Cont'd
Injunctions, §2-1403.07.
Insurance.
Discrimination based upon AIDS test,
§§31-1601 to 31-1610.
Unfair trade practices, §§31-2231.01 to
31-2231.25.
See INSURANCE.
Investigation of complaints
regarding, §2-1403.05.
Judges.
Affiliation with discriminatory
organization, CJC Canon 3.6.
Bias, prejudice or harassment
prohibited, CJC Canon 2.3.
Impartiality generally, CJC Canon 2.
Jury selection, §11-1903.
Landlord and tenant, §42-3505.05.
Leave of absence.
Right to sick and safe leave.
Discharge or discrimination
prohibited, §32-131.08.
Licensed places.
Admission to, §§47-2901 to 47-2911.
Licenses, §§2-1402.67, 2-1403.17.
Marital status discrimination.
Prohibition of, §2-1401.01.
Matriculation discrimination.
Prohibition of, §2-1401.01.
Metropolitan police not allowed to
enforce discriminatory laws,
§5-133.11.
Motor vehicles.
Insurance, §2-1402.71.
Rentals, §2-1402.72.
National origin discrimination.
Prohibition of, §2-1401.01.
No-fault motor vehicle insurance,
§31-2409.
Occupational safety and health,
§32-1117.
Office of Human Rights, §§2-1411.01
to 2-1411.06.
Pay equity and training commission,
§§32-601 to 32-609.
Personal appearance discrimination.
Prohibition of, §2-1401.01.
Persons with disabilities.
See DISABILITIES, PERSONS WITH.
Place of residence or business
discrimination.
Prohibition of, §2-1401.01.
Police and firefighters retirement
and disability.
Widows' and orphans' pensions.
Equalization of, §5-744.

DISCRIMINATION —Cont'd

Political affiliation discrimination.
Prohibition of, §2-1401.01.

Pregnancy, childbirth, or related conditions.
Discrimination based on, §2-1401.05.

Private right of action, §2-1403.16.

Private vehicles-for-hire.
Zero-tolerance, §50-301.29a.

Program on work, employment, and responsibility (POWER),
§4-205.19i.

Prohibited acts, §§2-1402.01 to 2-1402.73.

Public accommodations, §2-1402.31.

Public utility charges, §§1-204.93, 34-1101.

Race discrimination.
Prohibition of, §2-1401.01.

Real estate transactions.
Unlawful discriminatory practices in, §§2-1402.21 to 2-1402.24.

Records, §2-1402.52.

Religious beliefs.
See RELIGIOUS BELIEFS.

Rental housing providers.
Discrimination against elderly tenants and families with children, §42-3505.05.

Reports, §2-1403.01.

Retaliation, §2-1402.61.

Seniority system exceptions,
§2-1402.12.

Severability of provisions, §2-1401.04.

Sex discrimination.
Benefit programs for District employees, §1-607.07.
Educational institutions.
Exceptions for, §2-1402.42.
Type of prohibited discrimination, as, §2-1401.01.

Sexual orientation discrimination.
Prohibition of, §2-1401.01.

Smokers.
Employment discrimination against, §7-1703.03.

Source of income discrimination.
Prohibition of, §2-1401.01.

Substance abuse and mental illness coverage, §31-3105.

Subterfuge.
Real estate transactions.
Unlawful discriminatory practices in, §2-1402.21.

Temporary assistance for needy families (TANF) program,
§4-205.19i.

DISCRIMINATION —Cont'd

Tenant assistance program,
§42-3509.01.

Threatening, injuring, intimidating, or interfering with persons in order to deprive them of due process, §§22-3312.02 to 22-3312.04.

Types of, §2-1401.01.

Unemployment status, §§32-1361 to 32-1368.
Applicability, §32-1368.
Definitions, §32-1361.
Effective date, §32-1368.
Enforcement of provisions, §32-1365.
Exemptions, §32-1364.
Penalties for violations, §32-1366.
Prohibited, §32-1362.
Retaliation, §32-1363.
Rules, §32-1367.

Unspecified practices with discriminatory effects,
§2-1402.68.

Workplace fraud.
Employer's retaliation, §32-1331.10.

DISEASES.
AIDS.
See AIDS.

Cancer.
District of Columbia general hospital hospice program, §§4-1101 to 4-1105.
Mammograms, §§31-2901 to 31-2903.
Prevention and monitoring, §§7-301 to 7-304.

Contagious, communicable, or infectious diseases.
See COMMUNICABLE DISEASES.

Emergency.
Public health emergency executive order, §7-2304.01.

Homozygous sickle cell disease,
§§7-831 to 7-840.

Malignant neoplastic diseases, prevention and monitoring,
§§7-301 to 7-304.

Metabolic disorders in newborns, screening for, §§7-831 to 7-840.

Neoplastic diseases, malignant,
§§7-301 to 7-304.

Occupational diseases and workplace safety, §32-1510.

Ophthalmia in newborns, §§7-801 to 7-804.

Plants and plant diseases, §§8-301 to 8-305.

DISEASES —Cont'd
Presumption as to disability or death resulting from.
Fire and emergency medical services employees, §5-654.
Public health emergency executive order, §7-2304.01.
Vector-borne disease control, §§8-2131.01 to 8-2131.09.
See VECTOR-BORNE DISEASE CONTROL.

DISFIGUREMENT, MALICIOUS, §22-406.

DISMISSAL OF ACTIONS.
Abandonment of prosecution, §23-102.
Anti-SLAPP, §16-5502.
Appeals, D.C. courts, DCCtApp Rule 13.
Appeals, federal cases.
Content of notice of appeal, FRAP 3(c).
Failure to file briefs, FRAP 31(c).
Voluntary dismissal, FRAP 42.
Appearance at trial.
Failure to appear, CivPro Rule 39-I.
Attachment after judgment, CivPro Rule 69-I.
Order dismissing attachment and garnishment, CivPro Form CA 109.
Bankruptcy.
Adversary proceedings, USDistDCBank Rule 7041-1.
Dismissal of involuntary petitions, USDistDCBank Rules 1013-1, 1017-2.
Class actions, CivPro Rule 23.
Unincorporated associations, CivPro Rule 23.2.
Collection actions, CivPro Rule 40-III.
Competence to proceed.
Incompetent criminal defendants.
Failure of defendant to obtain competence, §24-531.08.
Condemnation of property, CivPro Rule 71A.
Corporations.
Derivative actions, §29-305.54.
Costs of previously dismissed action, CivPro Rule 41.
Counterclaims, CivPro Rule 41.
Criminal proceedings, CrimPro Rule 48.
Assignment of felony cases and related cases, CrimPro Rule 105.

DISMISSAL OF ACTIONS —Cont'd
Criminal proceedings —Cont'd
Errors or omissions in indictment, CrimPro Rule 7.
Objections to grand jury, CrimPro Rule 6.
Cross-claims, CivPro Rule 41.
Death of party, CivPro Rule 25.
Default judgments.
Non-compliance with procedural rules, CivPro Rule 55.
Derivative actions by shareholders, CivPro Rule 23.1.
Domestic relations actions, DomRel Rule 41.
Judgment of dismissal, DomRel Rule 50.
Jurisdiction lacking, DomRel Rule 12.
Reciprocal enforcement of support proceedings, DomRel Rule 401.
Domestic violence unit proceedings, DomesticViolence Rule 10.
Ethics and government accountability, §1-1162.16.
Hearing commissioner proceedings.
Motions to review orders and judgments, CivPro Rule 73.
Incompetent criminal defendants.
Competence to proceed.
Failure of defendant to obtain competence, §24-531.08.
Intellectual disability proceedings, MentalRetardation Rule 17.
Intrafamily proceedings.
Domestic violence unit proceedings, DomesticViolence Rule 10.
Involuntary dismissal, CivPro Rule 41.
Failure to prosecute action, CivPro Rule 41-I, USDistCt LCvR 83.23.
Jurisdiction lacking, CivPro Rule 12.
Domestic relations actions, DomRel Rule 12.
Juvenile proceedings, JuvProc Rule 48.
Landlord and tenant court, LandlordTenant Rules 11, 12, 14-I.
Motion to dismiss, CivPro Form CA 19.
Nonprofit corporations.
Derivative actions, §29-411.05.
Parties.
Death of party, CivPro Rule 25.
Misjoinder not grounds for dismissal, CivPro Rule 20.
Real party in interest not prosecuting action, CivPro Rule 17.
Domestic relations actions, DomRel Rule 17.

DISMISSAL OF ACTIONS —Cont'd
Pretrial conferences.
Failure to appear, CivPro Rule 16-II.
Prosecution of action.
Failure to prosecute, CivPro Rule 41-I, USDistCt LCvR 83.23.
Receiver appointed, CivPro Rule 66.
Domestic relations actions, DomRel Rule 66.
Reciprocal enforcement of support proceedings, DomRel Rule 401.
Small claims court, SmallClaims Rule 12.
Subrogation cases, CivPro Rule 40-III.
Tax proceedings, Tax Rule 13.
Third party claims, CivPro Rule 41.
Voluntary dismissal, CivPro Rule 41.
Domestic relations actions, DomRel Rule 41.

DISMISSAL OF EMPLOYEE.
See TERMINATION OF EMPLOYMENT.

DISORDERLY CONDUCT, §22-1321.
Prosecutions, §22-1809.

DISORDERLY HOUSES.
Houses of prostitution.
See PROSTITUTION.

DISPLACED FAMILIES.
Landlord and tenant.
Relocation assistance for displaced tenants, §§42-3507.01 to 42-3507.05.
Temporary assistance for needy families (TANF) program, §4-205.19l.
Victims of crime.
Housing on temporary basis, VictComp Rule 29.

DISPLACED TENANTS.
Relocation assistance, §§42-3507.01 to 42-3507.05.
Urban renewal, due to.
See URBAN RENEWAL.

DISPLACED WORKERS, §§32-101 to 32-103.
Applicability of provisions, §32-101.
Enforcement of provisions, §32-103.
Temporary assistance for needy families (TANF) program, §4-205.19l.
Transition benefits for displaced public officers and employees, §§1-624.21 to 1-624.24.
Transition employment period, §32-102.

DISPOSABLE CARRYOUT BAGS.
Retail stores.
Credit for consumer-provided bags, §8-102.03.
Fees, §8-102.03.
Recycling requirements, §8-102.02.
Rulemaking authority, §8-102.04.
Violations, §8-102.04.

DISPOSABLE FOOD SERVICE WARE, MANAGEMENT, §§8-1531 to 8-1537.
Compostable or recyclable food service ware.
Compostable, defined, §8-1531.
List of vendors offering, §8-1534.
Required (not funded), §8-1533.
Definitions, §8-1531.
Enforcement, §8-1537.
Evaluation of food service ware litter in the Anacostia River, §8-1536.
Expanded polystyrene food service products.
Prohibited, §8-1532.
Rules, §8-1537.

DISSOCIATION.
Limited cooperative associations, §§29-1011.01 to 29-1011.03.
Effect of, §29-1011.02.
Events causing, §29-1011.01.
Personal representatives.
Powers, §29-1011.03.
Powers, §29-1011.01.
Limited liability company members, §§29-806.01 to 29-806.03.
Effect of, §29-806.03.
Events causing, §29-806.02.
Powers of members, §29-806.01.
Wrongful dissociation, §29-806.01.
Limited partnerships, §§29-706.01 to 29-706.07.
See LIMITED PARTNERSHIPS.
Partners, §§29-606.01 to 29-606.03.
See PARTNERSHIPS.

DISSOLUTION OF BANKS AND FINANCIAL INSTITUTIONS, §26-103.

DISSOLUTION OF BUSINESS ORGANIZATIONS.
Cooperative associations, §29-934.
Corporations, §§29-312.01 to 29-312.40.
General provisions.
See BUSINESS ORGANIZATIONS.

DISSOLUTION OF BUSINESS ORGANIZATIONS —Cont'd
Limited cooperative associations, §§29-1012.01 to 29-1012.13.
  See LIMITED COOPERATIVE ASSOCIATIONS.
Limited liability companies, §§29-807.01 to 29-807.07.
Limited partnerships, §§29-708.01 to 29-708.11.
Nonprofit corporations, §§29-412.01 to 29-412.30.
  See NONPROFIT CORPORATIONS.
Partnerships, §§29-608.01 to 29-608.12.
  See PARTNERSHIPS.
Professional corporations, §29-516.
Series trusts, §29-1204.04.
Statutory trusts, §§29-1208.01 to 29-1208.06.
Title insurers, §31-5031.09.
Unincorporated nonprofit associations, §29-1124.

DISSOLUTION OF CHARTER SCHOOLS.
Mandatory dissolution, §38-1802.13a.

DISSOLUTION OF PROPERTY RIGHTS.
Divorce or annulment, §16-910.

DISTANCE EDUCATION.
Higher education licensure commission.
  Postsecondary educational institutions incorporated in or outside of District.
    Delivery of online instruction, §38-1309.01.

DISTILLERY PUBS.
Alcoholic beverage licenses, §25-125.

DISTRACTED DRIVING, §§50-1731.01 to 50-1731.10.
Definitions, §50-1731.02.
Educational information, §50-1731.08.
Penalties for violations, §50-1731.06.
Prohibition, §50-1731.03.
Questions included on drivers' license exam, §50-1731.08.
Report of police officer, §50-1731.07.
Restricted use of mobile telephones, §50-1731.04.
  Certain operators, §50-1731.05.
Rule making, §50-1731.10.
Statistical data reports, §50-1731.09.

DISTRESSED RENTAL PROPERTIES.
Improvement of, §§42-3508.04, 42-3508.05.

DISTRICT COURT, §§11-501 to 11-521.
See UNITED STATES DISTRICT COURT FOR THE DISTRICT OF COLUMBIA.

DISTRICT DEPARTMENT OF THE ENVIRONMENT, §§8-151.01 to 8-151.15.
See ENVIRONMENTAL PROTECTION.

DISTRICT DEPARTMENT OF TRANSPORTATION (DDOT), §§50-921.01 to 50-921.22.
See TRANSPORTATION.

DISTRICT OF COLUMBIA.
Acquisition of excess property to develop seat of government, §§16-1331 to 16-1337.
  Appropriations for purchase, §16-1335.
  Condemnation of excess, §16-1336.
  Construction of provisions, §16-1337.
  Generally, §16-1331.
  Method of acquiring, §16-1331.
  Retention for public use of excess, §16-1334.
  Sale of excess, §16-1332.
    Notice, §16-1333.
Boundaries, §1-101.
Buildings of.
  See PUBLIC BUILDINGS.
Campaign finance.
  General provisions.
    See CAMPAIGN FINANCE.
Capitalsaurus dinosaur.
  Official dinosaur, §1-161.
Charter.
  Amendment of, §1-203.03.
  Preamble, §1-203.01.
  Referendum, §§1-207.01 to 1-207.04.
Cherry.
  Official fruit of the District of Columbia, §1-171.
Chief technology officer, §§1-1401 to 1-1406.
Claims against the District.
  General provisions, §§2-401 to 2-425.
    See CLAIMS AGAINST THE DISTRICT.
Commissioner and assistant commissioner of District.
  Vacancy resulting from abolition of office, §1-207.16.

DISTRICT OF COLUMBIA —Cont'd

Comprehensive plan, §§1-306.01 to 1-306.07.

Housing linkage requirement of housing element, §§1-306.31 to 1-306.45.

Congress, US Const Art I §8.

Applicability of federal laws to delegate, §1-402.

Delegate to the house of representatives, §§1-401, 1-402.

Home Rule act.

Reservation of Congressional authority, §§1-206.01 to 1-206.04.

Constitutional provisions, US Const Art I §8.

Constitution of the state of New Columbia.

Approval and ratification, §1-132.

Text of proposed constitution. See Vol. 1.

Continuation of former corporation, §1-105.

Corporation for municipal purposes, constituted as, §1-102.

Continuation as body corporate, §1-207.17.

Costs charged to District, CivPro Rule 54.

Council.

See COUNCIL.

Counterclaims and cross-claims against District, CivPro Rule 13.

Creation of District, §§1-101 to 1-109.

Criminal appeals, §23-104.

Criminal justice coordinating council, §§22-4231 to 22-4244.

Customer service operations unit, §§1-327.31 to 1-327.34.

Daylight savings time as standard time for, §28-2711.

Default judgments against District, CivPro Rule 55.

Delinquent debts owed to, recovery, §§1-350.01 to 1-350.12.

See DEBTORS AND CREDITORS.

Discovery.

Expenses for non-compliance, CivPro Rule 37.

Domestic relations actions, DomRel Rule 37.

Discrimination.

District of Columbia government.

Applicability of chapter, §2-1402.73.

Donations.

Authority to accept, §1-329.01.

DISTRICT OF COLUMBIA —Cont'd

Elections.

General provisions, §§1-1001.01 to 1-1041.04.

See ELECTIONS.

Multilingual election materials, §§1-1031.01, 1-1031.02.

Emancipation day.

Defined, §32-1201.

Designated holiday, §§1-612.02, 28-2701.

Parade and fund, §§1-181 to 1-183.

Energy efficiency standards, §§8-1771.01 to 8-1771.06.

Energy plan, §§8-171.01 to 8-171.07, 8-1779.01 to 8-1779.03.

Approval, §8-1779.03.

Definitions, §8-171.02.

Energy reduction, §8-171.04.

Limitation on expenditures, §§8-1779.02.

Office of Energy, §8-171.04.

Policy declaration, §§8-171.01, 8-171.03.

Renewable energy study, §8-1775.01.

Review of, §8-1779.03.

Severability of provisions, §8-171.07.

Submission to Council and federal agencies, §8-1779.01.

Establishment of District, §§1-101 to 1-109.

Executive Secretary, §1-301.23.

Financial plan.

Five-year financial plan and report, §1-204.56c.

Flag.

Design, §§1-151, 1-152.

Advisory committee, §1-153.

Display, §§1-141 to 1-145.

Findings, §1-141.

Inside public buildings, §1-144.

Notice of provisions to commercial property owners, §1-145.

Requirements, §1-142.

Staff used, §1-143.

Donations and grants to defray expense of replacing existing flag, §1-154.

Former corporations.

Abolition of Georgetown and extension of general laws of Washington to, §1-107.

Anacostia, Uniontown's name changed to, §1-108.

Continuation of former corporation, §1-105.

DISTRICT OF COLUMBIA —Cont'd
Former corporations —Cont'd
Georgetown.
  See GEORGETOWN.
Records of former corporations as
  property of District, §1-106.
Successor corporation of Washington
  and Georgetown, District as,
  §1-104.
Washington.
  Abolition of City of Georgetown and
    extension of general laws of
    Washington to, §1-107.
  District of Columbia as successor
    corporation of, §1-104.
  Geographic area, §1-107.
  Territorial area, §1-107.
Geographic area of, §1-101.
Georgetown.
Acts relating to corporation of
  Georgetown.
  See Vol. 1.
Gifts.
Authority to accept, §1-329.01.
Home Rule act.
General provisions, §§1-201.01 to
  1-207.71.
  See HOME RULE.
**Immunity for year 2000 system
  failure,** §2-381.31.
Applicability, §2-381.32.
Indebtedness of, §47-102.
Injunctions.
Security requirement not applicable,
  CivPro Rule 65.
Interest.
Judgment rate on judgments against
  District, §28-3302.
Judgments and decrees.
Interest on judgments against District,
  §28-3302.
Leasing authority, §§1-301.01,
  1-301.91.
Liability, §1-109.
Mayor.
See MAYOR.
Merit system.
General provisions, §§1-601.01 to
  1-636.03.
  See MERIT SYSTEM.
New Columbia statehood initiative,
  §§1-129.21 to 1-129.35.
Notes in anticipation of revenues,
  §1-204.72.
Officers of corporation, §1-103.
Offices, abolition of and changes to,
  §1-301.69.

DISTRICT OF COLUMBIA —Cont'd
Official dinosaur, §1-161.
Official fruit.
Cherry, §1-171.
Official rock.
Potomac bluestone, §1-165.02.
Legislative findings, §1-165.01.
Offset program, §47-143.
Organizational chart, §1-315.06.
Pensions and retirement.
Employees retirement program
  management, §§1-701 to 1-753.
  See EMPLOYEES RETIREMENT
    PROGRAM MANAGEMENT.
Funds, §§1-801.01 to 1-821.01.
  See PENSIONS AND
    RETIREMENT.
Merit system, §§1-626.01 to 1-626.14.
  See PENSIONS AND
    RETIREMENT.
Retirement generally.
  See PENSIONS AND
    RETIREMENT.
**Permanent seat of federal
  government,** §1-207.17.
Potomac bluestone.
Official rock of District of Columbia,
  §§1-165.01, 1-165.02.
**Private use of designation,
  prohibition on,** §§22-3401 to
  22-3403.
Public contracts.
General provisions, §§2-201.01 to
  2-223.07.
  See PUBLIC CONTRACTS.
Public records management,
  §§2-1701 to 2-1714.
  See PUBLIC RECORDS
    MANAGEMENT.
**Records of former corporations as
  property of,** §1-106.
Reorganization of government,
  §§1-15-1 to 1-15-35, 1-315.01 to
  1-315.07.
  See REORGANIZATION OF
    DISTRICT OF COLUMBIA
    GOVERNMENT.
Reports, §§1-323.02, 1-323.03.
Revenue anticipation notes,
  §1-204.72.
RLA revitalization corporation,
  §1-202.01.
Self-government, §§1-201.01 to
  1-207.71.
  See HOME RULE.
Service of process on District.
Summons, CivPro Rule 4.

DISTRICT OF COLUMBIA —Cont'd
Statehood constitutional convention, §§1-121 to 1-128.
"State" includes District of Columbia, CivPro Rule 81.
Stay of proceedings, CivPro Rule 62.
Domestic relations actions, DomRel Rule 62.
Subrogation as to disability compensation for public officers and employees, §1-623.31.
Successor corporation of Washington and Georgetown, §1-104.
Surveyor of the District, §§1-1301 to 1-1329.
Territorial area of, §1-101.
Volunteers, use of, §§1-319.01 to 1-319.05.
Zoning conformity, §1-306.07.

DISTRICT OF COLUMBIA ALLEY DWELLING ACT, §§6-101.01 to 6-102.05.
See NATIONAL CAPITAL HOUSING AUTHORITY.

DISTRICT OF COLUMBIA BAR.
Accounts and accounting, DCBar Rule VIII.
Admission to bar, DCCtApp Rule 46.
False statements, etc., ProfCond Rule 8.1.
Amendment of rules, DCBar Rule XV.
Arbitration for fee disputes, DCBar Rule XIII.
Bar counsel, DCBar Rule XI.
Confidential files.
Access by trustees of client security fund, DCBar Appx C.
Board of governors, DCBar Rule IV.
Recommendations to the board of governors, DCBar Rule VI.
Board on professional responsibility, DCBar Rule XI.
By-laws, DCBar Rule IX.
Amendment, DCBar Rule XV.
Clients' Security Trust Fund, DCBar Rule XII.
Confidential files of bar counsel.
Access by trustees of client security fund, DCBar Appx C.
Restitution to fund by attorney, DCBar Rule XI.
Creation, DCBar Rule I.
Disbursements, DCBar Rule VIII.

DISTRICT OF COLUMBIA BAR —Cont'd
Disciplinary proceedings, DCBar Rule XI.
Authority to initiate proceedings, CivPro Rule 102.
False statements, etc., ProfCond Rule 8.1.
Family court proceedings generally, FamDiv Rule S.
Jurisdiction and choice of law, ProfCond Rule 8.5.
Dues, DCBar Rule II.
Effective date of rules, DCBar Rule XVI.
Executive attorney, DCBar Rule XI.
Executive committee, DCBar Rule V.
Fiduciary eligibility requirements, CivPro Rule 304.
Financial statements, DCBar Rule VIII.
Guardian ad litem to be member of bar, CivPro Rule 304.
Probate proceedings.
Death on or after July 1, 1995, Probate Rule 422.
Guardians, conservators, trustees, etc., involved, Probate Rule 202.
Interest on Lawyers Trust Account (IOLTA), DCBar Appx A, DCBar Rule X.
Verification of participation, DCBar Rule XIV.
Meetings of the bar, DCBar Rule VI.
Executive committee meetings, DCBar Rule V.
Membership, DCBar Rule II.
New admittees course, DCBar Rule II.
Officers, DCBar Rule III.
Powers of bar, DCBar Rule I.
Public expression of bar opinions, DCBar Rule V.
Purpose of bar, DCBar Rule I.
Recommendations to the board of governors, DCBar Rule VI.
Referendum procedures, DCBar Rule VII.
Registration of attorneys, DCBar Rule II.
Rules of professional conduct, DCBar Rule X, ProfCond Rules 1.0 to 9.1.
See ATTORNEYS AT LAW.

DISTRICT OF COLUMBIA CODE, §§45-102, 45-201.
Archives, filing acts and resolutions with, §2-604.

DISTRICT OF COLUMBIA CODE
—Cont'd
Definitions, §2-601.
Enrollment of acts and resolutions, §2-604.
Government notices in newspapers, §2-621.
History of the District of Columbia code.
See Vol. 1.
Interpretation of provisions, §§45-601 to 45-606.
See STATUTORY CONSTRUCTION.
Judicial notice of published acts and resolutions, §2-605.
Notice.
Government notice in newspapers of publication of, §2-621.
Judicial notice of published acts and resolutions, §2-605.
Preparation, printing, and publication, §45-102.
Publication requirements, §2-602.
Statutes-at-large, publication of, §2-603.

DISTRICT OF COLUMBIA CORRECTIONS INFORMATION COUNCIL, §24-101.

DISTRICT OF COLUMBIA COURT OF APPEALS.
See COURT OF APPEALS.

DISTRICT OF COLUMBIA CULTURAL PLAN, §39-231.

DISTRICT OF COLUMBIA EMANCIPATION DAY, §§1-181 to 1-183.
Defined, §32-1201.
Designated holiday, §§1-612.02, 28-2701.
Emancipation day parade and fund, §§1-181 to 1-183.

DISTRICT OF COLUMBIA GENERAL HOSPITAL.
Hospice program, §§4-1101 to 4-1105.
Human Services Department, under control of, §7-180.
Rates schedule, §47-2713.

DISTRICT OF COLUMBIA HEALTH PROFESSIONAL RECRUITMENT PROGRAM, §§7-751.01 to 7-751.16.
See HEALTH PROFESSIONAL RECRUITMENT PROGRAM.

DISTRICT OF COLUMBIA HOUSING AUTHORITY, §§6-201 to 6-229.
Assets.
Disposition on dissolution, §6-224.
Board of commissioners, §6-211.
Bonds, notes and other obligations, §§6-209, 6-210.
Financial disclosure and conflicts of interest, §6-220.
Conflicts of interest, §§6-220, 6-221.
Costs.
Exemption from court fees and costs, §6-208.
Definitions, §6-201.
Dissolution.
Disposition of assets, §6-224.
Drug and alcohol testing of employees, §6-217.
Employees.
Benefits, §6-216.
Drug and alcohol testing, §6-217.
Financial disclosure and conflicts of interest, §6-221.
Political activities.
Applicability of Hatch act, §6-218.
Status, §6-215.
Established, §6-202.
Executive director, §6-213.
Financial disclosure and conflicts of interest, §6-220.
Fees.
Exemption from court fees and costs, §6-208.
Fund, §6-202.
Housing choice voucher program, §6-228.
Intergovernmental cooperation, §6-225.
Legal representation, §6-206.
Limitation of actions against, §6-205.
Office of audit and compliance, §6-207.
Partnership program for affordable housing, §6-227.
Police department of authority, §6-223.
Powers, §6-203.
Bonds, notes and other obligations, §6-209.
Procurement, §6-219.
Property managers.
Local law exemption, §6-222.
Purposes, §6-202.
Rent supplement program, §6-226.
Capital-based assistance, §6-229.

DISTRICT OF COLUMBIA HOUSING AUTHORITY —Cont'd
Rent supplement program —Cont'd
Tenant-based assistance, §6-228.
Voucher assistance, §6-227.
Social services teams in public housing, §6-214.
Tax exemption, §6-204.
Tenant-based assistance, §6-228.
Zoning.
Inclusionary zoning.
Responsibilities, §6-1041.08.

DISTRICT OF COLUMBIA JOBS TRUST FUND, §2-219.04c.

DISTRICT OF COLUMBIA OFFICE OF DOCUMENTS.
Administrator, §§2-611, 2-612.
Documents to be filed with, §§2-554 to 2-562.
Duties and responsibilities, §2-612.
Establishment of, §2-611.
Organization and staff, §2-611.

DISTRICT OF COLUMBIA REGIONAL AIRPORTS AUTHORITY.
Metropolitan Washington airports authority, §§9-901 to 9-926, 9-1001 to 9-1011.
See METROPOLITAN WASHINGTON AIRPORTS AUTHORITY.

DISTRICT OF COLUMBIA SCHOOL OF LAW, §§38-1205.01 to 38-1205.12.
Audit of records, §38-1205.09.
Full faith and credit of District not pledged for, §38-1205.12.
Policy declaration, §38-1205.01.
Records, §38-1205.09.
Transfer of powers of board to University of the District of Columbia, §38-1202.11.
Tuition.
Mayor's stipends, §38-1205.11.
Preferential tuition for residents, §38-1205.10.

DISTRICT OF COLUMBIA UNIFORM LAW COMMISSION, §§3-1431 to 3-1433.
Establishment, §3-1431.
Membership, §3-1432.
Responsibilities and duties, §3-1433.

DISTRICT OF COLUMBIA VILLAGE.
Rates schedule, §47-2714.

DISTURBING THE PEACE, §§22-1301 to 22-1323.

DIVERSION PROGRAMS.
Alcoholic beverages.
Children and minors.
Purchase, possession, or consumption by, §25-1002.
Attorneys at law, DCBar Rule XI.
Mental health disclosures, §7-1204.03.

DIVIDENDS.
Banks and financial institutions, §26-106.
Captive insurance companies.
Special purpose financial captive insurance companies.
Dividends and distributions, §31-3932.09.
Health insurance ratemaking, §31-3311.02.
Property dividends, income tax on, §47-1811.03.
Title insurers, §31-5031.10.
Trust, mortgage and title corporations, §§26-1327, 26-1328.
Unclaimed property, §41-121.

DIVORCE.
Alienation of affections, abolition of action for, §16-923.
Annulment of marriage.
See ANNULMENT OF MARRIAGE.
Appointment of counsel, §16-918.
Child custody.
Generally.
See CHILD CUSTODY AND CHILD CUSTODY PROCEEDINGS.
Uniform child custody proceedings, §§16-4601.01 to 16-4605.03.
See CHILD CUSTODY AND CHILD CUSTODY PROCEEDINGS.
Criminal conversation, abolition of action for, §16-923.
Defaults, §16-919.
Effective date of decree, §16-920.
Equitable distribution of property, §16-910.
Evidence requirements, §16-919.
Family court proceedings, §11-1101.
Grounds for, §16-904.
Legal separation, causes for divorce arising after, §16-906.
Motor vehicle ownership determined by decree.
Motor vehicle titling tax.
Exemption, §50-2201.03.
Name change following, §16-915.
Name change upon divorce, DomRel Rule 13.

DIVORCE —Cont'd
Pendente lite relief, §16-911.
Prior to January 1, 1902, §16-922.
Procedure generally, DomRel Rules 1 to 406.
  See DOMESTIC RELATIONS ACTIONS.
Property rights, §16-910.
Registration, §7-216.
Residence requirements, §16-902.
Service by publication on nonresidents, §13-336.
Spousal support following, §§16-913, 16-916.
  Crime victims' compensation.
    Loss of support, VictComp Rule 30.
  Divorce, on grant of, §16-913.
  Interstate family support.
    General provisions, §§46-351.01 to 46-359.03.
      See INTERSTATE FAMILY SUPPORT.
  Reciprocal enforcement of support proceedings, DomRel Rule 401.
  Jurisdiction, retention of, §16-914.01.
  Leaving jurisdiction of court.
    Writ of ne exeat, DomRel Rule 406.
  Payment of moneys through court, DomRel Rule 403.
  Pendente lite, §16-911.
  Procedure generally, DomRel Rules 1 to 406.
    See DOMESTIC RELATIONS ACTIONS.
  Reciprocal enforcement of support proceedings, DomRel Rule 401.
Statutory rule against perpetuities.
  Agreements excluded from rule, §19-904.

DNA COLLECTION.
Qualifying offenses, §22-4151.

DNA TESTING.
Pre-conviction and post-conviction.
  Protection of innocence act, §§22-4131 to 22-4135.

DNR ORDERS.
Comfort care orders, §§7-651.01 to 7-651.16.
  See EMERGENCY MEDICAL SERVICES.

DOCKETING STATEMENT.
Appeals in federal cases, USCtApp Rule 12.
  Administrative review, USCtApp Rule 15.

DOCKETS.
Adoption proceedings, Adoption Rule 79.
Appeals, D.C. courts, DCCtApp Rule 12.
Appeals, federal cases, FRAP 12.
  Bankruptcy proceedings, FRAP 6(b).
  Book to be kept, FRAP 45(b).
  Computerized format, FRAP 45(b).
  Entries.
    Appendix.
      Arrangement, FRAP 30(d).
    Appendix to brief, FRAP 30(a).
    Certified copy transmitted in lieu of entire record, FRAP 11(e).
    Composition of record on appeal, FRAP 10(a).
  Permission under 28 USCS 1292(b), FRAP 5(d).
  Petition for writs of mandamus, prohibition, and other extraordinary writs, FRAP 21, USCtApp Rule 21.
  Representation statement.
    Attorneys at law, FRAP 12(b).
  Review of decisions of U.S. Tax court, FRAP 13(d).
Civil docket, CivPro Rule 79.
Criminal proceedings.
  Clerk to make entries in dockets, CrimPro Rule 55.
Domestic relations actions, DomRel Rule 79.
Garnishment.
  Prejudgment garnishment, §16-531.
Garnishment docket cards.
  Attachment of wages, CivPro Rule 69-II.
  Domestic relations actions, DomRel Rule 69.
Juries and jury trials.
  Docketing as jury trial, CivPro Rules 39, 79.
Tax petitions, Tax Rule 6.

DOCTOR-PATIENT PRIVILEGE.
Attorney discipline or disability proceedings.
  Waiver of privilege for reinstatement of incapacitated attorney, DCBar Rule XI, USDistCt LCrR 57.30, USDistCt LCvR 83.19.
Child abuse and neglect.
  Privilege not grounds for excluding evidence of, §4-1321.05.
Controlled substances, §48-931.01.

DOCTOR-PATIENT PRIVILEGE
—Cont'd
Witnesses.
Physicians and mental health
professionals, §14-307.

DOCTORS.
Health maintenance organizations.
General provisions, §§31-3401 to
31-3431.
See HEALTH MAINTENANCE
ORGANIZATIONS.
Health occupations boards.
General provisions, §§3-1201.01 to
3-1213.01.
See HEALTH OCCUPATIONS
BOARDS.
**Health occupations licensure,
registration or certification,**
§§3-1205.01 to 3-1205.24.
See HEALTH OCCUPATIONS
LICENSURE, REGISTRATION
OR CERTIFICATION.
**Hospital and medical services
corporations.**
General provisions, §§31-3501 to
31-3524.
See HOSPITAL AND MEDICAL
SERVICES CORPORATIONS.
Physicians generally.
See PHYSICIANS AND SURGEONS.

DOCUMENTS.
Authentication of official records.
See AUTHENTICATION OF
OFFICIAL RECORDS.
Business records.
See BUSINESS RECORDS.
Medical records, §§44-801 to 44-805.
Public records management,
§§2-1701 to 2-1714.
See PUBLIC RECORDS
MANAGEMENT.
Recorder of deeds.
General provisions, §§42-1202 to
42-1218.
See RECORDER OF DEEDS.
Records generally.
See RECORDS.
Registration of births, §§7-205 to
7-210.
Sealed records.
See SEALED RECORDS.
Vital records.
General provisions, §§7-201 to 7-228.
See VITAL RECORDS.

DOCUMENTS OF TITLE, §§28:7-101
to 28:7-702.
Agriculture.
Warehouse receipts.
Storage of commodities under
government bond, §28:7-201.
Alcoholic beverages.
Warehouse receipts.
Storage under government bond,
§28:7-201.
Alteration.
Bills of lading, §28:7-306.
Warehouse receipts, §28:7-208.
Applicability of provisions.
Effective date, §28:7-701.
Savings clause, §28:7-702.
Attachment of goods.
Goods covered by negotiable document,
§28:7-602.
Bills of lading.
Altered bills, §28:7-306.
Care owing from carrier, §28:7-309.
Consignments.
Reconsignment, §28:7-303.
Contractual limitation of carrier's
liability, §28:7-309.
Delivery of goods, §28:7-303.
Good faith delivery pursuant to bill,
§28:7-404.
Obligation of carrier to deliver,
§28:7-403.
Description of goods.
"Said to contain," §28:7-301.
"Shipper's weight, load and count,"
§28:7-301.
Destination bills, §28:7-305.
Diversion of goods, §28:7-303.
Duplicates, §28:7-402.
Generally, §§28:7-301 to 28:7-309.
Handling of goods.
Improper handling, §28:7-301.
Instructions.
Change, §28:7-303.
Irregularities in issue or conduct of
issuer, §28:7-401.
Liability.
Contractual limitation of carrier's
liability, §28:7-309.
Good faith delivery pursuant to bill,
§28:7-404.
Nonreceipt or misdescription of
goods, §28:7-301.
Lien of carrier, §28:7-307.
Enforcement, §28:7-308.
Negotiability, §28:7-104.
Overissue, §28:7-402.

DOCUMENTS OF TITLE —Cont'd
Bills of lading —Cont'd
Receipt of goods.
Liability for nonreceipt, §28:7-301.
Sets, §28:7-304.
Third party documents.
Prima facie evidence, §28:1-307.
Through bills and similar documents,
§28:7-302.
Citation of article.
Short title, §28:7-101.
Consignor and consignee.
Bills of lading.
Reconsignment, §28:7-303.
Construction and interpretation.
Relation of article to treaty, statute,
tariff, classification or regulation,
§28:7-103.
Contracts.
Bills of lading.
Limitation of carrier's liability,
§28:7-309.
Warehouse receipts.
Limitation of warehouse liability,
§28:7-204.
When adequate compliance with
obligations of commercial contract,
§28:7-509.
Crops.
Warehouse receipts.
Storage under government bond,
§28:7-201.
Definitions, §28:7-102.
Duly negotiated, §28:7-501.
General commercial code definitions,
§28:1-201.
Course of dealing, §28:1-303.
Reasonable time and seasonably,
§28:1-205.
Usage of trade, §28:1-303.
Index of definitions, §28:7-102.
Delivery of goods.
Bills of lading, §28:7-303.
Good faith delivery pursuant to bill,
§28:7-404.
Obligation of carrier to deliver,
§28:7-403.
Excuses, §28:7-403.
Negotiation and transfer.
Seller's stoppage of delivery.
Rights acquired in absence of due
negotiation, §28:7-504.
Warehouse receipts.
Good faith delivery pursuant to
receipt, §28:7-404.
Obligation of warehouse to deliver,
§28:7-403.

DOCUMENTS OF TITLE —Cont'd
Delivery of goods —Cont'd
Warranties, §28:7-507.
Description of goods.
Bills of lading.
Liability for misdescription,
§28:7-301.
"Said to contain," §28:7-301.
"Shipper's weight, load and count,"
§28:7-301.
Warehouse receipts.
Liability for misdescription,
§28:7-203.
Diversion of goods.
Bills of lading, §28:7-303.
Negotiation and transfer.
Rights acquired in absence of due
negotiation.
Effect of diversion, §28:7-504.
Duplicates, §28:7-402.
Electronic documents.
Control, §28:7-106.
Reissuance in alternative medium,
§28:7-105.
Endorsements.
Negotiation and transfer.
Delivery without endorsement,
§28:7-506.
Endorser not guarantor for other
parties, §28:7-505.
Right to compel endorsement,
§28:7-506.
Evidence.
Bills of lading.
Third party documents, prima facie
evidence, §28:1-307.
Forms.
Warehouse receipts, §28:7-202.
Fungible goods.
Warehouse receipts, §28:7-207.
General provisions, §§28:1-101 to
28:1-310.
See COMMERCIAL CODE.
Good faith.
Obligation of good faith, §28:1-304.
Guaranty.
Negotiation and transfer.
Endorser not guarantor for other
parties, §28:7-505.
Handling of goods.
Bills of lading.
Improper handling, §28:7-301.
Interpretation of provisions,
§§28:10-103, 28:10-104.
Liability.
Carrier's liability.
Contractual limitation of carrier's
liability, §28:7-309.

DOCUMENTS OF TITLE —Cont'd
Warehouse receipts —Cont'd
Liability.
Contractual limitation of warehouse liability, §28:7-204.
Good faith delivery of goods pursuant to receipt, §28:7-404.
Nonreceipt or misdescription of goods, §28:7-203.
Lien of warehouse, §28:7-209.
Enforcement, §28:7-210.
Negotiability, §28:7-104.
Overissue, §28:7-402.
Receipt of goods.
Liability for nonreceipt, §28:7-203.
Separation of goods, §28:7-207.
Termination of storage.
Option of warehouse, §28:7-206.
Terms.
Essential terms, §28:7-202.
Optional terms, §28:7-202.
Title defeated in certain cases, §28:7-205.
Who may issue, §28:7-201.
Warranties.
Negotiation or delivery, §28:7-507.
Collecting bank's warranties as to documents, §28:7-508.

DODD-FRANK WALL STREET REFORM AND CONSUMER PROTECTION ACT.
Filings under, USDistCt LCvR 85.

DOG BITES.
Civil liability, §8-1812.
Dangerous dog.
Generally, §§8-1901 to 8-1908.
See DANGEROUS DOGS.

DOG LEASH LAWS, §8-1808.

DOG PARKS.
At large does not include dog in dog park, §8-1801.
Defined, §8-1801.
Establishment, requirements, §8-1808.01.

DOGS.
Allowing animal to go at large, §8-1808.
Fierce or dangerous dogs, §22-1311.
Animal control, §§8-1801 to 8-1813.
Assisted housing.
Pet ownership restriction in assisted housing.
See PETS.

DOGS —Cont'd
Assisted housing for elderly or persons with disabilities.
Pet ownership restriction in assisted housing, §§8-2031 to 8-2035.
Commercial guard dogs, §§8-1841.01 to 8-1841.09.
Dangerous dogs, §§8-1901 to 8-1908.
See DANGEROUS DOGS.
Defending private property of owners from intruders.
Maintaining properly trained dog, §8-1808.
Feral dogs, §8-2206.
Fighting animals, §22-1009.
Penalty, §22-1006.01.
Urging dogs to fight or create disorder, §22-1310.
Guard dogs, commercial, §§8-1841.01 to 8-1841.09.
Defined, §8-1841.01.
Health examination, §8-1841.03.
Immunizations required, §8-1841.02.
Liability insurance, §8-1841.04.
License required, §8-1841.02.
Notice and contact information to mayor, §8-1841.05.
Retirement when unfit to work, §8-1841.03.
Rules, §8-1841.09.
Shelter and proper care requirements, §8-1841.07.
Sign alerting public to presence of dog, §8-1841.06.
Violation of provisions, §8-1841.08.
Guide dogs.
Defined, §7-1009.
Housing accommodations.
Full and equal access, §7-1006.
Public places accommodations and conveyances.
Right to be accompanied by, §7-1002.
Leash laws, §§1-303.41, 8-1808, 22-1311.
Liabilities of owners, §8-1812.
Licenses.
Fees, §8-1804.
Guard dogs, commercial, §8-1841.02.
Removing without permission of owner, §8-1808.
Police animals.
Harassing, interfering with, injuring or obstructing, §22-861.
Power to make regulations regarding, §1-303.41.

DOGS —Cont'd
School grounds.
Permitting on when school in session.
Leash required, §8-1808.

DOMESTIC LIFE INSURANCE COMPANIES, §§31-4401 to 31-4452.
Amendment of articles of incorporation, §31-4409.
Applicability of provisions, §31-4420.
Bonds, surety, §31-4402.
Capital stock.
Decreasing, §31-4411.
Increasing, §31-4410.
Payments for, §31-4413.
Records, §31-4415.
Requirements, §31-4408.
Rights and liabilities, §31-4412.
Transfers of, §31-4414.
Certificates of authority, §31-4403.
Classification of risks and members, §31-4433.
Commencement of issuance of policies after formation.
Time limits on, §31-4407.
Conflicts of interest, §31-4430.
Defined, §31-4202.
Directors, §§31-4421 to 31-4431.
Bylaws, power to make, §31-4422.
Election, §31-4421.
Cumulative voting, §31-4424.
Procedure, §31-4423.
Voting powers under group policies, §31-4425.
Liability, §31-4426.
Pecuniarily interested in transactions, §31-4428.
Proxies, limitations, §31-4421.
Qualifications, §31-4421.
Salaries, §31-4427.
Disbursements, vouchers or affidavits evidencing, §31-4439.
Examination of, §31-4406.
Filing requirements, §31-4402.
Formation, §§31-4401 to 31-4407.
Group policies.
Voting powers under, §31-4425.
Guaranteed contracts.
Variable or modified, §31-4442.
Mergers and consolidations, §§31-4443 to 31-4452.
Approval by mayor, §31-4447.
Approval by shareholders, §31-4449.
Articles, §31-4451.
Date completed, §31-4452.
Dissenting shareholders' rights, §31-4450.

DOMESTIC LIFE INSURANCE COMPANIES —Cont'd
Mergers and consolidations —Cont'd
Domestic and foreign insurers, §31-4446.
Effect, §31-4443.
Procedure for consolidation, §31-4445.
Procedure for merger, §31-4444.
Procedures before voting, §31-4448.
Mutual companies, §§31-4416, 31-4417.
Notice of formation, §31-4402.
Officers, §§31-4427 to 31-4431.
Election or appointment, §31-4429.
Pecuniarily interested in transactions, §31-4428.
Payments limited to stockholders and policyholders, §31-4428.
Records.
Capital stock, §31-4415.
Manner of keeping, §31-4440.
Reincorporations, §31-4418.
Stock and stockholders.
Capital stock. See within this heading, "Capital stock."
Election of directors, §§31-4421 to 31-4425.
Mergers and consolidations, §§31-4449, 31-4450.
Rights and liabilities, §31-4412.
Stock subscriptions, §§31-4404, 31-4405.
Surplus requirements, §31-4408.
Voting trust agreements, §31-4431.
Voting trust agreements, §31-4431.

DOMESTIC PARTNER BENEFITS, §§32-701 to 32-710.
Definitions, §32-701.
Domestic partnerships generally.
See DOMESTIC PARTNERSHIPS.
Enforcement of provisions, §32-703.
Existing rights and benefits, effect on, §32-710.
Public officers and employees, §§32-705, 32-706.
Records, §32-708.
Registration of partnership, §32-702.
Rules, §32-709.
Termination of partnership, §32-702.
Types of, §32-704.

DOMESTIC PARTNERSHIPS.
Adoption of children, §16-308.
Benefits, §§32-701 to 32-710.
See DOMESTIC PARTNER BENEFITS.
Bigamy, §22-501.

DOMESTIC PARTNERSHIPS
—Cont'd
Birth registration, §7-205.
Child support.
Definitions, §16-901.
College saving program.
Tax exemption, §47-4509.
Community property, §19-602.15.
Confidential communications,
§14-306.
Equal access to marriage, §46-401.
Income taxes.
Generally.
See INCOME TAXES.
Joint filing of returns, §47-1805.01.
Reciprocal rights of credit, §47-4440.
Refund offsets, §47-4432.
Inheritance and estate taxes.
Marriage equality estate tax
clarification, §1-301.153.
Intestate succession, §§19-101.01 to
19-101.06.
Definitions, §§19-115, 19-322.
Descent in fee simple, §19-301.
Devises or bequests, §§19-112 to
19-115.
Surplus distributed after payment to,
§19-305.
Whole, entitlement to, §19-302.
Intrafamily offenses.
Generally, §§16-1001 to 16-1034.
Joint bank accounts, §26-801.
Safe deposit boxes, §26-802.
Legitimacy and illegitimacy of
children, §§16-907, 16-908.
Marriage.
Equal access to marriage, §46-401.
Licenses.
Issuance to domestic partners,
§32-702.
Nonprobate transfers.
Definitions, §19-602.01.
Ownership during lifetime, §19-602.11.
Rights at death, §19-602.12.
Parentage proceedings, §§16-909 to
16-909.03.
Parent-child relationship, §§16-907,
16-908.
Perpetuities, rule against.
Agreements excluded, §19-904.
Powers of attorney, §21-2113.
Property rights and obligations,
§46-601.
Prostitution.
Causing domestic partner to live in
prostitution, §22-2708.

DOMESTIC PARTNERSHIPS
—Cont'd
Real property assessment.
Domestic partner defined, §47-802.
Sexual abuse.
No immunity from prosecution,
§22-3019.
Tenancy by the entirety, §19-602.15.
Tenants by the entirety, §§42-516,
46-601.
Termination.
Assignment and equitable distribution
of property, §16-910.
Pendente lite, §16-911.
Support, §§16-913, 16-916.
Witnesses, privileges, §§14-306,
14-309.
Wrongful death, §16-2701.

DOMESTIC RELATIONS.
Actions generally, DomRel Rules 1 to
406.
See DOMESTIC RELATIONS
ACTIONS.
Adoption.
See ADOPTION.
Age of majority.
Child support enforcement, §46-101.
Annulment of marriage.
See ANNULMENT OF MARRIAGE.
Child abuse and neglect.
See CHILD ABUSE AND NEGLECT.
Child custody.
General provisions.
See CHILD CUSTODY AND CHILD
CUSTODY PROCEEDINGS.
Parental kidnapping, §§16-1021 to
16-1026.
Child placement.
Adoption.
See ADOPTION.
Family homes, §§4-1401 to 4-1410.
Child support.
Enforcement of child support, §§46-201
to 46-231.
See CHILD SUPPORT
ENFORCEMENT.
General provisions, §§46-351.01 to
46-359.03.
See INTERSTATE FAMILY
SUPPORT.
Medical support enforcement,
§§46-251.01 to 46-251.10.
Reciprocal enforcement of support
proceedings, DomRel Rule 401.
Delinquent minors.
See DELINQUENT MINORS.

DOMESTIC RELATIONS —Cont'd
Dependent children.
See DEPENDENT CHILDREN.
Divorce.
See DIVORCE.
Dower.
See DOWER.
Durable powers of attorney,
§§21-2081 to 21-2085.
Family and medical leave, §§32-501
to 32-517.
Family court proceedings, FamDiv
Rules A to T.
See FAMILY COURT PROCEEDINGS.
Family violence, §§16-1031 to 16-1034.
Foster care, §§4-217.01 to 4-217.11.
Health care decisions, §§21-2201 to
21-2213.
Hospital discharge planning,
§§21-2231.01 to 21-2231.05.
Hospital discharge planning,
§§21-2231.01 to 21-2231.05.
Interstate compact for juveniles,
§§24-1101 to 24-1106.
**Interstate compact on placement of
children,** §§4-1421 to 4-1424.
Interstate family support.
General provisions, §§46-351.01 to
46-359.03.
See INTERSTATE FAMILY
SUPPORT.
Reciprocal enforcement of support
proceedings, DomRel Rule 401.
Intrafamily proceedings, §§16-1001 to
16-1034.
See INTRAFAMILY PROCEEDINGS.
Legal separation, §§16-904 to 16-906.
See LEGAL SEPARATION.
Legitimacy and illegitimacy,
§§16-907, 16-908.
Living wills, §§7-621 to 7-630.
Marriage.
General provisions, §§46-401 to
46-421.
See MARRIAGE.
Medical support enforcement,
§§46-251.01 to 46-251.10.
Neglect proceedings.
Generally.
See CHILD ABUSE AND
NEGLECT.
Termination of parental rights of
certain neglected children,
§§16-2351 to 16-2365.
See TERMINATION OF PARENTAL
RIGHTS.

DOMESTIC RELATIONS —Cont'd
Parentage proceedings.
General provisions, §§16-2341 to
16-2348.
See PARENTAGE PROCEEDINGS.
Parental kidnapping, §§16-1021 to
16-1026.
Post-nuptial agreements, §19-113.
Premarital agreements.
General provisions, §§46-501 to
46-510.
See PREMARITAL AGREEMENTS.
Simultaneous death act, §§19-501 to
19-506.
Spousal property rights, §46-601.
Surviving spouse.
See SURVIVING SPOUSES.
**Termination of parental rights of
certain neglected children,**
§§16-2351 to 16-2365.
See TERMINATION OF PARENTAL
RIGHTS.
Uniform child custody proceedings.
See CHILD CUSTODY AND CHILD
CUSTODY PROCEEDINGS.

DOMESTIC RELATIONS ACTIONS.
Amendment of rules, DomRel Rule 86.
Appeals.
Deposition pending appeal, DomRel
Rule 27.
Injunction pending appeal, DomRel
Rule 62.
Stay upon appeal, DomRel Rule 62.
Transcript on appeal, DomRel Rule
201.
Motion for free transcript, DomRel
Rule 54-II.
Assignment of cases, DomRel Rule 40.
Attachment before judgment,
DomRel Rule 64.
Attorneys at law, DomRel Rule 101.
Pretrial procedures, DomRel Rule 16-I.
Auditor-masters, DomRel Rule 53.
Bonds, surety.
Injunctions, DomRel Rule 71.
Proceedings against sureties, DomRel
Rule 71.
Child custody.
Uniform child custody proceedings,
§§16-4601.01 to 16-4605.03.
See CHILD CUSTODY AND CHILD
CUSTODY PROCEEDINGS.
Civil procedure rules.
Applicability of rules, DomRel Rule 1.
Collection of money judgments,
DomRel Rule 69.

DOMESTIC RELATIONS ACTIONS
—Cont'd
Commencement of action, DomRel
 Rule 3.
 Parentage proceedings, DomRel Rule
  405.
 Reciprocal enforcement of support
  proceedings, DomRel Rule 401.
Consolidation of actions, DomRel
 Rule 42.
Costs, DomRel Rule 54.
 Compelling discovery, DomRel Rule
  37.
 Failure to attend deposition, DomRel
  Rule 30.
 Offer of judgment, DomRel Rule 68.
 Waiver of costs, fees or security,
  DomRel Rule 54-II.
Counterclaims, DomRel Rule 13.
Cross-examination, DomRel Rule 43.
Definitions, DomRel Rule 2.
Deposits with court, DomRel Rule 67.
**Discovery and disclosure of
 information,** DomRel Rule 26.
 Collection of money judgment, DomRel
  Rule 69.
 Deadline for discovery requests,
  DomRel Rule 16-I.
 Depositions, DomRel Rules 30, 31.
  Appeal pending, DomRel Rule 27.
  Outside forum's jurisdiction, DomRel
   Rule 28.
  Persons before whom depositions
   may be taken, DomRel Rule 28.
  Pre-action depositions, DomRel Rule
   27.
  Use of depositions, DomRel Rules
   27, 32.
 Interrogatories, DomRel Rule 33.
  Attachment writ accompanying
   interrogatories, DomRel Rule
   64.
 Noncompliance, DomRel Rule 37.
 Physical and mental examination of
  persons, DomRel Rule 35.
 Production of documents and things,
  DomRel Rule 34.
 Requests for admission, DomRel Rule
  36.
 Stipulations regarding discovery
  procedure, DomRel Rule 29.
Dismissal of actions, DomRel Rule 41.
 Judgment of dismissal, DomRel Rule
  50.
 Reciprocal enforcement of support
  proceedings, DomRel Rule 401.

DOMESTIC RELATIONS ACTIONS
—Cont'd
Evidence, DomRel Rules 43, 44.
 Newly discovered evidence.
  Relief from judgment or order,
   DomRel Rule 60.
Exceptions unnecessary, DomRel
 Rule 46.
Findings by the court, DomRel Rule
 52.
Forms, DomRel Rule 84.
 Absent defendant.
  Order of publication, DomRel Form
   1.
 Certificate and order, DomRel Form
  15.
 Complaint for support, DomRel Form
  13.
 Employer's statement, DomRel Form
  6.
 Husband's financial statement,
  DomRel Form 4.
 Motion and affidavit, DomRel Form 2.
  Contempt, DomRel Form 7.
  Opposition to motion and affidavit,
   DomRel Form 3.
 Order for support, DomRel Forms 10,
  15.
 Parentage, DomRel Forms 11, 12.
 Petition for support, DomRel Form 9.
 Show cause order, DomRel Form 16.
 Testimony of plaintiff, DomRel Form
  14.
 Uncontested stipulation, DomRel Form
  8.
 Wife's financial statement, DomRel
  Form 5.
Harmless error, DomRel Rule 61.
Injunctions, DomRel Rule 65.
 Appeal pending, DomRel Rule 62.
Interpreters, DomRel Rule 43.
Intervention, DomRel Rule 24.
Joinder, DomRel Rules 18, 19.
Judges.
 Inability to proceed and recusal,
  DomRel Rule 63.
Judgments and decrees, DomRel Rule
 54.
 Amendment of judgment, DomRel
  Rule 59.
 Collection of money judgments,
  DomRel Rule 69.
 Conveyances, deed transfers, etc.,
  DomRel Rule 70.
 Declaratory judgments, DomRel Rule
  57.

DOMESTIC RELATIONS ACTIONS
—Cont'd
Judgments and decrees —Cont'd
Default judgments, DomRel Rule 55.
Judgment not to exceed demand,
DomRel Rule 54.
Dismissal of action, DomRel Rule 50.
Entry of judgment, DomRel Rule 58.
Findings of the court, DomRel Rule 52.
Foreign judgment enforcement,
DomRel Rule 72.
Harmless error, DomRel Rule 61.
Notice of judgment, DomRel Rule 77.
Offer of judgment, DomRel Rule 68.
Parentage proceedings, DomRel Rule
405.
Relief from judgment, DomRel Rule
60.
Stay to enforce judgment, DomRel
Rule 62.
Summary judgment, DomRel Rule 56.
Jury trials, FamDiv Rule L.
Law student practice, FamDiv Rule
M.
Leaving jurisdiction of court.
Writ of ne exeat, DomRel Rule 406.
Masters, DomRel Rule 53.
Motions generally, DomRel Rule 7.
Contempt, DomRel Form 7.
Form of motions, DomRel Form 2,
DomRel Rule 10.
Non-appearance at hearing, DomRel
Rule 12.
Opposition to motion and affidavit,
DomRel Form 3.
Signing, DomRel Rule 11.
New trial, DomRel Rules 59, 61.
Stay of proceedings, DomRel Rule 62.
**Notice of hearing and order
directing appearance,** DomRel
Rule 4, FamDiv Rule H.
Form, FamDiv Form 1.
Oaths, DomRel Rule 2.
Offers of judgment, DomRel Rule 68.
Parties, DomRel Rule 17.
Joinder, DomRel Rules 18, 19.
Proceedings for or against non-parties,
DomRel Rule 71.
Substitution of parties, DomRel Rule
25.
Payment of moneys through court,
DomRel Rule 403.
**Physical and mental examination of
persons,** DomRel Rule 35.
Pleadings.
Amended and supplemental pleadings,
DomRel Rule 15.

DOMESTIC RELATIONS ACTIONS
—Cont'd
Pleadings —Cont'd
Counterclaims, DomRel Rule 13.
Defenses and objections, DomRel Rule
12.
Form of pleadings, DomRel Rule 10.
General rules of pleading, DomRel
Rule 8.
Parentage proceedings, DomRel Rule
405.
Permitted pleadings, DomRel Rule 7.
Reciprocal enforcement of support
proceedings, DomRel Rule 401.
Signing, DomRel Rule 11.
Special matters, DomRel Rule 9.
Pretrial procedures, DomRel Rule
16-I.
Protective orders, DomRel Rule 26.
Receivers appointed by court,
DomRel Rule 66.
**Reciprocal enforcement of support
proceedings,** DomRel Rule 401.
Replevin actions, DomRel Rule 64.
Scope of rules, DomRel Rule 1.
Seizure of person or property,
DomRel Rule 64.
Separate trials, DomRel Rule 42.
Service of process, DomRel Rules 4, 5.
Attachment writs, DomRel Rule 64.
Subpoenas, DomRel Rule 45.
Settlement conferences, DomRel Rule
16-I.
Show cause orders, DomRel Rule 4.
Single form of action, DomRel Rule 2.
Social service referrals, DomRel Rule
404.
Status conferences, DomRel Rule 16-I.
Stays, DomRel Rule 62.
Stipulations, DomRel Rule 7.
Discovery procedures, DomRel Rule
29.
Uncontested stipulation, DomRel Form
8.
Subpoenas, DomRel Rule 45.
Summary judgment, DomRel Rule 56.
Summons, DomRel Rule 4.
Time computation or extension,
DomRel Rule 6.
Title of rules, DomRel Rule 1.
Transcripts, DomRel Rule 201.
Motion for free transcripts, DomRel
Rule 54-II.

DOMESTIC VIOLENCE.
Abused children.
See CHILD ABUSE AND NEGLECT.

DOMESTIC VIOLENCE —Cont'd
Arrest, §16-1031.
Immunity of law enforcement officer
making arrest, §16-1033.
Child abuse and neglect.
Counselors to report, §4-1321.02.
Collaborative law, §16-4015.
Confidential information.
Domestic violence counselors.
Disclosure prohibited, exceptions,
§§14-307, 14-310.
Crime victims' compensation.
Eligibility for compensation, VictComp
Rule 7.
Shelter and transitional housing for
victims of domestic violence fund,
§4-521.
Domestic violence counselors.
Child abuse and neglect.
Counselors to report, §4-1321.02.
Confidential communication between
victim and counselor.
Disclosure prohibited, exceptions,
§14-310.
Confidential information acquired in
professional capacity.
Disclosure prohibited without
consent of client, §14-307.
Defined, §14-310.
Domestic violence unit rules,
DomesticViolence Rules 1 to 14. See
within this heading, "Rules
governing proceedings in domestic
violence unit."
Fatality review board.
Access provided to certain information,
§16-1054.
Confidentiality of information,
§16-1056.
Definitions, §16-1051.
Destruction of records obtained,
§16-1054.
Duties, §16-1052.
Establishment, §16-1052.
Immunity from liability, §16-1057.
Members, §16-1053.
Rules promulgation, §16-1058.
Subpoenas, §16-1055.
Grants.
Grant-making authority for assisting
domestic violence victims.
Shelter and transitional housing for
victims of domestic violence
fund, §4-521.
Hotline.
Definitions, §4-551.

DOMESTIC VIOLENCE —Cont'd
Hotline —Cont'd
Established, §4-552.
Operation, §4-552.
Task force, §4-553.
**Immunity of law enforcement officer
making arrest, §16-1033.**
**Interstate enforcement of domestic
violence protection, §§16-1041 to
16-1048.**
See INTERSTATE ENFORCEMENT
OF DOMESTIC VIOLENCE
PROTECTION.
Intrafamily offenses.
Generally, §§16-1001 to 16-1034.
See INTRAFAMILY
PROCEEDINGS.
Leave of absence due to.
Employee sick leave generally,
§§32-131.01 to 32-131.16.
See LABOR AND EMPLOYMENT
RELATIONS.
**Parental kidnapping, §§16-1021 to
16-1026.**
See PARENTAL KIDNAPPING.
**Privacy protection in domestic
relations actions, §16-925.**
**Report of incident filed by law
enforcement officer, §16-1032.**
**Rules governing proceedings in
domestic violence unit,**
DomesticViolence Rules 1 to 14.
Appeals, DomesticViolence Rule 13.
Bench warrants, DomesticViolence
Rule 5.
Commencement of action,
DomesticViolence Rule 2.
Contempt, DomesticViolence Rule 12.
Continuances, DomesticViolence Rule
4.
Discovery, DomesticViolence Rule 8.
Dismissal of action, DomesticViolence
Rule 10.
Ex parte default hearings,
DomesticViolence Rule 5.
Failure to appear, DomesticViolence
Rule 5.
Hearings, DomesticViolence Rule 9.
Motions, DomesticViolence Rule 7.
Orders, DomesticViolence Rule 11.
Petition, DomesticViolence Rule 2.
Form of pleadings, DomesticViolence
Rule 6.
Service of process, DomesticViolence
Rule 3.
Pleadings, DomesticViolence Rule 6.

DOMESTIC VIOLENCE —Cont'd

Rules governing proceedings in domestic violence unit —Cont'd

Scope of rules, DomesticViolence Rule 1.

Service of process, DomesticViolence Rule 3.

Subpoenas, DomesticViolence Rule 14.

Temporary protection orders, DomesticViolence Rule 7A.

Shelter and transitional housing for victims of domestic violence fund, §4-521.

Stalking, §§22-3131 to 22-3135.

Training program for law enforcement officers, §16-1034.

Unemployment compensation, §§51-131 to 51-136.

DOMESTIC VIOLENCE COUNSELORS.

Child abuse and neglect.

Counselors to report, §4-1321.02.

Confidential communication between victim and counselor.

Disclosure prohibited, exceptions, §14-310.

Confidential information acquired in professional capacity.

Disclosure prohibited without consent of client, §14-307.

Defined, §14-310.

DOMICILE.

Residency.

See RESIDENCY.

DONATED FOOD.

Good faith immunity, §§48-301, 48-302.

DONOR LEAVE.

Government employees serving as organ or bone marrow donors, §1-612.03b.

DO NOT RESUSCITATE PROCEDURES.

Comfort care orders, §§7-651.01 to 7-651.16.

See EMERGENCY MEDICAL SERVICES.

DOOR-TO-DOOR SALES.

Hearing aid dealers.

Written consent of buyer required, §28-4005.

Home solicitation sales, §28-3811.

DOT.

Department of transportation, §§50-921.01 to 50-921.22.

See TRANSPORTATION.

DOUBLE JEOPARDY, US Const Amd 5.

DOUBLE RENT.

Claims for, §42-3211.

Refusal to surrender possession, for, §42-3207.

DOUGLAS KNOLL.

Real property tax exemptions, §47-1065.

DOWER.

Abolishment, §19-102.

Antenuptial agreements, §19-113.

Commutation of dower, CivPro Rule 307.

Probate proceedings, Probate Rule 6.

Prenuptial agreements, §19-113.

Will, devise or bequest to spouse in, §§19-112 to 19-114.

DOWNTOWN BUSINESS IMPROVEMENT DISTRICTS, §§2-1215.01 to 2-1215.71.

DRAFT, MILITARY.

Drivers' licenses and identification cards.

Selective Service registration upon application, §50-1401.01.

DRAFTS.

Contracts.

Sale of goods.

Documents against which draft is drawn.

When deliverable, §28:2-514.

Documentary drafts.

Bank deposits and collections.

Dishonor.

Duty to notify customer, §28:4-501.

Privilege of presenting bank to deal with goods, §28:4-504.

Reporting reasons, §28:4-503.

Generally, §§28:4-101 to 28:4-504.

See BANK DEPOSITS AND COLLECTIONS.

Presentment.

Duty to send, §28:4-501.

On arrival drafts, §28:4-502.

Negotiable instruments.

Generally, §§28:3-101 to 28:3-605.

See NEGOTIABLE INSTRUMENTS.

DRAM SHOP LIABILITY, §25-781.

DRAWBRIDGE OPENINGS.
Submarine cables used at, §9-1207.02.

DRINKING WATER.
Water and sewer authority.
Testing of drinking water,
§34-2202.06d.
Water quality assurance advisory
panel, §§34-2202.06e, 34-2202.06f.

DRIVE-BY SHOOTINGS.
Murder.
Aggravating circumstances,
§22-2104.01.

DRIVER EDUCATION PROGRAMS.
Schools and education, §§38-912,
38-913.
Issuance of rules, §38-912.01.

DRIVERLESS VEHICLES, §§50-2351
to 50-2354.

DRIVER LICENSE COMPACT,
§§50-1001, 50-1002.

DRIVERS' LICENSES.
Age requirements, §50-1401.01.
Anatomical gifts.
Generally, §§7-1531.01 to 7-1531.28.
See ANATOMICAL GIFTS.
Children and minors.
Alcoholic beverage offenses.
Suspension or revocation, §§25-1002,
50-1403.03.
Drug offenses, §50-1403.02.
Restrictions on, §50-1401.01.
Child support enforcement,
§46-225.01.
Commercial motor vehicles.
General provisions, §§50-401 to
50-409.
See COMMERCIAL DRIVERS'
LICENSES.
Counterfeit documentation.
Seizure of suspect documents,
§50-1401.04.
Definitions, §50-1301.02.
Disqualification, §50-1403.02.
Driver license compact, §§50-1001,
50-1002.
Driving under the influence.
License revocation, §50-2206.55.
Exemptions, §50-1401.02.
Expiration.
Notification, §50-1401.01a.
Fees, §50-1401.01.
Fraudulent documentation.
Seizure of suspect documents,
§50-1401.04.

DRIVERS' LICENSES —Cont'd
Identification card as option,
§50-1401.03.
Learner's permits, §50-1401.01.
Limited purpose driver's license,
permit, or identification card,
§50-1401.05.
Lost or stolen, §50-1401.01.
Mayor authorized to issue or renew,
§50-1401.01.
Military personnel, §50-1401.01.
Motor vehicle defined for purposes
of, §50-1401.01.
New permit following revocation,
§50-1403.01.
Nonresidents, §50-1401.02.
Penalties, §50-1401.01.
Alcohol and drug abuse, §§50-1403.02,
50-1403.03.
Disqualification, §50-1403.02.
Foreign convictions, suspensions for,
§50-1301.37.
Operation of vehicle in violation of
restrictions, §50-1401.01.
Operation of vehicle with expired
license, §50-1401.01.
Operation of vehicle with revoked or
suspended license, §50-1403.01.
Revocation, §§50-1403.01, 50-1403.02.
Suspension, §§50-1301.37, 50-1403.03.
Personal information from motor
vehicle records and accident
reports.
Prohibitions on release and use of,
§50-1401.01b.
Provisional licenses, §50-1401.01.
Revocation, §§50-1403.01, 50-1403.02,
50-1905 to 50-1907.
Driving under the influence,
§50-2206.55.
Seizure of suspect documents,
§50-1401.04.
Selective Service registration upon
application, §50-1401.01.
Suspension of license and
registration, §§50-1301.37,
50-1301.39, 50-1403.01.
Alcohol violations by minors,
§§25-1002, 50-1403.03.
Conditions for lifting, §50-1301.47.
Duration of, §50-1301.37.
Failure to surrender suspended license
and registration, §50-1301.74.
Fleeing from a law enforcement officer
in a motor vehicle, §50-2201.05b.
No-fault motor vehicle insurance
violations, §31-2413.

DRIVERS' LICENSES —Cont'd
Suspension of license and
  registration —Cont'd
  Nonpayment of judgment, for,
    §50-1301.43.
  Nonresidents' operating privileges,
    §50-1301.40.
  Proof of financial responsibility,
    pending, §50-1301.67.
  Surrender of license and registration,
    §50-1301.70.
Vehicle-for-hire drivers' licenses,
  §47-2829.
Veteran designation, §50-1401.01.
  Identification cards, §50-1401.03.

DRIVEWAYS.
Barbed-wire fences, §§9-1213.01 to
  9-1213.05.

DRIVING INSTRUCTORS.
License fee, §47-2842.

DRIVING UNDER THE
  INFLUENCE, §50-2206.11.
Amendment or repeal of provisions,
  effect, §50-2206.59.
Assessment of substance abuse
  history for treatment program
  options, §50-2206.54.
Blood tests.
  Admissibility for criminal proceeding,
    §50-2206.52c.
Boating under the influence.
  Chemical testing, §§50-1908 to
    50-1912.
    See BOATING UNDER THE
      INFLUENCE.
  Generally, §§50-2206.31 to 50-2206.36.
    See BOATING UNDER THE
      INFLUENCE.
Breath tests.
  Admissibility.
    Generally, §50-2206.52.
    Notification, §50-2206.52b.
    Presence or testimony of person
      maintaining instruments,
      §50-2206.52a.
  Preliminary test, §50-1904.01.
Chemical testing, §§50-1901 to
  50-1912.
  Admissibility of chemical tests.
    Blood or urine, §50-2206.52c.
    Generally, §50-2206.52.
    Notification, §50-2206.52b.
    Presence or testimony of person
      maintaining instruments,
      §50-2206.52a.

DRIVING UNDER THE INFLUENCE
  —Cont'd
Chemical testing —Cont'd
  After arrest, §50-1904.02.
  Availability of test results and
    information, §50-1904.
  Boating under the influence,
    §§50-1908 to 50-1912.
  Definitions, §50-1901.
  Failure to submit to testing, §50-1905.
  Hearing on revocation of license,
    §50-1906.
  Judicial review of revocation of license,
    §50-1907.
  Medical professionals, withdrawal of
    blood for test, §50-1903.
  Preliminary breath test, §50-1904.01.
  Presence or testimony of person
    maintaining breath instrument,
    §50-2206.52a.
  Refusal to submit to test, §50-1905.
  Revocation of license as penalty for
    failure to submit to test,
    §§50-1905 to 50-1907.
  Specimens for chemical testing,
    §50-1904.02.
    Refusal to submit, §50-1905.
  Watercraft, §§50-1908 to 50-1912.
Chief medical examiner.
  Responsibilities regarding blood and
    urine testing, §5-1419.
Commercial drivers, §§50-405.01,
  50-2206.12.
  Additional term of incarceration,
    §50-2206.17.
Definitions, §50-2206.01.
Diversion programs, §50-2206.53.
Drivers' license revocation for
  violations, §50-2206.55.
Evidence of impairment, §50-2206.51.
Fines collected, transfer to general
  fund, §50-2206.58.
Forensic sciences department.
  Certification and testing of breath
    alcohol equipment, §5-1501.07.
Horse-drawn vehicles.
  Operating under the influence,
    §50-2206.16.
Ignition interlock devices,
  §50-2201.05a.
Impaired driving, §50-2206.14.
Impoundment of vehicle, §50-2206.56.
Mandatory-minimum periods of
  incarceration, proof required,
  §50-2206.57.
Marijuana.
  Articulable suspicion, §48-921.02a.

DRIVING UNDER THE INFLUENCE
—Cont'd

Minor in vehicle, impaired driving with.
Additional penalty, §50-2206.18.

Offense generally, §50-2206.11.

Penalties, §50-2206.13.
Commercial vehicles.
Additional term of incarceration, §50-2206.17.
Drivers' license revocation, §50-2206.55.
Impaired driving, §50-2206.15.
Mandatory-minimum periods of incarceration, proof required, §50-2206.57.
Minor in vehicle, additional penalties, §50-2206.18.

Preliminary breath test, §50-1904.01.

Prosecution of violations, §50-2206.53.

Repeal of provisions, effect, §50-2206.59.

Substance abuse history assessment for treatment program options, §50-2206.54.

Urine tests.
Admissibility for criminal proceeding, §50-2206.52c.

Watercraft.
See BOATING UNDER THE INFLUENCE.

DRUG ABUSE.

Alcohol and drugs.
See ALCOHOL AND DRUG ABUSE.

Children and youth.
Juveniles and young adults, rehabilitation programs for, §24-612.
Pilot substance abuse program for youth, §§7-3101 to 7-3103.

Choice in drug treatment, §§7-3001 to 7-3015.
See SUBSTANCE ABUSE.

Controlled substances, §§48-901.02 to 48-931.02.
See CONTROLLED SUBSTANCES.

Corrections department.
Mandatory testing of Corrections Department employees, §§24-211.21 to 24-211.24.

Driving under the influence.
See DRIVING UNDER THE INFLUENCE.

Firearms.
Possession by addict unlawful, §22-4503.

DRUG ABUSE —Cont'd

Health insurance coverage, §§31-3101 to 31-3112.
See HEALTH INSURANCE.

Nurses.
Impaired nurses, treatment and rehabilitation, §§3-1251.01 to 3-1251.15.
See NURSES.

Prisons and prisoners.
Alcoholics, rehabilitation of, §§24-601 to 24-615.
See PRISONS AND PRISONERS.
Drug addicts, rehabilitation of, §§24-701 to 24-715.
See PRISONS AND PRISONERS.
Mandatory testing of Corrections Department employees, §§24-211.21 to 24-211.24.

DRUG AND ALCOHOL TESTING OF PUBLIC EMPLOYEES.

Commercial motor vehicle drivers, §1-620.11.

Corrections department employees, §§24-211.21 to 24-211.24.

Department of mental health and department of human services employees.
Mandatory testing for certain employees, §§1-620.21 to 1-620.25.

District employees who serve children.
Mandatory testing, §§1-620.31 to 1-620.37.

District of Columbia housing authority, §6-217.

Forensic sciences department.
Certification and testing of breath alcohol equipment, §5-1501.07.

DRUG-FREE ZONES, §48-904.07a.

DRUG MANUFACTURE AND DISTRIBUTION LICENSURE, §§48-701 to 48-715.

Application procedures, §48-704.

Cease and desist orders, §48-713.

Conditional license, §48-706.

Controlled substances, §§48-903.01 to 48-903.09.

Cosmetics exception, §48-715.

Crimes and offenses, §48-711.

Definitions, §48-701.

Denial of license, §48-710.

Embargoes, §48-713.

Fines, §48-712.

Inspections, §48-708.

DRUG MANUFACTURE AND DISTRIBUTION LICENSURE
—Cont'd
Issuance of rules and regulations, §48-714.
Out-of-state manufacturers, distributors, repackagers, or wholesalers, §48-707.
Penalties, §§48-711, 48-712.
Prohibited acts, §48-702.
Renewal of license, §48-705.
Requirement to have license, §48-703.
Revocation of license, §48-710.
Summary actions, §48-709.
Suspension of license, §48-710.

DRUG PARAPHERNALIA, §§48-1101 to 48-1104.
Definitions, §48-1101.
Factors in determining if object paraphernalia, §48-1102.
Prohibited acts, §§48-904.10, 48-1103.
Property subject to foreclosure, §48-1104.
Schools and education.
Distribution of needles or syringes near schools, §48-1121.

DRUG PREVENTION AND CHILDREN AT RISK TAX CHECK-OFF, §§47-1812.11b, 47-4001 to 47-4005.

DRUG-RELATED EVICTIONS, §§42-3601 to 42-3610.
Action for possession of rental unit used as drug haven, §42-3602.
Attorneys' fees and court costs, §42-3608.
Choice of remedies, §42-3609.
Complaint by tenant or resident association leading to, §42-3606.
Court costs and attorneys' fees, §42-3608.
Default judgment, §42-3605.
Definitions, §42-3601.
Hearings, §42-3604.
Injunctions, §42-3603.
Issuance of rules and regulations, §42-3610.
Mayor's authority and responsibility, §42-3607.
Preliminary injunction review, §42-3603.
Remedies other than, §42-3609.
Rulemaking authority, §42-3610.
Tenant complaints, §42-3606.

DRUG-RELATED NUISANCE ABATEMENT, §§42-3101 to 42-3114.
See CRIME-RELATED NUISANCE ABATEMENT.

DRUGS.
Adulteration of food or drugs.
General provisions, §§48-101 to 48-110.
See ADULTERATION OF FOOD OR DRUGS.
Assisted living residences.
Medication management, §§44-109.01 to 44-109.07.
Child abuse and neglect related to, §4-1301.06a.
Controlled substances.
Abuse of.
See ALCOHOL AND DRUG ABUSE.
General provisions, §§48-901.02 to 48-931.02.
See CONTROLLED SUBSTANCES.
Detention of addicts prior to trial, §23-1323.
Deteriorating drugs, §47-2885.13.
Embargoes, §48-713.
Intellectual disabilities, persons with.
See INTELLECTUAL DISABILITIES, PERSONS WITH.
Labeling requirements for prescriptions, §47-2885.14.
Licensure of manufacturers and distributors.
General provisions, §§48-701 to 48-715.
See DRUG MANUFACTURE AND DISTRIBUTION LICENSURE.
Medication advisory committee receiving gifts or remuneration prohibition act of 2008, §§48-842.01 to 48-842.04.
Mental health disclosures.
Federal regulation and monitoring of prescription drugs, §7-1208.02.
Mental retardation, persons with.
See INTELLECTUAL DISABILITIES, PERSONS WITH.
Off-label use of prescription medication.
Informed consent, §§48-841.01 to 48-841.04.
Oral prescriptions for controlled substances, §3-1210.06.

DRUGS —Cont'd
Overdose victim, seeking medical attention for.
Mitigating factor in sentencing for certain offenses, §7-403.
Peddling drugs, §§47-2885.17, 47-2885.17a.
Pharmaceutical detailing.
Evaluation of effectiveness of law licensing persons practicing, §§48-844.01 to 48-844.03.
Pharmaceutical education program establishment act of 2008.
Education of prescribers in publicly funded, contracted or subsidized health-care programs, §§48-843.01 to 48-843.04.
Pharmacists and pharmacies.
See PHARMACISTS AND PHARMACIES.
Possession of drug paraphernalia, §§48-904.10, 48-1101 to 48-1104.
Prescription drugs.
General provisions, §§48-701 to 48-833.09.
See PRESCRIPTION DRUGS.
Off-label use of prescription medication.
Informed consent, §§48-841.01 to 48-841.04.
Pharmaceutical education program establishment act of 2008.
Education of prescribers in publicly funded, contracted or subsidized health-care programs, §§48-843.01 to 48-843.04.
Public employee drug and alcohol testing.
Commercial motor vehicle drivers, §1-620.11.
Corrections department, §§24-211.21 to 24-211.24.
Department of mental health and department of human services employees, §§1-620.21 to 1-620.25.
District employees who serve children.
Mandatory testing, §§1-620.31 to 1-620.37.
District of Columbia housing authority, §6-217.
Rehabilitation programs, §24-610.
Returned drugs, §47-2885.13.
SafeRX evaluation act of 2008.
Pharmaceutical detailing.
Evaluation of effectiveness of law licensing persons practicing, §§48-844.01 to 48-844.03.

DRUGS —Cont'd
Samples, §47-2885.13.
Sexual offenses, use in committing, §§22-3002, 22-3004.
Student health care.
Medication, §§38-651.01 to 38-651.12.
See STUDENT HEALTH CARE.

DRUG TREATMENT CENTERS.
Schools, establishment near.
Notice given by mayor, §38-3201.

DRUNK DRIVING.
See DRIVING UNDER THE INFLUENCE.

DRY CLEANERS.
Artisan's lien, §§40-307.01 to 40-307.03.
Business licenses, §47-2817.
Pre-kindergarten programs.
Licensing of child-occupied facilities.
Dry cleaning establishments in close proximity, restrictions on licensing, §38-271.01.

DRY GOODS.
Sale by weight, §37-201.15.

DUE PROCESS, US Const Amds 5, 14.
Court employees.
Debts and erroneous payments made to employees, collection by executive officer.
Notice and hearing requirements, §11-1733.
Demolition or enclosure of deteriorated property, §§42-3173.01 to 42-3173.12.
Special education student rights.
Hearings, §§38-2572.01 to 38-2572.04.
Attorney abuses, §38-2572.04.
Evaluation and termination of hearing officers, §38-2572.03.
Selection of hearing officer, §38-2572.02.
Short title, §38-2572.01.
Requirements, §38-2571.03.
Testing integrity in public schools.
Sanctions for violations, §38-771.07.

DULLES INTERNATIONAL AIRPORT, §§9-801 to 9-813.
Acquisition of facilities, §9-803.
Administrator, §9-801.
Appropriations, §9-812.
Arrests, §9-808.
Condemnation proceedings, §9-803.
Construction of, §§9-801, 9-803.
Contracts for supplies or services, §9-806.

DULLES INTERNATIONAL AIRPORT —Cont'd
Definitions, §9-811.
Federal agency property transfers, §9-807.
Fines, §9-810.
Highways, §9-803.
Leases of space or property for, §9-805.
Metropolitan Washington airports authority, §§9-901 to 9-926, 9-1001 to 9-1011.
  See METROPOLITAN WASHINGTON AIRPORTS AUTHORITY.
Municipal services arrangements, §9-809.
Operation of, §§9-801, 9-804.
Penalties, §9-810.
Pool and fountain, money recovered from, §9-813.
Repair and maintenance, §§9-801, 9-804.
Sanitary sewer, §§34-2131 to 34-2134.
  Plan for interceptor and sewer line.
    Commissioner authorized to develop, §34-2131.
  Potomac interceptor.
    Acquisition of land, §34-2134.
    Appropriations, §34-2133.
    Charges for use, §34-2132.
    Construction and operation, §34-2132.
    Transfer of land from federal department or agency, §34-2134.
Selection of site for, §9-802.
Streets and alleys, §9-803.
United States Park Police, §9-808.

DUMPING, ILLEGAL.
See ILLEGAL DUMPING.

DURABLE POWERS OF ATTORNEY, §§21-2081 to 21-2085.
Custodial power of attorney.
  Parents authorized to create, §21-2301.
Defined, §21-2081.
Evidence, §21-2085.
Fiduciary appointed by court, relationship between attorney in fact and, §21-2083.
Healthcare decisions.
  See HEALTHCARE DURABLE POWERS OF ATTORNEY.
Heath-care decisions, §§21-2201 to 21-2213.
Incapacity, not affected by, §21-2082.

DURABLE POWERS OF ATTORNEY —Cont'd
Intervention proceedings, Probate Rules 301 to 361.
  See INTERVENTION PROCEEDINGS.
Living wills, §§7-621 to 7-630.
  See LIVING WILLS.
Mental health consumers.
  Right to execute power of attorney for health care, §7-1231.06.
Revocation of, §21-2084.
Uniform fiduciaries act, §§21-1701 to 21-1712.
  See FIDUCIARIES.
Uniform general powers of attorney, extent of durability of, §21-2102.

DURESS.
Trusts and trustees.
  Uniform trust code.
    Void trusts, §19-1304.06.

DUST SUPPRESSION.
Hazardous waste management, §8-1313.

DYEING ESTABLISHMENTS.
Business licenses, §47-2817.

E

EARLY CHILDHOOD AND SCHOOL-BASED BEHAVIORAL HEALTH INFRASTRUCTURE.
Comprehension plan, §2-1517.32.
Definitions, §2-1517.31.

EARLY CHILDHOOD EDUCATION, §§38-755.01 to 38-755.04.

EARLY INTERVENTION PROGRAM, §§7-863.01 to 7-863.04.
Citation of act, §7-863.01.
Establishment, §7-863.03.
Interagency coordinating council.
  Establishment, §7-863.03.
Mayor.
  Rulemaking, §7-863.04.
Purpose of act, §7-863.02.
Title of act, §7-863.01.
Transfer of personnel, property, records and funds to the Office of the State Superintendent of Education, §7-863.03a.

EARNED INCOME CREDIT.
Public assistance, providing information to recipients of, §4-205.82.

EARS.
Hearing aid dealers, §§28-4001 to 28-4007.
See HEARING AID DEALERS.

EASEMENTS.
Condominiums.
See CONDOMINIUMS.
Conservation easements, §§42-201 to 42-205.
See CONSERVATION EASEMENTS.
Public space.
Commemorative works, §9-204.16.

EASTERN AVENUE VIADUCT, §9-315.

EASTERN BRANCH.
United States title to lands or waters of, §10-102.

EASTERN MARKET.
Community advisory committee, §§37-101, 37-111.
Coordinated management, §37-102.
Definitions, §37-101.
Enforcement of provisions, §37-110.
Enterprise Fund, §37-103.
Insurance, §37-112.
Manager, §37-105.
Neighborhood vending in vicinity of, §37-109.
Operation of market, §37-104.
Policy declaration, §37-104.
Reports, §37-113.
Tenants.
Duties and requirements, §37-106.
Right of first refusal.
Existing inside operations, §37-107.
Existing sidewalk operations, §37-108.

EASTERN STAR CHARITABLE FOUNDATION.
Real property exempt from taxation, §47-1045.

EAST OF THE RIVER HIV/AIDS CAPACITY BUILDING INITIATIVE.
Effi Slaughter Barry AIDS/HIV initiative.
Designation as, §7-1612.
General provisions, §§7-1611 to 7-1617.

EAVESDROPPING.
Interception of wire or oral communications.
General provisions.
See INTERCEPTION OF ORAL OR WIRE COMMUNICATIONS.

E-CIGARETTES.
Vapor products.
Tobacco tax, §47-2401.

ECKINGTON ONE RESIDENTIAL PROJECT.
Tax abatement and exemption, §47-4618.

E-COMMERCE COMPANIES.
Qualified social electronic commerce companies tax abatements, §§47-1818.01 to 47-1818.08.
Applicability, §47-1818.07.
BAS agreements, §47-1818.03.
Certification, §47-1818.04.
Council approval, §47-1818.05.
Citywide joint business activity strategy agreements, §47-1818.03.
Certification, §47-1818.04.
Council approval, §47-1818.05.
Definitions, §47-1818.01.
First Source employment.
Applicability, §47-1818.07.
Mayor, delegation of authority, §47-1818.08.
Tax credits, §47-1818.02.
Exceptions, §47-1818.06.

ECONOMIC DEVELOPMENT, §§2-1201.01 to 2-1217.84.
Business improvement districts.
General provisions, §§2-1215.01 to 2-1215.71.
See BUSINESS IMPROVEMENT DISTRICTS.
Business incubator facilitation, §§2-1209.01 to 2-1209.14.
Economic development liaison office, §§2-1203.01 to 2-1203.03.
Economic development zone incentives.
General provisions, §§6-1501 to 6-1506.
See ECONOMIC DEVELOPMENT ZONE INCENTIVES.
Enterprise zone study commission, §§2-1211.01 to 2-1211.06.
Grants.
Deputy Mayor for planning and economic development, grant-making authority, §1-328.04.
Workforce investment council grants for job development, §1-328.05.
Grocery store development program, §§2-1212.21 to 2-1212.24.
Healthy food retail program, §§2-1212.31 to 2-1212.34.

ECONOMIC DEVELOPMENT
—Cont'd
National Capital Revitalization Corporation.
General provisions.
See NATIONAL CAPITAL REVITALIZATION CORPORATION.
Office of business and economic development, §§2-1201.01 to 2-1201.05.
Retail development incentives, §§2-1217.71 to 2-1217.84.
See RETAIL DEVELOPMENT INCENTIVES.
Tax increment financing.
General provisions, §§2-1217.01 to 2-1217.12.
See TAX INCREMENT FINANCING.
Walter Reed Medical Center site development, §§2-1227.01 to 2-1227.06.

ECONOMIC DEVELOPMENT SPECIAL ACCOUNT, §2-1225.21.

ECONOMIC DEVELOPMENT ZONE INCENTIVES, §§6-1501 to 6-1506.
Applicability of rules, §6-1505.
Businesses, for, §6-1504.
Establishment of zones, §6-1501.
Mayor's authority to issue rules, §6-1506.
Qualification for incentives, §6-1503.
Requirements for zones, §6-1502.

EDES HOME.
Real property exempt from taxation, §47-1026.

EDUCATION.
Adult education courses, §§38-1001 to 38-1003.
Adult literacy.
Reports, §38-192.01.
Alcoholic beverage licenses.
Manager's license, §25-120.
Programs, §25-121.
American sign language as foreign language course, §§38-2431 to 38-2433.
Animals used in classroom, §§8-1851.01, 8-1851.02.
Athletics plan, §38-824.02a.
Attendance.
Compulsory school attendance, §§38-201 to 38-213.
See COMPULSORY SCHOOL ATTENDANCE.

EDUCATION —Cont'd
Aviation high school courses, §§38-920 to 38-922.
Board of education.
General provisions.
See BOARD OF EDUCATION.
Business partnerships, §§38-1806.01 to 38-1806.09.
Charter schools.
General provisions.
See CHARTER SCHOOLS.
Colleges generally.
See UNIVERSITIES AND COLLEGES.
Community education courses, §§38-1001 to 38-1003.
Compulsory school attendance, §§38-201 to 38-213.
See COMPULSORY SCHOOL ATTENDANCE.
Content standards, §§38-1803.11 to 38-1803.15.
Continuing education courses, §§38-1001 to 38-1003.
Core curriculum, §§38-1803.11 to 38-1803.15.
Department of general services, §§38-924 to 38-926.
Detained and committed youth under supervision of DYRS, §38-3301.
Drug-free zones, §48-904.07a.
Education commission of the states, compact for, §§38-3001 to 38-3004.
Expulsion of students for weapons, §§38-231 to 38-235.
Foreign language requirements.
American sign language, §§38-2431 to 38-2433.
Free textbooks, §§38-701 to 38-706, 38-922.
Health care of students.
General provisions, §§38-601 to 38-651.12.
See STUDENT HEALTH CARE.
Higher education.
See UNIVERSITIES AND COLLEGES.
Higher education licensure commission, §§38-1301 to 38-1313.
See HIGHER EDUCATION LICENSURE COMMISSION.
Human papillomavirus vaccination.
Public education campaign, §7-1651.02.

EDUCATION —Cont'd
Immunization of school students, §§38-501 to 38-508.
Interstate compact on educational opportunity for military children. Time to obtain immunizations, §49-1101.05.
Insurance.
Unfair trade practices, §§31-2231.01 to 31-2231.25.
Metrorail and metrobus student fares.
General provisions, §§35-232 to 35-237.
See METRORAIL AND METROBUS.
National technical institute for the deaf, §§38-2401.11, 38-2401.12, 38-2402.01 to 38-2402.11.
See NATIONAL TECHNICAL INSTITUTE FOR THE DEAF.
Nonresident tuition, §§38-301 to 38-313.
Opportunity accounts.
Generally, §§1-307.61 to 1-307.74.
Use of funds to pay expenses, §1-307.68.
Parental leave to attend or participate in school-related event, §§32-1201 to 32-1206.
Pensions and retirement.
Food services department, §38-803.
Teachers, §§38-2001.01 to 38-2041.01.
See TEACHERS' RETIREMENT.
Post-secondary education.
See UNIVERSITIES AND COLLEGES.
Pregnant or parenting teens.
Public assistance for, §§4-205.61 to 4-205.66.
Promotion gates, §§38-1803.11 to 38-1803.15.
Qualification of educational personnel, interstate agreement on, §§38-2101 to 38-2104.
Reform program, §§38-1800.01 to 38-1803.21.
School-based budgeting and accountability, §§38-2801.01 to 38-2807.
Schools and education.
See SCHOOLS AND EDUCATION.
State board of education.
General provisions.
See BOARD OF EDUCATION.

EDUCATION —Cont'd
State education office.
Educational licensure commission. Transfer to state education office, §38-1313.
State superintendent of education, office of, §§38-2601 to 38-2612.
Teachers.
General provisions, §§38-1901 to 38-1923.
See TEACHERS.
Retirement of teachers, §§38-2001.01 to 38-2041.01.
See TEACHERS' RETIREMENT.
Textbooks.
Free textbooks, §§38-701 to 38-706, 38-922.
School officials prohibited from profiting on, §38-902.
Transportation.
Appropriations restrictions, §38-911.
Charter schools, §38-1802.08.
Disabled children, §38-913.
Metrorail and metrobus, student fares on, §§35-232 to 35-237.
See METRORAIL AND METROBUS.
World Class Schools Task Force, §§38-1803.11 to 38-1803.15.

EDUCATIONAL GOOD TIME CREDITS.
Prisons and prisoners, §24-221.01.

EDUCATIONAL SERVICE, §§1-525.01, 1-608.01a, 1-611.11, 1-623.45.

EDUCATIONAL STEPLADDER PROGRAM, §§32-1651 to 32-1653.
Unemployment compensation.
Eligibility for benefits, §51-109.01.

EDUCATION COMMISSION OF THE STATES, COMPACT FOR, §§38-3001 to 38-3004.

EDUCATION OMBUDSMAN, §§38-351 to 38-356.

EFFI SLAUGHTER BARRY HIV/AIDS INITIATIVE, §§7-1611 to 7-1617.
Coordinator, §7-1614.
Designation, §7-1612.
Findings by council, §7-1611.
Fund created to support initiative, §7-1617.
Funding allocation, §7-1616.
Grant award criteria, §7-1615.
Participant selection, §7-1615.

**EFFI SLAUGHTER BARRY
  HIV/AIDS INITIATIVE** —Cont'd
Purpose, §7-1613.

**800 KENILWORTH AVENUE N.E.
  REDEVELOPMENT PROJECT.**
Tax abatements, §47-4643.

EJECTMENT, §§16-1101 to 16-1124.
Adverse possession, §§16-1103,
  16-1113.
Attorneys' fees and costs, §16-1114.
Complaints in, §16-1103.
Damages, recovery of, §§16-1109 to
  16-1112, 16-1116 to 16-1120.
Defendants, §16-1101.
Enclosure, §16-1113.
Evidence, §16-1103.
  Proof necessary, §16-1104.
Expiration of title pending suit,
  §16-1112.
**Failure of tenant to give notice to
  landlord,** §16-1102.
Final judgment, conclusiveness of,
  §16-1115.
Furniture, recovery of, §16-1110.
Future actions, §16-1114.
Good faith improvements, §16-1116.
Improvements made by defendant,
  §§16-1116 to 16-1121.
  Assessment in case findings in favor of
    plaintiff, §16-1116.
  New trial as to assessment,
    §16-1117.
  Election of plaintiff if value of
    improvements exceeds damages,
    §16-1120.
  Judgment and writ of possession after
    payment for improvements,
    §16-1121.
  Judgment and writ of possession after
    plaintiff's refusal to pay excess or
    tender deed, §16-1123.
  Judgment and writ of possession after
    tender of deed and defendant's
    refusal to pay, §16-1122.
  Judgment for damages in excess of
    improvements, §16-1118.
  Judgment when improvements and
    damages equal, §16-1119.
  Notice that defendant claims benefit of
    permanent improvements,
    §16-1116.
Joint tenants, §16-1101.
Judgments and decrees, §§16-1114,
  16-1121 to 16-1123.
  After payment for improvements,
    §16-1121.

EJECTMENT —Cont'd
Judgments and decrees —Cont'd
  After plaintiff's refusal to pay excess
    or tender deed, §16-1123.
  After tender of deed and defendant's
    refusal to pay, §16-1122.
Jury, directions to, §16-1116.
Jury verdict, §16-1114.
Less than is claimed, recovery of,
  §16-1108.
**Mesne profits and damages,
  recovery of,** §16-1109.
**Mortgages and deeds of trust, legal
  title in,** §16-1105.
Nonpayment of rent, §16-1124.
Notice, §16-1116.
Performance of contract, §16-1106.
Proof necessary, §16-1104.
Propriety of actions in ejectment,
  §42-3210.
**Severalty, tenants occupying
  distinct parcels in,** §16-1107.
Tenants in common, §16-1101.
Verdict, §16-1114.
Waste, claims for, §42-3211.

ELDERLY.
Aged persons generally.
  See AGED PERSONS.

ELECTIONS, §§1-1001.01 to 1-1041.04.
Absentee ballots, §1-1001.09.
  Voting by military and overseas voters,
    §§1-1061.01 to 1-1061.20. See
    within this heading, "Voting by
    military and overseas voters."
Age.
  Persons eighteen years of age, US
    Const Amd 26.
  Right to vote not to be abridged on
    account of age, US Const Amd 26.
Appropriations, §1-1001.13.
Attorney general, §§1-204.35,
  1-1001.08.
Ballots, §§1-1001.08, 1-1001.09, 1-1313.
  Arrangement by party, §1-1001.08.
  Voting by military and overseas voters.
  Applications, §1-1061.07.
    Receipt of confirmation,
      §1-1061.14.
  Casting, §1-1061.10.
  Declarations accompanying,
    §1-1061.13.
  Federal write-in absentee ballots,
    §1-1061.11.
  Unvoted, transmission of,
    §1-1061.09.

ELECTIONS —Cont'd
Ballots —Cont'd
Voting by military and overseas voters
  —Cont'd
  Voted, receipt of.
    Confirmation, §1-1061.14.
Bar association.
  Board of governors, DCBar Rule IV.
  Officers, DCBar Rule III.
  Referendums, DCBar Rule VII.
Board of education, §1-1001.08.
Board of elections, §§1-1001.02 to
  1-1001.05, 1-1001.06.
  Chairman, §1-1001.03.
  Compensation, §1-1001.04.
  Composition, §1-1001.03.
  Created, §§1-1001.03, 1-1163.05.
  Defined, §1-1001.02.
  Duties, §1-1001.05.
  Independent agency, §1-1001.06.
  Prohibited activities, §1-1001.04.
  Qualifications, §1-1001.04.
  Reappointment, §1-1001.03.
  Removal, §1-1001.04.
  Term of office, §1-1001.03.
  Vacancies, §1-1001.03.
    Time for filling, §1-1001.04.
  Voting by military and overseas voters,
    §1-1061.04.
Campaign finance.
  General provisions.
    See CAMPAIGN FINANCE.
**Campaign signs, posters or other
  materials.**
  Damaging, defacing, or destroying,
    §1-1001.14.
Candidates.
  More than one office, for, §1-1001.15.
  Qualifications, §1-1001.08.
  Similarity in names.
    Clarification by board of elections,
      §1-1001.05.
Challenged or special ballots,
  §1-1001.09.
Circulators of nominating petitions.
  Criminal penalty for violations,
    §1-1001.08.
Congress.
  Payment of poll tax not required, US
    Const Amd 24.
  Proclamation by governor of names of
    members of congress elected.
  Judge of elections, returns,
    qualifications of members, US
    Const Art I §5.
Corrupt practices, §1-1001.14.

ELECTIONS —Cont'd
Council, §1-1001.08.
Council authority regarding,
  §1-207.52.
**Current officeholders as candidates
  for another office,** §1-1001.15.
Definitions, §1-1001.02.
Early voting centers, §1-1001.09.
Effective date of provisions,
  §1-1021.04.
Election reform fund, §1-1001.06a.
Electors, §1-1001.01.
  Candidate qualifications, §1-1001.08.
  Qualifications, §1-1001.08.
  Votes for President and Vice President
    counted as votes for, §1-1001.10.
Fraud and deceit, §1-1001.14.
**Government employees engaging
  political activities,** §§1-1171.01 to
  1-1171.07.
See POLITICAL ACTIVITIES BY
  GOVERNMENT EMPLOYEES.
Grants.
  Grants to promote voting rights and
    statehood, §1-328.03.
Home Rule act charter.
  Referendum, §§1-207.01 to 1-207.04.
House of representatives.
  Constitution of the United States.
    See HOUSE OF
      REPRESENTATIVES.
Initiative and referendum,
  §§1-204.101 to 1-204.107, 1-1001.16.
See INITIATIVE AND
  REFERENDUM.
Interference with, §1-1001.12.
Issuance of rules and regulations,
  §1-1021.02.
Judges.
  Campaign activities.
    Appointive office, CJC Canon 4.3.
    Candidates for nonjudicial office,
      CJC Canon 4.5.
    General rules, CJC Canon 4.1.
  Political and campaign activities, CJC
    Canon 4.
Judicial review of results, §1-1001.11.
Mail-ballot voting, §1-1001.08.
Mayor, §§1-204.21, 1-1001.08.
Mobile application.
  Defined, §1-1001.02.
Mobile device.
  Defined, §1-1001.02.
Multilingual materials, §§1-1031.01,
  1-1031.02.
**Multiple nominations for single
  candidate,** §1-1001.15.

ELECTIONS —Cont'd

Nomination process, §1-1001.08.

Observers.

Granting access to electoral process, §1-1001.09.

Poll tax.

Failure to pay poll or other tax.

Denial or abridgement of right to vote by reason of failure prohibited, US Const Amd 24.

Post-election audits, §1-1001.09a.

Presidential and vice-presidential elections.

Ballots, §1-1001.08.

Electors to vote by ballot, US Const Amd 12.

Board of elections.

Duties, presidential primary elections, §1-1001.05.

Electors.

Appointment, US Const Art II §1.

Congress may appoint time of choosing electors, US Const Art II §1.

Ballot.

Vote to be by ballot, US Const Amd 12.

Majority vote is necessary to elect president or vice-president, US Const Amd 12.

Vote.

How given and transmitted, US Const Amd 12.

National popular vote interstate agreement, §1-1051.01.

Presidential electors.

Political parties entitled to elect, §1-1001.08.

Qualifications.

Board of elections members, §1-1001.04.

Candidates, §1-1001.08.

Voters, §1-1001.07.

Recall of elected public officials, §§1-204.111 to 1-204.115, 1-1001.17.

See RECALL OF ELECTED PUBLIC OFFICIALS.

Recounts, §1-1001.11.

Reform fund, §1-1001.06a.

Registration of voters.

See VOTER REGISTRATION.

Residency requirements, §1-1041.04.

Right to vote, US Const Amds 15, 19, 26.

Secrecy requirements, §1-1001.09.

Suffrage.

Constitutional provisions, US Const Amds 15, 19.

ELECTIONS —Cont'd

Summary count of votes cast at precinct, §1-1001.09.

Summary log prepared by precinct captain, §1-1001.09.

Taxation.

Capitation tax, US Const Art I §9.

Denial or abridgement of right to vote.

Failure to pay poll or other tax, US Const Amd 24.

Tie votes, §1-1001.10.

Time and date for holding, §1-1001.10.

Timely actions, §1-1021.01.

Vacancy left by death or resignation of elected official, §1-1001.10.

Voter identification for voting, §1-1001.07.

Voter qualifications, §1-1001.07.

Voter registration.

See VOTER REGISTRATION.

Voters.

Age.

Persons eighteen years of age, US Const Amd 26.

Right to vote not to be abridged on account of age, US Const Amd 26.

Constitutional provisions, US Const Amds 14, 15, 19, 26.

Qualifications of voters.

Persons eighteen years of age, US Const Amd 26.

Voting by military and overseas voters, §§1-1061.01 to 1-1061.20.

Address of voter, §1-1061.05.

Electronic mail address, §1-1061.15.

Ballots.

Applications, §1-1061.07.

Receipt of confirmation, §1-1061.14.

Casting, §1-1061.10.

Declarations accompanying, §1-1061.13.

Federal write-in absentee ballots, §1-1061.11.

Unvoted, transmission of, §1-1061.09.

Voted, receipt of.

Confirmation, §1-1061.14.

Board role, §1-1061.04.

Citation of provisions, §1-1061.01.

Construction of provisions, §1-1061.17.

Definitions, §1-1061.02.

Elections covered by, §1-1061.03.

Electronic mail address, §1-1061.15.

ELECTIONS —Cont'd
Voting by military and overseas voters —Cont'd
Electronic signatures and, §1-1061.20.
Equitable relief, §1-1061.18.
Implementation of provisions, §1-1061.04.
Interpretation of provisions, §1-1061.17.
Notice of election, §1-1061.16.
Publication of notice of election, §1-1061.16.
Registration address, §1-1061.05.
Registration methods, §1-1061.06.
Voting procedures, §1-1001.09.
Voting rights.
Grants to promote voting rights and statehood, §1-328.03.
Voting systems.
Defined, §1-1001.02.
Post-election audits, §1-1001.09a.
Standards, §1-1001.09.
Ward boundaries, §1-1041.03.
Wards, §1-1011.01.
Ward task forces on Advisory Neighborhood Commission, §§1-1041.01, 1-1041.02.
Women.
Woman suffrage, US Const Amd 19.
Write in votes, §1-1001.08.

ELECTRICAL ENGINEER.
Office of, §2-132.

ELECTRIC COMPANY INFRASTRUCTURE IMPROVEMENT FINANCING, §§34-1311.01 to 34-1314.04.
Amendments.
Commission order authorizing underground project charges, §34-1313.13.
Expedited consideration of applications, §34-1313.16.
Projects plan, §34-1313.12.
Bonds.
Authorization, §34-1312.02.
Electric company liability, bonds not to constitute, §34-1312.12.
Financing and closing documents, §34-1312.06.
Indebtedness of district, bonds not to constitute, §34-1312.07.
Legal investment, bonds as, §34-1312.08.
Mayor's authority, bond details, §34-1312.04.
Payment and security, §34-1312.03.

ELECTRIC COMPANY INFRASTRUCTURE IMPROVEMENT FINANCING —Cont'd
Bonds —Cont'd
Sale of bonds, §34-1312.05.
Cash deposits.
Bonds in lieu of, §34-1314.03.
Council findings, §34-1311.02.
DDOT underground electric company infrastructure fund.
Establishment, §34-1312.01.
DDOT underground electric company infrastructure improvement property, §34-1312.09.
District's interest in property, §34-1312.10.
Defined terms, §34-1311.01.
Expedited consideration of applications, §34-1313.16.
Financial advisors.
Retaining services, §34-1313.03.
Financing orders, §§34-1312.01, 34-1313.01 to 34-1313.06.
Application for order, §34-1313.02.
Consideration of application, §34-1313.03.
Notice to public, §34-1313.03.
Commission authorizations, §34-1313.01.
Duration of effectiveness, §34-1313.05.
Irrevocability, §34-1313.04.
Issuance advice letter, §34-1313.03.
Limitation on commission action, §34-1313.06.
Findings, §34-1311.02.
Funding.
Commission and OPC, §34-1314.01.
Gas companies.
Recovery of gas plant relocation costs, §34-1314.04.
Judicial review of commission orders, §34-1313.18.
Permitting fees.
Waiver, §34-1314.03.
Reconsideration of commission orders, §34-1313.17.
Report to council.
Review and analysis, §34-1313.19.
Revenue collection, §34-1312.01.
Rules and regulations.
Commission's authority, §34-1314.02.
Selection and construction of projects, §§34-1313.07 to 34-1313.15.
Judicial review of commission orders, §34-1313.18.

ELECTRIC COMPANY INFRASTRUCTURE IMPROVEMENT FINANCING —Cont'd

Selection and construction of projects —Cont'd

Reconsideration of commission orders, §34-1313.17.

Triennial projects plan, §34-1313.07.

Amendment of plan, §34-1313.12.

Application expenses and costs.

Recovery by electric company, §34-1313.10.

Commission orders, §34-1313.10.

Amendment of order authorizing underground project charges, §34-1313.13.

Judicial review, §34-1313.18.

Reconsideration, §34-1313.17.

Contents of application and plan, §34-1313.08.

Discovery process, §34-1313.09.

Expedited consideration of applications, §34-1313.16.

Notice to public, §34-1313.09.

Tax exemption.

DDOT improvement charges, §34-1312.11.

Transfer of title to electric company, §34-1313.11.

Triennial projects plan. See within this heading, "Selection and construction of projects."

True-up mechanism.

Approval of schedule applying mechanism to improvement charges, §34-1313.14.

Underground project charges.

Amendment of commission order authorizing charges, §34-1313.13.

Annual adjustment.

Application for approval, §34-1313.15.

Use of improvements, §34-1313.11.

ELECTRICIANS.

Board of industrial trades, §§47-2853.06 to 47-2853.10.

Business licenses, §§47-2853.91 to 47-2853.93.

Eligibility, §47-2853.92.

Representations prohibited, §47-2853.93.

Scope of practice, §47-2853.91.

Electrical engineer, office of, §2-132.

ELECTRICIANS —Cont'd

Fees and permits, §47-2712.

ELECTRIC LIGHT AND POWER COMPANIES, §§34-1401 to 34-1408.

Additional charge for nonpayment of bills, §34-1407.

Advanced metering infrastructure.

Authorization, §34-1562.

Definitions, §34-1561.

Aggregation programs, §34-1515.

Commission powers and duties, §34-301.

Competitive billing, §34-1503.

Conduits.

Authorization to construct, §9-1207.03.

Ducts for fire and police wires, §34-1407.

Existing conduits, §34-1403.

Extensions, §§34-1401, 34-1406, 34-1407.

Mount Pleasant, §34-1401.

Permits to repair, extend, or enlarge, §34-1406.

Prohibitions regarding, §34-1402.

Use of conduits of others, §34-1408.

Construction of plant, permission for, §34-302.

Consumer protection.

Disconnection of service in extreme temperature, prohibition, §34-1506.01.

Retail electric competition and consumer protection, §§34-1501 to 34-1522.

Customer choice.

Implementation, §34-1502.

Definitions, §§34-206 to 34-221.

Disconnection of service in extreme temperature, prohibition, §34-1506.01.

Ducts for fire and police wires, §34-1407.

Excessive charges, §34-304.

Extensions.

Conduits, §§34-1401, 34-1406, 34-1407.

Overhead wires in Georgetown, §34-1401.

Extreme temperature, forecast of.

Disconnection of service, prohibition, §34-1506.01.

Horizontal property regimes.

Submetering, §§34-1551 to 34-1553.

ELECTRIC LIGHT AND POWER COMPANIES —Cont'd

Inaugural ceremonies of the President of the United States, §§2-804, 2-805, 2-825.

Infrastructure improvement financing, §§34-1311.01 to 34-1314.04.
  See ELECTRIC COMPANY INFRASTRUCTURE IMPROVEMENT FINANCING.

Inspections, §§2-131 to 2-133.

Inspector of gas and meters, §34-1601.
  Power to appoint and remove inspector and assistants from office, §34-305.

Low-income electricity customer discount program, §8-1774.14.

Meter inspections, §§34-303 to 34-306.

Municipal aggregation fund, §34-1515.

Net metering, §34-1518.

New generating facilities within District, §34-1516.

Overhead wires.
  East of Rock Creek, §34-1405.
  Existing wires, §34-1403.
  Extensions in Georgetown, §34-1401.
  Prohibitions regarding, §34-1402.
  West of Rock Creek, §34-1404.

Pepco cost-sharing fund for DC PLUG, §1-325.331.

Price of current, §34-1407.

Public awareness programs regarding energy providers, §34-808.01.

Public service commission.
  See PUBLIC SERVICE COMMISSION.

Renewable energy portfolio standards, §§34-1431 to 34-1439.
  See RENEWABLE ENERGY PORTFOLIO STANDARDS.

Renewable energy sources, §34-1517.

Retail electric competition and consumer protection, §§34-1501 to 34-1522.
  Aggregation programs, §34-1515.
  Community renewable energy.
    Definitions, §34-1501.
    Disclosures to consumers, §34-1521.
    Facilities, §34-1518.01.
    General provisions, §34-1518.
    Limitations on production or offsetting of electricity, §34-1518.01.

ELECTRIC LIGHT AND POWER COMPANIES —Cont'd

Retail electric competition and consumer protection —Cont'd
  Community renewable energy —Cont'd
    Net metering, §34-1518.
    Policy, §34-1501.01.
    Recovery of implementation costs, §34-1522.
    Safety and performance standards of facilities, §34-1518.
    Subscriptions, §34-1518.01.
  Competitive billing, §34-1503.
    Defined, §34-1501.
  Conformity with settlement agreement, §34-1520.
  Consumer protections, §34-1507.
  CREF credit rate.
    Defined, §34-1501.
  Customer choice.
    Defined, §34-1501.
    Implementation, §34-1502.
  Definitions, §34-1501.
  Disclosure of customer information, restrictions, §34-1507.
  Disconnection of service in extreme temperature, prohibition, §34-1506.01.
  Discrimination prohibited, §34-1507.
  Duties of electric company, §34-1506.
  Engaging in business of electricity supplier, §34-1513.
  Investigation of violations, §34-1508.
  Licensing requirements, §34-1505.
  Net metering, §34-1518.
  New generating facilities in District, §34-1516.
  Penalties for violations, §34-1508.
  Recovery of costs under public purpose programs, §34-1511.
  Remedial actions by District, §34-1512.
  Renewable energy sources, §34-1517.
  Role, duties, powers of commission, §34-1504.
  Sale of generation assets by electric company, §34-1519.
  Standard offer service, §34-1509.
  Transition costs and benefits, §34-1510.

Smart lighting study.
  Definitions, §8-1776.01.
  Reports, §8-1776.02.

Street lighting, §§9-501 to 9-510.
  See STREET LIGHTING.

Submetering, §§34-1551 to 34-1553.

ELECTRIC LIGHT AND POWER COMPANIES —Cont'd
Taxation, §47-2501.
Theft of utility service, §§22-3218.01 to 22-3218.04.

ELECTRIC PERSONAL ASSISTIVE MOBILITY DEVICES.
Defined, §50-2201.01.
Exemption from regulations governing motor vehicles, §50-2201.03a.
Operation and registration requirements, §50-2201.04a.
Regulation, §50-2201.03a.

ELECTRIC PIPES.
Drug paraphernalia, §§48-904.10, 48-1101 to 48-1104.

ELECTRIC SHOCK THERAPY.
Consent required, §7-1231.07.

ELECTRIC VEHICLES.
Motor vehicle registration.
Definition of electric vehicle, §50-1501.01.
Fees, §50-1501.03.
Generally, §50-1501.02.
Motor vehicle titling tax.
Exemption, §50-2201.03.

ELECTRIFICATION OF STEAM RAILROAD LINES, §§9-1207.01 to 9-1207.05.

ELECTROCONVULSIVE TREATMENT.
Consent required, §7-1231.07.

ELECTRONICALLY STORED INFORMATION.
Discovery, production, CivPro Rule 34.

ELECTRONIC CHATTEL PAPER.
Secured transactions.
Control, §28:9-105.
Perfection by control, §28:9-314.
Defined, §28:9-102.

ELECTRONIC CIGARETTES.
Vapor products.
Tobacco tax, §47-2401.

ELECTRONIC FILING, CivPro Appx II, CivPro Rule 5.
Bankruptcy court, USDistDCBank Appx D.
Criminal proceedings, USDistCt LCrR 49.
Mandatory eFiling in civil division, CivPro Appx III.
Complaints, CivPro Appx IV.

ELECTRONIC FILING —Cont'd
Mental illness, persons with.
Hospitalization, MentalHealth Rule 14.
United States District Court case management/electronic case filing system.
Criminal proceedings, USDistCt LCrR 49.

ELECTRONIC FUNDS TRANSFERS.
Generally, §§28:4A-101 to 28:4A-507.
See FUNDS TRANSFERS.
Money transmissions, §§26-1001 to 26-1027.
See MONEY TRANSMISSIONS.

ELECTRONIC MONITORING DEVICE.
Tampering by persons required to wear, §22-1211.

ELECTRONIC RECORDING.
Recorder of deeds, §§42-1231 to 42-1235.
Titling of motor vehicles.
Liens, electronic recording, §50-1218.

ELECTRONIC SERVICE OF PROCESS AND PAPERS, CivPro Appx II.
Appeals, federal cases, FRAP 25(c).
Additional time after service, FRAP 26(c).
Proof of service, FRAP 25(d).
Bankruptcy court, USDistDCBank Appx D.
Mandatory E-filing in civil division, CivPro Appx III.
Complaints, CivPro Appx IV.
United States District Court case management/electronic case filing system.
Criminal proceedings, USDistCt LCrR 49.

ELECTRONIC SIGNATURES IN GLOBAL AND NATIONAL COMMERCE ACT.
Business organizations.
Relation to, §29-107.04.
Collaborative law.
Relation to, §16-4022.
Commercial code.
Documents of title.
Relation of article to treaty, statute, tariff, classification or regulation, §28:7-103.
General provisions.
Effect of commercial code on act, §28:1-108.

ELECTRONIC SIGNATURES IN GLOBAL AND NATIONAL COMMERCE ACT —Cont'd

Uniform certificates of title for vessels.

Relation to, §50-1541.27.

Uniform real property transfers on death act.

Relation to, §19-604.19.

Voting by military and overseas voters.

Relation to, §1-1061.20.

ELECTRONICS, PORTABLE.

Insurance.

Portable electronics insurance, §§31-5051.01 to 31-5051.06.

See PORTABLE ELECTRONICS INSURANCE.

ELECTRONIC TRANSACTIONS, UNIFORM ACT, §§28-4901 to 28-4918.

Acknowledgment requirement, satisfaction, §28-4910.

Agreement to transaction required, §28-4904.

Application of provisions, §28-4903.

Attribution of signature, §28-4908.

Automated transactions, §28-4913.

Change in transmission, §28-4909.

Commercial code.

Documents of title.

Relation of article to treaty, statute, tariff, classification or regulation, §28:7-103.

Control of transferable records, §28-4915.

Definitions, §28-4901.

Error in transmission, §28-4909.

Evidentiary effect of transmission, §28-4912.

Governmental agencies.

Acceptance and distribution procedures, §28-4917.

Discretion of mayor as to application of provisions, §28-4916.

Interoperability standards for cooperation with state and federal agencies, §28-4918.

Legal effect of transaction, §28-4906.

Notarization requirement, satisfaction, §28-4910.

Posting or display of record, §28-4907.

Receipt of transmission.

Time and place, §28-4914.

Retention of records, §28-4911.

ELECTRONIC TRANSACTIONS, UNIFORM ACT —Cont'd

Scope of provisions, §28-4902.

Sending of transmission.

Time and place, §28-4914.

Transferable records, §28-4915.

Uniform construction, §28-4905.

Variation by agreement, §28-4904.

Writing required by law.

Effect of electronic transmission, §28-4907.

ELECTRONIC WASTE, §§8-1041.01 to 8-1041.12.

Agency responsibilities, §8-1041.06.

Confidential information, §8-1041.08.

Definitions, §§8-1031.08, 8-1041.01 to 8-1041.12.

Disposal ban, §8-1041.07.

Enforcement, §8-1041.12.

Extended manufacturer responsibility, generally, §§8-1041.01 to 8-1041.12.

Federal program.

Limitation in event of, §8-1041.11.

Fees, §8-1041.04.

Shortfall fees, §8-1041.04.

Goal for district, §8-1041.02.

Immunity from liability, §8-1041.09.

Manufacturer responsibilities, §8-1041.05.

Registration, §§8-1041.03, 8-1041.04.

Reports, §8-1041.10.

Rules, §8-1041.12.

Supervision, §8-1041.09.

Trade secrets, §8-1041.08.

Violations of act.

Civil fines and penalties, §8-1041.12.

ELECTROSHOCK THERAPY.

Intellectual disabilities, persons with.

Prohibited therapy, §7-1305.06.

ELEEMOSYNARY INSTITUTIONS.

See CHARITABLE INSTITUTIONS.

ELEMENTARY AND SECONDARY EDUCATION ACT OF 1965.

Charter schools, §38-1802.10.

ELEVATORS.

Contractors, mechanics and inspectors, §§47-2853.95 to 47-2853.99.

Business licenses.

Eligibility, §47-2853.96.

Fees, §47-2853.99.

Temporary licenses, §47-2853.98.

ELEVATORS —Cont'd
Contractors, mechanics and inspectors —Cont'd
Definitions, §47-2853.95.
Representations prohibited, §47-2853.97.
Rules and regulations, §47-2853.99.
Scope of practice, §47-2853.95.
Inspections, §2-139.
Power to issue regulations regarding, §1-303.44.
Smoking, §7-1703.
"No Smoking" signs, §7-1704.

THE ELIZABETH MINISTRY, INC. AFFORDABLE HOUSING INITIATIVE.
Real property tax exemption, §47-4657.

ELOIGNMENT.
Replevin, §§16-3712, 16-3713.

E-MAIL.
Cooperative associations.
Voting by electronic mail, §§29-915, 29-916.
Open meeting act.
E-mail exchanges not electronic meeting, §2-577.
Pleadings, motions and other filings.
Signer's e-mail address.
Required information, CivPro Rule 11.
Public records management.
Retention of electronic mail, §2-1706.
Spam deterrence, §§28-5001 to 28-5003.
Damages, §28-5003.
Definitions, §28-5001.
Prohibited acts, §28-5002.

EMANCIPATION DAY.
Defined, §32-1201.
Designated holiday, §§1-612.02, 28-2701.
Parade and fund, §§1-181 to 1-183.

EMBALMERS.
Crimes and offenses.
Failure to report certain deaths, §5-1406.
Suspicious deaths.
Duty to report certain deaths to medical examiner, §5-1405.
Failure to report certain deaths, §5-1406.

EMBALMING, §43-125.

EMBARGOES.
Drug manufacture and distribution licensure, §48-713.

EMBASSIES.
Foreign missions, §§6-1301 to 6-1315.
See FOREIGN MISSIONS.

EMBEZZLEMENT.
Security agents and brokers.
Grounds for disciplinary actions, §31-5602.07.

EMBLEMS.
District of Columbia flag.
Design, advisory commission, donation and grants to replace, §§1-151 to 1-154.
Display, §§1-141 to 1-145.
Insignia of police and fire and emergency medical services departments.
Unauthorized use, §22-1409.

EMERGENCIES.
Adult guardianship and protective proceedings jurisdiction act.
Special jurisdiction, §21-2401.04.
Cable television.
Use of system during emergencies or disasters, §34-1257.06.
Debris removal during emergency, §8-741.
Emergency and non-emergency telephone system assessments fund, §§34-1801 to 34-1806.
Emergency management.
General provisions, §§7-2201 to 7-2404.
See EMERGENCY MANAGEMENT.
Family emergency services program, §4-206.04.
Funeral directors, services during, §3-411.
Homeland security and emergency management agency, §§7-2201 to 7-2209.
See EMERGENCY MANAGEMENT.
Medical services.
See EMERGENCY MEDICAL SERVICES.
Mental illness, hospitalization of persons with, §§21-521 to 21-528.
See HOSPITALIZATION OF PERSONS WITH MENTAL ILLNESS.
Natural disaster consumer protection, §§28-4101 to 28-4103.

EMERGENCIES —Cont'd

911 systems.

Emergency and non-emergency telephone system assessments fund, §§34-1801 to 34-1806.

Public assistance.

See EMERGENCY PUBLIC ASSISTANCE.

Public procurements, §2-354.05.

Volunteer health practitioners, §§7-2361.01 to 7-2361.12.

See EMERGENCY VOLUNTEER HEALTH PRACTITIONERS.

EMERGENCY AND NON-EMERGENCY TELEPHONE SYSTEM ASSESSMENTS FUND, §§34-1801 to 34-1806.

Office of unified communications.

Transfer of authority and operations to office, §1-327.53.

EMERGENCY CRIME VICTIMS' COMPENSATION AWARDS, §4-510, VictComp Rule 37.

EMERGENCY HIGHWAY RELIEF, §9-109.01.

EMERGENCY HOSPITALIZATION.

Mental illness, persons with, §§21-521 to 21-528.

See HOSPITALIZATION OF PERSONS WITH MENTAL ILLNESS.

EMERGENCY MANAGEMENT, §§7-2201 to 7-2404.

Ambulance service fees, §5-416.

Animal emergency preparedness plan, §8-1861.01.

Appropriations, §7-2207.

Civil defense.

Defined, §7-2201.

Interstate civil defense compacts, §7-2209.

Compact.

Emergency management assistance compact, §§7-2331, 7-2332.

Council, transmission of emergency preparedness program to, §7-2303.

Defined terms.

Civil defense, §7-2201.

Emergency, §5-1306.

Emergency operations plan, §7-2301.

Public emergency, §7-2301.

Resource, §7-2301.

EMERGENCY MANAGEMENT —Cont'd

Emergency executive order, §§7-2304 to 7-2308.

Administrative Procedure Act, applicability of, §7-2308.

Duration of, §7-2306.

Issuance of, §7-2304.

Violation of, §7-2307.

Emergency management assistance compact, §§7-2331, 7-2332.

Fire and emergency medical services training for non-District personnel, §§5-431, 5-432.

Homeland security and emergency management agency.

Appointment of police or fire department member to, §§7-2203, 7-2204.

Director, §7-2202.

Establishment of, §7-2202.

Personnel, §7-2202.

Powers and duties, §7-2205.

Program for homeland security, §§7-2231.01 to 7-2231.10.

Reports, §7-2208.

Wages and salaries, §7-2202.

Homeland security commission, §§7-2271.01 to 7-2271.07.

Confidential information, §7-2271.05.

Confidential proceedings, §7-2271.04.

Definitions, §7-2271.01.

Destruction of records, §7-2271.06.

Duties, §7-2271.03.

Established, §7-2271.02.

Members, §7-2271.02.

Reports, §7-2271.07.

Homeland security program, §§7-2231.01 to 7-2231.10.

Definitions, §7-2231.02.

Development of program, §7-2231.03.

Findings of council, §7-2231.01.

Large buildings, security of, §7-2231.06.

Notice to public of emergencies, §7-2231.08.

Private entities, collaboration to improve preparedness, §7-2231.09.

Public employee security training program, §7-2231.05.

Public information and involvement, §7-2231.04.

Readiness exercises, §7-2231.07.

Scope of program, §7-2231.03.

Video interoperability for public safety program.

Rules for use of surveillance technology, §7-2231.10.

EMERGENCY MANAGEMENT
—Cont'd
Interstate civil defense compacts,
§7-2209.
Issuance of regulations, §7-2305.
Liability limitations, §7-2206.
Metropolitan police.
Citizens appointed as special police
without pay, §5-129.03.
Federal government control in
emergencies, §1-207.40.
Miss Utility, §34-2709.
Nuclear weapons freeze, §§7-2401,
7-2404.
Policy declaration, §7-2201.
**Power to issue regulations
regarding,** §1-303.42.
Price gouging prohibitions,
§§28-4101 to 28-4103.
**Program of public emergency
preparedness, establishment and
publication of,** §§7-2302, 7-2303.
Public emergencies, §§7-2301 to
7-2404.
**Public health emergency executive
order,** §7-2304.01.
**Recommendation of legislation
regarding,** §7-2305.
Regional programs and agreements,
§§7-2209, 7-2306.
Reports, §7-2208.
Two-way radio communications,
§§5-1306 to 5-1309.
**Wastewater disposal system,
emergency suspension of,**
§8-105.12.
Water pollution contingency plan,
§8-103.08.

**EMERGENCY MANAGEMENT
ASSISTANCE COMPACT,**
§§7-2331, 7-2332.

EMERGENCY MEDICAL SERVICES,
§§7-2341.01 to 7-2341.29.
Access to, §§31-2801, 31-2802.
Advertising restrictions, §7-2341.20.
Advisory committee, §7-2341.22.
Agencies.
Inspection powers of mayor,
§7-2341.13.
Liability insurance requirement,
§7-2341.09.
License requirement, §7-2341.03.
Medical director to oversee,
§7-2341.03.
**Appeal of decisions regarding
certification,** §7-2341.18.

EMERGENCY MEDICAL SERVICES
—Cont'd
Applicability of provisions,
§7-2341.02.
Automated external defibrillator.
Usage, §§44-231 to 44-235.
Certification.
Appeal of decisions, §7-2341.18.
Denial, suspension or revocation,
§7-2341.15.
Emergency medical technicians,
§5-441.
Flight emergency medical services
personnel, §7-2341.06.
Hearings.
Disciplinary action, §7-2341.17.
Instructors, §7-2341.08.
Liability insurance requirement,
§7-2341.09.
Personnel generally, §7-2341.05.
Previously issued certification or
license, §7-2341.11.
Provisional and restricted licenses and
certifications, §7-2341.10.
Licensees from other jurisdictions,
§7-2341.12.
Reciprocal certification, §7-2341.12.
Renewal, §7-2341.14.
Summary suspension, §7-2341.16.
Training facilities, §7-2341.07.
**Children abused, neglected, or
delinquent,** §16-2338.
Children, services for, §7-2341.21.
Comfort care orders.
Non-resuscitation procedures,
§§7-651.01 to 7-651.16.
**Continuation of existing actions and
proceedings,** §7-2341.28.
**Controlled substances administered
by EMT.**
Supervision required, §48-931.02.
Covered services, mandated,
§31-2802.
Crimes and offenses.
Failure to notify medical examiner of
certain deaths, §5-1406.
Obstruction, prevention, or
interference with request for
ambulance or emergency medical
assistance, §22-1931.
Dead bodies.
Duty to report certain deaths to
medical examiner, §5-1405.
Failure to report certain deaths,
§5-1406.
Death, presumptions as to, §§5-651 to
5-656.

EMERGENCY MEDICAL SERVICES
—Cont'd
Definitions, §§7-2341.01, 31-2801.
Disability benefits.
Presumptions, §§5-651 to 5-656.
Do not resuscitate procedures.
Comfort care orders, §§7-651.01 to
7-651.16.
Bracelet or necklace, §7-651.04.
Decision to resuscitate, §7-651.07.
Decision to withhold resuscitation,
§7-651.06.
Definitions, §7-651.01.
Effective date, §7-651.16.
EMS decision to resuscitate,
§7-651.07.
EMS decision to withhold
resuscitation, §7-651.06.
EMS personnel to recognize bracelet
or necklace, §7-651.04.
Execution and issuance, §7-651.02.
Execution as condition for receiving
health care services, §7-651.13.
Falsification, forgery, other actions
causing resuscitation to be
withheld causing death,
§7-651.12.
Fee charged by mayor, §7-651.14.
Form approved by mayor, §7-651.03.
Immunity from liability, §7-651.11.
Interventions to alleviate pain
where bracelet or necklace
defaced, §7-651.08.
Issuance by attending physician,
§7-651.02.
Life insurance not affected,
§7-651.13.
Person who may execute, §7-651.02.
Reciprocity, §7-651.09.
Religious or moral reasons person
unwilling or unable to comply,
§7-651.11.
Revocation, §7-651.05.
Rules, §7-651.15.
Statement included, §7-651.03.
Suicide or assisting in suicide
excluded, §7-651.13.
Training and education, §7-651.10.
Unlawful homicide, §7-651.12.
EMAC.
Advisory committee, §7-2341.22.
Emergency response vehicles.
Advertising of ambulance service,
§7-2341.20.
Inspections, §7-2341.13.
Liability insurance requirement,
§7-2341.09.

EMERGENCY MEDICAL SERVICES
—Cont'd
Emergency response vehicles
—Cont'd
License requirements, §7-2341.04.
Exemptions from provisions,
§7-2341.02.
**Fees for emergency ambulance
service,** §5-416.
**Fire and emergency medical
services training for non-District
personnel,** §§5-431, 5-432.
Firefighters.
Fire and emergency services
department personnel.
Service longevity, §5-544.01.
Transfer to uniformed firefighters.
Fire and emergency services
department personnel,
§§5-409.01, 5-544.01.
**Flight emergency medical services
personnel.**
Certification, §7-2341.06.
Good Samaritan act.
Immunity for rendering care or
assistance, §7-401.
**Government employer-assisted
housing program,** §§42-2501 to
42-2507.
Grandfather clause.
Previously issued certification or
license, §7-2341.11.
**Health-care durable powers of
attorney.**
Provision of emergency health care
without consent, §21-2212.
**HIV screening test while receiving
emergency medical services.**
Health care coverage, §31-2803.
Hospital discharge planning,
§§21-2231.01 to 21-2231.05.
**Immunity for rendering care or
assistance,** §7-401.
Injunction of violations, §7-2341.26.
Instructors.
Certification, §7-2341.08.
Insurance.
Liability insurance requirement,
§7-2341.09.
Liability insurance requirement,
§7-2341.09.
Licenses. See within this heading,
"Certification."
Mayor's powers and duties,
§7-2341.13.
Rulemaking, §7-2341.23.

EMERGENCY MEDICAL SERVICES
—Cont'd
Mental illness, hospitalization of persons with, §§21-521 to 21-528.
See HOSPITALIZATION OF PERSONS WITH MENTAL ILLNESS.
Obstruction, prevention, or interference with request for ambulance or emergency medical assistance, §22-1931.
Penalties for violations, §7-2341.24.
Pending actions and proceedings, §7-2341.28.
Presumptive disability or death, §§5-651 to 5-656.
Applicability, §5-656.
Cancer, §5-653.
Definitions, §5-651.
Disqualification from presumption, §5-655.
Heart disease or hypertension, §5-652.
Infectious disease, §5-654.
Maintaining eligibility, §5-655.01.
Physical examination, §5-655.01.
Preemployment physical examination, defined, §5-651.
Reporting requirements, §5-655.02.
Respiratory disease, §5-652.
Rules, §5-655.03.
Provisional and restricted licenses and certifications, §7-2341.10.
Licensees from other jurisdictions, §7-2341.12.
Reciprocal certification, §7-2341.12.
Repeal of existing provisions, §7-2341.27.
Rulemaking by mayor, §7-2341.23.
Training facilities.
Advertising restrictions regarding training, §7-2341.20.
Certification, §7-2341.07.
Inspections, §7-2341.13.
Instructor certification, §7-2341.08.
Liability insurance requirement, §7-2341.09.
Trauma care system, §7-2341.19.
Violations.
Injunctions, §7-2341.26.
Penalties, §7-2341.24.
Prosecutions, §7-2341.25.
Wages and salaries.
Fire and emergency medical services overtime settlement fund, §5-525.01.
Applicability, §5-525.02.

EMERGENCY ORDERS.
Collaborative law, §16-4007.
Guardianship of incapacitated persons, §21-2046.
Hospitalization of persons with mental illness.
Court orders, §§21-523 to 21-528.
EMERGENCY PUBLIC ASSISTANCE.
Burial assistance programs, §4-1001.
Crisis assistance and service program, §4-206.02.
Emergency shelter allowances, §4-206.05.
Family emergency services program, §4-206.04.
Motor vehicles.
Retention, §4-205.41.
Sexual assault victims, §§7-2121 to 7-2125.
EMERGENCY RESERVE FUND, §1-204.50a.
Short-term borrowing, §47-369.03.
EMERGENCY TEMPORARY RULES.
Occupational safety and health, §32-1109.
EMERGENCY VOLUNTEER HEALTH PRACTITIONERS, §§7-2361.01 to 7-2361.12.
Applicability of law, §7-2361.02.
Uniformity, §7-2361.12.
Credentialing, effect on, §7-2361.06.
Definitions, §7-2361.01.
Immunity, §7-2361.10.
Privileging, effect on, §7-2361.06.
Prohibited acts, §7-2361.07.
Reciprocity, §7-2361.05.
Registration systems, §7-2361.04.
Regulation of services, §7-2361.03.
Relation to other laws, §7-2361.08.
Rulemaking authority, §7-2361.09.
Statutory construction, §7-2361.12.
Workers' compensation coverage, §7-2361.11.
EMINENT DOMAIN, §§16-1301 to 16-1385.
Abandonment of proceedings by District, §16-1321.
Appraisal.
Objection, §16-1318.
Assignment of judge for, §16-1302.
Attached property, §§16-524, 16-525, 16-555.
Building lines, §§6-402, 6-403.

EMINENT DOMAIN —Cont'd
Compliant filed in name of District,
§16-1311.
Condemnation proceedings.
See CONDEMNATION
PROCEEDINGS.
Condominiums, §42-1901.06.
Constitution of the United States,
US Const Amd 5.
Convention center hotel,
§§10-1202.31 to 10-1202.33.
Declaration of taking, §16-1314.
Adjustment of charges, §16-1316.
Compensation ascertained and
awarded by judgment, §16-1314.
Deposit in registry of court upon filing
declaration, §16-1314.
Distribution of money deposited on
declaration of taking, §16-1315.
Interest as part of just compensation
awarded, §16-1314.
Surrender of property under
declaration, §16-1316.
Dulles International Airport, §9-803.
**Excess property for development of
seat of government,** §§16-1331 to
16-1337.
Excess property for United States,
§§16-1381 to 16-1385.
Highways, §§9-101.05, 9-101.09,
9-101.18.
Horizontal property regimes,
§42-2029.
**Juries for condemnation
proceedings,** §§16-1312, 16-1313.
Objections, §16-1317.
Jurisdiction, §§16-1301, 16-1303.
**Metropolitan Washington Airports
Authority,** §9-909.
Metrorail and metrobus.
Acquisition of mass transit bus
systems, §9-1113.06.
Washington metropolitan area transit
authority compact, §9-1107.01.
National Capital Housing Authority,
§6-101.02.
New jury trial.
Appraisement vacated and set aside,
§16-1318.
**New Town at Capital City Market
revitalization,** §6-1062.07.
Payment of amount awarded,
§16-1319.
Procedure for condemnation, CivPro
Rule 71A.
Complaint, CivPro Form CA 29.

EMINENT DOMAIN —Cont'd
Procedure for condemnation
—Cont'd
Notice, CivPro Form CA 28.
Railroads, §9-1203.06.
Real property for the District,
§§16-1311 to 16-1321.
Real property for United States,
§§16-1352 to 16-1368.
Additional court powers regarding,
§16-1368.
Adjustment of charges, §16-1355.
Appeals, §16-1365.
Condemnation proceedings, §§16-1352
to 16-1368.
Declaration of taking, §§16-1353 to
16-1355.
Deficiency judgments, §§16-1354,
16-1365.
Definition of acquiring authority,
§16-1351.
Evidence, §16-1360.
Judgments and decrees, §§16-1363 to
16-1365.
Jury trials, §§16-1356 to 16-1362.
Payment of compensation, §§16-1364,
16-1366.
Surrender of possession, §§16-1355,
16-1367.
Verdict, §16-1361.
Vesting of title, §16-1366.
**Real property tax special
assessments,** §47-1204.
**Settlements for real estate acquired
by,** §1-301.04.
Telegraph and telephone companies,
§34-1921.08.
Transfer of title, §16-1314.
Upon payment of award, §16-1319.
Verdict.
Fixing time for return, §16-1320.
**Washington convention and sports
authority,** §§10-1202.31 to
10-1202.33.
Wastewater treatment systems.
Compensation of property owners,
§8-205.
False claims for compensation, §8-205.
Witnesses, assessment officials as,
§14-308.

EMINENT PERSONS.
**Foreign doctors of eminence and
authority.**
Licensure of, §3-1205.09a.
Receptions for, §1-333.09.

EMISSIONS.
Alternative fuel technology.
Emission credit trading program,
§50-713.
Emission standards for, §50-707.
Inspection of motor vehicles,
§§50-1101 to 50-1110.
See MOTOR VEHICLE
REGISTRATION.
Low-emissions vehicle program.
Establishment.
Adoption of California standards
and compliance requirements,
§50-731.
Registering vehicles not in
compliance.
Prohibition, §50-732.

**EMMAUS REHABILITATION
PROJECT.**
Real property tax exemptions,
§47-1057.

**EMPLOYEE COMPENSATION
LIABILITY INSURANCE
COMPANIES.**
Rate approval, §31-5205.

**EMPLOYEES RETIREMENT
PROGRAM MANAGEMENT,**
§§1-701 to 1-753.
**Annual report for each retirement
program,** §1-732.
Fling and furnishing information to
participants, §1-734.
Appropriations, §1-724.
Benefit rights.
Furnishing to participant or
beneficiary, §1-735.
Breach of fiduciary duty, §1-742.
**Convictions preventing persons
from holding certain positions,**
§1-744.
Criminal penalties, §1-739.
Definitions, §1-702.
Investment of public funds in certain
companies doing business with
government of Iran, §1-336.01.
Investment of public funds in certain
companies doing business with
government of Sudan, §1-335.01.
Denial of claim for benefits, §§1-751
to 1-753.
Applicability of provisions, §1-752.
Compliance by mayor, §1-753.
Notice of denial, §1-751.
Review, §1-751.
When claim filed, §1-751.

**EMPLOYEES RETIREMENT
PROGRAM MANAGEMENT**
—Cont'd
Disclosure, §§1-731 to 1-739.
**District of Columbia Retirement
Board,** §1-711.
Fiduciary duty, breach, §1-742.
Fiduciary responsibilities of board,
§§1-741 to 1-748.
Fines, §1-739.
Funds.
Investment limitations, §1-721.
Iran, certain companies doing
business with government of,
§§1-336.01 to 1-336.06.
Sudan, certain companies doing
business with government of,
§§1-335.01 to 1-335.07.
Iran, investment in certain companies
doing business with government
of, §§1-336.01 to 1-336.06.
Judges' retirement fund, §1-714.
Management requirements, §1-715.
Payments from, §1-716.
Payments to.
Appropriations authorized as,
§1-724.
Federal and District governments,
from, §1-722.
Police and firefighters retirement and
disability, §1-712.
Sudan, investment in certain
companies doing business with
government of, §§1-335.01 to
1-335.07.
Teachers' retirement fund, §1-713.
Information about programs,
§§1-723, 1-734 to 1-738.
Iran.
Investment of public funds in certain
companies doing business with
Iran, §§1-336.01 to 1-336.06.
Actions taken by public fund,
§1-336.03.
Definitions, §1-336.01.
Identification of companies,
§1-336.02.
Indemnification of board members
and employees, §1-336.05.
Notice to scrutinized companies,
§1-336.03.
Reporting, §1-336.04.
Scrutinized companies list,
§1-336.02.
Penalties, §1-739.

EMPLOYEES RETIREMENT PROGRAM MANAGEMENT
—Cont'd
Police and firefighters retirement and disability.
General provisions, §§5-631 to 5-762.
See POLICE AND FIREFIGHTERS RETIREMENT AND DISABILITY.
Policy declaration, §1-701.
Public information, §1-736.
Records, §§1-731 to 1-739.
Retention, §1-737.
Reports, §§1-731 to 1-739.
Annual reports, §1-732.
Fling and furnishing information to participants, §1-734.
Iran, investment of public funds in certain companies doing business with, §1-336.04.
Participants benefit rights, §1-735.
Public information, §1-736.
Sudan, investment of public funds in certain companies doing business with government of, §1-335.04.
Retention of records, §1-737.
Sudan.
Investment of public funds in certain companies doing business with Sudanese government, §§1-335.01 to 1-335.07.
Definitions, §1-335.01.
Enforcement by mayor, §1-335.07.
Identification of companies, §1-335.02.
Indemnification of board members or employees, §1-335.05.
Reinvestment in certain companies with active business operations, §1-335.06.
Reporting, §1-335.04.
Required actions, §1-335.03.
Summary plan descriptions, §§1-733, 1-909.03.
Teachers' retirement fund, §1-713.

EMPLOYER-ASSISTED HOUSING PROGRAM, §§42-2501 to 42-2507.
See GOVERNMENT EMPLOYER-ASSISTED HOUSING PROGRAM.

EMPLOYER-PAID PERSONNEL SERVICES.
See EMPLOYMENT AGENCIES.

EMPLOYERS AND EMPLOYEES.
Labor and employment relations.
See LABOR AND EMPLOYMENT RELATIONS.

EMPLOYMENT AGENCIES, §§32-401 to 32-416.
Arbitration, §32-413.
Bonds, surety, §32-403.
Cease and desist orders, §32-412.
Definitions, §32-401.
Delegation of powers, §32-415.
Discrimination, §32-408.
Exemptions to provisions, §32-416.
Fines, §32-414.
Investigations, §32-410.
Issuance of rules and regulations, §32-415.
Licenses, §32-402.
Mediation, §32-413.
Notice, §32-404.
Operating requirements.
Employer-paid personnel services, §32-406.
Employment agencies, §32-404.
Employment counseling services, §32-405.
Job-listing services, §32-407.
Penalties, §32-414.
Privacy and confidentiality, §32-409.
Unemployment discrimination, §§32-1361 to 32-1368.
Applicability, §32-1368.
Definitions, §32-1361.
Effective date, §32-1368.
Enforcement of provisions, §32-1365.
Exemptions, §32-1364.
Penalties for violations, §32-1366.
Prohibited, §32-1362.
Retaliation, §32-1363.
Rules, §32-1367.
Witnesses, §32-411.

EMPLOYMENT DISCRIMINATION, §§2-1402.01 to 2-1402.13.
Backpay or frontpay awarded.
Income averaging for tax purposes, §47-1806.10.
Blind and visually impaired, §7-1005.
Equal employment opportunity.
See EQUAL EMPLOYMENT OPPORTUNITY.
Exceptions, §2-1402.12.
Income averaging for tax purposes.
Backpay or frontpay awarded, §47-1806.10.
Persons with disabilities, §7-1005.
Pregnant and nursing workers.
Reasonable accommodations for, §§32-1231.01 to 32-1231.15.
Records and reports, §2-1402.52.
Smokers, against, §7-1703.03.

EMPLOYMENT DISCRIMINATION
—Cont'd
Unemployment status, §§32-1361 to
32-1368.
Applicability, §32-1368.
Definitions, §32-1361.
Effective date, §32-1368.
Enforcement of provisions, §32-1365.
Exemptions, §32-1364.
Penalties for violations, §32-1366.
Prohibited, §32-1362.
Retaliation, §32-1363.
Rules, §32-1367.
Workplace smoking, §7-1703.03.

EMPLOYMENT OF MINORS,
§§32-201 to 32-224.
See CHILD LABOR.

EMPLOYMENT SERVICES
DEPARTMENT.
Job training and adult education
programs.
Quarterly reporting by department,
§32-771.
Pregnant and nursing workers,
reasonable accommodations for.
Administrative enforcement,
§32-1231.07.
Public education, services,
§32-1231.05.

EN BANC PROCEEDINGS.
Appeals, federal cases, FRAP 35,
USCtApp Rule 35.
Petitions for hearing or rehearing,
USCtApp Rule 35.
Petition for hearing or rehearing en
banc, DCCtApp Rule 35.

ENCLOSURE.
Deteriorated structures, §§42-3173.01
to 42-3173.12.
Ejectment, §16-1113.

ENCLOSURE REQUIREMENTS.
Cemeteries, §43-105.

END HOMELESSNESS FUND,
§1-325.261.

ENDORSEMENTS.
Bank deposits and collections.
Collection of items by depository and
collecting banks.
Items endorsed "pay any bank,"
§28:4-201.
Missing endorsements.
Supplying, §28:4-205.

ENDORSEMENTS —Cont'd
Documents of title.
Negotiation and transfer.
Delivery without endorsement,
§28:7-506.
Endorser not guarantor for other
parties, §28:7-505.
Right to compel endorsement,
§28:7-506.
Negotiable instruments.
Anomalous endorsement, §28:3-205.
Blank endorsement, §28:3-205.
Defined, §28:3-204.
Discharge of endorser, §28:3-605.
Fraudulent endorsement.
Responsibility of employer for
fraudulent endorsement of
employee, §28:3-405.
Generally, §28:3-205.
Imposters, §28:3-405.
Obligation of endorser, §28:3-415.
Reacquisition, §28:3-205.
Restrictive endorsements, §28:3-206.
Signatures.
Proof of signatures, §28:3-308.
Special endorsement, §28:3-205.
Transfer of security interests,
§28:3-204.

ENDOWMENT CONTRACTS.
Life insurance company pure
endowment contracts, filing,
§31-4705.

ENERGY CONSERVATION.
Bond issues, §§8-1778.21 to 8-1778.31.
Authorization, §8-1778.22.
Closing documents, §8-1778.26.
Debt cap, §8-1778.30.
Financing documents, §8-1778.26.
Limited liability, §8-1778.27.
Payment, §8-1778.23.
Personal liability, §8-1778.28.
Private lending institutions,
§8-1778.31.
Sales, §8-1778.25.
Security, §8-1778.23.
Terms, §8-1778.24.
Transcripts of proceedings, §8-1778.29.
Commercial property energy
conservation, §§8-1772.01 to
8-1772.04.
Definitions, §8-1772.01.
Penalties for violations, §8-1772.03.
Requirements, §8-1772.02.
Rules, §8-1772.04.

ENERGY CONSERVATION —Cont'd

District of Columbia energy plan,
§§8-171.01 to 8-171.07, 8-1779.01 to 8-1779.03.
See DISTRICT OF COLUMBIA.

Energy efficiency financing.
Definitions, §8-1778.01.
Public purpose, §8-1778.02.

Energy efficiency standards,
§§8-1771.01 to 8-1771.06.

Government energy reduction,
§8-1777.01.

Green buildings, §§6-1451.01 to 6-1451.11.
See GREEN BUILDINGS.

National capital energy fund.
Administrators.
Contract to obtain, §8-1778.45.
Oversight, §8-1778.44.
Establishment, §8-1778.41.
Loans.
Applications, §8-1778.42.
Approval, §8-1778.43.
Quality assurance program, §8-1778.46.
Rulemaking authority, §8-1778.48.
Workforce development and employment plan, §8-1778.47.

Real property taxes, special assessments, §§47-895.31 to 47-895.35.
See REAL PROPERTY TAXES.

Special energy assessment fund, §8-1778.21.

ENERGY EFFICIENCY STANDARDS, §§8-1771.01 to 8-1771.06.

Applicability of provisions, §8-1771.02.

Definitions, §§8-1771.01, 8-1771.06.

Enforcement, §8-1771.05.

Generally, §8-1771.03.

Liquid-immersed distribution transformers.
Electric company purchase of.
Public service commission rules, §§8-1771.06, 34-302.01.

New and revised standards, §8-1771.04.

Scope of provisions, §8-1771.02.

Testing of samples of products, §8-1771.05.

ENGINEERED SHARPS INJURY PROTECTION.
Safe needle distribution, §§7-2851 to 7-2858.

ENGINEERS.

Board of professional engineering, §§47-2853.06 to 47-2853.10.

Business licenses, §§47-2853.131 to 47-2853.133.
Eligibility, §47-2853.132.
Representations prohibited, §47-2853.133.
Scope of practice, §47-2853.131.

Public procurement, §2-356.04.

ENTAILED ESTATES.

Abolition and recognition as fee simple estates, §42-502.

ENTERPRISE ZONES.

Business improvement districts, §§2-1215.01 to 2-1215.71.
See BUSINESS IMPROVEMENT DISTRICTS.

Business incubator facilitation, §§2-1209.01 to 2-1209.14.

Homeowners in enterprise zones tax abatement, §§47-858.01 to 47-858.05.

Small and certified business enterprise development and assistance, §§2-218.01 to 2-218.75.
See SMALL AND CERTIFIED BUSINESS ENTERPRISE DEVELOPMENT AND ASSISTANCE.

Study commission, §§2-1211.01 to 2-1211.06.
Compensation, §2-1211.06.
Duties, §2-1211.04.
Established, §2-1211.03.
Findings, §2-1211.02.
Purposes, statement of, §2-1211.01.
Report, §2-1211.05.

ENTERTAINMENTS.

Alcoholic beverage licenses.
Arena licenses, §25-114.
Entertainment endorsements, §25-113a.
Temporary licenses, §25-115.

Business licenses, §§47-2820 to 47-2826.

Child labor, §32-206.

Made in DC program, §§2-1208.31 to 2-1208.35.

Police and firefighters assigned to theaters, §47-2820.

Race discrimination in admission to licensed places, §§47-2901 to 47-2911.

ENTITY TRANSACTIONS,
§§29-201.01 to 29-205.06.
Appraisal rights, §29-201.09.
Approval.
Alternative methods, §29-201.08.
Required, §29-201.04.
Bequests, devises, gifts or grants to merging entity.
Inures to surviving entity, §29-201.04.
Conversion.
See BUSINESS ORGANIZATIONS.
Definitions, §29-201.02.
Domestication, §§29-205.01 to 29-205.06.
See BUSINESS ORGANIZATIONS.
General provisions, §§29-201.01 to 29-201.09.
Interest exchanges, §§29-203.01 to 29-203.06.
See BUSINESS ORGANIZATIONS.
Mergers and consolidations, §§29-202.01 to 29-202.06.
See MERGERS AND CONSOLIDATIONS.
Nonexclusivity of provisions, §29-201.06.
Notice, §29-201.04.
Reference to extrinsic facts, §29-201.07.
Short title, §29-201.01.
Status of filings, §29-201.05.
Statutory construction, §29-201.03.

ENVIRONMENTAL COVENANTS,
§§8-671.01 to 8-671.14.
Actions.
Enforcement, §8-671.10.
Amendment.
Consent, §8-671.09.
Court action, §8-671.08.
Contents, §8-671.03.
Definitions, §8-671.01.
Duration, §8-671.08.
Electronic signatures in global and national commerce act.
Relation to federal act, §8-671.14.
Enforcement, §8-671.10.
Nature of rights, §8-671.02.
Notice, §8-671.06.
Substitute notice, §8-671.11.
Other instruments.
Effect on, §8-671.04.
Other land-use law.
Relationship of provisions to, §8-671.05.
Recordation, §8-671.07.
Registry, §8-671.11.

ENVIRONMENTAL COVENANTS
—Cont'd
Rulemaking, §8-671.12.
Subordination of interests, §8-671.02.
Termination, §8-671.08.
Consent, §8-671.09.
Uniformity of application and construction, §8-671.13.
Validity, §8-671.04.
Failure to provide notice.
Validity not affected, §8-671.06.

ENVIRONMENTAL HEALTH AGENCY.
Brownfield revitalization.
Hazardous substances releases.
Liability, cleanup, response, §§8-631.01 to 8-638.01.
See HAZARDOUS SUBSTANCES RELEASES.

ENVIRONMENTAL IMPACT STATEMENTS, §§8-109.01 to 8-109.12.
Adverse impact, finding of, §8-109.04.
Appeals, §8-109.08.
Defined terms pertinent to, §8-109.02.
Exemptions to requirements regarding, §8-109.06.
Fees, §8-109.12.
Interpretation of provisions, §8-109.10.
Issuance of rules and regulations regarding, §8-109.09.
Judicial review, §8-109.08.
Lead agencies, §§8-109.02, 8-109.07.
Policy declaration, §8-109.01.
Public utilities, §§34-2601 to 34-2604.
Requirements and procedures, §8-109.03.
Solid waste facilities, §8-109.11.
Supplemental, §8-109.05.

ENVIRONMENTAL PROGRAMS, SCHOOL, §§38-825.01 to 38-825.03.
Applicability of law, §38-828.02.
Environmental literacy program, §38-825.02.
Office, §38-825.01.
Rulemaking authority, §38-828.01.
School gardens program, §38-825.03.

ENVIRONMENTAL PROTECTION.
Air pollution, §§8-101.05 to 8-101.06.
See AIR POLLUTION.
Anacostia river cleanup and protection, §§8-102.01 to 8-102.07.
Anacostia river cleanup and protection fertilizer act, §§8-104.01 to 8-104.07.

ENVIRONMENTAL PROTECTION
—Cont'd
Anacostia river toxics remediation.
Remediation of contaminated
sediment, §8-104.31.
**Anacostia waterfront development
zone.**
Environmental standards, §§2-1226.31
to 2-1226.41.
See ANACOSTIA WATERFRONT
DEVELOPMENT ZONE.
Asbestos licensing and control,
§§8-111.01 to 8-111.14.
See ASBESTOS CONTRACTORS.
Cleanup of contaminated property.
Hazardous substances releases,
§§8-631.01 to 8-638.01.
See HAZARDOUS SUBSTANCES
RELEASES.
Department of the environment,
§§8-151.01 to 8-151.15.
Administrative division.
Director authorized to establish,
§8-151.06.
Appropriated funds.
Implementing chapter when
available, §8-151.15.
Brownfields redevelopment division.
Establishment authorized, duties,
§8-151.06.
Community programming and
education outreach division.
Establishment authorized, duties,
§8-151.06.
Compilation of laws and regulations
relating to environment.
Publication, supplementing,
§8-151.14.
Comprehensive natural resource
management and protection plan.
Duty of director to prepare and
submit to mayor and council,
§8-151.08.
Definitions, §8-151.01.
Director.
Appointment, compensation,
§8-151.04.
Authority, §8-151.07.
Duties, §8-151.08.
Successor to environmental related
authority, §8-151.05.
Energy management and air quality
control division.
Establishment authorized, duties,
§8-151.06.
Established, §8-151.03.

ENVIRONMENTAL PROTECTION
—Cont'd
Department of the environment
—Cont'd
Federal environmental laws,
regulations and standards.
Primacy to enforce, achieving,
§8-151.12.
Federal grants.
Authority of director to apply for
and receive, §8-151.07.
Grants office.
Establishment, duties, §8-151.09.
Government relations and policy
division.
Establishment authorized, duties,
§8-151.06.
Grants office.
Authority of director to establish,
§8-151.07.
Establishment, §8-151.09.
Natural resources and water quality
division.
Establishment authorized, duties,
§8-151.06.
Organization, §8-151.06.
Organizational plan.
Mayor to submit, time, §8-151.03.
Powers and duties, §8-151.03.
Purpose of chapter, §8-151.02.
Recycling and solid waste
management division.
Establishment authorized, duties,
§8-151.06.
Rulemaking, §§8-151.10, 8-151.11.
Continuation of rules of transferred
agencies, §8-151.11.
Smart lighting study.
Definitions, §8-1776.01.
Reports, §8-1776.02.
State of the environment report.
Duty of director submit to council,
§8-151.08.
Transfers to department, §8-151.03.
Continuation of rules of transferred
agencies, §8-151.11.
Environmental impact statements,
§§8-109.01 to 8-109.12.
See ENVIRONMENTAL IMPACT
STATEMENTS.
Fertilizer.
Anacostia river cleanup and protection
fertilizer act, §§8-104.01 to
8-104.07.
Innovation fund, §§1-325.221 to
1-325.226.

ENVIRONMENTAL PROTECTION
—Cont'd
Lead-hazard prevention and elimination, §§8-231.01 to 8-231.20.
See LEAD-HAZARD PREVENTION AND ELIMINATION.
Paint stewardship, §§8-233.01 to 8-233.06.
Pesticides.
General provisions, §§8-401 to 8-440.
See PESTICIDES.
Plastic and other disposable bags, §§8-102.02 to 8-102.04.
Radon contractor proficiency, §§28-4201 to 28-4203.
Releases of hazardous substances.
Liability, cleanup, response, §§8-631.01 to 8-638.01.
See HAZARDOUS SUBSTANCES RELEASES.
Smoking restrictions.
General provisions, §§7-1701 to 7-1731.
See SMOKING.
Stormwater management, §§8-152.01 to 8-153.01.
See STORMWATER MANAGEMENT.
Underground storage tanks.
General provisions, §§8-113.01 to 8-113.12.
See UNDERGROUND STORAGE TANKS.
Wastewater control.
General provisions, §§8-105.01 to 8-105.15.
See WASTEWATER DISPOSAL SYSTEM.
Phosphate cleaners, §§8-107.01 to 8-107.04.
Water pollution.
General provisions, §§8-103.01 to 8-103.20.
See WATER POLLUTION.

EPAMD.
Electric personal assistive mobility devices.
Defined, §50-2201.01.
Exemption from regulations governing motor vehicles, §50-2201.03a.
Operation and registration requirements, §50-2201.04a.
Regulation, §50-2201.03a.

EQUAL ACCESS FOR BLIND AND OTHER PERSONS WITH PHYSICAL DISABILITIES.
Employment, §7-1005.

EQUAL ACCESS FOR BLIND AND OTHER PERSONS WITH PHYSICAL DISABILITIES
—Cont'd
Housing, §7-1006.
Pedestrians who are blind or deaf.
Safety standards for drivers of motor vehicles, §7-1004.
Penalties, §7-1007.
Public places, accommodations, and conveyances, §§7-1001, 7-1002.

EQUAL EMPLOYMENT OPPORTUNITY, §§2-1402.01 to 2-1402.13.
Affirmative action.
See AFFIRMATIVE ACTION.
Affirmative action plans.
Merit system, §1-607.01.
Disabilities, persons with.
Equal employment opportunity, §1-607.02.
Merit system, §§1-607.01 to 1-607.08.
Religious beliefs, reasonable accommodation for, §1-607.01.
Reporting requirements, §2-1402.13.
Selection procedures, §§1-607.04 to 1-607.06.
Evidence of validity, §1-607.06.
Relation to job required, §1-607.05.
Statement of purpose, §1-607.04.
Sex discrimination in benefit programs, §1-607.07.
Small and certified business enterprise development and assistance, §§2-218.01 to 2-218.75.
See SMALL AND CERTIFIED BUSINESS ENTERPRISE DEVELOPMENT AND ASSISTANCE.
Veterans preferences, §1-607.03.

EQUAL PAY.
Pay equity and training commission, §§32-601 to 32-609.

EQUAL PROTECTION, US Const Amd 14.

EQUITY.
Uniform trust code.
Principles of equity, applicability, §19-1301.06.
Voting by military and overseas voters, §1-1061.18.

ERRORS AND MISTAKES.
See MISTAKE OR ERROR.

ESCAPE.

Competence to proceed.

Incompetent criminal defendants.

Hospital defendant order confined,
§24-531.13.

Correctional institution or officer,
§22-2601.

District guardianship of minor,
§4-125.

Extradition.

See EXTRADITION.

Incompetent criminal defendants.

Competence to proceed.

Hospital defendant order confined,
§24-531.13.

Juvenile offenders, §10-509.01a.

Juvenile residential facilities,
§10-509.01a.

Mental illness, persons with.

Hospitalization, MentalHealth Rule
11.

Public welfare institutions, §§4-125,
10-509.01a.

ESCHEAT.

Intestate succession, §19-701.

Surviving spouse and children.

Renunciation of devise and bequest,
§19-113.

ESCROW ACCOUNTS.

Condominiums, §42-1904.09.

**Continuing care retirement
communities.**

Entrance fee, §44-151.09.

Mortgage lenders and brokers,
§26-1115.

**Real estate brokers and
salespersons,** §42-1704.

Title insurance producers,
§31-5041.06.

Title insurers, §31-5031.14.

E-SIGN ACT.

Business organizations.

Relation to, §29-107.04.

ESTATES.

Decedents' estates.

See DECEDENTS' ESTATES.

Deed, created otherwise than by,
§28-3501.

Income tax on, §§47-1809.01 to
47-1809.10.

Powers of appointment, §§42-1001 to
42-1019.

See POWERS OF APPOINTMENT.

Powers of attorney, §21-2111.

ESTATES —Cont'd

Statute of frauds, §§28-3501 to
28-3505.

Sufferance, estates by, §28-3501.

ESTATES BY SUFFERANCE.

Estate created other than by deed,
§28-3501.

ESTATES IN LAND, §§42-501 to
42-523.

At will estates, §§42-504, 42-522.

Chattel interests, §42-504.

Chattels real, §§42-504, 42-505.

Conditions precedent or subsequent,
§42-504.

Coparcenary estates, abolition of,
§42-517.

**Entailed estates abolished and
recognized as fee simple estates,**
§42-502.

Expectancy, estates in, §§42-506,
42-508, 42-514, 42-515.

Fee simple estates.

See FEE SIMPLE ESTATES.

Freeholds, §§42-504, 42-505.

Future estates, §§42-305, 42-510 to
42-513.

Joint tenancies, §42-516.

Life estates.

Allowance for life estate, CivPro Rule
307.

Probate proceedings, Probate Rule 6.

Month to month, estates by, §42-521.

Personal property, applicable to,
§42-523.

Possession, estates in, §§42-506,
42-507.

Pur autre vie, estates for, §42-505.

Quarter to quarter, estates by,
§42-521.

Recognized estates, §42-501.

Reversions, §42-509.

Sufferance, estates by, §§28-3501,
42-504, 42-520.

Tenancies in common, §42-516.

Tenants by the entirety, §42-516.

Years, estates for.

Chattels real, recognition as, §42-504.

Defined, §42-518.

Estates expressed from year to year,
§42-519.

ESTATE TAXES.

General provisions, §§47-3701 to
47-3722.

See INHERITANCE AND ESTATE
TAXES.

ESTIMATED TAX.
Banks, financial institutions, and
  insurance companies, §47-2509.
Income taxes, §47-1812.14.

ETHANOL.
Alternative fuel technology, §§50-701
  to 50-715.
  See ALTERNATIVE FUEL
    TECHNOLOGY.

ETHICS.
Conduct, standards of.
  See CONDUCT, STANDARDS OF.

ETHICS AND GOVERNMENT
  ACCOUNTABILITY BOARD,
  §§1-1161.01 to 1-1164.01.
Advisory opinions, §1-1162.19.
Appeals, §1-1162.17.
Applicability of provisions,
  §1-1162.01a.
Budget, §1-1162.07.
Campaign finance, §§1-1163.01 to
  1-1163.38.
  See CAMPAIGN FINANCE.
Citations of provisions, §1-1162.01.
Compensation, §1-1162.03.
Complaint dismissal, §1-1162.16.
Composition, §1-1162.03.
Conflicts of interest, §1-1162.23.
Contempt, §1-1162.21.
Definitions, §1-1161.01.
Director powers, §1-1162.11.
Dismissals, §1-1162.16.
Disposition of presented evidence,
  §1-1162.15.
Establishment, §1-1162.02.
Financial interest disclosures,
  §1-1162.25.
Formal investigations, §1-1162.13.
Fund, §1-1162.10.
Hearings, §1-1162.14.
Honoraria limitations, §1-1162.26.
Investigations.
  Dismissal, §1-1162.16.
  Formal, §1-1162.13.
  Preliminary, §1-1162.12.
Lobbyists, §§1-1162.27 to 1-1162.32.
  See LOBBYING.
Meetings, §1-1162.04.
  Quorum, §1-1162.08.
Members, §1-1162.03.
  Compensation, §1-1162.05.
Meritless claims, §1-1162.16.
Penalties for violations, §1-1162.21.
  Public officials, §1-1162.22.
Preliminary investigations,
  §1-1162.12.

ETHICS AND GOVERNMENT
  ACCOUNTABILITY BOARD
  —Cont'd
Proposed legislation, §1-1162.09.
Quorum, §1-1162.08.
Removal of members, §1-1162.03.
Reports, §1-1162.20.
  Public, §1-1162.24.
Royalty limitations, §1-1162.26.
Rules, §1-1162.09.
Staff, §1-1162.06.
Subpoena enforcement, §1-1162.18.
Transition provisions, §1-1164.01.

EUTHANASIA, §7-630.
Health care durable powers of
  attorney, §21-2212.
Natural death act, §§7-621 to 7-630.
  See LIVING WILLS.

EVICTIONS, §42-3505.01.
Arbitration, §§42-3505.03, 42-3505.04.
Complaint for possession of real
  estate.
  Nonpayment of rent and other
    grounds for eviction,
    LandlordTenant Form 1C.
  Violation of obligations of tenancy or
    other grounds for eviction,
    LandlordTenant Form 1B.
Conciliation, §42-3505.03.
Drug-related, §§42-3601 to 42-3610.
  See DRUG-RELATED EVICTIONS.
Forcible entry and detainer.
  Generally, §§16-1501 to 16-1505.
Redemption of tenancy,
  LandlordTenant Rule 14-II.
Rental housing.
  Residential drug-related evictions,
    §§42-3601 to 42-3610.
  See DRUG-RELATED EVICTIONS.
  Retaliatory evictions.
  See LANDLORD AND TENANT.

EVIDENCE.
Adoption trials, Adoption Rule 43.
  Proof of official records, statutes, etc.,
    Adoption Rule 44.
  Transcript as evidence, Adoption Rule
    201.
Alibi of defendant.
  Criminal procedure, CrimPro Rule
    12.1.
  Delinquent minors, JuvProc Rule 12.1.
Annulment, §16-919.
Appeals, D.C. courts.
  Statement of proceedings and
    evidence, DCCtApp Rule 10.
    Administrative orders and decisions,
      DCCtApp Rule 17.

EVIDENCE —Cont'd

Appeals, federal cases.

Composition of record on review or enforcement of administrative orders, FRAP 16(a).

Record on appeal, FRAP 10(b).

References in briefs to, FRAP 28(e).

Statement of when no report made or transcript unavailable, FRAP 10(c).

Arbitration, Arbitration Rule IX.

Small claims court, SmallClaimsArb Rule 3.

Trial de novo, Arbitration Rule XI.

Attorneys at law.

Client giving false testimony, ProfCond Rule 3.3.

Discipline or disability proceedings, DCBar Rule XI.

Fairness to opposing party and counsel, ProfCond Rule 3.4.

Authentication of official records.

Adoption proceedings, Adoption Rule 44.

Civil cases, CivPro Rule 44.

Criminal cases, CrimPro Rule 27.

Delinquent minors, JuvProc Rule 27.

Domestic relations actions, DomRel Rule 44.

Foreign judgments, CivPro Rule 72.

Blood tests.

Parentage proceedings, DomRel Rule 405.

Burden of proof.

See BURDEN OF PROOF.

Business records, CivPro Rule 43-I.

Family court proceedings generally, FamDiv Rule Q.

Certified mail return receipts, §14-506.

Child abuse and neglect.

Factfinding hearings, NeglectProc Rule 19.

Initial appearance, NeglectProc Rule 14.

Privilege not grounds for excluding evidence of, §4-1321.05.

Termination of parental rights, NeglectProc Rule 38.

Child labor.

Age of child engaged in, §§32-210, 32-212.

Children and minors.

Sale of property by guardians, §21-150.

EVIDENCE —Cont'd

Competence to proceed.

Incompetent criminal defendants.

Statements made during examination, evaluation or treatment, §24-531.10.

Conservators.

Proceedings involving, §21-2003.

Contracts.

Sale of goods.

Breaches with respect to accepted goods, §28:2-607.

Disputed goods.

Preserving evidence, §28:2-515.

Parol or extrinsic evidence, §28:2-202.

Proof of market price, §28:2-723.

Admissibility of market quotations, §28:2-724.

Controlled substances, §48-905.03.

Credible evidence defined, §4-1301.02.

Criminal procedure, CrimPro Rule 26.

Alibi of defendant, CrimPro Rule 12.1.

Biological materials, preservation, §22-4134.

Depositions, CrimPro Rule 15.

Insanity defense, CrimPro Rule 12.2.

Notice of intent to use evidence, CrimPro Rule 12.

Pleas, plea discussions, etc., CrimPro Rule 11.

Preservation of evidence.

Biological materials, §22-4134.

Pretrial motions to suppress evidence, CrimPro Rule 12.

Death.

Absence for seven years as evidence of, §§14-701, 14-702.

Deeds, §14-502.

Delinquent minors.

See DELINQUENT MINORS.

Depositions.

See DEPOSITIONS.

Divorce, §16-919.

Documentary evidence, §§14-501 to 14-507.

Certified mail return receipts, §14-506.

Deeds, §14-502.

Municipal ordinances and regulations, §14-505.

Other methods of proof, §14-507.

Proof of records, §14-501.

Wills.

Copies, §14-502.

Force and effect of District wills probated elsewhere, §14-504.

EVIDENCE —Cont'd

Documentary evidence —Cont'd

Wills —Cont'd

Record prima facie evidence of contents and execution, §14-503.

Documents of title.

Bills of lading.

Third party documents, prima facie evidence, §28:1-307.

Domestic life insurance company disbursements, §31-4439.

Domestic relations actions, DomRel Rules 43, 44.

Newly discovered evidence.

Relief from judgment or order, DomRel Rule 60.

Parentage proceedings, DomRel Rule 405.

Transcripts, DomRel Rule 201.

Domestic violence counselors.

Disclosure of confidential communication between victim and counselor.

Prohibition, exceptions, §14-310.

Disclosure of confidential information acquired in professional capacity.

Prohibited without consent of client, §14-307.

Domestic violence unit proceedings.

Conduct of hearings, DomesticViolence Rule 9.

Driving under the influence.

Admissibility of chemical tests.

Blood or urine, §50-2206.52c.

Generally, §50-2206.52.

Notification, §50-2206.52b.

Presence or testimony of person maintaining instruments, §50-2206.52a.

Evidence of impairment, §50-2206.51.

Drug, firearm, or prostitution-related nuisance abatement.

Burden of proof, §42-3108.

Conviction not required to demonstrate existence of nuisance, §42-3108.

Reputation, §42-3109.

Witnesses, §42-3105.

Durable powers of attorney, §21-2085.

Ejectment, §16-1103.

Electronic transactions, uniform act.

Evidentiary effect of transmission, §28-4912.

Eminent domain as to real property for United States, §16-1360.

EVIDENCE —Cont'd

Execution of judgments, §15-308.

Expert testimony.

See EXPERT WITNESSES.

Fiduciary security transfers.

Appointment or incumbency of fiduciary, §28-2904.

Firearms dealers.

Use of evidence obtained from prohibited, §7-2504.09.

Foreign law.

Determination of foreign law, CivPro Rule 44.1, CrimPro Rule 26.1.

Adoption proceedings, Adoption Rule 44.

Domestic relations actions, DomRel Rule 44.

Guardianship of minors.

Sale of property of infants, §21-150.

Harmless error in admission or exclusion of evidence.

Adoption proceedings, Adoption Rule 61.

Civil procedure, CivPro Rule 61.

Criminal procedure, CrimPro Rule 52.

Domestic relations actions, DomRel Rule 61.

Juvenile proceedings, JuvProc Rule 52.

Health maintenance organizations.

Evidence of coverage requirements, §31-3407.

Hearsay.

See HEARSAY.

Impeachment, §§14-102, 14-305.

Incompetent criminal defendants.

Competence to proceed.

Statements made during examination, evaluation or treatment, §24-531.10.

Injunctions.

Evidence received with preliminary injunction application, CivPro Rule 65.

Insanity defense, §§24-501 to 24-503, CrimPro Rule 12.2.

Instruments, §14-502.

Insurance.

Policy or certificate as prima facie evidence, §28:1-307.

Insurers rehabilitation and liquidation proceedings.

Proof of claims in, §31-1334.

Interception of wire or oral communications, CrimPro Rule 41-I.

Interrogatories.

See INTERROGATORIES.

EVIDENCE —Cont'd

Interstate family support.
Assistance with discovery, §46-353.18.
Special rules of evidence and procedure, §46-353.16.

Investment securities.
Rules concerning certificated securities, §28:8-114.

Joint contracts, §16-2105.

Juvenile proceedings.
See DELINQUENT MINORS.

Leading questions, CivPro Rule 43.
Adoption proceedings, Adoption Rule 43.
Domestic relations actions, DomRel Rule 43.

Mail return receipts, certified, §14-506.

Market value.
Commercial code, §§28:2-723, 28:2-724.

Maternity, §16-909.

Mediation, §16-4203.

Medical examiners.
Records as, §5-1413.
Taking possession of, §5-1408.

Medical malpractice.
Benevolent gestures inadmissible, §16-2841.

Metropolitan police.
Electronic recording of interrogations.
Evidentiary presumption, §5-116.03.

Metropolitan police property clerk.
Materials held by, §5-119.17.

Motions, CivPro Rule 43.

Motor vehicle safety responsibility.
Certified copy of record as evidence, §50-1301.05a.

Municipal ordinances and regulations as, §14-505.

Negotiable instruments.
Dishonor, §28:3-505.

Newly discovered evidence.
Crime victims' compensation.
Request for reconsideration of determination, VictComp Rule 18.
Criminal procedure, CrimPro Rule 33.
Juvenile proceedings, JuvProc Rule 33.
Relief from judgment or order, CivPro Rule 60.
Domestic relations actions, DomRel Rule 60.

Nonresident testimony, §14-104.

Oaths and affirmations, under, §14-101.

Offers of proof, CivPro Rule 43.

EVIDENCE —Cont'd

Open court testimony, CivPro Rule 43.
Domestic relations actions, DomRel Rule 43.

Opinion evidence, human trafficking, §22-1839.

Ordinances, CivPro Rule 44-I.
Adoption proceedings, Adoption Rule 44.
Domestic relations actions, DomRel Rule 44.

Parentage proceedings, §§16-909 to 16-909.03.
Blood tests, §§16-2343 to 16-2343.02, DomRel Rule 405.

Parent-child relationship, §16-909.

Parol evidence.
Sales contracts.
Parol and extrinsic evidence, §28:2-202.

Perjury.
Sufficiency of evidence, §§23-323, 23-324.

Pleas, plea discussions, etc., CrimPro Rule 11.
Delinquent minors, JuvProc Rule 11.

Presumption of death, §§14-701, 14-702.

Probate proceedings, §§16-3103, 16-3110.

Public utilities investigations by Commission compelling incriminatory evidence, §34-610.

Rape shield law, §§22-3021, 22-3022.

Real estate tax sales.
Revised real property tax sale.
Certificate of sale, §47-1351.

Real property transfer tax, §47-907.

Records, §§14-501 to 14-507.
Business records, CivPro Rule 43-I.
Family court proceedings generally, FamDiv Rule Q.
Excluded evidence, CivPro Rule 43.
Domestic relations actions, DomRel Rule 43.
Proof of official record, CivPro Rule 44.
Adoption proceedings, Adoption Rule 44.
Criminal cases, CrimPro Rule 27.
Delinquent minors, JuvProc Rule 27.
Domestic relations actions, DomRel Rule 44.

Regulations, CivPro Rule 44-I.
Adoption proceedings, Adoption Rule 44.

EVIDENCE —Cont'd
Regulations —Cont'd
Domestic relations actions, DomRel Rule 44.
Reputation evidence, human trafficking, §22-1839.
Restraints of trade.
Judgment in favor of District as prima facie evidence, §28-4510.
Sales contracts.
Parol and extrinsic evidence, §28:2-202.
Search warrants.
Motion to suppress evidence, CrimPro Rule 41.
Juvenile proceedings, JuvProc Rule 41.
Simultaneous deaths.
Rules governing determination of death, §19-505.
Small claims court.
Arbitration, SmallClaimsArb Rule 3.
Conciliation, SmallClaims Conciliation Rule 2.
Statutes, CivPro Rule 44-I.
Adoption proceedings, Adoption Rule 44.
Domestic relations actions, DomRel Rule 44.
Stenographic report or transcript, CivPro Rule 80.
Adoption proceedings, Adoption Rule 201.
Domestic relations actions, DomRel Rule 201.
Surveyor of the District's records as evidence, §1-1311.
Tampering with physical evidence, §22-723.
Termination of parental rights.
Child abuse and neglect proceedings, NeglectProc Rule 38.
Transmission from different location, CivPro Rule 43.
Trespass.
Prima facie evidence of unlawful entry on property, §22-3302.
Trust.
Mortgage and title corporations' certificate of charter of incorporation as evidence of existence of, §26-1332.
Unlawful entry on property.
Prima facie evidence, §22-3302.
Vector-borne disease control, §8-2131.04.

EVIDENCE —Cont'd
Weights and measures.
Official certificate as prima facie evidence, §28:1-307.
Wills as, §§14-502 to 14-504.
Witnesses.
Expert witnesses.
See EXPERT WITNESSES.
General provisions.
See WITNESSES.
Workplace safety, §32-805.

EXAMINATIONS.
Attachments, oral examinations regarding, §§16-521, 16-552.
Banks and financial institutions, §26-102.
Bar examination, DCCtApp Rule 46.
College savings program.
Program manager, §47-4506.
Dietetics and nutrition, §§3-1207.01, 3-1207.02.
Domestic life insurance companies, §31-4406.
Foreign and alien life insurance companies, §31-4502.
Fraternal benefit societies, §31-5325.
Funeral directors, licensure of, §3-405.
Health occupations licensure, registration or certification, §3-1205.06.
Horizontal property regime books and records, §42-2015.
Insurance companies, §§31-1401 to 31-1407.
Insurance holding companies, §31-707.
Life and health insurance guaranty association, §31-5412.
Managing general agents examined as insurers, §31-1505.
Medical examinations.
See MEDICAL EXAMINATIONS.
Mortgage lenders and brokers, §26-1112.
National guard.
Officer's capability, §49-311.
Promotion of commissioned officers, §49-309.
2nd Lieutenants, §49-310.
Property and liability insurance guaranty association, §31-5511.
Reinsurance intermediaries, §31-1809.
Savings and loan acquisitions, §26-1214.

EXAMINATIONS —Cont'd
Title insurance producers,
§31-5041.03.
Workplace safety, §32-809.

EXCAVATIONS.
Flood hazards, §6-504.
Miss Utility, §§34-2701 to 34-2709.
See MISS UTILITY.
Unclaimed deposits for excavation work in public space.
Applicability of law, §41-141.01.

EXCEPTED SERVICE, §§1-609.01 to 1-609.08, 1-611.02, 1-611.04.

EXCEPTIONS FOR INSUFFICIENCY OF A PLEADING.
Abolished, CivPro Rule 7.

EXCHANGE ALLOWANCES.
Similar items.
Use of exchange allowances or sale proceeds to purchase, §1-301.92.

EXCISE TAX.
Residential real property transfer excise tax, §47-1401.
Titling of motor vehicles,
§§50-2201.03, 50-2201.22.

EXECUTION OF JUDGMENTS,
§§15-301 to 15-371, CivPro Rule 69.
Alias writs, §15-303.
Applicability of provisions, §15-301.
Appraisement of levied property,
§15-314.
Assignment of choses in action,
§§28-2301 to 28-2305.
Attachment and garnishment after judgment in aid of execution,
§§16-541 to 16-556.
Administrator, in hands of, §16-549.
Attorneys' fees and costs, §§16-542, 16-553.
Claims to attached property, §16-554.
Condemnation proceedings, §16-555.
Credits, attachment of, §16-546.
Defenses, §16-551.
Definition of judgment for purposes of, §16-541.
Eligible property, §16-544.
Executor, in hands of, §16-549.
Interlocutory order.
Sale under, §16-555.
Interrogatories, §16-552.
Issuance of attachment after judgment, §16-542.
Judgment against garnishee, §16-556.
Marshal, in hands of, §16-548.

EXECUTION OF JUDGMENTS
—Cont'd
Attachment and garnishment after judgment in aid of execution
—Cont'd
Multiple attachments against same debtor, §16-545.
Oral examinations, §16-552.
Preservation of property, §16-550.
Property subject to, §16-544.
Retention of attached property and credits by garnishee, §16-547.
Revival of judgment, §16-543.
Sale of property, §§16-550, 16-555.
Traverse of garnishee's answers, §16-553.
Trials, §§16-551, 16-553.
Bills and other evidence of debt.
Levy on, §15-312.
Bills of lading.
Lien on goods covered by a negotiable document, §28:7-602.
Chattels lawfully pledged for payment of debt.
Levy on equitable interest, §15-313.
Claims against estates, §20-914.
College savings program.
Seizure of accounts prohibited, §47-4510.
Cooperative associations.
Exemption of share and membership certificates, §29-928.
Criminal procedure, §16-709.
Death.
Execution of final decree after, §15-319.
Judgment debtor's death after delivery of writ, §15-309.
Marshal, death of, §15-315.
Definition of judgment for purposes of, §15-301.
Delivery of chattels, enforcing decrees for, §15-322.
Domestic relations actions, DomRel Rule 69.
Enforcement, §§15-320 to 15-323.
Equitable interest in chattels pledged.
Levy on, §15-313.
Evidence, §15-308.
Exemptions.
Attachment of property as debt for wages, §15-501.
Clothing, §15-503.
Earnings and other income, §15-503.
Householders, property of, §15-501.

EXECUTION OF JUDGMENTS
—Cont'd

Exemptions —Cont'd
Mortgages and deeds of trust, §15-502.
Notice, §15-521.
Tools, §15-503.
Transit, property in, §15-501.
Wages and salaries, §15-503.
Exempt property, §§15-501 to 15-503.
Foreign judgments, §§15-351 to 15-357.
See FOREIGN JUDGMENTS.
Foreign-money judgments, §§15-361 to 15-503.
See FOREIGN-MONEY JUDGMENTS.
Insurers rehabilitation and liquidation proceedings, §31-1355.
Interlocutory decrees, enforcing, §15-321.
Interpleader, §§15-521 to 15-524.
Issuance of writ after expiration of time period, §15-305.
Levy, property subject to, §§15-311 to 15-314.
Lien of execution, §15-307.
Marshal.
Death, removal, or disqualification. Effect of, §15-315.
Endorsement of date of receipt of writ, §15-308.
Remedy for erroneous sale in good faith, §15-317.
Money or evidences of debt.
Levy on, §15-312.
New judgment in lieu of, §15-306.
Notice of claim or exemption, §15-521.
Police and firefighters retirement and disability.
Funds not subject to execution, §5-723.05.
Probate proceedings, §16-3112.
Property subject to levy, §15-311.
Real property seizures, limitations on, §15-323.
Replevin, §15-524.
Return of writ, §15-304.
Sale of levied property, §§15-314 to 15-318.
Subrogation of purchaser after defective sale, §15-316.
Teachers' retirement.
Funds not subject to garnishment. Retirement after June 30, 1946, §38-2021.17.

EXECUTION OF JUDGMENTS
—Cont'd

Time period for, §15-302.
Warehouse receipts.
Lien on goods covered by a negotiable document, §28:7-602.

EXECUTIVE SECRETARY, §1-301.23.

EXECUTIVE SERVICE, §§1-523.01, 1-610.51 to 1-610.64.

EXECUTORS AND ADMINISTRATORS.
Accounts and accounting.
Bond of executor or administrator. Discharge only after accounting, §28-2504.
Action of account, §16-101.
Administrator included in use of term, §45-605.
Assignments for benefit of creditors.
Death of trustee or assignee, §28-2105.
Attachment by, §§16-516, 16-549.
Bonds, surety.
Discharge only after accounting, §28-2504.
Counterclaims by or against, §13-505.
Decedents' estates.
See DECEDENTS' ESTATES.
Deeds, form for, §42-601.
Disclaimer of property interests, §§19-1501 to 19-1518.
See DISCLAIMER OF PROPERTY INTERESTS.
Fiduciaries generally.
See FIDUCIARIES.
Fiduciary's bond, undertaking in lieu of, §16-601.
Fiduciary security transfers, §§28-2901 to 28-2909.
See FIDUCIARY SECURITY TRANSFERS.
Garnishment.
Post-judgment garnishment in aid of execution.
Money or property held by executor or administrator, §16-549.
Prejudgment garnishment.
Money or property in hands of executor or administrator, §16-516.
Personal representatives.
General provisions, §§20-401 to 20-406.
See PERSONAL REPRESENTATIVES.

EXECUTORS AND ADMINISTRATORS —Cont'd
Probate proceedings.
General provisions, §§16-3101 to 16-3112, Probate Rules 1 to 430. See PROBATE PROCEEDINGS.
Special administrators.
Appointment of, §20-531.
Bond, surety, §20-532.
Defined, §20-101.
Powers and duties, §20-533.
Termination of powers, §20-534.
Special promise to answer for debt or default of another, §28-3502.
Statute of frauds.
Special promise to answer damages out of own estate, §28-3502.
Wills.
See WILLS.

EXECUTORY CONTRACTS.
Children and minors, property of, §21-145.

EXHIBITS.
Appeals, federal cases.
Certified lists, filing as filing of record, administrative review or enforcement, FRAP 17(b).
Composition of record on appeal, FRAP 10(a).
Physical exhibits, use in argument, FRAP 34(g).
Record on appeal, FRAP 10(a), 11(b).
Reproduction in appendix, FRAP 30(e).
Bankruptcy proceedings, USDistDCBank Rule 9070-1.
Custody of exhibits.
Civil cases, USDistCt LCvR 79.2.
Criminal cases, CrimPro Rule 119, USDistCt LCrR 56.2.
Domestic relations actions.
Masters, DomRel Rule 53.
Depositions, CivPro Rule 30.
Adoption proceedings, Adoption Rule 30.
Domestic relations actions, DomRel Rule 30.
Pleadings, motions, etc., CivPro Rule 10.
Domestic relations actions, DomRel Rule 10.
Summary, CivPro Form CA 119.
Tax proceedings, Tax Rule 12.

EX-OFFENDERS.
Commission on reentry and ex-offender affairs, §24-1303.

EX-OFFENDERS —Cont'd
Definitions, §24-1301.
Hiring of ex-offenders.
Fair criminal record screening. Rules, §32-1346.
Office on ex-offender affairs, §24-1302.
Public works department to hire, §32-1351.

EX PARTE COMMUNICATIONS.
Judges, CJC Canon 2.9.

EXPECTANCY, ESTATES IN, §§42-506, 42-508, 42-514, 42-515.

EXPEDITED APPEALS, DCCtApp Rule 4.
Appeals, federal cases, USCtApp Rule 47.2.

EXPERIMENTAL TREATMENT AND RESEARCH.
Intellectual disabilities, persons with, §§7-1305.06, 7-1305.09.

EXPERT WITNESSES.
Appointment by court.
Criminal procedure, CrimPro Rule 28.
Hospitalization of persons with mental illness, MentalHealth Rule 12.
Juvenile proceedings, JuvProc Rule 28.
Child abuse and neglect proceedings, NeglectProc Rule 47.
Criminal cases, CrimPro Rule 28.
Insanity defense, CrimPro Rule 12.2.
Delinquent minors, §16-2339.
Alibi defense, JuvProc Rule 12.1.
Expert witnesses, JuvProc Rule 28.
Production of witness statements, JuvProc Rule 26.2.
Discovery.
Adoption proceedings, Adoption Rule 26.
Civil cases, CivPro Rule 26.
Criminal procedure, CrimPro Rule 16.
Delinquent minors, JuvProc Rule 16.
Domestic relations actions, DomRel Rule 26.
Use of deposition, CivPro Rule 32.
Hospitalization of persons with mental illness, MentalHealth Rules 12, 17.
Insanity defense, CrimPro Rule 12.2.

EXPLORATORY COMMITTEES.
Elections.
See ELECTIONS.

EXPLOSIVES.
Business licenses, §47-2814.

EXPLOSIVES —Cont'd
Capitol grounds, prohibited on,
  §10-503.16.
Destruction or injury of property,
  placed with intent to cause,
  §22-3305.
Molotov cocktails, §22-4515a.
Police and firefighters on bomb
  disposal duty, additional
  compensation for, §5-542.02.
Power to issue regulations
  regarding, §1-303.43.
Unlawful purposes, intended for,
  §22-4515a.
Weapons of mass destruction.
  False reports, §22-1319.
  Hoax weapons, §22-1319.
    False report, §22-1319.
  Manufacture or possession, §22-3154.
  Use, dissemination or detonation,
    §22-3155.

EX POST FACTO LAWS, US Const Art
  I §§9, 10.

EXPRESS WARRANTIES.
Leases, UCC, §28:2A-210.
  Third party beneficiaries, §28:2A-216.
Sale of goods, UCC, §28:2-313.
  Cumulation and conflict, §28:2-314.
  Exclusions, §§28:2-316, 28:2-316.01.
  Modification, §§28:2-316, 28:2-316.01.
  Third party beneficiaries, §28:2-318.

EXPUNGEMENT OF RECORDS.
Arrest records, §§16-801 to 16-807,
  CrimPro Rule 118.
  Alcoholic beverages.
    Children and minors, purchase,
      possession, or consumption by,
      §25-1002.
  Delinquent minors, JuvProc Rule 118.
Probation discharge, CrimPro Rule
  32.

EXTENSION OF TIME, CivPro Rule 6,
  CrimPro Rule 45.
Appeals, D.C. courts, DCCtApp Rule
  26.
Appeals, federal cases, FRAP 26,
  USCtApp Rule 26.
  Filing.
    Notice of appeal, FRAP 4, 26(b).
    Record on review or enforcement of
      administrative orders, FRAP
      17(a).
    Rehearing petition, FRAP 40(a).
    Rehearing petition, FRAP 40(a).

EXTENSION OF TIME —Cont'd
Appeals, federal cases —Cont'd
  Transmission of record on appeal,
    FRAP 11(b).
Domestic relations actions, DomRel
  Rule 6.
Hospitalization of persons with
  mental illness, MentalHealth Rule
  13.

EXTERMINATORS.
Bureau of rodent control,
  §§8-2101.01, 8-2101.02.
Rodent abatement program,
  §§8-2103.01 to 8-2103.05.

EXTORTION.
Aged persons, offenses committed
  against.
  Enhanced penalties, §22-3601.
Blackmail, §22-3252.
False personation with intent to
  extort money, §22-1402.
Prohibited acts, §22-3251.
Security agents and brokers.
  Grounds for disciplinary actions,
    §31-5602.07.
Threatening kidnapping, injury, or
  damage to property for purposes
  of, §22-1402.

EXTRADITION.
Appearances before the court,
  CrimPro Rule 40-I.
Arrest procedures for fugitives from
  justice, §23-702.
Arrest warrants for fugitives from
  justice, §23-701.
Confinement, §23-706.
  Period of detention, CrimPro Rule
    40-I.
Definitions, §23-707.
Delivering fugitive, CrimPro Rule
  40-I.
Foreign country, removal
  procedures and return to,
  §23-705.
Fugitives from justice.
  Constitutional provisions, US Const
    Art IV §2.
Interstate agreement on detainers,
  §§24-801 to 24-805.
  Definitions, §24-802.
  Enactment, §24-801.
  Enforcement and cooperation, §24-803.
  Regulation, §24-804.
  Right to alter, amend, repeal reserved,
    §24-805.

EXTRADITION —Cont'd
Preliminary examination, CrimPro
Rule 40-I.
Procedure, §23-704, CrimPro Rule 40-I.
Waiver of further proceedings,
CrimPro Rule 40-I.
Warrants for arrest of fugitives,
CrimPro Rule 40-I.

EXTRAORDINARY WRITS.
Appeals, federal cases, FRAP 21,
USCtApp Rule 21.
Certiorari, stay of mandate pending
application for, FRAP 41(d).

EXTRINSIC EVIDENCE.
Commercial code.
Sale of goods, §28:2-202.

F

FACEBOOK.
E-commerce companies.
Qualified social electronic commerce
companies tax abatements,
§§47-1818.01 to 47-1818.08.

**FACILITIES SERVICE REQUEST
FUND,** §10-551.07a.

FACSIMILE MACHINES.
Service of process.
Adoption proceedings, Adoption Rule
5.
Domestic relations actions, DomRel
Rule 5.

**FAIR PHONE CHARGES FOR
PRISONERS,** §§24-263.01 to
24-263.04.

FAIRS.
Alcoholic beverage licenses.
Temporary licenses, §25-115.
Business licenses, §47-2826.
Recycling, §47-2826.
Rental of public space.
Street festival one day rental,
§10-1102.01a.

FAIR TRADE.
Restraints of trade, §§28-4501 to
28-4518.
See RESTRAINTS OF TRADE.

FAIR TRIALS, CivPro Rule 203,
CrimPro Rule 53.
Judges.
Fairness and impartiality, CJC Canon
2.2.
Bias, prejudice or harassment
prohibited, CJC Canon 2.3.

FALSE FIRE ALARMS, §22-1319.

FALSE PERSONATION, §§22-1402 to
22-1406.

FALSE POLICE REPORTS, §5-117.05.

FALSE PRETENSES, §§22-1402 to
22-1406.

**FALSE REPORT OF WEAPON OF
MASS DESTRUCTION,** §22-1319.

FALSE STATEMENTS, §22-2405.
Air pollution, §8-101.05e.
Alcoholic beverage licenses.
False statements on applications,
§25-401.
Alcoholic beverages.
Advertising, §25-766.
Mortgage lenders and brokers,
§26-1114.
Tobacco.
Purchases by minors, §7-1721.03.

FALSE SWEARING, §22-2404.

**FAMILIAL STATUS OR
RESPONSIBILITIES
DISCRIMINATION.**
Prohibition of, §2-1401.01.
Real estate transactions.
Unlawful discriminatory practices in,
§2-1402.21.

FAMILY AND MEDICAL LEAVE,
§§32-501 to 32-517.
Adoption of child, §32-502.
Amount of leave, §32-502.
Applicability of provisions, §32-516.
Benefit protections, §32-505.
Birth of child, §32-502.
**Certification of serious health
condition,** §32-504.
Definitions, §32-501.
Domestic partner benefits, §§32-701
to 32-710.
See DOMESTIC PARTNER
BENEFITS.
Employment protections, §32-505.
Enforcement of provisions, §32-510.
Existing benefits, effect on, §32-513.
Foster care, §32-502.
**Generous leave policies,
encouragement of,** §32-514.
Investigations, §32-509.
Investigative authority, §32-508.
Issuance of rules and regulations,
§32-517.
Medical leave requirement, §32-503.
Notice, §32-511.

FAMILY AND MEDICAL LEAVE
—Cont'd
Paid leave and, §§32-502, 32-503.
**Parental leave to attend or
participate in school-related
event,** §§32-1201 to 32-1206.
Placement of child, §32-502.
Prohibited acts regarding, §32-507.
Reasons for, §32-502.
Relationship to other laws, §32-512.
Requirements, §32-502.
School employees, §32-506.
Serious health condition.
Certification regarding, §32-504.
Defined, §32-501.
Medical leave requirement and,
§32-503.
Reason for leave, §32-502.
Sick leave, §§32-502, 32-503.
Teachers, §32-506.

FAMILY COURT PROCEEDINGS.
Adoption.
See ADOPTION.
Alimony.
See SPOUSAL SUPPORT.
Alternative dispute resolution.
Use to greatest extent possible,
§11-1102.
Annulment of marriage.
See ANNULMENT OF MARRIAGE.
Appointed counsel.
Standards of practice, §11-1103.
**Case tracking and management
system.**
Integrated computerized system,
§11-1104.
Child abuse and neglect.
See CHILD ABUSE AND NEGLECT.
Child custody.
Interstate child custody proceedings.
See CHILD CUSTODY AND CHILD
CUSTODY PROCEEDINGS.
Child support.
See CHILD SUPPORT.
Continuances, FamDiv Rule G.
Court appointed counsel.
Standards of practice, §11-1103.
Court-appointed special advocates,
§§16-2371, 16-2372.
Criminal complaints.
Intrafamily offenses.
Generally, §§16-1001 to 16-1034.
See INTRAFAMILY
PROCEEDINGS.
Criminal matters transferred to,
§16-2307.

FAMILY COURT PROCEEDINGS
—Cont'd
Cross-jurisdictional units.
Assignment of proceeding to, §11-1101.
Delinquent minors.
See DELINQUENT MINORS.
**Disciplinary proceedings against
attorneys,** FamDiv Rule S.
Divorce.
See DIVORCE.
**Domestic relations actions
generally,** DomRel Rules 1 to 406.
See DOMESTIC RELATIONS
ACTIONS.
**Employees of court not to practice
law,** FamDiv Rule T.
Employer's statement, FamDiv Rule J.
Exclusive jurisdiction, §11-1101.
**Family friendly environment,
promotion,** §11-1104.
Fees, FamDiv Rule C.
Witness fees, FamDiv Rule F.
Financial statements, FamDiv Rule K.
Hearing commissioners, FamDiv Rule
D.
**Interstate child custody
proceedings.**
General provisions.
See CHILD CUSTODY AND CHILD
CUSTODY PROCEEDINGS.
Interstate family support.
General provisions, §§46-351.01 to
46-359.03.
See INTERSTATE FAMILY
SUPPORT.
Judges.
Assignment of family court judges.
Special rules, §11-908A.
Emergency assignment of judges,
§11-908A.
Magistrate judges.
Special rules, §11-1732a.
Number of judges serving on family
court, §11-908A.
One family, one judge requirement,
§11-1104.
Presenting matters in chambers or in
emergency, FamDiv Rule R.
Presiding judges.
Designation by chief judge of
superior court, §11-902.
Qualifications to be assigned as judge,
§11-908A.
Terms of judges assigned to court,
§11-908A.
Training, §11-1104.

FAMILY COURT PROCEEDINGS
—Cont'd
Jurisdiction.
Exclusive jurisdiction, §11-1101.
Retention, §11-1104.
Jury trials, FamDiv Rule L.
Law student practice, FamDiv Rule
M.
Legal separation.
See LEGAL SEPARATION.
Magistrate judges.
Special rules, §11-1732a.
**Notice of hearing and order
directing appearance,** FamDiv
Rule H.
Form, FamDiv Form 1.
Parentage proceedings.
General provisions, §§16-2341 to
16-2348.
See PARENTAGE PROCEEDINGS.
Recording of court proceedings,
FamDiv Rule N.
Records.
Business records, FamDiv Rule Q.
Sealing of records, FamDiv Rule P.
Forms, FamDiv Forms 2 to 6.
Report to congress, §11-1106.
Retention of jurisdiction, §11-1104.
Social services and related services,
§11-1105.
Social services liaison, §11-1105.
Spousal support.
See SPOUSAL SUPPORT.
Subpoenas, FamDiv Rule E.
Surrogate parenting contracts,
§§16-401, 16-402.
Termination of parental rights.
See TERMINATION OF PARENTAL
RIGHTS.
Witness fees, FamDiv Rule F.

**FAMILY EMERGENCY SERVICES
PROGRAM,** §4-206.04.

FAMILY HOMES, §§4-1401 to 4-1410.
Adoption proceedings, §4-1406.
Inability to pay costs, §4-1410.
Child-placing agencies.
Adoption proceedings, §4-1406.
Charges or compensation, §4-1410.
Confidentiality of record, §4-1405.
Custody and control of children,
§4-1405.
Defined, §4-1402.
Fees, §4-1410.
Licenses.
Application, §4-1404.

FAMILY HOMES —Cont'd
Child-placing agencies —Cont'd
Licenses —Cont'd
Disciplinary actions against licensee,
§4-1407.
Duration, §4-1404.
Failure to obtain license, §4-1408.
Issuance, §§4-1404, 4-1407.
Provisional license, §§4-1404,
4-1407.
Refusal to issue, §4-1407.
Reinstatement or reissuance,
§4-1407.
Required, §4-1402.
Parental rights vesting in agencies,
§4-1406.
Visitation by agencies, §4-1405.
Child protection register.
Agency required to check, §4-1407.01.
Effect of failure to check or maintain
information, §4-1407.01.
Department of health.
Inspections and investigations,
§4-1409.
Foreign agreements with agencies,
§4-1405.01.
**Interstate compact on placement of
children,** §§4-1421 to 4-1424.
Agreements with other state for
placement, §4-1423.
Authority to enter into and execute
compact, §4-1422.
Definitions, §4-1421.
Delinquent children.
Administrative hearing on
placement, review, §4-1424.
Parental rights.
Termination, §4-1406.
Vesting in agencies or mayor, §4-1408.
Public policy, §4-1401.
Violations of act, §4-1408.

FAMILY SUPPORT COUNCIL,
§7-761.12.

FARM-TO-SCHOOL PROGRAM,
§§38-823.01 to 38-823.03.
Applicability of law, §38-828.02.
Comprehensive plan, §38-823.01a.
Preferences for locally grown food,
§38-823.01.
Promotion of locally grown food,
§38-823.02.
Reports, §38-823.03.
Rulemaking authority, §38-828.01.

FARM WINERIES.
Licenses, §25-123.

FAR SOUTHEAST COMMUNITY ORGANIZATION.
Real property tax exemption, §47-1075.

F.A.S.
Sale of goods, UCC, §28:2-319.

FASHION ARTS AND EVENTS, COMMISSION ON, §§3-651 to 3-653.
Established, §3-651.
Meetings and procedures, §3-652.
Members, §3-652.
Powers, §3-653.
Programs and initiatives, §3-651.

FAX MACHINES.
Service of process.
Adoption proceedings, Adoption Rule 5.
Domestic relations actions, DomRel Rule 5.

FDR AMENDMENT, US Const Amd 22.

FEDERAL CITY COLLEGE, §§38-1101 to 38-1112.
Appropriation authorized to carry out provisions, §38-1106.
Board of higher education, §§38-1102 to 38-1104.
Consolidation of existing institutions, §38-1202.05.
Definitions, §38-1101.
Fiscal accountability requirements, §38-1105.
Grants to, §38-1110.
Interpretation of provisions, §38-1111.
Land-grant college, regarded as, §§38-1107, 38-1109, 38-1112.
Appropriation in lieu of donation of public lands, §38-1108.
University of the District of Columbia.
Successor institution, §§38-1201.01 to 38-1207.07.
See UNIVERSITY OF THE DISTRICT OF COLUMBIA.

FEDERAL CONTROL OF PRISON SYSTEM, §§24-101 to 24-142.
See PRISON SYSTEM, FEDERAL CONTROL.

FEDERAL ENDOWMENT PROGRAMS.
Gallaudet University, §38-2402.07a.

FEDERAL LABOR RELATIONS AUTHORITY PROCEEDINGS.
Appellate procedure.
Administrative orders.
Briefs and oral argument, USCtApp Rule 15.1.

FEDERAL OFFENDERS.
Superior court.
Detention and release, CrimPro Rule 40.

FEDERAL PROPERTY.
Height of buildings fronting on federal property, §§6-611.01, 6-611.02.
Real property exempt from taxation, §§47-1002, 47-1011.
Real property tax valuation of federal property, §§47-840, 47-841.
Sale of, §47-709.
Snow and ice removal from sidewalks adjacent to federal buildings, §9-603.
Zoning exemptions for federal public buildings, §6-641.15.

FEDERAL PROTECTIVE SERVICE.
Federal law enforcement officer cooperative agreements, §§5-301 to 5-303.
Lateral police career appointments, §§1-610.71 to 1-610.76.

FEDERAL RULES OF APPELLATE PROCEDURE.
See APPEALS, FEDERAL CASES.

FEDERAL SUPPLEMENTAL DISTRICT OF COLUMBIA PENSION FUND, §§1-811.01 to 1-811.06.
Annual payment into fund.
Determination, §1-811.03.
Methods for making, §1-811.04.
Discontinuation.
Special requirements, §1-811.05.
Established, §1-811.01.
Investment of assets, §1-811.01.
Termination, §1-811.06.
Use of amounts in fund, §1-811.02.

FEEL-GOOD BONDS.
Pay-for-success contracts, §§2-211.01 to 2-211.03.

FEES.
Abandoned and unlawfully parked vehicles.
Reclamation of impounded vehicle, §50-2421.09.

FEES —Cont'd

Adult education courses, §38-1002.

Alcohol and drug abuse treatment, §44-1207.

Alcoholic beverage licenses.
Revocation or suspension.
Not returnable, §25-821.
Schedules for, §§25-501 to 25-511.

Alcoholic beverages.
See ALCOHOLIC BEVERAGES.

Ambulance services, §5-416.

Animals, §8-1804.

Anti-SLAPP actions, §16-5504.

Appeals, D.C. courts, DCCtApp Rule 50-Fee Schedule.
Administrative orders and decisions, DCCtApp Rule 15.
Criminal procedure, CrimPro Rule 37.
Docketing fee, DCCtApp Rule 12.

Appeals, federal cases, USCtApp Appx I, USCtApp Rule 45.
Administrative orders, FRAP 15(e).
Clerks of court, USCtApp HPIP Rule II(d).
Docketing.
Notice of appeal, FRAP 3(e).
Petition for mandamus, prohibition, and other extraordinary writs, FRAP 21, USCtApp Rule 21.
Permissive appeals, FRAP 5(d).

Arbitration, Arbitration Rules IV, V.
Small claims court, SmallClaimsArb Rule 1.

Arbitration, revised act.
Authority to award, §16-4421.

Asbestos contractors, §8-111.10.

Assessment of, §1-301.01.

Attorneys.
See ATTORNEYS' FEES.

Auditor-masters, CivPro Rule 53-I.
Domestic relations actions, DomRel Rule 53.

Bail bondsmen, §23-1105.

Bar examination, DCCtApp Rule 46.

Bathing pools and beaches, §10-164.

Bicycle operators, commercial, §50-1632.

Bingo licenses, §3-1325.

Boards and commissions, §§1-321.03 to 1-321.06.

Boiler inspections, §§2-110, 2-115, 2-118.
Inspection fees, §§2-110, 2-115.

Building code inspections, §§6-703.01, 6-703.02.

Building permits, §§6-641.09, 6-661.01.

FEES —Cont'd

Business license renewal fees for armed forces personnel, waiver of, §1-301.01.

Business organizations.
Filing, §29-102.12.

Certificate of taxes and assessments due, §47-405.

Check cashing businesses.
Cashing checks, §26-317.
Examination of licensees, §26-311.01.
Licenses, §26-305.

Child custody proceedings.
Enforcement of foreign custody determinations, §16-4603.12.

Child-placing agencies, §4-1410.

Clinical health services, §44-731.

Collection of, §1-301.01.
Fee collection incentive fund, §1-325.61.

Commercial bicycle operators, §50-1632.

Commercial drivers' licenses, §50-408.

Community education courses, §38-1002.

Condominium registration, §42-1904.03.

Conservators' proceedings, notice of, §21-2034.

Construction codes.
Compliance letter fees, §6-1406.02.

Continuing education courses, §38-1002.

Controlled substances, §48-903.01.

Conversion of health care entities, §44-608.

Cooperative associations, §29-939.

Council records, fees for reproducing, §1-301.49.

Court costs.
See ATTORNEYS' FEES.

Court fees credited to District, §47-128.

Court fees for superior court actions, CivPro Rule 202.

Credit unions, §26-503.

Criminal procedure, §16-703.

DC One Card, §1-327.72.

Delinquent debts owed District, recovery, §1-350.03.

Disposable carryout bags, §8-102.03.

District fees to be paid into Treasury, §47-127.

District of Columbia housing authority.
Exemption from court fees and costs, §6-208.

FEES —Cont'd
Drivers' licenses, §50-1401.01.
Driving instructors.
  License fee, §47-2842.
Education courses for adults, community, and continuing education, §38-1002.
Electricians, §47-2712.
Electronic waste.
  Extended manufacturer responsibility, §8-1041.04.
Elevator contractors, mechanics and inspectors, §47-2853.99.
Emergency ambulance services, §5-416.
Emergency and non-emergency number telephone calling systems fund.
  Assessments to subscribers, §34-1803.
Entertainments.
  Fees for police and firefighter assignments, §47-2820.
Environmental impact statements, §8-109.12.
Examination of insurance companies, §31-1406.
Family court proceedings, FamDiv Rule C.
  Witness fees, FamDiv Rule F.
Family homes, placement of children in, §4-1410.
Fee collection incentive fund, §1-325.61.
Fiduciary accounts.
  Audit and examination, CivPro Rule 305.
Fire and casualty insurance licenses, §31-2502.41.
Fire and emergency medical services training for non-District personnel, §5-431.
Firearms dealer's license, §7-2504.02.
Firearms registration, §7-2502.05.
Foreign judgments, §15-355.
Foreign missions.
  Benefits, provision of, §6-1304.
  Unsatisfied judgments or damages, §6-1304.01.
Funeral directors, §3-404.
Green building fee, §6-1451.08.
Hazardous waste and toxic chemical release source reduction fund, §8-1320.
Health maintenance organizations, §31-3415.
Health occupations boards.
  Fee schedules set by, §3-1204.09.

FEES —Cont'd
Impounded vehicles.
  Abandoned and unlawfully parked vehicles.
    Reclamation of impounded vehicle, §50-2421.09.
  Storage of, §50-2201.21.
Indigent persons.
  Affidavit in support of motion to proceed in forma pauperis, CivPro Form CA 106.
  Subpoenas.
    Criminal cases, CrimPro Rule 17.
    Delinquent minors, JuvProc Rule 17.
Industrial revenue bonds, §§47-340.20 to 47-340.23.
Inspection of motor vehicles, §§50-1101, 50-1104.
Insurance company taxation.
  Filing, §47-2606.
  Licenses, §47-2603.
Insurance premium finance companies.
  Licenses.
    Issuance upon payment of fee, §31-1104.
Intellectual disabilities, persons with.
  Registration fees for administration by trained employees of medication to, §21-1206.
Interstate family support.
  Filing fees and other costs, prohibition, §46-353.13.
Judges.
  Accepting gifts or other things of value.
    Waiver of fees or charges, CJC Canon 3.14.
Jurors, §§11-1912, 15-718.
Landlord and tenant court, LandlordTenant Rule 15.
Layaway plans, §28-3818.
Library use by persons not eligible for free user's card, §39-103.
Licenses.
  Business licenses.
    See BUSINESS LICENSES.
  General provisions.
    See LICENSES.
Liens on motor vehicles and trailers.
  Recordation of lien, §50-1212.
  Releasing liens, §50-1213.
Life insurance companies, §§31-4302, 31-4303.
Lottery and charitable games control board.
  Bingo and raffle licenses, §3-1325.

FEES —Cont'd
Lottery and charitable games control board —Cont'd
Suppliers' licenses, §3-1327.
Low-level radioactive waste generator regulatory policy, §8-1503.
Markets, §37-205.02.
Marriage.
Authorization to solemnize, registration fee for, §46-406.
License fees, §15-717.
Domestic partners, §32-702.
Medical examiners, §5-1412.
Medical marijuana, §7-1671.10.
Mental health disclosures pursuant to collection of, §7-1203.04.
Metropolitan police services, prohibition on accepting fees for, §5-133.10.
Metropolitan Washington Airports Authority, §9-917.
Money lenders, §§26-905, 26-908.
Mortgage lenders' and brokers' licenses, §§26-1103, 26-1107.
Motor fuel tax and International Fuel Tax Agreement, §47-2354.
Motor vehicle registration.
See MOTOR VEHICLE REGISTRATION.
Notaries public.
License fees, §1-1201.
Penalty for charging higher than scheduled fees, §1-1214.
Schedule of fees charged by, §1-1213.
Parks and recreation, §10-213.01.
Pawnbrokers' licenses, §§47-2884.03 to 47-2884.06.
Pesticide registration fee, §8-438.
Pharmacists and pharmacies, §47-2885.19.
Plastic carryout bags, §8-102.03.
Plumbing inspections, §2-136.
Private vehicles-for-hire.
Charges, §50-301.29f.
Probate proceedings, §§15-707, 15-708.
Death before January 1, 1981, Probate Rule 24.
Compensation of personal representatives, Probate Rule 22.
Pro hac vice appearances, DCCtApp Rule 49.
Public auction permits, §47-2702.
Public utilities investigations, witnesses at, §§34-905, 34-910, 34-919.

FEES —Cont'd
Radon contractors' proficiency requirements, §28-4203.
Raffle licenses, §3-1325.
Recorder of deeds, §§42-1210, 42-1212, 42-1215.
Recreation board, §10-213.01.
Register of wills, §§11-2104, 11-2106.
Registration fees, setting, §§1-301.74, 1-301.75.
Rental housing.
Conversion on sale.
Application fees, §42-3402.05a.
Certification fees, §42-3402.05.
Conversion fees, §42-3402.04.
Rental property locator fees, §28-3819.
Rental unit fees, §42-3504.01.
Secured transactions.
Financing statements.
Filing, §28:9-503.
Assignment of security interests, §28:9-514.
Security and fire alarm contractors, §§7-2811, 7-2814.
Setting, §§1-301.74, 1-301.75.
Small claims court, §16-3903, SmallClaims Rule 14.
Arbitration, SmallClaimsArb Rule 1.
Conciliation, SmallClaims Conciliation Rule 1.
Solid waste facilities, §8-1057.
Solid waste reduction and recovery, §8-1031.11.
Special public safety fees, §§47-2751 to 47-2753.
State health planning and development agency, §44-420.
Streets and alleys, closing, §9-202.14.
Student health care examinations, §38-605.
Surveyor of the District, fee schedule for services of, §1-1329.
Tax proceedings.
Filing petitions, Tax Rule 4.
Titling of motor vehicles, §50-2201.03.
Traffic laws.
See TRAFFIC LAWS.
Traffic ticket adjudication, §50-2301.05.
Treasury, payment of District fees into, §47-127.
Vacant buildings.
Delinquent collection of fees, §42-3131.13.
Registration fee, §42-3131.09.

FEES —Cont'd
Vital records, §7-221.
Water and sewer authority.
Storm water fee, §34-2202.16.
Weights and measures, inspecting,
§37-201.03.
Well construction and maintenance.
Permit fees, §8-103.13b.
Wharfage fee, §10-501.02.
Witness fees.
See WITNESSES.
Zoning, §6-661.01.

FEE SIMPLE ESTATES.
Absolute, §42-503.
Decedents' estates, §42-701.
Entailed estates now recognized as,
§42-502.
Estates in land.
General provisions, §§42-501 to
42-523.
See ESTATES IN LAND.
Form of deed for, §42-601.
Horizontal property regimes,
§42-2006.
Qualified, §42-503.

FELONIES.
See CRIMES AND OFFENSES.

FELONY MURDER, §22-2101.

FEMS SPECIAL EVENTS FEE
FUND, §1-325.81.

FENCING STOLEN PROPERTY,
§§22-3231, 22-3232.

FERN STREET VIADUCT, §§9-315,
9-316.

FERTILIZER.
Anacostia river cleanup and
protection fertilizer act,
§§8-104.01 to 8-104.07.
Definitions, §8-104.02.
Enforcement, §8-104.07.
Fertilizer application requirements,
§8-104.03.
Fertilizer labeling requirements,
§8-104.05.
Fertilizer public education program,
§8-104.04.
Penalties, §8-104.06.
Rules, §8-104.07.
Short title, §8-104.01.

FESTIVALS.
Rental of public space.
Street festival one day rental,
§10-1102.01a.

FETAL DEATHS, §§7-213, 7-214.

FIDUCIARIES, §§21-1701 to 21-1712.
Accounts and accounting.
Bond of fiduciary.
Discharge only after accounting,
§28-2504.
Accounts and reports, CivPro Rule
305.
Actions by fiduciaries, CivPro Rule
17.
Domestic relations actions, DomRel
Rule 17.
Applicability of other laws, §21-1711.
Assignments.
Securities, §28-2903.
Bond issues of District, investments
in, §1-204.86.
Bonds and undertakings, CivPro Rule
303.
Bonds, surety.
Discharge of, §28-2504.
Discharge only after accounting,
§28-2504.
Undertaking in lieu of, §16-601.
Check drawn by fiduciary.
From deposit in name of principal,
§21-1707.
Payable to fiduciary, §21-1705.
Payable to third person, §21-1704.
Compensation, CivPro Rule 301.
Guardian ad litem in conservatorship
proceedings, CivPro Rule 302,
Probate Rule 224.
Conflicts of interest, CivPro Rule 304.
Probate proceedings.
Death on or after July 1, 1995,
Probate Rule 422.
Guardians, conservators, trustees,
etc., involved, Probate Rule 202.
Death of represented person, CivPro
Rule 305.
Default judgment against minor or
incompetent person, CivPro Rule
55.
Definitions, §§21-1701, 28-2901.
Deposit in name of fiduciary as
fiduciary, §21-1706.
Deposit in name of principal,
§21-1707.
Deposit in names of two or more
trustees, §21-1709.
Deposit to personal credit of certain
funds, §21-1708.
Disclaimer of property interests,
§§19-1501 to 19-1518.
See DISCLAIMER OF PROPERTY
INTERESTS.

FIDUCIARIES —Cont'd

Durable powers of attorney.
Relationship to person with, §21-2083.

Eligibility requirements, CivPro Rule 304.

Expenditures, CivPro Rule 305.

Foreclosure rescue services.
Fiduciary duties, §42-2433.

Guardians ad litem generally.
See GUARDIAN AD LITEM.

Guardianship of incapacitated persons, §§21-2041 to 21-2049.
See GUARDIAN AND WARD.

Guardianship of minors.
General provisions, §§21-101 to 21-182.
See GUARDIAN AND WARD.
Intervention proceedings, Probate Rules 301 to 361.
See INTERVENTION PROCEEDINGS.

Health maintenance organizations.
Fiduciary responsibilities of, §31-3405.

Hospital and medical services corporations boards of directors or trustees, §31-3520.

Income taxes, §47-1805.02.

Investments, CivPro Rule 306.
Probate proceedings.
All proceedings, Probate Rule 5.
Guardians, conservators, trustees, etc., involved, Probate Rules 222, 223.
Petition for approval of investment plan, Probate Form 3.
Petition for authority to invest, Probate Form 2.
Prudent investor act.
See PRUDENT INVESTOR ACT.

Judges.
Appointment to fiduciary positions, CJC Canon 3.8.

Mortgages and deeds of trust.
Foreclosure rescue services.
Fiduciary duties, §42-2433.

Negotiable instruments transferred by fiduciary, §21-1703.

Partners, fiduciary duties of, §29-604.07.

Payment or transfer of money or other property to, §21-1701.

Personal representatives' status as, §20-701.

Pharmacy benefits managers.
Fiduciary duties of, §48-832.01.

FIDUCIARIES —Cont'd

Power of attorney.
Nonresident or absent fiduciary, CivPro Rule 305.

Principal and income act, §§28-4801.01 to 28-4806.02.
See PRINCIPAL AND INCOME.

Probate proceedings generally.
See PROBATE PROCEEDINGS.

Property held in fiduciary capacity.
Appraisal, CivPro Rule 305.
Removal from District of Columbia, CivPro Rule 304.
Sale, CivPro Rule 305.

Prudent investor act.
See PRUDENT INVESTOR ACT.

Public officers and employees as, §1-615.04.

Real estate brokers and salespersons.
Fiduciary duties of, §§47-2853.191 to 47-2853.195.

Retirement Board responsibilities, §§1-741 to 1-748.

Retroactivity of provisions, §21-1710.

Security transfers, §§28-2901 to 28-2909.
See FIDUCIARY SECURITY TRANSFERS.

Statement of distribution and settlement, CivPro Rule 305.

Successor fiduciaries.
Guardian ad litem not required, CivPro Rule 304.

Transfer of securities, §§28-2901 to 28-2909.
See FIDUCIARY SECURITY TRANSFERS.

Transfers to minors by, §21-306.

Trustees' powers.
Prohibitions, §21-1722.

Trust, mortgage and title corporations.
See TRUST, MORTGAGE AND TITLE CORPORATIONS.

Trusts and trustees.
Uniform trust code.
Personal representatives, §19-1303.03.

Unclaimed property held by, §41-111.

Uniform fiduciaries act, §§21-1701 to 21-1712.

Unincorporated nonprofit associations.
Duties of managers, §29-1119.

Validity of right or title acquired from fiduciary in consideration of payment or transfer, §21-1702.

FIDUCIARY SECURITY TRANSFERS, §§28-2901 to 28-2909.

Adverse claims, §28-2905.

Application of chapter.
Territorial application, §28-2908.

Appointment of fiduciary.
Evidence of appointment, §28-2904.

Assignment.
Assignment of security by fiduciary, §§28-2903, 28-2904.
Defined, §28-2901.

Claim of beneficial interest.
Adverse claims, §28-2905.
Defined, §28-2901.

Conflict of laws.
Territorial application of chapter, §28-2908.

Corporation making transfer.
Nonliability of, §28-2906.

Corporations.
Defined, §28-2901.
Nonliability, §28-2906.

Definitions, §28-2901.

Evidence of fiduciary status, §28-2904.

Fiduciaries.
Defined, §28-2901.

Incumbency of fiduciary.
Evidence of incumbency, §28-2904.

Inheritance and estate taxes.
Chapter not affected by tax obligations, §28-2909.

Jurisdiction, §28-2908.

Liability.
Corporations, §28-2906.
Third persons, §28-2907.
Transfer agent, §28-2906.

Notice.
Adverse claims, §28-2905.
Fiduciary no longer acting as such, §28-2902.

Person.
Defined, §28-2901.

Registration of security in name of fiduciary, §28-2902.

Security.
Defined, §28-2901.

Taxation, §28-2909.

Tax obligations.
Not affected by chapter, §28-2909.

Third persons.
Nonliability, §28-2907.

Transfer.
Defined, §28-2901.

Transfer agent.
Defined, §28-2901.

FIDUCIARY SECURITY TRANSFERS —Cont'd
Transfer agent —Cont'd
Nonliability, §28-2906.

FIERI FACIAS.
Garnishment.
Post-judgment garnishment in aid of execution.
Sale of property under fieri facias, §16-555.
Prejudgment garnishment.
Condemnation and sale of property, §16-525.
Writ, CivPro Form CA 120.

FIGHTING OR BAITING FOWL OR ANIMALS, §22-1009.
Penalty, §22-1006.01.
Urging dogs to fight or create disorder, §22-1310.

FILLING STATIONS, §§36-301.01 to 36-305.02.
See GAS STATIONS.

FILM.
Business licenses, §47-2820.
Children and minors, §47-2820.
Deceptive labeling, §22-3214.01.
Police and firefighters assigned to theaters, §47-2820.
Recording device.
Unlawful operation of, §22-3214.02.
Theft, §§22-3214.01, 22-3214.02.

FINANCE LEASES.
Commercial code leases.
Generally, §§28:2A-101 to 28:2A-532.
See LEASES, UCC.

FINANCIAL AID ASSISTANCE.
College access assistance, §§38-2701 to 38-2706.
DC promise program, §§38-2751 to 38-2759.
See UNIVERSITIES AND COLLEGES.
District of Columbia School of Law.
Mayor's stipends, §38-1205.11.
Nurse training corps, §§38-1501 to 38-1503.
Opportunity accounts.
Generally, §§1-307.61 to 1-307.74.
Use for educational expenses, §1-307.68.
Police and firefighters.
Tuition expenses, §5-1305.
University of the District of Columbia.
Grants, §§38-1207.01 to 38-1207.07.

FINANCIAL EXPLOITATION OF VULNERABLE ADULTS AND ELDERLY PERSONS.
Criminal abuse, neglect and financial exploitation of vulnerable adults and elderly persons, §§22-931 to 22-938.
See CRIMINAL ABUSE, NEGLECT AND FINANCIAL EXPLOITATION OF VULNERABLE ADULTS AND ELDERLY PERSONS.

FINANCIAL INSTITUTIONS.
Department and commissioner of insurance, securities, and banking, §§26-551.01 to 26-551.25.
See BANKS AND FINANCIAL INSTITUTIONS.
Generally.
See BANKS AND FINANCIAL INSTITUTIONS.

FINANCIAL INSTITUTIONS ADVISORY BOARD, §§26-551.06 to 26-551.09.
Establishment, §26-551.06.
Members, §26-551.07.
Organization and operation, §26-551.08.
Statements of reasons for not following board's advice, §26-551.09.

FINANCIAL LITERACY COUNCIL, §§38-731.01 to 38-731.05.
Definitions, §38-731.01.
Duties, §38-731.05.
Established, §38-731.03.
Members, §38-731.04.
Plan for education in public schools, §38-731.02.
Reports, §38-731.05.

FINANCIAL OFFICER.
Office of chief financial officer.
See CHIEF FINANCIAL OFFICER.

FINANCIAL RESPONSIBILITY AND MANAGEMENT ASSISTANCE AUTHORITY, §§47-391.01 to 47-395.
Actions, §§47-391.04, 47-391.05.
Annual federal payment, deposit of, §47-392.05.
Applicability of District laws to, §47-391.08.
Application processes, review of, §47-395.

FINANCIAL RESPONSIBILITY AND MANAGEMENT ASSISTANCE AUTHORITY —Cont'd
Approval of financial plan and budget, §47-392.02.
Bond issues, §§47-392.11 to 47-392.15.
Amounts included in aggregate limits on District borrowing, §47-392.14.
Authority to issue, §47-392.11.
Debt service reserve fund, §§47-392.13, 47-392.14.
No full faith and credit of federal government, §47-392.15.
Pledge or grant of security interest in revenues, §47-392.12.
Borrowing restrictions, §47-392.04.
Chief management officer, §47-391.09.
Control periods, §47-392.09.
Definitions, §47-393.
Development of financial plan and budget by, §47-392.01.
Establishment of, §47-391.01.
Executive director, §47-391.02.
Fiscal year 1996 special rules, §47-392.08.
Funding, §47-391.06.
General assistance in achieving stability and efficiency, providing, §47-392.22.
Liability, exemption from, §47-391.04.
Noncompliance with financial plan and budget, §47-392.06.
Non-control year duties, §47-392.21.
Operating cash reserve fund, §47-392.02.
Organization and membership, §47-391.01.
Permit processes, review of, §47-395.
Personnel, §47-391.02.
Powers and duties, §§47-391.03, 47-392.21.
Recommendations of, §47-392.07.
Regulatory review, §47-395.
Reports by, §47-392.24.
Reports to, §§47-392.06, 47-392.23.
Review of District government activities, §47-392.03.
School property, disposition of, §47-392.25.
Submission of financial plan and budget, §47-392.02.
Submission of reports to, §1-204.56e.
Suspension of activities of, §47-391.07.

FINANCING STATEMENTS.
Recordation, §§41-201 to 41-204.

FINE ARTS COMMISSION.
Building heights, review of,
§§6-611.01, 6-611.02.

FINES AND CIVIL PENALTIES.
Abandoned and unlawfully parked
vehicles.
Purchaser of salvaged vehicle,
abandoning vehicle, §50-2421.10.
Second offense, §50-2421.09.
Tampering with, §50-2421.04.
Accessories after the fact, §22-1806.
Administrative fines, §§2-1801.01 to
2-1803.03.
See ADMINISTRATIVE FINES.
Adulteration of food or drugs,
§48-109.
Adult protective services, §7-1912.
Affrays, §22-1301.
Aggravated assault, §22-404.01.
Air pollution, §8-101.05c.
Airspace, rental of, §10-1121.10.
Alcoholic beverage licenses.
Civil penalties for violations, §25-830.
Failure to ascertain valid
identification, §25-783.
Influencing application process,
§25-434.
No specific penalty specified, §25-831.
Pregnant women, warnings for.
Failure to post, §25-712.
Alcoholic beverages.
Children and minors.
Delivery, offer, or making available
to, §25-785.
Purchase, possession, or
consumption by, §25-1002.
Generally.
See ALCOHOLIC BEVERAGES.
Importation of beverages into District,
§25-772.
Open container law, §25-1001.
Public intoxication, §25-1001.
Sale to minors or intoxicated persons,
§25-781.
All-terrain vehicles.
Operating on public property,
§50-2201.04b.
Alternative fuel technology, §§50-703,
50-712.
Ammunition.
Restricted pistol bullets, §7-2507.06.
Amounts credited to District,
§47-128.
Animals, §8-1811.
Release of animals, §8-1831.01.
Armed carjacking, §22-2803.

FINES AND CIVIL PENALTIES
—Cont'd
Arson.
Generally, §22-301.
Intent to defraud or injury, §22-302.
Malicious burning, etc., of other's
property, §22-303.
Asbestos contractors, §§8-111.09,
8-111.10.
Assault.
Common law assault, §22-404.
Police officer or firefighter, assault on,
§22-405.
Public officials, §22-851.
Resisting arrest, §22-405.01.
Assignments.
Contract to assign future salary or
wages, §28-2305.
Assisted living residences.
Civil penalties, §44-104.02.
Athlete agents, §47-2887.15.
Automated traffic enforcement,
§50-2209.02.
Collection of fines, §1-629.05.
Bail bondsmen, §§23-1108, 23-1111.
Banks and financial institutions,
§26-103.
Offering public utility bill payment
services, §26-111.
Barbed-wire fences, §9-1213.04.
Bicycle identifying numbers.
Tampering with or removing,
§22-3234.
Bicycle operators.
Commercial, §50-1634.
Helmet violations, §50-1605.
Bingo games, unauthorized.
Aiding and abetting, §3-1332.
Blind and visually impaired.
Interfering with or discriminating
against, §7-1007.
Blindness in newborns, prevention
of, §7-804.
Blocking passage.
Public or private building, enclosure,
road or sidewalk, §22-1307.
Boating under the influence,
§50-2206.32.
Impaired operation, §50-2206.34.
Minor in watercraft, §50-2206.36.
Refusal or failure to submit to
chemical testing, §50-1912.
Body artists, §47-2853.76d.
Criminal penalties, §47-2853.76e.
Boiler inspections, §2-114.
Regulatory violations, §2-114.

FINES AND CIVIL PENALTIES
—Cont'd
Bonfires, kindling, §22-1313.
Boxing and wrestling commission,
§3-608.
Breaking and entering vending
machines, §22-601.
Bribery, §§22-704, 22-712.
Witnesses, §22-713.
Building associations, §26-204.
Building code.
Requirements for fire prevention,
§6-703.06.
Burglary, §22-801.
Business licenses, §§47-2844, 47-2846.
Disposition of, §47-2851.13.
Unpaid fines, penalties, and interest.
Computer recordkeeping and
reporting system, §47-2866.
Definitions, §47-2861.
Issuance prohibited, §47-2862.
Right to appeal denial of license,
§47-2865.
Self-certification of lack of
outstanding debt, §47-2863.
Falsification of certification,
penalty, §47-2864.
Business organizations, §29-101.06.
Campaign finance, §1-1163.35.
Cancer prevention and monitoring,
§7-304.
Capitol grounds, §10-503.18.
Captive insurance companies.
Imposition by commissioner,
§31-3931.15.
Carjacking, §22-2803.
Cemeteries and cemetery
associations, §43-126.
Certified business enterprises.
Breach of subcontracting plans,
§2-218.48.
Charitable solicitations, §44-1712.
Check cashing businesses, §26-323.
Child abuse and neglect reports,
§4-1321.07.
Child care facilities, §7-2046.
Child fatality report.
Failure to make, §4-1371.14.
Child fatality review committee
investigations.
Unlawful disclosure of information,
§4-1371.11.
Child labor, §32-213.
Child prostitution, §22-2704.
Child protection register
disclosures, §4-1302.08.

FINES AND CIVIL PENALTIES
—Cont'd
Child restraint seats, §50-1706.
Child sexual abuse.
Assault with intent to commit,
§22-401.
Failure to report, §22-3020.54.
First and second degree, §§22-3008 to
22-3010.
Lewd, indecent, or obscene acts,
§22-1312.
Sexually suggestive conduct,
§22-3010.01.
Civil infractions, §§2-1801.01 to
2-1803.03.
See ADMINISTRATIVE FINES.
Clinical laboratories, §44-212.
Closing-out sales, §47-2106.
Collection of taxes.
Divulging information about returns,
§47-4406.
Collections agencies.
Use of "District" or similar
designation, §22-3402.
Commercial bicycle operators,
§50-1634.
Commercial counterfeiting, §22-902.
Commercial drivers' licenses,
§§50-405, 50-405.01.
Commercial piracy, §22-3214.
Communicable diseases, §7-140.
Compulsory school attendance,
§38-203.
Condominiums, §42-1904.17.
Conspiracy, §22-1805a.
Construction codes, §6-1406.
Consumer credit reporting agencies.
Consumer security freeze.
Willful violations, §28-3864.
Consumer credit service
organizations, §28-4607.
Consumer protection.
Department of consumer and
regulatory affairs, §28-3903.
Overcharging.
Natural disasters, §28-4103.
Violations, §28-3905.
Contributing to the delinquency of a
minor, §22-811.
Controlled substances.
Penalties generally.
See CONTROLLED SUBSTANCES.
Conversion of health care entities,
§44-609.
Council.
Electronic communications.
Disclosure, §1-301.44a.

FINES AND CIVIL PENALTIES
—Cont'd

Council —Cont'd
Investigations, obstruction of, §1-301.43.
Crime investigation records.
Penalties for willful or malicious tampering with records, §5-113.33.
Criminal background checks.
Child or youth services providers.
Disclosing confidential information, §4-1501.10.
Unlicensed health care personnel, §44-553.
Criminal offenses generally, §§22-3571.01, 22-3571.02.
Criminal procedure.
Disposition of, §16-707.
Imprisonment on nonpayment of, §16-706.
Wrongful conversion of, §16-708.
Criminal street gangs, §22-951.
Cruelty to animals, §22-1001.
Cruelty to children, §§22-1101, 22-1102.
Dangerous dogs, §8-1906.
Deceptive labeling, §22-3214.01.
Delinquent minors.
Contributing to the delinquency of a minor, §22-811.
Restitution, JuvProc Rule 112.
Dirt bikes.
Operating on public property, §50-2201.04b.
Disabled, injured, or sick animals.
Abandonment of, §22-1012.
Neglect of, §22-1011.
Disorderly conduct, §22-1321.
District funds invested or deposited in banks and financial institutions, §47-351.15.
District of Columbia or similar designation.
Private use of, §22-3402.
Domestic violence fatality review board.
Disclosure of confidential information, §16-1056.
Drivers' licenses.
See DRIVERS' LICENSES.
Driving under the influence, §50-2206.13.
Boating under the influence, §50-2206.32.
Impaired operation of watercraft, §50-2206.34.
Minor in watercraft, §50-2206.36.

FINES AND CIVIL PENALTIES
—Cont'd

Driving under the influence —Cont'd
Fines collected, transfer to general fund, §50-2206.58.
Impaired driving, §50-2206.15.
Minor in vehicle, additional penalties, §50-2206.18.
Drug-free zones, §48-904.07a.
Drug manufacture and distribution licensure, §§48-711, 48-712.
Due process, threatening, injuring, intimidating, or interfering with persons in order to deprive them of, §22-3312.04.
Dulles International Airport, §9-810.
Educational licensure commission, §38-1313.
Electronic waste.
Violations of act, §8-1041.12.
Emergency medical services, §7-2341.24.
Emergency price gouging, §28-4101.
Employees retirement program management, §1-739.
Employment agencies, §32-414.
Energy conservation for commercial property.
Penalties for violations, §8-1772.03.
Energy efficiency standards.
Violations, §8-1771.05.
Escape, §22-2601.
Ethics and government accountability, §1-1162.21.
Public officials, §1-1162.22.
Excavation or demolition.
Public utility damages caused by, §34-2707.
Excessive fines, US Const Amd 8.
Extortion.
Blackmail, §22-3252.
Generally, §22-3251.
Failure to appear, §§23-703, 23-1327.
False fire alarms, §22-1319.
False personation.
Public officer or minister, §§22-1403 to 22-1405.
False statements, §22-2405.
False swearing, §22-2404.
Financial exploitation of vulnerable adults and elderly persons, §22-937.
Fire and casualty insurance, §31-2502.42.
Firearms, §7-2507.06.
Criminally negligent storage, §7-2507.02.

FINES AND CIVIL PENALTIES
—Cont'd

Firearms —Cont'd

Enhanced penalties and fines for
carrying guns into gun free zones,
§22-4502.01.

Pistol, license to carry, §7-2509.10.

Registration violations, §7-2502.09.

Violations not specifically provided for,
§22-4515.

Fire balloons, §22-1317.

**Firefighter retirement while under
disciplinary investigation,**
§§5-1054, 5-1055.

Fire-standard-compliant cigarettes,
§7-1756.

Fish and game, §22-4331.

**Fleeing from a law enforcement
officer in a motor vehicle,**
§50-2201.05b.

Flood hazards, §6-506.

Food delivery vehicles.

Motor vehicle insurance for, §50-104.

Footways in public grounds.

Driving or riding on, §22-1318.

**Foreclosure rescue services and
transactions.**

Violations of provisions, §42-2435.

Forgery, §22-3242.

Goods, brands or packaging of,
§22-1502.

Fraternal benefit societies, §31-5332.

Fraud and deceit, §22-3222.

Checks, drafts, or orders intended to
defraud, §22-1510.

Credit card fraud, §22-3223.

Fraudulent registration in lodgings,
§22-3224.

Fraudulent advertising, §22-1513.

Funeral directors, §3-417.

Gambling.

Bookmaking, §22-1708.

Confidence games, §22-1706.

Keeping gaming premises, §§5-115.06,
22-1704, 22-1705.

Sports, §§22-1708, 22-1713.

Three-card monte, §22-1706.

Gambling by children and minors,
§§3-1334, 3-1335.

Gangs, §22-951.

Gas stations, §36-302.05.

Graffiti, §22-3312.04.

Abatement.

Collection, §42-3141.09.

Disposition of, §42-3141.08.

Liability for, §42-3141.07.

FINES AND CIVIL PENALTIES
—Cont'd

Grave robbery, §§3-206, 22-3303.

Gross sales tax, §§47-2014, 47-2027.

Promoters of special events, §47-2826.

**Guardianship of incapacitated
persons.**

Sexual abuse of a ward, §§22-3013,
22-3014.

Gun free zones.

Enhanced penalties and fines for
carrying guns into, §22-4502.01.

Habeas corpus violations, §16-1904.

Hazardous materials transportation,
§8-1404.

Terrorism prevention, §8-1425.

Hazardous substance releases,
§8-634.06.

Hazardous waste management,
§8-1311.

Healing arts practitioners.

Sexual abuse of patient or client,
§§22-3015, 22-3016.

Health care facilities, §44-509.

Interference with or obstruction of,
§§22-1314.01, 22-1314.02.

Unsafe disposal of pharmaceuticals,
§48-851.03.

Health data privacy.

Unlawful use or disclosure of
information, §§7-245, 7-246.

Health maintenance organizations,
§31-3423.

Health occupations boards,
§3-1205.14.

**Health occupations licensure,
registration or certification,**
§§3-1205.13a, 3-1210.07, 3-1210.09,
7-161.

**Healthy DC and health care
expansion fund and program.**

Violations, §4-636.

Disposition of fines, §4-637.

Helmet requirements, §§50-1605,
50-1651.

Effective date for enforcement,
§50-1652.

Helmet violations.

Bicycle operators and passengers,
§50-1605.

Highway work zones.

Moving infractions, §50-2201.04c.

Hiring of ex-offenders.

Fair criminal record screening,
§32-1344.

Historic districts, §6-1110.

FINES AND CIVIL PENALTIES
—Cont'd

Historic landmarks, §6-1110.

Home improvement contractors.
Bonding requirements, §47-2883.04.

Horse-drawn carriages, §8-2012.

Hospital and medical services corporations, §31-3521.

Hospitalization of persons with mental illness, §21-591.

Human tissue banks, §7-1541.04.

Human trafficking, §22-1837.

Identity theft, §22-3227.03.

Impaired driving, §50-2206.15.
Minor in vehicle, additional penalties, §50-2206.18.

Impaired operation of watercraft, §50-2206.34.
Minor in watercraft, §50-2206.36.

Implements of crime, possession of, §22-2501.

Imports.
Alcoholic beverages.
Importation of beverages into District, §25-772.

Inaugural ceremonies of the President of the United States, §§2-809, 2-827.

Insanitary buildings, §6-916.

Inspection of motor vehicles, §50-1106.

Insurance adjusters, §31-1631.07.

Insurance companies engaging in business without license or certificate of authority, §47-2604.

Insurance fraud, §§22-3225.04, 22-3225.14.

Insurance holding companies, §31-710.

Insurance producers, §31-1131.12.

Interception of oral or wire communications.
Possession, sale, etc., of intercepting devices, §23-543.

Interest, §28-3313.

Intermediate care facilities for persons with intellectual disabilities.
Assessment on facilities, §47-1274.

Interstate banking and branch banks, §26-707.02.

Intestate succession.
Allowances and exemptions.
Willful violations, §19-101.06.

Jury selection.
Confidentiality violations, §16-5103.

FINES AND CIVIL PENALTIES
—Cont'd

Juvenile curfew violations, §2-1543.

Juvenile records.
Unlawful disclosure, §16-2336.

Kidnapping, §22-1810.

Labor and employment relations.
Pregnant and nursing workers, reasonable accommodations for.
Penalties for violations, §32-1231.11.

Labor unions' label, brand, or mark.
Unauthorized use of, §36-102.

Landlord and tenant, §42-3509.01.

Law enforcement officers.
Assault on, §22-405.
Fleeing from a law enforcement officer in a motor vehicle, §50-2201.05b.
Resisting arrest, §22-405.01.

Lead-hazard prevention and elimination.
Penalties for violations, §§8-231.15, 8-231.16.

Lead poisoning.
Childhood lead poisoning screening and reporting, failure to comply, §7-871.05.

Leash law violations, §22-1311.

Leave of absence.
Right to sick and safe leave.
Failure to post notices, §32-131.09.
Penalties for violations, §32-131.12.

Lewd, indecent, or obscene acts, §22-1312.

Libraries, §39-105.

Lie detector tests, §32-903.

Life insurance companies, §31-4601.

Litter control, §8-807.
Refusal to be identified on notice of violation, §8-811.

Lobbying, §1-1162.32.

Loitering.
Unlawful assembly, §22-1321.

Long-term care insurance, §31-3612.

Long-term care ombudsman, §7-704.01.

Lotteries.
Promotion, sale or possession of tickets, §§22-1701 to 22-1703.

Lottery tickets.
Forged, altered, or counterfeit, §3-1333.

Managing general agents, §31-1506.

Marijuana, possession decriminalization.
Fines for civil violations, §48-1203.

Marriage, §46-421.
License return, failure to make, §46-413.

FINES AND CIVIL PENALTIES
—Cont'd
Mattresses, §8-505.
Medicaid.
Service provider fraud, §§4-802, 4-803.
Medical and dental colleges.
Failure to register, §38-1403.
Medication advisory committee receiving gifts or remuneration prohibition act.
Violations, §48-842.04.
Mental health disclosures, §§7-1207.01, 7-1207.02, 7-1208.01.
Mental illness, hospitalization of persons with, §21-591.
Metrorail and metrobus.
See METRORAIL AND METROBUS.
Milk container registration, §36-130.
Minimum wages, §32-1011.
Minors loitering around business establishments during school hours, permitting, §32-221.
Money lenders, §26-907.
Monte Carlo night parties, unauthorized.
Aiding and abetting, §3-1332.
Mortgage lenders and brokers, §26-1118.
Mortgages and deeds of trust.
Foreclosure rescue services and transactions.
Violations of provisions, §42-2435.
Motion picture theaters.
Operation of recording device, §22-3214.02.
Motor fuel tax.
See MOTOR FUEL TAX.
Motor vehicles.
Financing, §50-607.
Identification numbers, altering or removing, §22-3233.
Inspections, §50-1106.
Registration, §50-1501.04.
Safety impact assessment of fine reductions, §50-2111.
Safety responsibility violations, §50-1301.75.
Theft, §22-3215.
Unlawful entry, §22-1341.
Murder.
Solicitation of murder or other violent crimes, §22-2107.
National guard.
Absence from duty, §49-104.
Armament, equipment, and supplies, selling, pawning, etc., §49-205.

FINES AND CIVIL PENALTIES
—Cont'd
National guard —Cont'd
Use of fines, §49-906.
Natural disaster price gouging, §28-4101.
No-fault motor vehicle insurance, §31-2413.
Non-code offenses, §22-1807.
Notaries public charging higher than scheduled fees, §1-1214.
Obscenity, §22-2201.
Obstruction of justice, §22-722.
Interference with reports to or requests for assistance from law enforcement, medical providers, or child welfare agencies, §22-1931.
Tampering with physical evidence, §22-723.
Occupational safety and health, §§32-1120, 32-1121.
Occupations and professions licensure, §47-2853.27.
Official correspondence violations, §§2-708 to 2-710.
Open meetings act violation, §2-579.
Outdoor signs, §1-303.23.
Out-of-District property.
Violation of provisions regarding, §10-509.03.
Panhandling, §22-2304.
Parachutes, §22-1317.
Parentage proceedings.
Disclosure of information, §16-2348.
Parental kidnapping, §16-1024.
Paving stones.
Failure to replace, §9-1201.08.
Pawnbrokers, §47-2884.16.
Pedestrians.
Failure to stop and give right-of-way to, §50-2201.28.
Pensions and retirement funds, §1-909.08.
Perjury, §§22-2402, 22-2403.
Personal property taxes.
See PERSONAL PROPERTY TAXES.
Persons with disabilities.
Interfering with or discriminating against, §7-1007.
Pesticides, §8-418.
Education and control violations, §8-439.
Pharmaceutical detailing.
Penalties for practice without license, §3-1207.45.
Pharmacists and pharmacies, §47-2885.20.

FINES AND CIVIL PENALTIES
—Cont'd

Phosphate cleaners, §8-107.03.

Plants and plant diseases, §8-305.

Playing games in streets, §22-1308.

Polygraphs, §32-903.

Portable electronics insurance.
Penalties for violations of provisions, §31-5051.05.

Potomac river.
Throwing or depositing matter into, §§22-4402, 22-4403.

Power to set, §1-301.01.

Pregnant and nursing workers, reasonable accommodations for.
Penalties for violations, §32-1231.11.

Prescription drugs.
Marketing costs, disclosure of, §48-833.06.
Pharmacy benefits managers, §48-832.03.
Pricing, §48-804.01.

Price gouging during natural disasters, §28-4101.

Prison breach, §22-2601.

Prison contraband, §22-2603.03.

Prisoners, commutation for, §24-201.04.

Prisons and prisoners.
Hiring of ex-offenders.
Fair criminal record screening, §32-1344.

Private detectives.
Use of "District" or similar designation, §22-3402.

Privies, §8-604.

Procurement claims, false, §2-381.09.

Profane and indecent language, §22-1321.

Prostitution.
Child prostitution, §22-2704.
Compelling individual to live life of prostitution, §22-2706.
Domestic partners caused to live in, §22-2708.
House of prostitution.
Pandering, procuring, or pimping for, §22-2710.
Inducing or inciting an individual to engage in, §22-2705.
Operating bawdy or disorderly house, §22-2722.
Operating house of prostitution, §22-2712.
Pandering, procuring, or pimping, §22-2705.
Third persons, for, §22-2711.

FINES AND CIVIL PENALTIES
—Cont'd

Prostitution —Cont'd
Receiving money or valuables for arranging assignations, §22-2707.
Solicitation for purposes, §22-2701.
Spouses caused to live in, §22-2708.

Protective orders, violation, §16-1005.

Protests targeting a residence, §22-2752.

Public assistance, §§4-218.02, 4-218.05.

Publication of documents, §2-562.

Public contract whistleblower protection, §2-223.04.

Public officers and employees.
Corrupt influence, §§22-704, 22-712.
Threatening, stalking, assaulting, etc., §22-851.

Public or private building, enclosure, road or sidewalk.
Blocking passage, §22-1307.

Public utilities.
See PUBLIC UTILITIES.

Public welfare institutions.
Assisting children in leaving without authorization, §4-125.

Race discrimination in admission to licensed places, §§47-2901 to 47-2911.

Radon contractors' proficiency requirements, §28-4203.

Raffles, unauthorized.
Aiding and abetting, §3-1332.

Railroad transportation of animals, §22-1003.

Rape.
Various degrees of sexual abuse, §§22-3002 to 22-3006.

Real estate brokers and salespersons, §42-1708.

Real property taxes.
Nonpayment, §47-811.
Special energy assessments, §47-895.33.
Violations, §47-861.

Real property wet settlement act, §42-2407.

Recordation tax.
See RECORDATION TAX.

Recycling.
Construction and demolition waste recycling accountability, §8-1076.
Fairs and carnivals, §47-2826.

Regulations.
Additional penalties for violation of, §1-303.05.

FINES AND CIVIL PENALTIES
—Cont'd

Reinsurance intermediaries, §31-1810.

Rental housing conversion and sale, §42-3405.10.

Rental of public space, §10-1104.04.

Rental properties, §42-3509.01.

Rental unit alterations to occupied units after notice to vacate, §6-731.04.

Rent control, §42-3509.01.

Research animals, release, §8-1831.01.

Resisting arrest, §22-405.01.

Restraints of trade, §§28-4505, 28-4506.

Retail natural gas suppliers, §34-1671.11.

Rioting or inciting to riot, §22-1322.

Robbery.
Attempt to commit, §22-2802.

Salvage, flood and junk vehicles.
Unlawful acts, §50-1331.08.

Savings and loan acquisitions, §26-1215.

Schools and education.
Residency, establishment of.
False information, §38-313.
Testing integrity in public schools.
Sanctions for violations, §38-771.04.

Seat belts, §50-1806.

Second conviction of criminal offense, §22-1804.

Security agents and brokers.
Civil fines, §§31-5606.02, 31-5606.03.
Criminal fines, §31-5606.04.

Security and fire alarm contractors, §§7-2811, 7-2814.

Sex offender registration, §22-4015.

Sexual abuse.
Child sexual abuse.
Assault with intent to commit, §22-401.
First and second degree, §§22-3008 to 22-3010.
Lewd, indecent, or obscene acts, §22-1312.
Sexually suggestive conduct, §22-3010.01.
Various degrees of sexual abuse, §§22-3002 to 22-3006.

Sexual performances using minors, §22-3103.

Shoplifting, §27-102.

Signs advertising real property for rent or for sale, §42-1801.

FINES AND CIVIL PENALTIES
—Cont'd

Small and certified business enterprise development and assistance, §2-218.63.
Falsification of certificates of registration, §2-218.64.

Smoking, §7-1706.

Smoking in public places, §7-741.04.

Solicitation for purposes of prostitution, §22-2701.

Solicitation of murder or other violent crimes, §22-2107.

Stalking, §22-3134.
Public officials, §22-851.

Stay upon appeal, CrimPro Rule 38.

Stolen property.
Receiving stolen property, §22-3232.
Trafficking in stolen property, §22-3231.

Stormwater management.
Coal tar pavement product limitations, §8-153.01.

Street gangs, §22-951.

Street lighting.
Failure to provide or maintain, §§9-503, 9-505.

Subornation of perjury, §22-2403.

Surrogate parenting contracts, §16-402.

Taxation.
Generally.
See TAXATION.
Penalties generally, §§47-4211 to 47-4218.

Tax return preparers, §47-4217.

Telegraph and telephone companies, §§34-1911.03, 34-1921.03.

Telephone solicitation, §§22-3226.09, 22-3226.10.

Tenant assistance program, §42-3509.01.

Tenant organizations.
Violation of provisions, §42-3505.06.

Termination of parental rights.
Unlawful disclosures, §16-2364.

Terrorism prevention.
Hazardous materials transportation, §8-1425.

Theft, §22-3212.
Commercial piracy, §22-3214.
Deceptive labeling, §22-3214.01.
Generally, §22-3212.
Motor vehicle theft, §22-3215.
Shoplifting, §22-3213.
Taking property without right, §22-3216.

FINES AND CIVIL PENALTIES
—Cont'd

Threats to do bodily harm, §22-407.
Throwing stones and other missiles, §22-1309.
Title insurance producers, §31-5041.09.
Title insurers, §31-5031.21.
Tobacco.
  Minors.
    Purchases by, §7-1721.03.
    Sales to, §7-1721.02.
    Prohibited sellers, §7-1721.06.
    Self-service displays, §7-1721.04.
Tobacco master settlement agreement enforcement, §7-1803.06.
Tobacco tax.
  Civil penalties for violations, §47-2422.
Toilets, §8-604.
Trademark counterfeiting, §22-902.
Trafficking in human body parts, §7-1501.02.
Traffic laws, §50-2201.03.
  Safety impact assessment of fine reductions, §50-2111.
Traffic ticket adjudication, §§50-2301.05, 50-2303.04.
Transportation department, §50-921.19.
Trenches in highways, cutting, §9-431.02.
Trespass.
  Forcible entry and detainer, §22-3301.
  Unlawful entry on property, §22-3302.
Two-way radio communications, interference with, §5-1308.
Unauthorized use of, §22-3215.
Unclaimed property, §§41-135, 41-136.
Underground storage tanks, §8-113.09.
Unemployment compensation.
  Disposition of fines, §51-120.
  Employer payment of contributions, §51-104.
  Fraud and deceit, §51-119.
  Violations of provisions, §51-117.
Unemployment discrimination, §32-1366.
Unit pricing, §28-5209.
Universities and colleges.
  Campus police and security officers, assaults on, §22-405.
Urban forest preservation.
  Special trees, preservation, §8-651.04.
Usury, §28-3313.

FINES AND CIVIL PENALTIES
—Cont'd

Vacant buildings.
  Failure to register, §42-3131.10.
Vandalism.
  Art works, defacing, §22-3306.
  Boundary markers, destroying, §22-3309.
  Cross burning, §§22-3312.02, 22-3312.04.
  Defacing public or private property, §22-3312.01.
  Explosives placed with intent to destroy or injure property, §22-3305.
  Grave robbery, §22-3303.
  Milestones, removal of, §22-3320.
  Obstruction.
    Public highways, §§22-3321, 22-3322.
    Public roads, §22-3320.
    Railroad tracks, §22-3319.
  Printed material, defacing, §22-3306.
  Public records, defacing, §22-3307.
  Railings, destroying, §22-3314.
  Railroad track obstruction or displacement, §22-3319.
  Streets and alleys.
    Destroying or defacing building material for, §22-3313.
  Tombs, destroying, §22-3314.
  Trees and shrubbery, destroying, §22-3310.
  United States property, injury or destruction to, §22-3311.
  Vending machines and similar devices, §22-601.
  Water pollution, malicious, §22-3318.
Vector-borne disease control, §8-2131.08.
Vehicle identification numbers.
  Altering or removing, §22-3233.
Vending machines, breaking and entering, §22-601.
Veterinary facilities, §47-2888.07.
Vital records, §7-225.
Voyeurism, §22-3531.
Vulnerable adults and elderly persons.
  Criminal abuse, neglect and financial exploitation.
    Criminal penalties, §22-937.
Wages and salaries, §§32-1307, 32-1455.
Washington humane society, §44-1506.

FINES AND CIVIL PENALTIES
—Cont'd
Washington National Airport, §9-705.
Waste, illegal dumping, §8-902.
Wastewater disposal system,
§8-105.14.
Wastewater treatment systems.
Failure to make required connections,
§8-203.
Water pollution, §8-103.16.
Water supply and waterworks.
See WATER SUPPLY AND
WATERWORKS.
Weapons, §7-2507.06.
Enhanced penalties and fines for
carrying guns into gun free zones,
§22-4502.01.
Violations not specifically provided for,
§22-4515.
Weights and measures, §37-201.32.
Wet settlement act, §42-2407.
Whistleblower protection, §§1-615.55,
2-223.04.
Workplace fraud.
Complaints, investigation,
§32-1331.05.
Penalties for violation of provisions,
§32-1331.07.
Facilitating violation or evading
detection, §32-1331.13.
Recordkeeping by employers.
Notice of classification as
independent contractor.
Failure to notify, §32-1331.12.
Workplace safety, §32-812.
Youth residential facilities, §7-2108.

FINGERPRINTING.
Bail bondsmen.
Authorization of sureties, CrimPro
Rule 116.
Child and family services agency.
Criminal background checks.
Processing the check, §4-1305.05.
Firearms registration, §7-2502.04.
Insurance producer licensing.
Resident insurance producer license.
Applicants, §31-1131.06a.
Insurance, securities and banking,
background checks.
Confidentiality of information,
§31-633.
Definitions, §31-631.
Requirement of, §31-632.
Rules, §31-634.
Juvenile records, §16-2334.
Lottery and charitable games
control board members, §3-1304.

FINGERPRINTING —Cont'd
Police duties permitted before
appearance before court,
CrimPro Rule 5.
Taxicabs.
Fingerprinting fund, §50-301.23.

FIRE ALARMS.
Security and fire alarm contractors.
General provisions, §§7-2801 to
7-2815.
See SECURITY AND FIRE ALARM
CONTRACTORS.

FIRE AND CASUALTY INSURANCE,
§§31-2501.01 to 31-2502.42.
Actuarial opinion, summary, report,
§§31-2502.26a, 31-2502.26b.
Applicability of provisions,
§§31-2501.02, 31-2502.14.
Capital requirements, §31-2502.13.
Casualty and other insurance rates.
General provisions, §§31-2701 to
31-2714.
See INSURANCE.
Certificates of authority,
§§31-2502.02, 31-2502.03,
31-2502.21.
Cessation of business, §31-2502.04.
Definitions, §31-2501.03.
Discrimination, §31-2502.29.
Domestic companies, §§31-2501.03,
31-2502.15 to 31-2502.19.
Exclusive agency contracts,
§31-2502.19.
Fines, §31-2502.42.
Flood insurance.
Homeowner's and renter's insurance.
Notice that standard policy does not
cover flood damage,
§31-2502.28a.
Foreign and alien companies,
§§31-2502.20 to 31-2502.22.
Formation of domestic companies,
§31-2502.15.
Fraud and deceit, §31-2502.09.
Health and accident policy
provisions, §31-2502.28.
Horizontal property regimes,
§§42-2020 to 42-2022.
Insurance premium finance
companies, §§31-1101 to 31-1112.
Insurance underwriting, §§31-5001 to
31-5011.
Investments, §§31-1373.01 to
31-1373.12.
See INSURANCE INVESTMENTS.

FIRE AND CASUALTY INSURANCE
—Cont'd
Issuance of rules and regulations,
§31-2502.01.
Liability, borrowing or assuming,
§31-2502.17.
Licenses.
Exceptions, §31-2502.38.
Fees, §31-2502.41.
Unauthorized companies, procurement
of policies from, §31-2502.40.
Unlicensed persons, no compensation
of, §31-2502.31.
**Limitations on exposure to risks or
hazards,** §31-2502.12.
Lloyd's organizations, §31-2502.20a.
Motor vehicle insurance.
See MOTOR VEHICLE INSURANCE.
Mutual insurance companies,
§§31-2502.24, 31-2502.25.
Notice.
Homeowner's and renter's insurance.
Notice that standard policy does not
cover flood damage,
§31-2502.28a.
Notice that standard policy does not
cover losses from sewer line
backup, §31-2502.28b.
Penalties, §31-2502.42.
Policy forms, §31-2502.27.
Premium finance companies.
See INSURANCE PREMIUM
FINANCE COMPANIES.
**Property and liability insurance
guaranty association.**
General provisions, §§31-5501 to
31-5515.
See PROPERTY AND LIABILITY
INSURANCE GUARANTY
ASSOCIATION.
Public contracts, §2-205.02.
Rate and form filing requirements,
§31-2502.28.
Rates generally.
Casualty and other insurance rates.
General provisions, §§31-2701 to
31-2714.
See INSURANCE.
Records, §31-2502.01.
Reserves.
Actuarial opinion summary,
§31-2502.26a.
Confidentiality, §31-2502.26b.
Actuarial report, §31-2502.26a.
Confidentiality, §31-2502.26b.
Statement of actuarial opinion,
§31-2502.26a.
Public document, §31-2502.26b.

FIRE AND CASUALTY INSURANCE
—Cont'd
Sewer line backup.
Homeowner's and renter's insurance.
Notice that standard policy does not
cover losses from sewer line
backup, §31-2502.28b.
Types of, §31-2502.11.
Unauthorized companies,
§31-2502.39.
**Unlicensed persons, no
compensation of,** §31-2502.31.

**FIRE AND EMERGENCY MEDICAL
SERVICES DEPARTMENT.**
All Hazards/EMS specialists.
Designation as, §5-409.01.
Cadet programs, §5-418.
Police officer cadet program.
Preference for appointment,
§5-109.01.
Call center.
Office of unified communications.
Transfer of responsibilities and
duties to office, §1-327.53.
Disciplinary actions.
Commencement of action, §5-1031.
Procedure, §§5-1031 to 5-1057.
Retirement while under disciplinary
investigation, §§5-1051 to 5-1057.
Administrative review, §5-1056.
Applicability, §5-1057.
Completion of investigation,
§5-1052.
Conditional retirement, §§5-1053,
5-1054.
Definitions, §5-1051.
Payments of penalties and collection
of debts, §5-1055.
Penalties in lieu of discipline for
members in conditional
retirement, §5-1054.
Education and training program,
§5-441.
**Firefighter retirement while under
disciplinary investigation,**
§§5-1051 to 5-1057.
Integrated health care task force,
§5-404.02.
Medical director, §5-404.01.
Non-District personnel, training,
§§5-431, 5-432.
**Paramedics, EMTs and EMS
specialists.**
Lateral transfer to uniform
firefighters, §§5-409.01, 5-544.01.
Service longevity, §5-544.01.

FIRE AND EMERGENCY MEDICAL SERVICES DEPARTMENT —Cont'd
Public duty doctrine, §5-401.02.
State safety office, §5-401.01.
Streetcar safety oversight, §5-401.01.

FIREARM-RELATED NUISANCE ABATEMENT, §§42-3101 to 42-3114.
See CRIME-RELATED NUISANCE ABATEMENT.

FIREARMS, §§7-2501.01 to 7-2551.03, 22-4501 to 22-4517.
Addicts.
Unlawful possession of firearms, §22-4503.
Additional penalty for committing crime when armed, §22-4502.
Administrative disposition of violations, §7-2507.06.
Administrative procedure, §7-2507.09.
Ammunition.
See AMMUNITION.
Antique pistols, applicability of provisions, §22-4513.
Assault weapons manufacturing strict liability, §§7-2551.01 to 7-2551.03.
California roster of handguns determined not to be unsafe.
Designated unsafe pistols not on list.
Prohibitions on possession, sale or transfer, §7-2505.04.
Capitol grounds, prohibited on, §10-503.16.
Carrying, generally, §22-4504.01.
Lawful transportation, §22-4504.02.
Child abuse and neglect.
Injuries caused by a bullet.
Reporting requirements, §4-1321.02.
Concealed weapons, carrying, §§22-4504, 22-4505.
Confiscation by law enforcement officers, §22-4517.
Correctional treatment facility officers, private, §§24-261.01 to 24-261.02a.
Criminally negligent storage, §7-2507.02.
Dealers.
Criminal proceedings.
Ban on use of evidence obtained from dealers in, §7-2504.09.
Display of weapons or ammunition by, §7-2504.07.

FIREARMS —Cont'd
Dealers —Cont'd
Identification number on firearm required for sale by, §7-2504.08.
Licenses. See within this heading, "Dealers' licenses."
Responsibilities of, §7-2504.04.
Sale of pistol not microstamp-ready prohibited, §7-2504.08.
Dealers' licenses, §§7-2504.01 to 7-2504.10.
Application for, §7-2504.02.
Corrections to, §7-2504.03.
Dangerous weapons, dealers in, §47-2838.
Denial of, §7-2504.06.
False information, supplying, §7-2507.04.
Fees, §7-2504.02.
Issuance of, §7-2504.03.
Office of administrative hearings, jurisdiction, §2-1831.03.
Qualifications for, §7-2504.02.
Records, §7-2504.04.
Requirements regarding, §7-2504.01.
Revocation of, §§7-2504.05, 7-2504.06.
Time period, §7-2504.03.
Definitions, §§7-2501.01, 22-4501.
Designated unsafe pistols.
Prohibitions on possession, sale or transfer, §7-2505.04.
Destruction by law enforcement officers, §22-4517.
Disassembling, §7-2507.02.
Discharging unlawfully, §22-4503.01.
District as federal firearms licensee, §7-2504.10.
Drug, firearm, or prostitution-related nuisance abatement, §§42-3101 to 42-3114.
See CRIME-RELATED NUISANCE ABATEMENT.
Enhanced penalties and fines for carrying guns into gun free zones, §22-4502.01.
Estates, as part of, §7-2503.01.
False information given in purchasing, §22-4511.
Felons.
Unlawful possession of firearms, §22-4503.
Fines, §7-2507.06.
Firing ranges, §7-2507.03.
Forfeiture of conveyances transporting firearms, §7-2507.06a.

FIREARMS —Cont'd
Fraud and deceit, §7-2507.04.
Fund, Firearms Bounty, §7-2531.04.
Gun free zones, §22-4502.01.
Gun offender registry, §§7-2508.01 to
7-2508.07.
Health care providers.
Reporting firearms or weapons
injuries, §§7-2601 to 7-2603.
**Identification number on firearm
required for sale of,** §7-2504.08.
Identifying marks, alteration of,
§22-4512.
Inspector general, office of.
Employees making felony
investigations.
Authority to carry, §1-301.115a.
Interpretation of provisions,
§7-2507.08.
Law enforcement officers.
Concealed weapons, carrying,
§22-4505.
Possession of certain dangerous
weapons by, §22-4514.
Taking and destruction of dangerous
articles, §22-4517.
Locks, use of, §7-2507.02.
Machine guns.
Defined, §22-4501.
Manufacture of.
Assault weapons, §§7-2551.01 to
7-2551.03.
Prohibition of manufacture within
District, §7-2504.01.
Metropolitan police.
Ammunition feeding devices,
prohibition on transfer of,
§5-133.16.
Pistol match attendance, expenses for,
§5-133.15.
**Microstamping of semiautomatic
pistols,** §7-2505.03.
Sale of pistol not microstamp-ready
prohibited, §7-2504.08.
**Military, possession of certain
dangerous weapons by,** §22-4514.
Minors, access to.
Responsibilities regarding storage,
§7-2507.02.
Motor vehicles, transporting in,
§22-4504.02.
Penalties, §7-2507.06.
Physicians and hospitals.
Reporting of injuries caused by,
§§7-2601 to 7-2603.
Pistols.
Defined, §§7-2501.01, 22-4501.

FIREARMS —Cont'd
Pistols —Cont'd
Designation of pistol as not unsafe,
California roster.
Prohibitions on possession, sale or
transfer of pistols not on list,
§7-2505.04.
License to carry, §§7-2509.01 to
7-2509.11.
Applications, §7-2509.02.
Concealed pistol licensing review
board, §7-2509.08.
Definitions, §7-2509.01.
Drugs or alcohol, carrying while
impaired, §7-2509.06.
Duties of licensees, §7-2509.04.
Expiration and renewal, §7-2509.03.
Freedom of information exception,
§7-2509.09.
Issuance, §22-4506.
Penalties, §7-2509.10.
Prohibitions, §7-2509.07.
Revocation and suspension,
§7-2509.05.
Rulemaking, §7-2509.11.
Microstamping of semiautomatic
pistols, §7-2505.03.
Prohibition on registration of certain
pistols, §7-2502.02.
Registration.
Ballistics identification procedure,
§7-2502.03.
Limitation on number of pistols
registered, §7-2502.03.
Sale of pistol not microstamp-ready
prohibited, §7-2504.08.
Sales of certain pistols prohibited,
§22-4507.
Toy or antique pistols, applicability of
provisions, §22-4513.
**Possession of certain dangerous
weapons, prohibition of,**
§22-4514.
**Power to issue regulations
regarding,** §1-303.43.
**Private correctional treatment
facility officers,** §§24-261.01 to
24-261.02a.
**Property owners prohibiting
possession.**
Public or private property,
§22-4503.02.
Public education program,
§7-2507.07.
**Public officers and employees
designated to protect life and
property outside the District,**
§10-509.01.

FIREARMS —Cont'd
Registration, §§7-2502.01 to 7-2502.11.
Corrections to, §7-2502.07.
Criminal proceedings, ban on use of registration information in, §7-2502.11.
Denial of, §7-2502.10.
Expiration of certificates, §7-2502.07a.
False information, providing, §7-2507.04.
Fees, §7-2502.05.
Fingerprinting applicants, §7-2502.04.
Firing ranges, §7-2507.03.
Freedom of information exception, §7-2502.11a.
Gun offender registry, §§7-2508.01 to 7-2508.07.
Information required for, §7-2502.03.
In-person application required for, §7-2502.04.
Issuance of certificates, §7-2502.07.
Oath, signing of application under, §7-2502.05.
Office of administrative hearings, jurisdiction, §2-1831.03.
Photographing applicants, §7-2502.04.
Prohibition on registration for certain firearms, §7-2502.02.
Qualifications for, §7-2502.03.
Renewal of certificates, §7-2502.07a.
Requirements regarding, §7-2502.01.
Responsibilities of registrants, §7-2502.08.
Revocation of, §§7-2502.09, 7-2502.10.
Time period, §§7-2502.06, 7-2502.07.
Reporting injuries caused by, §§7-2601 to 7-2603.
Immunity from liability, §7-2603.
Nature and contents, §7-2602.
Required by physicians, hospitals and similar institutions, §7-2601.
Rifles.
Carrying within district, §22-4504.
Defined, §7-2501.01.
Short-barreled.
Defined, §7-2501.01.
Rulemaking to implement provisions, §7-2507.11.
Sales and transfers, §22-4508.
Designated unsafe pistols, prohibitions, §7-2505.04.
Identification number on firearm required for, §7-2504.08.
Illegal sales and distributions, §§7-2531.01 to 7-2531.04.
Permissible sales and transfers, §7-2505.02.

FIREARMS —Cont'd
Sales and transfers —Cont'd
Pistol not microstamp-ready, sale prohibited, §7-2504.08.
Prohibited sales and transfers, §7-2505.01.
Sawed-off shotguns.
Defined, §7-2501.01.
Prohibition on registration of, §7-2502.02.
Security, prohibition on use as, §7-2507.01.
Semiautomatic pistols.
Microstamping, §7-2505.03.
Severability of provisions, §7-2507.10.
Short-barreled rifles.
Defined, §7-2501.01.
Prohibition on registration of, §7-2502.02.
Shotguns, carrying within district, §22-4504.
Storage, §7-2507.02.
Strict liability.
Illegal sales and distributions, §§7-2531.01 to 7-2531.04.
Definitions, §7-2531.01.
Exemption, §7-2531.03.
Firearms bounty fund, §7-2531.04.
Generally, §7-2531.02.
Manufacturing assault weapons, §§7-2551.01 to 7-2551.03.
Definitions, §7-2551.01.
Exemption, §7-2551.03.
Generally, §7-2551.02.
Toy or antique pistols, applicability of provisions, §22-4513.
Transportation.
Lawful transportation generally, §22-4504.02.
When permitted to carry firearm, §22-4504.01.
Trigger locks, use of, §7-2507.02.
Unlawful discharge, §22-4503.01.
Unlawful possession, §22-4503.
Unloading, §7-2507.02.
Violations not specifically provided for, penalties, §22-4515.
Voluntary surrender of, §7-2507.05.
Weapons dealers, §§22-4509, 22-4510.
Weapons generally.
See WEAPONS.

FIRE BALLOONS, §22-1317.

FIRE DEPARTMENTS, §§5-401 to 5-419.
Age requirements, §5-403.
Aide to the fire marshal, §5-542.03.

FIRE DEPARTMENTS —Cont'd
Appointment of members, §5-402.
Appropriations, §5-406.
Arson.
Investigations, §5-417.01.
Reports, §5-417.
Assaults on firefighters, §22-405.
Awards for meritorious service,
§§5-901 to 5-904.
Bomb disposal duty, additional
compensation for, §5-542.02.
Boundaries, §5-401.
Buildings, use of, §5-412.
Cadet programs, §§5-418, 5-419,
38-912, 38-913.
Issuance of rules, §38-912.01.
Police officer cadet program.
Preference for appointment,
§5-109.01.
Cardiopulmonary resuscitation in
case of cardiac arrest.
Non-resuscitation procedures for EMS,
§§7-651.01 to 7-651.16.
See EMERGENCY MEDICAL
SERVICES.
Career service promotions,
§§1-608.01, 5-402.
Chief and deputy chiefs, §5-402.
Medical director.
Assistant fire chief, §5-404.01.
Right of entry to inspect premises for
compliance with fire code,
§5-417.02.
Construction of firefighting
apparatus in repair shop, §5-413.
Council approval required for
changes in fire protection,
§5-401.
Court duty, §5-1304.
Death, presumptions as to, §§5-651 to
5-656.
Demotions, §5-543.05.
Disability benefits.
Presumptions, §§5-651 to 5-656.
Disciplinary actions.
Commencement of action, §5-1031.
Procedure, §§5-1031 to 5-1057.
Retirement while under disciplinary
investigation, §§5-1051 to 5-1057.
Administrative review, §5-1056.
Applicability, §5-1057.
Completion of investigation,
§5-1052.
Conditional retirement, §§5-1053,
5-1054.
Definitions, §5-1051.

FIRE DEPARTMENTS —Cont'd
Disciplinary actions —Cont'd
Retirement while under disciplinary
investigation —Cont'd
Payments of penalties and collection
of debts, §5-1055.
Penalties in lieu of discipline for
members in conditional
retirement, §5-1054.
District institutions located outside
District, §5-415.
District, presence in, §5-410.
Division of District into companies,
§5-401.
Electrical ducts for fire and police
wires, §34-1407.
Emergency medical services.
See EMERGENCY MEDICAL
SERVICES.
Entertainments, assignment to,
§47-2820.
Equipment, §§5-406, 5-411.
Excepted service appointments,
§§1-608.01, 5-402.
Helicopter duty, additional
compensation for, §5-542.02.
Holidays, §§5-405, 5-521.01 to 5-521.03.
Compensation for working on,
§5-521.01.
Holiday defined, §5-521.02.
Homeland security and emergency
management agency, §§7-2203,
7-2204.
Hours of duty, §5-405.
Housing finance and assistance.
Government employer-assisted
housing program, §§42-2501 to
42-2507.
Inefficiency, removal for, §5-501.01.
Insignia of police and fire and
emergency medical services
departments.
Unauthorized use, §22-1409.
Investigations.
Firefighter retirement while under
disciplinary investigation.
Completion of disciplinary
investigations, §5-1052.
Leave.
Accrual or accumulation of, §5-409.
Off-duty days and holidays, §§5-405,
5-1304.
Record of leave taken, §5-408.
Sick leave, §5-408.
Limited duty status, §5-632.
Definitions, §5-631.

FIRE DEPARTMENTS —Cont'd
Limited duty status —Cont'd
Rules, §5-635.
Mayor, commissioning of officers by,
§1-301.76.
Medical assistance, §5-404.
Medical director, §5-404.01.
Medical leave.
Nonperformance of duty injuries and
illnesses, §5-634.
Performance of duty injuries and
illnesses, §5-633.
Meritorious service awards, §§5-901
to 5-904.
Militia, §49-404.
Notice of resignation, §5-407.
Off-duty days, §5-405.
Organization of, §5-404.
Overtime, §5-405.
Holidays, working on, §§5-521.01,
5-521.02.
Paramedics and emergency medical
technicians/specialists.
Fire and emergency services
department personnel.
Service longevity, §5-544.01.
Transfer to be uniformed firefighters.
Fire and emergency services
department personnel,
§§5-409.01, 5-544.01.
Physical examinations of members,
§5-451.
Pilot civilian technical services
program, §5-451.
Police and firefighters retirement
and disability.
Firefighter retirement while under
disciplinary investigation,
§§5-1051 to 5-1057.
General provisions, §§5-631 to 5-762.
See POLICE AND FIREFIGHTERS
RETIREMENT AND
DISABILITY.
Prehospital medical care and
transport, duties, §5-401.
Prerecorded transmittals to, §7-2803.
Presumptive disability or death,
§§5-651 to 5-656.
Cancer, §5-653.
Definitions, §5-651.
Disqualification from presumption,
§5-655.
Heart disease or hypertension, §5-652.
Infectious disease, §5-654.
Respiratory disease, §5-652.
Promotion of members, §§1-608.01,
5-402, 5-543.04.

FIRE DEPARTMENTS —Cont'd
Reciprocal agreements with other
fire departments, §5-414.
Records.
Leave taken, §5-408.
Redeployment of retirees, §5-762.
Residence requirements, §5-410.
Resignations, §5-407.
Retirement.
Firefighter retirement while under
disciplinary investigation,
§§5-1051 to 5-1057.
Administrative review, §5-1056.
Applicability, §5-1057.
Completion of disciplinary
investigations, §5-1052.
Conditional retirement, §5-1053.
Administrative review, §5-1056.
Payments of penalties, §5-1055.
Penalties in lieu of discipline,
§5-1054.
Definitions, §5-1051.
Payments of penalties.
Conditional retirement, §5-1055.
Penalties in lieu of discipline.
Conditional retirement, §5-1054.
Police and firefighters retirement and
disability.
General provisions, §§5-631 to 5-762.
See POLICE AND
FIREFIGHTERS
RETIREMENT AND
DISABILITY.
Right of entry of fire chief or fire
marshal.
Inspection of premises for compliance
with fire code, §5-417.02.
Salaries.
Police and firefighters, §§5-501.01 to
5-563.02.
See WAGES AND SALARIES.
Sanction of public venues for failure
to post seating capacity,
§5-417.02.
Scuba diving duty, additional
compensation for, §5-542.02.
Sick leave, §5-408.
Special assignments, §5-1304.
Strikes, §5-407.
Technicians, salary, §5-543.02.
Telegraph and telephone ducts for
fire and police wires, §34-1911.05.
Third-party contractors.
Quarterly reports, §5-401.
Transfers, §5-543.04.
Trial boards, §§5-1001 to 5-1011.

FIRE DEPARTMENTS —Cont'd
Tuition expenses for, §5-1305.
Two-way radio communications,
§§5-1306 to 5-1309.
Uniforms, §5-406.
Veterinary surgeon, §5-404.
Volunteer organization, extra
equipment for, §5-411.
Wages.
See WAGES AND SALARIES.
West End library and fire station
maintenance fund, §1-325.181.
Workweek, §§5-405, 5-1304.

FIRE ESCAPES.
Inspections, §2-139.

FIRE HYDRANTS.
Private hydrants, §§34-2410.01 to
34-2410.06.
Definitions, §34-2410.01.
Inspections, §34-2410.04.
Maintenance, §34-2410.03.
Ownership determinations,
§34-2410.05.
Responsibility agreements,
§34-2410.02.
Responsibility limitations,
§34-2410.06.
Water and sewer authority duties,
§34-2202.03.

FIREPLUG TAX, §§34-2409.01 to
34-2409.04.
Cessation upon introduction of
water into building or premises,
§34-2409.03.
Discontinuance of water service.
Levy upon, §34-2409.04.
Rates, §34-2409.02.
Special annual tax levied,
§34-2409.01.

**FIRE PROTECTION STUDY
COMMISSION,** §§3-1101 to 3-1108.
Cooperation of other agencies with,
§3-1105.
Definitions, §3-1101.
Duration of, §3-1102.
Establishment of, §3-1102.
Financing, §3-1102.
Gifts and donations, §3-1106.
Interdepartmental Advisory
Committee, §3-1107.
Meetings, §§3-1102, 3-1108.
Minutes of meetings, §3-1108.
Operational space provided for,
§3-1105.

**FIRE PROTECTION STUDY
COMMISSION** —Cont'd
Organization and membership,
§3-1102.
Powers and duties of, §3-1103.
Quorum, §3-1102.
Records, §3-1108.
Reimbursement of expenses of,
§3-1102.
Reports, §3-1103.
Residence requirements, §3-1102.
Sprinkler installation program.
Duties regarding, §3-1103.
Job training program combined with,
§3-1104.

FIRES AND FIRE PREVENTION.
Arson.
See ARSON.
Assisted living residences.
Fire safety requirements, §44-110.02.
Barbed-wire fences, §§9-1213.01,
9-1213.02.
Bonfires, §22-1313.
Building code.
See BUILDING CODE.
Compliance with fire code and
occupancy requirements,
§5-417.02.
Construction codes.
General provisions, §§6-1401 to
6-1409.
See CONSTRUCTION CODES.
Smoke detectors, §§6-751.01, 6-751.02.
See SMOKE DETECTORS.
False alarms, §22-1319.
Fire department.
General provisions, §§5-401 to 5-419.
See FIRE DEPARTMENTS.
Fire escapes.
See BUILDING CODE.
Fire protection study commission,
§§3-1101 to 3-1108.
See FIRE PROTECTION STUDY
COMMISSION.
Height of buildings, §§6-601.05 to
6-611.02.
See BUILDING CODE.
Smoke detectors, §§6-751.01, 6-751.02.
See SMOKE DETECTORS.
Vacant buildings, §§42-3131.05 to
42-3131.17.

**FIRE-STANDARD-COMPLIANT
CIGARETTES,** §§7-1751 to 7-1757.
Definitions, §7-1751.
Enforcement of provisions, §7-1756.
Exceptions to provisions, §7-1757.

FIRE-STANDARD-COMPLIANT CIGARETTES —Cont'd
Manufacturer's certification, §7-1754.
Required for sale of cigarettes, §7-1752.
Manufacturer's data retention and availability requirements, §7-1755.
Penalties for noncompliance, §7-1756.
Performance standard, §7-1753.
Rulemaking, §7-1757.
Sale of cigarettes.
Requirements, §7-1752.
Testing.
Method, §7-1753.
Requirements for sale of cigarettes, §7-1752.

FIREWORKS.
Business licenses, §47-2814.

FIRING OF EMPLOYEE.
See TERMINATION OF EMPLOYMENT.

FIRING RANGES, §7-2507.03.

FIRM OFFERS.
Leases, UCC, §28:2A-205.

FIRST AMENDMENT ASSEMBLIES.
Arrests, §5-331.07.
Documentation, §5-331.10.
Physical restraints.
Use on persons arrested, §5-331.11.
Release.
Notice to persons arrested of their options, §5-331.13.
Promptness, §5-331.12.
Citation of act, §5-331.01.
Construction of provisions, §5-331.17.
Definitions, §5-331.02.
Post-and-forfeit procedure, §5-335.01.
Dispersal.
General order to disperse, §5-331.07.
Handcuffs.
Use of physical restraints on persons arrested in connection with, §5-331.11.
Metropolitan police department.
Arrests, §5-331.07.
Documentation, §5-331.10.
Physical restraints.
Use on persons arrested, §5-331.11.
Release.
Notice to persons arrested of their release options, §5-331.13.

FIRST AMENDMENT ASSEMBLIES —Cont'd
Metropolitan police department —Cont'd
Arrests —Cont'd
Release —Cont'd
Prompt release of persons arrested, §5-331.12.
Chemical irritant.
Use of, §5-331.16.
General order to disperse, §5-331.07.
Handling of, and response to, by police, §5-331.07.
Training for, §5-331.15.
Identification of MPD personnel policing assemblies, §5-331.09.
Display of police identifying information, §5-337.01.
Investigations concerning first amendment activities.
General provisions, §§5-333.01 to 5-333.13.
See METROPOLITAN POLICE.
News media.
Police-media relations, §5-331.14.
Notice and approval process, §§5-331.01, 5-331.05.
Police lines, §5-331.08.
Policy of district.
Recognition and implementation by MPD, §5-331.04.
Post-and-forfeit procedure.
Amounts associated with misdemeanors, §5-335.02.
Enforcement, §5-335.01.
Reports, §5-335.03.
Riot gear.
Use of, §5-331.16.
Training for handling of, and response to, §5-331.15.
News media.
Police-media relations, §5-331.14.
Notice and plan approval process.
Generally, §5-331.05.
Processing of applications, §5-331.06.
Plastic cuffs.
Use of physical restraints on persons arrested in connection with, §5-331.11.
Policy of district, §5-331.03.
Recognition and implementation by MPD, §5-331.04.
Restrictions.
Reasonable time, place and manner restrictions, §5-331.04.
Title of act, §5-331.01.

FIRST SOURCE EMPLOYMENT,
§§2-219.01 to 2-219.05.
Office of first source compliance,
§§2-219.31 to 2-219.35.

FISCAL IMPACT STATEMENTS.
Chief financial officer.
Duties, §1-204.24d.
Council, §1-301.47a.

FISCAL YEAR, §1-204.41.
Schools and education.
Fiscal year 2006 educational
investments fund for District of
Columbia public schools and
public charter schools, §1-325.31.
**Tobacco settlement financing
corporation,** §7-1831.03.

FISH AND GAME, §§22-4328 to
22-4333.
Council, authority of, §22-4328.
Delegation of functions regarding,
§22-4332.
Fines, §22-4331.
Inspections, §22-4329.
Inspector of, §7-173.
Interior, Secretary of, §§22-4332,
22-4333.
Licenses, §§22-4328, 22-4329.
Liens after sale of forfeitures,
§22-4330.
Mayor's powers, delegation of,
§22-4332.
Penalties, §22-4331.
Prosecutions, §22-4331.
Protection of aquatic life.
While regulating against water
pollution, §8-103.03.
Protection of wildlife, §§8-2201 to
8-2211.
See WILDLIFE PROTECTION.
Secured transactions.
When security interest attaches,
§28:9-204.

FISH DEALERS, WHOLESALE.
Business licenses, §47-2827.

FISH MARKET, MUNICIPAL,
§37-205.01.

**FITNESS FOR A PARTICULAR
PURPOSE.**
Leases, UCC.
Implied warranties, §28:2A-213.
Sale of goods, UCC.
Implied warranty, §§28:2-315,
28:2-316, 28:2-316.01.

**FIVE-DAY RULE FOR
CONTINUANCES.**
Family court proceedings generally,
FamDiv Rule G.

FIXTURES.
Leases, UCC.
Defined, §28:2A-309.
Lessors' and lessees' rights when
goods become fixtures, §28:2A-309.
Secured transactions.
Defaults.
Procedure when fixtures involved,
§28:9-604.
Financing statement, §28:9-502.
Place of filing, §28:9-501.
Priority of security interests in,
§28:9-334.

**FLAG DESIGN ADVISORY
COMMISSION,** §1-153.

FLAGS.
District of Columbia.
Design, §§1-151, 1-152.
Advisory committee, §1-153.
Display, §§1-141 to 1-145.
Findings, §1-141.
Inside public buildings, §1-144.
Notice of provisions to commercial
property owners, §1-145.
Requirements, §1-142.
Staff used, §1-143.
Donations and grants to defray
expense of replacing flag, §1-154.

**FLEEING FROM A LAW
ENFORCEMENT OFFICER IN A
MOTOR VEHICLE,** §50-2201.05b.

**FLEEING FROM SCENE OF
ACCIDENT.**
Leaving after colliding, §50-2201.05c.

FLIES.
Vector-borne disease control,
§§8-2131.01 to 8-2131.09.
See VECTOR-BORNE DISEASE
CONTROL.

FLOOD CONTROL.
Building code, §§6-501 to 6-506.

FLOOD INSURANCE.
**Homeowner's and renter's
insurance.**
Notice that standard policy does not
cover flood damage, §31-2502.28a.

FLOODS.
**District of Columbia flood assistance
fund.**
Sunset, §8-105.75.

FLOODS —Cont'd
Flood hazards, §6-506.

FLOOD VEHICLES.
Generally, §§50-1331.01 to 50-1331.09.
See SALVAGE, FLOOD AND JUNK VEHICLES.

F.O.B.
Sale of goods, UCC, §28:2-319.
Bill of lading required in overseas shipments, §28:2-323.

FOOD.
Adulteration of food or drugs.
General provisions, §§48-101 to 48-110.
See ADULTERATION OF FOOD OR DRUGS.
Business licenses, §47-2827.
Cottage food businesses, §§7-742.01, 7-742.02.
Crime victims' compensation.
Temporary emergency food, VictComp Rule 29.
Donated food, good faith immunity, §§48-301, 48-302.
Flavorings and extracts.
Alcoholic beverage licenses.
Exceptions to license requirements, §25-103.
Fraud and deceit in sale of, §37-201.22a.
Gross sales tax, §47-2002.02.
Income tax credits.
Farm to food donations, §47-1806.14.
Corporations and financial institutions, §47-1807.12.
Unincorporated businesses, §47-1808.12.
Local food economy study, §48-411.
Markets.
See MARKETS.
Milk and milk products.
Registration of milk containers, §§36-121 to 36-157.
See MILK CONTAINER REGISTRATION.
Sale by weight, §37-201.14.
Sales.
Implied warranty of merchantability, §28:2-314.
School food services, §§38-801 to 38-809.
See SCHOOLS AND EDUCATION.
Urban gardens program, §§48-401 to 48-403.
Definitions, §48-401.

FOOD —Cont'd
Urban gardens program —Cont'd
Established, §48-402.
Limitation on expenditures, §48-402.02.
Rules for implementation of provisions, §48-403.
Urban farm land leasing initiative, §48-402.01.
Warranties.
Implied warranty of merchantability, §28:2-314.
Weights and measures, sold by, §§37-201.13 to 37-201.22a.

FOOD DELIVERY VEHICLES.
Inspection of motor vehicles, §50-102.
Motor vehicle insurance, §§50-101 to 50-105.
Motor vehicle registration, §50-102.

FOOD ESTABLISHMENTS.
Adulteration of food, §§48-101 to 48-110.

FOOD POLICY COUNCIL, §§48-311 to 48-315.
Applicability of chapter, §48-315.
Definitions, §48-311.
Director, §48-314.
Duties, §48-312.
Establishment, §48-312.
Members, §48-313.
Terms of members, §48-313.
Vacancies, §48-313.

FOOD SERVICE CONTRACTS.
Private contractor and subcontractor prompt payment act, §§27-131 to 27-136.
See PROMPT PAYMENT.

FOOD SERVICE WARE.
Disposable food service ware, management, §§8-1531 to 8-1537.

FOOD STAMPS.
Categorical eligibility, §4-261.02.
Definitions, §4-261.01.
Expansion, §§4-261.01 to 4-261.04.
LIHEAP heat and eat initiative, §4-261.03.
Locally funded minimum benefit, §4-261.04.
Misuse of, §§4-218.05, 4-218.06.
Supplemental nutrition assistance program (SNAP), §§4-261.21 to 4-261.23.

FOOTWAYS IN PUBLIC GROUNDS.
Driving or riding on, §22-1318.

FORCED LABOR.
Human trafficking, §§22-1831 to
22-1843.
See HUMAN TRAFFICKING.

FORCIBLE ENTRY AND DETAINER,
§§16-1501 to 16-1505.

FORECLOSURE.
Alcoholic beverage licenses.
Involuntary transfer of license,
§25-361.
Building and loan associations.
Foreclosure of advanced shareholder's
security, §26-214.
Foreclosure, residential mortgages.
Fund, §42-815.03.
Money lenders, §26-908.
Mortgages and deeds of trust.
Construction of provisions, §42-815.04.
Defense against foreclosure.
Equity practice followed, answer
establishing defense, §42-812.
Foreclosure rescue services, §§42-2431
to 42-2435.
Generally.
See MORTGAGES AND DEEDS OF
TRUST.
Notice of intention to foreclose,
§42-815.
Residential mortgage foreclosure
default, right to cure, §42-815.01.
Residential mortgage mediation,
§42-815.02.
Real estate tax sales.
Revised real property tax sale,
§§47-1370 to 47-1383.
See REAL ESTATE TAX SALES.
Real property tax sales, §47-1314.
Foreclosure on tax certificate,
§47-1303.04.
Rescue services, §§42-2431 to 42-2435.
**Residential mortgage foreclosure
default, right to cure,** §42-815.01.
Secured transactions.
Defaults.
Enforcement after default,
§28:9-601.

FOREIGN BILLS OF EXCHANGE.
Notaries public, §1-1207.

**FOREIGN CHILD-PLACING
AGENCIES.**
Agreements with, §4-1405.01.

FOREIGN CONSERVATORS.
Protection of property, §§21-2076,
21-2077.

FOREIGN CORPORATIONS.
Building associations, §26-206.
Insurance companies.
Conversion from domestic to foreign
insurers, §31-1703.
Department of insurance, securities,
and banking, filing financial
statements with, §31-204.
Fire and casualty insurance,
§§31-2502.20 to 31-2502.22.
Fraternal benefit societies, §§31-5326
to 31-5328.
Life insurance companies, §§31-4501,
31-4502.
See LIFE INSURANCE
COMPANIES.
Redomestication, §§31-1701 to
31-1705.
See INSURANCE COMPANIES.
Risk-based capital, §31-2010.
State of entry for non-United States
insurers, §§31-2201 to 31-2207.
Taxation, §47-2602.
Service of process, §§13-334, 13-335.
Summons, CivPro Rule 4.
Domestic relations actions, DomRel
Rule 4.
**Trust, mortgage and title
corporations,** §26-1335.

FOREIGN COUNTRIES.
**Adoption of child born outside
United States.**
New certificates of birth, §7-210.
**Adult guardianship and protective
proceedings jurisdiction act.**
International application, §21-2401.03.
Depositions in foreign countries,
CivPro Rule 28.
Adoption proceedings, Adoption Rule
28.
Domestic relations actions, DomRel
Rule 28.
Diplomatic offices, §§6-1301 to 6-1315.
See FOREIGN MISSIONS.
Extradition to, §23-705.
Gifts to United States officials, US
Const Art I §9.
Real property, ownership of, §42-902.
Rental of public space by,
§10-1101.02.

**FOREIGN DOCTORS OF
EMINENCE AND AUTHORITY.**
Licensure of, §3-1205.09a.

FOREIGN EXCHANGE PROGRAM.
Teachers, §§38-1921 to 38-1923.

FOREIGN INTERESTS.
Powers of attorney, §21-2117.

FOREIGN JUDGMENTS, §§15-351 to 15-357.
Definitions, §15-351.
Enforcement, CivPro Rule 72.
  Action to enforce judgment, §15-356.
  Domestic relations actions, DomRel Rule 72.
Fees, §15-355.
Filing, §§15-352, 15-353.
Foreign-money judgments, §§15-361 to 15-368.
  See FOREIGN-MONEY JUDGMENTS.
Interpretation of provisions, §15-357.
Limitation of actions, §12-307.
Notice of filing, §15-353.
Request to file judgment, CivPro Form CA 112.
Status of, §15-352.
Stays, §15-354.

FOREIGN LANGUAGES.
Election materials, multilingual, §§1-1031.01, 1-1031.02.
Services and documents, §§2-1931 to 2-1936.
  See FOREIGN LANGUAGE SERVICES AND DOCUMENTS.

FOREIGN LANGUAGE SERVICES AND DOCUMENTS, §§2-1931 to 2-1936.
Covered entities.
  Definition, §2-1931.
  Duties, §2-1934.
  Oral language services, provision of, §2-1932.
  Written language services, provision of, §2-1933.
Definitions, §2-1931.
Effective dates, §2-1936.
Language access director.
  Definition, §2-1931.
  Duties, §2-1935.
Oral language services.
  Definition, §2-1931.
  Provision by covered entities, §2-1932.
Written language services.
  Provision by covered entities, §2-1933.

FOREIGN LAW.
Determination of foreign law, CivPro Rule 44.1, CrimPro Rule 26.1.
  Adoption proceedings, Adoption Rule 44.

FOREIGN LAW —Cont'd
Determination of foreign law —Cont'd
  Domestic relations actions, DomRel Rule 44.

FOREIGN MISSIONS, §§6-1301 to 6-1315.
Administrative proceedings, §6-1308.
Benefits, provision of, §§6-1302, 6-1304.
Definitions, §§6-1302, 6-1304.01.
Enforcement, §6-1311.
Federal and state governments and political subdivisions, laws of, §§6-1307, 6-1310.
Fees.
  Benefits, provision of, §6-1304.
  Unsatisfied judgments or damages, §6-1304.01.
Immunities, §6-1310.
International organizations, applicability of rules to, §6-1309.
Liability insurance coverage, notice of lapse or termination of, §6-1304.01.
Location of, §6-1306.
Motor vehicles, vessels, and aircraft owned by members of, §6-1304.01.
Office of Foreign Missions, §6-1303.
Policy declaration, §6-1301.
Preemption, §6-1307.
Presidential approved procedures and guidelines, §6-1312.
Privileges, §6-1310.
Protective services for, §6-1313.
Real property, §6-1305.
Travel restrictions for members of, §6-1315.
United Nations employees, §6-1309.01.
Use in manner incompatible with status, §6-1314.
Zoning and foreign chanceries, §§6-651.01, 6-651.02.

FOREIGN-MONEY CLAIMS, §§15-901 to 15-914.
Applicability of provisions, §§15-913, 15-914.
Asserting, §15-905.
Conflict of laws, §15-912.
Conversions, §§15-901, 15-906, 15-907.
Currency revalorization, effect of, §15-911.
Defending, §15-905.
Definitions, §15-901.

FOREIGN-MONEY CLAIMS —Cont'd
Determining amount of money,
§15-904.
Determining money of the claim,
§15-903.
Determining United States dollar
value, §15-910.
Distribution proceedings, §§15-901,
15-907.
Enforcement of foreign judgments
as to, §15-909.
Interest, judgment and
prejudgment, §15-908.
Interpretation of provisions, §15-914.
Judgments and decrees, §15-906.
Money of the claim.
Defined, §15-901.
Determining, §15-903.
Relationship to other laws, §15-912.
Uniformity of application and
interpretation, §15-914.
Variation by agreement, §15-902.

FOREIGN-MONEY JUDGMENTS,
§§15-361 to 15-368.
Applicability of provisions, §15-363.
Definitions, §15-362.
Effect of recognition, §15-367.
Interpretation of provisions, §15-370.
Personal jurisdiction.
When not required, §15-365.
Procedure for recognition, §15-366.
Saving clause, §15-371.
Standards for recognition of foreign-
country judgment, §15-364.
Statute of limitations, §15-369.
Stay of proceedings pending appeal,
§15-368.
Uniformity of application and
interpretation, §15-370.

FOREIGN POWERS, PERSONS
DETAINED BY.
Property, protection of.
See CONSERVATORS.

FOREIGN STUDENTS.
Gallaudet University, §38-2402.10.

FOREIGN TRADE ZONES, §§36-501
to 36-504.
Application to establish, operate and
maintain, §36-502.
Authorized activities within zone,
§36-502.
Definitions, §36-501.
Jurisdiction.
Reservation of civil and criminal
jurisdiction, §36-504.

FOREIGN TRADE ZONES —Cont'd
Licenses.
Applicability of licensing, permitting
and taxation provisions, §36-503.
Metropolitan Washington Airports
Authority, §9-908.
Permits.
Applicability of licensing, permitting
and taxation provisions, §36-503.
Private corporations.
Defined, §36-501.
Public corporations.
Defined, §36-501.
Taxation.
Applicability of licensing, permitting
and taxation provisions, §36-503.

FORENSIC SCIENCES
DEPARTMENT, §§5-1501.01 to
5-1501.16.
Breath alcohol equipment.
Certification and testing, §5-1501.07.
Certification of breath alcohol
equipment, §5-1501.07.
Definitions, §5-1501.01.
Director.
Appointment, §5-1501.03.
Duties, §5-1501.04.
Establishment, §5-1501.02.
Metropolitan police.
Transfer of personnel, records,
functions and authority,
§5-1501.08.
Personnel, §5-1501.05.
Powers and duties, §5-1501.06.
Rules.
Continuity, §5-1501.16.
Rulemaking authority, §5-1501.15.
Science advisory board.
Establishment, §5-1501.11.
Functions, §5-1501.12.
Stakeholder council.
Establishment, §5-1501.13.
Functions, §5-1501.14.
Testing.
Breath alcohol equipment, §5-1501.07.
Negligence, misconduct,
misidentification or other error,
§5-1501.10.
Reexamination by independent experts
prohibited, §5-1501.09.
Transitional provisions, §§5-1501.08,
5-1501.16.

FOREST HAVEN, §§44-1401 to
44-1404.
Acquisition of site, construction of
buildings, §44-1401.

FOREST HAVEN —Cont'd
Control and supervision, §44-1402.
Name, §44-1402.
**Sale of products, disposition of
proceeds,** §44-1403.
Severability, §44-1404.
Title and jurisdiction over land,
§44-1401.

FORFEITURES.
Alcoholic beverages, contraband,
§25-911.
Building association stock, §26-213.
Civil asset forfeiture, §§41-301 to
41-315.
  Adoptive seizures, §41-311.
  Construction of statutes, §41-314.
  Contesting forfeiture, §41-305.
  Definitions, §41-301.
  Disposal of forfeited property, §41-310.
  Hearings.
    Post-seizure property retention
      hearings, §41-306.
    Pre-seizure hearings for real
      property, §41-303.
  Lenity, §41-314.
  Libel of information, §41-307.
  Mitigation, §41-313.
  Notice, §41-304.
  Proceedings, §41-308.
  Property subject to forfeiture, §41-312.
  Remission, §41-313.
  Reports, §41-312.
  Return of property, §41-309.
  Rulemaking, §41-315.
  Seizures, §41-303.
Civil procedure, CivPro Rule 71A-I.
Controlled substances, §48-905.02.
Criminal procedure.
  Bail and recognizance, §16-709.
  Wrongful conversion of, §16-708.
Drug paraphernalia, §48-1104.
Firearms, conveyances transporting,
§7-2507.06a.
Fish and game, §22-4330.
Fraternal benefit societies.
  Nonforfeiture benefits, §31-5317.
Gambling premises, §22-1705.
Good time credits of prisoners,
§24-221.04.
Habeas corpus violations, §§16-1904,
16-1905.
Horizontal property regimes,
§42-2023.
Human trafficking, §22-1838.
Illegal dumping, §8-905.

FORFEITURES —Cont'd
Interest.
  Usury.
    Forfeiture of interest, §28-3303.
Judgments and decrees, §15-102.
**Life insurance company
  nonforfeiture benefits,**
§§31-4705.01 to 31-4705.03.
Motor fuel tax, §47-2320.
Prisoners' good time credits,
§24-221.04.
Prostitution, §§22-2717, 22-2723.
**Public officers and employees
  refusing to testify,** §1-506.
**Tobacco master settlement
  agreement enforcement,**
§7-1803.06.
Tobacco tax, §47-2409.
Usury.
  Forfeiture of interest, §28-3303.

FORGERY.
Congress.
  Powers of congress, US Const Art I §8.
Definitions, §22-3241.
Fines, §22-3242.
Goods, brands or packaging of,
§22-1502.
Investment securities.
  Effect of unauthorized signature,
§28:8-205.
Letters of credit, §28:5-109.
Lottery tickets, §3-1333.
Penalties, §22-3242.
Prohibited acts, §22-3241.

FOR-HIRE VEHICLES.
Impoundment of vehicles, §50-331.
Taxicabs, §§50-301.01 to 50-301.34.
  See TAXICABS.

FORMS.
Answers.
  Defense under Rule 12(b), CivPro
    Form CA 20.
  Money had and received, CivPro Form
    CA 21.
Appeals, D.C. courts.
  Application for appeal, DCCtApp
    Forms 3, 4.
  Certificate of counsel, DCCtApp Rule
    28.
  In forma pauperis appeals.
    Affidavits, DCCtApp Form 7b.
    Waiver of prepayment of court costs
      and fees, motion for, DCCtApp
      Form 7a.
  Notice of appeal, CivPro Form CA 27,
    DCCtApp Forms 1, 2.

FORMS —Cont'd
Appeals, D.C. courts —Cont'd
Petition for review, DCCtApp Form 5.
Pro bono cases.
Certification of practice pro bono publico, DCCtApp Form 9.
Pro hac vice admission application, DCCtApp Form 8.
Release in criminal cases.
Information required, DCCtApp Form 6.
Appeals, federal cases.
Agency, board, commission, or officer, petition for review, FRAP Form 3.
Application for writ of mandamus, prohibition, etc., FRAP 21, USCtApp Rule 21.
Briefs, appendix, and other papers, FRAP 32, USCtApp Rule 32.
Certificate of compliance with brief form requirements, FRAP Form 6.
In forma pauperis, affidavit to accompany motion for leave to appeal, FRAP Form 4.
Notices of appeal from district court, FRAP Form 1.
Bankruptcy court decisions and orders, FRAP Form 5.
Notices of appeal from tax court, FRAP Form 2.
Papers.
Appeals by permission under 28 USCS 1292(b), FRAP 5(c).
Arbitration.
Motion for confirmation of awards, CivPro Form CA 107.
Attachment and garnishment.
Dismissal of action, CivPro Form CA 109.
Notice, CivPro Form CA 105.
Writ of attachment on wages, salary and commissions, CivPro Form CA 123.
Writ of attachment other than wages, salary and commissions, CivPro Form CA 122.
Bankruptcy.
Local official forms, USDistDCBank Appx A.
Bill of costs, CivPro Form CA 121.
Child custody.
Absent defendant.
Order of publication, DomRel Form 1.
Motion and affidavit, DomRel Form 2.
Contempt, DomRel Form 7.

FORMS —Cont'd
Child custody —Cont'd
Motion and affidavit —Cont'd
Opposition to motion and affidavit, DomRel Form 3.
Complaints.
Accounts, CivPro Form CA 4.
Claim for debt, CivPro Form CA 13.
Condemnation, CivPro Form CA 29.
Conversion, CivPro Form CA 11.
Declaratory relief, CivPro Form CA 18.
Fraudulent conveyance set aside, CivPro Form CA 13.
Goods sold and delivered, CivPro Form CA 5.
Interpleader, CivPro Form CA 18.
Money had and received, CivPro Form CA 8.
Answer to complaint, CivPro Form CA 21.
Money lent, CivPro Form CA 6.
Money paid by mistake, CivPro Form CA 7.
Negligence, CivPro Forms CA 9, CA 10.
Possession of real estate, LandlordTenant Form 1.
Promissory notes, CivPro Form CA 3.
Specific performance to convey land, CivPro Form CA 12.
Support and maintenance, DomRel Form 13.
Third party complaints, CivPro Form CA 22-A.
Condemnation.
Complaint, CivPro Form CA 29.
Notice, CivPro Form CA 28.
Contempt.
Support and maintenance.
Motion and affidavit for contempt, DomRel Form 7.
Custodial trusts.
Custodial trustee's receipt and acceptance, §19-1104.
Declaration of trust under District of Columbia's uniform custodial trust act, §19-1118.
Transfer under District of Columbia's uniform custodial trust act, §19-1118.
Declarations.
Unsworn declaration supplement, CivPro Form CA 101-A.
Delinquent minors.
Consent decree, JuvProc Form 4.
Detention order, JuvProc Form 1.

FORMS —Cont'd
Delinquent minors —Cont'd
Dispositional order.
  Commitment to social services
    administration, JuvProc Form 7.
  Medical or private placement,
    JuvProc Form 5.
  Probation, JuvProc Form 6.
Illustrative nature of forms, JuvProc
  Rule 58.
Release upon conditions order,
  JuvProc Form 3.
Sealing records.
  Motion to seal records, JuvProc
    Form 8.
  Notice of motion to seal records,
    JuvProc Form 9.
  Notice of opposition, FamDiv Form
    3.
  Notice of proposal, FamDiv Form 2.
  Order denying application, FamDiv
    Form 6.
  Order for hearing, FamDiv Form 4.
  Order to seal records, FamDiv Form
    5, JuvProc Form 10.
Shelter care order, JuvProc Form 2.
**Disbursements from the registry of
  the court,** CivPro Form CA 118.
Discovery.
Request for entry upon land for
  inspection, etc., CivPro Form CA
  24.
Requests for admission, CivPro Form
  CA 25.
Dismissal of action, CivPro Form CA
  19.
Attachment and garnishment, CivPro
  Form CA 109.
Documents of title.
Warehouse receipts, §28:7-202.
Domestic relations actions.
See DOMESTIC RELATIONS
  ACTIONS.
Exhibits summary, CivPro Form CA
  119.
Family court proceedings.
Notice of hearing and order directing
  appearance, FamDiv Form 1.
Sealing records, FamDiv Forms 2 to 6.
Fieri facias, writ of, CivPro Form CA
  120.
Financial account information,
  Probate Form 27.
Foreign judgments.
Request to file judgment, CivPro Form
  CA 112.

FORMS —Cont'd
Indigent persons.
Affidavit in support of motion to
  proceed in forma pauperis, CivPro
  Form CA 106, DCCtApp Form 7b.
Waiver of prepayment of court costs
  and fees, motion for, DCCtApp
  Form 7a.
International wills.
Certificate of authorized person,
  §18-705.
Interpleader, CivPro Form CA 18.
Complaint for interpleader, CivPro
  Form CA 18.
Counterclaim for interpleader, CivPro
  Form CA 21.
Intervention proceedings.
Compensation of guardian,
  conservator, etc., Probate Rule
  308.
Motion to intervene, CivPro Form CA
  23.
Intrafamily proceedings.
Notice of hearing and order directing
  appearance, FamDiv Form 1.
Joinder of parties.
Allegation of reason for omitting party,
  CivPro Form CA 26.
Judgments and decrees.
Application for entry of judgment,
  CivPro Form CA 110-A.
Consent judgment praecipe,
  LandlordTenant Forms 4, 4a.
  Addendum, list of repairs,
    LandlordTenant Form 4A.
Decision by the court, CivPro Form CA
  32.
Jury verdict, CivPro Form CA 31.
Jurisdiction.
Allegation of jurisdiction, CivPro Form
  CA 2.
Landlord and tenant court.
Affidavit of service by special process
  server, LandlordTenant Form 3.
Application for termination of stay and
  notice, LandlordTenant Form 5.
Complaint for possession of real
  estate.
  Commercial property,
    LandlordTenant Form 1D.
  Nonpayment of rent,
    LandlordTenant Form 1A.
  Other grounds for eviction in
    addition to nonpayment of
    rent, LandlordTenant Form
    1C.

FORMS —Cont'd

Landlord and tenant court —Cont'd

Complaint for possession of real estate
—Cont'd

Violation of obligations of tenancy or
other grounds for eviction,
LandlordTenant Form 1B.

Consent judgment praecipe,
LandlordTenant Forms 4, 4a.

Addendum, list of repairs,
LandlordTenant Form 4A.

Consent settlement agreement,
LandlordTenant Form 4b.

Addendum, list of repairs,
LandlordTenant Form 4A.

Notice of hearing, LandlordTenant
Form 1S.

Notice of intent to seek writ of
restitution, LandlordTenant Form
2.

Mediation.

General mediation order, CivPro Form
CA 117.

Medical consents.

Authorization for minor by adult
caregiver, §16-4901.

Merit system.

Petition for review of agency decision,
CivPro Agency Review Rule 1.

Motions, pro se.

Superior court, civil division, CivPro
Form CA 115.

Name changes.

Notice of application, CivPro Form CA
111.

Nonprobate transfers.

Contract of deposit, §19-602.04.

Orders of court.

General order, CivPro Form CA 116.

Parentage.

Order of filiation/support, DomRel
Form 12.

Petition to establish and provide
support, DomRel Form 11.

Parties.

Death of party.

Suggestion of death upon record,
CivPro Form CA 30.

Joinder of parties.

Allegation of reason for omitting
party, CivPro Form CA 26.

Personal representatives.

Administration of estates, §20-704.

Letters of administration, §20-504.

Post-conviction relief.

Superior court proceedings.

Motions involving Rule 9(b) issues,
PostConvRel Forms 1, 2.

FORMS —Cont'd

Post-conviction relief —Cont'd

Superior court proceedings —Cont'd

Motions to vacate, set aside or
correct sentence and judgment,
PostConvRel Forms 3, 4.

Pretrial statements, CivPro Form CA
103.

Probate proceedings.

See PROBATE PROCEEDINGS.

Probation.

Order imposing conditions, CrimPro
Form 1.

Pro bono cases.

Certification of practice pro bono
publico, DCCtApp Form 9.

Pro hac vice admission application,
DCCtApp Form 8.

Purpose of forms, CivPro Rule 84.

Real property.

Complaints.

Specific performance to convey land,
CivPro Form CA 12.

Condemnation.

Complaint, CivPro Form CA 29.

Notice, CivPro Form CA 28.

Discovery.

Entry upon land for inspection, etc.

Request for entry, CivPro Form
CA 24.

Form of deed, §§42-601, 42-602.

Landlord and tenant court.

Complaint for possession of real
estate, LandlordTenant Form 1.

Transfers on death.

Deeds, optional form, §19-604.16.

Revocation by instrument,
§19-604.17.

Replevin order, CivPro Form CA 108.

Requests for admission, CivPro Form
CA 25.

Secured transactions.

Financing statement, §28:9-502.

Service of process.

Notice and acknowledgment for service
by mail, CivPro Form CA 1-A.

Order for the substitution of
publication for personal service,
§13-338.

Out-of-District service, order of
publication, §13-339.

Settlement agreements.

Landlord and tenant court.

Consent settlement agreement,
LandlordTenant Form 4b.

Addendum, list of repairs,
LandlordTenant Form 4A.

FORMS —Cont'd
Settlement statements, CivPro Form
CA 102.
Small claims court claim statements,
§16-3902.
Automobile damage.
Collision, SmallClaims Forms 4, 5.
Custody of defendant, SmallClaims
Form 7.
Parked vehicle, SmallClaims Form
6.
Contract breach, SmallClaims Form 3.
Deficiency balance, SmallClaims Form
1.
Deposit return.
Apartment, SmallClaims Forms 9,
10.
Merchandise, SmallClaims Form 8.
General form, SmallClaims Form 11.
Holder in due course, SmallClaims
Form 2.
Stays.
Application for termination, CivPro
Form CA 110-B.
Subpoenas, CivPro Form CA 14.
Summons, CivPro Form CA 1.
Third party defendants, CivPro Form
CA 22-A.
Support and maintenance.
Absent defendant.
Order of publication, DomRel Form
1.
Certificate and order, DomRel Form
15.
Complaint for support, DomRel Form
13.
Employer's statement, DomRel Form
6.
Husband's financial statement,
DomRel Form 4.
Motion and affidavit, DomRel Form 2.
Contempt, DomRel Form 7.
Opposition to motion and affidavit,
DomRel Form 3.
Order for support, DomRel Forms 10,
15.
Parentage, DomRel Forms 11, 12.
Petition for support, DomRel Form 9.
Show cause order, DomRel Form 16.
Testimony of plaintiff, DomRel Form
14.
Uncontested stipulation, DomRel Form
8.
Wife's financial statement, DomRel
Form 5.
Third party practice.
Motion to bring in third party, CivPro
Form CA 22-B.

FORMS —Cont'd
Third party practice —Cont'd
Summons and complaint against third
party defendant, CivPro Form CA
22-A.
Traffic ticket adjudication.
Application for leave to appeal, CivPro
Agency Review Rule 2.
Transfers to minors.
Creation of custodial property,
§21-309.
Nomination of custodian for purposes
of, §§21-303, 21-309.
Unsworn declaration supplement,
CivPro Form CA 101-A.
Verification of pleadings, CivPro
Form CA 101.
Warehouse receipts, §28:7-202.
Witness certificate, CivPro Form CA
104.

FORT DAVIS PARK, §10-121.

FORT DUPONT PARK, §10-121.

**4427 HAYES STREET, N.E.
DEVELOPMENT PROJECT.**
Real property tax exemptions,
§47-4649.

FORUM.
Rental housing conversion and sale,
§§42-3405.03a, 42-3405.03b.

FORUM NON CONVENIENS,
§13-425.
Child custody proceedings,
§16-4602.07.

FOSTER CARE, §§4-217.01 to 4-217.11.
Administrative procedure, §4-217.03.
**Adoption incentive program and
special funds,** §§4-341 to 4-346.
**Assignment of support rights
required for,** §§4-217.07 to
4-217.11.
Child abuse and neglect.
Criteria for shelter care, NeglectProc
Rule 13.
Notice of shelter care, NeglectProc
Rule 6.
Child-placing agencies, §§4-1401 to
4-1410.
Condition of eligibility.
Assignment of support rights,
§4-217.07.
Cooperation in identifying and locating
parents, establishing paternity,
§4-217.08.
Exception, §4-217.09.

FOSTER CARE —Cont'd
Condition of eligibility —Cont'd
Cooperation in identifying and locating parents, establishing paternity —Cont'd
Refusal to cooperate after notice and opportunity, §4-217.10.
Social security number.
Applicant required to furnish, §4-217.07.
Cooperation requirements, §§4-217.07 to 4-217.11.
Delinquent minors, JuvProc Rules 105 to 107.
Forms, JuvProc Forms 1 to 3.
Determination of need, §4-217.05.
Family and medical leave, §32-502.
Family home placement, §§4-1401 to 4-1410.
Federal contributions, §4-217.04.
Identifying and locating parents, establishment of paternity.
Cooperation as condition of eligibility, §§4-217.08 to 4-217.10.
Interstate compact on placement of children, §§4-1421 to 4-1424.
Agreements with other state for placement, §4-1423.
Authority to enter into and execute compact, §4-1422.
Definitions, §4-1421.
Delinquent children.
Administrative hearing on placement, review, §4-1424.
Need, determining, §4-217.05.
Parents and parentage, locating and identifying, §§4-217.07 to 4-217.11.
Public welfare institutions, placement of children and minors in, §§4-118, 4-302.
Rights and responsibilities for youth in foster care, §§4-1303.71 to 4-1303.74.
Definition of youth, §4-1303.71.
Dissemination of information to youth and care providers, §4-1303.73.
Implementation plan for, §4-1303.74.
Guarantees provided by statement, §4-1303.72.
Implementation plans, §4-1303.74.
Rules to implement provisions, §4-1303.72.
Rights and responsibilities of foster parents, §§4-1303.81 to 4-1303.85.
Definitions, §4-1303.81.
Dissemination of rights and responsibilities information, §4-1303.83.

FOSTER CARE —Cont'd
Rights and responsibilities of foster parents —Cont'd
Implementation plan, §4-1303.84.
Rules, issuance, §4-1303.85.
Statements of rights and responsibilities, §4-1303.82.
Social Security numbers, §4-217.07.
Support rights.
Assignment condition for eligibility, §4-217.07.
Types of, §4-217.02.
Voluntary foster care registry, §4-1303.08.
Fund, §4-1303.09.

FOUNDATION LEVEL.
Uniform per student funding formula.
DCPS budget, §38-2907.01.
Education costs excluded from, §38-2907.
Public schools and public charter schools, §38-2903.
Revenue unavailability.
Procedure for adjusting appropriation, §38-2910.
Supplement.
At-risk students, §38-2905.01.
Special education, summer school and residential school students, §38-2905.

14W AND THE YMCA ANTHONY BOWEN PROJECT.
Real property tax exemptions, §47-4627.

FOURTH OF JULY.
Designated holiday, §§1-612.02, 28-2701.

FRANCHISES.
Gas stations.
Franchise purchase rights, §§36-304.11 to 36-304.15.
See GAS STATIONS.
Marketing agreements, §§36-303.01 to 36-303.07.
See GAS STATIONS.
Internet-related telecommunications.
Furnishing services for digitally-disadvantaged residents, §§34-1731.01 to 34-1731.11.
See INTERNET.
Taxes.
Income and franchise taxes, §§47-1801.01 to 47-1816.03.
See INCOME TAXES.

FRANCIS CASE MEMORIAL BRIDGE, §9-325.

FRANCIS SCOTT KEY BRIDGE, §9-311.

FRANKLIN SCHOOL.
Office purposes, used for, §38-403.

FRATERNAL BENEFIT SOCIETIES, §§31-5301 to 31-5335.
Amendments to laws, §31-5308.
Appeals, §31-5334.
Applicability of provisions, §31-5321.
Attachment of benefits, §31-5315.
Beneficiaries, §31-5314.
Benefit contracts, §31-5316.
Benefits provided by, §31-5313.
Bylaws, §31-5302.
Cash surrender value, §31-5317.
Certificates, §31-5322.
Definitions, §31-5301.
Examinations, §31-5325.
Exemptions, §31-5333.
Fines, §31-5332.
Foreign and alien societies, §§31-5326 to 31-5328.
Funds and assets, §31-5319.
Injunctions, §§31-5327, 31-5329.
Investments, §31-5318.
Laws of, §31-5308.
Liabilities, §31-5305.
Licenses, §§31-5324, 31-5328, 31-5330.
Liquidations, §31-5327.
Loans, §31-5317.
Location of principal office, §31-5304.
Mergers and consolidations, §31-5311.
Mutual life insurance company.
Conversion into, §31-5312.
Nonforfeiture benefits, §31-5317.
Nonprofit institutions operated by, §31-5309.
Operation for benefit of members, §31-5302.
Optional benefits, §31-5317.
Organization of, §31-5307.
Penalties, §31-5332.
Publications, §31-5325.
Qualifications for membership, §31-5303.
Receiverships, §31-5327.
Reinsurance arrangements, §31-5310.
Reports, §31-5323.
Severability of provisions, §31-5335.
Taxation, §31-5320.
Unfair trade practices, §31-5331.
Valuation standards for certificates, §31-5322.

FRATERNAL BENEFIT SOCIETIES —Cont'd
Waiver of laws, §31-5306.

FRAUD AND DECEIT.
Advertising, fraudulent, §22-1511.
Prosecution, §22-1512.
Aged persons.
Enhanced penalties for offenses committed against, §22-3601.
Aggregate amounts received determining grade of offense, §22-3202.
Ammunition, §7-2507.04.
Assignment for benefit of creditors, §28-2109.
Attorneys at law.
Candor toward the tribunal, ProfCond Rule 3.3.
Attornment, fraudulent, §42-3232.
Banks and financial institutions.
Fraudulent activity prohibited, §26-551.22.
Checks, drafts, or orders intended to defraud, §22-1510.
Closing-out sales, §47-2106.
Condominium public offering statement, §42-1904.02.
Continuing care retirement communities, §44-151.15.
Contracts.
Sale of goods.
Remedies for fraud, §28:2-721.
Controlled substances, §48-904.03.
Conveyances, §§28-3101 to 28-3111.
See FRAUDULENT TRANSFERS.
Credit card fraud, §22-3223.
Crime victims' compensation, §4-513.
False claims, VictComp Rule 41.
Debt collectors, §28-3814.
Decedents' estates, §20-108.01.
Definitions, §22-3201.
Discrimination, §2-1402.65.
Drivers' licenses.
Seizure of suspect documents, §50-1401.04.
Elections, §1-1001.14.
False personation, §§22-1402 to 22-1406.
Fines, §22-3222.
Fire and casualty insurance, §31-2502.09.
Firearms, §7-2507.04.
First degree fraud, §22-3221.
Aged persons, offenses committed against.
Enhanced penalties, §22-3601.

FRAUD AND DECEIT —Cont'd
First degree fraud —Cont'd
Continuing care retirement
communities, §44-151.15.
Fines and penalties, §22-3222.
Insurance fraud, §22-3225.02.
**Food sold by misrepresentation or
false advertising,** §37-201.22a.
Forgery, §§22-1502 to 22-1513.
Fraudulent transfers.
General provisions, §§28-3101 to
28-3111.
See FRAUDULENT TRANSFERS.
**Future performance, false promise
as to,** §22-3221.
Garnishment.
Prejudgment garnishment.
Fraudulent conveyances, §16-529.
**Grade of offense, aggregate amounts
received determining,** §22-3202.
**Health occupations licensure,
registration or certification,**
§§3-1210.04, 3-1210.05.
Hearing aid dealers.
Grounds for revocation or suspension,
§28-4006.
Human Rights Commission,
§2-1402.65.
Indictments and informations.
Intent to defraud, §23-322.
Insurance fraud, §§22-3225.01 to
22-3225.15.
See INSURANCE FRAUD.
**Insurers rehabilitation and
liquidation proceedings,**
§§31-1324, 31-1325.
Interest, §28-3312.
Jury selection, §11-1915.
Fraudulent interference or collusion
in, §22-1514.
Landlord and tenant, §42-3509.01.
Leases, UCC.
Effect of fraud on rights and remedies,
§28:2A-505.
Letters of credit, §28:5-109.
**Liens on motor vehicles and trailers,
false statements as to,** §50-1215.
Life insurance companies, §§31-4310
to 31-4314.
See LIFE INSURANCE COMPANIES.
Lottery tickets, §3-1333.
Marriage.
Consent obtained by fraud or deceit,
§46-403.
Medicaid service provider fraud,
§§4-801 to 4-805.

FRAUD AND DECEIT —Cont'd
**Metropolitan police, false reports
made to,** §5-117.05.
Mortgage lenders and brokers,
§26-1114.
Misrepresentation by name, §26-1120.
**Motor vehicle financing, false
statements in connection with,**
§50-606.
Multijurisdictional cases.
Referral to other law enforcement
agency, §22-3204.
Negotiable instruments.
Indorsements.
Responsibility of employer for
fraudulent indorsement by
employee, §28:3-405.
**Occupations and professions
licensure,** §47-2853.26.
Penalties, §22-3222.
Aged persons, offenses committed
against.
Enhanced penalties, §22-3601.
Perjury, §§22-2402 to 22-2405.
See PERJURY.
Personal property taxes, §47-1527.
Pesticides, §8-417.
Pleading special matters, CivPro Rule
9.
Domestic relations actions, DomRel
Rule 9.
Police and fire trial boards.
Willful false swearing before, §5-1002.
Procurement practices.
False claims against District,
§2-381.02.
Fines and penalties for false
representations, §2-381.09.
Prohibited acts, §22-3221.
Public assistance, §§4-205.69,
4-218.01.
Public auction permit requirements,
§47-2706.
Public officers and employees,
§1-615.05.
Public utilities.
False statements to secure approval
for stock issue for, §34-701.
**Recordation of false financing
statements,** §41-204.
Recordation tax, §42-1121.
Registration in lodgings, §22-3224.
Offenses committed in D.C.,
§22-3224.01.
Relief from judgment or order,
CivPro Rule 60.
Domestic relations actions, DomRel
Rule 60.

FRAUD AND DECEIT —Cont'd
Rental properties, §42-3509.01.
Rent control, §42-3509.01.
Rent, lien for, §42-3218.
Retirement communities.
Continuing care retirement
communities, §44-151.15.
School residency reports, §38-312.03.
Second degree fraud, §22-3221.
Aged persons, offenses committed
against.
Enhanced penalties, §22-3601.
Continuing care retirement
communities, §44-151.15.
Fines and penalties, §22-3222.
Insurance fraud, §22-3225.03.
Security agents and brokers.
Fraudulent transactions, §31-5605.02.
Grounds for disciplinary actions,
§31-5602.07.
Manipulation of market, §31-5605.03.
Misleading filings, §31-5605.04.
Unlawful representation, §31-5605.05.
Unlicensed or unregistered activity,
§31-5605.01.
Statute of frauds, §§28-3501 to
28-3505.
Taxation.
Penalties for fraud, §47-4212.
Recordation tax, §42-1121.
Telephone solicitation, §§22-3226.01
to 22-3226.15.
Tobacco tax, §§47-2406, 47-2409.
Trade practices.
Unlawful trade practices, §28-3904.
Transfers, §§28-3101 to 28-3111.
See FRAUDULENT TRANSFERS.
**Trust, mortgage and title
corporations,** §26-1320.
Trusts and trustees.
Uniform trust code.
Void trusts, §19-1304.06.
Unemployment compensation,
§51-119.
Unlawful trade practices, §28-3904.
Wastewater disposal systems.
Falsified information regarding,
§8-105.04.
Wastewater treatment systems.
False compensation claims regarding,
§8-205.
Water pollution, §8-103.16.
Weapons.
False information given in purchasing,
§22-4511.
Weights and measures, §§37-201.07,
37-201.22a.

FRAUD AND DECEIT —Cont'd
Wills, §18-112.
Workers' compensation, §32-1533.
Anti-fraud report, §32-1542.03.
Workplace fraud, §§32-1331.01 to
32-1331.12.
See WORKPLACE FRAUD.

FRAUDULENT CONVERSION.
Security agents and brokers.
Grounds for disciplinary actions,
§31-5602.07.

FRAUDULENT TRANSFERS,
§§28-3101 to 28-3111.
Actual intent construed, §28-3104.
Applicability of provisions, §28-3111.
Assignments for benefit of creditors.
Assignment to hinder or defraud
creditors, §28-2109.
Orders to prevent, §28-2106.
Bankruptcy and insolvency,
§28-3102.
**Complaint to set aside fraudulent
conveyance,** CivPro Form CA 13.
Construction of act.
Supplementary provisions, §28-3110.
Uniformity of application, §28-3111.
Creditors' remedies, §28-3107.
Definitions, §28-3101.
Insolvency, §28-3102.
Value, §28-3103.
Future creditors.
Actual intent, §28-3104.
Remedies, §28-3107.
Holders-in-due-course, §28-3108.
Interpretation of provisions,
§28-3111.
Joinder of claims and remedies,
CivPro Rule 18.
Limitation of actions, §28-3109.
Extinguishment of causes of action,
§28-3109.
Obligations.
When incurred, §28-3106.
When voidable, §28-3108.
Present creditors.
Actual intent, §28-3104.
Claim arose before transfer, §28-3105.
Fraudulent as to, §28-3105.
Remedies, §28-3107.
Present value transfer, §28-3103.
Remedies of creditors against,
§28-3107.
Statute of limitations.
Extinguishment of causes of action,
§28-3109.

FRAUDULENT TRANSFERS —Cont'd
Supplementary provisions
    regarding, §28-3110.
Time transfer made or obligation
    incurred, §28-3106.
Transfers.
    When made, §28-3106.
    When voidable, §28-3108.
Uniformity of application and
    interpretation, §28-3111.
Value, giving, §28-3103.
Voidability, factors affecting,
    §28-3108.

FREDERICK DOUGLASS
    MEMORIAL AND HISTORICAL
    ASSOCIATION (CEDAR HILL).
Real property exempt from taxation,
    §47-1025.

FREEBASE KITS.
Drug paraphernalia, §§48-904.10,
    48-1101 to 48-1104.

FREE CIGARETTES.
Prohibition on distribution of,
    §7-1731.

FREE CLINIC CAPTIVE
    INSURANCE COMPANY.
Dissolution, §1-307.94.

FREEDOM OF INFORMATION,
    §§2-531 to 2-540.
Access to public records, §2-532.
Administrative agency appeals,
    §2-537.
Agency votes.
    Recording of final votes, §2-535.
Appeal of denial of right to inspect
    record, §2-537.
Arbitrary or capricious violations.
    Criminal penalty, §2-537.
Child fatality or near fatality.
    Public disclosure of findings and
        information.
        Freedom of information act requests,
            §4-1303.35.
Citation of subchapter, §2-540.
Classified information.
    Exemptions from disclosure, §2-534.
Definitions, §2-539.
Denial of right to inspect record.
    Review by mayor, injunctive or
        declaratory relief, §2-537.
Disclosure of public information,
    §2-536.
Fees.
    Access to public records, §2-532.

FREEDOM OF INFORMATION
    —Cont'd
Firearms.
    License to carry pistol, §7-2509.09.
    Registration, §7-2502.11a.
Injunctive or declaratory relief.
    Denial of right to inspection, §2-537.
Letters of denial.
    Contents, §2-533.
Mayor's report to council, §2-538.
Oversight of disclosure activities.
    Mayor, §2-538.
Public contracts.
    Information required to be made
        public, §2-536.
Public policy, §2-531.
Short title, §2-540.
Staff manuals and instructions to
    staff.
    Information required to be made
        public, §2-536.
Statutory exemptions from
    disclosure, §2-534.
Unified economic development
    budget transparency and
    accountability disclosure,
    §2-1208.04.

FREEHOLDS, §§42-504, 42-505.
Press, US Const Amd 1.

FREEMASONS.
Real property exempt from taxation,
    §47-1045.

FREE TEXTBOOKS, §§38-701 to
    38-706.

FREE TRADE.
Restraints of trade, §§28-4501 to
    28-4518.
    See RESTRAINTS OF TRADE.

FREEZING OF ASSETS.
Financial exploitation of vulnerable
    adults and elderly persons.
    Injunction, restraining order and asset
        protection, §22-938.

FRESH PURSUIT, §§23-901 to 23-903.
Arrest in District by officers of other
    states, §23-901.
    Discharge, §23-902.
    Hearing without unnecessary delay,
        §23-902.
    Release or detention ordered to await
        requisition demanding extradition,
        §23-902.
Defined, §23-903.

FRIVOLOUS ACTIONS.

Appeals, D.C. courts, DCCtApp Rule 38.

Appeals, federal cases.
Damages for, FRAP 38.
Sanctions against attorneys, USCtApp Rule 38.

Attorney not to assert frivolous claims, ProfCond Rule 3.1.

Sanctions, CivPro Rule 11.
Appeals in federal cases, USCtApp Rule 38.
Domestic relations actions, DomRel Rule 11.
Hospitalization of persons with mental illness, MentalHealth Rule 14.

Special education student rights.
Restriction of practice by attorney based on pattern of frivolous pleadings, §38-2572.04.

FRONTPAY.

Employment discrimination award.
Income averaging for tax purposes, §47-1806.10.

FRUITS.

Cherry.
Official fruit of the District of Columbia, §1-171.

Weights and measures.
General provisions, §§37-201.13 to 37-201.22a.
See WEIGHTS AND MEASURES.

FUEL CELLS.

Renewable energy portfolio standards, §§34-1431 to 34-1439.

FUGITIVES FROM JUSTICE.

Arrest procedures, §23-702.

Arrest warrants on, §23-701.

Constitution of the United States, US Const Art IV §2.

Extradition.
General provisions, §§23-701 to 23-707.
See EXTRADITION.

Failure to appear, fines and penalties for, §§23-703, 23-1327.

Insanity defense, persons committed under, §24-501.

Limitation of actions, §23-113.

Public assistance, §4-205.70.

Rewards for information regarding, §24-201.27.

Sealing arrest records, §16-803.01.

FULL FAITH AND CREDIT.

Bond issues, §§1-204.82, 1-204.84, 47-392.15.

FULL FAITH AND CREDIT —Cont'd

Constitution of the United States, US Const Art IV §1.

District of Columbia School of Law, not pledged for, §38-1205.12.

District retirement funds, §1-819.06.

Foreign judgment enforcement, CivPro Rule 72.
Domestic relations actions, DomRel Rule 72.

Housing finance agency bond issues, not pledged for, §42-2704.08.

Marriages from other jurisdictions, recognition of, §46-405.01.

Out-of-state parentage determinations, §16-909.02.

FUNDS.

Academic certification and testing fund, §38-2602.

AccessRx fund, §48-831.10.

Addiction recovery fund, §7-3004.

Adoption support fund, §4-344.01.

Adoption voucher fund, §4-344.

Advisory neighborhood commission security fund, §1-309.14.

Alcoholic beverage regulation administration fund, §25-210.

Animal control license fees fund, §8-1804.

Annual federal payment.
Deposit of, §47-392.05.

Anti-graffiti mural assistance program fund, §1-325.101.

Anti-prostitution vehicle impoundment proceeds fund, §22-2725.

Appraisal education fund, §47-2853.154.

Arts and humanities enterprise fund, §39-205.01.

Audit of closed special funds, §47-131.

Automated external defibrillator registration fund, §44-234.

Bank fees special fund, §1-325.231.

Basic business license fund, §47-2851.13.

Benchmarking enforcement fund.
Green buildings, §6-1451.07a.

Bicycle sharing fund, §50-921.16.

BID parking abatement fund, §1-325.341.

Board of ethics and government accountability fund, §1-1162.10.

Board of pharmacy fund, §7-733.02.

Books from birth fund, §39-116.

FUNDS —Cont'd

Business improvement district litter cleanup assistance fund, §1-325.111.

Business improvement districts.
BID parking abatement fund, §1-325.341.

Capital access fund, §1-325.172.

Capital project support fund, §§1-325.151 to 1-325.156.

Career and technical education (CTE) grant program fund, §38-2612.

Charter schools.
Direct loan fund for charter school improvement, §38-1833.02.
District of Columbia public charter school board fund, §38-1802.14.

Chief tenant advocate rental accommodations fee fund, §42-3504.01.

Child care services assistance fund, §§7-2001 to 7-2008.

Children's Trust Fund, §§4-1341.01 to 4-1341.08.
See CHILD ABUSE AND NEGLECT.

Clean land fund.
Brownfield revitalization, §8-633.08.

Clients' Security Trust Fund, DCBar Rule XII.
Restitution to fund by attorney, DCBar Rule XI.

Commission on health disparities fund, §7-755.04.

Commodities cost reserve fund, §47-368.04.

Common lottery board fund, §38-195.

Community-based violence reduction fund, §1-325.121.

Community school fund, §38-754.04.

Construction and demolition waste recycling fund, §8-1077.

Construction Services Fund, §10-620.

Control, §§47-381 to 47-385.
Definitions, §47-382.
Findings, §47-381.
Grant applications.
Council consent, §47-385.
Notice of application, §47-384.
Procedure, §47-383.

Copying by District, working fund for, §47-135.

Corporate recordation fund, §29-102.13.

Council technology projects fund, §1-325.201.

FUNDS —Cont'd

Crime victims assistance fund, §4-515.01.

Crime victims' compensation fund, §4-515.

Dangerous structures on public space fund, §10-1181.04.

DC Circulator fund, §50-921.33.

DC-NET services support fund, §1-1432.

DCPL revenue-generating activities fund, §39-117.

DC promise fund, §38-2753.

DC Streetcar fund, §50-921.73.

DDOT stormwater retention credit fund, §50-921.22.

Debt service.
Deposit of revenues dedicated to, §47-368.05.

Delinquent debt fund, §1-350.04.

Department of behavioral health enterprise fund, §1-325.281.

Department of corrections reimbursement fund, §1-325.21.

Department of housing and community development unified fund, §42-2857.01.

Department of mental health enterprise fund, §7-1131.21.

Destination DC marketing fund, §1-325.301.

Direct loan fund for charter school improvement, §38-1833.02.

Disability compensation for public officers and employees, §1-623.42.

Disbursement control, §§47-381 to 47-385.

District department of transportation enterprise fund for transportation initiatives, §50-921.13.

District department of transportation special purpose revenue funds, §50-921.12.

District of Columbia auditor legal fund, §1-301.174.

District of Columbia health benefit exchange authority fund, §31-3171.03.

District of Columbia public charter school board fund, §38-1802.14.

Domestic violence.
Shelter and transitional housing for victims of domestic violence fund, §4-521.

Drug, firearm, or prostitution-related nuisance abatement fund, §42-3111.01.

FUNDS —Cont'd

Drug prevention and children at risk, §47-4002.

Duplicating by district.
Working fund for, §47-135.

Eastern Market Enterprise Fund, §37-103.

Economic development special account, §2-1225.21.

Effi Slaughter Barry Initiative Fund, §7-1617.

Election reform fund, §1-1001.06a.

Electric light and power companies.
Municipal aggregation fund, §34-1515.

Emancipation day fund, §1-183.

Emergency and non-emergency telephone calling systems fund, §§34-1802, 34-1803.03.
Assessments, §34-1803.
Prepaid wireless E911 charge.
Collection and remittance, §34-1803.02.

Emergency and non-emergency telephone system assessments fund, §§34-1801 to 34-1806.

Employees' Compensation Fund, §1-623.42.

Employees retirement program management, §§1-711 to 1-725.
See EMPLOYEES RETIREMENT PROGRAM MANAGEMENT.

End homelessness fund, §1-325.261.

Energy assistance trust fund, §§8-1774.11.

Facilities service request fund, §10-551.07a.

Federal Pension Fund, §§1-817.01 to 1-817.06.

Federal Pension Liability Trust Fund, §§1-807.01 to 1-807.06.

Federal securities, investment in, §47-133.

Federal Supplemental Fund, §§1-811.01 to 1-811.06.

Fee collection incentive fund, §1-325.61.

FEMS special events fee fund, §1-325.81.

Financial responsibility and management assistance authority.
General provisions, §§47-391.01 to 47-395.
See FINANCIAL RESPONSIBILITY AND MANAGEMENT ASSISTANCE AUTHORITY.

FUNDS —Cont'd

Fire and emergency medical services training fund, §5-432.

Firearms Bounty fund, §7-2531.04.

Fiscal year 2006 educational investments fund for District of Columbia public schools and public charter schools, §1-325.31.

Fitness fund, §7-125.

Foreclosure mediation fund, §42-815.03.

For-hire vehicles department.
Fingerprinting fund, §50-301.23.

Fund-type accounting, §§47-371 to 47-377.

General fund, §§47-129, 47-131.
Certification of accumulated general fund balance, §47-387.01.
Composition of, §1-204.50.
Debt service, deposit of revenues dedicated to, §47-368.05.
Establishment of, §47-131.
Maintenance of effort and matching funds, §§47-387.51, 47-387.52.
Motor fuel tax deposited into, §§47-2301, 47-2324.
Nursing home receivership special fund or account, §44-1002.09.
Occupations and professions licensure special account, §47-2853.11.
Parking, §50-2603.
Real property, correction of conditions violative of law, §42-3131.01.
Recreation board fees, §10-213.01.
Revenues credited to, §47-129.
Sanitary sewage works, §§34-2102, 34-2113.
Statehood Constitutional Convention, §1-127.
University of the District of Columbia material fund, §38-1204.05.
Water supply and waterworks rents paid into, §34-2401.14.

Graffiti abatement fund, §42-3141.08.

Grants, District applications for, §§47-382 to 47-385.

Greater Southeast community hospital capital equipment fund, §1-325.71.

Green building fund, §6-1451.07.

Guardianship fund, §21-2060.

Hazardous materials reimbursement fund, §8-1447.

Health care financing fund, §§7-1931 to 7-1933.

Health department.
Board of pharmacy fund, §7-733.02.

FUNDS —Cont'd
Health department —Cont'd
Health occupations regulation fund,
§7-733.
Health occupations regulation fund.
Health department, §7-733.
**Health professional recruitment
fund,** §7-751.15a.
**Healthy DC and health care
expansion fund,** §31-3514.02.
Healthy schools fund, §§38-821.01,
38-821.02.
**Higher education incentive grant
fund,** §38-274.03.
**Higher education licensure
commission site evaluation fund,**
§38-2607.
Highway funds, §§9-109.02 to
9-111.01a.
Highway trust fund.
Report on expenditures by mayor,
§9-111.31.
**Historic landmark-District
protection fund,** §6-1110.01.
**HIV/AIDS crisis area capacity
building fund,** §§1-325.51 to
1-325.53.
Home purchase assistance fund,
§§42-2601 to 42-2626.
See HOME PURCHASE ASSISTANCE
FUND.
**Home repair and improvement
program fund for senior citizens,**
§§42-2201 to 42-2207.
Hospital provider fee fund.
Medicaid hospital outpatient 2016-
2017 supplemental payment,
§44-661.12.
Housing assistance fund, §42-3531.09.
Housing first fund, §4-753.01a.
Housing production trust fund,
§§42-2801 to 42-2804.
**Howard Theatre redevelopment
project fund,** §2-1217.34b.
**H Street retail priority area grant
fund,** §1-325.172.
Income tax secured bond fund,
§47-340.27.
**Indoor mold assessment and
remediation fund,** §8-241.07.
Inmate welfare fund, §§24-281 to
24-284.
Innovation fund, §§1-325.221 to
1-325.226.
Insurance regulatory trust fund,
§§31-1201 to 31-1210.

FUNDS —Cont'd
**Interest on Lawyers Trust Account
(IOLTA),** DCBar Appx A, DCBar
Rule X.
Verification of participation, DCBar
Rule XIV.
Interest on public funds.
Bank fees special fund, §1-325.231.
Interim disability assistance fund,
§4-204.09.
IPW fund, §1-325.291.
**John A. Wilson building centennial
fund,** §10-1302.
**John A. Wilson building renovation
development trust fund,**
§§10-1333, 10-1336.
Judges' retirement fund, §§1-714,
1-821.01.
**Judicial retirement and survivors
annuity fund,** §11-1570.
**Lead service line priority
replacement assistance fund,**
§§34-2151, 34-2152.
Library development trust fund,
§39-113.
Litigation support fund, §1-301.86b.
**Local roads construction and
maintenance fund.**
Report on expenditures by mayor,
§9-111.31.
Local transportation fund,
§9-111.01a.
Deposits, §50-2607.
Lottery and charitable games fund,
§3-1312.
Low-income housing tax credit fund,
§42-2853.02.
Definitions, §42-2853.01.
**Maintenance of effort and matching
funds,** §§47-387.51, 47-387.52.
**Medicaid and special education
reform fund,** §§4-204.51 to
4-204.56.
**Medicaid hospital inpatient 2016-
2017 rate supplement.**
Hospital fund, §44-662.12.
**Medicaid hospital outpatient 2016-
2017 supplemental payment.**
Hospital provider fee fund, §44-661.12.
Medical liability captive trust fund,
§1-307.91.
**Metropolitan area transit authority
fund,** §§9-1108.01, 9-1108.02.
**Metropolitan police department
body-worn camera fund,**
§5-116.51.

FUNDS —Cont'd

Metropolitan Washington Airports Authority, §9-918.

Motor Vehicle Biennial Inspection Fund, §50-1102.

Motor vehicle registration.
Out-of-state vehicle registration special fund, §50-1501.03a.

Motor vehicles of District.
Working fund for repair and maintenance of, §47-134.

MPD overtime reimbursement fund, §47-2826.

Municipal aggregation fund, §34-1515.

National capital energy fund, §§8-1778.41 to 8-1778.48.
See ENERGY CONSERVATION.

Neighborhood parade and festival fund, §1-325.211.

New Columbia statehood fund, §§1-129.31 to 1-129.35.

New convention center hotel fund, §10-1221.03.

Not-for-profit hospital corporations fund, §44-951.03.

Nursing facility quality of care fund, §47-1262.

Nursing home receivership special fund or account, §44-1002.09.

Occupations and professions licensure special account, §47-2853.11.

Office of the people's counsel agency fund, §34-912.

Office of veterans' affairs fund, §49-1004.

Operating cash reserve, §47-392.02.

Organization of fund structure, §47-373.

Other post-employment benefits fund.
Actuarial statement and opinion, §1-621.09b.
Annual audit, §1-621.09e.
Calculation of District's payment, §1-621.09a.
District contribution, §1-621.09.

Out-of-state vehicle registration special fund, §50-1501.03a.

Parking.
Deposit of fees and moneys, §50-2607.
Establishment of parking system fund, §50-2510.
Mayor's use of funds, §50-2603.

Parking meter pay-by-phone transaction fee fund, §50-921.14.

FUNDS —Cont'd

Parks and recreation, §10-303.

Pay equity and training commission, §§32-607, 32-608.

Pay-for-success contract fund, §2-211.03.

Pensions and retirement, §§1-801.01 to 1-821.01.
See PENSIONS AND RETIREMENT.

Pepco cost-sharing fund for DC PLUG, §1-325.331.

Performance parking program fund, §50-2531.01.

Pesticide registration fund, §8-438.01.

Photocopying by District.
Working fund for, §47-135.

Photographing by District.
Working fund for, §47-135.

Police and firefighters retirement and disability, §§1-712, 1-903.01.

Police complaints, office of, §5-1115.

Pregnant workers protection fund, §32-1231.12.

Printing by District.
Working fund for, §47-135.

Prison industries fund, §§24-231.02, 24-231.03, 24-231.15.

Private security camera incentive fund, §7-2832.

Productivity Bank Fund, §§1-325.01, 1-325.02.

Public buildings.
Construction Services Fund, §10-620.

Public planning capital project fund, §1-325.11.

Public-private partnership administration fund, §2-272.04.

Public school capital improvement fund, §§38-2971.01 to 38-2971.04.

Public service commission agency fund, §34-912.

Public utilities depreciation fund, §34-1115.

Public vehicles-for-hire consumer service fund, §50-301.20.

Public works, §§9-401.07, 9-1209.04.

Real estate guaranty and education fund, §§42-1706, 42-1707.

Recorder of deeds automation and infrastructure improvement fund, §42-1214.

Recreation Enterprise Fund, §10-303.

Recycling.
Construction and demolition waste recycling fund, §8-1077.

FUNDS —Cont'd

Rehabilitations Loan Insurance Fund, §6-1006.

Renewable energy development fund, §34-1436.

Rent supplement fund, §6-226.

Schedule of, §47-214.

Schools.

At-risk supplemental allocation preservation fund, §1-325.35.

Common lottery board fund, §38-195.

Fiscal year 2006 educational investments fund for District of Columbia public schools and public charter schools, §1-325.31.

General services department, §38-925.

Healthy schools fund, §§38-821.01, 38-821.02.

Healthy tots fund, §38-282.

Higher education licensure commission site evaluation fund, §38-2607.

Medicaid and special education reform fund, §§4-204.51 to 4-204.56.

Private funds, use of, §38-121.01.

Public school capital improvement fund, §§38-2971.01 to 38-2971.04.

Schools modernization fund, §§1-325.41 to 1-325.45.

See SCHOOLS AND EDUCATION.

Schools technology fund, §1-325.251.

Special education enhancement fund, §38-2613.

State athletic activities, programs, and office fund, §§38-2671 to 38-2674.

Senior citizens' home repair and improvement program fund, §§42-2201 to 42-2207.

Shelter and transitional housing for victims of domestic violence fund, §4-521.

Skyland TIF fund, §2-1217.35b.

Small business capital access fund, §2-218.75.

Solid waste nuisance abatement fund, §8-807.01.

Southwest waterfront fund, §2-1217.133.

Special education.

Medicaid and special education reform fund, §§4-204.51 to 4-204.56.

Special education enhancement fund, §38-2613.

Special energy assessment fund, §8-1778.21.

Special funds and accounts.

Establishment of, §§1-204.50, 47-131.

FUNDS —Cont'd

Sports and entertainment fund, §10-1202.08b.

Sports facilities account, §10-1202.08c.

State health planning and development fund, §44-420.01.

Step Up program, §42-2622.

Sterilization fund, §8-1804.

Stevie Sellows quality improvement fund, §§47-1270 to 47-1278.

Stormwater permit compliance enterprise fund, §8-152.02.

Stormwater retention credit fund, §§10-551.07b, 50-921.22.

Streetscape loan relief fund, §1-325.191.

Student residency verification fund, §38-312.02.

Substance abuse.

Addiction recovery fund, §7-3004.

Supply schedule, purchase card, and training fund, §2-361.03.

Sustainable energy trust fund, §8-1774.10.

Sustainable transportation fund, §50-921.15.

Taxicabs, §50-301.20.

Fingerprinting fund, §50-301.23.

Public vehicles-for-hire consumer service fund, §50-301.20.

Teachers.

Teachers' retirement and annuity fund, §38-2021.02.

Teachers' retirement fund, §§1-713, 1-903.02.

Technology infrastructure services support fund, §1-1433.

Technology projects fund, §1-325.201.

Teen pregnancy prevention fund, §§1-325.321 to 1-325.326.

Authorization for grant-managing entity, §1-325.325.

Definitions, §1-325.321.

Duplicative projects, §1-325.326.

Established, §1-325.322.

Reporting requirements, §1-325.324.

Required information before approval, §1-325.323.

Telecommunications.

Emergency and non-emergency telephone system assessments fund, §§34-1801 to 34-1806.

Telephone solicitation.

Fraud prevention fund, §22-3226.14.

Tobacco Settlement Trust Fund, §§7-1811.01 to 7-1811.03.

FUNDS —Cont'd

Transportation infrastructure improvement fund, §9-107.53.

Transportation infrastructure project review fund, §50-921.17.

Unemployment compensation.
Deposits into fund, §51-106.
Establishment of fund, §51-102.

Uninsured motorist fund, §31-2408.01.

Universal Service Trust Fund, §34-2003.

University of the District of Columbia.
Debt collection fund, §38-1251.01.
Higher education incentive grant program fund, §38-274.03.
Material fund, §38-1204.05.

Vector-borne infectious disease control fund, §8-2131.07.

Vending regulation fund, §37-131.07.

Veterans appreciation scholarship fund, §1-325.141.

Vision zero pedestrian and bicycle safety fund, §50-921.20.

Vital records fees fund, §7-221.

Voluntary foster care registry fund, §4-1303.09.

Wage theft prevention fund, §32-1307.01.

Walter Reed redevelopment fund, §2-1227.06.

Walter Reed reinvestment fund, §2-1227.05.

Washington convention and sports authority fund, §10-1202.08.
Marketing fund, §10-1202.08a.

Washington convention center fund, §10-1203.07.

Washington metropolitan area transit authority.
WMATA operations support fund, §1-325.311.

Washington metropolitan area transit authority fund, §§9-1108.01, 9-1108.02.

Water and Sewer Enterprise Authority Fund, §§34-2202.07, 34-2202.41.

Waterfront Park at the Yards.
Maintenance fund, §10-1803.

West End library and fire station maintenance fund, §1-325.181.

Wetland and stream mitigation trust fund, §8-103.09.

WMATA momentum fund, §1-325.241.

FUNDS —Cont'd

WMATA momentum support fund, §1-325.311.

Workers' compensation.
Administration fund, §32-1541.
Special fund, §32-1540.

Workplace fraud fund, §32-1331.15.

Youth challenge participant support fund, §49-434.

FUNDS TRANSFERS, §§28:4A-101 to 28:4A-507.

Applicability of article, §28:4A-102.
Federal electronic fund transfer act.
Relationship between UCC provision and federal provision, §28:4A-108.

Attachment and garnishment.
Creditor process served on receiving bank, §28:4A-502.

Bank deposits and collections.
Generally, §§28:4-101 to 28:4-504.
See BANK DEPOSITS AND COLLECTIONS.

Beneficiary.
Defined, §28:4A-103.
Payment order misdescription, §28:4A-207.

Beneficiary's bank.
Defined, §28:4A-103.
Payment orders.
Misdescription, §28:4A-208.
Obligation to pay and give notice to beneficiary, §28:4A-404.
Payment to beneficiary, §28:4A-405.
Set-off by, §28:4A-502.

Choice of law, §28:4A-507.

Citation of title, §28:4A-101.

Conflict of laws.
Choice of law, §28:4A-507.
Federal electronic fund transfer act.
Relationship between UCC provision and federal provision, §28:4A-108.
Federal reserve regulations and operating circulars, §28:4A-107.

Creditor process served on receiving bank, §28:4A-502.

Definitions.
Agreement for electronic presentment, §28:4-110.
Authorized account, §28:4A-105.
Bank, §28:4A-105.
Beneficiary, §28:4A-103.
Beneficiary's bank, §28:4A-103.
Creditor process, §28:4A-502.
Customer, §28:4A-105.

FUNDS TRANSFERS —Cont'd
Payment orders —Cont'd
Time of acceptance, §28:4A-209.
Time received, §28:4A-106.
Transmission through communications system, §28:4A-206.
Transmission through funds-transfer system, §28:4A-206.
Unauthorized payment orders.
Duty of customer to report, §28:4A-204.
Refund of payment, §28:4A-204.
Verified payment orders, §28:4A-202.
Unenforceability of, §28:4A-203.
Scope of article, §28:4A-102.
Service of process.
Creditor process on receiving bank, §28:4A-502.
Setoff by beneficiary's bank, §28:4A-502.
Short title, §28:4A-101.
Statutory construction.
Federal electronic fund transfer act.
Relationship between UCC provision and federal provision, §28:4A-108.
Taxes, payment, §47-4402.
Title of article, §28:4A-101.
Transitional provisions, §§28:11-101 to 28:11-108.
See COMMERCIAL CODE.

FUNERAL DIRECTORS, §§3-401 to 3-421.
Appeals, §3-410.
Apprenticeship terms and conditions, §3-407.
Board of funeral directors, §§47-2853.06 to 47-2853.10.
Change of address, §3-416.
Child death.
Reports, §4-1371.12.
Courtesy cards for directors licensed in Maryland or Virginia, §3-415.
Crimes and offenses.
Failure to report certain deaths, §5-1406.
Definitions, §3-402.
Direct supervision by director, services requiring, §3-414.
Emergencies, services during, §3-411.
Emergency medical transport services, §3-411.
Examinations for licensure, §3-405.
Fees, §3-404.
Fines, §3-417.

FUNERAL DIRECTORS —Cont'd
Hearings, §3-409.
Human tissue banks, §7-1541.06.
Immediate supervision, services requiring, §3-421.
Injunctions, §3-419.
Licenses, §§3-405 to 3-416.
Courtesy cards for directors licensed in Maryland or Virginia, §3-415.
Denial of, §3-408.
Examinations for licensure, §3-405.
Issuance of, §3-406.
Qualifications for, §3-405.
Renewal of license, §3-406.
Revocation of license, §3-408.
Suspension of license, §3-408.
Maryland, licensed in, §3-415.
Medical examiner.
Duty to report certain deaths to medical examiner, §5-1405.
Failure to report certain deaths, §5-1406.
Penalties, §3-417.
Policy declaration, §3-401.
Possession of human remains, taking, §§3-412, 3-413.
Disputes, §3-413.01.
Priority of next of kin claiming human remains, §3-413.
Prohibited acts, §3-411.
Prosecutions, §3-418.
Qualifications, §3-405.
Reciprocity, §3-405.
Reports.
Child death, §4-1371.12.
Rules, §3-420.
Suspicious deaths.
Duty to report certain deaths to medical examiner, §5-1405.
Failure to report certain deaths, §5-1406.
Virginia, licensed in, §3-415.

FUNERAL EXPENSES.
Claims against estates, §20-907.
Crime victims' compensation, VictComp Rule 25.
Request for information, VictComp Rule 15.
Police and firefighters retirement and disability, §5-720.
Public assistance claims, §§4-214.01 to 4-214.04.
Public officers and employees, §1-623.34.

FUNERAL HEARSES.
Business licenses, §47-2829.

FUNGIBLE GOODS.

Buyer in the ordinary course of business.

Delivery by warehouseman, §28:7-205.

Duplicate receipt or bill.

Rights conferred, §28:7-402.

Warehouse.

Duty to keep goods separate, §28:7-207.

Liability for commingling goods, §28:7-207.

FURLOUGH.

Prisons and prisoners.

Resocialization furlough program, §§24-251.01 to 24-251.08.

FUTURE ADVANCES.

Secured transactions, §28:9-204.

Priority of security interests, §28:9-323.

Security interest in, §28:9-204.

FUTURE ESTATES, §§42-510 to 42-513.

Commencement at future day, §42-510.

Conditional limitation.

Commencement on contingency, §42-511.

Contingent future estate, §42-512.

Defined, §42-510.

Estates created to take effect in alternative, §42-513.

Remainder.

Commencement upon expiration of precedent estate, §42-511.

Vested future estate, §42-512.

FUTURE INTERESTS.

Estates in land.

General provisions, §§42-501 to 42-523.

See ESTATES IN LAND.

G

GAG ORDERS, CivPro Rule 203, CrimPro Rule 53.

Child abuse and neglect proceedings, NeglectProc Rule 45.

Juvenile proceedings, JuvProc Rule 53.

GALACTOSEMIA, §§7-831 to 7-840.

GALA HISPANIC THEATRE.

Real property tax exemptions, §47-4660.

GALLAUDET UNIVERSITY,

§§38-2301 to 38-2402.11.

Appropriation for indigent blind children formerly instructed at, §38-2301.

Appropriations, §38-2402.11.

Audits, §38-2402.03.

Board of trustees, §38-2401.03.

Charitable solicitations, §§44-1701 to 44-1714.

See CHARITABLE SOLICITATIONS.

Continuation of Gallaudet College as, §38-2401.01.

Definitions, §38-2402.01.

Elementary school program, §§38-2401.04, 38-2401.05.

Evaluations, §38-2402.05.

Federal endowment programs, §38-2402.07a.

Foreign students, §38-2402.10.

Gifts, §38-2402.02.

International students, §38-2402.10.

Liaison for educational programs, §38-2402.06.

Management of institutional funds.

General provisions.

See PRUDENT INVESTOR ACT.

Monitoring, §38-2402.05.

Oversight activities, §38-2402.09.

Property rights, §§38-2302, 38-2401.02.

Report on Convention of American Instructors of the Deaf, §38-2304.

Reports, §§38-2402.04, 38-2402.05.

Scholarship program, §38-2402.08a.

School programs, §§38-2401.04, 38-2401.05.

Secondary education program, §§38-2401.04, 38-2401.05.

Student health care.

General provisions, §§38-601 to 38-651.12.

See STUDENT HEALTH CARE.

Supervision of, §38-2303.

Transfer of property to, §38-2302.

Universities and colleges.

General provisions.

See UNIVERSITIES AND COLLEGES.

GALLERY PLACE PROJECT.

Sales tax exemption, §47-2005.

Tax and fee abatements, §2-1217.31.

GAMBLING, §§22-1701 to 22-1718.

Action to recover losses at gaming, §16-1702.

Relief from further penalty upon repayment, §16-1703.

GAMBLING —Cont'd

Alcoholic beverage license transfer restrictions, §25-316.

Athletic contests, §§22-1708, 22-1713.

Bookmaking, §22-1708.

Cheating at, §16-1704.

Confidence games, §22-1706.

Definitions.
Gaming premises, §22-1705.
Gaming tables, §22-1707.

Fines, §22-1705.

Forfeiture of gambling premises, §22-1705.

Gaming contracts invalid, §16-1701.

Gaming tables.
Defined, §22-1707.
Setting up or keeping, §22-1704.

Inducing gaming play, §22-1704.

Keeping gaming premises, §§5-115.06, 22-1704, 22-1705.

Legalized gambling, §§22-1716 to 22-1718.
Advertising and promotion, §22-1718.
Bingo, raffles, Monte Carlo night parties for educational and charitable purposes.
Permissible activities, §22-1717.
Lotteries and daily numbers games operated for and by District.
Permissible activities, §22-1717.
Sale of tickets and slips, §22-1718.
Permissible gambling activities, §22-1717.
Statement of purposes, §22-1716.

Liens on gambling premises, §22-1705.

Lotteries.
See LOTTERIES.

Lottery and charitable games control board.
General provisions, §§3-1301 to 3-1336.
See LOTTERY AND CHARITABLE GAMES CONTROL BOARD.

Monte Carlo night parties, §3-1322.01.

Penalties, §22-1705.

Pools, §22-1708.

Records, §22-1714.

Sports, §§22-1708, 22-1713.

Three-card monte, §22-1706.

Witness immunity, §22-1714.

GAME LAWS, §§22-4328 to 22-4333.
See FISH AND GAME.

GAMES ESTABLISHMENTS.

Business licenses, §47-2821.

GAMES PLAYED IN STREET, §22-1308.

GAMING.

Action to recover losses at gaming, §16-1702.
Relief from further penalty upon repayment, §16-1703.

Gambling.
General provisions, §§22-1701 to 22-1718.
See GAMBLING.

Gaming contracts invalid, §16-1701.

Lotteries.
See LOTTERIES.

Lottery and charitable games control board.
General provisions, §§3-1301 to 3-1336.
See LOTTERY AND CHARITABLE GAMES CONTROL BOARD.

Monte Carlo night parties, §3-1322.01.

GANGS.

Contributing to the delinquency of a minor, §22-811.

Crime victims' compensation.
Eligibility for compensation, VictComp Rule 7.

Criminal street gangs, §22-951.

Joint working group.
Gang and crew intervention, §2-1531.01.

Metropolitan police.
School safety division.
Protection of students from gang and crew violence, §§5-132.01 to 5-132.21.

GAP-CLOSING ACTIONS.

Budgets and budget estimates, §§47-318.03, 47-318.04.

GARAGE KEEPERS.

Reporting requirements regarding vehicles damaged in accidents, §50-2201.06.

GARAGE KEEPERS' LIENS, §§40-102 to 40-105.

Motor vehicles, liens for storage, repairs, and supplies for, §40-102.

Sales associated with.
Enforcement of lien by sale, §40-103.
Proceeds, application of, §40-104.

Storage, liens for.
Allowance of, §40-102.
Limitations on, §40-105.

GARBAGE COLLECTION.

Debris removal during public service event, emergency or training operation, §8-741.

Facilities, purchase or lease of, §8-741.

Illegal dumping, §§8-901 to 8-906.
See ILLEGAL DUMPING.

Litter control, §§8-801 to 8-812.
See LITTER CONTROL.

Municipal function, recognized as, §8-741.

Noise violations, §8-731.
Rules, §8-732.

Real property taxes, §47-872.

Tips and gratuities, §8-741.

Trash compactor grant program, §§8-751 to 8-753.

GARNISHMENT, §§16-501 to 16-584.

Alimony.
Enforcement of alimony pendente lite, §16-911.

College savings program.
Seizure of accounts prohibited, §47-4510.

Compensation of victims of violent crime.
Exemption of award, §4-507.

Cooperative associations.
Exemption of share and membership certificates, §29-928.

Definitions.
Post-judgment garnishment in aid of execution, §16-541.
Wages, §16-571.

Dismissal of attachment, CivPro Form CA 109.

Docket cards.
Attachment of wages, CivPro Rule 69-II.
Domestic relations actions, DomRel Rule 69.

Fraternal benefit societies.
Prohibition, §31-5315.

Insurance.
Insurers rehabilitation and liquidation procedures, §31-1355.
Life insurance.
Disability benefits.
Exemption from legal process, §31-4716.01.
Group life policies or proceeds.
Exemptions from legal process, §31-4717.

Judgments.
Generally, CivPro Rule 69-II.

GARNISHMENT —Cont'd

Police and firefighters retirement and disability.
Funds not subject to execution, §5-723.05.

Post-judgment garnishment in aid of execution.
Applicability of provisions, §16-541.
Claims to attached property, §16-554.
Condemnation of property.
Sale under fieri facias, §16-555.
Costs, §16-542.
Credits, §16-546.
Defending against the attachment, §16-551.
Definitions, §16-541.
Interrogatories to garnishee, §16-552.
Issuance, §16-542.
Judgment against garnishee, §16-556.
Judgments in favor of defendant may be attached, §16-548.
Money or property held by marshal, §16-548.
Money or property in hands of executors and administrators, §16-549.
Multiple attachments against same judgment debtor, §16-545.
Oral examination, §16-552.
Preservation of property, §16-550.
Property subject to garnishment, §16-544.
Retention of property or credits by garnishee, §16-547.
Revival of judgment unnecessary, §16-543.
Sale of property, §§16-550, 16-555.
Scire facias unnecessary, §16-543.
Traverse of garnishee's answers, §16-553.

Prejudgment garnishment.
Affidavits, §16-501.
Bonds, surety, §§16-501, 16-505.
Claims to attached property, §16-523.
Condemnation of attached property, §§16-524, 16-525.
Contracts.
Damages for breach, §16-501.
Costs, §16-522.
Debts, §16-501.
Discharge of garnishee, §16-524.
Defenses by garnishee, §16-519.
Dockets, §16-531.
Executors and administrators.
Money or property in hands of executor or administrator, §16-516.

GARNISHMENT —Cont'd
Prejudgment garnishment —Cont'd
Fieri facias.
Sale of condemned property, §16-525.
Fraudulent conveyances, §16-529.
Grounds, §16-501.
Index of garnishment, §16-531.
Interrogatories to garnishee, §16-521.
Traverse of answers, §16-522.
Judgment against garnishee, §16-526.
Protection of garnishee, §16-528.
Judgments may be garnished, §16-515.
Liens, §16-507.
Money or property held by marshal, §16-515.
Nonresident wages, §16-512.
Notice, §16-502.
Oral examination of garnishee, §§16-521, 16-522.
Other remedies of judgment creditor.
Effect of subchapter, §16-532.
Partnership interest or credits, §16-511.
Retention of property or credits by garnishee, §16-511.
Personal property, §16-501.
Other property may be garnished in replevin action, §16-517.
Property subject to garnishment, §16-507.
Undertaking by defendant or person in possession, §16-509.
Plaintiff prevails, §16-527.
Release of property or credits from attachment, §16-510.
Sufficiency of undertaking, §16-510.
Preservation of property, §16-518.
Proceedings in superior court, §16-533.
Property subject to garnishment, §16-507.
Publication of notice, §16-502.
Receivers.
Appointment to take possession of property, §16-518.
Release of property or credits from garnishment, §16-510.
Replevin.
Other property may be garnished in replevin action, §16-517.
Representative capacity of property holder, §16-514.
Sale of property, §16-518.
Service of process, §16-502.
Trial.
Defending against, §16-520.

GARNISHMENT —Cont'd
Prejudgment garnishment —Cont'd
Trial —Cont'd
Time for trial of issues, §16-530.
Trial on traverse of garnishee's answers, §16-522.
Two or more property holders, §16-514.
Undertaking by defendant or person in possession, §16-509.
Plaintiff prevails, effect of judgment, §16-527.
Release of property or credits from attachment, §16-510.
Sufficiency of undertaking, §16-510.
Wages.
Advance payment void, §16-513.
Nonresidents.
Levy and attachment upon wages of nonresident, §16-512.
Prohibition of prejudgment garnishment, §16-583.
Public assistance.
Payments not subject to garnishment, §4-215.01.
Public officers and employees.
Compensation subject to garnishment for child support, maintenance or alimony payments, §1-507.
Real property.
Property subject to garnishment, §16-507.
Salaries and wages.
Amount garnished.
Percentage limitations, §16-572.
Applicability of subchapter, §16-582.
Definitions, §16-571.
Discharge from employment for garnishment prohibited, §16-584.
Hindering just claims as reason for obtaining judgment.
Quashing attachment, §16-580.
Medical assistance program.
Recoupment of amounts spent on child medical care, §1-307.43.
No salary or salary inadequate for services rendered.
Payments by employer-garnishee, §16-579.
Percentage limitations, §16-572.
Prejudgment garnishment prohibited, §16-583.
Advance payment void, §16-513.
Nonresidents.
Levy and attachment upon wages of nonresident, §16-512.

GARNISHMENT —Cont'd
Salaries and wages —Cont'd
Priority, §16-572.
Quashing attachment where judgment obtained to hinder just claims, §16-580.
Receipts of amount collected.
Creditor on judgment to file receipts in court, §16-574.
Resignation or dismissal of employee.
Lapse of attachment, §16-576.
Rules of procedure, §16-581.
Superior court judgments.
Lapse, §16-578.
Validity, §16-578.
Support and maintenance.
Applicability of percentage limitations to judgment for support, §16-577.
Withholding and making payments, §16-573.
Failure of employer to pay percentages, §16-575.
Percentage limitations, §16-573.
Superior court.
Judgments.
Generally, CivPro Rule 69-II.
Prejudgment garnishment.
Proceedings in superior court, §16-533.
Wages.
Lapse of superior court judgments, §16-578.
Validity of superior court judgments, §16-578.
Support orders, enforcement, §16-571.01.
Teachers' retirement.
After June 30, 1946.
Funds not assignable or subject to execution, §38-2021.17.
Writ of attachment on wages, salary and commissions, CivPro Form CA 123.
Writ of attachment other than wages, salary and commissions, CivPro Form CA 122.

GAS COMPANIES.
Commission powers and duties, §34-301.
Construction of plant, permission for, §34-302.
Consumer protection.
Disconnection of service in extreme temperature, prohibition, §34-1671.06a.

GAS COMPANIES —Cont'd
Consumer protection —Cont'd
Retail natural gas suppliers, §34-1671.08.
Applicability of consumer protection laws, §34-1671.13.
Daily inspection requirement, §34-1605.
Definitions, §§34-209, 34-210.
Disconnection of service in extreme temperature, prohibition, §34-1671.06a.
Excessive charges, §34-304.
Extreme temperature, forecast of.
Disconnection of service in extreme temperature, prohibition, §34-1671.06a.
Inspector of gas and meters, §34-1601.
Power to appoint and remove inspector and assistants from office, §34-305.
Laboratories for testing gas, §§34-1602 to 34-1604.
Licenses.
Retail natural gas suppliers, §34-1671.05.
Suspension, revocation or rescission, §34-1671.11.
Low-income gas customer discount program, §8-1774.15.
Meter inspections, §§34-303 to 34-306.
Public service commission.
See PUBLIC SERVICE COMMISSION.
Rates, maximum, §34-1608.
Refusal to pay bills.
Additional charge for nonpayment, §34-1608.
Excessive charges as defense to, §34-304.
Removal of meters due to, §34-1606.
Reports, §34-1607.
Retail natural gas suppliers, §§34-1671.01 to 34-1671.14.
Anticompetitive conduct and conditions.
Monitoring markets, §34-1671.14.
Complaints, §34-1671.10.
Consumer education program, §34-1671.07.
Consumer protections, §34-1671.08.
Applicability of other consumer protections laws, §34-1671.13.
Disconnection of service in extreme temperature, prohibition, §34-1671.06a.

GAS COMPANIES —Cont'd
Retail natural gas suppliers —Cont'd
Cumulative nature of rights and
remedies, §34-1671.12.
Definitions, §34-1671.02.
Duties of gas companies, §34-1671.06.
Information provided to commission,
§34-1671.09.
Jurisdiction.
Consent to, §34-1671.04.
Public service commission,
§34-1671.10.
Legislative findings, §34-1671.01.
Licensing, §34-1671.05.
Suspension, revocation or rescission,
§34-1671.11.
Monitoring markets for
anticompetitive conduct and
conditions, §34-1671.14.
Penalties for violations, §34-1671.11.
Reports.
Annual financial report,
§34-1671.09.
Market monitoring, §34-1671.14.
Rulemaking, §§34-1671.03, 34-1671.08.
Violations.
Penalties, §34-1671.11.
Street lighting, §§9-501 to 9-510.
See STREET LIGHTING.
Taxation, §47-2501.
**Testing and inspecting
requirements,** §§34-1601 to
34-1608.
Annual reports to Congress, §34-1607.
Daily inspections, §34-1605.
Laboratory for testing gas, §34-1602.
Additional laboratories, §34-1603.
Officer of company present at tests,
§34-1604.
Removal of meters for neglect or
refusal to pay amount due,
§34-1606.
Theft of utility service, §§22-3218.01
to 22-3218.04.

GAS-FITTERS.
Business licenses, §§47-2853.121 to
47-2853.123.
Licenses, §2-135.

GAS MAINS.
Public works, §9-401.03.

GASOLINE PUMPS, AUTOMATIC.
Weights and measures, §37-201.18.

GAS STATIONS, §§36-301.01 to
36-305.02.
Advisory board, §36-304.01.

GAS STATIONS —Cont'd
Automatic gasoline pumps,
§37-201.18.
Business licenses, §47-2814.
Coercion.
Conversion to limited service.
Prohibited acts by distributors,
§36-304.01.
Conversions to limited service,
§36-304.01.
Costs.
Franchise purchase rights, §36-304.14.
Definitions, §36-301.01.
Exemptions, §36-302.04.
Fines, §36-302.05.
Franchise purchase rights,
§§36-304.11 to 36-304.15.
Application of law, §36-304.15.
Costs, §36-304.14.
Definitions, §36-304.11.
Duty of good faith, §36-304.13.
Exemptions, §36-304.15.
Injunctions, §36-304.14.
Remedies for violations, §36-304.14.
Right of first refusal, §36-304.12.
**Gasoline and fuel pump octane
measurement,** §37-201.18a.
Good faith.
Franchise purchase rights, §36-304.13.
Injunctions, §36-302.05.
Franchise purchase rights, §36-304.14.
Interpretation of provisions,
§36-305.01.
Issuance of rules and regulations,
§36-302.04.
**Jobbers, producers, refiners and
manufacturers.**
Restriction on operating, §36-302.02.
Limited service conversions,
§36-304.01.
Marketing agreements, §§36-303.01 to
36-303.07.
Applicability of provisions, §36-303.07.
Civil actions, §36-303.06.
Defined, §36-301.01.
Disclosures required for, §36-303.02.
Remedies, §36-303.06.
Remedies of retail dealer, §36-303.04.
Sale, assignment, or transfer,
§36-303.05.
Termination, cancellation, or failure to
renew, §36-303.03.
Terms and conditions, §36-303.01.
**Nondiscrimination requirements for
wholesalers,** §36-302.03.
Notice of violations, §36-302.05.

GAS STATIONS —Cont'd
Penalties, §36-302.05.
Policy declaration, §36-305.01.
Registration, §36-302.01.
Reports, §36-302.04.
Restrictions on operation of,
§§36-302.02, 36-302.04.
Right of first refusal.
Franchise purchase rights, §36-304.12.
Security requirements, §36-301.21.
Public service announcement,
§36-301.22.
Severability of provisions, §36-305.02.

GATEWAY MARKET CENTER AND RESIDENCES.
Real property tax exemptions,
§47-4621.

GAY COUPLES.
Domestic partner benefits.
General provisions, §§32-701 to
32-710.
See DOMESTIC PARTNER
BENEFITS.
Domestic partnerships.
See DOMESTIC PARTNERSHIPS.
Inheritance and estate taxes.
Marriage equality estate tax
clarification, §1-301.153.
Office of lesbian, gay, bisexual,
transgender, and questioning
affairs, §§2-1381 to 2-1384.

GAY, LESBIAN, BISEXUAL, AND TRANSGENDER AFFAIRS, OFFICE OF, §§2-1381 to 2-1384.

GENDER IDENTITY OR EXPRESSION.
Bias-related crimes, §§22-3701 to
22-3704.
Change of name or gender,
§§16-2501, 16-2503.
Insurance.
Discrimination based upon AIDS test,
§§31-1601 to 31-1610.
Unfair trade practices, §§31-2231.01 to
31-2231.25.

GENERAL COOPERATIVE ASSOCIATION ACT OF 2010,
§§29-901 to 29-939.
See COOPERATIVE ASSOCIATIONS.

GENERAL CORPORATIONS,
§§29-301.01 to 29-314.02.
See CORPORATIONS.

GENERAL FUND, §§47-129, 47-131.
Certification of accumulated general
fund balance, §47-387.01.

GENERAL FUND —Cont'd
Composition of, §1-204.50.
Debt service, deposit of revenues
dedicated to, §47-368.05.
Establishment of, §47-131.
Maintenance of effort and matching
funds, §§47-387.51, 47-387.52.
Motor fuel tax deposited into,
§§47-2301, 47-2324.
Nursing home receivership special
fund or account, §44-1002.09.
Occupations and professions
licensure special account,
§47-2853.11.
Parking, §50-2603.
Real property, correction of
conditions violative of law,
§42-3131.01.
Recreation board fees, §10-213.01.
Revenues credited to, §47-129.
Sanitary sewage works, §§34-2102,
34-2113.
Statehood Constitutional
Convention, §1-127.
University of the District of
Columbia material fund,
§38-1204.05.
Water supply and waterworks rents
paid into, §34-2401.14.

GENERAL LICENSE LAW,
§§47-2805.01 to 47-2881.
See BUSINESS LICENSES.

GENERALLY ACCEPTED ACCOUNTING PRINCIPLES (GAAP), §§47-372, 47-374.

GENERAL OBLIGATION BONDS,
§§1-204.61 to 1-204.90.

GENERAL PARTNERSHIPS,
§§29-601.01 to 29-611.01.
See PARTNERSHIPS.

GENERAL POWERS OF ATTORNEY,
§§21-2101 to 21-2118.
See POWERS OF ATTORNEY.

GENERAL PUBLIC ASSISTANCE (GPA).
Termination of, §4-202.01a.

GENERAL SERVICES, DEPARTMENT OF, §§10-551.01 to
10-551.10.
Director.
Appointment, §10-551.03.
Duties and powers, §10-551.03.
Head of department, §10-551.01.
Established, §10-551.01.

GENERAL SERVICES,
DEPARTMENT OF —Cont'd
Functions, §10-551.01.
Organizational functions, §10-551.02.
Transfers to department, §10-551.04.
Funds.
Facilities service request fund,
§10-551.07a.
Stormwater retention credit fund,
§10-551.07b.
Green building priority, §10-551.06.
Inventory of real property assets,
§10-551.05.
Organizational functions, §10-551.02.
Real estate brokerage or real estate
consulting services.
Contract with representative to
provide, §10-551.07.
Rules to implement chapter,
§10-551.08.
See Forever Foundation-Evans
Campus.
Modernization or new construction.
Authority to direct and manage,
§10-551.10.
Transfers to department, §10-551.04.
Transition process, §10-551.09.

GENERIC DRUGS, §§48-803.01 to
48-803.05.
See PRESCRIPTION DRUGS.

GENETIC TESTING.
Parentage, establishing, §16-909.01.

GEORGETOWN.
Abolition of City of Georgetown and
extension of general laws of
Washington to, §1-107.
Acts relating to corporation of
Georgetown.
See Vol. 1.
Alcoholic beverage licenses.
Special restrictions for Georgetown
historic district, §25-339.
Beatty and Hawkins's addition to
Georgetown.
Street connections for, §9-101.07.
District of Columbia as successor
corporation of, §1-104.
Electric overhead wires, extensions
to, §34-1401.
Former Georgetown Reservoir site,
§10-136.
Historic landmarks and districts.
Old Georgetown district, §§6-1201 to
6-1207.
Old Georgetown Market, §§6-1206,
6-1207.

GEORGIA COMMONS.
Real property transfer tax
exemptions.
Housing and retail elements,
§47-4610.

GEOTHERMAL ENERGY.
Renewable energy portfolio
standards, §§34-1431 to 34-1439.
Sustainable energy, §§8-1773.01 to
8-1774.16.
See SUSTAINABLE ENERGY.

GET DC RESIDENTS TRAINING
FOR JOBS NOW, §§38-1011.01 to
38-1011.05.
See JOB TRAINING PROGRAMS.

GHOST IN THE ATTIC STATUTE.
Disclosures real estate brokers,
salespersons not required to
make, §47-2853.198.

GIFT CERTIFICATES.
Unclaimed property, §41-114.

GIFTS.
Alcoholic beverage licenses.
Manufacturers.
Gifts and loans for manufacturer
prohibited, §25-735.
Wholesalers.
Gifts and loans for wholesaler
prohibited, §25-736.
Alcohol rehabilitation program,
§24-615.
Anatomical gifts.
General provisions, §§7-1531.01 to
7-1531.28.
See ANATOMICAL GIFTS.
Human tissue banks, §§7-1541.01 to
7-1551.01.
See HUMAN TISSUE BANKS.
Board of Education, §38-907.
Cemeteries and cemetery
associations.
Dedication of land for use as cemetery,
§43-112.
Constitution of the United States.
Foreign presents to United States
officials, US Const Art I §9.
Corporations.
Powers, §29-303.02.
Fire protection study commission.
Gifts and donations to commission,
§3-1106.
Foreign presents to United States
officials, US Const Art I §9.
Gallaudet University, §38-2402.02.

GIFTS —Cont'd
Home purchase assistance fund,
§42-2602.
Housing finance agency, §42-2704.01.
Libraries.
Mayor allowed to accept, §39-101.
Medication advisory committee
receiving gifts or remuneration
prohibition act of 2008,
§§48-842.01 to 48-842.04.
Metropolitan police prohibited from
accepting, §5-133.10.
Nonprofit corporations.
Powers, §29-403.02.
School buildings and grounds.
Repairs and maintenance of,
§§38-1805.61, 38-1805.71.
Schools and education, §§38-907,
38-910.
Senior citizens' home repair and
improvement program fund,
§42-2203.
Transfers to minors, §21-304.
Uniform gifts to minors act.
Repeal of, §21-324.
Transfers to minors act, §§21-301 to
21-324.
See TRANSFERS TO MINORS.
United States.
Foreign presents to United States
officials, US Const Art I §9.
University of the District of
Columbia, §38-1204.03.

GLEN DALE HOSPITAL.
Rates schedule, §47-2715.

GLOBAL POSITIONING SYSTEM.
Detection device.
Tampering by persons required to
wear, §22-1211.

GOLD.
Public auction permit requirements,
§47-2705.

GOLDEN RULE PLAZA, INC.
Real property tax exemptions,
§47-1079.

GONORRHEA.
Treatment for sexual partners,
§§7-2081.01 to 7-2081.04.

GOOD FAITH.
Appeals, federal cases.
In forma pauperis proceedings, FRAP
24.
Commercial code.
Disclaimer of good faith obligation by
agreement prohibited, §28:1-302.

GOOD FAITH —Cont'd
Commercial code —Cont'd
Obligation generally, §28:1-304.
Ejectment.
Good faith improvements, §16-1116.
Gas stations.
Franchise purchase rights, §36-304.13.

GOOD SAMARITANS ACT, §§7-401 to
7-403.

GOOD TIME CREDITS.
Felonies committed on or after
August 5, 2000, §24-403.01.
Misdemeanors committed on or
after August 5, 2000, §24-403.02.
Prisons and prisoners, §§24-221.01 to
24-221.06.

GOVERNMENT ACCOUNTABILITY
BOARD, §§1-1161.01 to 1-1164.01.
See ETHICS AND GOVERNMENT
ACCOUNTABILITY BOARD.

GOVERNMENT EMPLOYER-
ASSISTED HOUSING
PROGRAM, §§42-2501 to 42-2507.
Additional assistance available to
government and public charter
school employees, §42-2506.
Deferred payment loans made
available to participants,
§42-2505.
Definitions, §42-2501.
District's contribution, §42-2504.
Down payment and closing costs.
Required savings by participants to
cover, §42-2504.
Eligibility, §42-2503.
Established, §42-2502.
Rules, §42-2507.
Savings required of participant,
§42-2504.

GOVERNMENT ETHICS ACT OF
2011, §§1-1162.01 to 1-1162.32.

GPS.
Detection device.
Tampering by persons required to
wear, §22-1211.

GRADE CROSSING ELIMINATION
PROJECTS, §§9-107.04, 9-1201.15.
Construction of viaducts and
subways, §9-1201.15.
Authority of mayor, §9-1203.05.
Fern Street viaduct, §9-316.
Lamond, §9-318.
Michigan Avenue, §§9-320, 9-322.
Switch connections, §9-1205.03.

GRAFFITI.
Abatement, §§42-3141.01 to 42-3141.11.
  Answer, §42-3141.06.
  Costs.
    Collection, §42-3141.09.
    Disposition of, §42-3141.08.
    Liability for, §42-3141.07.
  Deemed authorization to abate,
    §42-3141.04.
  Definitions, §42-3141.01.
  Expedited hearing, §42-3141.06.
  Fines and civil penalties.
    Collection, §42-3141.09.
    Disposition of, §42-3141.08.
    Liability for, §42-3141.07.
  Fund, §42-3141.08.
  Materials, §42-3141.10.
  Notice of violation, §42-3141.05.
  Notice to abate, §42-3141.03.
  Nuisance, §42-3141.02.
  Requirements, §42-3141.02.
  Rulemaking authority, §42-3141.11.
Anti-graffiti mural assistance
  program fund, §1-325.101.
Definitions, §22-3312.05.
Minors.
  Parental liability, §22-3312.04.
Real property.
  Correction of conditions violative of
    law, §§42-3131.01 to 42-3131.03.
Restitution, §22-3312.04.

GRAND JURIES, §§11-1911, 11-1916,
  CrimPro Rule 6, USDistCt LCrR
  6.1.
Capital or infamous crimes, US Const
  Amd 5.
Discovery of transcripts, CrimPro
  Rule 16.
  Delinquent minors, JuvProc Rule 16.
Indictments, §16-702.
Presentments, CrimPro Rule 109.
Prosecutor's ethical responsibilities,
  ProfCond Rule 3.8.
Time for action to be undertaken by,
  §23-102.
War.
  Presentment dispensable in certain
    cases, US Const Amd 4.

GRANDPARENTS.
Child custody.
  Third-party custody, §§16-831.01 to
    16-831.13.
    See CHILD CUSTODY AND CHILD
      CUSTODY PROCEEDINGS.

GRANDPARENTS —Cont'd
Deeds between grandparent and
  grandchild.
  Exemptions from recordation tax,
    §42-1102.
Intestate succession, §19-312.
Temporary assistance for needy
  families.
  Grandparent caregiver subsidies,
    §§4-251.01 to 4-251.07.

GRANTS.
Administration of grants, §§1-328.11
  to 1-328.17.
  Applicability, §1-328.12.
  Award of grants, §1-328.13.
  Definitions, §1-328.11.
  Eligibility, §1-328.15.
  Reporting, §1-328.16.
  Requirements, §1-328.14.
  Transparency of process for issuing
    and managing, §1-328.17.
American Recovery and
  Reinvestment Act of 2009, under.
  Jobs listing, §2-219.52.
  Reports, §2-219.51.
Arts, cultural and educational
  facilities.
  Economic assistance to, §§39-401 to
    39-405.
Authority, limitations on, §47-368.06.
Budgets.
  Acceptance of grant amounts not
    included in annual budget,
    §1-204.46b.
Career and technical education
  (CTE) grant program, §38-2611.
Child development home satellite
  programs.
  Grants to develop, §4-414.
City Market at O Street tax
  increment financing.
  Grant authorization, §2-1217.33m.
Communicable and chronic disease
  prevention and treatment fund,
  §7-736.02.
DC promise grant awards, §§38-2756,
  38-2757.
Department of corrections inmate
  and returning citizen assistance
  grant, §24-211.71.
District applications for, §§47-382 to
  47-385.
Domestic violence victims, §4-521.
Economic development.
  Deputy Mayor for planning and
    economic development, grant-
    making authority, §1-328.04.

GRANTS —Cont'd
Economic development —Cont'd
Workforce investment council grants for job development, §1-328.05.
Elections.
Grants to promote voting rights and statehood, §1-328.03.
Eligibility, §1-328.15.
Funds provided by federal government.
Definitions, §47-382.
Findings, §47-381.
Grant applications.
Council consent, §47-385.
Notice of application, §47-384.
Procedure, §47-383.
Get DC Residents Training for Jobs Now, §38-1011.04.
Health care financing fund, §7-1932.
Health department, §7-736.01.
Higher education incentive grant fund, §38-274.03.
Historic landmarks.
Targeted homeowner grant program, §6-1110.02.
Home purchase assistance fund, §42-2602.
Housing finance agency providing, §42-2703.07.
Housing production trust fund, §§42-2801 to 42-2804.
Job opportunity bank.
General provisions, §§32-751 to 32-756.
LGBTQ homeless youth training grant fund, §2-1384.
Limitations on authority, §47-368.06.
Local grants-in-aid, urban renewal transfers not considered to be, §§6-321.07, 6-341.05.
Mayor, planning and planning implementation, §1-328.02.
Deputy Mayor for planning and economic development, grant-making authority, §1-328.04.
Rules, authority to implement, §1-328.02a.
Metrorail and metrobus acquisition of mass transit bus systems, §§9-1113.03 to 9-1113.05.
Planning mission of mayor, §1-328.02.
Deputy Mayor for planning and economic development, grant-making authority, §1-328.04.
Rules, authority to implement, §1-328.02a.

GRANTS —Cont'd
Powers of appointment executed by, §42-1018.
Pre-kindergarten programs.
High quality standards for existing programs.
Assistance grants, §38-272.03.
Teachers, workforce development.
Higher education incentive grant program, §38-274.01.
Public assistance applications.
Income status for purposes of, §4-205.29.
Public defender service, §2-1607.
Rehabilitation services program.
Authority, §32-331.01.
Remainders, §42-3231.
Reporting, §1-328.16.
Requirements.
Administration of grants, §1-328.14.
Applicability, §1-328.12.
Award of grants, §1-328.13.
Eligibility, §1-328.15.
Reporting, §1-328.16.
Senior citizens' home repair and improvement program fund, §42-2203.
Soil and water conservation, §8-1710.
Statehood.
Grants to promote voting rights and statehood, §1-328.03.
Stormwater management.
Grant program to employ low impact development or best management practices, §8-152.04.
Transparency of process for issuing and managing, §1-328.17.
Trash compactor grant program, §§8-751 to 8-753.
Universities and colleges.
DC leveraging educational assistance partnership program, §38-2733.
University of the District of Columbia tuition grants, §§38-1207.01 to 38-1207.07.
Voting rights.
Grants to promote voting rights and statehood, §1-328.03.
Water quality, research grants for, §8-103.12.
Workforce investment council.
Authority to make grants for job development, §1-328.05.
World Class Schools Task Force, §38-1803.11.

GRATUITIES.
Garbage collection, §8-741.

GRATUITIES —Cont'd
Minimum wage for persons receiving, §32-1003.

GRAVE ROBBERY, §§3-206, 22-3303.

GRAY MARKET CIGARETTES.
Tobacco tax, §47-2419.
Applicability of provisions, §47-2426.
Penalties, §47-2421.
Seizure as contraband, §47-2423.

GREATER SOUTHEAST COMMUNITY HOSPITAL.
Capital equipment fund, §1-325.71.
Real property tax abatement, §47-1050.

GREEN BUILDINGS, §§6-1451.01 to 6-1451.11.
Advisory council, §6-1451.09.
Anacostia waterfront development zone.
Green building standards, §2-1226.35.
Benchmarking enforcement fund, §6-1451.07a.
Bonds, surety, §6-1451.05.
Compliance review, §6-1451.04.
Construction codes.
Revisions for green building practices, §6-1412.
Definitions, §6-1451.01.
Department of general services.
Priority, §10-551.06.
Energy star benchmarking, §§6-1451.02, 6-1451.03.
Exemptions, §6-1451.10.
Financial security, §6-1451.05.
Green building fee, §6-1451.08.
Green building fund, §6-1451.07.
Incentive program.
Bond of applicants, §6-1451.05.
Performance bond of applicants, §6-1451.05.
Mayor.
Compliance review, §6-1451.04.
Exemptions, granting, §6-1451.10.
Rulemaking, §6-1451.11.
New construction.
Requirements, §§6-1451.02, 6-1451.03.
Performance bond, §6-1451.05.
Private leasing of public property, §6-1451.02.
Privately-owned buildings, §6-1451.03.
Privately-owned buildings and projects, §6-1451.03.
Publicly financed buildings, §6-1451.02.

GREEN BUILDINGS —Cont'd
Publicly-owned buildings, §6-1451.02.
Publicly-owned, leased and financed buildings and projects, §6-1451.02.
Recycling.
Construction and demolition waste recycling accountability, §§8-1071 to 8-1077.
Rulemaking, §6-1451.11.
Tenant improvements, §6-1451.02.

GREEN PUBLIC PROCUREMENTS, §2-361.01.

GRIEVANCE PROCEDURES.
Health benefit plans, §§44-301.01 to 44-304.01.
See HEALTH BENEFITS PLANS.
Merit system, §§1-616.51 to 1-616.54.

GROCERIES.
Alcoholic beverages.
Tasting permits, §25-118.
Business licenses, §47-2827.
Supermarket tax incentives, §§47-3801 to 47-3805.

GROCERY STORE DEVELOPMENT PROGRAM, §§2-1212.21 to 2-1212.24.
Ambassador program, §2-1212.23.
Established, §2-1212.21.
Participation, §2-1212.22.
Rules, §2-1212.41.
Zoning incentives, §2-1212.24.

GROSS NEGLIGENCE.
Child abuse and neglect.
Reasonable and prudent parent standard.
Damages for application or failure to apply, §4-1303.03f.
Metropolitan police Property Clerk, §5-119.11.

GROSS SALES TAX, §§47-2001 to 47-2027.
Alcoholic beverages, §47-2002.02.
Rate of tax, §47-2002.
Anacostia river clean up and protection fund.
Exemption, §47-2005.
Annual returns, §47-2017.
Appeals, §47-2021.
Assumption of tax by vendor, §47-2014.
Ballpark sales taxes, §47-2002.05.
Beverages, §47-2002.02.
Verizon center, §47-2002.06.

GROSS SALES TAX —Cont'd
CareFirst.
Tax credit for wages, sales tax
exemption, §47-4602.
**Carver 2000 low-income and senior
housing project.**
Exemption, §47-4605.
Casual and isolated sales.
Exempt sales, §47-2005.
**Charity auction by nonprofit
teaching hospital.**
Exemption, §47-2005.
Collection of taxes, §§47-2002.03,
47-2002.07, 47-2004, 47-2007.
Council powers, §47-2024.
Credit for expenses of collecting,
§47-2004.
DC-USA project.
Exemptions, §47-4606.
Deficiencies, §47-2019.
Definitions, §47-2001.
Exemptions, §§47-2005, 47-2006.
Fines, §47-2027.
Food, §47-2002.02.
Verizon center, §47-2002.06.
**Food or drink prepared for
immediate consumption.**
Rate of tax, §47-2002.
Fuel.
Exempt sales, §47-2005.
Government sales, exemption,
§47-2005.
Interest, §47-2027.
Issuance of rules and regulations,
§§47-2008, 47-2023.
Jenkins Row Development.
Exemption, §47-4603.
Lincoln Square Theater.
Exemption, §47-4601.
Lodging places, §47-2002.02.
Lot 878, square 456.
Exemption, §47-4604.
Mayor's powers, §§47-2023, 47-2024.
Medical equipment.
Exempt sales, §47-2005.
Medical marijuana, §47-2002.
Monthly returns, §47-2015.
Motor vehicles.
Exempt sales, §47-2005.
Rental vehicles, §47-2002.02.
Rate of tax, §47-2002.
Parkside Terrace project.
Tax exemption, §47-4607.
Payment of, §47-2016.
Penalties, §§47-2014, 47-2027.
Presumptions, §47-2010.
Certificate of mayor regarding
violations, §47-2027.

GROSS SALES TAX —Cont'd
Priority over other property taxes,
§47-2012.
**Privacy and confidentiality of
returns,** §47-2018.
Promoters of special events.
Duties, §47-2826.
Rates, §47-2002.
Reciprocity of returns, §47-2018.
Refunds, §§47-2014, 47-2020.
Registration, §47-2026.
Reimbursement of vendor for,
§47-2003.
Rental vehicles, §47-2002.02.
Rate of tax, §47-2002.
Returns, §47-2015.
Annual, §47-2017.
Monthly, §47-2015.
Privacy and confidentiality, §47-2018.
Reciprocity, §47-2018.
**Separate statement apart from price
of item,** §47-2009.
Special event promoters.
Obligations and responsibilities,
§47-2002.04.
Street vendors, §§47-2002.01, 47-2003.
Telecommunications companies.
Exempt sales, §47-2005.
Vendor collection of, §47-2004.
Verizon center sales tax, §47-2002.06.
**Washington convention and sports
authority, transfers to,**
§47-2002.03.

GROUPON.
E-commerce companies.
Qualified social electronic commerce
companies tax abatements,
§§47-1818.01 to 47-1818.08.

GUAM.
Acknowledgment of deed, §42-111.

GUARANTY COMPANIES.
See INSURANCE COMPANIES.

GUARD DOGS, §§8-1841.01 to
8-1841.09.

GUARDIAN AD LITEM, §§21-2031,
21-2033.
Accounts and accounting.
Bond of guardian.
Discharge only after accounting,
§28-2504.
Adoption proceedings.
Appointment and compensation,
§16-316.

GUARDIAN AD LITEM —Cont'd
Appointment for prosecution of action, CivPro Rule 17.
Domestic relations actions, DomRel Rules 17, 101.
Bar membership required, CivPro Rule 304.
Intervention proceedings, Probate Rule 306.
Probate proceedings.
Death on or after July 1, 1995, Probate Rule 422.
Guardians, conservators, trustees, etc., involved, Probate Rule 202.
Bonds, surety.
Discharge only after accounting, §28-2504.
Child abuse and neglect proceedings.
Appointment of counsel, NeglectProc Rule 42.
Shelter care hearing or initial appearance, NeglectProc Rule 12.
Child taken into custody.
Appointment, §16-2312.
Reports to court, NeglectProc Rule 21.
Child custody proceedings.
Third-party custody.
Court authorized to appoint, §16-831.06.
Decedents' estates.
Conflicts.
Appointment of guardian for person with a legal disability, §20-108.
Fiduciaries generally.
See FIDUCIARIES.
Fiduciary security transfers, §§28-2901 to 28-2909.
See FIDUCIARY SECURITY TRANSFERS.
Intellectual disabilities, persons with.
Filing petition for commitment, MentalRetardation Rule 4A.
Intervention proceedings, Probate Rule 306.
Compensation, Probate Rule 308.
Limited liability companies.
Dissolution.
Claims, court proceedings on.
Appointment of guardian ad litem for unknown claimants, §29-807.07.

GUARDIAN AD LITEM —Cont'd
Partnerships.
Dissolution.
Court proceedings regarding claims, appointment of guardian ad litem for unknown claimants, §29-608.10.
Probate proceedings, Probate Rule 209.
Death between January 1, 1981 and June 30, 1995, Probate Rule 122.
Death on or after July 1, 1995, Probate Rule 422.
Guardians, conservators, trustees, etc., involved, Probate Rule 202.
Statutory trusts.
Dissolution, court proceedings on claims.
Appointment of guardian to represent unknown claimants, §29-1208.06.
Successor fiduciaries.
Guardian ad litem not required, CivPro Rule 304.

GUARDIAN AND WARD.
Actions by guardians, CivPro Rule 17.
Domestic relations actions, DomRel Rule 17.
Adult guardianship and protective proceedings jurisdiction, §§21-2401.01 to 21-2405.03.
Communication between courts, §21-2401.04.
Cooperation between courts, §21-2401.05.
Definitions, §21-2401.02.
Electronic signatures in global and national commerce act, relation to, §21-2405.02.
International application of chapter, §21-2401.03.
Jurisdiction.
Appropriate forum, §21-2402.06.
Conduct as reason to decline jurisdiction, §21-2402.07.
Declining to exercise jurisdiction, §§21-2402.06, 21-2402.07.
Definitions, §21-2402.01.
Exclusive and continuing jurisdiction, §21-2402.05.
Exclusive basis for jurisdiction of court, §21-2402.02.
Exercise of jurisdiction, §21-2402.03.
Multiple states, proceedings in, §21-2402.09.

GUARDIAN AND WARD —Cont'd
Adult guardianship and protective proceedings jurisdiction —Cont'd
Jurisdiction —Cont'd
Notice of proceeding, §21-2402.08.
Significant connection factors, §21-2402.01.
Special jurisdiction, §21-2402.04.
Registration and recognition of orders from other states.
Effect of registration, §21-2404.03.
Guardianship orders, §21-2404.01.
Protective orders, §21-2404.02.
Short title, §21-2401.01.
Testimony of witness taken in another state, §21-2401.06.
Transfer of guardianship or conservatorship.
From another state, §21-2403.02.
To another state, §21-2403.01.
Transitional provision, §21-2405.03.
Uniformity of application and construction, §21-2405.01.
Bonds, surety.
Minors, guardianship of, §§21-114 to 21-118.
Conservators.
General provisions, §§21-2001 to 21-2034.
See CONSERVATORS.
Court appointment of guardians.
Incapacitated persons, guardianship of, §§21-2041 to 21-2045.
Minors, guardianship of, §21-103.
Default judgment against infant or incompetent person, CivPro Rule 55.
Durable powers of attorney.
General provisions, §§21-2081 to 21-2085.
See DURABLE POWERS OF ATTORNEY.
Intervention proceedings, Probate Rules 301 to 361.
See INTERVENTION PROCEEDINGS.
Fiduciaries generally, §§21-1701 to 21-1712.
See FIDUCIARIES.
Fiduciary security transfers.
General provisions, §§28-2901 to 28-2909.
See FIDUCIARY SECURITY TRANSFERS.
Guardians ad litem.
See GUARDIAN AD LITEM.

GUARDIAN AND WARD —Cont'd
Incapacitated persons, guardianship of, §§21-2041 to 21-2049.
Acceptance of appointment by guardian, §21-2045.
Actions by guardians, CivPro Rule 17.
Domestic relations actions, DomRel Rule 17.
Attorneys at law.
Appointment of counsel.
Temporary guardians, §21-2046.
Seeking appointment of guardian for client with diminished capacity, ProfCond Rule 1.14.
Conflicts of interest, §21-2043.
Court appointment of, §§21-2041 to 21-2045.
Decedents' estates, guardian ad litem for, §20-108.
Default judgment against incompetent person, CivPro Rule 55.
Durable powers of attorney.
General provisions, §§21-2081 to 21-2085.
See DURABLE POWERS OF ATTORNEY.
Intervention proceedings, Probate Rules 301 to 361.
See INTERVENTION PROCEEDINGS.
Eligibility for guardianship, §21-2043.
Emergency and health care guardians.
Powers, §21-2047.02.
Emergency orders, §21-2046.
Fiduciaries generally.
See FIDUCIARIES.
Findings of court, §21-2044.
Inheritances, §20-1107.
Insanitary buildings.
Incompetent or incapacitated persons owning, §6-909.
Interstate compact on mental health, §§7-1101 to 7-1106.
Intervention proceedings, Probate Rules 301 to 361.
See INTERVENTION PROCEEDINGS.
Landlord and tenant, §42-3228.
Leases, §42-3228.
Limitations, §21-2047.01.
Mandatory court review, §21-2045.01.
Mental health consumer's rights.
Emergency appointment of guardian, §7-1231.07.
Notice of guardianship proceeding, §§21-2042, 21-2045.
Temporary guardians, §21-2046.

GUARDIAN AND WARD —Cont'd
Incapacitated persons, guardianship of —Cont'd
Order of appointment by court, §21-2044.
Powers and duties, §21-2047.
Limitations, §21-2047.01.
Priorities as to guardianship, §21-2043.
Removal of guardian, §21-2049.
Resignation of guardian, §21-2049.
Sexual abuse of wards.
Defenses to sexual abuse of, §22-3017.
First degree sexual abuse of, §22-3013.
Second degree sexual abuse of, §22-3014.
Successor guardian, appointment of, §21-2049.
Temporary guardians, §21-2046.
Removal, §21-2049.
Termination of guardianship, §§21-2048, 21-2049.
Termination of incapacity, §21-2049.
Trusts and trustees.
Uniform trust code.
Personal representatives, §19-1303.03.
Uniform fiduciaries act, §§21-1701 to 21-1712.
See FIDUCIARIES.
Workers' compensation, §32-1512.
Intervention proceedings, Probate Rules 301 to 361.
See INTERVENTION PROCEEDINGS.
Jurisdiction.
Adult guardianship and protective proceedings jurisdiction, §§21-2401.01 to 21-2405.03. See within this heading, "Adult guardianship and protective proceedings jurisdiction."
Landlord and tenant, §§42-3225 to 42-3228.
Minors, guardianship of, §§21-101 to 21-182.
Actions by guardians, CivPro Rule 17.
Domestic relations actions, DomRel Rule 17.
Actions involving minors, settlement of, §21-120.
Ancillary guardian of nonresident minor, §§21-111, 21-112.
Bonds, surety, §§21-114 to 21-118.
Additional bond required, §21-117.

GUARDIAN AND WARD —Cont'd
Minors, guardianship of —Cont'd
Bonds, surety —Cont'd
Allowances made prior to giving of, §21-119.
Counter security, §21-118.
Guardian of estate, §21-115.
Loss in consequence of suretyship, §21-118.
Parents of child entitled to property, §21-114.
Single bond for several wards, §21-116.
Child custody.
Uniform child custody proceedings, §§16-4601.01 to 16-4605.03.
See CHILD CUSTODY AND CHILD CUSTODY PROCEEDINGS.
Court appointment of, §21-103.
Default judgment against minors, CivPro Rule 55.
Education of child.
Amounts expended for, §21-143.
Sale of principal for, §21-147.
Fiduciaries generally.
See FIDUCIARIES.
Indigent children, §§21-181, 21-182.
Injunction against interference with minor's estate, §21-113.
Intervention proceedings, Probate Rules 301 to 361.
See INTERVENTION PROCEEDINGS.
Landlord and tenant, §§42-3225 to 42-3228.
Leases on property of infants, §21-156.
Maintenance and education of child.
Amounts expended for, §21-143.
Sale of principal for, §21-147.
Marriage.
Consent to marriage by guardian, §46-411.
Spouse of minor as guardian, §§21-107, 21-109.
Mortgages on property of infants, §21-157.
Natural guardians, §21-101.
Neglect or refusal of guardian to provide for child under 14, §22-1102.
Nonresident guardians, §21-110.
Nonresident minors, §21-111.
Number of wards, limits on, §21-103.
Permanent guardianship, §§16-2381 to 16-2399. See within this heading, "Permanent guardianship."

GUARDIAN AND WARD —Cont'd
Minors, guardianship of —Cont'd
 Preferences regarding, §21-107.
 Probate proceedings.
  Guardians, conservators, trustees,
   etc., involved, Probate Rules 201
   to 225.
   See PROBATE PROCEEDINGS.
 Property of infants.
  Accounting requirements, §21-143.
  Amounts expended for education
   and maintenance, §21-143.
  Best interests of ward.
   Management with regard to,
    §21-143.
  Executory contract, subject to,
   §21-145.
  Final account on majority, §21-158.
  Inventory of, §21-142.
  Leases, §21-156.
  Liens, §§21-144, 21-152.
  Mortgages, §21-157.
  Possession of, §21-141.
  Powers and duties regarding,
   §21-143.
  Separate guardian of estate of
   minor, §§21-106, 21-115.
  Transfers to minors, §§21-301 to
   21-324.
   See TRANSFERS TO MINORS.
  Wages and salaries for managing,
   §21-143.
 Sale of property of infants.
  Contested sales, §§21-148 to 21-151.
  Decree of sale, §21-151.
  Evidence as to propriety of, §21-150.
  Exchanges, §21-153.
  Liens, §21-152.
  Maintenance and education.
   Sale of principal for, §21-147.
  Parties to procedure, §21-149.
  Procedure for sale or exchange of
   real property, §21-148.
  Property held jointly with adult,
   §21-146.
  Ratification of sale by court,
   §21-154.
  Remainders and reversions, §21-155.
  Terms and conditions, §21-152.
 Selection by minor, §21-108.
 Service of process on minors, §13-332.
 Sexual abuse of wards.
  Defenses to sexual abuse of,
   §22-3017.
  First degree sexual abuse of,
   §22-3013.

GUARDIAN AND WARD —Cont'd
Minors, guardianship of —Cont'd
 Sexual abuse of wards —Cont'd
  Second degree sexual abuse of,
   §22-3014.
 Spouse of minor as, §§21-107, 21-109.
 Standby guardianship, §§16-4801 to
  16-4810. See within this heading,
  "Standby guardianship."
 Termination of, §§21-104, 21-118.
 Testamentary guardians, §§21-102,
  21-105.
 Transfers to minors, §§21-301 to
  21-324.
  See TRANSFERS TO MINORS.
 Trusts and trustees.
  Uniform trust code.
   Personal representatives,
    §19-1303.03.
  Uniform fiduciaries act, §§21-1701 to
   21-1712.
   See FIDUCIARIES.
 Wages and salaries, §21-143.
 Workers' compensation, §32-1512.
Permanent guardianship, §§16-2381
 to 16-2399.
 Adjudicatory hearings, §§16-2386,
  16-2388.
 Appeal of guardianship order,
  §16-2392.
 Conduct of hearing, §16-2387.
 Confidentiality of records, §16-2393.
 Construction of act, §16-2381.
 Court retention of jurisdiction,
  §16-2390.
 Criteria for establishing, §16-2383.
 Definitions, §16-2382.
 Effect of guardianship order, §16-2389.
 Enforcement of guardianship order,
  §16-2395.
 Finality guardianship order, §16-2392.
 Grounds for creating, §16-2383.
 Interlocutory order of guardianship,
  §16-2397.
 Modification of guardianship order,
  §16-2395.
 Motions, §16-2384.
 Notice, §16-2386.
 Parties, §16-2385.
 Public policy, §16-2381.
 Relocation of child, §16-2391.
 Subsidy payments, §16-2399.
 Successor guardian, §16-2398.
 Support from child's parent, §16-2396.
 Termination of guardianship order,
  §16-2395.

GUARDIAN AND WARD —Cont'd
Permanent guardianship —Cont'd
Unlawful disclosures, §16-2394.
Sexual abuse of wards.
Defenses to sexual abuse of, §22-3017.
First degree sexual abuse of, §22-3013.
Second degree sexual abuse of,
§22-3014.
Standby guardianship, §§16-4801 to
16-4810.
Alternate guardian.
Court approval, §16-4806.
Authority, §16-4804.
Best interest of child.
Court approval, rebuttable
presumption, §16-4806.
Capacity to serve as guardian.
Rebuttable presumption, §16-4806.
Challenging, §16-4809.
Concurrent authority.
Designator maintaining, §16-4804.
Court approval, §16-4806.
Death of designator.
Guardian legal custodian of child,
§16-4804.
Definitions, §16-4802.
Designation, §16-4803.
Documentation attached to petition,
§16-4805.
Effect of filing petition, §16-4807.
Findings of council, §16-4801.
Hearing on approval, §16-4806.
Notice of filing, §16-4808.
Order of court approving, §16-4806.
Parental rights not divested, §16-4804.
Petition for approval, §16-4805.
Rebuttable presumption.
Court approval in best interest of
child, §16-4806.
Guardian capable of serving,
§16-4806.
Revocation, repudiation or rescission,
§16-4810.
Summary approval, §16-4806.
Summons, notice of filing by, §16-4808.
Temporary legal authority, §16-4807.
Termination of guardian's authority,
§16-4804.
Withdrawal of consent acknowledging
debilitation.
Termination of guardian's authority,
§16-4804.
Witnesses.
Designation, §16-4803.
Termination of guardianship.
Incapacitated persons, guardianship
of, §§21-2048, 21-2049.

GUARDIAN AND WARD —Cont'd
Termination of guardianship
—Cont'd
Minors, guardianship of, §§21-104,
21-118.
Transfers to minors, §§21-301 to
21-324.
See TRANSFERS TO MINORS.
Trusts and trustees.
Uniform trust code.
Personal representatives,
§19-1303.03.
**Uniform adult guardianship and
protective proceedings
jurisdiction act,** §§21-2401.01 to
21-2405.03. See within this heading,
"Adult guardianship and protective
proceedings jurisdiction."
Uniform fiduciaries act, §§21-1701 to
21-1712.
See FIDUCIARIES.
Workers' compensation, §32-1512.

GUIDE DOGS.
Defined, §7-1009.
Housing accommodations.
Full and equal access, §7-1006.
**Public places accommodations, and
conveyances.**
Right to be accompanied by, §7-1002.

GUIDES.
Business licenses, §47-2836.

GUILTY PLEAS, CrimPro Rule 11.
Delinquent minors, JuvProc Rules 11,
12.
Withdrawal of plea, JuvProc Rule 32.
**Hearing commissioners' power to
accept plea,** CrimPro Rule 117.
Presence of defendant, CrimPro Rule
43.
Withdrawal of plea, CrimPro Rule 32.

GUN-FREE ZONES, §22-4502.01.

GUN OFFENDER REGISTRY,
§§7-2508.01 to 7-2508.07.
Certification and order, §7-2508.04.
Compliance as condition of release,
§7-2508.07.
Definitions, §7-2508.01.
Duty to register, §7-2508.02.
FOIA exception, §7-2508.05.
Forms, §7-2508.06.
Penalties for violations, §7-2508.07.
Registration period, §7-2508.03.
Rulemaking authority, §7-2508.06.
Sharing registration information,
§7-2508.05.

GUN OFFENDER REGISTRY
—Cont'd
Superior court duties, §7-2508.04.
Verification of information,
§7-2508.02.

GUNS.
See FIREARMS.

GUTTERS AND CURBS.
Assessments, §§9-401.04, 9-411.01 to
9-411.04, 9-421.02.

GYMNASIUM MEMBERSHIPS.
Consumer credit, §28-3817.

GYNECOLOGISTS.
Closed claim analysis.
Medical malpractice claims, §31-2991.

H

HABEAS CORPUS, §§16-1901 to
16-1909.
Alcoholics, rehabilitation of.
Commitment by court order.
Challenge of order, §24-607.
Appeals, federal cases, FRAP 22,
USCtApp Rule 47.2.
Certificate of appealability, FRAP
22(b).
Certificate of probable cause, necessity
of, FRAP 22(b).
Custody of prisoners, FRAP 23.
Modification of initial order respecting
custody, FRAP 23(d).
Original writ, application for, FRAP
22(a).
Recognizance, FRAP 23(b), (c).
Release of prisoners, FRAP 23(b), (c).
Service, notice of filing of notice of
appeal as of right, FRAP 3(d).
Bail and recognizance, §16-1906.
Committees.
Right of other persons to writ,
§16-1908.
Competence to proceed.
Incompetent criminal defendants.
Establishing eligibility for release,
§24-531.13.
Constitution of the United States.
Habeas corpus not to be suspended,
US Const Art I §9.
Court of appeals.
Criminal cases.
Release in criminal cases, DCCtApp
Rule 9.
Disobedience of writ, §16-1903.

HABEAS CORPUS —Cont'd
District court, USDistCt LCvR 9.2.
Writs directed to federal officers and
employees, §16-1901.
Evasion of writ.
Suspected evasion, §16-1903.
Family court proceedings.
Actions seeking custody of minor
children.
Exclusive jurisdiction, §11-1101.
Writs directed to nonfederal officers
and employees, §16-1901.
Forfeitures.
Failure to produce or make return,
§16-1904.
Refusal or neglect to provide copy of
warrant or commitment.
Forfeiture to detain party, §16-1905.
Guardians.
Right of third person to writ,
§16-1908.
Incompetent criminal defendants.
Competence to proceed.
Establishing eligibility for release,
§24-531.13.
Inquiry into cause of detention,
§16-1906.
Issuance and return of writ,
§16-1901, CivPro Rule 81.
Pleadings.
Traversing return, §16-1907.
Release, §16-1906.
Release pending appeal, DCCtApp
Rule 9.
Return, §16-1902.
Failure to make, §16-1904.
Inquiry into cause of detention,
§16-1906.
Traversing return, §16-1907.
Rules of civil procedure.
Applicability of rules, CivPro Rule 81.
Sentences.
Motions to attack sentence, §23-110.
Service of process, §16-1902.
Statutory construction, §16-1909.
Suspension.
Prohibited, US Const Art I §9.
Third parties.
Right of other persons to writ,
§16-1908.
Warrants.
Right to copy of commitment,
§16-1905.
Witnesses, §16-1907.

HABITUAL OFFENDERS.
Commercial counterfeiting, §22-902.

HABITUAL OFFENDERS —Cont'd
Controlled substances, §48-904.08.
Prostitution.
Solicitation for purposes, §22-2701.
Sentencing.
Third felony conviction, §22-1804a.
Sexual performances using minors, §22-3103.
Trademark counterfeiting, §22-902.

HADLEY MEMORIAL HOSPITAL.
Real property tax abatement, §47-1050.

HAIRDRESSERS.
Business licenses, §§47-2809, 47-2810.

HALFWAY HOUSES.
Public assistance recipients, §4-205.49.
Schools, establishment near.
Notice given by mayor, §38-3201.

HANDICAPPED PERSONS.
Judges.
Commission on judicial disabilities and tenure, §§11-1521 to 11-1530.
See COMMISSION ON JUDICIAL DISABILITIES AND TENURE.
Persons with disabilities generally.
See DISABILITIES, PERSONS WITH.

HARASSMENT.
Judges.
Prohibited, CJC Canon 2.3.
Police animals.
Harassing, interfering with, injuring or obstructing, §22-861.

HARBORS AND PORTS.
Crimes and offenses related to, §§22-4402 to 22-4404.

HARDSHIP PETITIONS.
Rent control, §§42-3502.06, 42-3502.12.

HARMLESS ERROR.
Adoption proceedings, Adoption Rule 61.
Civil cases, CivPro Rule 61.
Criminal procedure, CrimPro Rule 52.
Delinquent minors, JuvProc Rule 52.
Domestic relations actions, DomRel Rule 61.
Plea procedures, CrimPro Rule 11.

HATCH ACT, §§1-625.01, 1-625.02.
District of Columbia housing authority.
Applicability to employees of, §6-218.

HATE CRIMES, §§22-3701 to 22-3704.
Bias-related crime, §22-3703.

HATE CRIMES —Cont'd
Civil action regarding, §22-3704.
Collection and publication of data on, §22-3702.
Cross-burning, §22-3312.02.
Definitions, §22-3701.
Due process, threatening, injuring, intimidating, or interfering with persons in order to deprive them of, §§22-3312.02 to 22-3312.04.
Emblems of certain types, displaying, §22-3312.02.
Hoods or masks, wearing, §22-3312.03.
Murder prosecutions.
Aggravating circumstance, §22-2104.01.
Sentencing.
Aggravating circumstances.
Offense committed because of victim's race, color, religion, national origin or sexual orientation, §24-403.01.

HAZARD INSURANCE.
Fire and casualty insurance, §§31-2501.01 to 31-2502.42.
See FIRE AND CASUALTY INSURANCE.

HAZARDOUS FINANCIAL CONDITIONS.
Insurance company standard for determining, §§31-2101 to 31-2103.

HAZARDOUS SUBSTANCES.
Defined, §§8-103.01, 8-109.02.
Lead-hazard prevention and elimination, §§8-231.01 to 8-231.20.
See LEAD-HAZARD PREVENTION AND ELIMINATION.
Prohibition on discharge into sewers, §8-103.07.
Transportation of hazardous materials.
See HAZARDOUS WASTE MANAGEMENT.
Wastewater disposal systems, §8-105.06.

HAZARDOUS SUBSTANCES RELEASES, §§8-631.01 to 8-638.01.
Actions.
Compelling compliance, §8-634.07.
Contribution, §8-634.09.
Cleanup.
Assistance, §8-637.04.

HAZARDOUS SUBSTANCES RELEASES —Cont'd
Cleanup —Cont'd
Environmental savings account program, §8-637.03.
Incentives.
Real property tax credits or reduction, §§8-637.01, 8-637.02.
Voluntary cleanup program, §§8-633.01 to 8-633.08.
Comprehensive response plan, §8-634.01.
Contribution actions, §8-634.09.
Cost reimbursements, §8-634.02.
Criminal penalties for violations, §8-632.01.
Defenses to liability for causing release, §8-632.02.
Definitions, §8-631.02.
Entry rights, §8-634.04.
Environmental savings account program, §8-637.03.
Financial assistance for cleanup and redevelopment, §8-637.04.
Findings and declaration of purposes, §8-631.01.
Fines.
Violations of chapter, §8-632.01.
Grants.
Financial assistance for cleanup and redevelopment, §8-637.04.
Information access, §8-634.03.
Inspection rights, §8-634.04.
Institutional control, DDOE, §8-635.01.
Judicial review, §§8-634.11, 8-636.03.
Liability of person causing or contributing to release, §8-632.01.
Defenses, §8-632.02.
Non-responsible person, new contamination, §8-632.03.
Limitation of actions, §8-634.10.
Non-responsible person.
Liability for new contamination, §8-632.03.
Notice of lawful release, §8-632.01.
Penalties for provisions violations, §8-634.06.
Real property tax credits or reduction.
Cleanup incentives, §§8-637.01, 8-637.02.
Report of lawful release, §8-632.01.
Response plan, §8-634.01.
Costs, §8-634.02.
Reviews, §8-634.05.

HAZARDOUS SUBSTANCES RELEASES —Cont'd
Responsible person.
Liability of person causing or contributing to release, §8-632.01.
Defenses, §8-632.02.
Rules, §8-638.01.
Sampling, §8-634.04.
Settlement authority, §8-634.08.
Time for reporting lawful release, §8-632.01.
Unlawful to release hazardous substance, §8-632.01.
Voluntary cleanup program, §§8-633.01 to 8-633.08.
Certification of completion, §8-633.06.
Public notice, §8-636.01.
Clean land fund, §8-633.08.
Cleanup action plan, §8-633.03.
Public notice, §8-636.01.
Cleanup standards, §8-633.05.
DDOE responsibilities, §8-633.01.
Eligibility to participate, §8-633.02.
Established, §8-633.01.
Fee of applicant, bond and other security to participate, §8-633.04.
Incentives.
Real property tax credits or reduction, §§8-637.01, 8-637.02.
Public involvement plans, §8-636.02.
Real property tax credits or reduction.
Incentives, §§8-637.01, 8-637.02.
Requirements for participating, §8-633.02.
Withdrawal, §8-633.07.

HAZARDOUS WASTE MANAGEMENT, §§8-1301 to 8-1322.
Access for inspections, §8-1307.
Appeals, §8-1308.
Asbestos licensing and control, §§8-111.01 to 8-111.14.
See ASBESTOS CONTRACTORS.
Definitions, §8-1302.
Disposable food service ware, §§8-1531 to 8-1537.
Dust suppression, §8-1313.
Fines, §8-1311.
Guarantors.
Actions against, §8-1314.
Hazardous materials transportation, §§8-1401 to 8-1405, 8-1421 to 8-1426, 8-1441 to 8-1447.
Definition of hazardous materials, §8-1402.
Fines, §8-1404.

**HAZARDOUS WASTE
MANAGEMENT** —Cont'd
Hazardous materials transportation
—Cont'd
Inspections, §§8-1403.01, 8-1403.02.
Issuance of rules and regulations
regarding, §8-1405.
Penalties, §8-1404.
Policy declaration, §§8-1301, 8-1401.
Program for, §8-1403.
Releases, §8-1404.01.
Rulemaking, §8-1426.
Strict liability for releases during
transport, §§8-1441 to 8-1447.
Action to recover costs, §8-1444.
Applicability of liability, §8-1442.
Costs recoverable by District,
§8-1443.
Defenses, §8-1445.
Definitions, §8-1441.
Punitive damages, §8-1446.
Reimbursement fund, §8-1447.
Scope of liability, §8-1442.
Terrorism prevention.
Definitions, §8-1422.
Legislative findings, §8-1421.
Penalties, §8-1425.
Permits, §§8-1421, 8-1424.
Prohibited shipments, §8-1423.
Illegal dumping, §§8-901 to 8-906.
See ILLEGAL DUMPING.
Injunctions, §8-1310.
Inspections, §8-1307.
**Low-level radioactive waste
generator regulatory policy,**
§§8-1501 to 8-1506.
**Notice of presence of hazardous
waste,** §8-1307.
Penalties, §8-1311.
Permits.
Requirements for, §8-1303.
Suspension or revocation, §8-1309.
Pesticides.
General provisions, §§8-401 to 8-440.
See PESTICIDES.
Plan requirements, §§8-1304, 8-1318.
Policy declaration, §8-1301.
Road treatments, §8-1313.
Rules and regulations regarding,
§8-1305.
Severability of provisions, §8-1312.
Toxic source reduction, §§8-1315 to
8-1322.
Definitions, §8-1302.
Fees, §8-1320.
Identification of major generators,
§8-1316.

**HAZARDOUS WASTE
MANAGEMENT** —Cont'd
Toxic source reduction —Cont'd
Issuance of rules and regulations,
§8-1322.
Plans for, §8-1318.
Privacy and confidentiality of business
information, §8-1321.
Reports, §8-1317.
**Transportation of hazardous
materials,** §§8-1401 to 8-1405,
8-1421 to 8-1426, 8-1441 to 8-1447.
See within this heading, "Hazardous
materials transportation."
Variances, §8-1306.

HEALTH.
Adult protective services, §§7-1901 to
7-1913.
See ADULT PROTECTIVE
SERVICES.
AIDS, §§7-1601 to 7-1606.
See AIDS.
Alcoholic beverage licenses.
Health and safety violations.
Summary revocation or suspension,
§25-826.
Animal control, §§8-1801 to 8-1813.
See ANIMALS.
Assisted living residences,
§§44-101.01 to 44-113.01.
See ASSISTED LIVING
RESIDENCES.
Automated external defibrillators.
Usage, §§44-231 to 44-235.
Bisphenol-A restrictions, §§8-108.01,
8-108.04, 8-108.05.
Blind and visually impaired.
See BLIND AND VISUALLY
IMPAIRED.
Board of Health (defunct), §§7-174 to
7-177.
Cancer prevention and monitoring,
§§7-301 to 7-304.
Child abuse and neglect, §§4-1301.02
to 4-1362.
See CHILD ABUSE AND NEGLECT.
**Child welfare and juvenile justice
behavioral health infrastructure.**
Family resource guide, §2-1517.51.
Reports, §2-1517.52.
Clinical laboratories, §§44-201 to
44-213.
See CLINICAL LABORATORIES.
Commissioner of Public Health,
§7-101.
Commission on aging, §§7-504.01 to
7-504.10.

HEALTH —Cont'd
Communicable diseases.
  See COMMUNICABLE DISEASES.
**Dairies and dairy farms, inspector
  of,** §7-179.
Data privacy.
  Generally, §§7-241 to 7-248.
    See HEALTH DATA PRIVACY.
  Mental health disclosures, §§7-1201.01
    to 7-1208.07.
    See MENTAL HEALTH
      DISCLOSURES.
Death, §§7-601 to 7-630.
  See DEATH.
**Denial of treatment due to inability
  to pay,** §47-2716.
Department of health.
  See HEALTH DEPARTMENT.
Drainage of lots, §§8-201 to 8-205.
**Early childhood and school-based
  behavioral infrastructure,**
  §§2-1517.31, 2-1517.32.
Emergency.
  Public health emergency executive
    order, §7-2304.01.
Emergency medical services.
  See EMERGENCY MEDICAL
    SERVICES.
Environmental quality.
  See ENVIRONMENTAL
    PROTECTION.
Examinations.
  See MEDICAL EXAMINATIONS.
Federal government restaurants,
  §7-2701.
Firearms regulation, §§7-2501.01 to
  7-2551.03.
  See FIREARMS.
**Fish and other marine products,
  inspector of,** §7-173.
Flame retardants.
  Prohibitions on chlorinated flame
    retardants, §8-108.02a.
  Replacement of regulated flame
    retardants, §8-108.02b.
Garbage collection.
  See GARBAGE COLLECTION.
Hazardous waste management.
  General provisions, §§8-1301 to
    8-1322.
    See HAZARDOUS WASTE
      MANAGEMENT.
Health care financing fund, §§7-1931
  to 7-1933.
**Health care safety net
  administration,** §§7-1401 to
  7-1405.01.

HEALTH —Cont'd
**Health Care System Development
  Commission,** §§7-2901 to 7-2906.
Health emergency.
  Public health emergency executive
    order, §7-2304.01.
**Healthy DC and health care
  expansion fund and program,**
  §§4-631 to 4-638.
  See HEALTHY DC AND HEALTH
    CARE EXPANSION FUND AND
    PROGRAM.
Human Services, Department of,
  §§7-103 to 7-171.
  See HUMAN SERVICES,
    DEPARTMENT OF.
Illegal dumping.
  See ILLEGAL DUMPING.
**Inability to pay, denial of treatment
  due to,** §47-2716.
Inspections and inspectors.
  Dairies and dairy farms, §7-179.
  Fish and other marine products,
    §7-173.
  Human Services Department
    inspectors, §7-103.
  Livestock, §7-179.
Litter control, §§8-801 to 8-812.
  See LITTER CONTROL.
Livestock, inspector of, §7-179.
Long-term care facilities.
  Nursing homes.
    General provisions, §§44-1001.01 to
      44-1005.01.
Long-term care ombudsman,
  §§7-701.01 to 7-706.01.
  See LONG-TERM CARE
    OMBUDSMAN.
Malignant neoplastic diseases.
  Prevention and monitoring, §§7-301 to
    7-304.
Mattresses, §§8-501 to 8-508.
Mental health.
  See MENTAL HEALTH.
Metabolic disorders in newborns.
  Screening for, §§7-831 to 7-840.
Mosquito control and abatement,
  §8-2141.01.
Needles.
  Safe needle distribution.
    Sharps injury protection, §§7-2851
      to 7-2858.
Neoplastic diseases.
  Malignant, §§7-301 to 7-304.
Newborns.
  Newborn screening, §§7-831 to 7-840.
  See NEWBORNS.

HEALTH —Cont'd
Newborns —Cont'd
Ophthalmia in newborns, §§7-801 to
7-804.
See NEWBORNS.
Occupational safety and health.
See OCCUPATIONAL SAFETY AND
HEALTH.
Office on aging, §§7-503.01 to 7-503.06.
**Ordinances of board of health
legalized,** §7-174.
Alteration, amendment, repeal, §7-177.
Force and effect, exemption from
enforcement, §7-176.
Titles, §7-175.
**Parole for medical and geriatric
reasons,** §§24-461 to 24-468.
See PAROLE.
Perchloroethylene in dry cleaning,
§§8-108.03 to 8-108.05.
**Physical fitness, health and
nutrition, mayor's council,**
§§7-121 to 7-126.
Administrative support, §7-123.
Executive committee, §7-126.
Fitness fund, §7-125.
Fitness report, §§7-122, 7-124.
Meetings, §7-121.
Membership, §7-121.
Mission, §7-121.
Powers and duties, §7-122.
Plants and plant diseases, §§8-301 to
8-305.
See PLANTS AND PLANT
DISEASES.
**Polybrominated diphenyl ethers
prohibitions,** §§8-108.02, 8-108.04,
8-108.05.
Privacy of health information.
Generally, §§7-241 to 7-248.
See HEALTH DATA PRIVACY.
Mental health disclosures, §§7-1201.01
to 7-1208.07.
See MENTAL HEALTH
DISCLOSURES.
Privies, §§8-601 to 8-604.
**Public Health Coordination
Advisory Committee,** §7-154.
Public Health, Department of.
See PUBLIC HEALTH,
DEPARTMENT OF.
Public officers and employees.
Workplace wellness.
Healthy food and beverage
standards for government
property, §1-541.02.

HEALTH —Cont'd
Public officers and employees
—Cont'd
Workplace wellness —Cont'd
Policy, §1-541.01.
Radiation control.
Low-level radioactive waste generator
regulatory policy, §§8-1501 to
8-1506.
See RADIATION CONTROL.
Rates adjustment, §47-2717.
Regulations.
Rules and powers regarding,
§1-303.03.
**Restaurants run by federal
government,** §7-2701.
Safe needle distribution.
Sharps injury protection, §§7-2851 to
7-2858.
Schools.
Health and wellness programs,
§§38-826.01 to 38-826.05.
Health education, §§38-824.01 to
38-824.05.
Healthy schools fund, §§38-821.01,
38-821.02.
Healthy youth and schools
commission, §§38-827.01 to
38-827.04.
Sharps injury protection.
Safe needle distribution, §§7-2851 to
7-2858.
Spas, §28-3817.
Strokes, §§44-1151 to 44-1159.
See STROKES.
Students, §§38-601 to 38-651.12.
See STUDENT HEALTH CARE.
**Temporary assistance for needy
families (TANF) program,**
§4-205.19j.
Tobacco Settlement Trust Fund,
§§7-1811.01 to 7-1811.03.
Toilets, §§8-601 to 8-604.
Trafficking in human body parts,
§§7-1501.01 to 7-1501.03.
Tuberculosis sanatoria, §7-180.
Vital records.
General provisions, §§7-201 to 7-228.
See VITAL RECORDS.
Waterclosets, §§8-601 to 8-604.
**Youth behavioral health
epidemiology reports.**
Citation of provisions, §2-1517.01.
Definitions, §2-1517.02.

**HEALTH AND WELLNESS
PROGRAMS, SCHOOL,**
§§38-826.01 to 38-826.05.

HEALTH BENEFIT EXCHANGE AUTHORITY, §§31-3171.01 to 31-3171.18.
Advisory board, §31-3171.07.
Applicability, §31-3171.18.
Certification as qualified health benefit plan, §31-3171.09.
Conflicts of interest, §31-3171.10.
Definitions, §31-3171.01.
Dissolution, liquidation, termination, §31-3171.15.
Distribution of individual and small group plans, §31-3171.09a.
District of Columbia health benefit exchange authority fund, §31-3171.03.
Duties, §31-3171.04.
Establishment, §31-3171.02.
Executive board, §31-3171.05.
  Conflicts of interest, §31-3171.10.
  Powers and duties, §31-3171.06.
Executive director, §31-3171.08.
Exemption from individual responsibility requirement and penalty, §31-3171.04.
Health carriers seeking certification of plans.
  Requirements, §31-3171.09.
Immunity of executive and advisory board members, officers and employees, §31-3171.12.
Implementation, §31-3171.16.
Insurance producers.
  Sale, solicitation, and negotiation by producers, §31-3171.09b.
Mayor's powers, §31-3171.14.
Open meetings, §31-3171.11.
Powers, §31-3171.04.
Purpose, §31-3171.02.
Relation to other laws, §31-3171.13.
Rules, §31-3171.17.
Sale, solicitation, and negotiation by producers, §31-3171.09b.
Staff, §31-3171.08.
  Conflicts of interest, §31-3171.10.

HEALTH BENEFITS PLANS.
Child health screening.
  General provisions, §§7-875.01 to 7-875.06.
Clinical trials insurance coverage, §§31-2993.01 to 31-2993.03.
Grievance procedures, §§44-301.01 to 44-304.01.
  Assessment of insurers to cover administrative costs, §44-301.09.
  Compliance with regulations and standards, §44-304.01.

HEALTH BENEFITS PLANS —Cont'd
Grievance procedures —Cont'd
  Definitions, §44-301.01.
  Department of insurance, securities and banking, appeals of rescissions to, §44-301.06a.
  Establishment of grievance system, §44-301.03.
  External appeals process, §44-301.07.
  External review system, use by plans not subject to district regulation, §44-301.11.
  Female health services, direct access to specialists for, §44-302.03.
  Formal internal review, §44-301.06.
  Independent review organizations. Certification and general requirements, §44-301.08.
  Insurer to provide procedures to members, §44-301.04.
  Medicare, inapplicability, §44-301.02.
  Plans not subject to district regulation, use of external review system, §44-301.11.
  Process for bringing grievance, §44-301.04.
  Provider leaving plan, notice to member by insurer, §44-303.01.
  Referrals to specialists, standing referrals, §44-302.02.
  Reports of insurers, §44-301.10.
  Retaliation prohibited by insurer, §44-301.03.
  Specialist acting as primary care provider, §44-302.01.
Health benefit exchange authority, §§31-3171.01 to 31-3171.18.
  See HEALTH BENEFIT EXCHANGE AUTHORITY.
Health care ombudsman program.
  General provisions, §§7-2071.01 to 7-2071.12.
  See HEALTH CARE OMBUDSMAN PROGRAM.
Health insurance generally.
  See HEALTH INSURANCE.
Telehealth reimbursement, §§31-3861 to 31-3863.
Voluntary withdrawal by plan carriers, §§31-3151 to 31-3154.

HEALTHCARE ALLIANCE.
Requirements, §7-2071.10.
Retaliatory acts prohibited, §7-2071.09.

HEALTH-CARE ASSISTANCE REIMBURSEMENT, §§4-601 to 4-609.
See MEDICAID.

HEALTHCARE DURABLE POWERS OF ATTORNEY, §§21-2201 to 21-2213.
Abortions, §21-2211.
Certification of incapacity, §21-2204.
Consent, authority to grant, refuse or withdraw, §21-2210.
Convulsive therapy, §21-2211.
Definitions, §21-2202.
Designation of, §21-2205.
Emergency health care.
Provision without consent, §21-2212.
Euthanasia, §21-2212.
Form for creating, §21-2207.
Health care providers requesting patients to execute, §21-2209.
Intellectual disabilities, persons with.
Health care decision-makers, §7-1305.07a.
Interpretation of provisions, §21-2213.
Limitations as to, §21-2211.
Lobotomies, §21-2211.
Mental health consumers.
Right to execute, §7-1231.06.
Mercy killing, §21-2212.
Policy declaration, §21-2201.
Powers and duties of attorney in fact, §21-2206.
Presumption of capacity, §21-2203.
Psycho-surgery, §21-2211.
Revocation of, §21-2208.
Shock treatments, §21-2211.
Sterilization, §21-2211.
Substituted consent for, §21-2210.

HEALTHCARE ENTITY CONVERSION ACT, §§44-601 to 44-610.
Approval of conversion, §44-603.
Charitable trust to safeguard charitable assets.
Establishment, governance, §44-604.
Conversion fee, §44-608.
Declaratory judgment, §44-607.
Definitions, §44-602.
Enforcement, §44-609.
Findings, §44-601.
Mandatory condition precedent, §44-605.
Process of review, §44-606.
Rules, §44-610.

HEALTHCARE ENTITY CONVERSION ACT —Cont'd
Violations and penalties, §44-609.

HEALTH CARE FACILITIES.
Childhood lead poisoning screening and reporting, §§7-871.01 to 7-871.06.
Crimes and offenses.
Failure to report certain deaths, §5-1406.
Criminal background checks for unlicensed personnel, §§44-551 to 44-554.
Dead bodies.
Duty to report certain deaths to medical examiner, §5-1405.
Failure to report certain deaths, §5-1406.
Disposal of unused pharmaceuticals.
Prohibited methods of disposal, §48-851.03.
Enjoining violation, §44-509.
Fines, §44-509.
Health care entity conversion act, §§44-601 to 44-610.
Health maintenance organizations.
General provisions, §§31-3401 to 31-3431.
See HEALTH MAINTENANCE ORGANIZATIONS.
Hospitals.
See HOSPITALS.
Inspections, §44-505.
Interference with or obstruction of, §§22-1314.01, 22-1314.02.
Lead poisoning.
Childhood lead poisoning screening and reporting, §§7-871.01 to 7-871.06.
Licensure, §§44-501 to 44-509.
Penalties, §44-509.
Reports, §44-508.
Smoking, §7-1703.
"No Smoking" signs, §7-1704.
State health planning and development agency.
General provisions, §§44-401 to 44-421.
See STATE HEALTH PLANNING AND DEVELOPMENT AGENCY.
Unlawful operation, penalty, §44-509.
Unused pharmaceuticals.
Prohibited methods of disposal, §48-851.03.

HEALTH CARE FINANCE DEPARTMENT, §§7-771.01 to 7-771.11.
Chief financial officer.
Appointment and duties, §7-771.06.
Definitions, §7-771.01.
Director.
Appointment, §7-771.04.
Duties, §7-771.05.
Establishment, §7-771.02.
General counsel.
Appointment and duties, §7-771.06.
Organization, §7-771.06.
Personnel authority.
Temporary, §7-771.08.
Powers and duties, §7-771.07.
Procurement authority.
Temporary, §7-771.08.
Purpose, §7-771.03.
Transition process, §7-771.09.
Continuation of rules and regulations, §7-771.11.
Date of transfer of assets and authority, §7-771.10.
Violence prevention and health equity office, establishment, §7-781.

HEALTH CARE FINANCING FUND, §§7-1931 to 7-1933.

HEALTH CARE OMBUDSMAN PROGRAM, §§7-2071.01 to 7-2071.12.
Accessible services to be provided, §7-2071.04.
Administration, §7-2071.02.
Advisory council, §7-2071.11.
Confidentiality of information, §7-2071.07.
Data collection and reporting, §7-2071.06.
Definitions, §7-2071.01.
Establishment, §7-2071.02.
Evaluation, §7-2071.03.
Funding, §7-2071.12.
Health benefits plans.
Requirements, §7-2071.10.
Retaliatory acts prohibited, §7-2071.09.
HealthCare alliance.
Requirements, §7-2071.10.
Retaliatory acts prohibited, §7-2071.09.
Immunity, §7-2071.08.
Public outreach, §7-2071.05.
Retaliation.
Prohibited acts, §7-2071.09.

HEALTH CARE PROVIDERS.
Child neglect reports, §§4-1321.01 to 4-1321.07.
Correctional facilities.
Transferring from public to private, §24-261.02b.
Definitions of health occupations, §3-1201.02.
Emergency volunteer health practitioners, §§7-2361.01 to 7-2361.12.
See EMERGENCY VOLUNTEER HEALTH PRACTITIONERS.
Fetal alcohol spectrum disorder reporting, §4-1321.02.
Firearms or weapons injuries.
Reporting, §§7-2601 to 7-2603.
Good Samaritan Act, §§7-401, 7-402.
Health care durable powers of attorney.
Requesting patients to execute, §21-2209.
Health occupations boards.
General provisions, §§3-1201.01 to 3-1213.01.
See HEALTH OCCUPATIONS BOARDS.
Health occupations licensure, registration or certification, §§3-1205.01 to 3-1205.24.
See HEALTH OCCUPATIONS LICENSURE, REGISTRATION OR CERTIFICATION.
Indemnification of District medical employees, §2-415.
Lead poisoning.
Childhood lead poisoning screening and reporting, §§7-871.01 to 7-871.06.
Limitations of liability for providing medical assistance, §§7-401, 7-402.
Medicaid fraud, §§4-801 to 4-805.
Office of Medicaid operations reform, §§4-204.11 to 4-204.16.
Physicians and surgeons.
See PHYSICIANS AND SURGEONS.
Veterinarians, §§3-1208.61 to 3-1208.65.
See VETERINARY MEDICINE.

HEALTH CARE SAFETY NET ADMINISTRATION, §§7-1401 to 7-1405.01.
Assumption of liabilities of public benefit corporation, §7-1403.
Contract for comprehensive health care services, §7-1405.

HEALTH CARE SAFETY NET ADMINISTRATION —Cont'd
Established, §7-1401.
Responsibilities, §7-1401.
Rules, §7-1405.01.
Transfers from public benefit corporation, §7-1402.

HEALTH CARE SYSTEM DEVELOPMENT COMMISSION, §§7-2901 to 7-2906.
Compensation and expenses, §7-2903.
Duties, §7-2904.
Established, §7-2901.
Membership, qualifications, term of office, §7-2902.
Office space and staffing, §7-2906.
Purpose, §7-2901.
Recommendations for development health care system, §7-2904.
Approval, §7-2905.

HEALTH CLINICS.
Fee schedule for, §44-731.
Lead poisoning.
Childhood lead poisoning screening and reporting, §§7-871.01 to 7-871.06.
Medical liability captive insurance agency, §§1-307.81 to 1-307.95.
See MEDICAL LIABILITY CAPTIVE INSURANCE AGENCY.

HEALTH DATA PRIVACY, §§7-241 to 7-248.
Agency duties on receipt of request for information, §7-244.
AIDS health care records, §7-1605.
Data system to store and share information, §7-243.
Definitions, §7-241.
Disclosure of information, §7-242.
Penalty for unlawful disclosure, §§7-245, 7-246.
Application of penalty under other law, §7-247.
Limitation on information disclosed, §7-242.
Mental health disclosures, §§7-1201.01 to 7-1208.07.
See MENTAL HEALTH DISCLOSURES.
Permissible use and disclosure of information, §7-242.
Rules promulgation, §7-248.
Service provider request for information, §7-244.
Substance abuse.
Choice in drug treatment program, §7-3006.

HEALTH DATA PRIVACY —Cont'd
Unlawful use or disclosure of information, penalties, §§7-245, 7-246.
Application of penalty under other law, §7-247.

HEALTH DEPARTMENT.
AIDS/HIV education and outreach, §§7-1631 to 7-1633.
Athletic concussion program.
Materials development and distribution, §7-2871.04.
Board of pharmacy fund, §7-733.02.
Breastfeeding mothers, rights of.
Duties of department, §2-1402.83.
Cemetery superintendents.
Registration of, §43-118.
Child and family services agency, §§4-1301.02 to 4-1362.
See CHILD ABUSE AND NEGLECT.
Child and infant screening.
Newborn heart screening, §§7-857.01 to 7-857.04.
Director.
Clerks to director, §7-106.
Disparities.
Commission on health disparities, §§7-755.01 to 7-755.04.
Commission on health disparities fund, §7-755.04.
Establishment, §7-755.01.
Functions and duties, §7-755.02.
Powers and procedure, §7-755.03.
Commission on health equity, §§7-756.01 to 7-756.03.
Fees.
Public laboratory fees, §7-734.
Regulatory powers, §7-731.
Deposit of fees, §7-733.01.
Functions, §§7-731 to 7-737.
Grants, §7-736.01.
Health care ombudsman program, §§7-2071.01 to 7-2071.12.
See HEALTH CARE OMBUDSMAN PROGRAM.
Health care safety net administration, §§7-1401 to 7-1405.01.
Health occupations regulation fund, §7-733.
Human papillomavirus vaccination.
Effectiveness and risks.
Department of health certification, §7-1651.03.
Inspections, §§7-731, 7-741.02.
Newborn heart screening, §§7-857.01 to 7-857.04.

HEALTH DEPARTMENT —Cont'd

Nurse staffing agencies, §§44-1051.01 to 44-1051.18.
See NURSE STAFFING AGENCIES.

Overdose, education and outreach regarding, §7-403.

Powers.
Regulatory powers, §7-731.

Prescription drugs.
Access to prescription drugs, §§48-831.01 to 48-831.42.
See PRESCRIPTION DRUGS.

Rules, §7-737.

Smoking in public places, §§7-741.01 to 7-741.07.

HEALTH EDUCATION, §§38-824.01 to 38-824.05.
See SCHOOLS AND EDUCATION.

HEALTH EMERGENCY.

Public health emergency executive order, §7-2304.01.

HEALTH EQUITY, COMMISSION ON, §§7-756.01 to 7-756.03.

HEALTH INSURANCE.

Casualty and other insurance rates.
General provisions, §§31-2701 to 31-2714.
See INSURANCE.

Chemotherapy pill coverage, §§31-2995.01 to 31-2995.03.
Definitions, §31-2995.01.
Group health plans, applicability, §31-2995.03.
Mandated insurance coverage, §31-2995.02.

Children and minors.
Dependent child coverage, §31-2996.02.
Habilitative services coverage, §§31-3271, 31-3272.

Children's health insurance program, §1-307.05.

Child support enforcement.
Medical support enforcement, §§46-251.01 to 46-251.10.

Claims for reimbursement by providers.
Payment, §§31-3131 to 31-3138.

Class of insurance discontinued, §§31-3011 to 31-3013.
Applicability of provisions, §31-3013.
Requirements, §31-3011.
Rules, §31-3012.

Clinical trials insurance coverage, §§31-2993.01 to 31-2993.03.
Covered trials, §31-2993.02.

HEALTH INSURANCE —Cont'd

Clinical trials insurance coverage —Cont'd
Defined terms, §31-2993.01.
Right to file grievance, independent review, §31-2993.03.

COBRA, §§31-3301.01 to 31-3303.14.
See HEALTH INSURANCE PORTABILITY AND ACCOUNTABILITY.

Colorectal cancer screening, coverage, §31-2931.

Consultation.
Referral required for consultation.
Uniform consultation referral forms, §§31-3231 to 31-3234.

Continuation of coverage, §44-303.01.

Continuation of coverage under employer's health benefits plan, §§32-731 to 32-734.
Converted policy, eligibility of employee, §32-732.
Cost for continued coverage, §32-732.
Definitions, §32-731.
Dependents' right to continue coverage, §32-732.
Effective date of provisions, §32-734.
Employee's right to continue coverage, §32-732.
Health benefits plan defined, §32-731.
Regulations, §32-733.
Termination of continued coverage, §32-732.
Time period of continued coverage, §32-732.

Credentialing intermediaries.
Uniform credentialing form, §§31-3251 to 31-3255.
Applicability, §31-3255.
Application to become credentialed, §31-3252.
Definitions, §31-3251.
Penalties, §31-3253.
Regulation, §31-3254.

Credit life, accident and health insurance.
General provisions, §§31-5101 to 31-5112.
See CREDIT LIFE, ACCIDENT AND HEALTH INSURANCE.

Dependent coverage, §§31-2996.01 to 31-2996.03.
Definitions, §31-2996.01.
Dependent child, §31-2996.02.
Defined, §31-2996.01.
Other dependent coverage not limited or altered, §31-2996.03.

HEALTH INSURANCE —Cont'd

Diabetes health insurance coverage,
§§31-3001 to 31-3004.
Applicability, §31-3004.
Definitions, §31-3001.
Nondiscrimination, §31-3003.
Payable benefits, §31-3002.
**Dispute as to legitimacy of claim or
amount of reimbursement.**
Reimbursement under health benefit
plans.
Notice, §31-3132.
**District of Columbia medical
assistance program,** §§1-307.02 to
1-307.06.
Medical assistance expansion program.
Establishment, §1-307.03.
Penalties, §1-307.02.
Supplementary programs, §1-307.04.
Domestic partner benefits, §§32-701
to 32-710.
See DOMESTIC PARTNER
BENEFITS.
Emergency medical services.
HIV screening test while receiving
emergency medical services,
§31-2803.
Reimbursement for, §§31-2801,
31-2802.
Requirement, §§31-2801, 31-2802.
Employer obligations, §1-307.42.
Employer's health benefits plans.
Continuation of employee's and
dependents' coverage, §§32-731 to
32-734.
Forms.
Standardized forms, §31-3201.
Gender equality in ratemaking,
§§31-3161 to 31-3163.
Applicability, §31-3163.
Requirements, §31-3161.
Rules, §31-3162.
**Grievance procedures for health
benefit plans,** §§44-301.01 to
44-304.01.
See HEALTH BENEFITS PLANS.
Group policies.
Chemotherapy pill coverage,
§31-2995.03.
Dependent child coverage,
§31-2996.02.
Optometrists, access to, §31-4724.
Prostate cancer screening.
Coverage, §§31-2951 to 31-2954.
Psychologists, access to, §31-4724.

HEALTH INSURANCE —Cont'd

**Habilitative services for children,
coverage for,** §§31-3271, 31-3272.
Health benefit exchange authority,
§§31-3171.01 to 31-3171.18.
See HEALTH BENEFIT EXCHANGE
AUTHORITY.
Health maintenance organizations.
General provisions, §§31-3401 to
31-3431.
See HEALTH MAINTENANCE
ORGANIZATIONS.
Health reform federal compliance,
§31-3461.
**Healthy DC and health care
expansion fund and program,**
§§4-631 to 4-638.
See HEALTHY DC AND HEALTH
CARE EXPANSION FUND AND
PROGRAM.
**HIV screening test while receiving
emergency medical services.**
Coverage, §31-2803.
Hormone replacement therapy.
Women's rights, §§31-3831 to 31-3837.
**Hospital and medical services
corporations,** §§31-3501 to
31-3524.
See HOSPITAL AND MEDICAL
SERVICES CORPORATIONS.
Ian's law, §§31-3011 to 31-3013.
Applicability of provisions, §31-3013.
Requirements, §31-3011.
Rules, §31-3012.
Insurer obligations, §1-307.41.
Interest for late payment of claim.
Reimbursement under health benefit
plans, §31-3132.
Liens.
Health care benefits lien reduction,
§31-3551.
**Life and health insurance guaranty
association.**
General provisions, §§31-5401 to
31-5416.
See LIFE AND HEALTH
INSURANCE GUARANTY
ASSOCIATION.
Long-term care insurance, §§31-3601
to 31-3612.
See LONG-TERM CARE
INSURANCE.
Mammograms, §§31-2901 to 31-2903.
Applicability, §31-2903.
Definitions, §31-2901.

HEALTH INSURANCE —Cont'd
Mammograms —Cont'd
Payable benefits, §31-2902.
Mastectomies.
Reconstructive surgery following
mastectomies.
Women's rights to health insurance
coverage, §§31-3831 to 31-3837.
Medical marijuana, coverage of,
§7-1671.12.
Medicare supplement insurance.
General provisions, §§31-3701 to
31-3710.
See MEDICARE SUPPLEMENT
INSURANCE.
Newborn health insurance.
General provisions, §§31-3801 to
31-3805.
See NEWBORN HEALTH
INSURANCE.
Newborn hearing screening, §§7-851
to 7-855.
Newborn heart screening, §§7-857.01
to 7-857.04.
Payment of claims for
reimbursement.
Claims by providers, §§31-3131 to
31-3138.
Prompt payment of claims.
Reimbursement under health benefit
plans, §31-3132.
Prostate cancer screening.
Applicability, §31-2953.
Coverage, §§31-2951 to 31-2954,
31-2952.
Definitions, §31-2951.
Regulations, §31-2954.
Provider panels.
Defined, §31-3131.
Reimbursement under health benefit
plans, §31-3134.
Public officers and employees,
§§1-621.01 to 1-621.17.
See MERIT SYSTEM.
Ratemaking, §§31-3311.01 to
31-3311.11.
Aggregate medical loss ratios,
§31-3311.02.
Annual filings, §31-3311.04.
Applicability of provisions,
§31-3311.10.
Approved rates rescinded, §31-3311.05.
Casualty and other insurance rates.
General provisions, §§31-2701 to
31-2714.
See INSURANCE.

HEALTH INSURANCE —Cont'd
Ratemaking —Cont'd
Definitions, §31-3311.11.
Dividends, §31-3311.02.
Essential health benefits,
§31-3311.03a.
Filings, §31-3311.04.
Gender equality, §§31-3161 to 31-3163.
Applicability, §31-3163.
Requirements, §31-3161.
Rules, §31-3162.
Loss ratio disclosure, §31-3311.03.
Post-claims underwriting, §31-3311.06.
Principles, §31-3311.01.
Prior approvals, §31-3311.06.
Rating bands, §31-3311.02.
Records, §31-3311.07.
Reports and recommendations,
§31-3311.08.
Rescinding approved rates,
§31-3311.05.
Rules, §31-3311.09.
Standards, §31-3311.01.
Underwriting ratemaking criteria,
§31-3311.03b.
Reconstructive breast surgery.
Women's rights, §§31-3831 to 31-3837.
Referral required for consultation.
Uniform consultation referral forms,
§§31-3231 to 31-3234.
Regulatory standards.
Authorized control level events,
§31-3451.05.
Company action level events,
§31-3451.03.
Confidentiality of information,
§31-3451.08.
Definitions, §31-3451.01.
Foreign health organizations,
§31-3451.09.
Hearing to challenge determination of
commissioner, §31-3451.07.
Immunity from liability, §31-3451.11.
Mandatory control level events,
§31-3451.06.
Notice, when effective, §31-3451.12.
RBC reports, §31-3451.02.
Regulatory action level events,
§31-3451.04.
Supplemental nature of provisions,
§31-3451.10.
Transitional provision, §31-3451.13.
Reimbursement for emergency
medical services, §§31-2801,
31-2802.
HIV screening test while receiving
emergency medical services,
§31-2803.

HEALTH INSURANCE —Cont'd
Reimbursement under health benefit plans, §§31-3131 to 31-3138.
Applicability of provisions, §31-3138.
Claims payment report, included in annual report, §31-3135.
Claim submitted by provider, time for, §31-3132.
Retroactive denial, §31-3133.
Definitions, §31-3131.
Denial of reimbursement.
Retroactive, §31-3133.
Dispute as to legitimacy of claim or amount of reimbursement.
Notice, §31-3132.
Good cause, failure to pay, §31-3132.
Health benefit plan defined, §31-3131.
Interest for late payment of claim, §31-3132.
Prompt payment of claims, §31-3132.
Provider panels, §31-3134.
Rebuttable presumption.
Claim received by insurer, §31-3132.
Record of receipt of claim, insurer's duty to maintain, §31-3132.
Retroactive denial of reimbursement, §31-3133.
Rules and regulations, adoption, §31-3137.
Time limit for reimbursement, §31-3132.
Violations, penalties, §31-3136.
Secured transactions.
Health-care-insurance receivables.
Defined, §28:9-102.
Third party assignments.
Modification of assigned contract, §28:9-405.
Small businesses, §31-3303.03.
Specialists as primary care providers, access to, §§44-302.01 to 44-302.03.
Female health services.
Direct access to specialists, §44-302.03.
Generally, §44-302.01.
Standing referrals, §44-302.02.
Spouse or domestic partner equity, §1-529.04.
Compliance with court orders, §1-523.03.
Stop-loss insurance for employers, §§31-3821, 31-3822.
Substance abuse and mental illness, §§31-3101 to 31-3112.
Alcohol abuse benefits, §31-3103.

HEALTH INSURANCE —Cont'd
Substance abuse and mental illness —Cont'd
Coverage, §§31-3102, 44-1209.
Definitions, §31-3101.
Discrimination, §31-3105.
Drug abuse benefits, §31-3103.
Excluded programs, §31-3112.
Filing requirements, §31-3109.
Health maintenance organizations, §31-3110.
Mayor's duties, §31-3111.
Mental illness benefits, §31-3104.
Nonhospital residential facilities.
Certification, §31-3106.
Defined, §31-3101.
Notice of coverage and benefits, §31-3108.
Outpatient treatment facilities.
Certification, §31-3106.
Defined, §31-3101.
Preservation of other benefits, §31-3107.
Rates, §31-3109.
Telehealth reimbursement, §§31-3861 to 31-3863.
Definitions, §31-3861.
Denial when services covered in person prohibited, generally, §31-3862.
Medicaid reimbursement, §31-3863.
Private reimbursement, §31-3862.
Termination of coverage, §44-303.01.
Uniform consultation referral forms, §§31-3231 to 31-3234.
Applicability, §31-3232.
Completion by provider, §31-3232.
Definitions, §31-3231.
Regulations, §31-3233.
Use of form adopted by commissioner, §31-3232.
Voluntary withdrawal by health benefit plan carriers, §§31-3151 to 31-3154.
Allocation of group and nongroup contracts among other carriers, §31-3152.
Appeals by carriers, §31-3153.
Application, §31-3152.
Definitions, §31-3151.
Notice, §31-3152.
Prior approval, §31-3152.
Procedures, §31-3152.
Rules and regulations, promulgation, §31-3154.

HEALTH INSURANCE —Cont'd
Women's rights regarding certain insurance coverage, §§31-3831 to 31-3837.
Contraception, full-year coverage, §31-3834.01.
Definitions, §31-3831.
Group health plans, applicability, §31-3837.
Hormone replacement therapy coverage, §31-3834.
Prohibitions, §31-3835.
Reconstructive surgery following mastectomies, §31-3832.
Notice of coverage, §31-3833.
Regulations, §31-3836.
Workers' compensation, §32-1507.

HEALTH INSURANCE PORTABILITY AND ACCOUNTABILITY, §§31-3301.01 to 31-3303.14.
Defined terms, §31-3301.01.
Group insurance, §§31-3301.01, 31-3303.01 to 31-3303.14.
Affiliation period, §§31-3303.12, 31-3303.13.
Applicability of provisions, §§31-3303.01, 31-3303.14.
Availability, §31-3303.06.
Coverage, §31-3303.05.
Disclosure, §31-3303.08.
Enrollment eligibility, §31-3303.09.
Exclusions, §31-3303.10.
Plan sponsors, §31-3303.04.
Preexisting conditions, §31-3303.07.
Renewability, §31-3303.03.
Size of group, determining, §31-3303.11.
Small employers, §31-3303.02.
Individual health insurance, §§31-3301.01 to 31-3302.09.
Applicability of provisions, §31-3302.08.
Fair market provision, §31-3302.06.
Financial capacity limits, §31-3302.03.
Guaranteed availability, §31-3302.01.
Interpretation of provisions, §31-3302.09.
Issuance of regulations, §31-3302.07.
Market requirements, §31-3302.04.
Network plans, §31-3302.02.
Renewability, §31-3302.05.

HEALTH MAINTENANCE ORGANIZATIONS, §§31-3401 to 31-3431.
Acquisitions, §31-3427.

HEALTH MAINTENANCE ORGANIZATIONS —Cont'd
Bankruptcy and insolvency.
Assessments protecting against, §31-3430.
Protection against, §§31-3412, 31-3430.
Rehabilitation, liquidation, or conservation, §31-3420.
Replacement coverage in event of, §31-3414.
Uncovered expenditures insolvency deposit, §31-3413.
Books and records, location, §31-3431.
Certificate of authority.
Issuance, §31-3403.
Operating without, §31-3402.
Suspension or revocation, §31-3419.
Claims for reimbursement by providers, §§31-3131 to 31-3138.
See HEALTH INSURANCE.
Clinical laboratories.
General provisions, §§44-201 to 44-213.
See CLINICAL LABORATORIES.
Clinical trials insurance coverage, §§31-2993.01 to 31-2993.03.
Compliance with other laws, §31-3408.01.
Conservation, §31-3420.
Continuation of coverage.
Employer's health benefits plans.
Employees and dependents, §§32-731 to 32-734.
Definitions, §31-3401.
Emergency medical services, reimbursement for, §§31-2801, 31-2802.
HIV screening test while receiving emergency medical services, §31-2803.
Employer's health benefits plans.
Continuation of coverage.
Employees and dependents, §§32-731 to 32-734.
Enforcement of provisions, §31-3423.
Enrollment period, §31-3414.
Establishment of, §31-3402.
Evidence of coverage requirements, §31-3407.
Fees, §31-3415.
Fiduciary responsibilities, §31-3405.
Filing rating information, §31-3415.
Fines, §31-3423.
Grievance procedures, §§44-301.01 to 44-304.01.
See HEALTH BENEFITS PLANS.

HEALTH MAINTENANCE ORGANIZATIONS —Cont'd

Group contracts, §31-3407.

HIV screening test while receiving emergency medical services, §31-2803.

Hospital and medical services corporations.
General provisions, §§31-3501 to 31-3524.
See HOSPITAL AND MEDICAL SERVICES CORPORATIONS.

Individual contracts, §31-3407.

Information provided to enrollees, §31-3409.

Interpretation of provisions, §31-3424.

Investments, §31-3411.

Issuance of rules and regulations, §31-3422.

Liquidation, §31-3420.

Medical records, §31-3426.

Mergers and consolidations, §31-3427.

Net worth requirements, §31-3412.

Point of service plans, §31-3429.

Powers and duties of, §§31-3404, 31-3417.

Premium tax, §31-3403.01.

Principal office, §31-3431.

Privacy and confidentiality, §31-3426.

Producers, regulation of, §31-3416.

Prostate cancer screening.
Coverage, §§31-2951 to 31-2954.

Public documents.
Filings and reports as, §31-3425.

Quality assurance program, §31-3406.

Records, §31-3425.

Rehabilitation, §31-3420.

Reimbursement, health benefits plans.
Claims by providers, §§31-3131 to 31-3138.
See HEALTH INSURANCE.

Relationship to other laws, §31-3424.

Reports, §31-3425.

Revocation of certificate of authority, §31-3419.

Specialists as primary care providers, access to, §§44-302.01 to 44-302.03.

HEALTH MAINTENANCE ORGANIZATIONS —Cont'd

State health planning and development agency.
General provisions, §§44-401 to 44-421.
See STATE HEALTH PLANNING AND DEVELOPMENT AGENCY.

Substance abuse and mental illness coverage, §31-3110.

Summary orders and provisions regarding, §31-3421.

Suspension of certificate of authority, §31-3419.

Taxation.
Premium tax, §31-3403.01.

Uncovered expenditures insolvency deposit, §31-3413.

Violations, §31-3423.

Voluntary withdrawal by health benefit plan carriers, §§31-3151 to 31-3154.

HEALTH OCCUPATIONS BOARDS, §§3-1201.01 to 3-1213.01.

Abolished boards, §§3-1212.01 to 3-1212.03.

Administrative procedure, §§3-1203.01, 3-1203.02.

Advisory committees, §§7-743.01 to 7-743.07.

Applicability of provisions, §3-1201.03.

Appropriations, §3-1213.01.

Cease and desist orders, §3-1205.16.

Chiropractic, board of, §3-1202.16.

Collaborative practice agreements.
Pharmacists and pharmacies, §3-1204.12.

Consecutive terms, limitations on, §3-1204.03.

Definitions, §§3-1201.01, 3-1201.02.

Dentistry, board of, §3-1202.01.

Dietetics and nutrition, board of, §3-1202.02.

Disposition of funds collected by, §3-1204.10.

Employees, §3-1204.07.
Compensation, §§3-1204.06, 3-1204.07.

Existing rules and orders, §3-1212.03.

Fee schedules, §3-1204.09.

Fines, §3-1205.14.

Licensures, registrations and certifications overseen by, §§3-1205.01 to 3-1205.24.

HEALTH OCCUPATIONS BOARDS
—Cont'd

Long-term care administration,
  board of, §3-1202.05.

Massage therapy, board of,
  §3-1202.15.

Mayor's duties regarding, §3-1203.02.

Medicine, board of, §3-1202.03.

Meetings of, §3-1204.05.

Members of abolished boards.
  Service as members of successor
    boards, §3-1212.02.

Nursing, board of, §3-1202.04.

Occupational therapy, board of,
  §3-1202.06.

Officers of, §3-1204.05.

Optometry, board of, §3-1202.07.

Pending actions and proceedings of
  abolished boards, §3-1212.03.

Pharmacists and pharmacies.
  Collaborative practice agreements,
    §3-1204.12.

Pharmacy, board of, §3-1202.08.

Physical therapy, board of,
  §3-1202.09.

Podiatry, board of, §3-1202.10.

Powers and duties, §3-1204.08.

Professional counseling, board of,
  §3-1202.13.

Psychology, board of, §3-1202.11.

Qualifications of board members,
  §3-1204.01.

Quorum, §3-1204.05.

Removal of members, §3-1204.04.

Reports, §3-1204.11.

Reprimands issued by, §3-1205.14.

Respiratory care, board of,
  §3-1202.14.

Social work, board of, §3-1202.12.

Summary actions, §3-1205.15.

Terms of board members,
  §§3-1204.02, 3-1204.03.

Transfers between boards,
  §3-1212.01.

Vacancies, filling, §3-1204.02.

Veterinary medicine, board of,
  §3-1202.21.

Wages and salaries, §3-1204.06.
  Employees' compensation, §3-1204.07.

HEALTH OCCUPATIONS
  LICENSURE, REGISTRATION
  OR CERTIFICATION, §§3-1205.01
  to 3-1205.24.

Access to patient or client records,
  §3-1210.11.

Acupuncture therapists, §3-1209.03.

HEALTH OCCUPATIONS
  LICENSURE, REGISTRATION
  OR CERTIFICATION —Cont'd

Advanced registered nursing,
  §§3-1206.01 to 3-1206.04.
  See NURSES.

Adverse events.
  Mandatory reporting, §7-161.

Appeals, §3-1205.20.

Application procedures, §3-1205.05.

Background checks of applicants,
  §3-1205.22.

Cease and desist orders, §3-1205.16.

Change of address of licensee,
  §3-1205.13.

Civil fines, fees, and penalties,
  §3-1210.09.

Crimes and offenses, §3-1210.07.

Denial of licensee, §3-1205.14.

Dental assistants, §3-1209.05.

Dentistry and dental hygiene.
  Teaching license, §3-1205.08b.

Dietetics and nutrition, §§3-1207.01,
  3-1207.02.

Disciplinary actions against
  physicians.
  Reports by physicians and health care
    providers, §3-1205.13a.

Display of license, §3-1205.13.

Endorsement of licenses issued by
  states, §3-1205.07.

Examinations, §3-1205.06.

Exemptions from requirements
  regarding, §3-1205.02.

Expiration of license, §§3-1205.10,
  3-1205.12.

Fines, §§3-1205.13a, 3-1210.07,
  3-1210.09, 7-161.

Foreign doctors of eminence and
  authority, §3-1205.09a.

Fraud and deceit, §§3-1210.04,
  3-1210.05.

Hearings regarding, §3-1205.19.

Impaired health professional.
  Voluntary limitation or surrender of
    license by, §3-1205.18.

Inactive status, §3-1205.11.

Injunctions, §3-1210.10.

Issuance of license, §3-1205.08.

Mandatory adverse event reporting,
  §7-161.

Marriage and family therapy,
  §§3-1208.31, 3-1208.32.

Massage therapy, regulation of to be
  approved by council, §3-1205.24.

HEALTH OCCUPATIONS LICENSURE, REGISTRATION OR CERTIFICATION —Cont'd
Medical malpractice judgments against physicians.
 Reports by physicians and health care providers, §3-1205.13a.
Misrepresentation, §3-1210.02.
Nursing assistive personnel, §3-1209.07.
Penalties.
 Civil, §3-1210.09.
 Criminal, §3-1210.07.
Practicing without a license, §3-1210.01.
 Misrepresentation, §3-1210.02.
Prior law, licenses issued under, §3-1201.04.
Professional counseling, §§3-1207.10 to 3-1207.12.
Prosecutions regarding, §3-1210.08.
Psychology associates, §3-1209.06.
Qualifications of applicants, §§3-1205.03, 3-1205.04.
Reciprocity, §3-1205.07.
Reinstatement.
 Expired license, 3-1205.12.
 Suspended or revoked license, §3-1205.21.
Renewal of license, §3-1205.10.
Requirements regarding, §3-1205.01.
Respiratory care practitioners, §§3-1207.21 to 3-1207.23.
Revocation of licensee, §§3-1205.14, 3-1205.21.
Scope of license, §3-1205.09.
Social workers, §§3-1208.01 to 3-1208.06.
States other than District.
 Endorsement of licenses issued by, §3-1205.07.
Summary actions, §3-1205.15.
Surrender of license, §3-1205.17.
Suspension of licensee, §3-1205.14.
 During incarceration, §3-1205.23.
Temporary license, §3-1205.08a.
Titles and terms prohibited as misrepresentation without license to practice, §3-1210.03.
Trauma technologists, §§3-1205.01 to 3-1205.24.
Voluntary limitation or surrender of license, §§3-1205.17, 3-1205.18.
Waiver of licensure requirements.
 Dietetics and nutrition, §3-1207.02.
 Professional counseling, §3-1207.12.

HEALTH OCCUPATIONS LICENSURE, REGISTRATION OR CERTIFICATION —Cont'd
Waiver of licensure requirements —Cont'd
 Respiratory care practitioners, §3-1207.21.
 Social workers, §3-1208.06.

HEALTH PROFESSIONAL RECRUITMENT PROGRAM, §§7-751.01 to 7-751.16.
Administration of program.
 Department of health, §7-751.03.
Amount of loans repaid by program, §7-751.08.
Bankruptcy.
 Damages for breach of service obligation contract.
 Not dischargeable, §7-751.13.
Beginning service after entering contract, §7-751.07.
Breach of service obligation contract, §7-751.13.
Change of service obligation site by participant, §7-751.14.
Compensation package.
 Participant responsible for negotiating, §7-751.10.
Conditions of participation, §7-751.07.
Contract with director and representative of service site.
 Breach, §7-751.13.
 Conditions of participation, provision of contract, §7-751.07.
 No-compete clause prohibited, §7-751.07.
 Renewal, §7-751.07.
 Waiver of contract terms and conditions.
  Mental or physical disability or death, §7-751.15.
Definitions, §7-751.01.
Disbursement of loan repayment funds to participants, §7-751.09.
Duties of department of health, §7-751.03.
Educational expenses.
 Program to pay for, §7-751.02.
Effective start date of obligated service, §7-751.07.
Eligibility for program, §7-751.04.
Establishment, §7-751.02.
Fund, §7-751.15a.

HEALTH PROFESSIONAL RECRUITMENT PROGRAM
—Cont'd
Illness, family leave, maternity leave, suspension from practice, termination of employment.
Suspension of service obligation without penalty, §7-751.15.
Loan repayments.
Disbursement of funds to participants, §7-751.09.
Maximum amount, schedule, §7-751.08.
Taxable as income, §7-751.11.
Local government loans and commercial loans.
Program to pay for, §7-751.02.
Mental or physical disability or death.
Waiver of contract terms and conditions, §7-751.15.
Penalties for early educational loan repayment.
Responsibility of applicant, §7-751.05.
Preferential consideration.
Selection for participation, §7-751.06.
Purpose, §7-751.02.
Release of information.
Applicant to execute release, §7-751.05.
Repayment of educational loans.
Terms and conditions.
Responsibility of applicant, §7-751.05.
Rulemaking, §7-751.16.
Schedule of loan repayments, §7-751.08.
Selection for participation.
Criteria, §7-751.06.
Service verification forms.
Participants required to submit, §7-751.12.
Surveys to ensure compliance.
Department may conduct, §7-751.12.
Suspension of service obligation without penalty.
Illness, family leave, maternity leave, suspension from practice, termination of employment, §7-751.15.
Tax implications for loan repayments, §7-751.11.
Transfer to another service site.
Termination of employment for reason beyond participant's control.
Requirement, time restriction, failure breach of contract, §7-751.14.

HEALTH PROFESSIONAL RECRUITMENT PROGRAM
—Cont'd
Tuition and required fees.
Program to pay for, §7-751.02.
Waiver of contract terms and conditions.
Mental or physical disability or death, §7-751.15.

HEALTH PROGRAMS ADMINISTERED BY GOVERNMENT.
Medication advisory committee receiving gifts or remuneration prohibition act of 2008, §§48-842.01 to 48-842.04.
Pharmaceutical education program establishment act of 2008.
Education of prescribers in publicly funded, contracted or subsidized health-care programs, §§48-843.01 to 48-843.04.

HEALTH SERVICES PLANNING.
State health planning and development agency.
General provisions, §§44-401 to 44-421.
See STATE HEALTH PLANNING AND DEVELOPMENT AGENCY.

HEALTH SPAS AND CLUBS.
Buyer's right to cancel, §28-3817.
Definitions, §28-3817.
Health occupations.
Exemptions from chapter provisions, §3-1201.03.
Sales restrictions, §28-3817.

HEALTH SYSTEMS PLAN (HSP).
State health planning and development agency, §44-404.

HEALTHY DC AND HEALTH CARE EXPANSION FUND AND PROGRAM, §§4-631 to 4-638.
Administration, §§4-632, 4-635.
Benefits, §4-634.
Contract requirements, §4-635.
Costs.
Annual premium costs, §4-634.
Definition of health insurer, §4-631.
Eligibility, §4-633.
Establishment, §4-632.
Fines and civil penalties.
Disposition of, §4-637.
Prohibited acts, §4-636.

HEALTHY DC AND HEALTH CARE EXPANSION FUND AND PROGRAM —Cont'd
Implementation, §4-635.
Prohibitions, §4-636.
Rulemaking, §4-638.

HEALTHY FOOD RETAIL PROGRAM, §§2-1212.31 to 2-1212.34.
Distribution, §2-1212.33.
Energy efficiency, §2-1212.34.
Established, §2-1212.31.
Requirements, §2-1212.32.
Rules, §2-1212.41.

HEALTHY SCHOOLS FUND, §38-821.01.
Applicability of law, §38-828.02.
Definitions, §38-821.01.
Establishment, §38-821.02.
Rulemaking authority, §38-828.01.

HEALTHY YOUTH AND SCHOOLS COMMISSION, §§38-827.01 to 38-827.04.

HEARING AID DEALERS, §§28-4001 to 28-4007.
Advertising.
Dishonest or misleading advertising. Grounds for revocation or suspension of registration, §28-4006.
Assistive technology device warranty, §§28-4031 to 28-4034.
Audiologists.
Defined, §28-4001.
Definitions, §28-4001.
Door-to-door sales.
Written consent of buyer required, §28-4005.
Fraud.
Grounds for revocation or suspension, §28-4006.
Guarantee.
Money-back guarantee required, §28-4004.
Hearing aids.
Defined, §28-4001.
Hearing test evaluation.
Defined, §28-4001.
Medical clearance, §28-4004.
Defined, §28-4001.
Money-back guarantee.
Required, §28-4004.
Office of consumer protection.
Powers and duties, §28-4002.

HEARING AID DEALERS —Cont'd
Otolaryngologist.
Defined, §28-4001.
Penalties.
Civil fines, penalties and fees, §28-4006.
Price list.
Required posting and availability, §28-4005.
Prohibitions, §28-4004.
Receipts.
Required contents, §28-4005.
Records.
Customer records required, §28-4005.
Registration, §28-4003.
Grounds for revocation or suspension, §28-4006.
Powers and duties of office of consumer protection, §28-4002.
Regulatory provisions, §28-4004.
Required practices, §28-4004.
Revocation of registration.
Grounds, §28-4006.
Severability of chapter, §28-4007.
Suspension of registration.
Grounds, §28-4006.
Telephone option.
Defined, §28-4001.
False or misleading advertising, §28-4006.
Telephone sales.
Written permission of buyer required, §28-4004.
Used hearing aid.
Defined, §28-4001.
Violations of chapter.
Civil fines, penalties and fees, §28-4006.
Grounds for revocation or suspension of registration, §28-4006.

HEARING AIDS.
Assistive technology device warranty, §§28-4031 to 28-4034.

HEARING COMMISSIONERS.
Assignment of civil actions to commissioners, CivPro Rule 40-I.
Child support, FamDiv Rule D.
Civil procedure, CivPro Rule 73.
Collection and subrogation cases, CivPro Rule 40-III.
Criminal procedure, CrimPro Rule 117.
Family court proceedings, FamDiv Rule D.
Parentage proceedings, DomRel Rule 405.

HEARING IMPAIRED.
Deaf persons generally.
See DEAF AND HEARING
IMPAIRED.
Gallaudet University.
General provisions, §§38-2301 to
38-2402.11.
See GALLAUDET UNIVERSITY.
Hearing aid dealers, §§28-4001 to
28-4007.
See HEARING AID DEALERS.
Interpreters, §§2-1901 to 2-1912.01.
See INTERPRETERS.
Newborn hearing screening, §§7-851
to 7-855.

HEARINGS.
Administrative hearings.
Office of administrative hearings,
§§2-1831.01 to 2-1831.18.
See ADMINISTRATIVE
HEARINGS, OFFICE OF.
Adoption.
Revocation of consent or
relinquishment, Adoption Rule 70.
Show cause hearings, Adoption Rule
39.
Alcoholic beverage licenses.
Summary revocation or suspension,
§25-826.
Arbitration, Arbitration Rule IX.
Small claims court, SmallClaimsArb
Rule 3.
Attachment.
Pre-judgment attachment, CivPro Rule
64-I.
Domestic relations actions, DomRel
Rule 64.
**Attorney discipline or disability
proceedings,** DCBar Rule XI,
USDistCt LCrR 57.27, USDistCt
LCrR 57.30, USDistCt LCvR 83.16,
USDistCt LCvR 83.19.
Child abuse and neglect.
Factfinding hearings, NeglectProc Rule
19.
Permanency hearings, NeglectProc
Rules 32 to 34.
Report of initial investigation,
NeglectProc Rule 7.
Presentation, NeglectProc Rule 14.
Review hearings, NeglectProc Rules 28
to 30.
Revocation of protective supervision,
NeglectProc Rule 26.
Termination of parental rights,
NeglectProc Rules 38, 39.

HEARINGS —Cont'd
Civil asset forfeiture.
Post-seizure property retention
hearings, §41-306.
Pre-seizure hearings for real property,
§41-303.
Competence to proceed.
Incompetent criminal defendants.
During and after treatment,
§24-531.06.
Initial determination, §24-531.04.
Court employees.
Debts and erroneous payments made
to employees, collection by
executive officer.
Notice and hearing requirements,
§11-1733.
Crime victims' compensation.
Appeal of determination, VictComp
Rule 20.
Default judgments, CivPro Rule 55.
Domestic relations actions, DomRel
Rule 55.
Defenses.
Domestic relations actions, DomRel
Rule 12.
Preliminary hearings, CivPro Rule 12.
**Delinquent minor hearings
generally.**
See DELINQUENT MINORS.
Domestic relations actions.
Attachment before judgment, DomRel
Rule 64.
Default judgments, DomRel Rule 55.
Defenses, DomRel Rule 12.
Injunctions and restraining orders,
DomRel Rule 65.
Motions, DomRel Rule 7.
Non-appearance at hearing, DomRel
Rule 12.
Replevin actions, DomRel Rule 64.
Emergency medical services.
Disciplinary action, §7-2341.17.
**Ethics and government
accountability,** §1-1162.14.
Extradition, CrimPro Rule 40-I.
Grand juries.
Closing of hearings, CrimPro Rule 6,
USDistCt LCrR 6.1.
**Hospitalization of persons with
mental illness.**
See HOSPITALIZATION OF
PERSONS WITH MENTAL
ILLNESS.
Human rights commission.
See HUMAN RIGHTS COMMISSION.

HEARINGS —Cont'd

Incompetent criminal defendants.

Competence to proceed.

During and after treatment,
§24-531.06.

Initial determination, §24-531.04.

Intellectual disabilities, persons with.

Commitment hearings.

Individuals who are not competent to refuse commitment, MentalRetardation Rule 4A.

Respondents found incompetent to participate in criminal proceedings, MentalRetardation Rule 4B.

Transfer of committed person, MentalRetardation Rule 5.

Juvenile proceedings generally.

See DELINQUENT MINORS.

Landlord and tenant court.

Motions.

Time of hearing, LandlordTenant Rule 13.

Notice of hearing.

Form, LandlordTenant Form 1S.

Protective orders, LandlordTenant Rule 12-I.

Marijuana, possession decriminalization.

Hearings for civil violations, §48-1213.

Mental illness, hospitalization of persons with.

See HOSPITALIZATION OF PERSONS WITH MENTAL ILLNESS.

Motions, CivPro Rule 12-I.

Oral hearings, USDistCt LCvR 78.1.

Scheduling, CivPro Rule 78-I.

Place of hearings in superior court, CivPro Rule 77.

Probate proceedings.

Defaults or irregularities.

Guardians, conservators, trustees, etc., involved, Probate Rule 207.

Personal representative's authority to act.

Death on or after July 1, 1995, Probate Rule 412.

Reconsideration of determinations.

Death between January 1, 1981 and June 30, 1995, Probate Rule 130.

Death on or after July 1, 1995, Probate Rule 430.

HEARINGS —Cont'd

Probation revocation or modification, CrimPro Rule 32.1, USDistCt LCrR 32.1.

Delinquent minors, JuvProc Rule 32.

Hearing commissioners, CrimPro Rule 117.

Public-private partnerships.

Review of requests for proposal, §2-273.03.

Replevin, CivPro Rule 64-II.

Domestic relations actions, DomRel Rule 64.

Sentencing hearings, CrimPro Rule 32.

Delinquent minors, JuvProc Rule 32.

Small claims court.

Arbitration, SmallClaimsArb Rule 2.

Conciliation, SmallClaims Conciliation Rule 2.

Tax proceeding motions, Tax Rule 9.

Temporary assistance for needy families.

Grandparent caregiver subsidies.

Termination of payments, §4-251.03.

Termination of parental rights.

Child abuse and neglect, NeglectProc Rules 38, 39.

Unauthorized practice of law committee, DCCtApp Rule 49.

Workplace fraud.

Hearings on violations, §32-1331.06.

HEARSAY.

Criminal procedure.

Probable cause determination, CrimPro Rule 5.

Sealing of arrest records, §16-805, CrimPro Rule 118.

Delinquent minors, JuvProc Rule 118.

Probable cause determination, CrimPro Rule 5.

Sealing of arrest records, §16-805.

Criminal procedure, CrimPro Rule 118.

Delinquent minors, JuvProc Rule 118.

HEART ATTACKS.

Automated external defibrillators.

Usage, §§44-231 to 44-235.

Non-resuscitation procedures for EMS.

Comfort care orders, §§7-651.01 to 7-651.16.

See EMERGENCY MEDICAL SERVICES.

HEART ATTACKS —Cont'd
Presumption as to disability or death resulting from.
Fire and emergency medical services employees, §5-652.

HEART BALM ACT.
Abolition of actions for alienation of affections, criminal conversation, breach of promise to marry, §16-923.

HEATING OIL COMPANIES.
Taxation, §47-2501.

HEIGHTS ON GEORGIA AVENUE PROJECT.
Real property tax exemptions, §§47-4628, 47-4630.

HELICOPTER DUTY.
Police and firefighters, additional compensation for, §5-542.02.

HELICOPTER LANDING PADS, §9-1211.01.

HELMETS.
Bicycle operators or passengers, §§50-1605, 50-1651.
Child safety helmet assistance program, §50-1608.
Child safety helmet education program, §50-1607.
Failure to wear.
Not negligence per se, contributory negligence, assumption of risk, §50-1606.
Required for certain vehicles, §§50-1605, 50-1651.
Effective date for enforcement, §50-1652.

HERBICIDES.
Plants and plant diseases.
General provisions, §§8-301 to 8-305.
See PLANTS AND PLANT DISEASES.

HERITAGE ISLAND.
National Children's Island, §§10-1401 to 10-1406.

HIGHER EDUCATION.
See UNIVERSITIES AND COLLEGES.

HIGHER EDUCATION LICENSURE COMMISSION, §§38-1301 to 38-1313.
Board of higher education.
Transfer of positions and funding formerly assigned to board, §38-1305.

HIGHER EDUCATION LICENSURE COMMISSION —Cont'd
Bond or security requirement per institution, §38-1311.
Chairperson, §38-1304.
Compensation, travel expenses, per diem, §38-1304.
Conditional exemption granted degree granting institution, §38-1310.
Criminal penalty for violation, §38-1312.
Definitions, §38-1302.
Deposit of revenues collected, §38-1306.
Educational services endorsement to basic business license.
Licenses issued as, §38-1306.
Established, §38-1303.
Evaluation of institution's facilities and programs, §38-1306.
Functions, §38-1307.
Higher education licensure commission site fund, §38-2607.
Institutions or activities excluded from chapter's coverage, §38-1310.
Licensure of degree granting institutions, §38-1306.
Meetings, §38-1304.
Number of members, §38-1304.
Panels, §38-1305.
Postsecondary educational institutions incorporated in or outside of District.
Delivery of online instruction, §38-1309.01.
Requirements, §38-1309.
Postsecondary education, standards concerning quality.
Purpose of chapter, §38-1301.
Purpose in licensing postsecondary educational institutions, §38-1303.
Purposes of chapter, §38-1301.
Quorum, §38-1304.
Reciprocity agreement.
Defined, §38-1302.
Requirements for postsecondary educational institutions incorporated in or outside of District, §38-1309.
Rules, §38-1306.
Supplemental funding, §38-1308.
Suspension or revocation of licenses, §38-1306.

HIGHER EDUCATION LICENSURE COMMISSION —Cont'd
Term, §38-1304.
Transfer of commission to state education office, §38-1313.
Vacancies, §38-1304.
Violations, criminal penalty, §38-1312.

HIGH SCHOOLS.
Aviation courses, §§38-920 to 38-922.
Schools generally.
See SCHOOLS AND EDUCATION.
Teachers.
See TEACHERS.

HIGH TECHNOLOGY COMPANIES.
Income taxes.
Credits, capital gains, §§47-1817.01 to 47-1817.08.
Definitions, §47-1817.01.
Returns, certification as, §47-1805.05.
Lease of real property, security deposit assistance.
Qualified high technology company, §§2-1221.01, 2-1221.02.
Real property taxes, §47-811.03.
Real property tax exemptions.
Interior renovation tax rebate, §47-4665.
Tax penalties, §47-4218.

HIGHWAY BRIDGE OVER POTOMAC RIVER, §9-307.

HIGHWAYS, §§9-101.01 to 9-101.18.
Abandonment of streets, reversion of title upon, §9-101.08.
Approval of new plans, §9-101.12.
Barbed-wire fences, §§9-1213.01 to 9-1213.05.
Beatty and Hawkins's addition to Georgetown, §9-101.07.
Blocking passage, §22-1307.
Bond issues.
Transportation infrastructure improvement GARVEE bonds, §§9-107.51 to 9-107.62.
Budgets and budget estimates, §47-209.
Center Leg Freeway (interstate 395) PILOT Area.
Real property taxes.
Payments in lieu of taxes, §47-4632.
Complete streets policy, §50-2381.
Condemnation proceedings, §§9-101.05, 9-101.09, 9-101.18.
Constitution of the United States.
Post roads, US Const Art I §8.

HIGHWAYS —Cont'd
Construction program authorization, §9-101.16.
Cost-transfer projects, §9-111.01c.
Cutting trenches in highways.
Permit requirements, §§9-433.01, 9-433.02.
District highway trust fund, §9-111.01.
Dulles International Airport, §9-803.
Emergency highway relief, §9-109.01.
Eminent domain.
General provisions, §§16-1301 to 16-1385.
See EMINENT DOMAIN.
Excess property for development of seat of government.
Retention for public use, §16-1334.
Excess property for United States.
Retention for public use, §16-1382.
Federal-aid highway program, §9-109.03.
Expeditious processing and execution of contracts, §9-109.03.
Revolving fund account, §9-109.03.
Federal government.
Assessment of costs for parkways, §9-1217.01.
Federally-aided projects, §§9-107.01 to 9-107.04.
Transportation infrastructure improvement GARVEE bonds, §§9-107.51 to 9-107.62.
Funds, §§9-109.02 to 9-111.01a.
District of Columbia highway trust fund, §9-111.01.
Local transportation fund, §9-111.01a.
Report by mayor.
Highway trust fund and local roads construction and maintenance fund expenditures, §9-111.31.
Grade crossing elimination projects, §9-107.04.
Innerloop Freeway System, §10-511.06.
Interstate highway system.
Provisions not applicable to, §9-103.06.
Jurisdiction, §9-101.02.
Klingle road, §§9-115.01, 9-115.02, 9-115.11.
Local transportation fund, §9-111.01a.
Mall, vehicular tunnel under, §10-511.07.
Maps, §§9-103.02, 9-103.03.
Massachusetts Avenue through grounds of Naval Observatory, §9-101.11.

HIGHWAYS —Cont'd
Mayor control of, §§9-101.01, 9-107.03.
Naming and renaming, §1-301.01.
Naval Observatory, §§9-101.10, 9-101.11.
New streets and alleys.
Highway plan submission, §9-203.08.
Notice of proposed plan, §9-101.06.
Obstruction, §§22-3320 to 22-3322.
Parkways.
General provisions.
See PARKWAYS.
Permanent highway plan, §9-103.01.
Post roads, US Const Art I §8.
Preparation of plans and maps, §9-103.02.
Public contracts, §9-107.03.
Public officers and employees working on, §47-209.
Public roads declared to be public highways, §9-101.03.
Public utility relocation expenses, §9-107.02.
Public works.
General provisions, §§9-401.01 to 9-401.18.
See PUBLIC WORKS.
Real property acquisitions and transfers, §9-101.18.
Repair and maintenance, §9-101.01.
Signs.
Installation of traffic control devices, §38-3101.
Soldiers' Home grounds, use of, §9-105.02.
Southwest Freeway, §9-101.17.
Streets and alleys.
General provisions, §§9-201.01 to 9-206.02.
See STREETS AND ALLEYS.
Subdivisions.
Conformity with recorded plans, §9-101.13.
Maps of highways, subdivisions adopted by reference from, §9-103.03.
Resubdivision affected by highway plan pending condemnation proceedings, §9-101.09.
Surveys, entry upon property for purposes of, §9-103.04.
Temporary waiver of non-federal share, §§9-109.01, 9-109.02.
Transportation infrastructure improvement GARVEE bonds, §§9-107.51 to 9-107.62.
Bond authorization, §9-107.52.

HIGHWAYS —Cont'd
Transportation infrastructure improvement GARVEE bonds —Cont'd
Chief financial officer's authority, §9-107.62.
Closing documents, §9-107.57.
Maintenance, §9-107.60.
Definitions, §9-107.51.
Details, §9-107.55.
Financing documents, §9-107.57.
Maintenance, §9-107.60.
Fund, §9-107.53.
Issuance, §9-107.56.
Liability of District and employees, §§9-107.58, 9-107.59.
Mayor's authority, §9-107.55.
Payment, §9-107.54.
Reports, §9-107.61.
Trenches, cutting, §§9-431.01, 9-431.02.
United States land, District authorized to use, §9-101.14.
Width of, §9-103.01.

HIGHWAY TRUST FUND.
Report on expenditures by mayor, §9-111.31.

HILL CENTER.
Real property tax exemption, §47-1087.

HIPAA COMPLIANCE.
Health data privacy, §§7-241 to 7-248.
See HEALTH DATA PRIVACY.
Mental health disclosures, §§7-1201.01 to 7-1208.07.
See MENTAL HEALTH DISCLOSURES.

HISTORIC DISTRICTS, §§6-1104 to 6-1108, 6-1201 to 6-1207.
Administrative procedures, §6-1112.
Alterations, §§6-1105, 6-1202.
Board of Review, §6-1203.
Definitions, §6-1102.
Demolitions, §6-1104.
Effective date of provisions, §6-1115.
Fines, §6-1110.
Historic districts and landmarks.
Old Georgetown Market, §§6-1206, 6-1207.
Historic preservation review board, §6-1103.
Insanitary buildings, §6-1111.
Interpretation of provisions, §6-1205.
Issuance of regulations, §6-1109.
New construction, §6-1107.

HISTORIC DISTRICTS —Cont'd
Old Georgetown district, §§6-1201 to 6-1207.
Penalties, §6-1110.
Policy declaration, §6-1101.
Preliminary review of projects, §6-1108.
Real property tax relief, §§47-842 to 47-844.
Remedies, §6-1110.
Reports, §6-1113.
Severability of provisions, §6-1114.
Subdivisions, §6-1106.
Unsafe structures, §6-1111.
Washington convention center.
Neighborhood demolition permits.
See WASHINGTON CONVENTION CENTER.

HISTORIC LANDMARKS, §§6-1101 to 6-1115.
Administrative procedures, §6-1112.
Alterations, §6-1105.
Definitions, §6-1102.
Demolitions, §6-1104.
Neglect.
Prevention of demolition by neglect, §6-1109.03.
District undertakings.
Effect.
Comment by historic preservation officer, §6-1108.02.
Effective date of provisions, §6-1115.
Fines, §6-1110.
Grants.
Targeted homeowner grant program, §6-1110.02.
Historic landmark-District protection fund, §6-1110.01.
Historic preservation review board, §6-1103.
Historic Rhodes Tavern, §§6-1131 to 6-1133.
Insanitary buildings, §6-1111.
Issuance of regulations, §6-1109.
Maintenance of property.
Duties of owner, §6-1109.02.
Neglect.
Prevention of demolition by neglect, §6-1109.03.
New construction, §§6-1105, 6-1107.
Notice to owners, §6-1109.04.
Old Georgetown Market, §§6-1206, 6-1207.
Penalties, §6-1110.
Policy declaration, §6-1101.
Preliminary review of projects, §6-1108.

HISTORIC LANDMARKS —Cont'd
Prohibited acts, §6-1109.01.
Public safety facilities.
Conceptual review, §6-1108.01.
Defined, §6-1102.
Real property tax relief, §§47-842 to 47-844.
Remedies, §6-1110.
Reports, §6-1113.
Severability of provisions, §6-1114.
Subdivisions, §6-1106.
Targeted homeowner grant program, §6-1110.02.
Unsafe structures, §6-1111.

HISTORIC PRESERVATION REVIEW BOARD, §6-1103.
Streets and alleys.
Closing, §9-202.02.

HISTORIC RHODES TAVERN, §§6-1131 to 6-1133.

HISTOTECHNOLOGY AND HISTOLOGIC TECHNICIANS.
Definition of practice, §3-1201.02.
Health occupations licensure, registration or certification, §§3-1205.01 to 3-1205.24.
Qualifications for licensure, §3-1207.61.
Exemption, §3-1207.63.
Transition provision, §3-1207.64.
Waiver, §3-1207.62.
Titles and terms prohibited as misrepresentation without license to practice, §3-1210.03.

HIT AND RUN.
Leaving after colliding, §50-2201.05c.

HIV AND AIDS, §§7-1601 to 7-1606.
See AIDS.

HOAX WEAPONS OF MASS DESTRUCTION, §22-1319.
Defined, §22-3152.

HOLDERS IN DUE COURSE.
Bank deposits and collections.
Depositary and collecting banks.
When bank gives value for purposes of holder in due course, §28:4-211.
Commercial paper.
Defenses against holder in due course, §28:3-305.
Discharge.
Effect of discharge against holder in due course, §§28:3-302, 28:3-601.

HOLDERS IN DUE COURSE —Cont'd
Commercial paper —Cont'd
Proof of status as, §28:3-308.
Fraudulent transfers, §28-3108.
Small claims court forms,
SmallClaims Form 2.

HOLDING COMPANIES.
Insurance, §§31-701 to 31-738.
See INSURANCE HOLDING
COMPANIES.

HOLIDAYS.
Appeals, federal cases.
Clerk of court's office closed, FRAP
45(a).
Computation of time, FRAP 26(a).
Business holidays.
Designation of, §28-2701.
Christmas day.
Designated holiday, §§1-612.02,
28-2701.
Computation of time, CivPro Rule 6,
CrimPro Rule 45.
Appeals, DCCtApp Rule 26.
Domestic relations actions, DomRel
Rule 6.
Hospitalization of persons with mental
illness, MentalHealth Rule 13.
Juvenile proceedings, JuvProc Rule 45.
Designated, §28-2701.
**District of Columbia emancipation
day.**
Designated holiday, §§1-612.02,
28-2701.
**Extension of time for performing
acts,** §28-2701.
Fire departments, §§5-405, 5-521.01 to
5-521.03.
Compensation generally, §5-521.01.
Holiday defined, §5-521.02.
Independence day.
Designated holiday, §§1-612.02,
28-2701.
Labor day, §§1-612.02, 28-2701.
Legal public holidays in District,
§1-612.02.
Martin Luther King's birthday,
§§1-504, 1-612.02, 28-2701.
Metropolitan police.
Working on.
Compensation generally, §5-521.01.
Holiday defined, §5-521.02.
Park police.
Working on, compensation, §5-521.03.
Recordation of instruments.
Extension of time for, §§42-1216,
42-1217.

HOLIDAYS —Cont'd
Secret service.
Working on, compensation, §5-521.03.
Tax collection, §47-412.01.
Time.
Extension of time for performing acts,
§28-2701.
**Wages of police and firefighters
working on,** §§5-521.01 to 5-521.03.
Compensation generally, §5-521.01.
Holiday defined, §5-521.02.
Secret service, park police,
applicability, §5-521.03.

HOME BUYING WARRANTIES.
Implied warranties.
Fitness for particular purpose,
§28:2-315.
Merchantability, §28:2-314.
Usage of trade, §28:2-314.

HOME CARE AGENCIES.
**Clinical privileges and staff
membership.**
Reduction, suspension, revocation, not
renewed.
Reporting, §44-508.
Standards, §44-507.
**Criminal background checks for
unlicensed personnel.**
Confidentiality, §44-552.
Rules, §44-554.
Unauthorized release, penalties,
§44-553.
Convictions prohibiting employment,
§44-552.
Definitions, §44-551.
Required, §44-552.
Enjoining violations, §44-509.
Fines and penalties, §44-509.
Inspections, §44-505.
Licenses, §§44-501 to 44-509.
Applications, §44-502.
Definitions, §44-501.
Inspection, §44-505.
Mayor's authority, §44-503.
Provisional and restricted licenses,
§44-506.
Requirements, §44-502.
Rules, §44-504.
Unlawful to operate without, §44-502.
Violations, penalties, enforcement,
§44-509.

HOME FOR AGED AND INFIRM.
Admission of paying patients,
§44-717.
Sale of surplus products, §44-716.

HOME HEALTH CARE ADMINISTRATOR.
Transition provisions.
Persons already practicing, §3-1210.05.

HOME IMPROVEMENT CONTRACTORS.
Bonding requirements, §§47-2883.01 to 47-2883.07.
Home improvement business.
Defined, §47-2883.01.
Licenses, §§47-2883.01, 47-2883.02.
Mayor's authority, §47-2883.06.
Payment as defense to lien by, §47-2883.03.
Penalties, §47-2883.04.
Prosecution of violations, §47-2883.05.
Severability of provisions, §47-2883.07.
Prohibited practices between lenders and contractors, §26-1152.08.

HOMELAND SECURITY AND EMERGENCY MANAGEMENT AGENCY, §§7-2201 to 7-2209.
See EMERGENCY MANAGEMENT.

HOMELAND SECURITY COMMISSION, §§7-2271.01 to 7-2271.07.
See EMERGENCY MANAGEMENT.

HOMELAND SECURITY PROGRAM, §§7-2231.01 to 7-2231.10.
See EMERGENCY MANAGEMENT.

HOMELESS SERVICES, §§4-751.01 to 4-756.04.
Administrative hearings, office of.
Fair hearings, §4-754.41.
Administrative review, §4-754.42.
Applicability of provisions, §4-754.01.
Client responsibilities, §4-754.13.
Client rights, §4-754.11.
Additional rights for clients in temporary shelter or supportive housing, §4-754.12.
Construction and interpretation.
No entitlement to services, §4-755.01.
Continuum of care, §4-753.01.
Client responsibilities, §4-754.13.
Client rights, §§4-754.11, 4-754.12.
Defined, §4-751.01.
Eligibility for services within, §4-753.02.
Contracts.
Authority of mayor, §4-756.01.
Definitions, §4-751.01.
Director to end homelessness, §4-756.03.

HOMELESS SERVICES —Cont'd
Discriminatory practices.
Limitations on use of District monies, §4-755.02.
District monies.
Limitations on use of, §4-755.02.
Eligibility for services within continuum of care, §4-753.02.
End homelessness fund, §1-325.261.
Entitlement to services not created, §4-755.01.
Fair hearings, §4-754.41.
Administrative review, §4-754.42.
First-priority homeless families.
Placement, §§4-753.05, 4-753.07.
Flexible rent subsidy pilot program, §4-751.05.
Housing first fund, §4-753.01a.
Interagency council on homelessness, §§4-752.01 to 4-752.03.
Established, §4-752.01.
Operation, §4-752.03.
Plan to end youth homelessness in district by 2020, §4-752.02a.
Powers and duties, §4-752.02.
LGBTQ homeless youth.
Additional standards for providers of shelter or supportive housing, §4-754.25a.
Grant program, §4-755.01.
Training grant fund, §2-1384.
Low barrier shelter.
Additional standards for providers of, §4-754.23.
Mayor.
Contracting authority, §4-756.01.
Director to end homelessness, §4-756.03.
Policies and procedures, §4-754.56.
Rulemaking authority, §4-756.02.
Monitoring and evaluation by mayor, §4-754.31.
Office of shelter monitoring, §4-754.51.
Powers and duties, §4-754.52.
Reports, §4-754.53.
Retaliation against person bringing complaint or providing information to.
Prohibited, §4-754.55.
Staff, §4-754.54.
Pay-for-success contracts, §§2-211.01 to 2-211.03.
Permanent supportive housing.
Placement of individuals and families, requirements, §4-753.06.

HOMELESS SERVICES —Cont'd
**Prevention of homelessness
  program,** §4-771.01.
Providers.
Inspection of premises by mayor,
  §4-754.31.
Mediation of disputes with clients,
  §4-754.39.
Program rules, §4-754.32.
  Notice of, §4-754.33.
  Suspension of services for failure or
    refusal to comply, §4-754.35.
Standards.
  Additional standards for providers of
    low barrier shelter, §4-754.23.
  Additional standards for providers of
    temporary shelter and
    supportive housing, §4-754.24.
  Additional standards for providers of
    transitional housing, §4-754.25.
  Common standards for all providers,
    §4-754.21.
  LGBTQ homeless youth, additional
    standards for providers of
    shelter or supportive housing,
    §4-754.25a.
  Severe weather shelters, additional
    standards for providers,
    §4-754.22.
  Training standards for all providers,
    §4-754.21a.
Suspension of services, §4-754.35.
  Alternative sanctions, §4-754.37.
  Emergency suspensions, §4-754.38.
  Fair hearing, §4-754.41.
    Administrative review, §4-754.42.
Termination of delivery of services to
  client, §4-754.36.
  Alternative sanctions, §4-754.37.
  Emergency terminations, §4-754.38.
  Fair hearing, §4-754.41.
    Administrative review, §4-754.42.
Transfer of clients, §4-754.34.
  Alternative sanctions, §4-754.37.
  Emergency transfers, §4-754.38.
  Fair hearing, §4-754.41.
    Administrative review, §4-754.42.
Rapid rehousing, FY2012 and 2013,
  §4-753.04.
Rent supplement program, §6-226.
Capital-based assistance, §6-229.
Rapid rehousing, FY2012 and 2013,
  §4-753.04.
Tenant-based assistance, §6-228.
Voucher assistance, §6-227.
Reports.
Interagency council on homelessness,
  §4-752.02.

HOMELESS SERVICES —Cont'd
Reports —Cont'd
Interim eligibility reporting
  requirements, §4-756.04.
Residency grace period, §4-753.03.
**Retaliation against person bringing
  complaint or providing
  information to office of shelter
  monitoring.**
Prohibited, §4-754.55.
Rulemaking.
Authority of mayor, §4-756.02.
Severe weather shelter.
Additional standards for providers of,
  §4-754.22.
Supportive housing.
Additional rights for clients in,
  §4-754.12.
Additional standards for providers of,
  §4-754.24.
LGBTQ homeless youth, §4-754.25a.
Temporary shelter.
Additional rights for clients in,
  §4-754.12.
Additional standards for providers of,
  §4-754.24.
Transfer of clients by providers,
  §4-754.34.
Alternative sanctions, §4-754.37.
Emergency transfers, §4-754.38.
Fair hearing, §4-754.41.
  Administrative review, §4-754.42.
Transitional housing.
Additional standards for providers of,
  §4-754.25.
Walter Reed Army Medical Center.
Reuse of facilities, §§10-1901 to
  10-1906.

HOMELESS SHELTERS.
Homeless services generally,
  §§4-751.01 to 4-756.04.
See HOMELESS SERVICES.
Office of shelter monitoring,
  §4-754.51.
Powers and duties, §4-754.52.
Reports, §4-754.53.
Retaliation against person bringing
  complaint or providing
  information to.
  Prohibited, §4-754.55.
Staff, §4-754.54.
Schools, establishment near.
Notice given by mayor, §38-3201.
Walter Reed Army Medical Center.
Reuse of facilities, §§10-1901 to
  10-1906.

HOME OWNERSHIP COUNSELING PROGRAM, §42-2651.

HOMEOWNER'S INSURANCE.
Fire and casualty insurance generally, §§31-2501.01 to 31-2502.42.

HOME PURCHASE ASSISTANCE FUND, §§42-2601 to 42-2626.
Appropriations, §§42-2602, 42-2605.
Audits, §42-2605.
Availability of funds from, §42-2603.
Council, §§42-2604, 42-2605.
Deposits to credit of, §42-2602.
First-time home buyers, §42-2604.
Gifts, §42-2602.
Grants, §42-2602.
Issuance of rules and regulations, §42-2604.
Loan agreement terms, §42-2604.
Mayor, §§42-2603, 42-2604.
Policy declaration, §42-2601.
Priority of allocations, §42-2604.
Repayment structure, revision by mayor, §42-2602.01.
Reports, §42-2605.
Residence requirements, §42-2604.
Step up program, §§42-2621 to 42-2626.
  Amount of assistance available under, §42-2624.
  Applicability of provisions, §42-2626.
  Audits, §42-2622.
  Condominium owners, §42-2622.
  Cooperative owners, §42-2622.
  Definitions, §42-2621.
  Eligible residents, §§42-2622, 42-2623.
  Establishment of, §42-2622.
  Funding for, §42-2622.
  Issuance of rules and regulations, §42-2625.
  Residence requirements, §42-2623.
  Single family homes, purchase of, §42-2622.
  Starter home owners, §42-2622.
  Use of funds, §42-2622.
Tenant organizations, §42-2604.
Unexpended balance at end of year, disposition of, §42-2601.
Use of, §§42-2601, 42-2603.

HOME PURCHASES.
Opportunity accounts.
  Generally, §§1-307.61 to 1-307.74.
  Use to purchase primary residence, §1-307.68.

HOME REPAIRS.
Public assistance, §4-211.01.

HOME RULE, §§1-201.01 to 1-207.71.
Board of education.
  Continued, §1-207.19.
Budgets and budget estimates, §§1-204.41 to 1-204.53.
  See BUDGETS AND BUDGET ESTIMATES.
Charter.
  Amendment of, §1-203.03.
  Preamble, §1-203.01.
  Referendum, §§1-207.01 to 1-207.04.
Compensation from more than one source, §1-207.33.
Conflict of laws, §1-207.61.
Congress.
  Reservation of authority, §§1-206.01 to 1-206.04.
Construction and interpretation of act, §1-207.61.
  Severability of provisions, §1-207.62.
Council, §§1-204.01 to 1-204.13.
Court system continued, §1-207.18.
Definitions, §1-201.03.
District of Columbia home rule act.
  See Vol. 1.
Effective dates of provisions, §1-207.71.
Elections.
  Charter referendum, §§1-207.01 to 1-207.04.
40th anniversary celebration and commemoration.
  Sunset, §1-137.08.
Generally.
  See COUNCIL.
Governmental reorganization, §§1-204.01 to 1-204.04.
Initiative and referendum, §§1-204.101 to 1-204.107.
  See INITIATIVE AND REFERENDUM.
Interpretation of provisions, §1-207.61.
Legislative power, §1-203.02.
Mayor, §§1-204.21 to 1-204.23.
  See MAYOR.
Pending actions and proceedings not abated, §1-207.15.
Purposes, §1-201.02.
Recall of elected public officials, §§1-204.111 to 1-204.115.
  See RECALL OF ELECTED PUBLIC OFFICIALS.
Referendum.
  Charter referendum, §§1-207.01 to 1-207.04.

HOME RULE —Cont'd
Referendum —Cont'd
Initiative and referendum, §§1-204.101 to 1-204.107.
See INITIATIVE AND REFERENDUM.
Reserve funds, §1-204.50a.
RLA revitalization corporation, §1-202.01.
Severability of provisions, §1-207.62.
Short title, §1-201.01.
Succession in government, §§1-207.11 to 1-207.19.
Abolition of existing government, §1-207.11.
Delegated functions, §1-207.12.
Transfer of existing statutes, rules and regulations, §1-207.14.
Transfer of functions, §1-207.12.
Transfer of personnel, property and funds, §1-207.13.
Transition period.
Temporary provisions, §§1-207.21 to 1-207.24.

HOME SALES.
Department of housing and community development.
Employer-assisted housing program, §§42-2501 to 42-2507.
See GOVERNMENT EMPLOYER-ASSISTED HOUSING PROGRAM.
For sale signs, §42-1801.
Low and moderate income families.
Home purchase assistance fund, §§42-2601 to 42-2626.
See HOME PURCHASE ASSISTANCE FUND.
Real estate brokers and salespersons.
General provisions, §§42-1701 to 42-1709.
See REAL ESTATE BROKERS AND SALESPERSONS.
Residential real property sales disclosures, §§42-1301 to 42-1311.
Amendment of disclosure, §42-1308.
Applicability of chapter, §42-1301.
Change in conditions after delivery, §42-1304.
Delivery of report or opinion by professional or expert, §42-1303.
Delivery of required information to transferee by public agency.
Transferor's liability, §42-1303.
Disclosure requirements, §42-1305.

HOME SALES —Cont'd
Residential real property sales disclosures —Cont'd
Duty to comply imposed on transferor only, §42-1311.
Errors, inaccuracies, omissions. Transferor's liability, §42-1303.
Good faith disclosure, §42-1306.
Inapplicability of chapter, §42-1301.
Indication of compliance with chapter by transferor, §42-1302.
Licensed agency of transferor deemed in compliance with license obligations, §42-1307.
Methods for delivering disclosure statement, §42-1309.
Obligations created by laws, §42-1307.
Real property disclosure statement.
Signature and delivery of written statement by transferor, §42-1302.
Required disclosures, §42-1305.
Scope of transferor's liability, §42-1303.
Termination by transferee.
Notice of termination delivered to transferor, time, §42-1302.
Waiver of right, §42-1302.
Transfer not invalid because of failure to comply, §42-1310.
Unknown or unavailable information at time disclosure required, §42-1304.
Seller disclosures, §§42-1301 to 42-1311.

HOME SOLICITATION SALES.
Buyer's right to cancel, §28-3811.
Defined, §28-3811.
Generally, §28-3811.

HOMESTEAD DEDUCTION.
Cooperative housing associations, §§47-850.01 to 47-850.04, 47-3503.
Houses and condominium units, §47-850.
Real property taxes.
Houses and condominium units, §47-850.

HOMESTEAD HOUSING PRESERVATION, §§42-2101 to 42-2111.
Abatement agreements, §42-2108.
Appropriations, §42-2110.
Definitions, §42-2103.
Establishment of program and program administration, §42-2104.

HOMESTEAD HOUSING PRESERVATION —Cont'd

Guidelines, §42-2106.

Inventory, §42-2105.

Notice, §42-2111.

Policy declaration, §§42-2101, 42-2102.

Privatization of title services, §42-2105.01.

Publications, §42-2105.

Reports, §42-2110.

Sales, §42-2107.

Technical training program, §42-2109.

Transfers of property, §42-2107.

HOMICIDE.

Assault with intent to kill, §22-401.

Autopsies.

Medical examiners, §§5-1401 to 5-1419.

See MEDICAL EXAMINERS.

Comfort care orders.

Non-resuscitation procedures for EMS.

Forgery, concealment, withholding or placement causing resuscitation to be withheld and death results, §7-651.12.

Crime investigation records.

Retention of records in open homicide investigations, §5-113.32.

Do not resuscitate procedures.

Comfort care orders.

Falsification, forgery, other actions causing resuscitation to be withheld causing death, §7-651.12.

Euthanasia, §7-630.

Inheritance barred by, §19-320.

Insurance policies, §19-320.

Living wills and, §7-630.

Manslaughter, §22-2105.

See MANSLAUGHTER.

Mercy-killing, §7-630.

Murder generally.

See MURDER.

Negligent homicide as traffic law, §50-2203.01.

HOMOCYSTINURIA, §§7-831 to 7-840.

HOMOSEXUALS.

Domestic partner benefits.

General provisions, §§32-701 to 32-710.

See DOMESTIC PARTNER BENEFITS.

Domestic partnerships.

See DOMESTIC PARTNERSHIPS.

HOMOSEXUALS —Cont'd

Office of lesbian, gay, bisexual, transgender, and questioning affairs, §§2-1381 to 2-1384.

HOMOZYGOUS SICKLE CELL DISEASE, §§7-831 to 7-840.

HONORARIA.

Boards and commissions, §§1-321.01, 1-321.02.

Ethics and government accountability, §1-1162.26.

Senator or representative elected to represent District, §1-131.

HOODS.

Wearing, §22-3312.03.

HORIZONTAL PROPERTY REGIMES, §§42-2001 to 42-2031.

Access to units for repairs, §42-2008.

Assessments, §42-2017.

Audits, §42-2015.

Board of commissioners.

Authority vested in, §42-2031.

Bylaws, §§42-2013, 42-2014.

Common elements.

Actions relating to, §42-2024.

Defined, §42-2002.

Indivisibility of, §42-2007.

Proportionate share of, §42-2023.

Transfer of unit to include share in, §42-2010.

Undivided shares, held in, §42-2006.

Use of, §42-2008.

Common profits and expenses, §42-2016.

Condominiums.

General provisions, §§42-1901.01 to 42-1904.18.

See CONDOMINIUMS.

Conflicts of law, §42-2027.

Conversions to condominiums.

Council allowed to prohibit, §42-2051.

Deeds for units, §42-2006.

Definitions, §42-2002.

Electricity.

Submetering, §§34-1551 to 34-1553.

Eminent domain, §42-2029.

Examination of books and records, §42-2015.

Fee simple estates, §42-2006.

Fixed market values, lack of, §42-2006.

Forfeitures, §42-2023.

Hazard insurance, §§42-2020 to 42-2022.

Identification of units, §42-2023.

HORIZONTAL PROPERTY REGIMES —Cont'd

Incidents of real property, units as, §42-2004.

Indemnification, §42-2018.

Individual units, transfer of, §42-2004.

Insurance requirements, §§42-2020 to 42-2022.

Interpretation of provisions, §§42-2029, 42-2031.

Issuance of rules and regulations, §42-2028.

Joint and several liability, §42-2018.

Joint tenants, §42-2005.

Liens.

Common expenses, §42-2016.

Individual units, only against, §42-2025.

Materialmen's liens, §42-2025.

Mechanics' liens, §42-2025.

Priority of, §§42-2017, 42-2019.

Removal of, §42-2025.

Supplemental method of enforcement, §42-2019.

Written statement of payments due under, §42-2019.

Mergers and consolidations, §42-2012.

Natural gas.

Submetering, §§34-1551 to 34-1553.

Partition, §42-2007.

Percentages of ownership, §42-2006.

Perpetuities, §42-2026.

Plat of subdivision, §42-2009.

Public utilities.

Submetering, §§34-1551 to 34-1553.

Reconstitution, §42-2012.

Reconstruction, §§42-2021, 42-2022.

Recordation of instruments.

Individual units, transfers of, §42-2004.

Ownership percentages, declaration of, §42-2006.

Plat of subdivision, §§42-2009, 42-2010.

Records, §42-2015.

Rental housing conversion and sale.

General provisions, §§42-3401.01 to 42-3405.13.

See RENTAL HOUSING.

Repair and maintenance.

Access to units for repairs, §42-2008.

Mandatory contribution to, §42-2016.

Subdivision.

Certification and recordation, §42-2009.

HORIZONTAL PROPERTY REGIMES —Cont'd

Subdivision —Cont'd

Establishment by, §42-2003.

Plat of, §§42-2009, 42-2010.

Taxation, §§42-2016, 42-2017, 42-2023, 42-2029.

Tenants by the entirety, §42-2005.

Tenants in common, §42-2005.

Termination of, §42-2011.

Unreasonable restraints on alienation, §42-2026.

Voting on percentage basis, §42-2006.

Waiver of regime, §42-2011.

Water supply and waterworks, §42-2030.

Zoning, §42-2028.

HORMONE REPLACEMENT THERAPY.

Women's rights to health insurance coverage, §§31-3831 to 31-3837.

HORSE-DRAWN CARRIAGES, §§8-2001 to 8-2013.

Care and use of horses in trade, §8-2005.

Carriage and equipment requirements, §8-2006.

Definitions, §8-2001.

Examination of horses by veterinarian, §8-2003.

Fines, §8-2012.

Identification cards required for owners, operators, and custodians, §8-2004.

Issuance of rules, §8-2013.

Loading zones, §8-2009.

Operating under the influence, §50-2206.16.

Public works.

Use of horse-drawn vehicles in, §9-1209.03.

Records, §8-2011.

Requirements and prohibitions regarding, §8-2002.

Sick or injured horses, §8-2010.

Stables, §8-2008.

Weather conditions and operation of, §8-2007.

HORSES.

Footways in public grounds, driving or riding on, §22-1318.

Horse-drawn carriages, §§8-2001 to 8-2013.

See HORSE-DRAWN CARRIAGES.

Public works, use in, §9-1209.03.

HOSPICE.
Anatomical gifts.
Duties regarding, §7-1531.13.
Decedent's body or parts, §7-1531.24.
Certificate requirement, §7-1531.26.
Rulemaking, §7-1531.27.
General provisions, §§7-1531.01 to 7-1531.28.
See ANATOMICAL GIFTS.
Clinical privileges and staff membership.
Reduction, suspension, revocation, not renewed.
Reporting, §44-508.
Standards, §44-507.
Criminal background checks for unlicensed personnel, §§44-551 to 44-554.
Confidentiality, §44-552.
Rules, §44-554.
Unauthorized release, penalties, §44-553.
Convictions prohibiting employment, §44-552.
Definitions, §44-551.
Required, §44-552.
District of Columbia general hospital hospice program, §§4-1101 to 4-1105.
Appropriations, §4-1103.
Definition, §4-1101.
Established, §4-1102.
Report, §4-1105.
Rules, §4-1104.
Enjoining violations, §44-509.
Fines and penalties, §44-509.
Licenses, §§44-501 to 44-509.
Applications, §44-502.
Definitions, §44-501.
Inspection, §44-505.
Mayor's authority, §44-503.
Provisional and restricted licenses, §44-506.
Requirements, §44-502.
Rules, §44-504.
Unlawful to operate without, §44-502.
Violations, penalties, enforcement, §44-509.

HOSPITAL AND MEDICAL SERVICES CORPORATIONS, §§31-3501 to 31-3524.
Appeals, §31-3522.
Applicability of other laws, §31-3503.
Board of directors or trustees.
Fiduciary duties of, §31-3520.

HOSPITAL AND MEDICAL SERVICES CORPORATIONS
—Cont'd
Board of directors or trustees
—Cont'd
Organization and membership, §31-3518.
Powers and duties, §31-3520.
Reports to, §31-3519.
Violations, penalties, and fines, §31-3521.
Certificates of authority.
Application for, §31-3504.
Requirements to obtain, §31-3505.
Claims for reimbursement by providers, §§31-3131 to 31-3138.
See HEALTH INSURANCE.
Clinical trials insurance coverage, §§31-2993.01 to 31-2993.03.
Community health reinvestment.
Compliance and implementation of obligations, §31-3506.01.
Excessive surplus, §31-3506.
Requirements, §31-3505.01.
Continuation of coverage.
Employer's health benefits plans.
Employees and dependents, §§32-731 to 32-734.
Definitions, §31-3501.
Emergency medical services.
HIV screening test while receiving emergency medical services, §31-2803.
Reimbursement for, §§31-2801, 31-2802.
Employer's health benefits plans.
Continuation of coverage.
Employees and dependents, §§32-731 to 32-734.
Exclusivity of provisions, §31-3502.
Fiduciary duties of board of directors or trustees, §31-3520.
Fines, §31-3521.
For-profit company, conversion to prohibited, §31-3515.
Group Hospitalization and Medical Services, Inc.
Regulatory authority of council, §31-3523.01.
Healthy DC and health care expansion fund and program, §§4-631 to 4-638, 31-3514.02.
Healthy DC fund and program, §31-3514.02.
HIV screening test while receiving emergency medical services.
Coverage, §31-2803.

HOSPITAL AND MEDICAL SERVICES CORPORATIONS
—Cont'd

Investments, §31-3510.
Issuance of rules and regulations, §31-3524.
Management contracts, §31-3517.
Mutual company, conversion to prohibited, §31-3516.
Penalties, §31-3521.
Prostate cancer screening.
  Coverage, §§31-2951 to 31-2954.
Provider contracts, filing, §31-3507.
Rates, filing, §31-3508.
Reimbursement, health benefits plans.
  Claims for reimbursement by providers, §§31-3131 to 31-3138.
  See HEALTH INSURANCE.
Reports.
  Board of directors or trustees, §31-3519.
  Mayor, §31-3513.
Reserves required, §31-3509.
Service agreements, §31-3517.
Stock company, conversion to, §31-3515.
Subscriber contracts.
  Filing, §31-3508.
  Group standard provisions, §31-3512.
Surplus.
  Notes, §31-3511.
  Requirements for, §31-3506.
Taxation, §§31-205, 31-3514.01.
  Deductions, §47-2608.
Transition provisions, §31-3523.
Violations, §31-3521.
Voluntary withdrawal by health benefit plan carriers, §§31-3151 to 31-3154.

HOSPITAL DISCHARGE PLANNING, §§21-2231.01 to 21-2231.05.

Construction of subchapter, §21-2231.04.
Definitions, §21-2231.01.
Hospital discharge plan, §21-2231.03.
Lay caregiver designation, §21-2231.02.
Rules, §21-2231.05.

HOSPITALIZATION OF PERSONS WITH MENTAL ILLNESS, §§21-501 to 21-592, MentalHealth Rules 1 to 17.

Appeal of final determination.
  Notice of right to appeal, MentalHealth Rule 6.

HOSPITALIZATION OF PERSONS WITH MENTAL ILLNESS
—Cont'd

Appointment of counsel, §21-543, MentalHealth Rule 12.
Emergency detention, MentalHealth Rule 2.
Prisoner's commitment to mental institution, MentalHealth Rule 10.
Arrest of person believed to be mentally ill, §21-521.
Civil procedure rules.
  Applicability, MentalHealth Rule 12.
Civil rights, retention, §21-564.
Commission on Mental Health, §§21-502, 21-503.
  Proceedings, MentalHealth Rule 3.
  Civil procedure rules, applicability of, MentalHealth Rule 12.
  Report, MentalHealth Rule 3.
  Court hearing on report, MentalHealth Rule 4.
Renewal of commitment.
  Judicial review, MentalHealth Rule 7.
Competence to proceed.
  Criminal defendants, §§24-531.01 to 24-531.13.
  See COMPETENCE TO PROCEED.
Confidentiality of transcripts, MentalHealth Rule 12.
Construction of rules, MentalHealth Rule 1.
Convalescent leave.
  Periodic review of committed person, MentalHealth Rule 8.
Court filings.
  Form, MentalHealth Rule 14.
  Signing of filings, MentalHealth Rule 15.
Court-ordered commitment, §§21-541 to 21-551.
  Appointment of counsel, §21-543.
  Attorney's compensation, §21-543.
  Bonds, surety, §21-550.
  Civil procedure rules, applicability of, MentalHealth Rule 12.
  Continuation, §21-543.
  Determination by commission, §21-544.
  Discovery.
    Limited discovery in a commitment trial, MentalHealth Rule 17.
  Dismissal of petition, §21-545.
  Emergency hospitalization, §§21-523 to 21-528.

**HOSPITALIZATION OF PERSONS
WITH MENTAL ILLNESS**
—Cont'd
Court-ordered commitment —Cont'd
Examinations, §21-546.
Hearings.
Civil procedure rules, applicability
of, MentalHealth Rule 12.
Commission, §21-542.
Report of commission, court
hearing on, MentalHealth
Rule 4.
Court or jury, §21-545.
Disposition hearing, MentalHealth
Rule 6.
Jury trials, §21-544.
Nonresidents, §21-551.
Notice to person for whom petition is
forwarded to court, §21-541.
Order of hospitalization, §21-545.
Petition for commitment, §21-541.
Petition for release, §§21-546, 21-547.
Recess for counsel to prepare or for
good cause, §21-543.
Release of patient, §§21-546, 21-549.
Renewal of commitment by
commission, §21-545.01.
Judicial review, MentalHealth Rule
7.
Reports, §21-544.
Commission on mental health,
MentalHealth Rule 3.
Court hearing on report,
MentalHealth Rule 4.
Revocation of outpatient status,
§21-548.
Rights of person affected, §§21-542 to
21-544.
Right to counsel, §21-543.
Superior court review of commission
determination.
Renewal of commitment status,
§21-545.01.
Witnesses, §§21-545, 21-547.
Crimes and offenses, §21-591.
Definitions, §21-501.
**Detention of person pending judicial
proceedings,** §21-528.
Discovery, MentalHealth Rule 17.
Disposition hearings and orders,
MentalHealth Rule 6.
Electronic filing, MentalHealth Rule
14.
Emergency detention proceedings,
MentalHealth Rule 2.
Medical and psychiatric care and
treatment for emergency
involuntary patient, §21-562.

**HOSPITALIZATION OF PERSONS
WITH MENTAL ILLNESS**
—Cont'd
Emergency hospitalization, §§21-521
to 21-528, MentalHealth Rule 2.
Admission to hospital, §21-522.
Court orders, §§21-523 to 21-528.
Determination by court, §21-524.
Hearing, §21-525.
Required for hospitalization beyond
48 hours, §21-523.
Detention of person pending judicial
proceedings, §21-528.
Examination of patient, §§21-522,
21-527.
Hearings, §21-525.
Minimum and maximum period of
detention, §§21-523, 21-526.
Release of patient, §21-527.
Escaped patients, return of, §21-592.
Escapees, return of, MentalHealth
Rule 11.
**Examinations of persons with
mental illness.**
Commission, by, §21-503.
Court-ordered hospitalization, §21-546.
Emergency hospitalization, §§21-522,
21-527.
Federal reservations, persons found in,
§21-906.
Qualified psychologists, by, §21-501.01.
Expert witnesses, MentalHealth Rules
12, 17.
**Federal reservations, persons found
in,** §§21-901 to 21-909.
Application for admission, §21-904.
Apprehension of persons believed to
have mental illness, §21-903.
Care in Veterans' Administration
facility, §21-908.
Commitments.
Application for admission, §21-904.
Apprehension of persons believed to
have mental illness, §21-903.
Examination of person committed,
§21-906.
Proceedings for adjudication,
§21-906.
Special commissioners committing,
§21-902.
Superintendent to receive persons
committed or apprehended,
§21-905.
Expenses of transfer, payment,
§21-909.
Hearings.
Apprehension of persons believed to
have mental illness, §21-903.

HOSPITALIZATION OF PERSONS WITH MENTAL ILLNESS
—Cont'd

Federal reservations, persons found in —Cont'd

Mental illness defined, §21-901.

Mentally ill person defined, §21-901.

Military personnel transferred to custody of service, §21-907.

Special commissioners.

Commitments by, §21-902.

Financial responsibility for care of hospitalized person, §21-586.

Fines, §21-591.

Forms used for, §21-588.

Hearings, §21-503.

Commission on Mental Health proceedings, MentalHealth Rule 3.

Court hearing on report, MentalHealth Rule 4.

Court-ordered commitment.

Commission, §21-542.

Court or jury, §21-545.

Disposition hearings, MentalHealth Rule 6.

Emergency hospitalization, §21-525, MentalHealth Rule 2.

Prisoner's commitment to mental institution, MentalHealth Rule 10.

Release proceedings, MentalHealth Rule 9.

Incompetency, notice regarding, §21-581.

Incompetent criminal defendants, §§24-531.01 to 24-531.13.

See COMPETENCE TO PROCEED.

Interim provisions for term of commitment, §21-589.01.

Law student practice, FamDiv Rule M.

Mail privileges and rights, §21-561.

Mayor, proceedings instituted by, §21-581.

Medical care and treatment, §21-562.

Medical records, §21-562.

Military, §§21-587, 21-907, 21-908.

Minors admitted in emergency.

Notice to parent or guardian, §21-522.

Minors released.

Notice to parent or guardian, §21-527.

Nonprotesting and voluntary hospitalization, §§21-511 to 21-514.

Release of voluntary patient, §21-512.

Notice.

Appeal, right to, MentalHealth Rule 6.

HOSPITALIZATION OF PERSONS WITH MENTAL ILLNESS
—Cont'd

Notice —Cont'd

Commission on Mental Health determinations, MentalHealth Rule 3.

Court-ordered commitment, §21-541.

Decision not to seek renewal of commitment, MentalHealth Rule 6.

Emergency detention proceedings, MentalHealth Rule 2.

Incompetency, notice regarding, §21-581.

Prisoners.

Commitment to mental institutions.

Notice of petition and hearing, MentalHealth Rule 9.

Release of patient, §21-527.

Penalties, §21-591.

Periodic review of committed person on convalescent leave, MentalHealth Rule 8.

Physicians, §§21-582, 21-583.

Pretrial conferences, MentalHealth Rule 16.

Prior to September 15, 1964, §§21-564, 21-589.

Prisoner's commitment to mental institution, MentalHealth Rule 10.

Escapees, MentalHealth Rule 11.

Prison, prohibition on confinement in, §21-585.

Property rights of patients, §21-564.

Psychiatric care and treatment, §21-562.

Psychiatric examinations, §§21-501.01, 21-503.

Psychiatrists, §21-583.

Qualified psychologists, §§21-501, 21-501.01, 21-582, 21-583.

Release of patient.

Court-ordered hospitalization, §§21-546, 21-549, MentalHealth Rule 9.

Emergency hospitalization, §21-527, MentalHealth Rule 2.

Federal reservations, persons found in, §21-904.

Nonprotesting patients, §21-514.

Notice of release, §21-527.

Statement of release, §21-565.

Voluntary patients, §21-512.

Renewal of commitment by commission, §21-545.01.

Judicial review, MentalHealth Rule 7.

HOSPITALIZATION OF PERSONS WITH MENTAL ILLNESS —Cont'd

Reports.
Commission on Mental Health, MentalHealth Rule 3.
Court hearing on report, MentalHealth Rule 4.
Court-ordered commitment, §21-544.
Restraints, use of, §21-563.
Revocation of outpatient status, §21-548.
Rights of patients, §§21-561 to 21-565.
Scope of rules, MentalHealth Rule 1.
Seclusion or restraints, freedom from, §21-563.
Service of process.
Commission on Mental Health reports, MentalHealth Rule 3.
Time for service by mail or service of affidavit, MentalHealth Rule 13.
Statement supplied to patient or relatives, §21-565.
Subpoenas, §21-503.
Support and maintenance, §21-586.
Time computation and enlargement, MentalHealth Rule 13.
Transfers, §§21-907, 21-909.
Trials.
Court-ordered commitment, §21-544.
Limited discovery in a commitment trial, MentalHealth Rule 17.
Mental illness and dangerousness issues, MentalHealth Rule 5.
Prisoner's commitment to mental institution, MentalHealth Rule 10.
Request for jury trial, MentalHealth Rule 4.
Veterans, §21-587.
Visitors, §21-561.
Voluntary and nonprotesting hospitalization, §§21-511 to 21-514.
Admission as voluntary patient, §21-511.
Application to become voluntary patient, §21-511.
Discharge planning, §21-512.
Hospitalization of nonprotesting patients, §21-513.
Release, §21-514.
Release, §21-512.
Hospitalized nonprotesting persons, §21-514.
Statement that person does not object to hospitalization, §21-513.

HOSPITALIZATION OF PERSONS WITH MENTAL ILLNESS —Cont'd

Voluntary and nonprotesting hospitalization —Cont'd
Voluntary outpatient treatment, §21-511.
Voluntary outpatient treatment, §21-511.
Witnesses, §21-503.
Court-ordered hospitalization, §§21-545, 21-547.
Expert witnesses, MentalHealth Rules 12, 17.
Fees, §21-584.
Physicians, psychiatrists, and qualified psychologists as, §21-584.

HOSPITAL LIENS, §§40-201 to 40-205.
Accident cases.
Recovery for services provided in, §40-201.
Docket for, §40-205.
Failure to pay, §40-203.
Notice, §40-202.
Records of hospital.
Examination of, §40-204.

HOSPITALS.
Alcoholic beverage licenses.
Exceptions to license requirements, §25-103.
Anatomical gifts.
Coordination of procurement and use, §7-1531.14.
Duties of hospitals, §7-1531.13.
Decedent's body or parts, §7-1531.24.
Certificate requirement, §7-1531.26.
Rulemaking, §7-1531.27.
General provisions, §§7-1531.01 to 7-1531.28.
See ANATOMICAL GIFTS.
Birthing hospitals.
Parentage acknowledgment programs required of, §16-909.03.
Childhood lead poisoning screening and reporting, §§7-871.01 to 7-871.06.
Clinical health services, fees for, §44-731.
Clinical laboratories.
General provisions, §§44-201 to 44-213.
See CLINICAL LABORATORIES.

HOSPITALS —Cont'd
Clinical privileges and staff membership.
Reduction, suspension, revocation, not renewed.
Reporting, §44-508.
Standards, §44-507.
Columbia Hospital for Women.
Conveyance of property to, §44-751.
Lien in favor of United States, §44-753.
Communicable diseases.
Treatment of, §44-701.
Contract care for indigents, §44-706.
Correction department's use of D.C. General Hospital's campus, §24-211.61.
Crimes and offenses.
Failure to report certain deaths, §5-1406.
Criminal background checks for unlicensed personnel, §§44-551 to 44-554.
Confidentiality, §44-552.
Rules, §44-554.
Unauthorized release, penalties, §44-553.
Convictions prohibiting employment, §44-552.
Definitions, §44-551.
Required, §44-552.
Dead bodies.
Duty to report certain deaths to medical examiner, §5-1405.
Failure to report certain deaths, §5-1406.
Denial of treatment due to inability to pay, §47-2716.
Discharge of patients.
Hospital discharge planning, §§21-2231.01 to 21-2231.05.
Discharge planning, §§21-2231.01 to 21-2231.05.
Construction of subchapter, §21-2231.04.
Definitions, §21-2231.01.
Hospital discharge plan, §21-2231.03.
Lay caregiver designation, §21-2231.02.
Rules, §21-2231.05.
District of Columbia General Hospital.
Hospice program, §§4-1101 to 4-1105.
Human Services Department, under control of, §7-180.
Rates schedule, §47-2713.

HOSPITALS —Cont'd
Emergency services.
Hospital and medical services corporations.
HIV screening test while receiving emergency medical services, §31-2803.
Reimbursed for emergency medical services, §§31-2801, 31-2802.
Indigent persons, §44-704.
Trauma care system, §7-2341.19.
Enjoining violations, §44-509.
Fines and penalties, §44-509.
Firearms or weapons injuries.
Reporting, §§7-2601 to 7-2603.
Glen Dale Hospital rates schedule, §47-2715.
Greater Southeast community hospital.
Capital equipment fund, §1-325.71.
Real property tax abatement, §47-1050.
Health care entity conversion act, §§44-601 to 44-610.
Health maintenance organizations.
General provisions, §§31-3401 to 31-3431.
See HEALTH MAINTENANCE ORGANIZATIONS.
Hospital and medical services corporations.
General provisions, §§31-3501 to 31-3524.
See HOSPITAL AND MEDICAL SERVICES CORPORATIONS.
Hospital discharge planning, §§21-2231.01 to 21-2231.05.
Inability to pay.
Denial of treatment due to, §47-2716.
Indigent persons.
Treatment and admission, §§44-704 to 44-706.
Lead poisoning.
Childhood lead poisoning screening and reporting, §§7-871.01 to 7-871.06.
Licenses, §§44-501 to 44-509.
Applications, §44-502.
Definitions, §44-501.
Inspection, §44-505.
Mayor's authority, §44-503.
Provisional and restricted licenses, §44-506.
Requirements, §44-502.
Rules, §44-504.
Unlawful to operate without, §44-502.

HOSPITALS —Cont'd
Liens, §§40-201 to 40-205.
Malpractice.
  Medical malpractice, §§16-2801 to 16-2841.
    See MEDICAL MALPRACTICE.
Medicaid.
  Hospital assessments.
    Expiration of provisions, §44-638.
  Hospital inpatient rate supplement 2016-2017, §§44-662.11 to 44-662.18.
    Definitions, §44-662.11.
    Federal determination of assessment, §44-662.16.
    Hospital fund, §44-662.12.
    Hospital provider fee, §§44-662.13, 44-662.14.
    Multi-hospital systems, closure, merger and new hospitals, §44-662.15.
    Quarterly notice and collection of fees and payments, §44-662.14.
    Rules, §44-662.17.
    Sunset provision, §44-662.18.
    Suspension and termination of assessment, §44-662.16.
  Hospital outpatient supplemental payment.
    Expiration of provisions, §44-659.
  Hospital outpatient supplemental payment 2016-2017, §§44-661.11 to 44-661.19.
    Definitions, §44-661.11.
    Hospital provider fee, §§44-661.13, 44-661.14.
    Hospital provider fee fund, §44-661.12.
    Multi-hospital systems, closure, merger and new hospitals, §44-661.17.
    Outpatient hospital access payments, §44-661.15.
    Quarterly notice and collection of fees and payments, §44-661.16.
    Rules, §44-661.18.
    Sunset provision, §44-661.19.
Medicaid, hospital assessments.
  See MEDICAID.
Mental illness, hospitalization of persons with, §§21-501 to 21-592, MentalHealth Rules 1 to 17.
  See HOSPITALIZATION OF PERSONS WITH MENTAL ILLNESS.
Needy patients.
  Cash payments to, §44-705.

HOSPITALS —Cont'd
Newborn hearing screening, §§7-851 to 7-855.
Newborn heart screening, §§7-857.01 to 7-857.04.
"No Smoking" signs, §7-1703.
Not-for-profit hospital corporations, §§44-951.01 to 44-951.18.
  See NOT-FOR-PROFIT HOSPITAL CORPORATIONS.
Parentage acknowledgment programs required of birthing hospitals, §16-909.03.
Patients.
  Hospital discharge planning, §§21-2231.01 to 21-2231.05.
  Stipends for, §44-707.
Prisons and prisoners.
  Correction department's use of D.C. General Hospital's campus, §24-211.61.
Providence Hospital established as teaching hospital for nurses and interns, §44-703.
Public lands.
  Reservation 13.
    Health care facility set aside, §10-1502.
Real property exempt from taxation, §47-1002.
Resident employees.
  Stipends for, §44-707.
St. Elizabeth's Hospital.
  Commitment of prisoners to mental institution, MentalHealth Rule 10.
  Escapees, MentalHealth Rule 11.
  Mental health services administration, §§44-901 to 44-922.
    See MENTAL HEALTH SERVICES ADMINISTRATION.
Smoking, §7-1703.
Strokes, §§44-1151 to 44-1159.
  See STROKES.
Surgery.
  See SURGERY.
Training.
  Benefits in lieu of salary, §44-708.
  Providence Hospital established as teaching hospital for nurses and interns, §44-703.
  Stipends for patients and resident employees, §44-707.
Trauma care system, §7-2341.19.
Violations, penalties, enforcement, §44-509.
Wages and salaries.
  Benefits in lieu of pay, §44-708.

HOSPITALS —Cont'd
Wages and salaries —Cont'd
Patients.
Stipends for, §44-707.
Resident employees.
Stipends for, §44-707.
Walter Reed Army Medical Center,
§§10-1901 to 10-1906.

HOTELS.
Alcoholic beverage licenses.
Mini bars, §25-723.
On-premises retailers, §25-113.
Convention center hotel,
§§10-1221.01 to 10-1221.13.
See CONVENTION CENTER HOTEL.
Generally, §§30-101 to 30-103.
See LODGING PLACES.
Labor-peace agreement for public participation in hotel projects,
§§32-851 to 32-856.
Smoking, §7-741.03.

HOTLINES.
Business licenses, §47-2881.
Domestic violence hotline, §§4-551 to 4-553.
Human trafficking, §22-1843.
School residency false information hotline, §38-312.01.

HOT PURSUIT, §§23-901 to 23-903.

HOURS OF WORK.
Building service employees.
Minimum work hours, §§32-1051.01 to 32-1051.17.
Fire departments, §5-405.
Metropolitan police, §5-1304.
Public officers and employees,
§1-612.01.
Secret Service Uniform Division,
§5-1304.
Student health nurse, §38-621.
United States park police, §5-1304.

HOUSE OF REPRESENTATIVES, US
Const Art I §§1, 2, 4, 5.
Absent members, US Const Art I §5.
Arrest of members, US Const Art I §6.
Compensation of members, US Const
Art I §6, Amd 27.
Debate, US Const Art I §6.
Elections, US Const Art I §§2, 4.
Judge of elections, returns and qualifications of members, US
Const Art I §5.
Qualifications of electors, US Const
Art I §2.

HOUSE OF REPRESENTATIVES
—Cont'd
Elections —Cont'd
Returns.
Judge of returns, US Const Art I §5.
Taxation.
Denial or abridgement of right to vote for failure to pay poll tax prohibited, US Const Amd 24.
Times, places and manner of holding, US Const Art I §4.
Expulsion of member, US Const Art I §5.
Freedom of speech, US Const Art I §6.
Holding other office, US Const Art I §6.
Impeachment, US Const Art I §2.
Journals, US Const Art I §§5, 7.
Libel and slander.
Privilege of members, US Const Art I §6.
Officers, US Const Art I §2.
Presidential elector.
Representative ineligible, US Const Art II §1.
Punishment of members, US Const Art I §5.
Qualifications.
Electors, US Const Art I §2.
Members, US Const Art I §2.
Judge of qualifications, US Const Art I §5.
Revenue bills, US Const Art I §7.
Rules of procedure, US Const Art I §5.
Speaker, US Const Art I §2.
Term, US Const Art I §2.
Vacancies in office, US Const Art I §2.
Vice-president of the United States.
Vacancy in office.
Confirmation on nomination of president, US Const Amd 25.

HOUSING.
Affordable housing clearinghouse directory, §§42-2131 to 42-2136.
Affordable housing development request for inclusion, §42-2134.
Agency submission of data to mayor, §42-2133.
Contents of inventory information, §42-2135.
Definitions, §§42-2131, 42-2151.01.
Inventory, §§42-2132, 42-2135.
List of developments, §42-2136.
Locator, §42-2132.
Affordable housing inventory comprehensive tracking plan.
Definitions, §42-2141.

HOUSING —Cont'd

Affordable housing inventory comprehensive tracking plan —Cont'd

Requirements for tracking, §42-2142.

Alterations to occupied units after notice to vacate, §§6-731.01 to 6-731.04.

Attorneys' fees and costs, §42-3509.02.

Building code.

General provisions, §§6-501 to 6-919. See BUILDING CODE.

Business licenses, §47-2828.

Child abuse and neglect.

Public housing resident managers. Reporting requirements, §4-1321.02.

Comprehensive housing strategy task force, §§6-1051 to 6-1054.

Comprehensive plan.

Housing linkage requirement of the housing element, §§1-306.31 to 1-306.45.

Condominiums.

General provisions, §§42-1901.01 to 42-1904.18. See CONDOMINIUMS.

Construction codes.

General provisions, §§6-1401 to 6-1409. See CONSTRUCTION CODES.

Conversion into lodging places, §42-3506.01.

Cooperative housing associations.

Interest.

Maximum rate on share, §28-3301.

Secondary financing.

Required conditions, §28-3301.

Correction of conditions violative of law, §§42-3131.01 to 42-3131.03.

Crime victims' compensation.

Temporary housing costs, VictComp Rule 29.

Definitions, §42-3501.03.

Demolition for construction or expansion of lodging places, §42-3506.02.

Department of housing and community development.

Chief financial officer, §1-301.141.

Employer-assisted housing program, §§42-2501 to 42-2507. See GOVERNMENT EMPLOYER-ASSISTED HOUSING PROGRAM.

Unified fund, §42-2857.01.

HOUSING —Cont'd

Disabilities, persons with.

Equal access for blind persons and other persons with physical disabilities, §7-1006.

Distressed properties, improvement of, §§42-3508.04, 42-3508.05.

District of Columbia housing authority, §§6-201 to 6-229. See DISTRICT OF COLUMBIA HOUSING AUTHORITY.

Drug, firearm, or prostitution-related nuisance abatement, §§42-3101 to 42-3114. See CRIME-RELATED NUISANCE ABATEMENT.

Drug-free zones.

Public housing, §48-904.07a.

Drug-related evictions, §§42-3601 to 42-3610. See DRUG-RELATED EVICTIONS.

Ejectment.

Generally, §§16-1101 to 16-1124. See EJECTMENT.

Fines, §42-3509.01.

Firearms.

Enhanced penalties and fines for carrying guns into gun free zones, §22-4502.01.

Fraud and deceit, §42-3509.01.

Height of buildings, §§6-601.05 to 6-611.02. See BUILDING CODE.

Home purchase assistance fund, §§42-2601 to 42-2626. See HOME PURCHASE ASSISTANCE FUND.

Homestead housing preservation, §§42-2101 to 42-2111. See HOMESTEAD HOUSING PRESERVATION.

Horizontal property regimes, §§42-2001 to 42-2031. See HORIZONTAL PROPERTY REGIMES.

Housing assistance fund, §42-3531.09.

Housing finance agency.

General provisions, §§42-2701.01 to 42-2706.05. See HOUSING FINANCE AGENCY.

Housing linkage requirement of the housing element.

Comprehensive plan, §§1-306.31 to 1-306.45.

Housing production trust fund, §§42-2801 to 42-2804.

Bond issues, §§42-2812.01 to 42-2812.12.

HOUSING —Cont'd
Housing redevelopment.
General provisions, §§6-311.01 to
6-341.05.
See URBAN RENEWAL.
Inspection of rental housing,
§42-3509.08.
**Lead service line priority
replacement assistance,**
§§34-2151 to 34-2156.
See LEAD SERVICE LINE PRIORITY
REPLACEMENT ASSISTANCE.
Locator fees, §28-3819.
Lodging places.
Conversion into, §42-3506.01.
Demolition for construction or
expansion of, §42-3506.02.
**Lower income home ownership tax
abatement and incentives,**
§§47-3501 to 47-3508.
Low-income housing tax credit,
§§47-4801 to 47-4812.
See LOW-INCOME HOUSING TAX
CREDIT.
Low-income housing tax credit fund,
§42-2853.02.
Definitions, §42-2853.01.
Metropolitan police.
Housing assistance and community
safety program, §§42-2901 to
42-2903.
Municipal center.
Buildings acquired for, §10-602.
National Capital Housing Authority.
General provisions, §§6-101.01 to
6-103.01.
See NATIONAL CAPITAL
HOUSING AUTHORITY.
National housing act, §28-3307.
New rental housing, §§42-3508.01 to
42-3508.03.
**Nonprofit affordable housing
developer tax relief,** §47-1005.02.
Opportunity accounts.
Generally, §§1-307.61 to 1-307.74.
Use to purchase primary residence,
§1-307.68.
Pay-for-success contracts, §§2-211.01
to 2-211.03.
**Pet ownership restriction in
assisted housing,** §§8-2031 to
8-2035.
Policy declaration, §§42-3501.01,
42-3501.02.
**Preservation and rehabilitation of
government-supported housing,**
§§42-2851.01 to 42-2851.08.

HOUSING —Cont'd
Real property exempt from taxation,
§47-1005.
Rental housing act, §§42-3501.01 to
42-3509.08.
See LANDLORD AND TENANT.
Rental housing conversion and sale.
General provisions, §§42-3401.01 to
42-3405.13.
See RENTAL HOUSING.
Rent stabilization program,
§§42-3502.01 to 42-3502.23.
See RENT CONTROL.
Rent supplement program, §6-226.
Capital-based assistance, §6-229.
Tenant-based assistance, §6-228.
Voucher assistance, §6-227.
**Senior citizens' home repair and
improvement program fund,**
§§42-2201 to 42-2207.
Appropriations, §42-2203.
Definitions, §42-2201.
Eligibility for loans, §42-2204.
Establishment of, §42-2202.
Financial sources for, §42-2203.
Gifts, §42-2203.
Grants, §42-2203.
Issuance of rules and regulations,
§42-2206.
Repayment of loans, §42-2205.
Reports, §42-2207.
**Single-room-occupancy housing
development incentives,**
§42-3508.06.
Smoke detectors, §§6-751.01, 6-751.02.
See SMOKE DETECTORS.
Surrender of possession, §§42-3207,
42-3212, 42-3222 to 42-3227.
**Tax abatement for new residential
developments,** §§47-857.01 to
47-857.10, 47-859.01 to 47-859.05.
Truth in affordability reporting.
Calculation and reporting of
affordability, §42-2151.02.
Definitions, §42-2151.01.
Vacant rental housing, §§42-3508.01
to 42-3508.03.
Water lines.
Lead service line priority replacement
assistance, §§34-2151 to 34-2156.
**Workforce housing production
program,** §§6-1061.01 to 6-1061.04.

**HOUSING AND COMMUNITY
DEVELOPMENT DEPARTMENT.**
Chief financial officer, §1-301.141.

HOUSING AND COMMUNITY DEVELOPMENT DEPARTMENT
—Cont'd
Rental accommodations and rental conversions and sales,
§§42-3502.03, 42-3502.04a.
Housing regulation administrator, §42-3502.04c.
Public accessible rent control housing clearinghouse, §42-3502.03c.
Transfer of functions to housing and community development department, §42-3502.04b.

HOUSING AND COMMUNITY DEVELOPMENT REFORM ADVISORY COMMISSION,
§§6-1031 to 6-1037.
Administrative and technical support, §6-1034.
Advisory groups, committees, subcommittees, §6-1034.
Chairperson, §6-1032.
Compensation and expenses, §6-1036.
Dissolution, §6-1037.
Establishment, §6-1032.
Funding, §6-1036.
Information necessary to carry out responsibilities.
Requesting, §6-1034.
Meetings, §6-1035.
Members, §6-1032.
Quorum, §6-1035.
Report, §6-1033.
Research, surveys, prepare reports, other duties.
Contracts for, §6-1034.
Responsibilities, §6-1033.
Short title, §6-1031.
Transcript of proceedings, §6-1035.

HOUSING ASSISTANCE FUND,
§42-3531.09.

HOUSING AUTHORITY.
District of Columbia housing authority, §§6-201 to 6-229.
See DISTRICT OF COLUMBIA HOUSING AUTHORITY.

HOUSING FINANCE AGENCY,
§§42-2701.01 to 42-2706.05.
Accounts and accounting.
Payments out of accounts, §42-2704.11.
Administrative procedure, §42-2705.01.
Advisory committee, §42-2705.02.
Audits, §42-2705.04.

HOUSING FINANCE AGENCY
—Cont'd
Board of directors, §§42-2702.02 to 42-2702.05.
Bond issues, §§42-2704.02 to 42-2704.10.
Allocation of authority, §42-2706.03.
Authority to make, §42-2704.02.
Council delegation of authority to issue, §42-2702.06.
District full faith and credit and taxing power not pledged on, §42-2704.08.
Legal investments and securities, status as, §42-2704.09.
Maximum price, §42-2704.05.
Negotiable instruments regardless of form or character, §42-2704.02.
Obligations of agency regarding, §42-2704.02.
Operating expenses, §42-2704.04.
Personal liability of directors and employees, lack of, §42-2704.02.
Revenue bonds.
Delegation of council authority to issue, §1-204.90.
Rights and remedies, no limitations on, §42-2704.07.
Sale of, §42-2704.03.
Self-purchase, §42-2704.05.
Tax exemptions, §42-2704.10.
Trust indenture to secure, §42-2704.04.
Bonds, surety, §42-2702.05.
Conflicts of interest, §42-2702.04.
Consultative services, providing, §42-2703.07.
Council.
Delegation of powers by, §42-2702.06.
Review and approval of proposals, §42-2702.07.
Definitions, §42-2701.02.
Delegation of powers, §42-2702.06.
Deposits, §42-2704.11.
Disclosures of board and employees, §42-2702.04.
Disposition of assets on, §42-2706.04.
Disposition of funds, §42-2704.01.
Eligible persons and eligible state or local government units.
Consultative services, §42-2703.07.
Defined, §42-2701.02.
Grants, §42-2703.07.
Loans, §42-2703.07.
Support programs assisting, §42-2703.05.

HOUSING FINANCE AGENCY
—Cont'd
Eligible persons and eligible state or local government units —Cont'd
Technical assistance, §42-2703.07.
Employees, §§42-2702.03, 42-2702.04.
Establishment of, §42-2702.01.
Executive director, §§42-2702.03, 42-2702.04.
Financial affairs, §§42-2704.01 to 42-2704.13.
Financial assistance, providing, §42-2703.05.
Gifts, §42-2704.01.
Grants, providing, §42-2703.07.
Homeownership program financing, §42-2703.03.
Housing projects.
Financing, §42-2703.02.
Rent control exemptions, §42-2703.08.
Interpretation of provisions, §42-2706.01.
Investment of funds, §§42-2704.06, 42-2704.13.
Issuance of rules and regulations, §42-2703.06.
Loans, providing, §§42-2703.05, 42-2703.07.
Management of funds, §42-2704.06.
Northern Ireland.
Investment of funds with companies doing business with, §42-2704.13.
Policy declaration, §42-2701.01.
Powers and duties, §§42-2703.01 to 42-2703.08.
Public accountability, §§42-2704.13 to 42-2705.04.
Receipt of funds, §42-2704.01.
Relationship to other laws, §42-2706.05.
Rent control exemption for housing projects assisted by, §42-2703.08.
Repayment of funds, §42-2704.01a.
Reports, §§42-2702.07, 42-2705.03.
Reserve funds, §42-2704.06.
Severability of provisions, §42-2706.02.
Special funds, §42-2704.06.
Sponsors.
Consultative services, §42-2703.07.
Defined, §42-2701.02.
Financial assistance, §42-2703.05.
Grants, §42-2703.07.
Loans, §§42-2703.05, 42-2703.07.

HOUSING FINANCE AGENCY
—Cont'd
Sponsors —Cont'd
Support programs assisting, §42-2703.05.
Technical assistance, §42-2703.07.
Support programs, §42-2703.05.
Tax exemptions, §42-2704.10.
Technical assistance, §42-2703.07.
Waiver of ban on participation by interested party, §42-2702.04.

HOUSING FIRST FUND, §4-753.01a.

HOUSING PRODUCTION TRUST FUND, §§42-2801 to 42-2804.
Annual report, §42-2803.01.
Board, §42-2802.01.
Bond issues, §§42-2812.01 to 42-2812.12.
Authorized delegates, §42-2812.08.
Defined, §42-2812.01.
Closing documents, §42-2812.07.
Defined, §42-2812.01.
Filing, §42-2812.11.
Definitions, §42-2812.01.
Financing documents, §42-2812.07.
Defined, §42-2812.01.
Filing, §42-2812.11.
Legislative findings, §42-2812.02.
Liability, §§42-2812.09, 42-2812.10.
New community initiative neighborhoods, §42-2812.03.
Payment, §42-2812.06.
Sale of bonds, §42-2812.05.
Security, §42-2812.06.
Terms of bonds, §42-2812.04.
Transcript of proceedings.
Transmission to secretary of council, §42-2812.12.
Coordination of programs, community outreach, §42-2803.
Definitions, §42-2801.
Established, §42-2802.
Maintenance of affordability, §42-2802.02.
New communities initiative, §42-2802.
Bond issues, §42-2812.03.
Rules, §42-2804.

HOUSING REDEVELOPMENT, §§6-311.01 to 6-341.05.
See URBAN RENEWAL.

HOWARD THEATRE REDEVELOPMENT PROJECT.
Definitions, §2-1217.151.

**HOWARD THEATRE
REDEVELOPMENT PROJECT
TIF AREA,** §§2-1217.34a to
2-1217.34n.
Bonds, §§2-1217.34d, 2-1217.34e.
District officials not personally liable,
§2-1217.34j.
Issuance, §2-1217.34f.
Fiscal impact of issuance,
§2-1217.34n.
Limited liability, §2-1217.34i.
Payment, §2-1217.34g.
Place copies filed, §2-1217.34k.
Security, §2-1217.34g.
Special obligations of district,
§2-1217.34i.
Transcript of proceedings relating to,
§2-1217.34l.
Creation, §2-1217.34c.
Definitions, §2-1217.34a.
Financing and closing documents,
§2-1217.34h.
Place copies filed, §2-1217.34k.
**Howard Theatre redevelopment
project fund,** §2-1217.34b.
**Implementation consistent with
authority of chief financial
officer,** §2-1217.34m.

HOWARD UNIVERSITY.
Real property exempt from taxation,
§47-1018.

HPV VACCINATION, §§7-1651.01 to
7-1651.05.

**H STREET N.E. PERFORMANCE
PARKING PILOT ZONE,**
§50-2532.01.

**H STREET, N.E. RETAIL PRIORITY
AREA INCENTIVE,** §§1-325.171 to
1-325.173.
Business development, §1-325.173.
Definitions, §1-325.171.
Fund, §1-325.172.

**H STREET RETAIL PRIORITY
AREA GRANT FUND.**
Grants.
Award of grants to qualified high
technology companies (QHTCs),
§1-325.172.

HUMAN BODY PARTS.
Trafficking in, §§7-1501.01 to
7-1501.03.

HUMANE SOCIETY.
Child abuse and neglect.
Humane officers.
Reporting requirements, §4-1321.02.

HUMANE SOCIETY —Cont'd
Cruelty to animals.
Prosecution of violations.
Duties of humane officers, §22-1006.
Taking possession of animals,
§22-1004.

**HUMAN IMMUNODEFICIENCY
VIRUS.**
HIV and AIDS generally.
See AIDS.

**HUMAN PAPILLOMAVIRUS
VACCINATION,** §§7-1651.01 to
7-1651.05.
Defined terms, §7-1651.01.
Effectiveness and risks.
Department of health certification,
§7-1651.03.
Public education campaign,
§7-1651.02.
Program, generally, §7-1651.04.
Public education campaign,
§7-1651.02.
Rules, authority to promulgate,
§7-1651.05.
School enrollment, requirements,
§7-1651.04.

**HUMAN RIGHTS AND BUSINESS
DEVELOPMENT, DEPARTMENT
OF,** §§2-1411.04, 2-1411.06.

HUMAN RIGHTS COMMISSION,
§§2-1401.01 to 2-1404.04.
Affirmative action, §2-1402.53.
Aiding and abetting discrimination,
§2-1402.62.
Bases for discrimination, §2-1401.01.
Coercion of discrimination,
§2-1402.61.
Complaints.
Procedure for handling, §§2-1403.02 to
2-1403.17.
Conciliation agreements, §2-1402.63.
Conciliation of complaints,
§2-1403.06.
Definitions, §2-1401.02.
Discrimination.
Exceptions for practices with
discriminatory effects.
See DISCRIMINATION.
District government.
Complaints filed against, §2-1403.03.
Educational institutions, §§2-1402.41,
2-1402.42.
Employment discrimination,
§§2-1402.01 to 2-1402.13.
See EMPLOYMENT
DISCRIMINATION.

HUMAN RIGHTS COMMISSION
—Cont'd
Enforcement of orders, §2-1403.15.
Equal employment opportunity,
§2-1402.01.
Equal opportunity, §2-1402.01.
Establishment, §2-1404.01.
Fraud and deceit, §2-1402.65.
Functions, §2-1404.02.
Hearings.
Conduct of, §2-1403.12.
Decision and order following,
§2-1403.13.
Enforcement of order, §2-1403.15.
Judicial review of results, §2-1403.14.
Notice, §2-1403.10.
Service of process, §2-1403.09.
Tribunal, §2-1403.11.
Housing accommodation
discrimination complaints.
Posting notice of, §2-1403.08.
Injunctions, §2-1403.07.
Interfering with, resisting, or
impeding, §2-1402.64.
Investigations, §2-1403.05.
Licenses, §§2-1402.67, 2-1403.17.
Mediation of complaints, §2-1403.04.
Meetings, §2-1404.04.
Membership, §2-1404.03.
Motor vehicles.
Insurance, §2-1402.71.
Rentals, §2-1402.72.
Notice.
Hearings, §2-1403.10.
Housing accommodation
discrimination complaints.
Posting notice of, §2-1403.08.
Prohibited discrimination, §2-1402.51.
Office of human rights, §§2-1411.01 to
2-1411.06.
Powers and duties, §2-1411.02.
Organization, §2-1404.04.
Persons with disabilities.
General provisions.
See DISABILITIES, PERSONS
WITH.
Policy declaration, §2-1401.01.
Powers of, §2-1403.01.
Pregnancy, childbirth, or related
conditions.
Discrimination based on, §2-1401.05.
Private right of action, §2-1403.16.
Prohibited acts of discrimination,
§§2-1402.01 to 2-1402.73.
Public accommodations, §2-1402.31.
Purpose, §2-1404.02.

HUMAN RIGHTS COMMISSION
—Cont'd
Real estate transactions.
Unlawful discriminatory practices in,
§§2-1402.21 to 2-1402.24.
Records and reports, §2-1402.52.
Religious beliefs.
See RELIGIOUS BELIEFS.
Reports, §2-1403.01.
Retaliation, §2-1402.61.
Service of process, §2-1403.09.
Severability of provisions, §2-1401.04.
Types of discrimination, §2-1401.01.
Unspecified practices with
discriminatory effects,
§2-1402.68.

**HUMAN SERVICES, DEPARTMENT
OF, §§7-103 to 7-171.**
Assistant director, §7-172.
Chief clerk, §7-171.
Chief Inspector, §7-171.
Child care facilities, §§4-401 to 4-414,
4-401 to 4-415.
Custody proceedings.
Social service referrals, DomRel Rule
404.
Department of disability services,
§§7-761.01 to 7-761.12.
See DISABILITY SERVICES,
DEPARTMENT ON.
Deputy to director, §7-171.
Director.
Assistant director, §7-172.
Deputy to, §7-171.
Reports, §7-105.
District of Columbia General
Hospital under control of, §7-180.
Drug and alcohol testing of
employees, §§1-620.21 to 1-620.25.
Contractor to perform test, §1-620.22.
Definitions, §1-620.21.
Employees tested, §1-620.22.
Grounds for termination, §1-620.25.
Implied consent of employees
operating motor vehicles,
§1-620.24.
Methods of testing, §1-620.23.
Notice of confirmed positive urinalysis,
§1-620.23.
Notice of implementation of program,
§1-620.22.
Random testing.
Employees subject to, §1-620.22.
Method of testing, §1-620.23.
Results turned over to law
enforcement, §1-620.25.

HUMAN SERVICES, DEPARTMENT OF —Cont'd

Drug and alcohol testing of employees —Cont'd

Treatment following positive test, §1-620.25.

Industrial home school, §§44-1301, 44-1302.

Inspectors, §§7-103 to 7-171.

Reports.

Director, §7-105.

Inspectors, §7-104.

Sanitary inspectors, §§7-103 to 7-171.

Tuberculosis sanatoria under control of, §7-180.

Visitations proceedings.

Social service referrals, DomRel Rule 404.

Youth rehabilitation services, department of.

Successor in interest to department of human services, §2-1515.09.

Transfers to, §2-1515.08.

HUMAN TISSUE BANKS, §§7-1541.01 to 7-1551.01.

Anatomical gifts.

General provisions, §§7-1531.01 to 7-1531.28.

See ANATOMICAL GIFTS.

Blood banks' authority to transfer blood components within District, §7-1551.01.

Cemeteries and cemetery associations, §§43-119, 43-125.

Definitions, §7-1541.02.

Exemptions, §7-1541.06.

Fines, §7-1541.04.

Funeral directors, §7-1541.06.

Interpretation of provisions, §7-1541.07.

Licenses, §7-1541.03.

Organ procurement organizations.

Authority of organization acting on behalf of tissue bank, §7-1541.05a.

Penalties, §7-1541.04.

Policy declaration, §7-1541.01.

Prosecutions regarding, §7-1541.04.

Removal of tissue immediately after death, §43-125.

Trafficking in human body parts, §§7-1501.01 to 7-1501.03.

HUMAN TRAFFICKING, §§22-1831 to 22-1843.

Attorneys' fees, §22-1840.

Benefiting financially from, §22-1836.

HUMAN TRAFFICKING —Cont'd

Children and minors, sex trafficking, §22-1834.

Commercial sex acts, §22-1833.

Costs, §22-1840.

Counselor privilege, §14-311.

Disclosure of confidential information prohibited without consent of client, §14-307.

Definitions, §22-1831.

Documents, unlawful conduct with respect to, §22-1835.

Fines and civil penalties, §22-1837.

Forced labor, §22-1832.

Forfeitures, §22-1838.

Hotline.

Public posting, §22-1843.

Labor, trafficking in, §22-1833.

Limitation of actions, §23-113.

Opinion evidence, §22-1839.

Private right of action, §22-1840.

Reputation evidence, §22-1839.

Sentencing, §22-1837.

Training program, §22-1842.

HUNTING.

Fish and game, §§22-4328 to 22-4333.

See FISH AND GAME.

HUSBAND AND WIFE.

Adoption of children by spouse of natural parent, §16-308.

Alimony.

See SPOUSAL SUPPORT.

Annulment of marriage.

See ANNULMENT OF MARRIAGE.

Divorce.

See DIVORCE.

Domestic violence, §§16-1031 to 16-1034.

Dower.

See DOWER.

Legal separation, §§16-904, 16-905, 16-909.

Marriage.

Annulment of marriage.

See ANNULMENT OF MARRIAGE.

General provisions, §§46-401 to 46-421.

See MARRIAGE.

Pensions and retirement.

Spouse or domestic partner equity, §§1-529.01 to 1-529.05.

Prostitution, caused to live in, §22-2708.

Real property taxes.

Transfers without consideration, exempt from tax, §47-802.

HUSBAND AND WIFE —Cont'd
Spousal privilege.
See SPOUSAL PRIVILEGE.

HYBRID MOTOR VEHICLES.
Motor vehicle registration.
Fees, §50-1501.03.
Motor vehicle titling tax.
Exemption, §50-2201.03.

HYDRANTS.
Water and sewer authority duties,
§34-2202.03.

HYDROELECTRIC POWER.
Renewable energy portfolio
standards, §§34-1431 to 34-1439.

HYPERTENSION.
Presumption as to disability or
death resulting from.
Fire and emergency medical services
employees, §5-652.

HYPOTHECATION.
Taxation, anticipation of, §1-301.70.

HYPOTHYROIDISM, §§7-831 to 7-840.

I

IAN'S LAW, §§31-3011 to 31-3013.
Applicability of provisions, §31-3013.
Requirements, §31-3011.
Rules, §31-3012.

ICE.
Sale by weight, §37-201.12.

ICE AND SNOW REMOVAL.
Sidewalks, §§9-601 to 9-607.

ICE CREAM SALOONS.
Price list.
Charging greater price, §47-2911.
Posting required, §47-2908.
Failure, §47-2911.
Transmission to assessor, §47-2909.
Well-behaved persons.
Required to serve, §§47-2907, 47-2910.
Failure to serve, §47-2911.

ICE PIPES OR CHILLERS.
Drug paraphernalia, §§48-904.10,
48-1101 to 48-1104.

ICF-IDD.
Stevie Sellows quality improvement
fund, §§47-1270 to 47-1278.

ICF-MR.
Stevie Sellows quality improvement
fund.
See INTERMEDIATE CARE
FACILITIES.

IDENTIFICATION.
Alcoholic beverage licenses.
Valid identification required, §25-783.

IDENTIFICATION CARDS.
Federally-accepted identification
card, §50-1401.03.
Limited purpose identification card,
§50-1401.05.
Selective Service registration upon
application, §50-1401.01.

IDENTIFYING NUMBERS.
Bicycles.
Commercial bicycle operators.
Identification numbers, §50-1632.
Tampering with or removing numbers,
§22-3234.
Business licenses, §47-2851.03b.
Firearms.
Identification number on firearm
required for sale of, §7-2504.08.
Motor vehicles.
Altering or removing motor vehicle
identification numbers, §22-3233.
Probate proceedings.
Exclusion of personal identification
from filed documents, Probate
Rule 5.1.
Social security numbers.
See SOCIAL SECURITY NUMBERS.

IDENTITY THEFT, §§22-3227.01 to
22-3227.08.
Consumer security breach
notification, §§28-3851 to 28-3853.
Consumer security freeze, §§28-3861
to 28-3864.
Definitions, §22-3227.01.
District of Columbia public record,
§22-3227.05.
Elements of offense, §22-3227.02.
Jurisdiction, §22-3227.06.
Limitation of prosecutions,
§22-3227.07.
Motor vehicle records and accident
reports.
Prohibitions on release and use of
personal information,
§50-1401.01b.

IDENTITY THEFT —Cont'd
Penalties, §22-3227.03.
Prohibited acts, §22-3227.02.
Public records.
Correction, §22-3227.05.
Reports.
Police reports, §22-3227.08.
Restitution, §22-3227.04.

IGNITION INTERLOCK DEVICES.
Driving under the influence,
§50-2201.05a.

ILLEGAL DUMPING, §§8-901 to
8-906.
Bounty on, §8-904.
Business licenses.
Unpaid fines or penalties.
Computer record-keeping and
reporting system, §47-2866.
Definitions, §47-2861.
Issuance of license prohibited,
§47-2862.
Right to appeal denial of license,
§47-2865.
Self-certification of lack of
outstanding debt, §47-2863.
Falsification of certification,
penalty, §47-2864.
Definitions, §8-901.
Enforcement of provisions
regarding, §8-903.
Forfeitures, §8-905.
Hazardous waste, §§8-901, 8-902.
Medical waste, §§8-901, 8-902.
Prohibitions regarding, §8-902.
Regulations, §8-906.
Solid waste, §§8-901, 8-902.

IMMIGRATION.
Appeals, federal cases.
Record for review in agency action.
Filing, USCtApp Rule 17.
Constitution of the United States,
US Const Art I §9.
Prisons and prisoners.
District compliance with federal
immigration detainers, §24-211.07.

IMMUNITY.
Adult protective services, §7-1908.
Aged persons.
Volunteer service credit program for,
§§7-531.01 to 7-531.11.
Anatomical gifts, §7-1531.17.
Decedent's body or parts.
Organ preservation, §7-1531.25.
Arbitration, revised act.
Arbitrators, §16-4414.

IMMUNITY —Cont'd
Attorney discipline or disability
proceedings, DCBar Rule XI.
Lawyer counseling panel, USDistCt
LCrR 57.31, USDistCt LCvR
83.20.
Automated external defibrillator.
Use, §44-233.
Autonomous vehicles, conversion of
vehicle into.
Limited liability of original
manufacturer, §50-2353.
Benefit corporations.
Directors.
Immunity from personal liability for
damages, §29-1303.01.
Officers.
Immunity from personal liability for
damages, §29-1303.03.
Bicycle insurance policies.
Cancellation or refusal to renew.
Good faith immunity, §50-534.
Child abuse and neglect.
Reasonable and prudent parent
standard.
Application or failure to apply,
§4-1303.03f.
Reports, making, §4-1321.04.
Child custody proceedings.
Special appearance immunity from
personal jurisdiction, §16-4601.08.
Child fatality reports.
Persons making, §4-1371.13.
Public disclosure of findings and
information, §4-1303.34.
Child fatality review committee
investigation.
Providing information to committee,
§4-1371.10.
Child sexual abuse reporting.
Immunity of person making good faith
report, §22-3020.55.
City Market at O Street tax
increment financing.
Bond issues.
Limited liability of District,
§2-1217.33i.
Personal liability of officials,
§2-1217.33j.
Clients' security trust fund trustees.
Staff and agents, DCBar Rule XII.
Collaborative law, §16-4017.
Limits, §16-4019.
Waiver and preclusion, §16-4018.
Comfort care orders.
Non-resuscitation procedures for EMS,
§7-651.11.

IMMUNITY —Cont'd

Constitution of the United States, US Const Art IV §2.

Council's legislative immunity, §1-301.42.

Criminal history records.
Limited liability for employers regarding criminal history of employees, §24-1351.

Delinquent minors, §16-2339.

Domestic violence fatality review board, §16-1057.

Donated food.
Good faith immunity, §§48-301, 48-302.

Do not resuscitate procedures.
Comfort care orders, §7-651.11.

Driving under the influence.
Impoundment of vehicle, liability for damages, §50-2206.56.

Electronic waste.
Extended manufacturer responsibility, §8-1041.09.

Emergency volunteer health practitioners, §7-2361.10.

Employment relations.
Limited liability for employers regarding criminal history of employees, §24-1351.

Examination of insurance companies, §31-1407.

Firearms or ammunition.
Reporting injuries caused by, §7-2603.
Voluntary surrender of, §7-2507.05.

Foreign missions, §6-1310.

Gambling crimes.
Witnesses to, §22-1714.

Health benefit exchange authority.
Executive and advisory board members, officers and employees, §31-3171.12.

Health care ombudsman program, §7-2071.08.

Health insurance.
Regulatory standards, §31-3451.11.

Insurance company risk-based capital, §31-2011.

Insurance fraud.
Immunity for reporting, §22-3225.13.

Insurance underwriting, §31-5007.

Intellectual disabilities, persons with.
Actions to compel rights, §§7-1305.13, 7-1305.14.

Interstate compact on educational opportunity for military children.
Interstate commission, §49-1101.11.

IMMUNITY —Cont'd

Interstate enforcement of domestic violence proceedings.
Immunity from liability, §16-1045.

Interstate family support.
Defense of immunity based on parent-child relationship, inapplicable, §46-353.16.
Enforcement of support order without registration.
Immunity from civil liability, §46-355.04.
Limited immunity of petitioner, §46-353.14.

Juvenile offenders, §16-2339.

Lawyer counseling panel, USDistCt LCrR 57.31, USDistCt LCvR 83.20.

Life and health insurance guaranty association, §31-5414.

Long-term care ombudsman, §7-702.07.

Mediators, USDistCt LCvR 84.3.

Medical liability captive insurance agency.
Liability for obligations of agency, §1-307.89.

Medical marijuana, §7-1671.11.

Metropolitan police property clerk, §§5-119.06, 5-119.11.

NAIC insurance regulatory information system, §31-1902.

Negligent operation of vehicles by District employees, §§2-412, 2-415.

Newborn safe haven, §4-1451.06.

Nonprofit corporations.
Employees, §29-406.91.
Volunteers, §29-406.90.

Non-resuscitation procedures for EMS.
Comfort care orders, §7-651.11.

Not-for-profit hospital corporations.
District's immunity from liability, §44-951.14.

Nurse's rehabilitation program.
Committee on impaired nurses, §3-1251.08.

Ombudsman for public education, §38-355.

Paint stewardship.
Immunity from liability, compliance with chapter, §8-233.05.

Prescription drug monitoring program, §48-853.08.

Private correctional treatment facilities, §24-261.04.

IMMUNITY —Cont'd
Property and liability insurance guaranty association, §31-5514.
Public utilities investigations, §34-610.
Qualified zone academy revenue bond project forward commitment approval act.
Bond issues.
Limited liability of District, §2-1217.112.
Personal liability of officials, §2-1217.113.
Rental housing commission.
Official acts, immunity for, §42-3502.02a.
Secured transactions.
Default.
Limitation on liability of secured party, §28:9-628.
Southwest waterfront bond financing.
Immunity of district officials, §2-1217.141.
State health planning and development agency, §44-417.
Student health care.
Medication, §38-651.11.
Weapons, reporting injuries caused by, §7-2603.
Year 2000 computer system failure, §2-381.31.
Applicability, §2-381.32.

IMMUNIZATION.
Human papillomavirus vaccination, §§7-1651.01 to 7-1651.05.
Pharmacists administering, §3-1202.08.
School students, §§38-501 to 38-508.
Interstate compact on educational opportunity for military children.
Time to obtain immunizations, §49-1101.05.

IMPAIRED DRIVING, §§50-2206.01 to 50-2206.59.
See DRIVING UNDER THE INFLUENCE.

IMPEACHMENT.
Constitution of the United States, US Const Art I §§2, 3, Art II §4, Art III §2.
President, US Const Art II §4.
Vice-president, US Const Art II §4.
Witnesses, §§14-102, 14-305.
Adverse party as witness, CivPro Rule 43.

IMPEACHMENT —Cont'd
Witnesses —Cont'd
Deposition's use in court proceedings, CivPro Rule 32.
Criminal procedure, CrimPro Rule 15.

IMPLEADER.
Third party practice, CivPro Rule 14.

IMPLIED CONSENT.
Driving under the influence.
Chemical testing generally, §§50-1901 to 50-1912.
See DRIVING UNDER THE INFLUENCE.
Testing public employees for alcohol or drugs.
Department of mental health and department of human services employees, §1-620.25.
Employees who operate motor vehicles, §1-620.24.
Mandatory drug and alcohol testing of certain employees who serve children.
Motor vehicles operators deemed to have given consent, §1-620.33.

IMPLIED WARRANTIES.
Assistive technology device, §28-4032.
Home buying warranties.
Fitness for particular purpose, §28:2-315.
Merchantability, §28:2-314.
Usage of trade, §28:2-314.
Leases, UCC.
Fitness for particular purpose, §28:2A-213.
Merchantability, §28:2A-212.
Third party beneficiaries, §28:2A-216.
Sale of goods, UCC.
Course of dealing or usage of trade, §28:2-314.
Cumulation and conflict, §28:2-317.
Exclusions, §§28:2-316, 28:2-316.01.
Fitness for a particular purpose, §§28:2-315, 28:2-316, 28:2-316.01.
Merchantability, §§28:2-316, 28:2-316.01.
Modification, §§28:2-316, 28:2-316.01.
Third party beneficiaries, §28:2-318.

IMPORTS AND EXPORTS.
Alcoholic beverages.
Importation of beverages into District, §25-772.

IMPORTS AND EXPORTS —Cont'd
Alcoholic beverages —Cont'd
Taxation.
Import permits, §25-904.
Transportation of liquor into District.
Importation permits, §25-119.
Constitution of the United States,
US Const Art I §§9, 10.
Fines.
Alcoholic beverages.
Importation of beverages into
District, §25-772.
Gray market cigarettes.
Tobacco tax, §47-2419.
Applicability of provisions, §47-2426.
Penalties, §47-2421.
Seizure as contraband, §47-2423.

IMPOUNDED ANIMALS, §8-1805.
Adoption of, §8-1807.
Food and water supplied to,
§22-1007.
Owner, release to, §8-1806.
Relief of, §22-1008.

IMPOUNDMENT OF VEHICLES.
Abandoned and unlawfully parked
vehicles, §50-2421.07.
Blue Plains Impoundment Lot,
jurisdiction over, §50-2405.
Driving under the influence,
§50-2206.56.
Fees for storing impounded vehicles,
§50-2201.21.
For-hire vehicles, §50-331.
Outstanding traffic violations,
§50-2201.03.
Prostitution-related offenses, vehicle
used in furtherance of, §22-2724.
Anti-prostitution vehicle impoundment
proceeds fund, §22-2725.
Taxicabs, §50-331.

IMPRISONMENT.
Arrests.
See ARRESTS.
Delinquent minors.
Detention and shelter care procedures,
JuvProc Rule 105.
Criteria used, JuvProc Rule 106.
Forms, JuvProc Forms 1 to 3.
Hearings, JuvProc Rule 107.
Detention by force, §22-3301.
Detention prior to trial, §23-1322.
Addicts, §23-1323.
Habeas corpus, §§16-1901 to 16-1909.
See HABEAS CORPUS.
Life imprisonment.
Murder.
First and second degree, §22-2104.

IMPRISONMENT —Cont'd
Life imprisonment without parole.
Murder.
First degree murder, §22-2104.
Killing law enforcement officer,
§22-2106.
Three strikes offenders, §22-1804a.
Prisons and prisoners.
See PRISONS AND PRISONERS.
Prison terms.
See PRISON TERMS.
Sentencing generally.
See SENTENCING.

INAUGURAL CEREMONIES.
President of the United States,
§§2-801 to 2-810, 2-821 to 2-829.
See PRESIDENT OF THE UNITED
STATES.

INAUGURATION DAY.
Designated holiday, §§1-612.02,
28-2701.
Extension of time for performing
acts, §28-2701.

INCANDESCENT REFLECTOR
LAMPS.
Energy efficiency standards.
General provisions, §§8-1771.01 to
8-1771.06.

INCAPACITATED PERSONS.
Adult protective services, §§7-1901 to
7-1913.
See ADULT PROTECTIVE
SERVICES.
Attorneys at law.
Clients with diminished capacity.
Client-lawyer relationship, ProfCond
Rule 1.14.
Custodial trusts.
Generally, §§19-1101 to 19-1120.
See CUSTODIAL TRUSTS.
Decedents' estates, guardian ad
litem regarding, §20-108.
Durable powers of attorney not
affected by incapacity, §21-2082.
Finding of incapacity, effect of,
§21-2004.
Guardians for.
See GUARDIAN AND WARD.
Healthcare durable powers of
attorney, §§21-2201 to 21-2213.
See HEALTHCARE DURABLE
POWERS OF ATTORNEY.
Hospital discharge planning,
§§21-2231.01 to 21-2231.05.

INCAPACITATED PERSONS —Cont'd
Incompetent criminal defendants.
Competence to proceed, §§24-531.01 to 24-531.13.
See COMPETENCE TO PROCEED.
Inheritances, §20-1107.
Insanitary buildings.
Owners of, §6-909.
Insanity defense, §§24-501 to 24-503.
Intellectual disabilities, persons with.
See INTELLECTUAL DISABILITIES, PERSONS WITH.
Landlord and tenant, §42-3228.
Leases, §42-3228.
Limitation of actions, §12-302.
Living wills, §7-626.
Marriage, §46-403.
Mental illness, persons with.
See MENTAL ILLNESS, PERSONS WITH.
Mental retardation, persons with.
See INTELLECTUAL DISABILITIES, PERSONS WITH.
Metropolitan police property clerk.
Custody of property of, §5-119.09.
Parents.
Standby guardianship for minor, §§16-4801 to 16-4810.
See GUARDIAN AND WARD.
Parole for medical and geriatric reasons, §§24-461 to 24-468.
See PAROLE.
Personal representatives, §20-524.
Property.
Protection of.
See CONSERVATORS.
Public assistance.
See PUBLIC ASSISTANCE.
Service of process on, §13-333.
Sexual offenses against, §§22-3003, 22-3005.
Witness testimony involving, §§14-301 to 14-305.

INCENTIVE AWARDS.
Public officers and employees, §§1-619.01 to 1-619.03.
Single-room-occupancy housing development, §42-3508.06.
Teachers' retirement, §38-2041.01.

INCEST, §22-1901.
Intrafamily offenses.
Generally, §§16-1001 to 16-1034.
See INTRAFAMILY PROCEEDINGS.
Limitation of actions, §23-113.

INCEST —Cont'd
Marriages void ab initio or by judicial decree, §§46-401.01, 46-402.

INCITEMENT.
Criminal offenses, §22-1805.
Prostitution, §22-2705.
Riots, §22-1322.

INCOME SOURCE DISCRIMINATION.
Prohibition of, §2-1401.01.

INCOME TAXES, §§47-1801.01 to 47-1816.03.
Accounting periods, §§47-1804.01 to 47-1804.03.
Computation of income, §47-1804.01.
Items of gross income included, §47-1804.02.
Adjusted gross income, §47-1803.02.
Allocation and apportionment.
Between or among organizations, trades, or businesses, §47-1810.03.
Combined reports, §47-1810.04.
Accounting rules, §47-1810.08.
Business income of combined group, determining, §47-1810.05.
Future deductions, §47-1810.08.
Reporting election, §47-1810.07.
Surety, designation of, §47-1810.06.
Water's edge reporting, §47-1810.07.
District and non-District income, §47-1810.02.
Purpose of chapter, §47-1810.01.
Appeals.
Right of appeal, §47-1815.01.
Bad debts.
Deduction, §47-1803.03.
Basis, §§47-1811.01 to 47-1811.04.
Bond issues.
Income tax secured bonds, §§47-340.26 to 47-340.36.
See INCOME TAX SECURED BONDS.
Bone marrow donation.
Corporation tax credit.
Paid leave to employee serving as bone marrow donor, §47-1807.08.
Unincorporated business tax credit.
Paid leave to employee serving as bone marrow donor, §47-1808.08.
Business expenses.
Deduction, §47-1803.03.
Charitable contributions.
Deduction, §47-1803.03.

INCOME TAXES —Cont'd
Check-off for contributions.
Anacostia River clean up and
protection fund tax check-off,
§47-1812.11d.
New Columbia statehood fund,
§47-1812.11c.
Public fund for drug prevention and
children at risk, §47-1812.11b.
Combined reporting.
Unitary businesses, §47-1805.02a.
Accounting rules, §47-1810.08.
Business income of combined group,
determining, §47-1810.05.
District and non-District income,
allocation and apportionment of,
§47-1810.04.
Future deductions, §47-1810.08.
Reporting election, §47-1810.07.
Surety, designation of, §47-1810.06.
Water's edge reporting, §47-1810.07.
Computation of income, §§47-1804.01,
47-1804.07.
Constitution of the United States,
US Const Amd 16.
Corporations, §§47-1805.02, 47-1807.01
to 47-1807.12.
E-commerce companies.
Qualified social electronic commerce
companies tax abatements,
§§47-1818.01 to 47-1818.08.
Cost-of-living adjustment.
Defined, §47-1801.04.
Credits.
Accounting period for, §47-1804.03.
Alternative fuel infrastructure credit.
Corporations, §47-1807.10.
Residents and nonresidents,
§47-1806.12.
Unincorporated businesses,
§47-1808.10.
Alternative fuel vehicle conversion
credit.
Corporations, §47-1807.11.
Residents and nonresidents,
§47-1806.13.
Unincorporated businesses,
§47-1808.11.
Corporations, §§47-1807.04 to
47-1807.12.
Employer-assisted home purchase
credit, §47-1807.07.
Farm to food donations, §47-1806.14.
Corporations and financial
institutions, §47-1807.12.
Unincorporated businesses,
§47-1808.12.

INCOME TAXES —Cont'd
Credits —Cont'd
Job growth credit, §§47-1807.51 to
47-1807.56.
Long term homeowner credit,
§§47-1806.09 to 47-1806.09f.
Allowable credit, §47-1806.09a.
Application for credit,
§§47-1806.09b, 47-1806.09f.
Carryover, §47-1806.09e.
Correction of error, §47-1806.09c.
Definitions, §47-1806.09.
Effective date, §47-1806.09f.
Fraud, §47-1806.09d.
Qualified high technology companies,
§§47-1817.01 to 47-1817.08.
Residents and nonresidents,
§47-1806.04.
Alternative fuel infrastructure
credit, §47-1806.12.
Alternative fuel vehicle conversion
credit, §47-1806.13.
Unincorporated businesses,
§§47-1808.07 to 47-1808.12.
Deductions, §47-1803.03.
Accounting period, §47-1804.03.
Depreciation, §47-1811.04.
Deficiencies and delinquencies,
§47-1812.05.
Definitions, §47-1801.04.
Qualified high technology companies,
§47-1817.01.
Unincorporated business, §47-1808.01.
Depreciation.
Deduction, §§47-1803.03, 47-1811.04.
District and non-District income,
allocation and apportionment of,
§§47-1810.01 to 47-1810.08.
Dividends, property, §47-1811.03.
Domestic production activities.
Deduction disallowed, §47-1803.03.
E-commerce companies.
Qualified social electronic commerce
companies tax abatements,
§§47-1818.01 to 47-1818.08.
Employees' trusts, §47-1809.10.
Employer-assisted home purchase
credit, §47-1807.07.
Employment discrimination award.
Backpay or frontpay.
Income averaging for tax purposes,
§47-1806.10.
Estates and trusts, §§47-1809.01 to
47-1809.10.
Classification as resident or
nonresident estate or trust.
Residency or situs of fiduciary not to
control, §47-1809.02.

INCOME TAXES —Cont'd
Estates and trusts —Cont'd
    Computation, §47-1809.04.
      Income for benefit of grantor,
        §47-1809.08.
      Net income, §47-1809.05.
      Revocable trusts, §47-1809.07.
      Taxable year of beneficiary different
        from estate or trust,
        §47-1809.06.
    Deductions from net income,
      §47-1809.05.
    Employees' trusts, §47-1809.10.
    Imposition of tax, §47-1809.03.
    In discretion of grantor defined,
      §47-1809.09.
    Nonresident estates and trusts
      defined, §47-1809.01.
    Resident estates and trusts defined,
      §47-1809.01.
Estimated tax, §47-1812.14.
Exemptions.
    Exempt organizations, §§47-1802.01 to
      47-1802.04.
      Effective date, §47-1802.03.
      Generally, §47-1802.01.
      Political organization taxes same as
        corporation, §47-1802.04.
      Regulations, §47-1802.02.
    Personal exemptions, §47-1806.02.
    Unincorporated businesses,
      §47-1808.04.
Federal return.
    Furnishing copy of, §47-1812.17.
Fiduciaries, §47-1805.02.
Fractional parts of dollar,
    §47-1804.07.
Gain or loss, determining,
    §47-1811.02.
Gross income, §47-1803.02.
    Accounting period in which items of
      gross income included,
      §47-1804.02.
    Deduction and credits taken,
      §47-1804.03.
Health insurance premiums.
    Deduction, §47-1803.03.
High technology companies.
    Credits, capital gains, §§47-1817.01 to
      47-1817.08.
Income averaging for tax purposes.
    Employment discrimination award.
      Backpay or frontpay, §47-1806.10.
Installment sale income, §47-1804.04.
Insurance premiums.
    Deduction, §47-1803.03.

INCOME TAXES —Cont'd
Interest paid.
    Deduction, §47-1803.03.
Internal revenue code changes,
    §47-1816.03.
Inventories, §47-1804.05.
Issuance of rules and regulations,
    §§47-1816.01 to 47-1816.03.
Itemized deductions, §47-1803.03.
Job growth credit, §§47-1807.51 to
    47-1807.56.
    Allowance, §47-1807.52.
      Corporations, §47-1807.09.
      Unincorporated businesses,
        §47-1808.09.
    Applications, §47-1807.54.
    Calculation, §47-1807.54.
    Cancellation, §47-1807.55.
    Certification, §47-1807.55.
    Definitions, §47-1807.51.
    Eligibility, §47-1807.53.
    Reports, §47-1807.55.
    Rulemaking authority, §47-1807.56.
Levies.
    Corporations, §47-1807.02.
Limited liability companies,
    §47-1808.06a.
Long-term health care insurance
    premiums.
    Deduction, §47-1803.03.
Long term homeowner credit,
    §§47-1806.09 to 47-1806.09f.
    Allowable credit, §47-1806.09a.
    Application for credit, §§47-1806.09b,
      47-1806.09f.
    Carryover, §47-1806.09e.
    Correction of error, §47-1806.09c.
    Definitions, §47-1806.09.
    Effective date, §47-1806.09f.
    Fraud, §47-1806.09d.
Losses.
    Deduction, §47-1803.03.
Lottery winnings, withholding,
    §47-1812.08.
Mayor's duties, §§47-1812.01,
    47-1812.04, 47-1816.03.
Net income, §47-1803.01.
Net operating loses.
    Deduction, §47-1803.03.
New Columbia statehood fund tax
    check-off, §47-1812.11c.
Nonresidents, §§47-1805.02, 47-1806.01
    to 47-1806.07.
Organ donation.
    Corporation tax credit.
      Paid leave to employee serving as
        organ donor, §47-1807.08.

INCOME TAXES —Cont'd
Organ donation —Cont'd
Unincorporated business tax credit.
Paid leave to employee serving as organ donor, §47-1808.08.
Partnerships, §§47-1805.02, 47-1808.06.
Payment of taxes, §47-1812.07.
Personal exemptions, §47-1806.02.
Policy declaration, §47-1810.01.
Principal and income.
Adjustments due to, §28-4805.06.
Payment, §28-4805.05.
Qualified high technology companies.
Certification as, §47-1805.05.
Credit, §§47-1817.01 to 47-1817.08.
Alternative method to determine status, §47-1817.01a.
Definitions, §47-1817.01.
Employment relocation costs, exception, §47-1817.02.
Imposition of tax, rate, §47-1817.06.
Retraining costs for disadvantaged employees, §47-1817.04.
Rollover of capital gain from qualified stock to other stock, §47-1817.07.
Sale or exchange of qualified high technology company investment, §47-1817.07a.
Severability, §47-1817.08.
Wages for qualified disadvantaged employees, §47-1817.05.
Wages for qualified employees, exception, §47-1817.03.
Rates.
Corporations, §47-1807.02.
Residents and nonresidents, §47-1806.03.
Unincorporated businesses, §47-1808.03.
Real estate investment trusts.
Deduction, §47-1803.03.
Real property taxes, §47-1806.06.
Records, §47-1812.02.
Registration, §47-1805.02.
Rejection of return, §47-1804.06.
Relocation assistance payments not subject to, §42-3403.05.
Repeal of 1939 law, §§47-1801.01 to 47-1801.04.
Crimes and penalties under prior law not affected, §47-1801.01a.
Definitions, §47-1801.04.
Effective date, §§47-1801.01, 47-1801.02.

INCOME TAXES —Cont'd
Repeal of 1939 law —Cont'd
Exception for certain purposes, §47-1801.01.
Existing rights and liabilities not affected, §47-1801.01a.
Returns and payments, §47-1801.03.
Residents, §§47-1805.02, 47-1806.01 to 47-1806.07.
Returns, §§47-1805.01 to 47-1805.05.
Confidentiality, §47-1805.04.
Disclosures, §47-1805.04.
Federal return, furnishing copy of, §47-1812.17.
Filing, §47-1805.03.
Forms, §47-1805.01.
Persons required to file, §47-1805.02.
Privacy and confidentiality, §47-1805.04.
Qualified high technology company.
Certification as, §47-1805.05.
Reciprocity, §47-1805.04.
Rejection of, §47-1804.06.
Revocable trusts, §47-1809.07.
Rules and regulation.
Generally, §47-1816.01.
Revenue Act of 1956, §47-1816.02.
Standard deduction, §47-1803.03.
Surtax.
Corporations, §47-1807.02.
Unincorporated businesses, §47-1808.03.
Taxable income, §47-1806.01.
Taxes paid.
Deduction, §47-1803.03.
Tax havens.
Defined, §47-1801.04.
Listed, §47-1801.04.
Tax return preparers, §47-4217.
Teachers.
Deductions, §47-1803.03.
Trusts and trustees, §§47-1809.01 to 47-1809.10.
Underpayments, §47-1812.05.
Unincorporated businesses, §§47-1808.01 to 47-1808.12.
Credit, §47-1808.07.
Business providing employees paid leave to serve as organ or bond marrow donor, §47-1808.08.
Farm to food donations, §47-1808.12.
Job growth tax credit, §47-1808.09.
Definitions, §47-1808.02.
Unincorporated business, §47-1808.01.
Exemption, §47-1808.04.

INCOME TAXES —Cont'd
Unincorporated businesses —Cont'd
Levy and rates, §47-1808.03.
Limited liability companies,
§47-1808.06a.
Partnerships, §47-1808.06.
Persons liable for payment,
§47-1808.05.
Unitary businesses.
Combined reporting, §47-1805.02a.
Accounting rules, §47-1810.08.
Business income of combined group,
determining, §47-1810.05.
District and non-District income,
allocation and apportionment of,
§47-1810.04.
Future deductions, §47-1810.08.
Reporting election, §47-1810.07.
Surety, designation of, §47-1810.06.
Water's edge reporting, §47-1810.07.
Whole dollar computation,
§47-1804.07.
Withholding, §47-1812.08.

INCOME TAX SECURED BONDS,
§§47-340.26 to 47-340.36.
Authorization, §47-340.28.
Closing documents, §47-340.32.
Filing, §47-340.35.
Definitions, §47-340.26.
Details, §47-340.29.
District officials, liability of,
§47-340.34.
Document maintenance, §47-340.35.
Financing documents, §47-340.32.
Filing, §47-340.35.
Fund, §47-340.27.
Issuance, §47-340.30.
Transcript of proceedings, §47-340.36.
Limited liability, §47-340.33.
Payment, §47-340.31.
Security, §47-340.31.
Transcript, transmission of,
§47-340.36.

INCOMPETENT CRIMINAL
DEFENDANTS.
Competence to proceed, §§24-531.01
to 24-531.13.
See COMPETENCE TO PROCEED.

INCREMENTS.
Unclaimed property, §41-121.

INDECENCY.
Lewd, indecent, or obscene acts,
§22-1312.

INDECENCY —Cont'd
Obscenity.
General provisions, §§22-2201 to
22-3104.
See OBSCENITY.
Minors, sexual performances
involving, §§22-3101 to 22-3104.
See CHILD SEXUAL ABUSE.

INDECENT LANGUAGE, §22-1321.

INDEMNIFICATION.
Administrative law judges,
commission on selection and
tenure of, §2-415.
Chesapeake Olympic games regional
authority, §2-1137.
Corporations.
Officers and directors, §§29-306.50 to
29-306.59.
See CORPORATIONS.
District medical employees, §2-415.
Employees retirement program
management.
Investment of public funds in certain
companies doing business with
Iran.
Indemnification of board members
and employees, §1-336.05.
Investment of public funds in certain
companies doing business with
Sudanese government.
Indemnification of board members or
employees, §1-335.05.
Horizontal property regimes,
§42-2018.
Insurance fraud, §22-3225.06.
Limited cooperative associations,
§29-1009.01.
Limited liability companies.
Managers and members, §29-804.08.
Limited partnerships.
General partners, §29-704.09.
Nonprofit corporations.
Officers and directors, §§29-406.50 to
29-406.58.
See NONPROFIT CORPORATIONS.
Partnerships.
Indemnification of partners,
§29-604.01.
Smoke and carbon monoxide
detectors.
Program to test and install detectors,
§6-751.05a.
Statutory trustees, §29-1205.09.
Title insurance producers,
indemnity deposits, §31-5041.06.

INDEMNIFICATION —Cont'd
Title insurers, indemnity deposits, §31-5031.14.
Unincorporated nonprofit associations.
Managers and members, §29-1123.

INDEPENDENCE DAY.
Appeals, federal cases, FRAP 26(a), 45(a).
Designated holiday, §§1-612.02, 28-2701.

INDEPENDENT CONTRACTORS.
Misclassification.
Workplace fraud, §§32-1331.01 to 32-1331.12.
See WORKPLACE FRAUD.

INDIANS.
Child custody proceedings.
Inapplicability of uniform act, §16-4601.03.
Taxation, US Const Art I §2, Amd 14.

INDICES.
Adoption proceeding records, Adoption Rule 79.
Arrest records, CrimPro Rule 118.
Delinquent minors, JuvProc Rule 118.
Superior court dockets, judgments, etc., CivPro Rule 79.
Domestic relations actions, DomRel Rule 79.

INDICTMENTS AND INFORMATIONS, §§23-301 to 23-331.
Amendment of information, CrimPro Rule 7.
Bill of particulars, CrimPro Rule 7.
Child sexual abuse.
Fictitious name indictments, §23-331.
Constitution of the United States, US Const Amd 5.
Death penalty cases, CrimPro Rule 7.
Defraud, sufficiency of intent to, §23-322.
Dismissal, CrimPro Rule 48.
Errors or omissions, CrimPro Rule 7.
Felonies, CrimPro Rule 7.
Fictitious name indictments.
First or second degree sexual abuse or child sexual abuse, §23-331.
Finding and return of indictment, CrimPro Rule 6.
Form and contents, CrimPro Rule 7.
Grand juries, §16-702.

INDICTMENTS AND INFORMATIONS —Cont'd
Joinder of offenses or defendants, CrimPro Rules 8, 13.
Pretrial request for severance, CrimPro Rule 12.
Relief from prejudicial joinder, CrimPro Rule 14.
Verdicts, CrimPro Rule 31.
Misdemeanors, CrimPro Rule 114.
Money.
Sufficiency of description of, §23-321.
Necessity, US Const Amd 5.
Perjury, sufficiency requirements, §§23-323, 23-324.
Sealed indictments, CrimPro Rule 6.
Sexual abuse.
Fictitious name indictments.
First or second degree sexual abuse, §23-331.
Subornation of perjury, sufficiency requirements, §23-324.
Sufficiency requirements, §§23-321 to 23-324.
Use of indictment or information, CrimPro Rule 7.
Waiver of indictment, CrimPro Rule 7.

INDIGENT PERSONS.
Access to justice initiative program, §§4-1701.01 to 4-1704.07.
See ACCESS TO JUSTICE INITIATIVE PROGRAM.
Adult protective services.
Representation, §7-1906.
Attorneys at law.
Right to counsel.
See RIGHT TO COUNSEL.
Collaborative law, §16-4010.
Deceased.
Cremation, §7-178.
Part of reservation 13 transferred for use as indigent burial ground, §10-135.
Public assistance, burial on, §§4-214.01 to 4-214.04.
Gallaudet.
Indigent blind children formerly instructed at, §38-2301.
Hospital admissions, §§44-704 to 44-706.
In forma pauperis proceedings.
Generally.
See IN FORMA PAUPERIS PROCEEDINGS.
Plan for furnishing representation to indigents, IndigentRep Rules I to IV.

INDIGENT PERSONS —Cont'd
Metabolic disorders, screening newborns for, §7-838.
Military affairs.
Enlistment of indigent children, §§21-181, 21-182.
Physicians to the poor.
Compensation of, §44-713.
Public assistance.
General provisions, §§4-201.01 to 4-221.01.
See PUBLIC ASSISTANCE.
Right to counsel.
Generally.
See RIGHT TO COUNSEL.
Plan for furnishing representation to indigents, IndigentRep Rules I to IV.
Student health care, §38-605.
Subpoenas.
Criminal cases, CrimPro Rule 17, USDistCt LCrR 17.1.
Delinquent minors, JuvProc Rule 17.

INDIRECT PURCHASERS.
Restraints of trade, §28-4509.

INDOOR CLEAN AIR ACT.
Smoking in public places, §§7-741.01 to 7-741.07.

INDOOR MOLD ASSESSMENT AND REMEDIATION, §§8-241.01 to 8-241.09.
Certification of professionals, §8-241.03.
Common law unaffected, §8-241.08.
Definitions, §8-241.01.
Fund, §8-241.07.
Private right of action, §8-241.06.
Residential property obligations, §8-241.04.
Rules and regulations, §8-241.09.
Standards, §8-241.02.
Violations, §8-241.05.

INDORSEMENTS.
See ENDORSEMENTS.

INDUSTRIAL HOME SCHOOL, §§44-1301 to 44-1304.

INDUSTRIAL LIFE INSURANCE, §§31-4801 to 31-4805.
Applicability of provisions, §31-4801.
Assignment, §31-4804.
Beneficiaries, §31-4805.
Claimants, §31-4805.
Defined, §31-4202.
Incontestability of policies, §31-4803.

INDUSTRIAL LIFE INSURANCE —Cont'd
Premiums, §31-4721.
Prohibited provisions, §31-4723.
Required provisions, §31-4722.
Validity of policies, §31-4802.

INDUSTRIAL REVENUE BONDS.
Fees, §§47-340.20 to 47-340.23.
Forward commitment program, §§47-340.01 to 47-340.16.
See BOND ISSUES.

INDUSTRIAL SAFETY.
Occupational safety and health.
General provisions, §§32-1101 to 32-1124.
Workers' compensation.
General provisions, §§32-1501 to 32-1545.
Workplace safety, §§32-801 to 32-812.
See WORKPLACE SAFETY.

INDUSTRY PLACEMENT FACILITY, §§31-5002 to 31-5011.

INFANTS.
See NEWBORNS.

INFECTIOUS DISEASES.
See COMMUNICABLE DISEASES.

IN FORMA PAUPERIS PROCEEDINGS.
Affidavit in support of motion, CivPro Form CA 106.
Appeals, D.C. courts, DCCtApp Forms 7a, 7b, DCCtApp Rule 24.
Appeals, federal cases, FRAP 24, USCtApp HPIP Rule VI, USCtApp Rule 24.
Affidavits, FRAP 24, FRAP Form 4.
Appendix, USCtApp HPIP Rule IX(b)(6).
Appointment of counsel, USCtApp HPIP Rule VI(d).
Compensation, USCtApp HPIP Rule VI(d)(4).
Duties in criminal cases, USCtApp HPIP Rule VI(d)(3).
Time and manner of appointment, USCtApp HPIP Rule VI(d)(1).
Withdrawal, USCtApp HPIP Rule VI(d)(2).
District court dismissal of suits brought in forma pauperis, USCtApp HPIP Rule VI(b).
Good faith, FRAP 24.
Leave to appeal, FRAP 24(a).
Procedural consequences of, USCtApp HPIP Rule VI(c).

IN FORMA PAUPERIS
  PROCEEDINGS —Cont'd
Appeals, federal cases —Cont'd
  When permitted, USCtApp HPIP Rule
    VI(a).
Attorneys' fees and costs, §15-712.
**Plan for furnishing representation
  to indigents,** IndigentRep Rules I
  to IV.
Subpoenas.
  Criminal cases, CrimPro Rule 17,
    USDistCt LCrR 17.1.
  Delinquent minors, JuvProc Rule 17.

INFORMATION TECHNOLOGY.
**Citywide technology support
  services,** §§1-1431 to 1-1433.
**Contractors contracting with
  District.**
  Apprenticeship programs, registration,
    §32-1431.

INFRACTIONS.
Administrative fines.
  Adjudication of traffic offenses,
    §§50-2301.01 to 50-2305.02.
    See TRAFFIC TICKET
      ADJUDICATION.
  General provisions, §§2-1801.01 to
    2-1803.03.
    See ADMINISTRATIVE FINES.

**INHERITANCE AND ESTATE
  TAXES,** §§47-3701 to 47-3722.
Amendment of returns, §47-3708.
**Amendment, repeal, or replacement
  of 1954 IRC,** §47-3721.
Apportionment, §47-3714.
Assessments, §§47-3717, 47-4312.
Certification of payment, §47-3710.
Chief financial officer.
  Marriage equality estate tax
    clarification, §1-301.153.
Compromises, §47-3704.
Credit, §47-3702.
Deficiencies, §47-3717.
Definitions, §47-3701.
Determination of taxes, §47-3717.
Fiduciary security transfers.
  Chapter not affected by tax
    obligations, §28-2909.
Filing, §§47-3705, 47-3707.
Final account, §47-3716.
Formula clauses, application of,
  §20-1108.
Income tax on estates, §§47-1809.01 to
  47-1809.10.
Issuance of rules and regulations,
  §47-3720.

INHERITANCE AND ESTATE TAXES
  —Cont'd
**Marriage equality estate tax
  clarification,** §1-301.153.
Mayor's authority, §§47-3704 to
  47-3721.
Nonresidents, §47-3703.
Payment of tax, §§47-3705, 47-3710.
Personal representatives.
  Defined, §47-3701.
  Liability of, §47-3712.
  Powers and duties, §47-3713.
Privacy and confidentiality,
  §47-3719.
Probate proceedings.
  Tax certificates.
    Death before January 1, 1981,
      Probate Rule 19.
    Death between January 1, 1981 and
      June 30, 1995, Probate Rule
      114.
    Death on or after July 1, 1995,
      Probate Rule 414.
Register of wills.
  Monthly report of, §47-3715.
Repeals, §§47-3721, 47-3722.
Reports.
  Amendment, repeal, or replacement of
    1954 IRC, §47-3721.
  Register of wills, §47-3715.
Residents, §47-3702.
Returns, §47-3705.
Tax certificates.
  Probate proceedings.
    Death before January 1, 1981,
      Probate Rule 19.
    Death between January 1, 1981 and
      June 30, 1995, Probate Rule
      114.
    Death on or after July 1, 1995,
      Probate Rule 414.
Transfer of estate, tax on, §47-3702.

INITIATIVE AND REFERENDUM,
  §§1-204.101 to 1-204.107, 1-1001.16.
Adoption of acts regarding,
  §1-204.107.
Applicability of provisions,
  §1-1021.03.
Approval of, §1-204.105.
Bar association referendums, DCBar
  Rule VII.
Defined, §1-204.101.
Home Rule act.
  Referendum, §§1-207.01 to 1-207.04.
Procedures, §§1-204.102, 1-1001.16.
Rejection of, §1-204.104.

INITIATIVE AND REFERENDUM
—Cont'd
Short title and summary required for, §1-204.106.
Statehood constitutional convention, §1-122.
Submission at election, §1-204.103.

INJUNCTIONS.
Alcoholic beverage licenses.
Cease and desist orders, §25-829.
Alcoholic beverage violations, places of, §25-805.
Assignments for benefit of creditors.
Assignment to hinder or defraud creditors, §28-2109.
Bankruptcy proceedings,
USDistDCBank Rule 7065-1.
Bees.
Enforcement of chapter, §8-1825.09.
Bills of lading.
Enjoining negotiation of document, §28:7-602.
Building code.
Failure to fireproof building.
Abatement of nuisance, §6-601.08.
Fire safety violations, §6-703.09.
Charitable solicitations.
Regulatory violations, §44-1712.
Child care facilities, §7-2048.
Cigarette sales below cost, §28-4525.
Construction codes, §6-1407.
Consumer credit reporting agencies.
Consumer security freeze.
Willful violations, §28-3864.
Consumer protection.
Restraining prohibited acts, §28-3909.
Conversion of health care entities, §44-609.
Corporations.
Appraisal and payment for shares, §29-311.50.
Judicial dissolution, §29-312.21.
Discrimination, §2-1403.07.
Domestic relations actions, DomRel Rule 65.
Appeal pending, DomRel Rule 62.
Drug, firearm, or prostitution-related nuisance abatement.
Bonds, surety, §42-3107.
Permanent, §42-3110.
Preliminary, §42-3104.
Violating, §42-3112.
Drug-related evictions, §42-3603.
Emergency medical services.
Injunction of violations, §7-2341.26.
Excavations or demolitions, improper, §34-2708.

INJUNCTIONS —Cont'd
Financial exploitation of vulnerable adults and elderly persons.
Injunction, restraining order and asset protection, §22-938.
Fire-standard-compliant cigarettes.
Enforcement of provisions, §7-1756.
Fraternal benefit societies, §§31-5327, 31-5329.
Funeral directors, §3-419.
Gas station violations, §36-302.05.
Franchise purchase rights, §36-304.14.
Guardians of minors interfering with minor's estate, §21-113.
Hate crimes, §22-3704.
Hazardous waste management, §8-1310.
Health occupations practiced unlawfully, §3-1210.10.
Human Rights Commission, §2-1403.07.
Insurance companies.
Unauthorized entities.
Administrative and judicial enforcement, §31-233.
Insurance holding companies, §31-709.
Insurers rehabilitation and liquidation proceedings, §31-1304.
Labor unions' label, brand, or mark, unauthorized use of, §36-102.
Lead-hazard prevention and elimination violations, §8-231.15.
Long-term care ombudsman, §7-705.01.
Medical and dental colleges, §38-1404.
Milk container registration, §36-131.
Nonprofit corporations.
Judicial dissolution, §§29-412.20, 29-412.21.
Nursing homes.
Discharge, transfer, or relocation of residents of, §44-1004.01.
Occupations and professions licensure, §47-2853.30.
Personal representatives.
Restraining acts, §20-521.
Pharmacists and pharmacies, §47-2885.20.
Preliminary injunctions, CivPro Rule 65, USDistCt LCvR 65.1.
Prescription drugs, excessive pricing, §28-4555.
Prostitution, houses of, §§22-2714, 22-2716.

INJUNCTIONS —Cont'd
Residential drug-related evictions.
Preliminary injunction review,
§42-3603.
Full hearing, §42-3604.
Restraints of trade, §§28-4507,
28-4508.
Relief for injuries to or within the
District of Columbia, §28-4507.
Relief for private parties, §28-4508.
Secured transactions.
Defaults.
Noncompliance with provisions,
§28:9-625.
Security agents and brokers.
Administrative cease and desist
orders, §31-5606.02.
Temporary and permanent injunction,
§31-5606.03.
Stay of proceedings, CivPro Rule 62.
Domestic relations actions, DomRel
Rule 62.
Temporary restraining orders,
CivPro Rule 65, USDistCt LCvR
65.1.
Domestic relations actions, DomRel
Rule 65.
Tenant organizations.
Violation of provisions, §42-3505.06.
**Title insurance producers, RESPA
violations,** §31-5041.10.
Title insurers, RESPA violations,
§31-5031.22.
**Tobacco master settlement
agreement enforcement,**
§7-1803.06.
Tobacco tax.
Enforcement of provisions, §47-2425.
Trade secrets, §36-402.
**Vulnerable adults and elderly
persons.**
Criminal abuse, neglect and financial
exploitation, §22-938.
Warehouse receipts.
Enjoining negotiation of document,
§28:7-602.
Wastewater disposal system,
§8-105.11.
Zoning.
Inclusionary zoning violations,
§6-1041.04.

IN-KIND RESOURCES.
Public assistance, §4-205.40.

INMATE WELFARE FUND, §24-281.
Audits, §24-282.
Committee, §24-284.

INMATE WELFARE FUND —Cont'd
Definitions, §24-281.
Establishment, §24-282.
Reports, §24-282.
Uses, §24-283.

INNERLOOP FREEWAY SYSTEM,
§10-511.06.

INNOVATION FUND, §§1-325.221 to
1-325.226.
Administration, §1-325.222.
Definitions, §1-325.221.
Duplicative projects.
Limitation, §1-325.226.
Eligibility to receive subgrant,
§1-325.223.
Established, §1-325.222.
Grant-managing entity.
Authorization, §1-325.225.
Defined, §1-325.221.
Limitation on duplicative projects,
§1-325.226.
Purposes, §1-325.222.
Reporting requirements, §1-325.224.

INSANITARY BUILDINGS, §§6-901 to
6-919.
Appropriations, §6-917.
Condemnation proceedings, §6-903.
Appeal from order, §§6-913, 6-914.
Board for the Condemnation of
Insanitary Buildings, §6-902.
Cancellation of condemnation order,
§6-906.
Condemnation Review Board, §6-902.
Destruction, removal, or concealment
of order attached to building,
§6-912.
Extensions, §6-906.
Failure of owner to comply with
condemnation order, §6-907.
Notice, §§6-903, 6-910.
Occupancy of condemned buildings,
§§6-903, 6-904.
Repair or demolition by owner, §6-905.
Review of order, §6-913.
Definitions, §6-918.
Fines, §6-916.
Historic districts and landmarks,
§6-1111.
**Incompetent or incapacitated
persons owning,** §6-909.
Inspections, §§6-901, 6-911.
Landlord and tenant.
Neglect of tenants or occupants,
§6-915.
Limitation of actions, §6-919.

INSANITARY BUILDINGS —Cont'd

Neglect by tenants or occupants, due to, §§6-913, 6-914.

Notice, §§6-903, 6-910.

Penalties, §6-916.

Prior law, actions under, §6-919.

Repair or demolition.
Assessment of costs against owner failing to ensure, §6-907.
Owner, by, §6-905.

Title disputes, §6-908.

Title to property, controversy over, §6-908.

INSANITY DEFENSE, §§24-501 to 24-503, CrimPro Rule 12.2.

Acquittal by reason of insanity, §24-501.

Commitment by reason of.
Expenses of, §24-501.
Release from confinement, §24-501.
Sentence, while serving, §24-502.
Trial, during, §24-501.

Restoration to sanity, §24-503.

Sexual psychopaths, §§22-3803 to 22-3811.
See SEXUAL PSYCHOPATHS.

INSIGNIA.

Police and fire and emergency medical services departments.
Unauthorized use, §22-1409.

Private vehicles-for-hire.
Trade dress requirements, §50-301.29d.

INSOLVENCY.
See BANKRUPTCY AND INSOLVENCY.

INSPECTIONS.

Administrative search warrants, CivPro Rule 204.

Adoption records, §16-311.

Asbestos contractors, §8-111.05.

Asphalts and cements.
Inspector of, §1-333.02.

Assisted living residences, §44-103.06.

Boiler inspections, §§2-101 to 2-118.

Building code.
See BUILDING CODE.

Buildings, §2-138.

Business improvement districts, §2-1215.12.

Business licenses, §§47-2851.03c, 47-2851.16.

Cable television.
Records, §34-1259.05.
Right to inspect, §34-1259.01.

INSPECTIONS —Cont'd

Central detention facility, §24-211.02.

Child care facilities, §7-2043.

Child labor, §32-214.

Child-placing agencies, §4-1409.

Clinical laboratories, §44-207.

Communicable diseases.
Access to premises regarding, §7-138.

Construction codes.
Third party plan review.
Third party inspectors, §6-1405.04.

Contracts.
Sale of goods.
Inspection of goods, §§28:2-512, 28:2-513.

Controlled substances, §48-905.05.

Director of Department of Licenses, Investigations, and Inspections, §1-301.03.

Drug manufacture and distribution licensure, §48-708.

Electricity supply in buildings, §§2-131 to 2-133.

Elevators, §2-139.

Emergency medical services.
Mayor's powers, §7-2341.13.

Eminent domain as to real property for United States, jury inspection of property, §16-1359.

False personation of inspectors of District departments, §22-1405.

Family homes, §4-1409.

Fire escapes, §2-139.

Fish and game, §22-4329.

Fish and other marine products, inspectors of, §7-173.

Gas companies.
Inspector of gas and meters, §34-1601.

Hazardous materials transportation, §§8-1403.01, 8-1403.02.

Hazardous substance releases, §8-634.04.

Hazardous waste management, §8-1307.

Health care facilities, §44-505.

Health department, §§7-731, 7-741.02.

Homeless services.
Premises of providers, §4-754.31.

Human Services Department inspectors, §7-103.

Juvenile records, §§16-2331 to 16-2333.02.

Lead-hazard prevention and elimination.
Right of entry and inspection, §8-231.05.

INSPECTIONS —Cont'd
Lead-hazard prevention and elimination —Cont'd
Risk assessment of property, §8-231.03.
Certification for entities performing, §8-231.10.
Lead paint in public buildings, §10-702.
Marriage license applications, §46-416.
Money lenders' registers, §26-904.
Mortgage lenders and brokers, §26-1112.
Motor fuel tax, §47-2307.
Motor vehicles, §§50-1101 to 50-1109.
See MOTOR VEHICLE REGISTRATION.
Nonpublic schools for students with disabilities, §38-2561.09.
Notice of attempted residential service, §2-140.
Nurse staffing agencies.
Inspection of offices and operations, §44-1051.16.
Occupational safety and health, §32-1112.
Parentage records, §16-2348.
Pharmacists and pharmacies, §47-2885.16.
Plumbing, §§2-134 to 2-137.
Prescription drug pricing, §48-804.03.
Private fire hydrants, §34-2410.04.
Public procurements, §2-354.18.
Rental housing, §42-3509.08.
Savings and loan acquisitions, §26-1214.
Security and fire alarm contractors, §7-2810.
Solid waste facilities, §8-1056.
Surveyor of the District.
Fee schedule for services of, §1-1329.
Taxicabs.
Public vehicle inspection officer training, §50-301.30.
Telegraph and telephone company equipment, §34-1911.05.
Transportation department.
Enforcement, §50-921.19.
Underground storage tanks, §8-113.08.
Unemployment compensation, §51-117.
Vector-borne disease control, §8-2131.03.

INSPECTIONS —Cont'd
Veterinary facilities, §47-2888.05.
Wastewater disposal systems, §8-105.08.
Water pollution and water quality, §8-103.15.
Weights and measures, §§37-201.03 to 37-201.06.
See WEIGHTS AND MEASURES.
Workplace fraud.
Complaints, investigation, §32-1331.05.
Youth residential facilities, §7-2105.

INSPECTOR GENERAL, OFFICE OF.
Annual budget for office, §1-301.115a.
Budget.
Adoption, §1-301.115a.
Creation of office within executive branch, §1-301.115a.
Financial statement and report for fiscal year.
Audit by inspector general, §1-204.48.
Inspector general.
Appointment, §1-301.115a.
Deadline, §1-301.115b.
Audits, §1-301.115a.
Compensation, §1-301.115a.
Contract with auditor not officer or employee of office, §1-301.115a.
Duties, §1-301.115a.
Head of office, §1-301.115a.
Powers, §1-301.115a.
Qualifications, §1-301.115a.
Term, §1-301.115a.
Transition rule, §1-301.115b.
Vacancy, §1-301.115a.
Investigators carrying out felony violations.
Authority, §1-301.115a.
Peer review of office, §1-301.115a.
Reprisal against person making complaint or furnishing information to office.
Prohibition, §1-301.115a.
Term, §1-301.115a.

INSTALLMENT CONTRACTS.
Leases, UCC.
Default.
Defined, §28:2A-103.
Lessee's rights and remedies, §28:2A-508.
Rejection and default, §28:2A-510.
Sale of goods, UCC, §28:2-612.

INSTALLMENT LOANS.
Actions.
Consumers' remedies, §28-3813.

INSTALLMENT LOANS —Cont'd
Actions —Cont'd
Creditors' actions, §28-3812.
Annual percentage rate.
Defined, §28-3308.
Assignment of earnings.
Prohibited, §28-3804.
Attorneys at law.
Fees.
Consumers' remedies, §28-3813.
Provision for attorneys' fees,
§28-3806.
Balloon payments, §28-3803.
Confession of judgment.
Authorization to confess judgment.
Prohibited, §28-3804.
Conflict of laws, §28-3816.
Consumer protection, §§28-3801 to
28-3819.
See CONSUMER PROTECTION.
Creditors' remedies.
Limitation on creditors' remedies,
§28-3812.
Cure of default by debtor, §28-3812.
Damages.
Consumers' remedies, §28-3813.
Debt collection.
Restriction on creditors and debt
collectors, §28-3814.
Default.
Limitation on creditors' remedies,
§28-3812.
Defenses.
Lender subject to defenses arising
from sales, §28-3809.
Definitions, §28-3802.
Direct motor vehicle installment loans,
§28-3603.
**Direct motor vehicle installment
loans,** §§28-3601 to 28-3603.
**Enforcement of consumer protection
provisions.**
Administrative enforcement, §28-3815.
Equal payments, §28-3803.
Finance charge.
Defined, §§28-3308, 28-3603.
Motor vehicles.
Direct motor vehicle installment
loans, §28-3602.
Permitted finance charge, §28-3308.
Interest.
Maximum rate, §28-3308.
Loan sharking.
Repayment unenforceable, §28-3812.

INSTALLMENT LOANS —Cont'd
Motor vehicles, §28-3602.
Applicable law, §28-3601.
Finance charge, §28-3602.
Notice.
Default.
Required notice by creditor,
§28-3812.
Prepayment, §28-3309.
Punitive damages.
Consumers' remedies for violations,
§28-3813.
**Redemption of collateral after
default,** §28-3812.
Remedies.
Consumers' remedies, §28-3813.
Creditors' remedies.
Limitation on creditors' remedies,
§28-3812.
Repossession of collateral, §28-3812.
Salaries.
Assignment of earnings prohibited,
§28-3804.
Unconscionable agreements,
§28-3812.
Violations.
Punitive damages, §28-3813.
Wages.
Assignment of earnings prohibited,
§28-3804.

INSTALLMENT PAYMENTS.
Child support withholding, §46-220.
Direct installment loans.
Consumer credit, §28-3809.
Finance charges on, §§28-3308,
28-3602.
Motor vehicles, §§28-3601 to 28-3603.
**Finance charges on direct
installment loans,** §28-3308.
Motor vehicle judgments,
§50-1301.50.
Small claims court, §16-3907.
Judgments, SmallClaims Rule 17.
Teachers, §38-1902.

INSTALLMENT SALE INCOME.
Income taxes, §47-1804.04.

INSTRUCTIONS TO JURY.
See JURY INSTRUCTIONS.

INSURANCE.
Adjuster licensing, §§31-1631.01 to
31-1631.12.
See INSURANCE ADJUSTER
LICENSING.

INSURANCE —Cont'd

Agents and brokers.

Managing general agents, §§31-1501 to 31-1506.

See INSURANCE AGENTS AND BROKERS.

Producer licensing generally, §§31-1131.01 to 31-1131.19.

See INSURANCE PRODUCER LICENSING.

AIDS.

Discrimination in providing insurance on bases of AIDS test, §§31-1601 to 31-1610.

Appeal by person testing positive under testing protocols, §31-1604.

Applicability, §31-1602.

Applicants diagnosed as having AIDS, §31-1605.

Consent to tests, §31-1606.

Contesting validity of policy or contract, §31-1607.

Definitions, §31-1601.

Disclosure restrictions, §31-1606.

Enforcement provisions, §31-1608.

Prohibited acts, §31-1603.

Discrimination in use of AIDS test, §31-1610.

Rules, §31-1609.

Testing standards and protocols, §31-1604.

Alcohol and drug abuse treatment, §44-1209.

Coverage.

Definitions, §31-3101.

Exemptions, §31-3105.

Policy coverage requirements, §31-3102.

Annual audited financial reports, §§31-301 to 31-314.

See INSURANCE COMPANIES.

Assisted living residences, §44-111.01.

Bicycle insurance policies, §§50-531 to 50-535.

Boiler inspections, §§2-107, 2-110.

Business transactions with producer controlled insurers, §§31-401 to 31-408.

See INSURANCE COMPANIES.

Bus shelters.

Franchisee, §9-1156.

Cable television franchise, §34-1256.04.

Captive insurance companies, §§31-3931.01 to 31-3931.23.

See CAPTIVE INSURANCE COMPANIES.

INSURANCE —Cont'd

Casualty and other insurance rates, §§31-2701 to 31-2714.

Child development homes liability coverage, §§31-4001 to 31-4003.

Definitions, §31-4001.

General provisions, §31-4002.

Liability coverage levels established by commissioner, §31-4003.

Motor vehicle liability insurance, §31-4002.

Optional liability and comprehensive coverage, §31-4002.

Choice in drug treatment program, §7-3007.

Claims against estates, §20-903.

Commercial guard dogs.

Liability insurance, §8-1841.04.

Common carriers, §35-301.

Community development programs, §6-1006.

Compacts.

Interstate insurance product regulation compact.

Authority to enter, §31-1391.

Compliance self-evaluation privilege, §§31-851 to 31-858.

Applicability, §31-858.

Burden of proof of applicability, §31-857.

Court-ordered disclosure of material, §§31-854, 31-855.

Definitions, §31-851.

Privileged information, §31-853.

Requests for disclosure, §31-856.

Scope of privilege, §31-852.

Condominiums, §42-1903.10.

Corporations.

Officers and directors, §29-306.57.

Credit for reinsurance, §§31-501 to 31-503.

Credit life, accident and health insurance.

General provisions, §§31-5101 to 31-5112.

See CREDIT LIFE, ACCIDENT AND HEALTH INSURANCE.

Demutualization, §§31-901 to 31-915.

See INSURANCE DEMUTUALIZATION.

Department of insurance, securities, and banking.

General provisions, §§31-101 to 31-108.

See INSURANCE, SECURITIES, AND BANKING, DEPARTMENT OF.

INSURANCE —Cont'd
Discovery of insurance agreements,
CivPro Rule 26.
No-fault motor vehicle insurance,
§31-2403.01.
**Discrimination based upon AIDS
test,** §§31-1601 to 31-1610.
See AIDS.
Domestic partner benefits, §§32-701
to 32-710.
See DOMESTIC PARTNER
BENEFITS.
Eastern Market, §37-112.
**Electronic delivery and posting of
documents,** §§31-651.01 to
31-651.03.
Emergency medical services.
Liability insurance requirement,
§7-2341.09.
Evidence.
Policy or certificate as prima facie
evidence, §28:1-307.
Fire, casualty and marine insurance.
Certificate of authority.
Issuance and renewal, §31-2502.02.
Revocation and suspension,
§31-2502.03.
General provisions, §§31-2501.01 to
31-2502.42.
See FIRE AND CASUALTY
INSURANCE.
Foreign mission liability insurance.
Termination or lapse of, §6-1304.01.
Fraternal benefit societies.
General provisions, §§31-5301 to
31-5335.
See FRATERNAL BENEFIT
SOCIETIES.
Guard dogs, commercial.
Liability insurance, §8-1841.04.
Health insurance.
General provisions.
See HEALTH INSURANCE.
Long-term care insurance, §§31-3601
to 31-3612.
See LONG-TERM CARE
INSURANCE.
Health maintenance organizations.
General provisions, §§31-3401 to
31-3431.
See HEALTH MAINTENANCE
ORGANIZATIONS.
High school cadets.
Arms issued to, §38-909.

INSURANCE —Cont'd
Holding companies.
General provisions, §§31-701 to
31-738.
See INSURANCE HOLDING
COMPANIES.
Homeowner's insurance.
Fire and casualty insurance generally,
§§31-2501.01 to 31-2502.42.
Homicide, §19-320.
Horizontal property regimes,
§§42-2020 to 42-2022.
**Hospital and medical services
corporations.**
General provisions, §§31-3501 to
31-3524.
See HOSPITAL AND MEDICAL
SERVICES CORPORATIONS.
Human papillomavirus vaccination,
§§7-1651.01 to 7-1651.05.
Industrial life insurance, §§31-4801 to
31-4805.
Industry placement facility,
§§31-5002 to 31-5011.
Insurance companies.
General provisions.
See INSURANCE COMPANIES.
Life insurance companies, §§31-4201
to 31-4603.
See LIFE INSURANCE
COMPANIES.
**Insurers rehabilitation and
liquidation proceedings.**
General provisions, §§31-1301 to
31-1357.
See INSURERS REHABILITATION
AND LIQUIDATION
PROCEEDINGS.
Internet.
Electronic delivery and posting of
documents, §31-651.03.
**Interstate banking and branch
banks,** §26-707.01.
**Interstate insurance product
regulation compact.**
Authority to enter, §31-1391.
Leases, UCC.
Leased goods, §28:2A-218.
**Life and health insurance guaranty
association.**
General provisions, §§31-5401 to
31-5416.
See LIFE AND HEALTH
INSURANCE GUARANTY
ASSOCIATION.

INSURANCE —Cont'd
Life insurance companies.
General provisions, §§31-4201 to
31-4603.
See LIFE INSURANCE
COMPANIES.
Limited liability companies.
Managers and members, §29-804.08.
Limited partnerships.
General partners, insurance on behalf
of, §29-704.09.
Living will as condition of, §7-628.
Long-term care insurance, §§31-3601
to 31-3612.
See LONG-TERM CARE
INSURANCE.
Manslaughter, §19-320.
Marine insurance.
Fire, casualty and marine insurance,
§§31-2501.01 to 31-2502.42.
See FIRE AND CASUALTY
INSURANCE.
Investments, §§31-1373.01 to
31-1373.12.
See INSURANCE INVESTMENTS.
Prohibitions, §31-2601.01.
**Medical liability captive insurance
agency,** §§1-307.81 to 1-307.95.
See MEDICAL LIABILITY CAPTIVE
INSURANCE AGENCY.
Medicare supplement insurance.
General provisions, §§31-3701 to
31-3710.
See MEDICARE SUPPLEMENT
INSURANCE.
Mental illness coverage.
Definitions, §31-3101.
Exemptions, §31-3105.
Policy coverage requirements,
§31-3102.
Metrorail and metrobus.
Washington metropolitan area transit
authority compact, §9-1107.01.
Mortgages and deeds of trust.
Casualty insurance premiums.
Requirements, §28-3301.
Motor vehicle insurance.
See MOTOR VEHICLE INSURANCE.
Motor vehicles.
Safety responsibility act, §§50-1301.01
to 50-1301.86.
See MOTOR VEHICLE SAFETY
RESPONSIBILITY.
Murder, §19-320.

INSURANCE —Cont'd
Newborn health insurance.
General provisions, §§31-3801 to
31-3805.
See NEWBORN HEALTH
INSURANCE.
No-fault motor vehicle insurance.
General provisions, §§31-2401 to
31-2408.01.
See NO-FAULT MOTOR VEHICLE
INSURANCE.
Nonprofit corporations.
Officers and directors, §29-406.57.
Partnerships.
Insurance against liability, §29-604.01.
Pesticide operators.
Liability insurance for, §8-407.
Portable electronics insurance,
§§31-5051.01 to 31-5051.06.
See PORTABLE ELECTRONICS
INSURANCE.
Powers of attorney, §21-2110.
Private vehicles-for-hire.
Insurance requirements, §50-301.29c.
Producer licensing generally,
§§31-1131.01 to 31-1131.19.
See INSURANCE PRODUCER
LICENSING.
**Property and liability insurance
guaranty association.**
General provisions, §§31-5501 to
31-5515.
See PROPERTY AND LIABILITY
INSURANCE GUARANTY
ASSOCIATION.
Public contracts, §§2-205.01, 2-205.02.
Public insurance adjuster licensing,
§§31-1631.01 to 31-1631.12.
See INSURANCE ADJUSTER
LICENSING.
Rates, §§31-2701 to 31-2714.
Additional powers of commissioner,
§31-2708.
Adjustment, §31-2704.
Applicability of chapter, §31-2702.
Classifications, establishment,
§31-2703.
Contesting commissioner's actions.
Judicial proceedings, §31-2710.
Cooperative and concerted action,
§31-2705.
Definitions, §31-2701.
Enforcement of regulations, §31-2708.
Examination of companies, §31-2708.

INSURANCE —Cont'd
Rates —Cont'd
Excessive, inadequate, discriminatory
rates prohibited, §31-2703.
Removal of discrimination, §31-2704.
Exemptions and limitations, §31-2714.
Filing requirements, §31-2704.
Grievance procedure, §31-2707.
Hearings.
Commissioner's authority, §31-2708.
Information furnished insured and
commissioner, §31-2707.
Making rates, §31-2703.
Medical malpractice insurance rates,
§31-2703.
Motor vehicle insurance rates,
§31-2703.
Past and prospective loss experience,
§31-2703.
Violations, §31-2709.
Reinsurance.
General provisions.
See REINSURANCE.
Intermediaries, §§31-1801 to 31-1810.
See REINSURANCE
INTERMEDIARIES.
Rental of public space, §10-1104.02.
Renter's insurance.
Fire and casualty insurance generally,
§§31-2501.01 to 31-2502.42.
Retirement Board liability, §1-743.
Risk retention groups.
General provisions, §§31-4101 to
31-4112.
See RISK RETENTION GROUPS.
Savings and loan acquisitions,
§26-1212.
School buildings and grounds.
Public liability insurance for,
§38-401.02.
Simultaneous deaths, §19-504.
Student loan insurance program,
§1-307.01.
Subrogation.
Procedural rules for subrogation cases,
CivPro Rule 40-III.
Substance abuse.
Choice in drug treatment program,
§7-3007.
**Substance abuse and mental illness
coverage,** §§31-3101 to 31-3112.
See HEALTH INSURANCE.
Taxicabs, §50-301.14.
Title insurance producers,
§§31-5041.01 to 31-5041.12.
See TITLE INSURANCE
PRODUCERS.

INSURANCE —Cont'd
Title insurers, §§31-5031.01 to
31-5031.24.
See TITLE INSURERS.
Unauthorized entities, §§31-231 to
31-233.
Underwriting, §§31-5001 to 31-5011.
Unfair trade practices, §§31-2231.01
to 31-2231.25.
Administrative remedy only.
Construction of chapter,
§31-2231.02.
Appeals of commissioner's decisions.
Judicial review, §31-2231.24.
Boycott, coercion, intimidation,
§31-2231.06.
Cease and desist orders, §31-2231.22.
Civil penalty.
Failure to comply with order,
§31-2231.22.
Claims history.
Failure to provide, §31-2231.16.
Complaints handling procedures.
Failure to maintain, §31-2231.18.
Defamation, §31-2231.05.
Definitions, §31-2231.01.
Discrimination, §§31-2231.11,
31-2231.13.
Examination and investigation,
§31-2231.22.
Existing right in law and equity.
Not limited or impaired,
§31-2231.02.
False advertising, §§31-2231.03,
31-2231.04.
False information, §31-2231.04.
False statements and entries,
§31-2231.08.
Favored agent or insurer.
Coercion of debtor, §31-2231.20.
Financial planning practices.
Insurance agent or broker,
§31-2231.15.
Hearings, §31-2231.23.
Inducements to purchase.
Stocks or securities, special or
advisory board contracts,
§31-2231.09.
Interlocking ownership, management,
§31-2231.14.
Misrepresentations, §31-2231.03.
Insurance applications, §31-2231.19.
Premiums.
Illegal dealing in, excess charges for
insurance, §31-2231.07.
Private cause of action not created.
Construction of chapter,
§31-2231.02.

INSURANCE —Cont'd
Unfair trade practices —Cont'd
Rebates.
Life, health and annuities,
§31-2231.12.
Property, causality, surety
insurance, §31-2231.13.
Records.
Failure to maintain marketing and
performance records,
§31-2231.10.
Regulations, §31-2231.25.
Settlement practices, §31-2231.17.
Twisting, §31-2231.21.
Untrue, misleading, deceptive
information, §31-2231.04.
Workers' compensation, §32-1538.

**INSURANCE ADJUSTER
LICENSING,** §§31-1631.01 to
31-1631.12.
**Adjustments, compliance with
contract and laws,** §31-1631.09.
Bond, surety, §31-1631.05.
Contracts, §31-1631.08.
Definitions, §31-1631.02.
Denial of license, §31-1631.07.
Exemptions from provisions,
§31-1631.12.
Issuance of license, §31-1631.04.
License requirement, §31-1631.03.
Qualifications, §31-1631.04.
Record keeping requirements,
§31-1631.06.
Revocation or suspension of license,
§31-1631.07.
Rules promulgation, §31-1631.10.
Short title, §31-1631.01.

INSURANCE ADMINISTRATION.
Abolition of, §31-108.
Transfer of materials from, §31-105.

**INSURANCE AGENTS AND
BROKERS.**
**Fingerprint-based background
checks.**
Confidentiality of information,
§31-633.
Definitions, §31-631.
Requirement of, §31-632.
Rules, §31-634.
Managing general agents, §§31-1501
to 31-1506.
Acts of agent considered to be acts of
insurer, §31-1505.
Contract provision requirements,
§31-1503.

**INSURANCE AGENTS AND
BROKERS** —Cont'd
Managing general agents —Cont'd
Definitions, §31-1501.
Examination of agent as insurer,
§31-1505.
Fines, §31-1506.
Liabilities, §31-1506.
Licenses, §31-1502.
Penalties, §31-1506.
Powers and duties of insurers
regarding, §31-1504.
Producer licensing generally,
§§31-1131.01 to 31-1131.19.
See INSURANCE PRODUCER
LICENSING.
Reinsurance intermediaries.
General provisions, §§31-1801 to
31-1810.
See REINSURANCE
INTERMEDIARIES.
Security agents and brokers.
General provisions, §§31-5601.01 to
31-5608.04.
See SECURITY AGENTS AND
BROKERS.
Title insurers, favored producers,
§31-5031.16.

**INSURANCE AND SECURITIES
REGULATION, DEPARTMENT
OF.**
Commissioner.
Captive insurance companies.
Financial examination, §31-3931.14.
Fine, imposition, §31-3931.15.
Judicial review of commissioner,
§31-3931.20.
Mandamus, §31-3931.20.
Regulations, §31-3931.21.
Revocation or suspension of
certificate of authority,
§31-3931.15.

INSURANCE COMPANIES.
**Acquisitions and disposition of
assets.**
Reporting, §31-1002.
**AIDS test, discrimination on
provision of insurance on basis
of,** §§31-1601 to 31-1610.
Annual audited financial reports,
§§31-301 to 31-314.
Adverse financial condition, notice of,
§31-308.
Applicability of provisions, §31-314.
Audit committee responsibilities,
§31-311.01.

INSURANCE COMPANIES —Cont'd
Annual audited financial reports
  —Cont'd
  Canadian and British companies,
    §31-313.
  Consolidated or combined, §31-306.
  Contents, §31-303.
  Definitions, §31-301.
  Effective date of provisions, §31-312.
  Exemptions, §31-312.
  Extension to file, §31-302.
  False or misleading statements,
    §31-311.02.
  Filing, §31-302.
  Independent certified public
    accountant.
    Designated to perform audit,
      §31-304.
    Letter of qualifications submitted
      by, §31-310.
    Qualifications of, §31-305.
    Scope of audit and report, §31-307.
    Workpapers of, §31-311.
  Management report.
    Internal control over financial
      reporting, §31-311.03.
  Notice of adverse financial condition,
    §31-308.
  Omissions, §31-311.02.
  Prohibited conduct, §31-311.02.
  Records, §31-311.
  Unremediated material weaknesses in
    internal controls.
  Written communication, §31-309.
**Application made by insured to be
  delivered with policy,** §31-5203.
Audit committees, §31-302.
  Independence of members, §31-311.01.
  Requirements, §31-311.01.
Boiler inspections by, §2-107.
**Business transactions with producer
  controlled insurers,** §§31-401 to
  31-408.
  Applicability of minimum standards
    for, §31-403.
  Applicability of provisions, §31-402.
  Audit committee, §31-405.
  Contract provision requirements,
    §31-404.
  Definitions, §31-401.
  Disclosure, §31-407.
  Penalties, §31-408.
  Reports, §31-406.
Capital requirements, §§31-208,
  31-5201, 31-5202.

INSURANCE COMPANIES —Cont'd
Captive insurance companies,
  §§31-3931.01 to 31-3931.23.
  See CAPTIVE INSURANCE
    COMPANIES.
Certificates of authority.
  See CERTIFICATES OF AUTHORITY.
**Conversion of mutual company to
  stock company.**
  General provisions, §§31-901 to
    31-915.
    See INSURANCE
      DEMUTUALIZATION.
**Conversion of reciprocal insurance
  company.**
  Mutual insurance company, §§31-751
    to 31-760.
Demutualization, §§31-901 to 31-915.
  See INSURANCE
    DEMUTUALIZATION.
**Department of insurance, securities,
  and banking.**
  Filing with, §§31-101 to 31-108.
**Discrimination based upon AIDS
  test,** §§31-1601 to 31-1610.
  See AIDS.
District.
  Principal office and records to be
    located in, §31-5204.
**Domestication of US branch of
  non-US insurer,** §§31-2301 to
  31-2307.
  Authorized, §31-2302.
  Definitions, §31-2301.
  Domestication agreement.
    Authorization and execution,
      §31-2304.
    Consummation, §31-2306.
    Prior written approval, §31-2303.
    Required, §31-2302.
  Final approval by commissioner,
    §31-2305.
  Prior written approval of
    domestication agreement,
    §31-2303.
  Regulations, §31-2307.
  Transfer of deposits, §31-2306.
  Withdrawal of trust assets, §31-2306.
Domestic life companies.
  Power of mutual company to borrow or
    assume liability, §31-4434.
**Domestic stock insurance
  companies,** §§31-601 to 31-604.
  Authority vested in mayor not
    affected, §31-604.
  Defined, §31-601.

INSURANCE COMPANIES —Cont'd
Domestic stock insurance companies
—Cont'd
Proxies, consents, authorization.
Rules and regulations, §31-602.
Purchase or sale of equity security.
Beneficial owners, §31-603.
Redomestication of foreign
corporations, §§31-1701 to
31-1705.
Revocation or suspension of certificate
of authority.
Violation of rules and regulations,
§31-602.
Statements filed by beneficial owners,
directors, officers, §31-603.
**Employee compensation liability
insurance companies, §31-5205.**
Examination of insurers, §§31-1401 to
31-1407.
Access to books, records, accounts, etc.,
§31-1403.
Authority to conduct, §31-1402.
Captive insurance companies,
§31-3931.14.
Conduct, §31-1403.
Confidentiality of working papers,
recorded information, documents,
etc., §31-1404.
Conflict of interest, examiners,
§31-1405.
Costs, §31-1406.
Definitions, §31-1401.
Examination warrant, §31-1403.
Foreign or alien insurers.
Reports in lieu of examination,
§31-1402.
Guidelines and procedures, §31-1403.
Hearings, §31-1404.
Immunity from liability, §31-1407.
Opening report for public inspection,
§31-1404.
Orders entered, requirements,
§31-1404.
Reports, §31-1404.
Scheduling, §31-1402.
Scope, §31-1402.
Foreign insurers.
Domestication of US branch of non-US
insurer, §§31-2301 to 31-2307.
Use of District as state of entry by
non-United States insurers,
§§31-2201 to 31-2207.
Additional requirements for US
branches, §31-2206.
Authorization, §31-2202.

INSURANCE COMPANIES —Cont'd
Foreign insurers —Cont'd
Use of District as state of entry by
non-United States insurers
—Cont'd
Commissioner's authority, §31-2207.
Definitions, §31-2201.
Reporting requirements for US
branches and non-US branches,
§31-2205.
Requirements before authorizing
entry, §31-2202.
Trust account established pursuant
to trust agreement, §31-2202.
Amount of trust assets required,
§31-2203.
Requirements for trust agreement,
§31-2204.
Hazardous financial conditions.
Standard for determining, §§31-2101
to 31-2103.
Corrective actions, §31-2102.
Generally, §31-2101.
Judicial review of determination,
§31-2103.
Making determination, §31-2101.
Health maintenance organizations.
General provisions, §§31-3401 to
31-3431.
See HEALTH MAINTENANCE
ORGANIZATIONS.
Holding companies.
General provisions, §§31-701 to
31-738.
See INSURANCE HOLDING
COMPANIES.
Human papillomavirus vaccination,
§§7-1651.01 to 7-1651.05.
**Independent certified public
accountant.**
Annual audited financial reports. See
within this heading, "Annual
audited financial reports."
**Insurance industry material
transactions disclosures,**
§§31-1001 to 31-1004.
Report requirements, §31-1001.
Acquisitions and disposition of
assets, §31-1002.
Confidentiality, §31-1004.
Nonrenewals, cancellations,
revisions of ceded insurance,
§31-1003.
Insurance regulatory trust fund,
§§31-1201 to 31-1210.
See INSURANCE REGULATORY
TRUST FUND.

INSURANCE COMPANIES —Cont'd
Insurers rehabilitation and liquidation proceedings.
General provisions, §§31-1301 to 31-1357.
See INSURERS REHABILITATION AND LIQUIDATION PROCEEDINGS.
Internal control over financial reporting.
Management report, §31-311.03.
Unremediated material weaknesses.
Written communication, §31-309.
Licenses, §§31-5201, 31-5202.
Fire and casualty insurance.
See FIRE AND CASUALTY INSURANCE.
Insurance holding companies, §31-713.
Insurance premium finance companies, §§31-1103 to 31-1105.
Reinsurance intermediaries, §31-1802.
Taxation, §§47-2603, 47-2604, 47-2607.
United States branches of non-United States insurers, §31-2206.
Life insurance companies.
Certificate of authority.
Investigation of qualifications, §31-4304.
Issuance, §31-4304.
Revocation or suspension, §31-4305.
General provisions, §§31-4201 to 31-4603.
See LIFE INSURANCE COMPANIES.
Liquidation proceedings, §§31-1301 to 31-1357.
See INSURERS REHABILITATION AND LIQUIDATION PROCEEDINGS.
Managing general agents, §§31-1501 to 31-1506.
See INSURANCE AGENTS AND BROKERS.
Material transactions disclosures, §§31-1001 to 31-1004.
Medical liability captive insurance agency, §§1-307.81 to 1-307.95.
See MEDICAL LIABILITY CAPTIVE INSURANCE AGENCY.
Mutual insurance company.
Conversion of reciprocal insurance company, §§31-751 to 31-760.
NAIC insurance regulatory information system, §§31-1901 to 31-1904.

INSURANCE COMPANIES —Cont'd
Premium finance companies, §§31-1101 to 31-1112.
See INSURANCE PREMIUM FINANCE COMPANIES.
Producer controlled insurers, business transactions with, §§31-401 to 31-408. See within this heading, "Business transactions with producer controlled insurers."
Reciprocal insurance company conversion, §§31-751 to 31-760.
Records.
Annual audited financial reports, §31-311.
District.
Principal office and records to be located in, §31-5204.
Domestic life insurance companies.
Capital stock, §31-4415.
Manner of keeping, §31-4440.
Fire and casualty insurance, §31-2502.01.
Insurance premium finance companies, §31-1106.
Insurance regulatory trust fund, §31-1207.
Life and health insurance guaranty association, §31-5411.
Property and liability insurance guaranty association, §31-5515.
Reinsurance intermediary-brokers, §31-1804.
Redomestication of foreign insurance company, §§31-1701 to 31-1705.
Approval as domestic insurer, §31-1702.
Captive insurance companies, §31-3931.17.
Conversion from domestic to foreign insurers, §31-1703.
Definitions, §31-1701.
Effect of, §31-1704.
Issuance of rules and regulations, §31-1705.
Rehabilitation proceedings, §§31-1301 to 31-1357.
See INSURERS REHABILITATION AND LIQUIDATION PROCEEDINGS.
Reinsurance credit, §§31-501 to 31-503.
Domestic ceding insurers, §31-501.

INSURANCE COMPANIES —Cont'd
Reports.
Annual audited financial reports, §§31-301 to 31-314. See within this heading, "Annual audited financial reports."
Annual tax and financial statements, §31-5202.
Business transactions with producer controlled insurers, §31-406.
Captive insurance companies.
Annual report, §31-3931.13.
Commissioner of insurance, securities and banking, §§31-206, 31-207.
Examination of insurance companies, §31-1404.
Insurance fraud, §22-3225.08.
Insurance industry material transactions disclosures, §§31-1001 to 31-1004.
Life and health insurance guaranty association, §31-5412.
Management report.
Internal control over financial reporting, §31-311.03.
Risk-based capital, §31-2002.
Reserves, §31-5201.
Risk-based capital, §§31-2001 to 31-2013.
Authorized control level event, §31-2005.
Company action level event, §31-2003.
Definitions, §31-2001.
Exemptions, §31-2009.
Foreign corporations, §31-2010.
Health insurers, regulatory standards, §§31-3451.01 to 31-3451.13.
See HEALTH INSURANCE.
Hearings, §31-2007.
Immunity, §31-2011.
Issuance of rules and regulations, §31-2009.
Mandatory control level event, §31-2006.
Notice, §31-2012.
Phase-in provisions, §31-2013.
Privacy and confidentiality, §31-2008.
Publications, §31-2008.
Ratemaking restrictions on use of, §31-2008.
Regulatory action level event, §31-2004.
Reports, §31-2002.
Confidentiality, §31-2008.
Prohibition on use in ratemaking, §31-2008.

INSURANCE COMPANIES —Cont'd
Risk-based capital —Cont'd
Supplemental nature of provisions, §31-2009.
Salvage, flood and junk vehicles.
Junk vehicle certificate.
Duty to apply for, time, §50-1331.02.
Salvage vehicles, salvage title.
Duty to apply for, time, §50-1331.02.
State of entry for non-United States insurers, §§31-2201 to 31-2207.
Subsidiaries of insurers, §31-702.
Tax and financial statements, §31-5202.
Taxation, §§31-205, 47-2601 to 47-2611.
Annual statements, §47-2606.
Banks and financial institutions, insurance companies, and public utilities, §§47-2502 to 47-2515.
Captive insurance companies.
Premiums collected, §31-3931.12.
Certificate of authority revoked for failure to pay, §47-2608.
Definitions, §47-2601.
Exemptions, §§47-2608, 47-2611.
Failure to file.
Revocation of license for, §47-2607.
Failure to pay, §§47-2608, 47-2609.
Fees.
Filing, §47-2606.
Licenses, §47-2603.
Filing, §47-2606.
Foreign countries.
Domicile of companies organized in, §47-2602.
Licenses, §§47-2603, 47-2604, 47-2607.
Marine insurance exclusion, §47-2608.
Nonprofit relief association exemptions, §47-2611.
Payment of tax, §47-2608.
Prosecutions, §47-2605.
Rates, §47-2608.
Reciprocity, §47-2610.
Title insurance producers, §§31-5041.01 to 31-5041.12.
See TITLE INSURANCE PRODUCERS.
Title insurers, §§31-5031.01 to 31-5031.24.
See TITLE INSURERS.
Unauthorized entities, §§31-231 to 31-233.
Administrative and judicial enforcement, §31-233.
Aiding or assisting authorized activity, §31-232.

INSURANCE COMPANIES —Cont'd
Unauthorized entities —Cont'd
Certificate of authority.
Activities not within scope of
certificate, §31-231.
Unclaimed property.
General provisions, §§41-101 to
41-142.
See UNCLAIMED PROPERTY.
Unfair trade practices, §§31-2231.01
to 31-2231.25.
See INSURANCE.
United States branch domestication,
§§31-2301 to 31-2307.

INSURANCE DEMUTUALIZATION,
§§31-901 to 31-915.
**Adoption of conversion plan by
board of directors,** §31-902.
**Adoption of revised articles of
incorporation,** §31-905.
Alternative conversion plan, §31-908.
**Approval of conversion plan by
commissioner,** §31-903.
**Approval of conversion plan by
members,** §31-904.
Conflicts of interest, §31-912.
Corporate existence, §31-911.
Costs and expenses of, §31-913.
Definitions, §31-901.
Effective date of conversion plan,
§31-909.
Limitation of actions, §31-915.
Notice requirements, §31-914.
**Optional provisions in conversion
plan,** §31-907.
**Policies issued after adoption of
plan and before effective date of
plan,** §31-910.
**Required provisions in conversion
plan,** §31-906.
**Securities issued in connection with
conversion plan,** §31-905.01.

INSURANCE FRAUD, §§22-3225.01 to
22-3225.15.
Definitions, §22-3225.01.
Enforcement authority, §22-3225.11.
False testimony, §22-3225.11.
Fines, §22-3225.04.
First degree, §22-3225.02.
Immunity for reporting, §22-3225.13.
Indemnification, §22-3225.06.
Investigations, §22-3225.08.
Misdemeanor, §22-3225.03a.
Offenses committed in D.C.,
§22-3225.15.
Penalties, §§22-3225.04, 22-3225.05.

INSURANCE FRAUD —Cont'd
Practitioners, §22-3225.07.
Solicitation prohibited, §22-3225.14.
Prevention and detection,
§22-3225.09.
**Promulgation of regulations
regarding,** §22-3225.10.
Reports, §22-3225.08.
Anti-fraud activity reporting,
§22-3225.12.
Restitution, §22-3225.05.
Second degree, §22-3225.03.

**INSURANCE HOLDING
COMPANIES,** §§31-701 to 31-738.
Acquisitions, §§31-703, 31-704.
Appeals, §31-714.
Confidentiality of records, §31-708.
Definitions, §31-701.
Examinations, §31-707.
Fines, §31-710.
Injunctions, §31-709.
Licenses, §31-713.
Liquidation proceedings, §§31-712,
31-734.
Management practices, §31-706.
Mandamus, writ of, §31-714.
Mergers and consolidations,
§§31-703, 31-704, 31-732.
Mutual holding companies, §§31-731
to 31-738.
Amendment of articles of
incorporation, §31-733.
Applicability of provisions, §31-735.
Formation of, §31-731.
Incorporation, §31-733.
Issuance of rules and regulations,
§31-738.
Limitation of actions, §31-737.
Liquidation, §31-734.
Membership interests, §§31-732,
31-735.
Mergers and consolidations, §§31-732,
31-737.01.
Notice requirements, §31-736.
Powers of, §31-735.
Reciprocal insurance company,
formation from, §31-752.
Rehabilitation, §31-734.
Stock company, conversion to, §31-759.
Penalties, §31-710.
Privacy and confidentiality, §31-708.
Producer controlled insurers.
Business transactions with, §§31-401
to 31-408.
See INSURANCE COMPANIES.
Receivers, §31-711.

INSURANCE HOLDING COMPANIES —Cont'd

Reciprocal insurance company conversion, §§31-751 to 31-760.

Action challenging validity or arising out of actions taken.

Limitation of actions, §31-758.

Definitions, §31-751.

Merger of policyholder membership interests, §31-753.

Mutual insurance company.

Conversion of mutual insurance holding company, §31-759.

Formation from reciprocal company, §31-752.

Incorporation as holding company, §31-754.

Membership interest not equity security, §31-756.

Power of resulting holding company to borrow or assume liability, §31-756.

Notice requirements.

Substantial compliance, §31-757.

Rehabilitation and liquidation, §31-755.

Rules, §31-760.

Recovery from liquidation or rehabilitation proceedings, §31-712.

Registration, §31-705.

Rehabilitation proceedings, §§31-712, 31-734.

Rules.

Authority to promulgate, §31-708.01.

Reciprocal insurance company conversion, §31-760.

Standards of practice for insurers as part of, §31-706.

Subsidiaries of insurers, §31-702.

Supervisory colleges, §31-707.01.

Violations, §31-710.

Voting securities, §31-709.

INSURANCE INVESTMENTS, §§31-1371.01 to 31-1375.01.

Applicability of provisions, §31-1371.01.

Board of directors, supervision, §31-1371.04.

Conflicts of interest, §31-1371.06.

Definitions, §31-1371.02.

Fire, casualty and marine insurers, §§31-1373.01 to 31-1373.12.

Additional investments, §31-1373.12.

Applicability of provisions, §31-1373.01.

INSURANCE INVESTMENTS —Cont'd

Fire, casualty and marine insurers —Cont'd

Derivative transactions, §31-1373.11.

Diversification requirements, §31-1373.03.

Dollar roll transactions, §31-1373.09.

Equity interests, §31-1373.06.

Foreign investments, §31-1373.10.

Investment pools, §31-1373.05.

Leases of personal property, §31-1373.07.

Mortgage loans, §31-1373.08.

Personal property, §31-1373.07.

Rated credit instruments, §31-1373.04.

Real estate, §31-1373.08.

Repurchase transactions, §31-1373.09.

Reserves required, §31-1373.02.

Securities lending, §31-1373.09.

Life insurance companies, §§31-1372.01 to 31-1372.12.

Additional investments, §31-1372.12.

Applicability of provisions, §31-1372.01.

Derivative transactions, §31-1372.10.

Diversification of assets and investments, §31-1372.02.

Dollar roll transactions, §31-1372.08.

Equity interests in business entities, §31-1372.05.

Foreign investments, §31-1372.09.

Investment pools, §31-1372.04.

Leases of personal property, §31-1372.06.

Limits on assets and investments, §31-1372.02.

Loans to policyholders, §31-1372.11.

Mortgage loans, §31-1372.07.

Personal property investments, §31-1372.06.

Rated credit instruments, acquiring, §31-1372.03.

Real estate, §31-1372.07.

Repurchase transactions, §31-1372.08.

Securities lending transactions, §31-1372.08.

Loans to officers or directors, §31-1371.06.

Prohibited investments, §31-1371.05.

Qualifications for investments, §31-1371.03.

Regulations promulgation, §31-1375.01.

Value of investment, §31-1371.07.

INSURANCE PLACEMENT,
§§31-5001 to 31-5011.
Administrative appeals, §31-5009.
Definition, §31-5002.
Delegation of functions by mayor,
§31-5011.
Establishment of industry
placement facility, §31-5003.
Immunity from liability.
Statements regarding insurability,
§31-5007.
Joint underwriting association,
§31-5005.
Annual report, §31-5008.
Judicial review, §31-5009.
Purpose of chapter, §31-5001.
Reinsurance reimbursement fund.
Assessment, charge to recover,
§31-5010.
Rules and regulations, §31-5004.
Supervision and regulation of
operations, §31-5006.

INSURANCE PREMIUM FINANCE
COMPANIES, §§31-1101 to
31-1112.
Applicability of provisions, §31-1101.
Cancellation of contracts, §31-1111.
Definitions, §31-1102.
Delinquency charges, §31-1110.
Form and content of agreements,
§31-1108.
Issuance of license, §31-1104.
Issuance of rules and regulations,
§31-1107.
Licenses, §§31-1103 to 31-1105.
Records, §31-1106.
Renewal of license, §31-1104.
Service charges, §31-1109.
Validity of agreements as secured
transactions, §31-1112.

INSURANCE PRODUCER
LICENSING, §§31-1131.01 to
31-1131.19.
Application for license, §31-1131.03.
Resident insurance producer license,
§31-1131.06.
Fingerprinting of applicant,
§31-1131.06a.
Appointed agents, §31-1131.14.
Assumed names, §31-1131.10.
Change of name, residency or
address, §31-1131.08a.
Commissions, acceptance or
payment, §31-1131.13.
Continuing education, §31-1131.07b.
Definitions, §31-1131.02.

INSURANCE PRODUCER
LICENSING —Cont'd
Denial of license, §31-1131.12.
Education.
Continuing education, §31-1131.07b.
Pre-licensing education, §31-1131.05a.
Exemptions, §31-1131.09.
Prelicensing education.
Title insurers, §31-1131.05b.
Examination, §31-1131.05.
Exemptions, §31-1131.09.
Exceptions, §31-1131.04.
Fingerprinting.
Resident insurance producer license.
Applicants, §31-1131.06a.
Issuance of license, §31-1131.07.
License requirement, §31-1131.03.
Nonresidents, §31-1131.08.
Promulgation of rules, §31-1131.18.
Reciprocity, §31-1131.16.
Renewal, §31-1131.07a.
Report of administrative or criminal
actions, §31-1131.17.
Revocation or suspension,
§31-1131.12.
Short title, §31-1131.01.
Temporary license, §31-1131.11.
Termination of business or
appointment, §31-1131.15.
Term of license, §31-1131.07a.
Transitional provision, §31-1131.19.

INSURANCE PRODUCT
REGULATION COMPACT.
Authority to enter interstate
compact, §31-1391.

INSURANCE REGULATORY TRUST
FUND, §§31-1201 to 31-1210.
Appeal from assessment, §31-1205.
Applicability of provisions, §31-1210.
Assessments, §31-1203.
Appeal, §31-1205.
Failure to pay share, §31-1204.
Audits, §31-1209.
Budgets and budget estimates,
§31-1202.
Bureau, §31-1208.
Continuing care retirement
community regulatory and
supervision trust fund account,
§§31-1202, 44-151.18.
Continuing obligations, §31-1206.
Definitions, §31-1201.
Establishment of, §31-1202.
Failure to pay assessment, §31-1204.
Funding, §31-1202.
Certified capital companies,
§31-5238.01.

INSURANCE REGULATORY TRUST FUND —Cont'd

Records, §31-1207.

Uses of, §31-1202.

INSURANCE, SECURITIES, AND BANKING, DEPARTMENT OF, §§31-101 to 31-208.

Abolition of predecessor, §31-108.

Banking regulatory trust fund.

Established, §31-107.

Bureau of banking and financial institutions.

Director, §31-106.

Established, §31-106.

Business statements filed with, §31-205.

Capital requirements, §31-208.

Commissioner.

Appeals to mayor from decisions of, §31-4332.

Appointment of, §31-104.

Duties, §31-202.

Organization of personnel and property, §31-106.

Enforcement of orders and actions of, §31-4313.

Insurance demutualization plan approval, §31-903.

Rate of pay.

Resolution indicating, §31-104.

Reports, §§31-206, 31-207.

United States branches of non-United States insurers.

Authority regarding, §31-2207.

Valuation of reserves by, §31-4701.

Workers' compensation rate filings, §32-1542.02.

Definitions, §31-101.

Establishment of, §31-102.

Fees and charges, collection of, §§31-4302, 31-4303.

Foreign companies or associations.

Financial statements of, §31-204.

Funding, §31-107.

Health benefit plan grievance procedures.

Appeals of rescissions to department, §44-301.06a.

Life insurance companies, §31-4301.

Organization of, §31-106.

Powers and duties, §§31-103, 31-202.

Rulemaking.

Regulations under Gramm-Leach-Bliley act, §31-121.

Taxation, §31-205.

Transfers of material to, §31-105.

INSURANCE UNDERWRITING.

Property insurance, §§31-5001 to 31-5011.

See FIRE AND CASUALTY INSURANCE.

INSURANCE UNFAIR TRADE PRACTICES, §§31-2231.01 to 31-2231.25.

See INSURANCE.

INSURERS REHABILITATION AND LIQUIDATION PROCEEDINGS, §§31-1301 to 31-1357.

Ancillary formal proceedings, §31-1351.

Ancillary summary proceedings, §31-1352.

Applicability of provisions, §31-1302.

Assessments, §31-1329.

Assets.

Domiciliary liquidator's proposal to distribute assets, §31-1332.

List of, §31-1323.

Attachment, §31-1355.

Audits, §31-1347.

Claims.

Disputed claims, §31-1337.

Distribution of claims, priority of, §31-1340.

Filing claims, §31-1333.

Nonresident claims against District insurers, §31-1353.

Priority of distribution of claims, §31-1340.

Proof of claims, §31-1334.

Resident claims against insurers domiciled in reciprocal states, §31-1354.

Secured creditors, claims by, §31-1339.

Special claims, §31-1335.

Surety, claims of, §31-1338.

Third party claims, §31-1336.

Void or voidable rights.

Claims by holders of, §31-1327.

Confidentiality of records, §31-1309.

Conservation of property of insurer, §31-1348.

Continuation of coverage, §31-1317.

Cooperation of officers, owners, and employees required, §31-1305.

Definitions, §31-1301.

Delinquency proceedings.

Commencement of, §31-1306.

Continuation of, §31-1306.

Operations during, conditions on, §31-1307.

Release from, conditions on, §31-1307.

INSURERS REHABILITATION AND LIQUIDATION PROCEEDINGS
—Cont'd

Disputed claims, §31-1337.

Dissolution of insurer, §31-1318.

Distribution of assets, §§31-1332, 31-1342.

Distribution of claims, priority of, §31-1340.

Execution of judgments, levy of, §31-1355.

Filing claims, §31-1333.

Foreign or alien insurer.
Liquidation of property, §31-1349.

Fraud and deceit, §§31-1324, 31-1325.

Fraudulent transfer, §§31-1324, 31-1325.

Garnishment, §31-1355.

Health maintenance organizations, §31-3420.

Holding companies, §§31-712, 31-734.

Information to other regulators and guaranty associations.
Duty to provide, §31-1309.01.

Injunctions, §31-1304.

Interstate priority, §31-1356.

Jurisdiction, §31-1303.

Liens, voidable, §31-1326.

Liquidation.
Actions by and against liquidator, §31-1322.
Agents' duties on notice of, §31-1321.
Assets list, §31-1323.
Continuation of coverage, §31-1317.
Dissolution of insurer, §31-1318.
Domiciliary liquidator's proposal to distribute assets, §31-1332.
Foreign or alien insurer, property, §31-1349.
Grounds for, §31-1315.
Interstate priority, §31-1356.
Notice, §31-1320.
Orders, §31-1316.
Other states, domiciliary liquidators in, §31-1350.
Powers of liquidator, §31-1319.
Property of insurer, §31-1348.
Foreign or alien insurer, §31-1349.
Recommendations of liquidator to court, §31-1341.
Records, §31-1346.
Reopening, §31-1345.
Termination of proceedings, §§31-1344, 31-1346.

Mutual holding companies, §31-734.

Nonresident claims against District insurers, §31-1353.

INSURERS REHABILITATION AND LIQUIDATION PROCEEDINGS
—Cont'd

Notice on liquidation, §31-1320.

Orders, §31-1304.

Preferences, voidable, §31-1326.

Premiums owed, recovery of, §31-1331.

Priority.
Distribution of claims, §31-1340.
Interstate, §31-1356.

Proof of claims, §31-1334.

Reciprocal insurance company conversions, §31-755.

Reciprocity.
Interstate priorities, §31-1356.
Resident claims against insurers domiciled in reciprocal states, §31-1354.
Subordination of claims for noncooperation, §31-1357.

Records, §31-1346.
Confidentiality of records, §31-1309.

Rehabilitation.
Actions by and against rehabilitator, §31-1313.
Grounds for allowing, §31-1310.
Orders, §31-1311.
Powers and duties of rehabilitator, §31-1312.
Termination of, §31-1314.

Reinsurer, liability of, §31-1330.

Reopening liquidation, §31-1345.

Resident claims against insurers domiciled in reciprocal states, §31-1354.

Secured creditors, claims by, §31-1339.

Setoffs, §31-1328.

Special claims, §31-1335.

Subordination of claims for noncooperation, §31-1357.

Surety, claims of, §31-1338.

Temporary seizure order, §31-1308.

Third party claims, §31-1336.

Unclaimed funds, §31-1343.

Venue, §31-1303.

Void or voidable rights.
Holders of, claims by, §31-1327.
Liens, voidable, §31-1326.
Preferences, voidable, §31-1326.

Withheld funds, §§31-1336, 31-1343.

INSURRECTION OR REBELLION.
Constitution of the United States,
US Const Art I §8.

INTAKE PROCEDURES.
Delinquent minors, JuvProc Rules
102, 103.

**INTELLECTUAL DISABILITIES,
PERSONS WITH,** §§7-1301.02 to
7-1306.05.
ABLE savings accounts, §§47-4901,
47-4902.
Abuse, §7-1305.10.
Actions to compel rights of,
§7-1305.13.
**Administration of medication by
trained employees,** §§21-1201 to
21-1206.
Definitions, §21-1201.
Issuance of rules and regulations,
§21-1204.
Registration fees for trained
employees, §21-1206.
Requirements of medication orders,
§21-1204.
Rules and regulations, §21-1205.
Self-administration, §21-1202.
Trained employees' program, §21-1203.
Adult protective services, §§7-1901 to
7-1913.
See ADULT PROTECTIVE
SERVICES.
Advocate, §7-1304.13,
MentalRetardation Rule 12.
Appeal of commitment, §§7-1304.10,
7-1304.12.
Appropriations, §7-1306.03.
Attorneys at law.
Clients with diminished capacity.
Client-lawyer relationship, ProfCond
Rule 1.14.
Commitment proceedings,
MentalRetardation Rule 11.
Commitment of persons.
General provisions, §§7-1303.01 to
7-1303.14, 21-1114, 21-1115.
See COMMITMENT OF PERSONS
WITH INTELLECTUAL
DISABILITIES.
Hearing and review procedures,
§§7-1304.01 to 7-1304.13.
See COMMITMENT OF PERSONS
WITH INTELLECTUAL
DISABILITIES.
**Comprehensive evaluation and
individual habilitation plan,**
§7-1305.04.
**Comprehensive evaluation and
rehabilitation plan,** §§7-1304.03,
7-1304.04.

**INTELLECTUAL DISABILITIES,
PERSONS WITH** —Cont'd
**Consent of customers required for
services,** §7-1305.06a.
Health care decision-makers,
substitute consent, §7-1305.07a.
Consumers' rights protection,
§§7-1231.01 to 7-1231.15.
See MENTAL HEALTH CONSUMERS
PROTECTION ACT OF 2001.
Conveyances, §42-820.
Convulsive therapy, §7-1305.06.
**Criminal abuse, neglect and
financial exploitation of
vulnerable adults and elderly
persons,** §§22-931 to 22-938.
See CRIMINAL ABUSE, NEGLECT
AND FINANCIAL
EXPLOITATION OF
VULNERABLE ADULTS AND
ELDERLY PERSONS.
**Default judgment against
incompetent person,** CivPro Rule
55.
Definitions, §7-1301.03.
Department of mental health,
§§7-1131.01 to 7-1131.21.
See MENTAL HEALTH
DEPARTMENT.
Deprivation of civil rights of,
§7-1305.14.
Diet, rights regarding, §7-1305.05.
Discharge.
Intellectually disabled person,
discharge on request of,
§7-1303.07.
Parent or guardian, discharge on
request of, §7-1303.08.
Residential care, from, §7-1303.10.
Drugs.
Administration by trained employees.
See within this heading,
"Administration of medication by
trained employees."
Rights regarding, §7-1305.05.
Self-administration, §21-1202.
Dually diagnosed individuals.
Coordination of services, §7-1305.15.
Education, authority of Board of,
§7-1306.04.
Effective date of provisions,
§7-1306.05.
Electroshock therapy, §7-1305.06.
Employment, §§7-1305.11, 7-1305.14.
Exercise, right to, §7-1305.05.
**Experimental treatment and
research,** §§7-1305.06, 7-1305.09.

INTELLECTUAL DISABILITIES, PERSONS WITH —Cont'd

Forest Haven, §§44-1401 to 44-1404.

Group homes.
Criminal background checks for unlicensed personnel, §§44-551 to 44-554.
Licenses, §§44-501 to 44-509.

Guardianship of incapacitated persons.
See GUARDIAN AND WARD.

Habitation and care, §7-1305.01.
Comprehensive evaluation and individual habilitation plan, §7-1305.04.
Comprehensive evaluation and rehabilitation plan, §§7-1304.03, 7-1304.04.
Payment for, §7-1303.11.
Skills, teaching, §7-1305.02.

Health care decision-makers, §7-1305.07a.

Hearings.
Court hearing required prior to commitment, §7-1303.12.

Informed consent requirement, §7-1305.06a.

Intermediate care facilities.
Stevie Sellows quality improvement fund, §§47-1270 to 47-1278.
See INTERMEDIATE CARE FACILITIES.

Interstate compact on mental health, §§7-1101 to 7-1106.

Labor, compelled to perform, §7-1305.11.

Landlord and tenant, §42-3228.
Lease under control of.
Cost of renewal, charge against estate or chargeable to leasehold, §42-3226.

Leases, §42-3228.

Least restrictive conditions requirement, §7-1305.03.

Licenses for group homes, §§44-501 to 44-509.

Living conditions for, §7-1305.02.

Mail, access to, §7-1305.05.

Medical attention, §7-1305.05.

Mental health information, §§7-1201.01 to 7-1208.07.
See MENTAL HEALTH DISCLOSURES.

Mental illness, persons with.
Dually diagnosed individuals.
Coordination of services, §7-1305.15.

INTELLECTUAL DISABILITIES, PERSONS WITH —Cont'd

Mistreatment, §7-1305.10.

Neglect, §7-1305.10.

Outpatient nonresidential rehabilitation, application for.
Application of persons with, §7-1303.03.
Parent or guardian's application for, §7-1303.05.

Payment.
Appeals, costs and expenses of, §7-1304.12.
Evaluation report and habilitation plan, §7-1304.04.
Habilitation and care, §7-1303.11.
Hearings, costs and expenses of, §7-1304.12.
Rights, actions to compel, §7-1305.13.

Policy declaration, §7-1301.02.

Power of attorney.
Health care decision-makers, §7-1305.07a.

Privacy and confidentiality rights, §§7-1305.05, 7-1305.12.

Psychological therapies prohibited for, §7-1305.06.

Psychotropic medication.
Health care decision-makers.
Data for assessment of needs, §7-1305.07a.
Informed consent requirement, §7-1305.06a.
Panel to review proposals to administer, §7-1305.06b.
Review for all DDS customers, §7-1305.06c.

Public assistance.
Protective payments on behalf of adult recipients, §4-212.03.

Records, §7-1305.11.

Religious beliefs, right to practice, §7-1305.05.
Psychotropic medication.
Refusal to consent for valid religious reasons, §7-1305.06b.

Residential care, discharge from, §7-1303.10.

Respite care.
Rules and regulations, §7-1303.14.

Restraints, use of, §7-1305.10.

Rules for implementation of provisions, §7-1306.03a.

Seclusion of, §7-1305.10.

Service of process.
Commitment to facility, MentalRetardation Rule 9.

INTELLECTUAL DISABILITIES, PERSONS WITH —Cont'd

Service of process —Cont'd

Domestic relations actions, DomRel Rule 4.

Summons, CivPro Rule 4.

Severability of provisions, §7-1306.02.

Sterilization of, §7-1305.08.

Stevie Sellows quality improvement fund.

Intermediate care facilities, §§47-1270 to 47-1278.

Substitution of parties, CivPro Rule 25.

Commitment proceedings, MentalRetardation Rule 4A.

Domestic relations actions, DomRel Rule 25.

Telephones, access to, §7-1305.05.

Time out procedures, §7-1305.10.

Transfers between facilities, §7-1303.09.

Visitors, right to, §7-1305.05.

Voluntary admission to facility, §7-1303.02, MentalRetardation Rule 3.

INTELLECTUAL PROPERTY.

Authors.

Protection of rights, US Const Art I §8.

Inventions, US Const Art I §8.

Trademarks, §§47-2855.01 to 47-2855.05.

Trade secrets.

General provisions, §§36-401 to 36-410.

See TRADE SECRETS.

INTERAGENCY COLLABORATION AND SERVICES INTEGRATION COMMISSION, §§2-1591 to 2-1597.

Authority of commission, §2-1594.

Database information, §2-1595.

Definitions, §2-1592.

Duties of commission, §2-1595.

Establishment, §2-1594.

Members, §2-1596.

Program requirements, §2-1595.

Purpose of commission, §2-1593.

Staff and administrative support, §2-1597.

Title of provisions, §2-1591.

INTERCEPTION OF ORAL OR WIRE COMMUNICATIONS, §§23-541 to 23-556.

Appeals by government regarding suppression of intercepted communications, §23-552.

INTERCEPTION OF ORAL OR WIRE COMMUNICATIONS —Cont'd

Applications for authorization to intercept, CrimPro Rule 41-I.

Assignment of cases, USDistCt LCrR 57.10.

Authorization or approval of, §§23-546 to 23-548.

Confiscation of devices, §23-544.

Damages, §23-554.

Definitions, §23-541.

Devices for purposes of, §23-543.

Disclosure of intercepted communications, §§23-551 to 23-553.

Federal law on, §23-556.

Inventory of records and information, §23-550.

Prohibited acts, §23-542.

Records, §§23-549, 23-550.

Reports, §23-555.

Suppression of intercepted communications, §§23-551 to 23-553.

Use of intercepted communications, CrimPro Rule 41-I.

INTEREST, §§28-3301 to 28-3315.

Acceleration clauses, §28-3312.

Actions.

Recovery of usury paid, §28-3304.

Parties compelled to testify, §28-3306.

Unlawful interest credited on principal debt, §28-3305.

Appeals, D.C. courts.

Interest on lower court judgment, DCCtApp Rule 37.

Appeals, federal cases.

Interest on judgments, FRAP 37.

Assessments for paving and resurfacing streets, §9-421.09.

Consumer credit transactions.

Rate of interest, applicability of provisions, §28-3301.

Contracts.

Maximum rate of interest, §28-3301.

Rate expressed in, §28-3301.

Cooperative housing organizations.

Maximum rate on share, §28-3301.

Council.

Changing rates of interest.

Council authorized to change, §28-3309.

Exemption of certain loans.

Council authorized to exempt, §28-3309.

INTEREST —Cont'd
Court ordered property sales, CivPro Rule 308.
Defined, §28-3311.
Direct installment loans.
Finance charges on, §28-3308.
District of Columbia.
Judgment rate on judgments against District, §28-3302.
Exemptions, §28-3307.
Finance charges on direct installment loans, §28-3308.
Financial literacy council, §§38-731.01 to 38-731.05.
Fines, §28-3313.
Foreign-money claims.
Judgment and prejudgment interest on, §15-908.
Forfeitures.
Usury.
Forfeiture of interest, §28-3303.
Fraud and deceit, §28-3312.
Gross sales tax, §47-2027.
Health benefits plans.
Late payment of provider reimbursement claim, §31-3132.
Installment loans.
Maximum rate, §28-3308.
Interest rate ceiling amendment act.
Rates. See within this heading, "Rates."
Intermediate care facilities for persons with intellectual disabilities.
Assessment on facilities, §47-1274.
Judgments and decrees, §§15-108 to 15-110, 28-3302.
Money lenders.
Maximum interest rates, §26-905.
Mortgages and deeds of trust.
Exempt mortgages, §§28-3307, 28-3309.
Maximum rate, §28-3301.
Prepayment.
No penalty after three years, §28-3301.
Motor fuel tax, §47-2316.
Motor vehicles.
Direct motor vehicle installment loans.
Maximum finance charge, §28-3602.
National housing act.
Exemption from interest in usury regulations, §28-3307.
Negotiable instruments, §28:3-112.
Nursing facilities.
Assessment on nursing facilities, §47-1264.

INTEREST —Cont'd
Pawnbrokers' rates, §§47-2884.08 to 47-2884.12.
Penalties, §28-3313.
Points.
Defined, §28-3301.
Limitation on charging, §28-3301.
Private right of action, §28-3314.
Procurement claims, §2-359.09.
Prompt payment.
Private contractor and subcontractor prompt payment act.
Failure to make prompt payments, §27-133.
Subcontractors, payments to, §27-135.
Public building construction project loans, §§10-612, 10-613.
Public contract quick payment provisions and interest penalty payments, §§2-221.02, 2-221.03.
Public funds.
Bank fees special fund, §1-325.231.
Rates, §§28-3301 to 28-3315.
Absent expressed contract, §28-3302.
Changes to, §28-3309.
Consumer protection, §28-3310.
Council authorized to change or exempt, §28-3309.
Exemptions, §§28-3307, 28-3309.
Expressed in contract, §28-3301.
Finance charges on direct installment loans, §28-3308.
Interest rate ceiling amendment act.
Consumer protection, §28-3310.
Definition of "interest," §28-3311.
Delinquent or late charges.
Requirements, §28-3310.
Penalties, §28-3313.
Right of action, §28-3314.
Statements furnished to borrower, §28-3310.
Unlawful practices, §28-3312.
Judgments and decrees, on, §28-3302.
Maximum rate.
Changing rates.
District council authorized to change, §28-3309.
Contracts, §28-3301.
Cooperative housing organizations, §28-3301.
Exemptions, §§28-3307, 28-3309.
Judgments and decrees, §28-3302.
Judgments against District of Columbia, §28-3302.
Mortgages and deeds of trust, §28-3301.

INTEREST —Cont'd
Rates —Cont'd
  Maximum rate —Cont'd
    Motor vehicle installment loans,
     §28-3602.
    No maximum rate, §28-3301.
    Revolving credit accounts, §28-3702.
    Usurious. See within this heading,
     "Usury."
Real estate tax sales.
  Revised real property tax sale,
   §47-1334.
Real property taxes.
  Overpayment, §47-811.02.
  Special assessments, §47-1203.
  Special energy assessments,
   §47-895.33.
Revolving credit accounts.
  Maximum charge, §28-3702.
Statements required, §28-3310.
Taxation.
  Overpayment of tax, §47-4202.
  Protest of assessment, §47-4312.
  Underpayment of tax, §47-4201.
    Corporations, financial institutions
     and unincorporated businesses,
     by, §47-4204.
    Individuals, by, §47-4203.
Unclaimed property.
  Crediting interest to owner's account,
   §41-121.
  Failure to deliver or pay, §41-135.
Usury.
  Action to recover usury paid, §28-3304.
    Parties compelled to testify,
     §28-3306.
    Unlawful interest credited on
     principal debt, §28-3305.
  Defined, §28-3303.
  Fines and penalties, §28-3313.
  Forfeiture of interest, §28-3303.
  Principal debt, deemed to be payment
   on, §28-3305.
  Private right of action, §28-3314.
  Recovery of usury paid, §28-3304.
  Testimony required regarding,
   §28-3306.
Waiver of rights, clauses containing,
  §28-3312.

**INTEREST ON LAWYERS TRUST
  ACCOUNT (IOLTA),** DCBar Appx
  A, DCBar Rule X, ProfCond Rule
  1.15.
Approved depositories, DCBar Rule
  XI.
Verification of participation, DCBar
  Rule XIV.

**INTERIM DISABILITY ASSISTANCE
  (IDA),** §4-204.07.
Category of public assistance,
  §4-202.01.
Disability, defined, §4-204.07.
Fund, §4-204.09.
Public policy, §4-204.07.

**INTERIM DISABILITY ASSISTANCE
  FUND,** §4-204.09.

INTERIOR DESIGNERS.
**Board of architecture and interior
  designers,** §§47-2853.06 to
  47-2853.10.
Business licenses, §§47-2853.101 to
  47-2853.103.
  Eligibility, §47-2853.102.
  Representations prohibited,
   §47-2853.103.
  Scope of practice, §47-2853.101.

INTERLOCUTORY ORDERS.
Appeals from, FRAP 5(a).

INTERMEDIARY INTERPRETERS,
  §§2-1901, 2-1905.

INTERMEDIATE CARE FACILITIES.
**Stevie Sellows quality improvement
  fund,** §§47-1270 to 47-1278.
  Appeals, §47-1276.
  Assessments, §47-1273.
    Federal determinations, §47-1278.
    Interest and penalties, §47-1274.
  Confidentiality of information,
   §47-1275.
  Definitions, §47-1270.
  Eligibility to receive payments,
   §47-1272.
  Establishment, §47-1271.
  Rulemaking authority, §47-1277.
  Termination of funding, §47-1272.
  Use of fund, §47-1271.

**INTERNATIONAL BANKING
  CORPORATIONS.**
Generally, §§26-631 to 26-643.
  See BANKS AND FINANCIAL
   INSTITUTIONS.

**INTERNATIONAL FUEL TAX
  AGREEMENT.**
Motor fuel tax.
  General provisions, §§47-2351 to
   47-2354.
    See MOTOR FUEL TAX.
  Motor fuel tax provisions subject to,
   §47-2301.01.

INTERNATIONAL HOUSE OF PANCAKES RESTAURANT 3221 DEVELOPMENT PROJECT.
Real property tax exemptions, §47-4651.

INTERNATIONAL LAW.
Congress.
Power to punish offenses against, US Const Art I §8.

INTERNATIONAL ORGANIZATIONS.
Foreign mission rules applicable to, §6-1309.

INTERNATIONAL REGISTRATION PLAN AGREEMENTS.
Motor vehicles.
General provisions, §§50-1507.01 to 50-1507.07.
See MOTOR VEHICLE REGISTRATION.

INTERNATIONAL STUDENTS.
Gallaudet University, §38-2402.10.

INTERNATIONAL WILLS, §§18-701 to 18-710.
Applicability of provisions, §18-702.
Attesting witnesses, §18-703.
Attorneys at law.
Persons authorized to act in relation to international wills, §18-709.
Central information center.
Registration, §18-710.
Certificate of authorized person.
Attorney at law person authorized to act, §18-709.
Evidentiary effect, §18-706.
Form, §18-705.
Date of will, §18-704.
Definitions, §18-701.
Formalities, §§18-703, 18-704.
Registry.
Central information center, §18-710.
Revocation, §18-707.
Signatures.
Attesting witnesses, §18-703.
Placement on document, §18-704.
Statutory construction, §18-708.
Statutory requirements, §18-703.
Uniformity of construction, §18-708.
Validity, §§18-702, 18-706.
Writing requirement, §18-703.

INTERNET.
Arbitration organizations.
Information to be available to public, §16-4430.

INTERNET —Cont'd
Compensating-use tax, §§47-2201 to 47-2214.
See COMPENSATING-USE TAX.
Definition of internet access service, §47-2201.
District of Columbia Code, rules, regulations, publications, Internet publications.
Respectful language modernization, §§2-631, 2-632.
Franchise agreement.
Furnishing services to digitally-disadvantaged residents, §§34-1731.01 to 34-1731.11.
Awarding agreement.
Procedure, §34-1731.03.
Selection of franchisee, §§34-1731.05, 34-1731.07.
Chapter not franchise agreement, §34-1731.10.
Compliance schedule.
Violations of agreement, §34-1731.06.
Definitions, §34-1731.02.
Digitally-disadvantaged areas, population, residents.
Definitions, §34-1731.02.
District held harmless, §34-1731.04.
Findings and purpose, §34-1731.01.
Human rights act compliance required, §34-1731.09.
Legal liability of franchisee, §34-1731.04.
Liability insurance.
Franchisee required to obtain, §34-1731.04.
Nonexclusive agreement, §34-1731.03.
Office of the chief technology officer.
Delegation of mayor's authority to, §34-1731.08.
Performance bond.
Requiring franchisee to obtain, §34-1731.04.
Procedure for entering into agreement, §34-1731.03.
Selection of franchisee, §§34-1731.05, 34-1731.07.
Responsibility of franchisee, §34-1731.03.
Selection of franchisee, §§34-1731.05, 34-1731.07.
Severability of provisions, §34-1731.11.
Termination of agreement, §34-1731.06.

INTERNET —Cont'd
Franchise agreement —Cont'd
Furnishing services to digitally-
disadvantaged residents —Cont'd
Term of agreement, §34-1731.03.
Violations of agreement.
Notice, termination of agreement,
§34-1731.06.
Insurance.
Electronic delivery and posting of
documents, §31-651.03.
Spam deterrence, §§28-5001 to
28-5003.
Damages, §28-5003.
Definitions, §28-5001.
Prohibited acts, §28-5002.
Tax on internet sales, §§47-3931 to
47-3933.
Definitions, §47-3931.
Exemptions, §47-3932.
Imposition of tax, §47-3932.
Scope, §47-3933.
Small vendor exemption, §47-3932.
Toll telecommunication service tax,
§§47-3901 to 47-3922.
See TOLL TELECOMMUNICATION
SERVICE TAX.
Voice over Internet Protocol.
Emergency and non-emergency
number telephone calling systems
assessments, §34-1803.

INTERNET COMPANIES.
Income taxes.
Qualified high technology companies.
Credits, capital gains, §§47-1817.01
to 47-1817.08.

INTERNS OF SURVEYORS.
Business licenses, §47-2853.113.

INTERPLEADER, §§15-521 to 15-524,
CivPro Rule 22.
Bills of lading.
Determination of conflicting claims,
§28:7-603.
Commercial code.
Documents of title.
Conflicting claims, §28:7-603.
Complaint for interpleader, CivPro
Form CA 18.
Counterclaim for interpleader,
CivPro Form CA 21.
Trial of right to property seized on
process of superior court,
§§15-521 to 15-524.
Action of replevin against officer
levying on property, §15-524.

INTERPLEADER —Cont'd
Trial of right to property seized on
process of superior court
—Cont'd
Docketing claim, §15-522.
Judgment, §15-523.
Manner of trial, §15-522.
Notice of claim or exemption, §15-521.
Warehouse receipts.
Determination of conflicting claims,
§28:7-603.

INTERPRETERS, §§2-1901 to
2-1912.01, CivPro Rule 43.
Adoption proceedings, Adoption Rule
43.
Commencement of proceedings.
Interpreter to be in full view, §2-1909.
Costs and fees, §2-1912.
Criminal procedure, §2-1902, CrimPro
Rule 28.
Definitions, §2-1901.
Domestic relations actions, DomRel
Rule 43.
Foreign language services and
documents, §§2-1931 to 2-1936.
See FOREIGN LANGUAGE
SERVICES AND DOCUMENTS.
Intermediary interpreters, §2-1905.
Interviewers.
Procedures to certify qualified
interviewers, §2-1912.01.
Juvenile proceedings, JuvProc Rule
28.
Notice of need for interpreter,
§2-1903.
Oath or affirmation, §2-1907.
Office of interpreter services,
§2-1911.
Privileged communications, §2-1908.
Qualifications.
Preliminary determination, §2-1904.
Procedures to certify qualified
interviewers, §2-1912.01.
Recording of proceedings, §2-1910.
Waiver of services of interpreter,
§2-1906.
When required, §2-1902.

INTERROGATORIES, CivPro Rule 33.
Adoption proceedings, Adoption Rules
33, 37.
Attachments, §§16-521, 16-522, 16-552.
Certificates regarding discovery,
CivPro Rule 5.
Criminal procedure, CrimPro Rule 15.

INTERROGATORIES —Cont'd

Domestic relations actions, DomRel Rules 33, 37.

Attachment writ accompanying interrogatories, DomRel Rule 64.

Failure to answer, CivPro Rule 37.

Adoption proceedings, Adoption Rule 37.

Domestic relations actions, DomRel Rule 37.

Filing of requests, CivPro Rule 5.

Garnishment.

Post-judgment garnishment in aid of execution, §16-552.

Prejudgment garnishment, §16-521.

Traverse of answers.

Trial of issue, §16-522.

General provisions governing discovery, CivPro Rule 26, USDistCt LCvR 26.2.

Model interrogatories, CivPro Appx I.

Responses, form of, USDistCt LCvR 30.4.

Restraints of trade.

Civil investigative demand, §28-4505.

Verdict accompanied by answer to interrogatories, CivPro Rule 49.

INTERSTATE BANKING AND BRANCH BANKS, §§26-702.01, 26-731 to 26-741.

Acquisitions, effect of, §§26-703, 26-706.01.

Administrative procedure, §26-712.

Agency agreements between affiliated depository institutions, §26-739.

Applicability of provisions, §§26-706, 26-710.

Application for status as, §§26-704, 26-706.01.

Cease and desist orders, §26-712.

Definitions, §26-732.

De novo branching, §§26-733, 26-734.

District state banks.

Establishment of de novo branch or acquisition of branch outside District, §26-733.

Interstate merger transactions, §26-736.

Duties of superintendent, §26-702.01.

Enforcement of provisions, §§26-707, 26-714, 26-740.

Establishment and maintenance of branches.

District state banks, §26-733.

Out-of-state banks, §26-734.

INTERSTATE BANKING AND BRANCH BANKS —Cont'd

Establishment and maintenance of branches —Cont'd

Superintendent's authority, §26-735.

Exceptions, §26-703.

Fines, §26-707.02.

Hearings, §26-713.

Impact of provisions, review of, §26-709.

Insurance requirements, §26-707.01.

International banking corporations.

Branch bank establishment, §26-635.

Interstate merger transactions.

District state banks, §26-736.

Out-of-state banks, §26-737.

Superintendent's authority, §26-738.

Issuance of rules and regulations, §26-739.

Jurisdiction, §26-707.

Out-of-state banks.

Establishment of de novo branch or acquisition of branch within District, §26-734.

Interstate merger transactions, §26-737.

Policy declaration, §26-731.

Prohibited acts, §26-705.

Regional interstate banking, §§26-702 to 26-714.

Review of impact of provisions, §26-709.

Savings and loan acquisitions, §§26-1201 to 26-1217.

See SAVINGS AND LOAN ACQUISITIONS.

Women-owned banks, §26-711.

INTERSTATE CHILD CUSTODY PROCEEDINGS.

Uniform child custody proceedings act, §§16-4601.01 to 16-4605.03.

See CHILD CUSTODY AND CHILD CUSTODY PROCEEDINGS.

INTERSTATE COMMERCE.

Congress, US Const Art I §§8, 9.

Partnerships.

Applicability of law, §29-601.07.

Public utilities.

Withdrawal of authority of Interstate Commerce Commission over, §34-807.

INTERSTATE COMPACTS.

Child placement.

Interstate compact on placement of children, §§4-1421 to 4-1424.

Agreements with other state for placement, §4-1423.

INTERSTATE COMPACTS —Cont'd

Sewerage.

Agreements with Maryland and Virginia, §1-204.87.

Taxation.

Multistate tax compact, §§47-441 to 47-445.

Washington metropolitan area transit authority safety regulation.

Joint state oversight agency for creation of rail fixed guideway system, §§9-1109.01 to 9-1109.07.

Woodrow Wilson bridge and tunnel compact, §§9-1115.01 to 9-1115.04.

INTERSTATE DEPOSITIONS AND DISCOVERY, §§13-441 to 13-448.

Application of law.

Pending actions, §13-448.

Uniformity, §13-447.

Definitions, §13-442.

Rules of court, §§13-445, 13-446.

Short title, §13-441.

Statutory construction, §13-447.

Subpoenas.

Applications, §§13-443, 13-446.

Issuance, §13-443.

Protective orders, §13-446.

Rules of court, §§13-445, 13-446.

Service of process and papers, §13-444.

INTERSTATE ENFORCEMENT OF DOMESTIC VIOLENCE PROTECTION.

Construction of provisions, §16-1047.

Definitions, §16-1041.

Immunity from liability, §16-1045.

Judicial enforcement, §16-1042.

Non-judicial enforcement, §16-1043.

Other remedies not precluded, §16-1046.

Registration of orders, §16-1044.

Transitional provision, §16-1048.

INTERSTATE FAMILY SUPPORT, §§46-351.01 to 46-359.03.

Attorneys at law.

Private counsel, employment of, §46-353.09.

Citation of act, §46-351.01.

Communications between tribunals, §46-353.17.

Construction of act.

Applicability, §46-359.03.

Title of act, §46-351.01.

Uniform application and construction, §46-359.01.

INTERSTATE FAMILY SUPPORT —Cont'd

Convention support proceedings, §§46-357.01 to 46-357.13.

Applicability of subchapter, §46-357.02.

Contest of registered convention support order, §46-357.07.

Definitions, §46-357.01.

Direct request, §46-357.05.

English translation.

Record in original language, §46-357.13.

Foreign support agreement, §46-357.10.

Modification of convention child-support order, §46-357.11.

Office of the Attorney General.

Initiation by office of support proceeding under Convention, §46-357.04.

Relationship to United States central authority, §46-357.03.

Partial enforcement of registered convention support order, §46-357.09.

Personal information, limitation on use, §46-357.12.

Recognition and enforcement of registered convention support order, §46-357.08.

Record in original language, §46-357.13.

Registration of Convention support order, §46-357.06.

Defenses.

Nonparentage as defense, §46-353.15.

Spousal privilege, inapplicable, §46-353.16.

Definitions.

Convention support proceeding, §46-357.01.

General definitions, §46-351.02.

Depositions.

Special rules of evidence, §46-353.16.

Discovery.

Assistance with discovery, §46-353.18.

Electronic transmission of documentary evidence, §46-353.16.

Establishment of support order, §46-354.01.

Evidence.

Assistance with discovery, §46-353.18.

Copies of documents and records.

Evidentiary effect, §46-353.16.

INTERSTATE FAMILY SUPPORT
—Cont'd
Evidence —Cont'd
Special rules of evidence and
procedure, §46-353.16.
Fees and costs.
Filing fees and other costs,
prohibition, §46-353.13.
Identifying information.
Nondisclosure in exceptional
circumstances, §46-353.12.
Immunity.
Defense of immunity based on parent-
child relationship, inapplicable,
§46-353.16.
Limited immunity of petitioner,
§46-353.14.
**Income-withholding order of
another state or foreign support
order.**
Employer's compliance with income-
withholding order, §§46-355.01 to
46-355.07.
Administrative enforcement of
orders, §46-355.07.
Contest of obligor, §46-355.06.
Employer's receipt of income-
withholding order of another
state, §46-355.01.
Immunity from civil liability,
§46-355.04.
Penalties for noncompliance,
§46-355.05.
Two or more income-withholding
orders, §46-355.03.
Registration for enforcement of
support orders, §§46-356.01 to
46-356.04.
Choice of law, §46-356.04.
Effect of registration for
enforcement, §46-356.03.
Procedure to register order,
§46-356.02.
Registration of order, §46-356.01.
Initiating tribunal.
Communications between tribunals,
§46-353.17.
Duties of initiating tribunal,
§46-353.04.
Initiation of proceedings, §46-353.01.
Interstate rendition, §§46-358.01,
46-358.02.
Conditions, §46-358.02.
Grounds, §46-358.01.
Jurisdiction.
Child support orders.
Controlling child-support order,
determination of, §46-352.07.

INTERSTATE FAMILY SUPPORT
—Cont'd
Jurisdiction —Cont'd
Child support orders —Cont'd
Two or more obligees, §46-352.08.
Continuing, exclusive jurisdiction.
Enforcing child-support order,
§46-352.06.
Modifying child-support order,
§46-352.05.
Modifying spousal-support order,
§46-352.11.
Credit for payments, §46-352.09.
Initiating and responding tribunal of
state, §46-352.03.
Nonresidents.
Bases for jurisdiction over,
§46-352.01.
Subject to personal jurisdiction,
§46-352.10.
Personal jurisdiction.
Duration of, §46-352.02.
Nonresident subject to, §46-352.10.
Simultaneous proceedings, §46-352.04.
Minor parent.
Proceedings by, §46-353.02.
Nonparentage as defense, §46-353.15.
Nonresidents.
Jurisdiction.
Bases for jurisdiction over,
§46-352.01.
Subject to personal jurisdiction,
§46-352.10.
Physical presence in District.
Not required establish, enforce,
modify, etc., support order,
§46-353.16.
Office of the Attorney General.
Convention support proceeding.
Relationship to United States
central authority, §46-357.03.
Defined, §46-351.02.
Duties, §§46-353.08, 46-353.10.
Enforcement agency of District,
§§46-351.03, 46-351.04.
State information agency, designation,
§46-353.10.
Parentage proceedings.
Physical presence in District.
Not required to determine parentage
of child, §46-353.16.
Proceeding to determine parentage,
§46-354.02.
Voluntary acknowledgment of
paternity.
Admissible to establish parentage of
child, §46-353.16.

INTERSTATE FAMILY SUPPORT
—Cont'd
Petition or comparable pleading.
Filing with appropriate tribunal,
§46-353.01.
Nondisclosure of identifying
information, §46-353.12.
Pleadings and accompanying
documents, §46-353.11.
Receipt by inappropriate tribunal,
§46-353.06.
Proceeding by minor parent,
§46-353.02.
**Receipts and disbursement of
payments,** §46-353.19.
**Reciprocal enforcement of support
proceedings,** DomRel Rule 401.
**Registration of support order for
enforcement,** §§46-356.01 to
46-356.16.
Child-support order of another state,
§§46-356.09 to 46-356.14.
Effect of registration for
modification, §46-356.10.
Jurisdiction to modify order when
parties reside in the District,
§46-356.13.
Modification of order, §46-356.11.
Notice to issuing tribunal of
modification, §46-356.14.
Procedure to register for
modification, §46-356.09.
Recognition of modified order,
§46-356.12.
Choice of law, §46-356.04.
Contest of validity or support,
§§46-356.05 to 46-356.08.
Confirmed order, §46-356.08.
Notice of registration of order,
§46-356.05.
Procedure to contest validity or
enforcement of registered
support order, §46-356.06.
Registration or enforcement,
§46-356.07.
District enforcement of registered
order, §46-356.01.
Effect of registration, §46-356.03.
Foreign child-support order,
§§46-356.15, 46-356.16.
Application of chapter, §46-351.05.
Jurisdiction to modify, §46-356.15.
Procedure to register for
modification, §46-356.16.
Out-of-state support orders,
§46-356.01.

INTERSTATE FAMILY SUPPORT
—Cont'd
**Registration of support order for
enforcement** —Cont'd
Procedure to register order,
§46-356.02.
Responding tribunal.
Application of law of the District,
§46-353.03.
Communications between tribunals,
§46-353.17.
Duties and powers, §46-353.05.
Self-incrimination, right against.
Adverse inference from refusal to give
testimony, §46-353.16.
Support enforcement agency.
Administrative enforcement of orders,
§46-355.07.
Credit for payments, §46-352.09.
Defined, §46-353.02.
Duties, §46-353.07.
Enforcement agency of District,
§§46-351.03, 46-351.04.
Establishment of support order,
§46-354.01.
Proceedings under chapter,
§46-353.01.
Receipts and disbursement of
payments, §46-353.19.
**Support proceedings under
Convention.**
Application of chapter, §46-351.05.
Witnesses.
Special rules of evidence and
procedure, §46-353.16.

INTERSTATE HIGHWAY SYSTEM.
Provisions not applicable to,
§9-103.06.

**INTERSTATE INSURANCE
PRODUCT REGULATION
COMPACT.**
Authority to enter, §31-1391.

INTERSTATE PRIVILEGES.
Rental vehicle tax, §50-1505.02.

INTERVENTION PROCEEDINGS,
CivPro Rule 24-I.
Accounts and accounting.
Conservators, Probate Rule 330.
Audits, Probate Rule 331.
Termination of conservatorship,
Probate Rule 334.
Adoption proceedings, Adoption Rule
24.
Appeals, D.C. courts.
Administrative orders and decisions,
DCCtApp Rule 15.

INTERVENTION PROCEEDINGS
—Cont'd

Appeals, federal cases.
Administrative review, FRAP 15(d).
Briefs, USCtApp HPIP Rule IX(a)(4).
Docketing statement of intervenor, USCtApp Rule 12.

Attorneys at law, Probate Rule 304.
Compensation, Probate Rule 308.
Fifteen-day temporary guardians, Probate Rule 341.
General intervention proceedings, Probate Rule 321.
Guardian ad litem, Probate Rule 306.
Missing person conservatorship or protective orders, Probate Rule 350.

Bankruptcy proceedings, USDistDCBank Rule 7024-1.

Briefs for intervenors, UsCtApp Rule 28.

Child custody.
De facto parent motion to intervene, §16-831.03.
Third-party motion to intervene, §16-831.02.

Compensation of guardians, conservators, etc., Probate Rule 308.

Conservators.
Accounts, Probate Rule 330.
Audit of accounts, Probate Rule 331.
Appraisals, Probate Rule 333.
Bonds, Probate Rule 332.
Compensation, Probate Rule 308.
Conservatorship plans, Probate Rule 329.
Continuation of existing conservatorship proceedings, Probate Rule 301.
Foreign conservators, Probate Rule 361.
Inventories, Probate Rule 329.
Missing persons, Probate Rules 350, 351.
Reports, Probate Rule 330.
Termination of conservatorship, Probate Rule 334.

Court costs, Probate Rule 310.

Creditor's claims, Probate Rule 307.

Death of ward.
Suggestions of death, Probate Rule 328.
Termination of conservatorship, Probate Rule 334.

Discovery, Probate Rule 312.

INTERVENTION PROCEEDINGS
—Cont'd

Domestic relations actions, DomRel Rule 24.

Effective date of rules, Probate Rule 301.

Examiners, Probate Rules 321, 326.
Missing person conservatorship or protective orders, Probate Rule 350.

Fifteen-day temporary guardians, Probate Rules 341 to 361.

Forfeiture of property, CivPro Rule 71A-I.

Form of motion, CivPro Form CA 23.

Guardian ad litem, Probate Rule 306.
Compensation, Probate Rule 308.

Hearings, Probate Rule 321.
Petition.
Notice, Probate Rules 311, 321, 325.

Merit system.
Review of agency decision, CivPro Agency Review Rule 1.

Notice.
See NOTICE.

Parties, Probate Rule 303.

Petitions.
Compensation of guardians, conservators, etc., Probate Rule 308.
Fifteen-day temporary guardians, Probate Rule 341.
Form and contents, Probate Rule 302.
General intervention proceedings, Probate Rules 321, 322.
Missing persons.
Conservators or protective orders, Probate Rule 350.
Notice.
Hearings, Probate Rules 311, 321, 325.
Permission to participate in proceedings, Probate Rule 303.
Request by interested person for notice, Probate Rule 304.
Rule to show cause for recovery of property, Probate Rule 313.
Service of petitions, Probate Rules 311, 321, 325.
Termination of conservatorship, Probate Rule 334.
Termination of guardianship, conservatorship, or protective arrangement, Probate Rule 321.

Pleadings, Probate Rule 302.
Missing person conservatorship or protective orders, Probate Rule 350.

INTERVENTION PROCEEDINGS —Cont'd

Pleadings —Cont'd

Pre-hearing pleadings in general intervention proceedings, Probate Rule 321.

Pretrial statements, Probate Rule 321.

Removal of fiduciary, Probate Rule 309.

Reports.

Conservators, Probate Rule 330.

Termination of conservatorship, Probate Rule 334.

Guardians, Probate Rule 328.

Rule to show cause for recovery of property, Probate Rule 313.

Scope of rules, Probate Rule 301.

Service of process.

See SERVICE OF PROCESS AND PAPERS.

Six-month temporary guardians, Probate Rule 323.

Termination of conservatorship, Probate Rule 334.

Termination of guardianship, conservatorship, or protective arrangement.

Petitions, Probate Rule 321.

Service of petition and notice, Probate Rule 311.

Visitors, Probate Rules 321, 327.

Missing person conservatorship or protective orders, Probate Rule 350.

INTESTATE SUCCESSION, §§19-101.01 to 19-701.

Advancements, effect of, §19-319.

Alien ancestor, descent through, §19-321.

Antenuptial agreements, §19-113.

Brothers and descendants of brothers, §§19-309, 19-310, 19-315.

Child equivalent to adopted child in instruments, §16-313.

Children.

Antenuptial, §19-318.

Born out of wedlock, §§19-316, 19-318.

Equal shares, entitlement to, §19-306.

Posthumous, §19-314.

Collateral relatives, §19-311.

Death of distributee before distribution, §19-313.

Descent in fee simple, §19-301.

District.

Escheatment of property to, §19-701.

Escheat, §19-701.

INTESTATE SUCCESSION —Cont'd

Exempt property, §19-101.03.

Family allowance, §19-101.04.

Grandchildren, §19-307.

Grandmothers and grandfathers, §19-312.

Half-blood and whole-blood kin.

No distinction between, §19-315.

Homestead allowance, §19-101.02.

Minor children not in custody of surviving spouse.

Equitable apportionment, §19-101.05.

Murder or manslaughter.

Succession barred by, §19-320.

Nonprobate transfers on death, §§19-601.01 to 19-603.11.

See NONPROBATE TRANSFERS.

Parents, §19-308.

Posthumous children, §19-314.

Prenuptial agreements, §19-113.

Probate proceedings.

General provisions, §§16-3101 to 16-3112, Probate Rules 1 to 430.

See PROBATE PROCEEDINGS.

Siblings and descendants of siblings, §§19-309, 19-310, 19-315.

Simultaneous deaths, §§19-501 to 19-506.

Sisters and descendants of sisters, §§19-309, 19-310, 19-315.

Statutory rule against perpetuities, §§19-901 to 19-907.

Surplus distributed after payment to surviving spouse, §19-305.

Surviving spouse or domestic partner and children, §§19-101.01 to 19-101.06.

Applicability of provisions, §19-101.01.

Equitable apportionment.

Minor children not in custody of surviving spouse, §19-101.05.

Exempt property, §19-101.03.

Family allowance, §19-101.04.

Homestead allowance, §19-101.02.

Surplus distributed after payment to, §19-305.

Whole, entitlement to, §19-302.

Willful violations, §19-101.06.

TOD security registration, §§19-603.01 to 19-603.11.

See NONPROBATE TRANSFERS.

Trust estates, §19-317.

Uniform TOD security registration, §§19-603.01 to 19-603.11.

See NONPROBATE TRANSFERS.

INTOXICATED PERSONS.
Alcohol and drug abuse, §§44-1201 to 44-1210.
See ALCOHOL AND DRUG ABUSE.
Boats and other watercraft operated under the influence of alcohol, §§50-2206.31 to 50-2206.36.
Chemical testing, §§50-1908 to 50-1912.
Body artists.
Consent, §47-2853.76e.
Driving under the influence.
See DRIVING UNDER THE INFLUENCE.
Marijuana.
Consumption in public space or impairment, §48-911.01.
Public intoxication, §§24-604, 25-1001.
Marijuana, §48-911.01.
Sale of alcoholic beverages to, §25-781.
Vessels operated under the influence of alcohol, §§50-2206.31 to 50-2206.36.
Chemical testing, §§50-1908 to 50-1912.

INTRAFAMILY PROCEEDINGS, §§16-1001 to 16-1034.
Complaint of criminal conduct, §16-1002.
Definitions, §16-1001.
Domestic violence, §§16-1031 to 16-1034.
Rules governing proceedings in domestic violence unit, DomesticViolence Rules 1 to 14.
Hearings, §§16-1004, 16-1005.
Interstate enforcement of domestic violence protection, §§16-1041 to 16-1048.
See INTERSTATE ENFORCEMENT OF DOMESTIC VIOLENCE PROTECTION.
Jurisdiction to file petition, §16-1006.
Landlord and tenant.
Victims of intrafamily offenses.
Duties of housing provider as to protection of, §42-3505.08.
Notice of lease termination by tenant who is victim, §42-3505.07.
Notice of hearing and order directing appearance, §16-1004, FamDiv Rule H.
Form, FamDiv Form 1.
Parental kidnapping, §§16-1021 to 16-1026.

INTRAFAMILY PROCEEDINGS —Cont'd
Petition for civil protection, §§16-1003 to 16-1006.
Jurisdiction to file petition, §16-1006.
Rules governing proceedings in domestic violence unit, DomesticViolence Rules 1 to 14.
Private right of action, §16-1002.
Protection orders, §16-1005.
Temporary orders.
Exparte issuance, duration, extension, §16-1004.
Subpoenas, FamDiv Rule E.
Temporary protection order.
Exparte issuance, duration, extension, §16-1004.

INVASION.
Congress, US Const Art I §8.
Constitution of the United States, US Const Art I §§8 to 10, Art IV §4.

INVASION OF PRIVACY.
Freedom of information act exemption.
Information of personal nature, §2-534.

INVENTIONS, US Const Art I §8.

INVENTORIES.
Administration of estate, §§20-711 to 20-715.
Affordable housing.
Comprehensive tracking plan for affordable housing inventory.
Definitions, §42-2141.
Requirements for tracking, §42-2142.
Assignments for benefit of creditors.
Inventory of estate required, §28-2101.
Children and minors.
Property of, §21-142.
Conservators appointed for protection of property, §21-2064.
Controlled substances, §48-903.06.
Decedents' estates.
Death between January 1, 1981 and June 30, 1995, Probate Rule 109.
Waiver of filing inventories, Probate Rule 115.
Death on or after July 1, 1995, Probate Forms 12, 13, Probate Rule 409.
Waiver of filing inventories, Probate Form 18, Probate Rule 415.
Department of general services.
Real property assets, §10-551.05.

INVENTORIES —Cont'd

Guardians, conservators, trustees, etc., Probate Rule 204.

Conservators, Probate Rule 329.

Missing persons, Probate Rule 351.

Failure to file inventory, Probate Rule 207.

Homestead housing preservation program, §42-2105.

Income taxes, §47-1804.05.

INVESTIGATIONS.

Adoption of children, §§16-307, 16-308.

Adulteration of food or drugs, §48-105.

Adult protective services, §7-1904.

Alcoholic beverage licenses.

Examination of books, records and premises, §25-802.

Alcoholic beverages.

Examination of books, records and premises, §25-802.

Arson, §5-417.01.

Asbestos contractors, §8-111.05.

Attorney discipline or disability proceedings, DCBar Rule XI, USDistCt LCrR 57.27, USDistCt LCvR 83.16.

Charitable institutions, §§44-709, 44-710.

Check cashing businesses, §§26-308, 26-320.

Child abuse and neglect, §§4-1301.06, 4-1301.09.

Child-placing agencies, §4-1409.

Condominiums, §42-1904.13.

Registration, §42-1904.05.

Consumer protection.

Complaint procedures, §28-3905.

Department of consumer and regulatory affairs.

Powers, §28-3903.

Council investigations.

Obstruction of, §1-301.43.

Power to investigate, §1-204.13.

Council powers, §5-1021.

Criminal background checks.

Corrections Department employees, §24-211.41.

Unlicensed health care personnel, §§44-551 to 44-554.

Criminal investigators assigned to United States Attorney, powers of, §23-109.

Delinquent minors.

Intake procedures, JuvProc Rule 102.

INVESTIGATIONS —Cont'd

Director of Department of Licenses, Investigations, and Inspections, §1-301.03.

Discrimination, complaints regarding, §2-1403.05.

Employment agencies, §32-410.

Energy efficiency standards.

Enforcement, §8-1771.05.

Ethics and government accountability.

Dismissal, §1-1162.16.

Formal, §1-1162.13.

Preliminary, §1-1162.12.

Family and medical leave, §32-509.

Investigative authority, §32-508.

Family homes, §4-1409.

Human Rights Commission, §2-1403.05.

Insurance companies.

Unauthorized entities, §31-233.

Insurance fraud, §22-3225.08.

Judges.

Independent investigations prohibited, CJC Canon 2.9.

Life estates, proceedings to discover death of tenant, §16-1154.

Litter control, §8-803.

Long-term care ombudsman, §7-702.05.

Mattresses, §8-507.

Mayor's powers, §5-1021.

Medical examiners, investigations of deaths by, §5-1405.

Metropolitan police department.

Investigations concerning first amendment activities, §§5-333.01 to 5-333.13.

See METROPOLITAN POLICE.

Money lenders, §26-906.

Mortgage lenders and brokers, §26-1112.

Municipal matters, §5-1021.

Nurse staffing agencies.

Inspection of offices and operations, §44-1051.16.

Occupational safety and health, §32-1112.

Police complaints, office of, §5-1111.

Pretrial services agency, by, §23-1303.

Probation, §24-303.

Procurement claims, §§2-381.03, 2-381.07.

Public utilities.

See PUBLIC SERVICE COMMISSION.

INVESTIGATIONS —Cont'd
Public Welfare, Board of, §§4-112, 4-117.
Rental housing conversion and sale, §42-3405.05.
Restraints of trade, §28-4505.
Civil investigative demand, §28-4505.
Security agents and brokers.
Administrative files and records, §31-5607.07.
Subpoena power, §31-5606.01.
Teachers, §38-111.
Unauthorized practice of law committee, DCCtApp Rule 49.
Vector-borne disease control, §8-2131.03.
Water pollution, §8-103.19.
Workplace fraud.
Complaints, investigation, §32-1331.05.

INVESTMENT ADVISERS.
Repeal of act, §31-5608.04.
Security agents and brokers.
General provisions, §§31-5601.01 to 31-5608.04.
See SECURITY AGENTS AND BROKERS.

INVESTMENT COMPANIES.
Statutory trusts.
Independent trustees, §29-1205.12.

INVESTMENTS.
Arts, cultural and educational facilities.
Economic assistance to, §§39-401 to 39-405.
Banks and financial institutions.
District funds invested in, §§47-351.01 to 47-351.16.
Bond issues of District.
Fiduciary investments in, §1-204.86.
Captive insurance companies, §31-3931.07.
Corporations.
Powers, §29-303.02.
District of Columbia funds, §§47-351.01 to 47-351.16.
Fiduciaries, CivPro Rule 306.
Probate proceedings.
All proceedings, Probate Rule 5.
Guardians, conservators, trustees, etc., involved, Probate Forms 2, 3, Probate Rules 222, 223.
Prudent investor act.
See PRUDENT INVESTOR ACT.
Financial literacy council, §§38-731.01 to 38-731.05.

INVESTMENTS —Cont'd
Fraternal benefit societies, §31-5318.
Funds invested in federal securities, §47-133.
Health maintenance organizations, §31-3411.
Hospital and medical services corporations, §31-3510.
Housing finance agency funds, §42-2704.06.
Insurance investments, §§31-1371.01 to 31-1375.01.
See INSURANCE INVESTMENTS.
Iran.
Employees retirement program management.
Investment of public funds in certain companies doing business with government of Iran, §§1-336.01 to 1-336.06.
Medical liability captive trust fund, §1-307.91.
Nonprofit corporations.
Powers, §29-403.02.
Professional corporations.
Powers, §29-505.
Prudent investor act.
See PRUDENT INVESTOR ACT.
Security agents and brokers.
General provisions, §§31-5601.01 to 31-5608.04.
See SECURITY AGENTS AND BROKERS.
Sudan.
Employees retirement program management.
Investment of public funds in certain companies doing business with government of Sudan, §§1-335.01 to 1-335.07.
Trustees.
Prudent investor act.
See PRUDENT INVESTOR ACT.

INVESTMENT SECURITIES, §§28:8-101 to 28:8-601.
Acquisition of security or interest therein, §28:8-104.
Adverse claims.
Defined, §28:8-102.
Notice, §28:8-105.
Securities intermediary and others not liable to adverse claimant, §28:8-115.
Security entitlements.
Assertion of adverse claim against entitlement holder, §28:8-502.

INVESTMENT SECURITIES —Cont'd
Adverse claims —Cont'd
  Security entitlements —Cont'd
    Rights of purchaser of security
      entitlement from entitlement
      holder, §28:8-510.
Alteration of security certificate,
  §28:8-206.
Applicable law, §28:8-110.
Certificated and uncertificated
  securities.
  Delivery, §28:8-301.
  Rights of purchaser, §28:8-302.
Choice of law, §28:8-110.
Citation of article.
  Short title, §28:8-101.
Clearing corporations.
  Defined, §28:8-102.
  Rules, §28:8-111.
Completion of security certificate,
  §28:8-206.
Control, §28:8-106.
  What constitutes, §28:8-106.
Creditor's legal process, §28:8-112.
Defenses.
  Issuers defenses.
    Generally, §28:8-202.
    Notice of defense, §§28:8-202,
      28:8-203.
Definitions, §28:8-102.
  Appropriate evidence of appointment
    or incumbency, §28:8-402.
  General commercial code definitions,
    §28:1-201.
    Course of dealing, §28:1-303.
    Reasonable time and seasonably,
      §28:1-205.
    Usage of trade, §28:1-303.
  Guaranty of the signature, §28:8-402.
  Index of definitions, §28:8-102.
  Issuers, §28:8-201.
  Overissue, §28:8-210.
  Protected purchaser, §28:8-303.
  Securities account, §28:8-501.
Destroyed security certificates.
  Notification to issuer, §28:8-406.
  Replacement, §28:8-405.
Entitlement orders.
  Defined, §28:8-102.
  Effectiveness, §28:8-107.
Evidence.
  Rules concerning certificated
    securities, §28:8-114.
Financial assets.
  Acquisition of financial asset or
    interest therein, §28:8-104.

INVESTMENT SECURITIES —Cont'd
Financial assets —Cont'd
  Defined, §28:8-102.
  Rules for determining whether certain
    obligations and interests are
    securities or financial assets,
    §28:8-103.
  Security interests arising in purchase
    or delivery of, §28:9-206.
General provisions, §§28:1-101 to
  28:1-310.
  See COMMERCIAL CODE.
Indorsements, §28:8-304.
  Defined, §28:8-102.
  Effectiveness, §28:8-107.
  Guaranteeing indorsement.
    Effect, §28:8-306.
Instructions, §28:8-305.
  Assurance that instructions are
    effective, §28:8-402.
  Defined, §28:8-102.
  Effectiveness, §28:8-107.
  Guaranteeing instruction.
    Effect, §28:8-306.
Interpretation of provisions,
  §§28:10-103, 28:10-104.
Issuers.
  Defenses.
    Generally, §28:8-202.
    Notice of defense, §§28:8-202,
      28:8-203.
  Defined, §28:8-201.
  Liens, §28:8-209.
  Registration.
    Demand that issuer not register
      transfer, §28:8-403.
    Duty to register transfer, §28:8-401.
    Notification to issuer of lost,
      destroyed or wrongfully taken
      security certificate, §28:8-406.
  Responsibility, §28:8-202.
  Rights with respect to registered
    owners, §28:8-207.
  Transfer restrictions.
    Effect, §28:8-204.
Issues.
  Overissues.
    Defined, §28:8-210.
    Effect, §28:8-210.
Liens.
  Issuer's lien, §28:8-209.
Lost security certificates.
  Notification to issuer, §28:8-406.
  Replacement, §28:8-405.

INVESTMENT SECURITIES —Cont'd
Negotiable instruments.
General provisions, §§28:3-101 to
28:3-605.
See NEGOTIABLE
INSTRUMENTS.
Notice.
Adverse claims, §28:8-105.
Defects or defenses, §§28:8-202,
28:8-203.
Overissues.
Defined, §28:8-210.
Effect, §28:8-210.
Purchasers.
Adverse claims.
Notice, §§28:8-304, 28:8-305.
Bona fide purchasers.
Rights acquired, §28:8-301.
Title acquired, §28:8-302.
Delivery to purchaser, §28:8-303.
Notice of adverse claims, §§28:8-304,
28:8-305.
Protected purchaser, §28:8-303.
Rights acquired, §28:8-302.
Right to requisites for registration of
transfer, §28:8-307.
Registration.
Assurance that endorsements or
instructions are effective,
§28:8-402.
Authenticating trustee.
Obligations, §28:8-407.
Issuers.
Demand that issuer not register
transfer, §28:8-403.
Duty to register transfer, §28:8-401.
Notification to issuer of lost,
destroyed or wrongfully taken
security certificate, §28:8-406.
Rights with respect to registered
owners, §28:8-207.
Purchaser's right to requisites for
registration of transfer, §28:8-307.
Registrar.
Obligations, §28:8-407.
Replacement of lost, destroyed or
wrongfully taken security
certificates, §28:8-405.
Signature of registrar.
Effect, §28:8-208.
Transfer agent.
Obligations, §28:8-407.
Wrongful registration, §28:8-404.
Savings clause, §28:8-601.
Secured transactions.
Attachment and enforceability of
security interests, §28:9-203.

INVESTMENT SECURITIES —Cont'd
Secured transactions —Cont'd
Financial asset.
Security interest arising in purchase
or delivery of, §28:9-206.
Security entitlements.
Priority among security interests
and entitlement holders,
§28:8-511.
Securities and financial assets.
Rules for determining, §28:8-103.
Securities intermediaries.
Defined, §28:8-102.
Liability.
Not liable to adverse claimant,
§28:8-115.
Purchaser for value.
Status as, §28:8-116.
Security entitlements.
Acquisition from securities
intermediary, §28:8-501.
Change of entitlement holders
position to other form of
security holding.
Duty of securities intermediary,
§28:8-508.
Compliance with entitlement order.
Duty of securities intermediary,
§28:8-507.
Duties of securities intermediary,
§§28:8-504 to 28:8-509.
Exercise of rights as directed by
entitlement holder.
Duty of securities intermediary,
§28:8-506.
Financial asset held by securities
intermediary.
Duties of securities intermediary
as to, §§28:8-504 to 28:8-506.
Maintenance, §28:8-504.
Property interest of entitlement
holder in, §28:8-503.
Payments and distributions.
Duty of securities intermediary
with respect to, §28:8-508.
Security agents and brokers.
General provisions, §§31-5601.01 to
31-5608.04.
See SECURITY AGENTS AND
BROKERS.
Security entitlements.
Adverse claims.
Assertion of adverse claim against
entitlement holder, §28:8-502.
Rights of purchaser of security
entitlement from entitlement
holder, §28:8-510.

INVESTMENT SECURITIES —Cont'd
Security entitlements —Cont'd

Defined, §28:8-102.

Purchaser of security entitlement from entitlement holder.

Rights, §28:8-510.

Rights of purchaser, §28:8-510.

Securities account.

Defined, §28:8-501.

Securities intermediaries.

Acquisition from securities intermediary, §28:8-501.

Change of entitlement holders position to other form of security holding.

Duty of securities intermediary, §28:8-508.

Compliance with entitlement order.

Duty of securities intermediary, §28:8-507.

Duties of securities intermediary, §§28:8-504 to 28:8-509.

Exercise of rights as directed by entitlement holder.

Duty of securities intermediary, §28:8-506.

Financial asset held by securities intermediary.

Duties of securities intermediary as to, §§28:8-504 to 28:8-506.

Maintenance, §28:8-504.

Property interest of entitlement holder in, §28:8-503.

Payments and distributions.

Duty of securities intermediary with respect to, §28:8-508.

Security interests.

Priority among security interests and entitlement holders, §28:8-511.

Signatures.

Authenticating trustee's, registrar's or transfer agent's signature.

Effect, §28:8-208.

Evidentiary rules concerning certificated securities, §28:8-114.

Guaranteeing signature.

Effect, §28:8-306.

Unauthorized signature on security certificate.

Effect, §28:8-205.

Statute of frauds.

Inapplicability of statute of frauds, §28:8-113.

Title of article.

Short title, §28:8-101.

INVESTMENT SECURITIES —Cont'd
Transfer.

Agent's signature.

Effect, §28:8-208.

Delivery, §28:8-301.

Issuers' restrictions.

Effect, §28:8-204.

Transitional provisions, §§28:11-101 to 28:11-108.

See COMMERCIAL CODE.

Trusts and trustees.

Authenticating trustee.

Registration of securities.

Obligations, §28:8-407.

Signature.

Effect, §28:8-208.

Uncertificated securities.

Statement, §28:8-408.

Warranties.

Direct holding, §28:8-108.

Effect of signature of authenticating trustee.

Registrar or transfer agent, §28:8-208.

Indirect holding, §28:8-109.

Wrongfully taken security certificates.

Notification to issuer, §28:8-406.

Replacement, §28:8-405.

IOLTA.
Interest on Lawyers Trust Account, DCBar Appx A, DCBar Rule X, ProfCond Rule 1.15.

Approved depositories, DCBar Rule XI.

Verification of participation, DCBar Rule XIV.

IRAN.
Employees retirement program management.

Investment of public funds in certain companies doing business with government of Iran, §§1-336.01 to 1-336.06.

THE ISRAEL SENIOR RESIDENCES.
Real property tax exemptions, §47-4659.

J

JAILS.
Cap on prisoners housed at District of Columbia jail, §24-201.61.

JAILS —Cont'd

Corrections, department of.
General provisions, §§24-211.01 to 24-211.41.
See CORRECTIONS, DEPARTMENT OF.

Federal authority.
Transfer of prison system to, §§24-101 to 24-142.
See PRISON SYSTEM, FEDERAL CONTROL.

Habeas corpus.
General provisions, §§16-1901 to 16-1909.
See HABEAS CORPUS.

Juvenile offenders.
See JUVENILE OFFENDERS.

Parole.
General provisions, §§24-401c to 24-468.
See PAROLE.

Prison industries.
General provisions, §§24-231.01 to 24-231.15.
See PRISON INDUSTRIES.

Prisons and prisoners.
Cap on prisoners housed at District of Columbia jail, §24-201.61.
Escaped prisoners.
See FUGITIVES FROM JUSTICE.
General provisions, §§24-201.02 to 24-261.05.
See PRISONS AND PRISONERS.

Private correctional treatment facilities, §§24-261.01 to 24-261.05.

Probation.
See PROBATION.

Sex offender registration.
General provisions, §§22-4001 to 22-4017.
See SEX OFFENDER REGISTRATION.

Youth offenders.
See JUVENILE OFFENDERS.

JAMES REESE EUROPE POST NO. 5, AMERICAN LEGION.
Real property exempt from taxation, §47-1046.

JENKINS ROW DEVELOPMENT.
Taxation exemption, §47-4603.

JEWELRY.
Public auction permit requirements, §47-2705.

JOB GROWTH TAX CREDIT, §§47-1807.51 to 47-1807.56.

JOB LISTING SERVICES.
Employment agencies.
General provisions, §§32-401 to 32-416.
See EMPLOYMENT AGENCIES.

JOB OPPORTUNITY BANK, §§32-751 to 32-756.
Administration, §32-752.
Agreement by grantee, §32-755.
Applications for grants, §32-754.
Definitions, §32-751.
Eligibility for grants, §32-753.
Establishment, §32-752.
Performance evaluation of grantees, §32-756.
Priorities for grants, §32-754.

JOBS FOR DISTRICT OF COLUMBIA GRADUATES PROGRAM, §38-1806.07.

JOBS TRUST FUND.
District of Columbia jobs trust fund, §2-219.04c.

JOB TRAINING PROGRAMS.
Employment services department.
Job training and adult education programs.
Quarterly reporting by department, §32-771.

Fire protection study commission.
Sprinkler installation program, combined with, §3-1104.

Get DC Residents Training for Jobs Now, §§38-1011.01 to 38-1011.05.
Establishment, §38-1011.01.
Funding.
Federal aid, §38-1011.04.
Grants, §38-1011.04.
Local funds, §38-1011.04.
Rules and regulations, §38-1011.05.
Technical instruction and expertise, §38-1011.03.

Innovation fund, §§1-325.221 to 1-325.226.

Opportunity accounts.
Generally, §§1-307.61 to 1-307.74.
Use for training of account holder, §1-307.68.

JOHN A. WILSON BUILDING, §§10-1301, 10-1331 to 10-1336.
Administration of foundation, §10-1335.
Bicycle parking.
Increase in bicycle parking requirements, §50-1641.03.

JOHN A. WILSON BUILDING
—Cont'd
Board of directors, §10-1334.
Centennial fund, §10-1302.
Designation of, §10-1301.
Establishment of foundation for,
§10-1332.
Fund, §§10-1333, 10-1336.
Policy declaration, §10-1331.
Sunset provision regarding fund,
§10-1336.
Taxation without representation
federal tax pay-out message
board, §10-1701.

JOHN PHILIP SOUSA BRIDGE,
§9-306.

JOINDER OF CLAIMS.
Arbitration, revised act.
Consolidation of proceedings,
§16-4410.
Civil procedure, CivPro Rule 18.
Criminal procedure.
Indictments or information for trial,
§23-312.
Offenses, joinder of, §23-311.
Prejudicial joinder, relief from,
§23-313.

JOINDER OF PARTIES, CivPro Rules
19, 20.
Allegation of reason for omitting
party, CivPro Form CA 26.
Appeals, DCCtApp Rule 3.
Administrative orders and decisions,
DCCtApp Rule 15.
Child custody proceedings,
§16-4602.05.
Condemnation of property, CivPro
Rule 71A.
Counterclaims and cross-claims,
CivPro Rule 13.
Interpleader, CivPro Form CA 21.
Criminal procedure, CrimPro Rules 8,
13.
Defendants, joinder of, §23-311.
Discharge or acquittal of joint
defendant in order to be witness,
§23-107.
Prejudicial joinder, relief from,
§23-313.
Pretrial requests for severance,
CrimPro Rule 12.
Relief from prejudicial joinder,
CrimPro Rule 14.
Verdicts, CrimPro Rule 31.

JOINDER OF PARTIES —Cont'd
Delinquent minors, JuvProc Rules 8,
13.
Relief from prejudicial joinder,
JuvProc Rule 14.
Domestic relations actions, DomRel
Rule 19.
Interpleader, CivPro Rule 22.
Complaint for interpleader, CivPro
Form CA 18.
Counterclaim for interpleader, CivPro
Form CA 21.
Misjoinder and nonjoinder, CivPro
Rule 21.

JOINT ACCOUNTS, §§26-801 to
26-804.

JOINT CONTRACTS, §§16-2101 to
16-2106, 28-3504.
Death of defendant after action
brought.
Representation, §16-2104.
Death of party.
Executors, administrators, heirs bound
by contract, §16-2102.
Definition, §16-2101.
Judgment rendered if others not
joined, §16-2105.
Proof of joint liability unnecessary,
§16-2105.
Separate composition or
compromise with creditors,
§16-2106.
Service of process on some of
parties to contract.
Judgment against parties served not
extinguishment or merger of
action, §16-2103.

JOINTLY HELD PROPERTY.
Disclaimer of property interests.
Rights of survivorship in, §19-1507.

JOINT SEIZIN.
Legal estate, §42-1502.

JOINT TENANTS.
Ejectment, §16-1101.
Estates in land, §42-516.
Horizontal property regimes,
§42-2005.
Simultaneous deaths, §19-503.
Waste of real property, §42-1604.

JOINT UNDERWRITING
ASSOCIATION, §31-5005.

JOINT VENTURES.
Prison industries, §§24-231.04,
24-231.06.

JOURNALS.
Congress, US Const Art I §§5, 7.

JOYRIDING.
Unauthorized use of motor vehicles,
§22-3215.

JUBILEE HOUSING RESIDENTIAL
RENTAL PROJECT.
Real property tax exemptions,
§47-4633.

JUDGES, §§11-1501 to 11-1505.
Abusing prestige of judicial office.
Avoiding, CJC Canon 1.3.
Administrative appointments, CJC
Canon 2.13.
Administrative law judges.
Office of administrative hearings,
§§2-1831.01 to 2-1831.18.
See ADMINISTRATIVE
HEARINGS, OFFICE OF.
Affiliation with discriminatory
organization, CJC Canon 3.6.
Appeals, federal cases.
Complaints against judges, USCtApp
HPIP Rule II(e).
Generally, USCtApp HPIP Rule
I(b)(1).
Masters, appointment of, FRAP 48.
Promulgation of rules by, FRAP 47.
Single judge to entertain motions,
FRAP 27(c).
Staffs, USCtApp HPIP Rule I(b)(2).
Writs of mandamus and prohibition
directed to, FRAP 21, USCtApp
Rule 21.
Appearance of impropriety.
Avoidance, CJC Canon 1.
Appearances.
Governmental bodies, appearances
before.
Conflicts with office, avoiding, CJC
Canon 3.2.
Appointments, §11-1501.
Administrative appointments, CJC
Canon 2.13.
Governmental position.
Conflicts with office, avoiding, CJC
Canon 3.4.
Arbitrator.
Acting as, avoiding conflicts with
office, CJC Canon 3.9.
Assignment of cases, CivPro Rule 40-I,
USDistCt LCrR 57.8 to USDistCt
LCrR 57.15, USDistCt LCvR 40.1 to
USDistCt LCvR 40.9.
Civil I calendar, CivPro Rule 40-II.

JUDGES —Cont'd
Assignment of cases —Cont'd
Collection and subrogation cases,
CivPro Rule 40-III.
Domestic relations actions, DomRel
Rule 40.
Bias, CivPro Rule 63-I.
Adoption proceedings, Adoption Rule
63.
Domestic relations actions, DomRel
Rule 63.
Probate proceedings.
Death between January 1, 1981 and
June 30, 1995, Probate Rule
126.
Prohibited, CJC Canon 2.3.
Campaign activities.
Appointive office, CJC Canon 4.3.
Candidates for nonjudicial office, CJC
Canon 4.5.
General rules, CJC Canon 4.1.
Character witness, acting as.
Conflicts with office, avoiding, CJC
Canon 3.3.
Chief judges.
Designation of, §§1-204.31, 11-1503.
Responsibilities of, §11-1702.
United States District Court,
USDistCt LCrR 57.14, USDistCt
LCvR 40.7.
Coercion.
Coercing parties into settlement
prohibited, CJC Canon 2.6.
Comments on pending cases, CJC
Canon 2.10.
Commission on judicial disabilities
and tenure, §§11-1521 to 11-1530.
See COMMISSION ON JUDICIAL
DISABILITIES AND TENURE.
Communication with jurors, CJC
Canon 2.8.
Compensation of judges.
Accepting gifts or other things of
value, CJC Canon 3.13.
Extrajudicial activities, CJC Canon
3.12.
Reimbursement of expenses, CJC
Canon 3.14.
Reporting requirements, CJC Canon
3.15.
Competence and diligence, CJC
Canon 2.5.
Complaints against judges, USDistCt
LCrR 57.16, USDistCt LCvR 40.10.
Attorneys to report judicial misconduct
to appropriate authority, ProfCond
Rule 8.3.

JUDGES —Cont'd
Complaints against judges —Cont'd
Rules of the judicial council governing complaints of judicial misconduct or disability, USCtApp Appx III.
Compliance with the law, CJC Canon 1.1.
Condemnation proceedings, assignment for, §16-1302.
Confidence in judiciary.
Promoting, CJC Canon 1.2.
Conflicts with office.
Avoiding, CJC Canon 3.
Constitution of the United States.
Compensation, US Const Art III §1.
Tenure, US Const Art III §1.
Cooperation with other judges, CJC Canon 2.5.
Court of appeals, §§11-702 to 11-709.
Decisions.
Responsibility for, CJC Canon 2.7.
Decorum, CJC Canon 2.8.
Disability of judge, CJC Canon 2.14.
Discipline or removal of judges.
Cooperation of judge with authorities, CJC Canon 2.16.
Disclosure of nonpublic information, CJC Canon 3.5.
Discrimination.
Affiliation with discriminatory organization, CJC Canon 3.6.
Bias, prejudice or harassment prohibited, CJC Canon 2.3.
Impartiality generally, CJC Canon 2.
Disqualification, CJC Canon 2.11.
Dual office holding.
Appointment to governmental position.
Conflicts with office, avoiding, CJC Canon 3.4.
Fiduciary positions, appointment to, CJC Canon 3.8.
Participation in educational, charitable, civic, etc. activities, CJC Canon 3.7.
Elections.
Political and campaign activities, CJC Canon 4.
Ex parte communications, CJC Canon 2.9.
External influences.
Avoidance, CJC Canon 2.4.
Extrajudicial activities.
Activities prohibited, CJC Canon 3.1.
Conflicts with office, avoiding, CJC Canon 3.

JUDGES —Cont'd
Fairness and impartiality, CJC Canon 2.2.
Bias, prejudice or harassment prohibited, CJC Canon 2.3.
Family court proceedings generally.
Presenting matters in chambers or in emergency, FamDiv Rule R.
Fees.
Accepting gifts or other things of value.
Waiver of fees or charges, CJC Canon 3.14.
Fiduciary positions.
Appointment to, CJC Canon 3.8.
Financial, business or remunerative activities.
Avoiding conflicts with office, CJC Canon 3.11.
Financial statements, §11-1530.
Findings of the court.
See JUDGMENTS AND DECREES.
Gifts.
Accepting gifts or other things of value, CJC Canon 3.13.
Reporting requirements, CJC Canon 3.15.
Waiver of fees or charges, CJC Canon 3.14.
Government appearance or consultation.
Conflicts with office, avoiding, CJC Canon 3.2.
Harassment.
Prohibited, CJC Canon 2.3.
Impairment of lawyer or judge, CJC Canon 2.14.
Impartiality, competence and diligence, CJC Canon 2.
Bias, prejudice or harassment prohibited, CJC Canon 2.3.
Impartiality and fairness, goals, CJC Canon 2.2.
Impropriety and appearance of impropriety.
Avoiding, CJC Canon 1.
Inability to proceed, CivPro Rule 63.
Adoption proceedings, Adoption Rule 63.
Criminal procedure, CrimPro Rule 25.
Delinquent minors, JuvProc Rule 25.
Domestic relations actions, DomRel Rule 63.
Independent investigations.
Prohibited, CJC Canon 2.9.
Judicial Conference of the District of Columbia, DCCtApp Rule 50.

JUDGES —Cont'd
Judicial nomination commission,
§1-204.34.
Designation of chief judge of court of
District, §1-204.31.
Law practice.
Prohibited, avoiding conflicts with
office, CJC Canon 3.10.
Loans.
Accepting gifts or other things of
value, CJC Canon 3.13.
Reporting requirements, CJC Canon
3.15.
Magistrate judges, §11-1732.
Family court and domestic violence
unit.
Special rules, §11-1732a.
Generally.
See MAGISTRATE JUDGES.
Management of investments.
Avoiding conflicts with office, CJC
Canon 3.11.
Mediation.
Dispute resolution compliance judge,
USDistCt LCvR 84.10.
Judge acting as mediator, avoiding
conflicts with office, CJC Canon
3.9.
Mental impairment.
Disability of judge, CJC Canon 2.14.
Misconduct of others.
Response to misconduct of another,
CJC Canon 2.15.
Motions practice, CivPro Rule 12-I,
USDistCt LCvR 40.8.
Nomination and appointment,
§1-204.33.
Oaths, US Const Art VI.
Pensions and retirement, §§11-1561
to 11-1572.
See JUDICIAL RETIREMENT.
Performance of duties of office.
Impartiality, competence and diligence,
CJC Canon 2.
Physical impairment.
Disability of judge, CJC Canon 2.14.
Political activities, CJC Canon 4.
Appointive office, CJC Canon 4.3.
Candidates for nonjudicial office, CJC
Canon 4.5.
General rules, CJC Canon 4.1.
Practice of law.
Prohibited, avoiding conflicts with
office, CJC Canon 3.10.
Precedence given to duties of office,
CJC Canon 2.1.

JUDGES —Cont'd
Prejudice, CivPro Rule 63-I.
Adoption proceedings, Adoption Rule
63.
Domestic relations actions, DomRel
Rule 63.
Probate proceedings.
Death between January 1, 1981 and
June 30, 1995, Probate Rule
126.
Prohibited, CJC Canon 2.3.
Public statements on pending cases,
CJC Canon 2.10.
Qualifications of, §11-1501.
Reappointment, §1-204.33.
Recusal.
Disqualification, CJC Canon 2.11.
Reimbursement of expenses.
Accepting gifts or other things of
value, CJC Canon 3.14.
Reporting requirements, CJC Canon
3.15.
Removal or suspension, §§1-204.32,
11-1526.
Retirement of judges.
Generally, §§11-1561 to 11-1572.
See JUDICIAL RETIREMENT.
Involuntary retirement, §1-204.32.
Mandatory retirement, §1-204.31.
Service by, §§11-1504, 11-1565.
Right to be heard.
Ensuring, CJC Canon 2.6.
Rules of civil procedure.
Judicial directives, CivPro Rule 83.
Settlements.
Coercing parties into settlement
prohibited, CJC Canon 2.6.
Substance abuse.
Disability of judge, CJC Canon 2.14.
Superior court, §§11-903 to 11-910.
Supervisory duties, CJC Canon 2.12.
Suspension with entitlement to
retirement salary, §1-204.32.
Suspension without salary, §1-204.32.
Suspension with salary, §1-204.32.
Tenure, §§11-1502, 11-1521 to 11-1530.
Term of judge of court of District,
§1-204.31.
United States courts, US Const Art III
§1.
Complaints against judges.
Rules of the judicial council
governing complaints of judicial
misconduct or disability,
USCtApp Appx III.
Vacation, §11-1505.

JUDGES —Cont'd
Waiver of fees or charges.
Accepting gifts or other things of value, CJC Canon 3.14.
Reporting requirements, CJC Canon 3.15.
Witnesses.
Conflicts with office, avoiding, CJC Canon 3.3.

JUDGMENT AS A MATTER OF LAW, CivPro Rule 50.
Domestic relations actions, DomRel Rule 50.

JUDGMENT N.O.V., CivPro Rule 50.

JUDGMENTS AND DECREES, §§15-101 to 15-111.
Acquittal, CrimPro Rule 29.
Juvenile proceedings, JuvProc Rule 29.
Adoption decrees, Adoption Rules 7, 52.
Entry of decree, Adoption Rule 58.
Relief from decree, Adoption Rule 60.
Adoption of children.
Final decrees of, §§16-309, 16-310.
Amending judgment, CivPro Rule 59.
Domestic relations actions, DomRel Rule 59.
Annulment of marriage, §16-903.
Appeals, D.C. courts, DCCtApp Rule 36.
Appeals, federal cases.
Affirmance, reversal, etc., costs, FRAP 39(a).
Briefs.
Citing judicial dispositions, USCtApp Rule 32.1.
Conviction, release pending appeal, FRAP 9(b).
Entry of, FRAP 36.
Administrative orders, judgment enforcing, FRAP 19.
Issuance of mandate after, FRAP 41(b).
Interest, FRAP 37.
Notice of, FRAP 45(c).
Settlements of judgment enforcing administrative orders, FRAP 19.
Application for entry of judgment, CivPro Form CA 110-A.
Arbitration, Arbitration Rule X.
Modification or correction of award, Arbitration Rule XIII.
Objections, Arbitration Rule XII.
Small claims court, SmallClaimsArb Rules 5, 6.

JUDGMENTS AND DECREES —Cont'd
Arbitration, revised act.
Judgment on award, §16-4425.
Assignment, §28-2301.
Attachment after judgment, CivPro Rule 69-I.
Domestic relations actions, DomRel Rule 69.
Wages, CivPro Rule 69-II.
Attorneys' fees and costs in enforcement of, §15-111.
Bonds, surety, §15-106.
Child support.
Hearing commissioner's judgment, FamDiv Rule D.
Cigarette sales below cost, §28-4526.
Claims against the District.
Interest on judgments against District, §28-3302.
Class actions, CivPro Rule 23.
Confession of judgment, CivPro Rule 68-I.
Consent judgments, CivPro Rule 68-I.
Delinquent minors, JuvProc Rule 104.
Form, JuvProc Form 4.
Landlord and tenant court, LandlordTenant Rule 11-I.
Consent judgment praecipe, LandlordTenant Forms 4, 4a.
Addendum, list of repairs, LandlordTenant Form 4A.
Constitution of the United States.
Full faith and credit clause, US Const Art IV §1.
Proof, US Const Art IV §1.
Conveyances to enforce judgment, CivPro Rule 70.
Domestic relations actions, DomRel Rule 70.
Copies kept by clerk of court, CivPro Rule 79.
Certified copies, CivPro Rule 79-I.
Domestic relations actions, DomRel Rule 79.
Criminal procedure, CrimPro Rule 32.
Arrest of judgment, CrimPro Rule 34.
Clerical mistakes, CrimPro Rule 36.
Findings of the court, CrimPro Rule 23.
Declaratory judgments, CivPro Rule 57.
Complaint for interpleader and declaratory relief, CivPro Form CA 118.
Default judgments.
See DEFAULT JUDGMENTS.

JUDGMENTS AND DECREES
—Cont'd
Deficiency judgments.
Proof of deficiency, CivPro Rule 55-II.
Delinquent minors, JuvProc Rule 32.
Clerical mistakes, JuvProc Rule 36.
Consent decrees, JuvProc Rule 104.
Form, JuvProc Form 4.
Findings of the court, JuvProc Rule 31.
Demand for judgment, CivPro Rule 54.
District of Columbia.
Interest on judgments against District, §28-3302.
Domestic relations actions generally.
See DOMESTIC RELATIONS ACTIONS.
Ejectment, §16-1114.
Eminent domain as to real property for United States, §§16-1363 to 16-1365.
Entry of judgment, CivPro Rule 58.
Appeals, DCCtApp Rule 36.
Application for entry, CivPro Form CA 110-A.
Date of entry, CrimPro Rule 55.
Domestic relations actions, DomRel Rule 58.
Termination of stay, CivPro Rule 62-II.
Execution of judgments.
See EXECUTION OF JUDGMENTS.
Expiration of, §15-102.
Family court proceedings generally.
Hearing commissioners, FamDiv Rule D.
Domestic relations actions, DomRel Rule 70.
Final judgment, US Const Art IV §1.
Forcible entry and detainer, §§16-1503, 16-1505.
Foreign judgments, §§15-351 to 15-357.
See FOREIGN JUDGMENTS.
Foreign missions.
Fee for unsatisfied judgments or damages, §6-1304.01.
Foreign-money claims, §15-906.
Foreign-money judgments, §§15-361 to 15-503.
See FOREIGN-MONEY JUDGMENTS.
Forfeitures, §15-102.
Form of judgment.
Decision by the court, CivPro Form CA 32.

JUDGMENTS AND DECREES
—Cont'd
Form of judgment —Cont'd
Jury verdict, CivPro Form CA 31.
Fraudulent transfers.
Protection of transferee, §28-3108.
Full faith and credit clause, US Const Art IV §1.
Harmless error.
Adoption proceedings, Adoption Rule 61.
Civil procedure, CivPro Rule 61.
Criminal procedure, CrimPro Rule 52.
Domestic relations actions, DomRel Rule 61.
Juvenile proceedings, JuvProc Rule 52.
Plea procedures, CrimPro Rule 11.
Insurance.
Judgments against District of Columbia, §28-3302.
Rate, §28-3302.
Intellectual disability proceedings.
Entry of judgment, MentalRetardation Rule 16.
Interest, §§15-108 to 15-110.
Contracts, §§15-109, 15-110.
Damages, §15-109.
Judgments against District of Columbia, §28-3302.
Liquidated debt, judgment for, §15-108.
Rate of interest, §28-3302.
Tort cases, §15-109.
Interstate child custody proceedings.
See CHILD CUSTODY AND CHILD CUSTODY PROCEEDINGS.
Joint contracts, §16-2105.
Judgment as a matter of law, CivPro Rule 50.
Domestic relations actions, DomRel Rule 50.
Jury trials.
Judgment on jury verdict, CivPro Form CA 31.
Landlord and tenant court.
Consent judgments, LandlordTenant Rule 11-I.
Default judgments, LandlordTenant Rule 11.
Entry of judgment, LandlordTenant Rule 14.
Liens, §§15-102, 15-104.
Liquidated debt.
Interest on judgment for, §15-108.

JUDGMENTS AND DECREES
—Cont'd
Medical malpractice.
Judgments against physicians.
Reports by physicians and health
care providers, §3-1205.13a.
Mistakes, CivPro Rule 60, CrimPro
Rule 36.
Domestic relations actions, DomRel
Rule 60.
Harmless error. See within this
heading, "Harmless error."
Multiple claims or parties, CivPro
Rule 54.
Domestic relations actions, DomRel
Rule 54.
Stay of proceedings, CivPro Rule 62.
Domestic relations actions, DomRel
Rule 62.
Negotiable instruments.
Confession of judgment not to affect
negotiability, §28:3-112.
Notice of judgments, CivPro Rule 77.
Appeals, DCCtApp Rule 36.
Domestic relations actions, DomRel
Rule 77.
Form, CivPro Form CA 110-A.
Offer of judgment, CivPro Rule 68.
Domestic relations actions, DomRel
Rule 68.
Parentage proceedings, DomRel Rule
405.
Penal sums, §15-106.
Pleadings.
Judgment on the pleadings, CivPro
Rule 12.
Domestic relations actions, DomRel
Rule 12.
Special matters, CivPro Rule 9.
Domestic relations actions, DomRel
Rule 9.
Probate proceedings.
Finality of judgment, Probate Rule 8.
Quo warranto, §§16-3545, 16-3546.
Real estate tax sales.
Revised real property tax sale.
Foreclosure, §§47-1378 to 47-1382.
Relief from judgment, CivPro Rule 60.
Domestic relations actions, DomRel
Rule 60.
Harmless error. See within this
heading, "Harmless error."
Restraints of trade.
Judgment in favor of District of
Columbia as prima facie evidence,
§28-4510.

JUDGMENTS AND DECREES
—Cont'd
Revival, order of, §15-103.
Sale of property pursuant to,
§15-105.
Setoffs, §15-107.
Small claims court, §§16-3907,
16-3908, SmallClaims Rule 16.
Installment payment, SmallClaims
Rule 17.
Stay of proceedings.
See STAYS.
Summary judgment.
See SUMMARY JUDGMENT.
Termination of parental rights,
§§16-2361, 16-2362.
Time period for enforcement of,
§15-101.

**JUDICIAL CONFERENCE OF THE
DISTRICT OF COLUMBIA,**
DCCtApp Rule 50.
Appeals, federal cases, USCtApp Rule
47.3.

**JUDICIAL NOMINATION
COMMISSION,** §1-204.34.
**Designation of chief judge of court
of District,** §1-204.31.

JUDICIAL NOTICE.
Bankruptcy proceedings,
USDistDCBank Rule 9073-1.
Published acts and resolutions,
§2-605.

JUDICIAL POWER OF DISTRICT,
§§1-204.31 to 1-204.34.

JUDICIAL RETIREMENT, §§11-1561
to 11-1572.
**Commission on judicial disabilities
and retirement,** §§11-1521 to
11-1530.
See COMMISSION ON JUDICIAL
DISABILITIES AND TENURE.
Computation of retirement salary,
§11-1564.
Definitions, §11-1561.
Denial of claim for benefits.
Procedure, §§1-751 to 1-753.
Deposits into fund for, §11-1563.
Elections.
Crediting other service for, §11-1564.
Survivor annuity, §11-1566.
Eligibility for, §11-1562.
Fund, §§1-714, 1-821.01, 11-1570.
Increases in amount of salary,
§11-1571.

JUDICIAL RETIREMENT —Cont'd
Involuntary retirement, §11-1526.
Issuance of rules and regulations,
§11-1572.
Lump-sum credits, §11-1563.
Reform Act, superseding, §11-1572.
Service by retired judges, §§11-1504,
11-1565.
Survivor annuity, §§11-1566 to
11-1569.
Election, §11-1566.
Additional opportunity to make,
§§11-1568.02, 11-1568.03.
Lump-sum payment, §11-1566.
Order of precedence, §11-1569.
Payment of annuity, §§11-1568,
11-1569.
Payments to fund, §11-1567.
Revocation of election, §§11-1568.01,
11-1568.03.
Service of judge, §11-1568.
Termination, §11-1566.
Widow or widower simultaneously
receiving other annuity, §11-1568.
Tax proceedings, §47-3302.
Withholding from wages and
salaries for, §11-1563.

JUDICIAL RETIREMENT AND
SURVIVORS ANNUITY FUND,
§11-1570.

JUDICIAL REVIEW.
D.C. courts.
See APPEALS, D.C. COURTS.
Federal cases.
See APPEALS, FEDERAL CASES.

JUDICIARY SQUARE.
Detention facility construction,
§§24-1201 to 24-1203.
Steam furnished to buildings in,
§10-501.03.

JUNK VEHICLES.
Generally, §§50-1331.01 to 50-1331.09.
See SALVAGE, FLOOD AND JUNK
VEHICLES.
General provisions, §§50-2401 to
50-2406.
See ABANDONED VEHICLES.

JURIES AND JURY TRIALS.
Advisory juries, CivPro Rule 39.
Alternate jurors.
Criminal procedure, CrimPro Rule 24.
Appearance at trial.
Failure to appear as consent to no
jury, CivPro Rule 38-II.

JURIES AND JURY TRIALS —Cont'd
Attachment after judgment.
Other claims to property, CivPro Rule
69-I.
Bankruptcy proceedings,
USDistDCBank Rule 9015-1.
Communications with jurors,
USDistCt LCrR 24.2, USDistCt
LCvR 47.2.
Condemnation proceedings as to
real property for the District,
§§16-1312 to 16-1320.
Constitution of the United States.
Jury of vicinage, US Const Amd 6.
Contempt.
Criminal contempt, CrimPro Rule 42.
Criminal procedure, §16-705, CrimPro
Rules 23, 24.
Certification to criminal assignment
commissioner, CrimPro Rule 102.
Continuance at arraignment, CrimPro
Rule 102.
Polling jury, CrimPro Rule 31.
Presence of defendant at impaneling of
jury, CrimPro Rule 43.
Declaratory judgments.
Right to trial by jury, CivPro Rule 57.
Demand for trial by jury, CivPro Rule
38.
Default judgment.
Withdrawal of jury demand after
default, CivPro Rule 55-I.
Granting of trial by jury, CivPro Rule
39.
Landlord and tenant court,
LandlordTenant Rule 6.
Small claims court, SmallClaims Rule
6.
Docketing as jury trial, CivPro Rule
39.
Domestic relations actions, FamDiv
Rule L.
Ejectment, §§16-1114, 16-1116.
Eminent domain as to real property
for United States, §§16-1356 to
16-1362.
Examination of prospective jurors,
CivPro Rule 47, CrimPro Rule 24.
Excusing juror, CivPro Rule 47.
Family court proceedings, FamDiv
Rule L.
Grand juries.
See GRAND JURIES.
Instructions to the jury.
See JURY INSTRUCTIONS.
Judgment on jury verdict, CivPro
Form CA 31.

JURIES AND JURY TRIALS —Cont'd
Jury of vicinage, US Const Amd 6.
Landlord and tenant court,
LandlordTenant Rule 6.
Masters generally, CivPro Rules 53 to
53-II.
**Mental illness, hospitalization of
persons with,** MentalHealth Rule
16.
Court-ordered hospitalization, §21-544.
Request for trial by jury,
MentalHealth Rule 4.
Number of attorneys, CivPro Rule
39-II, USDistCt LCrR 44.2,
USDistCt LCvR 83.3.
Number of jurors, CivPro Rule 48.
Criminal procedure, CrimPro Rule 23.
Peremptory challenges, CivPro Rule
47-I.
Criminal procedure, CrimPro Rule 24.
Prosecutor's ethical responsibilities,
ProfCond Rule 3.4.
Polling jury, CrimPro Rule 31.
Quo warranto, §16-3544.
Right to trial by jury, CivPro Rule 38.
Selection of jurors.
See JURY SELECTION.
Small claims court, §16-3905,
SmallClaims Rule 6.
Superior court fees, §15-714.
Verdicts.
See VERDICTS.
Voir dire, CivPro Rules 24, 47.
Presence of criminal defendant,
CrimPro Rule 43.
Waiver of trial by jury, CivPro Rule
38.
Failure to appear for trial, CivPro
Rule 38-II.

JURISDICTION.
Administrative hearings, office of,
§2-1831.03.
Adoption of children, §16-301.
Allegation of jurisdiction, CivPro
Form CA 2.
Annulment, §11-1101.
Anti-terrorism act of 2002.
Jurisdiction and venue to prosecute,
§22-3156.
Appeals, federal cases.
Administrative agency cases, USCtApp
HPIP Rule III(a)(2).
Collateral review of local court
decisions, USCtApp HPIP Rule
III(a)(4).
Commencing appeal, USCtApp HPIP
Rule III(a).

JURISDICTION —Cont'd
Appeals, federal cases —Cont'd
District court cases, USCtApp HPIP
Rule III(a)(1).
Original jurisdiction, USCtApp HPIP
Rule III(a)(3).
Rules not to affect, FRAP 1.
Arbitration, revised act.
Jurisdiction to enforce agreement,
§16-4426.
Armory board, §3-303.
**Attorney discipline or disability
proceedings,** DCBar Rule XI,
ProfCond Rule 8.5.
Blue Plains Impoundment Lot,
§50-2405.
Boxing and wrestling commission,
§3-605.
Business organizations.
Registered agents, §29-104.14.
**Child abduction prevention
measures,** §16-4604.05.
Child abuse and neglect cases,
§16-2303.
Child custody, §§11-1101, 16-914.01.
Abduction prevention measures,
§16-4604.05.
Decline for reason of conduct,
§16-4602.08.
Exercise of personal jurisdiction,
§16-4601.07.
Immunity from personal jurisdiction,
§16-4601.08.
Initial child-custody jurisdiction,
§§16-4602.01 to 16-4602.03.
Third-party custody proceedings,
§16-831.12.
Child support, §§11-1101, 16-914.01.
Closing-out sales, §47-2108.
Compulsory school attendance,
§38-213.
Contract appeals board, §2-360.03.
Court of appeals, §§1-204.31, 11-721 to
11-723.
Courts-martial, §§49-504, 49-506.
Delinquent minors, §16-2303.
**Dismissal of action for lack of
jurisdiction,** CivPro Rule 12.
Domestic relations actions, DomRel
Rule 12.
Divorce, §11-1101.
Eminent domain, §§16-1301, 16-1303.
Family court proceedings, §11-1101.
Retention, §11-1104.
**Federal benefit payments under
District programs,** §1-815.02.

JURISDICTION —Cont'd
Fiduciary security transfers,
§28-2908.
Foreign-money judgments.
When personal jurisdiction not
required, §15-365.
Foreign trade zones.
Reservation of civil and criminal
jurisdiction, §36-504.
For-hire vehicles department,
§50-301.07.
Forum, inconvenience of, §13-425.
Fraudulent registration in lodgings,
§22-3224.01.
Guardian and ward.
Minors, guardianship of.
Permanent guardianship.
Court retention of jurisdiction,
§16-2390.
Uniform adult guardianship and
protective proceedings jurisdiction
act, §§21-2401.01 to 21-2405.03.
See GUARDIAN AND WARD.
Hearing commissioners.
Criminal proceedings, CrimPro Rule
117.
Highways, §9-101.02.
Identity theft, §22-3227.06.
Inconvenient forum, §13-425.
Insurance fraud, §22-3225.15.
Insurers rehabilitation and
liquidation proceedings,
§31-1303.
Interstate banking and branch
banks, §26-707.
Interstate child custody
proceedings.
See CHILD CUSTODY AND CHILD
CUSTODY PROCEEDINGS.
Intrafamily proceedings.
Petition for protection, §16-1006.
Long-arm statute, §§13-401 to 13-434.
See LONG-ARM STATUTE.
MacArthur Boulevard, §9-1201.01.
Marriage, §11-1101.
Metropolitan Washington Airports
Authority, §9-922.
Metrorail and metrobus.
See METRORAIL AND METROBUS.
Military courts, §§49-504, 49-506.
Motor vehicle registration,
international registration plan
agreements, §50-1507.04.
Nonresidents.
Suits against state, US Const Amd 11.
Office of administrative hearings,
§2-1831.03.

JURISDICTION —Cont'd
Parental kidnapping, §16-1023.
Parole, §24-131.
Personal jurisdiction, bases for,
§§13-421 to 13-425.
See LONG-ARM STATUTE.
Pornography.
Nonconsensual pornography, §22-3057.
Potomac River Bridges Towing
Compact, §9-1117.03.
Procurement practices.
Action for violations by attorney
general or qui tam plaintiff,
§2-381.03.
Prohibition, writ of, DCCtApp Rule
21.
Reformatory prisoners, §24-201.02.
Registered agents, §29-104.14.
Shoplifting, §27-105.
Small claims court, §11-1321.
Spousal support, §16-914.01.
Superior court, §§1-204.31, 11-921 to
11-925, 11-1101, 11-1201.
Rules not affecting jurisdiction, CivPro
Rule 82.
Support and maintenance, §11-1101.
Tax claims, §11-1201.
Terrorism.
Anti-terrorism act of 2002.
Jurisdiction and venue to prosecute,
§22-3156.
Transfers of jurisdiction over.
Parks and recreation.
See PARKS AND RECREATION.
Transfers to minors, §21-302.
Trust, mortgage and title
corporations, §26-1334.
Trusts and trustees.
Uniform trust code.
Trustee and beneficiary,
§19-1302.02.
Tunnel under Capitol grounds and
botanic gardens, §10-511.03.
Uniform adult guardianship and
protective proceedings
jurisdiction act, §§21-2401.01 to
21-2405.03.
See GUARDIAN AND WARD.
United States District Court for the
District of Columbia.
See UNITED STATES DISTRICT
COURT FOR THE DISTRICT OF
COLUMBIA.

JUROR FEES, §§11-1912, 15-718.

JURY DUTY.
Metropolitan police exempted from,
§5-133.09.

JURY INSTRUCTIONS.
Criminal procedure, CrimPro Rule 30.
Objections, CivPro Rule 51, CrimPro
    Rule 30.
Requests for instructions, CivPro
    Rule 51.
Special verdicts and interrogatories,
    CivPro Rule 49.
Time of giving instructions, CivPro
    Rule 51.

JURY SELECTION, §§11-1901 to
    11-1918, 16-5101 to 16-5104,
    USDistCt LCrR 24.1, USDistCt
    LCvR 47.1.
Challenges to jurors, §23-105.
Challenging, §11-1910.
Confidentiality of information,
    §16-5102.
    Penalties for violations, §16-5103.
Court coordination and cooperation
    regarding, §11-1917.
Deferral from service, §11-1909.
Definitions, §§11-1902, 16-5101.
Discrimination prohibited in,
    §11-1903.
District of Columbia government
    agency source lists, §16-5104.
Eminent domain as to real property
    for United States, §16-1357.
Employment protections, §11-1913.
Examination of prospective jurors,
    CivPro Rule 47, CrimPro Rule 24.
Exclusion from service, §11-1908.
Fraud and deceit, §11-1915.
Fraudulent interference or
    collusion, §22-1514.
Government agency source lists,
    §16-5104.
Grand juries, §§11-1911, 11-1916.
Identifying information.
    Confidentiality, §16-5102.
    Penalties for violations, §16-5103.
    Defined, §16-5101.
Jury system plan, §§11-1901, 11-1904.
Length of service, §11-1911.
Master juror list, §§11-1901, 11-1905.
Peremptory challenges, CivPro Rule
    47-I, CrimPro Rule 24.
    Prosecutor's ethical responsibilities,
        ProfCond Rule 3.4.
Petit juries, §11-1911.
Policy declaration, §11-1901.
Presence of criminal defendant,
    CrimPro Rule 43.
Qualifications of jurors, §11-1906.
Random selection, §§11-1901, 11-1904.

JURY SELECTION —Cont'd
Records, §11-1914.
Severability of provisions, §11-1918.
Summoning prospective jurors,
    §11-1907.

JURY TAMPERING, §22-1514.

JUVENILE CURFEW, §§2-1541 to
    2-1543.

JUVENILE HISTORY.
Release prior to trial, conditions of,
    §23-1333.

JUVENILE JUSTICE REFORM
    COMMISSION.
Establishment, §2-1533.01.
Members, §2-1533.01.
Reports, §2-1533.02.

JUVENILE OFFENDERS, §§24-901 to
    24-941.
Appeal of no-further-benefit notice,
    §24-905.
BOOT CAMP, §§24-921 to 24-932.
    See BOOT CAMP.
Commission on juvenile justice
    reform.
    Establishment, §2-1533.01.
    Members, §2-1533.01.
    Reports, §2-1533.02.
Community service, §24-903.
Compulsory school attendance.
    Tenth unexcused absence.
        Referrals to social services agencies,
            §38-208.
Conditional release, §24-904.
Contributing to delinquency of
    minor, §22-811.
Conviction set aside by
    unconditional discharge, §24-906.
Criminal prosecution, transfer for,
    §16-2307.
Definitions, §24-901.
Delinquent minors.
    See DELINQUENT MINORS.
Discharge and release, §24-904.
    Conviction set aside by unconditional
        discharge, §24-906.
Employment, education or housing
    application.
    Juvenile's right to refuse disclosure of
        delinquency history, §16-2335.
Escape from facility, §10-509.01a.
Facilities for, §24-902.
Family court.
    Criminal matters transferred to,
        §16-2305.02.

JUVENILE OFFENDERS —Cont'd

Family court —Cont'd

Delinquency, neglect or children in need of supervision proceedings, §§16-2301 to 16-2340.

First degree murder.

Sentencing, §22-2104.

Hate crimes.

Parental liability for damages, §22-3704.

Immunity, §16-2339.

Initial proceedings before the court.

Statement by the court, CrimPro Rule 5.

Intrafamily offenses.

Generally, §§16-1001 to 16-1034.

See INTRAFAMILY PROCEEDINGS.

Issuance of rules and regulations, §24-907.

No-further-benefit notice, §24-905.

Oak Hill youth center.

Closure and transfer of operations, §24-941.

Probation, §24-903.

Procedure, JuvProc Rules 1 to 119.

See DELINQUENT MINORS.

Release, §24-904.

Responsibility for, §24-907.

School grounds.

Expulsion of students for bringing weapons onto, §38-232.

Sentencing options, §24-903.

Service of process, §16-2306.

Sexual abuse of prisoner.

First degree, §22-3013.

Second degree, §22-3014.

Summons and process, §16-2306.

Superior court, family court.

Delinquency, neglect or children in need of supervision proceedings, §§16-2301 to 16-2340.

Unconditional discharge, §§24-904, 24-906.

Witnesses, §16-2339.

Youth rehabilitation, §§24-901 to 24-907.

K

KEEP DC WORKING.

Shared work unemployment compensation program, §§51-171 to 51-178.

See UNEMPLOYMENT COMPENSATION.

KEGS.

Alcoholic beverages, §25-753.

KELSEY GARDENS.

Property tax exemption.

Redevelopment project, §47-4625.

KEROSENE SALES OR STORAGE.

Business licenses, §47-2814.

KIDNAPPING, §§22-1810, 22-2001.

Aged persons, offenses committed against.

Enhanced penalties, §22-3601.

Child custody proceedings.

Abduction prevention measures, §§16-4604.01 to 16-4604.10.

See CHILD CUSTODY AND CHILD CUSTODY PROCEEDINGS.

Conduct constituting, §22-2001.

Felony murder, §22-2101.

Human trafficking, §§22-1831 to 22-1843.

See HUMAN TRAFFICKING.

Parental kidnapping, §§16-1021 to 16-1026.

KINDERGARTEN, §38-2807.

KINGMAN ISLAND.

National Children's Island, §§10-1401 to 10-1406.

KING TOWERS RESIDENTIAL HOUSING RENTAL PROJECT.

Real property tax exemption, §§47-4638, 47-4639.

KIPP DC.

Real property tax exemption, §47-1081.

Shaw campus, §47-1085.

KLINGLE ROAD, §§9-115.01, 9-115.02, 9-115.11.

KLINGLE VALLEY, CONNECTICUT AVENUE BRIDGE OVER, §9-313.

KOREAN LANGUAGE.

Foreign language services and documents, §§2-1931 to 2-1936.

See FOREIGN LANGUAGE SERVICES AND DOCUMENTS.

Government publications translated in.

Publications concerning health, safety and welfare of Asian and Pacific Islander resident, §2-1375.

KU KLUX KLAN.

Symbols and activities associated with, §§22-3312.02 to 22-3312.04.

L

LABELING.
Alcoholic beverage containers.
Keg restrictions, §25-753.
Alcoholic beverages, §25-752.
Deceptive, §22-3214.01.
Generic drug substitutes, §48-803.05.
Labor unions' label, brand, or mark, §§36-201 to 36-203.
Adoption authorized, §36-201.
Filing and registration, §36-201.
Unauthorized use, §36-202.
Criminal penalty for violation, §36-203.
Mattresses, §8-503.
Prescription drugs, §47-2885.14.

LABOR AND EMPLOYMENT RELATIONS.
Apprentices.
General provisions, §§32-1402 to 32-1413.
See APPRENTICES.
Attorneys at law.
Discrimination in employment, ProfCond Rule 9.1.
Noncomplete agreements, ProfCond Rule 5.6.
Blind and visually impaired.
Employment opportunities, §§32-301 to 32-305.
Breastfeeding.
Pregnant and nursing workers, reasonable accommodations for, §§32-1231.01 to 32-1231.15.
Broadcasting industry employment contracts, §§32-531 to 32-533.
Child labor.
General provisions, §§32-201 to 32-224.
See CHILD LABOR.
Programs for employment and training of domiciliaries of District, §32-241.
Crime victims' compensation.
Loss of earnings, VictComp Rule 28.
Request for employment information, VictComp Rule 14.
Criminal history records.
Limited liability of employers regarding criminal history of employees, §24-1351.
DC Streetcar service.
Labor negotiations with employees of program, §50-921.75.

LABOR AND EMPLOYMENT RELATIONS —Cont'd
Displaced workers, §§32-101 to 32-103.
See DISPLACED WORKERS.
District participation in real property developments.
Labor-peace agreement.
Contents, §32-853.
Definitions, §32-852.
Determination of need, §32-852.
Exceptions to applicability, §32-854.
Legislative findings, §32-851.
Limitations on requirements, §32-855.
Notice required in bid invitation, §32-856.
Domestic partner benefits, §§32-701 to 32-710.
See DOMESTIC PARTNER BENEFITS.
Educational stepladder program, §§32-1651 to 32-1653.
Employment agencies.
General provisions, §§32-401 to 32-416.
See EMPLOYMENT AGENCIES.
Equal employment opportunity.
Merit system.
Review of agency decision, CivPro Agency Review Rule 1.
Evaluation of summer youth employment program, §32-244.
Family and medical leave.
General provisions, §§32-501 to 32-517.
See FAMILY AND MEDICAL LEAVE.
Family court proceedings.
Employer's statement, FamDiv Rule J.
Domestic relations actions, DomRel Form 6.
First source employment, §§2-219.01 to 2-219.05.
Office of first source compliance, §§2-219.31 to 2-219.35.
Immunity of employers regarding criminal history of employees, §24-1351.
Independent contractors.
Misclassification.
Workplace fraud, §§32-1331.01 to 32-1331.12.
See WORKPLACE FRAUD.
Industrial safety.
General provisions, §§32-801 to 32-812.
See WORKPLACE SAFETY.

**LABOR AND EMPLOYMENT
RELATIONS** —Cont'd
Involuntary servitude.
Constitution of the United States, US
Const Amds 13, 15.
Job training.
Employment services department.
Job training and adult education
programs.
Quarterly reporting by
department, §32-771.
Fire protection study commission.
Sprinkler installation program,
combined with, §3-1104.
Get DC Residents Training for Jobs
Now, §§38-1011.01 to 38-1011.05.
Opportunity accounts.
Generally, §§1-307.61 to 1-307.74.
Use for training of account holder,
§1-307.68.
Jury selection.
Employment protections, §11-1913.
Lie detector tests, §§32-901 to 32-903.
Employer or prospective employer
administering in connection with
employment.
Civil liability of employer violating
provisions, §32-903.
Contract or arbitration provisions
prohibited, §32-903.
Criminal penalty for violation,
§32-903.
Definitions, §32-901.
Prohibition, exceptions, §32-902.
Violation invasion of privacy,
§32-903.
**Limited liability of employers
regarding criminal history of
employees,** §24-1351.
Marijuana testing.
Preemployment limitations, §§32-931,
32-932.
Minimum wages.
General provisions, §§32-1001 to
32-1015.
See MINIMUM WAGES.
Noncompete agreements.
Attorneys at law, ProfCond Rule 5.6.
Broadcasting industry employment
contracts, §§32-531 to 32-533.
Nurse staffing agencies, §§44-1051.01
to 44-1051.18.
See NURSE STAFFING AGENCIES.
Occupational safety and health.
General provisions, §§32-1101 to
32-1124.
See OCCUPATIONAL SAFETY AND
HEALTH.

**LABOR AND EMPLOYMENT
RELATIONS** —Cont'd
**Office of labor relations and
collective bargaining,** §1-531.01.
Funding for provided in budget,
§1-531.02.
**Parental leave to attend or
participate in school-related
event,** §§32-1201 to 32-1206.
Pay equity and training commission,
§§32-601 to 32-609.
Persons with disabilities.
Employment opportunities, §§32-301
to 32-305.
Rehabilitation services program.
Establishment, §32-331.
Grant and contract authority,
§32-331.01.
Rulemaking to implement, §32-332.
**Plans for delivery of workforce
development services,** §32-243.
Polygraphs, §§32-901 to 32-903.
Pre-apprenticeship program,
§32-1332.
**Pregnant and nursing workers,
reasonable accommodations for,**
§§32-1231.01 to 32-1231.15.
Administrative enforcement,
§32-1231.07.
Applicability, §32-1231.15.
Civil action, enforcement by,
§32-1231.09.
Interest and collection on amounts
due, §32-1231.10.
Construction and interpretation of
chapter, §32-1231.14.
Definitions, §32-1231.01.
DOES.
Administrative enforcement,
§32-1231.07.
Contesting determination.
Hearing by office of administrative
hearings, §32-1231.08.
Public education, services,
§32-1231.05.
Effective date, §32-1231.15.
Employee right of action, §32-1231.06.
Fines and civil penalties, §32-1231.11.
Interest and collection on amounts
due, §32-1231.10.
Hearing by office of administrative
hearings.
Contesting determination by DOES,
§32-1231.08.
Interest and collection on amounts
due, §32-1231.10.

LABOR AND EMPLOYMENT RELATIONS —Cont'd
Pregnant and nursing workers, reasonable accommodations for —Cont'd
Notice of rights to employees, §32-1231.04.
Penalties for violations, §32-1231.11.
Pregnant workers protection fund, §32-1231.12.
Prohibitions, §32-1231.03.
Reasonable accommodation.
Defined, §32-1231.01.
Prohibited conduct, §32-1231.03.
Provision of, required, §32-1231.02.
Rules, implementing chapter, §32-1231.13.
Prisons and prisoners.
Hiring of ex-offenders.
Fair criminal record screening, §§32-1341 to 32-1345.
Public employment service, §§1-202.04, 32-241.
Office of labor relations and collective bargaining, §1-531.01.
Funding for provided in budget, §1-531.02.
Public officers and employees.
Merit system, §§1-601.01 to 1-636.03.
See MERIT SYSTEM.
Recordkeeping requirements.
Paid leave, §32-131.10b.
Restraints of trade.
Exclusion of labor from chapter, §28-4504.
Right to sick and safe leave, §§32-131.01 to 32-131.16. See within this heading, "Sick leave."
Shared work unemployment compensation program, §§51-171 to 51-178.
See UNEMPLOYMENT COMPENSATION.
Sick leave, §§32-131.01 to 32-131.16.
Accrual of leave, §32-131.02.
Administration, §32-131.10.
Cause of action for violations, §32-131.12.
Certification.
Paid leave supported by, §32-131.04.
Civil penalty, §32-131.12.
Definitions, §32-131.01.
Discharge or discrimination by employer, §32-131.08.
Effective date, §32-131.16.
Effect of other laws, §32-131.11.

LABOR AND EMPLOYMENT RELATIONS —Cont'd
Sick leave —Cont'd
Employers with paid leave policies, §32-131.05.
Encouragement of more generous paid leave policies, §32-131.07.
Existing employment benefits, effect, §32-131.06.
Hardship exemption, §32-131.14.
Interference with right provided, §32-131.08.
Notice by employee, §32-131.03.
Notice of rights, posting requirements, §32-131.09.
Paid leave, §32-131.02.
Posting provisions, §32-131.08.
Prohibited acts, §32-131.08.
Public education and outreach, §32-131.15a.
Recordkeeping requirements, §32-131.10b.
Report by District auditor, §32-131.15.
Request of employee, §32-131.03.
Rules, §32-131.13.
Statute of limitations and tolling.
Civil complaints, §32-131.10a.
Violations.
Civil penalty, §32-131.12.
Smoking in workplace, §7-1703.
Employment discrimination on basis of tobacco use, §7-1703.03.
"No Smoking" signs, §7-1704.
Regulation of smoking in, §7-1703.02.
Strikes.
See STRIKES.
Transitional employment program, §32-1331.
Transportation benefits.
Reducing single occupancy vehicle use by encouraging transit benefits, §§32-151 to 32-153.
Definitions, §32-151.
Failure to provide, penalties, §32-152.
Required benefits, §32-152.
Rulemaking, §32-152.
Unemployment compensation.
General provisions, §§51-101 to 51-151.
See UNEMPLOYMENT COMPENSATION.
Wages and salaries.
General provisions, §§32-1301 to 32-1311.
See WAGES AND SALARIES.

LABOR AND EMPLOYMENT RELATIONS —Cont'd
Wages and salaries —Cont'd
Minimum wages, §§32-1001 to 32-1015.
See MINIMUM WAGES.
Workers' compensation.
General provisions, §§32-1501 to 32-1545.
See WORKERS' COMPENSATION.
Workforce investment implementation, §§32-1601 to 32-1661.
Workplace fraud, §§32-1331.01 to 32-1331.12.
See WORKPLACE FRAUD.
Workplace safety.
General provisions, §§32-801 to 32-812.
See WORKPLACE SAFETY.
Workplace smoking, §7-1703.
Employment discrimination on basis of tobacco use, §7-1703.03.
"No Smoking" signs, §7-1704.
Regulation of smoking in, §7-1703.02.
Year-round program to provide training and work experience, §32-242.

LABORATORIES.
Clinical laboratories, §§44-201 to 44-213.
See CLINICAL LABORATORIES.
Fees.
Public laboratory fees, §7-734.
Gas company testing, §§34-1602 to 34-1604.
Lead poisoning.
Childhood lead poisoning screening and reporting, §§7-871.01 to 7-871.06.
Fees, §7-734.
Medical laboratories and medical laboratory technicians.
See MEDICAL LABORATORIES AND MEDICAL LABORATORY TECHNICIANS.
Metropolitan police mobile laboratory, §5-133.13.
Rabies.
Fees, §7-734.
Sexually transmitted diseases.
Fees, §7-734.
Tuberculosis.
Fees, §7-734.

LABOR DAY.
Appeals, federal cases, FRAP 26(a), 45(a).

LABOR DAY —Cont'd
Designated holiday, §§1-612.02, 28-2701.
Extension of time for performing acts, §28-2701.

LABOR UNIONS.
Label, brand, or mark, §§36-201 to 36-203.
Adoption of label authorized, §36-201.
Filing and registration, §36-201.
Unauthorized use of registered label, §36-202.
Criminal penalty for violation, §36-203.
Metropolitan police, §5-123.01.
Registration of labor union labels, §§36-201 to 36-203.
Standards of conduct for, §1-617.03.

LADING, BILLS OF.
Attachment.
Goods covered by a negotiable document, §28:7-602.
Damages.
Limitations of liability, §28:7-309.
Documents of title.
Generally, §§28:7-101 to 28:7-702.
See DOCUMENTS OF TITLE.
Injunctions.
Enjoining negotiations of document, §28:7-602.
Interpleader.
Determination of conflicting claims, §28:7-603.
Lost and unclaimed property.
Missing bills, §28:7-601.
Overpayment liabilities, §47-112.

LAME DUCK AMENDMENT.
Congress.
Changing meeting of congress, US Const Amd 20.

LAND-GRANT COLLEGES, §§38-1107, 38-1109, 38-1112, 38-1201.02.

LANDLORD AND TENANT, §§42-3201 to 42-3232, 42-3501.01 to 42-3509.08.
Access to dwelling unit by housing provider, §42-3505.51.
Actions.
General provisions, LandlordTenant Forms 1 to 5, LandlordTenant Rules 1 to 16.
See LANDLORD AND TENANT COURT.

LANDLORD AND TENANT —Cont'd

Aged tenants, discrimination against, §42-3505.05.

Alterations or renovations to rental units.

Recovery of possession for purpose of making, §42-3505.01.

Arbitration to resolve disputes arising between housing providers and tenants.

Conciliation and arbitration service, §42-3505.03.

Arbitration of disputes not settled by conciliation and arbitration service, §42-3505.04.

Arrears of rent.

Claims for, §42-3211.

Consolidation of actions for possession and, §42-3212.

Life lease or demise for life, §42-3220.

Attorneys' fees and costs, §42-3509.02.

At will tenancies, §42-3203.

Bicycle parking spaces requirements, §50-1641.05.

Cable television.

Interference by landlord with installation, maintenance, etc., §34-1261.01.

Chief tenant advocate rental accommodations fee fund, §42-3504.01.

Children and minors, §§42-3225 to 42-3228.

Commercial tenancy.

Notice to quit, §42-3202.

Death of tenant.

Proceedings to discover, §§16-1151 to 16-1158.

See LIFE ESTATES.

Deed, lack of, §42-3221.

Definitions, §42-3501.03.

Disabled tenants, discrimination against, §42-3505.05.

Discrimination, §42-3505.05.

Displaced tenants, relocation assistance for, §§42-3507.01 to 42-3507.05.

Disputes arising between housing providers and tenants.

Conciliation and arbitration service, §42-3505.03.

Arbitration of disputes not settled by conciliation and arbitration service, §42-3505.04.

LANDLORD AND TENANT —Cont'd

Distressed property, §§42-3508.01, 42-3508.04 to 42-3508.06.

Distress for rent, §42-3217.

Domestic violence victims.

Duties of housing provider as to protection of, §42-3505.08.

Notice of lease termination by tenant who is victim, §42-3505.07.

Double rent.

Claims for, §42-3211.

Refusal to surrender possession, for, §42-3207.

Drug-related evictions.

Action for possession of rental unit, §42-3602.

Choice of remedies, §42-3609.

Court costs and attorney's fees, §42-3608.

Default judgment, §42-3605.

Definitions, §42-3601.

Full hearing on preliminary injunction, §42-3604.

Mayor's authority and responsibility, §42-3607.

Preliminary injunction review, §42-3603.

Rulemaking authority, §42-3610.

Tenant complaints, §42-3606.

Ejectment.

Generally, §§16-1101 to 16-1124.

See EJECTMENT.

Elderly tenants.

Discrimination against prohibited, §42-3505.05.

Emergency access.

Access to dwelling unit by housing provider, §42-3505.51.

Evictions.

See EVICTIONS.

Families with children.

Discrimination against prohibited, §42-3505.05.

Fines, §42-3509.01.

Forcible entry and detainer.

Generally, §§16-1501 to 16-1505.

For rent signs, §42-1801.

Fraud and deceit, §42-3509.01.

Fraudulent attornment, §42-3232.

Guardianship of incapacitated persons, §42-3228.

Housing code violation by tenant.

Access by housing provider to dwelling unit, §42-3505.51.

Incompetent or incapacitated persons, §42-3228.

LANDLORD AND TENANT —Cont'd

Infant or person with mental disability.
Lease under control of.
Cost of renewal.
Charge against estate or chargeable to leasehold, §42-3226.
New lease, §42-3225.
Lease valid and legal, §42-3228.
Same nature as surrendered lease, §42-3227.
Surrender, §42-3225.

Insanitary buildings.
Neglect of tenants or occupants, §§6-913 to 6-915.

Inspection of rental housing, §42-3509.08.

Intellectual disabilities, persons with, §42-3228.
Lease under control of.
Cost of renewal, charge against estate or chargeable to leasehold, §42-3226.

Intrafamily offenses.
Victims.
Duties of housing provider as to protection of, §42-3505.08.
Notice of lease termination by tenant who is victim, §42-3505.07.

Landlord and tenant branch.
General provisions, LandlordTenant Forms 1 to 5, LandlordTenant Rules 1 to 16.
See LANDLORD AND TENANT COURT.

Lead-hazard prevention and elimination.
Access to dwelling unit, tenant to provide, §8-231.06.
Disclosures for certain older properties, §8-231.04.
Notice to tenant of order to eliminate lead-hazards, §8-231.03.
Relocation during elimination of lead-hazards, §8-231.03.
Right to provide information to mayor concerning hazards, §8-231.07.

Liens for rent, §§42-3213 to 42-3218.
Attachment, issuance, §42-3215.
Distress, §42-3217.
Enforcement, §42-3214.
Entry, executing officer's power, §42-3215.
Execution on property subject to lien by another.
Payment required, §42-3216.

LANDLORD AND TENANT —Cont'd

Liens for rent —Cont'd
Fraudulent removal, conveyance, concealment of property, §42-3218.
Time of existence, §42-3213.

Master-metered apartment buildings.
See PUBLIC UTILITIES.

Mental disability.
Lease under control of person with, §§42-3222 to 42-3228.
Leases deemed good and valid, §42-3223.
Money received for renewal paid to guardian, §42-3224.
New lease, §42-3222.
Surrender of lease, §42-3222.

Mental illness, persons with, §42-3228.
Lease under control of.
Cost of renewal, charge against estate or chargeable to leasehold, §42-3226.

Month to month tenants, §42-3202.

Moving and storage assistance program.
Tenants displaced due to nonpayment of rent, §42-3505.01.

New rental housing, §§42-3508.01 to 42-3508.03.

Notice of termination.
Alternative notice, agreement by parties, §42-3208.
Expiration of notice, effect, §42-3206.
Not recalled without consent, §42-3206.
Tenancies at will, §42-3204.
Tenancies by sufferance, §42-3205.

Notice to quit.
Alternative notice, agreement by parties, §42-3208.
Commercial tenancy, §42-3202.
Expiration of notice, effect, §42-3206.
Month to month or quarter to quarter, §42-3202.
Not recalled with out consent, §42-3206.
Refusal to surrender possession, §42-3207.
Service, §42-3207.
Unnecessary for lease of certain term, §42-3201.

Office of tenant advocate, §§42-3531.01 to 42-3531.10.

Organization.
Right of tenants to organize, §42-3505.06.

LANDLORD AND TENANT —Cont'd
Partition.
  See PARTITION.
Policy declaration, §§42-3501.01,
  42-3501.02.
**Power or appointment to devise
  inheritance given to tenant with
  limited estate,** §42-1008.
Prior acts, supersedure of,
  §42-3509.03.
Public utilities.
  Water and sewer authority.
    Rates and charges.
      Passing increases along to tenant,
        §34-2202.16.
Quarter to quarter tenants, §42-3202.
**Real and personal property leased
  together, recovery of,** §42-3209.
**Reasonable notice, reasonable
  purpose, reasonable time.**
  Access to dwelling unit by housing
    provider, §42-3505.51.
Receivership.
  Tenants health, safety or security
    threatened by violation,
    §§42-3651.01 to 42-3651.08.
Refusal to surrender possession,
  §42-3207.
**Relocation assistance for displaced
  tenants,** §§42-3507.01 to
  42-3507.05.
  Advisory services, §42-3507.04.
  Calculation of amount and payment of
    assistance, §42-3507.03.
  Eligibility for assistance, §42-3507.02.
  Notice of right to assistance,
    §42-3507.01.
  Tenant hot line, §42-3507.05.
Remainders, §42-3231.
Renewal of lease, §§42-3222 to
  42-3228.
**Renovations or alterations to rental
  unit.**
  Recovery of possession for purpose of
    making, §42-3505.01.
Rental housing locators.
  Consumer protection provisions,
    §28-3819.
Rental unit fees, §42-3504.01.
Rent stabilization program,
  §§42-3502.01 to 42-3502.23.
  See RENT CONTROL.
Rent supplement program, §6-226.
  Capital-based assistance, §6-229.
  Tenant-based assistance, §6-228.
  Voucher assistance, §6-227.

LANDLORD AND TENANT —Cont'd
Residential drug-related evictions,
  §§42-3601 to 42-3610.
  See DRUG-RELATED EVICTIONS.
**Retaliation against tenant
  exercising rights,** §42-3505.02.
Reversions, §§42-3230, 42-3231.
Right of tenants to organize,
  §42-3505.06.
**Search of premises over tenant's
  objection.**
  Need for administrative search
    warrant, §42-3509.08.
Service of process, §42-3509.04.
**Single-room-occupancy housing
  development incentives,**
  §42-3508.06.
Snow and ice removal, §§9-601 to
  9-607.
Sufferance, tenants by, §42-3204.
Sunset provision.
  Rental housing act, §42-3509.07.
Superior court.
  Landlord and tenant branch.
    Forms, LandlordTenant Forms 1 to
      5.
    Rules of court, LandlordTenant
      Rules 1 to 16.
    See LANDLORD AND TENANT
      COURT.
Surrender of possession, §§42-3207,
  42-3212, 42-3222 to 42-3227.
Tenant assistance program,
  §§42-3503.01 to 42-3503.08.
  Aged persons, §42-3503.03.
  Amount of payments, calculating,
    §42-3503.04.
  Appropriations, §42-3503.02.
  Approval of rental units, §42-3503.05.
  Attorneys' fees and costs, §42-3509.02.
  Authority to enter into contracts for
    payments, §42-3503.03.
  Continuing eligibility after expiration
    date, §42-3503.06.
  Definitions, §42-3503.01.
  Discrimination, §42-3509.01.
  Eligibility for, §42-3503.03.
  Establishment of, §42-3503.02.
  Fines, §42-3509.01.
  Funding, §42-3503.02.
  Obligations of payment recipients,
    §42-3503.05.
  Persons with disabilities, §42-3503.03.
  Security deposits, §42-3503.05.
  Tax exemption of payments,
    §42-3503.08.

LANDLORD AND TENANT —Cont'd
Tenant assistance program —Cont'd
Termination of eligibility, §42-3503.07.
Tenant organizations, §42-3505.06.
Tenant receivership.
Violation threatening tenants health,
safety or security, §§42-3651.01 to
42-3651.08.
Final account, §42-3651.07.
Grounds for appointment,
§42-3651.02.
Notice and hearing requirements,
§42-3651.04.
Petition, §42-3651.03.
Powers and duties of receiver,
§42-3651.05.
Purpose of receivership,
§42-3651.01.
Termination, §42-3651.06.
Underleases, §42-3229.
**Under-tenant of life tenant, recovery
of rent from, §42-3219.**
Use and occupation actions,
§42-3221.
**Vacant rental housing, §§42-3508.01
to 42-3508.03.**
**Waiver or release of notice to quit or
notice of termination, §42-3208.**
Water and sewer authority.
Rates and charges.
Passing increases along to tenant,
§34-2202.16.
**Water and sewer services amnesty
program.**
Administrative review, §34-2305.
Appointment of receiver, §34-2304.
Services in tenant's own name,
§34-2303.

LANDLORD AND TENANT COURT.
Attorneys at law.
Limitation of cases, LandlordTenant
Rule 8.
Representation by attorney or law
student, LandlordTenant Rule 9.
Certification to civil division,
LandlordTenant Rule 1.
Pending motions and discovery,
LandlordTenant Rule 13-I.
Civil procedure rules' application,
LandlordTenant Rule 2.
Clerk of court.
Preliminary proceedings by clerk,
LandlordTenant Rule 11.

LANDLORD AND TENANT COURT
—Cont'd
Commencement of actions,
LandlordTenant Rule 3.
Receivers.
Properties subject to court-ordered
receiverships, LandlordTenant
Rule 3-I.
Complaints, LandlordTenant Rule 3.
Form, LandlordTenant Form 1.
Receivers.
Properties subject to court-ordered
receiverships, LandlordTenant
Rule 3-I.
Verified complaint for possession of
real property.
Commercial property,
LandlordTenant Rule 1D.
Filing instructions,
LandlordTenant Rule 1D.1.
Sample form, LandlordTenant
Rule 1D.1.
Nonpayment of rent,
LandlordTenant Rule 1A.
Filing instructions,
LandlordTenant Rule 1A.1.
Sample forms, LandlordTenant
Rule 1A.1.
Nonpayment of rent and other
grounds for eviction,
LandlordTenant Rule 1C.
Filing instructions,
LandlordTenant Rule 1C.1.
Sample form, LandlordTenant
Rule 1C.1.
Violation of obligations of tenancy or
other grounds for eviction,
LandlordTenant Rule 1B.
Filing instructions,
LandlordTenant Rule 1B.1.
Sample form, LandlordTenant
Rule 1B.1.
Consent judgments, LandlordTenant
Rule 11-I.
Consent settlement agreement,
LandlordTenant Form 4b.
Addendum, list of repairs,
LandlordTenant Form 4A.
Praecipe, LandlordTenant Forms 4, 4a.
Addendum, list of repairs,
LandlordTenant Form 4A.
Construction of rules, LandlordTenant
Rule 1.

LANDLORD AND TENANT COURT
—Cont'd

Continuances, LandlordTenant Rule 11.

Costs, LandlordTenant Rule 15.
Service of process, LandlordTenant Rule 4.

Default judgments, LandlordTenant Rule 11.
Redemption of tenancy, LandlordTenant Rule 14-II.

Discovery, LandlordTenant Rule 10.
Certification to civil division, LandlordTenant Rule 13-I.

Dismissal of actions, LandlordTenant Rules 11, 12, 14-I.

Entry of judgment, LandlordTenant Rule 14.
Default judgments, LandlordTenant Rule 11.
Redemption of tenancy, LandlordTenant Rule 14-II.

Fees, LandlordTenant Rule 15.

Jury demand, LandlordTenant Rule 6.

Motions, LandlordTenant Rule 13.
Certification to civil division, LandlordTenant Rule 13-I.
Protective orders, LandlordTenant Rule 12-I.
Stay of execution, LandlordTenant Rule 16.

Notice to tenant of payment required to avoid eviction, LandlordTenant Form 6.

Pleadings, LandlordTenant Rules 3, 5.
Complaint for possession of real estate, LandlordTenant Form 1.

Preliminary proceedings, LandlordTenant Rule 11.

Protective orders, LandlordTenant Rule 12-I.
Information sheet, LandlordTenant Form 8.

Receivership.
Properties subject to court-ordered receiverships, LandlordTenant Rule 3-I.

Redemption of tenancy, LandlordTenant Rule 14-II.

Scope of rules, LandlordTenant Rule 1.

Service of process, LandlordTenant Rule 4.
Affidavit of service by special process server, LandlordTenant Form 3.

LANDLORD AND TENANT COURT
—Cont'd

Settlement or compromise.
Consent settlement agreement, LandlordTenant Form 4b.
Addendum, list of repairs, LandlordTenant Form 4A.

Stays, LandlordTenant Rule 16.
Application for termination of stay, LandlordTenant Form 5.
Application to stay writ of restitution, LandlordTenant Form 9.

Summary judgment, LandlordTenant Rules 13, 14.

Time of sessions, trials, etc., LandlordTenant Rule 7.
Motion hearings, LandlordTenant Rule 13.
Postponing trial because of attorney's schedule, LandlordTenant Rule 8.

Trials, LandlordTenant Rule 12.

Writs of restitution, LandlordTenant Form 10, LandlordTenant Rule 16.
Application to stay writ, LandlordTenant Form 9.
Notice of intention to seek writ, LandlordTenant Form 2.

LAND USE PLANNING.

Condominiums, §42-1901.05.

Zoning.
General provisions, §§6-621.01 to 6-661.02.
See ZONING.

LANIER, CATHY L.

Police chief.
Length of service award, §5-544.01.
Separation pay, §1-610.58.
Term of office, §5-105.01.
Voluntary retirement, §5-712.

LARCENY.

Theft generally, §§22-3201 to 22-3216.
See THEFT.

LATINO COMMUNITY DEVELOPMENT, §§2-1301 to 2-1341.

Appropriations, §2-1341.

Commission on Latino community development, §§2-1321 to 2-1330.
Chairperson, §2-1327.
Compensation and expenses, §2-1328.
Composition, §2-1322.
Established, §2-1321.
Functions, §2-1330.

**LATINO COMMUNITY
DEVELOPMENT** —Cont'd
**Commission on Latino community
development** —Cont'd
Qualifications, §2-1323.
Rules of procedure, §2-1326.
Staff, §2-1329.
Term, §2-1324.
Vacancies, §2-1325.
Definitions, §2-1302.
Office on Latino affairs, §§2-1311 to
2-1313.
Established, §2-1311.
Executive director, §2-1312.
Functions, §2-1313.
Staff, §2-1312.
Policy declaration, §2-1301.

LAUNDRIES.
Business licenses, §47-2817.

LAW ENFORCEMENT OFFICERS.
**Advance information passed
regarding raids or arrests,**
§23-1109.
Alcoholic beverage licenses.
Assault on police officer, government
inspector or investigator.
Summary revocation or suspension,
§25-826.
Availability for inspection, §25-711.
Alcoholic beverages.
Reports.
Incident reports, §25-804.
Animals.
Harassing, interfering with, injuring
or obstructing police animal,
§22-861.
Assaults, §22-405.
Alcoholic beverage licenses.
Assault on police officer, government
inspector or investigator.
Summary revocation or
suspension, §25-826.
Resisting arrest, §22-405.01.
**Bomb disposal duty, additional
compensation for,** §5-542.02.
Cadet programs, §§38-912, 38-913.
Issuance of rules, §38-912.01.
Capitol police.
See CAPITOL POLICE.
Child abuse and neglect reports,
§4-1321.02.
Concealed weapons, carrying,
§22-4505.
Court duty, §5-1304.
Courthouse protection force.
Wages and salaries, §47-201.

LAW ENFORCEMENT OFFICERS
—Cont'd
Crimes and offenses.
Failure to notify medical examiner of
certain deaths, §5-1406.
Crime victims' compensation.
Responsibilities regarding, §4-517.
Dead bodies.
Duty to report certain deaths to
medical examiner, §5-1405.
Failure to report certain deaths,
§5-1406.
Delinquent minors.
Taking into custody, §16-2309.
Demotions, §5-543.05.
**District of Columbia housing
authority police department,**
§6-223.
Domestic violence, handling,
§§16-1031 to 16-1034.
Entertainments, assignment to,
§47-2820.
False personation of police officer,
§§22-1404, 22-1406.
**Federal law enforcement officer
cooperative agreements,** §§5-301
to 5-303.
Firearms.
Concealed weapons, carrying,
§22-4505.
Possession of certain dangerous
weapons by, §22-4514.
Taking and destruction of dangerous
articles, §22-4517.
**Fleeing from a law enforcement
officer in a motor vehicle,**
§50-2201.05b.
**Foreign missions, protective
services for,** §6-1313.
Hazardous materials.
Stopping and inspecting vehicles
carrying, §8-1403.01.
**Helicopter duty, additional
compensation for,** §5-542.02.
Housing finance and assistance.
Government employer-assisted
housing program, §§42-2501 to
42-2507.
Inefficiency, removal for, §5-501.01.
**Interception of wire or oral
communications.**
Applications for authorization to
intercept, CrimPro Rule 41-I.
Lateral police career appointments,
§§1-610.71 to 1-610.76.

LAW ENFORCEMENT OFFICERS
—Cont'd
Medical assistance.
Police and firefighters medical care reimbursement, §§5-601 to 5-609.
See MEDICAL ASSISTANCE.
Memorial for, §§5-1331 to 5-1333.
Mental health disclosures.
Authorized disclosures, §7-1203.05a.
Meritorious service awards, §§5-901 to 5-904.
Merit system.
Lateral police career appointments, §§1-610.71 to 1-610.76.
Metropolitan police.
General provisions, §§5-101.01 to 5-133.21.
See METROPOLITAN POLICE.
Metropolitan Washington Airports Authority, §9-907.
Motor vehicle insurance.
Enforcement of compulsory insurance requirements.
General provisions, §§5-114.01 to 5-114.04.
Murder of, §22-2106.
Mutual aid.
Reciprocal agreements between police departments, §§2-209.01 to 2-209.04.
National Law Enforcement Heroes Memorial, §§5-1331 to 5-1333.
Obstructing, preventing, or interfering with reports of criminal offenses, §22-1931.
Off-duty days and holidays, §§5-405, 5-1304.
Office of police complaints.
General provisions, §§5-1101 to 5-1115.
See OFFICE OF POLICE COMPLAINTS.
Pawnbrokers' premises and books, access to, §47-2884.11.
Police code, §§5-103.01, 5-103.02.
Prerecorded transmittals to, §7-2803.
Preservation of evidence.
Protection of innocence act, §22-4134.
Prison guards.
Deadly force.
Correctional treatment facilities, §24-261.02.
Private detectives, §§5-121.01 to 5-121.05.
Promotion, §5-543.04.
Public officers and employees designated to protect life and property outside the District, §10-509.01.

LAW ENFORCEMENT OFFICERS
—Cont'd
Reciprocal agreements between police departments, §§2-209.01 to 2-209.04.
Mutual aid agreements authorized, §2-209.01.
Personnel benefits, §2-209.03.
Required provisions, §2-209.02.
Supervision of non-District police in District, §2-209.04.
Redeployment of retirees, §§5-761, 5-762.
Registration of out-of-state officers, §§5-1201, 5-1202.
Reports.
Alcoholic beverages.
Incident reports, §25-804.
Resisting arrest, §22-405.01.
Runaway children.
Taking child into custody, §16-2309.
Salaries.
See WAGES AND SALARIES.
Scuba diving duty, additional compensation for, §5-542.02.
Special assignments, §5-1304.
Transfers, §5-543.04.
Truants.
Authority over, §38-207.
Taking into custody, §16-2309.
Tuition expenses for, §5-1305.
Two-way radio communications, §§5-1306 to 5-1309.
United States park police, §§5-201 to 5-208.
See UNITED STATES PARK POLICE.
United States secret service.
Lateral police career appointments, §§1-610.71 to 1-610.76.
Police and firefighters retirement and disability, §5-703.
Wages and salaries for uniformed division, §5-545.01.
Conversion to 2001 standards, §5-561.02.
Locality-based comparability adjustments, freeze, §5-563.02.
Wages.
See WAGES AND SALARIES.
Warrantless arrests by, §23-581.
Weapons.
Concealed weapons, carrying, §22-4505.
Possession of certain dangerous weapons by, §22-4514.
Taking and destruction of dangerous articles, §22-4517.

LAW ENFORCEMENT OFFICERS
—Cont'd
Weights and measures.
Police powers of Director of,
§37-201.24.
Workweek, §5-1304.

LAW FIRMS.
Imputed disqualification, ProfCond
Rule 1.10.
Government to private employment,
ProfCond Rule 1.11.
Name of firm, ProfCond Rule 7.5.
**Non-lawyers sharing fees, managing
firm, etc.,** ProfCond Rule 5.4.
**Partner's or supervisory lawyer's
responsibilities,** ProfCond Rule
5.1.
Non-lawyer assistants, ProfCond Rule
5.3.
Sale of law practice, ProfCond Rule
1.17.
**Subordinate lawyer's
responsibilities,** ProfCond Rule
5.2.

LAW REVISION COMMISSION,
§§45-301 to 45-305.
Annual report, §45-303.
Appropriations, §45-304.
Duties, §45-302.
Effective date of provisions, §45-305.
Establishment, §45-301.
Members, §45-301.
Powers, §45-301.
Terms of office and vacancies,
§45-301.

LAW STUDENT PRACTICE, CivPro
Rule 101, USDistCt LCrR 44.3,
USDistCt LCvR 83.4.
Appeals, D.C. courts, DCCtApp Rule
48.
Appeals, federal cases.
Appearance by, FRAP 46(g), USCtApp
Rule 46.
Assignment of counsel, CrimPro Rule
44-I.
Family court proceedings, FamDiv
Rule M.
Landlord and tenant court,
LandlordTenant Rule 9.
Small claims court, SmallClaims Rule
9.
Subpoenas.
Criminal cases, CrimPro Rule 17.
Delinquent minors, JuvProc Rule 17.

LAWYER COUNSELING PANEL,
USDistCt LCrR 57.31, USDistCt
LCvR 83.20.

LAYAWAY PLANS.
Buyer's right to cancel, §28-3818.
Consumer credit, §28-3818.
Default by seller, §28-3818.
Definitions, §28-3818.
Fees and charges, §28-3818.
Generally, §28-3818.

**LEAD-HAZARD PREVENTION AND
ELIMINATION,** §§8-231.01 to
8-231.20.
Abatement permits, §8-115.07.
**Access to dwelling unit, tenant to
provide,** §8-231.06.
Accreditation of training providers,
§8-231.12.
**Action against District not
authorized by provisions,**
§8-231.17.
**Certification for entities performing
lead-based paint activities,**
§8-231.10.
Accreditation of training providers,
§8-231.12.
Denial, suspension or revocation,
§8-231.14.
Civil penalties for violations,
§8-231.15.
**Conflicts of interest in conducting
clearance examinations,**
§8-231.11.
Criminal penalties for violations,
§8-231.16.
Definitions, §8-231.01.
Delegation of authority, §8-231.20.
**Disclosures for certain older
properties,** §8-231.04.
**Elimination of lead-hazards
identified by examination or
assessment,** §8-231.03.
Enforcement of provisions,
§§8-231.18a, 8-231.20.
**Federal regulations, incorporating
by reference,** §8-231.18.
**Information provided by tenant to
mayor concerning hazards.**
Right to provide, §8-231.07.
Injunction of violations, §8-231.15.
Lead-safe work practices, §8-231.11.
Order to eliminate lead-hazards,
§8-231.03.
Owner's concurrent obligations,
§8-231.08.

LEAD-HAZARD PREVENTION AND ELIMINATION —Cont'd
Presumed lead-based paint identified.
Notice of violation, §8-231.03.
Property to be free of lead-based paint or glaze, §8-231.02.
Public building inspections, §10-702.
Recordkeeping and disclosure of records, §8-231.13.
Relocation during elimination of lead-hazards, §8-231.03.
Remedies under common law applicable, §8-231.19.
Renovation work.
Lead-safe work practices applicable, §8-231.11.
Right of entry and inspection, §8-231.05.
Risk assessment of property, §8-231.03.
Certification for entities performing, §8-231.10.
Rulemaking, §8-231.18.
Safe work practice standards, §8-231.11.
Service of notices, §8-231.15.
Student health care, §§38-602, 38-610.
Training on performing lead-based paint activities.
Accreditation of training providers, §8-231.12.
Violations.
Civil penalties, §8-231.15.
Criminal penalties, §8-231.16.
Denial, suspension or revocation of certifications, §8-231.14.
Injunctions, §8-231.15.
Service of notice, §8-231.15.

LEADING QUESTIONS, CivPro Rule 43.
Adoption proceedings, Adoption Rule 43.
Domestic relations actions, DomRel Rule 43.

LEAD LEVEL WATER TESTING.
Multiple dwelling residences, §§42-3251 to 42-3255.
Definitions, §42-3251.
Rules and procedures, §42-3254.
Testing generally, §42-3252.
Violations, §42-3253.
Civil fines, penalties, fees, §42-3255.

LEAD PIPE REPLACEMENT FUNDING, §§34-2151 to 34-2156.

LEAD POISONING.
Childhood lead poisoning screening and reporting, §§7-871.01 to 7-871.06.
Definitions, §7-871.02.
Enforcement, §7-871.04.
Requirements, §7-871.03.
Rules, §7-871.06.
Short title, §7-871.01.
Violations, penalties, §7-871.05.
Laboratory services.
Fees, §7-734.

LEAD SERVICE LINE PRIORITY REPLACEMENT ASSISTANCE, §§34-2151 to 34-2156.
Eligibility, §34-2153.
Fund, §§34-2151, 34-2152.
Grant administration, §34-2154.
Liability of District, §34-2156.
Rulemaking, §34-2155.

LEARNFARE, §4-205.65.

LEASEHOLD CONDOMINIUMS, §§42-1902.10, 42-1902.29.

LEASE-PURCHASE AGREEMENTS, §§42-3671.01 to 42-3671.14.
Advertising, §42-3671.10.
Civil remedies for consumers, §42-3671.12.
Limitation of action, §42-3671.13.
Consumer rights, §42-3671.02.
Definitions, §42-3671.01.
Disclosures, §§42-3671.03, 42-3671.04.
Not required for extension, §42-3671.09.
Early purchase option.
Consumer rights, §42-3671.02.
Extension.
Disclosure not required, §42-3671.09.
Lost, stolen, damaged, destroyed property.
Consumer rights, §42-3671.02.
Maintenance and servicing of property during lease, §42-3671.05.
Consumer rights, §42-3671.02.
Manufacturer's express warranty.
Consumer rights, §42-3671.02.
New agreement.
Renegotiated agreement, §42-3671.09.
Price tag or card, §42-3671.11.
Prohibited provisions in agreement, §42-3671.06.
Receipt for each payment, §42-3671.08.

LEASE-PURCHASE AGREEMENTS
—Cont'd
Reinstatement of agreement without losing rights or options,
§42-3671.07.
Renegotiation.
Existing agreement satisfied and replaced by new agreement, §42-3671.09.
Termination of agreement.
Consumer rights, §42-3671.02.
Unintentional violation and timely adjustment of error, §42-3671.14.

LEASES.
Airspace.
General provisions, §§10-1121.01 to 10-1121.13.
See RENTAL OF AIRSPACE.
Capital review and debt affordability committee, §§47-336 to 47-340.
Children and minors, §§42-3225 to 42-3228.
Property of, §21-157.
Commercial code leases.
Generally, §§28:2A-101 to 28:2A-532.
See LEASES, UCC.
Convention center hotel.
Land lease authority for hotel, §§10-1202.21 to 10-1202.24.
District government, §§1-301.01, 1-301.91.
Dulles International Airport, space or property for, §9-805.
Form of, §42-601.
Garbage collection and disposal facilities, §8-741.
General provisions, §§28:1-101 to 28:1-310.
See COMMERCIAL CODE.
Guardianship of incapacitated persons, §42-3228.
Guardianship of minors, §§42-3225 to 42-3228.
Incompetent or incapacitated persons, §42-3228.
Intellectual disabilities, persons with, §42-3228.
Interpretation of provisions, §§28:10-103, 28:10-104.
Landlord and tenant, §§42-3201 to 42-3232, 42-3501.01 to 42-3509.08.
See LANDLORD AND TENANT.
Liens on motor vehicles and trailers, §50-1217.

LEASES —Cont'd
Mental illness, persons with, §42-3228.
Metropolitan Washington Airports Authority, §§9-1004, 9-1009.
Navy Yard track connection, §9-1203.02.
Parks and recreation, §§10-103, 10-143, 10-213.
Personalty leases, §§28:2A-101 to 28:2A-532.
See LEASES, UCC.
Private correctional treatment facilities, exemptions for, §24-261.05.
Public space.
Airspace.
General provisions, §§10-1121.01 to 10-1121.13.
See RENTAL OF AIRSPACE.
General provisions, §§10-1101.01 to 10-1104.08.
See RENTAL OF PUBLIC SPACE.
Over or under 9th Street Southwest, §1-301.01.
Public structures in public space, §§10-1141.01 to 10-1141.07.
Qualified high technology company.
Master lease of real property, security deposit assistance, §§2-1221.01, 2-1221.02.
Recreation board, §10-213.
Renewal of lease, §§42-3222 to 42-3228.
RLA revitalization corporation, leases of real property by, §§6-321.04, 6-341.02.
Surrender of possession, §§42-3207, 42-3212, 42-3222 to 42-3227.
Tenant receivership.
Violation threatening health, safety or security of tenants, §§42-3651.01 to 42-3651.08.
Transitional provisions, §§28:11-101 to 28:11-108.
See COMMERCIAL CODE.
Underleases, §42-3229.
Washington convention and sports authority.
Land lease authority for hotel, §§10-1202.21 to 10-1202.24.
Washington National Airport, space or property for, §9-703.
Wills devising land to include leaseholds, §18-304.

LEASES, UCC —Cont'd
Supply contracts.
Beneficiaries.
Lessee under finance lease,
§28:2A-209.
Defined, §28:2A-103.
Lessee under finance lease as
beneficiary, §28:2A-209.
Termination.
Defined, §28:2A-103.
Effect on rights and remedies,
§28:2A-505.
Third parties.
Standing to sue for injury to goods,
§28:2A-531.
Warranties.
Third party beneficiaries,
§28:2A-216.
Title of article.
Short title, §28:2A-101.
Title to goods, §28:2A-302.
Infringement.
Warranty against, §28:2A-211.
Transitional provisions, §§28:11-101
to 28:11-108.
See COMMERCIAL CODE.
Unconscionability, §28:2A-108.
Waiver.
Claims, rights after default or breach
of warranty, §28:2A-107.
Generally, §28:2A-208.
Objections by lessee to goods,
§28:2A-514.
Warranties, §§28:2A-211 to 28:2A-213.
Breach of warranty.
Damages, §§28:2A-508, 28:2A-519.
Notice of claim or litigation
answerable over, §28:2A-516.
Waiver or renunciation of rights
after breach, §28:2A-107.
Cumulation and conflict, §28:2A-215.
Damages.
Breach of warranty, §§28:2A-508,
28:2A-519.
Exclusion, §28:2A-214.
Express warranties.
Generally, §28:2A-210.
Third party beneficiaries,
§28:2A-216.
Implied warranties.
Fitness for particular purpose,
§28:2A-213.
Merchantability, §28:2A-212.
Third party beneficiaries,
§28:2A-216.
Infringement.
Warranty against, §28:2A-211.

LEASES, UCC —Cont'd
Warranties —Cont'd
Interference with goods.
Warranty against, §28:2A-211.
Merchantability.
Implied warranties, §28:2A-212.
Modification, §28:2A-214.
Third party beneficiaries, §28:2A-216.

LEASH LAWS, §§1-303.41, 8-1808,
22-1311.

LEAVE OF ABSENCE.
Annual leave bank, §§1-612.04 to
1-612.11.
See ANNUAL LEAVE BANK.
Charter schools.
Employees of DC public schools
accepting positions at,
§38-1802.07.
Compensatory time off.
Merit system compensation policy,
§1-611.03.
Disability compensation.
Election to use leave instead of,
§1-623.18.
Restoration of leave, §1-623.43.
Discipline and grievance process.
Administrative leave or forced leave
under, §1-616.54.
Domestic violence.
Employee sick leave generally,
§§32-131.01 to 32-131.16.
See LABOR AND EMPLOYMENT
RELATIONS.
Employee sick leave generally,
§§32-131.01 to 32-131.16.
See LABOR AND EMPLOYMENT
RELATIONS.
Family and medical leave, §§32-501
to 32-517.
See FAMILY AND MEDICAL LEAVE.
Family leave, §1-612.03c.
Fire departments.
Record of leave taken, §5-408.
Sick leave, §5-408.
Holidays.
See HOLIDAYS.
Public officers and employees,
§§1-612.03 to 1-612.11.
Donor leave.
Organ or bone marrow donors,
§1-612.03b.
Voluntary leave transfer program,
§§1-612.31 to 1-612.38.
Sick leave.
Disability compensation, election to
use instead of, §1-623.18.

LEAVE OF ABSENCE —Cont'd
Sick leave —Cont'd
Employee sick leave generally,
  §§32-131.01 to 32-131.16.
  See LABOR AND EMPLOYMENT
  RELATIONS.
Fire departments, §5-408.
Public officers and employees,
  §1-612.03.
**Teachers' retirement credit for
  unpaid leave,** §§38-2021.01a,
  38-2061.02.
Universal leave system, §§1-610.61,
  1-612.03a.
Voluntary leave transfer program,
  §§1-612.31 to 1-612.38.

LEGACIES.
General provisions.
  See WILLS.

**LEGAL AID AGENCY
  REDESIGNATED AS PUBLIC
  DEFENDER SERVICE,** §§2-1601,
  2-1608.

LEGAL ESTATE.
Cestui que use, in, §42-1501.
**Effect of purchase for value without
  notice of trust,** §42-1503.
Joint seizin, §42-1502.

LEGAL NOTICE.
Forfeiture of property, CivPro Rule
  71A-I.
Service by publication, CivPro Rule
  4-I.

LEGAL SEPARATION.
Divorce arising after, causes for,
  §16-906.
Enlargement of, §16-905.
Grounds for, §16-904.
Revocation of, §16-905.
Statutory rule against perpetuities.
  Agreements excluded from rule,
  §19-904.

LEGAL SERVICE, §§1-608.51 to
  1-608.65, 1-608.51 to 1-608.66.
Applicability of provisions, §1-608.62.
Appointment of attorneys, §1-608.54.
Budgets, §1-608.65.
Certificate of good standing.
  Attorneys employed at level DS-13 or
  above, §1-608.81.
**Continuing education and skills
  maintenance requirements,**
  §1-608.57.
Definitions, §1-608.51.

LEGAL SERVICE —Cont'd
Disciplinary actions, §1-608.56.
Establishment of, §1-608.52.
Mayor's office of legal counsel,
  §1-608.51a.
Performance management system,
  §1-608.57.
Privileges.
  Attorney-client privilege, applicability,
  §1-608.66.
Reports, §1-608.60.
Residence requirements, §1-608.59.
Rulemaking authority, §1-608.61.
Senior executive attorney service,
  §1-608.53.
Subordinate agencies.
  Payment of compensation to former
  subordinate agency attorneys,
  §1-608.63.
  Transfer of attorneys, employees and
  property to subordinate agencies,
  §1-608.64.
Supervision of attorneys, §1-608.55.
Wages and salaries, §1-608.58.

LEGAL SERVICE ORGANIZATIONS.
Attorney serving as director, officer,
  etc., ProfCond Rule 6.3.

LEGITIMACY OF CHILDREN.
Defined terms, §16-907.
Intestate succession, §§19-316, 19-318.
**Parent and child relationship not
  affected by status,** §16-908.

LEMON LAW, §§50-501 to 50-510.
Arbitration, §§50-503, 50-509.
Definitions, §50-501.
Disclosure.
  Rights of consumer, §50-504.
  Used vehicles, damages or defects in,
  §50-505.
Enforcement, suspension of, §50-510.
Issuance of rules and regulations,
  §50-508.
Limitation of actions, §50-507.
Odometer readings, §50-506.
Remedies, §§50-502, 50-507.
Rights of consumer, §§50-504, 50-507.
Suspension of enforcement of,
  §50-510.

LENITY.
Civil asset forfeiture, §41-314.

LESSER INCLUDED OFFENSES,
  CrimPro Rule 31.
Juvenile proceedings, JuvProc Rule
  31.

LETTERHEAD.
Attorneys at law, ProfCond Rule 7.5.
LETTERS OF CREDIT, §§28:5-101 to 28:5-120.
Adviser, §28:5-107.
  Defined, §28:5-102.
Amendment, §28:5-106.
  Cancellation, §28:5-106.
  Duration, §28:5-106.
Applicability of provisions, §28:5-118.
Applicant.
  Defined, §28:5-102.
  Subrogation, §28:5-117.
Assignment of proceeds, §28:5-114.
Choice of law and forum, §28:5-116.
Citation of article.
  Short title, §28:5-101.
Condominiums.
  Escrow deposits, §42-1904.09.
Confirmer, §28:5-107.
  Defined, §28:5-102.
Consideration, §28:5-105.
Construction of code, §§28:10-103, 28:10-104.
Contracts for sale of goods, §28:2-325.
Definitions, §28:5-102.
  General commercial code definitions, §28:1-201.
    Reasonable time and seasonably, §28:1-205.
  Index of definitions, §28:5-102.
  Proceeds of a letter of credit, §28:5-114.
Dishonor.
  Defined, §28:5-102.
  Remedies for wrongful dishonor, §28:5-111.
Forgery, §28:5-109.
Formal requirements, §28:5-104.
Fraud, §28:5-109.
General provisions, §§28:1-101 to 28:1-310.
  See COMMERCIAL CODE.
Good faith.
  Obligation of good faith, §28:1-304.
Interpretation of provisions, §§28:10-103, 28:10-104.
Issuance, §28:5-106.
Issuer.
  Defined, §28:5-102.
  Rights and obligations, §28:5-108.
  Subrogation, §28:5-117.
Negotiable instruments.
  General provisions, §§28:3-101 to 28:3-605.
    See NEGOTIABLE INSTRUMENTS.

LETTERS OF CREDIT —Cont'd
Nominated person, §28:5-107.
  Defined, §28:5-102.
  Subrogation, §28:5-117.
Remedies, §28:5-111.
Sales.
  Contracts for sale of goods, §28:2-325.
Savings clause, §28:5-119.
Scope of article, §28:5-103.
Security interest, §28:5-120.
Signatures, §28:5-104.
Statute of limitations, §28:5-115.
Subrogation.
  Issuer, applicant and nominated person, §28:5-117.
Title of articles.
  Short title, §28:5-101.
Transfer, §28:5-112.
  Operation of law, §28:5-113.
Transitional provisions, §§28:11-101 to 28:11-108.
  See COMMERCIAL CODE.
Warranties, §28:5-110.

LETTERS OF MARQUE AND REPRISAL, US Const Art I §§8 to 10.

LEVIES.
Claims against estates, §20-914.
Execution of judgments, §§15-311 to 15-314.
Income taxes.
  Corporations, §47-1807.02.
Nonresident wages, on, §16-512.
Personal property taxes.
  See PERSONAL PROPERTY TAXES.
Public works assessments for paving and resurfacing streets.
  Pro rata levy of, §9-421.01.
Real property taxes, §47-811.

LEVY COURT.
Ordinances, §45-402.

LIBEL AND SLANDER.
Congress.
  Privilege of members, US Const Art I §6.

LIBELS OF INFORMATION.
Forfeiture of property, CivPro Rule 71A-I.
  Civil asset forfeiture, §41-307.

LIBRARIES, §§39-101 to 39-124.
Appeals, federal cases.
  Generally, USCtApp HPIP Rule I(a)(5).
  Librarians, USCtApp HPIP Rule I(b)(6).

LIBRARIES —Cont'd
Appropriations for expenses.
Mayor authorized to seek, §39-106.
Board of trustees, §§39-104, 39-105.
Gifts, authority to accept, §39-107a.
Books and other library materials account, §39-114.
Books from birth program, §39-115.
Books from birth fund, §39-116.
Branches of, §39-102.
Children and minors.
Books from birth program, §39-115.
Books from birth fund, §39-116.
Circulation records.
Confidentiality of, §39-108.
DCPL revenue-generating activities fund, §39-117.
Drug free zones, §48-904.07a.
Enhancement task force.
Membership, §39-112.
Entitlement to use, §39-103.
Establishment of, §39-101.
Facility planning and construction, §10-1031.
Federal executive.
Books no longer used by, §39-123.
Fees to join, §39-103.
Fines, §39-105.
Firearms.
Enhanced penalties and fines for carrying guns into gun free zones, §22-4502.01.
Free library user's card.
Obtaining, §39-103.
Gifts, authority to accept.
Board of trustees, §39-107a.
Mayor, §39-101.
Government publications.
Designated depository of, §39-124.
Library development trust fund, §39-113.
Procurement authority.
Board of trustees, §39-105.
Profits, use of, §39-107.
Purchase of library-related items, §39-107.
Records as to circulation of books.
Confidentiality of, §39-108.
Rent of library-related items, §39-107.
Sale of library-related items, §39-107.
Schools and education, §§38-1901, 38-2807.
Transfer of books to, §39-123.
Use of, §39-103.
West End library and fire station maintenance fund, §1-325.181.

LICENSE PLATES.
Motor vehicle registration.
Generally.
See MOTOR VEHICLE REGISTRATION.

LICENSES.
Alcoholic beverages.
See ALCOHOLIC BEVERAGES.
Ambulatory surgical facilities, §§44-501 to 44-509.
Anesthesiologist assistants, §§3-1206.31, 3-1206.32.
Animals, §8-1804.
Circus, carnival or other special event animals, display of, §8-1808.
Commercial animal care or breeder license, §§8-1821.01, 8-1821.02.
Guard dogs, commercial, §8-1841.02.
Armed forces personnel.
Waiver of business license renewal fees for, §1-301.01.
Asbestos contractors, §§8-111.02 to 8-111.06.
See ASBESTOS CONTRACTORS.
Assisted living residences, §§44-103.01 to 44-103.05, 44-103.07.
Revocation or suspension, §§44-104.01, 44-104.04.
Attorneys at law.
Admission to bar, DCCtApp Rule 46.
False statements, etc., ProfCond Rule 8.1.
Disbarment, DCBar Rule XI.
Banks and financial institutions.
International banking corporations.
Application, §26-636.
Required, §26-635.
Boards and commissions, §§1-321.03 to 1-321.06.
Boxing and wrestling commission, §3-606.
Business licenses, §§47-2805.01 to 47-2881.
See BUSINESS LICENSES.
Cemetery purposes.
Licensing of lands for, §43-115.
Check cashing businesses.
See CHECK CASHING BUSINESSES.
Child care facilities.
See CHILD CARE FACILITIES.
Child-placing agencies, §§4-1402, 4-1404, 4-1407.
Cigarette sales below cost.
Suspension or revocation of license for, §28-4525.
Cigarettes, sales, §47-2404.

LICENSES —Cont'd
Clinical laboratories, §44-202.
Community residence facilities, §§44-501 to 44-509.
Continuing care providers, §§44-151.02, 44-151.03.
Controlled substances.
Supervision of administration of, §48-931.02.
Cooperative associations.
Fees, §29-939.
Cytotechnology, §§3-1207.61 to 3-1207.64.
Dangerous dogs, §8-1907.
Delinquent debts owed District, recovery, §1-350.07.
Dietetics and nutrition, §§3-1207.01, 3-1207.02.
Director of Department of Licenses, Investigations, and Inspections, §1-301.03.
Discrimination, §§2-1402.67, 2-1403.17.
Discrimination in admission to licensed places, §§47-2901 to 47-2911.
Driving instructors.
License fee, §47-2842.
Drug manufacture and distribution licensure, §§48-701 to 48-715.
See DRUG MANUFACTURE AND DISTRIBUTION LICENSURE.
Emergency medical services.
Agencies, §7-2341.03.
Appeal of decisions regarding certification, §7-2341.18.
Denial, suspension or revocation, §7-2341.15.
Emergency response vehicles, §7-2341.04.
Flight emergency medical services personnel certification, §7-2341.06.
Hearings, §7-2341.17.
Instructor certification, §7-2341.08.
Liability insurance requirement, §7-2341.09.
Personnel certification, §7-2341.05.
Previously issued certification or license, §7-2341.11.
Provisional and restricted licenses and certifications, §7-2341.10.
Reciprocal certification, §7-2341.12.
Renewal, §7-2341.14.
Summary suspension, §7-2341.16.
Training facilities, certification, §7-2341.07.

LICENSES —Cont'd
Employment agencies, §32-402.
Fees.
Authority regarding, §§1-301.74, 1-301.75.
Bingo licenses, §3-1325.
Business license renewal fees for armed forces personnel.
Waiver of, §1-301.01.
Business licenses.
See BUSINESS LICENSES.
Check cashing businesses, §26-305.
Commercial drivers' licenses, §50-408.
Drivers' licenses, §50-1401.01.
Fire and casualty insurance licenses, §31-2502.41.
Firearms dealer's license, §7-2504.02.
Insurance companies, §47-2603.
Lottery and charitable games control board.
Bingo and raffle licenses, §3-1325.
Suppliers' licenses, §3-1327.
Marriage license fees, §15-717.
Mortgage lenders' and brokers' licenses, §26-1107.
Motor fuel importers, §47-2303.
Notaries public, license fees, §1-1201.
Pawnbrokers' licenses, §§47-2884.03 to 47-2884.06.
Pharmacists and pharmacies, §47-2885.19.
Raffle licenses, §3-1325.
Refunds, §47-1318.
Setting, §§1-301.74, 1-301.75.
Firearms dealers.
See FIREARMS.
Fish and game, §§22-4328, 22-4329.
Food stamps.
Business license or permit suspended, revoked, or denied for trafficking in, §4-218.06.
Foreign trade zones.
Applicability of licensing, permitting and taxation provisions, §36-503.
Fraternal benefit societies, §§31-5324, 31-5328, 31-5330.
Funeral directors, §§3-405 to 3-416.
See FUNERAL DIRECTORS.
Gas-fitters, §2-135.
Health care facilities, §§44-501 to 44-509.
Health occupations licensure, registration or certification, §§3-1205.01 to 3-1205.24.
See HEALTH OCCUPATIONS LICENSURE, REGISTRATION OR CERTIFICATION.

LICENSES —Cont'd

Higher education licensure commission, §§38-1301 to 38-1313.
See HIGHER EDUCATION LICENSURE COMMISSION.

Histotechnology, §§3-1207.61 to 3-1207.64.

Home care agencies, §§44-501 to 44-509.

Home improvement contractors, §47-2883.01.

Hospices, §§44-501 to 44-509.

Hospitals, §§44-501 to 44-509.

Hotline, §47-2881.

Human Rights Commission, §§2-1402.67, 2-1403.17.

Human tissue banks, §7-1541.03.

Inaugural ceremonies of the President of the United States, §§2-802, 2-806.

Insurance companies.
See INSURANCE COMPANIES.

Insurance holding companies, §31-713.

Insurance premium finance companies, §§31-1103 to 31-1105.

Insurance producers, §§31-1131.01 to 31-1131.19.
See INSURANCE PRODUCER LICENSING.

Intellectual disabilities, persons with.
Group homes for, §§44-501 to 44-509.

Lottery and charitable games control board.
See LOTTERY AND CHARITABLE GAMES CONTROL BOARD.

Managing general agents, §31-1502.

Marriage.
See MARRIAGE.

Marriage and family therapy, §§3-1208.31, 3-1208.32.

Marriage license fees, §15-717.

Medical laboratories, §§3-1207.61 to 3-1207.64.

Money lenders.
See MONEY LENDERS.

Money transmissions.
See MONEY TRANSMISSIONS.

Money transmitters, §§26-1001 to 26-1027.

Mortgage lenders and brokers.
See MORTGAGE LENDERS AND BROKERS.

Motor vehicle business licenses.
See MOTOR VEHICLES.

LICENSES —Cont'd

Motor vehicle financing, §50-603.

Natural gas suppliers.
Retail natural gas supplier licensing, §§34-1671.01 to 34-1671.14.
See GAS COMPANIES.

Notaries public, §1-1201.

Nude dancers not allowed on premises licensed to sell alcoholic beverages, §25-113.

Nursing homes, §§44-501 to 44-509.

Pawnbrokers, §§47-2884.02 to 47-2884.07.

Pesticides, §§8-403 to 8-406, 8-410.

Pharmaceutical detailing.
Qualifications, §3-1207.42.
Waiver of requirements, §3-1207.43.

Pharmacists and pharmacies, §§47-2885.03 to 47-2885.10.

Pharmacy technicians, §§3-1207.51 to 3-1207.58.

Playgrounds.
Temporary structures on reservations used as, §10-125.

Plumbers, §2-135.

Portable electronics insurance.
Vendors, §31-5051.02.

Pre-kindergarten programs.
Licensing of child-occupied facilities.
Dry cleaning establishments in close proximity.
Restrictions on licensing, §38-271.01.

Price scales.
Posting requirements, §§47-2907 to 47-2911.

Professional counseling, §§3-1207.10 to 3-1207.12.

Public auction permit requirements, §47-2704.

Public insurance adjuster licensing, §§31-1631.01 to 31-1631.12.
See INSURANCE ADJUSTER LICENSING.

Race discrimination in admission to licensed places, §§47-2901 to 47-2911.

Refunds of fees for, §47-1318.

Reinsurance intermediaries, §31-1802.

Renal dialysis facilities, §§44-501 to 44-509.

Respiratory care, §§3-1207.21 to 3-1207.23.

Risk retention groups, §31-4111.

LICENSES —Cont'd

Security agents and brokers,
§§31-5602.01 to 31-5602.11.
See SECURITY AGENTS AND
BROKERS.

Security and fire alarm contractors.
Alarm agents, §7-2805.
Alarm dealers, §7-2804.

Social workers, §§3-1208.01 to
3-1208.06.

**State health planning and
development agency.**
Certificates of need as condition
precedent for, §44-415.

Taxicabs, §50-301.19.

Tidal basin boathouses, §10-151.

Title insurance producers.
Requirements, §31-5041.02.
Revocation or suspension, §31-5041.09.

Title insurers.
Requirements, §31-5031.02.
Revocation or suspension, §31-5031.21.

Underground storage tanks,
§8-113.06.

Veterinary facilities, §§47-2888.01 to
47-2888.08.
See VETERINARY FACILITIES.

Waste, writ of.
Prohibition of waste without written
license, §42-1602.

Weapons dealers, §§22-4509, 22-4510.

Wildlife control operator, §8-2204.
Conditions for issuance, §8-2205.
Fees, §8-2209.
Suspension or revocation, §8-2208.

Youth residential facilities, §§7-2102,
7-2107.

LIE DETECTOR TESTS.

**Employer or prospective employer
administering in connection
with employment.**
Civil liability of employer violating
provisions, §32-903.
Contract or arbitration provisions
prohibited, §32-903.
Criminal penalty for violation,
§32-903.
Definitions, §32-901.
Prohibition, exceptions, §32-902.
Violation invasion of privacy, §32-903.

LIENS.

Artisan's lien, §§40-307.01 to
40-307.03.

Assignments for benefit of creditors.
Priorities not affected, §28-2107.

LIENS —Cont'd

Attachment, §§16-507, 16-523.
Pre-judgment attachment, CivPro Rule
64-I.
Domestic relations actions, DomRel
Rule 64.

Attorneys' fees, ProfCond Rule 1.8.

Carriers, §28:7-307.
Enforcement, §28:7-308.

**Charitable institutions'
appropriations as liens on
property,** §44-711.

Children and minors.
Property of, §§21-144, 21-152.

Child support enforcement, §46-224.

Claims against estates, §20-903.

Collection of taxes.
Lien for taxes, §§47-4421 to 47-4423.

Columbia Hospital for Women,
§44-753.

Condominiums.
See CONDOMINIUMS.

**Delinquent debts owed District,
recovery,** §1-350.05.

Documents of title.
Carrier's lien, §28:7-307.
Enforcement, §28:7-308.
Warehouse lien, §§28:7-209, 28:7-210.

Enforcement, §40-303.08.

Execution of judgments, §15-307.

Federal tax liens.
Recorder of deeds, §42-1215.

Fish and game law forfeitures,
§22-4330.

Gambling premises, §22-1705.

Garage keepers' liens, §§40-102 to
40-105.

Health care benefits lien reduction,
§31-3551.

Home improvement contractors.
Payment as defense to lien by,
§47-2883.03.

Horizontal property regimes.
See HORIZONTAL PROPERTY
REGIMES.

Hospital liens, §§40-201 to 40-205.

**Insurers rehabilitation and
liquidation proceedings,**
§31-1326.

**Intermediate care facilities for
persons with intellectual
disabilities.**
Assessment on facilities, §47-1274.

Investment securities.
Issuer's lien, §28:8-209.

Judgments and decrees, §§15-102,
15-104.

LIENS —Cont'd
Landlord's lien for rent, §§42-3213 to 42-3218.
Leases, UCC.
Defined, §28:2A-103.
Priority of certain liens arising by operation of law, §28:2A-306.
Priority of liens arising by attachment or levy on security interests, §28:2A-307.
Litter control, §8-807.
Liveryman's lien, §40-101.
Mechanics' and materialmen's lien.
General provisions, §§40-301.01 to 40-307.03.
See MECHANIC'S LIENS.
Medicaid health-care assistance reimbursement, §4-606.
Motor vehicles.
Metropolitan police property clerk. Sale by, §5-119.10.
Titling of motor vehicles and trailers, §§50-1201 to 50-1218.
See MOTOR VEHICLES.
Nursing facilities.
Assessment on nursing facilities, §47-1264.
Police and firefighters medical care reimbursement, §5-604.
Public utilities, §34-501.
Real estate tax sales, §§47-1303.04, 47-1312.
Revised real property tax sale, §47-1331.
Rent, §§42-3213 to 42-3218.
Self-service storage facilities.
Rent, labor, or other charges, §40-403.
Enforcement of lien, §40-404.
Southwest waterfront special assessment district.
Unpaid special assessments, §47-895.04.
Stormwater management.
Failure to reimburse user fees, §8-152.03.
Subcontractor's liens.
General provisions, §§40-303.01 to 40-303.20a.
See SUBCONTRACTOR'S LIENS.
Vacant buildings.
Delinquent collection of fees, §42-3131.13.
Warehouse lien, §28:7-209.
Enforcement, §28:7-210.
Wastewater and sewage works, §34-2110.

LIENS —Cont'd
Water supply and waterworks, §34-2407.02.
Workers' compensation, §32-1518.

LIFE AND HEALTH INSURANCE GUARANTY ASSOCIATION, §§31-5401 to 31-5416.
Advertising, §31-5416.
Affiliates, §31-5411.
Assessments, §§31-5406, 31-5410.
Bankruptcy and insolvency, §§31-5409, 31-5411.
Board of directors, §31-5404.
Coverage, §31-5402.
Credit for assessments made, §31-5410.
Default, §31-5415.
Definitions, §31-5401.
Disbursement of assets, §31-5411.
Establishment of, §31-5403.
Examinations, §31-5412.
Immunity, §31-5414.
Interpretation of provisions, §31-5411.
Limitations on coverage, §31-5402.
Mayor's powers and duties, §31-5408.
Operating plan, §31-5407.
Powers and duties, §31-5405.
Records, §31-5411.
Reports, §31-5412.
Stay of proceedings, §31-5415.
Tax exemption for, §31-5413.
Termination or liquidation, §31-5411.

LIFE ESTATES.
Allowance for life estate, CivPro Rule 307.
Probate proceedings, Probate Rule 6.
Arrears of rent, §42-3220.
Death of tenant.
Proceedings to discover, §§16-1151 to 16-1158.
Evicted person.
Recovery of profits by, §16-1156.
Failure to produce life tenant as ordered, §16-1153.
Holding over, §16-1158.
Investigations outside the District regarding, §16-1154.
Order to produce life tenant, §16-1152.
Petition, §16-1151.
Preservation of rights of life tenant, §16-1157.
Restoration of property to life tenant, §16-1155.

LIFE ESTATES —Cont'd
Estates in land.
General provisions, §§42-501 to 42-523.
See ESTATES IN LAND.
Form of deed for, §42-601.
Remainder to heirs of life tenant, §42-703.
Sales, §§42-1401 to 42-1404.
Proceeds of sale, §42-1403.
Verified bill to apply for sale, §42-1402.
Under-tenant of life tenant, recovery of rent from, §42-3219.

LIFE IMPRISONMENT.
Murder.
First and second degree, §22-2104.
Without parole.
Murder.
First degree murder, §22-2104.
Killing law enforcement officer, §22-2106.
Three strikes offenders, §22-1804a.

LIFE INSURANCE.
Casualty and other insurance rates.
General provisions, §§31-2701 to 31-2714.
See INSURANCE.
Comfort care orders.
Non-resuscitation procedures for EMS.
Execution not to effect life insurance, §7-651.13.
Credit life, accident and health insurance, §§31-5101 to 31-5112.
Domestic life insurance companies, §§31-4401 to 31-4452.
See DOMESTIC LIFE INSURANCE COMPANIES.
Domestic partner benefits, §§32-701 to 32-710.
See DOMESTIC PARTNER BENEFITS.
Do not resuscitate orders.
Comfort care orders.
Execution not to affect, §7-651.13.
Executive service, §1-610.63.
Industrial life insurance, §§31-4801 to 31-4805.
See INDUSTRIAL LIFE INSURANCE.
Insurance companies.
General provisions.
See INSURANCE COMPANIES.
Life insurance companies, §§31-4201 to 31-4603.
See LIFE INSURANCE COMPANIES.

LIFE INSURANCE —Cont'd
Insurance investments.
Life insurance companies, §§31-1372.01 to 31-1372.12.
See INSURANCE INVESTMENTS.
Life and health insurance guaranty association.
General provisions, §§31-5401 to 31-5416.
See LIFE AND HEALTH INSURANCE GUARANTY ASSOCIATION.
Public officers and employees.
See MERIT SYSTEM.
Rates.
Casualty and other insurance rates.
General provisions, §§31-2701 to 31-2714.
See INSURANCE.

LIFE INSURANCE COMPANIES, §§31-4201 to 31-4603.
Actuarial opinion of reserves, §31-4901.
Advertising, §31-4310.
Annuity contracts, filing, §31-4705.
Appeals, §31-4332.
Applicability of provisions, §§31-4201, 31-4727.
Assessments prohibited, §31-4331.
Bonds, surety, §§31-4315 to 31-4317.
Cash surrender values, §31-4705.01.
Certificate of authority, §31-4403.
Investigation of qualifications, §31-4304.
Issuance, §31-4304.
Revocation or suspension, §31-4305.
Classes of business to be kept separate, §31-4702.
Definitions, §31-4202.
Department of insurance, securities, and banking, §31-4301.
Deposit of securities by, §§31-4315 to 31-4317.
Amount, §31-4315.
Deposit outside district, §31-4315.
Type of securities, §31-4316.
Withdrawal, §31-4317.
Disability benefits.
Exemption of benefits from legal process, §31-4716.01.
Domestic life insurance companies.
General provisions, §§31-4401 to 31-4452.
See DOMESTIC LIFE INSURANCE COMPANIES.
Effective date of provisions, §31-4730.

LIFE INSURANCE COMPANIES
—Cont'd
Enforcement of commissioner's orders or actions, §31-4313.
Excess fees, charges, and taxes charged to, §31-4303.
Exemption of benefits from legal process.
Disability benefits, §31-4716.01.
Group policies, §31-4717.
Fees and charges, collection of, §§31-4302, 31-4303.
Filing requirements, §31-4712.
Fines, §31-4601.
Foreign and alien life insurance companies, §§31-4501, 31-4502.
Approval of, §31-4501.
Defined, §31-4202.
Examinations, §31-4502.
Filing requirements, §31-4501.
Mergers and consolidations of domestic companies with, §31-4446.
Trustees of alien companies, §31-4502.
Foreign government entities.
Policy provisions required by, §31-4709.
Form of, §31-4712.
Forms, filing and approval of, §31-4708.
Fraternal benefit societies converted into mutual life insurance companies, §31-5312.
Fraud and deceit, §§31-4310 to 31-4314.
Alien companies, §31-4310.
Application for policy.
False statements regarding, §31-4314.
Group policies, §31-4711.
Exemption of benefits from legal process, §31-4717.
Individual policies taken out by group insured, §31-4711.01.
Individual policies.
Group policies, persons insured under, §31-4711.01.
Industrial life insurance, §§31-4801 to 31-4805.
See INDUSTRIAL LIFE INSURANCE.
Insurance regulatory trust fund, §§31-1201 to 31-1210.
See INSURANCE REGULATORY TRUST FUND.
Interpretation of provisions, §31-4729.

LIFE INSURANCE COMPANIES
—Cont'd
Issuance of regulations, §31-4728.
Language simplification requirements, §§31-4725, 31-4726.
Loans, §§31-4705.04, 31-4707.
Minors contracting with, §31-4330.
Nonforfeiture benefits, §§31-4705.01 to 31-4705.03.
Participating and nonparticipating policies.
Issuing, §31-4702.
Penalties, §31-4601.
Policy provisions, §31-4712.
Foreign government entities.
Policy provisions required by, §31-4709.
Group policies, §31-4711.
Nonforfeiture benefits and cash surrender value, §31-4705.01.
Standard nonforfeiture law, §§31-4705.02, 31-4705.03.
Prohibited, §31-4704.
Required, §31-4703.
Premiums.
Calculating, §31-4720.
Extension of time to pay, §31-4706.
Industrial life policies, §31-4721.
Paid to agents, disposition of, §31-4329.
Proceeds of policy held under trust or agreement, §31-4719.
Pure endowment contracts, filing, §31-4705.
Reserves.
Actuarial opinion of reserves, §31-4901.
Calculating, §31-4720.
Merit system special contingency reserve, §1-622.13.
Valuation of, §31-4701.
Rights of parties under policies, §31-4716.
Severability of provisions, §31-4603.
Standard nonforfeiture law, §§31-4705.02, 31-4705.03.
Subpoenas, §31-4312.
Unclaimed property.
See UNCLAIMED PROPERTY.
Valuation of reserves, §31-4701.

LIGHTING.
Outside city limits, §1-305.03.

LIMITATION OF ACTIONS, §§12-301 to 12-311.
Adoption.
Invalidation of decree, Adoption Rule 60.

LIMITATION OF ACTIONS —Cont'd
Appeals, §17-307.
Asbestos exposure.
Actions for death or injury caused by, §12-311.
Attorney discipline or disability proceedings, DCBar Rule XI.
Bank deposits and collections, §28:4-111.
Child abuse and neglect, §§16-2322, 16-2330.
Child sexual abuse, §23-113.
Claims against estates, §§20-902, 20-903.
Condominium warranties, §42-1903.17.
Continuing care retirement communities.
Action for violations, §44-151.14.
Contracts.
Sale of goods.
Breach of contract, §28:2-725.
Limitations by agreements may be reduced to less than one year, §28:2-725.
Court of appeals, §17-307.
Criminal proceedings, §23-113.
Identity theft, §22-3227.07.
Tax prosecutions, §47-4108.
Custodial trustees, claims for relief against, §19-1116.
Defendant absent or concealed, §12-303.
Delinquent minors, §§16-2322, 16-2330.
Disability, incapacity, or minority of plaintiff, §12-302.
District of Columbia housing authority.
Actions against, §6-205.
Estate of decedent.
Actions against, §12-305.
Execution of judgments.
Time period for, §15-302.
Federal benefit payments under District programs.
Actions regarding, §1-815.02.
Felonies, §23-113.
Foreign judgments, §12-307.
Foreign-money judgments, §15-369.
Fraudulent conveyances, §28-3109.
Fraudulent transfers.
Extinguishment of causes of action, §28-3109.
Fugitives from justice, §23-113.
Hazardous substances releases, §8-634.10.

LIMITATION OF ACTIONS —Cont'd
Human trafficking, §23-113.
Incest, §23-113.
Insanitary buildings, §6-919.
Insurance demutualization, §31-915.
Judgments and decrees.
Relief from judgment or order, CivPro Rule 60.
Domestic relations actions, DomRel Rule 60.
Time period for enforcement of, §15-101.
Lease-purchase agreements.
Consumer remedies, §42-3671.13.
Lemon law, §50-507.
Letters of credit, §28:5-115.
Limitation of actions, §§12-301 to 12-311.
See LIMITATION OF ACTIONS.
Limited liability partnerships.
Action for improper distributions, §29-610.03.
Mechanic's liens.
Subcontractor's lien, commencement of suit, §40-303.13.
Medical malpractice.
Notice of intention to file suit.
Extension of statute of limitations, §16-2803.
Misdemeanors, §23-113.
Murder, §23-113.
Mutual insurance holding companies, §31-736.
Negotiable instruments, §28:3-118.
No-fault motor vehicle insurance, §31-2411.
Parentage proceedings, §16-2342.
Partnerships.
Dissolution.
Barred claims against dissolved partnership, §§29-608.08, 29-608.09.
Pensions and retirement funds, §1-911.02.
Premarital agreements, §46-508.
Prisoners, §12-302.
Procurement claims, §2-381.05.
Action seeking relief from retaliatory actions, §2-381.04.
Quo warranto, §16-3548.
Real property.
Actions for death or injury caused by defective or unsafe improvements to, §12-310.
Recall of elected public officials, §1-204.113.

LIMITATION OF ACTIONS —Cont'd
Reciprocal insurance company
   conversion, §31-758.
Restraints of trade, §28-4511.
Retirement Board fiduciary
   responsibilities, §1-746.
Sales, §28:2-725.
Security agents and brokers.
   Civil liability, §31-5606.05.
   Criminal prosecution, §31-5606.04.
Sexual abuse, §23-113.
Sick leave violations.
   Civil complaints, §32-131.10a.
Statutory trusts.
   Improper distribution, §29-1206.16.
Stays by court or by statute, §12-304.
Taxation.
   Collection, §47-4302.
   Credits, §§47-4304, 47-4304.01.
   Liability for payment, §47-4301.
   Refunds, §47-4304.
   Suspension of limitations periods,
    §47-4303.
   Tax prosecutions, §47-4108.
Telephone solicitation, §22-3226.12.
Trade secrets, §36-406.
Trusts and trustees.
   Revocable trusts.
    Limitation on action contesting
     validity, §19-1306.04.
   Uniform trust code.
    Judicial proceedings, §19-1310.05.
Unclaimed property, §41-129.
United States.
   Actions by, §12-308.
Unliquidated damages actions
   against District, §12-309.
Warehouse receipts.
   Contractual limitation of warehouse
    liability, §28:7-204.
Workplace fraud.
   Private right of action to enforce
    provisions, §32-1331.09.
Wrongful death, §16-2702.

LIMITED COOPERATIVE
   ASSOCIATIONS, §§29-1001.01 to
   29-1015.08.
Actions, §29-1001.05.
   Members, §§29-1013.01 to 29-1013.06.
    See within this heading,
    "Members."
   Special litigation committee,
    §29-1013.06.
Administrative dissolution.
   Generally, §§29-106.01 to 29-106.04.
    See BUSINESS ORGANIZATIONS.

LIMITED COOPERATIVE
   ASSOCIATIONS —Cont'd
Allocations of profits and losses,
   §29-1010.04.
Antitrust.
   Relation to law, §29-1001.08.
Approval of entity transaction,
   §29-1001.13.
Articles of organization, §29-1003.02.
   Amendment.
    Filing, §29-1004.07.
    Restatement, §29-1004.06.
    Filing, §29-1004.07.
Business transactions of member
   with association, §29-1001.11.
Bylaws, §29-1003.04.
Contributions, §29-1010.01.
   Agreements, §29-1010.03.
   Valuation, §29-1010.02.
Conversion, merger or
   domestication.
   Approval of entity transaction,
    §29-1001.13.
Definitions, §29-1001.02.
Derivative actions, §29-1013.01.
Directors, §§29-1008.01 to 29-1008.23.
   Action without meeting, §29-1008.12.
   Best interests of association,
    §29-1008.20.
   Committees, §29-1008.17.
   Compensation, §29-1008.10.
   Conflicts of interest, §29-1008.19.
   Election, §29-1008.04.
   Information rights, §29-1008.21.
   Liability, §29-1008.18.
   Meetings, §29-1008.11.
    Notice, §29-1008.13.
     Waiver, §29-1008.14.
    Quorum, §29-1008.15.
   No liability for obligations of
    association, §29-1008.02.
   Number of, §29-1008.01.
   Qualifications, §29-1008.03.
   Removal of, §29-1008.07.
   Resignation of, §29-1008.06.
   Standards of conduct, §29-1008.18.
   Suspension of, §29-1008.08.
   Terms of office, §29-1008.05.
   Vacancies in office, §29-1008.09.
   Voting, §29-1008.16.
Discontinuances in member actions.
   Approval, §29-1013.04.
Disposition of assets, §§29-1014.01 to
   29-1014.04.
   Member approval, §29-1014.02.
   Not required, §29-1014.01.

**LIMITED COOPERATIVE
  ASSOCIATIONS** —Cont'd
Disposition of assets —Cont'd
  Member approval —Cont'd
    Requirements, §29-1014.04.
  Notice, §29-1014.03.
Dissociation, §§29-1011.01 to
  29-1011.03.
  Effect of, §29-1011.02.
  Events causing, §29-1011.01.
  Personal representatives.
    Powers, §29-1011.03.
  Powers, §29-1011.01.
Dissolution, §§29-1012.01 to
  29-1012.13.
  Authority, §29-1012.01.
  Court proceedings on claims,
    §29-1012.10.
  Distributions upon, §29-1012.07.
  Judicial dissolution, §29-1012.03.
  Known claims, §29-1012.08.
  Nonjudicial dissolution, §29-1012.02.
  Other claims, §29-1012.09.
  Rescission, §29-1012.13.
  Statement of dissolution, §29-1012.11.
  Voluntary dissolution.
    Approval, §29-1012.05.
    Before commencement of activity,
      §29-1012.04.
  Winding up, §29-1012.06.
Distributions, §29-1010.05.
  Dissolution, upon, §29-1012.07.
  Improper distributions.
    Liability, §29-1010.08.
  Limitations, §29-1010.07.
  Redemption or repurchase,
    §29-1010.06.
Duration of, §29-1001.04.
Entity transactions, approval,
  §29-1001.13.
Filing, §§29-1002.01 to 29-1002.03.
  Articles of organization.
    Amendment, §29-1004.07.
    Restatement, §29-1004.07.
  Delivery to mayor, §29-1002.01.
  Generally, §§29-102.01 to 29-102.13.
    See BUSINESS ORGANIZATIONS.
  Inaccurate information in filed record.
    Liability, §29-1002.03.
  Judicial orders, §29-1002.02.
  Mergers and consolidations,
    §29-1015.05.
Foreign entities.
  Generally, §§29-105.01 to 29-105.12.
    See BUSINESS ORGANIZATIONS.
Formation, §§29-1003.01 to 29-1003.04.

**LIMITED COOPERATIVE
  ASSOCIATIONS** —Cont'd
General provisions, §§29-1001.01 to
  29-1001.13.
Governing law, §29-1001.06.
Improper distributions.
  Liability, §29-1010.08.
**Inaccurate information in filed
  record.**
  Liability, §29-1002.03.
Indemnification, §29-1009.01.
Investor members.
  Membership interests, §29-1006.02.
  Voting, §29-1005.13.
Judicial dissolution, §29-1012.03.
Liability.
  Directors, §29-1008.18.
    No liability for obligations of
      association, §29-1008.02.
  Improper distributions, §29-1010.08.
  Inaccurate information in filed record,
    §29-1002.03.
  Members.
    No liability for obligations of
      association, §29-1005.04.
Marketing contracts, §§29-1007.01 to
  29-1007.04.
  Authorization, §29-1007.01.
  Breach of contract, §29-1007.04.
  Defined, §29-1007.01.
  Duration of, §29-1007.03.
  Effect of, §29-1007.02.
Meetings of directors, §29-1008.11.
  Notice, §29-1008.13.
    Waiver, §29-1008.14.
  Quorum, §29-1008.15.
Meetings of members.
  Annual meetings, §29-1005.06.
  Notice, §29-1005.08.
    Waiver, §29-1005.09.
  Special meetings, §29-1005.07.
Members, §§29-1005.01 to 29-1005.17.
  Actions, §§29-1013.01 to 29-1013.06.
    Derivative actions, §29-1013.01.
    Discontinuances.
      Approval, §29-1013.04.
    Pleading, §29-1013.03.
    Proceeds and expenses, §29-1013.05.
    Proper plaintiff, §29-1013.02.
    Settlement or compromise.
      Approval, §29-1013.04.
    Special litigation committee,
      §29-1013.06.
  Action without meeting, §29-1005.16.
  Becoming member, §29-1005.02.
  Business transactions of member with
    association, §29-1001.11.

LIMITED COOPERATIVE ASSOCIATIONS —Cont'd

Members —Cont'd

Classes of, §29-1005.17.

Information rights, §29-1005.05.

Investor members.

Voting, §29-1005.13.

Meetings.

Annual meetings, §29-1005.06.

Notice, §29-1005.08.

Waiver, §29-1005.09.

Special meetings, §29-1005.07.

No agency created by reason of becoming member, §29-1005.03.

No liability for obligations of association, §29-1005.04.

Number of, §29-1005.01.

Patron members.

Districts and delegates, §29-1005.17.

Voting, §§29-1005.11, 29-1005.12.

Quorum, §29-1005.10.

Voting.

Method of, §29-1005.15.

Requirements, §29-1005.14.

Membership interests, §§29-1006.01 to 29-1006.05.

Charging orders, §29-1006.05.

Dual capacity, §29-1001.12.

Investor members, §29-1006.02.

Patron members, §29-1006.02.

Personal property, §29-1006.01.

Security interests, §29-1006.04.

Setoffs, §29-1006.04.

Transferability, §29-1006.03.

Mergers and consolidations, §§29-1015.01 to 29-1015.08.

Amendment or abandonment, §29-1015.04.

Approval, §§29-1015.03, 29-1015.04.

Approval of entity transaction, §29-1001.13.

Authorization, §29-1015.02.

Consolidations, §29-1015.07.

Definitions, §29-1015.01.

Effective date, §29-1015.05.

Effect of, §29-1015.06.

Nonexclusivity of provisions, §29-1015.08.

Plans, §29-1015.02.

Required filings, §29-1015.05.

Names.

Generally, §§29-103.01 to 29-103.04.

See BUSINESS ORGANIZATIONS.

Requirements, §29-103.02.

Nature of, §29-1001.03.

Nonjudicial dissolution, §29-1012.02.

LIMITED COOPERATIVE ASSOCIATIONS —Cont'd

Notice.

Meetings of directors, §29-1008.13.

Waiver, §29-1008.14.

Meetings of members, §29-1005.08.

Waiver, §29-1005.09.

Officers.

Appointment, §29-1008.22.

Powers, §29-1008.22.

Removal of, §29-1008.23.

Resignation of, §29-1008.23.

Organic rules.

Amendment, §§29-1004.01 to 29-1004.07.

Approval, §29-1004.05.

Authority, §29-1004.01.

Notice, §29-1004.02.

Voting.

District, class or voting group, §29-1004.04.

Method, §29-1004.03.

Effect of, §29-1001.09.

Organization of, §29-1003.03.

Organizers, §29-1003.01.

Patron members.

Districts and delegates, §29-1005.17.

Membership interests, §29-1006.02.

Voting, §§29-1005.11, 29-1005.12.

Pleading in member actions, §29-1013.03.

Powers, §29-1001.05.

Proceeds and expenses in member actions, §29-1013.05.

Proper plaintiff in member actions, §29-1013.02.

Purposes of, §29-1001.04.

Records, §29-1001.10.

Registered agents.

Generally, §§29-104.01 to 29-104.14.

See BUSINESS ORGANIZATIONS.

Required information, §29-1001.10.

Requirements for formation, §29-1003.02.

Restraints of trade.

Relation to law, §29-1001.08.

Settlement or compromise in member actions.

Approval, §29-1013.04.

Short title, §29-1001.01.

Special litigation committee, §29-1013.06.

Statement of dissolution, §29-1012.11.

Statement of termination, §29-1012.12.

Statutory construction, §29-1001.07.

LIMITED COOPERATIVE ASSOCIATIONS —Cont'd
Voluntary dissolution.
Approval, §29-1012.05.
Before commencement of activity, §29-1012.04.
Voting.
Amendment of organic rules.
District, class or voting group, §29-1004.04.
Method, §29-1004.03.
Investor members, §29-1005.13.
Members.
Method of, §29-1005.15.
Requirements, §29-1005.14.
Winding up, §29-1012.06.

LIMITED LIABILITY COMPANIES, §§29-801.01 to 29-810.01.
Actions, §29-801.05.
Dissolution.
Claims, court proceedings on, §29-807.07.
Members, §§29-808.01 to 29-808.06.
See within this heading, "Members."
Administrative dissolution.
Generally, §§29-106.01 to 29-106.04.
See BUSINESS ORGANIZATIONS.
Certificates of organization, §29-802.01.
Amendment, §29-802.02.
Restatement, §29-802.02.
Contributions.
Form, §29-804.02.
Liability, §29-804.03.
Definitions, §29-801.02.
Derivative actions, §29-808.02.
Direct actions by members, §29-808.01.
Dissociation of members, §§29-806.01 to 29-806.03.
Effect of, §29-806.03.
Events causing, §29-806.02.
Powers of members, §29-806.01.
Wrongful dissociation, §29-806.01.
Dissolution, §§29-807.01 to 29-807.07.
Claims, court proceedings on, §29-807.07.
Distributions upon, §29-807.05.
Events causing, §29-807.01.
Known claims, §29-807.03.
Other claims, §29-807.04.
Rescission of dissolution, §29-807.06.
Winding up, §§29-807.01, 29-807.02.
Distributions.
Dissolution, upon, §29-807.05.

LIMITED LIABILITY COMPANIES —Cont'd
Distributions —Cont'd
Liability, §29-804.06.
Limitations, §29-804.05.
Right to, §29-804.04.
Domestication, §§29-809.06 to 29-809.11.
Authorization, §29-809.06.
Consent, §29-809.07.
Effect of, §29-809.09.
Nonexclusivity of provisions, §29-809.11.
Plans, §29-809.06.
Required filings, §29-809.08.
Restrictions, §29-809.10.
Duration of, §29-801.04.
Filing.
Delivery to mayor, §29-802.03.
Generally, §§29-102.01 to 29-102.13.
See BUSINESS ORGANIZATIONS.
Inaccurate information in filed records, §29-802.05.
Judicial orders, §29-802.04.
Mergers and consolidations, §29-809.04.
Foreign entities.
Generally, §§29-105.01 to 29-105.12.
See BUSINESS ORGANIZATIONS.
Formation, §§29-802.01 to 29-802.06.
General provisions, §§29-801.01 to 29-801.09.
Governing laws, §29-801.06.
Inaccurate information in filed records, §29-802.05.
Income tax, §47-1808.06a.
Indemnification, §29-804.08.
Information rights, §29-804.10.
Insurance, §29-804.08.
Knowledge, §29-801.03.
Liability.
Contributions, §29-804.03.
Distributions, §29-804.06.
Inaccurate information in filed records, §29-802.05.
Managers, §29-803.04.
Members, §29-803.04.
Management, §29-804.07.
Manager-managed limited liability companies, §29-804.07.
Managers.
Advancement of costs and fees, §29-804.08.
Indemnification, §29-804.08.
Information rights, §29-804.10.
Insurance, §29-804.08.

LIMITED LIABILITY COMPANIES
—Cont'd

Managers —Cont'd
Liability, §29-803.04.
Manager-managed limited liability companies, §29-804.07.
Reimbursement, §29-804.08.
Series, §29-802.06.
Standards of conduct, §29-804.09.
Member-managed limited liability companies, §29-804.07.
Members.
Actions, §§29-808.01 to 29-808.06.
Derivative actions, §29-808.02.
Direct actions, §29-808.01.
Pleading, §29-808.04.
Proceeds and expenses, §29-808.06.
Proper plaintiff, §29-808.03.
Settlement of derivative action, court approval required, §29-808.06.
Special litigation committees, §29-808.05.
Advancement of costs and fees, §29-804.08.
Becoming member, §29-804.01.
Indemnification, §29-804.08.
Information rights, §29-804.10.
Insurance, §29-804.08.
Liability, §29-803.04.
Member-managed limited liability companies, §29-804.07.
Not deemed agents, §29-803.01.
Reimbursement, §29-804.08.
Series, §29-802.06.
Standards of conduct, §29-804.09.
Mergers and consolidations, §§29-809.01 to 29-809.05.
Amendment or abandonment, §29-809.03.
Articles of merger, §29-809.04.
Authorization, §29-809.02.
Consent, §29-809.03.
Definitions, §29-809.01.
Effective date, §29-809.04.
Effect of, §29-809.05.
Filing, §29-809.04.
Nonexclusivity of provisions, §29-809.11.
Plans, §29-809.02.
Required filings, §29-809.04.
Restrictions, §29-809.10.
Names.
Generally, §§29-103.01 to 29-103.04.
See BUSINESS ORGANIZATIONS.

LIMITED LIABILITY COMPANIES
' —Cont'd

Names —Cont'd
Requirements, §29-103.02.
Nature of, §29-801.04.
Notice, §29-801.03.
Operating agreements, §29-801.07.
Members, effect on, §29-801.08.
Third parties, effect on, §29-801.09.
Partnership converted to.
Real property taxes.
Transfers exempt from tax, §47-802.
Personal property.
Transferable interests as, §29-805.01.
Pleading in actions by members, §29-808.04.
Powers, §29-801.05.
Proceeds and expenses in actions by members, §29-808.06.
Purposes of, §29-801.04.
Real property taxes.
Partnership converted to.
Transfers exempt from tax, §47-802.
Registered agents.
Generally, §§29-104.01 to 29-104.14.
See BUSINESS ORGANIZATIONS.
Relations of members and managers to each other and to LLC, §§29-804.01 to 29-804.10.
Relations of members and managers to other persons, §§29-803.01 to 29-803.04.
Requirements for formation, §29-802.01.
Series, §29-802.06.
Short title, §29-801.01.
Signing of records.
Delivery to mayor, §29-802.03.
Judicial orders, §29-802.04.
Special litigation committees, §29-808.05.
Standards of conduct, §29-804.09.
Statement of authority, §29-803.02.
Statement of denial, §29-803.03.
Transferable interests, §§29-805.01 to 29-805.04.
Authority, §29-805.02.
Charging orders, §29-805.03.
Personal property, §29-805.01.
Personal representatives.
Powers, §29-805.04.
Series, §29-802.06.
Transitional provisions, §29-810.01.
Winding up, §§29-807.01, 29-807.02.

LIMITED LIABILITY COMPANIES
—Cont'd
Wrongful dissociation, §29-806.01.

**LIMITED LIABILITY
   PARTNERSHIPS.**
Distributions.
   Liability for improper distributions,
      §29-610.03.
   Limitations, §29-610.02.
**Indebtedness, effect on
   distributions,** §29-610.02.
Names.
   Requirements, §29-103.02.
**Reinstatement following
   administrative revocation of
   statement of qualification,**
   §29-610.05.
   Appeal of denial of reinstatement,
      §29-610.06.
Statement of qualification,
   §29-610.01.
   Administrative revocation, §29-610.04.
   Reinstatement, §29-610.05.
      Appeal of denial of reinstatement,
         §29-610.06.

LIMITED PARTNERSHIPS,
   §§29-701.01 to 29-711.01.
Actionable conduct.
   Liability, §29-704.03.
Actions, §29-701.05.
   Dissolution.
      Court proceedings, §29-708.11.
   General partners, §29-704.05.
   Partners, §§29-709.01 to 29-709.06.
      Derivative actions, §29-709.02.
         Settlement, court approval
            required, §29-709.05.
      Direct actions, §29-709.01.
      Pleading, §29-709.04.
      Proceeds and expenses, §29-709.05.
      Proper plaintiffs, §29-709.03.
      Special litigation committee,
         §29-709.06.
Administrative dissolution.
   Generally, §§29-106.01 to 29-106.04.
      See BUSINESS ORGANIZATIONS.
**Business transactions of partner
   with partnership,** §29-701.11.
Certificates of limited partnership,
   §29-702.01.
   Amendment, §29-702.02.
   Restatement, §29-702.02.
Consent, §29-701.13.
Contributions.
   Dissolution, upon, §29-708.09.
   Form of, §29-705.01.

LIMITED PARTNERSHIPS —Cont'd
Contributions —Cont'd
   Liability for, §29-705.02.
Definitions, §29-701.02.
Derivative actions by partners,
   §29-709.02.
Direct actions by partners,
   §29-709.01.
Disposition of assets, §29-708.09.
Dissociation, §§29-706.01 to 29-706.07.
   Distributions upon, §29-705.05.
   General partners, §29-706.03.
      Effect of, §29-706.05.
      Liability, §§29-706.06, 29-706.07.
      Powers, §29-706.04.
      Power to bind partnership before,
         §29-706.06.
      Wrongful dissociation, §29-706.04.
   Limited partners, §29-706.01.
      Effect of, §29-706.02.
Dissolution, §§29-708.01 to 29-708.11.
   Claims against partnership,
      proceedings, §29-708.11.
   Contributions upon, §29-708.09.
   Court proceedings, §29-708.11.
   Disposition of assets, §29-708.09.
   General partners.
      Liability after, §29-708.05.
      Power to bind partnership after,
         §29-708.04.
   Judicial dissolution, §29-708.02.
   Known claims, §29-708.06.
   Nonjudicial dissolution, §29-708.01.
   Other claims, §29-708.07.
   Power to bind partnership after,
      §29-708.04.
   Rescission of dissolution, §29-708.10.
   Winding up, §29-708.03.
Distributions, §§29-705.03 to
   29-705.09.
   Dissociation, upon, §29-705.05.
   Improper distributions.
      Liability, §29-705.09.
   In kind, §29-705.06.
   Interim distributions, §29-705.04.
   Limitations, §29-705.08.
   Right to, §29-705.07.
   Sharing, §29-705.03.
Dual capacity, §29-701.12.
Duration of, §29-701.04.
Filing.
   Delivery to mayor, §29-702.04.
   Generally, §§29-102.01 to 29-102.13.
      See BUSINESS ORGANIZATIONS.
   Inaccurate information in filed record,
      §29-702.06.

LIMITED PARTNERSHIPS —Cont'd
Filing —Cont'd
Judicial orders, §29-702.05.
Mergers and consolidations,
§29-710.04.
Foreign entities.
Generally, §§29-105.01 to 29-105.12.
See BUSINESS ORGANIZATIONS.
Formation of, §§29-702.01 to 29-702.06.
General partners, §§29-704.01 to
29-704.09.
Actionable conduct.
Liability of partnership, §29-704.03.
Actions, §29-704.05.
Advancement of fees and expenses,
§29-704.09.
Agents, §29-704.02.
Becoming general partner, §29-704.01.
Dissociation, §29-706.03.
Effect of, §29-706.05.
Liability, §§29-706.06, 29-706.07.
Powers, §29-706.04.
Power to bind partnership before,
§29-706.06.
Wrongful dissociation, §29-706.04.
Dual capacity, §29-701.12.
Indemnification, §29-704.09.
Information rights, §29-704.07.
Insurance on behalf of, §29-704.09.
Liability, §29-704.04.
After dissolution, §29-708.05.
Dissociation, §§29-706.06, 29-706.07.
Insurance on behalf of general
partner, §29-704.09.
Mergers and consolidations, after,
§29-710.08.
When claims barred, §29-708.08.
Management rights, §29-704.06.
Mergers and consolidations.
Liability after, §29-710.07.
Power to bind partnership after,
§29-710.08.
Power to bind partnership after
dissolution, §29-708.04.
Reimbursement, §29-704.09.
Standards of conduct, §29-704.08.
General provisions, §§29-701.01 to
29-701.13.
Governing law, §29-701.06.
Improper distributions.
Liability, §29-705.09.
**Inaccurate information in filed
record,** §29-702.06.
In kind distributions, §29-705.06.
Interim distributions, §29-705.04.
Judicial dissolution, §29-708.02.

LIMITED PARTNERSHIPS —Cont'd
Knowledge, §29-701.03.
Liability.
Actionable conduct of general
partners, §29-704.03.
Contributions, §29-705.02.
General partners, §29-704.04.
After dissolution, §29-708.05.
Dissociation, §§29-706.06, 29-706.07.
Mergers and consolidations, after,
§29-710.08.
When claims barred, §29-708.08.
Improper distributions, §29-705.09.
Inaccurate information in filed record,
§29-702.06.
Limited partners, §29-703.03.
Limited partners, §§29-703.01 to
29-703.06.
Becoming limited partner, §29-703.01.
Dissociation, §29-706.01.
Effect of, §29-706.02.
Dual capacity, §29-701.12.
Duties, §29-703.05.
Erroneous belief, §29-703.06.
Information rights, §29-703.04.
Liability due to conduct as limited
partner, §29-703.02.
No agency relationship created by
limited partnership, §29-703.02.
No liability for partnership
obligations, §29-703.03.
Mergers and consolidations,
§§29-710.01 to 29-710.08.
Amendment or abandonment,
§29-710.03.
Articles of merger, §29-710.04.
Authorization, §29-710.02.
Consent, §29-710.03.
Definitions, §29-710.01.
Effective date, §29-710.04.
Effect of, §29-710.05.
Filing, §29-710.04.
General partners.
Liability after, §29-710.07.
Power to bind partnership after,
§29-710.08.
Plans, §29-710.02.
Required filings, §29-710.04.
Restrictions, §29-710.06.
Names.
Generally, §§29-103.01 to 29-103.04.
See BUSINESS ORGANIZATIONS.
Requirements, §29-103.02.
Nature of, §29-701.04.
Nonjudicial dissolution, §29-708.01.

LIMITED PARTNERSHIPS —Cont'd
Notice, §29-701.03.
  Dissolution.
    Claims against partnership,
      proceedings, §29-708.11.
Partnership agreements.
  Amendments, §29-701.09.
  Assent by person becoming partner,
    §29-701.08.
  Creation of agreement, §29-701.08.
  Effect of, §29-701.07.
  Nonwaivable provisions, §29-701.07.
  Third parties, effect on, §29-701.09.
Pleading in actions by partners,
  §29-709.04.
Powers, §29-701.05.
Proceeds and expenses in actions by
  partners, §29-709.05.
Proper plaintiffs in actions by
  partners, §29-709.03.
Proxy arrangements, §29-701.13.
Purposes of, §29-701.04.
Records, §29-701.10.
Registered agents.
  Generally, §§29-104.01 to 29-104.14.
  See BUSINESS ORGANIZATIONS.
Required information, §29-701.10.
Requirements for formation,
  §29-702.01.
Short title, §29-701.01.
Signing of records.
  Delivery to mayor, §29-702.04.
  Judicial orders, §29-702.05.
Statement of termination, §29-702.03.
Transferable interests, §§29-707.01 to
  29-707.04.
  Charging order against interest for
    unsatisfied judgment, §29-707.03.
  Creditors' rights, §29-707.03.
  Effect of, §29-707.02.
  Personal property, §29-707.01.
  Personal representatives.
    Powers, §29-707.04.
Transitional provisions, §29-711.01.
Winding up, §29-708.03.
Wrongful dissociation, §29-706.04.

LIMOUSINES.
Impoundment of vehicles, §50-331.
Non-resident taxi and limousine
  driver vehicle registration fee,
  §50-1501.03.
Taxicabs.
  General provisions, §§50-301.01 to
    50-301.34.
  See TAXICABS.

LINCOLN SQUARE THEATER.
Sales and use tax exemption,
  §47-4601.

LINKED DEPOSITS.
District funds invested or deposited
  in banks and financial
  institutions, §47-351.09.

LIQUIDATED DEBT.
Interest on judgment for, §15-108.

LIQUIDATION.
Banks and financial institutions,
  §26-103.
Captive insurance companies.
  Special purpose financial captive
    insurance companies, §31-3932.12.
Credit union loans, §26-503.
Fraternal benefit societies, §31-5327.
Insurers rehabilitation and
  liquidation proceedings,
  §§31-1301 to 31-1357.
  See INSURERS REHABILITATION
    AND LIQUIDATION
    PROCEEDINGS.
Title insurers, §31-5031.09.

LIQUOR.
Generally.
  See ALCOHOLIC BEVERAGES.

LIQUOR WAREHOUSES.
Warehouse receipts.
  Storage under government bond,
    §28:7-201.

LIS PENDENS NOTICE, §42-1207.

LITERACY.
Adult literacy.
  Reports, §38-192.01.
  Workforce investment implementation,
    §32-1661.

LITERARY RIGHTS.
Attorney drafting instruments
  giving attorney rights, ProfCond
  Rule 1.8.

LITTER AND SOLID WASTE
  REDUCTION.
Alcoholic beverage licenses.
  Litter control, §25-726.

LITTER CONTROL, §§8-801 to 8-812.
Answer to notice, §8-804.
Appeals, §8-809.
Business improvement district litter
  cleanup assistance fund,
  §1-325.111.

LITTER CONTROL —Cont'd
Business licenses.
  Unpaid fines or penalties.
    Computer record-keeping and
      reporting system, §47-2866.
    Definitions, §47-2861.
    Issuance of license prohibited,
      §47-2862.
    Right to appeal denial of license,
      §47-2865.
    Self-certification of lack of
      outstanding debt, §47-2863.
      Falsification of certification,
        penalty, §47-2864.
Enforcement regulations, §8-802.
  Offenders to be identified on notice of
    violation, §8-811.
  Reporting on number of violations,
    §8-812.
Fines, §8-807.
Hearing examiners, §8-808.
Hearings, §8-805.
Investigations, §8-803.
**Issuance of rules and regulations
  regarding,** §8-810.
Liens, §8-807.
Notice of nuisance, §§8-803, 8-804.
**Offenders to be identified on notice
  of violation,** §8-811.
Policy declaration, §8-801.
Regulatory penalties, §8-807.
Reinspections, §8-806.
Reporting on number of violations,
  §8-812.
**Solid waste nuisance abatement
  fund,** §8-807.01.

LIVERYMAN'S LIEN, §40-101.

LIVESTOCK.
Cruelty to animals.
  General provisions, §§22-1001 to
    22-1013.
    See CRUELTY TO ANIMALS.
Inspector of, §7-179.
Secured transactions.
  When security interest attaches,
    §28:9-204.
Veterinarians, §§3-1208.61 to
  3-1208.65.
  See VETERINARY MEDICINE.

LIVING WAGE ACT, §§2-220.01 to
  2-220.11.
Adjustment of wage rate, §2-220.03.
Applicability of act, §2-220.11.
  Exemptions, §2-220.05.
Citation of act.
  Short title, §2-220.01.

LIVING WAGE ACT —Cont'd
Contracts.
  Contents, §2-220.04.
  Subcontractors.
    Notice to, §2-220.04.
Definitions, §2-220.02.
Enforcement, §2-220.08.
Exemptions, §2-220.05.
Notice, §2-220.06.
  Subcontractors, §2-220.04.
Records, §2-220.07.
Requirements as to payment,
  §2-220.03.
  Waiver of requirements, §2-220.09.
Rulemaking, §2-220.10.
Title of act.
  Short title, §2-220.01.
Waiver of requirements, §2-220.09.

LIVING WILLS, §§7-621 to 7-630.
Competency of declarant, §7-626.
Crimes and offenses, §§7-627, 7-628.
Definitions, §7-621.
Euthanasia, §7-630.
Execution of, §7-622.
Form of declaration, §7-622.
Healthcare decisions.
  General provisions.
    See HEALTHCARE DURABLE
      POWERS OF ATTORNEY.
Heath-care decisions.
  General provisions, §§21-2201 to
    21-2213.
Insurance, as condition of, §7-628.
Intent of declarant, §7-626.
**Limitations and restrictions on
  effect of,** §7-623.
Medical liability, §7-627.
Mercy-killing, §7-630.
**Other legal rights and
  responsibilities, effect on,**
  §§7-629, 7-630.
Persons qualified to execute, §7-622.
Revocation of, §7-624.
Sample declaration, §7-622.
Suicide, compliance not regarded as,
  §7-628.
Terminal condition.
  Defined, §7-621.
  Diagnosis of, §7-625.
**Transfer of patient to care of
  physician able to comply with,**
  §7-627.

LLCS, §§29-801.01 to 29-810.01.
See LIMITED LIABILITY COMPANIES.

LLOYD'S ORGANIZATIONS.
Fire and casualty insurance,
  §31-2502.20a.

LOAN CORPORATIONS.
Regulatory provisions, §§26-1301 to 26-1336.
See TRUST, MORTGAGE AND TITLE CORPORATIONS.

LOAN OFFICERS, §§26-1101 to 26-1121.
See MORTGAGE LENDERS AND BROKERS.

LOAN ORIGINATORS, §§26-1101 to 26-1121.
See MORTGAGE LENDERS AND BROKERS.

LOANS.
Alcoholic beverage licenses.
Manufacturers.
Gifts and loans for manufacturer prohibited, §25-735.
Wholesalers.
Gifts and loans for wholesaler prohibited, §25-736.
Arts, cultural and educational facilities.
Economic assistance to, §§39-401 to 39-405.
Capital access program.
Ineligible loans, §2-1210.05.
Minimum requirements, §2-1210.04.
Sale of enrolled loan on secondary market, §2-1210.05.
Community development, §6-1006.
Community development by financial institutions, §§26-431.01 to 26-431.08.
Complaint for money lent, CivPro Form CA 6.
Completion of capital projects authorized or appropriated prior to October 1, 1983, §1-207.23.
Consumer protection, §§28-3801 to 28-3819.
See CONSUMER PROTECTION.
Corporations.
Powers, §29-303.02.
Direct installment loans.
Consumer credit, §28-3809.
Finance charges on, §§28-3308, 28-3602.
Motor vehicles, §§28-3601 to 28-3603.
Fraternal benefit societies, §31-5317.
Government employer assisted housing program, §§42-2501 to 42-2507.

LOANS —Cont'd
Health professional recruitment program.
Generally, §§7-751.01 to 7-751.16.
See HEALTH PROFESSIONAL RECRUITMENT PROGRAM.
Home purchase assistance fund, §§42-2601 to 42-2626.
See HOME PURCHASE ASSISTANCE FUND.
Housing finance agency providing, §42-2703.07.
Housing production trust fund, §§42-2801 to 42-2804.
Judges.
Accepting gifts or other things of value, CJC Canon 3.13.
Reporting requirements, CJC Canon 3.15.
Life insurance companies, §§31-4705.04, 31-4707.
Loan officers, §§26-1101 to 26-1121.
See MORTGAGE LENDERS AND BROKERS.
Loan originators, §§26-1101 to 26-1121.
See MORTGAGE LENDERS AND BROKERS.
Money lenders, §§26-901 to 26-912.
See MONEY LENDERS.
Mortgage lenders and brokers, §§26-1101 to 26-1121.
See MORTGAGE LENDERS AND BROKERS.
Mortgages and deeds of trust.
General provisions, §§42-804 to 42-820.
See MORTGAGES AND DEEDS OF TRUST.
Low and moderate income families, §§42-2601 to 42-2626.
See HOME PURCHASE ASSISTANCE FUND.
National capital energy fund.
Applications, §8-1778.42.
Approval, §8-1778.43.
National Capital Housing Authority loans by District, §6-102.05.
Nonprofit corporations.
Officers and directors, §29-406.32.
Powers, §29-403.02.
Pawnbrokers, §§47-2884.08 to 47-2884.16.
Points.
Definition of point, §28-3301.
Limitation on points, §28-3301.

LOANS —Cont'd
Poverty lawyer loan repayment assistance program, §§4-1704.01 to 4-1704.07.
See ACCESS TO JUSTICE INITIATIVE PROGRAM.
Productivity Bank Fund, §§1-325.01, 1-325.02.
Public assistance applications, income status for purposes of, §4-205.29.
Public building construction projects, §§10-603 to 10-620.
See PUBLIC BUILDINGS.
Real property wet settlement act, §§42-2401 to 42-2407.
Senior citizens' home repair and improvement program fund, §§42-2201 to 42-2207.
See HOUSING.
Soil and water conservation, §8-1710.
Streetscape loan relief fund, §1-325.191.
Student loans.
Collection of taxes.
Refund offsets.
Applicability of provisions, §47-4436.
Protest and notice, §47-4433.
Right to credit overpayments, §47-4431.
Health professional recruitment program.
Generally, §§7-751.01 to 7-751.16.
See HEALTH PROFESSIONAL RECRUITMENT PROGRAM.
Insurance program, §1-307.01.
Wet settlement act, §§42-2401 to 42-2407.

LOAN SHARKS.
Installment loans.
Repayment unenforceable, §28-3812.
Repayment unenforceable through civil processes, §28-3812.

LOBBYING, §§1-1162.27 to 1-1162.32.
Definitions, §1-1161.01.
Exceptions to registration requirements, §1-1162.28.
Form for registration, §1-1162.29.
Penalties, §1-1162.32.
Prohibited activities, §1-1162.31.
Registration requirements.
Persons required, §1-1162.27.
Reports.
Activities, §1-1162.30.

LOBOTOMIES.
Health care durable powers of attorney, §21-2211.

LOCAL BUSINESSES.
Small and certified business enterprise development and assistance, §§2-218.01 to 2-218.75.
See SMALL AND CERTIFIED BUSINESS ENTERPRISE DEVELOPMENT AND ASSISTANCE.

LOCAL EXCHANGE CARRIERS (LECS).
Telecommunications competition.
See TELECOMMUNICATIONS COMPETITION.

LOCAL GOVERNMENTS.
See POLITICAL SUBDIVISIONS.

LOCAL GRANTS-IN-AID.
Urban renewal transfers not considered to be, §§6-321.07, 6-341.05.

LOCAL ROADS CONSTRUCTION AND MAINTENANCE FUND.
Report on expenditures by mayor, §9-111.31.

LOCAL TRANSPORTATION FUND, §9-111.01a.
Deposits, §50-2607.

LOCK PICKS.
Implements of crime.
Possession of, §22-2501.

LODGING PLACES, §§30-101 to 30-103.
Compensating-use tax, §47-2202.01.
Convention center hotel, §§10-1221.01 to 10-1221.13.
See CONVENTION CENTER HOTEL.
Conversion of rental housing into, §42-3506.01.
Demolition of rental housing in order to construct or expand, §42-3506.02.
Discrimination.
Admission, §47-2902.
Recovery of fine, §47-2904.
Complaints.
Posting of notice in housing accommodation, §2-1403.08.
Defined, §2-1401.02.
Equal opportunities, §2-1402.01.
Unlawful discriminatory practices.
Generally, §2-1402.31.

LODGING PLACES —Cont'd
Fires and fire prevention.
Generally.
See FIRES AND FIRE
PREVENTION.
Fraudulent registration, §22-3224.
Offenses committed in D.C.,
§22-3224.01.
Gross sales tax, §47-2002.02.
**Liability for personal property of
guests, §30-101.**
**Liens on personal property of guests
for amount due, §30-102.**
Sales.
Satisfaction of lien on amounts due by
sale of personal property of guests,
§30-102.
Unclaimed personal property, §30-103.
Well-behaved persons.
Required to serve, §47-2907.

LOITERING.
Blocking passage, §22-1307.
**Minors loitering around business
establishments during school
hours, §32-221.**
Unlawful assembly, §22-1321.

**LONG-ARM STATUTE, §§13-401 to
13-434, CivPro Rule 4.1.**
Business organizations.
Registered agents, §29-104.14.
Conduct.
Personal jurisdiction based on,
§13-423.
Enduring relationship.
Personal jurisdiction based on,
§13-422.
Inconvenient forum, §13-425.
Interpretation of provisions, §13-402.
Minimum contacts.
Factors establishing, §13-423.
**Out-of-District service and
authorization of exercise of
personal jurisdiction, §13-424.**
**Person defined for purposes of,
§13-421.**
Registered agents, §29-104.14.
Relationship to other laws, §13-401.
**Service of process outside District
under, §§13-431 to 13-434.**
Individuals eligible to make service,
§13-432.
Manner of service and proof, §13-431.
Service on designated individuals,
§13-433.
Summons, CivPro Rule 4.
Criminal procedure, CrimPro Rule 4.

LONG-ARM STATUTE —Cont'd
Summons —Cont'd
Domestic relations actions, DomRel
Rule 4.
**Tortuous conduct, personal
jurisdiction based on, §13-423.**

LONG-TERM CARE FACILITIES.
**Board of long-term care
administration, §3-1202.05.**
Nursing homes.
General provisions, §§44-1001.01 to
44-1005.01.
See NURSING HOMES.

**LONG-TERM CARE INSURANCE,
§§31-3601 to 31-3612.**
Definitions, §31-3601.
Denial of claims, §31-3609.01.
Disclosures, §31-3606.
Fines for violations, §31-3612.
Group long-term care insurance.
Associations.
Minimum number of members,
§31-3607.
Defined, §31-3601.
Policies issued in other states,
§31-3604.
Income tax deduction.
Premiums paid for long-term health
care insurance, §47-1803.03.
Incontestability period, §31-3609.
Issuance.
Who may issue, §31-3603.
Nonforfeiture benefits, §31-3610.
Defined, §31-3601.
Reports.
Monthly reports, §31-3608.
Rules and regulations, §31-3611.
Scope of provisions, §31-3602.
Standards, §31-3605.

**LONG-TERM CARE OMBUDSMAN,
§§7-701.01 to 7-706.01.**
**Access to facilities and records,
§§7-702.06, 7-703.01, 7-703.02.**
Access to ombudsman.
Knowingly denying, §7-704.01.
Appointment of, §7-702.02.
Damages, civil action for, §7-705.02.
Definitions, §7-701.01.
Enforcement of provisions, §7-704.01.
Experience requirements, §7-702.03.
Facilities, access to, §7-703.01.
Fines, §7-704.01.
Immunity, §7-702.07.
Injunctions, §7-705.01.
Investigations, §7-702.05.

LONG-TERM CARE OMBUDSMAN
  —Cont'd
Issuance of rules and regulations regarding, §7-706.01.
Penalties, §7-704.01.
Policy declaration, §7-702.01.
Powers and duties of, §7-702.04.
Privacy and confidentiality, §7-702.06.
Records.
  Access to, §7-703.02.
  Privacy and confidentiality, §7-702.06.
Retaliation.
  Filing complaint or providing information, §7-704.01.
Training requirements, §7-702.03.
Vacancy in position, §7-702.02.
Visits to the home of a resident, §7-703.03.

LORTON CORRECTIONAL COMPLEX.
Bureau of prisons.
  Transfer of system to federal authority, §24-101.
Transfer of land to county authorities, §24-101.

LOST INSTRUMENTS.
Documents of title, §28:7-601.

LOTTERIES.
Advertising and promoting, §22-1718.
Arrests for keeping lottery ticket sale premises, §5-115.06.
Child support.
  Interception of prizes for delinquent payments of, §46-224.01.
Common lottery board, §38-194.
Common lottery board fund, §38-195.
Legalized lotteries, §§22-1716 to 22-1718.
Lotteries and daily numbers games operated by and for District.
  Permissible activities, §22-1717.
Lottery and charitable games control board, §§3-1301 to 3-1336.
Permission of sale of tickets on premises, §22-1703.
Possession of tickets for, §§22-1701, 22-1702.
Promotion of, §22-1701.
Sale of tickets for, §§22-1701, 22-1718.

LOTTERY AND CHARITABLE GAMES CONTROL BOARD, §§3-1301 to 3-1336.
Aiding and abetting unauthorized bingo games, raffles, or Monte Carlo Night parties, §3-1332.

LOTTERY AND CHARITABLE GAMES CONTROL BOARD
  —Cont'd
Audits, §3-1319.
Bingo card standards, §3-1330.
Bingo games, §§3-1322 to 3-1332.
Bonds, surety, §3-1304.
  Bingo and raffle licenses, §3-1325.
  Bingo and raffle operators, §3-1325.
  Suppliers, §3-1327.
Budgets and budget estimates, §3-1311.
Charitable Games Division, §3-1310.
Children and minors, gambling by, §§3-1334, 3-1335.
City Lottery and Numbers Game Division, §3-1310.
Committees and subcommittees, §3-1302.
Competitive bid contracts, §3-1336.
Conflicts of interest, §3-1305.
Depositories, §3-1317.
Deputy director, §3-1303.
Designation of responsible individual to utilize receipts of bingos and raffles, §3-1325.
Disclosure, §3-1302.
Divisions within, §3-1310.
Enforcement of provisions, §3-1306.
Establishment of, §3-1301.
Executive director, §3-1303.
Fees.
  Bingo and raffle licenses, §3-1325.
  Suppliers' licenses, §3-1327.
Fingerprinting members, §3-1304.
Forged, counterfeit, or altered tickets, §3-1333.
Fund, §3-1312.
Income tax withholding, §47-1812.08.
Ineligibility.
  Recipients of prizes or purchasers of tickets, §3-1320.
  Suppliers' licenses, persons ineligible for, §3-1328.
Issuance of rules and regulations, §§3-1306, 3-1321, 3-1324.
Licenses.
  Bingo games, §§3-1323, 3-1325.
  Fees for bingos and raffles, §3-1325.
  Monte Carlo night parties, §3-1323.
  Raffles, §§3-1323, 3-1325.
  Sales agents, §3-1315.
  Suppliers, §§3-1326 to 3-1328.
  Suspension or revocation, §3-1331.
Monte Carlo night parties, §§3-1322 to 3-1332.

LOTTERY AND CHARITABLE GAMES CONTROL BOARD —Cont'd

Oaths and affirmations, §§3-1302, 3-1308.

Operational requirements.
Daily numbers games, §3-1314.
Lotteries, §3-1313.

Organization and membership, §3-1301.

Quorum, §3-1302.

Raffles, §§3-1322 to 3-1332.

Records, §§3-1309, 3-1327.

Reports.
Annual report of board, §3-1307.
Sales agents' reports of receipts and transactions, §3-1316.

Rules and regulations.
Issuance, §§3-1306, 3-1321, 3-1324.

Sale of tickets, §3-1315.

Sales agents.
Accounts and reports, §3-1316.
Licenses, §3-1315.

Subpoenas, §3-1308.

Suppliers.
Bingo card standards, §3-1330.
Bingo equipment and supplies, §3-1326.
Bonds, surety, §3-1327.
Fees, §3-1327.
Ineligibility for license, §3-1328.
Licenses, §§3-1326 to 3-1328.
Price lists, §3-1327.
Prohibited activities, §3-1329.
Records, §3-1327.

Testimony, power to take, §3-1308.

Unclaimed prizes, disposition of, §3-1318.

Voting procedures, §3-1302.

Wages and salaries, §3-1301.

LOUISE HOME.

Real property exempt from taxation, §47-1012.

LOW AND MODERATE INCOME RESIDENTS.

Access to justice initiative program, §§4-1701.01 to 4-1704.07.
See ACCESS TO JUSTICE INITIATIVE PROGRAM.

Community development by financial institutions, §§26-431.01 to 26-431.08.

LOW AND MODERATE INCOME RESIDENTS —Cont'd

Home ownership tax abatement and incentives, §§47-3501 to 47-3508.

Homestead housing preservation, §§42-2101 to 42-2111.
See HOMESTEAD HOUSING PRESERVATION.

Housing finance agency.
General provisions, §§42-2701.01 to 42-2706.05.
See HOUSING FINANCE AGENCY.

Housing preservation and protections, §§42-2851.01 to 42-2851.08.

Housing tax credit fund, §§42-2853.01, 42-2853.02.

Internet-related telecommunications.
Franchise agreement.
Furnishing services to digitally-disadvantaged residents, §§34-1731.01 to 34-1731.11.
See INTERNET.

Real property taxes.
Deferral.
Low-income property owners, §47-845.02.
Low-income senior property owners, §47-845.03.
Resale restricted properties.
Assessments, §47-820.02.

Rent supplement program, §6-226.
Capital-based assistance, §6-229.
Tenant-based assistance, §6-228.
Voucher assistance, §6-227.

Senior citizens' home repair and improvement program fund, §§42-2201 to 42-2207.

Sustainable energy, §§8-1773.01 to 8-1774.16.
See SUSTAINABLE ENERGY.

LOWELL SCHOOL.

Real property exempt from taxation, §47-1049.

LOW-EMISSIONS VEHICLE PROGRAM.

Establishment.
Adoption of California emissions standards and compliance requirements, §50-731.

Vehicle not in compliance.
Registering prohibited, §50-732.

LOWER INCOME HOME OWNERSHIP TAX ABATEMENT AND INCENTIVES, §§47-3501 to 47-3508.

Certification of program providing low income rental housing, §47-3507.

Cooperative housing association.
Exemption from real property tax.
Property transfer to qualified homeowner, §47-3503.

Exemption from deed recordation tax, §47-3503.
Administration and enforcement, §47-3504.

Exemption from transfer tax, §47-3503.
Administration and enforcement, §47-3504.

Findings, §47-3501.

Qualification as lower income homeownership household, §47-3502.

Regulations, §47-3508.

Resident management corporations.
Requirements to qualify for exemptions, §47-3506.01.

LOW-INCOME HOUSING PRESERVATION AND PROTECTIONS ACT, §§42-2851.01 to 42-2851.08.

Acceptance of section 8 vouchers required, §42-2851.06.

Assignment of District's first right to purchase, §42-2851.04.

Definitions, §42-2851.02.

District's first right to purchase.
Sale of federally-assisted housing, §42-2851.04.

Enforcement, §42-2851.07.

Inspection of housing accommodations.
Discontinued participation, §42-2851.03.

Intention not to continue participation in federal assistance program.
Notice required upon opting out, §42-2851.03.

Notice of pending expiration date, §42-2851.03.

Notice required upon opting out, §42-2851.03.

Penalties for noncompliance, §42-2851.07.

Qualified areas, determination, §42-2851.08.

LOW-INCOME HOUSING PRESERVATION AND PROTECTIONS ACT —Cont'd

Relocation services to tenants.
Discontinued participation by owner, §42-2851.05.

Sale of federally-assisted housing.
District's first right to purchase, §42-2851.04.

Section 8 assistance considered income for nondiscrimination and minimum income purposes, §42-2851.06.

Short title, §42-2851.01.

LOW-INCOME HOUSING TAX CREDIT, §§47-4801 to 47-4812.

Additional filings, §47-4805.

Compliance, §47-4807.

Definitions, §47-4801.

Efficiency, §47-4809.

Eligibility, §47-4803.

Establishment, §47-4802.

Expiration of, §47-4808.

Look-back requirement, §47-4811.

Recapture, §47-4804.

Rules and regulations, §47-4812.

Transfer, sale, or assignment, §47-4806.

User fees, §47-4810.

LOW-INCOME HOUSING TAX CREDIT FUND, §42-2853.02.

Definitions, §42-2853.01.

LOW-LEVEL RADIOACTIVE WASTE GENERATOR REGULATORY POLICY, §§8-1501 to 8-1506.

LUMP-SUM CREDITS.
Judicial retirement, §11-1563.

LUMP-SUM PAYMENTS.
Disability compensation for public officers and employees, §1-623.31.

Program on work, employment, and responsibility (POWER).
Diversion payments under, §4-205.81.

Public assistance, §§4-205.30, 4-205.33.

LUNATICS.
Hospitalization of persons with mental illness.
General provisions, §§21-501 to 21-592.
See HOSPITALIZATION OF PERSONS WITH MENTAL ILLNESS.

LUNATICS —Cont'd
Incompetent or incapacitated persons.
See INCAPACITATED PERSONS.
Intellectual disabilities, persons with.
See INTELLECTUAL DISABILITIES, PERSONS WITH.
Mental illness, persons with.
See MENTAL ILLNESS, PERSONS WITH.

LUTHER STATUTE ASSOCIATION.
Real property exempt from taxation, §47-1019.

M

MACARTHUR BOULEVARD.
Jurisdiction, §9-1201.01.

MACE AND OTHER SELF-DEFENSE SPRAYS, §§7-2502.12 to 7-2502.14.

MADE IN DC PROGRAM, §§2-1208.31 to 2-1208.35.

MAGISTRATE JUDGES, §11-1732.
Collection and subrogation cases, CivPro Rule 40-III.
Family court and domestic violence unit.
Special rules, §11-1732a.
Intellectual disability proceedings, MentalRetardation Rule 2.
Mediation.
Consent cases, USDistCt LCvR 84.4.
Powers and duties, USDistCt LCrR 57.17, USDistCt LCvR 72.1.
Referrals to magistrate judges.
Civil cases for all purposes, USDistCt LCvR 73.1.
Matters for hearing and recommendation, USDistCt LCrR 59.2, USDistCt LCvR 72.3.
Misdemeanor cases, USDistCt LCrR 58.
Motions and pretrial matters, USDistCt LCrR 59.1, USDistCt LCvR 72.2.

MAIL.
Appeals, federal cases.
Additional time to act after service by, FRAP 26(c).
Briefs and appendices, time deemed filed, FRAP 25(a).
Copy of opinion to parties, FRAP 36.
Notice of appeal, decisions of U.S. tax court, FRAP 13(b).

MAIL —Cont'd
Appeals, federal cases —Cont'd
Service.
Additional time to act after, FRAP 26(c).
Generally, FRAP 25(a).
Notice of filing of notice of appeal as of right, FRAP 3(d).
Papers.
Generally, FRAP 25(c).
Cooperative association voting by, §§29-915, 29-916.
Corporations.
Methods of sending notice and other communications, §29-301.03.
Elections.
Mail-ballot voting, §1-1001.08.
Evidence.
Certified mail return receipts as, §14-506.
Intellectual disabilities, persons with.
Access to mail, §7-1305.05.
Mental illness, persons with.
Hospitalized, §21-561.
Official mail, §§2-701 to 2-710.
Authorized use by elected officials, §2-707.
Definitions, §2-701.
Fine or confinement for violations, §2-708.
Deposit of fines, §2-710.
Unintentional violations, §2-709.
Inspection of agency mail, §2-704.
Marking requirements on envelopes, §2-703.
Mayor and chairman and members of council.
Use of official mail, §2-705.
Official business.
Marking requirements on envelopes, §2-703.
Permissible use by elected officials, §2-706.
Permitted categories, §2-702.
Prohibited use by elected officials, §2-706.
Rules to implement law, §2-704.
Unintentional violations, §2-709.
Use of envelopes to enclosed materials not permitted.
Prohibition, §2-704.
Use of expedited services.
Prohibition, §2-704.
Service of process by mail.
See SERVICE OF PROCESS AND PAPERS.

MAIL —Cont'd
Vacant buildings.
  Notice by mail, §42-3131.05a.

MAIL-IN VOTER REGISTRATION APPLICATION FORMS, §1-1001.07.

MAIL ORDER PHARMACIES.
Prescription drug pricing.
  General provisions, §§48-801.01 to 48-804.51.
    See PRESCRIPTION DRUGS.

MAJORITY, AGE OF.
Child support enforcement, §46-101.

MALICE.
Arson.
  Malicious burning of another's property, §22-303.
Disfigurement, malicious, §22-406.
  Aged persons, offenses committed against.
    Enhanced penalties, §22-3601.
  Crime investigation records.
    Retention of records in open investigations, §5-113.32.
Pleading special matters, CivPro Rule 9.
  Domestic relations actions, DomRel Rule 9.
Water pollution with malicious intent, §22-3318.

MALIGNANT NEOPLASTIC DISEASES.
Prevention and monitoring, §§7-301 to 7-304.
Reporting, §§7-301 to 7-304.

MALL.
Vehicular tunnel under, §10-511.07.

MALPRACTICE.
Attorneys at law.
  Agreements or settlement with client, ProfCond Rule 1.8.
  Censure, suspension or disbarment for cause, §11-2502.
Medical malpractice, §§16-2801 to 16-2841.
  See MEDICAL MALPRACTICE.

MAMMOGRAMS.
Health insurance coverage, §§31-2901 to 31-2903.
  Applicability, §31-2903.
  Definition, §31-2901.

MAMMOGRAMS —Cont'd
Health insurance coverage —Cont'd
  Payable benefits, §31-2902.

MANAGED HEALTH CARE.
Health maintenance organizations.
  General provisions, §§31-3401 to 31-3431.
    See HEALTH MAINTENANCE ORGANIZATIONS.
Hospital and medical services corporations.
  General provisions, §§31-3501 to 31-3524.
    See HOSPITAL AND MEDICAL SERVICES CORPORATIONS.

MANAGEMENT OF INSTITUTIONAL FUNDS.
Prudent investor act.
  See PRUDENT INVESTOR ACT.

MANAGEMENT OF PROPERTY.
National Capital Housing Authority, §6-101.01.

MANAGEMENT SUPERVISORY SERVICE, §§1-609.51 to 1-609.58.

MANDAMUS, DCCtApp Rule 21.
Appeals, federal cases, FRAP 21, USCtApp Rule 21.
Captive insurance companies, §31-3931.20.
Insurance holding companies, §31-714.
Nursing homes.
  Discharge, transfer, or relocation of residents of, §44-1004.02.
Writ abolished, CivPro Rule 81.

MANDARIN ORIENTAL HOTEL PROJECT.
Fee deferral, §2-1217.32.
Real property tax exemptions, §§47-902, 47-1002.
Sales tax exemption, §47-2005.

MANDATE OF COURT OF APPEALS, DCCtApp Rule 41.

MANDATES.
Appeals, federal cases, FRAP 41, USCtApp Rule 41.
  Clerk to insert costs in, FRAP 39(d).
  Contents, FRAP 41(a).
  Effective date, FRAP 41(c).
  Interest on judgment, FRAP 37.
  Petition of party for rehearing en banc not to stay, FRAP 35(c).

MANDATES —Cont'd
Appeals, federal cases —Cont'd
Staying of mandate, FRAP 41(d).
When issues, FRAP 41(b).

MANSLAUGHTER, §22-2105.
Aged persons, offenses committed against.
Enhanced penalties, §22-3601.
Inheritance barred by, §19-320.
Insurance policies, §19-320.

MAPLE SYRUP URINE DISEASE, §§7-831 to 7-840.

MAPS.
Highways, §§9-103.02, 9-103.03.
Purchase and sale of, §1-301.01.
Streets and alleys.
Official map of, §9-203.09.

MARIJUANA.
Boating under the influence.
Articulable suspicion, §48-921.02a.
Consumption in public space prohibited, §48-911.01.
Driving under the influence.
Articulable suspicion, §48-921.02a.
Impairment prohibited, §48-911.01.
Medical marijuana, §§7-1671.01 to 7-1671.13.
See MEDICAL MARIJUANA.
Possession decriminalization, §§48-1201 to 48-1213.
Civil violations, §48-1203.
Adjudications, §48-1211.
Hearings, §48-1213.
Fines for civil violations, §48-1203.
Hearings.
Civil violations, §48-1213.
Identification of offenders.
Providing name and address to police officer, §48-1202.
Notice of violation.
Answer to notice, §48-1212.
Providing name and address to police officer, §48-1202.
One ounce or less.
Possession or transfer without remuneration, §48-1201.
Search warrants.
Articulable suspicion, §48-921.02a.
Substance abuse prevention and treatment fund, §48-1204.
Preemployment limitations on marijuana testing, §§32-931, 32-932.
Search warrants.
Articulable suspicion, §48-921.02a.

MARIJUANA —Cont'd
Youth rehabilitation services, department of.
Limitations on use of positive test, §2-1515.05.

MARINE INSURANCE.
Fire, casualty and marine insurance.
General provisions, §§31-2501.01 to 31-2502.42.
See FIRE AND CASUALTY INSURANCE.
Investments, §§31-1373.01 to 31-1373.12.
See INSURANCE INVESTMENTS.
Prohibitions, §31-2601.01.

MARITAL STATUS DISCRIMINATION.
Prohibition of, §2-1401.01.

MARKETING AGREEMENTS.
Gas stations, §§36-303.01 to 36-303.07.

MARKETS.
Assignment of employees, §37-205.01.
Destination DC marketing fund, §1-325.301.
Disposition of receipts for occupation, §37-205.02.
Eastern market, §§37-101 to 37-113.
See EASTERN MARKET.
Fees for occupation of stalls, §37-205.02.
Municipal fish market, §37-205.01.
Public markets.
Vending regulation, §37-131.06.
Public officers and employees, §37-205.01.

MARRIAGE, §§46-401 to 46-421.
Actions, effect on, §12-104.
Age of consent, parties under, §46-403.
Alienation of affections, abolition of action for, §16-923.
Annulment.
See ANNULMENT OF MARRIAGE.
Antenuptial agreements, §19-113.
Bigamy, §§22-501, 46-401.01.
Blood test.
Privacy and confidentiality, §46-420.
Breach of promise, abolition of action for, §16-923.
Children and minors.
Age of consent, parties under, §46-403.
Guardian of minor, spouse as, §§21-107, 21-109.
Clerk of superior court.
Examination of license applicants by, §46-410.

MARRIAGE —Cont'd

Consent to.

Fraud and deceit, obtained by, §46-403.

Inability to consent due to age or mental capacity, §46-403.

Parent or guardian, consent of, §46-411.

Criminal conversation, abolition of action for, §16-923.

Divorce.

See DIVORCE.

Domestic relations actions generally, DomRel Rules 1 to 406.

See DOMESTIC RELATIONS ACTIONS.

Dower, right of.

See DOWER.

Equal access to marriage, §46-401.

Examination of license applicants by clerk of superior court, §46-410.

Fees.

Authorization to solemnize, registration fee for, §46-406.

License fees, §15-717.

Domestic partners, §32-702.

Fines and civil penalties, §46-421.

License return, failure to make, §46-413.

Fraud and deceit.

Consent obtained by, §46-403.

Guardian.

Consent to marriage by, §46-411.

Spouse of minor as, §§21-107, 21-109.

Incestuous, §§46-401.01, 46-402.

Incompetent or incapacitated persons, §46-403.

Inheritance and estate taxes.

Marriage equality estate tax clarification, §1-301.153.

Judicial decree, void by, §46-402.

Jurisdiction other than District.

Illegal marriage entered into in, §46-405.

License fees, §15-717.

Domestic partners, §32-702.

Licenses.

Clerk of superior court, duties of, §46-410.

Domestic partners, issuance to, §32-702.

Forms, §46-412.

Public inspection of applications, §46-416.

Records, §46-414.

MARRIAGE —Cont'd

Licenses —Cont'd

Return.

Failure to make, §46-413.

Form of, §46-412.

Social security numbers filed with application, §46-416.01.

Officiants, §46-406.

Other jurisdictions, recognition of marriages from, §46-405.01.

Parental consent, §46-411.

Prenuptial agreements, §§19-113, 46-501 to 46-510.

Prior to January 1, 1902, §16-922.

Prison terms, violations, §46-421.

Prohibited marriages, §§46-401.01 to 46-405.

Property rights, §46-601.

Recognition of marriages from other jurisdictions, §46-405.01.

Records.

Licenses, §46-414.

Public inspection of license applications, §46-416.

Vital records, marriage registration, §7-215.

Registration, §7-215.

Religious societies not required to solemnize, §46-406.

Separation of spouses.

See LEGAL SEPARATION.

Solemnization, §46-406.

Statute of frauds.

Agreement made upon consideration of marriage, §28-3502.

Support of spouses.

See SPOUSAL SUPPORT.

Validity of alleged marriage, denial of, §16-921.

Void.

Ab initio, §46-401.01.

Date of decree, from, §46-403.

Judicial decree, by, §46-402.

Premarital agreements, effect on, §46-507.

MARRIAGE AND FAMILY THERAPY.

Board of, §3-1202.17.

Definition of practice of, §3-1201.02.

Licenses, §§3-1208.31, 3-1208.32.

Titles and terms prohibited as misrepresentation without license to practice, §3-1210.03.

MARTIN LUTHER KING, JR.'S BIRTHDAY.

Appeals, federal cases, FRAP 45(a).

MARTIN LUTHER KING, JR.'S BIRTHDAY —Cont'd

Designated holiday, §§1-504, 1-612.02, 28-2701.

Extension of time for performing acts, §28-2701.

MARYLAND.

Dulles International Airport Sanitary Sewer.

Acquisition of land for, §34-2134.

Funeral directors licensed in, §3-415.

Metrorail and metrobus.

Adopted regional system, §§9-1111.01 to 9-1111.17.

See METRORAIL AND METROBUS.

Compact for mass transportation, §§9-1103.01 to 9-1103.07.

Interstate agreement on, §9-1101.01.

Joint state oversight agency, §§9-1109.01 to 9-1109.07.

Washington metropolitan area transit authority compact, §§9-1107.01 to 9-1107.12.

Police departments.

Reciprocal agreements between, §§2-209.01 to 2-209.04.

Sewerage agreement with, §2-207.01.

Temporary assistance for needy families (TANF).

Amounts adjusted to meet local programs, §4-205.51a.

Wastewater and sewage works agreements with, §1-204.87.

Water supply for territory within Washington Suburban Sanitary District, §34-2401.16.

MARYLAND AVENUE.

Railroad sidings, §9-1201.10.

MASKS.

Protests targeting a residence, §§22-2751, 22-2752.

Wearing, §22-3312.03.

MASONS.

Real property exempt from taxation, §47-1045.

MASSACHUSETTS AVENUE AND NAVAL OBSERVATORY, §9-101.11.

MASSAGE PARLORS.

Business licenses, §47-2811.

MASSAGE THERAPY.

Board of, §3-1202.15.

Definition of practice of, §3-1201.02.

MASSAGE THERAPY —Cont'd

Health occupations boards.

General provisions, §§3-1201.01 to 3-1213.01.

See HEALTH OCCUPATIONS BOARDS.

Health occupations licensure, registration or certification, §§3-1205.01 to 3-1205.24.

See HEALTH OCCUPATIONS LICENSURE, REGISTRATION OR CERTIFICATION.

Regulation of licensed massage therapy facilities to be approved by council, §3-1205.24.

Titles and terms prohibited as misrepresentation without license to practice, §3-1210.03.

MASS TRANSIT.

Blocking passage, §22-1307.

Equal access to public conveyances, §7-1002.

Metrorail and metrobus, §§9-1101.01 to 9-1115.04, 35-201 to 35-253.

See METRORAIL AND METROBUS.

MASTECTOMIES.

Reconstructive surgery following mastectomies.

Women's rights to health insurance coverage, §§31-3831 to 31-3837.

MASTER FACILITIES PLANNING AND PROGRAM COORDINATION ADVISORY COMMITTEE, §§10-1031, 10-1032.

MASTERS, CivPro Rule 53.

Appeals, federal cases.

Appointment of, FRAP 48.

Deposit for expenses, CivPro Rule 53-II.

Domestic relations actions, DomRel Rule 53.

Fees, CivPro Rule 53-I, USDistCt LCvR 53.1.

Probate proceedings.

Sale of real property.

Death before January 1, 1981, Probate Rule 18.

MATERIAL WITNESSES.

Release of, §23-1326.

MATERNITY CENTERS.

Criminal background checks for unlicensed personnel, §§44-551 to 44-554.

Health-care facility licensure, §§44-501 to 44-509.

MATERNITY CENTERS —Cont'd
Newborn hearing screening, §§7-851
to 7-855.
Newborn heart screening, §§7-857.01
to 7-857.04.

MATRICULATION
DISCRIMINATION.
Prohibition of, §2-1401.01.

MATTRESSES.
Business licenses, §47-2818.
Manufacture, renovation, sale,
§§8-501 to 8-508.
Administration of chapter, §8-506.
Definitions, §8-501.
Guaranty by manufacture.
Defense to prosecution of dealer,
§8-504.
Investigators, §8-507.
Label requirements, §8-503.
Violations, penalties, §8-505.
Prosecution of manufacturers outside
District, §8-504.
Seizure and destruction of mattresses,
§8-508.
Unlawful acts, §8-502.
Violations, penalties, §8-505.
Violations, penalties, §8-505.

MAYHEM, §22-406.
Aged persons, offenses committed
against.
Enhanced penalties, §22-3601.
Assault with intent to commit,
§22-402.
Crime investigation records.
Retention of records in open
investigations, §5-113.32.
Felony murder, §22-2101.

MAYOR.
Accounting supervision and control,
§1-204.49.
Additional power rather than
limitation of power.
Statutes construed as conveying,
§1-301.05.
Airspace, use of, §10-1121.02.
Alcoholic beverage license fees.
Alteration.
Proposal by mayor, §25-502.
Alcoholic beverages tax, §§25-907,
25-908.
Alcoholics, rehabilitation of,
§§24-603, 24-609, 24-613.
Alternative fuel technology report,
§50-704.01.

MAYOR —Cont'd
Asbestos contractors.
Responsibilities regarding, §8-111.12.
Assisted living residences.
Appeals from actions of mayor,
§44-112.01.
Rulemaking, §44-113.01.
Automated data processing
responsibilities, §2-213.02.
Bicycle registry.
Establishment, §50-1611.
Bond, prohibited from being surety
on, §1-317.01.
Borrowing funds for capital
projects, §47-335.01.
Bridges.
Control of, §9-301.
Budget submissions by, §47-318.01.
Bureau of traffic adjudication.
Study on improving quality of
adjudications, §2-1831.18.
Capital funds.
Expending on operating expenses,
prohibition, §1-301.77.
Capital projects money.
Borrowing funds for capital projects,
§47-335.01.
Use for operating expenses, limitation,
§1-301.77.
Capitol grounds.
Responsibilities regarding, §10-503.11.
Casey Mansion.
Designated as official residence,
§1-331.10.
Cemetery purposes.
Licensing of lands for, §43-115.
Charitable institutions.
Responsibilities regarding, §§44-709,
44-710.
Charitable solicitations.
Powers and duties regarding,
§44-1702.
Chief financial officer.
Appointment, §1-204.24b.
Office of chief financial officer
generally.
See CHIEF FINANCIAL OFFICER.
Removal, §1-204.24c.
Child care facilities.
Powers and duties regarding, §7-2036.
Supplemental payments by Mayor,
§4-404.01.
Child welfare and juvenile justice
behavioral health infrastructure.
Family resource guide, §2-1517.51.
Reports, §2-1517.52.

MAYOR —Cont'd
Cigarette sales below cost.
Rulemaking authority, §28-4527.
Clinical laboratories advisory board,
§44-206.
Commissioning of officers by,
§1-301.76.
Community development program.
Annual preparation and submission of,
§6-1002.
Compensation, determination.
Mayor and council compensation
advisory committee, §§1-611.51 to
1-611.57.
See MAYOR AND COUNCIL
COMPENSATION ADVISORY
COMMITTEE.
**Comprehensive Plan for the
National Capital,** §§1-306.01 to
1-306.07.
Housing linkage requirement of the
housing element, §§1-306.31 to
1-306.45.
Condominium provisions.
Administration of, §42-1904.12.
**Consumer credit service
organizations.**
Rules and regulations, §28-4608.
Consumer protection.
Administrative enforcement, §28-3815.
Customer service operations unit,
§§1-327.31 to 1-327.34.
**Deputy Mayor for planning and
economic development.**
Grant-making authority, §1-328.04.
**Deputy Mayor for public safety and
justice.**
Report on felony crime statistics,
§1-301.191.
**District of Columbia corporation,
officer of,** §1-103.
Drivers' licenses.
Authorized to issue or renew,
§50-1401.01.
Drug addicts.
Examination of, §24-703.
Drug-related evictions.
Responsibilities regarding, §42-3607.
Early intervention program.
Rulemaking, §7-863.04.
E-commerce companies.
Qualified social electronic commerce
companies tax abatements.
Mayor, delegation of authority,
§47-1818.08.

MAYOR —Cont'd
**Economic development zone
incentives.**
Authority to issue rules regarding,
§6-1506.
Election of, §§1-204.21, 1-1001.08.
Designating employee to solicit, accept
or receive contributions while on
leave, §1-1171.02.
Emergency executive order, §§7-2304
to 7-2308.
Emergency management.
Recommendation of legislation
regarding, §7-2305.
Energy efficiency standards.
Enforcement, §8-1771.05.
Energy reduction plan, §8-1777.01.
Execution of laws.
Responsibilities regarding, §1-301.76.
Executive service.
Subordinate agency heads in the
executive service.
Mayoral nominees, §1-523.01.
Expenditure estimates by, §47-311.
Expenditures.
Approval of, §1-333.10.
Fee-setting authority, §§1-301.74,
1-301.75.
**Film DC economic incentive grant
fund.**
Rulemaking, §2-1204.12.
Financial duties of, §§1-204.48,
1-204.49, 47-318.01 to 47-318.05a.
Financial reports by, §47-310.01.
Fish and game powers.
Delegation of, §22-4332.
**Fund-type accounting
responsibilities,** §47-375.
Government attorneys.
Mayor's office of legal counsel,
§1-608.51a.
Grants for planning mission,
§1-328.02.
Rules, authority to implement,
§1-328.02a.
Green buildings.
Compliance review, §6-1451.04.
Exemptions, granting, §6-1451.10.
Rulemaking, §6-1451.11.
Gross sales tax, §§47-2023, 47-2024.
Health care financing fund.
Grants from, §7-1932.
Health occupations boards.
Duties regarding, §3-1203.02.
Highways, control of, §§9-101.01,
9-107.03.

MAYOR —Cont'd
Highway signs.
Mayoral authority to install, §38-3101.
Highway trust fund expenditures.
Report, §9-111.31.
Home improvement contractors.
Bonding requirements, §47-2883.06.
Homeless services.
Policies and procedures, §4-754.56.
Home purchase assistance fund,
§§42-2603, 42-2604.
Honoraria, §1-321.01.
Hospitalization of persons with
mental illness, proceedings
instituted by, §21-581.
Human papillomavirus vaccination.
Rules, authority to promulgate,
§7-1651.05.
Impact statements, §1-301.61.
Income taxes, §§47-1812.01,
47-1812.04, 47-1816.03.
Inheritance and estate taxes,
§§47-3704 to 47-3721.
Inspector general.
Appointment, §1-301.115a.
Investigation of municipal matters,
§5-1021.
Judiciary square detention facility
construction, §24-1203.
Libraries.
Appropriations for expenses.
Authorized to seek, §39-106.
Gifts.
Allowed to accept, §39-101.
Life and health insurance guaranty
association.
Powers and duties regarding,
§31-5408.
Local roads construction and
maintenance fund expenditures.
Report, §9-111.31.
Mayor and council compensation
advisory committee, §§1-611.51 to
1-611.57.
See MAYOR AND COUNCIL
COMPENSATION ADVISORY
COMMITTEE.
Medical assistance program,
§§1-307.02 to 1-307.06.
Metropolitan police.
Duties of mayor regarding, §5-101.03.
Powers regarding, §5-127.01.
Special detail of privates, §5-133.03.
Metrorail and metrobus.
Duties regarding.
See METRORAIL AND
METROBUS.

MAYOR —Cont'd
Minimum wages, §§32-1005 to 32-1007.
See MINIMUM WAGES.
Motor vehicle financing.
See MOTOR VEHICLE FINANCING.
Motor vehicle registration.
See MOTOR VEHICLE
REGISTRATION.
Motor vehicle safety responsibility,
§§50-1301.03, 50-1301.04.
National Capital Housing Authority.
Powers regarding, §1-202.02.
911 system.
Unauthorized use, §1-327.56a.
Nominees put forward by, §1-523.01.
Notaries public.
Appointment of, §1-1201.
Nursing home residents.
Transfer or discharge of, §§44-1003.05
to 44-1003.09.
Oaths and affirmations.
Authority to administer, §§1-301.22,
5-1021.
Office of cable television, film,
music, and entertainment,
§§34-1252.01 to 34-1252.03.
Office of Medicaid operations
reform, §§4-204.11 to 4-204.16.
Office of unified communications,
§§1-327.51 to 1-327.57.
Offices.
Abolition of and changes to, §1-301.69.
Operating expenses.
Capital projects money not to be used
for, §1-301.77.
Overdose data, duties regarding,
§7-403.
Paint stewardship.
Mayor's responsibilities, §8-233.04.
Rules, §8-233.06.
Pardons and respites.
Power to grant, §1-301.76.
Parking.
Powers regarding, §50-2603.
Pawnbrokers.
Attorney for, §47-2884.03.
Performance based budgets,
§47-308.01.
Capital asset replacement schedule,
§47-308.04.
Performance accountability reporting,
§47-308.03.
Relevant performance measures,
§47-308.02.
Permit review, §1-306.06.
Personal property taxes, §47-1535.

MAYOR —Cont'd

Pharmacists and pharmacies.
Duties regarding, §47-2885.18.

Physical fitness, health and nutrition, mayor's council, §§7-121 to 7-126.
Administrative support, §7-123.
Executive committee, §7-126.
Fitness fund, §7-125.
Fitness report, §§7-122, 7-124.
Meetings, §7-121.
Membership, §7-121.
Mission, §7-121.
Powers and duties, §7-122.

Planning and planning implementation grants, §1-328.02.
Deputy Mayor for planning and economic development, grant-making authority, §1-328.04.
Rules, authority to implement, §1-328.02a.

Planning functions, §1-204.23.

Police and firefighters medical care reimbursement.
Duty to promulgate rules and regulations for, §5-605.

Police and firefighters retirement and disability.
Duties regarding, §§5-721, 5-724.

Political contributions.
Designating employee to solicit, accept or receive contributions while on leave, §1-1171.02.

Powers and duties generally, §§1-204.22, 1-301.01.
Additional governmental powers, §1-301.86b.

Prison work release program.
Responsibilities regarding, §§24-241.08, 24-241.09.

Property and liability insurance guaranty association.
Powers and duties of mayor regarding, §31-5507.

Public assistance.
Duties and powers regarding, §§4-202.02, 4-202.03, 4-202.05.

Public lands.
Exchanges, §§10-903, 10-904.
Sales, §10-801.

Public safety and justice.
Office of deputy mayor, §1-301.191.

Public schools, seal, §38-155.

Public Service Commission not affecting authority of, §34-809.

Public welfare institutions.
Children and minors in, §§4-114, 4-302.

MAYOR —Cont'd

Radon contractor proficiency.
Duties, §§28-4201 to 28-4203.

Real estate tax sales.
Regulations, §47-1321.

Real property taxes, §47-839.
Assessments.
Duties regarding, §47-821.
Special assessments, §§47-1203, 47-1206.

Receptions for eminent persons, §1-333.09.

Recordation tax.
See RECORDATION TAX.

Recorder of deeds, §42-1218.

Recreation board.
Relationship to, §10-223.

Recycling.
Construction and demolition waste recycling accountability.
Rules and regulations, §8-1074.

Regulations.
Power to enforce.
Building regulations, §1-303.04.
Dogs, keeping and leashing of, §1-303.41.
Firearms, explosives and weapons, §1-303.43.
Police regulations, §1-303.01.
Protection of life, health, and property, §1-303.03.
Publication, §1-303.02.

Residence.
Casey mansion.
Designated as official residence, §1-331.10.
Mayor's official residence commission, §§1-331.01 to 1-331.05.

Retail development incentives.
Retail priority areas, designation of, §2-1217.73.
Rules.
Promulgation of rules and regulations, §2-1217.83.

School buildings and grounds.
Power to raze, §38-156.

Streetcar plan, §9-1208.01.

Streets and alleys.
Closing, §9-202.02.
Opening, extending, widening, or straightening, §9-203.02.

Subpoena powers, §1-301.21.

Tax court.
Referrals to, §47-3309.

Telegraph and telephone companies.
Powers and duties regarding, §§34-1911.01, 34-1921.01.

MAYOR —Cont'd

Temporary assistance for needy families.

Grandparent caregiver subsidies, §§4-251.01 to 4-251.07.

Traffic.

Authority to make rules regarding, §50-2201.03.

Transportation infrastructure improvement GARVEE bonds.

Authority of mayor, §9-107.55.

Closing documents, §9-107.57.

Financing documents, §9-107.57.

Issuance, §9-107.56.

Trash collection noise violations, §8-731.

Tunnel under Capitol grounds and botanic gardens, §10-511.03.

Unclaimed property.

Determination of claims regarding, §41-125.

Issuance of rules regarding, §41-138.

Unemployment compensation, §51-127.

Unsafe structures or excavations.

Power to take immediate action regarding, §6-801.

Urban forest preservation.

Responsibilities of mayor, §8-651.03.

Vacancy.

Filling, §1-204.21.

Vacant and abandoned property.

Special disposal procedures for certain properties.

Duties of mayor, §§10-831 to 10-839.

Wages and salaries, §§1-204.21, 1-611.09.

Wastewater disposal system.

Authority to establish, §8-105.06.

Water supply and waterworks.

Powers regarding, §§1-204.88, 34-2401.01 to 34-2401.03, 34-2401.26.

Weights and measures.

Power to remove device from service, §37-201.33.

Woodrow Wilson bridge and tunnel compact, §9-1115.01.

Workers' compensation.

See WORKERS' COMPENSATION.

Workforce housing production program.

Report on, §6-1061.02.

Work-related travel of government employees.

Report from Mayor to Council, §50-211.07.

MAYOR —Cont'd

Youth advisory council, §§2-1561 to 2-1564, 2-1565.01 to 2-1565.06.

Youth behavioral health epidemiology reports.

Citation of provisions, §2-1517.01.

Definitions, §2-1517.02.

Youth leadership institute, §§2-1571 to 2-1574.

Youth rehabilitation services, department of.

Powers, §2-1515.07.

Zoning powers and duties, §6-661.01.

Inclusionary zoning, §§6-1041.03, 6-1041.07.

Reports, §6-1041.09.

MAYOR AND COUNCIL COMPENSATION ADVISORY COMMITTEE, §§1-611.51 to 1-611.57.

Composition and term, §1-611.52.

Council action, §1-611.57.

Duties, §1-611.53.

Establishment, §1-611.51.

Meetings and hearings, §1-611.55.

Powers, §1-611.56.

Reports, §1-611.54.

MAYOR'S OFFICIAL RESIDENCE COMMISSION, §§1-331.01 to 1-331.05.

Compensation, §1-331.04.

Composition, §1-331.04.

Contracts for funding, §1-331.04.

Contributions and grants, §1-331.04.

Definitions, §1-331.02.

Duties, §1-331.03.

Establishment, §1-331.03.

Findings, §1-331.01.

Meeting, quorum, §1-331.04.

MAYOR'S YOUTH LEADERSHIP INSTITUTE, §§2-1571 to 2-1574.

Definitions, §2-1571.

Eligibility, §2-1573.

Established, §2-1572.

Rules, §2-1574.

MEADOWOOD FARM LAND EXCHANGE.

Lorton correctional complex, §24-101.

MEASLES.

Immunization of school students, §§38-501 to 38-508.

Interstate compact on educational opportunity for military children.

Time to obtain immunizations, §49-1101.05.

MEASURING DEVICES, §§37-201.01 to 37-201.33.
See WEIGHTS AND MEASURES.

MEAT AND MEAT PRODUCTS.
Sales.
Weights, measures and markets, §37-201.19.

MECHANIC'S LIENS, §§40-301.01 to 40-307.03.
Artisan's lien, §§40-307.01 to 40-307.03.
Commencement of suit, §40-303.13.
Discharge of, §§40-303.15 to 40-303.18.
Payment of amount claimed by owner, §40-303.16.
Prior to bringing of suit, §40-303.17.
Satisfaction, entry of, §40-303.15.
Sureties as party to suit, §40-303.18.
Enforcement, §40-303.08.
Artisan's lien, §§40-307.02, 40-307.03.
Equity, bill in, §40-307.03.
Sale, by. See within this heading, "Sales associated with."
Ground subject to, determining extent of, §40-303.14.
Horizontal property regimes, §42-2025.
Limitation of actions.
Subcontractor's lien, commencement of suit, §40-303.13.
Payment of amount claimed by owner, §40-303.16.
Priority of lien, §40-303.07.
Prompt payment, private contractors and subcontractors.
Prohibition on requiring waiver of right to claim mechanics' lien, §27-134.
Regulations, promulgation, §40-303.20a.
Sales associated with, §§40-303.09 to 40-303.12.
Artisan's lien, §40-307.02.
Decree of sale, §40-303.09.
Deficiency of, §40-303.20.
Distribution of proceeds, §40-303.11.
More than one building, §40-303.12.
Priority of satisfaction out of proceeds, §40-303.10.
Regulation, §40-303.20a.
Satisfaction of claim, entry of, §40-303.15.
Subcontractor's liens, §§40-303.01 to 40-303.20a.
See SUBCONTRACTOR'S LIENS.
Sureties as party to suit, §40-303.18.

MECHANIC'S LIENS —Cont'd
Wharves and lots, §40-305.01.
MEDIA COVERAGE.
Attorneys at law.
Trial publicity, ProfCond Rule 3.6.
Superior court proceedings, CivPro Rule 203, CrimPro Rule 53.
Child abuse and neglect proceedings, NeglectProc Rule 45.
Juvenile proceedings, JuvProc Rule 53.
United States District Court proceedings, USDistCt LCrR 53.1.1, USDistCt LCvR 83.1.
Nonparties to case.
Application for relief in a criminal case, USDistCt LCrR 57.6.

MEDIA RIGHTS TO STORY.
Attorney drafting instruments giving attorney rights, ProfCond Rule 1.8.

MEDIATION.
Admissibility of evidence, §16-4203.
Adoption.
Post-adoption contact agreements, §4-361.
Appeals, federal cases.
Docketing of appeals, USCtApp HPIP Rule IV(d).
Mediation program, USCtApp Appx I.
Applicability of provisions, §16-4213.
Arbitration.
General provisions, §§16-4401 to 16-4432.
See ARBITRATION.
Attorneys at law.
Lawyer serving as a third-party neutral, ProfCond Rule 2.4.
Confidentiality of information, §16-4207.
Confidential mediation statements, USDistCt LCvR 84.6.
Medical malpractice, §16-2827.
Proceedings, USDistCt LCvR 84.9.
Conflicts of interest, §16-4208.
Definitions, §16-4201.
International commercial mediation, §16-4210.
Discovery, §16-4203.
Discrimination, complaints of, §2-1403.04.
Electronic signatures in global and national commerce, relationship, §16-4211.
Employment agencies, §32-413.
Foreclosure, residential mortgages, §42-815.02.

MEDIATION —Cont'd
General mediation order, CivPro
   Form CA 117.
Homeless services.
  Providers.
    Resolution of disputes with clients,
     §4-754.39.
International commercial mediation,
   §16-4210.
Judges.
  Acting as mediators, CJC Canon 3.9.
Medical malpractice, §§16-2821 to
   16-2827.
  See MEDICAL MALPRACTICE.
Merit system, §1-606.06.
Participation, §16-4209.
Police complaints, office of, §5-1110.
Privilege against disclosure,
   §16-4203.
  Exceptions, §16-4205.
  Waiver and preclusion, §16-4204.
Scope of provisions, §16-4202.
Uniformity in application and
   construction, §16-4212.
United States District Court.
  See UNITED STATES DISTRICT
    COURT FOR THE DISTRICT OF
    COLUMBIA.

MEDICAID.
Disability services, department on.
  Medicaid services, §7-761.07.
District of Columbia medical
   assistance program, §§1-307.02 to
   1-307.06.
  Council review of plan Federal
    financial assistance under Title
    XIX, §1-307.02.
Expansion of eligibility.
  Program to be established, §4-205.80.
Financing.
  Medicaid and special education reform
    fund, §§4-204.51 to 4-204.56.
Fraud and deceit by service
   providers, §§4-801 to 4-805.
Health-care assistance
   reimbursement, §§4-601 to 4-609.
  Compromises, §4-605.
  Definitions, §4-601.
  Enforcement of rights, §4-604.
  Issuance of rules, §4-608.
  Liens, §4-607.
  Notice, §4-606.
  Preservation of existing rights, §4-609.
  Right to reimbursement, §§4-602,
    4-609.
  Setoffs, §4-603.

MEDICAID —Cont'd
Health-care assistance
   reimbursement —Cont'd
  Settlements, §4-605.
  Waiver of rights, §4-604.
Hospital assessments.
  Expiration of provisions, §44-638.
Hospital inpatient rate supplement
   2016-2017, §§44-662.11 to 44-662.18.
  Definitions, §44-662.11.
  Federal determination of assessment,
    §44-662.16.
  Hospital fund, §44-662.12.
  Hospital provider fee, §§44-662.13,
    44-662.14.
  Multi-hospital systems, closure,
    merger and new hospitals,
    §44-662.15.
  Quarterly notice and collection of fees
    and payments, §44-662.14.
  Rules, §44-662.17.
  Sunset provision, §44-662.18.
  Suspension and termination of
    assessment, §44-662.16.
Hospital outpatient supplemental
   payment.
  Expiration of provisions, §44-659.
Hospital outpatient supplemental
   payment 2016-2017, §§44-661.11 to
   44-661.19.
  Definitions, §44-661.11.
  Hospital provider fee, §§44-661.13,
    44-661.14.
  Hospital provider fee fund, §44-661.12.
  Multi-hospital systems, closure,
    merger and new hospitals,
    §44-661.17.
  Outpatient hospital access payments,
    §44-661.15.
  Quarterly notice and collection of fees
    and payments, §44-661.16.
  Rules, §44-661.18.
  Sunset provision, §44-661.19.
Medicaid and special education
   reform fund, §§4-204.51 to
   4-204.56.
Nursing facilities reimbursement,
   §§4-204.61, 4-204.62.
Office of Medicaid operations
   reform, §§4-204.11 to 4-204.16.
  Citation of part, §4-204.11.
  Defined terms, §4-204.12.
  Director.
   Defined, §4-204.12.
  Effective date, §4-204.16.
  Establishment, §4-204.13.

MEDICAID —Cont'd
Office of Medicaid operations reform
—Cont'd
Powers and duties, §4-204.14.
Purposes, §4-204.14.
Rules, §4-204.15.
Short title, §4-204.11.
Pharmaceutical education program establishment act of 2008.
Education of prescribers in publicly funded, contracted or subsidized health-care programs, §§48-843.01 to 48-843.04.
Powers of attorney, §21-2114.
Public assistance, §§4-204.05, 4-204.05a.
Service provider fraud, §§4-801 to 4-805.
Spousal maintenance needs allowance, §1-307.02a.
Telehealth reimbursement.
Medicaid reimbursement, §31-3863.

MEDICAID AND SPECIAL EDUCATION REFORM FUND, §§4-204.51 to 4-204.56.
Annual report, §4-204.56.
Definitions, §4-204.52.
Distribution, §4-204.55.
Establishment, §4-204.53.
Purposes, §4-204.54.
Short title, §4-204.51.

MEDICAID ELIGIBILITY EXPANSION ACT OF 2001, §4-205.80.

MEDICAL AND DENTAL COLLEGES, §§38-1401 to 38-1419.
Definitions, §38-1419.
Failure to register, §38-1403.
Financial assistance for, §§38-1411 to 38-1419.
Definitions, §38-1419.
Grants from secretary of education.
Amount, §38-1412.
Applications, §§38-1413, 38-1417.
Authorized to make, §38-1412.
Payment, §38-1415.
Regulations, §38-1414.
Payments by mayor to private medical dental colleges, §§38-1416, 38-1418.
Purpose of subchapter, §38-1411.
Grants from Secretary of Education, §§38-1412 to 38-1415.
Injunctions, §38-1404.
Payment of grants to, §§38-1415 to 38-1418.

MEDICAL AND DENTAL COLLEGES
—Cont'd
Permits, §§38-1401, 38-1402.
Registration, §§38-1401 to 38-1405.
Repeal of provisions and charters for inconsistency, §38-1405.

MEDICAL AND GERIATRIC PAROLE, §§24-461 to 24-468.
Authority of Board of Parole over, §24-463.
Criteria for geriatric release, §24-465.
Criteria for medical release, §24-464.
Definitions, §24-461.
Exceptions to eligibility, §24-467.
Exclusion of conditions present at time of sentence, §24-462.
Parole.
General provisions, §§24-401c to 24-468.
See PAROLE.
Public assistance, eligibility for, §24-466.
Suspension of sentence, §24-468.

MEDICAL ASSISTANCE.
Child and family services agency, ordered by, §4-1303.05.
Denial due to inability to pay, §47-2716.
Disability compensation, as part of, §1-623.03.
District of Columbia medical assistance program, §§1-307.02 to 1-307.06.
Fire departments, §5-404.
Good Samaritans act, §§7-401 to 7-403.
Inability to pay, denial due to, §47-2716.
Intellectual disabilities, persons with, §7-1305.05.
Limitations of liability for providing, §§7-401, 7-402.
Medicaid.
Health-care assistance reimbursement, §§4-601 to 4-609.
See MEDICAID.
Service provider fraud, §§4-801 to 4-805.
Mental illness, persons with, hospitalized, §21-562.
Police and firefighters medical care reimbursement, §§5-601 to 5-609.
Appropriations, §5-609.
Compromises, §5-606.
Definitions, §5-601.

MEDICAL ASSISTANCE —Cont'd
Police and firefighters medical care reimbursement —Cont'd
Effect on other recovery rights, §5-607.
Enforcement of right to recover costs, §5-603.
Liens to enforce right to recover costs, §5-604.
Mayor's duty to promulgate rules and regulations for, §5-605.
Retroactivity, §5-608.
Third person, District's right to recover costs from, §5-602.
Waiver or release of claims, §5-606.
Public officers and employees, §1-620.07.
Rates adjustment, §47-2717.
United States Park Police, §5-204.
Workers' compensation, §32-1507.

MEDICAL CONSENT.
Authorization for minor by adult caregiver, §16-4901.

MEDICAL DIRECTIVES.
Healthcare decisions.
General provisions.
See HEALTHCARE DURABLE POWERS OF ATTORNEY.
Heath-care decisions.
General provisions, §§21-2201 to 21-2213.
Hospital discharge planning, §§21-2231.01 to 21-2231.05.
Mental health.
Declaration of advance instructions, §7-1231.06.
Natural death act generally, §§7-621 to 7-630.
See LIVING WILLS.

MEDICAL EXAMINATIONS.
Adoption proceedings, Adoption Rule 35.
Child abuse and neglect, §4-1301.08.
Communicable diseases.
Persons believed to be carriers of, §7-135.
Delinquent minors, §16-2315.
Disability compensation claims, §1-623.20.
Discovery, CivPro Rule 35.
Domestic relations actions, DomRel Rule 35.
Drug abuse, §§24-703, 24-705, 24-710.
Hospitalization of persons with mental illness.
See HOSPITALIZATION OF PERSONS WITH MENTAL ILLNESS.

MEDICAL EXAMINATIONS —Cont'd
Juvenile proceedings, JuvProc Rule 110.
Transfer for criminal prosecution, JuvProc Rule 108.
Marriage license applicants, §46-410.
No-fault motor vehicle insurance, §31-2411.
Physical or mental examination of person.
Adoption proceedings, Adoption Rule 35.
Attorneys at law.
Incompetent or incapacitated attorneys, DCBar Rule XI, USDistCt LCrR 57.30, USDistCt LCvR 83.19.
Civil cases, CivPro Rule 35.
Criminal cases, CrimPro Rule 16.
Delinquent minors, JuvProc Rule 16.
Domestic relations actions, DomRel Rule 35.
Insanity defense, CrimPro Rule 12.2.
Juvenile proceedings, JuvProc Rule 110.
Transfer for criminal prosecution, JuvProc Rule 108.
Police and firefighters retirement and disability, §5-721.
Preliminary examination of criminal defendant, CrimPro Rule 5.
Delinquent minors, JuvProc Rule 10.
Program on work, employment, and responsibility (POWER), §4-205.74.
Psychiatric examinations.
Court-ordered, §7-1204.01.
Sexual psychopaths, §22-3806.
Student health care, §§38-602 to 38-605.

MEDICAL EXAMINERS, §§5-1401 to 5-1419.
Anatomical gifts.
Chief medical examiner.
Cooperation with procurement organizations, §7-1531.21.
Decedent whose body is under jurisdiction of.
Facilitation of anatomical gift from, §7-1531.22.
Appointments, §5-1402.
Autopsies, §§5-1409, 5-1410, 5-1414.
Child abuse and neglect reports, §4-1321.02.
Child death.
Reports, §4-1371.12.

MEDICAL EXAMINERS —Cont'd
Confidential medical records.
Issuance of subpoena by chief medical examiner, §5-1407.
Coroner's former duties, continuation of, §5-1404.
Court order.
Autopsies performed under, §5-1414.
Crimes and offenses.
Failure to notify of deaths, §5-1406.
Evidence.
Records as, §5-1413.
Taking possession of, §5-1408.
Expenses of delivery of body, §5-1411.
Fees, §5-1412.
Impaired driving, blood and urine testing related to.
Responsibilities of chief medical examiner, §5-1419.
Investigations of deaths by, §5-1405.
Issuance of death certificate.
No removal of tissue or embalming until after, §43-125.
Notice of investigation of deaths, §5-1406.
Pathologist other than medical examiner performing autopsy, §5-1410.
Personnel, services, and facilities, §5-1403.
Possession of evidence and property, taking, §5-1408.
Qualifications of, §5-1402.
Records, §§5-1410, 5-1412, 5-1413.
Release of body by, §5-1411.
Reports, §§5-1408, 5-1412.
Child death, §4-1371.12.
Subpoenas for confidential medical records.
Issuance by chief medical examiner, §5-1407.
Transfer of personnel, property and records.
Office of chief medical examiner, §5-1416.
Wages and salaries, §5-1402.

MEDICAL EXPENSES.
Crime victims' compensation, VictComp Rule 24.
Request for information, VictComp Rule 13.
Opportunity accounts.
Emergency withdrawals for expenses, §1-307.69.
Generally, §§1-307.61 to 1-307.74.

MEDICAL EXPENSES —Cont'd
Opportunity accounts —Cont'd
Use to pay emergency medical costs, §1-307.68.

MEDICAL FACILITIES.
Clinical laboratories.
General provisions, §§44-201 to 44-213.
See CLINICAL LABORATORIES.
Health care facilities.
Generally.
See HEALTH CARE FACILITIES.
Health maintenance organizations.
General provisions, §§31-3401 to 31-3431.
See HEALTH MAINTENANCE ORGANIZATIONS.
Hospitals.
See HOSPITALS.
State health planning and development agency.
General provisions, §§44-401 to 44-421.
See STATE HEALTH PLANNING AND DEVELOPMENT AGENCY.

MEDICAL LABORATORIES AND MEDICAL LABORATORY TECHNICIANS.
Definition of practice, §3-1201.02.
Health occupations licensure, registration or certification, §§3-1205.01 to 3-1205.24.
Qualifications for licensure, §3-1207.61.
Exemption, §3-1207.63.
Transition provision, §3-1207.64.
Waiver, §3-1207.62.
Titles and terms prohibited as misrepresentation without license to practice, §3-1210.03.

MEDICAL LEAVE.
Domestic partner benefits, §§32-701 to 32-710.
See DOMESTIC PARTNER BENEFITS.
Family and medical leave.
General provisions, §§32-501 to 32-517.
See FAMILY AND MEDICAL LEAVE.

MEDICAL LIABILITY CAPTIVE INSURANCE AGENCY, §§1-307.81 to 1-307.95.
Administration of agency, §1-307.84.

MEDICAL LIABILITY CAPTIVE INSURANCE AGENCY —Cont'd

Advisory council, §1-307.85.
  Liability for obligations of agency, §1-307.89.
Authority, §1-307.83.
Authority of the agency, §1-307.85.
Captive manager, §1-307.84.
  Liability for obligations of agency, §1-307.89.
Captive trust fund, §§1-307.82, 1-307.91.
Coverage offered, §1-307.90.
Definitions, §1-307.81.
Established, §1-307.82.
Exemption from certain laws, §1-307.92.
Exemption from procurement and merit personnel laws, §1-307.92.
Financial report, §1-307.86.
Free clinic captive insurance company dissolution, §1-307.94.
Fund, §1-307.91.
Inspection and examination by commissioner, §1-307.86.
Insurance coverage, §1-307.90.
Liability for obligations of agency, §1-307.89.
Limit of agency's liability, §1-307.82.
Personnel of district to be available, §1-307.83.
Plan of operation, §§1-307.86, 1-307.87.
Purpose, §1-307.82.
Risk officer.
  Administration of agency, §1-307.84.
  Advisory council, §1-307.85.
  Annual report, §1-307.88.
  Liability for obligations of agency, §1-307.89.
Rules for implementation of provisions, §1-307.93.
Scope of authority, §1-307.83.
Short title, §1-307.95.
Trust fund, §1-307.91.

MEDICALLY UNDERSERVED AREAS.

Health professional recruitment program, §§7-751.01 to 7-751.16.
  See HEALTH PROFESSIONAL RECRUITMENT PROGRAM.

MEDICAL MALPRACTICE, §§16-2801 to 16-2841.

Actions.
  Evidence.
    Benevolent gestures inadmissible, §16-2841.

MEDICAL MALPRACTICE —Cont'd

Actions —Cont'd
  Mediation, §§16-2821 to 16-2827.
  Notice of intention to file suit, §16-2802.
    Exceptions.
      Unknown or unlicensed defendant, §16-2804.
    Extension of statute of limitations, §16-2803.
Closed claim analysis.
  Obstetrician/gynecologist malpractice claims, §31-2991.
Confidentiality of information.
  Mediation, §16-2827.
Definitions, §16-2801.
Evidence.
  Benevolent gestures inadmissible, §16-2841.
Judgments against physicians.
  Reports by physicians and health care providers, §3-1205.13a.
Limitation of actions.
  Notice of intention to file suit.
    Extension of statute of limitations, §16-2803.
Mediation, §§16-2821 to 16-2827.
  Attendance at session, §16-2824.
  Confidentiality, §16-2827.
  Costs, §16-2822.
  Mediators, §16-2823.
    Report, §16-2826.
  Requirement, §16-2821.
  Statements by parties, §16-2825.
Medical liability captive insurance agency, §§1-307.81 to 1-307.95.
  See MEDICAL LIABILITY CAPTIVE INSURANCE AGENCY.
Notice of intention to file suit, §16-2802.
  Exceptions.
    Unknown or unlicensed defendant, §16-2804.
  Extension of statute of limitations, §16-2803.

MEDICAL MARIJUANA.
Advisory committee, §7-1671.09.
Authorization, §7-1671.02.
Board of medicine, recommendations regarding, §3-1202.03.
Crimes and offenses, §7-1671.08.
Cultivation centers.
  Fees, §7-1671.10.
  Regulation of, §7-1671.06.
  Rolling papers, sale of, §48-1103.

MEDICAL MARIJUANA —Cont'd
Definitions, §7-1671.01.
Dispensaries.
  Fees, §7-1671.10.
  Regulation of, §7-1671.06.
  Rolling papers, sale of, §48-1103.
Dispensing.
  Authorization, §7-1671.02.
  Restrictions, §7-1671.03.
Fees, §7-1671.10.
Gross sales tax, §47-2002.
Health insurance coverage,
    §7-1671.12.
Immunity, §7-1671.11.
Possession.
  Authorization, §7-1671.02.
  Cultivation centers, by, §7-1671.06.
  Dispensaries, by, §7-1671.06.
Program, §7-1671.05.
Recommendations of physicians,
    §7-1671.04.
  Board of medicine, review by,
    §7-1671.07.
Rulemaking authority, §7-1671.13.
Use.
  Authorization, §7-1671.02.
  Restrictions, §7-1671.03.

MEDICAL RECORDS, §§44-801 to
    44-805.
AIDS.
  Privacy and confidentiality of medical
    records and information
    regarding, §7-1605.
Definitions, §44-801.
Disclosure, §44-802.
Health data privacy, §§7-241 to 7-248.
  See HEALTH DATA PRIVACY.
Health maintenance organizations,
    §31-3426.
Mental health disclosures,
    §§7-1201.01 to 7-1208.07.
  See MENTAL HEALTH
    DISCLOSURES.
Mental illness, persons with,
    hospitalized, §21-562.
Peer review.
  Liability for actions or
    recommendations, §44-803.
  Use of reports, records, statements in
    judicial and administrative
    proceedings, §44-805.
Privacy and confidentiality, §44-804.
Secure manner.
  Maintenance of mental health records
    in, §§7-1206.01 to 7-1206.03.

MEDICAL RECORDS —Cont'd
Student health care, §38-607.
Subpoena for confidential records.
  Issuance by chief medical examiner,
    §5-1407.

MEDICAL SERVICES
    CORPORATIONS.
Hospital and medical services
    corporations.
  General provisions, §§31-3501 to
    31-3524.
  See HOSPITAL AND MEDICAL
    SERVICES CORPORATIONS.

MEDICAL TECHNOLOGISTS.
Definition of practice, §3-1201.02.
Health occupations licensure,
    registration or certification,
    §§3-1205.01 to 3-1205.24.
Qualifications for licensure,
    §3-1207.61.
  Exemption, §3-1207.63.
  Transition provision, §3-1207.64.
  Waiver, §3-1207.62.
Titles and terms prohibited as
    misrepresentation without
    license to practice, §3-1210.03.

MEDICAL WASTE.
Illegal dumping, §§8-901 to 8-906.
  See ILLEGAL DUMPING.

MEDICARE.
Health benefit plan.
  Grievance procedures not applicable
    to, §44-301.02.
Powers of attorney, §21-2114.

MEDICARE SUPPLEMENT
    INSURANCE, §§31-3701 to
    31-3710.
Applicability of provisions, §31-3702.
Definitions, §31-3701.
Disclosure, §31-3705.
Filing requirements.
  Advertising, §31-3708.
  Master policy and certificate,
    §31-3706.
Issuance of rules and regulations,
    §§31-3703, 31-3710.
Loss ratio standards, §31-3704.
Master policy and certificate.
  Filing, §31-3706.
Policy provision standards, §31-3703.
Remedies for violations, §31-3709.
Right to return and refund.
  Notice of, §31-3707.

MEDICATION ADVISORY COMMITTEE.
Receiving gifts or remuneration prohibition act, §§48-842.01 to 48-842.04.
Acceptance of gift or remuneration by committee member.
Prohibition, §48-842.03.
Definitions, §48-842.02.
Medication advisory committee defined, §48-842.02.
Medication samples.
Offering or accepting not prohibited, §48-842.03.
Offer of gift or remuneration by pharmaceutical company.
Prohibition, §48-842.03.
Short title, §48-842.01.
Violation, fine, §48-842.04.

MEDICATIONS.
AccessRX pharmaceutical resource center, §§48-831.41, 48-831.42.
Assisted living residences.
Medication management, §§44-109.01 to 44-109.07.
Medication advisory committee receiving gifts or remuneration prohibition act of 2008, §§48-842.01 to 48-842.04.
Pharmacists and pharmacies.
General provisions, §§47-2885.01 to 47-2885.23.
See PHARMACISTS AND PHARMACIES.
Prescription drugs.
General provisions, §§48-701 to 48-833.09.
See PRESCRIPTION DRUGS.

MEDICINE, PRACTICE OF.
Board of medicine, §3-1202.03.
Defined, §3-1201.02.
Physicians and surgeons.
See PHYSICIANS AND SURGEONS.

MEGAN'S LAW.
Sex offender registration, §§22-4001 to 22-4017.

MEMBER-GOVERNED CORPORATIONS, §29-401.50.

MEMBERSHIP EXCHANGES, §§29-409.01 to 29-409.08.
See NONPROFIT CORPORATIONS.

MEMORIAL DAY.
Appeals, federal cases, FRAP 26(a), 45(a).

MEMORIAL DAY —Cont'd
Designated holiday, §§1-612.02, 28-2701.

MEMORIALS.
Metropolitan police memorial fountain, §5-1301.
National Law Enforcement Heroes Memorial, §§5-1331 to 5-1333.

MENTAL ANGUISH.
Sale of goods.
Buyer damages for non-conforming goods, §28:2-714.

MENTAL EXAMINATIONS.
Adoption proceedings, Adoption Rule 35.
Attorneys at law.
Incompetent or incapacitated attorneys, DCBar Rule XI, USDistCt LCrR 57.30, USDistCt LCvR 83.19.
Civil procedure, CivPro Rule 35.
Criminal procedure, CrimPro Rules 12.2, 120.
Domestic relations actions, DomRel Rule 35.
Juvenile proceedings, JuvProc Rule 110.
Transfer for criminal prosecution, JuvProc Rule 108.

MENTAL HEALTH.
Advanced instructions for health treatment.
Execution by consumer, §7-1231.06.
Behavioral health department, §§7-1141.01 to 7-1141.09.
See BEHAVIORAL HEALTH DEPARTMENT.
Behavioral health ombudsman program, §7-1131.19.
Behavioral health resource guide, §7-1131.18.
Civil rights.
Retention by consumers, §7-1231.12.
Commitment of persons with intellectual disabilities.
General provisions, §§7-1303.01 to 7-1303.14.
See COMMITMENT OF PERSONS WITH INTELLECTUAL DISABILITIES.
Hearing and review procedures, §§7-1304.01 to 7-1304.13.
Conditions required for delivery of services, §7-1231.04.

MENTAL HEALTH —Cont'd
Confidentiality of consumer's mental health records, §7-1231.10.
Consent to services and supports.
Consumer's informed consent, requirement, §7-1231.07.
Administering medication, §7-1231.08.
Intellectual disabilities, persons with, §7-1305.06a.
Health care decision-makers, substitute consent, §7-1305.07a.
Youth receiving services and supports, §7-1231.14.
Consumers' rights protection, §§7-1231.01 to 7-1231.15.
See MENTAL HEALTH CONSUMERS PROTECTION ACT OF 2001.
Criminal abuse, neglect and financial exploitation of vulnerable adults and elderly persons, §§22-931 to 22-938.
Denial of treatment due to inability to pay, §47-2716.
Department, §§7-1131.01 to 7-1131.21.
See MENTAL HEALTH DEPARTMENT.
Disability services, department on, §§7-761.01 to 7-761.12.
See DISABILITY SERVICES, DEPARTMENT ON.
Disclosure of information, §§7-1201.01 to 7-1208.07.
See MENTAL HEALTH DISCLOSURES.
Durable power of attorney for health care.
Right of consumer to execute, §7-1231.06.
Electroconvulsive treatment.
Administering to consumer, §7-1231.07.
Grievances by consumers, §7-1231.11.
Hospitalization of persons with mental illness.
General provisions, §§21-501 to 21-592, MentalHealth Rules 1 to 17.
See HOSPITALIZATION OF PERSONS WITH MENTAL ILLNESS.
Inability to pay, denial of treatment due to, §47-2716.

MENTAL HEALTH —Cont'd
Intellectual disabilities, persons with.
General provisions, §§7-1301.02 to 7-1306.05.
See INTELLECTUAL DISABILITIES, PERSONS WITH.
Interstate compact on mental health, §§7-1101 to 7-1106.
Administrator, §7-1102.
Arrangements necessary to discharge District's financial obligations, §7-1104.
Authority to enter into compact, §7-1101.
Consultation with immediate family of proposed transferee, §7-1105.
Distributions of copies of chapter, §7-1106.
Supplemental agreements.
Authority to enter into, §7-1103.
Medication, §7-1231.08.
Minors receiving services and supports.
Consent, §7-1231.14.
Nurses.
Impaired nurses, treatment and rehabilitation, §§3-1251.01 to 3-1251.15.
See NURSES.
Privacy of consumer information, §7-1231.10.
Rates adjustment, §47-2717.
Rights of consumers of mental health services, §§7-1231.01 to 7-1231.15.
See MENTAL HEALTH CONSUMERS PROTECTION ACT OF 2001.
Seclusion and restraint of consumers.
Freedom from, §7-1231.09.
Service plans.
Consumer participation in development, §7-1231.05.
Sexual psychopaths, §§22-3803 to 22-3811.
See SEXUAL PSYCHOPATHS.
Youth behavioral health program, §7-1131.17.

MENTAL HEALTH CONSUMERS PROTECTION ACT OF 2001, §§7-1231.01 to 7-1231.15.
Access to information by consumer, §7-1231.10.

MENTAL HEALTH CONSUMERS PROTECTION ACT OF 2001
—Cont'd

Access to services free of discrimination, §7-1231.04.

Action for monetary damages to monetary damages those currently existing.
Not created, §7-1231.15.

Civil rights retained, §7-1231.13.

Conditions required in delivery of services, §7-1231.04.

Confidentiality of information and records, §7-1231.10.

Consent to services and supports, §7-1231.07.

Correction of inaccurate information, §7-1231.10.

Declaration for advance instructions for mental health treatment, §7-1231.06.

Definitions, §7-1231.02.

Durable power of attorney for health care, §7-1231.06.

Evaluation of services and support, participation, §7-1231.11.

Grievance resolution process.
Providers to adopt, §7-1231.12.

Individual plan of care, §7-1231.05.

Medication, administration, §7-1231.08.

Participation in development of service plans, §7-1231.05.

Persons committed to care of department by order of court in criminal proceeding.
Rights not abridged, §7-1231.03.

Presumption of legal competence, §7-1231.13.

Respectful treatment, §7-1231.04.

Rights of consumers generally, §7-1231.04.

Seclusion and restraint, freedom from, §7-1231.09.

Service planning, §7-1231.05.

Sexual orientation change efforts for minors, §7-1231.14a.

Short title, §7-1231.01.

Youth receiving services and support, §7-1231.14.

MENTAL HEALTH DEPARTMENT,
§§7-1131.01 to 7-1131.21.

Approval of Medicaid state plan amendment, §7-1131.15.

MENTAL HEALTH DEPARTMENT
—Cont'd

Behavioral health department.
Transfer of authority, functions, property and personnel, §7-1141.07.

Behavioral health ombudsman program, §7-1131.19.

Behavioral health resource guide, §7-1131.18.

Chief clinical officer, §7-1131.07.

Chief financial officer, §7-1131.06.

Consumer and family affairs officer, §7-1131.09.

Consumers' rights protection, §§7-1231.01 to 7-1231.15.
See MENTAL HEALTH CONSUMERS PROTECTION ACT OF 2001.

Definitions, §7-1131.02.

Director, §7-1131.05.

Drug and alcohol testing of employees.
Mandatory testing for certain employees, §§1-620.21 to 1-620.25.

Eligibility requirements.
Locally funded mental health rehabilitation services, §7-1141.02.

Established, §7-1131.03.

Funding.
Statement of anticipated funding, §7-1151.01.

General counsel, §7-1131.08.

Intragovernmental youth investment collaborative.
System of mental health care sub-council, §7-1131.11.

Nurse training program, §7-1131.20.

Office of Corporation Counsel, §7-1131.13.

Partnership council, §7-1131.10.

Powers and duties, §7-1131.04.

Purposes, §7-1131.03.

Rehabilitation services, locally funded.
Eligibility requirements, §7-1141.02.

Rules promulgation, §7-1131.14.

Statement of anticipated funding, §7-1151.01.

System of mental health care sub-council.
Intragovernmental youth investment collaborative, §7-1131.11.

Title of act, §7-1131.01.

Transfer of functions, property and personnel from commission on mental health services, §7-1131.12.

MENTAL HEALTH DEPARTMENT
—Cont'd
Youth behavioral health program,
§7-1131.17.
Youth rehabilitation services.
Transfers to, §7-1131.16.

MENTAL HEALTH DISCLOSURES,
§§7-1201.01 to 7-1208.07.
Access, client rights regarding.
Employees and other persons,
§7-1206.02.
Judicial action to compel access,
§7-1205.04.
Limitation of access by mental health
professional, §§7-1205.02,
7-1205.03.
Review by independent mental health
professional in case of limitation
of access, §7-1205.03.
Right to access, §7-1205.01.
Audits, for, §7-1203.05.
Authorization to disclose by client,
§§7-1202.01 to 7-1202.07.
Client 18 years of age or over.
Power to grant authorization,
§7-1202.05.
Client under age of 18.
Power to grant authorization,
§7-1202.05.
Disclosure upon voluntary
authorization, §7-1202.01.
Form of authorization, §7-1202.02.
Further disclosure only upon
authorization, §7-1202.03.
Limited disclosure to third party
payors, §7-1202.07.
Refusal or limitation of disclosure of
client's information.
Authority of mental health
professional, §7-1202.06.
Revocation of authorization,
§7-1202.04.
Client consent, disclosures
involving, §§7-1202.01 to
7-1202.07.
Commission on Mental Health,
authority of, §7-1208.03.
Conflicts of law, §§7-1208.02,
7-1208.06.
Correct information, right to,
§7-1205.05.
Correctional institutions,
§7-1203.05a.

MENTAL HEALTH DISCLOSURES
—Cont'd
Court-related disclosures,
§§7-1204.01 to 7-1204.05.
Access of client to records.
Judicial action to compel,
§7-1205.04.
Actions, §7-1204.03.
Anonymity in records of court,
requesting, §7-1204.05.
Civil commitment proceedings,
§7-1204.02.
Pretrial release, probation, parole,
supervised release or diversion,
§7-1204.03.
Psychological examinations, court-
ordered, §7-1204.01.
Redisclosure, §7-1204.04.
Crimes and offenses, §7-1207.02.
Definitions, §7-1201.01.
Effective date of provisions,
§7-1208.07.
Emergency basis for, §7-1203.03.
Exceptions to prohibited
disclosures, §§7-1201.02, 7-1203.01
to 7-1203.06.
Federal law, §§7-1208.02, 7-1208.06.
Fees, collection of, §7-1203.04.
Fines, §§7-1207.01, 7-1207.02,
7-1208.01.
General rules, §7-1201.04.
Group sessions, §7-1206.03.
Law enforcement officials,
§7-1203.05a.
Law, required by, §7-1203.02.
Limitation of authorized
disclosures, §§7-1202.06,
7-1202.07.
Notice, §§7-1206.02, 7-1206.03.
Penalties, §§7-1207.01, 7-1207.02,
7-1208.01.
Personal notes, §7-1201.03.
Prescription drugs.
Federal regulation and monitoring of,
§7-1208.02.
Program evaluation, for, §7-1203.05.
Prohibited disclosures, §7-1201.02.
Records.
Notation of disclosure in records,
§7-1201.04.
Redisclosure.
Court order, by, §7-1204.04.
Exceptions to rules regarding,
§7-1203.06.

MENTAL HEALTH DISCLOSURES
—Cont'd
Redisclosure —Cont'd
Initial authorization by client, following, §7-1202.03.
Requirements regarding, §7-1201.03.
Research purposes, §7-1203.05.
Revocation of authorization to disclose, §7-1202.04.
Secure manner, maintenance of records in, §§7-1206.01 to 7-1206.03.
Third-party payors, disclosures to, §7-1202.07.
Waivers and releases, prohibition on, §7-1208.04.
Within mental health facility, §7-1203.01.

MENTAL HEALTH PROFESSIONALS.
Child abuse and neglect reports, §4-1321.02.
Witnesses, §14-307.

MENTAL HEALTH SERVICES ADMINISTRATION, §§44-901 to 44-922.
Appropriations, §44-908.
Buy-American provisions, §44-909.
Client enterprise program, §§44-921, 44-922.
Congressional review of plan, §44-904.
Definitions, §44-902.
Development of plan, §44-903.
Employees.
Conditions of employment for, §44-906.
Transitional provisions, §44-905.
Forest Haven, §§44-1401 to 44-1404.
Policy declaration, §44-901.
Procurement practices, §44-909.
Transitional provisions.
Employees, §44-905.
Property, §44-907.

MENTAL ILLNESS, PERSONS WITH.
Adult protective services, §§7-1901 to 7-1913.
See ADULT PROTECTIVE SERVICES.
Alcoholics, rehabilitation of, §24-608.
Annulment of marriage.
Persons allowed to institute proceedings, §46-404.

MENTAL ILLNESS, PERSONS WITH
—Cont'd
Attorneys at law, DCBar Rule XI, USDistCt LCrR 57.30, USDistCt LCvR 83.19.
Clients with diminished capacity.
Client-lawyer relationship, ProfCond Rule 1.14.
Bank deposits and collections.
Incompetence of customer.
Authority of payor or collecting bank, §28:4-405.
Competence to proceed.
Criminal defendants, §§24-531.01 to 24-531.13.
See COMPETENCE TO PROCEED.
Consumers' rights protection, §§7-1231.01 to 7-1231.15.
See MENTAL HEALTH CONSUMERS PROTECTION ACT OF 2001.
Conveyances by and for individuals with mental disabilities, §42-820.
Crime victims' compensation.
Mental health expenses, VictComp Rule 24.
Criminal abuse, neglect and financial exploitation of vulnerable adults and elderly persons, §§22-931 to 22-938.
See CRIMINAL ABUSE, NEGLECT AND FINANCIAL EXPLOITATION OF VULNERABLE ADULTS AND ELDERLY PERSONS.
Declaration of advance instructions, §7-1231.06.
Default judgment against incompetent person, CivPro Rule 55.
Department of mental health, §§7-1131.01 to 7-1131.21.
See MENTAL HEALTH DEPARTMENT.
Dually diagnosed individuals.
Coordination of services, §7-1305.15.
Federal reservations, persons found in.
See HOSPITALIZATION OF PERSONS WITH MENTAL ILLNESS.
Firearms.
License to carry pistol, §7-2509.02.
Guardianship of incapacitated persons.
See GUARDIAN AND WARD.
Hearings.
See HEARINGS.

MENTAL ILLNESS, PERSONS WITH
—Cont'd
Hospitalization of persons with mental illness.
General provisions, §§21-501 to 21-592, MentalHealth Rules 1 to 17.
See HOSPITALIZATION OF PERSONS WITH MENTAL ILLNESS.
Incompetent criminal defendants.
Competence to proceed, §§24-531.01 to 24-531.13.
See COMPETENCE TO PROCEED.
Insanity defense, §§24-501 to 24-503, CrimPro Rule 12.2.
Procedures for mental examination, CrimPro Rule 120.
Intellectual disabilities, persons with.
Dually diagnosed individuals.
Coordination of services, §7-1305.15.
Interstate compact on mental health, §§7-1101 to 7-1106.
Judges.
Mental impairment, disability of judge, CJC Canon 2.14.
Landlord and tenant, §42-3228.
Lease under control of.
Cost of renewal, charge against estate or chargeable to leasehold, §42-3226.
Leases, §42-3228.
Nurses.
Impaired nurses, treatment and rehabilitation, §§3-1251.01 to 3-1251.15.
See NURSES.
Prisons and prisoners.
Hospitalization, §21-585, MentalHealth Rule 10.
Escapees, MentalHealth Rule 11.
Service of process.
Domestic relations actions, DomRel Rule 4.
Summons, CivPro Rule 4.
Sexual psychopaths, §§22-3803 to 22-3811.
Standing trial in criminal case.
Procedures for mental examination, CrimPro Rule 120.
Substance abuse and mental illness coverage, §§31-3101 to 31-3112.
See HEALTH INSURANCE.
Substitution of parties, CivPro Rule 25.
Domestic relations actions, DomRel Rule 25.

MENTAL ILLNESS, PERSONS WITH
—Cont'd
Volunteer Service Credit Program, §§7-531.01 to 7-531.11.
Vulnerable adults and elderly persons.
Criminal abuse, neglect and financial exploitation, §§22-931 to 22-938.

MENTAL RETARDATION, PERSONS WITH, §§7-1301.02 to 7-1306.05.
See INTELLECTUAL DISABILITIES, PERSONS WITH.

MERCHANTABILITY, WARRANTY OF.
Commercial code.
Sale of goods.
Implied warranty, §28:2-314.
Exclusion or modification, §§28:2-316, 28:2-316.01.

MERCHANT BANKS, §§26-831.01 to 26-831.22.
Business activities, policies, §26-831.10.
Capital requirements, §26-831.08.
Certificate of authority, §§26-831.04 to 26-831.06.
Revocation or limitation of exercise of powers under certificate, §26-831.05.
Charter.
Application, §26-831.03.
Conservators.
Appointment, §26-831.18.
Authority to borrow money, §26-831.20.
Bond, §26-831.18.
Expenses, reimbursement, §26-831.18.
Qualifications, §26-831.18.
Rights, powers, privileges, §26-831.19.
Termination of conservatorship, §26-831.21.
Definitions, §26-831.02.
Lien on property or assets of bank voidable, §26-831.16.
Liquidation, §26-831.11.
Powers and authority, §26-831.07.
Receivers.
Appointment by superior court, §26-831.14.
Bond, §26-831.14.
Duties and powers, §26-831.15.
Maintenance and disposal of records, §26-831.17.
Petition to appoint, §26-831.14.
Report, §26-831.14.

MERCHANT BANKS —Cont'd
Receivers —Cont'd
  Taking possession of banks, books and
    records, §26-831.15.
Rules, §26-831.22.
Structure and organization,
  §26-831.09.
Taking possession, §§26-831.12,
  26-831.13.
Transfers voidable, §26-831.16.

MERCHANTS.
Consumer protection.
  Definition of merchant, §28-3901.
Dishonored checks.
  Civil recovery for, §28-3152.
  Definition of merchant, §28-3151.
Natural disaster consumer
  protection, §§28-4101 to 28-4103.
Shoplifting.
  General provisions, §§22-3213, 27-101
    to 27-106.
  See SHOPLIFTING.

MERCY-KILLING, §7-630.
Healthcare durable powers of
  attorney.
  General provisions, §§21-2201 to
    21-2213.
    See HEALTHCARE DURABLE
      POWERS OF ATTORNEY.
Natural death act, §§7-621 to 7-630.
  See LIVING WILLS.

MERGERS AND CONSOLIDATIONS,
  §§29-202.01 to 29-202.06.
Amendment or abandonment,
  §29-202.04.
Approval, §29-202.03.
Authorization, §29-202.01.
Condominiums, §42-1903.19.
Corporations, §§29-309.01 to
  29-309.08.
  See CORPORATIONS.
Domestic life insurance companies,
  §§31-4443 to 31-4452.
Effect of, §29-202.06.
Fraternal benefit societies, §31-5311.
Health maintenance organizations,
  §31-3427.
Horizontal property regimes,
  §42-2012.
Insurance holding companies,
  §§31-703, 31-704, 31-732.
Limited cooperative associations,
  §§29-1015.01 to 29-1015.08.
  See LIMITED COOPERATIVE
    ASSOCIATIONS.

MERGERS AND CONSOLIDATIONS
  —Cont'd
Limited liability companies,
  §§29-809.01 to 29-809.05.
  See LIMITED LIABILITY
    COMPANIES.
Limited partnerships, §§29-710.01 to
  29-710.08.
  See LIMITED PARTNERSHIPS.
Metrorail and metrobus, §34-217.
Mutual insurance holding
  companies, §§31-732, 31-737.01.
Nonprofit corporations, §§29-409.01
  to 29-409.08.
  See NONPROFIT CORPORATIONS.
Plans, §29-202.02.
Professional corporations.
  Restrictions, §29-512.
Public utilities, §§34-504, 34-1001,
  35-271.
  See PUBLIC UTILITIES.
Reciprocal insurance companies,
  §31-752.
Statement of merger, §29-202.05.
Statutory trusts, §§29-1207.01 to
  29-1207.06.
  See STATUTORY TRUSTS.
Unincorporated nonprofit
  associations, §29-1126.

MERIDIAN HILL PARK, §10-108.

MERIDIAN PUBLIC CHARTER
  SCHOOL.
Real property tax exemption,
  §47-1088.

MERITORIOUS GOOD TIME
  CREDITS.
Prisons and prisoners, §24-221.01a.

MERIT SYSTEM, §§1-601.01 to
  1-636.03.
Adverse action.
  Appeal of agency decision resulting in,
    §1-606.03.
Annual leave bank, §§1-612.04 to
  1-612.11.
  See ANNUAL LEAVE BANK.
Appeals, §§1-606.01 to 1-606.11, CivPro
  Agency Review Rule 1.
  Disciplinary grievances and appeals,
    §1-616.52.
  Final agency decision affecting
    performance rating, §1-606.03.
  Labor-management relations under
    merit system, §1-617.13.
  Office of employee appeals, §§1-606.01
    to 1-606.11.

MERIT SYSTEM —Cont'd

Applicability of provisions
 regarding, §§1-602.01 to 1-602.06.
Appropriations, §1-633.01.
Arbitration, §1-606.07.
Attorneys' fees and costs, §§1-606.08,
 1-617.03.
Audits.
 Other post-employment benefits fund,
  annual audit, §1-621.09e.
Board of education.
 Delegation of authority, §1-604.03.
 Educational employees, applicability
  to, §1-602.03.
 Non-educational employees.
  Preference for resident applicants,
   §1-602.03.
Boards and commissions,
 compensation, §1-611.08.
Career service, §§1-608.01, 1-611.02,
 1-611.04, 1-623.45.
 Creation, §1-608.01.
 Reduction-in-force procedures,
  §1-608.01.
Civil Service Commission assistance
 with, §1-207.34.
Classification system, §§1-611.01 to
 1-611.21.
Compensatory time off, §1-611.03.
Conduct by employees.
 Conflicts of interest, §1-618.02.
 Nepotism prohibited, §1-618.04.
 Standards, §1-618.01.
Conduct, standards of.
 Disability compensation proceedings,
  §1-623.25.
 Labor unions, for, §1-617.03.
Conflicts of interest, §§1-615.05,
 1-618.02.
Continuation of statutes, rules, and
 regulations, §1-632.01.
Corrections departments,
 meritorious service awards for,
 §§5-901 to 5-904.
Covered employees, §§1-602.01 to
 1-602.06.
Death benefits, §1-623.33.
Debt setoffs for employees,
 §§1-629.01 to 1-629.04.
Definitions, §1-603.01.
Development of unified systems for
 all employees, §1-602.05.
Director of personnel, §1-604.02.
Disability compensation, §§1-623.01
 to 1-623.47.
 Adjustment after recovery from third
  party, §1-623.32.

MERIT SYSTEM —Cont'd

Disability compensation —Cont'd
 Adjustments, §1-623.41.
 Administered by mayor, §1-623.02a.
 Aliens, §§1-623.37, 1-623.38.
 Appeals, §1-623.28.
 Assignment of claims, §1-623.30.
 Attendant services, §1-623.11.
 Attorneys' fees and costs, §1-623.27.
 Authority over, transfer of, §1-623.46.
 Beneficiaries of awards unpaid at
  death, §1-623.09.
 Change of condition.
  Modification of award, §1-623.24.
 Claim, requirement to make,
  §1-623.21.
 Computation of amount, §1-623.14.
 Continuation of pay, §1-623.18.
 Credit given rights and benefits.
  Resumption of employment,
   §1-623.45.
 Death benefits, §1-623.33.
 Definitions, §1-623.01.
 Dependents, augmented compensation
  for, §1-623.10.
 Earning capacity, determining,
  §1-623.15.
 Earnings report, §1-623.06b.
 Employees' compensation fund,
  §1-623.42.
 Exceptions, §1-623.02.
 Functions of program, §1-623.02b.
 Fund, §1-623.42.
 Funeral expenses, §1-623.34.
 Hearing on claim, §1-623.24.
 Increases, §1-623.13.
  Adjustments, §1-623.41.
 Issuance of rules and regulations
  regarding, §1-623.44.
 Leave of absence.
  Election to use up, §1-623.18.
  Restoration of, §1-623.43.
 Limitations on right to, §1-623.16.
 Lump-sum payments, §1-623.35.
 Maximum monthly amounts,
  §1-623.12.
 Medical benefits and services,
  §1-623.03.
 Medical examinations, §1-623.23.
 Mental stress or emotional condition,
  §1-623.02.
 Minimum monthly amounts,
  §1-623.12.
 Misconduct at proceedings regarding,
  §1-623.25.
 Modification of award.
  Change of condition, §1-623.24.

MERIT SYSTEM —Cont'd
Disability compensation —Cont'd
Modified work program, §1-623.47.
Nonresidents, §1-623.37.
Notice, §1-623.19.
Oaths and affirmations, §1-623.26.
Outside United States, injury
   occurring, §1-623.36.
Overpayments, recovery of, §1-623.29.
Partial disability, §1-623.06.
Period of payments, §1-623.06a.
Proceedings as to claims, §1-623.24.
Reasons for providing, §1-623.02.
Reductions.
   Basic compensation, §1-623.13.
   Subsequent injury to same member,
      §1-623.08.
   Third party, adjustment after
      recovery from, §1-623.32.
Re-employment, §1-623.45.
Reopening of claim, §1-623.22.
Reports.
   Earnings report, §1-623.06b.
   Injury or death, §1-623.20.
Representation by counsel, §1-623.27.
Resumption of employment.
   Credit given, §1-623.45.
Right to receive.
   Limitations on, §1-623.16.
   Time of accrual of right, §1-623.17.
Schedule of compensation, §1-623.07.
Students, §1-623.39.
Subpoenas, §1-623.26.
Subrogation of District, §1-623.31.
Subsequent injury to same member,
   reduction of compensation for,
   §1-623.08.
Suspension of payments, §1-623.13.
Third party, adjustment after recovery
   from, §1-623.32.
Time limits.
   Accrual of right, §1-623.17.
   Making claim, §§1-623.22, 1-623.24.
Total disability, §1-623.05.
Transportation of body, §1-623.34.
Vocational rehabilitation, §§1-623.04,
   1-623.11.
Witnesses, examination of, §1-623.26.
**Disability income protection
   program.**
Establishment of, §1-622.15.
Study, §1-622.02.
Discipline and grievance process,
   §§1-616.51 to 1-616.54.
Administrative leave and enforced
   leave, §1-616.54.

MERIT SYSTEM —Cont'd
Discipline and grievance process
   —Cont'd
Alternative dispute resolution,
   §1-616.53.
Appeal from removal, reduction in
   grade, suspension, §1-616.52.
Contesting reprimand or suspension
   as grievance, §1-616.52.
Negotiated grievance procedure,
   §1-616.52.
Rules and regulations.
   Issuance to establish disciplinary
      system, §1-616.51.
   Prompt handling of grievances,
      §1-616.53.
Time limit on presenting grievance,
   §1-616.53.
**Displaced employees, transition
   benefits for,** §§1-624.21 to 1-624.24.
Administration of subchapter,
   §1-624.23.
Fiscal year 1996, §§1-624.21, 1-624.22.
Reports, §1-624.24.
**District of Columbia housing
   authority.**
Hatch act.
   Applicability to employees, §6-218.
   Status of employees, §6-215.
**Drug and alcohol testing of
   employees.**
Department of human services,
   §§1-620.21 to 1-620.25.
   Commercial motor vehicle drivers,
      §1-620.11.
   Contractor to perform test,
      §1-620.22.
   Definitions, §1-620.21.
   Employees tested, §1-620.22.
   Grounds for termination, §1-620.25.
   Implied consent of employees
      operating motor vehicles,
      §1-620.24.
   Methods of testing, §1-620.23.
   Notice of confirmed positive
      urinalysis, §1-620.23.
   Notice of implementation of
      program, §1-620.22.
   Random testing.
      Employees subject to, §1-620.22.
      Method of testing, §1-620.23.
      Results turned over to law
         enforcement, §1-620.25.
   Treatment following positive test,
      §1-620.25.
District employees who serve children,
   §§1-620.31 to 1-620.37.
   Definitions, §1-620.31.

MERIT SYSTEM —Cont'd
Drug and alcohol testing of employees —Cont'd
District employees who serve children —Cont'd
Employees tested, §1-620.32.
Employment contingent upon receipt of satisfactory drug test, §1-620.35.
Grounds for termination, §1-620.35.
Implied consent of employees operating motor vehicles, §1-620.33.
Methods of testing, §1-620.34.
Notice of confirmed positive urinalysis, §1-620.34.
Notice of implementation of program, §1-620.32.
Opportunity to seek treatment, §1-620.35.
Policy issued in advance of implementation, §1-620.35.
Private contract and licensed providers, §1-620.36.
Random testing, §1-620.32.
Methods of testing, §1-620.34.
Turning result over to law enforcement, §1-620.35.
Rules, §1-620.37.
Educational employee governed by chapter, §1-602.03.
Educational service, §§1-525.01, 1-608.01a, 1-611.11, 1-623.45.
Effective date of provisions, §1-636.02.
Employee debt setoffs, §§1-629.01 to 1-629.04.
Employee development, §1-613.01.
Employees of district on date chapter becomes effective.
Status, §1-602.04.
Enforced leave, placement on.
Appeal of agency action resulting in, §§1-606.03, 1-616.54.
Equal employment opportunity, §§1-607.01 to 1-607.08.
Excepted service, §§1-609.01 to 1-609.08, 1-611.02, 1-611.04.
Appointments to, §1-609.03.
Conversion rights, §1-609.02.
Creation, §1-609.01.
Domicile requirements, §1-609.06.
Expenses paid.
Hard to fill excepted service position, §1-609.03.
Hard to fill excepted service position.
Expenses paid, §1-609.03.

MERIT SYSTEM —Cont'd
Excepted service —Cont'd
Hired noncompetitively, §1-609.01.
List of positions to be filled.
Publication, §1-609.03.
Nature of positions, §1-609.02.
No job tenure or protection, §1-609.05.
Number of employees, §1-609.03.
Officeholders who serve at the pleasure of the appointing authority, §1-609.08.
Performance incentives for exceptional service, authorized, §1-609.03.
Publication of persons appointed to positions, §1-609.03.
Qualifications for positions, §1-609.01.
Redelegation of authority to appoint, §1-609.03.
Separation pay, §1-609.03.
Special appointments, §1-609.04.
Statutory officeholders, §1-609.08.
Transitional provisions, §1-609.07.
Executive service, §§1-523.01, 1-610.51 to 1-610.64.
Appointment in other service position after separation.
Time limit, §1-610.60.
Domicile requirement, §1-610.59.
Established, §1-610.51.
Life insurance benefits, §1-610.63.
Pay of person holding position on October 21, 1998, §1-610.54.
Pay plan, §1-610.53.
Pay schedule, §1-610.52.
Performance incentives, §1-610.57.
Preemployment travel expenses, §1-610.55.
Public safety pay schedule, §1-610.52a.
Relocation expenses, §1-610.55.
Retirement benefits, §1-610.62.
Scope of provisions, §1-610.51.
Separation from service.
Appointment to other service position following.
Time limit, §1-610.60.
Separation pay, §1-610.58.
Subordinate agency heads.
Employment contracts with, §1-610.64.
Nomination of persons to service as, §1-610.51.
Temporary housing allowance, §1-610.55.
Universal leave, §1-610.61.
Existing right retained, §1-602.04.
Fiduciary status of public officers and employees, §1-615.04.

MERIT SYSTEM —Cont'd
Findings, §1-601.01.
Fire departments, meritorious service awards for, §§5-901 to 5-904.
Fraud, §1-615.05.
Funeral expenses, §1-623.34.
Governing laws.
  Continuation of statutes, rules, and regulations, §1-632.01.
  Express retention of statutes, rules, and regulations, §1-632.06.
  Interpretation of provisions, §1-632.08.
  Police and firefighters, exceptions for, §1-632.03.
  Repeal of existing laws, §1-632.07.
  Supersession of existing statutes, rules, and regulations, §§1-632.02, 1-632.07.
Grievance process, §§1-616.51 to 1-616.54.
Hatch Act, §§1-625.01, 1-625.02.
  District of Columbia housing authority.
    Applicability to employees, §6-218.
Health benefits, §§1-621.01 to 1-621.17.
  Analysis of health care costs, §1-301.151.
  Audits, §1-621.12.
  Continuation of coverage, §1-621.14.
  Contracting authority providing, §1-621.04.
  Definitions, §1-621.03.
  District benefits, §1-621.02.
  District contribution, §1-621.09.
  Domestic partnerships, §32-706.
  Electing coverage, §1-621.07.
  Eligibility to receive, §1-621.13.
  Employee deductions and withholdings for, §1-621.08.
  Evaluating, §1-621.12.
  Federal benefits, §1-621.01.
  Information about, §1-621.10.
  Issuance of rules regarding, §1-621.13.
  Other post-employment benefits fund.
    Actuarial statement and opinion, §1-621.09b.
    Advisory committee, §§1-621.51 to 1-621.54.
    Annual audit, §1-621.09e.
    Annual report, §1-621.09f.
    Calculation of District's payment, §1-621.09a.
    District contribution, §1-621.09.
    Reprogramming of funds, §1-621.09f.
  Other post-employment benefits system, §§1-621.09b to 1-621.09e.
    Annual audit of fund, §1-621.09e.

MERIT SYSTEM —Cont'd
Health benefits —Cont'd
  Other post-employment benefits system —Cont'd
    Benefits system defined, §1-621.09b.
    Information about, §1-621.09c.
    Studies, preparation by enrolled actuary, §1-621.09d.
  Post-employment benefits, §1-621.17.
  Post-retirement benefit plans.
    Information on, §1-621.16.
  Public safety overtime bank, §1-301.151.
  Reports, §1-621.12.
  Restored employees, coverage of, §1-621.11.
  Types of benefits, §1-621.06.
  Types of plans, §1-621.05.
Holidays, §1-612.02.
  Legal private holidays, §1-612.02a.
Hours of work, §1-612.01.
Implementation task force, §1-636.03.
Incentive awards, §§1-619.01 to 1-619.03.
  Authority to grant, §1-619.01.
  Limitation, §1-619.02.
  Pilot programs, §1-619.03.
Interpretation of provisions, §1-632.08.
  Conforming amendments and repealers, §§1-632.01 to 1-632.08.
  Effective date, §1-636.02.
  Severability, §1-635.01.
Labor-management relations, §§1-617.01 to 1-617.18.
  Agreements and contracts, §1-617.15.
  Bargaining units, determining, §1-617.09.
  Costs, payment of, §1-617.13.
  Deduction of union dues and fees, §1-617.07.
  Elections, §1-617.10.
  Employee rights, §1-617.06.
  Enforcement of provisions, §1-617.13.
  Establishment of program, §1-617.02.
  Exclusive recognition, §§1-617.10, 1-617.11.
  Impasse resolution machinery, §1-617.02.
  Judicial review, §1-617.13.
  Management rights, §1-617.08.
  Policy declaration, §1-617.01.
  Public school employee evaluation system not subject to collective bargaining, §1-617.18.
  Remedies, §1-617.13.

MERIT SYSTEM —Cont'd
Labor-management relations
—Cont'd
Selection of exclusive representatives,
§1-617.10.
Standards of conduct for labor
organizations, §1-617.03.
Strikes, §1-617.05.
Subjects of collective bargaining,
§1-617.08.
Sunshine provisions, §1-617.12.
Timeliness of decisions regarding,
§1-617.14.
Unfair labor practices, §1-617.04.
Wages and salaries, §§1-602.06,
1-617.16, 1-617.17.
Lateral police career appointments,
§§1-610.71 to 1-610.76.
Law enforcement officers.
Lateral police career appointments,
§§1-610.71 to 1-610.76.
Leave of absence, §§1-612.03 to
1-612.11.
Enforced leave, placement on.
Appeal of agency action resulting in,
§§1-606.03, 1-616.54.
Voluntary leave transfer program,
§§1-612.31 to 1-612.38.
Legal service, §§1-608.51 to 1-608.66.
See LEGAL SERVICE.
Life insurance, §§1-622.01 to 1-622.16.
Accounting requirements, §1-622.12.
Additional coverage, option to
purchase, §1-622.07.
Automatic coverage, §1-622.06.
Claims, §1-622.08.
Contracting authority, §1-622.05.
Definitions, §1-622.04.
Description of benefits, §1-622.06.
District benefits, §1-622.03.
Eligibility for, §1-622.14.
Employee deductions, withholdings,
and payments, §1-622.10.
Employer contributions, §1-622.11.
Executive service, §1-610.63.
Federal benefits, §1-622.01.
Group insurance amounts, §1-622.07.
Issuance of rules regarding, §1-622.14.
Post-employment benefits, §1-622.16.
Reports, §1-622.12.
Special contingency reserve, §1-622.13.
Termination of, §1-622.09.
Viatical settlements, §1-622.08.
Limited application of chapter,
§1-602.02.
Management supervisory service,
§§1-609.51 to 1-609.58.
Competitive appointments, §1-609.53.

MERIT SYSTEM —Cont'd
Management supervisory service
—Cont'd
Composition, §1-609.52.
Employment-at-will, §1-609.54.
Pay, §1-609.56.
Residency preference, §1-609.57.
Skills, maintenance and enhancement,
§1-609.55.
Transition provisions, §1-609.58.
Managers' accountability, §§1-614.11
to 1-614.14.
Performance plans, §1-614.12.
Development, §1-614.14.
Performance reports, §1-614.13.
Development, §1-614.14.
Mayor, nominees put forward by,
§1-523.01.
Mediation, §1-606.06.
Military differential pay.
Call to active duty as result of
operation enduring freedom,
§1-611.03.
Nepotism, §1-618.04.
New personnel system, development,
§1-602.05.
Occupational safety and health,
§§1-620.01 to 1-620.08.
Officeholders.
Excepted service, §1-609.08.
Office of employee appeals,
§§1-606.01 to 1-606.11.
Appeal procedures, §1-606.03.
Arbitration, §1-606.07.
Attorney fees, §1-606.08.
Authority, §1-606.02.
Duties, §1-606.02.
Enforcement of order, §1-606.09.
Established, §1-606.01.
Hearing procedures, §1-606.04.
Mediation and settlement, §1-606.06.
Members, §1-606.01.
Public hearings, §1-606.10.
Rules, issuance, §§1-606.05, 1-606.11.
Office of personnel, §§1-604.01 to
1-604.08.
Personnel authority, §1-604.06.
Transfer of functions, property and
funds to, §1-604.07.
**Other post-employment benefits
fund advisory committee,**
§§1-621.51 to 1-621.54.
Composition, §1-621.52.
Duties, §1-621.53.
Established, §1-621.51.
Meetings, §1-621.54.

MERIT SYSTEM —Cont'd
Other post-employment benefits fund advisory committee —Cont'd
Records, §1-621.54.
Terms of office, §1-621.52.
Overtime, §1-611.03.
Public safety overtime bank, §1-301.151.
Pensions and retirement.
Executive service, §1-610.62.
General provisions, §§1-626.01 to 1-626.14.
See PENSIONS AND RETIREMENT.
Performance management system, §§1-613.51 to 1-613.53, 1-614.11 to 1-614.14.
Personal surety bonds, §1-630.01.
Personnel authority, §1-604.06.
Pilot classification and compensation personnel programs, §1-611.21.
Police departments, meritorious service awards for, §§5-901 to 5-904.
Police officers and firefighters.
Appointments after effective date, §1-632.03.
Policy declaration, §§1-601.01, 1-601.02.
Political rights of employees, §§1-625.01, 1-625.02.
Privacy of personnel records, §§1-622.01 to 1-622.08.
Private sector employees.
Assignment to work for District government.
Special rules, §1-627.06.
Public employee relations board, §§1-605.01 to 1-605.04.
Public safety executive service.
Pay schedule, §1-610.52a.
Public safety overtime bank.
Health benefits, §1-301.151.
Purpose, §1-601.02.
Reciprocal agreements, §§1-628.01 to 1-628.05.
Authorized, §1-628.01.
Courts, §1-628.03.
Disciplinary appeals, agreements, §1-628.05.
Required agreements, §1-628.02.
Transit commission, §1-628.04.
Records management, §§1-631.01 to 1-631.08.
Access of employees to records, §1-631.05.

MERIT SYSTEM —Cont'd
Records management —Cont'd
Disclosures, §§1-631.03 to 1-631.08.
Exchange of personnel information, §1-631.08.
Issuance of rules and regulations, §1-631.01.
Policy declaration, §1-631.01.
Privacy and confidentiality, §§1-631.03 to 1-631.08.
Rules and regulations governing disclosure, §1-631.04.
Transfer of personnel files, §1-631.07.
United States Civil Service Commission, §1-631.02.
Reductions in force, §§1-624.01 to 1-624.09.
Abolishment of positions for fiscal year 2000, §1-624.08.
Appeals, §§1-606.03, 1-624.04.
Board of education procedures, §1-525.01.
Career service procedures, §1-608.01.
Displaced employees, transition benefits for, §§1-624.21 to 1-624.24.
Identification of positions for abolishment, §1-624.08.
Policy declaration, §1-624.01.
Procedural requirements, §1-624.02.
Responsibility for final determination, §1-624.03.
Severance pay, §1-624.09.
Removal.
Appeal of agency action resulting in, §1-606.03.
Repeal of existing laws, §1-632.07.
Review of, §§1-611.05, 1-611.06.
Review of agency decision, CivPro Agency Review Rule 1.
Final decision affecting performance rating, §1-606.03.
Petition for review, CivPro Agency Review Rule 1.
Rules and regulations.
Appropriate personnel authority.
Who may issue for specific agency personnel, §§1-604.04, 1-604.06.
Implementation by appropriate personnel authority, §1-604.06.
Issuance of rules and regulations affecting employees, §§1-604.04, 1-604.05.
Safety.
Occupational safety and health, §§1-620.01 to 1-620.08.

MERIT SYSTEM —Cont'd

Selection procedures, §§1-607.04 to 1-607.06.

Setoff.

Collection of employee debts owing District, §§1-629.03, 1-629.04.

Erroneous payments made to employees, §1-629.02.

Waiver, §1-629.01.

Settlements, §1-606.06.

Severability of provisions, §1-635.01.

Severance pay, §1-624.09.

Student employees.

Disability compensation, §1-623.39.

Supersession of existing statutes, rules, and regulations, §§1-632.02, 1-632.07.

Supersession provisions, §1-602.06.

Suspension.

Appeal of agency action resulting in, §1-606.03.

Temporary assignment of District employees, §§1-627.01 to 1-627.06.

Assignment implemented by written agreement, §1-627.05.

Participation in program of personnel interchange, §1-627.01.

Policy, §1-627.01.

Special rules governing assignment of private sector employees to District, §1-627.06.

Status of employee of other government or organizations, §1-627.03.

Status of employee while on assignment, §1-627.02.

Travel expenses, §1-627.04.

Transition benefits for displaced employees, §§1-624.21 to 1-624.24.

University of the District of Columbia.

Applicability of, §1-602.03.

Delegation of authority, §1-604.03.

Preference for resident applicants.

Non-educational employees, §1-602.03.

Voluntary leave transfer program, §§1-612.31 to 1-612.38.

Wages and salaries, §§1-611.03 to 1-611.21.

Washington convention and sports authority personnel, not available to, §10-1202.16.

Water and Sewer Authority, §34-2202.15.

Whistleblower protection, §§1-615.51 to 1-615.59.

MESNE PROFITS AND DAMAGES.

Ejectment, §16-1109.

Rent, separate actions for, §16-1111.

Separate actions for rent or damages, §16-1111.

MESSENGER SERVICES.

Commercial bicycle operators, §§50-1631 to 50-1634.

METABOLIC DISORDERS.

Newborn screening, §§7-831 to 7-840.

METHANE.

Renewable energy portfolio standards, §§34-1431 to 34-1439.

METHANOL.

Alternative fuel technology, §§50-701 to 50-715.

See ALTERNATIVE FUEL TECHNOLOGY.

METROPOLITAN POLICE, §§5-101.01 to 5-133.21.

Actions taken based on citizen complaints, §5-1112.

Affiliations, prohibited, §5-123.01.

Age requirements, §5-105.07.

Agreement obligating service.

Candidates for appointment to execute, §5-107.01a.

Alcoholic beverage licenses.

Reimbursable details, §25-798.

Ammunition feeding devices, prohibition on transfer of, §5-133.16.

Appointment of officers and members, §5-105.01.

Eligibility for appointment, §§5-107.01, 5-107.04.

Appropriations.

Band, §5-131.05.

Uniforms, §5-111.03.

Armory, barriers and restricted zones at, §3-343.

Arrests, §§5-115.01 to 5-115.07.

See ARRESTS.

Assault on member of police force, §22-405.

Resisting arrest, §22-405.01.

Assignments of officers and members, §5-105.01.

Awards for meritorious service, §§5-901 to 5-904.

Band, §§5-131.01 to 5-131.05.

Appropriations, §5-131.05.

Detailing officers to participate, §5-131.02.

Park police officers, §5-131.03.

METROPOLITAN POLICE —Cont'd
Band —Cont'd
 Establishment authorized, §5-131.01.
 Purposes, §5-131.01.
 Retirement of director.
  Law applicable, §5-131.04.
Bicycle identification numbers.
 Duty to check recovered bicycle's
  number with bike registry,
  §50-1611.
Body-worn camera fund, §5-116.51.
Body-worn camera program,
  §§5-116.31 to 5-116.33.
 Established, §5-116.31.
 Funding, §5-116.31.
 Reporting requirements, §5-116.33.
 Rulemaking requirement, §5-116.32.
Bomb disposal duty, additional
  compensation for, §5-542.02.
Bonds, surety, §5-133.12.
Boundaries, §5-101.02.
Cadet program, §§5-109.01, 5-109.02.
Call center.
 Office of unified communications.
  Transfer of responsibilities and
   duties to office, §1-327.53.
Capitol police, detailed to,
  §§10-505.01 to 10-505.07.
Career service promotions,
  §§1-608.01, 5-105.01.
Carotid artery holds, §5-125.03.
Chief of Police.
 Alcoholic beverage licenses.
  Suspension or revocation at request
   of chief of police, §25-827.
 Appointment, §5-105.01.
 Depositing of seized currency.
  Granting exception to requirements,
   §23-532.
  Rulemaking authority, §23-533.
 Duty of members to obey and respect,
  §5-127.03.
 Electronic recording of interrogations.
  General order establishing
   additional procedures,
   §5-116.02.
 Reports, §5-133.08.
Child abuse and neglect reports,
  handling of, §4-1301.05.
Child custody proceedings.
 Enforcement of foreign custody
  determinations, §§16-4603.16,
  16-4603.17.
Chokeholds, §§5-125.01 to 5-125.03.
Community crime prevention team,
  §5-132.31.

METROPOLITAN POLICE —Cont'd
Community policing working group,
  §5-132.32.
Complaints against police.
 Office of police complaints.
  General provisions, §§5-1101 to
   5-1115.
  See OFFICE OF POLICE
   COMPLAINTS.
Conditional retirement.
 Retirement while under disciplinary
  investigation, §§5-801 to 5-807.
Conduct, standards of, §5-127.01.
Constables, powers of, §5-127.04.
Continuing education for sworn
  members, §5-107.02.
Contract for fleet management
  services.
 Privatization contract, §2-381.42.
Council powers regarding, §5-127.01.
Court duty, §5-1304.
Creation of, §5-101.01.
Crime investigation records,
  §§5-113.31 to 5-113.34.
 Definitions, §5-113.31.
 Penalties for willful or malicious
  tampering with records, §5-113.33.
 Records retention schedule, §5-113.34.
 Retention of records and preservation
  of evidence, §5-113.32.
Criminal records, §§5-113.02 to
  5-113.04.
Currency.
 Depositing of seized currency,
  §§23-531 to 23-534.
Demotions, §5-543.05.
Detection of crime, expenditures for,
  §5-133.14.
Detective Bureau, assistant to
  Inspector commanding,
  §5-105.06.
Disciplinary actions.
 Retirement while under disciplinary
  investigation, §§5-801 to 5-807.
 Applicability, §5-807.
 Completion of investigation, §5-802.
 Conditional retirement, §5-803.
  Penalties in lieu of discipline for
   members on, §5-804.
  Challenge of imposition,
   administrative review,
   §5-806.
  Payment, §5-805.
 Definitions, §5-801.
Disciplinary authority of, §5-1114.
Discriminatory laws, no
  enforcement of, §5-133.11.

METROPOLITAN POLICE —Cont'd

Duties of officers and members,
§§5-105.05, 5-127.03.

Electronic recording of interrogations, §§5-116.01 to 5-116.03.

Eligibility for appointment,
§§5-107.01, 5-107.04.

Emergencies.
Citizens appointed as special police without pay, §5-129.03.
Federal control during, §1-207.40.

Escorts and other law enforcement services.
Reimbursement for, §5-129.71.

Examination of certain business and records.
During searches for stolen property or suspected offenders, §5-117.03.
Interference with police, §5-117.04.
Property pledged to pawnbrokers, §5-117.03.

Excepted service appointments,
§§1-608.01, 5-105.01.

Excepted service sworn employees' compensation system.
Time mayor to submit, §1-609.03.

Expenses.
Crime prevention and detection, §5-133.14.
Pistol match attendance, §5-133.15.

False reports made to, §5-117.05.

Federal agencies, cooperative agreements with, §5-133.17.
Federal officers making arrest for nonfederal offenses, §5-301.
Restrictions, §5-302.
Priority at scene of crime.
Procedures establishing, §5-303.
Public information program as to power to make arrests, §5-303.

Federal control in emergencies,
§1-207.40.

Federal property, protection of,
§5-133.05.

Fees for services, prohibition on accepting, §5-133.10.

Firearms.
Ammunition feeding devices, prohibition on transfer of, §5-133.16.
Pistol match attendance, expenses for, §5-133.15.

First amendment assemblies.
General provisions, §§5-331.01 to 5-331.17, 5-335.01, 5-337.01.
See FIRST AMENDMENT ASSEMBLIES.

METROPOLITAN POLICE —Cont'd

First amendment assemblies —Cont'd
Investigations concerning first amendment activities.
General provisions, §§5-333.01 to 5-333.13. See within this heading, "Investigations concerning first amendment activities."

Fleet management services.
Privatization contract, §2-381.42.

Forensic sciences department.
Transfer of personnel, records, functions and authority, §5-1501.08.

Gifts, prohibition on accepting,
§5-133.10.

Government employer-assisted housing program, §§42-2501 to 42-2507.

Helicopter duty, additional compensation for, §5-542.02.

Holidays.
Off-duty days and holidays, §5-1304.
Working on, compensation, §5-521.01.
Holiday defined, §5-521.02.

Homeland security and emergency management agency, §§7-2203, 7-2204.

Housing assistance and community safety program, §§42-2901 to 42-2903.
Community police presence, §42-2903.
Definitions, §42-2901.
Rental assistance, §42-2902.

Insignia of police and emergency medical services departments.
Unauthorized use, §22-1409.

Interrogations.
Electronic recording, §§5-116.01 to 5-116.03.

Investigations concerning first amendment activities, §§5-333.01 to 5-333.13.
Authorization for, §5-333.05.
Authorized public activities by MPD members, §5-333.10.
Citation of act, §5-333.01.
Construction of provisions, §5-333.13.
Definitions, §5-333.02.
Files, §5-333.11.
Auditing, §5-333.12.
Informants.
Defined, §5-333.02.
Use of, §5-333.07.
Monitoring and auditing of, §5-333.12.

METROPOLITAN POLICE —Cont'd
**Investigations concerning first
    amendment activities** —Cont'd
Policy on, §5-333.04.
Preliminary inquiries.
    Authorization for, §§5-333.05,
        5-333.06.
    First amendment assemblies,
        §5-333.09.
    Monitoring and auditing of,
        §5-333.12.
    Rules for, §5-333.08.
    Techniques and procedures,
        §5-333.07.
Purpose of act, §5-333.03.
Rules for, §5-333.08.
Scope of act, §5-333.03.
Techniques and procedures, §5-333.07.
Termination of, §5-333.05.
Title of act, §5-333.01.
**Joint operations command
    center/Synchronized operations
    command center.**
Video surveillance regulations,
    §5-133.19.
Jury duty, exemption from, §5-133.09.
Labor unions, §5-123.01.
Lateral police career appointments,
    §§1-610.71 to 1-610.76.
Appointment by mayor as class 1
    private, pay, §1-610.72.
Definitions, §1-610.71.
Leave accrual, §1-610.74.
Retirement benefits, §1-610.75.
    Credit for prior law enforcement
        service, §1-610.76.
Treatment as officer hired after
    September 30, 1987, §1-610.73.
Limited duty status, §5-632.
Definitions, §5-631.
Rules, §5-635.
Mayor.
Commissioning of officers by,
    §1-301.76.
Duties of, §5-101.03.
Powers of, §5-127.01.
Special detail of privates, §5-133.03.
Medical assistance.
Police and firefighters medical care
    reimbursement, §§5-601 to 5-609.
    See MEDICAL ASSISTANCE.
Medical leave.
Nonperformance of duty injuries and
    illnesses, §5-634.
Performance of duty injuries and
    illnesses, §5-633.

METROPOLITAN POLICE —Cont'd
Members, §§5-105.01, 5-105.05.
Eligibility for appointment, §§5-107.01,
    5-107.04.
Physical examinations, §5-107.02a.
Memorial fountain, §5-1301.
Military service and seniority rights,
    §5-1302.
Exemption from military service,
    §5-133.09.
Rank or grade, preservation of,
    §5-1303.
Wages and salaries, effect on, §5-1303.
Mobile laboratory, §5-133.13.
Motor vehicle insurance.
Enforcement of compulsory insurance
    requirements.
    General provisions, §§5-114.01 to
        5-114.04.
**Motor vehicle theft prevention
    teams,** §5-133.21.
Musicians, §§5-131.01 to 5-131.05.
**National Crime Information System,
    participation in,** §5-113.04.
Notice.
Property clerk notice to owners,
    §5-119.06.
Release of prisoners, §5-113.05.
Resignation of officers, §5-123.01.
Oaths and affirmations, §§5-105.03,
    5-119.05, 5-127.02.
Obligated service.
Agreement executed by candidates for
    appointment, term, leaving early,
    reimbursement, §5-107.01a.
Off-duty days and holidays, §5-1304.
Office of police complaints.
General provisions, §§5-1101 to 5-1115.
    See OFFICE OF POLICE
        COMPLAINTS.
Officers, §§5-105.01, 5-105.05.
Organization of, §5-105.05.
Overtime.
Holidays, working on, §§5-521.01,
    5-521.02.
Uniformed members at rank of
    inspector or above.
    Prohibited, §1-611.03.
Patrol services areas system,
    §5-101.04.
**Pawnbrokers, secondhand
    merchandise dealers, watch and
    jewelry auctioneers, etc.**
Examination of books and premises
    during investigations, §§5-117.02
    to 5-117.04.

METROPOLITAN POLICE —Cont'd

Physical examinations, §5-107.02a.

Pistol match attendance, expenses for, §5-133.15.

Police and firefighters retirement and disability.
General provisions, §§5-631 to 5-762. See POLICE AND FIREFIGHTERS RETIREMENT AND DISABILITY.

Police code, §§5-103.01, 5-103.02.

Police vehicles.
Proceeds from sale of excess vehicles, §5-133.18.

Powers of, §5-127.04.

Prevention of crime, expenditures for, §5-133.14.

Private detectives, §§5-121.01 to 5-121.05.

Private motor vehicles, use of, §5-133.02.

Private property details, §5-129.02.

Privatization contract.
Fleet management services, §2-381.42.

Probation period for officers and members, §5-105.04.

Promotion of officers and members, §§1-608.01, 5-105.01, 5-543.04.

Property clerk, §§5-119.01 to 5-119.19.
Abandoned property, §§5-119.18, 5-119.19.
Acquittal of arrested person, return of property to, §§5-119.07, 5-119.08.
Animals, sale of unclaimed, §5-119.12.
Custody of lost, stolen, or abandoned property, §5-119.02.
Damages to property, §5-119.11.
Deceased persons, property of, §5-119.09.
Depositions, certification of, §5-119.05.
Evidence, use as, §5-119.17.
Fees for protecting property, §5-119.09.
Immunity, §§5-119.06, 5-119.11.
Incompetent or incapacitated persons, custody of property of, §5-119.09.
Large quantities of goods held for sale, §5-119.16.
More than one claimant to property, §5-119.06.
Notary Public, powers of, §5-119.04.
Oaths and affirmations, administration of, §5-119.05.
Perishable property, §§5-119.13, 5-119.15.
Public auction, sale of property at, §5-119.10.

METROPOLITAN POLICE —Cont'd

Property clerk —Cont'd
Records, §5-119.03.
Returning property to owners, §§5-119.06 to 5-119.09.
Sale of property, §§5-119.09 to 5-119.16.
Storage of property by, §5-119.09.
Transmittal of property taken into custody to, §5-119.09.
Trial, return to owner prior to, §§5-119.14 to 5-119.16.

Prosecution of arrested persons, §5-115.07.

Qualifications, §§5-107.01, 5-107.04.
Physical examinations, §5-107.02a.

Records, §5-113.01.
Contacts, frisks and stops, §5-113.01.
Crime investigation records, §§5-113.31 to 5-113.34.
Definitions, §5-113.31.
Penalties for willful or malicious tampering with records, §5-113.33.
Records retention schedule, §5-113.34.
Retention of records and preservation of evidence, §5-113.32.
Criminal records, §§5-113.02 to 5-113.04.
Destruction of, §5-113.07.
Preservation of, §5-113.07.
Property Clerk, §5-119.03.
Public inspection of, §5-113.06.

Reimbursable details.
Alcoholic beverage licenses, §25-798.

Release of prisoners, notice of, §5-113.05.

Reports.
Chief of Police, §5-133.08.

Reports by other police to, §5-113.03.

Reserve corps, §5-129.51.

Resignations, §5-123.01.

Resisting arrest, §22-405.01.

Retirement while under disciplinary investigation, §§5-801 to 5-807.

RFK Stadium, barriers and restricted zones at, §3-343.

Rulemaking authority.
Depositing of seized currency, §23-533.

Salaries.
Police and firefighters, §§5-501.01 to 5-563.02.
See WAGES AND SALARIES.

METROPOLITAN POLICE —Cont'd
School safety division, §§5-132.01 to 5-132.21.
  Comprehensive plan on school security, §5-132.04.
  Contracts related to school security.
    Requests for proposals.
      Authority to issue, §5-132.05.
  Definitions, §5-132.01.
  Effective date of provisions, §5-132.06.
  Establishment, §5-132.02.
  Functions, §5-132.02.
  Gang and crew violence, protection of students from, §5-132.02.
  Memorandum of agreement, §5-132.04.
  School safe passage emergency zones, §5-132.21.
  School security personnel.
    Defined, §5-132.01.
    Training, §5-132.03.
Scuba diving duty, additional compensation for, §5-542.02.
Seized currency.
  Depositing of seized currency, §§23-531 to 23-534.
Service obligation.
  Agreement executed by candidates for appointment, term, leaving early, reimbursement, §5-107.01a.
Service of process by, §13-302.01.
Service of process upon sworn member.
  Actions arising out of performance of duties.
    Rules establishing procedure, issuance, requirements, §5-105.09.
Sexual assault response.
  Duties, §4-561.07.
  Monitoring by chief of police, §4-561.08.
  Reports, §4-561.09.
Special assignments, §5-1304.
Special details.
  Band, §5-131.02.
  Citizens appointed without pay, §5-129.03.
  Mayor's detail of privates, §5-133.03.
  Property of individual or corporation, protection of, §5-129.02.
Standards and training board, §§5-107.03, 5-107.04.
Strikes, §5-123.01.
Subdivisions, §5-101.02.
Technicians, salary, §5-543.02.
Trachea holds, §5-125.03.

METROPOLITAN POLICE —Cont'd
Trial boards, §§5-133.06, 5-1001 to 5-1011.
Two-year term of obligated service.
  Agreement executed by candidates for appointment, leaving early, reimbursement, §5-107.01a.
Uniforms, §5-111.01.
  Appropriations for, §5-111.03.
  United States flag, display of, §5-111.02.
Vacancies, filling, §5-105.01.
Video recordings.
  Video surveillance regulations, §5-133.19.
Wages.
  See WAGES AND SALARIES.
Watchmen at municipal building.
  Not detailed, §5-133.04a.
Witnesses, detention of, §5-115.05.
Workweek, §5-1304.
Wrongful arrest cases.
  Legal assistance for police involved in, §5-115.04.

METROPOLITAN WASHINGTON AIRPORTS AUTHORITY, §§9-901 to 9-926, 9-1001 to 9-1011.
Audits, §9-919.
Authorization of, §9-903.
Bond issues, §§9-910, 9-1006.
  Credit of District not pledged, §9-915.
  Legal investment, §9-914.
  Marketability, §9-913.
  Pledge of funds, §9-912.
  Refunding bonds, §9-911.
  Securities for public deposit, §9-914.
Conflicts of law, §9-926.
Construction projects, §9-1005.
Contract liability, §9-922.
Definitions, §9-1003.
Eminent domain, §9-909.
Establishment of, §9-902.
Federal employees, §9-1007.
Fees, §9-917.
Foreign trade zone, operation of, §9-908.
Funds, §9-918.
Improvements, making, §9-1005.
Interpretation of provisions, §§9-924, 9-925.
Issuance of rules and regulations, §9-906.
Jurisdiction, §9-922.
Leases of airports, §§9-1004, 9-1009.
Membership and organization, §§9-904, 9-1006.

METROPOLITAN WASHINGTON AIRPORTS AUTHORITY —Cont'd
Nonstop flight requirements, §9-1011.
Police powers of, §9-907.
Policy declaration, §§9-1001, 9-1002.
Powers and duties, §§9-905, 9-1006.
Procurement practices, §9-923.
Real property acquisitions, §9-909.
Relationship to other laws, §9-1008.
Remedies, §9-920.
Repair and maintenance, §9-1005.
Separability of provisions, §9-1010.
Tax exemption, §9-921.
Tort liability, §9-922.

METRORAIL AND METROBUS,
§§9-1101.01 to 9-1115.04, 35-201 to 35-253.
Acquisition of mass transit bus systems, §§9-1113.01 to 9-1113.07.
Capital grant assistance, §9-1113.03.
Comptroller General of United States.
Authority of, §9-1113.07.
Condemnation proceedings.
Jurisdiction for, §9-1113.06.
Immediate grants, §9-1113.04.
Mayor authorized to pay District's share of cost of, §9-1113.02.
Policy declaration, §9-1113.01.
Repayment of advances, §9-1113.05.
Adopted regional system, §§9-1111.01 to 9-1111.17.
Appropriations.
Arlington cemetery and Smithsonian transit stations, §9-1111.10.
Authorization for, §9-1111.08.
Bond issues.
District contributions, funding, §1-204.89.
Guarantee of obligations, §9-1111.06.
Lawful investments, obligations as, §9-1111.09.
Payment on bonds, §9-1111.12.
Construction.
Approval of, §9-1111.04.
Federal contributions for, §§9-1111.11, 9-1111.14.
Definitions, §9-1111.01.
District contributions, §§1-204.89, 9-1111.03.
Excess revenues, §9-1111.05.
Federal contributions to, §§9-1111.02, 9-1111.11, 9-1111.14.
Local participating governments' revenue sources, §9-1111.13.
Metrorail/Metrobus account.
Establishment of, §9-1111.15.

METRORAIL AND METROBUS —Cont'd
Adopted regional system —Cont'd
Metrorail/Metrobus account —Cont'd
Reports, §9-1111.16.
Persons with disabilities.
Facilities for, §9-1111.17.
Aerial wires, §§9-1171 to 9-1174.
Assessment reports, §9-1174.
Authorized, §9-1171.
Planning requirements, §9-1173.
Wire-free zones, §9-1172.
Alternative fuel technology, §§50-701 to 50-715.
See ALTERNATIVE FUEL TECHNOLOGY.
Appropriations.
Adopted regional system.
Arlington cemetery and Smithsonian transit stations, §9-1111.10.
Authorization of appropriations, §9-1111.08.
Compact for mass transportation, §9-1103.03.
Rail rapid transit, §9-1105.02.
Washington metropolitan area transit authority compact, §9-1107.07.
Bond issues.
Adopted regional system. See within this heading, "Adopted regional system."
Washington metropolitan area transit authority compact, §9-1107.01.
Woodrow Wilson bridge and tunnel compact, §9-1115.03.
Bus stops.
Smoking, §7-1703.
Certificate required for competitive lines, §35-201.
Compact for mass transportation, §§9-1103.01 to 9-1103.07.
Amendments to, §9-1103.03.
Appropriations, §9-1103.03.
Congressional consent given.
For entry into compact, §9-1103.01.
To effectuate amendments, §9-1103.02.
Congressional right to alter, amend, or appeal, §9-1103.07.
Covenant enshrining, §9-1103.01.
Effect on other laws, §9-1103.04.
Enforcement, §9-1103.06.
Jurisdiction, §9-1103.06.
Mayor's duties regarding, §9-1103.03.
Review of Transit Commission orders, §9-1103.06.

METRORAIL AND METROBUS
—Cont'd
Compact for mass transportation
—Cont'd
Strikebreaking, use for, §9-1103.05.
Condemnation proceedings.
Acquisition of mass transit bus
systems, §9-1113.06.
Conduct, standards of, §§35-251 to
35-253.
Crimes and offenses.
Enhanced penalties for offenses
committed against transit
operators and station managers,
§22-3751.01.
Notice of enhanced penalties,
§35-261.
Offenses for which penalties apply,
§22-3752.
DC Circulator bus service,
§§50-921.31 to 50-921.38.
Definitions, §§34-216, 34-217.
Disused tracks, §35-211.
Duct lines, §35-206.
Entry by rear exit door, §35-216.
**Failure to pay fare or present valid
transfer,** §35-216.
**Fenders, street cars required to
have,** §35-204.
Fines and penalties.
Disused tracks, failure to remove,
§35-211.
Insufficiency of maintenance of
services and equipment, §35-202.
Misconduct or unlawful conduct,
§35-253.
Transfers, unlawful use of, §35-207.
Interpretation of provisions.
Washington metropolitan area transit
authority compact, §9-1107.01.
Interstate agreement program,
§9-1101.01.
Joint state oversight agency,
§§9-1109.01 to 9-1109.07.
Amendments to interstate agreement,
§9-1109.05.
Authorization of interstate agreement,
§9-1109.02.
Definitions, §9-1109.01.
District program in place of,
§9-1109.07.
District representatives.
Appointment of, §9-1109.03.
Procurement practices law
inapplicable to, §9-1109.06.
Requirements for interstate
agreement, §9-1109.04.

METRORAIL AND METROBUS
—Cont'd
Jurisdiction.
Acquisition of mass transit bus
systems.
Condemnation proceedings for,
§9-1113.06.
Compact for mass transportation,
§9-1103.06.
Potomac River Bridges Towing
Compact, §9-1117.03.
Washington metropolitan area transit
authority compact, §9-1107.10.
Washington metropolitan area transit
commission.
Review of orders of, §9-1107.01.
Labor and employment relations.
Transportation benefits.
Reducing single occupancy vehicle
use by encouraging transit
benefits, §§32-151 to 32-153.
**Maintenance of services and
equipment,** §35-202.
Mayor's duties.
Acquisition of mass transit bus
systems.
Authorized to pay District's share of
cost of, §9-1113.02.
Compact for mass transportation,
§9-1103.03.
Joint state oversight agency.
Authorization of interstate
agreement regarding,
§9-1109.02.
Washington metropolitan area transit
authority compact, §§9-1107.07,
9-1107.09.
Woodrow Wilson bridge and tunnel
compact, §9-1115.01.
Mergers and consolidations, §34-217.
Michigan Avenue viaduct, use of,
§9-321.
Misconduct on, §§35-251 to 35-253.
**National Capital transportation
agency transfers to Washington
metropolitan area transit
authority compact,** §9-1107.09.
**National capital transportation
program,** §9-1101.01.
**New York Avenue metrorail benefit
area.**
Special assessment district, §§47-881
to 47-885.
**Potomac river bridges towing
compact,** §§9-1117.01 to 9-1117.05.
Prosecutions, information as to,
§35-203.

METRORAIL AND METROBUS
—Cont'd
Public service commission.
See PUBLIC SERVICE
COMMISSION.
Rail rapid transit, §§9-1105.01 to
9-1105.03.
Rail requirements, §35-209.
Reciprocal trackage agreements,
§35-208.
Free transfers under, §35-212.
Unlawful use of another's
underground line, §35-210.
**Refusal of transportation to
violators of rules,** §35-252.
Reports, §35-215.
Safety regulation, §§9-1109.01 to
9-1109.07. See within this heading,
"Joint state oversight agency."
Severability of provisions.
Rail rapid transit, §9-1105.03.
Washington metropolitan area transit
authority compact, §9-1107.01.
Smoking, §7-1703.
"No Smoking" signs, §7-1704.
Stops.
Smoking, §7-1703.
Student fares, §§35-232 to 35-237.
Certification of eligibility required for,
§§35-234, 35-235.
Charter school students, §38-1802.08.
Discount cards, §35-234.
Eligibility for, §§35-233, 35-235.
Issuance of rules and regulations
regarding, §35-237.
Need requirements, §35-235.
Rates, §35-233.
Subsidies for, §§35-232, 35-236.
Tokens and tickets, §35-234.
Transfers, §35-233.
Validity of, §35-233.
**Sufficient cars, power, and
equipment,** §35-202.
Tokens and tickets.
Forgery, §22-3242.
Student fares, §35-234.
Transfers.
Failure to present valid transfer,
§35-216.
Forgery, §22-3242.
Reciprocal agreements, §§35-208,
35-212.
Student fares, §35-233.
Unlawful use of, §35-207.
Transfer tickets.
Unlawful disposition, acceptance and
use, §35-207.
Prosecution on information, §35-203.

METRORAIL AND METROBUS
—Cont'd
Underground lines of others.
Unlawful use of, §35-210.
Unlawful conduct, §§35-251 to 35-253.
**Washington metropolitan area
transit authority compact,**
§§9-1107.01 to 9-1107.12.
Amendment of United States and
District laws and reorganization
plans by, §9-1107.11.
Amendments, §§9-1107.02 to
9-1107.08.
Appropriations, §9-1107.07.
Bond issues, §9-1107.01.
Budget, §9-1107.01.
Condemnation proceedings,
§9-1107.01.
Conflicts of interest, §9-1107.01.
Congressional consent, §9-1107.01.
Title III amendments to articles I
and XVI, §9-1107.06.
Title III amendments to articles I,
III, VII, IX, XI, XIV, and XVI,
§9-1107.04.
Title III amendments to articles XII
and XVI, §9-1107.05.
Council authority to amend,
§§9-1107.02, 9-1107.03.
Funds, §9-1107.01.
Insurance, §9-1107.01.
Interpretation of provisions,
§9-1107.01.
Jurisdiction, §9-1107.10.
Mayor's duties, §§9-1107.07, 9-1107.09.
Reservation of right to alter, amend, or
repeal, §9-1107.12.
Severability of provisions, §9-1107.01.
Technical amendments, §9-1107.08.
Terms of compact, §9-1107.01.
Transfers from National Capital
Transportation Agency to,
§9-1107.09.
**Washington metropolitan area
transit authority fund,**
§§9-1108.01, 9-1108.02.
**Washington Metropolitan Area
Transit Commission.**
Jurisdiction of, §9-1107.01.
Review of Transit Commission orders,
§9-1103.06.
**Woodrow Wilson bridge and tunnel
compact,** §§9-1115.01 to 9-1115.04.

MICE.
Bureau of rodent control,
§§8-2101.01, 8-2101.02.

MICE —Cont'd
Rodent abatement program, §§8-2103.01 to 8-2103.05.

MICHIGAN AVENUE.
Abandonment of portion of, §9-105.03.
Grade crossing elimination projects, §§9-320, 9-322.
Plats, §9-105.04.
Relocation of, §§9-105.01, 9-105.04.
Right-of-way for Washington Railway and Electric Company, §9-101.15.
Viaduct, §§9-320, 9-321.

MILITARY AFFAIRS, §§49-101 to 49-1006.
Business licenses.
  Waiver of business license renewal fees for armed forces personnel, §1-301.01.
Child custody rights during deployment, §16-914.02.
Commander-in-chief, US Const Art II §2.
Congress.
  Appropriation powers for army or navy, US Const Art I §8.
Courts-martial.
  General provisions, §§49-501 to 49-509.
  See COURTS-MARTIAL.
Differential pay.
  District employee called to active duty. Operation Enduring Freedom, §1-611.03.
Direct-reduction loans for veterans, §42-3002.
Disabled American Veterans property as real property exempt from taxation, §47-1003.
Drivers' licenses for military personnel, §50-1401.01.
Hospitalization of persons with mental illness, §§21-587, 21-907, 21-908.
Indigent children, enlistment of, §§21-181, 21-182.
Interstate compact on educational opportunity for military children, §§49-1101.01 to 49-1101.20.
  See SCHOOLS AND EDUCATION.
Junior Reserve Officers' Training Program, §38-158.
Mental illness, hospitalization of persons with, §§21-587, 21-907, 21-908.

MILITARY AFFAIRS —Cont'd
Metropolitan police.
  Exemption from military duty, §5-133.09.
  Rank or grade, preservation of, §5-1303.
  Seniority rights and military service of, §5-1302.
  Wages and salaries, effect of service on, §5-1303.
Militia.
  See MILITIA.
Mortgages and deeds of trust.
  Servicemen's readjustment, §§42-3001, 42-3002.
Motor vehicles.
  Drivers' licenses for military personnel, §50-1401.01.
  Registration for disabled American veterans, §50-1503.01.
National guard.
  General provisions, §§49-101 to 49-906.
  See NATIONAL GUARD.
Police and firefighters retirement and disability.
  Credit for active military naval service, §5-742.
  Federal benefit payments affected by purchase of military service credit, §1-803.02.
Powers of attorney, §21-2114.
President of the United States.
  Commander-in-chief, US Const Art II §2.
Real property exempt from taxation.
  National Guard Association, §47-1042.
  Veterans.
    See VETERANS.
Recorder of deeds recording service and discharge certificates, §42-1215.
Schools and education.
  See SCHOOLS AND EDUCATION.
Servicemembers civil relief act.
  Default judgments, CivPro Rule 55-II, LandlordTenant Rules 11, 14.
  Affidavit, CivPro Form CA 114.
  Instruction sheet for Form CA 114, CivPro Form CA 114.1.
Veterans.
  See VETERANS.
Visitation rights during deployment, §16-914.02.
Voting by overseas military, §§1-1061.01 to 1-1061.20.
  See ELECTIONS.

MILITARY AFFAIRS —Cont'd
Weapons otherwise prohibited,
§22-4514.
Wills, §18-107.

MILITIA.
Calling out, §49-405.
Commander-in-Chief, President of
United States as, §49-409.
Courts-martial.
General provisions, §§49-501 to
49-509.
See COURTS-MARTIAL.
Duties of, §49-404.
Enrollment in.
Exempted persons, §49-402.
Enrollment requirements, §49-401.
Fire departments, §49-404.
List of persons liable to enrollment,
§49-403.
National guard.
General provisions, §§49-101 to
49-906.
See NATIONAL GUARD.
Police departments, §49-404.
Reserve corps of National Guard,
§49-407.

MILK AND MILK PRODUCTS.
Registration of milk containers,
§§36-121 to 36-157.
See MILK CONTAINER
REGISTRATION.
Sale by weight, §37-201.14.

MILK CONTAINER REGISTRATION,
§§36-121 to 36-157.
Applicability of provisions, §36-129.
Defacing or destroying registered
containers, §§36-123, 36-153.
Definitions, §§36-128, 36-151.
Description of milk container, filing
and publication of, §§36-121,
36-152.
Existing registrants, preservation of
rights of, §36-127.
Fines, §36-130.
Injunctions, §36-131.
Issuance of rules and regulations,
§36-156.
Person defined for purposes of,
§36-128.
Prosecutions, §§36-125, 36-130, 36-155.
Recorder of deeds, powers and
duties of, §36-156.
Refusal to surrender registered
container to registrant, §§36-124,
36-154.

MILK CONTAINER REGISTRATION
—Cont'd
Search warrants, §36-155.
Superior court proceedings,
§§36-125, 36-155.
Title to registered mark, acquiring,
§36-126.
Torts, §36-157.
Types of container, §36-129.
Unauthorized sale or use of
registered containers, §§36-122,
36-153.

MINES AND MINERALS.
Contracts.
Sales.
Applicability of sales chapter of
commercial code, §28:2-107.
Principal and income.
Mineral rights, §28-4804.11.
Secured transactions.
Description of land, §28:9-203.
When security interest attaches,
§28:9-204.

MINIATURE SPOONS.
Drug paraphernalia, §§48-904.10,
48-1101 to 48-1104.

MINIMUM WAGES, §§32-1001 to
32-1015.
Administrative actions, §32-1012.01.
Annual adjustments, §32-1003.
Civil actions, §32-1012.
Collective bargaining, §32-1014.
Definitions, §32-1002.
Disabilities, workers with, §32-1003.
Employers' duties, §32-1008.
Exceptions, §32-1004.
Fines, §32-1011.
Gratuities, employees receiving,
§32-1003.
Investigations, §32-1007.
Issuance of rules and regulations,
§32-1006.
Mayor.
Authority of, §32-1005.
Investigatory powers of, §32-1007.
Regulatory powers of, §32-1006.
Reporting to council, §32-1007.
Notice of act, posting and
distribution, §32-1009.
Tipped wages, §32-1009.01.
Overtime.
Time and a half, §32-1003.
Penalties, §32-1011.
Policy declaration, §32-1001.
Rate, §32-1003.

MINIMUM WAGES —Cont'd
Records, §32-1008.
Remedies, §32-1011.01.
Requirements, §32-1003.
Revised wage orders, §32-1015.
Security officer working in office building, §32-1003.
Office building defined, §32-1002.
Security officer defined, §32-1002.
Violations, §32-1010.
When persons deemed employed in District, §32-1003.

MINISTER-PENITENT PRIVILEGE, §14-309.

MINISTERS.
See RELIGION, MINISTERS OF.

MINORITY-OWNED BUSINESSES.
Community development by financial institutions, §§26-431.01 to 26-431.08.
Minority and women-owned business assessment program, §§2-214.01, 2-214.02.

MINORITY-OWNED SAVINGS AND LOAN ASSOCIATIONS, §26-1217.

MINORS.
See CHILDREN AND MINORS.

MIRANDA WARNINGS.
Initial proceedings before the court.
Statement by the court, CrimPro Rule 5.

MIRROR IMAGE RULE.
Contracts for sale of goods.
Variation of rule, §28:2-207.

MISCONDUCT.
See CONDUCT, STANDARDS OF.

MISDEMEANORS.
See CRIMES AND OFFENSES.

MISREPRESENTATIONS.
See FRAUD AND DECEIT.

MISSING PERSONS.
Child abuse and neglect proceedings.
Service of process where parent missing, NeglectProc Rule 11.
Child and family services agency.
Reports of missing children, §4-1323.01.
Conservators, Probate Rules 350, 351.
Interstate compact for juveniles, §§24-1101 to 24-1106.
Alteration, amendment or repeal of provisions, §24-1106.

MISSING PERSONS —Cont'd
Interstate compact for juveniles —Cont'd
Compact administrator, §24-1103.
Congressional findings, §24-1101.
Construction of compact, §24-1105.
Enforcement, §24-1104.
Entry into and execution of compact, §24-1102.
Protective orders, Probate Rule 350.

MISS UTILITY, §§34-2701 to 34-2709.
Damages.
Excavation or demolition, caused by, §34-2706.
Liability and civil penalties, §34-2707.
Definitions, §34-2701.
Emergency digs, §34-2709.
Excavation or demolition.
Damage caused by, §34-2706.
Definitions, §34-2701.
Emergency digs, §34-2709.
Mandamus or injunction against improper digs, §34-2708.
Notice required prior to, §34-2704.
Requirements for, §34-2705.
Mandamus or injunction against improper digs, §34-2708.
Notice prior to excavation or demolition, §34-2704.
One-call center.
Defined, §34-2701.
Formation of, §34-2702.
Operation of, §34-2702.
Permit drawings, availability of, §34-2703.

MISTAKE OR ERROR.
Adoption proceedings, Adoption Rules 60, 61.
Complaint for money paid by mistake, CivPro Form CA 7.
Delinquent minors.
Clerical mistakes in judgments, orders, etc., JuvProc Rule 36.
Harmless error and plain error, JuvProc Rule 52.
Petitions, JuvProc Rule 7.
Depositions, CivPro Rule 32.
Domestic relations actions, DomRel Rule 32.
Harmless error.
Adoption proceedings, Adoption Rule 61.
Civil procedure, CivPro Rule 61.
Criminal procedure, CrimPro Rule 52.
Plea procedures, CrimPro Rule 11.

MISTAKE OR ERROR —Cont'd
Harmless error —Cont'd
  Domestic relations actions, DomRel
    Rule 61.
  Juvenile proceedings, JuvProc Rule 52.
Indictments and informations,
  CrimPro Rule 7.
Judgments and orders, CivPro Rule
  60, CrimPro Rule 36.
  Domestic relations actions, DomRel
    Rule 60.
  Harmless error. See within this
    heading, "Harmless error."
Plain error.
  Criminal procedure, CrimPro Rule 52.
  Juvenile proceedings, JuvProc Rule 52.
Pleading special matters, CivPro Rule
  9.
  Domestic relations actions, DomRel
    Rule 9.
Plea procedures, CrimPro Rule 11.
Probate proceedings.
  Clerical mistakes in rulings,
    judgments, etc.
    Death between Jan. 1, 1981 and
      June 30, 1995, Probate Rule
      130.
    Death on or after July 1, 1995,
      Probate Rule 430.

MISTRIALS.
Comments before order, CrimPro
  Rule 26.3.
  Delinquent minors, JuvProc Rule 26.3.
Witness statements.
  Failure to produce statement, CrimPro
    Rule 26.2.
  Delinquent minors, JuvProc Rule
    26.2.

MOBILE TELECOMMUNICATIONS
  SERVICES.
Toll telecommunication service tax.
  Defined, §47-3901.
  Special rules for, §47-3922.

MOLD.
Indoor mold assessment and
  remediation, §§8-241.01 to
  8-241.09.
  See INDOOR MOLD ASSESSMENT
    AND REMEDIATION.

MOLOTOV COCKTAILS, §22-4515a.
Unlawful conduct, §22-4515a.

MONEY.
Congress.
  Powers of congress, US Const Art I
    §§8, 10.

MONEY —Cont'd
Defined, §28:1-201.
Metropolitan police.
  Currency.
    Depositing of seized currency,
      §§23-531 to 23-534.
Presumed abandonment of, §41-105.
Sufficiency of description for
  criminal indictments and
  informations, §23-321.

MONEY DECREES.
Assignment of choses in action,
  §28-2301.

MONEY LENDERS, §§26-901 to
  26-912.
Amounts of loans, §§26-904, 26-905.
Annual statements, §26-904.
Bonds, surety, §26-902.
Complaint for money lent, CivPro
  Form CA 6.
Complaint procedures, §26-906.
Damages provisions in contracts,
  §26-909.
Deductions from principal, §26-905.
Enforcement of provisions, §26-911.
Exemptions from provisions,
  §§26-910, 26-912.
Fees, §§26-905, 26-908.
Fines, §26-907.
Foreclosures, §26-908.
Inspection of registers, §26-904.
Interest rates, §26-905.
Investigations, §26-906.
Issuance of rules and regulations,
  §26-911.
Licenses.
  Applications for, §§26-902, 26-903.
  Bonds, surety.
    Accompanying application for
      license, §26-903.
  Denial, suspension, or revocation,
    §26-906.
  Requirement to have, §26-901.
Notice of death or discontinuation
  of business, §26-901.
Penalties.
  Contracts may not hold penalty
    provisions, §26-909.
  Violation of provisions, §26-907.
Receipts and statements provided to
  borrower, §26-905.
Records, §§26-904, 26-905.
Register, requirement to keep,
  §26-904.
Reports, §26-904.
Resident agent required for, §26-901.

MONEY LENDERS —Cont'd
Service of process, §26-901.
Severability of provisions, §26-912.
Taxation, §26-901.

MONEY ORDERS.
Fraudulent, §22-1510.
Metropolitan police.
Depositing of seized currency,
§§23-531 to 23-534.
Presumed abandonment of, §41-105.

MONEY TRANSMISSIONS, §§26-1001
to 26-1027.
**Authorized delegate, conducting
business through.**
Conduct, §26-1017.
Contracts, §26-1016.
Revocation or suspension, §26-1018.
Cease and desist proceedings,
§26-1022.
Changes in control of licensee,
§26-1012.
Civil penalties, §26-1021.
Criminal penalties, §26-1023.
Definitions, §26-1001.
Examination of licensee, §26-1013.
Exemptions from chapter, §26-1003.
Hearings and procedures.
Law governing, §26-1020.
Jurisdiction of courts of District.
Consent to, §26-1025.
Liability of licensee, §26-1019.
License to engage in business.
Application, §26-1006.
Contesting denial, §26-1009.
Fee, §26-1008.
Hearing on denial, §26-1009.
Notice application complete,
§26-1009.
Time limit for approving or denying,
§26-1009.
Bond or other security, §26-1007.
Investigation of application, §26-1009.
Issuance, §26-1009.
Not transferable or assignable,
§26-1002.
Persons engaged in selling payment
instruments under repealed
chapter 31, §26-1002.
Qualifications, §26-1004.
Renewal, §26-1010.
Required, §26-1002.
Separate license for cashing of checks
not required, §26-1026.
Suspension or revocation, §26-1015.
On-site examination of licensee,
§26-1013.

MONEY TRANSMISSIONS —Cont'd
Permissible investments.
Amount required of licensee, waiver,
§26-1005.
Held in trust, §26-1005.
Receipts to customers required,
§26-1027.
Records.
Keeping, preservation, destruction,
§26-1014.
Reports.
Annual report, §26-1010.
Special reporting requirements,
§26-1011.
Rules, §26-1024.
Violations.
Civil penalties, §26-1021.
Criminal penalties, §26-1023.
Enforcement, §26-1022.

MONOPOLIES.
Cigarette sales below cost, §§28-4521
to 28-4527.
See CIGARETTES.
Restraints of trade, §§28-4501 to
28-4518.
See RESTRAINTS OF TRADE.

MONROE STREET BRIDGE, §9-310.

MONTE CARLO NIGHTS.
**Lottery and charitable games
control board,** §§3-1322 to 3-1332.
**Operated for educational and
charitable purposes.**
Advertising and promoting, §22-1718.
Permissible activity, §22-1717.

MONTH TO MONTH, ESTATES BY,
§42-521.

MONTROSE PARK, §10-109.

**MORTGAGE LENDERS AND
BROKERS,** §§26-1101 to 26-1121.
Acquisition of control, §26-1105.
Actions for violation.
Mortgage protection violations,
§26-1153.01.
Administrative penalties.
Mortgage protection provision,
§26-1153.03.
Administrative procedure, §26-1119.
Advertising, §26-1116.
Assignee liability, §26-1153.05.
Bonds, surety, §26-1103.
Change of place of business,
§26-1108.
Confidentiality of information,
§26-1120.01.

MORTGAGE LENDERS AND BROKERS —Cont'd

Damages for violation.
Mortgage protection violations, §26-1153.01.
Definitions, §26-1101.
Mortgage loan protection, §26-1151.01.
Disclosures of loans, §26-1113.
Dual capacity, acting in, §26-1114.
Enforcement of provisions, §26-1118.
Mortgage protection provision, §26-1153.02.
Escrow accounts, §26-1115.
Evasive business tactics, §26-1117.
Examinations, §26-1112.
Exemptions from provisions, §26-1102.
False statements, §26-1114.
Filing requirements, §26-1152.21.
Final decision.
Mortgage protection provision, §26-1153.04.
Fraud, §26-1114.
Hearings, §26-1119.
Inspections, §26-1112.
Investigations, §26-1112.
Issuance of rules and regulations, §26-1121.
Licenses.
Acquisition of control, requirements for, §26-1105.
Application for, §26-1103.
Bonds, surety, §26-1103.
Denial of, §26-1106.
Expiration, §26-1107.
Fees, §§26-1103, 26-1107.
Issuance of, §26-1104.
Renewal, §26-1107.
Requirements regarding, §26-1103.
Surrender of, §26-1111.
Suspension or revocation, §26-1118.
Median family income.
Availability to lenders, §26-1152.23.
Misrepresentation by name, §26-1120.
Names, limitations on, §26-1120.
Nationwide mortgage licensing system and registry, §§26-1161.01 to 26-1161.11.
Defined, §26-1102.
Information challenge process, §26-1120.03.
Reports, §26-1120.02.
Notice.
Dual capacity, acting in, §26-1114.
Orders, §26-1119.

MORTGAGE LENDERS AND BROKERS —Cont'd

Orders, §26-1119.
Penalties, §26-1118.
Predatory loans or lending activities, §26-1114.
Prohibited acts, §§26-1114, 26-1152.01 to 26-1155.01.
Advance payments, §26-1152.16.
Advance waivers, §26-1152.17.
Applicability, §§26-1151.02, 26-1152.01, 26-1155.01.
Arbitration.
Oppressive mandatory arbitration clauses, §26-1152.18.
Balloon payments, §26-1152.13.
Borrower not able to make scheduled payments.
Lender making loan anyway, §26-1152.02.
Charges in bad faith, §26-1152.10.
Credit scores, unfair use, §26-1152.06.
Default, encouraging, §26-1152.05.
Default, increasing interest rate, §26-1152.09.
Disclosure notice.
Failure to timely send, §26-1152.11.
Favorable payment record.
Failing to report, §26-1152.07.
Financing origination or discount points and fees.
Refinancing loan, §26-1152.04.
Home improvement contracts, §26-1152.08.
Negative amortization, §26-1152.15.
No call provision, §26-1152.14.
Prepayment premium, fee or charge, §26-1152.12.
Single premium credit insurance.
Selling with covered loan, §26-1152.03.
Steering, §26-1152.06.
Purchaser or assignee of covered loan.
Liability, §26-1153.05.
Records, §26-1109.
Red flag disclosure notice.
Right to obtain counseling, §26-1152.19.
Regulatory provisions, §§26-1301 to 26-1336.
See TRUST, MORTGAGE AND TITLE CORPORATIONS.
Remedies for violation.
Mortgage protection violations, §26-1153.01.

MORTGAGE LENDERS AND BROKERS —Cont'd

Reports, §26-1110.

Nationwide mortgage licensing system and registry, §26-1120.02.

Right to obtain counseling.

Red flag disclosure notice, §26-1152.19.

Rules, §26-1154.01.

Settlement service providers.

List of suspect service providers, §26-1152.22.

Unfair or deceptive practices, §26-1114.

Verification that brokers licensed, §26-1152.20.

Violation of provisions, §26-1117.

Mortgage protection provision, §26-1153.01.

Administrative penalties, §26-1153.03.

Unlawful trade practices, §28-3904.

MORTGAGE LOAN PROTECTION, §§26-1151.01 to 26-1155.01.

See MORTGAGE LENDERS AND BROKERS.

MORTGAGES AND DEEDS OF TRUST, §§42-804 to 42-820.

Casualty insurance premiums.

Payments, §28-3301.

Children and minors.

Conveyances or assurances by, §§42-808, 42-809.

Property of, §21-158.

Servicemen's readjustment, §42-3001.

Commercial code.

Secured transactions, §§28:9-101 to 28:9-809.

See SECURED TRANSACTIONS.

Consumer protection.

Credit line deeds of trust, §28-3904.

Cooperative associations.

Powers, §29-905.

Corporations.

Powers, §29-303.02.

Credit line deeds of trust, §§42-2301 to 42-2303.

Death of mortgagee or trustee.

Appointment of trustee, §42-811.

Deed of release, petition, §42-819.

Deed of release.

Death of mortgagee or trustee, §42-819.

Defendant filing request and plaintiff filing admission.

Decree or order, §42-806.

MORTGAGES AND DEEDS OF TRUST —Cont'd

Defense against foreclosure.

Equity practice followed, answer establishing defense, §42-812.

Deficiency judgment.

Sale of property, §42-816.

Department of housing and community development.

Employer-assisted housing program, §§42-2501 to 42-2507.

Ejectment cases, legal title in mortgagee or trustee, §16-1105.

Estate of mortgagee or trustee, §42-803.

Execution, acknowledgment and recordation, §42-801.

Duty of recorder of deeds, §42-802.

Execution of judgment, property exempt from, §15-502.

Financing statements.

Mortgage as financing statement, §28:9-502.

Foreclosure.

Defense against foreclosure.

Equity practice followed, answer establishing defense, §42-812.

Mediation, residential mortgages, §42-815.02.

Construction of provisions, §42-815.04.

Fund, §42-815.03.

Notice of intention to foreclose, §42-815.

Rescue services, §§42-2431 to 42-2435.

Definitions, §42-2431.

Fiduciary duties, §42-2433.

Penalties for violations, §42-2435.

Private right of action, §42-2434.

Prohibited transactions and practices, §42-2432.

Residential mortgage foreclosure default, right to cure, §42-815.01.

Form of, §42-601.

Insurance.

Casualty insurance premiums.

Requirements, §28-3301.

Interest.

Exempt mortgages, §§28-3307, 28-3309.

Maximum rate, §28-3301.

Prepayment.

No penalty after three years, §28-3301.

Loan officers, §§26-1101 to 26-1121.

See MORTGAGE LENDERS AND BROKERS.

MORTGAGES AND DEEDS OF TRUST —Cont'd

Loan originators, §§26-1101 to 26-1121.
  See MORTGAGE LENDERS AND BROKERS.
Low and moderate income families.
  Home purchase assistance fund, §§42-2601 to 42-2626.
    See HOME PURCHASE ASSISTANCE FUND.
Mental illness, persons with.
  Conveyances or assurances, §42-820.
Mortgage lenders and brokers.
  General provisions, §§26-1101 to 26-1121.
    See MORTGAGE LENDERS AND BROKERS.
  Regulatory provisions, §§26-1301 to 26-1336.
    See TRUST, MORTGAGE AND TITLE CORPORATIONS.
Mortgage loan protection, §§26-1151.01 to 26-1155.01.
  See MORTGAGE LENDERS AND BROKERS.
National housing act.
  Exemption from interest in usury regulations, §28-3307.
New trustee.
  Petition for, §42-814.
Non-conventional mortgage loans.
  Defined, §26-1101.
  Disclosures, required, §26-1113.
Nonprofit corporations.
  Powers, §29-403.02.
Notice.
  Intention to foreclose, §42-815.
Penalties.
  Prepayment penalty.
    No penalty after three years, §28-3301.
Pending actions, §§42-805 to 42-807.
Points.
  Defined, §28-3301.
  Limitation on charging, §28-3301.
Prepayment.
  No penalty after three years, §28-3301.
Professional corporations.
  Powers, §29-505.
Qualified fee simple.
  Estate of mortgagee or trustee, §42-803.
Real estate taxes.
  Payments to lenders, §28-3301.

MORTGAGES AND DEEDS OF TRUST —Cont'd

Real property credit line deeds of trust.
  Consumer protection.
    Unlawful trade practices, §28-3904.
Recordation of instruments.
  Residential real estate transfers, §§47-1401, 47-1431 to 47-1433.
Recordation tax, §42-1104.
Redemption rights, §§42-807, 42-810.
Release of, §42-818.02.
Residential mortgage foreclosure default, right to cure, §42-815.01.
Residential real property seller disclosures, §§42-1301 to 42-1311.
  See HOME SALES.
Sale.
  Amount paid by creditor if purchaser, §42-817.
  Application to fix terms and determine notice, §42-815.
  Commission to mortgagee or trustee, §42-818.
  Deficiency judgment, §42-816.
Second mortgages.
  Required conditions, §28-3301.
Secured transactions.
  Commercial code, §§28:9-101 to 28:9-809.
    See SECURED TRANSACTIONS.
Service by publication on nonresidents, §13-336.
Servicemen's readjustment, §§42-3001, 42-3002.
Statute of frauds.
  Declaration, grant.
    An assignment of trust, §28-3503.
  Declaration, grant and assignment of trust, §28-3503.
Successor trustee.
  Appointment, §42-813.
Survival of mortgagee's or trustee's title, §42-804.
Tax sales.
  Levy for failure to pay.
    Real property, transfer of deed, §47-4475.
Tracking addresses for, §42-818.01.
Wet settlement act, §§42-2401 to 42-2407.
  Action by person suffering loss because of violation, §42-2407.
  Applicability, §42-2402.
  Civil fines, penalties, fees.
    Imposing for violation, §42-2407.

MORTGAGES AND DEEDS OF TRUST —Cont'd

Wet settlement act —Cont'd

Definitions, §42-2401.

Disbursement of loan funds to settlement agent.

Lender's duty, §42-2403.

Disbursement of settlement proceeds.

Duty of settlement agent, time, §42-2405.

Duties of owners and brokers, §42-2404.

Duty of lender, §42-2403.

Duty of settlement agent, §42-2405.

Failure to comply not to affect validity of loan documents, §42-2406.

Interest on loan.

Lender not to charge until disbursement of loan funds, §42-2403.

Redecoration of documents required to be recorded.

Duty of settlement agent, §42-2405.

MOSQUITOES.

Control and abatement, §8-2141.01.

Vector-borne disease control, §§8-2131.01 to 8-2131.09.

See VECTOR-BORNE DISEASE CONTROL.

MOTELS, §§30-101 to 30-103.

See LODGING PLACES.

MOTION PICTURES.

Business licenses, §47-2820.

Children and minors, §47-2820.

DC film incentive fund, §2-1204.11d.

Deceptive labeling, §22-3214.01.

Definitions, §2-1204.11c.

Film DC economic incentive grant fund, §2-1204.12.

Film DC special account fund, §2-1204.11d.

Infrastructure incentives, §2-1204.11b.

Police and firefighters assigned to theaters, §47-2820.

Production incentives, §2-1204.11a.

Production permits, §2-1204.11d.

Recording device, unlawful operation of, §22-3214.02.

Theft, §§22-3214.01, 22-3214.02.

MOTIONS.

Acquittal, CrimPro Rule 29.

Juvenile proceedings, JuvProc Rule 29.

MOTIONS —Cont'd

Address of signer.

Information required on pleadings, motions and other filings, CivPro Rule 11.

Adoption.

See ADOPTION.

Appeals, D.C. courts, DCCtApp Rule 27.

Form and copies of motions, DCCtApp Rule 32.

Indigent persons.

Proceedings in forma pauperis, DCCtApp Rule 24.

Stays pending appeal, DCCtApp Rule 8.

Appeals, federal cases, FRAP 27, USCtApp Rule 27.

Administrative orders.

Motion for stay pending review of administrative orders, filing, FRAP 18, USCtApp Rule 18.

Admission of attorney to practice, FRAP 46(a).

Brief of amicus curiae, leave to file, FRAP 29.

Clerk may dispose of certain motions, FRAP 27(e).

Consolidation of appeals, FRAP 3(b).

Dismissal of appeal.

Failure to file briefs, FRAP 31(c).

Record for hearing in court of appeals, FRAP 11(g).

Disposition by clerk, USCtApp HPIP Rule VII(c).

Disposition by merits panel, USCtApp HPIP Rule VII(e).

Disposition by panel, USCtApp HPIP Rule VII(d).

Distribution of orders, USCtApp HPIP Rule VII(f).

Expedite consideration of appeal, USCtApp HPIP Rule VIII(b).

Extensions of time, FRAP 26(b).

Filing notice of appeal as of right, FRAP 4.

Transmission of record on appeal, FRAP 11(b).

Filing, FRAP 25(a).

Formal requirements, USCtApp HPIP Rule VII(a).

Form of papers, FRAP 32(c).

Intervention.

Administrative review or enforcement, FRAP 15(d).

Leave to proceed in forma pauperis, FRAP 24.

MOTIONS —Cont'd
Appeals, federal cases —Cont'd
Oral arguments.
Amicus curiae, FRAP 29.
Postponement of, FRAP 34(b).
Preliminary hearing in court of appeals, record for, FRAP 11(g).
Procedural orders, motions for, FRAP 27(b).
Processing, USCtApp HPIP Rule VII(b).
Release in criminal cases, FRAP 9, USCtApp HPIP Rule VIII(c).
Remand, USCtApp HPIP Rule VIII(e).
Single judge, power to entertain, FRAP 27(c).
Stay or injunction pending appeal, FRAP 8, USCtApp HPIP Rule VIII(a), USCtApp Rule 8.
Summary disposition, USCtApp HPIP Rule VIII(g).
Suspension of rules, FRAP 2.
Transfer, USCtApp HPIP Rule VIII(f).
Unsealing sealed records, USCtApp HPIP Rule VIII(h).
Voluntary dismissal, FRAP 42, USCtApp HPIP Rule VIII(d).
Arbitration, Arbitration Rule VIII, CivPro Rule 70-I.
Confirmation of award, CivPro Form CA 107.
Pending motions at time of assignment, Arbitration Rule VI.
Attachment.
Quashing pre-judgment attachment, CivPro Rule 64-I.
Domestic relations actions, DomRel Rule 64.
Attorneys at law.
Signing of motions, CivPro Rule 11.
Attorneys' fees, CivPro Rule 54.
Domestic relations actions, DomRel Rule 54.
Bankruptcy proceedings.
Motion practice, USDistDCBank Rule 9013-1.
Child abuse and neglect proceedings, NeglectProc Rule 43.
Revocation or modification of terms of protective supervision, NeglectProc Rule 26.
Civil I calendar designation, CivPro Rule 40-II.
Class actions.
Certification motions, CivPro Rule 23-I, USDistCt LCvR 23.1.

MOTIONS —Cont'd
Criminal procedure.
See CRIMINAL PROCEDURE.
Defenses, CivPro Rule 12.
Domestic relations actions, DomRel Rule 12.
Delinquent minors, JuvProc Rule 47-I.
Pretrial motions, JuvProc Rule 12.
Sealing records, FamDiv Rule P, JuvProc Rule 118.
Form, JuvProc Form 8.
Search warrants.
Return of property and suppression of evidence, JuvProc Rule 41.
Transfer for criminal prosecution, JuvProc Rule 108.
Witness statement production, JuvProc Rule 26.2.
Directed verdicts, CivPro Rule 50.
Domestic relations actions, DomRel Rule 50.
Discovery.
Certification of good faith effort to resolve dispute, CivPro Rule 26.
Compelling discovery, CivPro Rule 37.
Adoption proceedings, Adoption Rule 37.
Domestic relations actions, DomRel Rule 37.
Conferences, CivPro Rule 26.
Enlargement of time for discovery, CivPro Rule 26.
Domestic relations actions, DomRel Rule 26.
Dismissal of action, CivPro Form CA 19.
Domestic relations actions, DomRel Rule 7.
Contempt, DomRel Form 7.
Form of motions, DomRel Form 2, DomRel Rule 10.
Non-appearance at hearing, DomRel Rule 12.
Opposition to motion and affidavit, DomRel Form 3.
Signing, DomRel Rule 11.
Domestic violence unit, DomesticViolence Rule 7.
E-mail address of signer.
Information required on pleadings, motions and other filings, CivPro Rule 11.
Evidence on motions, CivPro Rule 43.
Family court proceedings generally.
Sealing records, FamDiv Rule P.
Form and content, CivPro Rules 7, 12-I, USDistCt LCrR 47, USDistCt LCvR 7.

MOTIONS —Cont'd
Guardianship of minors.
Permanent guardianship.
Contents and filing, §16-2384.
Hearing commissioner proceedings.
Review of orders and judgments,
CivPro Rule 73, CrimPro Rule
117.
**Intellectual disabilities, persons
with.**
Commitment to intellectual disability
facility, MentalRetardation Rule
10.
**Interception of wire or oral
communications.**
Suppression of intercepted
communications, CrimPro Rule
41-I.
Intervention, CivPro Rule 24,
USDistCt LCvR 7.
Adoption proceedings, Adoption Rule
24.
Appeal of administrative orders and
decisions, DCCtApp Rule 15.
Form, CivPro Form CA 23.
Judgments and decrees.
Amending judgment, CivPro Rule 59.
Domestic relations actions, DomRel
Rule 59.
Judgment as a matter of law, CivPro
Rule 50.
Domestic relations actions, DomRel
Rule 50.
Judgment on the pleadings, CivPro
Rule 12.
Domestic relations actions, DomRel
Rule 12.
Relief from judgment or order, CivPro
Rule 60.
Domestic relations actions, DomRel
Rule 60.
Juvenile proceedings generally.
Application, JuvProc Rule 47.
Landlord and tenant court,
LandlordTenant Rule 13.
Application to stay writ of restitution,
LandlordTenant Form 9.
Certification to civil division,
LandlordTenant Rule 13-I.
Protective orders, LandlordTenant
Rule 12-I.
Stay of execution, LandlordTenant
Rule 16.
Matter taken under advisement,
CivPro Rule 12-I.
Adoption proceedings, Adoption Rule
52.

MOTIONS —Cont'd
Matter taken under advisement
—Cont'd
Child abuse and neglect proceedings,
NeglectProc Rule 43.
Juvenile proceedings, JuvProc Rule
47-I.
Mental illness, persons with.
Hospitalization of persons with mental
illness, MentalHealth Rule 14.
More definite statement, CivPro Rule
12.
Domestic relations actions, DomRel
Rule 12.
New trial.
Adoption proceedings, Adoption Rule
60.
Domestic relations actions, DomRel
Rules 59, 62.
Small claims court, CrimPro Rule 33,
SmallClaims Rule 16.
Opposing points and authorities,
USDistCt LCrR 47, USDistCt LCvR
7.
Oral hearings, USDistCt LCvR 78.1.
Parties.
Substitution of parties, CivPro Rule
25.
Pleadings generally.
See PLEADINGS.
Post-conviction proceedings.
Superior court proceedings,
PostConvRel Rules 1 to 12.
See POST-CONVICTION
PROCEEDINGS.
Pro se.
Superior court, civil division, CivPro
Form CA 115.
Required information, CivPro Rule
11.
Scheduling of hearings, CivPro Rule
78-I.
Search warrants.
Return of property and suppression of
evidence, CrimPro Rule 41.
Juvenile proceedings, JuvProc Rule
41.
Signatures, CivPro Rule 11.
Adoption proceedings, Adoption Rules
10, 11.
Domestic relations actions, DomRel
Rules 10, 11.
Sanctions for improper signing, CivPro
Rule 11.
Small claims court, SmallClaims Rule
13.
Certification to civil division,
SmallClaims Rule 13-I.

MOTIONS —Cont'd

Statement of points and authorities, USDistCt LCrR 47, USDistCt LCvR 7.

Striking pleading, CivPro Rule 12.
Domestic relations actions, DomRel Rule 12.

Summary judgment, CivPro Rule 56, USDistCt LCvR 7, USDistCt LCvR 56.1.
See SUMMARY JUDGMENT.

Surety liability enforcement, CivPro Rule 65.1.
Appeals, DCCtApp Rule 8.

Tax proceedings, Tax Rule 9.

Telephone number of signer.
Information required on pleadings, motions and other filings, CivPro Rule 11.

Termination of parental rights, §16-2354, NeglectProc Rules 35, 36.

Third party practice.
Motion to bring in third party, CivPro Form CA 22-B.

Time limits, CivPro Rule 12-I, USDistCt LCvR 7.

Vulnerable adults and elderly persons.
Criminal abuse, neglect and financial exploitation.
Ex parte motions for injunctive relief, §22-938.

MOTOR FUEL TAX, §§47-2301 to 47-2354.

Appeals, §47-2319.

Assessments.
Procedures, §47-2316.
Street paving, for, §§47-2323, 47-2324.

Bonds, surety, §47-2303.

Continuation after fiscal year end of uncompleted projects funded by, §47-2322.

Continuation of uncompleted projects, §47-2325.

Contraband, §47-2320.

Definitions, §47-2302.

Determination of tax, §47-2316.

Disposition of, §47-2301.

Erroneous or illegal collections, §47-2318.

Exemption of fuel exported from District, §47-2309.

Forfeitures, §47-2320.

General Fund, deposit in, §§47-2301, 47-2324.

Inspections, §47-2307.

MOTOR FUEL TAX —Cont'd

Interest, §47-2316.

International Fuel Tax Agreement, §§47-2351 to 47-2354.
Audits, §47-2353.
Defined, §47-2302.
Fees, §47-2354.
Reciprocity, §47-2351.
Registration, §47-2352.
Subject to provisions of, §47-2301.01.

Interpretation of provisions, §§47-2313, 47-2314.

Invoices, §47-2305.

Issuance of rules and regulations, §§47-2315, 47-2321.

Itemized statement, acceptance of fuel without, §47-2308.

Liability, §47-2316.

Licenses of importers, §47-2303.

Payment of tax, §47-2306.

Penalties and fines.
Forfeitures, §47-2320.
Interest, §47-2316.
Itemized statement, acceptance of fuel without, §47-2308.

Personal property tax, §47-2314.

Prosecution of violations, §47-2312.

Rates, §47-2301.

Records, §§47-2305, 47-2307.

Refunds, §47-2318.

Report of amounts sold, monthly, §47-2304.

Reports, §47-2304.

Sale of confiscated fuel or vehicles, §47-2320.

Savings clauses, §47-2322.

Searches, §47-2320.

Seizures, §47-2320.

Severability of provisions, §47-2322.

Uncompleted projects.
Continuation, §47-2325.

United States agency selling fuel in District, §47-2311.

MOTORIZED WHEELCHAIRS.

Assistive technology device warranty, §§28-4031 to 28-4034.

MOTOR OIL, USED.

Prohibition on discharge into sewers, §8-103.07.

MOTOR VEHICLE ACCIDENTS.

Aged persons (50 years of age and older), §§50-2001 to 50-2003.
Approval of accident prevention courses for, §50-2002.
Certificate of completion of accident prevention courses for, §50-2002.

MOTOR VEHICLE ACCIDENTS
—Cont'd
Aged persons (50 years of age and older) —Cont'd
Insurance discounts for completion of accident prevention courses for, §50-2003.
Need for accident prevention courses for, §§50-2001 to 50-2003.
Policy declaration, §§50-2001 to 50-2003.
Garage keepers required to report vehicles damaged in accidents, §50-2201.06.
Leaving after colliding, §50-2201.05c.
Major crash review task force, §50-1831.
Negligent operation of vehicles by District employees, §§2-412, 2-415.
Object falling or flying from vehicle, §50-2201.05d.
Open access to collision data and information, §§50-1951.01 to 50-1951.07.
Bicycle and pedestrian safety.
Biennial report on improving, §50-1951.07.
Citizen petitions for traffic calming measures.
Publication of information, §50-1951.05.
Collision data, publication of, §50-1951.02.
Collision, defined, §50-1951.01.
Definitions, §50-1951.01.
Highest frequency of collisions that injure or kill pedestrians.
Annual report on locations, §50-1951.06.
Occupation of public space, public rights of way and public structures.
Publication of permit information, §50-1951.04.
Personal information from motor vehicle records and accident reports.
Prohibitions on release and use of, §50-1401.01b.
Safety responsibility act.
General provisions, §§50-1301.01 to 50-1301.86.
See MOTOR VEHICLE SAFETY RESPONSIBILITY.

MOTOR VEHICLE ACCIDENTS
—Cont'd
Scrap vehicle title certification, §§50-2701 to 50-2708.
See SCRAP VEHICLE TITLE AUTHORIZATION.
Senior citizen accident prevention course certification, §§50-2001 to 50-2003.
Small claims court forms.
Custody of defendant, SmallClaims Form 7.
One defendant, SmallClaims Forms 4, 5.
Parked vehicle, SmallClaims Form 6.
Two defendants, SmallClaims Form 5.
Vehicle insurance enforcement.
Traffic accident reports.
Inclusion of insurance information, §5-114.03.

MOTOR VEHICLE FINANCIAL RESPONSIBILITY.
See MOTOR VEHICLE SAFETY RESPONSIBILITY.

MOTOR VEHICLE FINANCING, §§50-601 to 50-610.
Adjusting finance charges, §50-602.
Bonds, surety, §50-603.
Computing finance charges, §50-602.
Council powers, §50-605.
Dealers, licensing and bonding of, §50-603.
Definitions, §50-601.
Delegation of mayor's powers, §50-604.
Economic conditions determining finance charges, §50-602.
False statements, §50-606.
Finance charges, §§50-601, 50-602.
Liability insurance, §50-603.
Licensing and bonding of dealers, §50-603.
Maximum finance charge, §50-602.
Mayor's powers, §50-603.
Additional and supplementary authority, §50-609.
Delegation of, §50-604.
Penalties, §50-607.
Prosecutions for violations, §50-608.
Severability of provisions, §50-610.
Titling of motor vehicles.
Liens on vehicles and trailers.
See TITLING OF MOTOR VEHICLES.

MOTOR VEHICLE INSURANCE.
Aged persons (50 years of age and older).
Discounts for completion of accident prevention courses for, §50-2003.
Discrimination, §2-1402.71.
Enforcement of compulsory insurance requirements, §§5-114.01 to 5-114.04.
Definitions, §5-114.01.
Demand for proof of insurance, §5-114.02.
Proof of insurance.
Defined, §5-114.01.
Demand for, §5-114.02.
Report by metropolitan police department, §5-114.04.
Traffic accident reports.
Inclusion of insurance information, §5-114.03.
Financial responsibility, certificate of insurance as proof of, §§50-1301.53 to 50-1301.59.
Food delivery vehicles, §§50-101 to 50-105.
Definitions, §50-101.
Driver safety program, §50-103.
Fines, §50-104.
Issuance of rules, §50-105.
Penalties, §50-104.
Requirements regarding, §50-102.
Judgment, insurer found obligated to pay, §50-1301.46.
No-fault insurance.
General provisions, §§31-2401 to 31-2408.01.
See NO-FAULT MOTOR VEHICLE INSURANCE.
Private vehicles-for-hire, §50-301.29c.
Property and liability insurance guaranty association.
General provisions, §§31-5501 to 31-5515.
See PROPERTY AND LIABILITY INSURANCE GUARANTY ASSOCIATION.
Safety responsibility act.
General provisions, §§50-1301.01 to 50-1301.86.
See MOTOR VEHICLE SAFETY RESPONSIBILITY.
Self-insurers, §50-1301.79.
Taxicabs, §50-301.14.

MOTOR VEHICLE REGISTRATION, §§50-1501.01 to 50-1507.07.
Anacostia river commemorative plates, §8-102.07.

MOTOR VEHICLE REGISTRATION
—Cont'd
Charter buses, §50-1501.02.
International registration plan agreements.
Procedures for registration, §50-1507.03.
Penalties, §50-1501.04.
Child support enforcement, §46-225.01.
Clean cars.
Establishment of low-emissions vehicle program.
Registering vehicle not in compliance.
Prohibition, §50-732.
Council powers, §50-1501.05.
Counterfeit, stolen or fraudulent tags, §50-1501.04.
Dealers' proof of ownership certificates, §50-1501.02.
Dealers' registration certificates and tags, §50-1501.02.
Definitions, §50-1501.01.
Department of Motor Vehicles.
General provisions, §§50-901 to 50-907.
See MOTOR VEHICLES.
Disabled American veterans, §50-1503.01.
Domicile in District.
Required for issuance of certificate, exceptions, §50-1501.02.
Duplicate certificates and identification tags, §50-1501.02.
Duration of, §50-1501.02.
Electric vehicles, §50-1501.02.
Emissions.
Inspection of motor vehicles.
Self-service exhaust emissions testing pilot program, §50-1110.
Expiration, §50-1501.02.
Synchronizing inspection and registration, §50-1501.03.
Fees, §50-1501.03.
Classification, §50-1501.03.
Inspection of motor vehicles, §§50-1101, 50-1104.
Installment payments, §50-1501.03.
International registration plan agreements, §50-1507.06.
Setting, §50-1501.03.
Title fees, §50-2201.03.
Use of proceeds from, §50-1501.03.
Food delivery vehicles, §50-102.
Inaugural ceremonies of the President of the United States, §§2-802, 2-822.

MOTOR VEHICLE REGISTRATION
—Cont'd
Inspection of motor vehicles,
§§50-1101 to 50-1109.
Appropriations for inspection facilities,
§50-1103.
Assault of public vehicle inspection
officer, §22-404.02.
Aggravated assault, §22-404.03.
Biennial Inspection Fund, §50-1102.
Definition of motor vehicle for
purposes of, §50-1108.
Exemption from fees, §50-1104.
Expiration of sticker, notification,
§50-1109.
Synchronizing inspection and
registration, §50-1501.03.
Fees, §§50-1101, 50-1104.
Fleeing from public vehicle inspection
officer in public for-hire vehicle,
§50-301.34.
Food delivery vehicles, §50-102.
Mayor, regulations established by,
§50-1107.
Penalties, §50-1106.
Taxicabs.
Public vehicle inspection officer
training, §50-301.30.
Unsafe or uninspected vehicles,
§50-1105.
Vehicle inspection task force,
§§50-1121, 50-1122.
**International registration plan
agreements,** §§50-1507.01 to
50-1507.07.
Audits, §50-1507.05.
Definitions, §50-1507.01.
Fees, §50-1507.06.
Interjurisdictional and
intrajurisdictional privileges,
§50-1507.04.
Mayor establishing rules and
procedures for, §§50-1507.03,
50-1507.07.
Procedures for registration,
§50-1507.03.
Reciprocity, §§50-1507.01, 50-1507.02.
Rulemaking requirements,
§50-1507.07.
Low-emissions vehicle program.
Registering vehicle not in compliance.
Prohibition, §50-732.
Mayor.
Authorization to issue rules,
§50-1501.02.
Inspection of motor vehicles
regulations established by,
§50-1107.

MOTOR VEHICLE REGISTRATION
—Cont'd
Mayor —Cont'd
International registration plan
agreements, establishing rules
and procedures for, §§50-1507.03,
50-1507.07.
Rental vehicle tax registration
procedures, setting, §§50-1501.02,
50-1503.01.
**Out-of-state vehicle registration
special fund,** §50-1501.03a.
Penalties, §50-1501.04.
Inspection of motor vehicles, §50-1106.
Rental vehicle tax, §§50-1505.01 to
50-1505.04.
Definitions, §50-1505.01.
Interstate and intrastate privileges
extended to rental vehicles,
§50-1505.02.
Mayor's authority to establish
procedure for, §50-1505.03.
Procedure for registration,
§50-1505.03.
Requirement to register, §50-1501.02.
**Sale of five or more vehicles in a
year,** §50-1501.31.
Seizure of vehicles, §50-1501.04.
**Special use certificate and special
use identification tags,**
§50-1501.02.
**Surrender of suspended
registration,** §§50-1301.70,
50-1301.74.
**Suspension of license and
registration.**
See DRIVERS' LICENSES.
Suspension or revocation.
Rules, promulgation, §50-1501.02.
Taxicabs.
Public vehicle inspection officer
training, §50-301.30.
Titling.
See TITLING OF MOTOR
VEHICLES.
Trailers, §50-1501.02.
Inspection, §§50-1101 to 50-1109. See
within this heading, "Inspection of
motor vehicles."
**Transfer of registration to defeat
purpose of motor vehicle safety
responsibility requirements,**
§50-1301.69.
Unlawful acts, §50-1501.04.
Unregistered vehicles.
Operating, unlawful, §50-1501.04.

MOTOR VEHICLE REGISTRATION —Cont'd

Validity of, §50-1501.02.

Veterans' license plates, §50-1501.02a.

Vintage license plates, §50-1501.02.

MOTOR VEHICLE RENTALS.
See RENTAL VEHICLES.

MOTOR VEHICLES.

Abandoned vehicles.
Junk vehicle removal, §§50-2401 to 50-2406.
Unlawfully parked vehicles, §§50-2421.01 to 50-2421.15.

Accidents.
See MOTOR VEHICLE ACCIDENTS.

Aggressive driving, §50-2204.

Alternative fuel technology, §§50-701 to 50-715.
See ALTERNATIVE FUEL TECHNOLOGY.

Armed carjacking, §22-2803.

Autonomous vehicles, §§50-2351 to 50-2354.

Blind pedestrians, safety standards regarding, §7-1004.

Bureau of traffic adjudication.
Study on improving quality of adjudications, §2-1831.18.

Business licenses.
Parking establishments, §47-2832.01.
Public space, vehicles hauling goods from, §47-2831.
Rental vehicles, §47-2830.
Repairs, §47-2832.
Vehicles for hire, §47-2829.

Carjacking, §22-2803.

Child restraint seats, §§50-1701 to 50-1708.
General provisions.
See SEAT BELTS.

Clean cars.
Low-emissions vehicle program.
Establishment.
Adoption of California standards and compliance requirements, §50-731.
Registering vehicle not in compliance.
Prohibition, §50-732.

Cover requirements for loose debris or cargo, §50-2101.

Deaf pedestrians, safety standards regarding, §7-1004.

Decedents' estates, §20-357.

Department of Motor Vehicles, §§50-901 to 50-907.
Regulations, §50-921.

MOTOR VEHICLES —Cont'd

Direct installment loans, §§28-3601 to 28-3603.

Discrimination.
Insurance, §2-1402.71.
Rentals, §2-1402.72.

District vehicles, working fund for repair and maintenance of, §47-134.

Driver education programs in schools, §§38-912, 38-913.
Issuance of rules, §38-912.01.

Driverless vehicles, §§50-2351 to 50-2354.

Driver license compact, §§50-1001, 50-1002.

Drivers' licenses.
See DRIVERS' LICENSES.

Driving under the influence.
See DRIVING UNDER THE INFLUENCE.

Emergency public assistance.
Retention of vehicle, §4-205.41.

Emergency response vehicles.
License requirements, §7-2341.04.

Fine reductions, safety impact assessment, §50-2111.

Firearms.
Transportation in vehicle, §22-4504.02.
Forfeiture of conveyances transporting, §7-2507.06a.

Fleeing from a law enforcement officer in a motor vehicle, §50-2201.05b.

Footways in public grounds, driving or riding on, §22-1318.

Foreign missions, owned by members of, §6-1304.01.

For-hire vehicles.
Rental vehicles generally.
See RENTAL VEHICLES.
Taxicabs, §§50-301.01 to 50-301.34.
See TAXICABS.

Gross sales tax.
Exempt sales, §47-2005.

Hauling permits for multiaxle vehicles, §§6-703.01, 6-703.02.

Identification numbers.
Altering or removing, §22-3233.

Impaired operation or driving, §§50-2206.01 to 50-2206.59.
See DRIVING UNDER THE INFLUENCE.

Impoundment.
See IMPOUNDMENT OF VEHICLES.

MOTOR VEHICLES —Cont'd
Inspection of motor vehicles,
§§50-1101 to 50-1109.
See MOTOR VEHICLE
REGISTRATION.
Installment sales of motor vehicles,
§28-3602.
Applicable law, §28-3601.
Finance charges, §28-3602.
Interest.
Direct motor vehicle installment loans.
Maximum finance charge, §28-3602.
Leaving after colliding, §50-2201.05c.
Lemon law.
General provisions, §§50-501 to
50-510.
See LEMON LAW.
Licenses.
Drivers' licenses.
See DRIVERS' LICENSES.
Liens.
Metropolitan police property clerk,
sale by, §5-119.10.
Titling of motor vehicles and trailers,
§§50-1201 to 50-1218.
See TITLING OF MOTOR
VEHICLES.
**Loose debris or cargo, cover
requirements for,** §50-2101.
Low-emissions vehicle program.
Establishment.
Adoption of California standards
and compliance requirements,
§50-731.
Registering vehicles not in compliance.
Prohibition, §50-732.
Metropolitan police.
Theft prevention teams, §5-133.21.
Use of private motor vehicles by
police, §5-133.02.
Military personnel.
Drivers' licenses, §50-1401.01.
Registration for disabled American
veterans, §50-1503.01.
Motor fuel tax.
General provisions, §§47-2301 to
47-2354.
See MOTOR FUEL TAX.
**Multiaxle vehicles, hauling permits
for,** §§6-703.01, 6-703.02.
New car warranties, §§50-501 to
50-510.
See LEMON LAW.
Nonresidents.
See NONRESIDENTS.
Object falling or flying from vehicle,
§50-2201.05d.

MOTOR VEHICLES —Cont'd
**Operating records, availability of
abstracts of,** §50-1301.05.
Certified copy as evidence,
§50-1301.05a.
Pedestrian advisory council,
§50-1931.
Prostitution.
Impoundment of vehicle used in
prostitution-related offense,
§22-2724.
Anti-prostitution vehicle
impoundment proceeds fund,
§22-2725.
Public assistance.
Retention of vehicle, §4-205.41.
Public officers and employees.
Mandatory drug and alcohol testing of
certain employees who serve
children.
Motor vehicles operators deemed to
have given consent, §1-620.33.
Reimbursement for use of private
vehicle on official business, §1-509.
Public-owned vehicles, §§50-202 to
50-205.
Bicycle safety enhancements, §50-205.
EPA miles per gallon requirement,
§50-203.
Fleet management, §§50-211.01 to
50-211.07.
Official use, §50-202.
Restrictions on use, §50-204.
Public vehicles for hire.
Taxicabs, §§50-301.01 to 50-301.34.
See TAXICABS.
Public works, use in, §9-1209.03.
Registration of vehicles.
General provisions, §§50-1501.01 to
50-1507.07.
See MOTOR VEHICLE
REGISTRATION.
Inspection, §§50-1101 to 50-1109.
See MOTOR VEHICLE
REGISTRATION.
International registration plan
agreements, §§50-1507.01 to
50-1507.07.
See MOTOR VEHICLE
REGISTRATION.
Rental vehicle tax, §§50-1505.01 to
50-1505.04.
See MOTOR VEHICLE
REGISTRATION.
Regulations of the department,
§50-921.

MOTOR VEHICLES —Cont'd
Rentals.
See RENTAL VEHICLES.
Repairs, business licenses for,
§47-2832.
Safety responsibility act.
General provisions, §§50-1301.01 to
50-1301.86.
See MOTOR VEHICLE SAFETY
RESPONSIBILITY.
Salvage, flood and junk vehicles,
§§50-1331.01 to 50-1331.09.
See SALVAGE, FLOOD AND JUNK
VEHICLES.
Seat belts.
General provisions, §§50-1801 to
50-1807.
See SEAT BELTS.
Taxation.
Motor fuel tax, §§47-2301 to 47-2354.
See MOTOR FUEL TAX.
Taxicabs.
General provisions, §§50-301.01 to
50-301.34.
See TAXICABS.
Theft, §22-3215.
Metropolitan police.
Motor vehicle theft prevention
teams, §5-133.21.
Motor vehicle theft prevention
commission, §§3-1351 to 3-1358.
Definitions, §3-1351.
Established, §3-1352.
Financial statement and report,
§3-1355.
Members, §3-1353.
Powers, §3-1354.
Purpose, §3-1352.
Use of budget authority, §3-1358.
Traffic ticket adjudication.
General provisions, §§50-2301.01 to
50-2305.02.
See TRAFFIC TICKET
ADJUDICATION.
Transfer upon death, §20-357.
Unauthorized use of, §22-3215.
Unlawful entry, §22-1341.
Vehicle identification numbers.
Altering or removing, §22-3233.
Vehicle inspection task force,
§§50-1121, 50-1122.
Warranties.
New car warranties, §§50-501 to
50-510.
See LEMON LAW.

**MOTOR VEHICLE SAFETY
RESPONSIBILITY,** §§50-1301.01
to 50-1301.86.
Abstract of operating record,
§50-1301.05.
Administration, §50-1301.03.
**Aged persons accident prevention
courses.**
General provisions, §§50-2001 to
50-2003.
See MOTOR VEHICLE
ACCIDENTS.
**Agent of owner, operator deemed to
be,** §50-1301.08.
Appropriations, §50-1301.80.
Bonds.
Clerk of superior court may approve,
CivPro Rule 77-II.
Defaults.
Judgment, payment of, §50-1301.51.
Nonresident insurance carriers,
§50-1301.56.
Definitions, §§50-1301.02, 50-1301.35,
50-1301.36.
Enforcement, §50-1301.03.
Financial responsibility.
Cancellation of certificate of insurance,
§50-1301.68.
Certificate of insurance as proof of,
§§50-1301.53 to 50-1301.59.
Filing, §50-1301.54.
Nonresidents, §50-1301.55.
Required information, §50-1301.54.
Definition of proof of, §50-1301.35.
Each registered vehicle, required for,
§50-1301.52.
Effect of proof of, §50-1301.37.
Information furnished to injured
persons, §50-1301.06.
Methods of providing proof,
§50-1301.53.
Nonresidents, §50-1301.55.
Other or alternate proof, right to
require, §50-1301.67.
Owner of motor vehicle giving proof
for others, §50-1301.65.
Requirement of proof of, §§50-1301.34,
50-1301.39.
Substitution of proof, §50-1301.66.
Suspension of license until proof
provided, §50-1301.47.
Waiver of need to file proof,
§50-1301.68.
Government vehicles, §§50-1301.37,
50-1301.44.
Headings, effect of, §50-1301.77.

MOTOR VEHICLE SAFETY RESPONSIBILITY —Cont'd

Insurer obligated to pay judgment, §50-1301.46.

Interpretation of provisions, §50-1301.85.

Judgment.
Bankruptcy, discharge in, §50-1301.48.
Consent to retention of license, registration, or operating privileges, §50-1301.45.
Default on payment, §50-1301.51.
Defined, §50-1301.36.
Government vehicles exempted from nonpayment provisions, §50-1301.44.
Installment payments, §50-1301.50.
Insurer obligated to pay, §50-1301.46.
Nonresidents, against, §50-1301.42.
Payment of, §§50-1301.47, 50-1301.49, 50-1301.50.
Reporting nonpayment, §50-1301.41.
Suspension for nonpayment, §§50-1301.43, 50-1301.47.

Jurisdiction, §50-1301.76.

Mayor's responsibilities regarding, §§50-1301.03, 50-1301.04.

Nonpayment of judgments, reporting, §50-1301.41.

Nonresidents.
See NONRESIDENTS.

Operator deemed to be agent of owner, §50-1301.08.

Penalties, §50-1301.75.

Prevention of other actions at law, §50-1301.84.

Prior law, effect on, §50-1301.82.

Records.
Certified copy as evidence, §50-1301.05a.
Financial responsibility information, §50-1301.06.
Operating records, availability of abstracts of, §50-1301.05.

Reorganization Plan No. 5 of 1952, effect of, §50-1301.81.

Retroactivity of provisions, §50-1301.83.

Review of orders and acts by mayor, §50-1301.04.

Self-insurers, §50-1301.79.

Severability, §50-1301.86.

Superior court's jurisdiction, §50-1301.76.

MOTOR VEHICLE SAFETY RESPONSIBILITY —Cont'd

Suspension of license and registration, §§50-1301.37 to 50-1301.40.
Certain convictions, §§50-1301.37, 50-1301.39.
Duration, §50-1301.38.
Foreign convictions, §50-1301.37.
Nonresidents' operating privileges, §50-1301.40.

Transfer of registration to defeat purposes of, §50-1301.69.

MOTOR VEHICLES DEPARTMENT, §§50-901 to 50-907.

Anatomical gifts.
Donor registry.
Transfer of information, §7-1531.19c.

Bureau of traffic adjudication.
Study on improving quality of adjudications, §2-1831.18.

Director.
Powers and duties, §50-901.

Establishment of, §50-901.

Function of, §50-904.

Organization and structure of, §§50-903, 50-906.

Policy declaration, §50-902.

Reorganization of personnel, property, records, and appropriations transferred to, §50-906.

Ticket adjudication ombudsman, §50-907.

Transfer of personnel, property, records, and appropriations to, §50-905.

MOTOR-VOTER REGISTRATION, §1-1001.07.

MOVIES.
See MOTION PICTURES.

MOVING AND RELOCATION.

Crime victims' compensation.
Moving expenses, VictComp Rule 34.

Displaced tenants, relocation assistance for, §§42-3507.01 to 42-3507.05.

Public assistance for moving expenses, §§4-211.04, 4-211.05.

Rental housing conversion and sale relocation assistance, §§42-3403.01 to 42-3403.09.
Expiration of provisions, §42-3403.09.

MOVING AND RELOCATION
—Cont'd
Rental housing conversion and sale relocation assistance —Cont'd
Housing assistance payments, §42-3403.04.
Income tax exemption for payments, §42-3403.05.
Notice to tenant of intent to convert, §42-3403.06.
Office to coordinate programs and serve as clearinghouse for information, §42-3403.08.
Relocation payments, §42-3403.02.
Services for low-income tenants moving from converted housing, §42-3403.03.
Tax exemption for payments, §42-3403.05.
Tenant rights, §42-3403.06.
Title of provisions, §42-3403.01.
Streets and alleys closed.
Relocation assistance due to, §9-202.09.

MULTILINGUAL ELECTION MATERIALS, §§1-1031.01, 1-1031.02.

MULTIPLE-PARTY ACCOUNTS.
Nonprobate transfers on death, §§19-601.01 to 19-602.27.
See NONPROBATE TRANSFERS.

MULTISTATE BAR EXAMINATION, DCCtApp Rule 46.

MULTISTATE PROFESSIONAL RESPONSIBILITY EXAMINATION, DCCtApp Rule 46.

MULTISTATE TAX COMPACT, §§47-441 to 47-445.

MULTIYEAR CAPITAL IMPROVEMENTS PLAN, §§1-204.44, 47-339.

MUMPS.
Immunization of school students, §§38-501 to 38-508.
Interstate compact on educational opportunity for military children.
Time to obtain immunizations, §49-1101.05.

MUNICIPAL CENTER, §§10-601, 10-602.

MUNICIPAL FISH MARKET, §37-205.01.

MUNICIPAL GOVERNMENTS.
See POLITICAL SUBDIVISIONS.

MURDER, §§22-2101 to 22-2107.
Aged persons, offenses committed against.
Enhanced penalties, §22-3601.
Aiding and abetting, §22-2101.
Certain crimes, purposeful killing while perpetrating, §§22-2101, 22-2102.
Defined, §22-2101.
Felony murder, §22-2101.
First degree murder.
Killing in the commission of certain crimes, §22-2101.
Killing law enforcement officer, §22-2106.
Limitation of actions, §23-113.
Penalties, §22-2104.
Placing obstructions upon or displacement of railroad, §22-2102.
Prison terms, §22-2104.
Release prior to trial, §23-1325.
Sentencing procedure for, §22-2104.01.
What constitutes, §22-2101.
Inheritance barred by, §19-320.
Insurance policies, §19-320.
Law enforcement officer, §22-2106.
Limitation of actions, §23-113.
Manslaughter, §22-2105.
Penalties, §22-2104.
Aged persons, offenses committed against.
Enhanced penalties, §22-3601.
Solicitation of murder or other violent crimes, §22-2107.
Railroad obstructions or displacements, §22-2102.
Release prior to trial in first degree murder cases, §23-1325.
Second degree murder.
Conduct constituting, §22-2103.
Limitation of actions, §23-113.
Penalties, §22-2104.
Prison terms, §22-2104.
Sentencing procedure, §22-2103.
What constitutes, §22-2103.
Solicitation of murder or other violent crimes, §22-2107.

MURDER FOR HIRE.
First degree murder prosecutions.
Aggravating circumstances, §22-2104.01.

MUSEUM OF CITY OF WASHINGTON, §§39-301 to 39-309.
Board of directors, §§39-304, 39-305.
Cooperation of government, §39-306.
Corporate powers, §39-303.
Dissolution, §39-307.
Duties, §39-301.
Established, §39-301.
Official cultural institution, §39-301.
Retention of council authority, §39-309.
Service of process, §39-302.
Tax status, §39-308.

MUSEUMS.
City of Washington, museum of, §§39-301 to 39-309.
Real property exempt from taxation, §47-1002.

MUSIC.
Historic music cultural institutions.
Property tax exemption, §47-4662.

MUSICIANS.
Metropolitan police, §§5-131.01 to 5-131.05.
National guard, §49-903.

MUSIC PIRACY, §22-3214.

MUTUAL AID.
Reciprocal police mutual aid agreements, §§2-209.01 to 2-209.04.

MUTUAL INSURANCE COMPANIES.
Conversion of mutual company to stock company.
General provisions, §§31-901 to 31-915.
See INSURANCE DEMUTUALIZATION.
Demutualization, §§31-901 to 31-915.
See INSURANCE DEMUTUALIZATION.
Domestic life insurance companies, §§31-4416 to 31-4419, 31-4434.
Fire and casualty insurance, §§31-2502.24, 31-2502.25.
Fraternal benefit societies converted into mutual life insurance companies, §31-5312.
Holding companies, §§31-731 to 31-738.
See INSURANCE HOLDING COMPANIES.
Hospital and medical services corporations not to convert to, §31-3516.

N

NAIC INSURANCE REGULATORY INFORMATION SYSTEM, §§31-1901 to 31-1904.

NAMES.
Appeals in federal cases, USCtApp Rule 1.
Name or title of public officer substituted as party, FRAP 43(c).
Business organizations, §§29-103.01 to 29-103.04.
Foreign entities.
Noncomplying names, §29-105.06.
Permitted names, §29-103.01.
Registration of, §29-103.04.
Requirements, §29-103.02.
Reservation of, §29-103.03.
Captive insurance companies, §31-3931.10.
Change of name, CivPro Rule 205.
Divorce, DomRel Rule 13.
Insurance producer licensing, §31-1131.08a.
Notice of application, CivPro Form CA 111.
Deeds, §42-405.
Divorce.
Change of name upon divorce, DomRel Rule 13.
Law firms, ProfCond Rule 7.5.
Personal names, changing, §§16-2501, 16-2503.
Pleadings to contain names of parties or attorneys, CivPro Rule 10-I, USDistCt LCvR 5.1, USDistCt LCvR 11.1.
Criminal proceedings, USDistCt LCrR 49.
Real estate organizations, names prohibited for, §47-2853.185.
Schools, §§38-904, 38-905.
Streets and alleys.
See STREETS AND ALLEYS.

NATIONAL AIRPORT.
Ronald Reagan Washington national airport, §§9-701 to 9-707.
See RONALD REAGAN WASHINGTON NATIONAL AIRPORT.

NATIONAL BIKE REGISTRY.
Voluntary registration of bicycle through, §50-1611.

NATIONAL CAPITAL ENERGY FUND, §§8-1778.41 to 8-1778.48.
See ENERGY CONSERVATION.

NATIONAL CAPITAL HOUSING AUTHORITY, §§6-101.01 to 6-103.01.

Acquisition of property by, §6-101.01.

Agency of government, established as, §1-202.02.

Alley dwellings, notice to owners of, §6-101.06.

Appropriations, §6-101.03.

Condemnation proceedings, §6-101.02.

Contributions by District to housing projects of, §6-102.04.

Definitions, §§6-101.07, 6-102.01.

Designation of agency for, §6-101.02.

Housing projects.
Contributions by District to, §6-102.04.
Defined, §6-102.01.
Low-rent, §6-103.01.
Power of authority regarding, §6-102.02.

Improvements made by, §6-101.01.

Loans by District, §6-102.05.

Low-rent housing projects, §6-103.01.

Management of property, §6-101.01.

Mayor's authority, §1-202.02.

Plans, approval or disapproval of, §6-101.02.

Policy declaration, §6-101.01.

Powers of, §§6-101.01 to 6-101.03, 6-102.02.

Public housing agency, considered to be, §6-102.03.

Rental properties, §6-101.01.

Replatting by, §6-101.01.

Reports, §§6-101.04, 6-101.05.

Sale of property, §6-101.01.

NATIONAL CAPITAL PLANNING COMMISSION, §§2-1001 to 2-1011.

Acquisition of rights to real property, §10-101.

Appropriations, §§2-1008, 2-1010.

Budget estimates, §2-1011.

Committees, §2-1002.

Comprehensive Plan for the National Capital, §§1-306.01 to 1-306.07, 2-1003.
Housing linkage requirement of the housing element, §§1-306.31 to 1-306.45.

Duties and powers, §2-1002.

Establishment of, §2-1002.

Organization, §2-1002.

Personnel, §2-1002.

Policy declaration, §2-1001.

Predecessor agencies.
Transfers from, §2-1007.

NATIONAL CAPITAL PLANNING COMMISSION —Cont'd

Proposed developments and projects.
Consultation regarding, §2-1004.

Real property.
Acquisition of, §2-1009.

Reports, §2-1011.

Streets and alleys.
Closing, §§9-202.02, 9-202.03.

Transfers from predecessor agencies, §2-1007.

Zoning.
Board of Zoning adjustment, §6-641.07.
Platting and subdivisions, §2-1006.
Regulations.
Comments on, §§2-1006, 6-641.05.

NATIONAL CAPITAL REVITALIZATION CORPORATION.

Reorganization, §§2-1225.01 to 2-1225.42.
Assets and liabilities, transfer, §2-1225.11.
Capital funds, §2-1225.22.
Contracts and procurement, §2-1225.13.
Dissolution of boards, §2-1225.01.
Economic development special account, §2-1225.21.
Eminent domain authority not impaired, §2-1225.41.
Skyland eminent domain area, §2-1225.42.
Employees, §2-1225.02.
Transition to District control, §2-1225.02.
Urban renewal plan modifications, §2-1225.31.

Tax increment financing, §2-1217.11.

NATIONAL CAPITAL SERVICE AREA, §1-207.39.

NATIONAL CAPITAL TRANSPORTATION PROGRAM.

Interstate agreement, §9-1101.01.

NATIONAL CHILDREN'S ISLAND, §§10-1401 to 10-1406.

Comprehensive and Anacostia waterfront framework plans, §10-1406.

Definitions, §10-1401.

Property transfer, §10-1402.
Effect, §10-1404.

NATIONAL CHILDREN'S ISLAND
—Cont'd
Property transfer —Cont'd
Lands transferred and easements
granted, §10-1403.
Savings provision, §10-1405.

**NATIONAL COMMUNITY
REINVESTMENT COALITION.**
Real property tax exemptions,
§47-1071.

**NATIONAL CRIME INFORMATION
SYSTEM.**
Metropolitan police participation in,
§5-113.04.

**NATIONAL EDUCATION
ASSOCIATION.**
Real property exempt from taxation,
§§47-1036, 47-1036.01.

NATIONAL GUARD, §§49-101 to
49-906.
Adjutant General, §49-304.
Annual inspection and muster,
§49-215.
Armament, equipment, and supplies.
Annual inspection and muster,
§49-215.
Armories, §49-214.
Army of United States, issued by,
§49-201.
Deductions for lost property, §49-906.
Defective accounts.
Surveying officer to fix
responsibility, §49-208.
Dismissal, return on, §49-206.
Estate of officer, liability of, §§49-210,
49-211.
Failure to return property, §49-207.
Fines and penalties for selling,
pawning, or retaining, §49-205.
Fort Leslie J. McNair, use of, §49-216.
Lost equipment, liability for, §§49-203,
49-906.
Pawning of, §49-205.
Personal liability for, §§49-203, 49-210,
49-211.
Personal property, §49-213.
Promotion, return on, §49-206.
Purchase of, §49-217.
Reissue of, §49-202.
Retention by member of guard,
§49-205.
Retirement, return on, §49-206.
Return of, §§49-204, 49-206 to 49-211.
Sales of, §49-205.
Surveying officer, §§49-207 to 49-209.

NATIONAL GUARD —Cont'd
Armament, equipment, and supplies
—Cont'd
Uniforms, §§49-212, 49-906.
Verification of return of, §49-207.
Armory, §§3-301 to 3-344.
See ARMORY BOARD.
Battalions.
Naval battalion, §49-806.
Rulemaking by, §49-803.
Business licenses.
Waiver of business license renewal
fees for armed forces personnel,
§1-301.01.
Commander-in-chief, US Const Art II
§2.
Commanding General, §§49-301,
49-805.
Commissioned officers, §§49-301 to
49-313.
Adjutant General, §49-304.
Capability, examination for, §49-311.
Commanding General, §§49-301,
49-805.
Date of commissions, §49-802.
Discharge or dismissal, §49-313.
Duties of, §49-801.
Mayor, commissioning by, §1-301.76.
Noncommissioned staff, §49-302.
Officers, commissioning of, §49-305.
Promotions, examination for, §49-309.
Retirement, §§49-309, 49-312.
Second lieutenant.
Appointments to grade of, §49-308.
Appointments to grades above,
§49-307.
Examinations for, §49-310.
Staff department officers, §49-306.
Staff officers, §§49-302, 49-303.
Uniforms, §49-906.
Vacancies, §§49-303, 49-307.
Companies.
Disbanding of companies below
minimum strength, §49-408.
Rulemaking by, §49-803.
Courts-martial.
General provisions, §§49-501 to
49-509.
See COURTS-MARTIAL.
Designation as, §49-406.
Disability.
Excuse from duty for, §49-104.
Retirement of commissioned officer for,
§49-309.
**Disbanding of companies below
minimum strength,** §49-408.

NATIONAL GUARD —Cont'd
Discharge or dismissal.
Commissioned officers, §49-313.
Discharge without honor, §49-601.
Dishonorable discharge, §49-602.
Enlisted personnel, §§49-601, 49-602.
Noncommissioned officers, §49-701.
Return of armament, equipment, and
supplies on, §49-206.
**Disciplinary system of United States
Army, use of,** §49-804.
Drills, §49-101.
Field exercise system of United States
Army, use of, §49-804.
Prescription of, §49-102.
Duties, §49-101.
Encampments, §49-101.
Annual camp duty requirements,
§49-107.
Musicians on duty during, §49-903.
Rules for, §49-106.
Enlisted personnel, §§49-601, 49-602.
Examinations.
Officer's capability, §49-311.
Promotion of commissioned officers,
§49-309.
2nd Lieutenants, §49-310.
**Field exercise system of United
States Army, use of,** §49-804.
Fines and penalties.
Absence from duty, §49-104.
Armament, equipment, and supplies,
selling, pawning, or retaining,
§49-205.
Use of fines, §49-906.
Fort Leslie J. McNair, use of, §49-216.
**Morale, welfare, and recreation
association,** §§49-431 to 49-434.
Donations, §49-431.
Military corporation for social
purposes, §49-432.
Purpose, §49-431.
Unit and company funds, §49-433.
Youth challenge participant support
fund, §49-434.
Musicians, §49-903.
Naval battalion, §49-806.
Noncommissioned officers.
Appointment of, §49-701.
Discharge or dismissal, §49-701.
Reduction to ranks, §49-701.
Staff officers, §49-302.
Parades, §49-101.
Right-of-way of, §49-105.
Rules for, §49-106.
Pay and allowances, §§49-901 to
49-906.
Active service pay, §49-901.

NATIONAL GUARD —Cont'd
Pay and allowances —Cont'd
Deductions, §49-906.
Estimate of amount required annually,
§49-905.
General expenses, allowances for,
§49-902.
Musicians, §49-903.
Subsistence stores, §49-904.
Personal property, §49-213.
President of the United States, US
Const Art II §2.
Promotions.
Examinations for promotion of
commissioned officers, §49-309.
Return of armament, equipment, and
supplies on, §49-206.
**Reduction to ranks of
noncommissioned officers,**
§49-701.
Regiments, rulemaking by, §49-803.
Reserve corps, §49-407.
Retirement.
Commissioned officers, §49-312.
Disability, for, §49-309.
Return of armament, equipment, and
supplies on, §49-206.
Riot suppression, §49-103.
**Rulemaking by companies,
battalions, or regiments,** §49-802.
Second lieutenant.
Appointments to grade of, §49-308.
Appointments to grades above,
§49-307.
Examinations for, §49-310.
Staff officers, §§49-302, 49-303.
Subsistence stores, §49-904.
Tuition assistance benefits, §49-807.
United States Army.
Armament, equipment, and supplies
issued by, §49-201.
Disciplinary system, use of, §49-804.
Field exercise system, use of, §49-804.
Volunteers, composed of, §49-406.
**Youth challenge participant support
fund,** §49-434.

NATIONAL GUARD ASSOCIATION.
Real property exempt from taxation,
§47-1042.

NATIONAL HOUSING ACT.
Interest.
Exemption from interest in usury
regulations, §28-3307.
Mortgages and deeds of trust.
Exemption from interest in usury
regulations, §28-3307.

NATIONAL HOUSING ACT —Cont'd
Usury.
Exemption from interest in usury
regulations, §28-3307.

**NATIONAL LABOR RELATIONS
BOARD PROCEEDINGS.**
Appellate procedure.
Briefs and oral argument, FRAP 15.1,
USCtApp Rule 15.1.

**NATIONAL LAW ENFORCEMENT
HEROES MEMORIAL, §§5-1331 to
5-1333.**
Design and construction, §5-1332.
Establishment, §5-1331.
Expenses, §5-1333.

**NATIONAL LAW ENFORCEMENT
MUSEUM.**
Sales and use tax credit, §47-4622.

**NATIONAL ORIGIN
DISCRIMINATION.**
Insurance.
Unfair trade practices, §§31-2231.01 to
31-2231.25.
Prohibition of, §2-1401.01.

NATIONAL PARK SERVICE.
Park Police.
General provisions, §§5-201 to 5-208.
See UNITED STATES PARK
POLICE.
**Parks and recreation, §§10-101 to
10-308.**
See PARKS AND RECREATION.
**Recreation board, relationship to,
§10-223.**
**Steam heat furnished to District
buildings, §§10-501.03, 10-501.04.**

NATIONAL PUBLIC RADIO, INC.
Real property taxes.
Abatement of taxes, §47-4615.

**NATIONAL SCHOOL LUNCH ACT
PROGRAMS, §38-806.**

**NATIONAL TECHNICAL INSTITUTE
FOR THE DEAF.**
Agreement, §38-2401.12.
**Appropriations, §§38-2402.05,
38-2402.11.**
Audit, §38-2402.03.
Authority, §38-2401.11.
**Federal endowment programs,
§38-2402.07a.**
Gifts, §38-2402.02.
International student.
Limited enrollment, §38-2402.10.

**NATIONAL TECHNICAL INSTITUTE
FOR THE DEAF** —Cont'd
**Liaison for educational programs,
§38-2402.06.**
**Monitoring and evaluation of
activities, §38-2402.05.**
Oversight activities, §38-2402.09.
Report, §38-2402.04.
**Scholarships to deaf individuals for
careers in deaf education,
§38-2402.08a.**

NATIONAL WOMAN'S PARTY.
**Real property exempt from taxation,
§47-1040.**

**NATIONWIDE MORTGAGE
LICENSING SYSTEM AND
REGISTRY, §§26-1161.01 to
26-1161.11.**
Defined, §26-1102.
**Information challenge process,
§26-1120.03.**
Reports, §26-1120.02.

NATIVE AMERICANS.
Child custody proceedings.
Inapplicability of uniform act,
§16-4601.03.
Taxation, US Const Art I §2, Amd 14.

**NATURAL DEATH ACT, §§7-621 to
7-630.**
See LIVING WILLS.

**NATURAL DISASTER CONSUMER
PROTECTION, §§28-4101 to
28-4103.**
**Declaration of state of emergency,
§28-4102.**
Natural disaster.
Defined, §28-4101.
Normal average retail price.
Defined, §28-4101.
Overcharging, §28-4102.
Person.
Defined, §28-4101.
Sanctions, §28-4103.

NATURAL DISASTERS.
Price gouging, §§28-4101 to 28-4103.

**NATURALIZATION, US Const Art I
§§8, 9.**

NATURAL RESOURCES.
**Comprehensive natural resource
management and protection
plan.**
Duty of director of DDOE to prepare
and submit to mayor and council,
§8-151.08.

NATUROPATHY.
Advisory committee, §7-743.04.
Board of medicine.
  Advisory committee on naturopathic
    medicine, §3-1202.03.
Definition of practice of
  naturopathic medicine,
  §3-1201.02.
Health occupations boards.
  General provisions, §§3-1201.01 to
    3-1213.01.
  See HEALTH OCCUPATIONS
    BOARDS.
Health occupations licensure,
  registration or certification,
  §§3-1205.01 to 3-1205.24.
  See HEALTH OCCUPATIONS
    LICENSURE, REGISTRATION
    OR CERTIFICATION.
Naturopathic medicine.
  Disclosures required, §3-1206.22.
  Scope of practice, §3-1206.21.
Titles and terms prohibited as
  misrepresentation without
  license to practice, §3-1210.03.

NAVAL BATTALION.
National Guard, §49-806.

NAVAL LODGE BUILDING, INC.
Real property tax exemptions,
  §47-1097.

NAVAL OBSERVATORY.
Industrial home school, §44-1303.
Massachusetts Avenue and, §9-101.11.
Public thoroughfare within 1000
  feet, prohibition of, §9-101.10.

NAVAL SERVICE.
Police and firefighters retirement
  and disability.
  Credit for active military naval
    service, §5-742.

NAVY YARD TRACK CONNECTION.
Sale or lease of, §9-1203.02.

NAZI SWASTIKAS.
Displaying, §22-3312.02.

NECESSARY PARTIES.
Allegation of reason for omitting
  party, CivPro Form CA 26.
Joinder, CivPro Rule 19.
  Domestic relations actions, DomRel
    Rule 19.

NEEDLE EXCHANGE PROGRAMS,
  §48-1103.01.

NEEDLES.
Drug paraphernalia, §§48-904.10,
  48-1101 to 48-1104.
Schools and education.
  Distribution of needles or syringes
    near schools, §48-1121.
Sharps injury protection.
  Safe needle distribution, §§7-2851 to
    7-2858.

NEEDLESTICKS.
Sharps injury protection.
  Safe needle distribution, §§7-2851 to
    7-2858.

NE EXEAT WRITS.
Domestic relations actions, DomRel
  Rule 406.

NEGLECTED CHILDREN.
See CHILD ABUSE AND NEGLECT.

NEGLIGENCE.
Animals.
  Sick, injured, or disabled, §22-1011.
Appeals, D.C. courts.
  Time for filing notice upon showing
    excusable neglect, DCCtApp Rule
    4.
Appeals, federal cases.
  Extension of time to file notice of
    appeal as of right, FRAP 4.
Arrest, neglectful failure to make,
  §5-115.03.
Carriers.
  Contractual limitation of liability.
    Bill of lading, §28:7-309.
  Duty of carrier.
    Carrier issuing bill of lading,
      §28:7-309.
Child abuse and neglect, §§4-1301.02
  to 4-1362.
  See CHILD ABUSE AND NEGLECT.
Child restraint seats, §50-1707.
Comparative negligence.
  Bank deposits and collections.
    Unauthorized signature or
      alteration, customer's duty to
      report, §28:4-406.
Complaint for negligence, CivPro
  Forms CA 9, CA 10.
Death, causing, §§16-2701 to 16-2703.
Generic drug substitutes, §48-803.05.
Helmets.
  Failure of bicycle operator or
    passenger to wear, §50-1606.
Insanitary buildings, §6-915.
Intellectual disabilities, persons
  with.
  Neglect of, §7-1305.10.

NEGLIGENCE —Cont'd

Metropolitan police property clerk,
§5-119.11.

Negotiable instruments.
Contributing to forged signature alteration of instrument, §28:3-406.

Non-motorized user contributory negligence, §§50-2204.51 to 50-2204.53.

Operation of vehicles by District employees, §§2-412, 2-415.

Public officers and employees, §2-416.

Relief from judgment or order, CivPro Rule 60.
Domestic relations actions, DomRel Rule 60.

Seat belts, §50-1807.

Traffic laws, negligent homicide, §§50-2203.01, 50-2203.02.

Uniform commercial code.
Bill of lading.
Duty of carrier, §28:7-309.

Vulnerable adults and elderly persons.
Criminal abuse, neglect and financial exploitation.
Criminal negligence, §22-934.

Wrongful death.
Generally, §§16-2701 to 16-2703.
See WRONGFUL DEATH.

NEGOTIABLE INSTRUMENTS,
§§28:3-101 to 28:3-605.

Acceptance.
Defined, §28:3-409.
Drafts, §28:3-409.
Acceptance varying drafts, §28:3-410.
Obligation of acceptor, §28:3-413.
Incomplete drafts, §28:3-409.
Mistake, §28:3-418.
Obligation of acceptor, §28:3-413.
Operation of, §28:3-409.
Presentment.
Time allowed for acceptance, §28:3-501.
Unaccepted draft.
Drawee not liable, §28:3-408.
Varying of draft, §28:3-410.
Writing required, §28:3-409.

Accommodation party.
Discharge of secondary obligors, §28:3-605.
Reimbursement, §28:3-419.
Signing for accommodation, §28:3-419.

NEGOTIABLE INSTRUMENTS
—Cont'd

Accord and satisfaction.
Use of instrument, §28:3-311.

Actions.
Accrual of actions, §28:3-118.
Limitation of actions, §28:3-118.

Alteration of instruments.
Effect of, §28:3-407.
Negligence contributing to, §28:3-406.
What constitutes, §28:3-407.

Ambiguous terms, §28:3-114.

Applicability of article, §28:3-102.

Bearer.
Payable to bearer, §28:3-109.

Bills of lading.
General provisions, §§28:7-101 to 28:7-702.
See DOCUMENTS OF TITLE.

Cancellation.
Discharge, §28:3-604.

Cashier's checks.
Defined, §28:3-104.
Lost, destroyed or stolen cashier's check, §28:3-312.
Payment.
Obligation of issuer, §28:3-412.
Refusal to pay, §28:3-411.

Certificates of deposit.
Defined, §28:3-104.

Certified checks.
Defined, §28:3-409.
Lost, destroyed or stolen certified check, §28:3-312.
Refusal to pay, §28:3-411.

Checks.
Defined, §§28:3-104, 28:3-312.

Citation of article.
Short title, §28:3-101.

Claims in recoupment, §28:3-305.

Claim to the instrument, §28:3-306.

Conflict of laws, §28:3-102.

Consideration.
Absence of, §28:3-303.
Defined, §28:3-303.

Consumer credit sales.
Seller not permitted to take negotiable instrument, §28-3807.

Consumer protection.
Prohibited in consumer credit sales, §28-3807.

Consumer transactions.
Defenses and claims in recoupment.
Applicable provisions, §28:3-305.
Defined, §28:3-103.

Contradictory terms, §28:3-114.

NEGOTIABLE INSTRUMENTS
—Cont'd
Conversion.
Innocent representatives, §28:3-420.
When instrument converted,
§28:3-420.
Date.
Antedating, §28:3-113.
Failure to date, §28:3-113.
Postdating, §28:3-113.
Defenses.
Burden of establishing signature and
status of holder as due course,
§28:3-308.
Generally, §28:3-305.
Definitions, §28:3-103.
Acceptance, §28:3-409.
Alteration, §28:3-407.
Certified check, §28:3-409.
Checks, §§28:3-104, 28:3-312.
Claimant, §28:3-312.
Declaration of loss, §28:3-312.
Obligated bank, §28:3-312.
Consideration, §28:3-303.
Employee.
Fraudulent endorsement, §28:3-405.
Fiduciary, §28:3-307.
Fraudulent endorsement, §28:3-405.
Holder in due course, §28:3-302.
Incomplete instrument, §28:3-115.
Indorsement, §28:3-204.
Instruments, §28:3-104.
Issue, §28:3-105.
Negotiation, §28:3-201.
Person entitled to enforce, §28:3-301.
Presentment, §28:3-501.
Represented person, §28:3-307.
Responsibility.
Fraudulent endorsement, §28:3-405.
Demand.
Date of payment, §28:3-113.
Overdue instruments, §28:3-304.
Destroyed instruments.
Cashier's check, teller's check or
certified check, §28:3-312.
Enforcement, §28:3-309.
Discharge.
Accord and satisfaction.
Use of instrument, §28:3-311.
Cancellation, §28:3-604.
Certification of check, §28:3-310.
Effect of discharge, §28:3-601.
Generally, §28:3-601.
Holder in due course.
Effect of discharge against,
§28:3-601.

NEGOTIABLE INSTRUMENTS
—Cont'd
Discharge —Cont'd
Payment.
Discharge upon payment, §28:3-602.
Tender of payment, §28:3-603.
Renunciation, §28:3-604.
Secondary obligors, §28:3-605.
Dishonor.
Evidence of dishonor, §28:3-505.
Generally, §28:3-502.
Notice of dishonor, §§28:3-503 to
28:3-505.
Obligation of drawer, §28:3-414.
Obligation of indorser, §28:3-415.
When instrument is dishonored,
§28:3-502.
Documents of title.
General provisions, §§28:7-101 to
28:7-702.
See DOCUMENTS OF TITLE.
Drafts.
Acceptance, §§28:3-409, 28:3-410,
28:3-413.
Dishonor, §28:3-502.
Unaccepted drafts.
Drawee not liable on, §28:3-408.
**Effect of instrument on obligation
for which taken,** §28:3-310.
Evidence.
Dishonor, §28:3-505.
Notice of dishonor, §28:3-505.
Fictitious payees, §28:3-404.
Fiduciaries.
Breach of fiduciary duty.
Notice, §28:3-307.
Defined, §28:3-307.
Transfers by, §21-1703.
Foreign money.
Instrument payable in, §28:3-107.
Fraud.
Indorsements.
Responsibility of employer for
fraudulent indorsement by
employee, §28:3-405.
General provisions, §§28:1-101 to
28:1-310.
See COMMERCIAL CODE.
Holder in due course.
Defined, §28:3-302.
Discharge.
Effect of discharge against holder in
due course, §28:3-306.
Proof of status as, §28:3-308.
Small claims court forms, SmallClaims
Form 2.

NEGOTIABLE INSTRUMENTS
—Cont'd
Identification.
Person to whom instrument payable, §28:3-110.
Incomplete instruments, §28:3-115.
Indorsement.
Anomalous indorsement, §28:3-205.
Blank indorsement, §28:3-205.
Defined, §28:3-204.
Discharge of secondary obligors, §28:3-605.
Fraud.
Responsibility of employer for fraudulent indorsement of employee, §28:3-405.
Generally, §28:3-204.
Imposters, §28:3-404.
Obligation of indorser, §28:3-415.
Reacquisition, §28:3-207.
Restrictive indorsements, §28:3-206.
Signatures.
Proof of signature, §28:3-308.
Special indorsement, §28:3-205.
Transfer of security interest, §28:3-204.
Interest.
Payment, §28:3-112.
Rate, §28:3-112.
Interpretation of provisions, §§28:10-103, 28:10-104.
Issue.
Defined, §28:3-105.
Letters of credit.
General provisions, §§28:5-101 to 28:5-120.
See LETTERS OF CREDIT.
Liability of parties.
Employers.
Responsibility for fraudulent indorsement by an employee, §28:3-405.
Fictitious payees, §28:3-404.
Imposters, §28:3-404.
Signatures.
Authorized representative, §28:3-402.
Person not liable unless signature appears, §28:3-401.
Signing of instrument, §28:3-401.
Unaccepted draft.
Drawee not liable, §28:3-408.
Limitation of actions, §28:3-118.
Lost instruments.
Cashier's check, teller's check or certified check, §28:3-312.

NEGOTIABLE INSTRUMENTS
—Cont'd
Lost instruments —Cont'd
Enforcement, §28:3-309.
Metropolitan police.
Depositing of seized currency, §§23-531 to 23-534.
Mortgages and deeds of trust.
General provisions, §§42-804 to 42-820.
See MORTGAGES AND DEEDS OF TRUST.
Negligence.
Contributing to forged signature alteration or alteration of instrument, §28:3-406.
Negotiability.
Incomplete instruments, §28:3-115.
Other writings affecting instrument, §28:3-117.
Negotiation.
Defined, §28:3-201.
Rescission, §28:3-202.
Notes.
Dishonor, §28:3-502.
Notice.
Breach of fiduciary duty, §28:3-307.
Third parties.
Right to defend action, §28:3-119.
Notice of dishonor.
Delay.
Excused delay, §28:3-504.
Evidence of, §28:3-505.
Excused notice of dishonor, §28:3-504.
Generally, §28:3-503.
Protests, §28:3-505.
When necessary, §28:3-503.
Order.
Payable to order, §28:3-109.
Unconditional.
When order unconditional, §28:3-106.
Other agreements affecting instrument, §28:3-117.
Payment.
Bearer.
Payable to bearer, §28:3-109.
Demand.
Date of payment, §28:3-113.
Discharge, §§28:3-602, 28:3-603.
Foreign money, §28:3-107.
Identification of person to whom instrument payable, §28:3-110.
Interest, §28:3-112.
Mistakes, §28:3-418.
Money.
Foreign currency, §28:3-107.

NEGOTIABLE INSTRUMENTS
—Cont'd
Payment —Cont'd
Obligation of issuer.
Note or cashier's check, §28:3-412.
Order.
Payable to order, §28:3-109.
Overdue instruments, §28:3-304.
Place of payment, §28:3-111.
Refusal to pay.
Cashier's checks, teller's checks and certified checks, §28:3-411.
Time.
When payable at definite time, §28:3-108.
Place of payment, §28:3-111.
Presentment.
Acceptance.
Time allowed for acceptance, §28:3-501.
Defined, §28:3-501.
Dishonor.
When instrument is dishonored, §28:3-502.
Excused presentment, §28:3-504.
How made, §28:3-501.
Place of presentment, §28:3-501.
Rights of party to whom presentment made, §28:3-501.
Time of presentment, §28:3-501.
Warranties, §28:3-417.
Presentment warranties, §28:4-208.
Promises.
Unconditional.
When promise unconditional, §28:3-106.
Recoupment.
Claims in recoupment, §28:3-305.
Remotely created consumer items.
Defined, §28:3-103.
Presentment warranties, §28:3-417.
Transfer warranties, §28:3-416.
Renunciation.
Discharge, §28:3-604.
Rescission.
Negotiation subject to rescission, §28:3-202.
Restrictive indorsements, §28:3-206.
Secondary obligors.
Defined, §28:3-103.
Discharge, §28:3-605.
Signatures.
Accommodation party, §28:3-419.
How made, §28:3-401.
Imposters, §28:3-404.
Liability.
Person not liable unless signature appears, §28:3-401.

NEGOTIABLE INSTRUMENTS
—Cont'd
Signatures —Cont'd
Liability —Cont'd
Signature by authorized representative, §28:3-402.
Negligence.
Contributing to forged signature, §28:3-406.
Proof of signature, §28:3-308.
Representative.
Signature by authorized representative, §28:3-402.
Trade or assumed name, §28:3-401.
Unauthorized signature, §28:3-403.
Ratification, §28:3-403.
Small claims court.
Surrender of instruments, SmallClaims Rule 16.
Stolen instruments.
Cashier's check, teller's check or certified check, §28:3-312.
Enforcement, §28:3-309.
Teller's checks.
Defined, §28:3-104.
Lost, destroyed or stolen teller's check, §28:3-312.
Refusal to pay, §28:3-411.
Third parties.
Notice of right to defend action, §28:3-119.
Title of article.
Short title, §28:3-101.
Transfer.
Generally, §28:3-203.
Reacquisition, §28:3-207.
Rights vested in transferee, §28:3-203.
Warranties on transfer, §28:4-207.
Transitional provisions, §§28:11-101 to 28:11-108.
See COMMERCIAL CODE.
Traveler's checks.
Defined, §28:3-104.
Refusal to pay, §28:3-411.
Unconditional promises or orders, §28:3-106.
Value.
Issued or transferred for value, §28:3-303.
Warehouse receipts.
General provisions, §§28:7-101 to 28:7-702.
See DOCUMENTS OF TITLE.
Warranties.
Presentment, §§28:3-417, 28:3-418, 28:4-208.

NEGOTIABLE INSTRUMENTS
—Cont'd
Warranties —Cont'd
Transfers, §§28:3-416, 28:4-207.

NEIGHBORHOOD PARADE AND FESTIVAL FUND, §1-325.211.

NEIGHBORHOOD PLANNING COUNCILS.
Youth services.
See YOUTH SERVICES.

NEIGHBORHOOD WATCH MEMBERS.
Enhanced penalty for committing certain crimes against, §22-3602.

NEOPLASTIC DISEASES, MALIGNANT.
Prevention and monitoring, §§7-301 to 7-304.

NEPOTISM, §1-618.04.

NEUTERING OF ANIMALS, §8-1810.

NEWBORN HEALTH INSURANCE, §§31-3801 to 31-3805.
Applicability of provisions, §31-3804.
At-home postpartum treatment, §31-3802.01.
Casualty and other insurance rates.
General provisions, §§31-2701 to 31-2714.
See INSURANCE.
Exclusions, §31-3805.
In-patient postpartum treatment, §31-3802.01.
Notice of birth, §31-3803.
Payable benefits, §31-3801.
Premium payments, §31-3803.

NEWBORN HEARING SCREENING, §§7-851 to 7-855.

NEWBORN HEART SCREENING, §§7-857.01 to 7-857.04.

NEWBORNS.
At-home postpartum treatment, §31-3802.01.
Blindness, preventing screening, §§7-801 to 7-804.
Inflammation of the eyes, report, treatment, §7-802.
Treatment by other than registered physician, §7-803.
Violations, penalty, §7-804.
Breastmilk bank and lactation support, §§7-881.01 to 7-881.11.

NEWBORNS —Cont'd
Health insurance coverage, §§31-3801 to 31-3805.
See NEWBORN HEALTH INSURANCE.
Hearing screening, §§7-851 to 7-855.
Definitions, §7-851.
Health benefit plans, reimbursement, §7-853.
Effective date, §7-855.
Rules, §7-854.
Screening programs, §7-852.
Effective date, §7-855.
Heart screening, §§7-857.01 to 7-857.04.
Critical congenital heart disease screening, §7-857.02.
Defined terms, §7-857.01.
Health benefit plan reimbursement, §7-857.03.
Rules, §7-857.04.
Metabolic disorders, screening for, §§7-831 to 7-840.
Appropriation, §7-839.
Committee on metabolic disorders, §7-835.
Annual report, §7-837.
Duties, §7-836.
Costs, assumption by District, §7-838.
Definitions, §7-832.
Effective date, §7-840.
Neonatal testing, §7-833.
Principles governing screening, §7-834.
Purpose, §7-831.
Ophthalmia in newborns, §§7-801 to 7-804.
Safe haven, §§4-1451.01 to 4-1451.08.

NEWBORN SAFE HAVEN, §§4-1451.01 to 4-1451.08.
Definitions, §4-1451.01.
Immunity, §4-1451.06.
Parental rights, §4-1451.05.
Placement, §4-1451.04.
Rules and regulations, §4-1451.08.
Signage, §4-1451.03.
Status reports, §4-1451.07.
Surrender, §4-1451.02.

NEW CAR WARRANTIES, §§50-501 to 50-510.
See LEMON LAW.

NEW COLUMBIA.
State of New Columbia.
Text of proposed constitution.
See Vol. 1.

NEW COLUMBIA COMMUNITY LAND TRUST.
Real property tax exemptions, §47-1072.

NEW COLUMBIA STATEHOOD FUND.
Statehood Delegation members.
Use of funds by, §§1-129.32, 1-129.35.

NEW COLUMBIA STATEHOOD INITIATIVE, §§1-129.21 to 1-129.35.

NEW COMMUNITIES INITIATIVE.
Bond authorization, §42-2812.03.
Housing production trust fund, §42-2802.

NEW EVIDENCE.
Protection of innocence act, §§22-4131 to 22-4135.

NEW HOME WARRANTIES.
Implied warranties.
Fitness for particular purpose, §28:2-315.

NEWLY DISCOVERED EVIDENCE.
Crime victims' compensation.
Request for reconsideration, VictComp Rule 18.
Criminal procedure, CrimPro Rule 33.
Juvenile proceedings, JuvProc Rule 33.
Relief from judgment or order, CivPro Rule 60.
Domestic relations actions, DomRel Rule 60.

NEW RESIDENTIAL DEVELOPMENTS.
Tax abatement, §§47-857.01 to 47-857.10, 47-859.01 to 47-859.05.

NEWS MEDIA PRIVILEGE, §§16-4701 to 16-4704.

NEWSPAPER CARRIERS.
Child labor, §§32-201, 32-215.

NEWSPAPERS.
Court sales of property.
Notice of sale, CivPro Rule 308.
Probate proceedings, Probate Rule 203.
Forfeiture of property.
Notice of forfeiture, CivPro Rule 71A-I.
Homestead housing preservation program.
List of properties available for transfer, §42-2108.

NEWSPAPERS —Cont'd
Name changes.
Notice of application, CivPro Rule 205.
Service by publication, CivPro Rule 4-I.
Probate proceedings.
Death between Jan. 1, 1981, and June 30, 1995, Probate Rule 128.
Death on or after July 1, 1995, Probate Rule 428.
Sale of property by guardians, conservators, trustees, etc., involved, Probate Rule 203.
Taxation.
Levy for failure to pay.
Notice of seizure for sale, §47-4472.

NEW TOWN AT CAPITAL CITY MARKET REVITALIZATION, §§6-1062.01 to 6-1062.07.
Authority and responsibility of deputy mayor for economic development, §6-1062.05.
Definitions, §6-1062.02.
Developer to work with office of planning and other agencies, §6-1062.04.
Development and conceptual plan, §6-1062.06.
Eminent domain, §6-1062.07.
Findings, §6-1062.03.
Short title, §6-1062.01.

NEW TRIAL, CivPro Rule 59, CrimPro Rule 33.
Adoption proceedings, Adoption Rule 60.
Domestic relations actions, DomRel Rules 59, 61.
Stay of proceedings, DomRel Rule 62.
Eminent domain.
Objections or exceptions to appraisement, §16-1318.
Real property for United States.
Fixing date for new trial, §16-1362.
Harmless error.
Adoption proceedings, Adoption Rule 61.
Civil procedure, CivPro Rule 61.
Criminal procedure, CrimPro Rule 52.
Plea procedure, CrimPro Rule 11.
Domestic relations actions, DomRel Rule 61.
Juvenile proceedings, JuvProc Rule 52.
Judgment as a matter of law, CivPro Rule 50.

NEW TRIAL —Cont'd

Juvenile proceedings, JuvProc Rule 33.

Small claims court, SmallClaims Rule 16.

Stay of proceedings, CivPro Rule 62.
Domestic relations actions, DomRel Rule 62.

NEW YEAR'S DAY.

Appeals, federal cases, FRAP 26(a), 45(a).

Designated holiday, §§1-612.02, 28-2701.

Extension of time for performing acts, §28-2701.

NEW YORK AVENUE METRORAIL BENEFIT AREA, §§47-881 to 47-885.

NEXT FRIEND.

Actions by next friend, CivPro Rule 17.
Domestic relations actions, DomRel Rule 17.

NIGHTCLUBS.

Alcoholic beverage licenses.
Brew pub licenses, §25-117.
Georgetown historic district.
Special restrictions, §25-339.
On-premises retailers, §25-113.
Entertainment endorsements, §25-113a.
Wine pub permits, §25-124.

Smoking, §7-741.02.

911 SYSTEMS.

Authorized use of 911 call system, §1-327.56a.

Emergency and non-emergency telephone system assessments fund, §§34-1801 to 34-1806.

Prepaid wireless E911 charge.
Collection and remittance, §34-1803.02.

NOBILITY.

Titles of prohibited, US Const Art I §§9, 10.

NO-FAULT MOTOR VEHICLE INSURANCE, §§31-2401 to 31-2408.01.

Arbitration, §31-2405.

Assignment of right to future benefits, §31-2410.

Attorneys' fees and costs, §31-2410.

Availability of, §31-2406.

NO-FAULT MOTOR VEHICLE INSURANCE —Cont'd

Cancellation or nonrenewal of policy, §31-2409.

Consumer protection provisions, §31-2409.

Deductibles, §31-2410.

Definitions, §31-2402.

Discovery.
Pre-litigation discovery of insurance, §31-2403.01.

Discrimination, §§31-2409, 31-2410.

Drivers' license, suspension of, §31-2413.

Fines, §31-2413.

Good-faith mistakes, §31-2411.

Limitation of actions, §31-2411.

Medical examinations, §31-2411.

Notice of proposed settlement for policy limits upon waiver of subrogation, §31-2407.01.

Penalties, §31-2413.

Personal injury protection.
Availability of, §§31-2404, 31-2406.
Defined, §31-2404.
Elements of, §31-2404.
Lawsuit restrictions on persons with, §31-2405.
Overdue payments, interest on, §31-2410.
Payment priorities, §31-2407.

Policy declaration, §31-2401.

Pre-litigation discovery of insurance, §31-2403.01.

Requirement to have insurance, §31-2403.

Subrogation, §31-2411.
Notice of proposed settlement for policy limits upon waiver of subrogation, §31-2407.01.

Taxicabs, requirements waived for, §31-2411.

Uninsured motorist fund, §31-2408.01.

Violations, §31-2413.

NOISE RESTRICTIONS.

Alcoholic beverage licenses, §25-725.
Orientation classes for new licensees and general public, §25-212.

NOLLE PROSEQUI, CrimPro Rule 110.

NOLO CONTENDERE PLEAS, CrimPro Rule 11.

Hearing commissioners' power to accept plea, CrimPro Rule 117.

NOLO CONTENDERE PLEAS
—Cont'd
Presence of defendant, CrimPro Rule 43.
Withdrawal of plea, CrimPro Rule 32.

NONCOMPETE AGREEMENTS.
Attorneys at law, ProfCond Rule 5.6.
Broadcasting industry employment contracts, §§32-531 to 32-533.

NONDELIVERY.
Commercial code.
  Sale of goods.
    Buyer's damages for nondelivery, §28:2-713.

NONPROBATE TRANSFERS,
  §§19-601.01 to 19-603.11.
Agent on accounts.
  Designation, §19-602.05.
  Payment to designated agent, §19-602.24.
Allowances.
  Liability of nonprobate transferees for creditor claims and statutory allowances, §19-601.02.
Construction of act, §19-601.01.
  Limitation on scope, §19-602.02.
  Multiple party accounts, §19-602.06.
Contractual arrangements,
  §19-602.04.
Creditor claims.
  Liability of nonprobate transferees for creditor claims and statutory allowances, §19-601.02.
Definitions, §19-602.01.
  TOD security registration, §19-603.01.
Financial institutions, protection of,
  §§19-602.21 to 19-602.27.
  Authority of financial institution, §19-602.21.
  Designated agent, payment to, §19-602.24.
  Discharges from claims, §19-602.26.
  Multiple-party accounts, payment on, §19-602.22.
  POD designation, payment on, §19-602.23.
  Setoffs or liens, §19-602.27.
Inapplicability of act, §19-602.02.
Minor beneficiaries.
  Payment by financial institution, §19-602.25.
Multiple-party accounts.
  Alteration of rights, §19-602.13.
  Applicability of provisions, §19-602.06.
  Community property, §19-602.15.

NONPROBATE TRANSFERS —Cont'd
Multiple-party accounts —Cont'd
  Designation of agent, §19-602.05.
  Effect of transfer, §19-602.14.
  Existing accounts, §19-602.03.
  Ownership during lifetime, §19-602.11.
  Payment by financial institution, §19-602.22.
  Rights on death, §19-602.12.
  Tenancy by the entireties, §19-602.15.
  Types of accounts, §19-602.03.
POD designations.
  Alteration of rights, §19-602.13.
  Community property, §19-602.15.
  Contractual form, §19-602.04.
  Defined, §19-602.01.
  Effect of transfer, §19-602.14.
  Ownership during lifetime, §19-602.11.
  Payment by financial institution, §19-602.23.
  Rights on death, §19-602.12.
  Tenancy by the entireties, §19-602.15.
  Types of accounts, §19-602.02.
Single party accounts, §19-602.02.
  Contractual form, §19-602.04.
TOD security registration,
  §§19-603.01 to 19-603.11.
  Applicability of provisions, §19-603.11.
  Conditions of registration, §19-603.10.
  Definitions, §19-603.01.
  Forms of registration, §19-603.10.
  Nontestamentary transfer on death, §19-603.09.
  Ownership on death of owner, §19-603.07.
  Registering entity, protection of, §19-603.08.
  Registration in beneficiary form, §§19-603.01 to 19-603.06.
    Applicable law, §19-603.03.
    Effect of, §19-603.06.
    Form of, §19-603.05.
    Joint tenancy ownership, §19-603.02.
    Origination of, §19-603.04.
    Sole or joint tenancy ownership, §19-603.02.
  Terms of registration, §19-603.10.
Uniform real property transfers on death, §§19-604.01 to 19-604.19.

NONPROFIT ASSOCIATIONS, UNINCORPORATED, §§29-1101 to 29-1127.
Administrative dissolution.
  Generally, §§29-106.01 to 29-106.04.
  See BUSINESS ORGANIZATIONS.

NONPROFIT ASSOCIATIONS,
  UNINCORPORATED —Cont'd
Claims, assertion of, §29-1109.
Definitions, §29-1102.
Dissolution, §29-1124.
Distributions.
  Prohibitions, §29-1122.
Duration of, §29-1105.
Filing.
  Generally, §§29-102.01 to 29-102.13.
  See BUSINESS ORGANIZATIONS.
Foreign entities.
  Generally, §§29-105.01 to 29-105.12.
  See BUSINESS ORGANIZATIONS.
Governing law, §29-1104.
Indemnification, §29-1123.
Judgment or order against
  association.
  Effect of, §29-1110.
Legal entity separate from members,
  §29-1105.
Liability, §29-1108.
Managers.
  Advancements, §29-1123.
  Compensation, §29-1122.
  Distributions.
    Prohibitions, §29-1122.
  Duties, §29-1119.
  Indemnification, §29-1123.
  Information rights, §29-1121.
  Management rights, §29-1118.
  Reimbursement, §29-1123.
  Selection, §29-1118.
Meetings, §29-1120.
  Members, §29-1113.
Members.
  Admission, suspension, dismissal or
    expulsion, §29-1115.
  Advancements, §29-1123.
  Approval, §29-1112.
  Compensation, §29-1122.
  Distributions.
    Prohibitions, §29-1122.
  Duties, §29-1114.
  Indemnification, §29-1123.
  Interests not transferable, §29-1117.
  Meetings, §29-1113.
  Not deemed agents, §29-1111.
  Reimbursement, §29-1123.
  Resignation of, §29-1116.
  Voting, §29-1113.
Mergers and consolidations,
  §29-1126.
Names.
  Generally, §§29-103.01 to 29-103.04.
  See BUSINESS ORGANIZATIONS.

NONPROFIT ASSOCIATIONS,
  UNINCORPORATED —Cont'd
Pay-for-success contracts, §§2-211.01
  to 2-211.03.
Personal property.
  Ownership and transfer, §29-1106.
  Transitional provisions, §29-1127.
Powers, §29-1105.
Real property.
  Ownership and transfer, §29-1106.
  Statement of authority, §29-1107.
  Transitional provisions, §29-1127.
Registered agents.
  Generally, §§29-104.01 to 29-104.14.
  See BUSINESS ORGANIZATIONS.
Short title, §29-1101.
Statutory construction, §29-1103.
Termination of, §29-1125.
Transitional provisions, §29-1127.
Voting.
  Members, §29-1113.
Winding up, §29-1125.

NONPROFIT CORPORATIONS,
  §§29-401.01 to 29-401.03.
Actions, §29-403.02.
Administrative dissolution.
  Generally, §§29-106.01 to 29-106.04.
  See BUSINESS ORGANIZATIONS.
Admission of members, §§29-404.01 to
  29-404.03.
  Consideration, §29-404.03.
  Not required, §29-404.01.
  Procedures, §29-404.02.
Articles of incorporation.
  Amendment, §§29-408.01 to 29-408.09.
    Articles of amendment, §29-408.06.
    Authority, §29-408.01.
    Before issuance of memberships,
      §29-408.02.
    Effect of, §29-408.09.
    Membership corporations,
      §29-408.03.
    Nonmembership corporations,
      §29-408.05.
    Reorganization, upon, §29-408.08.
    Special rights, §29-408.40.
    Voting, §29-408.04.
  Contents, §29-402.02.
  Filing, §29-402.03.
  Restatement, §29-408.07.
Attorney general.
  Notice, §29-401.60.
Board of directors, §§29-406.01 to
  29-406.12. See within this heading,
  "Directors."

NONPROFIT CORPORATIONS
—Cont'd
Bylaws.
  Amendment, §§29-408.20 to 29-408.23.
    Authority, §29-408.20.
    Effect of, §29-408.23.
    Member approval, §29-408.22.
    Quorum, §29-408.21.
    Special rights, §29-408.40.
    Voting, §29-408.21.
  Contents, §29-402.06.
Conflicting interest transactions,
  §29-406.70.
Contracts.
  Officers.
    Contract rights, §29-406.44.
  Powers, §29-403.02.
Custodians.
  Judicial dissolution, §29-412.22.
Definitions, §29-401.02.
Delegates, §29-404.30.
Derivative actions, §§29-411.01 to
  29-411.09.
  Attorney's fees, §29-411.07.
  Costs, §29-411.07.
  Defined, §29-411.01.
  Demand, §29-411.03.
  Discontinuances, §29-411.06.
  Dismissal of actions, §29-411.05.
  Foreign corporations, §29-411.08.
  Notice, §29-411.09.
  Settlement or compromise, §29-411.06.
  Standing, §29-411.02.
  Stays, §29-411.04.
Directors, §§29-406.01 to 29-406.91.
  Action without meeting, §29-406.21.
  Advisory committees, §29-406.25.
  Board, §§29-406.01 to 29-406.12.
  Business opportunities, §29-406.80.
  Compensation, §29-406.11.
  Conflicting interest transactions,
    §29-406.70.
  Designated bodies, §29-406.12.
  Election, §§29-405.27, 29-406.04.
  Indemnification, §§29-406.50 to
    29-406.58. See within this
    heading, "Indemnification."
  Insurance, §29-406.57.
  Liability, §29-406.31.
    Unauthorized distributions,
      §29-406.33.
  Loans, §29-406.32.
  Meetings of directors, §§29-406.20 to
    29-406.25. See within this
    heading, "Meetings of directors."
  Number of, §29-406.03.

NONPROFIT CORPORATIONS
—Cont'd
Directors —Cont'd
  Powers, §29-406.01.
  Qualifications, §29-406.02.
  Records.
    Inspection, §29-413.05.
  Removal of.
    Judicial proceedings, §29-406.09.
    Members, §29-406.08.
  Requirements, §29-406.01.
  Resignation of, §29-406.07.
  Standards of conduct, §29-406.30.
  Terms of office, §29-406.05.
    Staggered terms, §29-406.06.
  Vacancies in office, §29-406.10.
  Voluntary dissolution, §29-412.01.
    Duties, §29-412.09.
  Voting, §29-406.24.
Disposition of assets, §§29-410.01 to
  29-410.03.
  Member approval, §29-410.02.
    Not required, §29-410.01.
  Restrictions, §29-410.03.
Dissolution, §§29-412.01 to 29-412.30.
  Deposit of assets with mayor,
    §29-412.30.
  Judicial dissolution, §§29-412.20 to
    29-412.23.
  Voluntary dissolution, §§29-412.01 to
    29-412.09. See within this
    heading, "Voluntary dissolution."
Distributions.
  Prohibitions, §29-404.40.
  Unauthorized distributions.
    Liability, §29-406.33.
Domestication, §§29-407.01 to
  29-407.06.
  Abandonment, §29-407.06.
  Approval, §29-407.03.
  Articles of domestication, §29-407.04.
  Authorization, §29-407.02.
  Definitions, §29-407.01.
  Effect of, §29-407.05.
  Plans, §29-407.02.
Duration of, §29-403.02.
Emergency powers, §29-403.03.
Employees.
  Immunity, §29-406.91.
Filing.
  Generally, §§29-102.01 to 29-102.13.
    See BUSINESS ORGANIZATIONS.
Financial provisions, §§29-404.40 to
  29-404.43.
  Compensation, §29-404.41.
  Debt, §29-404.42.

NONPROFIT CORPORATIONS
—Cont'd
Financial provisions —Cont'd
Distributions.
Prohibitions, §29-404.40.
Private foundations, §29-404.43.
Security interests, §29-404.42.
Financial statements, §29-413.20.
Foreign entities.
Generally, §§29-105.01 to 29-105.12.
See BUSINESS ORGANIZATIONS.
Fraternal benefit societies.
Nonprofit institutions operated by,
§31-5309.
General powers, §29-403.02.
Gifts.
Powers, §29-403.02.
Hospitals.
Not-for-profit hospital corporations,
§§44-951.01 to 44-951.18.
See NOT-FOR-PROFIT HOSPITAL
CORPORATIONS.
Immunity.
Employees, §29-406.91.
Volunteers, §29-406.90.
Incorporation, §29-402.03.
Incorporators, §29-402.01.
Voluntary dissolution, §29-412.01.
Indemnification, §§29-406.50 to
29-406.58.
Advancements, §29-406.53.
Court-ordered, §29-406.54.
Authorization, §29-406.55.
Court-ordered indemnification,
§29-406.54.
Definitions, §29-406.50.
Determinations, §29-406.55.
Mandatory indemnification,
§29-406.52.
Officers, §29-406.56.
Permissible indemnification,
§29-406.51.
Variation of, §29-406.58.
Insurance, §29-406.57.
Insurance companies.
Tax exemption for nonprofit relief
associations, §47-2611.
Investments.
Powers, §29-403.02.
Judicial dissolution, §§29-412.20 to
29-412.23.
Constructive trust, §29-412.20.
Custodians, §29-412.22.
Decree of dissolution, §29-412.23.
Grounds, §29-412.20.
Injunctions, §§29-412.20, 29-412.21.

NONPROFIT CORPORATIONS
—Cont'd
Judicial dissolution —Cont'd
Procedures, §29-412.21.
Receivers, §§29-412.20 to 29-412.22.
Liability.
Directors, §29-406.31.
Unauthorized distributions,
§29-406.33.
Preincorporation transactions,
§29-402.04.
Loans.
Officers and directors, §29-406.32.
Powers, §29-403.02.
**Lower income home ownership tax
abatement and incentives,**
§§47-3505, 47-3506.
Management of institutional funds.
General provisions.
See PRUDENT INVESTOR ACT.
Meetings of directors, §§29-406.20 to
29-406.25.
Action without meeting, §29-406.21.
Notice, §29-406.22.
Waiver, §29-406.23.
Quorum, §29-406.24.
Regular meetings, §29-406.20.
Special meetings, §29-406.20.
Voting, §29-406.24.
Meetings of members, §§29-405.01 to
29-405.09.
Action by ballot, §29-405.09.
Action without meeting, §29-405.04.
Annual meetings, §29-405.01.
Conduct of, §29-405.08.
Court-ordered meetings, §29-405.03.
Notice, §29-405.05.
Waiver, §29-405.06.
Quorum.
Transitional provisions, rules for
existing corporations,
§29-414.04.
Record date, §29-405.07.
Regular meetings, §29-405.01.
Special meetings, §29-405.02.
Member-governed corporations,
§29-401.50.
Members, §§29-404.01 to 29-404.22.
Action without meeting, §29-405.04.
Admission of members, §§29-404.01 to
29-404.03.
Consideration, §29-404.03.
Not required, §29-404.01.
Procedures, §29-404.02.
Bylaws.
Amendment.
Approval, §29-408.22.

NONPROFIT CORPORATIONS
—Cont'd
Members —Cont'd
Meetings of members, §§29-405.01 to 29-405.09. See within this heading, "Meetings of members."
Purchase of memberships, §29-404.22.
Records.
Inspection, §29-413.02.
Resignation of, §29-404.20.
Rights and obligations of members, §§29-404.10 to 29-404.14.
Creditors' rights, §29-404.14.
Differences, §29-404.10.
Dues, assessments and fees, §29-404.13.
Third parties, §29-404.12.
Transfers, §29-404.11.
Suspension of, §29-404.21.
Termination of memberships, §29-404.21.
Voting by members, §§29-405.20 to 29-405.28. See within this heading, "Voting by members."
Membership exchanges, §§29-409.01 to 29-409.08. See within this heading, "Mergers and membership exchanges."
Mergers and membership exchanges, §§29-409.01 to 29-409.08.
Abandonment, §29-409.08.
Approval, §29-409.04.
Articles of merger or membership exchange, §29-409.06.
Authorization, §§29-409.02, 29-409.03.
Controlled corporations, §29-409.05.
Definitions, §29-409.01.
Effect of, §29-409.07.
Membership exchanges, §29-409.03.
Mergers, §29-409.02.
Plans, §§29-409.02, 29-409.03.
Mortgages and deeds of trust.
Powers, §29-403.02.
Names.
Generally, §§29-103.01 to 29-103.04. See BUSINESS ORGANIZATIONS.
Requirements, §29-103.02.
Notice, §29-401.03.
Attorney general, §29-401.60.
Derivative actions, §29-411.09.
Exceptions, §29-413.06.
Meetings, §29-405.05.
Waiver, §29-405.06.
Meetings of directors, §29-406.22.
Waiver, §29-406.23.

NONPROFIT CORPORATIONS
—Cont'd
Notice —Cont'd
Methods of notice or other communications, §29-401.03.
Review of contested corporate actions, §29-401.23.
Officers, §§29-406.40 to 29-406.44.
Contract rights, §29-406.44.
Duties, §29-406.41.
Indemnification, §29-406.56.
Insurance, §29-406.57.
Loans, §29-406.32.
Removal of, §29-406.43.
Requirements, §29-406.40.
Resignation of, §29-406.43.
Standards of conduct, §29-406.42.
Organization of, §29-402.05.
Pay-for-success contracts, §§2-211.01 to 2-211.03.
Pensions and retirement.
Powers, §29-403.02.
Perpetual existence, §29-403.02.
Personal property.
Powers, §29-403.02.
Pledges.
Powers, §29-403.02.
Powers.
Emergency powers, §29-403.03.
General powers, §29-403.02.
Ultra vires, §29-403.04.
Preincorporation transactions.
Liability, §29-402.04.
Purposes of, §29-403.01.
Real property.
Powers, §29-403.02.
Tax-exempt status, §47-1002.
Receivers.
Judicial dissolution, §§29-412.20 to 29-412.22.
Records, §§29-413.01 to 29-413.07.
Inspections.
Court-ordered, §29-413.04.
Directors, §29-413.05.
Members, §29-413.02.
Scope of right, §29-413.03.
Membership lists, §29-413.07.
Retention, §29-413.01.
Reference to extrinsic facts, §29-401.04.
Registered agents.
Generally, §§29-104.01 to 29-104.14. See BUSINESS ORGANIZATIONS.
Religious corporations, §29-401.40.
Reports, §29-413.20.
Required approvals, §29-401.05.

NONPROFIT CORPORATIONS
—Cont'd
Review of contested corporate actions, §§29-401.20 to 29-401.23.
Definitions, §29-401.20.
Notice, §29-401.23.
Orders, §29-401.22.
Petitions, §29-401.22.
Proceedings prior to corporate action, §29-401.21.
Rights and obligations of members, §§29-404.10 to 29-404.14.
Creditors' rights, §29-404.14.
Differences, §29-404.10.
Dues, assessments and fees, §29-404.13.
Third parties, §29-404.12.
Transfers, §29-404.11.
Seals.
Powers, §29-403.02.
Short title, §29-401.01.
Special rights, §29-408.40.
Transitional provisions, §§29-414.01 to 29-414.04.
Cumulation of votes, §29-414.03.
Existing domestic corporations, application to, §29-414.01.
Foreign corporations, application to, §29-414.02.
Quorum for existing nonprofits, §29-414.04.
Registered foreign corporations, §29-401.02.
Ultra vires, §29-403.04.
Unauthorized distributions.
Liability, §29-406.33.
Voluntary dissolution, §§29-412.01 to 29-412.09.
Approval, §29-412.02.
Articles of dissolution, §29-412.03.
Court proceedings on claims, §29-412.08.
Directors, §29-412.01.
Duties, §29-412.09.
Effect of, §29-412.05.
Incorporators, §29-412.01.
Known claims, §29-412.06.
Other claims, §29-412.07.
Revocation, §29-412.04.
Volunteers.
Immunity, §29-406.90.
Voting agreements, §29-405.40.
Voting by directors, §29-406.24.
Voting by members, §§29-405.20 to 29-405.28.
Acceptance of votes, §29-405.23.

NONPROFIT CORPORATIONS
—Cont'd
Voting by members —Cont'd
Articles of incorporation.
Amendment, §29-408.04.
Bylaws.
Amendment, §29-408.21.
Directors.
Election, §29-405.27.
Entitlement, §29-405.21.
Inspectors, §29-405.28.
Members list, §29-405.20.
Multiple voting groups, §29-405.25.
Proxy arrangements, §29-405.22.
Quorum, §29-405.24.
Alteration, §29-405.26.
Requirements, §29-405.24.
Alteration, §29-405.26.
Single voting groups, §29-405.25.

NONRESIDENTS.
Attachment of wages of, §16-513.
Attorneys' fees and costs, §§15-703, 15-711.
Compensating-use tax and nonresident vendors, §47-2204.
Depositions, §14-104.
Disability compensation for public officers and employees, §1-623.37.
Employers.
Unemployment compensation.
Service of process for purposes of, §51-105.
Fiduciaries.
Power of attorney, CivPro Rule 305.
Probate proceedings, Probate Rules 14, 106.
Probate proceedings.
Death before Jan. 1, 1981, Probate Rule 14.
Death between Jan. 1, 1981, and June 30, 1995, Probate Rule 106.
Death on or after July 1, 1995, Probate Rule 406.
Guardianship of minors, §21-110.
Nonresident guardians, §21-110.
Nonresident minors, §21-111.
Hospitalization of persons with mental illness, court-ordered, §21-550.
Income taxes, §§47-1805.02, 47-1806.01 to 47-1806.07.
Inheritance and estate taxes, §47-3703.
Inheritances, §20-1107.
Insurance producer licensing, §31-1131.08.

NONRESIDENTS —Cont'd
**Insurers rehabilitation and
liquidation proceedings.**
Claims against District insurers,
§31-1353.
Interstate family support.
Jurisdiction.
Bases for jurisdiction over,
§46-352.01.
Subject to personal jurisdiction,
§46-352.10.
Physical presence in District.
Not required to establish, enforce,
modify, etc., support order,
§46-353.16.
Jurisdiction.
Suits against state, US Const Amd 11.
Motor vehicles.
Defaults by insurance carriers,
§50-1301.56.
Drivers' licenses, §50-1401.02.
Financial responsibility, proof of,
§50-1301.55.
Judgments against nonresidents
involving, §50-1301.42.
Service of process, §50-1301.07.
Suspension of operating privileges,
§50-1301.40.
No-fault motor vehicle insurance,
§31-2403.
Real property.
Ownership of real property, §§42-902,
42-903.
Service of process on, §13-336.
Suits against state, US Const Amd 11.
Tuition at District schools, §§38-301
to 38-313.
Wastewater treatment systems,
§8-204.
Witnesses, §14-104.

**NON-RESUSCITATION
PROCEDURES FOR EMS.**
Comfort care orders, §§7-651.01 to
7-651.16.
See EMERGENCY MEDICAL
SERVICES.

**NONSTOP FLIGHT
REQUIREMENTS.**
Washington National Airport,
§9-1011.

NORTHERN IRELAND.
**Housing finance agency investment
of funds with companies doing
business with,** §42-2704.13.

NO SMOKING SIGNS.
**Defacement, removal, or failure to
post,** §7-1706.
Elevators, §7-1704.
Enforcement, §7-1705.
Generally, §7-1704.
Health care facilities, §7-1703.
Property owners, §7-1703.04.

NOTARIAL ACTS, §§42-141 to 42-148.

NOTARIES PUBLIC, §§1-1201 to
1-1217.
Affidavits, taking, §1-1210.
Appointment by mayor, §1-1201.
Appropriations, §1-1217.
**Banks and financial institutions,
associated with,** §26-110.
Bills of exchange, foreign or inland,
§§1-1207, 1-1208.
Bonds, surety, §1-1203.
Certificates issued by mayor to,
§1-1216.
Certifications by, §1-1210.
Conflicts of interest, §1-1201.
Death of, custody of records on,
§1-1215.
Depositions, taking, §1-1210.
**Execution, exemption of seal and
official documents from,** §1-1206.
False personation before, §22-1403.
Fees.
Licenses, §1-1201.
Penalty for charging higher than
scheduled fees, §1-1214.
Schedule of fees charged, §1-1213.
**Filing signature and impression of
seal,** §1-1205.
Foreign bills of exchange, §1-1207.
Issuance of rules regarding, §1-1201.
Licenses, §1-1201.
Metropolitan police property clerk,
§5-119.04.
Oaths and affirmations.
Administering, §1-1210.
Taking, §1-1203.
Out-of-District effects of acts,
§1-1209.
Promissory notes, §1-1208.
Records, §§1-1211, 1-1212, 1-1215.
**Resignation or removal of, custody
of records on,** §1-1215.
Seal, §§1-1204 to 1-1206.
Signature, filing, §1-1205.
Term of office, §1-1202.
Uniform notarial acts, §§42-141 to
42-148.
Certificate of notarial act.
Notarial act evidenced by, §42-147.

NOTARIES PUBLIC —Cont'd
Uniform notarial acts —Cont'd
  Certificate of notarial act —Cont'd
    Short forms, §42-148.
  Definitions, §42-141.
  Foreign notarial acts, §42-146.
  In taking acknowledgments, §42-142.
    Certificate, short form, §42-148.
  In taking verification upon oath or
    affirmation, §42-142.
    Certificate, short form, §42-148.
  In witnessing or attesting signature,
    §42-142.
    Certificate, short form, §42-148.
  Notarial act defined, §42-141.
  Notarial act performed in District,
    §42-143.
  Notarial act performed in other
    jurisdictions of United States,
    §42-144.
  Notarial act performed under federal
    authority, §42-145.
  Notarial officer defined, §42-141.
  Persons who may perform notarial
    acts.
    Act performed under federal
      authority, §42-145.
    Foreign notarial acts, §42-146.
    Other jurisdictions of United States,
      §42-144.
    Within District, §42-143.
  Satisfactory evidence person is
    person's whose true signature
    appears on document, §42-142.

NOTES.
Assignments.
  Nonnegotiable notes, §28-2303.
Complaint on a promissory note,
  CivPro Form CA 3.
Fiduciary security transfers,
  §§28-2901 to 28-2909.
  See FIDUCIARY SECURITY
    TRANSFERS.
Negotiable instruments.
  General provisions, §§28:3-101 to
    28:3-605.
  See NEGOTIABLE
    INSTRUMENTS.
Notaries public, §1-1208.

**NOT-FOR-PROFIT HOSPITAL
  CORPORATIONS,** §§44-951.01 to
  44-951.18.
Action against corporation.
  Notice requirements, §44-951.14.
Attorney general, office of.
  Representation of corporation,
    §44-951.14.

**NOT-FOR-PROFIT HOSPITAL
  CORPORATIONS** —Cont'd
Board of directors, §§44-951.04,
  44-951.05.
Budget, §44-951.09.
Chief executive officer, §44-951.05.
Chief financial officer.
  Authority, §44-951.18.
Debt obligations, §44-951.16.
Definitions, §44-951.01.
**Employees of United Medical
  Center.**
  Transfer, §44-951.10.
Establishment of corporation,
  §44-951.02.
Fiscal year, §44-951.05.
Fund, §44-951.03.
General counsel, §44-951.15.
Governance, §44-951.05.
Health care professionals.
  Continuation of privileges to practice,
    §44-951.17.
Immunity from liability.
  District of Columbia, §44-951.14.
Notice requirements.
  Action against corporation, §44-951.14.
Outside counsel, §44-951.14.
Personnel system, §44-951.08.
Powers of corporation, §44-951.06.
Procurement law.
  Inapplicability, §44-951.11.
Purpose of corporation, §44-951.02.
Reports, §44-951.13.
Tax exemption, §44-951.12.
**Transfer of assets under deed of
  trust,** §44-951.07.

NOT GUILTY PLEAS, CrimPro Rule
  11.
Delinquent minors, JuvProc Rule 12.
Presence of defendant, CrimPro Rule
  43.

NOTICE.
**Abandoned and junk vehicles taken
  into custody,** §50-2622.
**Abandoned and unlawfully parked
  vehicles.**
  Impoundment, §50-2421.07.
  Removal from private property,
    §50-2421.05.
  Removal from public space,
    §50-2421.04.
  Scrap vehicle title authorization,
    §50-2702.
Abandoned property, §41-118.
Actions.
  Pendency of action (lis pendens),
    §42-1207.

NOTICE —Cont'd

Address of party changed, CivPro
Rule 10-I.
Small claims court, SmallClaims Rule
3.
**Administrative fines, infractions
incurring,** §2-1802.01.
Adoption of children, §16-306.
Adoption proceedings, Adoption Rules
4, 52.
Constitutional questions, Adoption
Rule 24.
Depositions, Adoption Rules 30, 31.
Determination of foreign law, Adoption
Rule 44.
Withdrawal of attorney, Adoption Rule
101.
Alcoholic beverage control board.
Application proceedings, §25-421.
Alcoholic beverage licenses.
Applications.
Notice of proceedings, §§25-421 to
25-423.
Employees.
Notice of criminal conviction,
§25-702.
Enforcement actions, §25-804.
Manager's license.
Traffic offenses.
Notice to board of conviction,
§25-701.
Moratoria on licenses, §25-353.
Revocation or suspension, §25-828.
Alibi of defendant.
Criminal procedure, CrimPro Rule
12.1.
Delinquent minors, JuvProc Rule 12.1.
Alley dwellings, notice to owners of,
§6-101.06.
Animal control violations, §8-1813.
Appeals, D.C. courts.
Constitutional questions, DCCtApp
Rule 44.
Docketing of appeal, DCCtApp Rule
12.
Fee for filing in criminal case,
CrimPro Rule 37.
Judgments and opinions, DCCtApp
Rule 36.
Notice of appeal, DCCtApp Rules 3, 4.
Forms, CivPro Form CA 27,
DCCtApp Forms 1, 2.
Right to appeal.
Criminal cases, CrimPro Rule 32.
Delinquent minors, JuvProc Rule 32.
Hearing commissioners, CrimPro
Rule 117.

NOTICE —Cont'd

Appeals, D.C. courts —Cont'd
Right to appeal —Cont'd
Hospitalization of persons with
mental illness, MentalHealth
Rule 6.
Prisoner's commitment to mental
institution, MentalHealth
Rule 10.
Transcript on appeal, CrimPro Rule
36-I.
Appeals, federal cases.
Argument, FRAP 34(b).
Decisions, USCtApp HPIP Rule XII(e).
Entry of judgment, date of, FRAP 36.
Filing of record.
Appeal, FRAP 12(c).
Review or enforcement of
administrative orders, FRAP
17(a).
Motion for stay or injunction, FRAP
8(a), 18.
Oral argument, USCtApp HPIP Rule
XI(a).
Orders or judgments, FRAP 45(c).
Partial transcript ordered, notice to
appellee, FRAP 10(b).
Release in criminal cases, appeal or
motion, FRAP 9(a).
Sanction against attorney for inclusion
of unnecessary material in
appendix to brief, FRAP 30(b).
Arbitration.
Evidence at hearings, Arbitration Rule
IX.
Removal of case from arbitration,
Arbitration Rule II.
Arbitration, revised act, §16-4402.
Initiation of proceeding, §16-4409.
Judicial relief, application for,
§16-4405.
Arrests.
Duty to make known to duty officer,
§5-115.02.
Return notice, §5-115.02.
Assignment for benefit of creditors,
§28-2110.
Notice to creditors, §28-2110.
Assisted living residences.
Residents' rights, §44-105.08.
Attachment, §16-502, CivPro Form CA
105.
Pre-judgment attachment, CivPro Rule
64-I.
Domestic relations actions, DomRel
Rule 64.

NOTICE —Cont'd
Attorneys at law.
  Bar association.
    Meetings of the bar, DCBar Rule VI.
    Membership status, DCBar Rule II.
  Discipline or disability proceedings,
    DCBar Rule XI, USDistCt LCrR
    57.26, USDistCt LCrR 57.28,
    USDistCt LCvR 83.15, USDistCt
    LCvR 83.17.
  Sale of law practice, ProfCond Rule
    1.17.
  Suspension or removal from assigned
    counsel list, CrimPro Rule 44-I.
    Juvenile proceedings, JuvProc Rule
    44.
Automated traffic enforcement,
  §50-2209.03.
**Bail bondsmen, notice to prisoners
  of authorized,** §23-1106.
Bankruptcy.
  Creditors and other interested parties,
    USDistDCBank Rule 2002-1.
    Undeliverable addresses,
      USDistDCBank Appx F.
  Electronic case filing.
    Bounced back ECF e-mails,
      USDistDCBank Appx G.
  United States, federal agencies, and
    District of Columbia,
    USDistDCBank Rule 2002-2.
Banks and financial institutions.
  Investigation by commissioner,
    §26-551.13.
Barbed-wire fences, removal of,
  §§9-1213.03, 9-1213.05.
Bees.
  Written warning notice of violation.
    Enforcement of chapter, §8-1825.09.
Birth, §31-3803.
Building code fire safety measures.
  See BUILDING CODE.
Cable television operators.
  Construction, public notice,
    §34-1257.05.
Child abuse and neglect.
  Custody, taking child into, NeglectProc
    Rule 6.
  Disposition hearings, NeglectProc Rule
    20.
  Initial appearance, NeglectProc Rule
    5.
  Motion based orders, NeglectProc Rule
    43.
  Permanency hearing, NeglectProc Rule
    32.

NOTICE —Cont'd
Child abuse and neglect —Cont'd
  Permanency planning notice,
    NeglectProc Rule 12.
  Review hearings, NeglectProc Rule 28.
  Right to appeal.
    Termination of parental rights,
      NeglectProc Rule 39.
  Shelter care hearing, NeglectProc Rule
    6.
Child custody proceedings.
  Child-custody determination,
    §16-4602.05.
  Enforcement of foreign custody
    determinations.
    Registration requirements,
      §16-4603.05.
Child labor, §32-202.
**Child Protection Register, persons
  identified in,** §4-1302.05.
Child support enforcement.
  See CHILD SUPPORT
    ENFORCEMENT.
**Claims against estates, action
  required on,** §20-908.
Class actions, CivPro Rule 23-I,
  USDistCt LCvR 23.1.
Code of District of Columbia.
  Government notice in newspapers of
    publication of, §2-621.
  Judicial notice of publication of,
    §2-605.
Compulsory school attendance.
  Parents, notice.
    Tenth unexcused absence as trigger
      for notice to parents, §38-207.
  Police and superintendent of
    education.
    Tenth unexcused absence as trigger
      for notice, §38-208.
Condemnation of property, CivPro
  Rule 71A.
  Form, CivPro Form CA 28.
Condominiums.
  See CONDOMINIUMS.
Conservators' proceedings.
  See CONSERVATORS.
Consumer credit reporting agencies.
  Consumer security breach notification.
    Notification of security breach.
      Conduct constituting notice,
        §28-3852.
      Defined, §28-3851.
      Electronic notice, §28-3851.
      Rights and remedies, §28-3853.
  Consumer security freeze.
    Notice of rights, §28-3863.

NOTICE —Cont'd
Consumer credit sales.
Default.
Required notice by creditor,
§28-3812.
Consumer protection.
Complaint procedures, §28-3905.
Default.
Required notice by creditor,
§28-3812.
Contempt.
Criminal contempt, CrimPro Rule 42.
Contested cases, §2-509.
Contesting validity of will, §20-305.
Cooperative associations.
Meetings, §29-911.
Corporations, §29-301.03.
Appraisal and payment for shares,
§29-311.12.
Demand, §29-311.11.
Right to, §29-311.10.
Common address, §29-301.22.
Meetings of directors, §29-306.22.
Waiver, §29-306.23.
Meetings of shareholders, §29-305.05.
Waiver, §29-305.06.
Methods of sending notice and other
communications, §29-301.03.
Records.
Exception, §29-313.06.
Court employees.
Debts and erroneous payments made
to employees, collection by
executive officer.
Notice and hearing requirements,
§11-1733.
Credit line deeds of trust, §42-2302.
Crime victims' compensation.
Appeal of determination, VictComp
Rule 20.
Determination of claim, VictComp
Rule 17.
Criminal procedure.
Alibi of defendant, CrimPro Rule 12.1.
Assignment or transfer of case,
CrimPro Rule 107.
Contempt, CrimPro Rule 42.
Insanity defense, CrimPro Rule 12.2.
Intent to use evidence, CrimPro Rule
12.
Right to appeal, CrimPro Rule 32.
Hearing commissioners, CrimPro
Rule 117.
Transcript on appeal, CrimPro Rule
36-I.
Victim impact statements, CrimPro
Rule 32.

NOTICE —Cont'd
Custodial trustee.
Resignation, §19-1113.
DC Circulator bus service.
Enhanced penalties for offenses
committed against transit
operators and station managers.
Notice of enhanced penalties,
§35-261.
**Dead bodies, notice of distribution
of, §3-203.**
Death, §32-1513.
**Debt service requirement to be
noted on real property tax bills,
§§47-336 to 47-340.**
Decedents' estates, §20-103.
**Deeds, notice of name and address
change for, §42-405.**
Default judgments, CivPro Rule 55.
Domestic relations actions, DomRel
Rule 55.
Delinquent minors.
Alibi, JuvProc Rule 12.1.
Depositions, JuvProc Rule 15.
Detention and shelter care procedures,
JuvProc Rule 105.
Government's intent to use evidence,
JuvProc Rule 12.
Notice of initial appearance, JuvProc
Rule 9.
Right to appeal, JuvProc Rule 32.
Sealing arrest records, FamDiv Rule P.
Forms, FamDiv Form 9, JuvProc
Forms 2, 3.
Termination of dispositional orders,
JuvProc Rule 32.
Transfer for criminal prosecution,
JuvProc Rule 108.
Depositions.
Criminal procedure, CrimPro Rule 15.
Delinquent minors, JuvProc Rule 15.
Oral examination, CivPro Rule 30,
USDistCt LCvR 30.1.
Adoption proceedings, Adoption Rule
30.
Domestic relations actions, DomRel
Rule 30.
Pre-action depositions, CivPro Rule 27.
Domestic relations actions, DomRel
Rule 27.
Waiver of errors and irregularities,
CivPro Rule 32.
Written questions, CivPro Rule 31.
Adoption proceedings, Adoption Rule
31.
Domestic relations actions, DomRel
Rule 31.

NOTICE —Cont'd

Derivative actions by shareholders.
Compromise or settlement, CivPro
Rule 23.1.

Disability compensation for public officers and employees, §1-623.19.

Disbarment, DCBar Rule XI.

Discovery.
Depositions. See within this heading,
"Depositions."
Physical or mental examination of
person, CivPro Rule 35.

Discrimination.
See HUMAN RIGHTS COMMISSION.

Displaced tenants' right to relocation assistance,
§42-3507.01.

Domestic life insurance companies, formation of, §31-4402.

Domestic relations actions.
Default judgments, DomRel Rule 55.
Depositions, DomRel Rules 30, 31.
Hearing and order directing
appearance, DomRel Rule 4,
FamDiv Rule H.
Form, FamDiv Form 1.
Injunctions and restraining orders,
DomRel Rule 65.
Judgments and orders, DomRel Rule
77.
Withdrawal of appearance, DomRel
Rule 101.
Writ of ne exeat, DomRel Rule 406.

Durable powers of attorney, revocation of, §21-2084.

Ejectment, §16-1116.
Failure of tenant to give notice to
landlord of, §16-1102.

Elections.
Voting by military and overseas voters,
§1-1061.16.

Electronic transactions, uniform act.
Error in transmission, §28-4909.

Emergency management.
Homeland security program.
Notice to public of emergencies,
§7-2231.08.

Emergency medical services.
Disciplinary action, §7-2341.17.

Eminent domain, CivPro Form CA 28.

Employees retirement program management.
Investment of public funds in certain
companies doing business with
Iran.
Actions to be taken regarding
scrutinized companies,
§1-336.03.

NOTICE —Cont'd

Employment agencies, §32-404.

Environmental covenants, §8-671.06.
Substitute notice, §8-671.11.

Execution of judgments.
Notice of claim or exemption in,
§15-521.

Family and medical leave, §32-511.

Family court proceedings generally.
Hearing commissioner's judgment,
FamDiv Rule D.
Notice of hearing and order directing
appearance, FamDiv Rule H.
Form, FamDiv Form 1.
Sealing of records, FamDiv Rule P.
Forms, FamDiv Forms 2, 3.

Fiduciaries.
Claims by guardian ad litem against
estate, CivPro Rule 302.
Compensation for extraordinary
services, CivPro Rule 301.
Probate proceedings generally. See
within this heading, "Probate
proceedings."

Fiduciary security transfers.
Adverse claims, §28-2905.
Fiduciary no longer acting as such,
§28-2902.

Fire department notice of resignation, §5-407.

Fire prevention, building code requirements for.
See BUILDING CODE.

First amendment assemblies.
Notice and approval process,
§§5-331.01, 5-331.05.

Foreign judgments, filing, §15-353.

Foreign law raised at trial, CivPro
Rule 44.1, CrimPro Rule 26.1.
Adoption proceedings, Adoption Rule
44.
Domestic relations actions, DomRel
Rule 44.

Foreign missions.
Liability insurance, termination or
lapse of, §6-1304.01.
Real property transactions, §6-1305.

Forfeiture of property, CivPro Rule
71A-I.
Civil asset forfeiture, §41-304.

Gas station violations, §36-302.05.

General obligation bonds, §1-204.63.

Grand juries.
Petition for disclosure, CrimPro Rule
6.

NOTICE —Cont'd

Guardian ad litem.

Conservatorship proceedings.

Claims by against estate, CivPro Rule 302.

Probate proceedings.

Motion or petition for compensation, Probate Rules 122, 224, 422.

Guardian and ward.

Adult guardianship and protective proceedings jurisdiction act.

Notice of proceedings, §21-2402.08.

Incapacitated persons, guardianship of, §§21-2042, 21-2045.

Temporary guardians, §21-2046.

Minors, guardianship of.

Permanent guardianship.

Service of process, §16-2386.

Standby guardianship.

Filing of petition, §16-4808.

Hazardous waste, presence of, §8-1307.

Health benefit plan carriers.

Voluntary withdrawal by health benefit plan carriers, §31-3152.

Highway plan, §9-101.06.

Historic landmarks, §6-1109.04.

Homeland security program.

Notice to public of emergencies, §7-2231.08.

Homeless services.

Client rights, §4-754.11.

Providers.

Program rules, §4-754.33.

Homestead housing preservation, §42-2111.

Hospitalization of persons with mental illness.

Appeals, D.C. courts.

Right to appeal, MentalHealth Rule 6.

Prisoner's commitment to mental institution, MentalHealth Rule 10.

Court-ordered commitment petitions, §21-541.

Incompetency, notice regarding, §21-581.

Release, notice of, §21-527.

Hospital liens, §40-202.

Housing accommodation discrimination complaints, §2-1403.08.

Human Rights Commission.

See HUMAN RIGHTS COMMISSION.

Immunization of school students, §38-503.

NOTICE —Cont'd

Injunctions, CivPro Rule 65.

Injury, §32-1513.

Insanitary buildings, §§6-903, 6-910.

Insanity defense, CrimPro Rule 12.2.

Inspections, §2-140.

Installment loans.

Default.

Required notice by creditor, §28-3812.

Insurance company annual audited financial reports, §31-308.

Insurance company risk-based capital, §31-2012.

Insurance demutualization, §31-914.

Insurance producer licensing.

Revocation or suspension, §31-1131.12.

Termination of business or appointment, §31-1131.15.

Intellectual disabilities, persons with.

Discharge from facility, MentalRetardation Rule 6.

Transfer of committed person, MentalRetardation Rule 5.

Interpreters, need for, §2-1903.

Interstate compact on educational opportunity for military children.

Notice and service, §49-1101.13.

Interstate family support.

Registration child-support order of another state for enforcement.

Notice to issuing tribunal of modification, §46-356.14.

Registration of support order for enforcement.

Notice of registration of order, §46-356.05.

Intervention proceedings.

Appeal of administrative orders and decisions, DCCtApp Rule 15.

Compensation of guardian, conservator, etc., Probate Rule 308.

Conservators.

Account of conservator, Probate Rule 330.

Missing persons, Probate Rule 350.

Constitutional case, CivPro Rule 24-I.

Domestic relations actions, DomRel Rule 24.

Hearings, Probate Rules 311, 321, 325.

Hearings on petitions.

Missing person conservatorship or protective order, Probate Rule 350.

NOTICE —Cont'd
Intervention proceedings —Cont'd
Removal of fiduciary hearings, Probate Rule 309.
Request by interested person for notice, Probate Rule 304.
Service, Probate Rules 311, 321, 325.
Intrafamily proceedings, §16-1004.
Notice of hearing and order directing appearance, FamDiv Rule H.
Form, FamDiv Form 1.
Investment securities.
Adverse claims, §28:8-105.
Defects or defenses, §§28:8-202, 28:8-203.
Judgments and decrees, CivPro Rule 77.
Appeals, DCCtApp Rule 36.
Domestic relations actions, DomRel Rule 77.
Form, CivPro Form CA 110-A.
Judicial notice of published acts and resolutions, §2-605.
Juvenile offenders, no-further-benefit notice, §24-905.
Landlord and tenant.
Commercial tenancy, §42-3202.
Notice to quit or notice of termination of lease, §§42-3201 to 42-3208.
Landlord and tenant court.
Hearing notice, LandlordTenant Form 1S.
Notice to tenant of payment required to avoid eviction, LandlordTenant Form 6.
Stays, LandlordTenant Rule 16.
Form, LandlordTenant Form 5.
Lead-hazard prevention and elimination.
Access to dwelling unit, tenant to provide, §8-231.06.
Notice to tenant of hazards, §8-231.03.
Violations, service of notice, §8-231.15.
Leave of absence.
Right to sick and safe leave, §32-131.03.
Posted notices, §32-131.09.
Liens.
Hospital liens, §40-202.
Mechanic's liens, §40-301.02.
Subcontractor's liens, notice to owner, §40-303.03.
Limited liability companies, §29-801.03.
Limited partnerships.
Dissolution.
Claims against partnership, proceedings, §29-708.11.

NOTICE —Cont'd
Liquidation of insurers, §31-1320.
Lis pendens, §42-1207.
Litter, notice of nuisance regarding, §§8-803, 8-804.
Low-income housing preservation and protections act.
Opting out of program, §42-2851.03.
Marijuana, possession decriminalization.
Notice of violation, §§48-1202, 48-1212.
Mechanic's liens, §40-301.02.
Medicaid health-care assistance reimbursement, §4-606.
Medical examiners.
Notice of investigation of deaths by, §5-1406.
Medical malpractice.
Notice of intention to file suit, §16-2802.
Exceptions.
Unknown or unlicensed defendant, §16-2804.
Extension of statute of limitations, §16-2803.
Medicare supplement insurance.
Right to return and refund, §31-3707.
Meetings.
Open meeting act, §2-576.
Mental health disclosures, §§7-1206.02, 7-1206.03.
Mental illness, persons with.
Hospitalization.
Commission on Mental Health determinations, MentalHealth Rule 3.
Emergency detention proceedings, MentalHealth Rule 2.
Prisoner's commitment to mental institution, MentalHealth Rule 10.
Right to appeal notice, MentalHealth Rules 6, 10.
Metropolitan police.
See METROPOLITAN POLICE.
Metrorail and metrobus.
Enhanced penalties for offenses committed against transit operators and station managers.
Notice of enhanced penalties, §35-261.
Minimum wages, §32-1009.
Tipped wages, §32-1009.01.
Missing persons.
Hearing for conservatorship or protective order, Probate Rule 350.

NOTICE —Cont'd

Miss Utility, §34-2704.

Money lenders, death or discontinuation of business of, §26-901.

Mortgage lenders and brokers.
Dual capacity, acting in, §26-1114.
Orders, §26-1119.

Mutual insurance holding companies, §31-736.

Name changes, CivPro Rule 205.
Application for change, CivPro Form CA 111.

Negotiable instruments.
Breach of fiduciary duty, §28:3-307.
Notice of dishonor, §§28:3-503 to 28:3-505.
Third parties.
Right to defend action, §28:3-119.

Newborn health insurance, notice of birth for, §31-3803.

No-fault motor vehicle insurance.
Cancellation of or refusal to renew policy, §31-2409.

Nurse staffing agencies.
Change in ownership or other information, §44-1051.10.

Nursing homes.
Discharge, transfer, or relocation of residents, §§44-1003.02, 44-1003.06, 44-1003.07, 44-1003.11.
Receiverships, §44-1002.04.

Occupational safety and health, §32-1122.

Open meeting act, §2-576.

Orders of court, CivPro Rule 77.
Domestic relations actions, DomRel Rule 77.

Parental leave, §32-1206.

Partnerships.
Dissolution.
Known claims against dissolved partnership, §29-608.08.
Other claims against dissolved partnership, §29-608.09.

Paving and resurfacing streets and alleys, §9-421.09.

Pawnbroker's sale of pawn or pledge, §47-2884.14.

Personal representative, appointment of, §20-704.

Pesticides.
Notice to abutting properties before application, §8-403.05.

Plea agreements, CrimPro Rule 11.

NOTICE —Cont'd

Pregnant or parenting teens.
Failing to meet home living requirement for public assistance, §4-205.64.
School attendance requirement, failure to meet, §4-205.66.

Price scales, posting requirements, §§47-2907 to 47-2911.

Prisoners.
Use of restraints on pregnant women, §24-276.04.

Probate proceedings.
All proceedings, Probate Rule 4.
Death before Jan. 1, 1981.
Accounts of administrators, executors and collectors, Probate Rule 19.
Petitions for probate and administration, Probate Rules 10 to 12.
Death between Jan. 1, 1981, and June 30, 1995, Probate Rule 103.
Accounts of personal representatives, Probate Rule 116.
Action on claims, Probate Rule 111.
Guardian ad litem motions for compensation, Probate Rule 122.
Publication of notices, Probate Rule 128.
Death on or after July 1, 1995.
Accounts of personal representatives, Probate Form 19, Probate Rule 416.
Action on claims, Probate Form 15, Probate Rule 411.
Appointment of personal representative, Probate Form 10, Probate Rule 403.
Extension of appointment, Probate Rule 429.
Foreign personal representatives, Probate Form 24, Probate Rule 427.
Termination of appointment, Probate Rule 423.
Creditors' notice, Probate Form 10, Probate Rule 403.
Guardian ad litem motions for compensation, Probate Rule 422.
Hearings on petition for authority to act, Probate Rule 412.
Publication of notices, Probate Rule 428.
Standard probate notice, Probate Form 9, Probate Rule 403.

NOTICE —Cont'd

Probate proceedings —Cont'd

Death on or after July 1, 1995 —Cont'd

Verification and certificate of notice, Probate Form 11, Probate Rule 403.

Guardians, conservators, trustees, etc., involved.

Account filed, Probate Rule 204.

Compensation of representatives, Probate Rules 224, 225.

Defaults or irregularities, Probate Rule 207.

Sale of property, Probate Rule 203.

Revocable trust.

Claims against trust, Probate Rule 213.

Existence of trust, Probate Rule 212.

Procedural requirements, CivPro Rule 83.

Public assistance.

Discontinuation of, §4-205.55.

Right to hearing, §§4-210.01, 4-210.04.

Public contract whistleblower protection, §2-223.05.

Public lands.

Exchanges, §10-902.

Sale, §10-801.

Public participation in rulemaking, §2-505.

Public space.

Abatement of dangerous conditions, §10-1181.02.

Public utilities.

Rate application or change in condition of service, §34-909.

Purchasing groups, §31-4107.

Quo warranto, §16-3542.

Real estate tax sales, §§47-1301, 47-1302, 47-1313.

Revised real property tax sale.

Agencies to be notified, §47-1340.

Foreclosure, §§47-1372, 47-1375.

Notice of delinquency, §47-1341.

Public notice, §47-1342.

Purchase by district, post-sale notice, §47-1353.01.

Redemption of property, §47-1361.

Real property tax assessments, §47-824.

Correction, §47-825.01a.

Proposed supplemental assessment, §47-829.

Southeast water and sewer improvement benefit district, §47-893.

NOTICE —Cont'd

Real property taxes.

Service of notice, §47-804.

Related cases, CivPro Rule 42, USDistCt LCrR 57.12, USDistCt LCvR 40.5.

Relocation assistance, displaced tenants' right to, §42-3507.01.

Rental housing conversion and sale.

Conversion or offer of sale, §42-3404.13.

Notice to tenant of intent to convert, §42-3403.06.

Rejection of parties, §42-3405.04.

Revocations, §42-3405.07.

Time certain notices, §42-3404.02.

Replevin, §16-3709.

Restraining orders, CivPro Rule 65.

Risk retention groups, §§31-4103, 31-4107.

Sale of property.

Court ordered sales, CivPro Rule 308.

Probate proceedings, Probate Rule 203.

Schools and education.

Immunization of school students.

See SCHOOLS AND EDUCATION.

Interstate compact on educational opportunity for military children.

Notice and service, §49-1101.13.

Scrap vehicle title authorization, §50-2702.

Security agents and brokers.

Licensing.

Notice filing procedures, §31-5602.03.

Unlawful representation, §31-5605.05.

Registration by notification, §31-5603.02.

Federal covered securities, §31-5603.08.

Security and fire alarm contractors' violations, §7-2812.

Service of process.

Notice and acknowledgment for service by mail, CivPro Form CA 1-A.

Service of process by publication, §§13-335 to 13-341.

Settlement or compromise.

Civil jury cases, notice of settlement in, USDistCt LCvR 47.1.

Sidewalk construction.

Prior to designing and constructing new sidewalks, §9-425.02.

Small claims court.

Conciliation, SmallClaims Conciliation Rule 2.

NOTICE —Cont'd

Small claims court —Cont'd

Forms.

Automobile damage, SmallClaims Forms 4 to 7.

Contract breach, SmallClaims Form 3.

Deficiency balance, SmallClaims Form 1.

Deposit return, SmallClaims Forms 8 to 10.

General form, SmallClaims Form 11.

Holder in due course, SmallClaims Form 2.

Small claims court action, §16-3902.

Southwest waterfront special assessment district, §47-895.04.

State health planning and development agency.

Health systems plan publication, §44-404.

Statutory trusts.

Constructive notice, §29-1201.07.

Known claims against dissolved statutory trust, §29-1208.04.

Other claims against dissolved statutory trust, §29-1208.05.

Stays.

Landlord and tenant court, LandlordTenant Rule 16.

Termination of stay, CivPro Form CA 110-B.

Landlord and tenant court, LandlordTenant Form 5.

Streets and alleys.

See STREETS AND ALLEYS.

Subcontractor's liens, notice to owner, §40-303.03.

Substance abuse and mental illness coverage and benefits, §31-3108.

Taxation.

Bulk sales, determination of tax liability, §§47-4461 to 47-4463.

Corporations, personal liability of officers, §47-4491.

Levy for failure to pay, §47-4471.

Notice of seizure for sale, §47-4472.

Tax proceedings, §47-3308.

Telephone number of party changed, CivPro Rule 10-I.

Small claims court, SmallClaims Rule 3.

Termination of parental rights, §16-2357.

Child abuse and neglect proceedings.

Right to appeal, NeglectProc Rule 39.

NOTICE —Cont'd

Title insurance producers, requirements, §31-5041.05.

Title insurers, requirements, §31-5031.12.

Towing and storage notice.

Scrap vehicle title authorization, §50-2702.

Traffic ticket adjudication.

Moving infractions, §50-2302.04.

Parking, standing, stopping, and pedestrian infractions, §50-2303.03.

Electronic notice, §50-2303.08.

Transcripts released for appeal, CivPro Rule 201.

Trust, mortgage and title corporation application for charter of incorporation, §26-1306.

Trusts and trustees.

Statutory trusts.

Constructive notice, §29-1201.07.

Known claims against dissolved statutory trust, §29-1208.04.

Other claims against dissolved statutory trust, §29-1208.05.

Uniform trust code.

Methods and waiver, §19-1301.09.

Qualified beneficiaries, §19-1301.10.

Unclaimed abandoned property, §41-118.

Urban forest preservation.

Notice of removal of trees on public space, §8-651.05.

Vacant buildings.

Designation as vacant.

Notice of designation and right to appeal, §42-3131.11.

Notice by mail, §42-3131.05a.

Registration.

Denial or revocation of registration, §42-3131.08.

Vaults, removal of unsafe, §10-1103.06.

Vector-borne disease control.

Public health nuisances, notice of, §8-2131.05.

Victim impact statements, CrimPro Rule 32.

Victims of crime, rights of, §23-1902.

Voluntary leave transfer program.

Approval or disapproval of transfer, §1-612.35.

Voting by military and overseas voters, §1-1061.16.

NOTICE —Cont'd
Wastewater treatment systems.
Connection requirements, §8-202.
Water supply and waterworks violations, §34-2401.21.
Weeds, removal of, §8-302.
Wells, abandonment, §8-103.13a.
Whistleblower protection, §§1-615.57, 2-223.06.
Workers' compensation, §32-1536.
Notice of injury or death, §32-1513.
Youth rehabilitation services department.
Use of restraints, §2-1515.54.
Zoning regulation amendments, public hearings required for, §6-641.03.

NOTICE OF APPEAL, DCCtApp Rules 3, 4.
As of right, FRAP 3, 4.
Death of party, filing notice of appeal, FRAP 43(a).
Decisions of U.S. Tax court, FRAP 13, FRAP Form 2.
Docketing fee, FRAP 3(e).
Forms, CivPro Form CA 27, DCCtApp Forms 1, 2.
Bankruptcy court, FRAP Form 5.
District court, FRAP Form 5.
District court orders, FRAP Form 1.
Tax court orders, FRAP Form 2.
Substitution of parties before or after filing, FRAP 43(a).

N STREET VILLAGE.
Real property tax exemptions, §47-1092.

NUCLEAR WEAPONS FREEZE, §§7-2401, 7-2404.

NUDE DANCERS.
Alcoholic beverage licenses.
Exceptions, §25-371.
Legitimate theater, §25-372.
Performance space, §25-372.
Grandfather clause, §25-371.
Moratorium on nude dancing establishments, §§25-371 to 25-374.
Prohibited generally, §§25-113, 25-371.
Transfer of location of establishment, §25-374.
Transfer of ownership of establishment, §25-373.

NUISANCES.
Alcoholic beverage violations, places of, §25-805.

NUISANCES —Cont'd
Aquatic life creating.
Power of mayor to protect against, §8-103.03.
Boilers, §2-113.
Building code.
Failure to fireproof building, §6-601.08.
Building height violations, §6-601.08.
Drug, firearm, or prostitution-related nuisance abatement, §§42-3101 to 42-3114.
See CRIME-RELATED NUISANCE ABATEMENT.
Graffiti abatement.
Correction of conditions violative of law, §§42-3131.01 to 42-3131.03.
Generally, §§42-3141.01 to 42-3141.11.
See GRAFFITI.
Helicopter landing pads, §9-1211.01.
Litter, notice of nuisance regarding, §8-803.
Prostitution.
Drug, firearm, or prostitution-related nuisance abatement, §§42-3101 to 42-3114.
See CRIME-RELATED NUISANCE ABATEMENT.
Houses of prostitution.
See PROSTITUTION.
Real property.
Correction of conditions violative of law, §§42-3131.01 to 42-3131.03.
Real property tax.
Special assessments for removal of, §47-1205.
Solid waste facilities, §8-1060.
Unsafe structures as dangerous nuisances, §6-804.
Correction of conditions violative of law, §§42-3131.01 to 42-3131.03.
Vector-borne disease control, §§8-2131.01 to 8-2131.09.
See VECTOR-BORNE DISEASE CONTROL.

NUNCUPATIVE WILLS, §18-107.

NURSE-MIDWIVES.
Newborn heart screening, §§7-857.01 to 7-857.04.

NURSES.
Advanced registered nursing, §§3-1206.01 to 3-1206.04.
Authorized acts, §§3-1206.01, 3-1206.04.
Collaboration, §§3-1206.01, 3-1206.03.

NURSES —Cont'd
Advanced registered nursing
  —Cont'd
  Definition of practice of, §3-1201.02.
  Titles and terms prohibited as
    misrepresentation without license
    to practice, §3-1210.03.
Alcohol and drug abuse.
  Rehabilitation program, §§3-1251.01 to
    3-1251.15.
Board of Nursing, §3-1202.04.
**Cardiopulmonary resuscitation in
  case of cardiac arrest.**
  Non-resuscitation procedures for EMS,
    §§7-651.01 to 7-651.16.
  See EMERGENCY MEDICAL
    SERVICES.
Child abuse and neglect reports,
  §4-1321.02.
Child death.
  Reports, §4-1371.12.
Controlled substances.
  Administering, supervision required,
    §48-931.02.
Crimes and offenses.
  Failure to report certain deaths,
    §5-1406.
Dead bodies.
  Duty to report certain deaths to
    medical examiner, §5-1405.
  Failure to report certain deaths,
    §5-1406.
Defined terms.
  Advanced registered nursing, practice
    of, §3-1201.02.
  Practical nursing, §3-1201.02.
  Registered nursing, §3-1201.02.
Drug abuse.
  Rehabilitation program, §§3-1251.01 to
    3-1251.15.
**Emergency volunteer health
  practitioners, §§7-2361.01 to
  7-2361.12.**
  See EMERGENCY VOLUNTEER
    HEALTH PRACTITIONERS.
Health occupations boards.
  General provisions, §§3-1201.01 to
    3-1213.01.
  See HEALTH OCCUPATIONS
    BOARDS.
**Health occupations licensure,
  registration or certification,**
  §§3-1205.01 to 3-1205.24.
  See HEALTH OCCUPATIONS
    LICENSURE, REGISTRATION
    OR CERTIFICATION.

NURSES —Cont'd
**Health professional recruitment
  program, §§7-751.01 to 7-751.16.**
  See HEALTH PROFESSIONAL
    RECRUITMENT PROGRAM.
**Impaired nurses, treatment and
  rehabilitation, §§3-1251.01 to
  3-1251.15.**
  Admission to program voluntary,
    §3-1251.09.
  Closed proceedings before committee,
    §3-1251.07.
  Committee on impaired nurses.
    Closed proceedings, §3-1251.07.
    Established, §3-1251.02.
    Immunity from liability, §3-1251.08.
    Meetings, §3-1251.03.
    Membership, §3-1251.02.
    Minutes of meetings, confidentiality,
      §3-1251.03.
    Powers and duties, §3-1251.05.
    Quorum, §3-1251.03.
    Records, privileged and confidential,
      §3-1251.03.
    Reports to board, §3-1251.14.
    Rules, promulgation, §3-1251.15.
    Staff, §3-1251.04.
  Confidentiality of records, §3-1251.11.
  Contract setting forth requirements
    for participation, §3-1251.09.
  Definitions, §3-1251.01.
  Designated treatment facilities.
    Qualification as, §3-1251.10.
  Destruction of records, time,
    §3-1251.11.
  Disciplinary action.
    Failure to comply with requirements
      and conditions of contract,
      §3-1251.09.
  Disclosure of records relating to
    impaired nurse.
    Restrictions, §3-1251.07.
  Eligibility for participation,
    §3-1251.09.
  Informational booklet, publication,
    §3-1251.13.
  License voluntarily limited or
    surrendered, §3-1251.09.
  Notice of programs procedures.
    Receipt by nurses requesting to
      participate in program,
      §3-1251.06.
  Nurses leaving district and applying
    for job in another state,
    §3-1251.12.
  Privileged and confidential.
    Minutes of committee meetings,
      §3-1251.03.

NURSES —Cont'd
Impaired nurses, treatment and rehabilitation —Cont'd
Privileged and confidential —Cont'd
Proceeding before committee, §3-1251.07.
Records of committee, §3-1251.03.
Disclosure, restrictions, §3-1251.07.
Records maintenance, §3-1251.11.
Records transferred to another state.
Nurse participant leaving District for another state, §3-1251.12.
Referral by self-report or complaint, §3-1251.09.
Transfer of participating nurse to another state's program, §3-1251.12.
Malpractice.
Medical malpractice, §§16-2801 to 16-2841.
See MEDICAL MALPRACTICE.
Mental health department training program, §7-1131.20.
Mental illness.
Rehabilitation program, §§3-1251.01 to 3-1251.15.
Nursing assistive personnel.
Board of nursing, §3-1202.04.
Definition of practice by, §3-1201.02.
Health occupations licensure, registration or certification, §3-1209.07.
Titles and terms prohibited as misrepresentation without license to practice, §3-1210.03.
Public assistance.
Nursing care in home of relative, §4-205.47.
Rehabilitation program, §§3-1251.01 to 3-1251.15.
Reports.
Child death, §4-1371.12.
Scholarships.
Nurse training corps, §§38-1501 to 38-1503.
School nurses, §38-621.
Health and wellness programs, §38-826.04.
Staffing agencies, §§44-1051.01 to 44-1051.18.
See NURSE STAFFING AGENCIES.
Titles and terms prohibited as misrepresentation without license to practice, §3-1210.03.
Training corps, §§38-1501 to 38-1503.

NURSE'S REHABILITATION PROGRAM.
Impaired nurses, treatment and rehabilitation, §§3-1251.01 to 3-1251.15.
See NURSES.

NURSE STAFFING AGENCIES, §§44-1051.01 to 44-1051.18.
Change in ownership or other information, §44-1051.10.
Definitions, §44-1051.02.
Enforcement as result of inspection or investigation, §44-1051.16.
Sanctions authorized, §44-1051.18.
Inspection of offices and operations, §44-1051.16.
Licenses.
Application.
Initial license, §44-1051.04.
Denial, §44-1051.07.
Expiration, §44-1051.05.
Failure to renew, §44-1051.06.
Initial license application, §44-1051.04.
Provisional licenses, §44-1051.08.
Publication of license status, §44-1051.09.
Renewal, §44-1051.06.
Required, §44-1051.03.
Restricted licenses, §44-1051.08.
Revocation or suspension, §44-1051.07.
Verification of credentials.
Home health or personal care aides, §44-1051.12.
Nursing personnel, §44-1051.11.
Operational procedures, §44-1051.15.
Publication of license status, §44-1051.09.
Reporting of disciplinary action, §44-1051.14.
Rules and regulations, §44-1051.17.
Services by unauthorized personnel, §44-1051.13.
Short title, §44-1051.01.
Verification of credentials.
Home health aides, §44-1051.12.
Nursing personnel, §44-1051.11.
Operational procedures, §44-1051.15.
Personal care aides, §44-1051.12.
Services by unauthorized personnel, §44-1051.13.
Violations, sanctions authorized, §44-1051.18.

NURSE TRAINING CORPS, §§38-1501 to 38-1503.
Administered by department of human services, §38-1502.

NURSE TRAINING CORPS —Cont'd
**Contract by student in exchange for
    financial aid,** §38-1501.
Criteria for selection, §38-1501.
Established, §38-1501.
Financial aid provided by corps,
    §38-1501.
Rules, §38-1503.

**NURSING HOME
    ADMINISTRATORS.**
Health occupations boards.
    General provisions, §§3-1201.01 to
        3-1213.01.
    See HEALTH OCCUPATIONS
        BOARDS.
**Health occupations licensure,
    registration or certification,**
    §§3-1205.01 to 3-1205.24.
    See HEALTH OCCUPATIONS
        LICENSURE, REGISTRATION
        OR CERTIFICATION.

NURSING HOMES, §§44-1001.01 to
    44-1005.01.
Administration.
    Board of long-term care
        administration, §3-1202.05.
    Definition of practice of nursing home
        administration, §3-1201.02.
Alcoholic beverage licenses.
    Exceptions to license requirements,
        §25-103.
Assessment on nursing facilities,
    §§47-1261 to 47-1269.
    Action to enforce, §47-1264.
    Appeals, §47-1266.
    Audit of information, §47-1265.
    Confidential information, §47-1265.
    Definitions, §47-1261.
    Determination, §47-1263.
    Effective date, §47-1269.
    Failure to pay or file report, §47-1264.
    False information or report, §47-1264.
    Federal determination, §47-1268.
    Interest and penalties, §47-1264.
    Lien, §47-1264.
    Null and void, §47-1268.
    Nursing facility quality of care fund,
        §47-1262.
    Rate, §47-1263.
    Rules, §47-1267.
    Summons, §47-1265.
    Uniform amount per licensed bed,
        §47-1263.
Court monitor, appointment of,
    §44-1002.10.

NURSING HOMES —Cont'd
Crimes and offenses.
    Failure to report certain deaths,
        §5-1406.
**Criminal background checks for
    unlicensed personnel,** §§44-551 to
    44-554.
Dead bodies.
    Duty to report certain deaths to
        medical examiner, §5-1405.
    Failure to report certain deaths,
        §5-1406.
Definitions, §44-1001.01.
**Discharge, transfer, or relocation of
    residents,** §§44-1003.01 to
    44-1003.13.
    Appeals, §44-1003.12.
    Assistance with, §44-1003.10.
    Closure of facility, §44-1003.11.
    Discussion and counseling prior to,
        §44-1003.04.
    Emergency transfer or discharge by
        mayor, §44-1003.08.
    Exemption from provisions,
        §44-1003.12.
    Hearings, §§44-1003.03, 44-1003.09.
    Involuntary, grounds for, §§44-1003.01
        to 44-1003.04.
    Mayor, grounds for transfer or
        discharge by, §§44-1003.05 to
        44-1003.09.
    Notice, §44-1003.02.
    Planning, §44-1003.10.
    Private right of action regarding,
        §§44-1004.01 to 44-1004.05.
**District of Columbia Village, rates
    schedule for,** §47-2714.
Issuance of rules and regulations,
    §44-1005.01.
Lead poisoning.
    Childhood lead poisoning screening
        and reporting, §§7-871.01 to
        7-871.06.
Licenses, §§44-501 to 44-509.
Long-term care ombudsman,
    §§7-701.01 to 7-706.01.
    See LONG-TERM CARE
        OMBUDSMAN.
Medicaid reimbursement, §§4-204.61,
    4-204.62.
Notice.
    Discharge, transfer, or relocation of
        residents, §§44-1003.02,
        44-1003.06, 44-1003.07,
        44-1003.11.
    Receiverships, §44-1002.04.

NURSING HOMES —Cont'd
Public assistance for recipients in,
§4-205.49.
Quality of care fund, §47-1262.
Receiverships, §§44-1002.01 to
44-1002.10.
Appointment of receiver, §§44-1002.04,
44-1002.05.
Court monitor, appointment of,
§44-1002.10.
Ex parte appointment of receiver,
§§44-1002.04, 44-1002.05.
Final accounting for, §44-1002.08.
Hearings, §44-1002.04.
Notice, §44-1002.04.
Petitions for, §44-1002.03.
Policy declaration, §44-1002.01.
Powers and duties, §44-1002.06.
Reasons for, §44-1002.02.
Special fund or account, §44-1002.09.
Termination of, §44-1002.07.

NUTRITION.
Mayor's council on physical fitness,
health and nutrition, §§7-121 to
7-126.
Administrative support, §7-123.
Executive committee, §7-126.
Fitness fund, §7-125.
Fitness report, §§7-122, 7-124.
Meetings, §7-121.
Membership, §7-121.
Mission, §7-121.
Powers and duties, §7-122.
Schools, §§38-822.01 to 38-822.07.
See SCHOOLS AND EDUCATION.

O

OAK HILL CEMETERY COMPANY.
Real property exempt from taxation,
§47-1015.

OAK HILL YOUTH CENTER.
Closure and transfer of operations,
§24-941.

OATHS.
Affirmation in lieu of oath, CivPro
Rule 43.
Domestic relations actions, DomRel
Rule 2.
Appeals in federal cases.
Attorneys, admission to practice,
FRAP 46(b).
Clerks of court of appeals, FRAP 45(a).
Assignments for benefit of creditors.
Examination of assignor under oath,
§28-2106.

OATHS —Cont'd
Attorney general, administration by,
§1-301.88.
Attorneys at law.
Admission to the bar, DCCtApp Rule
46.
Auditor for District of Columbia.
Powers and duties, §1-301.173.
Authority to administer, §§1-301.22,
5-1021.
Boiler inspections, §2-104.
Boiler inspectors, §2-104.
Campaign finance, §1-1163.37.
Congress.
Oath of office, US Const Art VI.
Constitution of the United States.
Congress, US Const Art VI.
Governor, US Const Art VI.
Lieutenant governor, US Const Amd
14.
House of representatives.
United States, US Const Art VI.
Public officers, US Const Art VI.
Senate.
United States, US Const Art VI.
Council's power to administer,
§§1-204.13, 1-301.22, 5-1021.
Court of appeals.
Judges' oaths, §11-704.
Power of court to administer, §11-742.
Depositions, CivPro Rule 30.
Adoption proceedings, Adoption Rule
30.
Domestic relations actions, DomRel
Rule 30.
Disability compensation
proceedings for public officers
and employees, §1-623.26.
Domestic relations actions, DomRel
Rule 2.
Eminent domain as to real property
for United States, oaths of jurors
in trials regarding, §16-1358.
Evidence given under, §14-101.
Executive officer of District of
Columbia courts, §11-1704.
False swearing.
General provisions, §22-2404.
Police and fire trial boards, before,
§5-1002.
Firearms registration, §7-2502.05.
Interpretation of provisions,
affirmation to be included in
references to oaths, §45-606.
Interpreters, §2-1907.
Judges, US Const Art VI.

OATHS —Cont'd

Lieutenant governor, US Const Art VI, Amd 14.

Lottery and charitable games control board, §§3-1302, 3-1308.

Mayor's powers, §§1-301.22, 5-1021.

Medicaid service provider fraud, §4-804.

Metropolitan police, §§5-105.03, 5-119.05, 5-127.02.

Notaries public.
  Administering oaths, §1-1210.
  Taking oaths, §1-1203.

Personnel authority, §1-604.08.

Police and fire trial boards, §5-1011.

Public officers and employees, required of, §1-501.

Public Parking Authority, §50-2505.

Public utilities.
  Commission oaths and affirmations, §34-801.
  Investigations by Commission, §34-918.

Register of wills, §11-2102.

Searches and seizures.
  Warrants.
    Supported by oath or affirmation, US Const Amd 4.

Superior court judges.
  Judges' oaths, §11-905.
  Power to administer oaths, §11-945.

Surveyor of the District, §1-1302.

Tax assessor, §47-602.

Trust, mortgage and title corporations as fiduciaries, §26-1311.

Unsworn declaration supplement, CivPro Form CA 101-A.

Vice-president of the United States, US Const Art VI, Amd 14.

Weights and measures, Director of, §37-201.02.

Workplace safety, §32-805.

OBJECTIONS.

Appeals, federal cases.
  Bill of costs, FRAP 39(d).
  Statement when transcript unavailable, service of objections, FRAP 10(c).

Arbitration, Arbitration Rule XII.
  Applications, CivPro Rule 70-I.

Conservator's account, Probate Rule 331.

Criminal procedure.
  Pretrial motions, CrimPro Rule 12.

Delinquent minors, JuvProc Rule 12.
  Depositions, JuvProc Rule 15.

OBJECTIONS —Cont'd

Delinquent minors —Cont'd
  Exceptions unnecessary, JuvProc Rule 51.

Discovery.
  Depositions, CivPro Rule 30.
    Admissibility of depositions, CivPro Rule 32.
    Adoption proceedings, Adoption Rules 30, 32.
    Criminal procedure, CrimPro Rule 15.
    Delinquent minors, JuvProc Rule 15.
    Domestic relations actions, DomRel Rules 30, 32.
  Interrogatories, CivPro Rule 33.
    Adoption proceedings, Adoption Rule 33.
    Domestic relations actions, DomRel Rule 33.
  Requests for admission, CivPro Rule 36.
    Adoption proceedings, Adoption Rule 36.
    Domestic relations actions, DomRel Rule 36.

Eminent domain.
  Appraisement, §16-1318.
  Jurors, §16-1317.

Exceptions unnecessary, CivPro Rule 46, CrimPro Rule 51.
  Domestic relations actions, DomRel Rule 46.
  Juvenile proceedings, JuvProc Rule 51.

Grand juries, CrimPro Rule 6.

Guardian and ward.
  Adult guardianship and protective proceedings jurisdiction act, §21-2401.03.

Intellectual disabilities, persons with.
  Discharge from facility, MentalRetardation Rule 6.

Intervention proceedings.
  Appearances by retained counsel, Probate Rule 305.
  Conservator's account, Probate Rule 331.
  General intervention proceedings, Probate Rule 322.
  Guardianship reports, Probate Rule 328.

Jury instructions, CivPro Rule 51, CrimPro Rule 30.

Master's report, CivPro Rule 53.
  Domestic relations actions, DomRel Rule 53.

OBJECTIONS —Cont'd
Offers of proof, CivPro Rule 43.
Parentage proceedings.
Blood tests, DomRel Rule 405.
Probate proceedings.
Compensation of conservators and guardians of minors, Probate Rule 225.
Subpoenas.
Inspection or copying of materials, CivPro Rule 45.
Domestic relations actions, DomRel Rule 45.
Transcripts released for appeal, CivPro Rule 201.
Adoption proceedings, Adoption Rule 201.
Domestic relations actions, DomRel Rule 201.

OBSCENITY, §§22-2201 to 22-3104.
Cable television.
Compliance with obscenity laws, §34-1264.01.
Definitions, §22-2201.
Disturbances of the peace, §22-1312.
Fines, §22-2201.
Language, profane or indecent, §22-1321.
Lewd, indecent, or obscene acts, §22-1312.
Minors, sexual performances involving, §§22-3101 to 22-3104.
See CHILD SEXUAL ABUSE.
Nonconsensual pornography, §§22-3051 to 22-3057.
Affirmative defenses, §22-3056.
Definitions, §22-3051.
Exclusions, §22-3055.
First degree unlawful publication, §22-3053.
Jurisdiction, §22-3057.
Second degree unlawful publication, §22-3054.
Unlawful disclosure, §22-3052.
Penalties, §22-2201.
Prohibited acts, §§22-1312, 22-2201.

OBSTETRICIANS/GYNECOLOGISTS.
Closed claim analysis.
Medical malpractice claims, §31-2991.

OBSTRUCTION OF JUSTICE, §§22-721 to 22-723.
Conduct constituting, §22-722.

OBSTRUCTION OF JUSTICE —Cont'd
Reports to or requests for assistance from law enforcement, medical providers, or child welfare agencies.
Obstruction, prevention, or interference with, §22-1931.

OCCUPATIONAL DISEASE.
Workers' compensation, §32-1510.

OCCUPATIONAL SAFETY AND HEALTH, §§32-1101 to 32-1124.
Administration, §32-1107.
Appeals, §32-1116.
Applicability of provisions, §§32-1102, 32-1124.
Board, §32-1105.
Citations for violations of standards, §32-1114.
Claims against the District, §32-1122.
Commission, §32-1106.
Crimes and offenses, §32-1121.
Definitions, §32-1101.
Discrimination, §32-1117.
Emergency temporary rules, §32-1109.
Employer and employee duties, §32-1103.
Enforcement of provisions.
Authority to enforce, §32-1107.
Court proceedings, §32-1116.
Procedures, §32-1115.
Fines, §§32-1120, 32-1121.
Health services, §1-620.07.
Imminent danger, §32-1118.
Industrial safety.
General provisions, §§32-801 to 32-812.
See WORKPLACE SAFETY.
Inspections, §32-1112.
Investigations, §32-1112.
Judicial review and enforcement, §32-1116.
Notice, §32-1122.
Office of, §32-1123.
Penalties, §32-1121.
Plan for, §32-1104.
Privacy and confidentiality, §32-1119.
Public officers and employees, §§1-620.01 to 1-620.08.
Authority of mayor, §1-620.04.
Employee rights, §1-620.05.
Extent of coverage, §1-620.02.

OCCUPATIONAL SAFETY AND HEALTH —Cont'd

Public officers and employees —Cont'd

Minimal standards, §1-620.03.

Public policy, §1-620.01.

Records, §1-620.08.

Records, §§1-620.08, 32-1113.

Reports, §32-1113.

Standards, §32-1108.

Summary actions regarding imminent danger, §32-1118.

Temporary assistance for needy families (TANF) program, §4-205.19j.

Temporary variances, §32-1110.

Trade secret disclosures, §36-410.

Trade secrets, §32-1119.

Training, §1-620.06.

Variances.

Permanent, §32-1111.

Temporary, §32-1110.

OCCUPATIONAL THERAPY.

Board of, §3-1202.06.

Definition of practice of, §3-1201.02.

Health occupations boards.

General provisions, §§3-1201.01 to 3-1213.01.

See HEALTH OCCUPATIONS BOARDS.

Health occupations licensure, registration or certification, §§3-1205.01 to 3-1205.24.

See HEALTH OCCUPATIONS LICENSURE, REGISTRATION OR CERTIFICATION.

Titles and terms prohibited as misrepresentation without license to practice, §3-1210.03.

ODOMETER READINGS.

Lemon law requirements, §50-506.

OFFER AND ACCEPTANCE.

Leases, UCC.

Firm offers, §28:2A-205.

Generally, §28:2A-206.

Sale of goods, UCC, §28:2-206.

Auctions, §28:2-328.

Firm offers, §28:2-205.

OFFER OF JUDGMENT, CivPro Rule 68.

Domestic relations actions, DomRel Rule 68.

OFFERS OF PROOF, CivPro Rule 43.

OFFICE OF ADMINISTRATIVE HEARINGS, §§2-1831.01 to 2-1831.18.

See ADMINISTRATIVE HEARINGS, OFFICE OF.

OFFICE OF ASIAN AND PACIFIC ISLANDER AFFAIRS, §§2-1371 to 2-1376.

OFFICE OF BICYCLE TRANSPORTATION AND SAFETY, §50-1603.

OFFICE OF BUSINESS AND ECONOMIC DEVELOPMENT, §§2-1201.01 to 2-1201.05.

OFFICE OF CABLE TELEVISION, FILM, MUSIC, AND ENTERTAINMENT, §§34-1252.01 to 34-1252.03.

OFFICE OF DISABILITY RIGHTS, §2-1431.03.

Mayor's committee on persons with disabilities.

Transfer of functions to office, §2-1431.06.

Office of risk management.

Transfer of functions to office, §2-1431.06.

Powers and duties, §2-1431.04.

OFFICE OF FIRST SOURCE COMPLIANCE, §§2-219.31 to 2-219.35.

Definitions, §2-219.32.

Established, §2-219.33.

Executive director, §2-219.35.

Powers and duties, §2-219.34.

Short title, §2-219.31.

OFFICE OF HUMAN RIGHTS, §§2-1411.01 to 2-1411.06.

Establishment of, §2-1411.01.

Human Rights and Business Development, Department of, §§2-1411.04, 2-1411.06.

Interfering with, resisting, or impeding, §2-1402.64.

Language access director.

Duties, §2-1935.

Organization of, §2-1411.05.

Policy declaration, §2-1411.02.

Powers and duties, §§2-1401.02, 2-1403.01, 2-1411.03, 2-1411.05.

Transfers to, §2-1411.04.

OFFICE OF INTERPRETER SERVICES, §2-1911.

OFFICE OF LABOR RELATIONS AND COLLECTIVE BARGAINING.
Funding for provided in budget, §1-531.02.
Reimbursement for representation, §1-531.01.

OFFICE OF LESBIAN, GAY, BISEXUAL, TRANSGENDER, AND QUESTIONING AFFAIRS, §§2-1381 to 2-1384.
Advisory committee, §2-1382.
Definitions, §2-1381.
Director, §2-1383.
Established, §2-1382.
Homeless youth training grant fund, §2-1384.
Staff, §2-1383.

OFFICE OF MEDICAID OPERATIONS REFORM, §§4-204.11 to 4-204.16.

OFFICE OF PEOPLE'S COUNSEL, §§34-804, 34-1118.
Funds.
Office of the people's counsel agency fund, §34-912.

OFFICE OF PERSONNEL, §§1-604.01 to 1-604.08.
Director of personnel, §1-604.02.

OFFICE OF POLICE COMPLAINTS, §§5-1101 to 5-1115.
Actions, §5-1112.
Authority of office, §5-1107.
Conciliation of complaints, §5-1110.
Definitions, §5-1103.
Dismissal of complaints, §§5-1108, 5-1113.
Establishment of board, §5-1104.
Establishment of office, §5-1105.
Executive director, §§5-1105, 5-1106.
Funds, §5-1115.
Investigation of complaints, §5-1111.
Freedom of information act exemption.
Investigation records, §2-534.
Mediation of complaints, §5-1110.
Policy declaration, §§5-1101, 5-1102.
Processing of complaints, §5-1107.
Referral of complaints to United States Attorney, §5-1109.
Types of complaints handled, §5-1107.

OFFICE OF PUBLIC-PRIVATE PARTNERSHIPS, §§2-272.01 to 2-272.04.

OFFICE OF REGISTRAR OF TITLES AND TAGS, §50-2201.24.

OFFICE OF TENANT ADVOCATE, §§42-3531.01 to 42-3531.10.
Chief tenant advocate, §42-3531.06.
Rental accommodations fee fund, §42-3504.01.
Definitions, §42-3531.04.
Duties, §42-3531.07.
Establishment, §42-3531.05.
Findings, §42-3531.03.
Housing assistance fund, §42-3531.09.
Purpose, §42-3531.02.
Rulemaking, §42-3531.10.
Short title, §42-3531.01.
Tenant bill of rights, §42-3531.07.

OFFICE OF THE CHIEF FINANCIAL OFFICER.
See CHIEF FINANCIAL OFFICER.

OFFICE OF THE CITY ADMINISTRATOR.
Master facilities planning and program coordination advisory committee, §§10-1031, 10-1032.

OFFICE OF UNIFIED COMMUNICATIONS, §§1-327.51 to 1-327.57.
Coordination with agencies, §1-327.56.
Definitions, §1-327.51.
Establishment, §1-327.52.
Functions, §1-327.54.
911 system, authorized use, §1-327.56a.
Organization, §1-327.55.
Rulemaking, §1-327.57.
Transfer of responsibilities and duties to, §1-327.53.

OFFICE OF VETERANS' AFFAIRS, §§49-1001 to 49-1006.
See VETERANS' AFFAIRS, OFFICE OF.

OFFICE OF VOCATIONAL EDUCATION AND SKILLS TRAINING.
University of the District of Columbia, §§38-1208.01 to 38-1208.06.

OFFICE ON AGING, §§7-503.01 to 7-503.06.

OFFICE ON EX-OFFENDER AFFAIRS, §24-1302.

OFFICIAL DINOSAUR OF THE DISTRICT OF COLUMBIA.
Capitalsaurus dinosaur, §1-161.

OFFICIAL FRUIT OF THE DISTRICT OF COLUMBIA.
Cherry, §1-171.

OFFICIAL INSIGNIA.
Police and fire and emergency medical services departments.
Unauthorized use, §22-1409.

OFFICIAL MAIL, §§2-701 to 2-710.
See MAIL.

OFFICIAL ROCK OF THE DISTRICT OF COLUMBIA.
Potomac bluestone, §1-165.02.
Legislative findings, §1-165.01.

OFF-LABEL INFORMED CONSENT ACT OF 2008.
Prescription medication.
Off-label use, §§48-841.01 to 48-841.04.

OFFSHORE FACILITIES.
Defined, §8-103.01.
Water pollution.
Discharges of, §8-103.08.
Spill prevention and cleanup plans, §8-103.10.

OIL AND GAS.
Contracts.
Sales.
Applicability of sales chapter of commercial code, §28:2-107.
Secured transactions.
Description of land, §28:9-203.
When security interest attaches, §28:9-204.

OLD GEORGETOWN AREA, §§6-1201 to 6-1207.
See HISTORIC DISTRICTS.

OLYMPIC GAMES.
Chesapeake Regional Olympic Games Authority, §§2-1131 to 2-1138.

OMBUDSMAN.
Behavioral health ombudsman program, §7-1131.19.
Long-term care ombudsman, §§7-701.01 to 7-706.01.
See LONG-TERM CARE OMBUDSMAN.
Public education, §§38-351 to 38-356.

ONE CALL, §§34-2701 to 34-2709.
See MISS UTILITY.

ONE CARD SERVICE SUPPORT, §§1-327.71 to 1-327.73.

ONE FEE RULE.
Witness fees, CrimPro Rule 113.
Family court proceedings, FamDiv Rule F.

ONSHORE FACILITIES.
Defined, §8-103.01.
Water pollution.
Discharges of, §8-103.08.
Spill prevention and cleanup plans, §8-103.10.

OPEN CONTAINER LAW.
Alcoholic beverages, §25-1001.
On-premises retailer knowingly allowing customer to exit with an open container, §25-113.

OPEN GOVERNMENT OFFICE, §§2-591 to 2-593.
Director, §2-594.
Duties, §2-592.
Established, §2-591.
Powers, §2-592.

OPENING ESTATES, §§20-301 to 20-357.
Abbreviated probate proceeding, §§20-311, 20-312, 20-331.
Application of provisions, §20-301.
Appointment of personal representative, §§20-301, 20-303.
Claims against estate prior to opening, §20-901.
Contesting validity of will, §20-305.
Finality of probate proceedings, §20-331.
Foreign personal representatives, §§20-341 to 20-344.
Necessity of probate for, §20-302.
Petition for probate, §20-304.
Probate proceedings.
See PROBATE PROCEEDINGS.
Small estates, §§20-351 to 20-357.
Standard probate proceeding, §§20-321 to 20-324, 20-331.

OPEN MEETINGS, §§2-571 to 2-579, 2-571 to 2-580.
Action for violation, §2-579.
Administrative procedure, §1-207.42.
Advisory neighborhood commissions.
Report as to whether provisions should apply, §2-575.
Alcoholic beverage control board, §25-204.01.
Closed meeting, §2-575.
Construction of subchapter, §2-573.

OPEN MEETINGS —Cont'd
Copies of record of meeting, §2-578.
Council meetings.
Adoption of rules to ensure policy met, §2-575.
Definitions, §2-574.
Electronically recorded, §2-578.
E-mail exchanges.
Not electronic meeting, §2-577.
Emergency meetings.
Notice, §2-576.
Statement of explanation, §2-577.
Enforcement of provisions, §2-579.
Ethic and government accountability board, §1-1162.04.
Quorum, §1-1162.08.
Fine for violation, §2-579.
Health benefit exchange authority, §31-3171.11.
Keeping attendees below quorum to avoid open meeting requirement.
Prohibition, §2-575.
Meeting deemed open to public, §2-575.
Notice, §2-576.
Open meeting act.
Short title, §2-571.
Procedures, §2-577.
Public policy, §2-572.
Public-private partnerships.
Review of requests for proposal, §2-273.03.
Record of, §2-578.
Remedies for violation, §2-579.
Rules of construction, §2-573.
Schedule of meetings.
Public body to adopt, §2-576.
Short title, §2-571.
Statement of public policy, §2-572.
Training manual for members of public bodies, §2-580.
Video or telephone conference, other electronic means.
Holding meetings, §2-577.

OPERATING ENGINEERS.
Business licenses, §§47-2853.211 to 47-2853.213.

OPERATORS' PERMITS.
See DRIVERS' LICENSES.

OPHTHALMIA.
Blindness in newborns, prevention of, §§7-801 to 7-804.

OPINION EVIDENCE.
Human trafficking, §22-1839.

OPPORTUNITY ACCOUNT OFFICE, §1-307.62.

OPPORTUNITY ACCOUNTS, §§1-307.61 to 1-307.74.
Administration of programs.
Proposals by organizations, §1-307.63.
Responsibility of administering organization, §1-307.64.
Amount limit, §1-307.66.
Death of account holder.
Disposition, §1-307.70.
Definitions, §1-307.61.
Eligibility to open account, §1-307.66.
Emergency withdrawal, §1-307.69.
Establishment of accounts by financial institutions, §1-307.65.
Matching funds, §1-307.67.
Opportunity account office, §1-307.62.
Public assistance program calculations.
Exclusion of account from, §1-307.72.
Reports, §1-307.74.
Reserve fund account.
Use of funds in for administrative expenses, §1-307.71.
Rules, §1-307.73.
Use of account funds, §1-307.68.

OPTOMETRY.
Board of, §3-1202.07.
Definition of practice of, §3-1201.02.
Health insurance, group policies, §31-4724.
Health occupations boards.
General provisions, §§3-1201.01 to 3-1213.01.
See HEALTH OCCUPATIONS BOARDS.
Health occupations licensure, registration or certification, §§3-1205.01 to 3-1205.24.
See HEALTH OCCUPATIONS LICENSURE, REGISTRATION OR CERTIFICATION.
Titles and terms prohibited as misrepresentation without license to practice, §3-1210.03.

ORAL ARGUMENTS.
Appeals, D.C. courts, DCCtApp Rule 34.
Amicus curiae, DCCtApp Rule 29.
Appeals, federal cases, FRAP 34, USCtApp Rule 34.
Amici curiae, USCtApp HPIP Rule XI(e).

ORAL ARGUMENTS —Cont'd
Appeals, federal cases —Cont'd
Appellee not heard, failure to file brief, FRAP 31(c).
Argument time, USCtApp HPIP Rule XI(c).
Rule 34(j) dispositions, USCtApp HPIP Rule XI(c)(2).
Screening by the panel, USCtApp HPIP Rule XI(c)(1).
Briefs, FRAP 28(a).
Federal labor relations authority proceedings, USCtApp Rule 15.1.
Form and content, USCtApp HPIP Rule XI(f).
Mandamus, prohibition, etc., petition for writ of, FRAP 21, USCtApp Rule 21.
Motions.
Amicus curiae, FRAP 29.
National labor relations board proceedings, FRAP 15.1, USCtApp Rule 15.1.
Notice, USCtApp HPIP Rule XI(a).
Number of counsel, USCtApp HPIP Rule XI(d).
Order and content of argument, FRAP 34(c).
Permissive appeals, FRAP 5(b).
Petition for extraordinary writ, FRAP 21, USCtApp Rule 21.
Postponements, USCtApp HPIP Rule XI(b).
Procedures, USCtApp HPIP Rule XI(h).
Transcription of arguments, USCtApp HPIP Rule XI(i).
Weather closings, USCtApp HPIP Rule XI(g).
Closing arguments.
Criminal procedure, CrimPro Rule 29.1.
Traffic ticket adjudication.
Appeal of board decisions, CivPro Agency Review Rule 2.

ORAL COMMUNICATIONS.
Interception of wire or oral communications.
General provisions, §§23-541 to 23-556.
See INTERCEPTION OF ORAL OR WIRE COMMUNICATIONS.

ORAL CONTRACTS, §28-3504.
Sales.
Modification of written contract for sale, §28:2-209.

ORAL CONTRACTS —Cont'd
Special promise to answer for debt or default of another, §28-3502.

ORDERS OF COURT.
Adoption, Adoption Rules 4, 7.
Show cause orders, Adoption Rule 39.
Appeals, federal cases.
Answer to petition for writ of mandamus, prohibition, etc., order directing, FRAP 21, USCtApp Rule 21.
Briefs.
Citing judicial dispositions, USCtApp Rule 32.1.
Extension of time to file petition for rehearing, FRAP 40(a).
Hearing or rehearing en banc, FRAP 35.
Interlocutory orders, appeals from by permission under 28 USCS 1292(b), FRAP 5(a).
Notice of, clerk to serve, FRAP 45(c).
Prehearing or appeal conference, recitation of action at, FRAP 33.
Transfer of custody pending review in habeas corpus proceedings, FRAP 23(a).
Arrest records.
Sealing records. See within this heading, "Sealing of records."
Bail bondsmen.
Authorization of sureties, CrimPro Rule 116.
Bankruptcy proceedings.
Proposed orders, USDistDCBank Rule 9072-1.
Child abuse and neglect.
Custody orders, NeglectProc Rule 4A.
Ex parte orders, NeglectProc Rule 4.
Disposition orders, NeglectProc Rule 25.
Inspection and disclosure of neglect records, NeglectProc Rule 46.
Permanency hearings, NeglectProc Rule 34.
Pretrial orders, NeglectProc Rule 17.
Review hearings, NeglectProc Rule 30.
Shelter care, NeglectProc Rule 15.
Termination of parental rights, NeglectProc Rule 39.
Class actions, CivPro Rule 23.
Clerks of court.
Orders grantable by clerk, CivPro Rule 77-II.
Appeals, DCCtApp Rule 27.
Conservatorship, CivPro Rule 310.

ORDERS OF COURT —Cont'd
Copies kept by clerk of court, CivPro
Rule 79.
Certified copies, CivPro Rule 79-I.
Domestic relations actions, DomRel
Rule 79.
Date of entry, CrimPro Rule 55.
Delinquent minors.
Clerical mistakes, JuvProc Rule 36.
Custody orders, JuvProc Rule 4.
Detention order, JuvProc Form 1.
Dispositional orders, JuvProc Rule 32.
Forms, JuvProc Forms 5 to 7.
Inspection of records, JuvProc Rule 55.
Release upon conditions, JuvProc
Form 3.
Sealing arrest records, FamDiv Rule P,
JuvProc Rule 118.
Forms, FamDiv Forms 4 to 6,
JuvProc Form 10.
Shelter care order, JuvProc Form 2.
Transfer for criminal prosecution,
JuvProc Rule 108.
Discovery.
Criminal procedure, CrimPro Rule 16.
Delinquent minors, JuvProc Rule 16.
Domestic relations actions.
Absent defendant.
Order of publication, DomRel Form
1.
Certificate and order, DomRel Form
15.
Motions, DomRel Rule 7.
Notice of order, DomRel Rule 77.
Physical or mental examination of
person, DomRel Rule 35.
Pretrial orders, DomRel Rule 16-I.
Reciprocal enforcement of support
proceedings, DomRel Rule 401.
Relief from orders, DomRel Rule 60.
Replevin actions, DomRel Rule 64.
Show cause orders, DomRel Form 16,
DomRel Rule 4.
Support orders, DomRel Forms 10, 12.
Exceptions unnecessary, CivPro Rule
46, CrimPro Rule 51.
Domestic relations actions, DomRel
Rule 46.
Juvenile proceedings, JuvProc Rule 51.
Fair trials in superior court, CivPro
Rule 203, CrimPro Rule 53.
Family court proceedings generally.
Sealing of records, FamDiv Rule P.
Forms, FamDiv Forms 4 to 6.
Gag orders, CivPro Rule 203, CrimPro
Rule 53.
Juvenile proceedings, JuvProc Rule 53.

ORDERS OF COURT —Cont'd
General order, CivPro Form CA 116.
Guardianship of minors.
Permanent guardianship orders,
§§16-2381 to 16-2399.
See GUARDIAN AND WARD.
Harmless error.
Adoption proceedings, Adoption Rule
61.
Civil cases, CivPro Rule 61.
Criminal procedure, CrimPro Rule 52.
Domestic relations actions, DomRel
Rule 61.
Juvenile proceedings, JuvProc Rule 52.
Intellectual disability proceedings.
Commitment to facility.
Entry of judgment,
MentalRetardation Rule 16.
Individuals who are not competent
to refuse commitment,
MentalRetardation Rule 4A.
Respondents found incompetent to
participate in criminal
proceedings, MentalRetardation
Rule 4B.
**Interception of wire or oral
communications,** CrimPro Rule
41-I.
Intervention proceedings.
Removal of fiduciary.
Show cause orders, Probate Rule
309.
Mediation.
General mediation order, CivPro Form
CA 117.
Mental illness, persons with.
Hospitalization.
Escaped patient's return to hospital,
MentalRetardation Rule 10.
Mistakes, CivPro Rule 60, CrimPro
Rule 36.
Adoption decrees, Adoption Rule 60.
Domestic relations actions, DomRel
Rule 60.
Harmless error. See within this
heading, "Harmless error."
Motions practice.
Providing proposed form of order,
CivPro Rule 12-I.
Nonparties to action.
Enforcement of orders favoring
nonparties, CivPro Rule 71.
Domestic relations actions, DomRel
Rule 71.
Notice of orders, CivPro Rule 77.
Domestic relations actions, DomRel
Rule 77.

ORDERS OF COURT —Cont'd
Pretrial orders, CivPro Rule 16,
USDistCt LCvR 16.3.
Domestic relations actions, DomRel
Rule 16-I.
Probate proceedings.
Abbreviated probate orders, Probate
Form 3.
Appointment of special administrator
to open safe deposit box, Probate
Rule 7.1.
Extension of appointment of personal
representative, Probate Form 17,
Probate Rule 429.
Personal representative's authority to
act, Probate Rule 412.
Rule to show cause.
Death between Jan. 1, 1981, and
June 30, 1995, Probate Rule
113.
Death on or after July 1, 1995,
Probate Rule 413.
Guardians, conservators, trustees,
etc., involved, Probate Rule 211.
Termination of appointment of
supervised personal
representative, Probate Form 22,
Probate Rule 423.
Probation.
Delinquent minors, JuvProc Form 6.
Form of order imposing conditions,
CrimPro Form 1.
Protective orders.
Generally.
See PROTECTIVE ORDERS.
**Reciprocal enforcement of support
proceedings,** DomRel Rule 401.
Relief from order, CivPro Rule 60.
Domestic relations actions, DomRel
Rule 60.
Harmless error. See within this
heading, "Harmless error."
Replevin, CivPro Rule 64-II.
Domestic relations actions, DomRel
Rule 64.
Form, CivPro Form CA 108.
Restraining orders, CivPro Rule 65.
Scheduling orders, CivPro Rule 16,
USDistCt LCvR 16.4.
Provided by moving party, CivPro
Rule 12-I.
Sealing of records, CrimPro Rule 118.
Delinquent minors, FamDiv Rule P,
JuvProc Rule 118.
Forms, FamDiv Forms 4 to 6,
JuvProc Form 10.

ORDERS OF COURT —Cont'd
Sealing of records —Cont'd
Family court proceedings generally,
FamDiv Rule P.
Forms, FamDiv Forms 4 to 6.
Termination of parental rights.
Child abuse and neglect, NeglectProc
Rule 39.
Veterans' estates.
Filing orders affecting estates, CivPro
Rule 5-I.

ORDINANCES.
**Board of health ordinances
legalized,** §§7-174 to 7-177.
Code of the District of Columbia.
Compilation.
Full force and effect, §45-402.
General provisions, §§45-102, 45-201.
See CODE OF THE DISTRICT OF
COLUMBIA.
Evidence, CivPro Rule 44-I.
Adoption proceedings, Adoption Rule
44.
Domestic relations actions, DomRel
Rule 44.

ORGAN DONATION.
Anatomical gifts, §§7-1531.01 to
7-1531.28.
See ANATOMICAL GIFTS.
Corporations.
Tax credit.
Provision of paid leave to employee
serving as donor, §47-1807.08.
**Government employee serving as
donor.**
Donor leave, §1-612.03b.
Human tissue banks, §§7-1541.01 to
7-1551.01.
See HUMAN TISSUE BANKS.
Trafficking in human body parts,
§§7-1501.01 to 7-1501.03.
Unincorporated businesses.
Tax credit.
Provision of paid leave to employee
serving as donor, §47-1808.08.

ORGANIZED CRIME.
**Interception of wire or oral
communications,** CrimPro Rule
41-I.

ORGAN TRAFFICKING, §§7-1501.01
to 7-1501.03.

**OTO HOTEL AT CONSTITUTION
SQUARE.**
Real property tax exemptions,
§47-4631.

OTOLARYNGOLOGISTS, §§28-4001 to 28-4007.

OUTDOOR ADVERTISING, §§1-303.21 to 1-303.23.

OUTHOUSES.
Permit to maintain privy by means other than connection to sewage system, §8-602.

OUT-OF-DISTRICT PROPERTY.
Collateral accepted for appearance before Magistrate regarding violations, §10-509.04.
Designation of employees to protect life and property on, §10-509.01.
Fines for violation of provisions regarding, §10-509.03.
Issuance of rules and regulations regarding, §10-509.02.
Juvenile facilities, escape from, §10-509.01a.
Penalties for violation of provisions regarding, §10-509.03.
Reciprocal agreements regarding, §10-509.05.

OUT-OF-STATE CHILD CUSTODY PROCEEDINGS.
See CHILD CUSTODY AND CHILD CUSTODY PROCEEDINGS.

OUT-OF-STATE LAW ENFORCEMENT OFFICERS AND AGENCIES.
Arrests in District made by, §23-901.
Reciprocal agreements, §§2-209.01 to 2-209.04.
Registration of, §§5-1201, 5-1302.

OUT-OF-STATE PARENTAGE DETERMINATIONS, §16-909.02.

OUT-OF-STATE TERMINATION OF PARENTAL RIGHTS, §16-2365.

OUT-OF-STATE WITNESSES.
Compelling attendance at hearings, §§23-1501 to 23-1504.

OVERCROWDING IN PRISONS.
Cap on prisoners housed at District of Columbia jail, §24-201.61.
Central detention facility.
Maximum number of inmates, §24-201.71.
New housing or facilities used as prisons.
Requirements, §24-201.72.

OVERDOSE.
Seeking medical attention for victim of drug overdose.
Mitigating factor in sentencing for certain offenses, §7-403.

OVERNIGHT SHELTER.
Emergency shelter allowances, §4-206.05.

OVERPAYMENTS.
Disability compensation for public officers and employees, §1-623.29.
Police and firefighters retirement and disability, §5-721.
Rental of public space, §10-1103.04a.

OVERTIME.
Merit system compensation policy, §1-611.03.
Minimum wage law.
Time and a half, §32-1003.
Police and firefighters, §§5-405, 5-1304.
Public officers and employees.
Exemption of district employees on compressed schedule from federal overtime requirements, §1-510.
Public safety overtime bank, §1-301.151.

P

PACKAGING.
Forgery, §22-1502.
Phosphate cleaners, §8-107.02.

PAGES.
Schools and education, §38-152.

PAINT.
Lead-hazard prevention and elimination, §§8-231.01 to 8-231.20.
See LEAD-HAZARD PREVENTION AND ELIMINATION.
Paint stewardship, §§8-233.01 to 8-233.06.
Assessment, §8-233.02.
Confidentiality of information, §8-233.05.
Definitions, §8-233.01.
Enforcement, §8-233.06.
Immunity from liability, compliance with chapter, §8-233.05.
Mayor's responsibilities, §8-233.04.
Rules, §8-233.06.
Producer paint stewardship plan required, §8-233.02.

PAINT —Cont'd
Paint stewardship —Cont'd
Retailer obligations, §8-233.03.
Rules, §8-233.06.

PANAMA CANAL ZONE.
Acknowledgment of deed, §42-111.

PANDERING.
Prostitution.
General provisions, §§22-2701 to
22-2725.
See PROSTITUTION.

PANHANDLING, §§22-2301 to 22-2306.
Definitions, §22-2301.
**Disclosure of arrests and
convictions for,** §22-2306.
Fines, §22-2304.
Penalties, §22-2304.
Permitted acts, §22-2303.
Prohibited acts, §22-2302.
Prosecutions, §22-2305.

PARACHUTES.
Crimes and offenses, §22-1317.

PARADES.
Capitol grounds, on, §10-503.17.
Emancipation day parade, §1-182.

PARAMEDICS.
**Cardiopulmonary resuscitation in
case of cardiac arrest.**
Non-resuscitation procedures for EMS,
§§7-651.01 to 7-651.16.
See EMERGENCY MEDICAL
SERVICES.
Certification, §5-441.
Transfer to be uniform firefighters.
Fire and emergency services
department personnel, §§5-409.01,
5-544.01.

PARDONS.
Constitution of the United States,
US Const Art II §2.
Mayor.
Power to grant pardons and respites,
§1-301.76.
President, US Const Art II §2.
Three strikes rule, §22-1804a.

PARENTAGE IDENTIFICATION,
§4-217.08.

PARENTAGE PROCEEDINGS,
§§16-2341 to 16-2348.
Acknowledgment.
Voluntary acknowledgment,
§§16-909.01, 16-2342.01.
Birth records, §§16-909.04, 16-2345.

PARENTAGE PROCEEDINGS
—Cont'd
Artificial insemination.
Presumptions and proof of parentage,
§16-909.
Birth as proof of maternity, §16-909.
Birth records agencies.
Voluntary parentage acknowledgment
program, §16-909.04.
Blood tests, DomRel Rule 405.
Child custody.
Uniform child custody proceedings,
§§16-4601.01 to 16-4605.03.
See CHILD CUSTODY AND CHILD
CUSTODY PROCEEDINGS.
Child support enforcement.
IV-D agency generally, §§46-226.01 to
46-227.
See CHILD SUPPORT
ENFORCEMENT.
Child support pendente lite,
§16-2349.01.
Commencement of action, DomRel
Rule 405.
Death of respondent, §16-2347.
Defaults, §16-2343.03.
Disclosure, §16-2348.
**Divorce and annulment proceedings,
establishing parentage in
context of,** §§16-907 to 16-909.03.
Domestic abuse victims.
Privacy protection in proceedings,
§16-925.
**Domestic relations actions
generally,** DomRel Rules 1 to 406.
See DOMESTIC RELATIONS
ACTIONS.
Estate, liability of, §16-2347.
Failure to respond, DomRel Rule 405.
Genetic testing.
Establishing, §§16-909.01, 16-2343.
Hearing commissioners, DomRel Rule
405.
Inspection of records, §16-2348.
Interpreters, §2-1902.
Interstate family support.
General provisions, §§46-351.01 to
46-359.03.
See INTERSTATE FAMILY
SUPPORT.
Physical presence in District.
Not required to determine parentage
of child, §46-353.16.
Proceeding to determine parentage,
§46-354.02.

PARENTAGE PROCEEDINGS
—Cont'd
Interstate family support —Cont'd
Voluntary acknowledgment of
paternity.
Admissible to establish parentage of
child, §46-353.16.
Judgment of parentage, DomRel Rule
405.
Jury trial, no right to, §16-2343.04.
Limitation of actions, §16-2342.
New birth record, issuance of,
§16-2345.
Order of filiation/support, DomRel
Form 12.
Petition to establish and provide
support, DomRel Form 11.
Privacy and confidentiality,
§16-2348.
Public excluded from, §16-2344.
Records, §16-2348.
Social Security numbers, inclusion of,
§16-2349.
Right to counsel, §16-2341.
Surrogate parenting contracts,
§§16-401, 16-402.
Tax returns or other tax
information.
Disclosure for parentage purposes,
§47-1805.04.
Termination of parental rights.
General provisions, §§16-2351 to
16-2365.
See TERMINATION OF PARENTAL
RIGHTS.
Tests to establish parentage,
§§16-2343 to 16-2343.02.
Admissibility of tests, §16-2343.01.
Genetic testing, §§16-909.01, 16-2343.
Voluntary acknowledgment of
parentage, §§16-909.01,
16-2342.01.
Birth records, §§16-909.04, 16-2345.
Voluntary parentage
acknowledgment program.
Birth records agencies, §16-909.01.
Mayoral designation of other sites,
§16-909.05.

PARENTAL KIDNAPPING, §§16-1021
to 16-1026.
Defense to prosecution, §16-1023.
Definitions, §16-1021.
Expenses incurred in returning
child, §16-1023.
Law enforcement officer taking
child into custody, return,
§16-1023.

PARENTAL KIDNAPPING —Cont'd
Petition filed by person in violation
of section 1022, §16-1023.
Prohibited acts, §16-1022.
Continuous offenses, §16-1023.
Expungement of records relating to
conviction, §16-1026.
Penalties, §16-1024.
Prosecutions, §16-1025.
Venue for prosecution, §16-1023.

PARENTAL LEAVE TO ATTEND OR
PARTICIPATE IN SCHOOL-
RELATED EVENT, §§32-1201 to
32-1206.
Administrative enforcement,
§32-1204.
Amount of leave, §32-1202.
Civil action to enforce, §32-1205.
Definitions, §32-1201.
Denial of leave, §32-1202.
Employment benefits or seniority
not affected, §32-1203.
Notice of provisions, §32-1206.
Notification to employer, §32-1202.
School-related event defined,
§32-1201.

PARENT AND CHILD.
Adoption.
General provisions, §§16-301 to
16-317, Adoption Rules 1 to 201.
See ADOPTION.
Anatomical gifts.
Who may make gift.
Before donor's death, §7-1531.03.
Decedent's body or parts,
§7-1531.08.
Born out of wedlock.
Defined, §16-907.
Breastmilk bank and lactation
support, §§7-881.01 to 7-881.11.
Child labor.
Applications for street trade badges.
Consent of parent, guardian, etc.,
§32-217.
Custodial power of attorney.
Parents authorized to create,
§21-2301.
Death of parent.
Standby guardianship for child,
§§16-4801 to 16-4810.
See GUARDIAN AND WARD.
Deeds between parent and child.
Exemptions from recordation tax,
§42-1102.
Domestic violence.
General provisions, §§16-1031 to
16-1034.

PARENT AND CHILD —Cont'd
Foster care.
General provisions, §§4-217.01 to
4-217.11.
See FOSTER CARE.
Guardianship of minors.
General provisions, §§21-101 to
21-182.
See GUARDIAN AND WARD.
Intervention proceedings, Probate
Rules 301 to 361.
See INTERVENTION
PROCEEDINGS.
Standby guardianship, §§16-4801 to
16-4810.
See GUARDIAN AND WARD.
Incapacity of parent.
Standby guardianship for child,
§§16-4801 to 16-4810.
See GUARDIAN AND WARD.
Incest, §22-1901.
Intestates' estates.
Generally, §§19-101.01 to 19-701.
See INTESTATE SUCCESSION.
Intrafamily proceedings, §§16-1001 to
16-1006.
See INTRAFAMILY PROCEEDINGS.
Kidnapping.
Parental kidnapping, §§16-1021 to
16-1026.
Legitimacy of children.
Definitions, §16-907.
Intestate succession, §§19-316, 19-318.
Parent and child relationship not
affected by status, §16-908.
Marriage.
Annulment.
Persons allowed to institute
annulment proceedings,
§46-404.
Consent of parent or guardian,
§46-411.
Legitimacy of child.
Relationship not dependent on
marriage, §16-908.
Parentage proceedings.
General provisions, §§16-2341 to
16-2348.
See PARENTAGE PROCEEDINGS.
Parental kidnapping, §§16-1021 to
16-1026.
See PARENTAL KIDNAPPING.
Personal representatives.
Trusts and trustees.
Uniform trust code, §19-1303.03.
Real property taxes.
Transfers without consideration,
exempt from tax, §47-802.

PARENT AND CHILD —Cont'd
Surrogate parenting contracts,
§16-401.
**Termination of parental rights of
certain neglected children.**
General provisions, §§16-2351 to
16-2365.
See TERMINATION OF PARENTAL
RIGHTS.
Trusts and trustees.
Uniform trust code.
Personal representatives,
§19-1303.03.

PARENT LOCATOR SERVICE.
Child support enforcement,
§46-224.02.

**PARENT-TEACHER
CONFERENCES,** §38-1809.01.

PARKING, §§50-2601 to 50-2624.
**Abandoned and unlawfully parked
vehicles,** §§50-2421.01 to
50-2421.15.
**Adams Morgan taxicab zone pilot
program,** §50-2536.
Appropriations, §50-2608.
Armory board, §3-304.
**Ballpark performance parking pilot
zone,** §50-2532.
Barbed-wire fences, §§9-1213.01 to
9-1213.05.
Bicycle parking, §§50-1641.01 to
50-1641.09.
See BICYCLES.
Building lines, §6-405.
Business improvement districts.
BID parking abatement fund,
§1-325.341.
Congressional parking, §§50-2201.03,
50-2631.
**Contractors, daytime parking
permit,** §50-2635.
Declaration of necessity regarding,
§50-2601.
Definitions, §50-2602.
Departments and agencies.
Motor Vehicle Parking Agency,
§50-2608.
Districts, §50-2511.
Facilities.
Business licenses, §47-2832.01.
Constructing and maintaining,
§50-2603.
Defined, §50-2602.
Establishment of, §50-2605.
Property for, acquiring and disposing
of, §50-2603.

PARKING —Cont'd
Federal property, §50-2624.
Fees.
Deposit into fund, §50-2607.
Rates, setting, §50-2603.
Funds.
Deposit of fees and moneys into fund,
§50-2607.
Establishment of parking system fund,
§50-2510.
Mayor's use of funds, §50-2603.
H Street N.E. performance parking
pilot zone, §50-2532.01.
Mayor's powers regarding, §50-2603.
Meters, §50-2603.
Breaking and entering, §22-601.
Fee moratorium, exceptions,
§50-2633.01.
Motor vehicle parking agency,
§50-2608.
Mount Pleasant visitor pass pilot
program, §50-2537.
Neighborhood commercial centers,
§50-2634.
Parks and recreation, §10-106.
Penn Quarter/Chinatown
performance parking pilot zone,
§50-2532.02.
Performance parking zones,
§§50-2531 to 50-2535.
Ballpark performance parking pilot
zone, §50-2532.
Columbia Heights retail performance
parking pilot zone, §50-2533.
Expenditure of generated revenues,
§50-2534.
Fund, §50-2531.01.
H Street NE performance parking
pilot zone, §50-2532.01.
Penn Quarter/Chinatown performance
parking pilot zone, §50-2532.02.
Purpose, §50-2531.
Reporting requirements and oversight,
§50-2535.
Policy declaration, §50-2601.
Property for parking facilities,
acquiring and disposing of,
§50-2603.
Public parking authority.
General provisions, §§50-2501 to
50-2514.
See PUBLIC PARKING
AUTHORITY.
Rates, establishment of, §50-2603.
Records and data for planning
purposes, availability of,
§50-2606.

PARKING —Cont'd
Residential parking protections.
Rules, §50-2552.
Ward 1 enhanced residential parking
program, §50-2551.
Rulemaking, council review,
§50-2610.
Signs advertising real property for
rent or for sale, §42-1801.
Small claims court forms.
Damage to parked vehicle,
SmallClaims Form 6.
Street repairs and improvements,
§50-2603.
Traffic ticket adjudication for
parking infractions.
See TRAFFIC TICKET
ADJUDICATION.
Unlawfully parked or abandoned
vehicles, §§50-2421.01 to
50-2421.15, 50-2637.
Ward 1 enhanced residential
parking program, §50-2551.
Rules, §50-2552.

PARKING METER PAY-BY-PHONE
TRANSACTION FEE FUND,
§50-921.14.

PARKING METERS, §50-2603.
Breaking and entering, §22-601.
Fee moratorium, exceptions,
§50-2633.01.

PARK PLACE AT PETWORTH,
HIGHLAND PARK, AND
HIGHLAND PARK PHASE II
PROJECTS.
Real property tax exemptions,
§47-4629.

PARK POLICE.
General provisions, §§5-201 to 5-208.
See UNITED STATES PARK POLICE.
Wages and salaries.
Holidays, working on, §5-521.03.
Locality-based comparability
adjustments, freeze, §5-563.02.
Termination of special salary rates,
§5-563.01.

PARKS AND RECREATION, §§10-101
to 10-308.
Acquisition of rights to real
property, §10-101.
Adoption of parks, §10-304.
Anacostia Park, §10-155.
Anacostia River, United States title
to lands or waters of, §10-102.

PARKS AND RECREATION —Cont'd
Athletic field permit coordination committee, §10-308.
Authority of Director of Department of Recreation and Parks, §10-137.01.
Automated external defibrillators, usage, §§44-231 to 44-235.
Bathing pools and beaches, §§10-162 to 10-165.
Beach Parkway.
Exchange of property to extend, §10-117.
Dedication and conveyances, §10-118.
Power of Secretary of Interior to sell not curtailed, §10-119.
Budget and budget estimates, §10-214.
Building, Congressional approval required for, §10-128.
Burial ground for indigent persons, part of reservation 13 transferred for, §10-135.
Canals, public spaces resulting from filling in of, §10-139.
Care of public grounds.
Division of park services, §10-166.
Issuance of rules and regulations for, §10-137.
Carriageways, §10-138.
Child and adult food program funding.
Use of department facilities, §38-284.
Children's island development plan, §§10-1431, 10-1432.
Composition of park system, §10-104.
Construction, Congressional approval required for, §10-128.
Control of park system, §10-104.
Department of parks and recreation, §§10-137.01, 10-137.02, 10-166, 10-302.
Division of park services, §10-166.
Dog parks.
At large does not include dog in dog park, §8-1801.
Defined, §8-1801.
Establishment, requirements, §8-1808.01.
Domestic tour bus program, §50-1531.
Eastern Branch, United States title to lands or waters of, §10-102.
Excess property for development of seat of government.
Retention for public use, §16-1334.

PARKS AND RECREATION —Cont'd
Excess property for United States.
Retention for public use, §16-1382.
Federal government.
Property exchanges with, §§10-114 to 10-119.
Transfer of jurisdiction between District and federal government, §§10-111, 10-112.
Fees, §10-213.01.
Former Georgetown Reservoir site, §10-136.
Fort Davis Park, §10-121.
Fort Dupont Park, §10-121.
Fund, §10-303.
Fundraising for recreational facilities, §§10-301 to 10-308.
Glover Parkway and children's playground, §§10-156, 10-157.
Indigent burial ground.
Part of reservation 13 transferred for, §10-135.
Leases, §§10-103, 10-143, 10-213.
Mega recreation centers, §10-305.
Meridian Hill Park, §10-108.
Montrose Park, §10-109.
National Children's Island, §§10-1401 to 10-1406.
Parking, §10-106.
Park Police.
General provisions, §§5-201 to 5-208.
See UNITED STATES PARK POLICE.
Parks and recreation department, §§10-137.01, 10-137.02, 10-166, 10-302.
Parkways.
See PARKWAYS.
Permits.
Athletic field permit coordination committee, §10-308.
Piney Branch Parkway, §10-146.
Playgrounds.
Drug free zones, §48-904.07a.
Excess property for development of seat of government.
Retention for public use, §16-1334.
Excess property for United States.
Retention for public use, §16-1382.
Firearms.
Enhanced penalties and fines for carrying guns into gun free zones, §22-4502.01.
Glover Parkway and children's playground, §§10-156, 10-157.
Issuance of rules and regulations, §10-127.

PARKS AND RECREATION —Cont'd
Playgrounds —Cont'd
Leasing land for, §10-103.
National Children's Island, §§10-1401 to 10-1406.
Temporary structures on reservations used as, §10-125.
Use of public grounds for, §10-124.
Washington Aqueduct land, §10-126.
Policies and programs division, §10-166.01.
Potomac Park, §§10-147 to 10-151.
Boathouses on banks of tidal reservoir. Licenses, §10-151.
Construction of lagoon, artificial body of water or speedway.
Restriction on expenditure of money, §10-149.
Control, §10-148.
Established, §10-147.
Parkway connecting park with Zoological and Rock Creek Parks, §§10-152, 10-153.
Temporary occupancy by Department of Agriculture, §10-150.
Potomac River, United States title to lands or waters of, §10-102.
Public Works Department, §10-166.
Recreation Assistance Board.
Rules, §10-307.
Recreation board, §§10-201 to 10-226. See RECREATION BOARD.
Repair and maintenance, §10-224.
Reports, §10-215.
Reservations.
Playgrounds.
Temporary structures on reservations used as, §10-125.
Transfer of jurisdiction. See within this heading, "Transfer of jurisdiction."
Widening roadways, §10-123.
Rock Creek Park, §§10-140 to 10-145.
Acceptance of dedicated property, §10-144.
Control, §10-142.
Duties of director of National Park Service, §10-142.
Established, §10-140.
Leasing authorized, disposition of proceeds, §10-143.
Protection of Rock Creek, §10-145.
Regulations, §10-142.
Total area of lands acquired, §10-141.
United States title to lands or waters of, §10-102.

PARKS AND RECREATION —Cont'd
Sidewalks, §10-138.
Small parks at street intersections outside original city limits, §10-107.
Sponsorship of parks, §10-304.
Squares 612 and 613, §10-120.
Street portions set aside as parks, §9-1201.06.
Superintendent of Recreation, §10-212.
Swimming, §§10-162 to 10-165.
Theodore Roosevelt Island, §§10-158 to 10-161.
Tidal basin (Potomac Park), §§10-147 to 10-151.
Toilet facilities, §§10-133, 10-134.
Traffic laws, §§10-105, 50-2201.07.
Transfer of jurisdiction.
Division of park services, §10-166.
Federal and District governments, between, §§10-111, 10-112.
Letters of transfer and acceptance, §10-129.
Reservation 8, §10-132.
Reservation 13, §10-135.
Reservation 32, §10-130.
Reservation 185, §10-122.
Reservation 290, §10-131.
Washington Aqueduct land transferred for playground purposes, §10-126.
Water Street, §10-110.
Whitehaven Parkway, §§10-113 to 10-116.
Boundaries, §10-113.
Exchange of federal property, §10-114.
Exchange with property owners, §10-115.
Plats prepared, §10-116.
Widening roadways, §10-123.
Zoological Park and Rock Creek Park with Potomac Park.
Parkway connecting, §§10-152 to 10-154.

PARKSIDE PARCEL E AND J MIXED-INCOME APARTMENTS.
Real property tax exemptions, §47-4658.

PARKSIDE TERRACE DEVELOPMENT PROJECT.
Tax exemptions, §47-4607.

PARKWAYS.
Beach Parkway, property exchange to extend, §§10-117 to 10-119.

PARKWAYS —Cont'd

Glover Parkway and children's playground, §§10-156, 10-157.

Piney Branch Parkway, §10-146.

Whitehaven Parkway, §§10-113 to 10-116.

Boundaries, §10-113.

Zoological Park and Rock Creek Park with Potomac Park.

Connecting, §§10-152 to 10-154.

PAROLE, §§24-401c to 24-468.

Application for, §24-401c.

Appropriations, §24-134.

Arrest for violation of, §§24-405, 24-406.

Authorization of, §24-404.

Board of Parole (District).

Medical and geriatric parole, authority over, §24-463.

Board of Parole (federal), §24-409.

BOOT CAMP juveniles, post-camp supervision of, §24-931.

Court Services and Offender Supervision Agency, §24-133.

Credit for time served in custody or on parole, §§24-221.03, 24-406.

Custody of parolees, §24-404.

Detection device.

Tampering by persons required to wear, §22-1211.

Discharge from, §24-404.

Educational good time credits, §24-221.01.

Eligibility for, §24-408.

Federal control of prison system, under, §§24-131 to 24-134.

Federal Parole Board, §24-409.

Felonies committed on or after August 5, 2000, §24-403.01.

Geriatric parole, §§24-461 to 24-468.

See within this heading, "Medical and geriatric parole."

Health, parole for reasons of, §§24-461 to 24-468.

Hearing following arrest for violation of, §24-406.

Inconsistent laws regarding, repeal of, §24-407.

Indeterminate sentences, §24-403.

Interstate parole and probation compact, §§24-451 to 24-453.

Authority of mayor to execute, §24-451.

Definitions, §24-452.

Severability, §24-453.

Jurisdiction, §24-131.

PAROLE —Cont'd

Life sentences, §24-403.

Maximum sentences, §24-403.

Medical and geriatric parole, §§24-461 to 24-468.

Authority of Board of Parole over, §24-463.

Criteria for geriatric release, §24-465.

Criteria for medical release, §24-464.

Definitions, §24-461.

Exceptions to eligibility, §24-467.

Exclusion of conditions present at time of sentence, §24-462.

Public assistance, eligibility for, §24-466.

Suspension of sentence, §24-468.

Mental health disclosures, §7-1204.03.

Minimum sentences, §24-403.

Murder.

First degree murder, §22-2104.

Pretrial services agency, §24-132.

Public assistance denied to parole violators, §4-205.70.

Repeal of inconsistent laws regarding, §24-407.

Reports on eligibility for, §24-221.05.

Sexual psychopaths, §22-3809.

Termination of legal custody over parolee prior to end of sentence, §24-404.

Violation of, §24-405.

PAROL EVIDENCE.

Sale of goods.

Contracts, §28:2-202.

Sales.

Written contract for sale.

Modification, §28:2-209.

Special promise to answer for debt or default of another, §28-3502.

PARTIAL DISABILITY.

Disability compensation for public employees, §1-623.06.

PARTIES.

Adoption proceedings, Adoption Rule 17.

Death or incompetency of party, Adoption Rule 25.

Appeals, D.C. courts.

Definition of "appellant" and "appellee," DCCtApp Rule 1.

Substitution of parties, DCCtApp Rule 43.

Appeals, federal cases.

Multiple appellants or appellees, briefs in cases involving, FRAP 28(i).

PARTIES —Cont'd

Appeals, federal cases —Cont'd

Non-appearance of parties, decision on briefs, FRAP 34(e).

Petition for hearing or rehearing en banc, FRAP 35(b).

References in briefs to, FRAP 28(d).

Statutes challenged on constitutional grounds.

Federal statute, FRAP 44(a).

State statute, FRAP 44(b).

Substitution of parties, FRAP 43.

Capacity.

Law determining capacity, CivPro Rule 17.

Domestic relations actions, DomRel Rule 17.

Pleading special matters, CivPro Rule 9.

Domestic relations actions, DomRel Rule 9.

Child abuse and neglect proceedings, NeglectProc Rule 10.

Child custody proceedings.

Appearances of parities and child, §16-4602.10.

Children and minors, CivPro Rule 17.

Domestic relations actions, DomRel Rule 17.

Class actions, CivPro Rule 23.

Collaborative law, §16-4011.

Death of party, CivPro Rule 25.

Adoption proceedings, Adoption Rule 25.

Domestic relations actions, DomRel Rule 25.

Suggestion of death upon the record, CivPro Form CA 30.

Domestic relations actions.

See DOMESTIC RELATIONS ACTIONS.

Guardianship of minors.

Permanent guardianship.

Motions for joinder or intervention, §16-2385.

Sale of property of infants, §21-149.

Incompetent persons, CivPro Rule 17.

Adoption proceedings, Adoption Rule 25.

Default judgment against incompetent person, CivPro Rule 55.

Domestic relations actions, DomRel Rule 17.

Substitution of parties, CivPro Rule 25.

Domestic relations actions, DomRel Rule 25.

PARTIES —Cont'd

Interpleader, CivPro Rule 22.

Complaint for interpleader, CivPro Form CA 18.

Counterclaim for interpleader, CivPro Form CA 21.

Intervention proceedings, Probate Rule 303.

Joinder of parties generally.

See JOINDER OF PARTIES.

Lis pendens notice, §42-1207.

Multiple party judgments, CivPro Rule 54.

Domestic relations actions, DomRel Rule 54.

Stay of proceedings, CivPro Rule 62.

Domestic relations actions, DomRel Rule 62.

Necessary parties.

Allegation of reason for omitting party, CivPro Form CA 26.

Joinder, CivPro Rule 19.

Domestic relations actions, DomRel Rule 19.

Next friend actions, CivPro Rule 17.

Domestic relations actions, DomRel Rule 17.

Nonparty to action.

Application for relief in a criminal case by persons not parties, USDistCt LCrR 57.6.

Enforcement of orders favoring non-parties, CivPro Rule 71.

Domestic relations actions, DomRel Rule 71.

Pleadings.

Name of parties, CivPro Rule 10, USDistCt LCvR 11.1.

Criminal proceedings, USDistCt LCrR 49.

Domestic relations actions, DomRel Rule 10.

Signature of party, CivPro Rule 11.

Real party in interest, CivPro Rule 17.

Domestic relations actions, DomRel Rule 17.

Substitution of parties, CivPro Rule 25.

Adoption proceedings, Adoption Rule 25.

Appeals, DCCtApp Rule 43.

Condemnation proceedings, CivPro Rule 71A.

Deposition's use not affected by substitution, CivPro Rule 32.

Domestic relations actions, DomRel Rule 25.

PARTIES —Cont'd
Substitution of parties —Cont'd
Intellectual disability proceedings,
MentalRetardation Rule 4A.
Third party practice, CivPro Rule 14.
Motion to bring in third party, CivPro
Form CA 22-B.
Summons and complaint against third
party defendant, CivPro Form CA
22-A.
Transfer of interest, CivPro Rule 25.
Domestic relations actions, DomRel
Rule 25.
United States.
Actions to which United States a
party, US Const Art III.
Usury.
Action to recover usury paid.
Parties compelled to testify,
§28-3306.

PARTITION.
Accounting by tenant in common,
§16-2901.
Horizontal property regimes,
§42-2007.
Parties to, §16-2901.
Service by publication on
nonresidents, §13-336.
Waste, writ of.
Joint tenants and tenants in common.
Action against cotenant, §42-1604.

PARTNERSHIPS, §§29-601.01 to
29-611.01.
Accounts, §29-604.01.
Settlement of, §29-608.07.
Actionable conduct.
Liability, §29-603.05.
Actions, §§29-603.07, 29-604.08.
Administrative dissolution.
Generally, §§29-106.01 to 29-106.04.
See BUSINESS ORGANIZATIONS.
Agents of partnership, partners as,
§29-603.01.
Appeals, federal cases.
Corporate disclosure statements,
FRAP 26.1, USCtApp Rule 26.1.
Applicability of law, §29-601.07.
Attachment of partnership interests,
§16-511.
Bankruptcy.
Petitions, USDistDCBank Rule 1004-1.
Becoming a partner, §29-604.02.
Campaign finance contributions,
§1-1163.34.
Class actions.
Unincorporated associations, CivPro
Rule 23.2.

PARTNERSHIPS —Cont'd
Continuation beyond definite term
or undertaking, §29-604.09.
Contributions.
Form, §29-604.03.
Liability for, §29-604.04.
Settlement of, §29-608.07.
Definitions, §29-601.02.
Dissociation of partners, §§29-606.01
to 29-606.03.
Effect of, §29-606.03.
Events causing, §29-606.01.
Power of dissociated partner to bind
partnership, §29-607.02.
Continued use of partnership name,
§29-607.05.
Statement of dissociation,
§29-607.04.
Powers of partner, §29-606.02.
When business not wound up,
§§29-607.01 to 29-607.05.
Liability of dissociated partner,
§29-607.03.
Purchase of dissociated partner's
interest, §29-607.01.
Wrongful dissociation, §29-606.02.
Dissolution, §§29-608.01 to 29-608.12.
Barred claims against dissolved
partnership, §§29-608.08,
29-608.09.
Liability of partners, §29-608.11.
Continuation of partnership,
§29-608.02.
Court proceedings regarding claims,
§29-608.10.
Distributions before dissolution and
winding up, §29-604.05.
Events causing, §29-608.01.
Known claims against dissolved
partnership, §29-608.08.
Liability of partner after, §29-608.06.
Other claims against dissolved
partnership, §29-608.09.
Partner's power to bind partnership
after, §29-608.04.
Rescission of dissolution, §29-608.12.
Settlement of accounts and
distributions, §29-608.07.
Statement of dissolution, §29-608.05.
Unknown claims against dissolved
partnership, §29-608.09.
Winding up, §29-608.03.
Distributions in kind, §29-604.05.
Execution of statements, §29-601.05.
Fiduciary duties of partners,
§29-604.07.

PARTNERSHIPS —Cont'd
Filing.
  Court action to require person to sign
    or file record, §29-601.10.
  Generally, §§29-102.01 to 29-102.13.
    See BUSINESS ORGANIZATIONS.
  Inaccurate information in filed record,
    liability for, §29-601.11.
  Statements, §29-601.05.
Foreign commerce.
  Applicability of law, §29-601.07.
Foreign entities.
  Generally, §§29-105.01 to 29-105.12.
    See BUSINESS ORGANIZATIONS.
Formation of, §29-602.02.
  Becoming a partner, §29-604.02.
General provisions, §§29-601.01 to
  29-601.11.
Governing law, §29-601.06.
Income taxes, §§47-1805.02,
  47-1808.06.
Indemnification of partners,
  §29-604.01.
Insurance against liability,
  §29-604.01.
Interest exchanges, §29-609.05.
Interstate commerce.
  Applicability of law, §29-601.07.
Knowledge, §29-601.03.
Legal entity, §29-602.01.
Liability.
  Actionable conduct, §29-603.05.
  Barred claims against dissolved
    partnership.
    Liability of partners, §29-608.11.
  Contributions, §29-604.04.
  Dissociation of partners when business
    not wound up, §29-607.03.
  Dissolution.
    Liability of partner after,
      §29-608.06.
  Inaccurate information in filed record,
    liability for, §29-601.11.
  Insurance against liability, §29-604.01.
  Partners, §29-603.06.
  Purported partners, §29-603.08.
Limited liability partnerships.
  General provisions.
    See LIMITED LIABILITY
      PARTNERSHIPS.
Limited partnerships, §§29-701.01 to
  29-711.01.
  See LIMITED PARTNERSHIPS.
Management rights, §29-604.01.
Mergers and consolidations,
  §§29-609.01 to 29-609.06.
  Definitions, §29-609.01.

PARTNERSHIPS —Cont'd
Mergers and consolidations —Cont'd
  Effect of, §29-609.03.
  Interest exchanges, §29-609.05.
  Nonexclusivity of provisions,
    §29-609.06.
  Plans, §29-609.02.
  Statement of merger, §29-609.04.
Names.
  Generally, §§29-103.01 to 29-103.04.
    See BUSINESS ORGANIZATIONS.
Nature of partnership, §§29-602.01 to
  29-602.04.
Notice, §29-601.03.
  Dissolution.
    Known claims against dissolved
      partnership, §29-608.08.
    Other claims against dissolved
      partnership, §29-608.09.
Partnership agreements.
  Amendments, §29-601.09.
  Assent to agreement by person
    becoming partner, §29-601.08.
  Creation and enforcement of,
    §29-601.08.
  Effect of, §29-601.04.
  Ineffective provisions, §29-601.09.
  Nonwaivable provisions, §29-601.04.
  Permissible and nonpermissible
    provisions, §29-601.04.
  Third parties, effect on, §29-601.09.
Personal property.
  Transferable interests of partners as,
    §29-605.02.
Professional corporations.
  Powers, §29-505.
Profits and losses, §29-604.01.
Property, §§29-602.03, 29-602.04.
  Partner not deemed co-owner of,
    §29-605.01.
  Transfer of, §29-603.02.
Public-private partnerships,
  §§2-271.01 to 2-275.01.
  See PUBLIC-PRIVATE
    PARTNERSHIPS.
Purported partners.
  Liability, §29-603.08.
Recording of statements, §29-601.05.
Registered agents.
  Generally, §§29-104.01 to 29-104.14.
    See BUSINESS ORGANIZATIONS.
Reimbursements and advancements,
  §29-604.01.
**Relations of partners to each other
  and to partnership,** §§29-604.01 to
  29-604.09.

PARTNERSHIPS —Cont'd
Relations of partners to other persons, §§29-603.01 to 29-603.08.
Rights and duties of partners, §29-604.01.
Information, §29-604.06.
Schools and education, §§38-1806.01 to 38-1806.09.
Service of process on partnership.
Domestic relations actions, DomRel Rule 4.
Summons, CivPro Rule 4.
Short title, §29-601.01.
Signatures.
Court action to require person to sign or file record, §29-601.10.
Liability for inaccurate information in filed record, §29-601.11.
Standards of conduct, §29-604.07.
Statement of denial, §29-603.04.
Statement of partnership authority, §29-603.03.
Transferable interests of partners, §§29-605.01 to 29-605.05.
Charging orders, §29-605.04.
Deceased partner, power of legal representative, §29-605.05.
Partner not deemed co-owner of partnership property, §29-605.01.
Personal property, §29-605.02.
Transfer of, §29-605.03.
Transitional provisions, §29-611.01.
Uniform fiduciaries act, §§21-1701 to 21-1712.
See FIDUCIARIES.
Winding up, §29-608.03.
Distributions before dissolution and winding up, §29-604.05.
Wrongful dissociation, §29-606.02.

PARTY WALLS, §§1-1325 to 1-1328.
Adjusting lines of buildings, §1-1328.
Certification and recording location, §1-1327.
Payment of reasonable price, §1-1325.
Wall extending over lot line, §1-1326.

PASSENGER VEHICLES FOR HIRE.
Business licenses, §47-2829.
Taxicabs.
See TAXICABS.

PATENTS.
Congress, US Const Art I §8.
Inventions.
Constitutional provisions, US Const Art I §8.

PATERNITY PROCEEDINGS.
See PARENTAGE PROCEEDINGS.

PAWNBROKERS, §§47-2884.01 to 47-2884.19.
Advertising, §47-2884.08.
Ammunition prohibited as pawns, §7-2507.01.
Appeals, §47-2884.07.
Attorney, appointment of mayor as, §47-2884.03.
Capital requirements, §47-2884.03.
Definitions, §47-2884.01.
Enforcement of provisions, §47-2884.07.
Exceptions, §47-2884.18.
Excessive consideration prohibited, §47-2884.10.
Firearms prohibited as pawns, §7-2507.01.
Interest rates.
Excessive consideration prohibited, §47-2884.10.
Maximum rate, §47-2884.09.
Investigation by mayor, §47-2884.09.
Issuance of rules and regulations, §47-2884.17.
Law enforcement officers allowed access to premises and books, §47-2884.11.
Licenses, §§47-2884.02 to 47-2884.07.
Application for, §47-2884.03.
Appointment of mayor as attorney required for, §47-2884.03.
Display of, §47-2884.05.
Fees, §§47-2884.03 to 47-2884.06.
Issuance of, §47-2884.05.
Notice to advisory neighborhood commissions prior to issuance, §47-2884.03.
Renewal, §47-2884.06.
Requirement to have, §47-2884.02.
Revocation or suspension, §47-2884.06.
Loans, §§47-2884.08 to 47-2884.16.
Books containing loans transactions required, §47-2884.11.
Instruments evidencing loan made in violation invalid and unenforceable, §47-2884.10.
Loans made outside District, §47-2884.10.
Memorandum of loan transaction, §47-2884.12.
Payment at anytime, §47-2884.09.
Right to rescind, §47-2884.09.
Mayor as attorney, §47-2884.03.

PAWNBROKERS —Cont'd

Metropolitan police examination of premises, books, and pledged property, §§5-117.02 to 5-117.04.

Name or place of business, transfer or change of, §47-2884.05.

Notice of sale of pawn or pledge, §47-2884.14.

Penalties, §47-2884.16.

Rates and charges.

Advertising, stating in, §47-2884.08.

Excessive consideration prohibited, §47-2884.10.

Records, §§47-2884.07, 47-2884.11.

Return of pawn or pledge, §47-2884.16.

Rules and regulations, §47-2884.17.

Sale of pawn or pledge, §§47-2884.13 to 47-2884.15.

Severability of provisions, §47-2884.19.

Sign or emblem, display of, §47-2884.02.

Surplus from sale of pawn or pledge, §47-2884.15.

PAY.

See WAGES AND SALARIES.

PAYDAY LOANS.

Check cashing businesses, §§26-301 to 26-323.

See CHECK CASHING BUSINESSES.

PAY EQUITY AND TRAINING COMMISSION, §§32-601 to 32-609.

PAY-FOR-SUCCESS CONTRACTS, §§2-211.01 to 2-211.03.

Authorization, §2-211.02.

Contents, §2-211.02.

Definitions, §2-211.01.

Fund, §2-211.03.

PAYMENT ON DEATH (POD) ACCOUNTS.

TOD security registration, §§19-603.01 to 19-603.11.

See NONPROBATE TRANSFERS.

PAYMENTS IN LIEU OF TAXES, §47-1052.

Generally, §§1-308.01 to 1-308.10.

See BOND ISSUES.

Lots 826 and 831, square 491, §47-1064.

Southwest waterfront.

PILOT/TIF area, §47-4616.

PAY TELEPHONE SERVICE PROVIDERS.

Public service commission.

Rules and regulations, power to prescribe, §34-1831.

PEACE, DISTURBING, §§22-1301 to 22-1323.

PEDDLING DRUGS, §§47-2885.17, 47-2885.17a.

PEDESTRIANS.

Advisory council, §50-1931.

Bicycle and pedestrian priority area program, §50-2371.

Blind pedestrians, safety standards regarding, §7-1004.

Complete streets policy, §50-2381.

Deaf pedestrians, safety standards regarding, §7-1004.

Identification of pedestrian offenders, §50-2303.07.

Motor vehicle accidents.

Open access to data and information.

General provisions, §§50-1951.01 to 50-1951.07.

Non-motorized user contributory negligence, §§50-2204.51 to 50-2204.53.

Parking, standing, stopping, and pedestrian infractions, §§50-2303.01 to 50-2303.11.

See TRAFFIC TICKET ADJUDICATION.

Public structures in public space.

Safe accommodation for pedestrians and cyclists required when path is obstructed, §§10-1141.03, 10-1141.04.

Right-of-way at crosswalks, §50-2201.28.

Special signs for failure to yield to pedestrian, §50-2201.30.

PEEPING TOMS.

Voyeurism, §22-3531.

PEER REVIEW.

Medical records, §§44-801 to 44-805.

PENALTIES.

Fines.

See FINES AND CIVIL PENALTIES.

Forfeitures.

See FORFEITURES.

PENN QUARTER/CHINATOWN PERFORMANCE PARKING PILOT ZONE, §50-2532.02.

PENNSYLVANIA AVENUE BRIDGE,
§9-304.

PENSIONS AND RETIREMENT,
§§1-626.01 to 1-626.14.
Alienation of benefits, §1-911.03.
Annual report, §1-905.02.
Civil actions, §§1-626.14, 1-747, 1-748.
Contracting authority, §1-626.06.
Contribution requirements.
  Employer and employee, §1-626.09.
Corporations.
  Powers, §29-303.02.
Creditable service.
  Defined for purposes of vesting
    pursuant to §1-626.10(b),
    §1-626.04.
Definitions, §1-626.04.
Denial of claim for benefits, §§1-751
    to 1-753.
District benefits, §§1-626.03, 1-626.05.
Early distribution.
  Income tax withholding, §47-1812.08.
Effect of other laws, §1-911.04.
Eligibility to participate, §§1-626.07,
    1-626.08.
Employees retirement program
    management, §§1-701 to 1-753.
  See EMPLOYEES RETIREMENT
    PROGRAM MANAGEMENT.
Executive service, §1-610.62.
Existing systems, §1-626.02.
Federal benefit payments under
    District programs.
  Actions to enforce rights, claims or
    provisions of chapter, §1-815.01.
  Jurisdiction and venue, §1-815.02.
  Statute of limitations, §1-815.03.
  Alternative financing measures,
    §1-819.02.
  Amount of, §1-805.01.
  Coordination of actions, §1-819.01.
  Denial of payments, §1-805.02.
  Description of, §1-803.02.
  District of Columbia federal pension
    fund, §§1-817.01 to 1-817.06.
  Annual federal payments, §1-817.04.
  Applicability of other provisions,
    §1-817.06.
  Established, §1-817.01.
  Investment of assets, §1-817.01.
  Transfer of assets and obligations,
    §1-817.03.
  Trustee to administer, §1-817.05.
  Use of amounts in fund, §1-817.02.

PENSIONS AND RETIREMENT
  —Cont'd
Federal benefit payments under
    District programs —Cont'd
  District of Columbia federal pension
    liability trust fund, §§1-807.01 to
    1-807.06.
  ERISA.
    Treatment of fund, §1-807.04.
  Established, §1-807.01.
  Internal Revenue Code.
    Treatment of fund, §1-807.04.
  Investment of assets, §1-807.01.
  Termination, §1-807.06.
  Transfer of assets and obligations of
    district pension funds,
    §1-807.03.
  Trustee to administer fund,
    §1-807.05.
  Use of amounts in fund, §1-807.02.
  District responsibilities, §§1-809.01,
    1-809.02.
  Effect on other statutes, §1-819.04.
  Eligibility for, §1-805.01.
  Enforcement of provisions, §§1-815.01
    to 1-815.04.
  Federal supplemental District of
    Columbia pension fund, §§1-811.01
    to 1-811.06.
  Annual payment into fund.
    Determination, §1-811.03.
    Methods for making, §1-811.04.
  Discontinuation.
    Special requirements, §1-811.05.
  Established, §1-811.01.
  Investment of assets, §1-811.01.
  Termination, §1-811.06.
  Use of amounts in fund, §1-811.02.
  Full faith and credit of United States,
    backed by, §1-819.06.
  Funds.
    Federal Pension Fund, §§1-817.01 to
      1-817.06.
    Federal Pension Liability Trust
      Fund, §§1-807.01 to 1-807.06.
    Federal Supplemental Fund,
      §§1-811.01 to 1-811.06.
  Interim payments, §1-903.05.
  Issuance of rules and regulations,
    §1-819.03.
  Military service credit considered in
    benefit amount, §1-803.02.
  Misappropriation of fund federal
    crime, §1-815.04.
  Obligation to make, §1-803.01.
  Records, §1-805.03.

PENSIONS AND RETIREMENT
—Cont'd
Federal benefit payments under District programs —Cont'd
Replacement plan, §§1-809.02, 1-905.01 to 1-905.03.
Reports, §§1-813.01, 1-813.02.
Severability of provisions, §1-819.07.
Verification of benefit determinations, §1-805.04.
Financial disclosure by retirement board, §1-905.01.
Funds, §§1-801.01 to 1-821.01.
Actuarial statement, §1-907.04.
Audits, §1-903.06.
Bonds, surety, §1-909.09.
Definitions, §1-801.02.
Disclosure requirements, §§1-909.01 to 1-909.05.
Enforcement of provisions, §§1-911.01 to 1-911.04a.
Federal Pension Fund, §§1-817.01 to 1-817.06.
Federal Pension Liability Trust Fund, §§1-807.01 to 1-807.06.
Federal Supplemental Fund, §§1-811.01 to 1-811.06.
Fines, §1-909.08.
Investment limitations, §§1-721, 1-907.01.
Iran.
Certain companies doing business with government of Iran, §§1-336.01 to 1-336.06.
Sudan.
Certain companies doing business with government of Sudan, §§1-335.01 to 1-335.07.
Iran.
Investment in certain companies doing business with government of Iran, §§1-336.01 to 1-336.06.
Judges' retirement fund, §§1-714, 1-821.01.
Limitation of actions, §1-911.02.
Management requirements, §§1-715, 1-903.03.
Payments from, §§1-716, 1-903.04.
Payments to.
Appropriations authorized as, §1-724.
Federal and District governments, from, §§1-722, 1-907.02, 1-907.03.
Penalties, §1-909.08.
Police and firefighters retirement and disability, §§1-712, 1-903.01.

PENSIONS AND RETIREMENT
—Cont'd
Funds —Cont'd
Policy declaration, §§1-801.01, 1-901.01.
Records, §1-909.07.
Reports, §§1-813.01, 1-813.02, 1-909.02 to 1-909.06.
Sudan.
Investment in certain companies doing business with government of Sudan, §§1-335.01 to 1-335.07.
Teachers' retirement fund, §§1-713, 1-903.02.
Information about programs, §§1-723, 1-734 to 1-738, 1-907.05.
Issuance of rules and regulations regarding, §1-626.08.
Judicial retirement, §§11-1561 to 11-1572.
See JUDICIAL RETIREMENT.
Nonprofit corporations.
Powers, §29-403.02.
Payment of benefits, §1-626.12.
Police and firefighters retirement and disability.
General provisions, §§5-631 to 5-762.
See POLICE AND FIREFIGHTERS RETIREMENT AND DISABILITY.
Policy declaration, §1-626.01.
Powers of attorney, §21-2115.
Public disclosure, §1-909.05.
Replacement plan, §1-809.02.
Replacement program for covered employees, §1-905.01.
Eligibility and benefit determinations, §1-905.02.
Tax treatment, §1-905.03.
Reports.
Annual report, §1-905.02.
Participants and beneficiaries, §1-909.04.
Schools and education.
Food services department, §38-803.
Teachers, §§38-2001.01 to 38-2041.01.
See TEACHERS' RETIREMENT.
Section 401(a) Trust, §1-626.11.
Spouse or domestic partner equity, §§1-529.01 to 1-529.05.
Compliance with court orders, §1-523.03.
Summary descriptions of plans, §§1-733, 1-909.03, 1-909.04.
Disclosure to public, §1-909.05.

PENSIONS AND RETIREMENT
—Cont'd
Trustee, duties and liabilities of,
§1-626.13.
Vesting, §1-626.10.
Under previous District of Columbia
retirement program, §1-527.01.

PEOPLE'S COUNSEL.
Funds.
Office of the people's counsel agency
fund, §34-912.
Office of the People's Counsel,
§§34-804, 34-1118.

**PEPCO COST-SHARING FUND FOR
DC PLUG,** §1-325.331.

**PEPPER SPRAYS AND OTHER
SELF-DEFENSE SPRAYS,**
§§7-2502.12 to 7-2502.14.

**PERCHLOROETHYLENE IN DRY
CLEANING,** §8-108.05.

PEREMPTORY CHALLENGES,
CivPro Rule 47-I.
Prosecutor's ethical responsibilities,
ProfCond Rule 3.4.

PERFORMANCE BASED BUDGETS,
§47-308.01.
Capital asset replacement schedule,
§47-308.04.
Performance accountability
reporting, §47-308.03.
Relevant performance measures,
§47-308.02.

**PERFORMANCE MANAGEMENT
SYSTEM.**
Collective bargaining, public school
employee evaluation system not
subject to, §1-617.18.
Departments and agencies,
performance accountability,
§§1-204.56a to 1-204.56e.
Public officers and employees,
§§1-613.51 to 1-613.53, 1-614.11 to
1-614.14.
Established, §1-613.51.
Purposes, §1-613.52.
Transition provisions, §1-613.53.

PERFORMANCE PARKING ZONES,
§§50-2531 to 50-2535.
Ballpark performance parking pilot
zone, §50-2532.
Columbia Heights retail
performance parking pilot zone,
§50-2533.

PERFORMANCE PARKING ZONES
—Cont'd
Expenditure of generated revenues,
§50-2534.
Fund, §50-2531.01.
H Street NE performance parking
pilot zone, §50-2532.01.
Penn Quarter/Chinatown
performance parking pilot zone,
§50-2532.02.
Purpose, §50-2531.
Reporting requirements and
oversight, §50-2535.

PERJURY, §§22-2402 to 22-2405.
Alcoholic beverage control board.
False swearing before board, §25-442.
Defined, §22-2402.
Evidence under oath or affirmation,
§14-101.
False statements, §22-2405.
False swearing.
General provisions, §22-2404.
Police and fire trial boards, willful
false swearing before, §5-1002.
Insurance fraud.
False testimony, §22-3225.11.
Medicaid service provider fraud,
§4-804.
Security agents and brokers.
Grounds for disciplinary actions,
§31-5602.07.
Subornation of, §§22-2403, 23-324.
Sufficiency of evidence for criminal
indictments and informations,
§§23-323, 23-324.
Trust, mortgage and title
corporations, §26-1320.

PERMANENT GUARDIANSHIP.
Guardianship of minors, §§16-2381 to
16-2399.
See GUARDIAN AND WARD.

PERMISSIVE APPEALS.
Appeals, federal cases, FRAP 5,
USCtApp Rule 5.

PERMITS.
Alcoholic beverages.
See ALCOHOLIC BEVERAGES.
Animals, §8-1809.
Circus, carnival or other special event
animals, display of, §8-1808.
Athletic field permit coordination
committee, §10-308.
Boxing and wrestling commission,
§3-606.

PERMITS —Cont'd

Building lines.
Permits for extensions of buildings beyond, §§6-404, 6-405.

Building permits.
Cancellation of, §6-661.02.
Fees for, §6-661.01.
Requirement to have, §§6-641.09, 6-661.01.

Business licenses.
General provisions, §§47-2805.01 to 47-2881.
See BUSINESS LICENSES.

Child labor.
Theatrical permits, §32-206.
Vacation permits, §§32-207 to 32-211.
Work permits, §§32-207 to 32-211, 32-219.

Conduits, §§1-301.01, 34-1406.

Construction projects, riparian permits for, §47-2711.

Delinquent debts owed District, recovery, §1-350.07.

Drivers' licenses.
See DRIVERS' LICENSES.

Electricians, §47-2712.

Electric light and power company conduits, §34-1406.

Financial Responsibility and Management Assistance Authority review of permit processes, §47-395.

Flood hazards, §§6-501, 6-504.

Food stamps.
Business license or permit suspended, revoked, or denied for trafficking in, §4-218.06.

Foreign trade zones.
Applicability of licensing, permitting and taxation provisions, §36-503.

Hauling permits for multiaxle vehicles, §§6-703.01, 6-703.02.

Hazardous materials transportation.
Terrorism prevention, §§8-1421, 8-1424.

Hazardous waste management.
Requirement for permit, §8-1303.
Suspension or revocation of permit, §8-1309.

Highways.
Cutting trenches in highways, §§9-433.01, 9-433.02.

Hotline, §47-2881.

Lead-hazard prevention and elimination.
Abatement permits, §8-115.07.

PERMITS —Cont'd

Mayor's review of, §1-306.06.

Medical and dental colleges, §§38-1401, 38-1402.

Miss Utility permit drawings, availability of, §34-2703.

Motion picture and television production permits, §2-1204.11d.

Multiaxle motor vehicles, hauling permits for, §6-703.01.

Outhouses.
Permit to maintain privy by means other than connection to sewage system, §8-602.

Parks and recreation.
Athletic field permit coordination committee, §10-308.

Paving stones, removal of, §9-1201.04.

Pipes, laying, §1-301.01.

Privies.
Permit to maintain privy by means other than connection to sewage system, §8-602.

Public auction permits, §§47-2701 to 47-2708.
See PUBLIC AUCTIONS.

Public space.
Commemorative works, §9-204.17.

Public space over or under 9th Street Southwest, §1-301.01.

Public space, public rights of way, and public structures, occupation of, §10-1141.03.
Waiver or reduction of permit fees, §10-1141.03a.

Riparian permits, §47-2711.

Septic tanks.
Permit to maintain privy by means other than connection to sewage system, §8-602.

Solid waste facility permits, §§8-1051 to 8-1063.
See SOLID WASTE FACILITY PERMITS.

State health planning and development agency certificates of need as condition precedent for, §44-415.

Streets and alleys.
Building lines, permits for extensions of buildings beyond, §6-404.

Telegraph and telephone companies, §34-1911.02.

Trenches in highways, cutting, §§9-431.01, 9-431.02.

PERMITS —Cont'd

Tunnel construction, §1-301.01.

Underground public spaces, rental of, §§10-1103.01 to 10-1103.06.

Washington convention center.

Neighborhood demolition permits.
See WASHINGTON CONVENTION CENTER.

Water pollutants, permits to discharge, §8-103.06.

PERPETUITIES.

Horizontal property regimes, §42-2026.

Statutory rule against perpetuities, §§19-901 to 19-907.

Abolition of common law rule, §19-906.

Construction of rule, §19-907.

Creation of nonvested property, §19-902.

Exclusions, §19-904.

Nonvested property interest.
Criteria for divestiture, §19-901.
Reformation, §19-903.

Power of appointment.
When created, §19-902.

Prospective application, §19-905.

Uniformity of application, §19-907.

PERSONAL APPEARANCE DISCRIMINATION.

Insurance.

Unfair trade practices, §§31-2231.01 to 31-2231.25.

Prohibition of, §2-1401.01.

PERSONAL DELIVERY DEVICES PILOT PROGRAM, §§50-1551 to 50-1555.

Definitions, §50-1551.

Establishment, §50-1552.

Operation, §50-1555.

Registration, §§50-1553, 50-1554.

PERSONAL FITNESS TRAINERS.

Registration requirements, §3-1209.08.

Titles and terms prohibited as misrepresentation without license to practice, §3-1210.03.

Transition provisions.

Persons already practicing, §3-1210.05.

PERSONAL INJURY PROTECTION.

Health care benefits lien reduction, §31-3551.

No-fault motor vehicle insurance.

Availability of, §§31-2404, 31-2406.

Defined, §31-2404.

PERSONAL INJURY PROTECTION —Cont'd

No-fault motor vehicle insurance —Cont'd

Elements of, §31-2404.

Lawsuit restrictions on persons with, §31-2405.

Overdue payments, interest on, §31-2410.

Payment priorities, §31-2407.

PERSONAL PROPERTY.

Access to public records, §42-1206.

Attachment, §16-509.

Attorneys at law.

Safekeeping client's property, ProfCond Rule 1.15.
Approved depositories, DCBar Rule XI.

Conveyances.

Court ordered sales of property, CivPro Rule 308.

Judgment enforcement, CivPro Rule 70.

Probate proceedings.
Death before Jan. 1, 1981, Probate Rule 17.
Guardians, conservators, trustees, etc., involved, Probate Rules 203, 222, 223.

Cooperative associations.

Powers, §29-905.

Corporations.

Powers, §29-303.02.

Disclaimer of property interests, §§19-1501 to 19-1518.

See DISCLAIMER OF PROPERTY INTERESTS.

Estates in land provisions applicable to, §42-523.

See ESTATES IN LAND.

Fiduciaries generally.

Removal of property from District of Columbia, CivPro Rule 304.

Leases.

Commercial code leases, §§28:2A-101 to 28:2A-532.
See LEASES, UCC.

Limited cooperative associations.

Membership interests as, §29-1006.01.

Limited liability companies.

Transferable interests as, §29-805.01.

Limited partnerships.

Transferable interests as, §29-707.01.

Lodging places.

Liability for loss of or damage to, §30-101.

PERSONAL PROPERTY —Cont'd
Lodging places —Cont'd
Liens on property of guests for
amounts due, §30-102.
Unclaimed personal property, sale of,
§30-103.
Nonprofit corporations.
Powers, §29-403.02.
Partnerships.
Transferable interests of partners as,
§29-605.02.
Powers of attorney, §21-2105.
Probate proceedings.
Sale of personal property.
Death before Jan. 1, 1981, Probate
Rule 17.
Guardians, conservators, trustees,
etc., involved, Probate Rules
203, 222, 223.
Professional corporations.
Powers, §29-505.
Public auction permit requirements,
§§47-2703, 47-2705.
Recordation of financing statements,
§§41-201 to 41-204.
Records.
Public access, §42-1206.
**Recovery of real and personal
property leased together,**
§42-3209.
Replevin.
See REPLEVIN.
Self-service storage facilities,
§§40-401 to 40-405.
Taxation.
Compensating-use tax, §§47-2201 to
47-2214.
See COMPENSATING-USE TAX.
General provisions, §§47-1508 to
47-1535.
See PERSONAL PROPERTY
TAXES.
Unclaimed property.
General provisions, §§41-101 to
41-142.
See UNCLAIMED PROPERTY.
**Unincorporated nonprofit
associations.**
Ownership and transfer, §29-1106.
Transitional provisions, §29-1127.

PERSONAL PROPERTY TAXES,
§§47-501, 47-1508 to 47-1535.
Annual levy of, §47-1522.
Appeals, §47-1533.
Assessments, §§47-1528, 47-4312.
Banks and financial institutions,
§47-2510.

PERSONAL PROPERTY TAXES
—Cont'd
Collection of taxes, §47-1527.
Compensating-use tax.
General provisions, §§47-2201 to
47-2214.
See COMPENSATING-USE TAX.
Corcoran Gallery exempt from,
§§47-1016, 47-1017.
Deficiencies, §47-1528.
Definitions, §47-1521.
Distraint or levy.
Annual levy, §47-1522.
Enforcement of provisions, §47-1527.
Exemptions, §47-1508.
Corcoran Gallery of Art, §§47-1016,
47-1017.
Sheridan tapestries, §47-1013.
Extensions, §47-1524.
Failure to file, §47-1527.
Filing, §47-1524.
Fraud and deceit, §47-1527.
Hearings, §47-1528.
Issuance of rules and regulations,
§47-1535.
Levies.
Annual levy, §47-1522.
Mayor's powers, §47-1535.
Motor fuel tax, §47-2314.
Person defined for purposes of,
§47-1521.
Procedures, §§47-1521 to 47-1535.
Railroad rolling stock, §47-1512.
Reports, §47-1523.
Return, form of, §47-1524.
Sales.
Annual levy, §47-1522.
Seizures.
Annual levy, §47-1522.
Sheridan tapestries exempt from,
§47-1013.
Valuation of property, §47-1523.

PERSONAL REPRESENTATIVES,
§§20-401 to 20-406.
Accounting duties.
See ADMINISTRATION OF
ESTATES.
Appeals in federal cases.
Substitution as party, FRAP 43(a).
Appointment of, §§20-301, 20-303,
20-501, 20-704.
Appraisals, §§20-711 to 20-715.
Assistants, §20-744.
Attorneys' fees and costs, §20-752.
Bond, surety, §20-502.
Breach of fiduciary duty, §20-743.

PERSONAL REPRESENTATIVES
—Cont'd
Change in probate proceeding, termination of powers due to, §20-527.
Claims against, §20-1303.
Claims against estates, action required on, §20-908.
Commencement of powers and duties, §20-505.
Confirmatory acts after closure of estate, §20-1305.
Conflicts of interest, §20-743.01.
Copersonal representatives, §§20-512, 20-513.
Court orders, §§20-701.01, 20-742.
Death, §20-524.
Defined, §20-101.
Devolution of property at death to, §20-105.
Disclaimer of property interests, §§19-1501 to 19-1518.
See DISCLAIMER OF PROPERTY INTERESTS.
Distributions.
Children and minors, to, §20-1106.
Effect of, §20-1104.
Expeditious settlement and distribution of estate, duty of, §20-701.01.
Fiduciary of incompetent or incapacitated nonresident, to, §20-1107.
Improper, §20-1104.
In kind, §§20-1102, 20-1103.
Petition for, §20-1105.
Title of, §20-1104.
Employees of estate, §§20-744, 20-753.
Excluded persons, §20-303.
Expeditious settlement and distribution of estate by, §20-701.01.
Expenses of litigation, §20-752.
Fiduciaries generally.
See FIDUCIARIES.
Fiduciary status of, §20-701.
Filing revised or corrected documents, §20-705.
Foreign personal representatives, §§20-341 to 20-344.
Copy of appointment.
Filing if administering estate with property in District, §20-341.
Creditor's statement of claim, §20-343.
Death taxes.
Responsibility for paying, §20-343.

PERSONAL REPRESENTATIVES
—Cont'd
Foreign personal representatives
—Cont'd
Letters in District.
Not required to obtain, §20-341.
Order directing transfer of property, §20-344.
Personal or leasehold property.
Failure to transfer leasehold property to persons entitled, §20-344.
Removal, §20-343.
Powers, §20-342.
Publication of notice, §20-343.
Real property.
Failure to transfer to persons entitled, §20-344.
Lease or transfer, §20-343.
Incompetency or incapacity, §20-524.
Inventory, §§20-711 to 20-715.
Letters issued to, §§20-503, 20-504.
Limited cooperative associations.
Dissociation.
Powers, §29-1011.03.
Limited liability companies.
Transferable interests.
Powers, §29-805.04.
Limited partnerships.
Transferable interests.
Powers, §29-707.04.
Ministerial acts after closure of estate, §20-1305.
Multiple personal representatives, §§20-511 to 20-513.
Order of priority for appointment of, §20-303.
Persons assisting or dealing with, §20-744.
Possession and control of estate, taking, §20-702.
Powers and duties, §§20-701, 20-741.
Accounting duties.
See ADMINISTRATION OF ESTATES.
Breach of fiduciary duty, §20-743.
Commencement of, §20-505.
Court order, power to proceed without, §20-701.01.
Expeditious settlement and distribution of estate, §20-701.01.
Improper exercise of, §20-743.
Possession and control of estate, taking, §20-702.
Special administrators, §20-533.
Successor representatives, §20-511.

PERSONAL REPRESENTATIVES
—Cont'd
Powers and duties —Cont'd
Supervised administration, §20-404.
Surviving copersonal representative,
§20-513.
Suspension of, §20-521.
Termination of. See within this
heading, "Termination of powers."
Probate proceedings.
General provisions, §§16-3101 to
16-3112, Probate Rules 1 to 430.
See PROBATE PROCEEDINGS.
Records and accounts.
See ADMINISTRATION OF
ESTATES.
Removal of, §20-526.
Resignation of, §20-525.
**Review of employment or
compensation,** §20-753.
Self-notice not required of, §20-103.
Small estates, §20-354.
Administration generally, §§20-351 to
20-357.
Statutory rule against perpetuities,
§§19-901 to 19-907.
Successor personal representatives,
§§20-511 to 20-513, 20-715.
Supervised administration, §§20-401
to 20-406.
Accounting duties, §§20-721 to 20-726.
Appraisal, §§20-712, 20-713.
Change from or to, §20-403.
Closing of estate, §20-1301.
Defined, §§20-101, 20-401.
Interim orders, §20-405.
Petition for, §20-403.
Powers and duties, §20-404.
Procedures, §20-402.
Reappraisal, §20-713.
Supplemental inventory, §20-713.
Termination of, §20-405.
Waiver of audit of accounts, §20-732.
Waiver of duty to file inventory,
§20-731.
Surcharges, §20-701.
**Surviving copersonal
representative,** §20-513.
Suspension of powers, temporary,
§20-521.
Termination of powers, §20-522.
Change in probate proceeding, due to,
§20-527.
Closing of estate, §20-1301.
Death or disability of representative,
§20-524.

PERSONAL REPRESENTATIVES
—Cont'd
Termination of powers —Cont'd
Effect of termination, §20-523.
Removal, §20-526.
Resignation, §20-525.
Special administrators, §20-534.
Supervised administration, §20-405.
Temporary restraints, §20-521.
**Terms and conditions of
appointment,** §20-501.
Trusts and trustees.
Uniform trust code, §§19-1303.01 to
19-1303.05.
Agents, §19-1303.03.
Appointment by court, §19-1303.05.
Consent of person represented,
§19-1303.01.
Conservators, §19-1303.03.
Fiduciaries, §19-1303.03.
Guardians, §19-1303.03.
Holder of general testamentary
power of appointment,
§19-1303.02.
Parents, §19-1303.03.
Person having substantially
identical interest, §19-1303.04.
Powers and duties generally,
§19-1303.01.
Uniform fiduciaries act, §§21-1701 to
21-1712.
See FIDUCIARIES.
Uniform trust code, §§19-1303.01 to
19-1303.05.
Unsupervised administration,
§20-406.
Accounting duties, §20-734.
Appraisal, §20-713.01.
Change from or to, §20-403.
Closing of estate, §§20-735, 20-1301.
Defined, §20-101.
Inventory, §20-713.01.
Wages and salaries, §§20-751, 20-753.
PERSONNEL, OFFICE OF, §§1-604.01
to 1-604.08.
Director of personnel, §1-604.02.
Personnel authority, §1-604.06.

PERTUSSIS.
Immunization of school students,
§§38-501 to 38-508.
Interstate compact on educational
opportunity for military children.
Time to obtain immunizations,
§49-1101.05.

PEST CONTROL.
Bureau of rodent control,
§§8-2101.01, 8-2101.02.

PEST CONTROL —Cont'd
Rodent abatement program,
§§8-2103.01 to 8-2103.05.

PESTICIDES, §§8-401 to 8-440.
Administrative procedure, §8-411.
Applicability of law to governmental
entities and public applicators,
§8-407.
Control of plant diseases and
insects, §8-304.
Cooperative agreements, §8-416.
Definitions pertaining to, §§8-401,
8-431.
Denial, suspension, modification, or
revocation of certification or
license, §8-410.
Disposal, §8-414.
Education and control, §§8-431 to
8-440.
Applicator reporting requirements,
§8-437.
Definitions, §8-431.
Exemptions from restrictions, §8-434.
Integrated pest management
education, §8-435.
Lists of pesticides classified as
restricted-use or nonessential,
§8-432.
Nonessential pesticides.
Classification as, §8-432.
Prohibited applications, §8-433.
Penalties for violations, §8-439.
Prohibited applications, §8-433.
Exemptions, §8-434.
Registration fee, §8-438.
Report on effectiveness of pesticide
programs, §8-436.
Restricted-use pesticides.
Classification as, §8-432.
Exemptions from restrictions,
§8-434.
Prohibited applications, §8-433.
Rulemaking to implement provisions,
§8-440.
Enforcement of rules and
regulations, §§8-411, 8-412.
Fines, §8-418.
Forms.
Notice of pesticide application,
§8-403.01.
Governmental entities and public
applicators.
Applicability of chapter, §8-408.
Information supplied customers,
§8-403.01.
Integrated pest management
education, §8-435.

PESTICIDES —Cont'd
Liability insurance, §8-407.
Licensing and certification, §§8-403
to 8-406, 8-410.
Multi-unit property residents and
tenants.
Information to be supplied to before
application of pesticides,
§8-403.02.
Nonessential pesticides.
Classification as, §8-432.
Prohibited applications, §8-433.
Notice.
Abutting properties, notice before
application, §8-403.05.
Pesticide application, form, §8-403.01.
Penalties, §§8-418, 8-439.
Pesticide applicators, §8-403.
Reporting requirements, §8-437.
Pesticide dealers, §8-405.
Pesticide operators, §8-406.
Prohibited and unlawful acts, §8-417.
Prohibited applications, §8-433.
Exemptions, §8-434.
Reciprocity, §8-415.
Records, §8-409.
Reduced-risk pesticides and
methods of pest control,
§8-403.04.
Registered technicians, §8-404.
Registration fee, §8-438.
Registration fund, §8-438.01.
Registration pesticides, §8-402.
Reports, §§8-409, 8-413.
Restricted-use pesticides.
Classification as, §8-432.
Exemptions from restrictions, §8-434.
Prohibited applications, §8-433.
Severability of provisions, §8-419.
Signs posted for exterior
application, §8-403.03.
Storage, §8-414.
Trade secret disclosures, §36-410.

PET CARE FACILITIES.
Commercial animal care or breeder
license, §8-1821.02.

PETITIONS.
Adoption, Adoption Rule 7.
Form, §16-305.
Appeals, D.C. courts.
Administrative orders and decisions,
DCCtApp Rule 15.
Extraordinary writs, DCCtApp Rule
21.
Form and copies of petitions,
DCCtApp Rule 32.

PETITIONS —Cont'd
Appeals, D.C. courts —Cont'd
Reconsideration of application for appeal, DCCtApp Rule 6.
Rehearing by division, DCCtApp Rule 40.
Rehearing, rehearing en banc, or initial hearing en banc, DCCtApp Rule 35.
Appeals, federal cases.
Administrative review, FRAP 15.
Extension of time to file prohibited, FRAP 26(b).
Hearing or rehearing en banc, FRAP 35(b).
Joint petition.
Administrative review, FRAP 15(a).
Mandamus, prohibition, and other extraordinary writs, FRAP 21, USCtApp Rule 21.
Motions practice generally, USCtApp Rule 27.
Permission to appeal under 28 USCS 1292(b).
Extension of time to file prohibited, FRAP 26(b).
Permissive appeals, FRAP 5.
Certificate of parties and amici attached, USCtApp Rule 5.
Discovery statement attached, USCtApp Rule 5.
Rehearing, USCtApp Rule 35.
Review of administrative order, FRAP Form 3.
Attorney discipline or disability proceedings, DCBar Rule XI, USDistCt LCrR 57.27, USDistCt LCvR 83.16.
Bar association.
Referendum procedures, DCBar Rule VII.
Child abuse and neglect, NeglectProc Rule 9.
Reading of petition, NeglectProc Rule 12.
Verified complaint requirement, §16-2305, JuvProc Rule 3.
Conservatorship, CivPro Rule 310.
Guardian ad litem's compensation, CivPro Rule 302, Probate Rule 224.
Missing persons, Probate Rule 350.
Constitution of the United States.
Right of, US Const Amd 1.
Custodial trust accounting by trustee, §19-1115.

PETITIONS —Cont'd
Custodial trust beneficiary incapacitated.
Incapacity determination, §19-1110.
Delinquent minors, JuvProc Rules 7, 12.
Initiation of judicial actions, §16-2305.
Probation revocation, JuvProc Rule 32.
Reinstituting charges, JuvProc Rule 5.
Dependent children.
Verified complaint requirement, §16-2305, JuvProc Rule 3.
Depositions.
Pre-action depositions, CivPro Rule 27.
Domestic relations actions, DomRel Rule 27.
Fiduciaries.
Accounts and reports.
Approval without reference to Auditor-Master, CivPro Rule 305.
Compensation, CivPro Rules 301, 302.
Probate proceedings, Probate Rules 224, 225.
Guardian ad litem's compensation, CivPro Rule 302, Probate Rule 224.
Guardianship of minors.
Standby guardianship.
Approval of guardianship, §16-4805.
Intellectual disability proceedings.
Commitment.
Individuals who are not competent to refuse commitment, MentalRetardation Rule 4A.
Respondents found incompetent to participate in criminal proceedings, MentalRetardation Rule 4B.
Objection to discharge from facility, MentalRetardation Rule 6.
Intervention proceedings.
See INTERVENTION PROCEEDINGS.
Mandamus, DCCtApp Rule 21.
Mental illness, persons with.
Hospitalization.
Escapees, MentalHealth Rule 11.
Prisoner's commitment to mental institution, MentalHealth Rule 10.
Merit system.
Review of agency decision, CivPro Agency Review Rule 1.
Form of petition, CivPro Agency Review Rule 1.
Missing persons.
Conservators or protection orders, Probate Rule 350.

PETITIONS —Cont'd
Parentage establishment, DomRel Form 11.
Probate proceedings.
Custodianship of minors, Probate Rules 231, 232.
Death before Jan. 1, 1981, Probate Rule 10.
Sale of real property, Probate Rule 18.
Death between Jan. 1, 1981, and June 30, 1995.
Claims against estate, Probate Rule 110.
Minors receiving distributions, Probate Rule 108.
Petition for probate, Probate Rule 102.
Rule to show cause for recovery of property, Probate Rule 113.
Termination of appointment of personal representative, Probate Rule 123.
Death on or after July 1, 1995, Probate Rule 403.
Claims against estate, Probate Form 14, Probate Rule 410.
Court order for authority to act, Probate Rule 412.
Guardian ad litem's compensation, Probate Rule 422.
Minors receiving distributions, Probate Rule 408.
Petitions for probate, Probate Form 2.
Rule to show cause for recovery of property, Probate Rule 413.
Termination of appointment of supervised personal representative, Probate Form 21, Probate Rule 423.
Guardians, conservators, trustees, etc., involved.
Appointment of guardian, Probate Rule 221.
Compensation of fiduciaries, Probate Rules 224, 225.
Expenditure authorization, Probate Form 1.
Investment authorization and approval, Probate Forms 2, 3.
Rule to show cause for recovery of property, Probate Rule 211.
Prohibition, writ of, DCCtApp Rule 21.
Protection orders.
Missing persons, Probate Rule 350.

PETITIONS —Cont'd
Real property taxes.
Reclassification, §47-813.
Right to petition for redress of grievances, US Const Amd 1.
Support and maintenance, DomRel Form 9.
Parentage proceedings, DomRel Form 11.
Tax proceedings, Tax Form 1, Tax Rule 6.
Fee for filing, Tax Rule 4.

PETIT JURIES, §11-1911.

PETS.
Animal control, §§8-1801 to 8-1813.
See ANIMALS.
Cruelty to animals.
General provisions, §§22-1001 to 22-1013.
See CRUELTY TO ANIMALS.
Dangerous dogs, §§8-1901 to 8-1908.
See DANGEROUS DOGS.
Dogs.
Generally.
See DOGS.
Pet care facilities.
Commercial animal care or breeder license, §8-1821.02.
Pet ownership restriction in assisted housing, §§8-2031 to 8-2035.
Definitions, §8-2031.
Discrimination by reason of owning pets, §8-2032.
Ownership policy, §8-2032.
Removal of pets constituting threat or nuisance, §8-2033.
Rules, §8-2035.
Violation civil infraction, fine, §8-2034.
Veterinary facilities, §§47-2888.01 to 47-2888.08.
See VETERINARY FACILITIES.
Veterinary medicine, §§3-1208.61 to 3-1208.65.
See VETERINARY MEDICINE.

PHARMACEUTICAL COMPANIES.
Gifts or remuneration to medication advisory committees.
Prohibition, §§48-842.01 to 48-842.04.

PHARMACEUTICAL DETAILING.
Evaluation of effectiveness of law licensing persons practicing, §§48-844.01 to 48-844.03.
Definitions, §48-844.02.

PHARMACEUTICAL DETAILING
—Cont'd
Evaluation of effectiveness of law licensing persons practicing
—Cont'd
Information required to be evaluated, §48-844.03.
Repeal or amendment of law.
Use of evaluation to determine, §48-844.03.
SafeRX evaluation act of 2008.
Short title, §48-844.01.
Time for submission of report, §48-844.03.

PHARMACEUTICAL EDUCATION PROGRAM, §§48-843.01 to 48-843.04.
Applicability, §48-843.04.
Established, §48-843.03.
Evidence-based program, §48-843.03.
Pharmaceutical product defined, §48-843.02.
Prescribers participating in publicly funded, contracted or subsidized health-care programs.
Education, §48-843.03.
Purposes, §48-843.03.
Short title, §48-843.01.

PHARMACISTS AND PHARMACIES, §§47-2885.01 to 47-2885.23.
Appeals, §47-2885.21.
Applicability of provisions, §3-1210.06.
Board of pharmacy, §3-1202.08.
Fund, §7-733.02.
Safe disposal of drugs, public education program, §48-851.02.
Bulk sales or transfers, §47-2885.12.
Collaborative practice agreements, §3-1202.08.
Health occupations boards, §3-1204.12.
Consultation with recipients or caregivers, §3-1210.06a.
Definitions, §§3-1201.02, 47-2885.02.
Deteriorating drugs, §47-2885.13.
Disposal of unused pharmaceuticals, §§48-851.01 to 48-851.04.
Employees, §47-2885.11.
Fees, §47-2885.19.
Health occupations boards.
Collaborative practice agreements, §3-1204.12.
General provisions, §§3-1201.01 to 3-1213.01.
See HEALTH OCCUPATIONS BOARDS.

PHARMACISTS AND PHARMACIES
—Cont'd
Health occupations licensure, registration or certification, §§3-1205.01 to 3-1205.24.
See HEALTH OCCUPATIONS LICENSURE, REGISTRATION OR CERTIFICATION.
Immunizations and vaccinations, administering, §3-1202.08.
Injunctions, §47-2885.20.
Inspections, §47-2885.16.
Interns.
Registration of, §47-2885.06.
Supervision of, §3-1210.06.
Labeling requirements for prescriptions, §47-2885.14.
Licenses, §§47-2885.03 to 47-2885.10.
Denial, suspension, or revocation, §47-2885.10.
Fees, §47-2885.19.
Pharmacy technicians, §§3-1207.51 to 3-1207.58.
Requirements regarding, §§47-2885.03, 47-2885.08.
Licensure of manufacturers and distributors.
General provisions, §§48-701 to 48-715.
See DRUG MANUFACTURE AND DISTRIBUTION LICENSURE.
Malpractice.
Medical malpractice, §§16-2801 to 16-2841.
See MEDICAL MALPRACTICE.
Mayor's duties regarding, §47-2885.18.
Operation of pharmacy by pharmacist, §47-2885.09.
Oral prescriptions for controlled substances, §3-1210.06.
Peddling drugs, §§47-2885.17, 47-2885.17a.
Penalties, §47-2885.20.
Pharmaceutical detailing.
Code of ethics, §3-1202.08.
Continuing education, §3-1207.44.
Definitions, §3-1201.02.
Licenses.
Qualifications, §3-1207.42.
Waiver of requirements, §3-1207.43.
Penalties for practice without license, §3-1207.45.
Scope of practice, §3-1207.41.
Unlawful activities, §3-1207.41.
Pharmacy technicians, §§3-1207.51 to 3-1207.58.
Ancillary services, §3-1207.57.

PHARMACISTS AND PHARMACIES
—Cont'd
Pharmacy technicians —Cont'd
Authority to provide services,
§§3-1207.55, 3-1207.57.
Definitions, §3-1207.51.
Name tag designating title,
§3-1207.53.
Trainees, §3-1207.54.
Registration.
Qualifications, §3-1207.52.
Required, §3-1207.52.
Rulemaking to implement provisions,
§3-1207.58.
Supervision of, §3-1210.06.
Titles and terms prohibited as
misrepresentation without license
to practice, §3-1210.03.
Trainees, §3-1207.54.
Waiver of educational or examination
requirement, §3-1207.56.
Physicians and surgeons.
Collaborative practice agreements,
§3-1202.08.
Policy declaration, §47-2885.01.
Prescription drugs.
Forgery for prescription forms,
§22-3242.
General provisions, §§48-701 to
48-833.09.
See PRESCRIPTION DRUGS.
**Prior regulations, effect of new laws
on,** §47-2885.23.
Prohibited acts, §47-2885.03.
Prosecution of violations regarding,
§47-2885.20.
Records, §§3-1210.06a, 47-2885.15.
Registered pharmacy technicians,
§§3-1207.51 to 3-1207.58.
Registration, §3-1210.06.
Registration of interns, §47-2885.06.
Returned drugs, §47-2885.13.
Sample drugs, §47-2885.13.
Severability of provisions,
§47-2885.22.
**Titles and terms prohibited as
misrepresentation without
license to practice,** §3-1210.03.
**Unused pharmaceutical safe
disposal,** §§48-851.01 to 48-851.04.
Definitions, §48-851.01.
Health care facilities.
Prohibited methods of disposal,
§48-851.03.
Mail-in program, §48-851.02.
Public education campaign,
§48-851.02.

PHARMACISTS AND PHARMACIES
—Cont'd
**Unused pharmaceutical safe
disposal** —Cont'd
Recommendations to mayor,
§48-851.02.
Rulemaking, §48-851.04.
**PHARMACY BENEFITS
MANAGERS.**
**Definition of pharmacy benefits
manager,** §48-831.02.
**Transparent business practices
among,** §§48-832.01 to 48-832.03.
Fiduciary duty, §48-832.01.
Compliance required, §48-832.02.
Enforcement, §48-832.03.
PHENYLKETONURIA, §§7-831 to
7-840.
PHILANTHROPIC BONDS.
Pay-for-success contracts, §§2-211.01
to 2-211.03.
PHILIPPINE ISLANDS.
Acknowledgment of deed, §42-112.
PHLEBOTOMY.
**Health occupations licensure,
registration or certification,**
§§3-1205.01 to 3-1205.24.
Registration, §3-1209.12.
**Titles and terms prohibited as
misrepresentation without
license to practice,** §3-1210.03.
PHOSPHATE CLEANERS, §§8-107.01
to 8-107.04.
Wastewater disposal system,
§§8-107.01 to 8-107.04.
PHOTO-COP, §§50-2209.01 to
50-2209.11.
PHOTOCOPYING.
Fund for District, §47-135.
PHOTOGRAPHS.
Child abuse and neglect, §4-1301.08.
Crime investigation records.
Retention of records in open
investigations, §5-113.32.
Firearms registration, §7-2502.04.
**Media coverage of superior court
proceedings,** CivPro Rule 203,
CrimPro Rule 53.
Child abuse and neglect proceedings,
NeglectProc Rule 45.
Juvenile proceedings, JuvProc Rule 53.
**United States District Court
proceedings,** USDistCt LCrR
53.1.1, USDistCt LCvR 83.1.

PHYSICAL EDUCATION, §§38-824.01 to 38-824.05.
See SCHOOLS AND EDUCATION.

PHYSICAL EVIDENCE, TAMPERING WITH, §22-723.

PHYSICAL EXAMINATIONS.
See MEDICAL EXAMINATIONS.

PHYSICAL EXHIBITS.
Appeals, federal cases.
Use in argument, FRAP 34(g).

PHYSICAL FITNESS.
Mayor's council on physical fitness, health and nutrition, §§7-121 to 7-126.
Administrative support, §7-123.
Executive committee, §7-126.
Fitness fund, §7-125.
Fitness report, §§7-122, 7-124.
Meetings, §7-121.
Membership, §7-121.
Mission, §7-121.
Powers and duties, §7-122.

PHYSICAL THERAPY.
Assistants, references to, §3-1212.04.
Board of, §3-1202.09.
Definition of practice of, §3-1201.02.
Health occupations boards.
General provisions, §§3-1201.01 to 3-1213.01.
See HEALTH OCCUPATIONS BOARDS.
Health occupations licensure, registration or certification, §§3-1205.01 to 3-1205.24.
See HEALTH OCCUPATIONS LICENSURE, REGISTRATION OR CERTIFICATION.
Titles and terms prohibited as misrepresentation without license to practice, §3-1210.03.

PHYSICIAN ASSISTANTS.
Advisory committee, §7-743.05.
Board of medicine.
Advisory committee on physician assistants, §3-1202.03.
Definition of practice by, §3-1201.02.
Health occupations boards.
General provisions, §§3-1201.01 to 3-1213.01.
See HEALTH OCCUPATIONS BOARDS.

PHYSICIAN ASSISTANTS —Cont'd
Health occupations licensure, registration or certification, §§3-1205.01 to 3-1205.24.
See HEALTH OCCUPATIONS LICENSURE, REGISTRATION OR CERTIFICATION.
Health professional recruitment program, §§7-751.01 to 7-751.16.
See HEALTH PROFESSIONAL RECRUITMENT PROGRAM.
Titles and terms prohibited as misrepresentation without license to practice, §3-1210.03.

PHYSICIAN-PATIENT PRIVILEGE.
Attorney discipline or disability proceedings.
Waiver of privilege for reinstatement of incapacitated attorney, DCBar Rule XI, USDistCt LCrR 57.30, USDistCt LCvR 83.19.
Child abuse and neglect.
Privilege not grounds for excluding evidence of, §4-1321.05.
Controlled substances, §48-931.01.
Witnesses.
Physicians and mental health professionals, §14-307.

PHYSICIANS AND SURGEONS.
Alcoholic beverage licenses.
Exceptions to license requirements, §25-103.
Cardiopulmonary resuscitation in case of cardiac arrest.
Non-resuscitation procedures for EMS, §§7-651.01 to 7-651.16.
See EMERGENCY MEDICAL SERVICES.
Child abuse and neglect reports, §§4-1321.01 to 4-1321.07.
Child death.
Report required, §4-1371.12.
Comfort care orders.
Non-resuscitation procedures for EMS, §§7-651.01 to 7-651.16.
See EMERGENCY MEDICAL SERVICES.
Crimes and offenses.
Failure to report certain deaths, §5-1406.
Dead bodies.
Duty to report certain deaths to medical examiner, §5-1405.

PHYSICIANS AND SURGEONS
—Cont'd
Dead bodies —Cont'd
Failure to report certain deaths,
§5-1406.
**Disciplinary actions against
physicians.**
Reports by physicians and health care
providers, §3-1205.13a.
**Emergency medical care and
assistance.**
Emergency volunteer health
practitioners, §§7-2361.01 to
7-2361.12.
See EMERGENCY VOLUNTEER
HEALTH PRACTITIONERS.
Good Samaritan act, §7-401.
Firearms or weapons injuries.
Reporting, §§7-2601 to 7-2603.
**Foreign doctors of eminence and
authority.**
Licensure of, §3-1205.09a.
Good Samaritan act, §7-401.
Health maintenance organizations.
General provisions, §§31-3401 to
31-3431.
See HEALTH MAINTENANCE
ORGANIZATIONS.
Health occupations boards.
General provisions, §§3-1201.01 to
3-1213.01.
See HEALTH OCCUPATIONS
BOARDS.
**Health occupations licensure,
registration or certification,**
§§3-1205.01 to 3-1205.24.
See HEALTH OCCUPATIONS
LICENSURE, REGISTRATION
OR CERTIFICATION.
**Health professional recruitment
program,** §§7-751.01 to 7-751.16.
See HEALTH PROFESSIONAL
RECRUITMENT PROGRAM.
**Hospital and medical services
corporations.**
General provisions, §§31-3501 to
31-3524.
See HOSPITAL AND MEDICAL
SERVICES CORPORATIONS.
**Hospitalization of persons with
mental illness,** §§21-582, 21-583.
Immunity.
Rendering emergency medical care
and assistance, §7-401.
Lead poisoning.
Childhood lead poisoning screening
and reporting, §§7-871.01 to
7-871.06.

PHYSICIANS AND SURGEONS
—Cont'd
Malpractice.
Medical malpractice, §§16-2801 to
16-2841.
See MEDICAL MALPRACTICE.
**Medical marijuana,
recommendations of physicians,**
§7-1671.04.
Board of medicine, review by,
§7-1671.07.
Medicine, board of, §3-1202.03.
Medicine, definition of practice of,
§3-1201.02.
Pharmacists and pharmacies.
Collaborative practice agreements,
§3-1202.08.
Poor.
Compensation of physicians to,
§44-713.
Practice by physicians-in-training.
Defined, §3-1201.02.
Fees, §3-1313.
Reports.
Child abuse and neglect, §§4-1321.01
to 4-1321.07.
Child death, §4-1371.12.
Surgical assistants.
Advisory committee on surgical
assistants, §3-1202.03.
Authority and scope of practice,
§3-1206.41.
Renewal of license, §3-1206.42.
**Titles and terms prohibited as
misrepresentation without
license to practice, §3-1210.03.**
Voluntary leave transfer program.
Application to receive transferred
leave.
Certification by physician of serious
health condition, §1-612.33.

PICNICS.
Alcoholic beverage licenses.
Temporary licenses, §25-115.

PIERCING.
Body art establishments.
Business licenses, §47-2809.01.

PILOT AGREEMENTS.
Lots 826 and 831, square 491,
§47-1064.
Payments in lieu of taxes, §47-1052.
Generally, §§1-308.01 to 1-308.10.
See BOND ISSUES.
**Rhode Island Metro Plaza PILOT
agreement.**
Sales tax exemption, §47-4613.

PIMPING.
Prostitution.
General provisions, §§22-2701 to 22-2725.
See PROSTITUTION.

PINEY BRANCH PARKWAY, §10-146.

PINTEREST.
E-commerce companies.
Qualified social electronic commerce companies tax abatements, §§47-1818.01 to 47-1818.08.

PIPELINES.
Defined as public utility, §34-214.
Permits.
Revocable permits for construction of conduits and pipes, §1-301.01.
Safety violations, §34-706.
Water supply and waterworks.
Acquisition of lands and rights of way for pipelines authorized, §§34-2401.19, 34-2411.03.
Damaging or defacing pipelines, §34-2401.22.
Mayor's power to lay pipes, §34-2401.01.
Repair and maintenance.
Authorized, §8-205.
Unlawful tapping, §§34-2401.20 to 34-2401.22.

PIPES.
Permits to lay, §1-301.01.
Service pipes as public works, §9-401.03.
Water supply and waterworks.
Unauthorized opening of mains or pipes, §34-2401.24.

PIRACY.
Audiovisual works, §§22-3214.01, 22-3214.02.
Commercial piracy, §22-3214.
Deceptive labeling, §22-3214.01.
Motion pictures, §§22-3214.01, 22-3214.02.
Music piracy, §§22-3214 to 22-3214.02.
Powers of congress, US Const Art I §8.
Proprietary information, §22-3214.
Sound recordings, §§22-3214 to 22-3214.02.

PISTOL MATCHES.
Metropolitan police attendance, expenses for, §5-133.15.

PISTOLS.
See FIREARMS.

PLACE OF RESIDENCE OR BUSINESS DISCRIMINATION.
Prohibition of, §2-1401.01.

PLAIN ERROR, CrimPro Rule 52.
Delinquent minors, JuvProc Rule 52.

PLANTS AND PLANT DISEASES, §§8-301 to 8-305.
Control of diseases and insects, §8-304.
Fines, §8-305.
Penalties, §8-305.
Weeds.
Duty to remove, §8-301.
Mayor's duty to remove, §8-302.
Notice to remove, §8-302.
Prosecutions regarding, §8-303.

PLASTIC AND OTHER DISPOSABLE ITEMS.
Disposable food service ware, management, §§8-1531 to 8-1537.
Retail stores, plastic and disposable bags.
Credit for consumer-provided bags, §8-102.03.
Fees, §8-102.03.
Recycling requirements, §8-102.02.
Rulemaking authority, §8-102.04.
Violations, §8-102.04.

PLATS.
Subdivisions.
Legal office of record, §1-1305.

PLAYGROUNDS.
Drug free zones, §48-904.07a.
Excess property for development of seat of government.
Retention for public use, §16-1334.
Excess property for United States.
Retention for public use, §16-1382.
Firearms.
Enhanced penalties and fines for carrying guns into gun free zones, §22-4502.01.
Glover Parkway and children's playground, §§10-156, 10-157.
Issuance of rules and regulations, §10-127.
Leasing land for, §10-103.
National Children's Island, §§10-1401 to 10-1406.
Parks and recreation generally, §§10-101 to 10-308.
See PARKS AND RECREATION.
Smoking, §7-1703.
"No Smoking" signs, §7-1704.

PLAYGROUNDS —Cont'd
Temporary structures on reservations used as, §10-125.
Use of public grounds for, §10-124.
Washington Aqueduct land, §10-126.

PLEADINGS.
Abolished pleadings, CivPro Rule 7.
Addresses and names of parties and attorneys, CivPro Rule 11, USDistCt LCvR 5.1, USDistCt LCvR 11.1.
 Criminal proceedings, USDistCt LCrR 49.
Adoption, Adoption Rule 7.
 Amended and supplemental pleadings, Adoption Rule 15.
 Form and content, Adoption Rules 10, 11.
Affidavits, CivPro Rule 9-I.
Amendments, CivPro Rule 15, USDistCt LCrR 47, USDistCt LCvR 7, USDistCt LCvR 15.1.
 Adoption proceedings, Adoption Rule 15.
 Condemnation of property, CivPro Rule 71A.
 Domestic relations actions, DomRel Rule 15.
Answers.
 See ANSWERS.
Appeals, federal cases.
 Appendix, FRAP 30(a).
 Composition of record on review or enforcement of administrative orders, FRAP 16(a).
Attachments, USDistCt LCvR 5.1.
 Criminal proceedings, USDistCt LCrR 49.
Attorneys at law.
 Signing of pleadings, CivPro Rule 11, USDistCt LCvR 5.1, USDistCt LCvR 11.1.
 Criminal proceedings, USDistCt LCrR 49.
Capacity, CivPro Rule 9.
 Domestic relations actions, DomRel Rule 9.
Class actions, CivPro Rule 23-I, USDistCt LCvR 23.1.
Commencement of actions generally.
 See COMMENCEMENT OF ACTIONS.
Complaints.
 See COMPLAINTS.
Condemnation of property, CivPro Rule 71A.

PLEADINGS —Cont'd
Conditions of the mind, CivPro Rule 9.
 Domestic relations actions, DomRel Rule 9.
Conditions precedent, CivPro Rule 9.
 Domestic relations actions, DomRel Rule 9.
Construction and interpretation.
 Domestic relations actions, DomRel Rule 8.
Construction of pleadings, CivPro Rule 8.
Corporate disclosure statements, CivPro Rule 7.1, USDistCt LCrR 44.6, USDistCt LCvR 7.1.
Counterclaims.
 See COUNTERCLAIMS.
Criminal procedure, CrimPro Rule 12.
Cross-claims, CivPro Rule 13.
Damages.
 Special damages, CivPro Rule 9.
Default judgments, CivPro Rule 55.
 Domestic relations actions, DomRel Rule 55.
Defenses and objections, CivPro Rule 12.
 Domestic relations actions, DomRel Rule 12.
Derivative actions by shareholders, CivPro Rule 23.1.
Dilatory pleadings, CivPro Rule 11.
 Domestic relations actions, DomRel Rule 11.
 Hospitalization of persons with mental illness, MentalHealth Rule 14.
Domestic relations actions generally.
 See DOMESTIC RELATIONS ACTIONS.
E-filing, CivPro Appx II, CivPro Rule 5.
 Bankruptcy court, USDistDCBank Appx D.
 Mandatory E-filing in civil division, CivPro Appx III.
 Complaints, CivPro Appx IV.
 United States District Court case management/electronic case filing system.
  Criminal proceedings, USDistCt LCrR 49.
Electronic signatures, CivPro Rule 5.
Electronic transmission, USDistCt LCvR 5.1.
E-mail address of signer.
 Information required on pleadings, motions and other filings, CivPro Rule 11.

PLEADINGS —Cont'd
Failure to deny averment, CivPro
Rule 8.
Filing with court, CivPro Rule 5,
USDistCt LCvR 5.1.
Criminal proceedings, USDistCt LCrR
49.
E-filing, CivPro Appx II, CivPro Rule
5.
Bankruptcy court, USDistDCBank
Appx D.
Mandatory E-filing in civil division,
CivPro Appx III.
United States District Court case
management/electronic case
filing system.
Criminal proceedings, USDistCt
LCrR 49.
Form and content, CivPro Rules 8,
10-I, USDistCt LCvR 5.1.
Criminal proceedings, USDistCt LCrR
49.
Domestic relations actions, DomRel
Rules 8, 10.
Forms.
See FORMS.
Fraud, CivPro Rule 9.
Domestic relations actions, DomRel
Rule 9.
Frivolous, dilatory, etc., pleadings,
CivPro Rule 11, ProfCond Rule 3.1.
Domestic relations actions, DomRel
Rule 11.
Hospitalization of persons with mental
illness, MentalHealth Rule 14.
Interpleader, CivPro Rule 22.
Complaint for interpleader, CivPro
Form CA 18.
Counterclaim for interpleader, CivPro
Form CA 21.
Intervention proceedings.
See INTERVENTION
PROCEEDINGS.
Joinder of parties.
Reasons for nonjoinder, CivPro Rule
19.
Allegation of reason for omitting
party, CivPro Form CA 26.
Judgment on the pleadings, CivPro
Rule 12.
Domestic relations actions, DomRel
Rule 12.
Judgments by courts, tribunals, etc.,
CivPro Rule 9.
Domestic relations actions, DomRel
Rule 9.

PLEADINGS —Cont'd
Jury trials.
Demand for trial by jury endorsed
upon pleading, CivPro Rule 38.
Juvenile proceedings, JuvProc Rule
12.
Landlord and tenant court,
LandlordTenant Rules 3, 5.
Mental illness, persons with.
Hospitalization.
Form of court filings, MentalHealth
Rule 14.
Signatures, MentalHealth Rule 15.
Mistake, CivPro Rule 9.
Domestic relations actions, DomRel
Rule 9.
More definite statement motions,
CivPro Rule 12.
Domestic relations actions, DomRel
Rule 12.
Motions generally.
See MOTIONS.
**Names and addresses of parties and
attorneys,** USDistCt LCvR 5.1,
USDistCt LCvR 11.1.
Criminal proceedings, USDistCt LCrR
49.
Official documents or acts, CivPro
Rule 9.
Domestic relations actions, DomRel
Rule 9.
Paper requirements, CivPro Rule 10-I,
USDistCt LCvR 5.1.
Parentage proceedings, DomRel Rule
405.
Parties.
Addresses and names of parties and
attorneys, CivPro Rule 11,
USDistCt LCvR 5.1, USDistCt
LCvR 11.1.
Criminal proceedings, USDistCt
LCrR 49.
Permitted pleadings, CivPro Rule 7.
Domestic relations actions, DomRel
Rule 7.
Place as an issue, CivPro Rule 9.
Domestic relations actions, DomRel
Rule 9.
Probate proceedings.
Exclusion of personal identification
from filed documents, Probate
Rule 5.1.
Verification of pleadings, Probate Rule
3.
**Reciprocal enforcement of support
proceedings,** DomRel Rule 401.

PLEADINGS —Cont'd
Required information, CivPro Rule
11.
Sealed or confidential documents,
CivPro Rule 5-III, USDistCt LCvR
5.1.
Criminal proceedings, USDistCt LCrR
49.
Service of process.
See SERVICE OF PROCESS AND
PAPERS.
Signatures, CivPro Rule 11.
Adoption proceedings, Adoption Rules
10, 11.
Hospitalization of persons with mental
illness, MentalHealth Rule 14.
Small claims court, SmallClaims Rules
3, 5.
Stipulations generally.
See STIPULATIONS.
Striking pleadings.
Unsigned pleadings, CivPro Rule 11.
Striking portion of pleadings, CivPro
Rule 12.
Domestic relations actions, DomRel
Rule 12.
Summary judgment.
See SUMMARY JUDGMENT.
Summons.
See SUMMONS AND PROCESS.
Supplemental pleadings, CivPro Rule
15.
Adoption proceedings, Adoption Rule
15.
Domestic relations actions, DomRel
Rule 15.
Tax proceedings.
Filing of documents, Tax Rule 4.
Form and style of papers, Tax Rule 4.
Telephone number of signer.
Information required on pleadings,
motions and other filings, CivPro
Rule 11.
Third party practice, CivPro Rule 14.
Motion to bring in third party, CivPro
Form CA 22-B.
Summons and complaint against third
party defendant, CivPro Form CA
22-A.
Time issues, CivPro Rule 9.
Domestic relations actions, DomRel
Rule 9.
Verification, CivPro Rule 9-I, USDistCt
LCvR 5.1, USDistCt LCvR 11.2.
Criminal proceedings, USDistCt LCrR
49.

PLEADINGS —Cont'd
Verification —Cont'd
Form, CivPro Form CA 101.
Probate proceedings, Probate Rule 3.
Veterans' estates.
Filing pleadings or orders affecting
estates, CivPro Rule 5-I.

PLEAS IN CRIMINAL CASES,
CrimPro Rule 11.
Delinquent minors, JuvProc Rules 11,
12.
Withdraw of plea, JuvProc Rule 32.
**Hearing commissioners' power to
accept pleas,** CrimPro Rule 117.
Presence of defendant, CrimPro Rule
43.
**Withdrawal of guilty or nolo
contendere plea,** CrimPro Rule 32.
Delinquent minors, JuvProc Rule 32.

PLEDGES.
Corporations.
Powers, §29-303.02.
Nonprofit corporations.
Powers, §29-403.02.

**PLENARY PROCEEDING,
DIRECTION OF.**
Probate proceedings, §§16-3105,
16-3106.

PLEUROPNEUMONIA, §1-333.01.

PLUMBERS.
Board of industrial trades,
§§47-2853.06 to 47-2853.10.
Business licenses, §§47-2853.121 to
47-2853.123.
Eligibility, §47-2853.122.
Representations prohibited,
§47-2853.123.
Scope of practice, §47-2853.121.
Construction codes.
See CONSTRUCTION CODES.
Licenses, §2-135.

PLUMBING INSPECTIONS, §§2-134
to 2-137.

PNEUMOCONIOSIS.
Workers' compensation, §32-1510.

PODIATRY.
Board of, §3-1202.10.
Definition of practice of, §3-1201.02.
Health occupations boards.
General provisions, §§3-1201.01 to
3-1213.01.
See HEALTH OCCUPATIONS
BOARDS.

PODIATRY —Cont'd

Health occupations licensure, registration or certification, §§3-1205.01 to 3-1205.24.
See HEALTH OCCUPATIONS LICENSURE, REGISTRATION OR CERTIFICATION.

Titles and terms prohibited as misrepresentation without license to practice, §3-1210.03.

POINT OF SALE TERMINALS, §§26-131.01 to 26-131.13.
See AUTOMATED TELLER MACHINES.

POINT OF SERVICE PLANS.

Health maintenance organizations, §31-3429.

POISON.

Assault with intent to, §22-401.

Lead-hazard prevention and elimination, §§8-231.01 to 8-231.20.
See LEAD-HAZARD PREVENTION AND ELIMINATION.

POLICE AND FIREFIGHTERS RETIREMENT AND DISABILITY, §§5-631 to 5-762.

Age requirements, §5-712.

Amount of benefits.
Determination of amount of pension relief, §5-743.
Limits, §5-723.01.

Appropriations, §5-732.

Assignment of funds prohibited, §5-723.05.

Benefits.
Computation, §5-723.01.
Limits on amount, §5-723.01.
Minimum distributions, §5-723.03.

Board, §5-722.

Burial expenses, §5-720.

Capitol police, §10-505.04.

Computation of benefits, §5-723.01.

Conditional retirement.
Police retirement while under disciplinary investigation, §§5-801 to 5-807.

Contributions.
Made by mistake, §5-706.
Maximum amount, §5-723.01.

Cost-of-living adjustments (COLA), §§5-718, 5-719.

Creditable service, §§5-704, 5-705.

Death benefits, distribution, §5-723.01.

POLICE AND FIREFIGHTERS RETIREMENT AND DISABILITY —Cont'd

Deductions, §§5-706, 5-717.

Deferred annuities, §5-717.

Definitions, §§5-631, 5-701.

Delegation of functions by mayor, §5-724.

Denial of claim for benefits.
Procedure, §§1-751 to 1-753.

Deposits, §§5-706, 5-741.

Disability retirement for disability incurred or aggravated in performance of duty, §§5-710, 5-711.

Disability retirement for disability not incurred in performance of duty, §5-709.

Disciplinary actions.
Firefighter retirement while under disciplinary investigation, §§5-1051 to 5-1057.

Distributions.
Minimum amount, §5-723.03.

Earning capacity, restoration of, §5-714.

Employment, reporting, §5-721.

Equalization of widows' and orphans' pensions, §5-744.

Executions, funds exempt from, §5-723.05.

Existing rights and reliefs, not affecting, §§5-731, 5-747.

Federal law, eligibility for benefits under, §5-733.

Federal payments, reduction in, §1-725.

Firefighter retirement while under disciplinary investigation, §§5-1051 to 5-1057.

Forfeitures, application of, §5-723.04.

Fund, §§1-712, 1-903.01.

Funeral expenses, §5-720.

Increases in amounts, §5-745.

Injuries sustained in performance of duty, §§5-633, 5-707 to 5-708.01, 5-710.

Involuntary separation from service due to injury or disease, §5-713.

Limited duty status, §§5-631 to 5-635.

Limits on amount of benefits, §5-723.01.

Longevity compensation.
Inclusion for purpose of retirement annuity calculations, §5-723.02.

Mayor's duties, §§5-721, 5-724.

POLICE AND FIREFIGHTERS RETIREMENT AND DISABILITY
—Cont'd
Medical examination requirements, §5-721.
Medical expenses, payment of.
Active members, §5-707.
Injuries sustained in performance of duty, §5-708.01.
Total disability retirees, §5-708.
Medical leave.
Non-performance of duty injuries, §5-634.
Performance of duty injuries, §5-633.
Military or naval service, credit for, §5-742.
Federal benefit payments affected by purchase of military service credit, §1-803.02.
Misconduct.
Police retirement while under disciplinary investigation, §§5-801 to 5-807.
Officers retired prior to July 1, 1953, §5-746.
Optional retirement at 25 years of service and 50 years of age, §5-712.
Overpayments, §5-721.
Payment of moneys, §§5-633, 5-707 to 5-708.01, 5-723, 5-741.
Recovery from disability, §§5-714, 5-715.
Redeployment of retirees, §§5-761, 5-762.
Reduction in federal payments to, §1-725.
Reduction of annuity, §§5-714, 5-723.
Refunds, §§5-706, 5-717.
Resignation.
Police retirement while under disciplinary investigation, §§5-801 to 5-807.
Rollover payments, §5-706.
Secret Service, §5-703.
Survivors, §§5-702, 5-716, 5-744, 5-747.
Suspension of annuity, §5-714.
Waiver or release of annuity, §5-723.

POLICE BRUTALITY.
Chokeholds, §§5-125.01 to 5-125.03.
Office of police complaints.
General provisions, §§5-1101 to 5-1115.
See OFFICE OF POLICE COMPLAINTS.

POLICE CODE, §§5-103.01, 5-103.02.

POLICE COMPLAINTS, OFFICE OF, §§5-1101 to 5-1115.
See OFFICE OF POLICE COMPLAINTS.

POLICE DEPARTMENTS.
Capitol police.
See CAPITOL POLICE.
District of Columbia housing authority police department, §6-223.
Metropolitan police.
General provisions, §§5-101.01 to 5-133.21.
See METROPOLITAN POLICE.
Park Police.
General provisions, §§5-201 to 5-208.
See UNITED STATES PARK POLICE.

POLICE OFFICERS.
Capitol police.
See CAPITOL POLICE.
Generally.
See LAW ENFORCEMENT OFFICERS.
Metropolitan police.
General provisions, §§5-101.01 to 5-133.21.
See METROPOLITAN POLICE.
Office of police complaints.
General provisions, §§5-1101 to 5-1115.
See OFFICE OF POLICE COMPLAINTS.
United States park police, §§5-201 to 5-208.
See UNITED STATES PARK POLICE.

POLIOMYELITIS.
Immunization of school students, §§38-501 to 38-508.
Interstate compact on educational opportunity for military children.
Time to obtain immunizations, §49-1101.05.

POLITICAL ACTIVITIES BY GOVERNMENT EMPLOYEES, §§1-1171.01 to 1-1171.07.
Activity authorized, §1-1171.02.
Applicability, §1-1171.07.
Candidate defined, §1-1171.01.
Definitions, §1-1171.01.
Designation of employee to solicit, accept or receive contributions while on leave.
Mayor and members of council, §1-1171.02.
Employee defined, §1-1171.01.

POLITICAL ACTIVITIES BY GOVERNMENT EMPLOYEES —Cont'd

Enforcement, §1-1171.04.

On duty defined, §1-1171.01.

Partisan defined, §1-1171.01.

Partisan political group defined, §1-1171.01.

Political activity defined, §1-1171.01.

Political contribution defined, §1-1171.01.

Political party defined, §1-1171.01.

Political purpose defined, §1-1171.01.

Prohibitions, §§1-1171.02, 1-1171.03.

While on duty, §1-1171.03.

Requesting subordinates to participate in campaign or make contribution.

Prohibition, §1-1171.02.

Rules, §1-1171.06.

Sanctions for violations, §1-1171.04.

POLITICAL PARTIES.

Campaign practices.

General provisions.

See CAMPAIGN FINANCE.

Child labor.

Political literature, distribution of, §32-215.

Discrimination.

Political affiliation discrimination, prohibition of, §2-1401.01.

Discrimination based on political affiliation.

Insurance.

Unfair trade practices, §§31-2231.01 to 31-2231.25.

Elections.

Board of elections, §§1-1001.02 to 1-1001.06.

Campaign practices.

See CAMPAIGN FINANCE.

General provisions, §§1-1001.01 to 1-1041.04.

See ELECTIONS.

Recall of elected public officials, §§1-204.111 to 1-204.115.

See RECALL OF ELECTED PUBLIC OFFICIALS.

Government employees engaging political activities, §§1-1171.01 to 1-1171.07.

See POLITICAL ACTIVITIES BY GOVERNMENT EMPLOYEES.

Public officers and employees.

Political rights of, §§1-625.01, 1-625.02.

POLITICAL PARTIES —Cont'd

Teachers.

Political rights of, §1-625.02.

POLITICAL SUBDIVISIONS.

Airspace structures of federal and District governments, §10-1121.11.

Charter schools.

Federal agency assistance, §38-1802.15.

Compacts between the states or with foreign powers, US Const Art I §10.

Constitution of the United States.

Admission of new states, US Const Art IV §3.

Bill of attainder, US Const Art I §10.

Bills of credit, US Const Art I §10.

Commerce, US Const Art I §§8, 9.

Compacts between the states or with foreign powers, US Const Art I §10.

Contracts.

Impairing obligations of contracts, US Const Art I §10.

Controversies between citizens of different states, US Const Art III §2.

Controversies between states, US Const Art III §2.

Duties and imposts, US Const Art I §10.

Equal suffrage in senate, US Const Art V.

Exports, US Const Art I §§9, 10.

Ex post facto laws, US Const Art I §10.

Full faith and credit clause, US Const Art IV §1.

Gold and silver coin tender in payment of debts, US Const Art I §10.

Impairing obligations of contracts, US Const Art I §10.

Imports and exports, US Const Art I §10.

Invasion.

Protection against, US Const Art IV §4.

Legal tender, US Const Art I §10.

Letters of marque or reprisal, US Const Art I §10.

Limitations on powers of the state, US Const Art I §10.

Money.

Coining money, US Const Art I §10.

POLITICAL SUBDIVISIONS —Cont'd
Constitution of the United States
—Cont'd
New states, US Const Art IV §3.
Powers, US Const Art I §10.
Reserved to state, US Const Amd
10.
Protection and aid of states, US Const
Art IV §4.
Republican form of government
guaranteed, US Const Art IV §4.
Reservation of powers to state, US
Const Amd 10.
Right to coin money, US Const Art I
§10.
Suits against, US Const Amd 11.
Tender in payment of debts, US Const
Art I §10.
Tonnage, US Const Art I §10.
Treaties, US Const Art I §10.
Troops or ships of war in time of
peace, US Const Art I §10.
War, US Const Art I §10.
Contracts.
Impairing obligations of contracts, US
Const Art I §10.
Customs.
Exportations from any state.
Duties not to be laid on, US Const
Art I §9.
State may not impose without consent
of congress, US Const Art I §10.
**Energy plan submitted to federal
agencies,** §8-1779.01.
**Fairfax County Sewage Delivery
System and Capacity Purchase
Agreement,** §24-106.
Foreign missions.
Preemption of laws regarding,
§§6-1307, 6-1310.
Foster care.
Federal financial participation in,
§4-217.04.
Highway projects, federally-aided,
§§9-107.01 to 9-107.04.
Invasion.
Protection against, US Const Art IV
§4.
Liability of United States, §1-109.
**Library as designated depository of
government publications,**
§39-124.
Maryland.
See MARYLAND.
Metropolitan police.
Cooperative agreements, §5-133.17.

POLITICAL SUBDIVISIONS —Cont'd
Metropolitan police —Cont'd
Emergencies, control by federal
government in, §1-207.40.
Federal property, protection of,
§5-133.05.
**Metropolitan Washington Airports
Authority.**
Federal employees, §9-1007.
Metrorail and metrobus.
Adopted regional system, §§9-1111.01
to 9-1111.17.
See METRORAIL AND
METROBUS.
Compact for mass transportation,
§§9-1103.01 to 9-1103.07.
Interstate agreement on, §9-1101.01.
Joint state oversight agency,
§§9-1109.01 to 9-1109.07.
Washington Metropolitan area transit
authority Compact, §§9-1107.01 to
9-1107.12.
**Motor vehicle safety responsibility
and government vehicles,**
§§50-1301.37, 50-1301.44.
Nobility, titles of.
Titles of nobility prohibited, US Const
Art I §§9, 10.
Parking.
Federal property, §50-2624.
Park Police.
General provisions, §§5-201 to 5-208.
See UNITED STATES PARK
POLICE.
Parks and recreation.
See PARKS AND RECREATION.
**Placement of orders with federal
departments and agencies,**
§1-301.01.
**Police and firefighters retirement
and disability.**
Eligibility for benefits under federal
law, §5-733.
Reciprocal arrangements with.
See RECIPROCITY.
**Rental of public space by
governments,** §10-1101.02.
Republican form of government.
Guaranteed to states, US Const Art IV
§4.
**Restaurants run by federal
government.**
Health regulations, §7-2701.
Secret Service.
See UNITED STATES SECRET
SERVICE DIVISION.

POLITICAL SUBDIVISIONS —Cont'd
**Services furnished between Federal
  and District governments,**
  §1-207.37.
United States Army.
  See NATIONAL GUARD.
Virginia.
  See VIRGINIA.
**Water supply and waterworks
  supplied to United States
  Government,** §34-2401.25.

POLL TAX.
Failure to pay poll or other tax.
  Denial or abridgement of right to vote,
    US Const Art I §9, Amd 24.

POLLUTION.
Air pollution, §§8-101.05 to 8-101.06.
  See AIR POLLUTION.
Water pollution, §§8-103.01 to
  8-103.20.
  See WATER POLLUTION.

**POLYBROMINATED DIPHENYL
  ETHERS,** §§8-108.02, 8-108.04,
  8-108.05.

POLYGRAPHS, §§32-901 to 32-903.

POLYSOMNOGRAPHY.
Advisory committee, §7-743.06.
Board of medicine.
  Advisory committee on
    polysomnography, §3-1202.03.
Definitions, §3-1201.02.
**Health occupations licensure,
  registration or certification,**
  §§3-1205.01 to 3-1205.24.
  See HEALTH OCCUPATIONS
    LICENSURE, REGISTRATION
    OR CERTIFICATION.
**Titles and terms prohibited as
  misrepresentation without
  license to practice,** §3-1210.03.

POLYSTYRENE.
**Disposable food service ware,
  management,** §§8-1531 to 8-1537.

POOL BUYING GROUPS.
Alcoholic beverages.
  Creation, §25-122.
  Importation permits, §25-119.
    Fee, §25-511.
  Retail agent permits.
    Applications, §25-411.
  Sales licenses, §25-102.

POOL TABLES.
Business licenses, §47-2821.

POOR PERSONS.
See INDIGENT PERSONS.

**POPULAR NAMES AND SHORT
  TITLES.**
Abandoned vehicles.
  Removal and disposition of abandoned
    and other unlawfully parked
    vehicles reform act, §50-2421.01.
**Abatement of dangerous conditions
  on public space,** §§10-1181.01 to
  10-1181.07.
ABLE savings accounts, §§47-4901,
  47-4902.
AccessRX act, §§48-831.01 to
  48-831.42.
Access to justice for bicyclists,
  §50-1621.
**Act for the regulation of credit life
  insurance and credit accident
  and health insurance,** §31-5101.
**Act to secure the attendance of
  witnesses from without a state
  in criminal proceedings,**
  §§23-1501 to 23-1504.
**Adoption incentive program and
  special funds,** §§4-341 to 4-346.
**Adult guardianship and protective
  proceedings jurisdiction act,**
  §§21-2401.02 to 21-2401.06.
**Anacostia River cleanup and
  protection fertilizer act,**
  §8-104.01.
**Anacostia waterfront environmental
  standards act,** §2-1226.31.
Anatomical gift revision act of 2008,
  §§7-1531.01 to 7-1531.28.
Anti-terrorism act, §22-3151.
Automated teller machine act,
  §26-131.01.
Automated traffic enforcement,
  §§50-2209.01 to 50-2209.11.
Autonomous vehicles, §§50-2351 to
  50-2354.
Baby drop-off law.
  Newborn safe haven, §§4-1451.01 to
    4-1451.08.
Banks and financial institutions.
  General provisions of the 21st century
    financial modernization act,
    §26-551.01.
  Merchant bank act, §26-831.01.
  Universal bank certification act,
    §26-1401.01.
Bees.
  Sustainable urban agriculture
    apiculture act of 2012, §8-1825.01.

0

0# INDEX

0**POPULAR NAMES AND SHORT TITLES** —Cont'd

Benefit corporation act of 2012, §29-1301.01.

Bicycle and pedestrian priority area program, §50-2371.

Bicycles.
Complete streets policy, §50-2381.

Bicyclists.
Access to justice for bicyclists, §50-1621.

Boating under the influence.
Chemical testing, §50-1908.
Offense generally, §50-2206.31.

Boiler inspection act, §2-101.

Bonus pay and special awards pay act of 2016, §§1-551.01 to 1-551.06.

Bullying, §§2-1535.01 to 2-1535.09.

Business corporation act of 2010, §29-301.01.

Business organizations code, §29-101.01.

Business organizations code general provisions act of 2010, §29-101.01.

Campaign finance, §1-1163.01.

Captive insurance agency establishment act of 2008, §1-307.95.

Chief tenant advocate.
Office of the chief tenant advocate establishment act, §42-3531.01.

Child abduction prevention act, §16-4604.01.

Child fatality review committee establishment act, §4-1371.01.

Childhood lead poisoning screening and reporting act, §7-871.01.

Colleges and universities.
Public postsecondary education reorganization act, §38-1201.01.

Commercial code, §28:1-101.
Bank deposits and collections, §28:4-101.
Documents of title, §28:7-101.
Funds transfers, §28:4A-101.
General provisions, §28:1-101.
Investment securities, §28:8-101.
Leases, §28:2A-101.
Letters of credit, §28:5-101.
Negotiable instruments, §28:3-101.
Sales, §28:2-101.
Secured transactions, §28:9-101.

Community development act, §26-431.01.

Community schools incentive act, §38-754.01.

POPULAR NAMES AND SHORT TITLES —Cont'd

Complete streets policy, §50-2381.

Compulsory school attendance, §§38-201 to 38-213.

Condominiums.
Horizontal property regimes act, §42-2001.

Construction and demolition waste recycling accountability, §8-1071.

Credit life insurance and credit accident and health insurance.
Act for the regulation of credit life insurance and credit accident and health insurance, §31-5101.

Criminal abuse, neglect, and financial exploitation of vulnerable adults and the elderly act of 2000, §22-931.

Criminal background checks for the protection of children act, §4-1501.01.

Customer service operations establishment act, §1-327.31.

Dc streetcar service, §50-921.71.

Death.
Presumptive disability or death of emergency medical services or fire department employees, §5-651.

Department of corrections inmate and returning citizen assistance grant, §24-211.71.

Department of mental health establishment amendment act, §7-1131.01.

Department on disability services establishment act, §7-761.01.

Disabilities, persons with.
Criminal abuse, neglect, and financial exploitation of vulnerable adults and the elderly act of 2000, §22-931.
Department on disability services establishment act, §7-761.01.

Disclaimer of property interests act, §19-1501.

Distracted driving safety act, §50-1731.01.

Dog leash laws, §§1-303.41, 8-1808, 22-1311.

Driverless vehicles, §§50-2351 to 50-2354.

Driving under the influence, §50-2206.01.
Chemical testing, §50-1901.
Diversion programs, §50-2206.53.

00I-934

POPULAR NAMES AND SHORT TITLES —Cont'd

Early childhood education act, §38-755.01.

Early intervention program establishment act, §7-863.01.

Early warning and support system act, §38-751.01.

Emergency medical services.
Presumptive disability or death of emergency medical services or fire department employees, §5-651.

Entity transactions act of 2010, §29-201.01.

Fiduciaries act, §21-1712.

Fire and casualty act, §31-2501.01.

Fire departments.
Presumptive disability or death of emergency medical services or fire department employees, §5-651.

First amendment assemblies act, §5-331.01.

First source compliance act, §2-219.31.

Foster care.
Rights and responsibilities for youth in foster care, §4-1303.71.

Freedom of information act, §2-540.

General cooperative association act of 2010, §29-901.

General license law, §§47-2805.01 to 47-2881.

General provisions of the 21st century financial modernization act, §26-551.01.

Good Samaritans act, §§7-401 to 7-403.

Government ethics act, §1-1162.01.

Government ethics act of 2011, §§1-1162.01 to 1-1162.32.

Health benefits plans grievance procedures, §§44-301.01 to 44-304.01.

Health occupations licensure, registration or certification, §3-1205.01.

Hit and run.
Leaving after colliding, §50-2201.05c.

Home Rule act, §1-201.01.

Horizontal property act, §42-2001.

Hospital discharge planning, §§21-2231.01 to 21-2231.05.

Housing and community development reform advisory commission act, §6-1031.

Ian's law, §§31-3011 to 31-3013.

POPULAR NAMES AND SHORT TITLES —Cont'd

Impaired driving, §50-2206.01.

Implied consent.
Boating under the influence, §50-1908.
Driving under the influence, §50-1901.

Incarceration to incorporation entrepreneurship program, §2-1210.55.

Insurance producer licensing act, §31-1131.01.

Interagency collaboration and services integration commission establishment act, §2-1591.

Interstate compact on educational opportunity for military children, §§49-1101.01 to 49-1101.20.

Interstate depositions and discovery act, §13-441.

Interstate family support, §§46-351.01 to 46-359.03.

Lead poisoning.
Childhood lead poisoning screening and reporting act, §7-871.01.

Leash laws, §§1-303.41, 8-1808, 22-1311.

Lemon law, §§50-501 to 50-510.

Life insurance act, §31-4201.

Living wage act, §2-220.01.

Low-income housing preservation and protections act, §42-2851.01.

Made in DC program, §§2-1208.31 to 2-1208.35.

Medicaid.
Medicaid and special education reform fund establishment act, §4-204.51.
Office of Medicaid operations reform establishment act, §4-204.11.

Medical examiners, §5-1401.

Medication advisory committee receiving gifts or remuneration prohibition act, §48-842.01.

Megan's law.
Sex offender registration, §§22-4001 to 22-4017.

Mental health consumers' rights protection act, §7-1231.01.

Mental health department.
Department of mental health establishment amendment act, §7-1131.01.

Merchant bank act, §26-831.01.

Metropolitan police.
Police investigations concerning first amendment activities act, §5-333.01.

**POPULAR NAMES AND SHORT
TITLES** —Cont'd

Series trusts, §§29-1204.01 to
29-1204.05.

**Small and certified business
enterprise development and
assistance,** §2-218.01.

SOAR act, §38-1853.01.

Solar for All program, §8-1774.16.

Streetcars.
DC streetcar service, §50-921.71.

**Sustainable urban agriculture
apiculture act of 2012,** §8-1825.01.

Taxicabs.
Public vehicles for hire, §§50-301.01 to
50-301.34.

Telehealth reimbursement, §31-3861.

Testing integrity act, §§38-771.01 to
38-771.07.

Traffic act, §50-2201.01.

Trash compactor grant program,
§§8-751 to 8-753.

Trusts and trustees.
Uniform trust code, §19-1301.01.

UCC, §28:1-101.

Unauthorized entities act of 2006,
§§31-231 to 31-233.

Unemployment compensation act,
§51-126.

**Uniform adult guardianship and
protective proceedings
jurisdiction act,** §§21-2401.02 to
21-2401.06.

**Uniform anatomical gift revision act
of 2008,** §§7-1531.01 to 7-1531.28.

**Uniform certificates of title for
vessels,** §§50-1541.01 to 50-1541.28.

**Uniform child abduction prevention
act,** §16-4604.01.

Uniform child custody proceedings,
§§16-4601.01 to 16-4605.03.

Uniform collaborative law act,
§16-4001.

Uniform commercial code, §28:1-101.
Bank deposits and collections,
§28:4-101.
Documents of title, §28:7-101.
Funds transfers, §28:4A-101.
General provisions, §28:1-101.
Investment securities, §28:8-101.
Leases, §28:2A-101.
Letters of credit, §28:5-101.
Negotiable instruments, §28:3-101.
Sales, §28:2-101.
Secured transactions, §28:9-101.

**POPULAR NAMES AND SHORT
TITLES** —Cont'd

Uniform custodial trust law,
§§19-1101 to 19-1120.

**Uniform disclaimer of property
interests act,** §19-1501.

Uniform electronic transactions act,
§§28-4901 to 28-4918.

Uniform fiduciaries act, §21-1712.

**Uniform foreign-country money
judgments recognition act of
2011,** §15-361.

Uniform general power of attorney,
§§21-2101 to 21-2118.

**Uniform interstate depositions and
discovery act,** §13-441.

**Uniform interstate family support
act,** §§46-351.01 to 46-359.03.

Uniform law commission, §§3-1431 to
3-1433.

**Uniform limited cooperative
association act of 2010,**
§29-1001.01.

**Uniform limited liability company
act of 2010,** §29-801.01.

**Uniform limited partnership act of
2010,** §29-701.01.

Uniform mediation act, §§16-4201 to
16-4213.

**Uniform military and overseas
voters act,** §1-1061.01.

**Uniform nonprobate transfers on
death act of 2000,** §§19-601.01 to
19-603.11.

Uniform partnership act of 2010,
§29-601.01.

Uniform principal and income act,
§28-4801.01.

**Uniform prudent management of
institutional funds,** §§44-1631 to
44-1639.

**Uniform real property transfer on
death act,** §§19-604.01 to 19-604.19.

**Uniform statutory trust entity act of
2010,** §29-1201.01.

Uniform TOD security registration,
§§19-603.01 to 19-603.11.

Uniform trust code, §19-1301.01.

**Uniform unincorporated nonprofit
association act of 2010,** §29-1101.

**Uniform unsworn foreign
declarations act,** §16-5301.

**Unit pricing requirements act of
2012,** §28-5201.

Universal bank certification act,
§26-1401.01.

POPULAR NAMES AND SHORT TITLES —Cont'd

Vulnerable adults.

Criminal abuse, neglect, and financial exploitation of vulnerable adults and the elderly act of 2000, §22-931.

Workforce investment implementation, §§32-1601 to 32-1661.

Workplace fraud, §32-1331.01.

Youth behavioral health epidemiology report act, §2-1517.01.

PORNOGRAPHY.

Child pornography.

Sexual performances using minors, §§22-3101 to 22-3104.

Obscenity.

General provisions, §§22-2201 to 22-3104.

See OBSCENITY.

PORTABLE ELECTRONICS INSURANCE, §§31-5051.01 to 31-5051.06.

Compensation of employees or authorized representatives, §31-5051.02.

Definitions, §31-5051.01.

Disclosures, §31-5051.02.

Limited lines licensing of vendors, §31-5051.02.

Suspension or revocation of ability of employees or authorized representatives to act under license.

Penalties for violations of provisions, §31-5051.05.

Modification of coverage, §31-5051.04.

Penalties for violations of provisions, §31-5051.05.

Premiums.

Billing and collection, §31-5051.03.

Termination of coverage for nonpayment of premium, §31-5051.04.

Reporting violation of provisions, §31-5051.05.

Rulemaking to implement provisions, §31-5051.06.

Supervising entity.

Defined, §31-5051.01.

Duties, §31-5051.02.

PORTABLE ELECTRONICS INSURANCE —Cont'd

Suspension of right to transact business.

Penalties for violations of provisions, §31-5051.05.

Termination of coverage, §31-5051.04.

Training.

Limited lines licensing of vendors, §31-5051.02.

Vendors.

Defined, §31-5051.01.

Licensing, §31-5051.02.

Reporting violation of provisions, §31-5051.05.

POSSESSION, ESTATES IN, §§42-506, 42-507.

POST-ADOPTION CONTACT AGREEMENTS, §4-361.

POST-CONVICTION DNA TESTING, §§22-4131 to 22-4135.

POST-CONVICTION PROCEEDINGS.

Appeals, federal cases.

Direct criminal appeals not delayed to handle postconviction proceedings in district court, USCtApp Rule 47.5.

Superior court proceedings, PostConvRel Rules 1 to 12.

Answers, PostConvRel Rule 5.

Appeal, time of, PostConvRel Rule 11.

Applicability of rules of criminal and civil procedure, PostConvRel Rule 12.

Appointment of counsel, PostConvRel Rule 4.

Evidentiary hearing, PostConvRel Rule 8.

Consideration by judge, PostConvRel Rule 4.

Delayed motions, PostConvRel Rule 9.

Discovery, PostConvRel Rule 6.

Evidentiary hearing, PostConvRel Rule 8.

Filing motion, PostConvRel Rule 3.

Forms.

Motions involving Rule 9(b) issues, PostConvRel Forms 1, 2.

Motion to vacate, set aside or correct sentence and judgment, PostConvRel Forms 3, 4.

Motions, PostConvRel Rule 2.

Answers, PostConvRel Rule 5.

POST-CONVICTION PROCEEDINGS —Cont'd
Superior court proceedings —Cont'd
Motions —Cont'd
Consideration by judge, PostConvRel Rule 4.
Delayed or successive motions, PostConvRel Rule 9.
Filing motion, PostConvRel Rule 3.
Record, expansion of, PostConvRel Rule 7.
Scope of rules, PostConvRel Rule 1.
Service of process, PostConvRel Rule 3.
Successive motions, PostConvRel Rule 9.

POSTHUMOUS CHILDREN.
Decedents' estates, §42-704.
Intestate succession, §19-314.

POSTING, SERVICE BY.
Adoption proceedings, Adoption Rule 4.
Domestic relations actions, DomRel Rule 4.
Landlord and tenant court, LandlordTenant Rule 4.

POST OFFICE.
Constitutional provisions, US Const Art I §8.

POSTSECONDARY EDUCATIONAL DEGREE GRANTING INSTITUTIONS.
Requirements, licensure, §§38-1301 to 38-1313.
See HIGHER EDUCATION LICENSURE COMMISSION.

POTENTIALLY DANGEROUS DOGS, §§8-1901 to 8-1908.
See DANGEROUS DOGS.

POTOMAC BLUESTONE.
Official rock of District of Columbia, §§1-165.01, 1-165.02.

POTOMAC INTERCEPTOR (DULLES INTERNATIONAL AIRPORT SANITARY SEWER), §§34-2131 to 34-2134.

POTOMAC PARK, §§10-147 to 10-151.
Boathouses on banks of tidal reservoir.
Licenses, §10-151.
Construction of lagoon, artificial body of water or speedway.
Restriction on expenditure of money, §10-149.

POTOMAC PARK —Cont'd
Control, §10-148.
Established, §10-147.
Parkway connecting park with Zoological and Rock Creek Parks, §§10-152, 10-153.
Temporary occupancy by Department of Agriculture, §10-150.

POTOMAC RIVER.
Highway Bridge over, §9-307.
Throwing or depositing matter into, §§22-4402, 22-4403.
United States title to lands or waters of, §10-102.

POTOMAC RIVER BASIN COMPACT, §§8-1601, 8-1602.

POTOMAC RIVER BRIDGES TOWING COMPACT, §§9-1117.01 to 9-1117.05.
General provisions, §9-1117.01.
Jurisdiction over vehicles towed or removed, §9-1117.03.
Parties to act on own authority, §9-1117.04.
Power and authority of parties, §9-1117.02.
Withdrawal, §9-1117.05.

POUND.
Animals.
Impounded animals, §§8-1805 to 8-1807.

POUR-OVER TRUSTS.
Wills, devises and bequests, §18-306.

POVERTY LAW.
Access to justice initiative program, §§4-1701.01 to 4-1704.07.
See ACCESS TO JUSTICE INITIATIVE PROGRAM.
Attorneys at law.
Right to counsel.
See RIGHT TO COUNSEL.
Indigent persons generally.
See INDIGENT PERSONS.
In forma pauperis proceedings.
Generally.
See IN FORMA PAUPERIS PROCEEDINGS.
Plan for furnishing representation to indigents, IndigentRep Rules I to IV.
Low and moderate income areas.
Community development by financial institutions, §§26-431.01 to 26-431.08.

POVERTY LAW —Cont'd
Low and moderate income residents.
See LOW AND MODERATE INCOME RESIDENTS.
Lower income home ownership tax abatement and incentives,
§§47-3501 to 47-3508.
Low-income housing preservation and protections act, §§42-2851.01 to 42-2851.08.
Low-income housing tax credit fund,
§42-2853.02.
Definitions, §42-2853.01.
Public assistance.
General provisions, §§4-201.01 to 4-221.01.
See PUBLIC ASSISTANCE.

POWER BOATS.
Bridges, requirements for going under, §9-309.

POWERS OF APPOINTMENT,
§§42-1001 to 42-1019.
Absolute power.
Limited estate, owner of, §42-1005.
No remainder on grantee's estate, §42-1007.
Unlimited estate, owner of, §42-1006.
Beneficial power, §42-1004.
Liability in equity, §42-1010.
Definition of power, §42-1001.
Devise, executed by, §42-1018.
Direct reference to power, execution without, §42-1019.
Disclaimer of property interest.
Appointee, object or taker in default of exercise.
Disclaimer by, §19-1510.
Generally, §§19-1501 to 19-1518.
See DISCLAIMER OF PROPERTY INTERESTS.
Power of appointment or other power not held in fiduciary capacity.
Rules applicable to disclaimer, §19-1509.
Distribution between beneficiaries,
§42-1015.
General power, §42-1002.
In trust, §42-1011.
Grant, executed by, §42-1018.
Limited estate.
Absolute power given to owner of, §42-1005.
Power to devise inheritance given to tenant with, §42-1008.
Power to devise inheritance given to tenant with limited estate,
§42-1008.

POWERS OF APPOINTMENT
—Cont'd
Reservation of power by grantor,
§42-1009.
Special power, §42-1003.
Liability in equity, §42-1010.
Tenant with limited estate, power to devise inheritance given to,
§42-1008.
Trust powers.
Execution for benefit of creditors and assignees, §42-1016.
General power in trust, §42-1011.
Grantee's right of selection of objects of trust, §42-1014.
Imperative nature of, §42-1013.
Special power in trust, §42-1012.
Will, executed by, §42-1018.
Written instrument required for execution of, §42-1017.

POWERS OF ATTORNEY, §§21-2101 to 21-2118.
Acknowledgment of deed, §42-101.
Applicability provisions, §21-2118.
Banks and financial institutions,
§21-2108.
Beneficiary transactions generally,
§21-2111.
Business operations, §21-2109.
Claims and litigation, power to settle, §21-2112.
Commodity transactions, §21-2107.
Custodial power of attorney.
Parents authorized to create, §21-2301.
Disclaimer of property interests,
§§19-1501 to 19-1518.
See DISCLAIMER OF PROPERTY INTERESTS.
Durability under uniform general powers, §21-2102.
Durable powers of attorney,
§§21-2081 to 21-2085.
See DURABLE POWERS OF ATTORNEY.
Estates, §21-2111.
Existing and future interests, applicable to, §21-2117.
Fiduciaries.
Nonresident or absent fiduciary, CivPro Rule 305.
Probate proceedings, Probate Rules 14, 106.
Foreign interests, §21-2117.
Governmental programs, §21-2114.

POWERS OF ATTORNEY —Cont'd

Healthcare decisions.

General provisions.

See HEALTHCARE DURABLE
POWERS OF ATTORNEY.

Heath-care decisions.

General provisions, §§21-2201 to
21-2213.

Insurance, §21-2110.

Interpretation of provisions,
§§21-2103 to 21-2118.

Intervention proceedings, Probate
Rules 301 to 361.

See INTERVENTION
PROCEEDINGS.

Medicaid, §21-2114.

Medicare, §21-2114.

Mental health consumers' rights,
§7-1231.06.

Military affairs, §21-2114.

Option transactions, §21-2107.

Parent and child.

Custodial power of attorney.

Parents authorized to create,
§21-2301.

Pensions and retirement, §§21-2114,
21-2115.

Personal property, §21-2105.

Probate proceedings.

Intervention proceedings, Probate
Rules 301 to 361.

See INTERVENTION
PROCEEDINGS.

Nonresident or absent fiduciary.

Death before Jan. 1, 1981, Probate
Rule 14.

Death between Jan. 1, 1981, and
June 30, 1995, Probate Rule
106.

Real property, §21-2104.

Security transactions, §§21-2106,
21-2107.

Social Security, §21-2114.

Statutory form for assigning,
§21-2101.

Stock and bond transactions,
§§21-2106, 21-2107.

Support and maintenance, §21-2113.

Tax matters, §21-2116.

Trusts and trustees, §21-2111.

**Uniform application and
interpretation of provisions,**
§21-2118.

Uniform fiduciaries act, §§21-1701 to
21-1712.

See FIDUCIARIES.

PRACTICE OF LAW.

Admission to the bar, DCCtApp Rule
46.

False statements, etc., ProfCond Rule
8.1.

Attorney general.

Forfeiture of position, §1-301.84.

Bar association.

See DISTRICT OF COLUMBIA BAR.

Court employees not to practice law.

Court of appeals, DCCtApp Rule 50.

Superior court, CivPro Rule 103.

Family division, FamDiv Rule T.

Lawyers generally.

See ATTORNEYS AT LAW.

**Non-lawyers sharing fees, managing
firm, etc.,** ProfCond Rule 5.4.

Restrictions on right to practice,
ProfCond Rule 5.5.

Unauthorized practice, DCCtApp
Rule 49, ProfCond Rule 5.5.

PRACTITIONERS.

Defined, §22-3225.01.

Health care practitioners.

General provisions, §§3-1201.01 to
3-1213.01.

See HEALTH OCCUPATIONS
BOARDS.

Health occupations licensure,
registration or certification,
§§3-1205.01 to 3-1205.24.

See HEALTH OCCUPATIONS
LICENSURE, REGISTRATION
OR CERTIFICATION.

Insurance fraud by, §§22-3225.07,
22-3225.14.

PRAECIPE.

Adoption proceedings.

Withdrawal of attorney by praecipe,
Adoption Rule 101.

Continuing effect of praecipe,
CrimPro Rule 112.

Domestic relations actions.

Withdrawal of attorney by praecipe,
DomRel Rule 101.

Landlord and tenant court.

Consent judgment praecipe,
LandlordTenant Forms 4, 4a.

Addendum, list of repairs,
LandlordTenant Form 4A.

**Scheduling order, praecipe
requesting,** CivPro Form CA 113.

PRECIOUS STONES.

Public auction permit requirements,
§47-2705.

PRE-CONVICTION DNA TESTING, §§22-4131 to 22-4135.

PREEXISTING CONDITIONS.
Defined terms, §31-3301.01.
Health insurance portability and accountability.
Group insurance provisions, §31-3303.07.

PREGNANCY.
Alcoholic beverage warnings, §25-712.
Breastmilk bank and lactation support, §§7-881.01 to 7-881.11.
Crime victims' compensation.
Medical expenses, VictComp Rule 24.
Discrimination based on, §2-1401.05.
Employment.
Reasonable accommodations for pregnant and nursing workers, §§32-1231.01 to 32-1231.15.
Labor and employment relations.
Reasonable accommodations for pregnant and nursing workers, §§32-1231.01 to 32-1231.15.
Prisoners.
Use of restraints on pregnant women, §§24-276.01 to 24-276.04.
Surrogate parenting contracts, §16-402.
Teenage pregnancy.
Public assistance.
Pregnant or parenting teens, §§4-205.61 to 4-205.66.
Teen pregnancy prevention fund, §§1-325.321 to 1-325.326.
Authorization for grant-managing entity, §1-325.325.
Definitions, §1-325.321.
Duplicative projects, §1-325.326.
Established, §1-325.322.
Grant-managing entity.
Authorization, §1-325.325.
Eligibility for grants, §§1-325.322, 1-325.323.
Limitation on duplicative projects, §1-325.326.
Reporting requirements, §1-325.324.
Reporting requirements, §1-325.324.
Required information before approval, §1-325.323.
Youth rehabilitation services department.
Use of restraints on pregnant youths, §§2-1515.51 to 2-1515.54.

PREGNANCY DISCRIMINATION, §2-1401.05.

PREHEARING CONFERENCE.
Appeals, federal cases, FRAP 33.

PREJUDICE OF JUDGE, CivPro Rule 63-I.
Adoption proceedings, Adoption Rule 63.
Domestic relations actions, DomRel Rule 63.
Probate proceedings.
Death between Jan. 1, 1981, and June 30, 1995, Probate Rule 126.
Prohibited, CJC Canon 2.3.

PRE-KINDERGARTEN PROGRAMS, §§38-271.01 to 38-275.01.
Discipline.
Out-of-school discipline, §38-273.03.
Early childhood development coordinating council, §38-271.07.
Enhancement and expansion of programs, §§38-271.01 to 38-271.07.
Administration of services, §38-271.02.
Capacity audit, §38-271.04.
Definitions, §38-271.01.
Duties of OSSE, §38-271.02.
Early childhood development coordinating council, §38-271.07.
Funding, §38-271.06.
Quality evaluation of current programs, §38-271.03.
Report to council, §38-271.05.
Expansion to universal pre-k.
Enrollment eligibility and priority, §38-273.02.
Evaluation of capacity, §38-273.01.
Implementation plan, §38-273.01.
Funding, §38-2807.
Enhancement and expansion of programs, §38-271.06.
High quality standards for existing programs.
Assistance grants, §38-272.03.
Audit of program in relation to high quality standards, §38-272.02.
Development, §38-272.01.
Licensing of child-occupied facilities.
Dry cleaning establishments in close proximity.
Restrictions on licensing, §38-271.01.
Out-of-school discipline, §38-273.03.
Rulemaking, §38-275.01.
State education office, §38-2602.

PRE-KINDERGARTEN PROGRAMS
—Cont'd
Teachers, workforce development.
Higher education incentive grant
program, §38-274.01.
Transfer of authority, §38-274.01a.
Higher education incentive scholarship
award program, §38-274.02.
Transfer of authority, §38-274.01a.

PRELIMINARY INJUNCTIONS,
CivPro Rule 65, USDistCt LCvR
65.1.

PREMARITAL AGREEMENTS,
§§19-113, 46-501 to 46-510.
Amendment, §46-505.
Construction, §46-510.
Content, §46-503.
Definitions, §46-501.
Effective date, §46-509.
**Effective upon marriage or domestic
partnership,** §46-504.
Enforcement, §46-506.
Formalities, §46-502.
Limitation of action, §46-508.
Revocation, §46-505.
Statutory rule against perpetuities.
Exclusions from rule, §19-904.
**Void marriage or domestic
partnership,** §46-507.

PREMIUM PAY.
Police and firefighters, §5-1304.

PREMIUMS.
Corporate income tax credit for,
§47-1807.05.
**Insurance premium finance
companies,** §§31-1101 to 31-1112.
Life insurance companies.
See LIFE INSURANCE COMPANIES.
Newborn health insurance, §31-3803.
Portable electronics insurance.
Billing and collection, §31-5051.03.
Termination of coverage for
nonpayment of premium,
§31-5051.04.
Premium finance companies.
See INSURANCE PREMIUM
FINANCE COMPANIES.
**Rehabilitation and liquidation
proceedings.**
Recovery of premiums owed in,
§31-1331.

PRENUPTIAL AGREEMENTS,
§§19-113, 46-501 to 46-510.

**PREPAID COLLEGE TUITION AND
SAVINGS,** §§47-4501 to 47-4512.
See COLLEGE SAVINGS PROGRAM.

**PREPONDERANCE OF THE
EVIDENCE.**
**Child abuse and neglect
proceedings.**
Factfinding hearings, NeglectProc Rule
19.
Crime victims' compensation.
Appeal of determination, VictComp
Rule 20.
**Enhanced penalties for certain
offenses against aged persons
and minors.**
Affirmative defense to be proved by
preponderance of evidence,
§22-3601.

PRESCRIPTION DRUGS.
Access to prescription drugs,
§§48-831.01 to 48-833.09.
AccessRx for the elderly, §§48-831.21
to 48-831.23.
AccessRx for uninsured District
residents, §§48-831.31 to
48-831.33.
AccessRx pharmaceutical resource
center, §§48-831.41, 48-831.42.
AccessRx program, §§48-831.01 to
48-831.42.
Administration of program,
§48-831.03.
Third-party administration,
§48-831.13.
Agreements with other jurisdictions
and entities, §48-831.16.
Cost containment, §48-831.04.
Definitions, §48-831.02.
Eligibility, §48-831.11.
AccessRx for low-income elderly,
§48-831.22.
AccessRx for uninsured District
residents, §48-831.32.
Establishment of program,
§48-831.03.
AccessRx for low-income elderly,
§48-831.21.
AccessRx for uninsured District
residents, §48-831.31.
Fund, §48-831.10.
Legislative findings, §48-831.01.
Manufacturers and labelers.
Publication of participation,
§48-831.09.
Method of prescribing or ordering
drugs, §48-831.12.

PRESCRIPTION DRUGS —Cont'd
Access to prescription drugs —Cont'd
AccessRx program —Cont'd
Operation of program, §48-831.07.
Rebates.
Agreements, §48-831.05.
Amount of rebates, §48-831.06.
Discrepancies in rebate amounts,
§48-831.08.
Reports, §48-831.15.
Rulemaking, §48-831.17.
Waiver of federal law, §48-831.14.
Marketing costs, disclosure of,
§§48-833.01 to 48-833.09.
Annual report by manufacturer or
labeler, content, §48-833.03.
Confidentiality of information,
§48-833.05.
Penalties, §48-833.06.
Reports, §§48-833.02 to 48-833.04,
48-833.08.
Requirement to disclose costs,
§48-833.01.
Rulemaking, §48-833.07.
Pharmacy benefits managers.
Defined, §48-831.02.
Transparent business practices
among, §§48-832.01 to
48-832.03.
Controlled substances, §48-903.08.
Oral prescriptions for, §3-1210.06.
Disposal of unused pharmaceuticals,
§§48-851.01 to 48-851.04.
Excessive pricing, §§28-4551 to
28-4555.
Forgery for prescription forms,
§22-3242.
Generic drug substitutes, §§48-803.01
to 48-803.05.
Dispensing, §48-803.02.
Conditions, §48-803.03.
Notice, §48-803.03a.
Formulary, §48-803.01.
Negligence.
Evidence of, §48-803.05.
Practice of medicine.
Evidence of, §48-803.05.
Recording and labeling, §48-803.04.
Therapeutic interchange list,
§48-803.01.
**Intellectual disabilities, persons
with.**
Administration of medication by
trained employees, §§21-1201 to
21-1206.
See INTELLECTUAL
DISABILITIES, PERSONS
WITH.

PRESCRIPTION DRUGS —Cont'd
**Labeling requirements for
prescriptions,** §47-2885.14.
Forgery for prescriptions, §22-3242.
List of most commonly used drugs,
§48-801.01.
**Medication advisory committee
receiving gifts or remuneration
prohibition act of 2008,**
§§48-842.01 to 48-842.04.
Mental health disclosures.
Federal regulation and monitoring of,
§7-1208.02.
Monitoring, §§48-853.01 to 48-853.10.
Confidentiality of information,
§48-853.05.
Definitions, §48-853.01.
Director's authority, §48-853.02.
Disclosure of information.
Criteria, §48-853.05.
Indicators of misuse, §48-853.07.
Unlawful disclosure, §48-853.09.
Dispensers.
Delegating access to database,
§48-853.04.
Reporting requirements, §48-853.03.
Immunity from liability, §48-853.08.
Interoperability.
Information exchange with other
monitoring programs,
§48-853.06.
Misuse.
Criteria for indicators of misuse,
§48-853.07.
Program objectives, §48-853.02.
Reporting requirements.
Dispensers, §48-853.03.
Rules, §48-853.10.
**Off-label use of prescription
medication,** §§48-841.01 to
48-841.04.
Adverse licensure determination.
Failure to comply with
requirements.
Use for determining, §48-841.04.
Definitions, §48-841.02.
Explanation to patient.
Required before prescribing or
administering, §48-841.03.
Failure to comply with requirements,
§48-841.04.
Information provided patient.
Required before prescribing or
administering, §48-841.03.
Off-label informed consent act of 2008.
Short title, §48-841.01.

PRESCRIPTION DRUGS —Cont'd
Off-label use of prescription medication —Cont'd
Off-label use defined, §48-841.02.
Requirements before prescribing, administering or furnishing medication, §48-841.03.
Pharmaceutical detailing.
Evaluation of effectiveness of law licensing persons practicing, §§48-844.01 to 48-844.03.
Pharmaceutical education program establishment act of 2008.
Education of prescribers in publicly funded, contracted or subsidized health-care programs, §§48-843.01 to 48-843.04.
Pharmacy benefits managers.
Defined, §48-831.02.
Transparent business practices among, §§48-832.01 to 48-832.03.
Pricing, §§48-801.01 to 48-804.51.
Advertising, §48-802.01.
Cease and desist orders, §48-804.03.
Definitions, §48-804.51.
Enforcement of provisions, §§48-804.01 to 48-804.03.
Excessive pricing, §§28-4551 to 28-4555.
Burden of proving price not excessive, §28-4554.
Civil remedies, §28-4555.
Definitions, §28-4552.
Determination of excessiveness, §28-4554.
Legislative findings, §28-4551.
Violation, §28-4553.
Fines and penalties for violations, §48-804.01.
Generic drug substitutes, §§48-803.01 to 48-803.05.
Inspections, §48-804.03.
Interference with disclosure of price information, §48-802.01.
Posting prices, §§48-801.01 to 48-801.06.
Completion and display of posters, §48-801.03.
Consumer information to reflect actual charges, §48-801.06.
List of commonly used drugs, §48-801.01.
Posters furnished pharmacies, contents, §48-801.02.
Services and drugs furnished at posted prices, §48-801.05.

PRESCRIPTION DRUGS —Cont'd
Pricing —Cont'd
Quotation of prices, services, charges, §48-801.04.
Records, §48-804.03.
Restraints of trade, §48-804.02.
SafeRX evaluation act of 2008.
Pharmaceutical detailing.
Evaluation of effectiveness of law licensing persons practicing, §§48-844.01 to 48-844.03.
Student health care.
Medication, §§38-651.01 to 38-651.12.
See STUDENT HEALTH CARE.
Substitutes, §§48-803.01 to 48-803.05.
Dispensing, §48-803.02.
Conditions, §48-803.03.
Notice, §48-803.03a.
Formulary, §48-803.01.
Negligence.
Evidence of, §48-803.05.
Practice of medicine.
Evidence of, §48-803.05.
Recording and labeling, §48-803.04.
Therapeutic interchange list, §48-803.01.
Therapeutic equivalents, §§48-803.01 to 48-803.05.
Unused pharmaceutical safe disposal, §§48-851.01 to 48-851.04.
Definitions, §48-851.01.
Health care facilities.
Prohibited methods of disposal, §48-851.03.
Mail-in program, §48-851.02.
Public education campaign, §48-851.02.
Recommendations to mayor, §48-851.02.
Rulemaking, §48-851.04.

PRESENCE OF CRIMINAL DEFENDANT, CrimPro Rule 43.
Delinquent minors, JuvProc Rule 43.
Detention or shelter care hearings, JuvProc Rule 107.
Transfer for criminal prosecution hearings, JuvProc Rule 109.

PRESENTMENTS, CrimPro Rule 109.

PRESIDENTIAL INAUGURAL CEREMONIES, §§2-801 to 2-810, 2-821 to 2-829.

PRESIDENT OF THE UNITED STATES.
Additional compensation, authority to grant, §1-333.07.

PRESIDENT OF THE UNITED STATES —Cont'd

Age, US Const Art II §1.

Aliens.

Ineligible for presidency, US Const Art II §1.

Ambassadors and consuls, US Const Art II §§2, 3.

Appointment of officers, etc., US Const Art II §2.

Approval of laws, US Const Art I §7.

Approval of order, resolution or vote of congress, US Const Art I §7.

Bribery, US Const Art II §4.

Commander-in-chief, US Const Art II §2.

Compensation, US Const Art II §1.

Congress.

Adjourning congress, US Const Art II §3.

Convening congress, US Const Art II §3.

Declaration of president's disability.

Determination of issue, US Const Amd 25.

By two-thirds vote of both houses, US Const Amd 25.

Messages to congress, US Const Art II §3.

Special sessions of congress, US Const Art II §3.

Death.

Duty of congress, US Const Art II §1.

President-elect.

Provision in case of, US Const Amd 20.

Succession upon death, US Const Amd 25.

Disability, US Const Art II §1.

Declaration by president.

Inability to perform duties, US Const Amd 25.

Declaration by vice-president and other officers, US Const Amd 25.

Determination of issue by congress, US Const Amd 25.

Duties, US Const Art II §3.

Declaration by president of inability to perform duties, US Const Amd 25.

Transmittal to senate and house of representatives, US Const Amd 25.

Elections.

Ballots.

Electors to vote by ballot, US Const Amd 12.

PRESIDENT OF THE UNITED STATES —Cont'd

Elections —Cont'd

Electors, §1-1301, US Const Art II §1, Amds 12, 14, 20.

Appointment, US Const Art II §1.

Majority vote of electors, US Const Amd 12.

National popular vote interstate agreement, §1-1051.01.

Voting by military and overseas voters, §1-1061.03.

Eligibility, US Const Art II §1.

Execution of laws, US Const Art II §3.

Executive power, US Const Art II §1.

Failure to qualify, US Const Amd 20.

Foreign missions, §6-1312.

Impeachment, US Const Art II §4.

Inability, US Const Art II §1.

Inaugural ceremonies, §§2-801 to 2-810, 2-821 to 2-829.

Applicability of provisions, §§2-807, 2-828.

Appropriations, §§2-810, 2-823.

Definitions, §§2-801, 2-821.

Effective period of special regulations and licenses, §2-827.

Electrical facilities, §§2-804, 2-805, 2-825.

Enforcement of provisions, §2-808.

Federal grounds, use of, §§2-803, 2-824.

Fines, §§2-809, 2-827.

Issuance of regulations, §§2-802, 2-806, 2-822.

Licenses, §§2-802, 2-806.

Overhead wires, §2-805.

Penalties, §§2-809, 2-827.

Public spaces, use of, §§2-803, 2-824.

Registration tags for motor vehicles, §§2-802, 2-822.

Telecommunications facilities, §2-826.

Inauguration.

Designated holiday, §§1-612.02, 28-2701.

Limitation on terms, US Const Amd 22.

Message to congress, US Const Art II §3.

Ministers.

Receiving, US Const Art II §3.

Opinions from executive officers in executive departments, US Const Art II §2.

Pardons, US Const Art II §2.

Powers of president, US Const Art II §§2, 3.

PRESIDENT OF THE UNITED STATES —Cont'd

Public officers.

Commissions, US Const Art II §3.

Qualifications, US Const Art II §1.

Removal, US Const Art II §§1, 4.

Succession upon removal, US Const Amd 25.

Resignation, US Const Art II §1.

Succession upon resignation, US Const Amd 25.

Signing bills, US Const Art I §7.

State of the Union address, US Const Art II §3.

Statutes.

Approval of laws by president, US Const Art I §7.

Veto, US Const Art I §7.

Succession to office, US Const Art II §1, Amd 20.

Upon death, resignation or removal of president, US Const Amd 25.

Supreme court.

Appointment of justices, US Const Art II §2.

Terms of office, US Const Art II §1, Amds 20, 21.

Limitation on terms, US Const Amd 22.

Time of taking office, US Const Amd 20.

Treason, US Const Art II §4.

Treaties, US Const Art II §2.

Vacancies during senate recess, US Const Art II §2.

Veto, US Const Art I §7.

PRESS.

Attorneys at law.

Trial publicity, ProfCond Rule 3.6.

Constitution of the United States.

Freedom of press, US Const Amd 1.

Superior court proceedings, CivPro Rule 203, CrimPro Rule 53.

Child abuse and neglect proceedings, NeglectProc Rule 45.

Juvenile proceedings, JuvProc Rule 53.

PRESSURE VESSELS.

Boiler inspections, §§2-101 to 2-118.

See BOILER INSPECTIONS.

PRESUMPTIONS.

Abandoned and unlawfully parked vehicles.

Disposal of unclaimed vehicle.

Owners' and lienholders' remedies, §50-2421.11.

PRESUMPTIONS —Cont'd

Anatomical gifts.

Validity of document of gift, §7-1531.18.

Boating under the influence.

Refusal or failure to submit to chemical testing, §50-1911.

Capacity as to health care decisions, §21-2203.

Child custody.

Third-party custody actions.

Inter-family offense, family member who has committed.

Presumption that custody not in best interests of child, §16-831.08.

Parental custody presumption, §16-831.05.

Rebuttal.

Burden of proof, §16-831.06.

Findings necessary to rebut, §16-831.07.

Child support.

Application of guideline, §16-916.01.

Civil asset forfeiture, §41-308.

Commercial code general provisions.

Effect to be given presumption by trier of fact, §28:1-206.

Competence of defendant, §24-531.04.

Conservators.

Competence of individuals, §21-2002.

Consumer credit service organizations.

Exemption or exception, §28-4606.

Contracts.

Sale of goods.

Breaches with respect to accepted goods, §28:2-607.

Decedents' estates, §20-104.

Emergency medical services.

Presumptive disability or death, §§5-651 to 5-656.

Extradition.

Complaint of fugitivity, CrimPro Rule 40-I.

Fire departments.

Presumptive disability or death, §§5-651 to 5-656.

General obligation bonds, §1-204.64.

Gross sales tax, §47-2010.

Certificate of mayor regarding violations, §47-2027.

Health care durable powers of attorney.

Order of priority, rebutting, §21-2210.

PRESUMPTIONS —Cont'd

Metropolitan police.
Electronic recording of interrogations. Evidentiary presumption, §5-116.03.

Real property taxes.
Property occupied, §47-813.

Real property transfers, compulsory recordation of, §47-1432.

Real property transfer tax, §47-907.

Reckless driving, §50-2201.04.

Standby guardian appointed for child, §16-4806.

Theft of electric or natural gas utility service.
Presumptions and rebuttal evidence, §22-3218.03.

Workers' compensation, §32-1521.

Workplace fraud.
Employer-employee relationship, presumption, §32-1331.04.

PRETRIAL CONFERENCES, CivPro Rule 16-II, USDistCt LCvR 16.5.

Adoption proceedings, Adoption Rule 16.

Appeals, federal cases.
Prehearing conference, FRAP 33.

Attorney discipline or disability proceedings, DCBar Rule XI.

Authority to set conference, CivPro Rule 309.

Child abuse and neglect proceedings, NeglectProc Rule 17.

Criminal procedure, CrimPro Rule 17.1.
Closure of pretrial proceedings, USDistCt LCrR 17.2.

Delinquent minors, JuvProc Rule 17.1.

Discovery conferences, USDistCt LCvR 16.3.

Domestic relations actions, DomRel Rule 16-I.

Mental illness, persons with.
Hospitalization, MentalHealth Rule 16.

Motions practice.
Scheduling order provided by movant, CivPro Rule 12-I.

Probate proceedings.
Contested estate cases, Probate Rule 407.
Death between Jan. 1, 1981, and June 30, 1995, Probate Rule 107.
Guardians, conservators, trustees, etc., involved, Probate Rule 208.

Tax proceedings, Tax Rule 11.
Failure to attend, Tax Rule 13.

PRETRIAL CONFERENCES —Cont'd

Tax proceedings —Cont'd
Status conferences, Tax Rule 10.

PRETRIAL SERVICES AGENCY,
§§23-1301 to 23-1309.

Assault on officer or employee, §22-405.

Bail and recognizance.
General provisions, §§23-1321 to 23-1333, USDistCt LCrR 46.1.
See BAIL AND RECOGNIZANCE.

Bail bondsmen.
General provisions, §§23-1101 to 23-1112.
See BAIL BONDSMEN.

Bail determinations.
Defined, §23-1302.
Reports used in making, §23-1303.

Budget estimates, §23-1308.

Chief assistant, §23-1306.

Definitions, §23-1302.

Director, §§23-1304, 23-1305.

Executive committee, §23-1304.

Interviews with detainees, §23-1303.

Investigations by, §23-1303.

Parole, §24-132.

Personnel, §§23-1304 to 23-1306.

Privacy and confidentiality of information obtained by, §23-1303.

Reference to Bail Agency deemed to be reference to, §23-1309.

Reports, §§23-1303, 23-1307.

PRETRIAL STATEMENTS, CivPro Form CA 103.

PRICE GOUGING.

Natural disasters, §§28-4101 to 28-4103.

PRICE LISTS.

Retail business posting requirements, §§47-2907 to 47-2911.

PRICE SCALES.

Posting requirements, §§47-2907 to 47-2911.

PRIEST-PENITENT PRIVILEGE,
§14-309.

PRINCE HALL FREEMASON AND EASTERN STAR CHARITABLE FOUNDATION.

Real property exempt from taxation, §47-1045.

PRINCIPAL AND INCOME,
§§28-4801.01 to 28-4806.02.
Adjustments between principal and income.
Powers of trustee, §28-4801.04.
Taxes, §28-4805.06.
Allocations to principal generally,
§28-4804.04.
Annuities, allocation, §28-4804.09.
Application of provisions,
§28-4806.01.
Existing trusts and estates,
§28-4806.02.
Apportionment.
Beginning and end of income interest.
Right to income, §28-4803.01.
Upon death of decedent,
§28-4803.02.
When interest begins, §28-4803.02.
When interest ends, §28-4803.03.
Asset-backed securities, receipts from, §28-4804.15.
Character of receipt from entity,
§28-4804.01.
Construction of provisions,
§28-4806.01.
Decedents' estates.
Beneficiaries, distributions,
§28-4802.02.
Determination and distribution of
income, §28-4802.01.
Deferred compensation, allocation,
§28-4804.09.
Definitions, §28-4801.02.
Depreciation.
Transfers from income to principal,
§28-4805.03.
Derivatives, receipts from,
§28-4804.14.
Disbursements from income,
§28-4805.01.
Disbursements from principal,
§28-4805.02.
Distributions.
Decedents' estates or terminating
interests, §28-4802.01.
Beneficiaries, §28-4802.02.
Receipts of income from trust or
estate, §28-4804.02.
Fiduciary duties generally,
§28-4801.03.
Income taxes.
Adjustments due to, §28-4805.06.
Payment, §28-4805.05.
Insubstantial allocations resulting from receipts, §28-4804.08.

PRINCIPAL AND INCOME —Cont'd
Insurance policy distributions,
allocation, §28-4804.07.
Liquidating assets, allocation,
§28-4804.10.
Marital deductions not productive of income, §28-4804.13.
Mineral rights, §28-4804.11.
Obligations to pay money, receipts from, §28-4804.06.
Options, receipts from, §28-4804.14.
Property not productive of income,
§28-4804.13.
Rental property, receipts from,
§28-4804.05.
Separate accounting for business activities, §28-4804.03.
Short title, §28-4801.01.
Terminating income interests,
§§28-4802.01, 28-4802.02.
Timber receipts, §28-4804.12.
Transfers from income to principal.
Depreciation purposes, §28-4805.03.
Reimbursement of principal,
§28-4805.04.
Transitional provisions, §28-4806.03.
Trustee's power to adjust,
§28-4801.04.

PRINTED WORKS.
Defacement of, §22-3306.
District of Columbia Code, §45-102.
Fund for District printing, §47-135.

PRIORITY OF SECURITY INTERESTS.
Collection of taxes.
Lien for taxes, §47-4423.
Secured transactions.
Accessions, §28:9-335.
Agricultural liens.
Agricultural liens on same
collateral, §28:9-322.
Filed financing statement providing
certain incorrect information.
Agricultural lien perfected by,
§28:9-338.
Interests that take priority over or
take free of, §28:9-317.
Law governing, §28:9-302.
Buyer of goods, §28:9-320.
Certificate of title.
Security interest in goods covered
by, §28:9-337.
Chattel paper or instrument.
Priority of purchaser, §28:9-330.
Commingled goods, §28:9-336.

PRIORITY OF SECURITY INTERESTS —Cont'd

Secured transactions —Cont'd

Conflicting security interests, §28:9-322.

Consignee.

Rights and title with respect to creditors and purchasers, §28:9-319.

Crops.

Security interest in, §28:9-334.

Deposit account, §28:9-327.

Transfer of funds from, §28:9-332.

Filed financing statement providing certain incorrect information.

Security interest perfected by, §28:9-338.

Financial asset.

Priority of certain interests in, §28:9-331.

Fixtures.

Security interest in, §28:9-334.

Future advances, §28:9-323.

Investment property, §28:9-328.

Law governing, §28:9-301.

Agricultural liens, §28:9-302.

Deposit accounts, §28:9-304.

Goods covered by certificate of title, §28:9-303.

Investment property, §28:9-305.

Letter-of-credit rights, §28:9-306.

Lessee of goods in ordinary course of business, §28:9-321.

Letter-of-credit right, §28:9-329.

Law governing, §28:9-306.

Licensee of general intangible, §28:9-321.

Liens arising by operation of law, §28:9-333.

New debtor.

Security interests created by, §28:9-326.

Purchase-money security interests, §28:9-324.

Purchasers of instruments, documents and securities under other provisions.

Priority of rights of, §28:9-331.

Sale of right to payment, §28:9-318.

Subordination.

Priority subject to, §28:9-339.

Transfer of money.

Transferee takes money free of security interest, §28:9-332.

Transferred collateral, §28:9-325.

Transition provisions, §28:9-709.

PRIORITY OF SECURITY INTERESTS —Cont'd

Secured transactions —Cont'd

Unperfected security interest.

Interests that take priority over or take free of, §28:9-317.

Taxation.

Levy for failure to pay.

Proceeds from sale, §47-4477.

PRISON BREACH, §22-2601.

PRISON GUARDS.

Deadly force.

Correctional treatment facilities, §24-261.02.

PRISON INDUSTRIES, §§24-231.01 to 24-231.15.

Accounting requirements, §24-231.11.

Administrative procedure, §24-231.04.

Advertising and marketing, §24-231.05.

Deductions from wages, §24-231.11.

Definitions, §24-231.01.

Employment of prisoners in, §24-231.08.

Fund, §§24-231.02, 24-231.03, 24-231.15.

Government-enterprise component, §24-231.04.

Joint venture component, §§24-231.04, 24-231.06.

Profits, disposition of, §24-231.14.

Reports, §24-231.13.

Rights, privileges, and entitlements not created by program, §24-231.09.

Sales, §24-231.05.

Taxation, §24-231.05.

Transfer of assets to fund, §24-231.15.

Unemployment compensation, §24-231.10.

Use of fund revenues, §24-231.03.

Wages and salaries, §§24-231.10, 24-231.11.

Workers' compensation, §24-231.12.

PRISON OVERCROWDING.

Cap on prisoners housed at District of Columbia jail, §24-201.61.

Central detention facility.

Maximum number of inmates, §24-201.71.

New housing or facilities used as prisons.

Requirements, §24-201.72.

PRISONS AND PRISONERS,
§§24-201.02 to 24-261.05.
Alcoholics, rehabilitation of, §§24-601 to 24-615.
Applicability of provisions, §24-608.
Chronic alcoholics not afflicted with mental illness, §24-608.
Coordination of treatment programs, §24-606.
Cost of treatment, payment for, §24-614.
Court-ordered commitments, §24-607.
Definitions, §24-602.
Detoxification centers, §24-604.
Gifts and donations for, §24-615.
Inpatient centers, §24-605.
Intoxication in public, §24-604.
Involuntary detention, §24-605.
Juveniles and young adults, §24-612.
Mayor's responsibilities, §§24-603, 24-609, 24-613.
Outpatient treatment, §24-606.
Persons with mental illness, §24-608.
Policy declaration, §24-601.
Prison inmates, §24-611.
Public education and information programs, §§24-603, 24-605.
Public officers and employees, §24-610.
Recovery, likelihood of, §24-606.
Voluntary admission to inpatient centers, §24-605.
Appeals, federal cases.
Appeal as of right, when taken, FRAP 4(c).
Filing and service, FRAP 25(a).
Habeas corpus proceedings, FRAP 22, 23.
See HABEAS CORPUS.
Assault on officer or employee of penal or correctional institution, §22-405.
Attorneys at law.
Solicitation of clients in prisons, ProfCond Rule 7.1.
Bail bondsmen visiting places of detention, §23-1107.
Capital cases, execution of judgments in, §24-201.17.
Central detention facility.
Inspections, §24-211.02.
Maximum number of inmates, §24-201.71.
Processing and release of prisoners, §24-211.02a.
Children and minors.
See JUVENILE OFFENDERS.

PRISONS AND PRISONERS —Cont'd
Children with parents in prison.
Public assistance, §4-205.20.
Chronic alcoholics. See within this heading, "Alcoholics, rehabilitation of."
Combination of Washington Asylum and Jail, §24-201.07.
Commitment to prison, §§24-201.08, 24-201.13.
Contraband on prison grounds.
Definitions, §22-2603.01.
Detention of persons on grounds, §§22-2603.01 to 22-2603.04.
Employee's failure to report violation, §22-2603.02.
Penalties, §22-2603.03.
Prohibited acts, §22-2603.02.
Correctional officers.
Assault on officer or employee of penal or correctional institution, §22-405.
Deadly force.
Correctional treatment facilities, §24-261.02.
Correctional treatment facilities, §§24-261.01 to 24-261.05.
Deadly and non-deadly force, use, §24-261.02.
Exemptions from leasing and property taxes, §24-261.05.
Firearms registered by private operators, §24-261.02a.
Health professional transferring from government to private operator, §24-261.02b.
Immunity from liability, §24-261.04.
Indemnification insurance, §24-261.04.
Inmates deemed in legal custody, §24-261.03.
Rules, §24-261.01.
Corrections, department of.
General provisions, §§24-211.01 to 24-211.41.
See CORRECTIONS, DEPARTMENT OF.
Corrections information council, §24-101.01.
Court services and offender supervisions agency.
Federal agency, §24-133.
Credit for time served in custody or on parole, §24-221.03.
Crimes and offenses.
Failure to report certain deaths, §5-1406.

PRISONS AND PRISONERS —Cont'd
Death.
Duty to report certain deaths to medical examiner, §5-1405.
Failure to report certain deaths, §5-1406.
Discharge and release of prisoners.
Central detention facility, §24-211.02a.
District, within, §24-201.06.
Drug addicts, §§24-709, 24-710, 24-715.
Juvenile offenders, §24-904.
Conviction set aside by unconditional discharge, §24-906.
Payments for prisoners on, §24-201.28.
Work release program. See within this heading, "Work release program."
DNA testing.
Protection of innocence act, §§22-4131 to 22-4135.
Drug addicts, rehabilitation of, §§24-701 to 24-715.
Authority of Surgeon General as to, §24-713.
Confinement of patient, §24-708.
Cost of treatment, §24-714.
Criminals, patients not deemed to be, §24-711.
Definitions, §24-702.
Discharge and release of patient, §§24-709, 24-710, 24-715.
Examination of patient, §§24-703, 24-705, 24-710.
Hearings, §§24-706, 24-707.
Mayor, examination by, §24-703.
Physician, examination by, §24-705.
Policy declaration, §24-701.
Public health service hospitals, admittance to, §24-714.
Right of patients to council, §24-704.
Drug offenders.
Non-violent drug offenders, treatment instead of jail.
See DRUG ABUSE.
Educational good time credits, §24-221.01.
Employees of prisons.
See CORRECTIONS, DEPARTMENT OF.
Employment of prisoners, §§24-201.12, 24-231.08.
Escape, §22-2601.
Mental illness, hospitalization of persons with, MentalHealth Rule 11.

PRISONS AND PRISONERS —Cont'd
Escaped prisoners.
See FUGITIVES FROM JUSTICE.
Ex-offenders.
Commission on re-entry and ex-offender affairs, §24-1303.
Definitions, §24-1301.
Hiring of ex-offenders.
Fair criminal record screening, §§32-1341 to 32-1345.
Complaints, filing, §32-1343.
Conditional offers of employment, withdrawal, §32-1342.
Definitions, §32-1341.
Exceptions, §32-1342.
Inquiries into certain arrests, accusations, and convictions, §32-1342.
Penalties, §32-1344.
Remedy exclusive, no private cause of action, §32-1343.
Reporting requirements, §32-1345.
Office on ex-offender affairs, §24-1302.
Public works department to hire, §32-1351.
Extradition proceedings, confinement of persons under, §23-706.
Federal authority, transfer of prison system to.
See PRISON SYSTEM, FEDERAL CONTROL.
Federal penitentiaries, District prisoners maintained in, §24-201.25.
Fines, commutation of, §24-201.04.
Fines in criminal procedures, imprisonment on nonpayment of, §16-706.
Fugitives.
See FUGITIVES FROM JUSTICE.
Furlough program. See within this heading, "Resocialization furlough program."
Good behavior credits, §24-221.01c.
Good time credits, §§24-221.01 to 24-221.06.
Administration of, §24-221.02.
Credit for time served in custody or on parole, §24-221.03.
Educational good time credits, §24-221.01.
Exceptions for minimum terms, §24-221.06.
Felonies committed on or after August 5, 2000, §24-403.01.

PRISONS AND PRISONERS —Cont'd
Good time credits —Cont'd
Forfeitures, §24-221.04.
Good behavior, §24-221.01c.
Limitations on, §24-221.01b.
Meritorious good time credits,
§24-221.01a.
Misdemeanors committed on or after
August 5, 2000, §24-403.02.
Rehabilitation program participation,
§24-221.01c.
Reports, §24-221.05.
Special project participation,
§24-221.01c.
Work detail participation, §24-221.01c.
Grounds of jail, increase in,
§24-201.21.
Habeas corpus.
General provisions, §§16-1901 to
16-1909.
See HABEAS CORPUS.
Health care, delivery of, §24-1401.
**Health care providers transferring
from public to private
correctional facilities,**
§24-261.02b.
HIV testing of inmates, §§22-3901 to
22-3903.
Hospitals.
Correction department's use of D.C.
General Hospital's campus,
§24-211.61.
Housing standards.
Cap on prisoners housed at District of
Columbia jail, §24-201.61.
Inspection of facilities, §24-211.02.
Immigration.
District compliance with federal
immigration detainers, §24-211.07.
Inmate welfare fund, §§24-281 to
24-284.
Interstate agreement on detainers,
§§24-801 to 24-805.
Interstate corrections compact,
§§24-1001, 24-1002.
Jail housing.
Cap on prisoners housed at District of
Columbia jail, §24-201.61.
**Judiciary Square detention facility
construction,** §§24-1201 to
24-1203.
Definitions, §24-1201.
Mayor's responsibilities, §24-1203.
Requirements, §24-1202.
**Jurisdiction over Reformatory
prisoners,** §24-201.02.

PRISONS AND PRISONERS —Cont'd
Juvenile offenders.
BOOT CAMP, §§24-921 to 24-932.
See BOOT CAMP.
General provisions, §§24-901 to
24-907.
See JUVENILE OFFENDERS.
Youth rehabilitation, §§24-901 to
24-907.
Labor and employment relations.
Hiring of ex-offenders.
Fair criminal record screening,
§§32-1341 to 32-1345.
Limitation of actions, §12-302.
Marshal of District.
Commitment of prisoners by,
§24-201.13.
Delivery of prisoners to, §24-201.14.
Mental health disclosures.
Authorized disclosures, §7-1203.05a.
Mental illness, persons with.
Hospitalization, §21-585,
MentalHealth Rule 10.
Escapees, MentalHealth Rule 11.
Meritorious good time credits,
§24-221.01a.
More than one year, sentence of,
§24-201.02.
**New housing or facilities used as
prisons.**
Requirements, §24-201.72.
**Non-violent drug offenders,
treatment instead of jail.**
See DRUG ABUSE.
Overcrowding, §§24-201.61, 24-201.71,
24-201.72.
Parole.
General provisions, §§24-401c to
24-468.
See PAROLE.
Personnel.
See CORRECTIONS, DEPARTMENT
OF.
Phone calls by prisoners.
Operator assisted calls.
Fair charges, §§24-263.01 to
24-263.04.
Place of imprisonment, §§24-201.02,
24-201.26.
Pregnant women.
Use of restraints, §§24-276.01 to
24-276.04.
Prison breach, §22-2601.
Prison industries.
General provisions, §§24-231.01 to
24-231.15.
See PRISON INDUSTRIES.

PRISONS AND PRISONERS —Cont'd

Prison overcrowding.

Cap on prisoners housed at District of Columbia jail, §24-201.61.

Central detention facility.

Maximum number of inmates, §24-201.71.

New housing or facilities.

Requirements, §24-201.72.

Private correctional treatment facilities, §§24-261.01 to 24-261.05.

Deadly and non-deadly force, use, §24-261.02.

Exemptions from leasing and property taxes, §24-261.05.

Firearms registered by private operators, §24-261.02a.

Health professional transferring from government to private operator, §24-261.02b.

Immunity from liability, §24-261.04.

Indemnification insurance, §24-261.04.

Inmates deemed in legal custody, §24-261.03.

Rules, §24-261.01.

Probation.

See PROBATION.

Public assistance for children with parents in prison, §4-205.20.

Rated design capacity, §24-201.72.

Records.

Detoxification centers, §24-604.

Resocialization furlough program, §24-251.05.

Rehabilitation program participation.

Good time credits, §24-221.01c.

Release of prisoners. See within this heading, "Discharge and release of prisoners."

Repair and maintenance of prisons, §24-201.23.

Reports.

BOOT CAMP, §24-932.

Good time credits, §24-221.05.

Parole eligibility, §24-221.05.

Prison industries, §24-231.13.

Resocialization furlough program, §§24-251.05, 24-251.07.

Restraints, use on pregnant women, §24-276.03.

Superintendent of Washington Asylum and Jail, §24-201.16.

Resocialization furlough program, §§24-251.01 to 24-251.08.

Administrative procedure, §24-251.04.

PRISONS AND PRISONERS —Cont'd

Resocialization furlough program —Cont'd

Authority to grant furloughs, §24-251.02.

Council, report to, §24-251.07.

Definitions, §24-251.01.

Eligibility for furlough, §24-251.02.

Institutional review committees for, §24-251.06.

Reasons for granting furloughs, §24-251.03.

Records, §24-251.05.

Reports, §§24-251.05, 24-251.07.

Severability of provisions, §24-251.08.

Twelve hours, furloughs longer than, §24-251.03.

Restraints, use of, §§24-276.01 to 24-276.04.

Definitions, §24-276.01.

Notice, §24-276.04.

Places of confinement, §24-276.02.

Pregnant women, generally, §§24-276.01 to 24-276.04.

Reports, §24-276.03.

Rewards for escaped prisoners, §24-201.27.

Safekeeping of prisoners, accountability for, §24-201.15.

Schools.

Correctional facility established near school.

Notice given by mayor, §38-3201.

Sex offender registration.

General provisions, §§22-4001 to 22-4017.

See SEX OFFENDER REGISTRATION.

Special project participation.

Good time credits, §24-221.01c.

Staff.

See CORRECTIONS, DEPARTMENT OF.

Subsistence of prisoners, payment for, §§24-201.22 to 24-201.25, 24-211.06.

Superintendent of Washington Asylum and Jail.

Appropriation for position, failure to make, §24-201.17.

Capital cases, execution of judgments in, §24-201.17.

Reports, §24-201.16.

Safekeeping of prisoners, accountability for, §24-201.15.

Wages and salaries, §47-201.

PRISONS AND PRISONERS —Cont'd
Telephone calls by prisoners.
Fair phone charges, §§24-263.01 to
24-263.04.
Prohibited charges in government
contracts, §24-263.02.
Rate for operator-assisted calls,
§§24-263.01, 24-263.04.
Report on survey and exploration for
alternative communications
plans, §24-263.03.
Surcharge or commission prohibited,
§24-263.01.
**Transfer of prison system to federal
authority,** §§24-101 to 24-142.
See PRISON SYSTEM, FEDERAL
CONTROL.
Transfers between prisons.
Penitentiary to reformatory,
§24-201.02.
Washington Asylum and Jail to
Workhouse, §24-201.03.
Truth in sentencing commission,
§§24-111 to 24-114.
Truth-in-sentencing requirements.
Designation of penal or correctional
facility.
Felons sentenced pursuant to,
§24-101.
United States prisoners, §§24-201.10,
24-211.06.
**United States reimbursed for
maintenance of District inmates,**
§§24-201.24, 24-201.25.
**Unjust imprisonment claims against
District,** §§2-421 to 2-425.
Wages and salaries.
Prison industries, §§24-231.10,
24-231.11.
Work release program, §§24-241.06,
24-241.07.
Work detail participation.
Good time credits, §24-221.01c.
Work release program, §§24-241.01 to
24-241.10.
Commissioners, authority of,
§24-241.09.
Conditions for actual release, setting,
§24-241.03.
District, participants not agent,
employee, or servant of,
§24-241.10.
Establishment of, §24-241.01.
Issuance of rules and regulations,
§24-241.04.
Mayor's responsibilities, §§24-241.08,
24-241.09.

PRISONS AND PRISONERS —Cont'd
Work release program —Cont'd
Recommendations and orders
regarding involvement in,
§24-241.02.
Support payments, §24-241.07.
Suspension or revocation of
participation in, §24-241.05.
Wages and salaries, §§24-241.06,
24-241.07.
Youth offenders.
See JUVENILE OFFENDERS.

**PRISON SYSTEM, FEDERAL
CONTROL,** §§24-101 to 24-142.
Bureau of prisons, §24-101.
Corrections trustee, §§24-102, 24-105.
**District residents given priority
consideration as employees,**
§24-103.
**Exemption from personnel and
budget ceilings,** §24-142.
Liability issues, §24-105.
Litigation responsibility, §24-105.
Parole, §§24-131 to 24-134.
Trustees.
Corrections trustee, §§24-102, 24-105.
Exemption from personnel and budget
ceilings, §24-142.
Reemployed annuitant trustee,
§24-141.
Truth in sentencing commission,
§§24-111 to 24-114.

PRISON TERMS.
**Abandoned and unlawfully parked
vehicles.**
Purchaser of salvaged vehicle,
abandoning vehicle, §50-2421.10.
Accessories after the fact, §22-1806.
Adult protective services, §7-1912.
Affrays, §22-1301.
Aggravated assault, §22-404.01.
Airspace, rental of, §10-1121.10.
Alcoholic beverage licenses.
Influencing application process,
§25-434.
No specific penalty specified, §25-831.
Alcoholic beverages.
Children and minors.
Delivery, offer, or making available
to, §25-785.
Open container law, §25-1001.
Public intoxication, §25-1001.
Ammunition.
Restricted pistol bullets, §7-2507.06.
Animal fighting, §22-1006.01.
Armed carjacking, §22-2803.

PRISON TERMS —Cont'd
Arson.
Generally, §22-301.
Intent to defraud or injury, §22-302.
Malicious burning, etc., of other's
property, §22-303.
Asbestos contractors, §8-111.09.
Assault, §22-401.
Assault with a dangerous weapon,
§22-402.
Common law assault, §22-404.
Offense of any kind, intent to commit,
§22-403.
Police officer or firefighter, assault on,
§22-405.
Public officials, §22-851.
Resisting arrest, §22-405.01.
Bigamy, §22-501.
Blocking passage.
Public or private building, enclosure,
road or sidewalk, §22-1307.
Boating under the influence,
§50-2206.32.
Impaired operation of watercraft,
§50-2206.34.
Minor in watercraft, §50-2206.36.
Boiler inspections.
Regulatory violations, §2-114.
**Breaking and entering vending
machines,** §22-601.
Bribery, §§22-704, 22-712.
Witnesses, §22-713.
**Building code requirements for fire
prevention,** §6-703.06.
Burglary, §22-801.
Cancer prevention and monitoring,
§7-304.
Capitol grounds, §10-503.18.
Carjacking, §22-2803.
Child abuse and neglect.
Failure to make required report,
§4-1321.07.
Child care facilities, §7-2046.
Child prostitution, §22-2704.
Child sexual abuse.
Aggravating circumstances, §22-3020.
Assault with intent to commit,
§22-401.
First and second degree, §§22-3008 to
22-3010.
Lewd, indecent, or obscene acts,
§22-1312.
Sexually suggestive conduct,
§22-3010.01.
Citizen patrol members.
Enhanced penalty for committing
certain crimes against, §22-3602.

PRISON TERMS —Cont'd
Collection of taxes.
Divulging information about returns,
§47-4406.
Collections agencies.
Use of "District" or similar
designation, §22-3402.
Commercial counterfeiting, §22-902.
Commercial piracy, §22-3214.
Communicable diseases, §7-140.
Conspiracy, §22-1805a.
Kidnapping, §22-2001.
Construction codes, §6-1406.
Contraband on prison grounds,
§22-2603.03.
**Contributing to the delinquency of a
minor,** §22-811.
Corrupt influence, §§22-704, 22-712.
Credit card fraud, §22-3223.
Criminal offenses generally,
§§22-3571.01, 22-3571.02.
Criminal street gangs, §22-951.
Cruelty to animals, §22-1001.
Cruelty to children, §§22-1101,
22-1102.
Disabled, injured, or sick animals.
Abandonment of, §22-1012.
Neglect of, §22-1011.
Disfigurement, malicious, §22-406.
Disorderly conduct, §22-1321.
Driving under the influence,
§50-2206.13.
Boating under the influence,
§50-2206.32.
Impaired operation of watercraft,
§50-2206.34.
Minor in watercraft, §50-2206.36.
Commercial drivers.
Additional term of incarceration,
§50-2206.17.
Impaired driving, §50-2206.15.
Minor in vehicle, additional
penalties, §50-2206.18.
Mandatory-minimum periods of
incarceration, proof required,
§50-2206.57.
Emergency medical services,
§7-2341.24.
Escape, §22-2601.
Extortion.
Blackmail, §22-3252.
False personation with intent to extort
money, §22-1402.
Generally, §22-3251.
False fire alarms, §22-1319.
False personation.
Public officer or minister, §§22-1403 to
22-1405.

PRISON TERMS —Cont'd

False statements, §22-2405.

False swearing, §22-2404.

Firearms, §7-2507.06.

Concealed weapons, carrying, §§22-4504, 22-4505.

Unlawful possession, §22-4503.

Fire balloons, §22-1317.

Fish and game, §22-4331.

Fleeing from a law enforcement officer in a motor vehicle, §50-2201.05b.

Flood hazards, §6-506.

Footways in public grounds, driving or riding on, §22-1318.

Foreclosure rescue services and transactions.

Violations of provisions, §42-2435.

Forgery, §22-3242.

Goods, brands or packaging of, §22-1502.

Fraud and deceit.

Checks, drafts, or orders intended to defraud, §22-1510.

Credit card fraud, §22-3223.

First and second degree, §22-3222.

Fraudulent registration in lodgings, §22-3224.

Insurance fraud, §22-3225.04.

Fraudulent advertising, §22-1513.

Funeral directors.

Regulatory violations, §3-417.

Gambling.

Bookmaking, §22-1708.

Confidence games, §22-1706.

Keeping gaming premises, §§5-115.06, 22-1704, 22-1705.

Sports, §§22-1708, 22-1713.

Three-card monte, §22-1706.

Gambling by minors, §§3-1334, 3-1335.

Gangs, §22-951.

Graffiti, §22-3312.04.

Grave robbery, §22-3303.

Guardianship of incapacitated persons.

Sexual abuse of a ward, §§22-3013, 22-3014.

Hazardous waste management, §8-1311.

Healing arts practitioners.

Sexual abuse of patient or client, §§22-3015, 22-3016.

Health care facilities.

Interference with or obstruction of, §§22-1314.01, 22-1314.02.

PRISON TERMS —Cont'd

Health care practitioners, §3-1210.07.

Health data privacy.

Unlawful use or disclosure of information, §7-246.

Historic landmarks, §6-1110.

Identity theft, §22-3227.03.

Impaired driving, §50-2206.15.

Minor in vehicle, additional penalties, §50-2206.18.

Impaired operation of watercraft, §50-2206.34.

Minor in watercraft, §50-2206.36.

Incest, §22-1901.

Insanitary buildings, §6-916.

Insurance fraud, §22-3225.04.

Interception of oral or wire communications.

Possession, sale, etc., of intercepting devices, §23-543.

Jury selection.

Confidentiality violations, §16-5103.

Juvenile records.

Unlawful disclosure, §16-2336.

Kidnapping, §§22-1810, 22-2001.

Lewd, indecent, or obscene acts, §22-1312.

Loitering.

Unlawful assembly, §22-1321.

Lottery tickets.

Forged, altered, or counterfeit, §3-1333.

Promotion, sale or possession of tickets, §§22-1701 to 22-1703.

Malicious disfigurement, §22-406.

Manslaughter, §22-2105.

Marriage, violations, §46-421.

Mattresses, §8-505.

Mayhem, §22-406.

Assault with intent to commit, §22-402.

Mental health disclosures, §7-1207.02.

Minimum wages, §32-1011.

Mortgages and deeds of trust.

Foreclosure rescue services and transactions.

Violations of provisions, §42-2435.

Motion picture theaters.

Operation of recording device, §22-3214.02.

Motor vehicles.

Identification numbers, altering or removing, §22-3233.

Theft, §22-3215.

Unlawful entry, §22-1341.

PRISON TERMS —Cont'd

Murder.

Assault with intent to commit, §22-401.

First and second degree, §§22-2104, 22-2104.01.

Killing law enforcement officer, §22-2106.

Second degree murder, §22-2103.

Solicitation of murder or other violent crimes, §22-2107.

Non-code offenses, §22-1807.

Obscenity, §22-2201.

Obstruction of justice, §22-722.

Interference with reports to or requests for assistance from law enforcement, medical providers, or child welfare agencies, §22-1931.

Tampering with physical evidence, §22-723.

Official correspondence violations, §§2-708, 2-709.

Panhandling, §22-2304.

Parachutes, §22-1317.

Parentage proceedings.

Disclosure of information, §16-2348.

Pedestrians.

Failure to stop and give right-of-way to, §50-2201.28.

Perjury, §§22-2402, 22-2403.

Poison.

Assault with intent to poison, §22-401.

Potomac river.

Throwing or depositing matter into, §§22-4402, 22-4403.

Prison breach, §22-2601.

Prison contraband, §22-2603.03.

Private detectives.

Use of "District" or similar designation, §22-3402.

Privies, §8-604.

Profane and indecent language, §22-1321.

Prostitution.

Child prostitution, §22-2704.

Compelling individual to live life of prostitution, §22-2706.

Domestic partners caused to live in, §22-2708.

House of prostitution.

Operating, §§22-2712, 22-2722.

Pandering, procuring, or pimping for, §22-2710.

Inducing or inciting an individual to engage in, §22-2705.

Pandering, procuring, or pimping, §22-2705.

Third persons, for, §22-2711.

PRISON TERMS —Cont'd

Prostitution —Cont'd

Receiving money or valuables for arranging assignations, §22-2707.

Solicitation for purposes, §22-2701.

Spouses caused to live in, §22-2708.

Protective orders, violation, §16-1005.

Public officers and employees.

Threatening, stalking, assaulting, etc., §22-851.

Public or private building, enclosure, road or sidewalk.

Blocking passage, §22-1307.

Railroad transportation of animals, §22-1003.

Rape.

Various degrees of sexual abuse, §§22-3002 to 22-3006.

Rental of public space, §10-1104.04.

Rental unit alterations to occupied units after notice to vacate, §6-731.04.

Resisting arrest, §22-405.01.

Rioting or inciting to riot, §22-1322.

Robbery, §22-2801.

Assault with intent to commit, §22-401.

Attempt to commit, §22-2802.

Sex offender registration, §22-4015.

Sexual abuse.

Aggravating circumstances, §22-3020.

Assault with intent to commit, §22-401.

Child sexual abuse.

Assault with intent to commit, §22-401.

First and second degree, §§22-3008 to 22-3010.

Lewd, indecent, or obscene acts, §22-1312.

Sexually suggestive conduct, §22-3010.01.

Various degrees of sexual abuse, §§22-3002 to 22-3006.

Solicitation for purposes of prostitution, §22-2701.

Solicitation of murder or other violent crimes, §22-2107.

Stalking, §22-3134.

Public officials, §22-851.

Stolen property.

Receiving stolen property, §22-3232.

Trafficking in stolen property, §22-3231.

Street gangs, §22-951.

PRISON TERMS —Cont'd
Subornation of perjury, §22-2403.
Telephone solicitation fraud,
§22-3226.10.
Termination of parental rights.
Unlawful disclosures, §16-2364.
Theft.
Commercial piracy, §22-3214.
Generally, §22-3212.
Taking property without right,
§22-3216.
Unauthorized use, §22-3215.
Threats to do bodily harm, §22-407.
Three strikes offenders, §22-1804a.
Tobacco master settlement
agreement enforcement,
§7-1803.06.
Tobacco sales to minors, §7-1721.02.
Toilets, §8-604.
Trademark counterfeiting, §22-902.
Trespass.
Forcible entry and detainer, §22-3301.
Unlawful entry on property, §22-3302.
Unauthorized use of, §22-3215.
Vandalism.
Art works, defacing, §22-3306.
Boundary markers, destroying,
§22-3309.
Cross burning, §§22-3312.02,
22-3312.04.
Defacing public or private property,
§22-3312.01.
Explosives placed with intent to
destroy or injure property,
§22-3305.
Grave robbery, §22-3303.
Milestones, removal of, §22-3320.
Obstruction.
Public highways, §22-3321.
Public roads, §22-3320.
Railroad tracks, §22-3319.
Printed material, defacing, §22-3306.
Public records, defacing, §22-3307.
Railings, destroying, §22-3314.
Railroad track obstruction or
displacement, §22-3319.
Streets and alleys.
Destroying or defacing building
material for, §22-3313.
Tombs, destroying, §22-3314.
Trees and shrubbery, destroying,
§22-3310.
United States property, injury or
destruction to, §22-3311.
Vending machines and similar devices,
§22-601.

PRISON TERMS —Cont'd
Vandalism —Cont'd
Water pollution, malicious, §22-3318.
Vehicle identification numbers.
Altering or removing, §22-3233.
Vending machines, breaking and
entering, §22-601.
Vital records, §7-225.
Voyeurism, §22-3531.
Wages and salaries.
Employer's failure to pay, §32-1307.
Washington National Airport, §9-705.
Water pollution, §8-103.16.
Youth residential facilities, §7-2108.

PRIVACY AND CONFIDENTIALITY.
Cable television operators.
Protection of customer privacy,
§34-1260.02.
Confidentiality of information.
See CONFIDENTIALITY OF
INFORMATION.
Filings with the court, CrimPro Rule
49.1.
Health data privacy.
Generally, §§7-241 to 7-248.
See HEALTH DATA PRIVACY.
Mental health disclosures, §§7-1201.01
to 7-1208.07.
See MENTAL HEALTH
DISCLOSURES.
Invasion of privacy.
Freedom of information act exemption.
Information of personal nature,
§2-534.
Privileged information.
See PRIVILEGES.
Probate proceedings.
Exclusion of personal identification
from filed documents, Probate
Rule 5.1.

PRIVATE CLUBS.
Business licenses, §47-2827.

PRIVATE CONTRACTOR AND
SUBCONTRACTOR PROMPT
PAYMENT ACT, §§27-131 to
27-136.
See PROMPT PAYMENT.

PRIVATE DETECTIVES, §§5-121.01 to
5-121.05.
Acting without compliance of law,
§5-121.03.
Actions.
Suits by injured parties against,
§5-121.01.

PRIVATE DETECTIVES —Cont'd
Arrest.
Acceptance of money, §5-121.05.
Duty in making, §5-121.02.
Bonds, surety, §5-121.01.
Business licenses, §47-2839.
Compromise of felony, §5-121.05.
Definition of detective, §47-2839.
District of Columbia or similar
designation, prohibition of,
§§22-3401 to 22-3403.
Escape, permitting, §5-121.05.
Laws governing police as to persons,
property, money.
Applicability, §5-121.04.
Regulation of, §47-2839.
Security agencies, §47-2839.01.
Withholding information, §5-121.05.

PRIVATE ENTITIES.
Automated traffic enforcement
system, §50-2209.03.
District of Columbia or similar
designation, prohibition of,
§§22-3401 to 22-3403.

PRIVATE FIRE HYDRANTS,
§§34-2410.01 to 34-2410.06.
Definitions, §34-2410.01.
Inspections, §34-2410.04.
Maintenance, §34-2410.03.
Ownership determinations,
§34-2410.05.
Responsibility agreements,
§34-2410.02.
Responsibility limitations,
§34-2410.06.

PRIVATE RIGHT OF ACTION.
Alternative fuel technology suits,
§50-706.
Decedents' estates, §20-107.
Discrimination complaints,
§2-1403.16.
Human Rights Commission,
§2-1403.16.
Interest, §28-3314.
Long-term care ombudsman,
§§7-705.01 to 7-705.03.
Low-level radioactive waste
generator regulatory policy,
§8-1505.
Nursing homes.
Discharge, transfer, or relocation of
residents of, §§44-1004.01 to
44-1004.05.
Restraints of trade, §28-4508.
Underground storage tanks,
§8-113.11.

PRIVATE RIGHT OF ACTION
—Cont'd
Usury, §28-3314.
Water pollution, §8-103.19.

PRIVATE SCHOOLS.
Nonpublic schools for students with
disabilities, §§38-2561.01 to
38-2561.16.
See SPECIAL EDUCATION.

PRIVATE VEHICLES-FOR-HIRE,
§§50-301.29a to 50-301.29g.
Applications.
Registration of operators, §50-301.29b.
Booking rides.
Operator requirements, §50-301.29e.
Certification, §50-301.29g.
Charges, §50-301.29f.
Criminal background checks.
Operators, §50-301.29a.
Registration of operators, §50-301.29b.
Discrimination.
Zero-tolerance, §50-301.29a.
Enforcement, §50-301.29g.
General requirements, §50-301.29a.
Impoundment of vehicles, §50-331.
Insurance requirements, §50-301.29c.
Operator requirements, §50-301.29e.
Records, §50-301.29a.
Registration of operators,
§§50-301.29a, 50-301.29b.
Rules, §50-301.29g.
Safety inspections, verification,
§50-301.29a.
Trade dress requirements,
§50-301.29d.

PRIVATIZATION.
Alcohol and drug abuse.
Residential treatment of, §44-1203.01.
Bureau of prisons.
Transfer of system to federal
authority, §24-101.

PRIVIES, §§8-601 to 8-604.
Permit to maintain, §8-602.
Regulation of waste disposal
systems, §8-603.
Violations, penalties, §8-604.
Water closets connected with sewer
and water main required, §8-601.

PRIVILEGES.
Adult protective services.
Waiver of privilege by professionals
regarding, §7-1911.
Arrest.
Congress, US Const Art I §6.

PRIVILEGES —Cont'd
Child abuse and neglect.
Privilege not grounds for excluding evidence of, §4-1321.05.
Clients' Security Trust Fund.
Claims submitted to fund, DCBar Rule XII.
Collaborative law, §16-4017.
Limits, §16-4019.
Waiver and preclusion, §16-4018.
Commission on judicial disabilities and tenure.
Disclosure of proceedings of, §11-1528.
Domestic violence counselors.
Disclosure of confidential communication between victim and counselor.
Prohibition, exceptions, §14-310.
Disclosure of confidential information acquired in professional capacity.
Prohibited without consent of client, §14-307.
Foreign missions, §6-1310.
Human trafficking counselors, §14-311.
Disclosure of confidential information prohibited without consent of client, §14-307.
Insurance compliance self-evaluation privilege, §§31-851 to 31-858.
Applicability, §31-858.
Burden of proof of applicability, §31-857.
Court-ordered disclosure of material, §§31-854, 31-855.
Definitions, §31-851.
Privileged information, §31-853.
Requests for disclosure, §31-856.
Scope of privilege, §31-852.
Interception of wire or oral communications, CrimPro Rule 41-I.
International motor vehicle registration plan agreements.
Interjurisdictional and intrajurisdictional privileges, §50-1507.04.
Interpreters, §2-1908.
Interstate privileges and rental vehicle tax, §50-1505.02.
Legal service.
Attorney-client privilege, applicability, §1-608.66.
Mediation, §16-4203.
Exceptions, §16-4205.

PRIVILEGES —Cont'd
Mediation —Cont'd
Waiver and preclusion, §16-4204.
News media privilege, §§16-4701 to 16-4704.
Physician-patient privilege.
Attorney discipline or disability proceedings.
Waiver of privilege for reinstatement of incapacitated attorney.
See PHYSICIAN-PATIENT PRIVILEGE.
Reports, prohibitions, §16-4206.
Sexual assault victim advocates, §14-312.
Disclosure of confidential information prohibited without consent of client, §14-307.
Spousal privilege.
See SPOUSAL PRIVILEGE.
Subpoenas.
Quashing or modifying subpoena, CivPro Rule 45.
Domestic relations actions, DomRel Rule 45.
Witness statements.
Production of statements.
Criminal procedure, CrimPro Rule 26.2.
Delinquent minors, JuvProc Rule 26.2.
Juvenile proceedings, JuvProc Rule 32.
Probation modification hearings, CrimPro Rule 32.1.
Release from custody or detention, CrimPro Rule 46.
Sentencing hearings, CrimPro Rule 32.

PROBABLE CAUSE.
Arrest warrants, CrimPro Rule 4.
Child abuse and neglect proceedings, NeglectProc Rule 14.
Extradition, CrimPro Rule 40-I.
Hearings to determine, CrimPro Rule 5.
Interception of wire or oral communications.
Authorized interception, CrimPro Rule 41-I.
Probation revocation hearings, CrimPro Rule 32.1.

PROBATE DIVISION, SUPERIOR COURT.
General Provisions, §§16-3101 to 16-3112, Probate Rules 1 to 430.
See PROBATE PROCEEDINGS.

PROBATE DIVISION, SUPERIOR COURT —Cont'd

Intervention proceedings, Probate Rules 301 to 361.

See INTERVENTION PROCEEDINGS.

Register of wills.

General provisions, §§11-2101 to 11-2106.

See WILLS.

Matters presented to register of wills.

All proceedings, Probate Rule 2.

Death between Jan. 1, 1981, and June 30, 1995, Probate Rule 101.

Disclaimers, Probate Rule 6.1.

PROBATE PROCEEDINGS, §§16-3101 to 16-3112, Probate Rules 1 to 430.

Abbreviated probate proceeding, §§20-311, 20-312, 20-331.

Admission of will to probate as conclusive evidence, §16-3110.

Appeals, Probate Rule 8.

Stays pending appeal, Probate Rule 9.

Arbitration, §16-3111.

Attachment, §§16-3104 to 16-3107.

Attorneys' fees and costs, §§16-3106, 16-3112.

Civil procedure rules applicable, Probate Rule 1.

Contempt proceedings, §16-3103.

Custodianship of minors, Probate Rules 231, 232.

Death before Jan. 1, 1981.

Accounts of administrators, executors and collectors, Probate Rule 19.

Assignments, Probate Rule 21.

Collector of estate, Probate Rule 13.

Accounts, Probate Rule 19.

Compensation of personal representatives, Probate Rules 19, 22.

Contested estate cases, Probate Rule 15.

Definitions, Probate Rule 25.

Delinquent fiduciaries, Probate Rule 23.

Exhibition of assets, Probate Rule 20.

Fees, Probate Rule 24.

Nonresident fiduciaries, Probate Rule 14.

Petitions for probate and administration, Probate Rule 10.

Notice requirements, Probate Rules 11, 12.

Sale of property.

Personal property, Probate Rule 17.

PROBATE PROCEEDINGS —Cont'd

Death before Jan. 1, 1981 —Cont'd

Sale of property —Cont'd

Real property, Probate Rule 18.

Securities' registration and appraisal, Probate Rule 16.

Death between Jan. 1, 1981, and June 30, 1995.

Accounts of personal representatives.

Audit of accounts, Probate Rules 117, 118.

Generally, Probate Rule 114.

Notice of filing accounts, Probate Rule 116.

Special administrators, Probate Rule 119.

Waiver of filing accounts, Probate Rule 115.

Appraisals, Probate Rule 109.

Assignment of rights, Probate Rule 120.

Bond of personal representative, Probate Rule 104.

Claims against estate, Probate Rule 110.

Compensation of personal representative.

Guardian ad litem, Probate Rule 122.

Requests for compensation, Probate Rule 124.

Contested estate cases, Probate Rule 107.

Court costs, Probate Rule 125.

Delinquent fiduciaries, Probate Rule 121.

Foreign personal representative's appointment, Probate Rule 127.

Guardians ad litem, Probate Rule 122.

Inventory, Probate Rule 109.

Waiver of filing inventories, Probate Rule 115.

Judge's bias or prejudice, Probate Rule 126.

Minors receiving distributions, Probate Rule 108.

Nonresident special administrators and personal representatives, Probate Rule 106.

Notice requirements, Probate Rule 103.

Action on claims, Probate Rule 111.

Publication of notices, Probate Rule 128.

Petition for probate, Probate Rule 102.

Reconsideration of determinations, Probate Rule 130.

PROBATE PROCEEDINGS —Cont'd
**Death between Jan. 1, 1981, and
June 30, 1995** —Cont'd
Register of wills.
Matters presented to register of
wills, Probate Rule 101.
Rule to show cause for recovery of
property, Probate Rule 113.
Special administrators, Probate Rules
105, 106.
Accounts, Probate Rule 119.
Costs in special administration
proceedings, Probate Rule 125.
Termination of appointment of
personal representative, Probate
Rule 123.
Death on or after July 1, 1995.
Abbreviated probate orders, Probate
Form 3.
Accounts of personal representatives.
Audit of accounts, Probate Rule 418.
Waiver of audit, Probate Form 20,
Probate Rule 417.
Generally, Probate Rule 414.
Notice of filing accounts, Probate
Form 19, Probate Rule 416.
Special administrators, Probate Rule
419.
Waiver of filing accounts, Probate
Form 18, Probate Rule 415.
Action on claims, Probate Form 15,
Probate Rule 411.
Admission of lost or destroyed will,
Probate Rule 403.
Appointment of personal
representative.
Consent to appointment, Probate
Form 4, Probate Rule 402.
Contesting appointment, Probate
Rule 407.
Extension of appointment, Probate
Forms 16, 17, Probate Rule 429.
Foreign personal representatives,
Probate Forms 24, 25, Probate
Rule 427.
Notice of appointment, Probate
Form 10, Probate Rule 403.
Termination of appointment, Probate
Forms 21, 22, Probate Rule 423.
Appraisals, Probate Rule 409.
Limited use of appraisals, Probate
Rule 412.
Assignment of rights, Probate Rule
420.
Bond of personal representative,
Probate Forms 5, 8, Probate Rules
404, 412.

PROBATE PROCEEDINGS —Cont'd
Death on or after July 1, 1995
—Cont'd
Certificates of completion, Probate
Form 23, Probate Rule 426.
Claims against estate, Probate Form
14, Probate Rule 410.
Compensation of personal
representative, etc., Probate Rule
424.
Guardian ad litem, Probate Rule
422.
Contested estate cases, Probate Rule
407.
Court costs, Probate Form 1, Probate
Rule 425.
Court order for authority to act,
Probate Rule 412.
Creditors' notice, Probate Form 10,
Probate Rule 403.
Custody of will, securing, Probate Rule
403.
Delinquent fiduciaries, Probate Rule
421.
Forms accepted for filing, Probate Rule
401.
Guardians ad litem, Probate Rule 422.
Heirs and legatees.
General information for heirs and
legatees, Probate Appx.
Intestacy, finding of after will has been
filed, Probate Rule 403.
Inventory, Probate Forms 12, 13,
Probate Rule 409.
Waiver of filing inventories, Probate
Form 18, Probate Rule 415.
Minors receiving distributions, Probate
Rule 408.
Nonresident special administrators
and personal representatives,
Probate Rule 406.
Petitions for probate, Probate Form 2.
Publication of notices, Probate Rule
428.
Reconsideration of determinations,
Probate Rule 430.
Responsive pleadings, Probate Rule
403.
Rule to show cause for recovery of
property, Probate Rule 413.
Special administrators, Probate Rule
405.
Accounts, Probate Rule 419.
Delinquent special administrators,
Probate Rule 421.
Nonresidents, Probate Rule 406.

PROBATE PROCEEDINGS —Cont'd
Death on or after July 1, 1995
—Cont'd
Standard probate notice, Probate Form
9, Probate Rule 403.
Verification and certification of notice
by personal representative,
Probate Form 11, Probate Rule
403.
Witnesses.
Securing witnesses, Probate Rule
403.
Default or irregularity.
Closing case despite problems, Probate
Rule 7.
Guardians, conservators, trustees, etc.,
involved, Probate Rule 207.
Expenditure or sale violations,
Probate Rules 222, 223.
Disclaimers.
Contents, Probate Rule 6.1.
Filing with court, Probate Rule 6.1.
Enforcement, §§16-3107 to 16-3109.
Evidence, §§16-3103, 16-3110.
Execution of judgment, §16-3112.
**Failure to appear or give evidence
before court,** §§16-3103 to 16-3105.
Fees, §§15-707, 15-708.
Finality of, §§20-324, 20-331, Probate
Rule 8.
Financial account numbers.
Exclusion of personal identification
from filed documents, Probate
Rule 5.1.
Forms.
Certificate of notice of existence of
revocable trust, Probate Rule 212.
Custodianship of minors.
Order for rule to show cause,
Probate Rule 232.
Death before Jan. 1, 1981.
Consent to account, Probate Rule 19.
Death between Jan. 1, 1981, and June
30, 1995.
Accounting-related forms, Probate
Rules 115 to 117.
Action on claims, Probate Rule 111.
Appointment of personal
representative notice, Probate
Rules 103, 127.
Claims against estate, Probate Rule
110.
Creditor notice, Probate Rule 103.
Foreign personal representative's
appointment, Probate Rule 127.
Inventory-related forms, Probate
Rules 109, 115.

PROBATE PROCEEDINGS —Cont'd
Forms —Cont'd
Death between Jan. 1, 1981, and June
30, 1995 —Cont'd
Request for compensation of
personal representative, Probate
Rule 124.
Standard probate notice, Probate
Rule 103.
Termination of appointment
petitions, Probate Rule 123.
Death on or after July 1, 1995.
Abbreviated probate orders, Probate
Form 3.
Accounting-related forms, Probate
Forms 18 to 20, Probate Rules
415 to 417.
Action on claim notice, Probate
Form 15, Probate Rule 411.
Appointment of personal
representative.
Consent to appointment, Probate
Form 4, Probate Rule 402.
Extension of appointment, Probate
Forms 16, 17, Probate Rule
429.
Foreign personal representatives,
Probate Forms 24, 25, Probate
Rule 427.
Notice of appointment, Probate
Form 10, Probate Rule 403.
Termination of appointment,
Probate Forms 21, 22, Probate
Rule 423.
Bond of personal representative,
Probate Forms 5 to 8, Probate
Rule 404.
Certificates of completion, Probate
Form 23, Probate Rule 426.
Claims against estate, Probate Form
14, Probate Rule 410.
Creditors' notice, Probate Form 10,
Probate Rule 403.
Forms acceptable for filing, Probate
Rule 401.
Inventory-related forms, Probate
Forms 12, 13, Probate Rule 409.
Waiver of filing inventories,
Probate Form 18, Probate
Rule 415.
Petitions for probate, Probate Form
2.
Rule to show cause order, Probate
Rule 413.
Standard probate notice, Probate
Form 9, Probate Rule 403.

PROBATE PROCEEDINGS —Cont'd
Forms —Cont'd
  Death on or after July 1, 1995
      —Cont'd
    Verification and certificate of notice,
        Probate Form 11, Probate Rule
        403.
    Financial account information, Probate
        Form 27.
    Guardians, conservators, trustees, etc.,
        involved.
    Account filing and consent notices,
        Probate Rule 204.
    Compensation of conservators and
        guardians of minors, Probate
        Rule 225.
    Expenditure authorization petitions,
        Probate Form 1.
    Investment authority and approval
        petitions, Probate Forms 2, 3.
    Rule to show cause order, Probate
        Rule 211.
  Revocable trust.
    Claims against, Probate Rule 213.
    Notice of existence of, Probate Rule
        212.
  Safe deposit boxes, appointment of
      special administrator to open,
      Probate Rule 7.1.
**Guardians, conservators, trustees,
    etc., involved.**
  Accounts, Probate Rules 204, 221.
    Costs for accounts, Probate Rule
        206.
    Failure to file account, Probate Rule
        207.
    Fiduciaries authorized to file
        consents, Probate Rule 205.
  Appointment of fiduciary, Probate
      Rules 202, 209.
    Contesting appointment, Probate
        Rule 208.
    Guardian ad litem in
        conservatorship proceedings,
        Probate Rule 224.
    Guardians, Probate Rule 221.
  Appraisal of property, Probate Rule
      204.
    Failure to file appraisal, Probate
        Rule 207.
  Bonds and undertakings, Probate Rule
      201.
  Compensation of fiduciaries.
    Conservators and guardians of
        minors, Probate Rule 225.
    Fiduciaries authorized to file
        consents, Probate Rule 205.

PROBATE PROCEEDINGS —Cont'd
**Guardians, conservators, trustees,
    etc., involved** —Cont'd
  Compensation of fiduciaries —Cont'd
    Guardian ad litem in
        conservatorship proceedings,
        Probate Rule 224.
  Conflicts of interest, Probate Rule 202.
  Contested cases, Probate Rule 208.
  Custodianship of minors, Probate
      Rules 231, 232.
  Expenditures, Probate Rules 222, 223.
    Petition for authority to expend
        funds, Probate Form 1.
  Guardians ad litem, Probate Rules
      202, 209.
    Conservatorship proceedings,
        Probate Rule 224.
  Intervention proceedings, Probate
      Rules 301 to 361.
    See INTERVENTION
        PROCEEDINGS.
  Inventories, Probate Rule 204.
    Failure to file inventory, Probate
        Rule 207.
  Investments, Probate Rules 222, 223.
    Petition for approval of investment
        plan, Probate Form 3.
    Petition for authority to invest,
        Probate Form 2.
  Irregularities and defaults, Probate
      Rule 207.
    Expenditure and sale violations,
        Probate Rules 222, 223.
  Nonresident fiduciaries, Probate Rule
      202.
  Rule to show cause for recovery of
      property, Probate Rule 211.
  Sale of property, Probate Rules 203,
      222, 223.
  Service of process, Probate Rule 210.
    Rule to show cause petitions and
        orders, Probate Rule 211.
Hearings.
  See HEARINGS.
**Identification of probate court as
    superior court,** §16-3101.
Intervention proceedings, Probate
    Rules 301 to 361.
  See INTERVENTION
      PROCEEDINGS.
Investments by fiduciaries.
  All proceedings, Probate Rule 5.
  Guardians, conservators, trustees, etc.,
      involved, Probate Rules 222, 223.
    Petition for approval of investment
        plan, Probate Form 3.

PROBATE PROCEEDINGS —Cont'd
Investments by fiduciaries —Cont'd
  Guardians, conservators, trustees, etc.,
    involved —Cont'd
    Petition for authority to invest,
      Probate Form 2.
  Ordering investment of funds,
    §16-3108.
Necessity of probate, §20-302.
**Notice requirements in all
  proceedings,** Probate Rule 4.
**Opening of will before delivery to
  probate court,** §18-110.
Personal identification.
  Exclusion of personal identification
    numbers from filed documents,
    Probate Rule 5.1.
Petition for probate, §20-304.
Plenary proceeding, direction of,
  §§16-3105, 16-3106.
Purpose of rules, Probate Rule 1.
Register of wills.
  General provisions, §§11-2101 to
    11-2106.
  See WILLS.
  Matters presented to register of wills.
    All proceedings, Probate Rule 2.
    Death between Jan. 1, 1981, and
      June 30, 1995, Probate Rule
      101.
    Disclaimers, Probate Rule 6.1.
    Revocable trust.
      Notice of claims against, Probate
        Rule 213.
      Notice of existence of, Probate
        Rule 212.
Revocable trusts.
  Claims against, Probate Rule 213.
  Existence, notice of, Probate Rule 212.
**Revocation of letters for
  noncompliance.**
  Failure to order to invest funds,
    §16-3108.
Safe deposit boxes.
  Appointment of special administrator
    to open safe deposit box, Probate
    Rule 7.1.
Scope of rules, Probate Rule 1.
Sequestration, §§16-3104 to 16-3107.
Settlement of accounts, §16-3102.
Small estates.
  Administration, §§20-351 to 20-357.
  See SMALL ESTATES.
Social security numbers.
  Exclusion of personal identification
    numbers from filed documents,
    Probate Rule 5.1.

PROBATE PROCEEDINGS —Cont'd
Standard probate proceeding,
  §§20-321 to 20-324, 20-331.
  Action on petition, §20-324.
  Affidavits of due execution, form,
    §20-324.
  Defined, §20-321.
  Instituted by filing petition, §20-321.
  Notice of request, §20-323.
  Order after proof of due execution,
    §20-324.
  Proof of due execution, §20-324.
  Register filing petition, §20-321.
  When mandatory, §20-322.
Stays, Probate Rule 9.
Summons, §16-3103.
**Trust, mortgage and title
  corporations,** §26-1334.
Verification of pleadings, Probate
  Rule 3.

PROBATION, §§24-303 to 24-306.
**Attorney discipline or disability
  proceedings,** DCBar Rule XI.
Continuation of, §24-304.
Delinquent minors, JuvProc Rule 32.
  Detention or shelter care, JuvProc
    Rule 107.
  Forms, JuvProc Forms 3, 6.
  Preliminary probation conferences for,
    §16-2305.
  Revocation of probation, §16-2327.
Detection device.
  Tampering by persons required to
    wear, §22-1211.
Discharge from, §24-304, CrimPro
  Rule 32.
Expiration of order, §24-304.
**Interstate parole and probation
  compact,** §§24-451 to 24-453.
  Authority of mayor to execute,
    §24-451.
  Definitions, §24-452.
  Severability, §24-453.
Investigations, §24-303.
Juvenile offenders, §24-903.
Medical and geriatric parole.
  Suspension of sentence and imposition
    of probation, §24-468.
Mental health disclosures,
  §7-1204.03.
Metropolitan police, §5-105.04.
Modification, §24-304, CrimPro Rule
  32.1, USDistCt LCrR 32.1.
Order imposing conditions, CrimPro
  Form 1.
Psychiatric services, §24-306.

PROBATION —Cont'd

Public assistance denied to probation violators, §4-205.70.

Reports, §24-303.

Revocation, §24-304, CrimPro Rule 32.1, USDistCt LCrR 32.1.

Hearing commissioners, CrimPro Rule 117.

Sentencing option, CrimPro Rule 32.

Suspension of imposition or execution of sentence, §16-710.

Stay upon appeal, CrimPro Rule 38.

PRO BONO CASES, ProfCond Rule 6.1.

Appearances by attorneys, CivPro Rule 101.

Certification of practice pro bono publico, DCCtApp Form 9.

Civil pro bono panel, USDistCt LCvR 83.11.

Unauthorized practice of law exceptions, DCCtApp Rule 49.

PROCUREMENT PRACTICES.

Acquisition planning, §2-361.05.

Appeals. See within this heading, "Contract appeals board."

Applicability of provisions, §§2-351.02, 2-351.05, 2-352.01.

Architectural services, §2-356.04.

Attorney general for District of Columbia.

Authority for procurement of goods and services, §1-301.88b.

Contingency fee contracts, §1-301.86a.

Procurement claims, §2-381.03.

Auctions, §2-354.09.

Audits, §2-354.18.

Bidding process.

Cancellation of solicitation, §2-354.14.

Competitive sealed bidding, §2-354.02.

Cancellation of solicitation, §2-354.14.

Stipends, §2-361.02.

Competitive sealed proposals, §2-354.03.

Cancellation of solicitation, §2-354.14.

Stipends, §2-361.02.

Requirements, §2-354.02.

Security, §2-357.01.

Stipends, §2-361.02.

Blind and visually impaired.

Employment opportunities for, §32-305.

Bonds, surety, §§2-357.01 to 2-357.06.

Construction bids, §2-357.01.

PROCUREMENT PRACTICES —Cont'd

Bonds, surety —Cont'd

Construction performance and payment bonds, §2-357.02.

Fiscal responsibility, §2-357.06.

Forms and copies, §2-357.03.

Forms of, §2-357.04.

Requiring, §2-357.05.

Cancellation of solicitation, §2-354.14.

Certification of contractors, §2-353.01.

Chief procurement officer (CPO).

Appointment, §2-352.03.

Duties, §2-352.04.

Chief technology officer, §§1-1401 to 1-1406.

Functions, §1-1403.

Organization functions, §1-1405.

Claims against the District.

Employer interference with employee disclosures, §2-381.04.

Claims for violations, §§2-359.08, 2-381.01 to 2-381.10.

Action for violations by attorney general or qui tam plaintiff, §2-381.03.

Adjustment of civil penalties for inflation, §2-381.10.

Appeals. See within this heading, "Contract appeals board."

Barred actions, §2-381.03.

Civil investigative demands, §2-381.07.

Definitions, §2-381.01.

District action against contractor.

Generally, §2-359.06.

Interest, §2-359.09.

False claims, §§2-381.02, 2-381.09.

Inflation adjustment of penalties, §2-381.10.

Interest, §2-359.09.

Interpretation of provisions, §2-381.06.

Investigations, §§2-381.03, 2-381.07.

Limitation of actions, §2-381.05.

Qui tam plaintiff, actions by, §2-381.03.

Relation back of pleadings for purposes of statute of limitations, §2-381.05.

Relief from retaliatory actions, §2-381.04.

Remedies, §2-381.06.

Severability of provisions, §2-381.06.

Collusion, §2-354.15.

Confidentiality of information, §2-354.17.

PROCUREMENT PRACTICES
—Cont'd
Construction bonds.
Payment bonds, §2-357.02.
Performance bonds, §2-357.02.
Construction of provisions, §2-351.01.
Construction projects and related services, §§2-356.01 to 2-356.04.
Architectural and engineering services, §2-356.04.
Authorized, §2-356.01.
Estimate of construction costs, §2-356.05.
Performance and payment bonds, §2-357.02.
Prequalification, §2-356.03.
Security, §2-357.01.
Security in non-construction service contracts, §2-357.02a.
Source selection methods, §2-356.02.
Contingency fee contracts, §1-301.86a.
Contingent fees, §2-354.16.
Continuation of provisions, §2-362.02.
Contract appeals board, §§2-360.01 to 2-360.08.
Creation, §2-360.01.
Decisions, §2-360.05.
Judicial review, §2-360.07.
Jurisdiction, §2-360.03.
Members, §2-360.02.
Powers, §2-360.06.
Procedures, §2-360.08.
Protest procedures, §2-360.08.
Right to appeal, §2-360.04.
Contractors.
Capacity determinations, §2-353.02.
Debarment or suspension of contractor, §2-359.07.
Standards, §2-353.01.
Contracts, §§2-355.01 to 2-355.04.
Authorized, §2-355.03.
Cost-plus-a-percentage-of-cost contracts, §2-355.01.
Cost-reimbursement contracts, §2-355.02.
Improper contracts, §2-359.02.
Multiyear contracts, §2-355.04.
Oral agreements, §2-359.01.
Punitive damages, §2-359.05.
Sovereign immunity, §2-359.04.
Termination, §2-359.03.
Cooperative purchasing, §2-354.11.
Cost benefit analyses.
Training for contracting manager or officer performing, §2-381.43.

PROCUREMENT PRACTICES
—Cont'd
Cost-plus-a-percentage-of-cost contracts, §2-355.01.
Cost-reimbursement contracts, §2-355.02.
Debarment or suspension of contractor, §2-359.07.
Definitions, §2-351.04.
Disclosures by employee to board.
Employer interference, §2-381.04.
District of Columbia housing authority, §6-219.
Electronic inventory control system, §2-358.03.
Electronic transactions, §2-381.21.
Reverse auctions, §2-381.23.
Solicitations and responses to solicitations, §2-381.22.
Emergency procurements, §2-354.05.
Employee conduct standards, §2-359.10.
Employer interference with employee disclosures, §2-381.04.
Engineering services, §2-356.04.
Exemption from provisions, §2-351.05.
Exemptions from competitive bidding process, §2-354.13.
Fleet management services in Metropolitan Police Department.
Privatization, §2-381.42.
Fraud and deceit.
False claims against District, §2-381.02.
Fines and penalties for false representations, §2-381.09.
Function closely associated with an inherently governmental function.
Defined, §2-351.04.
Good faith, §2-351.03.
Green procurement, §2-361.01.
GSA schedules, §2-354.10.
Human care procurements, §2-354.06.
Inherently governmental functions.
Contracts for performance, prohibition, §2-352.05a.
Defined, §2-351.04.
Inspections, §2-354.18.
Inspector general.
Creation and duties of office, §1-301.115a.
Term, §1-301.115a.
Labor organization.
Defined, §2-351.04.

PROCUREMENT PRACTICES
—Cont'd
Lottery and charitable games control board, §3-1336.
Mental health services administration, §44-909.
Metropolitan Police Department.
Fleet management services.
Privatization, §2-381.42.
Metropolitan Washington Airports Authority, §9-923.
Multiyear contracts, §2-355.04.
New contracts with costs more than existing contracts for same goods or services, §2-381.41.
Office of contracting and procurement, §§2-352.01 to 2-352.06.
Authority, §2-352.01.
Chief procurement officer.
Appointment, §2-352.03.
Duties, §2-352.04.
Inherently governmental functions.
Contracts for performance, prohibition, §2-352.05a.
Privatization contracts, §2-352.05.
Review of contracts, §2-352.02.
Multiyear contracts and contracts in excess of one million dollars, §2-352.02.
Training, §2-352.06.
Ombudsman for contracting and procurement, §2-352.07.
Oral agreements, §2-359.01.
Payment bonds, §2-357.02.
Performance bonds, §2-357.02.
Persons with disabilities.
Employment opportunities for, §32-305.
Planning, §2-361.05.
Prequalification, §2-354.20.
Construction projects and related services, §2-356.03.
Price reasonableness, §2-354.19.
Privatization contracts, §2-352.05.
Proposals, §2-354.03.
Cancellation of solicitation, §2-354.14.
Stipends, §2-361.02.
Public contracts.
General provisions, §§2-201.01 to 2-223.07.
See PUBLIC CONTRACTS.
Public-private partnerships, §§2-273.01 to 2-273.09.
Punitive damages, §2-359.05.
Repealed provisions, §2-352.01.

PROCUREMENT PRACTICES
—Cont'd
Request for proposals, §2-354.03.
Cancellation of solicitation, §2-354.14.
Stipends, §2-361.02.
Responsible contractor determinations, §2-353.02.
Restricted period.
Defined, §2-351.04.
Retaliation.
Employer interference with employee to disclosures to board, §2-381.04.
Reverse auctions, §2-354.09.
Review of contracts, §2-352.02.
Rules, §2-361.06.
Security, §§2-357.01 to 2-357.06.
Bond forms and copies, §2-357.03.
Construction bids, §2-357.01.
Construction performance and payment bonds, §2-357.02.
Fiscal responsibility, §2-357.06.
Forms, §2-357.04.
Requiring, §2-357.05.
Similar items, use of exchange allowances or sale proceeds to purchase, §1-301.92.
Small and certified business enterprise development and assistance.
See SMALL AND CERTIFIED BUSINESS ENTERPRISE DEVELOPMENT AND ASSISTANCE.
Small purchases, §2-354.07.
Sole source procurements, §2-354.04.
Source selection and contract formation, §§2-354.01 to 2-354.20.
Auctions, §2-354.09.
Audits, §2-354.18.
Cancellation of solicitation, §2-354.14.
Collusion, §2-354.15.
Competitive sealed bids, §2-354.02.
Cancellation of solicitation, §2-354.14.
Security, §2-357.01.
Competitive sealed proposals, §2-354.03.
Cancellation of solicitation, §2-354.14.
Confidentiality of information, §2-354.17.
Construction projects and related services, §2-356.02.
Contingent fees, §2-354.16.
Cooperative purchasing, §2-354.11.
Emergency procurements, §2-354.05.

PROCUREMENT PRACTICES
—Cont'd
Source selection and contract formation —Cont'd
Exemptions from competition, §2-354.13.
GSA schedules, §2-354.10.
Human care procurements, §2-354.06.
Inspections, §2-354.18.
Methods, §2-354.01.
Prequalification, §2-354.20.
  Construction projects and related services, §2-356.03.
Price reasonableness, §2-354.19.
Prohibited contacts during source selection, §2-354.01a.
Reverse auctions, §2-354.09.
Small purchases, §2-354.07.
Sole source procurements, §2-354.04.
Special pilot procurements, §2-354.08.
Supply schedules, §2-354.12.
Transparency in contracting, §2-361.04.
Sovereign immunity, §2-359.04.
Special pilot procurements, §2-354.08.
Stipends, §2-361.02.
Supply management, §§2-358.01 to 2-358.05.
Electronic inventory control system, §2-358.03.
Rules, §2-358.01.
Surplus goods, §2-358.02.
  Surplus property disposition agreements, §2-358.02a.
Supply schedule, purchase card, and training fund, §2-361.03.
Supply schedules, §2-354.12.
Surplus goods, §2-358.02.
Surplus property disposition agreements, §2-358.02a.
Surplus property sales fund, §2-358.05.
Training.
Contracting manager or office performing cost benefit analysis, §2-381.43.
Training institute, §2-352.06.
Transparency, §2-361.04.
Water and Sewer Authority, §§34-2202.03, 34-2202.14.

PROCURING PROSTITUTION.
See PROSTITUTION.

PRODUCE.
Sale by weight, §37-201.15.

PRODUCER CONTROLLED INSURERS.
Business transactions.
Insurance companies.
  See INSURANCE COMPANIES.

PRODUCER LICENSING ACT, §§31-1131.01 to 31-1131.19.
See INSURANCE PRODUCER LICENSING.

PRODUCTIVITY BANK FUND, §§1-325.01, 1-325.02.

PRODUCT LIABILITY.
Asbestos cases.
Civil I calendar cases, CivPro Rule 40-II.

PROFANE AND INDECENT LANGUAGE, §22-1321.

PROFESSIONAL BAIL BONDSMEN, §§23-1101 to 23-1112.
See BAIL BONDSMEN.

PROFESSIONAL CORPORATIONS, §§29-501 to 29-516.
Administrative dissolution.
Generally, §§29-106.01 to 29-106.04.
  See BUSINESS ORGANIZATIONS.
Applicability of law, §29-503.
Certificates of share, §29-511.
Definitions, §29-501.
Directors.
Number of, §29-507.
Qualifications, §29-508.
Disqualified professionals, §29-513.
Dissolution, §29-516.
Filing.
Generally, §§29-102.01 to 29-102.13.
  See BUSINESS ORGANIZATIONS.
Foreign entities.
Generally, §§29-105.01 to 29-105.12.
  See BUSINESS ORGANIZATIONS.
Incorporation, §29-506.
Investments.
Powers, §29-505.
Liabilities, §29-510.
Mergers and consolidations.
Restrictions, §29-512.
Mortgages and deeds of trust.
Powers, §29-505.
Names.
Generally, §§29-103.01 to 29-103.04.
  See BUSINESS ORGANIZATIONS.
Requirements, §29-103.02.
Officers.
Qualifications, §29-508.
Perpetual existence, §29-516.

PROFESSIONAL CORPORATIONS
—Cont'd
Personal property.
Powers, §29-505.
Powers, §29-505.
Professional relationships.
Effect on, §29-510.
Proxy arrangements.
Prohibitions, §29-509.
Purposes of, §29-505.
Real property.
Powers, §29-505.
Registered agents.
Generally, §§29-104.01 to 29-104.14.
See BUSINESS ORGANIZATIONS.
Shares and shareholders.
Certificates of share, §29-511.
Disposition by disqualified, deceased
or incompetent shareholder,
§29-514.
Qualifications of shareholders,
§29-508.
Redemption price, §29-515.
Transfer of shares, §29-511.
Short title, §29-501.
Statutory construction, §29-504.

PROFESSIONAL COUNSELING.
Addiction counselors, §§3-1208.51 to
3-1208.54.
Board of, §3-1202.13.
Definition of practice of, §3-1201.02.
Health occupations boards.
General provisions, §§3-1201.01 to
3-1213.01.
See HEALTH OCCUPATIONS
BOARDS.
Health occupations licensure,
registration or certification,
§§3-1205.01 to 3-1205.24.
See HEALTH OCCUPATIONS
LICENSURE, REGISTRATION
OR CERTIFICATION.
Licenses, §§3-1207.10 to 3-1207.12.
Qualifications for licensure,
§3-1207.10.
Titles and terms prohibited as
misrepresentation without
license to practice, §3-1210.03.
Transition, §3-1207.11.
Waiver of licensure requirements,
§3-1207.12.

PROFESSIONAL ENGINEERS.
See ENGINEERS.

PROFESSIONAL SPORTS.
Business licenses, §47-2823.

PROFESSIONAL SPORTS —Cont'd
Child labor, §32-206.

PROFESSIONS AND
OCCUPATIONS.
Boards.
Health occupations boards,
§§3-1201.01 to 3-1213.01.
See HEALTH OCCUPATIONS
BOARDS.
Non-health related, §§47-2853.06 to
47-2853.10.
Business licenses.
General provisions, §§47-2805.01 to
47-2881.
See BUSINESS LICENSES.
Engineers.
General provisions.
See ENGINEERS.
Health care practitioners.
General provisions, §§3-1201.01 to
3-1213.01.
See HEALTH OCCUPATIONS
BOARDS.
Health occupations licensure,
registration or certification,
§§3-1205.01 to 3-1205.24.
See HEALTH OCCUPATIONS
LICENSURE, REGISTRATION
OR CERTIFICATION.
Health occupations boards.
General provisions, §§3-1201.01 to
3-1213.01.
See HEALTH OCCUPATIONS
BOARDS.
Notaries public.
General provisions, §§1-1201 to
1-1217.
See NOTARIES PUBLIC.
Pawnbrokers.
General provisions, §§47-2884.01 to
47-2884.19.
See PAWNBROKERS.
Pharmacists and pharmacies.
General provisions, §§47-2885.01 to
47-2885.23.
See PHARMACISTS AND
PHARMACIES.
Pharmacy technicians, §§3-1207.51 to
3-1207.58.
See PHARMACISTS AND
PHARMACIES.
Professional bail bondsmen.
General provisions, §§23-1101 to
23-1112.
See BAIL BONDSMEN.

PROFESSIONS AND OCCUPATIONS
—Cont'd
Security agents and brokers.
General provisions, §§31-5601.01 to
31-5608.04.
See SECURITY AGENTS AND
BROKERS.
Security and fire alarm contractors.
General provisions, §§7-2801 to
7-2815.
See SECURITY AND FIRE ALARM
CONTRACTORS.
Veterinarians, §§3-1208.61 to
3-1208.65.
See VETERINARY MEDICINE.

**PROGRAM ON WORK,
EMPLOYMENT, AND
RESPONSIBILITY (POWER).**
Amount of assistance received,
§4-205.78.
Discrimination prohibitions,
§4-205.19i.
Diversion payments, §4-205.81.
**Earned income credit information,
providing,** §4-205.82.
Eligibility, §§4-205.72, 4-205.72a,
4-205.73, 4-205.75.
Entitlement not created by,
§4-205.79.
Establishment of, §§4-202.01, 4-205.72,
4-205.72a.
**Failure to participate in self-
sufficiency activities,** §4-205.77.
Income eligibility standards,
§4-205.10.
Lump-sum payments, §4-205.81.
Medical review procedures,
§4-205.74.
Need determinations, §4-205.11.
**Privacy and confidentiality of
applicant information,** §4-209.04.
Redetermination of eligibility,
§4-205.75.
**Self-sufficiency activities
requirement,** §§4-205.76, 4-205.77.
Support payments, §4-205.19.
TANF recipients, §4-205.73.
**Training and employment costs and
expenses,** §4-205.50.

PRO HAC VICE APPEARANCES,
CivPro Rule 101, CrimPro Rule 115,
USDistCt LCrR 44.1, USDistCt
LCvR 83.2.
Adoption proceedings, Adoption Rule
101.

PRO HAC VICE APPEARANCES
—Cont'd
**Application for admission pro hac
vice,** DCCtApp Form 8.
Domestic relations actions, DomRel
Rule 101.
Juvenile proceedings, JuvProc Rule
115.
**Unauthorized practice of law
exceptions,** DCCtApp Rule 49.

PROHIBITION, WRIT OF, DCCtApp
Rule 21.
Appeals in federal cases, FRAP 21,
USCtApp Rule 21.
Directed to judge, FRAP 21.

PROMISSORY NOTES.
Assignments.
Nonnegotiable notes, §28-2303.
Complaint on a promissory note,
CivPro Form CA 3.
Negotiable instruments generally,
§§28:3-101 to 28:3-605.
See NEGOTIABLE INSTRUMENTS.
Notaries public, §1-1208.

PROMOTIONS.
Fire departments, §§1-608.01, 5-402,
5-543.04.
**Meritorious service awards for fire,
police, and corrections
departments,** §5-903.
Metropolitan police, §§1-608.01,
5-105.01, 5-543.04.
National guard.
Examinations for promotion of
commissioned officers, §49-309.
Return of armament, equipment, and
supplies on, §49-206.

PROMPT PAYMENT.
Health benefits plans.
Claims for reimbursement by
providers, §31-3132.
**Private contractor and
subcontractor prompt payment
act,** §§27-131 to 27-136.
Applicability.
Effective date, §27-136.
Contractors.
Defined, §27-131.
Contractors' bonds.
Prohibition on requiring waiver of
right to sue on contractor's
bond, §27-134.
Contracts.
Defined, §27-131.
Definitions, §27-131.

PROMPT PAYMENT —Cont'd
Private contractor and subcontractor prompt payment act —Cont'd
Effective date, §27-136.
Failure to make prompt payments, §27-133.
Subcontractors, payments to, §§27-134, 27-135.
Interest.
Failure to make prompt payments, §27-133.
Subcontractors, payments to, §27-135.
Liens.
Prohibition on requiring waiver of right to claim mechanics' lien, §27-134.
Owners.
Defined, §27-131.
Subcontractors.
Defined, §27-131.
Time for payments, §27-132.
Failure to make prompt payments, §27-133.
Undisputed amounts.
Defined, §27-131.
Failure to make prompt payments.
Subcontractors, payments to, §27-135.
Time for payments, §27-132.
Failure to make prompt payments, §27-133.

PROPERTY AND LIABILITY INSURANCE GUARANTY ASSOCIATION, §§31-5501 to 31-5515.
Applicability of provisions, §31-5502.
Assessments, §31-5513.
Board of directors, §31-5504.
Definitions, §31-5501.
Detection and prevention of insolvencies, §31-5510.
Establishment of, §31-5503.
Examinations, §31-5511.
Immunity, §31-5514.
Nonduplicative recovery, §31-5509.
Operating plan, §31-5506.
Paid claims, effect of, §31-5508.
Powers and duties of association, §31-5505.
Powers and duties of mayor regarding, §31-5507.
Rates, recognition of assessments in, §31-5513.
Records, §31-5515.

PROPERTY AND LIABILITY INSURANCE GUARANTY ASSOCIATION —Cont'd
Stay of proceedings, §31-5515.
Tax exemption, §31-5512.

PROPERTY INSURANCE UNDERWRITING, §§31-5001 to 31-5011.

PROPERTY MANAGERS.
Business licenses.
Eligibility, §47-2853.142.
Representations prohibited, §47-2853.143.
Scope of practice, §47-2853.141.
Fiduciary duties, §47-2853.195.
Real estate brokers and salespersons, §§42-1701 to 42-1709.
See REAL ESTATE BROKERS AND SALESPERSONS.

PRO SE LITIGANTS.
Appeals, DCCtApp Rule 42.
Attorneys at law.
Dealings with unrepresented persons, ProfCond Rule 4.3.
Domestic relations actions, DomRel Rule 101.
Hospitalization of persons with mental illness.
Signing of pleadings, MentalHealth Rule 14.
Signing of papers by party not represented by attorney, CivPro Rule 11.

PROSTATE CANCER SCREENING.
Health insurance coverage, §§31-2951 to 31-2954.
Applicability, §31-2953.
Coverage, §31-2952.
Definitions, §31-2951.
Regulations, §31-2954.

PROSTITUTION, §§22-2701 to 22-2725.
Abatement of nuisances.
Bonds, surety, §22-2719.
Costs, §22-2715.
Declaration of house of prostitution as nuisance, §22-2713.
Delivery of premises, order for, §22-2719.
Dismissal of complaint, §22-2715.
Disposition of proceeds of sale, §22-2718.

PROSTITUTION —Cont'd

Abatement of nuisances —Cont'd

Drug, firearm, or prostitution-related nuisance abatement, §§42-3101 to 42-3114.

    See CRIME-RELATED NUISANCE ABATEMENT.

Forfeiture of property, §22-2717.

Injunctions, §§22-2714, 22-2716.

Order of abatement, §22-2717.

Prosecutions, §22-2715.

Release of, §22-2719.

Sale of property as nuisance, §§22-2717, 22-2718.

Tax for maintaining nuisance, §22-2720.

Temporary injunction, §22-2714.

Trial for, §22-2715.

Violation of injunction, §22-2716.

Alcoholic beverage license transfer restrictions, §25-316.

Arrest for keeping bawdy house, §5-115.06.

Child abuse and neglect.

Reporting requirements, §4-1321.02.

Child prostitution, §22-2704.

Compelling, §§22-2705, 22-2706.

Debt, for, §22-2709.

Spouse caused to live in prostitution, §22-2708.

Threats, duress, or detention, §§22-2705, 22-2706, 22-2709.

Conditions imposed on persons found guilty of, §22-2703.

Definitions, §22-2701.01.

Domestic partners caused to live in, §22-2708.

Enforcement of rules regarding, §22-2703.

Forfeitures, §§22-2717, 22-2723.

House of prostitution.

Arrest for keeping, §5-115.06.

Debt, detention of person in disorderly house for, §22-2709.

Fines and penalties for keeping, §22-2722.

Operating, §22-2712.

Pandering, procuring, or pimping for, §22-2710.

Human trafficking, §§22-1831 to 22-1843.

    See HUMAN TRAFFICKING.

Inciting, inducing, or compelling engagement in, §22-2705.

PROSTITUTION —Cont'd

Motor vehicles.

Impoundment of vehicle used in prostitution-related offense, §22-2724.

Anti-prostitution vehicle impoundment proceeds fund, §22-2725.

Nuisances.

Drug, firearm, or prostitution-related nuisance abatement, §§42-3101 to 42-3114.

    See CRIME-RELATED NUISANCE ABATEMENT.

Pandering, procuring, or pimping, §22-2705.

House of prostitution, for, §22-2710.

Receiving money or valuables for arranging assignations, §22-2707.

Spouses caused to live in prostitution, §22-2708.

Third persons, for, §22-2711.

Prohibited acts, §22-2701.

Spouses caused to live in, §22-2708.

Suspension of sentence for, §22-2703.

PROSTITUTION-RELATED NUISANCE ABATEMENT, §§42-3101 to 42-3114.

See CRIME-RELATED NUISANCE ABATEMENT.

PROTECTION OF INNOCENCE ACT, §§22-4131 to 22-4135.

PROTECTIVE ORDERS.

Adult guardianship and protective proceedings jurisdiction act, §§21-2401.01 to 21-2405.03.

See GUARDIAN AND WARD.

Adult protective services.

Ex parte temporary protection orders, §7-1907.

Provisional protection orders, §7-1906.

Attorney discipline or disability proceedings.

Confidentiality, DCBar Rule XI.

Detection device.

Tampering by persons required to wear, §22-1211.

Discovery, CivPro Rules 26, 37.

Adoption proceedings, Adoption Rule 26.

Criminal procedure, CrimPro Rule 16.

Delinquent minors, JuvProc Rule 16.

Domestic relations actions, DomRel Rule 26.

PROTECTIVE ORDERS —Cont'd
Domestic violence.
Alternative discovery methods, DomesticViolence Rule 8.
Appearances.
Failure of respondent to appear at hearing, DomesticViolence Rule 5.
Criminal charges.
Effect of bringing, DomesticViolence Rule 1.
Criminal contempt proceedings.
Discovery, DomesticViolence Rule 8.
Discovery, DomesticViolence Rule 8.
Duration and extension, DomesticViolence Rule 11.
Motion for modification and/or extension, DomesticViolence Rule 7.
Motion for contempt.
Violation of protection order, DomesticViolence Rule 7.
Motion for modification and/or extension, DomesticViolence Rule 7.
Proof required for order, DomesticViolence Rule 9.
Remedies available, DomesticViolence Rule 11.
Temporary protection orders.
Criminal charges.
Effect of bringing, DomesticViolence Rule 1.
Criminal contempt proceedings.
Discovery, DomesticViolence Rule 8.
Hearing on motion, DomesticViolence Rule 7A.
Scope of order, DomesticViolence Rule 7A.
Service upon respondent required, DomesticViolence Rule 7A.
Uniform child custody proceedings, §§16-4601.01 to 16-4605.03.
See CHILD CUSTODY AND CHILD CUSTODY PROCEEDINGS.
Financial exploitation of vulnerable adults and elderly persons.
Injunction, restraining order and asset protection, §22-938.
Intrafamily proceedings, §16-1005.
Temporary protection orders, §16-1004.
Landlord and tenant court,
LandlordTenant Rule 12-I.
Information sheet, LandlordTenant Form 8.

PROTECTIVE ORDERS —Cont'd
Missing persons, Probate Rule 350.
Temporary restraining orders,
CivPro Rule 65, USDistCt LCvR 65.1.
Uniform adult guardianship and protective proceedings jurisdiction act, §§21-2401.01 to 21-2405.03.
See GUARDIAN AND WARD.

PROTESTS TARGETING A RESIDENCE, §§22-2751, 22-2752.
Warrantless arrest, §23-581.

PROVIDENCE HOSPITAL.
Teaching hospital for nurses and interns, §44-703.

PROXY ARRANGEMENTS.
Cooperative associations.
Prohibitions, §29-914.
Corporations, §29-305.22.
Limited partnerships, §29-701.13.
Nonprofit corporations, §29-405.22.
Professional corporations.
Prohibitions, §29-509.

PRUDENT INVESTOR ACT.
Fiduciaries, CivPro Rule 306.
Probate proceedings, Probate Rule 5.
Uniform prudent investor act, §§19-1309.01 to 19-1309.06.
Compliance, determination, §19-1309.05.
Considerations, §19-1309.02.
Diversification of investments, §19-1309.03.
Duties upon accepting trusteeship, §19-1309.04.
General rule, §19-1309.01.
Prudent investor rule, §19-1309.01.
Risk and return objectives, §19-1309.02.
Standard of care, §19-1309.02.
Language invoking standard, §19-1309.06.

PRUDENT MANAGEMENT OF INSTITUTIONAL FUNDS, §§44-1631 to 44-1639.
Applicability of chapter, §44-1637.
Appropriation for expenditure or accumulation of endowment fund, §44-1633.
Compliance, determination of, §44-1636.
Construction and interpretation, §44-1639.

PRUDENT MANAGEMENT OF INSTITUTIONAL FUNDS —Cont'd

Definitions, §44-1631.

Delegation of management and investment functions, §44-1634.

Electronic signatures.
Relation to electronic signatures in global and national commerce act, §44-1638.

Modification of restrictions, §44-1635.

Release of restrictions, §44-1635.

Standard of conduct, §44-1632.

PRUDENT MAN STANDARD.

Trusts and trustees.
Powers and duties of trustees, §19-1308.04.

PSYCHIATRIC EXAMINATIONS.

Court-ordered, §7-1204.01.

Hospitalization of persons with mental illness.
See HOSPITALIZATION OF PERSONS WITH MENTAL ILLNESS.

Sexual psychopaths, §22-3806.

PSYCHIATRIC SERVICES.

Probation, §24-306.

PSYCHOLOGICALLY IMPACTED PROPERTY.

Disclosures real estate brokers, salespersons not required to make, §47-2853.198.

PSYCHOLOGY.

Board of, §3-1202.11.

Child abuse and neglect reports.
Psychologists required to make, §4-1321.02.

Child death.
Reports, §4-1371.12.

Definition of practice of, §3-1201.02.

Health insurance, group policies, §31-4724.

Health occupations boards.
General provisions, §§3-1201.01 to 3-1213.01.
See HEALTH OCCUPATIONS BOARDS.

Health occupations licensure, registration or certification, §§3-1205.01 to 3-1205.24.
See HEALTH OCCUPATIONS LICENSURE, REGISTRATION OR CERTIFICATION.

PSYCHOLOGY —Cont'd

Intellectual disabilities, persons with.
Psychological therapies used on, §7-1305.06.

Psychology associates.
Board of psychology, §3-1202.11.
Health occupations licensure, registration or certification, §3-1209.06.
Requirements, §3-1209.06.
Titles and terms prohibited as misrepresentation without license to practice, §3-1210.03.

Reports.
Child death, §4-1371.12.

Titles and terms prohibited as misrepresentation without license to practice, §3-1210.03.

PSYCHO-SURGERY.

Health care durable powers of attorney, §21-2211.

PSYCHOTROPIC MEDICATION.

Intellectual disabilities, persons with.
Health care decision-makers.
Data for assessment of needs, §7-1305.07a.
Informed consent requirement, §7-1305.06a.
Panel to review proposals to administer, §7-1305.06b.
Review for all DDS customers, §7-1305.06c.

PUBLIC ACCESS CORPORATION, §34-1253.02.

PUBLIC ACCOMMODATIONS.

Equal access to, §7-1002.

PUBLIC ASSISTANCE, §§4-201.01 to 4-221.01.

Administrative procedure, §4-202.02.

Amount of payment, §§4-208.01 to 4-208.05.
Determination, §4-208.01.
For assistance unit, §4-205.52.
Generally, §4-208.04.
Method, §4-208.01.
Repayment by former GPA recipient, §4-208.05.
Supplemental payments, §4-208.02.
Underpayment, §4-208.03.

Appeal.
Notification of right to judicial review, §4-210.13.

PUBLIC ASSISTANCE —Cont'd
Application for, §§4-205.19, 4-205.26 to 4-205.31.
  Veteran applicants, §4-126.
Appropriations, §4-219.01.
Assignment of public assistance, §4-215.01.
Assignment of support payments, §§4-213.01, 4-213.05, 4-213.06, 4-217.07 to 4-217.11.
Attorneys' fees and costs.
  In forma pauperis proceedings, §15-712.
Availability of income and resources, §4-205.38.
Categories of, §4-201.01.
Changes in policy, §4-210.16.
Children and minors.
  Child care facilities, §§4-401 to 4-415.
    See CHILD CARE FACILITIES.
  Crisis management, §§4-203.01 to 4-203.04.
  Foster care, §§4-217.01 to 4-217.11.
    See FOSTER CARE.
  General assistance for children program, §4-205.05a.
  Institutionalization.
    See PUBLIC WELFARE, BOARD OF.
  Pregnant or parenting teens, §§4-205.61 to 4-205.66.
  Prison, parents in, §4-205.20.
  Protective or vendor payments on behalf of dependent children, §4-212.02.
  Temporary assistance for needy families (TANF).
    See TEMPORARY ASSISTANCE FOR NEEDY FAMILIES (TANF).
  Unemployed parents, §4-205.21.
Class actions, §4-210.16.
Community residence facilities, recipients in, §4-205.49.
Confidentiality of applicant's or recipient's information, §4-209.04.
Congress.
  Power of congress to provide for general welfare, US Const Art I §8.
Constitution of the United States.
  General welfare.
    Powers of congress, US Const Art I §8.
Contracts.
  Pay-for-success contracts, §§2-211.01 to 2-211.03.

PUBLIC ASSISTANCE —Cont'd
Correction of challenged policy, §4-210.16.
Crimes and offenses, §§4-218.01 to 4-218.06.
Crisis assistance and service program, §4-206.02.
Definitions, §§4-201.01, 4-205.05.
Delegation of mayor's functions, §4-202.03.
Disability assistance.
  Interim program, §4-204.08.
Earned income, §4-205.39.
Earned income credit information, providing, §4-205.82.
Eligibility documents.
  Improper use of, §4-218.03.
Eligibility for, §§4-205.01, 4-205.26 to 4-205.31.
  Determination, §4-208.01.
  Failure to request hearing or submit information to clarify, §4-205.57.
Emergency assistance.
  See EMERGENCY PUBLIC ASSISTANCE.
Entitlements not created by, §4-220.03.
Estates, claims against, §4-214.01.
Family emergency services program, §4-206.04.
Fines, §§4-218.02, 4-218.05.
Food stamp coupons.
  Business license or permit suspended, revoked, or denied for trafficking in food stamps, §4-218.06.
  Misuse of, §§4-218.05, 4-218.06.
Foster care, §§4-217.01 to 4-217.11.
  See FOSTER CARE.
Fraud and deceit, §§4-205.69, 4-218.01.
Fugitive felons, §4-205.70.
Funeral expenses.
  Allowance, §4-214.04.
  Payment, §4-214.03.
General assistance for children program, §4-205.05a.
General public assistance (GPA).
  Repayments by recipients, §4-208.05.
  Termination of, §4-202.01a.
Grants, income status of, §4-205.29.
Halfway houses, recipients in, §4-205.49.
Hearings, §§4-205.56 to 4-205.59, 4-210.01 to 4-210.19.
  Assistance received during pendency of action, §4-210.19.

PUBLIC ASSISTANCE —Cont'd
Hearings —Cont'd
Class action, §4-210.16.
Final decisions by mayor's agent,
    §4-210.12.
    Filing decisions, §4-210.15.
Grounds for granting, §4-210.02.
Hearing officers, §4-210.03.
    Findings, conclusions,
        recommendations, §4-210.11.
Major objectives of process, §4-210.02.
Medical issues, §4-210.06.
Notice of right to hearing, §4-210.01.
Notice provisions of section 4-205.54
    applicable, §4-210.18.
Procedure enumerated, §4-210.10.
Request, §4-210.05.
    Administrative review, §4-210.07.
    Method of making request,
        §4-210.04.
    Notification of right to request,
        §4-210.04.
    Time limit, §4-210.09.
    While absent from District,
        §4-210.14.
Right to hearing, §4-210.01.
Time, date, place, §4-210.08.
Waiver of privilege of confidentiality,
    §4-210.17.
Home living requirement, §4-205.63.
Home repairs, §4-211.01.
Incapacitated persons.
Defined terms, §4-205.42.
Payments to, §4-212.01.
Protective or vendor payments on
    behalf of dependent children,
    §4-212.02.
Protective payments on behalf of adult
    recipients, §4-212.03.
Income and amount of assistance,
    determining, §§4-205.28 to
    4-205.41.
Income and resources
    determinations, §4-205.37.
In-kind resources, §4-205.40.
Institutionalization.
See PUBLIC WELFARE, BOARD OF.
Investigation of applicants,
    §§4-209.01, 4-209.04.
Issuance of rules and regulations,
    §4-202.05.
Loans, income status of, §4-205.29.
Lump-sum payments and
    settlements, §§4-205.30, 4-205.33.
Mayor's duties and powers,
    §§4-202.02, 4-202.03, 4-202.05.

PUBLIC ASSISTANCE —Cont'd
Medicaid, §§4-204.05, 4-204.05a.
More than one assistance payment.
Families receiving, §4-205.28.
Motor vehicles.
Retention of, §4-205.41.
Moving expenses, §§4-211.04, 4-211.05.
Net payment received, §4-205.32.
Nonabatement of causes of action,
    §4-220.02.
Nonrevival of previously repealed or
    superseded laws, §4-220.01.
Notice of discontinuation, §4-205.55.
Notice of right to hearing, §§4-210.01,
    4-210.04.
Nursing care in home of relative.
Person receiving, §4-205.47.
Nursing homes.
Recipients in, §4-205.49.
Opportunity accounts.
Exclusion from program calculations,
    §1-307.72.
Parole for medical and geriatric
    reasons, §24-466.
Parole violators, §4-205.70.
Pay-for-success contracts, §§2-211.01
    to 2-211.03.
Payments, making, §§4-208.01 to
    4-208.05.
Penalties, §§4-218.02, 4-218.05.
Pendency of action.
Assistance received, §4-210.19.
Persons with disabilities. See within
    this heading, "Incapacitated
    persons."
Privacy and confidentiality of
    applicant information, §4-209.04.
Probation violators, §4-205.70.
Program on work, employment, and
    responsibility (POWER).
See PROGRAM ON WORK,
    EMPLOYMENT, AND
    RESPONSIBILITY (POWER).
Prosecution of violations regarding,
    §§4-218.02, 4-218.04.
Reconsideration of grants of,
    §4-205.53.
Records, §4-216.01.
Relocation of recipients to another
    jurisdiction, §4-205.04.
Repayments by General Public
    Assistance (GPA) recipients,
    §4-208.05.
Requirement to apply for, §4-205.31.
Residence requirements, §§4-205.02
    to 4-205.04, 4-205.69.

PUBLIC ASSISTANCE —Cont'd
Residency determination, §4-205.03.
Residency requirements, §4-205.02.
Rights not created by, §4-220.03.
Severability of provisions, §4-221.01.
Sexual assault victims, emergency
    care, §§7-2121 to 7-2125.
Social security.
  See SOCIAL SECURITY.
Special living arrangements,
    recipients with, §4-205.49.
SSI/SSDI outreach, access and
    recovery (SOAR) pilot program,
    §4-271.01.
Standards of assistance, §§4-205.48,
    4-205.52.
Subpoenas, §4-218.04.
Supplemental nutrition assistance
    program (SNAP), §§4-261.21 to
    4-261.23.
  Reports, §4-261.23.
  Simplified self-employment deduction,
    §4-261.22.
  Transitional benefits, §4-261.21.
Supplemental payments, §4-208.02.
Support assignment, §§4-213.01,
    4-213.05, 4-213.06, 4-217.07 to
    4-217.11.
Temporary assistance for needy
    families (TANF).
  See TEMPORARY ASSISTANCE FOR
    NEEDY FAMILIES (TANF).
Termination or reduction of,
    §§4-205.53 to 4-205.59.
  Additional information considered,
    §4-205.58.
  Failure to request hearing or submit
    information to clarify eligibility,
    §4-205.57.
  Information from source other than
    recipient, §4-205.56.
  Timely notice of discontinuance,
    §4-205.55.
Time limits, failure to determine
    eligibility within, §4-205.27.
Training and employment costs and
    expenses, §4-205.50.
Transferability, lack of, §4-215.01.
Underpayments, correcting,
    §4-208.03.
Unemployment compensation.
  General provisions, §§51-101 to
    51-151.
  See UNEMPLOYMENT
    COMPENSATION.
Veterans.
  Assistance application forms, §4-126.

PUBLIC ASSISTANCE —Cont'd
Witnesses in prosecutions, §4-218.04.
Work incentive allowances, §4-205.36.

PUBLICATION.
Administrative procedure for
    publication of documents,
    §§2-504, 2-551 to 2-562.
Administrator, filing of documents
    to be published with, §2-556.
Appeals.
  Publication of opinions, DCCtApp Rule
    36.
Certification of published
    documents, §2-560.
Code of the District of Columbia,
    §2-602.
Court information and statistics,
    §11-1744.
District of Columbia Code, §45-102.
District of Columbia Municipal
    Regulations, §§2-552, 2-555, 2-557.
District of Columbia Office of
    Documents, §§2-554 to 2-562.
District of Columbia Register,
    §2-553.
Elections.
  Voting by military and overseas voters,
    §1-1061.16.
Errors in published documents,
    correcting, §2-559.
Fines regarding publication of
    documents, §2-562.
Garnishment.
  Prejudgment garnishment, §16-502.
Homestead housing preservation
    program.
  List of properties, §42-2105.
Legal effectiveness of published
    documents, §2-558.
Legal effectiveness of publishing
    acts and resolutions, §2-602.
Official, §2-504.
Partnerships.
  Dissolution.
    Notice of claims against dissolved
      partnership, §§29-608.08,
      29-608.09.
Penalties regarding publication of
    documents, §2-562.
Presumption created by publication
    of documents, §2-561.
Probate proceedings.
  Notices.
    Death before Jan. 1, 1981, Probate
      Rule 11.

PUBLICATION —Cont'd
Probate proceedings —Cont'd
Notices —Cont'd
Death between Jan. 1, 1981, and June 30, 1995, Probate Rule 128.
Death on or after July 1, 1995, Probate Rule 428.
Revocable trust, existence of, Probate Rule 212.
Real property assessments, §47-823.
Regulations, §1-303.02.
Replevin, return of writ.
Publication against defendant, §16-3706.
Service of process by publication, §§13-335 to 13-341, CivPro Rule 4-I.
Adoption proceedings, Adoption Rule 4.
Condemnation actions, CivPro Rule 71A.
Domestic relations actions, DomRel Rule 4.
Statutes-at-large, §2-603.
Statutory trusts.
Notice of claims against dissolved statutory trust, §29-1208.05.
Towing and storage notice.
Scrap vehicle title authorization, §50-2702.
Transcripts of meetings, §1-207.42.
United States District Court.
Notices relating to proceedings, USDistCt LCvR 83.22.
Rules.
Amendments, USDistCt LCrR 57.1, USDistCt LCvR 1.1, USDistCt LCvR 83.21.
Voting by military and overseas voters, §1-1061.16.

PUBLIC AUCTIONS.
Business licenses for auctioneers, §47-2808.
Jewelry and valuables, hours of sale restricted for, §47-2705.
Metropolitan police property clerk.
Sale of property at, §5-119.10.
Permit requirements, §§47-2701 to 47-2708.
Applications for permits, §47-2702.
Fees, §47-2702.
Fraud and deceit, §47-2706.
Interpretation of provisions, §47-2708.
Jewelry and valuables, hours of sale restricted for, §47-2705.
Personal property, §§47-2703, 47-2705.

PUBLIC AUCTIONS —Cont'd
Permit requirements —Cont'd
Prosecutions, §47-2707.
Suspension of license for violations, §47-2704.
Personal property, §§47-2703, 47-2705.
Real estate tax sales, §47-1301.
Stock and stockholders, public auction permits, §§47-2701 to 47-2708.
Trust, mortgage and title corporation stock sold at public auction on failure to pay over capital stock, §26-1317.

PUBLIC BATHS.
Business licenses, §47-2812.

PUBLIC BENEFIT CORPORATIONS, §§29-1301.01 to 29-1304.01.
See BENEFIT CORPORATIONS.

PUBLIC BUILDINGS.
Acquisitions of real property for, §10-604.
Appropriations for repairs and improvements, §10-703.
Bicycle parking, §§50-1641.01 to 50-1641.09.
See BICYCLES.
Blocking passage, §22-1307.
Construction loans, §§10-603 to 10-620. See within this heading, "Loans for construction projects."
Construction Services Fund, §10-620.
Control of, §10-507.01.
District government buildings.
Bicycle parking.
Mayor's report, §50-1641.04.
Federal buildings, zoning exemptions for, §6-641.15.
Funds.
Construction Services Fund, §10-620.
Graffiti abatement, §§42-3141.01 to 42-3141.11.
See GRAFFITI.
Height of buildings, §§6-601.05 to 6-611.02.
See BUILDING CODE.
Improvements, §§10-702, 10-703.
John A. Wilson building.
General provisions, §§10-1301, 10-1302, 10-1331 to 10-1336, 10-1701.
See JOHN A. WILSON BUILDING.
Labor-peace agreement for public participation in hotel projects, §§32-851 to 32-856.

PUBLIC BUILDINGS —Cont'd
Lead paint inspections, §10-702.
Loans for construction projects,
§§10-603 to 10-620.
Authorization to borrow money from
United States, §10-607.
Authorized projects, §§10-603, 10-608,
10-614, 10-619.
Capital needs, construction program to
meet, §10-619.
Construction Services Fund, §10-620.
Interest, §§10-612, 10-613.
Limitations on borrowing, §10-611.
Office of Recorder of Deeds, building
for, §§10-614 to 10-617.
Plans and specifications, §10-618.
Real property acquisitions, funds for,
§10-604.
Reimbursement of funds from
Treasury to Federal Emergency
Administration of Public Works,
§10-605.
Repayments, §§10-609, 10-616.
Reports, §§10-606, 10-610, 10-617.
Master facilities planning and
program coordination advisory
committee, §§10-1031, 10-1032.
Municipal center, §§10-601, 10-602.
National children's island, §§10-1401
to 10-1406.
Rental of airspace.
General provisions, §§10-1121.01 to
10-1121.13.
See RENTAL OF AIRSPACE.
Rental of public space.
General provisions, §§10-1101.01 to
10-1104.08.
See RENTAL OF PUBLIC SPACE.
Public structures in public space,
§§10-1141.01 to 10-1141.07.
Repair and maintenance, §§10-702,
10-703.
Reports on construction projects
and loans, §§10-606, 10-610,
10-617.
Steam heat furnished to, §§10-501.03,
10-501.04.
Walter Reed Army Medical Center,
§§10-1901 to 10-1906.
Washington convention and sports
authority.
General provisions, §§10-1202.01 to
10-1221.15.
See WASHINGTON CONVENTION
AND SPORTS AUTHORITY.
PUBLIC CHARTER SCHOOLS.
See CHARTER SCHOOLS.

PUBLIC CONTRACTS, §§2-201.01 to
2-223.07.
Automatic data processing,
§§2-213.01, 2-213.02.
Bonds, surety, §§2-201.01 to 2-201.11.
Child care facilities, §4-409.
Conflicts of interest, §1-207.32.
Contractor's bond, §2-201.01.
Debarment.
Workplace fraud.
Debarment for repeat violations,
§32-1331.11.
Deferred compensation program,
§47-3603.
Disapproved contracts.
Settlement agreements.
Limitations, §2-402.
Employment agreement with
District government, §2-219.03.
Expenditures in excess of $1,000,000
contracts involving, §1-204.51.
Federal and District governments,
provision of services between,
§1-207.37.
Fire insurance, §2-205.02.
First source employment, §§2-219.01
to 2-219.05.
Office of first source compliance,
§§2-219.31 to 2-219.35.
Highways, §9-107.03.
Hospital care for indigents, §44-706.
Indigents, hospital care for, §44-706.
Insurance, §§2-205.01, 2-205.02.
Laborers and materialmen.
Certified copy of bond and contract
supplied to, §2-201.03.
Right to sue on payment bonds,
§2-201.02.
Living wage act, §§2-220.01 to
2-220.11.
See LIVING WAGE ACT.
Maryland, sewerage agreement
with, §2-207.01.
Multi-year contracts, §1-204.51.
One year, contracts extending
beyond, §1-204.51.
Paving and resurfacing streets and
alleys, §§9-401.16, 9-401.17.
Procurement practices.
See PROCUREMENT PRACTICES.
Public-private partnerships,
§§2-271.01 to 2-275.01.
See PUBLIC-PRIVATE
PARTNERSHIPS.
Quick payment provisions, §§2-221.01
to 2-221.06.
Claims, filing, §2-221.04.

PUBLIC CONTRACTS —Cont'd
Quick payment provisions —Cont'd
Defined terms, §2-221.01.
Discounted prices, §2-221.03.
Disputed payments, §2-221.04.
Interest penalty payments, §§2-221.02, 2-221.03.
Change order clause, §2-221.02.
Failure to pay discounted price within specified period, §2-221.03.
Filing of claims, §2-221.04.
Receipt and payment dates.
Determining, §2-221.06.
Rental contracts.
Interpreting, §2-221.06.
Reports, §2-221.05.
Rental contracts.
Interpretation of provisions, §2-221.06.
Repair and maintenance of streets and alleys, §9-401.16.
Retents, §2-203.01.
School food services and security services, §38-157.
Sewerage agreements, §§2-207.01, 2-207.02.
Small and certified business enterprise development and assistance.
See SMALL AND CERTIFIED BUSINESS ENTERPRISE DEVELOPMENT AND ASSISTANCE.
Special hiring agreements, §2-219.03a.
Street lighting, not required for, §9-504.
Virginia, sewerage agreement with, §2-207.02.
Wages.
Living wage act, §§2-220.01 to 2-220.11.
See LIVING WAGE ACT.
Whistleblower protection, §§2-223.01 to 2-223.07.
Workplace fraud.
Debarment for repeat violations, §32-1331.11.
Mayor's authority to enforce provisions, §32-1331.11.

PUBLIC CONVENIENCES.
Parks and recreation facilities, §§10-133, 10-134.
Toilets.
Generally, §§8-601 to 8-604.

PUBLIC CONVEYANCES.
Blocking passage, §22-1307.

PUBLIC CONVEYANCES —Cont'd
Equal access to, §7-1002.
Metrorail and metrobus, §§9-1101.01 to 9-1115.04, 35-201 to 35-253.
See METRORAIL AND METROBUS.

PUBLIC DEFENDER SERVICE, §§2-1601 to 2-1608.
Board of trustees.
Composition, §2-1603.
Deputy director, §2-1604.
Director, §2-1604.
Eligibility for representation.
Financial eligibility, §2-1602.
Legal aid agency.
Designation of agency as service, §2-1601.
Personnel.
Compensation, §2-1605.
Persons who may be represented.
Enumeration, §2-1602.
Public grants and private contributions, §2-1607.
Reports.
Annual report of trustees, §2-1606.
Court reports, §11-1731.
Right to counsel.
See RIGHT TO COUNSEL.

PUBLIC EDUCATION AND INFORMATION PROGRAMS, §2-536.
Alcoholics, rehabilitation of, §§24-603, 24-605.
Animal education and spaying and neutering incentive program, §8-1810.
Bicycles, §§50-1601 to 50-1609.
Business licenses, §47-2851.06.
Child restraint seats, §50-1708.
Child support enforcement, §46-230.
Consumer and regulatory affairs department complaint procedures, §28-3904.
Courts, §11-1744.
Dangerous dogs, §8-1907.
Emergency preparedness, §§7-2302, 7-2303.
Firearms, §7-2507.07.
Metrorail and metrobus prosecutions, §35-203.
Seat belts, §50-1805.
Smoking, §7-1709.

PUBLIC EMPLOYEE RELATIONS BOARD, §§1-605.01 to 1-605.04.
Compensation, §1-611.12.
Establishment, §1-605.01.

PUBLIC EMPLOYEE RELATIONS BOARD —Cont'd
Members, §1-605.01.
Powers, §1-605.02.
Publication of decisions, §1-605.04.
Transition procedures, §1-605.03.

PUBLIC EMPLOYMENT SERVICE, §1-202.04.

PUBLIC GROUNDS, FOOTWAYS IN.
Driving or riding on, §22-1318.

PUBLIC HEALTH, DEPARTMENT OF.
Assistant Director of Public Health, §7-172.
Director of, §7-153.
Establishment of, §7-151.
Organization of, §7-152.
Public Health Coordination Advisory Committee, §7-154.

PUBLIC HEALTH EMERGENCY EXECUTIVE ORDER, §7-2304.01.

PUBLIC INFORMATION AND EDUCATIONAL PROGRAM.
Alcohol and drug abuse prevention, §44-1206.
Controlled substances, §48-905.04.
Rental housing conversion and sale, §42-3403.08.

PUBLIC INSURANCE ADJUSTER LICENSING, §§31-1631.01 to 31-1631.12.
See INSURANCE ADJUSTER LICENSING.

PUBLIC INTOXICATION, §§24-604, 25-1001.
Marijuana, §48-911.01.

PUBLIC LANDS.
Capitol Hill community garden land trust.
Real property tax exemption, §47-1054.
Crispus Attucks development corporation.
Real property tax exemptions, §47-1058.
Emmaus rehabilitation project.
Real property tax exemptions, §47-1057.
Exchange of District-owned land, §§10-901 to 10-904.
Council authority to effect, §10-901.
Mayor's authority.
Execution of deed, §10-903.

PUBLIC LANDS —Cont'd
Exchange of District-owned land —Cont'd
Mayor's authority —Cont'd
Payment or receipt of moneys as part of, §10-904.
Notice of, §10-902.
Labor-peace agreement for public participation in hotel projects, §§32-851 to 32-856.
National Children's Island, §§10-1401 to 10-1406.
Notice.
Exchanges, §10-902.
Sale, §10-801.
Parks and recreation, §§10-101 to 10-308.
See PARKS AND RECREATION.
Reservation 13.
Allocation of funds, §10-1505.
Approval of draft master plan, §10-1501.
Benefit area, §10-1503.
Health care facility set aside, §10-1502.
Real property tax exemption, §47-1055.
Special taxing district, §10-1504.
Rosedale conservancy.
Real property tax exemption, §47-1056.
Sale of public lands, §§10-801 to 10-806.
Approval of, §10-801.
Authorization to sell.
Mayor, §10-801.
Secretary of Interior, §10-804.
Definition of real property for purposes of, §10-801.01.
Deposit of proceeds, §10-802.
Description of property to be sold, §10-801.
Execution of deeds, §10-803.
Expenses of, §§10-802, 10-806.
Hearings, §10-801.
Notice of, §10-801.
Resolutions, §10-801.
Solicitation for bids, §10-805.
Subsidies, §10-834.
Time for sale of certain land, §10-801.
Unused and underutilized public school buildings, §10-803.01.
Trees.
Removal, notice attached to tree, §10-731.

PUBLIC LIBRARIES, §§39-101 to
39-124.
See LIBRARIES.

**PUBLIC OFFICERS AND
EMPLOYEES.**
Affirmative action plans, §§1-521.01
to 1-521.08.
Available workforce defined for
purposes of, §1-521.01.
Continuing responsibilities, §1-521.06.
Development of agency plans,
§1-521.02.
Diversity, actual and planned,
§1-521.03.
EEO officers and specialists,
nonuniformed, §1-521.08.
EEO program, §§1-521.05, 1-521.06.
Merit system, §1-607.01.
Policy declaration, §1-521.01.
Projection of hires and promotions,
§1-521.04.
Statement of number of hires,
promotions, and terminations,
§1-521.07.
Submission of agency plans, §1-521.02.
Alcohol and drug abuse.
Rehabilitation programs, §24-610.
Annual leave bank, §§1-612.04 to
1-612.11.
See ANNUAL LEAVE BANK.
Antideficiency provisions, §47-105.
Appeals in federal cases.
Death or separation from office.
Substitution, FRAP 43(c).
Successor in public office.
Substitution as party, FRAP 43(c).
Appropriations, §1-503.
Arrest powers, §10-509.01.
Assault, §22-851.
**Attorney general for District of
Columbia.**
Authority over personnel, §1-301.88a.
Auditor.
See AUDITOR FOR DISTRICT OF
COLUMBIA.
**Bail bond business, involvement
with,** §§23-1103, 23-1104, 23-1109.
Bonds, surety, §47-103.
Prohibited from being surety on bond,
§1-317.01.
Surety bonds on officers and
employees, §1-207.37.
**Bonus pay and special awards pay
act of 2016,** §§1-551.01 to 1-551.06.
Bribery, §§22-704, 22-712.
Career service, §1-608.01.

**PUBLIC OFFICERS AND
EMPLOYEES** —Cont'd
Chief financial officer.
See CHIEF FINANCIAL OFFICER.
Chief management officer, §47-391.09.
Chief technology officer, §§1-1401 to
1-1406.
Child care facilities, §§4-901 to 4-905.
Child care bureau, §4-902.
Closing facility and relocating
children, §4-905.
Management of designated areas,
§4-904.
Necessity for providing, §4-901.
Reassessment of need of facility,
§4-905.
Requisites for space set aside in
government buildings, §4-903.
**Children of, transportation in
District-owned vehicles,**
§1-333.08.
**Claims against the District,
nonliability in,** §§2-411 to 2-416.
Closing-out sales, §47-2107.
Conflicts of interest, §§1-615.05,
1-618.02.
Corrections, department of.
See CORRECTIONS, DEPARTMENT
OF.
Corrupt influence, §22-704.
Courts.
See COURTS.
Criminal history checks, §§1-620.41
to 1-620.44.
Definitions, §1-620.41.
Implementation of provisions,
§1-620.44.
Limitations on disqualification,
§1-620.43.
Pre-employment inquiries, §1-620.42.
Custodians of property, reports by,
§1-502.
Death benefits, §1-623.33.
Debt set-offs, §§1-629.01 to 1-629.04.
Deferred compensation program,
§§1-611.17, 47-3601 to 47-3604.
Annual report, §47-3604.
Contract for services, §47-3603.
Eligibility to participate, §47-3601.
Established, §47-3601.
Regulations, §47-3602.
**Designation to protect life and
property outside the District,**
§10-509.01.
Disabilities, persons with.
Equal employment opportunity,
§1-607.02.

PUBLIC OFFICERS AND EMPLOYEES —Cont'd

Disability compensation, §§1-623.01 to 1-623.47.
See MERIT SYSTEM.
Disbursing officer, §§47-111, 47-113 to 47-116.
See DISBURSING OFFICER.
District of Columbia corporation, officers of, §1-103.
Domestic partner benefits, §§32-705, 32-706.
Donor leave.
Organ or bone marrow donors, §1-612.03b.
Drug and alcohol testing.
Commercial motor vehicle drivers, §1-620.11.
Corrections department, §§24-211.21 to 24-211.24.
Department of mental health and department of human services employees.
Mandatory testing, §§1-620.21 to 1-620.25.
District employees who serve children.
Mandatory testing, §§1-620.31 to 1-620.37.
District of Columbia housing authority, §6-217.
Rehabilitation programs, §24-610.
Educational service, §§1-525.01, 1-608.01a.
Elections.
Government employees engaging in political activities, §§1-1171.01 to 1-1171.07.
Emergency management.
Homeland security program.
Public employee security training program, §7-2231.05.
Employee deferred compensation program, §§47-3601 to 47-3604.
Employer-assisted housing program, §§42-2501 to 42-2507.
See GOVERNMENT EMPLOYER-ASSISTED HOUSING PROGRAM.
Erroneous payments to, §§1-629.01, 1-629.02.
Expenditures, approval of, §1-333.10.
Expenses, §47-313.01.
False personation, §§22-1403 to 22-1405.
Family leave, §1-612.03c.
Fiduciaries, as, §1-615.04.

PUBLIC OFFICERS AND EMPLOYEES —Cont'd

Firearms, authorized to carry, §10-509.01.
Fire departments.
See FIRE DEPARTMENTS.
Foreign office or title, US Const Art I §9.
Fraud and deceit, §1-615.05.
Funeral expenses, §1-623.34.
General provisions, §§1-501 to 1-510.
Gifts from foreign states, US Const Art I §9.
Hatch act.
Political activity authorized, §1-1171.02.
Health insurance, §§1-621.01 to 1-621.17.
See MERIT SYSTEM.
Highway workers, §47-209.
Holidays, §1-612.02.
Homeland security program.
Public employee security training program, §7-2231.05.
Hours of work, §1-612.01.
Incentive awards, §§1-619.01 to 1-619.03.
Industrial revenue bond forward commitment program, no personal liability for, §47-340.10.
Intimidation, §22-851.
Leave of absence, §§1-612.03 to 1-612.11.
Donor leave.
Organ or bone marrow donors, §1-612.03b.
Voluntary leave transfer program, §§1-612.31 to 1-612.38.
Life insurance, §§1-622.01 to 1-622.16.
See MERIT SYSTEM.
Markets, §37-205.01.
Martin Luther King, Jr.'s Birthday designated as holiday for, §1-504.
Mayor, commissioning of officers by, §1-301.76.
Medical assistance, §1-620.07.
Medical examiners.
General provisions, §§5-1401 to 5-1419.
See MEDICAL EXAMINERS.
Merit system.
General provisions, §§1-601.01 to 1-636.03.
See MERIT SYSTEM.
Review of agency decision, CivPro Agency Review Rule 1.
Petition for review, CivPro Agency Review Rule 1.

PUBLIC OFFICERS AND EMPLOYEES —Cont'd

Metropolitan police.
See METROPOLITAN POLICE.

Motor vehicles.
Mandatory drug and alcohol testing of certain employees who serve children.
Consent deemed given, §1-620.33.
Reimbursement for use of private vehicle on official business, §1-509.

Multiple office-holding.
Congress, US Const Art I §6.

Negligence, §2-416.

Nepotism, §1-618.04.

Notaries public, §§1-1201 to 1-1217.
See NOTARIES PUBLIC.

Oaths and affirmations required of, §1-501.

Office of labor relations and collective bargaining, §1-531.01.
Funding for provided in budget, §1-531.02.

Overpayment liabilities, §47-112.

Overtime.
Exemption of district employees on compressed schedule from federal overtime requirements, §1-510.

Parties.
Substitution of parties, CivPro Rule 25.
Appeals, DCCtApp Rule 43.
Domestic relations actions, DomRel Rule 25.

Pensions and retirement.
Employees retirement program management, §§1-701 to 1-753.
See EMPLOYEES RETIREMENT PROGRAM MANAGEMENT.
Food services department, §38-803.
Judicial disabilities and tenure, §§11-1521 to 11-1530.
See COMMISSION ON JUDICIAL DISABILITIES AND TENURE.
Judicial retirement, §§11-1561 to 11-1572.
See JUDICIAL RETIREMENT.
Police and firefighters retirement and disability, §§5-631 to 5-762.
See POLICE AND FIREFIGHTERS RETIREMENT AND DISABILITY.
Teachers, §§38-2001.01 to 38-2041.01.
See TEACHERS' RETIREMENT.

Performance management system, §§1-613.51 to 1-613.53, 1-614.11 to 1-614.14.
Established, §1-613.51.

PUBLIC OFFICERS AND EMPLOYEES —Cont'd

Performance management system —Cont'd
Purposes, §1-613.52.
Transition provisions, §1-613.53.

Political activities, government employees engaging in, §§1-1171.01 to 1-1171.07.
Activity authorized, §1-1171.02.
Applicability, §1-1171.07.
Candidate defined, §1-1171.01.
Definitions, §1-1171.01.
Designation of employee to solicit, accept or receive contributions while on leave.
Mayor and members of council, §1-1171.02.
Employee defined, §1-1171.01.
Enforcement, §1-1171.04.
On duty defined, §1-1171.01.
Partisan defined, §1-1171.01.
Partisan political group defined, §1-1171.01.
Political activity defined, §1-1171.01.
Political contribution defined, §1-1171.01.
Political party defined, §1-1171.01.
Political purpose defined, §1-1171.01.
Prohibitions, §§1-1171.02, 1-1171.03.
While on duty, §1-1171.03.
Requesting subordinates to participate in campaign or make contribution.
Prohibition, §1-1171.02.
Rules, §1-1171.06.
Sanctions for violations, §1-1171.04.

Political rights, §§1-625.01, 1-625.02.

President of the United States.
Commissions, US Const Art II §3.

Prison personnel, §24-201.11.

Prison work release program participants not regarded as, §24-241.10.

Private sector employees.
Assignment to work for District government.
Special rules, §1-627.06.

Procurement.
Employee conduct, §2-359.10.

Protection of District public officials, §22-851.

Public defender service.
General provisions, §§2-1601 to 2-1608.
See PUBLIC DEFENDER SERVICE.

PUBLIC OFFICERS AND EMPLOYEES —Cont'd

Public records management, §§2-1701 to 2-1714.
See PUBLIC RECORDS MANAGEMENT.

Public works, for, §§9-1209.01 to 9-1209.04.

Quo warranto.
General provisions, §§16-3501 to 16-3548.
See QUO WARRANTO.

Recall, §§1-204.111 to 1-204.115.
See RECALL OF ELECTED PUBLIC OFFICIALS.

Recorder of deeds.
General provisions, §§42-1202 to 42-1218.
See RECORDER OF DEEDS.

Records, §§1-631.01 to 1-631.08.
See MERIT SYSTEM.

Reduction in number of, §1-301.69.

Reductions in force, §§1-624.01 to 1-624.24.
See MERIT SYSTEM.

Refusal to testify, forfeiture of office for, §1-506.

Register of wills, §§11-2101 to 11-2106.
See REGISTER OF WILLS.

Religious beliefs, reasonable accommodation for, §1-607.01.

Religious test for office.
Prohibited, US Const Art VI.

Reports, §1-502.

Residency.
Agency heads.
District residency requirement, §1-515.01.
Board of education.
Non-educational employees.
Preference for district residents, §1-602.03.
Board of elections.
Applicants for positions within board.
Preference for district residents, §1-1001.05.
Charter schools.
Preference for district residents.
Employees of DC public schools applying for positions at, §38-1802.07.
Public charter school board.
Applicants for positions within board, §38-1802.14.

PUBLIC OFFICERS AND EMPLOYEES —Cont'd

Residency —Cont'd
District of Columbia housing authority.
Applicants for positions within authority.
Preference for district residents, §6-215.
Executive director required to be district resident, §6-213.
Lottery and charitable games control board.
Applicants for positions within authority.
Preference for district residents, §3-1303.
Executive director required to be district resident, §3-1303.
Office of employee appeals.
Applicants for positions within office.
Preference for district residents, §1-606.01.
Office of zoning.
Applicants for positions within office.
Preference for district residents, §6-623.02.
Director required to be district resident, §6-623.02.
People's counsel.
Required to be district resident, §34-804.
Preference for district residents, §1-515.01.
Board of education.
Non-educational employees, §1-602.03.
Board of elections.
Applicants for positions within board, §1-1001.05.
Career service, §1-608.01.
Charter schools.
Employees of DC public schools applying for positions at, §38-1802.07.
Public charter school board.
Applicants for positions within board, §38-1802.14.
District of Columbia housing authority.
Applicants for positions within authority, §6-215.
District of Columbia retirement board, §1-711.

PUBLIC OFFICERS AND EMPLOYEES —Cont'd
Residency —Cont'd
Preference for district residents —Cont'd
Educational service, §1-608.01a.
Lottery and charitable games control board.
Applicants for positions within authority, §3-1303.
Office of employee appeals.
Applicants for positions within office, §1-606.01.
Office of zoning.
Applicants for positions within office, §6-623.02.
Public parking authority.
Applicants for positions within authority, §50-2506.01.
Public service commission.
Applicants for positions within commission, §34-806.
Teachers.
Charter schools.
Employees of DC public schools applying for positions at, §38-1802.07.
University of the District of Columbia.
Non-educational employees, §1-602.03.
Washington convention and sports authority.
Applicants for positions within authority, §10-1202.16.
Water and sewer authority.
Applicants for positions within authority, §34-2202.15.
Public parking authority.
Applicants for positions within authority.
Preference for residents, §50-2506.01.
Public service commission.
Applicants for positions within commission.
Preference for district residents, §34-806.
Retirement board.
Preference for district residents, §1-711.
Washington convention and sports authority.
Applicants for positions within authority.
Preference for district residents, §10-1202.16.

PUBLIC OFFICERS AND EMPLOYEES —Cont'd
Residency —Cont'd
Washington convention and sports authority —Cont'd
President and chief executive officer required to be district resident, §10-1202.07.
Water and sewer authority.
Applicants for positions within authority.
Preference for district residents, §34-2202.15.
General manager required to be district resident, §34-2202.06.
Review of personnel practices, §1-511.
Selection procedures, §§1-607.04 to 1-607.06.
Evidence of validity, §1-607.06.
Relation to job required, §1-607.05.
Statement of purpose, §1-607.04.
Severance pay, §1-624.09.
Sewer maintenance workers, §47-208.
Sex discrimination in benefit programs, §1-607.07.
Soil and water conservation district, §8-1705.
Stalking of, §22-851.
Surveyor of the District, §§1-1301 to 1-1329.
See SURVEYOR OF THE DISTRICT.
Tax-favored and pre-tax benefits, §1-611.19.
Temporary assignment of, §§1-627.01 to 1-627.06.
Temporary commission on pay equity and training.
General provisions, §§32-601 to 32-609.
Temporary employees for public works, §§9-1209.01, 9-1209.02.
Unclaimed property held by, §41-112.
United States.
Appointment, US Const Art II §2.
Bribery, US Const Art II §4.
Commissions, US Const Art II §3.
Emoluments, US Const Art I §9.
Holding more than one office, US Const Art I §6.
Impeachment, US Const Art II §4.
Ineligibility of members of congress, US Const Art I §6.
Presents from foreign states, US Const Art I §9.

PUBLIC OFFICERS AND EMPLOYEES —Cont'd
United States —Cont'd
Appointment —Cont'd
Presidential electors.
Eligibility, US Const Art II §1.
Religious tests, US Const Art VI.
Removal, US Const Art II §4.
Treason, US Const Art II §4.
Vacancies, US Const Art II §2.
Vacancies in office.
President.
Appointments during senate recess, US Const Art II §2.
Veterans preferences, §1-607.03.
Voluntary leave transfer program, §§1-612.31 to 1-612.38.
Wages and salaries, §§1-611.03 to 1-611.21.
Living wage act, §§2-220.01 to 2-220.11.
See LIVING WAGE ACT.
Weapons, authorized to carry, §10-509.01.
Whistleblower protection, §§1-615.51 to 1-615.59.
Workplace wellness.
Healthy food and beverage standards for government property, §1-541.02.
Policy, §1-541.01.

PUBLIC-OWNED VEHICLES.
Bicycle safety enhancements, §50-205.
EPA miles per gallon requirement, §50-203.
Fleet management, §§50-211.01 to 50-211.07.
Acquisition of vehicle, authority for, §50-211.05.
Agencies provisions applicable to, §50-211.02.
Alternative fuel, plan to expand use of, §50-211.06.
Council exempt from requirements, §50-211.02.
Definitions, §50-211.01.
Exempt agencies, §50-211.02.
Goals of program, §50-211.04.
Independent fleet manager, designation, §50-211.02.
Passenger vehicle allocations.
Acquisition rules, §50-211.05.
Real cost of ownership, §50-211.04.
Report from Mayor to Council, §50-211.07.

PUBLIC-OWNED VEHICLES —Cont'd
Official use, §50-202.
Restrictions on use, §50-204.

PUBLIC PARKING AUTHORITY, §§50-2501 to 50-2514.
Board of directors, §50-2504.
Bond issues.
Authority to issue revenue bonds, §50-2512.
Tax exemption for, §50-2513.
Conflicts of interest, §50-2514.
Definitions, §50-2502.
Employees.
Residency status, §50-2506.01.
Establishment of, §50-2503.
Executive director, §50-2506.
Financial disclosure statements by board members, §50-2505.
Oaths and affirmations, §50-2505.
Parking districts, §50-2511.
Parking System Fund, §50-2510.
Policy declaration, §§50-2501, 50-2503.
Powers of, §50-2507.
Property.
Acquisition and use of, §50-2508.
Transfer of property interest between District and Authority, §50-2509.
Residency status of applicants for hire, §50-2506.01.
Revenue bonds, authority to issue, §50-2512.

PUBLIC PLANNING CAPITAL PROJECT FUND, §1-325.11.

PUBLIC-PRIVATE PARTNERSHIP ADMINISTRATION FUND, §2-272.04.

PUBLIC-PRIVATE PARTNERSHIPS, §§2-271.01 to 2-275.01.
Applicability of chapter, §2-275.01.
Compliance with federal and D.C. law, §2-273.08.
Construction and interpretation, §2-275.01.
Definitions, §2-271.01.
Dispute resolution, §2-273.07.
Legal rights, §2-273.07.
Office of public-private partnerships, §§2-272.01 to 2-272.04.
Budget, §2-272.03.
Establishment, §2-272.01.
Public-private partnership administration fund, §2-272.04.
Rules, §2-274.01.

PUBLIC-PRIVATE PARTNERSHIPS
—Cont'd
Office of public-private partnerships
—Cont'd
Staff, §2-272.02.
Pay-for-success contracts, §§2-211.01
to 2-211.03.
Pre-qualification, §2-273.02.
Procurement, §§2-273.01 to 2-273.09.
Compliance with federal and District
law, §2-273.08.
Prequalification, §2-273.02.
Public-private partnership
agreements, §2-273.06.
Dispute resolution, §2-273.07.
Legal rights, §2-273.07.
Requests for information, §2-273.01.
Requests for proposals, §2-273.03.
Review, §2-273.05.
Transparency, §2-273.09.
Unsolicited proposals, §2-273.04.
Public-private partnership
agreements, §2-273.06.
Dispute resolution, §2-273.07.
Legal rights, §2-273.07.
Requests for information, §2-273.01.
Requests for proposal, §2-273.03.
Review of requests, §2-273.05.
Rules, §2-274.01.
Solicitation through requests for
proposals, §2-273.03.
Transparency, §2-273.09.
Unsolicited proposals, §2-273.04.

PUBLIC RECORDS MANAGEMENT,
§§2-1701 to 2-1714.
Access to public records, §§2-531 to
2-540.
Administrator, duties and
responsibilities of, §2-1703.
Applicability of provisions, §2-1714.
Budget, §2-1712.
Civil actions, §2-1713.
Copies, printouts, and photocopies,
§2-1708.
Defacement of public records,
§22-3307.
Definitions, §2-1701.
Disposition disposal, §§2-1705, 2-1709.
E-mail, rules for retention, §2-1706.
Enforcement of provisions, §2-1713.
Establishment of agencies and
offices for, §2-1702.
Expenditures, §2-1712.
Freedom of information, §§2-531 to
2-540.
Maintenance of public records,
§2-1706.

PUBLIC RECORDS MANAGEMENT
—Cont'd
Privacy and confidentiality, §2-1707.
Records disposition committee,
§2-1705.
Reports, §§2-1704, 2-1711.
Right to examine public records,
§2-1710.
Vital records, §§7-201 to 7-228.
See VITAL RECORDS.

PUBLIC SAFETY AND JUSTICE.
Innovation fund, §§1-325.221 to
1-325.226.
Office of deputy mayor, §1-301.191.

PUBLIC SCHOOLS.
Advertising.
Event sponsorships, §38-174.01.
Agency, cabinet-level, §§38-171 to
38-175.
Agency performance measures,
§38-121.02.
Board of Education.
General provisions.
See BOARD OF EDUCATION.
Chancellor.
Budget and budget estimates,
§38-2831.
Generally, §38-174.
Charter schools.
General provisions.
See CHARTER SCHOOLS.
College access assistance, §§38-2701
to 38-2706.
Compulsory school attendance,
§§38-201 to 38-213.
See COMPULSORY SCHOOL
ATTENDANCE.
DC promise program, §§38-2751 to
38-2759.
See UNIVERSITIES AND
COLLEGES.
DCPS.
Cabinet-level agency, §§38-171 to
38-175.
Department of education, §§38-191 to
38-193.
Ombudsman for public education,
§§38-351 to 38-356.
Educational data warehouse system,
§38-2609.
Evaluation of schools.
Department of education, §38-193.
Event sponsorships, §38-174.01.
Financial management reform,
§§38-1801.01 to 38-1801.03.
Plan, §38-2951.

PUBLIC SCHOOLS —Cont'd
Financial management reform
—Cont'd
Task force, §38-2952.
Fiscal year 2006 educational investments fund for District of Columbia public schools and public charter schools, §1-325.31.
Health care of students.
General provisions, §§38-601 to 38-651.12.
See STUDENT HEALTH CARE.
Interagency collaboration and services integration commission, §§2-1591 to 2-1597.
Metrorail and metrobus student fares.
General provisions, §§35-232 to 35-237.
See METRORAIL AND METROBUS.
Ombudsman for public education, §§38-351 to 38-356.
Pensions and retirement.
Food services department, §38-803.
Teachers, §§38-2001.01 to 38-2041.01.
See TEACHERS' RETIREMENT.
Private funds, use of, §38-121.01.
Schools generally.
See SCHOOLS AND EDUCATION.
State Board of Education.
General provisions.
See BOARD OF EDUCATION.
State superintendent of education, office of, §§38-2601 to 38-2612.
Superintendent of schools.
Posers and duties, §§38-131, 38-132.
Teachers.
General provisions, §§38-1901 to 38-1923.
See TEACHERS.
Retirement of teachers, §§38-2001.01 to 38-2041.01.
See TEACHERS' RETIREMENT.
Testing integrity, §§38-771.01 to 38-771.07.
See TESTING INTEGRITY IN PUBLIC SCHOOLS.
Youth advisory council, §§2-1561 to 2-1564, 2-1565.01 to 2-1565.06.

PUBLIC SERVICE COMMISSION.
Annual report by, §34-1119.
Appeals, §§34-604 to 34-609, 34-901.
Commission authority to rescind order after appeal filed, §34-608.
Commission orders and decisions in force pending appeal, §34-607.

PUBLIC SERVICE COMMISSION
—Cont'd
Appeals —Cont'd
Exclusive method of review, §34-609.
Jurisdiction of court of appeals to hear and determine appeal from commission orders and decision, §34-605.
Limited to questions of law, §34-606.
Petition for appeal, §34-605.
Procedure, §34-605.
Suspension of effective date of order, §34-607.
Appliances and equipment, fixing standards for, §34-1120.
Application for instructions as to elements of value, §34-604.
Reconsideration, §34-604.
Appropriations, §34-805.
Authorities not affected by powers of, §34-809.
Balance sheet supplied to, §34-1113.
Blank forms, preparation of, §34-1111.
Business conduct of utilities, §34-903.
Commissioners, §§34-202, 34-801.
Complaints.
Direct damage to claimant, complaints not involving, §34-913.
Hearing conducted as though complaint filed, §34-916.
Separate hearings for complaints, §34-913.
Utilities, made by, §34-917.
Compliance, compelling, §34-1103.
Composition, §34-801.
Costs and expenditures, ascertaining, §34-1105.
Defined, §34-201.
Destruction of apparatus or appliance belonging to, §34-707.
Distribution transformers.
Liquid-immersed distribution transformers.
Electric company purchase of.
Rules of commission, §§8-1771.06, 34-302.01.
Duties and powers of, §1-204.93.
Electric light and power companies, powers and duties regarding, §§34-301 to 34-306.
Elements of value.
Application to court of appeals for instruction, §34-604.
Reconsideration, §34-604.

PUBLIC SERVICE COMMISSION
—Cont'd
Eligibility to serve on, §34-801.
Employees of, §34-806.
Energy providers, public awareness programs regarding, §34-808.01.
Expenses, §34-806.
Investigation, valuation, litigation. Payment, §34-912.
Factors considered in discharging duties, §34-808.02.
Failure to obey orders of, §34-706.
Form of books and records, prescription of, §34-1110.
Gas companies, powers and duties regarding, §§34-301 to 34-306.
Retail natural gas suppliers, §34-1671.03.
Hearings.
Complaint filed, conducted as though, §34-916.
Formal hearing requirement, §34-908.
Notice, §§34-908, 34-916.
Oaths and affirmations, §34-918.
Separate hearings for complaints, §34-913.
Summary investigations, following, §34-915.
Time and place, setting, §34-909.
Witnesses, attendance of, §34-910.
Inspector of gas and meters.
Appointment and removal of assistants from office, §34-305.
Investigation of accidents, §34-401.
Investigations by Commission, §34-802.
Accidents, §34-401.
Agents conducting investigation, §34-906.
Attorney general, duties of, §34-905.
Compelling incriminatory evidence, §34-610.
Contempt proceedings, §34-918.
Deposition, testimony by, §34-920.
Disclosure of information and documents, §34-1118.
Discriminatory, unjust, or unreasonable rates, §34-908.
Expenses, responsibility for, §34-912.
Immunity, §34-610.
Officers of utilities, examining, §34-904.
Record of proceedings, §§34-921, 34-922.
Records and accounts, production of, §§34-904 to 34-907.

PUBLIC SERVICE COMMISSION
—Cont'd
Investigations by Commission
—Cont'd
Stenographer, §34-921.
Summary investigations, §§34-914, 34-915.
Time and place, setting, §34-909.
United States Attorney, duties of, §34-905.
Violations by utilities, §34-402.
Joint rates.
Defined, §34-211.
Schedule of, §34-1126.
Liquid-immersed distribution transformers.
Electric company purchase of. Rules of commission, §§8-1771.06, 34-302.01.
New construction information conveyed to, §34-1116.
Notice.
Hearings, §§34-908, 34-916.
People's Counsel, served on, §34-1118.
Rate applications or changes in conditions of service, §§34-909, 34-1127.
Rate schedule, change in, §34-1127.
Reasonable rates order, §34-911.
Oaths and affirmations, §34-801.
Office of the General Counsel, §34-803.
Office of the People's Counsel, §§34-804, 34-1118.
Office of the people's counsel agency fund, §34-912.
Officers of utilities, examining, §34-904.
Orders for repairs, improvements, and services, §34-808.
Pay telephone service providers.
Rules and regulations, power to prescribe, §34-1831.
Powers and duties, §34-802.
Public service commission agency fund, §34-912.
Quorum, §34-802.
Rates and charges.
Appeals, §§34-604 to 34-609, 34-901.
Approval of rate charges, §34-601.
Authority to regulate rates, §§34-601, 34-709.
Changes in form of rate schedule, §34-1130.
Changes in rate schedule, §§34-601, 34-901, 34-1123, 34-1127.

PUBLIC SERVICE COMMISSION
—Cont'd
Rates and charges —Cont'd
Commission's authority to regulate,
§§34-601, 34-709.
Continuation of existing rates,
§34-901.
Discriminatory, unjust, or
unreasonable charges, §§1-204.93,
34-1101.
Established rates, demanding or
receiving more or less than,
§§34-702, 34-901, 34-1129.
Facilities, reduced rates for consumers
furnishing, §34-703.
Filing schedule of, §§34-901, 34-1123
to 34-1128.
In force requirement, §34-603.
Joint rates, schedule of, §34-1126.
New schedules, filing, §34-1128.
Notice of changes, §§34-909, 34-1127.
Orders of Commission, required to
conform to, §§34-601, 34-602.
Prescription of changes in form of rate
schedule, §34-1130.
Public availability of rate schedule,
§34-1125.
Reasonableness requirement,
§§34-603, 34-911.
Rules and regulations affecting,
§34-1124.
Sanitary sewer service, §§34-2107 to
34-2112.
Separate hearings for complaints as
to, §34-913.
Sliding scale, §34-1117.
Summaries, providing, §34-1128.
Water and Sewer Authority,
§34-2202.16.
Water supply and waterworks.
See WATER SUPPLY AND
WATERWORKS.
Record of investigatory proceedings,
§§34-921, 34-922.
Records and accounts, examining,
§34-904.
Reimbursement fee.
Payment of expenses of investigation
or litigation, §34-912.
**Renewable energy portfolio
standards,** §§34-1431 to 34-1439.
See RENEWABLE ENERGY
PORTFOLIO STANDARDS.
Retail natural gas suppliers.
Licensing and consumer protection,
§§34-1671.01 to 34-1671.14.
See GAS COMPANIES.

PUBLIC SERVICE COMMISSION
—Cont'd
Rules and regulations, §34-902.
Distribution transformers.
Liquid-immersed distribution
transformers.
Electric company purchase of,
§§8-1771.06, 34-302.01.
Submetering, §34-1552.
Submetering.
Rulemaking, §34-1552.
Telecommunications competition,
§§34-2001 to 34-2008.
See TELECOMMUNICATIONS
COMPETITION.
Toll telecommunication service tax,
§§47-3901 to 47-3922.
See TOLL TELECOMMUNICATION
SERVICE TAX.
Valuation of property, §§34-1106 to
34-1108.
**Withdrawal of authority of
Interstate Commerce
Commission,** §34-807.
Witnesses at investigations.
Attendance of, §§34-905, 34-910.
Deposition, testimony by, §34-920.
Fees, §34-919.

PUBLIC SPACE.
Abatement of dangerous conditions,
§§10-1181.01 to 10-1181.07.
Dangerous structures on public space
fund, §10-1181.04.
Definitions, §10-1181.01.
Enforcement, §10-1181.07.
Fees, assessment of, §10-1181.05.
Private structures.
Costs of correcting, §10-1181.03.
Notice of unsafe conditions,
§10-1181.02.
Rules, §10-1181.06.
**Alcoholic beverages, drinking or
possession of open container of,**
§25-1001.
Canals, filling in of, §10-139.
Capitol grounds, §§10-503.01 to
10-503.26.
See CAPITOL GROUNDS.
Commemorative works, §§9-204.11 to
9-204.19.
Applications process.
Expiration of approval, §9-204.19.
Guidelines for considering
application, §9-204.15.
Proposal by sponsor, §9-204.14.
Committee.
Establishment, §9-204.12.

PUBLIC SPACE —Cont'd

Commemorative works —Cont'd

Committee —Cont'd

Powers and duties, §9-204.13.

Definitions, §9-204.11.

Deposit of maintenance fees, §9-204.18.

Easement to sponsor, §9-204.16.

Issuance of permits, §9-204.17.

Dangerous conditions, abatement of, §§10-1181.01 to 10-1181.07.

Designation of official names, §9-204.22.

Equal access to, §§7-1001, 7-1002.

Inaugural ceremonies of the President of the United States, use for, §§2-803, 2-824.

Naming, §9-204.09.

Designation of official names, §9-204.22.

Symbolic names.

Designation for public spaces, streets and alleys, §§9-204.23, 9-204.24.

9th Street Southwest, over or under, §1-301.01.

Peddling drugs in, §§47-2885.17, 47-2885.17a.

Permits, §47-2718.

Railroads extended through, §9-1203.04.

Rental of airspace.

General provisions, §§10-1121.01 to 10-1121.13.

See RENTAL OF AIRSPACE.

Rental of public space.

General provisions, §§10-1101.01 to 10-1104.08.

See RENTAL OF PUBLIC SPACE.

Public structures in public space, §§10-1141.01 to 10-1141.07.

Snow and ice removal from sidewalks adjacent to public property, §9-602.

Symbolic names.

Designation for public spaces, streets and alleys, §§9-204.23, 9-204.24.

Vaults.

See VAULTS.

PUBLIC TRANSPORTATION.

Blocking passage, §22-1307.

Equal access to public conveyances, §7-1002.

Metrorail and metrobus, §§9-1101.01 to 9-1115.04, 35-201 to 35-253.

See METRORAIL AND METROBUS.

PUBLIC TRIAL, US Const Amd 6.

PUBLIC UTILITIES.

Access.

Telecommunications competition.

Buildings, §34-2005.

Public ways, §34-2004.

Testing appliances and equipment, access to premises for, §34-1122.

Accidents.

Investigation, duty to report, §34-401.

Accounts. See within this heading, "Records and accounts."

Actions.

Pending actions not affected by new laws, §34-406.

Anacostia River, private conduits in, §34-2504.

Appeals, §§34-604 to 34-609, 34-901.

Commission authority to rescind order after appeal filed, §34-608.

Commission orders and decisions in force pending appeal, §34-607.

Exclusive method of review, §34-609.

Jurisdiction of court of appeals to hear and determine appeal from commission orders and decision, §34-605.

Limited to questions of law, §34-606.

Petition for appeal, §34-605.

Procedure, §34-605.

Suspension of effective date of order, §34-607.

Appliances and equipment.

Adequate and serviceable standards, §34-1120.

Examination and testing, §34-1121.

Entry of premises, §34-1122.

Material and equipment, §34-1122.

Regulations for testing, §34-1120.

Banks and financial institutions offering bill payment services, §26-111.

Board of directors, §34-404.

Boiler inspections.

Exemption, §2-131.

Cable television.

General provisions, §§34-1251.01 to 34-1264.06.

See CABLE TELEVISION.

Certification required to provide services and facilities, §34-1101.

Child support orders.

Furnishing IV-D agency with financial information, §34-1131.

Commission.

See PUBLIC SERVICE COMMISSION.

PUBLIC UTILITIES —Cont'd
Commodities cost reserve fund,
§47-368.04.
Common carrier defined for
purposes of, §34-203.
Complaints.
See PUBLIC SERVICE
COMMISSION.
Conduits.
Electric light and power companies.
See ELECTRIC LIGHT AND
POWER COMPANIES.
Private conduits. See within this
heading, "Private conduits."
Consolidation or reorganization,
stock issued for purposes of,
§34-504.
Construction.
Accounts, keeping, §34-1116.
Costs and expenditures, tracking,
§34-1105.
New construction information
conveyed to Commission,
§34-1116.
Contempt proceedings related to
investigations, §34-918.
Corporations.
Defined, §34-204.
Costs and expenditures to construct
and maintain, §34-1105.
Daily default constituting separate
and distinct offense, §34-708.
Definitions, §§34-201 to 34-221,
42-3301.
Depreciation, §34-1115.
Destruction of apparatus or
appliance belonging to
Commission, §34-707.
Direct damage to claimant,
complaints not involving,
§34-913.
Discriminatory, unjust, or
unreasonable charges, §1-204.93.
Dividends.
Sliding scale, §34-1117.
Electric light and power companies,
§§34-1401 to 34-1408.
See ELECTRIC LIGHT AND POWER
COMPANIES.
Enforcement, §34-402.
Environmental impact statements,
§§34-2601 to 34-2604.
Definitions, §34-2602.
Purpose, §34-2601.
Requirements, §34-2603.
Rules, §34-2604.

PUBLIC UTILITIES —Cont'd
Expenses of commission
investigations or litigation.
Reimbursement fee.
Payment, §34-912.
Extensions.
Defined, §34-208.
Electric light and power companies.
Conduits, §§34-1401, 34-1406,
34-1407.
Overhead wires in Georgetown,
§34-1401.
Telecommunications companies.
Conduits, §§34-1911.01, 34-1921.01.
Overhead wires, §34-1901.01.
False statements to secure approval
for stock issue, §34-701.
Fines and penalties.
Banks and financial institutions
offering public utility bill payment
services, §26-111.
Commission orders, failure to obey,
§34-706.
Cumulative nature of, §34-711.
Daily default constituting separate
and distinct offense, §34-708.
Destruction of apparatus or appliance
belonging to Commission, §34-707.
Disposition of, §34-710.
Duties, failure to perform, §34-706.
Established rates, demanding or
receiving more or less than,
§34-702.
Excavation or demolition, damages
caused by, §34-2707.
Facilities, reduced rates for consumers
furnishing, §34-703.
False statements to secure approval
for stock issue, §34-701.
Information, failure or refusal to
furnish, §34-705.
Master-metered apartment buildings,
§42-3304.
Pipeline safety violations, §34-706.
Prosecutions for violations, §34-731.
Rebates, §34-704.
Records, failure to keep, §34-705.
Stock and securities, §34-507.
Telegraph and telephone companies,
§§34-1911.03, 34-1921.03.
Waiver or release, §34-711.
Water supply and waterworks.
See WATER SUPPLY AND
WATERWORKS.
Gas companies.
See GAS COMPANIES.

PUBLIC UTILITIES —Cont'd
Governing laws.
Applicability of law, §§34-101, 34-102.
Congressional reservation of right to alter, amend, or repeal, §34-407.
Existing laws, continuing force of, §34-405.
Interpretation of provisions, §§34-403, 34-732.
Severability of provisions, §34-403.
Hearings.
See PUBLIC SERVICE COMMISSION.
Highway construction, relocation expenses for, §9-107.02.
Horizontal property regimes.
Submetering, §§34-1551 to 34-1553.
Information, failure or refusal to furnish, §34-705.
Inspector of gas and meters.
Power to appoint and remove inspector and assistants from office, §34-305.
Interpretation of provisions regarding, §§34-403, 34-732.
Interstate Commerce Commission, withdrawal of authority of, §34-807.
Investigations.
See PUBLIC SERVICE COMMISSION.
Liens, §34-501.
Location of offices and records, §34-1112.
Master-metered apartment buildings, §§42-3301 to 42-3307.
Definitions, §42-3301.
Delinquent accounts, §42-3303.
Fines and penalties, §42-3304.
Issuance of rules and regulations regarding, §42-3307.
Name of tenant, opportunity to receive service in, §42-3302.
Payments made by tenants, §42-3302.
Remedies, §42-3305.
Termination of service, §§42-3304, 42-3306.
Mergers and consolidations, §§34-504, 34-1001, 35-271.
Notice.
Rate application or change in condition of service, §34-909.
Oaths and affirmations.
Commission, taken by, §34-801.
Investigations by Commission, §34-918.

PUBLIC UTILITIES —Cont'd
Office of the General Counsel, §34-803.
Office of the People's Counsel, §§34-804, 34-1118.
Officers of utilities, examination by Commission, §34-904.
Offices and records, location of, §34-1112.
Other companies' equipment, use of, §34-1102.
Penalties. See within this heading, "Fines and penalties."
Pipeline company defined, §34-213.
Pipeline safety violations, §34-706.
Private conduits, §§34-2501 to 34-2504.
Anacostia River, in, §34-2504.
Conditions required for permission to lay, §34-2501.
Penalty for refusal to remove, §34-2502.
Right to alter, amend, or repeal rules regarding, §34-2503.
Prosecutions for violations, §34-731.
Public service commission.
See PUBLIC SERVICE COMMISSION.
Public works for, §9-401.03.
Rates and charges.
See PUBLIC SERVICE COMMISSION.
Rebates, §34-704.
Records and accounts.
Allocation of items to accounts, §34-1114.
Audit, §34-1114.
Balance sheet, §34-1113.
Blank forms, preparation of, §34-1111.
Closing of accounts annually, §34-1113.
Construction accounts, §34-1116.
Contents, §34-1118.
Depreciation account, §34-1115.
Examination by Commission, §34-904.
Failure to keep, §34-705.
Form of books and records, §34-1110.
Investigated utilities, disclosure of information and documents by, §34-1118.
Investigations by Commission, production for, §§34-904 to 34-907.
Location of, §34-1112.
Responsibility for furnishing, §34-1118.
Separate accounts, §34-1109.
Subpoenas, §§34-905, 34-918.

PUBLIC UTILITIES —Cont'd

Records and accounts —Cont'd

Uniform accounts, §34-1109.

Reimbursement fee.

Payment of expenses of commission investigation or litigation, §34-912.

Renewable energy portfolio standards, §§34-1431 to 34-1439.

See RENEWABLE ENERGY PORTFOLIO STANDARDS.

Reorganization or consolidation, stock issued for purposes of, §34-504.

Reports.

Accidents, §34-401.

Annual report by Commission, §34-1119.

Contents, §34-1118.

Costs and expenditures, §34-1105.

Responsibility for furnishing, §34-1118.

Revaluation of property, §34-1108.

Roadworks, §§9-431.01, 9-431.02.

Sale and merger of utilities, §34-1001.

Sales, §§34-504, 34-1001, 35-271.

Schedule of rates.

See PUBLIC SERVICE COMMISSION.

Securities, §§34-501 to 34-507.

Services and facilities.

Certification required to provide, §34-1101.

Definition of services, §34-215.

Discriminatory, unjust, or unreasonable charges for, §§1-204.93, 34-1101.

Reduced rates for consumers furnishing facilities, §34-703.

Severability of provisions, §34-403.

Sliding scale of rates and dividends, §34-1117.

Stock and securities, §§34-502 to 34-507.

Certificate of authority to issue, §§34-502, 34-503.

False statements to secure approval for stock issue, §34-701.

Fines and penalties, §34-507.

Proceeds, use of, §34-505.

Reorganization or consolidation, for purposes of, §34-504.

Void in absence of compliance with law, §34-506.

Street railways.

See METRORAIL AND METROBUS.

PUBLIC UTILITIES —Cont'd

Submetering, §§34-1551 to 34-1553.

Subpoenas, §§34-905, 34-918.

Summary investigations, §§34-914, 34-915.

Sustainable energy, §§8-1773.01 to 8-1774.16.

See SUSTAINABLE ENERGY.

Taxation, §§47-2501, 47-2501.01, 47-2511 to 47-2515.

Telecommunications companies, §§34-1701 to 34-2008.

See TELECOMMUNICATIONS COMPANIES.

Testing appliances and equipment, §§34-1120 to 34-1122.

Theft of utility service, §§22-3218.01 to 22-3218.04.

Trenches in highways, cutting, §§9-431.01, 9-431.02.

Unclaimed property.

General provisions, §§41-101 to 41-142.

See UNCLAIMED PROPERTY.

Underground facilities protection, §§34-2701 to 34-2709.

See MISS UTILITY.

Valuation of property, §§34-1106 to 34-1108.

Application to court of appeals for instruction, §34-604.

Reconsideration, §34-604.

Fair market value at time property valued, §34-1106.

Notice and hearing, §34-1107.

Revaluation, §34-1108.

Statement of valuation filed, §34-1107.

Vaults used for installations, §10-1103.08.

Wastewater and sewage works.

General provisions, §§34-2101 to 34-2134.

See WASTEWATER AND SEWAGE WORKS.

Water and sewer services amnesty program.

Administrative review, §34-2305.

Appointment of receiver, §34-2304.

Services in tenant's own name, §34-2303.

Water supply and waterworks.

General provisions, §§34-2401.01 to 34-2401.27.

See WATER SUPPLY AND WATERWORKS.

PUBLIC WAYS.

Defined, §34-2001.

PUBLIC WAYS —Cont'd
Rights of ways generally.
See RIGHTS OF WAY.
Surveyor of the District recording,
§1-1314.
**Telecommunications competition
and access to,** §34-2004.

PUBLIC WELFARE, BOARD OF,
§§4-105 to 4-126.
Board of Charities.
Transfer of powers connected with,
§§4-110, 4-120.
Budgets and budget estimates,
§4-121.
Children and minors.
Adoption of, §4-302.
Adoption subsidy, §4-301.
Assignment to public institution,
§§4-203.02, 4-203.04.
Commitment of, §§4-118, 4-119.
Custody of, §4-302.
Dependent children.
Duties and powers of board, §4-124.
Discharge from guardianship, §4-123.
Escape of, §§4-125, 10-509.01a.
Foster care, placement in, §§4-118,
4-302.
Investigations, §4-117.
Limitations on number of, §4-115.
Maintenance in public institution,
§4-203.03.
Mayor's powers regarding, §§4-114,
4-302.
Placement of, §§4-118, 4-302.
Privacy and confidentiality, §4-117.
Records, §4-117.
Removal or escape of child without
authorization.
Assisting in, §4-125.
Studies of, §4-117.
Types of children supervised in public
welfare, §4-116.
Wards, visitation of, §4-122.
Youth residential facilities, §§7-2101 to
7-2108.
Conflicts of interest, §4-113.
Congressional appropriations.
Supervision over institutions
supported by, §4-111.
Dependent children.
Duties and powers of board, §4-124.
Director of Public Welfare, §4-105.
Institutions.
Admissions to, §4-108.
List of, §4-106.
Records, §4-108.

PUBLIC WELFARE, BOARD OF
—Cont'd
Investigations of institutions,
§§4-112, 4-117.
**List of institutions under control of
board,** §4-106.
New institutions, §4-112.
**Personnel under supervision of
board,** §4-107.
Visitation of wards, §4-122.

PUBLIC WORKS, §§9-401.01 to
9-401.18.
Apprenticeship programs.
Registration by contractors and
subcontractors contracting with
District, §32-1431.
Appropriations, §9-401.07.
Assessments.
Curbs and gutters, §§9-401.04,
9-411.01 to 9-411.04, 9-421.02.
Paving and resurfacing streets and
alleys. See within this heading,
"Assessments for paving and
resurfacing streets."
Repayments from permit fund,
§9-401.07.
Sidewalks, §9-401.04.
**Assessments for paving and
resurfacing streets.**
Abutting property exemptions,
§9-401.18.
Amount assessed, §9-421.01.
Applicability to assessments levied
before 1885, §9-421.13.
Cancellation, §9-421.11.
Collection of, §9-421.09.
Computation of, §9-421.04.
Costs of paving streets, §9-401.10.
Curbs and gutters, §§9-401.04,
9-411.01 to 9-411.04, 9-421.02.
Exceptions and exemptions,
§§9-401.18, 9-421.03, 9-421.05 to
9-421.07.
Gutters and curbs, §§9-401.04,
9-411.01 to 9-411.04, 9-421.02.
Heater method, resurfacing by,
§9-421.07.
Interest on, §9-421.09.
Limitations on, §9-421.04.
Owner's expense, prior improvement
made at, §9-421.06.
Prior payment of assessment,
§9-421.05.
Property abutting 2 or more streets,
§§9-411.03, 9-421.08.
Pro rata levy of, §9-421.01.

PUBLIC WORKS —Cont'd

Assessments for paving and resurfacing streets —Cont'd

Protest by property owner, §9-421.10.

Reassessments, §9-421.11.

Refunds, §9-421.11.

Severability of provisions, §9-421.12.

Capital project support fund, §§1-325.151 to 1-325.156.

Construction projects, §9-401.01.

Costs of, payment for, §9-401.01.

Curbs and gutters, assessments, §§9-401.04, 9-411.01 to 9-411.04, 9-421.02.

Employees, §§9-1209.01 to 9-1209.04.

Ex-offenders.

Department to hire, §32-1351.

Fleet management administration, §§50-211.01 to 50-211.07.

See PUBLIC-OWNED VEHICLES.

Funds, §9-1209.04.

Gas mains, §9-401.03.

Gutters and curbs, assessments, §§9-401.04, 9-411.01 to 9-411.04, 9-421.02.

Horses and horse-drawn vehicles, §9-1209.03.

Motor vehicles, use of, §9-1209.03.

Parks and recreation, §10-166.

Paving and resurfacing streets and alleys, §§9-401.09, 9-421.01 to 9-421.13.

Assessments. See within this heading, "Assessments for paving and resurfacing streets."

Bituminous macadam, using, §9-401.13.

Heater method of resurfacing, using, §9-421.07.

Motor fuel tax assessment for, §§47-2323, 47-2324.

Notice requirements, §9-421.09.

Portable asphalt plant, using, §9-401.14.

Public contract limitations, §§9-401.16, 9-401.17.

Railroads contributing to cost of, §9-1203.07.

Repair and maintenance contracts, §9-401.17.

Use of unexpended allotments in succeeding year, §9-401.15.

Width of pavement, §9-401.11.

Permits.

Repayments from Permit Fund, §9-401.07.

PUBLIC WORKS —Cont'd

Permits —Cont'd

Trenches in highways, cutting, §§9-431.01, 9-431.02.

Public-private partnerships, §§2-271.01 to 2-275.01.

See PUBLIC-PRIVATE PARTNERSHIPS.

Public utilities features, §9-401.03.

Repairs and maintenance, §9-401.01.

Service pipes, §9-401.03.

Sewer connections, §§9-401.03, 9-401.08.

Sidewalks.

Assessments, §9-401.04.

Improvements, §9-401.06.

Repair and maintenance, §9-401.06.

Street railway tracks, removal of, §9-401.02.

Streets and alleys.

Assessments for paving and resurfacing. See within this heading, "Assessments for paving and resurfacing streets."

Minor changes in roadway width, §9-401.12.

Paving and resurfacing. See within this heading, "Paving and resurfacing streets and alleys."

Repairs and improvements to alleys, §9-401.06.

Schedules of street improvements, §9-401.05.

Trenches, cutting, §9-431.01.

Width of pavement, §9-401.11.

Technical and special employees, temporary employment of, §9-1209.01.

Temporary employees, §§9-1209.01, 9-1209.02.

Trenches in highways, cutting, §§9-431.01, 9-431.02.

Water mains, §§9-401.03, 9-401.08.

PUERTO RICO.

Acknowledgment of deed, §42-112.

PUNITIVE DAMAGES.

Consumer credit reporting agencies.

Consumer security freeze.

Willful violations, §28-3864.

Consumer credit sales.

Violations of chapter, §28-3813.

Consumer credit service organizations.

Violations of provisions, §28-4607.

Consumer protection.

Violations of chapter, §§28-3813, 28-3905.

PUNITIVE DAMAGES —Cont'd
Debt collectors.
Violation of restrictions, §28-3814.
Hate crimes, §22-3704.
Hazardous waste management.
Hazardous materials transportation.
Strict liability for releases during
transport, §8-1446.
Installment loans.
Consumers' remedies for violations,
§28-3813.
Procurement claims, §§2-359.05,
2-381.02.
Real property, waste of, §42-1601.
Revolving credit accounts.
Violations, §28-3813.

PUR AUTRE VIE, ESTATES FOR,
§42-505.

**PURCHASE MONEY DEED OF
TRUST.**
Recordation tax on deeds.
General provisions, §§42-1101 to
42-1124.
See RECORDATION TAX.

PURCHASE MONEY MORTGAGE.
Recordation tax on deeds.
General provisions, §§42-1101 to
42-1124.
See RECORDATION TAX.

**PURCHASE MONEY SECURITY
INTERESTS.**
Secured transactions, §28:9-103.
Priority, §28:9-324.

PURCHASING GROUPS.
Risk retention groups, §§31-4106 to
31-4110.
See RISK RETENTION GROUPS.

PURSE SNATCHING, §22-2801.

PYROXYLIN.
Business licenses, §47-2815.

Q

**QUALIFIED HIGH TECHNOLOGY
COMPANY.**
Income taxes.
Credits, capital gains, §§47-1817.01 to
47-1817.08.
Definitions, §47-1817.01.
Returns, certification as, §47-1805.05.
**Lease of real property, security
deposit assistance,** §§2-1221.01,
2-1221.02.

**QUALIFIED HIGH TECHNOLOGY
COMPANY** —Cont'd
Real property taxes, §47-811.03.
Real property tax exemptions.
Interior renovation tax rebate,
§47-4665.
Tax penalties, §47-4218.

QUALIFIED THEATER COMPANY.
Payment in lieu of taxes, §47-1052.

**QUALIFIED ZONE ACADEMY
REVENUE BOND PROJECT
FORWARD COMMITMENT
APPROVAL ACT.**
Bonds.
Allocation of available real property
tax revenues, §2-1217.109.
Authorization, §2-1217.103.
Financing and closing documents,
§2-1217.107.
Information reporting, §2-1217.115.
Limited liability of District,
§2-1217.112.
Maintenance of documents,
§2-1217.114.
Payment, §2-1217.106.
Personal liability of officials,
§2-1217.113.
Sale of bonds, §2-1217.105.
Security, §§2-1217.106, 2-1217.110.
Terms and conditions, §2-1217.104.
Definitions, §2-1217.102.
Delegation of authority, §2-1217.111.
Disclaimer, §2-1217.116.
Eligible projects, determination of,
§2-1217.108.
Severability, §2-1217.117.
Short title, §2-1217.101.

QUARANTINES.
Carriers of communicable diseases,
§§7-134 to 7-136.

QUARTERING SOLDIERS, US Const
Amd 3.

**QUARTER TO QUARTER, ESTATES
BY,** §42-521.

QUESTIONS OF LAW.
Certification of questions of law,
DCCtApp Rule 22.

QUICK PAYMENT ACT.
**Prompt payment of private
contractors and subcontractors
generally,** §§27-131 to 27-136.
See PROMPT PAYMENT.
Public contracts, §§2-221.01 to
2-221.06.

QUIET ENJOYMENT, COVENANT OF.
Real property, §42-606.

QUIET TITLE.
Adverse possession, §16-3301.

QUI TAM ACTIONS.
Procurement violations, §2-381.03.

QUO WARRANTO, §§16-3501 to 16-3548.
Corporate directors and trustees, actions against, §16-3547.
Damages, §16-3548.
Defaults, §16-3543.
District officers, actions against, §§16-3521 to 16-3523.
Deemed civil action, §16-3521.
Ex rel. proceedings, §16-3522.
Parties who may institute, §16-3522.
Persons against whom issued, §16-3521.
Refusal of Attorney General or United States Attorney to act, §16-3523.
Judgments and decrees, §§16-3545, 16-3546.
Jury trials, §16-3544.
Limitation of actions, §16-3548.
Notice, §16-3542.
Petition, §16-3541.
Pleadings, §16-3544.
Proceedings against directors and trustees, §16-3547.
Rules of civil procedure.
Applicability of rules, CivPro Rule 81.
United States officers, actions against, §§16-3501 to 16-3503.
Ex rel. proceedings, §16-3502.
Parties who may institute, §16-3502.
Persons against whom issued, §16-3501.
Proceedings deemed civil action, §16-3501.
Refusal of Attorney General or United States Attorney to act, §16-3503.
Verdict, §16-3545.

R

RABBITS.
Selling baby rabbits, restrictions, §8-1808.

RABIES.
Laboratory services.
Fees, §7-734.

RACE DISCRIMINATION.
Insurance.
Unfair trade practices, §§31-2231.01 to 31-2231.25.
Licensed places, admission to, §§47-2901 to 47-2911.
Pay equity and training commission, §§32-601 to 32-609.
Prohibition of, §2-1401.01.

RACIAL MINORITIES.
Affirmative action.
Condominiums, §42-1904.14.
Equal employment opportunity, §§2-1402.01 to 2-1402.13.
Public officers and employees, §§1-521.01 to 1-521.08.
See PUBLIC OFFICERS AND EMPLOYEES.
Constitution of the United States, US Const Amds 14, 15.
Discrimination generally.
See DISCRIMINATION.
Human rights commission, §§2-1401.01 to 2-1404.04.
See HUMAN RIGHTS COMMISSION.

RADIATION CONTROL.
Low-level radioactive waste generator regulatory policy, §§8-1501 to 8-1506.
Definitions, §8-1501.
Fees, §8-1503.
Issuance of rules and regulations regarding, §8-1506.
Private right of action, §8-1505.
Registration, §8-1503.
Reports, §8-1502.
Nuclear weapons freeze, §§7-2401, 7-2404.

RADIATION DISEASES.
Workers' compensation, §32-1510.

RADIO.
Child labor.
Theatrical permits, §32-206.
Compelled disclosures, §§16-4701 to 16-4704.
Emergency two-way radio communications.
Definition of "emergency," §5-1306.
Unlawful acts, §§5-1307, 5-1308.
Free flow of information, §§16-4701 to 16-4704.
Metrorail and metrobus.
Playing on public transit, §35-251.
News media privilege, §§16-4701 to 16-4704.

RADIO —Cont'd
Presidential inaugural ceremonies.
Installation of communication
facilities, §2-826.
Superior court proceedings, media
coverage of, CivPro Rule 203,
CrimPro Rule 53.
Child abuse and neglect proceedings,
NeglectProc Rule 45.
Juvenile proceedings, JuvProc Rule 53.
Toll telecommunication service tax,
§§47-3901 to 47-3922.
See TOLL TELECOMMUNICATION
SERVICE TAX.
United States District Court
proceedings.
Broadcasting in the courthouse,
USDistCt LCrR 53.1.1, USDistCt
LCvR 83.1.

RADON CONTRACTOR
PROFICIENCY, §§28-4201 to
28-4203.
Requirements, §28-4201.
Rulemaking, §§28-4202, 28-4203.

RAFFLES.
Lottery and charitable games
control board, §§3-1322 to 3-1332.
Operated for educational and
charitable purposes.
Advertising and promoting, §22-1718.
Permissible activities, §22-1717.

RAIDS, POLICE.
Advance information passed
regarding, §23-1109.

RAILROADS, §§35-101 to 35-124.
Abandonment of substation, §35-121.
Alcoholic beverage licenses.
On-premises retailers, §25-113.
Taxation, §25-905.
Animals transported by rail,
§22-1003.
Branch tracks, spurs, or sidings,
§9-1203.03.
Bridges.
See BRIDGES.
Buzzards Point track extensions,
§9-1203.01.
Commercial drivers.
Stopping at railroad crossings,
§50-405.01.
Condemnation proceedings,
§9-1203.06.
Congressional right to alter, amend,
or appeal provisions, §35-124.

RAILROADS —Cont'd
Electrification of steam railroad
lines, §§9-1207.01 to 9-1207.05.
Approval of plans, §9-1207.01.
Authorization, §9-1207.01.
Construction of electrical conduit
system authorized, §9-1207.03.
Jurisdiction of Department of Army,
mayor, Interstate Commerce
Commission not limited,
§9-1207.04.
Liability of railroad companies for
injuries, §9-1207.05.
Submarine cables at drawbridge
openings, §9-1207.02.
Grade crossing elimination projects.
See GRADE CROSSING
ELIMINATION PROJECTS.
Injuries, liability for, §9-1207.05.
Murder charges based on
obstruction or displacement of,
§22-2102.
Navy Yard track connection, sale or
lease of, §9-1203.02.
New York Avenue.
Construction of switch connections,
§§9-1205.01 to 9-1205.05.
Authorized, §9-1205.01.
Grade crossing, §9-1205.03.
Mayor's authority not abridged,
§9-1205.04.
Plans approved by mayor,
§9-1205.02.
Reservation of right to amend, alter,
repeal, §9-1205.05.
Personal property taxes on rolling
stock, §47-1512.
Prohibited on certain streets,
§9-1201.02.
Public space, extension through,
§9-1203.04.
Real property taxes, §§47-836 to
47-838.
Reversion of property to District,
§35-123.
Right to alter, amend, or repeal
provisions, §§9-1203.09, 9-1205.05.
Sidings.
Branch tracks, spurs, or sidings,
§9-1203.03.
Extension into business use lots,
§9-1201.11.
South of Virginia and Maryland
Avenues, §9-1201.10.
Stations, additional, §9-1201.12.
Steam railroad lines, electrification
of, §§9-1207.01 to 9-1207.05.

RAILROADS —Cont'd
Street lighting, §9-509.
Street railroads.
Metrorail and metrobus.
General provisions, §§35-201 to
35-253.
See METRORAIL AND
METROBUS.
Public utilities, defined for purposes
of, §§34-216, 34-217.
**Streets and alleys, repair or paving
of,** §9-1203.07.
**Streets to be under or over railroad
tracks,** §9-1201.14.
Substation, abandonment of, §35-121.
Switch connections, constructing,
§§9-1205.01 to 9-1205.05.
Tracks, additional, §9-1201.12.
Unclaimed property, disposition of.
Sale authorized by court order,
§35-102.
Sale of unclaimed freight and baggage,
§35-101.
Sale proceeds, disposition of, §35-103.
**Union Station and terminals, right
to use,** §9-1201.13.
**Use of track extensions by other
carriers,** §9-1203.08.
Viaducts.
See VIADUCTS.
Waiting rooms on platforms, §35-122.
Walkways, §35-123.

RAMSEY, CHARLES H.
Police chief.
Separation pay, §1-610.58.
Term of office, §5-105.01.
Voluntary retirement, §5-712.

**RANDALL SCHOOL
DEVELOPMENT PROJECT.**
Real property tax exemptions,
§47-4626.

RAPE.
Generally, §§22-3001 to 22-3024.
See SEXUAL ABUSE.
Sex offender registration, §§22-4001
to 22-4017.
See SEX OFFENDER
REGISTRATION.

RAPE SHIELD LAW, §§22-3021 to
22-3024.

RAPID TRANSIT.
Metrorail and metrobus.
General provisions, §§35-201 to
35-253.
See METRORAIL AND
METROBUS.

RATS.
Bureau of rodent control,
§§8-2101.01, 8-2101.02.
Rodent abatement program,
§§8-2103.01 to 8-2103.05.

RBC (RISK BASED CAPITAL).
**Health insurance regulatory
standards,** §§31-3451.01 to
31-3451.13.
See HEALTH INSURANCE.
Insurance companies generally,
§§31-2001 to 31-2013.
See INSURANCE COMPANIES.

REAL ESTATE.
See REAL PROPERTY.

**REAL ESTATE AND BUSINESS
CHANCE LICENSEES,** §§42-1701
to 42-1709.
See REAL ESTATE BROKERS AND
SALESPERSONS.

REAL ESTATE APPRAISERS.
Appraisal education fund,
§47-2853.154.
Board of real estate appraisers,
§§47-2853.06 to 47-2853.10.
Business licenses, §§47-2853.151 to
47-2853.154.
Appraisal education fund,
§47-2853.154.
Eligibility, §47-2853.152.
Prohibited representations,
§47-2853.153.
Required, §47-2853.153.
Scope of practice, §47-2853.151.

**REAL ESTATE BROKERS AND
SALESPERSONS,** §§42-1701 to
42-1709.
Board of real estate, §§47-2853.06 to
47-2853.10.
Business licenses, §§47-2853.161 to
47-2853.198.
Affiliation, automatic suspension of
license through, §47-2853.186.
Brokers, §§47-2853.161 to
47-2853.163.
Eligibility, §47-2853.162.
Representations prohibited,
§47-2853.163.
Scope of practice, §47-2853.161.
Change of status, §47-2853.182.
Disclosure, §§47-2853.196,
47-2853.198.
Exemptions, §47-2853.181.
Fiduciary duties, §§47-2853.191 to
47-2853.195.

**REAL ESTATE BROKERS AND
SALESPERSONS** —Cont'd
Business licenses —Cont'd
Fund for real estate guaranty and
education, payment into,
§42-1706.
Names prohibited for real estate
businesses, §47-2853.185.
Organizations, licensing, §47-2853.183.
Place of business, §47-2853.184.
Prohibited acts, §47-2853.197.
Revocation or suspension,
§47-2853.187.
Salespersons, §§47-2853.171 to
47-2853.173.
Eligibility, §47-2853.172.
Representations prohibited,
§47-2853.173.
Scope of practice, §47-2853.171.
Transfer of license, §47-2853.182.
Crimes and offenses, §42-1708.
Definitions, §42-1702.
Disclosure, §§47-2853.196, 47-2853.198.
Disclosure requirements, §42-1703.
Discriminatory practices, §2-1402.23.
Escrow accounts, §42-1704.
Fiduciary duties, §§47-2853.191 to
47-2853.195.
Representing buyer, §47-2853.192.
Representing landlord of leased
property, §47-2853.193.
Representing seller, §47-2853.191.
Representing tenant, §47-2853.194.
Fines, §42-1708.
**Fund for real estate guaranty and
education.**
Applications for payment from,
§42-1707.
Determination of amount paid into,
§42-1706.
License requirement to pay into,
§42-1706.
Management of, §42-1707.
Maximum payment from, §42-1707.
Licenses. See within this heading,
"Business licenses."
Policy declaration, §42-1701.
Powers and duties, §42-1703.
Prohibited acts, §47-2853.197.
Savings clauses, §42-1709.
**Written listing contract
requirement,** §42-1705.

REAL ESTATE TAX SALES, §§47-847,
47-1301 to 47-1321.
Actions, §47-1313.
Advertising, §47-1309.

REAL ESTATE TAX SALES —Cont'd
Amount payable on, §47-1315.
Assessor's duties regarding,
§§47-1310, 47-1311.
Assignment, §47-1303.04.
Revised real property tax sale.
Certificate of sale, §§47-1349,
47-1354.
Certificate of sale, §47-1304.
Revised real property tax sale,
§§47-1348 to 47-1351.
Assignment, §§47-1349, 47-1354.
Evidence, §47-1351.
Recordation, §47-1350.
Void certificate of sale, §47-1355.
Computational errors, effect of,
§47-1316.
Condemnation proceedings,
§47-1204.
Confirmation of sale, §47-1315.
Deeds, §§47-1303.03, 47-1304.
Definitions, §47-1303.01.
Revised real property tax sale,
§47-1330.
**Delinquent taxpayers prohibited
from bidding at,** §47-1320.
Delivery of deed to purchaser,
§47-1315.
Deposits required from purchasers,
§47-1304.
Disposition of proceeds, §47-1319.
Invalid sales, §47-1308.
Liens, §§47-1303.04, 47-1312.
Revised real property tax sale,
§47-1331.
List of sold property, §47-1311.
Notice, §§47-1301, 47-1302, 47-1313.
Revised real property tax sale. See
within this heading, "Revised real
property tax sale."
**Private sale of unimproved
residential real property bid off
in name of District,** §47-1303.02.
Procedures for sale, §§47-1303,
47-1314.
Public auction, at, §47-1301.
Revised real property tax sale,
§47-1346.
Redemption of property, §§47-1304 to
47-1319.
Lien for taxes and assessments,
§47-1312.
Revised real property tax sale,
§§47-1360 to 47-1366.
Time period, §47-1307.
Regulations, §47-1321.

REAL ESTATE TAX SALES —Cont'd
Revised real property tax sale,
§§47-1330 to 47-1385.
Accountings, §47-1340.
Applicability of provisions, §47-1385.
Bad check, payment by, §47-1342.01.
Certificate of redemption, §47-1361.
Certificate of sale, §§47-1348 to
47-1351.
Assignment, §§47-1349, 47-1354.
Evidence, §47-1351.
Recordation, §47-1350.
Void certificate of sale, §47-1355.
Certification of taxes due agencies,
§47-1340.
Construction of provisions, §47-1384.
Definitions, §47-1330.
Energy efficiency loan foreclosures,
§47-1336.
Deed of purchaser, §47-1382.
Foreclosure, §§47-1370 to 47-1383.
Deed of purchaser, §47-1382.
Final order, §47-1378.
Judgments, §§47-1378 to 47-1382.
Notice, §§47-1372, 47-1375.
Obtaining possession, §47-1383.
Parties, §§47-1371, 47-1373.
Payment and compliance with terms
of judgment as to payments,
§47-1382.
Presumption of validity of taxes and
sale, §47-1376.
Redemption of property.
Complaints by purchasers to
foreclose the right of
redemption, §47-1370.
Fixing amount necessary for
redemption after action to
foreclose filed, §47-1362.
Judgment bars redemption only in
real property described
therein, §47-1381.
Reimbursement of purchaser for
expenses by redeeming party,
§47-1377.
Reopening judgments, §47-1379.
Service of process, §47-1374.
Setting aside sale, judgment,
§47-1380.
Interest, §47-1334.
Lien on real property.
Tax as, §47-1331.
Mayor.
Cancellation of sale by, §47-1366.
Regulations, §47-1335.
Sale of all properties, §47-1332.

REAL ESTATE TAX SALES —Cont'd
Revised real property tax sale
—Cont'd
Notice.
Agencies to be notified, §47-1340.
Foreclosure, §§47-1372, 47-1375.
Notice of delinquency, §47-1341.
Public notice, §47-1342.
Redemption of property, §47-1361.
Other taxes and liabilities.
Payment by purchaser, §47-1354.
Parcels of real property.
Sale as entirety, §47-1343.
Payment by bad check, §47-1342.01.
Personal property of owner.
Sale not affected, §47-1344.
Possessory interests.
Sale of real property subject to,
§47-1345.
Post-judgment equity distribution,
§47-1382.01.
Procurement.
Sale not subject to, §47-1333.
Public auction.
Sale at, §47-1346.
Purchase by district, §47-1352.
Post-sale notice, §47-1353.01.
Right to sell or foreclose, §47-1353.
Purchase price.
Payment at tax sale, §47-1347.
Redemption of property, §§47-1360 to
47-1366.
Assessment during redemption
period, §47-1364.
Cancellation of sale, §47-1366.
Certificate, §47-1361.
Fixing amount necessary for
redemption after action for
foreclosure file, §47-1362.
Notice to purchaser, §47-1361.
Payments required, §47-1361.
Receiver, appointment, §47-1363.
Right, §47-1360.
Rights of owners and purchasers
during redemption period,
§47-1363.
Tenant or person with less than fee
simple interest paying taxes and
levies.
Credit out of rents, §47-1365.
Rents.
Credit out of rents for tenant or
person with less than fee simple
interest paying taxes or levies,
§47-1365.
Sale of improvements only, §47-1345.

REAL ESTATE TAX SALES —Cont'd
Revised real property tax sale
—Cont'd
Transition provisions, §47-1385.
Special assessments, §§47-1203 to
47-1205.
Surplus amounts, §§47-1307, 47-1315.
Time period for redemption,
§47-1306.
Transfer of title to new
homeowners, §47-848.

REAL ESTATE TRANSACTIONS,
UNLAWFUL DISCRIMINATORY
PRACTICES, §§2-1402.21 to
2-1402.24.
Blockbusting, §2-1402.22.
Broker or salesperson.
Discrimination by, §2-1402.23.
Definitions, §2-1401.02.
Exceptions, §2-1402.24.
Families with children.
Discrimination against, §2-1402.21.
Housing accommodation
discrimination complaints.
Posting notice of, §2-1403.08.
Persons with disabilities.
Discrimination against, §2-1402.21.
Steering, §2-1402.22.
Subterfuge, use of, §2-1402.21.

REAL PARTY IN INTEREST, CivPro
Rule 17.
Domestic relations actions, DomRel
Rule 17.

REAL PROPERTY.
Access to public records, §42-1206.
Acknowledgments, §§42-101, 42-111,
42-112.
See ACKNOWLEDGMENTS.
Acquisition and disposal by District.
Eliminating slum or blight,
§§42-3171.01 to 42-3171.04.
Special disposal procedures for certain
properties, §§10-831 to 10-839.
Adverse possession.
Ejectment, §§16-1103, 16-1113.
Quiet title, §16-3301.
After-acquired real property as
devises and bequests, §18-305.
Alien ownership, §§42-901, 42-902.
Assessments.
Correction of conditions violative of
law, §42-3131.01.
Costs, §47-211.
Attachment, §16-508.
Bonds, surety, §42-409.

REAL PROPERTY —Cont'd
Building associations.
Exchanging real property for federal
bonds, §26-232.
Purchase by, §26-215.
Business improvement districts.
Exempt real property in, §2-1215.21.
Cemetery associations' power to
acquire and sell, §43-102.
Cestui que use.
Legal estate in, §42-1501.
Condemnation proceedings.
See CONDEMNATION
PROCEEDINGS.
Condominiums.
General provisions, §§42-1901.01 to
42-1904.18.
See CONDOMINIUMS.
Conservation easements, §§42-201 to
42-205.
See CONSERVATION EASEMENTS.
Contingent interests.
Sale of, §§42-1401 to 42-1404.
Contracts relating to, §42-409.
Cooperative associations.
Powers, §29-905.
Corporations.
Powers, §29-303.02.
Correction of conditions violative of
law, §§42-3131.01 to 42-3131.03.
Covenants.
Encumbered land.
Against having, §42-607.
Environmental covenants, §§8-671.01
to 8-671.14.
See ENVIRONMENTAL
COVENANTS.
Further assurances, §42-608.
Meaning of use of term, §42-603.
Quiet enjoyment, §42-606.
Credit line deeds of trust, §§42-2301
to 42-2303.
Decedents' estates, §§42-701 to 42-705.
Uniform real property transfers on
death, §§19-604.01 to 19-604.19.
Deeds.
See DEEDS.
Demolition of deteriorated property,
§§42-3173.01 to 42-3173.12.
Department of general services.
Inventory of real property assets,
§10-551.05.
Department of housing and
community development.
Employer-assisted housing program,
§§42-2501 to 42-2507.

REAL PROPERTY —Cont'd
Disclaimer of property interests,
§§19-1501 to 19-1518.
See DISCLAIMER OF PROPERTY
INTERESTS.
Discovery.
Entry upon land for inspection, etc.,
CivPro Rule 34.
Domestic relations actions, DomRel
Rule 34.
Request for entry, CivPro Form CA
24.
Landlord and tenant court,
LandlordTenant Rule 10.
Certification to civil division,
LandlordTenant Rule 13-I.
Dower.
Commutation of dower, CivPro Rule
307.
Probate proceedings, Probate Rule 6.
Drainage of lots, §§8-201 to 8-205.
**Drug, firearm, or prostitution-
related nuisance abatement,**
§§42-3101 to 42-3114.
See CRIME-RELATED NUISANCE
ABATEMENT.
Easements.
Condominiums.
See CONDOMINIUMS.
Conservation easements, §§42-201 to
42-205.
See CONSERVATION
EASEMENTS.
Public space.
Commemorative works, §9-204.16.
Ejectment, §§16-1101 to 16-1124.
See EJECTMENT.
**Electronic signatures in global and
national commerce act.**
Transfers on death.
Relation to, §19-604.19.
Eminent domain, §§16-1301 to
16-1385.
See EMINENT DOMAIN.
Encumbered land.
Covenants against having, §42-607.
Environmental covenants, §§8-671.01
to 8-671.14.
See ENVIRONMENTAL
COVENANTS.
Estates in land.
Allowance for life estate, CivPro Rule
307.
Probate proceedings, Probate Rule 6.
General provisions, §§42-501 to
42-523.
See ESTATES IN LAND.

REAL PROPERTY —Cont'd
Execution of judgments, §15-323.
Forcible entry and detainer,
§§16-1501 to 16-1505.
Foreign governments.
Ownership by, §42-901.
Foreign missions, §6-1305.
Form of deed, §§42-601, 42-602.
Forms.
Complaints.
Specific performance to convey land,
CivPro Form CA 12.
Condemnation.
Complaint, CivPro Form CA 29.
Notice, CivPro Form CA 28.
Discovery.
Entry upon land for inspection, etc.
Request for entry, CivPro Form
CA 24.
Landlord and tenant court.
Complaint for possession of real
estate, LandlordTenant Form 1.
Transfers on death.
Deeds, optional form, §19-604.16.
Revocation by instrument,
§19-604.17.
For sale or rent signs, §42-1801.
Fraudulent transfers.
General provisions, §§28-3101 to
28-3111.
See FRAUDULENT TRANSFERS.
Further assurances.
Covenants for, §42-608.
Future estates, §§42-510 to 42-513.
Commencement at future day,
§42-510.
Conditional limitation.
Commencement on contingency,
§42-511.
Contingent future estate, §42-512.
Defined, §42-510.
Estates created to take effect in
alternative, §42-513.
Remainder.
Commencement upon expiration of
precedent estate, §42-511.
Vested future estate, §42-512.
General warranties, §42-604.
Highways.
Acquisitions and transfers for
purposes of, §9-101.18.
Home purchase assistance fund,
§§42-2601 to 42-2626.
See HOME PURCHASE ASSISTANCE
FUND.

REAL PROPERTY —Cont'd

Homestead housing preservation,
§§42-2101 to 42-2111.
See HOMESTEAD HOUSING
PRESERVATION.

Horizontal property regimes,
§§42-2001 to 42-2031.
See HORIZONTAL PROPERTY
REGIMES.

Housing finance agency.
General provisions, §§42-2701.01 to
42-2706.05.
See HOUSING FINANCE AGENCY.

Housing production trust fund,
§§42-2801 to 42-2804.

Joint seizin, §42-1502.

Judgment enforcement, CivPro Rule
70.
Domestic relations actions, DomRel
Rule 70.

Landlord and tenant.
General provisions, §§42-3201 to
42-3232, 42-3501.01 to 42-3509.08.
See LANDLORD AND TENANT.

**Limitation of actions for death or
injury caused by defective or
unsafe improvements to,** §12-310.

Limited interests, sale of, §§42-1401
to 42-1404.

**Metropolitan Washington Airports
Authority acquiring,** §9-909.

Mortgages and deeds of trust.
General provisions, §§42-804 to
42-820.
See MORTGAGES AND DEEDS OF
TRUST.

**National Capital Planning
Commission acquisition of,**
§2-1009.

Nonprofit corporations.
Powers, §29-403.02.

Nonresidents.
Ownership by nonresidents, §42-903.

Nonresidents' vacant property.
Resident agent required for, §42-903.

Ownership, §§42-901 to 42-903.

Parks.
Acquisition of rights to real property
related to, §10-101.

**Pleadings in actions involving real
property,** CivPro Rule 3-I.
Landlord and tenant court,
LandlordTenant Rules 3, 5.
Complaint for possession of real
estate, LandlordTenant Form 1.

REAL PROPERTY —Cont'd

Powers of appointment.
General provisions, §§42-1001 to
42-1019.
See POWERS OF APPOINTMENT.

Powers of attorney, §21-2104.

**Private correctional treatment
facilities.**
Exemptions for, §24-261.05.

Privies, §§8-601 to 8-604.

Probate proceedings.
Costs attributable to real estate in
District, Probate Rule 425.
Sale of real property.
Death before Jan. 1, 1981, Probate
Rule 18.
Death between Jan. 1, 1981, and
June 30, 1995, Probate Rule
112.
Guardians, conservators, trustees,
etc., involved, Probate Rules
203, 222, 223.
Value of real estate.
Death between Jan. 1, 1981, and
June 30, 1995, Probate Rule
109.
Death on or after July 1, 1995,
Probate Rule 409.

Professional corporations.
Powers, §29-505.

Public buildings, acquisition for,
§10-604.

Public lands.
See PUBLIC LANDS.

**Purchase for value without notice of
trust.**
Effect of, §42-1503.

Quiet enjoyment, covenant of,
§42-606.

Quiet title, §16-3301.

**Real estate brokers and
salespersons.**
General provisions, §§42-1701 to
42-1709.
See REAL ESTATE BROKERS AND
SALESPERSONS.

Recordation tax on deeds.
General provisions, §§42-1101 to
42-1124.
See RECORDATION TAX.

Recorder of deeds.
General provisions, §§42-1202 to
42-1218.
See RECORDER OF DEEDS.

Records.
Public access, §42-1206.

REAL PROPERTY —Cont'd
Rental housing conversion and sale.
General provisions, §§42-3401.01 to
42-3405.13.
See RENTAL HOUSING.
**Residential real property seller
disclosures,** §§42-1301 to 42-1311.
See HOME SALES.
**Senior citizens' home repair and
improvement program fund,**
§§42-2201 to 42-2207.
**Settlements for real estate acquired
by purchase or condemnation,**
§1-301.04.
Soil characteristics information,
§42-608.
Statute of frauds, §§28-3501 to
28-3505.
Contract or sale of real estate,
§28-3502.
Declaration.
Grant and assignment of trust,
§28-3503.
Streets and alleys.
Opening, extending, widening, or
straightening, §9-203.02.
Taxation.
General provisions, §§47-801 to
47-895.35.
See REAL PROPERTY TAXES.
Property exempt from taxation,
§§47-1001 to 47-1097.
See REAL PROPERTY TAX
EXEMPTIONS.
Real estate tax sales, §§47-847,
47-1301 to 47-1385.
See REAL ESTATE TAX SALES.
Real estate transfer tax, §§47-901 to
47-920.
See REAL PROPERTY TRANSFER
TAX.
Residential real property transfer
excise tax.
Compulsory recordation of transfers,
§§47-1431 to 47-1433.
Toilet facilities, §§8-601 to 8-604.
Transfers on death, §§19-604.01 to
19-604.19.
Allowances.
Statutory allowances, liability for,
§19-604.15.
Applicability of subchapter,
§19-604.03.
Uniformity, §19-604.18.
Beneficiaries.
Creditor claims, liability for,
§19-604.15.

REAL PROPERTY —Cont'd
Transfers on death —Cont'd
Beneficiaries —Cont'd
Disclaimer by beneficiary,
§19-604.14.
Statutory allowances, liability for,
§19-604.15.
Capacity of transferor, §19-604.08.
Citation of act, §19-604.01.
Construction.
Uniformity, §19-604.18.
Creditor claims.
Liability for, §19-604.15.
Deeds.
Authorized, §19-604.05.
Effect, during transferor's life,
§19-604.12.
Effective, when, §19-604.10.
Effect, upon transferor's death,
§19-604.13.
Form, optional form, §19-604.16.
Nontestamentary, §19-604.07.
Notice, delivery, acceptance,
consideration not required,
§19-604.10.
Requirements, §19-604.09.
Revocable, §19-604.06.
Revocation by instrument,
§19-604.11.
Form, §19-604.17.
Definitions, §19-604.02.
Disclaimer by beneficiary, §19-604.14.
Recordation, §19-1512.
Effective date, §19-604.03.
Electronic signatures in global and
national commerce act.
Relation to, §19-604.19.
Forms.
Deed, optional form, §19-604.16.
Revocation by instrument,
§19-604.17.
Nonexclusivity, §19-604.04.
Other methods of transfer,
nonexclusivity, §19-604.04.
Requirements of deeds, §19-604.09.
Revocation by instrument, §19-604.11.
Form, §19-604.17.
Rights under deed.
Effect of deed during transferor's
life, §19-604.12.
Effect of deed during upon
transferor's death, §19-604.13.
Short title, §19-604.01.
**Trust, mortgage and title
corporations,** §§26-1312, 26-1314.
Trust or confidence of real estate.
Declaration or creation of, §28-3503.

REAL PROPERTY —Cont'd
Uniform real property transfers on death, §§19-604.01 to 19-604.19.
Unincorporated nonprofit associations.
Ownership and transfer, §29-1106.
Statement of authority, §29-1107.
Transitional provisions, §29-1127.
Universities and colleges.
Exempt from taxation, §§47-1002, 47-1018.
Urban renewal.
See URBAN RENEWAL.
Vacant and abandoned property.
Special disposal procedures for certain properties, §§10-831 to 10-839.
Walter Reed Army Medical Center.
Transfer of real property, §§10-1904, 10-1905.
Warranties.
Special warranties, §42-605.
Void as to heirs, §42-609.
Waste, §§42-1601 to 42-1604, 42-3211.
Watercloset requirements, §§8-601 to 8-604.
Wet settlement act, §§42-2401 to 42-2407.
See MORTGAGES AND DEEDS OF TRUST.

REAL PROPERTY TAXES, §§47-801 to 47-895.35, 47-4601 to 47-4665.05.
Abatement.
Act introduced granting.
Analysis required, §47-4701.
Guidance from chief financial officer, §47-4703.
Requirements, §47-4701.
Applicability, §47-4704.
Certification of continuing eligibility, §47-4702.
Guidance from chief financial officer, §47-4703.
E-commerce companies.
Qualified social electronic commerce companies tax abatements, §§47-1818.01 to 47-1818.08.
Effective date, §47-4704.
800 Kenilworth Avenue N.E. redevelopment project, §47-4643.
Exempt property.
Abatement or refund of tax assessed against exempt property, §47-1008.
Greater Southeast Community Hospital, §47-1050.
Hadley Memorial Hospital, §47-1050.

REAL PROPERTY TAXES —Cont'd
Abatement —Cont'd
High technology commercial real estate database and service providers, §47-4630.
Homeowners in enterprise zones tax abatement, §§47-858.01 to 47-858.05.
Lower income home ownership tax abatement and incentives, §§47-3501 to 47-3508.
National Public Radio, Inc, §47-4615.
New residential development, §§47-857.01 to 47-857.10, 47-859.01 to 47-859.05.
Notice and appeal rights, §47-859.04a.
Nonprofit corporations locating in emerging commercial neighborhoods, §§47-857.11 to 47-857.16.
Applications, §47-857.13.
Caps, §47-857.15.
Certifications, §47-857.13.
Definitions, §47-857.11.
Reports, §47-857.14.
Requirements, §47-857.12.
Rulemaking authority, §47-857.16.
Penalty and interest, §47-811.04.
Rental housing.
Conversion and sale, §42-3402.09.
New or rehabilitated vacant units, §42-3508.02.
Section 8 and other affordable housing, §§47-865, 47-866.
Special assessments, §47-1203.
The Advisory Board Company, §§47-4665.01 to 47-4665.05.
2323 Pennsylvania Avenue, S.E. redevelopment project, §47-4640.
Urban Institute properties, §47-4624.
Additions to existing structures, §47-829.
Adjustments.
Credit against tax, annual adjustment, §47-872.
Cooperative housing associations, §47-873.
Administrative review.
Reclassification, §47-813.
Aged persons.
Deferral for low-income senior property owners, §47-845.03.
Reduced liability for, §47-863.
Agricultural use, reduced liability, §47-868.

REAL PROPERTY TAXES —Cont'd
Appeals.
Generally.
See APPEALS, D.C. COURTS.
Not deemed adjudicated under administrative procedure provisions, §47-877.
Applicability of other provisions, §47-875.
Applicability of provisions, §47-825.03.
Assessments, §§47-820 to 47-828.
Appeals, §47-825.01a.
Assessed value, §47-820.
Assessors.
Appointment of, §47-821.
Powers and duties, §47-835.
Real estate tax sales, §§47-1310, 47-1311.
Baltimore and Ohio Railroad Company, §47-837.
Class actions as to, §47-827.
Cooperative housing associations, §47-820.01.
Correction, administrative or clerical, §47-825.01a.
Estimated assessment roll, §47-823.
Assessed value of real property listed on, §47-820.
Estimated market value.
Assessed value, §47-820.
Frequency of, §47-820.
Homestead deduction.
Recent assessment changed as result of appeal, §47-820.
Information submitted by property owners, §47-821.
Listing of assessed values, §47-823.
Mayor's duties, §47-821.
Name, address and number in which assessment is made, §47-822.
Notice, §47-824.
Corrections, §47-825.01a.
Proposed supplemental assessment, §47-829.
Office of tax and revenue.
Duties of, §47-835.
Omitted properties, §47-831.
Preliminary roll, §47-823.
Public access to information, §47-823.
Publication of assessments in newspaper, §47-823.
Real property tax appeals commission, §47-825.01a.
Reassessment or redistribution, §§47-834, 47-839.

REAL PROPERTY TAXES —Cont'd
Assessments —Cont'd
Resale restricted properties, §47-820.02.
Sales ratio studies, §47-823.
Special assessments, §§47-1201 to 47-1207. See within this heading, "Special assessments."
Subdivisions, §§47-832 to 47-835.
Supplemental assessments, §47-829.
Appeal, §47-830.
Violation of provisions as to, §47-828.
Washington termination, §47-837.
Banks and financial institutions, §47-2514.
Bureau of National Affairs and tax deferrals, §47-845.01.
Capital review and debt affordability committee, §§47-336 to 47-340.
Capper/Carrollsburg PILOT.
Payments in lieu of taxes, §47-4611.
Center Leg Freeway (interstate 395) PILOT Area.
Payments in lieu of taxes, §47-4632.
Charter schools.
Public charter school rebate.
School leasing facility from entity subject to tax, §47-867.
Class actions as to, §47-827.
Classes of property, §47-813.
Comparison of rates and burdens with other.
Jurisdictions, §§47-817 to 47-819.
Complaints, §§47-829, 47-830.
Supplemental assessments, §§47-829, 47-830.
Computation of tax, §§47-872, 47-873.
Cooperative housing associations, §47-873.
Condemnation proceedings, special assessments, §47-1204.
Constitution square development project.
Tax abatements, §47-4612.
Cooperative housing associations, §§47-820.01, 47-850, 47-873.
Homestead deduction, §§47-850.01 to 47-850.04.
Transfers exempt from tax, §47-802.
Credits against tax, §47-872.
Cooperative housing associations, §47-873.
Owner-occupant residential tax credit, §47-864.
Section 8 and other affordable housing, §§47-865, 47-866.

REAL PROPERTY TAXES —Cont'd
**Debt service requirement to be
noted on bills,** §47-340.
Deferral of payments, §§47-845 to
47-846.01, 47-862, 47-1202.01.
Definitions, §§47-802, 47-803, 47-871.
Delinquent tax sales, §§47-1301 to
47-1321.
Revised real property tax sale,
§§47-1330 to 47-1385.
See REAL ESTATE TAX SALES.
**Designation of property for
assessment,** §§47-701 to 47-709.
Daily transcript of designations,
§47-703.
Numbering of squares, lots, blocks,
parcels, §47-701.
Official designation, §47-702.
Record of designations, §47-701.
Sale of federal property.
Report to proper official, §47-709.
System used outside city, §47-704.
Daily transcripts, §47-707.
Numbering of squares, lots, blocks,
parcels, §§47-704, 47-705.
Office designation, §47-708.
Plat books, §47-706.
Disposition of, §47-811.
**800 Kenilworth Avenue N.E.
redevelopment project.**
Tax abatements, §47-4643.
Energy assessments, §§47-895.31 to
47-895.35.
Collections, §47-895.33.
Definitions, §47-895.31.
Deposit of revenues, §47-895.35.
Fines and civil penalties, §47-895.33.
Interest, §47-895.33.
Levy, §47-895.32.
Notice, §47-895.33.
Real property tax sales.
Energy efficiency loan foreclosures,
§47-1336.
Deed of purchaser, §47-1382.
Termination, §47-895.34.
Enterprise zones.
Homeowners in enterprise zones tax
abatement, §§47-858.01 to
47-858.05.
**Enumerated reports adopted as
comparison of rates and burdens
with other jurisdictions,**
§47-818.01.
Exempt households.
Defined, §47-863.

REAL PROPERTY TAXES —Cont'd
Exempt property, §§47-1001 to
47-1097.
See REAL PROPERTY TAX
EXEMPTIONS.
Federal property valuations,
§§47-840, 47-841.
Real estate included, §47-840.
Return, §47-840.
Valuation made by persona designated
by Secretary of Interior, §47-841.
**Fees for production of records, data
and maps,** §47-876.
Fines.
Nonpayment, §47-811.
Forgiveness of, §§47-846.01,
47-1202.01.
Garbage collection services, §47-872.
**Government property made
available to person for non-
exempt purposes,** §47-1005.01.
Government transfers.
Exempt from tax, §47-802.
Hearings, §47-825.03.
Historic federal property valuations,
§§47-840, 47-841.
Historic property tax relief, §§47-842
to 47-844.
Agreements for maintenance and use
of buildings, §47-844.
Assessment of officially designated
buildings, §47-842.
Eligibility, §47-843.
**Homeowners in enterprise zones tax
abatement,** §§47-858.01 to
47-858.05.
Certified list of qualified properties,
§47-858.05.
Computation, §47-858.05.
Definitions, §47-858.01.
Effective date, §47-858.05.
Requirements, §47-858.02.
Substantial rehabilitation of single-
family residential property,
§47-858.03.
Tax credit, §47-858.04.
Homestead.
Residential property tax relief,
§§47-850.01 to 47-850.04.
**Homestead deduction for houses
and condominium units,** §47-850.
Recent assessment changed as result
of appeal, §47-820.
Housing improvements.
Section 8 and other affordable
housing.
Abatement of tax, §§47-865, 47-866.

REAL PROPERTY TAXES —Cont'd
Housing priority area A.
Tax abatement for new housing
projects in, §47-857.04.
Mixed-income housing projects,
§47-857.06.
Husband and wife.
Transfers without consideration,
exempt from tax, §47-802.
**Improvements to existing
structures,** §47-829.
Income taxes, §47-1806.06.
Interest.
Special assessments, §47-1203.
Waiver of interest owed, §47-811.04.
International organizations,
§47-1005.01.
Issuance of rules and regulations,
§§47-814, 47-862, 47-874.
**King towers residential housing
rental project.**
Exemption, §47-4631.
Levies, §47-811.
Limited liability companies.
Partnership converted to.
Transfers exempt from tax, §47-802.
Mayor's duties.
See MAYOR.
National Public Radio, Inc.
Abatement of taxes, §47-4615.
**New residential development tax
abatement,** §§47-857.01 to
47-857.10.
Abatement caps, §47-857.09.
Appeal of intent to impose penalty,
§47-857.09a.
Definitions, §47-857.01.
Downtown housing projects,
§47-857.03.
Mixed income projects, §47-857.05.
Housing projects in housing priority A,
§47-857.04.
Mixed income projects, §47-857.06.
Mixed income housing projects in
higher cost and other qualified
areas, §§47-857.07, 47-857.08.
New developments in NoMA.
Abatement caps, §47-859.04.
Appeal of imposition of penalty,
§47-859.04a.
Definitions, §47-859.01.
New housing projects in NoMA,
§47-859.03.
Notice of intent impose penalty,
§47-859.04a.
Requirements, §47-859.02.

REAL PROPERTY TAXES —Cont'd
**New residential development tax
abatement** —Cont'd
New developments in NoMA —Cont'd
Rules, §47-859.05.
Notice of intent impose penalty,
§47-857.09a.
Regulations, §47-857.10.
Requirements, §47-857.02.
New structures, §§47-829, 47-830.
**New York avenue Metrorail benefit
area.**
Special assessment districts, §§47-881
to 47-885.
Nonpayment fines, §47-811.
Notice.
Assessments.
Correction, §47-825.01a.
Proposed supplemental assessment,
§47-829.
New residential developments,
§47-859.04a.
Nuisances, removal of, §47-1205.
Omitted properties, §47-831.
Overpayment, §47-811.02.
**Owner-occupant residential tax
credit,** §47-864.
Parent and child.
Transfers without consideration,
exempt from tax, §47-802.
Payment of taxes, §§47-811, 47-1203.
Condemnation proceedings, §47-1204.
Nuisances, removal of, §47-1205.
Special assessments, §47-1203.
Payments in lieu of taxes, §47-1052.
Center Leg Freeway (interstate 395)
PILOT Area, §47-4632.
Lots 826 and 831, square 491,
§47-1064.
Penalties, §47-861.
Nonpayment of taxes, §47-811.
Waiver of penalty, §47-811.04.
Persons with disabilities.
Reduced liability for, §47-863.
Petitions.
Reclassification, §47-813.
PILOT.
Payments in lieu of taxes, §47-1052.
Policy declaration, §47-801.
Presumptions.
Property occupied, §47-813.
Property exempt from taxation.
General provisions, §§47-1001 to
47-1097.
See REAL PROPERTY TAX
EXEMPTIONS.

REAL PROPERTY TAXES —Cont'd
Property occupied.
Presumption, §47-813.
**Qualified high technology
companies,** §47-811.03.
Railroads, §§47-836 to 47-838.
Rates.
Comparison of rates and burdens with
other jurisdictions, §§47-817 to
47-819.
Establishment, §47-812.
Publication, §§47-815, 47-820.
Special tax rates, §47-812.
Submission, §§47-815, 47-816, 47-820.
Reassessment or redistribution,
§47-834.
Reclassification, §47-813.
Recordation of instruments.
Residential real estate transfers,
§§47-1401, 47-1431 to 47-1433.
Records.
Examination of books and records,
§47-4313.
Time and place, §47-4314.
Requirement of retention, §47-4311.
Refund of taxes erroneously paid,
§47-1317.
**Rental housing conversion and sale,
abatement for,** §42-3402.09.
Resale restricted properties.
Assessments, §47-820.02.
Residential property tax relief,
§§47-850.01 to 47-850.04.
Contract with collection agency,
§47-850.02.
Homestead deduction.
Cooperative housing associations,
§47-850.01.
House and condominiums, §47-850.
New residential development tax
abatement, §§47-857.01 to
47-857.10.
No homestead when multiple
homestead claimed, §47-850.04.
Notice that property no longer
qualified, §47-850.02.
One-time filing, §47-850.02.
Property owing because of erroneous
or improper deduction, §47-850.02.
Single-family residential property
deductions, §47-850.
Transfer of homestead to revocable
trust, §47-850.03.
Resident management corporations.
Transfers exempt from tax, §47-802.
Sales of delinquent property.
Generally, §§47-1301 to 47-1321.
See REAL ESTATE TAX SALES.

REAL PROPERTY TAXES —Cont'd
Sales of delinquent property —Cont'd
Revised real property tax sale,
§§47-1330 to 47-1385.
See REAL ESTATE TAX SALES.
Secured transfers.
Transfers exempt from tax, §47-802.
Senior households.
Deferral for low-income seniors,
§47-845.03.
Reduced tax liability, §47-863.
Service of notice, §47-804.
**Single-family residential property
deductions,** §47-850.
**Southeast water and sewer
improvement benefit district.**
Special assessment district, §§47-891
to 47-894.
**Southwest waterfront special
assessment district,** §§47-895.01 to
47-895.06.
See SOUTHWEST WATERFRONT.
Special assessments, §§47-1201 to
47-1207.
Abatement, §47-1203.
Adjustment, §47-1203.
Appeals, §47-1202.
Capitol, improvement of streets
around, §47-1207.
Condemnation proceedings, §47-1204.
Deferrals, §47-1202.01.
Energy assessments, §§47-895.31 to
47-895.35.
Forgiveness of, §47-1202.01.
Interest, §47-1203.
Mayor's powers and duties, §47-1203.
Mayor's reassessment powers,
§47-1206.
New York avenue metrorail benefit
area.
Special assessment districts,
§§47-881 to 47-885.
New York avenue Metrorail benefit
area.
Application of assessment, §47-884.
Definitions, §47-881.
Establishment of special assessment
district, §47-882.
Levy, protest, termination, §47-883.
Regulations, §47-885.
Notice of levy of, §47-1203.
Nuisances, removal of, §47-1205.
Payment of taxes, §47-1203.
Protests against, §47-1202.
Public improvements, for, §47-1201.
Reduction, §47-1203.

REAL PROPERTY TAXES —Cont'd
Special assessments —Cont'd
Sale of delinquent property, §§47-1203 to 47-1205.
Southeast water and sewer improvement benefit district.
Special assessment district, §§47-891 to 47-894.
Southwest waterfront special assessment district, §§47-895.01 to 47-895.06.
Waterfront park at the yards, §§47-895.21 to 47-895.24.
Subdivisions, §§47-832 to 47-835.
Tax return preparers.
Fines and penalties, §47-4217.
The Advisory Board Company.
Tax abatement, §§47-4665.01 to 47-4665.05.
Transfer tax on real property.
General provisions, §§47-901 to 47-920.
See REAL PROPERTY TRANSFER TAX.
Trusts and trustees.
Transfers to revocable trust, exempt from tax, §47-802.
2323 Pennsylvania Avenue, S.E. redevelopment project.
Tax abatements, §47-4640.
Types of real estate, §§47-813, 47-829.
Unsubdivided tracts, §47-833.
Waterfront park at the yards special assessment district, §§47-895.21 to 47-895.24.
Wax museum project.
Tax abatement, §47-857.06.

REAL PROPERTY TAX EXEMPTIONS, §§47-1001 to 47-1097.
Abatement, §47-1008.
Act introduced granting exemption.
Analysis required, §47-4701.
Guidance from chief financial officer, §47-4703.
Requirements, §47-4701.
Adams Morgan hotel development project, §47-4652.
Affordable Housing Opportunities, Inc., §§47-1078, 47-1084, 47-1086.
Alabama Avenue affordable rental housing project, §47-4641.
Allen Chapel A.M.E. senior residential rental project, §47-4641.
American Academy of Achievement, §47-1093.

REAL PROPERTY TAX EXEMPTIONS —Cont'd
American Association of University Women, §47-1041.
American College of Cardiology, §47-1059.
American Institute of Architects Foundation, §47-1044.
American Legion, §§47-1035, 47-1046.
American Psychological Association.
Lot 146, square 677, §47-1069.
AMVETS (American Veterans of World War II), §47-1038.
Appalachian state university.
Lot 42 in square 871, §47-1068.
Appeals of assessments, §47-1009.
ARCH training center, §47-1047.
Art galleries, §47-1002.
Beulah Baptist Church, §47-4654.
Board of education property, §47-1027.
Bolling Air Force Base housing, §47-1080.
Bread for the City Community Garden, §47-1062.
Brentwood retail center, §47-4608.
Building Bridges Across the River, Inc. properties, §47-1083.
Campbell Heights project, §47-4632.
Capitol Hill community garden land trust, §47-1054.
Lot 0109 in square 1100, §47-1061.
Carver 2000 low-income and senior housing project, §47-4605.
Catholic University of America's soldiers' and airmen's home, §47-1066.
Cedar Hill (Frederick Douglass Memorial and Historical Association), §47-1025.
Cemeteries, §§47-1002, 47-1015.
Center for Public Administration and Service, §47-1010.01.
Central union mission development project, §47-4651.
Certification of continuing eligibility, §47-4702.
Guidance from chief financial officer, §47-4703.
Charitable institutions, §§47-1002, 47-1010.01.
Chesapeake and Ohio canal, §47-1014.
Cincinnati, Society of the, §47-1037.
Classes of property, §47-813.
Colonial Dames of America, §47-1004.

REAL PROPERTY TAX EXEMPTIONS —Cont'd

Cooperative housing associations.
Property transfer to qualified lower income homeowner, §47-3503.
Administration and enforcement, §47-3504.
Corcoran Gallery of Art, §§47-1016, 47-1017.
Crispus Attucks development corporation, §47-1058.
Daughters of 1812, §47-1033.
Daughters of American Revolution, §§47-1028 to 47-1032.
Lots 4, 5, 6, 7 and 11, §47-1032.
Lots, 8, 9, 10 and square 173, §47-1028.
Lots 12 through 16, §47-1030.
Lots 23 through 28, §47-1031.
Square 173, §47-1029.
D.C. teachers federal credit union, §47-1053.
DC-USA project, §47-4606.
Denials of exemption, appealing, §47-1009.
Department of the District of Columbia Veterans of foreign Wars.
Lot 0040, square 5167, §47-1063.
Disabled American Veterans, §47-1003.
District property, §§47-1002, 47-1011.
Douglas Knoll, §47-1065.
Douglass Knoll rehabilitation project, §47-1065.
Eastern Star Charitable Foundation, §47-1045.
Eckington One residential project, §47-4618.
Edes Home, §47-1026.
The Elizabeth Ministry, Inc. affordable housing initiative, §47-4657.
Emmaus rehabilitation project, §47-1057.
Far Southeast Community Organization, §47-1075.
Federal property, §§47-1002, 47-1011.
14W and the YMCA Anthony Bowen project, §47-4627.
4427 HAYES street, N.E. development project, §47-4649.
Frederick Douglass Memorial and Historical Association (Cedar Hill), §47-1025.
Freemasons, §47-1045.

REAL PROPERTY TAX EXEMPTIONS —Cont'd

GALA Hispanic Theatre, §47-4660.
Gateway Market Center and residences, §47-4621.
Golden Rule Plaza, Inc. properties, §47-1079.
Golden Rule rehabilitation project, §47-1065.
Greater Southeast community hospital, §47-1050.
Hadley memorial hospital, §47-1050.
Heights on Georgia avenue, §47-4628.
Hill Center, §47-1087.
Hospitals, §47-1002.
Howard University, §47-1018.
International house of pancake restaurant 3221 development project, §47-4650.
The Israel senior residences, §47-4659.
Issuance of rules and regulations, §47-1010.
James Reese Europe Post No. 5, American Legion, §47-1046.
Jubilee Housing residential rental project, §47-4633.
Jubilee Ontario Apartments, LP, Lot 805, Square 2565, §47-1099.
Kelsey Gardens redevelopment project, §47-4625.
King Towers residential housing rental project, §§47-4638, 47-4639.
King Towers residential housing rental property, §47-4631.
KIPP DC property, §47-1081.
Shaw campus, §47-1085.
List of, §47-1002.
Lot 878, square 456, §47-4604.
Louise Home, §47-1012.
Lowell School, §47-1049.
Luther Statute Association, §47-1019.
Masons, §47-1045.
Meridian Public Charter School, §47-1088.
Military affairs.
National Guard Association, §47-1042.
Veterans. See within this heading, "Veterans."
Museums, §47-1002.
National Community Reinvestment Coalition, §47-1071.
National Education Association, §§47-1036, 47-1036.01.
National Guard Association, §47-1042.

REAL PROPERTY TAX
EXEMPTIONS —Cont'd
National Woman's Party, §47-1040.
Naval Lodge Building, Inc, §47-1097.
New Columbia community land
    trust, §47-1072.
Nonprofit affordable housing
    developers, §47-1005.02.
Nonprofit corporations, §47-1002.
N Street Village, §47-1092.
Oak Hill cemetery company,
    §47-1015.
OTO Hotel at Constitution Square,
    §47-4631.
Park Place at Petworth, Highland
    Park, and Highland Park Phase
    II projects, §47-4629.
Parkside parcel E and J mixed-
    income apartments, §47-4658.
Parkside Terrace development
    project, §47-4607.
Prince Hall Freemason and Eastern
    Star Charitable Foundation,
    §47-1045.
Publication of listing of, §47-1001.
Qualified high technology
    companies.
  Interior renovation tax rebate,
    §47-4665.
Randall School development project,
    §47-4626.
Red Cross, §47-1006.
Refunds, §47-1008.
Religious institutions, §47-1002.
  St. Mark's Episcopal Church,
    §47-1020.
  YMCA (Young Men's Christian
    Association), §47-1024.
  Young Women's Christian Association,
    §§47-1022, 47-1023.
  Young Women's Christian Home,
    §47-1021.
Rental property of exempt
    institutions and organizations,
    §47-1005.
Reports.
  Use of exempt property, §47-1007.
Reservation 13, §47-1055.
Rosedale conservancy, §47-1056.
St. Mark's Episcopal Church,
    §47-1020.
St. Martin's apartments project,
    §47-4620.
St. Paul Senior Living at Wayne
    Place, §47-4642.
Samuel J. Simmons NCBA Estates
    No. 1 limited partnership.
  Lot 8, square 2855, §47-4646.

REAL PROPERTY TAX
EXEMPTIONS —Cont'd
School buildings and grounds,
    §§47-1002, 47-1049.
SeVerna, §47-1095.
Shakespeare Theatre, §47-1048.
Soccer stadium tax abatements,
    §47-4663.
Society of the Cincinnati, §47-1037.
Sons of the American Revolution,
    §47-1034.
So Others Might Eat, Inc., §47-1078.
Southeast Neighborhood house.
  Lots 0808, 0904 and 0905 in square
    5802, §47-1060.
Studio theatre housing, §47-1082.
Supreme Council of Scottish Rite
    Free Masonry, §47-1094.
Teachers federal credit union,
    §47-1053.
Theatre Downtown, Inc., §47-1074.
The Heights on Georgia Avenue,
    §47-4630.
Third and H Streets, N.E.
    development project, §47-4634.
Thirteenth Church of Christ,
    §47-4644.
Tibetan community property,
    §47-4661.
Tregaron Conservancy, §47-1077.
Triangle community garden,
    §47-1073.
2 M street, N.E. development
    project, §47-4648.
Types of exempt property, §47-1002.
United House of Prayer for All
    People.
  Kitchen or feeding facilities, §47-1086.
Universal Holiness Church, §47-4653.
Universities and colleges, §§47-1002,
    47-1018.
Veterans.
  American Legion, §§47-1035, 47-1046.
  AMVETS (American Veterans of World
    War II), §47-1038.
  Disabled American Veterans, §47-1003.
  Veterans of Foreign Wars (VFW),
    §47-1039.
View 14 project, §47-4623.
Wagner Gainsville rehabilitation
    project, §47-1065.
Walker Jones/Northwest One Unity
    health center, §47-4619.
Walter Reed military housing,
    §47-1070.
Washington ballet, §47-4655.

**REAL PROPERTY TAX
  EXEMPTIONS** —Cont'd
Way of the Cross Church of Christ,
  §47-1067.
Whitman-Walker Clinic, Inc,
  §47-4664.
Women.
  American Association of University
    Women, §47-1041.
  National Woman's Party, §47-1040.
Woodrow Wilson House, §47-1043.
Wooly Mammoth theatre, §47-1051.
**YMCA (Young Men's Christian
  Association),** §47-1024.
  Community investment initiative,
    §47-1092.
**Young Women's Christian
  Association,** §§47-1022, 47-1023.
Young Women's Christian Home,
  §47-1021.

REAL PROPERTY TAX SALES,
  §§47-1301 to 47-1321.
  See REAL ESTATE TAX SALES.

REAL PROPERTY TRANSFER TAX,
  §§47-901 to 47-920.
Administration, §47-920.
Appeals, §47-914.
Burden of proof, §47-907.
**Carver 2000 low-income and senior
  housing project.**
  Exempt transfers, §47-4605.
**Compulsory recordation of
  transfers,** §§47-1431 to 47-1433.
Computation of, §47-904.
Definitions, §47-901.
Disposition of collected taxes,
  §47-919.
**East of the river hospital tax
  exemptions,** §47-4614.
Evidence, §47-907.
Exempt transfers, §47-902.
  Carver 2000 low-income and senior
    housing project, §47-4605.
  East of the river hospital tax
    exemptions, §47-4614.
  Georgia Commons.
    Housing and retail elements,
      §47-4610.
  New convention center hotel project,
    §47-4609.
**Fair market value of property as
  basis for,** §47-904.
Georgia Commons.
  Exempt transfers.
    Housing and retail elements,
      §47-4610.

REAL PROPERTY TRANSFER TAX
  —Cont'd
Issuance of rules and regulations,
  §§47-916, 47-920.
**Lease or ground rent for at least 30
  years.**
  Computation of tax, §47-903.
Liability of transferor, §47-903.
**New convention center hotel
  project.**
  Exempt transfers, §47-4609.
Nominal consideration, transfer for.
  Rate of tax, §47-903.
No or minimal consideration,
  §47-904.
Payment of tax.
  Time for, §47-903.
Presumptions, §47-907.
Rates, §47-903.
**Residential real property transfer
  excise tax,** §§47-1401, 47-1431 to
  47-1433.
**Returns required to accompany
  deed,** §47-903.

REBATES.
Consumer credit sales.
  Referral sales, §28-3810.
Public utilities, §34-704.
**Title insurance producers,
  prohibited,** §31-5041.07.
Title insurers, prohibited,
  §31-5031.15.

REBUILT VEHICLES.
Generally, §§50-1331.01 to 50-1331.09.
  See SALVAGE, FLOOD AND JUNK
    VEHICLES.

**RECALL OF ELECTED PUBLIC
  OFFICIALS,** §§1-204.111 to
  1-204.115, 1-1001.17.
Adoption of acts regarding,
  §1-204.115.
Definition of recall, §1-204.111.
Limitation of actions, §1-204.113.
Procedures, §§1-204.112, 1-1001.17.
Vacancy left by, filling, §1-204.114.
When official considered removed,
  §1-204.114.

RECEIVERS.
Action of account, §16-101.
Attachments, §16-518.
Banks and financial institutions,
  §26-103.
Corporations.
  Judicial dissolution, §§29-312.21,
    29-312.22.

RECEIVERS —Cont'd
Corporations —Cont'd
Shareholders.
Appointment, §29-305.70.
Dismissal of action, CivPro Rule 66.
Domestic relations actions, DomRel
Rule 66.
**Fiduciary's bond, undertaking in
lieu of,** §16-601.
Fraternal benefit societies, §31-5327.
Garnishment.
Prejudgment garnishment.
Appointment to take possession of
property, §16-518.
Insurance holding companies,
§31-711.
Landlord and tenant court.
Properties subject to court-ordered
receiverships, LandlordTenant
Rule 3-I.
Nonprofit corporations.
Judicial dissolution, §§29-412.20 to
29-412.22.
Nursing homes, §§44-1002.01 to
44-1002.10.
See NURSING HOMES.
Real estate tax sales.
Revised real property tax sale.
Redemption of property, §47-1363.
Rules governing receivers, CivPro
Rule 66.
Stay of proceedings, CivPro Rule 62.
Tenant receivership.
Violation threatening health, safety or
security of tenants, §§42-3651.01
to 42-3651.08.
Uniform fiduciaries act, §§21-1701 to
21-1712.
See FIDUCIARIES.

RECEIVING STOLEN PROPERTY,
§22-3232.

RECEPTIONS.
Eminent persons, §1-333.09.

RECESS OF TRIAL.
Witness statement examination.
Criminal cases, CrimPro Rule 26.2.
Delinquent minors, JuvProc Rule 26.2.

RECIPROCITY.
**Attorney discipline or disability
proceedings,** DCBar Rule XI,
USDistCt LCrR 57.27, USDistCt
LCvR 83.16.
Child support enforcement.
Medical support enforcement.
Medical support notice, §46-251.03.

RECIPROCITY —Cont'd
Collection of taxes.
Refund offsets.
Reciprocal rights of credit, §47-4440.
Comfort care bracelet or necklace.
Non-resuscitation procedures for EMS.
Recognition of bracelets issued in
Virginia or Maryland, §7-651.09.
**Delinquent debts owed District,
recovery,** §1-350.08.
Do not resuscitate procedures.
Comfort care orders, §7-651.09.
Emergency medical services.
Reciprocal certification, §7-2341.12.
**Emergency volunteer health
practitioners,** §7-2361.05.
**Fire departments, reciprocal
agreements between,** §5-414.
Funeral directors, §3-405.
Gross sales tax returns, §47-2018.
**Health occupations licensure,
registration or certification,**
§3-1205.07.
Income tax returns, §47-1805.04.
Insurance companies.
Reciprocal insurance company
conversion, §§31-751 to 31-760.
Taxation, §47-2610.
Insurance producer licensing,
§31-1131.16.
**Insurers rehabilitation and
liquidation proceedings.**
Interstate priorities, §31-1356.
Resident claims against insurers
domiciled in reciprocal states,
§31-1354.
Subordination of claims for
noncooperation, §31-1357.
**International motor vehicle
registration plan agreements,**
§§50-1507.01, 50-1507.02.
**Marriages from other jurisdictions,
recognition of,** §46-405.01.
Merit system.
Temporary assignment of District
employees, §§1-627.01 to 1-627.06.
**Metrorail and metrobus reciprocal
trackage agreements,** §§35-210,
35-212.
**Motor fuel tax and International
Fuel Tax Agreement,** §47-2351.
Out-of-District property, §10-509.05.
Pesticides, §8-415.
Police departments.
Reciprocal agreements between,
§§2-209.01 to 2-209.04.

RECIPROCITY —Cont'd
Taxation.
Multistate tax compact, §§47-441 to 47-445.
Reciprocal recovery of taxes, §§47-431 to 47-433.
Unclaimed property laws, §41-134.
Unemployment compensation, §51-116.

RECKLESS DRIVING, §50-2201.04.

RECOGNIZANCE.
Appellate procedure.
Release of prisoner pending review of habeas corpus decision, FRAP 23.

RECONSTRUCTIVE BREAST SURGERY.
Women's rights to health insurance coverage, §§31-3831 to 31-3837.

RECORDATION OF INSTRUMENTS.
Assignment for benefit of creditors, §28-2103.
Bonds, surety.
Relating to land, §42-409.
Building associations, §26-201.
Children and minors, conveyances by, §42-408.
Condominiums, §42-1902.01.
See CONDOMINIUMS.
Conservators appointed for protection of property, letters of, §21-2067.
Contracts relating to land, §42-409.
Deeds.
Recordation tax on deeds, §§42-1101 to 42-1124.
See RECORDATION TAX.
Recorder of deeds, §§42-1202 to 42-1218.
See RECORDER OF DEEDS.
Disclaimer of interests in property, §19-1515.
Electronic recording, §§42-1231 to 42-1235.
Applicability of provisions, §42-1234.
Construction of provisions, §42-1234.
Definitions, §42-1231.
Recorder of deeds, powers and duties, §42-1233.
Relation to federal law, §42-1235.
Validity of electronic documents and digitized images, §42-1232.
Environmental covenants, §8-671.07.
Extension of time for recordation due to Saturdays, Sundays, and legal holidays, §§42-1216, 42-1217.

RECORDATION OF INSTRUMENTS —Cont'd
False personation with intent to extort money, §22-1402.
Financing statements, §§41-201 to 41-204.
Effect of recordation, §41-201.
False statements, §41-204.
Filing, §41-201.
Indexing, §41-201.
Released instruments, disposal of, §41-203.
Termination statements, §§41-202, 41-204.
Void or lapsed instruments, disposal of, §41-202.
First recorded deed, preference for, §42-406.
Horizontal property regimes, §42-2006.
See HORIZONTAL PROPERTY REGIMES.
Improperly executed or acknowledged instruments, §42-407.
Real estate tax sales.
Revised real property tax sale. Certificate of sale, §47-1350.
Real property transfers, compulsory recordation of, §§47-1431 to 47-1433.
Recorder of deeds.
General provisions, §§42-1202 to 42-1218.
See RECORDER OF DEEDS.
Residential real estate transfers, §§47-1401, 47-1431 to 47-1433.
Streets and alleys, closing procedures, §§9-202.12, 9-202.13.
Subdivision maps and plats, §42-410.
Trustees of infants, conveyances by, §42-408.
Trust, mortgage and title corporation charters of incorporation, §26-1307.

RECORDATION OF PROCEEDINGS.
Arbitration hearings, Arbitration Rule IX.
Crime victims' compensation.
Appeal of determination, VictComp Rule 20.
Depositions, CivPro Rule 30.
Adoption proceedings, Adoption Rule 30.
Domestic relations actions, DomRel Rule 30.

RECORDATION OF PROCEEDINGS —Cont'd

Depositions —Cont'd

Use of expert's videotaped deposition, CivPro Rule 32.

Grand jury proceedings, CrimPro Rule 6.

Discovery of transcripts, CrimPro Rule 16.

Delinquent minors, JuvProc Rule 16.

Interception of wire or oral communications, CrimPro Rule 41-I.

Interpreters, §2-1910.

Probation revocation hearings, CrimPro Rule 32.1.

Superior court proceedings, CivPro Rule 201.

Family division, FamDiv Rule N.

RECORDATION TAX, §§42-1101 to 42-1124.

Appeals, §42-1114.

Appropriations, §42-1124.

Burden of proof as to exemptions, §42-1107.

Carver 2000 low-income and senior housing project.

Exemption, §47-4605.

Collection of taxes, §42-1122.

Conservation easements exempt from, §42-202.

Definitions, §§42-1101, 42-1102.02.

Deposits, §42-1122.

East of the river hospital tax exemptions, §47-4614.

Enforcement of provisions, §42-1108.01.

Exemptions, §§42-1102, 42-1102.01, 42-1107.

Carver 2000 low-income and senior housing project, §47-4605.

Georgia Commons.

Housing and retail elements, §47-4610.

New convention center hotel project deeds, §47-4609.

Extension of time for filing, §42-1103.

Fair market value shown on return, §42-1104.

Fines and penalties.

Stamps, illegal acts relating to, §42-1121.

Fractional amounts, §42-1119.

Fraud and deceit, §42-1121.

RECORDATION TAX —Cont'd

Georgia Commons.

Exemptions.

Housing and retail elements, §47-4610.

Issuance of rules and regulations, §42-1117.

Lack of consideration, §42-1104.

Liability for, §42-1103.

Mayor.

Issuance of rules and regulations, §42-1117.

Mortgages and deeds of trust, §42-1104.

New convention center hotel project deeds.

Exemptions, §47-4609.

Penalties.

Stamps, illegal acts relating to, §42-1121.

Rates, §42-1103.

Secondary market, sale or assignment of instruments on, §42-1102.01.

Severability of provisions, §42-1123.

Stamps and other devices.

Evidence of collection of tax, as, §42-1119.

Fractional devices, elimination of, §42-1119.

Illegal acts regarding, §42-1121.

Transfer of economic interest, §42-1102.02.

Waiver or release, §42-1103.

Whole-dollar rounding, §42-1119.

RECORDER OF DEEDS, §§42-1202 to 42-1218.

Appropriations, §42-1213.

Automation and infrastructure improvement fund, §42-1214.

Collector of taxes, deposit of fees with, §42-1212.

Construction loan for office of, §§10-614 to 10-617.

Advancements authorized, §10-614.

Annual report, §10-617.

Purposes for which advancement used, §10-615.

Repayment of advancements, §10-616.

Electronic recording, §§42-1231 to 42-1235.

Employees of, §42-1202.

Equipment purchases, §§42-1202, 42-1208.

Extension of time for recordation, §42-1217.

RECORDER OF DEEDS —Cont'd

Federal tax liens, §42-1215.

Fees.

Authority of mayor to adjust, §42-1218.

Deposit with collector of taxes, §42-1212.

Federal tax lien recordation, §42-1215.

Schedule of, §42-1210.

Fund for automation and infrastructure improvement, §42-1214.

Hospital lien docket, §40-205.

Liens on motor vehicles and trailers.

Demanding unavailable certificate, §50-1209.

Duties of Recorder, §50-1211.

Mayor, §42-1218.

Military service and discharge certificates, §42-1215.

Milk container registration powers and duties, §36-156.

Public access to records, §42-1206.

Recopying records for preservation purposes, §42-1209.

Saturdays, Sundays, and legal holidays, §§42-1216, 42-1217.

Surcharges, §42-1211.

Taxation.

Recordation tax on deeds, §§42-1101 to 42-1124.

See RECORDATION TAX.

Typewriter purchases and preference for typewritten records, §42-1208.

RECORDING DEVICES.

Motion picture theater, unlawful operation in, §22-3214.02.

RECORDS.

Access to public records, §§2-531 to 2-540.

Real and personal property records, §42-1206.

Administration of estate.

See ADMINISTRATION OF ESTATES.

Adoption, §16-311, Adoption Rules 79, 79-I, FamDiv Rule P.

Alcoholic beverage control board, §25-205.

Alcoholic beverage licenses, §25-773.

Credit sales.

Delivery and payment, §25-733.

Examination of books, records and premises, §25-802.

RECORDS —Cont'd

Alcoholic beverage licenses —Cont'd

Noise restrictions.

Complaints, §25-725.

Alternative fuel technology, §50-703.

Annulment registration, §7-216.

Appeals, D.C. courts.

Record on appeal.

See APPEALS, D.C. COURTS.

Appeals, federal cases.

Availability, USCtApp HPIP Rule II(b)(2).

Electronic public access to information, USCtApp HPIP Rule II(b)(3).

Arbitration hearings, Arbitration Rule IX.

Archives, filing acts and resolutions with, §2-604.

Arrest records.

Sealing records.

See SEALED RECORDS.

Asbestos contractors, §8-111.11.

Assisted living residences.

Resident records, §44-106.06.

Attorneys at law.

Client's property, ProfCond Rule 1.15.

Discipline or disability proceedings, DCBar Rule XI.

Auditor for District of Columbia, §1-204.55.

Authentication of official record.

Adoption proceedings, Adoption Rule 44.

Civil cases, CivPro Rule 44.

Criminal cases, CrimPro Rule 27.

Delinquent minors, JuvProc Rule 27.

Domestic relations actions, DomRel Rule 44.

Bail bondsmen, CrimPro Rule 116.

Records kept by, §23-1108.

Visiting places of detention, §23-1107.

Banks and financial institutions.

International banking corporations, §26-640.

Examination by commissioner, §26-641.

Birth records, §§7-205 to 7-210.

See VITAL RECORDS.

Boiler inspections, §2-112.

Business improvement districts, §2-1215.12.

Business records, CivPro Rule 43-I.

Family court proceedings generally, FamDiv Rule Q.

Cemeteries and cemetery associations, §43-117.

RECORDS —Cont'd

Check cashing businesses, §26-318.
Child abuse and neglect.
   Inspection and disclosure, NeglectProc
      Rule 46.
   Juvenile records. See within this
      heading, "Juvenile records."
   Sealing of records, FamDiv Rule P.
   Forms, FamDiv Forms 2 to 6.
Child and family services agency.
   Privacy and confidentiality,
      §4-1303.06.
   Unauthorized disclosure, §4-1303.07.
Child labor, §§32-202, 32-218.
Collection of taxes, §47-408.
   Account books for, §47-404.
Condominiums, §42-1903.14.
Conservators appointed for
     protection of property, §§21-2064,
   21-2065, 21-2067.
Constitution of the United States.
   Full faith and credit clause, US Const
      Art IV §1.
   Proof, US Const Art IV §1.
Controlled substances, §48-903.06.
Corporations, §§29-313.01 to
   29-313.07.
   See CORPORATIONS.
Correcting errors, CrimPro Rule 36.
Council.
   Fees for reproducing, §1-301.49.
Courts, §§11-1745, 11-1746.
   Custody and removal, USDistCt LCvR
      79.1.
Crime investigation records,
     §§5-113.31 to 5-113.34.
   Definitions, §5-113.31.
   Penalties for willful or malicious
      tampering with records, §5-113.33.
   Records retention schedule, §5-113.34.
   Retention of records and preservation
      of evidence, §5-113.32.
Crime victims' compensation.
   Appeal of determination, VictComp
      Rule 20.
Death registration, §§7-211 to 7-214,
   7-224.
Defacement of public records,
   §22-3307.
Delinquent minors, JuvProc Rule 55.
   Clerical mistakes in judgments,
      orders, etc., JuvProc Rule 36.
   Proof of official record, JuvProc Rule
      27.
   Sealing arrest records, FamDiv Rule P,
      JuvProc Rule 118.
     Forms, FamDiv Forms 2 to 6,
       JuvProc Forms 8 to 10.

RECORDS —Cont'd

Detoxification centers, §24-604.
Disbarment, DCBar Rule XI.
Discrimination, §2-1402.52.
District of Columbia School of Law,
   §38-1205.09.
Divorce registration, §7-216.
Domestic life insurance companies.
   See DOMESTIC LIFE INSURANCE
      COMPANIES.
Domestic partner benefits, §32-708.
Domestic violence, §16-1032.
Electronic transactions, uniform act,
   §§28-4901 to 28-4918.
Employees retirement program
     management, §§1-731 to 1-739.
Employer recordkeeping
     requirements.
   Paid leave, §32-131.10b.
Employment discrimination,
   §2-1402.52.
Evidence, as, §§14-501 to 14-507.
Excluded evidence, CivPro Rule 43.
   Domestic relations actions, DomRel
      Rule 43.
Expungement of official records.
   Arrest records, §§16-801 to 16-807,
      CrimPro Rule 118.
   Alcoholic beverages.
     Children and minors, purchase,
       possession, or consumption
       by, §25-1002.
   Delinquent minors, JuvProc Rule
      118.
   Probation discharge, CrimPro Rule 32.
Family court proceedings generally.
   Business records, FamDiv Rule Q.
   Sealing of records, FamDiv Rule P.
   Forms, FamDiv Forms 2 to 6.
Final votes of agencies, §2-535.
Fire and casualty insurance,
   §31-2502.01.
Firearms dealers, §7-2504.04.
Fire protection study commission,
   §3-1108.
First source employment.
   Modernization of recordkeeping,
      §2-219.04a.
Forgery of public records, §22-3242.
Freedom of information, §§2-531 to
   2-540.
Full faith and credit clause, US
   Const Art IV §1.
Gambling, §22-1714.
Generic drug substitutes, §48-803.05.
Health insurance ratemaking,
   §31-3311.07.

RECORDS —Cont'd

Health maintenance organizations, §31-3425.

Hearing aid dealers.
Customer records required, §28-4005.

Horizontal property regimes, §42-2015.

Horse-drawn carriages, §8-2011.

Hospital liens.
Permission to examine hospital records for purposes of, §40-204.

Identity theft.
Correction of public records, §22-3227.05.

Income taxes, §47-1812.02.

Indictments and informations.
Sealed records, CrimPro Rule 6.

Industrial revenue bond forward commitment program, §47-340.11.

Insurance companies.
See INSURANCE COMPANIES.

Intellectual disabilities, persons with, §7-1305.11.

Interception of oral or wire communications, §§23-549, 23-550, CrimPro Rule 41-I.

Interrogatories.
Option to produce business records, CivPro Rule 33.
Domestic relations actions, DomRel Rule 33.

Jury selection, §11-1914.

Juvenile records, §16-2331.
Absconding juveniles, §16-2333.02.
Case records, §16-2331.
Disclosure, §§16-2331 to 16-2333.02, 16-2336.
Employment, education or housing application.
Juvenile's right to refuse disclosure, §16-2335.
Fingerprints, §16-2334.
Inspections, §§16-2331 to 16-2333.02.
Permitted disclosures, §§16-2331 to 16-2333.02.
Police and other law enforcement records, §16-2333.
Police law enforcement records, §16-2334.
Privacy and confidentiality, §§16-2331 to 16-2333.02.
Sealing of, §16-2335.
Actual innocence, §16-2335.02.
Social records, §16-2332.
Transcripts of proceedings, §16-2329.
Unlawful disclosure, §16-2336.

RECORDS —Cont'd

Landlord and tenant court.
Interview and judgment officer proceedings, LandlordTenant Rule 11-I.

Lead-hazard prevention and elimination, §8-231.13.

Library circulation records, confidentiality of, §39-108.

Life and health insurance guaranty association, §§31-5409, 31-5411.

Living wage act, §2-220.07.

Long-term care ombudsman.
Access to records, §7-703.02.
Privacy and confidentiality, §7-702.06.

Lottery and charitable games control board, §§3-1309, 3-1327.

Marriage registration, §7-215.

Medical examiners, §§5-1410, 5-1412, 5-1413.

Mental health disclosures.
Notation of disclosure in records, §7-1201.04.

Metropolitan police.
See METROPOLITAN POLICE.

Minimum wages, §32-1008.

Money lenders, §§26-904, 26-905.

Mortgage lenders and brokers, §26-1109.

Motor fuel tax, §§47-2305, 47-2307.

Motor vehicle safety responsibility, §§50-1301.05, 50-1301.06.
Certified copy as evidence, §50-1301.05a.

Nonprofit corporations, §§29-413.01 to 29-413.07.
See NONPROFIT CORPORATIONS.

Notaries public, §§1-1211, 1-1212, 1-1215.

Occupational safety and health, §32-1113.

Occupational safety and health for public officers and employees, §1-620.08.

Open meetings, §2-578.

Parentage proceedings, §16-2348.

Parking data, §50-2606.

Pawnbrokers, §§47-2884.07, 47-2884.11.

Pensions and retirement District programs, federal benefit payments under, §1-805.03.

Pensions and retirement funds, §1-909.07.

Personal property records.
Public access, §42-1206.

RECORDS —Cont'd
Personnel files, District employees, §§1-631.01 to 1-631.08.
See MERIT SYSTEM.
Pesticides, §8-409.
Pharmacists and pharmacies, §§3-1210.06a, 47-2885.15.
Pleas in criminal cases, CrimPro Rule 11.
Delinquent minors, JuvProc Rule 11.
Prescription drug pricing, §48-804.03.
Proof of official record, CivPro Rule 44.
Adoption proceedings, Adoption Rule 44.
Criminal cases, CrimPro Rule 27.
Delinquent minors, JuvProc Rule 27.
Domestic relations actions, DomRel Rule 44.
Property and liability insurance guaranty association, §31-5515.
Public assistance, §4-216.01.
Public officers and employees, §§1-631.01 to 1-631.08.
See MERIT SYSTEM.
Public records management, §§2-1701 to 2-1714.
See PUBLIC RECORDS MANAGEMENT.
Public space, public rights of way, and public structures, permits to occupy, §10-1141.05.
Public utilities.
See PUBLIC UTILITIES.
Public welfare institutions, §4-109.
Children and minors, §4-117.
Real property records.
Public access, §42-1206.
Recorder of deeds.
General provisions, §§42-1202 to 42-1218.
See RECORDER OF DEEDS.
Register of wills, §§11-2101 to 11-2106.
Reinsurance intermediary-brokers (RB), §31-1804.
Resocialization furlough program, §24-251.05.
Schools and education.
See SCHOOLS AND EDUCATION.
Sealing records.
See SEALED RECORDS.
State health planning and development agency, §44-405.
Superior court records.
Management of records.
See SUPERIOR COURT.

RECORDS —Cont'd
Surveyor of the District, §§1-1306 to 1-1310.
Tax assessor, §47-601.
Taxation, §§47-502, 47-601.
Examination of books and records, §47-4313.
Time and place, §47-4314.
Liability of taxpayer to maintain records, §47-4311.
Teachers' retirement.
Prior to June 30, 1946, §38-2001.14.
Termination of parental rights, §§16-2363, 16-2364.
Title insurance producers, retention requirements, §31-5041.04.
Title insurers, retention requirements, §31-5031.20.
Tobacco tax, §§47-2408, 47-2418.
Transcripts.
See TRANSCRIPTS.
Trusts and trustees.
Uniform trust code.
Electronic records and signatures, §19-1311.02.
Unclaimed property, §41-130.
Unemployment compensation, §51-117.
Vital records, §§7-201 to 7-228.
See VITAL RECORDS.
Wages and salaries, §32-1306.
Weapons dealers, §22-4510.
Weights and measures, inspections of, §37-201.06.
Workers' compensation, §32-1531.
Workplace fraud.
Employer recordkeeping requirements, §32-1331.12.
Workplace safety, §32-808.
Zoning, §6-641.08.

RECOUPMENT.
Child health care expenses, §1-307.43.
Negotiable instruments.
Claims in recoupment, §28:3-305.
Secured transactions.
Banks and financial institutions.
Security interests in deposit accounts, §28:9-340.

RECREATIONAL FACILITIES.
Smoking, §7-1703.
"No Smoking" signs, §7-1704.

RECREATION AND PARKS, DEPARTMENT OF, §§10-137.01, 10-166, 10-302.

RECREATION ASSISTANCE BOARD.
Rules, §10-307.

RECREATION BOARD, §§10-201 to 10-226.
Board of Education, relationship to, §10-223.
Budget and budget estimates, §10-214.
Community Center and Playgrounds Department, §§10-221, 10-226.
Comprehensive program, development of, §10-213.
Control of lands, buildings, and facilities by, §10-222.
Employees, §10-212.
Establishment of, §10-201.
Expenditures, supervision and direction of, §10-211.
Fees, §10-213.01.
Issuance of rules and regulations by, §10-206.
Leases, §10-213.
Liability, §10-203.
Mayor, relationship to, §10-223.
Meetings of, §10-207.
National Park Service, relationship to, §10-223.
Officers, §10-206.
Organization and membership, §10-202.
Policy determinations by, §10-211.
Reimbursable services arrangements with other agencies, §10-225.
Repair and maintenance, §10-224.
Reports, §10-215.
Superintendent of Recreation, §10-212.
Transfer of funds, §§10-221, 10-224.
Vacancies, filling, §10-204.
Volunteers, §10-212.
Wages and salaries, §10-205.

RECREATION THERAPY.
Board of occupational therapy, §3-1202.06.
Health occupations licensure, registration or certification, §§3-1205.01 to 3-1205.24.
See HEALTH OCCUPATIONS LICENSURE, REGISTRATION OR CERTIFICATION.

RECUSAL OF JUDGE, CJC Canon 2.11, CivPro Rule 63-I.
Adoption proceedings, Adoption Rule 63.

RECUSAL OF JUDGE —Cont'd
Arbitrators, Arbitration Rule IV.
Domestic relations actions, DomRel Rule 63.

RECYCLING.
Carnivals, §47-2826.
Construction and demolition waste recycling accountability, §§8-1071 to 8-1077.
Certification of facilities, §8-1072.
Revocation of certification, §8-1075.
Use of certified facilities required, §8-1073.
Compliance, §8-1073.
Definitions, §8-1071.
Fees to recover costs, §8-1072.
Fine schedule, notice, §8-1076.
Fund, §8-1077.
List of certified facilities on website, §8-1072.
Mayor.
Rules and regulations, §8-1074.
Penalties, §8-1076.
Revocation of certification, §8-1075.
Rules and regulations, §8-1074.
Disposable carryout bags, §8-102.02.
Electronic waste, extended manufacturer responsibility, §§8-1041.01 to 8-1041.12.
See ELECTRONIC WASTE.
Fairs, §47-2826.
Fines.
Fairs and carnivals, §47-2826.
Plastic carryout bags, §8-102.02.
Solid waste management reduction and recovery, §§8-1031.01 to 8-1031.14.
See SOLID WASTE REDUCTION AND RECOVERY.

REDACTED FILINGS.
Privacy protection for filings made with the court, CrimPro Rule 49.1.

RED CROSS.
Real property exempt from taxation, §47-1006.

REDRESS OF GRIEVANCES.
Petition for, US Const Amd 1.

REDUCTION OF SENTENCE.
Application for, §24-401c.

REDUCTIONS IN FORCE.
Public officers and employees, §§1-624.01 to 1-624.24.
See MERIT SYSTEM.

REFEREES.
Masters generally, CivPro Rules 53 to 53-II.
  Domestic relations actions, DomRel Rule 53.

REFERENDUM, §§1-204.101 to 1-204.107.
See INITIATIVE AND REFERENDUM.

REFERRAL SALES.
Consumer credit, §28-3810.

REFERRALS TO ATTORNEY, ProfCond Rule 7.1.

REFRIGERATOR MECHANICS.
Board of industrial trades, §§47-2853.06 to 47-2853.10.
Business licenses, §§47-2853.201 to 47-2853.203.
  Eligibility, §47-2853.202.
  Representations prohibited, §47-2853.203.
  Scope of practice, §47-2853.201.

REFRIGERATORS.
Walk-in refrigerators or freezers.
  Energy efficiency standards.
    General provisions, §§8-1771.01 to 8-1771.06.

REFUNDS.
Assessments for paving and resurfacing streets, §9-421.11.
Assessments held void, §2-403.
Business license fees, §47-2849.
Compensating-use tax, §47-2209.
Fees, unearned, §1-321.03.
Gross sales tax, §§47-2014, 47-2020.
License fees, §47-1318.
Medicare supplement insurance.
  Notice of right to return and refund, §31-3707.
Motor fuel tax, §47-2318.
Police and firefighters retirement and disability, §§5-706, 5-717.
Public utilities refunds, unclaimed, §41-108.
Real property exempt from taxation, §47-1008.
Real property taxes erroneously paid, §47-1317.
Rental of public space, §§10-1102.02, 10-1103.04.
Tax proceedings.
  Erroneously collected tax, §47-3306.
  Overpayments, §47-3310.
Tobacco tax, §47-2412.
Unemployment compensation, §51-108.

REFUNDS —Cont'd
Water supply and waterworks.
  Overpaid assessments, §34-2401.09.
  Rents, erroneous payment of, §34-2401.10.

REGIONAL INTERSTATE BANKING, §§26-702 to 26-714.
Regional bank holding companies.
  Acquisitions, §26-702.
United States branch domestication, §§31-2301 to 31-2307.
Use of women-owned banks, §26-711.

REGIONAL SAVINGS AND LOAN ACQUISITIONS, §26-1202.

REGISTERED AGENT ACT OF 2010, §§29-104.01 to 29-104.14.
See BUSINESS ORGANIZATIONS.

REGISTERED AGENTS, §§29-104.01 to 29-104.14.
See BUSINESS ORGANIZATIONS.

REGISTERED INVESTMENT COMPANIES.
Statutory trusts.
  Independent trustees, §29-1205.12.

REGISTER OF BLIND PERSONS, §§7-901 to 7-904.

REGISTER OF WILLS.
Appointment, qualifications, oath, compensation, §11-2102.
Continuation of office, §11-2101.
Costs and other money collected.
  Turned over to financial officer, §11-2106.
Deputies and other employees, §11-2105.
Fee or other reward for giving advice.
  Prohibited, §11-2104.
Monthly report of, §47-3715.
Powers and duties, §11-2104.
Practice of law prohibited, §11-2104.
Probate proceedings.
  Clerk's duties, performing, §11-2103.
  General provisions, §§11-2101 to 11-2106.
  See WILLS.
  Matters presented to register of wills.
    All proceedings, Probate Rule 2.
    Death between Jan. 1, 1981, and June 30, 1995, Probate Rule 101.
  Powers and duties, §11-2104.

REGISTRATION.
Alcoholic beverages in kegs, §25-753.

REGISTRATION —Cont'd
Annulment registration, §7-216.
Apprentices.
Agreements, §32-1409.
Apprenticeship.
Programs, §32-1431.
Athlete agents, §§47-2887.01 to 47-2887.18.
Beverage bottles, §§36-101, 36-102.
Bicycles, §50-1611.
Blind persons, §§7-901 to 7-904.
Burials, §43-117.
Campaign finance.
Candidate statements, §1-1163.12.
Candidate statements, §1-1163.12.
Cemetery superintendents, §43-118.
Charitable solicitations, §§44-1703, 44-1704.
Child abuse and neglect.
Child-placing agencies required to check enumerated registers for, §4-1407.01.
Compensating-use tax, §47-2212.
Condominiums, §§42-1904.01 to 42-1904.18.
See CONDOMINIUMS.
Constitution of the United States.
Full faith and credit clause, US Const Art IV §1.
Consumer credit service organizations, §28-4602.
Requirements, §28-4602.
Revocation or suspension of registration.
Procedural requirements, §28-4606.
Statement, §28-4602.
Controlled substances.
Dispensers, distributors, manufacturers, §§48-903.01 to 48-903.09.
Dangerous dogs, §8-1904.
Deaths, §§7-211 to 7-214.
Divorce registration, §7-216.
Domestic partnerships, §32-702.
Electronic waste.
Extended manufacturer responsibility, §§8-1041.03, 8-1041.04.
Engineers.
See ENGINEERS.
Fees, authority regarding, §§1-301.74, 1-301.75.
Fiduciary security transfers, §28-2902.
Firearms, §§7-2502.01 to 7-2502.11.
See FIREARMS.
Firing ranges, §7-2507.03.

REGISTRATION —Cont'd
First source employment register, §2-219.02.
Fraudulent registration in lodgings, §22-3224.
Offenses committed in D.C., §22-3224.01.
Full faith and credit clause, US Const Art IV §1.
Gas stations, §36-302.01.
Gross sales tax, §47-2026.
Guardian and ward.
Adult guardianship and protective proceedings jurisdiction act.
Orders from other states, §§21-2404.01 to 21-2404.03.
Health occupations.
See HEALTH OCCUPATIONS LICENSURE, REGISTRATION OR CERTIFICATION.
Hearing aid dealers, §28-4003.
Grounds for revocation and suspension, §28-4006.
Powers and duties of office of consumer protection, §28-4002.
Income taxes, §47-1805.02.
Insurance holding companies, §31-705.
Intellectual disabilities, persons with.
Administration by trained employees of medication to, §21-1203.
Intellectual disabilities, persons with, administration by trained employees of medication to, §21-1206.
Interstate family support.
Registration of support order for enforcement, §§46-356.09 to 46-356.16.
See INTERSTATE FAMILY SUPPORT.
Investment securities.
Assurance that endorsements or instructions are effective, §28:8-402.
Issuers.
Notification to issuer of lost, destroyed or wrongfully taken security certificate, §28:8-406.
Rights with respect to registered owners, §28:8-207.
Purchaser's right to requisites for registration of transfer, §28:8-307.
Replacement of lost, destroyed or wrongfully taken security certificates, §28:8-405.

REGISTRATION —Cont'd

Investment securities —Cont'd

Signature of registrar.

Effect, §28:8-208.

Kegs, §25-753.

Low-level radioactive waste generator regulatory policy, §8-1503.

Marriage registration, §7-215.

Medical and dental colleges, §§38-1401 to 38-1405.

Milk containers, §§36-121 to 36-157.

See MILK CONTAINER REGISTRATION.

Motor fuel tax and International Fuel Tax Agreement, §47-2352.

Motor vehicles.

See MOTOR VEHICLE REGISTRATION.

Out-of-state law enforcement officers, §§5-1201, 5-1302.

Pesticides.

Registered technicians, §8-404.

Registration pesticides, §8-402.

Pharmacists and pharmacies, §3-1210.06.

Pharmacy interns, §47-2885.06.

Purchasing groups, §31-4107.

Rent control, §42-3502.05.

Security agents and brokers, §§31-5603.01 to 31-5603.09.

See SECURITY AGENTS AND BROKERS.

Self-defense sprays, §7-2502.14.

Sex offenders.

General provisions, §§22-4001 to 22-4017.

Solid waste reduction and recovery.

Collector registration, §8-1031.06.

TOD security registration, §§19-603.01 to 19-603.11.

See NONPROBATE TRANSFERS.

Trade names, §§47-2855.01 to 47-2855.05.

Underground storage tanks, §§8-113.06, 8-113.07.

Vacant buildings, §§42-3131.05 to 42-3131.17.

See VACANT BUILDINGS.

Vital records.

See VITAL RECORDS.

Voting by military and overseas voters, §1-1061.05.

Methods, §1-1061.06.

Wills, §§11-2101 to 11-2106.

REGISTRY OF THE COURT.

Disbursements from, CivPro Form CA 118.

REHABILITATION OF BUILDINGS.

Building rehabilitation code, §6-1410.

Advisory council, §6-1411.

REHABILITATION OF INSURERS.

Captive insurance companies.

Special purpose financial captive insurance companies, §31-3932.12.

Insurers rehabilitation and liquidation proceedings, §§31-1301 to 31-1357.

See INSURERS REHABILITATION AND LIQUIDATION PROCEEDINGS.

REHABILITATION SERVICES PROGRAM.

Grant and contract authority, §32-331.01.

Individuals with disabilities.

Establishment, §32-331.

Rulemaking to implement, §32-332.

REINSURANCE.

Captive insurance companies, §31-3931.08.

Special purpose financial captive insurance companies, §31-3932.11.

Credit for, §§31-501 to 31-503.

Allowed domestic ceding insurer, §31-501.

Qualified United States financial institutions, §31-503.

Reduction from liability.

Reinsurance ceded by domestic insurer to assuming insurer, §31-502.

Fraternal benefit societies, §31-5310.

REINSURANCE INTERMEDIARIES, §§31-1801 to 31-1810.

Definitions, §31-1801.

Examinations, §31-1809.

Fines, §31-1810.

Liabilities, §31-1810.

Licenses, §31-1802.

Reinsurance intermediary-brokers (RB).

Books and records, §31-1804.

Contract provision requirements, §31-1803.

Defined, §31-1801.

Duties of insurers using, §31-1805.

REINSURANCE INTERMEDIARIES
—Cont'd
Reinsurance intermediary-managers (RM).
Contract provision requirements, §31-1806.
Defined, §31-1801.
Duties of reinsurers using, §31-1808.
Prohibited acts, §31-1807.

RELEASE IN CRIMINAL CASES.
Appeals in federal cases, FRAP 9, 22, 23, USCtApp Rule 9.
Record for preliminary hearing in court of appeals, FRAP 11(g).

RELEASE OF HAZARDOUS SUBSTANCES.
Liability, cleanup, response, §§8-631.01 to 8-638.01.
See HAZARDOUS SUBSTANCES RELEASES.

RELEVANCY.
Discovery scope and limits, CivPro Rule 26.

RELIGION, MINISTERS OF.
Constitution of the United States.
Jurisdiction of actions affecting, US Const Art III §2.
False personation, §22-1404.
Health occupations.
Exemption of clergy from chapter provisions, §3-1201.03.
Interception of wire and oral communications.
Interception of communications of practicing clergymen, §23-547.
Militia.
Exemption from service, §49-402.
Real property tax.
Exemption of pastoral residences from tax, §47-1002.
Solemnization of marriage.
Failure to return certificate, §46-413.
Generally, §46-406.
Witnesses, §14-309.

RELIGIOUS BELIEFS.
Children treated solely by spiritual means, §4-1321.06.
Communicable diseases, persons relying on spiritual means to cure, §7-141.
Do not resuscitate procedures.
Comfort care orders.
Religious or moral reasons person unwilling or unable to comply, §7-651.11.

RELIGIOUS BELIEFS —Cont'd
Immunization for school students.
Exemption from certification, §38-506.
Intellectual disabilities, persons with.
Right to practice religious beliefs, §7-1305.05.
Psychotropic medication.
Refusal to consent for valid religious reasons, §7-1305.06b.
Marriage.
Solemnization, §46-406.
Prohibition of discrimination based on, §2-1401.01.
Reasonable accommodation by employers.
General provisions, §2-1402.11.
Public officers and employees, §1-607.01.
Religious tests, US Const Art VI.
Student health care, §38-603.

RELIGIOUS CORPORATIONS, §29-401.40.

RELIGIOUS INSTITUTIONS.
Acts relation to governing bodies of, §45-403.
Appropriations, §44-715.
Real property.
Exempt from taxation, §47-1002.
See REAL PROPERTY TAX EXEMPTIONS.
Wastewater and sewage works, §34-2111.

RELIGIOUS SYMBOLS.
Defacing or burning, §22-3312.02.

RELOCATION.
See MOVING AND RELOCATION.

REMAINDERS.
Landlord and tenant, §42-3231.

REMANDS.
Appeals, federal cases, USCtApp Rule 41.
Calendar.
Scheduling of cases.
Cases on remand to this court, USCtApp HPIP Rule X(e)(3).
Motions for remand, USCtApp HPIP Rule VIII(e).
Terminating case, USCtApp HPIP Rule XIII(a)(3).

RENAL DIALYSIS FACILITIES.
Criminal background checks for unlicensed personnel, §§44-551 to 44-554.

RENAL DIALYSIS FACILITIES
—Cont'd
Licenses, §§44-501 to 44-509.

**RENEWABLE ENERGY PORTFOLIO
STANDARDS,** §§34-1431 to
34-1439.
Applicable to electricity sales,
§34-1432.
Commission to implement, §34-1432.
Compliance fee.
Failure to file compliance report,
§34-1434.
**Compliance report by electricity
suppliers,** §34-1434.
**Cost recovery by distribution
company,** §34-1435.
Definitions, §§34-1431, 34-1440.
**Energy from tier one renewable
source.**
Renewable energy credits, §34-1433.
**Energy from tier two renewable
source.**
Renewable energy credits, §34-1433.
Energy portfolio reports, §34-1434.
Generally, §34-1432.
**Home improvement financing for
solar or renewable energy,**
§8-1774.13.
Meeting standard.
Renewable energy credits, §§34-1432,
34-1433.
Pass through of costs incurred,
§34-1435.
Renewable energy credits, §34-1433.
Compliance, submission as evidence of,
§34-1438.
Diminished or extinguished, §34-1439.
Period of existence, §34-1438.
Sale or transfer, §34-1438.
Standard met by obtaining, §34-1432.
**Renewable energy development
fund,** §34-1436.
Renewable energy study, §8-1775.01.
Renewable energy tracking system,
§34-1437.
**Rules, duties and powers of
commission,** §34-1439.
Solar generation goals, reporting on,
§34-1434.
Solar system standards, §34-1432.
Tier two renewable source.
Defined, §34-1431.
RENT.
Arrears.
Claims for, §42-3211.

RENT —Cont'd
Arrears —Cont'd
Consolidation of actions for possession
and, §42-3212.
Life lease or demise for life, §42-3220.
Distress for, §42-3217.
Ejectment.
Damages, recovery of, §§16-1109 to
16-1112, 16-1116 to 16-1120.
Nonpayment of rent, §16-1124.
Fraud and deceit to defeat lien,
§42-3218.
Landlord and tenant, generally,
§§42-3201 to 42-3232, 42-3501.01 to
42-3509.08.
See LANDLORD AND TENANT.
Liens for, §§42-3213 to 42-3218.
**Metropolitan police housing
assistance and community safety
program,** §§42-2901 to 42-2903.
Rent supplement program, §6-226.
Capital-based assistance, §6-229.
Tenant-based assistance, §6-228.
Voucher assistance, §6-227.
Tenant assistance program,
§§42-3503.01 to 42-3503.08.
See LANDLORD AND TENANT.
Under-tenant of life tenant, §42-3219.
Water supply and waterworks,
§34-2401.07.

RENTAL BICYCLES.
Information on rental forms,
§50-1612.

RENTAL HOUSING.
**Access to dwelling unit by housing
provider,** §42-3505.51.
**Arbitration to resolve disputes
arising between housing
providers and tenants.**
Conciliation and arbitration service,
§42-3505.03.
Disputes not settled by conciliation
and arbitration service,
§42-3505.04.
Conversion on sale, §§42-3401.01 to
42-3405.13.
Actions, §42-3405.03.
Declaratory relief, §42-3405.03a.
Forum and standard of review,
§42-3405.03b.
Administrative proceedings,
§42-3405.08.
Aged tenants, §42-3402.08.
Appeals, §42-3405.09.
Applicability of Rental Housing Act of
1985, §42-3401.04.

RENTAL HOUSING —Cont'd
Conversion on sale —Cont'd
Certification of compliance with
provisions, §42-3402.02.
Continuing housing crisis, annual
declaration of, §42-3405.12.
Conversion procedures, §§42-3402.01
to 42-3402.11.
Cooperative conversions, §42-3402.06.
Definitions, §§42-3401.03, 42-3402.04,
42-3404.02.
Enforcement of provisions,
§42-3405.06.
Exceptions to provisions, §§42-3402.10,
42-3404.12.
Exemption from provisions,
§42-3402.02.
Expiration of provisions, §§42-3402.10,
42-3403.09, 42-3404.12.
Fees.
    Application fees, §42-3402.05a.
    Certification fees, §42-3402.05.
    Conversion fees, §42-3402.04.
Fines, §42-3405.10.
Forum, §§42-3405.03a, 42-3405.03b.
Impairment, tenants with,
§42-3402.08.
Interpretation of provisions,
§42-3405.11.
Investigations, §42-3405.05.
Issuance of rules and regulations,
§42-3405.01.
Lodging places, conversion of rental
housing into, §42-3506.01.
Notice.
    Conversion or offer of sale,
        §42-3404.13.
    Rejection of parties, §42-3405.04.
    Revocations, §42-3405.07.
    Time certain notices, §42-3404.02.
Opportunity of District to purchase,
§§42-3404.31 to 42-3404.37.
    Assignment of right to purchase,
        §§42-3404.31, 42-3404.36.
    Exercise of right to purchase,
        §42-3404.34.
    Five or more units, accommodations
        with, §42-3404.31.
    Limitations on District as owner
        after completion of purchase,
        §42-3404.33.
    Limitations on opportunity to
        purchase, §42-3404.32.
    Negotiation of contract, §42-3404.34.
    Rules, §42-3404.37.
    Tenant rights, §42-3404.35.

RENTAL HOUSING —Cont'd
Conversion on sale —Cont'd
Opportunity of tenant to purchase,
§§42-3404.02 to 42-3404.13.
    Assignment of right to purchase,
        §42-3404.06.
    Contract negotiations for sales,
        §42-3404.05.
    Definitions, §42-3404.02.
    Exceptions to provisions,
        §42-3404.12.
    Exercise of right to purchase,
        §42-3404.06.
    Expiration of provisions,
        §42-3404.12.
    First refusal, right of, §42-3404.08.
    Five or more units, accommodations
        with, §42-3404.11.
        Registration of tenant
            organization, §42-3404.02a.
    Intent to file petition, notice of,
        §42-3404.02.
    Notice.
        Conversion or offer of sale,
            §42-3404.13.
        Time certain notices, §42-3404.02.
    Offer of sale, §§42-3404.03,
        42-3404.13.
    Sale procedures, §§42-3404.02 to
        42-3404.13.
    Single-family residences,
        §42-3404.09.
    Third party rights in sale
        procedures, §42-3404.04.
    Transfer, notice of, §42-3404.02.
    Two to four units, accommodations
        with, §42-3404.10.
    Waiver of right to purchase,
        §42-3404.07.
Penalties, §42-3405.10.
Policy declaration, §§42-3401.01,
42-3401.02.
Prerequisites to conversion,
§42-3402.02.
Publications, §42-3405.01.
Public information and educational
programs, §42-3403.08.
Real property tax abatement,
§42-3402.09.
Rejection of parties, §42-3405.04.
Relocation assistance, §§42-3403.01 to
42-3403.09.
Retroactive conversion, §42-3402.11.
Revocations, §42-3405.07.
Severability of provisions, §42-3405.13.
Short title, §42-3402.01.

RENTAL HOUSING —Cont'd
Conversion on sale —Cont'd
Task force, §42-3405.10a.
Tenant election to convert,
§42-3402.03.
Tenant rights to relocation assistance,
§42-3403.06.
TOPA application assistance pilot
program, §42-3404.14.
Weekends, time periods ending on,
§42-3405.02.
Death of tenant.
Proceedings to discover, §§16-1151 to
16-1158.
See LIFE ESTATES.
Discrimination.
Elderly residents and families with
children, §42-3505.05.
**Drug, firearm, or prostitution-
related nuisance abatement,**
§§42-3101 to 42-3114.
See CRIME-RELATED NUISANCE
ABATEMENT.
Drug-related evictions, §§42-3601 to
42-3610.
See DRUG-RELATED EVICTIONS.
Ejectment.
Generally, §§16-1101 to 16-1124.
See EJECTMENT.
Elderly tenant.
Discrimination against prohibited,
§42-3505.05.
Emergency access.
Access to dwelling unit by housing
provider, §42-3505.51.
Evictions.
Drug-related evictions, §§42-3601 to
42-3610.
See DRUG-RELATED EVICTIONS.
Forcible entry and detainer, §§16-1501
to 16-1505.
Generally.
See EVICTIONS.
Retaliatory evictions.
See LANDLORD AND TENANT.
Forcible entry and detainer,
§§16-1501 to 16-1505.
Housing code violation by tenant.
Access by housing provider to dwelling
unit, §42-3505.51.
Landlord and tenant.
General provisions, §§42-3201 to
42-3232, 42-3501.01 to 42-3509.08.
See LANDLORD AND TENANT.
**Master-metered apartment
buildings,** §§42-3301 to 42-3307.
See PUBLIC UTILITIES.

RENTAL HOUSING —Cont'd
Office of tenant advocate,
§§42-3531.01 to 42-3531.10.
**Reasonable notice, reasonable
purpose, reasonable time.**
Access to dwelling unit by housing
provider, §42-3505.51.
Rental housing locators.
Consumer protection provisions,
§28-3819.
Rent stabilization program,
§§42-3502.01 to 42-3502.23.
See RENT CONTROL.
Rent supplement program, §6-226.
Capital-based assistance, §6-229.
Tenant-based assistance, §6-228.
Voucher assistance, §6-227.
**Resolution of disputes arising
between housing providers and
tenants.**
Conciliation and arbitration service,
§42-3505.03.
Arbitration of disputes not settled
by conciliation and arbitration
service, §42-3505.04.
**Retaliation against tenant
exercising rights,** §42-3505.02.
Sunset provision.
Rental housing act, §42-3509.07.
Tenant organizations, §42-3505.06.
Tenant receivership.
Safety, health or security threatened,
§§42-3651.01 to 42-3651.08.
Violation threatening tenants health,
safety or security, §§42-3651.01 to
42-3651.08.
Final account, §42-3651.07.
Grounds for appointment,
§42-3651.02.
Notice and hearing requirements,
§42-3651.04.
Petition, §42-3651.03.
Powers and duties of receiver,
§42-3651.05.
Purpose of receivership,
§42-3651.01.
Termination, §42-3651.06.

RENTAL OF AIRSPACE, §§10-1121.01
to 10-1121.13.
**Airspace and structures deemed real
property for purposes of
taxation, water and sewer
charges,** §10-1121.07.
Applicability of provisions,
§10-1121.06.
Definitions, §10-1121.01.

RENTAL OF AIRSPACE —Cont'd
Deposits of rents and charges collected, §10-1121.08.
Exempted areas, §10-1121.13.
Expiration or termination of lease, §10-1121.09.
Federal and District construction of airspace structures without rental, §10-1121.11.
Fines, §10-1121.10.
Issuance of rules and regulations, §10-1121.10.
Mayor's authority as to use of airspace, §10-1121.02.
Recovery of use of leased airspace, §10-1121.12.
Removal or relocation of public or private facilities, §10-1121.05.
Requirements for execution of leases, §10-1121.04.
Taxation, §10-1121.08.
Terms and conditions required in leases, §10-1121.03.
Zoning, §10-1121.06.

RENTAL OF PUBLIC SPACE, §§10-1101.01 to 10-1104.08.
Below ground space, §§10-1103.01 to 10-1103.09.
Collection of payments, §§10-1103.02, 10-1103.07.
Definitions, §10-1101.01.
Failure to make payments, §10-1103.07.
Fee waiver, §10-1102.02a.
Fines, §10-1104.04.
Governments, not applicable to, §10-1101.02.
Insurance requirements, §10-1104.02.
Issuance of rules and regulations, §10-1104.01.
Minor use without payment, §10-1101.03.
On or above ground surface, §10-1102.01.
Overpayments, §10-1103.04a.
Payments, §§10-1102.02, 10-1103.04.
Fee waiver, §10-1102.02a.
Penalties, §10-1104.03.
Public structures in public space, §§10-1141.01 to 10-1141.07.
Definitions, §10-1141.01.
Enforcement, §10-1141.07.
Inapplicability, §10-1141.02.
Inspection and audit of books and records, §10-1141.05.

RENTAL OF PUBLIC SPACE
—Cont'd
Public structures in public space
—Cont'd
Obstructing sidewalk or other pedestrian or bicycle path, §§10-1141.03, 10-1141.04.
Permits for occupation of space, rights of way, public structures, §10-1141.03.
Waiver of reduction of permit fees, §10-1141.04.
Rules, §10-1141.04.
Surcharge authorization, §10-1141.06.
Refunds, §§10-1102.02, 10-1103.04.
Service of process, §10-1104.03.
Street festival one day rental, §10-1102.01a.
Subchapter not to affect former section 9-113.04, §10-1104.08.
Subsurface space, §§10-1103.01 to 10-1103.09.
Annual payment of rent, refunds, §10-1103.04.
Assessment and collection of rent for vault located on public property, §§10-1103.02, 10-1103.07.
Exemption of vault abutting single or two-family dwellings, §10-1103.09.
Failure to pay rent, §10-1103.07.
Overpayment, §10-1103.04a.
Permit for use of vault, §10-1103.01.
Removal of vault, §§10-1103.05, 10-1103.06.
Rent fixed by council, waiver, §10-1103.03.
Use of vault for utility installation or construction, §10-1103.08.
Taxation, §10-1103.07.
Underground space, §§10-1103.01 to 10-1103.09.
Use of property, §10-1102.03.
Vaults, §§10-1103.01 to 10-1103.09.
See VAULTS.

RENTAL PROPERTY.
Building code.
General provisions, §§6-501 to 6-919.
See BUILDING CODE.
Construction codes.
General provisions, §§6-1401 to 6-1409.
See CONSTRUCTION CODES.
Death of tenant.
Proceedings to discover, §§16-1151 to 16-1158.
See LIFE ESTATES.

RENTAL PROPERTY —Cont'd

District of Columbia housing authority.
General provisions, §§6-201 to 6-229.
See DISTRICT OF COLUMBIA HOUSING AUTHORITY.

Drug, firearm, or prostitution-related nuisance abatement, §§42-3101 to 42-3114.
See CRIME-RELATED NUISANCE ABATEMENT.

Drug-related evictions, §§42-3601 to 42-3610.
See DRUG-RELATED EVICTIONS.

Ejectment.
Generally, §§16-1101 to 16-1124.
See EJECTMENT.

Height of buildings, §§6-601.05 to 6-611.02.
See BUILDING CODE.

Landlord and tenant, §§42-3501.01 to 42-3509.08.
See LANDLORD AND TENANT.

Master-metered apartment buildings.
General provisions, §§42-3301 to 42-3307.
See PUBLIC UTILITIES.

Rental housing act, §§42-3501.01 to 42-3509.08.
See LANDLORD AND TENANT.

Rental housing conversion and sale.
General provisions, §§42-3401.01 to 42-3405.13.
See RENTAL HOUSING.

Rent stabilization program, §§42-3502.01 to 42-3502.23.
See RENT CONTROL.

Rent supplement program, §6-226.
Capital-based assistance, §6-229.
Tenant-based assistance, §6-228.
Voucher assistance, §6-227.

Residential drug-related evictions, §§42-3601 to 42-3610.
See DRUG-RELATED EVICTIONS.

Smoke detectors, §§6-751.01, 6-751.02.
See SMOKE DETECTORS.

RENTAL VEHICLES.

Business licenses, §47-2830.

Commercial code leases.
Generally, §§28:2A-101 to 28:2A-532.
See LEASES, UCC.

Compensating-use tax, §47-2202.01.

Crime victims' compensation,
VictComp Rule 33.

Discriminatory practices, §2-1402.72.

RENTAL VEHICLES —Cont'd

Gross sales tax, §47-2002.02.
Rate of tax on rental or leasing of vehicles, §47-2002.

Seat belts.
Child restraint seats, §50-1703.

Tax on, §§50-1505.01 to 50-1505.04.
See MOTOR VEHICLE REGISTRATION.

RENT CONTROL, §§42-3502.01 to 42-3502.23.

Abolition of rent ceilings, §42-3502.06.

Actions.
Tenant organization.
Right to assert claim in name of member, §42-3502.16a.

Adjustments, §§42-3502.06, 42-3502.16.

Aged persons, §§42-3502.06, 42-3502.08.

Appeals, §42-3502.19.

Applicability of provisions, §42-3502.05.

Attorneys' fees and costs, §42-3509.02.

Base rent, increases above, §42-3502.08.

Calculating rent charged, §42-3502.06.

Capital improvements.
Increase above base rent for, §42-3502.08.
Petition for, §42-3502.10.

Certificate of assurance issued with building permits, §42-3502.21.

Covered units, §42-3502.05.

Database.
Public accessible rent control housing clearinghouse, §42-3502.03c.

Definitions, §42-3501.01.

Disallowance in rent increase, circumstances leading to, §42-3502.05.

Disclosures to tenants, §42-3502.22.
New tenancies, §42-3502.13.

Exemptions, §§42-3502.05, 42-3502.09.

Facilities, increase or decrease in, §42-3502.11.

Fines, §42-3509.01.

Fraud and deceit, §42-3509.01.

Hardship petitions, §§42-3502.06, 42-3502.12.

Home and community-based services waiver provider.
Defined, §42-3501.03.

Housing finance agency projects exempt from, §42-2703.08.

RENT CONTROL —Cont'd

Newly covered units, rent charged for, §42-3502.09.

New tenancies.

Disclosures to tenant, §§42-3502.13, 42-3502.22.

Notice.

Adjustment procedure, §42-3502.16.

Housing provider to provide notice of certain events to rent administrator, §42-3502.05.

Persons with disabilities, §§42-3502.06, 42-3502.08.

Petition for adjustment, §42-3502.16.

Public accessible rent control housing clearinghouse, §42-3502.03c.

Registration, §42-3502.05.

Remedies, §42-3502.18.

Rent administrator, §42-3502.03.

Appointment and removal, §42-3502.03a.

Duties generally, §42-3502.04.

Qualifications and compensation, §42-3502.03b.

Rental accommodations and rental conversions and sales, §§42-3502.03, 42-3502.04a.

Housing regulation administrator, §42-3502.04c.

Transfer of functions to housing and community development department, §42-3502.04b.

Rental housing commission, §§42-3502.01 to 42-3502.02a.

Compensation of chairperson, §42-3502.01.

Continuation, §42-3502.01.

Immunity from liability for performance of official acts, §42-3502.02a.

Members, §42-3502.01.

Powers and duties, §42-3502.02.

Reports, §42-3502.20.

Comprehensive housing strategy report, §42-3502.23.

Security deposits, §42-3502.17.

Services, increase or decrease in, §42-3502.11.

Substantial rehabilitation, §§42-3501.03, 42-3502.14.

Tenant organization.

Right to assert claim in name of member, §42-3502.16a.

Termination for exemption from rent charged, §42-3502.09.

RENT CONTROL —Cont'd

Vacancies, §42-3502.13.

Voluntary agreements between tenants and housing provider, §42-3502.15.

RENTER'S INSURANCE.

Fire and casualty insurance generally, §§31-2501.01 to 31-2502.42.

RENT STABILIZATION PROGRAM, §§42-3502.01 to 42-3502.23.

See RENT CONTROL.

RENT SUPPLEMENT PROGRAM, §6-226.

Tenant-based assistance, §6-228.

Voucher assistance, §6-227.

RENT-TO-OWN.

Lease-purchase agreements, §§42-3671.01 to 42-3671.14.

See LEASE-PURCHASE AGREEMENTS.

Leases.

Commercial code leases, §§28:2A-101 to 28:2A-532.

See LEASES, UCC.

REORGANIZATION OF DISTRICT OF COLUMBIA GOVERNMENT, §§1-315.01 to 1-315.07.

Content and format of reorganization plan, §1-315.05.

Definitions, §1-315.02.

Process of reorganization, §1-315.03.

Effective date of reorganization plan, §1-315.04.

Government organization chart.

Transmittal, §1-315.06.

Motor vehicle safety responsibility provisions, effect on, §50-1301.81.

Preparation and transmittal of reorganization plan, §1-315.04.

Process of reorganization defined, §1-315.03.

Publication of reorganization plan, §1-315.04.

Purposes, §1-315.01.

Report on boards and commissions, §1-315.07.

REORGANIZATION PLANS BY YEAR.

1975.

Plan 2, Department of Transportation, Title 1 Ch 15 Subch I Pt A.

Plan 3, Department of Housing and Community Development, Title 1 Ch 15 Subch I Pt B.

REORGANIZATION PLANS BY
    YEAR —Cont'd
1978.
  Plan 1, Department of Labor, Title 1
    Ch 15 Subch II Pt A.
1979.
  Plan 2, Department of Human
    Services, Title 1 Ch 15 Subch III
    Pt A.
1980.
  Plan 1, Department of Employment
    Services, Title 1 Ch 15 Subch IV
    Pt A.
  Plan 3, employee health, safety and
    compensation, Title 1 Ch 15 Subch
    IV Pt B.
1982.
  Plan 1, Building and Zoning
    Regulation Administration, Title 1
    Ch 15 Subch V Pt A.
  Plan 2, Office of the Surveyor, Title 1
    Ch 15 Subch V Pt B.
1983.
  Plan 1, Department of Consumer and
    Regulatory Affairs, Title 1 Ch 15
    Subch VI Pt A.
  Plan 2, motor vehicle registration
    process consolidation, Title 1 Ch
    15 Subch VI Pt B.
  Plan 3, Recorder of Deeds, Title 1 Ch
    15 Subch VI Pt C.
  Plan 4, Department of Public Works,
    Title 1 Ch 15 Subch VI Pt D.
  Plan 5, Department of Administrative
    Services, Title 1 Ch 15 Subch VI
    Pt E.
1986.
  Plan 2, Board of Parole, Title 1 Ch 15
    Subch VII Pt A.
  Plan 3, Department of Human
    Services, Title 1 Ch 15 Subch VII
    Pt B.
1987.
  Plan 1, Department of Public and
    Assisted Housing, Title 1 Ch 15
    Subch VIII Pt A.
  Plan 2, issuance of grants under water
    pollution control act, Title 1 Ch 15
    Subch VIII Pt B.
1988.
  Plan 4, consolidation of functions with
    Metropolitan Police Department,
    Title 1 Ch 15 Subch IX Pt B.
1989.
  Plan 1, Department of Human Rights
    and Minority Business
    Development, Title 1 Ch 15 Subch
    X Pt A.

REORGANIZATION PLANS BY
    YEAR —Cont'd
1992.
  Plan 1, Unclaimed Property Unit
    within executive branch, Title 1
    Ch 15 Subch XI Pt A.
  Plan 2, Office of Tourism and
    Promotions, Title 1 Ch 15 Subch
    XI Pt B.
  Plan 3, Office of Banking and
    Financial Institutions, Title 1 Ch
    15 Subch XI Pt C.
1993.
  Plan 2, Office of the Assistant City
    Administrator for Human
    Resources Development, Title 1
    Ch 15 Subch XII Pt A.
  Plan 3, weatherization assistance
    program transferred to Energy
    Office, Title 1 Ch 15 Subch XII Pt
    B.
  Plan 4, Office of Economic
    Development, transfer of functions
    to, Title 1 Ch 15 Subch XII Pt C.
1995.
  Plan 1, Department of Corrections,
    consolidation of psychiatric
    services, Title 1 Ch 15 Subch XIII
    Pt A.
  Plan 2, transfer to Mayor of certain
    authority vested in Department of
    Human Services, Title 1 Ch 15
    Subch XIII Pt B.
1996.
  Plan 4, Department of Health, Title 1
    Ch 15 Subch XIV Pt A.
  Plan 7, Office of International Affairs,
    Title 1 Ch 15 Subch XIV Pt B.
1998.
  Plan 1, Office of Corporation Counsel
    and Department of Human
    Services, Title 1 Ch 15 Subch XV
    Pt A.
  Plan 5, Department of Human
    Services, Title 1 Ch 15 Subch XV
    Pt B.
2000.
  Historical preservation, reorganization
    2000, Title 1 Ch 15 Subch XVI Pt
    A.
2002.
  Plan 2, motor vehicle sales finance
    company, Title 1 Ch 15 Subch
    XVII Pt A.
2003.
  Plan 1, Office of Risk Management,
    Title 1 Ch 15 Subch XVIII Pt A.

REPAIR AND MAINTENANCE.
Aged persons, home repair and
improvement program fund for,
§§42-2201 to 42-2207.
Alleys, §9-401.06.
Armory, §3-303.
Bathing pools and beaches, §10-162.
Charter schools, §38-1802.09.
Condominiums.
General provisions, §42-1903.07.
Horizontal property regimes.
See HORIZONTAL PROPERTY
REGIMES.
Dulles International Airport, §§9-801,
9-804.
Electric conduits, permits to repair,
extend, or enlarge, §34-1406.
Firefighting apparatus, §5-413.
Garage keepers' liens for storage,
repairs, and supplies for motor
vehicles, §40-102.
Highways, §9-101.01.
Highway workers, §47-209.
Horizontal property regimes.
Access to units for repairs, §42-2008.
Mandatory contribution to, §42-2016.
Insanitary buildings, repair or
demolition of, §6-907.
Lighting outside city limits,
§1-305.03.
Metropolitan Washington Airports
Authority, §9-1005.
Metrorail and metrobus services
and equipment.
Fines and penalties for insufficiency of,
§35-202.
Motor vehicle repair business
license, §47-2832.
Motor vehicles of District.
Working fund for repair and
maintenance of, §47-134.
Parking facilities, §50-2603.
Parks and recreation, §10-224.
Prisons, §24-201.23.
Public assistance for home repairs,
§4-211.01.
Public buildings, §§10-702, 10-703.
Public records maintenance, §2-1706.
Public utilities commission orders
for repairs, improvements, and
services, §34-808.
Public works, §9-401.01.
Railroads contributing to cost of
repairing streets, §9-1203.07.
Recreation board, §10-224.
School buildings and grounds.
See SCHOOL BUILDINGS AND
GROUNDS.

REPAIR AND MAINTENANCE
—Cont'd
Senior citizens' home repair and
improvement program fund,
§§42-2201 to 42-2207.
See HOUSING.
Sewer maintenance workers,
§47-208.
Sewers, §1-305.01.
Sidewalks, §9-401.06.
Street lighting, §§9-501, 9-506.
Streets and alleys, §50-2603.
Public contracts for, §9-401.16.
Railroads contributing to cost of
repairing streets, §9-1203.07.
Telegraph and telephone companies.
Overhead wires, §§34-1911.06,
34-1921.06.
Poles, §§34-1911.04, 34-1911.06,
34-1921.06.
Theodore Roosevelt Island, §10-158.
Wastewater and sewage works,
§34-2109.
Wastewater treatment systems,
§8-205.
Water and sewer authority
operation and maintenance
account, §34-2202.41.

REPARATION.
Criminal procedure requiring,
§§16-711, 16-711.01.

REPLEVIN, §§15-524, 16-3701 to
16-3713, CivPro Rule 64-II.
Affidavit, §16-3703.
Attachments, §16-517.
Attorneys' fees and costs, §16-3701.
Bonds, surety, §16-3708.
Complaint of, §16-3702.
Damages, §§16-3710 to 16-3713.
Determination and measure of
plaintiff's damages, §16-3710.
Judgment for defendant and
determination of damages,
§16-3711.
Judgment where good eloigned,
§16-3713.
Verdict where good eloigned, §16-3712.
Defaults, §16-3707.
Demand prior to action, §16-3701.
Domestic relations actions, DomRel
Rule 64.
Eloignment, §§16-3712, 16-3713.
Form of order, CivPro Form CA 108.
Judgment for defendant and
determination of damages,
§16-3711.

REPLEVIN —Cont'd

Judgment where good eloigned, §16-3713.

Leases, UCC.
Replevy of goods, §§28:2A-508, 28:2A-521.

Motion for return of property, §16-3708.

Notice, §16-3709.

Possession of goods, officer's failure to obtain, §16-3705.

Publication against defendant, §16-3706.

Sales, UCC.
Buyer's right, §28:2-716.

Undertaking to abide by judgment of court on, §16-3704.

REPORTS.

Access to justice program, §4-1702.02.

Adoption of children, §16-307.

Adoption proceedings, Adoption Rule 7.
Physical or mental examination of person, Adoption Rule 35.

Adult literacy, §38-192.01.

Adult protective services, §§7-1903, 7-1913.

Advisory neighborhood commission, §1-309.13.

Aged persons, Volunteer Service Credit Program for, §§7-531.01 to 7-531.11.

Alcoholic beverage control board, §25-205.

Alcoholic beverage licenses, §25-771.
Incident reports, §25-804.

Alternative fuel technology, §§50-703, 50-704.01.

American Recovery and Reinvestment Act of 2009, grants under, §2-219.51.

Appeals, federal cases.
Statement of evidence or proceedings when no report made or transcript unavailable, FRAP 10(c).

Apprentices, §32-1404.

Armory board, §3-310.

Arson, §5-417.

Attachment of wages after judgment, CivPro Rule 69-II.

Attorney discipline or disability proceedings, DCBar Rule XI.
Misconduct by other attorney, ProfCond Rule 8.3.

REPORTS —Cont'd

Attorney general for District of Columbia.
Challenges to statutes, rule, regulation, program or policy, §1-301.89a.

Auditor for District of Columbia, §1-204.55.

Banks and financial institutions, §§26-101, 26-103.
Financial reports, §26-551.11.
International banking corporations, §26-640.

Benefit corporations.
Annual benefit report, §29-1304.01.

Bicycle parking.
District government buildings.
Mayor's report regarding parking at, §50-1641.04.

Blind persons, registration of, §§7-902, 7-904.

Boards and commissions, report on, §1-315.07.

BOOT CAMP, §24-932.

Budget monitoring committee, §47-319.04.

Building associations, §26-204.

Bullying, §2-1535.07.

Business improvement districts, §2-1215.13.

Business incubator facilitation, §2-1209.14.

Cable television operators, §34-1259.09.

Campaign finance, §1-1163.13.
Committees, §1-1163.09.
Receipts and expenditures, §1-1163.17.
Legal defense, §§1-1163.31, 1-1163.32.

Capital access program.
Financial institution reports, §2-1210.09.
Mayor's status report, §2-1210.10.

Captive insurance companies.
Annual report, §31-3931.13.

Certified business enterprises.
Agency reporting requirements, §2-218.53.

Charitable institutions, §§44-709, 44-710.

Charitable solicitations, §44-1706.

Charter schools.
Reports.
Annual report, §38-1802.04.

Chief financial officer.
Comprehensive annual financial report, §47-310.02.

REPORTS —Cont'd
Chief financial officer —Cont'd
Financial reporting, §1-301.155.
Child abuse and neglect.
Disposition reports.
Contents, NeglectProc Rule 22.
Filing, NeglectProc Rule 21.
Initial investigation, NeglectProc Rule 7.
Presentation, NeglectProc Rule 14.
Permanency hearings.
Contents, NeglectProc Rule 33.
Filing, NeglectProc Rule 32.
Predisposition study and report, §16-2319.
Review hearing reports.
Contents, NeglectProc Rule 29.
Filing, NeglectProc Rule 28.
Child and family services agency.
Reports of missing children, §4-1323.01.
Child care services assistance fund, §7-2008.
Child fatality.
Failure to make, §4-1371.14.
Immunity of persons making, §4-1371.13.
Persons required to make report, §4-1371.12.
Child support payments, delinquent, §46-225.
Civil asset forfeiture, §41-312.
Claims against the District, §2-404.
Clients' Security Trust Fund, DCBar Rule XII.
Collaborative law.
Mandatory reports, §16-4013.
Status reports, §16-4006.
College savings program.
Submission of audit report, §47-4512.
Commission on juvenile justice reform, §2-1533.02.
Comprehensive housing strategy task force, §§6-1054, 42-3502.23.
Compulsory school attendance.
Absences, end-of-year report, §§38-203, 38-209.
Truancy referrals and enforcement, §38-208.
Condominiums, §42-1904.07.
Conservators, Probate Rule 330.
Termination of conservatorship, Probate Rule 334.
Consumer protection.
Department of consumer and regulatory affairs, §28-3903.

REPORTS —Cont'd
Controlled substances, §48-905.06.
Convention of American Instructors of the Deaf.
Gallaudet University, §38-2304.
Cooperative housing associations, §47-820.01.
Corporations, §29-313.07.
Court of appeals judges, §11-709.
Courts, §§11-1730, 11-1731, 11-1745.
Crime victims' compensation, §4-514.
Eligibility for compensation, VictComp Rule 7.
Cruelty to animals, §22-1002.01.
Custodians of property, §1-502.
Dead bodies buried at public expense, §3-202.
Deferred compensation program, §47-3604.
Delinquent debts owed District, recovery, §1-350.11.
Delinquent minors.
Failure to appear at hearings, §16-2325.02.
Mental examination, results of, §16-2315, JuvProc Rule 110.
Predisposition investigation reports, §16-2319, JuvProc Rule 32.
Department of insurance, securities, and banking.
Filing with, §§31-101 to 31-108.
Deposits with superior court, CivPro Rule 67-I.
Domestic relations actions, DomRel Rule 67.
Director of department of the environment.
State of the environment report.
Duty of director to submit to council, §8-151.08.
Disability compensation.
Earnings report, §1-623.06b.
Injury or death leading to claim, §1-623.20.
Discovery.
Physical or mental examination of person, CivPro Rule 35.
Adoption proceedings, Adoption Rule 35.
Domestic relations actions, DomRel Rule 35.
Discrimination, §§2-1402.52, 2-1403.01.
Distracted driving.
Statistical data reports, §50-1731.09.
District funds invested or deposited in banks and financial institutions, §47-351.08.

REPORTS —Cont'd

District of Columbia, §§1-323.02, 1-323.03.

District of Columbia General Hospital hospice program, §4-1105.

Domestic relations actions.
Physical or mental examination of person, DomRel Rule 35.

Driver's license compact, §50-1002.

Early warning and support system, §38-751.05.

Eastern Market, §37-113.

Election ward task forces of advisory neighborhood commission, §1-1041.02.

Electric company infrastructure improvement financing, §34-1313.19.

Electronic waste.
Extended manufacturer responsibility, §8-1041.10.

Emergency and non-emergency number telephone calling systems fund, §34-1805.

Emergency management, §7-2208.
Homeland security commission, §7-2271.07.
Homeland security program, §7-2231.03.

Employees retirement program management, §§1-731 to 1-739, 1-909.02.
Investment of public funds in certain companies doing business with Iran, §1-336.04.
Sudan.
Investment of public funds in certain companies doing business with government of Sudan, §1-335.04.

Employment discrimination, §2-1402.52.

Enterprise Zone Study Commission, §2-1211.06.

Equal employment opportunity requirements, §2-1402.13.

Ethics and government accountability, §1-1162.20.
Public, §1-1162.24.

Examination of insurance companies, §31-1404.

Farm-to-school program, §38-823.03.

Fetal deaths, §7-213.

Fiduciaries, CivPro Rule 305.

Financial accountability reports for departments and agencies, §1-204.56b.

REPORTS —Cont'd

Financial literacy council, §38-731.05.

Financial reports by mayor, §47-310.01.

Financial Responsibility and Management Assistance Authority, by, §47-392.24.
Submission of reports to, §§1-204.56e, 47-392.06, 47-392.23.

Firearms, injuries caused by, §§7-2601 to 7-2603.

Fire protection study commission, §3-1103.

First amendment assemblies.
Post-and-forfeit procedure, §5-335.03.

First source employment, §2-219.04.

Fitness report.
Mayor's council on physical fitness, health and nutrition, §7-124.

Flood hazards, §6-503.

For-hire vehicles department.
Public vehicles-for-hire consumer service fund, §50-301.20.

Fraternal benefit societies, §31-5323.

Funeral directors.
Child death, §4-1371.12.

Gallaudet University, §§38-2402.04, 38-2402.05.

Gallaudet University report on Convention of American Instructors of the Deaf, §38-2304.

Garage keepers required to report vehicles damaged in accidents, §50-2201.06.

Gas companies, §34-1607.
Retail natural gas suppliers.
Annual financial report, §34-1671.09.

Gas stations, §36-302.04.

Guardianship reports, Probate Rule 328.

Hazardous waste and toxic chemicals, §8-1317.

Health benefit plan grievance procedures, §44-301.10.

Health benefit plans.
Claim payment reports.
Reimbursement of providers, §31-3135.

Health benefits for public employees, §1-621.12.

Health care facilities, §44-508.

Health insurance.
Regulatory standards.
RBC reports, §31-3451.02.

REPORTS —Cont'd
Health insurance ratemaking,
§31-3311.08.
Health maintenance organizations,
§31-3425.
Health occupations boards,
§3-1204.11.
Historic districts and landmarks,
§6-1113.
HIV/AIDS crisis area capacity
building fund, §1-325.53.
Homeland security commission,
§7-2271.07.
Homeland security program,
§7-2231.03.
Homeless services.
Interagency council on homelessness,
§4-752.02.
Interim eligibility reporting
requirements, §4-756.04.
Home purchase assistance fund,
§42-2605.
Homestead housing preservation,
§42-2110.
Hospital and medical services
corporations.
Board of directors or trustees, reports
to, §31-3519.
Mayor, reports to, §31-3513.
Hospitalization of persons with
mental illness, court-ordered,
§21-544, MentalHealth Rule 3.
Housing.
Affordable housing clearinghouse
directory.
Agency submission of data to mayor,
§42-2133.
Comprehensive housing strategy task
force, §§6-1054, 42-3502.23.
Housing finance agency,
§§42-2702.07, 42-2705.03.
Housing production trust fund
annual report, §42-2803.01.
Human rights, §2-1403.01.
Human Services, Department of,
§§7-104, 7-105.
Identity theft.
Police reports, §22-3227.08.
Income taxes, Internal Revenue
Code changes affecting,
§47-1816.03.
Industrial revenue bond forward
commitment program, §47-340.12.
Inheritance and estate taxes.
Amendment, repeal, or replacement of
1954 IRC, §47-3721.

REPORTS —Cont'd
Inheritance and estate taxes —Cont'd
Register of wills, §47-3715.
Injuries caused by firearms or
weapons, §§7-2601 to 7-2603.
Inmate welfare fund, §24-282.
Insurance companies.
See INSURANCE COMPANIES.
Insurance fraud.
Anti-fraud activity reporting,
§22-3225.12.
Insurance producers.
Administrative or criminal actions,
§31-1131.17.
Intellectual disabilities, persons
with.
Commitment.
Individuals who are not competent
to refuse commitment,
MentalRetardation Rule 4A.
Respondents found incompetent to
participate in criminal
proceedings, MentalRetardation
Rule 4B.
Psychotropic medication reviews,
§7-1305.06c.
Substitute consent activities,
§7-1305.07a.
Interception of oral or wire
communications, §23-555.
Interest payments, §28-3310.
Intervention proceedings.
Conservators, Probate Rule 330.
Termination of conservatorship,
Probate Rule 334.
Examiners, Probate Rule 326.
Guardianship reports, Probate Rule
328.
Job growth tax credit, §47-1807.55.
Joint Underwriting Association,
§31-5008.
Law enforcement officers.
Alcoholic beverages.
Incident reports, §25-804.
Law revision commission, §45-303.
Lead-hazard prevention and
elimination.
Clearance reports, §8-231.04.
Legal service, §1-608.60.
Life and health insurance guaranty
association, §31-5412.
Life insurance for public officers
and employees, §1-622.12.
Lobbying.
Activities, §1-1162.30.
Long-term care insurance.
Monthly reports, §31-3608.

REPORTS —Cont'd

Lottery and charitable games control board.
Annual report of board, §3-1307.
Sales agents' reports of receipts and transactions, §3-1316.

Low-level radioactive waste generator regulatory policy, §8-1502.

Marijuana testing.
Preemployment limitations, §32-932.

Masters, CivPro Rule 53.
Domestic relations actions, DomRel Rule 53.

Mediation.
Prohibitions, §16-4206.

Medical examiners.
Child death, §4-1371.12.

Medical liability captive insurance agency.
Financial report, §1-307.86.
Risk officer annual report, §1-307.88.

Mental health department.
See MENTAL HEALTH DEPARTMENT.

Mental illness, persons with.
Hospitalization, §21-544.
Commission on Mental Health reports, MentalHealth Rule 3.

Metabolic disorders, committee on, §7-837.

Metropolitan police.
Body-worn camera program, reporting requirements, §5-116.33.
Reports by other police to, §5-113.03.

Metrorail and metrobus, §35-215.

Metrorail/Metrobus account, §9-1111.16.

Missing children, §4-1323.01.

Money lenders' annual statements, §26-904.

Mortgage lenders and brokers, §26-1110.
Nationwide mortgage licensing system and registry, §26-1120.02.

Motor fuel tax, §47-2304.

Motor vehicle violation judgments, nonpayment of, §50-1301.41.

National Capital Housing Authority, §§6-101.04, 6-101.05.

National Capital Planning Commission, §2-1011.

Newborns, eye inflammation in, §7-802.

New Columbia statehood initiative.
Annual reports, §1-129.33.

REPORTS —Cont'd

Nonprofit corporations, §29-413.20.

Not-for-profit hospital corporations, §44-951.13.

Nurses.
Child death, §4-1371.12.

Nurse staffing agencies.
Reporting of disciplinary action, §44-1051.14.

Occupational safety and health, §32-1113.

Outplacement services for displaced public officers and employees, §1-624.24.

Parks and recreation, §10-215.

Pay equity and training commission, §§32-607, 32-608.

Pensions and retirement, federal benefit payments under District programs, §§1-813.01, 1-813.02.

Pensions and retirement funds, §§1-909.02 to 1-909.06.

Performance accountability reports for departments and agencies, §1-204.56b.

Performance based budgeting, §47-308.03.

Performance management system, §§1-614.13, 1-614.14.

Performance parking zones, §50-2535.

Personal property taxes, §47-1523.

Pesticides, §§8-409, 8-413.
Education and control.
Applicator reporting requirements, §8-437.
Report on effectiveness of pesticide programs, §8-436.

Phosphate cleaners, §8-107.02.

Physical and health education, §38-824.05.

Physicians and surgeons.
Child death, §4-1371.12.

Police and firefighters retirement and disability.
Employment reporting requirements and, §5-721.

Pre-kindergarten programs.
Enhancement and expansion of programs, §38-271.05.

Prescription drugs.
AccessRx program, §48-831.15.
Marketing costs, disclosure of, §§48-833.02 to 48-833.04, 48-833.08.
Monitoring program.
Dispenser requirements, §48-853.03.

REPORTS —Cont'd
Presumed abandoned property,
§41-117.
Pretrial services agency, §§23-1303,
23-1307.
Prison industries, §24-231.13.
Prisons and prisoners.
See PRISONS AND PRISONERS.
Probate proceedings.
Exhibition of assets.
Death before Jan. 1, 1981, Probate
Rule 20.
Probation, §24-303.
Producer controlled insurers.
Business transactions with, §31-406.
Psychologists.
Child death, §4-1371.12.
**Public building construction project
loans,** §§10-606, 10-610, 10-617.
**Public contract quick payment
provisions,** §2-221.05.
Public defender service, §2-1606.
Public officers and employees,
§1-502.
Public records management,
§§2-1704, 2-1711.
Public utilities.
See PUBLIC UTILITIES.
**Quarterly financial reports for
departments and agencies,**
§1-204.56d.
Real property taxes.
Use of exempt property, §47-1007.
Recreation board, §10-215.
Register of wills, §47-3715.
Rent control, §42-3502.20.
Resocialization furlough program,
§§24-251.05, 24-251.07.
Risk-based capital, §31-2002.
Savings and loan acquisitions,
§26-1214.
**Scholarships for opportunity and
results (SOAR) act.**
Reporting requirements, §38-1853.10.
School residency fraud, §38-312.03.
Schools and education.
See SCHOOLS AND EDUCATION.
Schools modernization fund.
Annual report, §1-325.45.
**Senior citizens' home repair and
improvement program fund,**
§42-2207.
Sentencing.
Presentence investigation reports,
CrimPro Rule 32, USDistCt LCrR
32.2.
Delinquent minors, JuvProc Rule 32.

REPORTS —Cont'd
**Sentencing, Advisory Commission
on,** §3-104.
Sexual offenses, §22-3023.
**Smoke and carbon monoxide
detectors.**
Report on detector and battery
program from previous year,
§6-751.05b.
Social workers.
Child death, §4-1371.12.
Soil and water conservation, §8-1709.
Solid waste facility permits, §8-1055.
Solid waste reduction and recovery,
§8-1031.13.
State education office.
Higher education financial aid
assistance, §38-2734.
**State health planning and
development agency,** §§44-405,
44-419.
State of the environment report.
Duty of director to submit to council,
§8-151.08.
Superior court judges, §11-909.
**Supplemental nutrition assistance
program (SNAP),** §4-261.23.
Tax abatement.
Nonprofit corporations locating in
emerging commercial
neighborhoods, §47-857.14.
Taxicabs.
See TAXICABS.
Teachers.
Child death, §4-1371.12.
Teen pregnancy prevention fund,
§1-325.324.
**Temporary assistance for needy
families,** §§4-205.19m, 4-205.54.
Grandparent caregiver subsidies.
Reports, §4-251.05.
Tobacco tax, §47-2408.
Toll telecommunication service tax,
§§47-3905, 47-3906.
Traffic ticket adjudication.
Reports to DPW and DDOT,
§50-2301.10.
Report to Council, §50-2301.08.
**Transportation infrastructure
improvement GARVEE bonds.**
Reports, §9-107.61.
**Trust, mortgage and title
corporations,** §§26-1308, 26-1318,
26-1319.
**Unclaimed property presumed
abandoned.**
See UNCLAIMED PROPERTY.

REPORTS —Cont'd
Unemployment compensation,
§51-117.
Domestic violence, §51-135.
**Unified economic development
budget transparency and
accountability,** §2-1208.02.
**United States branches of non-
United States insurers,** §31-2205.
**University of the District of
Columbia,** §38-1204.04.
Vacant and abandoned property.
Special disposal procedures for certain
properties, §10-838.
Voluntary leave transfer program.
Report of agency, §1-612.38.
**Washington Asylum and Jail,
Superintendent of,** §24-201.16.
Weapons, injuries caused by,
§§7-2601 to 7-2603.
Workers' compensation.
Annual report to Council, §32-1502.
Anti-fraud report, §32-1542.03.
Compliance report, §32-1542.04.
Employers, by, §32-1532.
Workplace safety.
Employer reports of injuries and
deaths, §32-808.
Minimum wage and industrial safety
board report to mayor, §32-811.
**Work-related travel of government
employees.**
Report from Mayor to Council,
§50-211.07.
**Youth behavioral health
epidemiology reports.**
Citation of provisions, §2-1517.01.
Definitions, §2-1517.02.
Youth development plan, §2-1583.
**Youth rehabilitation services
department.**
Use of restraints, §2-1515.53.

REPOSSESSION.
Consumer credit sales.
Repossession of collateral after
default, §28-3812.
Secured transactions.
Defaults.
Collateral.
Disposition after default,
§28-9-610.
Application of proceeds,
§28-9-615.
Notice before disposition,
§28-9-611.

REPOSSESSION —Cont'd
Secured transactions —Cont'd
Defaults —Cont'd
Collateral —Cont'd
Disposition after default —Cont'd
Notice before disposition,
contents and form,
§§28:9-613, 28:9-614.
Notice before disposition,
timeliness, §28:9-612.
Surplus or deficiency
calculations, §28:9-616.
Right to possession after default,
§28:9-609.

REPRESENTATION BY COUNSEL.
See RIGHT TO COUNSEL.

REPROGRAMMING POLICY.
Budgets and budget estimates,
§§47-361 to 47-366.

**REPUBLICAN FORM OF
GOVERNMENT.**
Guaranteed, US Const Art IV §4.

REPUDIATION.
Leases, UCC.
Anticipatory repudiation, §§28:2A-402,
28:2A-403.
Damages, §§28:2A-519, 28:2A-528.
Insecurity.
Failure to provide adequate
assurance of performance,
§28:2A-519.
Lessor's remedies, §28:2A-523.
Sale of goods, UCC.
Anticipatory repudiation, §§28:2-610,
28:2-611.
Proof of market price, §28:2-723.
Buyer's repudiation.
Enumeration of seller's remedies,
§28:2-703.
Seller's repudiation.
Buyer's remedies enumerated,
§28:2-711.

REPUTATION EVIDENCE.
Human trafficking, §22-1839.

REQUESTS FOR ADMISSION, CivPro
Rule 36.
Adoption proceedings, Adoption Rule
36.
Domestic relations actions, DomRel
Rule 36.
Form, CivPro Form CA 25.
**General provisions governing
discovery,** CivPro Rule 26,
USDistCt LCvR 26.2.

REQUESTS FOR ADMISSION
—Cont'd
Responses, form of, USDistCt LCvR 30.4.

REQUESTS FOR INFORMATION.
Public-private partnership administration fund, §2-273.01.

REQUESTS FOR PROPOSAL.
Public-private partnership administration fund, §2-273.01.

RESALE.
Condominiums, §42-1904.11.
Merchandise sold to minor for, §32-220.

RESALE RESTRICTED PROPERTIES.
Real property taxes.
Assessment, §47-820.02.

RESCISSION.
Corporations.
Appraisal and payment for shares, §29-311.50.
Leases, UCC, §28:2A-208.
Effect on rights and remedies, §28:2A-505.
Limited cooperative associations, §29-1012.13.
Limited liability companies, §29-807.06.
Limited partnerships, §29-708.10.
Partnerships, §29-608.12.
Sale of goods, UCC, §28:2-209.

RESCUE SQUADS.
Cardiopulmonary resuscitation in case of cardiac arrest.
Non-resuscitation procedures for EMS, §§7-651.01 to 7-651.16.
See EMERGENCY MEDICAL SERVICES.

RESEARCH ASSISTANTS.
Teachers, classified as, §38-1906.

RESERVE CORPS.
Junior Reserve Officers' Training Program, §38-158.
National Guard, §49-407.

RESERVE FUNDS, §1-204.50a.

RESIDENCY.
Annulment, §16-902.
Assignments for benefit of creditors.
Assignee, §28-2103.
Business incubator facilitation, priorities regarding, §2-1209.07.

RESIDENCY —Cont'd
Council.
Qualifications for holding office, §1-204.02.
Discrimination based upon, §2-1401.01.
District of Columbia housing authority.
Executive director required to be district resident, §6-213.
Preference for district residents. Applicants for positions within authority, §6-215.
Divorce, §16-902.
Elections, §1-1041.04.
Excepted service.
Domicile requirements, §1-609.06.
Executive service.
Domicile requirements, §1-610.59.
Fiduciary eligibility requirements, CivPro Rule 304.
Probate proceedings.
Guardians, conservators, trustees, etc., involved, Probate Rule 202.
Fire departments, §5-410.
Fire protection study commission, §3-1102.
Homeless services, §4-753.03.
Home purchase assistance fund, §42-2604.
Legal service, §1-608.59.
Management supervisory service, §1-609.57.
Mayor.
Qualifications of office, §1-204.21.
Office of zoning.
Director required to be district resident, §6-623.02.
Preference for district residents. Applicants for positions within office, §6-623.02.
People's counsel.
Required to be district resident, §34-804.
Public assistance, §§4-205.02 to 4-205.04, 4-205.69.
Public officers and employees.
See PUBLIC OFFICERS AND EMPLOYEES.
Public parking authority.
Preference for district residents. Applicants for positions within authority, §50-2506.01.
Schools and education.
Establishment of residency, §§38-309 to 38-312.
False information, §38-313.

RESIDENCY —Cont'd
Schools and education —Cont'd
Establishment of residency —Cont'd
False information hotline,
§38-312.01.
Proof of residency, §38-307.
Status reports, §38-312.03.
Student residency verification fund,
§38-312.02.
Step Up program, §42-2623.
**University of the District of
Columbia preferential tuition
rates,** §38-1204.07.
**Voting by military and overseas
voters,** §1-1061.05.
Methods, §1-1061.06.

**RESIDENTIAL DRUG-RELATED
EVICTIONS,** §§42-3601 to 42-3610.
See DRUG-RELATED EVICTIONS.

**RESIDENTIAL HOME SALES
DISCLOSURES,** §§42-1301 to
42-1311.
See HOME SALES.

**RESIDENTIAL REAL PROPERTY
TRANSFER EXCISE TAX.**
**Compulsory recordation of
transfers,** §§47-1431 to 47-1433.
Definitions, §47-1401.

**RESIDENT MANAGEMENT
CORPORATIONS.**
**Lower income home ownership tax
abatement and incentives,**
§§47-3505, 47-3506.
Real property taxes.
Transfers exempt from tax, §47-802.

RESIGNATION OF EMPLOYEE.
Attachment, lapse or dismissal of,
§16-576.

**RESIGNATION OF PERSONAL
REPRESENTATIVES,** §20-525.

**RESOCIALIZATION FURLOUGH
PROGRAM,** §§24-251.01 to
24-251.08.
See PRISONS AND PRISONERS.

RESPIRATORY ARREST.
**Non-resuscitation procedures for
EMS.**
Comfort care orders, §§7-651.01 to
7-651.16.
See EMERGENCY MEDICAL
SERVICES.

RESPIRATORY ARREST —Cont'd
**Presumption as to disability or
death resulting from.**
Fire and emergency medical services
employees, §5-652.

**RESPIRATORY CARE
PRACTITIONERS.**
Board of, §3-1202.14.
Definition of practice of, §3-1201.02.
Health occupations boards.
General provisions, §§3-1201.01 to
3-1213.01.
See HEALTH OCCUPATIONS
BOARDS.
**Health occupations licensure,
registration or certification,**
§§3-1205.01 to 3-1205.24.
See HEALTH OCCUPATIONS
LICENSURE, REGISTRATION
OR CERTIFICATION.
Licenses generally, §§3-1207.21 to
3-1207.23.
Renewal of license.
Eligibility, §3-1207.23.
**Titles and terms prohibited as
misrepresentation without
license to practice,** §3-1210.03.
Waiver of licensure requirements.
Demonstration of performance,
§3-1207.21.
Meeting educational requirements,
§3-1207.22.

RESTAURANTS.
Adulteration of food, §§48-101 to
48-110.
Alcoholic beverage licenses.
Brew pub licenses, §25-117.
On-premises retailers, §25-113.
Sidewalk cafe or summer garden
endorsements, §25-113a.
Wine pub permits, §25-124.
Business licenses, §47-2827.
Discrimination in admission,
§47-2902.
Recovery of fine, §47-2904.
**Federal government restaurants,
health regulations for,** §7-2701.
**Fire code and occupancy
requirements,** §5-417.02.
**Food delivery vehicles, motor
vehicle insurance for,** §§50-101 to
50-105.
Price list.
Charging greater price, §47-2911.

RESTAURANTS —Cont'd
Price list —Cont'd
Posting required, §47-2908.
Failure, §47-2911.
Transmission to assessor, §47-2909.
Smoking, §§7-741.03, 7-1703.01.
"No Smoking" signs, §7-1704.
Tax incentives, §§47-3801 to 47-3805.
Well-behaved persons.
Required to serve, §§47-2907, 47-2910.
Failure to serve, §47-2911.

RESTITUTION.
Attorney discipline or disability proceedings, DCBar Rule XI.
Contracts.
Sale of goods.
Buyer's remedies, §28:2-718.
Crime victims' compensation, VictComp Rule 40.
Criminal procedure requiring, §16-711.
Enforcement, §16-711.01.
Delinquent minors, §16-2320.01, JuvProc Rule 112.
Graffiti, §22-3312.04.
Historic landmarks.
Demolition of, §6-1110.
Identity theft, §22-3227.04.
Insurance fraud, §22-3225.05.
Insurance producers, §31-1131.12.
Landlord and tenant court.
Writs of restitution, LandlordTenant Form 10, LandlordTenant Rule 16.
Application to stay writ of restitution, LandlordTenant Form 9.
Not of intention to seek writ, LandlordTenant Form 2.
Security agents and brokers.
Enforcement of act, §31-5606.02.
Workplace fraud.
Penalties for violation of provisions, §32-1331.07.
Public contracts.
Mayor's authority to enforce provisions, §32-1331.11.

RESTRAINING ORDERS.
Cease and desist orders.
See CEASE AND DESIST ORDERS.
Injunctions.
See INJUNCTIONS.
Protective orders.
See PROTECTIVE ORDERS.

RESTRAINT OF PATIENTS.
Mental health consumer's rights, §7-1231.09.

RESTRAINTS OF TRADE, §§28-4501 to 28-4518.
Actions, §28-4507.
Indirect purchasers, §28-4509.
Judgment in favor of District of Columbia as prima facie evidence, §28-4510.
Limitation on actions, §28-4511.
Relief for private parties, §28-4508.
Remedies cumulative, §28-4514.
Assurance of discontinuance of, §28-4512.
Attorney general.
Civil investigative demand, §28-4505.
Attorneys at law.
Actions.
Attorneys' fees, §28-4507.
Charitable, educational and religious organizations.
Exclusion from chapter, §28-4504.
Cigarette sales below cost, §§28-4521 to 28-4527.
See CIGARETTES.
Civil investigative demand regarding, §28-4505.
Class actions, §28-4508.
Combinations, §28-4502.
Conspiracy to restrain trade, §28-4502.
Construction and interpretation.
Uniformity with federal antitrust statutes, §28-4515.
Contract to restrain trade.
Declared illegal, §28-4502.
Cooperation with federal government and states, §28-4513.
Cooperative agreements to prosecute, §28-4513.
Crimes and offenses, §28-4506.
Criminal enforcement, §28-4506.
Cumulativeness of remedies, §28-4514.
Damages, §§28-4507, 28-4508.
Indirect purchasers, §28-4509.
Injuries to or within the District of Columbia, §28-4507.
Relief for private parties, §28-4508.
Definitions, §28-4501.
Discontinuance of violations.
Assurance of discontinuance, §28-4512.
Discovery.
Civil investigative demand, §28-4505.
Enforcement.
Actions, §28-4507.
Assurance of discontinuance of violations, §28-4512.

RESTRAINTS OF TRADE —Cont'd
Enforcement —Cont'd
Civil investigative demand, §28-4505.
Criminal enforcement, §28-4506.
Evidence.
Judgment in favor of District of
Columbia as prima facie evidence,
§28-4510.
Exclusions, §28-4504.
Fines, §28-4506.
Indirect purchasers, §28-4509.
When deemed to be entered, §28-4509.
Injunctions, §§28-4507, 28-4508.
Relief for injuries to or within the
District of Columbia, §28-4507.
Relief for private parties, §28-4508.
Interpretation of provisions,
§28-4515.
Interrogatories.
Civil investigative demand, §28-4505.
Investigations, §28-4505.
Civil investigative demand, §28-4505.
Judgment in favor of District as
prima facie evidence of, §28-4510.
Labor.
Exclusion of labor from chapter,
§28-4504.
Limitation of actions, §28-4511.
Limited cooperative associations.
Relation to law, §29-1001.08.
Monopolization, §28-4503.
Prohibited, §28-4503.
Nonprofit charitable, etc.,
organizations.
Exclusion from chapter, §28-4504.
Penalties, §28-4506.
Criminal enforcement, §28-4506.
Failure to comply with civil
investigative demand, §28-4505.
Person.
Defined, §28-4501.
Policy declaration, §28-4501.
Prescription drug pricing,
§48-804.02.
Private right of action, §28-4508.
Purpose of chapter, §28-4501.
Relation of chapter to other law,
§28-4518.
Relationship to other laws, §28-4518.
Remedies of chapter cumulative,
§28-4514.
Severability of chapter, §28-4517.
Severability of provisions, §28-4517.
Statute of limitations, §28-4511.
Uniformity of interpretation,
§28-4515.

RESTRAINTS OF TRADE —Cont'd
Uniformity with federal antitrust
statutes, §28-4515.
Unions.
Exclusion of labor from chapter,
§28-4504.
United States.
Cooperation with federal government,
§28-4513.
Violations.
Criminal enforcement, §28-4506.
Washington metropolitan area
transit authority.
Exclusion from chapter, §28-4504.
Witnesses.
Civil investigative demand, §28-4505.

RESTRAINTS ON ALIENATION.
Condominiums, §42-1903.15.
Horizontal property regimes,
§42-2026.

RESTRICTED ZONES.
Armory and RFK stadium, at, §3-343.

RESTRICTIVE INDORSEMENTS.
Negotiable instruments, §28:3-206.

RESTROOMS.
Parks and recreation facilities,
§§10-133, 10-134.
Toilets generally, §§8-601 to 8-604.

RETAIL CIGARETTE SALES.
License, §47-2404.

RETAIL DEVELOPMENT
INCENTIVES, §§2-1217.71 to
2-1217.84.
Bond issues, §2-1217.77.
Default, §2-1217.80.
Details of bonds, §2-1217.78.
Liability, §2-1217.81.
Limitations on issuance, §2-1217.72.
Proceeds, use of, §2-1217.75.
Security for bonds, §2-1217.79.
Construction and interpretation,
§2-1217.84.
Definitions, §2-1217.71.
Effect of chapter, §2-1217.82.
Funding agreements, §2-1217.75.
Retail priority areas.
Corridor revitalization programs,
§2-1217.73b.
Defined, §2-1217.71.
Designation, §2-1217.73.
Downtown retail priority area
demonstration project,
§2-1217.73a.
Rules of operation, §2-1217.74.
Defined, §2-1217.71.

RETAIL DEVELOPMENT INCENTIVES —Cont'd
Rules promulgation, §2-1217.83.
Streetscape loan relief fund, §1-325.191.
Tax increment revenues, allocation of, §2-1217.76.

RETAIL INSTALLMENT SALES.
Consumer protection, §§28-3801 to 28-3819.
See CONSUMER PROTECTION.

RETAIL NATURAL GAS SUPPLIER LICENSING AND CONSUMER PROTECTION, §§34-1671.01 to 34-1671.14.
See GAS COMPANIES.

RETAIL SERVICE STATIONS, §§36-301.01 to 36-305.02.
See GAS STATIONS.

RETAIL STORES.
Smoking restrictions, §7-1703.
"No Smoking" signs, §7-1704.

RETALIATION.
Bullying, §2-1535.05.
Discriminatory, §2-1402.61.
Unemployment status, §32-1363.
Health benefit plan grievance procedures.
Retaliation prohibited by insurer, §44-301.03.
Health care ombudsman program.
Prohibited acts, §7-2071.09.
Homeless services.
Office of shelter monitoring.
Retaliation against person bringing complaint or providing information to.
Prohibited, §4-754.55.
Leave of absence.
Right to sick and safe leave.
Discharge or discrimination prohibited, §32-131.08.
Procurement practices.
Claims for violations, relief from retaliatory actions, §2-381.04.
Employer interference with employee to disclosures to board, §2-381.04.
Rental housing.
Tenant exercising rights, §42-3505.02.
Smoking in public places.
Employee rights and protections, §7-741.06.

RETALIATION —Cont'd
Testing integrity in public schools.
Districtwide assessments.
LEA administration.
Prohibition of retaliation against whistleblowing activities, §38-771.02.
Unemployment status discrimination, §32-1363.
Wages and salaries.
Complaints about violations, prohibited, §32-1311.
Workers' compensation, §32-1542.
Workplace fraud.
Employer's retaliation, §32-1331.10.

RETENTS.
Public contracts, §2-203.01.

RETIREMENT.
Employees retirement program management, §§1-701 to 1-753.
See EMPLOYEES RETIREMENT PROGRAM MANAGEMENT.
Judicial retirement, §§11-1561 to 11-1572.
See JUDICIAL RETIREMENT.
Opportunity accounts, §§1-307.61 to 1-307.74.
Pensions and retirement.
General provisions, §§1-626.01 to 1-626.14.
See PENSIONS AND RETIREMENT.
Police and firefighters retirement and disability.
General provisions, §§5-631 to 5-762.
See POLICE AND FIREFIGHTERS RETIREMENT AND DISABILITY.
Schools and education.
Food services department, §38-803.
Teachers, §§38-2001.01 to 38-2041.01.
See TEACHERS' RETIREMENT.
Teachers.
General provisions, §§38-2001.01 to 38-2041.01.
See TEACHERS' RETIREMENT.

RETROACTIVE LAWS.
Ex post facto laws.
Prohibited, US Const Art I §§9, 10.

RETROACTIVITY.
Fiduciaries, provisions regarding, §21-1710.

RETROACTIVITY —Cont'd

Motor vehicle safety responsibility provisions, §50-1301.83.

Police and firefighters medical care reimbursement, §5-608.

Police and firefighters, wages and salaries of, §5-545.05.

Rental housing conversion and sale, §42-3402.11.

Simultaneous death provisions, §19-506.

Unclaimed property provisions, §41-142.

REVENUE ANTICIPATION NOTES.

General obligation bonds, §1-204.72.

REVENUE BONDS, §1-204.90.

Bond issues generally.
See BOND ISSUES.

Deposit and investments of District funds.
General provisions, §§47-351.01 to 47-351.16.
See BUDGETS AND BUDGET ESTIMATES.

Fiduciary security transfers, §§28-2901 to 28-2909.
See FIDUCIARY SECURITY TRANSFERS.

Housing finance agency, §§42-2704.02 to 42-2704.10.
See HOUSING FINANCE AGENCY.

Metropolitan Washington Airports Authority, §§9-910 to 9-916, 9-1006.

Metrorail and metrobus.
See METRORAIL AND METROBUS.

Transfer of securities by fiduciaries, §§28-2901 to 28-2909.
See FIDUCIARY SECURITY TRANSFERS.

Washington convention and sports authority, §§10-1202.09 to 10-1202.14.

Water and Sewer Authority.
See WATER AND SEWER AUTHORITY.

REVERSIONS.

Abandonment of streets, §9-101.08.

Estates in land, §42-509.

Landlord and tenant, §§42-3230, 42-3231.

REVISED WAGE ORDERS, §32-1015.

REVIVAL, ORDER OF.

Judgments and decrees, §15-103.

REVOCABLE TRUSTS.

Income tax, §47-1809.07.

Probate proceedings.
Claims against revocable trust, Probate Rule 213.
Notice of existence of revocable trust, Probate Rule 212.

Trustees.
Directions, power to direct or take directions, §19-1308.08.

Uniform trust code, §§19-1306.01 to 19-1306.04.

REVOLVING CREDIT ACCOUNTS, §§28-3701, 28-3702.

Actions.
Consumers' remedies, §28-3813.
Limitation on creditors' remedies, §28-3812.

Attorneys at law.
Consumers' remedies.
Attorneys' fees, §28-3813.

Consumer credit, §§28-3801 to 28-3819.
See CONSUMER CREDIT.

Consumer protection, §§28-3801 to 28-3819.
See CONSUMER PROTECTION.

Credit cards.
See CREDIT CARDS.

Cross-collateral.
Debts secured by cross-collateral, §28-3805.

Damages.
Consumers' remedies, §28-3813.

Definitions, §§28-3701, 28-3802.

Determination of debt secured by various security interests, §28-3805.

Interest.
Maximum charge, §28-3702.

Punitive damages.
Violations, §28-3813.

Remedies.
Consumers' remedies, §28-3813.
Limitation on creditors' remedies, §28-3812.

Service charge.
Amount and computation, §28-3702.

Violations.
Punitive damages, §28-3813.

REWARDS.

Escaped prisoners, §24-201.27.

Illegal dumping bounty, §8-904.

RFK STADIUM.

Armory board, §§3-322 to 3-330.
See ARMORY BOARD.

RHODE ISLAND METRO PLAZA PILOT AGREEMENT.
Payments in lieu of taxes.
Sales tax exemption, §47-4613.

RIDESHARING SERVICES.
Private vehicles-for-hire,
§§50-301.29a to 50-301.29g.
Public vehicles for hire exclusive of taxicabs and limousines,
§50-301.29.

RIGHT OF FIRST REFUSAL.
Condominiums, §42-1903.15.
Gas stations.
Franchise purchase rights, §36-304.12.
Rental housing conversion and sale,
§42-3404.08.

RIGHTS OF ENTRY.
Boiler inspectors, §2-111.
Lead-hazard prevention and elimination, §8-231.05.
Underground storage tanks,
§8-113.08.
Water pollution and water quality.
Inspections, §8-103.15.

RIGHTS OF WAY.
Bicycles and pedestrians.
Public structures in public space blocking sidewalks, lanes or paths, §§10-1141.03, 10-1141.04.
Bridges over canals and railways,
§9-302.
Buses.
Right of way at intersections, §50-2201.29.
Cable television.
Public service commission.
Regulation of rights of way, §34-1253.03.
Cemeteries, through, §1-1315.
Conservation easements, §§42-201 to 42-205.
See CONSERVATION EASEMENTS.
Crosswalks, at, §50-2201.28.
Special signs for failure to yield to pedestrian, §50-2201.30.
Easements.
Conservation easements, §§42-201 to 42-205.
See CONSERVATION EASEMENTS.
Eminent domain.
General provisions, §§16-1301 to 16-1385.
See EMINENT DOMAIN.

RIGHTS OF WAY —Cont'd
Michigan Avenue right-of-way for Washington Railway and Electric Company, §9-101.15.
National Guard parades, §49-105.
Permits to occupy public rights of way, §10-1141.03.
Revenue.
Inclusion in budget submission, §47-305.01.
Water supply and waterworks acquisition of lands and rights of way for pipelines, §34-2401.19.

RIGHT TO ASSEMBLE, US Const Amd 1.

RIGHT TO BEAR ARMS, US Const Amd 2.

RIGHT TO BE HEARD.
Judges.
Ensuring, CJC Canon 2.6.

RIGHT TO COUNSEL, US Const Amd 6.
Annulment cases, appointment of counsel in, §16-918.
Arbitration, revised act, §16-4416.
Assignment of counsel, CrimPro Rule 44-I, USDistCt LCrR 57.22, USDistCt LCvR 83.10.
Grounds for declining appointment, ProfCond Rule 6.2.
Hospitalization of persons with mental illness, §21-543, MentalHealth Rule 12.
Emergency detention, MentalHealth Rule 2.
Prisoner's commitment to mental institution, MentalHealth Rule 10.
Indigent persons, plan for furnishing representation to, IndigentRep Rules I to IV.
Juvenile proceedings, JuvProc Rule 44.
Child abuse and neglect, §16-2304, NeglectProc Rule 42.
Advisement of right, NeglectProc Rule 12.
Compensation of appointed attorney, §16-2326.01.
Child custody cases, appointment of counsel in, §16-918.
Third-party custody cases, §16-831.06.
Children, court-appointed special advocates for, §§16-2371, 16-2372.
Civil pro bono panel, USDistCt LCvR 83.11.

RIGHT TO COUNSEL —Cont'd
Court-appointed special advocates for children, §§16-2371, 16-2372.
Court-ordered commitment of persons with mental illness, appointment, compensation, §21-543.
Criminal defendants, §§11-2601 to 11-2608.
Appointment of counsel for, §§11-2602, 11-2603.
Appropriations, §11-2608.
Budgets and budget estimates, §11-2607.
Duration of appointment of counsel for, §11-2603.
Funds available for payment for, §11-2606.
Investigative, expert or other services. Providing, compensation, §11-2605.
Payment for representing, §11-2604.
Public defender service, §§2-1601 to 2-1608.
Services adjunct to counsel, §11-2605.
Services other than counsel's.
Right to, compensation, §11-2605.
Substitution of appointment of counsel for, §11-2603.
Delinquent minors, JuvProc Rule 44.
Disability compensation claims for public officers and employees, §1-623.27.
Divorce cases, appointment of counsel in, §16-918.
Domestic relations actions, DomRel Rule 101.
Drug addicts, rehabilitation of, §24-704.
Family court proceedings.
Standards of practice for appointed counsel, §11-1103.
Grounds for declining appointment, ProfCond Rule 6.2.
Indigent persons, plan for furnishing representation to.
Administration and oversight of plan, IndigentRep Rule I.
Appointment of counsel.
Court of appeals procedures, IndigentRep Rule III.
Superior court procedures, IndigentRep Rule II.
Court of appeals procedures, IndigentRep Rule III.
Determining need for counsel.
Court of appeals procedures, IndigentRep Rule III.

RIGHT TO COUNSEL —Cont'd
Indigent persons, plan for furnishing representation to —Cont'd
Determining need for counsel —Cont'd
Superior court procedures, IndigentRep Rule II.
Effective date of plan, IndigentRep Rule IV.
Expenses.
Court of appeals procedures, IndigentRep Rule III.
Superior court procedures, IndigentRep Rule II.
Table of guideline fees, IndigentRep Form.
Purpose of plan, IndigentRep Rule I.
Superior court procedures, IndigentRep Rule II.
Intellectual disabilities, persons with.
Commitment to mental health facility, §7-1304.02, MentalRetardation Rule 11.
Joint representation, CrimPro Rule 44.
Juvenile proceedings, JuvProc Rule 44.
Mental illness, persons with.
Hospitalization, §21-543, MentalHealth Rule 12.
Emergency detention proceedings, MentalHealth Rule 2.
Prisoner's commitment to mental institution, MentalHealth Rule 10.
Pleas in criminal cases.
Advice to defendant, CrimPro Rule 11.
Delinquent minors, JuvProc Rule 11.
Post-conviction proceedings.
Superior court proceedings.
Appointment of counsel, PostConvRel Rules 4, 8.
Sexual psychopaths, §22-3805.
Students practicing law, CrimPro Rule 44-I.
Termination of parental rights, §16-2304, NeglectProc Rule 42.
Advisement of right, NeglectProc Rule 12.
Compensation of appointed attorney, §16-2326.01.
RIGHT TO DIE.
Healthcare durable powers of attorney.
See HEALTHCARE DURABLE POWERS OF ATTORNEY.

RIGHT TO DIE —Cont'd
Heath-care durable powers of
attorney, §§21-2201 to 21-2213.
Natural death act, §§7-621 to 7-630.
See LIVING WILLS.

**RIGHT TO PETITION FOR
REDRESS OF GRIEVANCES,** US
Const Amd 1.

RIGHT TO VOTE, US Const Amds 14,
15, 26.

RIOT OR INCITEMENT TO RIOT,
§22-1322.

RIPARIAN PERMITS, §47-2711.

RISK MANAGEMENT.
Report by office of city
administrator, §2-431.

RISK RETENTION GROUPS,
§§31-4101 to 31-4112.
Authority over, administrative and
procedural, §31-4110.
Chartered out of District, §31-4103.
Chartered within the District,
§31-4102.
Countersignatures, §31-4105.
Definitions, §31-4101.
District court orders regarding,
§31-4112.
Licenses, §31-4111.
Notice, §§31-4103, 31-4107.
Purchasing groups, §§31-4106 to
31-4110.
 Authority over, administrative and
  procedural, §31-4110.
 Exemptions, §31-4106.
 Notice, §31-4107.
 Registration, §31-4107.
 Restrictions on, §31-4108.
 Taxation, §31-4109.
Restrictions on, §§31-4104, 31-4108.
Taxation of purchasing groups,
§31-4109.

**RLA REVITALIZATION
CORPORATION.**
Leases of real property by,
§§6-321.04, 6-341.02.
Urban renewal.
 General provisions, §§6-311.01 to
  6-341.05.
 See URBAN RENEWAL.

ROACH CLIPS.
Drug paraphernalia, §§48-904.10,
48-1101 to 48-1104.

ROADS.
Eminent domain.
 General provisions, §§16-1301 to
  16-1385.
 See EMINENT DOMAIN.
Highways.
 See HIGHWAYS.
Michigan Avenue.
 See MICHIGAN AVENUE.
Parkways.
 See PARKWAYS.
Public works.
 General provisions, §§9-401.01 to
  9-401.18.
 See PUBLIC WORKS.
Streets and alleys, §§9-201.01 to
 9-206.02.
 See STREETS AND ALLEYS.

ROBBERY, §§22-2801 to 22-2803.
Aged persons, offenses committed
against.
 Enhanced penalties, §22-3601.
Armed robbery.
 Felony murder, §22-2101.
Assault with intent to rob, §22-401.
Attempt to commit, §22-2802.
Carjacking, §22-2803.
Defined, §22-2801.
Implements of crime, possession of,
§22-2501.
Prohibited acts, §22-2801.
Security agents and brokers.
 Grounds for disciplinary actions,
  §31-5602.07.

**ROBERT F. KENNEDY MEMORIAL
STADIUM.**
Armory board, §§3-322 to 3-330.
See ARMORY BOARD.

ROBOTIC CARS.
Autonomous vehicles, §§50-2351 to
50-2354.

ROCHAMBEAU BRIDGE, §9-308.

ROCK CREEK.
Bridges over, §9-303.
Protection of Rock Creek and
tributaries, §10-145.
Throwing or depositing matter into,
§22-4403.
United States title to lands or
waters of, §10-102.

ROCK CREEK PARK, §§10-140 to
10-145.
Acceptance of dedicated property,
§10-144.

ROCK CREEK PARK —Cont'd
Control, §10-142.
Duties of director of National Park Service, §10-142.
Established, §10-140.
Leasing authorized, disposition of proceeds, §10-143.
Protection of Rock Creek, §10-145.
Regulations, §10-142.
Total area of lands acquired, §10-141.

RODENT CONTROL.
Bureau of rodent control, §§8-2101.01, 8-2101.02.
Rodent abatement program, §§8-2103.01 to 8-2103.05.
  Corrective actions, §8-2103.04.
  Definitions, §8-2103.01.
  Harborage prohibited, §8-2103.05.

ROLLER SKATES.
Helmet requirement for riders.
  Persons under 16 years, §50-1651.

ROLLING PAPERS.
Drug paraphernalia, §§48-1101 to 48-1104.

RONALD REAGAN WASHINGTON NATIONAL AIRPORT, §§9-701 to 9-707.
Administrator, §9-702.
Arrests, §9-704.
Boundaries of, §9-701.
Collateral deposited by violators, §9-706.
Definitions, §9-701.
Fines, §9-705.
Leasing space or property for, §9-703.
Metropolitan Washington airports authority, §§9-901 to 9-926, 9-1001 to 9-1011.
  See METROPOLITAN WASHINGTON AIRPORTS AUTHORITY.
Municipal services agreements, §9-707.
Nonstop flight requirements, §9-1011.
Penalties, §9-705.
United States Park Police, §9-704.

ROOSEVELT (BUSINESS) HIGH SCHOOL, §38-408.

ROSEDALE CONSERVANCY.
Real property tax exemptions, §47-1056.

ROYALTIES.
Ethics and government accountability, §1-1162.26.

RUBBISH COLLECTION.
Garbage collection.
  See GARBAGE COLLECTION.

RUBELLA.
Immunization of school students, §§38-501 to 38-508.
  Interstate compact on educational opportunity for military children.
  Time to obtain immunizations, §49-1101.05.

RULE AGAINST PERPETUITIES, §§19-901 to 19-907.

RUNAWAY CHILDREN.
Contributing to the delinquency of a minor, §22-811.
Interstate compact for juveniles, §§24-1101 to 24-1106.
  Alteration, amendment or repeal of provisions, §24-1106.
  Compact administrator, §24-1103.
  Congressional findings, §24-1101.
  Construction of compact, §24-1105.
  Enforcement, §24-1104.
  Entry into and execution of compact, §24-1102.
Taking child into custody, §16-2309.

RUNOFF.
Stormwater management, §§8-152.01 to 8-153.01.
  See STORMWATER MANAGEMENT.

S

SAFE DEPOSIT BOXES.
Joint accounts, §26-802.
Probate proceedings.
  Appointment of special administrator to open safe deposit box, Probate Rule 7.1.
Unclaimed property in.
  See UNCLAIMED PROPERTY.

SAFE DEPOSIT CORPORATIONS.
Regulatory provisions, §§26-1301 to 26-1336.
  See TRUST, MORTGAGE AND TITLE CORPORATIONS.

SAFE HAVEN FOR NEWBORNS, §§4-1451.01 to 4-1451.08.
See NEWBORN SAFE HAVEN.

SAFE NEEDLE DISTRIBUTION, §§7-2851 to 7-2858.
Definitions, §7-2851.
Effective date, §7-2857.

SAFE NEEDLE DISTRIBUTION
—Cont'd
Report of exposure incident, §7-2853.
Rules, §7-2855.
Sale, distribution, possession, use of sharp.
Requirements, §7-2852.
Severability, §7-2857.
Violations, penalties, §7-2854.

SAFERX EVALUATION ACT OF 2008.
Pharmaceutical detailing.
Evaluation of effectiveness of law licensing persons practicing, §§48-844.01 to 48-844.03.

ST. ELIZABETH'S HOSPITAL.
Commitment of prisoners to mental institution, MentalHealth Rule 10.
Escapees, MentalHealth Rule 11.
Mental health services administration, §§44-901 to 44-922.
See MENTAL HEALTH SERVICES ADMINISTRATION.

ST. MARK'S EPISCOPAL CHURCH.
Real property exempt from taxation, §47-1020.

ST. MARTIN'S APARTMENTS PROJECT.
Real property tax exemptions, §47-4620.

ST. PAUL SENIOR LIVING AT WAYNE PLACE.
Real property tax exemption, §47-4642.

SALE OF GOODS, UCC, §§28:2-101 to 28:2-725.
Acceptance of goods.
What constitutes, §28:2-606.
Action for price.
Seller's remedies, §28:2-709.
Affirmations.
Express warranties, §28:2-313.
Antecedent breach.
Effect of cancellation or rescission on claims, §28:2-720.
Anticipatory repudiation, §28:2-610.
Proof of market price, §28:2-723.
Retraction, §28:2-611.
Approval.
Sale on approval, §§28:2-326, 28:2-327.
Assignment of rights, §28:2-210.
Assortment of goods.
Buyer's option, §28:2-311.

SALE OF GOODS, UCC —Cont'd
Assurance of performance.
Right to adequate assurance, §28:2-609.
Auction sales, §28:2-328.
Breach of obligations.
Antecedent breach.
Effect of cancellation or rescission on claims, §28:2-720.
Installment contracts, §28:2-612.
Limitation of actions, §28:2-725.
Notice requirements, §28:2-607.
Burden of proof.
Breaches with respect to accepted goods, §28:2-607.
Cancellation of contract.
Buyer's remedies.
Enumerated, §28:2-711.
Seller's remedies, §28:2-703.
C. & F. terms, §§28:2-320, 28:2-321.
Casualty to identified goods, §28:2-613.
C.I.F. terms, §§28:2-320, 28:2-321.
Citation of article, §28:2-101.
Collateral contracts.
Remedies for breach not impaired, §28:2-701.
Complaint for goods sold and delivered, CivPro Form CA 5.
Consignment sales, §28:2-326.
Construction and interpretation.
Cancellation.
Effect of term on claims for antecedent breach, §28:2-720.
Course of performance, §28:1-303.
Delivery of goods.
Absence of specified place for delivery, §28:2-308.
Time for delivery.
Absence of specified time, §28:2-309.
Open price terms, §28:2-305.
Rescission.
Effect of term on claims for antecedent breach, §28:2-720.
Risks.
Allocation or division, §28:2-303.
Shipment of goods.
Time for shipment.
Absence of specified time, §28:2-309.
Cooperation respecting performance, §28:2-311.
Course of dealing.
Implied warranties, §28:2-314.
Cover.
Buyer's procurement of substitute goods, §28:2-712.

SALE OF GOODS, UCC —Cont'd
Shipment and delivery —Cont'd
Tender of delivery —Cont'd
Cure by seller of improper tender, §28:2-508.
Effect of seller's tender, §28:2-507.
Excuse by failure of presupposed conditions, §§28:2-615, 28:2-616.
Manner of seller's tender, §28:2-503.
Time for shipment or delivery.
Absence of specified time, §28:2-309.
Warranty of condition on arrival, §28:2-321.
Withholding delivery.
Seller's remedies, §28:2-703.
Specific performance.
Right of buyer, §28:2-716.
Statute of frauds, §28:2-201.
Statute of limitations, §28:2-725.
Substituted performance, §28:2-614.
Termination of contract.
Contracts of indefinite duration, §28:2-309.
Definition of "termination," §28:2-106.
Notice of termination, §28:2-309.
Third party actions.
Who can sue third parties for injury to goods, §28:2-722.
Timber.
Applicability of chapter, §28:2-107.
Title of article.
Short title, §28:2-101.
Title to goods.
Passing of title, §28:2-401.
Power to transfer title, §28:2-403.
Reservation for security, §28:2-401.
Warranty of title, §28:2-312.
Transfer of goods.
Requisites, §28:2-105.
Transitional provisions, §§28:11-101 to 28:11-108.
See COMMERCIAL CODE.
Unconscionability, §28:2-302.
Unfinished goods.
Seller's right to salvage, §28:2-704.
Usage of trade.
Implied warranties, §28:2-314.
Waiver of executory portion of contract, §28:2-209.
Warranties.
Damages for breach, §28:2-714.
Express warranties.
Cumulation and conflict, §28:2-317.
Exclusions, §§28:2-316, 28:2-316.01.
Generally, §28:2-313.
Modification, §§28:2-316, 28:2-316.01.

SALE OF GOODS, UCC —Cont'd
Warranties —Cont'd
Implied warranties.
Course of dealing or usage of trade, §28:2-314.
Cumulation and conflict, §28:2-317.
Exclusions, §§28:2-316, 28:2-316.01.
Fitness for a particular purpose, §28:2-315.
Exclusion or modification, §§28:2-316, 28:2-316.01.
Merchantability, §28:2-314.
Exclusion or modification, §§28:2-316, 28:2-316.01.
Modification generally, §§28:2-316, 28:2-316.01.
Infringement of enjoyment of goods.
Warranty of title and against infringement, §28:2-312.
Merchantability, §28:2-314.
Exclusion or modification, §28:2-316.
Title.
Warranty of title and against infringement, §28:2-312.

SALES.
Abandoned property, §41-122.
Alcoholic beverages.
See ALCOHOLIC BEVERAGES.
Ammunition.
Permitted sales and transfers, §7-2505.02.
Prohibited sales and transfers, §7-2505.01.
Artisan's liens, associated with, §40-307.02.
Assignments for benefit of creditors.
Disposal of assets, §28-2106.
Assistive technology devices.
Implied warranty, §§28-4031 to 28-4034.
Attached property, §§16-518, 16-525, 16-550, 16-555.
Bicycles.
Information on voluntary registration provided purchaser, §50-1611.
Capitol grounds, on, §10-503.14.
Cemetery associations.
Power to acquire and sell real property, §43-102.
Sale on execution, not liable to, §43-111.
Use of proceeds from sale of lots, §43-106.
Children and minors, property of.
See GUARDIAN AND WARD.

SALES —Cont'd

Cigarette sales below cost, §§28-4521 to 28-4527.

See CIGARETTES.

Coal, charcoal, or coke, §37-201.11.

Commercial code.

Sale of goods, §§28:2-101 to 28:2-725.

See SALE OF GOODS, UCC.

Complaint for specific performance to convey land, CivPro Form CA 12.

Condominiums, offer of disposition of, §§42-1904.01 to 42-1904.18.

See CONDOMINIUMS.

Consumer protection, §§28-3801 to 28-3819.

See CONSUMER PROTECTION.

Contingent interests, §§42-1401 to 42-1404.

Contracts.

Sale of goods, §§28:2-101 to 28:2-725.

See SALE OF GOODS, UCC.

Court ordered sales of property, CivPro Rule 308.

Probate proceedings. See within this heading, "Probate proceedings."

Dead bodies, §§3-206, 22-3303.

District sales of animals and materials, proceeds from, §47-132.

Estate property, §20-703.

Evidence.

Contracts.

Parol and extrinsic evidence, §28:2-202.

Excess property for development of seat of government, §§16-1332, 16-1333.

Execution of judgments, levied property pursuant to, §§15-314 to 15-318.

Federal property, §47-709.

Fiduciaries.

Sale of estate property, CivPro Rule 305.

Probate proceedings. See within this heading, "Probate proceedings."

Firearms.

See FIREARMS.

Fish and game law forfeitures, §22-4330.

Food.

Implied warranty of merchantability, §28:2-314.

Food, sale of unwholesome.

See FOOD.

SALES —Cont'd

Foreign missions, real property transactions by, §6-1305.

Forest Haven products, §44-1403.

For sale signs, §42-1801.

Fraudulent conveyances.

Complaint to set aside, CivPro Form CA 13.

Garage keepers' liens, associated with, §§40-103, 40-104.

General obligation bonds, §1-204.74.

Public or private sale of, §1-204.66.

Health spas, §28-3817.

Home for Aged and Infirm.

Sale of surplus products of, §44-716.

Homestead housing preservation, §42-2107.

Housing finance agency bond issues, §42-2704.03.

Industrial home school products, §44-1304.

Industrial revenue bond forward commitment program, §47-340.05.

Intercepting devices, §23-543.

Judgment enforcement, CivPro Rule 70.

Domestic relations actions, DomRel Rule 70.

Judgments and decrees, property sold pursuant to, §15-105.

Liens, satisfaction of.

Artisan's liens, §40-307.02.

Garage keepers' liens, §§40-103, 40-104.

Mechanic's liens.

General provisions, §§40-303.09 to 40-303.12.

Life estates, §§42-1401 to 42-1404.

Limitation of actions, §28:2-725.

Limited interests, §§42-1401 to 42-1404.

Lodging places.

Satisfaction of lien on amounts due by sale of personal property of guests, §30-102.

Unclaimed personal property, §30-103.

Lottery and charitable games control board tickets, §3-1315.

Lottery tickets, §22-1701.

Maps, §1-301.01.

Mechanic's liens, sales associated with.

General provisions, §§40-303.09 to 40-303.12.

See MECHANIC'S LIENS.

Metropolitan police property clerk.

Sale of property by, §§5-119.09 to 5-119.16.

SALES —Cont'd

Mortgages and deeds of trust.
Foreclosure sales.
  See MORTGAGES AND DEEDS OF
    TRUST.

Motor fuel tax contraband, §47-2320.

National Capital Housing Authority,
§6-101.01.

National Guard equipment, selling,
pawning, or retaining, §49-205.

Navy Yard track connection,
§9-1203.02.

Parol and extrinsic evidence.
Sales contracts, §28:2-202.

Pawnbrokers, §§47-2884.13 to
47-2884.15.

Personal property taxes, distraint or
levy.
See PERSONAL PROPERTY TAXES.

Pharmacies, bulk sales or transfers
by, §47-2885.12.

Phosphate cleaners, §§8-107.02,
8-107.03.

Pistols, §22-4507.

Prison industries program,
§24-231.05.

Probate proceedings.
Death before Jan. 1, 1981.
  Personal property, Probate Rule 17.
  Real property, Probate Rule 18.
Death between Jan. 1, 1981, and June
  30, 1995, Probate Rule 112.
Guardians, conservators, trustees, etc.,
  involved, Probate Rules 203, 222,
  223.

Prostitution, houses of, §§22-2717,
22-2718.

Publications, §1-301.01.

Public lands, §§10-801 to 10-806.
See PUBLIC LANDS.

Public utilities, §§34-504, 34-1001,
35-271.

Railroads, disposition of unclaimed
property by, §§35-101 to 35-103.

Real property taxes, sale of
delinquent property for,
§§47-1301 to 47-1321.
See REAL ESTATE TAX SALES.

Registered beverage bottles,
unauthorized sale of, §36-102.

Registered milk containers,
unauthorized sale of, §§36-122,
36-153.

Rental housing conversion and sale.
General provisions, §§42-3401.01 to
  42-3405.13.
See RENTAL HOUSING.

SALES —Cont'd

Residential home sales disclosures,
§§42-1301 to 42-1311.
See HOME SALES.

Residential real property.
Seller disclosures, §§42-1301 to
  42-1311.

Revised real property tax sale,
§§47-1330 to 47-1385.
See REAL ESTATE TAX SALES.

Secondary market, sale or
assignment of instruments on,
§42-1102.01.

Security agents and brokers.
General provisions, §§31-5601.01 to
  31-5608.04.
  See SECURITY AGENTS AND
    BROKERS.

Self-service storage facilities.
Lien for rent, labor or other charges.
Enforcement of lien, §40-404.

Similar items, use of exchange
allowances or sale proceeds to
purchase, §1-301.92.

State health planning and
development agency certificates
of need, §44-411.

Street sweepings, §1-305.02.

Taxation, anticipation of, §1-301.70.

Tickets of sale, §37-201.10.

Tobacco, §§7-1721.01 to 7-1721.07.
See TOBACCO.

Trust, mortgage and title
corporation capital stock,
§26-1317.

Unclaimed abandoned property,
§§30-103, 41-122.

Unlawful trade practices, §28-3904.

Unsafe structures sold for
nonpayment of cost to correct,
§6-806.

Weighing and measuring devices,
§37-201.23.

Weights and measures, §§37-201.01 to
37-201.33.
See WEIGHTS AND MEASURES.

SALES AND USE TAX.

Streamlined sales and use tax
agreement, §§1-301.121 to
1-301.128.
Authority to enter into agreement,
  §1-301.123.
Authority to participate in multistate
  negotiations, §1-301.122.
Benefits and effect, §1-301.127.
Construction with laws of the District,
  §1-301.124.

SALES AND USE TAX —Cont'd
Streamlined sales and use tax agreement —Cont'd
Effect, §1-301.127.
Liability of sellers or third parties, §1-301.128.
Prerequisites for entering into agreement, §1-301.125.
Purpose, §1-301.126.
Verizon center sales tax, §47-2002.06.

SALES ON ACCOUNTS.
Commercial code.
General provisions, §§28:9-101 to 28:9-809.
See SECURED TRANSACTIONS.

SALES TAXES.
Ballpark sales taxes, §47-2002.05.
Compensating-use tax, §§47-2201 to 47-2214.
See COMPENSATING-USE TAX.
Gross sales tax, §§47-2001 to 47-2027.
See GROSS SALES TAX.
Rhode Island Metro Plaza Pilot Area.
Payments in lieu of taxes, sales tax exemption, §47-4613.
Verizon center sales tax, §47-2002.06.

SALVAGE, FLOOD AND JUNK VEHICLES, §§50-1331.01 to 50-1331.09.
Authority of department to designate vehicles, §50-1331.04.
Definitions, §50-1331.01.
Flood vehicles.
Defined, §50-1331.01.
Fees, §50-2201.03.
Indication on title.
Authority of department, application by owner or lessor, §50-1331.04.
Notification of flood status prior to transfer.
Duty, §50-1331.03.
Junk vehicles.
Defined, §50-1331.01.
Flattened, baled, shredded or destroyed.
Surrender of title or certificate, §50-1331.07.
Insurance companies.
Junk vehicle certificate.
Duty to apply for, time, §50-1331.02.
Junk vehicle certificate.
Duty of owner to apply for, time, §50-1331.02.

SALVAGE, FLOOD AND JUNK VEHICLES —Cont'd
Junk vehicles —Cont'd
Junk vehicle certificate —Cont'd
Issuance, §50-1331.04.
Lessor.
Junk vehicle certificate.
Duty to apply for, time, §50-1331.02.
Persons acquiring.
Junk vehicle certificate.
Duty to apply for, time, §50-1331.02.
Titling or registering, §50-1331.07.
Fees, §50-2201.03.
Transfer of ownership.
Limitation, §50-1331.07.
Use and transfer restrictions, §50-1331.07.
Penalties, §50-1331.08.
Rules and regulations, §50-1331.09.
Salvage vehicles.
Defined, §50-1331.01.
Insurance companies.
Salvage certificate.
Duty to apply for, time, §50-1331.02.
Lessor.
Salvage certificate.
Duty to apply for, time, §50-1331.02.
Persons acquiring.
Salvage title.
Duty to apply for, time, §50-1331.02.
Rebuilt salvage vehicles.
Rebuilt salvage title.
Issuance, transfer through, §50-1331.06.
Registration, prohibition, §50-1331.05.
Salvage title.
Duty of owner to apply for, time, §50-1331.02.
Fees, §50-2201.03.
Issuance, §50-1331.04.
Transfer through, §50-1331.05.
Use and transfer restrictions, §50-1331.05.
Rebuilt salvage vehicles, §50-1331.06.
Unlawful acts, §50-1331.08.

SAME-SEX COUPLES.
Domestic partner benefits.
General provisions, §§32-701 to 32-710.
See DOMESTIC PARTNER BENEFITS.

SAME-SEX MARRIAGE.
Equal access to marriage, §46-401.

SAMOA.
Acknowledgment of deed, §42-111.

SAMPLES.
Sales warranties.
Express warranties by sample, §28:2-313.

SAMUEL J. SIMMONS NCBA ESTATES NO. 1 LIMITED PARTNERSHIP.
Lot 8, square 2855.
Real property tax exemptions, §47-4646.

SANCTIONS.
Adoption proceedings, Adoption Rule 16.
Discovery, Adoption Rule 37.
Air pollution, §8-101.05f.
Appeals, DCCtApp Rule 38.
Authority to initiate disciplinary proceedings, CivPro Rule 102.
Child support enforcement, §46-225.01.
Discovery, CivPro Rules 26, 37, USDistCt LCvR 26.2.
Adoption proceedings, Adoption Rule 37.
Domestic relations actions, DomRel Rule 37.
Frivolous, dilatory, etc., actions, CivPro Rule 11.
Appeals, DCCtApp Rule 38.
Domestic relations actions, DomRel Rule 11.
Hospitalization of persons with mental illness, MentalHealth Rule 14.
Landlord and tenant court.
Protective orders.
Late, partial or missed payments into court registry, LandlordTenant Rule 12-I.
Notice of procedural requirements, CivPro Rule 83.
Parentage proceedings.
Failure to submit to blood test, DomRel Rule 405.
Pretrial conferences, CivPro Rule 16-II.
Domestic relations actions, DomRel Rule 16-I.
Tax proceedings, Tax Rule 13.
Witness statements.
Failure to produce statement.
Criminal cases, JuvProc Rule 26.2.

SANCTIONS —Cont'd
Witness statements —Cont'd
Failure to produce statement —Cont'd
Juvenile proceedings, JuvProc Rule 32.
Probation modification hearings, CrimPro Rule 32.1.
Release from custody or detention, CrimPro Rule 46.
Sentencing hearings, CrimPro Rule 32.

SANITARY SEWAGE WORKS, §§34-2101 to 34-2134.
See WASTEWATER AND SEWAGE WORKS.

SATURDAYS.
After twelve o'clock noon.
Designated holiday, §28-2701.
Extension of time for performing acts, §28-2701.
Appeals, federal cases.
Clerk's office not open except as provided by local rule or order, FRAP 45(a).
Computation of time, FRAP 26(a).
Banks and financial institutions.
Designated holiday, §28-2701.
Building and loan associations.
Designated holiday, §28-2701.
Computation of time, CivPro Rule 6, CrimPro Rule 45.
Appeals, DCCtApp Rule 26.
Domestic relations actions, DomRel Rule 6.
Hospitalization of persons with mental illness, MentalHealth Rule 13.
Juvenile proceedings, JuvProc Rule 45.
Savings and loan associations.
Designated holiday, §28-2701.
Tax collection, §47-412.01.

SAVINGS ACCOUNTS.
ABLE savings accounts, §§47-4901, 47-4902.
Opportunity accounts, §§1-307.61 to 1-307.74.

SAVINGS AND LOAN ACQUISITIONS, §§26-1201 to 26-1217.
Application for, §26-1206.
Authorization.
Nonregional acquisitions, §26-1205.
Regional acquisitions, §26-1202.
Branches, regional, §§26-1203, 26-1204.

SAVINGS AND LOAN ACQUISITIONS —Cont'd

Continued operation of existing associations and holding companies, §26-1210.

Conversion from federal to state charter, effect of, §26-1211.

Cooperative agreements, §26-1214.

Definitions, §26-1201.

District status of associations controlled by non-District holding companies, §26-1208.

Examinations, §26-1214.

Exemptions from provisions, §26-1213.

Federal associations, exclusion of, §26-1213.

Fines, §26-1215.

Inspections, §26-1214.

Insurance requirements, §26-1212.

Issuance of rules regarding, §26-1209.

Minority-owned associations, §26-1217.

Nonregional acquisitions, §26-1205.

Prohibited acts, §26-1207.

Regional acquisitions, §26-1202.

Registered agent requirement, §26-1216.

Remedies, §26-1215.

Reports, §26-1214.

Use of minority-owned associations, §26-1217.

SAVINGS AND LOAN ASSOCIATIONS.

Acquisition of, §§26-1201 to 26-1217.
See SAVINGS AND LOAN ACQUISITIONS.

Direct-reduction loans for veterans, §42-3002.

Mortgages and deeds of trust.
General provisions, §§42-804 to 42-820.
See MORTGAGES AND DEEDS OF TRUST.

Saturdays.
Designated holiday, §28-2701.

Servicemen's readjustment for mortgages and deeds of trust, §§42-3001, 42-3002.

Unclaimed property.
General provisions, §§41-101 to 41-142.
See UNCLAIMED PROPERTY.

SAVINGS CLAUSES, §45-404.

Business licenses, §47-2847.

SAVINGS CLAUSES —Cont'd

Business organizations, §29-107.05.

Foreign-money judgments, §15-371.

Interpretation of provisions, §45-404.

Motor fuel tax, §47-2322.

Real estate brokers and salespersons, §42-1709.

Taxation of banks, financial institutions, insurance companies, and public utilities, §47-2512.

Traffic laws, §50-2201.08.

SCARIFICATION.

Body art establishments.
Business licenses, §47-2809.01.

Body artists.
Business licenses, §§47-2853.76a to 47-2853.76e.

SCHEDULING CONFERENCES, CivPro Rule 16, USDistCt LCrR 57.2, USDistCt LCvR 16.4.

Adoption proceedings, Adoption Rule 16.
Show cause hearings, Adoption Rule 39.

Authority to set conference, CivPro Rule 309.

Failure to appear, CivPro Rule 16-II.

Order provided by movant, CivPro Rule 12-I.

Probate proceedings.
Contested estate cases.
Death between Jan. 1, 1981, and June 30, 1995, Probate Rule 107.
Death on or after July 1, 1995, Probate Rule 407.
Guardians, conservators, trustees, etc., involved, Probate Rule 208.

SCHOLARSHIPS.

District of Columbia School of Law mayor's stipends, §38-1205.11.

Gallaudet University, §38-2402.08a.

Nurse training corps, §§38-1501 to 38-1503.

Pre-kindergarten programs.
Teachers, workforce development.
Higher education incentive scholarship award program, §38-274.02.

Scholarships for opportunity and results (SOAR) act, §§38-1853.01 to 38-1853.14.
Achievement reports, §38-1853.10.
Activities reports, §38-1853.10.

SCHOLARSHIPS —Cont'd
Scholarships for opportunity and results (SOAR) act —Cont'd
Administrative expenses.
Use of funds, §38-1853.07.
Appropriation, §38-1853.14.
Congressional findings, §38-1853.02.
Definitions, §38-1853.13.
Enrolling in another school.
Use of funds, §38-1853.07.
Evaluation of performance of students, §38-1853.09.
Funds to public schools and charter schools, §38-1853.04.
Applications, §38-1853.05.
Conditions of receipt of funds, §38-1853.11.
Nondiscrimination and other requirements, §38-1853.08.
Priorities in awarding grants, §38-1853.06.
Use of funds, §38-1853.07.
New participating schools.
Use of funds, §38-1853.07.
Nondiscrimination and other requirements, §38-1853.08.
Opportunity scholarships.
Applications for grants, §38-1853.05.
Award of grants, §38-1853.04.
Priorities in awarding grants, §38-1853.06.
Use of funds, §38-1853.07.
Parental assistance.
Use of funds, §38-1853.07.
Parents, reports to, §38-1853.10.
Personal information, disclosure prohibited, §38-1853.10.
Purpose, §38-1853.03.
Religiously affiliated schools, §38-1853.08.
Reporting requirements, §38-1853.10.
Short title, §38-1853.01.
Single sex schools, classes or other activities, §38-1853.08.
Special rules, §38-1853.12.
Student academic assistance.
Use of funds, §38-1853.07.
Student performance evaluation, §38-1853.09.
Testing requirements, §38-1853.08.
Transition provisions, §38-1853.12.
Teachers, workforce development.
Higher education incentive scholarship award program.
Transfer of authority, §38-274.01a.
University of the District of Columbia tuition grants, §§38-1207.01 to 38-1207.07.

SCHOOL BUILDINGS AND GROUNDS, §§38-401 to 38-409.
Automated external defibrillators, usage, §§44-231 to 44-235.
Budgets and budget estimates, §§47-202, 47-203.
Business High School, §38-408.
Charter schools, §38-1802.09.
Sharing facilities with public schools, §38-1831.01.
Construction projects, §38-402.
Entrances, §38-409.
Exclusive use of property for school purposes, §38-407.
Facilities master plan, §§38-1805.52, 38-2803.
Financial Responsibility and Management Assistance Authority, disposition by, §47-392.25.
Firearms.
Enhanced penalties and fines for carrying guns into gun free zones, §22-4502.01.
Franklin School used for office purposes, §38-403.
Leasing or purchasing public school facilities.
Preferences to eligible entities, §38-1802.09.
Lot 11, in square 141, §38-407.
Lot 14, in square 263, §§38-404, 38-405.
Lowell School real property exempt from taxation, §47-1049.
Mayor's power to raze, §38-156.
Public liability insurance, §38-401.02.
Real property exempt from taxation, §§47-1002, 47-1049.
Repairs and maintenance.
Charter schools, §38-1802.09.
Control of, §38-402.
Custodial employees, §38-903.
Definitions, §38-1805.50.
Facilities master plan, §§38-1805.52, 38-2803.
Gifts, §§38-1805.61, 38-1805.71.
Waivers, §38-1805.61.
Reports, §38-401.01.
Roosevelt (Business) High School, §38-408.
Sale of public lands.
Unused and underutilized public school buildings, §10-803.01.
Use of school buildings, §§38-401 to 38-409.

SCHOOL BUSES.
Business licenses, §47-2829.
Motor fuel tax.
Inapplicability of chapter provisions, §47-2313.
Restricted use of mobile telephones, §50-1731.05.

SCHOOL DISTRICTS.
State board of education.
Wards comprising districts, §38-2651.

SCHOOL LUNCH PROGRAM, §§38-801 to 38-809.

SCHOOLS AND EDUCATION.
Absences.
Attendance zone boundaries, §38-221.
Compulsory school attendance, §§38-201 to 38-213.
End-of-year reports by schools, §38-203.
Reporting to child and family services agency, §4-1321.02.
Accountability plans, §38-2806.
Adult education courses, §§38-1001 to 38-1003.
Employment services department.
Job training and adult education programs.
Quarterly reporting by department, §32-771.
Uniform per-student funding formula, §§38-2901 to 38-2914.
Advertising.
Event sponsorships, §38-174.01.
State athletic activities, programs, and office fund.
Advertisements and sponsorships, §38-2671.
Turkey Bowl revenue generation and sponsorship, §38-2981.
After-school programs.
Funding, §38-2931.
Agency performance measures, §38-121.02.
Allocation of funds to each school system, §38-2804.
Alternative educational programs.
Students expelled for weapons offenses, §38-233.
Americanization, evening, and summer schools, §38-1903.
Animals used in classroom, §§8-1851.01, 8-1851.02.
Appropriations, §§38-911, 38-914, 38-915, 38-1806.08.
Transfer of appropriation balance, §38-1204.05.

SCHOOLS AND EDUCATION
—Cont'd
Assessment of students, §38-2610.
Athletic concussion program, §§7-2871.01 to 7-2871.05.
Defined terms, §7-2871.01.
Materials development and distribution, §7-2871.04.
Removal from athletic activity.
Athletes suspected of sustaining concussion, §7-2871.02.
Return to athletic activity.
Athletes suspected of sustaining concussion, §7-2871.02.
Rules, §7-2871.05.
Training program, §7-2871.03.
Athletic equity, §§38-841.01 to 38-841.08.
Additional school requirements, §38-841.04.
Definitions, §38-841.01.
District of Columbia state athletic association.
Responsibility, §38-841.06.
Gender equity review committee, §38-841.04.
Nondiscrimination required, §38-841.02.
Recordkeeping, §38-841.04.
Reporting, §38-841.03.
Rules, §38-841.08.
Title IX athletic coordinators.
Designation, §38-841.05.
Title IX athletic equity strategic plans, §38-841.07.
Athletic events.
Medical coverage, requirement, §38-621.
State athletic activities, programs, and office fund, §§38-2671 to 38-2674.
Advertisements and sponsorships, §38-2671.
Applicability, §38-2674.
Effective date, §38-2674.
Established, §38-2672.
Purposes, §38-2672.
Rules, §38-2673.
Sources of revenue, §38-2672.
Turkey Bowl revenue generation and sponsorship, §38-2981.
At-risk students.
DCPS budget, §38-2907.01.
Supplement to foundation level funding, §38-2905.01.
Attendance.
Attendance zone boundaries, §38-221.

SCHOOLS AND EDUCATION
  —Cont'd
Attendance —Cont'd
  Compulsory school attendance,
    §§38-201 to 38-213.
    See COMPULSORY SCHOOL
      ATTENDANCE.
Audit.
  Calculation of number of students,
    §38-1804.02.
**Automated external defibrillators,
  usage,** §§44-231 to 44-235.
Aviation high school courses,
  §§38-920 to 38-922.
Behavioral health.
  Early childhood and school-based
    behavioral health infrastructure,
    §§2-1517.31, 2-1517.32.
Board of Education.
  General provisions.
    See BOARD OF EDUCATION.
BOOT CAMP, §24-924.
Budgets and budget estimates,
  §§38-1804.01, 38-1807.53.
  DCPS budget, §38-2907.01.
  Submission of budgets, §38-2831.
Buildings and grounds, §§38-401 to
  38-409.
  See SCHOOL BUILDINGS AND
    GROUNDS.
Bullying, §§2-1535.01 to 2-1535.09.
  See BULLYING.
Business partnerships, §§38-1806.01
  to 38-1806.09.
  Access to state of the art educational
    technology.
    Duty of private, nonprofit,
      §38-1806.04.
  Appropriations, §38-1806.08.
  District education and learning
    technologies advancement council.
    Duty of private, nonprofit to
      establish, membership, duties,
      §38-1806.04.
  District employment and learning
    center.
    Duty of private, nonprofit,
      §38-1806.04.
  Duties of superintendent, §38-1806.02.
  Grant to private nonprofit corporation.
    Eligibility to receive, §38-1806.03.
  Jobs for D.C. graduates program.
    Established by private, nonprofit
      corporation, §38-1806.07.
  Long-term technology plan.
    Duty of private, nonprofit,
      §38-1806.04.

SCHOOLS AND EDUCATION
  —Cont'd
Business partnerships —Cont'd
  Matching funds.
    Private, nonprofit corporation to
      provide, §38-1806.05.
  Purpose, §38-1806.01.
  Report by private, nonprofit
    corporation, §38-1806.06.
  Sense of congress relating to
    continuation, §38-1806.09.
  Termination of federal support,
    §38-1806.09.
  Workforce preparation.
    Duty of private, nonprofit,
      §38-1806.04.
Cadet programs. See within this
  heading, "Military affairs."
**Capital improvements to public
  schools.**
  Expenditure accountability.
    Audits, §38-2973.05.
    Disadvantaged businesses
      contracting requirements,
      compliance, §38-2973.04.
  Fund, §§38-2971.01 to 38-2971.04.
    Establishment, §38-2971.01.
    Facility management organizational
      strategy, §38-2971.04.
    General fund, offsetting revenue
      reductions to, §38-2972.01.
    Use, §38-2971.03.
Capital request, §38-919.
**Career and technical education
  (CTE) grant program,** §38-2611.
  Program fund, §38-2612.
Census of students.
  Funding purposes, §38-159.
  School attendance purposes, §38-204.
Ceremonial expenses, §38-914.
Certificates of immunization,
  §38-502.
  Attendance without certificate,
    §38-505.
  Exemptions, §38-506.
  Notice of missing certificate, §38-504.
Charter schools.
  General provisions.
    See CHARTER SCHOOLS.
Child abuse and neglect reports,
  §4-1321.02.
**Child and adult food program
  funding,** §§38-281 to 38-285.
  Applicability, §38-285.
  Child development facilities,
    participation, §38-282.01.

SCHOOLS AND EDUCATION
 —Cont'd
**Child and adult food program
 funding** —Cont'd
Definitions, §38-281.
Department of Parks and Recreation
 facilities, §38-284.
Effective date, §38-285.
Healthy Tots Fund, §38-282.
Office of state superintendent of
 education requirements, §38-283.
Child development facilities.
Child and adult food program.
 Office of state superintendent of
 education (OSSE) requirements,
 §38-283.
Participation in, §38-282.01.
Class size limitations, §38-109.
Collective bargaining.
Public school employee evaluation
 system not subject to, §1-617.18.
College access assistance, §§38-2701
 to 38-2706.
Common lottery board, §38-194.
Common lottery board fund, §38-195.
Community education courses,
 §§38-1001 to 38-1003.
Community input, §38-919.
Community schools.
Administration, §38-754.03.
Citation of provisions, §38-754.01.
Definitions, §38-754.02.
Fund establishment, §38-754.04.
Rules, §38-756.01.
Compulsory school attendance.
Attendance zone boundaries, §38-221.
Generally.
 See COMPULSORY SCHOOL
 ATTENDANCE.
**Consumer education and
 information,** §28-3906.
Content standards, §§38-1803.11 to
 38-1803.15.
Continuing education courses,
 §§38-1001 to 38-1003.
Core curriculum, §§38-1803.11 to
 38-1803.15.
**Correctional facility established
 near school.**
Notice given by mayor, §38-3201.
Counselors, §38-2807.
Counts of students.
Per student funding formula.
 Weighting at grade levels, §38-2904.
Crossing guards, §38-3101.
Custodial employees, §§38-903,
 38-1903, 38-1907.

SCHOOLS AND EDUCATION
 —Cont'd
DC promise program, §§38-2751 to
 38-2759.
See UNIVERSITIES AND
 COLLEGES.
Demographic analysis, §38-919.
Department of education, §§38-191 to
 38-193.
Authority, §38-191.
Establishment, §38-191.
Evaluation of schools, §38-193.
Ombudsman for public education,
 §§38-351 to 38-356.
Special education reporting, §38-192.
Department of general services,
 §§38-924 to 38-926.
Disabled children, §38-913.
Interstate compact on educational
 opportunity for military children.
 Comparable services for students
 with disabilities, §49-1101.06.
Nonpublic schools for students with
 disabilities, §§38-2561.01 to
 38-2561.16.
See SPECIAL EDUCATION.
Discriminatory practices,
 §§2-1401.01, 2-1402.41, 2-1402.42.
Athletic equity, §§38-841.01 to
 38-841.08.
**District of Columbia interscholastic
 athletic association (DCIAA).**
Turkey Bowl revenue generation and
 sponsorship, §38-2981.
**District of Columbia public schools
 (DCPS) funds.**
Relocation and use, §38-2955.
Driver education programs, §§38-912,
 38-913.
Issuance of rules, §38-912.01.
Drug-free zones, §48-904.07a.
Drug paraphernalia.
Distribution of needles or syringes
 near schools, §48-1121.
**Drug treatment centers established
 near.**
Notice given by mayor, §38-3201.
**Early childhood and school-based
 behavioral health infrastructure,**
 §§2-1517.31, 2-1517.32.
Early childhood education.
Citation of provisions, §38-755.01.
Definitions, §38-755.02.
Requirements and goals, §38-755.03.
Rules, §38-756.01.
Tracking and monitoring, §38-755.04.

SCHOOLS AND EDUCATION
—Cont'd

Early warning and support system.
Citation of provisions, §38-751.01.
Definitions, §38-751.02.
Pilot, §38-751.03.
Report, §38-751.05.
Rules, §38-756.01.
Survey, §38-751.04.
Educational data warehouse system,
§38-2609.
Education commission of the states,
compact for, §§38-3001 to 38-3004.
Adoption, §38-3001.
Bylaws filed with mayor, §38-3004.
Compact provisions, §38-3002.
District commission members,
§38-3003.
District membership approved,
§38-3001.
Environmental programs, §§38-825.01
to 38-825.03.
Applicability of law, §38-828.02.
Environmental literacy program,
§38-825.02.
Office, §38-825.01.
Rulemaking authority, §38-828.01.
School gardens program, §38-825.03.
Evaluation of schools.
Department of education, §38-193.
Expenses, §§38-914, 38-915.
Expulsion of students for weapons,
§§38-231 to 38-235.
Alternative educational programs,
eligibility for, §38-233.
Family and medical leave, §32-506.
Farm-to-school program, §§38-823.01
to 38-823.03.
Applicability of law, §38-828.02.
Comprehensive plan, §38-823.01a.
Preferences for locally grown food,
§38-823.01.
Promotion of locally grown food,
§38-823.02.
Reports, §38-823.03.
Rulemaking authority, §38-828.01.
Financial literacy education,
§38-731.02.
Financial management reform,
§§38-1801.01 to 38-1801.03.
Plan, §38-2951.
Task force, §38-2952.
Firearms.
Enhanced penalties and fines for
carrying guns into gun free zones,
§22-4502.01.

SCHOOLS AND EDUCATION
—Cont'd

Firearms —Cont'd
Expulsion of students for weapons,
§§38-231 to 38-235.
Fire department members.
Tuition expenses, §5-1305.
Firefighter cadet programs, §§38-912,
38-913.
Issuance of rules, §38-912.01.
Fiscal year, §1-204.41.
Fiscal year 2006 educational
investments fund for District of
Columbia public schools and
public charter schools, §1-325.31.
Food services, §§38-801 to 38-809.
Appropriations, §§38-805, 38-809.
Audit of accounts, §38-807.
Board of education powers, §38-802.
Contracts, §§38-157, 38-1807.51.
Department of food services, §38-801.
Creation, §38-801.
Deposits of revenues and receipts,
§38-804.
Distribution of commodities, §§38-808,
38-809.
Equipment appropriations, §38-805.
National school lunch act programs,
§38-806.
Foundation level.
Public education finance reform
commission, §38-2914.
Uniform per student funding formula.
DCPS budget, §38-2907.01.
Education costs excluded from,
§38-2907.
Public schools and public charter
schools, §38-2903.
Supplement.
At-risk students, §38-2905.01.
Special education, summer school
and residential school
students, §38-2905.
Free textbooks, §§38-701 to 38-706,
38-922.
Limitation on purchases, §38-704.
Funding.
After-school programs, §38-2931.
Annual budgets, §38-1804.01.
Appropriations, §§38-911, 38-914,
38-915.
At-risk supplemental allocation
preservation fund, §1-325.35.
Budget submission requirements,
§38-2831.
Business partnerships.
Matching funds, §38-1806.05.

SCHOOLS AND EDUCATION
—Cont'd
Funding —Cont'd
Capital request, §38-919.
Census of students for purposes of, §38-159.
Common lottery board fund, §38-195.
Fiscal year 2006 educational investments fund for District of Columbia public schools and public charter schools, §1-325.31.
Healthy tots fund, §38-282.
Higher education licensure commission site evaluation fund, §38-2607.
Innovation fund, §§1-325.221 to 1-325.226.
Number of students.
Calculating, §§38-159, 38-1804.02.
Payment procedures, §38-1804.03.
Policy declaration, §38-916.
Private funds, use of, §38-121.01.
Public education finance reform commission, §38-2914.
Public hearings, §38-917.
Public school capital improvement fund, §§38-2971.01 to 38-2971.04.
Schools modernization fund, §§1-325.41 to 1-325.45. See within this heading, "Schools modernization fund."
Schools technology fund, §1-325.251.
State athletic activities, programs, and office fund, §§38-2671 to 38-2674.
TANF fund sharing, §38-2931.
Turkey Bowl revenue generation and sponsorship, §38-2981.
Uniform per-student funding formula, §§38-2901 to 38-2914.
Adjusting appropriations in case of revenue unavailability, §38-2910.
Applicability, §38-2902.
DCPS budget, §38-2907.01.
Definitions, §38-2901.
Education costs excluded from formula.
Payments to, §38-2907.
Foundation level, §38-2903.
Per capita funding.
Supplement to foundation level funding, §38-2905.
Public charter schools.
Facilities allowance, §38-2908.
Payments to, §38-2906.02.
Public education finance reform commission, §38-2914.

SCHOOLS AND EDUCATION
—Cont'd
Funding —Cont'd
Uniform per-student funding formula —Cont'd
Revision of formula, §38-2911.
Services provided on equal basis, §38-2913.
Student counts, §38-2906.
Supplemental foundation level funding, §§38-2905, 38-2905.01.
Variations from uniformity, §38-2912.
Weightings applied to counts of students enrolled at certain grade levels, §38-2904.
Gallaudet University.
Appropriation for indigent blind children formerly instructed at, §38-2301.
Elementary school program, §§38-2401.04, 38-2401.05.
Secondary education program, §§38-2401.04, 38-2401.05.
Generally.
Compulsory school attendance, §§38-201 to 38-213.
General services department, §§38-924 to 38-926.
Gifts, §§38-907, 38-910.
Guardianship of minors responsible for maintenance and education of child.
Amounts expended, §21-143.
Sale of principal, §21-147.
Half way house established near school.
Notice given by mayor, §38-3201.
Heads of department, §§38-109, 38-1908.
Health and wellness programs, §§38-826.01 to 38-826.05.
Applicability of law, §38-828.02.
Local wellness policies, §38-826.01.
Nurses, §38-826.04.
Rulemaking authority, §38-828.01.
School health centers, §38-826.03.
School health profiles, §38-826.02.
Tobacco-free school campuses, §38-826.05.
Health care of students, §§38-601 to 38-651.12.
See STUDENT HEALTH CARE.
Healthy schools fund.
Applicability of law, §38-828.02.
Definitions, §38-821.01.

SCHOOLS AND EDUCATION
—Cont'd
Healthy schools fund —Cont'd
Establishment, §38-821.02.
Rulemaking authority, §38-828.01.
Healthy tots fund, §38-282.
Healthy youth and schools commission, §§38-827.01 to 38-827.04.
Administrative and technical support, §38-827.04.
Applicability of law, §38-828.02.
Establishment, §38-827.01.
Members, §38-827.02.
Rulemaking authority, §38-828.01.
Rules of procedure, §38-827.03.
Higher education licensure commission, §§38-1301 to 38-1313.
See HIGHER EDUCATION LICENSURE COMMISSION.
Higher education licensure commission site evaluation fund, §38-2607.
Homeless shelter established near school.
Notice given by mayor, §38-3201.
Human papillomavirus vaccination.
School enrollment, requirements, §7-1651.04.
Immunization of school students, §§38-501 to 38-508.
Human papillomavirus vaccination.
School enrollment, requirements, §7-1651.04.
Interstate compact on educational opportunity for military children.
Time to obtain immunizations, §49-1101.05.
Immunization plan, §38-507.
Innovation fund, §§1-325.221 to 1-325.226.
Interagency collaboration and services integration commission, §§2-1591 to 2-1597.
Interstate compact on educational opportunity for military children, §§49-1101.01 to 49-1101.20. See within this heading, "Military affairs."
Job training.
Employment services department.
Job training and adult education programs.
Quarterly reporting by department, §32-771.
Fire protection study commission.
Sprinkler installation program, combined with, §3-1104.

SCHOOLS AND EDUCATION
—Cont'd
Job training —Cont'd
Get DC Residents Training for Jobs Now, §§38-1011.01 to 38-1011.05.
Opportunity accounts.
Generally, §§1-307.61 to 1-307.74.
Use for training of account holder, §1-307.68.
Junior reserve officers' training program, §38-158.
Kindergarten, §38-2807.
Librarians, §§38-1901, 38-2807.
Long-term reform plan, §38-1801.01.
Lotteries.
Common lottery board, §38-194.
Common lottery board fund, §38-195.
Management systems, §38-1807.51.
Metropolitan police.
School safety division, §§5-132.01 to 5-132.21.
See METROPOLITAN POLICE.
Metrorail and metrobus student fares.
General provisions, §§35-232 to 35-237.
See METRORAIL AND METROBUS.
Military affairs.
Instructors for junior reserve officers' training program, §38-158.
Insurance for arms issued to high school cadets, §38-909.
Interstate compact on educational opportunity for military children, §§49-1101.01 to 49-1101.20.
Adoption of compact, §49-1101.01.
Amendment of compact, §49-1101.16.
Applicability, §49-1101.04.
Binding effect, §49-1101.19.
Children subject to compact, §49-1101.04.
Conflict of laws, §49-1101.19.
Construction of provisions, §49-1101.18.
Course placement, §49-1101.06.
D.C. interstate compact council, §49-1101.20.
Default of member state, §49-1101.13.
Definitions, §49-1101.03.
Deployment of parent or legal guardian.
Excused absence to visit, §49-1101.06.

SCHOOLS AND EDUCATION
—Cont'd
Military affairs —Cont'd
Interstate compact on educational
opportunity for military children
—Cont'd
Disabilities, students with.
Comparable services for,
§49-1101.06.
Dispute resolution, §49-1101.13.
Dissolution of compact, §49-1101.17.
Effectiveness of compact,
§49-1101.16.
Eligibility to be member state,
§49-1101.16.
Enforcement of compact,
§49-1101.13.
Enrollment of student, §49-1101.05.
Graduation requirements,
§49-1101.08.
Immunizations, time to obtain,
§49-1101.05.
Interstate commission.
Bylaws, §49-1101.11.
Committees, §49-1101.09.
Defense of actions, §49-1101.11.
Dispute resolution, §49-1101.13.
Established, §49-1101.09.
Financing of activities,
§49-1101.14.
Immunity, §49-1101.11.
Meetings, §49-1101.09.
Officers elected, §49-1101.11.
Organization and operation,
§49-1101.11.
Powers and duties, §49-1101.10.
Rulemaking functions,
§49-1101.12.
Local agency participation,
§49-1101.15.
Membership of state councils,
§49-1101.15.
Notice and service, §49-1101.13.
Oversight and enforcement of
compact, §49-1101.13.
Parental consent, power of attorney
for, §49-1101.07.
Purpose of compact, §49-1101.02.
Reinstatement following withdrawal,
§49-1101.17.
Release of educational records,
§49-1101.05.
Severability of provisions,
§49-1101.18.
Special power of attorney relative to
guardianship, §49-1101.07.

SCHOOLS AND EDUCATION
—Cont'd
Military affairs —Cont'd
Interstate compact on educational
opportunity for military children
—Cont'd
State council, §49-1101.20.
Tuition charges for transitioning
student, §49-1101.07.
Withdrawal of member state,
§49-1101.17.
Police officer and firefighter cadet
programs, §§38-912, 38-913.
Issuance of rules, §38-912.01.
Supplies issued by military.
No bond required, §38-908.
**My School DC EdFest sponsorship
and advertising,** §38-196.01.
Name changes, §§38-904, 38-905.
**National technical institute for the
deaf,** §§38-2401.11, 38-2401.12,
38-2402.01 to 38-2402.11.
See NATIONAL TECHNICAL
INSTITUTE FOR THE DEAF.
Needs evaluation for facilities,
§38-918.
**Nonpublic schools for students with
disabilities,** §§38-2561.01 to
38-2561.16.
See SPECIAL EDUCATION.
Nonresident tuition, §§38-301 to
38-313.
Notice.
Immunization of school students,
§38-503.
Certificate missing, §38-504.
Number of students.
Calculating, §§38-159, 38-1804.02.
Nurses, §38-621.
Health and wellness programs,
§38-826.04.
Nutrition, §§38-822.01 to 38-822.07.
Additional requirements, §38-822.03.
Applicability of law, §38-828.02.
Central kitchen, §38-822.04.
Fundraising, requirements,
§38-822.06.
Goals, §38-822.01.
Prizes, requirements, §38-822.06.
Public disclosure, §38-822.05.
Rulemaking authority, §38-828.01.
Standards, §38-822.02.
Triennial review, §38-822.07.
Vending machines, requirements,
§38-822.06.

SCHOOLS AND EDUCATION
—Cont'd
Office of state superintendent of education (OSSE) requirements.
Child and adult food program funding, §38-283.
Child development facilities, §38-283.
Official expenses, §38-915.
Ombudsman for public education, §§38-351 to 38-356.
Authority and powers, §38-354.
Charter schools, cooperation with, §38-1802.04.
Duties, §38-353.
Establishment, §38-351.
Limitation of liability, §38-355.
Prohibited acts, §38-355.
Qualifications, §38-352.
Terms of office, §38-351.
Opportunity accounts.
Generally, §§1-307.61 to 1-307.74.
Use for educational expenses, §1-307.68.
Pages, §38-152.
Parental leave to attend or participate in school-related event, §§32-1201 to 32-1206.
Parent-teacher conferences, §38-1809.01.
Pensions and retirement.
Food services department, §38-803.
Teachers, §§38-2001.01 to 38-2041.01.
See TEACHERS' RETIREMENT.
Per capita funding.
Calculation of number of students, §38-1804.02.
Payments to public charter schools, §38-2906.02.
Public school enrollment census, §38-159.
Student count, resident students, §38-2906.
Uniform per student funding formula.
Supplement to foundation level funding, §§38-2905, 38-2905.01.
Personnel files, §38-2802.
Per student funding formula, §§38-2901 to 38-2914.
Physical and health education, §§38-824.01 to 38-824.05.
Access to public facilities, §38-824.04.
Applicability of law, §38-828.02.
Goals, §38-824.01.

SCHOOLS AND EDUCATION
—Cont'd
Physical and health education
—Cont'd
Reports, §38-824.05.
Requirements, §§38-824.02, 38-824.03.
Rulemaking authority, §38-828.01.
Police department members.
Tuition expenses, §5-1305.
Police officer cadet programs, §§38-912, 38-913.
Issuance of rules, §38-912.01.
Postsecondary preparation plan.
Citation of provisions, §38-752.01.
Definitions, §38-752.02.
Requirements, §38-752.03.
Rules, §38-756.01.
Pregnant or parenting teens.
Public assistance for, §§4-205.61 to 4-205.66.
Pre-kindergarten programs, §§38-271.01 to 38-275.01, 38-2807.
Prisons and prisoners.
Educational good time credits for, §24-221.01.
Private schools.
Nonpublic schools for students with disabilities, §§38-2561.01 to 38-2561.16.
See SPECIAL EDUCATION.
Promotion and retention of students, §§38-781.01 to 38-781.06.
Definitions, §38-781.01.
Principal's authority, §38-781.02.
Reporting requirements, §38-781.03.
Review and appeal of retention decisions, §38-781.04.
Rules, §38-781.06.
Summer school, §38-781.05.
Promotion gates, §§38-1803.11 to 38-1803.15.
Public education finance reform commission, §38-2914.
Public schools agency, §§38-171 to 38-175.
Authority of mayor, §38-172.
Budget requirements, §38-173.
Chancellor, §38-174.
Establishment, §38-171.
Rules and regulations, §38-172.
Transfer of board functions to mayor, §38-175.

SCHOOLS AND EDUCATION
—Cont'd
**Qualification of educational
    personnel.**
    Interstate agreement on, §§38-2101 to
        38-2104.
**Qualified zone academy revenue
    bond project forward
    commitment approval act,**
    §§2-1217.101 to 2-1217.108.
    See QUALIFIED ZONE ACADEMY
        REVENUE BOND PROJECT
        FORWARD COMMITMENT
        APPROVAL ACT.
Records.
    Access to fiscal and staffing data,
        §38-1807.52.
    Food services accounts.
        Audit, §38-807.
    Medical records of students, §38-607.
    Personnel files, §§38-1807.52, 38-2802.
    Teachers' retirement.
        Prior to June 30, 1946, §38-2001.14.
Reform implementation plans,
    §38-2805.
Reform program, §§38-1800.01 to
    38-1803.21.
Reports.
    Absences, end-of-year report, §38-203.
    Business partnerships, §38-1806.06.
    Calculation of number of students,
        §38-1804.02.
    Capital request.
        Demographic analysis and
            community input in, §38-919.
    Enrollments and withdrawals,
        §38-205.
    Expulsion of students for weapons,
        §38-235.
    Lead poisoning tests, §38-610.
    Reforms, §§38-1801.02, 38-1801.03.
    School buildings and grounds,
        §38-401.01.
    Students, promotion and retention,
        §38-781.03.
    Suspension or expulsion of students,
        §38-236.
    Testing integrity in public schools.
        Authorized personnel,
            responsibilities, §38-771.03.
**Research assistants classified as
    teachers,** §38-1906.
Reservation 277-F, §38-906.
Residency.
    Establishment of residency, §38-308.
        Documentation to established,
            §38-309.

SCHOOLS AND EDUCATION
—Cont'd
Residency —Cont'd
    Establishment of residency —Cont'd
        False information, §38-312.
            Hotline, §38-312.01.
        Unable to confirm, procedures
            established, §38-311.
        Proof of residency, §38-307.
        Status reports, §38-312.03.
Sale of public lands.
    Unused and underutilized public
        school buildings, §10-803.01.
Schedule A submission, §38-160.
**School-based budgeting and
    accountability,** §§38-2802 to
    38-2807.
School buildings and grounds,
    §§38-401 to 38-409.
    See SCHOOL BUILDINGS AND
        GROUNDS.
School gardens program, §38-825.03.
School nurses, §38-621.
Schools modernization fund,
    §§1-325.41 to 1-325.45.
    Annual report, §1-325.45.
    Bonds.
        Authorization to issue, §1-325.43.
        Use of revenue, criteria, §1-325.44.
    Budget submission requirements,
        §1-325.42.
    Established, §1-325.41.
    Review of funding priorities,
        §1-325.45.
Security services.
    Contracting out, §§38-157, 38-1807.51.
Select adult.
    Community and continuing education
        courses, §§38-1001 to 38-1003.
Smoking.
    Educational facility, §7-1703.
    "No Smoking" signs, §7-1704.
    Tobacco-free school campuses,
        §38-826.05.
Special education.
    Disabled children, §38-913.
        Nonpublic schools, §§38-2561.01 to
            38-2561.16.
        See SPECIAL EDUCATION.
    Foundation level.
        Uniform per student funding
            formula.
            Supplement, §38-2905.
    Medicaid and special education reform
        fund, §§4-204.51 to 4-204.56.
    Task force, §§38-2551 to 38-2555.

SCHOOLS AND EDUCATION
—Cont'd
Special education —Cont'd
Uniform per-student funding formula,
§§38-2901 to 38-2914.
Sports events.
Medical coverage, requirement,
§38-621.
Turkey Bowl revenue generation and
sponsorship, §38-2981.
State Board of Education.
General provisions.
See BOARD OF EDUCATION.
**State superintendent of education,
office of,** §§38-2601 to 38-2612.
Street safety education, §38-3401.
Student advocate, office of, §§38-371
to 38-374.
Chief advocate, §38-372.
Duties, §38-373.
Public education resource centers,
§38-374.
Student counts.
Per student funding formula.
Weighting at grade levels, §38-2904.
Student health care, §§38-601 to
38-651.12.
See STUDENT HEALTH CARE.
Students.
Assessments, §38-2610.
Promotion and retention, §§38-781.01
to 38-781.06. See within this
heading, "Promotion and retention
of students."
Solicitation of gifts from, §§38-907,
38-910.
Truancy prevention resource guide,
§38-2602.
Summer school.
Foundation level.
Uniform per student funding
formula.
Supplement, §38-2905.
Promotion criteria, students failing to
meet, §38-781.05.
Uniform per-student funding formula,
§§38-2901 to 38-2914.
TANF fund sharing, §38-2931.
Teachers.
General provisions, §§38-1901 to
38-1923.
See TEACHERS.
Retirement of teachers, §§38-2001.01
to 38-2041.01.
See TEACHERS' RETIREMENT.

SCHOOLS AND EDUCATION
—Cont'd
Technical education.
Career and technical education (CTE)
grant program, §38-2611.
Program fund, §38-2612.
Technology.
Schools technology fund, §1-325.251.
Testing integrity, §§38-771.01 to
38-771.07.
See TESTING INTEGRITY IN
PUBLIC SCHOOLS.
Textbooks.
Evaluation, time period, §38-701.
Free textbooks, §§38-701 to 38-706,
38-922.
Board authorized to sell or
exchange, §38-705.
Books remain property of District,
§38-702.
Certification that each student
issued books and supplies,
§38-701.
Duty to issue books and supplies
without charge, §38-701.
Evaluation that textbooks meet
goals and objectives, §38-701.
Expenses, §38-706.
Only recommended and approved
books and supplies purchased,
§38-704.
Parents and guardians liable for
damage, §38-703.
Refundable deposit, §38-701.
Regulations to implement
provisions, §38-701.
Refundable deposit, §38-701.
School officials prohibited from
profiting on, §38-902.
Tobacco-free school campuses,
§38-826.05.
Traffic control, §38-3101.
Traffic control devices.
Installation, §38-3101.
**Transfer of public schools realty
office to office of public
education facilities,** §38-471.
Transportation.
Appropriations restrictions, §38-911.
Charter schools, §38-1802.08.
Disabled children, §38-913.
Metrorail and metrobus, student fares
on, §§35-232 to 35-237.
See METRORAIL AND
METROBUS.
Truancy prevention resource guide,
§38-2602.

SCHOOLS AND EDUCATION
—Cont'd
Tuition of nonresidents, §§38-301 to 38-313.

Amount fixed by State Education Office, §38-302.

Authority not affected by reorganization plan, §38-304.

Definitions, §38-301.

Deposit of payments, §38-302.

Establishment of residency, §38-308.

Documentation submitted, §38-309.

Residency fraud investigation, report, §38-313.

Unable to confirm, procedures established, §38-311.

False information or statements, §§38-303, 38-312.

False information hotline, §38-312.01.

Penalty, §38-312.

Free tuition, §§38-307, 38-308.

Interstate compact on educational opportunity for military children.

Tuition charges for transitioning student prohibited, §49-1101.07.

Other primary caregiver.

Document to establish status as, §38-310.

Unable to confirm, procedures established, §38-311.

Proof of residency, §38-306.

Regulations determining tuition requirements, §38-303.

Required of nonresidents, §38-302.

Rules, §38-313.

Student residency verification fund, §38-312.02.

Venue for prosecutions of violation, §38-303.

Turkey Bowl revenue generation and sponsorship.

Limitations, §38-2981.

Uniform per-student funding formula, §§38-2901 to 38-2914.

Unused and underutilized public school buildings.

Sale of public lands, §10-803.01.

Use of school buildings, §§38-401 to 38-409.

Weapons.

Enhanced penalties and fines for carrying guns into gun free zones, §22-4502.01.

Expulsion of students for, §§38-231 to 38-235.

SCHOOLS AND EDUCATION
—Cont'd
Whole school-day sessions requirement, §38-901.

World Class Schools Task Force, §§38-1803.11 to 38-1803.15.

Youth advisory council, §§2-1561 to 2-1564, 2-1565.01 to 2-1565.06.

SCHOOLS TECHNOLOGY FUND, §1-325.251.

SCIENTIFIC EXPERIMENTS ON ANIMALS, §22-1012.

SCIRE FACIAS.
Garnishment.

Post-judgment garnishment in aid of execution.

Revival of judgment unnecessary, §16-543.

Writ abolished, CivPro Rule 81.

SCOOTERS.
Helmet requirement for riders.

Persons under 16 years, §50-1651.

SCRAP VEHICLE TITLE AUTHORIZATION, §§50-2701 to 50-2708.
Applicability of provisions, §50-2708.

Definitions, §50-2701.

Issuance of scrap title, §50-2705.

Notice of removal of vehicle, §50-2702.

Reclamation.

Effect of failure to reclaim, §50-2705.

Procedure, §50-2704.

Time limit, §50-2703.

Repeals of other laws or regulations, effect of, §50-2707.

Rulemaking, §50-2706.

SCUBA DIVING DUTY.
Police and firefighters.

Additional compensation for, §5-542.02.

SEALED RECORDS, CivPro Rule 5-III.
Adoption record, §16-311, Adoption Rule 79-I, FamDiv Rule P.

Appeals, federal cases, USCtApp Rule 47.1.

Appendix containing matters under seal, USCtApp HPIP Rule IX(b)(7).

Briefs containing material under seal, USCtApp HPIP Rule IX(a)(10).

Cases with records under seal, USCtApp HPIP Rule III(k).

SEALED RECORDS —Cont'd
Appeals, federal cases —Cont'd
Motion to unseal, USCtApp HPIP Rule VIII(h).
Post-decision procedures.
Terminating case.
Disposal of sealed records, USCtApp HPIP Rule XIII(a)(5).
Arrest records, §§16-801 to 16-807, CrimPro Rule 118.
Actual innocence as grounds, §16-802.
Availability of sealed records, §16-806.
Decriminalized or legalized offenses, §16-803.02.
Definitions, §16-801.
Delinquent minors, FamDiv Rule P, JuvProc Rule 118.
Motion to seal records, JuvProc Form 8.
Notice of motion to seal records, JuvProc Form 9.
Notice of opposition, FamDiv Form 3.
Notice of proposal, FamDiv Form 2.
Order denying application, FamDiv Form 6.
Order for hearing, FamDiv Form 4.
Order to seal records, FamDiv Form 5, JuvProc Form 10.
Fugitives from justice, §16-803.01.
Grounds, §§16-802, 16-803.
Hearing, §16-805.
Motions, §16-804.
Dismissal or denial, §16-805.
Grounds, §§16-802, 16-803.
Response to, §16-805.
Savings provision, §16-807.
Child abuse and neglect, FamDiv Rule P.
Forms, FamDiv Forms 2 to 6.
Child custody proceedings.
Verified initial pleading.
Jeopardy in disclosing identifying information, §16-4602.09.
Criminal records, §§16-801 to 16-807, CrimPro Rule 118.
Actual innocence as grounds, §16-802.
Availability of sealed records, §16-806.
Decriminalized or legalized offenses, §16-803.02.
Definitions, §16-801.
Delinquent minors, FamDiv Rule P, JuvProc Rule 118.
Motion to seal records, JuvProc Form 8.

SEALED RECORDS —Cont'd
Criminal records —Cont'd
Delinquent minors —Cont'd
Notice of motion to seal records, JuvProc Form 9.
Notice of opposition, FamDiv Form 3.
Notice of proposal, FamDiv Form 2.
Order denying application, FamDiv Form 6.
Order for hearing, FamDiv Form 4.
Order to seal records, FamDiv Form 5, JuvProc Form 10.
Fugitives from justice, §16-803.01.
Grounds for sealing.
Actual innocence, §16-802.
Cases other than actual innocence, §16-803.
Hearing, §16-805.
Motions, §16-804.
Dismissal or denial, §16-805.
Grounds, §§16-802, 16-803.
Response to, §16-805.
Savings provision, §16-807.
Family court proceedings, FamDiv Rule P.
Forms, FamDiv Forms 2 to 6.
Juvenile record, §16-2335.
Actual innocence, §16-2335.02.
Pleadings, USDistCt LCvR 5.1.
Criminal proceedings, USDistCt LCrR 49.
Records on appeal, DCCtApp Rule 12.

SEAL OF COURT.
Appellate procedure, USCtApp Rule 1.

SEALS.
Cooperative associations.
Powers, §29-905.
Corporations.
Powers, §29-303.02.
Nonprofit corporations.
Powers, §29-403.02.

SEARCHES AND SEIZURES.
Administrative search warrants, CivPro Rule 204.
Civil asset forfeiture, §§41-301 to 41-315.
See FORFEITURES.
Civil remedies.
Seizure of person or property, CivPro Rule 64.
Domestic relations actions, DomRel Rule 64.
College savings program.
Seizure of accounts prohibited, §47-4510.

SEARCHES AND SEIZURES —Cont'd
Constitution of the United States,
US Const Amd 4.
**Controlled substances search and
seizure without warrant,**
§48-921.01.
Currency.
Metropolitan police.
Depositing of seized currency,
§§23-531 to 23-534.
Motor fuel tax, §47-2320.
Oaths.
Warrants.
Supported by oath or affirmation,
US Const Amd 4.
Summons, CivPro Rule 4.

SEARCH WARRANTS, §§23-521 to
23-525.
Alcoholic beverages, illegal, §25-803.
Any hour of day or night.
Execution of warrant.
Requesting in application, §23-522.
Application for warrant, §23-522,
CrimPro Rule 41.
Juvenile proceedings, JuvProc Rule 41.
Contents, CrimPro Rule 41.
Juvenile proceedings, JuvProc Rule 41.
Controlled substances, §§48-921.01,
48-921.02.
Marijuana, articulable suspicion,
§48-921.02a.
Cruelty to animals, §22-1005.
Definitions, §23-501.
Disposition of seized property,
§23-525, CrimPro Rule 41.
Juvenile proceedings, JuvProc Rule 41.
Execution, §§23-523, 23-524, CrimPro
Rule 41.
Juvenile proceedings, JuvProc Rule 41.
**Interception of wire or oral
communications.**
General provisions, §§23-541 to
23-556, CrimPro Rule 41-I.
See INTERCEPTION OF ORAL OR
WIRE COMMUNICATIONS.
Issuance, §22-1005, CrimPro Rule 41.
Juvenile proceedings, JuvProc Rule 41.
Probable cause required, US Const
Amd 4.
Juvenile proceedings, JuvProc Rule
41.
Leased housing.
Tenant objection to inspection of
premises.
Need for administrative search
warrant, §42-3509.08.

SEARCH WARRANTS —Cont'd
Marijuana.
Articulable suspicion, §48-921.02a.
Milk container registration, §36-155.
Oath or affirmation, US Const Amd 4.
Probable cause.
Required, US Const Amd 4.
**Property or persons subject to
seizure,** CrimPro Rule 41.
Juvenile proceedings, JuvProc Rule 41.
Superior court, §11-941.
**Tenant objection to inspection of
premises.**
Need for administrative search
warrant, §42-3509.08.
Time of execution of, §23-523.
Water pollution and water quality.
Inspections, §8-103.15.

SEAT BELTS, §§50-1801 to 50-1807.
Applicability of law.
Child restraint seats, §50-1705.
General provisions, §50-1804.
Child restraint seats, §§50-1701 to
50-1708.
Age of child required to be restrained,
§50-1703.
Applicability of law, §50-1705.
Child passenger safety fund.
Administration, §50-1704.01.
Child passenger safety program,
§50-1703.01.
Administration, §50-1704.01.
Civil action for damages, no basis for,
§50-1706.
Definitions, §50-1702.
Federal safety standards, required to
meet, §50-1704.
Fines, §50-1706.
Fitting stations.
Child passenger safety program,
§50-1703.01.
Funds.
Administration, §50-1704.01.
Installation.
Child passenger safety program,
§50-1703.01.
Issuance of rules on, §50-1708.
Loan program, §50-1708.
Negligence and contributory
negligence, §50-1707.
Penalties, §50-1706.
Policy declaration, §50-1701.
Public information program, §50-1708.
Rental car companies, §50-1703.
Requirements regarding use of,
§50-1703.

SEAT BELTS —Cont'd
Civil action for damages, no basis for.
Child restraint seats, §50-1706.
General provisions, §50-1807.
Definitions.
Child restraint seats, §50-1702.
General provisions, §50-1801.
Enforcement of law, §50-1806.
Exceptions to required use of, §50-1802.
Federal standards required for.
Child restraint seats, §50-1704.
General provisions, §50-1802.
Negligence and contributory negligence.
Child restraint seats, §50-1707.
General provisions, §50-1807.
Penalties, lack of, §50-1806.
Public education program, §50-1805.
Required use of, §50-1802.
Standards, §50-1803.

SEAT OF GOVERNMENT.
Acquisition of excess property to develop seat of government, §§16-1331 to 16-1337.

SECLUSION OF PATIENTS.
Mental health consumer's rights, §7-1231.09.

SECONDARY MARKET.
Sale or assignment of instruments on, §42-1102.01.

SECONDHAND DEALERS.
Business licenses, §47-2837.
Disciplinary action against licensees, §47-2844.

SECRETARY OF INTERIOR.
Additional compensation, authority to grant, §1-333.07.
Fish and game, §§22-4332, 22-4333.
Highways.
Real property acquisitions and transfers for purposes of, §9-101.18.
Public lands, authorized to sell, §10-801.
Robert F. Kennedy Memorial Stadium.
Authority to acquire property for, §3-322.
Steam heat furnished to District buildings, §§10-501.03, 10-501.04.

SECRETARY OF THE DISTRICT OF COLUMBIA, OFFICE OF.
Grants to promote voting rights and statehood, §1-328.03.

SECRET SERVICE.
Federal law enforcement officer cooperative agreements, §§5-301 to 5-303.
Holidays, working on, compensation, §5-521.03.
Lateral police career appointments, §§1-610.71 to 1-610.76.
Police and firefighters retirement and disability, §5-703.
Wages and salaries for uniformed division, §5-545.01.
Conversion to 2001 standards, §5-561.02.
Locality-based comparability adjustments, freeze, §5-563.02.

SECTION EIGHT HOUSING, §§42-3503.01 to 42-3503.08.
Preservation and rehabilitation of government-supported housing, §§42-2851.01 to 42-2851.08.
See LANDLORD AND TENANT.

SECURED TRANSACTIONS, §§28:9-101 to 28:9-809.
Accessions.
Perfection and priority of security interest in, §28:9-335.
Accounting.
Defined, §28:9-102.
Request for, §28:9-210.
After-acquired property, §28:9-204.
Security interest in, §28:9-204.
Agricultural liens.
Default.
Time of default, §28:9-606.
Defined, §28:9-102.
Perfection and priority.
Filed financing statement providing certain incorrect information.
Priority of agricultural lien perfected by, §28:9-338.
Filing.
When required to perfect lien, §28:9-310.
Interests that take priority over or take free of agricultural lien, §28:9-317.
Law governing, §28:9-302.
Priorities among agricultural liens on same collateral, §28:9-322.

SECURED TRANSACTIONS —Cont'd
Agricultural liens —Cont'd
Perfection and priority —Cont'd
When perfected, §28:9-308.
Ammunition prohibited as security,
§7-2507.01.
Applicability of provisions,
§§28:9-109, 28:9-110.
Assignments.
Filing officer's duties, §28:9-514.
Attachment of security interest,
§28:9-203.
Effect on delegation of performance
and assignment of rights,
§28:9-210.
Financial asset.
Security interest arising in purchase
or delivery of, §28:9-206.
Perfection.
Security interests perfected upon
attachment, §28:9-309.
Bank deposits and collections.
Depositary and collecting banks.
Collection of items.
Security interests of collecting
banks.
Items accompanying documents
and proceeds, §28:4-210.
Documentary drafts.
Dishonor.
Privilege of presenting bank to
deal with goods.
Security interest for expenses,
§28:4-504.
Banks and financial institutions.
Defined, §28:9-102.
Rights of banks and financial
institutions.
Control agreement.
Refusal to enter into or disclose
existence of, §28:9-342.
Deposit accounts, §§28:9-340,
28:9-341.
Security interests in deposit accounts.
Control agreements.
Rights of banks and financial
institutions with respect to
agreements, §28:9-342.
Perfection and priority, §28:9-304.
Rules of priority, §28:9-327.
Rights and duties of banks and
financial institutions, §28:9-341.
Set-off or recoupment, §28:9-340.
Transfer of funds from deposit
account, §28:9-332.

SECURED TRANSACTIONS —Cont'd
Chattel paper.
Electronic chattel paper.
Control, §28:9-105.
Perfection by control, §28:9-314.
Defined, §28:9-102.
Perfection of security interests in,
§28:9-312.
Purchaser of chattel paper or
instrument.
Priority, §28:9-330.
Citation of article.
Short title, §28:9-101.
Citation of provisions, §28:9-101.
Collateral.
Control of collateral.
Rights and duties of secured party
having, §§28:9-207, 28:9-208.
Default.
Acceptance in full or partial
satisfaction of obligation,
§§28:9-620 to 28:9-622.
Disposition after default, §§28:9-610
to 28:9-617.
Redemption.
Right to redeem collateral,
§28:9-623.
Transfer of record or legal title,
§28:9-619.
Description.
Sufficiency, §28:9-108.
Disposition.
Permissible, §28:9-205.
Rights of secured party on,
§28:9-315.
Without accounting, §28:9-205.
List of collateral.
Request regarding, §28:9-210.
Possession of collateral.
Rights and duties of secured party
having, §28:9-207.
Rights and duties when collateral in
secured party's possession,
§28:9-207.
Title immaterial, §28:9-202.
Transferred collateral.
Priority of security interests in,
§28:9-325.
Use.
Without accounting, §28:9-205.
Use permissible, §28:9-205.
Commingled goods, §28:9-336.
Construction and interpretation.
Leases article of UCC.
Security interests arising under,
§28:9-110.

SECURITIES —Cont'd
Registration.
Fiduciaries.
Registration in name of a fiduciary, §28-2902.
Security agents and brokers.
Exempt securities, §§31-5604.01 to 31-5604.06.
See SECURITY AGENTS AND BROKERS.
General provisions, §§31-5601.01 to 31-5608.04.
See SECURITY AGENTS AND BROKERS.
TOD security registration, §§19-603.01 to 19-603.11.
See NONPROBATE TRANSFERS.
Transfers.
Fiduciary security transfers, §§28-2901 to 28-2909.
See FIDUCIARY SECURITY TRANSFERS.

SECURITIES ACT, §§31-5601.01 to 31-5608.04.
Administration of act, §§31-5607.01 to 31-5607.09.
Adverse agency action.
Judicial review, §31-5608.03.
Civil and criminal liability, §§31-5606.01 to 31-5606.05.
Conformity with federal law, §31-5601.02.
Definitions, §31-5601.01.
Electronic filings, §31-5607.09.
Exemption from registration, §§31-5604.01 to 31-5604.06.
Fraudulent and prohibited practices, §§31-5605.01 to 31-5605.05.
Licensing requirements, §§31-5602.01 to 31-5602.11.
Public policy, §31-5601.02.
Registration of securities, §§31-5603.01 to 31-5603.09.
Repeal of prior acts, §31-5608.04.
Scope of act, §31-5608.01.

SECURITY AGENCIES, §47-2839.01.

SECURITY AGENTS AND BROKERS, §§31-5601.01 to 31-5608.04.
Administrative procedures act.
Applicability, §31-5607.08.
Appellate review.
Commissioner's decisions, §31-5608.03.
Canadian brokers-dealers.
Defined, §31-5601.01.

SECURITY AGENTS AND BROKERS —Cont'd
Canadian brokers-dealers —Cont'd
Limited registration, §31-5602.10.
Civil liability, §31-5606.05.
Commissioner.
Administration of act, §31-5607.01.
Administrative cease and desist orders, §31-5606.02.
Applicability of administrative procedures act, §31-5607.08.
Confidentiality of information, §31-5607.03.
Consent to service of process, §31-5607.06.
Defined, §31-5601.01.
Enforcement of act, §31-5606.02.
Ethical violations, §31-5607.02.
Injunctive relief, §31-5606.03.
Interagency cooperation, §31-5607.04.
Investigative powers, §31-5606.01.
Judicial review of actions and decisions, §31-5608.03.
Public access to information, §31-5607.03.
Register of applications, §31-5607.07.
Rulemaking authority, §31-5607.05.
Securities dealing prohibition, §31-5607.02.
Subpoena power, §31-5606.01.
Criminal liability, §31-5606.04.
Deceptive trade practices, §§31-5605.01 to 31-5605.05.
Definitions, §31-5601.01.
Electronic filings, §31-5607.09.
Federal covered securities.
Registration, §31-5603.07.
Federal law.
Intergovernmental coordination, §31-5601.02.
Fingerprint-based background checks.
Confidentiality of information, §31-633.
Definitions, §31-631.
Requirement of, §31-632.
Rules, §31-634.
Fraudulent transactions, §31-5605.02.
Investment adviser representatives.
Continuing education, rule or order providing for, §31-5602.11.
Licensing, §§31-5602.01 to 31-5602.11.
Application process, §31-5602.03.
Books and records.
Audit and inspection, §31-5602.06.
Broker-dealer and agent, §31-5602.01.

SECURITY AGENTS AND BROKERS
—Cont'd
Licensing —Cont'd
Disciplinary action.
Grounds, §31-5602.07.
Filing fee, §31-5602.03.
Grounds for disciplinary action,
§§31-5602.07, 31-5602.08.
Investment adviser and investment
adviser representative,
§31-5602.02.
Lack of qualification.
Grounds for disciplinary action,
§31-5602.08.
Notice filing procedures, §31-5602.03.
Unlawful representation,
§31-5605.05.
Post-licensing requirements,
§31-5602.04.
Successor firms, §31-5602.05.
Unlawful representation, §31-5605.05.
Withdrawal, §31-5602.09.
Manipulation of market, §31-5605.03.
Misleading filings, §31-5605.04.
Prior act.
Transitional provisions, §31-5608.04.
Public policy, §31-5601.02.
Registration of securities,
§§31-5603.01 to 31-5603.09.
Abandonment, §31-5603.09.
Coordination, registration by,
§§31-5603.03, 31-5603.06.
Disciplinary action, §31-5603.07.
Exempt securities, §§31-5604.01 to
31-5604.06.
Federal covered securities,
§31-5603.08.
Indefinite amount of securities.
Offer and sale of, §31-5603.05.
Mandatory, §31-5603.01.
Notification, registration by,
§§31-5603.02, 31-5603.06.
Qualification, registration by,
§§31-5603.04, 31-5603.06.
Registration statement.
Generally, §31-5603.06.
Required, §31-5603.01.
Unlawful representation, §31-5605.05.
Withdrawal, §31-5603.09.
Scope of act, §31-5608.01.
Securities exempt from registration,
§§31-5604.01 to 31-5604.06.
Additional exempt securities or
transactions, §31-5604.03.
Coordination of exemptions,
§31-5604.06.

SECURITY AGENTS AND BROKERS
—Cont'd
Securities exempt from registration
—Cont'd
Enumeration, §31-5604.01.
Exempt transactions, §31-5604.02.
Filing sales and advertising literature,
§31-5604.05.
Listing, §31-5604.01.
Revocation of exemptions, §31-5604.04.
Unlawful representation, §31-5605.05.
Unlicensed or unregistered activity,
§31-5605.01.

SECURITY AND FIRE ALARM
CONTRACTORS, §§7-2801 to
7-2815.
Alarm agents.
Defined, §7-2802.
Licensing, §7-2805.
Alarm dealers.
Defined, §7-2802.
Licensing, §7-2804.
Responsibilities and duties of, §7-2806.
Alarm systems.
Defined, §7-2802.
Standards for, §7-2808.
Alarm users.
Defined, §7-2802.
Responsibilities and duties of, §7-2807.
Definitions, §7-2802.
Exceptions to provisions, §7-2809.
Fees, §§7-2811, 7-2814.
Fines, §§7-2811, 7-2814.
Inspections, §7-2810.
Issuance of rules and regulations,
§7-2815.
Licensing.
Alarm agents, §7-2805.
Alarm dealers, §7-2804.
Notice of violations, §7-2812.
Policy declaration, §7-2801.
Prerecorded transmittals to police
and fire departments, §7-2803.
Severability of provisions, §7-2815.
Trials, §7-2813.

SECURITY CAMERAS.
Private security camera system
incentive program.
Established, §7-2831.
Private security camera incentive
fund, §7-2832.

SECURITY DEPOSIT ASSISTANCE
PROGRAM.
Qualified high technology company,
§2-1221.01.

SECURITY DEPOSITS.
Apartments.
Return of deposit, SmallClaims Form 10.
Rent-controlled units, §42-3502.17.
Tenant assistance program, §42-3503.05.

SECURITY OFFICERS.
Minimum wage.
Officers working in office building, §32-1003.
Office building defined, §32-1002.
Security officer defined, §32-1002.

SECURITY SERVICES.
School security services.
Contracting out, §§38-157, 38-1807.51.

SEE FOREVER FOUNDATION-EVANS CAMPUS.
Modernization or new construction.
Department of general services, §10-551.10.

SEEING-EYE DOGS.
Definition of guide dog, §7-1009.
Housing accommodations.
Full and equal access, §7-1006.
Public places accommodations, and conveyances.
Right to be accompanied by, §7-1002.

SEIZURES.
College savings program.
Seizure of accounts prohibited, §47-4510.
Controlled substances search and seizure without warrant, §48-921.01.
Insurers rehabilitation and liquidation proceedings.
Temporary seizure order, §31-1308.
Motor fuel tax, §47-2320.
Personal property taxes, distraint or levy for.
See PERSONAL PROPERTY TAXES.
Taxation.
Levy for failure to pay.
Notice of seizure for sale, §47-4472.
Storage of seized property, §47-4473.
Tobacco tax, §47-2409.
Trail of right to property seized on process of superior court, §§15-521 to 15-524.
Action for replevin against officer levying on property, §15-524.
Docketing claim, §15-522.
Judgment, §15-523.

SEIZURES —Cont'd
Trail of right to property seized on process of superior court —Cont'd
Manner of trial, §15-522.
Notice of claim or exemption, §15-521.

SELECTIVE SERVICE.
Drivers' licenses and identification cards.
Registration upon application, §50-1401.01.

SELF-DEFENSE SPRAYS, §§7-2502.12 to 7-2502.14.
Definition, §7-2502.12.
Possession, §7-2502.13.
Registration, §7-2502.14.

SELF-DRIVING CARS.
Autonomous vehicles, §§50-2351 to 50-2354.

SELF-GOVERNMENT.
Home Rule act, §§1-201.01 to 1-207.71.
See HOME RULE.

SELF-INCRIMINATION.
Constitution of the United States, US Const Amd 5.
Delinquent minors, JuvProc Rule 111.
Interstate family support.
Adverse inference from refusal to give testimony, §46-353.16.
Witnesses, US Const Amd 5.

SELF-SERVICE STORAGE FACILITIES, §§40-401 to 40-405.
Care, custody and control of personal property in storage, §40-405.
Definitions, §40-401.
Liens.
Rent, labor or other charges, §40-403.
Enforcement of lien, §40-404.
Prohibited acts, §40-402.
Sales.
Lien for rent, labor or other charges.
Enforcement of lien, §40-404.

SENATE.
Absent members, US Const Art I §5.
Adjournment, US Const Art I §§5, 7, Art II §3.
Arrest of members, US Const Art I §6.
Compensation of members, US Const Art I §6, Amd 27.
Debate, US Const Art I §§4, 6.
Elections.
Electors, US Const Amds 14, 17.

SENATE —Cont'd

Elections —Cont'd

Judge of elections, returns and qualifications of members, US Const Art I §5.

Qualifications of electors, US Const Amd 17.

Times, places and manner of holding, US Const Art I §4.

Equal suffrage in senate, US Const Art V.

Expulsion of member, US Const Art I §5.

Freedom of speech, US Const Art I §6.

Holding other office, US Const Art I §6.

Impeachment, US Const Art I §3.

Journals, US Const Art I §§5, 7.

Libel and slander.

Privilege of members, US Const Art I §6.

Officers, US Const Art I §3.

President.

Pro tempore, US Const Art I §3.

Presidential elector.

Senator ineligible, US Const Art II §1.

Punishment of members, US Const Art I §5.

Qualifications.

Electors, US Const Amd 17.

Members, US Const Art I §3.

Judge of qualifications, US Const Art I §5.

Revenue bills, US Const Art I §7.

Rules of procedure, US Const Art I §5.

Vice-president of the United States.

Vacancy in office.

Confirmation of president, US Const Amd 25.

SENIOR CITIZENS.

Aged persons generally.

See AGED PERSONS.

Assisted living residences, §§44-101.01 to 44-113.01.

See ASSISTED LIVING RESIDENCES.

Criminal abuse, neglect and financial exploitation of vulnerable adults and elderly persons, §§22-931 to 22-938.

Home repair and improvement program fund.

Housing.

See HOUSING.

SENIORITY SYSTEMS.

Exceptions for practices with discriminatory effects, §2-1402.12.

SENTENCING.

Accessories after the fact, §22-1806.

Affrays, §22-1301.

Aged persons, certain offenses committed against.

Enhanced penalties, §22-3601.

Aggravated assault, §22-404.01.

Aggravating circumstances, §24-403.01.

Aliens, §16-713.

Allocution, CrimPro Rule 32.

Ammunition.

Restricted pistol bullets, §7-2507.06.

Armed carjacking, §22-2803.

Assault, §22-401.

Common law assault, §22-404.

Dangerous weapon, assault with, §22-402.

Offense of any kind, intent to commit, §22-403.

Police officer or firefighter, assault on, §22-405.

Public officials, §22-851.

Resisting arrest, §22-405.01.

Bigamy, §22-501.

Boating under the influence, §50-2206.32.

Impaired operation of watercraft, §50-2206.34.

Minor in watercraft, §50-2206.36.

Bonfires, kindling, §22-1313.

Bribery, §§22-704, 22-712.

Witnesses, §22-713.

Burglary, §22-801.

Carjacking, §22-2803.

Child prostitution, §22-2704.

Children, crimes of violence committed against.

Enhanced penalties, §22-3611.

Child sexual abuse.

Aggravating circumstances, §22-3020.

Assault with intent to commit, §22-401.

First and second degree, §§22-3008 to 22-3010.

Lewd, indecent, or obscene acts, §22-1312.

Sexually suggestive conduct, §22-3010.01.

SENTENCING —Cont'd
Child support orders.
Modification or suspension of support
payments.
Individuals being sentenced to
period of imprisonment subject
to support order, §23-112a.
Petition, when deemed filed,
§46-204.
Citizen patrol members.
Enhanced penalties, §22-3602.
Collections agencies.
Use of "District" or similar
designation, §22-3402.
Commercial counterfeiting, §22-902.
Commercial piracy, §22-3214.
Commission, §§3-101 to 3-108.
See SENTENCING AND CRIMINAL
CODE REVISION COMMISSION.
Concurrent sentences, §23-112.
Consecutive sentences.
Criminal proceedings, §23-112.
Theft, §22-3203.
**Consecutive sentence unless
otherwise provided,** CrimPro Rule
32.
Conspiracy, §22-1805a.
Kidnapping, §22-2001.
Constitution of the United States,
US Const Amd 8.
Capital punishment, US Const Amd 5.
Contraband on prison grounds,
§22-2603.03.
**Contributing to the delinquency of a
minor,** §22-811.
Correction of sentence, CrimPro Rule
35.
Corrupt influence, §§22-704, 22-712.
Counsel's statement prior sentence,
§23-103.
**Credit for time served in custody or
on parole,** §24-221.03.
**Criminal offenses, penalties
generally,** §§22-3571.01,
22-3571.02.
Criminal street gangs, §22-951.
Cross burning, §§22-3312.02,
22-3312.04.
Cruelty to animals, §22-1001.
Cruelty to children, §§22-1101,
22-1102.
Death penalty.
Constitution of the United States, US
Const Amd 5.
Indictments and information.
Offenses to be prosecuted by
indictment, CrimPro Rule 7.

SENTENCING —Cont'd
Death penalty —Cont'd
Stay of execution upon appeal,
CrimPro Rule 38.
Deceptive labeling, §22-3214.01.
Definite term, §24-403.01.
Delinquent minors, JuvProc Rule 32.
Disabled, injured, or sick animals.
Abandonment of, §22-1012.
Neglect of, §22-1011.
Disfigurement, malicious, §22-406.
Disorderly conduct, §22-1321.
Driving under the influence,
§50-2206.13.
Boating under the influence,
§50-2206.32.
Impaired operation of watercraft,
§50-2206.34.
Minor in watercraft, §50-2206.36.
Commercial drivers.
Additional term of incarceration,
§50-2206.17.
Impaired driving, §50-2206.15.
Minor in vehicle, additional
penalties, §50-2206.18.
Mandatory-minimum periods of
incarceration, proof required,
§50-2206.57.
Enhanced or additional penalties.
Children, crimes of violence committed
against, §22-3611.
Child sexual abuse, §22-3020.
Citizen patrol member, §22-3602.
Committing crime when armed,
§22-4502.
Gun free zones, carrying guns into,
§22-4502.01.
Regulations, additional penalties for
violation of, §1-303.05.
Release prior to trial, offenses
committed during, §23-1328.
Senior citizen victims, §22-3601.
Sexual offenses, §22-3020.
Escape, §22-2601.
Extortion.
Blackmail, §22-3252.
False personation with intent to extort
money, §22-1402.
Generally, §22-3251.
False fire alarms, §22-1319.
False personation.
Public officer or minister, §§22-1403 to
22-1405.
False statements, §22-2405.
False swearing, §22-2404.
**Felonies committed after August 5,
2000,** §24-403.01.

SENTENCING —Cont'd
Felonies committed on or after August 5, 2000, §24-403.01.
Firearms, §7-2507.06.
Concealed weapons, carrying, §§22-4504, 22-4505.
Unlawful possession, §22-4503.
Fire balloons, §22-1317.
Fish and game, §22-4331.
Fleeing from a law enforcement officer in a motor vehicle, §50-2201.05b.
Footways in public grounds, driving or riding on, §22-1318.
Forgery, §22-3242.
Goods, brands or packaging of, §22-1502.
Fraud and deceit.
Checks, drafts, or orders intended to defraud, §22-1510.
Credit card fraud, §22-3223.
First and second degree, §22-3222.
Fraudulent registration in lodgings, §22-3224.
Fraudulent advertising, §22-1513.
Gambling.
Bookmaking, §22-1708.
Confidence games, §22-1706.
Keeping gaming premises, §§5-115.06, 22-1704, 22-1705.
Sports, §§22-1708, 22-1713.
Three-card monte, §22-1706.
Gangs, §22-951.
Good time credit, §24-403.01.
Grave robbery, §22-3303.
Guardianship of incapacitated persons.
Aggravating circumstances, §22-3020.
Sexual abuse of a ward, §§22-3013, 22-3014.
Guidelines, §3-105.
Habitual offenders.
Third felony conviction, §22-1804a.
Hate crimes.
Aggravating circumstances.
Offense committed because of victim's race, color, religion, national origin or sexual orientation, §24-403.01.
Healing arts practitioners.
Aggravating circumstances, §22-3020.
Sexual abuse of patient or client, §§22-3015, 22-3016.
Health care facilities.
Interference with or obstruction of, §§22-1314.01, 22-1314.02.

SENTENCING —Cont'd
Hearing commissioners' powers, CrimPro Rule 117.
Human trafficking, §22-1837.
Impaired driving, §50-2206.15.
Minor in vehicle, additional penalties, §50-2206.18.
Impaired operation of watercraft, §50-2206.34.
Incest, §22-1901.
Indeterminate sentences and parole, §24-403.
Interception of oral or wire communications.
Possession, sale, etc., of intercepting devices, §23-543.
Juvenile offenders, sentencing options for, §24-903, JuvProc Rule 32.
Kidnapping, §§22-1810, 22-2001.
Law enforcement officers.
Assault on, §22-405.
Resisting arrest, §22-405.01.
Leash law violations, §22-1311.
Lewd, indecent, or obscene acts, §22-1312.
Life sentences and parole, §24-403.
Loitering.
Minors loitering around business establishments during school hours, §32-221.
Unlawful assembly, §22-1321.
Lotteries.
Promotion, sale or possession of tickets, §§22-1701 to 22-1703.
Manslaughter, §22-2105.
Maximum sentences and parole, §24-403.
Minimum sentences.
Good time credit exception, §24-221.06.
Parole, §24-403.
Minors.
Contributing to the delinquency of, §22-811.
Juvenile offenders, sentencing options for, §24-903, JuvProc Rule 32.
Violent crimes committed against. Enhanced penalties, §22-3611.
Misdemeanors committed on or after August 5, 2000, §24-403.02.
Motion picture theaters.
Operation of recording device, §22-3214.02.

SENTENCING —Cont'd
Motions attacking, §23-110.
Rules governing proceedings under
section 23-110, PostConvRel Rules
1 to 12.
See POST-CONVICTION
PROCEEDINGS.
**Motor vehicle identification
numbers.**
Altering or removing, §22-3233.
Motor vehicles.
Theft, §22-3215.
Unauthorized use of, §22-3215.
Unlawful entry, §22-1341.
Murder.
Assault with intent to commit,
§22-401.
First and second degree, §§22-2104,
22-2104.01.
Killing law enforcement officer,
§22-2106.
Second degree murder, §22-2103.
Solicitation of murder or other violent
crimes, §22-2107.
Non-code offenses, §22-1807.
Obscenity, §22-2201.
Obstruction of justice, §22-722.
Interference with reports to or
requests for assistance from law
enforcement, medical providers, or
child welfare agencies, §22-1931.
Tampering with physical evidence,
§22-723.
**Overdose, seeking medical attention
for victim.**
Mitigating factor in sentencing for
certain offenses, §7-403.
Panhandling, §22-2304.
Parachutes, §22-1317.
Perjury, §§22-2402, 22-2403.
**Place of imprisonment for sentences
of more than one year,**
§24-201.02.
Playing games in streets, §22-1308.
Potomac river.
Throwing or depositing matter into,
§§22-4402, 22-4403.
Presence of defendant, CrimPro Rule
43.
Delinquent minors, JuvProc Rule 43.
Presentence investigations, CrimPro
Rule 32, USDistCt LCrR 32.2.
Prison breach, §22-2601.
Prison contraband, §22-2603.03.
Private detectives.
Use of "District" or similar
designation, §22-3402.

SENTENCING —Cont'd
Probation, CrimPro Rule 32, USDistCt
LCrR 32.1.
Delinquent minors, JuvProc Rule 32.
Detention and shelter care, JuvProc
Rule 107.
Forms, JuvProc Forms 3, 6.
Revocation or modification, §24-304,
CrimPro Rule 32.1, USDistCt
LCrR 32.1.
Stay upon appeal, CrimPro Rule 38.
Suspension of imposition or execution
of sentence, §16-710.
Profane and indecent language,
§22-1321.
Pronouncement, CrimPro Rule 32.
Prostitution.
Child prostitution, §22-2704.
Compelling individual to live life of
prostitution, §22-2706.
Domestic partners caused to live in,
§22-2708.
House of prostitution.
Pandering, procuring, or pimping
for, §22-2710.
Inducing or inciting an individual to
engage in, §22-2705.
Operating bawdy or disorderly house,
§22-2722.
Operating house of prostitution,
§22-2712.
Pandering, procuring, or pimping,
§22-2705.
Third persons, for, §22-2711.
Receiving money or valuables for
arranging assignations, §22-2707.
Solicitation for purposes, §22-2701.
Spouses caused to live in, §22-2708.
Suspension of sentence, §22-2703.
Public officers and employees.
Threatening, stalking, assaulting, etc.,
§22-851.
**Public or private building,
enclosure, road or sidewalk.**
Blocking passage, §22-1307.
Railroad transportation of animals,
§22-1003.
Rape.
Aggravating circumstances, §22-3020.
Various degrees of sexual abuse,
§§22-3002 to 22-3006.
Recommendations by council,
§24-112.
Reduction of sentence, CrimPro Rule
35.
Substance abuse treatment program.
Completion, persons sentenced for
nonviolent offenses, §24-403.01.

SENTENCING —Cont'd
Release pending sentence, CrimPro Rule 46.
Remedies on motions attacking, §23-110.
Resisting arrest, §22-405.01.
Rioting or inciting to riot, §22-1322.
Robbery, §22-2801.
  Attempt to commit, §22-2802.
Senior citizen victims.
  Enhanced penalties, §22-3601.
Sentencing guidelines, §3-105.
Sexual abuse.
  Aggravating circumstances, §22-3020.
  Child sexual abuse.
    Assault with intent to commit, §22-401.
    First and second degree, §§22-3008 to 22-3010.
    Lewd, indecent, or obscene acts, §22-1312.
    Sexually suggestive conduct, §22-3010.01.
  Various degrees of sexual abuse, §§22-3002 to 22-3006.
Sexual performances using minors, §22-3103.
Shoplifting, §22-3213.
Solicitation for purposes of prostitution, §22-2701.
Solicitation of murder or other violent crimes, §22-2107.
Stalking, §22-3134.
  Public officials, §22-851.
Statement by defendant before sentencing, CrimPro Rule 32.
Statements prior to imposing, §23-103.
Stolen property.
  Receiving stolen property, §22-3232.
  Trafficking in stolen property, §22-3231.
Street gangs, §22-951.
Subornation of perjury, §22-2403.
Substance abuse treatment program.
  Completion, reduction of sentence.
    Persons sentenced for nonviolent offenses, §24-403.01.
Supervised release, §24-403.01.
Suspension of imposition or execution of sentence, §16-710.
  Medical and geriatric parole.
    Suspension of sentence and imposition of probation, §24-468.
Theft.
  Commercial piracy, §22-3214.

SENTENCING —Cont'd
Theft —Cont'd
  Consecutive sentences, §22-3203.
  Deceptive labeling, §22-3214.01.
  Generally, §22-3212.
  Shoplifting, §22-3213.
  Taking property without right, §22-3216.
  Unauthorized use, §22-3215.
Threats to do bodily harm, §22-407.
Three strikes offenders, §22-1804a.
Throwing stones and other missiles, §22-1309.
Time of sentence, CrimPro Rule 32.
Tobacco sales to minors, §7-1721.02.
Trademark counterfeiting, §22-902.
Trespass.
  Forcible entry and detainer, §22-3301.
  Unlawful entry on property, §22-3302.
Truth in sentencing commission, §§24-111 to 24-114.
  Data collection, §24-113.
  Duties, §24-112.
  Enactment of amendments based on recommendations, §24-114.
  Recommendations, §24-112.
Universities and colleges.
  Campus police and security officers, assaults on, §22-405.
Vandalism.
  Art works, defacing, §22-3306.
  Boundary markers, destroying, §22-3309.
  Cross burning, §§22-3312.02, 22-3312.04.
  Defacing public or private property, §22-3312.01.
  Explosives placed with intent to destroy or injure property, §22-3305.
  Grave robbery, §22-3303.
  Milestones, removal of, §22-3320.
  Obstruction.
    Public highways, §22-3321.
    Public roads, §22-3320.
    Railroad tracks, §22-3319.
  Printed material, defacing, §22-3306.
  Public records, defacing, §22-3307.
  Railings, destroying, §22-3314.
  Railroad track obstruction or displacement, §22-3319.
  Streets and alleys.
    Destroying or defacing building material for, §22-3313.
  Tombs, destroying, §22-3314.
  Trees and shrubbery, destroying, §22-3310.

SENTENCING —Cont'd
Vandalism —Cont'd
United States property, injury or
destruction to, §22-3311.
Vending machines and similar devices,
§22-601.
Water pollution, malicious, §22-3318.
Vehicle identification numbers.
Altering or removing, §22-3233.
Victim impact statements, §23-103,
CrimPro Rule 32.
Victims' bill of rights, §23-1904.
Voluntary sentencing guidelines,
§3-105.
Voyeurism, §22-3531.
Weapons.
Armed criminal offenses.
Additional penalty, §22-4502.

**SENTENCING AND CRIMINAL
CODE REVISION COMMISSION,**
§§3-101 to 3-108.
Budget, §3-107.
Comprehensive study, §3-104.
Cooperative agreements, §3-108.
Correctional impact analysis, §3-106.
Duties, §3-101.
Employees, §3-107.
Establishment, §3-101.
Guidelines, §3-105.
Hearings, §3-103.
Meetings and hearings, §3-103.
Meetings of, §3-103.
Membership, §3-102.
Reports, §3-104.
Voluntary sentencing guidelines,
§3-105.

SEPARATION OF SPOUSES.
Divorce arising after, causes for,
§16-906.
Enlargement of, §16-905.
Grounds for, §16-904.
Revocation of, §16-905.

SEPTIC TANKS.
**Permit to maintain privy by means
other than connection to sewage
system,** §8-602.

SEQUESTRATION.
Probate proceedings, §§16-3104 to
16-3107.

SERIES TRUSTS, §§29-1204.01 to
29-1204.05.
Authorization, §29-1204.01.
Claims pertaining to series trusts,
§29-1204.05.

SERIES TRUSTS —Cont'd
Dissolution, §29-1204.04.
Duties of trustee, §29-1204.03.
Liability, §29-1204.02.

SERVICE BY POSTING.
Adoption proceedings, Adoption Rule
4.
Domestic relations actions, DomRel
Rule 4.
Landlord and tenant court,
LandlordTenant Rule 4.

SERVICE BY PUBLICATION.
Civil proceedings, §§13-335 to 13-341,
CivPro Rule 4-I.
Corporations, §13-335.
**Default, failure to appear in
obedience to order,** §13-340.
**Entry of order, judgment, decree
against nonresident or absent
defendant upon proof of notice
by publication,** §13-340.
**Nonresidents, absent defendants,
unknown heirs and devisees,**
§13-336.
Order of publication, §§13-338 to
13-340.
Out-of-District service, §§13-335 to
13-341.
**Personal service outside District in
lieu of,** §13-337.
**Persons unknown to be living or
dead and unknown heirs and
devisees,** §13-341.
Probate proceedings.
Death between Jan. 1, 1981, and June
30, 1995, Probate Rule 128.
Death on or after July 1, 1995,
Probate Rule 428.
Sale of property by guardians,
conservators, trustees, etc.,
involved, Probate Rule 203.

**SERVICE OF PROCESS AND
PAPERS,** §§13-301 to 13-341.
Absent defendants, on, §13-336.
Adoption, Adoption Rule 5.
Motions, Adoption Rule 8.
Notice of adoption proceedings,
Adoption Rule 4.
Time for service, Adoption Rule 6.
Affidavits.
Landlord and tenant court.
Affidavit of service by special
process server, CivPro Rule 6.

SERVICE OF PROCESS AND PAPERS —Cont'd

Affidavits —Cont'd

Time for service, CivPro Rule 6, CrimPro Rule 45.

Hospitalization of persons with mental illness, MentalHealth Rule 13.

Juvenile proceedings, JuvProc Rule 45.

Appeals, D.C. courts, DCCtApp Rule 25.

Administrative orders and decisions, DCCtApp Rule 15.

Briefs, DCCtApp Rule 31.

Appeals, federal cases, FRAP 25, USCtApp Rule 25.

Acknowledgment, service of papers, FRAP 25(d).

Administrative review or enforcement, FRAP 15(c).

Appendix to briefs, FRAP 30(a).

Application for enforcement of administrative orders, FRAP 15(c).

Briefs, FRAP 31.

Cross appeals, FRAP 28.1(f).

District courts, appeals from judgments and orders, FRAP 3(d).

Electronic service, FRAP 25(c).

Additional time after service, FRAP 26(c).

Proof of service, FRAP 25(d).

Filed papers, service of, required, FRAP 25(b).

Motion for stay or injunction pending appeal, USCtApp Rule 8.

Notice.

Orders or judgments by clerk, FRAP 45(c).

Notice of appeal.

Appeal as of right, FRAP 3(d).

Review of decisions of U.S. Tax Court, FRAP 13(c), FRAP Form 2.

Petition.

Administrative review or enforcement, FRAP 15(c).

Mandamus, prohibition or other extraordinary writs, FRAP 21, USCtApp Rule 21.

Rehearing, FRAP 40(b).

Proof of service, FRAP 25(d).

Statement of appellant when no transcript available, FRAP 10(c).

Arbitration.

Objections to applications, CivPro Rule 70-I.

SERVICE OF PROCESS AND PAPERS —Cont'd

Assistance tribunals and litigants outside District, §13-434.

Athlete agents.

Mayor appointed agent for service, §47-2887.02.

Attachment, §16-502.

Attorneys at law.

Discipline or disability proceedings, DCBar Rule XI, USDistCt LCrR 57.27, USDistCt LCvR 83.16.

Service upon attorney, CivPro Rule 5.

Domestic relations actions, DomRel Rule 5.

Banks and financial institutions.

International banking corporations.

Registered office and agent, §26-637.

Briefs, DCCtApp Rule 31.

Business licenses violations.

Cease and desist orders, §47-2844.01.

Business organizations.

Registered agents, §29-104.12.

Child abuse and neglect, NeglectProc Rule 11.

Motions, NeglectProc Rule 43.

Child custody proceedings.

Enforcement of foreign custody determinations.

Service of petition and order, §16-4603.09.

Child fatality review committee.

Subpoenas, §4-1371.07.

Children and minors, on, §13-332.

Children's Trust Fund, §4-1341.05.

Child support enforcement, §46-206.

City of Washington museum, §39-302.

Claims against the District, §2-401.

Collection actions, CivPro Rule 40-III.

Condemnation of property, CivPro Rule 71A.

Insanitary buildings, nonresident owners of.

Registered agent, appointment of, §6-910.

Conservators.

Accounts and reports, Probate Rule 330.

Plans and inventories, Probate Rule 329.

Missing persons, Probate Rule 350.

Contempt proceedings, CivPro Rule 4.1.

Corporations, foreign or domestic, §§13-334, 13-335.

Court rule, according to, §13-331.

SERVICE OF PROCESS AND PAPERS —Cont'd

Courts subject to, §13-301.

Criminal procedure, §16-703, CrimPro Rule 49.

Motions, CrimPro Rules 45, 47-I.

Summons, CrimPro Rules 4, 9.

Delinquent minors, JuvProc Rule 49.

Motions procedure, JuvProc Rule 47-I.

Summons and other notices of hearings, JuvProc Rule 9.

Time for service, JuvProc Rule 45.

Discovery.

Certificates regarding discovery.

Domestic relations actions, DomRel Rule 5.

Depositions.

Notice, USDistCt LCvR 30.1.

Outside District of Columbia, CivPro Rule 28-I.

Pre-action depositions, CivPro Rule 27, DomRel Rule 27.

Written questions, CivPro Rule 31.

Interrogatories, CivPro Rule 33.

Documents requiring service, CivPro Rule 5.

Domestic relations actions, DomRel Rules 4, 5.

Attachment writs, DomRel Rule 64.

Parentage proceedings, DomRel Rule 405.

Subpoenas, DomRel Rule 45.

Domestic violence unit proceedings, DomesticViolence Rule 3.

Electronic filing, CivPro Appxs II, III.

Complaints, CivPro Appx IV.

Facsimile machines.

Adoption proceedings, Adoption Rule 5.

Domestic relations actions, DomRel Rule 5.

Filing papers, CivPro Rule 5.

Domestic relations actions, DomRel Rule 5.

Forcible entry and detainer, §16-1502.

Foreign corporations, §§13-334, 13-335.

Forms.

Out-of-District service, order of publication, §13-339.

Garnishment.

Prejudgment garnishment, §16-502.

Guardians.

Fifteen-day temporary guardians, Probate Rule 341.

SERVICE OF PROCESS AND PAPERS —Cont'd

Guardianship of minors.

Permanent guardianship.

Notice, §16-2386.

Standby guardianship.

Notice of filing, §16-4808.

Guardians of minors, on, §13-332.

Habeas corpus, §16-1902.

Human rights commission, §2-1403.09.

Incompetent or incapacitated persons, on, §13-333.

Insanitary buildings, condemnation of.

Nonresident owners.

Registered agent, appointment of, §6-910.

Intellectual disabilities, persons with.

Commitment to intellectual disability facility, MentalRetardation Rule 9.

International banking corporations.

Registered office and agent, §26-637.

Interpleader, CivPro Rule 22.

Interrogatories, CivPro Rule 33.

Interstate compact on educational opportunity for military children.

Notice and service, §49-1101.13.

Intervention proceedings.

Conservators.

Accounts and reports, Probate Rule 330.

Plans and inventories, Probate Rule 329.

Termination of conservatorship, Probate Rule 334.

Fifteen-day temporary guardians, Probate Rule 341.

Missing persons, Probate Rule 350.

Notice of hearings on petitions, Probate Rule 311.

General intervention proceedings, Probate Rules 322, 325.

Petition and notice, Probate Rules 311, 321, 325.

Petition for compensation, Probate Rule 308.

Reports by guardians, Probate Rule 328.

Juvenile causes, §16-2306.

Landlord and tenant.

Affidavit of service by special process server, LandlordTenant Form 3.

Generally, §42-3509.04, LandlordTenant Rule 4.

**SERVICE OF PROCESS AND
PAPERS** —Cont'd
Landlord and tenant —Cont'd
Notice to quit, §42-3206.
**Lead-hazard prevention and
elimination.**
Violations, service of notice, §8-231.15.
Long-arm statute, under, §§13-431 to
13-434.
Mailing.
Additional time after service by mail,
CivPro Rule 6, CrimPro Rule 45.
Adoption proceedings, Adoption Rule
6.
Appeals, DCCtApp Rule 26.
Domestic relations actions, DomRel
Rule 6.
Hospitalization of persons with
mental illness, MentalHealth
Rule 13.
Juvenile proceedings, JuvProc Rule
45.
Adoption proceedings, Adoption Rules
4, 5.
Time for service, Adoption Rule 6.
Attorney discipline or disability
proceedings, DCBar Rule XI,
USDistCt LCrR 57.27, USDistCt
LCvR 83.16.
Notice and acknowledgment for service
by mail, CivPro Form CA 1-A.
Small claims court, SmallClaims Rule
4.
Summons, CivPro Rule 4.
Domestic relations actions, DomRel
Rule 4.
Marshal, by, §13-302.
Mental illness, persons with.
Hospitalization.
Commission on mental health
reports, MentalHealth Rule 3.
Time for service by mail or service of
affidavit, MentalHealth Rule 13.
Metropolitan police, by, §13-302.01.
**Metropolitan police, upon sworn
member.**
Actions arising out of performance of
duties.
Rules establishing procedure,
issuance, requirements,
§5-105.09.
Money lenders, §26-901.
Motor vehicles of nonresidents,
§50-1301.07.
Nonresidents, on, §13-336.
Numerous defendants, CivPro Rule 5.

**SERVICE OF PROCESS AND
PAPERS** —Cont'd
Out-of-District service.
Individuals eligible to make service,
§13-432.
Long-arm statute, §§13-431 to 13-434.
Manner of service, proof, §13-431.
Personal service, §13-337.
Publication, by, §§13-335 to 13-341.
Service upon designated individual or
individuals, §13-433.
Parentage proceedings, DomRel Rule
405.
**Personal service in lieu of
publication,** §§13-337, 13-338.
Persons eligible to serve process,
CivPro Rule 4.1.
Child abuse and neglect proceedings,
NeglectProc Rule 11.
Small claims court, SmallClaims Rule
4.
Subpoenas.
Civil cases, CivPro Rule 45.
Criminal cases, CrimPro Rule 17.
Delinquent minors, JuvProc Rule 17.
Domestic relations actions, DomRel
Rule 45.
Summons, CivPro Rule 4.
Domestic relations actions, DomRel
Rule 4.
Post-conviction proceedings.
Superior court proceedings,
PostConvRel Rule 3.
Posting.
Adoption proceedings, Adoption Rule
4.
Domestic relations actions, DomRel
Rule 4.
Landlord and tenant court,
LandlordTenant Rule 4.
Probate proceedings.
Death before Jan. 1, 1981.
Accounts of administrators,
executors and collectors, Probate
Rule 19.
Contested estate cases, Probate Rule
15.
Petitions for probate or
administration, Probate Rules
10 to 12.
Death between Jan. 1, 1981, and June
30, 1995.
Foreign personal representative's
agent to accept service, Probate
Rule 127.
Notice of action on claim, Probate
Rule 111.

SERVICE OF PROCESS AND PAPERS —Cont'd
Probate proceedings —Cont'd
Death on or after July 1, 1995.
Foreign personal representative's agent to accept service, Probate Form 25, Probate Rule 427.
Notice of action on claim, Probate Rule 411.
Rule to show cause petitions and orders, Probate Rule 413.
Guardians, conservators, trustees, etc., involved, Probate Rule 210.
Contested estate cases, Probate Rule 208.
Rule to show cause petitions and orders, Probate Rule 211.
Procurement practices.
Action for violations by qui tam plaintiff, §2-381.03.
Proof of delivery.
Certified mail return receipts, §14-506.
Proof of service, CivPro Rule 5-I, USDistCt LCvR 5.3.
Adoption proceedings, Adoption Rules 4, 5.
Appeals, DCCtApp Rule 25.
Child abuse and neglect proceedings, NeglectProc Rule 11.
Collection and subrogation cases, CivPro Rule 40-III.
Criminal proceedings, USDistCt LCrR 49, USDistCt LCrR 49.2.
Domestic relations actions, DomRel Rules 4, 5.
Intellectual disability proceedings, MentalRetardation Rule 9.
Intervention proceedings.
Notice of hearings on petitions, Probate Rule 311.
Probate proceedings.
Rule to show cause petitions and orders, Probate Rules 211, 413.
Small claims court, SmallClaims Rule 4.
Subpoenas, CivPro Rule 45.
Domestic relations actions, DomRel Rule 45.
Summons, CivPro Rule 4.
Publication, §§13-335 to 13-341, CivPro Rule 4-I.
Adoption proceedings, Adoption Rule 4.
Condemnation actions, CivPro Rule 71A.
Corporations, §13-335.

SERVICE OF PROCESS AND PAPERS —Cont'd
Publication —Cont'd
Default, failure to appear in obedience to order, §13-340.
Domestic relations actions, DomRel Rule 4.
Entry of order, judgment, decree against nonresident or absent defendant upon proof of notice by publication, §13-340.
Nonresidents, absent defendants, unknown heirs and devisees, §13-336.
Order of publication, §§13-338 to 13-340.
Personal service outside District in lieu of, §13-337.
Persons unknown to be living or dead and unknown heirs and devisees, §13-341.
Quiet title, §16-3301.
Real estate tax sales.
Revised real property tax sale. Foreclosure, §47-1374.
Real property taxes.
Service of notice, §47-804.
Registered agents, §29-104.12.
Rental of public space, §10-1104.03.
Replevin actions, CivPro Rule 64-II.
Domestic relations actions, DomRel Rule 64.
Security agents and brokers.
Commissioner.
Consent to service of process, §31-5607.06.
Small claims court, SmallClaims Rule 4.
Costs, SmallClaims Rule 15.
Specifications of other laws for, §13-331.
Subpoenas.
Adoption proceedings, Adoption Rule 45.
Civil cases, CivPro Rule 45.
Criminal procedure, CrimPro Rule 17, USDistCt LCrR 17.1.
Delinquent minors, JuvProc Rule 17.
Domestic relations actions, DomRel Rule 45.
Subrogation cases, CivPro Rule 40-III.
Summons, CivPro Rule 4.
Child abuse and neglect proceedings, NeglectProc Rule 11.
Criminal procedure, CrimPro Rules 4, 9.

SERVICE OF PROCESS AND PAPERS —Cont'd

Summons —Cont'd

Delinquent minors, JuvProc Rule 9.

Domestic relations actions, DomRel Rule 4.

Termination of parent and child relationship, NeglectProc Rule 36.

Superior court, §11-943.

Sureties.

Proceedings against sureties, CivPro Rule 65.1.

Appeals, DCCtApp Rule 8.

Domestic relations actions, DomRel Rule 71.

Tax proceedings, Tax Rule 5.

Petitions, Tax Rule 6.

Termination of parent and child relationship.

Service of motion, NeglectProc Rule 36.

Third party practice, CivPro Rule 14.

Time of service, CivPro Rule 6, CrimPro Rule 45.

Collection and subrogation cases, CivPro Rule 40-III.

Domestic relations actions, CivPro Rule 4, DomRel Rule 6.

Hospitalization of persons with mental illness, MentalHealth Rule 13.

Juvenile proceedings, JuvProc Rule 45.

Summons, CivPro Rule 4.

Tobacco master settlement agreement enforcement.

Agent for service of process, §7-1803.04.

Tribunals outside District.

Assistance in serving persons found in District, §13-434.

Unemployment compensation, service of process on nonresident employers for purposes of, §51-105.

Unknown persons, on, §§13-336, 13-341.

Veteran's estate affected, CivPro Rule 5-I.

When required, CivPro Rule 5.

SERVICE PIPES.

Public works, §9-401.03.

SERVICE STATIONS, §§36-301.01 to 36-305.02.

See GAS STATIONS.

SESSIONS OF COURT.

Appellate procedure, USCtApp Rule 1.

SETOFFS.

Counterclaims by way of, §13-501.

Ejectment for nonpayment of rent, §16-1124.

Insurers rehabilitation and liquidation proceedings, §31-1328.

Judgments and decrees, §15-107.

Limited cooperative associations.

Membership interests, §29-1006.04.

Medicaid health-care assistance reimbursement, §4-603.

Nonprobate transfers.

Financial institutions, §19-602.27.

Public officers and employees.

Employee debt setoffs, §§1-629.01 to 1-629.04.

Secured transactions.

Banks and financial institutions.

Security interests in deposit accounts, §28:9-340.

Small claims court, §16-3904.

SETTLEMENT CONFERENCES, CivPro Rule 16.

Authority to set conference, CivPro Rule 309.

Domestic relations actions, DomRel Rule 16-I.

Failure to appear, CivPro Rule 16-II.

Probate proceedings.

Contested estate cases.

Death between Jan. 1, 1981, and June 30, 1995, Probate Rule 107.

Death on or after July 1, 1995, Probate Rule 407.

Guardians, conservators, trustees, etc., involved, Probate Rule 208.

SETTLEMENT OR COMPROMISE.

Alcoholic beverage licenses.

Protest hearings.

Advisory neighborhood commissions.

Settlement agreements submitted to board, §25-609.

Settlement agreements, §25-446.

Enforceable provisions, §25-446.01.

Unenforceable provisions, §25-446.02.

Settlement conference, §25-445.

Appeals, federal cases.

Judgments enforcing administrative orders, FRAP 19.

Attorneys at law.

Communication of offer of settlement with client, ProfCond Rule 1.4.

SETTLEMENT OR COMPROMISE
—Cont'd
Attorneys at law —Cont'd
Discipline or disability proceedings,
DCBar Rule XI.
Malpractice claims, ProfCond Rule 1.8.
Multiple clients, ProfCond Rule 1.8.
Scope of representation, ProfCond
Rule 1.2.
Claims against the District, §§2-402,
2-404, 2-406.
Class actions, CivPro Rule 23.
Unincorporated associations, CivPro
Rule 23.2.
Collection of taxes.
Compromise as to liability, §47-4404.
Consumer protection.
Complaints.
Settlement of complaints, §28-3905.
Corporations.
Derivative actions, §29-305.55.
Court employees.
Debts and erroneous payments made
to employees, collection by
executive officer.
Compromise of claim to collect debt,
§11-1733.
Derivative actions by shareholders,
CivPro Rule 23.1.
Hazardous substance releases,
§8-634.08.
Inheritance and estate taxes,
§47-3704.
Judges.
Coercing parties into settlement
prohibited, CJC Canon 2.6.
Landlord and tenant court.
Consent settlement agreement,
LandlordTenant Form 4b.
Addendum, list of repairs,
LandlordTenant Form 4A.
Limited cooperative associations.
Member actions.
Approval, §29-1013.04.
Limited liability companies.
Settlement of derivative action, court
approval required, §29-808.06.
Limited partnerships.
Derivative actions, court approval
required for settlement,
§29-709.05.
Malpractice claims.
Legal malpractice, ProfCond Rule 1.8.
**Medicaid health-care assistance
reimbursement,** §4-605.
Merit system, §1-606.06.

SETTLEMENT OR COMPROMISE
—Cont'd
Nonprofit corporations.
Derivative actions, §29-411.06.
**Notice of settlement in civil jury
cases,** USDistCt LCvR 47.1.
**Police and firefighters medical care
reimbursement,** §5-606.
Probate proceedings, §16-3102.
Procurement practices.
Claims for violations.
Settlement of action brought by qui
tam plaintiff, §2-381.03.
**Real estate acquired by purchase or
condemnation,** §1-301.04.
Real property wet settlement act,
§§42-2401 to 42-2407.
Settlement statements, CivPro Form
CA 102.
Small claims court, §16-3906.
Statutory trusts.
Derivative actions, settlement
requiring court approval,
§29-1206.13.
Tobacco Settlement Trust Fund,
§§7-1811.01 to 7-1811.03.
Trusts and trustees.
Uniform trust code.
Nonjudicial settlement agreements,
§19-1301.11.
Wet settlement act, §§42-2401 to
42-2407.

SEVERANCE PAY.
Public officers and employees,
§1-624.09.

SEVERNA.
Real property tax exemptions,
§47-1095.

SEWAGE WORKS.
**Southeast water and sewer
improvement benefit district.**
Special assessment district, §§47-891
to 47-894.
Wastewater and sewage works,
§§34-2101 to 34-2134.
See WASTEWATER AND SEWAGE
WORKS.
Wastewater disposal systems,
§§8-105.01 to 8-105.15.
See WASTEWATER DISPOSAL
SYSTEM.
Wastewater treatment systems,
§§8-201 to 8-205.
See WASTEWATER TREATMENT
SYSTEMS.

SEWAGE WORKS —Cont'd
Water and sewer authority,
§§34-2201.01 to 34-2202.41.
See WATER AND SEWER
AUTHORITY.

SEX DISCRIMINATION.
Athletic equity.
Schools and education, §§38-841.01 to
38-841.08.
**Benefit programs for District
employees,** §1-607.07.
**Educational institutions, exceptions
for,** §2-1402.42.
**Grammatical gender, construction
of,** §45-603.
Insurance.
Unfair trade practices, §§31-2231.01 to
31-2231.25.
Pay equity and training commission,
§§32-601 to 32-609.
Prohibition of, §2-1401.01.
Schools and education.
Athletic equity, §§38-841.01 to
38-841.08.
Teachers.
Masculine pronoun to include both
male and female, §38-112.
Wages and salaries, §38-1901.

SEX OFFENDER REGISTRATION,
§§22-4001 to 22-4017.
Address.
Change of, §22-4009.
Age of consent, §22-4016.
Certification duties.
Court services and offender
supervision agency, §22-4008.
Superior court, §22-4003.
Community notification, §22-4011.
Consent, §22-4016.
Corrections, department of.
Duties, §22-4005.
Court services.
Certification function, §22-4008.
Registration function, §22-4007.
Definitions pertinent to, §22-4001.
Department of mental health.
Duties, §22-4006.
Dispute resolution procedures.
Superior court, §22-4004.
Duties of sex offenders, §22-4014.
Education duties, §22-4011.
Freedom of information act,
§22-4017.
Immunity, §22-4013.
Interagency coordination, §22-4012.

SEX OFFENDER REGISTRATION
—Cont'd
**Maintenance and release of
information,** §22-4010.
Mandatory release, §22-4015.
Offender supervision agency.
Certification function, §22-4008.
Registration function, §22-4007.
Penalties, §22-4015.
Registration function.
Court services and offender
supervision agency, §22-4007.
Registration period, §22-4002.

SEX TRAFFICKING.
Human trafficking, §§22-1831 to
22-1843.
See HUMAN TRAFFICKING.

SEXUAL ABUSE.
**Aged persons, offenses committed
against.**
Enhanced penalties, §22-3601.
Child custody and visitation.
Prohibition where child conceived as
result of sexual abuse, §16-914.
Child sexual abuse generally.
See CHILD SEXUAL ABUSE.
First degree sexual abuse, §22-3002.
Aggravating circumstances, §22-3020.
Limitation of actions, §23-113.
Reporting requirements, §4-1321.02.
Sexual abuse of a minor.
Arranging for a sexual contact with a
real or fictitious child,
§22-3010.02.
First degree, §22-3009.01.
Secondary education students,
§22-3009.03.
Second degree, §22-3009.02.
Secondary education students,
§22-3009.04.

SEXUAL ASSAULT RESPONSE,
§§4-561.01 to 4-561.16.
Chief of police.
Monitoring of MPD, §4-561.08.
Definitions, §4-561.01.
**Forensic examination kits and
specimens.**
Payment for kits, §4-561.03.
Processing, §4-561.02.
Hospitals.
Forensic examination kits and
specimens, billing, §4-561.03.
Independent expert consultant,
§4-561.04.
Duties, §4-561.05.

SEXUAL ASSAULT RESPONSE
—Cont'd
Independent expert consultant
—Cont'd
Reports, §4-561.06.
Reviews, §4-561.06.
MPD.
Duties, §4-561.07.
Monitoring by chief of police,
§4-561.08.
Reports, §4-561.09.
No private right of action, §4-561.16.
OCME.
Reports.
Sexual assault forensic examination
kits, §4-561.10.
Toxicology samples, §4-561.11.
Reports.
Independent expert consultant,
§4-561.06.
MPD, §4-561.09.
OCME.
Sexual assault forensic examination
kits, §4-561.10.
Toxicology samples, §4-561.11.
Reviews.
Independent expert consultant,
§4-561.06.
**Sexual assault response team
(SART).**
Case review subcommittee, §4-561.14.
Duties and responsibilities, §4-561.13.
Establishment, §4-561.12.
Membership, §4-561.12.
Sexual assault victim advocates,
§23-1909.
Disclosure of confidential information
prohibited without consent of
client, §14-307.
Privileged communications, §14-312.
**Sexual assault victim rights task
force, §4-561.15.**
Time limits.
Forensic examination kits and
specimens, processing, §4-561.02.
Victims' rights, §§23-1907 to 23-1911.
Access to information, §23-1910.
Definitions, §23-1907.
Multiple victims, §22-3020.
Past behavior of victim, admissibility
of evidence of, §§22-3021, 22-3022.
Private right of action, §23-1911.
Rights of victims, §23-1908.
Sexual assault response, §§4-561.01 to
4-561.16.

SEXUAL ASSAULT RESPONSE
—Cont'd
Victims' rights —Cont'd
Sexual assault victim advocates,
§23-1909.
Disclosure of confidential
information prohibited without
consent of client, §14-307.
Privileged communications, §14-312.
**SEXUAL ASSAULT VICTIM
ADVOCATES, §23-1909.**
**Disclosure of confidential
information prohibited without
consent of client, §14-307.**
Privileged communications, §14-312.
**SEXUALLY TRANSMITTED
DISEASES.**
AIDS.
Discrimination in AIDS insurance,
§§31-1601 to 31-1610.
Health care, §§7-1601 to 7-1606.
Human papillomavirus.
Vaccination, §§7-1651.01 to 7-1651.05.
See HUMAN PAPILLOMAVIRUS
VACCINATION.
Laboratory services.
Fees, §7-734.
Treatment for sexual partners,
§§7-2081.01 to 7-2081.04.
Defined terms, §7-2081.01.
Expedited partner therapy,
§7-2081.02.
Information provided to partners,
§7-2081.02.
Liability of health care practitioners,
§7-2081.03.
Liability of health care practitioners,
§7-2081.03.
Rules, §7-2081.04.
**SEXUAL OFFENSES, §§22-3001 to
22-3024.**
Aggravating circumstances, §22-3020.
Aiding and abetting, §22-3020.
**Alienation of affections, abolition of
action for, §16-923.**
**Arranging for a sexual contact with
a real or fictitious child,
§22-3010.02.**
**Assault with intent to commit sexual
abuse, §22-401.**
Attempts to commit, §22-3018.
Bigamy, §22-501.
**Breach of promise, abolition of
action for, §16-923.**
Child custody and visitation.
Prohibition where child conceived as
result of sexual abuse, §16-914.

SEXUAL OFFENSES —Cont'd
Child sexual abuse.
  See CHILD SEXUAL ABUSE.
Crime investigation records.
  Retention of records in open
    investigations, §5-113.32.
Crime victims' compensation.
  Eligibility for compensation, VictComp
    Rule 7.
Criminal conversation, abolition of
  action for, §16-923.
Defenses to, §22-3007.
Definitions, §22-3001.
  Voyeurism, §22-3531.
Domestic partnerships.
  No immunity from prosecution,
    §22-3019.
  Privileges inapplicable, §22-3024.
Drugs, use of, §§22-3002, 22-3004.
Emergency care for sexual assault
  victims, §§7-2121 to 7-2125.
First degree sexual abuse, §22-3002.
  Child sexual abuse, §22-3008.
  Indictments.
    Fictitious name indictments,
      §23-331.
  Minors, §22-3009.01.
  Patients or clients, §22-3015.
  Secondary education students,
    §22-3009.03.
  Wards, §22-3013.
Force or threat of force, use of,
  §§22-3002 to 22-3005.
Fourth degree sexual abuse,
  §22-3005.
Guardians, sexual abuse of wards.
  Defenses, §22-3017.
  First degree, §22-3013.
  Second degree, §22-3014.
Human trafficking, §§22-1831 to
  22-1843.
  See HUMAN TRAFFICKING.
Incest, §22-1901.
Incompetent or incapacitated
  persons, against, §§22-3003,
  22-3005.
Indictments.
  Fictitious name indictments.
    First or second degree sexual abuse
      or child sexual abuse, §23-331.
Misdemeanor sexual abuse, §22-3006.
Multiple perpetrators, §22-3020.
Multiple victims, §22-3020.
Obscenity.
  See OBSCENITY.
Past behavior of victim,
  admissibility of evidence of,
  §§22-3021, 22-3022.

SEXUAL OFFENSES —Cont'd
Patient or client.
  Defenses to sexual abuse of, §22-3017.
  First degree sexual abuse of, §22-3015.
  Second degree sexual abuse of,
    §22-3016.
Prostitution.
  General provisions, §§22-2701 to
    22-2725.
  See PROSTITUTION.
Rape Shield Law, §§22-3021 to
  22-3024, 22-3022.
Reasonable fear, placing victim in,
  §§22-3002 to 22-3005.
Reporting, §22-3023.
Second degree sexual abuse,
  §22-3003.
  Child sexual abuse, §22-3009.
  Indictments.
    Fictitious name indictments,
      §23-331.
  Minors, §22-3009.02.
  Patients or clients, §22-3016.
  Secondary education students,
    §22-3009.04.
  Wards, §22-3014.
Sexual assault response, §§4-561.01 to
  4-561.16.
  See SEXUAL ASSAULT RESPONSE.
Sexual psychopaths, §§22-3803 to
  22-3811.
  See SEXUAL PSYCHOPATHS.
Spousal immunity, lack of, §22-3019.
Spousal privilege inapplicable to,
  §22-3024.
Third degree sexual abuse, §22-3004.
Victims of crime, §§23-1907 to 23-1911.
  Access to information, §23-1910.
  Definitions, §23-1907.
  Multiple victims, §22-3020.
  Past behavior of victim, admissibility
    of evidence of, §§22-3021, 22-3022.
  Private right of action, §23-1911.
  Rights of victims, §23-1908.
  Sexual assault response, §§4-561.01 to
    4-561.16.
  Sexual assault victim advocates,
    §23-1909.
  Disclosure of confidential
    information prohibited without
    consent of client, §14-307.
  Privileged communications, §14-312.
Voyeurism, §22-3531.
Wards, sexual abuse of.
  Defenses to sexual abuse of, §22-3017.
  First degree sexual abuse of, §22-3013.

SEXUAL OFFENSES —Cont'd
Wards, sexual abuse of —Cont'd
Second degree sexual abuse of, §22-3014.

SEXUAL ORIENTATION DISCRIMINATION.
Insurance.
Discrimination based upon AIDS test, §§31-1601 to 31-1610.
Unfair trade practices, §§31-2231.01 to 31-2231.25.
Prohibition of, §2-1401.01.

SEXUAL PSYCHOPATHS, §§22-3803 to 22-3811.
Commitment to an institution, §22-3808.
Criminal law not affected by statutes regarding, §22-3811.
Definitions, §22-3803.
Discharge of committed person, §22-3809.
Filing of statement regarding, §22-3804.
Hearings, §§22-3807, 22-3808.
Parole, §22-3809.
Psychiatric examinations, §22-3806.
Right to counsel, §22-3805.
Stay of criminal proceedings against, §22-3810.

SHAKESPEARE THEATRE.
Real property exempt from taxation, §47-1048.

SHARE DATA CENTER, §47-317.07.

SHARED WORK UNEMPLOYMENT COMPENSATIONS PROGRAM, §§51-171 to 51-178.
See UNEMPLOYMENT COMPENSATION.

SHARE EXCHANGES, §§29-309.01 to 29-309.08.
See CORPORATIONS.

SHARPS INJURY PROTECTION.
Safe needle distribution, §§7-2851 to 7-2858.
Definitions, §7-2851.
Effective date, §7-2857.
Report of exposure incident, §7-2853.
Rules, §7-2855.
Sale, distribution, possession, use of sharp.
Requirements, §7-2852.
Severability, §7-2857.
Violations, penalties, §7-2854.

SHELLEY'S CASE RULE.
Abolition of, §42-703.

SHELTER AND TRANSITIONAL HOUSING FOR VICTIMS OF DOMESTIC VIOLENCE FUND, §4-521.

SHELTERS.
Animals.
Impounded animals, §§8-1805 to 8-1807.
Domestic violence.
Shelter and transitional housing for victims of domestic violence fund, §4-521.
Emergency.
Public assistance.
Emergency shelter allowances, §4-206.05.

SHERIDAN TAPESTRIES.
Personal property tax exemption, §47-1013.

SHIPS.
See BOATS AND OTHER WATERCRAFT.

SHOCK TREATMENTS.
Health care durable powers of attorney, §21-2211.

SHOPLIFTING, §§22-3213, 27-101 to 27-106.
Attorney's fees and costs, §27-106.
Criminal procedure, §27-103.
Damages, §27-102.
Definitions, §27-101.
Fines, §27-102.
Jurisdiction, §27-105.
Liability for, §27-102.
Merchant election of remedies, §27-104.
Merchant's recovery of civil damages, §§27-101 to 27-106.

SHOPPING MALLS.
Smoking, §7-1703.
"No Smoking" signs, §§7-1703.04, 7-1704.

SHORT TITLES.
See POPULAR NAMES AND SHORT TITLES.

SIBLINGS AND DESCENDANTS OF SIBLINGS.
Intestate succession, §§19-309, 19-310, 19-315.

SICK ANIMALS.
Abandonment of, §22-1012.

SICK ANIMALS —Cont'd

Horse-drawn carriage trade horses,
§8-2010.

Neglect of, §22-1011.

SICK LEAVE.

Disability compensation, election to use instead of, §1-623.18.

Employee sick leave generally,
§§32-131.01 to 32-131.16.
See LABOR AND EMPLOYMENT
RELATIONS.

Family and medical leave, §§32-502,
32-503.

Fire departments, §5-408.

Public officers and employees,
§1-612.03.

Right to sick and safe leave,
§§32-131.01 to 32-131.16.
See LABOR AND EMPLOYMENT
RELATIONS.

SICKLE CELL ANEMIA, §§7-831 to
7-840.

SICKLE HEMOGLOBINOPATHY,
§§7-831 to 7-840.

SIDEWALKS.

Affected advisory neighborhood commissions.
Weight given recommendations,
§9-425.02.

Assessments, §9-401.04.

Barbed-wire fences, §§9-1213.01 to
9-1213.05.

Blocking passage, §22-1307.

District department of transportation.
Exemption from design and
installation requirements,
§9-425.03.

Health of existing trees.
Preserving, §9-425.02.

Improvements, §9-401.06.

Installation requirements, §9-425.01.

Notice to parties in affected ward.
Prior to designing and constructing
new sidewalks, §9-425.02.

Parks and recreation, §10-138.

Previous materials considered for design and installation,
§9-425.02.

Prioritized installation, §9-425.01.

Repair and maintenance, §9-401.06.

Roads lacking sidewalks on both sides.
Installation required, §9-425.01.

SIDEWALKS —Cont'd

Roads missing sidewalks but not undergoing major construction.
Prioritized installation, §9-425.01.

Signs advertising real property for rent or for sale, §42-1801.

Snow and ice removal, §§9-601 to
9-607.
Owners or occupants of abutting
property, §9-411.01.
Sidewalks adjacent to federal
buildings, §9-411.03.
Sidewalks adjacent to public property,
§9-411.02.
Temporary use of sand and ashes,
§9-411.04.

Vending regulation, §§37-131.01 to
37-131.10.
See VENDING REGULATION.

SIGNATURES.

Adoption proceedings.
Pleadings, motions, etc., Adoption
Rules 10, 11.

Appeals.
Notice of appeal, DCCtApp Rule 3.

Business organizations.
Filing.
Signing as affirmation, §29-102.09.

Discovery.
Depositions.
Adoption, Adoption Rule 30.
Domestic relations actions, DomRel
Rule 30.
Requests, responses, and objections,
CivPro Rule 26.

Domestic relations actions.
Pleadings, motions, etc., DomRel Rules
10, 11.

Electronically filed documents,
CivPro Rule 5.
Hospitalization of persons with mental
illness, MentalHealth Rule 14.

Electronic signatures in global and national commerce act.
See ELECTRONIC SIGNATURES IN
GLOBAL AND NATIONAL
COMMERCE ACT.

Electronic transactions, uniform act,
§§28-4901 to 28-4918.

International wills.
Attesting witnesses, §18-703.
Placement on document, §18-704.

Investment securities.
Authenticating trustee's, registrar's or
transfer agent's signature.
Effect, §28:8-208.

SIGNATURES —Cont'd
Investment securities —Cont'd
Evidentiary rules concerning
certificated securities, §28:8-114.
Guaranteeing signature.
Effect, §28:8-306.
Unauthorized signature on security
certificate.
Effect, §28:8-205.
Letters of credit, §28:5-104.
Limited liability companies.
Signing of records.
Delivery to mayor, §29-802.03.
Judicial orders, §29-802.04.
Limited partnerships.
Signing of records.
Delivery to mayor, §29-702.04.
Judicial orders, §29-702.05.
Mediation.
Electronic signatures in global and
national commerce, relationship
with uniform mediation act,
§16-4211.
Negotiable instruments.
General provisions, §§28:3-101 to
28:3-605.
See NEGOTIABLE
INSTRUMENTS.
Partnerships.
Court action to require person to sign
or file record, §29-601.10.
Liability for inaccurate information in
filed record, §29-601.11.
Pleadings, motions, etc., CivPro Rule
11.
Adoption proceedings, Adoption Rules
10, 11.
Domestic relations actions, DomRel
Rules 10, 11.
E-Filing system.
Documents filed electronically,
CivPro Rule 5.
Hospitalization of persons with
mental illness, MentalHealth
Rule 14.
Hospitalization of persons with mental
illness, MentalHealth Rule 15.
Electronically filed documents,
MentalHealth Rule 14.
Statutory trusts.
Signing of records, §29-1202.03.
Inaccurate information in filed
records.
Liability of person signing or
causing another to sign,
§29-1202.05.

SIGNATURES —Cont'd
Statutory trusts —Cont'd
Signing pursuant to judicial order,
§29-1202.04.
Subpoenas, CivPro Rule 45.
Domestic relations actions, DomRel
Rule 45.

SIGNS, §§1-303.21 to 1-303.23.
Alcoholic beverage licenses.
Advertising, §§25-763 to 25-766.
Application proceedings.
Posted notice outside of
establishment, §25-423.
Legal drinking age, §25-713.
Posting of license, §25-711.
Pregnant women, warnings for,
§25-712.
Proof of valid identification, §25-713.
Revocation or suspension, notice,
§25-828.
**Crosswalks, special signs for failure
to yield to pedestrians in,**
§50-2201.30.
Gas stations.
Security requirements, §36-301.21.
Graffiti abatement, §§42-3141.01 to
42-3141.11.
See GRAFFITI.
Highway signs.
Construction or work zones.
Notice of increased fines and
penalties, §50-2201.04c.
Mayoral authority to install, §38-3101.
Newborn safe haven, §4-1451.03.
"No Smoking" signs.
Defacement, removal, or failure to
post, §7-1706.
Elevators, §7-1704.
Generally, §7-1704.
Health care facilities, §7-1703.
Property owners, §7-1703.04.
Pawnbrokers, §47-2884.02.
Rental housing.
For rent signs, §42-1801.
Residential home sales.
For sale signs, §42-1801.
**Strict traffic enforcement zone, signs
identifying District as,**
§50-2201.31.
Unit pricing.
Display of price, §28-5207.
Work zones on roads and highways.
Notice of increased fines and penalties,
§50-2201.04c.

SILICOSIS.
Workers' compensation, §32-1510.

SILVER.
Public auction permit requirements, §47-2705.

SIMULTANEOUS DEATHS, §§19-501 to 19-509.
Claims of entitlement.
Personal liability of recipient, §19-507.
Protection of payors, bona fide purchases and third parties, §19-507.
Construction of act, §§19-508, 19-509.
Co-owners with right of survivorship.
Defined, §19-501.
Survival by 120 hours, §19-504.
Definitions, §19-501.
Determination of death, §19-505.
Evidence of death or status, §19-505.
Survival by 120 hours.
Co-owners with right of survivorship, §19-504.
Exceptions to requirement, §19-506.
Governing instruments, requirement of, §19-503.
Probate laws, requirement under, §19-502.
Uniformity of construction, §19-508.

SINGLE-ROOM-OCCUPANCY HOUSING.
Development incentives, §42-3508.06.

SISTERS AND DESCENDANTS OF SISTERS.
Intestate succession, §§19-309, 19-310, 19-315.

SKATEBOARDS.
Helmet requirement for riders.
Persons under 16 years, §50-1651.

SKATING RINKS.
Business licenses, §47-2820.
Children and minors, §47-2820.
Police and firefighters assigned to, §47-2820.

SKYLAND TIF AREA, §§2-1217.35a to 2-1217.35l.
Available sales tax revenues base year determinations, §2-1217.35c.
Bond issues.
Authorization, §2-1217.35d.
District officials not personally liable on, §2-1217.35j.
Information reporting, §2-1217.35l.
Issuance, §2-1217.35g.
Limited liability, §2-1217.35i.
Maintenance of documents, §2-1217.35k.

SKYLAND TIF AREA —Cont'd
Bond issues —Cont'd
Payment, §2-1217.35e.
Security, §2-1217.35e.
Terms and conditions, §2-1217.35f.
Closing documents, §2-1217.35h.
Creation, §2-1217.35c.
Definitions, §2-1217.35a.
Financing documents, §2-1217.35h.
Fund, §2-1217.35b.

SLAVERY.
Civil War amendments, US Const Amds 13 to 15.
Human trafficking, §§22-1831 to 22-1843.
See HUMAN TRAFFICKING.
Importation, US Const Art I §9, Amd 14.
Congressional apathy to prohibit, US Const Art I §9.
Prohibition, US Const Amd 13.
Compensation, illegal and void, US Const Amd 14.
Runaway slaves.
Congressional authority to return, US Const Art IV §2, Amd 13.
Suffrage, US Const Amd 15.
Taxation, US Const Art I §§2, 9, Amd 14.
Three-fifths rule, US Const Art I §2, Amd 14.

SLAYER'S ACT, §19-320.

SLEDS.
Helmet requirement for riders.
Persons under 16 years, §50-1651.

SLUDGE FROM WASTEWATER TREATMENT FACILITIES.
Use of, §8-103.14.

SLUM CLEARANCE.
Acquisition and disposal by District.
Eliminating slum or blight, §§42-3171.01 to 42-3171.04.
Community development.
General provisions, §§6-1001 to 6-1007.
See COMMUNITY DEVELOPMENT.
Housing and community development reform advisory commission, §§6-1031 to 6-1037.
Demolition of deteriorated property, §§42-3173.01 to 42-3173.12.
Housing redevelopment.
General provisions, §§6-311.01 to 6-341.05.
See URBAN RENEWAL.

SLUM CLEARANCE —Cont'd
National Capital Housing Authority.
General provisions, §§6-101.01 to
6-103.01.
See NATIONAL CAPITAL
HOUSING AUTHORITY.

**SMALL AND CERTIFIED BUSINESS
ENTERPRISE DEVELOPMENT
AND ASSISTANCE,** §§2-218.01 to
2-218.75.
Audits of certificates of registration,
§2-218.65.
Capital access fund, §2-218.75.
**Capital improvements to public
schools.**
Expenditure accountability,
§38-2973.04.
Certified business enterprises.
Bid and proposals.
Identification of business in,
§2-218.64.
Preferences, §2-218.43.
Breach of subcontracting plan,
§2-218.48.
Certification, §§2-218.61 to 2-218.65.
Application, §2-218.61.
Required, §2-218.61.
Certified joint ventures, §2-218.39a.
Contracting and procurement goals of
agencies, §2-218.41.
Required programs, procedures,
policies, §2-218.42.
Disadvantaged business enterprises,
§2-218.33.
Eligibility for certification, §§2-218.31
to 2-218.39a.
Enforcement, §2-218.48.
Against agency, §2-218.52.
Local business enterprises, §2-218.31.
Local manufacturing businesses,
§2-218.39.
Mandatory set-asides.
Follow-on and renewable
acquisitions, §2-218.45a.
Pilot program, §2-218.49.
Small contracts, §2-218.44.
Supply schedule, §2-218.45.
Performance and subcontracting
requirements, §2-218.46.
Policies and procedures to maximize
participation, §2-218.49.
Principal offices located in enterprise
zone, §2-218.37.
Regional governmental entities,
§2-218.55.
Reporting requirements, §§2-218.53,
2-218.54.

**SMALL AND CERTIFIED BUSINESS
ENTERPRISE DEVELOPMENT
AND ASSISTANCE** —Cont'd
Certified business enterprises
—Cont'd
Resident owed businesses, §2-218.35.
Longtime resident businesses,
§2-218.36.
Small business enterprises, §2-218.32.
Unbundling requirement, §2-218.47.
Veteran owned business, §2-218.38.
Waiver of subcontracting
requirements, §2-218.51.
Certified joint ventures, §2-218.39a.
**Complaints against business
enterprises,** §2-218.63.
Contracts and procurement,
§§2-218.41 to 2-218.55.
Crimes and offenses.
Falsification of certificates of
registration, §2-218.64.
Definitions, §2-218.02.
**Department of small and local
business development,** §§2-218.11
to 2-218.13.
Director, §2-218.12.
Established, §2-218.11.
Functions, §2-218.13.
Organization, §2-218.13.
Record keeping, §2-218.24.
Transfers, §2-218.14.
Eligibility for certification.
Disadvantaged business enterprises,
§2-218.33.
Local business enterprises, §2-218.31.
With principal offices located in an
enterprise zone, §2-218.37.
Local manufacturing business
enterprises, §2-218.39.
Longtime resident businesses,
§2-218.36.
Resident-owned businesses, §2-218.35.
Small business enterprises, §2-218.32.
Veteran-owned business enterprises,
§2-218.38.
**Equity and development
participation,** §2-218.49a.
Exemptions, §2-218.55.
**Falsification of certificates of
registration,** §2-218.64.
Fines and civil penalties, §2-218.63.
Falsification of certificates of
registration, §2-218.64.
Identification of enterprises,
§2-218.64.
**Minority and women-owned
business assessment program,**
§§2-214.01, 2-214.02.

SMALL AND CERTIFIED BUSINESS ENTERPRISE DEVELOPMENT AND ASSISTANCE —Cont'd
Programs.
Requirements for programs, §§2-218.41 to 2-218.55.
Record keeping, §2-218.24.
Regional governmental entities.
Exemptions, §2-218.55.
Repealed provisions, §2-218.82.
Reports.
Agency reporting requirements, §2-218.53.
Department reporting requirements, §2-218.54.
Review of program, §2-218.71.
Rulemaking, §2-218.72.
Small business capital access fund, §2-218.75.
Stabilization and job creation strategy, §§2-218.66 to 2-218.69.
Plans, §2-218.68.
Procurement training and assistance, §2-218.69.
Services to certified business enterprises, §2-218.66.
Volunteer Corps of Executives and Entrepreneurs, §2-218.67.
Title of act, §2-218.01.
Triennial review of program, §2-218.71.
Volunteer Corps of Executives and Entrepreneurs, §2-218.67.

SMALL BUSINESSES.
Economic development zone incentives.
General provisions, §§6-1501 to 6-1506.
See ECONOMIC DEVELOPMENT ZONE INCENTIVES.
Health insurance, §31-3303.03.
Small and certified business enterprise development and assistance, §§2-218.01 to 2-218.75.
See SMALL AND CERTIFIED BUSINESS ENTERPRISE DEVELOPMENT AND ASSISTANCE.

SMALL BUSINESS FINANCING.
Community development by financial institutions, §§26-431.01 to 26-431.08.

SMALL CLAIMS COURT, §§16-3901 to 16-3910.
Applicability of other laws and provisions, §16-3901.

SMALL CLAIMS COURT —Cont'd
Arbitration, §11-1322.
Awards, SmallClaimsArb Rule 5.
Recording award, SmallClaimsArb Rule 6.
Consent statements, SmallClaimsArb Rule 2.
General provisions, SmallClaimsArb Rule 1.
Hearings, SmallClaimsArb Rule 3.
Withdrawal or discontinuance, SmallClaimsArb Rule 4.
Attorneys at law.
Arbitration, SmallClaimsArb Rule 3.
Representation by attorney or law student, SmallClaims Rule 9.
Attorneys' fees and costs, §§16-3902, 16-3903, 16-3909.
Certification to civil division, SmallClaims Rule 8.
Pending motions and discovery, SmallClaims Rule 13-I.
Civil procedure rules applicable, SmallClaims Rule 2.
Commencement of actions, §16-3902, SmallClaims Rule 3.
Conciliation, §11-1322.
All parties appear voluntarily, SmallClaims Conciliation Rule 3.
Availability of conciliation, SmallClaims Conciliation Rule 1.
Certification by superior court judge, SmallClaims Conciliation Rule 4.
One party applying, SmallClaims Conciliation Rule 2.
Continuances, SmallClaims Rule 7.
Continuation as branch of superior court, §§11-1301 to 11-1323.
Costs, SmallClaims Rule 15.
Attorneys' fees, SmallClaims Rule 19.
Counterclaims, §16-3904.
Daily sessions, §11-1302.
Default judgments, §§16-3902, 16-3906, SmallClaims Rule 11.
Discovery, SmallClaims Rule 10.
Certification to civil division, SmallClaims Rule 13-I.
Dismissal of action, SmallClaims Rule 12.
Enforcement of judgments, §16-3907.
Fees, §16-3903, SmallClaims Rule 14.
Arbitration, SmallClaimsArb Rule 1.
Conciliation, SmallClaims Conciliation Rule 1.
Form of claim.
Automobile damage.
Collision, SmallClaims Forms 4, 5.

SMALL CLAIMS COURT —Cont'd
Form of claim —Cont'd
Automobile damage —Cont'd
Custody of defendant, SmallClaims
Form 7.
Parked vehicle, SmallClaims Form
6.
Contract breach, SmallClaims Form 3.
Deficiency balance, SmallClaims Form
1.
Deposit return.
Apartment, SmallClaims Forms 9,
10.
Merchandise, SmallClaims Form 8.
General form, SmallClaims Form 11.
Holder in due course, SmallClaims
Form 2.
Form of statement, §16-3902.
Installment payments, §16-3907.
Judgments and decrees, §§16-3907,
16-3908, SmallClaims Rule 16.
Installment payment, SmallClaims
Rule 17.
Jurisdiction, §11-1321.
Jury demand, SmallClaims Rule 6.
Jury trials, §16-3905.
Motions, SmallClaims Rule 13.
Certification to civil division,
SmallClaims Rule 13-I.
New trials, SmallClaims Rule 16.
Notice, §16-3902.
Pleadings, SmallClaims Rule 5.
Form of claim. See within this
heading, "Form of claim."
Preliminary proceedings by clerk,
SmallClaims Rule 11.
Proceedings, §16-3906, SmallClaims
Rule 12.
Time of trials, SmallClaims Rule 7.
Rights of judgment creditor,
§16-3910.
Scope of rules, SmallClaims Rule 1.
Service of process, SmallClaims Rule
4.
Costs, SmallClaims Rule 15.
Setoffs, §16-3904.
Settlements, §16-3906.
Stays, §16-3907, SmallClaims Rule 16.
Vacating stay, SmallClaims Rule 11.
Summary judgment, SmallClaims
Rule 13.
Superior court, §§16-3901 to 16-3910.
**Time of sessions, office hours, and
trials,** SmallClaims Rule 7.
**Transfer of cases between small
claims and superior court,**
§11-1323.

SMALL CLAIMS COURT —Cont'd
Wages and salaries, §16-3908,
SmallClaims Rule 18.

SMALL ESTATES.
Administration, §§20-351 to 20-357.
After-discovered property, §20-355.
Amount for estate to be administered
as small estate, §20-351.
Applicability of other provisions of
title, §20-356.
Attorney, representation by not
required, §20-354.
Bond not required, §20-354.
Commission, not entitled to, §20-354.
Distribution, §20-354.
Duties of personal representative,
§20-354.
Motor vehicles, transfer of title,
§20-357.
Notice, §20-353.
Petition, §20-352.
Proceedings after petition, §20-353.

SMOKE DETECTORS.
Definitions, §6-751.01.
Owners, duties, §6-751.02.
**Program to test and install
detectors,** §6-751.05a.
Funding and purchase of detectors and
batteries, §6-751.05c.
Report on program from previous year,
§6-751.05b.
Requirements regarding, §6-751.02.

SMOKING, §§7-1701 to 7-1731.
Cessation programs, §7-1709.
Cigarette sales below cost, §§28-4521
to 28-4527.
Definitions, §7-1702.
Drug paraphernalia, §§48-904.10,
48-1101 to 48-1104.
Education programs, §7-1709.
**Enforcement of requirements
regarding,** §7-1705.
Exceptions to provisions, §7-1708.
Existing law, effect on, §7-1710.
Fines, §7-1706.
Fire-standard-compliant cigarettes,
§§7-1751 to 7-1757.
**Free cigarettes, prohibition on
distribution of,** §7-1731.
Minors.
Purchase of tobacco by, §7-1721.03.
Sale of tobacco to, §7-1721.02.
No smoking signs, posting, §7-1704.
Penalties, §7-1706.
Policy declaration, §7-1701.

SMOKING —Cont'd
Prohibitions and restrictions,
  §7-1703.
  Health department, §7-741.02.
Public places.
  Health department regulations,
    §§7-741.01 to 7-741.07.
Restaurants, §7-1703.01.
Schools.
  Tobacco-free school campuses,
    §38-826.05.
Severability of provisions, §7-1707.
Tobacco tax.
  General provisions, §§47-2401 to
    47-2426.
  See TOBACCO TAX.
Workplaces.
  Prohibition of employment
    discrimination on basis of tobacco
    use, §7-1703.03.
  Regulation of smoking in, §7-1703.02.

SMOKING IN PUBLIC PLACES.
Definitions, §7-741.01.
Economic hardship waiver,
  §7-741.05.
Employee rights and protections,
  §7-741.06.
Exemptions, §7-741.03.
Inspections, §7-741.02.
Penalties, §7-741.04.
Prohibitions, §7-741.02.
Rulemaking to implement, §7-741.07.

SNAP, §§4-261.21 to 4-261.23.
See SUPPLEMENTAL NUTRITION
  ASSISTANCE PROGRAM (SNAP).

SNOW AND ICE REMOVAL.
Sidewalks, §§9-601 to 9-607.
  Abutting property, removal by owner
    or occupant, §9-601.
  Federal buildings, sidewalks adjacent
    to, §9-603.
  Public property, sidewalks adjacent to,
    §9-602.
  Rules, implementation, §9-607.

SOAPS.
Phosphate cleaners, §§8-107.01 to
  8-107.04.

**SOCCER STADIUM
  DEVELOPMENT.**
Not funded, §§10-1603.01 to
  10-1603.08.
Tax abatements, §47-4663.

SOCIAL IMPACT INVESTING.
Pay-for-success contracts, §§2-211.01
  to 2-211.03.

SOCIAL MEDIA.
Consumer protection.
  Unlawful trade practices, §28-3904.
**Qualified social electronic commerce
  companies.**
  Tax abatements, §§47-1818.01 to
    47-1818.08.

SOCIAL SECURITY.
Child support.
  Effect of receipt of SSDI by child,
    §16-916.01.
Powers of attorney, §21-2114.
**SSI/SSDI outreach, access and
  recovery (SOAR) pilot program,**
  §4-271.01.
Unemployment compensation,
  §§51-101 to 51-151.
  See UNEMPLOYMENT
    COMPENSATION.

SOCIAL SECURITY NUMBERS.
Birth registration, §7-205.01.
Business licenses, §47-2805.02.
Child support enforcement.
  Inclusion in records, §46-205.01.
Foster care, §4-217.07.
Parentage records.
  Inclusion of number, §16-2349.
Probate proceedings.
  Exclusion of personal identification
    from filed documents, Probate
    Rule 5.1.

SOCIAL WORK.
Associates, §3-1208.01.
Board of, §3-1202.12.
Child abuse and neglect reports.
  Social workers required to make,
    §4-1321.02.
Child death.
  Reports, §4-1371.12.
Definition of practice of, §3-1201.02.
Director of social services, §11-1722.
  Abused, neglected, and delinquent
    children.
    Additional powers regarding,
      §16-2337.
Graduate social workers, §3-1208.02.
Health occupations boards.
  General provisions, §§3-1201.01 to
    3-1213.01.
  See HEALTH OCCUPATIONS
    BOARDS.
**Health occupations licensure,
  registration or certification,**
  §§3-1205.01 to 3-1205.24.
  See HEALTH OCCUPATIONS
    LICENSURE, REGISTRATION
    OR CERTIFICATION.

SOCIAL WORK —Cont'd

Independent clinical social workers,
§3-1208.04.

Independent social workers,
§3-1208.03.

Licenses, §§3-1208.01 to 3-1208.06.

Malpractice.
Medical malpractice, §§16-2801 to
16-2841.
See MEDICAL MALPRACTICE.

Reports.
Child death, §4-1371.12.

**Titles and terms prohibited as
misrepresentation without
license to practice,** §3-1210.03.

Transition to licensed status,
§3-1208.05.

Waiver of license requirements,
§3-1208.06.

SOCIETY OF THE CINCINNATI.

Real property exempt from taxation,
§47-1037.

SODA FOUNTAINS.

Price list.
Charging greater price, §47-2911.
Posting required, §47-2908.
Failure, §47-2911.
Transmission to assessor, §47-2909.

Well-behaved persons.
Required to serve, §§47-2907, 47-2910.
Failure to serve, §47-2911.

**SOIL AND WATER CONSERVATION
DISTRICTS,** §§8-1701 to 8-1721.

Annual work plan, §8-1708.

Budget, §8-1711.

Chair of District, §8-1705.

Composition of District, §8-1704.

Cooperative agreements, §8-1709.

Definitions, §8-1702.

Documentary function of District,
§8-1709.

Employees of District, §8-1705.

Establishment of District, §8-1703.

Grants, §8-1710.

Limitations on authority of District,
§8-1712.

Loans, §8-1710.

Long-range program, §8-1708.

Meetings of District, §8-1705.

Policy declarations, §8-1701.

Powers of District, §8-1707.

Public hearings, §8-1709.

Reestablishment of District, §8-1721.

Reports, §8-1709.

Terms of District members, §8-1714.

**SOIL CHARACTERISTICS
INFORMATION.**

Contracts required to contain,
§42-608.

SOLAR ENERGY.

**Renewable energy portfolio
standards,** §§34-1431 to 34-1439.

Solar for All program, §8-1774.16.

Sustainable energy, §§8-1773.01 to
8-1774.16.
See SUSTAINABLE ENERGY.

SOLDIERS' HOME.

Highways, use of grounds for,
§9-105.02.

SOLICITATIONS.

Business licenses, §47-2835.

Charitable solicitations, §§44-1701 to
44-1714.
See CHARITABLE SOLICITATIONS.

Consumer credit, §28-3811.

Gangs, §22-951.

Home solicitation sales, §28-3811.

Insurance fraud, §22-3225.14.

Murder.
Penalty for solicitation of murder or
other violent crimes, §22-2107.

Panhandling, §§22-2301 to 22-2306.

Prostitution, §22-2701.

Public-private partnerships.
Requests for proposal, §2-273.03.

**School students, gifts and donations
solicited from,** §§44-1701 to
44-1714.

SOLICITORS.

Alcoholic beverage licenses, §25-116.

SOLID WASTE FACILITY PERMITS,
§§8-1051 to 8-1063.

Application for, §8-1054.

Definitions, §8-1051.

Fees, §8-1057.

Hearings, §8-1059.

Inspections, §8-1056.

Issuance of rules and regulations,
§8-1058.

Moratorium on, §8-1063.

Nuisance charges, §8-1060.

Open solid waste facilities.
Defined, §8-1051.
Prohibition of, §8-1052.

Operating requirements, §8-1055.

Penalties, §8-1060.

Remedies, §8-1060.

Reports, §8-1055.

Requirement to have permit,
§8-1053.

SOLID WASTE FACILITY PERMITS
—Cont'd
**Transfer Facility Site Selection
Advisory Panel,** §§8-1061, 8-1062.

SOLID WASTE MANAGEMENT.
Disposable food service ware,
§§8-1531 to 8-1537.
Electronic waste, §§8-1041.01 to
8-1041.12.
See ELECTRONIC WASTE.
**Environmental impact statements
required for facilities,** §8-109.11.
Garbage collection.
General provisions.
See GARBAGE COLLECTION.
Illegal dumping, §§8-901 to 8-906.
See ILLEGAL DUMPING.
Litter control.
Generally, §§8-801 to 8-812.
See LITTER CONTROL.
Recycling.
Construction and demolition waste
recycling accountability, §§8-1071
to 8-1077.
Generally.
See RECYCLING.
Solid waste facility permits, §§8-1051
to 8-1063.
See SOLID WASTE FACILITY
PERMITS.
Reduction and recovery, §§8-1031.01
to 8-1031.14.
See SOLID WASTE REDUCTION
AND RECOVERY.
**Solid waste disposal cost recovery
special account,** §1-325.91.

**SOLID WASTE NUISANCE
ABATEMENT FUND,** §8-807.01.

**SOLID WASTE REDUCTION AND
RECOVERY,** §§8-1031.01 to
8-1031.14.
Adequate waste collection,
§8-1031.04.
Collector obligations, §8-1031.05.
Collector registration, §8-1031.06.
Contract and licensing authority,
§8-1031.10.
Definitions, §8-1031.01.
Enforcement, §8-1031.14.
Enforcement training, §8-1031.09.
Fees, §8-1031.11.
**Interagency waste reduction
working group,** §8-1031.08.
Office of Waste Diversion, §8-1031.07.
Reports, §8-1031.13.

**SOLID WASTE REDUCTION AND
RECOVERY** —Cont'd
Rules, §8-1031.14.
Solid waste diversion fund,
§8-1031.12.
Source separation, §8-1031.03.
**Sustainable solid waste management
hierarchy,** §8-1031.02.

**SONS OF THE AMERICAN
REVOLUTION.**
Real property exempt from taxation,
§47-1034.

SO OTHERS MIGHT EAT, INC.
Real property tax exemptions,
§47-1078.

SOUND RECORDINGS.
Piracy, §22-3214.

**SOURCE OF INCOME
DISCRIMINATION.**
Prohibition of, §2-1401.01.

SOUTH DAKOTA AVENUE BRIDGE,
§9-312.

**SOUTHEAST NEIGHBORHOOD
HOUSE.**
Real property tax exemptions.
Lots 0808, 0904 and 0905 in square
5802, §47-1060.

**SOUTHEAST WATER AND SEWER
IMPROVEMENT BENEFIT
DISTRICT.**
Special assessment district, §§47-891
to 47-894.
Application of assessment, §47-894.
Definitions, §47-891.
Establishment, §47-892.
Levy of special assessment, §47-893.

**SOUTHWEST AREA
REDEVELOPMENT,** §9-101.17.

SOUTHWEST FREEWAY.
Highways, §9-101.17.

SOUTHWEST WATERFRONT.
Bond financing, §§2-1217.131 to
2-1217.151.
Affordable housing, §2-1217.151.
Authorization for bonds, §2-1217.135.
Closing documents, §2-1217.139.
Definitions, §2-1217.131.
Financing documents, §2-1217.139.
Findings of council, §2-1217.132.
Fund, §2-1217.133.
Immunity of district officials,
§2-1217.141.

SOUTHWEST WATERFRONT
—Cont'd
Bond financing —Cont'd
Obligations of district, limitation of
liability, §2-1217.140.
Payment in lieu of taxes, applicability,
§2-1217.143.
Payment of debt service, §2-1217.136.
PILOT/TIF area, §2-1217.134.
Sale of bonds, §2-1217.138.
Terms and conditions of bonds,
§2-1217.137.
Transcript of proceedings, §2-1217.142.
PILOT/TIF area, §47-4616.
Special assessment district,
§§47-895.01 to 47-895.06.
Application of special assessment,
§47-895.06.
Collection of special assessments,
§47-895.04.
Contesting amount of special
assessment, §47-895.04.
Definitions, §47-895.01.
Establishment, §47-895.02.
Levy of special assessment,
§47-895.03.
Notice, §47-895.04.
Liens.
Unpaid special assessments,
§47-895.04.
Notices, §47-895.04.
Termination of special assessment,
§47-895.05.

SOVEREIGN IMMUNITY.
Claims against the District, §§2-401
to 2-425.
Procurement contract claims,
§2-359.04.

SPAM E-MAIL.
Deterrence, §§28-5001 to 28-5003.
Damages, §28-5003.
Definitions, §28-5001.
Prohibited acts, §28-5002.

SPANISH.
**Complaint for forcible entry and
detainer.**
Summons and process, §16-1501.
**Foreign language services and
documents,** §§2-1931 to 2-1936.
See FOREIGN LANGUAGE
SERVICES AND DOCUMENTS.

SPAYING OF ANIMALS, §8-1810.

SPECIAL EDUCATION.
Department of education.
Special education reporting, §38-192.

SPECIAL EDUCATION —Cont'd
Disabled children, §38-913.
Foundation level.
Uniform per student funding formula.
Supplement, §38-2905.
**Medicaid and special education
reform fund,** §§4-204.51 to
4-204.56.
Nonpublic schools.
Assessment and placement of students
with disabilities, §38-2561.02.
Certificate of approval, §38-2561.07.
Compliance, §38-2561.08.
Denial, revocation, refusal to renew,
or suspension, §38-2561.11.
Inspection, §38-2561.09.
Renewal, §38-2561.10.
Refusal to renew, §38-2561.11.
Compliance with provisions,
§38-2561.08.
Definitions, §38-2561.01.
Dispute resolution, §38-2561.05.
Funding of students, §38-2561.03.
Placement of students, §38-2561.04.
Special education schools or
programs by other District of
Columbia agencies, §38-2561.03.
Individualized education plan.
Defined, §38-2561.01.
Participation of public local
education system in
development or review,
§38-2561.06.
Placement of students, §38-2561.02.
Funding, §38-2561.04.
Rate-setting, §38-2561.12.
Reconsideration, §38-2561.13.
Panel, §38-2561.14.
Reporting requirements, §38-2561.16.
Rulemaking to implement provisions,
§38-2561.15.
**Office of state superintendent of
education,** §38-2614.
Special education enhancement fund,
§38-2613.
Student rights, §§38-2571.01 to
38-2573.01.
Definitions, §38-2571.02.
Due process hearings, §§38-2572.01 to
38-2572.04.
Evaluation and termination of
hearing officers, §38-2572.03.
Restriction of practice by attorney
based on pattern of frivolous
pleadings, §38-2572.04.
Selection of hearing officer,
§38-2572.02.

SPECIAL EDUCATION —Cont'd
Student rights —Cont'd
Due process hearings —Cont'd
Short title, §38-2572.01.
Due process requirements,
§38-2571.03.
Procedural protections, §§38-2571.01
to 38-2571.04.
Rules, §38-2573.01.
Short title, §38-2571.01.
Transfer of rights, §38-2571.04.
Task force, §§38-2551 to 38-2555.
Development of reform plan, §38-2553.
Established, §38-2551.
Functions, §38-2552.
Members, §38-2554.
Memorandum of understanding,
§38-2555.
**Uniform per-student funding
formula,** §§38-2901 to 38-2914.

SPECIAL INDORSEMENTS.
Negotiable instruments, §28:3-205.

SPECIAL LEGAL CONSULTANTS,
DCCtApp Rule 46.

SPECIAL MASTERS, CivPro Rules 53
to 53-II.
Appeals, federal cases.
Appointment of, FRAP 48.
Domestic relations actions, DomRel
Rule 53.

SPECIAL PUBLIC SAFETY FEE,
§§47-2751 to 47-2753.
Collection, §47-2752.
Computation, §47-2752.
Definitions, §47-2751.
Enforcement, §47-2753.
Perfected security interest in fee,
§47-2752.
Remission, §47-2752.

**SPECIAL PURPOSE FINANCIAL
CAPTIVE INSURANCE
COMPANIES,** §§31-3932.01 to
31-3932.15.
See CAPTIVE INSURANCE
COMPANIES.

SPECIFIC PERFORMANCE.
Cable television, §34-1263.02.
**Complaint for specific performance
to convey land,** CivPro Form CA
12.
Sale of goods.
Commercial code.
Buyer's right to specific
performance, §28:2-716.

SPECIFIC PERFORMANCE —Cont'd
Security agents and brokers.
Civil liability, §31-5606.04.

SPEECH.
Anti-SLAPP, §§16-5501 to 16-5505.
Applicability of provisions, §16-5505.
Definitions, §16-5501.
Dismissal motions, §16-5502.
Fees and costs, §16-5504.
Quash motions, §16-5503.
Freedom of speech, US Const Amd 1.
Members of congress, US Const Art I
§6.

SPEECH-LANGUAGE PATHOLOGY.
Assistants.
Registration, §3-1209.10.
Transition provisions, persons already
practicing, §3-1212.05.
**Board of audiology and speech-
language pathology,** §3-1202.18.
Clinical fellows.
Registration, §3-1209.11.
Transition provisions, persons already
practicing, §3-1212.05.
**Health occupations licensure,
registration or certification,**
§§3-1205.01 to 3-1205.24.
See HEALTH OCCUPATIONS
LICENSURE, REGISTRATION
OR CERTIFICATION.
Practice of, defined, §3-1201.02.
Qualifications for licensure,
§3-1208.41.
Renewal of license, §3-1208.41.
**Titles and terms prohibited as
misrepresentation without
license to practice,** §3-1210.03.

SPEEDING.
Evaluation of speed limits,
§50-2201.32.
Traffic laws, §§50-2201.04, 50-2203.03.

SPEEDY TRIAL.
Constitution of the United States,
US Const Amd 6.
Dismissal of criminal proceedings,
CrimPro Rule 48.
United States District Court,
USDistCt LCrR 45.1.

SPENDTHRIFT PROVISIONS.
Disclaimer of property interests.
Power to disclaim, §19-1505.

SPIRITUAL BELIEFS.
See RELIGIOUS BELIEFS.

SPLIT-INTEREST TRUSTS, §21-1801.

SPORTS.
Alcoholic beverage licenses.
Arena licenses, §25-114.
Athletic concussion program,
§§7-2871.01 to 7-2871.05.
Defined terms, §7-2871.01.
Materials development and
distribution, §7-2871.04.
Removal from athletic activity.
Athletes suspected of sustaining
concussion, §7-2871.02.
Return to athletic activity.
Athletes suspected of sustaining
concussion, §7-2871.02.
Rules, §7-2871.05.
Training program, §7-2871.03.
Business licenses, §47-2823.
Child labor, §32-206.
Coaches.
Child abuse and neglect.
Reporting requirements, §4-1321.02.
**District of Columbia interscholastic
athletic association (DCIAA).**
Turkey Bowl revenue generation and
sponsorship, §38-2981.
Gambling, §§22-1708, 22-1713.
Interscholastic athletic events.
Medical coverage, requirement,
§38-621.
**Soccer stadium development (not
funded),** §§10-1603.01 to
10-1603.08.

SPORTS AGENTS, §§47-2887.01 to
47-2887.18.

SPORTS ARENA.
See DC ARENA.

SPOUSAL PRIVILEGE.
Child abuse and neglect.
Privilege not grounds for excluding
evidence of, §4-1321.05.
Confidential communications,
§14-306.
Interstate family support.
Inapplicable to proceedings under
chapter, §46-353.16.
Sexual offenses.
Inapplicable to, §22-3024.
No immunity for, §22-3019.
Witness testimony and, §14-306.

SPOUSAL PROPERTY RIGHTS,
§46-601.

SPOUSAL SUPPORT, §16-916.
Crime victims' compensation.
Loss of support, VictComp Rule 30.

SPOUSAL SUPPORT —Cont'd
Divorce, on grant of, §16-913.
Domestic partnerships, termination,
§§16-913, 16-916.
Interstate family support.
General provisions, §§46-351.01 to
46-359.03.
See INTERSTATE FAMILY
SUPPORT.
Reciprocal enforcement of support
proceedings, DomRel Rule 401.
Jurisdiction, retention of, §16-914.01.
Leaving jurisdiction of court.
Writ of ne exeat, DomRel Rule 406.
Payment of moneys through court,
DomRel Rule 403.
Pendente lite, §16-911.
Procedure generally, DomRel Rules 1
to 406.
See DOMESTIC RELATIONS
ACTIONS.
**Reciprocal enforcement of support
proceedings,** DomRel Rule 401.

SPOUSES.
See HUSBAND AND WIFE.

**SPRINKLER INSTALLATION
PROGRAM.**
Fire protection study commission.
Duties of commission regarding,
§3-1103.
Job training program combined with,
§3-1104.

STADIUM.
Ballpark.
See BALLPARK.
RFK stadium.
Armory board, §§3-322 to 3-330.
See ARMORY BOARD.
Soccer stadium development.
Tax abatements, §47-4663.
**Soccer stadium development (not
funded),** §§10-1603.01 to
10-1603.08.

STALKING, §§22-3131 to 22-3135.
Definitions, §22-3132.
Elements of offense, §22-3133.
Fines for violations, §22-3134.
Jurisdiction, §22-3135.
Prison terms, §22-3134.
Public officials, §22-851.

STANDARD OF PROOF.
See BURDEN OF PROOF.

STANDBY GUARDIANSHIP,
§§16-4801 to 16-4810.
See GUARDIAN AND WARD.

STANDING.
Alcoholic beverage licenses.
Protests, §25-601.
Corporations.
Derivative actions, §29-305.51.
Leases, UCC.
Claims.
Third parties.
Standing to sue for injury to
goods, §28:2A-531.
Nonprofit corporations.
Derivative actions, §29-411.02.

START UP COSTS FOR BUSINESS.
Opportunity accounts.
Generally, §§1-307.61 to 1-307.74.
Use for, §1-307.68.

STATE EDUCATION OFFICE.
DC leveraging educational
assistance partnership program.
Program administration, §38-2732.
Educational licensure commission.
Transfer to state education office,
§38-1313.

STATE HEALTH PLANNING AND
DEVELOPMENT AGENCY,
§§44-401 to 44-421.
Certificates of need, §§44-406 to
44-420.
Administrative appeal, §44-413.
Appeals, §§44-412 to 44-414.
Condition precedent for license or
permit, §44-415.
Duration of, §44-411.
Exempt activities, §44-407.
Assisted living residences,
§44-110.12.
Expedited administrative review,
§44-408.
Fees, §44-420.
Health care entity conversion approval
as condition precedent for,
§44-605.
Judicial review, §44-414.
Modification of, §44-411.
Moratorium on applications for,
§44-418.
Procedures and criteria for review,
§§44-409, 44-410.
Proceeding without certificate,
§44-416.
Reconsideration of decisions, §44-412.
Requirements, §44-406.
Sale or transfer of, §44-411.
Definitions, §44-401.
Establishment of, §44-402.

STATE HEALTH PLANNING AND
DEVELOPMENT AGENCY
—Cont'd
Fees, §44-420.
Fund, §44-420.01.
Health planning data system
(HPDS), §44-405.
Health systems plan (HSP), §44-404.
Immunity, §44-417.
Issuance of rules and regulations,
§44-421.
Powers and duties, §44-402.
Records, §44-405.
Reports, §§44-405, 44-419.
State health planning and
development fund, §44-420.01.
Statewide health coordinating
council, §44-403.
Violations and penalties for
noncompliance, §44-416.

STATEHOOD.
Budgets and budget estimates.
Statehood initiatives budgeting,
§1-301.154.
Chief financial officer.
Statehood initiatives budgeting,
§1-301.154.
Constitutional convention, §§1-121 to
1-128.
Appropriations, §1-127.
Call of convention, §1-123.
Composition of convention, §1-124.
Duties of convention, §1-123.
Election of delegate candidates,
§1-124.
Initiative.
Purpose, §1-121.
Question presented to voters,
§1-122.
Severability, §1-127.
Constitution for the State of New
Columbia.
Approval and ratification, §1-132.
Text of proposed constitution.
See Vol. 1.
Grants to promote voting rights and
statehood, §1-328.03.
Home Rule 40th anniversary
celebration and commemoration.
Sunset, §1-137.08.
Income tax.
New Columbia statehood fund tax
check-off, §47-1812.11c.
New Columbia statehood initiative,
§§1-129.21 to 1-129.35.
Annual reports, §1-129.33.

STATEHOOD —Cont'd
New Columbia statehood initiative
   —Cont'd
   Definitions, §1-129.21.
   Establishment of New Columbia
      statehood commission, §1-129.31.
   Establishment of New Columbia
      statehood fund, §1-129.32.
   New Columbia statehood commission
      and New Columbia statehood
      fund, §§1-129.31 to 1-129.35.
   Office of the statehood delegation,
      §1-129.22.
   Tax-exempt status, §1-129.34.
   Use of funds by delegation members,
      §1-129.35.
**Senators or representatives elected
   to represent District.**
   Campaign finance reform and conflict
      of interest act.
      Applicability of act, §1-135.
   Honoraria, §1-131.

STATES.
Maryland.
   See MARYLAND.
Political subdivisions.
   See POLITICAL SUBDIVISIONS.
Virginia.
   See VIRGINIA.

**STATE SUPERINTENDENT OF
   EDUCATION, OFFICE OF,**
   §§38-2601 to 38-2612.
Adult education.
   Supervision, §38-2608.
Adult education program.
   Supervision, §38-2608.
Chief state school officer, §38-2601.
Duties, §38-2601.01.
Early intervention program.
   Transfer of personnel, property,
      records and funds to the Office of
      the State Superintendent of
      Education, §7-863.03a.
Educational data warehouse system.
   Development, §38-2609.
Educator evaluations, §38-2615.
**Enhancement and expansion of
   pre-k programs,** §§38-271.01 to
   38-271.07.
Established, §38-2601.
**Existing state agency
   responsibilities,** §38-2606.
**Headed by state superintendent of
   education,** §38-2601.
**Higher education licensure
   commission site fund,** §38-2607.

**STATE SUPERINTENDENT OF
   EDUCATION, OFFICE OF**
   —Cont'd
Responsibilities, §38-2602.
Short-term SEO plan.
   Contents, §38-2604.
   Process for formulation, §38-2603.
Special education, §38-2614.
   Special education enhancement fund,
      §38-2613.
Student assessments.
   Developing and administering,
      §38-2610.
Teachers.
   Educator evaluations, §38-2615.
Testing integrity in public schools.
   Definition of OSSE, §38-771.01.
   Duties and responsibilities of office,
      §38-2602.
**Transfer of state level functions
   from board of education,**
   §38-2602.01.
Transition plan, §§38-2605, 38-2605.01.

STATUS CONFERENCES, CivPro
   Rule 16.
Adoption proceedings, Adoption Rule
   16.
Authority to set conference, CivPro
   Rule 309.
Domestic relations actions, DomRel
   Rule 16-I.
Failure to appear, CivPro Rule 16-II.
   Tax proceedings, Tax Rule 13.
Tax proceedings, Tax Rules 10, 13.

STATUTE OF FRAUDS, §§28-3501 to
   28-3505.
Acknowledgment of contract,
   §28-3504.
**Acknowledgment of debt incurred
   during infancy,** §28-3505.
Estate created other than by deed,
   §28-3501.
Estates by sufferance.
   Estate created other than by deed,
      §28-3501.
Executors and administrators.
   Special promise to answer damages
      out of own estate, §28-3502.
Investment securities.
   Inapplicability of statute of frauds,
      §28:8-113.
Joint contractors.
   New promise or acknowledgment of
      contract, §28-3504.
Marriage.
   Agreement made upon consideration of
      marriage, §28-3502.

STATUTE OF FRAUDS —Cont'd

Minors.

New promise or acknowledgment of debt incurred during infancy, §28-3505.

Mortgages and deeds of trust.

Declaration, grant and assignment of trust, §28-3503.

New promise, §28-3504.

Debt incurred during infancy, §28-3505.

Performance one year after agreement, §28-3502.

Public procurements, §2-359.01.

Real property.

Contract or sale of real estate, §28-3502.

Declaration, grant and assignment of trust, §28-3503.

Special promise to answer for debt or default of another, §28-3502.

Trusts and trustees.

Declaration, grant and assignment of trust, §28-3503.

STATUTE OF LIMITATIONS.
See LIMITATION OF ACTIONS.

STATUTORY CONSTRUCTION,
§§45-601 to 45-606.

Acts of Congress, §45-401.

Administrator included in executor, §45-605.

Admiralty, principles of, §45-401.

Adulteration of food or drugs, §48-110.

Affirmations included in oaths, §45-606.

Bank deposits and collections, §§28:10-103, 28:10-104.

Behavioral health department, §7-1141.09.

Benefit corporations, §29-1301.03.

Bulk transfers, §§28:10-103, 28:10-104.

Business licenses, §47-2807.

Business organizations.

Uniformity, §29-107.03.

Child abuse and neglect.

Construction of rules, NeglectProc Rule 2.

City of Washington, ordinances of, §45-402.

Civil asset forfeiture, §41-314.

Civil procedure rules.

Scope of rules, CivPro Rule 1, USDistCt LCvR 1.1.

Closing-out sales, §47-2110.

Collaborative law, §16-4021.

STATUTORY CONSTRUCTION —Cont'd

Commission for law revision, §§45-301 to 45-305.

Common law, §45-401.

Common trust funds, §26-403.

Communicable diseases, §7-144.

Community development, §6-1007.

Condominiums.

See CONDOMINIUMS.

Conservation easements, §42-205.

Conservators, §21-2001.

Constitution of the United States.

Effect of enumeration of rights, US Const Amd 9.

Construction codes, §6-1404.

Convention center and sports arena, §47-398.05.

Crimes, repeal.

Common law crime not reinstated, §45-401.

Criminal procedure rules, CrimPro Rule 2, USDistCt LCrR 1.1.

Delinquent minors.

Rules for juvenile proceedings, JuvProc Rule 2.

Drug, firearm, or prostitution-related nuisance abatement, §42-3113.

Emergency volunteer health practitioners, §7-2361.12.

Entity transactions, §29-201.03.

Environmental impact statements, §8-109.10.

Equity, §45-401.

Excess property for development of seat of government, retention for public use, §16-1337.

Excess property for United States, §16-1385.

Executor, administrator included in, §45-605.

Federal City College, §38-1111.

Firearms, §7-2507.08.

Foreign judgments, §15-357.

Foreign-money claims, §15-914.

Foreign-money judgments, §15-370.

Fraudulent conveyances, §28-3111.

Fraudulent transfers, §§28-3110, 28-3111.

Funds transfers, §§28:10-103, 28:10-104.

Federal electronic fund transfer act. Relationship between UCC provision and federal provision, §28:4A-108.

STATUTORY CONSTRUCTION
—Cont'd
Fund-type accounting, §47-376.
Gas stations, §36-305.01.
Gender constructions, §45-603.
General rules, §§45-601 to 45-606.
Habeas corpus, §16-1909.
Health care durable powers of attorney, §21-2213.
Health insurance portability and accountability.
Individual health insurance provisions, §31-3302.09.
Health maintenance organizations, §31-3424.
Historic districts, §6-1205.
Home Rule act, §1-207.61.
Horizontal property regimes, §§42-2029, 42-2031.
Hospitalization of persons with mental illness.
Construction of rules, MentalHealth Rule 1.
Housing finance agency, §42-2706.01.
Human tissue banks, §7-1541.07.
Intellectual disabilities, persons with.
Rules for intellectual disability proceedings, MentalRetardation Rule 1.
Interstate compact for juveniles, §24-1105.
Interstate depositions and discovery, §13-447.
Landlord and tenant court rules, LandlordTenant Rule 1.
"Law" includes statutes and judicial decisions, CivPro Rule 81.
Law revision commission, §§45-301 to 45-305.
Laws remaining in force, §§45-401 to 45-404.
Life and health insurance guaranty association, §31-5411.
Life insurance companies, §31-4729.
Limited cooperative associations, §29-1001.07.
Long-arm statute, §13-402.
Mediation, §16-4212.
Merit system.
See MERIT SYSTEM.
Metropolitan Washington Airports Authority, §§9-924, 9-925.
Metrorail and metrobus.
See METRORAIL AND METROBUS.
Motor fuel tax, §§47-2313, 47-2314.

STATUTORY CONSTRUCTION
—Cont'd
Motor vehicle safety responsibility, §50-1301.85.
Negotiable instruments, §§28:10-103, 28:10-104.
Nonrevival of statutes, §45-501.
Oaths and affirmations, §45-606.
"Officer" of United States, CivPro Rule 81.
Person, partnerships and corporations included in uses of, §45-604.
Pleadings, CivPro Rule 8.
Domestic relations actions, DomRel Rule 8.
Powers of attorney, §§21-2103 to 21-2118.
Premarital agreements, §46-510.
Probate proceedings.
Death before Jan. 1, 1981, Probate Rule 25.
Death between Jan. 1, 1981, and June 30, 1995.
Waiver of formal audit of account, Probate Rule 117.
Death on or after July 1, 1995.
Waiver of filing inventories and accounts, Probate Rule 415.
Waiver of formal audit of account, Probate Rule 417.
Professional corporations, §29-504.
Prudent management of institutional funds, §44-1639.
Public auction permit requirements, §47-2708.
Public-private partnership administration fund, §2-275.01.
Public utilities, §§34-403, 34-732.
Religious institutions, governing provisions of, §45-403.
Rental contracts, §2-221.06.
Rental housing conversion and sale, §42-3405.11.
Restraints of trade, §28-4515.
Uniformity with federal antitrust statutes, §28-4515.
Retail development incentives, §2-1217.84.
Sales, UCC, §§28:10-103, 28:10-104.
Savings clauses, §45-404.
Secured transactions, §§28:10-103, 28:10-104.
Severability, §45-201.
Simultaneous deaths, §19-506.
Singular usage held to include plural, §45-602.

STATUTORY CONSTRUCTION
—Cont'd
"State" includes District of Columbia, CivPro Rule 81.
"Statute of United States" includes acts locally applicable, CivPro Rule 81.
Statutory trusts.
Rules of construction, §29-1201.06.
Termination of parental rights, §16-2351.
Title insurance producers, §31-5041.12.
Title insurers, §31-5031.24.
Trade secrets, §36-408.
Unclaimed property, §41-141.
Unincorporated nonprofit associations, §29-1103.
Unsworn foreign declarations, §16-5307.
Voting by military and overseas voters, §1-1061.17.
Washington Technical Institute, §38-1111.
Witness fees, CrimPro Rule 113.
Family court proceedings, FamDiv Rule F.
Zoning, §6-641.11.

STATUTORY RULE AGAINST PERPETUITIES, §§19-901 to 19-907.

STATUTORY TRUSTS, §§29-1201.01 to 29-1209.01.
Actions, §29-1203.08.
Beneficial owners.
Derivative actions, §29-1206.10.
Complaint, contents, §29-1206.12.
Proceeds, costs and fees, §29-1206.13.
Proper plaintiff, §29-1206.11.
Settlement requiring court approval, §29-1206.13.
Special litigation committee, §29-1206.14.
Direct actions, §29-1206.09.
Trust management and trustees, §29-1205.03.
Administrative dissolution.
Generally, §§29-106.01 to 29-106.04.
See BUSINESS ORGANIZATIONS.
Applicability of law, §29-1201.05.
As entity, §29-1203.02.
Beneficial owners, §§29-1206.01 to 29-1206.16.
Actions.
Derivative actions, §29-1206.10.
Complaint, contents, §29-1206.12.

STATUTORY TRUSTS —Cont'd
Beneficial owners —Cont'd
Actions —Cont'd
Derivative actions —Cont'd
Proceeds, costs and fees, §29-1206.13.
Proper plaintiff, §29-1206.11.
Settlement requiring court approval, §29-1206.13.
Special litigation committee, §29-1206.14.
Direct actions, §29-1206.09.
Beneficial interests, §29-1206.01.
Redemption of, §29-1206.05.
Charging orders, §29-1206.06.
Consent, §29-1206.02.
Contributions, §29-1206.03.
Distributions, §29-1206.04.
Liability for improper distribution, §29-1206.16.
Limitations, §29-1206.15.
Indebtedness of trust due to distributions at parity with indebtedness to creditors, §29-1206.15.
Information rights, §29-1206.08.
Transactions with, §29-1206.07.
Voting, §29-1206.02.
Certificates of trust, §29-1202.01.
Amendment, §29-1202.02.
Restatement, §29-1202.02.
Constructive notice, §29-1201.07.
Contributions.
Beneficial owners, §29-1206.03.
Debts.
Liability, §29-1203.04.
Definitions, §29-1201.02.
Dissolution, §§29-1208.01 to 29-1208.06.
Articles of dissolution, §29-1208.02.
Court proceedings on claims, §29-1208.06.
Events causing, §29-1208.01.
Known claims, §29-1208.04.
Other claims, §29-1208.05.
Series trusts, §29-1204.04.
Winding up, §29-1208.03.
Distributions.
Beneficial owners, §29-1206.04.
Liability for improper distribution, §29-1206.16.
Limitations, §29-1206.15.
Duration of, §29-1203.06.
Filing.
Generally, §§29-102.01 to 29-102.13.
See BUSINESS ORGANIZATIONS.

STATUTORY TRUSTS —Cont'd
Filing —Cont'd
Inaccurate information in filed records.
    Liability, §29-1202.05.
Mergers and consolidations,
    §29-1207.04.
Pursuant to judicial order,
    §29-1202.04.
Foreign entities.
Generally, §§29-105.01 to 29-105.12.
    See BUSINESS ORGANIZATIONS.
Formation of, §29-1202.01.
General provisions, §§29-1201.01 to
    29-1201.07.
Governing instruments, §29-1201.03.
Governing law, §29-1203.01.
Liability.
Debts, §29-1203.04.
Improper distribution, §29-1206.16.
Series trusts, §29-1204.02.
Mandatory rules, §29-1201.04.
Mergers and consolidations,
    §§29-1207.01 to 29-1207.06.
Amendment or abandonment,
    §29-1207.03.
Articles of merger, §29-1207.04.
Authorization, §29-1207.02.
Consent, §29-1207.03.
Definitions, §29-1207.01.
Effective date, §29-1207.04.
Effect of, §29-1207.05.
Filing, §29-1207.04.
Nonexclusivity of provisions,
    §29-1207.06.
Plans, §29-1207.03.
Required filings, §29-1207.04.
Names.
Generally, §§29-103.01 to 29-103.04.
    See BUSINESS ORGANIZATIONS.
Requirements, §29-103.02.
Notice.
Constructive notice, §29-1201.07.
Known claims against dissolved
    statutory trust, §29-1208.04.
Other claims against dissolved
    statutory trust, §29-1208.05.
Property, §29-1203.07.
No creditor rights, §29-1203.05.
Power to hold, §29-1203.07.
Title, §29-1203.07.
Purposes of, §29-1203.03.
Registered agents.
Generally, §§29-104.01 to 29-104.14.
    See BUSINESS ORGANIZATIONS.
Rules of construction, §29-1201.06.
Series trusts, §§29-1204.01 to
    29-1204.05.
Authorization, §29-1204.01.

STATUTORY TRUSTS —Cont'd
Series trusts —Cont'd
Claims pertaining to series trusts,
    §29-1204.05.
Dissolution, §29-1204.04.
Duties of trustee, §29-1204.03.
Liability, §29-1204.02.
Short title, §29-1201.01.
Signing of records, §29-1202.03.
Inaccurate information in filed records.
    Liability of person signing or
    causing another to sign,
    §29-1202.05.
Signing pursuant to judicial order,
    §29-1202.04.
Statutory construction.
Rules of construction, §29-1201.06.
Transitional provisions, §29-1209.01.
Trust management and trustees,
    §§29-1205.01 to 29-1205.12.
Advancements, §29-1205.09.
Delegation by trustees, §29-1205.11.
Direction of trustees, §29-1205.10.
Exoneration, §29-1205.09.
Indemnification, §29-1205.09.
Information rights of trustees,
    §29-1205.08.
Interested transactions, §29-1205.07.
Protection of persons dealing with
    trustees, §29-1205.04.
Reasonable reliance, §29-1205.06.
Registered investment companies.
    Independent trustees, §29-1205.12.
Reimbursement, §29-1205.09.
Standards of conduct, §29-1205.05.
Trustees.
    Actions, §29-1205.03.
    Authority, §29-1205.01.
    Powers, §29-1205.02.
Winding up, §29-1208.03.

STAYS.
**Administrative procedure, appeals
    from,** §17-304.
Adoption proceedings, Adoption Rule
    62.
Appeals, D.C. courts.
See APPEALS, D.C. COURTS.
Appeals, federal cases.
Criminal cases, FRAP 8(c).
Mandate, FRAP 41, USCtApp Rule 41.
    Pending application for certiorari,
    FRAP 41(d).
Pending appeal, FRAP 8, USCtApp
    Rule 8.
    Administrative orders, FRAP 18,
    USCtApp Rule 18.

STAYS —Cont'd

Appeals, federal cases —Cont'd

Pending appeal —Cont'd

Record for preliminary hearing in court of appeals, FRAP 11(g).

Petition of party for rehearing en banc not to stay mandate, FRAP 35(c).

Arbitration.

Removal of arbitrator, Arbitration Rule IV.

Removal of case from arbitration, Arbitration Rule II.

Arbitration, revised act.

Motion to stay arbitration, §16-4407.

Bankruptcy.

Relief from automatic stay, USDistDCBank Rule 4001-1.

Child custody proceedings.

Verified initial pleading.

Failure to furnish required information, §16-4602.09.

Civil procedure, CivPro Rule 62.

Collaborative law, §16-4006.

Corporations.

Derivative actions, §29-305.53.

Criminal procedure, CrimPro Rule 38.

Hearing commissioner proceedings, CrimPro Rule 117.

Domestic relations actions, DomRel Rule 62.

Family court proceedings generally.

Hearing commissioner proceedings, FamDiv Rule D.

Foreign judgments, §15-354.

Foreign-money judgments, §15-368.

Hearing commissioner proceedings.

Review of orders and judgments, CivPro Rule 73, CrimPro Rule 117.

Landlord and tenant court, LandlordTenant Rule 16.

Application for termination of stay, LandlordTenant Form 5.

Application to stay writ of restitution, LandlordTenant Form 9.

Life and health insurance guaranty association, §31-5415.

Limitation of actions and stays by court or by statute, §12-304.

Mandate of court of appeals, DCCtApp Rule 41.

Merit system.

Review of agency decision, CivPro Agency Review Rule 1.

Nonprofit corporations.

Derivative actions, §29-411.04.

STAYS —Cont'd

Probate proceedings, Probate Rule 9.

Property and liability insurance guaranty association, §31-5515.

Sexual psychopaths, stay of criminal proceedings against, §22-3810.

Small claims court, §16-3907, SmallClaims Rule 16.

Vacating stay, SmallClaims Rule 11.

Supersedeas bonds, CivPro Rule 62-I, DCCtApp Rules 7, 8.

Administrative orders and decisions reviewed, DCCtApp Rule 19.

Termination of stay, CivPro Rule 62-II.

Application for termination, CivPro Form CA 110-B.

Landlord and tenant court, LandlordTenant Form 5.

Domestic relations actions, DomRel Rule 62.

STEAM AND OTHER OPERATING ENGINEERS.

Business licenses, §§47-2853.211 to 47-2853.213.

Eligibility, §47-2853.212.

Representations prohibited, §47-2853.213.

Scope of license, §47-2853.211.

STEAM BOILERS.

Boiler inspections, §§2-101 to 2-118.

See BOILER INSPECTIONS.

STEAM HEAT.

District buildings, furnished to, §§10-501.03, 10-501.04.

STEAM RAILROAD LINES.

Electrification of, §§9-1207.01 to 9-1207.05.

STENOGRAPHERS.

See COURT REPORTERS.

STEP UP PROGRAM, §§42-2621 to 42-2626.

See HOME PURCHASE ASSISTANCE FUND.

STERILIZATION.

Animals.

Spaying and neutering incentive program for, §8-1810.

Sterilization fund, §8-1804.

Health care durable powers of attorney, §21-2211.

Intellectual disabilities, persons with, §7-1305.08.

STEVIE SELLOWS QUALITY IMPROVEMENT FUND.
Intermediate care facilities for persons with intellectual disabilities, §§47-1270 to 47-1278.
See INTERMEDIATE CARE FACILITIES.

STIPULATIONS.
Adoption, Adoption Rule 8.
Discovery procedures, Adoption Rule 29.
Appeals.
Record on appeal, DCCtApp Rule 10.
Appeals, federal cases.
Correction of record on review or enforcement of administrative orders, FRAP 16(b).
Dismissal of appeal in district court, FRAP 42(a).
Parts of record to be retained in district court, FRAP 11(f).
Record or parts thereof to be filed, administrative review or enforcement, FRAP 17(b).
Bankruptcy proceedings, USDistDCBank Rule 9071-1.
Child abuse and neglect proceedings.
Disposition, NeglectProc Rule 23.
Fact-finding, NeglectProc Rule 18.
Discovery procedures, CivPro Rule 29.
Adoption proceedings, Adoption Rule 29.
Domestic relations actions, DomRel Rule 29.
Dismissal of actions, CivPro Rule 41.
Domestic relations actions, DomRel Rule 7.
Discovery procedures, DomRel Rule 29.
Uncontested stipulation, DomRel Form 8.
Form of stipulation, CivPro Rule 7-I, USDistCt LCrR 57.3, USDistCt LCvR 16.6.
Master's report, CivPro Rule 53.
Domestic relations actions, DomRel Rule 53.

STOCK AND STOCKHOLDERS.
Building associations.
See BUILDING ASSOCIATIONS.
Commercial code.
Investment securities, §§28:8-101 to 28:8-601.
See INVESTMENT SECURITIES.

STOCK AND STOCKHOLDERS
—Cont'd
Cooperative associations.
Certificates of share.
Contents, §29-925.
Exemption for legal process, §29-928.
Issuance, §29-925.
Recall, §29-927.
Transfer of shares, §29-926.
Corporations, §§29-304.01 to 29-305.70.
See CORPORATIONS.
Derivative actions by shareholders, CivPro Rule 23.1.
Domestic life insurance companies.
See DOMESTIC LIFE INSURANCE COMPANIES.
Fiduciary security transfers, §§28-2901 to 28-2909.
See FIDUCIARY SECURITY TRANSFERS.
Forgery of stock certificate, §22-3242.
Investment securities.
Commercial code, §§28:8-101 to 28:8-601.
See INVESTMENT SECURITIES.
Personal property regarding stock transactions, §§21-2106, 21-2107.
Professional corporations.
Certificates of share, §29-511.
Disposition by disqualified, deceased or incompetent shareholder, §29-514.
Qualifications of shareholders, §29-508.
Redemption price, §29-515.
Transfer of shares, §29-511.
Public auction permits, §§47-2701 to 47-2708.
Public utilities.
See PUBLIC UTILITIES.
Trust, mortgage and title corporations.
See TRUST, MORTGAGE AND TITLE CORPORATIONS.
Unclaimed stock in business associations, §41-109.

STOCK INSURANCE COMPANIES, §§31-601 to 31-604.
Conversion of mutual company to stock company.
General provisions, §§31-901 to 31-915.
See INSURANCE DEMUTUALIZATION.

STOCK INSURANCE COMPANIES
—Cont'd
Mutual holding companies
converted to, §31-759.

STOCK TRANSFER ACT, §§28-2901 to
28-2909.

STOLEN PROPERTY.
Defined, §22-3201.
Receipt of property stolen outside
District, §22-1808.
Receiving, §22-3232.
Secondhand dealers, §47-2844.
Trafficking in, §22-3231.

STONE THROWING, §22-1309.

STORAGE.
Alcoholic beverages, §25-754.
Warehouse receipts.
Storage under government bond,
§28:7-201.
Firearms, §7-2507.02.
Landlord and tenant.
Tenants displaced due to nonpayment
of rent.
Moving and storage assistance
program, §42-3505.01.
Liens for storage.
Allowance of, §40-102.
Limitations on, §40-105.
Motor vehicles.
Garage keepers' liens, §40-102.
Pesticides, §8-414.
Self-service storage facilities,
§§40-401 to 40-405.
Underground storage tanks.
General provisions, §§8-113.01 to
8-113.12.
See UNDERGROUND STORAGE
TANKS.

STORMWATER MANAGEMENT,
§§8-152.01 to 8-153.01.
Administration, §8-152.01.
Advisory panel, §8-152.05.
Best management practices.
Grant program to employ, §8-152.04.
Coal tar pavement product
limitations, §8-153.01.
Compliance by other agencies,
§8-152.01.
Environmental management system,
§8-152.01.
General services department.
Stormwater retention credit fund,
§10-551.07b.
Grant program to employ low
impact development or best
management practices, §8-152.04.

STORMWATER MANAGEMENT
—Cont'd
Liens.
Failure to reimburse user fees,
§8-152.03.
Low impact development.
Grant program to employ, §8-152.04.
Permit compliance enterprise fund,
§8-152.02.
User fee discount program, §8-152.03.

STORMWATER RETENTION
CREDIT FUND, §§10-551.07b,
50-921.22.

STRAY DOGS.
Animal control, §§8-1801 to 8-1813.

STREAMLINED SALES AND USE
TAX AGREEMENT, §§1-301.121 to
1-301.128.

STREETCAR PLAN, §9-1208.01.

STREETCARS.
DC Streetcar service, §§50-921.71 to
50-921.77.
See DC STREETCAR SERVICE.

STREET FESTIVALS.
Rental of public space.
Street festival one day rental,
§10-1102.01a.

STREET GANGS, §22-951.
Contributing to the delinquency of a
minor, §22-811.
Crime victims' compensation.
Eligibility for compensation, VictComp
Rule 7.
Joint working group.
Gang and crew intervention,
§2-1531.01.
Metropolitan police.
School safety division.
Protection of students from gang
and crew violence, §§5-132.01 to
5-132.21.

STREET LIGHTING, §§9-501 to 9-510.
Failure to provide or maintain,
§§9-503, 9-505.
Gas mains extended for
maintenance of, §9-506.
Hours of, §9-507.
Increase in, §9-510.
Overhead wires, on, §9-502.
Public contracts not required for,
§9-504.
Railroads, §9-509.
Rates, §9-501.

STREET LIGHTING —Cont'd
Repair and maintenance, §§9-501, 9-506.
Testing, §9-503.
Washington Terminal Company, §9-508.

STREET RAILWAYS AND BUS LINES.
Metrorail and metrobus.
General provisions, §§35-201 to 35-253.
See METRORAIL AND METROBUS.
Prohibition on further laying of street railways, §9-1201.03.
Removal of street railway tracks, §9-401.02.

STREETS AND ALLEYS, §§9-201.01 to 9-206.02.
Advisory neighborhood commission.
Closing procedures, §9-202.02.
Naming of public spaces, §9-204.07.
Assessments for parkways, §9-1217.01.
Avenues, designation of, §9-204.02.
Barbed-wire fences, §§9-1213.01 to 9-1213.05.
Blocking passage, §22-1307.
Building lines, §§6-401 to 6-406.
Business streets denomination, §9-1201.05.
Cleaning, §1-305.01.
Closing procedures.
Advisory neighborhood commission, §9-202.02.
Applications for, §9-202.06.
Authority of Council, §9-202.01.
Conditions, subject to, §9-202.09.
Damages awards, §9-202.11.
Disposition of property following, §9-202.08.
Fees, §9-202.14.
Historic Preservation Review Board, §9-202.02.
Issuance of, §9-202.15.
Judicial proceeding upon objections to, §9-202.11.
Mayor's actions prior to, §9-202.02.
National Capital Planning Commission, §§9-202.02, 9-202.03.
Notice.
Affected property owners' notice of approval of closing, §9-202.10.
Public hearing, §§9-202.06, 9-202.07.
Objections, filing, §9-202.11.
Plat, §§9-202.12, 9-202.13.

STREETS AND ALLEYS —Cont'd
Closing procedures —Cont'd
Property owners affected by.
Notice of approval of closing, §9-202.10.
Objections and damages awards, §9-202.11.
Relocation assistance for, §9-202.09.
Public hearing.
Duties of applicant, §9-202.06.
Notice, §9-202.07.
Required, §9-202.04.
Inapplicability, §9-202.05.
Recordation, §§9-202.12, 9-202.13.
Relocation assistance following, §9-202.09.
Repealed laws, condemnations or closings pursuant to, §9-206.01.
Complete Streets policy, §50-2381.
Condemnation proceedings.
Construction materials, §9-1219.01.
Opening, extending, widening, or straightening, §9-203.02.
Repealed laws.
Condemnations or closings pursuant to, §9-206.01.
Cost of street extension assessed as benefits, §9-1217.01.
Definitions, §9-201.01.
Designation of official names.
Official name, defined, §9-201.01.
Procedural requirements, §9-204.21.
Public spaces other than alley or street, §§9-204.22, 9-204.24.
Destroying or defacing building material for, §22-3313.
Dulles International Airport, §9-803.
Eminent domain.
General provisions, §§16-1301 to 16-1385.
See EMINENT DOMAIN.
Excess property for development of seat of government.
Retention for public use, §16-1334.
Excess property for United States.
Retention for public use, §16-1382.
Extending. See within this heading, "New streets and alleys."
Games played in street, §22-1308.
Grade crossing elimination projects.
See GRADE CROSSING ELIMINATION PROJECTS.
Hazardous waste management of road treatments, §8-1313.
Highways generally.
See HIGHWAYS.

STREETS AND ALLEYS —Cont'd
Improvements, §50-2603.
Issuance of rules and regulations,
§9-206.02.
Lettered streets, §9-204.02.
Map, official, §9-203.09.
Naming of public spaces.
Advisory neighborhood commission,
§9-204.07.
Alleys, §9-204.03.
Boards and commissions.
Rights of, §9-204.09.
Council authority over, §9-204.01.
Deceased persons.
Restriction on use of names of,
§9-204.05.
Designation of official names.
Official name, defined, §9-201.01.
Procedural requirements, §9-204.21.
Public spaces other than alley or
street, §§9-204.22, 9-204.24.
Duplicative names.
Prohibition of, §§9-204.03a, 9-204.04.
Living persons.
Prohibition on use of names of,
§9-204.05.
Notice to affected property owners,
§9-204.08.
Symbolic names, §9-204.03a.
Designation for public spaces,
streets and alleys, §§9-204.23,
9-204.24.
System of designation as avenues,
numbered streets, and lettered
streets, §9-204.02.
**National capital housing authority
notice to alley dwellers,**
§6-101.06.
New streets and alleys, §§9-203.01 to
9-203.09.
Condemnation proceedings, §9-203.02.
Dedications of land.
Acceptance of, §9-203.03.
Highway plan submission, §9-203.08.
Improvement of street, §§9-203.06,
9-203.07.
Mayor's authority regarding,
§9-203.01.
Minor streets.
Dimensional requirements for,
§9-203.04.
Official street map, inclusion on,
§9-203.09.
Property line and building restriction
line.
Area between, §9-203.05.

STREETS AND ALLEYS —Cont'd
New streets and alleys —Cont'd
Real property acquisition for purposes
of, §9-203.02.
Notice.
Closing procedures.
Affected property owners' notice of
approval of closing, §9-202.10.
Public hearings, §§9-202.06,
9-202.07.
Naming of public spaces.
Notice to affected property owners,
§9-204.08.
Paving and resurfacing, §9-421.09.
Numbered streets, §9-204.02.
Obstructions, §§22-3320 to 22-3322.
Removal of, §9-1201.07.
**Occupation or appropriation,
improper,** §9-1201.09.
Parks, parts of streets set aside as,
§9-1201.06.
Parkways.
See PARKWAYS.
Paving.
See PUBLIC WORKS.
Paving stones.
Failure to replace, §9-1201.08.
Removal of, §9-1201.04.
Playing games in streets, §22-1308.
**Property line and building
restriction line, area between,**
§9-203.05.
Public works.
See PUBLIC WORKS.
**Railroads prohibited on certain
streets,** §9-1201.02.
Regulation of alleys, §1-1323.
Repair and maintenance, §50-2603.
Public contracts for, §9-401.16.
Railroads contributing to cost of
repairing streets, §9-1203.07.
**Repealed laws, condemnations or
closings pursuant to,** §9-206.01.
Resurfacing.
See PUBLIC WORKS.
Schedules of street improvements,
§9-401.05.
Straightening. See within this heading,
"New streets and alleys."
Streetcar plan, §9-1208.01.
Street lighting, §§9-501 to 9-510.
See STREET LIGHTING.
Surveyor of the District and alleys,
§1-1323.
Sweepings, sale of, §1-305.02.
**Telegraph and telephone poles in
alleys,** §§34-1911.04, 34-1921.04.

STREETS AND ALLEYS —Cont'd
Width of.
Height of buildings controlled by
street width, §6-601.05.
Highways, §9-103.01.
Minor changes in, §9-401.12.
Park space or reservations used for
widening streets, §10-123.
Paving and resurfacing, §9-401.11.

**STREETSCAPE LOAN RELIEF
FUND,** §1-325.191.

STREET VENDORS.
Child labor, §§32-215 to 32-220.
Gross sales tax, §§47-2002.01, 47-2003.
Minimum sales tax, §§47-2002.01,
47-2004.

STRICT LIABILITY.
Firearms.
Illegal sales and distributions,
§§7-2531.01 to 7-2531.04.
Manufacturing assault weapons,
§§7-2551.01 to 7-2551.03.
Hazardous materials transportation.
Strict liability for releases during
transport, §§8-1441 to 8-1447.
See HAZARDOUS WASTE
MANAGEMENT.

STRIKES.
Fire departments, §5-407.
Metropolitan police, §5-123.01.
**Metrorail and metrobus compact for
mass transportation.**
Use for strikebreaking, §9-1103.05.
Public officers and employees.
Strikes prohibited for, §1-617.05.

STROKES, §§44-1151 to 44-1159.
Applicability of chapter, §44-1159.
Confidentiality of information,
§44-1157.
**Continuous improvement in quality
of care,** §44-1156.
Definitions, §44-1151.
Designation of hospitals, §44-1152.
List of hospitals and publication,
§44-1154.
Suspension and revocation, §44-1153.
**Pre-hospital care protocol and
training,** §44-1155.
Public information, §44-1157.
Rulemaking, §44-1158.

STUDENT HEALTH CARE, §§38-601
to 38-651.12.
Administration, §38-608.
Definitions, §38-601.
Medication, §38-651.01.

STUDENT HEALTH CARE —Cont'd
Drugs.
Medication, §§38-651.01 to 38-651.12.
See within this heading,
"Medication."
**Duty of responsible person to obtain
treatment,** §38-606.
**Exclusion from school for
noncompliance,** §38-604.
Fees for examinations, §38-605.
Indigent persons, §38-605.
Lead paint poisoning, §§38-602,
38-610.
Liability, §38-609.
Medication.
Immunity from liability, §38-651.11.
Medical examinations, §§38-602 to
38-605.
Medical records, §38-607.
Medication, §§38-651.01 to 38-651.12.
Administration of medication.
Employee or agent of school,
§38-651.05.
Emergency circumstances,
§38-651.06.
Training program for, §38-651.04.
Self-administration by student,
§38-651.02.
Misuse, §38-651.10.
Training program for agents and
employees of school, §38-651.04.
Definitions, §38-651.01.
Discipline of students.
Self-administration for purpose
other than own treatment,
§38-651.10.
Emergency circumstances.
Administration of medication,
§38-651.06.
Emergency response information.
Posting, §38-651.07.
Immunity from liability, §38-651.11.
Medication action plan, §38-651.03.
Denial by school, §38-651.10.
Keeping in accessible location,
§38-651.08.
Required for possession and self-
administration by student,
§38-651.02.
Possession by student, §38-651.02.
Records, §38-651.08.
Rulemaking, §38-651.12.
Self-administration by student,
§38-651.02.
Misuse, §38-651.10.
Storage, §38-651.09.

STUDENT HEALTH CARE —Cont'd
Medication —Cont'd
Student access to epinephrine,
§38-651.04a.
**Noncompliance, notice, exclusion
from school, fine, §38-604.**
Notice of noncompliance, §38-604.
Religious beliefs, §38-603.
School nurses, §38-621.

**STUDENT LOAN INSURANCE
PROGRAM, §1-307.01.**

STUDENT LOANS.
Collection of taxes.
Refund offsets.
Applicability of provisions, §47-4436.
Protest and notice, §47-4433.
Right to credit overpayments,
§47-4431.
Financial aid assistance generally.
See FINANCIAL AID ASSISTANCE.
**Health professional recruitment
program.**
Generally, §§7-751.01 to 7-751.16.
See HEALTH PROFESSIONAL
RECRUITMENT PROGRAM.

STUDIO THEATRE HOUSING.
**Real property tax exemption,
§47-1082.**

STYROFOAM.
**Disposable food service ware,
management, §§8-1531 to 8-1537.**

SUBCONTRACTORS.
**Private contractor and
subcontractor prompt payment
act, §§27-131 to 27-136.**

**SUBCONTRACTOR'S LIENS,
§§40-303.01 to 40-303.20a.**
Advance payments.
Insufficiency of, §40-303.06.
Commencement of suit, §40-303.13.
Discharge of.
General provisions, §§40-303.15 to
40-303.18.
See MECHANIC'S LIENS.
Enforcement, §40-303.08.
**Entitlement of subcontractor to lien,
§40-303.01.**
Ground subject to.
Determining extent of, §40-303.14.
Limitations on, §40-303.02.
Notice to owner, §40-303.03.
Owners.
Duties of, §40-303.04.
Notice to, §40-303.03.

SUBCONTRACTOR'S LIENS —Cont'd
Owners —Cont'd
Payment of amount claimed,
§40-303.16.
Personal actions against, §40-303.19.
**Payment of amount claimed by
owner, §40-303.16.**
Priority of lien, §40-303.07.
**Regulations, promulgation,
§40-303.20a.**
Sales associated with.
General provisions, §§40-303.09 to
40-303.12.
See MECHANIC'S LIENS.
Satisfaction of claim.
Entry of, §40-303.15.
Sureties as party to suit, §40-303.18.
Terms and conditions.
Liens subject to, §40-303.02.
Subcontractor entitled to know,
§40-303.05.
Subject to, §40-303.02.

SUBDIVISIONS.
Certified plat, §1-1320.
Highways.
Conformity with recorded plans,
§9-101.13.
Maps of highways.
Subdivisions adopted by reference
from, §9-103.03.
Resubdivision affected by highway
plan pending condemnation
proceedings, §9-101.09.
Historic districts, §6-1106.
Historic landmarks, §6-1106.
Horizontal property regimes.
See HORIZONTAL PROPERTY
REGIMES.
Legal record of, §1-1321.
Metropolitan police, §5-101.02.
**National Capital Planning
Commission platting and
subdivisions, §2-1006.**
Plats.
Legal office of record, §1-1305.
**Real property taxes, §§47-832 to
47-835.**
**Recordability of maps or plats,
§42-410.**
Surveyor of the District.
See SURVEYOR OF THE DISTRICT.

SUBMARINE CABLES.
Drawbridge openings, §9-1207.02.

**SUBORNATION OF PERJURY,
§§22-2403, 23-324.**

SUBPOENAS.

Adoption proceedings, Adoption Rule 45.

Alcoholic beverage control board.
Witnesses, §25-443.

Alcoholic beverage licenses.
Hearings, §25-443.

Arbitration, revised act.
Witnesses, §16-4417.

Athlete agents.
Issuance for relevant material, §47-2887.02.

Attachment after judgment, CivPro Rule 69-I.

Attorney discipline or disability proceedings, DCBar Rule XI.

Attorney general's powers, §1-301.88c.
Consumer protection matters, authority to issue, §1-301.88d.

Auditor for District of Columbia.
Powers and duties, §1-301.173.

Banks and financial institutions.
Investigation by commissioner, §26-551.13.

Charitable solicitations.
Prosecutions, §44-1712.

Chief medical examiner.
Confidential medical records, §5-1407.

Child abuse and neglect proceedings, FamDiv Rule E.

Child fatality review committee, §4-1371.07.

Civil procedure, CivPro Rule 45.

Consumer protection.
Department of consumer and regulatory affairs.
Power to subpoena, §28-3903.

Continuing care retirement communities.
Investigations of providers.
Issuance authorized, §44-151.12.

Controlled substances, §48-905.07.

Council's power to issue, §1-204.13.

Criminal procedure, CrimPro Rule 17, USDistCt LCrR 17.1.

Delinquent minors, JuvProc Rule 17.

Depositions, CivPro Rule 30, CrimPro Rule 17.

Disability compensation proceedings for public officers and employees, §1-623.26.

Domestic relations actions, DomRel Rule 45.

Domestic violence fatality review board, §16-1055.

SUBPOENAS —Cont'd

Domestic violence unit proceedings, DomesticViolence Rule 14.

Ethics and government accountability board enforcement, §1-1162.18.

Family court proceedings generally, FamDiv Rule E.

Form, CivPro Form CA 14.

Hospitalization of persons with mental illness, §21-503.

Interstate depositions and discovery.
See INTERSTATE DEPOSITIONS AND DISCOVERY.

Intrafamily proceedings, FamDiv Rule E.

Life insurance companies, §31-4312.

Lottery and charitable games control board, §3-1308.

Mayor's powers, §1-301.21.

Medicaid service provider fraud, §4-804.

Police and fire trial boards, §5-1003.

Public assistance, §4-218.04.

Public utilities investigations, §§34-905, 34-918.

Rules of civil procedure.
Applicability of rules, CivPro Rule 81.

Superior court, §11-942.

Unclaimed property records, §41-130.

Wages and salaries, §32-1306.

Water pollution and water quality, §8-103.15.

Workplace fraud.
Complaints, investigation, §32-1331.05.

Workplace safety, §32-805.

SUBROGATION.

Bonds, surety, §16-4102.

Child support enforcement.
Subrogation of District regarding, §46-203.

Crime victims' compensation, §4-509, VictComp Rule 40.

Disability compensation for public officers and employees, §1-623.31.

Execution of judgments.
Subrogation of purchaser after defective sale pursuant to, §15-316.

Health care benefits lien reduction, §31-3551.

Letters of credit.
Issuer, applicant and nominated person, §28:5-117.

SUBROGATION —Cont'd

Medicaid health-care assistance reimbursement, §§4-601 to 4-609. See MEDICAID.

No-fault motor vehicle insurance, §31-2411.

Notice of proposed settlement for policy limits upon waiver of subrogation, §31-2407.01.

Procedural rules for subrogation cases, CivPro Rule 40-III.

SUBSTANCE ABUSE.

Access to recovery voucher program, §7-3003.01.

Addiction recovery fund, §7-3004.

Alcohol and drug abuse.

General provisions, §§44-1201 to 44-1210. See ALCOHOL AND DRUG ABUSE.

Child abuse and neglect.

Exposure of children to drug-related activity, §§4-1301.06a, 4-1301.07.

Children and youth.

Juveniles and young adults, rehabilitation programs for, §24-612.

Pilot substance abuse program for youth, §§7-3101 to 7-3103.

Choice in drug treatment, §§7-3001 to 7-3015.

Access to recovery voucher program, §7-3003.01.

Addiction recovery fund, §7-3004.

Administration, §7-3005.

Administration of drug treatment choice program, §7-3005.

Aftercare plan, §7-3011.

Amount of benefits received by clients, §7-3008.

Certification of providers, §§7-3005.01, 7-3009.

Comprehensive plan to develop District's treatment and prevention infrastructure, §7-3012.

Confidential records, §7-3006.

Definitions, §7-3002.

Entitlement to treatment not created, §7-3008.

Establishment of drug treatment choice program, §7-3003.

Evaluation of programs, §7-3013.

Legislative findings, §7-3001.

No insurance benefits available for treatment, §7-3007.

Priority for enrollment, §7-3008.

SUBSTANCE ABUSE —Cont'd

Choice in drug treatment —Cont'd

Procurement authority, §7-3005.01.

Provider agreement or other arrangements, §7-3005.01.

Purpose of drug treatment choice program, §7-3003.

Quality assurance, §7-3010.

Residency requirement, §7-3007.

Rules, §7-3015.

Controlled substances, §§48-901.02 to 48-931.02. See CONTROLLED SUBSTANCES.

Driving under the influence.

See DRIVING UNDER THE INFLUENCE.

Firearms.

Possession by addict unlawful, §22-4503.

Health insurance coverage, §§31-3101 to 31-3112. See HEALTH INSURANCE.

Judges.

Disability of judge, CJC Canon 2.14.

Pay-for-success contracts, §§2-211.01 to 2-211.03.

Pilot substance abuse program for youth.

Establishment, §7-3101.

One-year support, §7-3102.

Rules, §7-3103.

Prisons and prisoners.

Alcoholics, rehabilitation of, §§24-601 to 24-615. See PRISONS AND PRISONERS.

Drug addicts, rehabilitation of, §§24-701 to 24-715. See PRISONS AND PRISONERS.

Mandatory testing of corrections department employees, §§24-211.21 to 24-211.24.

Residential housing.

Drug, firearm, or prostitution-related nuisance abatement, §§42-3101 to 42-3114. See CRIME-RELATED NUISANCE ABATEMENT.

Drug-related evictions, §§42-3601 to 42-3610. See DRUG-RELATED EVICTIONS.

Treatment and prevention.

General provisions, §§44-1201 to 44-1210. See ALCOHOL AND DRUG ABUSE.

SUBSTITUTE DRUGS, §§48-803.01 to 48-803.05. See PRESCRIPTION DRUGS.

SUBSTITUTE TEACHERS, §§38-1909, 38-1910.

SUBSTITUTION OF PARTIES.
Appeals in federal cases, FRAP 43.
Civil actions, §12-102.

SUBWAYS.
Baltimore and Ohio tracks near Chestnut Street, Fern Place, and Piney Branch Road, under, §9-323.
Cedar Street, §9-319.
Grade crossing elimination projects, as part of, §9-1201.15.
Authority of mayor, §9-1203.05.
Van Buren Street, §9-317.

SUBWAY SYSTEM.
Metrorail and metrobus, §§9-1101.01 to 9-1115.04.
See METRORAIL AND METROBUS.

SUDAN.
Employees retirement program management.
Investment of public funds in certain companies doing business with government of Sudan, §§1-335.01 to 1-335.07.
See EMPLOYEES RETIREMENT PROGRAM MANAGEMENT.

SUFFERANCE, ESTATES BY, §§28-3501, 42-504, 42-520.

SUFFERANCE, TENANTS BY, §42-3204.

SUFFOCATION.
Non-resuscitation procedures for EMS.
Comfort care orders, §§7-651.01 to 7-651.16.
See EMERGENCY MEDICAL SERVICES.

SUFFRAGE, US Const Art V, Amds 14, 15, 19, 26.

SUGGESTIONS OF DEATH.
Guardianship, Probate Rule 328.
Party substitution, CivPro Form CA 30.

SUICIDE.
Living wills.
Compliance with, §7-628.
Non-resuscitation procedures for EMS.
Comfort care orders.
Not deemed, §7-651.13.

SUICIDE —Cont'd
Non-resuscitation procedures for EMS —Cont'd
Not deemed suicide, §7-651.13.

SUMMARY ACTIONS.
Administrative fines, §2-1801.06.
Asbestos contractors, §8-111.07.
Child care facilities, §7-2041.
Drug manufacture and distribution licensure, §48-709.
Health occupations licensure, registration or certification, §3-1205.15.
Occupational safety and health.
Imminent danger regarding, §32-1118.
Underground storage tanks, §8-113.10.

SUMMARY JUDGMENT, CivPro Rule 56.
Appeals.
Summary disposition motions, DCCtApp Rule 27.
Bankruptcy proceedings, USDistDCBank Rule 7056-1.
Domestic relations actions, DomRel Rule 56.
Landlord and tenant court, LandlordTenant Rules 13, 14.
Motions practice, CivPro Rule 12-I, USDistCt LCvR 7, USDistCt LCvR 56.1.
Small claims court, SmallClaims Rule 13.

SUMMER SCHOOL.
Foundation level.
Uniform per student funding formula. Supplement, §38-2905.
Uniform per-student funding formula, §§38-2901 to 38-2914.

SUMMONS AND PROCESS, §§23-561 to 23-563.
Attachment after judgment, CivPro Rule 69-I.
Child abuse and neglect proceedings, NeglectProc Rule 11.
Civil actions, CivPro Rule 4.
Contents of, §23-561.
Criminal procedure, CrimPro Rule 4.
Indictments and informations, CrimPro Rule 9.
Reprosecution, CrimPro Rule 4-I.
Delinquent minors, JuvProc Rule 9.
Reinstituting charges, JuvProc Rule 5.
Transfer for criminal prosecution, JuvProc Rule 108.

SUMMONS AND PROCESS —Cont'd
Domestic relations actions, DomRel Rule 4.
Execution of, §23-562.
Forcible entry and detainer, §§16-1501, 16-1502.
Form, §23-561, CivPro Form CA 1.
Third party defendants, CivPro Form CA 22-A.
Guardianship of minors.
Standby guardianship.
Notice of filing by summons, §16-4808.
Issuance of, §23-561.
Juvenile causes, §16-2306.
Landlord and tenant court,
LandlordTenant Form 1S.
Probate proceedings, §16-3103.
Contested estate cases.
Death before Jan. 1, 1981, Probate Rule 15.
Death between Jan. 1, 1981, and June 30, 1995, Probate Rule 107.
Death on or after July 1, 1995, Probate Rule 407.
Guardians, conservators, trustees, etc., involved, Probate Rule 208.
Return, §23-562.
Service of process.
Generally, §§13-301 to 13-341.
See SERVICE OF PROCESS AND PAPERS.
Long-arm statute, §§13-401 to 13-434.
See LONG-ARM STATUTE.
Publication, service by.
See SERVICE BY PUBLICATION.
Taxation.
Power of mayor to summons taxpayers, §47-4310.
Third party defendants, CivPro Form CA 22-A.

SUNDAYS.
Computation of time, CivPro Rule 6, CrimPro Rule 45.
Appeals, DCCtApp Rule 26.
Domestic relations actions, DomRel Rule 6.
Hospitalization of persons with mental illness, MentalHealth Rule 13.
Juvenile proceedings, JuvProc Rule 45.
Tax collection, §47-412.01.

SUPERINTENDENT OF EDUCATION, OFFICE OF, §§38-2601 to 38-2612.
Enhancement and expansion of pre-k programs, §§38-271.01 to 38-271.07.

SUPERINTENDENT OF SCHOOLS.
Posers and duties, §§38-131, 38-132.

SUPERIOR COURT, §§11-901 to 11-947.
Administration by chief judge, §11-906.
Administration of the estate.
General provisions, §§20-701 to 20-753.
See ADMINISTRATION OF ESTATES.
Adoption.
General provisions, §§16-301 to 16-317.
See ADOPTION.
Arbitration.
Civil adoption rules.
See ARBITRATION.
General provisions, §§16-4401 to 16-4432.
See ARBITRATION.
Arrest warrants, §11-941.
Assignment of cases, CivPro Rule 40-I.
Civil I calendar, CivPro Rule 40-II.
Collection and subrogation cases, CivPro Rule 40-III.
Domestic relations actions, DomRel Rule 40.
Assignment of judges, §11-908.
Family court judges, special rules, §11-908A.
Attachment.
See ATTACHMENT.
Attachment and garnishment of wages, §16-578.
Attachment proceedings, §16-533.
Branches.
Dividing divisions into, §11-902.
Chief judge, §§11-906, 11-907.
Child custody, §11-925.
Child support enforcement.
General provisions, §§46-201 to 46-231.
See CHILD SUPPORT ENFORCEMENT.

SUPERIOR COURT —Cont'd

Child support enforcement —Cont'd

Interstate family support, §§46-351.01 to 46-359.03.

See INTERSTATE FAMILY SUPPORT.

Medical support enforcement, §§46-251.01 to 46-251.10.

Civil division proceedings.

See ACTIONS.

Civil docket, CivPro Rule 79.

Conflicting schedules, CivPro Rule 104.

Civil jurisdiction, §11-921.

Claims against the estate.

General provisions, §§20-901 to 20-914.

See CLAIMS AGAINST ESTATES.

Clerks, §§11-910, 46-410.

Family division, FamDiv Rule B.

Hours of clerk's office, CivPro Rule 77-I.

Criminal division, CrimPro Rule 56.

Domestic relations actions, DomRel Rule 77.

Family division, FamDiv Rule B.

Landlord and tenant branch, LandlordTenant Rule 7.

Small claims and conciliation branch, SmallClaims Rule 7.

Tax division, Tax Rule 1.

Notice of orders and judgments, CivPro Rule 77.

Domestic relations actions, DomRel Rule 77.

Orders grantable by clerk, CivPro Rule 77-II.

Practice of law prohibited, CivPro Rule 103.

Family division, FamDiv Rule T.

Records management. See within this heading, "Records management."

Closing-out sales, §47-2108.

Commencement of action.

See COMMENCEMENT OF ACTIONS.

Compulsory school attendance, §38-213.

Conducting proceedings outside District.

Emergency authority, §11-911.

Contempt powers, §11-944.

Continuation, §§1-207.18, 11-901.

Continuous session of court, CivPro Rule 6-I.

Costs, §§15-709, 15-711, 15-713, 15-714.

SUPERIOR COURT —Cont'd

Court of appeals.

Application for allowance of appeals from, §17-301.

Assignment of judges to and from, §§11-705, 11-707.

Orders and judgments, jurisdiction over, §11-721.

Crime victims' compensation, §§4-501 to 4-518, VictComp Rules 1 to 41.

See CRIME VICTIMS' COMPENSATION.

Criminal division.

Assignment section, CrimPro Rule 101.

Authorization of sections, CrimPro Rule 1.

Branches, CrimPro Rule 1.

Creation of sections, CrimPro Rule 100.

District of Columbia section, CrimPro Rule 102.

Traffic section, CrimPro Rule 103.

Criminal division proceedings.

See CRIMINAL PROCEDURE.

Criminal finance office.

Hours of office, CrimPro Rule 56.

Criminal jurisdiction, §11-923.

Criminal procedure.

Criminal division proceedings.

See CRIMINAL PROCEDURE.

Issuance of rules and regulations, §16-701.

Decedent estates.

General provisions, §§20-101 to 20-109.

See DECEDENTS' ESTATES.

Delay of proceedings.

Emergency authority, §11-947.

Deposits with court, CivPro Rule 67-I.

Domestic relations actions, DomRel Rule 67.

Descent and distributions.

General provisions, §§19-101.01 to 19-701.

See INTESTATE SUCCESSION.

Designation of judges, §11-908.

Dismissal of actions.

See DISMISSAL OF ACTIONS.

Divisions, §11-902.

Domestic relations proceedings.

General rules for domestic relations proceedings.

See DOMESTIC RELATIONS ACTIONS.

Parentage proceedings, §§16-2341 to 16-2348.

See PARENTAGE PROCEEDINGS.

SUPERIOR COURT —Cont'd

Domestic violence.

Generally, §§16-1001 to 16-1034.
See INTRAFAMILY
PROCEEDINGS.

Rules governing domestic violence unit
proceedings, DomesticViolence
Rules 1 to 14.

Durable powers of attorney.

General provisions, §§21-2081 to
21-2085.
See DURABLE POWERS OF
ATTORNEY.

Intervention proceedings, Probate
Rules 301 to 361.
See INTERVENTION
PROCEEDINGS.

Ejectment, §§16-1101 to 16-1124.
See EJECTMENT.

Eminent domain.

General provisions, §§16-1301 to
16-1385.
See EMINENT DOMAIN.

Jurisdiction over, §16-1303.

Employees not to practice law,
CivPro Rule 103.

Family division, FamDiv Rule T.

Estates in land.

General provisions, §§42-501 to
42-523.
See ESTATES IN LAND.

Family court.

Branches and sections, FamDiv Rule
A.

Clerks, FamDiv Rule B.

Fees, FamDiv Rule C.

General rules.
See FAMILY COURT
PROCEEDINGS.

Hearing commissioners, FamDiv Rule
D.

Proceedings generally, §§16-2301 to
16-2372.
See FAMILY COURT
PROCEEDINGS.

Federal offenders.

Detention and release, CrimPro Rule
40.

**Federal Rules of Civil Procedure
and Federal Rules of Criminal
Procedure, use of,** §11-946.

Fees, CivPro Rule 202.

Garnishment.

See GARNISHMENT.

SUPERIOR COURT —Cont'd

Guardian and ward.

Adult guardianship and protective
proceedings jurisdiction act,
§§21-2401.01 to 21-2405.03.
See GUARDIAN AND WARD.

Incapacitated persons, guardianship
of, §§21-2041 to 21-2049.
See GUARDIAN AND WARD.

Intervention proceedings, Probate
Rules 301 to 361.
See INTERVENTION
PROCEEDINGS.

Minors, guardianship of, §§21-101 to
21-182.
See GUARDIAN AND WARD.

Habeas corpus.

General provisions, §§16-1901 to
16-1909.
See HABEAS CORPUS.

Hours of court, CivPro Rule 77.

Landlord and tenant branch,
LandlordTenant Rule 7.

Small claims and conciliation branch,
SmallClaims Rule 7.

Tax division, Tax Rule 1.

Intellectually disabled commitment.

General provisions.
See COMMITMENT OF PERSONS
WITH INTELLECTUAL
DISABILITIES.

Interpreters, §§2-1901 to 2-1912.01.
See INTERPRETERS.

Interstate family support.

General provisions, §§46-351.01 to
46-359.03.
See INTERSTATE FAMILY
SUPPORT.

Intestate succession.

General provisions, §§19-101.01 to
19-701.
See INTESTATE SUCCESSION.

Intrafamily proceedings, §§16-1001 to
16-1034.
See INTRAFAMILY PROCEEDINGS.

Judges, §§11-903 to 11-910.

Chief judge.
Designation, term, §1-204.31.

Mandatory retirement, §1-204.31.

Nomination and appointment,
§1-204.33.

Reappointment, §1-204.33.

Removal, suspension, involuntary
retirement, §1-204.32.

SUPERIOR COURT —Cont'd
Judges —Cont'd
Term, §1-204.31.
Judicial Conference of the District of Columbia, DCCtApp Rule 50.
Judicial power of District vested in, §§1-204.31, 11-101.
Jurisdiction, §§1-204.31, 11-921 to 11-925, 11-1101, 11-1201.
Rules not affecting jurisdiction, CivPro Rule 82.
Jury selection, coordination and cooperation regarding, §11-1917.
Jury trial deposits, §15-713.
Jury trials.
See JURIES AND JURY TRIALS.
Juvenile proceedings.
Crimes by juvenile offenders, §§24-901 to 24-941.
See JUVENILE OFFENDERS.
General rules for juvenile proceedings.
See DELINQUENT MINORS.
Limitation of actions.
General provisions, §§12-301 to 12-311.
See LIMITATION OF ACTIONS.
Magistrate judges, §11-1732.
Family court and domestic violence unit.
Special rules, §11-1732a.
Media coverage of proceedings, CivPro Rule 203, CrimPro Rule 53.
Attorneys publicizing trials, ProfCond Rule 3.6.
Child abuse and neglect proceedings, NeglectProc Rule 45.
Juvenile proceedings, JuvProc Rule 53.
Meetings of judges, §11-909.
Mental health proceedings.
General provisions, §§21-501 to 21-592.
See HOSPITALIZATION OF PERSONS WITH MENTAL ILLNESS.
General rules for mental health proceedings.
See HOSPITALIZATION OF PERSONS WITH MENTAL ILLNESS.
Milk container registration, §§36-125, 36-155.
Motor vehicle safety responsibility jurisdiction, §50-1301.76.
Neglect proceedings.
General rules for neglect proceedings.
See CHILD ABUSE AND NEGLECT.

SUPERIOR COURT —Cont'd
Neglect proceedings —Cont'd
Termination of parental rights, §§16-2351 to 16-2365.
See TERMINATION OF PARENTAL RIGHTS.
Oaths and affirmations.
Judges' oaths, §11-905.
Power to administer oaths, §11-945.
Opening the estate.
General provisions, §§20-301 to 20-357.
See OPENING ESTATES.
Parentage proceedings.
General provisions, §§16-2341 to 16-2348.
See PARENTAGE PROCEEDINGS.
Personal representatives.
General provisions, §§20-401 to 20-406.
See PERSONAL REPRESENTATIVES.
Place of trials, CivPro Rule 77.
Powers of appointment.
General provisions, §§42-1001 to 42-1019.
See POWERS OF APPOINTMENT.
Practice of law before the court, CivPro Rules 101 to 104.
Pretrial conferences.
See PRETRIAL CONFERENCES.
Private right of action.
See PRIVATE RIGHT OF ACTION.
Probate proceedings.
General provisions, §§16-3101 to 16-3112.
See PROBATE PROCEEDINGS.
General rules for the probate division.
See PROBATE PROCEEDINGS.
Intervention proceedings, Probate Rules 301 to 361.
See INTERVENTION PROCEEDINGS.
Register of wills, §§11-2101 to 11-2106.
See WILLS.
Quo warranto.
General provisions, §§16-3501 to 16-3548.
See QUO WARRANTO.
Recording of proceedings, CivPro Rule 201.
Family division, FamDiv Rule N.
Records management.
Adoption proceeding records, Adoption Rule 79.
Civil cases, CivPro Rule 79-I.

SUPERIOR COURT —Cont'd
Records management —Cont'd
Criminal cases.
Removal of records, CrimPro Rule
55-I.
Domestic relations actions, DomRel
Rule 79.
Juvenile proceedings, JuvProc Rule 55.
Register of wills, §§11-2101 to 11-2106.
See REGISTER OF WILLS.
Replevin.
General provisions, §§16-3701 to
16-3713.
See REPLEVIN.
Reports of judges, §11-909.
Scheduling conflicts, CivPro Rule 104.
Seal, §11-901.
Search warrants, §11-941.
Secretaries, §11-910.
Service of process, §11-943.
Generally, §§13-301 to 13-341.
See SERVICE OF PROCESS AND
PAPERS.
Long-arm statute, §§13-401 to 13-434.
See LONG-ARM STATUTE.
**Small claims and conciliation
branch.**
General provisions, §§16-3901 to
16-3910.
See SMALL CLAIMS COURT.
Special administrators, §§20-531 to
20-534.
See PERSONAL
REPRESENTATIVES.
Stay of proceedings.
See STAYS.
Subpoena powers, §11-942.
**Supervised and unsupervised
administration.**
General provisions, §§20-401 to
20-406.
See PERSONAL
REPRESENTATIVES.
Tax division, CrimPro Rules 1, 104.
Abolition of other remedies, §11-1202.
Address and business hours, Tax Rule
1.
Exclusive jurisdiction, §§11-1201,
11-1202.
General rules for the tax division.
See TAX PROCEEDINGS.
Rules and regulations, §11-1203.
**Tax returns or other tax
information.**
Disclosure to, §§47-1805.04, 47-4406.

SUPERIOR COURT —Cont'd
Termination of parental rights.
General provisions, §§16-2351 to
16-2365.
See TERMINATION OF PARENTAL
RIGHTS.
Terms of court abolished, CivPro Rule
6-I.
Tolling of proceedings.
Emergency authority, §11-947.
Transfer of civil actions to or from,
§§11-503, 11-922.
**United States District Court for the
District of Columbia.**
Removal of cases to or from, §§11-503,
11-922.
Wages and salaries of judges,
§11-904.
**Washington metropolitan area
transit authority violations.**
Jurisdiction over, §11-924.
Wills.
General provisions, §§18-101 to
18-308.
Witness fees, §15-714.
Youth residential facilities, §§7-2101
to 7-2108.
See YOUTH RESIDENTIAL
FACILITIES.
Youth services, §§2-1501 to 2-1511.
See YOUTH SERVICES.

SUPERMARKETS.
Business licenses, §47-2827.
Tax incentives, §§47-3801 to 47-3805.

SUPERSEDEAS BONDS, CivPro Rule
62-I, DCCtApp Rules 7, 8.
**Administrative orders and decisions
reviewed,** DCCtApp Rule 19.

SUPERVISED RELEASE.
Detection device.
Tampering by persons required to
wear, §22-1211.
Mental health disclosures,
§7-1204.03.
Sentencing offender to, §24-403.01.

**SUPPLEMENTAL NUTRITION
ASSISTANCE PROGRAM
(SNAP),** §§4-261.21 to 4-261.23.
Reports, §4-261.23.
**Simplified self-employment
deduction,** §4-261.22.
Transitional benefits, §4-261.21.

**SUPPLY SCHEDULE, PURCHASE
CARD, AND TRAINING FUND,**
§2-361.03.

SUPPORT AND MAINTENANCE, §16-916.

Attachment and garnishment of wages.
Enforcement of support orders, priority, §16-571.01.
Percentage limitations, §16-577.

Child abuse and neglect proceedings, §16-2325.

Child support enforcement.
General provisions, §§46-201 to 46-231.
See CHILD SUPPORT ENFORCEMENT.
Medical support enforcement, §§46-251.01 to 46-251.10.
Reciprocal enforcement of support proceedings, DomRel Rule 401.

Crime victims' compensation.
Loss of support, VictComp Rule 30.

Delinquent minors, §16-2325.

Domestic partnerships, termination, §§16-913, 16-916.

Family court proceedings, §11-1101.

Forms.
Absent defendant.
Order of publication, DomRel Form 1.
Certificate and order, DomRel Form 15.
Complaint for support, DomRel Form 13.
Employer's statement, DomRel Form 6.
Husband's financial statement, DomRel Form 4.
Motion and affidavit, DomRel Form 2.
Contempt, DomRel Form 7.
Opposition to motion and affidavit, DomRel Form 3.
Order for support, DomRel Forms 10, 15.
Parentage, DomRel Forms 11, 12.
Petition for support, DomRel Form 9.
Show cause order, DomRel Form 16.
Testimony of plaintiff, DomRel Form 14.
Uncontested stipulation, DomRel Form 8.
Wife's financial statement, DomRel Form 5.

Guardianship of minors responsible for maintenance and education of child.
Amounts expended, §21-143.
Sale of principal, §21-147.

SUPPORT AND MAINTENANCE —Cont'd

Hearing commissioners, FamDiv Rule D.

Interstate family support.
General provisions, §§46-351.01 to 46-359.03.
See INTERSTATE FAMILY SUPPORT.
Reciprocal enforcement of support proceedings, DomRel Rule 401.

Leaving jurisdiction of court.
Writ of ne exeat, DomRel Rule 406.

Medical support enforcement, §§46-251.01 to 46-251.10.

Mental illness, persons with, hospitalized, §21-586.

Powers of attorney, §21-2113.

Procedure generally, DomRel Rules 1 to 406.
See DOMESTIC RELATIONS ACTIONS.

Program on work, employment, and responsibility (POWER), §4-205.19.

Public assistance, responsible relatives of persons on, §§4-213.01, 4-213.05, 4-213.06, 4-217.07 to 4-217.11.

Public officers and employees.
Wages subject to attachment and garnishment for, §1-507.

Reciprocal enforcement of support proceedings, DomRel Rule 401.

Spousal support.
See SPOUSAL SUPPORT.

Temporary assistance for needy families (TANF) program, §4-205.19.

SUPREME COUNCIL OF SCOTTISH RITE FREE MASONRY.

Real property tax exemptions, §47-1094.

SUPREME COURT OF THE UNITED STATES.

Chief justice presides in impeachment of president, US Const Art I §3.

D.C. Circuit court of appeals.
Review by Supreme Court, USCtApp HPIP Rule XIII(c).

Judicial power invested in, §11-101.

Jurisdiction, US Const Art III §2.

Justices.
Appointment, US Const Art II §2.
Compensation, US Const Art III §1.

SUPREME COURT OF THE UNITED STATES —Cont'd

Justices —Cont'd

Tenure, US Const Art III §1.

Mandate of court of appeals.

Stay of mandate pending application for certiorari, DCCtApp Rule 41.

Supreme law of the land, US Const Art VI.

U.S. Court of appeals for the DC Circuit.

Review by supreme court, USCtApp HPIP Rule XIII(c).

SURCHARGES.

Personal representatives, §20-701.

Public space, public rights of way, and public structures, permits to occupy, §10-1141.06.

Recorder of deeds, §42-1211.

SURGEON GENERAL.

Drug addicts, rehabilitation of, §24-713.

SURGERY.

Breast surgery.

Reconstructive surgery following mastectomies.

Women's rights to health insurance coverage, §§31-3831 to 31-3837.

Health insurance.

Mastectomies.

Reconstructive surgery following mastectomies.

Women's rights to health insurance coverage, §§31-3831 to 31-3837.

Hospital discharge planning, §§21-2231.01 to 21-2231.05.

Mastectomies.

Reconstructive surgery following mastectomies.

Women's rights to health insurance coverage, §§31-3831 to 31-3837.

Psycho-surgery.

Health care durable powers of attorney, §21-2211.

Reconstructive breast surgery.

Women's rights to health insurance coverage, §§31-3831 to 31-3837.

SURGICAL ASSISTANTS.

Advisory committee, §7-743.07.

Authority and scope of practice, §3-1206.41.

Board of medicine.

Advisory committee on surgical assistants, §3-1202.03.

SURGICAL ASSISTANTS —Cont'd

Health occupations licensure, registration or certification, §§3-1205.01 to 3-1205.24.

See HEALTH OCCUPATIONS LICENSURE, REGISTRATION OR CERTIFICATION.

Renewal of license, §3-1206.42.

Supervising surgeon, defined, §3-1206.41.

Transition provisions, §3-1206.43.

SURROGATE PARENTING CONTRACTS, §§16-401, 16-402.

SURSUM CORDA.

Bond issues.

New communities initiative, §42-2812.03.

SURVEYOR OF THE DISTRICT, §§1-1301 to 1-1329.

Adjusting building lines, §1-1328.

Alleys, §1-1322.

Appointment of, §1-1301.

Assistant surveyor.

Appointment of, §1-1303.

Duties of, §1-1304.

Boundaries, §§1-1318, 1-1319.

Cemeteries.

Platting and surveying, §§43-103, 43-116.

Rights of way through, §1-1315.

Changes, entering and recording, §1-1318.

Condominium plat and plans filed with, §42-1902.14.

District surveying work conducted without charge, §1-1316.

Employees of, §1-1303.

Evidence, transcripts of records as, §1-1311.

Fee schedule, §1-1329.

Highways, entry upon property for purposes of surveying, §9-103.04.

Lots.

Boundaries, marking, §1-1319.

Record of, §1-1307.

Wall of house extending over lot line, §1-1326.

Oaths and affirmations, §1-1302.

Party walls, §§1-1325 to 1-1328.

Adjusting lines of buildings, §1-1328.

Certification and recording location, §1-1327.

Payment of reasonable price, §1-1325.

Wall extending over lot line, §1-1326.

Plats.

Admission to record, §1-1313.

SURVEYOR OF THE DISTRICT
—Cont'd
Plats —Cont'd
Certification, §1-1320.
Orders regulating, §1-1313.
Scale of, §1-1310.
Prompt execution of court surveying orders, §1-1317.
Property of District, records as, §1-1308.
Public ways, recording, §1-1314.
Real property taxes, designation of property for assessment, §§47-701 to 47-709.
Records, §§1-1306 to 1-1310.
Retention of records, §1-1306.
Rights of way through cemeteries, §1-1315.
Squares.
Excess or deficiency in measurement, apportioning, §1-1324.
Record of, §1-1307.
United States squares, subdivision of, §1-1312.
Streets and alleys, closing procedures, §9-202.12.
Subdivisions.
Admission to record, §1-1313.
Certified plat, §1-1320.
Dimensions, §1-1321.
Legal record of, §1-1321.
Orders regulating, §1-1313.
References made to, §1-1322.
United States squares, subdivision of, §1-1312.
Transfer of records on vacancy in office, §1-1308.
Typewritten records, §1-1309.
Wages and salaries, §1-1301.

SURVEYS AND SURVEYORS.
Business licenses, §§47-2853.111 to 47-2853.114.
Eligibility, §47-2853.112.
Interns, §47-2853.113.
Representations prohibited, §47-2853.114.
Scope of practice, §47-2853.111.
Old Georgetown district.
Survey authorized, §6-1204.
Surveyor of the District, §§1-1301 to 1-1329.
See SURVEYOR OF THE DISTRICT.

SURVIVAL OF ACTIONS.
Death of party, §12-101.
Appeals in federal cases, FRAP 43.

SURVIVING SPOUSES.
Defined, §47-1801.04.
Intestate succession, §§19-101.01 to 19-101.06.
Applicability of provisions, §19-101.01.
Equitable apportionment.
Minor children not in custody of surviving spouse, §19-101.05.
Exempt property, §19-101.03.
Family allowance, §19-101.04.
Homestead allowance, §19-101.02.
Surplus distributed after payment to, §19-305.
Whole, entitlement to, §19-302.
Willful violations, §19-101.06.
Police and firefighters retirement and disability.
Survivor benefits generally, §§5-702, 5-716, 5-744, 5-747.
Spousal devises or bequests, §19-112.

SURVIVORSHIP.
Disclaimer of property interests.
Rights of survivorship in jointly held property, §19-1507.

SUSTAINABLE ENERGY, §§8-1773.01 to 8-1774.16.
Contracting with sustainable energy utility, §8-1774.01.
Implementation of contract, §8-1774.05.
Structure of contract, §8-1774.02.
Definitions, §8-1773.01.
Demand-side programs proposed by electric company, §8-1774.07.
Energy assistance trust fund, §8-1774.11.
Energy consumption data.
Provision upon request, §§8-1774.07, 8-1774.08.
Gas company information, §8-1774.08.
Home improvement financing for solar or renewable energy, §8-1774.13.
Incentive program for renewable energy, §8-1774.09.
Low-income electricity customer discount program, §8-1774.14.
Low-income gas customer discount program, §8-1774.15.
Sustainable energy branding, §8-1774.06.
Sustainable energy trust fund, §8-1774.10.
Sustainable energy utility advisory board, §§8-1774.03, 8-1774.04.

SUSTAINABLE TRANSPORTATION FUND, §50-921.15.

SUSTAINABLE URBAN AGRICULTURE APICULTURE ACT OF 2012, §§8-1825.01 to 8-1825.09.
See BEES.

SWIMMING, §§10-162 to 10-165.

SWIMMING POOLS.
Business licenses, §47-2824.
Drug free zones, §48-904.07a.
Firearms.
Enhanced penalties and fines for carrying guns into gun free zones, §22-4502.01.

SYRINGES.
Drug paraphernalia, §§48-904.10, 48-1101 to 48-1104.
Needle exchange programs, §48-1103.01.
Safe needle distribution, §§7-2851 to 7-2858.
Schools and education.
Distribution of needles or syringes near schools, §48-1121.

T

TAGGING.
See GRAFFITI.

TAMPERING WITH PHYSICAL EVIDENCE, §22-723.

TANGIBLE PERSONAL PROPERTY.
Compensating-use tax on, §§47-2201 to 47-2214.
See COMPENSATING-USE TAX.

TARGETS.
Persons or animals used as, §47-2841.

TATTOOS.
Body art establishments.
Business licenses, §47-2809.01.
Body artists.
Business licenses, §§47-2853.76a to 47-2853.76e.

TAVERNS.
Alcoholic beverage licenses.
Brew pub licenses, §25-117.
Georgetown historic district.
Special restrictions, §25-339.
On-premises retailers, §25-113.
Wine pub permits, §25-124.
Georgetown historic district.
Alcoholic beverage licenses.
Special restrictions, §25-339.

TAVERNS —Cont'd
Smoking, §§7-741.02, 7-741.03.

TAX ASSESSOR, §§47-601, 47-602.

TAXATION.
Abatement.
See ABATEMENT.
Administrative hearings, office of.
Assessments, protest of, §47-4312.
Airspace, rental of, §10-1121.08.
Alcoholic beverages, §§25-901 to 25-911.
Appeals, §25-910.
Beer, §25-902.
Collection and payment, §§25-903, 25-908.
Common carriers, §25-905.
Exemptions, §25-906.
Fines and penalties.
Contraband, seizure and forfeiture of, §25-911.
Failure to pay tax, §25-907.
Generally.
See ALCOHOLIC BEVERAGES.
Importation permits, §25-904.
Personal debt, liability deemed as, §25-907.
Protests, §25-907.
Refunds, §25-909.
Wine and spirits, §25-901.
Anticipation by sale or hypothecation, §1-301.70.
Antideficiency provisions, §47-105.
Assessments.
See ASSESSMENTS.
Ballpark fee, §§47-2761 to 47-2763.
Ballpark sales taxes, §47-2002.05.
Banks and financial institutions.
General provisions, §§47-2503 to 47-2515.
See BANKS AND FINANCIAL INSTITUTIONS.
Beer, §25-902.
Board of education.
Real property exempt from taxation, §47-1027.
Bonding companies, §47-2502.
Bond issues, tax exemption for, §1-204.85.
Bonds, surety.
Stay of collection, §47-4452.
Books.
Examination of books and records.
Time and place for, §47-4314.
Brew pubs, §25-902.
Bulk sales.
Failure to notify, §47-4462.

TAXATION —Cont'd
Bulk sales —Cont'd
Notice required, §47-4461.
Personal liability for tax, §47-4463.
Business improvement districts,
§§2-1215.15, 2-1215.17.
Collection and disbursement of BID
taxes, §2-1215.15.
Business licenses.
Past due taxes.
Computer record-keeping and
reporting system, §47-2866.
Definitions, §47-2861.
Issuance prohibited, §47-2862.
Right to appeal denial of license,
§47-2865.
Self-certification of lack of
outstanding debt, §47-2863.
Falsification of certification,
penalty, §47-2864.
Cable television, §47-2501.01.
Capitation tax.
Constitutional provisions, US Const
Art I §9, Amd 24.
Elections.
Denial or abridgement of the right
to vote for failure to pay poll tax
prohibited, US Const Amd 24.
Captive insurance companies.
Premiums collected, §31-3931.12.
CareFirst.
Tax credit for wages, sales tax
exemption, §47-4602.
**Cemetery associations, exemption
of,** §43-111.
Certified capital companies.
Premium tax credit.
See CERTIFIED CAPITAL
COMPANIES.
Check-offs.
Drug prevention and children at risk,
§§47-4001 to 47-4005.
Chief financial officer.
Revenue estimates and other revenue
duties, §1-204.24d.
Tax increment financing, authorization
to enter into financing documents,
§2-1217.02.
Tax preference review, §1-301.157.
Transparency, §1-301.156.
Children's Trust Fund, §4-1341.08.
City of Washington museum.
Tax exemptions for, §39-308.
Collection of taxes.
General provisions, §§47-401 to
47-433.
See COLLECTION OF TAXES.

TAXATION —Cont'd
Collection of taxes —Cont'd
Tax compliance simplification act,
§§47-4401 to 47-4491.
See COLLECTION OF TAXES.
College savings program, §§47-4501
to 47-4512.
Common trust funds, §26-402.
Compensating-use tax.
General provisions, §§47-2201 to
47-2214.
See COMPENSATING-USE TAX.
Condominiums.
See CONDOMINIUMS.
Congress.
Powers of congress, US Const Art I §8.
Constitution of the United States.
Capitation tax, US Const Art I §9.
Elections.
Denial or abridgement of right to
vote for failure to pay poll tax
prohibited, US Const Amd 24.
Excises.
Powers of congress, US Const Art I
§8.
Exports, US Const Art I §§9, 10.
Income tax, US Const Amd 16.
Limitations on powers of states, US
Const Art I §10.
Powers of congress, US Const Art I §8.
Revenue bills, US Const Art I §7.
Cooperative associations, §29-939.
**Corporations, personal liability of
officers,** §47-4491.
Criminal provisions, §§47-4101 to
47-4111.
Attempt to evade or defeat tax,
§47-4101.
Attempt to interfere with revenue
laws, §47-4107.
Construction of provisions, §47-4109.
Failure to collect or pay over tax,
§47-4102.
Failure to pay tax. make return, keep
records or supply information,
§47-4103.
Fraud and false statements, §47-4106.
Fraudulent withholding information,
failure to supply information to
employer, §47-4105.
To employees, §47-4104.
Informants, payment of expenses,
§47-4111.
Limitations period on prosecutions,
§47-4108.
Mayor's regulatory authority,
§47-4110.

TAXATION —Cont'd

Criminal provisions —Cont'd

Rewards for informants, §47-4111.

Special agents for office of tax and revenue, §47-4108.01.

Deeds.

Recordation tax on deeds, §§42-1101 to 42-1124.

See RECORDATION TAX.

Department of insurance, securities, and banking, §31-205.

District of Columbia housing authority.

Exemption, §6-204.

Diversion of tax money, unlawful, §47-104.

East of the river hospital tax exemptions, §47-4614.

Economic development zone incentives.

General provisions, §§6-1501 to 6-1506.

See ECONOMIC DEVELOPMENT ZONE INCENTIVES.

Elections.

Capitation tax, US Const Art I §9.

Denial or abridgement of right to vote. Failure to pay poll or other tax, US Const Amd 24.

Electric light and power companies, §47-2501.

Emergency and non-emergency number telephone calling systems fund.

Assessments to subscribers, §34-1803.

Estate, §§47-3701 to 47-3722.

See INHERITANCE AND ESTATE TAXES.

Estimated tax.

Banks, financial institutions, and insurance companies, §47-2509.

Income taxes, §47-1812.14.

Excess money raised via, disposition of, §47-503.

Federal tax liens.

Recorder of deeds, §42-1215.

Fiduciary security transfers, §28-2909.

Chapter not affected by tax obligations, §28-2909.

Financial institutions.

Requests for information about delinquent obligor, §47-4481.

Fines.

Real property taxes, nonpayment of, §47-811.

TAXATION —Cont'd

Fines —Cont'd

Tax return preparers, §47-4217.

Fiscal year, §1-204.41.

Foreign trade zones.

Applicability of licensing, permitting and taxation provisions, §36-503.

Fraternal benefit societies, §31-5320.

Fraud and deceit.

Penalties for fraud, §47-4212.

Gas companies, §47-2501.

General obligation bonds, payment of, §1-204.81.

Gross sales tax.

General provisions, §§47-2001 to 47-2027.

See GROSS SALES TAX.

Heating oil companies, §47-2501.

Homeowners in enterprise zones tax abatement, §§47-858.01 to 47-858.05.

Horizontal property regimes, §§42-2016, 42-2017, 42-2023, 42-2029.

Hospital and medical service corporations, §§31-205, 31-3514.01.

Deductions, §47-2608.

Housing finance agency, tax exemptions for, §42-2704.10.

Income and franchise taxes.

General provisions, §§47-1801.01 to 47-1816.03.

See INCOME TAXES.

Income tax secured bonds, §§47-340.26 to 47-340.36.

See INCOME TAX SECURED BONDS.

Indebtedness of District of Columbia, §47-102.

Indians.

Constitutional provisions, US Const Art I §2, Amd 14.

Informants, payment of expenses, §47-4111.

Inheritance and estate taxes, §§47-3701 to 47-3722.

See INHERITANCE AND ESTATE TAXES.

Insurance companies, §31-205.

General provisions, §§47-2502 to 47-2515.

See INSURANCE COMPANIES.

Interest.

Overpayment of tax, §47-4202.

Protest of assessment, §47-4312.

TAXATION —Cont'd

Interest —Cont'd

Underpayment of tax, §47-4201.

Corporations, financial institutions and unincorporated businesses, by, §47-4204.

Individuals, by, §47-4203.

Internet tax, §§47-3931 to 47-3933.

Definitions, §47-3931.

Exemptions, §47-3932.

Imposition of tax.

Sales made via internet, §47-3932.

Scope, §47-3933.

Small vendor exemption, §47-3932.

Jenkins Row Development.

Exemption, §47-4603.

Jeopardy assessments, §47-4451.

Levy for failure to pay.

Certificate of sale, §47-4475.

Evidence of right to sell, §47-4476.

Distraint generally, §47-4471.

Wrongful distraint action, §47-4479.

Financial institutions.

Requests for information about delinquent obligor, §47-4481.

Legal effect of sale, §47-4476.

Notice of seizure for sale, §47-4472.

Proceeds from sale, §47-4477.

Real property, transfer of deed, §47-4475.

Evidence of right to sell, §47-4476.

Redemption of property, §47-4474.

Refusal to surrender levied property, §47-4480.

Release of levy, §47-4478.

Return of property after release, §47-4478.

Sale of seized property, §47-4472.

Storage of seized property, §47-4473.

Wrongful distraint action, §47-4479.

Life and health insurance guaranty association.

Tax exemption for, §31-5413.

Limitation of actions.

Collection, §47-4302.

Credits, §§47-4304, 47-4304.01.

Liability for payment, §47-4301.

Refunds, §47-4304.

Suspension of limitations periods, §47-4303.

Lincoln Square Theater.

Sales and use tax exemption, §47-4601.

Local exchange providers (LECs), §34-2007.

Lower income home ownership tax abatement and incentives, §§47-3501 to 47-3508.

TAXATION —Cont'd

Low-income housing tax credit, §§47-4801 to 47-4812.

See LOW-INCOME HOUSING TAX CREDIT.

Marine insurance exclusion, §47-2608.

Metropolitan Washington Airports Authority, exemption of, §9-921.

Money lenders, §26-901.

Motor fuel tax.

General provisions, §§47-2301 to 47-2354.

See MOTOR FUEL TAX.

Multistate tax compact, §§47-441 to 47-445.

Adopted, §47-441.

Audits, §47-443.

Existing laws and regulations not affected, §47-442.

Form, §47-441.

Implementation subject to appropriation, §47-445.

Rules and regulations, §47-444.

New Columbia statehood initiative.

Tax-exempt status, §1-129.34.

New residential development tax abatement, §§47-857.01 to 47-857.10, 47-859.01 to 47-859.05.

Not-for-profit hospital corporations.

Exemption, §44-951.12.

Nursing facilities.

Assessment, §§47-1261 to 47-1269.

"Officer" of United States includes IRS officers, CivPro Rule 81.

Payments in lieu of taxes, §47-1052.

Bond issues, §§1-308.01 to 1-308.10.

See BOND ISSUES.

Penalties.

Corporations, personal liability of officers, §47-4491.

Failure to file or pay, §47-4213.

Fraud, §47-4212.

Frivolous returns, §47-4216.

Preparers of returns, §47-4217.

Protest of assessment, §47-4312.

Qualified high technology company, §47-4218.

Returns intended to delay or impede, §47-4216.

Substantial underpayment penalty, §47-4211.

Waiver or abatement, §47-4221.

Pensions and retirement replacement plan, §1-905.03.

TAXATION —Cont'd
Personal property taxes.
General provisions, §§47-1508 to 47-1535.
See PERSONAL PROPERTY TAXES.
PILOT.
Payments in lieu of taxes, §47-1052.
Bond issues, §§1-308.01 to 1-308.10.
See BOND ISSUES.
Poll taxes, US Const Art I §9.
Prohibited, US Const Amd 24.
Powers of attorney as to tax matters, §21-2116.
Powers of congress, US Const Art I §8.
Prison industries program, §24-231.05.
Privatization of administration and collection, §47-317.04a.
Property and liability insurance guaranty association.
Tax exemption for, §31-5512.
Property exempt from taxation.
General provisions, §§47-1001 to 47-1097.
See REAL PROPERTY TAX EXEMPTIONS.
Prostitution, tax for maintaining nuisance of house of, §22-2720.
Public officers and employees.
Tax-favored and pre-tax benefits for, §1-611.19.
Public utilities, §§47-2501, 47-2501.01, 47-2511 to 47-2515.
Purchasing groups, §31-4109.
Radio, §47-2501.01.
Rates, §§47-501, 47-503, 47-504.
Real property taxes.
See REAL PROPERTY TAXES.
Real property tax sales.
General provisions, §§47-1301 to 47-1321.
See REAL ESTATE TAX SALES.
Real property transfer tax.
General provisions, §§47-901 to 47-920.
See REAL PROPERTY TRANSFER TAX.
Reciprocal recovery of taxes, §§47-431 to 47-433.
Definitions, §47-433.
Multistate tax compact, §§47-441 to 47-445.
Right of District to sue in states.
Mayor's authority to secure services, §47-432.

TAXATION —Cont'd
Reciprocal recovery of taxes —Cont'd
Right of states to sue in District.
Proof of authority, §47-431.
Recordation of instruments.
Residential real estate transfers, §§47-1401, 47-1431 to 47-1433.
Recordation tax on deeds, §§42-1101 to 42-1124.
See RECORDATION TAX.
Recorder of deeds.
Federal tax liens, §42-1215.
Records, §§47-502, 47-601.
Examination of books and records, §47-4313.
Time and place, §47-4314.
Liability of taxpayer to maintain records, §47-4311.
Reform of taxes.
Procedure and priority, §47-181.
Rental of public space, §10-1103.07.
Rental vehicle tax.
General provisions, §§50-1505.01 to 50-1505.04.
See MOTOR VEHICLE REGISTRATION.
Retail development incentives, §§2-1217.71 to 2-1217.84.
See RETAIL DEVELOPMENT INCENTIVES.
Return preparers.
Penalties, §47-4217.
Returns.
Income taxes.
See INCOME TAXES.
Revenue bills, US Const Art I §7.
Revision of taxes.
Procedure and priority, §47-181.
Rhode Island Metro Plaza PILOT Area.
Payments in lieu of taxes, sales tax exemption, §47-4613.
Sales taxes.
Compensating-use tax, §§47-2201 to 47-2214.
See COMPENSATING-USE TAX.
Gross sales tax, §§47-2001 to 47-2027.
See GROSS SALES TAX.
Social media.
Qualified social electronic commerce companies tax abatements, §§47-1818.01 to 47-1818.08.
Special agents for office of tax and revenue, §47-4108.01.
Special assessments, §§47-1201 to 47-1207.

TAXATION —Cont'd
Special public safety fee, §§47-2751 to 47-2753.
Summons of taxpayer.
Powers of mayor, §47-4310.
Supermarkets, restaurants or retail stores.
Tax incentives, §§47-3801 to 47-3805.
Definitions, §47-3801.
Rules, §47-3804.
Supermarket real property tax rebate, §47-3805.
Tax exemption, §47-3802.
Tax assessor, §§47-601, 47-602.
Tax return preparers.
Penalties, §47-4217.
Tax returns.
Income taxes.
See INCOME TAXES.
Tax revision commission, §§47-461 to 47-464.
Telecommunications companies, §47-2501.
Telegraph and telephone companies, §47-2501.
Television, §47-2501.01.
Tenant assistance program payments, tax exemption for, §42-3503.08.
Title corporations, §47-2502.
Tobacco tax.
General provisions, §§47-2401 to 47-2426.
See TOBACCO TAX.
Toll telecommunication service tax.
General provisions, §§47-3901 to 47-3922.
See TOLL TELECOMMUNICATION SERVICE TAX.
Trust, loan, mortgage, safe deposit and title corporations, §§47-2502, 47-2511 to 47-2515.
See BANKS AND FINANCIAL INSTITUTIONS.
Trusts and trustees.
Tax savings, §19-1308.14.
Uniform trust code.
Modification to achieve settlor's tax objectives, §19-1304.16.
Verizon center sales tax, §47-2002.06.
Video services, §47-2501.01.
Waiver or abatement.
Abatement of unpaid taxes, §47-4222.
Reasonable cause for underpayment, §47-4221.
Washington Stock Exchange, §47-2504.

TAXATION —Cont'd
Water and Sewer Authority exemption from District taxation, §34-2202.20.
Water supply and waterworks.
Assessments for constructing mains and sewers, §§34-2405.01 to 34-2405.08.
Water supply and waterworks taxes.
Uniformity of taxes, §34-2401.07.

TAXATION WITHOUT REPRESENTATION.
Federal tax pay-out message board, §10-1701.
Flag of district, inclusion on, §1-152.

TAX COURT.
Appeals from, USCtApp HPIP Rule III(d).
Docketing of appeal, USCtApp HPIP Rule IV(a).
Review of decisions of, FRAP 13.
Applicability of other rules, FRAP 14.
Leave to proceed in forma pauperis, FRAP 24(b).
Notice of appeal, FRAP Form 2.

TAX DIVISION, SUPERIOR COURT.
See TAX PROCEEDINGS.

TAX ENFORCEMENT ACT OF 1982, §47-3410.

TAX EVASION.
Penalties, §47-4101.

TAXICABS, §§50-301.01 to 50-301.34.
Accessible taxicabs, §50-301.25.
Digital dispatch for individuals with disabilities, §50-301.25a.
Training of employees and operators, §50-301.25b.
Adams Morgan taxicab zone pilot program, §50-2536.
Blanket bond or blanket policy, §50-301.15.
Blind and visually impaired.
Digital dispatch for individuals with disabilities, §50-301.25a.
Bonds, surety, §50-301.15.
Business licenses, §47-2829.
Carsharing service, §§50-301.29a to 50-301.29g.
Citations, §50-332.
Complaints, §50-301.32.
Criminal offenses against drivers.
Enhanced penalties, §22-3751.
Offenses for which penalties apply, §22-3752.

TAXICABS —Cont'd
Deaf and hearing impaired.
Digital dispatch for individuals with
disabilities, §50-301.25a.
Definitions, §50-301.03.
Disabilities, persons with.
Accessible taxicabs, §50-301.25.
Digital dispatch for individuals with
disabilities, §50-301.25a.
Training of employees and operators,
§50-301.25b.
Dispatch services, §50-301.31.
**Dome light and taxicab smart meter
system installation businesses,**
§50-301.33.
Enforcement of laws, §50-332.
Equipment.
Dispatch services, §50-301.31.
Existing regulations, effect of,
§50-301.18.
Findings, §50-301.01.
**Fleeing from public vehicle
inspection officer,** §50-301.34.
For-hire vehicles department,
§§50-301.04 to 50-301.11.
Complaints, §50-301.32.
Director, §50-301.05.
Duties and powers of, §50-301.07.
Establishment of, §50-301.04.
Fingerprinting fund, §50-301.23.
For-hire vehicles advisory council,
§50-301.10a.
Hearing examiner.
Appointment, duties, appeals,
§50-301.09b.
Impoundment of vehicles, §50-331.
Internal rules, §50-301.10.
Jurisdiction of, §50-301.07.
Membership of, §50-301.05.
Organization of, §50-301.06.
Procedures, §50-301.10.
Regulation authority, §50-301.13.
Reports, §50-301.11.
Fuel-efficient taxicabs, §50-301.27.
Funds.
Fingerprinting fund, §50-301.23.
Public vehicles-for-hire consumer
service fund, §50-301.20.
Hack stands, §1-301.71.
Impoundment of vehicles, §50-331.
Inspection of vehicles.
Fleeing from public vehicle inspection
officer, §50-301.34.
Public vehicle inspection officer
training, §50-301.30.
Insurance, §50-301.14.

TAXICABS —Cont'd
Licenses, §50-301.19.
Loitering of public vehicles for hire,
§50-301.28.
Metered taxicabs, §50-381.
Dome light and taxicab smart meter
system installation businesses,
§50-301.33.
Modernization, §50-301.26.
Motor vehicle equipment.
Dome light and taxicab smart meter
system installation businesses,
§50-301.33.
Motor vehicle registration.
Public vehicle inspection officer
training, §50-301.30.
**No-fault motor vehicle insurance,
requirements waived for,**
§31-2411.
**Non-resident taxi and limousine
driver vehicle registration fee,**
§50-1501.03.
Policy declaration, §§50-301.01,
50-301.02.
Private vehicles-for-hire,
§§50-301.29a to 50-301.29g.
**Public vehicles-for-hire consumer
service fund.**
Establishment, §50-301.20.
**Public vehicles for hire exclusive of
taxicabs and limousines,**
§50-301.29.
Purposes, §50-301.02.
Rates and rate structures.
Guidelines for, §50-301.17.
Review of, §50-301.17.
Regulation authority, §50-301.13.
Reports.
Citations, §50-332.
For-hire vehicles department,
§50-301.11.
Ridesharing services.
Public vehicles for hire exclusive of
taxicabs and limousines,
§50-301.29.
Sinking funds, §50-301.15.
Stands, §1-301.71.

TAX INCREMENT FINANCING,
§§2-1217.01 to 2-1217.12.
Allocation of tax increments,
§2-1217.05.
**Approval of development project by
Council,** §2-1217.04.
Bond issues, §§2-1217.02, 2-1217.06.
Certification of development project,
§2-1217.03.

TAX INCREMENT FINANCING
—Cont'd
**City Market at O Street tax
increment financing,** §§2-1217.33a
to 2-1217.33m.
See CITY MARKET AT O STREET
TAX INCREMENT FINANCING.
Convention center hotel.
Creation of TIF area, §10-1221.04.
DC ballpark TIF area, §2-1217.12.
Default in payment on bonds,
§2-1217.08.
Definitions, §2-1217.01.
**Howard Theatre Redevelopment
Project TIF Area,** §§2-1217.34a to
2-1217.34n.
See HOWARD THEATRE
REDEVELOPMENT PROJECT
TIF AREA.
**H Street, N.E. retail priority area
incentive,** §§1-325.171 to 1-325.173.
Liability issues, §2-1217.10.
**National Capital Revitalization
Corporation,** §2-1217.11.
See NATIONAL CAPITAL
REVITALIZATION
CORPORATION.
Public inspection of bond order,
§2-1217.09.
Retail development incentives,
§§2-1217.71 to 2-1217.84.
See RETAIL DEVELOPMENT
INCENTIVES.
Security for bonds, §2-1217.07.
Skyland TIF area, §§2-1217.35a to
2-1217.35l.
See SKYLAND TIF AREA.
Southwest waterfront.
PILOT/TIF area, §47-4616.
**Southwest waterfront bond
financing,** §§2-1217.131 to
2-1217.151.
See SOUTHWEST WATERFRONT.
Transfer of authority regarding,
§2-1217.11.
Union Market District, §§2-1217.36a
to 2-1217.36d.

TAX PROCEEDINGS, §§47-3301 to
47-3310.
Answers, Tax Rule 7.
Replies, Tax Rule 8.
Applicable rules.
Civil proceedings, Tax Rule 3.
Criminal proceedings, Tax Rule 2.
Assessment appeals, §47-3303.
Burden of proof, Tax Rule 12.

TAX PROCEEDINGS —Cont'd
**Computations by parties for entry of
decision,** Tax Rule 14.
Conferences.
Failure to appear, Tax Rule 13.
Pretrial conferences, Tax Rule 11.
Status conferences, Tax Rule 10.
Definitions, §47-3301.
Exhibits, Tax Rule 12.
Filing of documents, Tax Rule 4.
Form and style of papers, Tax Rule 4.
Hearings, §47-3303.
Motions, Tax Rule 9.
Notice, §47-3308.
Overpayments, §47-3310.
Petitions, Tax Form 1, Tax Rule 6.
Fee for filing, Tax Rule 4.
Procedures, §47-3304.
Prohibited lawsuits, §47-3307.
Real property tax appeals, §47-3305.
Referral of cases by mayor, §47-3309.
Refunds.
Erroneously collected taxes, §47-3306.
Overpayments, §47-3310.
Representation, Tax Rule 3.
Retirement of judges, §47-3302.
Service of process, Tax Rule 5.
Petitions, Tax Rule 6.
Superior court jurisdiction,
§§11-1201 to 11-1203.
Trials, Tax Rule 12.
Failure to appear, Tax Rule 13.

TAX REFUNDS.
Alcoholic beverage taxes, §25-909.
Bankruptcy proceedings.
Refunds to debtors, USDistDCBank
Rule 6070-1.

TAX RETURN PREPARERS,
§47-4217.

TAX REVISION COMMISSION,
§§47-461 to 47-464.
Authority, §47-464.
Compensation and expenses, §47-463.
Composition, §47-463.
Director, §47-463.
Established, §47-462.
Findings, §47-461.
Functions, §47-462.
Quorum, §47-464.
Reports.
Submission of recommendations,
§47-462.
**Special fund established for receipt
of operating donations.**
Administration, §47-464.

TAX SALES.
Alcoholic beverage licenses.
Involuntary transfer of license, §25-361.

TAX-SHELTERED ANNUITIES.
Teachers' retirement, §38-2023.16.

TEACHERS, §§38-1901 to 38-1923.
Aeronautics, §38-921.
Americanization, evening, and summer schools, §38-1903.
Board of Education.
General provisions.
See BOARD OF EDUCATION.
Charter schools.
Employees of DC public schools accepting positions at, §38-1802.07.
Child abuse and neglect reports, §4-1321.02.
Child death.
Reports, §4-1371.12.
Clerks, employment as, §38-1901.
Family and medical leave, §32-506.
Federal credit union.
Real property tax exemptions, §47-1053.
Foreign exchange program, §§38-1921 to 38-1923.
Heads of department, §§38-109, 38-1908.
Head teachers, §38-109.
Higher education licensure commission, §§38-1301 to 38-1313.
Highly effective teacher incentive.
Expiration of subchapter, §38-753.05.
Rules, §38-756.01.
Housing finance and assistance.
Government employer-assisted housing program, §§42-2501 to 42-2507.
Income tax deductions, §47-1803.03.
Installment payments, §38-1902.
Interstate agreement on qualification of educational personnel, §§38-2101 to 38-2104.
Authority to enter into agreement, §38-2101.
Contents of agreement, §38-2101.
Contracts made on behalf of District pursuant to agreement.
Filing, §38-2103.
Governor defined, §38-2104.
Superintendent designated state official, §38-2102.
Investigations of, §38-111.
Librarians, employment as, §38-1901.

TEACHERS —Cont'd
Masculine pronoun to include both male and female, §38-112.
Parent-teacher conferences, §38-1809.01.
Pensions and retirement.
Fund, §§1-713, 1-903.02.
General provisions, §§38-2001.01 to 38-2041.01.
See TEACHERS' RETIREMENT.
Personnel files, §38-2802.
Political rights, §1-625.02.
Pre-kindergarten programs.
Teachers, workforce development.
Higher education incentive grant program, §38-274.01.
Higher education incentive scholarship award program, §38-274.02.
Preservation of school-based staff positions, §38-1807.57.
Qualification of educational personnel.
Interstate agreement on, §§38-2101 to 38-2104.
Reports.
Child death, §4-1371.12.
Research assistants classified as, §38-1906.
Retired teachers as substitutes, §38-1910.
Sex discrimination.
Masculine pronoun to include both male and female, §38-112.
Wages and salaries, §38-1901.
State Board of Education.
General provisions.
See BOARD OF EDUCATION.
State superintendent of education, office of.
Educator evaluations, §38-2615.
Substitutes, §§38-1909, 38-1910.
Testing integrity in public schools.
Sanctions for violations, §38-771.04.
Trials, §38-111.
Vacancies, §38-1904.
Vocational education, §38-1905.
Wages and salaries.
Foreign exchange program participants, §38-1922.
Installment payments, §38-1902.
Research assistants classified as teachers for purposes of, §38-1906.
Retirement, salary deductions for, §38-2001.01.
Sex discrimination, §38-1901.

TEACHERS COLLEGE.
Federal city college.
Board of higher education.
Assumption of control by, §38-1103.
Transfer of functions, personnel, etc., §38-1202.08.
University of the District of Columbia.
Attendance by foreign students, §38-161.
Board of trustees.
Transfer of functions, personnel, etc., to, §38-1202.08.
College reorganized into University of the District of Columbia, §38-1201.02.
Successor institution, §§38-1201.01 to 38-1207.07.
See UNIVERSITY OF THE DISTRICT OF COLUMBIA.
Tuition charged students, §38-305.

TEACHERS' RETIREMENT, §§38-2001.01 to 38-2041.01.
After June 30, 1946, §§38-2021.01 to 38-2023.16.
Age at retirement, §38-2021.03.
Annuities, §§38-2021.01 to 38-2023.16.
Applicability of provisions, §38-2021.18.
Assignment of funds, §38-2021.17.
Computation of annuity, §§38-2021.05 to 38-2021.08, 38-2021.21 to 38-2023.01.
Internal Revenue Code limits, §38-2021.27.
Credited service requirements, §§38-2021.01a, 38-2021.03, 38-2061.02.
Purchase of service credits, §38-2021.26.
Death of teacher, §§38-2021.09, 38-2021.10, 38-2021.23, 38-2023.02.
Deferred annuity, §38-2021.09.
Deposit of deductions, §38-2021.01.
Disability retirement, §§38-2021.04, 38-2021.06.
Distributions.
Minimum distributions, required, §38-2021.07a.
Effective date of annuities, §38-2023.03.
Employment of retired teachers, §38-2061.01.
Excessing or other involuntary separation, §38-2021.03.

TEACHERS' RETIREMENT —Cont'd
After June 30, 1946 —Cont'd
Forfeitures.
Disposition, §38-2021.15a.
Fund, §38-2021.02.
Increase in annuity, §§38-2021.23, 38-2023.01, 38-2023.04, 38-2023.12, 38-2023.13.
Effective date, §38-2023.03.
Interest computations, §38-2023.14.
Involuntary retirement, §38-2021.03.
Price index adjustments, §38-2021.21.
Recomputation of annuity, §§38-2021.19, 38-2023.11.
Rollovers, §38-2021.26.
Salary deductions, §§38-2021.01, 38-2021.11.
Tax-sheltered annuity program, §38-2023.16.
Termination of employment, §§38-2021.09, 38-2021.12.
Unmarried widows or widowers, annuity for, §38-2023.02.
Unpaid leave, credit for, §§38-2021.01a, 38-2061.02.
Vesting, §38-2021.03.
Voluntary retirement, §38-2021.03.
Waiver or revocation of annuity, §38-2023.15.
Attachment.
Retirement of public school teachers.
Funds not subject to garnishment.
Retirement after June 30, 1946, §38-2021.17.
Denial of claim for benefits.
Procedure, §§1-751 to 1-753.
Employment of retired teachers, §§38-1910, 38-2061.01.
Execution.
Retirement of public school teachers.
Funds not subject to garnishment.
Retirement after June 30, 1946, §38-2021.17.
Garnishment.
Retirement of public school teachers.
Funds not subject to garnishment.
Retirement after June 30, 1946, §38-2021.17.
Retirement before June 30, 1946, §38-2001.17.
Incentive program, §38-2041.01.
Maximum benefit computations, §38-2021.27.
Prior to June 30, 1946.
Age of retirement, §38-2001.03.
Annuities, §§38-2001.01, 38-2001.05, 38-2001.18, 38-2001.19.

TEACHERS' RETIREMENT —Cont'd
Prior to June 30, 1946 —Cont'd
Appropriations, §38-2001.07.
Assignment, funds not subject to, §38-2001.17.
Credited service requirements, §§38-2001.03, 38-2001.06, 38-2001.08.
Death of teacher, §§38-2001.10, 38-2001.10a.
Deposit of amounts in United States Treasury, §38-2001.02.
Disability retirement, §§38-2001.04 to 38-2001.06.
Issuance of rules and regulations, §38-2001.16.
Records, §38-2001.14.
Refund of deductions, §38-2001.09.
Salary deductions for, §§38-2001.01, 38-2001.11.
Termination of employment, §38-2001.12.
Substitute teachers, retired teachers as, §38-1910.

TECHNOLOGY FUND.
Council technology projects fund, §1-325.201.
Schools technology fund, §1-325.251.

TECHNOLOGY SUPPORT SERVICES.
Citywide technology support services, §§1-1431 to 1-1433.
DC One Card, §§1-327.71 to 1-327.73.

TEENAGE PREGNANCY.
Public assistance.
Pregnant or parenting teens, §§4-205.61 to 4-205.66.
Teen pregnancy prevention fund, §§1-325.321 to 1-325.326.
Authorization for grant-managing entity, §1-325.325.
Definitions, §1-325.321.
Duplicative projects, §1-325.326.
Established, §1-325.322.
Reporting requirements, §1-325.324.
Required information before approval, §1-325.323.

TELECOMMUNICATIONS.
Assistive technology device warranty, §§28-4031 to 28-4034.
Compensating-use tax, §§47-2201 to 47-2214.
See COMPENSATING-USE TAX.
Competition, §§34-2001 to 34-2008.
See TELECOMMUNICATIONS COMPETITION.

TELECOMMUNICATIONS —Cont'd
Emergency and non-emergency telephone system assessments fund, §§34-1801 to 34-1806.
Inaugural ceremonies of the President of the United States, §2-826.
Interception of, §§23-541 to 23-556.
See INTERCEPTION OF ORAL OR WIRE COMMUNICATIONS.
Internet-related telecommunications franchise agreement.
Furnishing services to digitally-disadvantaged residents, §§34-1731.01 to 34-1731.11.
See INTERNET.
911 systems.
Emergency and non-emergency telephone system assessments fund, §§34-1801 to 34-1806.
Office of unified communications, §§1-327.51 to 1-327.57.
Pay telephone service providers.
Public service commission.
Rules and regulations, power to prescribe, §34-1831.
Prisoner phone calls.
Operator assisted calls.
Fair charges, §§24-263.01 to 24-263.04.
Telecommunications companies.
General provisions, §§34-1701 to 34-2008.
See TELECOMMUNICATIONS COMPANIES.
Toll telecommunication service tax, §§47-3901 to 47-3922.
See TOLL TELECOMMUNICATION SERVICE TAX.
Voice over Internet Protocol.
Emergency and non-emergency number telephone calling systems assessments, §34-1803.
Wireless network antennae franchise agreement.
Internet-related telecommunications.
Furnishing services to digitally-disadvantaged residents, §§34-1731.01 to 34-1731.11.
See INTERNET.

TELECOMMUNICATIONS COMPANIES, §§34-1701 to 34-2008.
Automated telephone dialing system ban, §34-1701.

TELECOMMUNICATIONS COMPANIES —Cont'd

Competition, §§34-2001 to 34-2008.
See TELECOMMUNICATIONS COMPETITION.

Condemnation proceedings, §34-1921.08.

Conduits.
Condemnation proceedings, §34-1921.08.
Ducts for fire and police wires, §34-1911.05.
Extensions, §§34-1911.01, 34-1921.01.
Inspection requirements, §§34-1911.05, 34-1921.05.
Plans of, §§34-1911.02, 34-1921.02.
Poles to eventually be replaced by, §34-1911.04.
Public parks or reservations, in, §34-1921.04a.

Definitions, §§34-201 to 34-221.

Ducts for fire and police wires, §34-1911.05.

Emergency and non-emergency telephone system assessments fund, §§34-1801 to 34-1806.

Extensions.
Conduits, §§34-1911.01, 34-1921.01.
Overhead wires, §34-1901.01.

Fines, §§34-1911.03, 34-1921.03.

Gross sales tax.
Exempt sales, §47-2005.

Inspection requirements, §§34-1911.05, 34-1921.05.

Mayor's powers and duties regarding, §§34-1911.01, 34-1921.01.

Overhead lines.
Inspection requirements, §34-1911.05.

Overhead wires.
Additional wiring, §34-1901.01.
Extensions, §34-1901.01.
Inspection requirements, §§34-1911.05, 34-1921.05.
Removal of, §§34-1911.01, 34-1921.01.
Repairs and renewals, §§34-1911.06, 34-1921.06.

Pay telephone service providers.
Public service commission.
Rules and regulations, power to prescribe, §34-1831.

Penalties, §§34-1911.03, 34-1921.03.

Permit requirements, §34-1911.02.

Poles.
Alleys, in, §§34-1911.04, 34-1921.04.
Conduits, to eventually be replaced by, §§34-1911.04, 34-1921.04.

TELECOMMUNICATIONS COMPANIES —Cont'd

Poles —Cont'd
Erection and maintenance of, §34-1911.04.
Removal of, §§34-1911.01, 34-1911.02, 34-1921.01, 34-1921.02.
Repairs and renewals, §§34-1911.04, 34-1911.06, 34-1921.06.

Prisoner phone calls.
Operator assisted calls.
Fair charges, §§24-263.01 to 24-263.04.

Public service commission.
See PUBLIC SERVICE COMMISSION.

Right to alter, amend or repeal rules regarding, §§34-1911.07, 34-1921.07.

Taxation, §47-2501.

Toll telecommunication service tax, §§47-3901 to 47-3922.
See TOLL TELECOMMUNICATION SERVICE TAX.

TELECOMMUNICATIONS COMPETITION, §§34-2001 to 34-2008.

Access.
Public ways, §34-2004.

Actions, §34-2003.01.

Alternative regulation or forbearance of regulation.
Petition, plan, approval, §34-2002.

Definitions, §34-2001.

Exemptions to applicability of rules, §34-2006.

Implementation of rules, §34-2008.

Local exchange carriers (LECs).
Defined, §34-2001.
Regulation of, §34-2002.
Taxation of, §34-2007.

Public ways.
Access to, §34-2004.
Defined, §34-2001.

State of business operations.
Filing, exemption from certificate of public convenience and necessity requirement, §34-2002.

Tariffs.
Filing and maintaining, LECs and competitive service providers, §34-2002.

Universal services.
Defined, §34-2001.
Trust Fund, §34-2003.

VoIP act, study and report of effect on consumers, §34-2008.

TELEHEALTH REIMBURSEMENT,
§§31-3861 to 31-3863.
Definitions, §31-3861.

TELEPHONE AND TELEGRAPH COMPANIES.
See TELECOMMUNICATIONS COMPANIES.

TELEPHONES.
Coin telephones.
Breaking and entering, §22-601.
Debt collection practices.
Time for making telephone calls, §28-3814.
Depositions by telephone.
Adoption proceedings, Adoption Rule 30.
Domestic relations actions, DomRel Rule 30.
Fraud prevention.
Telephone solicitation, §§22-3226.01 to 22-3226.15.
Hearing aid dealers.
Telephone sales.
Written permission of buyer required, §28-4004.
Pleadings.
Parties' telephone numbers required, CivPro Rule 10-I.
Adoption proceedings, Adoption Rule 11.
Small claims court, SmallClaims Rule 3.
Signer's telephone number required, CivPro Rule 11.
Pretrial conferences.
Domestic relations actions, DomRel Rule 16-I.
Sales by telephone.
Hearing aid dealers.
Written permission of buyer required, §28-4004.

TELEPHONE SOLICITATION,
§§22-3226.01 to 22-3226.15.
Abusive acts, §22-3226.08.
Actions for damages, §22-3226.11.
Bonds, surety required, §22-3226.03.
Security in lieu of bond, §22-3226.04.
Certificate of registration.
Application, §22-3226.02.
Required, §22-3226.02.
Compensation for making charitable solicitations prohibited, §44-1708.
Criminal penalties, §22-3226.10.
Deceptive acts, §22-3226.07.
Definitions, §22-3226.01.

TELEPHONE SOLICITATION
—Cont'd
Disclosures required, §22-3226.15.
Exemptions from bond and registration, §22-3226.05.
Fines and civil penalties, §22-3226.09.
Fraud prevention fund, §22-3226.14.
Limitation of actions, §22-3226.12.
Private right of action, §22-3226.11.
Security in lieu of bond, §22-3226.04.
Targeting elderly or aged persons, §22-3226.09.
Task force to combat fraud, §22-3226.13.
Unlawful acts, §22-3226.06.

TELEVISION.
Broadcasting industry employment contracts, §§32-531 to 32-533.
Cable television.
General provisions, §§34-1251.01 to 34-1264.06.
See CABLE TELEVISION.
Electronic waste, §§8-1041.01 to 8-1041.12.
See ELECTRONIC WASTE.
News media privilege, §§16-4701 to 16-4704.
Production permits, §2-1204.11d.
Superior court proceedings, media coverage of, CivPro Rule 203, CrimPro Rule 53.
Child abuse and neglect proceedings, NeglectProc Rule 45.
Juvenile proceedings, JuvProc Rule 53.
Taxation, §47-2501.01.
United States District Court proceedings.
Broadcasting in the courthouse, USDistCt LCrR 53.1.1, USDistCt LCvR 83.1.

TELLER'S CHECKS.
Defined, §28:3-104.
Refusal to pay, §28:3-411.

TEMPORARY ASSISTANCE FOR NEEDY FAMILIES (TANF).
Aliens, §4-205.24.
Amounts under $10, §4-205.51.
Application for, §4-205.19.
Child care facilities, §§4-401 to 4-415.
See CHILD CARE FACILITIES.
Child's eligibility for, §4-205.18.
Child support rights of persons receiving public assistance assigned to District, §4-205.19.
Comparative review procedures, §4-205.51a.

TEMPORARY ASSISTANCE FOR NEEDY FAMILIES (TANF)
—Cont'd
Cooperation requirements, §§4-217.07 to 4-217.11.
Crisis management, §§4-203.01 to 4-203.04.
Custodial relatives other than parents, §4-205.23.
Deemed parent income, consideration of, §4-205.22.
Discrimination prohibition, §4-205.19i.
Displacement of workers, prohibition of, §4-205.19l.
District of Columbia housing authority.
General provisions, §§6-201 to 6-229.
See DISTRICT OF COLUMBIA HOUSING AUTHORITY.
Section eight housing, §§42-3503.01 to 42-3503.08.
District of Columbia medical assistance program, §§1-307.02 to 1-307.06.
Drug felons, §4-205.71.
Earned income credit information, providing, §4-205.82.
Establishment of, §4-202.01.
Exemptions to rules regarding, §4-205.19g.
Failure to comply with requirements.
Job readiness requirements, §4-205.19c.
Job search requirements, §4-205.19c.
Penalties, §4-205.19f.
Work participation requirements, §4-205.19e.
Family assessment plan, §4-205.19n.
Foster care, §§4-217.01 to 4-217.11.
See FOSTER CARE.
Grandparent caregiver subsidies, §§4-251.01 to 4-251.07.
Amount of subsidy, §4-251.04.
Construction of provisions, §4-251.07.
Definitions, §4-251.01.
Eligibility, §4-251.03.
Establishment of pilot program, §4-251.02.
Godparents.
Transfer of subsidy, §4-251.03a.
Recertification of eligibility, §4-251.03.
Relative caregivers.
Transfer of subsidy, §4-251.03a.
Reports, §4-251.05.

TEMPORARY ASSISTANCE FOR NEEDY FAMILIES (TANF)
—Cont'd
Grandparent caregiver subsidies
—Cont'd
Rules issuance by mayor, §4-251.06.
Termination of payments, §4-251.03.
Transfer of subsidy, §4-251.03a.
Waiver of eligibility requirements, §4-251.03.
Health and safety standards, §4-205.19j.
Home living requirement for pregnant or parenting teens, §§4-205.61 to 4-205.66.
Impact of reductions, §4-205.11c.
Income eligibility standards, §4-205.10.
Redetermination, §4-205.19a.
Job readiness assistance, §4-205.50.
Job search and job readiness programs, §4-205.19h.
Job search assistance, §4-205.50.
Job search requirements, §§4-205.19b, 4-205.19c.
Local programs in Virginia and Maryland.
Adjustment of amounts to compare to, §4-205.51a.
Medicaid.
General provisions.
See MEDICAID.
Medicare.
Medicare supplement insurance, §§31-3701 to 31-3710.
See MEDICARE SUPPLEMENT INSURANCE.
Need determinations, §4-205.11.
Overnight shelter.
See HOMELESS SERVICES.
Parents and parentage, locating and identifying, §§4-217.07 to 4-217.11.
Payment for work activity, treatment of, §4-205.13a.
Persons included in assistance unit, §4-205.15.
Pregnant or parenting teens, §§4-205.61 to 4-205.66.
Pregnant women, §4-205.43.
Prison, children with parents in, §4-205.20.
Privacy and confidentiality of applicant information, §4-209.04.
Program on work, employment, and responsibility (POWER) eligibility of recipients of, §4-205.73.

TEMPORARY ASSISTANCE FOR NEEDY FAMILIES (TANF)
—Cont'd
Prospective determination of eligibility, §4-205.25.
Public assistance.
Emergency assistance.
See EMERGENCY PUBLIC ASSISTANCE.
General provisions, §§4-201.01 to 4-221.01.
See PUBLIC ASSISTANCE.
Public Welfare, Board of.
General provisions, §§4-105 to 4-126.
See PUBLIC WELFARE, BOARD OF.
Redetermination of eligibility, §4-205.19a.
Reduction in benefits for long-term recipients, §§4-205.11b, 4-205.11c.
Relative caregiver subsidies, §§4-251.01 to 4-251.07.
Reports, §§4-205.19m, 4-205.54.
Schools and education.
TANF fund sharing, §38-2931.
Section eight housing, §§42-3503.01 to 42-3503.08.
Self-sufficiency and work programs, §4-205.19h.
Stepparent income, consideration of, §4-205.22.
Supplemental nutrition assistance program (SNAP), §§4-261.21 to 4-261.23.
Reports, §4-261.23.
Simplified self-employment deduction, §4-261.22.
Transitional benefits, §4-261.21.
Support payments, §4-205.19.
Teenage parents, §§4-205.61 to 4-205.66.
Time limit on receipt of benefits under, §4-205.11a.
Training and employment costs and expenses, §4-205.50.
Unemployed parents, §4-205.21.
Unemployment compensation.
General provisions, §§51-101 to 51-151.
See UNEMPLOYMENT COMPENSATION.
Universal service delivery model, §4-205.51b.
Workers' compensation, §4-205.19k.
Work incentive allowances, §4-205.36.
Work participation assistance, §4-205.50.

TEMPORARY ASSISTANCE FOR NEEDY FAMILIES (TANF)
—Cont'd
Work participation requirements, §§4-205.19d, 4-205.19e.

TENANT ADVOCATE, OFFICE OF, §§42-3531.01 to 42-3531.10.
See OFFICE OF TENANT ADVOCATE.

TENANT ASSISTANCE PROGRAM, §§42-3503.01 to 42-3503.08.
See LANDLORD AND TENANT.

TENANT ORGANIZATIONS, §42-3505.06.
Home purchase assistance fund, §42-2604.
Rental housing conversion and sale.
Five or more units, accommodations with.
Registration of a tenant organization, §42-3404.02a.
Right to assert claim on behalf of members, §42-3502.16a.

TENANTS BY THE ENTIRETY.
Domestic partnerships, §§42-516, 46-601.
Estates in land, §42-516.
Horizontal property regimes, §42-2005.
Simultaneous deaths, §19-503.

TENANTS IN COMMON.
Ejectment, §16-1101.
Estates in land, §42-516.
Horizontal property regimes, §42-2005.
Partition.
See PARTITION.
Waste of real property, §42-1604.

TENDER, LEGAL, US Const Art I §10.

TENURE.
Judges, §§11-1502, 11-1521 to 11-1530.

TERMINALLY ILL.
Brain death, §§7-601 to 7-630.
Hospice program, §§4-1101 to 4-1105.
Living wills, §§7-621 to 7-630.
See LIVING WILLS.

TERMINATION OF EMPLOYMENT.
Attachment and garnishment of wages.
Deliberate termination due to, §16-584.
Lapse or dismissal on termination, §16-576.
Child support withholding, §46-216.

TERMINATION OF EMPLOYMENT
—Cont'd
Payment of wages upon, §32-1303.
Public officers and employees.
Reductions in force, §§1-624.01 to
1-624.24.
See MERIT SYSTEM.
Teachers' retirement.
After June 30, 1946, §§38-2021.09,
38-2021.12.
Prior to June 30, 1946, §38-2001.12.

**TERMINATION OF PARENTAL
RIGHTS,** §§16-2351 to 16-2365.
Adjudicatory hearings, §16-2359,
NeglectProc Rule 38.
Appeal of grant or denial of petition.
Expedited review in court of appeals,
§11-721.
Attorneys at law.
Appointment of counsel, §16-2304,
NeglectProc Rule 12.
Compensation of appointed counsel,
§16-2326.01, NeglectProc Rule 42.
Attorneys' fees and costs,
§16-2326.01, NeglectProc Rule 42.
**Best interests of child, for reasons
of,** §16-2353.
Child custody.
Uniform child custody proceedings,
§§16-4601.01 to 16-4605.03.
See CHILD CUSTODY AND CHILD
CUSTODY PROCEEDINGS.
Definitions, §16-2352.
Disclosure, §16-2364.
Disposition of child after, §16-2360.
Effect of decree, §16-2361.
**Family homes, placement of
children in,** §4-1406.
Hearings.
Adjudicatory, §16-2359, NeglectProc
Rule 38.
Conduct of, §16-2358.
Interpretation of provisions,
§16-2351.
Judgments and decrees, §§16-2361,
16-2362.
Motion for, §16-2354, NeglectProc
Rules 35, 36.
Notice of proceedings, §16-2357.
**Out-of-state jurisdictions, decrees
by,** §16-2365.
Parties to proceedings, §16-2356.
Policy declaration, §16-2351.
Privacy and confidentiality,
§§16-2363, 16-2364.
Reasons for, §16-2353.

**TERMINATION OF PARENTAL
RIGHTS** —Cont'd
Records, §§16-2363, 16-2364.
Review hearings, NeglectProc Rule 39.
Consideration of termination,
§16-2355.
Service of motion, NeglectProc Rule
36.
Status conference, NeglectProc Rule
37.

TERRITORIES.
Constitution of the United States,
US Const Art IV §3.

TERRORISM.
Alien terrorist removal court.
Appeals from, USCtApp Rule 47.6.
Anti-terrorism act of 2002, §§22-3151
to 22-3156.
Appeals in federal cases.
Alien terrorist removal court, appeals
from, USCtApp Rule 47.6.
Definitions, §22-3152.
Hazardous materials transportation,
§§8-1421 to 8-1426.
Jurisdiction and venue to prosecute,
§22-3156.
Penalties, acts of terrorism, §22-3153.
**Prosecution for first or second
degree murder constituting act
of terrorism.**
Commenced at any time, §23-113.
**Response plan or vulnerability
assessment.**
Freedom of information exemption,
§2-534.
Weapons of mass destruction.
Defined, §22-3152.
Manufacture or possession, §22-3154.
Public health emergency executive
order, §7-2304.01.
Use, dissemination, detonation,
§22-3155.

TEST ANSWER AND QUESTION.
**Freedom of information act
exemptions,** §2-534.

**TESTING INTEGRITY IN PUBLIC
SCHOOLS,** §§38-771.01 to
38-771.07.
Alteration of responses.
Authorized personnel, prohibited acts,
§38-771.03.
Assisting students with answers.
Authorized personnel, prohibited acts,
§38-771.03.

TESTING INTEGRITY IN PUBLIC SCHOOLS —Cont'd

Authorized personnel.
Defined, §38-771.01.
Responsibilities, §38-771.03.

Cell phones.
Authorized personnel, prohibited acts, §38-771.03.

Definitions, §38-771.01.

Districtwide assessments.
Defined, §38-771.01.
LEA administration, §38-771.02.

Electronic devices.
Authorized personnel, prohibited acts, §38-771.03.

Photocopying test materials.
Authorized personnel, prohibited acts, §38-771.03.

Practice testing with secure materials.
Authorized personnel, prohibited acts, §38-771.03.

Rulemaking to implement provisions, §38-771.06.

Sanctions for violations, §38-771.04.
Administrative review, §38-771.05.
Due process, §38-771.07.

State superintendent of education, office of.
Definition of OSSE, §38-771.01.
Duties and responsibilities of office, §38-2602.

Unapproved electronic devices.
Authorized personnel, prohibited acts, §38-771.03.

TETANUS.
Immunization of school students, §§38-501 to 38-508.
Interstate compact on educational opportunity for military children.
Time to obtain immunizations, §49-1101.05.

TEXTBOOKS, §§38-701 to 38-706, 38-922.
Free textbooks.
Limitation on purchases, §38-704.

THANKSGIVING DAY.
Appeals in federal cases, FRAP 26(a), 45(a).
Designated holiday, §§1-612.02, 28-2701.
Extension of time for performing acts, §28-2701.

THEATRE DOWNTOWN, INC.
Property tax exemption, §47-1074.

THEATRICAL PERFORMANCES.
Alcoholic beverage licenses.
Nudity.
Exception to license restrictions for legitimate theater, §25-372.
Business licenses, §47-2820.
Child labor, §32-206.
Children and minors attending, §47-2820.
Nudity.
Alcoholic beverage licenses.
Exception to license restrictions for legitimate theater, §25-372.
Police and firefighters assigned to theaters, §47-2820.

THEFT, §§22-3211 to 22-3216.
Aged persons, offenses committed against.
Enhanced penalties, §22-3601.
Aggregate amounts received determining grade of offense, §22-3202.
Audiovisual works, §§22-3214.01, 22-3214.02.
Burglary, §22-801.
Cable television.
Cable theft, §34-1264.02.
Commercial piracy, §22-3214.
Consecutive sentences, §22-3203.
Criminal trespass, via, §§22-3301 to 22-3311.
See VANDALISM.
Deceptive labeling of sound recordings or audiovisual works, §22-3214.01.
Definitions, §§22-3201, 22-3211.
Documents of title.
Stolen records, §28:7-601.
Fencing stolen property, §§22-3231, 22-3232.
Fines, §22-3212.
Grade of offense, aggregate amounts received determining, §22-3202.
Implements of crime, possession of, §22-2501.
Investment securities.
Notification to issuer of wrongfully taken security certificate, §28:8-406.
Replacement of wrongfully taken security certificate, §28:8-405.
Motion pictures, §§22-3214.01, 22-3214.02.
Motor vehicle identification numbers.
Altering or removing, §22-3233.

THEFT —Cont'd
Motor vehicles.
  Metropolitan police.
    Motor vehicle theft prevention
      teams, §5-133.21.
  Theft prevention commission, §§3-1351
    to 3-1358.
    Definitions, §3-1351.
    Established, §3-1352.
    Financial statement and report,
      §3-1355.
    Members, §3-1353.
    Powers, §3-1354.
    Purpose, §3-1352.
    Use of budget authority, §3-1358.
  Unauthorized use of, §22-3215.
Multijurisdictional cases.
  Referral to other law enforcement
    agency, §22-3204.
Music piracy, §§22-3214 to 22-3214.02.
Penalties, §22-3212.
  Aged persons, offenses committed
    against.
    Enhanced penalties, §22-3601.
Prohibited acts, §22-3211.
Proprietary information, piracy of,
  §22-3214.
Robbery, §§22-2801 to 22-2803.
  See ROBBERY.
Shoplifting, §§22-3213, 27-101 to
  27-106.
  See SHOPLIFTING.
Sound recordings, §§22-3214 to
  22-3214.02.
Stolen property.
  Defined, §22-3201.
  Receiving, §22-3232.
  Trafficking in, §22-3231.
Taking property without right,
  §22-3216.
Trust, mortgage and title
  corporations, misappropriation
  of moneys from, §26-1320.
Utility service, §§22-3218.01 to
  22-3218.04.
  Definitions, §22-3218.01.
  Penalties, §22-3218.04.
  Presumption and rebuttal evidence,
    §22-3218.03.
  Unlawful acts, §22-3218.02.
Wage theft prevention fund,
  §32-1307.01.

THEODORE ROOSEVELT ISLAND,
  §§10-158 to 10-161.

THIRD PARTIES.
Business license inspections,
  §47-2851.16.

THIRD PARTIES —Cont'd
Captive insurance companies.
  Special purpose financial captive
    insurance companies.
    Contested case by a third party,
      §31-3932.14.
Check drawn by fiduciary payable
  to third person, §21-1704.
Child custody.
  Third-party custody, §§16-831.01 to
    16-831.13.
    See CHILD CUSTODY AND CHILD
      CUSTODY PROCEEDINGS.
Insurers rehabilitation and
  liquidation proceedings,
  §31-1336.
Mental health disclosures to payors,
  §7-1202.07.
Merit system disability
  compensation adjustment after
  recovery from, §1-623.32.
Pandering, procuring, or pimping
  for third persons, §22-2711.
Police and firefighters medical care
  reimbursement rights, §5-602.
Rental housing conversion and sale,
  §42-3404.04.
Sale of goods, UCC.
  Warranties.
    Third party beneficiaries, §28:2-318.
  Who can sue third parties for injury to
    goods, §28:2-722.
Secured transactions.
  Rights of third parties, §§28:9-401 to
    28:9-409.
  See SECURED TRANSACTIONS.
Transfers to minors.
  Claims by third persons to custodial
    property, §21-317.
  Exemption of third persons from
    liability, §21-316.
  Liability to third persons, §21-317.
  Third persons assisting with, §21-316.
Workers' compensation liability,
  §32-1535.

THIRD PARTY PRACTICE, CivPro
  Rule 14.
Default judgments applicable, CivPro
  Rule 55.
Dismissal of actions, CivPro Rule 41.
Joinder of claims and remedies,
  CivPro Rule 18.
Motion to bring in third party,
  CivPro Form CA 22-B.
Summons and complaint against
  third party defendant, CivPro
  Form CA 22-A.

INDEX

THIRTEENTH CHURCH OF CHRIST.
Tax exemption, §47-4644.

THREATS.
Assault, §22-404.
Bodily harm, §22-407.
Common-law assault, §§22-404, 22-3312.02.
Creditors and debt collectors, §28-3814.
Due process, deprivation of, §§22-3312.02 to 22-3312.04.
Extortion, threats of kidnapping, injury, or damage to property for purposes of, §22-1810.
Gangs, §22-951.
Sexual offenses, §§22-3002 to 22-3005.
Unlawful trade practices, §28-3904.

THREE-CARD MONTE, §22-1706.

THREE-STRIKES RULE.
Felony convictions, §22-1804a.

THROWING STONES OR OTHER MISSILES, §22-1309.

TIBETAN COMMUNITY PROPERTY.
Real property tax exemptions, §47-4661.

TICKS.
Vector-borne disease control, §§8-2131.01 to 8-2131.09.
See VECTOR-BORNE DISEASE CONTROL.

TIDAL BASIN (POTOMAC PARK), §§10-147 to 10-151.

TIF.
See TAX INCREMENT FINANCING.

TIME.
Administrative search warrants.
Execution of warrants, CivPro Rule 204.
Adoption.
Periods of time contained in rules, Adoption Rule 6.
Revocation of consent or relinquishment, Adoption Rule 70.
Appeals.
Administrative orders and decisions, DCCtApp Rule 17.
Applications for appeal, DCCtApp Rules 5, 6.
Brief filing, DCCtApp Rule 31.
Docketing of appeal, DCCtApp Rule 12.

TIME —Cont'd
Appeals —Cont'd
Hearing commissioner orders and judgments, CivPro Rule 73, CrimPro Rule 117.
Notice of appeal filed, DCCtApp Rule 4.
Oral argument, DCCtApp Rule 34.
Petitions for rehearing, DCCtApp Rule 35.
Record on appeal, DCCtApp Rule 10.
Review of administrative orders and decisions, DCCtApp Rule 17.
Transmission of record, DCCtApp Rule 11.
Arbitration.
Discovery, Arbitration Rule VII.
Hearings, Arbitration Rule IX.
Modification or correction of award, Arbitration Rule XIII.
Objections, Arbitration Rule XII.
Trial de novo, Arbitration Rule XI.
Attachment.
Post-judgment attachment issues, CivPro Rule 69-I.
Pre-judgment attachment issues, CivPro Rule 64-I.
Brief filing, DCCtApp Rule 31.
Child abuse and neglect proceedings.
Disposition hearings, NeglectProc Rule 20.
Factfinding hearings, NeglectProc Rule 19.
Initial appearance, NeglectProc Rule 5.
Motions, NeglectProc Rule 43.
Petition.
Time for filing, NeglectProc Rule 9.
Shelter care hearing, NeglectProc Rule 8.
Computation of time, CivPro Rule 6.
Appeals, DCCtApp Rule 26.
Civil cases, CivPro Rule 6.
Criminal procedure, CrimPro Rule 45.
Delinquent minors, JuvProc Rule 45.
Domestic relations actions, DomRel Rule 6.
Hospitalization of persons with mental illness, MentalHealth Rule 13.
Intellectual disability proceedings, MentalRetardation Rule 8C.
Crime victims' compensation.
Appeal of determination, VictComp Rule 20.
Criminal procedure, CrimPro Rule 45.
Alibi notice, CrimPro Rule 12.1.

TIME —Cont'd

Criminal procedure —Cont'd

Arrest of judgment, CrimPro Rule 34.

Motions filing, CrimPro Rule 47-I.

Preliminary examination of defendant, CrimPro Rules 5, 110.

Probation revocation hearings, CrimPro Rule 32.1.

Sealing arrest records, CrimPro Rule 118.

Daylight-saving time, §28-2711.

Default judgments.

Entry of judgment, CivPro Rule 55.

Delinquent minors.

Computation of time, JuvProc Rule 45.

Transfer for criminal prosecution.

Time to conduct transfer hearing and enter order, JuvProc Rule 108.

Discovery, CivPro Rule 26, USDistCt LCvR 26.2.

Arbitration, Arbitration Rule VII.

Depositions, CivPro Rule 26, USDistCt LCvR 26.2.

Domestic relations actions, DomRel Rule 26.

Dismissal of actions, CivPro Rule 41.

Domestic relations actions.

Amended or supplemental pleadings, DomRel Rule 15.

Amendment of judgment, DomRel Rule 59.

Computation or extension of time, DomRel Rule 6.

Defenses and objections, DomRel Rule 12.

New trial motions, DomRel Rule 59.

Offer of judgment, DomRel Rule 68.

Pleading time issues, DomRel Rule 9.

Extension of time, CivPro Rule 6, CrimPro Rule 45.

Appeals, DCCtApp Rule 26.

Domestic relations actions, DomRel Rule 6.

Hospitalization of persons with mental illness, MentalHealth Rule 13.

Fiduciaries.

Accounts and reports, CivPro Rule 305.

Grand juries.

Time for action to be undertaken by, §23-102.

Hearing commissioner proceedings.

Appeal of orders and judgments, CivPro Rule 73, CrimPro Rule 117.

TIME —Cont'd

Holidays.

Extension of time for performing acts, §28-2701.

Intellectual disabilities, persons with.

Filing reports for commitment.

Individuals who are not competent to refuse commitment, MentalRetardation Rule 4A.

Respondents found incompetent to participate in criminal proceedings, MentalRetardation Rule 4B.

Periodic review of commitment orders, MentalRetardation Rule 7.

Judge's bias or prejudice.

Filing affidavit, CivPro Rule 63-I.

Probate proceedings, Probate Rule 126.

Judgments and decrees.

Arrest of judgment, CrimPro Rule 34.

Motion to amend judgment, CivPro Rule 59.

Domestic relations actions, DomRel Rule 59.

Jury instructions, CivPro Rule 51.

Landlord and tenant court.

Sessions, trials, hearings, etc., LandlordTenant Rule 7.

Motion hearings, LandlordTenant Rule 13.

Postponing trial because of attorney's schedule, LandlordTenant Rule 8.

Mental illness, persons with.

Hospitalization.

Court hearings on commission reports, MentalHealth Rule 4.

Merit system.

Review of agency decision, CivPro Agency Review Rule 1.

Motions practice, CivPro Rule 12-I.

New trial motions, CivPro Rule 59.

Criminal procedure, CrimPro Rule 33.

Domestic relations actions, DomRel Rule 59.

Juvenile proceedings, JuvProc Rule 33.

Offer of judgment, CivPro Rule 68.

Domestic relations actions, DomRel Rule 68.

Pleadings.

Defenses, CivPro Rule 12.

Domestic relations actions, DomRel Rule 12.

Special matters, CivPro Rule 9.

Domestic relations actions, DomRel Rule 9.

TIME —Cont'd
Post-conviction relief.
Superior court proceedings.
Time for appeal, PostConvRel Rule
11.
Probation revocation hearings,
CrimPro Rule 32.1.
Sealing of records.
Criminal procedure, CrimPro Rule
118.
Delinquent minors, FamDiv Rule P,
JuvProc Rule 118.
Family court proceedings generally,
FamDiv Rule P.
Search warrants.
Time of execution, CrimPro Rule 41.
Juvenile proceedings, JuvProc Rule
41.
Sentencing, CrimPro Rule 32.
Correction or reduction of sentence,
CrimPro Rule 35.
Delinquent minors, JuvProc Rule 32.
Service of process, CivPro Rule 6,
CrimPro Rule 45.
Collection and subrogation cases,
CivPro Rule 40-III.
Domestic relations actions, DomRel
Rules 4, 6.
Hospitalization of persons with mental
illness, MentalHealth Rule 13.
Juvenile proceedings, JuvProc Rule 45.
Summons, CivPro Rule 4.
Small claims court.
Sessions, office hours, and trials,
SmallClaims Rule 7.
Traffic ticket adjudication.
Appeal of board decisions, CivPro
Agency Review Rule 2.

TIME LIMITS.
See LIMITATION OF ACTIONS.

TIME OFF.
See LEAVE OF ABSENCE.

TINTED WINDOWS.
Traffic laws prohibiting, §50-2207.02.

TIPS AND GRATUITIES.
Garbage collection, §8-741.
Minimum wage for persons
receiving gratuities, §32-1003.

TIRES.
Business licenses for tire dealers,
§47-2832.02.

TISSUE REMOVAL.
Body art establishments.
Business licenses, §47-2809.01.

TISSUE REMOVAL —Cont'd
Body artists.
Business licenses, §§47-2853.76a to
47-2853.76e.

TITLE.
Boats and other watercraft.
Uniform certificates of title for vessels,
§§50-1541.01 to 50-1541.28.
See BOATS AND OTHER
WATERCRAFT.
Contracts.
Sale of goods.
Warranty of title, §28:2-312.
Divesting title to enforce judgment,
CivPro Rule 70.
Domestic relations actions, DomRel
Rule 70.
Eminent domain.
Transfer of title, §16-1319.
Insanitary buildings.
Title disputes, §6-908.
Landlord and tenant court.
Plea of title, LandlordTenant Rule 5.
Mortgages and deeds of trusts.
Survival of title, §42-804.
Motor vehicles.
See TITLING OF MOTOR
VEHICLES.
Statutory trust property, §29-1203.07.
Streets and alleys.
Abandonment of streets.
Reversion of title, §9-101.08.
Trusts and trustees.
Title to trust property.
Uniform trust code, §19-1304.18.

TITLE CORPORATIONS.
Regulatory provisions, §§26-1301 to
26-1336.
See TRUST, MORTGAGE AND TITLE
CORPORATIONS.

TITLE INSURANCE PRODUCERS,
§§31-5041.01 to 31-5041.12.
Applicability of law, §31-5041.12.
Audits, §31-5041.03.
Closing accounts, §31-5041.06.
Commitments, §31-5041.05.
Definitions, §31-5041.01.
Education, prelicensing education,
§31-1131.05b.
Errors and omissions policy.
Requirements for licenses,
§31-5041.02.
Escrow accounts, §31-5041.06.
Examinations, §31-5041.03.
Favored producers, §31-5031.16.

TITLE INSURANCE PRODUCERS
—Cont'd

Fee splitting prohibited, §31-5041.07.
Fines and civil penalties, §31-5041.09.
Indemnity deposits, §31-5041.06.
Injunctions, RESPA violations,
§31-5041.10.
Licenses.
Requirements, §31-5041.02.
Revocation or suspension, §31-5041.09.
Notice requirements, §31-5041.05.
Prelicensing education, §31-1131.05b.
Prohibited acts.
Fee splitting, §31-5041.07.
Rebates, §31-5041.07.
RESPA violations, §31-5041.10.
Rebates prohibited, §31-5041.07.
Records, retention requirements,
§31-5041.04.
RESPA violations, §31-5041.10.
Rulemaking authority, §31-5041.11.
Settlement accounts, §31-5041.06.
Statutory construction, §31-5041.12.
Title insurers using services of,
§31-5031.13.
Underwriting contracts, §31-5041.08.

TITLE INSURERS, §§31-5031.01 to
31-5031.24.

Admitted assets, §31-5031.07.
Applicability of law, §31-5031.24.
Authorized activities, §31-5031.03.
Capital requirements, §31-5031.05.
Commitments, §31-5031.12.
Definitions, §31-5031.01.
Dissolution, §31-5031.09.
Diversification, §31-5031.11.
Dividends, §31-5031.10.
Escrow accounts, §31-5031.14.
Favored producers, §31-5031.16.
Fee splitting, prohibited, §31-5031.15.
Fines and civil penalties, §31-5031.21.
Forms, filings, §31-5031.18.
Indemnity deposits, §31-5031.14.
Injunctions, RESPA violations,
§31-5031.22.
Insolvency, §31-5031.09.
Licenses.
Requirements, §31-5031.02.
Revocation or suspension, §31-5031.21.
Limitations on powers, §31-5031.04.
Liquidation, §31-5031.09.
Notice requirements, §31-5031.12.
Powers, limitations on, §31-5031.04.
Prohibited acts.
Fee splitting, §31-5031.15.
Rebates, §31-5031.15.

TITLE INSURERS —Cont'd
Prohibited acts —Cont'd
RESPA violations, §31-5031.22.
Rates, filings, §31-5031.17.
Ratings bureaus, filings, §31-5031.19.
Rebates, prohibited, §31-5031.15.
Records, retention requirements,
§31-5031.20.
Reserves, §31-5031.08.
RESPA violations, §31-5031.22.
Rulemaking authority, §31-5031.23.
Single risk limit, §31-5031.06.
Statutory construction, §31-5031.24.
Surplus requirements, §31-5031.05.
Title insurance producers, using
services of, §31-5031.13.

TITLE IX.
Schools and education.
Athletic equity, §§38-841.01 to
38-841.08.

TITLES OF NOBILITY.
Prohibited, US Const Art I §§9, 10.

TITLING OF MOTOR VEHICLES.
Boats and other watercraft.
Uniform certificates of title for vessels,
§§50-1541.01 to 50-1541.28.
See BOATS AND OTHER
WATERCRAFT.
Denial of title due to lien statement
on application, §50-1206.
Excise tax, §§50-2201.03, 50-2201.22.
Fees, §50-2201.03.
Liens on motor vehicles and trailers,
§§50-1201 to 50-1218.
Applications for certificates, required
to be shown by, §50-1206.
Appropriations, §50-1216.
Assignment of lien, §§50-1208,
50-1209.
Certificate of title, lien required to
appear on, §50-1202.
Definitions, §50-1201.
Denial of title due to incorrect
statement on application,
§50-1206.
Electronic creation, recordation and
transfer, §50-1218.
Entry of lien.
Nonavailable certificates, §50-1209.
Nonentry, situations involving,
§50-1204.
Previously-issued certificates, on,
§50-1207.
Requirements regarding, §50-1203.
False statements as to, §50-1215.

TITLING OF MOTOR VEHICLES
—Cont'd
Liens on motor vehicles and trailers
—Cont'd
Fees.
See FEES.
Holder of first lien, certificate sent to,
§§50-1206 to 50-1208.
Instrument creating lien, §50-1204.
Leased vehicles, §50-1217.
Lost certificates, §50-1211.
Nonavailable certificates, §50-1209.
Perfection of security interest, when
effective, §50-1202.
Priority of lien, §50-1203.
Recordation.
Electronic recordation, §50-1218.
Fees, §50-1212.
Recorder of deeds.
See RECORDER OF DEEDS.
Satisfaction of lien, §50-1210.
Violations related to, §50-1215.
**Office of Registrar of Titles and
Tags,** §50-2201.24.
Salvage, flood and junk vehicles.
Generally, §§50-1331.01 to 50-1331.09.
See SALVAGE, FLOOD AND JUNK
VEHICLES.
Scrap vehicle title authorization,
§§50-2701 to 50-2708.
See SCRAP VEHICLE TITLE
AUTHORIZATION.

TOBACCO.
Cigarette sales below cost, §§28-4521
to 28-4527.
Crimes and offenses.
Minors, sales to, §7-1721.02.
Prohibited sellers, §7-1721.06.
Self-service displays, §7-1721.04.
Fines and civil penalties.
Minors.
Purchases by, §7-1721.03.
Sales to, §7-1721.02.
Prohibited sellers, §7-1721.06.
Self-service displays, §7-1721.04.
Fire-standard-compliant cigarettes,
§§7-1751 to 7-1757.
Minors.
False identification, use of, §7-1721.03.
Purchases by, §7-1721.03.
Sales to, §7-1721.02.
Tobacco-free school campuses,
§38-826.05.
Rolling papers.
Drug paraphernalia, §§48-1101 to
48-1104.

TOBACCO —Cont'd
Sales, §§7-1721.01 to 7-1721.07.
Definitions, §7-1721.01.
Fines and civil penalties, §7-1721.07.
Minors.
False identification, use of,
§7-1721.03.
Purchases by, §7-1721.03.
Sales to, §7-1721.02.
Package requirements, §7-1721.05.
Prohibited sellers, §7-1721.06.
Self-service displays, §7-1721.04.
Schools.
Tobacco-free school campuses,
§38-826.05.
Smoking, §§7-1701 to 7-1731.
See SMOKING.
Tobacco tax.
General provisions, §§47-2401 to
47-2426.
See TOBACCO TAX.

**TOBACCO MASTER SETTLEMENT
AGREEMENT,** §§7-1831.01 to
7-1831.06.
Enforcement, §§7-1803.01 to 7-1803.07.
Agent for service of process,
§7-1803.04.
Certifications by manufacturers,
§7-1803.03.
Civil actions brought by District,
§7-1803.07.
Construction and interpretation,
§7-1803.07.
Definitions, §7-1803.02.
Directory of brand families,
§7-1803.03.
Penalties for violations, §7-1803.06.
Purpose of act, §7-1803.01.
Qualified escrow fund, §7-1803.05.
Reports of wholesalers, §7-1803.05.
Review of determinations, §7-1803.07.
Requirements generally, §7-1801.02.
**Sale of rights under master
settlement agreement,**
§§7-1831.02, 7-1831.04.
Tobacco settlement financing,
§§7-1831.01 to 7-1831.06.
Definitions, §7-1831.01.
Establishment of tobacco settlement
financing corporation, §7-1831.03.
Purchase agreement, §7-1831.02.
Sale of rights under master settlement
agreement, §§7-1831.02,
7-1831.04.
Severability, §7-1831.05.
Tobacco settlement trust fund,
§§7-1811.01 to 7-1811.03.

TOBACCO SETTLEMENT FINANCING CORPORATION.
Board of directors, §7-1831.03.
Bond issues.
Revenue bonds.
Delegation of council authority to issue, §§1-204.90, 7-1831.03.
Establishment, §7-1831.03.
Powers and duties, §7-1831.03.
Purpose, §7-1831.03.

TOBACCO SETTLEMENT TRUST FUND, §§7-1811.01 to 7-1811.03.
Establishment, §7-1811.01.
Use of funds, §7-1811.03.

TOBACCO TAX, §§47-2401 to 47-2426.
Appeals, §47-2413.
Applicability of enforcement provisions, §47-2426.
Assessments, §47-2410.
Civil penalties for violations, §47-2422.
Deficiencies, §47-2410.
Definitions, §47-2401.
Effective date of provisions, §47-2417.
Enforcement of provisions, §47-2425.
Exemptions, §47-2403.
Filing and documentation, §47-2420.
Forfeitures, §47-2409.
Fraud and deceit, §§47-2406, 47-2409.
Government sales exemption, §47-2403.
Gray-market cigarettes, §47-2419.
Applicability of provisions, §47-2426.
Penalties for violations, §47-2421.
Seizure as contraband, §47-2423.
Issuance of regulations, §47-2415.
Licenses, §47-2404.
Payment of tax, §§47-2402, 47-2418.
Penalties, §47-2409.
Rates, §47-2402.
Records, §§47-2408, 47-2418.
Refunds, §47-2412.
Reports, §47-2408.
Returns, §47-2408.
Seizures, §47-2409.
Severability of provisions, §47-2416.
Stamps.
Defined, §47-2401.
Effective date, purchased or held prior to, §47-2418.
Imposition of tax via, §47-2402.
Offenses related to, §47-2406.
Redemption of, §§47-2407, 47-2411.
Transportation of cigarettes, §47-2405.

TOBACCO TAX —Cont'd
Underpayments, §47-2410.
Unfair trade practices, §47-2424.
Weight-based excise tax, §47-2402.01.

TOD SECURITY REGISTRATION, §§19-603.01 to 19-603.11.
See NONPROBATE TRANSFERS.

TOILETS, §§8-601 to 8-604.
Parks and recreation facilities, §§10-133, 10-134.

TOLL TELECOMMUNICATION SERVICE TAX, §§47-3901 to 47-3922.
Alternative reporting method, §47-3906.
Amendments, §47-3920.
Applicability of provisions, §47-3920.
Assessments, §§47-3908, 47-4312.
Credit, §47-3907.
Deductions, §47-3903.
Deficiencies, §47-3908.
Definitions, §47-3901.
Determination of tax by mayor, §47-3908.
Effective date, §47-3921.
Exemptions, §47-3904.
Issuance of rules and regulations, §47-3919.
Mobile telecommunications services.
Defined, §47-3901.
Special rules, §47-3901.
Payment of tax, §47-3905.
Rates, §47-3902.
Repeals, §47-3920.
Reports, §§47-3905, 47-3906.
Returns, §47-3905.
Severability of provisions, §47-3920.

TONGUE BIFURCATION.
Body art establishments.
Business licenses, §47-2809.01.
Body artists.
Business licenses, §§47-2853.76a to 47-2853.76e.

TOOLS OF A TRADE.
Execution of judgment, property exempt from, §15-503.

TOOTHPASTE.
Phosphate cleaners, §§8-107.01 to 8-107.04.

TORTS.
Claims against the District.
General provisions, §§2-401 to 2-425.
See CLAIMS AGAINST THE DISTRICT.

TORTS —Cont'd
Comparative negligence.
Bank deposits and collections.
Customer's duty to report
unauthorized signature or
alteration, §28:4-406.
Condominiums.
Liability of association and declarant,
§42-1903.09.
Contributory fault.
Bank deposits and collections.
Customer's duty to report
unauthorized signature or
alteration, §28:4-406.
Damages generally.
See DAMAGES.
Dangerous dog.
Defined, §8-1901.
Dog bites, §8-1812.
Generally, §§8-1901 to 8-1908.
See DANGEROUS DOGS.
District volunteers.
Tort liability, §1-319.03.
Dog bites, §8-1812.
Good Samaritan law, §7-401.
Immunity generally.
See IMMUNITY.
Judgments.
Interest on judgment for damages in
tort, §15-109.
Marriage.
Effect of marriage on civil litigation,
§46-601.
Property rights.
Effect of marriage on property
rights, §46-601.
Negligence generally.
See NEGLIGENCE.
Nuisances.
Drug, firearm, or prostitution-related
nuisance abatement, §§42-3101 to
42-3114.
See CRIME-RELATED NUISANCE
ABATEMENT.
Generally.
See NUISANCES.
Prostitution, abatement of houses of,
§§22-2713 to 22-2720.
See PROSTITUTION.
Secured transactions.
Secured party not obligated in tort,
§28:9-402.
Strict liability.
Illegal sales and distributions,
§§7-2531.01 to 7-2531.04.
Manufacturing assault weapons,
§§7-2551.01 to 7-2551.03.

TORTS —Cont'd
Trademarks and trade names.
Registration of containers for
beverages composed principally of
milk.
Actions in tort permissible, §36-157.
**Washington metropolitan airports
authority.**
Tort liability, §9-922.
Wrongful death.
General provisions, §§16-2701 to
16-2703.
See WRONGFUL DEATH.

TOURISM.
IPW fund, §1-325.291.

TOWING SERVICES.
**Rules governing business of
furnishing.**
Promulgation, violation, criminal
penalty, §47-2850.
Scrap vehicle title authorization,
§§50-2701 to 50-2708.
See SCRAP VEHICLE TITLE
AUTHORIZATION.

TOXIC WASTE, §§8-1301 to 8-1322.
See HAZARDOUS WASTE
MANAGEMENT.

TOY VEHICLES.
Helmet requirement for riders.
Persons under 16 years, §50-1651.

TRACHEA HOLDS.
Metropolitan police prohibitions,
§5-125.03.

TRADE AND COMMERCE.
**Business and economic
development.**
General provisions, §§2-1201.01 to
2-1217.84.
See BUSINESS AND ECONOMIC
DEVELOPMENT.
Business improvement districts.
General provisions, §§2-1215.01 to
2-1215.71.
See BUSINESS IMPROVEMENT
DISTRICTS.
Business incubator facilitation,
§§2-1209.01 to 2-1209.14.
Business licenses.
General provisions, §§47-2805.01 to
47-2881.
See BUSINESS LICENSES.
**Commerce and business in the
states.**
Constitutional provisions, US Const
Art I §§8, 9.

TRADE AND COMMERCE —Cont'd

Economic development liaison office, §§2-1203.01 to 2-1203.03.

Economic development zone incentives.
General provisions, §§6-1501 to 6-1506.
See ECONOMIC DEVELOPMENT ZONE INCENTIVES.

Enterprise zone study commission, §§2-1211.01 to 2-1211.06.

Foreign trade zones, §§36-501 to 36-504.
See FOREIGN TRADE ZONES.

National capital revitalization corporation.
General provisions.
See NATIONAL CAPITAL REVITALIZATION CORPORATION.

Office of business and economic development, §§2-1201.01 to 2-1201.05.

Restraints of trade, §§28-4501 to 28-4518.
See RESTRAINTS OF TRADE.

Retail development incentives, §§2-1217.71 to 2-1217.84.
See RETAIL DEVELOPMENT INCENTIVES.

Tax increment financing.
General provisions, §§2-1217.01 to 2-1217.12.
See TAX INCREMENT FINANCING.

Unlawful trade practices, §28-3904.

TRADEMARK COUNTERFEITING, §§22-901, 22-902.

TRADE NAMES.
Attorneys at law, ProfCond Rule 7.5.
Definitions, §47-2855.01.
Registration, §§47-2855.01 to 47-2855.05.
Amendment, §47-2855.03.
Cancellation, notice, §47-2855.03.
Execution, §47-2855.02.
Failure to complete, effect, §47-2855.03.
Fees, §47-2855.04.
Collection and deposit, §47-2855.05.
Required, §47-2855.02.
Rules, §47-2855.04.
Secured transactions.
Name of debtor and secured party, §28:9-503.

TRADE SECRETS, §§36-401 to 36-410.
Applicability of provisions, §§36-408, 36-409.
Attorneys' fees and costs, §36-404.
Damages, §36-403.
Definitions, §36-401.
Disclosures, §36-410.
Electronic waste.
Extended manufacturer responsibility, §8-1041.08.
Freedom of information act exemptions, §2-534.
Injunctions, §36-402.
Interpretation of provisions, §36-408.
Limitation of actions, §36-406.
Occupational safety and health, §32-1119.
Occupational safety and health-related disclosures, §36-410.
Pesticide-related disclosures, §36-410.
Privacy and confidentiality, §36-405.
Relationship to other laws, §36-407.
Subpoenas.
Quashing or modifying subpoena, CivPro Rule 45.
Domestic relations actions, DomRel Rule 45.
Uniformity of application and interpretation, §36-408.

TRAFFIC CONTROL DEVICES.
Bicycles.
Pedestrian crossing signals, crossing with, §50-2201.04d.
Mayoral authority to install, §38-3101.
Strict enforcement zone, signs identifying District as, §50-2201.31.

TRAFFICKING, HUMAN, §§22-1831 to 22-1843.
See HUMAN TRAFFICKING.

TRAFFICKING IN HUMAN BODY PARTS, §§7-1501.01 to 7-1501.03.

TRAFFICKING IN STOLEN PROPERTY, §22-3232.

TRAFFIC LAWS, §§50-2201.01 to 50-2209.03.
Adjudication of traffic tickets, §§50-2301.01 to 50-2305.02.
See TRAFFIC TICKET ADJUDICATION.
Aggressive driving, §50-2204.
All-terrain vehicles.
Defined, §50-2201.02.

TRAFFIC LAWS —Cont'd
All-terrain vehicles —Cont'd
Operating on public property,
§50-2201.04b.
Registration not required,
§50-2201.04b.
**Appeal of excise tax assessment on
titling vehicles, §50-2201.22.**
Automated traffic enforcement,
§§50-2209.01 to 50-2209.11.
Autonomous vehicles, §§50-2351 to
50-2354.
Bicycles.
Pedestrian crossing signals, crossing
with, §50-2201.04d.
Capitol police, §10-503.25.
Child restraint seats.
General provisions, §§50-1701 to
50-1708.
See SEAT BELTS.
Common carriers, §50-2201.03.
Congress.
Parking, §§50-2201.03, 50-2631.
Tags, §§50-2201.25, 50-2201.26.
**Curb loading zone management
program, §50-2651.**
Implementation, §50-2652.
Definitions, §50-2201.02.
**Department of Transportation,
establishment of, §50-2201.03.**
Director of vehicles and traffic,
§50-2201.03.
Dirt bikes.
Defined, §50-2201.02.
Operating on public property,
§50-2201.04b.
Registration not required,
§50-2201.04b.
Distracted driving, §§50-1731.01 to
50-1731.10.
See DISTRACTED DRIVING.
Driverless vehicles, §§50-2351 to
50-2354.
Driving under the influence.
See DRIVING UNDER THE
INFLUENCE.
**Electric personal assistive mobility
devices.**
Defined, §50-2201.01.
Exemption from regulations governing
motor vehicles, §50-2201.03a.
Operation and registration
requirements, §50-2201.04a.
Regulation, §50-2201.03a.
**Enforcement, interstate agreements
on, §50-2201.23.**

TRAFFIC LAWS —Cont'd
Fees.
Storing impounded vehicles,
§50-2201.21.
Titling of motor vehicles, §50-2201.03.
Fines, §50-2201.03.
Safety impact assessment of fine
reductions, §50-2111.
**Fleeing from a law enforcement
officer in a motor vehicle,**
§50-2201.05b.
**Garage keepers required to report
vehicles damaged in accidents,**
§50-2201.06.
Impaired operation or driving,
§§50-2206.01 to 50-2206.59.
See DRIVING UNDER THE
INFLUENCE.
Impoundment of vehicles.
Abandoned and unlawfully parked
vehicles, §50-2421.07.
Blue Plains Impoundment Lot,
jurisdiction over, §50-2405.
Fees for storing impounded vehicles,
§50-2201.21.
For-hire vehicles, §50-331.
Outstanding violations, for,
§50-2201.03.
Prostitution-related offenses, vehicle
used in furtherance of, §22-2724.
Taxicabs, §50-331.
**Interstate agreements on
enforcement, §50-2201.23.**
Leaving after colliding, §50-2201.05c.
**Legal rate of speed, immoderate
speed not dependent on,**
§50-2203.03.
Loading zone management program,
§50-2651.
Implementation, §50-2652.
**Mayor's authority to make rules
regarding, §50-2201.03.**
Motor vehicle accidents.
See MOTOR VEHICLE ACCIDENTS.
Negligent homicide, §§50-2203.01,
50-2203.02.
Object falling or flying from vehicle,
§50-2201.05d.
Parking.
General provisions, §§50-2601 to
50-2624.
See PARKING.
**Parking meter fee moratorium,
exceptions, §50-2633.01.**
Parks and recreation, §§10-105,
50-2201.07.

TRAFFIC LAWS —Cont'd
Pedestrian advisory council,
§50-1931.
Pedestrian crossing signals.
Bicycles, crossing with, §50-2201.04d.
Reckless driving, §50-2201.04.
Registration of vehicles.
General provisions, §§50-1501.01 to
50-1507.07.
See MOTOR VEHICLE
REGISTRATION.
Inspection, §§50-1101 to 50-1109.
See MOTOR VEHICLE
REGISTRATION.
International registration plan
agreements, §§50-1507.01 to
50-1507.07.
See MOTOR VEHICLE
REGISTRATION.
Rental vehicle tax, §§50-1505.01 to
50-1505.04.
See MOTOR VEHICLE
REGISTRATION.
Repeal of prior laws, §50-2201.08.
Reports.
Garage keepers required to report
vehicles damaged in accidents,
§50-2201.06.
Safety responsibility act.
General provisions, §§50-1301.01 to
50-1301.86.
See MOTOR VEHICLE SAFETY
RESPONSIBILITY.
Savings clause, §50-2201.08.
Seat belts.
Child restraint seats, §§50-1701 to
50-1708.
See SEAT BELTS.
General provisions, §§50-1801 to
50-1807.
See SEAT BELTS.
Severability of provisions,
§50-2201.09.
Speeding, §§50-2201.04, 50-2203.03.
Evaluation of speed limits,
§50-2201.32.
**Strict enforcement zone, signs
identifying District as,**
§50-2201.31.
Tinted windows, prohibition of,
§50-2207.02.
**Unlawfully parked or abandoned
vehicles,** §50-2637.
Work zones, moving infractions in,
§50-2201.04c.

TRAFFIC TICKET ADJUDICATION,
§§50-2301.01 to 50-2305.02.
**Administrative adjudication,
imposition of,** §50-2301.01.
Answer to notice of infraction.
Moving infractions, §50-2302.05.
Parking, standing, stopping, and
pedestrian infractions,
§50-2303.05.
Appeal of board decisions, CivPro
Agency Review Rule 2.
Application for leave to appeal, CivPro
Agency Review Rule 2.
Appeals.
Administrative review, §§50-2304.01 to
50-2304.05.
Appeals boards, establishment of,
§50-2304.01.
Judicial review, §50-2304.05.
Right to appeal, §50-2304.02.
Scope of administrative review,
§50-2304.03.
Time limits on, §50-2304.04.
**Authority to promulgate
regulations,** §50-2301.07.
**Automated parking enforcement
system,** §50-2303.02a.
Business licenses.
Unpaid fines or penalties.
Computer record-keeping and
reporting system, §47-2866.
Definitions, §47-2861.
Issuance of license prohibited,
§47-2862.
Right to appeal denial of license,
§47-2865.
Self-certification of lack of
outstanding debt, §47-2863.
Falsification of certification,
penalty, §47-2864.
Collateral security in traffic cases.
Reduction of security, CrimPro Rule
35.
Crosswalks, right-of-way at,
§50-2201.28.
Decriminalization, §50-2301.01.
Definitions, §50-2301.02.
Effective date of provisions,
§50-2305.02.
Fees, §50-2301.05.
Fines, §§50-2301.05, 50-2303.04.
**Fleet reconciliation program for
parking, standing, stopping, and
pedestrian infractions,**
§50-2303.04a.
Hearing examiners, §50-2301.04.

TRAFFIC TICKET ADJUDICATION
—Cont'd
Hearings.
Automated traffic enforcement,
§50-2209.02.
Moving infractions, §50-2302.06.
Parking, standing, stopping, and
pedestrian infractions,
§50-2303.06.
Lessor's liability for fine or penalty,
§50-2303.04.
Liability for penalties imposed,
§50-2303.04.
Moving infractions, §§50-2302.01 to
50-2302.06.
Answer to notice of infraction,
§50-2302.05.
Applicability of rules, §§50-2302.01 to
50-2302.06.
Exceptions to applicability,
§§50-2302.02, 50-2302.03.
Hearings, §50-2302.06.
Notice of infraction, §50-2302.04.
Serious offenders, exceptions for,
§50-2302.03.
Notice of infraction.
Automated traffic enforcement,
§50-2209.02.
Collection of fines, §1-629.05.
Moving infractions, §50-2302.04.
Parking, standing, stopping, and
pedestrian infractions,
§50-2303.03.
Operation of traffic section of
criminal division, CrimPro Rule
103.
Parking, standing, stopping, and
pedestrian infractions,
§§50-2303.01 to 50-2303.11.
Answer to notice of infraction,
§50-2303.05.
Appeal of decision after liability
affirmed on reconsideration,
§50-2303.11.
Applicability of rules, §50-2303.01.
Automated parking ticket enforcement
system, §50-2303.02a.
Civil liabilities for, §50-2303.04.
Collection of fines, §1-629.05.
Electronic notice, §50-2303.08.
Fines and penalties, §50-2303.04.
Fleet reconciliation program,
§50-2303.04a.
Hearings, §50-2303.06.
Identification of pedestrian offenders,
§50-2303.07.

TRAFFIC TICKET ADJUDICATION
—Cont'd
Parking, standing, stopping, and
pedestrian infractions —Cont'd
Notice of infraction, §50-2303.03.
Electronic notice, §50-2303.08.
Reconsideration of decision,
§50-2303.11.
Serious offenders, exception for,
§50-2303.02.
Vacation of deemed admission,
§50-2303.05.
Pedestrians.
Identification of pedestrian offenders,
§50-2303.07.
Infractions and pedestrian infractions.
See within this heading, "Parking,
standing, stopping, and pedestrian
infractions."
Right-of-way at crosswalks,
§50-2201.28.
Reports to DPW and DDOT,
§50-2301.10.
Report to council on, §50-2301.08.
Review of records, §50-2301.09.
Serious offenders.
Moving infractions.
Exceptions for, §50-2302.03.
Parking, standing, stopping, and
pedestrian infractions,
§50-2303.02.
Severability of provisions,
§50-2305.01.
Study of parking infraction
adjudications, §50-2301.11.
Ticket adjudication ombudsman,
§50-907.
Time, computation of, §50-2301.06.
Traffic division of criminal division.
Authorization of sections, CrimPro
Rule 1.
Creation, CrimPro Rule 100.
Duties and operation, CrimPro Rule
103.
Operation of traffic section of criminal
division, CrimPro Rule 103.

TRAILERS.
Defined, §50-1501.01.
Inspection, §§50-1101 to 50-1109.
Liens on trailers.
See TITLING OF MOTOR
VEHICLES.
Motor vehicle registration,
§50-1501.02.
Utility trailers, rental.
Defined, §50-1505.01.

TRAILERS —Cont'd
Utility trailers, rental —Cont'd
Procedure for registering, §50-1505.03.

TRAINING.
Athletic concussion program,
§7-2871.03.
BOOT CAMP, §24-924.
Court employees, nonjudicial,
§11-1728.
Domestic violence.
Handling, §16-1034.
Employment and training of
domiciliaries of District, §32-241.
Evaluation of summer youth
employment program, §32-244.
Homestead housing preservation
technical training program,
§42-2109.
Hospitals, §§44-703, 44-707.
Human trafficking, §22-1842.
Innovation fund, §§1-325.221 to
1-325.226.
Junior Reserve Officers' Training
Program, §38-158.
Long-term care ombudsman,
§7-702.03.
Nurse training corps, §§38-1501 to
38-1503.
Occupational safety and health for
public officers and employees,
§1-620.06.
Plans for delivery of workforce
development services, §32-243.
Procurement practices.
Contracting manager or officer
performing cost benefit analysis,
§2-381.43.
Public assistance meeting costs and
expenses of, §4-205.50.
Public employment service,
§§1-202.04, 32-241.
Solid waste reduction and recovery,
§8-1031.09.
Year-round program to provide
training and work experience,
§32-242.

TRAINS.
Metrorail and metrobus, §§9-1101.01
to 9-1115.04.
See METRORAIL AND METROBUS.

TRANSCRIPTS.
Adoption proceedings, Adoption Rule
201.
Depositions, Adoption Rule 30.
Appeals, D.C. courts.
Administrative orders and decisions,
DCCtApp Rule 17.

TRANSCRIPTS —Cont'd
Appeals, D.C. courts —Cont'd
Domestic relations actions, DomRel
Rule 201.
Motion for free transcript, DomRel
Rule 54-II.
Indigent persons.
Proceedings in forma pauperis,
DCCtApp Rule 24.
Motion for free transcript, CivPro Rule
54-II.
Record on appeal, DCCtApp Rule 10.
Appeals, federal cases, FRAP 10(b).
Agreed statement as record on appeal,
FRAP 10(d).
Appellant's duty to order, FRAP 10(b).
Certified list, filing as constituting
filing of record, administrative
review or enforcement, FRAP
17(b).
Composition of record on appeal,
FRAP 10(a).
Correction of record on appeal, FRAP
10(e).
Modification of record on appeal,
FRAP 10(e).
Reporter's duty to prepare and file,
FRAP 11(b).
Statement of evidence when
unavailable, FRAP 10(c).
Transmitting the record on appeal,
FRAP 11.
Arbitration hearings, Arbitration Rule
IX.
Costs of litigation, CivPro Rule 54-I.
Crime victims' compensation.
Appeal of determination, VictComp
Rule 20.
Criminal proceedings, CrimPro Rule
36-I.
Correcting errors, CrimPro Rule 36.
Depositions, CivPro Rule 30.
Adoption proceedings, Adoption Rule
30.
Domestic relations actions, DomRel
Rule 201.
Depositions, DomRel Rule 30.
Motion for free transcript, DomRel
Rule 54-II.
Grand jury proceedings, CrimPro
Rule 6.
Discovery of transcripts, CrimPro Rule
16.
Delinquent minors, JuvProc Rule 16.
Mental illness, persons with.
Hospitalization.
Confidentiality of transcripts,
MentalHealth Rule 12.

TRANSCRIPTS —Cont'd

Releasing superior court transcripts, CivPro Rule 201, CrimPro Rule 36-I.

Stenographic reports.
Admissibility, CivPro Rule 80.
Adoption proceedings, Adoption Rule 201.
Domestic relations actions, DomRel Rule 201.

TRANSFER AGENTS.
Defined, §28-2901.

TRANSFERS OF FIREARMS.
See FIREARMS.

TRANSFERS ON DEATH.
Uniform real property transfers on death, §§19-604.01 to 19-604.19.

TRANSFERS TO MINORS, §§21-301 to 21-324.

Accounting duties of custodians, §21-319.

Applicability of provisions, §§21-302, 21-321, 21-323.

Bonds, surety, §21-315.

Care of custodial property, §21-312.

Claims by third persons to custodial property, §21-317.

Creation of custodial property, §21-309.

Death, resignation, or removal of custodian, §21-318.

Definitions, §21-301.

Effect of, §21-311.

Exercise of power of appointment, transfer by, §21-304.

Existing custodianships, effect of new provisions on, §21-322.

Expenses, §21-315.

Fiduciary transfers, §21-306.

Fraudulent transfers.
General provisions, §§28-3101 to 28-3111.
See FRAUDULENT TRANSFERS.

Gift, transfer by, §21-304.

Interpretation of provisions, §21-323.

Jurisdiction, §21-302.

Liability of custodians, §21-319.

Nomination of custodian for purposes of, §§21-303, 21-309.

Obligor, by, §21-307.

Powers and duties of custodian, §21-313.

Powers of appointment.
General provisions, §§42-1001 to 42-1019.
See POWERS OF APPOINTMENT.

TRANSFERS TO MINORS —Cont'd

Receipts, §21-308.

Resignation, death, or removal of custodian, §21-318.

Single custodianship requirement, §21-310.

Successor custodians, §21-318.

Termination of custodianship on majority, §21-320.

Third parties.
Claims by third persons to custodial property, §21-317.
Third persons assisting with transfer, §21-316.

Third persons assisting with, §21-316.

Trust, authorized by, §21-305.

Uniform Gifts to Minors Act, repeal of, §21-324.

Uniformity of application and interpretation of provisions, §21-323.

Use of custodial property, §21-314.

Validity of, §21-311.

Wages and salaries for custodians of, §21-315.

Will, authorized by, §21-305.

TRANSFER TAX ON REAL PROPERTY, §§47-901 to 47-920.
See REAL PROPERTY TRANSFER TAX.

TRANSFER WARRANTIES.
Commercial code, §28:4-207.

TRANSIENT LODGINGS, §§30-101 to 30-103.
See LODGING PLACES.

TRANSITIONAL EMPLOYMENT PROGRAM, §32-1331.

TRANSIT PASSES.
Labor and employment relations.
Transportation benefits.
Reducing single occupancy vehicle use by encouraging transit benefits, §§32-151 to 32-153.

TRANSIT RIDER ADVISORY COUNCIL, §§50-2361.01 to 50-2361.03.

TRANSPORTATION.
Alcoholic beverages.
Transportation into District, §25-772.
Importation permits, §25-119.

Bicycle transportation and safety, §§50-1601 to 50-1612.
See BICYCLES.

TRANSPORTATION —Cont'd
Capital project review and reconciliation, §§50-921.51 to 50-921.54.
Closing projects, §50-921.52.
Use of funds resulting from closure, §50-921.53.
Defined terms, §50-921.51.
Fund usage, §50-921.53.
Reports, §50-921.54.
Cigarettes, §47-2405.
Complete streets policy, §50-2381.
Congestion management study, §50-921.21.
Crime victims' compensation.
Transportation expenses, VictComp Rule 35.
DC Circulator bus service, §§50-921.31 to 50-921.38.
DC Streetcar service, §§50-921.71 to 50-921.77.
See DC STREETCAR SERVICE.
Department of transportation, §§50-921.01 to 50-921.22.
Administrative administration, §50-921.03.
Duties, §50-921.04.
Bike Sharing program and fund.
Fund created, §50-921.16.
Block parties, §§9-631 to 9-634.
Capital project review and reconciliation, §§50-921.51 to 50-921.54.
Congestion management study, §50-921.21.
Cost-transfer projects, §9-111.01c.
Definitions, §50-921.01a.
Director, §50-921.02.
Duties, §50-921.04.
Enforcement, §50-921.19.
Enterprise fund for transportation initiatives, §50-921.13.
Established, §50-921.01.
Fines and civil penalties, §50-921.19.
Head of department.
Director, §50-921.02.
Infractions, §50-921.19.
Inspections.
Enforcement, §50-921.19.
Office of director, §50-921.03.
Operations administration, §50-921.03.
Duties, §50-921.04.
Performance administration, §50-921.03.
Duties, §50-921.04.
Personal delivery devices pilot program, §§50-1551 to 50-1555.

TRANSPORTATION —Cont'd
Department of transportation —Cont'd
Project delivery administration, §50-921.03.
Duties, §50-921.04.
References to department or DOT.
Deemed to refer to district department or DDOT, §50-921.09.
Reorganization of personnel and property, §50-921.07.
Repeal of orders in conflict with chapter, §50-921.08.
Rules, §50-921.18.
Sidewalk design and installation requirements.
Exemption, §9-425.03.
Special purpose revenue funds, §50-921.12.
Stormwater retention credit fund, §50-921.22.
Successor to transportation related authority, §50-921.06.
Transfer of positions, personnel, property and records, §50-921.05.
Transportation infrastructure project review fund, §50-921.17.
Vision zero pedestrian and bicycle safety fund, §50-921.20.
Hazardous materials.
See HAZARDOUS WASTE MANAGEMENT.
Labor and employment relations.
Reducing single occupancy vehicle use by encouraging transit benefits, §§32-151 to 32-153.
Metrorail and metrobus, §§9-1101.01 to 9-1115.04.
See METRORAIL AND METROBUS.
Mulitmodal accessibility advisory council, §§50-2361.31, 50-2361.32.
Overpayment liabilities, §47-112.
Schools and education.
See SCHOOLS AND EDUCATION.
Stormwater retention credit fund, §50-921.22.
Transit rider advisory council, §§50-2361.01 to 50-2361.03.
Vision zero pedestrian and bicycle safety fund, §50-921.20.
Washington metropolitan area transit authority.
General provisions, §§1-628.04, 6-333.01, 28-4504.

TRANSPORTATION INFRASTRUCTURE IMPROVEMENT GARVEE BONDS, §§9-107.51 to 9-107.62.

TRANSSHIPMENT OF GOODS.
Uniform commercial code.
No arrival, no sale, §28:2-324.

TRASH COLLECTION.
See GARBAGE COLLECTION.

TRAUMA CARE SYSTEM, §7-2341.19.

TRAUMA TECHNOLOGISTS, §§3-1206.51 to 3-1206.53.
Board of medicine.
Advisory committee on trauma technologists, §3-1202.03.
Continuing medical education, §3-1206.52.
Health occupations licensure, registration or certification, §§3-1205.01 to 3-1205.24.
Qualifications for licensure, §3-1205.04.
Renewal of license, §3-1206.52.
Scope of practice, §3-1206.51.
Titles and terms prohibited as misrepresentation without license to practice, §3-1210.03.
Transition provisions, §3-1206.53.

TRAVEL ALLOWANCES.
Witness fees, CrimPro Rule 113.
Family court proceedings, FamDiv Rule F.

TRAVELER'S CHECKS.
Defined, §28:3-104.
Money transmitters, §§26-1001 to 26-1027.
See MONEY TRANSMISSIONS.
Presumed abandonment of, §41-105.
Refusal to pay, §28:3-411.

TRAVEL RESTRICTIONS.
Foreign missions, members of, §6-1315.

TREASON.
Constitution of the United States, US Const Art I §6, Art II §4, Art III §3.
Two witnesses required, US Const Art III §3.

TREASURER OF DISTRICT.
Duties, §1-204.24e.
Office of chief financial officer generally.
See CHIEF FINANCIAL OFFICER.

TREASURER OF DISTRICT —Cont'd
Vacancy in office of chief financial officer.
Treasurer as acting CFO, §1-204.24b.

TREASURY, UNITED STATES.
Borrowing from treasury in anticipation of revenues, §47-309.
Fees of District paid into, §47-127.
Offset program, §47-143.
Outstanding check amounts of disbursing officer.
Deposit of, §47-125.
Payment of, §47-126.
Recordation tax paid into, §42-1122.
Sales of animals and materials, proceeds from, §47-132.

TREATIES.
Supreme law of the land, US Const Art VI.

TREES AND TIMBER.
Contracts under UCC.
Applicability of sales chapter of commercial code, §28:2-107.
Principal and income.
Timber receipts, §28-4804.12.
Removal of tree on public lands.
Written notice attached to tree, §10-731.
Secured transactions.
Description of land, §28:9-203.
Financing statement, §28:9-502.
Place of filing, §28:9-501.
When security interest attaches, §28:9-204.

TREGARON CONSERVANCY.
Real property tax exemptions, §47-1077.

TRENCHES IN HIGHWAYS, CUTTING, §§9-431.01, 9-431.02.

TRESPASS, §§22-3301 to 22-3311.
See VANDALISM.

TRIAL OF RIGHT TO PROPERTY SEIZED ON PROCESS OF SUPERIOR COURT, §§15-521 to 15-524.
Action for replevin against officer levying on property, §15-524.
Docketing claim, §15-522.
Judgment, §15-523.
Manner of trial, §15-522.
Notice of claim or exemption, §15-521.

TRIALS.

Adoption, Adoption Rule 43.

Consolidation or bifurcation, Adoption Rule 42.

Proof of official record, statute, etc., Adoption Rule 44.

Arbitration.

Trial de novo, Arbitration Rule XI.

Assignment of cases.

See ASSIGNMENT OF CASES.

Attachment, §§16-506, 16-522, 16-530, 16-551, 16-552.

Civil I calendar, CivPro Rule 40-II.

Competence to proceed.

Incompetent criminal defendants, §§24-531.01 to 24-531.13.

See COMPETENCE TO PROCEED.

Conflicts in engagements.

Avoidance and resolution, USDistCt LCrR 57.5, USDistCt LCvR 16.2.

Consolidation, CivPro Rule 42, USDistCt LCvR 40.5.

Adoption, Adoption Rule 42.

Appeals, DCCtApp Rule 3.

Motions, DCCtApp Rule 27.

Assignment of criminal trials, CrimPro Rule 105.

Child abuse and neglect proceedings, NeglectProc Rule 3.

Domestic relations actions, DomRel Rule 42.

Constitution of the United States.

Public trial, US Const Amd 6.

Speedy trial, US Const Amd 6.

Continuances.

See CONTINUANCES.

Criminal procedure.

See CRIMINAL PROCEDURE.

Criminal trial by court or jury, §16-705, US Const Art III §2, Amds 6, 7.

Date of trial, CivPro Rule 40-I.

Demand for jury trial.

See DEMAND FOR TRIAL BY JURY.

Discovery.

See DISCOVERY.

Dismissal of actions.

See DISMISSAL OF ACTIONS.

Fair trials, CivPro Rule 203, CrimPro Rule 53.

Attorneys publicizing trial, ProfCond Rule 3.6.

Garnishment.

Post-judgment garnishment in aid of execution, §16-551.

Traverse of garnishee's answers, §16-553.

TRIALS —Cont'd

Garnishment —Cont'd

Prejudgment garnishment.

Defending against, §16-520.

Time for trial of issues, §16-530.

Trial on traverse of garnishee's answers, §16-522.

Harmless error, CivPro Rule 61, CrimPro Rule 52.

Adoption proceedings, Adoption Rule 61.

Domestic relations actions, DomRel Rule 61.

Juvenile proceedings, JuvProc Rule 52.

Plea procedure, CrimPro Rule 11.

Hospitalization of persons with mental illness.

Court-ordered commitment, §§21-541 to 21-551.

Mental illness and dangerousness issues, MentalHealth Rule 5.

Prisoner's commitment to mental institution, MentalHealth Rule 10.

Request for jury trial, MentalHealth Rule 4.

Incompetent criminal defendants.

Competence to proceed, §§24-531.01 to 24-531.13.

See COMPETENCE TO PROCEED.

Injunctions.

Preliminary injunction hearings consolidated with trial, CivPro Rule 65.

Interpreters, §§2-1901 to 2-1912.01, CivPro Rule 43.

Adoption proceedings, Adoption Rule 43.

Judges.

See JUDGES.

Jury trials.

See JURIES AND JURY TRIALS.

Landlord and tenant court, LandlordTenant Rule 12.

Time of trial, LandlordTenant Rule 7.

Postponing because of attorney's schedule, LandlordTenant Rule 8.

Masters, CivPro Rules 53 to 53-II.

Domestic relations actions, DomRel Rule 53.

Media coverage, CivPro Rule 203.

Attorneys publicizing trials, ProfCond Rule 3.6.

Child abuse and neglect proceedings, NeglectProc Rule 45.

TRIALS —Cont'd
Mental illness, persons with.
Hospitalization, MentalHealth Rule
16.
Court-ordered commitment,
§§21-541 to 21-551.
Jury trials, MentalHealth Rule 16.
Request for jury trial,
MentalHealth Rule 4.
Mental illness and dangerousness
issues, MentalHealth Rule 5.
Prisoner's commitment to mental
institution, MentalHealth
Rule 10.
New trial.
See NEW TRIAL.
Number of attorneys, CivPro Rule
39-II, USDistCt LCrR 44.2,
USDistCt LCvR 83.3.
Place of trials in Superior Court,
CivPro Rule 77.
Plain error.
Criminal procedure, CrimPro Rule 52.
Juvenile proceedings, JuvProc Rule 52.
Pretrial conferences.
See PRETRIAL CONFERENCES.
Publicizing trial, ProfCond Rule 3.6.
Public trial, US Const Amd 6.
Recess.
Witness statement examination.
Criminal cases, CrimPro Rule 26.2.
Delinquent minors, JuvProc Rule
26.2.
Related cases, CivPro Rule 42,
USDistCt LCrR 57.12, USDistCt
LCvR 40.5.
Replevin.
Expedited trials, CivPro Rule 64-II.
Domestic relations actions, DomRel
Rule 64.
Right of seized property, §§15-521 to
15-524.
See INTERPLEADER.
Separate trials, CivPro Rule 42.
Adoption, Adoption Rule 42.
Counterclaims and cross-claims,
CivPro Rule 13.
Domestic relations actions, DomRel
Rule 42.
Joinder of parties, CivPro Rule 20.
Small claims court, SmallClaims Rule
12.
New trial, SmallClaims Rule 16.
Time of trial, SmallClaims Rule 7.
Speedy trial, USDistCt LCrR 45.1, US
Const Amd 6.

TRIALS —Cont'd
Tax proceedings, Tax Rule 12.
Failure to appear, Tax Rule 13.
Teachers on trial, §38-111.
Verdicts.
See VERDICTS.

TRIANGLE COMMUNITY GARDEN.
Real property tax exemption,
§47-1073.

TRICHOMONIASIS.
Treatment for sexual partners,
§§7-2081.01 to 7-2081.04.

TRUANCY.
Compulsory school attendance,
§§38-201 to 38-213.
See COMPULSORY SCHOOL
ATTENDANCE.
**Contributing to the delinquency of a
minor.**
Encouraging, causing, or allowing
truancy, §22-811.
Prevention resource guide, §38-2602.

TRUST DEEDS.
Mortgages and deeds of trust.
General provisions, §§42-804 to
42-820.
See MORTGAGES AND DEEDS OF
TRUST.

**TRUST, MORTGAGE AND TITLE
CORPORATIONS,** §§26-1301 to
26-1336.
Bylaws, §26-1325.
Capital stock.
Calling, §26-1317.
Deposit of, §26-1316.
Fiduciary security, as, §26-1312.
Increase or decrease in, §26-1331.
Payment, §§26-1316, 26-1317.
Sale of stock at public auction on
failure to pay over, §26-1317.
Certificate.
Charter of incorporation, §§26-1307,
26-1332.
Evidence, certificate of charter of
incorporation as, §26-1332.
Intention of existing company to avail
itself of provisions, §26-1313.
Organization, §26-1304.
Charter of incorporation.
Certificate, §§26-1307, 26-1332.
Council authority regarding, §26-1305.
Duration of, §26-1315.
Evidence, certificate of charter of
incorporation as, §26-1332.

TRUST, MORTGAGE AND TITLE CORPORATIONS —Cont'd
Charter of incorporation —Cont'd
Notice of application for, §26-1306.
Recordation, §26-1307.
Classes of business formed to carry out, §26-1301.
Congressional right to amend or repeal, reservation of, §26-1336.
Directors or trustees.
Bylaws, power to make, §26-1326.
Dividend declarations, liability on, §§26-1327, 26-1328.
Election of, §26-1324.
Management by, §26-1324.
Officers, §26-1325.
Personal liability when liabilities exceed assets, §26-1329.
Report, liability for failure to produce, §26-1319.
Dividend declarations, §§26-1327, 26-1328.
Establishment of, §26-1301.
Existing companies, §§26-1313, 26-1351.
Fiduciaries.
Appointment as fiduciary, §26-1310.
Automatic substitution of, §26-1311.01.
Oaths and affirmations, §26-1311.
Security requirements, §§26-1312, 26-1333.
Stockholder, fiduciary not liable as, §26-1330.
Foreign corporations, §26-1335.
Formation of, §26-1301.
Fraud and deceit, §26-1320.
Jurisdiction, §26-1334.
Liability.
Corporation as trustee, §26-1309.
Dividend declarations, §§26-1327, 26-1328.
Fiduciary not liable as stockholder, §26-1330.
Fiduciary security, liability on, §26-1333.
Personal liability of directors or trustees when liabilities exceed assets, §26-1329.
Report, failure to produce, §26-1319.
Stockholders, §26-1322.
Misappropriation of moneys, §26-1320.
Officers, §26-1325.
Organization certificate, §26-1304.
Perjury, §26-1320.
Perpetual succession, trust companies to have, §26-1352.

TRUST, MORTGAGE AND TITLE CORPORATIONS —Cont'd
Perpetual, title companies becoming, §26-1351.
Policy declaration, §26-1301.
Powers and duties, §26-1309.
Probate court powers, §26-1334.
Real property, §§26-1312, 26-1314.
Recordation of charter of incorporation, §26-1307.
Reports, §§26-1308, 26-1318, 26-1319.
Security requirements for fiduciaries, §§26-1312, 26-1333.
Stock and stockholders.
Capital stock. See within this heading, "Capital stock."
Certificates, §26-1321.
Fiduciary not liable as stockholder, §26-1330.
Liability of stockholders, §26-1322.
Payment of, §26-1323.
Personal estate, deemed as, §26-1321.
Transferability, §26-1321.
Taxation, §47-2502.
General provisions, §§47-2503 to 47-2515.
See BANKS AND FINANCIAL INSTITUTIONS.
Theft, misappropriation of moneys as, §26-1320.

TRUSTS AND TRUSTEES.
ABLE savings accounts, §§47-4901, 47-4902.
Accounts and accounting.
Bond of trustee.
Discharge only after accounting, §28-2504.
Animals, trust for care of.
Uniform trust code.
Creation of trusts, §19-1304.08.
Artist protection.
Art work and proceeds of sale as trust property, §28-5102.
Dealer responsibilities, §28-5103.
Attorneys at law.
Clients' Security Trust Fund, DCBar Rule XII.
Restitution to fund by attorney, DCBar Rule XI.
Interest on Lawyers Trust Account (IOLTA), DCBar Appx A, DCBar Rule X, ProfCond Rule 1.15.
Approved depositories, DCBar Rule XI.
Verification of participation, DCBar Rule XIV.

TRUSTS AND TRUSTEES —Cont'd
Attorneys' fees and costs.
Judicial proceedings, §19-1310.04.
Bonds, surety.
Discharge only after accounting,
§28-2504.
Captive insurance companies.
Special purpose financial captive
insurance companies.
Trust requirements, §31-3932.08.
Certification of trust, §19-1310.13.
Charitable trusts, §21-1801.
Combination and division of trusts,
§19-1304.17.
Compensation of trustees,
§19-1307.08.
Condominium owners' associations
as trustees, §42-1903.21.
Consent.
Modification or termination by,
§19-1304.11.
Cotrustees, §19-1307.03.
Counterclaims, §13-504.
Creation of trusts.
Uniform trust code, §§19-1304.01 to
19-1304.09.
Custodial trusts.
Uniform law, §§19-1101 to 19-1120.
See CUSTODIAL TRUSTS.
Cy pres doctrine.
Uniform trust code.
Modification or termination,
§19-1304.13.
Death of trustee.
Vacancies in trusteeship, §19-1307.04.
Declaration, grant, and assignment
of, §28-3503.
Deeds, form for, §42-601.
Disclaimer of property interests.
Generally, §§19-1501 to 19-1518.
See DISCLAIMER OF PROPERTY
INTERESTS.
Interest not trust property.
Disclaimed interest would have
become trust property,
§19-1508.
Distribution of trust property.
Uniform trust code.
Revocable trusts, §19-1306.04.
Division of trusts, §19-1304.17.
Duress.
Uniform trust code.
Void trusts, §19-1304.06.
Effect of purchase for value without
notice of trust, §42-1503.
Employee benefit trust distributions,
unclaimed.
See UNCLAIMED PROPERTY.

TRUSTS AND TRUSTEES —Cont'd
Expenses of trustee.
Reimbursement, §19-1307.09.
Express trusts, §42-1503.
Fiduciaries.
Generally.
See FIDUCIARIES.
Uniform trust code.
Personal representatives,
§19-1303.03.
Fiduciary security transfers,
§§28-2901 to 28-2909.
See FIDUCIARY SECURITY
TRANSFERS.
Fraud.
Uniform trust code.
Void trusts, §19-1304.06.
Housing production trust fund,
§§42-2801 to 42-2804.
Income tax, §§47-1809.01 to
47-1809.10.
Intestate succession of trust estates,
§19-317.
Investments.
Prudent investor act.
See PRUDENT INVESTOR ACT.
Investment securities.
Authenticating trustee.
Registration of securities.
Obligations, §28:8-407.
Signature.
Effect, §28:8-208.
Jurisdiction.
Uniform trust code.
Trustee and beneficiary,
§19-1302.02.
Limitation of actions.
Revocable trusts.
Limitation on action contesting
validity, §19-1306.04.
Uniform trust code.
Judicial proceedings, §19-1310.05.
Management of institutional funds.
General provisions.
See PRUDENT INVESTOR ACT.
Mistakes, reformation to correct.
Uniform trust code, §19-1304.15.
Modification or termination of
trusts.
Distribution upon termination of trust,
§19-1308.17.
Uniform trust code, §§19-1304.10 to
19-1304.17.
Mortgages and deeds of trust.
Trustee or assignee for foreclosure.
See MORTGAGES AND DEEDS OF
TRUST.

TRUSTS AND TRUSTEES —Cont'd
Notice.
  Uniform trust code.
    Methods and waiver, §19-1301.09.
    Qualified beneficiaries, §19-1301.10.
Personal representatives.
  Uniform trust code, §§19-1303.01 to
    19-1303.05.
Powers and duties of trustees,
    §§19-1307.01 to 19-1307.09,
    19-1308.01 to 19-1308.17.
  Accepting trusteeship, §19-1307.01.
  Administration of trust in good faith,
    §19-1308.01.
  Bonds, surety, §19-1307.02.
  Breach of trust.
    Consent of beneficiary, §19-1310.09.
    Damages, §19-1310.02.
    Damages in absence of breach,
      §19-1310.03.
    Duty to redress, §19-1308.12.
    Remedies, §19-1310.01.
  Certification of trust, §19-1310.13.
  Collection of trust property from
    former trustee, §19-1308.12.
  Compensation, §19-1307.08.
  Control and direction of trust
    property, §19-1308.09.
  Costs of administration,
    reasonableness, §19-1308.05.
  Cotrustees, §19-1307.03.
  Declining trusteeship, §19-1307.01.
  Delegation of powers or duties,
    §19-1308.07.
  Directions, power to direct or take
    directions, §19-1308.08.
  Discretionary powers, §19-1308.14.
  Distribution upon termination of trust,
    §19-1308.17.
  Enforcement and defense of claims,
    §19-1308.11.
  Expenses, reimbursement,
    §19-1307.09.
  General powers, §19-1308.15.
  Good faith administration,
    §19-1308.01.
  Impartiality, §19-1308.03.
  Information and reporting,
    §19-1308.13.
  Liability of person dealing with
    trustee, §19-1310.12.
  Limitation on personal liability,
    §19-1310.10.
    General partners, §19-1310.11.
  Loyalty, duty of, §19-1308.02.
  Prudent administration, §19-1308.04.

TRUSTS AND TRUSTEES —Cont'd
Powers and duties of trustees
    —Cont'd
  Recordkeeping, §19-1308.10.
  Reliance on trustee, §19-1310.12.
  Removal of trustee, §19-1307.06.
    Delivery of property by former
      trustee, §19-1307.07.
  Reports, duty to inform and report,
    §19-1308.13.
  Resignation of trustee, §19-1307.05.
    Delivery of property by former
      trustee, §19-1307.07.
  Separation of trust property,
    §19-1308.10.
  Special skills or expertise, reliance,
    §19-1308.06.
  Specific powers, §19-1308.16.
  Tax savings, §19-1308.14.
  Vacancies in trusteeship, §19-1307.04.
  Waiver of liability, effect, §19-1310.08.
Powers of appointment.
  See POWERS OF APPOINTMENT.
Powers of attorney, §21-2111.
Principal and income act,
    §§28-4801.01 to 28-4806.02.
  See PRINCIPAL AND INCOME.
Probate proceedings.
  Proceedings involving trustees,
    Probate Rules 201 to 225.
  See PROBATE PROCEEDINGS.
Prudent investors.
  Uniform prudent investor act,
    §§19-1309.01 to 19-1309.06.
Real property taxes.
  Transfers to revocable trust, exempt
    from tax, §47-802.
Records.
  Uniform trust code.
    Electronic records and signatures,
      §19-1311.02.
Reliance on trustee, §19-1310.12.
Reliance on trust instrument,
    §19-1310.06.
Removal of trustee, §19-1307.06.
  Delivery of property by former trustee,
    §19-1307.07.
Resignation of trustee, §19-1307.05.
  Delivery of property by former trustee,
    §19-1307.07.
Revocable trusts.
  Income tax, §47-1809.07.
  Probate proceedings.
    Claims against revocable trust,
      Probate Rule 213.
    Notice of existence of revocable
      trust, Probate Rule 212.

TRUSTS AND TRUSTEES —Cont'd
Revocable trusts —Cont'd
Trustees.
Directions, power to direct or take directions, §19-1308.08.
Uniform trust code, §§19-1306.01 to 19-1306.04.
Secured transactions.
Name of debtor and secured party, §28:9-503.
Security transfers, §§28-2901 to 28-2909.
See FIDUCIARY SECURITY TRANSFERS.
Series trusts, §§29-1204.01 to 29-1204.05.
Authorization, §29-1204.01.
Claims pertaining to series trusts, §29-1204.05.
Dissolution, §29-1204.04.
Duties of trustee, §29-1204.03.
Liability, §29-1204.02.
Settlement or compromise.
Uniform trust code.
Nonjudicial settlement agreements, §19-1301.11.
Spendthrift provision.
Uniform trust code, §19-1305.02.
Enforceability, §19-1305.03.
Exception, §19-1305.03.
Split-interest trusts, §21-1801.
Statute of frauds.
Declaration, grant and assignment of trust, §28-3503.
Statutory rule against perpetuities, §§19-901 to 19-907.
Statutory trusts, §§29-1201.01 to 29-1209.01.
See STATUTORY TRUSTS.
Taxation.
Tax savings, §19-1308.14.
Uniform trust code.
Modification to achieve settlor's tax objectives, §19-1304.16.
Title to trust property.
Uniform trust code, §19-1304.18.
Transfers to minors authorized by trust, §21-305.
Undue influence.
Uniform trust code.
Void trusts, §19-1304.06.
Uniform custodial trust law, §§19-1101 to 19-1120.
See CUSTODIAL TRUSTS.
Uniform fiduciaries act, §§21-1701 to 21-1712.
See FIDUCIARIES.

TRUSTS AND TRUSTEES —Cont'd
Uniform prudent investor act, §§19-1309.01 to 19-1309.06.
Compliance, determination, §19-1309.05.
Considerations, §19-1309.02.
Diversification of investments, §19-1309.03.
Duties upon accepting trusteeship, §19-1309.04.
General rule, §19-1309.01.
Prudent investor rule, §19-1309.01.
Risk and return objectives, §19-1309.02.
Standard of care, §19-1309.02.
Language invoking standard, §19-1309.06.
Uniform trust code, §§19-1301.01 to 19-1311.03.
Actual knowledge, §19-1301.04.
Administration.
Costs of administration.
Reasonableness, §19-1308.05.
Uneconomic trusts, termination, §19-1304.14.
Court's role in administration of trust, §19-1302.01.
Event affecting administration or distribution.
Liability of trustees, §19-1310.07.
Good faith administration, §19-1308.01.
Principal place of administration, §19-1301.08.
Prudent administration, §19-1308.04.
Animals, trust for care of.
Creation of trusts, §19-1304.08.
Applicability.
Conflict of laws, §19-1301.05.
Effective date of chapter, §19-1311.03.
Scope of chapter, §19-1301.02.
Attachment.
Creditor's claims, §19-1305.01.
Breach of trust.
Consent of beneficiary, §19-1310.09.
Damages, §19-1310.02.
Damages in absence of breach, §19-1310.03.
Remedies, §19-1310.01.
Charitable purposes, §19-1304.05.
Citation of chapter, §19-1301.01.
Combination and division of trusts, §19-1304.17.
Common law of trusts, §19-1301.06.

TRUSTS AND TRUSTEES —Cont'd
Uniform trust code —Cont'd
  Conflict of laws, §19-1301.05.
    Governing law, §19-1301.07.
  Construction and interpretation,
    §19-1311.01.
  Control and direction of trust
    property, §19-1308.09.
  Costs of administration.
    Uneconomic trusts, termination,
      §19-1304.14.
  Court's role in administration of trust,
    §19-1302.01.
  Creation of trusts, §§19-1304.01 to
    19-1304.09.
    Animals, trust for care of,
      §19-1304.08.
    Charitable purposes, §19-1304.05.
    Duress, §19-1304.06.
    Fraud, §19-1304.06.
    Methods of creating, §19-1304.01.
    Noncharitable trust without
      ascertainable beneficiary,
      §19-1304.09.
    Oral trusts, evidence, §19-1304.07.
    Purposes, §19-1304.04.
      Charitable purposes, §19-1304.05.
    Recognition of trusts created in
      other jurisdictions, §19-1304.03.
    Requirements, §19-1304.02.
    Trusts created in other jurisdictions,
      §19-1304.03.
    Undue influence, §19-1304.06.
    Void trusts, §19-1304.06.
  Creditor's claims, §19-1305.01.
    Overdue distributions, §19-1305.06.
    Personal obligations of trustee,
      §19-1305.07.
    Settlor, claims against, §19-1305.05.
  Cy pres doctrine.
    Modification or termination,
      §19-1304.13.
  Damages.
    Absence of breach, §19-1310.03.
    Breach of trust, §19-1310.02.
  Death of trustee.
    Vacancies in trusteeship,
      §19-1307.04.
  Defined terms, §19-1301.03.
    Knowledge, §19-1301.04.
  Distribution of trust property.
    Event affecting administration or
      distribution.
      Knowledge of trustees,
        §19-1310.07.
    Revocable trusts, §19-1306.04.

TRUSTS AND TRUSTEES —Cont'd
Uniform trust code —Cont'd
  Division of trusts, §19-1304.17.
  Duress.
    Void trusts, §19-1304.06.
  Effective date of chapter, §19-1311.03.
  Electronic records and signatures,
    §19-1311.02.
  Equitable principles, §19-1301.06.
  Fraud.
    Void trusts, §19-1304.06.
  Illegal, impracticable impossible or
    wasteful.
    Modification or termination.
      Cy pres doctrine, §19-1304.13.
  Imputed knowledge, §19-1301.04.
  Judicial proceedings, §§19-1302.01,
    19-1302.02.
    Attorney's fees and costs,
      §19-1310.04.
    Limitation of actions, §19-1310.05.
    Reliance on trust instrument,
      §19-1310.06.
  Jurisdiction.
    Trustee and beneficiary,
      §19-1302.02.
  Knowledge.
    Defined, §19-1301.04.
  Limitation of actions, §19-1310.05.
  Mistakes, reformation to correct,
    §19-1304.15.
  Modification or termination,
    §§19-1304.10 to 19-1304.17.
    Approval or disapproval, proceedings
      for, §19-1304.10.
    Combination and division,
      §19-1304.17.
    Consent, modification or termination
      by, §19-1304.11.
    Cy pres doctrine, §19-1304.13.
    Distribution upon termination of
      trust, §19-1308.17.
    Illegal, impracticable impossible or
      wasteful.
      Cy pres doctrine, §19-1304.13.
    Inability to administer effectively,
      §19-1304.12.
    Mistakes, reformation to correct,
      §19-1304.15.
    Proceedings for approval or
      disapproval, §19-1304.10.
    Revocable trusts, §19-1306.02.
    Spendthrift provision.
      Not a material purpose,
        §19-1304.11.
    Tax objectives.
      Modification for settlor,
        §19-1304.16.

TRUSTS AND TRUSTEES —Cont'd
Uniform trust code —Cont'd
Modification or termination —Cont'd
Unanticipated circumstances,
§19-1304.12.
Uneconomic, §19-1304.14.
Notice.
Methods and waiver, §19-1301.09.
Qualified beneficiaries, §19-1301.10.
Oral trusts, evidence, §19-1304.07.
Overdue distributions.
Creditor's claims, §19-1305.06.
Personal representatives, §§19-1303.01
to 19-1303.05.
Agents, §19-1303.03.
Appointment by court, §19-1303.05.
Consent of person represented,
§19-1303.01.
Conservators, §19-1303.03.
Fiduciaries, §19-1303.03.
Guardians, §19-1303.03.
Holder of general testamentary
power of appointment,
§19-1303.02.
Parents, §19-1303.03.
Person having substantially
identical interest, §19-1303.04.
Powers and duties generally,
§19-1303.01.
Powers and duties of trustees,
§§19-1308.01 to 19-1308.17.
Principal place of administration,
§19-1301.08.
Purposes, §19-1304.04.
Recognition of trusts created in other
jurisdictions, §19-1304.03.
Records.
Electronic records and signatures,
§19-1311.02.
Reliance on trust instrument,
§19-1310.06.
Representation, §§19-1303.01 to
19-1303.05.
Revocable trusts, §§19-1306.01 to
19-1306.04.
Distribution of trust property,
§19-1306.04.
Limitation on action contesting
validity, §19-1306.04.
Revocation or amendment,
§19-1306.02.
Settlor's capacity, §19-1306.01.
Settlor's powers, §19-1306.03.
Trustees.
Directions, power to direct or take
directions, §19-1308.08.

TRUSTS AND TRUSTEES —Cont'd
Uniform trust code —Cont'd
Revocable trusts —Cont'd
Validity.
Limitation on action contesting,
§19-1306.04.
Withdrawal, power of, §19-1306.03.
Scope of chapter, §19-1301.02.
Settlement agreements.
Nonjudicial settlement agreements,
§19-1301.11.
Settlor.
Creditor's claims against settlor,
§19-1305.05.
Powers, §19-1301.05.
Revocable trusts.
Settlor's capacity, §19-1306.01.
Settlor's powers, §19-1306.03.
Short title, §19-1301.01.
Spendthrift provision, §19-1305.02.
Creditor's claims, §19-1305.01.
Overdue distributions,
§19-1305.06.
Enforceability, §19-1305.03.
Exception, §19-1305.03.
Not a material purpose, §19-1304.11.
Taxes.
Modification to achieve settlor's tax
objectives, §19-1304.16.
Title to trust property, §19-1304.18.
Transfer of principal place of
administration, §19-1301.08.
Trustees, §§19-1307.01 to 19-1307.09.
Accepting trusteeship, §19-1307.01.
Administration of trust in good
faith, §19-1308.01.
Attorney's fees and costs,
§19-1310.04.
Bonds, surety, §19-1307.02.
Breach of trust.
Consent of beneficiary,
§19-1310.09.
Damages, §19-1310.02.
Duty to redress, §19-1308.12.
Remedies, §19-1310.01.
Certification of trust, §19-1310.13.
Collection of trust property from
former trustee, §19-1308.12.
Compensation, §19-1307.08.
Control and direction of trust
property, §19-1308.09.
Costs of administration,
reasonableness, §19-1308.05.
Cotrustees, §19-1307.03.
Damages in absence of breach,
§19-1310.03.

TRUSTS AND TRUSTEES —Cont'd
Uniform trust code —Cont'd
Trustees —Cont'd
Death of trustee, §19-1307.04.
Declining trusteeship, §19-1307.01.
Delegation of powers or duties, §19-1308.07.
Directions, power to direct or take directions, §19-1308.08.
Discretionary powers, §19-1308.14.
Distribution upon termination of trust, §19-1308.17.
Enforcement and defense of claims, §19-1308.11.
Event affecting administration or distribution.
Liability of trustees, §19-1310.07.
Exculpation of trustees, §19-1310.08.
Expenses, reimbursement, §19-1307.09.
General powers, §19-1308.15.
Good faith administration, §19-1308.01.
Impartiality, §19-1308.03.
Information and reporting, §19-1308.13.
Knowledge of trustees.
Event affecting administration or distribution, §19-1310.07.
Liability in absence of breach, §19-1310.03.
Liability of person dealing with trustee, §19-1310.12.
Limitation of actions against trustees, §19-1310.05.
Limitation on personal liability, §19-1310.10.
General partners, §19-1310.11.
Loyalty, duty of, §19-1308.02.
Personal obligations of trustee, §19-1305.07.
Powers and duties, §§19-1308.01 to 19-1308.17.
Prudent administration, §19-1308.04.
Uniform prudent investor act, §§19-1309.01 to 19-1309.06.
Recordkeeping, §19-1308.10.
Reliance on trustee, §19-1310.12.
Reliance on trust instrument, §19-1310.06.
Removal of trustee, §19-1307.06.
Delivery of property by former trustee, §19-1307.07.
Reports, duty to inform and report, §19-1308.13.

TRUSTS AND TRUSTEES —Cont'd
Uniform trust code —Cont'd
Trustees —Cont'd
Resignation of trustee, §19-1307.05.
Delivery of property by former trustee, §19-1307.07.
Separation of trust property, §19-1308.10.
Special skills or expertise, reliance, §19-1308.06.
Specific powers, §19-1308.16.
Tax savings, §19-1308.14.
Uniform prudent investor act, §§19-1309.01 to 19-1309.06.
Vacancies in trusteeship, §19-1307.04.
Waiver of liability, effect, §19-1310.08.
Undue influence.
Void trusts, §19-1304.06.
Uniform application, §19-1311.01.
Uniform prudent investor act, §§19-1309.01 to 19-1309.06.
Void trusts, §19-1304.06.
Vacancies in trusteeship, §19-1307.04.

TRUTH IN SENTENCING COMMISSION, §§24-111 to 24-114.

TUBERCULOSIS.
Laboratory services.
Fees, §7-734.

TUBERCULOSIS SANATORIA, §7-180.
Children's tuberculosis sanatorium, §44-702.

TUGBOATS.
Bridges, requirements for going under, §9-309.

TUITION EXPENSES.
College access assistance, §§38-2701 to 38-2706.
DC promise program, §§38-2751 to 38-2759.
See UNIVERSITIES AND COLLEGES.
District of Columbia School of Law.
Mayor's stipends, §38-1205.11.
Preferential tuition for residents, §38-1205.10.
Health professional recruitment program.
Generally, §§7-751.01 to 7-751.16.
See HEALTH PROFESSIONAL RECRUITMENT PROGRAM.
National Guard.
Tuition assistance benefits, §49-807.

TUITION EXPENSES —Cont'd

Nonpublic schools.

Rate-setting, §38-2561.10.

Reconsideration, §38-2561.13.

Panel, §38-2561.14.

Nonresidents attending District schools, §§38-301 to 38-313.

Nurse training corps, §38-1501.

Opportunity accounts.

Generally, §§1-307.61 to 1-307.74.

Use for educational expenses, §1-307.68.

Police and firefighters, §5-1305.

Scholarships.

See SCHOLARSHIPS.

University of the District of Columbia.

Grants, §§38-1207.01 to 38-1207.07.

Residents, preferential tuition rates for, §38-1204.07.

TUNNEL CONSTRUCTION.

Permits, §1-301.01.

TUNNEL UNDER CAPITOL GROUNDS AND BOTANIC GARDENS, §§10-511.01 to 10-511.07.

Construction, §10-511.02.

Expense or liability not incurred by United States, §10-511.05.

Jurisdiction, control, responsibility for operation and control, §10-511.03.

Required, §10-511.01.

Restoration of grounds to original condition, §10-511.04.

Right, title, interest in United States, §10-511.03.

TURKEY BOWL.

District of Columbia interscholastic athletic association (DCIAA).

Revenue generation and sponsorship, §38-2981.

TURNOVER COMMISSION.

Conservators and guardians of minors in probate proceedings, Probate Rule 225.

TWITTER.

E-commerce companies.

Qualified social electronic commerce companies tax abatements, §§47-1818.01 to 47-1818.08.

TWO-DAY CONTINUANCE RULE.

Criminal proceedings, CrimPro Rule 111.

TWO-DAY CONTINUANCE RULE —Cont'd

Family court proceedings generally, FamDiv Rule G.

2 M STREET, N.E. DEVELOPMENT PROJECT.

Real property tax exemptions, §47-4648.

TWO-WAY RADIO COMMUNICATIONS, §5-1308.

2323 PENNSYLVANIA AVENUE, S.E. REDEVELOPMENT PROJECT.

Tax abatements, §47-4640.

U

ULTRA VIRES DEFENSE.

Corporations, §29-303.04.

Nonprofit corporations, §29-403.03.

UNANIMITY OF VERDICT, CivPro Rule 48, CrimPro Rule 31.

UNAUTHORIZED ENTITIES ACT OF 2006, §§31-231 to 31-233.

UNAUTHORIZED PRACTICE OF LAW, DCCtApp Rule 49, ProfCond Rule 5.5.

Appeals in federal cases.

Clerk or deputy clerk not to practice, FRAP 45(a).

Court employees, USCtApp Rule 1.

UNAUTHORIZED USE OF MOTOR VEHICLES, §22-3215.

UNCLAIMED PROPERTY, §§41-101 to 41-142.

Actions.

Compelling delivery, §41-133.

Reciprocal actions and agreements, §41-134.

Animals, metropolitan police property clerk sale of, §5-119.12.

Applicability of law, §41-141.

Unclaimed deposits for excavation work in public space, §41-141.01.

Appropriations, §41-139.

Banking organization.

Bank deposits and funds in, §41-106.

Crediting of dividends, interest, or increments to owner's account, §41-121.

Defined, §41-102.

Fiduciaries, property held by, §41-111.

Property of organizations in course of dissolution, §41-110.

UNCLAIMED PROPERTY —Cont'd
Banking organization —Cont'd
Safe deposit boxes.
Charges, payment of, §41-120.
Delivery or payment of contents,
§41-119.
Unclaimed contents of, §41-115.
Bills of lading.
Lost and missing bills, §28:7-601.
Business associations.
Defined, §41-102.
Property of associations in course of
dissolution, §41-110.
Stock and other intangible interests
in, §41-109.
Cash, presumed abandonment of,
§41-105.
Claims.
Determination by mayor, §41-125.
Filing, §41-124.
Judicial review of decision regarding,
§41-127.
State claim to recover property,
§41-126.
Crediting of dividends, interest, or
increments to owner's account,
§41-121.
Credit memos, §41-114.
Custody of, §§41-104, 41-120.
Declining to receive, §41-128.
Definitions, §41-102.
Delivery or payment of, §41-119.
Action to compel, §41-133.
Declining, §41-128.
Failure to pay or deliver, §41-135.
Deposit of funds from, §41-123.
Dividends credited to owner's
account, §41-121.
Documents of title.
Lost and missing documents,
§28:7-601.
Employee benefit trust distributions.
Defined, §41-102.
Presumed abandonment of, §41-113.
Enforcement, §41-136.
Escheat.
Intestate succession, §19-701.
Fiduciaries, property held by,
§41-111.
Fines, §§41-135, 41-136.
Gift certificates, §41-114.
Governing law.
Issuance of rules and regulations,
§41-138.
Retroactivity, §41-142.
Severability of provisions, §41-140.

UNCLAIMED PROPERTY —Cont'd
Governing law —Cont'd
Uniformity of application and
interpretation, §41-141.
Increments credited to owner's
account, §41-121.
Interest credited to owner's account,
§41-121.
Interest due to failure to pay or
deliver, §41-135.
Interpretation of provisions, §41-141.
Investment securities.
Notification to issuer of lost security
certificate, §28:8-406.
Replacement of lost security
certificates, §28:8-405.
Issuance of rules regarding, §41-138.
Life insurance companies.
Defined, §41-102.
Funds owing under life insurance
policies, §41-107.
Property distributable in course of
demutualization, rehabilitation or
reorganization, §41-107.01.
Limitation of actions, §41-129.
Location agreements, §41-137.
Lodging houses, left in, §30-103.
Mayor.
Determination of claims, §41-125.
Issuance of rules, §41-138.
Metropolitan police, property clerk.
See METROPOLITAN POLICE.
Money orders, presumed
abandonment of, §41-105.
Notice of abandoned property,
§41-118.
Payment of. See within this heading,
"Delivery or payment of."
Penalties, §41-135.
Policy declaration, §41-101.
Presumption of abandonment, what
constitutes, §41-103.
Public officers and agencies,
property held by, §41-112.
Public utilities.
Defined, §41-102.
Deposits and refunds held by, §41-108.
Railroads, disposition by, §§35-101 to
35-103.
Reciprocal actions and agreements,
§41-134.
Reclamation by owner, §41-120.
Records.
Confidentiality of, §41-131.
Examination of, §41-130.
Requirement to keep, §41-130.

UNCLAIMED PROPERTY —Cont'd
Records —Cont'd
  Retention of, §41-132.
  Subpoena of, §41-130.
Recovery agreements, §41-137.
Reimbursement of holder paying
    claim, §41-120.
Reports, §41-117.
  Declining to receive property following,
    §41-128.
  Payment or delivery and, §41-119.
  Verification of, §41-130.
Retroactivity of provisions, §41-142.
Safe deposit boxes.
  Charges, payment of, §41-120.
  Delivery or payment of contents,
    §41-119.
  Unclaimed contents of, §41-115.
Sale of, §§30-103, 41-122.
Severability of provisions, §41-140.
States.
  Claim to recover property by, §41-126.
  Reciprocal actions and agreements,
    §41-134.
Subpoenas of records, §41-130.
Traveler's checks, presumed
    abandonment of, §41-105.
Unclaimed deposits for excavation
    work in public space.
  Applicability of law, §41-141.01.
Wages, unpaid, §41-116.
Warehouse receipts.
  Lost and missing receipts, §28:7-601.

UNCONSCIONABILITY.
Sale of goods, UCC, §28:2-302.

UNDERDRAINING
    REQUIREMENTS.
Cemeteries, §43-105.

UNDERGROUND CONDUITS.
Conduit defined, §34-2001.
Permits, §§1-301.01, 34-1406.
Public utilities.
  Electric light and power companies.
    See ELECTRIC LIGHT AND
      POWER COMPANIES.
  Private conduits.
    See PUBLIC UTILITIES.
Telecommunications companies.
  See TELECOMMUNICATIONS
    COMPANIES.

UNDERGROUND FACILITIES.
Water pollution, §8-103.10.

UNDERGROUND RAIL LINES.
Metrorail and metrobus unlawful
    use of others' underground lines,
    §35-210.

UNDERGROUND STORAGE TANKS,
  §§8-113.01 to 8-113.12.
Access to, §8-113.08.
Certification, §§8-113.06, 8-113.07.
Corrective action, requiring,
  §8-113.08.
Definitions, §8-113.01.
Denial, revocation, or suspension of
    license or permit, §8-113.07.
Enforcement of rules regarding,
  §8-113.09.
Fines, §8-113.09.
Inspections, §8-113.08.
Interim prohibition for installation,
  §8-113.04.
Issuance of rules regarding,
  §8-113.12.
Licenses, §§8-113.06, 8-113.07.
Notice.
  Existence and specifications of tank,
    §8-113.02.
  Release notification requirements,
    §8-113.03.
Private right of action, §8-113.11.
Registration, §8-113.06.
Summary action, §8-113.10.
Water pollution, §8-103.10.

UNDERLEASES, §42-3229.

UNDERTAKINGS.
Attachment, §§16-509, 16-527.
Defined, §28-2501.
Fiduciary's bond, undertaking in
    lieu of, §16-601.
Replevin, undertaking to abide by
    judgment of court on, §16-3704.

UNDERWRITING.
Insurance, §§31-5001 to 31-5011.

UNDUE INFLUENCE.
Alcoholic beverage licenses.
  Manufacturers.
    Revocation or suspension.
      Undue influence of wholesaler or
        retailer, §25-824.
  Revocation or suspension.
    Wholesalers.
      Undue influence of retailer,
        §25-825.
Trusts and trustees.
  Uniform trust code.
    Void trusts, §19-1304.06.

UNEMPLOYMENT
    COMPENSATION, §§51-101 to
    51-151.
Actions, §51-121.

UNEMPLOYMENT COMPENSATION
—Cont'd
Additional benefits program, §51-107.
Administration, §§51-113, 51-114.
Administrative expenses, payment of, §51-114.
Amount of benefits, determining, §51-107.
Appeals, §§51-111, 51-112.
Audits, §51-122.
Average weekly wage.
Computation, §51-107.
Benefits.
Additional benefits program, §51-107.
Claims for, §51-111.
Dependent relatives, payment with respect to, §51-107.
Determining amount and duration, §51-107.
Disqualification for, §51-110.
Domestic violence claimants, §§51-131 to 51-136.
Eligibility for, §51-109.
Educational stepladder program participants, §51-109.01.
Extended benefit period, §51-107.
Payment of, §51-108.
Protection of, §51-118.
Qualification for, §51-107.
Shared work benefits.
Shared work unemployment compensation program, §§51-171 to 51-178.
Total amount, §51-107.
Benefits and refunds, payment of, §51-108.
Board, §51-121.
Child support, §51-118.
Claims for benefits, §51-111.
Collection of taxes.
Refund offsets.
Applicability of provisions, §47-4436.
Notice and protest, §47-4436.
Right to credit overpayment, §47-4431.
Computation of benefits, §51-107.
Computation of employer contributions, §51-103.
Congressional right to alter, amend, or repeal provisions, reservation of, §51-123.
Definitions, §51-101.
Deposits into fund, §51-106.
Disclosure, §51-113.
Domestic violence claimants, §51-136.
Disqualification for benefits, §51-110.

UNEMPLOYMENT COMPENSATION
—Cont'd
Domestic violence, §§51-131 to 51-136.
Disclosure of claimants' information, §51-136.
Employee awareness training, §51-134.
Experience rating accounts.
Benefits not to be charged to, §51-133.
Reports, §51-135.
Separation from employment due to domestic violence, §51-131.
Evidence required for payment of benefits, §51-132.
Duration of benefits, determining, §51-107.
Effective date, §51-125.
Eligibility for benefits, §51-109.
Educational stepladder program participants, §51-109.01.
Employer contributions, §51-103.
Computation tables, §51-103.
District of Columbia, by, §51-151.
Payment of, §51-104.
Employment defined for purposes of, §51-101.
Expenses of administration.
Source, §51-114.
Extended benefit period, §51-107.
Fines and penalties.
Disposition of fines, §51-120.
Employer payment of contributions, §51-104.
Fraud and deceit, §51-119.
Violations of provisions, §51-117.
Fraud and deceit, §51-119.
Fund.
Deposits into fund, §51-106.
Establishment of, §51-102.
Hearings, §51-111.
Inspections, §51-117.
Mayor, §51-127.
Nonresident employers, service of process on, §51-105.
Payment of benefits, §51-108.
Penalties. See within this heading, "Fines and penalties."
Prison industries, §24-231.10.
Reciprocity, §51-116.
Records, §51-117.
Refunds, §51-108.
Reports, §51-117.
Rights, protection of, §51-118.
Service of process on nonresident employers, §51-105.

UNEMPLOYMENT COMPENSATION
—Cont'd
Severability of provisions, §51-124.
**Shared work unemployment
compensation program,** §§51-171
to 51-178.
Affected unit defined, §51-171.
Definitions, §51-171.
Eligibility for shared work benefit,
§51-177.
Payment of benefit, §51-178.
Employer participation, §51-173.
Establishment, §51-172.
Reports relating to operation of plan.
Participating employers to furnish,
§51-173.
Rules and procedures.
Adoption, establishment, §51-172.
Shared work benefit.
Defined, §51-171.
Employees eligible for, §51-177.
Payment, §51-178.
Shared work plan.
Changed conditions.
Modification to meet, §51-176.
Defined, §51-171.
Effective date, §51-175.
Expiration, §51-175.
Modification, §51-176.
Seasonal or part-time employees.
Plan not used to subsidize,
§51-174.
Submission by employers
participating, §51-173.
Approval, §51-174.
Collective bargaining unit covered
by, approval, §51-174.
Termination, §51-175.
Short title of chapter, §51-126.
**"Unemployed" construed for
purposes of earnings,** §51-101.
Waiver or release of rights, §51-118.
Weekly benefit amount, §51-107.
Witnesses, §51-111.

**UNEMPLOYMENT
DISCRIMINATION,** §§32-1361 to
32-1368.
Applicability, §32-1368.
Definitions, §32-1361.
Effective date, §32-1368.
Enforcement of provisions, §32-1365.
Exemptions, §32-1364.
Penalties for violations, §32-1366.
Prohibited, §32-1362.
Retaliation, §32-1363.
Rules, §32-1367.

**UNFAIR INSURANCE TRADE
PRACTICES,** §§31-2231.01 to
31-2231.25.
See INSURANCE.

UNFAIR TRADE PRACTICES.
Cigarette sales below cost, §§28-4521
to 28-4527.
See CIGARETTES.
**Consumer and regulatory affairs
department complaint
procedures,** §28-3904.
Fraternal benefit societies, §31-5331.
Insurance, §§31-2231.01 to 31-2231.25.
See INSURANCE.
Mortgage lenders and brokers,
§26-1114.
Natural gas suppliers, §§34-1671.01 to
34-1671.14.
See GAS COMPANIES.
Restraint of trade.
General provisions, §§28-4501 to
28-4518.
See RESTRAINTS OF TRADE.
Tobacco tax, §47-2424.

**UNIFIED COMMUNICATIONS,
OFFICE OF,** §§1-327.51 to
1-327.57.
Emergency medical application.
Development to aid in providing
cardiopulmonary resuscitation,
§1-327.54a.
Interagency coordination, §1-327.56.
Organization.
Primary organizational functions,
§1-327.55.

**UNIFORM ACT TO SECURE THE
ATTENDANCE OF WITNESSES
FROM WITHOUT A STATE IN
CRIMINAL PROCEEDINGS,**
§§23-1501 to 23-1504.

**UNIFORM ADULT GUARDIANSHIP
AND PROTECTIVE
PROCEEDINGS JURISDICTION
ACT,** §§21-2401.01 to 21-2405.03.
See GUARDIAN AND WARD.

**UNIFORM ANATOMICAL GIFT
REVISION ACT OF 2008,**
§§7-1531.01 to 7-1531.28.

**UNIFORM CERTIFICATES OF
TITLE FOR VESSELS,**
§§50-1541.01 to 50-1541.28.
See BOATS AND OTHER
WATERCRAFT.

UNIFORM CHILD ABDUCTION
PREVENTION ACT, §§16-4604.01
to 16-4604.10.
See CHILD CUSTODY AND CHILD
CUSTODY PROCEEDINGS.

UNIFORM CHILD CUSTODY
PROCEEDINGS, §§16-4601.01 to
16-4605.03.
See CHILD CUSTODY AND CHILD
CUSTODY PROCEEDINGS.

UNIFORM COLLABORATIVE LAW
ACT, §§16-4001 to 16-4022.
See COLLABORATIVE LAW.

UNIFORM COMMERCIAL CODE,
§§28:1-101 to 28:11-108.
See COMMERCIAL CODE.

UNIFORM CUSTODIAL TRUST
LAW, §§19-1101 to 19-1120.
See CUSTODIAL TRUSTS.

UNIFORM DISCLAIMER OF
PROPERTY INTERESTS ACT,
§§19-1501 to 19-1518.
See DISCLAIMER OF PROPERTY
INTERESTS.

UNIFORM ELECTRONIC
TRANSACTIONS ACT, §§28-4901
to 28-4918.
See ELECTRONIC TRANSACTIONS,
UNIFORM ACT.

UNIFORM FIDUCIARIES ACT,
§§21-1701 to 21-1712.
See FIDUCIARIES.

UNIFORM FOREIGN-COUNTRY
MONEY JUDGMENTS
RECOGNITION ACT OF 2011,
§§15-361 to 15-368.
See FOREIGN-MONEY JUDGMENTS.

UNIFORM GENERAL POWER OF
ATTORNEY, §§21-2101 to 21-2118.
See POWERS OF ATTORNEY.

UNIFORM GIFTS TO MINORS ACT.
Repeal of, §21-324.

UNIFORM INTERSTATE
DEPOSITIONS AND
DISCOVERY ACT, §§13-441 to
13-448.
See INTERSTATE DEPOSITIONS AND
DISCOVERY.

UNIFORM INTERSTATE FAMILY
SUPPORT ACT, §§46-351.01 to
46-359.03.
See INTERSTATE FAMILY SUPPORT.

UNIFORM LAW COMMISSION,
§§3-1431 to 3-1433.

UNIFORM LIMITED COOPERATIVE
ASSOCIATION ACT OF 2010,
§§29-1001.01 to 29-1015.08.
See LIMITED COOPERATIVE
ASSOCIATIONS.

UNIFORM LIMITED LIABILITY
COMPANY ACT OF 2010,
§§29-801.01 to 29-810.01.
See LIMITED LIABILITY COMPANIES.

UNIFORM LIMITED PARTNERSHIP
ACT OF 2010, §§29-701.01 to
29-711.01.
See LIMITED PARTNERSHIPS.

UNIFORM MEDIATION ACT,
§§16-4201 to 16-4213.

UNIFORM MILITARY AND
OVERSEAS VOTERS ACT,
§§1-1061.01 to 1-1061.20.
See ELECTIONS.

UNIFORM NONPROBATE
TRANSFERS ON DEATH ACT
OF 2000, §§19-601.01 to 19-603.11.
See NONPROBATE TRANSFERS.

UNIFORM PARTNERSHIP ACT OF
2010, §§29-601.01 to 29-611.01.
See PARTNERSHIPS.

UNIFORM PER STUDENT
FUNDING FORMULA, §§38-2901
to 38-2914.

UNIFORM PRINCIPAL AND
INCOME ACT, §§28-4801.01 to
28-4806.02.
See PRINCIPAL AND INCOME.

UNIFORM PRUDENT
MANAGEMENT OF
INSTITUTIONAL FUNDS,
§§44-1631 to 44-1639.
See PRUDENT MANAGEMENT OF
INSTITUTIONAL FUNDS.

UNIFORM REAL PROPERTY
TRANSFERS ON DEATH,
§§19-604.01 to 19-604.19.

UNIFORMS.
Insignia of police and fire and
emergency medical services
departments.
Unauthorized use, §22-1409.
Private vehicles-for-hire.
Trade dress requirements,
§50-301.29d.

UNIFORM STATUTORY TRUST
ENTITY ACT OF 2010,
§§29-1201.01 to 29-1209.01.
See STATUTORY TRUSTS.

UNIFORM TOD SECURITY
REGISTRATION, §§19-603.01 to
19-603.11.
See NONPROBATE TRANSFERS.

UNIFORM TRUST CODE,
§§19-1301.01 to 19-1311.03.
See TRUSTS AND TRUSTEES.

UNIFORM UNINCORPORATED
NONPROFIT ASSOCIATION ACT
OF 2010, §§29-1101 to 29-1127.
See NONPROFIT ASSOCIATIONS,
UNINCORPORATED.

UNIFORM UNSWORN FOREIGN
DECLARATIONS ACT, §§16-5301
to 16-5308.
See UNSWORN FOREIGN
DECLARATIONS.

UNINCORPORATED BUSINESSES.
Income taxes, §§47-1808.01 to
47-1808.12.

UNINCORPORATED NONPROFIT
ASSOCIATIONS, §§29-1101 to
29-1127.
See NONPROFIT ASSOCIATIONS,
UNINCORPORATED.

UNINHABITABLE BUILDINGS,
§§6-901 to 6-919.
See BUILDING CODE.

UNINSURED MOTORIST FUND.
No-fault motor vehicle insurance,
§31-2408.01.

UNION MARKET DISTRICT.
Tax increment financing,
§§2-1217.36a to 2-1217.36d.
Declaration of intent, §2-1217.36c.
Defined terms, §2-1217.36a.
Findings of council, §2-1217.36b.
Future legal requirements,
§2-1217.36d.
Maximum amount of bonds,
§2-1217.36c.
Request for issuance of bonds,
§2-1217.36b.

UNIONS.
Labor unions.
See LABOR UNIONS.
Restraints of trade.
Exclusion of labor from chapter,
§28-4504.

UNION STATION.
Railroad companies' right to use,
§9-1201.13.

UNIONTOWN.
Anacostia, name changed to, §1-108.

UNITED HOUSE OF PRAYER FOR
ALL PEOPLE.
Real property tax exemption.
Kitchen or feeding facilities, §47-1086.

UNITED KINGDOM.
Insurance company annual audited
financial reports, §31-314.

UNITED NATIONS EMPLOYEES,
§6-1309.01.

UNITED STATES.
Actions against, US Const Art III §2.
Appeals in criminal cases, §23-104.
Appeals in federal cases.
Costs for and against, FRAP 39(b).
Appropriations, US Const Art I §9.
Bonds, surety.
Action on bond to United States,
§28-2503.
Costs charged to United States,
CivPro Rule 54.
Appeals, DCCtApp Rule 39.
Counterclaims and cross-claims
against United States, CivPro
Rule 13.
Criminal appeals, §23-104.
Criminal prosecutions.
Judicial determination of federal
venue, §23-101.
Customs.
Congress.
Power to lay and collect, US Const
Art I §8.
Duty of tonnage, US Const Art I §10.
Importation of persons, US Const Art I
§9.
Tonnage, US Const Art I §10.
Default judgments against United
States, CivPro Rule 55.
Discovery.
Expenses for non-compliance, CivPro
Rule 37.
Domestic relations actions, DomRel
Rule 37.
Gifts.
Foreign presents to United States
officials, US Const Art I §9.
Injunctions.
Security requirement not applicable,
CivPro Rule 65.

UNITED STATES —Cont'd
Judges.
  United States courts, US Const Art III §1.
Letters of marque and reprisal, US Const Art I §§8, 10.
"Officer" of United States includes IRS officers, CivPro Rule 81.
Parties.
  Actions to which United States a party, US Const Art III.
Post office.
  Constitutional provisions, US Const Art I §8.
Restraints of trade.
  Cooperation with federal government, §28-4513.
Securities.
  Federal covered securities.
    Registration by notice, §31-5603.08.
Service of process on United States.
  Summons, CivPro Rule 4.
"Statute of United States" includes acts locally applicable, CivPro Rule 81.
Statutes.
  Approval of laws by president, US Const Art I §7.
  Ex post facto laws, US Const Art I §§9, 10.
  Full faith and credit, US Const Art IV §1.
  Limitations on legislation, US Const Art I §9.
  Proof, US Const Art IV §1.
  Revenue bills, US Const Art I §7.
  Supreme law of land, US Const Art VI.
  Veto, US Const Art I §7.
Stay of proceedings, CivPro Rule 62.
  Domestic relations actions, DomRel Rule 62.
Suits against, US Const Art III §2.
Titles of nobility.
  Prohibited, US Const Art I §§9, 10.
Weights and measures.
  Constitutional provisions, US Const Art I §8.

UNITED STATES ATTORNEY.
Criminal investigators assigned to United States Attorney, powers of, §23-109.
Police complaints, office of.
  Referral of complaints to United States Attorney, §5-1109.

UNITED STATES ATTORNEY —Cont'd
Reimbursement for space costs of, §47-205.

UNITED STATES COURT OF APPEALS FOR THE DISTRICT OF COLUMBIA CIRCUIT.
Appeals in federal cases.
  See APPEALS, FEDERAL CASES.
District of Columbia court of appeals.
  Jurisdiction of appeal from, §11-301.
Judicial power invested in, §11-101.

UNITED STATES DEPARTMENT OF AGRICULTURE (USDA).
Potomac Park temporarily occupied by, §10-150.

UNITED STATES DISTRICT COURT FOR THE DISTRICT OF COLUMBIA, §§11-501 to 11-521.
Appeals from judgments and orders.
  Amendments, statement of appellant when no transcript available, FRAP 10(c).
  Appendix to briefs, inclusion of memoranda of law, FRAP 30(a).
  As of right.
    Civil cases, FRAP 4(a).
    Content of notice of appeal, FRAP 3(c).
    Criminal cases, FRAP 4(b).
    Filing notice of appeal, FRAP 3(a).
    How taken, FRAP 3, USCtApp HPIP Rule III(b)(1).
    Joint or consolidated appeals, FRAP 3(b).
    Service of notice of appeal, FRAP 3(d).
    Time to file notice of appeal, FRAP 4, USCtApp HPIP Rule III(b)(2).
    When taken, FRAP 4.
  Bankruptcy appeal, FRAP 6.
  Bond.
    Civil cases, FRAP 7.
    Stay or injunction pending appeal, FRAP 8(b).
  Clerk of court's duties, FRAP 3, 11(b).
  Copies.
    Record on appeal, FRAP 10(b).
  Costs.
    On appeal taxable, FRAP 39(e).
    Record on appeal, FRAP 10(b).
    Taxable costs, FRAP 39(e).

UNITED STATES DISTRICT COURT FOR THE DISTRICT OF COLUMBIA —Cont'd

Appeals from judgments and orders —Cont'd

Court reporter, duty to prepare and file transcript, FRAP 11(b).

Criminal justice act, record on appeal, FRAP 10(b).

Docketing appeal, FRAP 12, USCtApp HPIP Rule IV(a)(3).

Preliminary record on appeal and preparation of transcripts, USCtApp HPIP Rule IV(a)(1).

Evidence, record on appeal, FRAP 10(b).

Exhibits, record on appeal, FRAP 11(b).

Extension of time.
  Transmitting the record on appeal, FRAP 11(b).

Fees.
  Payment in appeals as of right, FRAP 3(e).

Filing of record.
  Partial record or certificate, FRAP 12(c).

In forma pauperis proceedings, FRAP 24(a).

Notice.
  Appeal, FRAP Forms 1, 5.
  Partial transcript ordered, notice to appellee of, FRAP 10(b).
  Transmission of record, notice to court of, FRAP 11(b).

Objections, statement of appellant when no transcript available, FRAP 10(c).

Partial transcript, FRAP 10(b).

Recollection of appellant, unavailable record, FRAP 10(c).

Record on appeal, FRAP 10 to 12.
  Bankruptcy proceedings, filing, FRAP 6(b).
  Filing, FRAP 5(d), 12.
  Permission under 28 USCS 1292(b), filing, FRAP 5(d).
  Transmission, FRAP 11.

Release in criminal cases, FRAP 9.

Reporter, duty to prepare and file transcript, FRAP 11(b).

Retention of record, FRAP 11(c).
  By stipulation of the parties, FRAP 11(f).

Service of process.
  Notice of appeal, FRAP 3(d).

UNITED STATES DISTRICT COURT FOR THE DISTRICT OF COLUMBIA —Cont'd

Appeals from judgments and orders —Cont'd

Service of process —Cont'd
  Statement of appellant when no transcript available, FRAP 10(c).

Stay or injunction pending, FRAP 8, USCtApp Rule 8.

Temporary retention of record in district court for use in preparing appellate papers, FRAP 11(c).

Title of action, docketing of appeal, FRAP 12(a).

Transcript of proceedings, FRAP 10(b), 11(b).

Transmission of record on appeal, FRAP 11, USCtApp HPIP Rule IV(a)(2).

Voluntary dismissal, FRAP 42.

Weight of record on appeal, FRAP 11(b).

Assignment of cases, USDistCt LCrR 57.8 to USDistCt LCrR 57.15, USDistCt LCvR 40.1 to USDistCt LCvR 40.9.
  See ASSIGNMENT OF CASES.

Attorneys at law.

Appearances, USDistCt LCrR 44.1, USDistCt LCrR 44.5, USDistCt LCvR 83.2, USDistCt LCvR 83.6.

Appointment of counsel, USDistCt LCrR 57.22, USDistCt LCvR 83.10.
  Civil pro bono panel, USDistCt LCvR 83.11.

Bar.
  Admission, USDistCt LCrR 57.21, USDistCt LCvR 83.8.
  Membership renewal, USDistCt LCrR 57.21.1, USDistCt LCvR 83.9.

Disciplinary action.
  Committee on grievances, USDistCt LCrR 57.25, USDistCt LCvR 83.14.
  Grounds, USDistCt LCrR 57.26, USDistCt LCrR 57.27, USDistCt LCvR 83.15, USDistCt LCvR 83.16.
  Notice to disciplinary authorities, USDistCt LCrR 57.26, USDistCt LCrR 57.28, USDistCt LCvR 83.15, USDistCt LCvR 83.17.

**UNITED STATES DISTRICT COURT
FOR THE DISTRICT OF
COLUMBIA** —Cont'd
Attorneys at law —Cont'd
Disciplinary action —Cont'd
Obligations of attorneys, USDistCt
LCrR 57.26, USDistCt LCvR
83.15.
Panel, USDistCt LCrR 57.24,
USDistCt LCvR 83.13.
Procedures, USDistCt LCrR 57.27,
USDistCt LCvR 83.16.
Reinstatement, USDistCt LCrR
57.27, USDistCt LCrR 57.29,
USDistCt LCrR 57.30, USDistCt
LCvR 83.16, USDistCt LCvR
83.18, USDistCt LCvR 83.19.
Rules of disciplinary enforcement,
USDistCt LCrR 57.23, USDistCt
LCvR 83.12.
Incompetent or incapacitated
attorneys, USDistCt LCrR 57.30,
USDistCt LCvR 83.19.
Lawyer counseling panel, USDistCt
LCrR 57.31, USDistCt LCvR
83.20.
Number of counsel, USDistCt LCrR
44.2, USDistCt LCvR 83.3.
Patent office practice.
Orders as to admission or exclusion,
review of, USDistCt LCvR 83.7.
Practice of law before the court,
USDistCt LCrR 44.1, USDistCt
LCvR 83.2.
Court employees, USDistCt LCrR
44.4, USDistCt LCvR 83.5.
Law students, USDistCt LCrR 44.3,
USDistCt LCvR 83.4.
Auditor, §11-521.
**Broadcasting, tape recording, and
photographs in the courthouse,**
USDistCt LCrR 53.1.1, USDistCt
LCvR 83.1.
**Case management/electronic case
filing system,** USDistCt LCvR 5.4.
Notice re bounced back ECF e-mails,
USDistDCBank Appx G.
Civil jurisdiction, §11-501.
Clerk of court.
Office, USDistCt LCrR 56.1, USDistCt
LCvR 77.1.
Criminal jurisdiction, §11-502.
Dismissal of actions.
Failure to prosecute, USDistCt LCvR
83.23.
**Dodd-Frank Wall Street reform and
consumer protection act.**
Filings under, USDistCt LCvR 85.

**UNITED STATES DISTRICT COURT
FOR THE DISTRICT OF
COLUMBIA** —Cont'd
Eminent domain, jurisdiction over,
§16-1301.
Judges.
Chief judge, duties of, USDistCt LCrR
57.14, USDistCt LCvR 40.7.
Complaints against judges, USDistCt
LCrR 57.16, USDistCt LCvR
40.10.
Rules of the judicial council
governing complaints of judicial
misconduct or disability,
USCtApp Appx III.
Magistrate judges.
See MAGISTRATE JUDGES.
Mediation.
Dispute resolution compliance judge,
USDistCt LCvR 84.10.
Motions judges, USDistCt LCvR 40.8.
Judicial council.
Rules governing complaints of judicial
misconduct or disability, USCtApp
Appx III.
Judicial power invested in, §11-101.
**Jury selection, coordination and
cooperation regarding,** §11-1917.
Magistrate judges.
See MAGISTRATE JUDGES.
Mediation.
Administration of program, USDistCt
LCvR 84.1.
Agreements, USDistCt LCvR 84.7.
Attendance requirements, USDistCt
LCvR 84.8.
Confidentiality of proceedings,
USDistCt LCvR 84.9.
Defined, USDistCt LCvR 84.2.
Dispute resolution compliance judge,
USDistCt LCvR 84.10.
Mediators.
Appointment, USDistCt LCvR 84.5.
Discretion, USDistCt LCvR 84.7.
Generally, USDistCt LCvR 84.3.
Limits on role of mediators,
USDistCt LCvR 84.2.
Process, USDistCt LCvR 84.7.
Referral to mediation, USDistCt LCvR
84.4.
Rules, purpose and scope of, USDistCt
LCvR 84.
Statements, USDistCt LCvR 84.6.
Records.
Custody and removal, USDistCt LCvR
79.1.

UNITED STATES DISTRICT COURT FOR THE DISTRICT OF COLUMBIA —Cont'd
Registry investment system, USDistCt LCvR 67.1.
Removal of cases to, §11-503.
Speedy trial, USDistCt LCrR 45.1.
Tax returns or other tax information.
Disclosure to, §47-1805.04.
Three-judge court.
Applications, USDistCt LCvR 9.1.
Assignment of cases, USDistCt LCvR 40.3.

UNITED STATES HOUSING ACT.
Preservation and rehabilitation of government-supported housing, §§42-2851.01 to 42-2851.08.

UNITED STATES MARSHALS.
Attachment by, §§16-515, 16-548.
Courts, service to, §11-1729.
Execution of judgments.
Death, removal, or disqualification. Effect of, §15-315.
Endorsement as to date of receipt of writ, §15-308.
Remedy for erroneous sale in good faith, §15-317.
Forfeiture of property, CivPro Rule 71A-I.
Prisoners.
Commitment of, §24-201.13.
Delivery to Marshal, §24-201.14.
Reimbursement for space costs of, §47-205.
Service of process, §13-302, CivPro Rule 4.1, CrimPro Rule 17.
Adoption proceedings, Adoption Rule 4.
Delinquent minors, JuvProc Rule 17.
Fees, CivPro Rule 202.
Summons, CivPro Rule 4.
Domestic relations actions, DomRel Rule 4.

UNITED STATES PARK POLICE, §§5-201 to 5-208.
Arrests, §5-206.
Authority to issue rules and regulations, §5-207.
Boundaries in District, §5-208.
Control of, §5-202.
Dulles International Airport, §9-808.
Equipment for, §5-203.
Federal law enforcement officer cooperative agreements, §§5-301 to 5-303.

UNITED STATES PARK POLICE —Cont'd
Holidays.
Working on, compensation, §5-521.03.
Lateral police career appointments, §§1-610.71 to 1-610.76.
Medical services for, §5-204.
Members of, §5-202.
Motorcycle service, §5-203.
Organization of, §5-202.
Powers and duties, §5-201.
Special appointments, §5-205.
Wages and salaries, §5-545.01.
Washington National Airport, §9-704.

UNITED STATES SECRET SERVICE DIVISION.
Federal law enforcement officer cooperative agreements, §§5-301 to 5-303.
Holidays.
Working on, compensation, §5-521.03.
Lateral police career appointments, §§1-610.71 to 1-610.76.
Police and firefighters retirement and disability, §5-703.
Wages and salaries for uniformed division, §5-545.01.
Conversion to 2001 standards, §5-561.02.
Holidays.
Working on, compensation, §5-521.03.
Locality-based comparability adjustments, freeze, §5-563.02.

UNIT PRICING, §§28-5201 to 28-5210.
Applicability of requirement, §28-5203.
Exemptions from requirement, §28-5205.
Consistency of pricing, §28-5208.
Definitions, §28-5202.
Display of price, §28-5207.
Exemptions from requirement, §28-5205.
Penalties for violations, §28-5209.
Presentation of price, §28-5207.
Rounding of prices, §28-5206.
Rulemaking to implement provisions, §28-5210.
Scope of provisions, §28-5203.
Exemptions from requirement, §28-5205.
Short title, §28-5201.
Signs.
Display of price, §28-5207.
Specificity of pricing, §28-5206.

UNIT PRICING —Cont'd
Tags.
  Display of price, §28-5207.
Terms for unit pricing, §28-5204.
Uniformity of pricing, §28-5208.

UNIVERSAL BANKS, §§26-1401.01 to
    26-1401.31.
**Acquisitions, merger, asset
    purchases,** §26-1401.29.
Articles of incorporation,
    §26-1401.28.
Bylaws, §26-1401.28.
Certificate of authority, §§26-1401.03
    to 26-1401.06.
  Application to be certified,
    §26-1401.03.
  Issuance, §26-1401.04.
  Revocation or subsequent limitation,
    §26-1401.05.
  Voluntary termination, §26-1401.06.
Conservator.
  Appointment, duties and powers,
    §§26-1401.23 to 26-1401.27.
Definitions, §26-1401.02.
Fees, commissioner may establish,
    §26-1401.30.
Insurance and securities,
    §26-1401.15.
Investments, §§26-1401.13, 26-1401.14.
Liquidation, §26-1401.16.
Loans, §26-1401.12.
**Possession, receivership,
    conservatorship, liquidation,**
    §§26-1401.16 to 26-1401.27.
  Commissioner taking possession,
    §26-1401.17.
    Resumption of business,
      §26-1401.18.
  Conservator.
    Appointment, qualifications,
      §26-1401.23.
    Authority to borrow money,
      §26-1401.26.
    Bond, §26-1401.23.
    Deposits received while bank in
      conservatorship, §26-1401.25.
    Rights, powers, privileges,
      §26-1401.24.
    Termination of conservatorship,
      §26-1401.27.
  Liquidation, §26-1401.16.
  Receiver.
    Appointment, §26-1401.19.
    Duties and powers, §26-1401.20.
    Grounds for seeking appointment,
      §26-1401.19.

UNIVERSAL BANKS —Cont'd
**Possession, receivership,
    conservatorship, liquidation**
    —Cont'd
  Receiver —Cont'd
    Lien or transfer of property
      voidable, §26-1401.21.
    Petition for appointment,
      §26-1401.19.
    Records, §26-1401.22.
Powers and authority, §§26-1401.07 to
    26-1401.11.
  Exercise of power exercised by other
    financial institutions, §26-1401.08.
  Limitations on powers, exception,
    §§26-1401.12 to 26-1401.15.
    Insurance and securities powers,
      §26-1401.15.
    Investment power, §§26-1401.13,
      26-1401.14.
    Loan power, §26-1401.12.
  Necessary or convenient powers,
    §26-1401.10.
  Parity of powers, §26-1401.08.
  Preexisting powers, §26-1401.07.
  Reasonably related or incidental
    activities, §26-1401.11.
  Specific powers, §26-1401.09.
Receiver.
  Appointment, duties and powers,
    §§26-1401.19 to 26-1401.22.
Rules, §26-1401.31.
Taking possession, §§26-1401.17,
    26-1401.18.

UNIVERSAL HOLINESS CHURCH.
Real property tax exemption,
    §47-4653.

UNIVERSAL LEAVE SYSTEM,
    §1-612.03a.
Executive service, §1-610.61.

UNIVERSITIES AND COLLEGES.
Charitable solicitations, §§44-1701 to
    44-1714.
  See CHARITABLE SOLICITATIONS.
College access assistance, §§38-2701
    to 38-2706.
  Assistance to University of District of
    Columbia, §38-2703.
  General requirements, §38-2705.
  Greater choices among institutions of
    higher education.
    Purpose, §38-2701.
  Limit on aggregate amount of federal
    funds, §38-2706.
  Private school program, §38-2704.

UNIVERSITIES AND COLLEGES
—Cont'd

College access assistance —Cont'd
Public school program, §38-2702.
Purpose, §38-2701.

College savings program, §§47-4501 to 47-4512.

DC leveraging educational assistance partnership program, §§38-2731 to 38-2733.
Administration, §38-2732.
Establishment, §38-2731.
Grant awards, §38-2733.

DC promise program, §§38-2751 to 38-2759.
Administration of program, §38-2752.
Adult education, §38-2757.
Applicability, §38-2759.
Conditions of participation, §38-2755.
Definitions, §38-2751.
Eligibility to participate, §38-2754.
Fund, §38-2753.
Grant awards, §38-2756.
Rules, §38-2758.

Dental colleges.
General provisions, §§38-1401 to 38-1419.
See MEDICAL AND DENTAL COLLEGES.

Disabilities, persons with.
ABLE savings accounts, §§47-4901, 47-4902.

Discriminatory practices, §§2-1402.41, 2-1402.42.

Drug free zones, §48-904.07a.

Educational stepladder program, §§32-1651 to 32-1653.

Federal City College.
General provisions, §§38-1101 to 38-1112.
See FEDERAL CITY COLLEGE.
Successor institution, §§38-1201.01 to 38-1207.07.
See UNIVERSITY OF THE DISTRICT OF COLUMBIA.

Financial aid assistance.
College access assistance, §§38-2701 to 38-2706.
DC promise program, §§38-2751 to 38-2759. See within this heading, "DC promise program."

Firearms.
Enhanced penalties and fines for carrying guns into gun free zones, §22-4502.01.

UNIVERSITIES AND COLLEGES
—Cont'd

Gallaudet University.
General provisions, §§38-2301 to 38-2402.11.
See GALLAUDET UNIVERSITY.

Higher education licensure commission, §§38-1301 to 38-1313.

Howard University real property exempt from taxation, §47-1018.

Land-grant colleges, §§38-1107, 38-1109, 38-1112, 38-1201.02.

Law school, §§38-1205.01 to 38-1205.12.
See DISTRICT OF COLUMBIA SCHOOL OF LAW.

Management of institutional funds.
General provisions.
See PRUDENT INVESTOR ACT.

Medical colleges.
General provisions, §§38-1401 to 38-1419.
See MEDICAL AND DENTAL COLLEGES.

National technical institute for the deaf, §§38-2401.11, 38-2401.12, 38-2402.01 to 38-2402.11.
See NATIONAL TECHNICAL INSTITUTE FOR THE DEAF.

Nonresident tuition, §§38-301 to 38-313.

Opportunity accounts.
Generally, §§1-307.61 to 1-307.74.
Use for educational expenses, §1-307.68.

Police and security officers, assaults on, §22-405.

Providence Hospital established as teaching hospital for nurses and interns, §44-703.

Real property.
Exempt from taxation, §§47-1002, 47-1018.

Savings program, §§47-4501 to 47-4512.

Student health care.
General provisions, §§38-601 to 38-651.12.
See STUDENT HEALTH CARE.

Taxation.
College savings program, §§47-4501 to 47-4512.

University of the District of Columbia.
General provisions, §§38-1201.01 to 38-1207.07.
See UNIVERSITY OF THE DISTRICT OF COLUMBIA.

UNIVERSITIES AND COLLEGES
—Cont'd

Usury law, exemption from, §28-3315.

Veterans appreciation scholarship fund, §1-325.141.

Washington technical institute.
General provisions, §§38-1121 to 38-1125.
See WASHINGTON TECHNICAL INSTITUTE.
Successor institution, §§38-1201.01 to 38-1207.07.
See UNIVERSITY OF THE DISTRICT OF COLUMBIA.

UNIVERSITY OF THE DISTRICT OF COLUMBIA, §§38-1201.01 to 38-1207.07.

Advisory committee, §38-1204.02.

Appropriations, §§38-1203.01, 38-1204.05.

Board of trustees, §§38-1202.01 to 38-1202.11, 38-1204.01 to 38-1204.07.
Board of governors of District of Columbia School of Law.
Transfer of functions to trustees, §38-1202.11.
Board of higher education and vocational board.
Transfer of functions, property, personnel to trustees, §38-1202.08.
Chairperson and vice-chairperson, §38-1202.01.
Chief executive officer.
Nonvoting member, §38-1202.01.
Compensation and expenses, §38-1202.04.
Duties, §38-1202.06.
Established, §38-1202.01.
Members, §38-1202.01.
Powers, §38-1202.01.
Removal, §38-1202.03.
Responsibilities, §38-1202.01.
Suspension, §38-1202.03.
Term, §38-1202.01.
Termination of student member, §38-1202.03.

Budget and funding authority.
Duties of trustees, §38-1202.06.
Transfer to university, §38-1241.01.
UDC debt collection fund, §38-1251.01.

Chief executive officer.
Nonvoting member of board of trustees, §38-1202.01.
Selection, appointment, compensation.
Duties of trustees, §38-1202.06.

UNIVERSITY OF THE DISTRICT OF COLUMBIA —Cont'd

College access assistance, §§38-2701 to 38-2706.

Community college transition to independence advisory board.
Funding, §38-1271.03.
Membership, §38-1271.01.
Transition plan, §38-1271.02.

Consolidation of existing institutions, §38-1202.05.

Contracting power of board, §38-1204.05.

Council authority, §38-1204.06.

Debt collection fund, §38-1251.01.

Definitions, §38-1201.03.

District of Columbia School of Law.
Merged with and component of university, §38-1202.11.

Establishment.
Authority of trustees, §38-1202.01.
Duties of trustees, §38-1202.06.
Land grant university, §§38-1202.09, 38-1202.10.

Federal City College.
Predecessor institution, §§38-1101 to 38-1112.
See FEDERAL CITY COLLEGE.

Foreign students, attendance by, §38-161.

Funds.
Debt collection fund, §38-1251.01.
Higher education incentive grant program fund, §38-274.03.
Material fund, §38-1204.05.

Get DC Residents Training for Jobs Now, §§38-1011.01 to 38-1011.05.
See JOB TRAINING PROGRAMS.

Gifts, §38-1204.03.

Higher education incentive grant program, §38-274.01.
Fund, §38-274.03.
Transfer of authority, §38-274.01a.

Land grant university, §§38-1202.09, 38-1202.10.

Law school, §§38-1205.01 to 38-1205.12.
See DISTRICT OF COLUMBIA SCHOOL OF LAW.

Material fund, §38-1204.05.

Meetings of trustees, §38-1204.01.

Merit system.
Applicability of, §1-602.03.
Delegation of authority, §1-604.03.
Preference for resident applicants.
Non-educational employees, §1-602.03.

UNIVERSITY OF THE DISTRICT OF COLUMBIA —Cont'd
Office of vocational education and skills training, §§38-1208.01 to 38-1208.06.
Policy declaration, §38-1201.02.
Predecessor institution.
Federal City College, §§38-1101 to 38-1112.
See FEDERAL CITY COLLEGE.
Teachers college.
See TEACHERS COLLEGE.
Washington Technical Institute, §§38-1121 to 38-1125.
See WASHINGTON TECHNICAL INSTITUTE.
Reports, §38-1204.04.
Residents, preferential tuition rates for, §38-1204.07.
School of law, §§38-1205.01 to 38-1205.12.
Tuition expenses.
Grants, §§38-1207.01 to 38-1207.07.
Budget account, §38-1207.07.
Conditions of enrollment, §38-1207.03.
Criteria for eligibility, §38-1207.02.
Definitions, §38-1207.01.
Offering additional financial assistance and educational opportunities, §38-1207.06.
Previous recipient failing to remain in good academic standing.
Grants not awarded to, §38-1207.05.
Report on participation, §38-1207.04.
Residents, preferential tuition rates for, §38-1204.07.
Vocational education and skills training (VEST), §§38-1208.01 to 38-1208.06.
Executive director, §38-1208.05.
Funding, §38-1208.06.
Office of.
Definitions, §38-1208.01.
Establishment, §38-1208.02.
Responsibility, §38-1208.02.
Washington Technical Institute.
Predecessor institution, §§38-1121 to 38-1125.
See WASHINGTON TECHNICAL INSTITUTE.

UNJUST IMPRISONMENT.
Claims against the District, §§2-421 to 2-425.
Applicability to person entering guilty plea, §2-425.

UNJUST IMPRISONMENT —Cont'd
Claims against the District —Cont'd
Damages, §2-423.
Effective date, §2-424.
Proof required, §2-422.
Right to present claim, §2-421.

UNLAWFUL ASSEMBLY, §22-1321.
Capitol grounds, on, §10-503.17.

UNLAWFUL ENTRY ON PROPERTY, §22-3302.

UNLIQUIDATED DAMAGES.
Limitation of actions against District, §12-309.

UNMARRIED PARTNERS.
Benefits for, §§32-701 to 32-710.
See DOMESTIC PARTNER BENEFITS.

UNOCCUPIED STRUCTURES.
Demolition or enclosure of deteriorated structures, §§42-3173.01 to 42-3173.12.

UNSAFE STRUCTURES OR EXCAVATIONS, §§6-801 to 6-808.
See BUILDING CODE.

UNSANITARY BUILDINGS.
See INSANITARY BUILDINGS.

UNSWORN DECLARATION.
Supplement, CivPro Form CA 101-A.

UNSWORN FOREIGN DECLARATIONS, §§16-5301 to 16-5308.
Applicability of law, §16-5303.
Uniformity, §16-5307.
Definitions, §16-5302.
E-SIGN Act, relation to, §16-5308.
Form, §16-5306.
Required medium, §16-5305.
Short title, §16-5301.
Statutory construction, §16-5307.
Validity of, §16-5304.

UNUSED PHARMACEUTICAL SAFE DISPOSAL, §§48-851.01 to 48-851.04.
Definitions, §48-851.01.
Health care facilities.
Prohibited methods of disposal, §48-851.03.
Mail-in program, §48-851.02.
Public education campaign, §48-851.02.
Recommendations to mayor, §48-851.02.

UNUSED PHARMACEUTICAL SAFE DISPOSAL —Cont'd
Rulemaking, §48-851.04.

URBAN FOREST PRESERVATION.
Advisory council, §8-651.09.
Definitions, §8-651.02.
Enforcement of violations, §8-651.08.
Hazardous trees, §8-651.06.
　Defined, §8-651.02.
Heritage trees.
　Protection, §8-651.04a.
　Removal permit requirement, §8-651.04a.
Legislative findings, §8-651.01.
Mayor's responsibilities, §8-651.03.
Notice of removal of trees on public space, §8-651.05.
Program established, §8-651.03.
Special trees, preservation, §8-651.04.
Tree fund, §8-651.07.
Urban forestry advisory council, §8-651.09.

URBAN GARDENS PROGRAM, §§48-401 to 48-403.

URBAN INSTITUTE.
Real property tax abatement, §47-4624.

URBAN RENEWAL, §§6-311.01 to 6-341.05.
Community development, §§6-1001 to 6-1007.
　Housing and community development reform advisory commission, §§6-1031 to 6-1037.
Displaced persons.
　Authority to make regulations regarding, §6-331.04.
　Determining availability of housing for, §6-331.02.
　Housing for, §6-331.02.
　Payments to, §6-333.01.
　Relocation assistance office, §6-331.03.
　Relocation services for, §§6-331.01 to 6-333.02.
Housing for displaced persons, §6-331.02.
Leasing of real property, §§6-321.04, 6-341.02.
Local grant-in-aid, transfers not considered to be, §§6-321.07, 6-341.05.
Maine Avenue, transfer to agency of property near, §§6-321.01 to 6-321.08.
　Authorized, §6-321.01.

URBAN RENEWAL —Cont'd
Maine Avenue, transfer to agency of property near —Cont'd
Definitions, §6-321.08.
Lease of property, §6-321.04.
Necessity determination, §6-321.02.
Not local grant-in-aid, §6-321.07.
Not required to transfer property needed for municipal purposes, §6-321.06.
Transfer of jurisdiction to agency, §6-321.03.
Maryland Avenue and Virginia Avenue, transfer to RLA revitalization corporation of properties near, §§6-341.01 to 6-341.05.
Definitions, §6-341.05.
Lease or sale authorized, §6-341.02.
Transfer authorized, §6-341.01.
　Not local grant-in-aid, §6-341.04.
　Rights-of-way to District, §6-341.03.
Neighborhood redevelopment programs, §6-311.01.
Relocation assistance office, §6-331.03.
Relocation services for displaced persons, §§6-331.01 to 6-333.02.
Transfers of real property.
　Maine Avenue, transfer to agency of property near, §§6-321.01 to 6-321.08.
　Maryland Avenue and Virginia Avenue, transfer to RLA revitalization corporation of properties near, §§6-341.01 to 6-341.05.

USAGE OF TRADE.
Sale of goods, UCC.
Implied warranty, §28:2-314.

USURY, §§28-3301 to 28-3315.
Actions.
　Recovery of usury paid, §28-3304.
　　Parties compelled to testify, §28-3306.
　　Unlawful interest credited on principal debt, §28-3305.
Defined, §28-3303.
Fines and penalties, §28-3313.
Forfeiture of interest, §28-3303.
National housing act.
　Exemption from interest in usury regulations, §28-3307.
Parties.
　Action to recover usury paid.
　　Parties compelled to testify, §28-3306.

USURY —Cont'd
Principal debt, deemed to be payment on, §28-3305.
Private right of action, §28-3314.
Recovery of usury paid, §28-3304.
Testimony required regarding, §28-3306.
Universities and colleges exempt from laws on, §28-3315.
Witnesses.
Action to recover usury paid.
Parties compelled to testify, §28-3306.

UTILITY SERVICE THEFT.
Electric and natural gas, §§22-3218.01 to 22-3218.04.

V

VACANT AND ABANDONED PROPERTY.
Special disposal procedures for certain properties, §§10-831 to 10-839.
Closing on properties, §10-836.
Evaluation committee, §10-837.
Method of disposition, §10-832.
Minimum standards for disposition, §10-833.
Properties subject to disposition, §§10-831, 10-839.
Reports, §10-838.
Request for proposals, §10-832.
Contents, §10-833.
Evaluation criteria, §10-835.
Subsidies, §10-834.
Trespass.
Prima facie evidence, §22-3302.

VACANT BUILDINGS, §§42-3131.05 to 42-3131.17.
Administrative agency review.
Final decisions, §42-3131.15.
Appeals.
Administrative review and appeal, §42-3131.15.
Notice of vacancy designation and right to appeal, §42-3131.11.
Assessment as tax.
Unpaid fees, §42-3131.14.
Collection of unpaid fees, §42-3131.14.
Definitions, §42-3131.05.
Demolition or enclosure of deteriorated structures, §§42-3173.01 to 42-3173.12.

VACANT BUILDINGS —Cont'd
Liens.
Unpaid fees, §42-3131.14.
List, transmission by mayor, §42-3131.16.
Blighted vacant buildings, §42-3131.17.
Mail.
Notice by mail, §42-3131.05a.
Maintenance standards, §42-3131.12.
Posting identification of owner, §42-3131.13.
Registration.
Denial notice, §42-3131.08.
Exempt buildings, §42-3131.06.
Fees, §42-3131.09.
Penalty for failure to register, §42-3131.10.
Procedure, §42-3131.07.
Renewal, §42-3131.07.
Required, §42-3131.07.
Revocation notice, §42-3131.08.
Trespass.
Prima facie evidence, §22-3302.

VACATION OF JUDGMENTS.
Appellate procedure.
Costs, FRAP 39(a).
Procedural orders, determination of motions for, FRAP 27(b).

VACATION PERMITS.
Child labor, §§32-207 to 32-211.

VACATIONS.
Judges, §11-1505.

VAN BUREN STREET SUBWAY, §9-317.

VANDALISM, §§22-3301 to 22-3311.
Art works, defacing, §22-3306.
Boundary markers, destroying, §22-3309.
Burning crosses, §22-3312.02.
Cemeteries.
Grave robbery, §22-3303.
Railings, destroying, §22-3314.
Tombs, destroying, §22-3314.
Cross-burning, §22-3312.02.
Dead bodies, stealing and selling, §22-3303.
Detention by force, §22-3301.
Due process, threatening, injuring, intimidating, or interfering with persons in order to deprive them of, §§22-3312.02 to 22-3312.04.
Emblems of certain types, displaying, §22-3312.02.

VANDALISM —Cont'd
Explosives placed with intent to destroy or injure property, §22-3305.
Forced entry, §22-3301.
Graffiti.
See GRAFFITI.
Grave robbery, §22-3303.
Hoods, wearing, §22-3312.03.
Masks, wearing, §22-3312.03.
Milestones, removal of, §22-3320.
"No Smoking" signs, §7-1706.
Obstruction.
Public highways, §22-3321.
Public roads, §22-3320.
Railroad tracks, §22-3319.
Printed material, defacing, §22-3306.
Private property, defacing, §22-3312.01.
Public property, defacing, §22-3312.01.
Public records, defacing, §22-3307.
Public roads and highways.
Boundary markers, destroying, §22-3309.
Building material for streets, destroying or defacing, §22-3313.
Collection of fines for obstruction of highways, §22-3322.
Milestones, removal of, §22-3320.
Obstruction of highways, §22-3321.
Obstruction of roads, §22-3320.
Railroad track obstruction or displacement, §22-3319.
Religious symbols, defacing or burning, §22-3312.02.
Trees, shrubs and vines, §22-3310.
Unlawful entry, §22-3302.
Vending machines, breaking and entering, §22-601.
Wastewater disposal system.
Tampering and misuse, §8-105.05.
Water pollution, malicious, §22-3318.

VANPOOLS.
Labor and employment relations.
Transportation benefits.
Reducing single occupancy vehicle use by encouraging transit benefits, §§32-151 to 32-153.

VAPOR PRODUCTS.
Tobacco tax, §47-2401.

VARIANCES.
Child care facilities, §7-2037.
Condominiums, §42-1901.07.
Hazardous waste management, §8-1306.

VARIANCES —Cont'd
Occupational safety and health.
Permanent, §32-1111.
Temporary, §32-1110.

VARNUM STREET VIADUCT, §9-315.

VAULTS.
Rental of public space, §§10-1103.01 to 10-1103.09.
Abutting single-family or duplex dwelling, §10-1103.09.
Chief Financial Officer, waiver and compromise of interest and rent, §10-1103.07a.
Construction, used for, §10-1103.08.
Defined, §10-1101.01.
Delinquent taxes, §10-1103.07.
Interest on unpaid rent, §10-1103.07.
Payments, §10-1103.04.
Public utility installations, use for, §10-1103.08.
Removal of unsafe vaults, §§10-1103.05, 10-1103.06.
Rulemaking, §10-1103.10.
Services performed on, §10-1103.07.
Waiver and compromise of interest and rent, §10-1103.07a.

VECTOR-BORNE DISEASE CONTROL, §§8-2131.01 to 8-2131.09.
Abatement of public health nuisances, §8-2131.05.
Corrective action by the District, §8-2131.06.
Definitions, §8-2131.01.
Fund, §8-2131.07.
Inspections, §8-2131.03.
Penalties for violations, §8-2131.08.
Prohibited activities, §8-2131.02.
Public health nuisances.
Abatement, §8-2131.05.
Corrective action by the District, §8-2131.06.
Prima facie evidence, §8-2131.04.
Rules, §8-2131.09.

VEGETABLES.
Sale by weight, §37-201.15.

VEHICLE IDENTIFICATION NUMBERS.
Altering or removing, §22-3233.

VEHICLES FOR HIRE.
Business licenses, §47-2829.
Taxicabs.
See TAXICABS.

VENDING MACHINES, §37-201.09.
Breaking and entering, §22-601.

VENDING MACHINES —Cont'd
Cigarette sales, license, §47-2404.
Citywide vending task force,
§37-131.09.
Rulemaking, §37-131.10.
School nutrition, requirements,
§38-822.06.

VENDING REGULATION, §§37-131.01
to 37-131.10.
Assignment of vending locations,
§37-131.04.
Definitions, §37-131.01.
Fees, §37-131.07.
Fund, §37-131.07.
Locations designated for vending,
§37-131.03.
Assignment of vending locations,
§37-131.04.
Penalties for violations, §37-131.08.
Public markets, §37-131.06.
Public space, requirements for
vending from, §37-131.02.
Vending development zones,
§37-131.05.

VENEREAL DISEASES.
AIDS.
See AIDS.
Human papillomavirus.
Vaccination, §§7-1651.01 to 7-1651.05.
See HUMAN PAPILLOMAVIRUS
VACCINATION.
Laboratory services.
Fees, §7-734.

VENUE.
Anti-terrorism act of 2002.
Jurisdiction and venue to prosecute,
§22-3156.
Child care facilities.
Regulatory prosecutions, §7-2047.
Child custody proceedings.
Inconvenient forum, §16-4602.07.
Constitution of the United States,
US Const Art III §2.
Criminal procedure, CrimPro Rule 20.
Federal benefit payments under
District programs, §1-815.02.
Insurers rehabilitation and
liquidation proceedings,
§31-1303.
Terrorism.
Anti-terrorism act of 2002.
Jurisdiction and venue to prosecute,
§22-3156.

VERDICTS.
Criminal procedure, CrimPro Rule 31.
Presence of defendant, CrimPro Rule
43.
Directed verdicts, CivPro Rule 50.
Domestic relations actions, DomRel
Rule 50.
Stay of proceedings, CivPro Rule 62.
Ejectment, §16-1114.
Eminent domain.
Fixing time for return of verdict,
§16-1320.
Real property for United States,
§16-1361.
Interrogatories.
General verdict accompanied by
answer to interrogatories, CivPro
Rule 49.
Judgment on jury verdict, CivPro
Form CA 31.
Mental illness, persons with.
Hospitalization, MentalHealth Rule 5.
Prisoner's commitment to mental
institution, MentalHealth Rule
10.
Setting aside verdict.
Harmless error.
Adoption proceedings, Adoption Rule
61.
Civil procedure, CivPro Rule 61.
Criminal procedure, CrimPro Rule
52.
Domestic relations actions, DomRel
Rule 61.
Juvenile proceedings, JuvProc Rule
52.
Special verdicts, CivPro Rule 49.
Unanimity of verdict, CivPro Rule 48,
CrimPro Rule 31.

VERIFICATION OF PLEADINGS,
CivPro Rule 9-I.
Form, CivPro Form CA 101, USDistCt
LCvR 5.1, USDistCt LCvR 11.2.
Criminal proceedings, USDistCt LCrR
49.
Probate proceedings, Probate Rule 3.

VERIZON CENTER.
Gross sales tax, §47-2002.06.

VERMIN.
Bureau of rodent control,
§§8-2101.01, 8-2101.02.
Rodent abatement program,
§§8-2103.01 to 8-2103.05.

VESSELS.
See BOATS AND OTHER
WATERCRAFT.

VEST.
Office of vocational education and skills training, §§38-1208.01 to 38-1208.06.

VETERANS.
Direct-reduction loans, §42-3002.
Drivers' licenses.
Veteran designation, §50-1401.01.
Identification cards, §50-1401.03.
Estates of veterans.
Filing pleadings or orders affecting estate, CivPro Rule 5-I.
Hospitalization of persons with mental illness, §§21-587, 21-908.
License plates, §50-1501.02a.
Motor vehicle registration for disabled American veterans, §50-1503.01.
Office of veterans' affairs, §§49-1001 to 49-1006.
Preferences for veterans, §1-607.03.
Public assistance.
Assistance application forms, §4-126.
Real property exempt from taxation.
American Legion, §§47-1035, 47-1046.
AMVETS (American Veterans of World War II), §47-1038.
Department of the District of Columbia Veterans of foreign Wars.
Lot 0040, square 5167, §47-1063.
Disabled American Veterans, §47-1003.
Veterans of Foreign Wars (VFW), §47-1039.
Servicemen's readjustment for mortgages and deeds of trust, §§42-3001, 42-3002.
Veterans appreciation scholarship fund, §1-325.141.

VETERANS' AFFAIRS, OFFICE OF, §§49-1001 to 49-1006.
Benefits and claims.
Advocate support and informational services, purpose of office, §49-1003.
Definitions, §49-1001.
Director.
Appointment, responsibilities, compensation, delegation, §49-1002.
Established, §49-1002.
Fund, established, §49-1004.
Purposes, §49-1003.
Rulemaking, §49-1006.
Staff, authority to hire, §49-1002.

VETERANS' AFFAIRS, OFFICE OF
—Cont'd
Transfer of positions and property to office, §49-1005.

VETERANS' DAY.
Appellate procedure, FRAP 26(a), 45(a).
Designated holiday, §1-612.02.

VETERINARY FACILITIES, §§47-2888.01 to 47-2888.08.
Application for license, §47-2888.03.
Definitions, §47-2888.01.
Denial, suspension, or revocation of license, §47-2888.04.
Fees, §47-2888.03.
Inspections, §47-2888.05.
License requirement, §47-2888.02.
Penalties for violations, §47-2888.07.
Posting license on premises, §47-2888.03.
Renewal of license, §47-2888.03.
Rules, §47-2888.08.
Scope of operation.
Specifying, §47-2888.03.

VETERINARY MEDICINE, §§3-1208.61 to 3-1208.65.
Alcoholic beverage licenses.
Exceptions to license requirements, §25-103.
Animal licenses.
Issuance by veterinarian, §47-2888.06.
Board of veterinary medicine, §3-1202.21.
Executive director, §3-1202.22.
General supervision.
Defined, §3-1208.65.
Health occupations boards.
General provisions, §§3-1201.01 to 3-1213.01.
Health occupations licensure, registration or certification, §§3-1205.01 to 3-1205.24.
License requirement and exceptions, §3-1208.61.
Qualifications for license to practice, §3-1208.62.
Titles and terms prohibited as misrepresentation without license to practice, §3-1210.03.
Veterinary euthanasia technicians.
Certification, §3-1208.64.
Transition provisions.
Persons already practicing, §3-1212.05.
Veterinary technicians.
Certification, §3-1208.63.

VETERINARY MEDICINE —Cont'd
Veterinary technicians —Cont'd
Transition provisions.
Persons already practicing,
§3-1212.05.

VETERINARY SURGEON.
Fire departments, §5-404.

VETO.
Constitution of the United States,
US Const Art I §7.

VFW (VETERANS OF FOREIGN WARS).
Real property exempt from taxation,
§47-1039.

VIADUCTS.
Eastern Avenue, §9-315.
Fern Street, §§9-315, 9-316.
Grade crossing elimination projects, as part of, §9-1201.15.
Authority of mayor, §9-1203.05.
Michigan Avenue, §§9-320, 9-321.
Varnum Street, §9-315.

VIATICAL SETTLEMENTS.
Defined, §1-622.04.
Merit system, §1-622.08.

VICE-PRESIDENT OF THE UNITED STATES.
Age, US Const Amd 12.
Bribery, US Const Art II §4.
Death, US Const Art II §1.
Elections.
Electors.
Majority vote is necessary to elect
president or vice-president, US
Const Art II §1, Amd 12.
Voting by military and overseas voters,
§1-1061.03.
Failure to qualify, US Const Amd 20.
Impeachment, US Const Art II §4.
Oaths, US Const Art VI, Amd 14.
President of the senate, US Const Art
I §3.
Qualifications, US Const Amd 12.
Removal, US Const Art II §4.
Succession to office of president, US
Const Art II §1, Amds 20, 25.
Upon death, resignation or removal of
president, US Const Amd 25.
Treason, US Const Art II §4.

VICE-PRESIDENT OF THE UNITED STATES —Cont'd
Vacancy in office, US Const Art II §1,
Amd 20.
Nomination by president, US Const
Amd 25.
Confirmation by majority vote by
both houses of congress, US
Const Amd 25.
Voting by military and overseas voters, §1-1061.03.

VICIOUS DOGS, §§8-1901 to 8-1908.
See DANGEROUS DOGS.

VICTIM COMPENSATION, §§4-501 to
4-518, VictComp Rules 1 to 41.
See CRIME VICTIMS'
COMPENSATION.

VICTIM IMPACT STATEMENTS,
§23-103, CrimPro Rule 32.
Delinquency proceedings.
Disposition, §16-2320.
Predisposition reports, §16-2319,
JuvProc Rule 32.

VICTIMS OF CRIME.
Aged persons, certain offenses committed against.
Enhanced penalties, §22-3601.
Bill of rights, §§23-1901 to 23-1911.
Access to information, §23-1910.
Applicability, §23-1906.
Definitions, §§23-1905, 23-1907.
Expedited proceeding where child
called as witness, §23-1903.
Notice to victims, §23-1902.
Privacy and security, §23-1903.
Private right of action, §23-1911.
Rights enumerated, §23-1901.
At sentencing, §23-1904.
Sexual assault victim advocates,
§23-1909.
Disclosure of confidential
information prohibited without
consent of client, §14-307.
Privileged communications, §14-312.
Sexual assault victims, §23-1908.
Children, violent crimes committed against.
Enhanced penalties, §22-3611.
Community impact statements,
§23-1904.

VICTIMS OF CRIME —Cont'd
Crime victims' compensation, §§4-501
to 4-518, VictComp Rules 1 to 41.
See CRIME VICTIMS'
COMPENSATION.
Defined, §22-3001.
Delinquency proceedings.
Definition of victim, §16-2301.
HIV/AIDS testing.
Test results.
Respondent's results to be
disclosed to victim, §16-2315,
JuvProc Rule 110.
Impact statements, §§16-2319,
16-2320, JuvProc Rule 32.
Notice of disposition and post-
disposition hearings, §16-2317.
Rights of victim in delinquency
proceedings, §16-2340.
Domestic violence victims, grants
for, §4-521.
Domestic violence victims, leave of
absence.
Employee sick leave generally,
§§32-131.01 to 32-131.16.
See LABOR AND EMPLOYMENT
RELATIONS.
Emergency care for sexual assault
victims, §§7-2121 to 7-2125.
Compliance with provisions, §7-2125.
Definitions, §7-2121.
Duties of hospitals, §7-2123.
Training of personnel, §7-2124.
Information regarding antibiotics and
contraception, §7-2122.
HIV testing requests, §§22-3901 to
22-3903.
Delinquency proceedings.
Respondent's test results to be
disclosed to victim, §16-2315,
JuvProc Rule 110.
Impact statements, §23-103, CrimPro
Rule 32.
Delinquency proceedings.
Disposition, §16-2320.
Predisposition report, §16-2319,
JuvProc Rule 32.
Leave of absence, victims of
domestic violence.
Employee sick leave generally,
§§32-131.01 to 32-131.16.
See LABOR AND EMPLOYMENT
RELATIONS.
Minors, violent crimes committed
against.
Enhanced penalties, §22-3611.

VICTIMS OF CRIME —Cont'd
Office of victim services.
Domestic violence hotline, §§4-551 to
4-553.
Privacy of child victims, §23-1902.
Senior citizen victims, enhanced
penalties for, §22-3601.
Sexual assault response, §§4-561.01 to
4-561.16.
Chief of police.
Monitoring of MPD, §4-561.08.
Definitions, §4-561.01.
Forensic examination kits and
specimens.
Payment for kits, §4-561.03.
Processing, §4-561.02.
Hospitals.
Forensic examination kits and
specimens, billing, §4-561.03.
Independent expert consultant,
§4-561.04.
Duties, §4-561.05.
Reports, §4-561.06.
Reviews, §4-561.06.
MPD.
Duties, §4-561.07.
Monitoring by chief of police,
§4-561.08.
Reports, §4-561.09.
No private right of action, §4-561.16.
OCME.
Reports.
Sexual assault forensic
examination kits, §4-561.10.
Toxicology samples, §4-561.11.
Reports.
Independent expert consultant,
§4-561.06.
MPD, §4-561.09.
OCME.
Sexual assault forensic
examination kits, §4-561.10.
Toxicology samples, §4-561.11.
Reviews.
Independent expert consultant,
§4-561.06.
SART.
Case review subcommittee,
§4-561.14.
Duties and responsibilities,
§4-561.13.
Establishment, §4-561.12.
Membership, §4-561.12.
Sexual assault victim rights task force,
§4-561.15.

VICTIMS OF CRIME —Cont'd
Sexual assault response —Cont'd
Time limits.
Forensic examination kits and
specimens, processing,
§4-561.02.
Sexual assault victim advocates,
§23-1909.
Disclosure of confidential information
prohibited without consent of
client, §14-307.
Privileged communications, §14-312.
Sexual assault victims' rights,
§§23-1907 to 23-1911.
Access to information, §23-1910.
Definitions, §23-1907.
Emergency care for sexual assault
victims, §§7-2121 to 7-2125.
Multiple victims, §22-3020.
Past behavior of victim, admissibility
of evidence of, §§22-3021, 22-3022.
Private right of action, §23-1911.
Rights of victims, §23-1908.
Sexual assault victim advocates,
§23-1909.
Disclosure of confidential
information prohibited without
consent of client, §14-307.
Privileged communications, §14-312.
Sexual offenses, §§23-1907 to 23-1911.
Access to information, §23-1910.
Definitions, §23-1907.
Emergency care for sexual assault
victims, §§7-2121 to 7-2125.
Multiple victims, §22-3020.
Past behavior of victim, admissibility
of evidence of, §§22-3021, 22-3022.
Private right of action, §23-1911.
Rights of victims, §23-1908.
Sexual assault victim advocates,
§23-1909.

VIDEO RECORDINGS.
Depositions, CivPro Rule 30.
Adoption proceedings, Adoption Rule
30.
Domestic relations actions, DomRel
Rule 30.
Use of expert's videotaped deposition,
CivPro Rule 32.
Metropolitan police.
Video surveillance regulations,
§5-133.19.
Voyeurism, §22-3531.

VIDEO SERVICES.
Taxation, §47-2501.01.

VIDEO SURVEILLANCE.
Gas stations.
Security requirements, §36-301.21.

VIETNAMESE LANGUAGE.
**Foreign language services and
documents,** §§2-1931 to 2-1936.
See FOREIGN LANGUAGE
SERVICES AND DOCUMENTS.
**Government publications translated
in.**
Publications concerning health, safety
and welfare of Asian and Pacific
Islander resident, §2-1375.

VIEW 14 PROJECT.
Real property tax exemptions,
§47-4623.

VIOLENCE, DOMESTIC, §§16-1031 to
16-1034.

VIOLENT CRIME.
Compensation of victims, §§4-501 to
4-518, VictComp Rules 1 to 41.
See CRIME VICTIMS'
COMPENSATION.
Crime investigation records.
Retention of records in open
investigations, §5-113.32.
Gangs, §22-951.
Minors, violent crimes against.
Enhanced penalties, §22-3611.

VIRGINIA.
Bridges.
Obstructing bridges connecting
District of Columbia and Virginia,
§22-1323.
Dulles International Airport.
Municipal services arrangements,
§9-809.
Sanitary sewer, acquisition of land for,
§34-2134.
**Fairfax County Sewage Delivery
System and Capacity Purchase
Agreement,** §24-106.
Funeral directors licensed in, §3-415.
Metrorail and metrobus.
Adopted regional system, §§9-1111.01
to 9-1111.17.
See METRORAIL AND
METROBUS.
Compact for mass transportation,
§§9-1103.01 to 9-1103.07.
Interstate agreement on, §9-1101.01.
Joint state oversight agency,
§§9-1109.01 to 9-1109.07.
Washington metropolitan area transit
authority compact, §§9-1107.01 to
9-1107.12.

VIRGINIA —Cont'd
Police departments.
Reciprocal agreements between,
§§2-209.01 to 2-209.04.
Sewerage agreement with, §2-207.01.
**Temporary assistance for needy
families (TANF).**
Amounts adjusted to meet local
programs, §4-205.51a.
**Washington National Airport
municipal services agreements,**
§9-707.
**Wastewater and sewage works
agreements with,** §1-204.87.
Water supply and waterworks.
Arlington County, delivery of water to,
§34-2401.17.
Falls Church, delivery of water to,
§34-2411.01.

VIRGINIA AVENUE.
Railroad sidings, §9-1201.10.

**VISION ZERO PEDESTRIAN AND
BICYCLE SAFETY FUND,**
§50-921.20.

VISITATION.
Child abuse and neglect.
Disposition of child.
Parental visitations, §16-2323.
Child custody proceedings.
Temporary visitation, §16-4603.04.
Delinquent minors.
Custody, parental visitation of children
in, §16-2310.
**Military personnel during
deployment,** §16-914.02.
Public welfare, board of.
Visitation of wards, §4-122.
**Sexual abuse, child conceived as
result of.**
Prohibition on child custody or
visitation, §16-914.
Social service referrals, DomRel Rule
404.

VISITORS.
Appointment of, §21-2033.

VITAL RECORDS, §§7-201 to 7-228.
Adoption forms, §7-209.
Amendments to, §7-217.
Annulment registration, §7-216.
Birth registration, §§7-205 to 7-210.
Adoptions, §7-209.
New certificates of birth, obtaining,
§7-210.
Change of gender, amendment of birth
certificate, §16-2503.

VITAL RECORDS —Cont'd
Birth registration —Cont'd
Delays in filing for, §7-207.
Domestic partnerships, §7-205.
Facts of birth, judicial procedure to
establish, §7-208.
Matching birth and death certificates,
§7-224.
New certificates of birth, obtaining,
§7-210.
Parentage.
Voluntary acknowledgment,
§§16-909.04, 16-2345.
Parentage proceedings, following,
§16-2346.
Social Security numbers, §7-205.01.
Unknown parentage of infant, §7-206.
Burial registers held by cemeteries,
§43-117.
Child death.
Report to registrar, §4-1371.12.
Civil fines, penalties and fees.
Sanctions for infractions, §7-225.
Copies of, §§7-218, 7-220, 7-221.
Death registration, §§7-211 to 7-214,
7-224.
Definitions, §7-201.
Delayed filing.
Birth registration, §7-207.
Death registration, §7-212.
Divorce registration, §7-216.
Effective date of provisions, §7-228.
**Establishment of vital records
system,** §7-202.
False certification of document.
Criminal penalty, §7-225.
Fees, §7-221.
Fetal deaths, §§7-213, 7-214.
Fines, §7-225.
Fund, §7-221.
Issuance of regulations regarding,
§7-226.
Marriage registration, §7-215.
**Matching birth and death
certificates,** §7-224.
Parentage.
Voluntary acknowledgment,
§§16-909.04, 16-2345.
Penalties, §7-225.
**Persons required to furnish
information for,** §7-223.
Persons required to keep, §7-222.
Privacy and confidentiality, §7-219.
Registrar, §7-203.
Reproductions of, §§7-218, 7-220,
7-221.

VITAL RECORDS —Cont'd
Requirements regarding, §7-204.
Searches of, §7-221.
Severability of provisions, §7-227.
Violations.
  Penalties, §7-225.

VOCATIONAL EDUCATION.
Child labor.
  Minors under sixteen, §32-204.
Drug free zones, §48-904.07a.
Elementary and secondary
  education levels, §38-1905.
John A. Chamberlain Vocational
  School.
  Named, §38-905.
Teachers, §38-1905.
University of the District of
  Columbia.
  Former institution, §§38-1121 to
    38-1125.
    See WASHINGTON TECHNICAL
      INSTITUTE.
  Successor institution, §§38-1201.01 to
    38-1207.07.
    See UNIVERSITY OF THE
      DISTRICT OF COLUMBIA.
Washington Technical Institute,
  §§38-1121 to 38-1125.
  See WASHINGTON TECHNICAL
    INSTITUTE.

VOCATIONAL REHABILITATION.
BOOT CAMP, §24-924.
Disability compensation, as part of,
  §§1-623.04, 1-623.11.

VOIDABLE TITLE.
Sales.
  Power to transfer.
    Good faith purchaser, §28:2-403.

VOIR DIRE, CivPro Rule 47, CrimPro
  Rule 24.

**VOLUNTARY ACKNOWLEDGMENT
  OF PARENTAGE,** §§16-909.01,
  16-2342.01.
Birth records, §§16-909.04, 16-2345.

VOLUNTARY APPRENTICES,
  §§32-1402 to 32-1413.
  See APPRENTICES.

VOLUNTARY ASSIGNMENTS.
Assignments for benefit of creditors,
  §§28-2101 to 28-2110.
  See ASSIGNMENTS FOR BENEFIT
    OF CREDITORS.

VOLUNTARY CLEANUP PROGRAM.
Hazardous substances releases,
  §§8-631.01 to 8-638.01.
  See HAZARDOUS SUBSTANCES
    RELEASES.

**VOLUNTARY LEAVE TRANSFER
  PROGRAM,** §§1-612.31 to 1-612.38.
Accounting by agency, §1-612.36.
Accrual of normal leave suspended
  during period of use, §1-612.36.
Amount eligible for transfer,
  §1-612.34.
Application to receive transferred
  leave, §1-612.33.
Approval of transfer, §1-612.35.
Coercion, threats or intimidation
  prohibited, §1-612.37.
Definitions, §1-612.31.
Disapproval of transfer, §1-612.35.
Eligibility, §1-612.32.
Establishment by agency, §1-612.32.
Exclusion of agency from program,
  §1-612.32.
  Reporting requirements, §1-612.38.
Physician certification of serious
  health condition.
  When required, §1-612.33.
Report of agency, §1-612.38.
Request by contributor to transfer,
  §1-612.34.
Termination of leave, §1-612.36.
Unused leave, §1-612.36.
Use of transferred leave by
  recipient, §1-612.36.
When authorized, §1-612.32.

**VOLUNTEER FIRE
  ORGANIZATION.**
Extra equipment for, §5-411.

VOLUNTEERS.
Criminal background checks.
  Recreational volunteers.
    See PARKS AND RECREATION.
Emergency volunteer health
  practitioners, §§7-2361.01 to
  7-2361.12.
  See EMERGENCY VOLUNTEER
    HEALTH PRACTITIONERS.
Nonprofit corporations.
  Immunity, §29-406.90.
Recreation board, §10-212.
Utilization by government, §§1-319.01
  to 1-319.05.
  Conflicts of interest.
    Placing volunteer in positions likely
      to constitute, §1-319.03.

VOLUNTEERS —Cont'd
Utilization by government —Cont'd
Considered employees of district,
§1-319.03.
Definitions, §1-319.05.
Encouraged, §1-319.01.
Inapplicability to offices of United
States Marshal and United States
Attorney for district, §1-319.04.
Not eligible for benefits, §1-319.03.
Regulations, §1-319.02.
Tort liability of district, §1-319.03.
Volunteer service credit program,
§§7-531.01 to 7-531.11.
Advisory committees, §7-531.06.
Definitions, §7-531.01.
Demonstration projects, §7-531.07.
Eligible persons.
Defined, §7-531.01.
Establishment of pilot program,
§7-531.02.
Qualified immunity, §7-531.09.
Reimbursement of volunteers for
expenses, §7-531.08.
Reports, §7-531.11.
Rules, §7-531.10.
Service credits, §7-531.04.
Defined, §7-531.01.
Guarantee, §7-531.05.
Targeted services, §7-531.03.
Defined, §7-531.01.
Volunteers not considered employees
or agents, §7-531.08.
Volunteers not entitled to
compensation, §7-531.08.

VOLUNTEER SERVICE CREDIT
PROGRAM.
Aged persons, §§7-531.01 to 7-531.11.

VOTER REGISTRATION.
Application form, §1-1001.07.
Application to register, §1-1001.07.
Automatic registration, feasibility
report, §1-1001.07.
Board of elections, §1-1001.05.
Accepting application, §1-1001.07.
Challenges, §1-1001.07.
Duties, §1-1001.07.
Challenges, §1-1001.07.
Corrupt election practices,
§1-1001.14.
Election day registration, §1-1001.07.
False representations, §1-1001.14.
Faxed postcard applications,
§1-1001.07.
Interference with registration,
§1-1001.12.

VOTER REGISTRATION —Cont'd
Lists of qualified electors registered
to vote, §1-1001.07.
Mail-in registration, §1-1001.07.
Motor voter application forms,
§1-1001.07.
Notification form, §1-1001.07.
Objections, §1-1001.07.
Pre-registration before person's 18th
birthday, §1-1001.07.
Qualifications, §1-1001.07.
Time for registration, §1-1001.07.
Voter registration agency.
Defined, §1-1001.02.

VOTING BY MILITARY AND
OVERSEAS VOTERS, §§1-1061.01
to 1-1061.20.
See ELECTIONS.

VOTING RIGHTS.
Grants to promote voting rights and
statehood, §1-328.03.

VOTING SECURITIES.
Insurance holding companies,
§31-709.

VOTING TRUST AGREEMENTS.
Domestic life insurance companies,
§31-4431.

VOUCHERS.
Certification, liability for, §47-121.
Domestic life insurance company
disbursements, §31-4439.
Rent assistance program.
Capital-based assistance, §6-229.
Housing choice voucher program,
§6-228.
Tenant-based assistance, §6-228.
Voucher assistance, §6-227.
Youth services, §2-1507.

VOYEURISM, §22-3531.

VULNERABLE ADULTS AND
ELDERLY PERSONS.
Criminal abuse, neglect and
financial exploitation, §§22-931 to
22-938.
Civil penalties, §22-937.
Criminal negligence, §22-934.
Criminal penalties, §§22-936,
22-936.01.
Definitions, §22-932.
Elderly person.
Financial exploitation, §22-933.01.
Ex parte motions.
Injunctive relief, §22-938.

VULNERABLE ADULTS AND ELDERLY PERSONS —Cont'd
Criminal abuse, neglect and financial exploitation —Cont'd
Freezing assets of vulnerable adult or elderly person, §22-938.
Injunctive relief, §22-938.
Short title, §22-931.
Treatment by religious methods of healing.
Exception to criminal offense, §22-934.
Vulnerable adult.
Criminal abuse, §22-933.
Financial exploitation, §22-933.01.

W

WAGES AND SALARIES, §§32-1301 to 32-1311.
Administrative actions, §32-1308.01.
Retaliation prohibited, §32-1308.01.
Appropriations for, §1-503.
Appropriations for pay increases, §47-3403.
Assignment of choses in action, §28-2305.
Assignments.
Consumer credit sales or direct installment loans.
Assignment of earnings prohibited, §28-3804.
Contract to assign future salary or wages prohibited, §28-2305.
Attachment and garnishment, §16-516, CivPro Rule 69-II.
Advance payment of wages to avoid attachment, §16-513.
Amount collection, judgment creditor to file receipts of, §16-574.
Applicability of provisions, §16-582.
Definitions, §16-571.
Domestic relations actions, DomRel Rule 69.
Employer duties regarding, §16-573.
Employer failure to pay, §16-575.
Employer payment where employee's salary inadequate, §16-579.
Inadequacy of employee's salary, §16-579.
Nonresidents, §16-513.
Percentage limitations on, §§16-572, 16-577.
Priority of attachments, §16-572.
Prior to judgment, §16-583.
Quashing attachment obtained to hinder just claims, §16-580.

WAGES AND SALARIES —Cont'd
Attachment and garnishment —Cont'd
Records, §16-575.
Superior court judgments, §16-578.
Support orders.
Enforcement, §16-571.01.
Percentage limitations, §16-577.
Termination of employee.
Garnishment, termination for, §16-584.
Lapse or dismissal of attachment upon, §16-576.
Writ of attachment on wages, salary and commissions, CivPro Form CA 123.
Attorney general, §1-611.09.
Auditor for District of Columbia, §1-204.55.
Basic pay levels, §1-611.14.
Board of Education, §1-611.10.
Basic pay levels, §1-611.14.
Boards and commissions, §1-611.08.
Budget monitoring committee, §47-319.03.
Career services, §1-611.04.
Basic pay levels, §1-611.14.
Charitable solicitations over the phone.
Compensation prohibited, §44-1708.
Chief financial officer, §1-204.24b.
Child-placing agencies, §4-1410.
Civil actions based on statutory violations, §32-1308.
Retaliation prohibited, §32-1311.
Collective bargaining under merit system for public officers and employees, §§1-602.06, 1-617.16, 1-617.17.
Commission on judicial disabilities and tenure, §11-1524.
Conservators appointed for protection of property, §21-2060.
Consumer credit sales.
Assignment of earnings prohibited, §28-3804.
Consumer protection.
Assignment of earnings prohibited, §28-3804.
Corporate income tax credit for, §47-1807.04.
Council, §§1-204.03, 1-611.09.
Mayor and council compensation advisory committee, §§1-611.51 to 1-611.57.
See MAYOR AND COUNCIL COMPENSATION ADVISORY COMMITTEE.

WAGES AND SALARIES —Cont'd
Court employees, nonjudicial,
§11-1726.
Courthouse protection force, §47-201.
Court of appeals judges, §11-703.
Crime victims' compensation.
Loss of earnings, VictComp Rule 28.
Request for employment
information, VictComp Rule 14.
**Debt set-offs for public officers and
employees,** §§1-629.01 to 1-629.04.
Definitions, §32-1301.
Delegation of powers regarding,
§32-1309.
Direct deposit, §1-611.20.
Educational employees, §1-611.11.
Elected officials.
Mayor and council compensation
advisory committee, §§1-611.51 to
1-611.57.
See MAYOR AND COUNCIL
COMPENSATION ADVISORY
COMMITTEE.
Emergency medical services.
Fire and emergency medical services
overtime settlement fund,
§5-525.01.
Applicability, §5-525.02.
Enforcement of provisions, §32-1306.
**Erroneous payments to public
officers and employees,**
§§1-629.01, 1-629.02.
Excepted services, §1-611.04.
Basic pay levels, §1-611.14.
**Execution of judgment, property
exempt from,** §15-503.
Executive service, §§1-610.52 to
1-610.58.
Basic pay levels, §1-611.14.
**Family homes, placement of
children in,** §4-1410.
Fines, §32-1307.
**Fire and emergency medical
services overtime settlement
fund,** §5-525.01.
Applicability, §5-525.02.
Garnishment. See within this heading,
"Attachment and garnishment."
Guardianship of minors, §21-143.
Health occupations boards,
§3-1204.06.
Employees' compensation, §3-1204.07.
Holidays, working on, compensation.
Metropolitan police, fire department,
§5-521.01.
Holiday defined, §5-521.02.

WAGES AND SALARIES —Cont'd
Holidays, working on, compensation
—Cont'd
Metropolitan police, fire department
—Cont'd
Secret service, park police,
applicability, §5-521.03.
**Homeland security and emergency
management agency,** §7-2202.
Hospitals.
See HOSPITALS.
**Incentive awards for public officers
and employees,** §§1-619.01 to
1-619.03.
Installment loans.
Assignment of earnings prohibited,
§28-3804.
Interpreters, §2-1912.
Legal service, §1-608.58.
**Limitations on pay received by
public officers and employees,**
§1-611.16.
Living wage act, §§2-220.01 to
2-220.11.
See LIVING WAGE ACT.
**Lottery and charitable games
control board,** §3-1301.
Management supervisory service,
§1-609.56.
Mayor, §§1-204.21, 1-611.09.
**Mayor and council compensation
advisory committee,** §§1-611.51 to
1-611.57.
See MAYOR AND COUNCIL
COMPENSATION ADVISORY
COMMITTEE.
Medical examiners, §5-1402.
Merit system.
Compensation of employees,
§§1-611.01 to 1-611.21.
See MERIT SYSTEM.
General provisions, §§1-601.01 to
1-636.03.
See MERIT SYSTEM.
Minimum wages.
General provisions, §§32-1001 to
32-1015.
See MINIMUM WAGES.
National Guard.
See NATIONAL GUARD.
Park police, §5-545.01.
Holidays, working on, compensation,
§5-521.03.
Locality-based comparability
adjustments, freeze, §5-563.02.
Termination of special salary rates,
§5-563.01.

WAGES AND SALARIES —Cont'd

Pay equity and training commission,
§§32-601 to 32-609.
Applicability, §32-606.
Conduct of study and report by
consultant, §32-604.
Cooperation with consultant, §32-605.
Definitions, §32-601.
Design and methodology of study,
§32-603.
Final report by commission, §32-607.
Findings and recommendations of
consultant, §32-604.
Funding, §32-609.
Members of commission, §32-602.
Recommendations of mayor upon
review of final report, §32-608.
Selection of consultants, §32-603.
Temporary commission established,
§32-602.

Payment of wages.
Resignation of employee, upon,
§32-1303.
Suspension from work, upon,
§32-1303.
Termination of employment, upon,
§32-1303.
Unconditional payment of wages
conceded to be due, §32-1304.
When wages must be paid, §32-1302.

Penalties, §32-1307.

Personal representatives, §§20-751,
20-753.

Physicians to the poor, §44-713.

Police and firefighters, §§5-501.01 to
5-563.02.
Adjustments to compensation,
§5-542.01.
Aide to the fire marshal, §5-542.03.
Bomb disposal duty, additional
compensation for, §5-542.02.
Computation of rates of compensation,
§5-501.02.
Council authority to regulate,
§§5-545.04, 5-545.06a.
Decreases in compensation, §5-545.03.
Definitions, §5-1304.
Delegation of powers regarding,
§5-545.06.
Demotions, §5-543.05.
Helicopter duty, additional
compensation for, §5-542.02.
Holidays, working on, §§5-521.01 to
5-521.03.
Compensation generally, §5-521.01.
Holiday defined, §5-521.02.

WAGES AND SALARIES —Cont'd

Police and firefighters —Cont'd
Holidays, working on —Cont'd
Secret service, park police,
applicability, §5-521.03.
Increases, reasons for denying or
implementing, §5-501.01.
Length of service awards, §5-544.01.
Maximum compensation amount,
§5-541.01.
Military service, §5-1303.
Minimum rates, §5-543.01.
Overtime, §5-1304.
Fire and emergency medical services
overtime settlement fund,
§5-525.01.
Applicability, §5-525.02.
Park police, §5-545.01.
Holidays, working on, compensation,
§5-521.03.
Premium pay, §5-1304.
Promotions, §5-543.04.
Reappointments, rates for, §5-543.01.
Retroactive salary, §5-545.05.
Schedule of salaries, §5-541.01.
Scuba diving duty, additional
compensation for, §5-542.02.
Secret Service, §5-545.01.
Conversion to 2001 standards,
§5-561.02.
Holidays, working on, compensation,
§5-521.03.
Service step adjustments, §5-543.03.
Setting pay for, §1-611.13.
Technicians, §5-543.02.
Transfers, §5-543.04.
Workweek, §5-1304.

Prisons and prisoners.
Prison industries, §§24-231.10,
24-231.11.
Work release program, §§24-241.06,
24-241.07.

Public contracts.
Living wage act, §§2-220.01 to
2-220.11.
See LIVING WAGE ACT.

**Public defender service, attorneys
employed by,** §2-1605.

Public employee relations board,
§1-611.12.

Public officers and employees,
§§1-611.03 to 1-611.21.
Living wage act, §§2-220.01 to
2-220.11.
See LIVING WAGE ACT.

Records, §32-1306.

WAGES AND SALARIES —Cont'd
Recreation board, §10-205.
Register of wills, §11-2102.
Rental housing commission,
§42-3502.01.
Retaliation, §32-1311.
Secret service, §5-545.01.
  Conversion to 2001 standards,
    §5-561.02.
  Holidays, working on, compensation,
    §5-521.03.
  Locality-based comparability
    adjustments, freeze, §5-563.02.
Severance pay for public officers
  and employees, §1-624.09.
Signature by mark on payment of,
  §1-505.
Small claims court, §16-3908.
  Supplementary proceedings in wage
    claims, SmallClaims Rule 18.
Subpoenas, §32-1306.
Superintendent of Washington
  Asylum and Jail, §47-201.
Superior court judges, §11-904.
Surveyor of the District, §1-1301.
Teachers.
  See TEACHERS.
Teachers, setting pay for, §1-611.13.
Telephone charitable solicitations.
  Compensation prohibited, §44-1708.
Terminated employees, §47-392.26.
Transfers to minors, custodians of,
  §21-315.
Transparency, §§32-1451 to 32-1457.
  Applicability, §32-1457.
  Definitions, §32-1451.
  Enforcement, §32-1455.
  Exceptions, §32-1453.
  Prohibited actions of employer,
    §32-1452.
  Rules, §32-1456.
  Waiver of statutory provisions,
    §32-1454.
University of the District of
  Columbia, board of trustees.
  Educational employees.
    Basic pay levels, §1-611.14.
Unpaid wages as unclaimed
  property, §41-116.
Wage theft prevention fund,
  §32-1307.01.
Waiver of compensation by public
  officers and employees, §1-611.15.
Waiver of provisions not allowed as
  to, §32-1305.
Workplace fraud, §§32-1331.01 to
  32-1331.12.
  See WORKPLACE FRAUD.

WAITRESSES AND WAITERS.
Minimum wage for persons
  receiving gratuities, §32-1003.

WAIVER OR RELEASE.
Adult protective services.
  Waiver of privilege regarding, §7-1911.
Artist protection.
  Waiver of statutory provisions void,
    §28-5107.
Attachment.
  Release from, §16-510.
Business license renewal fees for
  armed forces personnel,
  §1-301.01.
Child abuse and neglect.
  Privilege not grounds for excluding
    evidence of, §4-1321.05.
Child care facilities overpayments,
  §4-408.
Conservators' notice requirements,
  §21-2032.
Costs.
  Civil procedure, CivPro Rule 54-II.
    Affidavit, CivPro Form CA 106.
    Application to proceed without
      prepayment of costs, fees or
      security, CivPro Form CA 106A.
Court employees.
  Debts and erroneous payments made
    to employees, collection by
    executive officer.
  Waiver of claim, §11-1733.
Decedents' estates.
  Accounts.
    Waiver of audit on, §20-732.
  Inventories.
    Waiver on filing, §20-731.
Dietetics and nutrition licenses,
  §3-1207.02.
Dietetics and nutrition
  practitioners.
  Examination, §3-1207.02.
Erroneous payments to public
  officers and employees, §1-629.01.
Health occupations licensure,
  registration or certification.
  See HEALTH OCCUPATIONS
    LICENSURE, REGISTRATION
    OR CERTIFICATION.
Home solicitation sales.
  Buyer's right to cancel, §28-3811.
Horizontal property regimes,
  §42-2011.
Housing finance agency waiver of
  ban on participation by
  interested party, §42-2702.04.

WAIVER OR RELEASE —Cont'd

Interest.

Waiver of rights regarding, §28-3312.

Interpreters, §2-1906.

Judges.

Waiver of fees or charges.

Accepting gifts or other things of
value, CJC Canon 3.14.

Reporting requirements, CJC
Canon 3.15.

Landlord and tenant.

Notice to quit or notice of termination,
§42-3208.

**Medicaid health-care assistance
reimbursement rights,** §4-603.

Mental health disclosures,
§7-1208.04.

**Motor vehicle financial
responsibility.**

Waiver of need to file proof of,
§50-1301.68.

News media privilege, §16-4704.

**No-fault motor vehicle insurance
requirements waived for
taxicabs,** §31-2411.

Nursing homes.

Discharge, transfer, or relocation of
residents of, §44-1004.05.

**Police and firefighters medical care
reimbursement,** §5-606.

**Police and firefighters retirement
and disability annuity,** §5-723.

Prostitution.

Order of abatement of nuisance of
house of, §22-2719.

Public utilities fines and penalties,
§34-711.

Recordation tax, §42-1103.

**Rental housing conversion and sale
rights,** §42-3404.07.

School buildings and grounds.

Repairs and maintenance of,
§38-1805.61.

Unemployment compensation rights,
§51-118.

**Wage provisions, waiver not allowed
as to,** §32-1305.

Wage transparency.

Waiver of statutory provisions,
§32-1454.

Workplace fraud.

Waiver of protections of law by
agreement.

Prohibition, §32-1331.08.

**WALKER JONES/NORTHWEST ONE
UNITY HEALTH CENTER.**

Real property tax exemptions,
§47-4619.

WALL STREET.

**Dodd-Frank Wall Street reform and
consumer protection act.**

Filings under, USDistCt LCvR 85.

**WALTER REED ARMY MEDICAL
CENTER,** §§10-1901 to 10-1906.

Advisory committee, establishment,
§10-1906.

Approval of plans, §10-1903.

Definitions, §10-1901.

Findings, §10-1902.

Purpose, §10-1902.

Transfer of real property, §§10-1904,
10-1905.

**WALTER REED MEDICAL CENTER
SITE DEVELOPMENT,**
§§2-1227.01 to 2-1227.06.

Definitions, §2-1227.01.

**Disposition of Walter Reed
redevelopment site, approval,**
§2-1227.04.

EDC agreement approval, §2-1227.03.

Findings, §2-1227.02.

Walter Reed redevelopment fund,
§2-1227.06.

Walter Reed reinvestment fund,
§2-1227.05.

**WALTER REED REDEVELOPMENT
FUND,** §2-1227.06.

**WALTER REED REINVESTMENT
FUND,** §2-1227.05.

WAR.

Articles of war, US Const Art I §8.

Congress.

Articles of war, US Const Art I §8.

Declaration of war, US Const Art I §8.

Declaration by congress, US Const
Art I §8.

Grand jury.

Presentment is dispensable in certain
cases, US Const Amd 5.

Quartering soldiers in homes, US
Const Amd 3.

State.

May not make without consent of
congress, US Const Art I §10.

Treason.

In levying against the United States,
US Const Art III §3.

WARD 1 ENHANCED RESIDENTIAL PARKING PROGRAM, §50-2551.

WARDS, CITY.

Alcoholic beverage licenses.
Restrictions in Ward 2, §25-345.
Restrictions in Ward 6, §25-346.
Restrictions in Ward 7, §25-342.
Restrictions in Ward 8, §25-343.

Boundaries of election wards, §1-1041.03.

Election ward task forces of advisory neighborhood commission, §§1-1041.01, 1-1041.02.

WAREHOUSE RECEIPTS.

Documents of title.
Generally, §§28:7-101 to 28:7-702.
See DOCUMENTS OF TITLE.

WAREHOUSES.

Alcoholic beverages.
Warehouse receipts.
Storage under government bond, §28:7-201.

Liens, §28:7-209.
Enforcement, §28:7-210.

Penalties.
Executions.
Liens or goods covered by a negotiable document, §28:7-602.
Lost and missing receipts, §28:7-601.

WARRANTIES.

Alcoholic beverages.
Implied warranty of merchantability, §28:2-314.

Assistive technology device.
Implied warranty, §28-4032.

Bank deposits and collections.
Presentment warranties, §28:4-208.
Transfer warranties, §28:4-207.

Beverages.
Implied warranty of merchantability, §28:2-314.

Bills of lading.
Collecting banks.
Warranties of collecting bank as to bills, §28:7-508.
Warranties on negotiation or delivery, §28:7-507.

Condominiums, §§42-1903.16, 42-1903.17.

Documents of title.
Negotiation or delivery, §28:7-507.
Collecting bank's warranties as to documents, §28:7-508.

WARRANTIES —Cont'd

Food.
Implied warranty of merchantability, §28:2-314.

Home sales, implied warranties.
Fitness for particular purpose, §28:2-315.
Merchantability, §28:2-314.
Usage of trade, §28:2-314.

Investment securities.
Direct holding, §28:8-108.
Effect of signature of authenticating trustee, registrar or transfer agent, §28:8-208.
Indirect holding, §28:8-109.

Leases, UCC.
Breach of warranty.
Damages, §§28:2A-508, 28:2A-519.
Notice of claim or litigation answerable over, §28:2A-506.
Waiver or renunciation of rights after breach, §28:2A-107.
Cumulation and conflict, §28:2A-215.
Damages.
Breach of warranty, §§28:2A-508, 28:2A-519.
Exclusion, §28:2A-214.
Express warranties.
Generally, §28:2A-210.
Third party beneficiaries, §28:2A-216.
Fitness for particular purpose.
Implied warranty, §28:2A-213.
Implied warranties.
Fitness for particular purpose, §28:2A-213.
Merchantability, §28:2A-212.
Third party beneficiaries, §28:2A-216.
Infringement.
Warranty against, §28:2A-211.
Interference with goods.
Warranty against, §28:2A-211.
Merchantability.
Implied warranty, §28:2A-212.
Modification, §28:2A-214.
Third party beneficiaries, §28:2A-216.

Letters of credit, §28:5-110.

Motor vehicles.
New car warranties, §§50-501 to 50-510.
See LEMON LAW.

Negotiable instruments.
Presentment warranties, §28:3-417.
Transfer warranties, §28:3-416.

Real property.
General warranties, §42-604.

WARRANTIES —Cont'd
Real property —Cont'd
  Special warranties, §42-605.
  Void as to heirs, §42-609.
Sale of goods, UCC.
  Cumulation and conflict, §28:2-314.
    Exclusions, §§28:2-316, 28:2-316.01.
    Modification, §§28:2-316, 28:2-316.01.
    Third party beneficiaries, §28:2-318.
  Damages for breach, §§28:2-317, 28:2-714.
  Express warranties, §28:2-313.
    Cumulation and conflict, §28:2-317.
    Exclusions generally, §§28:2-316, 28:2-316.01.
    Generally, §28:2-313.
    Modification generally, §§28:2-316, 28:2-316.01.
    Third party beneficiaries, §28:2-714.
  Implied warranties.
    Course of dealing or usage of trade, §28:2-314.
    Cumulation and conflict, §28:2-317.
    Exclusions generally, §§28:2-316, 28:2-316.01.
    Fitness for a particular purpose, §§28:2-315, 28:2-316.
      Exclusion or modification, §§28:2-316, 28:2-316.01.
    Merchantability, §28:2-316.
      Exclusion or modification, §§28:2-316, 28:2-316.01.
    Modification, §§28:2-316, 28:2-316.01.
    Third party beneficiaries, §28:2-318.
  Infringement of enjoyment of goods.
    Warranty of title and against infringement, §28:2-312.
  Merchantability, §28:2-314.
    Implied warranty, §§28:2-316, 28:2-316.01.
  Shipment and delivery of goods.
    Warranty of condition on arrival, §28:2-321.
  Third party beneficiaries, §§28:2-312, 28:2-318.
  Title.
    Warranty of title and against infringement, §28:2-312.
Samples.
  Sales warranties.
    Express warranties by sample, §28:2-313.
Warehouse receipts.
  Collecting bank.
    Warranties of collecting bank as to receipts, §28:7-508.

WARRANTIES —Cont'd
Warehouse receipts —Cont'd
  Warranties on negotiation or delivery, §28:7-507.
WARRANTLESS ARRESTS, §§23-581, 23-582.
Controlled substances, §48-921.01.
Cruelty to animals, arrest without warrant for, §22-1004.
Definitions, §23-501.
Persons other than law enforcement officers, by, §23-582.
WARRANTS.
Administrative search warrants, CivPro Rule 204.
Arrest warrants.
  See ARREST WARRANTS.
Child abduction prevention.
  Warrant to take physical custody of child, §16-4604.09.
Constitution of the United States.
  Searches and seizures.
    Conditions for issuance, US Const Amd 4.
Inspection of weights and measures without, §37-201.24.
Searches and seizures.
  Constitution of the United States.
    Conditions for issuance, US Const Amd 4.
Search warrants.
  See SEARCH WARRANTS.
WASHINGTON.
Abolition of City of Georgetown and extension of general laws of Washington to, §1-107.
District of Columbia as successor corporation of, §1-104.
Geographic area, §1-107.
Territorial area, §1-107.
WASHINGTON AQUEDUCT.
Playground purposes, §10-126.
WASHINGTON ASYLUM AND JAIL.
See PRISONS AND PRISONERS.
WASHINGTON BALLET.
Real property tax exemption, §47-4655.
WASHINGTON CHANNEL BRIDGE, §9-326.
WASHINGTON CONVENTION AND SPORTS AUTHORITY, §§10-1202.01 to 10-1221.15.
Armory board.
  Transfer of authority, §10-1202.02a.

WASHINGTON CONVENTION AND SPORTS AUTHORITY —Cont'd
Audits, §10-1203.05.
Board of directors, §§10-1202.05, 10-1202.06.
Bond issues, §§10-1202.09 to 10-1202.14.
  Convention center hotel, §§10-1202.04, 10-1202.09.
  Delegation of council authority to issue, §10-1202.09.
  District pledges, §10-1202.12.
  Power and authority to issue, §10-1202.10.
  Right to direct authority to purchase own bonds and notes, §10-1202.14.
  Sale, §10-1202.11.
Chief executive officer and general manager.
  References to, §10-1202.07a.
Compensating-use tax collected, §47-2202.02.
Convention center hotel.
  Bond issues, §§10-1202.04, 10-1202.09.
  Contracting requirements, §§10-1202.41 to 10-1202.44.
  Defined, §10-1202.01.
  Eminent domain, §§10-1202.31 to 10-1202.33.
  Financing, §§10-1221.01 to 10-1221.13.
  General provisions.
    See CONVENTION CENTER HOTEL.
  Land lease authority for hotel, §§10-1202.21 to 10-1202.24.
Definitions, §10-1202.01.
Effective date of provisions, §10-1203.06.
Eminent domain, §§10-1202.31 to 10-1202.33.
  Definitions, §10-1202.31.
  Exercise, §10-1202.33.
  Findings, §10-1202.32.
Establishment of, §10-1202.02.
Excess cash, transfers of, §10-1202.13.
Funds, §§10-1202.08, 10-1203.07.
  Marketing fund, §10-1202.08a.
  Sports and entertainment fund, §10-1202.08b.
  Sports facilities account, §10-1202.08c.
Gross sales tax transfers to, §47-2002.03.
Limitations on powers of, §10-1202.04.
Marketing fund and marketing service contracts, §10-1202.08a.

WASHINGTON CONVENTION AND SPORTS AUTHORITY —Cont'd
Merit personnel system not applicable to employees of, §10-1202.16.
Policy declaration, §10-1202.02.
Powers and duties, §§10-1202.03, 10-1202.04.
President and chief executive officer, §10-1202.07.
  References to, §10-1202.07a.
Sports and entertainment commission.
  Transfer of assets and obligations, §10-1202.02c.
  Transfer of authority, §10-1202.02b.
Taxes collected and transferred to fund, §10-1203.07.

WASHINGTON CONVENTION CENTER.
Authorizations, §§47-396.01 to 47-398.06.
Convention center hotel.
  General provisions.
    See CONVENTION CENTER HOTEL.
Expenditure of revenues for activities, §47-396.01.
Location of new center, §10-1202.15.
Redevelopment of existing site, §10-1202.15a.

WASHINGTON HUMANE SOCIETY, §§44-1501 to 44-1511.
Alter, amend, repeal provisions, power, §44-1510.
Arrest of violators at member's request, §44-1504.
Bylaws, §44-1503.
Cruelty to animals.
  Enforcement of laws, §44-1509.
Cruelty to children.
  Enforcement of laws, §44-1508.
Cruelty to children, prevention, §44-1507.
Fines, disposition, §44-1505.
Incorporation, §44-1501.
Name, §44-1501.
Officers, §44-1502.
Provisions effective throughout District, §44-1506.

WASHINGTON METROPOLITAN AREA TRANSIT AUTHORITY.
WMATA operations support fund, §1-325.311.

WASHINGTON METROPOLITAN AREA TRANSIT AUTHORITY COMPACT, §§9-1107.01 to 9-1107.12.
Restraints of trade.
Exclusion from chapter, §28-4504.
Superior court jurisdiction, §11-924.

WASHINGTON METROPOLITAN REGION DEVELOPMENT, §§2-1101 to 2-1105.
Congressional declaration, §2-1101.
Congressional policy, §2-1102.
Final report by Joint Committee on Washington Metropolitan Problems.
Study, §2-1104.
Priority projects, §2-1103.
Washington metropolitan region defined, §2-1105.

WASHINGTON NATIONAL AIRPORT.
See RONALD REAGAN WASHINGTON NATIONAL AIRPORT.

WASHINGTON RAILWAY AND ELECTRIC COMPANY.
Michigan Avenue right-of-way for, §9-101.15.

WASHINGTON'S BIRTHDAY.
Appeals in federal cases, FRAP 26(a), 45(a).
Designated holiday, §§1-612.02, 28-2701.
Extension of time for performing acts, §28-2701.

WASHINGTON STOCK EXCHANGE.
Taxation, §47-2504.

WASHINGTON TECHNICAL INSTITUTE, §§38-1121 to 38-1125.
Board of vocational education, §§38-1122 to 38-1124.
Facilities, §38-1124.
Members, §38-1122.
Powers and duties, §38-1123.
Consolidation of existing institutions, §38-1202.05.
Definitions, §38-1121.
Fiscal accountability requirements, §38-1125.
Interpretation of provisions, §38-1111.
Land-grant college, regarded as, §§38-1107, 38-1109, 38-1112.

WASHINGTON TECHNICAL INSTITUTE —Cont'd
University of the District of Columbia.
Successor institution, §§38-1201.01 to 38-1207.07.
See UNIVERSITY OF THE DISTRICT OF COLUMBIA.

WASHINGTON TERMINAL COMPANY.
Street lighting, §9-508.

WASTE AND WASTE DISPOSAL.
Compost drop-off program, §8-761.
Garbage collection.
See GARBAGE COLLECTION.
Hazardous waste management.
General provisions, §§8-1301 to 8-1322.
See HAZARDOUS WASTE MANAGEMENT.
Illegal dumping, §§8-901 to 8-906.
See ILLEGAL DUMPING.
Litter control.
Generally, §§8-801 to 8-812.
See LITTER CONTROL.
Low-level radioactive waste generator regulatory policy, §§8-1501 to 8-1506.
See RADIATION CONTROL.
Privies, §§8-601 to 8-604.
Real property, §§42-1601 to 42-1604, 42-3211.
Recycling.
Construction and demolition waste recycling accountability, §§8-1071 to 8-1077.
General provisions.
See RECYCLING.
Solid waste facility permits, §§8-1051 to 8-1063.
See SOLID WASTE FACILITY PERMITS.
Regulation of waste disposal systems, §8-603.
Solid waste management.
See SOLID WASTE MANAGEMENT.
Trash compactor grant program, §§8-751 to 8-753.

WASTE-TO-ENERGY.
Renewable energy portfolio standards, §§34-1431 to 34-1439.

WASTEWATER AND SEWAGE WORKS, §§34-2101 to 34-2134.
Advances for sanitary sewage works, §34-2103.

WASTEWATER AND SEWAGE WORKS —Cont'd

Amnesty program, §§34-2301, 34-2302.
  Rules, §34-2306.
Charitable institutions, §34-2111.
Contesting bill, §34-2305.
Council, authority of, §34-2114.
Definitions, §34-2101.
Delinquent account by owner or manager of rental unit.
  Appointment of receiver upon nonpayment of account, §34-2304.
Dulles International Airport Sanitary Sewer, §§34-2131 to 34-2134.
Fairfax County Sewage Delivery System and Capacity Purchase Agreement, §24-106.
Federal government, §34-2112.
Flood hazards, §6-503.
General Fund, use of, §§34-2102, 34-2113.
Liens, §34-2110.
Maintenance workers, §47-208.
Maryland, agreements with, §1-204.87.
Meters, §34-2109.
Potomac Interceptor (Dulles International Airport Sanitary Sewer), §§34-2131 to 34-2134.
Public service commission.
  See PUBLIC SERVICE COMMISSION.
Public works, sewer connections as, §§9-401.03, 9-401.08.
Rates and charges for sanitary sewer service, §§34-2107 to 34-2112.
Religious institutions, §34-2111.
Rental property.
  Delinquent account by owner or manager of rental unit.
  Appointment of receiver upon nonpayment of account, §34-2304.
  Housing, deferral or forgiveness of fees for new or rehabilitated vacant units, §42-3508.03.
  Opportunity for tenant to receive service in own name, §34-2303.
Repair and maintenance, §§1-305.01, 34-2109.
Rules, §34-2306.
Sanitary sewer service charge.
  Persons obligated to pay, §34-2108.
Virginia, agreements with, §1-204.87.

WASTEWATER DISPOSAL SYSTEM, §§8-105.01 to 8-105.15.
Administrative procedure, §§8-105.07, 8-105.10.
Appeals, §8-105.10.
Definitions, §8-105.02.
Drainage of lots, §§8-201 to 8-205.
Emergency suspension of service, §8-105.12.
Enforcement, §8-105.10.
Environmental controls, §§8-105.01 to 8-107.04.
Falsified information, §8-105.04.
Fines, §8-105.14.
Hazardous substances, §8-105.06.
Industrial users in significant noncompliance, §8-105.13.
Injunctions, §8-105.11.
Inspections, §8-105.08.
Issuance of regulations, §8-105.15.
Mayor's authority to establish, §8-105.06.
Misuse, §8-105.05.
Penalties, §8-105.14.
Phosphate cleaners, §§8-107.01 to 8-107.04.
Policy declaration, §8-105.01.
Privacy and confidentiality, §8-105.09.
Privies, §§8-601 to 8-604.
Prohibitive discharge limits, §8-105.06.
Requirements regarding, §8-105.06.
Special agreements regarding, §8-105.03.
Tampering, §8-105.05.
Water and sewer authority, authority of, §§8-105.07, 8-105.15.

WASTEWATER TREATMENT SYSTEMS, §§8-201 to 8-205.
Compensation of property owners for installations, §8-205.
Connection requirements, §§8-201 to 8-203.
Definitions, §8-205.
Drainage of lots into public sewers, §8-201.
Failure to make required connections, §§8-203, 8-204.
Nonresident lot owners, §8-204.
Notice.
  Connection requirements, §8-202.
Repair and maintenance, §8-205.
Sludge, use of, §8-103.14.

WASTE, WRIT OF, §§42-1601 to 42-1604.
Amercement, §42-1602.

WASTE, WRIT OF —Cont'd
Conditions, §42-1601.
Elements of cause of action,
§42-1601.
Joint tenants.
Action against cotenant, §42-1604.
Licenses.
Prohibition of waste without written
license, §42-1602.
Prohibition of waste, §42-1602.
Reversioner maintaining writ,
§42-1603.
Tenants in common.
Action against cotenant, §42-1604.

WATER AND SEWER AUTHORITY,
§§34-2201.01 to 34-2202.41.
Amnesty program, §§34-2301 to
34-2306.
Assets, §34-2202.07.
Assistance programs with fees,
§34-2202.16.
Board of directors, §§34-2202.04,
34-2202.05.
Bond issues.
Generally. See within this heading,
"Revenue bonds."
Revenue bonds.
Delegation of council authority to
issue, §1-204.90.
Budget, §1-204.45a.
Budgets and budget estimates,
§47-212.
Business licenses.
Unpaid fees.
Computer record-keeping and
reporting system, §47-2866.
Definitions, §47-2861.
Issuance of license prohibited,
§47-2862.
Right to appeal denial of license,
§47-2865.
Self-certification of lack of
outstanding debt, §47-2863.
Falsification of certification,
penalty, §47-2864.
Definitions, §34-2202.01.
Drinking water testing, §34-2202.06d.
Endocrine disruptor compounds.
Defined, §34-2202.01.
Remediation and continued testing,
§34-2202.06h.
Study and testing for presence in
wastewater, §34-2202.06g.
Water quality assurance advisory
panel, §§34-2202.06e, 34-2202.06f.
Establishment of, §34-2202.02.

WATER AND SEWER AUTHORITY
—Cont'd
Existing contracts or regional
agreements.
Not amended, altered, modified or
repealed by chapter, §34-2202.18.
Existing management structure to
serve as operator.
Until initial meeting of board,
§34-2202.17.
Fees.
Low impact design incentive program
and discounts, §34-2202.16a.
Storm water fee, §34-2202.16.
Financial management, §1-204.96.
Fund, §§34-2202.07, 34-2202.41.
General Manager, §34-2202.06.
Impervious surface fee discounts.
Retroactive, §34-2202.16a.
Lead level water testing.
Multiple dwelling residences,
§§42-3251 to 42-3255.
Lead service line priority
replacement assistance,
§§34-2151 to 34-2156.
See LEAD SERVICE LINE PRIORITY
REPLACEMENT ASSISTANCE.
Low impact design incentive
program and discounts,
§34-2202.16a.
Merit personnel system, §34-2202.15.
Operation and maintenance
account, §34-2202.41.
Personnel responsibilities, §1-204.96.
Policy declaration, §34-2201.01.
Powers and duties of, §34-2202.03.
Procurement, §§1-204.96, 34-2202.03,
34-2202.14.
Rates and charges, §34-2202.16.
Rental housing, deferral or
forgiveness of fees for new or
rehabilitated vacant units,
§42-3508.03.
Restriction of combined sewer flow
from adjoining states into
District, §34-2202.06.
Revenue bonds.
Defeasance of, §34-2202.13a.
Defined, §34-2202.01.
Delegation of Council authority to
issue, §34-2202.08.
District pledge not to limit or alter
rights of Authority regarding,
§34-2202.11.
District repayment option,
§34-2202.13.

WATER AND SEWER AUTHORITY
—Cont'd
Revenue bonds —Cont'd
Power of Authority to issue,
§34-2202.09.
Terms for sale of, §34-2202.10.
Storm water fee, §34-2202.16.
**Taxation by District, exemption
from,** §34-2202.20.
Testing of drinking water,
§34-2202.06d.
Transfer of functions to authority,
§34-2202.19.
Transition provisions for,
§§34-2202.07, 34-2202.17 to
34-2202.20.
Unregulated contaminants.
Defined, §34-2202.01.
Remediation and continued testing,
§34-2202.06h.
**Wastewater disposal system,
authority over,** §§8-105.07,
8-105.15.
**Water quality assurance advisory
panel,** §§34-2202.06e, 34-2202.06f.
WATER CLOSETS.
Parks and recreation facilities,
§§10-133, 10-134.
Toilets generally, §§8-601 to 8-604.
WATER DISPENSERS.
Bottle-type water dispensers.
Energy efficiency standards.
General provisions, §§8-1771.01 to
8-1771.06.
**WATERFRONT PARK AT THE
YARDS,** §§10-1801 to 10-1805.
Definitions, §10-1801.
Maintenance agreement.
Authorization, §10-1802.
Maintenance fund.
Creation, §10-1803.
Naming rights, §10-1805.
**Sales tax revenue attributable to
retail area.**
Allocation, §10-1804.
Special assessment district,
§§47-895.21 to 47-895.24.
Definitions, §47-895.21.
Deposit of revenues, §47-895.24.
Establishment of district, §47-895.22.
Levy of special assessment,
§47-895.23.
Protests, §47-895.23.
Termination of levy, §47-895.23.

WATER MAINS, §§34-2405.01 to
34-2405.08.
**Assessment against abutting
property,** §34-2405.01.
Disposition of funds collected,
§34-2405.07.
Levy, §34-2405.02.
Notice, §34-2405.03.
Payable in installments, §34-2405.04.
Property in County of Washington,
§34-2405.05.
Rate, §34-2405.02.
Re-levy, assessments declared void,
§34-2405.06.
Service sewer defined, §34-2405.08.
Erected at direction of mayor,
§34-2405.01.
WATER PIPES.
Drug paraphernalia, §§48-904.10,
48-1101 to 48-1104.
WATER POLLUTION, §§8-103.01 to
8-103.20.
Amount of discharge, §8-103.07.
Aquatic life, protection of, §8-103.03.
**Beneficial uses of waters, what
constitutes,** §8-103.04.
Civil actions, §8-103.18.
**Contingency plan for environmental
emergencies,** §8-103.08.
Definitions, §8-103.01.
Emergencies, contingency plan for,
§8-103.08.
Enforcement, §8-103.17.
**Exceptions to prohibited discharge
of pollutants,** §8-103.06.
Financial management system,
§8-103.09.
**Hazardous substances, prohibition
on discharge of,** §8-103.07.
Inspections, §8-103.15.
Investigations, §8-103.19.
Issuance of rules regarding,
§§8-103.19, 8-103.20.
Location of discharge, §8-103.07.
Malicious pollution of water,
§22-3318.
Monitoring requirements, §8-103.05.
Offshore or onshore facilities.
Defined, §8-103.01.
Discharges from, §8-103.08.
Spill prevention and cleanup plans,
§8-103.10.
Penalties, §8-103.16.
Permissible discharge of pollutants,
§8-103.06.

WATER POLLUTION —Cont'd
Permits to discharge pollutants,
§8-103.06.
Private right of action, §8-103.19.
Prohibited discharge of pollutants,
§8-103.02.
Quality of water.
See WATER QUALITY.
Reduction of pollutants, no
recognition of, §8-103.07.
Subpoenas, §8-103.15.
Underground tanks and facilities,
§8-103.10.
Vessels, discharged from, §8-103.08.
Wastewater disposal systems,
§§8-105.01 to 8-105.15.
See WASTEWATER DISPOSAL
SYSTEM.
Wells.
Construction, maintenance and
abandonment, §8-103.13a.
Permit fees, §8-103.13b.
Wetland and stream mitigation trust
fund, §8-103.09.

WATER QUALITY.
Construction bearing upon,
§8-103.13.
Inspections, §8-103.15.
Management plan, §8-103.11.
Research grants for, §8-103.12.
Subpoenas, §8-103.15.
Well construction, maintenance and
abandonment, §8-103.13a.
Permit fees, §8-103.13b.

WATER STREET.
Parks and recreation, §10-110.

WATER SUPPLY AND
WATERWORKS, §§34-2401.01 to
34-2401.27.
Acquisition of lands and rights of
way for pipelines, §34-2401.19.
Amnesty program, §§34-2301 to
34-2306.
Appropriations, §§1-204.88,
34-2401.26.
Arlington County, Virginia, delivery
of water to, §34-2401.17.
Assessments for constructing mains
and sewers, §§34-2405.01 to
34-2405.08.
Contract payments, §§1-204.88,
34-2401.26.
Council, powers of, §34-2401.03.
Definitions, §§34-2401.18, 34-2405.08.
Distribution systems outside
District, investigation of,
§34-2411.02.

WATER SUPPLY AND
WATERWORKS —Cont'd
Diversion outside District,
§34-2401.15.
Engineer's office, operations under
direction of, §§34-2401.02,
34-2401.03.
Environmental Services, role of
Department of, §34-2401.08.
Falls Church, Virginia, delivery of
water to, §34-2411.01.
Federal government, supplied to,
§34-2401.25.
Meters at federal connection,
installation, §34-2401.25a.
Fines and penalties.
Damaging or defacing water pipes,
§34-2401.22.
Opening mains or pipes, §34-2401.24.
Shutting off supply for nonpayment,
§34-2401.06.
Tapping water pipes, §34-2401.20.
Fireplug tax, §§34-2409.01 to
34-2409.04.
Fiscal year, §34-2401.04.
Horizontal property regimes,
§42-2030.
Industrial users, §34-2403.02.
Investigation of distribution systems
outside District, §34-2411.02.
Large-quantity consumers,
§34-2403.03.
Lead level water testing.
Multiple dwelling residences,
§§42-3251 to 42-3255.
Liens, §34-2407.02.
Mains, §§34-2405.01 to 34-2405.08.
Assessments for constructing,
§§34-2405.01 to 34-2405.08.
Public buildings, laying for use of,
§34-2401.23.
Public works, §§9-401.03, 9-401.08.
Service connections, §9-401.08.
Unauthorized opening of, §34-2401.24.
Maryland territory within
Washington Suburban Sanitary
District, delivery of water to,
§34-2401.16.
Mayor, powers of, §§1-204.88,
34-2401.01 to 34-2401.03,
34-2401.26.
Meters.
Large-quantity consumers,
§34-2403.03.
Notice of violations, §34-2401.21.
Penalties. See within this heading,
"Fines and penalties."

WATER SUPPLY AND WATERWORKS —Cont'd
Pipelines, acquisition of lands and rights of way for, §34-2401.19.
Prevention of water waste, §34-2403.01.
Public service commission.
See PUBLIC SERVICE COMMISSION.
Rates and charges.
  Advance collection, §34-2401.11.
  Collection of, §34-2401.04.
  Fireplug tax, §34-2409.02.
  Liens, §34-2407.02.
  Payment of, §34-2401.05.
  Remedies for nonpayment, §34-2407.03.
  Revenue, not to be source of, §34-2401.12.
  Shutting off supply for nonpayment, §§34-2401.06, 34-2407.01.
  Statement of account, issuance of, §34-2401.06.
Refunds.
  Overpaid assessments, §34-2401.09.
  Rents, erroneous payment of, §34-2401.10.
Remedies, §34-2407.03.
Rental housing, deferral or forgiveness of fees for new or rehabilitated vacant units, §42-3508.03.
Rents.
  General Fund, payment into, §34-2401.14.
  Refunds for erroneous payment of, §34-2401.10.
  Uniformity of, §34-2401.07.
Reservoirs, §§1-204.88, 34-2401.26.
Sewers.
  Assessments to erect, §§34-2405.01 to 34-2405.08.
  Service sewer defined, §34-2405.08.
Shutting off supply for nonpayment, §§34-2401.06, 34-2407.01.
Taxes.
  Assessments for constructing mains and sewers, §§34-2405.01 to 34-2405.08.
  Fireplug tax, §§34-2409.01 to 34-2409.04.
  Uniformity of, §34-2401.07.
Virginia.
  Arlington County, delivery of water to, §34-2401.17.
  Falls Church, delivery of water to, §34-2411.01.

WAY OF THE CROSS CHURCH OF CHRIST.
Real property tax exemptions, §47-1067.

WEAPONS, §§22-4501 to 22-4517.
Additional penalty for committing crime when armed, §22-4502.
Armed carjacking, §22-2803.
Armed criminal offenses.
  Additional penalty, §22-4502.
Assault with a dangerous weapon, §22-402.
Business licenses for dealers in dangerous weapons, §47-2838.
Capitol grounds, prohibited on, §10-503.16.
Child abuse and neglect.
  Injuries caused by a bullet, knife, or other sharp object.
  Reporting requirements, §4-1321.02.
Concealed weapons, carrying, §§22-4504, 22-4505.
Confiscation by law enforcement officers, §22-4517.
Constitution of the United States.
  Right to bear arms, US Const Amd 2.
Dangerous weapons, business licenses for dealers in, §47-2838.
Dealers, §§22-4509, 22-4510.
Definitions, §22-4501.
Destruction by law enforcement officers, §22-4517.
Enhanced penalties and fines for carrying guns into gun free zones, §22-4502.01.
Explosives as, §22-4515a.
False information given in purchasing, §22-4511.
Firearms.
  Generally, §§7-2501.01 to 7-2551.03.
  See FIREARMS.
Gun free zones, §22-4502.01.
Gun offender registry, §§7-2508.01 to 7-2508.07.
Health care providers.
  Reporting firearms or weapons injuries, §§7-2601 to 7-2603.
High school cadets, arms issued to, §38-909.
Identifying marks, alteration of, §22-4512.
Law enforcement officers.
  Concealed weapons, carrying, §22-4505.
  Possession of certain dangerous weapons by, §22-4514.

WEAPONS —Cont'd
Law enforcement officers —Cont'd
Taking and destruction of dangerous
articles, §22-4517.
Mace and other self-defense sprays,
§§7-2502.12 to 7-2502.14.
Military, possession of certain
dangerous weapons by, §22-4514.
Molotov cocktails, §22-4515a.
Unlawful conduct, §22-4515a.
Pepper sprays and other self-
defense sprays, §§7-2502.12 to
7-2502.14.
Possession of certain dangerous
weapons, prohibition of,
§22-4514.
Power to issue regulations
regarding, §1-303.43.
Public officers and employees
designated to protect life and
property outside the District,
§10-509.01.
Reporting injuries caused by,
§§7-2601 to 7-2603.
School buildings and grounds.
Enhanced penalties and fines for
carrying guns into gun free zones,
§22-4502.01.
Expulsion of students for weapons
brought onto, §§38-231 to 38-235.
Self-defense sprays, §§7-2502.12 to
7-2502.14.
Severability of provisions, §22-4516.
Violations not specifically provided
for, penalties, §22-4515.
Weapons of mass destruction.
Defined, §22-3152.
False reports, §22-1319.
Hoax weapons, §22-1319.
Manufacture or possession, §22-3154.
Public health emergency executive
order, §7-2304.01.
Use, dissemination or detonation,
§22-3155.

WEATHER.
Appeals, federal cases.
Court operation during inclement
weather, USCtApp HPIP Rule
II(b)(4).
Oral arguments.
Weather closings, USCtApp HPIP
Rule XI(g).
Electric light and power companies.
Disconnection of service in extreme
temperature, prohibition,
§34-1506.01.

WEATHER —Cont'd
Gas companies.
Disconnection of service in extreme
temperature, prohibition,
§34-1671.06a.
Horse-drawn carriages, operation of,
§8-2007.

WEEDS.
Plants and plant diseases, §§8-301 to
8-305.

WEEKENDS.
Computation of time, CivPro Rule 6,
CrimPro Rule 45.
Appeals, DCCtApp Rule 26.
Domestic relations actions, DomRel
Rule 6.
Hospitalization of persons with mental
illness, MentalHealth Rule 13.
Juvenile proceedings, JuvProc Rule 45.

WEIGHTS AND MEASURES,
§§37-201.01 to 37-201.33.
Automatic pumps, §§37-201.18,
37-201.20.
Bread, §37-201.13.
Coal, charcoal, or coke, sale of,
§37-201.11.
Condemnation tags, §§37-201.03,
37-201.04.
Congress, US Const Art I §8.
Constitution of the United States,
US Const Art I §8.
Cord of wood, §37-201.17.
Dairy products, §37-201.14.
Definitions, §§37-201.29, 37-201.30.
Department of Weights, Measures,
and Markets, §§37-201.01 to
37-201.03.
Director of Weights, Measures, and
Markets.
Bonds, surety, §37-201.02.
Definition of Director, §37-201.29.
Delegation of powers and duties to
assistants and inspectors,
§37-201.27.
Oaths and affirmations by, §37-201.02.
Police powers of, §37-201.24.
Powers and duties, §§37-201.03,
37-201.27.
Sale of measuring devices by,
prohibition of, §37-201.23.
Supervision of markets by, §37-201.28.
Dry goods, §37-201.15.
Dry measures, §§37-201.15, 37-201.16.
Eastern market, §§37-101 to 37-113.
See EASTERN MARKET.

WEIGHTS AND MEASURES —Cont'd
Evidence.
  Official certificate as prima facie
    evidence, §28:1-307.
Fees, §37-201.03.
  Registration and inspection,
    §37-201.33.
Fines, §37-201.32.
Food, §§37-201.13 to 37-201.22a.
Fraud and deceit, §§37-201.07,
  37-201.22a.
Fruits, §37-201.15.
Gasoline and fuel pumps.
  Automatic, §37-201.18.
  Octane measurement, §37-201.18a.
Gas stations, §§36-301.01 to 36-305.02.
  See GAS STATIONS.
Ice, §37-201.12.
Inspections.
  Commodities, §37-201.22.
  Condemnation tags, §§37-201.03,
    37-201.04.
  Fees, §37-201.33.
  Obstruction of or interference with,
    §37-201.05.
  Record of, §37-201.06.
  Repair, inspection required after,
    §37-201.04.
  Warrants, without, §37-201.24.
  Weighing and measuring devices,
    §§37-201.03 to 37-201.06.
Liquid measures, §37-201.18.
Markets.
  See MARKETS.
**Mayor, power to remove device from
  service,** §37-201.33.
Net weight, required use of,
  §37-201.08.
Penalties, §37-201.32.
Police powers of director, §37-201.24.
Produce, §37-201.15.
Pro rata sale of smaller quantities,
  §37-201.21.
Prosecutions, §37-201.32.
Quantity markings, §37-201.16a.
Record of inspections, §37-201.06.
Registration and inspection fees,
  §37-201.33.
Removal of devices from service.
  Mayor, power of, §37-201.33.
Repair, inspection required after,
  §37-201.04.
Retail service stations, §§36-301.01 to
  36-305.02.
  See GAS STATIONS.
**Sale of measuring devices by
  director,** §37-201.23.

WEIGHTS AND MEASURES —Cont'd
Sales tickets, §37-201.10.
Severability of provisions, §37-201.31.
Specifications, establishing,
  §37-201.25.
Tolerances, establishing, §37-201.25.
Ton defined for purposes of,
  §37-201.08.
United States.
  Constitutional provisions, US Const
    Art I §8.
Vegetables, §37-201.15.
Vending machines, §37-201.07.

WELFARE.
**District of Columbia housing
  authority.**
  General provisions, §§6-201 to 6-229.
  See DISTRICT OF COLUMBIA
    HOUSING AUTHORITY.
  Section eight housing, §§42-3503.01 to
    42-3503.08.
**District of Columbia medical
  assistance program,** §§1-307.02 to
  1-307.06.
Food stamps.
  Misuse of, §§4-218.05, 4-218.06.
General public assistance (GPA).
  Termination of, §4-202.01a.
Medicaid.
  General provisions.
  See MEDICAID.
Medicare.
  Medicare supplement insurance,
    §§31-3701 to 31-3710.
  See MEDICARE SUPPLEMENT
    INSURANCE.
Pay-for-success contracts, §§2-211.01
  to 2-211.03.
Public assistance.
  General provisions, §§4-201.01 to
    4-221.01.
  See PUBLIC ASSISTANCE.
Public welfare institutions.
  General provisions, §§4-105 to 4-126.
  See PUBLIC WELFARE, BOARD
    OF.
Section eight housing, §§42-3503.01 to
  42-3503.08.
**Temporary assistance to needy
  families.**
  General provisions, §§4-205.01 to
    4-205.19l.
  See TEMPORARY ASSISTANCE
    FOR NEEDY FAMILIES
    (TANF).

WELFARE —Cont'd
Workforce investment implementation, §§32-1601 to 32-1661.

WEST END LIBRARY AND FIRE STATION MAINTENANCE FUND, §1-325.181.

WET SETTLEMENT ACT, §§42-2401 to 42-2407.
Action by person suffering loss because of violation, §42-2407.
Applicability, §42-2402.
Civil fines, penalties, fees.
Imposing for violation, §42-2407.
Definitions, §42-2401.
Disbursement of loan funds to settlement agent.
Lender's duty, §42-2403.
Disbursement of settlement proceeds.
Duty of settlement agent, time, §42-2405.
Duties of owners and brokers, §42-2404.
Duty of lender, §42-2403.
Duty of settlement agent, §42-2405.
Failure to comply not to affect validity of loan documents, §42-2406.
Interest on loan.
Lender not to charge until disbursement of loan funds, §42-2403.
Redecoration of documents required to be recorded.
Duty of settlement agent, §42-2405.

WHARFAGE FEE, §10-501.02.

WHARF PROPERTY, §§10-501.01, 10-501.02.

WHARVES AND LOTS.
Liens on, §40-305.01.

WHEELCHAIRS.
Assistive technology device warranty, §§28-4031 to 28-4034.

WHISTLEBLOWER PROTECTION.
Health benefit plan grievance procedures.
Retaliation prohibited by insurer, §44-301.03.
Long-term care ombudsman.
Retaliation for filing complaint or providing information, §7-704.01.
Procurement practices.
Claims for violations, relief from retaliatory actions, §2-381.04.

WHISTLEBLOWER PROTECTION —Cont'd
Public contracts, §§2-223.01 to 2-223.07.
Applicability of provisions, §2-223.07.
Definitions, §2-223.01.
Discipline, §2-223.04.
Election of remedies regarding, §2-223.05.
Enforcement of provisions, §2-223.03.
Fines, §2-223.04.
Notice posting requirements, §2-223.06.
Prohibited actions, §2-223.02.
Remedies, §2-223.05.
Public officers and employees, §§1-615.51 to 1-615.59.
Applicability of provisions, §1-615.59.
Compensation restrictions for interference with rights, §1-615.58a.
Definitions, §1-615.52.
Discipline, §1-615.55.
Election of remedies regarding, §1-615.56.
Enforcement of provisions, §1-615.54.
Fines, §1-615.55.
Notice posting requirements, §1-615.57.
Policy declaration, §1-615.51.
Prohibited actions, §1-615.53.
Remedies, §§1-615.54, 1-615.56.
Rights and responsibilities of employees regarding, §1-615.58.
Testing integrity in public schools.
Districtwide assessments.
LEA administration.
Retaliation against whistleblowing activities, §38-771.02.

WHITE CANE SAFETY DAY, §7-1008.

WHITEHAVEN PARKWAY.
Boundaries, §10-113.
Exchange of federal property, §10-114.
Exchange with property owners, §10-115.
Plats prepared, §10-116.

WHITMAN-WALKER CLINIC, INC.
Real property tax exemptions, §47-4664.

WHOLESALE FISH DEALERS.
Business licenses, §47-2827.

WHOLESALERS.
Alcoholic beverage licenses, §25-111.

WHOLESALERS —Cont'd
Cigarette sales, license, §47-2404.
Drug manufacture and distribution licensure, §§48-701 to 48-715.
See DRUG MANUFACTURE AND DISTRIBUTION LICENSURE.

WHOOPING COUGH.
Immunization of school students, §§38-501 to 38-508.
Interstate compact on educational opportunity for military children.
Time to obtain immunizations, §49-1101.05.

WIFE-BEATING, §§16-1031 to 16-1034.

WILDLIFE.
Game laws, §§22-4328 to 22-4333.
See FISH AND GAME.
Protection of wildlife, §§8-2201 to 8-2211.
See WILDLIFE PROTECTION.

WILDLIFE PROTECTION, §§8-2201 to 8-2211.
Annual report.
Wildlife control operator license, §8-2207.
Complaints against wildlife control service providers, §8-2210.
Definitions, §8-2201.
Diseased wildlife, §8-2202.
Enforcement, §8-2211.
Euthanasia, §8-2202.
Feral dogs and cats, §8-2206.
Injunctions against violations, §8-2211.
Nonlethal means of control, §8-2202.
Notice to clients, §8-2203.
Recordkeeping requirements.
Wildlife control operator license, §8-2207.
Release of captured non-target wildlife, §8-2202.
Specific species, control of, §8-2206.
Transport of captured wildlife, §8-2202.
Traps and exclusion devices, §8-2202.
Wildlife control operator.
License, §8-2204.
Annual report, §8-2207.
Conditions for issuance, §8-2205.
Fees, §8-2209.
Recordkeeping requirements, §8-2207.
Suspension or revocation, §8-2208.
License fees, §8-2209.

WILDLIFE PROTECTION —Cont'd
Wildlife control service providers, §8-2202.
Complaints against, §8-2210.

WILLS, §§18-101 to 18-308.
Administration of the estate.
General provisions, §§20-701 to 20-753.
See ADMINISTRATION OF ESTATES.
Advancements, §18-307.
After-acquired real property, §18-305.
After-discovered property, §§20-355, 20-1304.
Antenuptial agreements, §19-113.
Appointment made by will in exercise of a power, §18-108.
Attestation required, §18-103.
Attorneys at law.
Drafting will giving attorney gift, ProfCond Rule 1.8.
Capacity to make, §18-102.
Child equivalent to adopted child in instruments, §16-313.
Claims against the estate.
General provisions, §§20-901 to 20-914.
See CLAIMS AGAINST ESTATES.
Closing the estate, §§20-1301 to 20-1305.
Concealing, §18-112.
Contesting validity of will, §20-305.
Probate proceedings.
Death before Jan. 1, 1981, Probate Rule 15.
Death between Jan. 1, 1981, and June 30, 1995, Probate Rule 107.
Death on or after July 1, 1995, Probate Rule 407.
Guardians, conservators, trustees, etc., involved, Probate Rule 208.
Conveyances of interests in real estate, §42-301.
Creditors as witnesses, §18-106.
Decedents' estates.
General provisions, §§20-101 to 20-109.
See DECEDENTS' ESTATES.
Definitions, §18-101.
Descent and distributions.
General provisions, §§19-101.01 to 19-701.
See INTESTATE SUCCESSION.
Destroying, §18-112.

WILLS —Cont'd

Devises and bequests, §§18-301 to 18-308.

Advancement as satisfaction of, §18-307.

After-acquired real property, §18-305.

Death of devisee legatee, §18-308.

General devise and bequest of all property, §18-303.

Lapsed or void, §18-308.

Leaseholds, devise of land to include, §18-304.

Murder or manslaughter, succession barred by, §19-320.

Pour-over trusts, §18-306.

Powers of appointment, §§42-1001 to 42-1019.

See POWERS OF APPOINTMENT.

Renunciation of, §19-113.

Spouses or domestic partners, §§19-112 to 19-115.

Witnesses, to, §§18-104, 18-105.

Estates in land.

General provisions, §§42-501 to 42-523.

See ESTATES IN LAND.

Evidence, as, §§14-502 to 14-504.

Forgery of will or codicil, §22-3242.

Fraud and deceit, §18-112.

Guardianship of minors, §§21-102, 21-105.

Inheritance and estate taxes.

General provisions, §§47-3701 to 47-3722.

See INHERITANCE AND ESTATE TAXES.

International wills, §§18-701 to 18-710.

See INTERNATIONAL WILLS.

Leasehold property, §18-304.

Legacies in. See within this heading, "Devises and bequests."

Living wills, §§7-621 to 7-630.

See LIVING WILLS.

Military affairs, §18-107.

Murder or manslaughter, succession barred by, §19-320.

Mutilating, §18-112.

Nuncupative, §18-107.

Opening before delivery to probate court, §18-110.

Opening the estate.

General provisions, §§20-301 to 20-357.

See OPENING ESTATES.

Oral wills, §18-107.

WILLS —Cont'd

Personal representatives, §§20-401 to 20-406.

See PERSONAL REPRESENTATIVES.

Posthumous children, §42-704.

Powers of appointment.

General provisions, §§42-1001 to 42-1019.

See POWERS OF APPOINTMENT.

Prenuptial agreements, §19-113.

Probate fees, §§15-707, 15-708.

Probate proceedings.

General provisions, §§16-3101 to 16-3112, Probate Rules 1 to 430.

See PROBATE PROCEEDINGS.

Real estate, conveyances of interests in, §42-301.

Register of wills, §§11-2101 to 11-2106.

See REGISTER OF WILLS.

Revival of revoked will, §18-109.

Revocation, §18-109.

Secreting, §18-112.

Simultaneous deaths, §§19-501 to 19-506.

Small estates, §§20-351 to 20-357.

See SMALL ESTATES.

Special administrators, §§20-531 to 20-534.

See PERSONAL REPRESENTATIVES.

Spousal devises, §19-112.

Statutory rule against perpetuities, §§19-901 to 19-907.

Supervised and unsupervised administration.

General provisions, §§20-401 to 20-406.

See PERSONAL REPRESENTATIVES.

Taking and carrying away, §18-112.

Transfers to minors authorized by, §21-305.

Withholding, §18-111.

Witnesses.

Creditors as, §18-106.

Devises and bequests to, §§18-104, 18-105.

Requirement to have, §18-103.

Written requirement, §18-103.

Nuncupative wills, §18-107.

Revocation of will in writing, §18-109.

WILSON BUILDING, §§10-1301, 10-1302, 10-1331 to 10-1336, 10-1701.

See JOHN A. WILSON BUILDING.

WIND ENERGY.
Renewable energy portfolio
  standards generally, §§34-1431 to
  34-1439.
  See RENEWABLE ENERGY
    PORTFOLIO STANDARDS.
Renewable energy study, §8-1775.01.
Sustainable energy, §§8-1773.01 to
  8-1774.16.
  See SUSTAINABLE ENERGY.

WINE FESTIVALS.
Tasting permits, §25-118.

WINE PUBS.
Permits, §25-124.

WIRE COMMUNICATIONS.
Compensating-use tax, §§47-2201 to
  47-2214.
  See COMPENSATING-USE TAX.
Interception of, §§23-541 to 23-556.
  See INTERCEPTION OF ORAL OR
    WIRE COMMUNICATIONS.
Telecommunications companies,
  §§34-1701 to 34-2008.
  See TELECOMMUNICATIONS
    COMPANIES.
Toll telecommunication service tax,
  §§47-3901 to 47-3922.
  See TOLL TELECOMMUNICATION
    SERVICE TAX.

WIRED CIGARETTE PAPERS.
Drug paraphernalia, §§48-904.10,
  48-1101 to 48-1104.

WIRELESS NETWORK ANTENNAE
  FRANCHISE AGREEMENTS.
Internet-related
  telecommunications.
  Furnishing digitally-disadvantaged
    residents, §§34-1731.01 to
    34-1731.11.
  See INTERNET.

WIRETAPPING.
Interception of wire or oral
  communications.
  General provisions, §§23-541 to
    23-556.
  See INTERCEPTION OF ORAL OR
    WIRE COMMUNICATIONS.

WITHHOLDING.
Child support enforcement via,
  §§46-207 to 46-223.
  See CHILD SUPPORT
    ENFORCEMENT.
Income taxes, §47-1812.08.

WITHHOLDING —Cont'd
Insurers rehabilitation and
  liquidation proceedings.
  Withheld funds, §§31-1336, 31-1343.

WITNESSES, §§14-301 to 14-311.
Actions to perpetuation testimony.
  Depositions not limiting power of court
    to entertain action, CivPro Rule
    27.
    Domestic relations actions, DomRel
      Rule 27.
Adverse party as witness, CivPro
  Rule 43.
  Adoption proceedings, Adoption Rule
    43.
Alcoholic beverage control board.
  Perjury.
    False swearing before board,
      §25-442.
  Subpoenas, §25-443.
Alcoholic beverage licenses.
  Hearings, §25-442.
  Subpoenas, §25-443.
Alibi of defendant.
  Criminal procedure, CrimPro Rule
    12.1.
  Delinquent minors, JuvProc Rule 12.1.
Arbitration, revised act.
  Subpoena and discovery procedures,
    §16-4417.
Assessment officials as witnesses in
  condemnation proceedings,
  §14-308.
Attorney as witness, ProfCond Rule
  3.7.
Bankruptcy proceedings,
  USDistDCBank Rule 9070-1.
Bribery of, §22-713.
Certificate of witnesses, CivPro Form
  CA 104.
Child fatality review committee.
  Compelling appearance, §4-1371.07.
Children and minors, corroboration
  of testimony not required for,
  §23-114.
Competency of witnesses, §§14-301 to
  14-311.
Condemnation proceedings,
  assessment officials as witnesses
  in, §14-308.
Constitution of the United States.
  Confrontation with witnesses, US
    Const Amd 6.
  Process to obtain, US Const Amd 6.
  Self-incrimination, US Const Amd 5.

WITNESSES —Cont'd
Constitution of the United States
—Cont'd
Treason.
Number in treason cases, US Const
Art III §3.
Courts-martial, §49-507.
Crime, conviction for, §14-305.
Criminal law and procedure.
Alibi of defendant, CrimPro Rule 12.1.
Preliminary examination hearings.
Cross-examination of adverse
witnesses, CrimPro Rule 5.
Production of witness statements,
CrimPro Rule 26.2.
Juvenile proceedings, JuvProc Rule
32.
Probation modification hearings,
CrimPro Rule 32.1.
Release from custody or detention,
CrimPro Rule 46.
Sentencing hearings, CrimPro Rule
32.
Right to be confronted by witness, US
Const Amd 6.
Cross-examination.
Adoption proceedings, Adoption Rule
43.
Adverse party as witness, CivPro Rule
43.
Criminal procedure.
Preliminary examination hearings,
CrimPro Rule 5.
Depositions, CivPro Rule 30.
Adoption proceedings, Adoption Rule
30.
Domestic relations actions, DomRel
Rule 30.
Dead persons.
Partner or other interested person,
death or incapacity of, §14-304.
Testimony against, §14-302.
Testimony by, §14-303.
Delinquent minors, §16-2339.
Alibi defense, JuvProc Rule 12.1.
Expert witnesses, JuvProc Rule 28.
Production of witness statements,
JuvProc Rule 26.2.
Rights of victims or eyewitnesses,
§16-2340.
Depositions.
See DEPOSITIONS.
**Disability compensation
proceedings for public officers
and employees, §1-623.26.**
Domestic partners, §§14-306, 14-309.

WITNESSES —Cont'd
Domestic violence counselors.
Disclosure of confidential
communication between victim
and counselor.
Prohibition, exceptions, §14-310.
Disclosure of confidential information
acquired in professional capacity.
Prohibited without consent of client,
§14-307.
**Drug, firearm, or prostitution-
related nuisance abatement,
§42-3105.**
Employment agencies, §32-411.
Evidence generally.
See EVIDENCE.
Examination of witness.
Adoption proceedings, Adoption Rule
43.
Adverse party as witness, CivPro Rule
43.
Expert witnesses.
See EXPERT WITNESSES.
**Fees, CivPro Rule 54-I, CrimPro Rule
113.**
Appointed expert witnesses.
Criminal procedure, CrimPro Rule
28.
Juvenile proceedings, JuvProc Rule
28.
Arbitration hearings, Arbitration Rule
IX.
Criminal defense witnesses, §23-106.
Cruelty to children or animals,
prosecutions involving, §15-715.
Family court proceedings, FamDiv
Rule F.
Public utilities investigations,
§§34-905, 34-910, 34-919.
Superior court, §15-714.
Unemployment compensation, §51-111.
Waiver of costs, CivPro Rule 54-II.
Workers' compensation, §32-1527.
**Gambling crimes, immunity for,
§22-1714.**
**Hospitalization of persons with
mental illness.**
See HOSPITALIZATION OF
PERSONS WITH MENTAL
ILLNESS.
**Human trafficking counselor
privilege, §14-311.**
Disclosure of confidential information
prohibited without consent of
client, §14-307.
Impeachment, §§14-102, 14-305.
Adoption proceedings, Adoption Rule
43.

WITNESSES —Cont'd
Impeachment —Cont'd
Adverse party as witness, CivPro Rule 43.
Deposition's use in court proceedings, CivPro Rule 32.
Criminal procedure, CrimPro Rule 15.
Incompetent or incapacitated persons.
Competency requirements, §§14-301, 14-305.
Partner or other interested person, death or incapacity of, §14-304.
Testimony against, §14-302.
Testimony by, §14-303.
International wills.
Attesting witnesses, §18-703.
Interpreters, §2-1902, CivPro Rule 43.
Adoption proceedings, Adoption Rule 43.
Interstate family support.
Special rules of evidence and procedure, §46-353.16.
Judges.
Acting as witnesses, avoiding conflicts with office, CJC Canon 3.3.
Juvenile offenders, immunity for, §16-2339.
Masters, CivPro Rule 53.
Domestic relations actions, DomRel Rule 53.
Material witnesses, release of, §23-1326.
Medicaid service provider fraud, §4-804.
Mental health professionals as, §14-307.
Mental illness, hospitalization of persons with.
See HOSPITALIZATION OF PERSONS WITH MENTAL ILLNESS.
Metropolitan police detention of, §5-115.05.
Nonresidents, §14-104.
Out-of-state witnesses, compelling attendance, §§23-1501 to 23-1504.
Certificate providing for attendance at criminal prosecutions in District, §23-1502.
Exemption from arrest, §23-1503.
Hearing on recall of witnesses by state courts, §23-1501.
Physician-patient privilege, §14-307.

WITNESSES —Cont'd
Probate proceedings.
Death on or after July 1, 1995.
Securing witnesses, Probate Rule 403.
Public assistance prosecutions, §4-218.04.
Public utilities investigations.
See PUBLIC SERVICE COMMISSION.
Religion, ministers of, §14-309.
Restraints of trade.
Civil investigative demand, §28-4505.
Spousal privilege, §14-306.
Statements by witnesses.
Production of statements.
Criminal cases, CrimPro Rule 26.2.
Delinquent minors, JuvProc Rule 26.2.
Juvenile proceedings, JuvProc Rule 32.
Probation modification hearings, CrimPro Rule 32.1.
Release from custody or detention, CrimPro Rule 46.
Sentencing hearings, CrimPro Rule 32.
Tax assessor, §47-602.
Treason.
Two witnesses required, US Const Art III §3.
Unemployment compensation, §51-111.
Usury, §28-3306.
Action to recover usury paid.
Parties compelled to testify, §28-3306.
Wills.
Attesting witnesses, §§18-104 to 18-106.
See WILLS.
Workers' compensation, §§32-1526, 32-1527.
Workplace safety, §32-805.
WMATA.
Restraints of trade.
Exclusion from chapter, §28-4504.
WOMEN.
American Association of University Women real property exempt from taxation, §47-1041.
Columbia Hospital for Women.
Conveyance of property to, §44-751.
Lien in favor of United States, §44-753.

WOMEN —Cont'd
Commission for women, §§3-701 to 3-704.
Constitution of the United States.
Woman suffrage, US Const Amd 19.
Elections.
Woman suffrage, US Const Amd 19.
Health benefits plans.
Grievance procedures.
Female health services, direct access to specialists for, §44-302.03.
Health insurance.
Rights regarding certain insurance coverage, §§31-3831 to 31-3837.
Labor and employment relations.
Reasonable accommodations for pregnant and nursing workers, §§32-1231.01 to 32-1231.15.
National Woman's Party real property exempt from taxation, §47-1040.
Suffrage, US Const Amd 19.

WOMEN-OWNED BANKS.
Interstate banking and branch banks, §26-711.

WOMEN-OWNED BUSINESSES.
Community development by financial institutions, §§26-431.01 to 26-431.08.
Minority and women-owned business assessment program, §§2-214.01, 2-214.02.

WOOD.
Weights and measures, §37-201.17.

WOODROW WILSON BRIDGE AND TUNNEL COMPACT, §§9-1115.01 to 9-1115.04.
Authority to enter into compact, §9-1115.01.
Contents of compact, §9-1115.03.
Part of law of District, §9-1115.04.
Preamble, §9-1115.02.

WOODROW WILSON HOUSE.
Real property exempt from taxation, §47-1043.

WORKERS' COMPENSATION, §§32-1501 to 32-1545.
Administration by mayor, §32-1502.
Administration fund, §32-1541.
Anti-fraud report, §32-1542.03.
Appeal of orders, §32-1522.
Compensation order review board, §32-1521.01.
Applicability of provisions, §32-1503.

WORKERS' COMPENSATION —Cont'd
Appropriations, §32-1543.
Asbestosis, §32-1510.
Assignment, §32-1517.
Attorney general appearing for mayor in court proceedings regarding, §32-1523.
Attorneys' fees and costs, §32-1530.
Average weekly wage, determining, §32-1511.
Bad faith.
Costs of proceedings, §32-1528.
Bonds, surety, §32-1534.
Business licenses.
Proof of coverage requirement, §47-2851.07.
Claims procedures, §32-1520.
Commencement of payment of, §32-1505.
Commission, §32-1542.01.
Compensation order review board, §32-1521.01.
Compliance.
Enforcement of employer compliance, §32-1542.04.
Costs.
Frivolous proceedings, §32-1528.
Creditors' claims, exempt from, §32-1517.
Death benefits, §32-1509.
Defaulted payments, collecting, §32-1519.
Definitions, §32-1501.
Disability income, §32-1508.
Compensation schedule.
Public officers and employees, §§1-623.01 to 1-623.47.
Discharge of employer liability by carrier, §32-1537.
Effective date of provisions, §32-1545.
Emergency volunteer health practitioners, coverage, §7-2361.11.
Enforcement of employer compliance, §32-1542.04.
Exclusiveness of liability and remedy, §32-1504.
Failure to secure payment, §32-1539.
Filing claims for, §32-1514.
Fraud and deceit, §32-1533.
Anti-fraud report, §32-1542.03.
Frivolous proceedings.
Costs, §32-1528.
Funds.
Administration fund, §32-1541.

WORKERS' COMPENSATION
—Cont'd
Funds —Cont'd
Special fund, §32-1540.
**Guardianship of incapacitated
persons,** §32-1512.
Guardianship of minors, §32-1512.
Health insurance, §32-1507.
Hearings, §32-1525.
Insurance, §32-1538.
Insurance study commission,
§32-1542.01.
Invalid agreements, §32-1516.
Liens for, §32-1518.
Maximum amount of compensation,
§32-1505.
Mayor.
Attorney general appearing for mayor
in court proceedings regarding,
§32-1523.
Hearings before, §32-1525.
Powers and duties of, §32-1529.
Medical benefits, §32-1507.
**Merit system disability
compensation.**
See MERIT SYSTEM.
Modification of awards, §32-1524.
Notice of injury or death, §32-1513.
Notice of secured compensation,
§32-1536.
Occupational disease, §32-1510.
Payment of, §32-1515.
Pneumoconiosis, §32-1510.
Presumptions, §32-1521.
Prison industries, §24-231.12.
Radiation diseases, §32-1510.
Rate filings, evaluating, §32-1542.02.
Records, §32-1531.
Reports.
Annual report to Council, §32-1502.
Anti-fraud report, §32-1542.03.
Compliance report, §32-1542.04.
Employers, by, §32-1532.
Retaliation, §32-1542.
Severability of provisions, §32-1544.
Silicosis, §32-1510.
Special fund, §32-1540.
Supplemental allowances, §32-1506.
**Temporary assistance for needy
families (TANF) program,**
§4-205.19k.
Third party liability for injury,
§32-1535.
Witnesses, §§32-1526, 32-1527.

**WORKFORCE HOUSING
PRODUCTION PROGRAM,**
§§6-1061.01 to 6-1061.04.
Approval of plan, §6-1061.03.
Findings, §6-1061.01.
Land trust, §6-1061.02.
Pilot program, §6-1061.02.
**Transfer of moneys from housing
production trust fund and
industrial revenue bond special
account,** §6-1061.04.
**WORKFORCE INTERMEDIARY
PILOT PROGRAM,** §2-219.04b.
**WORKFORCE INVESTMENT
COUNCIL,** §32-1603.
**Authority to make grants for job
development,** §1-328.05.
**WORKFORCE INVESTMENT
IMPLEMENTATION,** §§32-1601 to
32-1661.
Administrative entity, §32-1603.01.
Adult literacy task force, §32-1661.
Anti-displacement provisions,
§32-1608.
Approval of state plan by council,
§32-1604.
Career pathways innovation,
§32-1605.01.
Council findings, §32-1601.
**Council not to withhold information
from public,** §32-1613.
Definitions, §32-1602.
Educational stepladder program,
§§32-1651 to 32-1653.
Establishment, §32-1651.
Funding program, §32-1652.
Funding students, §32-1653.
Funding.
Educational stepladder program.
Funding program, §32-1652.
Funding students, §32-1653.
Use of funds for employment and
training services, §32-1610.
Grievance procedure, §32-1609.
Individual training accounts.
Limits on, §32-1631.
Mandatory partner programs,
§32-1611.01.
Participant eligibility criteria,
§32-1602.01.
References, §32-1612.01.
**Regional information sharing
system.**
Regional cooperation to produce,
§32-1612.

WORKFORCE INVESTMENT IMPLEMENTATION —Cont'd
Residency of participant, §32-1602.01.
Restrictions on assigning, placing or permitting to work, §32-1608.
Training services criteria and performance accountability, §32-1607.
Use of funds for employment and training services, §32-1610.
Workforce investment council, §32-1603.
Authority to make grants for job development, §1-328.05.
Youth activities, §32-1610.01.

WORK INCENTIVE ALLOWANCES, §4-205.36.

WORK PERMITS.
Child labor, §§32-207 to 32-211, 32-219.

WORKPLACE FRAUD, §§32-1331.01 to 32-1331.12.
Actions to enforce provisions.
Private right of action, §32-1331.09.
Applicability of provisions to construction services industry, §32-1331.02.
Backpay.
Private right of action to enforce provisions, §32-1331.09.
Damages.
Private right of action to enforce provisions, §32-1331.09.
Definitions, §32-1331.01.
Discrimination.
Employer's retaliation, §32-1331.10.
Employers.
Deemed employers.
Agents managing corporation, §32-1331.03.
Officers of corporation, §32-1331.03.
Defined, §32-1331.01.
Recordkeeping, §32-1331.12.
Evasion of detection of violation.
Penalty, §32-1331.13.
Exempt persons.
Presumption of employer-employee relationship.
Overcoming presumption, §32-1331.04.
Facilitating violation.
Penalty, §32-1331.13.
Fund.
Workplace fraud fund, §32-1331.15.
Hearings on violations, §32-1331.06.

WORKPLACE FRAUD —Cont'd
Independent contractors.
Misclassifying of individuals as independent contractors.
Prohibition of workplace fraud, §32-1331.04.
Notice by employer to persons classified as independent contractor, §32-1331.12.
Investigation of complaints, §32-1331.05.
Limitation of actions.
Private right of action to enforce provisions, §32-1331.09.
Penalties for violation of provisions, §32-1331.07.
Facilitating violation or evading detection, §32-1331.13.
Recordkeeping by employers.
Notice of classification as independent contractor.
Failure to notify, §32-1331.12.
Presumption of employer-employee relationship, §32-1331.04.
Public contracts.
Debarment for repeat violations, §32-1331.11.
Mayor's authority to enforce provisions, §32-1331.11.
Reinstatement.
Private right of action to enforce provisions, §32-1331.09.
Restitution.
Penalties for violation of provisions, §32-1331.07.
Public contracts.
Mayor's authority to enforce provisions, §32-1331.11.
Retaliation by employer, §32-1331.10.
Rulemaking to implement provisions, §32-1331.14.
Stop work orders.
Defined, §32-1331.01.
Penalties for violation of provisions, §32-1331.07.
Waiver of protections of law by agreement.
Prohibition, §32-1331.08.

WORKPLACE SAFETY, §§32-801 to 32-812.
Council power to make rules and regulations, §32-804.
Death reports, §32-808.
Definitions, §32-802.
Director of industrial safety, §32-807.
Employer duties, §32-808.

WORKPLACE SAFETY —Cont'd
Examinations, §32-809.
Fines, §32-812.
Injury reports, §32-808.
Issuance of rules and regulations, §32-804.
Minimum wage and industrial safety board.
  Director, §32-807.
  Evidence, taking, §32-805.
  Examination of place of employment, §32-809.
  Information furnished to, §32-808.
  Office space and supplies furnished to, §32-810.
  Powers and duties, §32-803.
  Report to mayor by, §32-811.
Oaths and affirmations, §32-805.
Occupational safety and health.
  General provisions, §§32-1101 to 32-1124.
    See OCCUPATIONAL SAFETY AND HEALTH.
Penalties, §32-812.
Policy declaration, §32-801.
Records, §32-808.
Reports.
  Employer reports of injuries and deaths, §32-808.
  Minimum wage and industrial safety board report to mayor, §32-811.
Smoking, §§7-1703.02, 7-1703.03.
Subpoenas, §32-805.
Variations from rules and regulations, §32-806.
Witnesses, §32-805.
Workers' compensation.
  General provisions, §§32-1501 to 32-1545.
    See WORKERS' COMPENSATION.

WORKPLACE SMOKING, §§7-1703.02, 7-1703.03.

WORK-PRODUCT OF ATTORNEY.
Discovery scope and limits, CivPro Rule 26.
  Adoption proceedings, Adoption Rule 26.
  Criminal procedure, CrimPro Rule 16.
  Delinquent minors, JuvProc Rule 16.
  Domestic relations actions, DomRel Rule 26.
Liens on client files, ProfCond Rule 1.8.

WORK RELEASE PROGRAM, §§24-241.01 to 24-241.10.
See PRISONS AND PRISONERS.

WORLD CLASS SCHOOLS TASK FORCE, §§38-1803.11 to 38-1803.15.
Appropriation, §38-1803.15.
Consultation in conducting duties, §38-1803.12.
Defined, §38-1803.11.
Federal personnel detailed to task force to assist in carrying out duties, §38-1803.14.
Grant authorized, §38-1803.11.
Public access to proceedings, §38-1803.13.
Recommendations requirements, §38-1803.11.
Transcripts of proceedings made available to public, §38-1803.13.

WRITINGS.
Authors.
  Protection of rights, US Const Art I §8.

WRITS.
Appeals.
  Extraordinary writs, DCCtApp Rule 21.
Attachment.
  See ATTACHMENT.
Audita querela.
  Abolished, CivPro Rule 60.
Coram nobis.
  Abolished, CivPro Rule 60.
Coram vobis.
  Abolished, CivPro Rule 60.
Execution of judgments, §§15-301 to 15-371.
  See EXECUTION OF JUDGMENTS.
Fieri facias, CivPro Form CA 120.
Habeas corpus.
  See HABEAS CORPUS.
Landlord and tenant court.
  Writs of restitution, LandlordTenant Form 10, LandlordTenant Rule 16.
    Application to stay writ of restitution, LandlordTenant Form 9.
    Not of intention to seek writ, LandlordTenant Form 2.
Mandamus, DCCtApp Rule 21.
  Appeals, federal cases.
    Petitions alleging unreasonable agency delay, USCtApp HPIP Rule III(g)(4).
    Petitions challenging district court transfers, USCtApp HPIP Rule III(g)(3).
  Insurance holding companies, §31-714.

WRITS —Cont'd
Mandamus —Cont'd
Nursing homes.
Discharge, transfer, or relocation of residents of, §44-1004.02.
Writ abolished, CivPro Rule 81.
Ne exeat writ.
Domestic relations actions, DomRel Rule 406.
Prohibition, DCCtApp Rule 21.
Replevin.
See REPLEVIN.
Scire facias abolished, CivPro Rule 81.

WRONGFUL ARRESTS.
Metropolitan police.
Legal assistance for police involved in, §5-115.04.

WRONGFUL DEATH, §§16-2701 to 16-2703.
Damages, §§16-2701, 16-2703.
Liability for wrongful death, §16-2701.
Limitation of actions, §§12-301, 16-2702.
Asbestos.
Injury or death caused by exposure to asbestos, §12-311.
Injury or death resulting from real property improvements, §12-310.
Parties.
Plaintiff, §16-2702.
Prior recovery precludes action, §16-2701.
Survival of actions, §12-101.

Y

YEARS, ESTATES FOR.
Chattels real, recognition as, §42-504.
Defined, §42-518.
Estates expressed from year to year, §42-519.

YEAR 2000 DISTRICT GOVERNMENT COMPUTER LIABILITY IMMUNITY.
Immunity for year 2000 system failure, §2-381.31.
Applicability, §2-381.32.

YMCA (YOUNG MEN'S CHRISTIAN ASSOCIATION).
Real property exempt from taxation, §47-1024.
Community investment initiative, §47-1092.

YOUNG WOMEN'S CHRISTIAN ASSOCIATION.
Real property exempt from taxation, §§47-1022, 47-1023.

YOUNG WOMEN'S CHRISTIAN HOME.
Real property exempt from taxation, §47-1021.

YOUTH APPRENTICESHIP ADVISORY COUNCIL, §32-1412.01.

YOUTH COUNCIL, §§2-1561 to 2-1564, 2-1565.01 to 2-1565.06.
Advisory council, §§2-1561 to 2-1564.
Composition, §2-1563.
Definitions, §2-1561.
Establish, §2-1562.
Organizational structure, §2-1564.
Composition, §2-1565.03.
Definitions, §2-1565.01.
Duties, §2-1565.02.
Established, §2-1565.02.
Funding, §2-1565.06.
Integration with learning standards, §2-1565.05.
Staff, §2-1565.04.

YOUTH DEVELOPMENT PLAN.
Executive working group, §2-1585.
Funding, §2-1584.
Realignment of funding priorities, §2-1584.
Goals for children, §2-1584.
Implementation, §2-1581.
Outcome measures, §2-1583.
Performance measures, §2-1583.
Realignment of funding priorities, §2-1584.
Reports, §2-1583.
Strategy update, §2-1582.

YOUTH LEADERSHIP INSTITUTE, §§2-1571 to 2-1574.

YOUTH OFFENDERS, §§24-901 to 24-941.
See JUVENILE OFFENDERS.

YOUTH REHABILITATION, §§24-901 to 24-907.

YOUTH REHABILITATION SERVICES, DEPARTMENT OF, §§2-1515.01 to 2-1515.54.
Assault on officer or employee, §22-405.
Behavioral health screenings and assessments, §2-1515.04a.

YOUTH REHABILITATION SERVICES, DEPARTMENT OF
—Cont'd
Child welfare and juvenile justice behavioral health infrastructure.
Family resource guide, §2-1517.51.
Reports, §2-1517.52.
Confidentiality of youth records, §2-1515.06.
Conflicting orders repealed, §2-1515.10.
Divisions, §2-1515.03.
Duties, §2-1515.05.
Educational services for committed and detained children, §38-3301.
Establishment, §2-1515.02.
Human services, department of.
Successor in interest to, §2-1515.09.
Transfers from, §2-1515.08.
Marijuana.
Limitations on use of positive test, §2-1515.05.
Mayor.
Powers, §2-1515.07.
Medicaid.
Report on eligibility, §2-1515.06a.
Mental health department.
Transfers from, §7-1131.16.
Offices, §2-1515.03.
Duties, §2-1515.04.
Organization, §2-1515.03.
Powers, §2-1515.05.
Delegation and redelegation of authority, §2-1515.09.
Pregnant youths.
Restraints, use of, §§2-1515.51 to 2-1515.54.
Purpose, §2-1515.02.
Restraints, use of, §§2-1515.51 to 2-1515.54.
Definitions, §2-1515.51.
Notice, §2-1515.54.
Places of confinement, §2-1515.52.
Pregnant youths, generally, §§2-1515.51 to 2-1515.54.
Reports, §2-1515.53.

YOUTH RESIDENTIAL FACILITIES, §§7-2101 to 7-2108.
Boards and committees of, §7-2104.
Definitions, §7-2101.
Enforcement of provisions, §7-2108.
Escape from, §10-509.01a.
Foster care, §§4-217.01 to 4-217.11.
See FOSTER CARE.
Inspections, §7-2105.
Issuance of rules regarding, §7-2103.

YOUTH RESIDENTIAL FACILITIES
—Cont'd
Licenses, §§7-2102, 7-2107.
Monitoring outplaced residents, §7-2106.
Penalties, §7-2108.
Remedies, §7-2108.
Therapeutic care.
Defined, §7-2101.
Monitoring residents placed in, §7-2106.

YOUTH SERVICES, §§2-1501 to 2-1511.
Accounting system, §2-1507.
Budget estimates, §2-1510.
Conflicts of interest, §2-1508.
Definitions, §2-1501.
Division of community-based programs for children and youth.
Establishment of, §2-1503.
Educational services for committed and detained youth, §38-3301.
Neighborhood planning councils.
Budget estimates, §2-1510.
Conflicts of interest, §2-1508.
Defined, §2-1501.
Elections, §2-1503.01.
Establishment of, §2-1503.01.
Financing, §2-1507.
Operational rules for, §2-1509.
Tenure on, §2-1503.01.
Office of youth advocacy, §§2-1504, 2-1505.
Office of youth opportunity services.
Abolition of, §2-1503.
Policy declaration, §2-1502.
Severability of provisions, §2-1511.
Transfers from office of youth opportunity services, §§2-1503, 2-1506.
Voucher system, §2-1507.

YWCA (YOUNG WOMEN'S CHRISTIAN ASSOCIATION).
Real property exempt from taxation, §§47-1022, 47-1023.

Z

ZEALOUS REPRESENTATION.
Attorneys at law, ProfCond Rule 1.3.

ZONING, §§6-621.01 to 6-661.02.
Airspace, rental of, §10-1121.06.
Alcoholic beverage license restrictions.
Retail licenses, §25-336.

ZONING —Cont'd
**Alcoholic beverage license
   restrictions** —Cont'd
Wholesale licenses, §25-337.
Appropriations, §6-641.13.
Assisted living residences.
Applicability to, §44-110.01.
**Ballpark parking structures not
   subject to zoning,** §1-306.07.
Board of Zoning Adjustment.
National Capital Planning
   Commission, §6-641.07.
Wages and salaries for members,
   §6-641.13.
Building permits, §§6-641.09, 6-661.01,
   6-661.02.
Certificates of occupancy, §6-641.09.
Commission.
Board of Zoning Adjustment,
   §6-641.07.
Establishment of, §6-621.01.
Organization of, §6-621.01.
Power to issue regulations, §6-641.01.
Wages and salaries for members,
   §6-641.13.
Condominiums, §42-1901.05.
**District of Columbia government
   subject to,** §1-306.07.
Enforcement, §6-641.10.
**Federal public buildings,
   exemptions for,** §6-641.15.
Fees, §6-661.01.
Foreign government chanceries,
   §§6-651.01, 6-651.02.
Helicopter landing pads, §9-1211.01.
Horizontal property regimes,
   §42-2028.
**Horse-drawn carriages, loading
   zones for,** §8-2009.
Inclusionary zoning, §§6-1041.01 to
   6-1041.09.
Certificate of compliance, §6-1041.05.
Civil infractions, §6-1041.04.
Definitions, §6-1041.01.
Housing authority.
   Responsibilities, §6-1041.08.
Injunction of violations, §6-1041.04.
Maximum rent and purchase prices for
   inclusionary units.
   Establishment, §6-1041.03.
Mayor.
   Powers and duties, §§6-1041.03,
      6-1041.07.
   Reports, §6-1041.09.
Purchase prices.
   Maximum rent and purchase prices
      for inclusionary units.
      Establishment, §6-1041.03.

ZONING —Cont'd
Inclusionary zoning —Cont'd
Rent.
   Maximum rent and purchase prices
      for inclusionary units.
      Establishment, §6-1041.03.
Reports.
   Mayor, §6-1041.09.
Students.
   Ineligibility to rent or purchase
      inclusionary unit, §6-1041.06.
Unlawful acts, §6-1041.02.
Interpretation of provisions,
   §6-641.11.
Maps, filing of, §6-641.08.
Mayor's powers and duties,
   §6-661.01.
Inclusionary zoning, §§6-1041.03,
   6-1041.07.
Reports, §6-1041.09.
**National Capital Planning
   Commission.**
Board of Zoning adjustment,
   §6-641.07.
Platting and subdivisions, §2-1006.
Regulations, comments on, §§2-1006,
   6-641.05.
**Nonconforming use of building,
   grandfathering of,** §6-641.06a.
Office of Zoning.
Establishment, §6-623.01.
Office of Planning activities, §6-623.04.
Organization of, §6-623.02.
Transfer of functions to, §6-623.03.
Records, §6-641.08.
Regulations.
Commission's power to issue,
   §6-641.01.
Enforcement, §6-641.10.
Existing regulations, force of,
   §6-641.03.
Federal public buildings, exemptions
   for, §6-641.15.
Filing of, §6-641.08.
Interpretation of provisions, §6-641.11.
National Capital Planning
   Commission comments on,
   §6-641.05.
Policy declaration, §6-641.02.
Publication of, §6-641.08.
Public hearings required for
   amendments or new regulations,
   §§6-641.03, 6-641.05.
Vote required for, §6-641.04.
Repeal of laws regarding, §6-641.14.
Schools and education.
Attendance zone boundaries, §38-221.

POPULAR NAMES INDEX

CAPTIVE INSURANCE AGENCY ESTABLISHMENT ACT OF 2008, §1-307.95.

CHIEF TENANT ADVOCATE.
Office of the chief tenant advocate establishment act, §42-3531.01.

CHILD ABDUCTION PREVENTION ACT, §16-4604.01.

CHILD FATALITY REVIEW COMMITTEE ESTABLISHMENT ACT, §4-1371.01.

CHILDHOOD LEAD POISONING SCREENING AND REPORTING ACT, §7-871.01.

CHILDREN AND YOUTH INITIATIVE ESTABLISHMENT ACT, §2-1551.

COLLEGES AND UNIVERSITIES.
Public postsecondary education reorganization act, §38-1201.01.

COMMERCIAL CODE, §28:1-101.
Bank deposits and collections, §28:4-101.
Documents of title, §28:7-101.
Funds transfers, §28:4A-101.
General provisions, §28:1-101.
Investment securities, §28:8-101.
Leases, §28:2A-101.
Letters of credit, §28:5-101.
Negotiable instruments, §28:3-101.
Sales, §28:2-101.
Secured transactions, §28:9-101.

COMMUNITY DEVELOPMENT ACT, §26-431.01.

COMMUNITY SCHOOLS INCENTIVE ACT, §38-754.01.

COMPLETE STREETS POLICY, §50-2381.

COMPREHENSIVE HOMICIDE ELIMINATION STRATEGY TASK FORCE, §22-4251.

COMPULSORY SCHOOL ATTENDANCE, §§38-201 to 38-213.

CONDOMINIUMS.
Horizontal property regimes act, §42-2001.

CONSTRUCTION AND DEMOLITION WASTE RECYCLING ACCOUNTABILITY, §8-1071.

CREDIT LIFE INSURANCE AND CREDIT ACCIDENT AND HEALTH INSURANCE.
Act for the regulation of credit life insurance and credit accident and health insurance, §31-5101.

CRIMINAL ABUSE AND NEGLECT OF VULNERABLE ADULTS ACT, §22-931.

CRIMINAL BACKGROUND CHECKS FOR THE PROTECTION OF CHILDREN ACT, §4-1501.01.

CUSTOMER SERVICE OPERATIONS ESTABLISHMENT ACT, §1-327.31.

D

DC STREETCAR SERVICE, §50-921.71.

DEATH.
Presumptive disability or death of emergency medical services or fire department employees, §5-651.

DEPARTMENT OF CORRECTIONS INMATE AND RETURNING CITIZEN ASSISTANCE GRANT, §24-211.71.

DEPARTMENT OF MENTAL HEALTH ESTABLISHMENT AMENDMENT ACT, §7-1131.01.

DEPARTMENT ON DISABILITY SERVICES ESTABLISHMENT ACT, §7-761.01.

DISABILITIES, PERSONS WITH.
Criminal abuse and neglect of vulnerable adults act, §22-931.
Department on disability services establishment act, §7-761.01.

DISCLAIMER OF PROPERTY INTERESTS ACT, §19-1501.

DISTRACTED DRIVING SAFETY ACT, §50-1731.01.

DOG LEASH LAWS, §1-303.41, §8-1808, §22-1311.

DRIVERLESS VEHICLES, §§50-2351 to 50-2354.

DRIVING UNDER THE INFLUENCE, §50-2206.01.
Chemical testing, §50-1901.

OPEN CONTAINER LAW —Cont'd
On-premises retailer knowingly
allowing customer to exit with
an open container, §25-113.

OPEN GOVERNMENT ACT, §2-591.

OPEN MEETINGS ACT, §2-571.

P

**PERSONAL DELIVERY DEVICES
PILOT PROGRAM,** §§50-1551 to
50-1555.

PESTICIDES, §§8-401 to 8-440.

**PHARMACEUTICAL EDUCATION
PROGRAM ESTABLISHMENT
ACT,** §48-843.01.

PHARMACY TECHNICIANS,
§3-1207.51.

PHOTO-COP, §§50-2209.01 to
50-2209.11.

**POLICE INVESTIGATIONS
CONCERNING FIRST
AMENDMENT ACTIVITIES ACT,**
§5-333.01.

**PORTABLE ELECTRONICS
INSURANCE,** §31-5051.01.

**POSTSECONDARY PREPARATION
PLAN,** §38-752.01.

PRESCRIPTION DRUGS.
Off-label informed consent act,
§48-841.01.
Pharmaceutical education program
establishment act, §48-843.01.
SafeRx evaluation act, §48-844.01.

PRINCIPAL AND INCOME ACT,
§28-4801.01.

**PRIVATE CONTRACTOR AND
SUBCONTRACTOR PROMPT
PAYMENT ACT,** §27-131.

PRODUCER LICENSING ACT,
§31-1131.01.

**PROFESSIONAL CORPORATION
ACT OF 2010,** §29-501.

**PROFESSIONAL ENGINEERS'
REGISTRATION ACT,**
§47-2886.01.

PUBLIC BENEFIT CORPORATIONS,
§29-1301.01.

**PUBLIC INSURANCE ADJUSTER
LICENSURE ACT,** §31-1631.01.

**PUBLIC POSTSECONDARY
EDUCATION
REORGANIZATION ACT,**
§38-1201.01.

**PUBLIC-PRIVATE PARTNERSHIP
ADMINISTRATION FUND,**
§2-272.04.

Q

**QUALIFIED ZONE ACADEMY
REVENUE BOND PROJECT
FORWARD COMMITMENT
APPROVAL ACT,** §2-1217.101.

R

RAPE SHIELD LAW, §§22-3021 to
22-3024.

**REAL PROPERTY TRANSFER ON
DEATH ACT,** §§19-604.01 to
19-604.19.

RECYCLING.
Construction and demolition waste
recycling accountability, §8-1071.

REGISTERED AGENT ACT OF 2010,
§29-104.01.

**RELOCATION AND HOUSING
ASSISTANCE ACT OF 1980,**
§42-3403.01.

**REMOVAL AND DISPOSITION OF
ABANDONED AND OTHER
UNLAWFULLY PARKED
VEHICLES REFORM ACT,**
§50-2421.01.

ROBOTIC CARS.
Autonomous vehicles, §§50-2351 to
50-2354.

S

SAFERX EVALUATION ACT,
§48-844.01.

**SALVAGE, FLOOD AND JUNK
VEHICLES,** §§50-1331.01 to
50-1331.09.

**SCHOLARSHIPS FOR
OPPORTUNITY AND RESULTS
ACT (SOAR ACT),** §38-1853.01.

SCHOOL REFORM ACT, §38-1800.01.